PUBLIC PAPERS OF THE PRESIDENTS
OF THE
UNITED STATES

PUBLIC PAPERS OF THE PRESIDENTS
OF THE
UNITED STATES

George W. Bush

2006

(IN TWO BOOKS)

BOOK I—JANUARY 1 TO JUNE 30, 2006

UNITED STATES GOVERNMENT PRINTING OFFICE
WASHINGTON : 2010

Published by the
Office of the Federal Register
National Archives and Records Administration

For sale by the Superintendent of Documents, U.S. Government Printing Office
• Internet: bookstore.gpo.gov • Phone: (202) 512–1800 • Fax: (202) 512–2250
• Mail: Stop SSOP, Washington, DC 20401

Foreword

This volume collects my speeches and papers from the first half of 2006.

As the year opened, I appeared before the Congress to deliver my annual State of the Union message. In this speech, I called for an ambitious agenda to strengthen our Nation's economy and ensure that our Nation remained competitive in the world. I proposed the Advanced Energy Initiative, a plan to harness the power of technology to reduce America's dependence on foreign sources of energy. I presented a strategy to reform health care for the 21st century by making it more affordable, portable, and efficient. And I introduced the American Competitiveness Initiative—a bold plan to support science and technology by investing in research and development, education, and entrepreneurship.

During these 6 months, I toured the Nation to promote these initiatives and other important domestic priorities. In March, I traveled to New Orleans to discuss the Federal Government's continued commitment to rebuilding communities devastated by Hurricane Katrina. During the spring, I visited a variety of States to encourage Americans to take part in the new Medicare prescription drug benefit. And as summer approached, I visited California, New Mexico, Nebraska, and Arizona to highlight the need for the Congress to pass comprehensive immigration reform.

On May 15, I addressed the Nation from the Oval Office on this vital issue. I said, "Our new immigrants are just what they've always been—people willing to risk everything for the dream of freedom. And America remains what she has always been: the great hope on the horizon, an open door to the future, a blessed and promised land. We honor the heritage of all who come here, no matter where they come from, because we trust in our country's genius for making us all Americans—one Nation under God."

During this period, we took decisive action on several key priorities for our Nation's future. In March, I signed the "USA PATRIOT Improvement and Reauthorization Act of 2005"—legislation that gave our country's intelligence and law enforcement officials vital tools to protect our citizens from threats such as international terrorists and drug dealers. In May, I was proud to sign into law a bill that extended tax relief for American families and businesses. And in June, I signed a proclamation creating the Northwestern Hawaiian Islands Marine National Monument—the largest single conservation area in the history of our country, and the largest fully protected marine area in the world.

This was a time when many talented and able Americans were appointed to the highest levels of the Federal Government. In January, Samuel Alito was confirmed by the United States Senate as the Supreme Court's newest Associate Justice. Less than a week later, Ben Bernanke was sworn in as our Nation's 14th Chairman of the Federal Reserve. In May, General Michael Hayden was appointed to be the new Director of the Central Intelligence Agency. And during this period, I also welcomed two new members to my cabinet—Dirk Kempthorne as Secretary of the Interior and Henry Paulson as Secretary of the Treasury.

As we focused on these key priorities at home, my Administration remained engaged in vital issues around the world. In March, the First Lady and I traveled to Afghanistan, India, and Pakistan to demonstrate America's commitment to strong partnerships in that vital region. While in Afghanistan, I was able to witness firsthand how America's men and women in uniform were combating radicalism and creating a more hopeful future for the Afghan people. After years under the radical Taliban regime, Afghanistan was transforming into a country where entrepreneurs had the freedom to pursue opportunity, journalists had the freedom to ask questions, and, at long last, girls had the freedom to receive an education. I praised this progress and let the Afghan people know that America's commitment to them remained firm.

Later that month, I visited Mexico, where I met with Mexican President Vicente Fox and Canadian Prime Minister Stephen Harper to discuss an agenda of security and prosperity for North America. In June, I attended a summit meeting between the United States and the European Union. On this trip, Laura and I visited Austria and Hungary, and I reaffirmed America's commitment to work with our European allies to promote peace, human rights, and democracy worldwide.

Finally, this period saw both setbacks and successes in the continued struggle for Iraq's future. Despite the destruction sparked by the terrorist bombing of a sacred Shiite mosque in Samarra, the Iraqi people banded together to form their first unity government in April. In May, Nouri Al-Maliki became Prime Minister of Iraq and presented his cabinet to the new government. And in June, United States military forces killed Abu Musab Al-Zarqawi, the operational commander of the terrorist movement in Iraq—a dramatic victory in the War on Terror.

Less than a week after Zarqawi was brought to justice, I made a surprise visit to Iraq, where I spent time with the men and women of our Armed Forces and met with the new Prime Minister. Upon my return, I told the American people, "I traveled to Baghdad to personally show our Nation's commitment to a free Iraq, because it is vital for the Iraqi people to know with certainty that America will not abandon them after we have come this far. The challenges that remain in Iraq are serious. We face determined enemies who remain intent on killing the innocent, and defeating these enemies will require more sacrifice and the continued patience of our country. But our efforts in Iraq are well worth it, the mission is necessary for the security of our country, and we will succeed." In the months to come, our country's patience would indeed be tested, but our determination to safeguard our Nation and help foster a free Iraq would prevail.

Preface

This book contains the papers and speeches of the 43d President of the United States that were issued by the Office of the Press Secretary during the period January 1–June 30, 2006. The material has been compiled and published by the Office of the Federal Register, National Archives and Records Administration.

The material is presented in chronological order, and the dates shown in the headings are the dates of the documents or events. In instances when the release date differs from the date of the document itself, that fact is shown in the textnote. Every effort has been made to ensure accuracy: Remarks are checked against a tape recording, and signed documents are checked against the original. Textnotes and cross references have been provided by the editors for purposes of identification or clarity. At the request of the Office of the Press Secretary, the Bush property known as Prairie Chapel Ranch in Crawford, Texas, is referred to simply as the Bush Ranch. Speeches were delivered in Washington, DC, unless indicated. The times noted are local times. All materials that are printed full-text in the book have been indexed in the subject and name indexes, and listed in the document categories list.

The Public Papers of the Presidents series was begun in 1957 in response to a recommendation of the National Historical Publications Commission. An extensive compilation of messages and papers of the Presidents covering the period 1789 to 1897 was assembled by James D. Richardson and published under congressional authority between 1896 and 1899. Since then, various private compilations have been issued, but there was no uniform publication comparable to the Congressional Record or the United States Supreme Court Reports. Many Presidential papers could be found only in the form of mimeographed White House releases or as reported in the press. The Commission therefore recommended the establishment of an official series in which Presidential writings, addresses, and remarks of a public nature could be made available.

The Commission's recommendation was incorporated in regulations of the Administrative Committee of the Federal Register, issued under section 6 of the Federal Register Act (44 U.S.C. 1506), which may be found in title 1, part 10, of the Code of Federal Regulations.

A companion publication to the Public Papers series, the Weekly Compilation of Presidential Documents, was begun in 1965 to provide a broader range of Presidential materials on a more timely basis to meet the needs of the contemporary reader. Beginning with the administration of Jimmy Carter, the Public Papers series expanded its coverage to include additional material as printed in the Weekly Compilation. That coverage provides a listing of the President's daily schedule and meetings, when announced, and other items of general interest issued by the Office of the Press Secretary. Also included are lists of the President's nominations submitted to the Senate, materials released by the Office of the Press Secretary that are not printed full-text in the book, and proclamations, Executive orders, and other Presidential documents released by the Office of the Press Secretary and published in the *Federal Register*. This information appears in the appendixes at the end of the book.

Volumes covering the administrations of Presidents Herbert Hoover, Harry S. Truman, Dwight D. Eisenhower, John F. Kennedy, Lyndon B. Johnson, Richard Nixon, Gerald R. Ford, Jimmy Carter, Ronald Reagan, George Bush, and William J. Clinton are also included in the Public Papers series.

The Public Papers of the Presidents publication program is under the direction of Frances D. McDonald, Managing Editor, Office of the Federal Register. The series is produced by the Presidential and Legislative Publications Unit. The Chief Editor of this book was Stacey A. Mulligan, assisted by William K. Banks, Loretta F. Cochran, Lois Davis, Kathleen M. Fargey, Stephen J. Frattini, Michael J. Forcina, Allison M. Gavin, Gwendolyn J. Henderson, Diane Hiltabidle, Alfred Jones, Joshua H. Liberatore, Heather N. McDaniel, Ashley Merusi, Amelia E. Otovo, Jennifer M. Partridge, D. Gregory Perrin, Matthew R. Regan, and Michael J. Sullivan.

The frontispiece and photographs used in the portfolio were supplied by the White House Photo Office. The typography and design of the book were developed by the Government Printing Office under the direction of Robert C. Tapella, Public Printer.

Raymond A. Mosley
Director of the Federal Register

David S. Ferriero
Archivist of the United States

Contents

Cabinet

Secretary of State .... Condoleezza Rice

Secretary of the Treasury .... John W. Snow
(resigned 6/30)
Henry M. Paulson, Jr.
(confirmed 6/28)

Secretary of Defense .... Donald H. Rumsfeld

Attorney General .... Alberto R. Gonzales

Secretary of the Interior .... Gale A. Norton
(resigned 3/31)
Dirk Kempthorne
(confirmed 5/26)

Secretary of Agriculture .... Mike Johanns

Secretary of Commerce .... Carlos M. Gutierrez

Secretary of Labor .... Elaine L. Chao

Secretary of Health and Human
Services .... Michael O. Leavitt

Secretary of Housing and Urban
Development .... Alphonso R. Jackson

Secretary of Transportation .... Norman Y. Mineta
(resigned 7/7)
Mary E. Peters
(confirmed 9/30)

Secretary of Energy .... Samuel W. Bodman

Secretary of Education .... Margaret Spellings

Secretary of Veterans Affairs .... R. James Nicholson

Secretary of Homeland Security .... Michael Chertoff

Chief of Staff .... Andrew H. Card, Jr.
(resigned 4/14)
Joshua B. Bolten
(appointed 4/14)

Administrator of the Environmental
Protection Agency .... Stephen L. Johnson

United States Trade Representative .... Robert J. Portman
(resigned 5/30)
Susan C. Schwab
(confirmed 6/8)

Director of the Office of Management
and Budget .... Joshua B. Bolten
(resigned 4/14)
Robert J. Portman
(confirmed 5/26)

Director of National Drug Control
Policy .... John P. Walters

Administration of George W. Bush

2006

Remarks to Reporters Following a Visit With United States Troops and an Exchange With Reporters in San Antonio, Texas
January 1, 2006

The President. Happy New Year to you all. Thanks. I can't think of a better way to start 2006 than here at this fantastic hospital, a hospital that's full of healers and compassionate people who care deeply about our men and women in uniform. It's also full of courageous young soldiers, marines, airmen—men and women—who are serving our country and making great sacrifice. I'm just overwhelmed by the great strength of character of not only those who have been wounded but of their loved ones as well. And so, thank you all for bringing great credit to our country.

As you can probably see, I have injured myself, not here at the hospital but in combat with a cedar. I eventually won. The cedar gave me a little bit of a scratch. As a matter of fact, the colonel asked if I needed first aid when she first saw me. I was able to avoid any major surgical operations here, but thanks for your compassion, Colonel.

I've been thinking long and hard about 2006. My hopes, of course, are for peace around the world. I'll continue to work as hard as I can to lay that foundation for peace. And also my hope is that this country remains as prosperous as it was in 2005. We had a very strong economy, and we'll work to keep the economy as strong as it possibly can, so anybody that wants to find a job can find one.

With that, I'll be glad to answer a couple of questions. Toby [Tabassum Zakaria, Reuters]—or, excuse me, Deb. You are Deb [Deb Riechmann, Associated Press], right?

Terrorist Surveillance Program

Q. Yes, sir. Mr. President, were you aware of any resistance to the launching of the NSA program at high levels of your administration, and if so, how did that influence your decision to approve it?

The President. First of all, the NSA program is an important program in protecting America. We're at war, and as the Commander in Chief, I've got to use the resources at my disposal, within the law, to protect the American people. And that's what we're doing.

The NSA program is one that listens to a few numbers, called from the outside of the United States in, of known Al Qaida or affiliate people. In other words, the enemy is calling somebody, and we want to know who they're calling and why. And that seems to make sense to me, as the Commander in Chief, if my job is to protect the American people.

This program has been reviewed, constantly reviewed, by people throughout my administration. And it still is reviewed. It has got—not only has it been reviewed by Justice Department officials, it's been reviewed by Members of the United States Congress. It's a vital, necessary program.

Now, some say, "Well, maybe this isn't a war. Maybe this is just a law enforcement operation." I strongly disagree. We're at war with an enemy that wants to hurt us again, and the American people expect the Commander in Chief to protect them, and that's exactly what I intend to do.

Toby.

U.S. Troop Levels in Iraq

Q. Mr. President, as we start the new year, what is your outlook for U.S. troop withdrawal from Iraq in 2006?

The President. The conditions on the ground will dictate our force level. As the Iraqis are able to take more of the fight to the enemy, our commanders on the ground will be able to make a different assessment about the troop strength. And I'm going to continue to rely upon those commanders, such as General Casey, who is doing a fabulous job and whose judgment I trust, and that will determine—his recommendations will determine the number of troops we have on the ground in Iraq.

Terrorist Surveillance Program

Q. In 2004, when you were doing an event about the PATRIOT Act, in your remarks you had said that any wiretapping required a court order and that nothing had changed. Given that we now know you had prior approval for this NSA program, were you in any way misleading?

The President. I was talking about roving wiretaps, I believe, involved in the PATRIOT Act. This is different from the NSA program. The NSA program is a necessary program. I was elected to protect the American people from harm. And on September the 11th, 2001, our Nation was attacked. And after that day, I vowed to use all the resources at my disposal, within the law, to protect the American people, which is what I have been doing and will continue to do. And the fact that somebody leaked this program causes great harm to the United States.

There's an enemy out there. They read newspapers. They listen to what you write. They listen to what you put on the air, and they react. And it seems logical to me that if we know there's a phone number associated with Al Qaida and/or an Al Qaida affiliate and they're making phone calls, it makes sense to find out why. They attacked us before; they will attack us again

if they can. And we're going to do everything we can to stop them.

Yes, Ed [Edwin Chen, Los Angeles Times].

Q. Mr. President, with this program, though, what can you say to those members of the public that are worried about violations of their privacy?

The President. Ed, I can say that if somebody from Al Qaida is calling you, we'd like to know why. In the meantime, this program is conscious of people's civil liberties, as am I. This is a limited program designed to prevent attacks on the United States of America. And I repeat, limited. And it's limited to calls from outside the United States to calls within the United States. But they are of known—numbers of known Al Qaida members or affiliates. I think most Americans understand the need to find out what the enemy is thinking, and that's what we're doing.

We're at war with a bunch of cold-blooded killers who will kill on a moment's notice. And I have a responsibility, obviously, to act within the law, which I am doing. It's a program that's been reviewed constantly by Justice Department officials, a program to which the Congress has been briefed, and a program that is, in my judgment, necessary to win this war and to protect the American people.

Last question. Mike [Mike Allen, Time].

U.S. Troops Wounded in Iraq

Q. Mr. President, in August you said that Katrina could—the effects of it could test the strongest faith. I'm sure of some of the things that you saw today, that's the case as well. What do you tell a young soldier or his young wife about how a loving God could permit or cause some of the things you saw today?

The President. First of all, Mike, I'm conscious not to be trying to substitute myself for God. I am, on the other hand, inspired by the mom who told me upstairs that she prays every day and believes in the miracle of healing, that I think we see God's work here every day. I think when you find nurses and doctors who work around the clock, who come in at a moment's notice to save a life, I happen to believe there's a lot of divine inspiration to that kind of dedication and work. The parents I saw or the wives I saw, many of them were in prayer on a regular basis for their loved one.

And, you know, war is terrible. There's horrible consequences to war; that's what you see in this building. On the other hand, we also see people who say, "I'd like to go back in, Mr. President." What we're doing is the right thing, because many of these troops understand that by defeating the enemy there, we don't have to face them here. And they understand that by helping a country in the Middle East become a democracy, we are, in fact, laying

the foundation for future peace. And my— as the Commander in Chief, I am resolved to make sure that those who have died in combat's sacrifice are not in vain. And I am resolved to make sure that these kids who are recovering here, that have suffered terrible injury, that their injuries are not in vain, by completing the mission and laying that foundation for peace for generations to come. And I'm optimistic we'll achieve that objective.

Thank you all very much.

NOTE: The President spoke at 12:05 p.m. at the Brooke Army Medical Center. In his remarks, he referred to Col. Lark Ford, USA, deputy commander for nursing, Brooke Army Medical Center; and Gen. George W. Casey, Jr., USA, commanding general, Multi-National Force—Iraq.

Remarks Following a Meeting on the PATRIOT Act
January 3, 2006

Earlier today, I spoke to Governor Manchin of West Virginia. I told him that Americans all across our country were praying for the miners who are trapped in the mine there in West Virginia. I told him that I appreciated the great outpouring of compassion from the West Virginia citizens toward those worried family members. I also assured him that the Federal Government will help the folks in West Virginia any way we can to bring those miners out of that mine, hopefully in good condition. And may God bless those who are trapped below the Earth, and may God bless those who are concerned about those trapped below the Earth.

I also have just met with folks on the frontline of fighting the war on terror. U.S. Attorneys from around the country have joined us. Folks from the FBI, whose job it is to protect the American people, are with us as well.

We're talking about the PATRIOT Act and how useful the PATRIOT Act has been to safeguard America and, at the same time, safeguard liberties of Americans. And yet, the PATRIOT Act is going to expire in 30 days. And these good folks, whose task it is to do everything they can to protect the American people from a terrorist enemy that wants to hit us again, is asking the United States Congress to give them the tools necessary to do their jobs. And I'm asking the Congress to do so as well.

The American people expect to be protected, and the PATRIOT Act is a really important tool for them to stay protected. You know, the Congress says to people in the administration, "How come you haven't connected the dots?" And the PATRIOT Act is an important way to help connect the dots to protect the people.

This PATRIOT Act was passed overwhelmingly by the United States Congress in 2001. Members from both parties came together and said, "We will give those on the frontline of protecting America the tools necessary to protect American citizens and, at the same time, guard the civil liberties of our citizens." For 4 years, that's what's happened. These good folks have used the PATRIOT Act to protect America. There's oversight on this important program. And now, when it came time to renew the act, for partisan reasons, in my mind, people have not stepped up and have agreed that it's still necessary to protect the country. The enemy has not gone away. They're still there. And I expect Congress to understand that we're still at war, and they've got to give us the tools necessary to win this war.

And so for the next 30 days, I look forward to working with Members of Congress and speaking to the American people as clearly as I can about the importance of renewing the PATRIOT Act.

Thank you.

NOTE: The President spoke at 1:42 p.m. in the Roosevelt Room at the White House. In his remarks, he referred to Gov. Joe Manchin III of West Virginia. The Office of the Press Secretary also released a Spanish language transcript of these remarks.

Remarks Following a Meeting on the War on Terror in Arlington, Virginia
January 4, 2006

Today our Nation mourns those who lost their lives in the mining accident in West Virginia. We send our prayers and heartfelt condolences to the loved ones whose hearts are broken. We ask that the good Lord comfort them in their time of need.

I want to thank the Governor of West Virginia for showing such compassion, and I want to thank those who risked their lives to save those miners for showing such courage. May God bless the good people of West Virginia.

I just finished an important meeting, a briefing with members of my national security team, a briefing hosted by Secretary Don Rumsfeld and General Pete Pace. We spent time talking about this war on terror, the global war on terror. And to make sure that my team understood the progress we've made and the challenges ahead, the Secretary asked three of our commanders to join in the briefing, Generals Abizaid, Casey, and General Dempsey.

I want to tell the American people that I am most impressed by the caliber of these generals. They are smart. They are capable. They are visionary, and they're working hard to win this global war. We also were able to speak to one of our fine Ambassadors, Ambassador Khalilzad from Baghdad, as well.

During our briefing, we talked about the areas of concern in this global war on terror, recognizing that the enemy, which has an ideology of hate and a desire to kill, lurks in parts around the world. I assured those generals that this administration would do everything in our power to bring these enemies to justice.

We also spent time talking about the two major fronts in this war on terror, and that would be Iraq and Afghanistan. In Iraq, 2005 was a year of progress toward meeting our goal of victory. If you really think about it, there was three important elections that took place and in an atmosphere that some predicted wouldn't yield democracy. We had the January elections; we had the Constitution elections; we had elections last December when nearly 11 million people defied the terrorists to vote. The turnout in that country was 70 percent. Part of our strategy for defeating the enemy in Iraq is for there to be a viable political process. And when 70 percent of the people show up to vote, that's a good sign. See, people are saying, "I want to participate in the democratic process." The Iraqis showed great courage.

Now, we look forward to the process, obviously, moving on. The formation of a unity government is going to be important to the stability of the future of Iraq. Before that happens, obviously, you've got to finish counting the votes. And that's going to happen over the next couple of weeks. And then the Government—well, they're beginning to form the Government under their new Constitution. It takes a two-third vote of the Parliament for certain top officials to assume office. And to form this inclusive government, the Iraqi leaders must compromise and negotiate and build consensus, and this is going to take some time.

What the American people will see during the weeks ahead is a political process unfold, that people will be making decisions not based upon who's got the biggest gun but who's got the capacity to rally the will of the people. And that's positive. Democracies are an important part of our winning the war on terror. Democracies yield an ideology that is based on an ideology that says people are free—free to choose. The ideology of the enemy says a few people will choose, and if you don't like what we tell you to believe in, we'll kill you or treat you harshly.

And I want the American people to remember what life was like for the poor people in Afghanistan under the Taliban. The Taliban had no hopeful vision. They're vision was, if you don't agree with us, we'll take you in the public square and whip you. They're vision was, women don't have rights. They're vision was a dark and dim vision, which stands in stark contrast to the vision based upon freedom and democracy.

The second part of our strategy is to—in Iraq, a strategy for victory, is to train the Iraqis so they can take the fight against

the few who would stop the progress of many. And during this election, we were briefed about the security forces during the election. The commanders talked about more than 215,000 Iraqi soldiers and police that secured the country. That was an increase, by the way, of 85,000 since January of 2005. General Casey labeled the performance of the troops as superb.

Before the elections, there was a number of joint operations to lay the groundwork for a peaceful election. The Iraqis were in the lead on election day. In other words, they were responsible for the security of the elections. We were in a position to help them, but they were responsible for securing the voting booths. And they did a fine job. The number of attacks during the election were down dramatically. They performed, and that's part of our calibrating whether or not the Iraqi troops are becoming more capable. Numbers are one thing, but the ability to perform is another. And during these elections, the Iraqi troops showed our commanders on the ground and showed the American people that they're becoming more and more capable of performing their duty to provide security to the Iraqi people.

Now, you've got to understand that just because the elections went forward that doesn't mean these Saddamists, Zarqawi types, are going to lay down their arms. They're not. There will still be violence, and there will still be some who believe that they can affect the political outcome of Iraq through violent means. We understand that. And we're going to stay on the offense against these—"we" being coalition forces as well as the Iraqi forces. But the recent elections have served as a real defeat for the rejectionists and the Saddamists and Al Qaida types. Sunni Arabs who had boycotted the process joined the process. And as they did so, those who want to stop the progress of freedom are becoming more and more marginalized inside of Iraq.

So in 2006, the mission is to continue to hand over more and more territory and more and more responsibility to Iraqi forces. A year ago, there was only a handful of Iraqi Army and police battalions ready for combat, ready to take the lead. Today, there are more than 125 Iraqi combat battalions fighting the enemy, and 50 of those are in the lead. That's progress. And it's important progress, and it's an important part of our strategy to win in Iraq. And as these forces become more battle-hardened and take the lead, we're going to see continued confidence in the Iraqi people of the Iraqis being able to defend themselves, and that's important. And as we see more of these Iraqi forces in the lead, we'll be able to continue with our desire, our stated strategy that says, as Iraqis stand up, we'll stand down.

The commanders have recently determined that we can reduce our combat forces in Iraq from 17 to 15 brigades. And the reason they were able to do so is because the Iraqis are more capable. The adjustment is underway. This adjustment will result in a net decrease of several thousand troops below the pre-election baseline of 138,000 U.S. troops in Iraq. The decrease comes in addition to the reduction of about 20,000 troops who were in Iraq to assist with security during the December elections.

Later this year, if Iraqis continue to make progress on the security and political sides that we expect, we can discuss further possible adjustments with the leaders of a new Government in Iraq. But my decisions will be based upon conditions on the ground and the recommendation of our commanders, not based by false political timetables in Washington, DC. I'm not going to let politics get in the way of doing the right thing in Iraq, and the American people have got to understand that.

We've also got the opportunity to change our composition of our forces inside Iraq. In 2006, we expect Iraqis will take more and more control of the battle space, and as they do so, we will need fewer U.S. troops to conduct combat operations

around that country. More of our forces will be dedicated to training and supporting the Iraqi units. In the coming year, we will continue to focus on helping Iraqis improve their logistics and intelligence capabilities so more Iraqi units can take the fight and can sustain themselves in the fight.

We're also going to spend a lot of time on police training. An important part of our strategy is not only to have a competent Iraqi Army but police forces that are capable of earning the confidence of the Iraqi citizens. To restore security, Iraq has got to have capable police forces. And the recent reports of abuses by some of the Iraqi police units are troubling, and that conduct is unacceptable. Our commanders understand that; the Secretary understands that; and I know that.

To stop such abuses and increase the professionalism of the Iraqi police, General Dempsey, who's in charge of training, and others are working with the Iraqis to continue making adjustments in the way the forces are trained. First, we're going to work with the Iraqi Government to increase the training Iraqi police recruits receive in human rights and the rule of law, so they understand the role of the police in a democratic society.

Second, we're training Iraqi police with a program that has been effective with the Iraqi Army. In other words, when we find something that works, we'll do it. And if we find something that's not working, we change; and that is to embed coalition transition teams inside Iraqi special police units. Embedding our folks inside Iraqi Army units has worked. One reason why these Iraqi units are better able to take the lead is because they've worked side by side with American specialists and experts, some of our best troops. And so, we're going to embed these type of soldiers with the Iraqi police forces as well.

These transition teams will be made up of our officers, as well as noncommissioned officers. The coalition teams will go in the field with the police. They'll provide real-time advice and important assistance on patrol and during operations. And between operations, they're going to train the Iraqi officers; they're going to help them become increasingly capable and professional so they can serve and protect all the Iraqi people without discrimination.

As we train not only the soldiers but the police, our special units will continue hunting down Al Qaida and their affiliates. See, Al Qaida thinks they can use Iraq as a safe haven from which to launch attacks. That's their stated objective. I'm not making this up. Nobody in the—this is what Zawahiri and Zarqawi discussed. They said, "Let's drive America out of Iraq so we can use Iraq as a safe haven." We're going to train Iraqis. We'll train their army and train their police, and at the same time, we've got some of the finest soldiers ever on the hunt to bring Zarqawi and his buddies to justice.

The second front is in Afghanistan. The second major front in this global war against these terrorists is in Afghanistan, where we've made steady progress on the road to democracy. President Karzai got elected. There's a sitting Parliament. I mean, it's amazing how far Afghanistan has come from the days of the Taliban. General Abizaid told us in our briefing that new democracy is being increasingly defended by a capable Afghan Army and police. The Afghan National Army is now nearly 27,000 soldiers who are trained and equipped. General Abizaid tells us these soldiers are tough in battle. They want to defend their homeland. There are some 55,000 Afghan police officers on the beat. They're taking the fight to the enemy. They're working side by side with coalition forces to protect this new democracy.

They're receiving a lot of international support through the NATO Alliance. The NATO-led international security assistance force has now about 9,000 troops in the country that represents all 26 NATO Allies and 10 non-NATO nations. In other words,

the international community is stepping up. Like they have in Iraq, they're stepping up in Afghanistan as well. In 2006, the force levels will increase by up to another 6,000 forces, to a total of approximately 15,000 personnel. In other words, you're going to see in 2006 an increase of international force inside of Afghanistan.

As NATO takes on a larger role in Afghanistan and as the capability of Afghan forces continues to grow, the United States will reduce force levels in Afghanistan from 19,000 to 16,500 this year. In other words, our strategy has been to provide a strong commitment to provide stability so democracy can flourish. And then as others, including Afghan troops as well as NATO troops, step in, we step back. We're going to continue to conduct antiterrorist operations in Afghanistan as well. This is a part of a global war against the terrorist network.

I said after September the 11th we would do everything in our power to bring justice to the enemy that attacked the American people, and I meant it. And part of chasing down the Taliban and Al Qaida is to find them where they hide. And just like in Iraq, we're going to have our special forces stay on the hunt. And we'll continue training at the same time.

There's a lot of work to be done in this war on terror, but the American people can be—rest assured this administration understands the task and understands the challenges and understands our obligation to protect you, to protect the American people.

During the past year, we lost some really good folks who wore the uniform of the United States of America. We pray for their loved ones. We pray for the comfort of those who had a sorrowful holiday season because a seat at the table was empty. And we vow to those that we will complete our mission: We will lay that foundation of peace for generations to come, that we'll do our duty to protect this country by not only bringing justice to an enemy that wants to do us harm but by spreading freedom and democracy.

Thank you very much.

NOTE: The President spoke at 11:24 a.m. at the Pentagon. In his remarks, he referred to Gov. Joe Manchin III of West Virginia; Gen. John P. Abizaid, USA, commander, U.S. Central Command; Gen. George W. Casey, Jr., USA, commanding general, Multi-National Force—Iraq; Lt. Gen. Martin E. Dempsey, USA, commander, Multi-National Security Transition Command—Iraq and NATO Training Mission—Iraq; U.S. Ambassador to Iraq Zalmay Khalilzad; senior Al Qaida associate Abu Musab Al Zarqawi; Ayman Al-Zawahiri, founder of the Egyptian Islamic Jihad and senior Al Qaida associate; and President Hamid Karzai of Afghanistan. The Office of the Press Secretary also released a Spanish language transcript of these remarks.

Statement on the Health of Prime Minister Ariel Sharon of Israel
January 4, 2006

Laura and I share the concerns of the Israeli people about Prime Minister Ariel Sharon's health, and we are praying for his recovery. Prime Minister Sharon is a man of courage and peace. On behalf of all Americans, we send our best wishes and hopes to the Prime Minister and his family.

Remarks Following a Meeting With Military and Diplomatic Leaders
January 5, 2006

It's been my honor to host former Secretaries of State and Secretaries of Defense from Republican administrations and Democratic administrations here at the White House. I've asked Secretary Rice and Secretary Rumsfeld and Ambassador Khalilzad and General Casey to bring these men and women up to date on our strategy for victory in Iraq.

I've also had a chance to listen to their concerns, their suggestions about the way forward. Not everybody around this table agree with my decision to go into Iraq, and I fully understand that. But these are good, solid Americans who understand that we've got to succeed now that we're there. And I'm most grateful for the suggestions that have been given. We take to heart the advice. We appreciate your experience, and we appreciate you taking time out of your day.

We have a dual-track strategy for victory. On the one hand, we will work to have a political process that says to all Iraqis, "The future belongs to you." And on the other hand, we'll continue to work on the security situation there. The main thrust of our success will be when the Iraqis are able to take the fight to the enemy that wants to stop their democracy, and we're making darn good progress along those lines.

Again, I want to thank you all for coming. I appreciate your interests. I appreciate you being such a solid citizen of our country.

NOTE: The President spoke at 10:31 a.m. in the Roosevelt Room at the White House. In his remarks, he referred to Gen. George W. Casey, Jr., USA, commanding general, Multi-National Force—Iraq. Participating in the meeting were former Secretaries of State Colin L. Powell, Madeleine K. Albright, Lawrence S. Eagleburger, James A. Baker III, George P. Shultz, and Alexander M. Haig, Jr.; and former Secretaries of Defense William S. Cohen, William J. Perry, Frank C. Carlucci, Harold Brown, James R. Schlesinger, Melvin R. Laird, and Robert S. McNamara.

Remarks to the United States University Presidents Summit on International Education
January 5, 2006

Thank you all. Madam Secretary, it's your building; you can give my speech if you want to. [*Laughter*]

But first, our Nation sends our deepest sympathies to Ariel Sharon. He lies immobilized in an Israeli hospital. We pray for his recovery. He's a good man, a strong man, a man who cared deeply about the security of the Israeli people and a man who had a vision for peace. May God bless him.

Madam Secretary, thanks for having me. I'm here to let the good folks know here how strongly I support the National Security Language Initiative. I've had a little problem with the language in the past, so— [*laughter*]—if you've got room in the initiative for me, let me know. [*Laughter*] Condi said, "Come on by. We've got a bunch of university presidents here." And I said, "Great, just so long as we don't have to compare transcripts." [*Laughter*] She's the Ph.D.; I'm the President. [*Laughter*]

She's a heck of a Secretary of State, though, and Don Rumsfeld is a heck of a Secretary of the Defense, and I want to thank you both for joining together on this initiative. It's interesting, isn't it, that the State Department and the Defense Department are sponsoring a language initiative. It says something about the world we live in. I felt certain that the Secretary of Education would be here. After all, we're talking about education, and I want to thank you for being here, Margaret. But I also find it's interesting you're sitting next to John Negroponte, who is the Director of National Intelligence.

In other words, this initiative is a broad-gauged initiative that deals with the defense of the country, the diplomacy of the country, the intelligence to defend our country, and the education of our people. And it's an important initiative, and I'm going to tell you why in a second. But thank you for joining your—together to make this happen.

I want to thank Deputy Secretary of State Bob Zoellick, and I want to thank the chairman of the Senate Foreign Relations Committee, Senator Lugar from Indiana. Senator Pat Roberts from Kansas is with us. I think you'll find this interesting: He has promoted the advanced study of foreign languages through the Pat Roberts Intelligence Scholars Program. Thanks for doing that. And I want to thank Congressman Rush Holt for being here as well. Thank you for coming, Rush. Thanks for taking time.

I appreciate all the ambassadors who are here. I'm scanning the room. I see a few familiar faces, and thanks for serving. What the heck are you doing here? Like, you're supposed to be—[*laughter*]—the deal was overseas. [*Laughter*]

We're living in extraordinary times. I wish I could report to you the war on terror was over. It's not. There is still an enemy that lurks, that wants to hurt us.

I hate to report that to the American people, but my duty is to lay it out as plainly as I possibly can. And that's the truth.

And so the fundamental question is, how do we win? What do we do? Well, in the short term, our strategy is to find them and bring them to justice before they hurt us. In other words, we've got to stay on the offense. We've got to be unyielding and never give them a, you know, a breath of fresh air, never give them a hope that they can succeed. It's the only way to do it. We must defeat them in foreign battlefields so they don't strike us here at home.

And that's one of the reasons why the Secretary of Defense is here. He wants his young soldiers who are on the frontlines of finding these killers to be able to speak their language and be able to listen to the people in the communities in which they live. That makes sense, doesn't it, to have a language-proficient military, to have people that can go into the far reaches of this world and be able to communicate in the villages and towns and rural areas and urban centers, to protect the American people.

We need intelligence officers who, when somebody says something in Arabic or Farsi or Urdu, knows what they're talking about. That's what we need. We need diplomats—when we send them out to help us convince governments that we've got to join together and fight these terrorists who want to destroy life and promote an ideology that is so backwards it's hard to believe. These diplomats need to speak that language.

So our short-term strategy is to stay on the offense, and we've got to give our troops, our intelligence officers, our diplomats all the tools necessary to succeed. That's what people in this country expect of our Government. They expect us to be wise about how we use our resources, and a good use of resources is to promote this language initiative in K through 12, in our universities. And a good use of resources is to encourage foreign language speakers from important regions of the world to come here and teach us how to speak their language.

You're going to hear a lot about the specifics of the program. What I'm trying to suggest to you, that this program is a part of a strategic goal, and that is to protect this country in the short term and protect it in the long term by spreading freedom. We're facing an ideological struggle, and we're going to win. Our ideology is a heck of a lot more hopeful than theirs.

You can't have an ideology that works if you say to half the population in a part of the world, "You have no rights." You can't say to a group of people, "My ideology is better than freedom, and if you speak out, you're going to get—you'll be tortured."

You see, freedom is the ideology that wins. We've got to have confidence in that as we go out. But you can't win in the long run for democracy unless you've got the capacity to help spread democracy. You see, we've got to convince people of the benefits of a free society. I believe everybody desires to be free. But I also know people need to be convincing—convinced—I told you I needed to go to language school. [*Laughter*] And you can't convince people unless you can talk to them. And I'm not talking to them right now directly; I'm talking through an interpreter on some of these Arabic TV stations.

But we need people in America who can go and say to people, "Living in freedom is not the American way of life; it is a universal way of life." We're not saying your democracy has to be like yours. We're just saying give your people a chance to live in a free society, give women a chance to live freely, give young girls a chance to be educated and realize their full potential.

And the best way to do that is to have those of us who understand freedom be able to communicate in the language of the people we're trying to help. In order to convince people we care about them, we've got to understand their culture and show them we care about their culture. When somebody comes to me and speaks Texan, I know they appreciate the Texas culture. [*Laughter*] I mean, somebody takes time to figure out how to speak Arabic, it means they're interested in somebody else's culture. Learning a language—somebody else's language is a kind gesture. It's a gesture of interest. It really is a fundamental way to reach out to somebody and say, "I care about you. I want you to know that I'm interested in not only how you talk but how you live."

In order for this country to be able to convince others, people have got to be able to see our true worth in our heart. And when Americans learn to speak a language, learn to speak Arabic, those in the Arabic region will say, "Gosh, America is interested in us. They care enough to learn how we speak."

One of the great programs we've got here in America in terms of people understanding how we think and how we act is these scholarships we provide to our universities. I know this isn't the topic the Secretary assigned me to talk about, but it's one I'm going to talk about anyway. We want young kids from around the world coming to our universities. It's in our national interest that we solve visa issues and make sure that—[*applause*].

We have been calibrating the proper balance after September the 11th, and I fully understand some of your frustrations, particularly when you say the balance wasn't actually calibrated well. But we're going to get it right, because the more youngsters who come to America to get educated, the more likely it is people in the world will understand the true nature of America.

You can't figure out America when you're looking on some of these TV stations—you just can't—particularly given the message that they spread. Arabic TV does not do our country justice. They put out some kind—sometimes put out propaganda that just is—just isn't right. It isn't fair, and it doesn't give people the impression of what we're about. You bring somebody here to college—it doesn't matter what's on TV—they see firsthand the compassion of the United States of America. They get to see firsthand that we don't discriminate based upon religion. They get to see firsthand the multicultural society in which we live, all united under the fabric of freedom. That's what they get to see.

And so I'm working with Condi, and she's working with others, to work with you, to make sure these youngsters are able to come to our universities. I'll tell you what's really neat, is to sit down with leaders from around the world, welcome them in the Oval Office or go to their office; they say, "You know, Mr. President, I went to Texas A&M," or, "I went to Stanford"—like President Toledo of Peru. I mean, it is—it makes it so much easier to conduct foreign policy and diplomacy when you've got that common ground of being able to talk about a university experience here in the United States. It makes it so much easier to be able to advance the interests of this country when you're dealing with a leader who doesn't have a preconceived notion about what America is all about, because he spent time studying here in the United States.

We're going to teach our kids how to speak important languages. We'll welcome teachers here to help teach our kids how to speak languages. But we're also going to advance America's interests around the world and defeat this notion about our—you know, our bullying concept of freedom, by letting people see what we're about. Let them see firsthand the decency of this country.

And so, Madam Secretary, in front of these presidents, you and I vow that we'll find that proper balance between security and letting people come to our universities for the good of this country.

I—there is no doubt in my mind we will win the war on terror. There's no doubt in my mind that Afghanistan will remain a democracy and serve as an incredible example. For those of you in education, you might remember, this was a country that refused to educate young girls. And now, young girls in most of Afghanistan are going to school.

Iraq—we'll succeed in Iraq. It's tough. And the reason it's tough is because a handful of killers wants to stop the advance of freedom for a reason. Democracy in the heart of the Middle East is a major defeat to their ideology and their ambitions.

And it's hard work. What you're seeing on your TV screen is hard work. But we've done, as Condi said, hard work before. We have defeated fascism in the past. We defeated communism in the past. And we will defeat this ideology of hatred, but it's going to take all the tools at our disposal.

One of the stories I like to share with people is this. I—one of my best buddies in international politics is Prime Minister Koizumi of Japan. He's an interesting person. Elvis was his favorite singer, for example. [*Laughter*] Every time I meet with him, it strikes me as an amazing fact of history that number 41, President 41, at age 18 fought the Japanese, and 43, his son, is sitting down with the Prime Minister working on keeping the peace. It's amazing to me. And something happened between 41 going into combat and 43 talking to the Prime Minister, whether it be about troops in Iraq to help this young democracy flourish in the heart of the Middle East, or whether it be dealing with the leader of North Korea who is starving his people to death, and how do we solve that? What do we do about it?

And what happened was that the Japanese adopted a Japanese-style democracy.

It wasn't an American-style democracy; it was Japanese-style democracy. And that society, that form of government was able to convert an enemy to an ally. And that's what's happening. I live it when I talk to the Prime Minister. I see it firsthand. It's a real part of my family's life.

Someday, an American President is going to sit down and thank this generation for having the willpower and the determination to see to it that democracy has a chance to flourish in a part of the world that is desperate for democracy. Someday, somebody is going to say—[*applause*]—somebody someday will say, we're able to more likely keep the peace because this generation of Americans had confidence in our capacity to work with others to spread freedom.

And that's what we're facing today, and the stakes are high. It's an exciting time to be here in Washington, DC. It's a fantastic opportunity to serve our country. And I want to thank those of you who are serving it in government, and I want to thank those of you who serve it through higher education. There's no greater gift to give a child than the chance to succeed and realize his or her dreams. And you're doing that.

Appreciate you giving me a chance to come by and tell you what's on my mind. May God bless our country.

NOTE: The President spoke at 3:50 p.m. at the Department of State. In his remarks, he referred to Prime Minister Ariel Sharon of Israel; President Alejandro Toledo of Peru; Prime Minister Junichiro Koizumi of Japan; and Chairman Kim Jong Il of North Korea.

Remarks to the Economic Club of Chicago in Chicago, Illinois
January 6, 2006

Thanks for the warm welcome. It's nice to be back. Congratulations to the White Sox, all you longtime White Sox fans and you recent converts. [*Laughter*] We choppered in—the Speaker said, "There's the home of the Cubs." I said, "Well, Mr. Speaker, maybe next year." [*Laughter*]

I did come here 3 years ago, and I appreciate the chance to come back. Three years ago, I came and said that we had an economic plan to help this country move forward after the devastating attacks, that we had an idea as to how to help this economy grow. And the cornerstone of that speech was to tell Congress they needed to accelerate the tax relief we passed. And they did, and the plan is working.

We got some new numbers today to show our economy added 108,000 jobs in December, and it's added more than 400,000 jobs in the last 2 months. The unemployment rate is down to 4.9 percent. Americans are going to work. This economy is strong, and we intend to keep it that way.

I appreciate the Economic Club of Chicago inviting speakers to come and talk about economics. I appreciate you giving me a chance to come back. I want to thank Miles White.

I'm proud to be traveling with the Speaker, Denny Hastert. He's a good, solid American. And he's doing a heck of a job as the Speaker of the House of Representatives. I appreciate being here with the senior Senator from the State of Illinois, Dick Durbin. I think the chairman is here—Mr. Chairman, Henry Hyde, thank you for being here, sir.

Congressman John Shimkus is here, from the south part of your State. Thanks for coming all the way up here. Congresswoman Judy Biggert is with us. Judy, good to see you. Thanks for coming. Congressman Mark Kirk is with us. I appreciate you all. You do what the Speaker tells you to do. [*Laughter*]

I appreciate Charlie Carey; he's the chairman of the Chicago Board of Trade. I just went there. A guy yelled out, in the corn pit, "Hook 'em, Horns!" [*Laughter*] So I hooked 'em—[*laughter*]—and now I own a lot of corn. [*Laughter*]

I want to thank the members of the Chicago Board of Trade. I thank Terry Duffy, who is the chairman of the board of the Chicago Merc, where I had the honor of traveling in March of 2001. Thank you all for giving me a chance to come.

The American economy heads into 2006 with a full head of steam. Our economy grew at more than 4 percent in the third quarter. We've been growing at nearly that rate for 2 years. The American consumer is confident. More Americans now own their home than at any time in our Nation's history. Minority homeownership is at a record high. Real disposable income is up. New orders for durable goods like machinery have risen sharply. Shipments of manufactured goods are up as well. Business activity in our manufacturing sector reported its 31st straight month of growth. Our small businesses are thriving. In 2005, the American economy turned in a performance that is the envy of the industrialized world. And we did this in spite of higher oil prices and natural disasters.

We're strong, and I'm optimistic about the future of this economy. And one reason I am is because of the rise of American productivity. We're an incredibly productive nation. Our productivity has been growing at 3.5 percent for the last 5 years. American workers are now more than 17 percent more productive than they were in 2001. And why is that important? That's important because productivity means America will remain the leader in the world. Productivity is important because it helps people live a better life.

From 1973 to 1995, productivity grew at 1.4 percent per year. At that rate, it would take 50 years to double the standard of living for Americans. Our economists now project that productivity will grow by 2.6 percent over the long term. And at that rate, we can double the standard of living of Americans nearly twice as fast. And that's important. We want to be able to compete, and we want our people being able to realize their dreams. In short, we're productive, we're innovative, we're entrepreneurial, and the role of government is to keep it that way.

Our goal in Washington has got to make sure America is the leader in the world when it comes to economic vitality, the best place to realize your dream in the world. And the best way to make sure economic opportunity reaches throughout our land is to make sure that we have economic growth. My administration has pursued and we'll continue to pursue progrowth economic policy. American businesses and farmers, workers, and entrepreneurs create the wealth in this country. Government does not create wealth. The role of government is to create an environment where the entrepreneurial spirit flourishes and where small businesses can grow to be big businesses and where people can dream about owning their own home and have it become a reality. That's the role of government.

In our economy, the most precious resource is the talent and ingenuity of the American people. And there's no limit to what the American people can achieve when they have the skill sets to compete and the freedom to make a better life for themselves and their family.

Our trust in the American people has brought us through some tough times. We've been through a lot. In the past 5 years, this economy has endured a stock market collapse, a recession, terrorist at-

tacks, corporate scandals, high energy costs, and natural disasters. They're all shocks to our economy, and they deserved swift action, firm resolve, and clear thinking.

Here's how I started to address—the perspective I took when it came time to addressing these challenges. I said, "The American economy grows when the American people are allowed to keep more of their own money so they can save and they can invest and they can spend as they see fit." So I called on the Congress, as I mentioned to you earlier, to cut the taxes, and Congress responded. It's been a while since that happened. Let me review what took place. [*Laughter*]

We lowered the taxes so Americans—so American families could thrive. We cut the taxes on the families by lowering the rates and by doubling the child credit and by reducing the marriage penalty. I can't imagine a Tax Code that penalizes marriage. It seems like to me we ought to be encouraging marriage through our Tax Code.

We thought it was unfair to say to a farmer and a small-business owner, "The Government is going to tax you twice." So we put the death tax on the road to extinction. We cut the taxes, and by doing so, we helped raise after-tax income for a person by 7 percent since I've been your President. Real after-tax income per person is up by 7 percent. And that's good for our families. We want our families to have more money in their pocket.

These tax cuts make a real difference in the lives of those who work hard in this country. By cutting taxes on income, we helped create jobs. You see, when people are allowed to keep more of their own money, it means they're going to demand more goods and services. And in the marketplace, somebody will produce that—those goods and services to meet demand. And when somebody meets the increased demand in the marketplace, it's more likely somebody is going to be able to find a job. Cutting taxes helps people find a job in the United States of America.

We cut taxes on small businesses. Most small businesses pay individual income tax rates, sole proprietorship or a limited partnership or a subchapter S corporation. So when you reduce individual rates, you're really increasing the amount of capital available for small businesses to expand. And that's important because 70 percent of the new jobs in America are created by small businesses. And when you couple the tax—reduction in tax rates with incentives for small businesses to invest in new equipment, you can understand why this economy is strong. The small-business sector of the United States of America is flourishing. The entrepreneurial spirit is widespread, and more and more Americans are starting their own company.

American families have benefited from the tax cuts on dividends and capital gains. Let me repeat that. American families all across this country have benefited from the tax cuts on dividends and capital gains. Half of American households—that's more than 50 million households—now have some investment in the stock market, either by owning shares in individual companies or through owning mutual funds. By cutting the taxes on dividends and capital gains, we have boosted confidence in our economy. More people have more money to invest. As a result, the stock market has added nearly $3 trillion in value.

I'll never forget going to an automobile manufacturing plant in Mississippi. It was a very diverse group of workers. I said, "How many of you own your own 401(k)?" In other words, "How many of you have a stock portfolio?" Nearly 90 percent held their hands up. When you cut taxes on capital gains and you cut taxes on dividends, you're helping the lineworkers in the automobile plant.

Part of making sure this economy grows is to understand who owns the wealth in the United States of America, and it's becoming widespread all throughout our soci-

ety. Cutting taxes has reduced—on capital gains and dividends has reduced the cost of capital. If you want your economy to grow, you want the cost of capital down. And reducing the cost of the capital has made it easier for investment, and investment has increased the productivity of the American worker, and the productivity increases for the American worker increased the standard of living for the American worker.

There's a mindset in Washington that says, "You cut the taxes, we're going to have less money to spend." Well, the growth, the economic vitality that has been set off by the tax cuts has been good for our Treasury. Since we cut taxes on income, tax revenues from income has jumped by 17 percent. Tax revenues from dividends and capital gains has increased an estimated 50 percent. By cutting the taxes on the American people, this economy is strong, and the overall tax revenues have hit at record levels.

Now, there are a lot of people in Washington that don't believe in tax cuts. As a matter of fact, they didn't believe the tax cuts would work. Critics said our economy was the worst since the Great Depression. The truth of the matter is, by cutting taxes when we did, we've had the fastest growing economy of any major industrialized nation. Critics said the tax cuts are ruining the economy. They're just wrong. The facts say otherwise.

Since we cut the taxes, household wealth is on the rise; people are doing better; we're creating jobs. One Democratic critic described the day the House voted for tax relief this way: She said, "Today the Congress of the United States will vote on a reckless, irresponsible tax plan that will undermine opportunity in our country." Since that Congresswoman had uttered those words, the economy has added more than 4.5 million new jobs.

By letting people keep more of what they earn, this economy is strong. Unfortunately, just as we're seeing the evidence of how the tax cuts have created jobs and opportunity, some in Washington are saying we need to raise your taxes. See, that's either by saying, "We're not going to make the tax cuts permanent"—in other words, they're going to expire—or, "Why don't we repeal the tax cuts right now." When you hear somebody say, "Let's don't make the tax cuts permanent," what they're telling the American worker and the American family is, "We're going to raise taxes on you." If that were to happen, a Chicago family of four making $50,000 would see Federal income taxes go up by nearly 50 percent.

Just as this economy is getting going, there are some in Washington who want to take the money out of your pocket. They think they can spend it better than you can. To keep this economy growing, to keep the entrepreneurial spirit alive, to make sure that the United States of America is the most productive nation in the world, the United States Congress must make the tax cuts permanent.

There's been a lot of discussion about the budget in Washington; there should be. You'll hear the folks say, "Why don't we just raise the taxes to balance the budget?" Folks, that's not the way Washington works. They will raise your taxes and increase Federal spending. The best way to deal with the budget deficit is to have progrowth policies in place and be fiscally sound with taxpayers' money.

Listen, we're at war. And by the way, we're going to win the war. And so long as we've got our kids—and so long as we've got our men and women in uniform in harm's way, this Government will support them with all the resources that are necessary to win that war. That means we've got to show extra discipline in other areas of the Federal budget.

Now, our budget has two kinds of spending—it's called discretionary spending and mandatory spending. And thanks to working with the Speaker and others, we've shown real progress on being fiscally wise when it comes to discretionary spending. We've now cut the rate of growth in nonsecurity discretionary spending each year since I've been in office. Last February, my budget proposed an actual cut in nonsecurity discretionary spending. It's the most disciplined budget proposal since Ronald Reagan was the President.

We ended or reduced about 90 low-priority or poorly performing Government programs. We cut nonsecurity discretionary spending and kept overall discretionary spending growth below the rate of inflation. That's what the American people want us to do. They want us to set priorities, be wise with the money. And by doing this, we are still on track to cut the Federal deficit in half by 2009.

The bigger challenge to this budget is the long-term deficits driven by mandatory spending, or what they call entitlements. And these entitlements include Social Security and Medicare, both of which are growing faster than our ability to pay for them. The costs of these programs are growing faster than the economy. The cost of these programs are growing faster than the rate of inflation. The costs of these programs are growing faster than the population is growing. It's unsustainable growth, because a lot of people like me are getting ready to retire. [*Laughter*] In my case, I turn 60 in 2008—that's a convenient date for me—[*laughter*]—62 in 2008, 60 this year, unfortunately.

Projected deficits of these programs when these baby boomers like me retire are fixing to grow and grow and grow. And we don't have enough people paying into the system to cover them. It's what's called unfunded liabilities. And they're a problem for our children and our grandchildren, and we can solve this problem. It just takes political will, political courage. We don't need to cut the programs; we need to slow their growth. That's what we need to do.

Oh, I know some in Washington would like me to stop talking about it. I'm not going to. I believe the role of the President of the United States—[*applause*]. I believe my role, and I believe all our roles in Washington is to confront problems now and not pass them on to future Presidents and future Congresses.

Congress has an opportunity to show its commitment to controlling entitlement spending when it comes back off its recess. Before Members of the House and the Senate left Washington, they agreed to rein in future spending on entitlements by nearly $40 billion. They did this by reforming programs and eliminating waste and reducing the rate of spending growth. Now Congress needs to finish the work on this important bill. And, Mr. Speaker, I want to thank you for your leadership on this important bill.

Listen, we got a lot of people in Washington who preach fiscal discipline and then they go on to vote against spending restraint. By passing the first reduction in the growth of entitlement spending in nearly a decade, Congress can send a clear signal that the people's Representatives can be good stewards of the people's money.

As we work to keep taxes low and restrain spending, we've also got other challenges. One big challenge we face is energy. Again, I want to thank the Speaker and the Congress for putting an energy bill on my desk that I signed that encourages conservation, alternative forms of energy, encourages the exploration for natural gas in environmentally friendly ways. It's a good start. But the truth of the matter is, technology is going to lead this country away from our dependence upon hydrocarbon, and the United States Government can help speed up technology.

In order to make sure this economy grows, we've got to have a reasonable health care system. I view the role of the Federal Government is to help the elderly. And we got good Medicare reforms done. And I believe the role of the Federal Government is to help the poor. And that's why we've got Medicaid. But I do not believe the role of the Federal Government is to tell doctors how to work and patients what to do. We need to make sure we connect the doc—the patient-doctor relationship to inventive programs like health savings accounts. This Congress needs to expand health savings accounts on behalf of good health care in America.

To make sure this is the most competitive country in the world, we've got to get rid of some of these junk lawsuits that are running capital out of America. We've got a real challenge; the trial bar is tough. You need to speak up. You need to let people understand the consequences of all these lawsuits.

Now, I want to thank the Speaker again, and the Senate; we got some legal reform done. We got a good class-action piece of legislation. We got good bankruptcy law. I hope that this year, we can get a good asbestos reform out of the United States Congress. But one thing is for certain: People around this country have got to understand we need a balanced legal system if Americans want to be able to find good-paying jobs.

A growing economy means we've got to have a private pension system that is fully funded and one in which those who pay into the private pension system keep the promises they make. I'm going to talk more about these issues as the legislative session begins.

I want to talk about two things real quick to make sure that this country remains the leader in the world when it comes to economic growth, and the first is education. We've got to make sure that our citizens have the skills they need to be able to fill the jobs which will be created in the 21st century. This country has a moral and an economic obligation, a moral and an economic interest in seeing that our people have the skills they need to succeed in a competitive world. You see, if we don't make sure our people have the skills they need in a competitive world, the jobs are going to go somewhere else. And that's what we've got to understand.

Making sure that people have got a good basis of education and capacity to fill the jobs which will actually exist really, it's important, particularly given the fact that our economy is one that is so dynamic and so vibrant that people are changing jobs all the time. Do you realize that if the recent pattern continues, the typical American worker will have held at least 10 jobs between the ages of 18 and 38? This job market of ours is churning. It's creating opportunity. We've got to have the skills to be able to fill these new jobs. And that's the challenge ahead of us. And having good skills begins with making sure our children can read and write and add and subtract. The best job training program begins early in life.

We came together in Congress—with the Congress and passed what's called the No Child Left Behind Act. I'd like to remind you about the spirit and the philosophy behind that act. It basically says, "Let's raise the standards, and let's measure." And the reason the Federal Government has got a right to call for measurements is because we spend a fair amount of money from Washington, DC, at the local level. And so we simply said, "If you're taking our money"—it's actually your money—[*laughter*]—"do you mind showing us whether or not the children can read or write?" I don't think that's too much to ask, is it? Unless you believe that certain kids can't learn to read and write.

I remember when I was the Governor of Texas, I found some school systems that simply, I guess, didn't believe that certain kids could read and write, so they just shuffled them through. They said, "It's much easier than taking on the tough task of analyzing and correcting, so let's just quit. Let's just say, okay, we'll just kind of socially promote you." It makes us look good on paper, but it's not treating American families well. And it's not setting that foundation to make sure our children can get the job skills necessary to fill the jobs of—

or the skills necessary to fill the jobs of the 21st century.

And so the No Child Left Behind Act came into being. And we're now measuring, and it's beginning to work. There's an achievement gap in America that is beginning to close. You know why I know? Because we're measuring. There's what's called the NAEP test. It's a standardized test across the country. It's called the Nation's Report Card. It gives us a chance to measure. It has shown that American children have made strong gains over the last 5 years, especially in the early grades. The results have showed that our fourth and eighth graders have improved math scores for not only Anglo students but African American students and Hispanic students. As a matter of fact, the math scores were the highest ever for African American kids and Hispanic kids. Overall scores for fourth grade reading matched the alltime high.

There is an achievement gap in America that is inexcusable, and it's beginning to close. And I think one of the main reasons it's closing is because we are now measuring. We're posting scores on the Internet for people to see, and we're saying to school districts, "If you've got a problem, correct it early, before it is too late. And if you can't figure out how to correct it, give parents a different option than keeping their child in a school which will not change and will not teach."

And tell your brother, tell your brother I appreciate his understanding of the need to challenge the status quo when it's failing the kids of Chicago.

And if you hear them talking about getting rid of the accountability standards, say to the local school folks, "Don't do it." You see, we've all got to challenge the soft bigotry of low expectations. We cannot revert to a system which quits on kids too early in life. As business leaders and community activists, you must stand strong for strong accountability systems and systems which correct problems early, before it is too late.

We've got a problem in our high schools. We're beginning to make progress at the elementary school level, over the 5 years, the test scores have risen. But we've got a problem in our high schools. Our high school American students rank below students from around the world when it comes to math and science. We measure fine in junior high grades, but for some reason, between junior high and high school, our kids are falling behind. And that's a problem. If we want to be competitive and if we want our children to be able to fill the jobs of the 21st century, we must do a better job in high school.

I think one place to start is to bring the spirit of No Child Left Behind, which is K through eight, into the high schools and insist upon measuring early and to say, "If you've got a problem, develop remediation programs today." Because we just can't guess anymore in America. If we want to be competitive, we've got to know, and we've got to measure.

We've got programs to bring professionals from math and science into the classrooms as adjunct teachers. We're going to help teachers—particularly in low-income schools—have the training they need to teach advanced placement courses. What I'm telling you is, is that we're going to take that very same spirit that's beginning to work in elementary school and put it in the high schools.

And then we've got to make sure our kids go to college. And that's one of the important programs that we've worked with both Republicans and Democrats alike in Congress, to increase the number of Pell grants available for students by a million people. And that's important.

One of the real assets in our country is the community college system. I spent a lot of time going to the community college system because, as I tell people, they're available; they're affordable; and unlike some institutions of higher education, they know how to change their curriculum to meet the needs of society.

In other words, what's interesting about the community college experience is that if you're living in an area where there's a need for health care workers, and you got a chancellor of the community college system that is any good, that person will devise a program with the local health care providers that will help train nurses or whatever is needed. I mean the health care—the community college system is a fabulous job training opportunity for the American people. It's a place to find—to match people's desire to work with the jobs that actually exist.

There's an interesting story about a woman named Julie Duckwitz here in this area. She had been a bookkeeper for 11 years, and she's a single mom—which happens to be the hardest job in America, by the way—and she's laid off. And she doesn't know what to do. You can imagine being a single mother with two kids—two young kids—and you get laid off your job.

Fortunately, she went to the job training counselors, and they steered her to Lake Land community college. Lake Land had received a Federal grant to help fund training programs, and she enrolled in a nursing program. Why? Because Lake Land understood there was a need for nurses. In other words, it's a demand-driven curriculum in the community college system. And they adjusted, not just for her, but for others. And she got a nursing degree. And she said, "Now I feel I can move upward. When I lost my old job, I was as high as I could go with that position, but health care offers me many more avenues for the future."

Gaining additional education to enhance your chance to get a job means more productivity. It means you're a more productive worker, which means higher pay, which means better news for the American economy. This Government must utilize our community college system to make sure people have the skills necessary to fill the jobs of the 21st century. I'm looking forward to Congress to fully fund my request for these job training grants to the community college system of our country.

I want to tell you one other thing, and then I'll let you eat. [*Laughter*] I want to talk about trade. It's a pretty controversial subject in some people's minds. Here's how I think about it. We're home to 5 percent of the world's population. That means that 95 percent of our potential customers live abroad. I believe this country ought to do everything it can to open up markets for our products overseas. I know it's going to be necessary to make sure this economy grows, short term and long term, to open up markets for our manufacturers, our farmers, and our entrepreneurs.

I believe that trade opens up opportunities for people here at home. Now, we've got some people in Washington who are what I call economic isolationists. They have a different point of view—good people, just a different philosophy. They don't believe trade is good. They believe that it's okay to wall ourselves off from the rest of the world. I disagree strongly. And that's why my administration has pursued free trade agreements around the globe and will continue to do that.

Do you realize that more than 350,000 people in Illinois have jobs that depend on exports? In other words, there's a market overseas; somebody is meeting the demand for the product or the good and service and are manufacturing right here in Illinois, which means somebody is working out there, because there's a market overseas. One in every five manufacturing jobs in this State is supported by exports.

Look, I know the manufacturing industry got hit hard here. All I had to do is listen to the Speaker every time I met him. He said, "We got a problem. The manufacturing base of this State is getting hit hard." He said, "What are you going to do about it?" I said, one thing I'm not going to do about it is deny opportunities for those who are able to export, and second, what we're going to do about it is make sure the playing field is level, make sure our manufac-

turers are treated fairly. That's all we can expect. We don't expect any special treatment, we just want to be treated fairly.

My view of trade is this: If we can get a level playing field, American workers and farmers and entrepreneurs can compete with anybody, anytime, anywhere in the world. And now we have a chance, through the World Trade Organization, the Doha round of the World Trade Organization, to see to it that this world trades more fairly and more freely.

And that's in our interests. I'm telling you, it's in the farmers' interests that we're selling soybeans in China. It's in our interests that we have a free-trading world. If we wall ourselves off from the rest of the world, a bunch of other folks are going to take the—take advantage of the opportunity of free trade.

This is an important issue for our country. We got to be confident in our ability to compete. We'll be tough when it comes to the policy to make sure you're treated fairly, but I refuse to allow walls to shut our producers and entrepreneurs off from opportunities around the world. Free and fair trade is an important cornerstone of strong and valid economic policy for the creation of jobs here in America.

So that's what I'm going to be talking about when it comes to our economy. We're doing fine, but I believe we can do even better. The right policies out of Washington, DC—policies that encourage growth, not stifle growth, policies that encourage entrepreneurship, not diminish the entrepreneurial hopes, policies that educate our folks so we can fill the jobs of the 21st century—will keep the United States the economic leader of the world. And that's the way I want it, and that's the way you should want it, and that's the way Members of the United States Congress on both political parties should want it as well.

I can't tell you how neat it is to travel the world and represent the United States of America. Ours is a land that is so unique, if you think about our country where a person can start off with nothing except a dream, can start off with just a hope, and own something, own your own business, own an opportunity to thrive. And that's what we're about. That's what we have been about, and that's what we must remain about.

We've got to still be the greatest hope for mankind on the face of this Earth. We are today, and with the right policies, we'll be tomorrow.

Listen, thanks for letting me come back. God bless.

NOTE: The President spoke at 11:44 a.m. in the Hilton Chicago. In his remarks, he referred to Miles White, CEO, chairman of the board, and director, Abbott Laboratories.

Statement on Signing the National Defense Authorization Act for Fiscal Year 2006
January 6, 2006

Today, I have signed into law H.R. 1815, the "National Defense Authorization Act for Fiscal Year 2006." The Act authorizes funding for the defense of the United States and its interests abroad, for military construction, and for national security-related energy programs.

Several provisions of the Act, including sections 352, 360, 403, 562, 818, and 2822, call for executive branch officials to submit to the Congress proposals for legislation, including budget proposals for enactment of appropriations, or purport to regulate or require disclosure of the manner in which the President formulates recommendations to the Congress for legislation. The executive branch shall implement these provisions in a manner consistent with the President's constitutional authority to supervise the unitary executive branch and to recommend for the consideration of the Congress such measures as the President judges necessary and expedient. Also, the executive branch shall construe section 1206(d) of the Act, which purports to regulate formulation by executive branch officials of proposed programs for the President to direct, in a manner consistent with the President's constitutional authority to supervise the unitary executive branch and to require the opinions of heads of executive departments. In addition, the executive branch shall con-

strue section 1513(d) of the Act, which purports to make consultation with specified Members of Congress a precondition to the execution of the law, as calling for but not mandating such consultation, as is consistent with the Constitution's provisions concerning the separate powers of the Congress to legislate and the President to execute the laws.

A number of provisions of the Act, including sections 905, 932, 1004, 1212, 1224, 1227, and 1304, call for the executive branch to furnish information to the Congress on various subjects. The executive branch shall construe such provisions in a manner consistent with the President's constitutional authority to withhold information the disclosure of which could impair foreign relations, national security, the deliberative processes of the Executive, or the performance of the Executive's constitutional duties.

Section 1222 of the Act refers to a joint explanatory statement of a committee of conference on a bill as if the statement had the force of law. The executive branch shall construe the provision in a manner consistent with the bicameral passage and presentment requirements of the Constitution for the making of a law.

The provisions in Title XIV in Division A of the Act are identical, except for a punctuation change in section 1405(b)(1)(B) and revisions in section 1406, to the corresponding provisions in Title X of Division A of the Department of Defense, Emergency Supplemental Appropriations to Address Hurricanes in the Gulf of Mexico, and Pandemic Influenza Act, 2006 (H.R. 2863 of the 109th Congress) (Public Law 109–148). The statement I issued upon signing H.R. 2863 into law on December 30, 2005, is incorporated herein by reference insofar as that statement referred to Title X of Division A of that Act.

GEORGE W. BUSH

The White House,
January 6, 2006.

NOTE: H.R. 1815, approved January 6, was assigned Public Law No. 109–163.

Letter to Congressional Leaders Transmitting a Notice of Intention To Enter Into a Free Trade Agreement With the Republic of Peru
January 6, 2006

Dear Mr. Speaker: (Dear Mr. President:)

Consistent with section 2105(a)(1)(A) of the Trade Act of 2002, (Public Law 107–210; the "Trade Act"), I am pleased to notify the Congress of my intention to enter into a free trade agreement with the Republic of Peru.

The United States-Peru Trade Promotion Agreement will generate export opportunities for U.S. farmers, ranchers, and companies, help create jobs in the United States, and help American consumers save money while offering them more choices. The Agreement will also benefit the people of Peru by providing economic opportunity and by strengthening democracy.

Consistent with the Trade Act, I am sending this notification at least 90 days in advance of signing the Agreement. My Administration looks forward to working with the Congress in developing appropriate legislation to approve and implement this Agreement.

Sincerely,

GEORGE W. BUSH

NOTE: Identical letters were sent to J. Dennis Hastert, Speaker of the House of Representatives, and Richard B. Cheney, President of the Senate. The related notice of January 6 is listed in Appendix D at the end of this volume.

The President's Radio Address
January 7, 2006

Good morning. As we begin 2006, we are hearing more good news about the American economy. This week, we learned that our economy added 108,000 jobs in December and has added over 400,000 jobs in the last two months. Our unemployment rate is now 4.9 percent, lower than the average rate of the 1970s, 1980s, and 1990s.

Our economy grew at more than 4 percent in the third quarter of 2005, and it has been growing at nearly that rate for 2 years. Productivity is high. Consumers are confident. And more Americans now own their homes than at any time in our Nation's history.

To keep our economy strong and secure the American Dream for future generations, leaders in Washington must make sound decisions. And one of the best decisions we made since I took office was to cut your taxes so you could keep more of your hard-earned money to save and spend as you see fit. We lowered tax rates to let workers keep more of their paychecks. We doubled the child credit. We reduced the marriage penalty. We also cut taxes on dividends and capital gains, and we created incentives for small businesses to invest in new equipment so they could expand and create new jobs.

Some people in Washington said these tax cuts would hurt the economy. The day the House voted for tax relief in May 2003, one Democratic leader declared it a "reckless and irresponsible tax plan that will undermine opportunity in our country." Since those words were spoken, our economy has added more than 4.6 million new jobs for the American people.

Unfortunately, just as we're seeing new evidence of how our tax cuts have created jobs and opportunity, some people in Washington are saying we need to raise your taxes. They want the tax cuts to expire in a few years or even repeal the tax cuts now. In either case, they want you to get a big tax hike. If we allow that to happen, a family of four making $50,000 would see their Federal income taxes go up by nearly 50 percent.

Inaction by the Congress will mean a tax increase on the American people. When you hear people in Washington say, "We don't need to make the tax relief permanent," what they're really saying is they're going to raise your taxes. To keep our economy growing, we need to ensure that you keep more of what you earn, and Congress needs to make the tax cuts permanent.

Our economy is also strong because we've been wise with taxpayers' dollars. We've now cut the rate of growth in nonsecurity discretionary spending each year I've been in office. Working with Congress,

last year, we ended or reduced about 90 low-priority or poorly performing Government programs, cut nonsecurity discretionary spending, and stayed on track to meet our goal of cutting the Federal deficit in half by 2009.

The bigger challenge to our budget is long-term deficits driven by mandatory spending or entitlements. We can solve this problem. We do not need to cut entitlements, but we do need to slow their growth. When Congress returns from its recess, it has an opportunity to show its commitment to controlling entitlement spending. Before Members of the House and Senate left Washington, they agreed to rein in future spending on entitlements by nearly $40 billion. Now Congress needs to finish its work on this important bill. By passing the first reduction in the growth of entitlement spending in nearly a decade, Congress will send a clear signal that the people's Representatives can be good stewards of the people's money.

As we work to keep your taxes low and restrain Federal spending, we have other challenges to address. A growing economy requires secure and affordable sources of energy, free and fair trade, legal reform and regulatory reform, and a health care system where workers can find affordable care. And we must ensure that all Americans get a good education so they will have the skills they need for the jobs of the 21st century.

In the months ahead, we will work on all these issues. By making choices that reward hard work and enterprise, we will keep the American economy prosperous and strong and guarantee opportunity for generations to come.

Thank you for listening.

NOTE: The address was recorded at 7:58 a.m. on January 6 in the Cabinet Room at the White House for broadcast at 10:06 a.m. on January 7. The transcript was made available by the Office of the Press Secretary on January 6 but was embargoed for release until the broadcast. The Office of the Press Secretary also released a Spanish language transcript of this address.

Message on the Observance of Eid al-Adha
December 21, 2005

I send greetings to Muslims around the world as you celebrate Eid al-Adha.

When God asked Abraham to sacrifice his son, Abraham placed his faith in God above all else. During Eid al-Adha, Muslims celebrate Abraham's devotion and give thanks for God's mercy and many blessings. Eid is also a time for demonstrating charity and reaching out to family, friends, and those in need.

America is blessed to have people of many religious beliefs who contribute to the diverse makeup of this country. Through generosity, compassion, and a commitment to faith, Muslim Americans have helped make our country stronger.

Laura and I send our best wishes for a joyous celebration. Eid Mubarak.

GEORGE W. BUSH

NOTE: This message was released by the Office of the Press Secretary on January 9. An original was not available for verification of the content of this message.

Remarks to Reporters Following a Meeting With Associate Justice-Designate Samuel A. Alito, Jr.
January 9, 2006

Good morning. I just had breakfast with Judge Alito. I told him I think he conducted himself with such dignity and class in the weeks leading up to the confirmation process, which begins today.

Sam Alito is imminently qualified to be a member of the bench. I'm not the only person who feels that way. The American Bar Association looked at his record, looked at his opinions, looked at his temperament, and came to the same conclusion, that he is well-qualified to be a Supreme Court judge.

Sam's got the intellect necessary to bring a lot of class to that Court. He's got a judicial temperament necessary to make sure that the Court is a body that interprets the law and doesn't try to write the law. And so I'm looking forward to your hearings. I know the American people will be impressed, just like I have been impressed and a lot of other Members of the Senate have been impressed.

And my hope, of course, is that the American people will be impressed by the process. It's very important that Members of the Senate conduct a dignified hearing. The Supreme Court is a dignified body; Sam is a dignified person. And my hope, of course, is that the Senate bring dignity to the process, give this man a fair hearing, and an up-or-down vote on the Senate floor.

Sam, good luck to you. Thanks for your agreement to serve. I appreciate you.

NOTE: The President spoke at 7:52 a.m. in the Rose Garden at the White House. The

Office of the Press Secretary also released a Spanish language transcript of these remarks.

Remarks on the No Child Left Behind Act in Glen Burnie, Maryland
January 9, 2006

Thank you all. Please be seated. Thanks for the warm introduction. It's great to be here with Laura. She is a fantastic mom. She understands something that's very interesting: All education begins at home. I can remember her reading to our little girls all the time. Occasionally, I did, too, but stumbled over a few of the words and might have confused them. [*Laughter*] Laura cares deeply about education, as do I.

Thank you all for coming. We're here at North Glen Elementary School because it is a center of educational excellence. That's why we're here. We're here to herald success. We're here to say—[*applause*].

It so happens this is the fourth anniversary of when I signed the No Child Left Behind Act. I think the No Child Left Behind Act is one of the most significant accomplishments in education in a long, long time. I want to thank both the Republicans and Democrats who worked together back then to get this piece of legislation passed. It is a really important piece of legislation that is working. And I'm here today to talk about the spirit of the No Child Left Behind Act, the evidence that says it's working, and my deep desire to work with Congress to make sure it continues to have the desired effect on children all across the country.

First, I want to welcome our Secretary of Education, Margaret Spellings. I've known her for a long time. She is a dear friend of mine who also happens to be a significant warrior when it comes to leaving no children behind in our society. She believes that I believe—like I believe, that

every single child can learn, and we've got to make sure that every child does learn. I want to thank you for your leadership, Margaret. You're doing a heck of a job as the Secretary of Education.

I want to thank the first lady, as well, for being here—Kendel, thanks for coming. Tell that old husband of yours, it's okay to sleep in occasionally. [*Laughter*]

Dutch, I want to thank you for being here—Congressman Ruppersberger's district—real proud you took time out of your life to be here. Thanks for coming. I also want to thank Congressman Wayne Gilchrest for being here as well. Wayne, appreciate you taking time.

I want to thank all the local and State officials who've joined us. I want to thank Nancy Mann, the superintendent of schools for this school district. Julie, thank you—the principal, Julie Little-McVearry, who is the—listen, let me say something—and by the way, Maurine Larkin, who is the former principal here.

One of the things that's interesting, that when you look at public schools, when you find centers of excellence, you always find a principal that is capable of setting high standards, working with teachers, demanding results and following through to make sure that the schools achieve the results. Every school requires a dedicated educational entrepreneur, someone willing to challenge the status quo if there's failure and being imaginative about how to achieve results. And you've got such principals here. Again, I want to congratulate Julie and Maurine for leading this school. You've done a heck of a job, and we're proud— we're proud to honor you.

We went to Laneie Taylor's fifth grade class. I see that they're here. Laneie, thank you—second-year teacher. Listen, schools succeed because they've got teachers that care. And I want to thank all the teachers who are here.

One of my predecessors as the Governor of Texas was Sam Houston. You may have heard of him, may not have heard of him— [*laughter*]—interesting old guy. He was the President of the Republic of Texas. He was a United States Senator. He was a Congressman from Tennessee. He was the Governor of Texas. He had done a lot of things. He led the battle of San Jacinto. I mean, he was a heck of a guy. They asked him, "Of all the things you've done in your life, what is the most important job?" He said, "Teacher." And so, all the teachers here, thanks for teaching. It is really an important job, and we appreciate your dedication in the classroom.

And to the parents of the students who come here, thanks for caring. Schools that succeed have got parents who are involved at the school. And so, whatever is working here in terms of parental involvement is— needs to be duplicated around this State and around the country, because parental involvement is a very important part of the success of schools around America.

So the No Child Left Behind Act—we got here to Washington, and I decided to make sure that the public school system in America met the promise of—and the hopes of our country. I understand how important it is to have a public school system work really well. A vibrant America is one in which the public schools provide a avenue for success. And it's really important we have a good public school system. It's been important in the past that the public school system function well, and it's going to be really important in the future.

Secondly, we have a moral obligation to make sure every child gets a good education. That's how I—it's a moral obligation to make sure that we herald success and challenge failure. It's not right to have a system that quits on kids. I mean, some schools may not think they're quitting on kids, but when you shuffle kids through the schools without determining whether or not they can read and write and add and subtract, I view that as quitting on kids. I called it the soft bigotry of low expectations. In other words, you believe certain children can't learn, so, therefore, just move them through. It's kind of a process world, isn't it? It's more important that somebody be shuffled through than it is to determine whether or not they're capable of meeting certain standards in certain grades.

And it troubled me to realize that in my own State of Texas, as well as other States, there wasn't that sense of urgency; there wasn't that sense of focus on results. It was kind of a process world we lived in. And we were beginning to realize that as a result of a process world, the kids were coming out of the school system that were—who were illiterate. And it wasn't right. It was morally wrong, in my judgment, not to challenge a system that wasn't achieving great national goals such as an illiterate—a literate workforce. See, we live in a competitive world. And we'd better make sure our—the future of this country has the got the capacity to compete in that world.

And the best place to start is to make sure every child can read and write and add and subtract. And so that was the spirit behind proposing the No Child Left Behind Act. And as I mentioned, there was a lot of nonpartisan cooperation, kind of a rare thing in Washington. But it made sense when it come to public schools.

The No Child Left Behind Act embodied these principles: First, there is a role for the Federal Government, a funding role. In other words, the Federal Government has committed and should be committed to helping Title I students, for example.

As a matter of fact, Title I program spending has increased 45 percent since 2001. There is what's called the elementary and secondary school program; that's up by 41 percent. In other words, there is a Federal dollar commitment, certainly not as big as the State government or as local government, nor should it be. I don't think you want the Federal Government funding all public schools. But I do think you want the Federal Government focusing money on certain aspects of public education.

I also believe that sometimes you can have so many goals there are no goals. In other words, there's just this kind of long list of goals, and so nothing gets accomplished. I'm the kind of person that believes that we ought to set specific goals, and one of the most specific goals we've set is that every child should be reading at grade level by the 3d grade and remain at grade level. That's a clear goal; it's easy to understand, there's no ambiguity with it. It says every child—not just some children, every child—ought to be reading at grade level by the 3d grade—no doubt— it's not the 2d or 10th; it's 3d—and remain there.

And so we back that goal up. And by the way, it's the understanding that if you can't figure out—if you can't read, you can't do math or science. Reading is the gateway to educational excellence. That's why I asked the kids in your classroom whether or not they read more than they watched TV. I was pleased to see a lot of hands went up. It's kind of a hard question to ask in this day and age, isn't it, particularly since we've got too many TV channels to begin with. [*Laughter*]

And so we quadrupled the amount of money available for what's called the Reading First Program. In other words, we set the goal, and the Federal Government has provided the money for certain parts of the education system around the country. We're not going to fund it all, but we're going to make targeted funding. And it's a good use of money, in my judgment.

On the other hand, it seems like to me if we're going to spend money, we ought to be asking the question, is it—are we getting the results for the money? In other words, once there's a commitment, a logical followup to that commitment is, why don't you show us whether or not we're meeting goals? So, in other words, let's measure, finally. And so the No Child Left Behind Act has said that in return for Federal money, we'll test 3 through 8. Children will be tested grades 3 through 8.

And why do we do that? Well, one is to figure out whether or not kids are learning. It's an interesting way to determine whether or not the curriculum you're using works. I remember when I was the Governor of Texas, there was a lot of debate about different types of curriculum, different ways to teach reading. You might remember those debates. They were full of all kinds of politics. The best way to cut through the political debate is to measure. The best way to say, the program I'm using is working, is because you're able to measure to determine whether or not it's working. That's what this school has done. They said, "We welcome accountability, because we believe our teachers are great, and the system we use can work."

Another reason to measure is so that the parents stay involved. You know, there's a lot of anecdotal evidence about parents believing that the school their kids go to is doing just fine. That's what you would hope if you were a parent. I mean, it's a natural inclination to say, "Gosh, my kid goes to a really good school. I like the principal. I like the teachers." But sure enough, in some cases, the performance might not have been up to par.

And so making sure there's an accountability system that the parents get to see is one that says to a parent, you know, if things aren't going so well, get involved with the school and help. Or if things are going well, make sure you thank the teachers. Make sure you take time out of your day to thank the person whose soul is invested in the future of your child. It's like the teachers right here in this school have invested their time and efforts to make sure the children learn to read. I bet there's nothing better than a teacher to have a thankful parent come up and say, "Thank you for making sure my daughter or my son has got the capacity to be able to succeed in this great country."

Measurement also is a way to let schools understand how they're doing relative to other schools, or school districts to see how they're doing relative to other school districts. In other words, if you're living in the school district here, and one school like this was doing fine, another one is not, it should provide an opportunity for the principal of that school or the parents of that school to say, "Wait a minute. Look at this school over here; it's doing fine. How come we're not?" You can't solve a problem until you diagnose it, is what I'm telling you. And our accountability system helps us all diagnose problems and solve them early, before it's too late.

One of the interesting parts of the No Child Left Behind Act was what's called supplemental service money. I don't know if you've used it here or not—bet you have to a certain extent. It basically says, if a child is falling behind, here is extra money from the Federal Government to help you catch up. If a child needs help in reading, we've diagnosed a problem early and said, let's make sure this child is not left behind. That's what it says.

This is a bill that says, in return for Federal money, we're going to measure; we'll adjust. We'll change to achieve the most important objective of all, to make sure every single child in America can read by the third grade and stay at grade level, that children can read and write and add and subtract.

Listen, I've been through this debate about testing. Again, I remember when I was the Governor of Texas, there was a lot of people saying, "How can you be for testing?" My answer is, how can you not be for testing? They said it was discriminatory to test. I said it's discriminatory not to test. If you can't know what a child—whether a child can read and write, how can you solve the problem? I've heard people say, "Oh, all you're doing is teaching to test." My answer is, if you teach a child how to read, they will pass the test. Accountability is crucial, in my judgment, for making sure the public school system meets the important goals of our society.

Having said all that, an important part of the No Child Left Behind Act is the understanding that one size does not fit all when it comes to public schools, and that the governance ought to be local. If you've noticed, I've never said the Federal Government is going to tell you how to teach. That would be the worst thing that could happen to the public school system. The worst possible thing is, we're sending you money and now we're going to tell you how to use it and how to teach and what curriculum to use. That's the opposite of the spirit of the No Child Left Behind Act. The No Child Left Behind Act understands there needs to be flexibility and local control of schools.

We did not design a Federal test. There was great pressure to say, let's have a Federal test. All that would mean, that once you have a Federal test, it could lead to local prescriptions for that test. We said the States ought to develop their own accountability systems, and that local people ought to have input into the design of the State at the—of local accountability systems. And so for those of you who think, well, the Federal Government has reached too far into the governance issue, it's just not true. It's not the case. As a matter of fact, quite the contrary; it makes sure that there was local control of schools. It made sure that the State had the option and opportunity to say to the local superintendent and principals, "Design your program that works. You're closest to the people; you listen to the parents; you see the issues firsthand in the neighborhood in which you live. Come up with a curriculum that meets your own needs."

The system is working. That's what's important for people to understand. And by the way, any attempt to roll back the accountability in Washington, DC, will be—I'll fight any attempt to do that. I'm just not going to let it happen. We're making too much progress. There's an achievement gap in America that's closing. We don't need achievement gaps in this country. It's not good for us to have achievement gaps where certain kids can read in fourth grade better than others. One of our goals has got to be to achieve that—close that achievement gap. And we're doing it. How do we know? Because we're measuring.

There's what they called the Nation's Report Card; it's the National Assessment of Educational Progress, NAEP. It's a way to kind of norm testing scores across States without having a national test. It's a way to determine whether or not the great State of Maryland is doing okay relative to your neighboring States, for example. It's a way for us to kind of get a glimpse about whether or not we're making progress toward achieving certain goals. In 2005, America's fourth graders posted the best scores in reading and math in the history of the test. That's positive. Ever since the test has been issued, 2005 was the best scores. If we didn't test, by the way, you could never say—I could never stand up and say this. I'd just be guessing, wouldn't I? It could be that we're doing fine—maybe not, maybe so.

African American fourth graders set records in reading and math in 2005. Hispanic fourth graders set records in reading and math. That's really good. It's important for our country that all children from all walks of life have the ability to realize the great promise of the country. The NAEP also showed that eighth graders earned the best math scores ever recorded; eighth grade Hispanic and African American stu-

dents achieved the highest math scores ever.

As I said, there's an achievement gap—we know because we measure—and it's closing, and that's positive. And our goal has got to be to continue to work to make sure there is no achievement gap in America.

Now, let me talk about North Glen Elementary School. I don't know if you—those of you interested in this school have paid attention to these results, but I would like to share some—[*applause*]—if I might, I'd like to share some statistics with you, and perhaps this will give you an indication about why Laura and I came here.

In 2003, 50 percent—57 percent of North Glen students scored proficient in reading—57 percent—and 46 percent were proficient in math. Now, that's unacceptable. Fifty-seven percent is a lousy number. Forty-six percent, obviously, is even worse. But it was unacceptable to the principals and the superintendent and the teachers, that's most important. And so they got after it, and they figured out how to make sure that goals were met.

I didn't spend a lot of time talking today to the principal about the different analysis that went on, but I bet it was pretty indepth. But one thing for certain is, the test in '03 said we better do something different. When we find out something is going right, let's stay on it, and if something is going wrong, let's change. That's what happened here, because guess what: In 2005, 82 percent of North Glen students were ranked proficient in reading, and 84 percent were ranked proficient in math.

It's great news, isn't it? It's a system that says, why don't we show everybody whether or not we can succeed. And if we're not, we'll change; and if we are, we now have a chance to have the old President come by and say thanks, you know. [*Laughter*]

Interestingly enough, in 2003, 45 percent of the African American students in this school rated proficient in reading; in 2005, 84 percent are proficient. In other words, this is a school that believes every child can learn. Not just certain children, every child. And then they work to see to it that it happens. This—the statistics I just announced—oh, by the way, in 2003, 35 percent of African American students rated proficient in math. You've got to know math if you're going to compete in this 21st century world. It's really important that math and science become a focal point of our high schools, for example. But it's not going to work if kids coming out of elementary school can't do math. Thirty-five percent of the African American students rated proficient in math; now it's 82 percent. It's a good score.

This is a fine school. We're here to herald excellence. We're here to praise the law that is working. I'm here to thank the teachers not only here but around the State of Maryland and around the country who are dedicating their lives to providing hope for our future. I want to thank the Members of Congress for working together on this vital piece of legislation, a piece of legislation that's laying the cornerstone for a hopeful tomorrow.

Laura and I's spirits are uplifted any time we go to a school that's working, because we understand the importance of public education in the future of our country. We also believe, strongly believe, that every child can learn, and with the right focus and right energy, every child will learn. And as every child learns, the future of this country will never have been brighter.

Thanks for a job well done. God bless the teachers here and the principal. God bless the parents. And may God bless the students as well. Thank you.

NOTE: The President spoke at 10:26 a.m. at North Glen Elementary School. In his remarks, he referred to Kendel S. Ehrlich, wife of Gov. Robert L. Ehrlich, Jr., of Maryland. The transcript released by the Office of the Press Secretary also included the remarks of the First Lady. The Office of the Press Secretary also released a Spanish language transcript of these remarks.

Remarks to the Veterans of Foreign Wars
January 10, 2006

Thank you all. Please be seated. Thanks for the warm welcome. It is an honor to stand with the men and women of the Veterans of Foreign Wars again. This is one of America's great organizations. I appreciate the proud and patriotic work you do across America. Thanks for your hard work in our Nation's Capital to make sure our Government listens to the concerns of our veterans.

Your members include veterans who served in World War II—I just happened to spend Christmas with one of your members—[*laughter*]—the Korean war, the Vietnam war, the Persian Gulf war, Panama, Bosnia, Kosovo, and many other operations. In the past 4 years, you've welcomed into your ranks new veterans who have defended liberty in places like Afghanistan and Iraq as a part of the global war on terror. No matter where you deployed or which century you wore the uniform, each of you stepped forward when America needed you most. And these days, first days of the year 2006, a grateful nation says, thank you for your service and the great example you set for today's men and women who wear the uniform.

I want to thank the commander in chief of the VFW, Jim Mueller. I had the honor of welcoming him to the Oval Office the other day, where we discussed issues important to our Nation's veterans and issues important to our Nation's security. He's a clear thinker. He's a patriot. I appreciate the invitation, Jim.

I'm also proud to be joined today by the Secretary of State, Condi Rice, the Secretary of the Department of Veterans Affairs, Jim Nicholson, Mr. Secretary.

Two Members of the United States Congress, one Republican and one Democrat, have joined us. [*Laughter*] Americans' quest for freedom and peace is a bipartisan quest, and I'm honored that Senator Pat Roberts is with us and Congressman Adam Schiff. Thank you both for coming.

Lieutenant General Bob Shea of the Joint Chiefs is with us today. As is my friend Lieutenant General Danny James, who was the Texas Adjutant General when I had the honor of being the commander in chief of the Texas Guard. [*Laughter*] Good to see you, Danny.

To all those who wear the uniform who are here, I particularly want to pay my respects to those wounded soldiers from Walter Reed. Thanks for serving. I'm proud you're here. And I want to report to our fellow citizens that we've got a fantastic health care system for those who wear the uniform. Any man or woman wounded in combat is removed immediately from the battlefield into the best possible care. I want to thank those at Walter Reed, those healers and helpers—not only at Walter Reed but at Bethesda and Brooke's, where I recently went—for the great compassion and great skill that they show in helping those who have been wounded on the battlefield. May God bless you all.

As veterans and soon-to-be veterans, you have placed the Nation's security before your own lives. You took an oath to defend our flag and our freedom, and you kept that oath underseas and under fire. All of us who live in liberty live in your debt, and we must never forget the sacrifice and the service of our veterans.

A new generation of Americans is carrying on your legacy, defending our Nation in another great struggle for freedom, the global war on terror. This war began with a sudden attack on September the 11th, 2001. That morning we saw the destruction our enemies intend for us, and we accepted new responsibilities. Like generations before us, we're taking the fight to those who attacked us and those who share their murderous vision for future attacks. Like generations before us, we have faced setbacks on the path to victory, yet we will fight this war with resolve and without wavering. And like generations before us, we will prevail.

Like earlier struggles for freedom, the war on terror is being fought on many battlefronts. Yet the terrorists have made it clear that Iraq is the central front in their war against humanity. And so we must recognize Iraq as the central front in the war against the terrorists.

Our goal in Iraq is victory. And in a series of speeches last December, I described the enemy we face in that country, our strategy to defeat them, and how we have adapted our tactics to meet changing conditions on the ground. Today I've come before you to discuss what the American people can expect to see in Iraq in the year ahead. We will see more tough fighting, and we will see more sacrifice in 2006 because the enemies of freedom in Iraq continue to sow violence and destruction. We'll also see more progress toward victory. Victory will come when the terrorists and Saddamists can no longer threaten Iraq's democracy. Victory will come when the Iraqi security forces can provide for the safety of their own citizens. Victory will come when Iraq is not a safe haven for terrorists to plot new attacks on our Nation.

And when victory comes and democracy takes hold in Iraq, it will serve as a model for freedom in the broader Middle East. History has shown that free nations are peaceful nations. And by helping Iraqis build a lasting democracy, we spread the hope of liberty across a troubled region. We will gain new allies in the cause of freedom. By spreading democracy and freedom, we're laying the foundation of peace for generations to come.

Our work in Iraq in 2006 will be focused on three critical areas. On the political side, we will help Iraqis consolidate the democratic gains they made last year and help them build democratic institutions, a unified government, and a lasting, free society. On the security side, we will stay on the offense against the terrorists and Saddamists. We will continue to strengthen the Iraqi security forces, with an emphasis on improving the capabilities of the Iraqi police, so that over the next 12 months, Iraqi forces can take control of more territory from our coalition and take the lead in the fight. And on the economic side, we will continue reconstruction efforts and help Iraq's new Government implement difficult reforms that are necessary to build a modern economy and a better life.

In all three aspects of our strategy—democracy and security and reconstruction—we're learning from our experiences, and we're fixing what hasn't worked. And in the year ahead, we will continue to make changes that will help us complete the mission and achieve the victory we all want.

On the political side, we've witnessed a transformation in Iraq over the past 12 months that is virtually without precedent. Think back to a year ago. At this time last year, the Iraqi people had an appointed government, no elected legislature, no permanent constitution, and no recent experience with free national elections. Just one year later, they have completed three successful nationwide elections.

Iraqis voted for a transitional government, drafted the most progressive, democratic Constitution in the Arab world, approved that Constitution in a national referendum, and elected a new Government under their new Constitution. Each successive election has seen less violence, bigger turnouts, and broader participation than the one before. One Iraqi voter in Tall 'Afar described the December elections this way:

"We want democracy. This is our answer to the decades of slavery we had before."

When the final election results come in, Iraqi leaders will begin working to form a new Government. And in the weeks ahead, Americans will likely see a good deal of political turmoil in Iraq as different factions and leaders compete for position and jockey for power. Our top commander in the region, General John Abizaid, has said he expects the coming weeks to produce "some of the hardest, bare-knuckle politics ever in the Arab world." We should welcome this for what it is: freedom in action.

Dictatorships seem orderly—when one man makes all the decisions, there is no need for negotiation or compromise. Democracies are sometimes messy and seemingly chaotic, as different parties advance competing agendas and seek their share of political power. We've seen this throughout our own history. We've seen this in other democracies around the world. Yet out of the turmoil in Iraq, a free government will emerge that represents the will of the Iraqi people, instead of the will of one cruel dictator.

Iraqis are undertaking this process with just a year's experience in democratic politics, and the legacy of three decades under one of the world's most brutal tyrannies still hangs over them. Many of the institutions and traditions we take for granted in America—from our party structures to our centuries' experience with peaceful transitions of power—are new to Iraq. So we shouldn't be surprised if Iraqis make some mistakes and face setbacks in their effort to build a Government that unites the Iraqi people.

Despite the obstacles they face, Iraqis have shown they can come together for the sake of national unity. Think about what happened after the January 2005 elections: Shi'a and Kurdish leaders who did well at the polls reached out to Sunni Arabs who failed to participate, giving them posts in the Government and a role in fashioning the new Constitution. Now Iraqis must reach out once again across political and religious and sectarian lines and form a Government of national unity that gives voice to all Iraqis.

Because Sunni Arabs participated in large numbers in the December elections, they will now have a bigger role in the new Parliament and more influence in Iraq's new Government. It's important that Sunnis who abandoned violence to join the political process now see the benefits of peaceful participation. Sunnis need to learn how to use their influence constructively in a democratic system to benefit their community and the country at large. And Shi'a and Kurds need to understand that successful free societies protect the rights of a minority against the tyranny of the majority.

The promise of democracy begins with free elections and majority rule, but it is fulfilled by minority rights and equal justice and an inclusive society in which every person belongs. A country that divides into factions and dwells on old grievances cannot move forward and risks sliding back into tyranny. Compromise and consensus and power sharing are the only path to national unity and lasting democracy. And ultimately, the success of Iraqi democracy will come when political divisions in Iraq are driven not by sectarian rivalries but by ideas and convictions and a common vision for the future.

When the new Iraqi Government assumes office, Iraq's new leaders will face some tough decisions on issues such as security and reconstruction and economic reform. Iraqi leaders will also have to review and possibly amend the Constitution to ensure that this historic document earns the broad support of all Iraqi communities. If the new Parliament approves amendments, these changes will be once again taken to the Iraqi people for their approval in a referendum before the end of the year. By taking these steps, Iraqi leaders will bring their nation together behind a strong democracy and help defeat the terrorists and the Saddamists.

America and our coalition partners will stand with the Iraqi people during this period of transition. We will continue helping Iraqis build an impartial system of justice so they can replace the rule of fear with the rule of law. We'll help Iraqi leaders combat corruption by strengthening Iraq's Commission on Public Integrity so Iraqis can build a transparent, accountable government. And we will help Iraq's new leaders earn the confidence of their citizens by helping them build effective government ministries.

It's especially important in the early months after Iraq's new Government takes hold, that its leaders demonstrate an ability to deliver measurable progress in the lives of the Iraqi people. So we will continue helping the new Government to develop their ministries to ensure they can lead effectively and produce real results for the Iraqi people.

The foreign terrorists and Saddamists will continue to fight this progress by targeting the citizens and institutions and infrastructure of a free Iraq. An enemy that sends suicide bombers to kill mourners at a funeral procession is an enemy without conscience. These killers will stop at nothing to undermine the new Government, divide the Iraqi people, and try to break their will. Yet with the recent elections, the enemies of a free Iraq have suffered a real defeat. The Saddamists and rejectionists are finding themselves increasingly marginalized, as Sunni Arabs who once rejected the political process are now participating in the democratic life of their country.

And as democracy takes hold in Iraq, the terrorists like Zarqawi and his Al Qaida associates are suffering major defeats. Zarqawi tried to stop the elections throughout the year 2005, and he failed. He tried to stop the writing and ratification of a new Constitution, and he failed. The advance of freedom is destroying his and Al

Qaida's greatest myth. These terrorists are not fighting on behalf of the Iraqi people against a foreign occupation; they are fighting the will of the Iraqi people expressed in free elections.

In the face of these thugs and terrorists and assassins, the Iraqi people have sent a clear message to the world: Iraqis will not cower before the killers, and the terrorists and regime loyalists are no match for the millions of Iraqis determined to live in liberty.

As we help Iraqis strengthen their new Government, we're also helping them to defend their young democracy. We're going to train the security forces of a free Iraq. We have been doing so, and we will continue to do so in 2006. Last November, I described many of the changes we made over the past year to improve the training of the Iraqi Army and the police. And we saw the fruits of those changes during the December elections. Iraqi forces took the lead in the election security. They were in the lead; we were there to help. They protected over 6,000 polling centers. They disrupted attacks, and they maintained order across the country.

Thanks in large part to their courage and skill, the number of attacks during the elections declined dramatically compared with last January's vote. One Iraqi general put it this way on election day: "All the time and money you have spent in training the Iraqi Army, you harvest it today."

The Iraqi security forces are growing in strength and in size, and they're earning the trust and confidence of the Iraqi people. And as Iraqis see their own countrymen defending them against the terrorists and Saddamists, they're beginning to step forward with needed intelligence. General Casey reports that the number of tips from Iraqis has grown from 400 in the month of March 2005 to over 4,700 last month and that some of the new intelligence is being passed by Iraqi civilians directly to Iraqi soldiers and police. Iraqis are gaining confidence that their security forces can defeat the enemy, and that confidence is producing the intelligence that is helping to turn the tide in freedom's way.

There's more work to be done in the year ahead. Our commanders tell me that the Iraqi Army and police are increasingly able to take the lead in the fight. Yet the Iraqi police still lag behind the army in training and capabilities. And so one of our major goals in 2006 is to accelerate the training of the Iraqi police. We'll focus our efforts on improving the performance of three categories of the Iraqi police. First, we will work to improve the Special Police under the Ministry of the Interior, who are fighting alongside the Iraqi Army against the terrorists and Saddamists. Second, we will expand and strengthen the border police charged with securing Iraq's frontiers. And third, we will increase our focus on training local station police, so they can protect their communities from the criminals and the terrorists.

The Interior Ministry's Special Police are the most capable of Iraq police forces. There are now about 19,000 Iraqi Special Police trained and equipped, which is near our goal for a complete force. Many of these Special Police forces are professional; they represent all aspects of society. But recently, some have been accused of committing abuses against Iraqi civilians. That's unacceptable. That's unacceptable to the United States Government; it's unacceptable to the Iraqi Government as well. And Iraqi leaders are committed to stopping these abuses. We must ensure that the police understand that their mission is to serve the cause of a free Iraq, not to address old grievances by taking justice into their own hands.

To stop abuses and increase the professionalism of all the Iraqi Special Police units, we're making several adjustments in the way these forces are trained. We're working with the Iraqi Government to increase the training Iraqi Special Police receive in human rights and the rule of law. We're establishing a new Police Ethics and

Leadership Institute in Baghdad that will help train Iraqi officers in the role of the police in a democratic system and establish clear lesson plans in professional ethics for all nine Iraqi police academies. To improve their capability, we will soon begin implementing a program that has been effective with the Iraqi Army, and that is partnering U.S. battalions with Iraqi Special Police battalions. These U.S. forces will work with and train their Iraqi counterparts, helping them become more capable and professional, so they can serve and protect all Iraqi's without discrimination.

Second, we're working to increase the number of border police that can defend Iraq's frontiers and stop foreign terrorists from crossing into that country. Iraqis now have about 18,000 border police on the job, manning land and sea and airports across the country. Our goal is to have a total of 28,000 Iraqi border police trained and equipped by the end of this year.

To better train Iraqi police, we've established a new customs academy in Basra. We're embedding border police transition teams with Iraqi units, made up of coalition soldiers and assisted by experts from our Department of Homeland Security. The Iraqi border police are growing increasingly capable and are taking on more responsibility. In November, these forces took the lead in protecting Iraq's Syrian border, with coalition forces playing a supporting role. In other words, they're beginning to take the lead and take responsibility for doing their duty to protect the new democracy. And as more skilled border police come on line, we're going to hand over primary responsibility for all of Iraq's borders to Iraqi border police later on this year.

Finally, we're helping Iraqis build the numbers and capabilities of the local station police. These are the Iraqi police forces that need the most work. There are now over 80,000 local police officers across Iraq, a little more than halfway toward our goal of 135,000. To improve the capabilities of these local police, we're taking a concept

that worked well in the Balkans and applying it to Iraq: partnering local Iraqi police stations with teams of U.S. military police and international police liaison officers, including retired U.S. police officers.

These officers will work with provincial police chiefs across Iraq and focus on improving local police forces in nine key cities that have seen intense fighting with the terrorists. By strengthening local police in these cities, we can help Iraqis provide security in areas cleared of enemy forces and make it harder for these thugs to return. By strengthening local police in these cities, we'll help them earn the confidence of the local population, which will make it easier for local leaders and residents to accelerate reconstruction and rebuild their lives.

The training of the Iraqi police is an enormous task, and frankly, it hasn't always gone smoothly. Yet we're making progress, and our soldiers see the transformation up close. Army Staff Sergeant Daniel MacDonald is a Philadelphia cop who helped train Iraqi police officers in Baghdad. He says this of his Iraqi comrades: "From where they were when we got here to where they are now, it's like two different groups of people. They're hyped-up; they look sharp; they're a lot better with their weapons. I'd take these guys out with me back home." If he's going to take them back home in Philadelphia, they must be improving. [*Laughter*]

As we bring more Iraqi police and soldiers on line in the months ahead, we will increasingly shift our focus from generating new Iraqi forces to preparing Iraqis to take primary responsibility for the security of their own country. At this moment, more than 35 Iraqi battalions have assumed control of their own areas of responsibility, including nearly half of the Baghdad province and sectors of south-central Iraq, southeast Iraq, western Iraq, and north-central Iraq. And in the year ahead, we will continue handing more territory to Iraqi forces, with the goal of having the Iraqis in control of more territory than the coalition by the end of 2006.

As Iraqi forces take more responsibility, this will free up coalition forces to conduct specialized operations against the most dangerous terrorists like Zarqawi and his associates so we can defeat the terrorists in Iraq, so we do not have to face them here at home. We will continue to hand over territory to the Iraqis so they can defend their democracy, so they can do the hard work, and our troops will be able to come home with the honor they have earned.

I've said that our strategy in Iraq can be summed up this way: As the Iraqis stand up, we will stand down. And with more Iraqi forces demonstrating the capabilities needed to achieve victory, our commanders on the ground have determined that we can decrease our combat forces in Iraq from 17 to 15 brigades by the spring of 2006. That's what they've decided. And when they decide something, I listen to them. This adjustment will result in a net decrease of several thousand troops below the preelection baseline of 138,000 U.S. troops in Iraq. This decrease comes in addition to the reduction of about 20,000 troops who were in Iraq largely to assist with the security during the December elections.

Later this year, if Iraqis continue to make progress on the security and political sides, we expect to discuss further possible adjustments with the leaders of Iraq's new Government. Having said this, all of my decisions will be based on conditions on the ground, not artificial timetables set by Washington politicians. Our commanders on the ground will have the forces they need to complete the mission and achieve victory in Iraq.

As we help Iraqis defend their democracy, we will continue to help Iraqis build their infrastructure and economy in the coming year. Iraqis face real challenges from the long-term economic damage caused by Saddam Hussein's regime. They face challenges because of acts of sabotage

by the enemies of a free Iraq. Yet despite these challenges, our coalition and Iraqi leaders have made progress in a number of areas: Iraq now has a stable currency, an independent stock exchange, an independent Central Bank. Iraqis have new investment laws to welcome foreign capital, tax and commercial laws to encourage private sector growth, and low-tariff trade regime that has opened Iraq's economy to the world. Under Saddam, private property was not protected. Today, Iraq's new Constitution guarantees private property rights that are the foundation of any free society.

Iraqi leaders are also beginning to make the tough choices necessary to reform their economy, such as easing gasoline subsidies. Until recently, Government subsidies put the price of fuel in Iraq at artificially low prices, really low prices. And that created incentives for black-market corruption and crime, and changing these subsidies is a necessary step on the path for economic reform. So Iraqi leaders have begun a series of price increases aimed at dismantling the gas subsidy system. That's hard political work. But gasoline subsidies, along with other subsidies, consume over half of Iraq's annual budget; it diverts critical resources from health care and education and infrastructure and security. Addressing these subsidies will allow Iraqi leaders to better provide for their people and build a modern economy.

One of the biggest challenges facing Iraq is restoring the country's oil and electric power infrastructure. These sectors were devastated by decades of neglect. And since liberation, terrorists have targeted these areas for destruction. As a result, oil and power production are below prewar levels. To help increase production, we're helping Iraqis better maintain their refineries, build their oil supply and transportation capabilities, improve their capacity to generate power, and better protect their strategic infrastructure.

The struggles with oil production and the shortage of electricity remain sources of frustration for the Iraqi citizens. Yet they're putting these challenges in perspective. Today, 7 in 10 Iraqis say their lives are going well. Nearly two-thirds expect things to improve even more in the next year. The vast majority of Iraqis prefer freedom with intermittent power to life in permanent darkness of tyranny and terror. Iraqis are optimistic about the future, and their optimism is justified.

To realize their dreams, the Iraqi people still need help. And in the coming year, the international community must step up and do its part. So far, other nations and international organizations have pledged more than $13 billion in assistance to Iraq. Iraqis are grateful for this promised aid, so is the United States. Yet many nations have been slow to make good on their commitments.

I call on all governments that have pledged assistance to follow through with their promises as quickly as possible, so the Iraqis can rebuild their country and provide a better future for their children. Many nations have still not returned all Iraqi assets frozen during the regime of Saddam Hussein. I call on all nations to return these assets to their rightful owners. The free people of Iraq own those assets, not the foreign governments.

Many of the world's smallest nations have been among the most generous. Last month, for example, Slovakia announced its plans to forgive 100 percent of Iraq's $145 million debt. This makes Slovakia only the third country, along with the United States and Malta, to write off Iraqi debt completely. More nations should do the same so the Iraq people are not held back by the crushing burden of debt accumulated by Saddam Hussein.

International lending institutions are also stepping forward with needed assistance. Last month, the International Monetary Fund approved Iraq's request for a $680 million loan to carry out economic reforms. The World Bank recently approved its first loan to Iraq in over 30 years, lending the Iraqi Government $100 million to improve the Iraqi school system and making up to $400 million available to fund water, electricity, roads, and sanitation projects.

The international community must meet its responsibilities in Iraq, and here in America, we have responsibilities as well. The coming year will test the character of our country and the will of our citizens. We have a strategy for victory, but to achieve that victory, we must have the determination to see this strategy through. The enemy in Iraq knows they cannot defeat us on the battlefield, and so they're trying to shake our will with acts of violence and force us to retreat. That means that our resolve in 2006 must stay strong. We must have the patience as Iraqis struggle to build democracy in a volatile region of the world. We must not allow the images of destruction to discourage us or obscure the real progress that our troops are making in Iraq. And we must continue to provide these troops with all the resources they need to defend our Nation and prevail in the global war on terror.

We face an added challenge in the months ahead. The campaign season will soon be upon us, and that means our Nation must carry on this war in an election year. There is a vigorous debate about the war in Iraq today, and we should not fear the debate. It's one of the great strengths of our democracy, that we can discuss our differences openly and honestly, even in times of war. Yet we must remember there is a difference between responsible and irresponsible debate, and it's even more important to conduct this debate responsibly when American troops are risking their lives overseas.

The American people know the difference between responsible and irresponsible debate when they see it. They know the difference between honest critics who question the way the war is being prosecuted and partisan critics who claim that we acted in Iraq because of oil or because of Israel or because we misled the American people. And they know the difference between a loyal opposition that points out what is wrong and defeatists who refuse to see that anything is right.

When our soldiers hear politicians in Washington question the mission they are risking their lives to accomplish, it hurts their morale. In a time of war, we have a responsibility to show that whatever our political differences at home, our Nation is united and determined to prevail. And we have a responsibility to our men and women in uniform, who deserve to know that once our politicians vote to send them into harm's way, our support will be with them in good days and in bad days, and we will settle for nothing less than complete victory.

We also have an opportunity this year to show the Iraqi people what responsible debate in democracy looks like. In a free society, there is only one check on political speech, and that's the judgment of the people. So I ask all Americans to hold their elected leaders to account and demand a debate that brings credit to our democracy, not comfort to our adversaries.

Support for the mission in Iraq should not be a partisan matter. VFW members come from all across the country and both sides of the political aisle, yet your position on the war is clear. In a recent resolution, the VFW declared, quote, "It is critical that the United States succeed in Iraq, which will result in stability and security in the region." I appreciate your support for the

mission in Iraq, and so do our troops in the fight. Your lives of service, from the first time you put on the uniform to this day, are a credit to our country and an inspiration to our military. A new generation of soldiers and sailors, airmen, marines, and coastguardsmen is now carrying out an urgent and noble mission, and they're doing so with the same determination and courage as you who came before them.

Some of our finest men and women have given their lives in freedom's cause. Others have returned home with wounds that the best medicine cannot heal. We hold all who sacrificed and their families in our thoughts and our prayers. And I'm going to make you this pledge: We will not waver, we will not weaken, and we will not back down in the cause they served. By their sacrifice, we are laying the foundation of freedom in a troubled part of the world. And by laying that foundation, we're laying the foundation of peace for generations to come.

Thank you for letting me come by today. God bless.

NOTE: The President spoke at 10:17 a.m. at the Omni Shoreham Hotel. In his remarks, he referred to Gen. John P. Abizaid, USA, commander, U.S. Central Command; former President Saddam Hussein of Iraq; and Gen. George W. Casey, Jr., USA, commanding general, Multi-National Force—Iraq. The Office of the Press Secretary also released a Spanish language transcript of these remarks.

Remarks on Signing the Trafficking Victims Protection Reauthorization Act of 2005
January 10, 2006

Thank you all. Please be seated. Thanks for coming. I appreciate you all being here. In a moment, I'll have the honor of signing

the Trafficking Victims Protection Reauthorization Act.

Human trafficking is an offense against human dignity, a crime in which human beings, many of them teenagers and young children, are bought and sold and often sexually abused by violent criminals. Our Nation is determined to fight and end this modern form of slavery. And this bipartisan bill will help expand our efforts to combat this brutal crime that steals innocence and destroys lives.

I want to thank the Members of the United States Congress who have joined me here. I appreciate Senator Sam Brownback, Chris Smith, Deborah Pryce, and Carolyn Maloney for their hard work on this important legislation.

I appreciate the Secretary of State, who has joined us here, and the Attorney General, Al Gonzales, and his wife.

In today's world, too often, human traffickers abuse the trust of children and expose them to the worst of life at a young age. It takes a perverse form of evil to exploit and hurt those vulnerable members of society. Human traffickers operate with greed and without conscience, treating their victims as nothing more than goods and commodities for sale to the highest bidder. Recent years, hundreds of thousands of people around the world have been trafficked against their will across international boundaries, and many have been forced into sexual servitude. Thousands of teenagers and young girls are trafficked into the United States every year. They're held hostage. They're forced to submit to unspeakable evil. America has a particular duty to fight this horror, because human trafficking is an affront to the defining promise of our country.

We're attacking this problem aggressively. Over the past 4 years, the Department of Homeland Security has taken new measures to protect children from sexual predators, as well as pornography and prostitution rings. The Department of Health and Human Services has partnered with faith-based and community organizations to form antitrafficking coalitions in 17 major cities across our country. The Department of Justice has more than tripled the number of cases brought against these traffickers.

The bill I sign today will help us to continue to investigate and prosecute traffickers and provide new grants to State and local law enforcement. Yet, we cannot put the criminals out of business until we also confront the problem of demand. Those who pay for the chance to sexually abuse children and teenage girls must be held to account. So we'll investigate and prosecute the customers, the unscrupulous adults who prey on the young and the innocent.

We also have a duty to reach out to victims of trafficking, some of whom were smuggled into this country as children. The legislation I sign today will help us provide important new services to these victims, including appointing a guardian for young victims and providing access to residential treatment facilities to help victims get a chance at a better life.

We'll continue to call on other nations to take action against trafficking within their own borders. Three years ago at the United Nations, I asked other governments to pass laws making human trafficking a crime. Since then, many have risen to the challenge. Secretary Rice and I will continue to press the others to rise to the challenge. We are working with the nations of Southeast Asia and others to crack down on sex tourism. America is a compassionate and decent nation, and we will not tolerate an industry that preys on the young and the vulnerable. The trade in human beings continues in our time, and we are called by conscience and compassion to bring this cruel practice to an end.

For those of you who've worked on this bill, thank you very much. For those of you who are involved in this important struggle, I appreciate your efforts, continue to do so. For those of you who are providing the compassionate care to those who've been affected by human trafficking, thank you for your love. And for those of you in Congress who've worked to make this reality, good work.

NOTE: The President spoke at 1:33 p.m. in Room 350 of the Dwight D. Eisenhower Executive Office Building. In his remarks, he referred to Rebecca Turner Gonzales, wife of Attorney General Alberto R. Gonzales. H.R. 972, approved January 10, was assigned Public Law No. 109–164.

Statement on Signing the Trafficking Victims Protection Reauthorization Act of 2005
January 10, 2006

Today, I have signed into law H.R. 972, the "Trafficking Victims Protection Reauthorization Act of 2005." This Act enhances our ability to combat trafficking in persons by extending and improving prosecutorial and diplomatic tools, and also adds new protections for victims.

Section 104(e)(2) purports to require the Secretary of State, prior to voting for a new or reauthorized peacekeeping mission under the auspices of a multilateral organization (or, in an emergency, as far in advance as is practicable), to submit to the Congress a specific report. The executive branch shall construe this reporting requirement in a manner consistent with the President's constitutional authority as Commander in Chief and the President's constitutional authority to conduct the Nation's foreign affairs.

GEORGE W. BUSH

The White House,
January 10, 2006.

NOTE: H.R. 972, approved January 10, was assigned Public Law No. 109–164.

Letter to Congressional Leaders on Continuation of the National Emergency Relating to Cuba and of the Emergency Authority Relating to the Regulation of the Anchorage and Movement of Vessels
January 10, 2006

Dear Mr. Speaker: (Dear Mr. President:)

Section 202(d) of the National Emergencies Act (50 U.S.C. 1622(d)) provides for the automatic termination of a national emergency unless, prior to the anniversary date of its declaration, the President publishes in the *Federal Register* and transmits to the Congress a notice stating that the emergency is to continue in effect beyond the anniversary date. In accordance with this provision, I have sent to the *Federal Register* for publication the enclosed notice, which states that the emergency declared with respect to the Government of Cuba's destruction of two unarmed U.S.-registered civilian aircraft in international airspace north of Cuba on February 24, 1996, as amended and expanded on February 26, 2004, is to continue in effect beyond March 1, 2006.

Sincerely,

GEORGE W. BUSH

NOTE: Identical letters were sent to J. Dennis Hastert, Speaker of the House of Representatives, and Richard B. Cheney, President of the Senate. This letter was released by the Office of the Press Secretary on January 11. The notice is listed in Appendix D at the end of this volume.

Remarks on the War on Terror and a Question-and-Answer Session in Louisville, Kentucky
January 11, 2006

The President. Thank you all. Please sit down. I think I will. Bad view. [*Laughter*] Thanks for having me. What I thought I'd do is maybe make some opening comments and answer any questions you got. I probably can't stay here all day, since I've got a job to do, but I'm interested in your opinions and your point of view.

I hope the questions are broader than the war on terror; if you want, you can ask me anything you want. We got an economy that's going good, and perhaps you want to know what we're going to do to keep it growing. You know, we got a health care system that needs reform. We got an energy problem in the United States. I mean, there's a lot of issues that I'd be more than happy to talk about.

I do want to talk about how to secure this country and keep the peace. Before I do, I want to thank Joe. He stole my line "Reagan-Bush"—[*laughter*]. It was going to work just fine, until he took it. [*Laughter*] But thank you for setting this up. Thanks a lot for the sponsors. I appreciate you all taking time out of your day, and I appreciate your interest.

Before I begin, I do want to say I married well. I'm sorry the First Lady isn't with me. She is a heck of a person. I love her dearly, and she sends her very best to our friends here in Louisville, Kentucky.

I thank the Governor for being here and the Lieutenant Governor. And I want to thank your mayor. The mayor showed me a pair of cufflinks that my dad gave him when he was the President and the mayor was the mayor. [*Laughter*] It looks like the mayor is going to outlast both Bushes. [*Laughter*]

I also want to thank Congresswoman Anne Northup. I call her a friend because she is one. She brings a lot of dignity to the halls of the United States Congress. I'm sure there are some folks here who don't necessarily agree with the party she's picked, and that's okay. But one thing you've got to agree with is she's honest; she's capable; and she's a decent, honorable soul. And I appreciate you. I want to thank Ron Lewis. He's a Congressman from Kentucky as well. And you let somebody slide across the border in Congressman Mike Sodrel. I appreciate both the Congressmen being here as well. I'm looking forward to working with you in the year 2006. We've got a lot to do.

Let me—I wish I didn't have to say this, but we're still at war, and that's important for the citizens of this Commonwealth to understand. You know, no President ever wants to be President during war. But this war came to us, not as a result of actions we took; it came to us as a result of actions an enemy took on September the 11th, 2001. And I vowed that day, starting when I was in Florida and got on the airplane to head across the country, that I would use everything in my power—obviously, within the Constitution—but everything in my power to protect the American people. That is the most solemn duty of Government, is to protect our people from harm.

And I vowed that we'd find those killers and bring them to justice, and that's what we're doing. We're on the hunt for an enemy that still lurks. I know because I'm briefed on a daily basis about the threats that face the United States of America. And my duty is to assess this world the way it is, not the way we'd like it to be. And there's a danger that lurks—and there's a danger that lurks because we face an enemy which cannot stand freedom. It's an enemy which has an ideology that does not believe in free speech, free religion, free dissent, does not believe in women's rights, and they have a desire to impose their ideology on much of the world.

Secondly, after September the 11th, not only did I vow to use our assets to protect the people by staying on the offense, by defeating an enemy elsewhere so we don't have to face them here at home, I also said that, "If you harbor a terrorist, if you provide safe haven to a terrorist, you're equally as guilty as the terrorist." And I meant it. And the Taliban in Afghanistan— a barbaric group of individuals who suppressed women, suppressed religious freedom, suppressed young girls—had harbored these terrorists. They provided safe haven. These folks were there plotting and planning a vicious attack against the United States of America in a safe haven called Afghanistan.

And so we took action. We took action because the Taliban refused to expel Al Qaida. And we took action because when an American President says something, he better mean it. In order to be able to keep the peace, in order to be able to have credibility in this world, when we speak, we better mean what we say, and I meant what we said. And we sent some brave souls into Afghanistan to liberate that country from the Taliban.

I also said, after September the 11th, that oceans no longer protected us. You know, when I was growing up, or other baby boomers here were growing up, we felt safe because we had these vast oceans that could protect us from harm's way. September the 11th changed all that. And so I vowed that we would take threats seriously. If we saw a threat, we would take threats seriously before they fully materialized, and I saw a threat in Saddam Hussein.

I understand that the intelligence didn't turn out the way a lot of the world thought it would be. And that was disappointing, and we've done something about it. We've reformed our intelligence services. But Saddam Hussein was a sworn enemy of the United States. He was on the nations-that-sponsor-terror list for a reason. I didn't put him on the list; previous Presidents put him on the list. And the reason why is because he was sponsoring terrorism. He was shooting at our airplanes. He had attacked his own people with chemical weapons. I mean, the guy was a threat.

I went to the United Nations; some of you were probably concerned here in Kentucky that it seemed like the President was spending a little too much time in the United Nations. But I felt it was important to say to the world that this international body that we want to be effective, spoke loud and clear not once, but 15-odd times to Saddam Hussein—said, "Disarm. Get rid of your weapons. Don't be the threat that you are, or face serious consequences." That's what the international body said. And my view is, is that in order for the world to be effective, when it says something, it must mean it.

We gave the opportunity to Saddam Hussein to open his country up. It was his choice. He chose war, and he got war. And he's not in power, and the world is better off for it.

The hardest decision I made as your President is to put troops into harm's way, because I understand the consequences. I see the consequences when I go to the hospitals. I see the consequences when I try to comfort the loved ones who have lost a son or a daughter in combat. I understand that full—firsthand: War is brutal.

And so I didn't take the decision lightly. Now that I've made the decision, we must succeed in Iraq. I've tried to explain to my fellow citizens, I can understand folks who said, "I wish you hadn't done that. We don't agree with your decision." Now that we're there, in my humble opinion, we have got to succeed.

I said I'd try to be short and answer your questions. I'm getting a little windy. [*Laughter*] But let me talk real quick about the goals in Iraq. The goal is victory, nothing short of victory. When you put these kids in harm's way, we owe them the best equipment, the best training, and a strategy for victory. And victory is a country that— where the Saddamists and the terrorists can't unwind the democracy. Victory is when Iraq is no longer a safe haven for the terrorists. Victory is—will be achieved when the Iraqis are able to defend their democracy.

In the last couple of weeks, I've been talking about the strategy to achieve victory. It's one thing to say we want victory; the other thing is, can you get there? And the answer is, absolutely, we can get there. And the strategy is threefold. One, there's a political strategy. First, let me make sure you understand the enemy. The enemy is, in our judgment, my judgment, three types of people. One, we call them rejectionists; these are Sunnis who had privileged status under Saddam Hussein, even though they were in the minority in the country. They had a pretty good deal because the tyrant was a Sunni and made sure that the Sunnis got special treatment, as opposed to the Shi'a or the Kurds. And they liked that kind of special treatment. They liked privileged status.

The second group is the Saddam loyalists. These are the thugs and people that basically robbed the country blind, and not only had privileged status but they were the all-powerful. And needless to say, they don't like it with their man sitting in prison and them no longer being able to exploit the people of Iraq. They're irritated.

Finally, the third group, and this is a dangerous group; it's Al Qaida and its affiliates. A guy named Zarqawi is the chief operating officer in Iraq on behalf of Al Qaida. Al Qaida has made it very clear their intentions in Iraq, which is to drive the United States out so they will have a base from which to operate to spread their ideology. That's what they have said. This is what Mr. Zawahiri said. It's important for those of us involved in trying to protect you to take the enemy seriously, to listen to their words closely. In other words, Al Qaida has made Iraq a front in the war on terror, and that's why we've developed a strategy for victory.

The first part of it is to have a political process that marginalizes the rejectionists and isolates the dissenters. And it's happening. Under any objective measurement, what took place last year in Iraq was remarkable, when you think about it. This country is a country that lived under the brutal dictatorship of Saddam Hussein, and last year they had elections for a transitional government. They wrote a Constitution and got the Constitution approved, and then had elections for a permanent Government under the new Constitution, all in one year. And every election had more participants. And most importantly, in the last election, the rejectionists who had sat out the first couple of elections—many Sunnis had sat out; they said, "We're not going to be involved in the political process"— got involved. Slowly but surely, those who were trying to stop the advance of democracy are becoming marginalized.

Secondly, this is a country, obviously, that has got brutal action; this enemy we face has got no conscience. They will kill innocent people in a heartbeat in order to achieve their objectives. And it's hard for Americans to deal with that. I understand that. It's hard for me to believe that there is such brutality in the world where people going to a funeral to mourn the dead, and a suicider shows up and kills people. It's hard for me to believe that we've got soldiers passing out candy to young kids, and a killer comes and kills the kids and the soldiers. It is beyond the imagination of most Americans, but it should say something about this enemy. They will go to no ends to defeat us, but they can't beat us on the battlefield. The only thing they can do is create these brutal scenes.

And they're trying to drive us out of Iraq, as I mentioned. And the best way to deal with them is train Iraqis so they can deal with them. And that's what's happening. There are two aspects of our training. And, listen, the training hasn't gone smoothly all the time. I mean, this is a war. And you're constantly adjusting your strategies and tactics—not strategies—tactics on the ground to meet an enemy which is changing.

And so the army is getting on its feet. We've turned over a lot of territory to the army. And they're good fighters; they really are. I spent a great deal of time with General Abizaid and General Casey; they were in Washington this past week. These are generals, you'd be happy to hear, who tell me the way it is, not the way they think I would like it to be. I can't tell you how good the caliber of our military brass and those in the field, by the way, all the way up and down the line, are good; they are good people. [*Inaudible*]—better trained, not just numbers. I'm talking about capacity to take the fight and stay in the fight. And as I've said, as the Iraqis stand up, we'll stand down. So the strategy, the security strategy is to let the Iraqis do the fighting. It's their country. The people have shown they want democracy; millions voted. And now part of the mission is to give this Government a security force which will help fight off the few who are trying to stop the hopes of the many.

One of the places where we've lagged is training police. There are three types of police. There's a national police force, kind of like a SWAT team, a national SWAT team, that can move; they're pretty well trained. They need some human rights training. In other words, part of the problem in Iraq is you've got people that are plenty irritated at what took place in the past, and they're going to use their positions of power to take revenge. You can't have a democracy in which the police don't enforce the rule of law but enforce their view of revenge. And so you got ethics training, rule of law training, all done by good troops who are embedded, who are side by side with this Iraqi police force. And it's getting better; it really is.

Secondly, you've got the Border Patrol. The reason why the border is necessary is because there's suiciders coming in from Syria into Iraq. And the Iraqis have got to be able to enforce their border in order to be able to protect their democracy.

And thirdly, you've got local police, and we're lagging in the local police. And the local police, it's just that, local. And so what we're going to do is use what worked in the Balkans and embed people in the local police units to teach them how to—effective enforcements of the law. And so, 2006 you're going to see a lot of police training and a lot of police focus.

Finally, there's the economic and reconstruction front. We started up grand projects in Iraq when we first got there, said we're going to build some grand projects. It turns out, a more effective use of reconstruction money was localized projects to empower those who were willing to take a risk for democracy with the capacity to say, "Follow me, your life is going to be better." By the way, democracy works in Iraq just like it does here; you're going to vote for somebody who thinks that they can bring character to the office and they're going to help your life. Same anywhere else. You're out there campaigning. They want to know, "What are you going to do for me?" And so part of the reconstruction effort was to focus on local reconstruction projects.

The Iraqi economy has got a great chance to succeed. They got oil and gas revenues. They had been having trouble getting some oil and gas revenues up to the levels we anticipated because of the infrastructure damage—done by Saddam Hussein, by the way—and because the terrorists, every time there's some progress, tend to blow things up. Now, having said that, they got these surveys—and I must confess I'm not much of a survey guy, but they got them—and most Iraqis are optimistic about the future. And as I said yesterday, they're willing to live with intermittent darkness, as opposed to the darkness—and freedom—as opposed to the darkness of tyranny. That's what you're seeing.

But this economy is going. Small businesses are flourishing. They got a—they had to deal with gasoline subsidies. Saddam Hussein, in order to make sure people kept him around and thought he was all right—they didn't have much choice, by the way, because he had a force behind him—but, nevertheless, he subsidized gasoline, which meant a lot of the central budget was going for subsidization of fuel, as opposed to education and health. And so the new Government made a difficult decision; they started floating that price of gasoline up a little higher, to take the pressure off their budget and to introduce markets, market-based forces into the economy.

It's not going to happen overnight. You can't go from a tightly controlled economy to an open market overnight, but it's happening. In other words, the Government is making difficult choices to help the entrepreneurial spirit begin to flourish.

And so things are good. I'm confident we'll succeed. And it's tough, though. The enemy has got one weapon, I repeat to you, and that's to shake our will. I just want to tell you, whether you agree with me or not, they're not going to shake my will. We're doing the right thing.

A couple of quick points, then I'll answer your questions. You hear a lot of talk about troop levels. I'd just like to give you my thinking on troop levels. I know a lot of people want our troops to come home. I do too. But I don't want us to come home

without achieving the victory. I mentioned to you—[*applause*]—we owe that to the mothers and fathers and husbands and wives who have lost a loved one. That's what I feel. I feel strongly that we cannot let the sacrifice—we can't let their sacrifice go in vain.

Secondly, I—these troop levels will be decided by our commanders. If you run a business, you know what I'm talking about when I say it's called delegating. You count on people to give you good advice. The best people to give any politician advice about whether or not we're achieving a military objective is the people you put out there on the ground. I told you I've got good confidence in these generals and the people who report to them. These are honest, honorable, decent, very capable, smart people, and they'll decide the troop levels. They hear from me: Victory. And I say to them, "What do you need to achieve victory?"

I don't know if you've noticed recently, but we're beginning to reduce presence in Iraq based upon the recommendation of our commanders. We've gone from 17 to 15 battalions. We kept up to about 60,000—160,000 troops in Iraq for the elections. We held over about 25,000 or so on a—that were to rotate out—to help in the elections. Those 25,000 are coming back, plus the reduced battalions. And people say, "Well, how about more for the rest of the year?" And the answer to that is, I'm going to do what they tell me to do. And that depends upon the capacity of the Iraqis to help us achieve victory.

And why is victory important? Let me just conclude by this point. You know, it's hard for some to—in our country to connect the rise of democracy with peace. This is an ideological struggle, as far as I'm concerned, and you defeat an ideology of darkness with an ideology of light and hope. History has proven that democracies yield the peace. If you really look at some of the past struggles where—in which the

United States has been involved, the ultimate outcome, the final product, was peace based upon freedom. Europe is whole, free, and at peace because of democracy.

One of the examples I like to share with people in order to make the connection between that which we're doing in Iraq today, and laying—what I call, laying the foundation of peace, is my relationship with Prime Minister Koizumi of Japan. And the reason I like to bring up this story is I find it amazing that my dad, old number 41, at the age of 18, fought the Japanese. They were the sworn enemy of the United States. Many in this audience, I know, had relatives in that war. They were the bitter enemy. They had attacked us, just like we were attacked on September the 11th. People in America said, "We'll do everything we can to defeat this enemy," and thousands of people lost their lives.

Laura and I were over in the Far East recently. I was sitting down at the table with the Prime Minister of our former enemy talking about how to keep the peace. We were talking about the spread of democracy in Iraq and in the Middle East as a way to counter an ideology that is backwards and hateful. We were talking about North Korea, how to keep the peace on the Korean Peninsula.

Isn't it amazing—at least it is to me—that some 60 years after an 18-year-old fighter pilot joined the Navy to fight the Japanese, his son is talking with the Prime Minister of the former enemy about keeping the peace. Something happened. And what happened was, Japan adopted a Japanese-style democracy. Democracies yield the peace. And I firmly believe, I firmly believe that years from now people are going to look back and say, "Thank goodness the new generation of Americans who rose to the challenge of a war against terror had faith in the capacity of freedom to help change the world." And someday, an American President is going to be talking to a duly elected leader from Iraq, talking about how to keep the peace for a generation to come.

I want to thank you all. That is the definition of a short speech. [*Laughter*] Probably hate to hear a long one. [*Laughter*] All right, I'll answer some questions. Start us off.

Progress in the War on Terror/Democracy

Mr. Joe Reagan. Mr. President, thank you very much. As I told you, we'd like to have some tough and challenging questions——

The President. ——Washington, DC, press conference?

Mr. Reagan. I thought you'd be at home here with that. We do want to keep these questions respectful, and we really do thank you for making the time to share this dialog with us; we really do.

You've talked a lot about history. In your State of the Union after September 11th, you defined this war as a war on terror. In history, our parents' generations had V–E Day and V–J Day. And in our time, we've seen the fall of the Berlin Wall and the end of the cold war. If you define this as a war on terror, will there ever be a V–T Day? And, if not, what do you need to do to prepare us to be able to go the duration?

The President. I also said that this is a different kind of war, the kind of war we've never faced before. We're not facing a nation-state per se; we're facing a shadowy network of people bound together by a common ideology that—by the way, the enemy knows no rules of war. They just—they kill innocent people.

And so, you're right, I did say it's a war. It's the first war of the 21st century, but I've been emphasizing it's a different kind of war. So I don't envision a signing ceremony on the USS *Missouri*. As a matter of fact, this is a war in which the enemy is going to have to be defeated by a competing system in the long run.

The short-term objective is to use our intelligence and our allies to hunt these people down. And we're getting—we're doing it. And we're on the—we got brave, brave souls, who, every single day, are trying to find the Al Qaida leadership and the network. We're doing—we've done a good job so far. If Usama bin Laden were the top guy, and Mr. Zawahiri—he was the person that put out the strategy, by the way, for Al Qaida, for everybody to see. I don't think he put it out for everybody to see. It just happened to be exposed for everybody to see eventually. But Abu Zubaydah, Khalid Sheikh Mohammed—there's a series of chief operators who are no longer a threat to the United States. I mean, we are dismantling the operators. And when we find them, we bring them to justice as quickly as we can.

That's the short-term strategy. There's also the strategy of making it clear, if you harbor a terrorist—the short-term strategy of dealing with threats before they come to hurt us—I say, before they fully materialize. One of the lessons of September the 11th is, when you see a threat out there, you can't assume that it's not going to come to our shore anymore. And so we've got to deal with it.

Obviously, the best way to deal with these kinds of threats is diplomatically. We're doing so in Iran. If somebody has got a question on Iran, I'll be glad to answer it in a minute. But that's what we're trying to get done. The military option is always the last option. The long-term victory will come by defeating the hopelessness and despair that these killers exploit with a system that is open and hopeful, and the only such system is a free system.

And I have got faith in the capacity of people to self-govern. Now, there is a point of view in this world by some that say, "Well, maybe certain kind of people can't self-govern"—which, by the way, was the attitude of some right after World War II—"The enemy can't possibly self-govern." The attitude was somewhat blinded by the fact that we were so angry at the Japanese

that no one could see a hopeful tomorrow for them.

I believe everybody desires to be free. That's what I believe, and I believe everybody has the capacity to self-govern. I'm not—never have I said nor do I believe that we are trying to impose our style of democracy on another country. It won't work. Each country has got its own cultures and own history and own tradition, and they ought to have their own style of democracy. But I do know that tyrants breed resentment and hatred. And I do know that if a person is—if they want to be free and not allowed to express their belief, it causes resentment, the breeding grounds for a terrorist movement which exploits the unsettled attitudes of the people.

So, in other words, it's not going to be that kind of—it's not the kind of war that you talked about earlier, and so the peace won't be the kind of peace that we're used to.

Thank you. Good question. Okay.

Terrorist Surveillance Program/PATRIOT Act

Q. I'd like to ask, recently in the media, you've been catching a lot of flak about that National Security Agency thing.

The President. Yes.

Q. There's people in our States and there's people that are in DC that will take and jeopardize what I feel is our national security and our troops' safety today for partisan advantage, for political advantage. They're starting an investigation in the Justice Department about the—looking into this, where these leaks came from. Is the Justice Department going to follow through and, if necessary, go after the media to take and get the answers and to shut these leaks up?

The President. First, let me talk about the issue you brought up, and it's a very serious issue. I did say to the National—it's called the NSA, National Security Agency, that they should protect America by taking the phone numbers of known Al

Qaida and/or affiliates and find out why they're making phone calls into the United States, and vice versa. And I did so because the enemy still wants to hurt us. And it seems like to me that if somebody is talking to Al Qaida, we want to know why.

Now, I—look, I understand people's concerns about Government eavesdropping, and I share those concerns as well. So obviously, I had to make the difficult decision between balancing civil liberties and, on a limited basis—and I mean limited basis— try to find out the intention of the enemy. In order to safeguard the civil liberties of the people, we have this program fully scrutinized on a regular basis. It's been authorized, reauthorized many times. We got lawyers looking at it from different branches of Government.

We have briefed the leadership of the United States Congress, both Republican and Democrat, as well as the leaders of the intelligence committees, both Republicans and Democrats, about the nature of this program. We gave them a chance to express their disapproval or approval of a limited program taking known Al Qaida numbers—numbers from known Al Qaida people—and just trying to find out why the phone calls are being made.

I can understand concerns about this program. Before I went forward, I wanted to make sure I had all the legal authority necessary to make this decision as your President. We are a rule—a country of law. We have a Constitution, which guides the sharing of power. And I take that—I put that hand on the Bible, and I meant it when I said I'm going to uphold the Constitution. I also mean it when I'm going to protect the American people.

I have the right as the Commander in Chief in a time of war to take action necessary to protect the American people. And secondly, the Congress, in the authorization, basically said the President ought to— in authorization of the use of troops—ought

to protect us. Well, one way to protect us is to understand the nature of the enemy. Part of being able to deal with this kind of enemy in a different kind of war is to understand why they're making decisions they're making inside our country.

So I want to thank you for bringing that up. There will be a lot of hearings and talk about that, but that's good for democracy, just so long as the hearings, as they explore whether or not I have the prerogative to make the decision I made, doesn't tell the enemy what we're doing. See, that's the danger.

The PATRIOT Act is up for renewal. That's another piece of legislation which is important to protect. Do you realize that the PATRIOT Act has given our FBI and intelligence services the same tools of sharing information that we have given to people that are fighting drug lords? In other words, much of the authorities that we ask for in the PATRIOT Act to be able to fight and win the war on terror has already been in practice when it comes to dealing with drug lords. And I can't tell you how important it is to reauthorize the legislation.

There's a lot of investigation, you're right, in Washington, which is okay. That's part of holding people to account in a democracy. But at one point in time the Government got accused of not connecting the dots. You might remember that debate; we didn't connect the dots. And all of a sudden, we start connecting the dots through the PATRIOT Act and the NSA decision, and we're being criticized. Now, you know, I got the message early: Why don't you connect dots? And we're going to. And we're going to safeguard the civil liberties of the people. That's what you've got to know.

That was a great question, thank you for asking it. I'm going to avoid the part on the press. [*Laughter*]

Threat of Terrorism/Separation of Church and State

Q. Mr. President, we hear a common expert opinion all the time that the terrorists are going to attack us; it's not a question of whether, it's a question of when. And, yes, that might happen. But the facts are that since 9/11, we haven't had any, so thank you.

And now to my question. You have said many a time to all those who will listen that the two major pillars of democracy are free and fair elections and the separation of church and state. However, historically and to date, a vast majority of the Islamists across nations do not believe in that simple fact of separation between church and state. Therefore, how can we help change their belief, that for democracy to succeed, certain elements must be in place? Thank you.

The President. It's a great question. First, let me say that the enemy hasn't attacked us, but they attacked others. Since September the 11th, there have been multiple attacks around the world. These guys are active. You might remember Beslan, an attack on Russian schoolchildren, just killed them coldblooded. I remember going to the G–8, and there were the attacks in London. You know, there's—are they Al Qaida, not Al Qaida? These are people that are inspired, at the very minimum, by Al Qaida. The enemy is active. They are. And we're just going to do everything we can to protect you.

Look, there have been—when you think about the Far East, democracy didn't exist for a long period of time. And so principles, such as separation of church and state, were foreign to a lot of people where democracy doesn't exist, until democracy begins to exist, and then it becomes a logical extension of democracy.

I made a foreign policy decision in the Middle East that said, "We can't tolerate the status quo any longer for the sake of inexpensive energy." In other words, there was a period of time when people said, "Let's just kind of deal with the situation as it is," sometimes tolerating strong men for a economic objective. I changed our foreign policy that said, that attitude of kind of accepting the things the way they are is going to lead to the conditions that will allow the enemy to continue to breed hatred and find suiciders and soldiers in their attempt to do harm.

What I'm telling you is, is that the part of the world where we've started this democracy initiative hasn't known democracy, except for in Israel and Lebanon. So to answer your question, it's going to be the spread of democracy, itself, that shows folks the importance of separation of church and state. And that is why the Constitution written in Iraq is an important Constitution, because it separates church and state for the first time in a modern-day constitution in Iraq.

The Iraqi example is going to spread. I believe that—one of the big issues in the Middle East is women's rights, the freedom of women, that they're not treated fairly. And yet, when you're guaranteed rights under a Constitution and people are able to see that life is improving, it will cause others to say, "I want the same kind of right."

Part of our strategy in order to keep the peace is to encourage the spread of democracy, and the enemy understands that. The enemy knows that a democracy, as it spreads, will help deal with issues such as the separation of—it will encourage the separation of church and state, will encourage women to rise up and say, "We want to be treated equally," will mean that mothers will be able to have confidence that their young daughter will have an opportunity to achieve the same as a young son. And those thoughts frighten the enemy. It's hard to believe, but it does.

So to answer your question, concepts that we take for granted in democracy are foreign because the system of government has yet to take hold. But when it takes hold, it will become—people will begin to understand the wisdom of that part of the democratic process.

Let's see, let me—kind of searching around. Yes, sir?

Immigration/Mexico-U.S. Border

The President. Hola—*en Mexico?*

Q. Monterrey. We went for Christmas, to spend Christmas with my family in Mexico. And, you know, my family, friends, media, President Fox, they're talking about the wall that the United States wants to build across the border with Mexico. My question for you is, what is your opinion or your position about that wall? And, you know, when people ask me how can I justify the answer to build a wall, other than saying, "We don't want you here," you know?

The President. Yes, great question.

Q. Thank you.

The President. His question is on immigration. Let me talk about immigration. We have an obligation to enforce our borders. There are people—[*applause*]—hold on— let me just—save it for a full answer. [*Laughter*] And we do for a lot of reasons. The main reason is security reasons, seems like to me. And security means more than just a terrorist slipping in. It means drugs. The mayor was telling me that there's a lot of crime around the country—he's been studying this—because of drug use. And who knows if they're being smuggled in from Mexico, but drugs do get smuggled in. So it's a security issue. It's more than just the war on terror security issue. It's the issue of being able to try to secure the lifestyle of our country from the use of drugs, drug importation, for example. A lot of things get smuggled across. Generally, when you're smuggling something, it's against the law. So we have an obligation of enforcing the border. That's what the American people expect.

Now, you mentioned wall. The intent is to use fencing in some areas, particularly in urban centers, where people have found it easy to cross illegally into the country. It is impractical to build a wall all the way up and down the border. Look, I was the old Governor of Texas; you can't build a wall up and down the entire length of the border of the United States. But you can find those border crossing points in high urban areas and use some construction. You can be able to put berms up in order to prevent people from smuggling people across the border. There are ways to use electronics to be able to help our Border Patrol agents detect people who are illegally coming into the country. And we're getting—we're kind of modernizing the border, I guess is the best way to put it.

I mean, there is an electronic wall, to a certain extent, on parts of our border where there may be an unmanned drone flying along that radios to a Border Patrol center that says, "Hey, we've got people sneaking across illegally; find them." The second aspect—and so we are going to enforce the border as best as we possibly can. It's our duty.

Secondly, one of the problems we've faced is that people get stopped, and they get let back out in society and say, "Come on back for your hearing." But guess what? They don't come back for the hearing. That's the catch-and-release. And we're trying to change that, particularly for those from Central America who've come up from Central America through Mexico and the United States.

The reason most people come is to work. I always have said that family values do not stop at the Rio Grande River. There are some jobs Americans will not do that are being filled by people who want to feed their families. And that's what's happening. And my attitude about that is, is that when you find a willing worker and a company who can't find an American to do the job, there ought to be a legal way, on a temporary basis, to fill that job.

And so let me finish real quick. It is compassionate—by the way, it is important to enforce the border. President Fox understands he's got to enforce his border in the south of Mexico, by the way, from people coming up from the south. It is compassionate to recognize why most people are here, and they're here to work.

It also makes sense to take pressure off the border by giving people a legal means, on a temporary basis, to come here, so they don't have to sneak across. Now, some of you all may be old enough to remember the days of Prohibition. I'm not. [*Laughter*] But remember, we illegalized whiskey, and guess what? People found all kinds of ways to make it and to run it. NASCAR got started—positive thing that came out of all that. [*Laughter*]

What you're having here is, you've created a—you've made it illegal for people to come here to work, that other Americans won't do, and guess what has happened? A horrible industry has grown up. You've got folks right here in Kentucky who are hiring people to do jobs Americans won't do, and you say, "Show me your papers," and they've been forged, and the employer doesn't know about it.

Part of making sure that immigration policy works is, you hold employers to account. But how can you hold them to account when they're being presented with forged documents? A whole forgery industry has grown up around this. We've got good, honorable people coming to work to put food on their tables, being stuffed in the back of 18-wheelers. We've got people being smuggled by what they call *coyotes* into the deserts and asked to walk across. And they're dying because they're trying to get to work, and they're being mistreated. In other words, this underground industry is creating a human condition that any American wouldn't accept. I mean, it's just not right.

And so I think, yes, absolutely enforce the border but, at the same time, have a recognition that people are going to come here to work if an American won't do the job, so let's make it legal on a temporary

basis. And I mean a temporary-worker's card that's tamper proof, that gives the employer satisfaction they're not breaking the law, that says, "You can come here for a period of time, and you go home."

Now, the big issue on this, besides enforcing the border, is amnesty. I am against amnesty. And the reason I am against amnesty—amnesty means automatic citizenship—I'm against automatic citizenship, in all due respect to others in our country that believe it's a good thing. And I'm against it because all that, in my judgment, would do would cause another 8 to 11 million people to come here to try to be able to get the same—hopefully, put the pressure on the system to create automatic citizenship. So I think the best solution is the one I just described. And it's an issue that's going to be important for the American people to conduct in a way that honors our values.

We value—every life is important. We hold everybody up to respect. We should, you know? But we're going to enforce our laws at the same time. And I think you can do both in a compassionate way. I appreciate you asking that question. Thank you.

Yes, ma'am.

Education/No Child Left Behind Act

Q. President Bush, I've been an educator in five States for 36 years.

The President. Thank you.

Q. Thank you. Right up there with national security, I think, is the issue of education of every single person in the United States. It's of crucial importance to our future. And given the challenges in the world, the fact that we have to keep this Nation secure in the future and that we have to deal with all sorts of threats—many of which we don't know—what do you think we need to do better in education to provide a well-educated citizenry that will meet those challenges and keep us secure?

The President. No, I appreciate it. Listen, part of security is economic security. And one way to make sure we're economically secure in a competitive world is to make sure every child gets a good education. It's a huge issue for America to make sure the public school system functions.

First, let me just say, the public school system is important for our country, and we want it to work. The public school system in the past has provided an avenue for success, and we've got to make sure we continue to do so.

Let me start with grades K through 12. We passed what's called the No Child Left Behind Act. It is a really good piece of legislation, at least, in my humble opinion. And the reason why is, it says every child can learn, and we expect every child to learn. In other words, in return for Federal money—and we've increased spending for Title I kids up somewhere about 40-something percent, and elementary and secondary school programs gone up 41 percent. Listen, I'm a local control guy, but I also am a results person, and I said we're spending a lot of money, particularly on poor kids. And I think it makes sense for the taxpayers to know whether or not those kids can read and write and add and subtract.

And so we said, "In return for receiving this money, you've got to test"—not the Federal Government is going to test—"You test. You design the test," Governors can figure out the right way to test, to determine whether or not children can read and write and add and subtract.

You can't solve a problem until you diagnose it. And I was worried—when I was the Governor of my own State, I was worried about a system that did not test. And so we were just kind of hoping things went well, and we're just going to shuffle through. And guess who gets shuffled through? Poor black kids get shuffled through. Young Latinos get shuffled through. You know, let's just kind of socially promote them. And so step one of making sure that the education system

works is to measure to determine whether it is working.

Step two is to correct problems early, before it's late. And so part of the No Child Left Behind bill is supplemental services money, per child, to help a child get up to speed at grade level by the appropriate time.

Step three is to be able to use the accountability system to determine whether the curriculum you're using is working. I don't know if you've had these debates here in Kentucky, but I can remember them a while ago; we were debating what kind of reading instruction works, and it was a hot debate. Everybody had their opinion. The best way to determine what kind of reading program works is to measure to determine what kind of reading program works.

Four, you've got to have your parents involved in your schools. The best way— one good way to get your parents involved is to put the scores out there for everybody to see. It's amazing how many people go to schools and say, "Gosh, my kid is going to a fabulous school," until they see the score for the school next door may be better.

Step five is—on the accountability system is what we call disaggregate results. Do you realize in the old accountability systems, they didn't bother to look at the African American kids stand-alone? They just kind of looked at everybody and assumed everybody was doing good. That is not good enough for the future of this country. If we expect every child to learn, we got to measure every child and analyze whether or not those children are learning.

Step six is to make sure local folks run the schools. I can remember talking about No Child Left Behind. I saw a lot of my friends in Texas glaze over: "He's going to Washington, and he's going to change. He's going to start telling us how to run the schools." Quite the contrary. The No Child Left Behind Act actually devolves power to the local level. All we say is, "You measure. You show us. And if there's something wrong, you figure out how to correct it." You don't want Washington, DC, telling people how to run their schools. And it's working. No Child Left Behind is working.

And how do we know? Because we're measuring. There's an achievement gap in America that's not right. And that's wrong. Not enough African American fourth grade kids could read at grade level. But it's increasing dramatically. Something is happening out there, thanks to good principals and good teachers and concerned parents and a system—and a system—that focuses on results. We've got to extend this to high schools.

Now, we've got a problem when it comes to math and science. Our kids test fine. Math and science eighth grade test lousy—math and science in high school—and that's a problem. In my State of the Union, I'm going to address this. I'm going to hold a little back here. But in order for us to be competitive, we better make darn sure our future has got the skills to fill the jobs of the 21st century.

It was one thing in the past to go to a public school, become literate, and then go out there and make a living with your back. That's not what's going to happen in the next 30 or 40 years. We've got to have children that are Internet savvy. We've got to have kids that are the best in science and engineering and math; otherwise, jobs are going to go to where the workforce is that got those skills. And that's the real challenge facing us.

Fantastic question. Thanks. I'm pandering, I know, but it is really one of the most important challenges we face.

And I'm looking forward to working with Congress to, one, build on No Child Left Behind. I will refuse to allow any weakening of accountability. I remember people saying to me, "It's racist to measure." I'm telling you, it's racist not to measure. That's what I think. They say, "You're teaching the test"—I'm telling you if a child can read, it can pass a reading comprehensive

test. And so accountability coupled with a smart use of resources to focus on math and science, I think, is the proper strategy to help deal with an issue that is an important issue for the future of this country.

Yes, ma'am.

Education/National Economy/Social Security Reform

Q. Hello, Mr. President. You just made a very poignant—about math and science. I am a—number one, I'd like to thank you for taking time to be here. I think all of us would reiterate that. I am a businessowner, and I am living the American Dream. And I would like to personally thank you for having a will that will not be broken, and the men and women of the Armed Forces that protect the freedoms that we have had and that we oftentimes take for granted and give us this way of life.

So as a businessowner, though, my greatest challenge is, I worked 20 years in the civil engineering arena before starting my companies. And the thing that is really frightening to me is our—we have a true weakness, a wave that's coming in both the engineering arena, the sciences, as well as construction—construction inspectors. There's going to be a huge—these baby boomers that are starting to retire, that knowledge base that's getting ready to go away, and there is no one to replace it that's compelling enough. What could you suggest that corporate America can do to help in this deficit?

The President. No, I appreciate it. First, thanks for owning your own business. I love being the President of a country where people can—I'm not saying you started with nothing, but, you know, have a dream and end up with owning your own business. As a matter of fact, the small-business sector of America is really the job creators of America. Things are going good when it comes to job creation, 4.5 million new jobs since April of 2003. A lot of it has to do with the fact that the entrepreneurial spirit is strong and vibrant and alive.

Corporate America—big corporate America does a good job of training people. It's in their interest. It would be helpful if they didn't have to spend so much time on training people by having a literate workforce to begin with: literate in math, literate in science, literate in all different aspects of what is going to be necessary to fill the skill base of the 21st century.

One of my initiatives, and one that I hope you're taking advantage of here in Kentucky, is the use of the community college system. The community college system is really an interesting part of our education network and fabric because the community colleges are available; in other words, they're plentiful. They are affordable, relative to the different kinds of higher education institutions. And interestingly enough, I'd like to describe them as they're market driven, if run properly. In other words, their curriculum can adjust.

And what you want is a community college system that works with the local industry and says—just take the health care industry. You know, we need a certain type of nurse practitioner, for example. Or we need x-ray technologists or whatever. And that you have a community college system that will help design the system that will enable a person to go from one industry to the next, where there's a bright future. So a lot of job training to make sure that people have the skills that you're talking about, they are transferable and trainable skills. But there needs to be the place where they can find those skills, particularly those who have already gotten out of college.

Do you realize that between age 18 and 38, it's estimated that a person will change jobs 10 times, coming down the future, which means that there's a lot of activity in our economy, a lot of vibrancy. But the danger is, is that people aren't going to have the skills that fill the jobs that keep us competitive. And the community college

system is a wonderful opportunity. The Federal Government can provide job training grants, which we do, 125 million last budget cycle; I'm asking for the same this budget cycle, if you don't mind, Members of Congress. [*Laughter*]

Let me talk about small businesses real quick. In order for America to be competitive, not only do we need a skilled workforce, we've got to have certainty in our Tax Code. In order to get this economy going out of a recession and a stock market collapse and scandals, I had called upon Congress, and they delivered meaningful tax relief. The worst thing that could happen when you're trying to plan your small business, or any business, is to wonder what the taxes are going to be like. You know, when old George W. leaves, are the taxes going to go—I mean, how do we plan for the future? I strongly urge the United States Congress, this year, to make all the tax relief we passed permanent.

People will say, "Well, how are you going to balance the budget?" Well, let me warn you that raising taxes doesn't necessarily equate to balancing budgets. As a matter of fact, in my judgment, if we raise the taxes, all that will mean is Congress will increase spending. The way to balance the budget is to set priorities and to hold people to account in Washington, which is what we're doing.

Now, the biggest increases in the budget, however, are not the discretionary accounts; they're what's called mandatory accounts. And that's the increase of Medicare and Social Security. And this is a big issue that I know you didn't ask me about, but I'm going to tell you anyway, my opinion. Because you mentioned baby boomer, and that happens to be me. And a lot of people like me, my age, are fixing to retire. I'm going to be 62 in 2008, which is a convenient year to turn 62. [*Laughter*] And a lot of them—and there are fewer people paying into the system. And the benefits I've been promised are going up faster than the rate of inflation. And we can't afford it, and we need to do something about it now.

One of the real drains and real threats to our economy is the inability of Congress to be able to confront the Medicare and Social Security issue, the unwillingness to take on the tough political job. I worked hard last year. I laid out a lot of solutions that I think will work. It didn't work. We've still got a problem. I'm going to keep talking about it. My job is to confront problems, as your President, and not just hope they go away. This one is not going away. And so we need to deal with the fact that a bunch of baby boomers are retiring with fewer workers paying into the system in order to make sure we're competitive, in order to make sure that we can balance the budgets.

Now, Congress took a good step in cutting mandatory spending by $40 billion over the next years. And that's important. By the way, that was just reforming the systems. It wasn't cutting meat out of the systems; it was reforming the systems so they work better. And then when you get back, you need to pass that—I know you will—in order to show the country that you've got the will necessary to take on the tough issues. And so, you didn't ask, and I told you. Anyway. [*Laughter*] Hope I can do something about it. I'm going to keep talking about it until we can get something done. It's really important. One of these days, more and more Americans are going to realize that the Congress has got to make something happen; otherwise, we're going to pass on a disaster for our kids. And that's just the truth. And, you know, the truth wins out when it's all said and done. So don't be surprised if I keep talking about it.

Yes, sir, and then I'll get the little guy up there.

Health Care Reform

Q. Mr. President, we'd like to talk about health care a little bit.

The President. Okay.

Q. As a small-business owner, like a lot of people in this room, we look at the dramatic cost increase that has been passed along, and that we all really struggle with. How do we provide our employees with health insurance that's comprehensive? And we all view you as a very pragmatic problem solver, and we'd like you to take this one on, sir.

The President. Okay, I am. Thank you. Here's my view of the role of the Federal Government. The Federal Government needs to help the poor, and we do that through a program called Medicaid. I was just talking to the Governor today about how best to get the Medicaid program in Kentucky able to meet the needs, both budget needs, but more importantly, the social needs.

The Federal Government made a commitment when Lyndon Baines Johnson was the President that we would take care of the elderly when it came to health care, and that's why it was important to reform Medicare, to make sure the Medicare system was a modern system.

There's two different issues in Medicare. One is the long-term structural problem of paying for Medicare as more baby boomers retire and fewer people paying in the system. But the short-term issue was to have a Medicare system that frankly was not modern enough. If you're going to make a commitment to your seniors, you've got to make sure the seniors have got modern medicine. And part of modern medicine was prescription drugs.

And so the new Medicare law that came into being in January of this year, for the first time incorporates prescription drug coverage available in Medicare, as a modernization of the system. The rest of the people ought to be encouraged to have affordable health care that really does put the consumer and the provider in touch with each other, I guess is the best way to put it. We need a more consumer-driven pricing mechanism in health care in order to be able to properly deal with the inflation you're talking about. One aspect of it is, people make purchases in the health care without really realizing there may be other options available to them.

We need to make sure we expand information technology. I am told—a lot of health care guys here can tell you—that the modernization of health care, when it comes to information technology, should save up to 20 to 25 percent of cost, as well as reducing a lot of medical errors. By that I mean, everybody ought to have an electronic medical record that you're able to transfer from provider to provider. You know, the day of a person carrying these thick files of medical paper, and most of the time it's hard to read because doctors can't write hardly at all, and—but it needs to be modernized. There's a lot of inefficiency, what I'm telling you, in the health care field, particularly when it comes to information sharing.

Thirdly, it seems like to me, and this is a—health care is a particular problem for small businesses, and I fully understand that. It's becoming an unmanageable cost, putting our CEOs of small businesses in the unfortunate position of saying, "I can't pay for you anymore."

Three ideas. First, health savings accounts, which is a new product passed as part of the new Medicare bill, which is an evolving product that enables a business and/or worker to be able to buy a catastrophic plan and put the incidental costs of medicine into the plan on a tax-free basis. That's a lot of words. Look into it, is what I'm telling you. And I think Congress needs to expand HSAs and their use and their tax advantages, relative to corporate taxation when it comes to health care. Look at them. I'm not kidding you. Take a look at health savings accounts. Any small-business owner in Kentucky ought to be looking—and Indiana ought to be looking.

Secondly, we must allow small businesses to pool risk across jurisdictional boundaries. These are called association health plans. In other words, a restauranteur in Kentucky ought to be allowed to put his or her employees in the same risk pool as a restauranteur in Texas in order to be able to get the economies of sharing risk, just like big companies are able to do. These are called association health plans.

Thirdly, one of the reasons why the cost of medicine is going up and the availability of medicine is declining, particularly in specialty fields like ob-gyn, is because of lawsuits. Make no mistake about it, medical liability lawsuits is driving up the cost of your insurance. Now, when I went to Washington, I said, "This is a local issue. This is something the Governors ought to figure out how to solve," until I began to analyze the cost of lawsuits on the Federal budget. And those costs go up as a result of increased premiums and what's called the defensive practice of medicine. If you're living in a society that's got a lot of lawsuits and you're worried about getting sued, you're going to practice extra medicine to make sure that if you do get sued, that you can say in the court of law, "I did not only everything expected, I did double what was expected, Your Honor. I'm innocent."

So the defensive practice of medicine runs up the cost that you pay at the Federal level. And so I decided to do something about it and proposed a piece of legislation—it got out of the House, and I want to thank you all for passing it—that says, "If you're injured, you're going to be taken care of," but we're not going to let these frivolous lawsuits run up the cost of medicine. There ought to be reasonable limits. There ought to be reasonableness in the legal system so that the small-business owner can get affordable health care.

And so there are three ideas that should address—I think it will address—your concerns. There is a philosophical struggle in Washington on this issue. There are some really decent people who believe that the

Federal Government ought to be the decider of health care, not just for the elderly, not just for the poor, but for all people. I strongly disagree. I believe the best health care system is one in which there is a direct connect between provider and customer, where there is transparency in the pricing system, where there is an information system that is modern and flows, and in which people are held to account for medical errors but not to the point where the cost of medicine has gotten out of control. Good question.

Little guy, how old are you?

Public Support for the War on Terror/ Responsible Debate

Q. Seven.

The President. See. That's good. [*Laughter*]

Q. How can people help on the war on terror?

The President. Well, that's the hardest question I've had all day. [*Laughter*]

First of all, I expect there to be an honest debate about Iraq, and welcome it. People can help, however, by making sure the tone of this debate is respectful and is mindful about what messages out of the country can do to the morale of our troops.

I fully expect in a democracy—I expect and, frankly, welcome the voices of people saying, you know, "Mr. President, you shouldn't have made that decision," or, you know, "You should have done it a better way." I understand that. What I don't like is when somebody said, "He lied," or, "They're in there for oil," or, "They're doing it because of Israel." That's the kind of debate that basically says the mission and the sacrifice were based on false premise. It's one thing to have a philosophical difference, and I can understand people being abhorrent about war. War is terrible. But one way people can help as we're coming down the pike in the 2006 elections, is remember the effect that rhetoric can have on our troops in harm's way

and the effect that rhetoric can have in emboldening or weakening an enemy.

So that was a good question. Thank you.

Let's see, yes, ma'am. I'm running out of time here. You're paying me a lot of money, and I've got to get back to work. [*Laughter*]

Progress in Iraq

Q. Thank you for taking the time with us.

The President. I'm thrilled to be here.

Q. Along with the 7-year-old, my question is, how is it that the people of Iraq, when polled, have more hope about their future than the rest of the world has, with regard to what we're doing in Iraq? How can we get the positive things that are happening in Iraq—how can we get everybody to know what's happening out there?

The President. Well, I appreciate that question. And obviously, I've thought long and hard about it. Part of my job is to make sure and to keep explaining and explaining and explaining in as realistic a way as possible about why we're there and why it's necessary, in order to remind the American people about the stakes involved. That's why I've come here, for example.

You don't want your Government running your press. That would be the worst thing that could happen. That would mean we have just fallen prey to exactly that which we're trying to liberate people from in Iraq. And my own judgment is that action on the ground will win the day. I mean, results will ultimately trump kind of the short-term glimpse at things. So my job and the job of those of us in the administration, the job of those who have made the decision to go in there—not just me but Members of Congress that voted to support our military must continue to explain and keep the American people engaged.

I am not surprised that Iraqis feel more confident about the future than Americans do. They were the ones who lived under the tyrant. They were the ones whose families got gassed by his chemical weapons. They were the ones who, if they spoke out, were harassed by a police state. It must be a magnificent feeling to be liberated from the clutches of a tyrant.

Secondly, much of life is normal in Iraq. And you talk to people who go there, and they come back and tell you that change is significant and palpable. People can see the difference; there's vibrancy. What we see, of course, is isolated incidents of terror. And as I mentioned earlier to you, it hurts—it hits our conscience. America is a wonderful country because we're a country of conscience. It bothers us to see not only our own troops die but it bothers us to see an Iraqi kid killed. That's the nature of our society; we don't treat life in a cavalier way. We believe in America—and it's one of the really beautiful things about America—that every life is precious. That's what we believe. And so I'm not surprised that there is a different attitude inside the country than our own.

Ultimately, here in America, success on the ground in Iraq—and I've defined what victory means before—will buoy the spirits of our people. And in the meantime, I've got to go to places like Louisville, Kentucky, and sit down and spend time giving it my best shot to describe to you my decisionmaking process, the philosophy behind which this Government is operating, and my optimism about our capacity to achieve our objective.

And my deep belief, my firm and deep belief is that the sacrifices being made today will inure to the benefit of our children and grandchildren. On the one hand, we have got to protect America, and we're working hard to do so. Every day you've got good citizens in your country making sacrifices to either find an enemy that's hiding somewhere or picking up information that we can use to protect us. In the long run, we have got to have faith in a great system of government that, over the ages, has proven to be the foundation for peace.

Listen, I want to thank you all for giving me a chance to come by. May God bless you all.

NOTE: The President spoke at 1:18 p.m. in the Kentucky International Convention Center. In his remarks, he referred to Joe Reagan, president and chief executive officer, Greater Louisville, Inc.; Gov. Ernie Fletcher and Lt. Gov. Stephen B. Pence of Kentucky; Mayor Jerry E. Abramson of Louisville, KY; former President Saddam Hussein of Iraq; Ayman Al-Zawahiri, founder of the Egyptian Islamic Jihad and senior Al Qaida associate; Gen. John P. Abizaid, USA, commander, U.S. Central Command; Gen. George W. Casey, Jr., USA, commanding general, Multi-National Force—Iraq; Usama bin Laden, leader of the Al Qaida terrorist organization; Abu Zubaydah, senior Al Qaida associate, who was captured in Pakistan on March 28, 2002; Khalid Sheikh Mohammed, senior Al Qaida leader responsible for planning the September 11, 2001, terrorist attacks, who was captured in Pakistan on March 1, 2003; Prime Minister Junichiro Koizumi of Japan; and President Vicente Fox Quesada of Mexico.

Remarks Prior to a Meeting of Small-Business Owners and Community Leaders in New Orleans, Louisiana
January 12, 2006

Mr. Mayor, thank you. It's good to be back in your city. I appreciate the Lieutenant Governor and Members of the United States Congress for being here as well. I particularly want to thank the small-business owners of New Orleans. I'm looking forward to hearing what you have to say about your traditions and your hopes and your frustrations. We all share the same goal, and that's to have this great city rise again, to be a shining part of the South.

It was in the past, and I think this can be a better city, and to this end, I've done a couple of things. One, I appointed my friend Don Powell to be down here to help implement the strategy developed by the mayor and the Governor and Lieutenant Governor. In other words, I believe the best strategy for the rebuilding of New Orleans and the revitalization of the parishes around New Orleans is for the local folks to design the strategy and to have the Federal Government become a partner.

And I want to thank you for putting a committee together; I know you did as well, Mitch. Powell's job is to come down and help interface and interact. I've told the people down here that the Federal Government has got a major role to play. So far we've appropriated or made available $85 billion in reconstruction and relief along the gulf coast. About 25 billion of that has been spent; there's $60 billion in the pipeline, thanks to the good work of the Members of the Congress and the United States Senate.

One issue I do want to touch on is the levees. Now, the mayor made it very clear to me that we need a Federal policy, a strong Federal policy on the levees in order to encourage investors and investment in New Orleans. In other words, if there's any doubt about levees, people wouldn't be willing to reinvest in this city. If we couldn't get people to reinvest in this city, the recovery wouldn't be as strong as we hope it to be.

Working with the Corps of Engineers, we've put forth a plan that said that the levee system will be stronger and better than the previous levee system. And we put a request in for $3.1 billion, plus money to study how possibly to make this

system even better. Unfortunately, at the very last minute in the appropriations process, some Members of Congress moved 1.4 billion of that 3.1 billion to projects not directly related to New Orleans and the surrounding area. And so, in order to make sure that this city gets the money necessary to make sure that the levees are stronger and better, Congress needs to restore that 1.4 billion directly into projects for New Orleans and the surrounding parishes. I'm looking forward to working with the Members of the Congress to make sure that that money is restored.

Secondly, I understand that one of the keys to success is going to be private-sector initiatives. That's why we've got the small-business owners here and the man responsible for making sure New Orleans is well represented to the rest of the country, and that is Stephen, who is a part of the Chamber. One way to make sure that the private sector leads the recovery for New Orleans is to make sure the tax laws encourage investment. And I want to thank the Members of Congress for passing the GO Zone legislation which encourages investment. And that will be helpful for the folks here.

And finally, I know housing is a particularly difficult issue, an important issue. You can't have a revitalized New Orleans unless people have a place to live. And we want to—we look forward to working with the mayor and the State on implementing the vision, but want to remind people that in the new appropriations bill I signed is $11.5 billion of CDBG money. In Mississippi, the Governor intends to use that money on uninsured housing—to pay for the uninsured folks who didn't have flood insurance. And the law is written so that the State, in working in conjunction with the local authorities, can spend that money in a way to help the recovery.

We're aware of the issues here. I'm looking forward to hearing more from you all about how we can continue to work together. I will tell you, the contrast between when I was last here and today, Stephen, is pretty dramatic. It may be hard for you to see, but from when I first came here to today, New Orleans is reminding me of the city I used to come to visit. It's a heck of a place to bring your family. It's a great place to find some of the greatest food in the world and some wonderful fun. And I'm glad you got your infrastructure back on its feet. I know you're beginning to welcome citizens from all around the country here to New Orleans. And for folks around the country who are looking for a great place to have a convention or a great place to visit, I'd suggest coming here to the great New Orleans.

Anyway, thank you all very much.

NOTE: The President spoke at 11:12 a.m. in the New Orleans Metropolitan Convention Center and Visitors Bureau, Inc. In his remarks, he referred to Gov. Kathleen Babineaux Blanco and Lt. Gov. Mitchell J. Landrieu of Louisiana; Donald E. Powell, Chairman, Federal Deposit Insurance Corporation, in his capacity as coodinator of Federal gulf coast relief efforts; Mayor C. Ray Nagin of New Orleans, LA; Stephen J. Perry, president and chief executive officer, New Orleans Metropolitan Convention and Visitors Bureau, Inc.; and Gov. Haley Barbour of Mississippi.

Remarks on Gulf Coast Reconstruction in Bay St. Louis, Mississippi
January 12, 2006

Thank you all. Please be seated. Haley said that it's protocol not to introduce the President. Well, that shows what he knows about protocol. [*Laughter*] He just introduced me. [*Laughter*] Thanks for having me back. My first observation is, it's good to see—to be able to look in people's eyes and not see them all bloodshot. [*Laughter*]

I can remember coming here, the times I came and looked hard in people's eyes and saw a sense of desperation and worry and deep, deep concern about the future. I'm sure there is still concern about the future, but the eyes have cleared up. There's a sense of optimism. There's a hope. There's a little bounce in people's step. I'm not surprised; the people down here have showed incredible courage. And I want to thank you for showing the rest of our country what it means to survive an incredible hardship with high spirits.

Your Governor has done a magnificent job. He went up to Washington—[*applause*]. You know, it's nice of him to give me the credit to sign the bill. It's nice of him to compliment Congressman Taylor,

who deserves to be complimented, and compliment—and Congressman Chip Pickering, both of whom are here, and I thank them for coming. It's wise of him to compliment Senator Lott and Senator Cochran. [*Laughter*] And he's right to compliment them. But the truth of the matter is, the person who deserve the biggest compliment, in my judgment, is the man who brought the will of the Mississippi people, the needs of the Mississippi people up to Washington, DC, and fashioned one heck of a piece of legislation for the people of this important State. Thank you, Governor, for your hard work.

And I want to thank Marsha for being here as well. I don't know how you put up with him for all these years. [*Laughter*] You must be a patient soul. But he married well, just like me. And speaking about that, Laura sends her best wishes to all of you all. She's looking forward to coming back down here. She's not going to believe the difference between the last time she was here and today.

It's hard sometimes, unless you've got a perspective. I have the perspective of having spent some time here but not all my time. And I can remember what was and now what is, and I can see what's going to be too. And it's going to be a better gulf coast of Mississippi.

I want to thank Roy Bernardi, who is the Deputy Secretary of HUD. He's going to have some stuff to do to make sure this part of the world rebounds. I like your mayors. They're down-to-earth people. They are good, solid people—Mayor Eddie Favre. You know, one time a buddy of mine said, when the baseball players and owners couldn't figure out an agreement and they went on strike and quit Major League Baseball, he said, "I'm never going back to a baseball game for 10 years." And I said, sure, you know. And he's a great baseball fan. And, sure enough, last year was his 10th year, and he finally went to a game. The reason I bring that up is Eddie said, "I'm not going to wear long pants"—[*laughter*]—and I'm saying to myself, "One of these days, the President is going to show up, and Eddie sure enough will put on long pants." [*Laughter*] I didn't know him very well. [*Laughter*] I arrived here at this important school, and he's got short pants on. Eddie, I like a man who sticks to his guns. [*Laughter*] Thanks for hosting us.

And so I'm standing in the White House at a Christmas reception, and in walks Tommy Longo. He's the mayor of Waveland, of course. And he had on a fantastic suit. [*Laughter*] I nearly fell out. [*Laughter*] Tommy Longo in a suit? [*Laughter*] I said, "Where did you get that thing?" He said, "It's amazing what you can find in the rubbish." [*Laughter*]

I've learned something about the mayors up and down the gulf coast. You've got some young mayors east of here who have been in office, what, 3 or 4 months, and the storm hit. They were incredibly tested—Pascagoula and other places. You got some veterans who have been around for a while, never dreamt they'd see a day like the day they saw. But whether they're veterans or rookies, all of them have stood strong. All of them have rallied with the first-responders. All of them have shown great compassion to the people. I am proud of your local mayors, your local governments, people like Rocky Pullman of the Hancock Board of Supervisors, the people working in these counties. You got some good folks down here. And one of the reasons why I'm confident about your recovery is because you've elected good people to take on the job.

Finally, I want to thank Brother Talbot and Brother Hingle of this fantastic school. Thanks for hosting us. Tommy Longo was in the class of '75. I hope that means you didn't lower your academic standards in that year. [*Laughter*] He and old Doc Blanchard, they told me. Doc Blanchard went here, in case you didn't know it, the Heisman Trophy winner who carried the leather for West Point. And one of the things the Brother told me, he said, "We wanted to make sure we saved the Heisman Trophy that Doc Blanchard had made sure was housed here at this facility." But I do want to thank you all for letting us come by. Thanks for your being in education, really an important part of the future of this State and this country, to make sure people get a good education.

I stood in Jackson Square early on in—after the storm hit, and I said, "We're not just going to survive but thrive." By that I meant, it's one thing to kind of ride it out; it's another thing to take out of the harm that came, convert this into a better life. I said, "We're not just going to cope, but we'll overcome." I meant what I said. I couldn't have said that if I didn't have confidence, though, in the people in the local area that have such a spirit to be able to do so.

I'm here to report to you some of the progress made and to let you know that people in faraway places like Washington, DC, still hear you and care about you.

Signing all the legislation I've signed, the Federal Government has committed 85 billion so far to helping folks and to help rebuild the gulf coast of our country. Of that 85 billion, about 25 billion has been spent. So 85 million [billion]° is available; 25 of it is already in the pipeline. That's 60 billion more coming your way.

Part of the strategy to make sure that the rebuilding effort after the recovery effort worked well was to say to people like Haley and the Governor of Louisiana and the mayor of New Orleans, "You all develop a strategy. It's your State. It's your region; you know the people better than people in Washington. Develop the rebuilding strategy." And the role of the Federal Government is to coordinate with you and to help.

I thought that was an important first statement to make when people began to wonder what life would be like after the storm hit. My view is, and a lot of my political philosophy is based on, the local folks know better than the folks in Washington, DC. I remember when Haley invited me down, and he said—I think we were in a tent at that time, and there wasn't a lot of electricity—it was like an old-time daytime revival without electricity. It was hot in the tent. It was the first meeting, I think, at least the first called meeting, of the commission headed by Jim Barksdale. Citizens from all walks of life, all occupations, all aimed at one thing: putting together a strategy that will help this part of the world become even better than it was before.

I have an obligation to make sure that the Federal Government responds and coordinates and stays in touch with not only the commission and the Governor but local folks as well. And I picked a fellow that I trust, a person who's had a lot of experience, a person who understands how people think down here; after all, he is from Texas. He understands urban life, and he

---

° White House correction.

understands rural life, and he knows the importance of county commissioners; you call them county supervisors, I guess. He's a guy who's a good listener, and he's got my full confidence. And that's my friend Don Powell who's with me today. He's going to be the Federal coordinator. His job is to come down here and listen and report back.

And I recognize there are some rough spots, and I'm going to mention some of them here in a minute, and we're going to work to make them as smooth as possible. The first challenge we had after the storm hit was to take care of the people that were displaced, millions of people, or over a million people evacuated and scattered. It was an amazing period in our history, when you think about it. One day people's lives are turned upside down, and they're looking for help, and they're looking for compassion, and they found it. People found it in churches, in synagogues, in community centers, in private homes. It's an amazing part of our history, when you think about it. It's like there's a great capacity to absorb hurt in our country, because we've got individuals that are so decent and honorable.

The Government had a role to play, and that was to get money in people's pockets. I mean, when you have to evacuate, you don't have time to plan. And so one of the first things we did was, we got $2,000 in people's pockets as quickly as possible, to help them. In other words, it was a response geared toward the individual. We had a special designation for all evacuees, so they can become available for Medicaid or family services or the Federal programs. The idea was to get a response as quickly as possible to people who are scattered all over the country so they could—to help get their feet on the ground.

We gave waivers to States. In other words, we kind of deregulated the system so States could respond quickly to the people who needed help. We provided 700,000 households with rental help. In other words, the goal is for people to be back in their homes, in a home they call their own. That's the goal. But in the meantime, we had to deal with people evacuated and people without homes. And so a part of the plan has been to provide temporary housing with rental vouchers; $390 million went out as HUD vouchers for a group of people that qualified.

I can remember people hollering for trailers. We became the largest consumer of trailers probably in the history of mankind. [*Laughter*] And I know it was slow to begin with. The production needed to be ramped up, and, frankly, the Government crowded out other purchasers in order to set priorities for people down in this part of the world. We've now put out 61,000 trailers, and there are more in the pipeline. I was asking Haley, does he have a feel for how many more we need, and he said, "We're getting close to the end, but there's still a need." And we understand that. And the manufacturing is making—we put cruise ships out at one point to help people house on a temporary basis, particularly in New Orleans, so that we could get the police and the firefighters a place to stay so they could do their job.

People ended up in hotel rooms. At one time there was about 80-some thousand people in hotel rooms. It's now down to 25,000 families in hotel rooms. We're in the process of trying to locate every single family and provide the rental assistance help for them, so they can move from the hotel into rental housing, all aimed, by the way, at providing some kind of housing until the permanent housing market takes off. We're trying to bridge from being an evacuee to a person in a place until their own home gets ready to move into.

And so what can we do? Well, first thing is, we can focus on repairing homes. That's not going to do you very good down here in Waveland. I understand that. Tommy and I and the Governor and Marsha just drove by; there's no homes to repair. It's just been flattened. That's what the people

of America have got to understand. Sometimes hurricanes go through, and, you know, there's a home and a structure you can maybe put a roof on or do something—not here. Our fellow citizens have got to know when this hurricane hit, it just obliterated everything. It just flattened it.

But in parts of the hurricane zone, there's repairs that can be done. FEMA assistance will help with that. SBA loans have gone out to about—for about $2.1 billion to help people repair their homes. Now, the most innovative approach, however, to getting the homes rebuilt is the CDBG grants that Haley Barbour negotiated on behalf of the people of Mississippi. That's government initials for, direct money to help people who weren't able to get their insurance to pay them off.

I remember being down in Biloxi. I think it was my first trip. And it was hot, and it was steamy. An old lady walked up to me and said to me—I said, "How are you doing?" And she looked at me and she said, "Not worth a darn." [*Laughter*] And I said, "Well, I don't blame you." She said, "I've been paying all my life for my insurance. Every time that bill came, I paid it, every single month. And all of a sudden the storm hit, Mr. President, and I came time to collect, and they told me no." And she was plenty unhappy, and she was looking for anybody she could be unhappy with, and I just happened to be the target. [*Laughter*] I think Gene was with me then; I might have shared the story with Gene about that.

One way to handle the issue—I know you got a lawsuit here; I'm not going to talk about the lawsuit. But Haley did something innovative, which was take the CDBG grants, a lot of money for Mississippi and going to help the people do the job that many think the insurance companies should have done in the first place.

Having said that, the Government has paid out $12 billion in flood insurance. For those who had flood insurance, the Government is making good on its—on the bargain with the people. If you got an FHA loan, your loan will be forgiven for a year. In other words, there is an attempt to try to make sure that things are being done so that we can—people can get back in their homes, and people can get to be rebuilding.

There's going to be a building boom down here; there just is. It's going to be an exciting time for people. One of the real challenges is whether or not people are going to have the skill set necessary to be able to meet the needs of the people. Are there going to be enough electricians, enough plumbers, enough roofers? But you're going to have yourself a building boom; you watch. There's going to be work; people are going to be working hard here.

And Don Powell and I, to this end, met with a group of leaders in Washington, DC, from building trade unions and businesses, and the whole idea was to come up with a strategy to make sure people have got the skills necessary to fill the jobs which are going to exist. See, our goal, and I know it's the Governor's goal, is to make sure the jobs first go to Mississippi people, when it comes to rebuilding this—[*applause*]—and Mississippi businesses. And we want this opportunity to be an opportunity where minority-owned businesses and women-owned businesses have a chance to flourish. An ownership society has got to be a part of a new vision, where people from all walks of life can say, "I'm owning my own business. I'm operating my own business. I'm owning my own home."

It's a fantastic opportunity. And—but it's not going to work unless people have the skill set necessary to be able to fill those jobs and to be able to provide for the— to meet the consumer demand. And so the idea is—and Powell is going to work on this strategy—is to work with your community college system or the building trades and have centers where people can go to learn how to get the skills necessary to fill the jobs which are coming. They're coming. It's going to be an exciting time down here, just so long as you're able to get enough material and enough labor.

One of the important—and by the way, speaking about jobs, not only we got to make sure people have the skills necessary to fill the jobs, the Federal Government has got a lot of facilities down here, and there's a lot of Federal employees in this part of the world. We're going to rebuild the Federal facilities so that the people will be able to work.

This recovery is going to be led by the private sector. However, the Federal Government is going to help, and $85 billion is a good—I would call that "help"—so far. But the truth of the matter is, the jobs and the quality of life, the recovery, is going to be led by the private sector. I was asking Haley about some of the industries down here, and he told me, for example, at the year end, a casino opened. I mean, it's remarkable. If you'd have seen what I—I'm sure you saw what it looked like up and down this coast, and all of the sudden, there's businesses, and people are thriving. People are beginning to work. It's happening. It's the private sector that's going to carry much of the recovery.

Congress did a smart thing, in my judgment—was to provide tax incentives for businesses who are in this part of the world. They provide tax incentives for small businesses to expense up to $200,000 of investment and private—and incentive for all businesses to provide a 50-percent bonus depreciation for investment made. What I'm telling you is, it's kind of economic talk for saying, if somebody spends money in an investment in this part of the world, they get a tax incentive to do so. In other words, if you're able to make the Tax Code attract capital so people invest, it means you're more likely to be able to find work here. It goes on. It's a smart idea, and again, I want to thank the Members of Congress for working on that. I think it's going to make a big difference.

If you're a small-business owner—we just met today, by the way, with some small-business owners in New Orleans. And one of the things that became loud and clear to me there was that because a lot of people haven't moved back into the area, and if you're a small-business owner, there's no customers, so you have no cash flow, which makes it awfully difficult to survive. There are SBA loans for this, and I understand for some the word "SBA" means "slow bureaucratic paperwork." [*Laughter*] I hear it loud and clear. I will tell you that SBA has put out about $470 million worth of SBA loans. In other words, the loans are going out.

But this small agency has been overwhelmed. And so Don Powell is working on an interesting idea, and that is to work with the local bankers, people who understand the local customer, as to how to become the agent for the SBA to get money out the door to help small businesses manage their cash flow needs until the customer base comes back.

The other thing that happened quickly—and I'm real proud of your folks down here—was that the energy sector rebounded unbelievably fast. This part of the world is really important for national security and economic security of the United States of America. Remember, when the storms hit, a lot of folks were really worried about the price of crude oil and gasoline. We, fortunately—we just did two things I thought were wise.

One, we suspended reformulated gasoline rules, which enabled us to import gasoline from Europe, which helped to take the pressure off the market. And the price of gasoline, although it went up, didn't go up nearly as high as a lot of people thought, and is now heading back down, thank goodness, for people who are working for a living. And the price of crude oil stayed reasonable because we opened up the Strategic Petroleum Reserve. I was confident in being able to do that because I knew how fast this industry could move

if just given a chance. The suspension of some regulations to help these refineries and these gas processing plants get up on their feet was important. In other words, if you can get government out of the way, amazing things can happen sometimes in the private—[*applause*].

And so I want to thank those of you who work in the energy industry for doing what you're doing. I remember going to the plant—I think Haley was with me—went to the plant in Pascagoula. And we had people there camped out there working as hard as they could to get the refineries up so that our citizens from all around the country would be able to have gasoline at a reasonable price. And these people worked hour after hour after hour and did the Nation a great service. In the meantime, we did our part, tried to do our part to make sure that we cleaned out the waterways so that the ships could move better. Our Coast Guard, by the way, provided invaluable service here in this part of the country.

Part of the recovery of this part of the world is going to be when you get your infrastructure up and running. And I can remember first choppering over here and seeing the incredible devastation done to the bridges and highways. First of all, there has been some incredible construction done. The Slidell Bridge there, to the west of you, got up in record time. It's amazing what happens when you provide a completion bonus for people doing work. [*Laughter*]

And I know you're concerned about the I–90 bridge, but they're getting ready to start on it, as I understand. And the bills I've signed provide $2.3 billion for repair of highways and bridges in this part of the world. That's going to provide not only jobs but it's going to make the quality of life come back to what it was. You're dependent upon good highways and good bridges in this part of the world. The Government recognized that and put the money out there, available for reimbursing the States when they get these highway projects moving.

One of the really interesting things that happened was education, how the country responded for the kids who have been moved around. And school districts all over America took children from Louisiana and Mississippi and helped educate them. It was really remarkable to watch the education system rise to the challenge. In the bill there is $1.6 billion worth of operating money. It was money to help these schools stay afloat; it was to reimburse school districts for taking in the children who had evacuated to their part of the world. That's in addition to the Federal commitment to replace every school. In other words, part of the commitment is that if your school got destroyed, the Federal Government will help rebuild the school or will rebuild the school.

Plus, we understood that there was a lot of kids that were going to higher education and these—higher education institutions were affected by the storm, obviously, and they were allowed to retain their Federal aid, even though children weren't going to school. In other words, we made a concerted effort to help these schools to cope with the crisis. We're going to make a concerted effort to help the schools deal with the long-term reconstruction as a result of the crisis.

Ninety-three percent of the schools here in Mississippi are up and running, and it's an amazing feat in 4 months time. It's a great credit, again, to your Governor and your education institution, but more importantly, it's a great credit to the teachers and superintendents and principals of your local schools.

Finally, the first issue I was confronted with as the President was debris. I remember the meeting very well when the mayor showed up and said, "We can't possibly say to our people things are going to get better so long as we got piles of debris lying around." It was not only a practical issue, but it was a psychological issue. And

I can understand—I mean, I understood right off the bat what they were talking about. And we had a slow start, because we had a little bit of a—we had an issue of how to get debris off of private property. And, thankfully, there was some creative work done here at the local and State level, with the Federal Government—it really was—as to how to deal with the liability issue.

I don't want to go into the law; I'm not even a lawyer. Got too many of them up there in Washington, anyway. But my point is, is that by listening to the local folks and by being flexible about how to deal with an important issue like debris, we're making pretty good progress. Out of 42 million cubic yards of debris, 27 million have been removed.

Now, there's still debris. It's estimated about 15 million cubic foot—cubic yards of debris left. But there's a certain momentum that's gathering. Haley believes that by the end of March, we can get most of the debris off of the public property. In other words, they're making progress.

Don Powell's job is, to the extent that the Federal Government is contracting out—we want to make sure that they just don't hustle when the President shows up, that they're hustling all the time, because the rebuilding and rebirth of this area is really going to depend in large measure to getting these lots clean, to getting your public access roads cleaned up, getting that debris out of people's sight. There's something—there's a certain confidence to be gained when you see this beautiful countryside cleared of the damage of Katrina. Things have changed a lot when it comes to debris. It looks a lot different, a whole lot different. And we got more work to be done, and we're going to stay on it until it gets done.

And so we've done a lot, and there's a lot more to do, but there's a certain optimism and hope that's coming. I hope you feel that. You've come a long way in 4 months. Seems like an eternity to you, I know. Seems like a lot of time for a lot of people to have gone through what you went through. Four months is not all that long, and a lot has happened in that 4-month period. And a lot more is going to happen in the next 4 months, and then the next 4 months. I can't wait to come back, and keep coming back and seeing the progress that's being made.

We've learned some lessons about Katrina, and we're going to analyze every lesson learned. Obviously, the Federal response in parts of this devastated area could have been a lot better. We want to know how to make them better. We want to make sure that when there's a catastrophe of any kind, this Government, at the Federal level, is capable of dealing with it, in conjunction with the State and local governments.

There's going to be some lessons learned about having agencies that get overwhelmed by a size of a storm, agencies whose job it is to help people get on their feet and maybe aren't able to do it quite as efficiently as some would like. Those are the lessons we're going to continually analyze. That's what you ought to expect of those of us who have been given the high honor of serving you, to constantly look for ways to do things better. And I just want to assure you, we are. We are.

But there's some other lessons learned where we don't need to change: the lesson of courage. We saw great courage. I'll never forget going to the hangar to see those Coast Guard kids that were flying those choppers. I think it's something like 30,000 citizens were saved by rescue efforts by Coast Guard men and local responders. And the people here on the frontlines of saving lives showed great courage during Katrina.

I remember seeing the determination of our citizens. One of the lessons learned is when people are determined, they can get things done. At the Pass Christian school system, for example, this is a place where they consolidated all the schools at the elementary school. It was kind of inconvenient, when you think about it, but the inconvenience didn't bother the people in charge of that school system. As a matter of fact, they viewed it as a fantastic opportunity to be able to come together and share—and that school was up and running, with broken windows and—but there wasn't a broken heart, and their spirit wasn't broken.

One of the lessons, of course, as I mentioned, is the compassion of our fellow citizens. Think about lonely folks being sent out, having all their property, their material goods destroyed, wondering what the future meant for them, and there's a loving family saying, "I love you, brother. I love you, sister." Think about a country where the compassion is so strong that a neighbor in need can find a stranger that wants to help them get their feet back on the ground.

One of the lessons of this storm is the decency of people, the decency of men and women who care a lot about their fellow citizens, whether they be elected officials or just folks on the ground here just trying to make somebody else's life even better than it was before. So we learned some lessons about how to respond, and we're going to change. But some of the lessons shouldn't change, and that is the decency and character of the American people.

It's been an amazing experience for you. You just got to know, though, that a lot of people in this country, many of whom have never been down here, care for you; they pray for you, and they're pulling for you. God bless.

NOTE: The President spoke at 1:47 p.m. at St. Stanislaus College. In his remarks, he referred to Gov. Haley Barbour of Mississippi, and his wife, Marsha; Mayor Edward A. Favre of Bay St. Louis, MS; Brothers Ronald Talbot, president, and Ronald Hingle, principal, St. Stanislaus College; Gov. Kathleen Babineaux Blanco of Louisiana; Mayor C. Ray Nagin of New Orleans, LA; James L.

Barksdale, chairman, Governor's Commission on Recovery, Rebuilding, and Renewal; and Donald E. Powell, Chairman, Federal Deposit Insurance Corporation, in his capacity as coordinator of Federal gulf coast relief efforts.

The President's News Conference With Chancellor Angela Merkel of Germany
January 13, 2006

President Bush. Thank you all. It's such an honor to welcome Chancellor Angela Merkel here to the White House. We just had a long visit. The first thing I did was ask everybody to leave the room except for the Chancellor. And we talked about our philosophy and our hopes. We talked about our desire to work together to accomplish important goals for the world, starting with peace. We share a deep desire to help those who suffer. We care about the hungry and the sick.

Germany is a valued ally. We've got a friendship that's important. We share common values based upon human rights and human decency and rule of law, freedom to worship and freedom to speak, freedom to write what you want to write.

We've got an important job ahead of us, to work on key issues like Iran. We spent some time talking about the Iranian issue and the desire to solve this issue diplomatically by working together.

We talked about the war on terror. I told the Chancellor that there's still an enemy that wants to do harm to the American people and others who like freedom, an enemy there that lurks, and that we've got to share information and share intelligence and work carefully to protect our peoples, that the threat is real, and that my obligation as the President of this country is to do everything in my power to protect the people, and we can't do it alone.

We talked about Eastern Europe and the Balkans. I thanked the Chancellor for Germany's contribution in Afghanistan. Afghanistan is a country that has gone from being ruled brutally by the Taliban, a group of people who have values the exact opposite of the values of Americans and the German people, to one that's now beginning to see the light of freedom. Democracy yields the peace, and it's important that democracy succeed in Afghanistan, and I want to thank the German people and the German Government for their contributions.

We talked about Iraq, and we've had our disagreements on Iraq, obviously. It's been a difficult issue in our relationship, and I fully understand that. But in spite of disagreements, we share the desire for the Iraqi people to live in freedom. I want to thank the German Government for help with reconstruction.

We talked about Israel and Palestine. Both of us care deeply about the health of Ariel Sharon, Prime Minister Sharon. We wish him all the very best and hope for his recovery. We also care deeply about the plight of the people in that part of the world, and we hope that there will be two states living side by side in peace.

We talked about NATO as the foundation of our collective defense and consultations. We talked about the importance of trade relations and business relations and commerce so that people on both sides of the Atlantic in our respective countries can find meaningful, high-paying jobs.

We talked about a lot, and the reason we talked about a lot is because we've got a lot in common. And the reason we talked about a lot, because there's a lot of issues in the world that require our intense co-operation and desire to work together. And I appreciate the candid conversation, and I appreciate the beginning of what's going to be an important relationship for the sake of our respective peoples.

Welcome.

Chancellor Merkel. Well, thank you very much. And let me say that we indeed had a very open, a very candid discussion, one that was characterized by a spirit of trust that builds on a long tradition of German-American relations. But I think that will open up, also, a new chapter, as I hope, in our relationship.

This is my first visit as Chancellor, heading a new Federal Government. And I explained that there are two objectives that we have set out for ourselves. First of all, as regards our domestic agenda, we would like to strengthen our economic force, our economic strength. We look at the challenges that globalization entails, and we would like to explain to our people that in order to meet the social challenges ahead, we need to be economically strong.

And I think there is a lot of common ground here because we are at one in thinking that, obviously, we ought not to fall back into isolationist tendencies. We know that these tendencies are there, for example, in the European Union. We think we ought to meet these challenges of competition head on. And I think what we need to do is we need to convince our people to believe in themselves and to believe that even in the face of the challenges of globalization, prosperity and social equality is possible.

Secondly, apart from the domestic component, Germany wants to be a reliable partner to our partners in the world but also to our partners in Europe. And in order to be able to do that—well, Europe, as you know is composed of smaller and larger nations. We talked about the European Union. We talked about the possibilities and the chances open to the European Union. And I think it's essential that those countries that feel that they share common ground as regard to values in the Western World stand together. And for Germany, I would like to say that throughout the period of the cold war, the fact that for more than 40 years, we believed in the value of freedom actually was the firm foundation for what was possible later on in European unification.

The fact that your father, sir—partnership and leadership, that was an incredible offer that was made to us by President Bush at the time. And I think that this is certainly in our vested interest to work together with you. What does that mean, "our vested interest"? It means that we face the challenges in the world today head on. It means that after the threat through the cold war is no longer with us, obviously, the threat of terrorism is certainly the greatest challenge to our security in the 21st century.

There may sometimes be differences as to the acuteness of the danger, as to what form it presents itself, how we actually also counteract here and how we face up to this matter. Afghanistan, for example, is a case in point. We are engaged, and we're committed to Afghanistan because we see that as a vested interest. We think it is only in our interest that the whole of this region is stabilized. The same goes for Iraq. Secure democratic structures ought to be in existence in Iraq. This is in our vested interest. In spite of the fact that we don't have troops on the ground there, stability there is in our very own vested interest, and we've shown that through commitments that we've entered on in other areas.

On the Balkans, the Balkans, too, their stability is the only promising sign which can actually ensure stability for the whole of the region. And NATO, for me, is the forum where we need to discuss, where we need to debate strategic issues and what we think is necessary as regards further military capabilities.

We also openly addressed that there sometimes have been differences of opinion. I mentioned Guantanamo in this respect. But I think that at the end of the day, what counts is that we come back to the situation where we openly address all of the issues, not only how we envisage the fight against terrorism, but I just mean a very broad-based debate, for example, on trade issues; how do we see our relationship with China; how do you see our relationship with Russia; what sort of strategic relationships do we want to forge as Western nations. And this is why I'm so happy about the fact that we were at one in saying we need to intensify our contacts further; we need to address all of these issues.

And I think a very successful chapter, for example, was opened over the past few days and weeks as regards Iran. To us Germans, too, it is totally unacceptable what Iran has said recently, for example, as regards the questioning the right of existence of Israel, the statements that were made with relevance to the Holocaust. And it's essential, we feel, that the EU–3, together with the United States, take a common position here, become active, that we try to persuade as many other countries as possible to join themselves to us, to ally themselves with us, and we will certainly not be intimidated by a country such as Iran.

I must say that I was greatly encouraged by our meeting here today, Mr. President, and I hope and trust that we shall continue our very good discussions, that we will further intensify them. We have every opportunity, I think, to intensify our economic relations, our business relations, relations in the area of research and development, in foreign policy. And I'm very, very pleased that we made such a good start here today.

President Bush. Terry [Terence Hunt, Associated Press].

Guantanamo Bay Detainees

Q. Thank you, Mr. President. Chancellor Merkel has said that the U.S. prison camp at Guantanamo should not be kept open indefinitely. Are you willing to close it down anytime soon? And Chancellor, what are your concerns about Guantanamo?

President Bush. Yes, she brought up the subject, and I can understand why she brought it up, because there's some misperceptions about Guantanamo. First of all, I urge any journalist to go down there and look at how the folks that are being detained there are treated. These are people picked up off a battlefield who want to do harm. A lot of folks have been released from Guantanamo.

Like the Chancellor, I'd like to see a way forward there. The way forward, of course, is ultimately through a court system. I think the best way for the court system to proceed is through our military tribunals, which is now being adjudicated in our courts of law—to determine whether or not this is appropriate path for a country that bases itself on rule of law, to adjudicate those held at Guantanamo.

The answer to your question is that Guantanamo is a necessary part of protecting the American people, and so long as the war on terror goes on, and so long as there's a threat, we will inevitably need to hold people that would do ourselves harm in a system that—in which people will be treated humanely, and in which, ultimately, there is going to be a end, which is a legal system. We're waiting for our own courts to determine how that's best to proceed.

Chancellor Merkel. Well, it is true that we addressed this issue openly, and I think it's, after all, only one facet in our overall fight against terrorism. I made it very clear that I completely share your assessment as regards the nature and dimension of this threat, and that the Federal Republic of Germany, just as other European countries, need to come up with convincing proposals as to how we ought to deal with detainees, for example, who do not feel bound by any law; and how we deal with people who come from countries where such state structures don't exist.

So I think what we need to address is how we further want to proceed. We need to, for example, find a reform of the international law in this respect, and I think the United Nations is indeed a good forum to do that. But I think that's part of a permanent dialog between our two countries, where we really need to debate how we wish to proceed further. And the basis and the common ground needs to be, we have shared values, and I have seen that this is a very best precondition, even though, from time to time, we may have differences of opinion here.

The President. Want to call on somebody?

Iran

Q. ——been discussed. Are you in favor of sanctions against Iran in the Security Council, and what kind of sanctions should that be? And another question is, in Germany, there's a discussion about intelligence, secret service people working in Baghdad during the Iraq war. From your knowledge, did the German intelligence help the U.S. before and during the Iraq war in Baghdad?

President Bush. I have no idea about the latter. [*Laughter*] You did say secret intelligence, right? [*Laughter*] I understand. I really—the truth of the matter is, the Chancellor brought this up this morning. I had no idea what she was talking about. The first I heard of it was this morning, truthfully.

Secondly, the first part of your question was Iran.

Q. Iran, sir.

President Bush. Okay, good. Sometimes when you mix them up, it throws us off balance, you know?

I'm not going to prejudge what the United Nations Security Council should do. But I recognize that it's logical that a country which has rejected diplomatic entreaties be sent to the United Nations Security

Council. I want to put it in this perspective: The U.N. Security Council is part of a diplomatic process started by Germany, France, and Great Britain representing the interests of a lot of countries like ourself, which made it abundantly clear to the Iranians that the development of the know-how and/or—a nuclear weapon was unacceptable. And the reason it's unacceptable is because Iran, armed with a nuclear weapon, poses a grave threat to the security of the world.

And countries such as ours have an obligation to step up, working together, sending a common message to the Iranians that it's their behavior—trying to clandestinely develop a nuclear weapon or using the guise of a civilian nuclear weapon program to get the know-how to develop a nuclear weapon—is unacceptable. And Germany has played an incredibly constructive role in this dialog, and I want to thank the Chancellor for continuing that dialog.

As I say, we're working very carefully together in consultation about how to proceed next. One of the things friends do is they spend time discussing strategies before we make a common statement about what next ought to happen. And we spent a fair amount of time today, and I know Condi Rice has spent a fair amount of time with the current Government about strategizing how best to achieve the objective. That's what we want to do. We want an end result to be acceptable, which will yield peace, which is that the Iranians not have a nuclear weapon in which to blackmail and/or threaten the world.

I want to remind you that the current President of Iran has announced that the destruction of Israel is an important part of their agenda. And that's unacceptable. And the development of a nuclear weapon seems like to me would make them a step closer to achieving that objective. And we have an obligation, in order to keep the peace, to work together to achieve the objective that we're trying to achieve through the current diplomatic process.

I don't know if you want to add to that brilliance or not. [*Laughter*]

Steve [Steve Holland, Reuters].

Q. Thank you, sir. If I could just follow up on that. China's U.N. Ambassador says referring Iran to the Security Council might complicate the issue. How hard is it going to be to get a——

President Bush. Say that again, Steve. I'm getting a little old. I'm getting old; I'm having trouble hearing.

Q. China's U.N. Ambassador——

President Bush. The Chinese Ambassador said what?

Q. It might complicate the issue if you refer Iran to——

President Bush. Might complicate the issue?

Q. Yes, sir—of how hard it's going to be. What's your timetable? Should the sanctions include the threat of military force?

President Bush. First of all, I want to repeat what I said before. We should not prejudge the strategy in the Security Council until they get to the Security Council. What we're doing now is beginning· to lay out the strategy of what happens in the Security Council. That's what friends do. We consult, we talk, we strategize as to how to achieve an important objective, which is not allowing an—for Iran not to have a nuclear weapon.

And you're going to see a lot of public discussion about this matter. And the Chinese, you know, have got an opinion; the Russians have an opinion; we have opinions; everybody has opinions. Our job is to form a common consensus. And so you're—this is what's called diplomacy. I know you know that, Steve. I don't mean to insult you. But diplomacy is out talking to friends, allies, and others about a common objective. This meeting has got a lot of diplomacy in it today, because this is a subject in which we've spent a lot of time. I'm very interested in the Chancellor's opinion on this subject.

We did talk about the Chinese statement. Our job is to make it clear to all parties that it is in the world's interest that Iran not have a nuclear weapon, in other words, share the same goal. Once that goal is established, it makes it easier to come up with the strategy to achieve the goal.

And so, of course, we'll reach out to the Chinese and remind them, once again, that it's not in their interest or the world's interest for the Iranians to develop the capacity to—and/or a nuclear—to build a weapon and/or to possess a weapon. And I just gave you one reason why.

Another reason why is, it's very important for nontransparent societies not to have the capacity to blackmail free societies. We're thinking about how to lay the foundation for peace. We must be proactive. And that's what you're seeing. You're seeing the evolution of a proactive diplomatic policy——

Q. What about——

President Bush. Military option?

Chancellor Merkel. Allow me, if I may, and give you my German perspective on the matter. What is essential and is crucial is that over the next—when we look at the next step to be taken by the EU–3 and the United States together in a genuine consultation process that where we say at one point in time, "We actually did everything we could." They refused it. Iran refused every offer we made, even the Russian offer. Now we refer this matter back to the Board of Governors of the IAEA. But they, too, do their utmost to try to enlist as large a number of member states to join in on a proposal that will then be made to the Iranians. And I think this is going to be absolutely crucial for the Iranians to see how serious we are about all of this.

So what is at stake now is what sort of attempt—and serious attempt—is taken by all of us. And we've seen it with Syria, that it does leave an impression. It does leave an impact, if as large a number of nations in this world as possible makes it abundantly clear we are not accepting a stance that says, in effect, the right of existence of Israel is questioned. "You are trying to lie to us. You are trying to cheat." This is something that we don't accept. And this is what we need to discuss: who is going to take which role, who is going to play which part, and what will be the final proposal? And then I think this has—it was what made this EU–3 approach so successful. They stood together, and they had one uniform position.

Thank you.

Germany-U.S. Relations

Q. A question addressed to you, Madam Chancellor, and then one to you, Mr. President. Chancellor, would you say that this visit today has opened up a new chapter in German-American relations? And how do you think this should look, better than with Chancellor Schroeder at the last year? [*Laughter*]

Chancellor Merkel. Well, for my part, I can say that there is every opportunity for us to further enhance our relations, and such enhancement of relations is founded on a shared experience, no doubt about this. Afghanistan was mentioned here; the Balkans were mentioned. And here, too, we're also able to tell you that, after all, we have been successful in WTO negotiations.

So what is important to me, I think, is to have as many international contacts as possible, because I think, to a very large part, misunderstandings occur when you don't meet often enough, when you don't talk to each other often enough. The President just pointed out how much intellectual effort has to go further into trying to come up with a convincing strategy as how to deal with Iran, and we can't resort to some kind of ivory tower and think for ourselves. We have to do it in exchange with others.

Secondly—and I do see a chance here, a climate of openness has to exist, an area where one says quite clearly and candidly to one another, "Well, there we agree; there we disagree." But there also has to be a climate of absolute trust, of reliability, where one stands by what one has agreed upon.

Thirdly, in spite of the great threat of terrorism that is the great threat to us in the 21st century, we need to point out that U.S.-Germany relations cannot only rest on fighting terrorism, but we have common interests. We have, for example, competitors, such as China and other countries, who don't abide by any rule. And we would like to see the rules kept. And now we need to find a common basis, a common approach, even though we sometimes may be, ourselves, competitors in certain business fields, for example, where we vie for orders.

So I see opportunities and I think that we need to be aware of the fact that after the end of the cold war, many of the contacts that existed in the past and also because of our cooperation as allies, that these cannot be taken for granted these days anymore. So it's going to be essential for us not to only talk at governmental level—it's a good experience, obviously—but that also our societies have to be engaged, that they have to understand that we need their contribution, too, to have good relations. And I think I made a little start in the right direction. So in about six months you may ask me again whether I've been able to add a few more chapters to it.

President Bush. We've got something in common; we both didn't exactly landslide our way into office. [*Laughter*]

I'm convinced that we will have a really important and good relationship.

First, I do want to send my best regards to Gerhard Schroeder. We spent a lot of time together, and we talked about important issues. Listen, there was room for agreement and room for disagreement. And I do hope he's doing well.

Our job now is to work together. We've got big interests. Germany is a really important country. It's right in the heart of

Europe; it's vital that Germany take the lead on a lot of issues. And I look forward to working with the Chancellor on common objectives. And my first impressions, with 45 minutes alone in the Oval Office, were incredibly positive. She's smart—[laughter]—she's plenty capable. She's got kind of a spirit to her that is appealing. She loves freedom.

I was particularly touched by hearing about her early life in Communist Germany. There's something uplifting to talk to somebody who knows the difference between just talking about tyranny and living in freedom and actually done it.

So we're going to have a very good relationship. And that's important for our respective people. I'm looking forward to consultations, visits, contacts, phone calls,

all the things you do. And now I'm going to take her to lunch. [*Laughter*]

Thank you.

Chancellor Merkel. Thank you.

NOTE: The President's news conference began at 11:37 a.m. in the East Room at the White House. In his remarks, he referred to Prime Minister Ariel Sharon of Israel; President Mahmud Ahmadi-nejad of Iran; China's Ambassador to the United Nations Wang Guangya; and former Chancellor Gerhard Schroeder of Germany. Chancellor Merkel and two reporters spoke in German, and their remarks were translated by an interpreter. The Office of the Press Secretary also released a Spanish language transcript of this news conference.

Remarks Following a Meeting Business Leaders on Central American Relief and Reconstruction Efforts
January 13, 2006

I want to thank Secretary Rice and Ambassador Hughes for joining three of our Nation's most distinguished business leaders here at the White House to discuss a very important project, and that's raising money for those affected by the storms and natural disaster in Guatemala and Honduras.

Ours is a Nation that when we see human suffering, we respond. And we responded at the governmental level, because we had our military help provide infrastructure and logistics and get supplies to people who were hurting. We helped through USAID. And now it's time for the private sector in our country to step up and support the efforts of those Guatemalans struggling to get their lives back together and those in Honduras doing the same thing.

The fund that's going to be raised is made up of private donations. People can find out more about it on what's called—

a web site called hurricaneaction.org. I think the site went up today, if I'm not mistaken. It's a place for people to come and access and to find out how they can join other Americans as to how to contribute. The money will go for things such as education of displaced families or infrastructure rebuilding, with a particular emphasis on reforestation or on microloans to help the economy get back on its feet in these countries.

So I want to thank you all very much for coming. I appreciate your interest. Thank you for traveling down to the region to take an assessment of the needs. And most importantly, thanks for coming back and calling our citizens to action. Appreciate it.

NOTE: The President spoke at 1:34 p.m. in the Oval Office at the White House. A tape was not available for verification of the content of these remarks.

The President's Radio Address
January 14, 2006

Good morning. Last October, I was proud to nominate Judge Sam Alito to be an Associate Justice on the Supreme Court of the United States. This week, Judge Alito testified before the Senate Judiciary Committee, and the American people saw a man of character and intelligence. He forthrightly answered questions with grace and composure and showed his personal humility and legal brilliance, qualities that have made him one of America's most accomplished and respected judges.

In his opening statement to the committee, Judge Alito offered an eloquent description of the proper role of a judge. He put it this way: "A judge cannot have any agenda; a judge cannot have any preferred outcome in any particular case. The judge's only obligation is to the rule of law. In every single case, the judge has to do what the law requires."

Judge Alito has embodied this understanding of a judge's proper role throughout his distinguished career. He has participated in thousands of appeals, and he has authored hundreds of opinions. His record shows that he strictly and fairly interprets the Constitution and laws and does not try to legislate from the bench or impose his personal preference on the people. As the American people saw this week, Judge Alito always approaches the law in a thoughtful, fair, and openminded way.

Throughout his life, Sam Alito has demonstrated a mastery of the law, great decency, and a strong commitment to public service. As a young man, he wore his country's uniform in the Army Reserve and achieved the rank of captain. Early in his legal career, he worked as a Federal prosecutor. As Assistant to the Solicitor General, Sam Alito argued 12 cases before the Supreme Court. He later served in the Justice Department's Office of Legal Counsel, where he provided constitutional advice for the President and the executive branch.

In 1987, President Reagan named Sam Alito the United States Attorney for the District of New Jersey, the top Federal prosecutor in one of the Nation's largest Federal districts. The Senate confirmed him by unanimous consent. In this important post, Sam Alito showed a passionate commitment to justice and the rule of law and earned a reputation for being both tough and fair. He moved aggressively against white-collar and environmental crimes, drug trafficking, organized crime, and violations of civil rights. In 1990, President Bush nominated Sam Alito for the United States Court of Appeals for the Third Circuit, and the Senate once again confirmed him by unanimous consent. He's served with distinction on that court for 15 years, and he has more prior judicial experience than any Supreme Court nominee in more than 70 years.

Sam Alito's brilliance, integrity, and accomplishments have gained him respect and praise from his colleagues and from attorneys across the political spectrum. This week, fellow judges from the Third Circuit publicly testified in support of his confirmation, and they praised his integrity and fairness. The American Bar Association gave Judge Alito a unanimous rating of "well-qualified," the ABA's highest possible rating. The ABA concluded that Judge Alito meets "the highest standards" of "integrity, professional competence, and judicial temperament." In the past, leading Democratic Senators have called the ABA's rating system the "gold standard" for judicial nominees.

During this week's hearings and over the course of his career, Judge Alito has demonstrated that he is eminently qualified to serve on our Nation's highest Court. I'm grateful to Senator Arlen Specter for his superb work in chairing the hearings. I also thank Judge Alito's wife, Martha, and the Alito children for their patience and dignity during the confirmation process.

Now the Senate has a duty to give Judge Alito a prompt up-or-down vote. I look forward to the Senate voting to confirm Sam Alito as 110th Justice of the Supreme Court. America is fortunate to have a man of his intellect and integrity willing to serve, and as a Justice on our Nation's highest Court, Sam Alito will make all Americans proud.

Thank you for listening.

NOTE: The address was recorded at 8 a.m. on January 13 in the Cabinet Room at the White House for broadcast at 10:06 a.m. on January 14. The transcript was made available by the Office of the Press Secretary on January 13 but was embargoed for release until the broadcast. The Office of the Press Secretary also released a Spanish language transcript of this address.

Remarks to Reporters Following a Visit to the National Archives and Records Administration
January 16, 2006

It seems fitting on Martin Luther King Day that I come and look at the Emancipation Proclamation in its original form. Abraham Lincoln recognized that all men are created equal. Martin Luther King lived on that admonition to call our country to a higher calling, and today we celebrate the life of an American who called Americans to account when we didn't live up to our ideals.

Allen, thanks for having me. I would strongly recommend our fellow citizens come to this house of archives, a house that archives a lot of our important documents. It's really an amazing place; it's really fascinating. I appreciate you and your staff—thanking you.

All right, thank you all. See you later today.

NOTE: The President spoke at 9 a.m. in the East Rotunda Gallery. In his remarks, he referred to Archivist of the United States Allen Weinstein. A tape was not available for verification of the content of these remarks.

Remarks at Georgetown University's "Let Freedom Ring" Celebration
January 16, 2006

Thank you all. Thanks for the kind introduction, and thanks for the invitation to be here. It's an honor to join you on this national holiday celebrating one of America's most important lives, Martin Luther King, Jr.

Every year on this day, we reflect on the great movement for civil rights that transformed our country. We remember leaders like Rosa Parks, who today is being honored with the John Thompson, Jr., Legacy of a Dream Award. And we recommit ourselves to working for the dream that Martin Luther King gave his life for: an America where the dignity of every person is respected, where people are judged not by the color of their skin—by the content of their character, and where the hope of a better tomorrow is in every neighborhood in this country.

I'm sorry Laura is not with me. She's leading a delegation to Liberia for the swearing-in of President Johnson Sirleaf, who, by the way, is the first elected woman President on the continent of Africa.

I want to thank Dr. DeGioia and the good folks at Georgetown University. I want to thank the members of my Cabinet who are here. By the way, Condoleezza Rice is not here, because she's with Laura. [*Laughter*] I want to thank Majority Leader Bill Frist and his wife, Karyn, other Members of Congress who are here. I appreciate Bruce Gordon, the president of the NAACP, for his strong leadership.

It is such an honor always to be in the presence of Dorothy Height. And I want to thank Tiffany Thompson for being here to represent her good dad—wondering where your brother was. [*Laughter*] DeGioia hired him, and he's working. [*Laughter*] Thank you all for being here.

When our Founders declared America's independence, they invoked the self-evident truth that all men are created equal. Our Constitution was written to put the principles of a free and equal society into practice. It is a living document. It required amendment to make sure that promise was fulfilled, amendments like the abolishment of slavery, the guarantee of equal protection, and the right to vote for all Americans. Dr. King called these documents America's great "Charters of Freedom," and he continued to trust in their power even when the practice of America did not live up to their promise.

As children of the South, Martin Luther King and Rosa Parks both came to the civil rights movement with long personal experience of the evils of discrimination and segregation. Dr. King called the daily humiliations endured by black Americans "the jangling discords of our Nation." And Rosa Parks famously experienced it when that bus driver had her arrested for refusing his order to give up her seat to a white man.

But Mrs. Parks and Dr. King shared a deep belief in a hopeful future. They strongly believed that segregation could not stand once it was held up to the light in all its ugliness. And because of their spirit and their work, the cruelty and humiliation of Jim Crow is a thing of the past.

As well, Martin Luther King, Jr., and Mrs. Parks's faith in the future reflected their faith in a Higher Being. Martin Luther King and Mrs. Parks both believed that the answer to hate and discrimination was love. Dr. King once wrote, "It is quite easy for me to think of a God of love, mainly because I grew up in a family where love was central and where lovely relationships were ever-present." Mrs. Parks was a devout member all her life of the African Methodist Episcopal Church and a woman who saw the face of God in every human being. These two leaders knew that freedom was not a grant of government but a gift from the Author of All Life.

So when they made their appeal to equal rights, they aimed straight for America's soul, and they roused the dozing conscience of a complacent nation. By calling us to be true to our founding promise of equality, Martin Luther King, Jr., and Mrs. Parks helped African Americans gain their God-given rights.

As leaders, Martin Luther King and Mrs. Parks believed their calling was to be involved, to be active, to work for change. Long before Mrs. Parks refused to move from her bus seat, she'd been active in community efforts to advance opportunities for African Americans and to register them to vote.

At the dawn of this new century, America can be proud of the progress we have made toward equality, but we all must recognize we have more to do. The reason to honor Martin Luther King is to remember his strength of character and his leadership but also to remember the remaining work. The reason to honor Mrs. Parks is not only to pay homage to her strength of character but to remember the ideal of active citizenship. Active citizens in the 1960s struggled hard to convince Congress to pass civil rights legislation that ensured the rights of all, including the right to vote. And Congress must renew the Voting Rights Act of 1965.

Martin Luther King did not live to celebrate his 40th birthday. Yet in the short time he walked upon this earth, he preached that all the powers of evil are ultimately no match for one individual armed with eternal truths. And one evening, on a bus ride home from work, a tired but brave woman named Rosa Parks proved that Dr. King was right.

And so today we honor Dr. Martin Luther King and Rosa Parks. We ask for God's blessings on their legacy, and we ask for God's blessings on our great Nation.

Thank you.

NOTE: The President spoke at 3:50 p.m. at the John F. Kennedy Center for the Performing Arts. In his remarks, he referred to President Ellen Johnson Sirleaf of Liberia; John J. DeGioia, president, Georgetown University; civil rights leader Dorothy I. Height; and former Georgetown University head men's basketball coach John Thompson, Jr., and his daughter, Tiffany, and son, John Thompson III.

Remarks Following a Meeting With Prime Minister Guy Verhofstadt of Belgium
January 17, 2006

President Bush. You're probably wondering what the Prime Minister is sharing with me. First of all, welcome. We're talking mountain biking; actually, he's talking about the Tour de France. He's a huge advocate and a follower of the bike scene around the world. He's also an avid mountain biker, and one of these days, he and I are going to ride. He's going to give me a lesson on how to ride a mountain bike.

First of all, welcome. Thanks for the wide-ranging discussion. I've been honored to know Guy for a long period of time. We have got a close relationship. And we talked about the importance of transatlantic relations, about how it's important for the United States to work with the European Union to reach common objectives and to help work together to make this world a more peaceful place and a better place for people.

We talked about bilateral relations, and the Prime Minister brought up an antiquated tax treaty that he believes needs to be looked at by our Government in order to facilitate trade between Belgium and the United States.

We talked about Africa, in particular, the Congo. And I want to thank you for your leadership, Mr. Prime Minister, on this very important issue. I told the Prime Minister my Government would work very closely with the Belgium Government to help the people of the Congo realize their full potential.

We had a wide-ranging discussion, as to be expected among friends, and it's been my honor to welcome him here. And I'm glad you're here.

Prime Minister Verhofstadt. Well, we had, in fact, a very good and intense discussion, not only about biking, that was only at the end, the biking, in the search of who can be the successor of Lance Armstrong. [*Laughter*] We have not made a final choice on who can be his successor.

But we had a very good, I think, discussion about transatlantic relationship. I'm very pleased that since our last meeting, we have started with this transatlantic informal meetings in New York and in Brussels. And it improves, I think, the relationship, the transatlantic relationship. There is certainly a lot of work still to do, and I think that common point of view and a common policy of the U.S. and of Europe on issues like the Middle East, like Iran, is certainly absolutely necessary and can improve this transatlantic relationship.

And we also discussed the need to have more reflection on future of North Atlantic Alliance, on the relationship between European defense and North Atlantic Alliance,

and maybe we can develop a number of initiatives with Belgium in Brussels on that issue.

About the Congo, it's very clear that we have to help. The transition period is, at this moment, successful. We hope for elections in April, a second round in June. But we have already discussed what after these elections. The international community has to continue to help and to seek good governance in the Congo and in Central Africa.

So that were, in any way, the most important elements, and then at the end, in fact, we shall start a negotiation with the American administration to have a new tax treatment between Belgium and the U.S., to avoid double taxation in the future.

Thank you.

President Bush. Good job. Thanks, Guy. Appreciate you.

NOTE: The President spoke at 10:02 a.m. in the Oval Office at the White House. Prime Minister Verhofstadt referred to 2005 Tour de France winner Lance Armstrong.

Statement on the Death of Sheikh Jabir al-Ahmad al-Jabir al-Sabah of Kuwait
January 17, 2006

I was deeply saddened to learn of the death of His Highness Sheikh Jabir al-Ahmad al-Sabah, the Amir of Kuwait. Sheikh Jabir was a friend and steadfast and reliable ally of the United States. He supported the U.S. service men and women who fought to liberate Kuwait and later Iraq from the aggression and tyranny of Saddam Hussein. Sheikh Jabir worked tirelessly to provide a better future for Kuwait's citizens and was the driving force

behind many reforms, including the establishment of a vibrant, elected Parliament and a free press. In his last months, he provided critical leadership to ensure that Kuwait's women achieved political rights. On behalf of the American people, Laura and I send our deepest condolences to Sheikh Jabir's family and to the Government and people of Kuwait on the passing of this historic leader.

Letter to Congressional Leaders on Review of Title III of the Cuban Liberty and Democratic Solidarity (LIBERTAD) Act of 1996
January 17, 2006

Dear _____ :

Consistent with section 306(c)(2) of the Cuban Liberty and Democratic Solidarity (LIBERTAD) Act of 1996 (Public Law 104–114)(the "Act"), I hereby determine and report to the Congress that suspension for 6 months beyond February 1, 2006, of the right to bring an action under title III of the Act is necessary to the national interests of the United States and will expedite a transition to democracy in Cuba.

Sincerely,

GEORGE W. BUSH

NOTE: Identical letters were sent to Richard G. Lugar, chairman, and Joseph R. Biden, Jr., ranking member, Senate Committee on Foreign Relations; Thad Cochran, chairman, and Robert C. Byrd, ranking member, Senate Committee on Appropriations; Henry J. Hyde, chairman, and Tom Lantos, ranking member, House Committee on International Relations; and Jerry Lewis, chairman, and David R. Obey, ranking member, House Committee on Appropriations.

Remarks Following a Meeting With Iraqi Citizens
January 18, 2006

Listen, thank you all for coming. It's been my honor to visit with folks who know firsthand the brutality of Saddam Hussein. These are folks who have suffered one way or the other because the tyrant was a law unto himself and was willing to deny people basic human rights. The stories here are compelling stories. They're stories of sadness and stories of bravery.

In the course of our discussion, we were also able to talk about what a contrast it is between a society which was willing to jail people, torture people, and beat people and kill people, to a society that is beginning to understand the fruits of democracy and freedom.

Last year was an amazing year in Iraq. Millions of people went to the polls to vote, first in January, then to ratify a Constitution, and then back to the polls again to elect a Government under the new Constitution. It's a testimony to the courage of the Iraqi people. Obviously, we still have got work to do and fully intend to do it.

And one of the interesting moments will come here this year when Saddam Hussein's trial is brought forth for the world to see, to see the butcherer, the person who brutalized many people or ordered the brutality of many people here at this table, get his due justice under rule of law.

And so I want to thank you all for coming. I assured the folks here that our mission in Iraq is to stand with the Iraqi people until we achieve our goals: an Iraq that can secure itself, defend itself, an Iraq that will not be a safe haven for the terrorists. And of all the countries in the Middle East, I'm convinced Iraq is going to lead that part of the world to a more democratic future. The Iraqi people are brave and courageous and smart people.

And so thank you for being here. Thank you for sharing your stories. I appreciate it very much.

NOTE: The President spoke at 11:50 a.m. in the Roosevelt Room at the White House. In his remarks, he referred to former President Saddam Hussein of Iraq. A tape was not available for verification of the content of these remarks.

Letter to Congressional Leaders on Continuation of the National Emergency With Respect to Terrorists Who Threaten To Disrupt the Middle East Peace Process
January 18, 2006

Dear Mr. Speaker: (Dear Mr. President:)

Section 202(d) of the National Emergencies Act (50 U.S.C. 1622(d)) provides for the automatic termination of a national emergency unless, prior to the anniversary date of its declaration, the President publishes in the *Federal Register* and transmits to the Congress a notice stating that the emergency is to continue in effect beyond the anniversary date. In accordance with this provision, I have sent to the *Federal Register* for publication the enclosed notice, stating that the emergency declared with respect to foreign terrorists who threaten to disrupt the Middle East peace process is to continue in effect beyond January 23, 2006. The most recent notice continuing this emergency was published in the *Federal Register* on January 21, 2005 (70 *FR* 3277).

The crisis with respect to the grave acts of violence committed by foreign terrorists who disrupt the Middle East peace process that led to the declaration of a national emergency on January 23, 1995, as ex-

panded on August 20, 1998, has not been resolved. Terrorist groups continue to engage in activities that have the purpose or effect of threatening the Middle East peace process and that are hostile to United States interests in the region. Such actions constitute an unusual and extraordinary threat to the national security, foreign policy, and economy of the United States. For these reasons, I have determined that it is necessary to continue the national emergency declared with respect to foreign terrorists who threaten to disrupt the Middle East peace process and to maintain in force the economic sanctions against them to respond to this threat.

Sincerely,

GEORGE W. BUSH

NOTE: Identical letters were sent to J. Dennis Hastert, Speaker of the House of Representatives, and Richard B. Cheney, President of the Senate. The notice is listed in Appendix D at the end of this issue.

Remarks on the National Economy and a Question-and-Answer Session in Sterling, Virginia
January 19, 2006

The President. Thanks for having me. Please be seated. Thanks for coming to say hello. What I thought I'd do is share some thoughts with you and then answer questions for a while. Before I do, I want to

thank Randy and the Loudoun County Chamber of Commerce for setting this up. I appreciate you all coming.

I've got something to say, and I hope you do as well, as we have a conversation about how to make sure this economy of ours continues to stay robust and strong, so people can find work and realize their dreams.

Before I talk about the economy, I do want to say Laura sends her regrets. She came home last night about 12:45. She just came back from Africa, where she and my daughter Barbara and Condi Rice went to witness the swearing-in of the first elected woman President on the continent of Africa. They had a great trip. She said it was an inspiring inauguration. I just wish she'd have tiptoed in a little quieter. [*Laughter*]

She's doing great. You know, one of the best things about the Presidency is how close our family has remained and how wonderful a wife and mother she is. And the American people are getting to see that.

Speaking about families, Chuck Kuhn's family is pretty remarkable, turns out his mother works for him. [*Laughter*] That's the opposite in my family. [*Laughter*] I need a little advice on how to—[*laughter*]—restructure the chain of command in the Bush family. [*Laughter*] But I love being here in a place where a guy who had a dream at age 17 years old—that's how old Chuck was when he started to act on his entrepreneurial instincts—said, "If I work hard and if I'm smart and if I figure out what the market wants, I can build something that I call my own." And 23 years later, we're standing, obviously, in what has become a very successful business enterprise, successful because he is thriving and expanding, successful because he has provided people a good place to make a living. And so I want to thank you, Chuck, for being a great entrepreneur.

I want to thank the folks who work here for setting this deal up. I'm here to talk about how to make sure that America is the place where the entrepreneur can succeed. That's what we're really here to discuss, isn't it? And it's a wonderful place to have that discussion.

Before we get there, I want to thank the attorney general, Bob McDonnell, of the State of Virginia—the Commonwealth of Virginia for being here. Appreciate you. He's sitting next to an old Governor buddy of mine, Bill Graves. He was the Governor of Kansas during the time I was the Governor of Texas. And I used to remind him he made a really smart move when he married a woman from Texas. [*Laughter*] Still married, aren't you? Yes. [*Laughter*] Good move—[*laughter*]—the best deal that's ever happened to you. It's great to see you. Bill is the president and CEO of the American Trucking Association.

I want to thank all the other State and local officials who are here, but most importantly, I want to thank the small-business owners who are here.

I was interested to find out that Loudoun County is the home of 10,000 small businesses, 80 percent of which have got 10 employees or less. It's pretty strong, isn't it? Amazing. Probably one of the reasons why you're growing so fast is that people realize this is a good place to take risk, and that's really the role of government, when you think about it.

I like to tell people the role of government is not to try to create wealth; that's not the role of government. Oh, sure, the role of government is to help the poor and help the elderly with medicine, but it's not to try to create overall wealth. The role of government is to create an environment in which people are willing to risk capital, to take risk, an environment in which people are willing to work to realize their dreams, just like here at this trucking company. That's the fundamental policy, the principle on which I'm basing my decisions as I ask Congress to think about how to make sure the economic growth that is now prevalent in America continues.

We have got a robust economy, but it wasn't necessarily going to be that way; when you think about what we've been through, it kind of helps point to what good policy may be. We've been through a stock market correction. We've been through corporate scandals, which affected the confidence of people. We have been through a terrorist attack, which hurt our economy. We have been through war. We've had significant natural disasters. All of which could have sent us into a downward spiral had we not put good policy in place.

We've overcome these issues, and I believe one of the main reasons why is because we let people keep more of their own money. I asked Congress for tax relief. I believe strongly that if the entrepreneurs of America have more money in their pocket, they will use it to expand their businesses. I believe more—very strongly that if a consumer has more money in their pocket, they will demand extra goods and services. And when somebody demands an extra good and service in a market economy, somebody is going to produce it to meet that demand.

And so I went to Congress and said, "Look, we've got problems; let's be aggressive about how we address it; let's cut the taxes on everybody." I remember the debate. They said only some people should have tax cuts. So we lowered rates for everybody. If you all have tax relief, everybody who pays taxes ought to get relief; you ought not to try to play favorites with who gets it and who doesn't get it.

We mitigated the damage of the marriage penalty. I always thought it was a little contradictory to have a Tax Code that discouraged marriage. Seems like to me we ought to encourage marriage in this country, and the Tax Code ought to encourage that.

We lowered taxes on dividends and capital gains because we want to encourage investment. We put the death tax on the road to extinction. The death tax is a punitive tax for small businesses and farmers and ranchers. It's a tax you pay; you know, you're paying income tax when you're making money. You're paying tax to the Government; that's fine. And then you die, and then your heirs get to pay it all over again,

and that doesn't seem fair. It seems like to me that you want a tax system that encourages families to be able to—a family member to pass their assets on to whomever they choose without the Government making it impossible to do so. And so the death tax was put on its way to extinction. I said, put on its way to extinction; the problem is the way the law was written. It's coming back to life in 2011, which is going to make some interesting estate issues, particularly in 2010.

We increased the child credit. We want to help families who have got children. One of the things that's really important for Congress to recognize is that most new jobs in America are created by small businesses. If you're interested in job growth, then you've got to be thinking about, where's the engine for growth? And it's the small-business owner. Seventy percent of new jobs in America are created by small-business owners and entrepreneurs. Many small businesses pay tax at the individual income tax level, sole proprietorships, subchapter S, you know. These are structures in which people are able to grow their businesses, but they're advantageous to the owners of business. And yet you pay individual income tax rates.

So when you hear me talking about, "We cut taxes on individuals," you also have to recognize we cut taxes on small businesses. And if you want there to be job creation to offset the trauma that our economy has been through, our country has been through, then it makes sense to say to the job creators, "Here's a little more money for you in your pocket."

We also encouraged investment. You might remember, we made it tax advantageous to increase investment in plant equipment if you're a small-business owner. All the policies that I'm describing to you were aimed at saying to the small-business sector, "We understand your importance; here's how to help you grow."

The other thing that you've got to understand in Washington is that you hear a lot of debate about the deficit, and it's an important debate, don't get me wrong. But in my judgment, the best way to solve the deficit is to grow the economy, not run up your taxes. See, there is a myth in Washington; they say, "All we've got to do is just raise the taxes a little bit, and we'll solve the deficit." No, that's not how it works. They're going to run up your taxes, but they're going to find new ways to spend the money and not solve the deficit. That's how Washington works.

The best way, it seems like to me, to solve the deficit is to keep progrowth tax policies in place and do something on the spending side. And so I'm working with Congress; and I want to thank the Speaker and the Leader for supporting and passing lean budgets. I say "lean" because we've got one aspect of our budget that is not going to be lean. And that is any time we've got a kid in harm's way, he or she is going to have the best equipment, best training, best possible pay. That's what we owe the families of our military.

But on nonsecurity discretionary spending, we've slowed it down every year I've been in office. And, actually, the nondiscretionary—nonsecurity discretionary spending—I'm from Texas—[*laughter*]—is lower in '06 than it was in '05. We've actually reduced nonsecurity discretionary spending. The issue for the budget is mandatory spending. See, that's when—that means you don't have discretion over it; it's fixed by formula. The two biggest programs we face, of course, are—for mandatory spending increases—are Medicare and Social Security. And we're going to have to do something about it, and a lot of folks in Washington don't want to do anything about it. It's too hard, politically.

I want to share some thoughts with you about my view of "too hard, politically." I think we're supposed to do the hard things, politically. I think the job of a President and jobs of leaders in Congress from both political parties should—confront problems now and not pass them on to future generations. And we've got a problem with Social Security and Medicare, and I'll tell you why. We've got a bunch of baby boomers like me getting ready to retire. As a matter of fact, I'm 62 years old in the year 2008. It's a perfect fit. [*Laughter*] And there are a lot of us. I'm looking at some of them here. And we've been promised greater benefits than previous generations.

The politicians that ran for office said, "Vote for me; I'll make sure your Social Security benefits go faster than the rate of inflation." And as a result of a lot of us retiring and fewer people paying the system, the deal is going broke. And it's hard for me to travel our country and look at hard-working people paying payroll taxes to a system that I know is going broke. And it should be hard for Republicans and Democrats on Capitol Hill as well.

And so I just want to assure you that no matter how hard it may seem for some, I'm going to keep talking about it. That's the job of a President, is to remind people of the challenges.

There's a long-term deficit issue as a result of a system which is out of balance and out of kilter, and we need to do something about it now. We have that obligation. The Senate has the chance—or the House now has the chance to pass a budget bill, or an appropriations bill, reconciliation bill that actually starts to cut mandatory spending by making reforms. The deal passed out of the House, passed out of the Senate. Now it has to go back to the House. And it would be a good-faith gesture on people from both political parties to say, "We see we've got a problem on mandatory spending; why don't we start reforming the system for the sake of future generations of Americans."

Things are going well, by the way, in the economy. We added 4.6 million new jobs since April of 2003. What I'm telling you is, the tax plan is working, and here's why I can say it to you without having to throw some hot air your way. Since April of 2003, 4.6 million new jobs have been created, not by government, but by entrepreneurs. We had a national unemployment rate of 4.9 percent; I think it's 2 percent, 2-point-something percent here in Loudoun County. But think about—[*applause*]—the economy grew at 4.1 percent in the third quarter. And that's in spite of high energy prices, or higher energy prices and two storms. Think about that. Think of how robust our economy is when it's growing at 4.1 percent in the third quarter of this year, in the face of storm and high energy prices. It's got to affect your business, doesn't it, all those high energy prices. And yet you're growing.

In other words, we've got an economy which is robust. The interesting statistic is the manufacturing activity has been up for 31 straight months. You hear a lot of talk about manufacturers and the trouble with manufacturers, and of course, there are some trouble. But we've had growth for 31 straight months. Productivity is up. That's a really important statistic for our country because productivity—as a worker becomes more productive, as the workforce is more productive, higher wages follow. That's just a fact of life.

Do you realize that from 1973 to 1995, productivity in America grew at 1.4 percent. At that rate, the standard of living doubles every 50 years. Today, our productivity is up, averaged 3.4 percent over the past 5 years. In other words, we're more productive as time goes on. Technology enables our workers to be more productive. Education enables our workers to be more productive. Smart business leaders are constantly trying to figure out how to make their companies more productive. The more productive a workforce is, the faster incomes go up.

So what I'm saying is, things are going fine. I mean, you know, we've got more minorities ever before in our country owning their own home. Homeownership is on the rise. And the fundamental question facing us is, what do we do to keep it going?

What do we do? Well, first thing is, Congress needs to make the tax relief permanent. You know, this relief is set to expire. The easy course is, of course, say, "Well, then just let it expire." That's a tax increase if the tax relief expires. When you hear people say, "Well, we're not going to make it permanent," what they're telling you is they're going to run up your taxes; that's what they're saying.

Failure to make tax relief permanent is a tax raise on the working people and the small businesses in this country. If you're a small-business owner, there's got to be certainty in the Tax Code. Congress needs to put themselves in the shoes of people who are trying to plan. Good businessowners, good small-business owners don't think, you know, 2 months in advance; they think years in advance. They're making capital schedules; they're thinking about how to grow their company; they're constantly strategizing. Uncertainty in the Tax Code makes it hard for the small-business sector to stay confident and to make investments. And when there is uncertainty, it makes it harder for this economy to show steady growth.

So people need to make this tax cut permanent so we don't take money out of your pocket. And we need to make the tax cuts permanent so there will be certainty when it comes time for small businesses to plan.

I understand there's a problem in health care, and I suspect during the question-and-answer, we'll get questions on health care. One of the biggest problems our small businesses have is the increase in health care. The role of government, in my judgment, is to take care of the poor through Medicaid and community health centers. The role of the government, in my judgment, is to take care of the elderly through a Medicare program which is modern and, by the way, provides choices for our seniors. But I also think the role of government is to encourage a direct relationship between the consumer/the patient, and the provider/the doctor, without a lot of go-between.

I think that—I know that small businesses should be allowed the same affordability of health care that big businesses get by being able to pool across jurisdictional boundaries, pool your risk. If you're a restaurant owner in here—Loudoun County and a restaurant owner in Crawford—I think there are a couple of restaurants here. [*Laughter*] If not, there will be. No, there is a good one, the coffee shop—I mean, Coffee Station, excuse me. But they should be allowed to pool their risk across jurisdictional boundaries. In other words, the larger the risk pool, the more employees you're able to get in a risk pool, the easier it is to manage your costs when it comes to health insurance. You can't do that now. And Congress should be allowed—encourage you to be able to pool risk.

An interesting product available is called health savings accounts. I strongly urge every small-business owner here to look at them. It's an innovative product that enables the small-business owner and the employee to combine, work together to come up with a plan where the employee owns it. It provides for a high deductible catastrophic plan, coupled with tax-free contributions in the plan, basically gives the consumer control over his or her medical decisions. The plan can grow tax-free, which is an encouragement for people to make wise decisions about how they treat their body. If you have a catastrophic event, the insurance kicks in and covers it. It's portable; if you change jobs, you can take it with you. It's a good—it's an interesting idea.

It certainly stands in stark contrast with a system in which the Federal Government gets to make the consumers decisions, or tells the providers what they can charge. It's the opposite of Federal control; it is patient control.

We need—do a lot on information technology. The health care industry is ineffi-cient in that you've still got people filing out forms with handwritten notes. And doctors can't write anyway—[*laughter*]—and it creates a lot of confusion, as you can imagine.

We need to have legal reform. I mean, you can't have a legal system—I mean, a medical system that's available and affordable when you've got your doctors being sued. Do you realize we've got a crisis when it comes to ob-gyns in America? These good docs who have got the great compassionate job of taking care of youngins, they're getting run out of business because of frivolous and junk lawsuits. It makes no sense.

When I first came to Washington, I said, you know, "This is a State issue." But the problem with all these junk lawsuits is that they cause doctors to practice defensive medicine. In other words, they prescribe more than they should because they're afraid of getting sued. And when you practice defensive medicine, it makes the cost of medicine go up. And when you couple that with increasing premiums, it costs us a lot of money at the Federal level, I'm talking billions a year as the result of junk lawsuits.

And good small-business owners have trouble affording health care; part of the reason why is because of these junk lawsuits. And so I've decided this is a national issue that requires a national response. We need medical liability reform in Washington, DC, so that health care is available and affordable.

Laura always says I get too long-winded when I come to one of these deals—[*laughter*]—and so I'll try to rein it in here. I've got something to say, though.

We've got do something about lawsuits, in general, not just medical lawsuits. One of the things I hear a lot from small-business owners is they're afraid of getting sued. I mean, we've got a society which is litigious in nature. People are just suing right and left. That makes it—that runs up the cost of staying in business. It makes it harder for people to work. Of course, if you have a legitimate lawsuit, you ought to get—you know, have your day in court. Everybody understands that. It's just these frivolous lawsuits.

And we're trying to do some things about it in Washington. We've got a class-action lawsuit reform passed. We're trying to get asbestos reform passed. We got bankruptcy passed. We got manufacturers liability passed when it comes to firearms. I mean, we're making some progress when it comes to lawsuit reform. I urge the attorney general here to—urge the Governor in the Commonwealth to pass good lawsuit reform as well. It's a really important issue for the vibrancy of our economy.

Now, energy, real quick—look, we're hooked on foreign sources of oil, and we need to do something about it, pure and simple. I've got a strong faith in technology being able to lead us away from a hydro-carbon society. It's going to take awhile. But the Federal Government has a role to invest in research and development. I envision a day when we're using corn, corn husks, different kind of grasses to be able to convert that into energy.

Down in Brazil, they've got enormous amounts of energy they get from their sug-arcane. Their automobiles are flex-fuel automobiles; they're able to convert from gasoline to ethanol made by sugarcane on an easy basis. I mean, it's coming. And the role of the Federal Government is to encourage these new technologies, to be able to make us less dependent on foreign sources of oil.

We need to be—we ought to have more nuclear power in the United States of America. It's clean; it's renewable; it's safer than it ever was in the past. And we need to be thinking about how we can use solar batteries better. I mean, there's a lot of things we can be doing. I'm confident that with the right policies and the right incentives, technology will help us diversify away from a hydrocarbon world.

But we've got plenty of certain kinds of hydrocarbons we can use—coal. I'm also convinced, with the right expenditure of money, that we'll be able to have zero-emissions coal-fired plants that will make us less dependent. Do you realize we've got about 250 years of coal here in America? It seems like to me a wise investment is to figure out how to use that coal in a way that heats your homes and fuels your businesses and, at the same time, protects the environment. So we have to think about how to incorporate new technologies to di-versify away from foreign sources of energy, not only for economic security but for national security purposes.

I want to talk real quick about trade. I believe it's important to open up markets. I think it's a mistake for this country to go isolationist when it comes to economic policy. Do you realize we're 5 percent of the world's population, which means 95 percent of the rest of them could be customers, so long as we've got a level playing field. My job is to make sure that if you're producing a product, that it has fair access to markets. We ought to treat people—people ought to treat us just like we treat them. And I'm a strong believer that if the playing field is level, this country can compete with anybody, anytime, anywhere. And if we can't, we ought to figure out why not. Competition is good, so long as it's fair competition.

And finally, I want to talk about edu-cation. As you expand your businesses, as they become—you know, as they change because of technology, you're going to need a workforce that is capable of filling the jobs. We've got to make sure we get edu-cation right in the United States; otherwise, the jobs of the 21st century are going to go somewhere else. This is a competitive world in which we live; there's no way to deny that there's competition in the world. We can play like it. We can put up, you know, foolish, short-term economic policies that will hurt the small-business sector, pro-tectionist policies. But it's a competitive world, and people are going to go to where the skill sets of the labor market are such that they'll be able to produce the products of the 21st century. It's a reality.

So what do you do about it? Well, the first thing you do about it is you make sure your kids at the elementary school get an education; teach them how to read, write, and add and subtract. The No Child Left Behind Act is a great piece of legislation. I think as small-business owners, you'll understand where I'm coming from. It says, you've got to measure to determine whether or not you're succeeding.

I was concerned when I was the Governor of Texas that we had an education system that didn't measure, and therefore, we didn't know. And oftentimes when you don't know whether a child can read and write and add and subtract, they just end up being shuffled through the system. I believe that we ought to measure. As a matter of fact, we are now measuring as a result of the No Child Left Behind Act that says, "We want to determine whether or not you can read at grade level by the third grade and whether or not you're grade level at the fourth grade and the fifth grade and so on. And if not, here's some money to help you make sure the child is up at grade level."

You cannot solve a problem until you diagnose a problem. And the No Child Left Behind Act is a diagnostic tool for local school districts. We're not telling you how to run your schools; that's up to you. We didn't design a Federal test; we just said, "You design an accountability system." And it's working. We have an achievement gap in America that is not right and needs to be closed. We have too many African American kids not reading at grade level, and they should be. And I say a lot of that is due to just moving kids through without determining early whether or not they've got the skills necessary to read, write, and add and subtract. And we're changing that. The achievement gap is closing. It's a really positive development. I

can tell you how I know, because we measure, and we solve problems early, before it's too late.

We've got to have these same high standards in high school, with an emphasis on math and science. We've got to use our community college systems to constantly upgrade the skills of people. As you know, the job market changes. And the easiest thing for a society is to have technological change; the hardest thing is to make sure that the education systems are flexible enough to help the job market change with technology.

Community college is a great asset in our country. They're available; they're affordable. And if they're run right, they have a curriculum that changes with the times. They're not one of these institutions to just stay stuck. They're an institution that says, "We're going to change our curriculum to be able to educate people for the jobs which actually exist." That's what we need to do, what I'm telling you.

So I'm going to go to Congress here pretty soon and call on them to put economic policy, energy policy, health policy in place that understands that this economy is strong, but we need to do the right things to keep it going, with the centerpiece of our economic policy being the small business in America.

Anyway, that's all I've got to tell you right now. I'll be glad to answer a few questions. Yes, sir.

Transportation

Q. [*Inaudible*]

The President. Thank you.

Q. [*Inaudible*]

The President. You have got a transportation problem here.

Q. [*Inaudible*]—northern Virginia. Downtime in traffic is loss of productive time for businesses, and it's time away from home and family for individuals. We don't get to use helicopters. [*Laughter*]

The President. Right. I won't in 3 years, either. [*Laughter*]

Q. How can the Federal Government help States and localities address transportation problems?

The President. We passed the highway bill, and it's set. Congress argued about it, and I argued with them about it. And it's a $270 billion-plus bill that is the law for a period of time, and now it's up to you to spend the money allocated to you by formula in a wise way. I think it's an issue where the Federal Government's responsibility is clear on the law. And that is that we take the gasoline taxes and pass them back to you, but you get to decide where the roads go. And that's probably the way it should be.

I was noticing that the inauguration—or the campaign for Governor here, part of the campaign was roads. And that's good; that's the way it should be. People say, "Vote for me; I'm going to do something about your roads," or, "I hear your problem with your roads." And so you want the decisionmaking about the roads to be here at the local level. But the Federal Government's role in highways is pretty well fixed for 5 or 6 years.

Yes, sir. Go ahead and yell it out.

Taxation/Public Accountability

Q. Yes, good morning. I'm a CPA here in Loudoun County.

The President. Right.

Q. [*Inaudible*]—prepare a couple hundred tax returns a year, and the IRS does not spend a lot of time auditing. The last administration turned the IRS into a customer service department. And here, the last 3 years, it's been reorganized. There's quite a few people that do not comply. I really think that the IRS needs to get out there and audit. I hope none of my clients are here. [*Laughter*]

The President. That's a very unbelievably interesting statement from a—[*laughter*]. No, but you've got a good point. Look, here's the point the man is saying. He's right. There are too many honest people—first of all, there are people who feel like

they don't have to pay taxes, and that's not fair to the millions of honest people who do. A tax system is—[*applause*].

Look, I don't know the inner workings of the IRS; I know there is strong enforcement. And with the millions of filings, I would suspect there's programs in place that highlight irregularities that then call up the audits. I don't think you can ever audit everybody, nor would you subscribe for everybody being audited who files a return. But if there's flagrant anomalies in reporting, I suspect they take a good look at it.

You'll be pleased to hear that I'm audited every year—[*laughter*]—one way or the other. More than happy to put out my income tax returns for my friends in the press to scrutinize. [*Laughter*] I see them nodding—yes, they love—[*laughter*]—as it should be, by the way, for people in public office. Those of us in public office have the high responsibility to uphold the integrity of the process. And people ought to be held to high standards. In Washington, DC, there needs to be high standards for conduct of public officials.

Yes, sir.

Homeownership/Market Adjustments

Q. [*Inaudible*]

The President. Homebuilder, good.

Q. [*Inaudible*]—substantially over the past housing boom. And I guess my question is, as the consequence of this great housing boom has increased the cost of housing so much, not only in this area but throughout the country, it's very difficult for me to envision my kids being able to afford a home, or even the workforce that drives much of, you know, our school systems and our police and fire forces—[*inaudible*]. How do you see the Federal Government helping this workforce out—[*inaudible*]—to be able to afford housing close to where their jobs are?

The President. Markets adjust, and the role of the government is to make sure the market is able to adjust in a way that is not precipitous and disruptive. When you have wage and price controls, for example, in history, it's tended to not allow the market to adjust in a smooth function, a smooth way. It doesn't function properly. And therefore, the consequences of government trying to either manage price or demand is very severe.

So to answer your question, one role of the government is to make sure that markets are given the flexibility to adjust in a way that doesn't cause major disruption. If houses get too expensive, people will stop buying them, which will cause people to adjust their spending habits.

Secondly, setting of interest rates affects your business. You'll be happy to hear that the White House doesn't set interest rates; the Federal Reserve Board sets interest rates. I get to name the Chairman; I named a good guy in Ben Bernanke. But it's their job to be independent from the political process and look at market forces—in all aspects of our economy—to determine the interest rate to be set. Obviously, they look at inflation, consumer demand, et cetera.

And so to answer your question, a simple answer is let the market function properly. Let the market function properly. I guarantee that your kind of question has been asked throughout the history of homebuilding; you know, prices for my homes are getting bid up so high that I'm afraid I'm not going to have any consumers—or my kid—and yet things cycle. That's just the way it works. Economies should cycle. We just don't want the cycles to be so severe that it gets disruptive so that, you know, you get thrown out of business, for example, or somebody gets thrown out of work.

Yes, ma'am.

Health Care Reform

Q. Thank you for coming to Loudoun County, Mr. President. I run a nonprofit that provides health care to the uninsured——

The President. Good.

Q. ——something near and dear to your heart—45 million uninsured people in the country, and of course, Loudoun County is no different. We provide health care free by volunteer physicians who are involved in a nonprofit, and it's a good private-public partnership. You talked about creating health—[*inaudible*]—as part of the health care delivery systems. We, too, are part of health care delivery systems. How do you see your role and the government's role in helping us do what we do, when we've discovered recently that we're not going away anytime in the near future?

The President. Yes. Well, first, I think there ought to be—well, first, there are tax incentives to encourage people to contribute to your nongovernmental organization, which is good. That's what we want. We want people to have a Tax Code such that if you give to your group or a church, synagogue, or mosque, or somebody whose job it is to help the unfortunate, you get a deduction for it.

Secondly, the uninsured is—first of all, there's the working uninsured; a lot of them work for small businesses because small businesses can't afford insurance. A small-business owner would like to pay for the insurance, but the cost of medicine is increasing.

And I just gave you two prescriptions for that. One is—well, a bunch of prescriptions—to help control the cost and enable small businesses to be able to manage the expense. If you stand alone as a small-business owner—10,000 businesses, 80 percent of which have got 10 employers or less—and you try to buy insurance as an employer of 10 people, it's going to cost you a heck of a lot more than if you try to buy insurance with your 10 people in a pool of 5,000 people. It's just the way insurance works. It's called spreading the risk.

There are some in the uninsured world who simply choose not to buy insurance. That would be your bulletproof 22-year-old person—you know, just out of college—

[*laughter*]—"I'm never going to be sick; nothing ever bad is going to happen. I just don't think I'm going to want any." [*Laughter*]

Health savings account is an interesting opportunity for the young 22-year-old healthy person, who is able to put money aside, tax-free, and watch that money grow, tax-free, and take the money out of the health savings account, tax-free, coupled with a high deductible catastrophic health plan. In other words, this is a product that will say to those who choose, here's an opportunity for you. You start putting aside $1,000 a year; in other words, you buy a high deductible policy with a $1,000 deductible, and you put the $1,000 cash— you do or your employer does, or however you negotiate it—that $1,000 grows. And it can grow to be pretty substantial, particularly as you're a healthy person, over a period of time, tax-free. And all of a sudden, you've got quite a nest egg.

I'm going to call on Congress, by the way, to make these health savings accounts more attractive, more portable, more individualized.

There are some who come to our country that don't have any health insurance but work. We've got immigrants coming that can't afford health care. Their employers— the type of job they have is one that doesn't lend itself to health care. One way the Government can help is to have community health centers as primary care facilities to deliver health care and take the pressure off the emergency rooms. We're expanding these a lot. In my judgment, it's a good use of taxpayers' money to provide health clinics for the poor and the indigent, so that they don't go to where the health care is more expensive, the emergency room, but go to where the health care—primary health is more manageable.

And so there's a series of ways to address the issue. But the truth of the matter is, Government policy has got to aim at the increasing cost of health care.

Part of the issue in Medicare is the projections of health care costs going up the way they are. The issues that small-business owners face in the short term is increasing premiums. And so we need medical liability reform to help address the costs. We need to encourage information technologies, and I'm told that there would be a significant reduction of medical costs as we modernize medicine and bring medicine into the 21st century through the use of information technology.

Health savings accounts encourage consumers to pay attention to price. There needs to be transparency in pricing. Do you realize the medical field is one where you don't do any comparative shopping? When you buy tile, I presume, for your house, you're out there shopping it. You know, say, look, what am I bid? You know, when you're buying pipe or things you put in the wall, insulation, you're out there bidding price. There's no transparency in pricing in medicine. You don't know whether the guy next door is going to offer a better deal when it comes to some kind of medical procedure.

It seems like to me the more transparency in pricing, the more likely it is consumers will have an input into the cost of health care. And so these are ways to address the cost of health care. Obviously, as health care costs—the rate of increase is manageable, there will be less people coming in to see you.

One of the reasons why the uninsured is going up, because the cost is going up. And so the Government needs to address the cost. There is a debate in Washington. Some will say the way to address the cost is to have the Federal Government be the decider, the decider for the consumer and the decider for the provider, and that will be—in my judgment—terrible for this country. And so this is—we're talking about a very important and interesting debate. And I'm going to continue pushing policies that address cost and empower the patient and the doctor into a relationship that is not only good for the patient but also one in which, I think, will affect the pricing mechanisms and the prices here in the country.

Yes, ma'am.

U.S. Armed Forces

Q. [*Inaudible*]—and we're proud of you Mr. President, and your——

The President. Keep it up, will you? [*Laughter*] About time.

Q. [*Inaudible*]

The President. Thank you. [*Laughter*] It's always good to have a plant in every audience, you know? [*Laughter*]

Q. Well, the timing of this opportunity is uncanny. I want to thank you for your unwavering support of the Veterans Administration. My father spent the last 2 years at the Martinsburg, West Virginia VA, where he was loved and respected and so well cared for. And we buried him 2 weeks ago in Arlington, and it struck me then how strong the promise still is for our veterans and our wonderful men and women of the service. And I thank you.

The President. Thanks. You know what I thought just when you said that at first? Our country is great because we've got a lot of people who have been willing to serve. It's really important that we keep an all-volunteer military. And one way to do that is to make sure that people are paid well, or as good as you can pay them; that they're trained well; that their loved ones have got adequate housing on the bases—in other words, family life is good; that the education systems work on our bases. But also after service, there is a health care system that will provide modern health care for them.

So thanks for bringing that up. The Volunteer Army is really an important part of our Nation, and it's a really important part of fighting this war on terror. We've got kids who know the stakes. They saw the attack on September the 11th. They have made a conscious decision to swear in to serve the country. So thanks for brining

that up. I just wanted to share that with you, to tell you that our troops are always on my mind; their families are always on my mind. And it's important to leave a legacy behind of a strong military based upon patriotic Americans saying, "I want to serve. I'm stepping up. Nobody is telling me to. I have made the decision to do so."

Yes, sir.

President's Personal Values/Leadership

Q. Good morning, Mr. President, thank you for being here. My son is one of those young men, at 18 years old almost—I hope I don't cry, but I——

The President. I hope you don't too, because I will as well, and then we—[*laughter*].

Q. Okay. He asked me to take him to the Army recruiter. He didn't drive yet, but he wanted to go to the Army recruiter to join the Army. He's in the National Guard in Christiansburg, Virginia. And he's also at the Virginia Tech Corps of Cadets.

The President. Oh, good, thanks. I know you're proud of him.

Q. Yes, I am.

The President. Good.

Q. He sends his best wishes to you.

The President. To the old Commander in Chief, that's a smart move, you know. [*Laughter*]

Q. He and I discussed a question, and I want to ask you. Most people in this room today are leaders of some type. I'm a leader of an adult education center for Marymount University. And my question to you is, how do you remain upbeat when you're surrounded by the burdens of leadership?

The President. Thanks. My faith and my family and my friends, for starters. I like going home to be with my family. I was teasing about Laura waking me up this morning at 12:45 a.m., but I'm glad she did. I take great pride in my little girls. I'm not going to talk about them too much; otherwise, these people will put it in the newspaper. And I'm trying—[*Laughter*]. Right, Jackson [David Jackson, USA Today]? I'm trying to spare them because I think that one of the hardest decisions about going into public life is exposing people you love to the public nature of public life.

I'm proud to tell you that my friends that I knew before I became in public office are still my friends. One of the coolest things to do in my Presidential work, one of the—[*laughter*]—seeing if you're paying attention up there—[*laughter*]—things I like to do is to welcome my buddies, and Laura feels the same way—people we grew up with—we both grew up in Midland, Texas. I remember having some of my friends that I went to first grade with, a guy I grew up across the street with, Michael Proctor, they came up to have dinner at the White House. You know, and they kind of walk in there. You can imagine what it's like. It's a great honor, pretty awe-inspiring deal. They walk in there and, kind of, "What are you doing here, Bush?" You know. [*Laughter*]

But I really like it. And they're my friends. They help me keep—help me remind myself that what's important is what you believe. And leaders have got to know the core principles on which you'll make decisions, and you can't change. There's a lot of temptation to change to try to make people want to like you. That's not the job of a leader. The job of a leader is to know where he or she wants to lead and know the principles on which you'll make decisions.

I take great comfort in having people around me who can walk in my office and tell me what's on their mind. Part of my job is—they say, "What's your job?" My job is, decisionmaker. I make a lot of decisions, obviously, some of which you've seen, and a lot of them you don't. And they're big ones and little ones, but you make a lot of decisions. And if you don't—if you're uncertain about all the facts surrounding a decision, you've got to rely upon people.

And you've then got to create an environment in which people are willing to come in and say, "Here's what's on my mind."

It's important at the Presidential level. It's important in business. You've got to have people comfortable about saying, "Here's what I think you ought to do, Mr. CEO." You've got to listen and have a— I've always believed in a flat organizational chart. I think the worst thing that can happen for decisionmakers is to get a filtered point of view.

And it's pretty hard as President, needless to say, but I've got a group of people around me that are empowered to walk in. Condi Rice, when she walks in, she comes in as a close friend, but as someone who knows that our friendship will be sustained, whether she agrees with me or not. Rumsfeld comes in—and he's a crusty old guy who—[*laughter*]—and he's got an opinion, and he tells it. And that's important. And that's the way it is throughout the White House.

I like to tell people, the first decision I made as President was this—the guy called me—I was at the Blair House looking at my Inaugural speech, trying to get comfortable with it, get ready to go; it was a pretty big event coming up, and wanted to make sure that it worked well. And he said, "Mr. President-elect, what color rug do you want in the Oval Office?" I said, "Man, this is going to be a decisionmaking experience. [*Laughter*] What color rug do I want in the Oval Office? "[*Laughter*] He said, "No, I'm not kidding you." Turns out Presidents design rugs. [*Laughter*] Or somebody designs them for them. And I said, "I don't know anything about rug designing," so I delegated to Laura. [*Laughter*]

Interestingly enough, the job of a leader is to think strategically. It's important for your businesses; it's important for the country. And so she said, "Tell me about the rug." And I said, "I want it to say, 'optimistic person comes here to work every day.' " It was the strategic thought for the rug. She figured out the colors. It looks like a sun, with nice, open colors. You walk into that Oval Office, I think you're going to say, it looks like, you know, this guy is optimistic. I'm optimistic—by the way, you can't lead your company and say, "Follow me, the world is not going to be good." You're not going to have a lot of employees say, "Great, I love working here," you know. [*Laughter*] It's got to be, "Follow me, the world is going to be better, and I have a plan to do it."

And one reason I'm optimistic is because I'm sustained by my faith, family, and friends. I'm also sustained by the fact that I believe strongly in the values of the United States of America: human rights, human dignity, individuals count, freedom is the future of the world. And I'm sustained by those beliefs.

And thanks for the question. It was an interesting question.

Yes.

Broadband Technology

Q. On behalf of the Loudoun County Board of Supervisors, we welcome you.

The President. Thanks. Thanks for having me. You don't look old enough to have run. [*Laughter*]

Q. I'm the youngest member of the board. [*Laughter*]

The President. Yes, is this your board, here?

Q. This is—[*inaudible*].

The President. Yes, you certainly are the youngest, I can—[*laughter*]. He's a pretty young guy too.

Q. And you probably know we've got health savings accounts for our county employees—[*inaudible*].

The President. Good move. Good move.

Q. But on transportation, one of the solutions that I've been putting forward is telework and expansion of broadband.

The President. Yes.

Q. [*Inaudible*]—so that people don't get caught in traffic. But Congress is contemplating revisions to the Telecommunication Act of '96 that would essentially shut down the options that States and localities are exploring to give broadband to every business and every home. So what is your thought on, as we are falling behind in the world on delivering broadband to businesses and homes and residences—what will you do to——

The President. Yes, I need to find out—it's interesting you said that because I laid out the opposite vision, which was that broadband ought to be available and accessible all throughout the country by a set period of time. I need to make sure I understand what you mean—Congress is trying to unwind that vision, because it sounds like you and I share—I believe you. Thank you for the heads-up. I'll take a look.

You're very smart to—part of the role of government is to create an environment in which people are willing to risk capital. Broadband expansion is part of creating an environment in which it will make it easier for people to be competitive in this part of the world. It's a brilliant idea. People are able to do so much more from their home, particularly if you've got the technology capable of carrying information.

You're right—want to make sure—you mentioned that other nations are ahead of us. True, we're catching up, and we'll do better, by the way. But if—part of making sure America is competitive is to make sure that we've got broadband available and accessible. One of the interesting questions we're going to have is the last-mile issue, and a lot of that, hopefully, will be changed, or at least options—more options will be available with the development of a dish that is capable of passing broadband over the air, as opposed to cable.

Good question. I need to check and see what you're talking about, and will. Thanks for bringing it up.

Yes, ma'am.

First Lady Laura Bush

Q. [*Inaudible*]

The President. Yes, well——

Q. ——who happens to be one of the best First Ladies we've had.

The President. Thank you. I thought you might say "top two," but you know— [*laughter*].

Q. Well, the top two.

The President. If not, I won't tell her. [*Laughter*]

Q. I was just wondering when we'll see our lovely First Lady run for the Senate in the——

The President. Never. [*Laughter*]

Q. Come on. Ask her, will you?

The President. No, I'm not going to ask her. Never. [*Laughter*] You know, I think— I'm pretty certain when I married her, she didn't like politics or politicians. [*Laughter*] She's a great lady. She's interested—she's not interested in running for office.

She is interested in literacy. We're going to meet with foundations later on today to encourage them to step in where government can't step in, in New Orleans and the gulf coast. Laura is coming to the meeting. And the reason why is she wants to help these schools get their libraries up. She was a school librarian, and she believes strongly in literacy.

I can remember her reading to the girls all the time. And I would encourage moms all over the country—and dads—to sit down and read to your young children over and over and over again. It's one of the lessons she taught me, right after she taught me how to read. [*Laughter*] She's great. Thank you for bringing her up. She's not going to run for office.

Yes, sir.

Democracy in the Middle East/Domestic Agenda

Q. Mr. President, my wife, Sandy, and I send our prayers and our appreciation for all that you're doing and these difficult issues that you're dealing with. I'm a grandfather, about your age, but I have——

The President. You got started earlier.

Q. I got started a little earlier. And I'm really proud of my family. You touched on a lot of issues that really affect us. We have a health care provider and an attorney in the building industry, in the defense industry, and a young grandson who is espousing to—[*inaudible*]—the Military Academy. We are very happy with the foundations that President Reagan and your father laid 23 years ago, about the time that— [*inaudible*]—started. We're building off of that today. We're living in that security, with a good defense system, and we have a strong economy, some of which extends from those days. Do you look forward— and what can I tell my grandchildren— do you look forward 20, 25 years from now and see a vision of America?

The President. Yes. I tell people this story a lot. When my dad was 18, he went to fight the Japanese. And some 60 years later, his son sits at the table with the Prime Minister of Japan to help keep the peace. Someday, I firmly believe that leaders in the broader Middle East will be duly elected and will be sitting down with future American Presidents to keep the peace.

So part of the vision for your children and grandchildren is to understand history and the power of democracy and freedom and liberty to change enemies into allies. And I talk about a lot in my speeches, laying the foundation of peace. And I firmly believe that what we're doing today is laying the foundation of peace.

I know that some say democracy can't take hold in parts of the world—"You're wasting your time, Mr. President." I strongly disagree with that. The natural rights of men and women—that's part of our founding—says that inherent in every soul, I believe implanted by a higher being, is the desire to live in freedom, no matter the color of your skin or the religion you embrace. And so part of the vision is to lay that foundation of peace by believing and acting on the principles that caused our own existence to be and on principles and values that have proven over time to yield the peace.

Think about Europe. It's hard for some of us to think about Europe because Europe didn't really affect our lives, did it, much. But if you look back over the recent history of the United States and the world, two world wars started in Europe. And today, Europe is whole, free, and at peace because of democracy, in my judgment. The Far East—[*applause*].

And the reason this is important is because we're in an ideological struggle. The enemy which attacked us on September the 11th was not just acting out of anger, although they were not acting out of hate, although I believe their hearts are hateful, but they were acting based upon an ideology.

The best way to make sure the American people understand what happens when their ideology takes hold is to think about life in Afghanistan under the Taliban. If you're a young girl in Afghanistan under the Taliban, you have no chance for success. You have no chance for education. If your mother speaks out in the public square, you get whipped—she would get whipped. These people have a vision that is the opposite of America. Their vision is, "Here is my view of religion, and if you don't agree with me, you're in trouble."

Our belief is, is that what matters is your view of religion; you can choose. The great freedom in America is the ability to choose your religion, to be religious or not religious. We're equally American—Jew, Muslim, Christian—we're all equally American in this country. That's the opposite of what these people think. They have got a strategy; they've got a goal, which is to spread this vision throughout the world, starting in the broader Middle East. I say it's to go from Spain to Indonesia, to establish their—a caliphate with their point of view. These are ideologues.

And so you defeat an ideology with a better ideology. If there's no competition, if there's a vacuum, if there's poverty, hunger, and anxiety and a vacuum is created because of that, this ideology will move in.

However, there is a competing ideology available. If there's an alternative for people to choose from, then all of a sudden, their march to their vision is impeded in the long run. And democracy is the alternative, liberty.

It's not American-style democracy. Japan didn't say, "Let's just look like America." Japan said, "We'll have a democracy that suits our needs." That's the way democracies develop. They develop with history and culture of the people in mind.

And so what you're seeing in Iraq is twofold: one, a commitment to defeat an enemy overseas so they don't hit us again, coupled with allowing these Iraqis to live a dream of being free. And it's tough work. It's tough because some of the enemy are these ideologues that are trying to stop the march of freedom. Some of them are people that are irritated because Saddam is not in power. They liked it being the, you know, the power elite. Some of them are wondering whether or not—the Sunni rejectionists are wondering whether or not they'll even have a say in the future government and, therefore, are nervous given the dynamics and the demographics. But some of them are people there intent upon destroying the advance of democracy because they understand—they know that they can't compete with liberty.

And the amazing thing that happened last year that I hope—at least gives me heart is that millions of Iraqis made a choice. They defied terrorists. We see them. The terrorists have got a weapon; it's called our TV screens. These people are coldblooded killers, I'm telling you. As you know, I don't need to tell you that. And what they're trying to do is they're trying to drive us out before democracy can take hold because they understand— I haven't talked to one so I'm not exactly sure—I'm putting words in somebody's mouth. I would suspect, though, deep in their soul, they understand they can't compete. Their ideology cannot compete with liberty.

And so to answer your question—it's a long answer, but it's an important question. The President has got to be thinking down the road. We've got a short-term battle we're going to win, but there's a long-term struggle as well. It's an ideological struggle.

At home, I think two things that I would like to be remembered for, and one is promoting ownership. I want people to own something. I want people owning their own small business. I want people owning their own homes. I think people ought to be allowed to own their own health care account and make decisions for what is best for them. And there ought to be incentives. I know a vibrant Social Security system is one in which people are able to take some of their own money if they so choose and put in a personal savings account so they can get a better rate of return on their own money than the Government can get through the Social Security trust. But more importantly, I want people owning something.

I'll never forget going to a Mississippi automobile manufacturing plant. And I was on—a lot of the floor workers there, you know. And I said, "How many of you own your own 401(k)?" Just needless to say, it was a very diverse audience. I don't know, I'd say 95 percent of the hands went up—men, women, black, white. I said, "How's it feel to own your own assets?"

See, one of the problems we've had that shows—what we found out in New Orleans—there's not—there wasn't a lot of—we take—some things we take for granted, like the generations passing assets from one generation to the next just didn't happen in the African American community, and should. We ought to encourage—we take that for granted, don't we? Some of us do. You know, you pass the house on. A lot of these people didn't own their own homes. A lot of them didn't have checking accounts. And yet one of the things we ought to encourage is systems—is reforms that enable somebody to own something so they can pass it on to their child. It's

part of creating stability and healthy families and strength. And so I want to be known as an ownership guy.

I also want to be known as the person that kept the de Tocqueville vision for America alive. De Tocqueville was a Frenchman. He came to America in the 1830s, and he studied America, and he came away impressed by our democracy, but really impressed by the fact that people came together to serve a greater cause through voluntary organizations. People said, well, how best to help—in a vibrant society, help a neighbor? And that is, they formed what you call voluntary organizations to help a neighbor in need. The great strength of this country is the fact that there are millions of loving souls in America who are willing to reach out to somebody in need.

I always say, government can't love; it's just not a loving organization. There are people who work for government who have love in their heart, but government, itself, is not loving. It ought to be law and justice. In my judgment, government ought to be constantly thinking about ways to rally what I call the armies of compassion, so that light can head into the dark corners of our country, so that people who have heard the call to love a neighbor are empowered to do so and encouraged to do so.

One of the most—I think one of the most important and interesting domestic initiatives, which I agree has created an interesting philosophical debate, is to allow faith-based programs and community-based programs to access Federal money in order to achieve the results we all want. I mean, for example, if you're trying to encourage people to quit drinking, doesn't it make sense to give people—somebody an alternative? He can maybe go to a Government counselor; or how about somebody who calls upon a higher being to help you quit drinking? All I care about is the results. And the Government ought to be——

So to answer—and that's a long answer, and, by the way, it's my last answer, because you're paying me a lot of money, or probably—[*laughter*]. I'm not going to argue about my salary. [*Laughter*] But I've got to get back to work. I do want to thank you for your interest. I hope you can tell I understand the importance of making sure America is entrepreneurial heaven.

You know, one of the things that I love when I travel the world is you can get a sense for the country by asking questions. One of the things about our country is it's a place where you can start with zero, you start with a dream and a good idea—in this case, a good mom and dad—and take risk and realize your dream. And it's really important we keep it that way forever.

America has got to be a place where dreamers can realize their dreams, and I love being in the midst of dreamers.

Thanks for letting me come by. God bless you all.

NOTE: The President spoke at 10:06 a.m. at JK Moving & Storage. In his remarks, he referred to Randy Minchew, chairman, Loudoun County Republican Committee; President Ellen Johnson Sirleaf of Liberia; Charles Kuhn, president, chief executive officer, and founder, JK Moving & Storage, Inc., and his mother, Shirley; Linda Graves, wife of former Gov. Bill Graves of Kansas; Gov. Timothy M. Kaine of Virginia; Prime Minister Junichiro Koizumi of Japan; and former President Saddam Hussein of Iraq.

Remarks Following a Meeting With Foundations Involved With Gulf Coast Recovery
January 19, 2006

Laura and I are so thankful that Dr. Francis and Leland Speed—Dr. Francis is from Louisiana; Mr. Leland Speed is from Mississippi—are here to brief not only Don Powell and myself and Laura but also members of the compassion community here in America. We've got charities from all across the country, foundations from all across the country who have come to listen to the needs of the good people in Mississippi and Louisiana and the gulf coast region.

Don and I talked about the commitment of the Federal Government; we've committed $85 billion thus far. But we also made it very clear that we're going to need the help of—the continued help, I might add, of America's charities and foundations. Part of making sure the money is spent well is to hear from the local folks about what is needed; how can we help; how best can the money be spent.

And that's exactly what we've done today. We're going to make sure that the Federal money is spent wisely and local money and charitable money is spent wisely as well, all aimed at making sure that the folks in Louisiana and Mississippi get back on their feet and this vital region of our country is up and running again. There's no doubt in my mind that out of this incredible devastation will come a better tomorrow.

And again, I want to thank all the people who have taken time out of your busy schedules to come and show your interest and represent your foundations and let the good folks know, in that troubled part of the world, that their voices of despair and concern are being heard all around the country.

So thank you all for coming. I appreciate it very much.

NOTE: The President spoke at 2:07 p.m. in Room 350 of the Dwight D. Eisenhower Executive Office Building. In his remarks, he referred to Norman Francis, chairman, Louisiana Recovery Authority; Leland Speed, director, Mississippi Development Authority; and Donald E. Powell, Chairman, Federal Deposit Insurance Corporation, in his capacity as coordinator of Federal gulf coast relief efforts. A tape was not available for verification of the content of these remarks.

The President's Radio Address
January 21, 2006

Good morning. This past Thursday, I visited a thriving company in Loudoun County, Virginia, named JK Moving & Storage. I met with the owners and workers and with small-business people from the area, and I discussed my agenda to keep America's economy growing and to help our small businesses stay vibrant and strong.

Our agenda for growing the economy and helping small businesses starts with wise tax policy. Our economy grows when American workers and families can keep more of their hard-earned money to spend, save, and invest as they see fit. Small businesses create most of the new jobs in our country, and tax relief helps them as well, because most small businesses pay taxes at individual income tax rates.

So after I took office, we cut taxes on everyone who pays income taxes, leaving more money in the hands of workers and families and giving small businesses more resources to expand and hire. We increased the tax incentives for small businesses to invest in new equipment, and we cut taxes on dividends and capital gains. We also put the death tax on the road to extinction, because farmers and small-business owners should not be taxed twice after a lifetime of work.

Thanks to tax relief, spending restraint, and the hard work of America's entrepreneurs and workers, our economy today is strong. We've added over 400,000 jobs in the last 2 months and over 4.6 million jobs since May 2003. Our unemployment rate is now 4.9 percent, lower than the average rate of the 1970s, 1980s, and 1990s. Our economy grew at 4.1 percent in the third quarter of 2005, and it has been growing at nearly that rate for 2 years. Real after-tax income has grown 7 percent per person since 2001. Productivity is high; inflation is contained; consumers are confident; and more Americans now own their homes than at any time in our Nation's history.

Unfortunately, just as we are seeing how our tax cuts have created jobs and opportunity, some in Washington want to repeal the tax relief. Others want to just let it expire in a few years. Either way, they want to raise your taxes. If that happens, families across America would see their taxes increase dramatically. Small businesses would also pay higher taxes, which would mean less money to hire workers and buy new equipment. To keep our economy growing and our small-business sector strong, we need to ensure that you keep more of what you earn, so Congress needs to make the tax cuts permanent.

For the sake of America's small businesses, workers, and families, we must also make health care more affordable and accessible. A new product known as health savings accounts helps control costs by allowing businesses or workers to buy low-cost insurance policies for catastrophic events and then save, tax free, for routine medical expenses. This year, I will ask Congress to take steps to make these accounts

99

more available, more affordable, and more portable. Congress also needs to pass association health plans, which allow small businesses across the country to join together and pool risk so they can buy insurance at the same discounts big companies get.

Our small businesses are confronting other challenges that we must address. Too many entrepreneurs face the threats of costly junk lawsuits. Last year, we passed bipartisan class-action reform to ease this burden. Now Congress needs to curb abusive asbestos litigation, pass medical liability reform to reduce the costs of frivolous litigation on our doctors and patients, and penalize those who abuse the legal system by repeatedly filing junk lawsuits.

Rising energy costs are also a concern for small businesses, so we're going to continue to work to develop new technologies and alternative and renewable fuels that will make us less dependent on foreign sources of energy. And we will continue to open up new markets for small businesses so they can sell their products and services overseas. On a level playing field, I know our workers, farmers, and businesses can compete with anybody, anytime, anywhere.

America's economy is strong and growing stronger. Small businesses have been a driving force behind the tremendous growth and job creation of recent years. By adopting sound policies that help our small businesses continue to grow and expand, we will keep the economy moving forward and extend prosperity and hope in our country.

Thank you for listening.

NOTE: The address was recorded at 7:50 a.m. on January 20 in the Cabinet Room at the White House for broadcast at 10:06 a.m. on January 21. The transcript was made available by the Office of the Press Secretary on January 20 but was embargoed for release until the broadcast. The Office of the Press Secretary also released a Spanish language transcript of this address.

Telephone Remarks to the March for Life
January 23, 2006

Nellie, thank you very much. I appreciate the invitation to speak. I'm calling from Manhattan, Kansas. [*Applause*] Sounds like you've got some good folks from Kansas there. I want to thank everybody there— if you're from Kansas or anywhere else in our country—for your devotion to such a noble cause.

You believe, as I do, that every human life has value, that the strong have a duty to protect the weak, and that the self-evident truths of the Declaration of Independence apply to everyone, not just to those considered healthy or wanted or convenient. These principles call us to defend the sick and the dying, persons with disabilities and birth defects, all who are weak and vulnerable, especially unborn children.

We're making good progress in defending these principles, Nellie, and you and I are working together, along with others, to build what I've called a culture of life. One of my first acts as the President was to ban the use of taxpayer money on programs that promote abortion overseas. I want to thank you all for getting that ban on partial-birth abortion to my desk, a bill I was proud to sign and a law which we are going to defend and are defending vigorously in our courts.

Because we acted, infants who are born despite an attempted abortion are now protected by law. Thanks to "Laci and

Conner's Law," prosecutors can now charge those who harm or kill a pregnant woman with harming or killing her unborn child as well.

We're vigorously promoting parental notification laws, adoption, teen abstinence, crisis pregnancy programs, and the vital work of our faith-based groups. We're sending a clear message to any woman facing a crisis pregnancy: We love you; we love your child; and we're here to help you.

There's more work to be done. The House has passed a bill to ensure that State parental involvement laws are not circumvented by those who take minors across State lines to have abortions. And the United States Senate needs to pass this bill so I can sign it into law.

We also must respect human life and dignity when advancing medical science, and we're making progress here as well. Last month, I signed a pro-life bill supporting ethical treatment and research using stem cells from umbilical cord blood. I also renew my call for Congress to ban all forms of human cloning. Because human life is a gift from our Creator and should never be used as a means to an end, we will not sanction the creation of life only to destroy it.

By changing laws, we can change our culture. And your persistence and prayers, Nellie, and the folks there with you, are making a real difference. We, of course, seek common ground where possible. We're working to persuade more of our fellow Americans of the rightness of our cause. And this is a cause that appeals to the conscience of our citizens and is rooted in America's deepest principles, and history tells us that with such a cause, we will prevail.

Again, Nellie, thank you for letting me come to speak to you. Tell everybody there that I ask for God's blessings on them and their families, and, of course, may God continue to bless our grand country.

NOTE: The President spoke at 11:40 a.m. from Manhattan, KS, to march participants on the National Mall in Washington, DC. In his remarks, he referred to Nellie J. Gray, president, March for Life Education and Defense Fund.

Remarks on the War on Terror and a Question-and-Answer Session in Manhattan, Kansas
January 23, 2006

The President. Thanks for the warm welcome. Thanks for inviting me here to give the Landon Lecture. For those students who are here, I want you to know I can remember what it was like to sit through lectures. [*Laughter*] I didn't particularly like it then. [*Laughter*] Some will take a little different approach. I'm here to tell you how I see the world and how I've made some of the decisions I've made and why I made them.

Before I get there, I want to thank the introducer. So he's on Air Force One; he says, "That's a cute-looking blue tie you have—[*laughter*]—but I strongly suggest, Mr. President"—[*laughter*]. I said, "I don't know, Senator, if I can take it; I'm worried about all those lobby laws or the lack of them." [*Laughter*] He said, "Fine, I'll just loan it to you." I said, "Well, now that you're helping me dress, you got any hints on how I ought to do my hair?" [*Laughter*]

Pat Roberts is a good man. He's got a great sense of humor. He loves the people of Kansas, and he loves Kansas State, and I'm proud to be with him on this stage.

And I'm proud to be here, as well, with the other United States Senator, Senator Sam Brownback, former president of the Kansas State student body.

I want to thank your Governor. Governor Sebelius, thanks for putting up with me, Roberts, and Brownback as we drove from the airport to here. One hour with the three of us required a lot of patience. [*Laughter*] I'm proud the Governor came with us, and I want to thank you.

I want to thank Congressman Jim Ryun, right from this district. I appreciate you being here, Congressman. I'm not interested in jogging with you. [*Laughter*] I also thank Congressman Dennis Moore and Congressman Jerry Moran, both fine Members of the United Stated Congress from the State of Kansas. Thank you all for coming.

I appreciate President Wefald for having me come. I know Laura was his first choice. [*Laughter*] That's why he's the head of such a fine institution; he's got good judgment. [*Laughter*] By the way, she sends her best. I married really well.

And I want to thank Charles Reagan and Edward Seaton. Charles is the chairman of the Landon Lecture Series. And Edward is the head of the patrons. He said to me, he said, "I so appreciate you believing in free speech; thanks for giving a free one." [*Laughter*] I want to thank Tom Herald, who is the faculty senate president. I want to thank all the faculty members who are here. Thanks for teaching. It's such a noble profession, and I appreciate you lending your expertise to help youngsters learn what is possible and how to think and how to be creative. And I want to thank the president of the student body, Michael Burns, for being here as well.

I appreciate the students being here. I particularly want to thank those who've come from the Last Chance Bar. [*Laughter*] Better than watching daytime TV, I guess. [*Laughter*] I appreciate your interest in your country. Looking forward to sharing some thoughts with you, and then I'll answer some questions.

Before I get there, I do want to pay tribute to our wonderful men and women in uniform. Thank you for serving our country.

You know, really one of the interesting things about being the President is to invite my guys, buddies I grew up with from Texas, to the White House. It's really neat to see how they react to the majesty of the White House and the Oval Office and the South Lawn and just the beauty of Washington. And most of them, after they get over the initial shock of seeing the White House, then come to the shock of wondering how in the heck I got there. [*Laughter*]

But they—oftentimes, they ask me, they say, "What's it like, being the President of the United States?" And my answer to them is, first, it's a huge honor. But secondly, if I had to give you a job description, it would be a decisionmaker. I make a lot of decisions. I make some that you see that, obviously, affect people's lives, not only here but around the world. I make a lot of small ones you never see, but have got consequence. Decisionmaker is the job description.

First of all, when you make decisions, you've got to stand on principle. If you're going to make decisions, you've got to know what you believe. I guess the best way to summarize me is I came from Texas, and I'm going back to Texas with the exact same values I had when I arrived in Washington, DC.

In order to make good decisions, you've got to rely upon the judgment of people you trust. I'll never forget the first decision I had to make as the President. I wasn't even sworn in yet, and a fellow called me on the phone and he said, "What color rug do you want to have in the Oval Office?" [*Laughter*] "You've got to be kidding me, man." [*Laughter*] He said, "No, what color rug would you like to have in the Oval Office?" I said, "I don't know." He said, well, it turns out that Presidents—you've just got to know, Presidents design their rugs. I said, "Well, to be honest with you, I don't know much about designing rugs."

So I called—I delegated—that's one of the things you do in decisionmaking. [*Laughter*] I said, "Laura, how about helping design the rug?" [*Laughter*] Part of being a decisionmaker, though, is you've got to help—you've got to think strategically. And so I said to her—she said, "What color do you want?" I said, "Make it say 'This optimistic person comes here to work every single day.' " You can't lead the Nation, you can't make good decisions unless you're optimistic about the future.

So for the students here, as you take over organizations or head out of college and become involved in your life, you've got to be optimistic about—if you're going to lead somebody. Imagine somebody saying, "Follow me; the world is going to be worse." [*Laughter*] That's not a very good organizing principle about which to lead people. I'm optimistic about our future, and the reason I am is because I believe so strongly in what America stands for: liberty and freedom and human rights and the human dignity of every single person.

Sometimes decisions come to your desk unexpectedly. Part of the job of a President is to be able to plan for the worst and hope for the best, and if the worst comes, be able to react to it. On September the 11th, the worst came. We got attacked. We didn't ask for the attack, but it came. I resolved on that day to do everything I can to protect the American people.

You know, a lot of us grew up thinking that oceans would protect us, that if there was a threat overseas, it really didn't concern us, because we were safe. That's what history had basically told us. Yes, there was an attack on Pearl Harbor, obviously, but it was a kind of hit and run, and then we pursued the enemy. A lot of folks—at least, my age, when I was going to college, I never dreamt that the United States

of America could be attacked. And in that we got attacked, I vowed then, like I'm vowing to you today, that I understand my most important priority. My most important job is to protect the security of the American people.

I knew right after September the 11th, though, that the attack would begin to fade in people's memories. I mean, who wants to constantly go through life thinking that you're going to get hit again? Who wants to, kind of, relive those days in your memory? As a matter of fact, I asked the American people to go on about your life. But given the fact that it's human nature to forget or try to put in the past, put the pain in the past, I want to assure you and our fellow Americans, I'm not going to put it in the past. The threat to the United States is forefront in my mind. I knew that at times people would say, you know, "It may be an isolated incident; let's just don't worry about it." Well, for me, it's not an isolated incident. I understand there is still an enemy which lurks out there.

And so part of my decisionmaking process, part of it, as you see when I begin to make decisions to protect you, to do my number-one priority, rests upon this fact: that there is an enemy which is relentless and desirous to bring harm to the American people because of what we believe in. See, we're in an ideological struggle. It's very important for the students here to understand that there is an enemy which has an ideology, and they're driven by an ideology. They make decisions based upon their view of the world, which is the exact opposite of our view of the world.

Perhaps the best way to describe their political vision is to remind you what life was like for people living in Afghanistan when the Taliban was running that country with Al Qaida as the parasite. If you were a young girl in that society, you had no chance to get educated. If you spoke out against the view of these folks, their religious view, you could be taken to the public square and whipped. In other words, there was not freedom. There wasn't freedom to worship the way you want to, just like we believe here in the United States of America. You can worship, you cannot worship in our country, and you're equally American. You can be a Christian, Jew, or Muslim, and you're equally American. It's the greatness of the United States of America which stands in stark contrast to what these ideologues believe.

Their vision of the world is dark and dim. They have got desires to spread a totalitarian empire. How do we know? Because they told us. Mr. Zawahiri, the number two in the Al Qaida network, told the world such. He might not have wanted us to read that particular thing he was sending, but nevertheless, we did. And he said that, "Here's our designs and our desires." In other words, these people have got an ideology and strategy to implement the ideology. They've got a—they have no heart, no conscience. They kill innocent men, women, and children to achieve their objective. These folks cannot be appeased. We can't hope that nice words will change their point of view.

And so the decision I made right off the bat is, we will find them, and we will hunt them down, and we will bring them to justice before they hurt America again. But that requires a different kind of response than the old days of nations fighting nations. First of all, I want to step back and just tell you—I probably—I hope I say this more than once, but committing U.S. troops into harm's way is the last option of the President. It's the hardest decision a President can make. And so when I'm telling you I made the decision, you all have got to understand, I did not take that decision lightly. I knew the consequences, but I also believed that the consequences of not acting against this enemy would mean I wasn't doing my job of working with others to protect the United States of America.

So we sent our men and women into harm's way, all volunteers. It is really im-portant for the United States of America to have an all-volunteer army. The best way to keep people volunteering in the Army is to make sure they got good pay, good training, good equipment, and good housing for their loved ones.

But since we're not able to track vast battalions or armadas, we've got to have intelligence, good intelligence, to help us locate the dark corners of the world where these people hide. A lot of the decisions I make and decisions future Presidents make will be based upon the capacity of our intelligence services to find the enemy and to understand the intentions of the enemy and to share information with our allies. This is a different kind of struggle and requires the best intelligence possible. That's why we're reevaluating, constantly reevaluating how best to use our intelligence services to be able to protect the American people.

We've got to be strong in diplomacy. Secretary Rice, who is a great diplomat— she followed another great diplomat in Colin Powell—they're constantly working to remind people about the stakes. Just like part of my job is to educate the American people about the threats we face, at a lecture series such as this, our Government must constantly remind our friends and allies the nature of the enemy and the stakes that all free countries face. There's a diplomatic effort that's constantly going on.

You can't run your network without money, and so we're working with our friends and allies to seize terrorist assets and choke off their funding sources. In other words, what I'm telling you is, we're using all assets at our disposal to protect you in a different kind of war. In order to make the right decision about how to win this war, it's important to understand the nature of the enemy and to take the enemy's word seriously and to understand their lethality and not let the kind of lull in the action lull us to sleep.

Secondly, right after they attacked us, I laid out a doctrine, and it said, "If you harbor a terrorist, you're equally as guilty as the terrorist." The reason I said that is because I understand that a terrorist network can sometimes burrow in society and can sometimes find safe haven from which to plot and plan. The perfect example of that was Afghanistan. For those of you who didn't pay much attention to the initial stages of this war, it became apparent to the world that Afghanistan became safe haven. You'll hear stories about people that went into Afghanistan to be trained: trained as to how to brutally kill people, trained in different methodologies, trained in how to communicate.

So, in other words, the enemy was able to burrow in and felt safe and confident and secure. And I understood in this different kind of war that we had to make it clear to any country that if they harbored a terrorist, they would be held to account. And when the American President speaks, it's really important for those words to mean something. And so when I said to the Taliban, "Get rid of Al Qaida," and they didn't, I made the difficult decision to commit our troops, to uphold the doctrine that if you harbor a terrorist, you're equally as guilty as the terrorist. And our kids went in, men and women alike, and liberated a country from the clutches of the barbaric regime, the Taliban.

And today, today in Afghanistan—think about what has happened in a brief period of time—today in Afghanistan, there is a fledgling democracy. Al Qaida no longer has run of the country. The Taliban is routed. There's an elected Parliament and a President dedicated to democratic institutions.

The doctrine still stands: If you harbor a terrorist, you're equally as guilty as the terrorists who commit murder.

Thirdly—and this is very important for the students to understand, and others—because oceans no longer protect us, the United States of America must confront threats before they cause us harm. In other words, in the old days, we could see a threat and say, "Well, maybe it will cause harm; maybe it won't." Those days changed, as far as I'm concerned. Threats must be taken seriously now, because geography doesn't protect us, and there's an enemy that still lurks.

And so early in my first term, I looked at the world and saw a threat in Saddam Hussein. And let me tell you why I saw the threat. First of all, there was an immediate threat because he was shooting at our airplanes. There was what's called no-fly zones; that meant the Iraqis couldn't fly in the zones. And we were patrolling with British pilots, and he was firing at us, which was a threat, a threat to the life and limb of the troops to whom I'm the Commander in Chief. He was a state sponsor of terror. In other words, the Government had declared, "You are a state sponsor of terror." And remember, we're dealing with terrorist networks that would like to do us harm.

There's a reason why he was declared a state sponsor of terror: because he was sponsoring terror. He had used weapons of mass destruction. And the biggest threat that this President and future Presidents must worry about is weapons of mass destruction getting in the hands of a terrorist network that would like to do us harm. That is the biggest threat we face. Airplanes were horrible; the attacks of aircraft were horrible. But the damage done could be multiplied if weapons of mass destruction were in the hands of these people.

The world thought Saddam Hussein had weapons of mass destruction. It wasn't just me or my administration. My predecessor thought he had weapons of mass destruction. And there's a logical reason why—the data showed that he would likely have weapons of mass destruction, and he'd use them. I told you, the last option for a President is to send troops into combat, and I was hoping that we could solve the issue, the threat, the threat to the United States by diplomatic means.

So I went to the United Nations. Secretary Powell carried our message to the

United Nations. It said—see, now, I actually gave a speech to the United Nations, you might remember, and I said to them, basically, how many resolutions is it going to take before this threat will take us seriously? I mean, we passed, I don't know, 14, 15 different resolutions. That's a lot of resolutions. Pretty soon, if you pass that many resolutions, somebody is going to say, "Well, they may not mean anything." I want this body to be effective. It's important for the world, when it speaks, that people listen.

And so we passed another resolution that said that Saddam is in—and it unanimously passed, and the reason why is because the world thought he was a danger. It said, "Disarm, disclose, or face serious consequences." I'm the kind of fellow, when I—when we say something, I mean it, like I told you before. And I meant it.

And so Saddam Hussein was given a choice. He chose war. And so we moved, and he was removed from power. And there is absolutely no doubt in my mind, America is safer for it, and the world is better off without Saddam Hussein.

A lot of people, I understand, disagreed with that decision, and that's what democracy is all about. That's what we believe in; we believe you can disagree. There's a custom in our country for people to express themselves, and it's good. It's what makes us a great country, that people can stand up and tell people what's on their mind. And we're going to keep it that way. It's very important for those who didn't agree with the decision, though, to understand the consequences of success in Iraq. It's really important we succeed for a lot of reasons.

And the definition of success, by the way, is for there to be a country where the terrorists and Saddamists can no longer threaten the democracy, and where Iraqi security forces can provide for the security of their own people, and where Iraq is not a safe haven from which the terrorists—Al Qaida and its affiliates—can plot attacks against America.

We got a strategy, and I'm going to keep talking about the strategy; it will yield a victory. And the strategy is political security and economic in nature. In economic, we're going to help them rebuild their country, help secure their oil supply so they'll have cash flow in order to invest in their people.

On the political front, you've seen it; you've seen what happened in one year's time. It's just amazing, I think. I guess we take it for granted; some of us do. I don't. The fact that people have gone from living under the clutches of a tyrant who ordered the murder of thousands of his own citizens, to a society in which people last year started voting for an interim government, voting for a Constitution, and then voting for a permanent Government under the new Constitution. The Government is now—they're beginning to form.

In other words, you're seeing a lot of sharp elbows, probably kind of like American politics seem to some people, a lot of throwing of sharp elbows. You didn't see a lot of elbows, political elbows being thrown under the tyrant, did you? That's because tyrants don't allow for the political process to evolve. But we're watching the political process evolve, made complicated by the fact that the terrorists still want to cause destruction and death as this Government is forming to try to stop it.

We got to step back and ask why. Why would they want to stop democracy? And the answer: Because democracy stands for the exact opposite of their vision. Liberty is not their credo. And they understand a defeat to their ideology by the establishment of a free Iraq will be a devastating blow for their vision.

And so the Iraqis are showing incredible courage. When somebody says, "If you vote, I'm going to get you," sometimes people maybe say, "Well, maybe I don't want to vote." Eleven million or so Iraqis went to the polls in defiance of these killers.

It's a magical moment in the history of liberty.

And then on the security front, our strategy can be summed up this way: As the Iraqis stand up, we'll stand down. Look, we want the Iraqis to be prepared to take the fight to the enemy. Let me talk about the enemy, real quick, in Iraq. There are what we call rejectionists. These are Sunnis that kind of like the fact that they—even though a minority inside the country—had the upper hand for a long period of time with Saddam. And they're worried about whether or not a Constitution that says it will protect minority rights actually will protect minority rights. But the good news is, more and more Sunnis started to vote. And if you watch the news, they're beginning to negotiate; they're beginning to see a better way. In other words, the political process is beginning to marginalize the remaining elements of those who are trying to stop the progress.

One of those elements is Saddamists. These are the thugs that kind of controlled the country. They loved power; they don't want to give it up. And they'd like to return to the good old days, which isn't going to happen.

And the other group, of course, is the Al Qaida types—Mr. Zarqawi, who wants us to leave Iraq. They want us to get out of Iraq so Iraq can be a safe haven. It is their stated objective: Don't worry, take your time, keep killing the innocent because America will lose its will. That's what the enemy has said. That's their words.

The way to defeat the enemy is for the political process to marginalize the rejectionists and for us to train the Iraqi forces so they can find the few that want to dash the hopes of the many. And that's what we're doing. Our strategy is twofold: We're on the hunt for the terrorists, and we're training Iraqis. And we're making decent progress. There are more and more Iraqi units in the fight. There's more and more country being turned over to the Iraqis. We got a lot of bases around Iraq,

and more of those bases are being given to the Iraqi troops.

This is the year that we'll not only continue to focus on the troops, we'll continue to train Iraqi police. We've seen some problems about what it means to have lived in a society where people want to seek revenge. In other words, they use their police—status as a police person to take it out on others because of past grievances. That's not acceptable to the United States of America, and it's not acceptable to most Iraqis either.

And so part of the training for police is not only to give them the capacity to handle the enemy but to make sure they understand human rights and ethics involved with police work. And so that's what you'll be seeing. You're going to see more Iraqi troops in the fight and more police providing security. And as a result, our commanders on the ground informed me that they thought we could reduce our troop level from the 168,000 that were there—165,000, more or less, that were there for the elections—below 138,000.

Now, I want to emphasize something to you. You heard me say, "Our commanders on the ground said." You see, sometimes in the political process, people feel beholden to polls and focus groups. You don't have to worry about me. I'm going to be listening to the people that know what they're talking about, and that's the commanders on the ground in Iraq. They'll make the decisions. They will give the advice. Conditions on the ground will dictate our force levels over the next year, but the strategy is what I said it is: We'll stay on the offense, and we'll give these brave Iraqis the skills and training necessary to defend their own democracy.

Look, this enemy cannot beat us. They cannot defeat us militarily. There's no chance. The one weapon they have, which is a lethal weapon, is the willingness to kill people. I remember the story—and it just broke my heart to think about the young soldier that was giving candy to a kid, and they set off the car bomb next to the kids. I mean, it's just—I cannot describe to you how brutal these people are. And they understand that their scenes will get on TV.

And I don't know if they can adequately understand the compassion of the American people, but we're compassionate. I told you one of the great beliefs of our country is every life matters, every person counts, whether it be a child here in America or a child in Iraq. And they understand. And so part of my decisionmaking process is to understand the strength of the enemy— the only strength they have—and continue to remind the people that is their only strength, and the only way we can lose is if we lose our nerve and our will. The American people are resolute. They are strong. And we're not going to lose our will to these thugs and murderers.

In the long term—in the short term, we'll stay on the offense; in the long term, the way to defeat these people is to spread liberty. As you study history, I want you to watch the effects of freedom around the world. One of my favorite ways to describe my belief in the capacity of freedom to help achieve peace—not only security for the American people but peace—is to give people the example of my dad and me, in terms of Japan.

My dad was an 18-year-old kid and went to fight the Japanese. I promise you, a lot of folks here's relatives did the same thing. They were called into action because the enemy had attacked us. They were the sworn enemy of the United States of America. It was a brutal war against the Japanese. Took a lot of lives—Japanese lives and American lives—to win that war. And today, like my recent trip to the Far East, I sit down with Prime Minister Koizumi, who is the Japanese Prime Minister, and talk about the peace. Now, think about that. I particularly want the students to think about what took place when 18-year-old President 41 was fighting the Japanese, and 59-year-old 43—that would be me—

is talking to the Prime Minister of the former enemy about peace. And you know what took place? A Japanese-style democracy came to be.

History has shown that democracies yield the peace. Europe is free, whole, and at peace because the nations are democratic. That wasn't always the case, obviously, in the 1900s. Two major wars were fought where a lot of Americans died, and yet systems and forms of government changed. And now Europe is completely different, in terms of security and peace. The Far East—I just mentioned the Japanese example. And that's what the enemy understands, and that's why they're so brutal and relentless. They understand the march of peace will be contagious. Part of my decisionmaking process is my firm belief in the natural rights of men and women, my belief that deep in everybody's soul is the desire to live free. I believe there's an Almighty, and I believe the Almighty's great gift to each man and woman in this world is the desire to be free. This isn't America's gift to the world; it is a universal gift to the world. And people want to be free.

And if you believe that and if you believe freedom yields the peace, it's important for the United States of America, with friends, to lead the cause of liberty. I'm not saying to any country, "You must have a democracy that looks like America." I am saying, "Free your people. Understand that liberty is universal, and help lay that foundation of peace for generations to come." Someday, an American President will be sitting down with elected leaders from a country like Iraq talking about how to keep the peace. This generation is rising to the challenge. We're looking at history. We understand our values, and we're laying that foundation of peace for generations to come.

We've also got to be diligent here at home. I'm getting ready to answer some questions. Laura said, "Whatever you do, don't get too windy." [*Laughter*]

We've created the Department of Homeland Security. We're reorganizing our intelligence services. I want you to know that every morning, I meet with the Director of National Intelligence or his Deputy, sometimes with the head of the CIA, and always with a briefer, CIA briefer that comes and gives me the latest intelligence and the analysis of intelligence. That's every morning in the White House, except for Sunday.

And the reason I do is because I told you early that my job is not to be complacent; my job is to be on the lookout, along with a lot of other people, I want you to know. We've got 800,000 State and first-responders that have been trained. Security is strong at the airports. I hope they stop taking off the shoes of the elderly. [*Laughter*] I must confess, they haven't taken off my shoes lately at the airport. [*Laughter*]

We're doing a lot of stuff, but I want to talk about two tools necessary to protect you. First, before September the 11th, our law enforcement and intelligence services weren't able to share information. For example, within the FBI, you had your law enforcement division and your intelligence division—and for a lot of reasons, if they had information about a potential terrorist, they couldn't share it. That's hard to fathom, but it's the truth. There was a wall built up, and there's a lot of reasons why the wall was built up, some of it historical, obviously, legal ramifications.

And I didn't think you could ask our frontline officers to defend us if they didn't have all the tools necessary to share intelligence and to share information—by the way, tools which have been granted to use in tracking down drug dealers, for example. My attitude was, if it's good enough—these tools are good enough to find a drug dealer, then they ought to be good enough to protect us from the new threats of the 21st century.

And so the Congress passed what's called the PATRIOT Act by huge majorities. They saw the threat, and they said, "Wait a

minute. Let's make sure that if we ask the administration and, more importantly, people in the administration to defend us, let's give them the tools necessary to defend us." Interestingly enough, the PATRIOT Act, some of its provisions, are set to expire. I like to remind people the PATRIOT Act may be set to expire, but the threats to the United States haven't expired. And exactly what has changed, I asked out loud, after the attack of September the 11th and today? Those tools are still needed for our law enforcement officers. I want you to know that this PATRIOT Act is under constant review, and there has been no documented abuses under the PATRIOT Act.

In other words, Congress, in its wisdom when it passed the Act, said, "We'll make sure that the civil liberties of the United States are protected as we give the tools to those who are asked to take the fight to the enemy, to protect us." Congress extended this PATRIOT Act to February the 3d. That's not good enough for the American people, it seems like to me. When they get back there, they need to make sure they extend all aspects of the PATRIOT Act to protect the American people.

The threat still exists, is my message to members of both political parties. The tools, if they were important right after September the 11th, they're still important in 2006. The enemy has not gone away.

Let me talk about one other program—and then I promise to answer questions—something that you've been reading about in the news lately. It's what I would call a terrorist surveillance program. After the enemy attacked us and after I realized that we were not protected by oceans, I asked people that work for you—work for me, "How best can we use information to protect the American people?" You might remember, there was hijackers here that had made calls outside the country, to somebody else, prior to the September the 11th attacks. And I said, "Is there anything more we can do within the law, within the Constitution, to protect the American people?" And they came back with a program—designed a program that I want to describe to you. And I want people here to clearly understand why I made the decision I made.

First, I made the decision to do the following things because there's an enemy that still wants to harm the American people. What I'm talking about is the intercept of certain communications emanating between somebody inside the United States and outside the United States; and one of the numbers would be reasonably suspected to be an Al Qaida link or affiliate. In other words, we have ways to determine whether or not someone can be an Al Qaida affiliate or Al Qaida. And if they're making a phone call in the United States, it seems like to me we want to know why.

This is a—I repeat to you, even though you hear words, "domestic spying," these are not phone calls within the United States. It's a phone call of an Al Qaida, known Al Qaida suspect, making a phone call into the United States. I'm mindful of your civil liberties, and so I had all kinds of lawyers review the process. We briefed Members of the United States Congress, one of whom was Senator Pat Roberts, about this program. You know, it's amazing, when people say to me, "Well, he was just breaking the law." If I wanted to break the law, why was I briefing Congress? [*Laughter*]

Federal courts have consistently ruled that a President has authority under the Constitution to conduct foreign intelligence surveillance against our enemies. Predecessors of mine have used that same constitutional authority. Recently there was a Supreme Court case called the Hamdi case. It ruled the authorization for the use of military force passed by the Congress in 2001; in other words, Congress passed this piece of legislation. And the Court ruled, the Supreme Court ruled that it gave the President additional authority to use what

it called "the fundamental incidents of waging war" against Al Qaida.

I'm not a lawyer, but I can tell you what it means. It means Congress gave me the authority to use necessary force to protect the American people, but it didn't prescribe the tactics. It said, "Mr. President, you've got the power to protect us, but we're not going to tell you how." And one of the ways to protect the American people is to understand the intentions of the enemy. I told you it's a different kind of war with a different kind of enemy. If they're making phone calls into the United States, we need to know why—to protect you.

And that's the world in which you live. I view it as a chance for—an historic opportunity to make this place better for your children and your grandchildren, "this place" being the world. I'm just confident that if we don't lose our will and stay strong and that as that liberty advances, people may look back at this lecture and other speeches by people who profess the same devotion to freedom that I've had, and say, you know, maybe they're just right. Maybe America, that was founded on natural rights of men and women, is a ticket for peace. Maybe that kind of view—that every person matters, that there are such things as human dignity and the basic freedoms that we feel—that becomes a huge catalyst for change for the better. These troops are defending you with all their might, but at the same time, they're beginning to help change that world by spreading liberty and freedom.

It's such an honor to be the President of the great country that we are, during such historic times, and I want to thank you for giving me a chance to describe to you some of the decisionmaking processes I've used to do my duty to defend the American people. God bless.

Be glad to answer some questions if you've got some. Thank you. I think there's some people with microphones and all that, that are going to be out there. Anybody has any questions? Any boys from the Last Chance Bar got any questions?

Q. [*Inaudible*] [*Laughter*]

Q. Mr. President.

The President. Thank you, yes. Yes, ma'am.

Trade/Beef Industry

Q. Mr. President, we salute what you have done, your aggressive stance on terrorism. But more than that, as you know, Kansas is a beef State. The number-one industry in the State of Kansas is beef production and beef processing. A strong beef industry indicates a strong Kansas, and it affects all of us. We sincerely appreciate your efforts in regaining our markets with Japan, your aggressive stance on trade. We support that tremendously. I wondered if you would just comment on what's happened recently.

The President. Yes, well, thanks. Thank you for your leadership. We think we grow pretty good beef in Texas too. [*Laughter*] Now is not the time to compare, of course. [*Laughter*]

Look, here's the thing: There's an interesting debate in the United States about markets, about whether or not we should aggressively seek markets or whether or not we should become protectionists. Protectionism means tariffs and policies that make it difficult for people to trade in the United States and for people in the United States to trade outside the United States. I'm a big believer in opening markets. There's a practical reason why. One is that we're 5 percent of the people, which means— in the world—that means 95 percent of the people are potential customers for U.S. farmers and ranchers and small businesses and entrepreneurs. And so what madam president—former president is referring to is that I have been very aggressive about opening up markets through trade agreements.

I'm a little concerned about trade agreements, though, because it's more and more difficult to get them passed out of the

United States Congress. It seems like they're becoming so political that people either are becoming protectionist or lose sight—are losing sight of the value about opening markets.

Look, if you're a cattle raiser in Kansas, you want to be able to sell your product in Japan or South Korea or China. I mean, people want the beef. And the problem we've recently had, as you mentioned, reflects what is necessary to make sure that trade works. And that is, if there are problems, like in this case, some beef coming out of Brooklyn, I think it was, and if the Japanese balk at opening their markets, we have got to be aggressive about explaining to people why our beef is safe. And so part of being—part of making sure that the ranchers, in this case, see the benefits of open markets is when a market gets open, to work hard to make sure that market stays open if there happens to be a problem, or a short-term problem.

Secondly is to make sure that we're treated fairly. And that part—when you see me arguing for trade agreements, a lot of times it means that a country is getting a better deal from us than we are from them. All I'm saying is, "Look, just treat us the way we treat you. If we open up our markets for your product, you open your markets for our products."

And so my—and I believe, and this is going to sound—let me just say to people, as you study the economics of how to make sure this economy continues to grow, one way to do it is to make sure the markets are available, that there be a level playing field. I believe we can compete with anybody, anytime, anywhere, so long as it's fair.

And obviously, one area where we're trying to keep those markets open is when it comes to beef. And we had the BSE, and one of the jobs of the Federal Government is to respond quickly to the BSE issue, is to try to settle people's nerves down so we can get those markets reopened. And when I went to see Prime

Minister Koizumi, as well as President Roh in South Korea, one of the items I discussed was, "You're missing out on some Kansas beef." [*Laughter*]

Sudan

Q. Thank you, Mr. President. One of the things that both of our Senate delegation has worked tirelessly on is the situation in the Sudan. Sudan was, of course, slated to be the chair of the African Union next year, which is—they have tried, much like the United Nations, to do something. Does the United States have a larger role to play in the Sudan and the entire sub-Saharan African region?

The President. Yes, great question. We have played an active—first of all, I do want to thank both Senators. I'm on treacherous ground here to kind of credit one versus the other, but I guess I will, since one of them is going to want a free meal going back to Washington—[*laughter*]—I guess both. Sam, I mean—Roberts is great on the issue, and Sam is the person I've been interfacing with the most, frankly, in the whole United States Senate, about his deep concern for life in the Sudan. Matter of fact, in the vehicle driving over here, he brought the issue up.

We have got an important role to play and have played it. I don't know if you remember the Danforth Commission, where Jack Danforth, the former Senator from Missouri, was my Envoy to the Sudan to help resolve the North-South conflict. And there was a peace agreement in place. And the peace agreement was set back, unfortunately, because—well, it's still intact, don't get me wrong, but the implementation was delayed somewhat because of John Garang's untimely death—he was the leader of the south of Sudan. So the important thing there is that we showed, through diplomacy, that it's possible to resolve differences and to begin to reduce the abhorrent issue of slavery.

As you now know, the issue in Sudan is—and by the way, one of the great

strengths of this country is our faith-based programs that rose up in indignation about the slavery that was taking place in the Sudan. Much of the first wave of help that went into the Sudan—some of it was Government—most of it was the response of the private sector, particularly the religious communities.

The issue now is Darfur. And when Colin was still the Secretary of State, he declared the policy of the U.S. and our deep concern that we are headed toward genocide. I think we're the only nation that has uttered those words thus far in Darfur. The strategy—and it's a very complex situation. It would take yet another lecture to give you all the kind of ins and outs. But suffice it to say that we are deeply concerned about poor folks who have been run out of their villages into refugee camps, who are still being threatened by Janjaweed militia and some rebellious groups that are trying to extract political gain through marauding and death and rape and destruction.

We've empowered the AU, and this is what your question really kind of—part of your question leads to—to provide forces on the ground, to provide stability. And what he's referring to is that the Sudanese Government is going to be the head of the African Union—that's what AU stands for—which would then put them the titular head of the troops on the ground. And obviously, that should be of concern—concern to us. It is a concern to us, and it should be a concern to the AU nations.

That issue has yet to be resolved as to whether or not Sudan will be the AU. This is an important issue. We will continue to work with Congress to provide aid, food aid, and help. We helped fly the AU troops into Sudan. We're watching it very carefully. We are considering different strategies as to how to make sure that there's enough protection, at least to get people help and protection and, at the same time, see if we can't try to broker the same kind of agreement we did North-South, with the

Darfur and the Government. Thank you for asking the question.

Yes, sir.

Iran/China

Q. What is your position, or would you comment on a long-term strategy with respect to the geopolitical ambitions of China and Iran?

The President. Yes, great question. First, let me start with Iran. I'm deeply concerned about Iran, as should a lot of people be concerned about Iran. I'm concerned when the country of Iran, their President announces his desire to see that Israel gets destroyed. Israel is our ally. We're committed to the safety of Israel, and it's a commitment we will keep.

Secondly, I'm concerned about a non-transparent society's desire to develop a nuclear weapon. The world cannot be put in a position where we can be blackmailed by a nuclear weapon. I believe it is very important for the Iranian Government to hear loud and clear from not only the United States but also from other nations around the world. I also want the Iranian people to hear loud and clear, and that is, we have no beef with you. We are worried about a Government that is transparent, whose aims and objectives are not peaceful. And therefore, we don't think that you should have the capacity to make a nuclear weapon.

The diplomatic strategy is being led right now by what's called the EU–3: France, Germany, and Great Britain. And they're doing a good job of keeping together a common message to say to the Iranians that we expect you to adhere to international norm. The next logical step, if the Iranians continue not to adhere to international norm or the demands of the free world, is to go to the United Nations Security Council.

At the same time, the development of Iraqi democracy is an important message to people inside of Iran. I told you what I believe. I believe everybody desires to be free. I believe women want to be treated equally. And I think that a message of democracy and freedom in that part of the world will embolden reformers. But this is a serious issue.

China is—we have a complex relationship with China. Unlike with Iran, which we sanctioned a long time ago, we've got a lot of relations with China. We've got trade relations with China. We have got diplomatic relations with China. I've met with the Chinese leadership quite often and will tell you my personal relations with Hu Jintao are warm, warm enough to be able to sit with him in private and talk about things that matter to me. And one thing that matters to me is the freedom of the Chinese people.

I think any time in the diplomatic arena, you want the President to be in a position where he can have a relationship where you can speak with candor and your words can be heard, as opposed to a relationship that gets so tense and so off-putting because of distrust. Nobody likes to be lectured in the public arena; let me put it to you that way. I don't like it, and I'm sure other leaders don't like it. And so I've worked hard to make sure that my personal diplomacy is such that I'm able to make certain points with the Chinese.

One such point is that, you know, treat us the way we treat you. You've got a trade imbalance with the United States. And if we don't get it under control, there could be a backlash here. And therefore, we expect you to treat our products the same way we treat you. And by the way, if you happen to dump—choose to dump products, like in textiles, we'll hold you to account under our law.

I talk about their currency with the Chinese. You've got to let your currency float. The market currency ought to be priced through market, not by government edict, which is—they're beginning to move a little bit on the currency, if you're paying attention to the issue.

Now, I went to church in China. And I was a little nervous, at first, frankly, about a licensed church. I wasn't sure whether or not I was going to go to a church or not a church, and went—Laura and I went with a guy named Luis Palau. And I was impressed by the spirit I felt in the church. And after it was over, I told Hu Jintao, I said, you know, "I'm a religious person, and the more free religion is in your country, the better off your society will be, and you shouldn't fear the church. You ought to come to the church. You know, you ought to see what I saw, which is peaceful people honoring something greater than themselves."

I would hope that China will continue to move in the—or move in the direction of human dignity. I talked to him about, of course, the Dalai Lama, talked to him about the Catholic Church's inability to get their bishops in. In other words, what I do is I press the freedom issue. We don't always agree with China, of course. It's a complex relationship, but it's one in which, in my judgment, it's best to be in a position where we can dialog and discuss things in order to keep relations on keel and keep peace in that part of the world.

It's really interesting: Do you realize that it takes China 25 million new jobs a year to stay even? Think about that—I'm out there blowing when we get 4 million in the past—since April of 2003—this guy needs to get 25 million a year. [*Laughter*] And Sam and I and Pat and the Governor were talking about the Chinese demand for energy. One reason they've got such a huge demand for energy is because they've got to grow their economy, 25 million people a year. And their economy is just beginning to modernize, so they're using a lot of raw materials. I'm kind of wandering here, but—which says two things to me, by the way; it's called a filibuster—[*laughter*]—it says we've got to diversify away from hydrocarbons in the United States of America.

When we were driving through the beautiful country coming here, I told the Governor and I told the two Senators I firmly believe a day is coming when we're going to be able to grow saw grass and convert that into energy. And secondly, we've got to share technology with China so that they become better users of energy and better protectors of the environment. It's a complex relationship that we spend a lot of time thinking about. And I appreciate your question very much. Hu Jintao is coming, I think, here pretty soon, to the United States. And as I say, I enjoy my visits—personal visits with him.

Yes, ma'am.

Iraqi Government

Q. Hello, Mr. President. I am an American Iraqi Kurd. I would like to salute you and salute all the troops are freeing 27 million people. They are free.

The President. Thank you.

Q. Mr. President, I would like to share this thought with all our Nation and everybody who is questioning what happened to the chemical weapons. Saddam burned 4,500 villagers. I lost more than 10 members of my family underground. We found their bones after, when we freed Iraq. Saddam himself and his people, his followers, they are chemical weapons. Please stop questioning the administration and their decision. It was the best decision anybody could take, freeing 27 million people.

The President. Okay, this is a question and answer period.

Q. Mr. President——

The President. I hate to cut you off. You're on a roll, but what's the question?

Q. Mr. President, all I could tell you, I have two members of my family—they are in the Iraqi Parliament. And both of them are women, my sister-in-law and my aunt. They are in the Iraqi Parliament. And I would like you to share this happiness with me and with all the Iraqi people. Thank you, Mr. President.

The President. Thank you. And here's my message—here's my message to your relatives in the Iraqi Parliament: Work to form a unity government, a government that includes the minorities in the country—a Shi'a, Kurd, and Sunni—no, no, no—[*laughter*]—no, no. [*Laughter*] Thank you. [*Laughter*].

Q. My husband is Sunni. My mother-in-law was a Christian, Catholic——

The President. All right. [*Laughter*]

Q. I have two kids——

The President. Thank you. Got a question? Only in America. Hold on. [*Laughter*]

Prime Minister Tony Blair of the United Kingdom

Q. I'm from the United Kingdom.

The President. Welcome.

Q. Thank you. Although I might be living here for a while now, and you haven't kicked me out, and I thank you very much for that. [*Laughter*]

The President. Write your Senator. [*Laughter*] Anyway, go ahead.

Q. Us British, we're a querulous people, and we know that we're one of your greatest supporters in the world, and Tony Blair, who I have the greatest respect for, is my leader. When you say, "Jump," he says, "How high?" At least, that's the perception of many of the British people. And when he agrees and does your bidding, then it weakens him on the homefront at home. And many people enjoy this, but some of the more vocal ones will say, "He's a yes-man." Have you discussed that with him, and do you have any——

The President. I appreciate that a lot. First, I'm aware that that is a criticism of Tony, and I just strongly disagree with that. Frankly, it's demeaning to his character and his strength of conviction. But I've heard the criticism, and it's just simply not the case.

Like you, I admire him a lot. He's an independent thinker. He and I share this interesting moment in history together, and we also share this deep belief that liberty will transform the world—it can transform the world. That's what we believe. In other words, there is a philosophical core of Tony Blair that I—belief, core beliefs that Tony and I share.

You know, sometimes we disagree on tactics. We try to work through what we—we've had a lot of disagreements. I mean, a classic came on the Kyoto treaty. You might remember the treaty. I said I just wasn't going to support it. I didn't think it was good for the American economy; I thought there was a better way to go about being good stewards of the environment. He disagreed with me. There's a series of issues where we—International Criminal Court is another good example. I think the International Criminal Court is something we shouldn't join. I just don't want unelected prosecutors prosecuting our troops or our diplomats in a court overseas. Tony disagreed strongly.

I can give you a series of examples where—but we agree strategically. And that's what's important. Look, I'm sorry that his relationship with me causes him political problems at home. Sometimes I can be a little allergic for people overseas, if you know what I mean. [*Laughter*] But I think I would classify our relationship as historic. You don't know this—I'm about to tell you something interesting—that we talk once a week, or try to. And it's a really interesting way to share just thoughts and concerns. And the British-U.S. relationship is unique. It's been unique in the past. It is unique today, and I'm convinced it will be unique in the future, for the good of the world.

But, no, I'm very aware of the political difficulties he's faced. By the way, when you make hard decisions, like Tony has made, and frankly, I've made, it creates angst. I mean, the easy route would have been to do nothing and just hope for the best. And that's why I admire Tony. Tony is a person of great courage.

I can remember—I'll tell you an anecdote—you didn't even ask, and I'm going to tell you. [*Laughter*] And it's been published in a book a guy wrote in Washington.

Tony was very worried about his Government. You might remember when the second resolution—we had the first resolution; then there was an argument about what "serious consequences" meant—I guess that's what the problem was. I kind of knew what it meant. He knew what it meant. Others, all of a sudden, had a different view of "serious consequences" when Saddam chose to not deal squarely with the world and not deal with the inspectors. He was worried about his Government, and so was I. And I told him one time, I said, "If you're worried about your Government"—I said, "You don't want your Government to fall, and if you're worried about it, just go ahead and pull out of the coalition, so you can save your Government."

And he said to me, he said, "I'm going to"—he said, "I have made my commitment on behalf of the great country of Britain, and I'm not changing my mind." Basically, what he told me, he said, "George," he said, "politics—I'm not interested in politics; what I'm interested in is doing the right thing." And that's why I admire Tony Blair; he'll do the right thing.

Good question. Yes, sir.

President's Personal Values/Leadership

Q. I have a question less with politics and more with leadership in general. You're in a situation where you're under a lot of flack, especially for your character. And that's something that, it seems to me, means a lot to you, as it does to many of us here. As a leader, as many of us are going to need to know here because we're going to be leaders in just a few years, what's the best way that you go about preparing yourself for attacks on your character, and how do you deal with others in those matters?

The President. Yes, I appreciate that. I would summarize it: faith, family, and friends. I am sustained mightily by the fact that millions of citizens—for whom I'll never get to thank personally—pray for me. It's hard for me to describe why I feel that way, why I'm so sustained. I guess it's just called faith. And I'm sustained by my family. And there's nothing better than going home to somebody who understands and is sympathetic and is part of—we're working together. I mean, Laura's job is just as important as mine in many ways.

The girls still love me. [*Laughter*] I really love them. And then there's my man, Barney, a little Scottish terrier. [*Laughter*] I say this—and Laura will be furious at me—he's the son I never had, you know? [*Laughter*]

I believe in what I'm doing. And I understand politics, and it can get rough. I read a lot of history, by the way, and Abraham Lincoln had it rough. I'm not comparing myself to Abraham Lincoln, nor should you think just because I mentioned his name in the context of my Presidency—I would never do that. He was a great President. But, boy, they mistreated him. He did what he thought was right.

A lot of politicians, a lot of Presidents have gone through some tough times in the Presidency, and I understand that. One of my biggest disappointments is the tone in Washington, DC. I've done my best to try to elevate the tone. I just—needless name-calling, to me, is beneath the dignity of the office of the President.

I also make time in my day not only for prayer but also—and my family, but also for exercise. I found that part of keeping a positive outlook is to kind of burn off that excess energy, you know what I'm saying? [*Laughter*] I work out. I try to work out 5 or 6 days a week. It's really important—if you feel that's important for your life—to schedule your life. In other words, I have trouble with people saying, "I'm so busy, I can't exercise." I don't think you're too busy for things that are important in your life, and you can figure out ways to make time in your life.

And so I'm the kind of guy—I'm not running too well these days; I'm not running hardly at all. It's kind of like my knees are like tires, you know, and they're bald.

[*Laughter*] I'm a mountain bike guy. And it's a fantastic experience.

I think to answer your—summarize your question, is to make sure that you've got good priorities in your life. By having good priorities in your life, it helps you keep perspective on your life. And perspective is very important as you assume responsibility. Thanks for the question.

Yes, ma'am.

Associate Justice-Designate Samuel A. Alito, Jr.

Q. Mr. President, I thank you for being here. I served under your father; he was my Commander in Chief during Desert Storm. And it was with great interest that I followed your campaign; my husband and I both are great fans of yours. I thank you for making the hard decisions, for making—not listening to the critics and keeping your campaign promises.

And I've been following the confirmation hearings of Judge Alito. And I certainly hope he's confirmed. I think he's a good man.

The President. Well, I appreciate that.

Q. But I'd like to kind of know how it stands right now.

The President. Yes, what's happening. First of all, I told the people—and thank you for your kind comments—and I told the people when I ran for President I would put people on the bench who would strictly interpret the Constitution—in other words, not use their position to write law. We've got legislators to write law; that's their job. The judges are to interpret law.

And Sam has been one of the picks I made for the Supreme Court, Sam Alito. He's a very, very smart, capable man. When you talk to Sam Alito, you think, "smart judge." He's written a lot of opinions. His judicial philosophy is clear, and his judicial temperament that is sound. That's why the American Bar Association gave him the highest possible rating. And now the question is, will Sam Alito be given an up-or-down vote on the Senate floor?

I don't know whether or not in our history there's ever been a filibuster of a Supreme Court judge. One, years ago, according to—Sam, by the way, is on the Judiciary Committee and helps conduct the hearings in a way that I thought has brought dignity to the process.

And so to answer your question, I don't know. You hear gossip about a filibuster, meaning a minority of Democrats—Senators could stop Alito from getting a vote. It would really—I didn't mean to slip; I'm not trying to be—[*laughter*]—I'm not taking political shots. It just so happens that it would be the Democrats who would try to not give him an up-or-down vote on the Senate floor. I think he deserves an up-or-down vote. I believe that if given an up-or-down vote, he'll be confirmed and the decisionmaking—you know, we're in the process now of hearing from the Democrat leadership.

There are 14 Senators, 7 from both political parties, who have vowed to try to prevent a filibuster from taking place without extraordinary circumstances. In other words, if there is extraordinary circumstance, they would agree to a filibuster. There has been no sign of any extraordinary circumstance, except for this extraordinary thing: He's extraordinarily capable to serve on the Supreme Court. And so thank you for your question on Sam. It's going to come to a head here pretty soon. I think the vote in the committee is—Wednesday is the vote in the Judiciary? Tomorrow, yes. You don't have to worry about it in the committee—the floor possibly later this week. That's great.

Okay, a couple more and then I've got to head back home. Yes, ma'am.

Social Security Reform

Q. Hi. First I'd like to say that when I was first able to cast my vote for President, it was my honor to vote for you—[*inaudible*]. Can you hear me?

The President. I like that part. [*Laughter*]

Q. My question is about Social Security.

The President. Social Security?

Q. Yes. What are your plans to make sure that it's still viable when all the students sitting here are of an age that it would make a difference in our lives? And also, do you have any advice for us to plan for the problems—[*inaudible*]?

The President. I couldn't hear the question, so I'll put the words in your mouth. [*Laughter*] I guess you asked, is the system going to be viable when you get—yes? No. [*Laughter*]

If I were you, I'd pay attention to the issue. And the reason why is because there's a lot of us getting ready to retire. There's a baby boomer bulge. I was born in '46, on the leading edge of what we call the baby boomers, and there's a lot of us getting ready to retire, which means you are going to have to pay for a lot more people in the system, plus we've been promised greater benefits than the previous generation. So the system is going to go broke unless we do something about it.

Last year I talked about doing something about it, and the Congress didn't do anything about it. So this year I'm going to talk about doing something about it and the next year something about it and the next year something about it. I have a duty to confront problems and not hope, you know, and just kind of—shuffling them along. And so this is a big issue; both Medicare and Social Security are big issues. They're big issues for long-term deficits, and they're big issues for the individuals who are going to be having to pay in the system for people like me. And the fix isn't all that hard.

What is first required is people setting aside needless politics in Washington, DC, and saying, "Why don't we come together and get something done for the sake of a future generation?" And we can make sure that this generation—that the up-and-coming generation—see, nothing changes if you're over 55. It's the young people paying into a broke system. By the way, they call it a Social Security trust; there's no "trust."

The money is paid, and it's spent on other programs, and all that's left in the Social Security is an IOU. And so it seems like to me that it's really important to kind of lay out all the facts on the table for people to determine whether or not there's a problem or not. And once they see a problem, then they ought to be calling on people on the phone, their elected representatives, saying, "Do something about it."

And I believe we can fix this problem by slowing down the rate of growth of benefits, not cutting benefits; benefits will increase. But the promises have been just too great, and we need to be frank about it. And we need to be open about it to make sure that we save the Social Security system for our younger generation.

I also happen to believe we have a fantastic opportunity to promote ownership in America. I believe younger workers ought to be able to take some of their own money and set it aside in a personal savings account. And the reason I believe that is, I think if you own an asset, it helps provide stability in American society. I am concerned that—I'm concerned at the low rate of return people get on their money through the Social Security—you know, quote, "Social Security trust." I know the power of compounding rate of interest. For those of you studying in economics, look it up. It says money grows exponentially over time. And if you put your money in just a safe series of instruments, it will grow. If you start saving at age 20, it grows quite dramatically over time, and then that's your nest egg. It's what you call—it's a part of a Social Security benefit system. Again, those of us who are retiring, I'm not talking about you, I'm talking about younger workers being given an option.

I'm also concerned about people in our society who've never owned anything. You know, I'm worried about—and I know that if you own—can you imagine a single mom working and able to put some of the money aside for herself if she wants and watch that grow with just safe investments over time, and when she retires, she's got a nest egg that she calls her own, that Government can't spend on another program, a nest egg that she can pass on to her loved one.

I mean, ownership and the ability to pass wealth from one generation to the next is an important part of busting the cycle of poverty, for example. And so this is a great opportunity to think differently about this very important program. And I appreciate you bringing it up, and thanks for being concerned about it. You need to be.

Yes, ma'am.

Q. [*Inaudible*]

The President. Do what?

Q. [*Inaudible*]

The President. Yes, I'll look at it. Thank you. Appreciate it. Is your return address on there so I can write you back? No? Okay. [*Laughter*] Make sure I get that.

Education

Q. I was just wanting to get your comments about education. Recently, $12.7 billion was cut from education, and I was just wanting to know how that's supposed to help our futures?

The President. Education budget was cut—say it again. What was cut?

Q. Twelve point seven billion dollars was cut from education, and I was just wanting to know how is that supposed to help our——

The President. At the Federal level?

Q. Yes.

The President. I don't think that—I don't think we've actually—for higher education? Student loans?

Q. Yes, student loans.

The President. Actually, I think what we did was reform the student loan program. We're not cutting money out of it. In other words, people aren't going to be cut off the program. We're just making sure it works better. It's part of the reconciliation package, I think she's talking about. Yes, it's a reform of the program to make sure it functions better. It is—in other words,

we're not taking people off student loans, we're saving money in the student loan program because it's inefficient. And so I think the thing to look at is whether or not there will be fewer people getting student loans. I don't think so. And secondly, on Pell grants, we're actually expanding the number of Pell grants through our budget.

But, great question. I think that the key on education is to make sure that we stay focused on how do we stay competitive into the 21st century. And I plan on doing some talking about math and science and engineering programs, so that people who graduate out of college will have the skills necessary to compete in this competitive world.

But I'm—I think I'm right on this. I'll check when I get back to Washington. But thank you for your question.

Yes, ma'am.

First Lady Laura Bush

Q. Again, I just wanted to thank you for coming. Your speech was very good. I'm a big admirer of your wife. I know that you said that your role as a President was as a decisionmaker, and I would like you to comment, please, on how your wife contributes to your decisionmaking process and how you confide in her. Thank you.

The President. Yes, thanks. Yes, she's great. She keeps—she tells me when I'm out of line. [*Laughter*]

First of all, Laura pays attention to what's going on. And so she offers her advice, and it's sound advice. She's a west Texas woman, born and raised in west Texas. Kind of a—I would say she brings common sense. Kind of remind people from here—reminds me of people here from Kansas, down-to-earth, no airs, commonsense point of view. And so I appreciate very much when she does give me her advice, which can be too frequent sometimes. [*Laughter*] Not true, honey. [*Laughter*]

It's like the time—she tells the story about the time when I was running for Congress in 1978 in west Texas, and she criticized one of my speeches, and I ran into the garage door. [*Laughter*] But the best—I guess the best way to describe it is, one, I value her judgment, and I know it comes from her heart. And I appreciate the perspective she brings. Common sense is just a very important part of being a decisionmaker. There is something reassuring to me when I get advice from somebody who's got the best interests in mind, has got my best interests in mind, as well as just this kind of down-to-earth read on the situation. And that's how I view my advice from Laura.

Plus, she does—I mean, I said some things—"wanted dead or alive"—and she said, you might be able to explain that a little—express yourself a little better than that, George W. [*Laughter*] And so we've got a great relationship. You know, when I married her, she really didn't like politics, and particularly—didn't care particularly for politicians either. And here she is, the First Lady of the United States. And she is good. Boy, I tell you, she's—when she speaks, she's very credible because she's a decent, credible person. And I love her a lot.

Yes. Is that a Washington National hat?

"Brokeback Mountain"

Q. Wisconsin, actually.

The President. Okay, yes.

Q. "W" is for Wisconsin. You're a rancher. A lot of us here in Kansas are ranchers. I was just wanting to get your opinion on "Brokeback Mountain," if you've seen it yet? [*Laughter*] You would love it. You should check it out.

The President. I haven't seen it. I'll be glad to talk about ranching, but I haven't seen the movie. [*Laughter*] I've heard about it. I hope you go—you know—[*laughter*]—I hope you go back to the ranch and the farm is what I'm about to say. I haven't seen it. [*Laughter*]

Nuclear Proliferation

Q. Mr. President, I have a question about the nuclear weapons the United States is keeping. It's around 3,000 nuclear weapons, so I want to know your opinion when you are going to destroy them.

The President. Do what, now? I didn't hear what you said.

Q. When you are going to——

The President. I can't hear you very well. I'm sorry. I'm not trying to avoid the question; I just didn't get it.

Q. United States has 3,000 nuclear weapons.

The President. Three thousand nuclear weapons.

Q. Yes. And I want to know your opinion about these weapons of mass destruction, that when the United States is going to destroy the nuclear weapons to prevail the peace in the world.

The President. Got it. No, I appreciate it. One of the first things I did as the President was to negotiate a reduction of nuclear—deployable nuclear weapons with Vladimir Putin. Actually, I think we had 6,000 at the time, and we agreed to reduce our nuclear—deployable nuclear arsenals to between 1,700 and 2,200. And we're in the process of doing that now. And then of course, there will be—another President can then evaluate where we are. So we're in the process of honoring what's called the Moscow Treaty.

A couple of more, and then I've got to hop. Yes, ma'am.

Immigration/Border Security

Q. Mr. President—[*inaudible*]—I know that the relationship between United States and Venezuela is no good. That's not my problem. My problem is—or the question I have for you is what are you doing in the borders? You know, we try to secure the United States for terrorism, I know. So we're trying to secure the borders, but as well, some of us who are Hispanics and professional sometimes are denied the opportunity to work and advance in the workplace because we are minorities.

What are you going to do? I represent—[*inaudible*]—what are you going to do provide the most secure job in which we serve the country, we serve the university? I can't complain in this university; I've been treated like royalty here. But when you work outside the university as a Hispanic, you are not look good enough because they think you come from Mexico.

I come from Venezuela, which is a different country, but all of us are Hispanics, and all of us embrace ourselves in America because America is—North America, the United States, in Central and South America, where one continents embrace each other. So what are you going to do to provide opportunities for the Hispanics who come to this country legally, like I did or who are illegal here? We should help them to get legal here, not provide directly a green card, but help them to become legal in step by step——

The President. Okay.

Q. ——like all of us have done. Thank you.

The President. Yes, I got the question. Immigration. [*Laughter*]

First of all, *bienvenidos*. And we have an obligation in this country to enforce our borders. And there's huge pressure on our borders. We've got a long border, obviously, with Mexico and a long border with Canada. And the biggest, most problematic area right now is the border with Mexico—California, Arizona, New Mexico, and Texas.

The issue is not only Mexican citizens who are coming across the border illegally, but it's other citizens who are coming across the border. And our obligation is to use a wise strategy to shut down the trafficking of anything illegal across the border. We're a country of law, and we must enforce the border. And we spend a lot of time in Washington, DC, analyzing the border issues and strategizing with Congress about how to do a better job including the following things: One, increasing the number of Border Patrol agents; two,

increasing the use of technology on the border, so that you can see people coming, through drones, for example, and then be able to rally the Border Patrol to stop people from crossing—coming across.

Some physical barriers, particularly in urban centers, are now being constructed. Some berms—there's parts of our border, where, literally, you can just drive across, I mean, there's nothing. You know, you just land, and in you come. And it's hard—the demarcation zone is different, and it makes it hard for people to enforce the border.

Secondly, when we detain somebody at the border, we've got to have a rational policy to help back up the people we're paying to enforce the border. And by that I mean, if you're somebody from Central America, for example, caught coming into our country, that the policy has been to give you a notification to report back to a judge, and they'll hear your case. Well, guess what? A lot of them don't come back. They're here because they're trying to better their lives, and they're going to move into our society as best as they can. And they're not going to return back. So we're ending what's called catch-and-release, and we're beginning to provide more detention space for our Border Patrol to be able to say to people, particularly from Central America and South America, "You've come illegally; we're sending you back home."

Thirdly, in terms of workers, we do have H1, H2B visa programs that we're constantly analyzing with the United States Congress. It makes sense that highly skilled workers, for example, be given work permits here in the United States if it helps us meet an economic objective. But I feel strongly that we need to take the worker program a step further, and I'll tell you why. I'm mindful that most people come here to work. There are a lot of people in your State dependent upon people coming here to work.

I tell you, I used to say that—when I was Governor of Texas—family values didn't stop at the Rio Grande River. And people, if they could make 50 cents and had mouths to feed or $5 and had mouths to feed, a lot of people would come to try find that $5 work. And so here's my position, and that is that if there is someone who will do a job an American won't do, then that person ought to be given a temporary-worker card to work in the United States for a set period of time.

I do not believe that any guest-worker program ought to contain amnesty, because I believe that if you granted amnesty to the people here working now that that would cause another 8 million people or so to come here. I do believe, however, it is humane to say to a person, "You're doing a job somebody else won't do; here is a temporary card to enable you to do the card."

The length of the stay here will be dependent upon the actions of the Congress. It's conceivable you could have a 3-year period with a renewal period. I've thought a lot about this issue; I just want you to know. And by the way, when you mention guest worker, a lot of people automatically spring to amnesty—all he wants to do is grant legal status—that's just not the case; I don't believe we ought to do that. But I do believe we ought to recognize there are people doing work others won't do.

And there's a lot of good employers here in Kansas employing these people, and the employers don't know whether or not somebody is here legally or not, because what's happened is, a whole kind of industry has sprung up around people coming here. And it's inhumane. It's inhumane for the people being trafficked into the United States, and it's not fair to employers who may be breaking the law.

And here's what I mean. You've got people being smuggled into the United States of America by these criminal networks. They're called *coyotes—coyotes*. And they're bringing them in the back of 18-wheelers—stuffing human beings to come and do work in America that Americans

won't do, in the back of 18-wheelers. You've got a whole forgery industry up and running, you know? And so these guys show up with documents that—so the employer says, "Well, you look legal to me." They don't know whether they're legal or not legal.

I think it is a—and I know that we've got a lot of our Border Patrol agents trying to catch people sneaking in the country. And so it seems like to me that why don't we recognize reality, give people worker cards on a temporary basis so somebody can come back and forth legally, with a tamper-proof card that will enable an employer to know whether or not they're hiring somebody who is illegal. And if we catch employers after that hiring somebody illegal, there's got to be a fine and a consequence.

And so a compassionate way to enforce our border is to give people a temporary-worker card without granting amnesty. That's a long answer to a very important problem that is—now is the time for the United States to take it on squarely, in a humane way, that recognizes the situation and deals with it in an upfront way. And I want to thank you for your question.

Look, I've got a dinner tonight. [*Laughter*] I'd like to be here for a longer period of time, but Laura is serving dinner for retiring Alan Greenspan, and I better not be late, otherwise all that advice, it will be kind of—have a little different tone to it. [*Laughter*] I've really enjoyed being here. I want to thank you for your courtesy for having me. Thank you for supporting a great university in Kansas State University.

May God bless you all, and may God continue to bless our country. Thank you very much.

NOTE: The President spoke at 11:51 a.m. in Bramlage Coliseum at Kansas State University . In his remarks, he referred to Gov. Kathleen Sebelius of Kansas; Jon Wefald, president, Kansas State University; President

Hamid Karzai of Afghanistan; senior Al Qaida associate Abu Musab Al Zarqawi; President Roh Moo-hyun of South Korea; President Mahmud Ahmadi-nejad of Iran; President Hu Jintao of China; and President Vladimir V. Putin of Russia.

Statement on the Death of President Ibrahim Rugova of Kosovo
January 23, 2006

I am deeply saddened by the death of President Ibrahim Rugova. For many years, President Rugova led the campaign for peace and democracy in Kosovo. He was a friend of the United States, and he earned the world's respect for his principled stand against violence. Throughout years of conflict, he was a voice of reason and moderation that helped Kosovo's people lay the groundwork for a peaceful future. The United States remains committed to working with the people of Kosovo to build a future that is stable, democratic, and prosperous. On behalf of the people of the United States, Laura and I extend our condolences to President Rugova's family and to the people of Kosovo.

Remarks Following Discussions With Prime Minister Shaukat Aziz of Pakistan
January 24, 2006

President Bush. Mr. Prime Minister, welcome. We have just had a wide-ranging discussion, which one should expect when we've got a strategic relationship like we have with Pakistan. I think the relationship with Pakistan is a vital relationship for the United States, and I want to thank the Prime Minister and thank the President for working closely with us on a variety of issues. We're working closely to defeat the terrorists who would like to harm America and harm Pakistan.

We talked about the importance of trade and commerce and investment, and we also talked about the world response to the terrible tragedy that Pakistan has gone through. It's hard to imagine the devastation. The country lost 75,000 people; 4 million people were made homeless. I was very pleased that the United States, our taxpayers, our military could contribute to helping the people of Pakistan recover.

They are our friends, and we consider this friendship to be a vital friendship for keeping the peace.

And so, Mr. Prime Minister, thank you for coming. I'm really looking forward to going to your country. I'll be traveling to India and Pakistan in March. And I want to thank you for your invitation and your hospitality in advance.

Prime Minister Aziz. Thank you, Mr. President. Thank you for receiving us. The United States and Pakistan have a multifaceted relationship, covering a host of areas. It goes back in history, and the people of Pakistan value the relationship very much.

Let me, at the outset, say that the assistance the United States has given to Pakistan—the Chinooks, the MASH hospitals, the engineers, and the financial assistance after the earthquake—has touched the hearts and minds of all Pakistanis—and including your private sector and civil society. We really appreciate what has been done, and it will help restore the lives of the people who've been impacted by the earthquake. A sense of caring and sharing always builds a better relationship between countries. And that's what we are seeing between Pakistan and the United States.

Mr. President, we have a multifaceted relationship, and our discussions today, which we'll continue later, have covered a host of areas: the economic side, trade and investment—we are very keen to expand that. Pakistan has a growing economy, and U.S. investors can take part in this growth.

We also strive for peace in our area. It's an area which has a lot of challenges, and we are pursuing peace with all our neighbors. We want a solution of all disputes, including the Kashmir dispute. We want to see a strong, stable Afghanistan. We are against proliferation of nuclear weapons by anybody, and we want to fight terrorism in all its forms and manifestations. There is no good terrorist or bad terrorist, and terrorism knows no borders. Our coalition with the United States in fighting terrorism is very important to all of the world and all of civil society.

We are delighted we are here to share this time with you, and the people of Pakistan and the President and all of our Cabinet and various stakeholders in Pakistan are looking forward to your visit, because we think that this is an important visit for building relations further between our two countries and serving the cause of peace in the world.

President Bush. Thank you, sir.

NOTE: The President spoke at 11:50 a.m. in the Oval Office at the White House. In his remarks, he referred to President Pervez Musharraf of Pakistan.

Remarks Following a Visit to the National Security Agency at Fort Meade, Maryland
January 25, 2006

Thank you very much. I just had a really interesting visit here at the National Security Agency, and I want to thank General Alexander and all the folks who work out here for their hospitality and their briefing. I gave a speech to the men and women who are dedicating their lives to serving the American people and preventing this country from being attacked again. I was also able to talk to folks who work for the NSA, via video. They're around the world— some are in Iraq, some in Afghanistan. And it's just such an honor to be able to tell these people that the work they do is vital and necessary, and I support them 100 percent.

Most of the accomplishments, of course, that happen out here have got to be secret. But I know the good work they're doing. And so I want to assure the American people that we are lucky to have such professional, smart people working day and night to protect us.

The National Security Agency is playing a crucial part in the war on terror. First of all, the good folks who work out here understand we are at war, and they know what we know—that we face determined enemies who will strike without warning. And they know what I know, that we must learn the intentions of the enemies before they strike. That's what they do here—they work to protect us. The efforts of the people out here are a crucial part in protecting the homeland, and they've been a crucial part in success in Iraq and Afghanistan as well.

Officials here learn information about plotters and planners and people who would do us harm. Now, I understand there's some in America who say, "Well, this can't be true—there are still people willing to attack." All I would ask them to do is listen to the words of Usama bin Laden and take him seriously. When he says he's going to hurt the American people again, or try to, he means it. I take it seriously, and the people of NSA take it seriously. And most of the American people take it seriously as well.

Part of the war on terror—we've seen that part of the terrorists' strategy is to place operatives inside of our country. They blend in with civilian population. They get their orders from overseas, and then they emerge to strike from within. We must be able to quickly detect when someone linked to Al Qaida is communicating with someone inside of America. That's one of the challenges of protecting the American people, and it's one of the lessons of September the 11th.

When terrorist operatives are here in America communicating with someone overseas, we must understand what's going on if we're going to do our job to protect the people. The safety and security of the American people depend on our ability to find out who the terrorists are talking to and what they're planning.

In the weeks following September the 11th, I authorized a terrorist surveillance program to detect and intercept Al Qaida communications involving someone here in the United States. This is a targeted program to intercept communications in which intelligence professionals have reason to believe that at least one person is a member or agent of Al Qaida or a related terrorist organization. The program applies only to international communications. In other words, one end of the communication must be outside the United States.

We know that two of the hijackers who struck the Pentagon were inside the United States communicating with Al Qaida operatives overseas. But we didn't realize they were here plotting the attack until it was too late.

Here's what General Mike Hayden said—he was the former Director here at NSA. He's now the Deputy Director of the National Intelligence—Deputy Director of National Intelligence—and here's what he said earlier this week: "Had this program been in effect prior to 9/11, it is my professional judgment that we would have detected some of the 9/11 Al Qaida operatives in the United States, and we would have identified them as such."

The 9/11 Commission made clear, in this era of new dangers, we must be able to connect the dots before the terrorists strike, so we can stop new attacks. And this NSA program is doing just that. General Hayden has confirmed that America has gained information from this program that would not otherwise have been available. This information has helped prevent attacks and save American lives. This terrorist surveillance program includes multiple safeguards to protect civil liberties, and it is fully consistent with our Nation's laws and Constitution. Federal courts have consistently ruled that a President has authority under the Constitution to conduct foreign intelligence surveillance against our enemies.

My predecessors have used the same constitutional authority on numerous occasions. And the Supreme Court has ruled that Congress gave the President additional authority to use the traditional tools—or "fundamental incidents"—of war in the fight against terror when Congress passed the authorization for the use of military force in 2001. These tools include surveillance to detect and prevent further attacks by our enemies. I have the authority, both from the Constitution and the Congress, to undertake this vital program. The American people expect me to protect their lives and their civil liberties, and that's exactly what we're doing with this program.

I'll continue to reauthorize this program for so long as our country faces a continuing threat from Al Qaida and related groups. This enemy still wants to do harm to the American people. We cannot let the fact that we have not been attacked lull us into the illusion that the threats to our Nation have disappeared. They have not disappeared; the terrorists are still active. And we've seen their activity in London and Madrid and Bali and Beslan and Amman and Baghdad and many other places since September the 11th. Just last week, as I mentioned earlier, we heard from Usama bin Laden. The terrorists will do everything they can to strike us. And I'm going to continue to do everything I can within my legal authority to stop them, and so are the good people here at NSA.

In the long run, we can be confident in the outcome of this struggle, because we've seen the power of freedom to defeat tyranny and terror before. And we can be confident because we know our military and law enforcement and homeland security and intelligence professionals are working day and night to protect us.

I'm grateful for the skill and dedication of the good folks who work out here. These are fine patriots, and they're making America safer. Thank you all very much.

NOTE: The President spoke at 2:10 p.m. In his remarks, he referred to Lt. Gen. Keith B. Alexander, USA, Director, National Security Agency; and Usama bin Laden, leader of the Al Qaida terrorist organization. The Office of the Press Secretary also released a Spanish language transcript of these remarks.

Remarks Following a Meeting With Former Clerks of Associate Justice-Designate Samuel A. Alito, Jr.
January 25, 2006

Thank you all very much. Thank you all for being here. I just finished a meeting in the Oval Office with a group of distinguished lawyers, many of whom come from different backgrounds, and they've got a wide range of political views. They share two things in common: They all clerked for Judge Sam Alito; and they strongly support his nomination to be an Associate Justice to the Supreme Court.

The relationship between a judge and a law clerk is extremely close. Each judge has only three or four clerks a year, and these clerks serve as the judge's aides and advisers. They provide legal research; they discuss and debate pending cases; and they see firsthand how the judge arrives at decisions.

These fine men and women with me today have worked side by side with Sam Alito, and they are uniquely qualified to assess what kind of Supreme Court Justice he would be. As the full Senate takes up Judge Alito's nomination, it is important for the American people to hear what his former clerks say about this fine judge and his approach to the law.

One of the clerks I met today who describes himself as a Democrat said this about Judge Alito: "He is meticulous in the way he goes about deciding cases. He's meticulous in the way he goes about finding what the law is. I can't think of better qualities for anyone to serve as a judge on the Supreme Court."

Another former clerk here today says this: "I am a Democrat who always voted Democrat, except when I vote for a Green candidate—but Judge Alito was not interested in the ideology of his clerks. He didn't decide cases based on ideology."

Another former clerk who described himself as a proud member of the NAACP and the ACLU says, "After a year of working closely with the Judge on cases concerning a wide variety of legal issues, I left New Jersey not knowing Judge Alito's personal beliefs on any of them."

Another former clerk who describes herself as a left-leaning Democrat told the Senate this about Sam Alito: "He's a man of great decency, integrity, and character. I believe very strongly he deserves to be confirmed as the Court's next Associate Justice."

Another of Judge Alito's former clerks worked for Senator Kerry's Presidential campaign. She said this about Judge Alito: "I learned in my year with Judge Alito that his approach to judging is not about personal ideology or ambition but about hard work and devotion to law and justice."

In case you were wondering, Judge Alito has also the support of Republican clerks. [*Laughter*] In fact, he has the strong support of all 54 of his former clerks, regardless of their political beliefs. Judge Alito has earned broad support from his fellow judges on the Third Circuit. Seven of them took the extraordinary step of testifying on his behalf before the Senate Judiciary Committee.

Former Chief Judge Ed Becker, who sat with Judge Alito on more than 1,000 cases, said this about his colleague: "I have never seen a chink in the armor of his integrity, which I view as total. He is a real judge deciding each case on the facts and the law, not his personal views, whatever they may be."

Another colleague on the Third Circuit who was appointed by President Clinton said this about Judge Alito: "He is a fair-minded man, a modest man, a humble man, and he reveres the rule of law." The judge went on to say, "If confirmed, Judge

Sam Alito will serve as a marvelous and distinguished Associate Justice."

All these brilliant legal minds are united in their strong support of Sam Alito. And in his confirmation hearings, the American people saw why. Judge Alito is openminded and principled. He gives every case careful attention, and he makes decisions based on the merits. Judge Alito understands that the role of a judge is to interpret the law, not to advance a personal or political agenda. Judge Alito is a man of character and integrity. Judge Alito will bring to the Supreme Court a broad range of experience and accomplishment.

Before he became a judge, Sam Alito served as a Federal prosecutor, Assistant to the Solicitor General, where he argued 12 cases before the Supreme Court; an attorney in the Justice Department's Office of Legal Counsel; and the U.S. Attorney for the District of New Jersey—the top Federal prosecutor in one of the Nation's largest Federal districts.

In 1990, Sam Alito was unanimously confirmed by the Senate to serve on the United States Court of Appeals for the Third Circuit. He now has more prior judicial experience than any Supreme Court nominee in more than 70 years. The American Bar Association gave Judge Sam Alito its highest possible rating, a unanimous well-qualified. It based its rating on its assessment of his integrity, professional competence, and judicial temperament.

In the past, leading Democrat Senators have called the ABA's rating the gold standard for judicial nominees. Yesterday, Ed Rendell, the Democratic Governor of Pennsylvania and former chairman of the Democratic National Committee, came out in support of Judge Sam Alito. Governor Rendell said he was not pleased with the way his fellow Democrats have handled Sam Alito's nomination and said that Democrats should vote to confirm him. Governor Rendell put it this way: "As long as a Supreme Court Justice has high academic qualifications and significant integrity—and Judge Alito certainly does—we should confirm him."

There's no doubt about Judge Alito's qualifications, his intellect, or his complete dedication to our Constitution and laws. He is exactly the kind of person Americans want on the Supreme Court.

The Senate has a constitutional responsibility to give every judicial nominee an up-or-down vote. In its 216-year history, the Senate has held an up-or-down vote on every Supreme Court nominee with a majority of Senate support. And I call on the United States Senate to put partisanship aside and give Judge Alito the up-or-down vote he deserves and to confirm him as the next Associate Justice of the Supreme Court.

I'm grateful to Judge Alito. And I appreciate his wonderful wife, Martha, and their children for their dignity throughout the confirmation process. America is fortunate that this good, humble man is willing to serve, and all of us look forward to seeing him take a seat on our Nation's highest Court.

Thank you all for being here. Appreciate it.

NOTE: The President spoke at 3:35 p.m. in Room 350 of the Dwight D. Eisenhower Executive Office Building.

The President's News Conference
January 26, 2006

The President. Sorry to interrupt. [*Laughter*] Thank you all very much. I look forward to answering some of your questions here in a minute. I'm also looking forward to going up to Capitol Hill next Tuesday to give my State of the Union Address. I thought it probably best not to practice my speech in front of you here, so you'll pay attention to it when I deliver it. But I do want to give you some thoughts about what I'm thinking about.

First, I recognize we live in a momentous time——

[*At this point, there was technical difficulty with a camera attached to the ceiling.*]

For those of you watching, we seem to have a mechanical flaw. [*Laughter*]

Q. That was an accident, right?

The President. Are you wearing your helmets?

Q. It's that renovation project.

The President. Exactly. [*Laughter*] I'll take it up with the First Lady. [*Laughter*]

I'm going to remind people we're living in historic times and that we have a chance to make decisions today that will help shape the direction of events for years to come. I'm going to continue to talk about an optimistic agenda that will keep—that will remind folks we've got a responsibility to lead. We've got a responsibility to lead to promote freedom and a responsibility to continue to put policies in place that will let us be a leader when it comes to the economy in the world.

I recognize this is an election year, but I believe that we can work together to achieve results. In other words, I think we can set aside the partisanship that inevitably will come with an election year and get some stuff done. And that's what I'm going to call Congress to do.

We've got—must work together to protect our Nation's security. I'm going to continue to do everything within my authority to protect the American people. We're going to stay on the offense in the war against terror. We'll hunt down the enemies in Afghanistan and in Iraq and elsewhere. We'll continue our terrorist surveillance program against Al Qaida. Congress must reauthorize the PATRIOT Act so that our law enforcement and intelligence and homeland security officers have the tools they need to rout out the terrorists—terrorists who could be planning and plotting within our borders. And we'll do all this and, at the same time, protect the civil liberties of our people.

We're going to continue to lead the cause of freedom in the world. The only way to defeat a dark ideology is through the hopeful vision of human liberty.

Here at home, we're also—we've got great opportunities. And to seize those opportunities, we have got to lead. Our economy is growing; it is strong. This economy has created millions of new jobs, yet it's an economy that is changing rapidly. And we live in a competitive world. And so policies must be put in place to recognize the competition of the global economy and prepare our people to be able to continue to compete so America can continue to lead.

Of course, we'll talk about fiscal policy in my State of the Union, talking about the Congress to be wise about how we spend the people's money and to make the tax cuts permanent.

I will talk about initiatives to make sure our health care and education and energy is—recognizes the realities of the world in which we live today and anticipates the problems of the world tomorrow so that we can remain competitive.

I will talk about the values that are important for our country. I'm going to remind people we show the character and compassion of America by taking focused action to confront disease and to help devastated areas of our country that have been—areas that have been devastated by natural disasters, and ensure that medical research is conducted in a manner that recognizes the dignity of every human life.

I look forward to the speech; I really do. As you can imagine, it's an interesting experience to walk out there and not only talk to Members of Congress but, as importantly, talk to the American people.

I'm also looking forward to the Senate finishing its business on the confirmation of Sam Alito. He's a man of character, and he's a man of integrity. He understands that the role of a judge is to interpret the law. He understands the role of a judge is not to advance a personal or political agenda. Yesterday I had an interesting experience standing with his law clerks, and I could—started reading the notes that, of course, were adequately prepared for me, and the first person said he's a Democrat who supports Alito; the second person was a person who voted Green that supported Alito; the third, a left-leaning woman Democrat who supported Alito; the fourth person I talked about was somebody who worked in the John Kerry campaign who supported Alito. I was wondering, where are all those Republican clerks? [*Laughter*]

My point is, is that he has broad support from people who know him, people from both political parties, because he's a decent man who's got a lot of experience, and he deserves an up-or-down vote on the floor of the Senate. I was interested in Ed Rendell's comments—he's the Governor of Pennsylvania. He was the former chairman of the Democrat National Committee. He did not like the way the debate was headed. He believed that Sam Alito should be confirmed, and so do I. The Senate needs to give him an up-or-down vote as quickly as possible.

Listen, thank you all for giving me a chance to share some thoughts with you. I'd be glad to answer some questions, starting with you, Terry [Terence Hunt, Associated Press].

Palestinian Elections/Hamas

Q. Mr. President, is Mideast peacemaking dead with Hamas's big election victory? And do you rule out dealing with the Palestinians if Hamas is the majority party?

The President. Peace is never dead because people want peace. I believe—and that's why I articulated a two-state solution early in my administration, so that—as a vision for people to work toward, a solution that recognized that democracy yields peace. And the best hope for peace in the Middle East is two democracies living side by side.

So the Palestinians had an election yesterday, and the results of which remind me about the power of democracy. You see, when you give people the vote, you give people a chance to express themselves at the polls. And if they're unhappy with the status quo, they'll let you know. That's the great thing about democracy; it provides a look into society.

And yesterday the turnout was significant, as I understand it. And there was a peaceful process as people went to the polls, and that's positive. But what was also positive is, is that it's a wake-up call to the leadership. Obviously, people were not happy with the status quo. The people are demanding honest government. The people want services. They want to be able to raise their children in an environment in which they can get a decent education and they can find health care.

And so the elections should open the eyes of the old guard there in the Palestinian Territories. I like the competition of ideas. I like people who have to go out and say, "Vote for me, and here's what I'm going to do." There's something healthy and—about a system that does that. And so the elections yesterday were very interesting.

On the other hand, I don't see how you can be a partner in peace if you advocate the destruction of a country as part of your platform. And I know you can't be a partner in peace if you have a—if your party has got an armed wing. And so the elections just took place. We will watch very carefully about the formation of the Gov-

ernment. But I will continue to remind people about what I just said, that if your platform is the destruction of Israel, it means you're not a partner in peace. And we're interested in peace.

I talked to Condi twice this morning. She called President Abbas. She also is going to have a conference call today about the Quartet—with the Quartet, about how to keep the process on the road to peace.

Steve [Steve Holland, Reuters].

Palestinian Democracy

Q. If I can follow up, sir.

The President. Yes.

Q. Are you cautioning Prime Minister Abbas not to resign? And——

The President. We'd like him to stay in power. I mean, we'd like to stay in office. He is in power; we'd like him to stay in office. Sorry to interrupt. I knew this was a two-part question, so I tried to head it off.

Q. Will this affect aid to the Palestinians? Will you be able to work with Hamas if they're—assuming they take on a large share of the Government?

The President. Well, I made it very clear that the United States does not support political parties that want to destroy our ally Israel and that people must renounce that part of their platform. But the Government hasn't formed yet. They're beginning to talk about how to form the Government. And your question on Abbas was a good one. And our message to him was, we would hope he would stay in office and work to move the process forward.

Again, I remind people, the elections—democracy is—can open up the world's eyes to reality by listening to people. And the elections—the election process is healthy for society, in my judgment. In other words, it's—one way to figure out how to address the needs of the people is to let them express themselves at the ballot box. And that's exactly what happened yesterday. And you'll hear a lot of people saying, "Well, aren't we surprised at the outcome," or this, that, or the other.

If there is corruption, I'm not surprised that people say, "Let's get rid of corruption." If government hadn't been responsive, I'm not the least bit surprised that people said, "I want government to be responsive."

And so that was an interesting day yesterday in the—as we're watching liberty begin to spread across the Middle East.

Let's see here. Yes, David [David Gregory, NBC News].

Q. Mr. President, good morning. I have a different question, but I'd like to pin you down on this point about Hamas because I don't think you've completely answered it. Are you ruling out dealing with a Palestinian Government comprised, in part, of Hamas?

The President. Dave, they don't have a Government yet, so you're asking me to speculate on what the Government will look like. I have made it very clear, however, that a political party that articulates the destruction of Israel as part of its platform is a party with which we will not deal.

Q. Okay, can I——

The President. No, it's——

Q. But, sir, I'm sorry——

The President. Well, it's unfair to the other people.

Q. No, I'm just following up——

The President. You're trying to hoard. [*Laughter*]

Q. I'm not trying—I have a question about New Orleans, sir.

The President. This is—I agree with you. I can see the expressions on your colleagues' faces that it's——

Q. Well, I hope it will be worth your time. [*Laughter*]

The President. They don't think so. [*Laughter*]

Gulf Coast Relief Efforts

Q. The administration has rejected a local plan to rebuild New Orleans, and your administrator down there, Don Powell, said that the focus for Federal money should be to rebuild for those 20,000 homeowners who were outside the flood plain. Critics, local officials say that that ignores so many people in New Orleans, the poorest of the poor, the hardest hit areas, people who didn't have flood insurance or didn't expect the levees to break. And they feel, sir, that this is a certain betrayal of your promise that New Orleans would rise again. So why did you reject it? And do you think that the people of New Orleans have to expect that there is a limit for the extent to which the city can be rebuilt?

The President. The Congress has appropriated $85 billion to help rebuild the gulf coast. And that is a good start; it's a strong start; it's a significant commitment to the people whose lives were turned upside down by that—by those—by that hurricane.

Secondly, we have said that we look forward to the time when each State develops its recovery plan. I, early on in the process, said it's important for the folks in Mississippi to come forward with a recovery plan. And it's important for New Orleans and the State of Louisiana to work together to develop a State recovery plan. And the reason I said that is because I was aware that folks in Congress will want to spend money based upon a specific strategy. In other words, we've got to get comfortable with how to proceed. Those plans haven't—the plan for Louisiana hasn't come forward yet, and I urge the officials, both State and city, to work together so we can get a sense for how they're going to proceed.

Now, having said that, I recognize there were some early things we needed to do to instill confidence. One of them was to say that we will make the levees stronger and better than before and study further strengthening of the levees. In other words, I recognize that people needed to be able to say, "Well, gosh, we can't even get started until we got a commitment from the Federal Government on the levees."

A lot of the money we're spending is prescribed by law, but we also went a step further and proposed to Congress, and they accepted, the CDGB money so that monies can actually go directly to individual families that need help. We'll continue to work with the folks down there. But I want to remind the people in that part of the world, $85 billion is a lot, and secondly, we were concerned about creating additional Federal bureaucracies, which might make it harder to get money to the people.

Q. But is there a limit, sir?

The President. John [John Roberts, CBS News].

Q. I have five questions, sir. I hope you'll indulge me. [*Laughter*]

The President. That's only two-and-a-half times more——

Terrorist Surveillance Program

Q. On the NSA eavesdropping program, there seems to be growing momentum in Congress to either modify the existing law or write some new law that would give you the latitude to do this and, at the same time, ensure that people's civil liberties are protected. Would you be resistant to the notion of new laws if Congress were to give you what you need to conduct these operations?

The President. The terrorist surveillance program is necessary to protect America from attack. I asked the very questions you asked, John, when we first got going. Let me tell you exactly how this happened. Right after September the 11th, I said to the people, what can we do—can we do more—"the people" being the operators, a guy like Mike Hayden—can we do more to protect the people? There's going to be a lot of investigation and a lot of discussion about connecting dots, and we have a responsibility to protect the people, so let's make sure we connect the dots. And so he came forward with this program. In other words, it wasn't designed in the White House; it was designed where you

expect it to be designed, in the NSA.

Secondly, I said, before we do anything, I want to make sure it's legal. And so we had our lawyers look at it—and as part of the debate, the discussion with the American people as to the legality of the program, there's no doubt in my mind it is legal.

And thirdly, will there be safeguards for the—to safeguard the civil liberties of the American people? There's no doubt in my mind there are safeguards in place to make sure the program focuses on calls coming from outside the United States in, with an Al Qaida—from a—with a belief that there's an Al Qaida person making the call to somebody here in the States, or vice versa—but not domestic calls.

So as I stand here right now, I can tell the American people the program's legal; it's designed to protect civil liberties; and it's necessary. Now, my concern has always been that in an attempt to try to pass a law on something that's already legal, we'll show the enemy what we're doing. And we've briefed Congress—Members of Congress. We'll continue to do that, but it's important for people to understand that this program is so sensitive and so important, that if information gets out to how it's—how we do it, how we run it, or how we operate, it will help the enemy.

And so, of course, we'll listen to ideas. But, John, I want to make sure that people understand that if it—if the attempt to write law makes this program—is likely to expose the nature of the program, I'll resist it. And I think the American people understand that. Why tell the enemy what we're doing if the program is necessary to protect us from the enemy? And it is. And it's legal. And we'll continue to brief Congress. And we review it a lot, and we review it not only at the Justice Department but with a good legal staff inside NSA.

Yes.

Lobbying Reform/Jack Abramoff Investigation

Q. What do you hear or your staff hear about releasing of photographs of Jack Abramoff with you, Mr. President? If you say you don't fear anything, tell us why you won't release them?

The President. She's asking about a person who admitted to wrongdoing and who needs to be prosecuted for that. There is a serious investigation going on, as there should be. The American people have got to have confidence in the ethics of all branches of Government. You're asking about pictures. I had my picture taken with him, evidently. I've had my picture taken with a lot of people. Having my picture taken with someone doesn't mean that, you know, I'm a friend with them or know them very well. I've had my picture taken with you—[*laughter*]—at holiday parties.

My point is, I mean, there's thousands of people that come through and get their pictures taken. I'm also mindful that we live in a world in which those pictures will be used for pure political purposes, and they're not relevant to the investigation.

Q. Do you know how many?

The President. I don't have any idea.

I'm coming your way. Carl [Carl Cameron, FOX News].

Iran

Q. Thank you, Mr. President. Good morning. On the subject of Iran, what parameters might the U.S. be willing to accept Iran having a nuclear power program? And to the extent that you've said in the past that the United States supports the Iranian people, would you support expedited legislation or a move that would send resources to such groups in Iran that might hasten regime change or democratic reform?

The President. I have made it clear that I believe that the Iranians should have a civilian nuclear program—power program under these conditions: that the material used to power the plant would be manufac-tured in Russia, delivered under IEEE—IAEA inspections—inspectors to Iran to be used in that plant, the waste of which will be picked up by the Russians and returned to Russia. I think that is a good plan. The Russians came up with the idea, and I support it.

And the reason why I think it makes sense is because I do believe people ought to be allowed to have civilian nuclear power. However, I don't believe nontransparent regimes that threaten the security of the world should be allowed to gain the technologies necessary to make a weapon. And the Iranians have said, "We want a weapon."

And it's not in the world's interest that they have a weapon. And so we are working hard to continue the diplomacy necessary to send a focused message to the Iranian Government, and that is, your desires for a weapon are unacceptable. Part of that is—part of that diplomacy was to provide an acceptable alternative to the Iranian desire to have a civilian nuclear power industry.

Secondly, we will support freedom movements all around the world. I constantly talked about today's reformers will be tomorrow's leaders, and therefore, we will work with groups that demand for people to be given the natural rights of men and women, and that right is to live in a free society.

Dana [Dana Bash, Cable News Network].

Lobbying Reform/Jack Abramoff Investigation

Q. Mr. President, you talked about Jack Abramoff in the context of pictures, but it may not necessarily just be about pictures. He also had some meetings with some of your staff. So you remember, you ran on the idea of restoring honesty and integrity to the White House. So why are you letting your critics, perhaps, attack you and paint you with, maybe, a guilt by association? Why not just throw open your books and say, look, here is——

The President. There is a serious investigation going on by Federal prosecutors, and that's their job. And they will—if they believe something was done inappropriately in the White House, they'll come and look, and they're welcome to do so. There's a serious investigation that's going on.

Q. But, sir, don't you want to tell the American people look, as I promised, this White House isn't for sale, and I'm not for sale?

The President. It's hard for me to say I didn't have pictures with the guy when I did. But I have also had pictures with thousands and thousands of people. I mean, people—it's part of the job of the President to shake hands and—with people and smile. [*Laughter*] And I do. And the man contributed to my campaigns, but he contributed, either directly or through his clients, to a lot of people in Washington. And this needs to be cleared up so the people have confidence in the system.

Yes, Peter [Peter Baker, Washington Post].

Palestinian Elections

Q. Mr. President, the U.S. Government has spent about $2 million to help promote the Palestinian Authority in the lead-up to this week's elections. I wonder, sir, whether you feel like it's consistent with your push to spread democracy around the world if the U.S. puts its thumb on the scale? Or are there moments when it's okay to compromise that because you want to keep organizations with a terrorist threat out of government?

The President. I talked to Secretary Rice about the story that you're referring to, and what she told me was, is that this money was part of a USAID package that had been in the pipeline for a while. The—kind of the allegation or the insinuation that we were funding a political effort just simply isn't the case, as far as I can tell.

Q. It was designed to promote the image of the Palestinian Authority among its own people——

The President. As I say, this money was part of a USAID package. We had—I proclaimed, I made it very clear that Jim Wolfensohn was going to be in the region with an economic aid package to help the Palestinian people. Our programs are aimed to help the people. And——

Q. I'm talking about who gets credit. Part of the thing was there would be no——

The President. Well, obviously—obviously——

Q. Credit would go to the Authority.

The President. Yes, well, our attempt was to help the Palestinian people through a active USAID program. And you saw the results of the election.

Q. Why, then, not disclose the USAID involvement?

The President. It is disclosed; you just disclosed it. [*Laughter*]

Elisabeth [Elisabeth Bumiller, New York Times]. Thank you. Are you trying to help the man out there?

Q. He's my colleague.

The President. Okay, good.

Terrorist Surveillance Program

Q. Members of your administration have said that the secret eavesdropping program might have prevented the September 11th attacks. But the people who hijacked the planes on September 11th had been in this country for years, having domestic phone calls and e-mails. So how, specifically, can you say that?

The President. Well, Michael Hayden said that, because he believes that had we had the capacity to listen to the phone calls from those from San Diego elsewhere, we might have gotten information necessary to prevent the attack. And that's what he was referring to.

Q. They were domestic calls——

The President. No, domestic outside—we will not listen inside this country. It is a call from Al Qaida, Al Qaida affiliates, either from inside the country out or outside the country in, but not domestically.

Jack Abramoff Investigation

Q. Can I ask you again, why won't you release the photos of yourself with Jack Abramoff?

The President. I just answered the question.

Yes.

Terrorist Surveillance Program

Q. Your explanation on the monitoring program seems to say that when the Nation is at war, the President, by definition, can order measures that might not be acceptable or even, perhaps, legal in peacetime. And this seems to sound like something President Nixon once said, which was, "When the President does it, then that means it is not illegal," in the areas involving national security. So how do the two differ?

The President. Well, I said yesterday that other Presidents have used the same authority I've had, to use technology to protect the American people. Other Presidents—most Presidents believe that during a time of war, that we can use our authorities under the Constitution to make decisions necessary to protect us.

Secondly, in this case, there is an act passed by Congress in 2001 which said that I must have the power to conduct this war using the incidents of war. In other words, we believe there's a constitutional power granted to Presidents as well as, this case, a statutory power. And I'm intending to use that power—Congress says, "Go ahead and conduct the war; we're not going to tell you how to do it." And part of winning this war on terror is to understand the nature of the enemy and to find out where they are so we can protect the American people.

There's going to be—there will be a constitution—there will be a legal debate about whether or not I have the authority to do this; I'm absolutely convinced I do. Our Attorney General has been out describing why. And I'm going to continue using my authority. That's what the American people expect.

Yes, Mark [Mark Smith, Associated Press Radio].

U.S. Armed Forces

Q. Mr. President, the Pentagon recently studied U.S. forces overseas and concluded that between Iraq and Afghanistan, that the military was very seriously overextended. Then Secretary Rumsfeld told us yesterday, well, that's really not what the study concluded. But this morning General Casey told us, in Iraq, U.S. forces there are stretched. Who's right here?

The President. I haven't seen General Casey's comments, his specific comments. I will tell you this, that after 5 years of war, there is a need to make sure that our troops are balanced properly, that threats are met with capability. And that's why we're transforming our military. The things I look for are the following: morale, retention, and recruitment. And retention is high; recruitment is meeting goals; and people are feeling strong about the mission, Mark. But I also recognize that we've got to make sure that our military is transformed. And that's what's taking place right now. We're transforming the United States Army so that capabilities and the threats are better aligned.

And I'll give—go ahead.

Q. It's not overextended then?

The President. The question is whether or not we can win victory in Iraq. Our troops will have what they—I mean, our commanders will have the troops necessary to do that. The question is, can we help keep the peace in a place like the Far East? Absolutely.

And let me use the Far East as an example of what I'm talking about. There was some 30,000 troops on the South Korean Peninsula. As you might remember, we reduced the amount of manpower, replaced it with technology. A lot of people—some people at the time said, "Well, wait a minute. They're lessening their commitment to peace and security in the Far East by moving people out." I made the case that, no, what we're doing is replacing manpower—we're transforming our military presence in South Korea to be able to meet the threats of the 21st century. And that's what you're seeing all throughout our military.

And so this is a time where we've been in theater for—been in this war against terror for 5 years and, at the same time, transforming. And I think if you look at what our commanders are saying and what are people like Pete Schoomaker are saying is that this transformation is going to make it more likely America will be able to continue in the out years of doing what we need to do to keep the peace.

Yes, Holly [Holly Rosenkrantz, Bloomberg News].

Federal Budget

Q. Mr. President, do you think you need to be more aggressive with vetoing or at least threatening to veto more spending bills this year? I mean, every year you say, "I want Congress to show spending restraint; this is important for our budget and our economy." But do you think they're doing enough? Do you need to be more aggressive——

The President. Yes, I do think they are when they meet our budget targets. And here's the way—hold on, let me finish, please. Here's the way it works. We sit down and say, "Here's what we'd like you to do. We'd like you to reduce nonsecurity discretionary spending." Or we present a budget target, and they meet them. They have met those targets.

And I am pleased that I've got a working relationship with the Speaker and Leader Frist and other Members of Congress to help meet those targets.

Go ahead; you've got a followup?

Q. So essentially, then, you think everything is going fine with the budget, and there's no need to use a veto or anything like that?

The President. Well, I'm fully prepared to use the veto if they overspend. They've got a chance now to continue to show the American people that they're willing to be—have fiscal discipline by voting on the reconciliation package in the House of Representatives. We've still got a lot of work to do, don't get me wrong. And I'll present a—in the process of laying out a budget that will continue to eliminate programs that don't work or that are duplicative in nature, one that says we can cut our deficit in half by 2009 and make sure the American people still get their tax relief.

We don't need to be running up the taxes right now, in my judgment. And I think it is—you know, people say, "Well, let's raise the taxes and balance the budget." That's not how it works. They're going to raise your taxes, and they're going to continue to expand the Government. And I understand that.

Now, in terms of how they spend the money once they meet the budget targets, that's going to be an interesting discussion on Capitol Hill. That's about this business about earmarks and people making special deals in the budget. And they need to—there needs to be earmark reform. And we look forward to working with responsible Members on the Hill about earmark reform.

Yes.

North Korea

Q. Mr. President, last year, your administration imposed a package of economic sanctions on North Korea. Now North Korea says it will not come back to the table in the nuclear talks unless those sanctions go. South Korea is warning of a dispute on the issue. Would you consider removing them, suspending them, making some gesture to get North Korea back to the negotiation table?

The President. Actually, I think what you're referring to is the fact that we're trying—that we are cutting off the transfer of monies generated by illicit activities. When somebody is counterfeiting our money, we want to stop them from doing that. And so we are aggressively saying to the North Koreans, "Just—don't counterfeit our money." And we are working with others to prevent them from illicit activities. That's different from economic sanctions.

Q. Fair enough.

The President. And no, we think it's very important for the North Koreans to come back to the table. There's a six-party talk framework that is hopeful and positive for them. It requires them to make some difficult decisions, and, of course, one of them is to get rid of their nuclear arsenal. But we're more than willing to—and want the six-party talks to continue forward. I think the framework is a framework that can eventually yield to a peaceful settlement of the issue. But the other issue is one that I just wanted to make sure I clarify for you why we're doing what we're doing.

Jonathan[*] [Joseph Curl, Washington Times]——

Q. You see this as completely separate then, sir?

The President. I think——

Q. There's no room to suspend them or——

The President. Well, if somebody is cheating on us, we need to stop it. I mean, the American people—if we know people are counterfeiting our money, they expect the Government to act. And there is no compromise when it comes to, you know, "Hey, come back to the table so you can counterfeit our money; just counterfeit 20s and not 100s, or whatever it is." I mean, no. We are going to uphold the law and protect the currency of the American people.

Jonathan.

---

[*] The President mistakenly referred to Joseph Curl as "Jonathan."

Terrorist Surveillance Program

Q. Stepping back from the immediate NSA debate that's going on right now, Vice President Cheney recently said that the White House is reasserting its executive power. Is the NSA program part of that effort? And what do you say to Democrats who charge that you are abusing your constitutional authority?

The President. I would say that there has been a historical debate between the executive branch and the legislative branch as who's got what power. And I don't view it as a contest with the legislative branch. Maybe they view it as a contest with the executive; I just don't. I view it—I view the decisions I've made, particularly when it comes to national security, as necessary decisions to protect the American people. That's how—that's the lens on which I analyze things, Jonathan. And I understand we're at war with an enemy that wants to hit us again. Usama bin Laden made that clear the other day, and I take his words very seriously. And I also take my responsibility to protect the American people very seriously.

And so we're going to do what is necessary, within the Constitution and within the law and, at the same time, guaranteeing people's civil liberties, to protect the people. And that's how I look at this debate. Now, there's all kinds of people taking a step back and saying, well, this is this, this is that. And I recognize throughout history, people—there have been a debate about legislative power and executive power. Part of the questions asked here today kind of reflect that debate.

And I'm going to leave that to the lawyers. I believe I've been hired by the people to do my job, and that's to protect the people, and that's what I'm going to do, mindful of my authorities within the Constitution, mindful of our need to make sure that we stay within the law, and mindful of the need to protect the civil liberties of the people.

Q. Mr. President, though—this is a direct followup to that—the FISA law was implemented in 1978, in part because of revelations that the National Security Agency was spying domestically. What is wrong with that law that you feel you have to circumvent it and, as you just admitted, expand Presidential power?

The President. May I—if I might, you said that I have to circumvent it. There—wait a minute. That's a—there's something—it's like saying, you know, "You're breaking the law." I'm not. See, that's what you've got to understand. I am upholding my duty and, at the same time, doing so under the law and with the Constitution behind me. That's just very important for you to understand.

Secondly, the FISA law was written in 1978. We're having this discussion in 2006. It's a different world. And FISA is still an important tool. It's an important tool. And we still use that tool. But also—and we—look—I said, "Look, is it possible to conduct this program under the old law?" And people said, "It doesn't work, in order to be able to do the job we expect us to do."

And so that's why I made the decision I made. And you know, "circumventing" is a loaded word, and I refuse to accept it, because I believe what I'm doing is legally right.

Bob [Bob Deans, Cox Newspapers]——

Q. There are going to be hearings on Capitol Hill starting February 6th regarding——

The President. Regarding that point, right. And Al Gonzales has recently given a speech laying out the administrative position, and I'm sure you analyzed it carefully. Deans.

U.S. Policy on Detainees in the War on Terror

Q. Sir, you said a few minutes ago the United States needs to continue to lead in the cause of freedom around the world, and yet in recent weeks, a couple of groups—Human Rights Watch and Amnesty International—have criticized the U.S. handling of terrorist suspects. They say that has undermined the U.S. voice as a champion of human rights and even, perhaps, undercut a generation of progress in human rights. And my question, sir, is, how do you respond to that?

The President. I haven't seen the report, but if they're saying we tortured people, they're wrong—period.

Q. Could you call on your Texas straight talk and make a clear and unambiguous statement today that no American will be allowed to torture another human being anywhere in the world at any time——

The President. Yes. No American will be allowed to torture another human being anywhere in the world. And I signed the appropriations bill with the McCain amendment attached on because that's the way it is. I know some have said, "Well, why did he put a qualifier in there?" And one reason why Presidents put qualifiers in is to protect the prerogative of the executive branch. You see, what we're always doing is making sure that we make it clear that the executive branch has got certain responsibilities. Conducting war is a responsibility in the executive branch, not the legislative branch.

But make no mistake about it, the McCain amendment is an amendment we strongly support and will make sure it's fully effective.

Let's see, Richard [Richard Benedetto, USA Today].

2006 Elections

Q. Mr. President, you mentioned earlier that this is an election year. Republicans are expressing great confidence that they're going to be able to take back the Congress.

The President. Who are?

Q. The Democrats, I mean, they're expressing——

The President. We already have the Congress. [*Laughter*]

Q. They say that they can use issues such as corruption and the war in Iraq and high energy prices against Republicans and against you. How much do you plan to go out and campaign——

The President. I'm looking forward on the campaign, but I'm also looking forward to reminding people we have a responsibility to get some things done. And that's part of what the State of the Union is going to be about, but, no, I'm looking forward to getting out there. I've got one more off-year campaign in me as a sitting President, and I'm looking forward to it, Richard. As you know, I like to get out and tell people what's on my mind, explain to people we're a party with ideas, we know how to lead, that—remind people of the stakes in the world in which we live, and that we have a plan to deal with them.

And we've got a good record here in Washington, DC, and I'm looking forward to talking about the economy, for example. That seems like a debate worthwhile having—not only what we have done to make sure that we've overcome a lot of hurdles but how to make sure policies are put in place that this economic growth continues, and remind people we've added a lot of jobs since April of 2003, that the economy is pretty strong this year given the fact— in spite of the fact there was high energy prices and storms. I look forward to debating people whether or not we ought to raise their taxes. I don't believe we should. Matter of fact, I think raising taxes will hurt the economy. And that's a debate I look forward to having with the people as we get closer to the 2006 elections.

And so, look, I don't blame people for saying, "I'm confident about the elections." Can you imagine right here at the election year saying, "I'm not very confident about the elections"? [*Laughter*] No wonder the Democrats are saying that.

But we've got a record—and a good one. And that's what I intend to campaign on, and explain to people why I've made the decisions I've made, and why they're nec-

essary to protect the American people, and why they've been necessary to keep this economy strong, and why the policies we've got will keep this economy strong in the future. And this election is about peace and prosperity. And I intend to get out there and campaign.

Abril—April [April Ryan, American Urban Radio Networks].

Q. Yes, Mr. President. Good morning.

The President. You're going to have to speak loudly because somebody took your seat. Your name was on my seating chart, and you're not sitting down.

Q. Isn't that a shame.

The President. Well, I mean, look, you're probably going to blame it on me. [*Laughter*]

Q. I'm going to let you pass that time.

The President. Just trying to rattle you before you get going.

Gulf Coast Response Investigation

Q. I know. Mr. President, as you're saying Hurricane Katrina and the aftermath is one of your top priorities——

The President. Yes.

Q. Why is it that this administration is not allowing the senior—your senior staff that you conversated with prior to Hurricane Katrina, during, and after to testify, to interview, or talk with congressional leaders? And why not push Michael Brown, who is now a private citizen, to go before them, as he is what many are calling a linchpin to the whole issue?

The President. Well, let me make sure you have the facts. We have given 15,000 pages of White House documents to the investigators, congressional investigators; some—I think it's 600,000 pages, administrative documents. We have sent a fellow named Rapuano to talk about—he's a White House staffer—to talk to the committee. There have been a lot of interviews. There have been public testimony.

As a matter of fact, we are so concerned about this that we've started our own investigation to make sure that lessons—that we understand the lessons learned from this. This is a problem we want to investigate thoroughly so we know how to better respond on behalf of the American people.

And so we're fully cooperative with the Members of the House in—of the Senate, and we'll do so without giving away my ability to get sound advice from people on my staff. You see, April, here's—and this is an issue that comes up all the time, and you might—we've had several discussions like this since I've been the President. If people give me advice and they're forced to disclose that advice, it means the next time an issue comes up, I might not be able to get unvarnished advice from my advisers. And that's just the way it works. But we've given thousands of pages of documents over for people to analyze.

Q. Does that include Michael Brown?

The President. Pardon me?

Q. Does that include Michael Brown?

The President. People who give me advice—it will have a chilling effect on future advisers if the precedent is such that when they give me advice that it's going to be subject to scrutiny.

Now, we've analyzed—we've given out all kinds of pages of documents for people, and we're cooperating with the investigators. And that's important for the American people to know. What's also important is we want to know how we can do a better job. And so we're having a lessons-learned investigation, led by Fran Townsend. And—anyway, we need to know.

Let's see here—yes, Mark [Mark Knoller, CBS Radio].

Lobbying Reform/Jack Abramoff Investigation

Q. Sir, back on lobbying—never mind about the photographs, but can you say whether—

The President. It's easy for a radio guy to say. [*Laughter*]

Q. Can you say, sir, whether you were lobbied by Jack Abramoff or other lobbyists, and what your policy is about lobbyists meeting with senior staff?

The President. You know, I, frankly, don't even remember having my picture taken with the guy. I don't know him. And this investigation will—needs to look into all aspects of his influence on Capitol Hill, and if there's some in the White House, I'm sure they're going to come and knock on the door. But I—I can't say I didn't ever meet him, but I meet a lot of people. And evidently, he was just like you were the other day, at a holiday party—came in, put—the grip-and-grin. They click the picture, and off he goes. And that's just—I take thousands of—I mean, somebody told me I maybe take over 9,000 pictures this holiday season. And he obviously went to fundraisers, but I've never sat down with him and had a discussion with the guy.

Q. Do you meet with lobbyists?

The President. I try not to. Have I ever met with one? Never having met with one is a—if I ever say that, sure enough, you'll go find somebody. But, no, I don't have them come in.

Now, when, for example, people are helping on issues, like on promoting trade, you bet we bring them in, and I say, "Thank you for promoting CAFTA," or, "Thanks for working on the vote," or, "Thanks for helping on tax relief." That may be—if you consider that a meeting, the answer is, yes, I'm sure I have, in a roomful of people, as we either thank people for success in policy or thank people for going out of their way to get a piece of legislation passed on the Hill.

Listen, thank you all very much. Looking forward to Tuesday evening. I hope you are as well. Thank you.

NOTE: The President's news conference began at 10:15 a.m. in the James S. Brady Press Briefing Room at the White House. In his remarks, he referred to President Mahmoud Abbas (Abu Mazen) of the Palestinian Authority; James D. Wolfensohn,

Quartet Special Envoy for Gaza Disengagement; Gen. George W. Casey, Jr., USA, commanding general, Multi-National Force—Iraq.; Usama bin Laden, leader of the Al Qaida terrorist organization; and Deputy Assistant to the President for Homeland Security Kenneth Rapuano. Reporters referred to Donald E. Powell, Chairman, Federal Deposit Insurance Corporation, in his capacity as coordinator of Federal gulf coast relief efforts; and Mike Brown, former Director, Federal Emergency Management Agency.

Remarks Following Discussions With Parliament Member Saad Hariri of Lebanon
January 27, 2006

It's my honor to welcome a Member of the Lebanese Parliament, Saad Hariri, here to the Oval Office. We've just had a very interesting and important discussion about our mutual desire for Lebanon to be free—free of foreign influence, free of Syrian intimidation, free to chart its own course.

The American people mourn the loss of life. I know it's been hard on you and your mom, who we had the honor of meeting in Paris, and your family to think about your dad, a man who cared about Lebanon a lot. It's very important for the investigation into your dad's death to go forward. We expect there to be a full and firm investigation, and the people who are responsible for your dad's death need to be held to account.

I want to thank you for your passion for the people of Lebanon. I was telling him I was raised in west Texas, and I can remember Lebanese-American Texans being such great citizens of our State and our country. Many people of Lebanese extraction want Lebanon to flourish and thrive, and so do I. It will be very important for the region for Lebanon's democracy to be able to reach its full potential. And there's no doubt in my mind, with the focused effort of the free world reminding Syria to uphold to U.N. Resolution 1559, we will be able to achieve the objective.

So I talked about a donors conference—he's going to work the world community to try to help organize a conference to help the Lebanese people get going. And we appreciate very much your suggestions and your advice.

In the meantime, welcome to the Oval Office. Thank you for your courage. I appreciate it very much. Thank you.

NOTE: The President spoke at 12 p.m. in the Oval Office at the White House. In his remarks, he referred to Nazek Hariri, widow of former Prime Minister Rafiq Hariri of Lebanon, who was assassinated on February 14, 2005, in Beirut.

The President's Radio Address
January 28, 2006

Good morning. The United States Senate is now considering my nomination of Judge Sam Alito to be an Associate Justice on the Supreme Court. As Americans saw in his confirmation hearings, Sam Alito is a man of great character and integrity. He has more prior judicial experience than any Supreme Court nominee in more than 70 years. He understands that the role of a judge is to strictly interpret the law, not to advance a personal or political agenda. And throughout his extraordinary career, Sam Alito has earned the tremendous respect of his colleagues and attorneys across the political spectrum.

This past Wednesday, I met with a distinguished group of 39 former law clerks to Judge Alito. During Judge Alito's 15 years on the bench, these fine men and women have worked side by side with him, providing legal research, discussing and debating pending cases, and seeing firsthand how he arrives at decisions. They are uniquely qualified to assess what kind of Supreme Court Justice Sam Alito would be, and they are united in their strong support of Judge Alito's nomination.

One of Judge Alito's former clerks, who describes herself as a left-leaning Democrat, says this about Sam Alito: "He's a man of great decency, integrity, and character. I believe very strongly he deserves to be confirmed as the Court's next Associate Justice." Another former clerk worked on Senator Kerry's Presidential campaign. She says this about Judge Alito: "His approach to judging is not about personal ideology or ambition but about hard work and devotion to law and justice." In fact, Judge Alito has the strong support of all 54 of his former clerks, regardless of their political beliefs. They know him well, and they know he'll make an outstanding Supreme Court Justice.

Judge Alito has also earned broad support from his fellow judges on the Third Circuit Court of Appeals. Seven of them took the extraordinary step of testifying on his behalf before the Senate Judiciary Committee. Former Chief Judge Ed Becker, who sat with Judge Alito on more than 1,000 cases, said this about his colleague: "He's a real judge, deciding each case on the facts and the law, not on his personal views." Another colleague on the Third Cir-

cuit who was appointed by President Clinton said this about Judge Alito: "He is a fair-minded man, a modest man, a humble man, and he reveres the rule of law." This judge went on to say that, if confirmed, Judge Alito "will serve as a marvelous and distinguished Associate Justice."

Judge Alito received the American Bar Association's highest possible rating, a unanimous "well-qualified." The ABA based its rating on its assessment of Judge Alito's integrity, professional competence, and judicial temperament. In the past, leading Democratic Senators have called the ABA rating the gold standard for judicial nominees.

This past week, Judge Alito gained the endorsement of Pennsylvania's Democratic Governor, Ed Rendell. Governor Rendell said he was not pleased with the partisan way some of his fellow Democrats have handled Sam Alito's nomination. Democratic Senator Robert Byrd of West Virginia announced he was voting for Judge Alito, and he said that many people in his State were calling the treatment of Judge Alito by some Democrats, quote, "an outrage and a disgrace," endquote. Another Democratic Senator expressed concern that the Senate confirmation process in recent years has become, quote, "overly politicized, to the detriment of the rule of law," quote.

The Senate has a constitutional responsibility to hold an up-or-down vote on Judge Alito's nomination. Throughout its 216-year history, the Senate has held an up-or-down vote on every Supreme Court nominee with majority Senate support. Judge Alito has demonstrated that he is eminently qualified to serve on our Nation's highest Court, and America is fortunate to have a man of his integrity and intellect willing to serve.

I'm grateful to Judge Alito, his wife, Martha, and the Alito children for their patience and dignity during the process. And I look forward to the Senate voting to confirm Judge Sam Alito as the 110th Justice of the Supreme Court.

Thank you for listening.

NOTE: The address was recorded at 7:50 a.m. on January 27 in the Roosevelt Room at the White House for broadcast at 10:06 a.m. on January 28. The transcript was made available by the Office of the Press Secretary on January 27 but was embargoed for release until the broadcast. The Office of the Press Secretary also released a Spanish language transcript of this address.

Letter to the Speaker of the House of Representatives Revising Budget Amendments for the Department of Veterans Affairs
January 28, 2006

Dear Mr. Speaker:

My Administration is committed to ensuring that our Nation's veterans continue to receive timely and high-quality health care.

On July 14, 2005, I submitted an FY 2006 budget amendment to the Congress of $1.977 billion to cover increased costs in the Department of Veterans Affairs medical care system. I did not designate the funds as an emergency requirement when I submitted the FY 2006 budget amendment. While I believe this funding should be categorized as part of the VA's base budget, it is critical that this funding be made available to meet veterans' needs. As a result, to provide the needed funds to veterans in a timely manner and consistent with the 2006 Military Quality of Life and Veterans Affairs Appropriations Act, Public Law 109–114, I hereby revise that request to designate $1.225 billion of the amount proposed in that amendment as an emergency requirement. I appreciate your cooperation in working with me to ensure the highest quality of care for our veterans.

Additional information on this action is set forth in the enclosed letter from the Director of the Office of Management and Budget. The details of the FY 2006 amendment were included in the previous transmittal.

Sincerely,

GEORGE W. BUSH

NOTE: This letter was released by the Office of the Press Secretary on January 30.

Remarks Following a Cabinet Meeting and an Exchange With Reporters
January 30, 2006

The President. I want to thank the members of my Cabinet for being here. We just had a really good discussion about the year 2006. Tomorrow night I'm going to be speaking to the Congress, giving the country my State of the Union Address. I can't tell you how upbeat I am about our future, so long as we're willing to lead.

We talked about how to make sure that America continues to spread the peace and to protect ourselves. I heard from the Secretary of Defense and Deputy Secretary of State about very positive initiatives, not only in the Middle East but in the Far East as well. We talked about how to make sure this economy of ours stays the strongest economy in the world and that we recognize we can't just sit back and hope for the best, that we've got to lead. And so we had a good discussion about matters such as health care and energy and education, all of which I'll address tomorrow night.

I'm looking forward to speaking to the country. We've got a lot to be proud of. We've got a lot of work to do. One of the things I will do is call for Congress and the executive branch to have a good, honest dialog but to speak candidly with each other, but to do so in a way that brings credit to the process. And I'll do my best to elevate the tone here in Washington, DC, so we can work together to achieve big things for the American people.

I'll answer a couple of questions. Nedra Pickler [Associated Press].

Iran

Q. Thank you, Mr. President. The talks between Iran and the EU–3 appear to be making little progress. A senior British official there said that they detect nothing new in their approach. What can be done now?

The President. Well, obviously, one option is to—for the Perm 5 to work together to bring Iran to the U.N. Security Council. That's an option. And we're going to continue to work with our friends and allies to present a united front to the Iranians. And the message is, give up your nuclear weapons ambitions. And the good news is, most of the world recognizes that Iran, being the nontransparent society that it is, a Government that had violated IAEA rules, is one that cannot be trusted with technology that could enable it to develop a nuclear weapon. And so we're united in our goal to keep the Iranians from having a weapon, and we're working on the tactics necessary to continue putting a united front out.

The other thing is that we want the people of Iran to be able to live in a free society. And so tomorrow night I am going to talk about this issue and make clear the policy of the United States.

Patsy [Patricia Wilson, Reuters].

Palestinian Elections/Hamas

Q. Mr. President, Israeli officials are seeking an international boycott of a Palestinian Government that includes Hamas. Do you support this? And if so, isn't that punishing the Palestinian people for exercising the democratic rights that you've called for in the region?

The President. The Hamas party has made it clear that they do not support the right of Israel to exist. And I have made it clear, so long as that's their policy, that we will not support a Palestinian Government made up of Hamas. We want to work with a government that is a partner in peace, not a government that is—whose declared intentions might be the destruction of Israel.

Secondly, this new democracy that's emerging in the Palestinian Territories must understand that you can't have a political party that also has got a armed wing to it; that democracies yield peace. And so the second half of our message to Hamas is, get rid of your arms; disavow terrorism; work to bring what you promised to the people of the Palestinian Territories. Listen, these folks ran on the campaign, "We're going to get rid of corruption," and that "We're going to provide services to the people," and that's positive. But what isn't positive is that they've got parts of their platform that will make it impossible for them to be a peaceful partner.

Thank you all very much.

NOTE: The President spoke at 11:06 a.m. in the Cabinet Room at the White House.

Statement on Senate Action To Vote on the Nomination of Samuel A. Alito, Jr., To Be an Associate Justice of the United States Supreme Court
January 30, 2006

I am pleased that a strong, bipartisan majority in the Senate decisively rejected attempts to obstruct and filibuster an up-or-down vote on Judge Sam Alito's nomination. The Senate has a constitutional responsibility to hold an up-or-down vote on every judicial nominee, and throughout its 216-year history, the Senate has held an up-or-down vote on every Supreme Court nominee with majority Senate support. Judge Alito is extraordinarily well-qualified to serve on our Nation's highest Court, and America is fortunate that this good and humble man is willing to serve. I look forward to the Senate voting to confirm Sam Alito as the 110th Justice of the Supreme Court.

Statement on the Death of Coretta Scott King
January 31, 2006

Laura and I are deeply saddened by the death of Coretta Scott King. Mrs. King was a remarkable and courageous woman and a great civil rights leader. She carried on the legacy of her husband, Dr. Martin Luther King, Jr., including through her extraordinary work at the King Center. Mrs. King's lasting contributions to freedom and equality have made America a better and more compassionate nation. Laura and I were fortunate to have known Mrs. King, and we will always treasure the time we spent with her. We send our condolences and prayers to the entire King family.

Statement on Senate Confirmation of Samuel A. Alito, Jr., To Be an Associate Justice of the United States Supreme Court
January 31, 2006

I am pleased that the Senate has voted to confirm Judge Sam Alito as the 110th Justice of the Supreme Court. Sam Alito is a brilliant and fair-minded judge who strictly interprets the Constitution and laws and does not legislate from the bench. He is a man of deep character and integrity, and he will make all Americans proud as a Justice on our highest Court. The son of an Italian immigrant, Judge Alito's appointment to the Supreme Court is the realization of the American dream for this good man and his family. I congratulate Judge Alito, his wife, Martha, the Alito children, and Judge Alito's mother, Rose, on this historic achievement and momentous day in the life of our country.

Judge Alito replaces Justice Sandra Day O'Connor. Justice O'Connor was the first woman ever to sit on the Supreme Court, and she is one of the most admired Americans of our time or any time. Our Nation is grateful to Justice O'Connor for her extraordinary and dedicated public service, and Laura and I wish her and John all the best.

Statement on Senate Confirmation of Ben S. Bernanke To Be Chairman of the Federal Reserve System
January 31, 2006

I am pleased that the Senate has voted to confirm Ben Bernanke to be the next Chairman of the Federal Reserve. Ben is a man of impeccable credentials, sound policy judgment, and strong character, and he will make an outstanding Chairman. Ben has provided wise counsel and good advice as a member of my economic team, and he will serve our Nation with great distinction at the Federal Reserve.

America's economy is strong for a lot of reasons, and one reason is the excellent work done by the men and women of the Federal Reserve. Under the leadership of Chairman Ben Bernanke, the Federal Reserve will continue to help provide Americans with a high quality of living.

Address Before a Joint Session of the Congress on the State of the Union
January 31, 2006

Thank you all. Mr. Speaker, Vice President Cheney, Members of Congress, members of the Supreme Court and diplomatic corps, distinguished guests, and fellow citizens: Today our Nation lost a beloved, graceful, courageous woman who called America to its founding ideals and carried on a noble dream. Tonight we are comforted by the hope of a glad reunion with the husband who was taken so long ago, and we are grateful for the good life of Coretta Scott King.

Every time I'm invited to this rostrum, I'm humbled by the privilege and mindful of the history we've seen together. We have gathered under this Capitol dome in moments of national mourning and national achievement. We have served America through one of the most consequential periods of our history, and it has been my honor to serve with you.

In a system of two parties, two chambers, and two elected branches, there will always be differences and debate. But even tough debates can be conducted in a civil tone, and our differences cannot be allowed to harden into anger. To confront the great issues before us, we must act in a spirit of good will and respect for one another, and I will do my part. Tonight the state of our Union is strong, and together we will make it stronger.

In this decisive year, you and I will make choices that determine both the future and the character of our country. We will choose to act confidently in pursuing the enemies of freedom, or retreat from our duties in the hope of an easier life. We will choose to build our prosperity by leading the world economy, or shut ourselves off from trade and opportunity. In a complex and challenging time, the road of isolationism and protectionism may seem broad and inviting, yet it ends in danger and decline. The only way to protect our people, the only way to secure the peace, the only way to control our destiny is by our leadership. So the United States of America will continue to lead.

Abroad, our Nation is committed to an historic, long-term goal: We seek the end of tyranny in our world. Some dismiss that goal as misguided idealism. In reality, the future security of America depends on it. On September the 11th, 2001, we found that problems originating in a failed and oppressive state 7,000 miles away could bring murder and destruction to our country. Dictatorships shelter terrorists, and feed resentment and radicalism, and seek weapons of mass destruction. Democracies replace resentment with hope, respect the rights of their citizens and their neighbors, and join the fight against terror. Every step toward freedom in the world makes our country safer, so we will act boldly in freedom's cause.

Far from being a hopeless dream, the advance of freedom is the great story of our time. In 1945, there were about two dozen lonely democracies in the world. Today, there are 122. And we're writing a new chapter in the story of self-government—with women lining up to vote in Afghanistan, and millions of Iraqis marking their liberty with purple ink, and men and women from Lebanon to Egypt debating the rights of individuals and the necessity of freedom. At the start of 2006, more than half the people of our world live in democratic nations. And we do not forget the other half—in places like Syria and Burma, Zimbabwe, North Korea, and Iran—because the demands of justice and the peace of this world require their freedom as well.

No one can deny the success of freedom, but some men rage and fight against it. And one of the main sources of reaction and opposition is radical Islam—the perversion by a few of a noble faith into an ideology of terror and death. Terrorists like bin Laden are serious about mass murder, and all of us must take their declared intentions seriously. They seek to impose a heartless system of totalitarian control throughout the Middle East and arm themselves with weapons of mass murder.

Their aim is to seize power in Iraq and use it as a safe haven to launch attacks against America and the world. Lacking the military strength to challenge us directly, the terrorists have chosen the weapon of fear. When they murder children at a school in Beslan or blow up commuters in London or behead a bound captive, the

terrorists hope these horrors will break our will, allowing the violent to inherit the Earth. But they have miscalculated: We love our freedom, and we will fight to keep it.

In a time of testing, we cannot find security by abandoning our commitments and retreating within our borders. If we were to leave these vicious attackers alone, they would not leave us alone. They would simply move the battlefield to our own shores. There is no peace in retreat, and there is no honor in retreat. By allowing radical Islam to work its will, by leaving an assaulted world to fend for itself, we would signal to all that we no longer believe in our own ideals or even in our own courage. But our enemies and our friends can be certain: The United States will not retreat from the world, and we will never surrender to evil.

America rejects the false comfort of isolationism. We are the nation that saved liberty in Europe and liberated death camps and helped raise up democracies and faced down an evil empire. Once again, we accept the call of history to deliver the oppressed and move this world toward peace. We remain on the offensive against terror networks. We have killed or captured many of their leaders. And for the others, their day will come.

We remain on the offensive in Afghanistan, where a fine President and a National Assembly are fighting terror while building the institutions of a new democracy. We're on the offensive in Iraq with a clear plan for victory.

First, we're helping Iraqis build an inclusive government, so that old resentments will be eased and the insurgency will be marginalized. Second, we're continuing reconstruction efforts and helping the Iraqi Government to fight corruption and build a modern economy, so all Iraqis can experience the benefits of freedom. And third, we're striking terrorist targets while we train Iraqi forces that are increasingly capable of defeating the enemy. Iraqis are showing their courage every day, and we are proud to be their allies in the cause of freedom.

Our work in Iraq is difficult because our enemy is brutal. But that brutality has not stopped the dramatic progress of a new democracy. In less than 3 years, the nation has gone from dictatorship to liberation, to sovereignty, to a Constitution, to national elections. At the same time, our coalition has been relentless in shutting off terrorist infiltration, clearing out insurgent strongholds, and turning over territory to Iraqi security forces. I am confident in our plan for victory; I am confident in the will of the Iraqi people; I am confident in the skill and spirit of our military. Fellow citizens, we are in this fight to win, and we are winning.

The road of victory is the road that will take our troops home. As we make progress on the ground and Iraqi forces increasingly take the lead, we should be able to further decrease our troop levels. But those decisions will be made by our military commanders, not by politicians in Washington, DC.

Our coalition has learned from our experience in Iraq. We've adjusted our military tactics and changed our approach to reconstruction. Along the way, we have benefited from responsible criticism and counsel offered by Members of Congress of both parties. In the coming year, I will continue to reach out and seek your good advice. Yet there is a difference between responsible criticism that aims for success and defeatism that refuses to acknowledge anything but failure. Hindsight alone is not wisdom, and second-guessing is not a strategy.

With so much in the balance, those of us in public office have a duty to speak with candor. A sudden withdrawal of our forces from Iraq would abandon our Iraqi allies to death and prison, would put men like bin Laden and Zarqawi in charge of a strategic country, and show that a pledge from America means little. Members of

Congress, however we feel about the decisions and debates of the past, our Nation has only one option: We must keep our word, defeat our enemies, and stand behind the American military in this vital mission.

Our men and women in uniform are making sacrifices and showing a sense of duty stronger than all fear. They know what it's like to fight house to house in a maze of streets, to wear heavy gear in the desert heat, to see a comrade killed by a roadside bomb. And those who know the costs also know the stakes. Marine Staff Sergeant Dan Clay was killed last month fighting in Fallujah. He left behind a letter to his family, but his words could just as well be addressed to every American. Here is what Dan wrote: "I know what honor is— it has been an honor to protect and serve all of you. I faced death with the secure knowledge that you would not have to. Never falter. Don't hesitate to honor and support those of us who have the honor of protecting that which is worth protecting."

Staff Sergeant Dan Clay's wife, Lisa, and his mom and dad, Sara Jo and Bud, are with us this evening. Welcome.

Our Nation is grateful to the fallen, who live in the memory of our country. We're grateful to all who volunteer to wear our Nation's uniform. And as we honor our brave troops, let us never forget the sacrifices of America's military families.

Our offensive against terror involves more than military action. Ultimately, the only way to defeat the terrorists is to defeat their dark vision of hatred and fear by offering the hopeful alternative of political freedom and peaceful change. So the United States of America supports democratic reform across the broader Middle East. Elections are vital, but they are only the beginning. Raising up a democracy requires the rule of law and protection of minorities and strong, accountable institutions that last longer than a single vote.

The great people of Egypt have voted in a multiparty Presidential election, and now their Government should open paths of peaceful opposition that will reduce the appeal of radicalism. The Palestinian people have voted in elections, and now the leaders of Hamas must recognize Israel, disarm, reject terrorism, and work for lasting peace. Saudi Arabia has taken the first steps of reform; now it can offer its people a better future by pressing forward with those efforts. Democracies in the Middle East will not look like our own, because they will reflect the traditions of their own citizens. Yet liberty is the future of every nation in the Middle East because liberty is the right and hope of all humanity.

The same is true of Iran, a nation now held hostage by a small clerical elite that is isolating and repressing its people. The regime in that country sponsors terrorists in the Palestinian territories and in Lebanon, and that must come to an end. The Iranian Government is defying the world with its nuclear ambitions, and the nations of the world must not permit the Iranian regime to gain nuclear weapons. America will continue to rally the world to confront these threats.

Tonight let me speak directly to the citizens of Iran: America respects you, and we respect your country. We respect your right to choose your own future and win your own freedom. And our Nation hopes one day to be the closest of friends with a free and democratic Iran.

To overcome dangers in our world, we must also take the offensive by encouraging economic progress and fighting disease and spreading hope in hopeless lands. Isolationism would not only tie our hands in fighting enemies, it would keep us from helping our friends in desperate need. We show compassion abroad because Americans believe in the God-given dignity and worth of a villager with HIV/AIDS or an infant with malaria or a refugee fleeing genocide or a young girl sold into slavery. We also show compassion abroad because regions overwhelmed by poverty, corruption, and despair are sources of terrorism

and organized crime and human trafficking and the drug trade.

In recent years, you and I have taken unprecedented action to fight AIDS and malaria, expand the education of girls, and reward developing nations that are moving forward with economic and political reform. For people everywhere, the United States is a partner for a better life. Shortchanging these efforts would increase the suffering and chaos of our world, undercut our long-term security, and dull the conscience of our country. I urge Members of Congress to serve the interests of America by showing the compassion of America.

Our country must also remain on the offensive against terrorism here at home. The enemy has not lost the desire or capability to attack us. Fortunately, this Nation has superb professionals in law enforcement, intelligence, the military, and homeland security. These men and women are dedicating their lives, protecting us all, and they deserve our support and our thanks. They also deserve the same tools they already use to fight drug trafficking and organized crime, so I ask you to reauthorize the PATRIOT Act.

It is said that prior to the attacks of September the 11th, our Government failed to connect the dots of the conspiracy. We now know that two of the hijackers in the United States placed telephone calls to Al Qaida operatives overseas. But we did not know about their plans until it was too late. So to prevent another attack—based on authority given to me by the Constitution and by statute—I have authorized a terrorist surveillance program to aggressively pursue the international communications of suspected Al Qaida operatives and affiliates to and from America.

Previous Presidents have used the same constitutional authority I have, and Federal courts have approved the use of that authority. Appropriate Members of Congress have been kept informed. The terrorist surveillance program has helped prevent terrorist attacks. It remains essential to the security of America. If there are people inside our country who are talking with Al Qaida, we want to know about it, because we will not sit back and wait to be hit again.

In all these areas—from the disruption of terror networks, to victory in Iraq, to the spread of freedom and hope in troubled regions—we need the support of our friends and allies. To draw that support, we must always be clear in our principles and willing to act. The only alternative to American leadership is a dramatically more dangerous and anxious world. Yet we also choose to lead because it is a privilege to serve the values that gave us birth. American leaders—from Roosevelt to Truman to Kennedy to Reagan—rejected isolation and retreat, because they knew that America is always more secure when freedom is on the march.

Our own generation is in a long war against a determined enemy, a war that will be fought by Presidents of both parties who will need steady bipartisan support from the Congress. And tonight I ask for yours. Together, let us protect our country, support the men and women who defend us, and lead this world toward freedom.

Here at home, America also has a great opportunity: We will build the prosperity of our country by strengthening our economic leadership in the world.

Our economy is healthy and vigorous and growing faster than other major industrialized nations. In the last 2½ years, America has created 4.6 million new jobs, more than Japan and the European Union combined. Even in the face of higher energy prices and natural disasters, the American people have turned in an economic performance that is the envy of the world.

The American economy is preeminent, but we cannot afford to be complacent. In a dynamic world economy, we are seeing new competitors like China and India, and this creates uncertainty, which makes it easier to feed people's fears. So we're seeing some old temptations return. Protec-

tionists want to escape competition, pretending that we can keep our high standard of living while walling off our economy. Others say that the government needs to take a larger role in directing the economy, centralizing more power in Washington and increasing taxes. We hear claims that immigrants are somehow bad for the economy, even though this economy could not function without them. All these are forms of economic retreat, and they lead in the same direction, toward a stagnant and second-rate economy.

Tonight I will set out a better path: an agenda for a nation that competes with confidence; an agenda that will raise standards of living and generate new jobs. Americans should not fear our economic future because we intend to shape it.

Keeping America competitive begins with keeping our economy growing. And our economy grows when Americans have more of their own money to spend, save, and invest. In the last 5 years, the tax relief you passed has left $880 billion in the hands of American workers, investors, small businesses, and families. And they have used it to help produce more than 4 years of uninterrupted economic growth. Yet the tax relief is set to expire in the next few years. If we do nothing, American families will face a massive tax increase they do not expect and will not welcome. Because America needs more than a temporary expansion, we need more than temporary tax relief, I urge the Congress to act responsibly and make the tax cuts permanent.

Keeping America competitive requires us to be good stewards of tax dollars. Every year of my Presidency, we've reduced the growth of nonsecurity discretionary spending, and last year, you passed bills that cut this spending. This year, my budget will cut it again and reduce or eliminate more than 140 programs that are performing poorly or not fulfilling essential priorities. By passing these reforms, we will save the American taxpayer another $14 billion next year and stay on track to cut the deficit in half by 2009.

I am pleased that Members of Congress are working on earmark reform, because the Federal budget has too many special interest projects. And we can tackle this problem together, if you pass the line-item veto.

We must also confront the larger challenge of mandatory spending, or entitlements. This year, the first of about 78 million baby boomers turn 60, including two of my dad's favorite people—me and President Clinton. [*Laughter*] This milestone is more than a personal crisis—[*laughter*]—it is a national challenge. The retirement of the baby boom generation will put unprecedented strains on the Federal Government. By 2030, spending for Social Security, Medicare, and Medicaid alone will be almost 60 percent of the entire Federal budget. And that will present future Congresses with impossible choices: staggering tax increases, immense deficits, or deep cuts in every category of spending. Congress did not act last year on my proposal to save Social Security, yet the rising cost of entitlements is a problem that is not going away. And every year we fail to act, the situation gets worse.

So tonight I ask you to join me in creating a commission to examine the full impact of baby boom retirements on Social Security, Medicare, and Medicaid. This commission should include Members of Congress of both parties and offer bipartisan solutions. We need to put aside partisan politics and work together and get this problem solved.

Keeping America competitive requires us to open more markets for all that Americans make and grow. One out of every five factory jobs in America is related to global trade, and we want people everywhere to buy American. With open markets and a level playing field, no one can outproduce or outcompete the American worker.

Keeping America competitive requires an immigration system that upholds our laws, reflects our values, and serves the interests of our economy. Our Nation needs orderly and secure borders. To meet this goal, we must have stronger immigration enforcement and border protection. And we must have a rational, humane guest-worker program that rejects amnesty, allows temporary jobs for people who seek them legally, and reduces smuggling and crime at the border.

Keeping America competitive requires affordable health care. Our Government has a responsibility to provide health care for the poor and the elderly, and we are meeting that responsibility. For all Americans, we must confront the rising cost of care, strengthen the doctor-patient relationship, and help people afford the insurance coverage they need.

We will make wider use of electronic records and other health information technology to help control costs and reduce dangerous medical errors. We will strengthen health savings accounts, making sure individuals and small-business employees can buy insurance with the same advantages that people working for big businesses now get. We will do more to make this coverage portable, so workers can switch jobs without having to worry about losing their health insurance. And because lawsuits are driving many good doctors out of practice, leaving women in nearly 1,500 American counties without a single ob-gyn, I ask the Congress to pass medical liability reform this year.

Keeping America competitive requires affordable energy. And here we have a serious problem: America is addicted to oil, which is often imported from unstable parts of the world. The best way to break this addiction is through technology. Since 2001, we have spent nearly $10 billion to develop cleaner, cheaper, and more reliable alternative energy sources. And we are on the threshold of incredible advances.

So tonight I announce the Advanced Energy Initiative—a 22-percent increase in clean-energy research at the Department of Energy—to push for breakthroughs in two vital areas. To change how we power our homes and offices, we will invest more in zero-emission coal-fired plants, revolutionary solar and wind technologies, and clean, safe nuclear energy.

We must also change how we power our automobiles. We will increase our research in better batteries for hybrid and electric cars and in pollution-free cars that run on hydrogen. We'll also fund additional research in cutting-edge methods of producing ethanol, not just from corn but from wood chips and stalks or switchgrass. Our goal is to make this new kind of ethanol practical and competitive within 6 years.

Breakthroughs on this and other new technologies will help us reach another great goal: to replace more than 75 percent of our oil imports from the Middle East by 2025. By applying the talent and technology of America, this country can dramatically improve our environment, move beyond a petroleum-based economy, and make our dependence on Middle Eastern oil a thing of the past.

And to keep America competitive, one commitment is necessary above all: We must continue to lead the world in human talent and creativity. Our greatest advantage in the world has always been our educated, hard-working, ambitious people. And we're going to keep that edge. Tonight I announce an American Competitiveness Initiative to encourage innovation throughout our economy and to give our Nation's children a firm grounding in math and science.

First, I propose to double the Federal commitment to the most critical basic research programs in the physical sciences over the next 10 years. This funding will support the work of America's most creative minds as they explore promising areas such as nanotechnology, supercomputing, and alternative energy sources.

Second, I propose to make permanent the research and development tax credit to encourage bolder private sector initiative

in technology. With more research in both the public and private sectors, we will improve our quality of life and ensure that America will lead the world in opportunity and innovation for decades to come.

Third, we need to encourage children to take more math and science, and to make sure those courses are rigorous enough to compete with other nations. We've made a good start in the early grades with the No Child Left Behind Act, which is raising standards and lifting test scores across our country. Tonight I propose to train 70,000 high school teachers to lead Advanced Placement courses in math and science, bring 30,000 math and science professionals to teach in classrooms, and give early help to students who struggle with math, so they have a better chance at good, high-wage jobs. If we ensure that America's children succeed in life, they will ensure that America succeeds in the world.

Preparing our Nation to compete in the world is a goal that all of us can share. I urge you to support the American Competitiveness Initiative, and together we will show the world what the American people can achieve.

America is a great force for freedom and prosperity. Yet our greatness is not measured in power or luxuries but by who we are and how we treat one another. So we strive to be a compassionate, decent, hopeful society.

In recent years, America has become a more hopeful nation. Violent crime rates have fallen to their lowest levels since the 1970s. Welfare cases have dropped by more than half over the past decade. Drug use among youth is down 19 percent since 2001. There are fewer abortions in America than at any point in the last three decades, and the number of children born to teenage mothers has been falling for a dozen years in a row.

These gains are evidence of a quiet transformation, a revolution of conscience, in which a rising generation is finding that a life of personal responsibility is a life of fulfillment. Government has played a role. Wise policies, such as welfare reform and drug education and support for abstinence and adoption have made a difference in the character of our country. And everyone here tonight, Democrat and Republican, has a right to be proud of this record.

Yet many Americans, especially parents, still have deep concerns about the direction of our culture and the health of our most basic institutions. They're concerned about unethical conduct by public officials and discouraged by activist courts that try to redefine marriage. They worry about children in our society who need direction and love, and about fellow citizens still displaced by natural disaster, and about suffering caused by treatable diseases.

As we look at these challenges, we must never give in to the belief that America is in decline or that our culture is doomed to unravel. The American people know better than that. We have proven the pessimists wrong before, and we will do it again.

A hopeful society depends on courts that deliver equal justice under the law. The Supreme Court now has two superb new members on its bench, Chief Justice John Roberts and Justice Sam Alito. I thank the Senate for confirming both of them. I will continue to nominate men and women who understand that judges must be servants of the law and not legislate from the bench.

Today marks the official retirement of a very special American. For 24 years of faithful service to our Nation, the United States is grateful to Justice Sandra Day O'Connor.

A hopeful society has institutions of science and medicine that do not cut ethical corners and that recognize the matchless value of every life. Tonight I ask you to pass legislation to prohibit the most egregious abuses of medical research: human cloning in all its forms; creating or implanting embryos for experiments; creating human-animal hybrids; and buying, selling, or patenting human embryos.

Human life is a gift from our Creator, and that gift should never be discarded, devalued, or put up for sale.

A hopeful society expects elected officials to uphold the public trust. Honorable people in both parties are working on reforms to strengthen the ethical standards of Washington. I support your efforts. Each of us has made a pledge to be worthy of public responsibility, and that is a pledge we must never forget, never dismiss, and never betray.

As we renew the promise of our institutions, let us also show the character of America in our compassion and care for one another.

A hopeful society gives special attention to children who lack direction and love. Through the Helping America's Youth Initiative, we are encouraging caring adults to get involved in the life of a child. And this good work is being led by our First Lady, Laura Bush. This year, we will add resources to encourage young people to stay in school, so more of America's youth can raise their sights and achieve their dreams.

A hopeful society comes to the aid of fellow citizens in times of suffering and emergency and stays at it until they're back on their feet. So far the Federal Government has committed $85 billion to the people of the gulf coast and New Orleans. We're removing debris and repairing highways and rebuilding stronger levees. We're providing business loans and housing assistance. Yet as we meet these immediate needs, we must also address deeper challenges that existed before the storm arrived.

In New Orleans and in other places, many of our fellow citizens have felt excluded from the promise of our country. The answer is not only temporary relief but schools that teach every child and job skills that bring upward mobility and more opportunities to own a home and start a business. As we recover from a disaster, let us also work for the day when all Americans are protected by justice, equal in hope, and rich in opportunity.

A hopeful society acts boldly to fight diseases like HIV/AIDS, which can be prevented and treated and defeated. More than a million Americans live with HIV, and half of all AIDS cases occur among African Americans. I ask Congress to reform and reauthorize the Ryan White Act and provide new funding to States, so we end the waiting lists for AIDS medicines in America. We will also lead a nationwide effort, working closely with African American churches and faith-based groups, to deliver rapid HIV tests to millions, end the stigma of AIDS, and come closer to the day when there are no new infections in America.

Fellow citizens, we've been called to leadership in a period of consequence. We've entered a great ideological conflict we did nothing to invite. We see great changes in science and commerce that will influence all our lives. Sometimes it can seem that history is turning in a wide arc toward an unknown shore. Yet the destination of history is determined by human action, and every great movement of history comes to a point of choosing.

Lincoln could have accepted peace at the cost of disunity and continued slavery. Martin Luther King could have stopped at Birmingham or at Selma and achieved only half a victory over segregation. The United States could have accepted the permanent division of Europe and been complicit in the oppression of others. Today, having come far in our own historical journey, we must decide: Will we turn back or finish well?

Before history is written down in books, it is written in courage. Like Americans before us, we will show that courage, and we will finish well. We will lead freedom's advance. We will compete and excel in the global economy. We will renew the defining moral commitments of this land. And so we move forward, optimistic about our country, faithful to its cause, and confident of the victories to come.

May God bless America.

NOTE: The President spoke at 9:12 p.m. in the House Chamber of the Capitol. In his remarks, he referred to Usama bin Laden, leader of the Al Qaida terrorist organization; senior Al Qaida associate Abu Musab Al Zarqawi; and President Hamid Karzai of Afghanistan. The Office of the Press Secretary also released a Spanish language transcript of this address.

Remarks in Nashville, Tennessee
February 1, 2006

The President. Thank you all very much. Thanks for coming. Please be seated.

Audience member. We love you—[*inaudible*].

The President. Thanks for being here. Yes. I can see—[*applause*]. Did you say you love Laura? So do I. You stole my line. [*Laughter*] Thanks for coming. This is an amazing experience to be here. I can see why my buddy Gatlin finds that extra note when he stands out here and sings. It's a fantastic hall. The last time Laura and I were here, we were honoring Mother and Dad for their 50th wedding anniversary. Mother thought he'd lost his mind when he said, "Honey, I want to celebrate the 50 years of marriage at the Grand Ole Opry." I said, "Gosh, you got good judgment, Dad, you know." [*Laughter*] So thanks for coming. I'm really thrilled to be here.

I should have probably come before I gave my speech. When I was on the plane flying down here, I thought, how cool would it be to give a State of the Union address in a Porter Wagoner outfit. [*Laughter*]

I do want to give you some of the thoughts behind what I said in my State of the Union. That's what I've come to do. You know, it's one thing to give the speech—I think it's important to come here to Nashville to tell people the reason why I said some of the things I said. I think it will help you understand why I have made some of the decisions I have made.

One of the interesting things about the Presidency is we get to entertain a lot, and my favorite—the favorite folks to entertain are the people that Laura and I grew up with. I like my buddies from west Texas. I liked them when I was young; I liked them when I was middle-age; I liked them before I was President; and I like them during President; and I like them after President. And it's fun to have them come to the White House. It's neat to show off this fantastic experience that Laura and I are being able to go through. When they first walk in there, they're amazed at the White House. And the second thing is, they're amazed I'm in the White House. [*Laughter*] And they always say, "What's it like to be President of the United States?" And after I say it's just a huge honor, which it is, I say, "If I could give you the job description, it would be decisionmaker." I have to make a lot of decisions. And today what I'd like to do is share with you why I have made decisions in the context of the State of the Union I gave last night.

Before I do, I really am thrilled Laura's traveling with me. She's a great First Lady. She is—[*applause*]. I'm proud to be traveling with your two United States Senators—the majority leader of the United States Senate, Bill Frist. He's a good man.

He's a good guy to deal with. He is doing a fantastic job of herding cats. [*Laughter*] And I'm proud to be here with Senator Lamar Alexander as well.

A little later on, I'm going to talk about a key component of the competitive agenda, and that is to make sure our folks are educated for the jobs of the 21st century. And I will tell you that Lamar had a lot to do with planting this in my mind. He's, as you know, made his fame here in Tennessee for being a great education Governor. You'll be pleased to hear he's carried over that passion into the Halls of the United States Senate. And so in case I forget to give him credit later on, he deserves a lot of credit for making sure that we're competitive in the 21st century.

I appreciate the members of the statehouse who are here. Thanks for serving. I appreciate those in local government who are here. I understand the mayor is here, Mayor Purcell. I appreciate you taking time out of your busy day. I know you didn't ask for any advice. My only advice is, fill the potholes. [*Laughter*] Works every time, Mayor. [*Laughter*]

I want to thank the good folks here at Gaylord Entertainment for letting me come by and just explain some things to the people of Tennessee. This is such a fantastic facility. I had been here before my mother and dad's 50th wedding anniversary when I was—happened to be involved in the baseball business. I can remember the winter meetings we held here. And we're still looking for two of our guys that worked for us. They got lost—[*laughter*]—in one of the 14 lobbies in this fantastic facility. It's a wonderful place.

I want to thank those of you who wear our Nation's uniform who have joined us today. We particularly want to recognize Lieutenant Colonel Dan Epright. He's in active duty, U.S. Air Force. He's on a 2-week leave from Iraq, where he's stationed in the International Zone in Baghdad as the American Forces Network—Iraq, commander. He's in his 20th year of active duty. I don't know where Colonel Epright is, but wherever you are, thanks for serving. Welcome back—Epright. Thank you very much. Is that your wife? I knew exactly where Epright was; I just forgot. [*Laughter*] And I'm proud that his wife is with him.

Yesterday I said something I really mean: As we give praise to our troops who wear the uniform, we must also remember to give praise to military families who support the troops.

Our state of the Union is strong. I say that because America is working hard to protect ourselves; we're spreading freedom; our economy is vigorous and strong as well. But there's some uncertainty in people's minds. People are uncertain, in spite of our strong union, because of war. And I understand that. I think it is—my job is as much educator in chief as it is Commander in Chief. And during times of uncertainty, it's important for me to do what I'm doing today, which is to explain the path to victory, to do the best I can to articulate my optimism about the future.

But I understand there's an anxiety about a time of war. That's natural, it seems like to me. Even though this economy is roaring—and it's strong, particularly when you think—recognize we've overcome a lot. This year alone we've overcome higher energy prices and natural disasters, and yet we really are the envy of the world. Our economy is the envy of the world. And yet people are changing jobs a lot, and there's competition from India and China, which creates some uncertainty.

My worry is, is that people see that uncertainty and decide to adopt isolationist policies or protectionist policies. In other words, in uncertain times, it's easy to— for people to lose confidence in the capacity of this country to lead and to shape our future.

Last night in my speech, I talked about a couple of themes. And one of the themes was that we must never lose sight of our capacity to lead this world toward peace, and that we must never fear—and we must

never fear competition. But, on the other hand, we've got to put solid policy in place to make sure that we can compete.

First, let me talk about foreign policy and why I'm concerned about isolationism. We're at war, see. A lot of my thinking in the speech I gave last night—and speeches that I have been giving—is based upon my understanding that we're at war. On September the 11th, 2001, I vowed to the American people that we would not rest and tire in order to protect us. And I have never forgotten that vow. As a matter of fact, every day of my Presidency, I think about this war. That's what you've got to understand. And so when you hear me give a speech and talk about the dangers to America, they are real, not imagined. Some would like us to look at the world the way we would hope it would be. My job as your President is to look at the world the way it is.

And I clearly see the threats to America. My job is to worry about those threats. That's not your job. We got a lot of people in Government worrying about those threats on your behalf, so you can go about your life. That's what we want. I knew after September the 11th, people would—they would tend to forget the nature of the enemy and forget the war, because it's natural. Who wants to live all your day worried about the next attack? That's my job, to worry about the attack. It's the job of the intelligence community and our military and law enforcement. That's what you pay us to do. But I also recognize that if we ever get weary or tired or uncertain and withdraw within our boundaries, the enemy is not going away.

The enemy is a bunch of coldblooded killers that have taken a great religion— taken parts of a great religion and converted it into an ideology that is—they perverted a great religion, and they have an ideology. We've been through ideological struggles in the past. We've had an ideological struggle against fascism and communism. And we're in that same kind of struggle now. That's what's important for the American people to understand. They have ambition. They want to spread their totalitarian empire.

People say, "What do you mean by that?" I say, the best thing to think about is what life was like in Afghanistan for the Taliban—under the Taliban, for the people under the Taliban. It's a life where young girls couldn't get an education. Think about that. You talk about a dark vision of the future—it's a life where if you didn't agree with their view of religion, you were punished. It's a life in which freedom of expression was not encouraged. It was a dim view of the world. That's what these people think like.

They have stated clearly their desire to hurt us. And we got to take what they say seriously. When the enemy says something, an enemy which attacked us brutally on September the 11th, I would hope you would want the people in Government to take their word seriously—which I do. They have said they want to drive us out of Iraq. They have said they want weapons of mass destruction. In other words, they've got an ideology that they want to spread, and they want us to retreat. That's what they have openly stated. And that is why it's essential that we remain active in the world and keep the lead for peace. We have the duty to protect the American people. And so our strategy is to never give in, and never be—and never—[applause]. It's to never lose heart. This enemy has got one weapon, and it's the weapon of fear.

What a fantastic country America is. We deeply care about every human life. The life of a child in Baghdad is precious. And so when we see these killers kill somebody—a young child outside a hospital where one of our soldiers is handing out candy—we weep, because Americans have a deep compassion for every human being. And the only weapon they have is to cause us to weep and lose our nerve. And as I said last night—it's something I truly believe—they don't understand the nature of

America. We love our freedom, and we will do everything in our power to defend our freedom.

And so we're on the hunt for Al Qaida, and we're going to stay on the hunt. And we will bring them to justice. No doubt in my mind—no doubt in my mind we are bringing them to justice. We're making great progress in dismantling Al Qaida, and the others who hide won't be able to hide long enough. We're using every asset in our power to keep them on the defense, to find them and bring them to justice.

Secondly, I said something that I meant early on in this war against these terrorists, and that is, is that—to countries, "If you harbor a terrorist, you're equally as guilty as the terrorist." In other words, one of the—[applause]. Because I understand that these terrorist networks need safe haven in order to plan and plot. We're not dealing with nation-states; we're dealing with an ideological movement that needs a nation in which to hide. And so we made it clear that if you're complicit with the murderers, you're just as guilty as the murderers themselves. And that's why we took the action in Afghanistan. We gave the Taliban an opportunity to get rid of Al Qaida. They chose not to, and we acted.

So, thirdly, when we see a threat, we've got to deal with the threat. I remember growing up in Midland—Gatlin grew up in Odessa, by the way, right down the road—or the Gatlins did. I was white collar; he was blue collar. Anyway—[laughter]. I'm President; he's a singer. Anyway—[laughter]. You can tell I like him, because when I put the needle out, it's a sign of affection. Just don't give him the mike. Anyway—[laughter].

When we grew up, oceans protected us, it seemed like. We felt pretty safe and secure from a attack on American soil. We were concerned about a nuclear threat, but nevertheless, we felt secure because we were isolated from threats, it seemed like. September the 11th changed my way of thinking. It changed my way of thinking on a lot of things, and one way it changed is that when we see a threat, we got to deal with it. We can't hope for the best. One of the lessons of September the 11th is we—threats should not be allowed to fully materialize; otherwise, it will cause harm to the American people.

I saw a threat in Iraq. The world saw a threat in Iraq. We gave Saddam Hussein a chance to deal with the world in good faith by honoring the United Nations Security Council resolutions. He chose—it was his choice; he chose to defy the resolutions. And so we took action. The world is safer and America is more secure without Saddam Hussein in power.

I recognize in a free society like ours, there can be and should be debate on big matters. I welcome the debate. But as I said last night to Congress, whether you agree or not agree with the decision, this country has one option, and that's victory in Iraq. I say that because the enemy has said they want to drive us out of Iraq and use it as safe haven. We've got to take the word seriously of those who want to do us harm.

I want to describe right quick our plans for victory in Iraq. First of all, anytime we put our troops in harm's way, we got to go in with victory in mind. And the victory is for Iraq to be a democracy that can sustain itself and govern itself and defend itself, a country which will be an ally in the war on terror, a country which will deny safe haven to the Al Qaida, and a country which will serve as a powerful example of liberty and freedom in a part of the world that is desperate for liberty and freedom.

The Iraqis have shown incredible courage and a strong desire to live in democracy. If you really think about last year, the year 2005, the progress toward democracy was remarkable. Anyway you look at it, it was remarkable. This young democracy has gone from tyranny—[*inaudible*]—a brutal dictator that killed or had killed thousands of people to a country which had

a transitional government in an election, to a country which wrote a progressive Constitution for the Middle East and had that Constitution ratified, to a country in which 11 million people voted in elections last December. You see, one of the things that—[*applause*]—one of the inherent parts of my foreign policy is my strong belief that liberty is universal, that everybody desires to be free, that freedom is not just a Western idea or an American idea; freedom is lodged in the soul of every person. I used—I put it—let me put it another way to you: I believe there's an Almighty, and I believe the Almighty's gift is freedom to every single person in this world.

And if you believe that—I'm just getting wound up here. [*Laughter*] I told Laura, I'd try to keep it under a couple hours. [*Laughter*] If you believe that, that freedom is universal, then it shouldn't surprise you that 11 million people, more or less, went to the polls. People want to be free, and the Iraqis are showing the world that.

Secondly, we've got to make sure their economy is able to function as good as possible so that people see the benefits of democracy. It's one thing to have elections; it's another thing for people to say, "Democracy is good for me; democracy is good for my family." And so we're working on reconstruction and fighting corruption and making sure that there are tangible benefits. And it's been difficult because the enemy is not only brutal in terms of killing people, the enemy is just relentless in trying to destroy infrastructure so that people cannot see the benefits of democracy.

And the third aspect—and it's one that I know is dear to the hearts of many people—is, how long will we be in Iraq? And the answer is this: It's a security aspect. And that is that if people want to be free and if 11 million people chose to vote, the question on people's mind is, is there a willingness for the Iraqis to defend their own freedom? And I will tell you, the answer we have seen, our commanders on the ground have seen, is, absolutely. Absolutely. There is great bravery amongst these Iraqi soldiers. Our job is to convert their desire to protect their new democracy into effective forces. And that's what we're doing.

We've changed our training patterns. When we first got in there—one of the things I talked about over the Christmas season or the holiday season—prior to the holiday season—was that we've adjusted. That's what happens. We see things, and we change. We've done things differently. When we first went in there, we helped train an army for an external threat. Well, sure enough, the external threat wasn't nearly as significant as the internal threat. And so we started adjusting our training tactics. And we got good advice from Members of the Senate and the House from both political parties who went to Iraq and came back and said, "Here's what we've seen." And so we're changing.

And the security forces of Iraq are up to about 230,000, more or less. But the question is not just numbers. I first asked about numbers. You'd read about these suiciders knocking people off that were trying to stand these recruiting stations, and so the question is, are you able to get recruits? If it's dangerous to sign up, are you able to sign people up? And the answer is, absolutely. People wanted to serve the Iraqi military, which is a good sign about whether or not we're succeeding in our mission in training folks to defend their freedom. And if they're willing to sign up in the face of suiciders, it says something about their desire to protect their country.

The second question is, can they do the job? Are we training them well enough so they can take the fight on their own? And the election was an interesting example where the Iraqis were in the lead, and the violence in the last election was significantly lower than the violence in the first election.

Today, by video, I met with my—I met not only in the room with my national security team, but we had the Ambassador and General Casey from Baghdad. And it's interesting to be able to communicate with your commanders on the ground in real time. And the reason I bring that up is that they are constantly updating the national security team and me about the effectiveness of these troops and how much territory we're turning over to the Iraqi troops.

What I have told the American people is, as the Iraqis stand up, we will stand down. As the Iraqis are capable of taking the fight to the enemy, we will reduce our troop levels. We have two less brigades there than we thought. In other words, these troops are being trained—the troops that we're training are more effective, more capable of taking the fight to the enemy. The commanders on the ground say, "We need less American presence."

Now, I'm going to talk—tell you something about timetables and withdrawals and all that business. It is a mistake to have a definitive timetable of withdrawal, because the enemy will react; the Iraqis will react. And it's not fair to our men and women who wear the uniform.

So I will make my decisions based upon what these commanders tell me. That's what you expect of the Commander in Chief. My job is to set the strategy. I just told you what victory is all about. We've defined victory. And now it's up to the commanders on the ground to help us achieve that victory. And if they say these Iraqis are capable of taking the fight, they're there firsthand to tell me that, and then we'll reduce our troops based upon their recommendation, not based upon the politics in Washington, DC.

Another reason—in other words, we can't be isolationists and win the war on terror. And we can't be isolationist, either, because it would prevent us from doing our duty around the world, and not only make this world a place where terrorists have trouble recruiting, but to live to that admonition, "To whom much is given, much is required."

159

Effective foreign policy is—recognizes that we can help change conditions on the ground to make life better for future generations of Americans. And I believe that helping defeat HIV/AIDS on the continent of Africa is—not only reflects the great compassion of America, but it will improve lives for generations of Americans to come. I believe defeating hopelessness and despair and helping others defeat poverty is in our national interest. I also know it reflects the deep character of the American people.

If this country were to become isolationist and withdraw and say we don't care about conditions of life elsewhere, we're not only ceding the ground to terrorists, we're not doing our duty as a compassionate nation.

Do you realize we feed a lot of the hungry in the world—and I'm proud of that record—that we're providing incredibly important lifesaving antiretroviral drugs to help defeat HIV/AIDS on the continent of Africa? There is a pandemic sweeping that continent, and the United States of America is leading the world in helping save lives. Do you realize that when the tsunami hit earlier this past year, it was the United States military that moved in and provided immediate help and aid and comfort and organization? Our choppers were flying rescue missions in Pakistan after the devastating earthquake. In my judgment, an active foreign policy, one that aids the suffering and helps the poor, is one that is in the interest of the United States of America, both short term and long term.

And finally, if we were to withdraw, not only would we cede ground to the terrorists and endanger this country, we would miss a fantastic opportunity to help spread liberty. In my speech, I mentioned Roosevelt and Kennedy, Truman, and Reagan. I did so because I wanted to remind the American people that these leaders were one that acted in confidence in our values. They understood when America led, not only was

America better off, but the world was. And we're spreading freedom now.

For those of you who are young, I want you to watch the spread of freedom in our world. It's amazing to see, when you think about it. The vote in Afghanistan was part of freedom's march. The vote in Iraq is part of freedom's march. People in Lebanon want to be free from Syria, and we're working—the Palestinians voted. Now, that election was an important election because it said what the people on the street wanted. They wanted clean government. They want people to pay attention to the education needs and their health needs. In order for us to—and Hamas, by the way, now has a choice to make. If they want to work with the United States of America, they must renounce their desire to destroy Israel; they must be a partner in peace.

Last night I spoke to the people of Iran—spoke first to the Government of Iran and said, "The world will continue to come together in unity to say you can't have nuclear weapons." But I also spoke to the people, because I believe that everybody desires to be free, and I just wanted to assure them that someday, that they will be able to have a choice in their Government, and the United States looks forward to a friendship with a free and democratic Iran.

Liberty is universal, but it's important also to understand that freedom and liberty yield the peace we all want. One reason to be active in the world is to spread peace. If the United States were to withdraw, we'd miss an opportunity to make this world a more peaceful place for generations to come.

I like to tell people about my relationship with Prime Minister Koizumi because it helps drive home the point about freedom yielding peace. You know, my dad and, I suspect, a lot of your relatives fought against the Japanese in World War II. They were the sworn enemy of the United States of America. If there are any World War II vets here, they'll tell you what it was like during that period of time. The Japanese attacked us, and we vowed to do everything in our power to defeat them. And we sent a lot of kids into battle, and we lost a lot of lives, and the Japanese lost a lot of lives. It was a brutal battle, and we won.

Interestingly enough, one of the people that I work closest with in the world is the Prime Minister of Japan. Isn't that interesting? At least it is to me. My dad fought them, and now his son is working to keep the peace with the Prime Minister of the country that he went to war against. And so what happened between when he was 18 and I'm sitting here at 59? I'll tell you what happened in between: Japan adopted a Japanese-style democracy. Freedom has the capacity to convert enemies into allies. Freedom has the capacity to lay—[*applause*]—freedom has that capacity to lay that foundation for peace for generations to come.

I believe we will be victorious in Iraq, and I know that by laying that foundation of peace in the Middle East, we'll be able to say, job well done. We have laid—we have made a better chance for peace for a generation of Americans coming up. Someday, an American President will be sitting down with a duly elected leader of Iraq, working on keeping that peace, and a new generation of Americans will say, thank goodness this generation accepted the responsibilities given to them.

Talk about a couple of other issues. There is a duty of us in Washington to protect you. One of the important aspects of protecting you is to make sure our law enforcement has all the tools necessary to do their job. Right after September the 11th, members of both political parties came together and said, "Let us make sure that we tear down walls between intelligence gathering service and law enforcement services in America so they can share information to connect dots and protect the people." And so they passed what's called the PATRIOT Act.

The PATRIOT Act is an important piece of legislation, in my judgment, because it says to folks, "Here's some tools that we use in other areas of law enforcement now applicable to intelligence, to protecting you." For example, some of the tools in the PATRIOT Act were already being used by people fighting off drug lords or Medicaid fraud, interestingly enough. The PATRIOT Act had safeguards designed in it where the programs were reviewed, and if people had complaints about abuse of civil liberty, they could bring them, and we would know whether or not the law was meeting intended consequences.

The law has worked. It's been a very important tool for our law enforcement officials. The PATRIOT Act is set to expire. The war against terrorists is not expiring. These people need the tools necessary to do their job. It's essential that Congress reauthorize the PATRIOT Act.

I want to take a little time to explain the terrorist surveillance program to you. First, if I was trying to pull a fast one on the American people, why did I brief Congress? In other words—[*applause*]. Right after September the 11th, it was apparent that there was some of the hijackers in the United States who were calling Al Qaida—Al Qaida operatives calling overseas. We don't know what they were talking about. Matter of fact, we found out about the calls after it was too late. But I was concerned about a system that wasn't doing everything we could to protect the American people, within the Constitution. And so, as you would hope that the Commander in Chief would do, I said to our operators, people responsible for protecting you, "Are we doing everything we can to protect you? Come up with other ways to connect the dots." And this terrorist surveillance program was designed by very capable operatives.

But before I implemented the program—I'm mindful of the fact that I took an oath to uphold the Constitution and the laws of the United States. So I had law-yers—the Attorney General and the Justice Department—look at what I was doing. I'm also mindful that people want to make sure the President safeguards civil liberties while we protect the country, that there needs to be a balance. And so this is a program—and I became comfortable with that balance and confident that I had the legal authority to do what I did.

And so let me tell you what I did without talking about the operating details. I'm sure you can understand why you don't want the President or anybody talking about the operating details. If you're at war and you're trying to stop an enemy from attacking you, why in the world would you want to tell the enemy what they're doing to stop them, because they'll adjust. So I've authorized NSA to listen to a phone call from outside the United States in, or inside the United States out. In other words, this is not a program where we're listening to phone calls inside the United States. One of the people making the call has to be Al Qaida, suspected Al Qaida, and/or affiliate.

This is a program in which we have briefed key Members of the Congress a lot of times. It is constantly reviewed by a legal team, constantly reviewed. It is constantly reviewed inside NSA by a legal team. We are safeguarding your liberties.

Federal courts have ruled that the President—a President has constitutional authority to use foreign intelligence surveillance against enemies. Previous Presidents have used the same constitutional authority I have. I've got statutory authority as well. The Congress passed the authorization to use military force against Al Qaida after September the 11th, and the Supreme Court, in a recent opinion, ruled that the President—the Congress gave me the authority to use what's called the "fundamental incidents of war." In other words, Congress authorized me to use force in the fundamental incidents of war, which means in this case, you can't defeat the enemy

until you know when the enemy is going to hit. And therefore, using this surveillance to find out the intention of the enemy is a fundamental incident of war to protect the American people. Let me put it to you in Texan: If Al Qaida is calling into the United States, we want to know.

Here's the challenge at home—we got a great economy. The American people are amazing when you unleash their creativity and talent. The entrepreneurial spirit of this country is strong when we reinforce that entrepreneurial spirit. Over the past 2½ years, this economy has created 4.6 million new jobs; the unemployment rate is 4.9 percent. Small businesses are flourishing. After-tax income since '01 is up 7 percent. Productivity is very high, which is important for quality of life and higher standards of living. Homeownership is at an alltime high; more minorities own a home today in America than ever before in our Nation's history. This economy is doing just fine.

But the question is, how do we stay competitive? What do we do to make sure, in a world in which competition is becoming fiercer and fiercer—what do we do to stay ahead of it? Now, some would say, "Protect yourselves by withdrawing from the world." I think that is a huge mistake. Protectionism doesn't work. Protectionism would default to other countries in the world. That's not the American way. America must be confident and lead and do what is necessary to keep us competitive.

And I've got some ideas for you. First, in order to make sure we're competitive, this economy has got to continue to grow. Last night I said an interesting statistic, at least I thought it was; otherwise, I wouldn't have said it, but—[*laughter*]. I said the tax relief we passed left $880 billion in the hands of American families and small businesses and entrepreneurs. See, my philosophy is that the more money you got, the more of your own money you keep, you will save and invest and spend, and that's how this economy grows. And the tax relief we passed is working because the American people are responding.

And so how do we make sure that we have economic vitality and growth. Well, one thing you don't want to do is take money out of—if it has worked, why take money out of your pocket? And the tax relief we passed is set to expire. If Congress doesn't do anything, your taxes are going to go up, which, in my judgment, would be bad for the economy. In order to keep America competitive, the Congress needs to make the tax relief permanent.

You'll hear folks say, "Well, we got to run up your taxes in order to balance the budget." That's not the way it works in Washington. They're going to raise your taxes so they can find new ways to spend your money. That's how it works. So I want the tax cuts permanent, and I want to work on the deficit by controlling Federal spending.

We can meet priorities. We can meet priorities. See, you got to set priorities in order to meet priorities. So long as we've got kids in harm's way, a priority will be to make sure our troops have what's necessary to do their job.

We got a plan to cut this deficit in half by 2009. It's just going to take Congress making some hard choices. Part of my job is to present a budget that gives them a chance to show how to cut that deficit in half by 2009. Looking forward to working with them on achieving this objective. [*Laughter*] But the long-term problem we got is the mandatory spending. And I want to spend a little time on it.

There's—we got a real issue with Social Security and Medicare. And the reason why is, guys like me are fixing to retire. I'm turning 62, retirement age, in 2008, which is a convenient coincidence. [*Laughter*] I'm looking around and I see some other baby boomers out there too. And we're going to stress the system. There's a lot of us getting ready to retire, a heck of a lot more than have been retired. And we've been promised a lot. And a lot of young guys

are going to be having to pay into a system that is flat going broke. That's the reality.

It's hard for me to be the President and look at young workers, young people coming into the workforce, paying payroll taxes into a system that I know is going broke. And it is. We've been promised too much, and too few people paying into the system. And now we need to do something about it, because this mandatory spending, these entitlement programs, are going to make it really hard for future Congresses and future taxpayers.

I tried last year with the Social Security plan. I thought my job was not only to raise the issue but to come up with some solutions. One of my first objectives was to explain to the American people, we got a problem. I believe that until Congress hears from the people that we got a problem that their attitude is going to be, "Nobody thinks we got a problem; why do anything about it?" People now know we got a problem.

Last night I said to Members of Congress the truth: We're not going to be able to solve this issue until we bring Republicans and Democrats together. It's a big issue solving the baby boomer—[*applause*]. We can get the job done. You don't have to cut benefits to people; you just got to slow them down so that the next generation can afford them. Do you realize my benefits or your benefits grow faster than the rate of inflation? I mean, in other words, there's ways to make it work. But it's going to require a new attitude in Washington, DC. There's too much politics up there. There's too much zero-sum. I want the Democrats on Capitol Hill to hear loud and clear: I want a bipartisan solution on mandatory and entitlement spending for the sake of future generations of Americans.

I want to talk about four other issues right quick. You still awake? [*Laughter*] They didn't come all the way to hear this, kind of getting shortchanged. I'll make it quick. It's important for us to stay competitive, to open up markets. The temptation is to shut markets down. I'm confident in our ability. I'm confident in our farmers; I'm confident in our entrepreneurs. I think the job—I know the job of the President is to work to open up markets and level the playing field. My attitude is this: We say to countries, "You treat us the way we treat you," and when they do, nobody can outcompete the American worker and farmer and entrepreneur.

A big issue is immigration. It's important for us to get this issue solved so that we can be competitive as we go out into the 21st century. First of all, the obligation of the Federal Government is to enforce our borders, is to make sure that—[*applause*]. And I want to thank Leader Frist for passing a strong appropriations bill to provide resources necessary for more Border Patrol technology along the border. Listen, the border is long, and it's not easy to enforce. But with proper use of technology, some physical barriers, I think we'll be able to do a much better job.

The second issue along the border, by the way, is that when we catch somebody sneaking into our country illegally, we just can't release them out into the system. We've got to have more detention space so that—it used to be they'd catch them, a lot of the folks, they'd say, "All right, check back in with your immigration judge here in 45 days." And the guy would say, "Yes, you bet—[*laughter*]—see you later." So we're changing that along the border.

I do want to talk about the worker issue. A lot of people here in America have come to do jobs Americans won't do. And they're here because they can make money for their families. I used to tell people in Texas that family values didn't stop at the Rio Grande River. If you're a mother or a dad and you want to put food on the table for your children, and you had the choice between $5 and $50, you'd head for $50 if you could.

I believe a very significant part of enforcing our border—make it easier for our Border Patrol to do the job—is to end this system that encourages smuggling and pressure on the border by people sneaking across, and saying if there is somebody that's willing to do a job an American won't do, let's give him a fool-proof pass so they can be here on a temporary basis.

Now, I'm against amnesty, and the reason I am is, I believe if you grant amnesty to people that are here, it will cause another wave of people to want to come. But I am for recognizing reality and saying that if you're doing a job, if you're an employer and you're looking for somebody to do a job an American won't do, then here is a card for a temporary worker. That's a humane way to treat the issue. I can't stand a system that has caused people to get stuffed in the back of 18-wheelers and they're driving across the desert. We have—because of our policy, we have caused there to be a whole smuggling industry and a forgery industry. If you're out there working and somebody shows up, and you can't find somebody to find work, and they show up and you say, "Show me your card"—you don't know whether it's real or not real. There's people forging cards in order to help these people find work.

We've got Border Patrol agents chasing people getting smuggled across the border to do work. If you are able to have a rational plan on a temporary-worker basis, it doesn't seem like to me—they're not going to have to try to sneak across the border, and our Border Patrol will be able to do a better job on drugs and terrorists and guns that are trying to be snuck in and out of this country. Immigration is an important issue, and I'm looking forward to working with Congress to get a job done on behalf of the American people.

I want to talk about health care right quick. The job of the Federal Government is to take care of the elderly and the poor. We're rolling out a Medicare plan that is going to make medicine for our seniors modern, up to date, and work well. It's a really important reform.

Listen, if you say, "We're going to provide medicine for our seniors," you need to provide the best medicine possible for our seniors. And that means including prescription drug coverage for the seniors. And that's what's happening. We got—millions of people are signing up for this program. We've been in it for about 4 weeks. We're going to correct problems. Most of the people signing up are finding out it's a good deal. I urge seniors to look at this program carefully and sign up.

We also have an obligation to the poor, which we're taking care of in Medicaid. But I want to give you another way of dealing with medicine other than having the Federal Government run it all, which I am unalterably opposed to. I think, one, we ought to have policies that encourage the doctor-patient relationship, strengthen that relationship. Secondly, we got to be wise about how we help control costs. One way to control costs is to spread information technology out—throughout the health care field.

Let me put it to you this way: Health care is kind of lagging behind when it comes to using modern technology. Think about it. You got docs still writing out those files. And they hand that file to you and say, "Take it down the hall." You're moving paper still in a paperless world. The problem is, not only are you moving paper, but doctors can't write in the first place. [*Laughter*] It creates inefficiencies in the system. There are too many medical errors. By spreading information technology, which—Bill Frist and I went to a hospital—I think it was here in Nashville—where they've got a modern information technology system being put in place. They're going to save 20 percent to 30 percent on health care costs. It's a rationale way of helping control health care without the Federal Government getting in your business.

I'm for allowing small businesses to pool risk across jurisdictional boundaries so they have the opportunity of buying health care at the same discount big businesses get.

I am big believer in health savings accounts. For those of you who don't know health savings accounts, investigate health savings accounts. They're an innovative way to make sure the doctor-patient relationship is strong, that people are in charge of making the health care decisions themselves, that there is an incentive to taking care of your body through good exercise and good nutrition. It's a way to save money tax-free in your health care and, at the same time, get coverage for catastrophic illness. These make sense for small businesses; they make sense for individuals. And I'm going to ask Congress to make them more available and more attractive for individual consumers all across the United States.

Finally, if you want to do something about availability of health care and affordability of health care, we have got to get the United States Senate to pass medical liability reform. You don't have to worry about Frist. No, he understands. We got a problem with ob-gyns. I said last night a statistic which should alarm the American people: There are 1,500 counties in America in which a woman can't find an ob-gyn. And a lot of that has to do with lawsuits driving good docs out of practice. This isn't right, folks. This isn't right. It's time for those Senators who are blocking that bill, those Senators who are representing the trial lawyers of America, to understand the damage they're doing to the health care industry of this country.

I'm just getting warmed up. [*Laughter*] In order to stay competitive, America must end its dependence on oil. When you're hooked on oil from the Middle East, it means you've got an economic security issue and a national security issue. And I spoke last night to some exciting opportunities here in America. I believe—I know that technology is going to enable us to diversify away from being dependent on hydrocarbon, from oil.

Let me talk about cars, and that's really the area where we can achieve a lot of independence. We use a lot of foreign oil in our automobiles, and we drive a lot. And people say, well, CAFE this and CAFE that. Actually, we have increased CAFE standards for certain types of vehicles during my administration, and that's important, as is giving people choice, and marketplace function is important. But most important of all, it seems like to me, if you recognize the fact that being dependent upon oil is a problem for the long term, then why don't we figure out how to drive our cars using a different type of fuel?

Now, let me talk about two things that we're working on. We spent—I said last night, we've spent $10 billion, since I've been President, on research, and we're close to some really interesting breakthroughs. One such breakthrough is advanced batteries, which will make the hybrid car or the electric car much more affordable and much more suitable to the consumer demands. You don't want your battery running out halfway between here and somewhere else.

But I do want to talk about ethanol right quick. You know, we're making ethanol out of corn right now. We're very close to a breakthrough where we'll be able to figure out how to make ethanol from other forms, other materials, like grasses, woods. Now, think about that. All of a sudden—we may be in the energy business by being able to grow grass on the ranch—[*laughter*]—and have it harvested and converted into energy. And that's what's close to happening. We're told that if we continue to focus on research, we'll be able to, within 6 years, have a competitive fuel to gasoline.

Now, people say, "Well, that's great. How about the automobile?" Will they be able to use it? Four-and-a-half million cars today are flex-fuel automobiles. In other words, they can either use gasoline or ethanol. So the technology is there for the automobile, and we're close to the technology of providing a competitive fuel to gasoline by converting that which we grow into fuel. It's coming. It's an exciting time. I can't wait to work with Congress to continue promoting this kind of research so that someday we're no longer dependent on Middle Eastern oil.

People say, "Well, why can't—once you get the fuel, why can't you just convert your fleet instantly?" We've got 200 million cars out there. It takes a while for new automobiles to become the main, dominant part of the automobile fleet. What I'm telling you is, is that we're close to some breakthroughs. These are exciting times. Technology is going to help keep this country competitive.

But the thing that's going to keep the country most competitive is making sure our workforce has got the skills to compete. This is a dynamic world. Whether the people want to recognize it or not, we're in a competitive world. Some will say, "It's so competitive; let's withdraw and protect ourselves." That's not my attitude. My attitude is if it's competitive, let's get in a position where we can out-compete the rest of the world. And the most important place is going to be to make sure our kids have got the skills to fill the jobs of the 21st century. If our kids don't have those skills, those jobs will go somewhere else.

And so this is the initiative that I praised Lamar about; it's called the America Competitiveness Initiative. It basically says that we're going to focus on research, both in public and private sector, to make sure that the technologies and skill base of our science and engineering community leads the world. It also recognizes that we've got to make sure our children have got math and science skills.

By the way, that starts with making sure children can read. One of Laura's most important initiatives and inherent in the No Child Left Behind Act is the absolute demand by our Government that schools teach every single child how to read by fourth grade—or third grade—and remain at grade level throughout their entire public school career.

One of the ways to make sure that our children have got math and science skills that will give them the basis on which to compete—and, by the way, when you test our scores relative to other children, we're doing just fine in elementary school, and we start slipping off in middle school, and we're not doing worth a darn in high school. And so one way to reverse that trend is to make sure our high school teachers have got the necessary skills to teach kids the skill sets to be able to compete. And so we believe that we can help train 70,000 high school teachers to lead Advanced Placement courses in math and science.

Advanced Placement works. AP is a vital program. If you study your AP results here in Tennessee schools, you'll see it makes a lot of sense. We want AP programs to be available to children from all walks of life so that they have the skills necessary to compete. We got a plan to get 30,000 math and science professionals to teach in our classrooms. And we want to make sure, just like we do on No Child Left Behind, that we focus on math as well, and we find math deficiencies early—we provide money to correct them. See, if you diagnose and don't correct, you're doing a child a disservice. If you don't diagnose, you're doing a child a disservice. The best thing to do is what we're doing, is diagnose and solve problems early, before they're too late. And that's what we're going to do in this very exciting initiative.

A couple of other things I want to talk about. What I just told you is how to stay competitive. See, we have a choice. We can withdraw and say, "Okay, you all go do your thing, and we'll just protect ourselves inside America," or we can compete. And I just laid out an agenda for America to lead. I believe that the way you enhance prosperity for the American people is you shape your own destiny. And America has been a leader and will continue to be a leader in the world economy.

What really matters in the long term is the character of the American people. The great strength of this country is the compassion of our citizens. It really is. I like to remind people that de Tocqueville got it right when he came and looked at America in the 1830s and recognized the voluntary associations. The ability for people to serve something greater than themselves was the strength of America then, and it's the strength of America now.

One of the reasons why I mentioned Laura last night and her program is not only I want her to get a little air time—[*laughter*]—but she's heading up a very important effort to encourage mentors to help say to a child, "I love you. What can I do to help you? How can I help you realize you need to make the right choices in life in order to succeed?"

I see a Scout there. The Scouting program is a great mentoring program. But there are all kinds of ways you can help, all kinds of ways you can help get involved with people's lives. Last night we honored some folks by putting them in the box there during the State of the Union. I guess it's an honor when you sit there and have to listen to an old guy for an hour. But anyway, nevertheless, they were there. And one of them was a young guy that was volunteering down there in—for those affected by the hurricanes.

One of the things about that hurricane is we're going to make sure that we analyze the response. And, as I said, we just didn't do as good a job as we should have done at all levels of government. As the head of the Federal Government, I take responsibility for that. But having said that, the response of the American people to these hurricanes was unbelievable. People were uprooted out of their homes. They were wandering out there, wondering whether or not anybody cared. And thousands of our fellow citizens had open arms and said, "I care about you. How can I help you?" It was a remarkable, remarkable thing to watch. It's reconfirmed my great faith in the American people.

The Government has got a role. As I mentioned last night, we've committed $85 billion to help the people get on their feet down there. We're going to stay with them. We'll help them. And the American people are helping them as well.

Another thing I talked about last night, to make sure that our country is hopeful and the spirits are up, is that when you look at Washington, you've got to be assured that people are upholding the integrity that you expect them to. I look forward to working with Congress on ethics reform. We have a solemn duty and an obligation to say to the American people that we will uphold the honor of the offices to which we have been elected.

I do want to say something about judges. I want to thank both Senators here for voting to confirm a good man. Laura and I are going to—if I can ever stop speaking here—[*laughter*]—we're going to go back and have a swearing-in ceremony for Judge Sam Alito. The reason I bring this up is that part of making sure America knows there's a hopeful tomorrow is that—a lot of Americans don't like it when judges kind of write the law. We've got plenty of legislators in Washington. Believe me, we've got plenty of legislators in Washington. And so I'm going to put judges on the bench who know the difference between interpreting the Constitution and trying to write the law. I'll continue to do that.

And so that's what's on my mind, and it took me an hour to tell you. [*Laughter*] I hope you get the sense of my optimism about the country. I told you mine is a decisionmaking job. I first learned that when the guy called me—I was getting ready to give my Inaugural Address, right before the swearing-in of the first Presidency—the first term. And a guy called me and said, "What color rug do you want in the Oval Office?" I said, "Man, this is a decisionmaking job." [*Laughter*]"What color rug do I want?" The second thing about decisionmaking is you've got to know when it's time to delegate. So, not knowing much about rug designing, I said, "Laura, give me a hand." [*Laughter*]

And the third thing about my job is you've got to set a strategic vision. I set the strategic vision last night for our country: active in the pursuit of our own security and the spread of freedom; confident in our ability to compete in the world; understanding we need to continually recommit ourselves to serving others. And so I said, "Laura, the only thing I want is that rug to say—you figure out how to say it— is, 'Optimistic person comes here to work every day.' " And she captured my spirit, because I am optimistic about our future.

Thanks for giving me a chance to share that optimism with you. God bless.

NOTE: The President spoke at 12:01 p.m. at the Grand Ole Opry House. In his remarks, he referred to entertainer Larry Gatlin of the Gatlin Brothers; entertainer Porter Wagoner; Mayor Bill Purcell of Nashville, TN; former President Saddam Hussein of Iraq; U.S. Ambassador to Iraq Zalmay Khalilzad; Gen. George W. Casey, Jr., USA, commanding general, Multi-National Force—Iraq; and Prime Minister Junichiro Koizumi of Japan.

Remarks at a Swearing-In Ceremony for Samuel A. Alito, Jr., as an Associate Justice of the United States Supreme Court
February 1, 2006

Good afternoon. Laura and I welcome you to the White House. Mr. Chief Justice, thank you for coming. Members of the Supreme Court, thank you all for being here. Members of the Senate, honored you're here. Ladies and gentlemen, appreciate you joining us on this historic occasion. This afternoon we're also honored by the presence of a strong and graceful woman, Mrs. Cissy Marshall. Thank you for coming, Mrs. Marshall.

Yesterday the United States Senate confirmed Sam Alito as the 110th Justice of the Supreme Court of the United States. Last night he looked pretty good in that black robe sitting there. [*Laughter*]

It's a proud day for Judge Alito and his entire family. We extend a special welcome to Martha, who has been at his side for more than 20 years. And with us, you can see his son, Phil, and daughter, Laura. If they're anything like our daughters, they're probably telling their dad how to behave and how to testify. [*Laughter*]

I appreciate Rosemary being with us today. And we're thinking of Sam's mom, Rose, who turned 91 in December. And of course, as we think of Rose, we think of her husband, Sam's late father. He came to our country as an immigrant from Italy in 1914. Sam Alito, Sr., instilled in his son a deep commitment to serving his fellow Americans. And I'm sure he's looking down with pride as Sam takes his place on the highest Court of the United States of America.

Sam Alito is replacing an extraordinary Justice, Sandra Day O'Connor. Justice O'Connor has been an admired member of the Supreme Court for 24 years. She has served our Nation with decency and spirit and great devotion, and I thank her on behalf of all the American people.

Sam, you've drawn quite a distinguished crowd here. I appreciate the Vice President being here, and Lynne. I want to thank the Attorney General and other members of my Cabinet who have joined us today. I want to thank the members of my team who have worked so hard to help Sam, particularly former Senator Dan Coats of Indiana.

I want to thank Secretary Mike Chertoff, who's with us. The reason I bring up Chertoff is they worked together, and Chertoff kind of put in a good word for Sam, you know—[*laughter*]—at a crucial moment. [*Laughter*]

I particularly want to thank the Members of the Senate who are here. I'm sorry I'm a little late. I've just come in from Tennessee. I got a little windy. And Senator Frist was with me. I appreciate you, Leader, for working hard to get this good man through. And thank you, Mitch McConnell, Senator McConnell, as well. I don't want to name all the Senators since we're running a little late, but I do want to mention the chairman of the Judiciary Committee, Arlen Specter, who did a heck of good job.

Judge Alito becomes Justice Alito. As he becomes Justice Alito, our Nation completes a process that was ordained by our Founders in Philadelphia more than 200 years ago. Under the Constitution, the President nominates and, by and with the consent—advice and consent of the Senate, appoints the Justices of the Supreme Court. This process has been carried out many times since the beginning of our democracy. And each new appointment represents a renewal of the promise of our country and our constitutional order.

Our Founders thought carefully about the role they wanted judges to play in the American Republic. They decided on a court system that would be independent from political or public pressure, with judges who serve for life. America expects members of our judiciary to be prudent in exercising judicial power and firm in defending judicial independence. So every member of the Supreme Court takes an oath to uphold the Constitution and administer justice faithfully and impartially. This is a solemn responsibility.

And the man we honor today has demonstrated his devotion to our courts and law through years of service to our country. Sam Alito has distinguished himself as a member of our military, a Federal prosecutor, Assistant to the Solicitor General, U.S. Attorney in New Jersey, and for the last 15 years, a highly respected judge on the Third Circuit Court of Appeals.

Sam Alito is known for his steady demeanor, careful judgment, and complete integrity. Throughout his career he has treated others with respect. In return, he has earned the admiration of his colleagues on the bench, the lawyers who have come before it, and, of course, a very devoted group of proud law clerks.

During the confirmation process, the American people saw a man of character and legal brilliance. Like our fellow citizens, I was impressed by the dignity Sam Alito and his family displayed during the Senate hearings, and by the thoughtful scholarship and reverence of the Constitution that have always defined his approach to the law.

A Supreme Court Justice must meet the highest standard of legal excellence, while serving with humility and fidelity to our founding promise of equal justice under the law. These are qualities Americans want in a Supreme Court Justice. These are qualities Americans see in Sam Alito. He will make a superb Justice of the Supreme Court, and I know this son of New Jersey will make all Americans proud.

Sam, I thank you for agreeing to serve our country again and for accepting this new call to duty.

Now I ask the Chief Justice of the United States, John Roberts, to please step forward and administer the oath.

NOTE: The President spoke at 4:22 p.m. in the East Room at the White House. In his remarks, he referred to Cecilia Marshall, wife of former Justice Thurgood Marshall. The transcript released by the Office of the Press Secretary also included the remarks of Associate Justice Alito.

Statement on House of Representatives Passage of Spending-Reduction Legislation
February 1, 2006

As I said last night, keeping America competitive requires us to be good stewards of taxpayer dollars. The House today passed a significant spending-reduction package that will curb the growth of entitlement spending for the first time in years and help us stay on track to cut the deficit in half by 2009. I look forward to signing this bill into law. The budget I propose next week will continue to build on the spending restraint we have achieved.

NOTE: The statement referred to S. 1932.

Statement on the New Freedom Initiative
February 1, 2006

Five years ago, I announced the New Freedom Initiative to build on the progress of the Americans with Disabilities Act and more fully integrate people with disabilities into all aspects of life. Since the announcement of this important initiative, we have expanded educational opportunities for children with disabilities and provided essential funding for the Individuals with Disabilities Education Act. We have launched disabilityinfo.gov to serve as an online resource for people with disabilities and their families, employers, service providers, and other community members. To provide expanded employment opportunities, we are assisting persons with disabilities by implementing the Ticket to Work program and strengthening training and employment services at One-Stop Career Centers.

As a result of these efforts, Americans with disabilities have greater access to the opportunities of America. My administration will continue to work to remove barriers that still confront Americans with disabilities and their families.

Remarks at the National Prayer Breakfast
February 2, 2006

The President. Thank you all. Please be seated. Thanks for the warm welcome. Laura and I are delighted to be here. This lovely personality said this morning, "Keep your remarks short." [*Laughter*]

I appreciate this prayer breakfast a lot, and I appreciate the spirit in which it was formed. Ike said he was living in the loneliest house in America—for what he got to say is, the rent is pretty good. [*Laughter*]

It's great to be here with distinguished guests from all around the world. Your Majesty and Prime Ministers and former Prime Ministers, friends with whom I have the honor to work, you're welcome here. I appreciate the fact that people from different walks of life, different faiths have joined us. Yet I believe we share one thing in common: We're united in our dedication to peace and tolerance and humility before the Almighty.

I want to thank Senators Pryor and Coleman for putting on this breakfast. I appreciate Senator Frist, Representative Blunt, Representative Pelosi, other Members of the United States Congress who've joined us on the dais and who are here for this breakfast. I thank the members of my Cabinet who are here. Get back to work. [*Laughter*]

I find it interesting that the music is from Arkansas. [*Laughter*] I'm glad it is, because they know how to sing down there. [*Laughter*]

You know, I was trying to figure out what to say about Bono. [*Laughter*]

Bono. Careful. [*Laughter*]

The President. And a story jumped to mind about one of these really good Texas preachers. And he got going in a sermon, and a fellow jumped up in the back and said, "Use me, Lord, use me." And the preacher ignored him and finished his sermon. Next Sunday, he gets up and cranking on another sermon, and the guy jumps up and says, "Use me, Lord, use me." And after the service, he walked up to him and said, "If you're serious, I'd like for you to paint the pews." Next Sunday, he's preaching; the guy stands up and says, "Use me, Lord, use me, but only in an advisory capacity." [*Laughter*]

So I've gotten to know Bono. [*Laughter*] He's a doer. The thing about this good citizen of the world is, he's used his position to get things done. You're an amazing guy, Bono. God bless you. God bless you.

It is fitting we have a National Prayer Breakfast, because our Nation is a nation of prayer. In America, we do not prescribe any prayer; we welcome all prayer. We're a nation founded by men and women who came to these shores seeking to worship the Almighty freely. From these prayerful beginnings, God has greatly blessed the American people, and through our prayers, we give thanks to the true source of our blessings.

Americans remain a prayerful people today. I know this firsthand. I can't tell you the number of times out there traveling our country, people walk up, total strangers, and say, "Mr. President, I'm praying for you and your family." It is one of the great blessings of the Presidency and one of the most wonderful gifts a person can give any of us who have the responsibility to govern justly. So I thank my fellow citizens for their gracious prayers and wonderful gifts.

Every day, millions of Americans pray for the safety of our troops, for the protection of innocent life, and for the peace we all hope for. Americans continue to pray for the recovery of the wounded and to pray for the Almighty's comfort on those who have lost a loved one. We give thanks daily for the brave and decent men and women who wear our Nation's uniform, and we thank their families as well.

In this country, we recognize prayer is a gift from God to every human being. It is a gift that allows us to come before our Maker with heartfelt requests and our deepest hopes. Prayer reminds us of our place in God's creation. It reminds us that when we bow our heads or fall to our knees, we are all equal and precious in the eyes of the Almighty.

In prayer, we're reminded we're never alone in our personal trials or individual suffering. In prayer, we offer our thanksgiving and praise, recognizing our lives, our talents, and all that we own ultimately flow from the Creator. And in these moments of our deepest gratitude, the Almighty reminds us that for those to whom much has been given, much is required.

In prayer, we open ourselves to God's priority, especially His charge to feed the hungry, to reach out to the poor, to bring aid to the widow or the orphan. By surrendering our will to God's will, we learn to serve His eternal purposes. Through prayer, our faith is strengthened, our hearts are humbled, and our lives are transformed. Prayer encourages us to go out into the world and serve.

In our country, we recognize our fellow citizens are free to profess any faith they choose, or no faith at all. You are equally American if you're a Hebrew—a Jew or a Christian or a Muslim. You're equally American if you choose not to have faith. It is important America never forget the great freedom to worship as you so choose.

Yes, what I've found in our country, that whatever our faith, millions of Americans answer the universal call to love your neighbor just like you'd like to be loved yourself. Over the past 5 years, we've been inspired by the ways that millions of Americans have answered that call. In the face of terrorist attacks and devastating natural disasters here and around the world, the American people have shown their faith in action again and again. After Katrina, volunteers from churches and mosques and synagogues and other faith-based and community groups opened up their hearts and their homes to the displaced. We saw an outpouring of compassion after the earthquake in Pakistan and the tsunami that devastated entire communities. We live up to God's calling when we provide help for HIV/AIDS victims on the continent of Africa and around the world.

In millions of acts of kindness, we have seen the good heart of America. Bono, the true strength of this country is not in our military might or in the size of our wallet; it is in the hearts and souls of the American people.

I was struck by the comment of a fellow who was rescued from the gulf coast and given shelter. He said, "I don't—I didn't think there was so much love in the world." This morning we come together to recognize the source of that great love. We come together before the Almighty in prayer, to reflect on God's will, to seek His aid, and to respond to His grace.

I want to thank you for the fine tradition you continue here today. I pray that our Nation will always have the humility to commend our cares to Providence and trust in the goodness of His plans.

May God bless you all.

NOTE: The President spoke at 9:09 a.m. at the Hilton Washington Hotel. In his remarks, he referred to musician and activist Bono.

Remarks in Maplewood, Minnesota
February 2, 2006

Thank you all. Please be seated. Thanks for coming. Appreciate the warm welcome. Got to take my Post-it note off my speech here. [*Laughter*] My fault. My fault. [*Laughter*] I should have cleaned off the podium. [*Laughter*] I saw that I could get—I see the Governor out there—he says, "You want to have some lunch?" I said, "Sure, what are you serving?" He said, "Lutefisk." [*Laughter*] I said, "No, I think I'll eat on Air Force One." [*Laughter*]

It's great to see you, Governor. Thanks for being here. Laura and I are delighted to be here at 3M. We're glad to be with the Governor and the first lady, Lieutenant Governor.

I was greeted by your chairman and CEO, George W. [*Laughter*] I'll just call you "W." [*Laughter*] Thanks for having me. I appreciate it. I want to thank Jay Ihlenfeld, the senior vice president, for the tour we just went on. I want to thank all the employees here for giving me a chance to come by and visit with you.

I really want to send a message to the United States of America that in order for us to keep the standard of living that we're accustomed to, that in order for us to be the leader in the world that we want to be, that we must remain a flexible, technologically based economy.

You know, it's amazing when you come to 3M to talk to George W. about the number of products you make and—products that people just take for granted, but products, many of which started in a laboratory as the result of a really smart, capable person making the technological advances necessary to get these products to market.

Innovation is a vital part of the future of the United States of America, and the fundamental question is, how do we keep our society innovative? That's what I'm here to talk about.

You know, one way for our fellow citizens to understand the importance of innovation and technology is just think about what has taken place over 25 years. Now, for a 59-year-old guy, that doesn't seem like much these days. If you're 26, it seems like a lot. Twenty-five years ago, most Americans used the typewriter. Isn't that interesting? Twenty-five years ago, they had such a thing as pay phones. [*Laughter*] Now we're using cell phones. Carbon paper was used. For those youngsters here, carbon paper was kind of a messy way to duplicate things. Now we're using laser printers. They had bank tellers that were distributing most money in those days. Twenty-five years ago, you had to go to the bank and say to the teller, "Good day, may I have some money?" Now you can go to the ATM machine.

Technology is changing the way we think. I don't know if you remember those awful trips when you had to drive with your family; you played the license plate game. [*Laughter*] Now we got the DVDs—[*laughter*]—right there in the car. Technology happens quickly if you remain an innovative society. And it's those technological improvements that help create high-paying jobs and enhances the standard of living of the American people.

Do you realize that economists say that as much as half of our Nation's economic growth in the last half-century is directly due to technological progress fueled by research and development, the kind of research and development you do right here? Think about that. One-half of the progress of our economy is due to research and development. Well, if that's the case, if that's the truth, we got to make sure we continue to encourage research and development.

Technology has enabled us to be the preeminent economy in the world. I think it's good that we're the preeminent economy in the world. I think it's good for the American people that we're in a leadership position. And the reason why I think it's good is because when you lead, your people benefit. By being a leader in the economy of the world, it means somebody is more likely to find work. And somebody is able to— likely to realize dreams and opportunity.

I say we're the preeminent economy in the world because the facts bear me out. We're growing faster than other industrial—major industrialized nations. We've added 4.6 million new jobs in 2½ years. That's more than Japan and the European Union combined. And the fundamental question is, one, do we want to remain the leader, and two, how do you do it?

There's some uncertainty in America today, and I can understand why. There's uncertainty when it comes to our economy. People are beginning to see competitors emerge, India and China. I'm a fellow who likes competition. I think it's good to have competition. I think it makes us do things better. But some people in our country look at competition and say, "Well, we can't possibly compete with China or India or other countries, and therefore, why don't we just think about walling ourselves off?" That's called protectionism. It's a trend that we need to worry about. See, there's uncertainty when people see jobs go overseas. I can understand that. Somebody's working hard all their life, and all of the sudden, the job gets moved overseas because of competition. That creates uncertainty in the workplace. And one of the reactions to that uncertainty could be, "Well, I'm tired of competing. Maybe what we need to do is instead of competing, just kind of leave ourselves apart from the world."

The United States of America has been through this before. This isn't a new thought. If you look at our history, our economic history, you'll find that we've been through periods of protectionism before. If you'll look at our foreign policy history, you'll find there's been periods of isolationism before. I think that—and so the first thing I want to share with you is, it's important for us not to lose our confidence in changing times. It's important for us not to fear competition but welcome it.

There's a global economy. The Internet has really changed a lot, when you think about it. It is—I happen to think it's good news that countries are becoming more wealthy; that through the global competition, that people's lives are improving. I believe that because most Americans—all Americans believe in the dignity of every human being. But I take a practical look at it, and so should you at 3M. You ought to say, "We welcome this developing world, this new economy, because as wealth spreads, there are new customers for our products." In other words, instead of saying, "We fear the competition; the global economy frightens us," the United States of America ought to say, "We want more people to be able to buy our products."

And so what I'm telling you is I think the role of government is to shape the future, not fear the future. And I think the role of a President is to say to the American people, "Be bold; be confident. And if we do the right things, we'll remain the leader in the world."

And here are the things I think we ought to do. First, I know we got to keep our economy growing. You can't be a world leader in the economy if your economy is flat. You can't be a world leader—world economic leader if your economy is flat. I mean, you got to have progrowth policies in place.

One of the interesting debates in Washington, DC, is, how do you encourage growth? Well, I'll give you my position. I think when people have more money in their pocket to save, earn, or spend, the economy grows. I think when a small-business person has more money to invest, the economy grows.

We passed tax relief. As I said in my State of the Union the other night, the tax relief that we passed left $880 billion in the hands of individuals and families and small businesses and entrepreneurs. And I believe that is why our economy is the most preeminent in the world.

And this—[*applause*]—and that tax relief is set to expire. And when it does, you're going to get a tax increase. There's—not only do I think it's wrong to take money out of your pocket at this point in our economic history, I also believe that uncertainty in the Tax Code makes it difficult for people to make wise decisions about investment. And I meant what I said to the Congress: In order to make sure this expansion is not temporary, they need to make sure that tax relief is permanent.

You'll hear them say, "Well, we need to raise taxes to balance the budget." That's not the way Washington works. They'll raise taxes to increase spending. That's the way it works. And so I think the best way to balance the budget is to have progrowth policies in place so these tax revenues remain strong, and be wise about how we spend your money. That's hard in Washington. Everybody has got a great idea about how to spend your money. But when you're running 3M Company or you're running your family budget, you learn how to set priorities. And that's what Congress must do.

I'm going to tell you something: If Congress does set its priorities—and we've got a few suggestions for them how to set the priorities—we can cut this deficit in half by 2009. The real issue on spending, though—and this is important, by the way; the current deficit is important, don't get me wrong. But if you're a younger person sitting out there, you need to worry about the long-term deficit caused by baby boomers like me fixing to retire. I don't know if you know this or not, but I turn 62, retirement age, in 2008. That's a convenient year for me to be in retirement. [*Laughter*]

And there's a lot of us getting ready to retire. And when we retire, this baby boom generation retires, we're going to put a big strain on Social Security and Medicare. Interestingly enough, my generation has been promised better benefits than the previous generation. And yet per worker, there's fewer people paying into the system to support me. We got a problem.

You know, it's really hard for me to realize we have a problem and travel around the country and look at younger workers paying payroll taxes into a system that I know is going bankrupt. It's not right for Members of Congress, by the way, to travel around the country and talk—and look at workers paying into a system that's going bankrupt and not tell the truth. We can fix this problem. This is a problem—we don't have to cut benefits of younger workers. We need to slow the rate of benefits down.

Do you realize the benefits grow faster than the rate of inflation? Congress over here—and people say, "Vote for me; I'm going to make sure the benefits grow faster than the rate of inflation." Listen, Social Security was meant to supplement income, retirement income, initially. And so what I'm telling you is, there's a solution to be had. Unfortunately, the atmosphere in Washington appears that there will be no solution because there's too much politics. And my call to members of both parties—and I mean this—is we need to set aside this needless politics in Washington, this zero-sum attitude, and fix mandatory spending so a younger generation of Americans can confidently contribute into a system that's going to—[*applause*].

If we live in a global economy—which we do—with competition, it's—the countries that are able to fix their entitlement programs will be the countries that remain competitive. Congress needs to remember that. When we fix this—and I'm confident we can, and I believe we will—when we reform the program, it will keep the United States of America competitive. Because if we don't, the majority of tax revenues will go to—there will have to be massive tax increases to pay for the promises, or significant cuts throughout our Government.

To keep us competitive, we've got to make sure we keep markets open. I told you—I'm telling you something you already know—61 percent of your revenue is as a result of sales from the United States elsewhere, which says to me—listen, my theory is this: If you're good at something, let's make sure we can sell it all around the world. And so I believe in open markets. As a matter of fact, I know that in order to keep us competitive in the 21st century, that the United States of America should be doing everything we can to open markets and level the playing field.

We've signed a lot of free trade agreements, and at the same time we've done so, we've said to countries, "Listen, treat us the way we treat you." That's all we ask; level the playing field. There is no doubt in my mind, American farmers and entrepreneurs and business people and 3M employees can compete with anybody, anytime, anywhere, so long as the rules are fair.

In my speech, I talked about a health care system that takes care of the elderly and takes care of the poor. We'll do that. But it needs to be a health care system, as well, in which there's transparency in pricing, information technology in the health care field to help reduce costs, a doctor-patient relationship that is the center of the decisionmaking, a plan that encourages preventative medicine. People need to be incented to make right choices with their bodies, in what they eat and how they exercise.

Another aspect of making sure that medicine is affordable and available is—listen, there's too many lawsuits. I said a startling statistic the other night: Do you realize there are 1,500 counties in America without an ob-gyn? Now, think about that. And the reason why is, a lot of good docs are getting run out of practice because of needless lawsuits. It's one thing to make sure that there's justice; it's another thing to have a system that encourages junk lawsuits that are running up your cost of medicine and running good docs out of practice. Congress needs to pass medical liability reform now.

And speaking about legal reform, you talk to people that take risk, one of the things they tell you about is these lawsuits hamper strong investment. If we want to be competitive, we've got to have balance in our legal system. Congress has the chance to send a signal again—we did a pretty good job on class-action lawsuits, but now they got a chance to do something on asbestos. And there's a bill going to be moving out of the Senate. It's time to send a clear message to investors and markets and employees that we've got to have a legal system, in regards to asbestos, that's fair to those who have actually been harmed and reasonable for those who need to pay.

I talked about energy the other day, and Tim mentioned it. I guess I shocked some people, being from Texas, to say we're addicted to oil, but we are, and it's a problem. It's a problem; it's a national security problem and an economic security problem. Touring here and seeing the great benefits of nanotechnology, I'm beginning to get a better sense of how nanotechnology plays into fuel cells, for example, and the capacity for us to have hydrogen automobiles. I know that technology will end up leading away from dependence on oil. I know it's going to happen. I'll tell you why I'm optimistic about it, is because the scientists there in Washington, those in the Energy Department, believe we're darn close to a couple of very important breakthroughs.

Before I get to them, I did talk about the need to use safe nuclear energy to power our plants. I mean, if you're worried about the environment, which I am, it seems like to make sense that we use nuclear power. It's renewable, and it's clean.

We're pretty close to some interesting breakthroughs on solar energy as well. I truly believe that with continued research and development, focusing on interesting technologies, that we'll have coal-fired plants that will be emitting zero emissions. And it's coming. And what I'm telling you is, is that technology is important for your jobs, but it's also important for the quality of life.

Automobiles—if we want to get rid of dependence on oil, we got to do something with automobiles. I mean, that's the place where we use a lot of oil. We got to change how we drive. We got to change how cars are powered. This administration has done some things on CAFE standards, but that recognizes that we're still dependent upon oil to manufacture our fuel. What I'm interested in doing is providing alternative choices for the consumers like ethanol or plug-in hybrid vehicles. We're close to some breakthroughs on battery technologies, that I'm sure some of you know about, to make these hybrid automobiles even better and more cost-effective for the American consumer.

I'm excited about ethanol. Now, we've been making ethanol out of corn, mainly. But now we got a chance, with breakthroughs in research and development, new technologies, to make ethanol out of switchgrass or wood products or weeds. And we're close. And I said the other night in the State of the Union, within 6 years, this kind of fuel ought to be competitive with gasoline.

Now, people say, "That's fine; how about the automobiles?" Well, I had an interesting experience. I went down to Brazil, and I saw President Lula down there. I don't know if you know this, but the vast majority of fuel to fuel the cars in Brazil is made from sugar. And guess who makes the cars that run on sugar? General Motors. So the technology is available for flex-fuel automobiles. As a matter of fact, I am told there's over 4 million flex-fuel automobiles operating in the United States today. And so the hope is and the belief is, is that with a breakthrough with these cellulosic technologies—big word for a history major—[*laughter*]—I don't want to try to spell it—[*laughter*]—the car industry has got the capacity to manufacture automobiles that can burn that stuff.

Now, people say, "Well, if you can get the technology and you got the cars, how come it takes until 2025 to reduce—significantly reduce dependence on the Middle Eastern oil?" Well, the answer is, we got a lot of automobiles, and it takes awhile for the fleet to turn over. Things just don't happen instantly when it comes to an automobile fleet.

And so—but what I'm telling you is, and what I'm telling the American people is, research is going to lead to an important breakthrough here, when it comes to our energy. I'm confident that we'll be able to say to the American people when this research is complete, that the United States is on our way to no dependence on oil from the Middle East.

I want to talk about another important issue, and I've come to 3M to highlight this issue. And the truth of the matter is, in order to stay competitive, we have got to lead the world in research and development, and got to lead the world in having people, scientists and engineers, that are capable of helping this America stay on the cutting edge of technology. And 3M is a perfect place to come.

There's an economic reason why we need to do this. The economic reason why we got to stay on the leading edge of technology is to make sure that people's standard of living here in America goes up—that's what it is. And there's a direct correlation by being the most innovative country in the world and how our citizens live.

Secondly, the second practical application to make sure we've got young scientists and engineers coming up is that if we don't have people that have got the skill set to fill the jobs of the 21st century, because we're in a global world and a competitive world, they're going to go somewhere else. And so I want to talk about an initiative to make sure America remains competitive.

The first element is, is that for the Federal Government to continue its role—oh, by the way, when we went on the tour, so I asked, "How are you doing?" "Fine." "What do you do?" "This." "Where did you get your education?" We met engineers and chemists and physicists. I didn't meet any history majors. [*Laughter*] I met people who are incredibly capable, smart thinkers that are able to take their brainpower and come up with ways to make practical products that change Americans' lives. And so—and the Federal Government has a role in this, and our taxpayers have got to understand, a good use of your taxpayers'

money is to promote research and development—research into the physical sciences.

Again, I'd repeat to you that if we can remain the most competitive nation in the world, it will benefit the worker here in America. People have got to understand, when we talk about spending your taxpayers' money on research and development, there is a correlating benefit, particularly to your children. See, it takes awhile for some of the investments to—that are being made with Government dollars to come to market. I don't know if people realize this, but the Internet began as the Defense Department project to improve military communications. In other words, we were trying to figure out how to better communicate. There was research money spent, and as a result of this sound investment, the Internet came to be.

The Internet has changed us. It's changed the whole world. It's an amazing example of what a commitment to research dollars can mean. The iPod—I'm a bike guy, and I like to plug in music on my iPod when I'm riding along to, hopefully, help me forget how old I am. [*Laughter*] But it was built—when it was launched, it was built on years of Government-funded research and microdrive storage or electrochemistry or single compression—signal compression. See, the nanotechnology research that the Government is helping sponsor is going to change the way people live.

And so what I said to the Congress was, "Let's be wise with taxpayers' money. Let's stay on the leading edge of technology and change, and let's reaffirm our commitment to scientific innovation." I think we ought to double the Federal commitment to the most basic critical research programs in physical sciences over the next decade.

This year alone, we're proposing $6 billion go to the National Science Foundation to fund research in physics and chemistry and material science and nanotechnology. We're proposing $4 billion goes to the Energy Department's Office of Science to build the world's most powerful civilian supercomputer. We're proposing $535 million to the Commerce Department's National Institute of Standards and Technology to research electronics information technologies and advanced computers.

I wouldn't be proposing this if I didn't believe that there will be tangible benefits for the American people. We may not see them tomorrow, but you're children will see them. We're staying on the leading edge of technology for a reason. If America doesn't lead, if we try to kind of forget that we're in a competitive world, generations of Americans won't be able to realize the standard of living that we've been able to realize.

Secondly, I also realize that, by far, the vast majority of research and development is done at the private level by companies—3M, you're spending a lot of money on research and development. So the Government can help, but the truth of the matter is, two-thirds of all research and development spending in America comes from the private sector. And so the fundamental question is, what can the Government do, if anything, to encourage that money to continue to be invested? If it makes sense to develop new technologies and the private sector provides most of the money for that, is there anything we can do to encourage this kind of investment?

And the answer is, yes, there is. There's something called the research and development tax credit. Interestingly enough—obviously, if you think about tax credit, it says if you spend money on research and development, the Tax Code—it treats you generously, more generously than if you didn't. It says, go ahead and do it; there's an advantage for you to make this decision. The problem is, it expired. The research and development tax credit expires in 2005. And so the Congress is saying, "Well, why don't we just temporarily extend it?" You cannot run a business and plan to make long-term investments if the incentive program is only temporary.

Congress needs to understand that nations like China and India and Japan and Korea and Canada all offer tax incentives that are permanent. In other words, we live in a competitive world. We want to be the leader in this world. And therefore, in my judgment, in order—one important part of staying the leader, when it comes to innovation and research and technology, is for the Congress to make the tax credit on research and development permanent.

Third part of the competitiveness agenda is to make sure our kids learn math and science. It's one thing to research, have incentives for money, but if you don't have somebody in that lab, like those chemists I met, we're not going to be that good. And so I got some ideas for the Congress to consider. The first is to emphasize math and science early, and to make sure that the courses are rigorous enough that our children can compete globally.

We made a pretty good start on, by the way, high standards with the No Child Left Behind Act. I was talking to—it about the Governor. He said, "People get a little nervous when Government says, 'Measure.' " And he didn't say that; he's reflecting the opinion of others. As the Governor of Texas, I remember that attitude too. But here's my attitude: If you spend money, doesn't it make sense to determine whether or not the results are halfway decent? As a taxpayer, it seems like that's something you'd want to know. It's certainly—it's part of, I'm sure, how 3M succeeds and continues to compete. You set high standards, and then you measure.

Well, I think schools ought to do the same thing. I don't think we ought to tell you how to design your test. I don't think we ought to dictate curriculum, but I do know, in return for Federal money, it makes sense to say, "Can the child read, write, add, and subtract when he or she is supposed to?" And so we're measuring in return for Federal money. That's the whole thing behind No Child Left Behind.

When I was the Governor of Texas, schools that didn't measure thought they were doing pretty well until—that's a natural assumption for a parent, right? "I'm happy. They're paying attention to me." And things are going fine, and then the child gets out there and has to take remedial reading courses in college. And so you've got to measure. I remember the debate in Texas. They said, "It's racist to measure." I said, "Uh-uh, it's racist not to measure." Think about a system that just shuffles kids through.

So we're making good progress at the early grades, particularly in reading and math. Matter of fact, America is competitive in math in the early grades. How do we know? Because we test. We test. And by the way, we make the test results known locally, and we compare tests State to State, so people can figure out—old Pawlenty can figure out how he's doing against other States. [*Laughter*] It's a nice tool if you're a reformist, by the way. See, if you believe in reform, it gives you leverage on a system that tends to be status quo-oriented.

The other thing that we did in No Child Left Behind, which makes a lot of sense, is there's supplemental service money. That means extra money so that when we find a child lagging behind in reading, that family got extra money for extra tutoring. In other words, we said, let's diagnose the problem and solve it early, before it's too late.

Accountability does a further thing that is important. It kind of helps resolve curriculum disputes. You might remember the old debates—at least I certainly remember them—over which kind—how do you teach reading. And there was this kind of theory and that kind of theory. Well, when you measure, it kind of makes it pretty clear which works and what doesn't work. We need to have the same emphasis in math that we have in reading, and the reason why is, is that because when you test early, we do fine in math, and yet when our kids start heading into junior high and high

school, it's clear they can't compete in the world. And now is the time to do something about it.

Well, so what do you do? What do you do? Well, the first thing, you've got to make sure your teachers have the skills necessary to be able to teach math and science. And I think the most practical way to do that is to teach teachers how to teach Advanced Placement. If you believe in high standards and if you want your kids to compete, a proven system is the AP programs. And they work. And therefore, we're going to ask Congress to appropriate money so that we can have a full-scale effort to train 70,000 teachers in how to teach AP.

Another way to make sure that we have high standards in math and science is to take the same approach we took in reading, and that is intervention early, but apply that to math in the sixth, seventh, and eighth grade. In other words, have supplemental service money, extra money, tutorial money, money that could be used at the public school or private school or tutoring service to say, when we find a child that's lagging behind in math in the junior high schools, let's intervene. Let's not let them slip. Let's make sure that same high standard we've achieved in the fourth grade applies throughout the junior high level. So you got intervention in junior high, teachers able to send that—spend that—get that curriculum right in high school.

The third thing we need to do is what you do here at 3M. And I want to applaud those scientists who are here who have gone in the classroom and said, "This is a good deal. You're not going to believe how exciting it is to be a physicist or a mathematician or a chemist. Let me tell you the practical applications of what it means to be a scientist and tell you what a—how cool a job it is, how exciting it is." See, these kids need somebody to walk in to their classrooms and say, "Follow me; follow my example." And so we've got a plan to help 30,000 adjunct professors— that would be you—to be able to go into the schools all across America and set a good example to excite kids about the potential.

One of the other things we're going to do that makes sense is to have a—what we call a national math panel. Again, we made great progress in reading, and one of the reasons why is that we've—there's a science to reading. I mean, it's not guesswork anymore. We've got a lot of really smart people, particularly out of NIH, that helped develop curriculum go-bys. We're not telling you what to use, but we are saying, "If you're interested in teaching every child to read, here are some things that are necessary to make it work." We want to do the same thing with the math curriculum so that every school district, if they so choose, has got a resource base in which to figure out what works.

Sometimes you have a good teacher sitting there, but they really don't understand what works when it teaches a child—how to teach a child math. And we believe we can figure it out. I believe we have figured it out, and now we'll make that available to school districts all around the country through the Governors and the States.

And so the initiative I just described is, America will remain competitive by being wise about how we encourage research and development but, most importantly, by making sure our kids have the skill sets for the jobs of the 21st century.

Now, in the meantime, there's another issue that I want to discuss right quick—two other quick issues, then you'll be liberated. [*Laughter*] One of them is, there are more high-tech jobs in America today than people available to fill them. And if that's—so what do we do about that? And I said—the reason it's important, and the American citizen has got to understand it's important, is if we don't do something about how to fill those high-tech jobs here, they'll go somewhere else where somebody can do the job. In other words, there are some who say, "We can't worry about competition. It doesn't matter; it's here. Don't

worry about it; do something about it. It's a real aspect of the world in which we live."

And so one way to deal with this problem, and probably the most effective way, is to recognize that there's a lot of bright engineers and chemists and physicists from other lands that are either educated here or received an education elsewhere but want to work here. And they come here under a program called H1B visas. And the problem is, is that Congress has limited the number of H1B visas that can come and apply for a job—a H1B visa holder can apply for a job at 3M. And I think it's a mistake not to encourage more really bright folks who can fill the jobs that are having trouble being filled here in America—to limit their number. And so I call upon Congress to be realistic and reasonable and raise that cap.

We'll educate our kids. That's the goal. Of course, we want every job that's ever generated in America filled by Americans, but that's not the reality today. In order for 3M to remain competitive, in order for this job base to remain strong, in order for us to be a leader in innovation, we got to be wise about letting kids come here who've got the skill sets needed to fill the jobs that help us remain the leader in the world.

And so what I'm telling you is, is that I'm an optimistic guy about America's future because I believe in our system, and I believe in the people. The government's role is to make sure that we're a flexible economy. Its role is to make sure that we apply our resources properly to make sure we're an innovative economy. And certainly, a very vital role at all levels of government is to make sure our children have the skill sets necessary to fill the jobs that will inevitably come in this changing world.

My belief is that we should not fear the future; we should shape it. America has a vital role to play as a leader. And the policies I just outlined will help us remain the leader that I think most Americans want us to be.

I appreciate 3M's leadership. I appreciate you employing so many people. I appreciate you making this a good place for people to come to work. I could tell it just in the pride of the voices of the researchers I met. Thanks for making this an environment where innovation succeeds and people are able to realize their full human capacity.

God bless you all, and may God continue to bless our country.

NOTE: The President spoke at 11:50 a.m. at 3M Corporate Headquarters. In his remarks, he referred to Gov. Timothy J. Pawlenty of Minnesota, and his wife, Mary; Lt. Gov. Carol Molnau of Minnesota; George W. Buckley, chairman, president, and chief executive officer, 3M; and President Luiz Inacio Lula da Silva of Brazil. The Office of the Press Secretary also released a Spanish language transcript of these remarks.

Statement on Negotiation of a Free Trade Agreement With South Korea
February 2, 2006

The United States and the Republic of Korea have a strong alliance and are bound together by common values and a deep desire to expand freedom, peace, and prosperity throughout Asia and the world. Today we seek to deepen the ties between our nations by negotiating a comprehensive U.S.-Republic of Korea Free Trade Agreement.

A free trade agreement with the Republic of Korea will provide important economic, political, and strategic benefits to both countries and build on America's engagement in Asia. The Republic of Korea is our seventh largest trading partner and seventh largest export market, and this free trade agreement advances our commitment to opening markets and expanding opportunities for America's farmers, ranchers, workers, and businesses.

Remarks in a Discussion on American Competitiveness in Rio Rancho, New Mexico
February 3, 2006

The President. Thank you all. Thanks for the warm welcome. Thanks for the Mexican food last night, Pete. [*Laughter*] I hope you picked up the tab. [*Laughter*] Laura and I are thrilled to be here. This is going to be an interesting discussion. What you're watching—what you'll watch is a way to talk about how to put good policy in place, not only through my voice but through the voices of many who are living exactly the

strategy that we want to implement for the rest of the country.

So I first want to welcome my wife, Laura. We don't get to travel that much——

The First Lady. Together.

The President. Together. We both were raised in west Texas and occasionally slipped across the border there to go to New Mexico. And every time we did, we were better for it. [*Laughter*] It's a great State.

Do you want to have a few words?

The First Lady. Well, I'm going to just speak and, as they say in the political business, step off the message a little bit. George is going to be talking today about what we can do to make sure our children are educated and our economy is competitive. But I also just want to remind everyone that earlier this week, he signed a proclamation to make February American Heart Month. And a lot of people are wearing their red tie or their red dress. I'm wearing my Red Dress pin today to remind the American people that heart disease is the number-one killer; it's the number-one killer among women in the United States.

A lot of women don't know that, and if they start to suffer the signs of a heart attack or the symptoms of a heart attack, they wait. They don't go to the emergency room like they might rush their husbands to the emergency room, but they don't go themselves as fast.

So I want to encourage Americans to remember that heart disease is the number-one killer, to talk to people about all the ways we can prevent heart disease through exercise, healthy eating, not smoking, seeing your doctor on a regular basis so you can find out if you have any early signs of heart disease.

The other thing that fits into the message that George is going to talk about is, we know that if our children have the chance to study more math and science, we'll have even more doctors, we can produce even more doctors, and many, many more medical breakthroughs.

So, remember that February is National Heart Month and take good care of your heart.

The President. Before we get started, I do want to recognize some folks. Obviously, Senator Domenici is here. I know you are very proud of his service in the United States Senate. What a good man he is. And

with him is Senator Bingaman, who is also doing a fine job.

What happened the other day was, I got a phone call from Domenici, and generally when someone of that—with that much power calls you, you say, "Yes, sir, Mr. Senator." [*Laughter*] And he said, "I want to come by, and I want to bring Jeff Bingaman with me and Senator Alexander." And I said, "Fine, come on over." And they come over the Oval Office and sit down and say, "Look, at your State of the Union, we want you to seriously consider announcing an agenda that we think is important to make this country competitive." And I said, "I'll consider it." One of the things you want to do when you're the President is kind of keep your cards close to your vest. [*Laughter*] I said, "I'll give that serious consideration, Senator."

But I knew prior to him coming in that he had looked at the same report I had seen, which is called the Augustine report. Craig Barrett, who I'm going to talk about here in a second, was on that committee. Chuck Vest—I don't know if Chuck is with us or not. We had dinner with Chuck last night, as well as Augustine—Norm Augustine, himself. But they're a group of distinguished citizens and scholars and businesspeople who started looking out beyond the immediate and asking the question, what does America need to do to remain the preeminent economy in the world so our people can have a good life? And they made some suggestions. And Jeff and Pete looked at it, fine-tuned it, brought me some ideas. And at the State of the Union, I talked about how to keep this country strong.

And want to give credit to the Senators. I also want to give credit to the Senators after they get the deal done too, see. [*Laughter*] And so I want to thank both Senators for being here.

I also want to thank the Congressman from this district, Tom Udall. Thank you, Mr. Congressman, for joining us. Proud you're here. Two other Congresspeople—

Heather Wilson—thank you for coming, Heather; appreciate you and Steve Pearce from eastern New Mexico. Is it Hobbs? Yes, Hobbs, that's right. [*Laughter*] Flying Eagles—that's the name of the basketball team.

I do want to thank the mayor, Jim Owen. Mr. Mayor, thank you for being here. I appreciate you coming. You're kind to take time out of your day.

Before I talk about the Intel family, I do want to recognize the vice president of the Navajo Nation, and his wife, Virginia—and that would be Frank Dayish. Frank is here. Good to see you again, Frank. The reason I want to bring up Frank and Virginia is that their daughter, Staff Sergeant Felissa Dayish, is with us. She has been to Iraq twice. Thank you for serving. God bless. I remember the pride that Frank had when he described his daughter's service to me. And I know you're doubly proud, Frank. Thanks for being here; proud you're here.

And finally, the Governor of the great State of New Mexico has joined us, Governor Bill Richardson. Governor, thank you for being here. Good to see you. I appreciate you coming. I know you're proud of the Intel facility and the Intel family, as you should be.

One of the things we're going to talk about is the importance of research and development and technology. And the people here in this part of the world understand that when you have a research and development facility that promotes modern technology, it improves the quality of the life of the community in which the facility exists. And that has been, really, Craig Barrett's credo as the CEO of this company. He wants to provide a product that people want to buy, obviously; otherwise, you're not going to be in business. [*Laughter*]

But he also understands there's something called corporate responsibility. It's in his interest that there be corporate responsibility in Intel. In other words, Intel can only be strong if it has a workforce that's capable of making sure this company is competitive in a global economy. And so I really want to say thanks to Craig and all the employees here for doing the following things—besides making a good product and providing jobs—to provide people from this company to teach in local schools.

And if corporate CEO is paying attention to this little seminar, I strongly urge you to follow the Intel example of making employees available to make sure math and science becomes an important part of the curriculum of the local schools. They provide internships for young students here to encourage them to become involved with math and science. They help train teachers. And we're going to talk a little bit about teacher training. And then they provide scholarships.

And so for those of you who work here, thanks for being such—so generous with your knowledge and your talent. And Craig, thanks for having us. It's not easy to host the President here. It kind of disrupts—[*laughter*]—disrupt—yes, I know. [*Laughter*]

A couple of points I want to make—and the reason why this subject is relevant, first, we've got a strong economy. Today you're going to see that in January, we added 193,000 new jobs, 81,000 new jobs—extra jobs were added as a result of upgrading the November and December numbers. And we got steady growth. And that's important. We want our people working. We want people to be able to realize opportunity and hope. And in order to do that, you got to have a growing economy, obviously.

And we've overcome a lot. I really ascribe that to, mainly, the entrepreneurial spirit of America is strong; the small-business sector is strong. I do happen to think good tax policy helped. I think keeping taxes low is an important way to make sure this economy continues to grow.

But what's interesting about the numbers is that beneath that, there's a certain amount of uncertainty amongst some in America; that, you know, we've got a lot of competition, and people begin to see an emerging China and India, and that makes people uncertain. It creates certain anxiety when they hear the stories about India and China beginning to grow robustly, or jobs going to India and China, or India and China consuming a lot of natural resources.

Secondly, there's a lot of turnover in the job market. People are changing jobs, and that creates uncertainty. And during times of uncertainty, we're—we get faced with certain choices. And there's a tendency throughout our history, our economic history and foreign policy history, to withdraw. Times of uncertainty sometimes encourage folks to say, "Well, why do we need to compete? Why don't we just come within ourselves? Why don't we protect ourselves off from the world? Why do we need to be trying to spread freedom when the world is a dangerous place? Why don't we just come home?"

And I strongly reject that notion, and I want to explain to you why. First of all, with an enemy that lurks, if we were to withdraw, it would only embolden the enemy and make this country less secure. If we were to withdraw from the world, it would be a missed opportunity to lay the foundation of peace for generations to come by spreading liberty and freedom. See, part of my foreign policy is this: I believe that there is an Almighty, and I believe that the Almighty's gift to everybody on the face of the Earth, regardless of where they live, regardless of their religion, is freedom. And I believe deep in everybody's soul is the deep desire to live in freedom. And I believe that this country, if it were to retreat, would miss an opportunity to help others realize their dream. And I also know that history has proven that free societies yield the peace that we all want.

Secondly, when it comes to competition, the world is going to be competitive whether we're in the mix or not. For example, this competitive world is going to demand a job skill set that is—that emphasizes math and science, which we'll talk about here in a second. And if our kids don't have the talents necessary to compete, those jobs won't go away; they'll just go to another country.

I mean, we're in a global competition. Here's my attitude: With the right policy, we can compete with anybody, anytime, anywhere. This has been the history of America, and it's going to be the future of America. We should not fear the future because we intend to shape it.

The American—this American economy leads the world, and we're going to continue to lead it. And here's how: good fiscal policy out of Washington, DC, making sure that this economy is flexible. In other words, when you say that, that means there's not a lot of rules and regulations that prohibit capital moving freely and people making investment.

We've got to have an energy policy that gets us off this dependence on Middle Eastern oil. I spent a lot of time on that before; I'm going to spend a little more time on it next week. But I'm going to tell you something: With research and development and technology, we can change the fuels we put in our cars, and we can become less dependent on unstable sources of energy overseas. And if we intend to be the leader of the world, we've got to do that. It's a goal that can be achieved, and it's a goal that's necessary.

I've talked about health care—and will continue—in the past. I want to talk about trade real quick, and then we're going to talk about the education initiative. Our panelists are beginning to wonder what, you know—[*laughter*]. It's called a filibuster. [*Laughter*] First, let us talk about trade. The first sign that the country is becoming protectionist is when we refuse to ratify trade agreements. That's a sign. It's an indication that the elected officials are beginning to get worried about the capacity of this country to compete. It's hard to get trade agreements through Congress, and I'm worried that that is an indication that we're losing our confidence.

But if you're working at Intel, you better be for open trade, because 80 percent of the products this company makes are sold overseas. Yesterday we were at 3M in Minnesota. It's a great United States company, very much like Intel. Sixty percent of the products they manufacture are overseas—or get sold overseas. We're 5 percent of the world's population, which means the rest of the 95 percent could be, and should be, customers to United States products, either grown or manufactured.

Now, the role of the government, it seems like to me, is to not only open up markets for our products but, at the same time, say to our competitors and/or other markets, "Treat us the way we treat you." That's all we ask. In other words, level the playing field. It is very important if this country is to remain competitive that we do not lose our nerve, that we open up markets for our products, that we level the playing field—because nobody can outcompete us when the rules are fair.

Now, let me talk about education. That's kind of the—that's part of the cornerstone of making us competitive, shaping our destiny, refusing to lose our great desire to continue to lead. But perhaps the most important thing of all is to make sure that we lead the world in innovation and technological development and make sure we have a workforce that has the skill sets necessary to do so. And that's really the heart of the American Competitive Initiative. And that's why we're here at Intel.

Again, I want to repeat to you: All the people who understand the connection between technology and jobs ought to be the people in this part of the world. I remember when this plant didn't exist—and neither did much of the neighborhood around

it. I mean, one of the most exciting things that's happened to the Albuquerque area is the arrival of Intel, not only because it's provided good jobs, but the spinoff of those jobs, the small businesses that have occurred as a result of—when this amazing center of brilliance came here.

I want to talk about three things, and then we'll start visiting. Here's some things, practical things the Government can do. First of all, the Government can't do everything. The Government is a partner. For those of you who think the Government can solve all problems, this is not the way it works. Most problems are solved locally. First—one thing the Government can do is to spend money on research. In other words, we can be a partner with enterprise.

Do you realize that the Internet came to be as a result of Federal Government research into basic sciences? In other words, research yields practical applications that improve people's live, is what I'm trying to say. And so I proposed to Congress that we double basic research programs in physical sciences over the next 10 years.

They tell me that by doing so, we'll be the leader in nanotechnology research. I'm just beginning to understand what that means. [*Laughter*] But the smart people tell you, if you're the leader in nanotechnology research, you'll be the leader in quality jobs and quality of life.

The second thing that the Congress needs to do is to encourage private investment in research and development. As a matter of fact, this makes sense. Most of the research done in the United States is done through the private sector. About two-thirds of it is done through private sector research; 15,000 companies take advantage of what's called the research and development tax credit. It's part of our Tax Code. It says, if you spend money on research, you'll be rewarded through the Tax Code.

Seems to make sense, if we're trying to encourage people to spend private sector dollars. The problem is, is that the research and development tax credit is only a temporary measure. And so you're a CEO of a major company like Intel or a CEO of a small company that's thinking about spending research dollars, and you're uncertain as to whether or not that research and development tax credit will be available.

People don't plan big amounts of money to invest on a short-term basis. It's important to provide stability in the Tax Code so that the planners and thinkers and investors have confidence that if they make an investment 5 years from now, the reason they made the investment in the first place—besides trying to improve product lines—the reason they made the tax—the reason they made the investment because of tax incentive will still exist. And so Congress needs to make the research and development tax credit a permanent part of our Tax Code to encourage more private sector research to keep America on the leading edge of innovation.

Finally—you'll be happy to hear—[*laughter*]—how do we make sure the folks who are going to be running this economy, our workers and entrepreneurs, have the skill set necessary to do so? How do we encourage people to stay focused on math and science? And that's really an important subject. I—here's what the Government can and should do.

First of all, we passed the No Child Left Behind Act. It's a great piece of legislation. It basically says, let's raise standards and measure. I can remember people said, "Why would you want the Government to cause people to measure?" I said, "Because we're spending a lot of money." If you're running a business and you're spending money, you want to measure. You want to look at results. People in America want to know, you see? And if a child can't read at the third grade, we want to know why. And we also want to be able to analyze curriculum to determine if that's one of the reasons why. And equally importantly,

by diagnosing, you're able to say, this child deserves extra help.

I strongly believe all government is locally controlled. However, I believe that it's the responsibility of government that spends money to say to those who designed the curriculum, "Please, show us whether or not you're achieving results; and if not, correct what you're doing, and solve problems early, before they're too late." We need to send that same spirit into—that we've got in reading in the No Child Left Behind Act into math.

Now, the positive news is that we're doing fine, relative to the rest of the world, in math in the early grades. And you know why we know? We measure. I can remember when I was Governor of Texas and we didn't measure, people would say, "Gosh, my schools are doing great"—until the kids graduated from school, and they couldn't read very well and then had to be re-educated at college. Measuring lets you know. Measuring lets you compare. And measuring lets us know how we're doing with the rest of the world. If we're in a competitive world, we want to make sure our students can compete.

And we're doing fine in the fourth grade. We're doing lousy in junior high. Something happens between elementary school, where our teachers are able to get the kids interested in math and they test well, to junior high. And that's where we ought to emphasize focus. In the early—in the initiative—in the reading initiative in No Child Left Behind, we say that if you're not up to grade level, there's extra money for you. It's called supplemental services. There's extra money to correct problems early, before they're too late.

We're now going to ask Congress to apply that same supplemental service to junior high kids in math. If the kids aren't testing well in math in junior high, in other words, if they're part of the falloff, let's intervene. Let's make sure there's tutorials available, after-school mathematics available, for these children so that they can remain competitive.

And they'll go to high school. So how can we help in high school? Well, one thing that we've learned is that our teachers have got to have the skill set necessary to teach the skills in math and science. And one effective program—and Laura and I are fixing to go to Dallas after this to herald this program—is an Advanced Placement program. And the Federal Government can be a partner in helping teachers train to be AP teachers. Advanced Placement works. Advanced Placement raises standards. Advanced Placement gives teachers the tools to teach kids to take this Advanced Placement test, which is a measurement. It's a go-by to determine how competitive our workforce can be in the 21st century.

And finally, we want to get 30,000 adjunct professors into classrooms. That's a fancy word for saying, we want engineers and chemists and physicists in places like Intel, or retired professionals, to go in the classroom and excite students about the possibility of math and science. That's what we need. We need role models. We need people walking into a classroom full of youngsters and say, "You're not going to believe how cool this profession is. You're not going to believe the horizons that will be available to you." And one of the things Craig has encouraged Intel to do is do just that.

And so here's an initiative that makes sense. Here's a chance for Republicans and Democrats to put aside all the foolishness that's going on in Washington and come together and get something done for the future of this country.

And I want to thank you all for giving me a chance to lay out the strategy. And now I want to turn this over to Craig Barrett. He's the CEO of this company. He himself—he probably won't tell you this, but I will—is an engineer, highly qualified engineer. I asked him last night where he

spent most of his youth. He said, "On the Stanford campus." And here he is now the CEO of one of the great companies. He was able to take his degree—for those of you who are interested in whether or not a degree makes sense—he took his engineering degree, and now he runs one of the world's preeminent companies. And he's sitting right here.

[At this point, Craig R. Barrett, chairman of the board, Intel Corp., made brief remarks.]

The President. I appreciate that. One of the good things about being the President is you tend to draw cameras. *[Laughter]* Good or bad, depending on your perspective. I hope people listening hear what Craig has just said, those particularly in CEO America, corporate America, that there is such a thing as corporate responsibility. He said, "I take this responsibility serious." It's in your interest, by the way, to help train a teacher. It's in your interest to provide a scholarship. It's in your interest to help a young group of Americans learn math and science because, after all, if you intend to stay in business, you better have a workforce that's capable.

And so thanks for setting such a good example. Thanks for joining us.

We're also joined today by Tom Hunter. He's the president of Sandia. The last time I was with him, we were standing out kind of in a desert area, and he fired up one of these new solar research beams. *[Laughter]* All I can tell you is I was glad I wasn't at the other end of the beam. *[Laughter]* But they're doing some good stuff when it comes to research and development here at Sandia.

Welcome. Thanks for being here. What's on your mind?

[Thomas Hunter, president, Sandia Corp., made brief remarks.]

The President. Tom, let me ask you something. I think it's very important for people listening to understand when you say nanotechnology, that it's got an application to their life. In other words, when the Federal Government says, "We're going to spend money on research," that the taxpayers got to understand that there's something—their life is going to improve. And the question is, how?

The other day, I was talking about how research is—I mean, how technology has changed our society, and I ended with the example: I remember driving across Texas playing the license plate game, and now they're driving across Texas listening—watching a DVD. And it all happened in 20 years.

But when you talk about supercomputing will have an application that could help somebody, or nanotechnology, share an example with people.

[*Mr. Hunter made further remarks.*]

The President. Yesterday we saw nanotechnology being applied to a fuel membrane that will go into a hydrogen-powered automobile at some point in time, which means we'll be using hydrogen as opposed to extract from oil, the byproduct of which will be water. And it's coming. And technology and research will help us achieve that. We want to be the ones with the hydrogen breakthrough. It means there will be jobs here for Americans that will improve your quality of life as well.

Okay, thanks. Good job.

Matt, welcome. Tell everybody what you do.

[*Matthias W. Pleil, faculty member, Albuquerque Technical Vocational Institute (TVI), made brief remarks.*]

The President. Wait, let me stop you a minute. NSF is the National Science Foundation. Don't speak in initials, because we're—[*laughter*].

Mr. Pleil. I'm originally from industry, and everything was an acronym. [*Laughter*]

The President. That's right. Imagine what it would be like if you were originally from government.

Mr. Pleil. They have longer acronyms. [*Laughter*]

The President. National Science Foundation. And you're doing what?

Mr. Pleil. I'm working creating educational materials for college students and also for college and high school teachers so that we can teach the future technologists about microsystems, which a lot of people don't know much about.

The President. Right. And microsystems are what?

Mr. Pleil. Well, microsystems are here and now, and they include the circuitry that Intel produces, but also micromachines, as well. And we're collaborating with Sandia National Labs. They're on the cutting edge of making surface micromachines, it's called. And I've been fortunate enough to work there part-time, learn from Sandia, and help them create educational materials that they use in their University Alliance program.

And we've also been able to train teachers at several workshops. So we're creating a group of folks now that are understanding microsystems and, hopefully, energizing the kids in school.

The President. And is there an interest—I mean, I presume with Intel being here, it serves as a magnet for kids to say, "Gosh, that's a good place to work. I need the skill set necessary, and TVI provides that skill set."

Mr. Pleil. Absolutely, Intel supported TVI over the years to create our semiconductor manufacturing technology program. We have a teaching clean room that was sponsored primarily by Intel, and many of our students go and work for Intel. In fact, one of my students is actually working in the lab, probably today.

The President. We hope so. [*Laughter*]

Mr. Pleil. He'd better be.

The President. It's interesting, isn't it—I want to kind of take off on what Matt was talking about. One of the really great assets we have in America is the community college or technical school system. And the reason why is, is that these schools tend to be market-driven. And by that I mean the curriculum adjusts to the needs of the local folks. And what he just said was, is that here's a job provider, here's an education institute; they collaborated to design a curriculum that actually means something to the graduate.

I'm not saying my history degree didn't mean anything. [*Laughter*] It did; it meant a lot. But nevertheless, if you're interested in work and you're getting out of school and you want to be trained in a job which actually exists, this collaboration is a vital part. And I urge communities all across the country to utilize their community college or their technical vocational schools to work with the local industry to design curriculum that matters.

And so one of the ways to make sure that we're competitive in the 21st century is to adequately utilize our community college system and make sure that they are incented to constantly adjust by working with the job providers.

And so thanks for bringing that up. It's an interesting idea, and I bet a lot of people in Albuquerque didn't even know this is going on. And for people who are looking to find work, you ought to look at the TVI as an opportunity. And the other thing people ought to do—you may be 35 years old or so; there's money to help you upgrade your job skills. And what education does, it enables you to become a more productive worker. And as your ability to be a more productive worker increases, so do your wages. Education adds—it makes it more likely you're going to have a higher wage. And that's what Matt is doing—I think that's what you just said. [*Laughter*]

Mr. Pleil. Yes, absolutely. Thank you.

The President. Good job. Now, we've got an interesting person here, Nicole Lopez. Nicole, welcome. Tell people your story, if you don't mind.

[*Nicole Lopez, senior, Rio Rancho High School, made brief remarks.*]

The President. You have learned to communicate. [*Laughter*] That was fantastic. So what are your dreams?

Ms. Lopez. I plan on going to the University of New Mexico and majoring in civil engineering.

The President. Fantastic. This isn't exactly on the subject, but it is kind of—Laura is involved, leading what's called Helping America's Youth. The whole spirit of the program is a mentor can make a difference in a person's life; that we can change America one heart at a time. A person can, by just taking time out of his or her life and surrounding somebody with love and compassion, can make a significant contribution to the country.

And so you just described the whole spirit of Helping America's Youth. You also just described the true strength of the country. Our country's strength is not our military or the size of our wallet; it's the fact that there are millions of people that have got great heart who want to improve somebody else's life, love a neighbor like they'd like to be loved themselves.

Nicole, so you're interested in sciences, obviously.

Ms. Lopez. Yes, I have found that math and science have become my niche. And it's my passion, and I want to continue it.

The President. Awesome. You know, a lot of people probably think math and science isn't meant for me—it kind of seems a little hard, algebra. I can understand that, frankly, but—[*laughter*]. I'm looking for a mentor, by the way. [*Laughter*] Both in math and English. [*Laughter*] But I hope people listening hear Nicole's story that, you know, take a look at math and science. I'm sure there's some—kind of the "nerd patrol." [*Laughter*] It's not; it's the future. That's what Nicole just said; she said the future is engineering and physics and chemistry and math.

Chris Baca—really good job, by the way. Thanks for coming. Appreciate it.

Chris Baca is with us. Chris, why don't you give everybody your job description.

[*Chris Baca, president and chief executive officer, Youth Development, Inc., made brief remarks.*]

The President. Clubhouses, go ahead and explain what that is.

Mr. Baca Clubhouses are—Intel has provided both mentors and equipment and actually a design for a clubhouse that involves using state of the art technology.

The President. You mean there's a physical plant that people go to where there's the latest technology?

Mr. Baca. Exactly it. And that's located right in a neighborhood where you won't— you wouldn't expect it to be.

The President. And you run the clubhouse?

Mr. Baca. Yes, sir. My program runs the clubhouse.

The President. I mean, the program. Good.

Mr. Baca. And so the kids can walk from—after school, we get these little kids dropping in. They don't even go home. They stop by. We help them do their homework, and then they can play.

[*Mr. Baca made further remarks.*]

The President. Great. Thanks, Chris. Chris just laid out the strategy, which is government, corporate, community involvement, all aiming at making sure that we save the lives of our children, and not only saves their lives but give them the skills necessary to be productive leaders into the 21st century.

You're right; old guys like us, we'd better be—count on the next generation to—[*laughter*]—now we got to make sure they got the skills. Finally, we want to make sure that we're in entrepreneurial heaven, and by that I mean that if you've got the instinct and the drive to start your own business, that you'll be comfortable in doing so. Government can't guarantee your product is successful. We can guarantee

you good legal policy, good tax policy, good regulator policy, and then go for it.

And one of the things that I notice about our country when I travel the world is we really are entrepreneurial heaven. We got people from all walks of life saying, "I want to realize my dream." One of them is Justin Sanchez.

Welcome, Justin. Let her rip.

[*Justin Sanchez, director of Semiconductor Operations, Advent Solar, Inc., made brief remarks.*]

The President. I think it's going to happen. I think what you're talking about is that one of these days our homes are going to be little sources of power, and to the extent that we have excess power, we'll feed it back into the grid.

Mr. Sanchez. That's right; that's absolutely correct.

The President. How far away are we from that, in terms of your thinking?

Mr. Sanchez. You know, solar is a technology that the time has come, and I think with some of the more recent innovations and some of the things that we're doing now, in the next 5 to 10 years, you could see that happen.

The President. One reason why it makes sense for the taxpayers to have research and development into solar energy, which we're doing through the Energy Department in collaboration with Sandia Labs, is because he's just describing a product that's going to come as a result of the research money spent. And that is, it's conceivable that you'll have a little unit on top of your house that will power your own house, and that to the extent that you don't use the power generated from the unit, you actually sell it back to the grid, so you become a mini powerplant.

Mr. Sanchez. Absolutely. A million mini powerplants.

The President. And what's the average age of your team, would you say?

Mr. Sanchez. Average age of the team? Well, that's a good question. Probably about thirty.

The President. Management team. Thirty?

Mr. Sanchez. Forty.

The President. Forty? Old guys.

Mr. Sanchez. Of the management team, or the team?

The President. Management team.

Mr. Sanchez. Management team, it's probably closer to 50.

The President. Really?

Mr. Sanchez. Yes.

The President. So you're bringing down the average.

Mr. Sanchez. Bringing down the average. [*Laughter*]

The President. We want Justin Sanchezes of the country to dream big dreams and to think big. Look at the product they're thinking about. I mean, this is a big idea. And there's people willing to risk capital on the idea, and you're willing to risk time in it.

Mr. Sanchez. Absolutely.

The President. And it's going to happen, isn't it?

Mr. Sanchez. It will happen.

The President. Yes, and America will be better off for it. This is a good way to end, for our people to understand there's a direct connection between research and development, technology, and quality of life. This country has a chance—in other words, it needs to make a choice: Are we going to lead, or are we going to fear the future? I hope after this discussion, people sitting around here and listening ought to realize we ought not to fear the future but shape the future and continue to be the leader. And by leading, our people will realize a more peaceful world and a more prosperous world and a chance to realize dreams. And that's what America has been all about in the past and it should be about in the future.

Listen, thank you all for the panel. It's been a great discussion. God bless.

NOTE: The President spoke at 9:10 a.m. at Intel New Mexico. In his remarks, he referred to Charles M. Vest, president, Massachusetts Institute of Technology; Norman R. Augustine, chair, National Academies' Committee on Prospering in the Global Economy of the 21st Century; and Mayor Jim Owen of Rio Rancho, NM.

Remarks Following a Visit to the School of Science and Engineering in Dallas, Texas
February 3, 2006

Let me say a few things, and then we want to get our picture with you, if that's all right. First of all, it's such an honor to be here at this school. Thank you all for coming. Every good school requires a couple of things: one, a good principal—thank you for doing that—and great teachers and good support. Mr. Superintendent, thanks for being here.

Laura and I are here because we believe it's important to spread AP classes all around the country. This is a unique place.

The students here are really impressive people. They have decided to focus on the sciences and math and engineering. And this school helps lift their sights; and one way it does so is to encourage them to take AP.

We want more AP students because we want more engineers and scientists that are able to compete with other students around the world. And so one thing the Government can do is help train 70,000 teachers all around the country so that they can teach students Advanced Placement.

We also want to encourage scientists and chemists and physicists to come into the classrooms all around the country to excite students about the possibilities of science and engineering. And the reason why is, in order for America to be a competitive nation in the years to come, we have got to have a workforce that is strong in engineering and science and physics. You know, some would hope that the competition around the world will go away; it's not going to. And so we have a choice to make: Do we want to retreat, become protectionist, or do we want to seize the moment and shape our future?

And so the American Competitiveness Initiative I've outlined says that America will continue to lead. We'll shape our fu-

ture, and we'll make sure our kids are well-versed in science and math and engineering.

Again, I want to thank you all for letting us come to your school. It's a fantastic school. It really does brighten my hopes about the future of the country to see you all and see your enthusiasm for the subjects and to listen to your very articulate explanations of the different courses you're studying. Thanks a lot. Appreciate it.

NOTE: The President spoke at 2:13 p.m. at Yvonne A. Ewell Townview Magnet Center. In his remarks, he referred to Richard White, principal, the School of Science and Engineering; and Michael Hinojosa, general superintendent, Dallas Independent School District.

The President's Radio Address
February 4, 2006

Good morning. This week in the State of the Union Address, I set forth my American Competitiveness Initiative. This plan will help our Nation to compete with confidence, raise the standard of living for our families, and generate new jobs for our citizens.

Generations of risk takers, inventors, and visionaries have made America the world's most prosperous and innovative nation. Just 25 years ago, most Americans used typewriters instead of computers, rotary phones instead of cell phones, and bank tellers instead of ATMs. Today, America is at the doorstep of even more technological advances. But we cannot afford to be complacent. We're seeing the rise of new competitors like China and India, who are making great strides in technology. In response, some people want to wall off our economy from the world. That is called protectionism. The American people should not

fear our economic future because we intend to shape our economic future.

To keep America the world's most competitive and innovative nation, we must continue to lead the world in human talent and creativity. My American Competitiveness Initiative will encourage innovation throughout our economy and give American children a firm grounding in math and science.

This initiative has three key elements. The first element is to double the Federal commitment to the most critical basic research programs in the physical sciences over the next decade. Most of the technological advances we enjoy today are the fruits of research investments made years ago, and many of these advances benefited from Government support. The increased funding I have proposed will support America's creative minds as they explore promising areas such as nanotechnology, supercomputing, and alternative energy sources. These investments will lead to new inventions that offer better choices for consumers and a better life for our citizens.

The second element of this new initiative is to encourage bolder private sector investment in technology, because the private sector remains America's greatest engine of innovation. The research and development tax credit gives businesses an incentive to invest in projects that could lead to new discoveries. Congress allowed this tax credit to expire at the end of 2005, and the House and Senate are now considering another temporary extension. But a temporary extension does not allow our innovators to plan and invest with certainty. Other countries offer permanent tax incentives for research and development. To keep America the world's leader in technology and innovation, Congress needs to make the tax credit for research and development permanent.

The third element of this initiative is to make sure our children learn the skills they will need to keep America the world's most innovative country. Math and science are critical to many of our country's fastest-growing industries, so we must encourage our children to take more math and science classes and make sure those classes are rigorous enough to compete with other nations. I'm proposing that we train 70,000 high school teachers to lead Advanced Placement courses in math and science, bring 30,000 math and science professionals to teach in classrooms, and give early help to students who struggle with math so they have a better chance at good, high-wage jobs. If we ensure that America's children succeed in life, they will ensure that America succeeds in the world.

The American Competitiveness Initiative will help our Nation remain the world's economic leader. By investing in research and development, unleashing the innovative spirit of America's entrepreneurs, and making sure that our economy has workers highly skilled in math and science, we will lay the foundation for lasting economic prosperity.

Thank you for listening.

NOTE: The address was recorded at 10:20 a.m. on February 3 at the Marriott Hotel Albuquerque in Albuquerque, NM, for broadcast at 10:06 a.m. on February 4. The transcript was made available by the Office of the Press Secretary on February 3 but was embargoed for release until the broadcast. The Office of the Press Secretary also released a Spanish language transcript of this address.

Statement on the International Atomic Energy Agency Board of Governors Vote To Report Iran to the United Nations Security Council
February 4, 2006

Today in Vienna, the International Atomic Energy Agency Board of Governors voted to report Iran to the United Nations Security Council. This important step sends a clear message to the regime in Iran that the world will not permit the Iranian regime to gain nuclear weapons.

The Security Council will now address the IAEA Board's finding of "Iran's many failures and breaches of its obligations to comply" with its Nuclear Nonproliferation Treaty Safeguards Agreement. We expect the Security Council to add its weight to the IAEA Board's calls for the Iranian regime to return to the Paris Agreement, suspending all enrichment and reprocessing activity; cooperate fully with the IAEA; and return to negotiations with the EU–3 of Great Britain, France, and Germany. Those steps are necessary for the regime to begin to restore any confidence that it is not seeking nuclear weapons under the cover of a civilian program.

Today's vote by the IAEA Board is not the end of diplomacy or the IAEA's role. Instead, it is the beginning of an intensified diplomatic effort to prevent the Iranian regime from developing nuclear weapons. We will continue working with our international partners to achieve that common objective. The path chosen by Iran's new leaders— threats, concealment, and breaking international agreements and IAEA seals—will not succeed and will not be tolerated by the international community. The regime's continued defiance only further isolates Iran from the rest of the world and undermines the Iranian people's aspirations for a better life.

I end with a message to the Iranian people. The action today by the IAEA Board of Governors is not about denying the Iranian people the benefits of civilian nuclear power. The EU–3 and Russia, with the support of the United States, have made the Iranian regime offers that would enable Iran to have a civil nuclear energy program. The international community's sole purpose in this vote is to prevent the acquisition of nuclear weapons by the regime. Iran's true interests lie in working with the international community to enjoy the benefits of peaceful nuclear energy, not in isolating Iran by continuing to develop the capability to build nuclear weapons.

Letter to Congressional Leaders Transmitting a Report on Digital Computer Exports
February 3, 2006

Dear _____ :

In accordance with the provisions of section 1211(d) of the National Defense Authorization Act for Fiscal Year 1998 (Public Law 105–85), I hereby notify you of my decision to establish a new level for the notification procedure for digital computers set forth in section 1211(a) of Public Law 105–85. The new level will be 0.75 WT (Weighted TeraFLOPS). In accordance with the provisions of section 1211(e), I hereby notify you of my decision to remove Bulgaria from the list of countries covered under section 1211(b). The attached report provides the rationale supporting these decisions and fulfills the requirements of Public Law 105–85, sections 1211(d) and (e).

I have made these changes based on the recommendation of the Departments of State, Defense, Commerce, and Energy.

Sincerely,

GEORGE W. BUSH

NOTE: Identical letters were sent to John W. Warner, chairman, Senate Committee on Armed Services; Richard C. Shelby, chairman, Senate Committee on Banking, Housing, and Urban Affairs; Duncan L. Hunter, chairman, House Committee on Armed Services; and Henry J. Hyde, chairman, House Committee on International Relations. This letter was released by the Office of the Press Secretary on February 6.

Remarks at a Swearing-In Ceremony for Ben S. Bernanke as Chairman of the Federal Reserve
February 6, 2006

Good morning. Thank you for the warm welcome here at the Federal Reserve. The Fed is one of our Government's most vital institutions. And today I congratulate a fine man and a distinguished public servant, Dr. Ben Bernanke, on becoming the 14th Chairman of the Federal Reserve.

It's good to be with Anna, Ben's wife, Alyssa and Joel, his sister Sharon, and the other members of the Bernanke family. Welcome. Thanks for being here. You probably didn't think your brother was going to amount to much. [*Laughter*]

I'm honored—members of my Cabinet who are here, Secretary Carlos Gutierrez, Deputy Secretary Bob Kimmitt. Members of Congress—Congressman Oxley, Congressman Frank—thank you all for coming. It's awfully generous of you both to be here. I appreciate Roger Ferguson, the Vice Chairman, other members of the Board of Governors; thank you for being here as well. Former Chairman Paul Volcker, thanks for coming today, sir. I've got something to say about the other former Chairman who is here, in a minute. [*Laughter*]

Since its creation in 1913, the Federal Reserve has helped bring stability and growth to our Nation's economy. Around the world, the Fed is a symbol of integrity and reliability. Its decisions set our Nation's monetary policy, ensure a sound banking system, and help contain the risks that can arrive in our financial markets. The Fed's actions touch the lives of all Americans, and the Chairman of the Federal Reserve must be a leader of unquestionable credentials, sound judgment, and impeccable character. Ben Bernanke meets those high standards, and he will be an outstanding Chairman of the Federal Reserve.

As Chairman, Ben follows in the footsteps of one of America's most respected public servants. Alan Greenspan is perhaps the only central banker ever to achieve what one publication called "rock star status." [*Laughter*] For almost two decades, Chairman Greenspan's prudence and wise policies have guided this Nation through major economic challenges, have kept inflation in check, and contributed to phenomenal economic growth and a better life for all our citizens.

Recently he said, "I have only just realized that I have been on 24-hour call for 18 years." Mr. Chairman, you can rest a little easier and know that a grateful nation thanks you for your extraordinary service.

Ben Bernanke now takes up Alan Greenspan's mantle. When I announced Ben's nomination last October, economists and leaders across the political spectrum responded positively. They praised him for his unsurpassed academic credentials, broad policy experience, and a reputation for consensus-building. The son of a pharmacist and a school teacher, Ben graduated from Harvard with top honors and earned a doctorate in economics from Massachusetts Institute of Technology. He rose through the academic ranks to become the chairman of the economics department at Princeton.

Ben is one of the most cited economists in the world and is recognized for his pathbreaking work in the field of monetary policy. Ben Bernanke also knows the Federal Reserve System. From 2002 to 2005, he served with distinction on the Fed's Board of Governors. Since last year, he has served as the Chairman of the Council of Economic Advisers at the White House. I came to trust his judgment, his calm demeanor, and his sly sense of humor. [*Laughter*]

Throughout his distinguished career, Ben has earned a reputation for intellectual rigor, integrity, and personal decency. He's earned the respect of the global financial community. Ben is an economist's economist, one of the most esteemed leaders in the field. He understands that economics is more than just crunching numbers; good economics embraces policies that unleash hope and hard work and the power of free people to be able to fashion and improve their lives. Ben Bernanke will work every day to keep America's economic prospects strong and prosperous. He'll be a superb Chairman.

Mr. Chairman, thank you for agreeing to serve. Congratulations.

NOTE: The President spoke at 10:04 a.m. at the Federal Reserve. In his remarks, he referred to former Chairman of the Federal Reserve Paul A. Volcker. The transcript released by the Office of the Press Secretary also included the remarks of Chairman Bernanke.

Remarks at a Dinner Honoring the Dance Theatre of Harlem
February 6, 2006

Good evening. Laura and I welcome you to the White House for what is going to be a very special evening. One of the interesting things about living here is that, on occasion, some of our Nation's finest artists come to perform. Nothing like having great performers in your living room. [*Laughter*] And tonight we're looking forward to a fantastic performance.

As we gather during African American History Month, tonight we honor the Dance Theatre of Harlem and its unique founder, Arthur Mitchell. America is blessed to have people like Arthur Mitchell in our midst. So, Arthur, thank you for coming; thank you for your care and concern for our Nation's youth; and thank you for being dogged in your determination to see that this program flourishes. And we're glad to be a part of seeing that the program does flourish.

Since its creation in 1969, the company has set a new standard for excellence in dance and has won international acclaim. The Dance Theatre of Harlem School has provided thousands of students the opportunity to study dance, some of whom we'll see tonight. The Dance Theatre's community outreach programs are now bringing arts education to people all across America and around the world.

For almost four decades, the Dance Theatre of Harlem has done a lot to enrich countless lives through its brilliant performances and educational efforts. And so tonight I offer a toast to the achievements and continued success of Arthur Mitchell and the Dance Theatre of Harlem.

NOTE: The President spoke at 7:56 p.m. in the State Dining Room at the White House.

Remarks at the Funeral Service for Coretta Scott King in Lithonia, Georgia
February 7, 2006

To the King Family, distinguished guests, and fellow citizens: We gather in God's house, in God's presence, to honor God's servant, Coretta Scott King. Her journey

was long and only briefly with a hand to hold. But now she leans on everlasting arms. I've come today to offer the sympathy of our entire Nation at the passing of a woman who worked to make our Nation whole.

Americans knew her husband only as a young man. We knew Mrs. King in all the seasons of her life, and there was grace and beauty in every season. As a great movement of history took shape, her dignity was a daily rebuke to the pettiness and cruelty of segregation. When she wore a veil at 40 years old, her dignity revealed the deepest trust in God and His purposes. In decades of prominence, her dignity drew others to the unfinished work of justice. In all her years, Coretta Scott King showed that a person of conviction and strength could also be a beautiful soul. This kind and gentle woman became one of the most admired Americans of our time. She is rightly mourned, and she is deeply missed.

Some here today knew her as a girl and saw something very special long before a young preacher proposed. She once said, "Before I was a King, I was a Scott." And the Scotts were strong and righteous and brave in the face of wrong. Coretta eventually took on the duties of a pastor's wife and a calling that reached far beyond the doors of the Dexter Avenue Baptist Church.

In that calling, Dr. King's family was subjected to vicious words, threatening calls in the night, and a bombing at their house. Coretta had every right to count the cost and step back from the struggle. But she decided that her children needed more than a safe home; they needed an America that upheld their equality and wrote their rights into law. And because this young mother and father were not intimidated, millions of children they would never meet are now living in a better, more welcoming country.

In the critical hours of the civil rights movement, there were always men and women of conscience at the heart of the drama. They knew that old hatreds ran deep. They knew that nonviolence might be answered with violence. They knew that much established authority was against them. Yet they also knew that sheriffs and mayors and Governors were not ultimately in control of events, that a greater authority was interested and very much in charge. The God of Moses was not neutral about their captivity. The God of Isaiah and the prophets was still impatient with injustice. And they knew that the Son of God would never leave them or forsake them.

But some had to leave before their time, and Dr. King left behind a grieving widow and little children. Rarely has so much been asked of a pastor's wife, and rarely has so much been taken away. Years later, Mrs. King recalled, "I would wake up in the morning, have my cry, then go in to them. The children saw me going forward."

Martin Luther King, Jr., had preached that unmerited suffering could have redemptive power. Little did he know that this great truth would be proven in the life of the person he loved the most. Others could cause her sorrow, but no one could make her bitter. By going forward with a strong and forgiving heart, Coretta Scott King not only secured her husband's legacy, she built her own. Having loved a leader, she became a leader. And when she spoke, America listened closely, because her voice carried the wisdom and goodness of a life well lived.

In that life, Coretta Scott King knew danger; she knew injustice; she knew sudden and terrible grief. She also knew that her Redeemer lives. She trusted in the Name above every name. And today we trust that our sister Coretta is on the other shore—at peace, at rest, at home. May God bless you, and may God bless our country.

NOTE: The President spoke at 1 p.m. at the New Birth Missionary Baptist Church.

Remarks Following Discussions With King Abdullah II of Jordan
February 8, 2006

President Bush. Your Majesty, welcome back. I have had two good discussions with His Majesty. Last night His Majesty and the Crown Prince came to have dinner with Laura and me and some Members of Congress, and we had a really good discussion. We had a little time by ourselves to talk strategically about the world and our deep desire for this world to be peaceful.

Of course, we talked about Iraq, Iran, the Palestinian Territories. And I appreciate your vision and your desire to achieve a better world for the people in your neighborhood.

We also talked about a topic that requires a lot of discussion and a lot of sensitive thought, and that is the reaction to the cartoons. I first want to make it very clear to people around the world that ours is a nation that believes in tolerance and understanding. In America, we welcome people of all faiths. One of the great attributes of our country is that you're free to worship however you choose in the United States of America.

Secondly, we believe in a free press. We also recognize that with freedom comes responsibilities. With freedom comes the responsibility to be thoughtful about others. Finally, I have made it clear to His Majesty, and he made it clear to me, that we reject violence as a way to express discontent with what may be printed in a free press. I call upon the governments around the world to stop the violence, to be respectful, to protect property and protect the lives of innocent diplomats who are serving their countries overseas.

And so, Your Majesty, thank you for coming. I'm proud to share the moment with you.

King Abdullah. Thank you very much for your kind words. And I would just like to echo what the President said. We've had some very fruitful discussions, and we're appreciative of the vision and the desire that the President has for peace and stability in our part of the world. He has always strived to make life better for all of us in the Middle East, and I tremendously appreciate that role.

The issue of the cartoons, again, and with all respect to press freedoms, obviously, anything that vilifies the Prophet Mohammed—peace be upon him—or attacks Muslim sensibilities, I believe needs to be condemned. But at the same time, those that want to protest should do it thoughtfully, articulately, and express their views peacefully. When we see protests—when we see destruction, when we see violence, especially if it ends up taking the lives of innocent people, is completely unacceptable. Islam, like Christianity and Judaism, is a religion of peace, tolerance, moderation.

And we have to continue to ask ourselves, what type of world do we want for our children? I too often hear the word used as, tolerance. And tolerance is such an awful word. If we are going to strive to move forward in the future, the word that we should be talking about is acceptance. We need to accept our common humanity and our common values. And I hope that lessons can be learned from this dreadful issue, that we can move forward as humanity, and truly try to strive together, as friends and as neighbors, to bring a better world to all.

President Bush. Thank you, Your Majesty. I appreciate you.

NOTE: The President spoke at 9:26 a.m. in the Oval Office at the White House. In his remarks, he referred to Crown Prince Hussein of Jordan.

Remarks to the Business and Industry Association of New Hampshire in Manchester, New Hampshire
February 8, 2006

The President. Thank you. Please be seated. Thank you for the welcome. It's good to be back here in New Hampshire. We had a little problem scheduling a room here in this State. It turns out, a lot of Judd's colleagues are prebooking for the '08 elections. [*Laughter*]

I really appreciate you giving me a chance to come by. I want to spend a little time on our economy. I want to talk about your money; I want to talk about the budget I submitted. I hope at the end of this discussion you'll have a better feel for why I make the decisions I've made. You know, one of the interesting things about my job is you get to make a lot of decisions. My buddies from Texas come up, and they say—after they get over the initial shock of me being in the White House in the first place—[*laughter*]—they say, "What's the job like? What's it like to be President of the United States?"

The best thing I can tell them is it's a job that requires decisionmaking. Decisionmaking is based upon—good decisionmaking is based upon standing for something, making decisions based upon certain principles that won't change even though the political circumstances may appear to be changing. Decisionmaking means listening to people, surrounding yourself with excellence. Decisionmaking means doing what you think is right, not what may be politically expedient.

And so today I hope I give you a sense of why I made some of the decisions that I made on the budget I've submitted to the Congress and why I believe it'll help the American people.

Before I begin, I do want to thank Judd. The guy is a great friend—he's a great friend of mine; he's a great friend of the people of New Hampshire. I've gotten to know him really well. He's a good man—

and he married well too, by the way. [*Laughter*] So did I. Laura sends her best. She's winging her way, by the way, to Italy to represent the United States at the Winter Games, which is pretty unusual for a woman who was raised in west Texas, where it rarely snows. [*Laughter*]

I'm also proud to be traveling today with Senator John Sununu. He, too, is a fine man and a great Senator for the people of New Hampshire. I'm proud to be here with the two Congressmen, Jeb Bradley and Charlie Bass. I'm looking forward to flying them back to Washington. It's amazing what people will do to get a free flight. [*Laughter*]

I want to thank the speaker who is here; Doug, thank you for being here. I remember going to your farm a while back. You know, I don't follow New Hampshire politics that closely these days, at least state-house politics, but I do know this is a guy who loves his family. And he's got a lot of family to love; I've met them all. Appreciated his hospitality.

I want to thank the president of the senate, Ted Gatsas, who is with us as well. Mr. Mayor, thank you for joining us today. The mayor said he just got elected; he's all excited and fired up. Just fill the potholes, Mayor, and everything will be fine. [*Laughter*]

I want to thank all the other State and local officials. I want to thank George Gantz. Thanks for the introduction. I asked him what his middle name was; I was hoping it was W. [*Laughter*] But it wasn't. But, anyway, George, thanks for introducing me, and thanks for having me here. I want to thank Mike Donahue and all the other members of the board of the Business and Industry Association of New Hampshire.

I also want to thank the bankers who are here. Thank you for allowing me to horn in on your meeting. I hope it's worth your while to have me. Most of all, thank you all for giving me a chance to come.

Let me first start off with our economy. It's strong, and it's getting stronger. That's how I see it. I say that because we're now in our fifth year of uninterrupted economic growth. Last year, this economy of ours grew at 3.5 percent, which is good; that's good, strong economic growth. We did so in the face of higher energy prices and natural disasters, which makes the growth even more extraordinary.

More Americans now own their home than ever before in our Nation's history. I love the fact that America is an ownership society. I think it's important for policy to promote ownership. Low interest rates, by the way, helps promote ownership. You'll be happy to hear that this administration doesn't intend to set the interest rates, but I did name somebody good, named Ben Bernanke, to head up the Fed, to replace Alan Greenspan, and I'm confident he will do a good job of being the Chairman of the Fed.

More minority families now own a home than ever before in our Nation's history as well. See, a hopeful society is one in which all people see a positive future. There's nothing better than saying, "I own my own home; welcome to my home."

Real after-tax income is up by 8 percent—nearly 8 percent per person since 2001. New orders for durable goods like machinery are rising, which is a good sign. Shipments of manufactured goods are up as well. The productivity of the United States was strong last year, and that's important. A productive society is one in which the standard of living rises. It's important for us to have policies in place that keep us the most productive society in the world.

Small businesses are thriving. We've added 4.7 million new jobs over the last 2½ years. The national unemployment rate is at 4.7 percent, the lowest level since July 2001. I was interested to see that your

unemployment rate is still unbelievably low; it's at 3.5 percent. A recent survey of your businesses says that nearly two-thirds of the CEOs expect revenues to increase this coming year. In other words, there's a positive feel here in New Hampshire and around a lot of parts of our country as well.

I like to say it's an exciting time for the economy. We're productive; we're innovative; we're entrepreneurial. And the role of government is to keep it that way. That's the role of the government. The global economy—we're the leader. We're growing faster than other major industrialized nations, and in the past 2½ years, we've created more jobs than the EU and Japan combined.

Now, one of the interesting things we face here in America is in spite of the numbers and the economic growth, there is uncertainty. Some of the uncertainty comes as a result of competition from places like India and China. The temptation with uncertainty and competition is to say, "We can't compete; let us kind of wall ourselves off." If you look at the history of the United States, the economic history, there have been periods of protectionism and isolationism, in the hopes that that will lead to a better lifestyle for our citizens. I strongly reject the notion of becoming a protectionist nation. I don't think this country ought to fear the future. I don't think we ought to fear competition. I know we ought to shape the future with good policies out of Washington, DC, and make sure that we're the preeminent economy in the world.

There's also, you know, kind of a debate in Washington about how to handle your money. There are some that—frankly, whose policies would make us look more like Europe than we should, and that is kind of a centralization of power. The surest way to centralize power is to take more of your own money to Washington. And so I want to talk a little bit about why our economic policies, in my judgment, should reject the centralization of power, particularly through the budget process, and let the folks at home make the decisions about their own money.

You see, government doesn't create wealth. A lot of my decisionmaking is based upon this principle: The role of government is not to try to create wealth but an environment in which the entrepreneur can flourish; is to create an environment in which people are willing to risk capital; an environment in which a person feels comfortable with making a decision to start their own business. That's the role of government. It's a role of government that says, "We trust people to spend their own money wisely."

And so in the State of the Union Address, which I gave last week, I outlined a series of steps that encompass that philosophy and steps that I believe that will keep America the preeminent economy in the world, the leader in the world, which is what we should be. If we want our people to prosper, if we want lifestyles to improve, if we want our standard of living to go up, America must remain the leader.

I've talked about health care and the importance for us to have a health care system that takes care of the elderly and the poor, but a health care system that strengthens the relationship between doctor and patient, a health care system that provides transparency into pricing, a health care system that uses information technology to bring the medical profession into the 21st century.

You know, some are going to say, "What do you mean by that?" Well, I mean, when you're writing your files by hand, it means you're not in the 21st century. And since most doctors can't write too well, there's a lot of information that didn't pass through—[*laughter*].

I've talked, as well, about the need to get legal reform in the medical industry. Look, we've got too many lawsuits, pure and simple. We've got a real problem in the country because docs and hospitals are

getting sued. A lot of good docs are being driven out of business. I said an appalling— a statistic that I think is appalling in my State of the Union. Do you realize there are 1,500 counties in America without an ob-gyn? And that's wrong. And one of the reasons that's happening is because there's too many lawsuits driving good docs out of practice. We need a medical liability system that is fair to medical providers in the United States of America.

When I first went to Washington, I thought it might be a State issue. And then I realized that all these lawsuits are causing doctors to practice defensive medicine as well as running up premiums, which costs the Federal Government a lot of money. And so I've decided this is a national issue that requires a national response. And the United States Senate needs to be pass medical liability reform this year.

Part of our plan for a patient-doctor system, one that gives you choices to make and counts on you for making rational choices, is to expand health savings accounts and make sure that individuals and small-business employees can buy insurance with the same tax advantages that people working for big businesses now get. And we're going to make sure those health savings accounts are portable. One of the things about our economy, which is interesting, is that there's a lot of turnover when it comes to jobs. People are changing jobs a lot, which creates uncertainty. And one way to deal with that uncertainty, to bring certainty to people in the workforce, is to make sure they can carry their health savings account with them from job to job, so they don't fear losing their health insurance.

So I've got a lot of ideas on health care that I'm going to be talking to the Nation about in the coming weeks. Also, as we continue to make sure this country is whole, we're going to make sure that we repair parts of our country that have been hurt by natural disaster. Thus far, the Federal Government has committed $85 billion to the folks who got hurt by Katrina. I went down there in Jackson Square, and I said, "The Federal Government is going to help you," and we are helping—$85 billion is a lot. It may not be all it takes, but I want to compliment the Congress for making a strong commitment to helping the people down there get on their feet and get this important part of our country up and running again.

I talked about a very important issue that I think surprised old Judd a little bit—you know, he knows I'm from Texas, a little concerned about my views on energy, I think, at times—prejudged me the wrong way. I meant what I said; we've got to get off our dependence on oil. To stay competitive, this country cannot be reliant upon oil from unstable parts of the world. And therefore—as I said in the State of the Union, we're spending $10 billion so far to come up with ways to wean ourselves off of oil.

I talked about clean coal technologies. We have got to promote safe nuclear power. We have got to continue our investment in solar energy. But I want to spend a little time—I mean, a little time—on making sure that you understand that I am serious when it comes to spending money so that—to be able to develop the technologies necessary to be able to convert saw grass and wood chips and refuse into energy. It's coming. We believe this technology is close to breakthrough status.

I also want to tell you something interesting that I didn't say in the speech, is that there's 4½ million automobiles on the road today that are flex-fuel automobiles that can switch from gasoline to ethanol already. In other words, the technology is available for the automobiles. When we have the breakthrough, when it comes in ethanol, I'm convinced that this country is going to become what we want it to be—not reliant upon Middle Eastern oil.

It's exciting times. It's important. This is not only an economic security issue, it is a national security issue. And we're intent

at the Federal Government to promote research dollars to see to it that we achieve this important objective.

I also talked about education. One of the things we've got to understand here in America is that if our children don't have the skills necessary to fill the jobs of the 21st century, those jobs are going to go somewhere else. We live in a competitive world, and as I told you, I recognize that competition creates uncertainty, but we've got to be certain about the goal to make sure our children are educated.

And so, laid out a math and science initiative, which embodies a lot of the principles in the No Child Left Behind Act, which basically says, "Look, we're going to measure, and if we determine that you're falling behind in middle school in math, we'll provide extra money so you can catch up." We need more AP teachers trained in the classrooms for our high schools. We're going to have 30,000 adjunct professors from private industry and/or retired scientists to go and excite our children about math and science.

And, as well, we've got to lead the world in basic research. I committed our Government to doubling the basic research for sciences over a 10-year period of time, as well as we've got to understand that most of the money invested in research is done at the private sector. And that's why we've got to make sure the research and development tax credit is permanent. You see, the research and development tax credit expires annually. Now, how can you possibly plan for an aggressive research budget if you're uncertain as to what the Tax Code is going to allow you to do? Congress has got to understand that CEOs of companies that are investing to make our life better can't make sound decisions with uncertainty in the Tax Code. And so they've got to make the research and development tax credit permanent.

And so there are some ways to make sure that we remain competitive. And I'm going to work with Members of Congress to make sure we get these initiatives passed.

Today I'm going to focus on the budget strategy. We're on our way to cutting our deficit in half by 2009. And I'm going to give you some ideas as to how we can do that. The budget strategy has three parts. The first part is to promote economic growth by keeping taxes low. The second part is to restrain spending. And the third part is to insist that Federal programs produce results. That may sound odd to you. [*Laughter*] But I'm going tell you how we—we've got interesting ideas how to promote results-oriented programs in Washington, DC.

First, we're going to keep the taxes low to make sure the economy growing—grows. My philosophy is this: When Americans are allowed to keep more of their own money to spend and save and invest, that helps the economy grow, and when the economy grows, people can find work. If entrepreneurs have more money in their pocket, they're going to use it to expand their businesses, which means somebody is more likely to find work. If consumers have more money in their pocket, they're likely to demand additional good or services. And in a marketplace economy when somebody demands a good or a service, somebody meets that demand with product or the service. And when that demand is met, it means somebody is more likely to find work. Cutting taxes means jobs for the American people.

We're a confident nation, and one reason we are is because we've overcome a lot. I want you to think about what this economy has been through in a relatively quick period of time. We've been through a recession, a stock market collapse, terrorist attacks, a war, and corporate scandals. And I told you how strong the economy was going. I think one of the reasons why this economy is as strong as it is, is because Congress wisely cut the taxes for the American taxpayers.

We lowered taxes, and in doing so, the message was and the philosophy is, you can spend your money better than the Government can spend its money. We want you making decisions for your families. We want you making investments. And so we cut taxes on families by lowering income tax rates and doubling the child credit. We reduced the marriage penalty. I've never understood a Tax Code that penalizes marriage. Seems like to me, we ought to be encouraging marriage in the Tax Code. We put the death tax on its way to extinction. My view is, is that if you're running a small business, you ought not to have to pay taxes twice, once while you're living and once after you die. If you're a farmer or a rancher, you ought to be allowed—the Tax Code ought to encourage you to be able to pass your property on to whomever you choose.

We cut taxes on small businesses. An interesting part of the debate that a lot of people in America haven't focused— didn't focus on is that when you're cutting individual income tax rates, you're also cutting a lot of taxes on small businesses. See, most small businesses are sole proprietorships or subchapter S corporations, and therefore, they pay tax at the individual income tax level. And so when you reduce all rates, you're really interjecting capital into the small-business sector of the country. And that's important because two-thirds of new jobs in America are created by small businesses. It makes sense, doesn't it, if you're worried about people finding work, if you're trying to overcome economic hardship, to fuel the engine of growth that will provide work—and that's the small-business sector of the United States.

One of the interesting things we did is we understand it's important to encourage investment, particularly for small businesses. And so we raised the amount of investment a small business can deduct immediately from $25,000 to $100,000. And why do you do that? Well, one, you want your small-business sector to remain productive. Investment yields enhanced productivity, which means it's easier to compete and stay in business. We want more productivity. Productivity will yield a higher lifestyle for the American citizens.

Secondly, we want people to invest because it means somebody is going to have to produce the product that they buy. And so this—raising the deduction had a positive effect not only in the small-business sector but throughout the economy. By the way, this deduction is set to expire, and so part of my budget proposal is to double the deduction to $200,000 to help small businesses and to make this a permanent part of the Tax Code so small-business entrepreneurs have security in planning.

We also lowered the taxes on dividends and capital gains. One of the interesting statistics, and why this is such an important initiative, is that half of America, now 50 million households, have some investment in the stock market. Think about that. Half the households in America have got a stake in the stock market. They either own shares in individual companies or through mutual funds. By cutting the taxes on dividends and capital gains, we helped add nearly $4 trillion in new wealth to the stock market. In other words, it invigorated the markets. That's positive, particularly if you're one of the one-half of the American family that owns stock. When those stocks go up, you see the value increase in your IRAs or your 401(k)s or your mutual funds.

These gains help American families. See, there's a correlation between cutting taxes on dividends and capital gains and increase in the market and increase in individual net worth. When that happens, that helps American families be able to afford a down payment for a home, or helps a family be able to afford a college tuition, or it helps a family in retirement enjoy a better life. In other words, there is a direct correlation between cutting taxes on the capital gains and dividends and quality of life all across America.

The tax relief on dividends and capital gains has also helped families that don't own stocks. And the reason why is, people out here understand—capital flows will tell you that cutting taxes on dividends and capital gains has reduced the cost of capital. That's economic talk for meaning the money that you borrowed doesn't cost you as much, and that helps investment. An economy in which there is ample investment is an economy in which people are able to find work. So this has been a positive part of our tax plan.

One of the interesting things that I hope you realize when it comes to cutting taxes is this tax relief not only has helped our economy, but it's helped the Federal budget. In 2004, tax revenues to the Treasury grew about 5.5 percent. That's kind of counterintuitive, isn't it? At least it is for some in Washington. You cut taxes and the tax revenues increase. See, some people are going to say, "Well, you cut taxes; you're going to have less revenue." No, that's not what happened. What happened was, we cut taxes, and in 2004, revenues increased 5.5 percent. And last year, those revenues increased 14.5 percent, or $274 billion. And the reason why is, cutting taxes caused the economy to grow, and as the economy grows, there is more revenue generated in the private sector, which yields more tax revenues.

Revenues from dividends and capital gains are up by an estimated 50 percent. Think about that. We cut the taxes, so if you got a dividend or you sell your stock after a period of time and pay capital gains—and the revenues from those two areas have gone up—the economy kicked into high gear, and we're getting more money in the Treasury.

Now, this tax relief I mentioned to you is set to expire. In other words, when Congress passed it, it wasn't permanent. Kind of like the R&D tax credit, it's kind of—it may be permanent, it may not be permanent, depending upon whether or not Congress acts.

If you're a small-business owner, that's not good for you, to be wondering what your taxes are going to look like. You cannot plan your future if you're a small-business owner if you wonder whether or not your tax rates are going to go up in the short term. I don't think families are looking forward to any tax increases. I think they agree with me. We've got plenty of money to spend in Washington, and we just need to make sure we set our priorities.

If Congress doesn't act, your taxes are going to go up—and you're not going to like it, and it's going to hurt the economy. And so Congress needs to make the tax relief we passed permanent.

You will hear the argument during the budget debates, you know, all the noise coming out of Washington, that you need to raise taxes in order to balance the budget. I've been there long enough to tell you, that's not the way Washington works. They're going to raise your taxes, and they're going to find new ways to spend your money. The best way to reduce the deficit is to make sure we have progrowth economic policies in place and be smart and wise about how we spend your money.

So the second thing I want to talk to you today about—the strategy behind the budget and the decisions I made for the budget—is how we can be wise with your money. In the State of the Union, I outlined priorities. One way you're wise with your money is you set priorities. You know what it's like to manage your own family budget. Of course, you'd like to take a vacation every week, you know, some exotic place; but you've got to set your priorities; you can't do that. You want to do this or do that, go to a fancy restaurant every night, but that's not setting priorities. Families set priorities. Individual Americans set priorities. Business people set priorities all the time when it comes to setting the budget, and that's what the Federal Government needs to do.

And the first priority of our Government is to make sure our troops in harm's way have all they need to complete their mission for the sake of peace.

The budget I've submitted has got other priorities; I mentioned some of them. A priority is to make sure that we help the folks down South get on their feet, those suffering from Hurricane Katrina. I talked about the need to have education as a priority, particularly in math and science. I talk about the priority to spend research money so we become less dependent on Middle Eastern oil. Those are priorities.

Now, when it comes to budget talk, there are two types of spending in Washington. There's called discretionary spending and mandatory spending. Discretionary spending is the kind of spending Congress votes on every year. Mandatory spending is the kind of spending that happens based upon fixed formula. We made good progress in discretionary spending. In the last year of the previous administration, nonsecurity discretionary spending rose by 15 percent. Every year of my Presidency, we've reduced the growth of that spending. And last year, Congress responded to my request and passed bills that actually cut nonsecurity discretionary spending.

There's no question, the war and the hurricanes have stressed our budget—all the more reason to set priorities and to be wise with your money. And so we submitted a budget. The budget I submitted this year proposes to cut discretionary spending that's not related to defense and homeland security. We will keep the growth in overall discretionary spending below the rate of inflation so we can cut the deficit in half by 2009.

One reason we're able to do so and meet priorities is because we've identified $14 billion in savings from programs that aren't performing very well at all. I'm going to talk a little bit later about that.

Now, the biggest challenge we've got, however—and this is very important for our citizens to understand—when it comes to deficits—the deficits, the unfunded liabilities inherent in our mandatory programs, such as Medicare and Social Security and Medicaid. And the reason why there's a lot of unfunded liabilities in those programs is because a baby boom generation is fixing to retire, and I'm one. As a matter of fact, I turn 62 in 2008, which is a convenient year for me to be retiring. [*Laughter*] Old Judd is a baby boomer. I think he's 7 months younger than I am.

And I'm looking around, and I see a couple of baby boomers out there. And we're getting ready to get into the system. And there is a lot of us. A huge number of retirees are getting ready to get on Social Security and Medicare. And there is not a lot of—relative to those of us who retire, the number of payers in the system is shrinking. And there's a burden. The math doesn't work. It's a problem, particularly for people who are going to be having to pay for baby boomers like me.

Medicare recently was modernized. I'm not talking about the recent modernization program—which is the right thing to do, by the way. If you make a commitment to America's seniors, which Lyndon Johnson did and this country has honored, then it makes sense to make sure the health care system you provide the seniors is modern and up to date. A commitment means a commitment of modern medicine, and that's precisely what we did when we provided prescription drug coverage for seniors.

Imagine a system that said, "We will pay for an invasive surgery but not for the drugs that will prevent the surgery from being needed in the first place." It didn't make sense. Medicare was old and antiquated, and I'm proud to have signed the reform. Twenty-four million seniors are now enrolled in this new program. Tens of thousands of more are signing up each day. The prescription drug benefit is saving the typical senior more than $1,100 on medicine a year. And the average expected premium that seniors pay has gone down by a third, from $37 per month to $25 a month. It's amazing what happens when you interject competition into the health care system.

But the real problem for Medicare is the long-term problem of baby boomers coming into the system. There is going to be 78 million of us. And interestingly enough, we've been promised greater benefits than the previous generation. People ran for office who said, "Vote for me; I'm going to make sure that you get a better Social Security deal or a Medicare deal." And sure enough, Congress passed that. Do you realize that if we don't do anything on fixing this problem—and by the way, if you're a senior, you don't have anything to worry about; you'll get your check. I'm talking about knowing the system is going broke and walking around this country and talking to people who are paying payroll taxes into a broke system. And that's not right. It just doesn't make any sense to me for us not to take care of this problem.

In 2030, spending on Social Security, Medicare, and Medicaid alone will be almost 60 percent of the entire Federal budget. I mean, there is a problem. One of the tricks in Washington is just to pass them on to future Congresses and future Presidents. That's not my style. I want to get something done. I believe the job of a President is to confront problems and not say, somebody else can take care of it. That's why I ran. That's why Judd ran and Sununu ran as well, by the way. And they're strong advocates of doing something about this before it's too late.

Listen, I understand that Congress didn't act last year on the Social Security proposal I laid out, but that's not stopping me from doing what I think is right. I see a problem. And so do the American people, by the way. They see a problem, and they expect us to put aside all that needless political rhetoric, that partisanship and get something done. And I'm serious about it.

So I'm looking forward to putting together a group of both Republicans and

Democrats in the Congress—from the Senate and the House—people who can get something done—and sitting down at the table and doing what the American people expect us to do and solve this problem for a generation of Americans that are coming up in our society.

In the meantime, we've got to do what we can do to make sure that we keep spending under control. Later today we're flying back to Washington, and I'm going to sign a bill that will rein in spending on entitlements, on mandatory spending, by nearly $40 billion over 5 years. And I applaud Judd and Members of the House and the Senate for putting fiscal sanity back into the budget. By the way, it's hard work up there to get everybody in the same direction. Everybody thinks their own program is special. And the noise can get a little loud up there when you're making some decisions that are apparently tough decisions for some.

Let me talk about the Medicaid decisions that was made. Medicaid is an important program. It's a program that's a part of our commitment to the poor and the elderly. People talked about how the decision to reform Medicaid was immoral. Well, it's not immoral to make sure that prescription drug pharmacists don't overcharge the system. You're a taxpayer, you expect the Medicaid person we're helping to be able to buy drugs at a reasonable cost. But it turns out that there was inflated markups for people who had Government help to buy drugs. That doesn't make any sense, so we reformed that. The people are still going to get their drugs, but the taxpayers aren't going to have to pay inflated prices. That seems to make sense, seems to be fair.

They talk about us slashing resources for the elderly. No, there are resources for the elderly in Medicaid, but what we did was, we said, "We're going to try to stop you from transferring assets from the parent to the child," so that the parent's apparent poverty enabled them to get on Medicaid.

That's not fair. You work hard for your money. We want to take care of the poor, but we don't want to reward people who game the Medicaid system. And so we saved money for the taxpayers by making rational reforms in Medicaid. We're able to keep the commitment to the poor, and that's important for you all to understand. And at the same time, by putting common-sense reforms in place, we saved the taxpayers $4.7 billion of entitlement reform.

Let me talk about the student loan program. I remember going to Kansas State recently, and a young lady stood up and asked me a question. She said, "Well, here you are on a college campus; why are you cutting our loans?" I said, well, I didn't think we were—as a matter of fact, I thought we were helping you get student loans. She was talking about the reforms within the budget I'm going to sign today.

Let me tell you what those reforms were. There were too many subsidies to folks who were providing loans to the students. And so we decided to reform those subsidies to make it more rational for the taxpayers and, at the same time, to help the students. By reducing the cost of lending, we saved the taxpayers $22 billion, of which $10 billion will be used to increase student loans. So here is an example of staying focused on the mission, providing money for loans and, at the same time, providing relief for the taxpayer.

The new budget I submitted builds on our progress in controlling mandatory spending by proposing another $65 billion in entitlement savings. I'm looking forward to working with Judd to get this passed out of the Senate and the House. It's an important part of maintaining fiscal discipline. Thirty-six-billion dollars of that comes from Medicare, and let me tell you how we achieve that.

The annual growth of Medicare spending is about 8.1 percent. Now, if you think about inflation, the growth in that program far exceeds inflation. And the budget I submitted suggests that we slow that growth down to 7.7 percent. That doesn't seem too unreasonable to me, if you're trying to bring fiscal sanity into Washington—to slow the growth of the program down from 8.1 percent to 7.7 percent. This isn't a cut. People call it a cut in Medicare. That's not a cut. It's slowing down the rate of growth. It's the difference between slowing your car down to go the speed limit or putting your car in reverse.

In Medicare, we believe that payments ought to be made to the individual we're helping, in a reasonable way. If there are productivity gains and savings to be had at the hospitals, for example, those savings ought to be given to the taxpayers, not to the hospitals. Reform means making health care providers bid and compete for services. That seems to make sense. Competition and bidding creates transparency in the process, but it also helps the taxpayers.

So we brought these reforms into place recognizing that the choices will be tough for Members of Congress—but necessary choices. That's what you expect, it seems like to me. You ought to expect us to ask the tough questions, to make sure the programs focus on the people we're trying to help and, at the same time, achieve savings, if possible to do.

Congress is working on earmark reform, and I appreciate that a lot. It's a necessary part of making sure the budget process is rational. I look forward to helping them. I've got some ideas of my own, in terms of budget reform.

One, I believe any time Washington makes a spending commitment that our children and grandchildren will not be able to afford, I propose that Congress offset those expenditures in entitlement spending. In other words, if they make a commitment to increase entitlement spending somewhere, they've got to decrease it elsewhere, in order to make sure we have rational budgeting.

Secondly, I believe we ought to sunset Federal programs. That means that they ought to be reviewed at a certain period of time to determine whether or not they're meeting the objectives that Congress set them out to be. And if not, get rid of them.

And finally, I'd like to have the line-item veto.

I mentioned to you getting good results. Let me talk about the last part of our budget strategy. We have worked hard to insist upon results. Perhaps the most vivid example of that is in the relationship between the Federal Government and the State government when it comes to public school education. I was always worried about a system that never asked the question, "Are we getting results for our money?" It's a legitimate question, particularly when it comes to schools.

When I was the Governor of Texas, I remembered what it was like to be the Governor of a State where people just got shuffled through, and we didn't know whether they could read or write, add and subtract, until it was too late. And it was a real problem, and it's been a problem throughout our society. And so we came to Washington with a spirit of innovation and reform—worked with Judd on that bill as well. I don't mean to be mentioning your name too often, Judd, but if it helps you, fine. [*Laughter*]

But we had a new spirit when it came to funding schools, and that is, in return for Federal money—I mean, we spend a fair amount of money, not nearly as much as State and local governments, of course. About 10 percent of all the money spent nationwide is spent at the Federal level—but in return for that money, I thought it made sense to say, "Why don't you show us whether or not a child can read." That seemed to make sense. It wasn't that difficult a request.

It turns out, it's a pretty difficult request politically. You know, "How dare you measure. All they're doing is teaching the test. It's racist to measure." No, it's racist not to measure. It's racist not to know whether a curriculum is working. It makes sense for the Federal Government to demand results for money spent.

We didn't tell the people of New Hampshire how to teach. We didn't design the test, nor should we have, from the Federal level. I believe in local control of schools. I believe in aligning—[*applause*]—but I darn sure want to know. And the interesting thing about these tests—we test three through eight, or we demand that the schools test three through eight. One of the parts of the test that I find most important, and I hope you do as well, is that when we find a child deficient in reading, that family gets supplemental services, extra help, where they can go get tutoring at a private or public institution. In other words, there's a focus on every child, making sure that we solve problems early, before it's too late. And you can't solve a problem unless you measure. We're going to apply that same thing to the math and sciences agenda, as I mentioned to you earlier.

And so that's the spirit of asking for reform. And so I've got a group of folks that are constantly analyzing whether or not the Federal Government is doing what you're doing—doing what you expect us to do. You realize we spend $2.7 trillion a year, and there are more than 1,000 Federal programs. That's a lot; that's a lot of programs. And it makes sense to make sure that they're working. See, good intentions aren't enough, as far as this administration is concerned. We're insisting that people show us, program managers show us, whether or not they're achieving—these programs achieve results.

Last 4 years, we've had what we call the President's Management Agenda. Employees have been working to help ensure that the programs are doing what we expect them to do. That's what they do. They spend a lot of time on this. We ask Federal managers to achieve good results at reasonable costs, and we measure them. The point is, is that if they can't prove they're achieving good results, then the programs,

in my judgment, ought to be eliminated and/or trimmed back. That's why I told you earlier, we found 141 such programs. And we did the same thing in last year's budget as well.

One of the interesting innovations that we have put forth is a new web site called expectmore.gov. It's a program where—it's a web site where we start to put the measurement results up for everybody to see. Nothing like transparency into the Federal bureaucracy to determine whether or not a program is working. And so I think you'll find it innovative—I do—that the White House has put this web site up. And you'll be able to see whether or not results are being achieved for the money spent.

I'll give you one example of what we're talking about. I'll give you two examples—one example of money poorly spent, and one example of money well-spent, as a part of this management initiative—the analyzation as to whether or not the programs are actually delivering results we want.

One of them is, the Department of Energy runs the natural gas technology program that is designed or was designed to help businesses increase natural gas supplies. That sounds reasonable, doesn't it? Let's have a program at the Federal Government that says to producers, produce more natural gas. The problem is when we found out—when we analyzed the program, we found that it's impact on production is minimal. It's not working. It sounds good. Somebody thought of it, had a good title to the bill, but it's not delivering results. The private sector has got better incentives to provide natural gas for you; it's called price, not the Federal Government's program.

And so I'm asking the erstwhile chairman to eliminate the program.

Senator Judd Gregg. It's done. [*Laughter*]

The President. If it was that easy, government would be a breeze, wouldn't it?

I'm going to talk about an example of something that is working, based upon our analysis, and these are called community health centers. Community health centers are run by HHS. Their mission is to provide effective health care for the poor and the indigent. It makes sense. If you don't believe in the nationalization of health care, which I don't, then it does make sense to provide good care for people—primary care for people that are poor or indigent.

And so community health centers, which was an idea during the previous administration, is one that we've embraced. We have found that these health care centers work really well. I don't know if you've got one in Manchester, but they're good. [*Applause*] You know what I'm talking about. And so they analyzed the cost relative to the benefit, and it's worthwhile to fund these. And so the budget that I'm submitting increases—has a 10 percent increase for community health centers.

And so that's it. That's why—I hope you get an idea of why I submitted the budget I submitted. You know, the budgets really, kind of, generally are numbers. They look at numbers, but you've got to understand I look behind the numbers and see quality of life issues. When I think about the budget, I think about making sure that the economy grows. You can't be the preeminent economy in the world if your economy doesn't grow.

When I think about the budget, I think about taxpayers and always remember whose money we spend in Washington. It's not our money; it's your money. When I think about the budget, I think about difficult issues like mandatory spending in So-

cial Security and Medicare and how we've got to have political will to not play "gotcha" with the issue but focus on solving it for a generation coming up. When I think about the budget, I think about people that suffer from Hurricane Katrina. When I think about the budget, I think about our troops that are doing everything they can to spread freedom and democracy so we're safe at home.

And so the budget—you'll hear numbers this, numbers that, but you've got to know that those of us who put it together really do see the human dimension behind good budgeting. Ours is a nation that is a generous nation and a compassionate nation. Ours is a nation that I truly believe can achieve anything we put our mind to. And in terms of our economic future, we shouldn't fear it, because we're going to shape it and continue to lead the world so that people who are in this country have got a high quality of life.

I really appreciate you giving me the chance to come back up here to New Hampshire. May God bless your wonderful State, and may God continue to bless our country.

NOTE: The President spoke at 11:33 a.m. at the Radisson Hotel Manchester-Center of New Hampshire. In his remarks, he referred to W. Douglas Scamman, Jr., speaker, New Hampshire State House of Representatives; Mayor Frank C. Guinta of Manchester, NH; George Gantz, chair, and Mike Donahue, chair-elect, board of directors, Business and Industry Association of New Hampshire.

Remarks on Signing the Deficit Reduction Act of 2005
February 8, 2006

Please be seated. Thanks for coming. Welcome to the White House. In a few moments, I will sign the Deficit Reduction Act of 2005. This important piece of legisla-

tion restrains Federal spending, and it will leave more money in the pockets of those who know how to use it best, the American people.

I appreciate the Vice President being here. Mr. Speaker, welcome, Leader Frist—thank you all for coming. Senator McConnell; Senator Santorum; Senator Judd Gregg, chairman of the Senate Budget Committee; Congressman John Boehner, the House majority leader; Roy Blunt, the House Majority Whip; Congressman Nussle, chairman of the House Budget Committee—I want to thank you all for coming. I appreciate the members of the Cabinet who are here, as well as all the Members of the United States Congress and the Senate who have come for this important bill signing.

Our economy is strong, and it's getting stronger. We're now entering our fifth year of uninterrupted economic growth, and last year, our economy grew at a healthy 3.5 percent. Real after-tax income is up nearly 8 percent per American since 2001. Productivity growth is high. Small businesses are thriving. America has added 4.7 million new jobs over the last 2½ years. The unemployment rate is down to 4.7 percent, the lowest level since July 2001.

Our economy leads the world, yet we cannot be complacent. To keep our economic momentum, we need to look at the challenges down the road and respond with wise policies now. And one of the most important policies we need to pursue is spending restraint in Washington, DC.

Earlier this week, I sent Congress a disciplined Federal budget for 2007, and this morning I traveled to New Hampshire with Chairman Gregg, Senator Sununu, Congressman Bass, and Congressman Bradley to discuss the new budget proposal in detail. The budget strategy begins with keeping taxes low so that Americans can spend, save, and invest more of their own money—and that will help keep our economy growing and creating jobs. My budget funds our priorities, starting with funding the United States military, promoting alternative sources of energy, investing in math and science education and basic research,

and helping to care for the poor and the elderly.

At the same time, my budget tightens the belt on Government spending. Every American family has to set priorities and live within a budget, and the American people expect us to do the same right here in Washington, DC.

The Federal budget has two types of spending, discretionary spending and mandatory spending. Discretionary spending is the kind of spending Congress votes on every year. Last year, Congress met my request and passed bills that cut discretionary spending not related to defense or homeland security. And this year, my budget again proposes to cut this spending. My budget also proposes again to keep the growth in overall discretionary spending below the rate of inflation, so we can stay on track to cut the deficit in half by 2009.

In the long run, the biggest challenge to our budget is mandatory spending, or entitlement programs like Medicare and Medicaid and Social Security. Entitlement spending is determined by a specific formula, and it rises automatically, year after year, unless the Congress intervenes. Together, Medicare, Medicaid, and Social Security are now growing faster than the economy, faster than the population, and nearly three times the rate of inflation. And the retirement of baby boom generation will put even more strains on these programs. By 2030, spending for Medicare, Medicaid, and Social Security alone will be almost 60 percent of the entire Federal budget. And that will leave future generations with impossible choices: staggering tax increases, immense deficits, or deep cuts in every category of spending.

Bringing entitlement spending under control is a critical priority of our Government. We need to slow the annual growth of entitlement programs to levels that we can afford; we do not need to cut these programs. There is an important distinction; it is the difference between slowing your car down to the speed limit or putting your car into reverse. By making wise reforms that will reduce the annual growth of mandatory spending, the Deficit Reduction Act will save taxpayers nearly $40 billion over the next 5 years; that's about $300 per taxpayer.

The Deficit Reduction Act is estimated to slow the pace of spending growth in both Medicare and Medicaid. Medicare is a Federal program that provides health care for older Americans. Medicaid is a program administered in conjunction with the States that provides health care for low-income Americans, family with children, and some seniors. These programs are providing vital services to millions of Americans in need, yet the costs of Medicare and Medicaid are straining budgets at both the State and Federal level. The bill I sign today restrains spending for entitlement programs, while ensuring that Americans who rely on Medicare and Medicaid continue to get the care they need.

The Deficit Reduction Act is estimated to reduce the growth in Medicare spending by more than $6 billion over the next 5 years. The bill, together with the Medicare act of 2003, requires wealthier citizens to pay higher premiums for their Medicare coverage. The savings created by this reform and others will make it possible to increase Federal funding for important areas like kidney dialysis and rural hospitals. With this bill, we're showing that we can keep the promise of Medicare and be good stewards of the taxpayers' money at the same time.

The Deficit Reduction Act will also reduce the growth in Medicaid spending by nearly $5 billion over the next 5 years. This bill helps restrain Medicaid spending by reducing Federal overpayment for prescription drugs. Taxpayers should not have to pay inflated markups for the medicine that the people on Medicaid depend. The bill gives Governors more flexibility to design Medicaid benefits that meet the needs of their States efficiently and affordably. The bill tightens the loopholes that allowed peo-

ple to game the system by transferring assets to their children so they can qualify for Medicaid benefits. Along with Governors of both parties, we are sending a clear message: Medicaid will always provide help for those in need, but we will never tolerate waste, fraud, or abuse.

The Deficit Reduction Act's reforms in Medicare and Medicaid are a step on the road to long-term stability for these important programs. Now, we need to continue finding ways to make Medicare and Medicaid more efficient. My budget next year proposes another $36 billion in savings on Medicare and more than a billion in savings on Medicaid. Budget proposals will slow the annual growth in Medicare over the next 5 years from 8.1 percent to 7.7 percent. That seems reasonable. And together with the bill I sign today, my budget will slow the average annual growth of Medicaid over the next 5 years from 6.9 percent a year to 6.6 percent a year. This is progress in the right direction, but these growth rates are still unsustainable.

In the long run, ensuring the stability of Medicare and Medicaid requires structural reform. So I have proposed a bipartisan commission to examine the full impact of baby boomer retirements on Medicare and Medicaid as well as Social Security. The commission will include Members of Congress from both political parties. It will recommend long-term solutions that will keep the promise of these vital programs while addressing their growing costs. I look forward to working with Congress to get this problem solved for generations to come.

As the Deficit Reduction Act delivers savings in mandatory spending, it also shows the compassion of America. This bill provides new resources for programs that serve some of our citizens with the greatest needs, including hurricane victims, children, and low-income families struggling to pay their heating bills.

The Deficit Reduction Act makes important improvements to Federal student loan programs. The bill cuts excess Government subsidies to lenders and makes other reforms that will help us reduce overall student loan costs by about $22 billion. With that money, we will save the taxpayers $12 billion—because we intend to increase student aid by 10 additional billion dollars. What I'm telling you is, the students are getting the money, and we're making the program a lot more efficient for the taxpayers.

The Deficit Reduction Act also reauthorizes welfare reform for another 5 years. Welfare reform has proved a tremendous success over the past decade. By insisting on programs that require work and self-sufficiency in return for Federal aid, we've helped cut welfare cases by more than half since 1996. Now we're building on that progress by renewing welfare reform with a billion-dollar increase in child care funding and new grants to support healthy marriage and responsible fatherhood programs.

One of the reasons for the success of welfare reform is a policy called charitable choice, which allows faith-based groups that provide social services to receive Federal funding without changing the way they hire. Ten years ago, Congress made welfare the first Federal program to include charitable choice. The bill I sign today will extend charitable choice for another 5 years and expand it to the new healthy marriage and responsible fatherhood programs. Appreciate the hard work of all who supported the extension of charitable choice, including the good-hearted men and women of the faith-based community who are here today. By reauthorizing welfare reform with charitable choice, we will help millions more Americans move from welfare to work and find independence and dignity and hope.

The message of the bill I sign today is straightforward: By setting priorities and making sure tax dollars are spent wisely, America can be compassionate and responsible at the same time. Spending restraint demands difficult choices, yet making those choices is what the American people sent us to Washington to do. One of our most important responsibilities is to keep this economy strong and vibrant and secure for our children and our grandchildren. We can be proud that we're helping to meet that responsibility today.

Now I ask the Members of the Congress to join me as I sign the Deficit Reduction Act of 2005.

NOTE: The President spoke at 3:31 p.m. in the East Room at the White House. S. 1932, approved February 8, was assigned Public Law No. 109–171.

Statement on Signing the Deficit Reduction Act of 2005
February 8, 2006

Today, I have signed into law S. 1932, the "Deficit Reduction Act of 2005." The Act reduces unnecessary spending of taxpayer dollars, reflecting a commitment to fiscal responsibility.

The executive branch shall construe section 1936(d)(2) of the Social Security Act as enacted by section 6034 of the Act, which purports to make consultation with a legislative agent a precondition to execution of the law, to call for but not mandate such consultation, as is consistent with the Constitution's provisions concerning the separate powers of the Congress to legislate and the President to execute the laws.

Sections 5006(b) and 5008(c) of the Act, and section 401A(a)(2)(C) of the Higher Education Act of 1965 as enacted by section 8003 of the Act, call for executive branch officials to submit legislative recommendations to the Congress. The executive branch shall construe such provisions in a manner consistent with the constitutional authority of the President to supervise the unitary executive branch and to recommend for congressional consideration such measures as the President shall judge necessary and expedient.

GEORGE W. BUSH

The White House,
February 8, 2006.

NOTE: An original was not available for the verification of the content of this statement.

Message to the Congress Reporting on the Executive Order on Blocking Property of Certain Persons Contributing to the Conflict in Cote d'Ivoire
February 8, 2006

To the Congress of the United States:

Consistent with subsection 204(b) of the International Emergency Economic Powers Act, 50 U.S.C. 1703(b) (IEEPA), and section 301 of the National Emergencies Act, 50 U.S.C. 1631 (NEA), I hereby report that I have issued an Executive Order (the "order") blocking the property of certain persons contributing to the conflict in Cote d'Ivoire. In that order, I declared a national emergency to deal with the unusual and extraordinary threat to the national security and foreign policy of the United States posed by that conflict, as described below.

The United Nations Security Council, in Resolution 1572 of November 15, 2004, expressed deep concern over the resumption of hostilities in Cote d'Ivoire, the public incitement of hatred and violence, and the repeated violations of the ceasefire agreement of May 3, 2003. United Nations Security Council Resolution (UNSCR) 1572 determined that the situation in Cote d'Ivoire poses a threat to international peace and security in the region and called on member States to take certain measures against persons responsible for the continuing conflict. The United Nations Security Council has continued to express serious concern at the persistence of the crisis in Cote d'Ivoire and of obstacles to the peace and national reconciliation process from all sides in UNSCRs 1643 of December 15, 2005, and 1652 of January 24, 2006.

Despite the intervention and efforts of the international community, there have been massacres of large numbers of civilians, widespread human rights abuses, significant political violence and unrest, and attacks against international peacekeeping forces in Cote d'Ivoire. Such activity includes the killing of large numbers of civilians in Korhogo in June 2004, and in Abidjan in March 2004; significant violence and unrest, including public incitements to violence, in Abidjan in November 2004; human rights violations, including extrajudicial killings, in western Cote d'Ivoire in April and June 2005; attacks on a police station and prison in July 2005 in Anyama and Agboville, and violent protests in Abidjan and attacks on U.N. and international nongovernmental organization facilities in western Cote d'Ivoire in January 2006. Also, notwithstanding the Linas-Marcoussis Agreement signed by the Ivorian political forces on January 24, 2003, the related ceasefire agreement of May 3, 2003, the Accra III Agreement of July 30, 2004, the Pretoria Agreement of April 6, 2005, and the Declaration on the Implementation of the Pretoria Agreement of June 29, 2005, consolidating the implementation of the Linas-Marcoussis peace and national reconciliation process, Ivorian parties have continued to engage in military operations and attacks against peacekeeping forces in Cote d'Ivoire leading to fatalities.

Pursuant to the IEEPA and the NEA, I have determined that these actions and circumstances constitute an unusual and extraordinary threat to the national security and foreign policy of the United States and declared a national emergency to deal with that threat and have issued an Executive Order to deal with the threat to U.S. national security and foreign policy posed by the situation in or in relation to Cote d'Ivoire.

The order blocks the property and interests in property in the United States, or in the possession or control of United States persons, of the persons listed in the Annex to the order, as well as of any person determined by the Secretary of the Treasury, after consultation with the Secretary of State,

- to constitute a threat to the peace and national reconciliation process in Cote d'Ivoire, such as by blocking the implementation of the Linas-Marcoussis, Accra III, and Pretoria Agreements;
- to be responsible for serious violations of international law in Cote d'Ivoire;
- to have directly or indirectly supplied, sold or transferred to Cote d'Ivoire arms or any related materiel or any assistance, advice, or training related to military activities; or
- to have publicly incited violence and hatred contributing to the conflict in Cote d'Ivoire.

The designation criteria will be applied in accordance with applicable domestic law, including where appropriate, the First Amendment to the United States Constitution. The order also authorizes the Sec-

retary of the Treasury, after consultation with the Secretary of State, to designate for blocking any person determined to have materially assisted, sponsored, or provided financial, material, or technological support for, or goods or services in support of, the activities listed above or any person listed in or designated pursuant to the order. I further authorized the Secretary of the Treasury, after consultation with the Secretary of State, to designate for blocking any person determined to be owned or controlled by, or acting or purporting to act for or on behalf of, directly or indirectly, any person listed in or designated pursuant to the order. The Secretary of the Treasury, after consultation with the Secretary of State, is also authorized to remove any persons from the Annex to the order as circumstances warrant.

I delegated to the Secretary of the Treasury, after consultation with the Secretary of State, the authority to take such actions, including the promulgation of rules and regulations, and to employ all powers granted to the President by the IEEPA and the United Nations Participation Act, as may be necessary to carry out the purposes of the order. All executive agencies are directed to take all appropriate measures within their authority to carry out the provisions of the order.

The order, a copy of which is enclosed, became effective at 12:01 a.m. eastern standard time on February 8, 2006.

GEORGE W. BUSH

The White House,
February 8, 2006.

NOTE: The Executive order is listed in Appendix D at the end of this volume.

Remarks to the National Guard Association of the United States
February 9, 2006

Please be seated. Thanks for that warm welcome. I'm delighted to be here with the men and women of the National Guard Association of the United States. For 128 years, the National Guard Association has been fighting for the citizen soldiers who fight for America. I appreciate your service, and I appreciate you supporting those that America depends on in times of crisis. Our Nation is safer because citizens are willing to put on the uniform and defend our freedom.

The first thing I want to tell you is America is grateful for the service of our guards men and women, and I'm proud to be their Commander in Chief.

I thank Brigadier General Bob Taylor for his service and for his introduction. I appreciate Congressman Jim Gibbons, who is with us today, from the great State of Nevada. Thanks for coming, Congressman. I'm proud you're here. Thanks for supporting the Guard.

I thank Brigadier General Steve Koper, retired president of the National Guard Association of the United States. General, thank you for greeting me. I'm proud to be here with Major General Roger Lempke, the president of the Adjutants General Association. I thank my friend Lieutenant General Danny James. One of the interesting things about my life, I've been the Commander in Chief twice: today and when I was the Governor of Texas. And Danny and I worked together for the good of our State. Thanks for coming, Danny; glad to see you brought your beautiful wife too.

I want to thank Lewis King; he's the Chief Warrant Officer, retired. He helped raise the money for this box, and I appreciate it very much, Lewis, and all those who contributed to it. I want to thank Charles Parks, the sculptor. Charles caught me before my hair went gray. [*Laughter*]

I also want to thank Lanny McNeely for joining us today; he's the head of the 147th Wing Guard at Ellington, where I used to serve. And I appreciate you coming, Colonel. Thanks for being here. Thanks for greeting me when I arrived there, on Air Force One there at Ellington—checking on my mother and father on a regular basis. I also want to thank Chuck Rodriguez, who's the TAG of Texas. When you're a Texan, you always got to make sure you pay attention to your fellow Texans.

And thank you all for having me. I want to share with you some thoughts about the war on terror. Before I do, I want to remind our country that the Guard has been fighting for America since before America was a nation. From the First Muster in 1636 to today's global war on terror, Americans have counted on the Guard to protect our land and defend our way of life. The role of the Guard in our military is unique. It's the only part of the Armed Forces that serves both the State and the Nation. And in the past year, Americans have witnessed the courage of our guards men and women at home and abroad.

When Hurricane Katrina struck the gulf coast last year, more than 40,000 guards men and women rushed to the impact zone; it was the largest stateside deployment in National Guard history. They conducted search and rescue operations, distributed food and water, provided emergency medical care, protected communities from criminality, and worked around the clock to repair homes and restore power. Guard units from all 50 States, three U.S. territories, and the District of Columbia provided assistance. And together, they saved lives and helped evacuate over 175,000 people stranded by the storm.

When the Pennsylvania National Guard came to repair the roof of a Louisiana woman, she said this to the soldiers: "That's a long way to come to help us. We're really grateful. You boys are going to heaven, I tell you." [*Laughter*] When tragedy strikes, Americans know they can count on the men and women of the National Guard.

As you protect your neighbors from natural disasters, you're also protecting the American people from terrorist dangers. Since September the 11th, 2001, more than 260,000 members of the National Guard have been mobilized for various missions in the war on terror. At this moment, guards men and women are training the Afghan National Army, standing watch over the world's most dangerous terrorists in Guantanamo Bay, Cuba, and taking the fight to the enemy in Iraq. Across the world and on every front, the men and women of the Guard are serving with courage and determination. And they're bringing us to victory in the global war on terror.

Your service is vital to the security of the country and the peace of the world, and that service would not be possible without the support of the Guard families. Guard loved ones miss their husband and wife or son and daughter; they worry when our guardspeople are deployed overseas. By standing behind our guards men and women, the families of the Guard serve our country as well, and America appreciates their service.

Our Nation also depends on the commitments of the employers of the guards men and women. In offices and schools and factories across America, organizations do without the talents of some really fine people that have been called upon to protect our Nation. Businesses that are putting patriotism ahead of profit deserve the gratitude of all Americans.

Each of the guards men and women have stepped forward to defend our country, and our country owes them something in return. We've taken a number of steps to improve the callup process so it's more respectful to the guards men and women and their families. In most cases, we're now giving you at least 30 days notification be-

fore mobilization so that you and your families have time to make arrangements. We're working to give you as much certainty as possible about the length of mobilizations so you can know when you will be able to resume civilian life. We're working to minimize the number of extensions and repeat mobilizations. We're working to ensure that you and your families are treated with the dignity they deserve.

We're also taking steps to improve the quality of life. We've expanded health care benefits for Guard and Reserve forces and their families, giving you access to the military's TRICARE system. We're also expanding access to education for America's citizen soldiers. I was proud to sign legislation providing our Guard and Reserve forces between 40 to 80 percent of education benefits available to Active-Duty Forces—depending on the length of their mobilization in the war on terror. We've also tripled the amount that can be paid for re-enlisting in the National Guard or Reserve. The last month, I signed into law a new retention bonus for guardsmen and reservists with critical skills needed in this war on terror. Our guardsmen and reservists are standing up for America, and you need to know that this administration supports you in your efforts.

We're working to give you the tools and resources you need to prevail in the war on terror and meet State and homeland security missions as well. Our 2007 budget that I just submitted to the Congress increases funding for our men and women of Armed Forces by $28.5 billion. That includes vital funds to help the National Guard meet its responsibilities during this war.

The Army National Guard currently has about 330,000 soldiers, and my 2007 budget funds the Guard at that level. As the Guard recruits above that level, we'll make certain that there is funding in place for every citizen who steps forward to wear the uniform. And to ensure that the Army and our Air National Guard are ready for any challenge, my budget more than doubles funding for equipment and modernization over the next 5 years. Any time we've got folks in harm's way, they deserve the best: the best pay possible, the best training possible, and the best equipment possible. It's a commitment this administration has made since I've been the Commander in Chief, and it's a commitment we will keep.

We remain a nation at war. I wish I could report, you know, a different sentence to you. But my job as the President of the United States is to keep the American people fully informed of the world in which we live. In recent months, I've spoken extensively about our strategy for victory in Iraq. Today I'm going to give you an update on the progress that we're making in the broader war on terror, the actions of our global coalition to break up terrorist networks across the world, plots we've disrupted that have saved American lives, and how the rise of freedom is leading millions to reject the dark ideology of the terrorists and laying the foundation of peace for generations to come.

On September the 11th, 2001, our Nation saw that vast oceans and great distances could no longer keep us safe. I made a decision that day that America will not wait to be attacked again. And since that day, we've taken decisive action to protect our citizens against new dangers. We're hunting down the terrorists using every element of our national power: military, intelligence, law enforcement, diplomatic, and financial. We're clarifying the choice facing every nation: In this struggle between freedom and terror, every nation has responsibilities, and no one can remain neutral.

Since September the 11th, we've led a broad coalition to confront the terrorist threat. Four weeks after the attacks, America and our allies launched military operations to eliminate the terrorists' principal sanctuary in the nation of Afghanistan. I told the world that if you harbor a terrorist, you're equally as guilty as the terrorists. And when an American President says

something, he better mean what he said; I meant what I said.

We removed a cruel regime that oppressed its people, brutalized women and girls, and gave safe haven to the terrorists who attacked America. Because we acted, the terror camps in Afghanistan have been shut down and 25 million people have tasted freedom, many for the first time in their lives. Afghanistan now has a democratically elected President, a new National Assembly, and the beginnings of a market economy. Women are working and starting their own businesses. Boys and girls are back in school. The Afghan people are building the institutions of a lasting democracy and the foundations of a hopeful future for their children and their grandchildren.

Afghanistan still faces serious challenges, from illicit drug trafficking to continued violence from Al Qaida and the remnants of the Taliban regime. So the international community is working together to help Afghanistan's young democracy succeed. Earlier this month, Prime Minister Tony Blair hosted over 40 nations and 9 international organizations for a conference in London, where they pledged $10.5 billion in aid to Afghanistan. With the help of 35 nations, NATO is leading the International Security Assistance Force in Afghanistan.

The United States, Britain, Norway, Germany, Italy, Spain, Lithuania, Canada, the Netherlands, and New Zealand are all leading Provincial Reconstruction Teams. These teams are helping the Afghan Government extend its authority and provide security in provinces all across the country. Our coalition has trained nearly 27,000 Afghan soldiers and more than 56,000 Afghan police, so they can take the fight to the terrorists and eventually provide security for this new democracy. Afghan forces are risking their lives to fight our common enemy, and coalition forces are proud to serve along with such courageous and bold and determined allies.

Our coalition is also working to root out and destroy terrorist networks all around the world. More than 90 nations—nearly half the world—are now cooperating in the global campaign to dry up terrorist financing, hunt down terrorist operatives, and bring terrorist leaders to justice.

Some said that an aggressive strategy of bringing the war to the terrorists would cost us international support; it would drive nations from our coalition. The opposite has happened. Today, more governments are cooperating in the fight against terror than ever before. And in one of the most significant developments of this war, many nations that once turned a blind eye to terror are now helping lead the fight against it.

A little over 4 years ago, Pakistan was only one of three countries in the world that recognized the Taliban regime in Afghanistan. Today, Pakistan forces are risking their lives in the hunt for Al Qaida. President Musharraf has faced several attempts on his life since his courageous decision to join the war on terror. Before September the 11th, terrorist supporters were operating with relative ease in Saudi Arabia, where fundraisers and facilitators were providing money and logistical support to Al Qaida. Since the Riyadh bombings in May of 2003, the Saudi Government has recognized that it is a prime target of the terrorists. And in the past 2½ years, Saudi forces have killed or captured nearly all of the terrorists on their most-wanted list. They've reduced the flow of money to terror groups and arrested hundreds of radical fighters bound for Iraq.

These governments are taking important steps to confront terror, and as they do, we will continue to encourage them to take the path of political reform. By respecting the rights and choices of their own people, these nations can marginalize the extremists, strengthen their societies, and eliminate the conditions that feed radicalism.

These and other governments around the world are stepping forward to fight the terrorists because they know the lives of their citizens are at stake. President Musharraf said something interesting: "Terrorism threatens to destabilize all modern societies. It cannot be condoned for any reason or cause. The people of Pakistan have suffered from terrorism, and we are making our contribution to the fight against terrorism." President Musharraf is right. In the war against terror, there is no separate peace, and no nation can stand on the sidelines.

By standing together, the United States and our partners are striking real blows against the enemy. Since September the 11th, 2001, our coalition has captured or killed Al Qaida managers and operatives in over two dozen countries. That includes many of Al Qaida's operational commanders, the senior leaders responsible for day-to-day planning of terrorist activities across the globe. In November 2001, our coalition forces killed Muhammad Atif with an air strike in Afghanistan. In March 2003, his replacement, Khalid Sheikh Mohammed, was captured in Pakistan. In May 2005, the man who took over for him, a terrorist named al-Libbi, was captured in South Asia.

The terrorists are living under constant pressure, and this adds to our security. When terrorists spend their days working to avoid death or capture, it's harder for them to plan and execute new attacks on our country. By striking the terrorists where they live, we are protecting the American homeland.

Since September the 11th, the United States and our coalition partners have disrupted a number of serious Al Qaida terrorist plots, including plots to attack targets inside the United States. Let me give you an example. In the weeks after September the 11th, while Americans were still recovering from an unprecedented strike on our homeland, Al Qaida was already busy planning its next attack. We now know that in October 2001, Khalid Sheikh Mohammed—the mastermind of the September the 11th attacks—had already set in motion a plan to have terrorist operatives hijack an airplane, using shoe bombs to breach the cockpit door, and fly the plane into the tallest building on the west coast. We believe the intended target was Liberty [Library]° Tower in Los Angeles, California.

Rather than use Arab hijackers as he had on September the 11th, Khalid Sheikh Mohammed sought out young men from Southeast Asia, whom he believed would not arouse as much suspicion. To help carry out this plan, he tapped a terrorist named Hambali, one of the leaders of an Al Qaida affiliated group in Southeast Asia called JI. JI terrorists were responsible for a series of deadly attacks in Southeast Asia, and members of the group had trained with Al Qaida. Hambali recruited several key operatives who had been training in Afghanistan. Once the operatives were recruited, they met with Usama bin Laden, and then began preparations for the west coast attack.

Their plot was derailed in early 2002 when a Southeast Asian nation arrested a key Al Qaida operative. Subsequent debriefings and other intelligence operations made clear the intended target and how Al Qaida hoped to execute it. This critical intelligence helped other allies capture the ringleaders and other known operatives who had been recruited for this plot. The west coast plot had been thwarted. Our efforts did not end there. In the summer of 2003, our partners in Southeast Asia conducted another successful manhunt that led to the capture of the terrorist Hambali.

As the west coast plot shows, in the war on terror, we face a relentless and determined enemy that operates in many nations, so protecting our citizens requires unprecedented cooperation from many nations as well. It took the combined efforts of several countries to break up this plot. By working together, we took dangerous terrorists off the streets; by working to-gether, we stopped a catastrophic attack on our homeland.

Across the world, our coalition is pursuing the enemy with relentless determination. And because of these efforts, the terrorists are weakened and fractured, yet they're still lethal. We cannot let the fact that America hasn't been attacked in 4½ years, since September the 11th, lull us into an illusion that the threats to our Nation have disappeared. They have not. Just last month, we heard Usama bin Laden declare his intention to attack America again. Our military, law enforcement, homeland security, and intelligence professionals take those threats very seriously, and they're working around the clock, day and night, to protect us. We are safer for their efforts, but we're not yet safe. America remains at risk, so we must remain vigilant. We will stay on the offensive. We will hunt down the terrorists, and we will never rest until this threat to the American people is removed.

We will continue to take the fight to the enemy. Yet we must also recognize in the long run, victory will require more than military means alone. Ultimately, the only way to defeat the terrorists is to defeat their dark vision of hatred and fear by spreading the hope of freedom to troubled regions of the world. The terrorists have an ideology. They share a hateful vision that rejects tolerance and crushes all dissent, a world where women are oppressed and children are indoctrinated and those who reject their ideology of violence and extremists are threatened and often murdered.

The terrorists have aims. They seek to impose their heartless ideology of totalitarian control throughout the Middle East and arm themselves with weapons of mass murder. Their stated goal is to overthrow moderate governments, take control of countries, and use them as safe havens to launch attacks against America. When an enemy states a goal and a strategy and tactics, we must take their word seriously.

° White House correction.

To achieve their aims, the terrorists need popular support. We know this from the terrorists' own words. In a letter to his chief of operations in Iraq, the terrorist Zawahiri wrote that popular support is, quote, "a decisive factor between victory and defeat. In the absence of this popular support, the movement would be crushed in the shadows." He went on to say, "Therefore, our planning must strive to involve the Muslim masses in the battle."

So a key part of the terrorists' strategy is to feed public resentment by convincing people across the Muslim world that the future holds just two choices: one of Islam and holiness and virtue; and one of Western decadence, immorality, and imperialism. They use every opportunity to promote this false choice. Sometimes they spread blatant lies about America. Other times, it is American mistakes—like the abuses of Abu Ghraib—that give them ammunition in their campaign to foment anti-Western sentiment and rally Muslims to support their dark ideology.

The problem for the terrorists is they cannot hide the inhumanity of their ideology. Because they lack the military strength to challenge us directly, they have turned to the weapon of fear. They seek to break our will with stunning acts of violence. They don't understand America. They cannot shake our will. We will stay on the hunt. We will never give in, and we will win this war on terror.

In the terrorists' campaign of violence and destruction, the majority of their victims since 9/11 have been innocent Muslims. When the people in the Arab world see Al Qaida murdering Iraqi children or blowing up mourners in an Iraqi mosque, their outrage grows. And as the terrorists spread violence in places like Riyadh and Istanbul and Sharm el-Sheikh and Jakarta and Bali, the people of those countries are starting to turn against the terrorists.

After terrorists bombed a Palestinian wedding at a hotel in Amman last November, thousands of Jordanians took to the street and rallied against Al Qaida. One protester carried a sign that read, "Jordan's Nine-Eleven." Others chanted, "This is not Islamic; this is terrorism!" The outrage even reached the Jordanian town of Zarqa, birthplace of the terrorist Zarqawi, who heads Al Qaida in Iraq and who was the mastermind of the Jordan bombing. A cousin standing outside the Al Qaida leader family home said this: "We hate him even more than other people do now." Zarqawi was even expelled by his own tribesmen, hundreds of whom declared in a letter to a Jordanian newspaper, quote, "We renounce his actions, pronouncements, or whatever he approves of. We disown him until judgment day."

Before the bombings, most Jordanians reportedly sympathized with Al Qaida. Today, only a minority sympathize with Al Qaida, and most Jordanians say its activities are not in conformity with the teachings of Islam. Similar shifts in public opinion are beginning to appear in other parts of the Muslim world. From Pakistan to Indonesia to Al Qaida's former home base of Afghanistan, more people now say they oppose the terrorists and their tactics.

These are positive signs, but we still have a long way to go. So we'll continue to oppose the terrorists' ideology by offering the hopeful alternative of political freedom and peaceful change. We're working to spread the hope of liberty across the broader Middle East, because we've learned the lessons of history: Free nations don't wage wars of aggression; they don't give safe haven to terrorists to attack other democracies. Free nations are peaceful nations. And when democracy takes hold, nations replace resentment with hope, respect the rights of their citizens and their neighbors, and join the fight against the terrorists. Every step toward freedom in the world makes this country safer, so across the world, the United States of America is acting boldly in freedom's cause.

We're standing with the brave people of Iraq as they risk their lives to build a strong democracy in the heart of the Middle East. And their courage is changing their country, and it's changing the region, and it's changing the world. Before January 2005 elections, the terrorists threatened anybody who voted with death. The Iraqi people defied the threats and went to the polls in that election and two other elections last year, each with larger and broader participation than the one that came before. Iraqis are rejecting terror; they're rejecting the violence. And they want to replace terror and violence with openness and democracy. They have made their decision, and the world saw their decision. They're showing the world that the terrorists' ideology cannot compete on a level playing field with the ideology of freedom.

Iraqis still face challenges, and they're serious. The terrorists and Saddamists continue to sow violence and terror, and they will continue fighting freedom's progress with all the hateful determination they can muster. The Iraqis still have to overcome long-standing ethnic and religious tensions, and they must build the institutions of a free society that will serve all the people, not narrow political or religious interests. These challenges ahead are complex and difficult, yet the Iraqis are determined to overcome them, and our coalition is determined to help the Iraqi people succeed.

We're carrying out a clear strategy for victory in Iraq. First, we're helping the Iraqis build an inclusive government, so that old resentments will be eased and the insurgency marginalized. Second, we're continuing reconstruction efforts and helping Iraqis build a modern economy, so all Iraqi citizens can experience the benefits of freedom. And third, we're striking the terrorist targets. We're after the terrorists, and at the same time, we're training Iraqi forces, which are becoming increasingly capable of defeating the enemy. The Iraqi forces show courage every day. We are proud to be the allies in the cause of freedom. As Iraqis stand up, America and our coalition will stand down.

Many of you are concerned about troop levels in Iraq. Those decisions will be made based upon conditions on the ground, based upon the recommendations of our military commanders, not based upon politics in Washington, DC.

The courage of Iraqis is inspiring others across the broader Middle East to claim their freedom as well. And the message is going forth, from Damascus to Tehran, that the future of the Middle East belongs to freedom. As liberty spreads in this vital region and freedom produces opportunity and hope for those who have not known it, the terrorist temptation will start to fall away. And as more nations claim their freedom, we will gain new allies in the war on terror and new partners in the battle for peace and moderation in the Muslim world.

Before that day comes, there will be more days of testing. The terrorists remain brutal and determined, and they still have some resources at their disposal. The attacks in London and Madrid and other cities are grim reminders of how lethal Al Qaida remains. Money is still flowing to radical mosques and madrassas, which are still turning out new terrorist recruits. Some countries, like Syria and Iran, still provide terrorists with support and sanctuary. And the terrorists are sophisticated at spreading propaganda and using spectacular attacks to dominate our evening news.

Yet from the vantage point of a terrorist sitting in a cave, the future seems increasingly bleak. Consider how the world looks 4½ years into the war on terror: The terrorists have lost their home base in Afghanistan and no longer have control of a country where they can train recruits and plot new attacks; many of their leaders are dead or in custody, and the rest of them are on the run; they've been reduced to using messengers to communicate; they're running low on funds and have been forced to beg the terrorists in Iraq to send money; countries that once allowed them free reign are now on the hunt.

Their efforts to divide the West have largely failed, and the vast majority of the world's governments are standing firm and working together in the fight against those terrorists. Iraqis are forming a unity government instead of giving into disunity, instead of fighting the civil war that the terrorists hoped to foment. Iraqi Sunnis are joining the political process. The success of democracy in Iraq and Afghanistan is inspiring calls for change across the region. And the terrorists' strategy of attacking innocent Muslims is beginning to backfire and expose them for what they are: murderers with no respect for human life and human dignity.

Despite the violence and the suffering the terrorists are wreaking, we're winning the war on terror. Yet victory will require more courage and sacrifice. In this war, we have said farewell to some very good men and women, including more than 360 heroes of the National Guard. We hold their loved ones in our hearts, and we lift them up in our prayers. These brave Americans gave their lives for a cause that is just and necessary for the security of our country. And their sacrifice is sparing millions from lives of tyranny and sorrow.

And now we will honor their sacrifice by completing the mission. And in this long run, we can be confident in the outcome of this struggle, because we've seen the power of freedom to defeat tyranny and terror before, and because we have on our side the greatest force for freedom in the history of the world: the men and women of the United States Armed Forces.

One of the great strengths of our military is that it's an all-volunteer army and all-volunteer force. And since the attacks of September the 11th, 2001, nearly 1.5 million Americans has stepped forward to put on our Nation's uniform, including nearly 290,000 who have joined the National Guard. Nearly 1.3 million more American troops have made the courageous decision to re-enlist and stay in the fight, including more than 350,000 members of the National Guard.

These brave Americans saw the future the terrorists intend for us, and they said, "Not on my watch." Four-and-a-half years into the fight, America's Armed Forces are determined, experienced, and ready for any challenge, and our Nation is blessed to have such brave defenders. All of you are bringing honor to the uniform and pride to our country and security to the American people. America will always be grateful for your service in the cause of freedom.

Thank you for letting me come today. God bless you and your families, and may God continue to bless our country.

NOTE: The President spoke at 10:03 a.m. at the National Guard Memorial Building. In his remarks, he referred to Brig. Gen. Robert V. Taylor, USA, assistant adjutant general, Michigan Army National Guard—Army, and chairman, National Guard Association of the United States; Lt. Gen. Daniel James, USAF, director, Air National Guard, and his wife, Dana; Maj. Gen. Charles G. Rodriguez, USA, adjutant general, Texas National Guard; President Hamid Karzai of Afghanistan; Prime Minister Tony Blair of the United Kingdom; President Pervez Musharraf of Pakistan; Abu Faraj al-Libbi, senior Al Qaida associate arrested in Pakistan on April 30, 2005; Nurjaman Riduan Isamuddin (also known as Hambali), Al Qaida's chief operational planner in Southeast Asia, who was captured in Thailand on August 11, 2003; Usama bin Laden, leader of the Al Qaida terrorist organization; and Ayman Al-Zawahiri, founder of the Egyptian Islamic Jihad and senior Al Qaida associate. The Office of the Press Secretary also released a Spanish language transcript of these remarks.

Remarks Following Discussions With President Lech Kaczynski of Poland
February 9, 2006

President Bush. Mr. President, welcome to the Oval Office. It's really good to have you here. We have just had a extensive discussion about important issues. After this press statement, we'll go have lunch and continue our discussions. And we've got a lot to discuss, because we're strong allies and friends. We're friends in liberty. We believe in peace.

I told the President it's amazing to be sitting with somebody who knows the difference between living in a society that is not independent and not free, and one that—and now he's the President of a free country. I thanked the President and the Polish people for their support of the democracy movement in Iraq.

We had a very interesting discussion about NATO and the European Union. You can be an active member of the EU, a loyal member of the EU, and a friend of the United States at the same time. I asked the President his advice on Ukraine. That's what friends do; they share information and share strategic thoughts.

We talked about the importance for commercial ties. We'll continue those discussions over lunch. The President of Poland comes to a country that respects Poland. There's a lot of Polish Americans that still got great pride for the homeland. We congratulate you on your victory and welcome you.

Thanks for coming.

President Kaczynski. President Bush has spoken of the subject of our talks. The first part has been extended, to a certain extent, and we will continue our discussions during lunch. We have discussed issues relating to NATO, the European Union, Belarus, Ukraine, and Russia and Iraq and Afghanistan. In other words, to speak—say very briefly, we've discussed all issues that both countries are interested in.

Mr. President and myself have discussed issues relating to freedom in Ukraine and Belarus. And the support of the United States for all actions that are leading to freedom in Ukraine and Belarus are very important for Poland at the same time. There have been certain signals that might lead to an improvement of relations between the Republic of Poland and the Russian Federation. We have no certainty yet, but these signals we have received, and we're hoping for an improvement in relations between Poland and Russia.

We shall continue our talks in a few minutes.

President Bush. Thank you, sir. Thank you.

NOTE: The President spoke at 11:57 a.m. in the Oval Office at the White House. President Kaczynski spoke in Polish, and his remarks were translated by an interpreter.

Statement on the Resignation of Claude Allen as Assistant to the President for Domestic Policy
February 9, 2006

Claude Allen has been a trusted adviser since 2001. As Deputy Secretary of Health and Human Services, he worked hard to improve the health and welfare of all Americans. During the past year, he has served as my top domestic policy adviser at the

White House and has helped develop policies that will strengthen our Nation's families, schools, and communities.

Claude is a good and compassionate man, and he has my deep respect and my gratitude. I thank him for his many years of principled and dedicated service to our country. Laura and I wish Claude, Jann, and their family all the best.

Remarks to the House Republican Conference in Cambridge, Maryland
February 10, 2006

Thank you all. Please be seated. Thank you very much. It's an honor to be back here again. Mr. Speaker, thank you for your leadership and your friendship. One of the real joys of being in Washington is to be able to work with Speaker Hastert. He is a straightforward—[*applause*]. Some of my buddies at home say, "What's he like?" I say, "He's a straightforward, no-nonsense kind of guy who's here to get things done." And, Mr. Speaker, thank you for your leadership and your friendship.

I congratulate the majority leader, John Boehner; looking forward to working with you, John. Congratulations to you. I appreciate Roy Blunt. He's a—right after I called Boehner from Air Force One, I called Blunt, and I said, "I want to say two things to you: One, thanks for waging the race for the majority leader; and second, thanks for passing the reconciliation package." He said, "If I could count votes as good on my race as I did on the reconciliation package"—[*laughter*]. But I appreciate a man who is gracious in defeat. But he's still got an important position, and I'm looking forward to working with you, Roy. Thank you.

I appreciate the rest of the folks up here. Thank you all for coming. It is an honor to serve our country with you. I hope you feel that way as well. There is nothing more heartwarming and exhilarating than to represent the good people of the United States of America here in Washington. I want to thank you all for your service. I particularly want to thank your families for your service to our country as well. The cause is noble and worthwhile.

A couple of things I want to say, and then I'll be glad to answer some of your questions. First, the state of our Union is strong, and it's getting stronger. And I want to thank you all for putting policies in place that, on the one hand, spread prosperity throughout the country and, at the same time, spread freedom and peace throughout the world.

You know, we've overcome a lot in this country. If you really think about what this economy has been through, it's amazing how resilient and flexible and strong our economy is. We're growing at faster rates than any major industrialized nation in the world. We've added over 4.5 million new jobs since April of 2003. The national unemployment rate is 4.7 percent. Productivity is high.

One of the things we've been working together is to promote an ownership society. More people own a home than ever before in our Nation's history. More minority families own a home than ever before in our Nation's history. Small businesses are thriving. The economic plan we put in place is working. And it starts with saying to the American people, "We trust you with your own money."

We've got a record, and it's a record of accomplishment. We have worked closely together to achieve results for the American people. We've been fiscally wise with the people's money. I want to thank you for that bill you sent me that I signed yesterday. It's hard work to cut out and cut back on programs that don't work. Every program sounds beautiful in Washington, DC, until you start analyzing the results. And I want to thank you for being wise with the people's money.

You know, you hear people in Washington, DC, saying, "Well, we've got to solve the deficit, and the best way to do it is raise the people's taxes." We understand that's not the way Washington works. What happens is, they'll raise your taxes and figure out new ways to spend your money. The best way to reduce the deficit is to keep progrowth policies in place and be wise with the taxpayers' money.

The House passed a good piece of legislation to help us secure our borders, and I want to thank you for that. The House passed good energy legislation last year. The House passed good tort reform last year, including class-action reform and bankruptcy. The House passed the PATRIOT Act last year. The House passed CAFTA last year. Last year was a year of accomplishment for the House of Representatives, thanks to the leadership here at the table.

And we're ready to lead again. We don't fear the future because we're going to shape the future of the United States of America. And that means supporting our troops in harm's way. I want to thank you for supporting the troops last year, and I look forward to working with you to support our troops this coming year.

We'll continue to lead. And I want to appreciate your steadfast support in the war on terror. Our most important responsibility is to protect the American people from harm. And I want to thank the Members of Congress for working with the administration to protect the American people from future attack.

You know, in my State of the Union— thanks for paying attention to it when I got up there the other day—[*laughter*]— I talked about how best to keep the country competitive. You know, some would lose confidence in the capacity of this country to lead, and kind of hide behind walls. That's not what we think. We're confident in America, and we're confident in our people, and we're confident that we can work together to put good policies in place that will keep this country the world's leader when it comes to the economy. So I'm looking forward to working with you to continue to be fiscally sound with the people's money and to put those tax cuts we put in place in a permanent status.

I'm looking forward to working with you on expanding health savings accounts so we can strengthen the doctor-patient relationship. I'm looking forward to working with you on making sure that we become less dependent on Middle Eastern oil by promoting alternative sources of energy. I'm looking forward to working with you on making sure our education system remains strong and our kids can learn math and science so we remain the most competitive nation in the world.

I'm looking forward to working with you, and I'm confident we'll continue the success we have had together. And so I've come to say thanks for your hard work in the past, and thanks for what we're going to do to make this country—to continue to be the greatest country on the face of the Earth.

God bless your work. May God continue to bless our country.

NOTE: The President spoke at 12:23 p.m. at the Hyatt Regency Chesapeake Bay.

The President's Radio Address
February 11, 2006

Good morning. Today I want to talk to you about the new Medicare prescription drug coverage that went into effect on January 1st of this year.

When I came into office, I found a Medicare system that was antiquated and not meeting the needs of America's seniors. The system would pay tens of thousands of dollars for a surgery but not a few hundred dollars for the prescription drugs that could have prevented the surgery in the first place. So working with Congress, we passed critical legislation that modernizes Medicare, provides seniors with more choices, and gives seniors better access to the prescription drugs they need.

Since the program went into effect 6 weeks ago, more than 24 million people with Medicare now have prescription drug coverage, and hundreds of thousands more are enrolling each week. The competition in the prescription drug market has been stronger than expected and is lowering costs for taxpayers and seniors alike. This year, the Federal Government will spend 20 percent less overall on the Medicare drug benefit than projected just last July. The average premium that seniors pay is a third less than had been expected—just $25 per month instead of $37 per month. And the typical senior will end up spending about half of what they used to spend on prescription drugs each year.

Last month in Oklahoma City, a senior named Dorothy Brown signed up for Medicare prescription drug coverage. Dorothy has six prescriptions, and previously she paid about $300 a month for her medicines. A Medicare enrollment counselor at a shopping mall helped Dorothy log on to the Medicare web site, where she typed the information on Dorothy's Medicare card and listed Dorothy's prescriptions. When the counselor was finished, the computer showed five different plans that fit Dorothy's needs. Dorothy chose the least expensive plan, and now, instead of paying $300 a month, she will pay about $36 a month for her medicines. As a result, Dorothy will save more than $3,000 this year.

For Dorothy and for the vast majority of our seniors, the new prescription drug program is working well. Still, when you make a big change in a program involving millions of people, there are bound to be some challenges, and this has been the case with the new drug coverage. Some people had trouble the first time they went to the pharmacy after enrolling. Information for some beneficiaries was not transferred smoothly between Medicare, drug plans, and the States. And in the early days of the drug coverage, waiting times were far too long for many customers and pharmacists who called Medicare or their drug plans to seek help.

Secretary of Health and Human Services Mike Leavitt has traveled to 18 States in the past 3 weeks to meet with Governors and make sure the prescription drug program is working for everyone, and we're making good progress. We're ensuring that drug plans have more up-to-date information on their beneficiaries, and we're improving data-sharing among Medicare, health plans, and the States. We have also extended the transition period from 30 days to 90 days, to guarantee that seniors do not go without the medicine they need as they switch to a new drug plan. We have also acted to ensure that phone calls to the Medicare help line are now answered with little or no waiting time, and we're working with insurers to help them do the same on their phone lines.

Despite early challenges, the results so far are clear: The new Medicare prescription drug plan is a good deal for seniors. If you're a Medicare recipient and have not yet signed up for prescription drug coverage, I encourage you to review your options and choose the plan that is right for you. Americans who have parents on Medicare should encourage and help them to sign up. Citizen groups, faith-based organizations, health professionals, and pharmacies across America are working to help answer questions. Seniors can also get information 24 hours a day by calling 1–800–MEDICARE or by visiting the official Medicare web site at medicare.gov.

Prescription drug coverage under Medicare has been available for just a few weeks, but its benefits will last for decades to come. I was proud to sign this Medicare reform into law. And because we acted, millions of American seniors are now saving money, getting the lifesaving drugs they need, and receiving the modern health care they deserve.

Thank you for listening.

NOTE: The address was recorded at 7:10 a.m. on February 10 in the Cabinet Room at the White House for broadcast at 10:06 a.m. on February 11. The transcript was made available by the Office of the Press Secretary on February 10 but was embargoed for release until the broadcast. The Office of the Press Secretary also released a Spanish language transcript of this address.

Remarks on Presenting the National Medals of Science and Technology
February 13, 2006

Thank you all. Please be seated. Thanks and welcome to the White House. It is an honor to be in the company of so many bright and distinguished Americans. Each of our honorees has been blessed with talent, and each has used their talent to the fullest.

The work we honor today has improved the lives of people everywhere. It has helped move our economy forward, and it's helped make sure that America is the leader of innovation in our world. The medals are our Nation's way of expressing gratitude to gifted and visionary citizens. I also appreciate the family members and friends who are here as well.

I want to thank members of my Cabinet who have joined us, Secretary Gutierrez, Secretary Bodman. I want to thank Dr. Jack Marburger, who is the Director of the Office of Science and Technology Policy. I thank David Sampson from Commerce for joining us. I want to thank Dr. Arden Bement, the Director of the National Science Foundation, who is with us, Dr. Kathie Olsen, the Deputy Director of the National Science Foundation. I want to thank the representatives from the National Science Foundation and members of the board of the National Science and Technology Medals Foundation. Those were the folks who decided that you won. [*Laughter*]

I thank Dr. Bill Jeffrey who is with us, Director of the National Institute of Standards and Technology. I want to thank the previous recipients of the National Medals of Science and Technology who've joined us. I thank my friends Congressman Sherry Boehlert, as well as Dave Reichert from the United States Congress for being here. Thank you both for coming. Most of all, thank you all for joining us.

The medals I'm about to present are the highest award a President can bestow for astounding achievement in science and technology. They recognize work that has helped expand the horizons of human knowledge. The National Medal of Science honors those whose research has enhanced our understanding of life and the world around us. And the National Medal of Technology recognizes innovators whose work keeps America on the cutting edge with discoveries that change the way we live.

The spirit of discovery is one of our national strengths. Our greatest resource has always been the educated, hard-working, ambitious people who call this country their home. From Thomas Edison's lightbulb to Robert Ledley's CAT scan machine, most of America's revolutionary inventions began with men and women with the vision to see beyond what is and the desire to pursue what might be.

Think back to how much this country has changed since the—since we first created the National Medal of Technology in 1980. Twenty-five years ago, most Americans used typewriters instead of computers. Most of us used pay phones instead of cell phones. Most of us used carbon paper instead of laser printers. Most of us had rolodexes—you might remember those—[*laughter*]. And on the long family trip, we'd play the license plate game—[*laughter*]—and now we're watching DVDs.

Many technologies that are in our laboratories today will bring cures and technologies that are beyond our imagination. And we will then wonder how we ever lived without them. These kinds of changes are the result of years of hard work by American innovators, like those we honor here today.

Over the years, National Science and Technology laureates have been responsible for breakthroughs that revolutionized telecommunications, discovered the structure of DNA, led to the invention of the microchip. These laureates have done work that have revolutionized organ transplants and led to development of global positioning systems and helped feed millions around the world.

Our Nation has a vital stake in the research and discovery that makes these advances possible. And so in my State of the Union, I encouraged our Nation to stay on the leading edge of technology and education. I've talked about an American Competitiveness Initiative that will double over the next 10 years the Federal commitment to the most critical, basic research programs in the physical sciences. I think that's a good use of taxpayers' money.

Six of today's eight science laureates have benefited from past investment in this kind of research. If we want this country to but—be the most competitive country in the world, we have got to spend money now to make sure we stay on the leading edge of technological change. We also got to recognize it's in the private sector where most money is spent on research and development, yet we unwisely have allowed the research and development tax credit to expire. If the United States expects to remain competitive in a global economy, we must encourage our private sector to continue to invest in leading-edge technologies, and therefore, we ought to make the research and development tax credit a permanent part of our Tax Code.

We can't be the leading country in the world in science and technology unless we educate scientists and young mathematicians. And so as part of the competitive initiative, I'm going to work with the Congress to make sure we extend the same standards in the No Child Left Behind Act that we apply to reading to math. The facts are that we're doing fine with fourth grade kids in math and science. The facts, also, are these, that we're falling off the face of the charts when it comes to eighth grade math, and we've got to change that. And one of the sure ways to change that is to apply special money for kids who need extra help in junior high for math and science.

We can't make sure our children have got math and science—fine math and science courses unless we've got teachers capable of teaching math and science. And one way to do that is to expand education to high school teachers in how to teach Advanced Placement. Advanced Placement programs work. They make a significant difference in the lives of our children. And so by making sure more teachers can teach AP, this country will be better off in making sure that we've got the future scientists and mathematicians living right here in the United States of America.

Another part of the initiative is to encourage school districts to recruit 30,000 math and science professionals to teach in our Nation's classrooms. I mean, we want young kids to think math and science are cool subjects, that it's okay to be a mathematician, that it's exciting to be a scientist. And there's no better way to make sure that young students are encouraged to take math and science than to have successful scientists explain to our students just the wonders of exploration.

You know, I was out in Albuquerque and had a good visit in Intel. They've got an interesting program. They provide incentives for their employees to go into the classrooms of local high schools and community colleges to say to youngsters, "Join us in these exciting fields." And the exciting jobs of the 21st century are going to be in math and science, and the American people must understand that if we don't educate our kids in math and science, the jobs are going to go elsewhere in the years to come. The competitive initiative recognizes we're great when it comes to research and development, and we intend to stay that way. But we've also got to be great when it comes to making sure our students have got the skills necessary to compete in the 21st century.

I appreciate the work that today's laureates are doing to inspire young scientists. We've got some young scientists from Benjamin Banneker High School with us. Thank you all for joining us. I appreciate you being here. I hope that you are inspired by the examples of excellence and success that you see right here in this ceremony today.

You know, it's interesting, people generally do not pursue a career in science or technology with the goal of fame. I'm kind of trying to change that today. [*Laughter*] The work of discovery is quiet and often solitary. Yet all Americans benefit from your imagination and your talent and your resolve. And so today we're here to say thanks for what you've done; thanks for helping improve the quality of life in this country; thanks for inspiring others. Congratulations on your medals, and now the military aide will read the citations.

[*At this point, Lt. Col. Christian Cabaniss, USMC, Marine Corps Aide to the President, read the citations, and the President presented the medals.*]

The President. Again, thank you for coming. Got a little reception back here for the honorees and their families. I'm proud to have you here in the White House. May God continue to bless our great Nation. Thank you.

NOTE: The President spoke at 10:45 a.m. in the East Room at the White House.

Remarks Following Discussions With United Nations Secretary-General Kofi Annan
February 13, 2006

President Bush. Mr. Secretary-General, thank you.

Secretary-General Annan. Thank you.

President Bush. As usual, we had a very constructive dialog. I always enjoy visiting with the Secretary-General. It gives us a chance to talk about our common interests and our desire for peace and liberty around the world.

We had a good discussion on Sudan, with particular emphasis on Darfur. I told the Secretary-General that Mrs. Garang was in to see me the other day and that we had a long discussion—she and I had a long discussion not only about the Darfur region but about implementing the north-south accords. And I appreciate the Secretary's leadership on that issue.

We talked about the broadened Middle East. And there's a lot to talk about. I am very optimistic, however, that democracy and liberty will prevail. And so I want to thank you for your interest and leadership on those particular issues.

We talked about U.N. reform, structural reform, management reform, as well as the reform of the Human Rights Commission. I was most interested in the Secretary-General's thoughts. I appreciate very much his leading on these issues, and we'll continue to work closely through Secretary Bolton— Ambassador Bolton with the Security Council and the United Nations.

And so, Mr. Secretary-General, thanks for coming. It's always a pleasure to welcome you here to the Oval Office. And the floor is yours.

Secretary-General Annan. Thank you very much, Mr. President. I also enjoy our periodic exchanges, and I'm very happy that we have agreed to work together on the Darfur issue, working with other governments from Europe, from Asia, and other regions, to ensure that we do have an effective security presence on the ground to protect the IDPs and ensure that humanitarian workers have access to those in need. And of course, this is an issue where all governments have to play their role.

On security—on the U.N. reform and Human Rights Council, I think the President and I agree that we need to reform the Human Rights Council, and it should be done as soon as possible. The President of the General Assembly, Jan Eliasson, is working very hard to ensure that we will have that done by this month, and that when the Human Rights Commission meets in Geneva, it will be in the process of transformation; it will not be business as usual. And I also thanked the President for all the support he's given us on U.N. reform, on the broader U.N. reform. And there are quite a lot of things that we're going to do.

We also discussed the Middle East and the Hamas elections and the need for transformation of Hamas into a political party along the lines that the Quartet had discussed. And I think there is an opportunity here for Hamas to transform itself into a political party and work with the international community and the Israeli Government.

We also touched on the issue of the nuclear issue in—of Iran. And here again, I hope the—between now and the time the Atomic Agency issues its next report, there will be indications and steps from the Iranian side to indicate that negotiations are not dead and that both sides can come back to the table and find a way out of this crisis. We need to be able to work to resolve it, and I hope there will be no steps taken to escalate this approach.

Thank you very much.

President Bush. I appreciate you. Good job. Thank you.

NOTE: The President spoke at 2:06 p.m. in the Oval Office at the White House. In his remarks, he referred to Rebecca Garang, Minister of Transportation, Roads, and Bridges, Government of Southern Sudan; and Ambassador John R. Bolton, U.S. Permanent Representative to the United Nations.

Remarks Honoring the 2005 World Series Champion Chicago White Sox
February 13, 2006

The President. Welcome. Thank you. Be seated. They may be playing basketball, but it's always baseball season here. [*Laughter*]

The last time the Chicago White Sox won the World Series was 1917. President Woodrow Wilson was living here. Reinsdorf, I don't know if you came here then or not. [*Laughter*] There were only eight teams in the American League, and the league leader hit a total of nine home runs. After 88 years of waiting, the White Sox have earned the right to be called world champs, and we're glad you're here.

I—first of all, I want to welcome Jerry Reinsdorf. Some of my most joyous times in my life have been during—as a baseball owner. Harold Baines may not have thought they were so joyous, since we never won much. [*Laughter*] And one of the reasons that I ended up in baseball with my partners is because of Jerry Reinsdorf's help, and I want to thank you for that now that we've got the team here. I know how much you love the game, and I know how much you love the Chicago White Sox. And so it had to be a thrilling moment for you and Eddie and the owners that were patient for all those years you didn't win. And so I congratulate you from the bottom of my heart, and thank you for your friendship. It's great to see you.

I appreciate Ken Williams, a man who obviously knows what he's doing, who is—was able to put a team together. It's easy to put stars on the field. The hard thing about baseball is to put people who can play together, and I congratulate you for being a great general manager.

I welcome Ed Farmer and the broadcasting team. Eddie, good to see you again. Thanks. I can see they all remember you—at least one person does. [*Laughter*]

It's good to be here with Bob DuPuy of baseball. I thought you're here to sign the lease, you know, but it's—[*laughter*]—another subject.

I do want to thank the members of my Cabinet who are here. It's great to see you all. I thought you all told me you were Red Sox fans. [*Laughter*]

I want to thank the—Senator Durbin and Senator Obama from the great State of Illinois, and Don Manzullo and Roy LaHood. Thank you all for coming.

I—my question to most of these folks is like, "Were you White Sox fans at the beginning of the season?" [*Laughter*]

Audience member. Yes, he puts us on the spot.

The President. Yes, he did. No, I'm not putting you on the spot. But I know one person—elected official who was a White Sox fan at the beginning of the season. As a matter of fact, he was a White Sox fan at the beginning of his life. He's been forever a White Sox fan. He is a great mayor of a great city, and that's the mayor, his honor, Dick Daley. Thanks for coming.

Roland Hemond—it's good to see you, Roland. Thank you. Just showing off my baseball knowledge. Anybody that knows—[*laughter*]—knows Roland Hemond knows something about baseball. And it's good to see Harold Baines and the other coaches.

I understand Ozzie is on vacation, which I fully understand. If he's a Caribbean guy, taking a look at the weather forecast up here yesterday would have made me not want to come as well. [*Laughter*] But I want to congratulate Ozzie Guillen, as well as the team and the staff, the coaching staff, and the managers, and all those who worked hard to make these guys ready to play. And I want to congratulate Ozzie on being a great manager, manager of the year, as well as becoming a United States citizen earlier this year. We're proud to have him as an American citizen.

I don't want to bring up the Sosa trade, so I won't—[*laughter*].

Audience member. Please don't.

The President. I won't. [*Laughter*] But it's great to see you. Harold Baines is one class act. I mean, that guy can not only hit, but he brought a lot of class into the clubhouse, and I'm really proud to see you here, Harold. Congratulations to you and the buddies you're working with.

And to the players, congratulations. We're really proud to have you here at the White House. It means a lot for baseball fans, White Sox fans, all across the country that you would take time to come and be honored here at the White House, and it's my great honor to honor you. It's a big deal to have you here.

The amazing thing about this team is you went wire to wire, which is really hard to do. You win one-nothing on opening day, and like, they're in your rearview mirror for the rest of the season. It takes a lot to win 99 games and to remain in the lead and not falter. And it says something about the character of the team that you put together and the character of the players.

The—I got a firsthand report from the World Series from two people I love dearly who had actually front-row seats, and that would be my mother and father. [*Laughter*] I'm not going to tell you who they were rooting for, but it didn't have much effect on the outcome of the series, I'll put it to you that way. [*Laughter*]

I was impressed as a baseball guy—at least somebody who follows it still, closely—that you had four complete games in a row in the playoffs. That's a good strategy, Jerry, to keep the bullpen—[*laughter*]—keep the bullpen fresh. [*Laughter*]

You know, there was great players, but nobody off the chart, if you know what I mean, which means you competed as a team. Jermaine Dye had an interesting quote that I think is worth sharing with people who are paying attention at this moment. He said, "From the start of spring training, everybody was hungry." He didn't say one player was hungry or a guy going into arbitration was hungry or a free agent for next year was hungry. He said everybody was hungry. They're—everybody wanted to go out there and win together. Everybody was pulling on the same rope. That's why you're the world champs. Everybody was pulling on the same rope. And that's what we're here to honor, a great championship team.

I congratulate Jermaine for being the MVP of the World Series. I congratulate Paul for being the MVP of the American League Championship Series. It must be a pretty cool feeling to hit a grand slam in the World Series. I didn't get one in Little League, much less the World Series. [*Laughter*] And you had a grand slam; you caught the last out of the season; and you witnessed the birth of your child all in the same month. Man, what a special month. The Lord has blessed you. That's why you're called "Mr. Soxtober." [*Laughter*]

I know the effect you had on White Sox fans, and it must have been electrifying. One women in her nineties said, "I've been a Sox fan all my life; I never thought I'd live to see the day." Think about that—think about the joy that you all put in the hearts of this 90-year-old person, and probably some young ones, too, that were pulling for the White Sox.

The people of Chicago turned out en masse not only because you were baseball champs but because you have brought some character to the city. I want to applaud the organization for supporting inner-city Little League. I think it's really important for this great state of baseball to reach out to people of all walks of life to make sure that the sport is inclusive. The best way to do it is to convince little kids how to—the beauty of playing baseball.

I appreciate the baseball fields you're building in Chicago, kind of little centers of hope, little diamonds of joy for people to come and be able to play the greatest game ever invented. I appreciate the Chicago White Sox Charities, your support of cancer research and cancer treatment in the metropolitan area. Most of all, I appreciate the fact that these players understand they're setting examples for young boys and girls all across Chicago as well as the country. You're setting the example that something—serving something greater than yourself is important in life; coming together as a team is a heck of a lot more important and satisfying than worrying about your own batting average or your own ERA.

And so here we are in the White House, Jerry, honoring the great Chicago White Sox. I'm proud to be with you. God bless your championship and God continue to bless the country.

Paul Konerko. Mr. President, on behalf of our organization and all the fans on the South Side and all over the world, we want to present you with this jersey and jacket.

The President. I thought you were going to give me a loan. [*Laughter*]

Jermaine Dye. And also, we know deep down you probably wish this was a Houston Astros jacket. [*Laughter*]

The President. Now wait a minute——

Mr. Dye. Hopefully, this will do.

Mr. Konerko. Thanks for having us here today.

The President. Actually it was a Texas Rangers jacket. [*Laughter*]

NOTE: The President spoke at 2:35 p.m. in the East Room at the White House. In his remarks, he referred to Jerry Reinsdorf, chairman, Harold Baines, bench coach, Eddie Einhorn, vice chairman, Ken Williams, general manager, Ed Farmer, radio broadcaster, Roland Hemond, executive adviser to the general manager, Ozzie Guillen, manager, Jermaine Dye, outfielder, and Paul Konerko, first baseman, Chicago White Sox; Robert A. DuPuy, president and chief operating officer, Major League Baseball; Representatives Donald A. Manzullo and Raymond H. LaHood of Illinois; Mayor Richard M. Daley of Chicago, IL; and Sammy Sosa, outfielder, Baltimore Orioles.

Remarks Honoring the University of Texas at Austin 2005 NCAA Football Champions
February 14, 2006

The President. Please be seated, except for you guys up there. [*Laughter*] Welcome to the White House. January 4, 2006, is a day that a lot of Texas fans will never forget. I called one of those Texas fans, who shall remain anonymous. I said, "How was it?" He said, "That game was the greatest day in my life." [*Laughter*] I said, "Well, how about your wedding?" [*Laughter*] He said, "Yes, that too." [*Laughter*]

I want to welcome Mack and Sally Brown here. Congratulations, Coach, for doing something that—[*applause*]—leading this group of great athletes to a victory that made a lot of Texans proud. I know

you made a person you admire proud, and a fellow who I wish were here today, but he's not, and that's Coach Darrell Royal. We send Coach Royal—we send him our very best, and you're following in his footsteps. It's a—you know, you've learned something about the press, in all due respect to those that are here—[*laughter*]— they tend to underestimate people sometimes—[*laughter*]—as I remember, they started calling you "Mr. February." Well, today, Mack, you're giving February—the title "Mr. February" a whole new meaning. This February you brought the national champs to the White House.

As you can see, you've brought out a lot of folks here to the South Lawn. We've never had quite a celebration this big here, and it's because there's a lot of Texas fans living here in Washington. But we've got some of the university officials with us. Mr. President, Bill Powers, it's good to see you, sir. I appreciate you coming, and your wife, Kim. It's good to see Mark Yudof and Judy, as well as Samara. Good to see you all again. I see the members of the board of regents, James Huffines and Rita Clements, other members of the board. Thank you for being here. DeLoss Dodds, I appreciate you doing a fine—there he is. Hi, DeLoss. Yes, sir.

I want to congratulate the coaching staff. One of the members of the staff has had an influence on my life. I might ask him to come up here—Mad Dog. My body is what it is today because of Mad Dog. [*Laughter*]

Jeff Madden. That's right.

The President. I appreciate you. He told me once—he said, "If you ever make it to Washington, I promise you, Mr. President-to-be, I'm coming up there with a team of champions." And he did. Congratulations. I didn't know you owned a suit. [*Laughter*]

Mr. Madden. I had to get one made.

The President. I didn't know they had one big enough. [*Laughter*]

But Jeff is——

Audience members. Oh. [*Laughter*]

The President. Yes. One reason the mighty Horns are here is because they were in good shape, and they were tough, and they were in good condition. And the reason they were was because of Jeff Madden and his belief in them as athletes and his willingness to work hard to get them in shape. And so you guys keep listening to him.

I want to thank the members of my Cabinet who are with us today. We appreciate you being here. I want to thank the Members of Congress—Senator Hutchison is a huge Texas fan—as well as Members of the House of Representatives. Thank you all for being here to welcome this great football team. Get back to work here quickly. [*Laughter*]

The—Mack can tell you what it takes to win, but one thing it takes is a team of great athletes playing together. That's how you win national championships. I suspect it's the difference between showing up and, you know, winning all but two and showing up and winning them all, is that people figured out how to put something greater than themselves on the line—in this case, the University of Texas football team. This was a team that—great power, great finesse. They were real quick.

But the thing that impressed me about the team and—you know, we can follow you here in Washington, DC, just as well as we can follow you in Crawford—is that this team never seemed—that they never figured out the word "lose." It never entered their vocabulary. Every time they walked on the field, you knew they were going to win. And perhaps one of the reasons why is because they were winners off the field as well.

I'm impressed by Ahmard Hall, who's the fullback. He—where is he? Where is Ahmard? There he is. He—I don't know if you know this or not, but he was a United States marine. Once a marine, always a marine. He served in Afghanistan and Kosovo. He entered the University of Texas on the GI bill. He's not only a fine blocker—you need to get him to Baltimore—[*laughter*]—he started something called "Momma Bear Cares," which sends packages to our troops overseas. Congratulations on being a great player, but more importantly, a great citizen.

Mike Garcia is with us. Where's Mike? There he is. Yes. I'm glad we're on the same side. [*Laughter*] Mike was involved in the Children's Miracle Network last spring. I take it you weren't a wide receiver.

Mike E. Garcia. Afraid not.

The President. The point is, is that this guy was good in the trenches of football, and he's good in the trenches of life by supporting people who need our help.

We've got some other—I don't know if you want to call them "big uglies" or not—but Kasey Studdard and Neale Tweedie and David Thomas. Where are those guys? Come on up here. The reason I—waiting on Neale to come down here. The reason these three guys are here—Will Allen was supposed to be with them, but I think he missed the flight. Slept in but—[*laughter*]—or study hall. [*Laughter*] These fellas took time out of their lives to go to the Austin Children's Hospital to bring some joy into a kid's life. You might have frightened them when they first saw you. [*Laughter*] But my point to you is, is that a championship football team is made up of people of character and decency.

One final athlete I want to recognize is, of course, Vince Young, the great quarterback who—[*applause*].

Head Coach Mack Brown. They didn't bring his suit.

The President. Oh, that's all right. He doesn't need a suit. [*Laughter*]

Mr. Brown. He was supposed to bring it—forgot.

The President. Yes, you can borrow a tie. [*Laughter*] I think Vince will tell you that the reason he got to where he is today is because of his teammates. One reason why Vince got to where he is, as well, is because he understands that the role of a star is to put something back in the community in which you were raised. I was impressed by his being involved in a program called LEAP, which means, learn, enjoy, and play. It's basically a chance for somebody like Vince to go in and say to some other—to a young child, "Here's what it takes to succeed in life." It's called mentoring. And all these athletes, whether they know it or not, are mentoring by the way they behave, by the example they set for young kids all across Texas and all across the country.

I want to congratulate Coach and Sally for setting the examples they've set for these players. They're instrumental in what's called the Rise School in Austin. It's a school that helps infants and toddlers and preschool children with developmental disabilities. They're very much involved with the Capital Campaign for the Helping Hands in Austin. They, like these players, are good citizens.

I also want to say congratulations to the coach for not only being a good—having a good football team, being able to raise these young men to butt heads harder than the other ones around the country, but nearly half the team earned a spot on the UT athletic director's honor roll for posting a 3.0 grade point average last fall.

This team won a lot of football games and won the national championship, but of the 32 seniors on the team, 28 will have earned their degrees by the end of this summer—and one of those, who hasn't quite earned it yet, made a promise to his mother. And Vince, I'd suggest you honor that promise to your mother—[*laughter*]—and get your degree by the end of this summer, which I know he will.

All in all, we're honored to have a great group of individuals, people who brought great pride to our State and pride to a great university. Welcome to Washington. Congratulations to the national champs, the University of Texas.

NOTE: The President spoke at 1:07 p.m. on the South Lawn at the White House. In his remarks, he referred to Darrell K. Royal, former head coach, Mike E. Garcia, Kasey W. Studdard, and William W. Allen, Jr., offensive guards, and Neale Tweedie and John David Thomas, tight ends, University of Texas at Austin football team; William Powers, Jr., president, University of Texas at Austin, and his wife, Kim Heilbrun; Mark G. Yudof, chancellor, University of Texas System, his wife, Judy, and his daughter, Samara; James R. Huffines, chairman, and Rita C. Clements, vice chairman, board of regents, University of Texas

C. Clements, vice chairman, board of regents, University of Texas System; DeLoss Dodds, men's athletic director, University of Texas at Austin; and Felicia Young, mother of quarterback Vince Young.

Statement on the Anniversary of the Death of Former Prime Minister Rafiq Hariri of Lebanon
February 14, 2006

One year ago today, former Lebanese Prime Minister Rafiq Hariri was assassinated. Mr. Hariri was a great Lebanese patriot who worked to rebuild a free, independent, and prosperous Lebanon after years of brutal civil war. Our thoughts are with the people of Lebanon as they mark this anniversary.

Lebanon has continued to make progress in the year since Mr. Hariri's murder, thanks to the foundation of freedom he laid and the determination of the Lebanese people. Lebanon has conducted a free and fair parliamentary election and begun economic reforms. Great challenges remain, and the United States will continue to stand with the people of Lebanon as they strive to build a free and democratic future.

Message to the Congress Transmitting a Report by the National Science Board
February 14, 2006

To the Congress of the United States:

Consistent with 42 U.S.C. 1863(j)(1), I transmit herewith a report prepared for the Congress and the Administration by the National Science Board entitled, "Science and Engineering Indicators—2006." This report represents the seventeenth in the series examining key aspects of the status of science and engineering in the United States.

GEORGE W. BUSH

The White House,
February 14, 2006.

Remarks on Health Care in Dublin, Ohio
February 15, 2006

Thank you all. Thanks for coming. Please be seated. Jack, thanks for the introduction; thanks for letting us convert your lobby into a—[*laughter*]—place to come and visit.

So I get on Air Force One this morning, I said, "Take me to Dublin"—the guy heads east. [*Laughter*] I said, "Nuh-uh, Dublin, Ohio." [*Laughter*] Proud to be here. Thanks for letting me come and visit with you. It's neat to be in "the house that Dave built." He was a great American.

George Voinovich and I were sharing Dave Thomas stories, particularly when he came and helped educate and lead the

Governors—that's when we were Governors—about adoption. And one of his great legacies is inspiring people to show the ultimate act of love, which is to adopt a child. The other great legacy is, leave behind a great company that is providing thousands with good jobs; another great legacy is to leave behind consumer choice. You can either get your three-quarter pound triple cheeseburger—[*laughter*]—or your salad. [*Laughter*]

I appreciate the fact that Wendy's understands that choice for the consumers is important. I also appreciate the fact that Wendy's understands that giving employees the opportunity to make rational choices in health care is an important part of having a workforce that is vigorous, active, and enthused about their jobs. And so today I'm here to talk about innovation in the health place, how we can make sure the health care system in the United States of America remains the best in the world.

And so, Jack, thanks for letting me come. Thanks for being an innovator. I love the entrepreneurial spirit of America. And the entrepreneurial spirit doesn't end if you happen to be a big company. As a matter of fact, it's important to remain entrepreneurial, no matter what your size is. And to have a company like Wendy's introduce HSAs, which I'm about to talk about, reminds me that the entrepreneurial spirit is alive and well here.

I appreciate the team, the management team, and all the employees for giving me a chance to come and visit. I will keep my remarks relatively short so you can get back to work. [*Laughter*]

Governor, thank you for coming. I appreciate Governor Bob Taft joining us. Yesterday I had the privilege of meeting with his wife, Hope. We were talking about how to rally the great armies of compassion around the United States to help provide love and help and concern for those amongst us who need love and help and concern.

I want to thank my friend Senator George Voinovich. I've known him for a long time. He's steady; he is capable; he is a great public servant. Thank you for being here, George.

I want to thank the Members of the United States Congress who managed to get a free flight on Air Force One—[*laughter*]—to come and join us. I'm better for the fact that you accompanied me; thank you. And that would be Pat Tiberi, the United States Congressman from this district. Congressman David Hobson is with us as well—as well as Congresswoman Deborah Pryce. Thank you all for coming today.

The speaker of the house is with us; Mr. Speaker, thanks for joining us. The president of the Ohio Senate is with us. Glad you guys are here; thanks for coming. I also want to mention Senator Steve Stivers, United States Senator, Lieutenant Colonel in the Ohio National Guard. He served a 12-month tour of duty in the Middle East and Africa. Appreciate your service. God bless you and your family, and God bless all our troops in harm's way.

I skipped the majority leader—I didn't mean to—Mr. Majority Leader, in fact, it's an oversight, you know? Thank you for being here, Larry Flowers. I want to thank the mayor of the city of Dublin for joining us. Appreciate you coming, Mayor. I'm honored you're here. Thanks for taking time out of your schedule.

I just met with some folks that work here at Wendy's—I'll talk about them later. But I also met with the owner of a restaurant here, Frank Ciotola. I met with Shawn Kessinger; he's the vice president of finance for the Ohio Credit League Union. I met with a farmer, Debbie Carr. We talked about health care from the perspective of small-business owners, entrepreneurs. I listened to their concerns; I listened to their solutions. And as I begin to give this address on the health care system, I want you to know that many of their thoughts are incorporated in what the vision is for good health care. Thanks for taking time to be here today.

Let me start by giving you kind of a state of the economy: It's strong. I recognize there's parts of Ohio that aren't necessarily as strong as other parts of the country. But from an overall perspective, when you look at the Nation's economy, it's strong, and it's getting stronger. And the reason I say that is because we're now in our fifth year of uninterrupted economic growth.

Last year, this economy, in spite of high energy prices and in spite of natural disasters, grew at 3.5 percent. We've—after-tax income of our people—and that matters a lot, you know, whether or not people have got money in their pocket after paying their taxes—is up 8 percent since 2001. Productivity is high. It's important to have high productivity growth in an economy because that's how economies improve their standard of living for their people. The more productive you are as a citizen or the more productive you are as the—as a company, the more likely it is you will generate higher revenues and higher quality of life.

And so productivity is increasing, which is a measurement of not only this country's competitiveness, but is a measure of whether or not life is improving for our citizens. Small businesses are thriving. That's really good news. Most new jobs in America are created by small businesses. And when the small-business sector is thriving, it means people are working. We've added 4.7 million new jobs over the last 2½ years. The national unemployment rate is 4.7 percent. That's low.

Things are improving here in Ohio. The unemployment rate is still 5.9 percent, but nevertheless, the trends are in good shape. You've gone from 6.4 percent to 5.9 percent. Obviously, there's still work to do. George and members of the delegation are concerned about trade that is fair and free. He wants the manufacturers here in Ohio to be treated fairly in places like China. I assured him I understand it's part of my

job. I'm going to India at the end of this month, and I'm going to make it clear to the Indians, "We will look forward to trading with you, but just treat us the way we treat you; that's all we ask." The reason I say that is because we can compete with anybody, anytime, anywhere, so long as the rules are fair.

The fundamental question is, how do we remain a leader in the world economy? You know, there's uncertainty in this economy of ours. People are changing work a lot—that kind of creates a sense of uncertainty. People see China and India out there looming as competitors, and the reaction with some is, "Let's don't compete; let's just kind of shut her down; let's get protectionist," or, "Why don't we isolate?" I have a different point of view. My attitude is, we shouldn't fear the future; we ought to shape the future. My attitude is, the United States of America must continue to be the leader in the world economy, for the good of our people.

And so here are some ways as to how to make sure this economy remains strong today and remains strong for years to come. And first, in order for us to be a leader in the world, we've got to remain a leader when it comes to technological developments. So I'm proposing to the Congress an American Competitiveness Initiative, which will double the basic research in basic sciences over the next 10 years.

And secondly, I recognize most research is done in the private sector, and yet the incentive for companies to invest in research, which yields technologies, which increases standard of living and makes sure our economy is on the leading edge, is through the research and development tax credit. It expires on an annual basis. It is very difficult for private sector to plan when a Tax Code is uncertain. And so Congress, in order to make sure that we invest in the future, should make the research and development tax credit a permanent part of our Tax Code.

Finally, in order to remain competitive, we've got to have kids who understand math and science. And so I laid out an initiative—[*applause*]—I spent some time talking about it last week. I'm going to continue talking about it. I'm looking forward to working with—this is an issue, by the way, where we can put aside needless politics, which tends to dominate Washington, DC, and focus on the good for the future of this country. I'm confident we can get something done on this very important education as well as research and technology issue.

In order to make sure we're competitive, we've got to be wise about your money. The tax relief we passed is working. In order to make sure America is the most competitive Nation in the world, we've got to keep your taxes low and be wise about how we spend your money, which means we've got to learn to set priorities in Washington, DC. We can't try to be all things to all people when it comes to spending your money. We're on the way to cutting this deficit in half by 2009, and I intend to keep us on track to cut the deficit in half by 2009.

But to be wise—to be competitive in the future, we've got to get off being hooked on Middle Eastern oil. In order for us to grow—[*applause*]—I said something in the State of the Union that probably surprised some of you. I said, we have a serious problem; we're addicted to oil. But I meant what I said. I fully understand that an economy that requires oil from parts of the world that—where some countries may not like us, puts our economic security at risk and puts our national security at risk. And I'm serious about working with members of both parties to advance technological research that will enable us to drive cars by using switchgrass as a base stock of ethanol—or wood chips, as well as the corn and soybeans we use today. I mean, I can't wait for the day, and I know future Presidents can't wait for the day, when some-body walks in with the farm report, and says, "Mr. President, the crops are up, and we're less dependent on Middle Eastern oil." And it's coming; it's coming.

To keep this country competitive, we need a health care system that provides Americans with high-quality care at good prices. And that's what I want to talk about today. The health care costs are rising sharply in America. If they continue rising the way are—they are, that will make us less competitive. Many Americans are worried that they're not going to get the treatments they need. Small businesses, in particular, are struggling to pay for health care for their employees. If two-thirds of the new jobs in America are created by small businesses and your small-business owner is struggling to keep their employee base because of health care, then we've got to do something about it. Workers have lost good coverage because they're changing jobs. I've told you, there's uncertainty in the marketplace because people are changing work. And if you fear about losing health care when you change work, it creates even more uncertainty.

More than 45 million Americans have no health insurance at all, and this is unacceptable for our country. We've got the best health care system in the world, make no mistake about it. The question is, how do we keep it that way? And I've got some ideas for you.

First of all, we've got to choose between two competing philosophies when it comes to health care. Behind all the rhetoric in Washington and all the proposals, there's really a philosophical debate. On the one hand, there's some folks who—good-hearted folks, good, decent folks who believe that Government ought to be making the decisions for the health care industry. And there are some of us who believe that the health care industry ought to be centered on the consumer.

I think as we kind of make our minds up about what philosophy works, it's important to look at the world health care systems. Other nations have adopted for Government control of health care for centralized decisionmaking when it comes to health care, which has created long waiting lines and quality of care not as good as the American system and a significant lag in technological development.

We've done a different path up to now in our Nation's history. We believe in private medicine that encourages innovation and change. That's been the cornerstone of American public health up until now. And we have a choice to make. I've made my choice; I'm going to lead the Congress to make sure that our health care system preserves America's system of private medicine, that we strengthen the relationship between doctors and patients, and that we make the benefits of private medicine more affordable and accessible for our citizens. That's our strategy.

Obviously, Government has a role to play. We have made a commitment to the poor and the elderly in the United States, and it's a commitment we're going to keep. When I got to Washington, I took a look at the Medicare system. It's a very important part of our Nation's health care system, and that is Medicare, except it was old and tired and hadn't been changed. It was a centrally-controlled system. I'll give you an example of what I meant by old and tired. This is a system that paid $28,000 for ulcer surgery—when you've got an ulcer, you check in the hospital—Medicare would write you a $28,000 check. It wouldn't pay the $500 necessary to prevent the ulcer from happening in the first place. In other words, medicine had began to— begun to change, and Medicare didn't change with it. One reason why is because it's centrally controlled; all decisions had to be made by people out of Washington, DC.

And so I worked with Members of the United States Congress to modernize the system. I said, "If we've got a commitment to our elderly, let's make the commitment a good one." We're not going to make the commitment and have it be a mediocre commitment; it ought to be a good, sound commitment. And we did. And we added the prescription drug benefit to Medicare that modernizes the system.

And at the same time, we gave seniors more options from which to choose. See, part of making sure a health care system works, seems like to me, the consumers ought to have more choice. In a centralized system, the Government makes the choice. In a private system that focuses on kind of the markets, people ought to have a choice. People ought to be able to be given different options from which to choose.

And so we did modernize the system. It's tough sledding up there in Washington to get things changed. [*Laughter*] People like the status quo at times. Twenty-four million Americans have now signed up to the new Medicare plan since January 1st. That's a lot of folks, 24 million. Hundreds of thousands are enrolling each week. Now, needless to say, when you have a change that size, there's going to be some things that need to be adjusted in the system. And you probably read about, kind of, the dual-eligible problem. I don't know if you've had that problem here in Ohio, Governor. We're dealing with it. Our job is to solve problems when they arise. When you have that big a shift, you can imagine there's going to be glitches. But by far, the vast majority of people are signing up to a program that's making a big difference in their lives.

Competition—in other words, when you have choices, it creates a sense of competition in the marketplace—is lowering costs for American seniors. The average premium that seniors now pay for the prescription drug benefit is a third less than what was expected. In other words, when we started rolling out the plan, it was expected that the prescription drug benefit would cost the seniors $37 a month. The actual cost is $25 a month. It's an interesting lesson about what can happen when you give people different options from which to choose.

The other thing that's important for you all to know is that the typical senior will end up spending about half of what he or she used to spend on prescription drugs. I mean, if you want the system to function well, it seemed like to me and others here that we ought to modernize the system to make it good for our seniors. It's working.

If you happen to have a mother or father or a neighbor who's a senior, I strongly urge you to get your loved one or your friend to call 1–800–MEDICARE or to go on the web at medicare.gov and help that person realize the great new options available to him or her.

Medicaid, as well, is a program that we take very seriously. It's a program aimed at helping the poor. It's administered in conjunction with States. It is health care for low-income families with children, poor seniors, and disabled Americans. It's a very important program. It needed to be restructured, however, in order to make the program actually work in a cost-effective way. And so we decided to work with the States to give Governors and folks at the local level more flexibility in how to structure the program to meet the needs at the local level.

See, in the past, if you had a good idea, if old Taft had a good idea, he had to come to Washington and beg permission for a waiver: "I, the Governor, was elected to do something good for the people. I'm worried about those who are qualified for Medicaid. Please give me permission to do what I think is right." The new bill I signed is one which will make the States—give States a lot more flexibility when it comes time to signing up people—to designing eligibility standards to providing what the programs ought to look like. In other words, it's flexibility, all aiming to make sure the Medicaid system works well.

We take the program seriously, but we fully understand what happens when the

bureaucracy becomes so encrusted that it's impossible to design programs that will actually meet States budgetary needs as well as the needs of the people. And we're remedying that fact.

The—I mentioned to you we have the goal of making sure that our budgets are responsible. One of—the budget I just signed or the bill I just signed and the budget I proposed is finally beginning to do something about the growth in Medicare and Medicaid. I want to describe to you a little bit about what we're doing.

Let me give you this story, kind of an analogy—there is a difference between slowing your car down to the speed limit or putting your car into reverse. I want you to think about that as I explain to you that, in working with the Congress, we have slowed Medicare growth down from 8.1 percent a year to 7.7 percent a year. In other words, we found ways to reform the system so that we can slow the growth rate down to make it—Medicare more affordable for future generations. We're not putting the car in reverse; we're just finding the speed limit.

Same thing with Medicaid. It grows—slow it down from 6.9 percent a year to 6.6 percent a year, which means just by slowing the growth rate down on those two important programs and, at the same time, making them more efficient and delivering better services, we're saving the taxpayers $104 billion over 5 years. I want to thank the Congress for working on this. You hear rhetoric, of course, that we're "starving the poor." The car is going the speed limit; it's not going backwards.

Now, the long-term solution for Medicare requires—and Social Security—requires an understanding that we've got a lot of baby boomers getting ready to retire. The true strain on our budget is really going to be the unfunded deficits caused by a baby boom generation retiring, with fewer workers to pay for guys like me. See? I mean, a lot of us are retiring. As a matter of fact, my retirement date is—I turn 62 on 2008, which is—[*laughter*]—pretty convenient time to retire. [*Laughter*] There's a lot of us, a whole lot of us. And there are fewer people paying in the system per person retiring.

And what's interesting—and you've got to know this—is that my generation has been promised greater benefits than a previous generation. So you can imagine when you start to think about the strain, a lot of us have been promised greater benefits with fewer people paying for us. And it's not going to work; it's simply not going to work.

I was very serious in the State of the Union—I explained this to George and the Congressmen—that I understand a solution to Social Security and Medicare in terms of dealing with a bulge of retirees is going to require a bipartisan solution. And I mean it to Members of Congress—I expect there to be a bipartisan effort to come up with a solution. Nothing will pass the House or the Senate unless there's agreement. And now is the time to put aside the politics that have stopped rational people from coming up with a rational answer to a very serious problem, to set it aside, sit down at the table, and solve this problem once and for all—so we can travel the country looking at young workers and saying, "You're not going to pay payroll taxes into a bust system anymore. You're going to pay payroll taxes into the system which will be around not only for baby boomers like me but for a young generation of Americans coming up." Now is the time for us to get something done.

I want to talk about another program that's working. One of the things that we've got to do is spend time in Washington actually measuring results of programs. You know, every title on a bill sounds just fantastic, you know. [*Laughter*] The problem is, is that every bill doesn't deliver the results it's supposed to. I will tell you about a program that does. It fits into a vision of a health care system where the Government does have responsibility, and that's community health centers.

One of the real strains on local hospitals and local health providers is the fact that the poor and the indigent use emergency rooms for primary care—it's an incredibly inefficient use of assets. It's an important use of assets if somebody can't find care and they need help—I'm not denigrating the people going to the emergency rooms, but I am saying there's a better way to be wise about how we spend your money and to solve a very important problem, and that is, have the emergency rooms be there for emergencies, and have primary care facilities like community health centers being there for primary care for the indigent and the poor.

Since I took office, we've opened or expanded about 800 health centers. There are now 3,700 of these centers around the United States serving 13 million Americans. It is a cost-effective way to provide primary care for those who need help. And I'm going to call upon Congress and work with Congress to put 400 more of those health centers in.

So what I'm telling you is, is that the Federal Government obviously has a role, to make sure the Medicare system is cost-effective and works well, make sure Medicaid is—works well and gives flexibility to States, and to expand community health centers.

I now want to talk to you about how the rest of us need to have a health care system, if you don't fall into those categories. What should the role of the Government be? And I believe the role of the Government ought to be to empower consumers to make choices. And so let me talk to you about five ideas I have to make sure that health care is more available and more affordable.

And the first one is to expand health savings accounts. We—I call them HSAs. When you hear me say HSA, that's kind of government-speak for health savings account. They—HSAs are helping to begin a movement away from what's called a third-party payer system to one where the consumer is very much involved in making wise purchases of health care. That's a very important philosophical point.

The traditional insurance today will cover your health care costs—most of your health care costs—in exchange for a high premium payment up front. The costs are generally shared by you and your employer. You may also pay a small deductible and copayment at the time of treatment. What's interesting about this system is that those payments cover only a fraction of the actual costs of health care, the rest of which are picked up by a third party, basically your insurance company.

It means most Americans have no idea what their actual cost of treatment is. You show up; you got a traditional plan; you got your downpayment; pay a little copay, but you have no idea what the cost is. Somebody else pays it for you. And so there's no reason at all to kind of worry about price. If somebody else is paying the bill, you just kind of—hey, it seems like a pretty good deal.

There's no pressure for an industry to lower price. And so what you're seeing is price going up. If you don't care what you're paying and the provider doesn't have any incentive to lower, the natural inclination is for the cost to go up. And the insurance companies, sure enough, pass on the costs—the increase in cost to you and your employer. That's what's happening.

The fundamental problem with traditional coverage is that there's no incentive to control how their health care dollars are spent. You don't have any incentive, whatsoever. And that's one of the cost drivers in our system. If we want to solve health care problems, if we want to make health care affordable and available, we've got to analyze and address the cost-drivers of health care. And there's one right there. If patients controlled how their health care dollars are spent, the result is better treatment at lower cost.

I'll give you an interesting example of a procedure called LASIK—laser eye surgeries. It's a good example of how the market can work when there's not a third-party payer involved. You might remember when LASIK first appeared, was approved about a decade ago for its use. It went through the process of getting a Government approval, and when approved, it was an opportunity for people to have their eyesight—feeling a little nervous about LASIK surgery when it first came out, and it was awfully expensive. Consumers began to, however, inquire as to why something costs the way it costs, how safe it was. Doctors felt more comfortable starting to offer more and more of the surgery. More providers came in the market; there was transparency of pricing. You might—I can remember billboards springing up with people advertising LASIK surgery. Today, the price of LASIK surgery has dropped dramatically. More people are getting the surgery; they're giving up their glasses and contact lenses.

The market is working. I think if you go back and look at the history of the pricing of LASIK surgery, the availability of LASIK surgery, you'll find that when consumers start showing up saying, "I want to know more information; I'm interested in this idea. How about—how does your cost compare to old Joe's over here"—the market began to adjust. LASIK surgery is now more widespread, at much more reasonable cost for consumers.

And so, how to affect those kinds of cost changes in the health care industry, that's what we're really here to discuss. And one way to do so is to—to make health care more responsive is through health savings accounts. Many people in our country don't know what a health savings account is. I will start to try to explain it here.

First, it is a part of our drive to make health care more consumer-driven. There's two components to a health savings account; one is low-cost catastrophic insurance coverage and a tax-free health savings account. Those are the two components of what I'm talking about. Catastrophic coverage protects you and the family in the event of devastating medical illness—if you're really sick, a catastrophic plan kicks in.

The health savings account portion of this product allows you and your employer to contribute tax-free to pay for routine medical costs. In other words, your company or yourself or a combination of the two makes a tax-free contribution into a health savings plan, a savings plan that you own. It's yours to call your own. And the savings within that plan are tax-free. In other words, you're not just going to put it under your pillow; you put it into a bank until you use it. The interest will be tax-free. Your money is growing.

It means that if you don't spend money in your savings account on health care, you can roll it over to the next year, tax-free. You have money growing for health care to pay incidental expenses; it's growing at a reasonable interest rate; it's yours you call your own. And if you don't spend it in a year, you can put it into the next year and the next year and the next year.

For many routine medical needs, HSAs mean you can shop around until you get the best treatment for the best price. In other words, it's your money; you're responsible for routine medical expenses; the insurance pays for the catastrophic care. You're responsible for paying for the portion of your health care costs up to your deductible. And so you—you talk to your doctor; you say, "Well, can't we find this drug at a little cheaper cost?" Or you go to a specialist, "Maybe we can do this a little better—old Joe does it for X; I'm going—why don't you try it for Y?" It allows you to choose treatment or tests that meet your needs in a way that you're comfortable with when it comes to paying the bills.

In other words, decisions about routine medical treatments are made by you and the doc, not by third-party people that you

never know. And all of a sudden, when you inject this type of thinking in the system, price starts to matter. You're aware of price. You begin to say, "Well, maybe there's a better way to do this and more cost-effective way."

The combined cost of catastrophic insurance coverage and HSA contributions are usually less expensive than traditional coverage. That's important to know. In other words, HSAs are making health care more affordable. By the way, these HSAs became expanded—George tried to do it in the mid-1990s, 1996 I think—yes—medical savings accounts, he called them. He couldn't get them going. People who had the business didn't want any competition, which sometimes happens in the marketplace. [*Laughter*] But he thought of the idea; it made sense. This really—these HSAs have kicked off big time because of the Medicare bill I signed. And they haven't been around a long time. They're just kind of a fresh product that the marketplace is becoming used to.

Forty percent of those who own HSAs have family incomes below $50,000 a year. In other words, if people are having trouble affording traditional insurance, all of a sudden, the HSA becomes a more affordable product. HSAs make a difference—are making health care more accessible to those without insurance. In the first year HSAs were available, more than a third of those who bought HSAs had been uninsured. In other words, as health care becomes more affordable, it makes it easier, obviously, for somebody who is uninsured to be able to pick up health insurance.

You know, a lot of young folks are uninsured. You might remember the days when you kind of felt like you were never going to get sick. [*Laughter*] So why should you buy insurance? Why do you need coverage? A lot of young folks are saying, "Wait a minute; this is a pretty good deal. If I'm going to stay healthy and can save a portion of that money, tax-free, and I'm not going to spend money on health care for a while, all of a sudden, a nest egg really begins to build." By the way, it's a nest egg they call their own; it's not something the Government—if there's excess money in your account, the Government can't take it away, or insurance can't take it away; it's yours. You own the thing. It's a vital part of kind of—a responsible society is when there's a sense of ownership in important parts of our economy.

Over the last 10 months, the number of HSAs has tripled. In other words, people are becoming aware. One of the reasons I'm here talking about HSAs at Wendy's is because you've decided to implement this product. I want people to be aware of it. The number of people who bought HSAs has gone from a million to 3 million. And I'm going to talk today about ways to make sure that HSAs are—even expand even further.

You know, I can remember the debate in Washington—I'm sure you can as well—I remember one person who said, "Health savings accounts are not a solution for the uninsured; they're regressive; they favor the wealthy." It's just not the facts. They've helped the uninsured, and a lot of folks with incomes under $50,000 are buying these plans. It's kind of basically saying, "If you're not making a lot of money, you can't make decisions for yourself." That's kind of a Washington attitude, isn't it: "We'll decide for you; you can't figure it out yourself." I think a lot of folks here at Wendy's would argue that that point of view is just simply backwards and not true.

People have said that expanding HSAs would fail to reduce health care costs. It's just not the case. I've just talked to Joe Cava—he knows what it's done to your costs. Wendy's decided to take on this product. They—you were facing double-digit increases in the cost of providing health care. That's a strain if you're a CEO. In order to have a workforce, you've got to have a workforce that's comfortable with the health care plan, and all of a sudden, it's beginning to take big bites out of the

balance sheet. It's hard to expand your business, it's hard to grow when more and more of your costs are being consumed by health care. And it provides a real tension for small-business owners or large business managers—how do you take care of your people? No corporation, no entity can run unless the people are taken care of and, at the same time, expand your business.

The company wanted to reduce projected health care increases. You didn't want to pass—keep passing on the high costs of—increasing costs to your employees. So they adopted HSAs. Nine—about 9,000 of Wendy's full-time employees and their families have got HSAs. In other words, Wendy's said, "Why don't we give people a chance to make health care decisions themselves?" They don't have some of the attitude in Washington. If you believe like Washington believes, you would never try an HSA because, "People can't decide for themselves," see. That's not what the folks here at Wendy's thought.

At the end of the first year with HSAs, more than 90 percent of Wendy's employees had positive balances in their savings accounts. In other words, there's a sharing ratio. The company paid—helped pay the premium for the catastrophic care. They shared the money that goes in to help pay for incidental or routine expenses. And—but 90 percent of the folks didn't use all the money for the routine expenses. It's kind of interesting that maybe it helps preventative medicine, I guess—when you're watching your own money, and you realize that if you take care of your body and you exercise and you don't do stupid things, you end up saving money. [*Laughter*] And when you save money, it's your money, not the company's money.

Medical claims through this company have decreased by 17 percent since they've implemented HSAs. It's an interesting statistic, I think. After more than 5 years of health care costs going at double-digit rates, Wendy's overall health care costs rose only by 1 percent last year. HSAs have had a positive effect. This has a positive effect on the individual employee; it's had a positive effect on the income statement of the company. They work.

They're doing—and, Jeff, you made a good—get the boy a raise. [*Laughter*] It's a—here's what he said—you know, never mind. He said, "We entered into this plan to use our money more wisely and to allow our employees to use their money wisely." Kind of an interesting corporate concept, to allow our employees to use their own— more money wisely. "It's making health care more transparent," Jeff says, "and making improved health more sustainable for our employees and for all the consumers of health care." I think he gets it. He gets the philosophy of having a consumer-driven system.

The savings have allowed Wendy's to raise the company's contribution to its employees' HSA accounts. By saving money on health insurance, it enables them to put more money into your account, which has got to be a heck of a good benefit, working for this company. It's your money now; it grows tax-free. It goes in tax-free; it grows tax-free; and you take it out tax-free.

The—I met with Marla Hipsher. Thanks for coming, Marla. She works here. She is a senior paralegal for 4 years. She was part of the briefing party that was there when I arrived. She is a single mom with a 24-year-old daughter and two teenage sons. As an aside, she has the toughest job in America, being a single mother. She obviously cares about her health care for herself and, more importantly, for her children. Marla's sons are on her HSA plan with her, which is a family plan. She enjoys the choice. She's comfortable with the control she has over her HSA. Marla's premiums with her HSA are 18 percent lower than the traditional plan she used to have at Wendy's. She's saving money. It makes it easier to do the hardest job in America, which is being a single mother. She likes her HSA so much, she's helping her 24-year-old daughter look into setting one up

herself. I—listen to your mother; it makes a lot of sense. [*Laughter*]

I want folks who don't understand HSAs to listen to what Marla has to say: "It has made me more informed, because you discuss it with your doctor now." She's talking about health care. "You want to know up front what it's going to cost and what you need to know. You become a better informed consumer." HSAs are working; they're working. And I'm looking forward to working with Congress to expand them to more Americans.

I'm going to talk about three ways to make them more attractive, so more people can have the benefits of an HSA, like Marla or the small-business owners we had. The greatest obstacle—one of the greatest obstacles to expansion of HSAs is the Tax Code. One problem is that under current law, employers and employees pay no income or payroll tax on any health insurance provided through the workplace. The health care plan here at Wendy's, you don't pay for it. It's a benefit that's not taxable. Those who buy their insurance on their own don't get the same tax break. That means that the self-employed, the unemployed, and workers at companies that do not provide insurance are at a disadvantage. The playing field isn't level. And so I believe that one thing Congress needs to do is to give Americans who purchase their own HSA policies the same tax breaks as those who get their health insurance from their employers.

Another problem is that under current law, the amount you can put into your HSA tax-free is limited to the amount of your deductible. But sometimes your out-of-pocket expenses are greater than your deductible. That's because at—on some catastrophic plans, there is an additional copay, and therefore, when you—you're paying after-tax dollars under the current law if you exceed the amount of money you spend beyond your deductible. We can change that. We can raise the cap on the amount of money you put into your HSA so it remains tax-free, so that all out-of-pocket expenses can be covered. That's the important—[*applause*].

And finally, HSAs—we want to make sure they meet the practical needs of today's workers. I told you, people are changing jobs. And one of the problems is a lot of folks fear that when they change jobs, they're going to lose their health care. And that means—people feel like they've got to get locked into a job because of health care, and that's not right. We need more flex—they need to be more thoughtful to our workers and recognize that this is a changing world in which we live. And so we ought to make sure people can take their own health savings account with them job to job.

Today, the savings in your health account—health savings account are portable; portable means you can take it job to job. So you've got savings in your own account; you can take it with you. But the health insurance that comes with the account you can't take with you, because of outdated laws and practices that prevent insurers from offering portable policies. So I believe that health insurers should be allowed to sell portable HSA policies nationwide.

You see, it's like car insurance. If you change jobs, you can take your car insurance with you. You can't take your insurance in your HSA with you. In order to make sure this economy works better, in order to make sure the health care system functions better for our workers, we've got to make sure portability in HSAs is consistent and real. It's going to make a difference in people's lives when Congress gets that done.

The second policy—way to make—making sure health care is affordable and accessible is to increase transparency in our health care system. To be smart consumers, you need to be informed consumers. It's hard to make wise choices unless you have information available. In order to spend your HSA dollars wisely, you need to know in advance what your options are. You need

to know the quality of doctors and hospitals in your area; you need to know the full extent of procedures that someone recommends to you.

You know, like when you buy a new car, you have access to consumer research on safety, you have access to information on reliability, you can compare price. There's performance data. You can become an informed consumer before you purchase your automobile. And that same sense of transparency and information ought to be available in health care. A modern health care system recognizes that people ought to be encouraged to shop for quality and price. So the health care industry and the insurance industry needs to provide reliable information about prices and quality on most common medical procedures.

Tomorrow I'm going to have a little visit with people in the insurance industry and the health care industry and the business industry to encourage transparency. I know Members of Congress are working on a bill. It would—better this be done with people saying, "Oh, we understand it's important to be transparent." There's always a bill out there in case the voluntarism is not quite as strong as it should be. [*Laughter*]

Third policy that's important is to apply modern information technology to our medical system. Doctors practice 21st century medicine; they still have 19th century filing systems. And this is an important issue. One reason it's an important issue, because when a doc writes their files by hand, you generally can't read the writing. [*Laughter*] That leads to inefficiency and error. In hospitals, there is more risk of preventable medical error when records are handwritten, instead of being cross-checked on a computer. Oftentimes doctors duplicate expensive tests because they do not have access to previous results. In other words, the medical system has not taken advantage of information technology like I'm sure Wendy's has, or other industries around the country.

And so I set a goal in 2004 that most Americans would have an electronic health record within 10 years. You'd have your own health record on a chip. And we're making pretty good progress toward that goal. Mike Leavitt is the Secretary of Health and Human Services. He's got a whole division inside HHS aiming towards getting information technology spread throughout health care.

First thing is, they've got to have a language that kind of can talk between a hospital in Dublin and a hospital in Crawford, you know? We don't have a hospital in Crawford. [*Laughter*] How about a hospital close to Crawford? [*Laughter*] And that's important, because there's a lot of different—the language needs to be standardized. And Mike's making pretty good progress on that.

And we're developing solutions for a nationwide health information network. One of the things I've insisted upon is that it's got to be secure and private. There's nothing more private than your own health records. So any system that works is one that is—it's your record; you decide the disclosure of your health records.

And let me give you an example about how such a system can work and what I'm trying to explain to you about how to help control costs and reduce medical errors. After Katrina hit, there was hundreds of veterans that had to be relocated. What's interesting is, is that the Veterans Department has already started this information technology modernization. There are medical—electronic medical records for veterans. And so when these poor folks got scattered around the country, they—the doctors and providers had access to the electronic records of our veterans.

So if a person had a diabetes issue, up pops on the screen the information, the latest test, the medicine being taken. It was an incredibly efficient way to make sure that the health care needs of our veterans were met during this time of catastrophe. It helped people fill out the prescription drugs of our seniors without fear of error. It helped a local doc say, "Well, gosh, look, you've been taking this medicine in the past; I'm going to prescribe it for you in the future, in order to make sure that your health care needs continue." If you have your own medical record, your own electronic medical record, and you get sick in a remote part of our country, people instantly see your blood type, the issues that you've faced in the past, really important information about your—about who you are and what you're going to need to help you.

And we're on our way to providing a nationwide information network. It's going to help save maybe 25 percent of the costs in medical care. I told you that one of the important things we've got to be worried about is how to deal with the cost-drivers, how to come up with ways to, practically, with a commonsense solution, deal with rising costs. One way is to modernize health care. Another way is to put consumers in charge of making decisions with transparency in pricing.

I want to talk a little bit about small businesses. The—obviously, I've told you once and I really mean it, I understand how important small businesses are for the economy. I also love the thought of America being a great place for entrepreneurship. There's nothing better than talking to somebody and saying, "I started my own business," or, "I own my own company." It's just—I love—it's refreshing to me. And it's just really an important part of the American experience. And obviously, as I mentioned, health care is a really important issue for small business. If you sat down with a roundtable of small businesses, the first issue that comes to their mind is, "I can't provide health care for my people. How do you expect me to stay in business when health care costs are driving us out?" Well, HSAs help a lot, and I really urge American small businesses to take a look at HSAs. They're good for Wendy's; they'll be good for you as well.

Here's another idea. One of the problems that small businesses have is that they enter into the market—they're trying to provide traditional insurance without any risk pool behind them. If you've got three people you're trying to insure, it's a heck of a lot more expensive then if you're trying to insure 3,000 people or 10,000 people. In other words, the more people that are in the risk pool, the lower the cost of traditional insurance is for a small business. And so I look forward to working with the Congress to expand what we call associated health plans. That's kind of Washington-speak for allowing small firms to band together to buy insurance at the same discounts that big companies get.

I'll give you an example. You've got yourself a family restaurant here in Dublin, Ohio. They've got 10 employees, and you try to go in the marketplace, and it's prohibitively expensive. It seems to make sense to me that the family restaurant in Dublin ought to team up with family restaurants all across the country, so that the employees provide one big risk pool to help lower the cost for small businesses. It is a practical way of helping small businesses that choose not to go into HSAs to be able to buy traditional insurance in a cost-effective way.

The bill passed the House of Representatives; it remains stuck in the United States Senate. I urge the Senate—I urge the Senate, for the sake of affordable health care for small businesses and their employees, to pass associated health plans.

I'll talk about one other issue. I hope you're hanging in there with me here. [*Laughter*] And that issue is one that I remember well when I was traveling your State, and that is the number of good docs that are getting driven out of practice because of frivolous lawsuits. If you're worried about affordabilty of health care and availability of health care, then you have got to be concerned about junk lawsuits. You just have to be, because a lot of docs and providers, thinking they're going to get

sued, practice what's called defensive medicine. They order tests; they write prescriptions that simply are not necessary so they can protect themselves from being sued in a court of law by a trial lawyer. That's just a fact of life.

I find interesting a quote from an emergency physician here. Here's what this person said, "In an effort to reduce our malpractice exposure"—that means, in an effort not to get sued—"we're being encouraged to overtreat, overtest, and overadmit patients." It has to be driving medical costs right out of the roof, and it is. It is.

In order to address the rising cost of health care, we've got to have a rational liability system. If you're harmed, you ought to have your day in court. You ought to—there ought to be justice for you, if you're injured. But we can write laws that make sure that you get your due claims without encouraging a plethora of junk lawsuits that is costing you a lot of money.

I'll tell you how it's costing you money. The cost of defensive medicine—in other words, practicing medicine that is otherwise not necessary—is estimated to cost our society $60 to $100 billion a year. It raises the cost of Medicare, Medicaid, Veterans Affairs, and other health programs by an estimated $28 billion a year.

You're paying it. You're working hard. You're putting money into the—paying your taxes, and $28 billion of those taxes goes to pay for the cost of frivolous and junk lawsuits. As equal—more importantly, in my judgment, actually, is that good docs are leaving the practice of medicine.

I said something in the State of the Union, and it's a startling statistic, if you really take time to think about it, and that is there are 1,500 counties in America without an ob-gyn. There are 15 counties in your State of Ohio without an ob-gyn. Now, that isn't right. I mean, these are good docs who are involved with the precious—the delivery of precious life. And they're getting sued—a lot. And they're leaving the practice, and it's putting a lot of women in a bind. Women are having to travel miles. There's nothing worse than being—having uncertainty at this very important time of life.

And we need to do something about it, you know. I thought when I got to Washington it was a State issue, Governor—not when I see the effect on the Federal budget of $28 billion a year, it's a national issue. It requires a national response. The House of Representatives passed a good piece of legislation. The trial lawyers have got it stuck in the United States Senate. For the sake of affordable health care and available health care, for the sake of good health care for our women across the United States of America, we need medical liability reform this year.

So that's what I wanted to talk about— [*laughter*]—ways to make health care more affordable and more available. I hope you can get a sense of my philosophy that when you trust the American people to make wise decisions about their health care, positive things happen. Free markets and competition transform our world. They have the power to transform our health care system. It's important to recognize—Wendy's recognized that when you introduced health savings accounts.

The agenda I just talked about, one I'm looking forward to working with both Democrats and Republicans in Congress, builds on the strengths of the private sector, recognizes what's good, and let's continue to build on that. It focuses on practical, market-based solutions. It offers the potential to deliver real improvements, genuine improvements in the lives of our fellow citizens.

The heart of the reform is that you got to trust the people of the United States of America. And I do. And I do. I want to thank you for giving me a chance to come by and visit with you. God bless you. God bless our country.

NOTE: The President spoke at 12:13 p.m. at Wendy's International, Inc. In his remarks, he referred to John T. "Jack" Schuessler, chairman and chief executive officer, and Jeffrey Cava, executive vice president of human resources and administration, Wendy's International, Inc.; Gov. Bob Taft of Ohio; Jon A. Husted, speaker, and Larry L. Flowers, majority leader, Ohio State House of Representatives; Bill M. Harris, president, and Steve Stivers, senator, Ohio State Senate; and Mayor Marilee Chinnici-Zuercher of Dublin, OH. The Office of the Press Secretary also released a Spanish language transcript of these remarks.

Remarks in a Discussion on Health Care Initiatives
February 16, 2006

The President. Thank you all. Thanks for the warm welcome. Thanks for coming. We're about to have a discussion about how this country can make sure our health care system is available and affordable. And I want to thank our panelists for joining us. It's an interesting way to describe and discuss policy. It's a lot better than me just getting up there and giving a speech—you don't have to nod. [*Laughter*]

Do you want to kick things off, Mark?

Mark B. McClellan. I'd be glad to. I'd like to welcome all of you to the Department of Health and Human Services. As you know, there are many people here who are working day and night to protect the public health, to help our health care system work better.

We have the privilege of working with the best health professionals in the world—

doctors, nurses, others who have some great ideas about delivering better care and about finding ways to do it with fewer complications and at a much lower cost. But in many ways, our health care policies haven't kept up with what our health care system can do, and we're going to spend some time talking about that today.

So, Mr. President, we're very pleased to have you here today to lead this discussion of some new ideas for improving our health care.

The President. Yes, thank you, Mark. Thanks. Mike Leavitt—where are you, Michael? Surely, he's here? [*Laughter*]

Dr. McClellan. He's in Florida, Mr. President.

The President. Oh, he's in Florida. Okay. Surfing. [*Laughter*] Actually, I saw him this morning—now don't make excuses for him. He's doing a heck of a job—he really is—and I hope you enjoy working for him.

I am really pleased that Nancy Johnson is here. Madam Congresswoman, thank you for coming. If you want to meet somebody in Congress who knows something about health care, talk to Nancy; she is a tireless advocate for making sure the health care systems are efficient and compassionate. And I really want to thank you for coming. It's a joy to work with you on these big issues.

I thank all the folks here at HHS. Thank you for working hard on behalf of our fellow citizens. You've got a tough and important job, and you're doing it well. One of the reasons why is because, you know, we've clearly defined roles of government—with the role of Government in health care. And one of the roles is to make sure our seniors have a modern, reformed Medicare system. And I want to thank those of you who are working on making sure that the Medicare system is explained to and available for seniors all across the country.

We did the right thing when it came to saying that if we're going to have a program for seniors, let's make sure it works as good as possible. And part of that meant

modernizing the system so it included a prescription drug benefit. It's not easy to sign up millions of people in a quick period of time to a new program, and there were some glitches. The good thing about this Department, and the good thing about Mike and Mark is that they have prioritized problems to be fixed and have gone around the country fixing them.

Millions of folks—about 25 million people have signed up for the new Medicare benefit. I don't know if you remember when we first had the discussions about the Medicare benefit, people said, "It will cost about $37 a month per beneficiary." One of the interesting reforms was not only making sure that medicine was modernized, but seniors actually were given choices to make in the program. And Mark's done a fine job of encouraging providers to be in the markets. And as a result of choice in the marketplace, the average per—anticipated cost is $27 a month.

In other words, giving people a decision to make is an important part of helping to keep control of cost. We have a third-party system—third-party payer system. When somebody else pays the bills, rarely do you ask price or ask the cost of something. I mean, it seems kind of convenient, doesn't it? You pay your premium; you pay your copay; you pay your deductible; and somebody pays the bills for you.

The problem with that is, is that there's no kind of market force. There's no consumer advocacy for reasonable price when somebody else pays the bills. And one of the reasons why we're having inflation in health care is because there is no sense of market. We're addressing the cost-drivers of health care, and this discussion today is a part of helping to make sure health care is affordable. And as it becomes affordable, it becomes more available, by the way.

A couple of ideas, other than the subject at hand, to make sure health care is affordable is—and we'll talk a little bit about information technology. I know there's a great initiative here at HHS to help bring the health care industry into the modern era by implementing information technology reforms. And for those of you working on the project, thanks, and we take it very seriously at the White House, and I know you take it seriously here.

Secondly, I want to thank those of you who are working on community health centers. One way to help control costs is to help people who are poor and indigent get costs in places that are much more efficient at delivery of health than emergency rooms. And so we're committed to expansion of community health centers. Again, thanks on that, Nancy, for helping in Congress. They work. We're measuring results, and the results are good results.

Thirdly, lawsuits are running up the cost of medicine. The practice of—the defensive practice of medicine or the practice of defensive medicine—I'm a Texan—[laughter]—it costs about 28 billion a year when doctors overprescribe, to make sure that they kind of inoculate themselves against lawsuit. It runs up Federal budgets. It costs the economy about 600 to 100 billion—60 to 100 billion a year.

And so we've got to do something about these junk lawsuits. I mean, they're running good people out of practice. I said a statistic the other day in the State of the Union that's got to startle you if you're involved with the health care delivery in America: 1,500 counties don't have an ob-gyn because lawsuits have driven a lot of good docs out of those counties. And that's not right.

And so we've got to get medical liability reform. The House has done a good job of passing it. It's stuck in the Senate. So for the sake of affordable and available health care and if—is to get a good, decent bill passed.

One other way to help control costs is to interject market forces, as I mentioned. And one way to do that is through what's called health savings accounts. Health savings accounts are an innovative product that

came, really, to be as a result of the Medicare bill that I was honored to sign. And they're an innovative account that combines savings on a tax-free basis with a catastrophic health care plan. We'll have some consumers here of health savings accounts that will describe how they work and whether or not they're working worth a darn.

But the key thing in a health savings account is you actually put a patient in charge of his or her decisions and—which we think is a vital aspect of making sure the health care system is not only modern, but a health care system in which costs are not running out of control. And part of making sure consumers, if they have a decision to make, can make rational decisions is for there to be transparency in pricing. In other words, how can you make a rational decision unless you fully understand the pricing options or the quality options. When you go buy a car, you know, you're able to shop and compare. And yet in health care, that's just not happening in America today.

And so one of the—this discussion is centered around encouraging consumer-based health care systems and strengthening private medicine through transparency and pricing and quality. And I hope you find this as interesting a discussion as I will.

I'm going to start off with Dr. Gail Wilensky. Do you know anything about health care? No. [Laughter] She knows a lot about health care. You've been working the health care industry for, what—tell us what you do.

[At this point, Gail Wilensky, senior fellow, Project HOPE, made brief remarks.]

The President. Thank you for the lead-in. We spend a lot of money at the Federal level, and you would expect that if we're sitting up here talking about transparency then we ought to do something about it. I mean, the Federal Government is the largest purchaser of health care—am I right—46 percent of all health care dollars.

Dr. McClellan. That's right.

The President. Okay. What are you going to do about it? [*Laughter*]

Dr. McClellan. Well, Mr. President, we are doing a lot about this already, as you know. With—before the Medicare drug benefit, Medicare provided a drug discount card for millions of seniors to enable them to save billions of dollars. And with that card, we made available information on discounted drug prices for all the prescription drugs and all the pharmacies around the country. Seniors use that information to keep prices down. They shopped, and we saw during the course of this program, savings actually increase over time.

The President. Yes.

Dr. McClellan. G1We also saw lots of seniors switching to drugs that they found out about that could meet their medical needs at a much lower cost.

The President. One thing a person watching out there—what we're talking about, for example, when it comes to putting information out on drugs, a brand name drug and a generic drug do the same thing, but there's a huge price differential. And what Mark is saying is, is that we made, as a result of our Government policies, the providers to provide a shopping list, a comparison for people to get on the Internet and find out whether they can buy a drug cheaper or not.

Dr. McClellan. That's right. And many people are saving 70 or 80 percent or more on their drug cost by switching to generics. You can get this information on the Internet. You can also get it by calling 1–800–MEDICARE. And we're doing the same thing with the drug benefit. And that's one reason the drug benefit costs now are so much lower than people expected, as you mentioned earlier.

We're trying to make more information available on hospital quality, on nursing home quality, on many other aspects of health care. But we can't do this alone;

we've got a public/private health care system, so we need to work with health professionals, with consumer groups, with business purchasers, and with the health plans in this country to get useful information out. We started to do that through collaborative efforts, like the Hospital Quality Alliance and the Ambulatory Care Quality Alliance. These are groups that include all of the different key stakeholders in our health care system working together to make useful information available on quality and cost.

Some of that's happened already, but I think with the leadership from the President and with the full backing of the Federal Government, we can move this effort along much more quickly and much more extensively to get information out about satisfaction with care, to get information out about outcomes of care and complications, and to get information out about cost. And, Mr. President, we're very pleased to be starting right now a new program that will be piloted in six large communities around the country, where all these different groups—the health professionals, business groups, Government organizations, including Medicare and the Agency for Health Care Research and Quality, and health plans—are going to be working together to make useful information available to consumers and health professionals in these communities about the quality and costs of their health care. And hopefully, we'll be able to move this project along very, very quickly.

The President. Good.

Dr. McClellan. We're working.

The President. Nice going. Yes, I know you are. You're working hard. Mark also has been responsive to some of the issues of the Medicare rollout. And they've been moving hard and traveling around the State. And thanks for responding to what's going to end up being a really, really important program for our seniors—let me say, a revitalized, important program for our seniors. It's going to make a big difference. Thanks for working so hard.

Robin Downey. What do you do, Robin?

Roberta "Robin" Downey. I'm head of product development for Aetna.

The President. Yes.

Ms. Downey. And I was instrumental in launching our HSA program. We've been doing consumer-directed plans since 2002. And so we're the first national plan to offer an HSA in the health plan arena.

The President. Good move. I bet you're really selling a lot of them.

Ms. Downey. Yes, we are. The adoption is higher in the HSA than it is in the HRA now. It's increasing, and I'm probably one of Aetna's first members in the HSA.

The President. You and I both. We own an HSA.

Ms. Downey. Yes, yes, both in it.

The President. Let me ask you something. Aetna, obviously, is a big health insurance company. Do you—obviously you've got an opinion on transparency, otherwise you wouldn't be sitting here—but give us from your perspective, from the insurance company's perspective, tell us what transparency means to you and how best we can work together to implement the transparency.

[*Ms. Downey, vice president and head of product development, Aetna, made brief remarks.*]

The President. Good. And I presume there was resistance at first?

Ms. Downey. Not resistance; they wanted to know why. I think physicians are wondering why the consumers need that kind of information. So they're getting used to that. And then they were actually pretty helpful when we were talking about how we were going to display it. They were saying, make it easy for the patients to understand, so they're helping us take the medical terminology, put it into layman's terms. They wanted to make sure it wasn't going to create more work for them; were people going to be calling their offices con-stantly. And that's what we want to do; we want to put it on the web site so they don't have to constantly call. So we want to provide easy access.

And so they were also concerned with, if you put cost information there, and you don't have quality, then people will price shop on cost alone, and they're very afraid of that—and they should be, because people should understand the——

The President. So how do you handle that?

Ms. Downey. We're marrying that now. We're going to expand that pilot. It was so successful, we're going to expand it into more locations in the fall of 2006, and we're going to be marrying that information with the quality information so the consumer can go out and see what the unit cost is, what the efficiency is, what the clinical quality is. And so they can look at the overall value. We're pretty pumped about it.

The President. Well, I appreciate you doing it. It must be exciting to be on the leading edge of an interesting innovation and to a—into health care.

Ms. Downey. Very much.

The President. It's hard to believe that ours is a market society in which people are able to shop based upon price and quality in almost every aspect of our life, with the exception of health care. And it's no wonder that we're dealing with what appears to be ever-increasing costs.

You know, it's really interesting, LASIK surgery is a good example of a procedure that was really didn't—was not a part of a third-party payer, just came to be. People could choose it if they wanted to choose it, could pay for it if they didn't want to—would pay for it themselves if they chose to use it. And more doctors started offering LASIK surgery. There was more information about LASIK surgery, and the price came down dramatically over time, and the quality was increasing. And now LASIK surgery is eminently affordable for a lot of people, because the market actually functioned. And I think what Robin is saying is that they're trying to introduce those same kind of forces in Cincinnati.

Thanks for doing what you're doing. I met with your old boss today. Maybe he's watching out there. [*Laughter*]

Ms. Downey. He talks to me just the way you talk to Mark—"just do it." [*Laughter*]

The President. A little bossy. [*Laughter*]

Ms. Downey. Yes. But you get stuff done.

The President. Yes, that's right.

Dan Evans is the president and CEO of Clarion Health Partners in Indianapolis, Indiana. Thanks for coming. They're doing some interesting things. He's a hospital guy.

Daniel F. Evans, Jr. Yes. We're—I'm the CEO of an academic medical center, so we have both a university and a hospital. We have 4,000 peer review projects ongoing right now, including——

The President. Tell everybody what a peer review project is.

[*Mr. Evans, president and chief executive officer, Clarion Health Partners, Inc., made brief remarks.*]

The President. So how easy is it to establish a matrix, or a—information for consumers to be able to really accurately understand?

[*Mr. Evans made further remarks.*]

The President. The—we're really talking about making sure each American has an electronic medical record, over which he or she has got control of the privacy. An interesting—another example was what happened—the Veterans Administration, by the way, has implemented electronic medical records. In other words, they're using modern technology to bring this important agency into the 21st century. A lot of files at your hospital still—probably not your hospital but the typical hospital—are handwritten.

Mr. Evans. Well, you know, what happens is, they may be electronic in the hospital, but handwritten in the doctor's office——

The President. Yes, and the doctors can't write anyways, so—[*laughter*].

Mr. Evans. Well, the pen is a very dangerous thing.

The President. Yes, it is.

Mr. Evans. Yes, as you well know. [*Laughter*]

The President. And so the idea is to modernize doctors' offices and hospitals and providers through information technology. And so the Veterans Department has done this. In other words, each veteran has got an electronic medical record. And so when Katrina hit, a lot of veterans were scattered, and they were just displaced. And you can imagine the trauma to begin with, and the trauma is compounded if you're worried about your record being lost somewhere, your medical record.

And fortunately, because the veterans at the Department had already acted, these medical records went with the patient, and a lot of veterans got instant help. And so a doc could just, you know, kind of download their record, take a look at what was prescribed before, take a look at other procedures, and boom, the medicine and the help was brought up to speed quickly, which is great. And I want to thank you for doing that.

Information technology is going to help change medicine in a constructive way, and it does dovetail with price and equality.

Yes. Getting kind of adrift of what we're talking about here? I hope so. If not, we'll go over to Jerry; she'll help—[*laughter*]. Jerry, welcome. Where do you live? What do you do?

Jerry W. Henderson. Mr. President, I live in Baltimore, Maryland.

The President. Welcome.

Ms. Henderson. And I am a nurse, and I've been in health care for over 30 years. And for the last 9 years, I've had the responsibility of running an ambulatory surgery center in Baltimore.

The President. Good. Called?

Ms. Henderson. The SurgiCenter of Baltimore.

The President. Very good. And tell us, you know, the transparency issue—you—we had a little visit ahead of time, so it's not the first time I've seen her; she gave me a little hint about what she was going to talk about. Go ahead and share with people—small clinic, relatively small clinic, big hospital guy, small clinic person.

[*Ms. Henderson, executive director, SurgiCenter of Baltimore, made brief remarks.*]

The President. Right. And the reason why they can't yet is because you happen to be on the leading edge of what is an important reform.

Ms. Henderson. I think so.

The President. Yes, it is. Well, so do the patients, more importantly. And thank you for sharing that with us.

You have—happen to have a patient here.

Ms. Henderson. I do.

The President. You've known Gail before?

Ms. Henderson. Gail Zanelotti was a patient at our center, and I think she'll tell you that probably it was a more convenient and comfortable and patient——

The President. You're not putting words in her mouth are you? [*Laughter*]

Ms. Henderson. No, no. But I bet she would tell you that. [*Laughter*]

Gail Zanelotti. It was more convenient and comfortable. [*Laughter*]

The President. It was? Very good. [*Laughter*]

Ms. Henderson. See? [*Laughter*]

The President. You were diagnosed with what?

Ms. Zanelotti. With bilateral breast cancer in October. And I had several procedures performed at the Surgical Center of Baltimore. And they treated me as if I were the main event. That's how I felt—socially, emotionally, physically. The whole gamut was covered. And I chose the surgeon first for quality and then went on to find the pricing and everything else through them——

The President. Sure.

Ms. Zanelotti. ——which they were very transparent about. It was a very positive experience. And I'm still in communication with them because—through the reconstructive process.

The President. Yes.

Ms. Zanelotti. And I would do it the same way again.

The President. And so how does—I mean, so you're the consumer. You walk in, obviously, pretty well traumatized to a certain extent. You've got this horrible disease that's attacked you. And you come to them, and they—and you're asking what questions?

Ms. Zanelotti. I saw the surgeon that night, and I think we were there at 10:30 p.m. at night.

The President. Oh, great.

Ms. Zanelotti. I mean, it's amazing how dedicated some of these doctors are. And then they take you through the process of different diagnostic steps that you have to take. And really, you see how curable things can be if it's caught early. And I was very lucky to be able to be faced with step-by-step approach to get back to my journey of full health.

The President. Good job. Congratulations.

Ms. Zanelotti. Thank you.

The President. You've got that sparkle in your eye, you know. [*Laughter*]

Ms. Zanelotti. Thank you. Very lucky.

The President. And so—no, I appreciate it. It's an interesting—the transparency reform is going to take place in both large entities and smaller entities, because consumers shouldn't be restricted to shopping only in a large entity or a small entity. "Shopping" isn't the right word, but you know what I mean—in other words, out there looking for the procedure that fits their needs at the right cost and the right price.

It almost doesn't matter if we have transparency if consumers, however, are not in a position to make decisions. In other words, if somebody is making the decision for you, transparency only matters to the decider.

And so Bruce is with us today—Bruce Goodwin. He's an HSA owner. Bruce, describe HSAs—well, first of all, tell us what you do.

William "Bruce" Goodwin. My company manufactures computer plate technology for the graphic arts printing business.

The President. How many employees?

Mr. Goodwin. We have 20 employees. We're a small company.

The President. Yes. By the way, two-thirds of new jobs in America are created by small businesses. And if a small business can't afford health care, it's pretty likely they're not going to be aggressive in expanding. And I presume you have some health care issues.

Mr. Goodwin. Well, I'm here as an employer who is concerned about health care costs for sure, and a strong advocate of health savings accounts. I'm a firm believer that for employers, health savings accounts is probably the best weapon we've got in the battle of these rapidly escalating health care costs. And I'm very much hopeful, and I appreciate very much your leadership in trying to help strengthen the health savings accounts.

The President. Yes, we'll talk about it in a minute. So tell people what a health savings account is. This is kind of a foreign language to everybody but the 3 million people who own one. It's just a new product. And it's just beginning to happen.

[*Mr. Goodwin, president, Glunz and Jensen, Inc., made brief remarks.*]

The President. An insurance plan with a health savings account is a high-deductible catastrophic plan coupled with a tax-free health savings account to pay routine medical costs up to the deductible. That's the way they're structured now. Many employees—I was at Wendy's yesterday. Wendy's has now got 9,000 employees using health savings accounts. The company pays for part of the premium, as well as the contribution into the cash account to be paid by the customer for routine medical expenses.

If you don't spend all your money in your cash account, you can save it tax-free and roll it over to the next year, and then you contribute again. Wendy's premiums rose this year, I think, at less than 2 percent—maybe even less than 1 percent, if I'm not mistaken. And they were increasing at double-digit rates—I hope I'm not exaggerating—they were going up quite dramatically, let me put it to you that way. And now their premiums were significantly lower. And the savings enabled them to put additional money into their employees' accounts, additional contributions.

It's an interesting concept, because all of a sudden, it puts an individual in charge of health care decisions. There's an incentive, by the way, for people to make rational choices about what they consume—like, if you don't smoke and drink, it's more likely you'll stay healthy and not spend money in your account. If you exercise—I'd strongly urge mountain biking—[*laughter*]—it helps you stay healthy. And by staying healthy, you actually save money. There's a remuneration for good choice.

And what Bruce is saying is that it's helped his business afford health care. It's helped a lot of small businesses. If you're a small-business owner, please look into health savings accounts for the good of your employees.

Interestingly enough, about a third of those who've purchased the new health savings accounts were uninsured. Many of the uninsured in America are young people, kind of the bulletproof syndrome—you're never going to get sick, so therefore, why buy insurance. Now, there's an incentive to buy insurance because it means you can save tax-free.

And so Bruce has used them, and it's— and he reports that he's able to better control his costs, which is really important for the small-business sector. And it's also important for the large-business sector to say to their employees, "Here is something that's really beneficial for you and your families because when you saved the money, it's your money." Savings in health care doesn't go to a third party entity; it goes to the consumer. It's a new concept that's just coming in to be.

In order for it to work, there has to be transparency. How can you expect somebody to make rational decisions in the marketplace if they don't see price and quality? It's going to be a very important— what we're talking here is a very important reform to really fit into a—making sure the private medicine aspect of our medical system remains the center of medicine.

There's a debate here in Washington about who best to make decisions. Some up here believe the Federal Government should be making decisions on behalf of people. I believe that consumers should be encouraged to make decisions on behalf of themselves. And health savings accounts and transparency go hand in hand.

There are some things we need Congress to do to make health savings accounts work even better than they are. One is to make sure that one's contributions into the health savings account is—can be—it will be equal to the deductible, plus any copays that may have to be made. In other words, we shouldn't cap the contribution, cash contribution at where it is; it needs to be raised.

Secondly, we need to make sure the Tax Code treats employees in large companies and employees in small companies equally when it comes to purchasing health savings accounts. And thirdly, and a key component of making sure health savings accounts works, that addresses one of the real concerns in our society, and that is people changing jobs but fearful of losing health care as they do change jobs, is to make sure health savings accounts are portable in all aspects, a health care plan that encompasses health savings accounts. Today, the rules enable one to take with them the cash balances in their health savings accounts but not the insurance in their health savings accounts. In order to make these plans truly portable, so as to bring peace of mind to people, we've got to make sure that health savings accounts are genuinely portable accounts.

I look forward to working with Congress to strengthen, not weaken, but strengthen these very important products that puts the doctor and the patient in the center of the health care decision. Today we've heard some interesting, innovative ideas that are taking place from the insurance industry to the providers to the Federal Government. And we will continue to implement transparency. And it's just the beginning. And I predict that when this—as this society becomes more transparent, as the consumers have more choice to make, you'll see better cost containment. And as we're able to contain costs, we achieve some great national objectives: One is to make sure health care is affordable, and two, make sure it's available.

I want to thank you all for coming to join us. It was an interesting discussion. Appreciate your time. God bless.

NOTE: The President spoke at 1:18 p.m. in the Great Hall at the U.S. Department of Health and Human Services.

Remarks Following Discussions With President Alvaro Uribe Velez of Colombia and an Exchange With Reporters
February 16, 2006

President Bush. Thank you all for coming. The President and I will make a statement. We'll be glad to take two questions per side.

Mr. President, *bienvenidos*. We're glad you're here.

First of all, the President and I are friends, and we are personal friends, and we're friends of freedom as well. Every time I visit with President Uribe, I am impressed by his strength of character and his belief in the future of his country. Mr. President, I'm proud that you're here. I want to thank you for the wide-ranging discussions we have had.

The President, of course, has got trade on his mind. I've explained to him very carefully that we are interested in a trade agreement that we will negotiate in good faith. The agreement must be good for the people of Colombia and—as well as the people of the United States. And I assured him that our trade negotiators will be fair in our approach.

So, Mr. President, thank you for your strength of character, and thank you for your friendship. And welcome here to the Oval Office.

[*At this point, President Uribe made remarks in Spanish.*]

President Bush. Si, senor.

Q. Senor Presidente——

President Bush. Hold on for a second. Hold on for a second. *Un momento, por favor.* [*Laughter*] You want to say it?

[*The interpreter then translated President Uribe's remarks as follows.*]

President Uribe. President Bush, this meeting has been very constructive, as it always is whenever we meet. I want to thank you, I want to thank the Government, and I want to thank the Congress and the people of the United States for their permanent interest in Colombia.

Our peoples have a relationship that is historic, and it's also a relationship that is close. We also have a convergence, a convergence that is based on democratic values and the belief that democracy needs security in order to build those values.

We have been negotiating an FTA for the last 23 months. All of us have come to this negotiation in good faith, and I'm sure that we will see a conclusion. This meeting has been good for democracy, and it has been good for the interests of our people, as well as for our shared war on terror and our war against the drugs that finance that terror.

Thank you.

President Bush. I understood you. [*Laughter*]

President Uribe. Thank you.

President Bush. Nedra [Nedra Pickler, Associated Press].

Vice President's Hunting Accident

Q. Yes, Mr. President, do you feel it was appropriate that the Vice President didn't reveal his shooting accident until the next day and through a private citizen? And do you think it was okay that he didn't talk to you about it, personally, until Monday?

President Bush. I thought the Vice President handled the issue just fine. He went through—and I thought his explanation yesterday was a powerful explanation. This is a man who likes the outdoors, and he likes to hunt. And he heard a bird flush, and he turned and pulled the trigger and saw his friend get wounded. And it was a deeply traumatic moment for him, and obviously, for the—it was a tragic moment for Harry Whittington.

And so I thought his explanation yesterday was a very strong and powerful explanation, and I'm satisfied with the explanation he gave.

Q. But are you satisfied about the timing?

President Bush. I'm satisfied with the explanation he gave.

Mr. President is about to ask somebody to ask a question.

Colombia–U.S. Free Trade Agreement

Q. Mr. President, is there going to be a free trade agreement with Colombia or not?

President Bush. Espero que si.

Q. Pronto? Soon?

President Bush. Vamos a ver. I spent time visiting with the President about the progress on negotiations. Free trade agreements are never easy to negotiate—*es muy dificile* and—because there's interests. He represents the people of your country very well. He's a good negotiator, as is his trade minister. They're strong in representing the interests of the people, whether they be farmers or manufacturers. And our people are good, strong negotiators too.

I'm very hopeful. I'm very hopeful we reach a conclusion. It's a—trade agreements are never easy, and that's what's very important to understand. But they—in my judgment—and by the way, I, too, have to convince the American people of the importance of trade agreements—in my judgment an agreement with this important country, Colombia, will be a very important agreement. And so we're working hard.

Steve [Steve Holland, Reuters].

Vice President's Hunting Accident

Q. Some Democrats say that this shooting episode has contributed to a perception of White House secrecy. What do you say to that, sir?

President Bush. I think people are making the wrong conclusion about a tragic accident. The Vice President was involved in a terrible accident, and it profoundly affected him. Yesterday when he was here in the Oval Office, I saw the deep concern he had about a person who he wounded. And he—again, I thought yesterday's explanation was a very strong and important explanation to make to the American people.

And now our concerns are directed toward the recovery of our friend. I knew Harry Whittington when I was the Governor of Texas, down there in Austin. He's a fine man. He was been involved in our State's politics for a long period of time. And, you know, my concern is for Harry, and I know the Vice President feels the same way.

Colombia–U.S. Free Trade Agreement

Q. President Bush, do you think the negotiators are making the link between the fact that it's important to prove legal economy as a way to fight against terror and illegal drugs?

President Bush. That's a great question. I believe that when we work together in a free trade, it strengthens markets and the appreciation for open markets, whether it be in Colombia or here at home. I believe free commerce between nations will enable countries—people in countries to realize their full potential. I think one of the things that's very important—I know the President is dedicated on—is a strategy on the one hand that says he will deal harshly with those who deal in drugs. But he also recognizes there needs to be economic activity to compete.

We've had a lot of discussions about crop substitution and microloans for people to be able to develop ways to make a living that is distinct from and different from being involved in the drug trade.

And so absolutely we understand the connection between trade of legal products in a free way between nations as a way to compete against illegal activities. I appreciate the President's leadership on working hard to make sure that Colombia is rid of narcotrafficking. It's a great country with a wonderful history. And the determination to rid the country of narcotrafficking will go down as a very important part of your nation's history, and we'll continue to say to the world Colombia is a great country with great enterprise and great hope and great opportunity.

So thank you for coming. *Adios.*

NOTE: The President spoke at 4:16 p.m. in the Oval Office at the White House. In his remarks, he referred to Harry M. Whittington, chairman, Texas Funeral Service Commission, who was injured on February 11 while hunting with the Vice President on a ranch in Corpus Christi, TX; and Minister of Commerce, Industry, and Tourism Jorge Humberto Botero of Colombia. President Uribe spoke in Spanish, and his remarks were translated by an interpreter.

Letter to the Speaker of the House of Representatives Transmitting a Request for Fiscal Year 2006 Supplemental Appropriations for Ongoing Military and Intelligence Operations and Selected Other International Activities
February 16, 2006

Dear Mr. Speaker:

Today, I am submitting a request for Fiscal Year 2006 supplemental appropriations of $72.4 billion for ongoing military and intelligence operations in support of Operation Iraqi Freedom, Operation Enduring Freedom, and selected other international activities. These funds support U.S. Armed Forces and Coalition partners as we advance democracy, fight the terrorists and insurgents, and train and equip Iraqi security forces so that they can defend their sovereignty and freedom. Already more than 35 Iraqi battalions have assumed control of their own areas of responsibility. This request provides the resources necessary to continue that effort so the Coalition can continue to hand over control of more territory to Iraqi forces.

In Afghanistan, our Armed Forces continue to track down terrorists, help the Afghan people rebuild their country, and train and equip Afghan security forces so that Afghanistan may continue to take control of its democratic future. Our coalition has trained many thousands of Afghan soldiers and police. These forces are risking their lives to fight our common enemy. This request provides the resources necessary to continue the train and equip effort so Afghan forces can eventually provide for the security of their own citizens.

The request includes funds to confront the threat from Improvised Explosive Devices and to improve the protection of our forces. In addition, the request addresses the need for substantial investment to repair or replace equipment worn out or lost in military operations. It also provides additional funding to cover the costs of restructuring the Army and Marine Corps into more agile, self-sustaining units that provide increased combat effectiveness critical to winning the Global War on Terror.

The request includes bonuses and incentive pay to properly compensate American troops for the sacrifices they make in defense of freedom. It also includes funds to cover enhanced benefits for survivors of all military members and provides for newly authorized benefits for those injured in combat.

The request also provides funds for the extraordinary security and operating costs associated with supporting U.S. diplomatic activity in Iraq and Afghanistan.

The request includes funds to help create political and economic stability in post-conflict areas, help Iraqis protect and sustain their infrastructure, and build Iraqi capacity at the national and provincial levels for better, more responsive, and transparent governance. The request also supports the successful Commander's Emergency Response program that enables military commanders to respond to urgent, small-scale, humanitarian relief and reconstruction needs in their area of responsibility. These counter-insurgency and stabilization activities help build civilian capabilities to ensure the transition to greater Iraqi self-reliance. Coupling increased civilian capacity with increased military capacity is essential to sustained progress in all realms—security, political, and economic—and is essential to neutralizing the insurgents and defeating the terrorists.

Finally, the supplemental requests funds for urgent, unanticipated needs to help re-lieve human suffering associated with a number of humanitarian crises, including Sudan and other parts of Africa, assistance for refugees, and the costs of humanitarian relief and reconstruction efforts in response to the devastating earthquake in Pakistan. The request also includes funding to address urgent democracy-promotion activities in Iran.

I hereby designate the specific proposals in the amounts requested herein as emergency requirements. This request reflects urgent and essential requirements. I ask the Congress to appropriate the funds as requested and promptly send the bill to me for signature. The details of the request are set forth in the enclosed letter from the Director of the Office of Management and Budget.

Sincerely,

GEORGE W. BUSH

Letter to the Speaker of the House of Representatives Transmitting a Request for Additional Funds To Support Recovery Efforts in the Gulf Coast
February 16, 2006

Dear Mr. Speaker:

Hurricane Katrina was one of the worst natural disasters in our Nation's history. Katrina devastated an area roughly the size of Great Britain. This devastation has required an unprecedented response by Federal, State, and local governments, as well as the private sector. So far, the Federal Government has committed more than $87 billion in spending and $8 billion in tax relief for the people of the Gulf Coast and New Orleans.

To provide additional resources to assist the region in its recovery, I ask the Congress to consider the enclosed requests, totaling $19.8 billion. This request includes critical funding to: replenish the Depart-ment of Homeland Security's Disaster Relief Fund in support of ongoing response efforts; support the Small Business Administration's Disaster Loan program; provide funding for the Community Development Block Grant program to support Louisiana's flood mitigation plans; achieve my commitment through the Corps of Engineers for stronger and better levee protection for New Orleans; and continue rebuilding of the region's Federal infrastructure.

I urge the Congress to act expeditiously on this request to ensure that the Federal response and recovery efforts continue uninterrupted. I designate this proposal in the amount requested herein as an emergency requirement.

The details of this request are set forth in the enclosed letter from the Director of the Office of Management and Budget.

Sincerely,

GEORGE W. BUSH

Remarks on the War on Terror and a Question-and-Answer Session in Tampa, Florida
February 17, 2006

The President. Thank you all. Please be seated. Thanks for the warm welcome. Thanks for the warm weather. [*Laughter*] It's nice to be back here. I just came from MacDill, where I was talking to General Abizaid and General Brown, and one of the things that's clear is folks there at MacDill really do appreciate the support that the citizens of the communities of Tampa and St. Pete and the surrounding area provide them. So I want to thank you all very much for being—[*applause*].

I'd like to share some thoughts with you and then answer questions as time allows, if you've got any. First, I send Laura's greetings. She's doing great, by the way. She's a fantastic First Lady and a—[*applause*]. She's obviously got to be a woman of enormous patience. [*Laughter*]

I appreciate Congressmen Adam Putnam, Bill Young, Mike Bilirakis, and Katherine Harris for being here today. Oh, there they are, yes. Proud to give them a ride on Air Force One. [*Laughter*] Some of them aren't going back, by the way. [*Laughter*] Mark Kennedy—is Mark here with us, from Minnesota? I think he was going to drop by—he supposedly was going to be here. You don't know him because he's from Minnesota, but I do, and he's a fine guy. [*Laughter*]

I want to thank my buddy Mel Sembler, Ambassador Sembler, who represented our country so well, once in Australia under 41, and then to Italy under 43—and Betty. I want to thank the chambers of both Tampa and St. Pete. I want to thank the mayors from Tampa and St. Pete—Mayor Iorio and Mayor Baker are with us. Thank you both for coming. Appreciate you being here.

I didn't mean to take you away from your work. Any excuse is a good one on Friday, right? [*Laughter*] So long as I keep the speech short. I want to thank members of the statehouse who are here. I want to thank you all for letting us use this beautiful facility. And thank you for coming.

First of all, the economy's in good shape; it's growing. I guess that's an easy thing to say in the State of Florida, when the unemployment rate is 3.3 percent. Pretty amazing, isn't it? I'm sure the Governor is going to try to take credit for it, you know. [*Laughter*] I'm not going to, because the role of government is to create an environment where the entrepreneurs can flourish and small businesses can grow.

And the fundamental question facing this country of ours is, how do we keep ourselves to be the economic leader of the world? It's really the interesting question. You know, in spite of the good economic numbers—4.7 percent unemployment around the country; our economy growing at over 3 percent, in the face of hurricanes as well as high gas prices; homeownership is an alltime high; small businesses are growing. In spite of all that, there's a certain sense of uncertainty. People are worried. They're worried because they're changing jobs a lot. They're worried because of competition from India and China. There's a certain sense of uncertainty.

And so we have a choice to make about our economy: Do we retreat in the face of uncertainty, or do we lead? And I will be working with the Congress, Members of—from both political parties, to be the leader of the world. And here's some ideas. One, keep taxes low. We can't be the economic leader of the world if we run up your taxes, and so we're going to keep them low.

And you'll hear a debate in Washington, DC, that says, "Well, we've got to run up your taxes to balance the budget." That's not the way it works in Washington. They will run up your taxes, and they'll figure out new ways to spend money. The best way to balance the budget is to keep the taxes low and be wise about how we spend your money. That's how we're going to balance the budget.

In order for us to be competitive and lead in the world, we've got to get off of Middle Eastern oil. I know it shocks some of you to hear a Texan say, "We're addicted to oil." And we are, and it's a problem. It's a problem. It's a national security problem, and it's an economic security problem to be reliant upon oil from parts of the world that may be unstable or parts of the world that simply don't like us. And so the best way to deal with that is to continue to foster new technologies because of research and development that will enable us to use different fuels in our cars, for example.

There's Kennedy right there. Good to see you, Kennedy. The reason I thought of him is because he's from a part of the world that's growing a lot of crops that can be converted into energy. We're close. We're close to technological breakthroughs that will enable us to convert wood chips and saw grass. We already convert sugar, corn, and soy into fuel. And think about that. If this technology comes true, which we believe it will, then pretty soon a President is going to say, "We're growing a lot of crops, and we're less dependent on Middle Eastern oil." There are 4.5 million cars today that are flex-fuel cars that can either run on gasoline or ethanol. In other words,

the technology is available inside the automobile. And it's coming.

And we're making some great breakthroughs on battery technology. Next week I'm going to travel around the country going to some of the most innovative places around our country that are providing new technologies to enable us to become less dependent on oil, which will keep us a leader in the world.

Another thing we need to do is to make sure that our health care system is modern. I want to talk real quick about Medicare here. First of all, I'm aware there's a lot of seniors in this State that rely upon Medicare. The Federal Government made a commitment to the seniors around the United States, starting with Lyndon Baines Johnson, that we would provide good health care to the seniors. And when I got to Washington, I found that we were not providing modern medicine. I mean, we would provide the money for ulcer surgery in old Medicare, but not the prescription drugs necessary to prevent the ulcer from happening in the first place. And that didn't seem to make sense to me. It's an old, centralized system that was not modern and was not fulfilling the promise we made.

And so I worked with Congress—Republicans and Democrats—to get a new bill out of Congress that said, "We're going to provide a prescription drug benefit, and as we do, we're going to give seniors more choices and more options from which to choose."

About 25 million seniors have signed up for this new plan since January 1st. That's a lot of folks in a quick period of time. And needless to say, when you make that kind of transition to a modern system, there's going to be some glitches. And our job is to fix those glitches. And that's what the Department of Health and Human Services, under Mike Leavitt, is doing. And it's important for our seniors to take advantage of this new program. Call 1–800–MEDICARE. Or if you've got a mom or a dad who's eligible for Medicare, sit down with them and explain the new benefit. It is a really good deal for America's seniors.

To make sure that health care works, we'll continue to take care of the poor. In other words, the Government has made a commitment to the elderly and the poor, but the Government has also got to understand, the best medicine is private medicine. And we should not get in between the doctors and the patients in America.

Finally, I want to spend a little time on education, briefly. First of all, No Child Left Behind Act is working. It's a piece of legislation that says, "We're going to raise the standards for every child, and we're going to measure to make sure children are meeting those standards." Can you imagine—you might remember the old— well, I'll tell you. When I was Governor of Texas, we had a system that didn't measure right early on. And guess what happened? We just shuffled kids through the system who couldn't read, and we found out too late. And that is a terrible system. It lets people down. And we're spending a lot of your money. It seems like to me, it makes sense to say, when we spend your money, we ought to insist upon results. Results are good for the taxpayers; more importantly, they're good for the students. So now we measure early, before it's too late, and we're correcting problems, before they're too late. And our kids are learning to read.

And we need to apply that same rigor to children in math and science, particularly in junior high. Fourth grade tests, our kids are doing fine compared to other countries. But there's a big dropoff when it comes to math and—mathematics, particularly in junior high. And so we need to apply that same standard. We'll measure in junior high, and if you need help, we'll provide it for you. And the reason why is, the jobs of the 21st century are going to require mastery in math and science and engineering. And if we don't make—and if we don't educate our kids, the jobs are going to go elsewhere, whether we like it or not. So

to make sure America remains the leader in the world, we're going to stay on the leading edge of research and development, and educate the young scientists of tomorrow, today.

And so, look, my attitude about the future is this, when it comes to the economy, and when it comes to foreign policy: We shouldn't fear it; let's shape the future. Let's be the leader tomorrow that we are today.

Now, we're living in historic times. But when you think about this world we're in, it is a time of challenge, and it's a time of opportunity. We've got the challenge to protect the American people. My most important duty is to protect you from harm. And we have an opportunity to lay the foundation of peace for generations to come.

I make a lot of decisions. My buddies in Texas, when they show up to Washington, after they get over the initial surprise that I'm still there—[*laughter*]—or got there in the first place—[*laughter*]— say, "Like, what's it like, you know? What is the job description? What's it like to be President?" And the best way to answer it is, I make a lot of decisions. And part of the reason's—my thinking was shaped on September the 11th, let me put it to you that way. And I think it's important for you to understand how the President thinks and why I make decisions I make, particularly decisions relating to war and peace.

I knew we're at war when they attacked us. As a matter of fact, I was down here in Florida. It didn't take long to figure out what was going on. And I vowed that day that I would not rest, so long as I was the President, in protecting the people. So a lot of my decisionmaking is based upon the attack. And I know we're at war, see— I knew it then, and the enemy has, unfortunately, proved me right because they continue to attack. In order to win the war against the enemy, you've got to understand the nature of the enemy.

First of all, these people are coldblooded killers, people who will kill the innocent in order to achieve a tactical objective and a strategic objective. They have no conscience. You can't negotiate with these people. You cannot reason with them. You must bring them to justice.

Secondly, they have an ideology; they believe in something. The best way to describe what they believe in is to think about what life was like in Afghanistan under the Taliban. These were people that saw to it that young girls didn't get educated. If you didn't agree with their view of religion, you were whipped in the public square. They tolerated no dissent, no different point of view—tearing down the—destroying the culture from the past. They had no sense of history other than their dim view of history. That's what they think.

And they have made it clear their objectives. You probably have read some of Zawahiri's writings, admonitions to his fellow fighters. They've made it clear that they believe the United States is soft and weak and that they can shake our will. They've made it clear that it's just a matter of time before we vacate parts of the world which they can then occupy in order to be able to plan, plot attacks against the United States of America. They have made it clear they're interested in weapons of mass destruction. In other words, they've laid out a strategy, you know, for the world to see.

And my job is to take that strategy seriously. My job is to see the world the way it is, not the way some would hope it would be. If 9/11 affected our thinking, then we've got to make sure when the enemy speaks, we take every single sentence that they say seriously and deal with it. And that's what we're doing.

So I want to share some of the strategy in winning this war on terror. Make no mistake about it, we're going to win the war on terror. We'll protect the American people.

First, when we see threats, we've got to deal with them. When I was growing up in west Texas, oceans protected us. You might remember some of those days. Old Mayor Martinez, I know he remembers those days when we felt pretty comfortable here in America that we could see a threat overseas, but oceans made it pretty clear that—to a lot of folks—that nothing would happen, you know. September 11th came along and made it clear that we are vulnerable, that the enemy can hit us if they want to.

And therefore, when you see a threat, you've got to deal with it. You can't take things for granted anymore. The best way to deal with this enemy is to defeat them overseas so we don't have to face them here at home and to stay on the hunt. And that's what we're doing.

And we've got a coalition of countries. I spent a lot of time reminding people about the nature of the war. Listen, the tendency for folks is to say, "Well, this really isn't a war." I can understand that. Who wants to walk around thinking there's a war about to hit us. I mean, that's my job to worry about it and not yours. How can you have an economy recover from a recession if people are afraid to risk capital because they're worried about thinking something is going to happen? And the same thing happens overseas. People kind of want to slip to the comfortable. They don't believe it's a war, some of them, and I understand that. And so we spend a lot of time reminding people that we've got to work together because the enemy can't stand what we stand for, and that's freedom. They just hate freedom. And so we've got a good coalition, and we're on the hunt. We're keeping the pressure on them. It's hard to plot and plan and execute attacks when you're on the run.

And so the first step of our strategy is defeat them there so we don't to have to face them here. And we've got some great Special Forces. I met the Special Forces command guy here—and there's great intelligence officers and wonderful coalition folks. We're cutting off their money. It makes it kind of hard to operate when you can't get your bank accounts full of money in order to—we're just doing a lot of stuff. And it's important for citizens to know that there's a constant, constant pressure. I think about it every day.

And we're making progress. Khalid Sheikh Mohammed, September the 11th plotter/planner, is incarcerated; his successor brought to justice. Slowly but surely, we're finding them where they hide, and they know we're on their trail.

Secondly, we got to deny them safe haven. These people can't operate without safe haven. It's an interesting war we're in. It's totally different from what we're used to because we're not facing nation-states; we're dealing with an enemy that is international in nature, that hides in states.

When the President says something like, "If you harbor a terrorist, you're equally as guilty as the terrorists," those words mean nothing unless you act upon them. And I said that to the people of Afghanistan—the Taliban. They didn't listen, and so we acted. And removing the Taliban is a clear signal that we won't tolerate safe haven. In other words, if you harbor the terrorist, you're just as guilty as the murderers. And that's a clear signal that the United States must continue to send in order to win the war on terror.

We saw a threat in Saddam Hussein. Obviously, this issue is one that has caused a lot of people to wonder about certain aspects, caused me to wonder about the capacity of our intelligence services to provide good intelligence. And that's why we're constantly working to reform the intelligence services, to make sure we get the best intelligence, because I thought there would be weapons of mass destruction, and so did everybody else in the world, and so did people in the United States Congress from both political parties—thought that

there would be weapons of mass destruction.

The United Nations and the United Nations Security Council thought there would be weapons of mass destruction. After all, they passed a unanimous resolution that said, "Disclose, disarm, or face serious consequences." In other words, we worked the diplomatic front.

And so when Saddam Hussein chose war—and believe me, he made the choice. The hardest thing for the President of the United States to do is commit troops into combat. It's the last option, the very last option. Except September the 11th taught me—and September the 11th taught me that we've got to take threats seriously. And the world saw a threat. This man was harboring terrorists. He was on the state sponsor of terrorists lists. I didn't put him on there; he was put on there by previous Presidents. He was firing at our pilots. He had invaded countries. He was a threat. And the world spoke with one voice and said, "Disclose, disarm, or face serious consequences." And when the United States says something, it must mean it. And we said, "Disclose, or face serious consequences." And when he wouldn't, he faced serious consequences. Removing Saddam Hussein has made America safer and the world a better place.

And we have a plan to achieve victory. Victory is a state, a democracy that can sustain itself and defend itself and join America in fighting the war on terror. That's the goal of victory. That's the definition of victory.

First, part of our strategy is a political strategy. I try to tell people how I make decisions. And part of making good decisions is you've got to believe something. You have a belief system that, by the way, can't alter because of politics or polls or focus groups or what somebody wants you to think. And I believe that freedom is universal. I believe that deep in everybody's soul is the desire to be free. That's what I believe. I don't believe freedom or liberty is confined here to Methodists from Texas. I believe everybody wants to be free—white, black, brown, Muslim, Jew, Christian, agnostic. I believe there is a deep desire for people to be free.

And if you believe that, then you have faith in people demanding freedom, if given a chance. And the Iraqis proved that theory right. Eleven million people went to the polls in the face of unbelievable terror, terrorist threats, and said, "I want to be free; let me vote; let me decide my future." And so on the political front, they're making progress because of the courage of the Iraqis.

And now the task at hand is to work with the—those who won votes in the new parliament to set up a unity government, one that is—can help deal with the grievances of the past, one that unites under the fabric of democracy. And that's what we're doing. I talked to the Ambassador, Zal Khalilzad, there yesterday. He's spent a lot of time working with making our position known that we want the Government to be a unified government.

Secondly, we're helping the country rebuild itself after years of neglect, so that people can see the benefits of democracy. And we started off initially with, kind of, these grand projects. We got the Congress to appropriate money, and we tried to build some great electricity-type renovations. And the enemy kept blowing them up, and so we've altered our strategy. One of the things that you've got to do in a situation like this is constantly adjust. You can't just get stuck in one kind of response mode. You've got to think and watch the enemy and adjust to the enemy in order to achieve an objective. And we're doing that. So now we've got much smaller-scale projects that are yielding instant results for the people on the ground, so people say, "Wait a minute—this democracy deal is a pretty good thing," you know.

Businesses are flourishing in Iraq. I mean, freedom is coming; freedom is coming. There's a determined enemy trying to stop it, of course. They can't stand freedom. I told you, they think the exact opposite we do. They don't believe that everybody desires to be free. They want everybody to live under their totalitarian thumb. That's what they want. Not America and our coalition, we want governments to be responsible and responsive to the people. That's what we believe in.

Thirdly, in order to achieve our objective, the Iraqis are going to have to fight the enemy. They've proven their worth, in terms of defying the terrorists when it comes to making the vote, and they're proving their desire to defend themselves against the enemy too. You know how I know? I'm listening to the people on the ground. I talk to our commanders a lot. They're the ones who are giving me the appraisal about how well these Iraqis are being trained.

An interesting measurement, right off the bat, however, was how the Iraqis responded to these attacks on the police stations and the recruiting stations. You remember that they had a series of attacks on the recruiting stations? Guess what my question was to them out there: Are there still people lining up to join up? If you're getting blown up line—standing in line, are they still coming? And the answer was, absolutely. And we're training them, and there's a command structure—command and control structure getting in place. And this military is getting better and better. We're turning over a lot of territory to the Iraqis. They now have two divisions, which is a lot of folks, that are capable of taking the fight nearly on their own. The training mission is working.

So on the security side, we're on the hunt. We're after Zarqawi. See, he wants us to leave. He believes we'll lose our nerve, so he can establish a safe haven in Iraq. And we're not going to let him do it. And so we've got great special operators and U.S. forces and coalition forces on the hunt. And at the same time, we're training the Iraqis.

There's a big debate in Washington about who gets to decide the troop levels. Well, those troop levels will be decided by this administration, and this administration is going to listen not to politicians but to the commanders on the ground of what we need on the ground in order to win this deal.

After I leave here, I'm going to go visit with a family of one of the fallen troops. I have to be able to look that person in the eye, and say, "The cause is just." I believe it is just and necessary. And I have to look that person in the eye and say that the sacrifice of your loved one will not go in vain, that we will complete the mission. And that's what I want to assure my fellow citizens. No matter what it looks like in Washington, DC, I'm committed to victory in Iraq so—to achieve peace.

And so in the short term, we're going to succeed in Iraq. We'll deny them safe haven. We'll stay on the hunt. But there has to be a long-term strategy as well, to win. And that long-term strategy is to liberate people and give them the chance to live under the greatest system of government ever, and that's democracy—because democracies respond to people.

You know, our foreign policy in the broader Middle East for a long period of time was just kind of, tolerate the status quo and hope for the best. It didn't work. The surface looked placid, but beneath the surface was brewing resentment and anger and fertile recruiting opportunities for those who have got a dark vision of the future. And so we're working to help the Iraqis develop a democracy.

Elections are only the beginning of democracy, not the end. Election is the beginning of a process where government listens to the people. In order to make sure democracy works, there has to be institution-building and support for young, fledgling democracies. And that's what you're seeing. This is an historic moment. The world is changing because freedom is on the march. And we shouldn't be discouraged about setbacks—short-term setbacks or the enemy's capacity to take innocent life, because we've seen democracy change the world in the past.

I think about all the wars fought in Europe over the past 100 years. A hundred years seems like a long time, probably, for the little guy there—me too. It seems like a while—I'm only 59 years old. But Americans shed a lot of blood in Europe, World War I and World War II. And yet the continent is—Europe is peaceful. You know why? Because there's democracies living side by side in peace. Democracies don't fight each other. Generally, people in a democracy don't campaign and say, "Vote for me; I promise you war." They say, "Vote for you—vote for me; I'll work for the peace. I want your children to grow up in a peaceful world." That's what people say to get elected.

Japan—one of my favorite analogies and stories about this is my friend Koizumi, Prime Minister of Japan. He's an interesting guy. I like him a lot. We spend time talking about the peace. He understands that democracy in the heart of the Middle East, a democracy in a part of the world that is desperate for freedom, is an important part of laying the foundation for peace. And so he committed Japanese troops to help the Iraqis rebuild their country and to provide security so they could rebuild their country.

What's amazing about this is that, like many whose relatives—like many here whose relatives fought against the Japanese, my dad did too. Isn't that interesting? Eighteen-year-old kid, Navy fighter pilot, country calls him; like thousands, he goes overseas to fight the sworn enemy, the Japanese. And today, this guy's son is sitting down with the Prime Minister of Japan working to keep the peace. And what happened in between was that a Japanese-style democracy grew. Democracies yield the peace. And what the youngsters here have to see that's happening is, we're laying that foundation for peace. Someday, when you're old and—older, I know you never think it's going to happen, but it does—you'll look back and say, "Maybe old George W. Bush and the United States Congress was right in keeping the faith that democracies can yield the peace we all want."

I got two other things—two other things I want to tell you, then I'll answer questions. We not only protect ourselves by keeping the pressure on the enemy and defeating them over there so we don't have to face them here at home, we've got to protect ourselves by doing smart things in America. I hope—I appreciate working with the mayors on homeland security issues. We're training a lot of first-responders and getting people ready in case something happens.

Secondly, in order to ask our folks on the frontline of protecting America to do the job, they've got to have all the tools. And the PATRIOT Act passed right after September the 11th—had a little problem getting it out of the United States Senate, it got kind of hung up there. My reminder to those Senators is that the bill may—about ready to lapse, but the threat isn't. And if people in Washington expect those on the frontline of protecting America to do their job, they got to give them the tools. The PATRIOT Act needs to be passed.

Finally, I made a decision that has been in the news lately, and I want to share with you my thinking, because it's an important decision. The—September the 11th made it clear to me that an enemy would do anything it could to hurt us. We're at war. And I understand some don't think that, that we're at war. There are good, decent Americans who believe that. I know that. This is not what I—I don't believe it, see. I got a different point of view. I asked our people on the ground there in Washington, is there anything more we can do to protect the American people? What can we do? The enemy wants to hit us; they're planning to hit us. Is there anything

we can do so I can go around the country saying, "Go about your business. We're taking care of your security for you"? I think most people would ask that question.

And General Mike Hayden of the NSA—he's a wonderful person—said he thought there was something more we could do. And he showed me the plans for this country to pick up conversation—listen to conversations from people outside the country, inside the country, who had an affiliation with Al Qaida or were Al Qaida. He said, "I think we can design a program, Mr. President, that will enable us to have quick response to be able to detect and deter a potential attack."

I said, that's interesting, General. I said, that makes a lot of sense to me. I said, you're not going to listen inside the country. "No, this is calls from outside the country in, or inside out, to people who we know or suspect are affiliated with Al Qaida." And I remember some of those phone calls coming out of California prior to the September the 11th attacks by the killers—just thinking maybe if we'd have listened to those on a quick-response basis, you know, it might have helped prevent the attacks.

My second question was, is it legal? See, I take that oath of office seriously—I've taken it twice as your President—to uphold the laws and the Constitution. And so we got lawyers all over Washington, as I'm sure you can imagine. [*Laughter*] I'm not one. I said, is it legal? I'm asking this to the Attorney General of the United States, the Legal Counsel in the White House; NSA has got lawyers. I mean, a lot of lawyers looked at this, and they said, "You bet, Mr. President, it's legal." And they gave me the legal ramifications. You'll see this all—this is part of the debate.

Thirdly, I knew I needed to tell Members of Congress. See, they like to be a part of the process. They're a co-equal branch of Government, and I recognize that, and I honor that. And so we briefed Members of the United States Congress on the full program so that they would know—appropriate Members of Congress, leaders, Republicans, and Democrats, leaders of the Intelligence Committee whose job it is to provide oversight on intelligence operations. They were abreast. Like my old buddy called me, he said, "You know something, if you're trying to pull one over on them, if you're trying to have an illegal program, why are you briefing the Congress?" I said, "Because I want people to know."

Unfortunately, we're having this discussion. It's too bad, because guess who listens to the discussion: the enemy. If you don't think we're at war, it doesn't matter then, does it? I know we're at war. And the enemy is adjusting. But I'm going to tell you something. I'm doing the right thing. Washington is a town that says, "You didn't connect the dots," and then when you do connect the dots, they say, "You're wrong." In order to protect America, if somebody is talking to Al Qaida, we want to know who they are and why they're talking to them.

Okay. That's what's on my mind. Now, what's on yours? Yes, sir. Go ahead and yell it.

Homeownership

Q. Mr. President, I just wanted to take an opportunity to tell you that I think our country is blessed to have you as our President.

The President. Thank you.

Q. That—we are very thankful that you don't make your decisions based on the polls, like previous Presidents have.

The President. Well, I appreciate that.

Q. And my comment is, is that I'm a homebuilder. I'm very happy right now.

The President. You've got to be. [*Laughter*]

Q. But I wanted to just keep you apprised that things are good now. The economy is good; interest rates are low. There are people that still can't afford homes in our country today. Affordable housing is very important. We, as homebuilders—I

serve on the Board of Directors of the National Association of Homebuilders.

The President. Well, good.

Q. We'll be up in Washington in about a month or so to see you guys. But we're concerned with the environment just as much as anyone else is, and—but there's got to be a balance to make sure that we can develop land and provide homes, affordable homes. And also, Congress is working on some things now that has an affect on financing and interest rates for people buying their first homes. And let's make sure that we have affordable homes for people.

My daughter is a school teacher here in Tampa, and it's important to people like her, people that protect us—the fire department, the sheriffs—they need homes. And the times are good now, and I was a builder when your friend Jimmy Carter was President, and interest rates weren't so good back then, and those were tough times. And I just want to tell you that I'm blessed to be here today with you in this room, and we all love you.

The President. Well, thanks. Let me talk about that. Thank you. You'll be happy to hear, I don't set interest rates. [*Laughter*] That's set by an independent body. And I just named a new Chairman of the Fed to do that. And he's a good fellow. And so if I were you, I'd be worried about interest rates, because when the interest rates go up, it makes it harder for your school teacher.

Well, there's help, to help certain folks who qualify with their downpayments. We want people owning their own home. See, that's—we want this to be an ownership society. We want people owning their own business; we want people owning their own home; we want people owning their own health account they can take with them from job to job like health savings accounts. And homeownership is high right now. More minorities own a home than ever before in our Nation's history, which is a fantastic statistic.

And—but interest rates matter, as does good tax policy. And, I know—maybe you're hinting at whether or not the mortgage deduction would be part of a plan. I don't think you have to worry about the mortgage deduction not being a part of the income tax law. But thank you for bringing that up.

Yes, sir. Go ahead and yell it. Let me get a mike for you.

Florida Coastline/Energy

Q. Mr. President, you mentioned a trip next week to visit the sources of renewable, additional technology to reduce our dependence on foreign oil. We have a not-so-renewable resource, which is our precious Florida coastline. And because of your great brother, we do have an unemployment rate of 3.3 percent. How can you work with us to protect our Florida shoreline——

The President. Yes.

Q. ——with respect to offshore drilling?

The President. Well, I made a commitment that nothing is going to happen within 100 miles of this coastline, and I'm honoring the commitment. I don't care what people might be saying—I guess maybe they quit saying it after the '04 campaign—but it's a commitment that this Government has—at least my Government has made, and I'm going to honor it. When we say 100 miles off the coastline, we don't mean 99 or 89, we mean 100. And so rest easy.

Now, the thing about—look, we've got to get off of hydrocarbons. We just do. And it's—I'm a believer in nuclear power. I think it's a—[*applause*]—maybe someday, and I think we'll—I'll figure out—I'll find out how close we are when I visit with some of these solar technology people, but it's very likely that you'll become a little power generator on—in your own home, and that the excess power that you do not use, you feed back in the grid. Hybrid batteries—batteries for plug-in hybrid automobiles are pretty close, they tell me. And

I'm going to see firsthand—sometimes the President gets the cook's tour, I know it—[*laughter*]—but nevertheless, I'm going to see firsthand.

And what's interesting is, is that a lot of people in urban areas are not going to drive more than 30 miles a day. And it's—so we're developing automobile engines that can run on electricity for 30 miles, and then if you go more, your gasoline kicks in. But it requires a battery that has got good storage capacity and is easy to recharge. It's coming.

And so there's a lot of technologies that are coming on the market, and we're spending money. And it's a good use of taxpayers' money, it seems like to me, to—in order to achieve some big objectives.

I'm going to India on March the 1st, around that period of time, and I believe that it's good policy for the United States to encourage these emerging economies to use clean energy, nuclear power, so as to help reduce demand for, kind of, nonrenewables. And so I'm going to talk to them about development of a civilian nuclear power industry. They're telling me China has got about 34 plants on the market, which is good. But this expansion of nuclear power—which is in our interests, by the way; it's in our interests because of the quality of the air; it's in our interests because it takes—reduces demand, kind of global demand—is going to create another issue, and that is, what are we going to do with this spent fuel? This country doesn't reprocess spent fuel; we should. Reprocessing spent fuel means that we're able to continue to reuse the base material that went through the burn the first time in a plant and reduce the amount that we have to then eventually store. And we chose not to do that in the late seventies because of proliferation concerns. I'm convinced we can work internationally to address those issues.

And so I'm just sharing with you—we got a full strategy to help us make us less dependent on energy—on foreign sources of energy.

Yes, sir.

Transportation

Q. Commissioner Reynolds from Winter Garden in the central part of the State.

The President. Oh, yes, I know where you are.

Q. Pressed into service by your brother, Honorable Jeb Bush.

The President. Is that good or bad?

Q. Well, it's been a riot, sir.

The President. If it's bad, take it up with him. [*Laughter*]

Q. I thought about calling him and asking him if he'd like to have the job back.

The President. That's right. [*Laughter*]

Q. The concerns from the central part of this State is, we've got a really unprecedented growth rate there in the middle part. The challenge is for mass transportation to free us from the oil that you talk about. Unfortunately, the proportionate share of funding that we're able to secure seems to be tied into porkbarrel, like light rail which does—Congressman Mica needs to buy into the fact that it's not realistic. So how do we—can get free from that so we can get direct funding——

The President. Yes.

Q. ——for mass transit?

The President. Yes. That will be something that you'll be able to effect 5 years from now, because I signed the highway bill, and it's done. And nobody wants to deal with it again until it expires, to be frank with you. But I understand—but what he's saying is, how come you just don't let Floridians decide how to spend the money that's supposed to go back to them? Why do you earmark parts of the bill? That's what you're saying. And I do think Congress needs to work on earmark reform. I'm just not one of these guys—if there's no hope, I got to let you know, brother. There ain't no hope. [*Laughter*] They're not going to revisit the highway bill. They're just not going to revisit the highway bill

until the highway bill expires. And then perhaps you can get the kind of—they can get the kind of reforms. As you know, I ain't going to be around. [*Laughter*]

Yes, sir. I've heard from Jeb on this issue, by the way.

Alternative Sources of Energy

Q. Mr. President, welcome back to Tampa.

The President. Thank you.

Q. And my question is, you've talked a lot about our addiction to oil today. You've also talked about advanced, alternative fuel sources, in particular for household vehicles as a potential mitigant to that dilemma. But we have a very robust, industrialized economy—air, rail, shipping, trucking—that has depended on oil, frankly, for generations to be successful and vibrant. So my question is, how do we maintain the most advanced, industrialized economy on Earth and actually reduce our dependency on oil going forward?

The President. Yes. Well, I believe—first of all, natural gas has driven a lot of our industrialized growth, as you know. And we are—we need to have—import liquefied natural gas if we're going to be modern and stay competitive.

Listen, we're going to need oil. The question is, are we able to reduce dependency from certain parts of the world? And I think that by relieving pressure on how we drive our cars, we'll, in fact, help segments of our economy that are going to take a while to diversify away from hydrocarbons, I guess is the best kind of macro look.

Things don't happen instantly; I understand that. But nevertheless, there are some practical ways that we can reduce our dependency, and it seems like to me, the most practical way is to change automobiles, change how we drive. In the short term, ethanol and hybrid batteries makes the most sense to me. It's the most practical way and most economic way to get—to begin the reduction of dependency.

Now, listen, we've got a large fleet—I told you, there's 4½ [million]° flex-fuel cars. That's good, except there's about 200 million cars. And it takes a while for fleets to renew. And so things don't happen instantly, but they will happen quicker as we continue to press for innovation and technology.

Ultimately, I believe that we're going to be using hydrogen to power our automobiles. But that's 15 years down the—for the technology to be applicable is 15 years down the road. And I guess what I'm not only—I guess I am, what I'm telling you is that we see technological breakthroughs pretty darn quick when it comes to ethanol and hybrid batteries, which is a positive development for the people. And it's an interesting thing about ethanol, is that the barriers to entry are pretty low, when it comes to manufacturing the—if the technology says that we can—yields the capacity to convert switchgrasses and refuses to ethanol, once that technological breakthrough comes, the barriers to entry are pretty low when it comes to building the manufacturing capacity that converts raw material to ethanol. Much different from a big cracker refinery. And so that's positive. So we've got the car technology, hopefully have the breakthrough technology on fuel, and then the infrastructure will follow.

And so what I'm saying is this is the most practical way to become less dependent on oil. And the economy will continue to function. But things are happening, by the way, in diesel. I don't know visiting your area—if any of you know something about trucking, you know that diesel, clean diesel engines are coming. We did a deal in my administration to work with diesel engine manufacturers to come up with a very low-emission engine that is now being applied in trucks, and it's going to make a difference—on Caterpillar tractors. We're getting there; we're getting there.

Thanks for the question.

° White House correction.

Yes, sir.

Spread of Democracy/America's Influence Abroad

Q. The dilemma, it seems to me, that we are facing in this country—I've had the opportunity to interface with people of Muslim countries, and the war is bad enough, and I applaud what you're doing because freedom is important, but what concerns me is if the youth in these nations are being taught that you and I and us Americans are, in fact, the devil incarnate or Satan himself—I guess my question is, what can we do about that, to win over the people, the children, the youth, so that the next generation will not be facing this same dilemma? I think this is an incredible problem.

The President. I appreciate that. First is to support and work with moderate governments, and there are a lot. The largest Muslim nation is Indonesia. And we're working closely with the President there to help promote a better understanding of different religions. I will be seeing President Musharraf, who I like, and he's a good fellow who understands that moderation is an important part of a hopeful future. And so support governments that practice moderation.

Secondly, provide assistance when assistance is needed. In my State of the Union, I said, we've got to reject isolationism. Isolationism is the tendency for a nation to withdraw and not feel an obligation to be involved in the world. And I—we cannot defend ourselves if we're isolationist. I just made the case. But I also believe—and part of my philosophy in the decisionmaking is that to whom much has been given, much is required. And therefore, when we see suffering in places like Pakistan or because of the tsunami, the United States of America is leading the way in.

And it helps. It helped a lot in Pakistan, for example, to see those choppers flying relief supplies up for poor folks who had been—whose lives had been just devastated. I can't remember the exact numbers, but President Musharraf told me; we're talking hundreds of thousands of people either dead, injured, or displaced. And there was the United States of America military flying in supplies. I believe John Abizaid—General Abizaid told me today that we turned over our MASH unit to the Pakistani Government to help so they could continue to provide aid and comfort.

And so there are practical ways. One is to support moderation, and two, help where help is needed. Our HIV/AIDS initiative, by the way, is a fantastic initiative. It is—I can't tell you how proud I am of the American people for supporting this. It is necessary for the United States of America to be taking the lead on this issue to save lives. If we say, human dignity matters and every life is precious, if that's part of a credo as a country, which it is—that's what we say. We say, "People matter; every human life is precious." Then those human lives apply not just here at home but on the continent of Africa or in Muslim countries. And there's a lot of Muslims in Africa who've seen the great compassion of the United States of America when it comes to helping to battle HIV/AIDS. There's a pandemic taking place. And you ought to be proud of this country, like I am, that we're filling that void of compassion and need and hope.

Yes. Right here. Yes. You're next. Yes. Yes, ma'am.

Helping America's Youth Initiative

Q. I know that you and First Lady Bush have talked much about our hurting generation of teens and our unproductive teens in our communities. Just wanted you to talk a little bit about the efforts being made with the work that you're doing in initiatives——

The President. Thanks.

Q. ——that will help that.

The President. I appreciate that. First, there's positive news. Teen pregnancies are

down; teen drug use is down. And that's positive. That's good—[*applause*]—because of people at the grassroots level—people at the grassroots level. I think one of the most important initiatives of this administration is to—is the Faith-Based and Community Initiative, which recognizes what de Tocqueville saw in the 1830s. He's a French guy who came over here—[*laughter*]—in case you don't remember. And he recognized that the great strength of America was the capacity for individualists—or the willingness of individualists to work together in what he called voluntary associations to make the community in which they live a better place. And he saw that in the 1830s.

It's a—what he saw is still the strength of our country, if you really think about it. You know, government can hand out money, but government cannot put a hope in a person's heart. A lot of people miss one of the basics ingredients of life, and that is love. And love happens when somebody puts an arm around a person and says, "What can I do to help you, brother or sister?"

And so part of our initiative in dealing with loneliness, discouragement, lack of self-esteem, is to encourage faith-based programs will—which all exist because they hear a universal call to love a neighbor, by the way—to have access to Federal money, in other words, level the playing field for grant money so that these programs—which have been set up to love somebody and provide love—have got equal access to Federal money. It's a really important initiative.

There are targeted monies, of course. There's monies aimed at the different community groups dealing with drug use. But I think the most important initiative of all is to empower groups that really do provide mentoring and care and decency on an individual basis for somebody who needs it. And it's happening. It's happening in America.

Yes.

277

Culture of Life

Q. Mr. President, it's an honor to be here with you today, and I thank you so much for the time that you take to share with us. I'm a 40-year-old father of a 3-year-old.

The President. There you go.

Q. And I'm also an adopted child. And it seems that anymore, through the results of legislation from the bench, that maybe the unsafest place for a child in this country is in his or her mother's womb. And my question for you is—and I commend you for your Supreme Court picks. I thank you for your bold stance in who you picked. My question is, with my son—this is the future of America. And my question is, where do you believe we're headed? Long after your term of serving us has ended and long after we've had other Presidents serve this country, where do you think we're headed in the areas of abortion, in the areas of traditional marriage, in the areas of faith and the foundations that this country was founded upon that are so under attack anymore? Where do you believe we're going?

The President. I'm an optimist. I believe we're headed toward a period of personal responsibility, where people understand that they're responsible for the decisions they make in life.

I just gave you some statistics. Abortions are down in America as well, by the way. People are—I—one of my jobs is to promote a culture of life. And I just told you every life is precious, and I meant it, whether it be here at home or on the continent of Africa where somebody's suffering from HIV/AIDS. And so I'm an optimist. I think people are beginning to understand that there is virtue in being personally responsible for the decisions you make in life.

And that—there's a—and cultures change, and it takes a while for cultures to change. All of us—I'm not going to peg anybody a certain age around here, but those of us born, like, around '46, '47, '48,

we've seen a culture change in our lifetime, if you really think about it. The culture changed, and it can change again. And I think these statistics that show that some problems that seemed incurable at one point in our history indicate that there is a cultural shift. A lot of it has to do with people being responsible. Some of it has to do with there's a religious awakening around many communities in the country, not just Christian religion, Jewish religion, Muslim religion. People are becoming religious in America. And that, in itself, helps people realize that you've got to be conscious of the decisions you make and mindful of the needs of others.

And—but we still got challenges. One of the things that obviously undermines good teaching at home is TV and some of the movies. But I remind people, they put "off" and "on" knobs on TVs for a reason. You don't have to go to a movie if you don't want to go to a movie. See, I think you can promote responsibility at home and still live in the free society where people are allowed to express themselves. And my advice to parents is, pay attention to the Internet. Part of the problem we have in our society is people aren't paying attention to their kids' habits. And when you've got your child on the Internet, make sure you know what that child is looking at, because that's your responsibility. It's not the government's responsibility to take care of your child; it's your responsibility to take care of that child.

President's Personal Values

Q. Thank you for being our President. We are all way better off and very safe——

The President. Thanks. It's my high honor, by the way.

Q. Thank you.

The President. I'm glad I did it.

Q. We appreciate it. How do you—earlier you shared with us some intimacy about how you make decisions, and I felt that was heartfelt. How do you keep it together? What do you really think about when the biggest story this week was Dick Cheney's hunting trip and not Al Gore blasting our troops and being treasonous in his regard to this war on terror in the Middle East? How do you keep it together?

The President. Well, I appreciate that. That's a loaded question. [*Laughter*] I keep it in perspective. There's a lot of noise in Washington. There's a lot of flattery; there's a lot of criticism; there's just a lot of noise. And I keep it in—I try to keep my life in perspective. I try to—I don't try to; I do keep my life in perspective. And I am focused on achieving certain objectives. Every day—I've said this, and I mean this—every day I think about how to protect America. Every day in the morning, first thing in the morning, I get briefed by our intelligence officers about potential threats. So every morning I'm aware of the world around us. And I told you that it's—9/11 changed my thinking. So my focus is there.

And, you know, I care deeply about troubled youth. I'm worried about Katrina victims. I'm worried about people that got moved out of their home, and they ended up somewhere else. Put yourself in their perspective. I said homeownership is valuable. We talked about homeownership here, how important it is—and somebody wakes up the next morning and their home is gone. And not only that, they ended up out in—somewhere else, you know. The good news is those people found love, which is a wonderful thing about our country. And I think about those kind of things.

So to answer your question—and I appreciate that—first, I'm wise enough not to fall into your trap because—[*laughter*]—there are some keen reporters paying attention to every word I'm saying. [*Laughter*] But I really don't let that bother me. I've got my perspective, and I've got my priorities. My faith is a priority. My family is a priority. Look, we got to deal with issues, of course, when they come up. That's part of the—it's part of Washington. It's part of being the President. There's—issues

come, and they go. And they and—but I hope that when it's all said and done, people see me as a strategic thinker and that I'm able to stay focused on a strategy that will leave behind peace and hope—peace around the world and hope not only around the world but equally importantly, here at home, so people have this sense of the greatness of America. It's a—we're a fantastic country.

Think about a country—when you really put America in perspective, ours is a country where somebody can come with nothing except drive and desire, and end up being able to raise a family and realize dreams. It is a fantastic land. And the great thing about America is it doesn't matter who you are, you know, if you got the drive and the desire and the willingness, you can make it in this country. And it's such a powerful—it's a powerful—that's a powerful statement to make. And that's the way we need to keep it, by the way. And so— I don't even know how I got there, but anyway. [*Laughter*]

Yes, ma'am.

Immigration/Social Security Reform

Q. In light of national security, some of us baby boomers are going to retire in the next 3 to 5 years.

The President. There you go. I know how you're thinking, baby. [*Laughter*] I'm right there with you. [*Laughter*]

Q. And the number of people replacing us is only at about 63 percent. So what are we going to do with immigration to make sure we have enough people to fill those positions?

The President. Yes, it's interesting. I thought you were going a different direction. [*Laughter*] I'm going to answer two questions. I thought you were taking me down that Social Security route, because it's a really interesting—that's a really interesting way to frame the immigration debate. Really is, I haven't heard it put that way.

Let me answer immigration first and then talk about the unfunded liabilities inherent in Medicare and Social Security as a result of baby boomers like me and you retiring with not enough people to pay it, to pay the bill.

First, immigration—there are a lot of people working here in America doing jobs Americans will not do. And that is a fact. And it's a—and as I told you, we deal with the way the world—the way it is, not the way we hope that it is, and therefore, how to deal with that issue; what do you do? You got people working here, doing jobs Americans won't do.

My attitude is, you recognize it for what it is, and you say, "You can do this on a temporary basis." You say, if there's a willing employer and a willing worker on a job an American won't do, then it's okay to fill that job, so long as you're not here permanently, so long as this is not—[*applause*]. And so I believe there ought to be a temporary-worker program. We've tried this in America before—pretty successful, at least in my own home State of Texas. You got people—old Red Putnam over there, he's got people—probably have been bringing people in to pick oranges for a while, I don't know. Agriculture relies upon a lot of people willing to do the work that others won't do. And it seems like to me that there ought to be a legal way to make this happen so that—but without creating a sense of amnesty or permanency.

And so, one, I have a deal with immigration rationally. Now, we've got an obligation to enforce our borders and our coastlines, and we're spending a lot of money to do so. The Texas border is long, and it's hard to enforce. I mean, it's a lot of miles, a lot of empty country. And so we're using new technologies, drones, infrared, some mounds, some fencing in cities, to try to make it harder for people to cross. But the truth of the matter is, a lot of our Border Patrol agents are chasing people who are coming here to work, see. And it seems like to me that if we could have

a rational system that would enable people to do this on a temporary basis, it would take the pressures off the borders. People would be able to come in here in a rational, legal way.

Now, as I told you, I'm not for amnesty. You got about 8 million-plus people here illegally. My worry is if they—all of a sudden legal citizens, then another 8 million comes. And I don't think that makes any sense. So in terms of immigration, I'm for border enforcement, and strong border enforcement, with a rational guest-worker program that's temporary in nature, where it's understood that you're working here for a period of time, then you're going back on home.

Now, I want to talk to you about what's happened as a result of the current program. When you make something illegal, and there's a—you know, people coming here to work; people figure out ways around it. I'm not old enough to remember the old whisky days of Prohibition, but I remember reading about it—people still made whisky because people wanted to drink it.

And so guess what's happening today? We've got people getting stuffed in the back of 18-wheelers, driving across hot desert to find jobs that, most often or not, Americans won't do. There's a whole smuggling industry as a result of making temporary work—not making it legal. A whole smuggling industry—*coyotes* they're called—and it's inhumane. It just is, any way you look at it.

You know, family values don't stop at the Rio Grande River. If you've got starving children and there's a job over here in America that pays you more than it does in Mexico that an American won't do, you'll come and do that job and get that money back to your family.

Secondly, one way to make immigration policy work is you've got to enforce the law. And so you've got to go to employers. I'm not going to come to your home building site—but anyway. [*Laughter*] You come to enforce the law, right? And so you're a homebuilder out here in the Tampa area; a bunch of people show up, roofers show up, and say, you know, "We're legal; here's my card." You're not in the business of telling me whether or not that's a forged document or not. You don't know. It looks real. And that's all you're expected—but I'm telling you, they're forging these documents. There's a whole underground industry. They're smuggling people, and they're forging documents. And our borders are being over—it makes it much harder to enforce. And so I think by having a rational plan—temporary worker, no amnesty—will expose these people runners and drug—document forgers for what they are. So that's my answer on immigration.

Now, Social Security and Medicare—they're giving me the hook, by the way; I've got another speech here in Florida. Laura said, "Whatever you do, don't be too windy." [*Laughter*] I didn't listen to her.

You bring up a huge problem, and that is, she identified something younger workers better be asking politicians to do something about, and that is, just to put it blunt, Social Security is going broke. And the reason why is a baby boom generation, like some of us here, are fixing to retire. And there's a lot of us, and we've been promised greater benefits than the previous generation, and there are fewer people paying in the system. And it's difficult——

Audience member. [*Inaudible*]

The President. ——and we're living longer, yes, thank you. [*Laughter*] Yes, cameras and everything, they're—leave your name with them. [*Laughter*] She's right, and we're living longer. I wish I'd have thought of that. [*Laughter*]

And we've got to do something about it, and I tried last year. The job of the President is not to pass problems on but to confront them. That's my job. That's what you expect people to do. And I'm going to continue trying. And so they said, "Well, we don't have a problem." Well,

one thing people now have recognized is we got a problem. I succeeded. Not only did I succeed, others succeeded too, in reminding—we've got the issue, talking it up.

People are now beginning to realize what you realize and I realize, that we're going to fine—it's just the people paying in the payroll taxes. Can you imagine looking at youngsters in the eye, and say, "Pay in the payroll taxes," and you know the system is going broke? That's not a good deal. And so in the State of the Union, I said, "Look, I tried it; I'm going to try it again," is basically what I said. This time I believe that we need to have a table with Republican and Democrats sitting around it, and sit down and get something done. This isn't going to pass unless it's—people from both parties can come up with something to do. There's just too much opposition one way or the other, unless there's a bipartisan solution. I believe the American people are pretty sick and tired of needless partisanship in Washington, DC, and I know they expect us to get some stuff done.

And so I just want to assure you, I'm going to keep trying and keep trying and keep trying because it's the right thing to do. It's the right thing to uphold the honor of our offices by confronting these problems now, and not saying, "It's okay for another President," or "It's okay for another Congress," and just keep shuffling it down the path. Now is the time to get it done, because the longer you wait, the worse the problem gets. Every year that goes by, the problem gets worse for a next generation of Americans.

Okay, I've got the hook. Listen, let me conclude—yes, ma'am. Anybody who makes that kind of noise——

Uganda/Sudan

Q. I did not do that.

The President. Okay, good. [*Laughter*]

Q. It's a small part of the world, but it's very important to me—I'm concerned about the children in northern Uganda who are the victims——

The President. Yes, warlords.

Q. ——of the rebel Joseph Kony.

The President. Yes.

Q. And I'm wondering if you can bring any pressure to bear on President Museveni to stop that 20-year war and free those children from the bondage that they're under.

The President. Really interesting question. She's talking about the—northern Uganda. There's a group called the Lord's Group that has been terrorizing both northern Uganda and southern Sudan. I talked to Mrs. Garang, John Garang's widow. John Garang was the head of the Sudanese in the southern part of the country that, by the way, became adopted by a church in Midland, Texas, my old hometown, interestingly enough. And early in my administration, I got Jack Danforth, a former United States Senator, to go and negotiate an agreement between northern Sudan and southern Sudan. And John Garang was a partner in peace. Unfortunately, he died in a helicopter accident about a year ago, I think. And the reason I bring this up is that there's no doubt it would be easier to deal with the Lord's Group if we were able to achieve peace between north and south Sudan. They take advantage of instability.

I have talked to this—I've talked about this issue with Mrs. Garang, as well as—now, there are peacekeepers in the region, by the way, U.N. peacekeepers on the north-south accord. I hope they're effective at helping the people of southern Sudan. I have talked to Museveni, President Museveni, about the issue as well, and I've been with him, I think, two or three times. I know on two occasions we've talked about this—and will continue to talk to him about it. It's—I'm very aware of the issue.

My hope is that by having a southern Sudanese—having the peace agreement negotiated between north and south so the southern Sudanese can begin to get their lives back in order, get the oil money moving that's guaranteed to them, will help

provide—help drive them out of any safe haven in the south, which will make it easier for all of us to deal. It's kind of a roundabout answer, but I'm aware of the problem, first of all. And secondly, I'm surprised that anybody in this audience would bring it up, and I thank you for that.

We also have got a major issue in Darfur, Sudan. I presume if you're worried about northern Uganda, you're also worried about western Sudan, as am I. The strategy there was to encourage African Union troops to try to bring some sense of security to these poor people that are being herded out of their villages and just terribly mistreated. We need more troops. It's—the effort was noble, but it didn't achieve the objective.

And so I'm in the process now of working with a variety of folks to encourage there to be more troops, probably under the United Nations. I talked to Kofi Annan about this very subject this week. But it's going to require a—I think a NATO stewardship, planning, facilitating, organizing, probably double the number of peacekeepers that are there now, in order to start bringing some sense of security. There has to be a consequence for people abusing their fellow citizens.

At the same time, part of the issue in the Darfur region is that the rebel groups are not united in their objectives. And so politically or diplomatically, we have to work to make sure there's one voice from which to speak, so that we can then create kind of the same agreement between Government in Darfur that was created between north and south. A lot of talk, but we've got a strategy, and it's of concern, to the point where our country was the first country to call what was taking place a genocide, which matters—words matter.

And so thank you for bringing up that part of the world. That's very interesting that you would have that on your mind. You're a decent soul, a decent soul.

All right, I've got to go. Thanks for your time. God bless. Appreciate it.

NOTE: The President spoke at 1:26 p.m. at the Port of Tampa. In his remarks, he referred to Gen. John P. Abizaid, USA, commander, U.S. Central Command; Gen. Bryan D. Brown, USA, commander, U.S. Special Operations Command; Betty Sembler, wife of U.S. Ambassador to Italy Melvin Sembler; Mayor Pam Iorio of Tampa, FL; Mayor Rick Baker of St. Petersburg, FL; Gov. Jeb Bush of Florida; Ayman Al-Zawahiri, founder of the Egyptian Islamic Jihad and senior Al Qaida associate; former Mayor Robert Martinez of Tampa, FL; U.S. Ambassador to Iraq Zalmay Khalilzad; senior Al Qaida associate Abu Musab Al-Zarqawi; President Susilo Bambang Yudhoyono of Indonesia; President Pervez Musharraf of Pakistan; President Yoweri Kaguta Museveni of Uganda; and Secretary-General Kofi Annan of the United Nations. A participant referred to Joseph Kony, leader of the Ugandan rebel group the Lord's Resistance Army.

Remarks at a Republican Party of Florida Dinner in Lake Buena Vista, Florida
February 17, 2006

Thank you all. Thanks for the warm welcome. Please be seated. Florida is a Republican State because Jeb Bush has done in office what he promised the citizens of Florida he would do. He has been a great Governor because he doesn't waver in the face of criticism, because he doesn't rely upon polls and focus groups to tell him what to think, and because he has a clear vision for a better future for the people of this State.

And on top of all that, he married well. I'm proud to be here with my sister-in-law, Columba Bush. I married well too. And Laura sends her love to Columba and Jeb and to our friends here in Florida.

It is so wonderful to be here to be able to thank the many people that helped me get to where I got and helped Jeb get to where he got. And, you know, you just can't take anything for granted in the political business. You can't say thanks enough, and particularly when I look around the room and see so many people that I know I can't thank enough. I'll try: Thank you from the bottom of our hearts for being here. Thank you for helping the party.

I'm proud to be here with Mel Martinez and Kitty—the United States Senator from the State of Florida. I want to thank Mel for standing strong with the administration and with me when it came time to ratify and confirm judges who would strictly interpret the Constitution, judges like Judge Roberts and Judge Alito. And it would sure be nice to have two United States Senators who would confirm conservative judges.

To that end, I welcome Congresswoman Katherine Harris. Thank you for coming. Congressman Ric Keller, Congressman Mike Bilirakis and Evelyn—where's Michael? There he is. Michael, good to see— flew down on Air Force One—kind of wanted a little comfortable ride back home. [*Laughter*] John Mica is with us, and Pat. John, thank you for being here. Ginny Brown-Waite and Harvey—where's Ginny Brown? Thank you for coming. I appreciate Toni Jennings, the Lieutenant Governor. The attorney general, Charlie Crist—thank you for coming, Charlie; the chief financial officer, Tommy Gallagher.

I guess I shouldn't feel too uncomfortable reading the names back to back, you know? [*Laughter*] Thanks for running. Good luck. [*Laughter*]

I appreciate Charlie Bronson, the commissioner of agriculture. Thanks for being here, Charlie. Members of the statehouse—

Senator Tom Lee, the president of the senate, as well as Allan Bense, the speaker of the house. It's good to see you, Allan. Thank you. Look, my only advice to the speaker and the president, just do what the Governor tells you. It's real easy. [*Laughter*] That's all it takes. [*Laughter*] Not exactly the way they do it in Washington. [*Laughter*]

I want to thank Carole Jean Jordan, the chairman of the Florida Republican Party. You'd have thought they gave you a better seat than that, you know, after all the hard work. I want to thank Al Austin, who is the finance chairman, and his wife, Beverly. They're great friends of Jeb and mine. Thank you, Al. Jim Blosser, finance cochairman—thank you, Jim. And Jim MacDougald—I appreciate you all being here. Thanks for coming.

Finally, I've got to say something about Rich Crotty. Now, you might remember, Rich raised a little fellow named Tyler. [*Laughter*] I don't know if you remember the moment or not, but I got up there to give what I thought was going to be a stemwinder of a speech, and Tyler went flat asleep. [*Laughter*] So I asked Rich, where is Tyler? He said, "Well, Mr. President, he's taking a nap in anticipation of this address." [*Laughter*] Crotty, give him my best.

I am amazed by this number: The unemployment rate in Florida is 3.3 percent. It's an amazing statistic. It's a tribute to people in office who understand the role of government is not to try to create wealth, but the role of government is to create an environment in which people are willing to risk capital, in which small businesses grow to be big businesses, in which people can realize their dreams.

Feeney, I forgot to mention you. [*Laughter*] I was thinking about entrepreneurship and looked right at you. [*Laughter*] This Florida economy is strong, and so is the economy around the United States. We've overcome a lot. We've overcome attacks and corporate scandals and stock market collapses. And yet we're growing—amazing growth last year, over 3 percent growth, in spite of the fact we had high energy prices and a devastating hurricane.

And the reason why is because people feel there's an incentive to work in America. The tax relief we passed is working, and the United States Congress needs to make that tax relief permanent.

You'll hear them say in Washington, "Well, we need to balance the budget." And they're right. But then they say, "We're going to raise the taxes to balance the budget." I just want to warn you that that's not the way Washington works. It may sound good in the newspapers, but Washington works this way: If you give them more money, they will spend it. A tax increase, raising your taxes will mean there is more money to spend in Washington, and this economy isn't going to grow as strong. No, the way to balance the budget is keep progrowth economic policies in place and be wise about how we spend your money.

There's uncertainty in our economy today. It's an interesting phenomenon, isn't it? You get unbelievable economic growth, and yet people are worried. They're worried about changing jobs and not having a health care plan they can take with them. They're worried about having the skill set necessary to find the jobs of the 21st century. People are worried about China and India. And any time people worry about an economy, the reaction sometimes in our country is to wall ourselves off from the world, is to be protectionist. That's the wrong attitude for the United States of America. America needs to be confident about the future because we intend to shape the future.

And that's what this Republican Party stands for. This Republican Party stands for leadership based upon sound principles. And let me share some ideas with you.

To keep this economy the leader in the world, we got to make sure we do something about all these frivolous and junk lawsuits that are making it hard to risk capital. And I applaud your Governor, and I urge the Florida Legislature to join him in enacting meaningful, real tort reform.

We can become independent from oil from the Middle East. In order to remain a competitive nation, in order to remain a world leader, this country has got to use technology to get us off being hooked on oil. I know that may sound strange from a guy from Texas. [*Laughter*] But I sit there and think about the world on a daily basis. I see what happens when there's instability in parts of the world from which we get our oil. Listen, we're close to some amazing technological breakthroughs that will enable us to drive automobiles fueled by ethanol or have a plug-in hybrid battery that will make it much easier for you to use electricity when it comes to driving your cars.

Our party stands for innovation. Our party stands for change. And our party is going to stand for economic and national security by doing something about our dependence on Middle Eastern oil.

We're getting some things done. One of the commitments this Federal Government has made is to take care of the elderly. And when we go to Washington, DC, and the commitment is to take care of the elderly, it seems like to me, we want to make sure we do it in a way that is modern. So I saw an old, tired, stale Medicare system there. You know, this Government of ours would pay thousands of dollars for ulcer surgery but not one dime for the prescription drugs that would prevent the ulcer surgery from being needed in the first place. That's a waste of your money, and it wasn't that—we weren't fulfilling a promise to our seniors. So we reformed Medicare. And today, seniors are getting modern medicine, thanks to the Republican Party.

And I want to tell you something. We've signed up 25 million people since January 1st for this new, reformed system. And sure, there's some glitches. But we're also the party that knows how to solve problems. And you mark my words: When seniors get settled in and realize what we have done for them, they will realize the Republican Party has delivered good medicine.

But we also know something else, that the best practice of medicine is in the private sector, and the most important relationship is between doctor and patient. And so we're going to continue to promote HSAs, health savings accounts, which puts patients in charge of their health care, and it helps small business afford insurance.

I want to say something about Jeb and education. This guy understands, and so does our party, that we must challenge the soft bigotry of low expectations if we want the United States to be the leader in the world's economy. You cannot allow a system to develop in education that just simply shuffles kids through and hopes for the best. It doesn't work. It just doesn't work.

I remember when I was Governor of Texas, and we saw these statistics about kids coming out of high school not able to read. I decided—I dedicated myself then, just like Jeb has dedicated himself as Governor of Florida, to stop this business of socially promoting kids. You know who suffers? Inner-city African American kids suffer; families who don't speak English as a first language suffer. Ours is a party that believes in high standards and excellence when it comes to education.

And so we've said something pretty easy for people to understand. We said, "We're going to spend your money, but we're going to insist that schools measure, because you can't solve problems unless you diagnose the problem." Ours is the party that says no child will left behind—be left behind, and we're delivering on the results.

And so we're going to take this attitude of high standards and accountability and apply it to math, particularly in junior high grades. If our kids do not have the skills of the 21st century, jobs are going to go somewhere else. In order for this country to remain competitive and the world leader, we must lead the world in research and development, and we must make sure we're educating the young scientists and engineers for the 21st century. And that's exactly what we're going to do.

I am always amazed to hear some talk about, well, you know, maybe the best days are behind us when it comes to our economy. You just got to know something about me. I think this country can do anything we put our mind to. I think we've got such a strong entrepreneurial spirit, such wonderful people, that we're a land of doers and accomplishers and risk takers, that just given the right impetus and the right leadership, this country will still remain the preeminent economic leader in the world. And that's good for our people, and that means a higher living—standard of living.

I said in my State of the Union, we must reject isolationism. You see, when you get nervous about things or get a little despondent, the tendency is not only to wall yourself off but to withdraw from the world. And in the 21st century, we can't afford to do that. We can't afford to do it because there's an enemy that still lurks, an enemy that wants to attack the American people.

Today in Tampa, I was trying to explain to people how I make decisions, and I said, 9/11 affected my way of thinking, because I made the determination that so long as I'm the President of the United States, I will use everything at my disposal to protect the American people. That is our most solemn duty. I knew the further we got away from 9/11, the more likely it is people would kind of get comfortable and forget the challenges. And that's good, actually. It's hard to have economic growth if you walk around wondering when the next attack is going to occur. My job and the job of those of us in Washington is to constantly worry on behalf of the American people and to act on behalf of the American people so the American people can go about their business.

In order to be able to defeat an enemy, you've got to understand the nature of the enemy. I will tell you, these people are fierce ideologues. They have a totalitarian view of the world. In other words, they want to decide how people think and act and how they worship the Almighty. It's their judgment that matters, not an individual's judgment. And they are nothing but coldblooded killers that kill innocent life at the drop of a hat in order to achieve their objectives.

They have clearly stated their objectives, and I hope you appreciate a President who listens carefully to the words of the enemy. See, my job is to see the world the way it is, not the way some would like it to be. And this enemy—[*applause*]. They have openly stated, it's just a matter of time for the United States to lose its nerve. To what end? They want to find safe haven in which to plan, plot, and strike the United States. They look forward to having safe haven in which they can develop weapons of mass destruction to use against our people. This is what the enemy has said.

They made a big mistake, however, when they attacked the United States. They roused a mighty nation that understands the stakes in this war on terror. And we will not relent, and we will not tire until we win the war on terror. So we're on the offense, and we will stay on the offense so long as I'm the President of the United States.

One of the lessons of September the 11th is, we've got to prevent attacks before they occur. There are some old enough out here to remember the era when oceans protected America, and if we saw a threat overseas, we could decide to deal with it if we wanted to, or not. But we no longer have that luxury. And so part of my thinking and part of my rationale for our policy is my clear understanding that we must defeat the enemy overseas so we do not face them here at home.

And that's what we're doing. We got a lot of good people on the hunt right now. It's hard to plot and plan if you're trying to hide from Special Forces of the United States military.

I also made it clear that if anybody harbors a terrorist, they're equally as guilty of murder; that if you provide safe haven for a terrorist organization, you're equally as guilty as the terrorist. And when the United States—and when the President of the United States says something, for the sake of peace and stability, he better mean it. And I meant it when I told the Taliban to kick Al Qaida out. They refused to listen, and the United States military and our coalition rid Afghanistan of one of the most barbaric regimes in the history of mankind, and America is safer for it.

The whole world thought Saddam Hussein had weapons of mass destruction. The United Nations Security Council voted resolution after resolution after resolution because they felt he had weapons of mass destruction. Members of the United States Senate, both Republicans and Democrats, felt he had weapons of mass destruction. Members of the United States Congress, both Republicans and Democrats, in voting to give me the right to use force to remove Saddam Hussein, felt he had weapons of mass destruction. So did I. And he didn't. But he had the capacity to make weapons of mass destruction. He was a state sponsor of terror. He was shooting at American airplanes. The decision I made was the right decision, and America is safer for it. [*Applause*]

Thank you all. And now we're implementing a strategy for victory, where Iran—I mean, Iraq becomes a ally in the war on terror, where this young democracy can sustain itself and defend itself, where this democracy becomes an example of hope for people in Iran and Syria, where this country can be an example for others who demand the natural rights of men and women.

I want to assure you this—that we have one goal in mind, and that's victory, and we're going to achieve it. And the Iraqi people are helping. Think about what happened in one year. We live in a world where, I guess, there's too many television stations or something—[*laughter*]—but there's a lot of opinion; that's for sure. [*Laughter*] But in one year's time, these people who were threatened by brutal terrorists went to the polls three time, every time in increasing numbers, with more and more people voting from different religious groups, saying loud and clear to the world, we love our freedom; we want to be free. The political part of our strategy is working.

And now you'll watch the formation of a government, and we're helping to make sure there's a unity government. But isn't it fun to watch a government being formed by people who had just finished living under the thumb of one of the most brutal tyrants in the history of mankind, Saddam Hussein?

Secondly, we'll help this country grow its economy by being wise about reconstruction money. We understand that in order for people to accept democracy, there has to be tangible benefits in their lives. But the good folks in Iraq are entrepreneurial, and businesses are beginning to flourish. Oh, I know sometimes it's hard to tell it, but it's happening.

And the final part of our strategy is, not only chase the terrorists down inside of Iraq but to train the Iraqis so they can take the fight to the enemy. And there are about 235,000 Iraqis now taking more and more control over their country. You know, one of the interesting measurements early on was when the enemy started bombing recruiting stations. I don't know if you remember that, but they'd drive by with a suicider or an IED and destroy people standing in line trying to serve their nation.

So one of the first questions I asked our commanders was, are you having any trouble finding anybody to sign up? The answer was, absolutely not. The people of Iraq want their freedom, and they're willing to stand up and defend their freedom. And the United States of America is proud to help them do so.

The enemy has got one weapon; they've got one weapon: their willingness to kill innocent life and have those images on the TV screen. The only way we can possibly lose is if we lose our nerve, and we're not going to lose our nerve so long as I am the Commander in Chief.

And the stakes are high, because not only are we defending ourself, not only are we preventing Iraq from becoming a safe haven for Al Qaida and their killers, we're helping spread freedom, which is an incredibly important part of achieving peace. I want the youngsters here to go back and think about the history of Europe over the last 100 years. Americans lost—America lost thousands of lives in World War I and World War II because of war on the European Continent. Today, there are no wars on the European Continent because of democracy. Democracies do not fight.

You can't imagine somebody saying, "Vote for me; I promise you war." [*Laughter*] Generally, the person doesn't get elected. [*Laughter*] People tend to run and say, "Vote for me; I'll promise to fight corruption," or, "Vote for me; I'll help your child get educated," or, "Vote for me; I'll help your health care system be modern." I believe that everybody in the world desires to be free. I believe there is an Almighty, and I believe the greatest gift of the Almighty, besides salvation, is freedom. And if you believe that—if you believe that, then you shouldn't be surprised that 11 million Iraqis have gone to the polls. And you shouldn't be surprised that Lebanon wants to be free. And you shouldn't be surprised that people are demanding their freedom in Afghanistan. Freedom is on the march, and we're laying the foundation of peace for generations to come.

I'm excited. I am excited to be your President. It has been a fantastic experience. I can't tell you how great it is to represent the United States of America around the world. We're a land of entrepreneurs and doers and dreamers. And when we find people that hurt, we help lead the world. One reason you don't become isolationists in this world is because—let me just say, to whom much has been given, much is required. And a lot has been given in the United States of America.

And the world requires our help in helping defeat HIV/AIDS on the continent of Africa, to feed the hungry, to provide relief in the outreaches of Pakistan, to help those who suffer from tsunami. No, ours is not only a nation laying the groundwork for peace, ours is a nation that's leading the world in compassionate help for people who suffer. We've got a great country. We've got a great country, and we're going to keep it great by making strong decisions that rally and play to the great strength of America, which is the hearts and souls of the American people.

Thanks for letting me be your President. Thanks for supporting Jeb. God bless. God bless America.

NOTE: The President spoke at 5:50 p.m. at Disney's Contemporary Resort. In his remarks, he referred to Kitty Martinez, wife of Senator Mel R. Martinez of Florida; Evelyn Bilirakis, wife of Representative Michael Bilirakis of Florida; Patricia Mica, wife of Representative John L. Mica of Florida; Harvey Waite, husband of Representative Ginny Brown-Waite of Florida; Jim MacDougald, finance cochairman, Florida Victory 2006; and Mayor Richard T. Crotty of Orange County, FL.

The President's Radio Address
February 18, 2006

Good morning. This coming week, I will visit Wisconsin, Michigan, and Colorado to discuss our strategy to ensure that America has affordable, reliable, and secure sources of energy. The best way to meet our growing energy needs is through advances in technology. So in my State of the Union Address, I announced the Advanced Energy Initiative. We will pursue promising technologies that will transform how we power our vehicles, businesses, and homes so we can reduce our Nation's dependence on foreign sources of energy.

This morning I want to speak to you about one part of this initiative: our plans to expand the use of safe and clean nuclear power. Nuclear power generates large amounts of low-cost electricity without emitting air pollution or greenhouse gases. Yet nuclear power now produces only about 20 percent of America's electricity. It has the potential to play an even greater role. For example, over the past three decades, France has built 58 nuclear powerplants and now gets more than 78 percent of its electricity from nuclear power. Yet here in America, we have not ordered a new nuclear powerplant since the 1970s. So last summer, I signed energy legislation that offered incentives to encourage the building of new nuclear plants in America. Our goal is to start the construction of new nuclear powerplants by the end of this decade.

As America and other nations build more nuclear powerplants, we must work together to address two challenges: We must dispose of nuclear waste safely, and we must keep nuclear technology and material out of the hands of terrorist networks and terrorist states.

To meet these challenges, my administration has announced a bold new proposal called the Global Nuclear Energy Partnership. Under this partnership, America will work with nations that have advanced civilian nuclear energy programs, such as France, Japan, and Russia. Together, we will develop and deploy innovative, advanced reactors and new methods to recycle spent nuclear fuel. This will allow us to produce more energy while dramatically reducing the amount of nuclear waste and eliminating the nuclear byproducts that unstable regimes or terrorists could use to make weapons.

As these technologies are developed, we will work with our partners to help developing countries meet their growing energy needs by providing them with small-scale reactors that will be secure and cost-effective. We will also ensure that these developing nations have a reliable nuclear fuel supply. In exchange, these countries would agree to use nuclear power only for civilian purposes and forego uranium enrichment and reprocessing activities that can be used to develop nuclear weapons. My new budget includes $250 million to launch this initiative. By working with other nations under the Global Nuclear Energy Partnership, we can provide the cheap, safe, and clean energy that growing economies need while reducing the risk of nuclear proliferation.

As we expand our use of nuclear power, we're also pursuing a broader strategy to meet our energy needs. We're investing in technologies like solar and wind power and clean coal to power our homes and businesses. We're also investing in new car technologies like plug-in hybrid cars and in alternative fuels for automobiles like ethanol and biodiesel.

Transforming our energy supply will demand creativity and determination, and America has these qualities in abundance. Our Nation will continue to lead the world in innovation and technology. And by building a global partnership to spread the benefits of nuclear power, we'll create a safer, cleaner, and more prosperous world for future generations.

Thank you for listening.

NOTE: The address was recorded at 7:37 a.m. on February 17 in the Cabinet Room at the White House for broadcast at 10:06 a.m. on

February 18. The transcript was made available by the Office of the Press Secretary on February 17 but was embargoed for release until the broadcast. The Office of the Press Secretary also released a Spanish language transcript of this address.

Remarks on Energy in Milwaukee, Wisconsin
February 20, 2006

John, thanks. Thanks for letting me come by to say hello. [*Laughter*] I've got something on my mind I want to share with you. First, happy President's Day. It turns out, most folks in Washington don't work on President's Day. [*Laughter*] The only one working is the President. [*Laughter*]

I want to talk to you about the fact that I think we're in an important moment in history and that we have a chance to transform the way we power our economy and how we lead our lives. That's what I'm here to talk about. It's a good place to come to talk about it because the truth of the matter is, in order to seize the moment, this country has got to remain technologically advanced.

Johnson Controls has been on the cutting edge of energy technology and other technologies for more than a century. And the innovators that work here and the smart folks who work here are on the leading edge of change, and that's why I've come. And there's a role for government to help, and I want to explain that role.

Before I do, again, I want to thank you, John. I want to thank all the folks who work for Johnson Controls. It's not easy to host the President. [*Laughter*]

I had the honor of touring the laboratory on the other side of town there, and it was really neat to see the engineers and the scientists and the Ph.D.s all working hard to apply their God-given talents to help this country remain on the leading

edge of technology. It reminded me of one of the challenges we have in America, and that's to make sure a new generation of our citizens are interested in science and engineering and physics. And part of making sure this country is the leader in the world, we've got to make sure our children are properly educated so they'll be ready for the jobs of the 21st century.

I want to thank Congresswoman Gwen Moore for joining us. I appreciate you coming; nice to see you. They tell me this is your congressional district, so it's awfully kind of you to let two other Congresspersons join us—that would be Congressman Mark Green and Congressman Paul Ryan. Thank you both for coming. We have eaten a lot of custard in the past. [*Laughter*] I'm still recovering, I want you to know. [*Laughter*]

I want to thank the speaker of the house who has joined us. The mayor of the great city of Milwaukee has joined us, and the county executive has joined us. Thank you all for coming; proud you're here.

By the way, it's always important, if any of you ever run for office, to always remember to recognize the sheriff. [*Laughter*] Sheriff Clarke, thank you for being here. Good to see you again. Thank you.

Our economy is strong. It's gaining steam too. We're now in our fifth year of uninterrupted economic growth. Last year, our economy grew at a healthy rate of 3.5 percent, in spite of high energy prices and devastating storms. Real after-tax income is up nearly 8 percent per American since 2001. And that's one of the explanations, one of the reasons why retail sales last month made their biggest gain in more than 4 years. Homeownership is at record levels. That's a good sign. We want people owning things in America. More minorities own a home than ever before in our Nation's history. America's unemployment rate is down to 4.7 percent. That's the lowest level since 2001. We've added 4.7 million new jobs over the last 2½ years. We're doing fine.

The fundamental question is, how do we keep doing fine? The challenge that faces us is, is how we make sure that the economic growth today carries over for tomorrow. And that's what I want to talk about. In order to understand what to do, you've got to understand what got us to where we are today. Part of it is keeping taxes low, by the way, and that's exactly what I intend to do so long as I'm the President, is keep taxes low. Part of it is being wise about how we spend our money. Part of it is understanding how technology plays in the future of the country.

Think back 25 years ago, in the start of the 1980s. It's not all that long ago, really. Some of us remember the eighties pretty clearly—[*laughter*]—a lot of kind of gray-haired folks here that lived through the eighties. [*Laughter*] Then most Americans used typewriters instead of the computers. They used pay phones—you remember what those were—instead of cell phones. They used carbon paper instead of laser printers, bank tellers instead of ATMs, and they played the license plate game on trips, as opposed to DVDs. [*Laughter*] Times have changed a lot in 25 years because of technology.

We're seeing new develops all the time—new developments. Advanced battery technology allows cell phones to last about 50 percent longer than they did just 5 years ago. In your laboratory, we're seeing—first-hand seeing the progress being made be-

cause of your scientists and engineers in lighter, more potent battery technology. Lightweight parts and better engines allow cars to travel 60 percent farther on a gallon of gas than they did three decades ago.

Technologies are helping this economy become more efficient. Listen to this: Over the last 30 years, our economy has grown three times faster than our energy consumption. The economy has grown three times faster than energy consumption. During that period of time, we created 56 million jobs while cutting air pollution by 50 percent. Technology is really important for the future of this country. And so in the State of the Union, I said that by using technology, we can help make sure this country remains a world leader. And that starts with making sure we change our energy habits.

I know it came as a shock to some to hear a Texan stand up there in front of the country and say, "We've got a real problem; America is addicted to oil." But I meant it, because it's a true fact, and we've got to do something about it now. Oil is the primary source of gasoline; it is the primary source of diesel; it is the primary source of jet fuel. And that means that oil accounts for virtually all energy consumption in the vital transportation sector of our economy.

The oil we consume in this important sector comes from foreign countries; most of it does. In 1985, three-quarters of the crude oil used in U.S. refineries came from America; today, that equation has changed dramatically. Less than half the crude oil used in our refineries is produced here at home. Sixty percent comes from foreign countries. Things have changed since 1985.

Some of the nations we rely on for oil have unstable governments or fundamental differences with the United States. These countries know we need their oil, and that reduces influence. It creates a national security issue when we're held hostage for energy by foreign nations that may not like us.

Energy is also part of our economic security as well. That's obvious. I mean, the global demand for oil has been rising faster than supply because there's new economies that are beginning to gin up, new economies growing, like China and India. Oil prices rise sharply when demand is greater than supply. And when they do, it strains your budgets. It hurts our families; it hurts our small entrepreneurs. It's like a hidden tax. And so we're vulnerable to high prices of oil, and we're vulnerable to sudden disruptions of oil. What I'm telling you is oil—the dependence upon oil is a national security problem and an economic security problem. And here's what we intend to do about it.

First, Congress passed a good energy bill last summer; I was pleased to sign it. It took a little bit of work. It's kind of hard to get things done in Washington; there's a lot of sharp partisan elbows up there these days. But we got something done, and it's a good bill. It encourages conservation and new technologies and alternative sources of energy. But there's a lot more that needs to be done.

The first thing that needs to be done is to make sure that there's an incentive for private business to invest in research and development. If technology is going to help us change our energy habits and change the way we live, it makes sense for the Government to incent people to invest in research and development. Right now we've got what we call a research and development tax credit, which is a major incentive for private companies such as yourselves to invest in research and development, which will yield new technologies. The problem is, is that the R&D tax credit expires. As a matter of fact, they've only renewed it on an annual basis.

Now, I don't know how in the heck Congress thinks that people can plan properly if they're uncertain as to whether or not the tax credit is going to exist. So therefore, if we want to be on the leading edge of research and development, then Congress needs to make the R&D tax credit a permanent part of the Tax Code.

Secondly, Government can help. Government provides about a third of the dollars for research and development. Two-thirds come from the private sector; one-third comes from the Government. And so I propose to double the Federal commitment to the most critical basic research programs in the physical sciences over the next decade.

Let me explain our strategy when it comes to energy. So in other words, part of our strategy is to make sure people continue to invest. The research you're doing at Johnson Labs will change people's lives appreciably. But we've got to continue to make sure we conduct research and development if we want to be a leader in the world. If we don't want to be a leader in the world, fine; we'll just quit. That's not how I view America. I want America to lead the world, because by leading the world when it comes to the economy, we're helping our people. We're making our people more productive, and productivity increases enhance standard of living, and increased standards of living means the American people are doing better.

Now, I laid out what's called an Advanced Energy Initiative. And a cornerstone of the initiative is a 22-percent increase in funding for clean energy research at the Department of Energy. And it's got two major goals, or two objectives: first, to transform the way we power our cars and trucks; and secondly, to transform the way we power our homes and offices.

So let me talk to you about the first one. Our Nation is on the thresholds of some new energy technologies that I think will startle the American people. It's not going to startle you here at Johnson Controls because you know what I'm talking about. [*Laughter*] You take it for granted. But the American people will be amazed at how far our technology has advanced in order to meet an important goal, which is to reduce our imports from the Middle

East by 75 percent by 2025 and eventually getting rid of our dependence totally.

The first objective is to change the way we power our cars and trucks. Today's cars and trucks are fueled almost exclusively by gasoline and diesel fuel, which, of course, comes from oil. To transform the way we power the vehicles, we have got to diversify away from oil. I just gave you a reason from a national security perspective as well as economic security perspective why reliance upon oil is not good for the United States.

And so here are three ways that we can do that, change our reliance from oil. First, invest in new kinds of vehicles that require much less gasoline. It's a practical thing to do. Secondly, find new fuels that will replace gasoline and, therefore, dependence on oil. And finally, develop new ways to run a car without gasoline at all.

The most promising ways to reduce gasoline consumption quickly is through hybrid vehicles. Hybrid vehicles have both a gasoline-powered engine and an electric battery based on technologies that were developed by the Department of Energy. In other words, this technology came to be because the Federal Government made a research commitment. That's why I think it's double—important to double research as we go down the next decade. The gasoline engine charges the battery, which helps drive the vehicle. And the twin sources of power allow hybrid cars and trucks to travel about twice as far on a gallon of fuel as gasoline-only vehicles. That is a good start, when something can go twice as far on a gallon of gasoline than the conventional vehicle can.

Hybrid vehicles are a good deal for consumers, and the American people are figuring it out. More than 200,000 hybrids were sold in the United States last year— the highest sales on record. There's growing demand for hybrid automobiles. And working with the Congress, we came up with an additional incentive, and that is, we provide a tax credit up to $3,400 per hybrid vehicle purchaser. In other words, we want to stimulate demand. In the marketplace, when there is demand, suppliers will meet that demand, and that's positive, because if you can go twice as far on a gallon of gasoline than otherwise, it means we're becoming less dependent on oil. Hybrid vehicles on the road today are delivering impressive gasoline savings.

But there is more to be done, and that's why I'm here at Johnson Controls, because engineers here are working on ways to replace the current hybrid battery technology with advanced lithium ion batteries that are now used in cell phones and laptops. These batteries are lighter; they are more powerful; and they can be recharged quickly. Using new lithium ion batteries, engineers will be able to design the next generation of hybrid vehicles, called plug-in hybrids, that can be recharged through a standard electrical outlet. Start picturing what I'm talking about: You've got your car; you pull in; you plug it right in the wall. [*Laughter*]

Development will make a big difference in the performance of hybrid cars and trucks. Instead of depending on the gasoline engine to recharge the electric battery, the plug-in hybrids will have fully charged batteries as soon as you get in the automobile. And that means plug-in hybrids will be able to travel much greater distances on electricity alone, thereby saving more gas for our consumers, thereby making us less dependent on oil.

The plug-in hybrid, they estimate, can initially go 40 miles on electricity alone. So you've got a lot of folks living in cities like Milwaukee, Wisconsin, who generally don't drive more than 40 miles a day. Therefore, within 40 miles, you'll be on electricity and using no gasoline. Eventually, plug-in hybrids with lithium ion batteries will be able to get 100 miles per gallon. And now all of a sudden, you're beginning to see the effects of this important technology on our national security and on our economic security, but more important, for the pocketbook of our consumers.

Plug-in hybrids are a really important part of the strategy I've announced, and we're going to provide $31 million to speed up research on these advanced technologiesSU; this is a 27-percent increase over current funding levels. In other words, we like to—the experts tell me this is a very good chance to have major breakthroughs, and we want to accelerate those breakthroughs. And, again, I want to thank you all for being on the leading edge of change.

We're also supporting the development of advanced fuels that can replace regular gasoline. Here again I'm talking to folks who know what I'm talking about; I'm talking about ethanol. You've got a lot of it here in Wisconsin because you've got corn. Ethanol is produced—primarily produced from corn; it's blended with gasoline to produce clean and efficient fuel. And blends with that ethanol concentration of less than 10 percent, ethanol can be used in any vehicle. With minor modifications— I emphasize "minor modifications"—cars and trucks can become what we call flex-fuel vehicles that run on a fuel blend called E–85, which is a mix of 85 percent ethanol and 15 percent gasoline. That's a positive development.

Ethanol, by the way, can be used in hybrid vehicles. So the more ethanol we use, the less crude oil we consume. And using ethanol has the added benefit of supporting our farmers. I like to kind of tease in a way, but beneath the tease is serious—it will be good one day when the President is given the crop report. [*Laughter*] It says, "Mr. President, corn is up—[*laughter*]— and we're less dependent on foreign sources of energy."

America produced a record 3.9 billion gallons of ethanol in 2005—was the record levels. That's twice the level produced when I got sworn in first time. There are five ethanol plants that are up and running here in Wisconsin, and more are coming. We offer a tax credit to ethanol blenders of 51 cents per gallon. We're committed

to ethanol. It makes sense. Ethanol benefits a lot of folks, but most importantly, it benefits those who are driving cars.

Now, we're on the edge of advancing additional ethanol production. New technology is going to make it possible to produce ethanol from wood chips and stalks and switchgrass and other natural materials. Researchers at the Energy Department tell me we're 5 or 6 years away from breakthroughs in being able to produce fuels from those waste products. In other words, we're beginning to—we're coming up with a way to make something out of nothing. And this is important because it's—economics are such that it's important to have your ethanol-producing factories or plants close to where the product is grown.

That's why E–85 has spread throughout the Midwest; that's where you're growing the corn. Pretty soon, you know, if you're able to grow switchgrass and convert that into ethanol, then you're going to have availability for ethanol in other parts of the country. I mean, there's a lot of stuff that gets thrown away that may be converted into fuel, but it's not just located in one part of the country; it's located around the country. And one of the goals is to make sure that ethanol is widespread. If we want to affect our consumption of oil, we want ethanol to be readily available for consumers outside certain parts of the—certain regions of the country.

And so we proposed spending $150 million for Government and private research into these homegrown fuels. It's an important initiative. We want to provide our consumers with reasonable, cost-effective ways to help us become less dependent on foreign sources of oil.

And we've got another initiative that I find interesting, and it's important. And that is, we're spending money—your hard-earned money—on research to develop a vehicle that will not use gasoline, and it won't produce any pollution whatsoever, and that's through hydrogen. When hydrogen is used in a device called a fuel cell, it can deliver enough electricity to power a car that emits pure water instead of exhaust fumes. It's an exciting new technology. We're a ways down the road from bringing it to fruition, but we are spending $1.2 billion over 5 years to research this important opportunity.

We're seeing some progress, by the way, when it comes to hydrogen fuel cells. They tell me that the cost of manufacturing hydrogen fuel cells has been cut in half, which is good. Research is taking place. There could be a new technology available so that when your children take their first driver's test—or when some of your children take their first driver's test, they will do so in a hydrogen-powered automobile.

And so those are three steps—three important steps—three steps in which we can help change our driving habits. And by changing our driving habits, we've changed our dependency on foreign sources of oil.

Now, the second objective of the Advanced Energy Initiative is to transform the way we power our homes and offices. And so we've got to diversify our electricity supply, is what I'm about to—I'll give you the bottom line first: We must diversify. Right now American electricity is generated by four principle sources: Coal accounts for about 50 percent; nuclear power, about 20 percent; natural gas, about 18 percent; and renewable sources like hydroelectric, solar, and wind power account for the rest.

The most versatile of these fuels is natural gas, and there we have a problem. We have a problem because natural gas is used for more than just heating your homes. Natural gas is important for—to help create fertilizer for farmers. Natural gas powers heavy duty machinery used for manufacturing and chemical production. In other words, there's a lot of uses for natural gas. And yet natural gas has become really popular for electricity generation in recent years, and the price has tripled recently. And these price increases obviously affect our farmers; they affect our ranchers; they affect our consumers.

And they affect our businesses. Businesses that rely upon natural gas feedstocks have found that in order to stay in business, they've got to move their plants closer to where vast quantities of natural gas are being discovered, and that's not here in the United States; that's elsewhere.

And so we've got to figure out how to confront this issue. And here's two ways to do it. First, we've got to make sure that we've got enough natural gas to meet our home heating and industrial needs. And one of the best ways to secure supply is to expand our ability to receive liquefied natural gas. It's a supercool form of natural gas that can be transported from overseas on tankers. Natural gas inside of America is generally transported by pipeline. Huge supplies of gas exist outside the reach of pipelines. And technology is being developed that can cool the gas. They can bring the gas over in tankers in liquefied form, deliquefy it, and put it into our pipeline system.

The problem is, is that we didn't have enough sites to set up terminals to receive the LNG. And until there's a place for the LNG to unload, the liquefied natural gas, what I'm talking about isn't going to come to fruition. And so one of the things in the energy bill that was important is it clarified Federal authority to site new receiving terminals for LNG. And that's good. In other words, if we need more natural gas to make sure that we take the pressure off the heating bills as well as meet our industrial needs, we've got to have places for the liquefied natural gas to come into the country.

And the bill also did another important thing, and that is to streamline permitting processes for onshore natural—off—onshore, offshore natural gas exploration. In other words, we've got to make it easier—and at the same time, protect our environment—to make sure that we can find natural gas that fits into the pipeline to help take the pressure off of price.

Secondly, we need to reduce our reliance on natural gas for electricity generation. In other words, we've got to substitute other forms of power for natural gas if we expect to be able to maintain a manufacturing base that relies upon natural gas. And the best way to do that is to expand our use of coal, nuclear power, and renewable sources of energy like wind and solar.

Let me start with coal. Coal is by far our country's most abundant and affordable energy resource. It's estimated we've got more than 250 years of reserves. That's a lot; that's a lot. And I'm sure you recognize this—or realize this, but in Wisconsin, when you flip on the light switch, there's a 75-percent chance that electricity is generated by coal-powered plants. In other words, you use it here in Wisconsin.

Coal has the potential to reduce our reliance on natural gas. The problem is, we've got to make sure that we can keep our commitment to the environment. Coal requires investment to make sure that we don't pollute our air. And that's the conundrum; that's the difficulty with coal. This country is—I told you we've reduced our air pollution by 50 percent, in spite of the fact that our economy has grown substantially. We want to continue that commitment.

I told folks when I was running for President the first time around that we would invest $2 billion over 10 years to promote clean coal technology. In other words, I believed, as did many others, that technology will help us deal with this dilemma. And we're on our way, by the way, to complete the promise several years ahead of schedule. In other words, we are committing research dollars to see if we can't use this abundant resource and, at the same time, protect our environment.

The coal research has helped pioneer more effective pollution controls. We're helping coal plant efficiency. We've also implemented new clean air regulations that use a cap and trade system, which gives utility companies incentives to continue investing in clean coal technology. Congress needs to pass my Clear Skies legislation.

But we're getting closer to an interesting, important goal—that by continuing to invest at the Federal level as well as encourage private investment, we will build the world's first powerplant to run on coal that produces zero emissions, by 2015. That will be a positive development for future generations of Americans.

I'd like to talk about nuclear power. Today, there are more than 100 nuclear plants in America that operate in 31 States, including right here in Wisconsin. The plants are producing electricity safely, and they don't emit any air pollution or greenhouse gases. America hasn't ordered a nuclear plant since the 1970s, and that's the result of litigation—or because of litigation and complex regulations.

It's interesting when you think about a country like France, however. They have built 58 plants since the 1970s; they get 78 percent of their electricity from nuclear power. It's an interesting contrast, isn't it? We haven't done anything since the seventies. This country has decided to recognize the importance of having renewable sources of energy that protect the environment, and 78 percent of their electricity comes from this form of energy. China has 8 nuclear plants in the works, by the way, and plans to build at least 40 more over the next two decades.

I'm going to India later on—at the beginning of next month, March 1st. I'm going to talk about a civilian nuclear power program for India. I'll tell you why I am in a minute, but first, let's talk about here at home.

I think we ought to start building nuclear powerplants again. I think it makes sense to do so. Technology is such that we can do so and say to the American people, "These are safe, and they're important." To encourage construction of nuclear powerplants, there's new Federal risk insurance for the first six new plants that will be built in the country. That's part of the energy bill I signed. This insurance helps protect the builders of these plants against lawsuits or bureaucratic obstacles and other delays beyond their control. In other words, there's an incentive to say, "Let's get six of them started."

The administration has also launched what's called Nuclear Power 2010 Initiative. It's a $1.1 billion partnership between the Government and industry to facilitate new plant orders. Chairman Nils Diaz of the Nuclear Regulatory Commission is taking steps to streamline the licensing process for new plant construction. In other words, we're analyzing barriers and hurdles and trying to eliminate them so we can start this process.

If we're trying to become less dependent on foreign sources of oil or energy like natural gas—we want to free up our natural gas to keep our manufacturing base intact—we need to move forward when it comes to alternative sources like nuclear power. And there's some encouraging results, and the mindset is beginning to change. After all, the mindset needed to change. We haven't built a plant since the 1970s. That's a fairly long period of time.

This time last year, only two companies were seeking to build nuclear powerplants; now nine companies have expressed a new interest in new—interest in new construction. They're considering as many as 19 new plants. This progress is going to help an important goal. We'll start building nuclear powerplants again by the end of this decade. As part of our strategy, as part of our way to make sure that the future is bright and that America remains a leader in the world, is to understand the promise of nuclear power.

We're also going to work with other nations to help them build nuclear power industries. And the reason why is, this is a global world in which we live, and demand for oil in China and India affects price here in America. And so, therefore, if we can help relieve the pressure off of demand for fossil fuels, it helps the entire world.

And so we've got some challenges, however, in dealing with this issue. And that's why I put together what's called a global nuclear energy partnership. It's a partnership that works with countries that have got advanced nuclear energy programs or civilian nuclear energy programs like France and Great Britain and Japan and Russia. And here are the objectives of the partnership.

First, supplier nations will provide fuel for nonsupplier nations so they can start up a civilian nuclear energy program. In other words, a lot of countries don't know how to enrich; a handful do. And it makes sense that we share that—share the benefits of our knowledge with others—but not share the knowledge, because there's concern about proliferation.

One of the concerns you hear from the critics of expanding nuclear power is, all this will do to create proliferation concerns. Well, here's one way to address those concerns—to say, "We'll provide the fuel for you, and we'll collect the fuel from you, by the way, and after we collect the fuel from you, we need to reprocess the spent nuclear material." By reprocessing, you can continue to use the fuel base, but equally importantly, we'll reduce the amount of nuclear waste that needs to be stored.

So here is an initiative that affects us here at home and an initiative that will help others develop nuclear power so they can generate their economic growth. We want people growing in the world. We want people—economies to be in good shape. And we also expect others to help us protect the environment as well.

Another electricity source with enormous potential is solar power. Today, Americans use small amounts of solar power, mainly to heat water or to power small consumer products like outdoor lights. After spending some time with you all here, I'm going over to Michigan to go to a company that manufactures thin film, photovoltaic cells.

That's kind of a fancy word for cells that can generate electricity directly from sunlight.

The technology—solar technology has the potential to change the way we live and work, if you really think about it. For example, roof makers will one day be able to create a solar roof that protects you from the elements and, at the same time, powers your house. And that's what these folks are working on.

The vision is this: That you will have—that the technology will become so efficient that you'll become a little power generator in your home and that if you don't use the energy you generate, you'll be able to feed it back into the electricity grid. The whole purpose of spending money on solar power—and we intend to spend $150 million next year in funding for both Government and private research—is to bring to market as quickly as possible this important and impressive technology. It's really going to help change the way we live—we think—and we want solar power to become competitive by 2015.

Another promising renewable is wind. You're getting—as Laura says, "When you speak too long, you're a little windy." [*Laughter*] I'm not saying I'm wind power—[*laughter*]—but I am telling you I recognize the importance of wind power. More than $3 billion worth of equipment to generate electricity from wind was installed in America last year. In other words, it's a new industry; it's beginning to grow; $3 billion is a good investment, good amount of investment. Obviously, people think there's potential when it comes to wind energy.

About 6 percent of the continental U.S. has been identified as highly suitable for construction of wind turbines. Some have estimated that this area alone has the potential to supply up to 20 percent of our Nation's electricity. In other words, they've identified 6 percent of the country's landmass as a good place for wind turbines that, if installed with the right technology,

could have a major effect on the electricity that we all use. So we're proposing additional money for research and development.

I think you're beginning to get the drift of what I'm talking about. We're on the edge of some amazing breakthroughs—breakthroughs all aimed at enhancing our national security and our economic security and the quality of life for the folks who live here in the United States. And so, therefore, now is the time for Congress to join me in spending this money. I think it's a good use of your money, to help us achieve major breakthroughs in how we live and how we can reduce our dependency on oil. This is an issue that Republicans and Democrats can and must come together on. It's an issue that—[*applause*].

Think about how your children or your grandchildren may be able to spend a President's Day in the future. If you're planning a trip to visit relatives, you can plug in your hybrid car the night before and drive the first 40 miles on your lithium ion battery. If you've got more distance to go, you can fill up at your local ethanol station. If you're in Wisconsin, you'll be filling it up with corn product. In Crawford, it may just be switchgrass. [*Laughter*] You may decide to travel in a hydrogen-powered minivan and refuel at a station with hydrogen generated by a local nuclear powerplant. When you finally make it to where you're going, you can sit at a house that is lit by clean coal or wind energy or solar-powered roof over your head.

We're close. We're close to having this vision realized in America. And by the way, this can all be done—the whole trip can be done without consuming a single drop of oil. It's within our reach. There was a lot of time when most Americans would never have imagined that we'd be traveling long distance in our automobile instead of a buggy or sending e-mails instead of letters. In the life of this Nation, we have seen incredible and rapid advances in technology—in the history of this country.

I believe the greatest advances are yet to come, and I want to thank the good folks here at Johnson for helping them come. Thanks for your time. God bless.

NOTE: The President spoke at 11:43 a.m. at Johnson Controls Building Efficiency Business. In his remarks, he referred to John M. Barth, chief executive officer, president, and director, Johnson Controls, Inc.; John G. Gard, speaker, Wisconsin State Assembly; Mayor Thomas M. Barrett of Milwaukee, WI; and Scott Walker, county executive, and Sheriff David A. Clarke, Jr., of Milwaukee County, WI.

Remarks Following a Tour of United Solar Ovonic in Auburn Hills, Michigan
February 20, 2006

I just had a interesting tour of United Solar here in the State of Michigan. I also had the honor of meeting the inventor of a lot of the technology and the machines here. A couple of things struck me. One, solar technology is commercial and—particularly because they've figured out ways to make long rolls of this photovoltaic technology. That's important to help us achieve a major goal, which is to become less dependent on foreign sources of oil.

I spent the day earlier in Wisconsin, where I was able to see some amazing technologies that will help us change the way we drive our automobiles. This technology right here is going to help us change the way we live in our homes. The ultimate goal is to have solar technology on your home, and that home will become a little power-generating unit unto itself, and that if you have extra electricity, that you could put it back in your grid, so you become a power producer, but you're using renewable sources of energy to power your homes and to fire up your refrigerators. And this is real. I really am thankful that the folks of this company gave me a chance to come and visit about it.

The role of the Government at this point is to continue to spend research dollars to help push technologies forward, is to get these technologies to be even more competitive in the marketplace. And I'm calling on Congress to join us on this most important energy initiative. As most folks know, there's a lot of needless politics in Washington, DC. There's a lot of finger pointing and a lot of zero-sum attitude amongst the people up there. And of all the issues, becoming less dependent on foreign sources of energy is an issue that we ought to be able to unite and show the American people we can work together to help advance the technologies that will change the world in which we live.

I am very excited about what I've seen here. I'm excited about the future, because we've got great inventors and great entrepreneurs here in our own country preparing for ways to enable the American people to get rid of our addition to oil. And that will not only enhance our economic security but enhance our national security as well.

Thank you very much.

NOTE: The President spoke at 4:18 p.m. In his remarks, he referred to Subhendu Guha, president and chief operating officer, United Solar Ovonic.

Remarks in a Discussion on Energy Conservation and Efficiency in Golden, Colorado
February 21, 2006

The President. Thank you all. Please be seated. Thanks for having me. I am honored to be at the National Renewable Energy Lab, which will be henceforth called NREL. [*Laughter*] I have come today to discuss unbelievable opportunities for our country to achieve a great national goal, and that is to end our addiction on oil.

I know it sounds odd for a Texan to say that. [*Laughter*] But I have spent a lot of time worrying about the national security implications of being addicted to oil, particularly from parts of the world where people may not agree with our policy or our way of life, and the economic security implications of being hooked on oil, particularly since the demand for oil is rising faster than the supply of oil. And any time that happens, it creates the conditions for what could be—price disruption and price spikes at home are like hidden taxes on the working people of our country.

And so we're here to discuss ways to achieve this really important national goal. And there's no better place to come than NREL, and I want to thank you all for hosting me. I appreciate—I really appreciate the scientists and dreamers and, more importantly, doers who work here to help achieve this important goal.

I recognize that there has been some interesting—let me say—mixed signals when it comes to funding. The issue, of course, is whether or not good intentions are met with actual dollars spent. Part of the issue we face, unfortunately, is that there are sometimes decisions made, but as a result of the appropriations process, the money may not end up where it was supposed to have gone. I was talking to Dan about our mutual desire to clear up any discrepancies in funding, and I think we've cleaned up those discrepancies. My message to those who work here is: We

want you to know how important your work is; we appreciate what you're doing; and we expect you to keep doing it; and we want to help you keep doing it.

I want to thank Dan. He's going to be saying some stuff here in a minute, so we're not going to—I'm just going to thank him. I want to thank your staff for hosting us. It's a pain to host the President. [*Laughter*] But anyway, you've done a fine job. And I want to thank the Governor of the State of Colorado, Bill Owens, for joining us. The United States Senator Ken Salazar—thanks for coming, Ken. I appreciate it. The Congressman from this district, Bob Beauprez—I appreciate you being here. The Congressman from the adjoining district, Mark Udall—Mark, there you go. Thanks for coming.

We got all kinds of people—we got the mayor—appreciate you coming, Mayor Baroch. Thanks for coming, mayor. Just fill the potholes. [*Laughter*] You got a great city; thanks for having us. I appreciate the statehouse folks, Senator Andy McElhany and Joe Stengel, from this district. I think that's right. Appreciate you coming. Thank you, Andy. Good to see you. I want to thank the directors—thank everybody. [*Laughter*]

So the challenge is, what do we do to achieve objectives? In other words, we set goals—so what do we need to do? What do we need to do as a nation to meet the goal? How can we fulfill our responsibilities that really say we understand the problems we face? So here's what we need to do.

First, we need to make sure we're the leader of technology in the world. I don't mean just relative to previous times in American history. I think this country needs to lead the world and continue to lead the world. And so, how do you do that? First, there's a Federal commitment to spending research dollars. In my State of the Union, I called on Congress to double the research in basic sciences at the Federal level. This will help places like NREL. It will continue this grand tradition of the Federal Government working with the private sector to spend valuable research money in order to make sure we develop technologies that keep us as the leader.

In order for us to achieve this national goal of becoming less dependent on foreign sources of oil, we've got to spend money. And the best place to do that is through research labs such as NREL. Now, we also got to recognize that two-thirds of the money spent on research in the United States comes from the private sector. See? So it's one thing for the Federal Government to make a commitment of doubling the funding over a 10-year period, but we've got to recognize that most of the money is done through corporate America, through the private sector.

And one thing that seems like a smart thing to do, for me, is to make the tax rules clear. The research and development tax credit expires on an annual basis. It doesn't make any sense to say to corporate America or the private sector, "Plan for the long run, but we're not going to tell you whether or not the Tax Code is going to be the same from year to year." And so, in order to encourage that two-thirds of the investment in the private sector— necessary to help us achieve national goals and objectives, one of which is to stay on the leading edge of innovation—is to have the research and development tax credit a permanent part of our Tax Code.

Now, in order to get us less addicted to oil, we got to figure out where we use oil, and that's pretty easy, when you think about it. We use a lot of oil for our transportation needs. And so if we can change the way we drive our cars and our trucks, we can change our addiction to oil. And laboratories such as this are doing unbelievably interesting work on helping us change

the way we drive our automobiles. And you're going to hear some interesting discussion with people who are on the frontlines of these technological changes.

Just—I want to tell the American people three ways that we can change the way we drive our automobiles. One is through the use of hybrid vehicles. And Congress wisely increased the tax credit available to those who purchase hybrid vehicles. In other words, we're trying to increase demand for hybrid vehicles. You can get up to a $3,400 tax credit now if you buy a hybrid vehicle. Hybrid vehicles are vehicles that use a gasoline engine to help charge a battery, and when the battery is charged, the battery kicks in, and if the battery gets low, the gasoline engine kicks back in to charge the battery. It's a hybrid—in other words, two sources of power for the engine.

The new technological breakthrough, however, is going to be when we develop batteries that are able to enable an automobile to drive, say, the first 40 miles on electricity alone. Those are what we call plug-in hybrid vehicles. And yesterday I was at Johnson Controls, which is one of the private-sector companies that are developing the new technologies to enable cars to be able to not need the gasoline engine to charge the battery. Now, that saves a lot of—you can begin to think about how this new technology is going to enable us to save on gasoline use, which makes us less dependent on crude oil, since crude oil is the feedstock for gasoline.

The idea is to have an automobile, say, that can drive 40 miles on the battery, as I mentioned. But if you're living in a big city, that's probably all you're going to need for that day's driving. And then you can get home and plug your car right into the outlet in your house. This is coming. I mean, we're close to this. It's going to require more research dollars. The budget I submitted to the Congress does have money in it for this type of research for new types of batteries. But I want the people to know we're close. The hybrid vehicles you're buying today are an important part of making sure you save money when it comes to driving. But they're going to change with the right research and development. Technology will make it so that the hybrid vehicles are even better in getting us less addicted on oil and making it good for the consumer's pocketbook.

Secondly, there is a fantastic technology brewing—I say brewing; it's kind of a catch on words here—[*laughter*]—called ethanol. I mean, it's—there's a lot of folks in the Midwest driving—using what's called E–85 gasoline. It means 85 percent of the fuel they're putting in their car is derived from corn. This is exciting news for those of us worried about addiction to oil. I mean, you grow a lot of corn; you're less dependent on foreign sources of energy. Using corn for fuel helps our farmers and helps our foreign policy at the same time. It's a good deal.

The problem is, we need more sources of ethanol. We need more—need to use different products than just corn. Got to save some corn to eat, of course. [*Laughter*] Corn flakes without corn is kind of—[*laughter*]. And so one of the interesting things happening in this laboratory and around the country is what's called the development of cellulosic ethanol. That's a fancy word for using switchgrass, corn—or wood products, stuff that you generally allow to decompose, to become a source of energy.

And as our fellow citizens begin to think to whether or not it makes sense to spend research, imagine—dollars on this technology, imagine people in the desert being able to grow switchgrasses that they can then convert into energy for ethanol for the cars that they're driving there in Arizona. I mean, all of a sudden, the whole equation about energy production begins to shift dramatically. And we're going to hear a lot about cellulosic ethanol.

Finally, hydrogen fuel cells—it's not a short-term solution or an intermediate-term solution, but it's definitely a long-term solution. It will help us achieve grand objectives: less dependence on oil and the production of automobiles that have zero emissions that could harm our air. And we'll talk a lot about hydrogen fuel cells.

Finally, I do want to talk about technologies that will enable us to change the way we power our homes and businesses, which is the second part of the strategy, the Advanced Energy Initiative strategy.

First of all, there's huge pressure on natural gas; people in Colorado know what I'm talking about. We've been using a lot of natural gas for the generation of electricity. And we got to change that. Natural gas is important for manufacturing. It's important for fertilizers. But to use it for electricity is causing enormous pressure, because we're not getting enough natural gas produced.

One way to alleve [alleviate] * the pressure on price is to expand the use of liquefied natural gas through new terminals. And I want to thank the Congress for passing new siting rights in the energy bill that will enable us to have more terminals for us to be able to receive liquefied natural gas from parts of the world that can produce it cheaply—liquefy it, and then ship it to the United States.

But the other way to take the price off of gas is to better use coal, nuclear power, solar and wind energy. Now, when you hear people say coal, it causes people to shudder, because coal—it's hard to burn it. But we have got—we're spending about $2 billion over a 10-year period to develop clean coal technologies. If technology can help the way we live, technology can certainly help change the way we utilize coal. And it's important that we spend money on new technologies so we can burn coal cleanly, because we got 250 years worth of coal reserves.

---

* White House correction.

One way to take the pressure off natural gas is to use coal more efficiently. We believe by 2015, we'll have developed the first zero-emission coal-fire electricity plant. We're making progress. We're spending money; research is good. The American taxpayers have got to know that by spending money on this vital research, that we're going to be able to use our abundant sources of coal in an environmentally friendly way and help with your electricity bills.

Secondly, we've got to use nuclear power more effectively and more efficiently. We haven't built a plant since the 1970s. You're seeing now, France has built a lot of plants since the 1970s. They get about 85 percent of their electricity from nuclear power. And technology has changed dramatically, and I believe we can build plants in a safe way and, at the same time, generate cost-effective electricity that does not—that the process of which won't pollute.

And so we've begun to, in the energy bill, begun to provide incentives for the nuclear power industry to start siting plants. It just doesn't make any sense to me that we don't use this technology if we're interested in becoming less dependent on foreign sources of energy and we want to protect our environment.

And finally, solar and wind technologies—we're also going to talk about that. NREL is doing a lot of important work on solar and wind technology. The vision for solar is, one day, each home becomes a little power unit unto itself, that photovoltaic processes will enable you to become a little power generator, and that if you generate more power than you use, you can feed it back into the grid.

I was, yesterday, in Michigan, and went to United Solar, and they've got some fantastic technologies. Dan was quick to remind me, others have fantastic technologies as well. [*Laughter*] I just hadn't seen them firsthand. But the American people need to know, with additional research dollars, which we're proposing to Congress, we're close to some important breakthroughs—to be able to use this technology to help folks power their homes by the Sun.

And finally, wind—we don't have a lot of turbines in Washington, but there's a lot of wind there, I can assure you of that. [*Laughter*] But there are parts of the country where there are turbines. They say to me that there's about 6 percent of the country that's perfectly suited for wind energy, and that if the technology is developed further, that it's possible we could generate up to 20 percent of our electricity needs through wind and turbine.

What I'm talking about is a comprehensive strategy. In other words, we're not relying upon one aspect of renewable energy to help this country become less dependent; we're talking about a variety of fronts. And we're willing to work with both the public sector and private sector to make sure that we achieve breakthroughs. And I'm fired up about it and so should the American people be. I mean, we're close to changing the way we live in an incredibly positive way. And therefore, I want to thank the folks at NREL for being a part of this exciting movement. It's got to be pretty interesting to be one of these guys working on how to make switchgrass go to fuel. I mean, it's got to make you feel good about your work, because you're doing the country a great service.

And so with that in mind, I've asked Dan Arvizu to join us. He's the director of the NREL. That means he's—that means you're the boss? [*Laughter*]

Dan Arvizu. Only part of the time.

The President. Only part of the time.

Mr. Arvizu. Until I get home. [*Laughter*]

The President. Why don't you tell the folks—that's a smart man. [*Laughter*] Why don't you tell the folks what you do here so people can understand.

[*At this point, Mr. Arvizu, director, National Renewable Energy Laboratory, made brief remarks.*]

The President. I think what he's saying is, one of these days, we're going to take wood chips—[*laughter*]—put them through the factory, and it's going to be fuel you can put in your car. Is that right?

Mr. Arvizu. That's absolutely true. [*Laughter*]

The President. Stuff that would normally—[*applause*]. That's the difference between a Ph.D. and the C student. [*Laughter*]

Mr. Arvizu. I didn't want to say that.

The President. Yes, right. [*Laughter*] Anyway, keep going. [*Laughter*]

Mr. Arvizu. One of the other areas that we're tremendously excited by is photovoltaics. You mentioned the photovoltaics.

The President. Explain what photovoltaics are. I threw it out there as kind of, you know, showing off, but tell people what it means.

Mr. Arvizu. Photovoltaics is actually the direct conversion of sunlight to electricity through a semiconductor material, and it's essentially what we use in computers for chips that power those things. And to a large degree, it's a technology that's been around a long time, but it has become much closer to commercialization. Now, in high-value markets, it is commercial today.

[*Mr. Arvizu continued his remarks.*]

The President. See, what's changed is, the global supply for fossil fuels is outstripping the—the global demand is outstripping the global supply. And so you're seeing a price of the feedstock of normal energy going up, and technology driving the price of alternatives down. And that's why this is a really interesting moment that we're going to see. It's changed a lot of thinking. The price of natural gas and the price of crude oil has absolutely made these competitive alternative sources of energy real. And the question is, do we have the technological breakthroughs to make it such that it can get to your gas tanks?

[*Mr. Arvizu made further remarks.*]

The President. Thank you, sir. Larry Burns, why don't you explain to folks what you do for a living.

Lawrence D. Burns. Well, I'm responsible for research and development and strategic planning for General Motors. And I've been doing that, working for General Motors, for 37 years, actually.

The President. Thirty-seven years?

Mr. Burns. Yes. I started out in kindergarten.

The President. Yes, I was going to say. [*Laughter*] You're obviously not in politics because your hair is not gray. [*Laughter*]

You know, it's interesting—I bet you people don't know this—a lot of people don't know—there are 4.5 million automobiles on the road today that can either burn gasoline or ethanol—called flex-fuel vehicles. Isn't that interesting? And people don't know that. In other words, the technology is available.

Pick it up from there. I'm trying to give you—[*laughter*].

[*Mr. Burns, vice president of research and development and strategic planning, General Motors, made brief remarks.*]

The President. Tell people what a flex-fuel vehicle is. What is it? Tell them what it is.

Mr. Burns. What it is, it's a vehicle that can burn both gasoline and E–85 ethanol. As you explained, it's 85 percent ethanol and 15 percent gasoline. So any mixture between gasoline and E–85, the vehicle can burn. And in fact, E–85 burns cleaner and yields higher horsepower than gasoline. It's renewable, and it can be homegrown. So we think it's an ideal fuel.

The President. Does it cost much——

Mr. Burns. Well, from a cost standpoint——

The President. ——to make the engine——

Mr. Burns. No, no, actually not. It's a pretty straightforward thing for us to do. The fuel injectors in your engine have to be changed, but this is one of the reasons we can do it in high volume and give our customers the choice for——

The President. In other words, this isn't something that's going to be real expensive to the consumer, if somebody wants a flex-fuel vehicle?

Mr. Burns. No, not in terms of the vehicle.

[*Mr. Burns continued his remarks.*]

The President. Yes, just one quick point—sorry to interrupt. But people are sitting there saying, "Well, okay, maybe you've manufactured the fuel from different sources, but do you have the automobiles to use it?" And the point is, the technology is already advanced. I mean, they're out there, people on the road using it. So the question is, now, can we get the fuel manufactured close to where people are driving flex-fuel vehicles, or vice versa, so that we can get this technology expanded throughout the country? Go ahead.

[*Mr. Burns made further remarks.*]

The President. That's great. We're spending $1.2 billion over a 5-year period on—or 10-year period for hydrogen research. I would warn folks that I think the hybrid battery and the ethanol technologies will precede hydrogen. Hydrogen is a longer-term opportunity. It's going to take awhile for hydrogen automobiles to develop, plus the infrastructure necessary to make sure people can actually have convenience when it comes to filling up your car with hydrogen. But nevertheless, I'm pleased to hear that GM is like—joining the Federal Government on the leading edge of technological change.

Mr. Burns. The important part about that battery, too, is it's a stepping stone to the fuel-cell vehicle. We'll imagine our fuel-cell vehicles will have some form of storing energy, because as your car slows down, you want to capture that energy and store it. So it's not like we're making one investment here that doesn't help another one. They all come together—the ethanol,

the batteries, and the fuel cells are really one in the same roadmap to get to the future that offers a lot of alternatives for our Nation.

The President. Great. Thanks for joining us.

Mr. Burns. Thank you.

The President. Patty Stulp.

Patty Stulp. Hi. Good morning, Mr. President.

The President. You've got an interesting business.

Ms. Stulp. I do, thank you. I blend ethanol for gasoline refiner.

The President. You blend ethanol for a gasoline refinery.

Ms. Stulp. Would you like me to tell you about it?

The President. I wish you would. [*Laughter*] Please don't ask me to tell you about it. [*Laughter*]

Ms. Stulp. I've been involved in the ethanol industry for over 20 years. I grew up on a farm in Yuma County. I need to point out that Yuma County is the number one corn-producing county in the Nation most years. I'm a fourth generation——

The President. Number one corn-producing county in the country.

Ms. Stulp. It's in Colorado.

The President. Really?

Ms. Stulp. We grow a lot of corn, about——

The President. That's not what they told me in Iowa, but that's all right. [*Laughter*] I believe you.

[*Ms. Stulp, president, Ethanol Management Co., made brief remarks.*]

The President. Well said. Our economy—a strong economy is one that needs a good farm economy. And the more markets there are for our farmers, the stronger the economy is going to be. And ethanol is just another market.

Ms. Stulp. Mr. President, we really appreciate your support of this program.

The President. Well, listen, it makes sense. Anybody who doesn't support it doesn't quite understand the problems we face. But thanks. Good job. You're a pioneer yourself.

Ms. Stulp. Thank you.

The President. Colorado is famous for pioneers. [*Laughter*]

Bill Frey, straight out of Delaware, is that right?

William Frey. Straight out of Delaware, yes.

The President. Welcome.

Mr. Frey. Thank you.

The President. Tell people what you do.

[*Mr. Frey, global business director, DuPont Biobased Materials, made brief remarks.*]

The President. Are you dedicating a lot of dollars to research and development? I know you are in general, but how about to alternative sources of energy?

Mr. Frey. Absolutely. Absolutely. And we're doing it in two regards. Most of the discussion so far has been around the issue of fuels as an output. We do a lot of work in terms of using cellulose-based or using corn-based raw materials to make materials as well.

[*Mr. Frey continued his remarks.*]

The President. Good. Let's see what I can ask you here. [*Laughter*] What is your relationship—what is the nature of the relationship with NREL? When you say you work with NREL, tell people how the private sector and government entities interface.

Mr. Frey. So everyone—people have mentioned biorefinery—I think probably everyone so far has mentioned biorefinery—and we're working very closely with NREL. NREL, of course, has had a number of years of being in the space looking at renewable energy, doing a lot of the foundation work that allows us to now look at how we're going to commercialize cellulosics. So we're doing a lot of work in the area of biorefinery with NREL, looking at how we can take a process which, today, has challenges associated with the

economics of doing it, so it's an issue of economic. It's not a technology issue; the technology works. It's the economics of that technology. So we're spending a lot of time on trying to solve those problems.

The President. Do you have people here from your company coming——

Mr. Frey. Actually, there are people meeting today offsite, because of this particular event. [*Laughter*]

The President. I said I was a pain. Look, I said it up front. [*Laughter*]

[*Mr. Frey made further remarks.*]

The President. Part of it's the process of converting the switchgrass to fuel, and part of it's to make sure the manufacturing process yields a cost-effective product. And that's a lot of what you're discussing, which is important.

Mr. Frey. And it's important, I think, also, for a lot of the constituents to know that there isn't an either/or situation as it relates to the type of work that we're doing with cellulose. There's some confusion at times, as to is cellulosic going to take the place of corn-based ethanol, and of course, it's not going to at all.

The President. The answer is, no. We have plenty of demand. I mean, there's going to be a lot of cars. We've only got 4.5 million cars—what are there, 220 million cars in America? And by the way, just to make sure everybody's expectations are set, our fleet is not going to change overnight. It takes awhile. When you get new technologies available for people to buy—hybrid vehicles or flex-fuel vehicles—it takes awhile to change a 220-million car fleet to a modern fleet.

And so what we're talking about is an evolution, so people don't have the expectations that overnight, there's going to be millions of people driving hybrid vehicles or—we want them to be. It's just going to—from a practical perspective, it takes awhile. Thanks.

[*Mr. Frey made further remarks.*]

The President. I think the Nation—part of this deal today is to help develop national will. Most Americans understand the problems. And so good, thanks for joining. You did a fine job. Tell them back—hello there in Delaware.

Mr. Frey. All right. I'm sure they're watching so——

The President. They're watching. Well, give them a wave.

Mr. Frey. Okay. [*Laughter*]

The President. Lori Vaclavik.

Lori Vaclavik. Vaclavik.

The President. Vaclavik. It's a very—you're an interesting addition to the panel. Besides being a fine person, tell people what you do. I think people will find this interesting.

[*Ms. Vaclavik, executive director, Habitat for Humanity of Metro Denver, made brief remarks.*]

The President. Great, thanks—well-spoken. If anybody in the Denver area wants to contribute to help somebody's life be better life, join Habitat for Humanity. I mean, it's—if you want to—the truth of the matter is, I was just thinking about—we're talking about power and power sources and everything; the true power of the country is the hearts and souls of citizens who volunteer to help change people's lives. So, thanks. Beautiful statement—using some technology to help somebody. But you're right; the great source of inspiration is the fact that we got a new homeowner. Yes, that's neat.

Welcome. Dale, step forth. [*Laughter*]

Dale Gardner. I'm here, sir.

The President. Good. Reporting for duty. Are you gainfully employed?

Mr. Gardner. I am. [*Laughter*] As long as you're kind to my boss, Mr. President. [*Laughter*]

The President. As long as Congress quits earmarking, anyway.

Mr. Gardner. Well, we could talk about that too. [*Laughter*] I am here at NREL,

but I directly support the hydrogen program back at the Department of Energy.

The President. Great.

[*Mr. Gardner, associate lab director for systems integration, National Renewable Energy Laboratory, made brief remarks.*]

The President. So, like if you got a 2-year-old child, when the person gets to be 12, maybe thinking about driving a car, all of a sudden, the technology becomes more real—pretty close. For a guy 59, 10 years is a lot. [*Laughter*] If you're 2, it's not all that much. [*Laughter*] It's conceivable that a 2-year-old today could be taking a driver's test in a hydrogen-powered automobile.

Keep going.

Mr. Gardner. So here's what we're doing. The major technological challenges—I can boil them up into three areas. There are many, but here is a good way to think about it. The first is production of hydrogen. Hydrogen, even though it's the most common element in the universe, here on Earth, it's not found freely. It's bound up into these larger molecules, and therefore, it takes us energy and dollars to break it free. So that's the main thing.

The President. One reason why we need to expand nuclear power is to be able to help manufacture ample quantities of hydrogen to help change the way we live.

Mr. Gardner. That's exactly right. We can take that electricity from a nuclear powerplant, electrolyze water, which just means break the hydrogen free from the oxygen, and then have it for a fuel source. So production is one of our big goals. And the goal there, of course, is to make the cost of the hydrogen competitive with gasoline today; otherwise, you and I won't want to buy it at the filling station.

The President. Correct.

Mr. Gardner. The second area is storage. This is really an interesting one. Because hydrogen is the simplest element, it has the complexity that affects us in terms of using hydrogen in vehicles. We have to go put hydrogen in a tank, just as we do gasoline. Well, because it's so light and its density is so low, it's really hard to pack enough of it into a tank that's not the size of your whole trunk, such that we can get 300 miles down the road. And for Larry to sell a car to one of us, we want to go at least 300 miles more, especially when you're driving in Texas—a long way between filling stations. [*Laughter*]

The President. Yes. And we want more than one seat in the automobile. [*Laughter*]

[*Mr. Gardner made further remarks.*]

The President. So you've been looking at this for 3 years. Is this like science fiction, or are we talking about something that you think will come to fruition?

Mr. Gardner. This is going to happen.

The President. Pretty exciting, isn't it?

Mr. Gardner. It's going to be out in the middle of the century. It's not going to be something that's going to happen in the next 15 or 20 years, but it's going to be the way our kids and our grandkids view the energy structure of our country. It's very exciting work.

The President. In 1981, I don't think anybody ever thought there would be such a thing as e-mail. Matter of fact, we were still writing letters longhand, if I recall. Typewriters were kind of the—now it's computer. It's amazing what research and development can do to the way we live; pay phones to cell phones in 20 years. I think what we're hearing is change of lifestyle in incredibly important ways in the research that's taking place.

You can't have—we live in an instant gratification world, so we got to be wise about how we make investments. Part of the strategy is intermediate term, part of the strategy is long term. And thanks for explaining an important long-term strategy. You did a fine job, kind of boiled it down, simplified it—point one, two, three. [*Laughter*]

Mr. Gardner. I heard what you said today on——

The President. That's good, yes. Thank you for joining us. Thanks for your work on that.

Finally, Pat Vincent, the president and CEO of——

Patricia K. Vincent. Public Service Company of Colorado.

The President. Great. Thanks for joining us.

Ms. Vincent. Thank you.

The President. You have a vested interest in all this.

[*Ms. Vincent, president and chief executive officer, Public Service Co. of Colorado, made brief remarks.*]

The President. First let me—before you—what is the main source of your power today?

Ms. Vincent. It's a mix between coal and natural gas.

The President. Coal—right, right—50–50?

Ms. Vincent. We have some nuclear in Minnesota, depends on the State. Here in Colorado, it's predominantly natural gas.

The President. And what States do you cover?

Ms. Vincent. We cover 10 States. We cover the panhandle of Texas.

The President. Do you?

Ms. Vincent. We do. Oklahoma——

The President. People paying their bills down there? [*Laughter*]

Ms. Vincent. They are; they are.

The President. That's good. A fine part of the country, I want to you know. Well, you don't need to name them all, a 10-State area.

Ms. Vincent. Yes, 10 States.

The President. And you're based where?

Ms. Vincent. I'm based here in Denver, and this is our largest utility company here—is in Colorado. And we have a wind source program that's been around since 1998.

[*Ms. Vincent continued her remarks.*]

The President. So, like, when you analyze the wind turbine technology, is it advancing rapidly? Is there more advances being made—or am I getting you out of your lane here?

Ms. Vincent. No, it's advancing rapidly. And what we're finding is like Dan talked about, the demand for solar—is that the demand for the turbines is starting to outstrip the supply. And a lot of it's going overseas. The production tax credit really helps us here because it kind of goes in boom and bust cycles, so that has really helped us levelize the demand and make them commercially feasible. And people like GE are making big strides in wind technology.

The President. Good.

Ms. Vincent. Second programs we have are with NREL, and we have two. And the first one is a wind to hydrogen program. And I don't know about your experience with wind, but it does blow intermittently here in Colorado and——

The President. It does in Washington too. [*Laughter*]

Ms. Vincent. I wasn't sure if it was all the time or just intermittently.

The President. Lately, all the time. [*Laughter*]

[*Ms. Vincent made further remarks.*]

The President. By the way, this may interest you if you are—these people manufacturing photovoltaic products can't make enough. I mean, the demand for these things is huge. And there's just not enough capacity. The plant we were at yesterday is going to double in size. They're making neat roofing materials, by the way. I'm not their marketing guy—[*laughter*]—just happens to be on my mind. What's interesting about the discussion is the utility industry needs alternative sources of energy in order

for them to be able to do their job. I think that's what you're saying.

Ms. Vincent. Yes, and it's good for our customers. It's good for the communities; it's good for us——

The President. Absolutely.

Ms. Vincent. ——our shareholders.

The President. It's good for your customers; it's good for you.

Ms. Vincent. Yes.

The President. And I know you feel that way. Managing peak electricity loads with alternative sources of energy makes a lot of sense.

Ms. Vincent. Yes, it does.

The President. Good. You did a fine job.

Ms. Vincent. Thank you.

The President. So that's why we're here, to talk about a variety of options to achieve a great national goal. And there's no doubt in my mind we're going to achieve it. And it's exciting. It's exciting times to be involved with all aspects of this strategy. And you heard some of our fellow citizens describe to you what they're doing to be a part of this giant effort to change the way we live, so that future generations of Americans will look back at this period and say, "Thank goodness there was yet another generation of pioneers and entrepreneurs willing to think differently on behalf of the country."

Thanks for coming. God bless. Good job.

NOTE: The President spoke at 9:19 a.m. at the National Renewable Energy Laboratory. In his remarks, he referred to Mayor Charles J. Baroch of Golden, CO; Colorado State Senator Andy McElhany; and Joe Stengel, minority leader, Colorado State House of Representatives. The Office of the Press Secretary also released a Spanish language transcript of these remarks.

Interview With Reporters Aboard Air Force One
February 21, 2006

The President. Thank you all for coming. A couple of points I want to make to you. First, I'm excited about the energy initiative. American people are beginning to see that we've made good progress on research and development. We've got more to do. We're close to some breakthroughs that will achieve an economic and national security objective.

And I've enjoyed traveling around and talking to these scientists and engineers that are really excited about how close we are to some technological breakthroughs. Today, talking to the two scientists involved with the cellulosic ethanol projects was exciting. These guys are pretty fired up about it all, and they realize we've got a chance to change our driving habits.

I do want to talk about this port issue. A foreign company manages some of our ports. They've entered into a transaction with another foreign company to manage our ports. This is a process that has been extensively reviewed, particularly from the point of view as to whether or not I can say to the American people, "This project will not jeopardize our security." It's been looked at by those who have been charged with the security of our country. And I believe the deal should go forward. This company operates all around the world. I have the list somewhere. We can get you the list. They're in Germany and else-where—Australia.

They—in working with our folks, they've agreed to make sure that their coordination with our security folks is good and solid. I really don't understand why it's okay for a British company to operate our ports but not a company from the Middle East, when our experts are convinced that port security is not an issue; that having worked with this company, they're convinced that these—they'll work with those who are in charge of the U.S. Government's responsi-

bility for securing the ports—they'll work hand in glove. I want to remind people that when we first put out the Container Security Initiative, the CSI, which was a new way to secure our ports, UAE was one of the first countries to sign up.

In other words, we're receiving goods from ports out of the UAE as well as where this company operates. And so I, after careful review of our Government, I believe the Government ought to go forward. And I want those who are questioning it to step up and explain why all of a sudden a Middle Eastern company is held to a different standard than a Great—British company. I'm trying to conduct foreign policy now by saying to people of the world, "We'll treat you fairly." And after careful scrutiny, we believe this deal is a legitimate deal that will not jeopardize the security of the country and, at the same time, send that signal that we're willing to treat people fairly.

Thirdly, I'm looking forward to my speech tomorrow about my trip to India and Pakistan. It's going to be an important trip, one where we'll work on a variety of issues with both countries—security, prosperity, and trade—working with India, of course, on energy security. It will be an important trip.

I'll answer some questions, and then we're getting ready to land.

Dubai Ports World/Homeland Security

Q. Mr. President, leaders in Congress, including Senator Frist, have said that they'll take action to stop the port control shift if you don't reverse course on it. You've expressed your thoughts here, but what do you say to those in Congress who plan to take legislative action?

The President. They ought to listen to what I have to say about this. They ought to look at the facts and understand the consequences of what they're going to do. But if they pass a law, I'll deal with it, with a veto.

Crude Oil Supply/Middle East

Q. Mr. President, on energy and foreign policy, some Saudi officials have said they're unhappy with being targeted about Middle Eastern oil, saying that you wanted to reduce dependence on Middle East oil. You've got a close relationship with King Abdullah.

The President. I do.

Q. He's been to see you. Have you heard something directly, yourself, from the Saudis?

The President. No, I haven't talked to His Majesty, but if I did, I would say, I hope you can understand that the relationship between supply and demand is so tight that any disruption on the supply side of energy causes our prices to go up, and spiking prices hurts our economy. And secondly, there are parts of the world where people would—that don't agree with our policy, namely Iran, for example. And that it's not in our interest to be dependent, when it comes to our economic security, and for that matter, national security, in a market that is volatile. And so hopefully, he'll understand.

Q. So you don't think they should take offense at the comments about Middle Eastern oil?

The President. I would think that he would be understanding that new technologies will enable us to diversify away from our reliance upon crude oil. As a matter of fact, it's not only a message for the United States; that's also a message for India and China. In order for these growing economies to be able to be competitive, they're going to have to learn how to use technologies that will enable them to meet the needs of their people, but also the international demands of the world for good environment, for example. The Nuclear Energy Initiative I'll be talking to the Indians about is an important initiative.

Dubai Ports World/Homeland Security

Q. The understatement today, and one of the concerns of lawmakers, seems to be that they want more of a briefing, and they want more details about the things that you know that have given you confidence that there aren't any national security implications with the port deal. Are you willing to either have your staff or to give any kind of briefing to leaders of Congress——

The President. Look at the company's record, Jim [Jim VandeHei, Washington Post], and it's clear for everybody to see. We've looked at the ports in which they've operated. There is a standard process mandated by Congress that we go through called the CFIUS process. I'm not exactly sure if there's any national security concerns in briefing Congress. I just don't know. I can't answer your question.

Q. It seems like—you've already heard from different administration officials, saying, not in as strong terms as you have today, that there aren't problems with this deal, that the deal should go forward. But they seem to want more of a briefing. Would you be willing to give any additional briefings, either——

The President. We'll be glad to send——

Q. ——either in a classified basis or——

The President. I don't see why not. Again, you're asking—I need to make sure I understand exactly what they're asking for.

Yes. Oh, you're not the press.

Counselor to the President Dan Bartlett. I could ask a question. You showed some strong leadership today—[*laughter*].

Q. Why is it so important to you, sir, that you take on this issue as a political fight? Clearly, there's bipartisan——

The President. I don't view it as a political fight. So do you want to start your question over? I view it as a good policy.

Q. Why is it—clearly——

The President. Are you talking about the energy issue?

Q. No, I'm sorry, the ports issue.

The President. It's not a political issue.

Q. But there clearly are members of your own party who will go to the mat against you on this.

The President. It's not a political issue.

Q. Why are you—to make this, to have this fight?

The President. I don't view it as a fight. I view it as me saying to people what I think is right, the right policy.

Q. What's the larger message that you're conveying by sticking to this UAE contract, by saying that you're not going to budge on this or you don't want to change policy?

The President. There is a process in place where we analyze—where the Government analyzes many, many business transactions to make sure they meet national security concerns. And I'm sure if you—careful review, this process yielded a result that said, yes, a deal should go forward.

One of my concerns, however, is mixed messages. And the message is, "It's okay for a British company, but a Middle Eastern company—maybe we ought not to deal the same way." It's a mixed message. You put interesting words in your question, but I just view—my job is to do what I think is right for the country. I don't intend to have a fight. If there's a fight, there is one but—nor do I view this as a political issue.

Q. I say it because you said you'd be willing to use the veto on it.

The President. I would. That's one of the tools the President has to indicate to the legislative branch his intentions. A veto doesn't mean fight or politics; it's just one of the tools I've got. I say veto, by the way, quite frequently in messages to Congress.

Palestinian Government/Hamas

Q. Mr. President, Israel is halting payments to the Palestinians—the tax monies. What do you think about that, and what is the next step?

The President. I'll just give you our Government's position, and that is, we have

said that—well, first of all, the U.S. Government doesn't give direct grants to Palestine. We go through the Palestinian Authority. We go through—we give grants through NGOs from our USAID to help people. But my statement still stands, that so long as Hamas does not recognize Israel's right to exist, my view is, we don't have a partner in peace and, therefore, shouldn't fund a government that is not a partner in peace. I thought the elections were important. I was one voice that said the elections should go forward on time.

But I recognized that, one, elections are the first step in many cases in evolution of a true democracy; and secondly, that elections show—give everybody a true look at how—what people are thinking on the street; and thirdly, though, that because the Palestinians spoke, doesn't necessarily mean we have to agree with the nature of—the party elected. And the party elected has said, "We're for the destruction of Israel." And our policy is, two states living side by side in peace. And therefore, it's hard to have a state living side by side in peace when your stated objective is the destruction of one of the states. So my policy still stands, what I said day one after the Hamas elections.

Medicare Reform

Q. Can I ask you about a domestic issue, the prescription drug benefit plan? A lot of Democrats are on recess, and they want to make a big campaign issue out of this this year. What makes you think that the problems that this program being rolled out has had are something other than just the glitches that you've described?

The President. I'm glad that they're making this an issue. This is—the reforms that we passed in the Medicare law were necessary and are going to change people's lives in a positive way. And I look forward to talking about this issue next fall, if that's one of the issues they want to talk about, because I understand the impact that this law is going to have on seniors. And millions have signed up, and millions are realizing the benefit of this program. And so it's—we have done the right thing in passing this law. Seniors are given different options. Seniors are going to get an extraordinarily good drug benefit. We have helped modernize Medicare. And looking forward to talking about it.

Good.

Press Secretary Scott McClellan. Thank you all.

The President. Pleasant experience working with you all.

NOTE: The interview began at 2:42 p.m. en route from Golden, CO, to Andrews Air Force Base, MD. In his remarks, the President referred to King Abdallah bin Abd al-Aziz Al Saud of Saudi Arabia. A tape was not available for verification of the content of this interview.

Remarks on Dubai Ports World
February 21, 2006

I've just come back from a really good trip to the Midwest and the West talking about our need to change how we use energy—very encouraged by the technology that I saw and inspired by the scientists and engineers that are working on these new technologies.

And I also want to address another issue I just talked to the press about on Air Force One, and that is this issue of a company out of the UAE purchasing the right to manage some ports in the United States from a British company. First of all, this is a private transaction. But it—according to law, the Government is required to make sure this transaction does not, in any way, jeopardize the security of the country. And so people responsible in our Government have reviewed this transaction.

The transaction should go forward, in my judgment. If there was any chance that this transaction would jeopardize the security of the United States, it would not go forward. The company has been cooperative with the United States Government. The company will not manage port security. The security of our ports will be—continue to be managed by the Coast Guard and Customs. The company is from a country that has been cooperative in the war on terror,

been an ally in the war on terror. The company operates ports in different countries around the world, ports from which cargo has been sent to the United States on a regular basis.

I think it sends a terrible signal to friends around the world that it's okay for a company from one country to manage the port but not a country that plays by the rules and has got a good track record from another part of the world, can't manage the port.

And so, look, I can understand why some in Congress have raised questions about whether or not our country will be less secure as a result of this transaction. But they need to know that our Government has looked at this issue and looked at it carefully. Again, I repeat, if there was any question as to whether or not this country would be less safe as a result of the transaction, it wouldn't go forward. But I also want to repeat something again, and that is, this is a company that has played by the rules, that has been cooperative with the United States, a country that's an ally in the war on terror, and it would send a terrible signal to friends and allies not to let this transaction go through.

I want to thank you for your interest in the subject.

NOTE: The President spoke at 3:50 p.m. on the South Lawn at the White House.

Remarks to the Asia Society
February 22, 2006

Thank you all. Madam President—it's got a nice ring to it. [*Laughter*] Thank you for your kind introduction; thank you for inviting me here. I'm honored to be here with the members of the Asia Society as you celebrate your 50th anniversary.

I came here today to talk about America's relationship with two key nations in Asia: India and Pakistan. These nations are undergoing great changes, and those changes are being felt all across the world. More than five centuries ago, Christopher Columbus set out for India and proved the world was round. Now some look at India's growing economy and say that that proves that the world is flat. [*Laughter*] No matter how you look at the world, our relationship with these countries are important. They're important for our economic security, and they're important for our national security.

I look forward to meeting with Prime Minister Singh in India and President Musharraf in Pakistan. We will discuss ways that our nations can work together to make our world safer and more prosperous by fighting terrorism, advancing democracy, expanding free and fair trade, and meeting our common energy needs in a responsible way.

I appreciate Ambassador Holbrooke. I appreciate your service to our country. Thanks for being the chairman of the Asia Society. Leo Daly is the chairman of the Asia Society of Washington. Leo, thank you. It's good to see you.

I appreciate the members of the diplomatic corps that have joined us today, in particular, Ambassador Sen from India and Ambassador Karamat from Pakistan. Thanks

for taking time out of your busy schedules to come and hear the President give a talk.

Fifty years ago, many Asian nations were still colonies; today, Asians are in charge of their own destinies. Fifty years ago, there were only a handful of democracies in Asia; today, there are nearly a dozen. Fifty years ago, most of Asia was mired in hopeless poverty; today, its economies are engines of prosperity. These changes have been dramatic, and as the Asian continent grows in freedom and opportunity, it will be a source of peace and stability and prosperity for all the world.

The transformation of Asia is beginning to improve the lives of citizens in India and Pakistan, and the United States welcomes this development. The United States has not always enjoyed close relations with Pakistan and India. In the past, the cold war and regional tensions kept us apart, but today, our interests and values are bringing us closer together. We share a common interest in promoting open economies that creates jobs and opportunities for our people. We have acted on common values to deliver compassionate assistance to people who have been devastated by natural disasters. And we face a common threat in Islamic extremism. Today I'm going to discuss America's long-term interests and goals in this important part of the world and how the United States can work together with India and Pakistan to achieve them.

The first stop on my trip will be India. India is the world's largest democracy. It is home to more than a billion people— that's more than three times the population of the United States. Like our own country,

India has many different ethnic groups and religious traditions. India has a Hindu majority and about 150 million Muslims in that country. That's more than in any other country except Indonesia and Pakistan. India's Government reflects its diversity. India has a Muslim President and a Sikh Prime Minister. I look forward to meeting with both of them. India is a good example of how freedom can help different people live together in peace. And this commitment to secular government and religious pluralism makes India a natural partner for the United States.

In my meetings with Prime Minister Singh, we'll discuss ways to advance the strategic partnership that we announced last July. Through this partnership, the United States and India are cooperating in five broad areas.

First, the United States and India are working together to defeat the threat of terrorism. Like the American people, the people of India have suffered directly from terrorist attacks on their home soil. To defeat the terrorists, our intelligence and law enforcement agencies are cooperating on a regular basis to make air travel more secure, increase the security of cyberspace, and prevent bioterrorist attacks. Our two governments are sharing vital information on suspected terrorists and potential threats, and these cooperative efforts will make the Indian Government more effective as a partner in the global war on terror and will make the people in both our countries more secure.

Secondly, the United States and India are working together to support democracy around the world. Like America, India overcame colonialism to establish a free and independent nation. President Franklin Roosevelt supported India in its quest for democracy, and now our two nations are helping other nations realize the same dream.

Last year we launched the Global Democracy Initiative, which is a joint venture between India and the United States to promote democracy and development across the world. Under this initiative, India and the United States have taken leadership roles in advancing the United Nations Democracy Fund. The fund will provide grants to governments and civil institutions and international organizations to help them administer elections, fight corruption, and build the rule of law in emergency democracy—in emerging democracies. We're also encouraging India to work directly with other nations that will benefit from India's experience of building a multiethnic democracy that respects the rights of religious minorities.

India's work in Afghanistan is a good example of India's commitment to emerging democracies. India has pledged $565 million to help the Afghan people repair the infrastructure and get back on their feet. And recently, India announced it would provide an additional $50 million to help the Afghans complete their National Assembly building. India has trained National Assembly staff, and it's developing a similar program for the Assembly's elected leaders. The people of America and India understand that a key part of defeating the terrorists is to replace their ideology of hatred with an ideology of hope. And so we will continue to work together to advance the cause of liberty.

Third, the United States and India are working together to promote global prosperity through free and fair trade. America's economic relationship with India is strong, and it's getting better. Last year, our exports to India grew by more than 30 percent. We had a trade surplus of $1.8 billion in services. India is now one of the fastest-growing markets for American exports, and the growing economic ties between our two nations are making American companies more competitive in the global marketplace. And that's helping companies create good jobs here in America.

The growing affluence of India is a positive development for our country. America accounts for 5 percent of the world's population. That means 95 percent of our potential customers live outside our borders. More than a billion of them live in India. We welcome the growing prosperity of the Indian people and the potential market it offers for America's goods and services.

When trade is free and fair, it benefits all sides. At the end of World War II, the United States chose to help Germany and Japan recover. America understood then that as other nations prosper, their growing wealth brings greater stability to their regions and more opportunities for products Americans manufacture and grow. The same is true today with developing nations such as India. As India's economy expands, it means a better life for the Indian people and greater stability for the region. It means a bigger market for America's businesses and workers and farmers.

The area of America's relationship with India that seems to receive the most attention is outsourcing. It's true that a number of Americans have lost jobs because companies have shifted operations to India. And losing a job is traumatic. It's difficult. It puts a strain on our families. But rather than respond with protectionist policies, I believe it makes sense to respond with educational polices to make sure that our workers are skilled for the jobs of the 21st century.

We must also recognize that India's growth is creating new opportunities for our businesses and farmers and workers. India's middle class is now estimated at 300 million people. Think about that. That's greater than the entire population of the United States. India's middle class is buying air-conditioners, kitchen appliances, and washing machines, and a lot of them from American companies like GE and Whirlpool and Westinghouse. And that means their job base is growing here in the United States of America. Younger Indians are acquiring a taste for pizzas from Domino's— [*laughter*]—Pizza Hut. And Air India ordered 68 planes valued at more than $11 billion from Boeing, the single largest commercial airplane order in India's civilian aviation history. Today, India's consumers associate American brands with quality and value, and this trade is creating opportunity here at home.

Americans also benefit when U.S. companies establish research centers to tap into India's educated workforce. This investment makes American companies more competitive globally. It lowers the cost for American consumers. Texas Instruments is a good example. Today, Texas Instruments employs 16,000 workers in America. It gets more than 80 percent of its revenues from sales overseas. More than 20 years ago, Texas Instruments opened a center in Bangalore, which is India's Silicon Valley. They did so to assist in analog chip design and digital chip design and related software development. The company says that their research centers in countries like India allow them to run their design efforts around the clock. They bring additional brainpower to help solve problems and provide executives in the United States with critical information about the needs of their consumers and customers overseas.

These research centers help Texas Instruments to get their products to market faster. It helps Texas Instruments become more competitive in a competitive world. It makes sense. The research centers are good for India, and they're good for workers here in the United States.

In the past decade, India has made dramatic progress in opening its markets to foreign trade and investment, but there's more work to be done. India needs to continue to lift its caps on foreign investment, to make its rules and regulations more transparent, and to continue to lower its tariffs and open its markets to American agricultural products, industrial goods, and services. We'll continue to work for agreements on these economic and regulatory reforms to ensure that America's goods and services are treated fairly. My attitude is this: If the rules are fair, I believe our companies and our farmers and our entrepreneurs can compete with anybody, anytime, anywhere.

India is an important—is a market for our products. India is also important as a partner in opening up world markets. As a new nation, India emphasized self-sufficiency and adopted strong protectionist policies. During this period, its economy stagnated and poverty grew. India now recognizes that a brighter future for its people depends on a free and fair global trading order. Today, the Doha round of trade talks at the World Trade Organization provides the greatest opportunity to lift hundreds of millions of people out of poverty and to boost economic growth across the world. The WTO members' aim is to complete the Doha round by the end of this year. India has played an important leadership role in the Doha talks, and we look to India to continue to lead as we work together for an ambitious agreement on services and manufacturing and agriculture.

Fourth, the United States and India are working together to improve human health and the environment and address the issue of climate change. So we've joined together to create the Asia-Pacific Partnership on Clean Development and Climate. Together with Australia and China and Japan and South Korea, we will focus on practical ways to make the best practices and latest energy technologies available to all—things like—technologies like zero-emission, coal-fired plants. As nations across the region adopt these practices and technologies, they will make their factories and powerplants cleaner and more efficient. We look forward to being an active partner in this partnership.

Fifth, the United States and India will work together to help India meet its energy needs in a practical and responsible way. That means addressing three key issues: oil, electricity, and the need to bring India's nuclear power program under international norms and safeguards.

India now imports more than two-thirds of its oil. As the economy—as its economy grows, which we're confident it will, it will need even more oil. The increased demand from developing nations like India is one of the reasons the global demand for oil has been rising faster than global supply. Rising demand relative to global supply leads to price increases for all of us.

To meet the challenge here in America, I have proposed what's called an Advanced Energy Initiative to make this company [country]° less reliant upon oil. As I said in the State of the Union, "We've got a problem; we're hooked on oil." And we need to do something about it.

And so we're spending money on research and development to develop cleaner and more reliable alternatives to oil, alternatives that will work, alternatives such as hybrid vehicles that will require much less gasoline, alternatives such as new fuels to substitute for gasoline, and alternatives such as using hydrogen to power automobiles. We will share these promising energy technologies with countries like India. And as we do so, it will help reduce stress on global oil markets and move our world toward cleaner and more efficient uses of energy.

India's rising economy is also creating greater demand for electricity. Nuclear power is a clean and reliable way to help meet this need. Nuclear power now accounts for nearly 3 percent of India's electricity needs, and India plans to increase the figure by—to 25 percent by 2050. And America wants to help.

My administration has announced a new proposal called the Global Nuclear Energy Partnership. Under this partnership, America will work with nations that have advanced civilian nuclear energy programs—such as Great Britain, France, Japan, and Russia—to share nuclear fuel with nations like India that are developing civilian nuclear energy programs. The supplier nations

---

° White House correction.

will collect the spent nuclear fuel, and the supplier nations will invest in new methods to reprocess the spent nuclear fuel so that it can be used for advanced new reactors. The strategy will allow countries like India to produce more electricity from nuclear power; it will enable countries like India to rely less on fossil fuels; it will decrease the amount of nuclear waste that needs to be stored and reduce the risk of nuclear proliferation.

To benefit from this initiative, India first needs to bring its civilian energy programs under the same international safeguards that govern nuclear power programs in other countries. And India and the United States took a bold step forward last summer when we agreed to a civil nuclear initiative that will provide India access to civilian nuclear technology and bring its civilian programs under the safeguards of the International Atomic Energy Agency.

This is not an easy decision for India, nor is it an easy decision for the United States, and implementing this agreement will take time, and it will take patience from both our countries. I'll continue to encourage India to produce a credible, transparent, and defensible plan to separate its civilian and military nuclear programs. By following through on our commitments, we'll bring India's civilian—civil nuclear program into international mainstream and strengthen the bonds of trust between our two great nations.

We have an ambitious agenda with India. Our agenda is also practical. It builds on a relationship that has never been better. India is a global leader as well as a good friend, and I look forward to working with Prime Minister Singh to address other difficult problems such as HIV/AIDS, pandemic flu, and the challenge posed by Iran's nuclear ambitions. My trip will remind everybody about the strengthening of a important strategic partnership. We'll work together in practical ways to promote a hopeful future for citizens in both our nations.

The second stop of my trip will be to Pakistan. Pakistan is a key ally in the war on terror. Pakistan is a nation of 162 million people. It has come a long way in a short period of time. Five years ago, Pakistan was one of only three nations that recognized the Taliban regime in Afghanistan. That all changed after September the 11th. President Musharraf understood that he had to make a fundamental choice for his people. He could turn a blind eye and leave his people hostage to terrorists, or he could join the free world in fighting the terrorists. President Musharraf made the right choice, and the United States of America is grateful for his leadership.

Within 2 days of the attack, the Pakistani Government committed itself to stop Al Qaida operatives at its border, share intelligence on terrorist activities and movements, and break off all ties with the Taliban Government in Kabul if it refused to hand over bin Laden and the Al Qaida leadership. President Musharraf's decision to fight the terrorists was made at great personal risk. He leads a country that the terrorists seek to use as a base of operations, and they take advantage of every opportunity to create chaos and destabilize the country. The terrorists have tried to assassinate President Musharraf on a number of occasions, because they know he stands in the way of their hateful vision for his country. He is a man of courage, and I appreciate his friendship and his leadership.

Pakistan now has the opportunity to write a new chapter in its history, and the United States wants to build a broad and lasting strategic partnership with the people of Pakistan. And in my meetings with President Musharraf, we'll be discussing areas that are critical to the American-Pakistan relationship.

First, the United States and Pakistan will continue our close cooperation in confronting and defeating the terrorists in the war on terror. Second, the United States and Pakistan understand that in the long run, the only way to defeat the terrorists is through democracy.

Pakistan still has a distance to travel on the road to democracy, yet it has some fundamental institutions that a democracy requires. Pakistan has a lively and generally free press. I'm confident I will hear from them on my trip to Pakistan. [*Laughter*] Occasionally, there's interference by security forces, but it's a strong press. Pakistanis are free to criticize their Government, and they exercise that right vigorously. There are a number of political parties and movements that regularly challenge the Government. President Musharraf remains committed to a moderate state that respects the role of Islam in Pakistani society while providing an alternative to Islamic radicalism. The United States will continue to work with Pakistan to strengthen the institutions that help guarantee civil liberties and help lay the foundations for a democratic future for the Pakistani people.

The United States and Pakistan both want the elections scheduled for next year to be successful. This will be an important test of Pakistan's commitment to democratic reform, and the Government in Islamabad must ensure that these elections are open and free and fair. The Pakistanis are taking this step toward democracy at a difficult time in their history. There are determined enemies of freedom attacking from within. We understand this struggle; we understand the pressure. And the United States will walk with them on their path to freedom and democracy.

The United States and Pakistan both want to expand opportunity for the Pakistani people. Opportunity starts with economic growth, and that is why President Musharraf has made economic reform a priority for his administration. These reforms have helped Pakistan's economy grow rapidly last year. There is strong economic vitality in that country, and we will help Pakistan build on that momentum.

We're taking several steps to open up markets and expand trade. And these include efforts to conclude a bilateral investment treaty that would establish clear and transparent rules to provide greater certainty and encourage foreign direct investment. By fostering economic development and opportunity, we will reduce the appeal of radical Islam and demonstrate that America is a steadfast friend and partner of the Pakistani people.

The United States and Pakistan are working together to improve educational opportunities for the Pakistani people. Young men in Pakistan need a real education that provides the skills required in the 21st century workplace. Pakistan needs to improve literacy for its women and help more Pakistani girls have the opportunity to go to school.

Last year, the United States provided $66 million to help improve Pakistani education, especially in the least developed regions of the country. This is money well spent. We're glad to partner with the Pakistan Government to help train primary school teachers and administrators and build new schools and adapt existing ones so that young girls can attend school. These funds also support the largest Fulbright program in the world—an educational exchange that brings Pakistani scholars to America and American scholars to Pakistan. By helping Pakistan increase the educational opportunities for its people, we'll help them raise their standard of living and help them marginalize the terrorists and the extremists.

The Pakistani people saw America's commitment to their future when we responded in their hour of need. When a devastating earthquake hit a remote area in the mountains of north Pakistan, it claimed more than 73,000 lives and displaced more than 2.8 million people from their homes. American relief workers were on the ground within 48 hours. Since then, we've pledged more than a half a billion dollars for relief and reconstruction, including $100 million in private donations from our citizens. These funds have helped to build 228 tent schools, improve shelter for over half a million people, and feed over a million folks. Our compassion is making a difference in the lives of the Pakistanis, and it's making a difference in how they view America.

The terrorists have said that America is the Great Satan. Today, in the mountains of Pakistan, they call our Chinook helicopters "angels of mercy." Across their country, the Pakistani people see the generous heart of America. Our response has shown them that our commitments to Pakistan are real and lasting. We care about the people in that important country. When they suffer, we want to help.

The great changes that are taking place inside India and Pakistan are also helping to transform the relationship between these two countries. One encouraging sign came after the earthquake, when India offered assistance to Pakistan, and President Musharraf accepted. India sent tents and blankets and food and medicine, and the plane that delivered the first load of supplies was the first Indian cargo aircraft to land in Islamabad since the 1971 war. India and Pakistan must take advantage of this opening to move beyond conflict and come together on other issues where they share common interests.

Good relations with America can help both nations in their quest for peace. Not long ago, there was so much distrust between India and Pakistan that when America had good relations with one, it made the other one nervous. Changing that perception has been one of our administration's top priorities, and we're making good progress. Pakistan now understands that it benefits when America has good relations with India. India understands that it benefits when America has good relations with Pakistan. And we're pleased that India and Pakistan are beginning to work together to resolve their differences directly.

India and Pakistan are increasing the direct links between their countries, including a rail line that has been closed for four decades. Trade between India and Pakistan grew to more than $800 million from July of 2004 to July of 2005—nearly double the previous year.

The Governments of India and Pakistan are now engaged in dialog about the difficult question of Kashmir. For too long, Kashmir has been a source of violence and distrust between these two countries. But I believe that India and Pakistan now have an historic opportunity to work toward lasting peace. Prime Minister Singh and President Musharraf have shown themselves to be leaders of courage and vision. On my visit, I will encourage them to address this important issue. America supports a resolution in Kashmir that is acceptable to both sides.

This is a sensitive time in South Asia. In Pakistan and other countries, images broadcast around the world have inflamed passions, and these passions have been cynically manipulated to incite violence. America believes that people have the right to express themselves in a free press. America also believes that others have the right to disagree with what's printed in the free press and to respond by organizing protests, so long as they protest peacefully. And when protests turn violent, governments have an obligation to restore the rule of law, protect lives and property, and ensure that diplomats who are serving their nations overseas are not harmed. We understand that striking the right balance is difficult, but we must not allow mobs to dictate the future of South Asia.

In this vital region, the stakes are high and the opportunities are unprecedented. With the end of the cold war and the fall of the Taliban, more and more people are looking forward to a future of freedom. As freedom spreads, it's bringing hope to hundreds of millions who know nothing but despair. And as freedom spreads, it's sweeping away old grievances and allowing people in central Asia and South Asia and beyond to take their rightful place in the community of nations.

This vision will take years to achieve, but we can proceed with confidence because we know the power of freedom to transform lives and cultures and overcome tyranny and terror. We can proceed with confidence because we have two partners—two strong partners—in India and Pakistan.

Some people have said the 21st century will be the Asian century. I believe the 21st century will be freedom's century. And together, free Asians and free Americans will seize the opportunities this new century offers and lay the foundation of peace and prosperity for generations to come.

May God bless India and Pakistan. May God continue to bless the United States.

NOTE: The President spoke at 10:47 a.m. at the Mandarin Oriental Hotel. In his remarks, he referred to Vishakha N. Desai, president, and Richard C. Holbrooke, executive committee chairman, Asia Society; Prime Minister Manmohan Singh, Ambassador to the U.S. Ronen Sen, and President A.P.J. Abdul Kalam of India; President Pervez Musharraf and Ambassador to the U.S. Jehangir Karamat of Pakistan; and Usama bin Laden, leader of the Al Qaida terrorist organization.

Interview With Pakistani Journalists
February 22, 2006

The President. Thanks for coming. I'm looking forward to going to Pakistan. I appreciate the courage of your President—I'm looking forward to my visit with President Musharraf. I'm trying to think of the number of times I have met with President Musharraf since I've been the President. I would say five or six, seven times. I remember our visit to Camp David.

Q. I was there.

The President. He is—were you there?

Q. Yes.

The President. I appreciate his courage. I appreciate the difficult job he has. I appreciate his commitment to joining the world in dealing with Islamic radicals who will murder innocent people to achieve an objective. I appreciate the fact that he has stood strong in the face of several attempts on his life. I also appreciate our relationship with Pakistan and his vision for a democracy in Pakistan. And so I'm looking forward to the trip. The Prime Minister was here several weeks ago. We had a very good talk. And he was laying the groundwork for what I think will be a constructive visit. Be glad to answer some questions.

Reaction to Prophet Muhammad Depictions

Q. Mr. President, I'll start with the cartoon controversy. You and your allies work very hard on bridging the gap between the Islamic and the Western world, but the publication of a few cartoons in a remote newspaper seems to have undone everything. Why?

The President. First of all, I think it's very important for people around the world to know that a free press is important for a democratic state; a free press—for peaceful states as well. Free press holds people to account. Free press makes sure that there is a check and a balance on people in power. Free press also must be a responsible press.

Secondly, I fully understand people taking—not liking the cartoons. On the other hand, I do not believe that people should use that as a pretext for violence, nor do I appreciate the fact that some are using—manipulating the anger over the cartoons to achieve political ends. And therefore, it's very important for governments to not allow policy to be set by those who are cynically manipulating the anger that some have felt over these cartoons.

Nuclear Energy in Developing Nations

Q. Mr. President, you have announced this global nuclear energy initiative, and this is the one that you have offered to India also. And you have spoken about the countries—countries like India can also get a benefit of this initiative. Do you have Pakistan in mind—Pakistan already saying that this offer to India is India-specific? Is it India-specific, or Pakistan can also be included in this initiative?

The President. Well, we are starting with India, and one of the primary reasons why is that India is in need of a diversification away from fossil fuels. India is consuming a lot of fossil fuel. That is driving up the price of—a part of the reasons why the price is rising. America uses a lot of fossil fuels. China is using more fossil fuels. India is using more fossil fuels, and it's affecting the price of energy in the United States and in India and in Pakistan. And so therefore, to the extent to which we can get these fast-growing, developing nations to use something other than fossil fuels, it's in the world's interest, and it's in Pakistan's interest as well.

Now—and so I would not view—some say, "Well, this is a zero-sum attitude by the United States," quite the contrary. It's the beginning of a policy that says, there will be a suppliers group of people who are capable of providing fuel stocks for a civilian nuclear power industry, countries that will then collect the spent fuel, reprocess it to be able to burn it in new types of reactors.

The purpose of this whole initiative, and beginning with countries like India, is to recognize that alternative sources of energy are going to be important for the development of a clean world and a world that becomes substantially less reliant on non-renewable sources of energy.

Q. But Pakistan can't be included in that?

The President. Well, as I said, this is just the beginning of a very long process.

Kashmir

Q. Mr. President, in your speech, you talked about Kashmir dispute, and you said that you would like India and Pakistan to take bilateral steps to resolve the dispute. Pakistan has made certain proposals, but they are not reciprocated by India. And it seems that this bilateral is not going anywhere; there's need for a third-party mediation or some sort of help. Do you have any specific proposals for that?

The President. First, I'd like to make sure I clarify my statement for all to read. America supports a solution that is acceptable to all sides—since you're probably the only person in the room that paid attention to my speech—the speech, as you know, I said, "to both sides." The language should be "all sides," because it recognizes that a solution must be acceptable to India, Pakistan, and those living within Kashmir.

Our position is one that says a dispute that has been so long in a nation's history can best be resolved when two nations make the determination to sit down and come up with a solution that is acceptable to all sides. Of course, during my discussions, I will encourage that dialog to go forward. I'm convinced that history changes, and as history changes, attitudes can change, circumstances change, and that we have a possibility to see this issue resolved by strong and courageous leaders.

I'm pleased to see the amount of trade that's taking place between India and Pakistan. It's a substantial increase from July of '04 to July of '05. I thought that the—the new transportation routes between India and Pakistan are hopeful signs.

And so the role of the United States, in our judgment, is one that will help lead to a settlement that is acceptable to all sides.

Democracy in Pakistan

Q. Mr. President, you also spoke about democracy in Pakistan; some distance has to be covered. And the Commonwealth has recently asked Mr. Musharraf—President

Musharraf that he must decide by 2007 whether he wants to continue as the Chief of Army Staff or as the President, one decision. Is the United States comfortable with a leader who is also the Chief of Army Staff in a democracy? Does it bother you that he—his contribution as the Chief of Army Staff?

The President. I've had discussions with the President quite frequently about his vision for a democratic Pakistan. And I am—I believe that he is headed for a—continue to head for—on the road of reform. And he understands the pressures being put on him. As you said, the Commonwealth spoke, and I believe that he's committed to having a reform process come to fruition, and I believe he's committed to free and open elections.

Iran

Q. Mr. President, there is another issue that is particularly sensitive for both India and Pakistan, which is that Iran—India-Iran-Pakistan gas pipeline. As we said, India—need alternative sources of energy. So is it possible that—decision, allow the construction of the pipeline?

The President. What's important is that India, Pakistan, and the United States work together to send a firm message to the Iranians that a development of a nuclear weapon is unacceptable. You know, we—energy supplies are important for India, and they're important for Pakistan. I fully understand that. But a country which has been unwilling to adhere to treaties that it's agreed to, a country the President of which has said the destruction of Israel is in—part of foreign policy, a country which has not told the truth when it comes to whether or not they're enriching uranium or not, is a country that free nations need to deal with in a diplomatic way. And the best thing that the Iranians can hear is a unified message from all of us.

Q. Does it mean that at some date you could decide to take military action against Iran? Would you——

The President. Diplomacy is our first option.

War on Terror

Q. Mr. President, the recent incident in which U.S. military made a strike in the Pakistani tribal area in the Bajaur area. This has happened before also, and there was some outrage in Pakistan that there was no remorse from the U.S. Government on the action. These actions, when they are taken, is it because—the unilateral action that the folks on the other side do not trust their colleagues on the side of the border, or it's the timing, is it intelligence, or the lack of operational capabilities on the side—on the Pakistani side, that such actions are taken?

The President. We are—we're partners in the war against terrorists, some of whom tried to kill your President. We coordinate. We're allies, and we coordinate—nor do we talk about sensitive antiterror operations. Of course, the United States mourns the loss of innocent life.

Pakistan-U.S. Trade Relations/Earthquake in Pakistan

Q. Mr. President, in your speech, you also—you spoke about importance of prosperity, and you talked about offering business—industry in Pakistan. Do you have anything specific in mind, such as Pakistan has been trying for some time to get an FTA?

The President. First step is a BIT, and we will discuss that—we will continue to discuss that. We discussed that during the Prime Minister's trip, and we will continue to pursue this avenue toward opening up additional opportunities, commercial opportunities between our respective countries.

First things first, however—there have been some preliminary discussions, as well, about perhaps some trading arrangements in the Western Provinces of Pakistan. These are preliminary discussions. We think it makes sense to have a discussion. Such an agreement, if—a commercial arrangement, investment arrangement would be beneficial not only to Pakistan but to Afghanistan as well. And so there's a variety of discussions we're having to continue to open up ways to encourage investment and commerce.

I must—I applaud the President's economic reform package. It's yielded some strong results. Pakistan's economy is growing, and that's positive. You know, one of the key things is that people see the benefits of democracy—the tangible benefits of democracy, besides being able to express themselves. Today I also referred to the Pakistan press, you might recall. I think I referred to you as lively, meaning that—at least the Pakistan press I've been exposed to has never been afraid to ask any questions, or never been intimidated, particularly with the open press conference. And I suspect it might be the same when I go next week.

So I want to talk about reconstruction aid right quick before you finish. It's very important for the people of Pakistan to—and this is where trade matters as well, and commerce matters as well, that they see that the United States is interested in the lives of the citizens. You know, sometimes in the way things get reported, our policies get disconnected from people's lives improving. And we want that to happen, because a prosperous Pakistan is—will be a great example, a country that believes in markets and educating people to fill the jobs of the 21st century, and a country that continues to deal with rules and regulations that make investment difficult at times, will show what's possible. And that's important.

When the disaster struck, it took our Government no time to move. And we moved a lot of equipment and a lot of manpower and a lot of aid, because we cared about the people that were suffering. I remember President Musharraf calling me on the phone at one point to thank me. And it was a genuine thanks, because

we were—as you know, we transferred a lot choppers, which were necessary to be able to move manpower and aid into remote regions of your country.

He also asked, would we make sure that beyond the recovery effort, that there was a commitment to help rebuild. And my answer was, yes. And the reason—it's important for your readers to understand, I said, yes, because this country cares about the families whose lives were turned upside down by this disaster. When we heard 73,000 people lost their life, it touched our hearts and our conscience. When we realized over 2 million people lost their homes, we cared about those who had been displaced.

And so our commitment is to the people of Pakistan, and it's a genuine, real, tangible commitment that the people of the country can see. I understand there's politics, and there's—there's people expressing their opinions. But one thing they can't argue with—those who want to be critical of the United States can't argue with a genuine, heartfelt commitment to the improvement of the lives of those folks in Pakistan who suffered a—suffered mightily as a result of the natural disaster.

Final question, Kamran. Kamran.

Q. Yes, Kamran.

The President. Kamran.

War on Terror/U.S. Visa Policy

Q. Mr. President, being an ally, there are some expectations. We captured the top lot of the Al Qaida, and 300 Pakistani soldiers died. There is a lot of expectation in Pakistan—you spoke about bilateral investment treaty and stuff, access to the market—more on access to the market. Are we moving towards free trade?

And secondly, Pakistani students, sir, having terrible problems getting visas to the U.S. And that's very important—folks not getting to the U.S. for education, and can you help us?

The President. A couple of points—one, there's no question that the Musharraf

Government is committed to working to get Al Qaida brought to justice. It was Al Qaida that tried to kill him more than one time. And he also recognizes Al Qaida's presence is destabilizing. Al Qaida doesn't care about the people of Pakistan. They don't care about helping people get a good education, realize the vast potential of Pakistan. They're there to create chaos and murder. And so I appreciate that, and I appreciate his firm resolve.

Secondly, we have been—there is a tangible benefit for the Government and the security of Pakistan in dealing with—using—sharing with, providing equipment. We resolved a long-simmering issue in the F–16s. I recognize it has been put on hold, but the Government's commitment is a real commitment. It changed policy, as you recall. It reversed something that took place in the past.

The BIT is a beginning of—it's a step toward what you talked about, advancing—additional trading.

I agree with you on the issue of education. First of all, there are a lot of Pakistan citizens here, and a lot of Pakistani Americans that are making vital contributions to our country, proud United States citizens who honor their heritage.

I agree with you that there ought to be more student exchanges. But this is not an issue just for Pakistani students; this is an issue for students from other parts of the world as well. We had a very restrictive visa policy right after 9/11. It was a—our visa policy was a natural reaction to a terrible event that took place. But by—it didn't take me long to realize that we were missing a great opportunity to have students from Pakistan see the real America. And there's no better place, no better way in many ways to see America than to come as a student, study at our institutions, but more importantly, interface with people the same age and realize that ours is an accepting culture.

Q. Absolutely.

The President. And we welcome Muslims. And we welcome people that may be different, and that there's no better ambassador for the American way of life and the attitudes—the true attitudes of the American citizens than to have somebody here who has seen firsthand what America is like and then go back home. Word of mouth is a pretty significant antidote to some of the propaganda that is being played out for others to hear. And so I agree with you, and we're—Condi Rice is very much involved with constantly revisiting the visa issue—student visa issue, in particular, and not only encouraging students to come here, but once they're here, not making it difficult for them to complete their education. In other words, there are some restrictions even after the students got here.

Finally, we are also—along these lines announced a very strong language initiative so that more people are capable of—will be capable of conversing with people in parts of the world where, frankly, we haven't had that much conversation in their native language—all aimed at creating a hospitable world. And this trip will help send a message to the people of Pakistan: One, we're proud of the Pakistani Americans who live here; two, we want this relation to continue on. It's a vital relationship. And as I say, I am pleased with my personal relationship with President Musharraf. I try to put myself in his shoes. He is— he's got a tough assignment. On the one hand, he's got people trying to kill him, and on the other hand, he's taking this country toward—further down the road of democracy, and in so doing, is dealing with—as we speak, dealing with people who are taking advantage of a free press.

And as I mentioned to you, I understand why people are reacting to that. It's very important, however, that they react in a way that does honor to the process and not resort to violence and destruction and, in some countries, to death.

And so looking forward to it. See you all there, I hope.

President's Upcoming Visit to Pakistan

Q. Mr. President, one last——

The President. Yes.

Q. About the visit, can you state if you ever think of canceling the visit——

The President. No, I'm not going to—never thought about canceling it.

Q. No?

The President. Of course not.

Q. Because——

The President. No, zero, zero chance.

U.S. Visa Policy

Q. So we are a good word for the students, they may get visas?

The President. Well, I think we're working it very hard to make sure. Obviously, Ambassador Crocker and the Embassy there is the conscience. I will pass this on to Condi when I talk to her just to make sure that she's—she's constantly calibrating and looking at the issue. We hear—believe we've had a lot of—there are a lot of folks here that—in America, and a lot of Embassies around the world hear from respective governments when there's backlogs and slowness. These voices that are concerned about whether or not there's access to our universities are heard loud and clear. Believe me, it's——

Q. Mr. President, best antidote is exposing people to American people.

The President. There you go.

Q. That's the best antidote you have.

The President. Well, thank you.

Q. Don't restrict that.

The President. Don't worry. Glad you're here. Good job.

NOTE: The interview was taped at 2:11 p.m. in the Roosevelt Room at the White House. In his remarks, the President referred to President Pervez Musharraf and Prime Minister Shaukat Aziz of Pakistan; and President Mahmud Ahmadi-nejad of Iran. A tape was not available for verification of the content of this interview.

Remarks at a Celebration of African American History Month
February 22, 2006

The President. Welcome. Please be seated. Thanks for coming. Welcome to the White House. So glad you could join us for the 80th—80th—celebration of America—African American History Month. We're here today to mark the achievements of African Americans in our country's history and to honor the contributions so many African Americans are making to our land today.

I appreciate the Vice President joining us. I want to thank the Secretary of Health and Human Services—[*laughter*]—he's constantly trying to promote himself—the Secretary of HUD, Alphonso Jackson. Looking sharp today. [*Laughter*] Keeping good company too, by the way. I want to thank the other members of my administration who have joined us.

I particularly want to pay my respects to Dr. Dorothy Height, president emeritus and founder—[*applause*]. I couldn't help but noticing A.C. Green. [*Laughter*] Thanks, A.C., for setting such a good example and using your position to help others. It's an honor you're here; really appreciate you coming.

This month, we gather to honor the generations of heroes who called on our Nation to live up to its founding promise of equality—people like Dorothy Height. The past year, we lost two of these heroes, women whose grace and determination helped change the path of American history, Rosa Parks and Coretta Scott King.

Mrs. Parks helped set in motion a national movement for equality and freedom when she refused a bus driver's order to give her seat to a white man. Mrs. King spent her life advancing the cause of civil rights for all Americans. The courage and the dignity of these women helped rouse the conscience of a complacent nation, and we will continue to work to make the America these women fought for uphold the promise to all.

The reason to honor these women is to pay homage to their character and their strength and to remember the ideal of active citizenship. In the 1960s, many active citizens struggled hard to convince Congress to pass civil rights legislation that ensured the rights of all—including the right to vote. That victory was a milestone in the history of civil rights. Congress must act to renew the Voting Rights Act of 1965.

When African American History Month began eight decades ago, it was based on the belief that if African Americans were to take their rightful place in American society, Americans of all races should learn about black contributions to our history. That conviction is every bit as true today as it was in 1926. Generations of African Americans have added to the unique character of our society. Our Nation is stronger and more hopeful as a result of those contributions.

America is a better place because of African American writers like Langston Hughes, Zora Neale Hurston, and W.E.B. DuBois. Our culture is richer, thanks to the talents of musicians like Nat King Cole, Lena Horne, and Dizzy Gillespie. We've been inspired by the achievements of African American scientists like George Washington Carver and baseball stars like Jackie Robinson. Our Nation is stronger because of the distinguished leadership of those like Supreme Court Justice Thurgood Marshall and our two most recent Secretaries of State, Colin Powell and Condoleezza Rice.

Thanks to the contributions of these leaders and many others, our Nation has made great progress toward racial equality, yet we've got to remember there is still more work to be done.

As we honor the achievements of black Americans across our land, we will keep striving to build an America where the dignity of every person is respected, where people are judged by the content of their character, and where the hope of the American Dream reaches every neighborhood and every citizen.

To ensure the promise of America reaches all our citizens, we have got to make sure that every child receives a quality education. The reason I worked so hard for the No Child Left Behind Act is because I believe that every child can learn, and I refuse to accept a school system that doesn't teach every child. And so we've raised the standards, and we measure. You cannot solve a problem unless you measure, and when we detect problems, we solve them early, before it's too late.

The No Child Left Behind Act is challenging the soft bigotry of low expectations, and it's having a positive result. Because we measure, because we hold people to account, we know this: that the most recent results of our Nation's Report Card show African American children are closing an achievement gap. And it's an achievement gap we must close if the promise of this country is going to reach every neighborhood.

Last year, African American 9-year-olds set records in reading and math. The gap between white and African American 9-year-olds in reading is the narrowest it's been in the history of the accountability system. Thirteen-year-old African American students achieved their highest math scores ever. We're making progress, and we're not going to stop until every single child has a quality education.

One way to ensure the promise of America reaches all of our citizens is to encourage ownership. We want people owning something. One way to help people realize their dreams is to encourage African Americans to own their own businesses. Last year, the Small Business Administration increased the number of loans to African American businesses by 42 percent. We're going to continue encouraging entrepreneurship throughout our country. Minority businesses are getting a better chance to compete for Federal contracts. More African Americans than ever before own their own businesses, and that's a hopeful statistic and an important signal that the American Dream is reaching beyond certain segments of our society.

Part of ownership is for people to own their own homes. I love the idea when somebody opens up the door of their house and says, "Welcome to my home; welcome to my piece of property." In 2002, Alphonso and I set a goal of having 5.5 [million]° new minority homeowners by the end of the decade. Since we set that goal, the number of minority homeowners has increased by 2.6 million. We're on track to reach our goal. Minority homeownership in the United States of America is at an alltime high.

As we celebrate African American History Month, we remember and thank the many African Americans who are defending our ideals as members of the United States Armed Forces, some of whom are with us here today. I thank these courageous men and women who are risking lives to protect us, to preserve our liberty. By bringing the promise of freedom to millions across the world, they are laying the foundation of peace for generations to come. God bless.

Service is a value that we all share, and today I am proud to recognize five citizens who are setting an example for all our fellow citizens. The President's Volunteer Service Award is the highest level of commendation a President can give in recognition of those who have contributed their time and their talent and their energy to helping others.

Today we honor five such souls who are working to improve their communities and help their fellow citizens. Each of them has heard a call to serve something greater than themselves. By answering that call, you are inspiring others to do the same.

The volunteers we recognize today are Carl Anderson from Washington; Karl'Nequa and Katie Ball from Jackson, Mississippi; Steve Ellis from the great State of Texas—[*laughter*]—and Joan Thomas from Smyrna, Georgia. Their efforts are helping to provide role models and mentors to inner-city girls, to encouraging youth volunteers to work with people with disabilities, to provide computer skills training in local schools and community centers, and providing college scholarships to underprivileged children.

Today we honor your service. We appreciate what you have done to lift the spirit of the country. We thank you for loving a neighbor just like you would like to be loved yourself. And I join all Americans in congratulating you and wishing you continued success.

And now, Commanders, if you all would read the citations.

[*At this point, Lt. Col. Christian Cabaniss, USMC, Marine Corps Military Aide to the President, read the citations, and the President presented the medals.*]

That's it. Thanks for coming. God bless. Appreciate you all.

NOTE: The President spoke at 3:13 p.m. in the East Room at the White House. In his remarks, he referred to civil rights leader Dorothy I. Height; and A.C. Green, Jr., former National Basketball Association forward.

° White House correction.

Statement on the Bombing of the Golden Mosque in Samarra, Iraq
February 22, 2006

On behalf of the American people, I extend my deepest condolences to the people of Iraq for the brutal bombing of the Golden Mosque in Samarra, one of the holiest sites in Shi'a Islam. The terrorists in Iraq have again proven that they are enemies of all faiths and of all humanity. The world must stand united against them and steadfast behind the people of Iraq. This senseless crime is an affront to people of faith throughout the world. The United States condemns this cowardly act in the strongest possible terms.

I ask all Iraqis to exercise restraint in the wake of this tragedy and to pursue justice in accordance with the laws and Constitution of Iraq. Violence will only contribute to what the terrorists sought to achieve by this act.

The United States stands ready to do all in its power to assist the Government of Iraq to identify and bring to justice those responsible for this terrible act. And the American people pledge to work with the people of Iraq to rebuild and restore the Golden Mosque of Samarra to its former glory.

Letter to Congressional Leaders on Extending Generalized System of Preferences Benefits to Liberia
February 22, 2006

Dear Mr. Speaker: (Dear Mr. President:)

I am writing to inform you of my intent to add Liberia to the list of beneficiary developing countries and to the list of least-developed beneficiary developing countries under the Generalized System of Preferences (GSP). I have carefully considered the criteria identified in sections 501 and 502 of the Trade Act of 1974, as amended. In light of these criteria, I have determined that it is appropriate to end the suspension of Liberia as a GSP beneficiary developing country and to extend least-developed beneficiary developing country benefits to Liberia.

This notice is submitted in accordance with section 502(f) of the Trade Act of 1974.

Sincerely,

GEORGE W. BUSH

NOTE: Identical letters were sent to J. Dennis Hastert, Speaker of the House of Representatives, and Richard B. Cheney, President of the Senate. The related proclamation of February 22 is listed in Appendix D at the end of this volume.

Letter to Congressional Leaders Transmitting a Report Relating to the Interdiction of Aircraft Engaged in Illicit Drug Trafficking
February 22, 2006

Dear Mr. Speaker: *(Dear Mr. President:)*

Consistent with the authorities relating to official immunity in the interdiction of aircraft engaged in illicit drug trafficking (Public Law 107–108, 22 U.S.C. 2291–4), and in order to keep the Congress fully informed, I am providing a report prepared by my Administration. This report address-es the matter of assistance for interdiction of aircraft engaged in illicit drug trafficking.

Sincerely,

GEORGE W. BUSH

NOTE: Identical letters were sent to J. Dennis Hastert, Speaker of the House of Representatives, and Richard B. Cheney, President of the Senate.

Interview With Indian Journalists
February 22, 2006

The President. Quick statement—I'll be glad to answer questions. I am really looking forward to my trip. It's the first trip to India for me and my wife. We had a great dinner here with the Prime Minister. I found him to be a very decent, honorable person with whom we established warm relations. And he—I just can't tell you how—what a kind person he was and, at the same time, represented his great country's interests very well.

I do want to make something clear in the speech I gave today. I said that—as to the Kashmir interest—issue, America supports a solution that is acceptable to all sides. As you might recall, in my remarks, I said, "to both sides." I would like the record to be so that the world hears me say, "all sides." I fully understand that the deal has to be acceptable to the Indians, Paks, as well as the citizens of Kashmir.

Okay?

India-U.S. Relations

Q. Yes. Mr. President, how and why has India come front and center to U.S. stra-tegic thinking now after being on the margins for so many years?

The President. Well, as you know, there was a history, particularly during the cold war, that made it difficult for our countries to establish a close relationship. However, things change in the world. And as the post-cold war thaw developed, as—attitudes began to shift.

Secondly, the Indian economy, as a result of more transparency and openness and trade, began to change. And as the Indian economy changed, it changed the commercial relationship between the United States and India.

Thirdly, there are some common threats that make it in our interests to work together—namely terrorism. As I said in my speech today, the United States has been attacked, but India certainly understands what it means to have suffering as a result of terrorist activities. And so there's common interests that have helped to change the relationship. And I intend to seize those interests, as does the Prime Minister, in order to foster what we've called a strategic relationship.

And in my speech today, I made it clear to the American people that this relationship is in our interests, and I described the various ways it was in our interests. I think the evolution of the relationship goes to show that the world is—changes, and it's never static. And so thank you for the question.

United Nations Security Council Membership

Q. Mr. President, if India's credentials are so good, why isn't the U.S. backing its candidacy for the U.N. Security Council?

The President. Well, let me make one other point, if you don't mind, that I should have made in my speech today, and that is that there are a lot of Indian Americans who made a tremendous contribution to our country as well. And there are a lot of—over the last—as the high-tech boom helped transform our society, a lot of the brain power behind that boom have been Indian Americans, as well as Indians educated here in America. And so the American people, as well, have begun to get kind of a different perspective on the great contributions that India can not only make to our own country but can make to the world.

Our position on the United Nations Security Council has been very clear. First, we support a U.N. Security Council reform, but we think it ought to happen after other institutions within the United Nations become reformed. What I was always worried about is that we would focus on the U.N. Security Council and nothing else would happen. And so we have—we have said to all parties concerned—I fully understand the Indian position just like other nations— that "we will take your case under consideration, but first things first."

And a classic case of the reform I'm talking about is the Human Rights Commission. It needed to be reformed. And what I was, again, worried about is that we'd

miss opportunity while focusing on the U.N. Security Council.

Civilian Nuclear Power Program in India

Q. Mr. President, when do you intend to take the U.S.-India nuclear deal before the Congress and before the Nuclear Supplies Group, which is part of the U.S. obligation?

The President. Yes, it is. As we speak, Nick Burns of the State Department is discussing this vital issue with Indian counterparts. We are working through what has been—as I said in the speech, a difficult issue for the Indian Government as well for the American Government. To change the past, the ways of the past, can be difficult at times.

I appreciate the Prime Minister's courage last July of laying out a way forward, which I support. And so first things first is to go to India and, hopefully, reach an agreement on separation and then bring that agreement back and start selling it to the Congress. It's—but we can't bring anything back until we've agreed to the agreement. And that's what's happening now. There's a spirit of good will and cooperation.

It's in our country's interest, by the way, to encourage India and aid India in its development of a civilian nuclear power program. The American people are beginning to see high prices of energy, but so are the Indian people. And the reason why is, is that there's growing economies—ours, India's, China's—which is adding to global demand for energy. And demand is outstripping supply, and then what happens, you see price.

And one way to help deal with price here at home and/or with India is to develop alternative ways to power homes and businesses as well as automobiles. I was sincere in my speech today when I said that we're dedicated to research and development to come up with alternative ways to use automobiles and want to share that technologies with other nations, particularly a nation like India, which has got huge potential and vast room for growth.

And it's in our mutual interests—I also made it clear that it's in our interests that the Indian economy prosper. And it's a very simple reason why. One, a prosperous country is one that is—particularly one that has shown its capacity to deal with a multiethnic and multireligious society—it will give India more opportunity to lead, particularly in parts of the world where people need to see how democracy can work and function in a proper way.

And secondly, the American people have got to understand a prosperous India is advantageous to our own industries. I mean, we want people buying American products. Indians want Americans buying Indian products. And that exchange of trade in a free and fair way is beneficial for workers and consumers.

And I said an amazing statistic today—at least I thought it was—300 million middle-class citizens in India. That's larger than the population of the United States. And so we shouldn't fear relations with India—matter of fact, we ought to welcome them and work on ways to strengthen them. That's really what the purpose of the trip is.

Q. Do you consider India to be a responsible nuclear nation?

The President. I do, particularly when they signed the IAEA safeguards, and they have a separation between their military and their civilian nuclear parts of their Government.

Iran

Q. Mr. President, would the United States have a problem if India continued to source oil and gas from Iran?

The President. I think people are going to have to buy their energy where they can get it. On the other hand, I do want to make it clear to the Indian people and the Indian Government that an Iran with a nuclear weapon will destabilize the world and that those of us who are for peace and stability must work in concert. So there's a difference between energy supply and working closely to achieve a very important objective.

And we will discuss this issue carefully with the Prime Minister. There is a consensus in the world, and that consensus is that an Iranian Government that has declared its—has said that Israel shouldn't exist, for example, and if it were to have a nuclear weapon, would be a danger to all of us. And I will continue to make that point with the Prime Minister.

A.Q. Khan

Q. Why has the U.S. not questioned A.Q. Khan, whose activities intersect proliferation and terrorism?

The President. Well, we were the nation that exposed the conspiracy to deal with—more than the conspiracy, the activities; let me rephrase that—we were the nation that exposed the activities of sharing technologies, sensitive technologies, nuclear weapons-related technologies. And we, of course, want to know as much about the A.Q. Khan network as possible. But had it not been for U.S. intelligence, coupled with British intelligence, this network never would have been exposed. And the light of day helps understand proliferation.

Civilian Nuclear Power Program in India

Q. Mr. President, why does India have to jump through the hoops to get a civilian nuclear agreement when its energy requirements are similar to China, another big, growing economy?

The President. There are the nuclear supplier group and the IAEA—in other words, the world has signed on to this. We think it's in India's interest to do so, as it pertains to its civilian nuclear power industry. It will give confidence to people. It will make it easier for the United States to work with India. This will be a confidence-building measure that we don't believe is an unrealistic request. And we do realize there will be separation between the military side and the civilian side. What we're working on is the civilian side.

Spread of Democracy

Q. Is the U.S. more comfortable dealing with dictators and monarchs?

The President. Do what now? Do I feel comfortable doing what?

Q. Dealing with dictators and monarchs?

The President. Do I feel comfortable dealing with them?

Q. No, the U.S.

The President. The U.S. feel comfortable with dealing with dictators?

Q. And monarchs.

The President. And monarchs? Well, I mean, I've got a great relationship with Her Majesty Queen Elizabeth of Great Britain. [*Laughter*] She's a lovely lady and a great figure in a country that's an important ally. And of course, that monarchy is very supportive of a free and open and democratic system.

You must take the words that I said in my second Inaugural Address very seriously, in that we must end tyranny in the 21st century. It's a goal that all of us can work on. India has got a unique role to play. I mean, when you really think about troubled spots, these are countries many times that are having difficulty dealing with what it means to honor minority rights and welcoming different religions within, kind of, a social and civil fabric.

And India has done a magnificent job of showing the world how democracy can work. And it's—India is—I'm confident the country will play a constructive role and can do so in a much better way—many times—than the United States can. I mean, after all, there are 150 [million]* Muslims living within the Indian democracy. We got a lot of Muslims in the United States, as well, which shows the world that it's— you're capable of honoring—worshiping God as you see fit, and you can do so

---

* White House correction.

in a free way and, at the same time, be a productive citizen of a state.

And India can help a lot. I was very impressed by its contribution to a new democracy in the neighborhood, and that's Afghanistan. India has provided $565 million of cash, recently pledged an additional $50 million to build the Afghan National Assembly building. And that's responsible— a responsible nation does that. And it's a— it goes to show—at least says to me that India understands that a democracy in our neighborhood will help yield peace, because if you study the history of the world, regions that had been in turmoil are now peaceful as a result of the evolution of democracy.

And one of the points I made in my address to the Asia Society is that there are—there's more democracies now in the region, which will make it easier for a current Prime Minister, future Prime Minister of India to help achieve the vision that we all want, which is a peaceful world.

India-U.S. Relations

Q. Mr. President, in this era of free-flow capital, why would—why are there so many restrictions about inflow of talent— human capital to the United States, who probably add wealth and knowledge——

The President. I appreciate that question. I am—you're talking about visa restrictions for highly educated citizens. I am for lifting those. I think we ought to raise the level of those who are either educated here and stay here and/or come meeting high—with high skill levels. It's in our interest. I've always been a proponent of that.

And likewise, I would hope that India would lift its investment caps. In other words—and part of the trip is to kind of work on ways to continue to develop this strategic relationship in a constructive way. It's a—you know, I said something interesting—at least I thought it was interesting—in the speech. I said, for a period of time, if you're a friend of Pakistan, you couldn't deal with India, and if you're a friend of India, you couldn't deal with Pakistan. And we have tried to change the relationships so that people recognize it's in their interest that the United States is a friend of Pakistan's, and people in Pakistan recognize it's in their interest that the United States is a friend of India's to help, if need be, reduce tensions.

Right now the level of tensions are, relatively speaking, down. I can remember when I first came into office. You might remember, there was a series of incidents that got everybody quite nervous, and we had shuttle diplomacy—Colin Powell. And it seems to me that there is a renewed commitment to resolving problems. I thought it was very interesting that trade between the two countries has doubled, that there's, you know, new transportation hubs. That's all very positive in terms of resolving issues.

You asked me about the relationship, how it's evolved, and I mentioned to you that as time passes sometimes and circumstances change, relationships are able to develop a new dynamic. I would hope that time and circumstantial change is enabling India and Pakistan to develop a new dynamic. It appears to be that way.

Final question.

President's Upcoming Visit to India

Q. Between a cricket match and a Bollywood movie, what would a——

The President. Cricket match and a——

Q. You like watching?

The President. What was the second?

Q. It's between a Bollywood movie and a cricket match.

The President. I'm a cricket match person. [*Laughter*] I appreciate it. As I understand it, I may have a little chance to learn something about cricket. It's a great pastime. [*Laughter*]

Q. But, Mr. President, you're going to India, but you're not visiting the Taj Mahal.

The President. I know. It means I'm going to have to——

Q. Have you broken a promise to the First Lady?

The President. No, it means I'm going to have to come back. It's a—I am disappointed with that. People who have seen the Taj Mahal say that it's—pictures don't do it justice. It's one of the great magnificent sites of the world. And look, if I were the scheduler, perhaps I'd be doing things differently. But you want me doing one thing. I'll be the President; we've got the scheduler being the scheduler. I'm going to miss a lot of the really interesting parts of your great country; I know that. I would hope that I would be invited back sometime after this trip.

Q. You could be in trouble with the "Desperate Housewife."

The President. Yes. Well, she's certainly the star of the family. She's really looking forward to going with me.

India

Q. Mr. President, what is your earliest memory of India?

Press Secretary Scott McClellan. We've got to go to the next one.

Q. What is your earliest memory of India and Indians?

The President. My best memory?

Q. Earliest.

The President. At least memory?

Press Secretary McClellan. Earliest.

The President. Earliest. [*Laughter*]

Q. Earliest.

The President. Gandhi. It's my first memory, as I think about India—you know, a person who was so spiritual that he captured the imagination of the entire world. He's proof positive that—throughout history there have been individuals that have had the capacity to shape thought and to influence and—beyond border. And he did that.

Q. You watched the movie?

The President. I watched that too. But that's—but my memory was earlier than that.

Thank you.

Q. Thank you very much.

The President. Enjoyed it.

NOTE: The interview was taped at 1:49 p.m. in the Roosevelt Room at the White House. In his remarks, the President referred to Prime Minister Manmohan Singh of India; A.Q. Khan, former head of Pakistan's nuclear weapons program; and former Secretary of State Colin L. Powell. The transcript was released by the Office of the Press Secretary on February 23. A tape was not available for verification of the content of this interview.

Remarks Following a Cabinet Meeting and an Exchange With Reporters
February 23, 2006

The President. Thank you all for coming. My Cabinet just met to get a report from Fran Townsend about the lessons learned from Hurricane Katrina. On September the 6th, I asked Fran to conduct a thorough review of the Federal response to Katrina and to make recommendations about how we can better respond in the future. I wasn't satisfied with the Federal response. Fran and her team produced a lessons-learned document, and she just briefed the Cabinet about lessons learned.

I reminded our Cabinet that hurricane season begins in June and that we will be tracking the implementations of the recommendations in this report. I want to thank her for her report. It's a good work. We will learn from the lessons of the past to better protect the American people.

We have made a strong commitment to people in the gulf coast, and we will honor that commitment as well. The report helps us anticipate how to better respond to future disasters. In the meantime, our commitment to rebuild and help rebuild Mississippi and Louisiana is ongoing and robust.

I'll be glad to answer some questions. Terry [Terence Hunt, Associated Press]. Two questions. You're the first questioner.

Bombing of the Golden Mosque in Samarra

Q. Mr. President, dozens of Sunni mosques have been attacked and scores of people have been killed after the bombing of the Golden Mosque. How serious is the danger of a civil war in Iraq?

The President. First of all, the people of the United States strongly condemn the destruction of the Golden Mosque. We believe in freedom to worship. And I understand the consternation and concern of Iraqi Shi'as when they see this most holy site wantonly destroyed.

I appreciate very much the leaders from all aspects of Iraqi society that have stood up and urged for there to be calm. They recognize two things—one, the Iraqi people want to live in a democracy. After all, 11 million people voted in the last election. In other words, given a choice of whether or not they want democracy or a different form of government, millions of people showed up to vote, making a clear statement to the Iraqi authorities as well as to the people of the world—they want democracy.

Secondly, the voices of reason from all aspects of Iraqi life understand that this bombing is intended to create civil strife, that the act was a evil act. The destruction of a holy site is a political act intending to create strife. And so I'm pleased with the voices of reason that have spoken out. And we will continue to work with those voices of reason to enable Iraq to continue on the path of a democracy that unites people and doesn't divide them.

Finally, I do want to assure the Iraqi people that the U.S. Government is serious in our commitment in helping to rebuild that holy site. We understand its importance to Iraqi society, and we want to stand side by side with the Government in making sure that beautiful dome is restored.

Caren [Caren Bohan, Reuters].

Dubai Ports World/Homeland Security

Q. Sir, do you wish you had known earlier about the Dubai Ports deal, and were you surprised by the controversy over it?

The President. The more people learn about the transaction that has been scrutinized and approved by my Government, the more they'll be comforted that our ports will be secure. Port security in the United States will be run by Customs—U.S. Customs—and the United States Coast Guard. The management of some ports, which heretofore has been managed by a foreign company, will be managed by another company from a foreign land. And so people don't need to worry about security. This deal wouldn't go forward if we were concerned about the security for the United States of America.

What I find interesting is that it's okay for a British company to manage some ports but not okay for a company from

a country that is also a valuable ally in the war on terror. The UAE has been a valuable partner in fighting the war on terror. A lot of goods are shipped from ports to the United States—managed by this company.

And again, I repeat to the American people, this wouldn't be going forward if we weren't certain that our ports would be secure. But I also want to remind folks that it's really important we not send mixed messages to friends and allies around the world as we combine—put together a coalition to fight this war on terror.

And so we'll continue to talk to people in Congress and explain clearly why the decision was made. Many of those doing the explanations are around this table, and I want to thank them for bringing a sense of calm to this issue, as people understand the logic of the decision.

Thank you all.

NOTE: The President spoke at 9:16 a.m. in the Cabinet Room at the White House. The Office of the Press Secretary also released a Spanish language transcript of these remarks.

Remarks at a Reception for Congressional Candidate Chris Chocola in Mishawaka, Indiana
February 23, 2006

Thank you all very much. Please be seated. Thanks for the warm welcome. I have grown to admire Chris Chocola a lot because he is a person who does in office what he said he would do during campaigns. He is a honest, decent, down-to-earth, practical man who deserves to be reelected to the United States Congress.

Chris is a rising star in the House of Representatives. And when you find a rising star, it makes a lot of sense to keep him serving you. So I want to thank you

all for recognizing talent when you see it. Thank you for backing this good man for his reelection. Thank you for coming today to give me a chance to say loud and clear, Chris is the right person for the Second Congressional District of Indiana.

And like me, he married well. [*Laughter*] It's great to see Sarah—and Caroline and Colin. You know, being in politics is hard on your family. But it sure does help when you, in my case, marry a good wife, and in Chris's case, marry a good wife too. And there's nothing better, by the way, in the political arena than going back home after a day when maybe some sharp elbows were flying, to a family that loves you more than anything. I think it's important to have somebody in the United States Congress who places his faith and his family as a priority in his life. And that's certainly what your Congressman Chris Chocola does. And I can't thank you enough for backing him.

I want to thank Bethel College for letting us come by; I want to thank your president, Steve Cramer. And I want to thank the students. I know there's some students listening to this speech—one, I'll try to keep it short so you can get back to class. [*Laughter*] And two, please take politics seriously. In our society, all of us have a duty to participate. And one way you participate is when elections come around, you go to the polls and do your civic duty by voting. Now, I hear too often, "My vote doesn't count." Your vote counts. And by the way, when you go into the booth, vote for him.

I want to thank all the organizers of this event. It's not easy to organize an event that has been this successful of this size. And so, for all of you who have worked so hard, thanks for taking time to support Chris. I want to thank Jack Hiler, former Member of the United States Congress, who is the chairman of Chris's campaign. I want to thank Murray Clark, the chairman of our Republican Party of the State of Indiana. The attorney general, Steve Carter, is with us. General Carter, thank you for coming. Appreciate you taking time out. Most of all, thank you for being here.

Before I get to my speech, I do want to thank the mayor, Jeff Rea. Jeff, thanks for coming. He gave me the key to the city. [*Laughter*] My only advice, Mr. Mayor, is pave the roads. [*Laughter*] And I know you will. [*Laughter*] I asked him, I said, "Do you like being mayor?" He said, "I love serving the people." And I don't see how you can be in public office if you don't love serving the people.

Chris loves serving the people of this district. Every time I'm with him, he's talking about the people of the Second Congressional District. He says, "I'm concerned about things; I'm worried about the small-business owner," or, "I want you to understand, Mr. President, how important Humvee is." I said, "I understand the importance of Humvee; you don't have to tell me that." [*Laughter*] He's talking about—all the time, talking about people who live here. And the reason why is because he cares about people. It's one thing to be espoused in policy; it's another thing to have, deep in your heart, the desire to help people help themselves.

One of the things about why I like working with Chris and people in Congress is that we're there for a reason. Some people in Washington just want to say, "Well, I held the office." But that's not why Chris ran. He didn't need to run. He is a successful small-business owner. Pleased to report he and I are not lawyers. For all your lawyers out there, that's all right. We need them. But we got plenty of them in Washington, DC. [*Laughter*] Seems like it makes sense to have somebody that knows how to run a business representing this important congressional district.

We're living during historic times. I wish I could report to you that the war on terror was over, but it's not. It's—these are serious times that require serious thought and serious purpose in order to do our most important duty, which is to protect the American people.

You know, my buddies in Texas, they come up to the White House quite frequently. And after they get over their initial shock that I'm there—[*laughter*]—they then ask me, "What's it like to be President of the United States?" And the best way to give a job description is it's—I make a lot of decisions. I'm a decisionmaker. And some of the decisions that—you'll see them; they're visible; they're big decisions. And some of them you'll never see. And I want to share with you the rationale as to why I made some of the decisions I've made, decisions that Chris has been strong to support for the good of the country.

My thinking about the world changed on September the 11th, 2001. You just got to know that, so that when you see me talking about why we're doing things we're doing for the country, just keep in mind that on that day, I vowed that I would use everything in my power to protect the American people; that I recognized the nature of the war we were in, and I recognized the nature of the enemy.

Let me talk about the enemy right quick. These are people who have no conscience, but they do have a philosophy. These aren't isolated cases of people that are acting out their anger. These are folks who have espoused an ideology that is the exact opposite of the United States of America. Perhaps the best way to describe their thinking is to remind you what life was like under the Taliban for people in Afghanistan. Life under the—in Afghanistan said that if you were a young girl you had no chance, no hope. As a matter of fact, you would never get educated. Life under the Taliban in Afghanistan said if you don't ascribe to the way we think about religion, you're subject to penalty—harsh penalty often, sometimes execution. In other words, there's no sense of freedom, no sense of individualism. It's all this kind of darkness prescribed by a few. It's totalitarianism at its worst.

They've made it clear their intentions. When the enemy speaks, you better have people in Congress and in the White House who takes their word seriously. See, some in Washington would like to look at the world the way they want it to be; our job is to look at the world the way it is and try to work to make it better.

And so the enemy has said, "Don't worry, America is soft and weak, and all we've got to do is use the one weapon we have, which is the capacity and willingness to kill innocent life, and they will lose their nerve." And the reason they want us to retreat from the world is because they want to find safe haven again from which they can plot and plan and attack and kill.

I told you September the 11th changed my frame of reference, changed my thinking. I am never going to give any quarter whatsoever to the enemy. We will stay on the hunt. We will be on the offense. And we will protect the American people by defeating them overseas so we do not have to face them here at home.

That's why it's important to have Members of Congress who understand that when we put any person in harm's way, he or she deserves the best training, the best equipment, the best support possible. Chris Chocola has been a strong backer of the men and women who wear the uniform of the United States of America.

I also recognize that if the enemy were able to find safe haven, that would make this country less secure. And so I put out a doctrine early on in this war, the first war of the 21st century—by the way, I wish I wasn't talking about war. No President ever says, "Gosh, I hope there's war." For those of you who are young here, I want you to know what I'm leading to is how to keep the peace and do my job that you expect me to do, which is to prevent the enemy from attacking again.

See, when I grew up, oceans would protect us. At least that's what we thought. You might remember the fifties and sixties. We'd see a threat overseas, and we were teenage kids and just didn't need to worry about it, did we, because oceans were there to protect us. That all changed on September the 11th. And so I've talked—two things to the American people—one, we've got to deny the terrorists safe haven; and secondly, we've got to deal with threats before they fully materialize.

In the old days, a threat could be there, and we could pick and choose, decide whether or not we needed to deal with it or not. That's no longer the case in the 21st century. And so I said to the people of Afghanistan, "You give up bin Laden;

give up Al Qaida," because they were providing safe haven. I said, "If you harbor a terrorist, you're equally as guilty as the terrorists." And when the President speaks, he better mean what he says. And I meant what I said, and they didn't give up Al Qaida, and we routed the Taliban, and 25 million people now live in freedom.

We saw a threat with Saddam Hussein. I wasn't the only person who saw the threat. The United States Congress saw the threat; Republicans and Democrats saw the same threat. The United Nations Security Council saw the same threat. The entire world saw that Saddam Hussein was a threat. He'd attacked his neighbors; he attacked U.S.—was attacking U.S. airplanes; he had used weapons of mass destruction; he had destroyed thousands of his own citizens. There are mass graves in Iraq because of his brutality. He was a threat. It was his choice to make: Disclose, disarm, or face serious consequences. He made the wrong choice. The world is better off without Saddam Hussein in power.

And I want to thank Chris for his strong support in this war on terror. It's important to have people who are clear-eyed in this battle. It's important never to send mixed signals to our troops in combat. It's important not to play politics with the issue of war and peace. And I appreciate his strong stand. That's not easy, by the way. I understand that. Nobody wants to go around bragging about being strong in a war. But he is. And you just got to know, it's vital to have this kind of strength in the Halls of Congress as we implement a plan for victory.

We have one option, and that is to achieve our victory. And we have such a plan, and it starts with making sure that we deny a safe haven to the terrorists in Iraq. We got a plan that, on the one hand, says that democracy can help heal old wounds. And the Iraqi people have stood up three times in the past 13 months and made it clear to the whole world that they want to live in democracy. Over 11 million

people voted in the face of terror. Their voices loud and clear, "We reject terrorism; we reject the dark view of the Al Qaida that want to use them as a safe haven."

And if you want to know how tough Al Qaida is, just look at—we don't know exactly who made the bombing of this incredibly important holy shrine in Iraq, but whoever did it is trying to stop the advance of freedom, because their ideology of darkness cannot stand the light that freedom brings to people around the world. The United States of America strongly condemns the destruction of a holy site. I firmly believe that whoever did this is not a religious person but an evil person. And I praise the leaders in Iraq who have urged for calm and who continue to make sure that Iraq stays on the road to democracy.

The second part of our strategy is to train the Iraqis so they can take the fight to the enemy. One of the interesting things early on in this war in Iraq, they started bombing these recruiting stations. So the first question I asked our commanders on the ground was, are you having any problem finding recruits? And the answer was, absolutely not. The people of Iraq want to be free, and we're training people to help them secure their freedom. And as the Iraqis stand up, we will stand down. Troop decisions will not be made by politicians in Washington, DC, but by commanders on the ground. And we've got a plan for victory, a victory we will achieve.

In the long run, the way to lay the foundation of peace for our children and grandchildren and defend the United States of America is the spread of liberty. I know some have questioned whether or not it made sense, in my second Inaugural Address, to put a goal for the 21st century to be the eradication of tyranny. I can't imagine anybody questioning whether or not we should work to eradicate tyranny. Part of my decisionmaking process is based upon this principle and belief: I believe there's an Almighty; I believe that freedom is a gift from the Almighty; I believe everybody, deep in their soul, desires to be free. And therefore, you should not be surprised—I wasn't—when eleven million Iraqis said, "I want to be free." Freedom is the best way to achieve peace in the long run.

If you look at our history, we had—a lot of your relatives have died in wars on the continent of Europe. And yet, because democracy spread in Europe, Europe is now whole, free, and at peace. My dad fought the Japanese. I'm sure some of your relatives did as well. They were the enemy of the United States of America in a brutal war. And yet today, I sit down at the table with Prime Minister Koizumi of Japan talking about how to keep the peace.

And what's the lesson to be learned? The lesson is this: That when a country adopts a democracy in their own style, reflecting their own history and their own traditions, they become a peaceful nation. Democracies do not war; democracies yield the peace. And someday, a duly elected leader from Iraq is going to be sitting down with an American President talking about how to keep the peace, and our children and grandchildren are going to be better off.

I want to talk about another decision I made that you've been reading about in the newspapers. Right after September the 11th, 2001, I called in people who have the responsibility of helping to protect this country. We've got some really fine people, by the way. Really good people on the frontlines of fighting off these terrorists. See, if you don't believe we're not at war, then I can understand why people were concerned about my decision with the NSA. But we are at war; there's an enemy that still lurks.

I spend every morning thinking about— at least every morning thinking about how to protect you. That's what you asked me to do; that's my job. It's really important for people in this country to know that the Government is working as hard as they can to protect the American people so you

can go about your business. It's hard to be a risk-taker if all you think about is war. See, you've hired a lot of us to think on your behalf.

And so I called in those on the frontline. I said, can we do anything more to protect the American people? What can we do? General Mike Hayden of the NSA is one fine public servant—came back, he said, "Mr. President, I think we can do a better job of picking up communications from an enemy before they attack so we can possibly respond." Mindful of that recommendation and mindful of the fact that I took the oath of office that said I will defend the Constitution and the laws of the United States—I called in the lawyers. I got a lot of them. [*Laughter*] I said, is what General Hayden recommended legal? Do I have the legal authority as the President of the United States to put this in practice—because it made a lot of sense, his recommendation. He said, "Mr. President, we have the capacity to listen to Al Qaida or suspected Al Qaida and their affiliates in making phone calls from outside the United States, inside the United States and vice versa."

It seemed to make sense to me that if somebody associated with the enemy is making a call inside the country, that it would be helpful to know why, in order to protect the American people. Lawyers came back and said, "You got the authority, Mr. President."

I then went and said, well, gosh, if we do go forward, I know there's going to be some consternation in the Halls of the United States Congress. So we briefed people responsible for intelligence and the leadership in both bodies, in both political parties. Just like my buddy in Texas said, "If you're trying to pull one over on them, why are you briefing the Congress?" [*Laughter*] "If you're doing something illegal, why did you call the Congress in and lay it for them to fully understand what we're doing to protect the American people?"

I wanted to share that with you. I think it's important for you to know why I make decisions. I'm confident what I'm doing—the decision I made is the right decision. If Al Qaida is calling in the United States, we want to know why.

We're also making decisions about how to keep this economy growing. One thing the people of this district ought to do is judge whether or not Chris's votes on creating an environment for capital to flourish is working or not. He said, look—he and I agree the role of government is not to create wealth but an environment in which small businesses can flourish, in which people can realize their dreams, in which capital moves more freely, so that people can find work.

And our plan is working. This economy of ours has been through a recession, an attack, a war, and corporate scandals, major storms last year, and high energy prices, and we grew at 3.5 percent. The national unemployment rate is 4.7 percent. We've added 4.7 million new jobs over the past 24 months—or a little longer than—2½ years. Productivity is at an alltime high. More people own a home today than ever before in our Nation's history. More minorities own a home today than ever before in our Nation's history.

Our progrowth economic policies are working, and it starts with keeping your taxes low. Cutting taxes was the right thing to do. And if we don't permanently keep these tax cuts in place, you're going to have a tax increase. And raising taxes is the wrong way to cause this economy to continue to grow.

I'm proud to have somebody like Chris who understands that when you have more money in your pockets to spend and save and invest, the economy grows. I've heard it—I'm sure you've heard all the talk in Washington. They said, "Look, we need to balance the budget, and therefore, let's raise the taxes." That's not how Washington works. They're going to raise your taxes, and they're going to figure out new ways

to spend your money. That's how Washington works. The best way to balance the budget is keep taxes low, grow the economy, and be wise about how we spend your money.

And I appreciate Chris's support of fiscal austerity, and he does a good job. Every program sounds like a brilliant program in Washington, but you got to set priorities with the people's money, and that's what we're doing. We're on a plan to cut the deficit in half by 2009, but the toughest deficit of all is the unfunded liabilities inherent in Medicare and Social Security.

And I recognize some of them in Washington don't want to touch that issue. By the way, it's a problem for both Republicans and Democrats. Sometimes if the issue looks too tough, the easiest thing to do is head for the hills. That's not the way Chris thinks. On Air Force One today, he said, "Mr. President, are you serious about continuing to discuss how to fix Social Security and Medicare?" And I said, "Absolutely, Chris." He understands what I know. Our job is to confront problems and not pass them on to future Presidents and future Congresses. And I intend to continue working with Chris on Social Security and Medicare reform.

You know, there's always a series of choices in Washington, DC, and I understand there's still uncertainty in the economy. And I understand why. There's a lot of changeover with new jobs, and you got some folks here in this district that lost work. And this troubles our fellow citizens, and it troubles me, and it troubles Chris. And we have a choice to make during this period of uncertainty, and that is whether or not we become protectionists and isolationists, or whether or not we're confident about the capacity of the United States to continue to lead the world's economy. And I'm proud to have a partner who ascribes to the latter philosophy.

Our view is this: We shouldn't fear the future because we intend to shape the future. And you shape the future with good tax policy and good spending policy. You shape the future with good legal policy. We got too many junk lawsuits making it hard for people to invest capital. We need legal reform in the United States of America if we intend to lead the world economy.

We intend to shape the future by encouraging research and development so this country remains the leading exporter and developer of new technologies. We're going to shape the future by changing our energy habits. I understand when an oil guy—I'm a guy from Texas—stands up and says, "We're addicted to oil," it caused people to take a second look. But I'm going to tell you something: Being addicted to oil puts us in an economic bind as well as a national security bind. And I intend to do something about it.

I'm glad to have a partner with Chris. We're going to spend money wisely—your money wisely on research and development so we can develop advanced new batteries, so you can plug in your car at night and be able to drive 40 miles on electricity, not using a drop of gasoline. We're going to continue to expand the use of ethanol. It makes sense, by the way, to use research and development—your dollars for research and development to figure out ways to burn—better ways to burn corn and wood chips and saw grass. I want it so the American agriculture sector is providing energy for United States automobiles, not unstable parts of the world providing energy for U.S. automobiles.

We've got an aggressive agenda. We believe in things. We're optimistic people. We believe in our philosophy, and we know you've sent us to Washington to produce results. And one of the really important areas, I know, for people in this part of the world is to make sure health care is available and affordable, particularly if you're a small-business owner. Everywhere I go small-business owners say, "It's tough for me to stay in business because I'm having trouble with my health care costs." And that's dangerous for the United States.

Two-thirds of all new jobs in the United States are produced by small-business owners, and so we got to do something about it.

I want to warn you, however, that there is a philosophical debate in Washington, and I would very—listen very carefully to the rhetoric during a political campaign. The debate is this, whether or not we should encourage market forces to help set price, or whether or not the Federal Government ought to be setting price. I strongly do not believe the Federal Government ought to be running our health care system, and neither does Chris Chocola. We believe that we ought to strengthen the doctor-patient relationship, bring transparency to pricing and medicine, encourage the development of information technology so medicine is modern.

In order to make sure health care is available and affordable, we've got to do something about these lawsuits—not necessarily in Indiana—but around the country that are running good docs out of business and running up the cost of medicine for the taxpayers.

We have passed what's called health savings accounts. It's a great new vehicle to add market pricing into medicine and to put doctors and patients in charge of medicine. I strongly urge people who have run the small businesses to take a look at health savings accounts. And I look forward to working with Chris to make health savings account more acceptable and more available as an important antidote to those who want to federalize health care.

I do want to talk about one aspect of health care that is a Federal responsibility, and that's Medicare. When I got to Washington, DC, I decided to do something about a health care system that had become stagnant and old as a result of Federal bureaucracies making decisions. I'll give you an example. The Government would pay your taxpayers' money—your money to help a person with an ulcer surgery. It may cost 50 grand; I don't know what ulcer surgeries cost. Fortunately, I haven't had one. But it costs a lot. But wouldn't pay a dime for the prescription drugs to prevent the ulcer surgery from happening in the first place. That seemed like the system was a little old to me and stale.

If you make a commitment to somebody, you got to make the commitment of excellence. And so I worked with Congress, Congressmen like Chris, to modernize Medicare, to provide a prescription drug benefit for our seniors. The Medicare modernization bill not only introduced HSAs but it gave seniors different options from which to choose. It's amazing what happens when you interject a sense of competition into a system. Do you realize that when we first analyzed the prescription drug benefit for seniors, they thought it was going to cost about $35 a month for the seniors? Because of competition, it's down to less than $28 a month. Competition works. Trusting people to make decisions works. Modernizing Medicare is an important, vital thing to have done. The Medicare bill I signed, that Chris supported, is going to make medicine for our seniors modern, and it's been necessary to do.

Good public policy is more than just talking about economic issues or cultural issues which matter to the United States as well. I'm proud to have a partner in promoting a culture of life in the United States of America. Banning partial-birth abortion was an important bill I signed and sends a signal that the United States of America should value all life in all forms.

The true strength of the United States of America is not our military strength or our economic strength, but it's the—the strength lies in the hearts and souls of our citizens. I am always astounded at the social entrepreneurship that takes place all around our country. I'm impressed by the thousands who have joined the armies of compassion to help bring hope where there's hopelessness and love where there's a lack of love.

Chris and I understand that the role of government is limited, and it's a fact that governments don't love. Governments can dispense law and justice but not love. And therefore, one of the most important initiatives of my tenure as your President has been to promote the Faith-Based and Community-Based Initiative, which recognizes governments should welcome people of faith in helping to solve the intractable problems of our society. We should not fear faith in America. We ought to say to those who want to love their neighbor just like they'd like to be loved themselves, "You should have equal access to Federal money, so long as you're helping to meet a Federal need." And we have a lot of need when it comes to saying to a brother or sister who's lost, "I love you. What can I do to help you?"

I've probably been going on a little too long. I hope the food's not getting cold. [*Laughter*] But I do tell you I'm proud to be here. I'm honored to stand by this good man. He's a fine, fine person and a great Member of the United States Congress who ran for a reason. And today I hope I can share some of the reasons why both he and I are proud to serve our country. I hope you can get a sense of philosophy behind why. We're not making up our minds based upon polls or focus groups. We're making up our mind based upon a philosophy and what we think is right for all the people of this country.

Please send him back to the United States Congress. He's necessary. He's important, and he's doing a fantastic job for the people of the Second Congressional District.

NOTE: The President spoke at 12:30 p.m. at Bethel College Indiana. In his remarks, he referred Sarah Chocola, wife of Representative Chris Chocola, and their children, Caroline and Colin; Indiana State Attorney General Steve Carter; Mayor Jeffrey L. Rea of Mishawaka, IN; Usama bin Laden, leader of the Al Qaida terrorist organization; and former President Saddam Hussein of Iraq.

Remarks to the American Legion
February 24, 2006

Thank you all. Please be seated. Thanks for the warm welcome. Mr. Commander, thank you for letting me come by and visit with you about the subject of how to keep the peace and protect the United States of America. I'm proud to be with my fellow Legionnaires. Always a pleasure to be in the midst of veterans who served our country. I see some people who are not quite veterans yet that are with us, members who are serving all branches of Government, and I thank you all for coming. I appreciate your interest in the direction this country must continue to lead in order to protect ourselves and promote the peace.

I want to thank Carol Van Kirk, who's the national president of the American Legion Auxiliary. Old Tom Bock is wise enough to always include the Auxiliary. He knows something about leadership. I want to thank Paul Hasz. I want to thank John Sommer, executive director. He spends quality time in the Oval Office, along with the commander. He's never shy to express his opinion, but that's what you pay him for. [*Laughter*]

I want to thank the chairman of the Senate Arms Services Committee, Senator John Warner. Senator, it means a lot to me and it means a lot to the folks here that you take time to come here to be with them. And I'm honored you're here. Thanks for coming.

The American Legion is one of America's great organizations. From your founding after World War I to today's war on terror, Legionnaires have fought for our freedom, and you fought for the brave veterans who defended our freedom as well. You served our country in uniform, and you serve our country in civilian life. The Legion was founded, in the words of your constitution, "to build a sense of individual obligation to the community, state, and nation." And when Hurricane Katrina struck our Nation's gulf coast, Legion posts all across America swung into action to help neighbors in need.

Take, for example, Post 338 in Bradner, Ohio. These good folks helped arrange medical transportation to reunite a sick child with his family after the family was forced apart because of the storm. Or Post 27 in DeRidder, Louisiana, which turned its bingo hall into an emergency shelter for 41 kidney dialysis patients and their caregivers and their loved ones.

I think it's very interesting what the post commander, Retired Navy Master Chief Bill Loftin, said—by the way, he said it when he was cooking hot meals and helped care for disabled evacuees. He put it this way: "This is for human life. That's what the Legion is all about." In times of crisis, our citizens know Legionnaires always come through, and I appreciate you.

Members of the American Legion are showing the heart of the Legion every single day, not just when catastrophe hits. Across America, Legionnaires and members of the Ladies Auxiliary volunteer in veterans hospitals, sponsor Scout troops and youth baseball, collect scholarship money for deserving students, including a special fund that the Legion established for the children of troops who've been killed in the war on terror. And I thank you for that as well.

Our Nation is grateful for your service on and off the battlefield. As you serve your fellow Americans in need, you're also strongly supporting the American flag. It was a Legion that helped draft our Nation's first flag code back in 1923. And Legionnaires have been working ever since to ensure the flag is cherished and protected. I appreciate your leadership of the Citizens Flag Alliance, and like you, I support a constitutional amendment to protect the American flag.

As veterans, you have placed the Nation's security before your own lives, and that sacrifice creates a debt that our country can never fully repay. Yet there are things Government can do, such as strongly support our veterans, and that's precisely what my administration is doing. The time when we're holding down discretionary spending, my 2007 budget—with my 2007 budget, my administration will have increased funding for our veterans by $35 billion since I took office, which is an increase of 75 percent.

We have made health care a top priority for my administration. With my 2007 budget, we'll increase VA's medical care budget by 69 percent since 2001. Our increased funding has given almost a million more veterans access to the VA medical care system. Since January 2002, disability claims are being processed 63 days faster than they were when I took office.

In the last 4 years, we've committed almost $3 billion to modernize and expanding VA facilities so that more veterans can get care closer to home. We're working to ensure that veterans with the greatest needs—those with service disabilities and lower incomes and special needs—are given priority. We're making sure that our men and women returning from combat are the first in line for treatment.

We're also getting results for veterans beyond the health care system. For more than a century, Federal law prohibited disabled veterans from receiving both their military retired pay and their VA disability compensation. Combat-injured and severely disabled veterans deserve better. I'm the first

President in more than 100 years to sign concurrent receipt legislation. And I thank the Legion for working on these issues.

Our Nation's debt extends not just to the veterans who served but also to the families who stood by them in war. I signed into law the Veterans Benefits Act, authorizing $1 billion in new and expanded benefits for disabled veterans, surviving spouses, and their children. The families of our veterans have served our country; our Nation will honor their service by standing with them in their time of need.

As veterans you know what it means to leave your family, put on the uniform, and head off to war. And today in Afghanistan and Iraq and other fronts in this war on terror, a new generation of service men and women is carrying on your legacy of selfless sacrifice and courage under fire. As they fight dangerous enemies in distant lands, I know that you share America's pride in them, and I thank all of you for your strong support of our troops in harm's way. Their service is needed in these dangerous times.

We remain a nation at war. The war reached our shores on September the 11th, 2001, when our Nation awoke to a sudden attack. Like generations before us, we have accepted new responsibilities, and we will confront these dangers with firm resolve.

Our most important duty is to defend the American people, and so we're taking the fight to those who attacked us. We're taking the fight to those who share their murderous vision for future attacks. We will take this fight to the enemy without wavering, and we will prevail.

The enemy we face is brutal and determined. The terrorists have an ideology; they share a hateful vision that rejects tolerance and crushes all dissent. They seek a world where women are oppressed, where children are indoctrinated, and those who reject their ideology of violence and extremism are threatened and often murdered.

The terrorists have aims. They seek to impose their heartless ideology of totalitarian control throughout the Middle East. They seek to arm themselves with weapons of mass murder. Their stated goal is to overthrow moderate governments, take control of countries, and then use them as safe havens to launch attacks against Americans and other free nations. To achieve their aims, the terrorists have turned to the weapon of fear. They don't have the military strength to beat us. They can't beat us on the battlefield. They just cannot defeat the United States military. And so they're trying to break our will with stunning acts of violence. The terrorists do not understand America. They're not going to shake our will. We will stay in the hunt. We will never give in, and we will prevail.

After the attacks of September the 11th, we have set forth a new strategy to do our duty to protect the American people. First, we're on the offensive, and we'll stay on the offensive, recognizing that we must defeat the terrorists abroad so we do not have to face them here at home.

Secondly, I've set a clear doctrine: America makes no distinction between the terrorists and the countries that harbor them. If you harbor a terrorist, you're just as guilty as the terrorists, and you're an enemy of the United States of America.

Thirdly, one of the clear lessons of September the 11th is that the United States of America must confront threats before they fully materialize. After September the 11th, I looked at the world and saw a clear threat in Saddam Hussein. Saddam Hussein was an enemy of the United States. He was firing at American military pilots patrolling the no-fly zones. He was a state sponsor of terror. He was in open defiance of more than a dozen United Nations resolutions. He had invaded his neighbors. He had brutalized his people. He had a history of using and producing weapons of mass destruction. Saddam defied the will of the world. And because we acted to remove this threat, Saddam Hussein is in prison,

he's on trial for his crimes, and the world is better for it.

Fourthly, we're advancing our security at home by advancing the cause of freedom across the world because, in the long run, the only way to defeat the terrorists is to defeat their dark vision of hatred and fear by offering the hopeful alternative of human freedom. That's what I want to talk to you about today—our forward strategy for freedom. I'll discuss why the advance of freedom is vital to our security and the peace of the world and how our efforts to spread liberty and democracy throughout the broader Middle East are progressing. I'm going to discuss with you our work to help the world's newest democracies build institutions of liberty that are the foundations for lasting peace. Our freedom agenda is based on a clear premise: The security of our Nation depends on the advance of liberty in other nations.

On September the 11th, 2001, we saw that problems originating in an oppressive state 7,000 miles away could bring murder and destruction to our country. We saw that dictatorships shelter terrorists and feed resentment and radicalism and threaten the security of free nations. We know throughout history that democracies can replace resentment with hope and respect the rights of their citizens and our neighbors and join together to fight in this global war against terror.

History has shown that free nations are peaceful nations. Think about all the bloodshed on the continent of Europe the past 100 years. In World War I and in World War II, there were bloody battles. Thousands of Americans went to Europe to fight in those wars and never came home. Democracy took hold in Europe, and today, Europe is whole, free, and at peace.

Think about the example of the Far East. You know, my dad, like many of your relatives, went off to fight the Japanese as an 18-year-old fighter pilot; 60 years later, his son is working with the Prime Minister of Japan to keep the peace. And what took place between war and friendship was the development of a Japanese-style democracy. As we march into the future, America must be confident in the capacity of democracies to yield the peace we all want.

We're committed to an historic long-term goal: To secure the peace of the world, we seek the end of tyranny in our world. Far from being a hopeless dream, the advance of freedom is the great story of our time. Just 25 years ago, at the start of the 1980s, there were only 45 democracies on the face of the Earth. Today, there are 122. And in the past 4 years alone, more than 110 million human beings have joined the ranks of the free.

In our time, we've witnessed revolutions of Rose and Orange and Purple and Tulip and Cedar, and these are just only the beginnings. Across the world, freedom is on the march, and we will not rest until the promise of freedom reaches people everywhere across the globe. It's in our national interest. It's important that we understand the capacity of freedom to yield the peace.

In the march of freedom, some of the most important progress is taking place in a region that has known—has not known the blessings of liberty, and that's the broader Middle East. Since September the 11th, 2001, the nation of Afghanistan has gone from the terror of the Taliban to a democratic Constitution, to successful Presidential elections, to the seating of a democratically elected Parliament.

In less than 3 years, the nation of Iraq has gone from living under the boot of a brutal tyrant to liberation, to sovereignty, to free elections, to a constitutional referendum, and to elections for a fully constitutional government.

By any standard or precedent of history, these two countries have made incredible progress on the road to a free society. America is inspired by Afghan and Iraqi determination to live in freedom.

Freedom's progress in Afghanistan and Iraq is inspiring millions around the world to demand their liberty as well. In Leb-

anon, in Kyrgyzstan, voters have gone to the polls to choose their leaders in free elections. In other nations across the broader Middle East, hope is stirring at the prospect of change, and change is going to come. In that region that has known decades of tyranny and oppression, we're seeing the rise of a new generation whose hearts burn for freedom, and they will have freedom.

As freedom spreads to new parts of the world, we're seeing something else as well, the uncertainty that often follows democratic change. Free elections are exhilarating events. Yet history teaches us that the path to a free society is long and not always smooth. I've seen that in our own history. In the years following the American Revolution, there were riots and uprisings and even a planned coup. In 1783, Congress was chased from Philadelphia by angry veterans demanding back pay, and Congress stayed on the run for 6 months. [*Laughter*] It was then that Congress learned, don't mess with America's veterans.

It's important to remember that our first effort at a governing charter, the Articles of Confederation, failed, and it took over a decade after independence before we adopted our Constitution and inaugurated George Washington as our first President. Other countries have had similar experiences. After the collapse of communism in Eastern and Central Europe, nations like Slovakia and Romania and Ukraine struggled for many years to overcome the legacy of oppression before freedom finally took root.

No nation in history has made the transition to a free society without setbacks and false starts. Free elections are an important step on the road to a free society, but they're the first step. What separates nations that succeed from those that falter is their progress in establishing a civil society based on free institutions. So, as we work for democratic change across the broader Middle East, we're also working to help new democracies establish the institutions that are the foundations of lasting free societies.

Our efforts in the broader Middle East have been guided by a clear principle. Democracy takes different forms in different cultures. Yet all cultures, in order to be successful, have certain common truths, universal truths—rule of law, freedom of speech, freedom of assembly, a free economy, freedom of women, and the freedom to worship. Societies that lay these foundations not only survive, but they thrive. Societies that don't lay these foundations risk backsliding into tyranny.

This principle has guided our efforts in Iraq. When our coalition arrived in Iraq, we found a nation where almost none of these basic foundations existed. Decades of brutal rule by Saddam Hussein had destroyed the fabric of Iraqi civil society. Under Saddam, Iraq was a country where dissent was crushed, a centralized economy enriched a dictator instead of the people, secret courts meted out repression instead of justice, and Iraqis were brutally oppressed by Saddam's security forces. And when Saddam Hussein's regime fled Baghdad, they left behind a country with few civic institutions in place to hold Iraqi society together.

So our coalition has worked to help the Iraqi people rebuild its civil society and the free institutions that sustain a democracy. And it has been very difficult work. Today, Iraq, though, does have a thriving free press, with hundreds of independent newspapers and magazines and talk radio shows where Iraqis openly debate the future course of their country. In spite of the difficulties, Iraq does have a emerging free market with an independent central bank and thousands of small businesses operating across the country.

Iraq is building an independent judiciary that is replacing the rule of a tyrant with the rule of law, and which is now holding Iraq's former dictator to account for his crimes against the Iraqi people. Iraqis have adopted one of the most progressive democratic constitutions in the Arab world with protections for minority rights and women's rights. Iraqis now enjoy freedom of association, as we saw in the December elections, when parties and coalitions openly campaigned for the vote of the Iraqi people.

We're carrying out our clear strategy of victory in Iraq. On the political side, we're helping Iraqis build a strong democracy so old resentments will be eased and the insurgency marginalized. On the economic side, we're continuing reconstruction efforts and helping Iraqis build a modern economy so all Iraqi citizens can experience the benefits of freedom.

And on the security side, we're striking terrorist targets and, at the same time, training Iraqis which are becoming increasingly capable of carrying the fight to the enemy. Our strategy in Iraq is, as the Iraqis stand up, we'll stand down. Troop levels on the ground will be decided by commanders on the ground, not by politicians in Washington, DC.

In all aspects of our strategy, we've learned from experiences. We've learned from the good advice of people like Chairman Warner. We're fixing what hadn't worked. We'll continue to make changes as necessary to complete the mission, to meet the objective, and that is a country which can sustain itself, defend itself, protect itself, and serve as a strong ally in the war on terror.

For every terrorist working to stop freedom in Iraq, there are many more Iraqis and Americans and troops from around the world working to defeat them. There's still a lot of work to be done. The enemies of a free Iraq are working to stop Iraq's democratic progress. Democracy scares them. They understand a democratic Iraq will be a major defeat in their totalitarian aims.

They're going to continue their campaign of violence and destruction. We saw their brutality again this week when terrorists bombed the Golden Mosque in Samarra.

That mosque is one of the holiest sites in Shi'a Islam. This senseless attack is an affront to people of faith throughout the world. The United States strongly condemns this cowardly act of terror and the subsequent attacks on other mosques and holy sites in Iraq. We'll do everything in our power to help the Iraqi Government identify and bring to justice those responsible for the terrorist acts.

This is a moment of choosing for the Iraqi people. This morning I talked to our Ambassador in Iraq, Zal Khalilzad, and General Casey. Zal is actively engaged with leaders of all political factions to ensure a common message of restraint and unity. He reports to me that the leaders are committed to stopping civil strife. The Government is taking concrete steps to determine how the attack happened and the necessary actions to help move the political process forward. The Ambassador reports many religious leaders are committed to a unified Iraq, a peaceful Iraq. The response by the Grand Ayatollah Sistani and many other leaders has been constructive and very important, and we appreciate their leadership. It's also been a test for the Iraqi security forces. General Casey reports that they're doing a fine job of enforcing curfew and working to restore order and calm.

We can expect the days—coming days will be intense. Iraq remains a serious situation. But I'm optimistic, because the Iraqi people have spoken, and the Iraqi people made their intentions clear. In December, more than 11 million Iraqis sent a clear message to the world and to the terrorists: They want their freedom. They want their country to be a democracy. Each of these elections that took place last year saw larger and broader participation than the one that came before. And with the results from the December elections in, the Iraqi leaders are now working to form a new Government under a new Constitution with different factions competing for position and jockeying for power.

Listen, the way ahead is going to require some patience as this process unfolds. The Iraqi Constitution requires two-thirds of the Parliament to form a government, which makes it harder to get agreement, but it helps ensure that all groups have a say in who governs them. The days ahead in Iraq are going to be difficult and exhausting. We're likely to see a lot of political bargaining. That doesn't happen under dictatorships. They seem orderly, particularly when one man makes all the decisions, and there is no need for negotiation or compromise.

In democracies, different party advance competing agendas, and they seek their share of power. And yet they reach accommodation and respond to the will of the people. And Iraqis are doing all this for the first time in the midst of violence and terrorist attacks. Yet out of negotiations now taking place in Iraq, a free government will emerge that will represent the will of the Iraqi people, instead of that of a cruel dictator, and that will help us keep the peace.

We're encouraging Iraqi leaders to reach out across political, religious, and sectarian lines and form a government that gives a voice to all Iraqis. And when a new Iraqi Government assumes office, Iraq's new leaders will face tough decisions on issues such as security and reconstruction and economic reform. This Government will need to provide effective leadership and earn the confidence of the Iraqi people by showing it can protect them. The Government will also need to put a stop to human rights abuses by security officers. By building free institutions and an inclusive society that provides minority rights, Iraqi leaders will bring the nation together, and this will help to defeat the terrorists and the Saddamists who are fighting Iraq's democratic progress.

Some critics have pointed out that the free elections in the Middle East have put political power in the hands of Islamics and extremists, in the case of the Palestinian elections, a notorious—notorious terrorist organization. Critics argue that our policies of promoting democracy are backfiring and destabilizing the region. I strongly disagree. First, their argument rests on the false assumption that the Middle East was a bastion of stability before the United States came in and disturbed the status quo by promoting democracy.

It was the status quo of the Middle East that led to the bombing of our Embassies in Kenya and Tanzania. It was the status quo in the Middle East that led to the attack of the USS *Cole* that killed 17 American sailors. It was the status quo in the Middle East that produced 19 hijackers and took planes and crashed them into the Pentagon and the World Trade Towers and killed nearly 3,000 innocent people on September the 11th, 2001. The status quo in the Middle East was dangerous and unacceptable, and our security demanded that we change it.

Secondly, the idea that lasting stability can be achieved by denying people a voice in the future control of their destiny is wrong. It is, in large part, because people in the Middle East have been denied legitimate means to express dissent that radical extremism has flourished. And it's only by giving people in the Middle East the freedom to express their opinions and choose their leaders that we will be able to defeat radical extremism. As liberty spreads in the broader Middle East, freedom will replace despair and hope. And over time, the terrorist's temptation will fall away.

Third, free societies do not take root overnight, especially in countries that have suffered from decades of tyranny and repression. It should come as no surprise that after 60 years of Western nations excusing and accommodating the lack of freedom in the Middle East, civil society in that region is not strong and those with the most extreme views are the most organized.

It will take time for the people of this region to build political parties and movements that are moderate in their views and capable of competing in a free democratic system. Yet free elections cannot wait for perfect conditions. Free elections are instruments of change. By giving people an opportunity to organize, express their views, and change the existing order, elections strengthen the forces of freedom and encourage citizens to take control of their own destiny.

Finally, as democracy takes root, the responsibilities of governing will have a moderating influence on those who assume power in free elections. It's easier to be a martyr than a mayor or a cabinet minister. When you're responsible for building roads and bridges and power stations and educating people and providing help, you're less likely to blow up health clinics and schools and bridges.

In democracies, elected leaders must deliver real change in people's lives, or the voters will boot them out at the next election time. This is a lesson that the leaders of Hamas will now have to learn, as they take power after their election victory in the Palestinian Territories. Hamas campaigned on a platform of fighting corruption and improving social services, and that is how a Hamas Government will be judged by the Palestinian people. The leaders of Hamas have a choice to make. If they want the help of America and the international community to build a prosperous, independent Palestinian state, they must recognize Israel, disarm, reject terrorism, and work for lasting peace. The international community must continue to make clear to Hamas that democratically elected leaders cannot have one foot in the camp of democracy and one foot in the camp of terror. The world is waiting to see what choice Hamas makes.

The international community is also speaking with one voice to the radical regime in Tehran. Iran is a nation held hostage by a small clerical elite that is isolating and repressing its people and denying them basic liberties and human rights. The Iranian regime sponsors terrorists and is actively working to expand its influence in the region. The Iranian regime has advocated the destruction of our ally Israel. And the Iranian regime is defying the world with its ambitions for nuclear weapons.

America will continue to rally the world to confront these threats, and Iran's aggressive behavior and pursuit of nuclear weapons is increasing its international isolation. When Iran's case was brought before the IAEA earlier this month, 27 nations voted against Iran, including Russia and China and India and Brazil and Sri Lanka and Egypt and Yemen. The only nations to support Iran were Syria, Cuba, and Venezuela. Now Iran's case will be taken up to the U.N. Security Council. The free world is sending the regime in Tehran a clear message: We're not going to allow Iran to have nuclear weapons.

The world's free nations are also worried because the Iranian regime is not transparent. You see, a nontransparent society that is the world's premier state sponsor of terror cannot be allowed to possess the world's most dangerous weapons. So, as we confront Iran's nuclear weapons ambitions, we're also reaching out to the Iranian people to support their desire to be free, to build a free, democratic, and transparent society.

To support the Iranian people's efforts to win their own freedom, my administration is requesting $75 million in emergency funds to support democracy in Iran. This is more than a fourfold increase over current levels of funding. These new funds will allow us to expand radio and television broadcasts into Iran. They will support reformers and dissidents and human rights activists and civil society organizers in Iran, so Iranians can organize and challenge the repressive policies of the clerical regime. They will support student exchanges, so we can build bridges of understanding between our people and expose more Iranians to life in a free society.

By supporting democratic change in Iran, we will hasten the day when the people of Iran can determine their own future and be free to choose their own leaders. Freedom in the Middle East requires freedom for the Iranian people, and America looks forward to the day when our Nation can be the closest of friends with a free and democratic Iran.

Freedom is on the march in the broader Middle East. The hope of liberty now reaches from Kabul to Baghdad to Beirut and beyond. Slowly but surely, we're helping to transform the broader Middle East from an arc of instability into an arc of freedom. And as freedom reaches more people in this vital region, we'll have new allies in the war on terror and new partners in the cause of moderation in the Muslim world and in the cause of peace.

Bringing greater freedom to nations in the Middle East is the work of generations, and the advance of liberty still faces determined enemies. The terrorists know the stakes in the struggle. They know that as more people in the region embrace freedom, they will lose their safe havens, lose their recruits, and lose the sources of funding they need to advance their hateful ideology. And so they'll continue to fight freedom's progress with all the murderous hatred they can muster. They will continue to create images of violence and suffering for the cameras. The terrorists know that the only way they can defeat us is to break our will and force our retreat. And that's not going to happen so long as I'm the President of the United States.

We will stay on the offense. We will continue to hunt down the terrorists wherever they hide. We'll continue to stand with the people of the Middle East as they step forward to claim their freedom. We can be confident in our cause because we have seen freedom conquer tyranny and secure the peace before. We've seen freedom arrive on waves of unstoppable progress to nations in Latin America and Asia and Africa and Eastern Europe. And now the hope of freedom is stirring in the Middle East, and no one should bet against it.

We can also have confidence in our cause—we have the greatest force for freedom in the history of the world on our side, the men and women of the United States Armed Forces. They are serving with courage and distinction on many fronts in the war on terror. And I know America's veterans feel a special bond with them as they defend freedom in foreign lands.

In this war, we've lost some really good men and women who left our shores to defend liberty and did not live to make the journey home. Others have returned from war with wounds the best medicine cannot heal. As veterans, you've lost friends and comrades in the field of battle, and you understand the sadness that has come to some of our Nation's military families. We pray for the families of the fallen, and we honor the memory of all who have given their lives in freedom's cause. And we will honor that memory by defeating the terrorists and spreading liberty and laying the foundation of peace for generations to come.

I appreciate the Legion's support for our troops in the fight. I appreciate the example you have set for those who wear the uniform today.

Before Veterans Day a few years ago, a group of soldiers serving in Iraq sent a letter to the American Legion Headquarters here in Washington. They wrote,

"Veterans of past wars will forever be in our hearts as American heroes. Their sacrifices give us courage, and their devotion reminds us of what we are fighting for." Our men and women on the frontlines are taking inspiration from the valor and courage that you've shown on the field of battle. When they face dark moments in the thick of the fight, they remember that you faced enemies as brutal and determined as those who threaten America today, and they remember how you prevailed. And now they're picking up your mantle and carrying on your fight. And like our veterans, they're bringing security to our citizens and freedom to the world.

Thank you for your idealism. I thank you for your dedication to God and country. May God bless our veterans. May God bless our troops in uniform. And may God continue to bless our country.

NOTE: The President spoke at 10 a.m. at the Capital Hilton Hotel. In his remarks, he referred to Tom Bock, national commander, and John Sommer, executive director, American Legion; Paul Hasz, commander, American Legion, District of Columbia; Prime Minister Junichiro Koizumi of Japan; and Gen. George W. Casey, Jr., USA, commanding general, Multi-National Force—Iraq. The Office of the Press Secretary also released a Spanish language transcript of these remarks.

Interview With Doordarshan of India
February 24, 2006

India-U.S. Relations

Q. Well, Mr. President, how is your strategy partnership with India is going to shape up during the forthcoming visit?

The President. Well, first of all, our strategic partnership had a great start, or a great impetus, when your Prime Minister came to visit here in Washington. We had a wonderful visit. And one of the important things about diplomacy is to get to know your counterpart. And I got to know the Prime Minister and admire him as really a decent fellow who is smart and capable.

And this visit will help foster not only the personal relationship, though, but a strategic partnership that is growing all the time. And it's one that is very important for the American people and, I think, the people of India. This relationship between the United States and India can produce good results for our people but also will enable us to achieve some international objectives as well.

Civilian Nuclear Power Program in India

Q. Well, in the context of excellent bilateral relations, which you have just mentioned, I think, what's your take on the civilian nuclear program?

The President. Well, it's a tough issue. It's a tough issue for the Prime Minister; I understand that, and it's a tough issue for me. I knew it was going to be a hard issue, because we have to convince—both of us have to convince our respective people it's in the interest to have a civilian nuclear program supported by the United States and India, as well as a civilian nuclear program that's separate from a military program in India.

And I understood the politics was going to be difficult, and there's still work to be done. We've just got to continue to come up with an agreement that both of us can live with. But the relationship is broader than just the civilian nuclear issue. I've told the American people, we want India to develop a civilian nuclear power program. We're all, kind of, connected globally, particularly when it comes to the price of energy. And the more nuclear power used by great emerging democracies and economies like India, the better off we'll all be.

Q. Well, there's an impression, as reflected in the U.S. media, that you are surrendering your interests while proposing to supply civilian nuclear technology to India. What do you tell them?

The President. Well, I tell them it's in the interests of the world that India have a nuclear power industry. On the other hand, it's also very important for India to understand our concerns about making sure that there's a—that a civilian program is separate from the military, and there's the IAEA safeguards. And again, we're breaking some new ground. I'm not surprised that it's difficult to reach a consensus. And we'll keep trying and working at it.

The key thing is, though, that the people of India understand that our relationship is a vital relationship. And it's vital on a variety of fronts. It's vital when it comes to commerce and trade and prosperity; it's vital on fighting the war on terror. I mean, the people of India know what terror is all about; you've been hit before. And it's vital on working together to achieve a more peaceful world. And so I'm really looking forward to this trip. It's going to be exciting for us.

War on Terror

Q. I think the—terrorism is one area—a joint working group has been working excellently, even before the unfortunate incident of 9/11, between India and U.S. But the terrorist training camps and training infrastructure in Pakistan-occupied Kashmir has not been totally dismantled. How about a—and from the Pak-Afghan border, sir, also, troops are being—your troops are being targeted. So how——

The President. Well, listen, I understand the war on terror is universal, and it's very important for all of us to work together to stop the advance and the goals of these terrorists. And you bring up Pakistan; it's an interesting moment in our relationships with each other. It used to be that if America were close to Pakistan, then the Indian Government——

Q. Yes, that zero-sum game, that is over.

The President. It was zero-sum. And now I think President Musharraf understands that it's important for me to have a good relationship with India and vice versa. Prime Minister Singh understands. And we do have a good relationship with both. But on my trip to Pakistan, I will of course talk about the terrorist activities, the need to dismantle terrorist training camps and to protect innocent life, because one of the real dangers of the terrorist movement is that they'll kill innocent people to achieve an objective. And India and President Musharraf, as well as our country, cares deeply about innocent life. We respect human life.

Trade With India

Q. Now about trade and commerce, which we are mentioning. Well, in your Asia Society speech—I attended; I heard it, was a spectacular speech you made.

The President. Thank you.

Q. So you talked about this Indian middle class, the 300 million, which is bigger than U.S.

The President. It is.

Q. Growing, emerging market and all that. But still, India right now contributes only 1.3 percent of your global export.

The President. Right.

Q. So what's the roadmap?

The President. Well, the roadmap is to continue to work for openness, opening markets on both sides. Listen, trade, again, this is an issue that takes time to develop. Our relationship is a growing relationship, and we're constantly addressing needs to make sure that markets are open. We are going to have a business CEO forum with India CEOs and American CEOs that will brief us on what more we can do together.

And we're democracies. I mean, India is a great democracy. And democracies, there's constant pressure against certain advances. People have their opinion, and people are allowed to express their opinion. And opening markets is difficult. It's difficult for a lot of countries, and it's not easy for America, either. But the purpose of the trip is to continue to work to open up markets because opening markets and free trade that's fair trade will benefit workers and families on both sides of the trading equation.

India-U.S. Relations

Q. Well, military-to-military relationship is again another success story, new heights. It is—every day it is reaching new heights.

The President. Yes.

Q. Marrying of technologies and understanding each other—and what about the same kind of cooperation in the field of defense industry?

The President. In what now?

Q. In defense industry, joint production with India, America, technology transfer.

The President. Well, as you know, there's a lot of technology transfer. And I quoted the example of Texas Instruments having a plant in India's silicon valley, a research center, and that's a classic case of technological transfer. Knowledge is technology, is the advancement of technology. And listen, this country has greatly benefited by Indian Americans, and Indians that have—with advanced degrees and degrees that have—unbelievably smart—engineering and different aspects of science and technology. And we welcome the presence of Indian students here in America, as well as the great contribution of our Indian Americans.

But technology transfers oftentimes require knowledge transfers, and one of the things about the relationship that has emerged is the fact there's a lot of knowledge transfer between private sectors and through research institutions, and that's positive.

President's Upcoming Visit to India

Q. Well, the last question—this is your first visit to India.

The President. It is.

Q. While preparing to visit India and political negotiations, have you discussed with Mrs. Bush how to negotiate hot Indian curry? [*Laughter*]

The President. Well, I'm going to have to—I'll have to try that on. I'll tell you afterwards. My one regret is that I'm not going to go see the Taj Mahal. And that's not the fault of the Indian Government; that's the fault of the George W. Bush schedulers. And obviously, it goes to show sometimes the President doesn't get all his wishes.

But I am really looking forward to going to the country. I am looking forward to meeting members of the Government. I'm looking forward to having private time with the Prime Minister. And I know Laura joins me in telling the Indian people, thanks for friendship, and we can't wait to come to your country.

Q. Thank you very much. And welcome to India, you and Mrs. Bush. And I think there will be many more visits after this.

The President. I hope so. Thank you, sir.

NOTE: The interview was taped at 11:18 a.m. in the Map Room at the White House for later broadcast, and it was embargoed by the Office of the Press Secretary until 9 p.m. In his remarks, the President referred to Prime Minister Manmohan Singh of India; and President Pervez Musharraf of Pakistan. A tape was not available for verification of the content of this interview.

Interview With Pakistan Television
February 24, 2006

Pakistan-U.S. Relations

Q. Mr. President, you are paying a visit to Pakistan at a very crucial juncture, at a time when changes are being experienced in the region. And people of Pakistan are pinning a lot of hope on your visit because they think many problems are there and your visit will play a very vital role in it. So what is your vision for making this trip more meaningful and productive?

The President. The first thing that's really important for people to understand is that relations between our countries oftentimes depend on the relations between the leaders. In other words, President Musharraf and I can set a tone for the relationship because of our capacity to talk to each other. And it's important to be with each other and to share concerns and to talk about ideas. And so one object of the trip is to continue what is a good relationship. A good relationship between me and the President tends to permeate throughout our Government.

Secondly, I—and one reason we've got a good relationship is we speak frankly with each other. Listen, I understand he has got a difficult job—made really difficult by the fact that people have tried to kill him, as you know. Extremists have decided that he is a obstacle to their vision and, therefore, have tried to kill him. And so he's not only a man who's shown great courage in the face of adversity, but he does have a vision of how to work together to achieve common objectives.

Secondly, I want the people of Pakistan to know that the American people care about them, that ours is a relationship that's much bigger than just the war on terror; that when our Chinooks flew supplies into the rural part of Pakistan, it wasn't out of a sense of just, kind of, pure diplomacy, it was out of a sense of care and concern about the individuals. And I understand sometimes people may have—wonder about our motives, wonder about America's true concerns. And this will give me a chance to speak to the people of Pakistan and say, "Look, we care for you," and remind people that in our country, there's great Pakistani Americans. We're a rich society because we've got people from around the world, including people who were born and raised in Pakistan and have now chosen

America as a home. And so it's a trip that's of good will and importance.

Q. Mr. President, there is a common perception that the relations between the United States and Pakistan have fluctuated in the past. So what measures would you suggest to make it more durable and sustainable for the days to come and the long-time perspective?

The President. Yes, that's a really good question, because, again, we want people to understand this relationship is a vital relationship that will exist throughout the years. One way we can do that is increase trade opportunities before our countries—between our countries. And we'll be talking about a bilateral investment treaty.

Secondly, student exchanges—and I understand there's been some issues with visas, and we've got to work through those, because I believe the more Pakistani youngsters who come to America to study will get to really see what America is all about. And as more Americans that go there to study—will see what Pakistan is all about.

And so there's ways for us, beyond the war on terror—and by the way, the war on terror is a critical aspect of our relationship; don't get me wrong. But the other thing that's interesting and I think important for the people of Pakistan to know is that President Musharraf, in his democracy initiative, can show the whole Muslim world, and the world itself, that it's possible to have a religious—that is not extreme and a state that listens to people and responds to the needs of people. And that's a really important message that Pakistan can show the world. And I will, of course, continue to talk to my buddy and my friend about his goals for a democratic Pakistan.

Kashmir

Q. Mr. President, an early solution to the whole issue of Kashmir, about which you have also mentioned in your speech at the Asia Society—that is vital for the region. So, in your view, being a close friend of both Pakistan and India, what role the United States can play in resolving this issue?

The President. Well, I started to play a role in my speech, and I spoke out on the issue and encouraged the President and the Prime Minister of India to continue down the road of solving the issue with a solution that's acceptable to all sides.

And that's very important. There's a temptation sometimes for countries to try to jump in the middle of dialog. I believe a lasting solution can be achieved. I've seen the progress that's been made in the relationship from when I first became President. You might remember an early time in my Presidency, there was real tension. And now, all of a sudden, there's some very encouraging signs—transportation exchanges—not transportation exchanges—new transportation opportunities, trade. In just my discussions with both the President and the Prime Minister, there appears to be a different attitude. And part of it has to do with trust, but there's got to be tangible progress; I recognize that. And so I will use my trip to urge the leadership to continue solving this issue, with the idea that it can be solved.

Pakistani Economy

Q. Mr. President, what economic incentive would you offer to Pakistan during the forthcoming visit?

The President. Well, trade is very important. And one of the steps on a robust trading relationship is what's called the Bilateral Investment Treaty, and that's an important part of the process. And believe me, every time the President talks to me, he's talking about markets, and I understand that. But he also understands that there's some steps needed before this robust trade.

I must applaud the President's vision for the Pakistan economy. And in our world, politics, there's a lot of talk and a lot of, kind of, big noise. But the truth of the matter is, what matters is results. And Pakistan's economy is strong, and that's good news. That's really good news for the people of Pakistan. First and foremost, because, obviously, if people can make a living and do well, they can see the benefits of democracy—tangible benefits of living in a system where people are free to express themselves, but where the marketplace is the economic determinant.

War on Terror

Q. Coming to another subject, what strategy the United States has adopted for conquering terrorism in Pakistan, in a very holistic manner?

The President. First of all, freedom defeats an ideology of hatred. And the enemy—I say "the enemy" because they'll kill—they—innocent Pakistanis; they kill innocent Americans. We need—more Muslims have died at the hands of Al Qaida and these extremists than anybody else. These—I don't view these people as religious people. I view them as people who have taken a great religion and kind of twisted it to meet their means.

And so they have a vision. And it's not a vision—it's a vision that doesn't recognize the freedom of people to worship. It's a vision that doesn't understand the—that recognize the importance of women in society or free speech. And so the way to defeat that vision is with a better vision, more hopeful, and democracy provides that vision.

We are in close coordination, of course, with the Government of Pakistan. We share a mutual interest. Nobody should want foreign fighters in their soil wreaking havoc. And it's hard for a part of a country to develop if there are people in that part of the country that are willing to kill innocent life to achieve an objective. And so we share short-term objectives with the Pakistani Government. We also share the long-term objective, and that is—that's freedom.

Q. Thank you very much, Mr. President.

The President. I'm looking forward to the trip. And I really appreciate you coming.

Q. Thank you very much. I'm grateful and honored.

The President. Thank you, sir.

NOTE: The interview was taped at approximately 11:20 a.m. in the Map Room at the White House for later broadcast, and it was embargoed by the Office of the Press Secretary until 9 p.m. In his remarks, the President referred to President Pervez Musharraf of Pakistan; and Prime Minister Manmohan Singh of India. A tape was not available for verification of the content of this interview.

The President's Radio Address
February 25, 2006

Good morning. On Sunday and Monday, I will meet with America's Governors during their annual gathering in Washington, DC. As a former Governor, I appreciate the work of these fine public servants. I look forward to talking with them about the challenges and opportunities facing their States and our Nation and discussing how leaders of both parties can work together to solve problems for our citizens.

One of the most important issues we will discuss is how to improve health care for the American people, and we have a good example in the Medicare system that provides health care coverage for our seniors. When I took office, I found a Medicare system that would pay tens of thousands of dollars for a surgery but not the money for the prescription drugs that could have prevented the surgery in the first place.

So working with Congress, we passed critical legislation that modernizes Medicare, provides seniors with more choices, and gives them better access to prescription drugs.

More than 25 million people with Medicare now have prescription drug coverage, and hundreds of thousands more are enrolling each week. This new coverage is saving seniors money on their drug premiums. The typical senior will end up spending about half of what they used to spend on prescription drugs each year.

Another issue I will discuss with Governors is how to keep America the most innovative and competitive nation in the world. In my State of the Union Address, I announced the American Competitiveness Initiative. Under this initiative, we will double the Federal commitment to the most critical basic research in the physical sciences over the next decade. We will also make the research and development tax credit permanent to encourage businesses and entrepreneurs to increase their investments in innovation. These investments will lead to new technologies that will offer a better life for our citizens and keep our economy strong.

My Competitiveness Initiative will also give American children a firm grounding in math and science to prepare them for the jobs of the 21st century. I propose that we train 70,000 additional high school teachers over the next 5 years to lead Advanced Placement courses in math and science and bring in 30,000 math and science professionals to teach in classrooms and give extra help to students who struggle with math. By ensuring that our children are prepared to succeed in life, we will ensure that America's economy succeeds in the world.

When I meet the Governors, I will also talk about our energy strategy. I propose an Advanced Energy Initiative to take advantage of new technologies. Under this initiative, we will change how we power our homes and offices by investing in clean coal technology, solar and wind power, and clean, safe nuclear energy. And we will change how we power our cars and trucks by investing in hybrid vehicles, pollution-free cars that run on hydrogen, and alternative fuels like ethanol and biodiesel. By applying the talent and innovative spirit of our citizens, we will move beyond a petroleum-based economy, protect our environment, and make America less dependent on foreign sources of energy.

I'll also discuss with Governors our progress in the war on terror. The States are playing a vital role in the war effort through the contributions of their National Guard units. During the past 2 years, many Governors have traveled to Iraq or Afghanistan to visit with the men and women from their States who are serving in freedom's cause. These Governors have seen firsthand the courage of our troops and their dedication to the mission. Last month, Arkansas Governor Mike Huckabee visited Iraq and Afghanistan with three of his fellow Governors. He said, "People back home need to realize just how proud they should be of our men and women here. It is obvious these troops remain upbeat and focused on ridding the world of terrorists."

To improve health care, keep America competitive, achieve greater energy independence, and protect our Nation, we must put aside politics and focus on what is best for the future of our country. America's Governors are good allies in this effort, and I look forward to working with them in the year ahead.

Thank you for listening.

NOTE: The address was recorded at 7:50 a.m. on February 24 in the Cabinet Room at the White House for broadcast at 10:06 a.m. on February 25. The transcript was made available by the Office of the Press Secretary on February 24 but was embargoed for release until the broadcast. The Office of the Press Secretary also released a Spanish language transcript of this address.

Remarks at a Dinner for the Nation's Governors
February 26, 2006

Good evening. Welcome to the White House. Laura and I are glad you're here. We really look forward to this evening. It's good to see some old friends, and I want to welcome two new Governors: Governor Corzine and Governor Tim Kaine. It happens to be his birthday. The first lady said he was tired of getting birthday songs, so we'll skip it. [*Laughter*]

We've also got some Governors here who will be here for the last time, some by choice, some by law. We thank you for your service. One of them happens to be Brother. Come on back, you know. But all of you who won't be back here, thank you for serving your States and our country.

I like being around Governors. Governors know how to set agendas; Governors know how to rally people to convince the legislature to get results; Governors are results-oriented people. So I picked a few for my Cabinet, including two Mikes: Mike Leavitt and Mike Johanns. They're doing great jobs. I appreciate the rest of my Cabinet being here, even though you aren't Governors. [*Laughter*] You're welcome to have a meal. [*Laughter*]

Look forward to working with you to help shape the future of the country. You know, I told the people, we don't need to fear the future because we intend to shape the future. And Governors play a big role in that. You got a big role in help-ing to protect our country, and I want to thank you for understanding we're still at war and that we need your solid support in defending our country. Our most important duty is to protect the American people.

Our economy is strong, and I mean to keep it that way, with good tax policy, both at the Federal and State level. We've got to make sure we're less dependent on foreign sources of oil to keep our economy strong. We've got to make sure that our education system—make sure every child is educated, and with special emphasis on math and science. This country is a great country, and we've led the world, and we'll continue to lead the world. And I look forward to working with you on such an agenda.

This is historic times, and I know you know that. And so I want to thank you for your service to our great Nation. I want to thank you for bringing dignity and honor to the offices you hold. And so now I'd like to offer a toast to the Governors of the United States.

NOTE: The President spoke at 8:03 p.m. in the State Dining Room at the White House. In his remarks, he referred to Gov. Jon S. Corzine of New Jersey; Gov. Timothy M. Kaine of Virginia and his wife, Anne Holton; and Gov. Jeb Bush of Florida.

Remarks to the National Governors Association Conference
February 27, 2006

Good morning. Thanks for coming. I enjoyed it last night; I hope you did too. It was a lot of fun. And thank you all for giving me a chance to come by. What I thought I'd do is say a few things and then answer some questions, if you have any.

We have got a chance to achieve some big things for the country, to lay the stage for peace and to keep America in the lead.

And these are goals that both Republicans and Democrats should share. You know, there's a lot of politics here in Washington, so it's—when you say, "Well, you know, it's a Republican goal to make America competitive," I just don't agree with that. It should be a national goal. It's a national goal to protect our people. And therefore, it requires a lot of collaboration throughout all aspects of government. And no better collaborators to implement good policy than our Governors. So thanks for giving me a chance to come and share some insights with you.

First, one question that ought to be confronting everybody is, how do we keep this economy of ours strong? A couple of notable exceptions, like our friends in Michigan and Ohio in particular, maybe Washington State, the overall economy is in great shape. People are working; productivity is up; people own their homes; small businesses are flourishing. And the fundamental question is, what can we do together to keep it that way? Part of it is to be wise with taxpayers' money.

I congratulate the States that have done a good job of increasing their surpluses; it's a good thing. I can remember a couple of years ago when we were a little worried about deficits at the State level. That's changed. Surplus and tax policy—wise with people's money—all go hand in hand in terms of making sure America remains competitive. I believe if you take money out of people's pockets, it hurts economic vitality and growth.

I know full well that in order for us to be competitive, two other things have to happen. One is, we've got to be less dependent on foreign sources of oil. Told the people, shocked them pretty much when I was standing up there as the guy from Texas saying, our dependency upon oil creates a problem. But I meant it. Dependency upon oil has created an economic problem for us. It challenges our economic security, because when demand for oil goes up relative to supply worldwide, it causes

the price at the pump to go up. It's like a hidden tax on our people when gasoline prices go up. Dependence on foreign sources of oil creates a national security problem. You hear parts of the world where there is disruption in oil supply as a result of local politics, for example; it affects the United States of America.

I spend a lot of time worrying about disruption of energy because of politics or civil strife in other countries or because tyrants control the spigots. And it's in our national interest that we become less dependent on oil. And so we've laid out a strong initiative to encourage Congress to continue to spend research and development money to enable us to power our automobiles through additional uses of ethanol, to expand E–85 beyond just the current regional—the region where it's being—where the corn is being grown, to be able to use other types of biomass to fuel our cars. We think we're very close to that kind of breakthrough. Hybrid batteries are going to make an enormous difference in our capacity to drive the first 40 miles in urban centers without the use of any gasoline. Hydrogen automobiles eventually are going to make a huge difference in enabling us to become less dependent on foreign sources of oil.

We've got to expand solar power. I went to a facility there in Michigan to see a fantastic company called United Solar. I don't mean to be pushing them, but nevertheless, they're making a great product. I remember going out to Colorado to the facility out there, the research facility on alternative uses of energy. We've got fantastic chances to advance this really important agenda, and we look forward to working with you to do so. It's one of these issues where when we continue to make these technological breakthroughs, we'll leave behind a better tomorrow for our children and grandchildren.

The other issue that I know we can work together and must work together is to make sure our children are not only educated in reading and writing but also in math and science. America must be competitive in the out years. We've got to have our—we've got to be educating the future physicists and engineers. And we look forward to working with you to help make math and science in our classrooms more of a reality.

As well, we're planning on doubling the amount of Federal research dollars for basic sciences. And recognizing that most of the research in the United States is done at the corporate level, to make the research and development tax credit a permanent part of the Tax Code. It's really hard to get our companies to invest in research and development if there's uncertainty in the Tax Code and Congress allows the R&D tax credit to lapse, and when it lapses, planners say, "Well, I'm not sure it's going to be around, so why do we want to make investment?" So making the R&D tax code [credit] * a permanent part of our Tax Code will help spur continued research and technology. Technology is going to help us stay competitive; it'll help us be the most productive society in the world, which means our people's standard of living is going to go up.

So here are some things we can work on to get rid of all of the, kind of, needless politics that tends to be dominating the landscape these days and focus on things that will help this country remain the leader in the world when it comes to the economy.

I also want to thank those of you who have set up faith-based offices. I'm sincere about working with State and local governments to rally the great armies of compassion. And I know that some 32 States have set up faith-based offices, and I appreciate you doing that. It's really an important part of making sure our social agenda is comprehensive and complete.

I wish I could report to you that the war on terror is over. It's not. An enemy

---

* White House correction.

still lurks. They're dangerous people, and it requires a comprehensive strategy to defeat, and part of it, of course, is making sure our homeland is secure. If you have any questions on the NSA decision, I'll be glad to give it to you—be glad to answer them.

The other part of the offense—of the strategy is to stay on the offense, is to keep them on the run. And to this end, I want to thank you for supporting our Guard troops. Many of you have been overseas and have seen our Guard troops in action. And I can't thank you enough for not only supporting the troops in harm's way but providing great comfort to their families as well.

Ultimately, the defeat of the terrorists is not only defeat them overseas so we don't have to face them here at home, but, as well, it's to spread liberty and freedom. And the freedom agenda is a powerful part of our country's desire to lay the foundation for peace. And it's making a difference. It's making a difference. I know one of the debates about the freedom agenda is, "Well, elections cause certain things to happen that you may not want to happen." No, elections are only the beginning of the process; they're not the end. Elections, plus a focused foreign policy effort that helps build the institutions of democracy, is what is going to be necessary to ultimately defeat the hateful ideology of those who would do our country harm.

It's an interesting debate that's going to take place here in Washington, or is taking place in Washington: Do elections cause radicalism or empower radicals? My answer is, the status quo empowered radicals. This notion that somehow the Middle East was a safe place for the last 30 years, because we didn't see, kind of, the turmoil that happens with elections, meant we were safe, I just totally disagree with that, kind of the—beneath the surface that appeared placid, the policymakers, was resentment and hatred and planning and plotting, all of which came home on September the 11th.

And I believe this country has got to be aggressive in our pursuit of democracy and liberty, based upon our firm belief that there are such things as the natural rights of men and women. After all, that's what caused our founding, that there is universality to liberty. And we shouldn't be surprised when 11 million Iraqis go to the polls and demand freedom in the face of unbelievable terrorist attacks. That shouldn't surprise America. We ought to say, we recognize that spirit. And it is that spirit that's ultimately going to be able to say, we've kept the peace for our children and grandchildren.

And so we can work together on these important issues, and I thank you for giving me a chance for me to come by and visit with you about them. Thank you.

NOTE: The President spoke at 11:05 a.m. in the State Dining Room at the White House.

Remarks at a Republican Governors Association Reception
February 27, 2006

The President. Thanks for the warm welcome. Be seated, unless you don't have a seat. [*Laughter*]

Mitt, thank you for that wonderful introduction. That columnist is pretty much alone in your State of Massachusetts— [*laughter*]—but I appreciate it. Appreciate your leadership of the RGA. I want to thank Sonny. I call him "Big Buddy Perdue." [*Laughter*] He is a big buddy. And I want to thank Matt Blunt as well and Melanie and Ann Romney. Thank you all very much for taking a strong leadership role.

One of the things you find out about successful Governors is they marry well. Same thing happens for Presidents. [*Laughter*] And I am married really well.

I want to thank you all for supporting people who know how to get things done. You know, in our line of work, there's a lot of talkers, sometimes there's not many doers; a lot of people who have got opinions, but oftentimes people can't roll up their sleeves and achieve agendas. And the folks you're supporting here today are people who know how to set agendas, make decisions based upon principle, and get things done on behalf of our country by running their State. Thank you for supporting them, and thank the Governors for being such strong leaders.

I enjoy working with the Governors. I know how these folks think. And they know what I know, that we are a nation at war. They are the commanders in chief of their respective National Guard units, many of which have been deployed overseas. And I want to thank our Governors and the first ladies for understanding the task ahead for our country, for supporting those who wear the uniform, and for reaching out to the families who worry about their loved ones. Our Governors, these Governors are on the frontline in the war against terror, and I thank you for your steadfast support.

They, like me, will never forget the lessons of September the 11th. Our Nation must never forget the lessons of September the 11th, for the greatest duty of our respective governments—Federal Government and State government—is to protect the American people. The security of our citizens is of paramount importance to my administration, to many in the Congress, as well as our Governors.

The way to win the war on terror is to stay on the offense, is to defeat the killers overseas so we do not have to face them here in America, is to be relentless in our pursuit, never give in, never give up, and keep the enemy on the run, which is precisely what we're doing.

In order to win the war on terror, it is really important for the President to speak clearly, and when he says something, means what he says. And so when I said to the world, if you harbor a terrorist, you're equally as guilty as the terrorist, I meant what I said, and the Taliban found out exactly that the United States of America keeps its word. And today, because we upheld that doctrine, America is a safer place. Al Qaida no longer has a safe haven in which to plan and plot an attack, and 25 million people are enjoying the fruits of liberty.

A lesson of September the 11th is that when we see a threat, we must take the threat seriously. When a lot of us were growing up, oceans—we felt oceans could protect us from harm; that if we saw a threat overseas, we could deal with it if we wanted to or not, because we were safe. September the 11th changed that forever. September the 11th taught us that when we see threats brewing or materializing, we must take them seriously. I saw a threat, the world saw a threat, people of both political parties in the United States Congress saw a threat, and that was Saddam Hussein. The world is better off without Saddam Hussein in power.

Many of our Governors have been to Iraq, and I thank them for supporting our troops in harm's way. We've got a strategy for victory in Iraq. Our strategy—our goal is to make sure that Iraq can govern itself and sustain itself and defend itself, will become an ally in the war on terror and not be a safe haven for Al Qaida, which wants to plan and plot and use the oil wealth to strike America again.

Our strategy is threefold. One, we'll help rebuild that country so people see the fruits of democracy. Two, we'll encourage a political system that will take into account the voices of the people. You saw what I saw; 11 million Iraqis made their voices abun-

dantly clear: "We want to be free"—in the face of terror. They decided to vote in overwhelming numbers.

The leaders of Iraq rejected this notion that a suicider and a thug and a terrorist can create civil war. They're interested in a unified government that will allow the people to express their will, a unified government that will give young mothers and fathers the hope that their children can grow up in a peaceful society.

The third part of our strategy is to train the Iraqis so they can take the fight to the enemy, and that's exactly what's happening. The Iraqis are standing up, and as they do, we will stand down. I know many of you are concerned about the troop levels. I know our Governors are worried about the troop levels in Iraq. Here's my response: I will determine the troop levels in Iraq, one, necessary to achieve victory, based upon the recommendations of our commanders, not based upon politics in Washington, DC.

Ours is an enemy that has no conscience, but they do have a philosophy. They're totalitarian in nature. They're fascist in their tactics. They will spare no life in order to achieve their objective. Their aims are clear. They believe the United States is weak and flaccid; it's only a matter of time before we withdraw and create vacuums into which their awful ideology can flow and in which they can achieve their objectives. They do not understand the United States of America. We will not flinch in the face of their terror. We will not let thugs and assassins determine the foreign policy of the United States. We will stay in the fight, and we will the fight for the security of the United States of America.

In the long run, the way to defeat an ideology of darkness is with an ideology of hope and light. And that ideology is based upon liberty, the fundamental rights of men and women to live in a free society. I believe—I believe that deep within everybody's soul is the desire to be free.

So I wasn't surprised when 11 million people voted. I wasn't surprised when the Afghans fought off the terrorists. I'm not surprised when people take to streets in Lebanon demanding their freedom. Freedom is on the march. And by having freedom on the march, we're laying the foundation of peace for generations to come.

It's not easy work. It's hard work. But this nation has done that kind of work before. I want to remind you that after World War II, America didn't abandon the world; we helped our enemies rebuild to become democracies. World War II and World War I cost our country dearly in the number of lives lost. But today, because we stuck with the principle that liberty is universal and democracies yield the peace, Europe is whole, free, and at peace.

And in Japan—you know, my dad went; many of your relatives have fought the Japanese. They were the sworn enemy of the United States of America. And yet today, some 60 years after World War II ended, I can sit down at the table with one of my close friends in the international arena, the Prime Minister of Japan, talking about keeping the peace. And what happened? Japan took on a Japanese-style democracy, and democracies and liberty convert enemies into allies. In order to lay the foundation of peace for generations to come, this country of ours must never forget the lessons of history and be confident in the universal values that can change the world to be a peaceful world.

And my fellow Governors understand that, and I appreciate your courage, and I appreciate your strong support. And I appreciate your steadfast will in the face of the enemy.

And here at home, we've got a strong agenda as well. Mitt was right; this economy of ours has overcome a lot. It's overcome recession and war and terrorist attacks and corporate scandals and hurricanes and high energy prices. Yet we're strong, and we're getting stronger. And one of the reasons why is, we understand that when you let people keep more of their own money, they will save and spend and invest and cause this economy to get going. Our economy grew at 3½ percent last year. Unemployment is 4.7 percent. We've added 4.7 million new jobs since August of 2003. Productivity is on the rise. Homeownership is at an alltime high. More minorities own a home today than ever before in our Nation's history.

And yet these are times of uncertainty. There's competition in the global economy. People are changing jobs quite often. There's kind of an unsettling feeling here in the United States of America. And the fundamental question is, what do we do as we head into the future? Some say, let us retreat; let's isolate ourselves from the world—or let's protect ourselves with artificial walls. That's not the attitude of me or our Governors. We're confident about the future because we intend to shape the future and keep the United States of America as the leading economy in the world.

To keep this economy growing, we've got to keep progrowth economic policies in place, not only at the Federal level but at the State level. You know, there's a lot of talk here in Washington about the deficit. I'm concerned about the deficit too. But don't fall prey to those who say, all you've got to do is raise the taxes and balance the budget—that's not how Washington works. Here's the way Washington works: They're going to run up your taxes, and they're going to figure out new ways to spend the money. The best way to deal with the deficit is keep taxes low. Congress needs to make the tax relief permanent.

On the one hand, you have progrowth economic policies that create economic wealth and generate new revenues for the Treasury. On the other hand, we've got to be wise about how we spend your money. I'm looking forward to working with Congress on yet another lean budget that focuses on priority, a budget that doesn't try to be all things to all people, a budget that recognizes we can cut our deficit in half by 2009 if we're fiscally sound with your money. And the Governors understand fiscal sanity. And I appreciate the surpluses you have. Don't be calling on us for any more money. [*Laughter*]

To keep this economy strong, we've got to make sure we have a flexible economy. And to make this economy stay the most competitive economy in the world, we've got to be smart about legal policy. We've got too many lawsuits in the United States of America, junk lawsuits that are driving capital away from job creation. We strongly believe in legal reform in order to make sure this economy remains the best economy in the world. I thank our Governors for tort reform.

We've got a problem: We're hooked on oil. I know that might surprise some of you to hear a Texan say that, but if we want to be the leading economy in the world, we have got to spend money on research and development to get us off of oil. Oil creates an economic problem for us. Because of rising demand in places like China and India relative to the supply of oil, we're finding it causes your price of gasoline to go up at the pump. That hurts our economy. Dependency upon oil also creates a national security issue.

Let me put it bluntly: Sometimes we rely upon oil from people that don't like us. And therefore, in order to make sure we're not only competitive but to make sure we're nationally secure, we have got to figure out new ways to power our automobiles, ways like ethanol and plug-in hybrid battery vehicles. And to make sure that we're less dependent on oil, we've got to have clean coal technology, nuclear power, as well as solar and wind power. This administration looks forward to working with the Governors to get us unhooked from foreign sources of energy.

Man, I've got a lot to say tonight, except Laura said, "Keep it short." [*Laughter*] I'm a wise man; I always listen to my wife. [*Laughter*]

But I do want to share another concern of mine, and that is, unless our children have got—are well-grounded in math and science, the jobs of the 21st century are going to go elsewhere. And our Governors understand that. Our Governors also understand that it's important for the Federal Government, as well as private companies, to invest in research and development so that we're always on the leading edge of technological change. And so I'm proposing to Congress that we double the Federal funding for basic research in the physical sciences. And I'm saying to Congress as clearly as I can, let's make the research and development tax credit a permanent part of the Tax Code so our corporations can accurately plan for investment that is necessary to make sure America is the most competitive nation in the world.

Finally, I look forward to working with our Governors to make sure the No Child Left Behind Act is fully implemented. The No Child Left Behind Act says, first of all, these guys know what to do when it comes to running the schools. We believe in local control of schools. But it does say, in return for Federal money, we expect there to be high standards and measurement to make sure every child learns how to read and write and add and subtract. And if we find a child who cannot read and write early on, we'll correct those problems early, before it's too late. We strongly believe every child in America should learn, and we expect every single school to teach.

And I look forward to working with our Governors to apply that same rigor of accountability, particularly in our junior high grades, for math and science. Because we believe and we know that not only can every child learn, but that when we ground our students in the skills necessary to be good engineers and good physicists and good chemists and good scientists, the United States of America will continue to be the preeminent economy in the world in the 21st century.

So ours is an agenda that is optimistic and hopeful. We believe in America. We believe in the ingenuity of the American people. We understand the power of this country lies in our people, not in our halls of Government. And we also understand the true strength of America lies in the hearts and souls of our citizens. And so I want to thank our Governors for setting up faith-based and community-based offices to help rally the vast numbers in the armies of compassion that help heal broken hearts, that surround people with love who are lonely.

See, we recognize that Government is not an agent of love; Government is law and justice. Government can hand out money, but it cannot put hope in a person's heart or sense of purpose in a person's life. That's done when a kind, decent soul who has heard the universal call to love a neighbor just like you'd like to be loved yourself opens his or her arms and helps mentor a child, helps somebody to read, helps somebody find food if they're hungry and shelter if they're homeless. Our Governors are on the forefront of a conservative and compassionate agenda, and I'm proud to stand with you.

So I've come to thank our Governors. And I've come to thank you all for helping our Governors. These are good, decent, honorable men and women who deserve your support, and you've given it. So thanks for doing it. I'm looking forward to working with our Governors to make this country to continue to be the greatest land on the face of the Earth. I love my job. They love their jobs. And collectively, we love representing the people of the United States of America. Thanks for coming, and God bless.

NOTE: The President spoke at 6:48 p.m. at the National Building Museum. In his remarks, he referred to Gov. Mitt Romney of Massachusetts and his wife, Ann; Gov. Sonny Perdue of Georgia; Gov. Matt Blunt of Missouri and his wife, Melanie; and Prime Minister Junichiro Koizumi of Japan.

Message to the Congress on Continuation of the National Emergency With Respect to Zimbabwe
February 27, 2006

To the Congress of the United States:

Section 202(d) of the National Emergencies Act (50 U.S.C. 1622(d)) provides for the automatic termination of a national emergency unless, prior to the anniversary date of its declaration, the President publishes in the *Federal Register* and transmits to the Congress a notice stating that the emergency is to continue in effect beyond the anniversary date. In accordance with this provision, I have sent to the *Federal Register* for publication the enclosed notice stating that the national emergency blocking the property of persons undermining democratic processes or institutions in Zimbabwe is to continue in effect beyond March 6, 2006. The most recent notice continuing this emergency was published in the *Federal Register* on March 4, 2005 (70 *FR* 10859).

The crisis constituted by the actions and policies of certain members of the Government of Zimbabwe and other persons to undermine Zimbabwe's democratic processes or institutions has not been resolved. These actions and policies pose a continuing unusual and extraordinary threat to the foreign policy of the United States. For these reasons, I have determined that it is necessary to continue this national emergency and to maintain in force the sanctions to respond to this threat.

GEORGE W. BUSH

The White House,

February 27, 2006.

NOTE: This message was released by the Office of the Press Secretary on February 28. The notice is listed in Appendix D at the end of this volume.

Remarks Following Discussions With Prime Minister Silvio Berlusconi of Italy and an Exchange With Reporters
February 28, 2006

President Bush. We'll have some opening statements. I will answer two questions from the U.S. side. The Prime Minister will answer two questions from the Italian side.

I welcome my friend to the Oval Office. Every time I meet with the Prime Minister my spirits are raised because he is such a positive, optimistic person. The Prime Minister is a strong leader. He's a man of his word. He has brought stability to the Italian Government. Obviously, it's important for an American President to be able to work with somebody in a consistent manner, and I appreciate the stability that the Prime Minister has brought to our close ally and friend.

We had a lot of discussion on important issues. We discussed the war on terror, and I thanked the Prime Minister for his strong leadership. We discussed the NATO role in Afghanistan. We discussed Iraq and the need for strong allies to continue to support the democracy movement there. I sought the Prime Minister's opinions on Iran. It was a very constructive dialog.

And finally, I want to thank the people of Italy for hosting the winter Olympics. You did a wonderful job. I know firsthand how good a job you did because my wife reported back. She loved her experience. And so congratulations to the Government and the people of Italy for hosting these magnificent games. And welcome.

Prime Minister Berlusconi. Thank you very much, Mr. President, for your words of appreciation which gave me a lot of satisfaction. On my behalf, I have to say that coming here and meeting the leader of a friendly country is the reason for me to go along the path that we decided to follow. It makes me firm in that.

The consensus and agreements which we always have stems from the fact that we share the same values. We both believe the problem affecting the world—is to spread democracy, because only through democracy there can be freedom, and only through freedom can human beings give the best of themselves.

Therefore, I think we can say that we're lucky because the biggest democracy of the world has such a leader who sees problems affecting the world so clearly and proceeds and follows so firmly in this direction. President Bush and the American people have found a firm and sound ally in my Government.

After 9/11, we both decided to carry out military operations in Afghanistan. And I think we both gave strong support in the reconstruction of Iraq and in the construction of democracy in that country. And we express our appreciation, and we're very close to the American people because of the many—I want to reassure President Bush and his people that when an American soldier dies for the cause of democracy and freedom in that country, we feel that and consider that as a loss for ourselves. But we will continue along this path because we are convinced, as President Bush has said, that only if all democratic states join together we can bring democracy and peace all over the world.

President Bush. Welcome. Tom [Tom Raum, Associated Press].

Iraq

Q. Mr. President, there was some more sectarian violence today in Iraq. There have been hundreds, maybe thousands, killed since the bombing of the mosque. Do you fear an all-out civil war? And will the events of Iraq of the last few days affect prospects for a U.S. drawdown?

And to the Prime Minister, do you still want to withdraw Italian troops by the end of the year?

President Bush. The United States strongly condemns the bombing of holy sites. We believe people should be allowed to worship freely. Obviously, there are some who are trying to sow the seeds of sectarian violence. They destroy in order to create chaos, and now the people of Iraq and their leaders must make a choice. The choice is chaos or unity. The choice is a free society or a society dictated by the—by evil people who will kill innocents.

This weekend, I spoke to seven of the Iraqi leaders. They understood the seriousness of the moment. They have made their choice, which is to work toward a unity government. The Iraqi people made their choice. Last December, 11 million people, in defiance of the terrorists and the killers, went to the polls and said, we want to be free.

Prime Minister Berlusconi. We have announced a plan to progressively withdraw our troops, which should be completed—we have to be completed by the end of this year. And this plan has been agreed upon also together with our allies and with the Iraqi Government. Because this what is going to be possible—why this will be possible.

President Bush. Yes.

Prime Minister Berlusconi. Why is this going to be possible? Because we have, all together with our allies, trained the Iraqi troops and the Iraqi soldiers and the law enforcement so that the Iraqi Government itself will be able to guarantee the security of its people through their own forces.

So as far as the Province which is under our control is concerned, we have 3,000 soldiers there, troops which will be withdrawn by the end of this year. But we have trained 10,000 law enforcement people who can guarantee the respect of peace.

Questions, Italian.

Italy-U.S. Relations

[*At this point, the reporter spoke in Italian, and the question was translated by an interpreter as follows.*]

Q. The first question is to President Bush. Should the center left win in Italy, since they have different views from President Berlusconi, will the relations between the United States and Italy continue to be as they are? Will they be proved worse?

And then with a question to Prime Minister Berlusconi—Prodi has just declared that President Bush has just organized for President—for Prime Minister Berlusconi a farewell party?

Prime Minister Berlusconi. You have a possibility to answer, no comment.

President Bush. That's right, yes. [*Laughter*] No, look, it's—obviously, there's an election. There must be an election, so the question is about pure politics. I have—my relationship is not a political relationship with this man; it's a strategic relationship. And this strategic relationship is important for both our peoples, and it's important to help lay the foundations for peace. Okay? [*Laughter*]

Caren [Caren Bohan, Reuters].

Dubai Ports World/Homeland Security

Q. Mr. President, since you're the final arbiter of the Dubai Ports deal, are you still inclined to approve it? And do you stand by your veto threat?

President Bush. My position hasn't changed to my message to the Congress. And I appreciate the fact that the companies concerned have asked the Congress for a review of all the security implications.

Let me just make something clear to the American people: If there was any doubt in my mind or people in my administration's mind that our ports would be less secure and the American people endangered, this deal wouldn't go forward. And I can understand people's consternation, because the first thing they heard was that a foreign company would be in charge of our port security, when in fact, the Coast Guard and Customs are in charge of our port security. Our duty is to protect America, and we will protect America.

On the other hand, this company is buying a British company that manages the ports. And by the way, there are a lot of foreign companies managing U.S. ports. And so my question to the Members of Congress as they review this matter is, one, please look at the facts, and two, what kind of signal does it send throughout the world if it's okay for a British company to manage the ports, but not a company that has been secure—been cleared for security purposes, from the Arab world? So I look forward to a good, consistent review. You don't need to interpret. That's a U.S. question.

One at a time.

Italy-U.S. Relations

[*The reporter spoke in Italian, and the question was translated by an interpreter as follows.*]

Q. Just a few minutes ago, President Bush praised stability. I would like to know from both of you what role did stability play in your personal relationship and in the relationship between the two countries?

President Bush. Well, first of all, a personal relationship is based upon mutual trust. And I have found Silvio to be a person of his word. Look, sometimes we don't agree, but at least you know where he stands. He is—and that matters, by the way, for a person to keep his word. In politics, people always try to look the easy—find the easy path. I like somebody who makes up his mind based upon principle.

And obviously, there's a practical reason why it's important to have stability. Because if a government is changing every year, it requires a person in my position to constantly have to reacquaint yourself. And that's what I meant by stability. It's much easier to make common policy when you're dealing with a person from one year to the next.

Prime Minister Berlusconi. As far as I'm concerned, I can only add that we brought into politics the values which pertain to the world of work and business, and the world of sport. Because in politics, people changing frequently their minds and positions are considered to be professional. [*Laughter*] While on the contrary in the world of business or the world of sports, a person who changes constantly his position and never keeps his promises is cornered or even set outside.

President Bush. Thank you. Thank you.

NOTE: The President spoke at 10:43 a.m. in the Oval Office at the White House. A reporter referred to Romano Prodi, candidate for Prime Minister of Italy. Prime Minister Berlusconi spoke partly in Italian, and those portions of his remarks were translated by an interpreter.

Remarks Following a Meeting With President Hamid Karzai of Afghanistan and an Exchange With Reporters in Kabul, Afghanistan
March 1, 2006

President Karzai. Well, such a wonderful moment for us in Afghanistan today to have our great friend, our great supporter, a man that helped us liberate, a man that helped us rebuild, a man that helped us move toward the future, President Bush, today with us in Afghanistan.

I conveyed upon President Bush's arrival to him that when the Afghan people come to know that you are here today—but when they see on the television that we did not provide you the kind of hospitality perhaps we want to provide you, I'll be in serious trouble. [*Laughter*] But I'll have a lot of explaining to do to the Afghan people.

Mr. President, welcome to Afghanistan. We owe a great, great deal in this country's rebuilding—peace, democracy, the strong steps toward the future—to your support, to your leadership, to the American people, and to the way you have given your hand to the Afghan people.

I'm not going to go into the details of all that you've done for us—it's from the defeat of terrorism, to peace in Afghanistan, to democracy, to reconstruction, to the success of the whole process. Thank you very much, Mr. President, and welcome to Afghanistan.

President Bush. Thank you, Mr. President. Thank you for having me. Laura and I are honored to be here. It's such a thrill to come to a country which is dedicating itself to the dignity of every person that lives here.

First of all, I want to thank you for the fantastic lunch we just had. I did get a taste of Afghanistan hospitality, and it's good. I appreciate you introducing me to many of the leaders of your Government. I'm impressed by their dedication to making sure the experience that you're going through, experience of growing a democ-

racy that honors and respects all, is successful.

One of the messages I want to say to the people of Afghanistan is, it's our country's pleasure and honor to be involved with the future of this country. We like stories of young girls going to school for the first time so they can realize their potential. We appreciate a free press. We are enthralled when we see an entrepreneurial class grow up where people are able to work and realize their dreams. We understand the importance of having a well-trained military dedicated to the sovereignty of the country and to the peace of the people. And we're impressed by the progress that your country is making, Mr. President. A lot of it has to do with your leadership.

Today I not only had a good, long visit with my friend, the President, but we had a good visit with a lot of the folks who make this Government work. From here, I'll go to cut a ribbon at our new Embassy. The Embassy should be a clear statement to the people of Afghanistan that we're dedicated to helping. And then I'm going to go out to the base and thank some of our troops who are here to protect our country and, at the same time, help the people of Afghanistan protect themselves.

One of the things I told Mr. President, told the members of your team and your Cabinet and the Government, is that people all over the world are watching the experience here in Afghanistan. I hope the people of Afghanistan understand that as democracy takes hold, you're inspiring others. And that inspiration will cause others to demand their freedom. And as the world becomes more free, the world will become more peaceful. And so I come as a friend, an ally, and a person like you, dedicated to peace. Thank you for having me.

President Karzai. Well, I guess we take some questions, Mr. President?

President Bush. Why don't we take a couple.

President Karzai. Two on each side?

President Bush. Sure.

President Karzai. All right.

President Bush. We'll start with the Afghans. Terry [Terence Hunt, Associated Press], please——

President Karzai. He's a guest. He's a guest.

President Bush. Guests first? You don't know who he is.

President Karzai. Please, go ahead.

President Bush. He's Terry by the way, AP. You might have seen him before.

President Karzai. Yes, we've seen him before.

President Bush. He asked you a very difficult question last time.

President Karzai. He did? Well——

President Bush. Hopefully, he'll tone it down some.

Usama bin Laden

Q. I'd like to ask you, Mr. President, there was a time when you talked about getting Usama bin Laden dead or alive. Why is he still on the loose 5 years later? And are you still confident that you'll get him?

President Bush. I am confident he will be brought to justice. What's happening is, is that we got U.S. forces on the hunt for not only bin Laden but anybody who plots and plans with bin Laden. There are Afghan forces on the hunt for not only bin Laden but those who plot and plan with him. We've got Pakistan forces on the hunt. And part of my message to President Musharraf is, is that it's important that we bring these people to justice. He understands that. After all, they've tried to kill him four times. So we've got a common alliance, all aimed at routing out people who are evildoers, people who have hijacked a great religion and kill innocent people in the name of that religion.

We're making progress of dismantling Al Qaida. Slowly but surely we're bringing the people to justice, and the world is better for it, as a result of our steady progress. You want to ask somebody?

President Karzai. Yes. I'll ask Reuters.

Q. Yes, please. Thank you, sir——

President Bush. Oh, no, no——

President Karzai. There's international Reuters; there's Afghan Reuters.

President Bush. He didn't mean to. Sorry.

Q. Mr. President, allow me to welcome you to Afghanistan first.

President Bush. Thank you.

Q. And I would like to ask you a couple of questions, if I may.

President Bush. Sure.

Afghanistan/Iran

Q. Regarding the worsening situation in Afghanistan, the Afghan Government says that most of the violence emanates from Pakistan. Will you be discussing in any way the issue of violence in Afghanistan with Pakistani authorities?

President Bush. Absolutely.

Q. And my second question is regarding Iran's nuclear program——

President Bush. Yes.

Q. Iran states that its nuclear program is for peaceful purposes, but you seem to doubt them. There seems to be some sort of standoff. Do you not think that the standoff will affect the security of the region, and do you think there is a way out of this standoff?

President Bush. Great. First, yes, I absolutely will bring up the cross-border infiltrations with President Musharraf. These infiltrations are causing harm to friends, allies, and cause harm to U.S. troops. And that will be a topic of conversation. It's an ongoing topic of conversation.

Secondly, Iran must not have a nuclear weapon. The most destabilizing thing that can happen in this region and in the world is for Iran to have a—develop a nuclear weapon. And so the world is speaking with one voice to the Iranians that it's okay for you to have a civilian power—nuclear power operation, but you shall not have the means, the knowledge, to develop a nuclear weapon.

And so we've joined with Russia as part of a diplomatic effort to solve this problem that says, Russia will provide enriched uranium to its civilian nuclear powerplant and will collect the uranium after it's been used in the plant.

I'll repeat to you: The most destabilizing thing that can happen is for Iran to have a nuclear weapon. And we will work with friends and allies to convince them not to.

Steven [Steve Holland, Reuters].

India

Q. Sir, you're going on to India from here. How close are you to sealing a nuclear agreement with India? And what does it mean for the trip if you don't get one?

President Bush. Our relationship with India is broader than our discussions about energy. Ours is a strategic relationship. It is a relationship that's got strong ties because of economics and our military, our desire to help democracies such as Afghanistan. Our people are talking to the Indians today on the plane, and we'll be doing so when we land in New Delhi about trying to come to an agreement on a civilian nuclear power agreement.

But as I said in my speech in Washington, this is a difficult issue. It's a difficult issue for the Indian Government; it's a difficult issue for the American Government. And so we'll continue to dialog and work, and hopefully, we can reach an agreement. If not, we'll continue to work on it until we do. It's in our interests and the interests of the United States. It's in the interests of countries around the world that India develop a nuclear power industry because that will help alleviate demand for fossil fuels. And by alleviating demand for fossil fuels, it takes the price off of gasoline at the pump. And so the faster the Indian economy grows, the more fuel they de-

mand; the more fuel they demand, it affects our gas prices; it affects your gas prices.

So what we're trying to do is have an international consortium that will enable countries to develop nuclear power industries in safe ways, ways that will prevent proliferation, and ways that will enable nations to meet their energy needs without excessive consumption of fossil fuels.

President Karzai. I will give a chance to the Afghan Television, for once.

Afghanistan-U.S. Cooperation

[*The reporter spoke in Dari, and the remarks were translated by an interpreter.*]

Q. Your Excellency President Bush, most welcome to Afghanistan and wish you a pleasant stay. The question is by a reporter from Afghanistan National Radio and Television. It has been 4 years since the presence of the international forces in Afghanistan. However, the security situation is increasingly deteriorating. What will be your long-term security policy to Afghanistan? And the second part of the question is, how will the U.S. policy be affected in regards to Afghanistan if Usama and Mullah Omar are captured?

President Bush. It's not a matter of if they're captured or brought to justice; it's when they're brought to justice. The United States is here at the request of an Afghan Government elected by the people. We signed an agreement in the Oval Office in Washington, DC, with the duly elected President of your country, President Karzai. It's an agreement that sets out a strategic relationship. It's an important relationship for our country. It's an important relationship for Afghanistan.

But it's important for the people of Afghanistan to recognize that we're here by mutual consent. We want to be here. We want to be here to help Afghanistan grow its democracy and to defeat those who will—can't stand the thought of freedom.

The President has talked to me a lot about this issue, assures me that the Government is sincere in its request that the United States and coalition help Afghanistan grow its democracy. Our commitment is firm. Our desire is to see this country flourish and set a great example not only in the neighborhood but around the world.

See, I hope people of Afghanistan understand the people of America have great— got great regard for human life and human dignity, that we care about the plight of people. We—when we saw the devastation in Pakistan, we were quick to respond with help because we care about people. When we heard 73,000 people lost their lives and 2.5 million people were displaced from their homes, it broke our hearts. When we see HIV/AIDS ravishing an entire continent of Africa, we care.

I'm going to repeat what I said before: We like stories, and expect stories, of young girls going to school in Afghanistan. It means a lot to the American people to hear the President say that. It means a lot for people to realize that there is an entrepreneurial class that's beginning to grow. We believe in hope, which is the exact opposite of the ideology of the bin Ladens of the world and the Taliban.

In our country, you can worship freely. You're equally American if you're a Christian, Muslim, Hindu, or Jew. You're equally American if you don't believe in an Almighty. Under the Taliban and Usama bin Laden, there is no religious freedom. You have no chance to express yourself in the public square without being punished. There is no capacity to realize your full potential. And so we're committed; we're committed to universal values. We believe—we believe everybody desires to be free. And we know that history has taught us that free societies yield peace. And that's what we want. We want peace for our children, and we want peace for the Afghan children as well.

President Karzai. Good. Wonderful. Great. Thank you very much.

President Bush. Thank you.

NOTE: The President spoke at 2:52 p.m. at the Presidential Palace. In his remarks, he referred to Usama bin Laden, leader of the Al Qaida terrorist organization; and President Pervez Musharraf of Pakistan. A reporter referred to Mullah Omar, head of the deposed Taliban regime in Afghanistan.

Remarks at a Dedication Ceremony for the United States Embassy in Kabul
March 1, 2006

Thank you for the warm welcome. I thought I'd just drop in to cut a ribbon. [*Laughter*] Ambassador, Laura and I are honored to join you. And Mr. President, thank you for joining us.

The President just hosted a great Afghan lunch. The hospitality of the Afghan people is well-known, and I enjoyed that hospitality, Mr. President. Thank you.

I appreciate the Secretary of State joining me. I'm proud to call Condi Rice

friend; America is proud to call her Secretary of State.

I appreciate Ron Neumann's service. There's nothing wrong with a son following in his father's footsteps. [*Laughter*] When we rolled by the old Embassy, he told me that it was his dad that cut the ribbon as the Ambassador from the United States to Afghanistan. And here we are about to open a brand new Embassy with a proud son and a great representative of our country, Ambassador Ron Neumann, cutting the ribbon.

History sometimes spins an interesting tale, doesn't it? And such a tale is being spun today of public service. I want to thank all of my fellow citizens for working so far away from home on an incredibly important mission. I want to thank the Embassy personnel, as well as our United States military personnel, for being on the frontline of freedom's march. I know it's a hard job, away from your families—a long way from your families, having just flown 17 hours to get here. But it's a vital mission. It's historic in its nature. This is the kind of mission that someday, the Secretary of State will be speaking to Foreign Service officers and relaying the stories and the tales and the toils of those who served in Afghanistan in 2006. And so I congratulate you on your hard work, and I thank you on behalf of a grateful nation.

I also want to thank the Foreign Service nationals who are here as well, those citizens of Afghanistan who are helping our folks to accomplish a big mission. I am struck by the story that our Embassy was kept open and guarded during the days of the Taliban. And when Afghanistan was liberated, there were Afghan nationals here to turn over the keys to the Embassy. For those of you who are guarding our Embassy, thank you. For those of you who carry on their legacy, I thank you as well. We welcome your help; we're honored with your presence today.

I've been honored to welcome Afghan citizens to Washington on a fairly regular basis. Laura and I have hosted brave men and women, who are dedicated to democracy and freedom, in Washington. One thing they always ask me—they ask me with their words, and they ask me with their stares, as they look into my eyes—is the United States firmly committed to the future of Afghanistan? That's what they want to know. My answer is, "Absolutely." It's in our Nation's interest that Afghanistan develop into a democracy. It's in the interests of the United States of America for there to be examples around the world of what is possible, that it's possible to replace tyrants with a free society in which men and women are respected, in which young girls can go to school to realize their full potential, in which people are able to realize their dreams.

And so my message to the people of Afghanistan is, take a look at this building. It's a big, solid, permanent structure, which should represent the commitment of the United States of America to your liberty. I firmly believe the work that we're doing together is laying the foundation of peace for generations to come. And I want to thank you for sharing that mission.

May God bless America and you and your families, and may God's blessings rain on the good people of Afghanistan.

NOTE: The President spoke at 3:31 p.m. In his remarks, he referred to President Hamid Karzai of Afghanistan.

Remarks to United States and Coalition Troops at Bagram Air Base, Afghanistan
March 1, 2006

Thanks for having us. Laura and I are honored to be here in Afghanistan with you. It's a real pleasure to be with our country's finest citizens. I want to thank

General Eikenberry and General Freakley and all those who are taking responsibility to make sure we complete our mission.

I particularly want to thank the members of the United States Army and Marines and Air Force and Navy who are here. Laura and I thank the civilian contractors who are here. I—really pleased to be with the 10th Mountain Division—"Climb to Glory."

I know it's not easy to be away from home, but I want you to understand that you're on the frontier of freedom, that you're involved with doing two important things. One is finding an enemy and bringing them to justice so they don't hurt our fellow citizens again. That mission requires steadfast determination. The enemy cannot defeat us militarily. The only thing they can do is to kill innocent lives and try to shake our will. But they don't understand the United States of America. We will never be intimidated by thugs and assassins. We will defeat the enemy and win the war on terror.

And the other thing you're doing is to help this new democracy not only survive but to flourish. Laura and myself and Secretary Condi Rice, who is with us here—step on over here. We just met with President Karzai. And my message to the people of Afghanistan is—was the following: One, it takes courage to get rid of a tyrant or tyrannical governments and to recognize that the future belongs to democracy. That's not easy work. It's hard to recognize that people ought to be allowed to worship freely and speak their minds freely after living under the grips of a tyrant.

Our other message was, is that the United States doesn't cut and run. When we make a commitment, we keep our commitments. It's in our national interest that the work you're doing here, the work of helping the Afghans develop a democracy—it's in the interests of your children and your grandchildren. Because, you see, democracies yield the peace we all want. History has taught us democracies don't war. You don't run for office in a democracy and say, "Please vote for me; I promise you war." [*Laughter*] You run for office

in democracies and say, "Vote for me; I'll represent your interests. Vote for me; I'll help your young girls go to school or the health care you get improved."

Democracies yield peace, and that's what we want. What's going to happen in Afghanistan is, a neighborhood that has been desperate for light instead of darkness is going to see what's possible when freedom arrives. What's going to happen in Afghanistan, it's going to send a signal, not only in the neighborhood but around the world, that freedom is the potential. The United States of America believes that freedom is universal. Freedom is not our gift to the world; freedom is the gift from an Almighty to every single person in this world.

I'm proud of our United States military. Many of you volunteered for service after September the 11th, 2001. You saw that our Nation was attacked, and when the country called upon you, you said, "Let me serve. Let me join in the fight to defeat the terrorists so attacks like that will never occur on our soil again." And that's what you're doing here in Afghanistan. You're helping to change this part of the world—and change the world with your courage and your sacrifice. I assure you that this Government of yours will not blink; we will not yield. We're on the right course, and the world is going to be a better place because of your service.

So we're here to thank you. I want you to e-mail and call your friends and, more important, your families, and tell them the old Commander in Chief showed up for a little bit, with a message of appreciation not only for you but for your loved ones as well. I ask for God's blessings on you and your mission, God's blessings on our country. Thank you for letting us come by.

NOTE: The President spoke at 4:37 p.m. at the Clam Shell. In his remarks, he referred to Lt. Gen. Karl W. Eikenberry, USA, commander, Combined Forces Command Afghanistan; Maj. Gen. Benjamin C. Freakley, USA, commander, 10th Mountain Division and Combined Joint Task Force 76; and President Hamid Karzai of Afghanistan.

Remarks Following a Meeting With American and Indian Business Leaders in New Delhi, India
March 2, 2006

Prime Minister Manmohan Singh of India. Mr. President, distinguished journalists, ladies and gentlemen, I've already welcomed President George Bush and Mrs. Laura Bush on this, their first visit to India. I would now like to welcome the U.S. CEOs who have traveled to India for this historic meeting.

The President and I have just concluded our official discussions, and I'm sure he shares my pleasure—[*inaudible*]—executive officers. The establishment of this group last year was an important initiative stated by the President—[*inaudible*]—in which the private sectors of our two countries could interact and build a roadmap for promoting cooperation. I would like to thank the two cochairs, Mr. William Harrison and Mr. Ratan Tata, and their colleagues for the excellent work done in preparing the report which they will now present.

I have been briefed on the main recommendations, and I am very happy to say that some of the recommendations are already reflected in the decisions which the President and I have issued today. I will have more to say on other recommendations a little later.

I now invite President Bush to share his thoughts and initiate the discussion. You have the floor, sir.

President Bush. Well, thank you, Mr. Prime Minister. I want to thank the CEOs for joining us from both India and the United States. Thank you all for coming.

The Prime Minister and I have had some really constructive dialog, starting in Washington, DC, and then here in New Delhi.

I would characterize our relationship as warm and results-oriented. Warm because he's a humble man who cares deeply about the people of India, and he's a good thinker. He can see beyond the horizon, which is necessary.

I say "results-oriented" because it's one thing to shake hands and smile for the cameras; it's another thing to actually deliver results on behalf of our people. I am a firm believer that relations with India are important to the United States. It's important for the people of the United States; it's important for people who want to work in the United States. And to the extent that we are able to achieve mutually beneficial goals, to eliminate barriers, and to hear from people who are actually on the frontlines creating jobs, I think is useful for those of us in government.

So I'm looking forward to this moment. One of the action steps that we agreed to take last July was to set up this forum. And, Mr. Prime Minister, it's good to see things happening. It's good to see results. And this is a result of an historic meeting, set of meetings.

And so I want to thank you for your hospitality. Thank you all for coming. I'm looking forward to hearing what folks have to say. And once you say it, once we figure out the roadblocks for further development, you have my commitment that we will work to remove those roadblocks.

Thanks for having me.

NOTE: The President spoke at 11:38 a.m. in the Hyderabad House. Prime Minister Singh referred to William B. Harrison, Jr., chairman of the board, JP Morgan Chase & Co.; and Ratan N. Tata, chairman, Tata Group.

Remarks Following Discussions With Prime Minister Manmohan Singh of India and an Exchange With Reporters in New Delhi
March 2, 2006

Prime Minister Singh. Shall I start?

President Bush. Please.

Prime Minister Singh. Mr. President, ladies and gentlemen of the press: President Bush and I have completed very cordial and productive discussions this morning. We reviewed the status of our cooperation, including the agenda that was set on July 18, 2005. The joint statement that will be shared with all of you today contains a number of announcements and initiatives that underline the significant progress in our relationship.

Many of the areas that our cooperation now covers are essential to India's national development. They include energy, agriculture, science and technology, trade and investment, high technology, health, and a clean environment. This is a highly ambitious agenda, one that is befitting our growing strategic partnership. When implemented, they will make a real difference to the lives of our people.

The President and I had an opportunity to review the global situation in our talks. As you're all aware, India and the United States are working together increasingly on global issues. This is not just good for our two countries but also benefits the international community, as we can complement each others' capabilities and share responsibilities. President Bush is admired for his strong position on terrorism. And I was particularly pleased that we agreed on the need to root out terrorism, of which India has been a major victim.

I'm particularly pleased that we have reached an understanding on the imple-

mentation of our agreement on civil nuclear cooperation of July 18, 2005. I have conveyed to the President that India has finalized the identification of civilian facilities to which we had committed. I was also happy to hear from the President that he now intended to approach the U.S. Congress to amend U.S. laws and the Nuclear Supplier Group to adjust its guideline. We will discuss with the International Atomic Energy Agency in regard to fashioning an appropriate India-specific safeguards agreement. You will appreciate I cannot say more now, while our Parliament is in session.

Before concluding, I would like to express my warm appreciation for the personal interest shown and the leadership role that President Bush has played in the transformation of our ties. I have met the President a number of times, and on each occasion, I have admired his vision, his resolve, and his commitment to strengthening our bilateral relations. Our discussion today make me confident that there are no limits to the Indo-U.S. partnerships.

May I invite you, Mr. President, now to make your remarks.

President Bush. Mr. Prime Minister, thank you very much. It's a joy to be here. Laura and I are really thankful for your hospitality, and I appreciate the lengthy and constructive dialog we just had on a wide range of issues. I particularly thank the CEOs from both the United States and India who have worked hard to help develop a way forward to make sure our relationship is constructive and long-lasting.

India and America have built a strategic partnership based upon common values. Our two democracies respect religious pluralism and the rule of law. We seek to foster economic development through trade and advancing the entrepreneurial spirit in both countries.

We're working as partners to make the world safer. India and America both suffered from terrorist attacks on our home soil. Terrorists attacked New Delhi. We're sharing information to protect each other. We have a common desire to enhance the security of our peoples. We're cooperating on the military front. We worked as partners in responding to the tsunami. I was struck, and so were the American people, that the Indian Air Force delivered Hurricane Katrina aid to an Air Force base in Little Rock, Arkansas. And for that, Mr. Prime Minister, thank you.

We are committed to promoting democracy worldwide. We are leaders in the United Nations Democracy Fund, which provides grants to help young democracies develop civil institutions in a free society. I particularly want to thank the Indian people and the Indian Government for supporting the new democracy in the neighborhood, and that being the democracy in Afghanistan, where you've pledged 565 million in reconstruction aid, plus 50 million for the new National Assembly building.

On Burma, we agree on the deplorable state of human rights in Burma, and all nations to seek the release of Aung San Suu Kyi. In Nepal, we agreed that the Maoists should abandon violence and that the King should reach out to the political parties to restore democratic institutions. In other words, our discussions are more than just friendly handshakes. We discuss important international relations. We're partners in peace. And that's in the interests of our own people, as well as the interests of people around the world.

On trade and investment, ties are growing. We're partners in expanding global trade. The United States is India's largest trading partner, and India is one of the United States fastest growing export markets. That's one of the reasons we met with the CEOs today, is to how to further trade and how to further commerce and how to further opportunities.

And, oh, by the way, Mr. Prime Minister, the United States is looking forward to eating Indian mangos. Part of liberalizing trade is to open up markets. And as a result of your leadership and our hard work, we are opening up markets. Our Agricultural Knowledge Initiative is an important initiative for both countries, where we'll fund joint agricultural research projects.

Prime Minister Singh and I established a trade policy forum to address bilateral trade issues. One of the areas we discussed today is how we can work together to make sure that the Doha negotiations end on a positive note. Trade is important. Trade is important for our peoples. Trade is important to help nations develop ways forward, help nations overcome poverty. And I appreciate your understanding of that, Mr. Prime Minister. I'm looking forward to working with you.

As the Prime Minister mentioned, we concluded an historic agreement today on nuclear power. It's not an easy job for the Prime Minister to achieve this agreement, I understand. It's not easy for the American President to achieve this agreement. But it's a necessary agreement. It's one that will help both our peoples.

Again, I applaud you for your courage and your leadership. I'm looking forward to working with our United States Congress to change decades of law that will enable us to move forward in this important initiative.

Also, we talked about the Advanced Energy Initiative that I'm proposing in my own country. Listen, the whole purpose of the Advanced Energy Initiative is to end our dependence on oil, and as we develop technologies that will enable us to do so, we look forward to working with India so we can achieve the same objectives. Dependency upon fossil fuels causes—particularly during times of shortage—causes prices to rise in both our countries. And it's in our interests that we share technologies to move away from the era of fossil fuels.

India and Pakistan have an historic opportunity to work toward lasting peace. Prime Minister Singh and President Musharraf have shown themselves to be leaders of courage and vision. And I encourage them to continue making progress on all issues, including Kashmir.

India and America are partners in addressing other global issues like HIV/AIDS and pandemic flu. In other words, this partnership of ours is substantive, and it's important, and it's strategic. And I thank the Prime Minister for working with me to advance this relationship in such a way that we can define our previous meetings and today's meeting as historic in nature. I'm confident that the relationship between India and the United States is good for the United States of America. I hope it's good for the people of India, and I know it's going to be good for laying the foundations of peace in this world of ours.

So, Mr. Prime Minister, thank you very much for having me.

Prime Minister Singh. It's a great honor, Mr. President, to have you.

Civilian Nuclear Power Program in India/United Nations Security Council Membership

Q. Thank you, Mr. Prime Minister. Thank you, Mr. President. Sir, since you have said that India-U.S. nuclear cooperation agreement is on, what we would like to know from you that how are you going to ensure that India's concerns and Indian scientific community's concerns regarding nonstop supply of fuel and also protecting India's three-phased nuclear research program?

And excuse me, sir, Mr. President, I have a question for you too, sir. Sir, you know,

everybody is saying that India and the United States are natural allies. And you have also said many times that our strategic partnership is based on common values, shared values. Sir, then why the largest democracy of the world is reluctant or not forthcoming to support—the oldest democracy of the world is not supporting the largest democracy of the world to have a permanent membership of the United Nations Security Council? This is an issue India would like to hear from you more, sir. Thank you. Thank you, Prime Minister.

Prime Minister Singh. You have asked me about the nuclear agreement. As I mentioned, we have reached a mutually satisfactory understanding with regard to carrying forward the process that was outlined in the July 18 statement which I and President Bush signed.

An important step forward is the preparation of a separation plan, a separation plan which separates the civilian nuclear program from the military program. That phase has been successfully completed. Now it is for the United States to go to the Congress for necessary amendments in U.S. laws. Also, the U.S. will approach the members of the Nuclear Supplier Groups, and thereafter we'll also have to go to the International Atomic Energy Agency for India-specific safeguards.

So we have made very satisfactory progress. And I thank the President for his initiative. But for his leadership, this day would probably have not come so soon.

President Bush. Thank you for your question on the U.N. Security Council. I'm not surprised you asked it. As a matter of fact, I gave an interview to a person from the India media in Washington, DC, prior to my trip, and that was one of the questions asked.

My answer hasn't changed, by the way, which is this: One, we support United Nations Security Council reform, and we're interested in different ways to reform the United Nations Security Council. My concern all along, however, is that if we only stick to the United Nations Security Council reform, we miss an opportunity to reform the United Nations overall. And so our position is, let's make sure reform overall moves forward as we think about the best way to reform the Security Council.

The United Nations is a very important international body. It's one that does, however, require better accountability and—accountability on how we spend money and accountability on getting results. One such area, for example, is the Human Rights Commission. The Human Rights Commission needs to be reformed in a way that actually is able to achieve significant results on behalf of the world.

And so we're openminded, and we're listening. But what we don't want to do is have a Security Council reform measure that causes the other reforms not to go forward.

Suzanne [Suzanne Malveaux, Cable News Network]. You probably need a microphone, unless you want to belt it out.

President's Upcoming Visit to Pakistan/War on Terror

Q. I'll try. Thank you, Mr. President. There are reports of multiple bombings out of Karachi, Pakistan, outside of the U.S. consulate, as well as the Marriott Hotel. What can you tell us about this? Will this impact your trip, your visit to that country? And how does this speak to Pakistan or even Musharraf's ability to contain terrorists?

President Bush. First of all, I've been briefed on the bombings. We have lost at least one U.S. citizen in a bombing, a Foreign Service officer, and I send our country's deepest condolences to that person's loved one and family. We also send the condolences to the people from Pakistan who lost their lives.

Terrorists and killers are not going to prevent me from going to Pakistan. My trip to Pakistan is an important trip. It's important to talk with President Musharraf about continuing our fight against terrorists. After

all, he has had a direct stake in this fight—four times the terrorists have tried to kill him.

The Prime Minister and I talked about the need to continue working together to fight the scourge of terrorism. People—these terrorists will kill innocent life just like that. They have no conscience. You can't negotiate with them; you can't reason with them. They must be brought to justice. The bombing that took place prior to my trip is an indication that there are—that the war on terror goes on and that free nations must come together to fight terrorism.

The way to defeat terrorism in the short run is to share intelligence and to take action. The way to defeat terrorism in the long run is to defeat the ideology of hate with an ideology of hope. And that's democracy. The great thing about being here in India is, it's a perfect opportunity to remind the world that it is possible for people of different religions to live peacefully together. That's precisely what this grand democracy has shown the world.

And my resolve has never been stronger about protecting our own people by working with other nations to answer the call to history. And the call to history now is to stand strong in the face of these terrorist attacks, and we will.

War on Terror/India-U.S. Relations

Q. President Bush, two questions for you. First——

President Bush. Only two? That's good.

Q. First, on the nuclear deal, how do you plan to sell the agreement to a very powerful nonproliferation lobby in Washington which has opposed the deal?

And second, on the issue of terrorism, in the context of today's bomb blasts in Karachi, how do you propose to work with India on terrorism, considering India considers that the epicenter of terrorism is in Pakistan?

President Bush. Well, one way we work together on terrorism is to make sure our intelligence services share information. The way you defeat terrorists is you—in the short term—is you anticipate and react to their motives and their actions through good intelligence.

We're involved in a different kind of war. This is a war where people hide and plot and plan and then, all of a sudden, emerge and kill. And so it requires a different response. And part of the response is to commit our intelligence services to sharing information. We spent some time talking about that issue today.

As well, I will send—bring the same message to President Musharraf, that we will continue to work with the President to share information to bring terrorists to justice. Terrorism is not prevalent only in this part of the world. It's prevalent in the Middle East as well. In the long run, terrorism will be defeated by giving people hope and opportunity as opposed to systems of government which breed resentment and provide—and as a result of that resentment, provide opportunity for these killers to recruit.

In terms of convincing the Congress, the first thing I will say to our Congress is that our relationship is changing to the better. You know, sometimes it's hard to get rid of history, and short-term history shows that the United States and India were divided. We didn't have much of a relationship. And as a result, there are laws on the books that reflect that. Now the relationship is changing dramatically. People in the United States have got to understand that trade with India is in our interests, that diplomatic relations with India is in our interests, that cultural exchanges with India are in our interest.

One of the things that helps make that case, of course, is the—there's a lot of Indian Americans making important contributions to our country. And we welcome those contributions. I think there needs to be more student exchanges between our countries. I think we ought to expand H1B

visas for Indian scientists and engineers and physicists and people in our country.

In other words, what I'm trying to explain to you is that it's a changing relationship, and part of that change is going to be how to deal with the nuclear issue. Now, proliferation is certainly a concern and a part of our discussions, and we've got a good faith gesture by the Indian Government that I'll be able to take to the Congress. But the other thing that our Congress has got to understand, that it's in our economic interests that India have a civilian nuclear power industry to help take the pressure off of the global demand for energy.

Obviously, nuclear power is a renewable source of energy, and the less demand there is for nonrenewable sources of energy like fossil fuels, the better off it is for the American people. Increasing demand for oil from America, from India and China, relative to a supply that's not keeping up with demand, causes our fuel prices to go up. And so to the extent that we can reduce demand for fossil fuels, it will help the American consumer.

And so there are several ways for me to make the case, which I'm kind of laying out for you now, so that—but this is what I'll be telling our Congress.

Axelrod [Jim Axelrod, CBS News].

Civilian Nuclear Power Program in India

Q. Mr. President, Mr. Prime Minister, following up on this just a touch, what kind of message, sir, does it send to the world that India, which has been testing as late as 1998, nuclear testing, and is not—has not signed the Nuclear Nonproliferation Treaty—is this a reward for bad behavior, as some critics suggest? And what kind of message does it send to other countries that are in the process of developing nuclear technology? Why should they sign the NPT if India is getting a deal without doing so, sir?

President Bush. What this agreement says is, things change, times change, that leadership can make a difference, and telling the world—sending the world a different message from that which is—what used to exist in people's minds.

I—listen, I've always said this was going to be a difficult deal for the Prime Minister to sell to his Parliament, but he showed great courage and leadership. And it's difficult for the American President to sell to our Congress, because some people just don't want to change and change with the times. I understand that. But this agreement is in our interests, and therefore, Jim, I'm confident we can sell this to our Congress as in the interest of the United States and, at the same time, make it clear that there's a way forward for other nations to participate in a—in civilian nuclear power in such a way as to address nonproliferation concerns.

India has charted a way forward. You heard the Prime Minister talk about going to the IAEA. That group exists to help safeguard the world from proliferation.

Listen, I proposed reprocessing agreements. That stands in stark contrast to current nuclear theology that we shouldn't reprocess for proliferation concerns. I don't see how you can advocate nuclear power in order to take the pressure off of our own economy, for example, without advocating technological development of reprocessing, because reprocessing will not only—reprocessing is going to help with the environmental concerns with nuclear power. It will make there—to put it bluntly, there will be less material to dispose.

And so I'm trying to think differently, not to stay stuck in the past, and recognize that by thinking differently, particularly on nuclear power, we can achieve some important objectives, one of which is less reliance on fossil fuels; second is to work with our partners to help both our economies grow; and thirdly is to be strong on dealing with the proliferation issues.

Well, Mr. Prime Minister, it's been a joy.

Prime Minister Singh. Thank you very much, Mr. President. We have made history today, and I thank you.

President Bush. Thank you, sir. Thank you.

NOTE: The President spoke at 12:26 p.m. in the Mughal Garden at the Hyderabad House. In his remarks, he referred to Aung San Suu Kyi, leader of the National League for Democracy of Burma; King Gyanendra Bir Bikram Shah Dev of Nepal; President Pervez Musharraf of Pakistan; and David Foy, a U.S. State Department official who was killed in a terrorist attack in Karachi, Pakistan, on March 2.

Remarks at a Luncheon Hosted by Prime Minister Manmohan Singh of India in New Delhi
March 2, 2006

Mr. Prime Minister and Mrs. Kaur, thank you for your hospitality. Mr. Prime Minister, I'm sorry you brought up the Taj Mahal. I've been hearing about it from Laura ever since I told her that we weren't going. But we pledged if you invite us back to come back, we'd love to see the magnificent part of your country that we will be unable to see this trip.

This is an historic trip. It's a chance to continue to build on the progress we made in Washington, DC, progress being a relationship that is—that lasts beyond our time in office. It's a relationship that is based upon our common values, that every person matters, every person belongs, and everybody should be able to worship as freely as they want to, the common values of recognizing the right to people to express themselves in a peaceful way.

Our relationship is one that's important for peace and prosperity in this world. It's important that we continue to work together to battle the terrorists, to give them no quarter, and to never yield. Terrorism has no place in democracy, and terrorism must be defeated for our children and grandchildren to be able to live in a peaceful world.

Our relationship is one based upon our belief that free and fair trade is in the interests of our people; that when trade moves freely and fairly, that people in our respective countries will be able to find good work and good jobs and improve their standard of living. I believe India has got a really important role to play in showing parts of the world what is possible when it comes to having people live side by side in peace. India is such a wonderful example of pluralism, of religious freedom, of human rights. This relationship of ours is a vital relationship; it's a strategic partnership.

And so Mr. Prime Minister, thank you very much for our dialogs and our work together. Thank you for your hospitality. I want to thank the leaders who are here with us today for taking time out of your busy schedules to welcome Laura and me and our delegation.

And so I too would like to propose a toast, a toast to the Prime Minister, his wife, and to the people of India.

NOTE: The President spoke at 1:39 p.m. in the Taj Palace. In his remarks, he referred to Kaur Gursharan, wife of Prime Minister Singh. The transcript released by the Office of the Press Secretary also included the remarks of Prime Minister Singh.

Remarks Following a Meeting With Religious Leaders in New Delhi
March 2, 2006

The President. We have just had a very important discussion about the role of religion, not only in India but the role that religion can play in helping the world become a more peaceful place. I want to thank the leaders here around the table. Leaders from different faiths have joined us to share with—their thoughts with me.

You know, one of the things that struck me during the conversation is, in India, is—it's a country that recognizes the importance of religion and welcomes interfaith dialog, understands the importance of faith and understands the importance of people of faith discussing thoughts and views that are deep in their hearts.

And we've had a—just a—you know, India is an amazing country. Just look around the table, and you'll see different religions represented. But everybody around the table also was so proud to be an Indian. In other words, their nationalism was equally important to them, as their religion.

We thank the——

Acharya Srivatsa Goswami. [Inaudible]— here to the world.

The President. Well, that's right. That's right. Thank you. Anyway, I just appreciate you all coming. Thank you for your kind words. And like you, I hope for peace, and like you, I'm proud to be here in India. It's a fantastic country.

Thank you.

NOTE: The President spoke at 4:23 p.m. at the Maurya Sheraton and Towers. Participating in the meeting was Acharya Srivatsa

Goswami, head of the Sri Caitanya Prema Samsthana.

Joint Statement Between the United States of America and India
March 2, 2006

President George W. Bush and Prime Minister Manmohan Singh today expressed satisfaction with the great progress the United States and India have made in advancing our strategic partnership to meet the global challenges of the 21st century. Both our countries are linked by a deep commitment to freedom and democracy; a celebration of national diversity, human creativity and innovation; a quest to expand prosperity and economic opportunity worldwide; and a desire to increase mutual security against the common threats posed by intolerance, terrorism, and the spread of weapons of mass destruction. The successful transformation of the U.S.-India relationship will have a decisive and positive influence on the future international system as it evolves in this new century.

Reviewing the progress made in deepening the global partnership between the United States and India since their Joint Statement of July 18, 2005, the President and the Prime Minister reaffirm their commitment to expand even further the growing ties between their two countries. Consistent with this objective, the two leaders wish to highlight efforts the United States and India are making together in the following areas, where they have:

For Economic Prosperity and Trade

(1) Agreed to intensify efforts to develop a bilateral business climate supportive of trade and investment by:
1. Welcoming the report of the U.S.-India CEO Forum, agreeing to consider its recommendations aimed at substantially broadening our bilateral economic relations, and directing the

Chairs of the Indo-U.S. Economic Dialogue to follow up expeditiously with the CEO Forum;
2. Endorsing the efforts of the U.S.-India Trade Policy Forum to reduce barriers to trade and investment with the goal of doubling bilateral trade in three years;
3. Agreeing to advance mutually beneficial bilateral trade and investment flows by holding a high-level public-private investment summit in 2006, continuing efforts to facilitate and promote foreign direct investment and eliminate impediments to it, and enhancing bilateral consultations on various issues including tariff and non-tariff barriers to trade in goods and services, and preventing the illicit use of the financial system.

(2) Sought to expand cooperation in agriculture by:
1. Launching the Knowledge Initiative on Agriculture with a three-year financial commitment to link our universities, technical institutions, and businesses to support agriculture education, joint research, and capacity building projects including in the area of biotechnology.
2. Endorsing an agreed workplan to promote bilateral trade in agriculture through agreements that: lay out a path to open the U.S. market to Indian mangoes, recognize India as having the authority to certify that shipments of Indian products to the United States meet USDA organic standards, and provide for discussions on current regulations affecting trade

in fresh fruits and vegetables, poultry and dairy, and almonds.

(3) Reaffirmed their shared commitment to completing the WTO Doha Development Agenda (DDA) before the end of 2006, and agreed to work together to help achieve this outcome.

For Energy Security and a Clean Environment

(1) Welcomed the successful completion of discussions on India's separation plan and looked forward to the full implementation of the commitments in the July 18, 2005 Joint Statement on nuclear cooperation. This historic accomplishment will permit our countries to move forward towards our common objective of full civil nuclear energy cooperation between India and the United States and between India and the international community as a whole.

(2) Welcomed the participation of India in the ITER initiative on fusion energy as an important further step towards the common goal of full nuclear energy cooperation.

(3) Agreed on India's participation in FutureGen, an international public-private partnership to develop new, commercially viable technology for a clean coal near-zero emission power project. India will contribute funding to the project and participate in the Government Steering Committee of this initiative.

(4) Welcomed the creation of the Asia Pacific Partnership on Clean Development and Climate, which will enable India and the U.S. to work together with other countries in the region to pursue sustainable development and meet increased energy needs while addressing concerns of energy security and climate change. The Partnership will collaborate to promote the development, diffusion, deployment and transfer of cleaner, cost-effective and more efficient technologies and practices.

(5) Welcomed India's interest in the Integrated Ocean Drilling Program, an international marine research endeavor that will contribute to long-term energy solutions such as gas hydrates.

(6) Noting the positive cooperation under the Indo-U.S. Energy Dialogue, highlighted plans to hold joint conferences on topics such as energy efficiency and natural gas, to conduct study missions on renewable energy, to establish a clearing house in India for coal-bed methane/coal-mine methane, and to exchange energy market information.

For Innovation and the Knowledge Economy

(1) Emphasizing the importance of knowledge partnerships, announced the establishment of a Bi-National Science and Technology Commission which the U.S. and India will co-fund. It will generate collaborative partnerships in science and technology and promote industrial research and development.

(2) Agreed that the United States and India would work together to promote innovation, creativity and technological advancement by providing a vibrant intellectual property rights regime, and to cooperate in the field of intellectual property rights to include capacity building activities, human resource development and public awareness programs.

(3) Agreed to continue exploring further cooperation in civil space, including areas such as space exploration, satellite navigation, and earth science. The United States and India committed to move forward with agreements that will permit the launch of U.S. satellites and satellites containing U.S. components by Indian space launch vehicles, opening up new opportunities for commercial space cooperation between the two countries.

(4) Welcomed the inclusion of two U.S. instruments in the Indian lunar mission Chandrayaan-1. They noted that memoranda of understanding to be signed by ISRO and NASA would be significant steps forward in this area.

(5) Welcomed the U.S. Department of Commerce's plan to create a license exception for items that would otherwise require an export license to end-users in India engaged solely in civilian activities.

For Global Safety and Security

(1) Noted the enhanced counter-terrorism cooperation between the two countries and stressed that terrorism is a global scourge that must be fought and rooted out in every part of the world.

(2) Welcomed the increased cooperation between the United States and India in the defense area, since the New Framework for the U.S.-India Defence Relationship was signed on June 28, 2005, as evidenced by successful joint exercises, expanded defence cooperation and information sharing, and greater opportunities to jointly develop technologies and address security and humanitarian issues.

(3) Reaffirmed their commitment to the protection of the free flow of commerce and to the safety of navigation, and agreed to the conclusion of a Maritime Cooperation Framework to enhance security in the maritime domain, to prevent piracy and other transnational crimes at sea, carry out search and rescue operations, combat marine pollution, respond to natural disasters, address emergent threats and enhance cooperative capabilities, including through logistics support. Both sides are working to finalize a Logistics Support Agreement at the earliest.

(4) Welcomed India's intention to join the Container Security Initiative aimed at making global maritime trade and infrastructure more secure and reducing the risk of shipping containers being used to conceal weapons of mass destruction.

(5) Reiterated their commitment to international efforts to prevent the proliferation of weapons of mass destruction.

(6) Building on the July 2005 Disaster Relief Initiative, noted the important disaster management cooperation and their improved capabilities to respond to disaster situations.

(7) Recognized the importance of capacity building in cyber security and greater cooperation to secure their growing electronic interdependencies, including to protect electronic transactions and critical infrastructure from cybercrime, terrorism and other malicious threats.

Deepening Democracy and Meeting International Challenges

(1) Recalled their joint launch of the UN Democracy Fund in September 2005 and offered the experience and expertise of both Governments for capacity building, training and exchanges to third countries that request such assistance to strengthen democratic institutions.

(2) Welcomed the decision of India and the United States to designate a representative to the Government Advisory Board of the International Centre for Democratic Transition (ICDT) located in Budapest to facilitate cooperative activities with ICDT.

(3) Agreed that the Virtual Coordination and Information Centres set up in September 2005 should be further strengthened and a bilateral meeting aimed at developing a practical programme for utilization of its services be held soon.

(4) Expressed satisfaction at the expedited USFDA drug approval processes that strengthen the combat against HIV/AIDS at the global level and encourage greater corporate participation to meet this challenge, including the establishment of the Indo-U.S. Corporate Fund for HIV/AIDS..

(5) Agreed to expand bilateral efforts and continue cooperation in the area of medical research and strengthen technical capacity in food and drug regulation in India as well as address the concern on avian influenza, including agreement to reach out to the private sector, develop regional communications strategies, and plan an in-region containment and response exercise. The President welcomed India's offer to host

the International Partnership on Avian and Pandemic Influenza meeting in 2007.

(6) Welcomed India's membership in the Coalition Against Wildlife Trafficking, a partnership through which we will collaborate in the fight against illegal trade in wildlife and wildlife parts; we also welcome the opportunity to strengthen longstanding work together on the conservation of wild-life through cooperation on park management and ecotourism.

President Bush thanked Prime Minister Singh and the people of India for the warmth of their reception and the generosity of their hospitality.

NOTE: An original was not available for verification of the content of this joint statement.

Joint Statement Between the United States of America and India on Trade
March 2, 2006

India and the United States agree that trade is essential to promoting global economic growth, development, freedom and prosperity.

We fully share the goal of completing the WTO Doha Development Agenda (DDA) before the end of 2006, and agree to work in partnership to help achieve this outcome.

During our discussions, we agreed to meet the task with ambition, determination and a readiness to contribute, consistent with our roles in global trade, and to keep the development dimension in focus. The system of trading rules to which our two great democracies have contributed immensely must be strengthened. Towards this global cause, we recommit ourselves and invite all key participants to demonstrate their leadership.

We agree that a successful Round depends upon progress in all areas of the negotiations if we are to meet our goal of promoting development through trade. We are committed to a DDA result consistent with the mandates already agreed that realize a substantial outcome in all three pillars of the agriculture negotiations (domestic support, export competition and market access); significant improvements in market opportunities in manufacturing and services; and appropriate disciplines, including transparency of regulatory practices in services. We also believe we should strengthen the rules that facilitate trade, where we have jointly made proposals. Work in all these areas must go hand in hand.

We agree to pursue an ambitious agenda for the first half of 2006, consistent with the important milestones that were set at the Hong Kong Ministerial for agriculture, manufacturing, services and other issues, and continuing to press for the goal of concluding the negotiations by the end of 2006.

We will continue to work to promote reform, respond to the concerns of developing countries, and create opportunities for growth for all. We are building the trading system of the future, where progressive liberalization and reform result in improvement in standards of living for all, in particular for the millions of poor across the developing world.

While working for a successful Doha Round, we also reaffirm our commitment to strengthen and deepen bilateral trading ties. We note with satisfaction the successful implementation of our initiative to create the U.S.-India Trade Policy Forum and the CEO Forum to this end, and in particular the achievements in the areas of agricultural trade, investment, trade in services, the reduction of tariff and non-tariff barriers to trade, and spurring innovation and creativity. We agree to promote innovation, creativity and technological advancement by providing a vibrant intellectual property rights regime. As two dynamic economies with many complementary interests, the U.S. and India will seek to enhance bilateral trade and investment ties by expanding private sector contacts, dismantling barriers to trade, building trade capacities and strengthening trade-promoting institutions.

NOTE: An original was not available for verification of the content of this joint statement.

Statement on Senate Passage of PATRIOT Act Reauthorization Legislation
March 2, 2006

I applaud the Senate for voting to renew the PATRIOT Act and overcoming the partisan attempts to block its passage. The terrorists have not lost the will or the ability to attack us. The PATRIOT Act is vital to the war on terror and defending our citizens against a ruthless enemy. This bill will allow our law enforcement officials to continue to use the same tools against terrorists that are already used against drug dealers and other criminals, while safeguarding the civil liberties of the American people.

Remarks at a State Dinner Hosted by President Abdul Kalam of India in New Delhi
March 2, 2006

Mr. President, Prime Minister, and distinguished guests, Laura and I thank you for such a warm welcome. Thank you for this wonderful dinner tonight. We're grateful for your hospitality, and we appreciate the opportunity to visit your beautiful country.

India is home to a proud civilization. Thousands of years ago, the people of this region built great cities, established trading routes with distant lands, and created wonders of art and architecture. Its reputation for wealth and wisdom attracted many brave explorers, one of them never did complete his journey, and he ended up in America.

Like India, America respects faith and family and is rich in diversity. Americans are proud that our Nation is home to more than 2 million individuals of Indian decent. Both our nations can take pride in their achievements. People from India serve with distinction in American businesses, in the sciences, and the arts. The contributions of our Indian American community have made America a better nation, and they've helped strengthen our ties with India.

The relationship between our two nations is strong, and it rests on a firm foundation. We share common interests rooted in common belief that freedom can change lives and transform nations. Today, our two democracies have formed a strategic partnership to bring the benefits of liberty to others, to expand global prosperity through free and fair trade, and to confront the challenges of our time. As great nations, we now have an opportunity to lead, and America values the leadership of the great nation of India.

Mr. President, again, Laura and I express our deepest heartfelt thanks. It's my honor now to toast to you, sir, and to the great nation of India.

NOTE: The President spoke at 8:45 p.m. at the Rashtrapati Bhavan. In his remarks, he referred to Prime Minister Manmohan Singh of India.

Remarks in a Discussion With Business Students in Hyderabad, India
March 3, 2006

The President. Thank you for the warm welcome. You know, as a Harvard Business School graduate, this isn't exactly how I went to class when I was there, but I am honored to be here at ISB.

Yesterday I had the honor of standing on the stage with your Prime Minister, talking about a new relationship between the United States and India. I am excited about our strategic partnership. I'm equally excited about the future of India. It is in the interest of the United States to be friends with India; it's in the interest of the United States to work for free and fair trade with India; it's in the interest of the United States that an entrepreneurial class grow in this great country. It's in the interest of India that an entrepreneurial class grow in this great country so that people can realize dreams and find good jobs.

You know, I said something really interesting—I thought interesting, otherwise, I wouldn't have said it—the other day in a speech I gave in Washington. There are—the middle class of India is 300 million people large. That's larger than the entire United States. And when America looks at India, America ought to look at India as a strategic partner in keeping the peace, a great democracy which is capable of having people from different religions live side by side in peace and harmony, and a wonderful opportunity to—with whom to trade.

One of the things that you can judge a country by is the vitality of the youth, and one of the reasons I really wanted to come to ISB was because I understand it's the center of excellence in education. It's a new school that is using innovative techniques to give people the tools necessary to succeed.

Yesterday I met with some Indian CEOs and American CEOs—kind of the old folks. Today I'm meeting with the CEOs of tomorrow, the people that are going to help drive this great engine of economic prosperity for India—for the good of the world, is how I view it.

And so thanks for letting me and the Ambassador come. Ambassador, thanks for setting this up. I want to thank Chairman Gupta, a fellow Harvard Business School graduate, who helped form this school. I want to thank the dean of this school, as well as the professors and faculty for being here as well, and the rest of the students—thanks for letting me come by to say hello. I think it would be interesting for you to tell me what's on your mind or ask me questions, the whole purpose of which is to help, kind of, foster this partnership that is developing on the political level so that people in my own country can see that there's folks just like themselves here in India working to realize dreams and create opportunities.

So whoever would like to begin, we can start. And if not, I'm just going to call on somebody—like you. [*Laughter*]

Globalization/Trade With India

Q. I guess I'll do the honors. Thank you for being here. I didn't graduate from ISB, but it seems like a great place. I graduated from Carnegie Melon in Pittsburgh.

The President. That's also a good place. [*Laughter*] I will tell you something: She's really smart—to go there. [*Laughter*] You don't go there unless you're smart. [*Laughter*]

Q. Anyways, so I'm from the IT industry, so let me ask a question relating to that—not just IT, I guess generally outsourcing. So India and China have experienced a lot of growth because of globalization and outsourcing, in general—IT outsourcing, in particular. And I live in the U.S., so I know that there is a lot of resistance in the media and also in the industry about outsourcing. But as entrepreneurs and as people who believe in capitalism, we feel that there's no other way to go but capitalism and globalization and outsourcing, et cetera. So does the government or—does it have a political strategy on how to manage, do a balancing act?

The President. I appreciate it. First of all, what do you do?

Q. I have a IT consulting company.

The President. Okay. One of the—the future of any country is to make sure women have got opportunity, and so I congratulate you for being a CEO.

Q. Thank you.

The President. By the way, I've got a strong woman who travels with me in the Secretary of State. [*Laughter*] I'm not trying to avoid your question, by the way. [*Laughter*]

People do lose jobs as a result of globalization, and it's painful for those who lose jobs. But the fundamental question is, how does a government or society react to that? And it's basically one of two ways. One is to say, "Losing jobs is painful; there-

fore, let's throw up protectionist walls." And the other is to say, "Losing jobs is painful, so let's make sure people are educated so they can find—fill the jobs of the 21st century." And let's make sure that there's progrowth economic policies in place. Now, what does that mean? That means low taxes; it means less regulation; it means fewer lawsuits; it means wise energy policy.

So I've taken the position—I've taken it as recently as my State of the Union, where I said, the United States of America will reject protectionism. We won't fear competition; we welcome competition. But we won't fear the future, either, because we intend to shape it through good policies.

And that's how you deal with in a global economy. You don't retrench and pull back. You welcome competition, and you understand globalization provides great opportunities. And the classic opportunity for our American farmers and entrepreneurs and small businesses to understand, there's a 300-million-person market of middle-class citizens here in India, and that if we can make a product they want, then it becomes—at a reasonable price—and then all of a sudden, people will be able to have a market here. And so—and people in America should, I hope, maintain their confidence about the future.

Thanks for the question. Good luck to you.

Yes, ma'am.

India-U.S. Relations/Investment

Q. I actually went to Wellesley College, and I'm actually a student at the ISB.

The President. Let me say something before you ask the question. One of the most important things for America is to make sure our universities and colleges are accessible to Indian students, because I find it really interesting the first two questioners have gone to school in the United States. There can be, sometimes, perceptions about our country that simply aren't the truth but, nevertheless, become stuck in people's minds. And one way to defeat those perceptions is to welcome people to the United States so you can see firsthand our good side and our bad side, and you can draw your own conclusions without being told what to think.

Sorry to interrupt.

Q. No problem. This is actually related to the point you just made about the market with the 300 million people. I actually run the non-profit club and social enterprise club here at the ISB, with a lot of help from the faculty from the Center of Entrepreneurship and the student body. And we're a fairly active group who are very—who believe in what we call compassionate capitalism, through providing for venture capital funding for the small businesses and social entrepreneurs so that they can innovate and actually self-sustain themselves by providing affordable goods and using a market-based model, rather than the traditional aid-based model.

So my question to you, Mr. President, is what do you feel and how do you feel that your Government will support India in this sort of bilateral partnership, whereby your investors can get a financial return, as well as create social impact in a developing country such as India?

The President. Well, there's two types of investments. One is private capital, which goes to places where people think they can get a reasonable return relative to risk. And Government can help assuage some concerns about risk by having transparency in policy, consistent law. One of the things you don't want to do is invest in a country, and then all of a sudden, laws change—or transparency into why people make decisions, or less bureaucratic hurdles in order to invest.

People look around at places to invest. In my country, for example, there's competition between the States. And if they see there's a lot of bureaucratic hurdles you have to get over in order to invest in one State versus another, people tend

to mitigate risk in order to maximize return.

There's also public investment, and through USAID and other aspects of our State Department, we do provide microfinancing—small loans to entrepreneurs.

Today I went over to the Agricultural Center and saw some of the benefits of not only good agricultural research but the concept of microloans to encourage entrepreneurship, particularly amongst women in rural India. And it's an effective program. And microloans have worked around the world.

And so one of the things we do through our State Department—ably led by Secretary Rice, I want you to know—is to encourage microloan financing.

Yes, sir.

Civilian Nuclear Power Program in India

Q. Yes, Mr. President. My company is based in the U.S., and we deal mostly with electronic components, exports to India. My question is, after this nuclear deal, do you think the same thing will come in electronics field? Like there are a lot of sanctions, export restrictions on shipping components to India. That same product they can buy at—they pay more, but they get it from Europe where there's no export restrictions.

The President. We're constantly reviewing what's called the Export Control List. And I thank you for bringing that up. And obviously, as this relationship changes, as a strategic partner, the folks involved with the Export Control List will be taking that into account.

Yesterday's energy agreement was an important agreement. It's important for the United States, and it's important for India. It's important for the United States because—in that we live in a global energy market when a fast-growing country like India consumes more fossil fuels, it causes the price of fossil fuels to go up not only in India but around the world, including the United States. And therefore, the extent to which we can help nations develop civilian nuclear power is in the nation's interest.

Secondly, India has been an excellent partner in nonproliferation over the past decades, and therefore, I can tell the American people that this is a important agreement to help deal with the proliferation issue.

For India, it makes sense because it will enable India to be able to meet electricity needs in a way that doesn't pollute the air. The United States and India and China must use technologies to do our duty to not only make sure our economies expand but also to be good stewards of the environment. And nuclear energy is a renewable source of energy in which there is zero greenhouse gases.

Yesterday was a—as I mentioned to you in our private meeting, yesterday was a way to put the cold war behind us and to move forward as strategic partners. And I want to congratulate your Prime Minister and the Indian Government for its—for working with me and our Government to show the world what's possible when people can come together and think strategically.

Yes, sir.

India-U.S. Relations

Q. Mr. President, I did my MBA in hospitality from Johnson and Wales, Rhode Island, and I loved every bit of it. I saw your speech on the Asia Society, and I thought it was very spectacular.

The President. Thank you. You can leave it right there. [*Laughter*] No, go ahead.

Q. My question is, India was never this important. Why has it become so important now?

The President. That's a really good question. I think India has always been an important country, but the problem is, international politics made it very difficult for previous Presidents and previous Prime Ministers to reach common agreement. As I said, we're getting rid of the cold war, and the truth of the matter is, the cold war caused the world to become pretty well divided. And if you're on one side of the divide, it was politically difficult to work with people on the other side of the divide.

That began to change, of course. And so I wouldn't say that India was not an important country up to now, because it was.

[*At this point, the public portion of the event concluded.*]

NOTE: The President spoke at 12:38 p.m. at the Indian School of Business. In his remarks, he referred to Prime Minister Manmohan Singh of India; U.S. Ambassador to India David C. Mulford; Rajat Gupta, chairman, and M. Rammohan Rao, dean, Indian School of Business. A portion of these remarks could not be verified because the tape was incomplete.

Remarks in New Delhi
March 3, 2006

Thank you. Thank you. Please be seated. Distinguished guests, *namaste*. Laura and I have been looking forward to this visit for a long time, and we're delighted to be in India.

Over the past 2 days, we've been grateful for your kind reception, touched by your warm hospitality, and dazzled by this vibrant and exciting land. I appreciate the opportunity to speak to the Indian people. I'm honored to bring the good wishes and the respect of the world's oldest democracy to the world's largest democracy.

Tonight we stand on the ruins of an ancient city that was the capital of an Indian kingdom thousands of years ago. Today, it is part of a modern Asian city that is the capital of one of the world's great nations. At the heart of a civilization that helped give the world mathematics, cutting-edge businesses now give us the technology of tomorrow. In the birthplace of great religions, a billion souls of varied faiths now live side by side in freedom and peace. When you come to India in the 21st century, you're inspired by the past, and you can see the future.

India in the 21st century is a natural partner of the United States because we are brothers in the cause of human liberty. Yesterday I visited a memorial to Mahatma Gandhi and read the peaceful words of a fearless man. His words are familiar in my country because they helped move a generation of Americans to overcome the injustice of racial segregation. When Martin Luther King arrived in Delhi in 1959, he said to other countries, "I may go as a tourist, but to India, I come as a pilgrim." I come to India as a friend.

For many years, the United States and India were kept apart by the rivalries that divided the world. That's changed. Our two great democracies are now united by opportunities that can lift our people and by threats that can bring down all our progress. The United States and India, separated by half the globe, are closer than ever before, and the partnership between our free nations has the power to transform the world.

The partnership between the United States and India has deep and sturdy roots in the values we share. Both our nations were founded on the conviction that all people are created equal and are endowed with certain fundamental rights, including freedom of speech, freedom of assembly, and freedom of religion. Those freedoms are enshrined in law through our written constitutions, and they are upheld daily by institutions common to both our democracies: an elected legislature, an independent judiciary, a loyal political opposition, and as I know well here in India, a lively free press.

In both our countries, democracy is more than a form of government; it is the central promise of our national character. We believe that every citizen deserves equal liberty and justice, because we believe that every life has equal dignity and value. We believe all societies should welcome people of every culture, ethnicity, and religion. And because of this enduring commitment, the United States and India have overcome trials in our own history. We're proud to stand together among the world's great democracies.

The partnership between the United States and India begins with democracy, and it does not end there. Our people share a devotion to family, a passion for learning, a love of the arts, and much more. The United States is the proud home of more than 2 million Americans of Indian descent, a figure that has more than tripled over the last 20 years. America is honored to welcome 500,000 Indian tourists and businesspeople to our country each year. And we benefit from 80,000 Indian students at our universities, more than we have from any other nation. Indian Americans have made tremendous contributions to my country in technology and medicine and business and countless other fields.

When I meet with the United States Congress, I talked to a brilliant Indian American who represents the State of Louisiana. I've returned the salute of Indian Americans who defend my nation in battle as members of the United States Armed Forces. And on a sad morning 3 years ago, we learned that a brave astronaut born in India had been lost aboard the space shuttle *Columbia*. I know that India will always be proud of Dr. Kalpana Chawla, and so will the United States of America.

Americans are spending more time in India as well, and it's easy to see why.

India is rich in history, culture, and activities—from the mountains of Delhi to the holy sites of Varanasi to the studios of Bollywood. Today I met with a fascinating group of students and farmers and entrepreneurs in Hyderabad—plus it was exciting to be in the hometown of Sania Mirza. To encourage more travel and more contact between our people, the United States intends to open a new consulate in Hyderabad. We'll also build a new, state-of-the-art American Center here in Delhi. By taking these steps, we'll continue to strengthen the ties between our two countries, our two democracies.

At the start of this young century, the United States of America and the Republic of India are working together to achieve two great purposes: to expand the circle of prosperity and development across the world and to defeat our common enemies by advancing the just and noble cause of human freedom.

Our first great purpose is to spread prosperity and opportunity to people in our own land, to millions who have not known it. The freedom that sustains India's democracy is now bringing dramatic changes to India's economy. Thanks to your country's wise economic reforms and advances in technology, unprecedented opportunities are coming to India, and you are seizing those opportunities.

India's innovative people have begun to look outward and connect to the global economy as never before. Today, India has more cell phones than land-line phones. And all that separates a business in Bangalore from a business in Boston is an e-mail, a text message, or video conference. Indian entrepreneurs have used these new connections to meet the demands of consumers and businesses all across the globe. As a result, your economy has more than doubled in size since you opened up your markets in 1991. And you've dramatically raised the living standards of your citizens. India's middle class now numbers 300 million people, more than the entire population of the United States.

America welcomes India's economic rise, because we understand that as other nations prosper, it creates more opportunity for us all. In a free economy, every citizen has something to contribute. That is why trade is such a powerful engine of prosperity and upward mobility. When markets are opened and the poor are given a chance to develop their talents and abilities, they can create a better life for their families, they add to the wealth of the world, and they can begin to afford goods and services from other nations. Free and fair trade is good for India, it's good for America, and it is good for the world.

In my countries, some focus only on one aspect of our trade relationship with India, outsourcing. It's true that some Americans have lost jobs when their companies moved operations overseas. It's also important to remember that when someone loses a job, it's an incredibly difficult period for the worker and their families. Some people believe the answer to this problem is to wall off our economy from the world through protectionist policies. I strongly disagree. My Government is helping Americans who have lost their jobs get new skills for new careers. And we're helping to create millions of new jobs in both our countries by embracing the opportunities of a global economy.

We see those opportunities here in India. Americans who come to this country will see Indian consumers buying McCurry meals from McDonald's, home appliances from Whirlpool. They will see Indian businesses buying American products, like the 68 planes that Air India recently ordered from Boeing. They will also see American businesses like General Electric and Microsoft and Intel, who are in India to learn about the needs of local customers and do vital research that makes their products more competitive in world markets. The United States will not give into the protectionists and lose these opportunities. For the sake of workers in both our countries, America will trade with confidence.

India has responsibilities as well. India needs to continue to lift its caps on foreign investment, to make its rules and regulations more transparent, and to continue to lower its tariffs and open its markets to American agricultural products, industrial goods and services. We also hope India will continue to work to ensure that its own people are treated fairly by enforcing laws that protect children and workers from trafficking and exploitation and abuse. By enforcing its laws and educating its people and continuing to open up its economy, India can assure that prosperity and opportunity of a growing economy reaches all segments of India's population.

The world also needs India's leadership to open up global markets. The Doha round of trade talks at the World Trade Organization provides the greatest opportunity to lift hundreds of millions of people out of poverty and boost economic growth in both our countries. The United States has been pushing for an ambitious agreement on services and manufacturing and agriculture. Prime Minister Singh and I share the goal of completing the Doha round by the end of this year, and we'll work together to achieve this goal. By completing Doha, we will help build a world that lives in liberty and trades in freedom and grows in prosperity, and America and India will lead the way.

By leading together, America and India can meet other global challenges. And one of the biggest is energy. Like America, India's growing economy requires growing amounts of electricity. And the cleanest and most reliable way to meet that need is through civilian nuclear power.

Last summer in Washington, America and India reached an agreement to share civilian nuclear technology and to bring India's civilian nuclear programs under the safeguards of the International Atomic Energy Agency. In our meetings this week, Prime Minister Singh and I agreed on a

plan to implement this historic initiative. Our agreement will strengthen the security and the economy of both our nations.

By applying the most advanced technology and international standards to India's civilian nuclear program, we will increase safety and reduce the risk of proliferation. And by helping India meet its energy needs, we will take the pressure off the price of fossil fuels for consumers in India and America and around the world. We'll help India be good stewards of our environment, and we will strengthen the bonds of trust between our two great nations.

America and India are also cooperating closely in agriculture. The United States worked with India to help meet its food needs in the 1960s, when pioneering American scientists like Norman Borlaug shared agricultural technology with Indian farmers. Thanks to your hard work, you have nearly tripled your food production over the past half-century. To build on this progress, Prime Minister Singh and I are launching a new Agricultural Knowledge Initiative. This initiative will invest $100 million to encourage exchanges between American and Indian scientists and promote joint research to improve farming technology. By working together, the United States and India will develop better ways to grow crops and get them to market and lead a second Green Revolution.

America and India are pursuing an historic agenda for cooperation in many other areas. We're working together to improve education and conservation and natural disaster response. We're cooperating closely in science and technology. And to promote the ties between American and Indian scientists, we're establishing a new $30 million science and technology commission that will fund joint research in promising areas like biotechnology.

We're working to improve health by confronting the threat of avian flu, reducing the spread of malaria and tuberculosis, and eliminating polio in India. Our nations also share the global challenge of HIV/AIDS. India must confront this challenge directly, openly, and at all levels of society. And as you do, America will be your partner in turning the tide against this terrible disease.

The United States and India have ambitious goals for our partnership. We have unprecedented opportunities in this world. We can look to the future with confidence because our relationship has never been better. America and India are global leaders, and we are good friends. And when we work together, there is no limit to what we can achieve.

The second great purpose is to confront the threats of our time by fighting terror and advancing freedom across the globe. Both our nations have known the pain of terror on our home soil. On September the 11th, 2001, nearly 3,000 innocent people were murdered in my country, including more than 30 who were born in India. Just over 3 months ago, terrorists struck the Parliament House here in Delhi, an attack on the heart of Indian democracy.

In both our countries, people have struggled to understand the reason for terrorist assaults on free societies. We've begun to learn some of the answers. The terrorists are followers of a violent ideology that calls for the murder of Christians and Hindus and Sikhs and Jews and vast numbers of Muslims who do not share their radical views.

The terrorists' goal is to impose a hateful vision that denies all political and religious freedom. Those terrorists lack the military strength to challenge great nations directly, so they use the weapon of fear. When terrorists murder innocent office workers in New York or kill shoppers at a market in Delhi or blow up commuters in London, they hope these horrors will break our will. They target democracies because they think we are weak, and they think we can be frightened into retreat. The terrorists have misunderstood our countries. America and

India love our freedom, and we will fight to keep it.

When your Prime Minister addressed the United States Congress, he said this: "We must fight terrorism wherever it exists, because terrorism anywhere threatens democracy everywhere." He is right. And so America and India are allies in the war against terror.

After the attacks of September the 11th, the Indian Navy provided vital support to Operation Enduring Freedom by relieving American ships securing the Strait of Malacca, and we thank the Indian Navy. Today, our nations are cooperating closely on critical areas like bioterrorism and airport security and cyber security. Our military cooperation is stronger than ever before. America and India are in this war together, and we will win this war together.

In the long run, the United States and India understand that winning the war on terror requires changing the conditions that give rise to terror. History shows us the way. From the East to West, we've seen that only one force is powerful enough to replace hatred with hope, and that is the force of human freedom. Free societies do not harbor terrorists or breed resentment. Free societies respect the rights of their citizens and their neighbors. Free societies are peaceful societies.

As your first Prime Minister, Prime Minister Nehru, once said: "Evil flourishes far more in the shadows than in the light of day." Together, America and India will bring the light of freedom to the darkest corners of our Earth.

Nearly 60 years have passed since India mounted a courageous fight for a free country of your own. The American people stood with you in the struggle for freedom. President Franklin Roosevelt was one of the first world leaders to support India's independence. Through the decades, India has built a strong democracy in which people from different faiths live together in freedom and peace.

India has a Hindu majority and one of the world's largest Muslim populations. India is also home to millions of Sikhs and Christians and other religious groups. All worship freely in temples and mosques and churches all across this great land. Indians of diverse backgrounds attend school together and work together and govern your nation together. As a multiethnic, multireligious democracy, India is showing the world that the best way to ensure fairness and tolerance is to establish the rule of law. The best way to counter resentment is to allow peaceful expression. The best way to honor human dignity is to protect human rights. For every nation divided by race, religion, or culture, India offers a hopeful path. If justice is the goal, then democracy is the way.

The world has benefited from the example of India's democracy. And now the world needs India's leadership in freedom's cause. As a global power, India has an historic duty to support democracy around the world. In Afghanistan, which I just visited on Wednesday, the world is beginning to see what India's leadership can accomplish. Since the Taliban was removed from power, India has pledged $565 million to help the Afghan people to get back on their feet. Your country has trained National Assembly staff, developing a similar program for the Assembly's elected leaders. You recently announced that you'll provide an additional $50 million to help the Afghans complete their National Assembly building. After so many years of suffering, the Afghan people are reclaiming a future of hope and freedom, and they will always remember that in their hour of need, India stood with them.

India is also showing its leadership in the cause of democracy by cofounding the Global Democracy Initiative. Prime Minister Singh and I were proud to be the first two contributors to this initiative to promote democracy and development across the world. Now India can build on this commitment by working directly with

nations where democracy is just beginning to emerge. As the world's young democracies take shape, India offers a compelling example of how to preserve a country's unique culture and history while guaranteeing the universal freedoms that are the foundation of genuine democracies.

India's leadership is needed in a world that is hungry for freedom. Men and women from North Korea to Burma to Syria to Zimbabwe to Cuba yearn for their liberty. In Iran, a proud people is held hostage by a small clerical elite that denies basic liberties, sponsors terrorism, and pursues nuclear weapons. Our nations must not pretend that the people of these countries prefer their own enslavement. We must stand with reformers and dissidents and civil society organizations and hasten the day when the people of these nations can determine their own future and choose their own leaders. These people may not gain their liberty overnight, but history is on their side.

Tonight I will leave India to travel to Pakistan, another important partner and friend of the United States. There was a time when America's good relations with Pakistan would have been a source of concern here in India. That day's passed. India is better off because America has a close relationship with Pakistan, and Pakistan is better off because America has a close relation with India. On my trip to Islamabad, I will meet with President Musharraf to discuss Pakistan's vital cooperation in the war on terror and our efforts to foster economic and political development so we can reduce the appeal of radical Islam. I believe that a prosperous, democratic Pakistan will be a steadfast partner for America, a peaceful neighbor for India, and a force for freedom and moderation in the Arab world.

The advance for freedom is the great story of our time. In 1945, just 2 years before India achieved independence, there were fewer than two dozen democracies on Earth. Today, there are more than 100, and democracies are developing and thriving from Asia to Africa to Eastern Europe to Latin America. The whole world can see that freedom is not an American value or an Indian value; freedom is a universal value, and that is because the source of freedom is a power greater than our own. As Mahatma Ghandi said, "Freedom is the gift of God and the right of every nation." Let us remember those words as we head into the 21st century.

In a few days, I'll return to America, and I will never forget my time here in India. America is proud to call your democracy a friend. We're optimistic about your future. The great Indian poet Tagore once wrote, "There's only one history—the history of man." The United States and India go forward with faith in those words. There's only one history of man—and it leads to freedom.

May God bless India.

NOTE: The President spoke at 6:42 p.m. at the Purana Qila. In his remarks, he referred to Prime Minister Manmohan Singh of India; professional tennis player Sania Mirza; and President Pervez Musharraf of Pakistan.

Remarks Following Discussions With President Pervez Musharraf of Pakistan and an Exchange With Reporters in Islamabad, Pakistan
March 4, 2006

President Musharraf. With your permission, Mr. President—ladies and gentlemen, it's indeed a great day. It's our honor, it's a proud privilege for Pakistan to receive President Bush, Mrs. Laura Bush, the First Lady, and such a large delegation from the United States. We are extremely glad that this has happened and the President is in our midst.

In our discussions, first of all, I expressed Pakistan's deepest regrets on the very sad incident of the killing of a United States diplomat in Karachi. We know that it has been timed very viciously to vitiate the atmosphere during the President's visit, but I'm very glad and I'm extremely grateful to the President for showing understanding and showing also the resolve not to let such terrorist acts interfere in the normal process of our strategic cooperation.

I also expressed Pakistan's gratitude to the President for the assistance that we got in the relief operations and the reconstruction activity of the earthquake in our hour of need. I don't think without the assistance of the Chinooks of United States and the medical teams, the hospitals, that we could have met the challenges of the relief operation in the earthquake. And we look forward to increased involvement—or sustained involvement of United States in assisting us in the reconstruction activity. So, our extreme gratitude to United States.

Ladies and gentlemen, Pakistan and United States have always had a strategic partnership, a strategic relationships all along. Today with my interaction with the President, we have revived and maybe further strengthened this relationship. We have laid the foundations of a very strong, sustainable, broad-based, and a long-term relationship between Pakistan and United States. And this relationship includes, first of all, commencing our United States-Pakistan strategic dialog in an institutional manner, creating an institutional methodology of doing that, and talking of—within this, talking of trade and investment, talking of defense relationships, cooperation in education, and above all, cooperation in our fight against terrorism and extremism.

I did express my gratitude to the President also for his efforts towards resolution of disputes in the region, to bring peace into the region, and a special reference to the resolution of the Kashmir dispute. I did request the President to remain involved in facilitating a resolution of all disputes including, obviously, the Kashmir dispute.

Last of all, I did touch on the very thorny issue of the act, blasphemous act against our Prophet, peace be upon him. I did express the concerns of the Muslim world, in general, who condemn such acts and who reject the issue of justifying these acts in the name of freedom of press. May I say that the President did show concern, and I'm extremely grateful to him for showing concern toward the sentiments of the Muslim world.

In the end, I would like to say that, again, that I look forward to an era of cooperation, of strategic relationships with you, with the United States. And may I add on a personal note, I look forward to sustaining this great friendship that I have developed with you, personally, Mr. President. Thank you very much again for coming to Pakistan and doing us this honor of hosting. Thank you very much.

President Bush. Mr. President, thank you. Laura and I are really glad to be here, and we want to thank you and Ms. Musharraf for your hospitality. We do have a good friendship. It was displayed last night when I got off Air Force One and your daughter was there to greet us. And that was a really kind gesture, and I thank you very much for that. I particularly thank your daughter for coming out.

We've had a—we're going to have a full day. We've just had a lengthy one-on-one discussion about common interests. Then we invited members of our Government in to continue our discussion. I'll talk a little bit about the earthquake relief—I mean, the—yes, the earthquake relief in a minute. But I am looking forward to the meeting with a cross-section of Pakistani society, which will take place later on today, and I'm particularly interested in cricket. I understand you've lined up a little cricket

exhibition for us, and maybe I'll take the bat, I don't know. We'll see. [*Laughter*] I'm kind of getting old these days.

Mr. President and I reaffirmed our shared commitment to a broad and lasting strategic partnership. And that partnership begins with close cooperation in the war on terror. President Musharraf made a bold decision for his people and for peace, after September the 11th, when Pakistan chose to fight the terrorists. The American people appreciate your leadership, Mr. President, and so do I.

Pakistan has captured or killed hundreds of Al Qaida terrorists. Pakistan has lost brave citizens in this fight. We're grateful to all who have given their lives in this vital cause. We honor the Pakistanis who continue to risk their lives to confront the terrorists. This week's bombing in Karachi shows again the war on terror goes on. America mourns the loss of all killed in the attack. We send our condolences to the family of David Foy, and we send our condolences, as well, to the families of the Pakistanis who lost their lives. We're not going to back down in the face of these killers. We'll fight this war, and we will win this war together.

Pakistan is an important partner in fighting proliferation. Pakistan agreed to join the Container Security Initiative, an international effort to stop the spread of dangerous material shipments. And I thank you for that, Mr. President. We'll continue to work together to ensure that the world's most dangerous weapons do not end up in the hands of the terrorists.

We support democracy in Pakistan. President Musharraf understands that in the long run, the way to defeat terrorists is to replace an ideology of hatred with an ideology of hope. And I thank you for your extensive briefing today on your plans to spread freedom throughout your country. President Musharraf envisions a modern state that provides an alternative to radicalism.

The elections scheduled for 2007 are a great opportunity for Pakistan. The President understands these elections need to be open and honest. America will continue to working with Pakistan to lay the foundations of democracy. And I appreciate your commitment.

Pakistan and India now have an historic opportunity to work toward lasting peace. President Musharraf and Prime Minister Singh have shown themselves to be leaders of courage and vision. I was reflecting with the President how much the atmosphere has changed since I first became inaugurated as President. You think back to 2001 and 2002, there was a lot of tension, a lot of concern. And yet the President has stood up and led the process toward better understanding, better exchanges with India. I encourage all sides to continue to make progress on important issues, including Kashmir.

We're proud to help our Pakistani friends recover from the devastation of the earthquake. We just saw a film of the earthquake. It is staggering what the people of this country have been through. It is unbelievable how many people lost their lives, how many people have lost their homes. And we're proud to help. We're proud to help a great Pakistan military take the lead. We're proud to stand with the NGOs and those who deliver compassion as this country rebuilds. We stand by our commitment, our pledge of one-half billion dollars for recovery and reconstruction.

We're cooperating to strengthen our economies. I congratulate the Government on its strong economic growth. We are in the process of working on a bilateral investment treaty that will encourage foreign investment and more opportunity for the people of Pakistan. We strongly support the President's vision of a reconstruction opportunity zone in remote areas of Pakistan and Afghanistan. This vision means that products manufactured in those zones would be eligible for duty-free entry into the United States. And so we're working to create such zones.

Our idea is to continue to work with our strong friend and ally, work to keep the peace, to win the war on terror, to help the spread of democracy and freedom, and to encourage vital economic development.

Finally, we look forward to continuing to work with the President on his vision to make sure that education is spread throughout this country, particularly for young girls. President Musharraf briefed us on his education plans today, and they're farsighted, and they're visionary. The United States looks forward to helping you, sir, implement that vision.

All in all, it's an honor to be here. Thanks for your hospitality. I'm looking forward to taking some questions.

Kashmir/Pakistan-U.S. Relations

Q. Thank you, President Musharraf.

President Bush, in your address to the Asia Society, you talked about a strategic partnership with Pakistan, as did President Musharraf just now. And, of course, you just mentioned the bilateral investment treaty. Could you list some possible tangible milestones in forging this relationship and taking it forward? And also, on Kashmir, what are your perceptions on how this can be resolved, given that you've met both the leaders of Pakistan and India now? Thank you.

President Bush. The best way for Kashmir to be resolved is for leaders of both countries to step up and lead. And that's exactly what President Musharraf has done, and that's what Prime Minister Singh has assured me he wants to do, and that is to resolve this situation.

Obviously, there needs to be some confidence in order for the countries to go forward, and therefore, the confidence-building measures that the governments have taken is beginning to bear fruits, in my judgment—increased trade, increased transportation. I thought it was interesting that the Indians sent supplies immediately upon the devastating natural disaster. In other words, things are—the atmosphere is changing.

However, in order for a deal to get done, it requires commitment at the leadership level. And in my perspective, I've seen the commitment, and the role of the United States is to continue to encourage the parties to come together.

The first part of the question was tangible evidence. Well, part of the tangible evidence of our relationship is a half-a-billion-dollars commitment to help this country rebuild; it's the $66 million last year to help implement the President's education initiative. It is the idea of developing reconstruction zones—I mean, trade zones in remote areas so that goods manufactured in those zones can get duty-free access to the United States, on the theory that economic vitality and economic prosperity for people in the remote regions of Pakistan will help defeat the terrorists and their hateful ideology.

Sam Bodman is coming, our Secretary of Energy, to work with Pakistan on Pakistan's energy needs. There's a variety of things we can continue to cooperate on. Perhaps the most important one of all is to defeat these terrorists, some of whom are lodged here in Pakistan, some of whom have tried to kill your President. And close cooperation is needed to defeat them.

Terry Hunt [Terence Hunt, Associated Press].

War on Terror

Q. Thank you, Mr. President. Mr. President, what would you like to see President Musharraf do in the war on terrorism that he's not doing now? Is the United States getting the access and the help that it needs to go after Al Qaida and Usama bin Laden?

President Bush. There's a lot of work to be done in defeating Al Qaida. The President and I know that. We've spent a good while this morning talking about the work that needs to be done. The best way to defeat Al Qaida is to find—is to share good intelligence to locate them and then to be prepared to bring them to justice. So, one, the first question that I always ask is whether or not our intelligence sharing is good enough, and we're working on it to make sure it's good enough. Intelligence is gathered by—in a lot of different ways, but the key thing is that, one, it be actionable, and two, it be shared on a real-time basis.

Secondly, in order for Pakistan to defend herself from Al Qaida, she must have equipment necessary to move quickly, without tipping off the enemy. The President is training up special forces teams to do just that. And so while we do have a lot of work to be done, it's important that we stay on the hunt. Part of my mission today was to determine whether or not the President is as committed as he has been in the past to bringing these terrorists to justice, and he is. He understands the stakes; he understands the responsibility; and he understands the need to make sure our strategy is able to defeat the enemy.

Do you want to say something to that?

President Musharraf. May I add to this, with your permission—the first element that one needs to be very clear is the intentions. I think it's very clear that the intentions of Pakistan and my intentions are absolutely clear that we are a very strong— we have a strong partnership on the issue of fighting terrorism. So the intentions should be very clear.

Then we need to strategize. We have strategized. We have strategized how to deal with terrorism, and then strategized also on how to deal with extremism, which is very different from terrorism. So we have strategized both. Then we need to come forward to the implementation part. Now, the implementation has to be strong also, with all the resolve. We are doing that also. So if at all there are slippages, it is possible in the implementation part. But as long as the intention is clear, the resolve is there, and the strategy is clear, we are moving forward toward to delivering, and we will succeed. That is what I think. Yes.

Energy/Pakistan-U.S. Relations

Q. My question is to President Bush. President Bush, you've talked about a strategic relationship with Pakistan. You've also talked about helping Pakistan economically, and you just mentioned that the Energy Secretary is going to be visiting Pakistan. So Pakistan has some general energy needs, and in that respect, the Iran-Pakistan-India gas pipeline seems to have hit some problems because of the opposition from the United States. So what are some specific options that you have to address Pakistan's energy concerns? And are you working on offering Pakistan a civilian nuclear deal? Thank you.

President Bush. As I mentioned, Secretary of Energy Sam Bodman will be here to work with the Pakistan Government. Our beef with Iran is not the pipeline; our beef with Iran is the fact that they want to develop a nuclear weapon. And I believe a nuclear weapon in the hands of the Iranians would be very dangerous for all of us. It would endanger world peace. So we're working very hard to convince the Iranians to get rid of their nuclear ambitions.

As to the civilian nuclear program, first of all, I understand—the President brought this issue up with me—that Pakistan has got energy needs because of a growing economy. And he explained to me the natural gas situation here in the country. We understand you need to get natural gas in the region, and that's fine.

Secondly, we discussed a civilian nuclear program, and I explained that Pakistan and India are different countries with different needs and different histories. So, as we proceed forward, our strategy will take in effect those well-known differences.

Toby [Tabassum Zakaria, Reuters].

Democracy in Pakistan

Q. Mr. President——

President Bush. Which one?

Q. Both of you can address this. Some critics——

President Bush. Trying to get you a question. [*Laughter*]

Q. Some critics say that Pakistan is not moving quickly enough on democratic reforms. And moves towards democracy has been one of the hallmarks of your administration. How do you respond to critics who say you are holding back on pressing President Musharraf on moves toward democracy because of its help in the war on terrorism? And I would also ask——

President Bush. Well, we discussed—we spent a lot of time talking about democracy in Pakistan, and I believe democracy is Pakistan's future. And we share a strong commitment to democracy. I just mentioned in my opening address the idea of making sure the elections go forward in 2007, and I discussed that with the President. President Musharraf has made clear that he intends to hold elections—I'll let him speak for himself on this issue, but democracy has been definitely a part of our agenda here, as it should be.

Secondly, one of the things that the President is constantly talking about is the ways to defeat extremism. We're talking about making sure that we work closely to bring the terrorists to justice, but in the long run, he understands that extremism can be defeated by freedom and democracy and prosperity and better education. And we spent a lot of time strategizing on that subject today.

I'll let you speak for yourself on the subject, though, Mr. President.

President Musharraf. Unfortunately, we are accused a lot on not moving forward on democracy. But as I understand democracy, we are a—may I venture to tell you what we've done in line with democracy to introduce sustainable democracy in Pakistan. The first ingredient of democracy, I believe, is the empowerment of the people. We have empowered the people of Pakistan now—they were never empowered before—by introducing a local government system where we have given the destiny of their areas for development, for welfare, for progress in their own hands through financial, political, and administrative involvement.

It also—democracy also means empowerment of women. It is the first time that we have empowered the women of Pakistan, by giving them a say in the political milieu of Pakistan. Today, there are over 30,000 women in the political hierarchy of Pakistan. We have empowered the minorities of Pakistan for the first time. They have got a joint election system, where previously they had a separate election system. Therefore, they have been mainstreamed in that every person standing for elections has to go to the minorities to ask for their votes now. Therefore, they feel more a part of the Pakistani culture and Pakistan society.

Then we have empowered also—we have liberated the media and the press. If you see this press today sitting around here, and the media, previously there was only one Pakistan television. Today, there are dozens of channels. All these people sitting around are the result of my democratization of Pakistan, opening the Pakistan society of the media—the print media and the electronic media, both. And they're totally liberated.

And then, finally—obviously, this is to do with freedom of speech and freedom of expression. And then, finally, is the issue of their having the right to vote and elect their own people. And that is what we do. Today, the Senate, the National Assembly, the Provincial assemblies and the—of the

local government is there. And they've been voted through absolute—franchise in a free and fair manner.

So, therefore, may I say that we have introduced the essence of democracy now in Pakistan. It has been done now. It never—all these things never existed before. What maybe you are talking of is merely the label, which probably you are inferring on to my uniform. Indeed, and without saying that you are inferring to it, yes, indeed, that is an issue which needs to be addressed. And I will follow constitutional norms. Even now I am following constitutional norms where I have been allowed to wear this uniform until 2007—being in uniform as the President of Pakistan. Beyond 2007, yes, indeed, this is an issue which has to be addressed, and it has to be addressed according to the Constitution of Pakistan. And I will never violate the Constitution of Pakistan.

So let me assure you that democracy will prevail. Sustainable democracy has been introduced in Pakistan and will prevail in Pakistan, especially beyond 2007. Long answer.

President Bush. Yes. Good job—important answer.

President Musharraf. Thank you very much.

President Bush. Very good job. Thank you again, sir.

NOTE: The President spoke at 12:45 p.m. at the Aiwan-e-Sadr. In his remarks, he referred to Sehba Musharraf, wife, and Ayla Raza, daughter, of President Musharraf; David Foy, a U.S. State Department official who was killed in a terrorist attack in Karachi, Pakistan, on March 2; and Prime Minister Manmohan Singh of India.

Remarks Prior to Discussions With Members of the Community in Islamabad
March 4, 2006

Secretary Rice and Ambassador Crocker and I want to thank members from the civil society and Members of Parliament for joining us. My trip to Pakistan is a really important trip. Pakistan is a strategic partner and a friend of the United States.

I want to thank those of you who have come to share with me and the Secretary and the Ambassador your thoughts about how the United States can better work with the people of Pakistan.

One of the signs of a modern society is the empowerment of women. And I want to thank the women who have joined us here today to share your thoughts. And we've got the head of a bank; we've got a Member of Parliament; we've got educators, heads of NGOs, businesspeople, that are all here to help us better understand the Pakistan society and how we can better interrelate.

Part of becoming closer friends is to listen, listen to concerns and to share our thoughts on common values. So we really want to thank you for being here. And thank you for your gracious hospitality to your country.

NOTE: The President spoke at 3:25 p.m. at the U.S. Embassy.

Joint Statement by President George W. Bush and President Pervez Musharraf of Pakistan: United States-Pakistan Strategic Partnership
March 4, 2006

President Bush and President Musharraf have affirmed the long-term, strategic partnership between their two countries. In 2004, the United States acknowledged its aspirations for closer bilateral ties with Pakistan by designating Pakistan as a Major Non-NATO Ally. The U.S.-Pakistan strategic partnership is based on the shared interests of the United States and Pakistan in building stable and sustainable democracy and in promoting peace and security, stability, prosperity, and democracy in South Asia and across the globe.

The two leaders are determined to strengthen the foundation for a strong, stable, and enduring relationship. This will require a significant expansion of U.S.-Pakistan bilateral economic ties, including mutual trade and investment. As a key step in this direction the United States and Pakistan are making meaningful progress toward concluding a Bilateral Investment Treaty.

Both leaders commit to working together with Afghanistan to make Pakistan and Afghanistan a land bridge linking the economic potentials of South Asia and Central Asia.

The American people feel profound sympathy for the victims of the tragic earthquake that struck on October 8, 2005. President Bush reaffirmed the United States' determination to stand by the Pakistani people as they recover and rebuild.

President Bush and President Musharraf reaffirm their condemnation of terrorism in all its forms and manifestations. Following the September 11 attacks, the United States and Pakistan joined international efforts to fight the scourge of terrorism. President Bush is grateful for President Musharraf's strong and vital support in the war on terror. The two leaders underscored the need for a comprehensive strategy for addressing the threat of terrorism and extremism. President Bush and President Musharraf will continue to work together to address political injustice, poverty, corruption, ignorance, and hopelessness. They resolve to maintain their close counterterrorism cooperation and to increase their efforts to reduce the threat of terrorism regionally and internationally.

The two leaders recognize the need to promote tolerance, respect and mutual understanding, and inter-faith harmony to strengthen appreciation of the values and norms common to the world's religions and cultures. The two leaders acknowledge with appreciation the various international initiatives in this regard including President Musharraf's concept of Enlightened Moderation. The two leaders agreed that acts that disturb inter-faith harmony should be avoided.

President Bush and President Musharraf support the peace process and composite dialogue between Pakistan and India for improvement of relations and resolution of disputes and building a better future in South Asia.

Both leaders share concern about the threat to global stability posed by the proliferation of Weapons of Mass Destruction (WMD) and the threat of terrorist groups acquiring such weapons. President Bush and President Musharraf commit to play leading roles in international efforts to prevent the proliferation of WMD, their delivery systems, and related technology and expertise.

Strategic Dialogue

President Bush and President Musharraf are launching a Strategic Dialogue under the Strategic Partnership. The Dialogue will be co-chaired by the U.S. Under Secretary of State for Political Affairs and Pakistan's Foreign Secretary. They will meet regularly to review issues of mutual interest.

In implementation of the strategic partnership, President Bush and President Musharraf commit both countries to undertake the following steps in the areas of economic growth and prosperity, energy, peace and security, social sector development, science and technology, democracy, and non-proliferation:

Economic Growth and Prosperity

- Establish and implement strong financial sector controls that can defend against illicit finance.
- Facilitate Pakistan's economic growth through increased trade and investment links with the United States and within the region and the global economy, including through an enhanced economic dialogue encompassing bilateral cooperation for Pakistan's economic development, regional economic cooperation, and the global economy.
- The United States will provide financial support for the establishment of a Center for Entrepreneurship in Pakistan under the Broader Middle East and North Africa (BMENA) Initiative. The Center will promote entrepreneurial training and skills development to young women and men to launch business initiatives that would generate employment opportunities.

Energy Cooperation

- Hold a High-Level Energy Meeting to inaugurate an energy working group, which will explore ways to meet Pakistan's growing energy needs and strengthen its energy security.
- Work together to develop public and private collaboration on a broad range of energy sources.

Peace and Security

- Build a robust defense relationship that advances shared security goals, promotes regional stability, and contributes to international security.

- Continue robust U.S. security assistance to meet Pakistan's legitimate defense needs and bolster its capabilities in the war on terror.
- Deepen bilateral collaboration in the fields of defense training, joint exercises, defense procurement, technology transfers, and international peace-keeping.
- Decide to increase the frequency of defense policy discussions to strengthen collaboration in the identified sectors.
- Work together to ensure the maintenance of peace, security, and stability in the South Asia region and beyond.
- Cooperate closely in international institutions, including bodies of the United Nations, on matters of mutual concern.

Social Sector Development

- Continue U.S. support in the health sector through collaborative projects and programs.
- Reinforce Pakistan's efforts to reform and expand access to its public education through continuing U.S. cooperation.
- Encourage educational programs and greater interaction and linkages between the research and academic institutions of the two countries.
- Promote exchange of students and scholars, fellowship programs, and strengthened research collaboration, including through institutional support for higher education and training.
- Establish a wide-ranging High Level Dialogue on Education to enhance and strengthen cooperation in the education sector.

Science and Technology

- Build capacity in Pakistan and work toward increased cooperation in science, technology, and engineering.
- Improve the quality, relevance, or capacity of education and research at Pakistan's institutions of higher education in the field of science and technology.
- Establish Pakistan-U.S. Joint Committee on Science and Technology to develop collaborative activities and relationships between the scientific and technological communities and institutions of both countries.
- Enhance institutional capacity of Pakistan in the area of environment through exchange of experts and developing linkages and collaborative projects with relevant U.S. institutions.

Democracy

- Support Pakistan as it develops strong and transparent democratic institutions and conducts free and fair elections to ensure sustainable democracy.

Non-proliferation

- Support Pakistan's non-proliferation efforts and strengthen its capabilities, by:
  - Supporting Pakistan's measures for implementation of its new export control law, including adoption of enforcement regulations and establishment of a new export licensing body; and
  - Providing U.S. assistance through the Department of Energy's Second Line of Defense Program (Megaports) and the Department of Homeland Security's Container Security Initiative.

Presidential Visit

- President Bush thanked President Musharraf and the people of Pakistan for the generous reception and warm hospitality accorded to him, Mrs. Laura Bush, and members of the Presidential delegation during their stay in Pakistan.

NOTE: An original was not available for verification of the content of this joint statement.

The President's Radio Address
March 4, 2006

Good morning. I have been traveling this past week in South Asia on a trip to Afghanistan, India, and Pakistan.

My first stop was Afghanistan, and I was thrilled to see firsthand the incredible transformation that has taken place there. Before September the 11th, 2001, Afghanistan was ruled by a cruel regime that oppressed its people, brutalized women, and gave safe haven to the terrorists who attacked America.

Today, the terror camps have been shut down, women are working, boys and girls are back in school, and 25 million people have now tasted freedom. The Afghan people are building a vibrant, young democracy that is an ally in the war on terror, and America is proud to have such a determined partner in the cause of freedom.

I was pleased to visit with President Karzai and members of his Cabinet and Government. I told them America will stand with the Afghan people as they build a free society and fight our common enemies, and we will see the mission through without wavering.

I was honored to visit our troops at Bagram Air Base who are serving on the frontlines of the war on terror. It was a privilege to thank them in person for their courage and for the sacrifice of their families back home. These fine Americans are standing watch for liberty halfway across the world, and I told them that all Americans were proud of them.

The next stop on my trip was India. Like America, India has endured terrorist attacks on its own soil. Like America, India is a democracy that understands the best way to ensure peace is to advance freedom. And like America, India is working to help nations like Afghanistan build the institutions of a free and democratic society.

Relations between the United States and India have never been better. One important aspect of this partnership is working together to meet the energy needs of our growing economies, especially through the use of clean and safe nuclear power. On my trip, the United States and India reached an historic agreement to share civilian nuclear technology as India brings its civilian nuclear programs under the safeguards of the International Atomic Energy Agency. This agreement is good for American security because it will bring India's civilian nuclear program into the international nonproliferation mainstream.

The agreement also is good for the American economy. The agreement will help meet India's surging energy needs, and that will lessen India's growing demand for other energy supplies and help restrain energy prices for American consumers.

Another important aspect of this partnership is the growing trade between our two countries. In the past 10 years, India has passed economic reforms that have opened its door to trade and helped raised the living standards for millions of its people. In my meetings with Prime Minister Singh, I made clear that trade between our countries must be free and fair. I know that America's workers can compete with anyone, anytime, anywhere, so long as the rules are fair.

Ultimately, the best way to create jobs for Americans is to expand markets for American products. Today, India is one of the fastest-growing export markets for goods, services, and crops. India has now a growing middle class that is estimated at 300 million people—more than the entire population of the United States. Middle class Indians are buying home appliances from American companies like Whirlpool. Younger Indians are enjoying McCurry meals from McDonald's. And Air India has recently ordered 68 planes from Boeing. Last year, our exports to India grew by more than 30 percent. And all this trade is creating jobs and opportunity in America. So we will continue to work to level the playing field for our workers, farmers, and businesses—and deliver a better life for all Americans.

The final stop on my trip was Pakistan, another important ally in the war on terror. After September the 11th, 2001, President Musharraf understood that he had to make a fundamental choice. He could turn a blind eye and leave his people hostage to the terrorists, or he could join the free world in fighting the terrorists.

President Musharraf made the right choice for his people, and America appreciates his leadership. Since he joined the fight against terror, President Musharraf has faced several attempts on his life, yet President Musharraf has not faltered. He understands that the terrorists are a threat to the peace and security of the Pakistani people and the world.

Our relations with Afghanistan, India, and Pakistan will enhance the security of our country. By working with these leaders and the people of these three nations, we're seizing the opportunities this new century offers and helping to lay the foundations of peace and prosperity for generations to come.

NOTE: The address was recorded at 9:05 a.m. on March 3 in the Muarya Sheraton Hotel and Towers in New Delhi, India, for broadcast at 10:06 a.m., e.s.t., on March 4. The transcript was made available by the Office of the Press Secretary on March 3 but was embargoed for release until the broadcast. Due to the 5-hour time difference, the radio address was broadcast after the President's midday remarks in Islamabad, Pakistan. In his address, the President referred to Prime Minister Manmohan Singh of India; and President Pervez Musharraf of Pakistan. The Office of the Press Secretary also released a Spanish language transcript of this address.

Remarks at a State Dinner Hosted by President Pervez Musharraf of Pakistan in Islamabad
March 4, 2006

Mr. President and Mrs. Musharraf and distinguished guests, Laura and I thank you for the warm and gracious welcome. It's such a pleasure to be here in Pakistan. We've had a fantastic day. I was fooled by a googly. [*Laughter*] Otherwise, I'd have been a better batsman. But it's been a full day, Mr. President, and your hospitality has overwhelmed us, and thank you.

I bring greetings from my fellow citizens, in particular the thousands of Pakistani Americans who call my land home, folks who have really made a tremendous contribution to the United States of America.

Our nations are strong allies, Mr. President. We're allies in the war on terror, and we're allies in laying the foundation of lasting peace. In the struggle in the war on terror, Pakistan and America has lost many good citizens. And we ask for God's blessings on their families. Pakistan's efforts to enhance peace and security have earned the respect and the admiration of the American people. When the terrorists are defeated and when the peace is won, our two nations will share the peace together.

The American people care deeply about the people of Pakistan. We watched with horror and great sorrow as last year's earthquake devastated this ancient land. Americans have experienced the trauma of natural disasters in our own country, and we've witnessed the power of friendship to rebuild lives and to restore hope. I'm proud of the U.S. relief efforts. I want to thank those officials who are here to help the people of Pakistan.

I'm pleased that our helicopters earned the name "angels of mercy" from those who were anxious for help in the mountains. I'm proud that our Government and businesses and private organizations and individual families also saw your need and gave their time and treasures to help rebuild this vital nation. Our donations reflect the compassion of our country, the respect we have for Pakistan. And we will make good on our donations, Mr. President.

America and Pakistan have confronted great challenges together, and we will continue to do so. Americans will support the Pakistani people as they take further steps toward democracy, expand educational opportunities for boys and girls, and create

prosperity through innovation and global trade. Pakistan has a bright future because of its proud people and because of the hard work of a strong leader. President Musharraf, you've proved yourself to be a man of courage and vision. I appreciate the honor of being your partner in working for peace and security.

And so, Mr. President, with gratitude for what we've accomplished and with optimism for what we will yet accomplish, I offer my respect to you, to your gracious wife, and to the people of Pakistan.

NOTE: The President spoke at 8:10 p.m. at the Aiwan-e-Sadr. In his remarks, he referred to Sehba Musharraf, wife of President Musharraf. The transcript released by the Office of the Press Secretary also included the remarks of President Musharraf.

Remarks at a Swearing-In Ceremony for Edward P. Lazear as Chairman of the Council of Economic Advisers
March 6, 2006

The President. Welcome. I'm here to swear in Ed Lazear as the Chairman of the Council of Economic Advisers. Thank you all for coming. Eddie has brought a lot of his family here. For the family members who are here, welcome; thanks for supporting the old boy. [*Laughter*] I particularly want to thank Vicki and Julie, as well as his mother, Rose, for being here. I'm really glad you all are here. Does he still listen to you, Rose? [*Laughter*]

Rose Lazear. Oh, yes. He's a good boy.

The President. That's a good boy. Well, I hope my mother is saying the same thing about me. [*Laughter*]

Eddie is an award-winning economist from Stanford University. He's been a part of the Hoover Institute. He's taught and lectured in Asia and the Middle East and Europe. He's advised Governments in the former Soviet Union and Eastern Europe

on economic reform. He's conducted pathbreaking research in the field of labor economics. He's applied his theories to real-world problems like education and immigration and compensation and productivity. He's well-rounded, and he's plenty smart.

He also understands how to get his message across. After all, he was voted teacher of the year at Stanford's Graduate School of Business. That's not an easy accomplishment. He's a founding editor of the Journal of Labor Economics. He's a good man, who has served with distinction before in Government. He served on my Advisory Panel on Federal Tax Reform. And he's going to be an outstanding Chairman of my Council of Economic Advisers.

He succeeds another outstanding economist who still bears the title of Chairman, and that's Ben Bernanke. He just wears his title over at another place here in

Washington. Eddie and Ben are part of a long line of talented economists who have served my administration as CEA Chairman, including Harvey Rosen, Greg Mankiw, and Glenn Hubbard. I want to thank Eddie for agreeing to serve our country. I appreciate his understanding of the important role he will play in my administration.

I appreciate those who are here from my administration. I see Carlos Gutierrez, the Secretary of Commerce. Carlos, welcome—Josh Bolten, a member of the Cabinet, the Office of Management and Budget. Senator Bob Bennett—thank you for coming, Senator. I really appreciate you taking time to be here. Congressman Jim Ryun and Anne are with us as well. Eddie told me he's a runner. Don't run with Ryun, Eddie.

Eddie leads my Council of Economic Advisers at an exciting time. It's a time of opportunity and a time of challenge. Today, the American economy is the envy of the world. Last year, our economy grew at a healthy 3.5 percent, faster than any other major industrialized nation. We've added more than 4.7 million new jobs during the last 2½ years. That's more than Japan and the European Union combined. Our unemployment rate is down to 4.7 percent. That's the lowest level since July of 2001. That's lower than the average of the 1970s, the 1980s, and the 1990s.

More Americans now own their homes than at any time in our history. More minority families own homes than any time in our Nation's history. This administration believes in ownership. We love the fact that somebody opens the door to their own piece of property, says, "Welcome to my piece of my property; welcome to my home."

Real after-tax income is up more than 8 percent per person since the beginning of 2001. New orders for durable goods, like machinery, have risen sharply. We've had 33 straight months of growth in our manufacturing sector. Productivity has grown

strongly over the last 5 years. Our small-business sector is thriving. America is productive; America is innovative; America is entrepreneurial. And I'm counting on Eddie's good advice to keep it that way.

We understand it's important to continue to promote progrowth economic policies and sound initiatives with one goal in mind, to keep America the economic leader in the world so our people can find jobs and realize their dreams.

Our economy grows when Americans have more of their own money to spend, save, and invest. In the last 5 years, we passed tax relief that left $880 billion in the hands of American workers and small businesses and families. And the American people have used that money to help produce more than 4 years of uninterrupted economic growth.

The tax relief that we passed is set to expire in the next few years. If we do nothing, American families will face a massive tax increase they do not expect and will not welcome. Because America needs more than a temporary expansion, we need more than temporary tax relief. So in my State of the Union, I called upon the United States Congress to make the tax relief we passed permanent.

I also outlined several other steps to keep this economy strong and growing. We need to address our dependence on foreign sources of oil. You might remember, I stood up in front of the country and said, "We have a real problem; we're addicted to oil." I meant what I said. I call upon Congress to join with this administration to pass the Advanced Energy Initiative that will fund research in cleaner, more reliable technologies like hydrogen and ethanol, so we become less dependent. For the sake of our national security and economic security, we must not be dependent on foreign sources of oil.

We need to ensure that Americans get the health care they need. And so we're working to make health coverage more affordable and available and portable through measures like health savings accounts and association health plans.

To maintain our edge in innovation and creativity, I proposed the American Competitiveness Initiative to promote cutting-edge research and to ensure that American children get math and science skills they need for the jobs of the 21st century.

One of the most important steps we need to take to keep this economy strong is to restrain Federal spending in Washington. That's hard to do. Everybody thinks their spending idea is a great idea. They all—all these spending ideas sound wonderful on paper. Here's our view: It's important for the Congress to set priorities. We are a nation at war, and one of the top priorities of this Government will continue to be to make sure our troops have the equipment they need to defend the United States and our citizens have what it takes to defend the homeland.

That means we must be careful about how we spend the taxpayers' money in other areas. In other words, we can't be all things to all people when it comes to spending the taxpayers' money. And we're making some good progress. Last year of the previous administration, nonsecurity discretionary spending rose by 15 percent. Every year of my Presidency, we've reduced the growth of this spending, and last year, at my request, Congress passed legislation that actually cut this spending. I thank them for their hard work.

Now I look forward to working on my—having them work on my 2007 budget that Josh Bolten is taking up to the Congress. This budget will save the taxpayers money, will cut—will continue to cut nonsecurity discretionary spending, and keep us on track to cut the deficit in half by 2009.

In the long run, the biggest challenge to our Nation's fiscal health is entitlement spending. I recently signed a bill to save nearly $40 billion over 5 years in entitlement spending. The 2000 [2006] ° budget

---

° White House correction.

we submitted proposes to save another $65 billion over 5 years. We don't need to cut this mandatory spending; we need to slow its growth. In other words, we don't need to put our cars into reverse; we just need to slow it to meet the speed limit.

As well, I'm deadly earnest in calling members of both parties together to work to pass—to propose something we can pass out of Congress that will modernize Social Security and Medicare. It's time for Congress to set aside needless partisan politics and focus on the future of our country with real, substantive entitlement reform.

We also need to do more to reform the way Washington spends people's money. Under the current system, Congress can slip spending provisions into large bills where they never get debated and never get discussed. Those are called earmarks. As a result, too many bills passed by Congress include unnecessary spending. These earmarks reflect special interests instead of the people's interest. I'm pleased that Congress is working on earmark reform, and I encourage Members of Congress to pass meaningful and real earmark reform.

Here's another idea for them: They need to give the President the line-item veto. Congress gave the President a line-item veto in 1996, but because with problems the way the law was written, the Supreme Court struck it down. That should not be the end of the story. So in my State of the Union, I called for new legislation creating a line-item veto that will meet Supreme Court standards. Today I'm sending Congress legislation that will meet standards and give me the authority to strip special interest spending and earmarks out of a bill and then send them back to Congress for an up-or-down vote. By passing this version of the line-item veto, the administration will work with the Congress to reduce wasteful spending, reduce the budget deficit, and ensure that taxpayer dollars are spent wisely.

Congress is on record, by the way, that the President should have the line-item veto authority. It has been approved previously. Forty-three Governors have this line-item veto in their States. Now it's time to bring this important tool for fiscal discipline to Washington, DC.

I'm really optimistic about the future of this country. I don't think there's any problem we can't tackle. It's really important as we put progrowth policies in place, to understand that the engine of growth is the ingenuity of the American people. I like to remind people: Government doesn't create wealth. Government creates an environment in which the entrepreneurial spirit can flourish, in which people can realize their dreams, in which small businesses can grow to be big businesses, in which the

newly arrived can have a chance to realize the great promise of our country.

Eddie understands that, and that's why I'm proud to have him by my side. And again, Eddie, thank you for agreeing to serve our great Nation. And now Andy Card will administer the oath of office.

NOTE: The President spoke at 10 a.m. in Room 450 of the Dwight D. Eisenhower Executive Office Building. In his remarks, he referred to Victoria Lazear, wife of Edward P. Lazear, and their daughter, Julie; Ben S. Bernanke, Chairman, Federal Reserve System; and Anne Ryun, wife of Representative Jim Ryun. The transcript released by the Office of the Press Secretary also included the remarks of Chairman Lazear.

Statement on Representative William M. Thomas's Decision Not To Seek Reelection
March 6, 2006

Congressman Bill Thomas is a friend and a man of great accomplishment who has been a very effective leader in the House of Representatives. As chairman of the House Ways and Means Committee, he helped pass legislation that has brought about strong job creation and economic growth, improved health care for people of all ages, and ensured that America continues to benefit from free and fair trade.

For the last 28 years, he has worked tirelessly for the people of the Bakersfield area in California and represented them with honor and distinction. I appreciate Bill's commitment and dedication to public service, and I look forward to working with him for the remainder of the session. I wish Sharon, Bill, and the entire Thomas family all the best in the future.

Message to the Congress Transmitting a Legislative Proposal To Give the President a Line-Item Veto
March 6, 2006

To the Congress of the United States:

In my State of the Union Address, I asked the Congress to give the President a line item veto. Today, I am sending the Congress a legislative proposal to give the

President line item authority to reduce wasteful spending. This legislation will help to limit spending and ensure accountability and transparency in the expenditure of taxpayer funds.

Although the Congress achieved significant spending restraint this past year, appropriations and other bills that are sent to my desk still contain spending that is not fully justified, is a low priority, or is earmarked to avoid the discipline of competitive or merit-based reviews. When this legislation is presented to me, I now have no ability to line out unnecessary spending. In 1996, the Congress gave the President a line item veto—an important tool to limit wasteful spending—but the Supreme Court struck down that version of the law in 1998.

My proposed legislation, the "Legislative Line Item Veto Act of 2006," would provide a fast-track procedure to require the Congress to vote up-or-down on rescissions proposed by the President. There has been broad bipartisan support for similar proposals in the past. Under this proposal, the President could propose legislation to re-scind wasteful spending, and the Congress would be obligated to vote quickly on that package of rescissions, without amendment. The same procedure would apply to new mandatory spending and to special interest tax breaks given to small numbers of individuals.

Forty-three Governors have a line item veto to reduce spending. The President needs similar authority to help control unjustified and wasteful spending in the Federal budget. I urge you to promptly consider and send me this legislation for enactment to reduce unnecessary spending and help achieve my goal of cutting the deficit in half by 2009.

GEORGE W. BUSH

The White House,
March 6, 2006.

Remarks at a Celebration of Women's History Month and International Women's Day
March 7, 2006

Thank you all. Thank you, Laura. Welcome to the White House. We like to call this the people's house. I want to remind people from around the world that we're only temporary occupants here, but we're trying to make the most of our time here.

I want to welcome you all as we celebrate Women's History Month and International Women's Day. Thanks for coming. We recognize the many contributions women have made to our country. We also honor those who have helped bring equality and freedom to women around the world.

A lot of strong women have influenced my life—[*laughter*]—beginning with my mother. [*Laughter*] She told me to say that, by the way. [*Laughter*] I am blessed to have a strong wife. And we are raising two young women to become independent, ca-pable risk takers—[*laughter*]—so that they can realize their dreams.

I have been blessed to have strong women in my Government. My administration is better off to have really capable women who feel comfortable marching in the Oval Office and giving the President their frank advice. [*Laughter*]

I want to thank Secretary of Labor Elaine Chao, who is with us; Secretary of Education Margaret Spellings—she's been giving me frank advice ever since I was the Governor of Texas. [*Laughter*] I want to thank Karen Hughes—Ambassador Karen Hughes, the Under Secretary for Public Diplomacy and Public Affairs. She's been really giving me a lot of advice. [*Laughter*] Paula Dobriansky, the Under Secretary for Democracy and Global Affairs; Harriet Miers, my attorney—by the way, for those of you who aren't familiar with America, it's always good to have a good attorney. [*Laughter*] Harriet Miers is my attorney. She gives me legal advice.

Fran Townsend is in charge of our—part of the National Security Council in charge of homeland security. Protecting our homeland is a vital part of America, and I rely upon a very capable, strong woman to give me good advice.

I want to thank my friend Pat Brister, who is the U.S. Representative to the United Nations Commission on the Status of Women, for joining us. Pat is—there she is—from Louisiana, where Laura and I will be tomorrow, by the way.

I want to thank Congresswoman Judy Biggert from the State of Illinois. She's with us. For those of you who are unfamiliar with our Congress, we have a lot of very capable women who are running for office and have become elected—and making a big difference in the Halls of Congress. I appreciate the members of the diplomatic corps who have joined us. Thank you all for coming. It's good to see so many ambassadors and ambassadresses here today. [*Laughter*]

I want to thank the members of the United States-Afghan Women's Council who are here. You all are making a significant difference in the lives of people who are beginning to feel the freshness of the light of democracy. And as Laura mentioned, we were in Afghanistan with President Karzai. And there's nothing better than being in a country that's beginning to realize the benefits of freedom; particularly, women who have been completely suppressed under the Taliban are now beginning to see the beautiful—breathe that beautiful air of a free society. And so I want to thank the members of the United States-Afghan Women's Council for being so diligent and caring and staying with this important issue—that issue being the freedom of women in Afghanistan.

I want to thank the members of the International Republican Institute and the National Endowment for Democracy. Thank you for hosting our international delegates. Thank you for helping them in their training exercises and sharing expertise and compassion. I want to thank the delegations from Afghanistan and Iraq and around the world for joining us today. You're welcome in the United States of America; I hope you feel that way.

The struggle for women's rights is a story of strong women willing to take the lead. That's particularly true in the United States of America, where women like Susan B. Anthony and Alice Stone Blackwell and Elizabeth Cady Stanton and Rosa Parks changed the course of our Nation's history. Our history was altered because strong women stood up and led. These women broke down barriers to equality. We weren't always an equal society in America, and it required strong leadership to help make America a more equal place. And we're a better place because of the leadership of women throughout our history.

Women today are shaping the future of America as scientists and entrepreneurs and teachers and astronauts. They serve our Nation with honor and distinction in our Armed Forces. The distinguished leadership of women like Secretary of State Condi Rice—where is she—she had an excused absence—[*laughter*]—and Justice Sandra Day O'Connor has helped open doors for women for future generations.

Across the world, the increasing participation of women in civic and political life has strengthened democracies. A democracy is strong when women participate in the society. The nation of Liberia recently elected its first woman President, and Laura and Secretary Rice were there to witness her swearing-in. I look forward to welcoming her to America, by the way.

Women lead Governments in Germany, in Chile, and the Philippines. In Rwanda, nearly half of the members of Parliament are women. And women are now holding more parliamentary seats in nations like Morocco and Jordan and Tunisia.

In the last 4 years, we have also seen women make great strides in Afghanistan and Iraq—countries where just a few years ago, women were denied basic rights and were brutalized by tyrants. Today in Afghanistan, girls are attending school. That speaks well for Afghanistan's future. Women hold about 20 percent of the seats in the National Assembly. Nobody could have dreamed that was possible 5 years ago. In last fall's elections, about 40 percent of the voters were women. In Iraq, women are voting in large numbers, and when the new Iraqi Parliament takes office, women will hold about one-quarter of the seats.

The United States is working to increase opportunities for women in these two emerging democracies. Through the Iraqi Women's Democracy Initiative, we're providing funds for Iraqi women to receive training in political leadership and learn about the legislative process, the judicial system, and how to defend and promote human rights.

In Afghanistan, we're helping women find ways to join the political process at the local level and to acquire the skills they need for advocacy and communication. We're working with the private sector in America to help Afghan women travel abroad to learn more about the political process and to be able to exchange ideas with fellow women, just like which is taking place here in America today.

Our work to help build vibrant and functioning democracies in Afghanistan and Iraq is part of a larger effort to encourage progress across the broader Middle East. We refuse to accept the status quo in the United States of America, particularly when we find women repressed. As women become a part of the democratic process, they help spread freedom and justice and, most importantly of all, hope for a future.

One important program is the Women's Democracy Network, which is holding its inaugural meeting this week in Washington. This conference provides an opportunity for women leaders around the world to connect with each other and serve as mentors for women in developing democracies so they can help shape the future of their nations.

As we work to advance the equality of women in the world's newest democracies, we must remember that many women in other countries around the world are still struggling for basic rights in places like Iran and North Korea and Burma. America will help women stand up for their freedom, no matter where they live.

Recently I welcomed two women from Belarus who were concerned about the repressive nature of their Government. We stand with the women in Belarus who advocate human rights in a runup to this month's election. America will continue to support courageous reformers around the world, women like Burmese dissident Aung San Suu Kyi, who has spent years under house arrest for her efforts to bring democracy to her nation.

We will continue to fight the threats to women across the world. We'll continue working with nations around the world to end the sexual exploitation and the trafficking of women and young girls. It breaks our hearts, our collective hearts, to realize many young girls are sold into sex slavery, and we will use our prestige to stop that evil process.

We will continue working to fight the transmission of HIV/AIDS. America is proud to lead the world in the struggle to defeat this pandemic. We understand that by defeating the pandemic of HIV/AIDS, we will help children and women, who have been disproportionately affected by this horrible pandemic.

We live in extraordinary times. These are exciting times. They are times that require a firm conviction in our beliefs that all people are created equal. We've seen the fall of brutal tyrants and the rise of democracy. We're also seeing women take their rightful place in societies that were once closed and oppressive. And the United States welcomes the arrival of women into these oppressive societies. There's no doubt in my mind, empowering women in new democracies will make those democracies better countries and help lay the foundation of peace for generations to come.

So Laura and I welcome you to the White House. We're really glad you're here. We're so glad you're here, we're about to throw a reception on your behalf. [*Laughter*] And we wish you to enjoy it.

May God bless everybody here. May God bless your families, and may God bless our respective nations. Thank you for coming.

NOTE: The President spoke at 10:44 a.m. in the East Room at the White House. In his remarks, he referred to President Hamid Karzai of Afghanistan; former Supreme Court Associate Justice Sandra Day O'Connor; President Ellen Johnson Sirleaf of Liberia; Chancellor Angela Merkel of Germany; President-elect Michelle Bachelet Jeria of Chile; President Gloria Macapagal-Arroyo of the Philippines; Irina Krasovskaya and Svyatlana Zavadskaya, widows of prodemocracy advocates who disappeared in Belarus; and Aung San Suu Kyi, leader of the National League for Democracy in Burma. The transcript released by the Office of the Press Secretary also included the remarks of the First Lady, who introduced the President. The Women's History Month proclamation of February 27 is listed in Appendix D at the end of this volume.

Remarks on Election Day in Crawford, Texas
March 7, 2006

The President. Thank you all.

Q. Was it worth coming?

The President. Yes, you bet. It's always good to come home to vote. And I urge all people to vote when given a chance. It's also good to be home in Texas—get a little rest here in my homestead and then heading over to New Orleans tomorrow and Mississippi.

Thank you all.

NOTE: The President spoke at 4:43 p.m. at the Crawford Fire Department. A tape was not available for verification of the content of these remarks.

Remarks Following a Tour of Recovery Efforts in the Areas Damaged by Hurricanes Katrina and Rita in New Orleans, Louisiana
March 8, 2006

I want to thank you all for coming. I want to thank Colonel Setliff for the tour that he just gave the Governor and the mayor and myself, along with Laura and part of our party. I want to thank Colonel Wagenaar for the aerial tour. We just flew over affected parts of Orleans Parish and Jefferson Parish and St. Bernard Parish, and getting a view of the progress that is being made.

I particularly want to thank my friend Don Powell for his hard work in coordinating Federal efforts with the Governor and the mayor. Governor Blanco and Mayor Nagin have been by my side when

I've come down here, and I really appreciate them being a part of the recovery efforts. I want to thank Walter Isaacson and David Voelker, the members of the Louisiana Recovery Authority. They were on Air Force One today to make sure I fully understood—understand the strategies that the local folks are putting in place to help the good people of this part of the world recover from the devastating storm.

You know, we just came from a neighborhood where people are fixing to—are in the process of cleaning up debris. We went there because the mayor and the Governor thought it was important for me to see firsthand the devastation of the storm in certain neighborhoods and the progress that is being made for cleaning up the debris. There's still a lot of work to be done, no question about it. And obviously, as the plan gets laid out and as the housing plan I'm fixing to discuss comes to fruition, people will feel more comfortable in granting the local authorities the right to remove debris from their homes to be cleaned up.

But I want to share a story about a fellow, Romalice Harris, I met. He was there—was part of the construction crew. I asked him, I said, "Where were you during the storm?" He said he felt like he could ride it out. He heard the evacuation orders but thought it would be all right to ride out the storm. He lived on the third floor of an apartment complex. And he described to me and the Governor and the mayor what it was like to see the water start to rise up to the second floor of the building. He and his three children and his wife and another relative were finally rescued by a boat.

I said, "What happened to you?" He said, "Well, I went to Salt Lake City, Utah." In other words, his is an example of what happened to the good folks in this part of the world. He watched the rising waters, and then he just had to abandon the part of the world he loves.

From there, the Federal Government helped fly him to Chicago, where he had some relatives—or a relative. He now has come back to work in the city he loves, New Orleans, with the hopes of rebuilding his life. His wife and children are still in Chicago; they're going to school there. But as he told us, he says he looks forward to bringing them home, bringing them back to Louisiana, to have his children educated right here. And I'm convinced he'll succeed. And our job at all levels of government is to provide the confidence and the help necessary so that people like Romalice Harris come home.

I appreciate the determination by the folks down here to rebuild. I fully understand, and I hope our country understands, the pain and agony that the people of New Orleans and Louisiana and the parishes surrounding New Orleans went through. But I think people would be impressed by the desire of the people in this part of the country to pick up and move on and rebuild. And that's why I'm so pleased that the Governor and the mayor have joined me, so we can discuss the importance of implementing a strategy that will help this part of the world rise again.

The first part of the strategy is to make sure these levees are strong. And we fully understand that if the people don't have confidence in the levee system, they're not going to want to come back. People aren't going to want to spend money or invest. I just got a briefing from the Army Corps of Engineers that said we're on schedule to repair the damage by the June 1st deadline. They're identifying and correcting design and construction deficiencies; so as we go into the start of the hurricane season, the levees will be equal or better than what they were before Katrina.

The corps is identifying areas that weren't damaged but that need additional attention. Over here you can see the—or one of the walls that are being built. I mean, there's a lot of concrete and a lot of steel being put in the ground to protect the levee system. By September of next year, additional improvements will be completed, bringing the entire levee system up to the full authorized design height, making it better and stronger than before.

Congress heard our message about improving the levees, but they shortchanged the process by about $1.5 billion. And so in order to help fulfill our promise on the levees, Congress needs to restore the $1.5 billion, to make this a real commitment, to inspire the good folks down here that they have a levee system that will encourage development and reconstruction.

As I mentioned, we went by the Ninth Ward to see the debris removal that was taking place. The vast majority of debris on public property has been removed. About 80 percent of the debris not related to demolition has been cleared. Most of the remaining debris is on private property, in yards or inside houses that need to be gutted or demolished. To get the debris, the residents need to give permission, in most cases, to the local authorities. And so they need to get back to their houses so they can decide what to keep and what to remove.

The problem is, obviously, many homeowners are still displaced. And that's why we're working at all levels of government to encourage evacuees to inspect their properties and to salvage what they can and to make decisions about the future.

Of course, the decisionmaking for the individual homeowners is going to be made easier when Congress funds the $4.2 billion that I asked them to fund for the State of Louisiana for housing purposes. Now, this $4.2 billion is in conjunction with the $6.2 billion of CDBG money for housing grants. The $4.2 billion request was done in a coordinated effort with State and local authorities.

The reason I thought this number made sense is because the number fits into a well-thought-out plan that has been together by the local folks. The housing plan has been coordinated by State authorities

with local authorities as well as with HUD authorities. In other words, we've all been working together to figure out how to come up with a housing plan that will restore the confidence of the people of this important part of our country. And in order to make sure that housing plan meets its goals, Congress should make sure that the $4.2 billion I requested goes to the State of Louisiana.

I'm also confident that this plan is solid right now. It's well-thought-out, and when it's submitted to HUD, because there's been close coordination, it should be approved on a timely basis.

And so again, I want to thank you all for inviting me to come back. I've always had a soft spot in my heart for Louisiana. Some of you might recall, I grew up across the line, over there in Texas, and really enjoyed my stay here when I came. I was pleased to see that the Mardi Gras parades went well, Mr. Mayor. As the mayor and the Governor described to me, it was as much of a homecoming as anything else. A lot of folks came back, came home. And that's what we want. We want people coming home. And the Federal Government will do our part, in conjunction with our State and local partners.

I ask for God's blessings on the people of this part of the world and thank the hard-working folks here for working around the clock to get this part of the country up and running again. Thank you.

Now, Laura is traveling with me. She's got a very important announcement she'd like to make as well.

NOTE: The President spoke at 10:33 a.m. at the Industrial Levee Canal. In his remarks, he referred to Col. Lewis F. Setliff III, USA, St. Louis district engineer, U.S. Army Corps of Engineers; Gov. Kathleen Babineaux Blanco of Louisiana; Mayor C. Ray Nagin of New Orleans, LA; Col. Richard P. Wagenaar, USA, New Orleans district engineer, U.S. Army Corps of Engineers; and Walter Isaacson, vice chairman of the board, and

David Voelker, board member, Louisiana Recovery Authority. The transcript released by the Office of the Press Secretary also included the remarks of the First Lady. The Office of the Press Secretary also released a Spanish language transcript of these remarks.

Remarks on Recovery Efforts in the Areas Damaged by Hurricanes Katrina and Rita in Gautier, Mississippi
March 8, 2006

Thank you all for coming. Laura and I are really honored to be back in Mississippi with the Governor and the first lady. And most of all, we're pleased to be with those who are helping to educate the young here on the gulf coast.

We, of course, want to thank those who are helping this important part of the country rebuild. Part of rebuilding the community is to make sure that the schools are able to function well and teach children how to read and write and add and subtract. Laura and I are committed to making sure no child is left behind anywhere in the United States of America.

Particularly want to thank the superintendent, the principal, and the teachers for helping this important part of the country recover from devastating storm.

And now it's my honor to introduce the First Lady, who is going to make an announcement.

NOTE: The President spoke at 12:22 p.m. at College Park Elementary School. In his remarks, he referred to Gov. Haley Barbour of Mississippi and his wife, Marsha; Wayne V. Rodolfich, superintendent, Pascagoula School District; and Suzanne Ros, principal, College Park Elementary School. The transcript released by the Office of the Press Secretary also included the remarks of the First Lady.

Remarks on New Home Construction in Gautier
March 8, 2006

The President. It's good to hear people hammering, isn't it?

Governor Haley Barbour. It really is. It's great for us in Mississippi.

The President. It is. People are building their lives back. And one of the reasons I've come down here is to remind people that there's still a lot of people hurting. And I talk to the Governor all the time about what we can do to make sure this part of the world rebuilds. It's great to see rebuilding.

Haley has been real good about talking to us about a variety of issues. I want to thank you for your leadership.

Gov. Barbour. Mr. President, thank you. Let me just say publicly, thank you. In the last day, President Bush and the Bush administration has made the fifth extension of the deadline for the Government to cover 100 percent of debris removal and other emergency measures. And this extension is to June 30th, when we ought to be through.

And first, I want to say thank you for that. You know, it's been a huge issue for these little communities, that they don't have any tax base, so thank you for that. That was made public yesterday. I'm glad to announce today that last night HUD approved our plan for our homeowner grant program. We intend to make $4 billion of community development block grant money from the Federal Government available to Mississippians, like Jerry and Elaine, so that they can rebuild their homes or build new homes, to get themselves out of the flood plain.

Tomorrow we have been allowed by HUD to post our plan. You can see it on our web site, mshomehelp—m-s-h-o-m-e-h-e-l-p—.gov, and we'll have to have a 2-week comment period, at the end of which we'll start taking applications. But somebody can go onto the web site now, Mr. President, or at noon tomorrow, and find out all the information they need to get, what all the rules are. And I'm pleased to say that the Akins qualify.

The President. That's good.

Gov. Barbour. They built this house up above the new flood plain, 25 feet above sea level, which is one of the requirements so that we reduce risks. And thank you for doing that.

The President. I always felt that it was really important to say to the Governor and to local folks, "Come to Washington with a plan to help people rebuild." I really didn't want the plan to be designed by Washington people; I wanted it to be designed by local folks. And Haley has put together a Mississippi plan. He not only put the plan together; he also came to Washington, DC, and helped get the plan funded—with the help of two fine United States Senators——

Gov. Barbour. The best pair of United States Senators in the country.

The President. ——and Members of the House. And so I want to congratulate you

and your team for putting together a good plan. Our job and our purpose is to help people like the Akins rebuild. And we want this part of the country rising up from the devastation. You know, people really didn't lose their spirit down here. But our job is to make sure that that spirit is able to, kind of, recapture the hope and optimism of the people and let that spirit flourish.

And I want to thank you for being a good leader. I appreciate you all having us. Listen, thanks. After all that work I've done, I'm thirsty. [*Laughter*]

Jerry Akins. Yes, sir. We have some lemonade, and we have some refreshments.

The President. You do? That's good. The other thing that's interesting is that we've got the Allens here from the Allen Brothers Construction Company. These are local folks——

Gov. Barbour. The Martins. [*Laughter*]

The President. The Martins. As I said, the Martins. You probably thought I said, the Allens. [*Laughter*] I said, the Martins. [*Laughter*]

You know, one of the interesting things is that there is going to be a lot of work, and here are the entrepreneurs with their sons helping to build this man's house. It's neat to be with them. Small businesses, if they seize the opportunity, are going to flourish. And that's what we want. These small construction companies are going to have work to do.

The other thing about the Martins, one of the boys won the Purple Heart in Iraq. There he is right there. It's my honor to congratulate him for serving the country. Thank you. At any rate——

The First Lady. Now we're going to present Jerry and Elaine a flag for your new house.

NOTE: The President spoke at 1:10 p.m. at a new home construction site.

Statement on the Proposed United States-Malaysia Free Trade Agreement
March 8, 2006

The United States and Malaysia share strong trade and investment ties and a commitment to generating prosperity through openness, democracy, and freedom. Today we seek to further strengthen the ties between our two countries by launching negotiations on a comprehensive U.S.-Malaysia Free Trade Agreement.

Once completed, a free trade agreement with Malaysia will generate significant commercial, economic, political, and strategic benefits to both countries. It will improve our ties with the Southeast Asia region and strengthen our engagement in Asia. Malaysia is our tenth-largest trading partner, and the United States is Malaysia's second-largest source of imports. A U.S.-Malaysia Free Trade Agreement will advance our commitment to opening markets around the world and expanding opportunities for America's farmers, ranchers, workers, and businesses.

Remarks Following a Meeting on Faith-Based and Community Initiatives
March 9, 2006

We just had a very interesting dialog here. I want to thank members of the faith community, the community-based action community, the corporate community, the foundation community for joining in a dialog about how we can continue to foster the good works of millions of our fellow citizens who deeply care about the future of our country and the plight of their fellow citizen.

One of the things that always strengthens my belief in our future is my understanding of how many acts of kindness take place on a daily basis in the United States, and it doesn't require any government edict or government law. People really care about the future of our country; millions of our citizens weep when they know somebody hurts. But nevertheless, there still needs to be focused efforts on encouraging more giving of money and time.

So I want to thank you all very much for joining us. Appreciate your being social entrepreneurs. I thank you for really strengthening the heart of the United States of America. Thank you.

NOTE: The President spoke at 11:49 a.m. at the Washington Hilton Hotel.

Remarks at the White House National Conference on Faith-Based and Community Initiatives
March 9, 2006

Thanks for coming. Appreciate you being here. Thanks for the warm welcome. This is the second White House National Conference on Faith-Based and Community Initiatives, and I appreciate your attendance. I take this conference very seriously, and I'm glad you do as well.

The last conference was in June of 2004. Some of you were probably wondering whether I'd be back for this conference.

[*Laughter*] For those of you who did think I was going to be back, it was just as matter of faith. [*Laughter*] I appreciate you being here. It's good to see some old faces—on some young people—and some new faces.

I want to thank my Secretary of Commerce, Carlos Gutierrez, for introducing me. I appreciate Secretary Elaine Chao, the Department of Labor; Secretary Jim Nicholson. It's a good sign when Cabinet members come. It shows a commitment beyond just the President.

I appreciate my friend Jim Towey. I don't know if you know Towey. There he is. His job has been to make sure that the Faith-Based and Community-Based Initiative becomes an integral part of the Government and that the White House effectively reaches out to people to assure them that if they participate in the faith-based initiative, they won't have to lose their faith. It's hard to be a faith-based program if you can't practice your faith, no matter what your faith may be. And I'm proud of the work that Towey has done.

Every time I talk about Towey, I always bring up the same old, tired line about him, but I might as well try it one more time. So he was Mother Teresa's lawyer. And I always wonder about a society where Mother Teresa actually needed a lawyer, you know? [*Laughter*] But she—they picked a good one in Towey.

I want to thank Acting Administrator Fred Schieck of the USAID. He's here because USAID must continue to reach out to faith-based programs in order to make sure that we fulfill missions around the world in a compassionate way. Stephen Goldsmith, who is the Chairman of the Corporation for National and Community Service, is with us. Steve, thanks for being here.

Congressman Tom Osborne—where is the Congressman? He's somewhere here. Anyway, I appreciate you coming, Congressman. Dr. Jim Billington, who is the head of the Library of Congress—Dr.

Billington, thank you for coming. Leaders in the armies of compassion—those would be your sergeants, your lieutenants, and a few generals—thank you all for joining. And I appreciate members of the corporate community who have joined us and foundation America that has joined us as well. This is an important conference.

We meet at a time of great hope for the country. In my State of the Union—I stated this, and I believe it firmly—that America is witnessing a quiet transformation, a revolution of conscience, in which a rising generation is finding that a life of personal responsibility is a life of fulfillment. Part of being personally responsible in America is to love a neighbor like you'd like to be loved yourself. And for those of you who are finding those who have heard the call to help interface with those in need, I thank you from the bottom of my heart. You represent the true strength of the United States of America.

Statistics matter, and you'll hear me talk about some of the results of the faith-based initiative. It's hard to be a results-oriented society unless you actually focus on results. I'd like to share some results with you to boost my belief that there is a quiet transformation taking place. Violent crime rates have fallen to their lowest level since the 1970s. Welfare cases have dropped by more than half. Drug use amongst youth is down 19 percent since 2001. There are fewer abortions in America than at any point in the last three decades. The number of children born to teenage mothers has fallen for a dozen years in a row. I attribute the success of these statistics to the fact that there are millions of our fellow citizens all working to help people who hurt, working toward a better tomorrow.

There's a lot of work to be done, obviously. We still have pockets of poverty where people wonder whether or not the American experience belongs to them. We have place where there is hopelessness and despair. We've got people that are homeless. We've got addicts trapped into a, what appears to them, I'm certain, kind of a never-ending cycle of despondency.

In answering the challenges, staying focused on helping change America one person at a time is a vital part of government, corporate America, philanthropic America, and the faith and community-based programs. It's got to be our continued focus. Even though statistics are improving, so long as we find anybody who hurts, we all should recognize that we hurt. It's the collective conscience of America that really helps define the nature of our country, and it gives me great optimism for the future of our country.

You know, it's interesting, as I—one of my jobs is to constantly herald our strengths. I think when people recognize if you deal with problems from your position of strength, it's more likely you'll be able to solve problems. And what's interesting about the conscience of our country is that it was first recognized by de Tocqueville. I often speak about Alexis de Tocqueville and his observations about what made America unique and different in the 1830s. He talked about voluntary associations of people all coming together to achieve a common good.

That's what you've done. You're representing voluntary associations of people all aiming to achieve the common good. And the common good is achieved in America when we help people who hurt, when we provide mentors for people who need love, when we provide food for those who are hungry, and we provide shelter for those who need shelter.

Our job is to make sure that the spirit that de Tocqueville saw is not only relevant today but stays alive and well throughout the 21st century. There's forever going to be a need of compassionate help in our society. And for those of you who are on the frontlines of social entrepreneurship, thank you for setting such a good example.

Part of this conference is to make sure that you receive encouragement. The other part is to make sure you've got the tools necessary to succeed. Part of the tools necessary to succeed is to help philanthropic America understand it's okay to support faith-based institutions.

We've got fantastic corporate foundations in America who recognize that we all ought to focus on results, not process, that the question government and private philanthropy ought to ask is, does the program get the results that we all want, as opposed to, what is the nature of the people trying to get results? When you focus on results, all of a sudden it becomes crystal-clear how best to spend resource dollars to achieve certain objectives.

And today I met with some folks earlier that talked about their foundations and how their foundations recognize the importance of achieving results—funding results-oriented programs, regardless of whether or not they're faith-based or not.

And for those of you who have set the example, I want to thank you very much, but the truth of the matter is that a recent survey of our Office of Faith-Based and Community Initiatives—headed by Towey—of 20 large corporate foundations found that only about 6 percent of their grants went to faith-based groups. I believe the results are better than that. I am confident that the faith community is achieving unbelievable successes in—throughout our country.

And therefore, I would urge our corporate foundations to reach beyond the norm, to look for those social entrepreneurs who have been—haven't been recognized heretofore, to continue to find people that are running programs that are making a significant difference in people's lives.

When we studied 50 large foundations, we found that one in five prohibited faith organizations from receiving funding for social service programs. In other words, there's a prohibition against funding faith programs from certain foundations in the country. I would hope they would revisit their charters. I would hope they'd take a look at achieving social objectives—make the priority the achievement of certain social objectives before they would make the decision to exclude some who are achieving incredible progress on behalf of our country.

I believe all of us, no matter what level of government we're in—Federal, State, and local—and I believe all of us, no matter if we're private or pubic, ought to allow religious organizations to compete for funding on an equal basis, not for the sake of faith, but for the sake of results.

The Tax Code can be—can encourage contributions. We had an interesting discussion from a person earlier that said that the level of giving in America is substantial, but it can be more. We all can do our part, individually, but the Tax Code can help as well. I've got some interesting ideas to help philanthropy here in America. One of them is to allow corporate America to deduct—take larger tax deductions for food donations.

If one of the issues—[*applause*]—it's kind of a specialized request, I admit it. But if one of the issues is to get food to the hungry, it makes sense to provide incentives for people who have got the wherewithal to be able to provide the resources to get the food headed toward the hungry in the first place. I think it will help those of you who are worried about getting food to people to know that providers of resources will be given an economic incentive to do that. That, hopefully, will make it easier for you to get the product to distribute.

Secondly, seniors now have to pay taxes on a portion of their individual retirement account savings, and so why not allow them to take part of that money and send it to charitable organizations, as opposed to paying tax on it. So let me give you some practical ways that the Government—[*applause*]. I hope the Senate and the House takes these initiatives seriously so that they recognize the Tax Code has got an important part of helping make sure that there's

more than just talk behind the Faith-Based and Community-Based Initiative.

Government has got a role to play. As you know, this has been quite a controversial subject here in the United States Congress. We believe in separation of church and state—the church shouldn't be the state, and the state shouldn't be the church. No question that's a vital part of the country, and that's a vital part of our heritage, and we intend to keep it that way. But when it comes to social service funding, the use of taxpayers' money, I think we're able to meet the admonition of separation of church and state and, at the same time, recognize that faith programs provide an important model of success. They help us achieve certain objectives in our country.

It used to be that groups were prohibited from receiving any Federal funding whatsoever because they had a cross or a star or a crescent on the wall. And that's changed, for the better. It's changed for the better for those who hurt in our society. And so now, when the government is making social service grants, money is rewarded to groups—awarded to groups that get the best results, regardless of whether they're a faith-based program or not. That's all people want. They want access to grant money on an equal basis, on a competitive basis, so there's no discrimination one way or the other.

I repeat to you, and I'm going to say this about five times, I'm sure: Our job in government is to set goals and to focus on results. If you're addicted to alcohol, if a faith program is able to get you off alcohol, we ought to say, "Hallelujah and thanks," at the Federal level.

One of the things I asked old Jim Towey to do was to let me know if we're making any progress. You know, a lot of people around the country say, "Politicians are good at talking, but sometimes they don't really follow through." It's kind of like, the check is in the mail. So I said, why don't you give us a score card, and I want to share with you some of the results that has taken place over the last year. The Federal Government awarded more than $2.1 billion in competitive social service grants to faith-based organizations last year. That's an increase of 7 percent over the previous year, and that is 11 percent of all Federal competitive social service grants. We're making progress about creating a level playing field for people to be comfortable in, one, applying for grants, and two, when receiving a grant—and then actually getting the money out the door to social service organizations.

For example, $780 million in grants was distributed through the Department of Health and Human Services. USAID gave $591 million worth of grants. These are the faith-based organizations—521 million through HUD. And so going from ground zero to today, we're making progress. I can tell you why; it's because we're measuring.

A lot of people were nervous about applying for grants. I can understand that, you know. They said, "Why in the world would I want to interface with the Federal Government? [*Laughter*] They may try to run my business. They may want to try to tell me how to conduct—how to run my program." We've done a good job, I think, through these different faith-based offices and throughout our Government of assuring people in the Government, don't— look, don't tell people how to run their business; accept the way they are, and focus on results. And part of the reason we had these conventions and these outreaches, regional outreaches, is to assure people that the role of the government is to fund, not to micromanage how you run your programs. I repeat to you: You can't be a faith-based program if you don't practice your faith.

We've launched some other initiatives which some of you are involved with—programs to help those who are addicted find treatment. We've talked about mentors for children of prisoners. And for those of you involved in the mentoring program for children of prisoners, I want to thank you on

behalf of a grateful nation. You are providing a fantastic service to help make sure the future is bright.

Can you imagine what it would be like growing up with your mom or dad in prison? Maybe some of you have. It's got to be a heartbreaking experience. And a lot of these kids just cry for love. And to help find a loving soul who is willing to embrace a child and to stay with that child is a wonderful contribution to the country, and it makes sense for the Federal Government to provide funding for such programs.

We are helping prisoners transition back into society. We want to help small service organizations gain capabilities. One of the things that some of you who have been involved with the faith-based community understand, that, you know, the big guys get rolling and kind of get a nice head of steam up, and there doesn't seem to be much focus on smaller organizations, some of which are just getting started. Our job is to make sure that the Compassion Fund helps startups. I don't want to sound like a business guy, but there are some people just getting started. They need tutoring; they need help. But they can provide a vital service.

One reason faith programs exist is because some good soul sees there's a demand. And they may not be the well-established organization, and it seems like to me, it's a proper use of resource to help startups, new social entrepreneurs, small social entrepreneurs get their feet on the ground to provide compassionate help, alongside the big ones. [*Applause*] There you go.

There's other targeted programs, as well as social service competitive grant money. And I'm sure you're being briefed on— I hope you're being briefed on all this during this conference. You ought to feel comfortable about making sure that your program has a chance to participate in a myriad of opportunities. We want you to do that. We welcome your participation. We want involvement.

The other thing is, we're trying to work hard is—to change the culture here in Washington. The faith-based program is relatively new, and it takes a while for cultures to change, and we want people throughout the bureaucracies to not fear the involvement of faith programs and community-based programs in the compassionate delivery of help. And one of the real challenges we have is at the State and local governmental level. We've made good progress, by the way, here at the Federal level on competitive grant money.

See, a lot of money that comes out of Washington is formula-driven. It just kind of flows out. And so sometimes that money goes to the States, and the States are the decisionmakers as to whether or not a faith program can be involved in the—in receiving that money to help meet social objectives. We are constantly working with Governors and mayors to convince them that having a faith-based office in their respective centers of responsibility will really help improve their State, as well as the—as well as their cities.

And there's progress being made there. I think there's something like 30 Governors have now got faith-based offices, and over 100 mayors have got faith-based offices. And to the extent that you can influence your mayor or your Governor, convince them to open up an office and make sure that some of the Federal money that flows to the States is open for competitive bidding for faith-based programs.

By the way, we just set up a new faith-based and community office in the Department of Homeland Security. Last month, I signed a bill extending what's called charitable choice. It's a mechanism by which these programs can go forward. And it's—one of the most important things about the legislation I signed, it allows faith-based groups to receive Federal funding without changing their hiring practices. This is going to stay around for another 5 years. In other words, the bill extended the life of the charitable choice provision in the welfare reform law by another 5 years.

I would hope Congress would recognize the importance of charitable choice and extend it forever. I mean, if it makes sense today, it makes sense forever.

You know, one of the things that really inspires me is when I get to meet folks who are on the frontline of changing America one soul at a time. And today I had the privilege of meeting a woman named Dana Ingram. She's with us. She is the founder of a faith-based housing and financial service organization in Hinesville, Georgia, called JC Vision. This is an organization that provides financial counseling and assistance in receiving credit and securing a home loan.

See, one of the things that I know is important for the future of the country is to promote ownership. I really like the idea when somebody opens the door of the place they're living and says, "Welcome to my home. Welcome to my piece of property." And this lady—and Dana is involved with counseling. Look, face it; when you look at a mortgage deal, all that fine print makes some people nervous. It makes me nervous. [*Laughter*] Of course, I'm in temporary housing. [*Laughter*]

When she first—a few years ago, her program served 500 people on a budget of less than $100,000. She applied for Federal funding. She said, "Yes, I'm a faith-based program, but I do believe that we can benefit from competitive grant money." And so she applied, and she was awarded a grant. Her budget is now $400,000. Now she's serving 10,000 people. The idea is to promote successful programs, to focus on whether or not these programs are successful, and if they are, encourage them. One way to encourage somebody is to have a little grant money available on a competitive basis—nothing more encouraging than to get some grant money. And so Dana is encouraged, and she's expanding her program.

One of the really successful programs in America is a program called Teen Challenge. I don't know if you're aware of Teen Challenge. So Pastor Arthur Stafford is with us. Arthur works at Teen Challenge New Haven. Notice I didn't say, "Mister." I said, "Pastor." Teen Challenge is a faith-based program.

And he is a—his program is aimed, like many of the Teen Challenge programs, at helping young folks overcome addiction to drugs, which oftentimes lead to crime and other problems. Not long ago, funding constraints limited how many people Teen Challenge in New Haven could host. And they spent—Arthur and his buddies spent a lot of time raising money for the program. For those of you who are on limited budgets who have got grand ambitions to save lives, you know how much time you can spend away from the task at hand toward finding money to sustain your programs. And so Arthur and Team Challenge competed for and earned a Federal grant through the Access to Recovery drug treatment program. For those of you involved in drug treatment, the Access to Recovery drug treatment program provides a good source of money for you. I recommend you applying for grants from that program.

And so what Arthur has said is that—when he got the money—"It's been a blessing to our ministry." I find that interesting, don't you—"It's been a blessing to our ministry. We're not worried about how to raise money all the time; we can focus on transforming lives."

And so today Matt Enriquez is with us. So Matt comes in to meet the President. I said, "How you doing, Matt?" He didn't speak—he looked a little nervous. [*Laughter*] Matt was addicted to drugs. He had spent time because of robbery. He was lost, and then he was found by people at Teen Challenge. He is now going to college.

Where are you, Matt? There he is. Where's Arthur? Pastor, stand up. [*Applause*] Yes, there you go. Get your Pastor, Matt. There he is. Thank you.

So Matt now goes to the Connecticut Culinary Institute. If you're looking for a cook, he's your man. [*Laughter*] Here's what he said: "The best thing about"—speaking about Teen Challenge—"is the love that's in the program. I had no idea what I wanted to do at all. This let me know what I wanted to do for the rest of my life."

See, government can pass law, and it can hand out money, but it cannot love. And so I want to thank—[*applause*]. I appreciate the examples—letting me use you as examples. America can change one heart at a time. Matt is living proof. America changes not only when a soul like Matt gets saved but the person who is involved with helping Matt also becomes a stronger and better citizen as well.

And now Matt goes on. See, Matt himself serves as a way to help change lives. Maybe Matt—maybe somebody is listening here. I don't know if this deal is on C–SPAN or not, but if it is, maybe somebody is out there, like Matt, who needs help and can find help at a Teen Challenge or another program, all aimed at helping somebody save lives.

Matt, I know when you get your deal going and making a good living as a cook, you yourself will turn and help find—somebody else find help too. So I appreciate you.

Our job is—for the next 3 years, is to continue to work with Congress to make sure that money is opened up to faith-based programs. Competitive grant money should not be earmarked. It should be open for competitive-based grants so that—[*applause*].

We'll continue to work with local and State officials to open up their programs to faith and community-based programs. I'm going to continue to work on individual choice programs. I like the idea of providing help for individuals by empowering them to be the decisionmaker. In other words, it makes a lot of sense to me to say to somebody who is trying to recover from a drug addiction, "Here's the money to help you; you go pick the program that suits your needs so you can solve your problem."

And so we got a lot of work to do to continue to encourage you to do the work you're doing. I am inspired by the love and compassion that I find as I travel the country. For those of you, by the way, who are involved with helping the Katrina folks, I want to thank you from the bottom of our Nation's heart for welcoming those who I'm sure felt lost and then felt welcomed when a total stranger embraced them in a typically American compassionate way. I assure you that as long as I'm the President, I will always recognize where the strength of this country lies, the true strength, and that's in the hearts and souls of our fellow citizens.

My hope is that the vision that de Tocqueville saw in 1830 is a vision that some observer will find still strong in America in the year 2030 and 2060 and beyond. Because so long as America is able to unleash the compassion of our country, will it be able to bring hope into dark corners of our country, places where there is no light, places where there's despair, places where people can realize their potential if given a chance.

And so I want to—for those of you who are a part of giving people a chance, for those of you who have heard the universal call, I thank you for your work and ask for God's blessings on your lives and on your work.

Thanks for coming. God bless.

NOTE: The President spoke at 11:58 a.m. at the Washington Hilton Hotel.

Remarks on Signing the USA PATRIOT Improvement and Reauthorization Act of 2005
March 9, 2006

Welcome. Thanks for the applause. Glad you're here in the people's house.

I'm going to sign—in a few moments I'll be signing the USA PATRIOT Improvement and Reauthorization Act. This is a really important piece of legislation. It is a piece of legislation that's vital to win the war on terror and to protect the American people.

The law allows our intelligence and law enforcement officials to continue to share information. It allows them to continue to use tools against terrorists that they used against—that they use against drug dealers and other criminals. It will improve our Nation's security, while we safeguard the civil liberties of our people. The legislation strengthens the Justice Department so it can better detect and disrupt terrorist threats. And the bill gives law enforcement

new tools to combat threats to our citizens from international terrorists to local drug dealers.

It is an important piece of legislation, and I thank those here who helped get it passed. I particularly want to thank the Attorney General, Al Gonzales. It's good to see former Attorney Generals here as well. I appreciate Secretary Mike Chertoff, Secretary John Snow, Ambassador Negroponte, Bob Mueller. Thank you all for coming. John Walters, appreciate you being here.

I particularly want to thank the Members of the Congress who are up here, starting with the Speaker of the House, Denny Hastert. Mr. Speaker, thanks for your leadership on this important piece of legislation. I do want to pay special tribute to Senator

Arlen Specter and Congressman Jim Sensenbrenner. These are the chairmen of the Judiciary Committees that got this legislation to this desk. Thank you all for your hard work. I appreciate you being here.

I want to thank Pat Roberts, who's with us; John Boehner, who's majority leader; Roy Blunt, the majority whip. I want to thank all the other Members of the Congress who have joined us, particularly Peter King, who is the chairman of the House Homeland Security Committee.

I want to thank all the State and local officials who are here. Chief Ramsey, it's good to see you. Appreciate you coming. Always be good to the local police chief. [*Laughter*]

America remains a nation at war. The war reached our shores on September the 11th, 2001. On that morning, we saw clearly the violence and hatred of a new enemy. We saw the terrorists' destructive vision for us when they killed nearly 3,000 men, women, and children.

In the face of this ruthless threat, our Nation has made a clear choice: We will confront this mortal danger; we will stay on the offensive; and we're not going to wait to be attacked again. Since September the 11th, 2001, we have taken the fight to the enemy. We've hunted terrorists in the mountains of Afghanistan, cities of Iraq, in the islands of Southeast Asia, and everywhere else they plot, plan, and train. Our men and women in uniform have brought down two regimes that supported terrorism. We liberated 50 million people. We've gained new allies in the war on terror.

As we wage the war on terror overseas, we're also going after the terrorists here at home, and one of the most important tools we have used to protect the American people is the PATRIOT Act. The PATRIOT Act closed dangerous gaps in America's law enforcement and intelligence capabilities, gaps the terrorists exploited when they attacked us on September the 11th.

The PATRIOT Act was passed with overwhelming bipartisan support. It strengthened our national security in two important ways. First, it authorized law enforcement and intelligence officers to share vital information. Before the PATRIOT Act, criminal investigators were often separated from intelligence officers by a legal and bureaucratic wall. The PATRIOT Act tore down the wall. And as a result, law enforcement and intelligence officers are sharing information, working together, and bringing terrorists to justice.

Secondly, the PATRIOT Act has allowed agents to pursue terrorists with the same tools they use against other criminals. Before the PATRIOT Act, it was easier to track the phone contacts of a drug dealer than the phone contacts of an enemy operative. Before the PATRIOT Act, it was easier to get the credit card receipts of a tax cheater than trace the financial support of an Al Qaida fundraiser. The PATRIOT Act corrected these double standards, and the United States is safer as a result.

Over the past 4 years, America's law enforcement and intelligence personnel have proved that the PATRIOT Act works. Federal, State, and local law enforcement have used the PATRIOT Act to break up terror cells in Ohio, New York, Oregon, and Virginia. We've prosecuted terrorist operatives and supporters in California and Texas, New Jersey, Illinois, Washington, and North Carolina.

The PATRIOT Act has accomplished exactly what it was designed to do. It has helped us detect terror cells, disrupt terrorist plots, and save American lives. The bill I sign today extends these vital provisions. It also gives our Nation new protections and added defenses.

This legislation creates a new position of Assistant Attorney General for National Security. This will allow the Justice Department to bring together its national security, counterterrorism, counterintelligence, and foreign intelligence surveillance operations under a single authority. This reorganization fulfills one of the critical recommendations of the WMD Commission. It will help our brave men and women in law enforcement connect the dots before the terrorists strike.

This bill also will help protect Americans from the growing threat of methamphetamine. Meth is easy to make. It is highly addictive. It is ruining too many lives across our country. The bill introduces common-sense safeguards that would make many of the ingredients used in manufacturing meth harder to obtain in bulk and easier for law enforcement to track.

For example, the bill places limits on large-scale purchases of over-the-counter drugs that are used to manufacture meth. It requires stores to keep these ingredients behind the counter or in locked display cases. The bill also increases penalties for smuggling and selling of meth. Our Nation is committed to protecting our citizens and our young people from the scourge of methamphetamine.

The PATRIOT Act has served America well, yet we cannot let the fact that America has not been attacked since September the 11th lull us into the illusion that the terrorist threat has disappeared. We still face dangerous enemies. The terrorists haven't lost the will or the ability to kill innocent folks. Our military, law enforcement, homeland security, and intelligence professionals are working day and night to protect us from this threat. We're safer for their efforts, and we'll continue to give them the tools to get the job done.

And now it's my honor to sign the USA PATRIOT Improvement and Reauthorization Act of 2005.

NOTE: The President spoke at 2:46 p.m. in the East Room at the White House. In his remarks, he referred to Charles H. Ramsey, chief, Metropolitan Police Department of Washington, DC. H.R. 3199, approved March 9, was assigned Public Law No. 109–177. The Office of the Press Secretary also released a Spanish language transcript of these remarks.

Statement on Signing the USA PATRIOT Improvement and Reauthorization Act of 2005
March 9, 2006

Today, I have signed into law H.R. 3199, the "USA PATRIOT Improvement and Re-authorization Act of 2005," and then S. 2271, the "USA PATRIOT Act Additional Reauthorizing Amendments Act of 2006." The bills will help us continue to fight terrorism effectively and to combat the use of the illegal drug methamphetamine that is ruining too many lives.

The executive branch shall construe the provisions of H.R. 3199 that call for furnishing information to entities outside the executive branch, such as sections 106A and 119, in a manner consistent with the President's constitutional authority to supervise the unitary executive branch and to withhold information the disclosure of which could impair foreign relations, national security, the deliberative processes of the Executive, or the performance of the Executive's constitutional duties.

The executive branch shall construe section 756(e)(2) of H.R. 3199, which calls for an executive branch official to submit to the Congress recommendations for legislative action, in a manner consistent with the President's constitutional authority to supervise the unitary executive branch and to recommend for the consideration of the Congress such measures as he judges necessary and expedient.

GEORGE W. BUSH

The White House,

March 9, 2006.

Remarks at the Georgia Republican Party's President's Day Dinner in College Park, Georgia
March 9, 2006

Thank you all. I appreciate you coming. Please be seated. Thanks for being here. I appreciate the warm reception. Thanks for letting me come back to Georgia. I'm proud to be here to help support the Republican Party of Georgia, which is changing this State for the better.

And I'm proud to be introduced by Sonny Perdue, who is doing a heck of a good job as the Governor of this State. So here's the thing I like about Sonny: One, he married well. [*Laughter*] Where's Mary? Oh, there she is. Hi, Mary, good to see you. Thanks for being here. Secondly, he said his favorite title in life is not "Governor" but "Big Buddy." [*Laughter*] You know who calls him "Big Buddy"? His grandkids. Sonny has got his priorities straight. I'm proud to call him friend, and I know you're proud to call him Governor.

By the way, Mary, Laura sends her very best and her love. Laura is a remarkable person. She is patient, especially to be married to me. [*Laughter*] One of the things that I love about being the President is, well, I've got a 45-second commute—[*laughter*]—and when I get home, there's a person there who is a wonderful partner in serving our country. She understands what I know: It's a huge honor to be the First Couple of the United States. And she is making an enormous difference in the lives of people in west Texas-type ways. And so she sends her love and sends her best.

I want to thank the—first of all, let me say something about your two United States Senators. They had votes, and that's good that they stayed there to do the job that you send them to do. I was incredibly proud to watch them help shepherd through two Supreme Court Justices I named. When I campaigned in Georgia, I said, "If you elect me to be President, I will name people to the bench who will strictly interpret the Constitution and not try to write laws from the bench." I did so with Chief Justice Roberts, Judge Alito. And Senator Saxby Chambliss and Johnny Isakson were strong supporters for those nominees.

I want to thank the Members of the United States Congress who have joined us here today: Nathan Deal from north Georgia; John Linder; Phil Gingrey; Lynn Westmoreland; and Tom Price. Thank you all for joining us. We spent some quality time on Air Force One flying down here. These are smart people. They never pass up a free flight when they're offered one. [*Laughter*] But I enjoy them. They're good folks—good, down-to-earth, decent folks serving the State of the Georgia in the United States Congress, and I'm proud to call them friends.

I want to thank Glenn Richardson, who is the speaker of the house. I want to thank Eric Johnson, the president pro tem of the State senate. I want to thank all those who are serving in the statehouse. It's a—it is an important job.

You know things are changing in Georgia when you say welcome to the speaker—[*laughter*]—and welcome to the leader of the senate. The Republican Party here has done a good job of establishing a grassroots political base that is not only helping people like me, but it's changing the statehouse for the better in the State of Georgia.

I want to thank Alec Poitevint, the mighty chairman and national committeeman of the great State of Georgia. Alec, good to see you, and Doreen is here. Alec has got his priorities straight. I've known him for a long period of time. We're quite familiar with each other. He said, "How many turkeys you got on your ranch?" I said, "I haven't been counting them lately." He says, "Well, I've been counting them on mine." The man's got his priorities straight. [*Laughter*]

I want to thank people who are running for office. I appreciate you willing to put your name on the line. I want to thank you for your willingness to get out and shake hands and tell people what you believe and speak from the heart. Two candidates running for the Lieutenant Governor with us, Casey Cagle and Ralph Reed, and I appreciate them both being here tonight.

Finally, I want to say something about two Mac—well, one Mac, one Max. [*Laughter*] One of the reasons I've come down here is to thank you for supporting two good folks who are running for the United States Congress, Mac Collins and Max Burns. I know them well. I know Mac's wife, Julie, and I know Max's wife, Lora. I've served with them before. I have seen what kind of people they are up close. They're principled gentlemen. They understand the risks to the world in which we live. They're smart with the people's money. I urge the people of Georgia to send Mac Collins and Max Burns back to the United States Congress. [*Applause*] I knew they were there somewhere.

And finally, I want to say something about Sonny. I think the people of this State need to judge your Governor based upon performance. He is a fellow who has performed. He's delivered results. He said he was going to do some things when he ran for the Governor of your State, and he did. I don't know if you remember, but when he took office, Georgia wasn't doing that well in the economy. Matter of fact,

you were losing jobs. I don't know if people remember in this great State, but when Sonny first came into office, he had a State deficit of $620 million. Today, Georgia's economy is on the march. You're increasing jobs; people are working; and you've got a surplus in the State treasury.

Now, Sonny knows how to get things done. And one of the main reasons I have come down here is to thank the good people of your State for electing such a good man to be the Governor of an important State. Sonny Perdue deserves to be reelected as the Governor of the State of Georgia.

We're living in historic times. We are a country still at war. I wish I could report—give you a different report. My job is to see the world the way it really is, not to see the world the way some would hope it would be. My job is—my thinking is, really—was defined on September the 11th—you've just got to know that.

Some of my buddies from Texas come over there to the White House, and they say, "What's it like to be the President?" First of all, I'm a person who is so honored to be sustained by the prayers of millions of people. It is—one of the truly great blessings of the Presidency is to be uplifted in prayer by people I never get to thank personally.

Secondly, I make a lot of decisions. It's a decisionmaking experience. Sonny will tell you, as the Governor of a State, you make decisions. That's what a chief executive officer does. In order to make decisions, you've got to make decisions based upon principle. And if not exactly sure what information you need, you've got to rely upon good people to give you information so you can make good decisions. A lot of my decisionmaking has come about as a result of the attack on our country. See, after that day, I vowed that I would do everything in my power to protect the United States of America from further attack.

That's why I'm proud to stand with Members of the United States Congress and candidates for Congress who understand our biggest job, our most important responsibility in Washington, is to protect the American people and never forget the lessons of September the 11th, 2001. I knew one of the challenges for our country would be, the farther we got away from that date, that day, that people would want to forget the trauma of the day and might be willing to forget the lessons learned on that day. I can assure you, these Members of Congress won't forget the lessons of that day, and neither will I.

And today I had the honor in the White House of signing an extension of the PATRIOT Act. We've asked brave souls to be on the frontline of fighting terrorists. They deserve every possible tool, while we safeguard the civil liberties of the United States of America. Thank you all for supporting the PATRIOT Act. We did the right thing in Washington.

After the attacks on the country, I did what you would expect me to do, and asked people who are on the frontlines of defending you whether or not there was—there's more we could be doing. What can we do more to protect the American people? I vowed on September the 11th I would do everything I can to protect the American people. I would rally the assets and resources and brain power of our country to protect you.

And so I called people in, and I said, "Is there anything else we could have done to prevent the attacks from September the 11th?" And a general named Mike Hayden said, "I believe there is, Mr. President. I believe we can design a system that will enable us to listen to a call from outside the country in, from a known Al Qaida affiliate or a suspected Al Qaida affiliate." I said, that makes sense, doesn't it? If the people inside the country that planned the attacks on the United States were making phone calls out, we'd want to know that prior to any attack.

And so I said, "Mike, show me how the system would work." I then called in law-

yers—and we've got a lot of them in Washington. [*Laughter*] By the way, two of my favorite lawyers are here today, Dan Coats and Connie Mack, former United States Senators who have been close to the White House on a variety of matters. So I'm not denigrating you two guys; I like lawyers. [*Laughter*] But we've got a lot of them—[*laughter*]—and some smart ones.

And I said, "Is the program that the NSA is recommending legal?" That's what you'd expect the President to do. You'd expect the President to ask, is there more we could do, and if the suggestion—if someone made a suggestion, the first question is, is it legal to do so? And they came back and said, "Mr. President, you have the authority to do this program"—in other words, it's legal.

Before I implemented the program, a program, by the way, which is limited in nature—phone calls coming from inside the country out and outside in, with one of the numbers being known Al Qaida, suspected Al Qaida, and affiliates—I then recognized that the United States Congress would be interested in this subject. So we briefed leaders from both parties, both chambers, on a program to protect the American people. We've kept them abreast more than one time, in a series of briefings, about a program that is necessary to protect the American people. As my buddy in Texas said, "If you're trying to do something illegal, why did you brief the Congress?" [*Laughter*]

What we're doing is the right thing. My thinking process, my decisionmaking, is based upon my understanding of the job of the President and the Federal Government—is to protect our people so we never have to go through what we went again. It is right; it is necessary to listen to Al Qaida. If Al Qaida is making a phone call into the United States of America or vice versa, we want to know why, in order to protect this country.

In order to protect this country, we must remember the lessons of September the

11th. And lesson number one is, we have got to stay on the offense against the terrorist network that would like to do harm to the United States of America, and we are. We are on the hunt. We've got some fantastic men and women who wear our Nation's uniform doing everything they can to find the terrorists before they can hurt us again. It's hard to plan and plot and destroy America if you're on the run. And we're bringing a lot of the killers to justice. And I will continue to insist that we pursue the killers to keep America safe.

The second lesson, since this is a different kind of war, is that if you harbor a terrorist, you're equally as guilty as the terrorist. We're dealing with a shadowy network. We're not fighting nation-states. We're fighting a group of coldblooded killers who adopted an ideology that's the exact opposite of America, that tries to find safe haven. And therefore, part of the strategy is to deny the enemy safe haven. And when the President says something, he better mean what he says, and I meant what I said when I said to the Taliban, "Give up Al Qaida." And when they refused, the United States of America removed a barbaric regime for our own security, and in so doing, however, we liberated 25 million people from the clutches of these barbaric people.

Another lesson of September the 11th is that we must deal with threats before they come to hurt us. You see, prior to September the 11th, 2001, a lot of folks assumed that we were safe in America. In other words, we could see a threat somewhere overseas, but we were fine. Oceans protected us; perhaps our might protected us. But that all changed for me on September the 11th, 2001. Whenever we see a threat, the United States of America must take them seriously. We cannot take threats for granted. I saw a threat; the world saw a threat; people in the United Nations Security Council saw a threat; Republicans on Capitol Hill saw a threat; Democrats on Capitol Hill saw a threat in Saddam Hussein.

And the reason they saw a threat—this is a man who at least had the capacity to manufacture weapons; he had used weapons of mass destruction; he was on the terrorist list of the United States of America; he killed thousands of his own citizens; he was firing at U.S. jets; and he invaded his neighbor. He was a threat, and getting rid of Saddam Hussein has made America safer and the world a better place.

And I'm proud to be on stage with people who understood the stakes and stand strong, particularly when we put men and women in harm's way. I'm proud to have people up here who understand that any time we put an American volunteer into harm's way, he or she deserves the best pay, the best training, and the best possible equipment.

We've got a strategy for victory in Iraq. Now, you got to understand, we're facing an enemy that can't beat us militarily, and they certainly can't beat us ideologically. And they've got one weapon, and their weapon is the willingness to kill innocent people and to have the horror on the TV screens, understanding full well that the American people are decent and compassionate people. That's the only weapon they have.

Their goal, their stated goal, is to drive the United States of America and allies out of the Middle East so they can spread their totalitarian vision. That's what they've said, and when the enemy says something, we got to take them seriously. They believe we're weak. They believe their tactics will cause us to run. The United States of America will not run in the face of thugs and assassins, and we're going to stand strong in support of people who expressed themselves last year at the ballot box in the face of incredible threats. Eleven million Iraqis said loud and clear to the world, "We reject civil war. We want our freedom, and we want our democracy." And America is proud to stand with them.

We have a political strategy, and that is to encourage the votes which took place last year under—and they ratified a Constitution, which is a modern constitution. A government should be a unified government that recognizes minority rights so that the people—when the people speak, government responds.

And secondly, we have a security strategy that says loud and clear that we want the Iraqis to take the fight to the enemy. As the Iraqis stand up, our troops will stand down. But I want to assure you, what I said in the State of the Union is what I mean. Troop levels in Iraq will be decided not by Washington, DC, politics but by the commanders on the ground. I will be making the military decisions necessary to win this war not based upon focus groups or opinion polls but based upon the solid, sound advice of a group of really fine military commanders.

Our objective is a country that can defend itself and sustain itself, a country that will not be a safe haven for Al Qaida and its terrorist network, a country which will be a ally in the war on terror, and a country will—which will serve as a powerful example for others in a part of the world that is desperate for freedom.

And so the ultimate way to achieve our objectives, which is to lay the foundation of peace for generations to come, is to help people live in liberty and help spread democracy. The people of the Middle East must understand that when I say democracy, I don't mean American-style democracy. I mean a democracy which reflects the values and the history and the tradition of the country in which democracy is spreading.

But I do believe in the universality of liberty. I personally believe there is an Almighty God, and I believe a gift from the Almighty God to every man and woman on the face of the Earth is freedom. Our country was formed based upon the natural rights of men and women, and we believe those natural rights extend to men and women all across the globe. The United States of America believes people desire to be free. And by freeing people, we are laying the foundation of peace for generations to come.

I've trotted this story out a lot, or my beliefs out a lot, about the effects of freedom. But let me try to explain for—particularly the youngsters here—about what I mean for laying the foundation for peace to come.

One of my best buddies in the international arena is Prime Minister Koizumi of Japan. What's interesting about that is 60 years ago, my dad, as an 18-year-old fighter pilot, Navy fighter pilot—and I'm sure many relatives of folks here fought the Japanese, because they were the sworn enemy. And this is one of the bloodiest of all wars. A lot of people lost their lives on both sides of this conflict. And yet today, the American President can speak to an audience in Atlanta, Georgia, and say, "I sit down at the table with Prime Minister Koizumi to keep the peace, to deal with some of the tough issues around the world. He's a partner in peace."

And so what happened? Something had to have happened between 18-year-old fighter pilot George H.W. Bush and George W. standing here as the President. And what happened was, Japan adopted a Japanese-style democracy. You see, democracies yield the peace, and someday, someday, if we do not lose our nerve and our will, an American President will be talking to a duly elected leader from Iraq, working together to keep the peace, and our children and grandchildren will be better off.

Now that you're stuck here, I'm going to tell you something else. [*Laughter*] Our economy has been through a lot in a relatively quick period of time. We've been through a recession; we've been through corporate scandals; we've been through a devastating attack on our country; we have dealt with war; we have dealt with high energy prices; and we have dealt with natural disasters, large natural disasters. Last year, our economy grew at 3.5 percent. The national unemployment rate is 4.7 percent. That's lower than the average rate of the 1970s, 1980s, and 1990s. We added 4.7 million new jobs over 2½ years. After-tax real income is up 8 percent. Productivity is at an alltime high. More people own a home than ever before in our Nation's history; more minority families own a home than ever before in our Nation's history. We're doing something right in Washington, DC, and you know what it is? We've unleashed the entrepreneurial spirit of the United States because of real, meaningful tax cuts. Republicans believe that the more money you have in the pocket, the more you save, invest, and spend, the better off this economy is.

The tax relief we passed and these Members voted for, these candidates voted for, is set to expire. And if it does, the American people are going to get a tax increase they don't expect and they don't want. In order to make sure this economy continues to grow, in order to make sure the entrepreneurial spirit continues to remain strong, in order to make sure the small-business sector of our economy is as strong as it is today, we need to make the tax relief permanent.

Now, I know what they're going to say. They're going to say, "How can you balance the budget if you cut the taxes?" People will say, "Well, we need to raise your taxes in order to balance the budget." That's not the way Washington works. What will happen is they will raise your taxes and figure out new ways to spend your money. The best way to balance the budget is to keep progrowth economic policies in place and be wise about how we spend your money. We're on our way to cutting that deficit in half by 2009, and I want to thank the Members up here for making the tough choices when it comes to our budget.

We got a choice to make in this country: Do we become a protectionist, isolated nation, or do we continue to lead? I made my choice. I believe America is better off

when America takes a leadership role in this world. I believe we should not fear our economic future, because we should shape it. Part of shaping the future is to keep taxes low. Part of shaping our future is to get rid of these junk and frivolous lawsuits that are running good capital out of America.

Part of shaping our future is to make sure we're not hooked on oil. I know that sounds odd for a Texan to say. [*Laughter*] But if you see the world from my perspective, I think you would agree with me. Being addicted to oil is a problem. When demand for hydrocarbons or fossil fuels goes up in developing parts of the world, it causes the price of gasoline to go up here at home. When parts of the world that don't like the United States of America threaten to withhold supplies of oil from the market, it creates a national security problem. And so I'm looking forward to working with Congress to diversify away from oil, to spend money on research and development so we can have plug-in hybrid automobiles that can drive the first 40 miles on electricity, to spend money to make sure that our technologies are able to help us develop ethanol. Look, we want our farmers in Georgia growing crops that can run our automobiles. We need to become less dependent on foreign sources of oil in order to be a competitive nation.

We need nuclear power and solar power and wind power. In order for this country to be competitive in the out years, in order for us to be confident about our national security, we have got to be less addicted to Middle Eastern oil, and I intend to lead that country this direction.

I want to talk to you about a couple of other things, about a competitiveness agenda. How do you stay competitive in a global economy? The key to making sure that America remains the leader in the world is to make sure our children are educated. You see, if our kids don't have the skills for the jobs of the 21st century, they're going to go somewhere else. That's just a fact of life. And so therefore, I told the United States Congress we need to work together to make sure that we're not only the leader in research and development, in technological development, but to make sure our children have got math and science skills so that we are educating the engineers of the future and the physicists of the future and the chemists of the future.

I want to congratulate Sonny Perdue for implementing the No Child Left Behind Act. I've heard all the debates about it; I'm sure you have as well: "How dare the Government measure?" Look, my attitude is, we're spending money. The taxpayer wants to know whether the money is well-spent. If you're spending money to teach a child to read and write, doesn't it make sense to measure, to determine whether or not the child is reading or writing? Doesn't it make sense to believe every child can read and demand that the school system teach every child to read? And how do you know? You measure. And if you find a child not reading early, I think it makes sense to provide additional help, additional money for each child, like we're doing through No Child Left Behind Act, so no child is left behind. No, Republicans should stand for high standards and the belief that every child can learn, and we ought to demand change where we find children trapped in schools that will not teach and will not change.

And we're getting results. We're getting results nationwide. There's an achievement gap in America that's not right. We've got too many of our African American kids and young Latino kids who can't read at grade level. But that's changing. See, we're measuring, we're correcting problems early, before it's too late. And that achievement gap is narrowing, and America is better off for it.

And we've got a problem when it comes to math. See, our fourth graders are testing fine in math but then falling off in the eighth grade. So what I want to do is apply the same rigor we've done for reading in the early grades to math in the middle grades to make sure that America is competitive, to make sure that our children have the skills necessary to fill the jobs of the 21st century. This country of ours should not fear the future. We ought to welcome the future and shape the future. And the United States of America must put policies in place to make sure that we're the leading economy in the world, for the sake of our people and the sake of people who want to find work. And that's exactly what I intend to do for this country.

And finally—you'll probably be happy to hear the word, "finally"—I'm going to continue to work with people on this stage to promote a culture of life in the United States of America. We believe every person matters, every person counts. We believe that—we believe in medicine and sound science, but we don't believe in taking life to promote science. We believe in upholding values that are important. We believe in the faith-based initiatives. We understand there are people in this part of the world and people all over our country who hurt.

We also understand the limitation of government. Government can hand out money, but it cannot put hope in a person's heart or a sense of purpose in a person's life. That's done when a loving individual finds a stranger in need or a child who needs to learn to read or a person addicted, says, "I love you, brother," or, "I love you, sister. What can I do to help you?" The greatest strength of the United States of America is not our military, and it's not the size of our wallet. The greatest strength of the United States of America lies in the hearts and souls of millions of our citizens who've heard the universal call to love a neighbor just like you'd like to be loved themselves and are doing that on a daily basis.

We've got millions of our citizens who are helping change America one heart, one soul, and one conscience at a time. And it's important for the Federal Government and the State government not to fear the armies of compassion but to support the armies of compassion as they help make this country a hopeful, optimistic place for every citizen who is honored to call themselves an American.

Listen, I love being your President. I love being back in Georgia. Thanks for giving me a chance to come back. Thanks for joining this great festival that celebrates the Republican Party of the great State of Georgia. And God bless.

NOTE: The President spoke at 6:22 p.m. at the Georgia International Convention Center. In his remarks, he referred to Gov. Sonny Perdue of Georgia, and his wife, Mary; and Alec Poitevint, State chairman and national committeeman, Georgia Republican Party, and his wife, Doreen.

Interview With Diana Moukalled of Future Television of Lebanon
March 9, 2006

Lebanese Freedom

Ms. Moukalled. Mr. President, thank you for receiving Future Television. As you know, head of U.N. inquiry, Serge Brammertz, will present his report to the Security Council in a few days. How should the international community respond if the report concluded that Syria did not fully cooperate with the inquiry, as previous efforts did?

The President. Our position is, is that we want to know the truth, and we expect all parties to be forthcoming with the truth. The truth is really important to help Lebanon meet a goal that we want for Lebanon, which is free of foreign interference, democratic and peaceful, so that people can realize dreams and so the great country of Lebanon can grow and prosper like I'm confident it can.

So the United States will constantly remind all parties that we seek the truth, and we expect parties, when asked about the truth, to be forthcoming with the truth. I'm worried about people who stall and hope that the world turns a blind eye to a terrible death. And we're not going to turn a blind eye. We will keep focused on this important issue, because we believe in the future of Lebanon.

Syrian Withdrawal From Lebanon

Ms. Moukalled. From what you say, many in Lebanon fear that there might be a deal between Washington and Damascus. In other words, if Damascus complied with Washington demands regarding Iraq, regarding Hizballah and Hamas, would you let the inquiry not reach its ultimate?

The President. Part of our desires for Damascus is, of course, to shut down terrorist bases in their country, and is, of course, to stop cross-border infiltration into Iraq, is, of course, to stop allowing people to find safe haven to plot and plan attacks in the neighborhood. But part of our demands was to—was 1559, which is, completely out of Lebanon. And so there are no deals. We are people who believe that when we say something, we've got to keep our word. And again, I repeat to you: I think that the light of truth is very important toward establishing a peace that we all want in the region.

I really do want young boys and girls in Lebanon to be able to grow up in a world free of violence. Lebanon is a fabulous country; Beirut is one of the great international cities of all time. And it's in the world's interest that this democracy survive, and not only survive but flourish and thrive. And so we don't—we really aren't going to deal away Lebanon's future.

U.S. Support for Lebanese Freedom

Ms. Moukalled. Regarding U.N. Resolution 1559, the Lebanese Government says that it wants to reach a true result with the issue through a national dialog——

The President. Yes.

Ms. Moukalled. ——and you have demanded repeatedly that Lebanon should implement this resolution. Will you give the Lebanese Government a chance to resolve this issue through national dialog, or you will exercise more pressure?

The President. I think it's very important that the national dialog process succeed. The truth of the matter is that peace in Lebanon is going to be achieved by Lebanese leaders, people in Lebanon who are dedicated to the future. The United States can—we can work; we can help; we can pressure Syria; or we can do things. But what we can't do is to force people to be courageous in the name of peace. That's up to Lebanon's people themselves—the people of Lebanon themselves. The Lebanese must stand up and say, "We demand a open and free and transparent society so we can live in peace."

We'll help, but courage comes from within people's souls. And we have been encouraged by courage being shown by those who believe in Lebanon's future.

Ms. Moukalled. Are you following the national dialog that's happening now in Lebanon?

The President. I am.

Ms. Moukalled. Many believe that without international efforts, this dialog will not succeed, where other parties think that the American pressure is keeping Lebanese from reaching an agreement.

The President. No, I hope—I believe that an agreement can be reached. I understand the talks have been suspended for a week, but they will be ongoing, and I think it's a very important part of the Lebanese folks putting aside past—the past and focusing on a bright future. And we will help, and we will encourage, but ultimately the decisions have to be made by the Lebanese citizens, that they want something better than violence and war and division.

Hizballah

Ms. Moukalled. The two controversial items are the ousting of President Emile Lahud and the disarming of Hizballah.

The President. Yes.

Ms. Moukalled. What's your comment? What——

The President. Our position is clear: 1559, which we strongly support, says that armed militias should be disarmed. And secondly, we believe that the President ought to be independent, ought to be someone who will strongly represent the interests of the Lebanese people.

Ms. Moukalled. The Lebanese Government considers Hizballah a resistance. What's your comment?

The President. My comment is, is that armed militias should disarm. And I think it's very important to understand that democracy—you can't have a democracy if political parties have their own armed force. Our position is that the Lebanese forces ought to be in control of the security of Lebanon, for the good of the people.

Lebanese Freedom

Ms. Moukalled. What's your position regarding ousting President Emile Lahud?

The President. Again, I repeat to you: I think the characteristics for the President ought to be somebody who is independent-minded, somebody who focuses on his— the future of the country, somebody who understands that foreign influences inside of a country can be very negative.

Spread of Democracy

Ms. Moukalled. Mr. President, as you know, the situation in Iraq is really deteriorating; the country is on the edge of a civil war. The support for U.S. policies among Arab public opinion is—it's minimal.

Many believe that you are focusing on Lebanon to divert attention from what's going on in Iraq, or it's a part of a whole scenario to control the region. Why did Lebanon get so much of your attention in the past year, whereas Syria controlled Lebanon for 30 years?

The President. Because I believe in democracy. I believe democracy yields peace. That's a historical—it's been proven throughout history that democracies yield the peace we all want. And I repeat to you: I want young boys and girls in Lebanon to grow up in peace. It's what I want.

I am—I want the same thing for Iraq. I want Iraq to be a democracy—not a U.S. democracy but a democracy that takes into the—the traditions, the Iraqi traditions and the history of Iraq, just like the Lebanese democracy will reflect the history of Lebanon and the traditions of Lebanon.

I believe there are such things as universal values, and I believe everybody desires to be free. And it's difficult in Iraq, no question about it. But I want—I want you to remember that the Iraqi people expressed their opinion last December about civil war. Eleven million people went to vote in difficult conditions saying, "We want freedom, and we want democracy. Give us a chance." And I'm convinced, ultimately, the people's will will win out and defeat those who want to try to create a civil war. Our position in the Middle East and throughout the Muslim world is that we want to be a partner in peace; we want to help people realize their potential.

And I hear the—I hear the language about the United States, that United States is anti-Islam. It's just not true. We view Islam as a religion of peace—or that the United States has got this design. But we'll protect ourselves. But the best way to protect ourselves ultimately is to encourage good relations amongst Muslim people and to encourage democracy. That's what we want. We want people to be able to be free. We want there to be minority rights and human rights; we want there to be

women's rights. We believe in societies where women have got a chance to realize their dreams. We want there to be good education and good health care, and to the extent that people want our help, we're willing to help.

Ms. Moukalled. But so far, you're not winning the hearts and minds of Arab people. Why not?

The President. Well, it's—there's a lot of negative news on TV. There's a—the enemy to democracy has got one tool, and that is the capacity and willingness to kill innocent people. And that shocks people. People of good conscience grieve when they see innocent life being taken by car bombs or when they read about beheadings.

And it's really important for those of us who believe in peace and the civilized world—it's not civilized to kill innocent people, nor do I think it's religious. It's very important for us to be steadfast and strong and have faith in the capacity of freedom to help answer people's desires and change society for the better.

My dream is for there to be a Palestinian state at peace with Israel. My dream is for Lebanon's democracy to flourish. My hope is that Iraq's democracy will serve as an example for others, and so people can realize their potential. And I believe this is going to happen. But there are people who want to stop that progress, and I know that. But I'm a firm believer in the future, and we'll continue to work in a way that tries to share our deepest desires to help people, that will try to combat some of the ugly news people see on the TV with positive policies that uplift lives, give people a chance.

Ms. Moukalled. Thank you, Mr. President. Unfortunately, we ran out of time.

The President. Well, thank you for coming.

Ms. Moukalled. Thank you.

The President. I'm honored you would come all the way from Beirut to interview me.

NOTE: The interview was taped at 10:40 a.m. in the Map Room at the White House for later broadcast. Ms. Moukalled referred to Serge Brammertz, commissioner, United Nations International Independent Investigation Commission into the assassination of former Prime Minister Rafiq Hariri of Lebanon; and President Emile Lahud of Lebanon. The transcript was released by the Office of the Press Secretary on March 10. A tape was not available for verification of the content of this interview.

Remarks at the National Newspaper Association Government Affairs Conference and a Question-and-Answer Session
March 10, 2006

The President. Thank you very much. Jerry likes to give a short introduction. [*Laughter*] I appreciate you letting me come by to visit with you some, and I look forward to answering some questions you might have. You can't come to a newspaper deal without answering questions. [*Laughter*]

First, I want to thank you all for being part of the backbone of democracy. You know, you can't have a democracy unless there is a free and vibrant press corps. I sometimes remind people I may not like what you print, but what you print is necessary to maintain a vibrant public forum where people feel comfortable about expressing themselves. And so thanks for what you do. I appreciate it very much.

I also recognize that not all the press is located in the big cities in America. I remember running for the United States Congress in 1978. I came in second in a two-man race, by the way. [*Laughter*] And I remember people telling me, "Whatever you do, you make sure you go knock on the door of the rural newspaper." If you're interested in finding out what's going on in the community, you not only go take questions, but you listen to what the people are saying. And I've never forgotten that lesson that good politics means paying attention to the people not only in the big cities but outside the big cities. It's one of the reasons I was grateful to accept your invitation. I'm looking forward to being here.

A couple of thoughts on my mind—first, obviously, your businesses thrive when the economy is good. And part of our job here in Washington is to make sure the environment for entrepreneurship and small businesses and the farmers and ranchers of this country is a strong environment. And this economy of ours has overcome a lot. We've overcome a recession and an attack, a national emergency, corporate scandals, a war, natural disasters. And we've overcome it, and the reason I say that is because the statistics say it—not just the politicians—but statistics: 3½ percent growth last year. The national unemployment rate as of today is 4.8 percent. That's lower than the average rate of the 1970s, 1980s, 1990s. Today we just learned that we've added 243,000 new jobs last month. That's about 5 million jobs over the past 2½ years. American workers are defying the pessimists. Our economy is strong. Productivity is up. Homeownership is up.

The fundamental question facing folks here in Washington and at the State governments is, what do you do to make sure that the economy remains strong? My philosophy can be summed up this way: The role of government is to create an environment in which the entrepreneurial spirit flourishes.

I believe one of the reasons we're having the economic success we're having is because we cut the taxes on the people. I believe that when somebody has more money in their pocket to save, invest, or spend, the economy benefits. The tax relief we passed is working. Parts of it are set to expire. I'm reminding the American people that if the Congress doesn't act, you're about to get hit with a tax increase you don't expect and most people don't want. So for the sake of economic vitality, to make sure this economy continues to grow and to make sure America is competitive in a global economy, Congress needs to make the tax relief permanent.

Now, some will say, "Well, we've got to raise taxes in order to balance the budget." That's not the way Washington works. Washington will raise your taxes and figure out new ways to spend your money; that's how it works.

The best way to balance the budget is to keep progrowth economic policies in place. In other words, keep the taxes low so the economy grows, which generates more revenues for the Treasury, and set priorities on the people's money. I've submitted a budget to the Congress which keeps us on track to cut the deficit in half by 2009.

Setting priorities is a difficult task for some in Washington. Every program sounds worthwhile. Everybody's spending request is necessary. But Congress needs to set priorities, needs to be wise about the people's money. And if they need some help, they ought to give me the line-item veto, and that way we can bring budget discipline, help keep budget discipline in Washington.

The long-term budget challenge is—it really has to do with mandatory spending, what's called mandatory spending. That's code word for Social Security and Medicare. Baby boomers like me are getting ready to retire. My retirement age happens in 2008, by the way, which is aligned perfectly. [*Laughter*] I talked about the issue last year. I'm going to keep talking about

the issue. The job of a President is to confront problems—that's why you put me up here—is to deal with problems, not to pass them on or hope somebody else takes care of it.

And we have a problem with Social Security and Medicare. We've got a lot of people retiring and not enough people paying into the system. We've been promised a lot of benefits, our generation, better benefits than the previous generation. And so Congress needs to join me in setting aside all the needless politics in Washington, DC, to come together and to present a solution to the American people so we can say we've done our job. I'm looking forward to working with Congress.

I said it in the State of the Union: I want people at the table. I meant it. I want Republicans and Democrats to come to the table, to come up with a solution. Part of the solution is going to be—the best way to describe it is like an automobile; if you're speeding, you slow your car down to get to the speed limit. You don't put it in reverse. We can fix the problem. We can come together and show the American people we're capable of dealing in a bipartisan way.

We also need bipartisanship when it comes to energy. I surprised some of you, and I'm sure some of my Texas friends here were somewhat surprised to hear me say, "We're addicted to oil, and that's a problem." [*Laughter*] And it is a problem. It's an economic problem—economic/security problem. When demand for fossil fuels goes up in India or China or elsewhere, it affects the price of gasoline in Granbury, Texas, Jerry.

When I'm sitting around the Oval Office talking about national security matters and somebody says, "Did you see what the Iranians said about consequences?"—really what they're talking about, I guess, is energy. So for national security purposes, we have got to become not addicted to oil.

And there are ways to do this—really interesting ways, exciting new technologies.

And Congress and the administration needs to work together to fund those new technologies. For example, it's possible to develop energy from saw grass. We know we can develop energy from sugar and corn; we're doing it in the Midwest. Those of you in the Midwest have seen the advent of the 85 pumps. Well, we need to be able to get ethanol out of other forms of biomass. And it's coming; we're close to some breakthroughs. We want people driving cars from fuels grown in America; that's what we want.

There's going to be hybrid batteries being developed that will enable you to plug in your car or your truck, and you'll be able to drive the first 40 miles on electricity. That's coming. It's called plug-in hybrid vehicles. That's going to be a part of making sure we're not addicted to oil.

Same on the electricity front. We can use wind power and electricity. These are all coming to the market because of research. They're becoming competitive forms of energy. We need nuclear power, in my judgment. It's a renewable source of energy that doesn't create greenhouse gases. We're spending a lot of money, by the way, on clean coal technology. We've got 250 years of coal here in the United States of America, and we can—we're developing technology so that we can burn the coal cleanly. In other words, we've got a comprehensive strategy to get us off oil, and looking forward to working with both Republicans and Democrats to get this passed.

One other issue, then I want to talk about the war on terror right quick; then I'll answer questions. Probably wondering whether I'm going to filibuster you. [*Laughter*]

We've got to make sure our children have the skills necessary to fill the jobs of the 21st century. If you're interested in talking about No Child Left Behind, you can ask me about it. I'm a firm believer. I believe it's changing public education for the better because we're measuring. And

we've got to use the same high standards that we've applied for reading in the early grades for math in the middle years, junior high. That's what we need to do.

And we need to spend research and development money at the Federal level so that we're always on the leading edge of technological change, that the United States is the leader of the world, and that we've got to make sure the research and development tax credit is a permanent part of the Tax Code, recognizing two-thirds of research dollars comes from the private sector.

One of the things—I guess what I'm telling you is, is that I don't fear the future for the United States because we intend to shape the future with good policies that keeps our economy flexible, entrepreneurial, that recognizes that small business is the backbone of job creation, that honors the contribution of our ranchers and farmers. I'm very optimistic about the economic future of the United States, and I'm looking forward to working with Congress to make sure the environment continues to encourage job growth.

We're at war. I wish I could report to you we weren't at war; we are. There's an enemy that still lurks, that would like to do serious harm to the United States. Much of my thinking, the decisions I have made, all revolve around that fateful moment when we got attacked. As concerned citizens, I'm going to share with you a little bit about why I have made decisions I have made. I'll be glad to answer any question you have along those decisions.

But I vowed after September—on September the 11th and after I would use all assets at our disposal to protect you. That is, by far, the most important job of the President, is to secure this homeland. There are lessons to have been learned after September the 11th. One of them is that we cannot take our security for granted. Listen, I understand that this is a different kind of war, and there are some in our country that may not believe there is a global war on terror. They may believe this is an isolated incident; I don't. I know we're at war with a jihadist movement that has got strategies and tactics to back up those strategies.

So we cannot take our security for granted. And we must remain on the offense, and we are. We're dismantling Al Qaida. It takes time. But whoever is the President of the United States after me must always keep the pressure on Al Qaida.

Secondly, we cannot let terrorists find safe haven. They found safe haven in Afghanistan, where they could plot and plan and attack. And therefore, it's very important for the United States to deny safe haven.

Thirdly, when we see a threat, we've got to take it seriously and never allow it to materialize. The first choice of any President ought to be to deal with issues diplomatically. And we dealt with the issue of Iraq diplomatically—Security Council resolution after Security Council resolution after Security Council resolution, until 1441, when the world spoke with a united voice that said to Iraq: "Disarm, disclose, or face serious consequences." Saddam Hussein chose otherwise. He was removed from power. And there's no doubt in my mind that the United States is more secure, and the world is better off without Saddam Hussein in power.

And now we must achieve a victory in Iraq by helping this country defend itself, secure itself, and become an ally in the war on terror. The enemy we face has got a powerful weapon. They can't defeat us militarily. They do not have an ideology that is appealing to people. But they do have the capacity to kill innocent life, and they're willing to do so, all attempting to shake our will and cause us to leave the Middle East, so they can find save haven from which to launch attacks. That is what they have said. And as your President, it is important for me to see the world the way it is, the realities of the world, not the way some would hope it would be.

We've got a three-part strategy in Iraq, that on the one hand says there is a— that politics can help achieve our objective. And the Iraqi people have said loud and clear—not in one election, but three elections during the past year—they want freedom. Eleven million people went to the polls in the face of terror and threats. There are some who are trying to, obviously, sow the seeds of sectarian strife. They fear the advancement of a democracy. They blow up shrines in order to cause this Iraqi democracy that is emerging to go backwards, to not emerge. That's what you're seeing on your TV screens. You're seeing the use of violence to try to create strife. And there's no question, this is a period of tension in Iraq.

The Iraqi forces responded well, however, which is the second part of our strategy, and that is to let the Iraqis take the fight to the enemy. It's up to Iraq to make the decision. They made the political decision, and now it's up to them to make the decision to defend their own security against those who would stop the march of democracy. And after the shrine bombing, while there was no question about it, there was attacks; nevertheless, the Iraqi forces moved. In 16 of the 18 Provinces, there was relative calm. And they performed, by and large, in good fashion.

I know people in your parts of the world wonder how long the troops are going to be there. They're going to be there so long as the commanders on the ground say they're necessary to achieve victory. But they're coming home as the Iraqis are more likely to be able to take the fight to the enemy.

And the third aspect is economic development. That includes wise reconstruction efforts, creation of a central bank, a sound currency, small businesses. And if we don't lose our nerve, I'm confident we'll achieve our objectives, and a democracy in the heart of the Middle East is going to help lay peace.

Part of winning this war on terror requires alliances. America has got a lot of friends in the war on terror. People understand the stakes. They understand that the bombings around the world were an indication of the plans that terrorists have for those of us who embrace freedom.

Obviously, you've been reading about the UAE issue. And I want to make a comment on that, the port issue. I'm sure that the decision by DP World was a difficult decision, to hand over port operations that they had purchased from another company. My administration was satisfied that port security would not have been undermined by the agreement. Nevertheless, Congress was still very much opposed to it. My administration will continue to work with the Congress to provide a greater understanding of how these transactions are approved, in other words, the process, and how we can improve that process in the future.

I'm concerned about a broader message this issue could send to our friends and allies around the world, particularly in the Middle East. In order to win the war on terror, we have got to strengthen our relationships and friendships with moderate Arab countries in the Middle East. UAE is a committed ally in the war on terror. They are a key partner for our military in a critical region.

And outside of our own country, Dubai services more of our military ships than any country in the world. They're sharing intelligence so we can hunt down the terrorists. They've helped us shut down a worldwide nuclear proliferation network run by A.Q. Khan. UAE is a valued and strategic partner. I'm committed to strengthening our relationship with the UAE and explaining why it's important to Congress and the American people.

Thank you for letting me come by. Be glad to answer some questions.

Yes, sir.

South Dakota Abortion Legislation

Q. Governor Mike Rounds signed a bill this week banning almost all abortions in South Dakota, sort of a frontal assault on the Constitution—[*inaudible*]. I wonder if you agree with this process that the State has taken.

The President. As a former Governor, I fully recognize that State legislatures will vote on matters that they think expresses the will of the local folks. Obviously, this bill he signed will work its way through the court system, and maybe someday be given a fair hearing in the Supreme Court. I don't know. I can't predict to you the course these legal challenges will take. I can assure you, however, if it does make it to the Supreme Court, the two people I nominated and who were approved were not picked because of any litmus test. They will interpret laws based upon the Constitution, is what they'll do. And so I followed this in the newspapers. I haven't talked to the Governor about it.

Health Care/Association Health Plans

Q. Mr. President——

The President. Yes, I meant to call on you first. I'm sorry. [*Laughter*] Don't hold it against the man from South Dakota.

Q. After that long introduction I gave you, I figured you owed me something.

The President. I do owe you one. [*Laughter*]

Q. This organization and its members are vitally interested in the passage of association health plans. And we wonder what the possibilities are for that.

The President. I appreciate that.

Q. And then as the next questions come around, we'll just hand this microphone around. So thank you.

The President. Look what you did. Fine with me. No, don't worry about it. I don't care. [*Laughter*] I don't have to deal with the guy. I'm fixing to leave. [*Laughter*] I'm going to go meet with President Toledo of Peru here after this.

The question is association health plans. First of all, I fully understand the pressures being put on small businesses because of rising health care costs. And therefore, good policy needs to address the rising cost of health care. I've got some ideas for you. I'll get to AHPs in a minute.

I think it's very important that there be more transparency in pricing in health care. It's really the only industry, when you think about it, where somebody else decides whether the price is worthwhile. The consumer isn't directly involved in health care decisions; a third-party payer is. And so there's really no interaction between the provider and the customer when it comes to health care.

I'm a big believer in what's called health savings accounts because it puts consumers in charge of health care decisions. And we strongly urge small businesses to look at this vehicle.

Secondly, the health care is an inefficient industry—when you really think about what information technology has done to your business, providing better productivity increases, as well as interesting challenges, by the way. The same productivity increases haven't happened in health care. I mean, you've got a guy writing down prescriptions by hand and/or files being written by hand, and doctors don't write so good anyway, which leads to medical error and inefficiencies.

So information technology, which we're now advancing here at the Federal level in conjunction with providers throughout the country to develop a common vocabulary so that eventually there will be electronic medical records with ample privacy protections available, will help wring out some of the costs of health care.

Health care costs are driven by frivolous lawsuits. Doctors practice defensive medicine in order to be able to withstand a court challenge. And a lot of times that practice of defensive medicine isn't necessary, except for legal reasons.

Secondly, lawsuits cause premiums to go up, which causes price to go up. And therefore, I'm a believer in medical liability reform at the Federal level. I wasn't when I first arrived in Washington; I thought States should handle it okay. But the problem is, is that it's estimated that these lawsuits and defensive practice of medicine and the rising premiums cause us to spend about $28 billion a year in additional Federal money through Medicaid and Medicare and veterans' benefits. And so I'm for medical liability at the Federal level.

Finally, AHPs makes a lot of sense. I am a strong backer. I believe small businesses ought to be able to pool risk across jurisdictional boundaries so they can get the same benefits from larger risk pools that big companies get. So I'm a believer in AHPs. I think we've got a pretty good chance this year—I hope so—to get it out of the—I know we got it out of the House; we've got to get it out of the Senate. So part of a comprehensive strategy for dealing with health care costs is to have AHPs as a part of a health care vision.

Yes, sir.

Postal Reform

Q. Mr. President, I've got a followup question about the small business—keeping small business healthy, that you referred to. Postal delivery rates are very important to community newspapers, much as you might know, I believe, Bonnie Mullens, of the McGregor Mirror and Crawford Sun down in your area. And we are——

The President. She didn't call you to go after a subscriber, did she? [*Laughter*]

Q. No, we just did a little research.

The President. Okay, good. Smart man. That's called due diligence. [*Laughter*]

Q. Postal reform, which has been going on in Congress for about 10 years, was really pushed forward by a commission that you appointed, and it was passed overwhelmingly by both Houses. And we have this bill going to conference in April or

May. There's some concern that the administration may want to oppose this bill or veto it if it's so-called not favorable to the Federal budget. But there are things in that bill that are very important to the newspaper industry. And part of that is the funding that keeps rates fair—because of some overpayment of military pensions—that we don't think should be put on the taxpayers, the rate payers. So we'd ask your support on behalf of us and Bonnie Mullens——

The President. Thank you.

Q. ——to support that bill as it's in the Congress if it comes to your desk, sir.

The President. As you know, we do support postal reform. And as you accurately noted, we've got the process started, and we look forward to working with Congress on an acceptable bill.

Frankly, this issue hasn't made it to my desk prior to me arriving at this meeting. And I'm mindful of the bill. I need to know more about the particulars before I make you a commitment one way or the other.

Yes, sir.

Iraq/Spread of Democracy

Q. Mr. President, what are our plans if civil war breaks out in Iraq?

The President. Yes. Step one is to make sure—do everything we can that there not be one. Secondly, I believe the Iraqi people have made a choice. It wasn't all that long ago that 11 million people went to the polls. It may seem like an eternity, but that was last December that people defied assassins, car bombers, threats, and said, "We want a democracy."

Secondly, the first real test for an interim government occurred when the Shias' shrine was blown up, the holy site. And while there's—as I said earlier, there was—no question there was violence and killing, the society took a step back from the abyss, and people took a sober reflection about what a civil war would mean.

I just got off of a teleconference with Ambassador Zal Khalilzad, as well as General Casey. They're obviously concerned about sectarian violence and the violence you see. They understand people are trying to create this tension, this ethnic tension. But they were also pleased with the response of the security forces. It wasn't perfect across the board. But nevertheless, in 16 of the 18 Provinces, I've mentioned that there was relative calm. Most of the violence was in the Baghdad area. It's the violence you're seeing on your TV screens.

And so the purpose is to make sure that we continue to remind the interim government that the people want democracy. One of the keys is going to be to get a unity government up and running, a government that reflects the diversity of the country. We talked about that today. We want the Iraqis to make that selection, of course. They are the ones who got elected by the people. They're the ones who must form the government.

But we are going to continue to remind them that the sooner they can get a unity government up and running, the more confidence the people will have in their future. So it's to take advantage of the desire of the Iraqis to live in a peaceful world and encourage government to continue to respond to fight off the desires of few people, fight off those who are trying to sow the seeds, and get a democracy going.

It's very important for the people in the Muslim world to understand that we understand there's a—we're dealing with a—that we want them to have a democracy that reflects their histories and their traditions. Iraqi democracy doesn't have to look like the United States, nor should it. But it's also important for people around the world to recognize that there are such things as the natural rights of men and women.

That's what we're founded on here in America. We believe in the universality of freedom. We believe people desire to be free, not just Americans, but universally. And that faith—at least my faith in the natural rights of men and women and the desire for people to be free was expressed at the ballot box. And it's that powerful statement that I believe will enable Iraq to develop a democracy.

A democracy in Iraq is important. It's important to deny safe haven to Al Qaida. Zawahiri made it clear—he's the number-two man in Al Qaida—that it's just a matter of time for America leaving. That's what he said. And the reason why that was important for him to say because they wanted to use Iraq as a place to plot/plan, as well as to spread their jihadist, their Islamist—radical Islamic view. They're totalitarians. That's what they are. And we've got to recognize them as such.

And so it's kind of a long-winded answer to my belief that we will succeed, and we must succeed. And the reason I say we will is because the Iraqis want us to succeed. They want to succeed.

There's a lot of talk about Iran. A free Iraq will inspire reformers in Iran. I believe the more women are empowered in the Middle East, like it's going to happen in Iraq, the more that will inspire others in the Middle East to demand their freedom.

Now, if you don't believe freedom is universal, then I can understand skepticism about what I just said. But I reject that notion that freedom is only available to some of us. I believe liberty is universally desired. And I know it's in our interest to help democracy spread.

I like to remind people about this historical parallel, and I've used it a lot. You've probably have heard it, so I beg your pardon for bringing it up again. But it's important for me to connect the idea of laying the foundation for peace with reality, and that reality is what we see in Europe today. There were two major world wars in Europe in the 1990s—I mean, the 1900s. And today, Europe is free and whole and at peace. And a lot of that has to do with the fact that the nations of Europe are democracies. Democracies don't war.

One of my best buddies in the international arena is Prime Minister Koizumi of Japan. What's interesting about that is my dad fought the Japanese—as did, I'm sure, your relatives, some of your relatives. And yet today I can tell the newspaper owners that I work with Koizumi to keep the peace. Democracy has the capacity to turn enemies into allies and cause, kind of, warring factions to come together. And it's hard work to help a democracy get hold, particularly if you had just left—lived under the thumb of a brutal tyrant, somebody who'd kill you in a moment—or get you killed in a moment's notice.

Remember, we discovered mass graves of a lot of people in Iraq. This guy—Saddam Hussein was brutal for the people of Iraq. And there's a lot of tension and a lot of rivalry. One of the big issues we're going to have to deal with is to make sure that people don't take revenge outside the rule of law. Militias that are, kind of, seeking revenge. And at any rate, I'm just trying to share with you some of my—the philosophical tenets of the decisions I have made and my optimism about the future and my hopefully realistic assessment about the necessity for us to achieve our objectives.

Remember, this is a global war on terror. We've got a strong ally in Pakistan fighting off Al Qaida. And Saudi Arabia and the Kingdom of Saudi has committed itself to fighting Al Qaida. Lebanon is now becoming a freer democracy, although we've still got work there to make sure foreign influence is—allow the Lebanese democracy to grow. Libya made a decision to get rid of its weapons programs. And there's—positive things are happening, and they need to happen on a global basis because this is a global war on terror.

Yes, ma'am.

Trade

Q. Thank you, Mr. President. Many of the things that you've mentioned today are affecting the State. We have a high unemployment rate. And of course, much of our economy is dependent upon the automobile industry.

The President. Right.

Q. General Motors is having problems with their health care plans, their pension plans, and of course, the issue of gas is definitely one—energy conservation. I know the auto industry has asked the administration for advice and for help in this problem. What role do you see the Federal Government playing in terms of some of the industries in the country that are partially problem-makers for your policies, as well for the people of our State?

The President. People have asked whether or not private companies that have made pension promises should be relieved of their responsibility. And my answer is, if you make a promise, you've got to keep it—that if you said, "I—company X, Y, Z—promise you this," it's up to the company to make good on the promise. I think that's a very important principle to state loud and clear.

One of the real issues that affects Michigan and people in Michigan is trade. They're concerned about trade. They're worried that trade has only benefited our friends but not our country. Let me take a step back and tell you I'm a free trader. I believe it's very important for this country to be opening markets. I'm confident that if the playing field is level, that we can compete with anybody. And therefore, one of the things I've tried to assure the people of Michigan is that not only am I free trader, I believe the rules ought to be fair. In other words, I would hope that American people say, "Just treat us fairly, and we've got the confidence to compete."

I know our farmers can compete. And for those of you who remember the price of soybean a couple of years ago, part of that is because we opened up markets. If you've got cattle men and women in your area, buying your newspapers, one of the things they constantly talk to me about is,

"Get those markets open; work with the Japanese to get that market open again." If you've got chicken growers—I remember one of the first discussions I had with Vladimir Putin in Russia was, "You made some promises on our chickens; open up your markets like you said you would do."

My point is, is that opening markets is good, so long as we're treated fairly. So I've constantly reminded the Chinese leadership that intellectual property rights needs to be protected; your currency needs to be floated; treat our people fairly. That's all we want. Our manufacturers need to have a level playing field.

And so I fully understand Michiganders' concerns about the trade arena. And I would think it would be a mistake if we become a protectionist nation. I thought so strongly about it that I put it in my State of the Union Address. I am worried about isolation and protectionism. To me, it's a lack of confidence in our ability to shape the future, and I think it would be wrong economic policy. And so I will continue to work to open up markets. But I fully am aware of the issues in Michigan.

Yes, sir.

Gulf Coast Reconstruction

Q. Mr. President, I publish in the southern and eastern suburbs of Baton Rouge, Louisiana.

The President. There you go.

Q. I know you've heard a lot of complaints from Louisiana and seen a lot of hands out. I would like to thank you for your personal interest and also for all the money. [*Laughter*]

My Congressman, Richard Baker, came up with the idea of employing a Federal entity to buy out property in New Orleans and sell it back into commerce selectively. It seemed to have a political consensus in Louisiana from both parties. It got to your office and was rejected.

The President. Correct.

Q. Can you talk a little bit about the problems that you see with Richard's plan?

And also, you're still about to send billions more down to us. How would you like to see that money handled, since you've been to us 10 times?

The President. Well, thank you. First of all, I want to thank the people of Baton Rouge for being so generous to the evacuees. I want to thank my fellow Texans for being generous to evacuees, and I'm sure people throughout—I'll bet you most of you are involved with communities that said, "Welcome." And that was a fantastic gesture of kindness by the American people, by the way.

I felt like there was a better approach to the housing issue. He's talking about a good fellow, a really good guy named Richard Baker, came up with a plan that basically had the Government buying the property, getting developers to develop the property, and to the extent that money was not recovered, the Government would basically be the banker.

Working with the folks—let me step back. Right off the bat, I knew it was important for Louisiana to develop its own plan, not have the Federal Government say, this is the—impose a plan, but to have the folks in Louisiana come up and develop a plan. We, obviously, have interfaced with them, because as you recognize, in kind of a cavalier way, "Thanks for all the money." [*Laughter*] Well, not "cavalier." You made sure you mentioned it, let me put it to you that way. [*Laughter*]

And Louisiana had the Baker plan but also was developing another plan, as well, and one that we agreed to. Governor Blanco has put together a citizens group of distinguished people—good, honorable people—who are working closely with the group that Mayor Nagin put together, to develop a plan that will take CDBG money, and money I've requested in the supplemental, to basically have money that goes directly to the homeowner. I like that idea better than the Government moving in and becoming the bank, as opposed to the Government providing money for individual homeowners to make decisions.

And the rules and the zoning laws attributable to that money are now being developed. But it's a very good concept, in my judgment. It's very important for Congress to make sure that the $4.2 billion, I think it was, request in the supplemental go to Louisiana, as I said down in New Orleans the other day.

Step one in the recovery in New Orleans has got to be to make sure that the levees are strong enough—equal to or better than pre-Katrina—in order for there to be confidence for the market, confidence for the homeowner to be able to rebuild in certain parts of New Orleans.

Secondly, it's important that as the levees are rebuilt and people gain confidence, that there be a rational development plan in place. I think a lot of taxpayers really don't want to pay money for people to rebuild in an area that's likely to be flooded again. And the people of New Orleans understand that, and the people of Louisiana understand that. That issue is being addressed.

Thirdly, it's very important that the Federal Government rebuild the infrastructure that we're obligated to rebuild in a timely fashion. Incredibly enough, the Slidell bridge, as I understand it, because of proper incentives, was built in record time, under budget. That may be a contradiction in terms when you hear a Federal official saying, "under budget, on time," but nevertheless, I believe that's what the Governor told me.

And so there is a comprehensive strategy in place that I'm comfortable with. Details need to be worked out, more details about dealing with the flood plain issue and how high the houses have to be rebuilt if people choose to rebuild there. I like the idea of funding people, of letting them make the decision.

By the way, Mississippi—and I don't know if we've got any folks from Mississippi here—but if you've ever been to the gulf coast of Mississippi since the storm, you'll know what I'm saying—it looked like a bomb blast. It just leveled, absolutely wiped out a lot of homes and property and some lives along there. And they developed a plan too—their own plan.

Louisiana is different from Mississippi. They came up with a Mississippi plan that has been funded. And they are now in the process of saying to homeowners, "We're helping you rebuild your lives." I went to a home where the guy building—rebuilding it on the beach. I forgot how high he's got it up, but it's high enough to meet new standards, new building standards.

Debris removal in both locations is—you just can't imagine how much debris was there. As you know, I'm not too poetic to begin with, so I'll probably not be able to describe it properly. Let me just say, it's a lot. [*Laughter*] I mean, a whole lot. And Mississippi has moved a lot of it off private and public land—I'm probably telling you more than you want to know.

I'll just give you an interesting public policy dilemma. When we first got down there, the Government will remove debris off public property but not private—will pay to remove debris off public property but not private property. The simplest way to explain why not is, you start moving debris off private property, and the guy shows up and says, "Where's my million-dollar necklace?" And so therefore, there needs to be a kind of a held-harmless statute, or a held-harmless agreement with local authorities. And so we've devised a perfectly legal way of saying that if you declare a health and safety hazard for particular blocks, then Government money will pay to clean up the land. A lot of Mississippi has been cleaned up because a lot of the local folks decided to take that tack.

Now, the problem in Louisiana, as far as debris cleanup, is that—like in the lower Ninth, a lot of people haven't come back to their homes yet to see the devastation. They've been displaced around the country. And until people are able to come home and until people are clear about what the rules will be and the funding mechanism will be, it's going to be—the debris removal will be slow. We've done a pretty effective job of cleaning debris off the public right-of-ways, public lands but not off the private lands. And so that's yet another deterrent to economic development.

So all this is coming together. My point—the funding is coming together; the levees are coming together; the rules about reconstruction are coming—or rebuilding are coming together; and the debris removal, albeit slow at this point in time, waiting for people to inspect their houses, will probably accelerate when people realize there's a way forward—long answer to a complicated problem.

We've got $100 billion that has been allocated for the region, which is going to create some interesting opportunities and further problems. One is going to be labor. People are going to be rebuilding down there a long time. If you're interested in making a living, go down there, and there will be a job. And we want the first people hired, of course, to be Mississippi people and Louisiana people. It's a great opportunity, by the way, for small business development. And I'm a believer—as you can tell, I'm an optimistic person. I believe that out of this terrible harm and grief is going to come a vibrant part—a vibrant economy.

You know, sales taxes receipts are, I think, almost equal to what they were last year in Mississippi. It's amazing, isn't it? There's great resiliency to the American people.

Anyway, thanks for asking. Yes, sir.

Democracy/Free Speech

Q. Aurora, Colorado—and in our town a teacher was suspended for remarks critical of your State of the Union message, made the talk shows, et cetera—compared you to Hitler and—actually, I've heard the tape and he didn't; he said, "Hitler-esque," but it's not the——

The President. He's not the only one. [*Laughter*]

Q. And it's not the content that my question is about. My question is about your sense of the free speech right in the classroom or in public to criticize you without being considered unpatriotic.

The President. Yes, I think people should be allowed to criticize me all they want, and they do. [*Laughter*] Now, what are you all laughing at over there? [*Laughter*] Don't cheer him on. [*Laughter*]

Look, there are some certain basic freedoms that we've got to protect. The freedom of people to express themselves must be protected. The freedom of people to be able to worship freely—that freedom is valuable. I tell people all the time, you're equally American if you're a Christian, Jew, or Muslim. You're equally American if you believe in an Almighty or don't believe in an Almighty; that's a sacred freedom.

The right for people to express themselves in the public square is a freedom. Obviously, there's limitations—if, for example, someone is inciting violence, or the destruction of property, or public—causing somebody harm. But the idea of being able to express yourself is a sacred part of our society. And that's what distinguishes us from the Taliban, and that's important for Americans to understand.

We're in an ideological struggle. And one way for people to connect the ideological struggle with reality is to think about what life was like for people under the rule of the Taliban. If you didn't agree with their view of religion, you were punished. If you tried to send your little girl to school, you were punished. These people have a backward view. I don't believe—I believe religion is peaceful. I believe people who have religion in their heart are peaceful people. And I believe these people have subverted a great religion to accomplish a political end.

And so thank you for bringing that up; I appreciate it. People say to me, my buddies in Texas, "How do you handle all this stuff?" After a while, you get used to it. [*Laughter*] But you have to believe in what you're doing, see. You have to believe in certain principles and beliefs. And you can't let the public opinion polls and focus groups, one, cause you to abandon what you believe and become the reason for making decisions.

My job is a job where I make a lot of decisions. And I decide big things and little things. And there are certain principles to decisionmaking. You make decisions—you know, you have to make a lot of decisions. And you don't put your finger in the air to figure out how to make a decision, and neither should the President of the United States. And you have to know what you believe.

Good decisionmaking rests on certain basic principles. I believe in the universality of freedom. I believe democracies lead to peace. I believe people ought to worship freely. I do believe there's an Almighty God that has spread freedom—making freedom available for everybody. I believe in private enterprise. I believe in free enterprise. I believe in high standards in education. These are basic beliefs that I'm not going to change.

And I know some would like me to change, but you can't be a good decisionmaker if you're trying to please people. You've got to stand on what you believe. That's what you've got to do if you're going to make decisions that are solid and sound. And I understand some of the things I've done are unpopular, but that's what comes with the territory.

If you're afraid to make decisions and you only worry about whether or not people in the classroom are going to say nice things about you, you're not leading. And I think we've got to lead. We've got to lead to spread the peace; we've got to lead to protect this country; and we've got to lead to make sure we're the preeminent economic power, so our people can benefit.

Yes, sir.

War on Terror/Iran/North Korea

Q. Who do you think the biggest threat is: Iran, North Korea, or China?

The President. Interesting question. The biggest threat to American security: Iran, North Korea, or China. Why did I call on you? [*Laughter*] No. It would be an Oklahoma guy, you know? [*Laughter*]

The biggest threat to American security, short-term, is Al Qaida. They would like to attack us again. I think about Al Qaida and their potential to attack all the time—all the time. That's what you want your President doing. My job is to basically insulate people from some concerns. You don't risk capital if you're worried about an attack coming tomorrow. You don't go confidently about your business if an attack is right around the corner. I understand that. But I think about it a lot. So step one—I'm changing your question: Would you please order the threats?—Al Qaida.

I said in an early speech there was an axis of evil, and it included Iran and North Korea. I said that, I think, help me out here, April—2002 perhaps? Yes, State of the Union. If it's not 2002, it's April's [April Ryan, American Urban Radio Networks] fault, because she nodded her head. [*Laughter*] Relatively early in my Presidency.

I did that because I'm concerned about totalitarian governments that are not transparent, that have stated their intentions to develop nuclear weapons. One of the real dangerous threats, of course, is the nexus of terrorist groups, nonstate groups that get a weapon of mass destruction, which is their stated objective. And so I'm concerned about that.

I'm concerned about—I would say they're equal, Iran and North Korea, as for a security threat, because any time there's a nontransparent regime without a free press to hold people to account, it creates an unpredictability in the world. The Iranian President has stated his desire to destroy our ally, Israel. So when you

start listening to what he has said, to their desire to develop a nuclear weapon, then you begin to see an issue of grave national security concern.

And therefore, it's very important for the United States to continue to work with others to solve these issues diplomatically—in other words, to deal with these threats today, and we are. We've got the EU–3—which is Great Britain, France, and Germany—diplomatic lingo, sorry—are basically taking the position for the free world to the Iranians, that said, "No nuclear weapon and no knowledge about how to make a nuclear weapon."

I talked to Vladimir Putin this week—or the Foreign Minister from Russia this week, about making sure that we're—Russia says the same thing. In other words, we want the Iranians to hear loud and clear that the world is speaking with one voice when it comes to their capacity to develop a nuclear weapon. Remember now, the reason we are where we are is because they had agreed to international norms and then were caught not adhering to the international norms. In other words, they basically tried to pull one over on the world. And to me, that's a warning signal we've got to take seriously.

Korea—the issue is one in which we tried to alter the relationship with the Koreans to be more than just the voice of the United States saying to the Koreans the same thing. And so we've now got China, South Korea, Russia, Japan, and the United States involved in what's called the six-party talks.

Ultimately, I think it's very important for the people in those countries to be able to live in a free society. If you believe liberty is universal, then you would hope liberty would spread to those countries as well.

The Chinese—you know, our relationship is a very interesting relationship with the Chinese. It's an amazing country, in many ways. It's a country that has got—it's got to create 25 million new jobs a year to stay even. Think about that. It's a country that has chosen the path, by and large, of markets and enterprise. They are an economic issue for us, and that's why we've got a huge deficit with them. And therefore, it's very important for the Government to, on the one hand, reject protectionism, but on the other hand, insist that their market is open and it be traded freely and fairly, like I answered the lady from Michigan. I don't view—China is a more—China is a strategic partner when it comes to trade, for example. And I can't say that about the other two countries. And so the relationship is different; it's a different relationship.

He's giving me the hook, because I've got to go see President Toledo. But anyway—yes, ma'am.

No Child Left Behind Act

Q. I represent the Tullahoma News, from Tullahoma, Tennessee. I have the very best job there. I'm the wife of the publisher.

The President. Yes. I don't know if Laura would say the same thing. [*Laughter*]

Q. But I wanted to know what you understand the complaints to be about your No Child Left Behind policy, and if you acknowledge those complaints as any weaknesses to the policy? How effective do you think that it is in spite of that?

The President. No, good question. I'm glad you brought up No Child Left Behind. The complaint is that, "How dare the Government cause us to measure"—one of the complaints—"Too much testing," you know. I heard that when I was the Governor of Texas. Jerry didn't editorialize there, I'm sure. [*Laughter*] Maybe you did.

You know, "How dare you test people who don't speak English as a first language." My answer to those concerns is that, how do you know if you don't test? How can you possibly tell whether a child is learning to read and write if you don't measure? When I was the Governor of our State, I was deeply concerned about a system where people would come to me and say, "You know what? We're getting kids in college that are not very literate." This kind of, just—social promotion was the culture and the norm.

If I were a newspaper owner, I'd want to make sure people could read. And one way to make sure people read is to measure early whether or not people can pass a test. I've heard people say, "All we're doing is teaching the test; you're causing people to teach the test." And my answer to that is, teaching a child to be literate will enable that child to pass the test. There's something fundamental about literacy.

Secondly, people said, "We believe in local control of schools, and the No Child Left Behind Act is not local control of schools." I strongly disagree. I believe in local control of schools. The No Child Left Behind Act said, "We're spending a lot of Federal money, particularly on Title I students; show us whether or not the money is being well spent."

We didn't say, "Here's the curriculum you must use; here are the class sizes you'll have." We didn't say, "We're going to design the test on your behalf." I fought off a national test, because I believed a national test would undermine local control of schools. All we said was, "Measure, and post your scores for everybody to see, and that you've got to be meeting a higher standard." In other words, we're holding people to standards. So I believe the No Child Left Behind Act honors local control of schools.

One of the classic debates that takes place at the local level is what curriculum to use. I'm sure some of you have been through the classic reading curriculum debates. They raged hot and heavy in the State of Texas for a while. And you'd have, this side would be yelling at that side. One way to make sure that your curriculum works is to measure. If a child is passing reading by using this curriculum, and another child is not passing reading when they use another curriculum, it provides a useful tool for the local newspaper, for example, to say, "We told you so; the curriculum is not working," or, "We told you so; the curriculum is working."

There's got to be accountability in the public school system. If you do not diagnose a problem, you can never solve the problem. And one of the things about No Child Left Behind which is important is that when we diagnose a reading problem early, there is supplemental service money to help that child be brought up to speed. That's why it's called No Child Left Behind. We believe every child can learn—every child. And therefore, this is a program that says we want accountability for the taxpayers' money. We'll provide extra help early on when we find a child who needs extra help. And it's working. That's the other thing that I would tell people. How do I know? Because we measure.

There's an achievement gap in America that is not right. When you measure at the fourth grade, Anglo kids did fine; African American and Latino kids didn't. And that's not fair, and it's not right. And so we've essentially ended social promotion in the early grades and said, we're going to correct problems. And it's working because that gap is narrowing. And the reason I can say that is because we measure.

Interestingly enough, when you, kind of, compare measurements internationally in math and science or math, we're doing fine in the fourth grade. We're falling off in the eighth grade. And so what I want to do is to apply the same rigor for reading that we did in the early grades to math in junior high. So in the eighth grades we get those scores and, kind of, lay that foundation for the sciences and the engineering—the physicists, so we can compete.

I'm a strong believer in No Child Left Behind. My Secretary of Education, my good buddy, Margaret Spellings, who helped me put a similar program in place in the State of Texas, is now the Secretary of Education. She's obviously listening to complaints about certain aspects of AYP. But we're not going to undermine the basic tenet that says we believe in high standards; we believe every child can learn; and we're going to measure. And when we see the status quo is unacceptable, we'll challenge the status quo. That's what you need to, and I'm sure you are doing that. It ought to be unacceptable to opinion makers when you find illiteracy. And you ought to demand change, not only for your own self interest but for the sake of this country. And so thanks for asking the question.

I've got to go. Listen, I'll be a diplomatic problem if I don't get over there on time. [*Laughter*] I'm honored you'd have me. Thanks for letting me come by and visit with you. God bless.

NOTE: The President spoke at 9:45 a.m. at the Wyndham Washington Hotel. In his remarks, he referred to Jerry Reppert, president, and Jerry Tidwell, vice president, National Newspaper Association; former President Saddam Hussein of Iraq; A.Q. Khan, former head of Pakistan's nuclear weapons program; U.S. Ambassador to Iraq Zalmay Khalilzad; Gen. George W. Casey, Jr., USA, commanding general, Multi-National Force—Iraq; Ayman al-Zawahiri, founder of the Egyptian Islamic Jihad and senior Al Qaida associate; President Vladimir V. Putin and Minister of Foreign Affairs Sergey V. Lavrov of Russia; Gov. Kathleen Babineaux Blanco of Louisiana; Mayor C. Ray Nagin of New Orleans, LA; President Mahmud Ahmadi-nejad of Iran; and President Alejandro Toledo of Peru.

Remarks Following Discussions With President Alejandro Toledo of Peru
March 10, 2006

President Bush. I am very pleased to welcome *mi amigo* back to the Oval Office. I have grown to admire President Toledo for his strength of character, his clear vision, his willingness to make difficult decisions, even sometimes when the popularity polls suggest he do something differently. Leadership requires strength of character, the willingness to make tough choices.

I admire my friend's record. Peru is on the verge of elections, and he'll be passing on to a successor a stable economy and stable political process. And that is a wonderful legacy—the first President in 50 years to be able to say, "I'm passing on a stable economy and a stable political process."

I admire the growth rate, the economic growth rate of Peru. It's the strongest growth rate in South America. I always admire this about my friend—he is—he says that one of his biggest goals was to reduce poverty, and he recognizes that while progress is being made—a lot of progress—that more needs to be done. He cares deeply about the people of Peru. He's a man of—he's got a *corazon gigante*.

I have enjoyed working with him. We accomplished some important missions, one of which was a free trade agreement between Peru and the United States was the result of his leadership and his vision.

And so it's with mixed emotions that I meet my friend. I'm pleased to be in the presence of an accomplished person, somebody who's led, and I'm going to miss working with him, because he's been a partner in peace.

And so, Mr. President, welcome to the Oval Office. It's an honor to have you back, and it's a joy to be with you. Welcome.

President Toledo. Thank you very much. You're very generous.

Let me say very briefly, Peru and Latin America are partners with the United States in more than just a free trade agreement. It's very important, the free trade agreement, because it generates jobs and enables to continue the sustained rates of economic growth, to reduce poverty. But we are also partners in spreading the democratic values in the region. We're also partners in the fight against narcotrafficking and terrorism. We are partners in the search of peace in the world. We are partners in trying to inculcate in the region that democracy is the imperfect way, but it's the best way that we have. We are partners in trying to convey the idea that being elected democratically is good, but it's insufficient; we need to govern democratically.

And I'm sure that after I finish and pass away the power to the next President, the Peruvians and Latin Americans do not want to go through this cycle that creates instability, that does not attract capital investment to continue growth, to generate jobs, to invest more in health, nutrition, and education, and to reduce poverty.

Mr. President, partnership means to focus seriously and deliver results in what we believe, but also means to have the degrees of tolerance to entertain our differences. And that's democracy, as practiced over here.

It has been a very productive relationship. I also have mixed feelings. And I would say publicly, you are my friend now, you will be my friend after I'm not President, and you will be my friend when you are no longer President. [*Laughter*]

The United States is a market of 290 million people, with an average income of $37,000 a year. It's a market that I will leave for the next President, and that means jobs, because that has to do with poverty. I don't believe in giving away fish, just a decent job and a quality education and health.

Mr. President, I hope that we soon will sign the free trade agreement and will continue working for the approval of that free trade agreement in our respective Congress.

I went through a tough time, but I'm stubborn. I'm a believer, a strong believer in my convictions. And I'm sure that the wisdom of Peruvians will, on April 9th— or May—will elect someone that believes in democracy, that believes in the stability to continue on, to build on our accomplishment, but correct our mistakes; that we cannot go back and forth, because the poor people cannot afford to wait so much.

Thank you very, very much for receiving us today. It has been a very productive meeting. I want to thank my collaborators. I'm not going away yet; I still have 5 more months. [*Laughter*] And we will continue working. We have done a good job, I think, of exchanging productive ideas in the meetings of APEC. APEC represents around 57 percent of the world economy, 46 percent of the world trade. And so in 2008, the next Peruvian President, he or she will receive you in Peru as a President of the APEC.

Thank you very, very much.

President Bush. Mi amigo, gracias. Thank you all.

NOTE: The President spoke at 11:53 a.m. in the Oval Office at the White House.

Statement on the Resignation of Gale Norton as Secretary of the Interior
March 10, 2006

Gale Norton has been a strong advocate for the wise use and protection of our Nation's natural resources and a valuable member of my administration for more than 5 years. As the first woman Secretary of the Interior, she served the Nation well with her vision for cooperative conservation, protection and improvement of our national parks and public lands, and environmentally responsible energy development on public lands and waters. She was instrumental in establishing my Healthy Forests Initiative that has helped make communities safer from catastrophic fire, while improving wildlife habitat. Gale played an influential role in shaping the Nation's offshore and onshore energy policies to help enhance America's domestic production. When Hurricane Katrina devastated the gulf coast region, she played a leading role in my administration's efforts to restore badly needed offshore energy production to avoid further supply disruption and higher energy costs for consumers. Because of her leadership and thoughtful attention to management, repairs, and maintenance issues, Americans will be able to better enjoy our great national parks and wildlife refuges for generations to come. I appreciate Gale's dedicated service to our country, and I wish Gale and John all the best.

Remarks Following a Briefing by the Joint Improvised Explosive Device Defeat Organization and an Exchange With Reporters
March 11, 2006

The President. Good morning. I want to thank General Meigs for being here to brief me about tactics on the ground in Iraq. One of the things that the Secretary and General Pace are constantly doing is briefing the Commander in Chief as to the nature of the enemy, what the enemy is trying to do to shake our will, and how we're adjusting, how we're constantly adapting our tactics on the ground to achieve a victory.

We face an enemy that will use explosive devices in order to shake our will, in order to foment violence in Iraq, in order to try to convince the American people that we can't win in Iraq. That's what they're trying to do. And the general has spent a lot of time thinking about the enemy's tactics and techniques and how our military can adjust to them.

So the briefing today was a series of briefing I get from our commanders on the ground, as well as our experts hired by the Pentagon, to let me know what we're doing, so I can let the American people know that we recognize the nature of this enemy. We're adjusting our tactics to defeat this enemy for the sake of peace, for the sake of the security of the United States of America, and for the sake of peace in the world.

And so, General, thank you for being here. I appreciate your time. I'll answer a couple of questions. Deb [Deb Riechmann, Associated Press].

Former Assistant to the President for Domestic Policy Claude Allen

Q. Mr. President, can you tell us your reaction to the arrest of your former Domestic Policy Adviser, Claude Allen?

The President. If the allegations are true, Claude Allen did not tell my Chief of Staff and legal counsel the truth, and that's deeply disappointing. If the allegations are true, something went wrong in Claude Allen's life, and that is really sad. When I heard the story last night, I was shocked. And my first reaction was one of disappointment, deep disappointment that—if it's true—that we were not fully informed. But it was also one—shortly thereafter, I felt really sad for the Allen family.

Caren [Caren Bohan, Reuters].

Republican Party/Dubai Ports World

Q. Sir, are you concerned about the rift that the Dubai Ports deal has opened within your own party?

The President. The Republican Party is united in our efforts to win the war on terror. The Republican Party is united in our efforts to keep this economy strong by keeping taxes low. The Republican Party is united in making us less dependent on foreign sources of oil.

I've read all the stories about this rift or that rift. That's typical Washington, it seems like to me. I am looking forward to continuing to work with the leadership in the United States Congress to pass an agenda that will keep America the economic leader of the world and will keep this country secure. And next fall, I'm looking forward to campaigning with our candidates. I'm convinced ours is the party that has got an agenda for the future, and ours is the party that has performed.

Stretch [Richard Keil, Bloomberg News].

Progress in Iraq

Q. Mr. President, are you concerned, with reference to the IEDs, are you concerned that the sophisticated weaponry our troops are facing now might be coming from foreign, neighboring countries? And if so, what are our courses going about——

The President. We're constantly gathering intelligence. We're monitoring influence. We are adjusting our tactics. We are—obviously, if there's any kind of influence from a foreign country that is disruptive, any kind of influence—if the Iranians are trying to influence the outcome of the political process or the outcome of the security situation there, we're letting them know our displeasure.

Our call is for those in the neighborhood to allow Iran—Iraq to develop a democracy. And that includes our call to Iran as well as to Syria. We have made our concerns known, and we will continue to make our concerns known. It's in the interests of the neighborhood that Iraq develop to be a peaceful democracy. It's important for countries to have stable, peaceful, prosperous countries on their border. Prosperity in one nation will help prosperity in other nations. It's important for our friends in the rest of the Middle East to help this new democracy.

And so, yes, we're interested in negative influence; we're also interested in positive influence. And we call on people to be a positive influence, to help this new democracy emerge. And I'm optimistic that the Iraqi people will overcome the challenges they face.

And my optimism is based upon reality on the ground. One, there were some people trying to, obviously, foment sectarian violence. Some have called it a civil war. But it didn't work. Secondly, I'm optimistic because the Iraqi security forces performed, in most cases, really well to provide security. All but two of the Provinces of Iraq, after the blowing up of the mosque, were settled. I'm positive and optimistic about the development that the Iraqi security forces are achieving.

I know we've got to do more work in the police forces; we have said that very clearly. General Casey has called the year 2006 "the year of police training," and we'll continue to work to train the police. I'm optimistic that the leadership recognizes that a sectarian violence will undermine the capacity for them to self govern. I believe we'll have a unity government in place that will help move the process forward. I fully recognize that the nature of the enemy is such that they want to convince the world that we cannot succeed in Iraq. I know we're going to succeed if we don't lose our will.

Thank you all.

NOTE: The President spoke at 8:46 a.m. in the Roosevelt Room at the White House. In his remarks, he referred to Gen. Montgomery Meigs, USA (Ret.), director, Joint Improvised Explosive Device Defeat Organization; and Gen. George W. Casey, Jr., USA, commanding general, Multi-National Force—Iraq.

The President's Radio Address
March 11, 2006

Good morning. This month will mark the 3-year anniversary of the start of Operation Iraqi Freedom, which liberated Iraq from the tyranny of Saddam Hussein. As this milestone approaches, I will be giving a series of speeches to update the American people on our strategy for victory in Iraq. I will discuss the progress we are making, the lessons we've learned from our experiences, and how we're fixing what has not worked.

On Monday I will give the first of these speeches, focusing on the security element of our strategy, the task of defeating the terrorists and training Iraqi security forces so they can take the lead in the fight and defend their own democracy.

The Iraqi security forces have made great strides in the past year, and they performed well after the recent bombing of the Golden Mosque of Samarra. This mosque is one of Shi'a Islam's holiest sites, and after it was bombed, bands of armed militia began exacting revenge with reprisal attacks on Sunni mosques and random violence that took the lives of hundreds of innocent Iraqis.

Immediately after the attack, Iraq's leaders came together and acted to restore calm and end the violence. They deployed Iraqi security forces to Baghdad and other areas threatened by violence. These forces moved rapidly and effectively to protect religious sites, enforce a curfew, and reestablish civil order where necessary. We commend them for their good work.

The situation in Iraq is still tense. Reports of kidnapings and executions are being taken very seriously. The Iraqi Government has made clear that such violent attacks cannot be tolerated. The vast majority of Iraqis have shown they want a future of freedom and peace.

By their response over the past 2 weeks and their participation in three successful elections last year, the Iraqi people have made clear they will not let a violent minority take that future away by tearing the country apart. And the Iraqi security forces have shown that they are capable of rising above sectarian divisions to protect the unity of a free Iraq.

The effective performance of the Iraqi security forces during this crisis showed that our hard work to build up and train these forces is paying off. In the coming months, we will help prepare more Iraqi battalions to take the lead in battle, and Iraqi forces will assume responsibility over more territory. Our goal is to have the Iraqis control more territory than the coalition forces by the end of this year. And as Iraqis assume responsibility over more territory, this frees American and coalition

forces to concentrate on hunting down high-value targets like the terrorist Zarqawi and his associates.

As we take the fight to the terrorists, they realize they cannot defeat us directly in battle, so they have resorted to brutal attacks against innocent Iraqis and American forces using improvised explosive devices, or IEDs. IEDs are homemade bombs that can be hidden in cars or by the side of a road and detonated remotely, using everyday devices like garage door openers and cordless phones.

These weapons are now the principal threat to our troops and to the future of a free Iraq. And to defeat this threat, my administration has established a new, high-level command at the Department of Defense, led by retired four-star General Montgomery Meigs. This weekend General Meigs is briefing me at the White House on our plan to defeat the threat of IEDs. We're harnessing every available resource, the ingenuity of our best scientists and engineers, and the determination of our military to defeat this threat. And we're not going to rest until this danger to our troops has been removed.

In the coming days, there will be considerable reflection on the removal of Saddam Hussein from power and our remaining mission in Iraq. The last 3 years have tested our resolve. The fighting has been tough. The enemy we face has proved to be brutal and relentless. We have changed our approach in many areas to reflect the hard realities on the ground. And the sacrifice being made by our young men and women who wear the uniform has been heartening and inspiring.

Amid the daily news of car bombs and kidnapings and brutal killings, I can understand why many of our fellow citizens are now wondering if the entire mission was worth it. I strongly believe our country is better off with Saddam Hussein out of power. Under Saddam Hussein, Iraq was an enemy of America who shot at our airplanes, had a history of pursuing and using weapons of mass destruction, threatened and invaded his neighbors, ordered the death of thousands of his citizens, and supported terrorism.

After the liberation of the Iraqi people, Al Qaida and their affiliates have made Iraq the central front on the war on terror. By helping the Iraqi people build a free and representative government, we will deny the terrorists a safe haven to plan attacks against America. The security of our country is directly linked to the liberty of the Iraqi people. This will require more difficult days of fighting and sacrifice, yet I am confident that our strategy will result in victory, and then our troops can come home with the honor they have earned.

Thank you for listening.

NOTE: The address was recorded at 7 a.m. on March 10 in the Cabinet Room at the White House for broadcast at 10:06 a.m. on March 11. The transcript was made available by the Office of the Press Secretary on March 10 but was embargoed for release until the broadcast. In his address, the President referred to former President Saddam Hussein of Iraq; senior Al Qaida associate Abu Musab Al Zarqawi; and Gen. Montgomery Meigs, USA (Ret.), director, Joint Improvised Explosive Device Defeat Organization. The Office of the Press Secretary also released a Spanish language transcript of this address.

Remarks Following Discussions With Prime Minister Mikulas Dzurinda of Slovakia
March 13, 2006

President Bush. Mr. Prime Minister, welcome. Thank you for coming. I always enjoy being with you because you're an optimistic, upbeat believer in the people of your country and the possibilities to work together to achieve peace. And so thanks for coming.

I admire the job you have done, and I admire the record that you have produced. A lot of times in politics, people are pretty good talkers, but they don't follow through. You have followed through.

We discussed a lot of issues. I thank the Prime Minister for his contributions to helping young democracies succeed, democracies in Afghanistan and Iraq. And I want to thank you for that.

We discussed the importance for transatlantic ties between the United States and not only Slovakia but also between the United States and Europe. And I assured him that those transatlantic ties are an important part of our policies here.

We talked about two issues that I found—that I know are important. One, of course, is the visa issue. The Prime Minister made it very clear that he expects there to be some progress on the visa issue, that he's—he represents the good people of Slovakia when he says to me that there needs to be a constant renewal of the process to make sure that it is fair. And I appreciate—I listened very carefully to my friend and can assure the people of Slovakia that we are working together to make the visa policy work better.

Secondly, he talked about the knowledge-based economy that he envisioned for his country. And I thought, first of all, it's very wise to—he recognizes the world and the challenges of the world and knows full well that as people gain knowledge, a country is going to end up being more competitive in the 21st century.

And so I—we strategized about ways to help Slovakia and the United States benefit

461

from exchanges, and particularly student exchanges, so that knowledge becomes a paramount part of our future.

And so, Mr. Prime Minister, thanks for your vision. And I also feel sorry for the fact that you broke your leg. This guy's a good runner. And so now I feel comfortable challenging you to a race. [*Laughter*] Had you been healthy, I wouldn't even had gotten on the same track with you. But I wish you a speedy recovery, and thanks again for coming to the United States.

Prime Minister Dzurinda. Thank you, Mr. President. My leg is broken, but my heart is happy. [*Laughter*] My heart is happy because we are friends and strong allies, America and Slovakia, America and the European Union. I am happy being here because we are good friends. President Bush visited us a year ago; he visited President of Russia, Mr. Putin, in Bratislava, and we remember this fantastic stay of President Bush in Slovakia.

We are good friends, and we share the responsibility for development in the world. I highly appreciate the leadership of President Bush in solving of global issues, the most hot and most complicated issues in the world. And I talked to President Bush

that transatlantic cooperation is and must stay the basis of our security. This is something like axis of stability, prosperity, and the future of both countries, but also the future of the democratic world.

As President Bush has already mentioned, we have some bilateral issues. I appreciate especially his State of Union, during which he announced a new program how to educate people, young generation. We want to do the same. We want to find a new way, thanks to which it would be possible to cooperate with the United States also in the area of science research and development, innovation, education. And I believe that we will discover these new ways.

Of course we spoke many issues of foreign policy, as usually. And I can only tell that our view is the same, and we will continue in this cooperation to advance freedom and democracy in the world.

Mr. President, thank you very, very much for being such a good leader.

President Bush. Thank you, sir.

NOTE: The President spoke at 10:35 a.m. in the Oval Office at the White House. Prime Minister Dzurinda referred to President Vladimir V. Putin of Russia.

Remarks to the Foundation for the Defense of Democracies
March 13, 2006

Thanks for the warm welcome. Cliff, thanks for the introduction. It's a pleasure to be with the Foundation for the Defense of Democracies. This organization was formed in the wake of the September the 11th attacks to fight the ideologies that drive terrorism. You recognized immediately that the war on terror is a struggle between freedom and tyranny and that the path to lasting security is to defeat the hateful vision the terrorists are spreading with the hope of freedom and democracy.

The foundation is making a difference across the world, and I appreciate the difference you're making. You have trained Iraqi women and Iranian students in the principles and practice of democracy. You've translated "democracy readers" into Arabic for distribution across the broader Middle East. You've helped activists across the region organize effective political movements so they can help bring about democratic change and ensure the survival of liberty in new democracies. By promoting democratic ideals and training a new generation of democratic leaders in the Middle East, you are helping us to bring victory in the war on terror, and I thank you for your hard work in freedom's cause.

I also want to thank the members of the Board of the Foundation for the Defense of the Democracies. I want to thank Steve Trachtenberg, the president of George Washington University, and his wife, Fran, for joining us today. Thanks for letting me come to your campus. I'm honored to be here. He informed me that my dad will be giving the graduation speech this year—[*laughter*]—and Mother is getting an honorary degree. [*Laughter*] Smart man.

Mr. Secretary, thanks for joining us. I'm proud that Secretary Rumsfeld is with us. I want to thank Senator Dick Lugar for being with us today. Mr. Chairman, proud you're here. Thanks for coming. I want to thank the Members of the United States Congress who have joined us: Congressman Lungren, Adam Schiff, Joe Wilson, Tom Cole, and Dan Boren. I appreciate you all taking time to be here today; it means a lot.

I want to thank the ambassadors who have joined us. I see two for certain, one from Jordan and one from Israel. Proud you both are here. If there's any other ambassadors here, I apologize for not introducing you, and you don't have as good a seat as these two guys. [*Laughter*]

The mission of this foundation is to defeat terror by promoting democracy, and that is the mission of my administration. Our strategy to protect America is based on a clear premise: The security of our Nation depends on the advance of liberty in other nations. On September the 11th, 2001, we saw that problems originating in a failed and oppressive state 7,000 miles away could bring murder and destruction to our country. We saw that dictatorships shelter terrorists, feed resentment and radicalism, and threaten the security of free nations. Democracies replace resentment with hope; democracies respect the rights of their citizens and their neighbors; democracies join the fight against terror. And so America is committed to an historic, long-term goal: To secure the peace of the world, we seek the end of tyranny in our world.

We are making progress in the march of freedom, and some of the most important progress has taken place in a region that has not known the blessings of liberty, the broader Middle East. Two weeks ago, I got a chance to visit Afghanistan and to see firsthand the transformation that has taken place in that country. Before September the 11th, 2001, Afghanistan was ruled by a cruel regime that oppressed its people, brutalized women, and gave safe haven to the terrorists who attacked America.

Today, the terror camps have been shut down; women are working; boys and girls are going to school; Afghans have voted in free elections—25 million people have had the taste of freedom. Taliban and Al Qaida remnants continue to fight Afghanistan's democratic progress. In recent weeks, they have launched new attacks that have killed Afghan citizens and coalition forces. The United States and our allies will stay in the fight against the terrorists, and we'll train Afghan soldiers and police so they can defend their country. The Afghan people are building a vibrant young democracy that is an ally in the war on terror, and America is proud to have such a determined partner in the cause of freedom.

Next week, we will mark the 3-year anniversary of the start of Operation Iraqi Freedom. In less than 3 years, the Iraqi people have gone from living under the boot of a brutal tyrant, to liberation, to sovereignty, to free elections, to a constitutional referendum, and last December, to elections for a fully constitutional government. In those December elections, over 11 million Iraqis—more than 75 percent of the Iraqi voting-age population—defied the terrorists to cast their ballots.

Americans were inspired by the images of Iraqis bringing elderly relatives to the polls, holding up purple ink-stained fingers, dancing in the streets, and celebrating their freedom. By their courage, the Iraqi people have spoken and made their intentions clear: They want to live in democracy, and they are determined to shape their own destiny.

The past few weeks, the world has seen very different images from Iraq, images of violence and anger and despair. We have seen a great house of worship, the Golden Mosque of Samarra, in ruins after a brutal terrorist attack. We've seen mass protests in response to provocation. We've seen reprisal attacks by armed militias on Sunni mosques and random violence that has taken the lives of hundreds of Iraqi citizens.

The terrorists attacked the Golden Mosque for a reason: They know that they lack the military strength to challenge Iraqi and coalition forces directly, so their only hope is to try and provoke a civil war. So they attacked one of Shi'a Islam's holiest sites, hoping to incite violence that would drive Iraqis apart and stop their progress on the path to a free society.

Immediately after the attack, I said that Iraq faced a moment of choosing. And in the days that followed, the Iraqi people made their choice. They looked into the abyss and did not like what they saw. After the bombing, most Iraqis saw what the perpetuators of this attack were trying to do. The enemy had failed to stop the January 2005 elections; they failed to stop the constitutional referendum; they failed to stop the December elections. And now they're trying to stop the formation of a unity government. By their response over the past 2 weeks, Iraqis have shown the world they want a future of freedom and peace, and they will oppose a violent minority that seeks to take that future away from them by tearing their country apart.

The situation in Iraq is still tense, and we're still seeing acts of sectarian violence and reprisal. Yet out of this crisis, we've also seen signs of a hopeful future. We saw the restraint of the Iraqi people in the face of massive provocation. Most Iraqis did not turn to violence, and many chose to show their solidarity by coming together in joint Sunni and Shi'a prayer services. We saw the leadership of Sunni and Shi'a clerics who joined together to denounce the bombing and call for restraint. Ayatollah Sistani issued a strong statement denouncing what he called sectarian sedition, and he urged all Iraqis—in his words—"not to be dragged into committing acts that would only please the enemies." We saw the capability of the Iraqi security forces, who deployed to protect religious sites, enforce a curfew, and restore civil order. We saw the determination of many of Iraq's leaders, who rose to the moment, came together, and acted decisively to diffuse the crisis.

Iraq's leaders know that this is not the last time they will be called to stand together in the face of an outrageous terrorist attack. Iraq's leaders know that they must put aside their differences, reach out across political, religious, and sectarian lines, and form a unity government that will earn the trust and the confidence of all Iraqis. Iraqis now have a chance to show the world that they have learned the lesson of Samarra: A country that divides into factions and dwells on old grievances risks sliding back into tyranny. The only path to a future of peace is the path of unity.

Soon the new Parliament will be seated in Baghdad, and this will begin the process of forming a government. Forming a new government will demand negotiation and compromise by the Iraqis; it will require patience by America and our coalition allies.

In the weeks ahead, Americans will likely see a good deal of political maneuvering in Iraq, as different factions and leaders advance competing agendas and seek their share of political power. Out of this process, a free government will emerge that represents the will of the Iraqi people, instead of the will of one cruel dictator.

The work ahead in Iraq is hard, and there will be more difficult moments. The Samarra attack was a clear attempt to ignite a civil war. And we can expect the enemy will try again, and they will continue to sow violence and destruction designed to stop the emergence of a free and democratic Iraq.

The enemies of a free Iraq are determined, yet so are the Iraqi people, and so are America and coalition partners. We will not lose our nerve. We will help the Iraqi people succeed. Our goal in Iraq is victory, and victory will be achieved when the terrorists and Saddamists can no longer threaten Iraq's democracy, when the Iraqi security forces can provide for the safety of their own citizens, and when Iraq is not a safe haven for terrorists to plot new attacks against our Nation.

We have a comprehensive strategy for victory in Iraq, a strategy I laid out in a series of speeches last year. Our strategy has three elements. On the political side, we are helping Iraqis build a strong democracy so that old resentments will be eased and the insurgency marginalized. On the economic side, we are continuing reconstruction efforts and helping Iraqis build a modern economy that will give all its citizens a stake in a free and peaceful Iraq. And on the security side, we are striking terrorist targets and training the Iraqi security forces, which are taking responsibility for more Iraqi territory and becoming increasingly capable of defeating the enemy. In the coming weeks, I will update the American people on our strategy, the progress we are making, the lessons we have learned from our experiences, and how we are fixing what hasn't worked.

Today I will discuss the third element of our strategy, the progress of our efforts to defeat the terrorists and train the Iraqi security forces so they can take the lead in defending their own democracy.

At the end of last year, I described in detail many of the changes we have made to improve the training of Iraqi security

forces, and we saw the fruits of those changes in recent days in Iraq. After the Samarra bombings, it was the Iraqi security forces—not coalition forces—that restored order. In the hours after the attack, Iraqi leaders put the Iraqi security forces on alert, canceling all leaves and heightening security around mosques and critical sites. Using security plans developed for the December elections, they deployed Iraqi forces in Baghdad and to other troubled spots.

Iraqi police manned checkpoints, increased patrols, and ensured that peaceful demonstrators were protected, while those who turned to violence were arrested. Public order brigades deployed as rapid reaction forces to areas where violence was reported. The 9th Mechanized Division of the Iraqi Army, which was in the midst of a major training event, regrouped and entered the Baghdad city gates, taking up assigned positions throughout the city with T–72 tanks and armored infantry vehicles. During the past 2 weeks, Iraqi security forces conducted more than 200 independent operations—each of them Iraqi-planned, Iraqi-conducted, and Iraqi-led.

Having Iraqi forces in the lead has been critical to preventing violence from spinning out of control. For example, on the day of the Samarra bombing, the Iraqi national police responded to an armed demonstration in an area immediately adjacent to Sadr City where an angry Shi'a crowd had surrounded the Sunni Al-Quds Mosque. The Iraqi brigade commander placed his troops—who were largely Shi'a—between the crowd and the mosque and talked to the crowd using megaphones and—calling for calm and urging them to disperse. After a 2-hour standoff, the crowd eventually left without incident, and the National Police remained in position overnight to guard the mosque until the threat was over. The fact that Iraqis were in the

lead and negotiating with their own countrymen helped diffuse a potential confrontation and prevented an escalation of
violence.

In another Baghdad neighborhood, a
similar situation unfolded. A group of
armed militia members had gone in and
occupied the Al-Nida Mosque. An Iraqi
Army brigade quickly arrived on the scene,
and the brigade commander negotiated
with the group and secured their peaceful
departure. Once again, because Iraqi forces
spoke their language and understood their
culture, they were able to convince the
Iraqi militia to leave peacefully.

Not all Iraqi units performed as well as
others, and there were some reports of
Iraqi units in Eastern Baghdad allowing militia members to pass through checkpoints.
But American commanders are closely
watching the situation, and they report
these incidents appear to be the exception,
not the rule. In the weeks since the bombing, the Iraqi security forces turned in a
strong performance. From the outset, Iraqi
forces understood that if they failed to
stand for national unity, the country would
slip into anarchy. And so they have stood
their ground and defended their democracy
and brought their nation through one of
its most difficult moments since liberation.

General Marty Dempsey, our top commander responsible for training the Iraqi
security forces, says this about their performance: "They were deliberate, poised,
even-handed, and professional. They engaged local tribal, political, and religious
leaders. They patiently but deliberately confronted armed groups to let them know
that they had control of the situation." He
went on to say, "I'm sure we will find instances where they could have performed
better, but in the face of immense pressure,
they performed very, very well." As a result
of their performance, the Iraqi security
forces are gaining the confidence of the
Iraqi people. And as the Iraqi security
forces make progress against the enemy,
their morale continues to increase.

When I reported on the progress of the
Iraqi security forces last year, I said that
there were over 120 Iraqi and police combat battalions in the fight against the
enemy, and 40 of those were taking the
lead in the fight. Today, the number of
battalions in the fight has increased to more
than 130, with more than 60 taking the
lead. As more Iraqi battalions come on line,
these Iraqi forces are assuming responsibility for more territory. Today, Iraqi units
have primary responsibility for more than
30,000 square miles of Iraq, an increase
of roughly 20,000 square miles since the
beginning of the year. And Iraqi forces are
now conducting more independent operations throughout the country than do coalition forces.

This is real progress, but there is more
work to be done this year. Our commanders tell me that the Iraqi police still
lag behind the army in training and capabilities, so one of our major goals in 2006
is to accelerate the training of the Iraqi
police. One problem is that some national
police units have been disproportionately
Shi'a, and there have been some reports
of infiltration of the National Police by militias. And so we're taking a number of
steps to correct this problem.

First, we have begun implementing a
program that has been effective with the
Iraqi Army—partnering U.S. battalions with
the Iraqi National Police battalions. These
U.S. forces are working with their Iraqi
counterparts, giving them tactical training
so they can defeat the enemy. And they
are also teaching them about the role of
a professional police force in a democratic
system, so they can serve all Iraqis without
discrimination.

Second, we are working with the Iraqi
leaders to find and remove any leaders in
the National Police who show evidence of
loyalties to militia. For example, last year,
there were reports that the Second Public
Order Brigade contained members of an
illegal militia who were committing abuses.
So last December, the Interior Ministry

leadership removed the Second Brigade commander and replaced him with a new commander, who then dismissed more than 100 men with suspected militia ties. Today, this Iraqi police brigade has been transformed into a capable, professional unit, and during the recent crisis after the Samarra bombing, they performed with courage and distinction.

Finally, we are working with Iraqis to diversify the ranks of the National Police by recruiting more Sunni Arabs. For example, the basic training class for the National Police public order forces that graduated last October was less than one percent Sunni. The class graduating in April will include many, many more Sunnis. By ensuring the public order forces reflect the general population, Iraqis are making the National Police a truly national institution, one that is able to serve, protect, and defend all the Iraqi people.

As more capable Iraqi police and soldiers come on line, they will assume responsibility for more territory, with the goal of having the Iraqis control more territory than the coalition by the end of 2006. And as Iraqis take over more territory, this frees American and coalition forces to concentrate on training and on hunting down high-value targets like the terrorist Zarqawi and his associates. As Iraqis stand up, America and our coalition will stand down. And my decisions on troop levels will be made based upon the conditions on the ground and on the recommendations of our military commanders, not artificial timetables set by politicians here in Washington, DC.

These terrorists know they cannot defeat us militarily, so they have turned to the weapon of fear. And one of the most brutal weapons at their disposal are improvised explosive devices, or IEDs. IEDs are bombs made from artillery shells, explosives, and other munitions that can be hidden and detonated remotely. After the terrorists were defeated in battles in Fallujah and Tall 'Afar, they saw that they could

not confront Iraqi or American forces in pitched battles and survive. And so they turned to IEDs, a weapon that allows them to attack from a safe distance, without having to face our forces in battle.

The principal victims of IED attacks are innocent Iraqis. The terrorists and insurgents have used IEDs to kill Iraqi children playing in the streets, shoppers at Iraqi malls, and Iraqis lining up at police and army recruiting stations. They use IEDs to strike terror in the hearts of Iraqis in an attempt to break their confidence in the free future of their country.

The enemy is also using IEDs in their campaign against U.S. and coalition forces in Iraq, and we are harnessing every available resource to deal with this threat. My administration has established a new, high-level organization at the Department of Defense, led by retired four-star General Montgomery Meigs. On Saturday, General Meigs along with the Secretary of Defense briefed me at the White House on our plan to defeat the threat of IEDs. Our plan has three elements: targeting, training, and technology.

The first part of our plan is targeting and eliminating the terrorists and bombmakers. Across Iraq, we are on the hunt for the enemy—capturing and killing the terrorists before they strike, uncovering and disarming their weapons before they go off, and rooting out and destroying bomb-making cells so they can't produce more weapons.

Because the Iraqi people are the targets—primarily the targets of the bombers, Iraqis are increasingly providing critical intelligence to help us find the bombmakers and stop new attacks. The number of tips from Iraqis has grown from 400 last March to over 4,000 in December. For example, just 3 weeks ago, acting on tips provided by local citizens, coalition forces uncovered a massive IED arsenal hidden in a location northwest of Baghdad. They found and confiscated more than 3,000 pieces of munitions in one of the largest weapons caches discovered in that region to date. Just 2 weeks ago, acting on intelligence from Iraqis, coalition forces uncovered a bomb-making facility northeast of Fallujah. They captured 61 terrorists at the facility and confiscated large numbers of weapons.

In all, during the past 6 months, Iraqi and coalition forces have found and cleared nearly 4,000 IEDs, uncovered more than 1,800 weapons caches and bomb-making plants, and killed or detained hundreds of terrorists and bombmakers. We're on the hunt for the enemy, and we're not going to rest until they've been defeated.

The second part of our plan is to give our forces specialized training to identify and clear IEDs before they explode. Before arriving in Iraq and Afghanistan, our combat units get training on how to counter the threat of IEDs. And to improve our training, last month, we established a new IED Joint Center of Excellence headquartered at Fort Irwin, California, where we're taking lessons learned from the IED fight in Iraq and sharing them with our troops in the field and those preparing to deploy. This new initiative will ensure that every Army and Marine combat unit headed to Afghanistan and Iraq is prepared for the challenges that IEDs bring to the battlefield.

Before deploying, our troops will train with the equipment they will use in the IED fight. They'll study enemy tactics and experience live-fire training that closely mirrors what they will see when they arrive in the zone of combat. Our goal with this training is to ensure that when our forces encounter the enemy, that they're ready.

The third part of our plan is to develop new technologies to defend against IEDs. We are putting the best minds in America to work on this effort. The Department of Defense recently gathered some—gathered 600 leaders from industry and academia, the national laboratories, the National Academy of Sciences, all branches of the military, and every relevant Government Agency to discuss technology solu-

tions to the IED threat. We now have nearly 100 projects underway. For security reasons, I'm not going to share the details of the technologies we're developing. The simple reason is, the enemy can use even the smallest details to overcome our defenses.

Earlier this year, a newspaper published details of a new anti-IED technology that was being developed. Within 5 days of the publication—using details from that article—the enemy had posted instructions for defeating this new technology on the Internet. We cannot let the enemy know how we're working to defeat him. But I can assure the American people that my administration is working to put the best technology in the hands of our men and women on the frontlines, and we are mobilizing resources against the IED threat.

I assured General Meigs that he will have the funding and personnel he needs to succeed. In 2004, the administration spent $150 million to fight the IED threat. This year, we're providing $3.3 billion to support our efforts to defeat IEDs. These investments are making a difference. Today, nearly half of the IEDs in Iraq are found and disabled before they can be detonated. In the past 18 months, we've cut the casualty rate per IED attack in half. More work needs to be done. Yet by targeting the bombmakers and training our forces and deploying new technologies, we will stay ahead of the enemy, and that will save Iraqi and American lives.

Some of the most powerful IEDs we're seeing in Iraq today includes components that came from Iran. Our Director of National Intelligence, John Negroponte, told the Congress, "Tehran has been responsible for at least some of the increasing lethality of anticoalition attacks by providing Shi'a militia with the capability to build improvised explosive devices" in Iraq. Coalition forces have seized IEDs and components that were clearly produced in Iran. Such actions—along with Iran's support for terrorism and its pursuit of nuclear weapons—

are increasingly isolating Iran, and America will continue to rally the world to confront these threats.

We still have difficult work ahead in Iraq. I wish I could tell you that the violence is waning and that the road ahead will be smooth. It will not. There will be more tough fighting and more days of struggle, and we will see more images of chaos and carnage in the days and months to come. The terrorists are losing on the field of battle, so they are fighting this war through the pictures we see on television and in the newspapers every day. They're hoping to shake our resolve and force us to retreat. They are not going to succeed.

The battle lines in Iraq are clearly drawn for the world to see, and there is no middle ground. The enemy will emerge from Iraq one of two ways, emboldened or defeated. The stakes in Iraq are high. By helping Iraqis build a democracy, we will deny the terrorists a safe haven to plan attacks against America. By helping Iraqis build a democracy, we will gain an ally in the war on terror. By helping Iraqis build a democracy, we will inspire reformers across the Middle East. And by helping Iraqis build a democracy, we'll bring hope to a troubled region, and this will make America more secure in the long term.

Since the morning of September the 11th, we have known that the war on terror would require great sacrifice, and in this war, we have said farewell to some very good men and women. One of those courageous Americans was Sergeant William Scott Kinzer, Jr., who was killed last year by the terrorists while securing polling sites for the Iraqi elections. His mom, Debbie, wrote me a letter. She said: "These words are straight from a shattered but healing mother's heart. My son made the decision to join the Army. He believed that what he was involved in would eventually change Iraq and that those changes would be re-

corded in history books for years to come. On his last visit home, I asked him what I would ever do if something happened to him in Iraq. He smiled at me with—his blue eyes sparkled, as he said, 'Mom, I love my job. If I should die, I would die happy. Does life get any better than this?'" His mom went on: "Please do not let the voices we hear the loudest change what you and Scott started in Iraq. Please do not let his dying be in vain. Don't let my son have given his all for an unfinished job. Please complete the mission."

I make this promise to Debbie and all the families of the fallen heroes: We will not let your loved ones dying be in vain. We will finish what we started in Iraq. We will complete the mission. We will leave behind a democracy that can govern itself, sustain itself, and defend itself. And a free Iraq in the heart of the Middle East will make the American people more secure for generations to come.

May God bless the families of the fallen. May God bless our troops in the fight. And may God continue to bless the United States of America.

NOTE: The President spoke at 1:16 p.m. in the Dorothy Betts Marvin Theatre at The George Washington University. In his remarks, he referred to Clifford D. May, president, Foundation for the Defense of Democracies; Jordan's Ambassador to the U.S. Karim Kawar; Israel's Ambassador to the U.S. Daniel Ayalon; former President Saddam Hussein of Iraq; Grand Ayatollah Ali al-Sistani, Iraqi Shiite leader; Lt. Gen. Martin E. Dempsey, USA, commander, Multi-National Security Transition Command—Iraq; senior Al Qaida associate Abu Musab Al Zarqawi; and Gen. Montgomery Meigs, USA (Ret.), director, Joint Improvised Explosive Device Defeat Organization. The Office of the Press Secretary also released a Spanish language transcript of these remarks.

Message to the Congress on Continuation of the National Emergency With Respect to Iran
March 13, 2006

To the Congress of the United States:

Section 202(d) of the National Emergencies Act (50 U.S.C. 1622(d)) provides for the automatic termination of a national emergency unless, prior to the anniversary date of its declaration, the President publishes in the *Federal Register* and transmits to the Congress a notice stating that the emergency is to continue in effect beyond the anniversary date. In accordance with this provision, I have sent the enclosed notice to the *Federal Register* for publication, stating that the Iran emergency declared on March 15, 1995, is to continue in effect beyond March 15, 2006. The most recent notice continuing this emergency was published in the *Federal Register* on March 14, 2005 (70 *FR* 12581).

The crisis between the United States and Iran constituted by the actions and policies of the Government of Iran that led to the declaration of a national emergency on March 15, 1995, has not been resolved. The actions and policies of the Government of Iran are contrary to the interests of the United States in the region and pose a continuing unusual and extraordinary threat to the national security, foreign policy, and economy of the United States. For these reasons, I have determined that it is necessary to continue the national emergency declared with respect to Iran and maintain in force comprehensive sanctions against Iran to respond to this threat.

GEORGE W. BUSH

The White House,
March 13, 2006.

NOTE: The notice is listed in Appendix D at the end of this volume.

Remarks Following a Meeting With Jason McElwain and an Exchange With Reporters in Rochester, New York
March 14, 2006

The President. First of all, it's great to be here in upstate New York. As you can see, a special person has greeted me at the airport.

Jason, mind if I call you J-Mac?

Jason McElwain. Yeah. [*Laughter*]

The President. I call him J-Mac. You call me George W. [*Laughter*]

But our country was captivated by an amazing story on the basketball court. I think it's a story of Coach Johnson's willingness to give a person a chance. It's a story of Dave and Debbie's deep love for their son, and it's a story of a young man who found his touch on the basketball court, which in turn, touched the hearts of citizens all across the country.

So I want to thank you for being here. You probably didn't realize the impact you were going to have on people all across America and around the world when you made those six 3s in a row. I've kind of gotten off the courts these days because I'm getting old, but if I got back on the courts, I'd need a lesson—[*laughter*]—on how to rotate that ball. But let me have that there, Coach.

James Johnson. Okay. There you go, sir.

[*At this point, the President held a sign with Jason's picture.*]

The President. Thank you. There you go. Kind of looks like you.

Anyway, thank you all for coming. God bless. I appreciate the wonderful story that's come out of your family.

Q. Mr. President, how did you hear about the story, and what's your reaction?

The President. Saw it on TV. Saw it on TV, and I wept, just like a lot of other people. It's just one of those stories that touched a lot of people's heart.

Q. Did somebody play it for you, or did you just see it?

The President. I can't remember exactly how it happened. Probably somebody played it for me, you know, being the President and all. But it's a wonderful tale. God bless.

NOTE: The President spoke at 10:50 a.m. at the Greater Rochester International Airport. In his remarks, he referred to Jason McElwain, an autistic student at Greece Athena High School who scored 20 points in his first varsity basketball game; and James Johnson, coach, Greece Athena High School boys basketball team.

Remarks in a Discussion on Medicare Prescription Drug Benefits in Canandaigua, New York
March 14, 2006

The President. Thank you all. Be seated. Thank you all very much. Thanks for coming. Thanks for the warm welcome. Thanks for giving me a chance to come and talk to you about an important issue for our seniors.

Before I get started, though, I do want to thank the folks here at Canandaigua Academy for letting me come by to say hello. The assistant principal, John LaFave, kindly greeted me behind stage here. As I understand, some of the students are here in the room, and some are watching. I'm glad to provide you a convenient excuse to get out of class. [*Laughter*] I want to thank the superintendent, Steve Uebbing, for greeting me as well.

For all the teachers who are here and are paying attention to this, thanks for being a teacher. It's a noble profession. It's an important—it's really important. And speaking about teachers, I married one. [*Laughter*] She sends her love. Laura W. Bush is a unique woman who is obviously a patient woman. [*Laughter*] When I married her, she was a public school librarian who wasn't that much interested in politics.

Now she's the First Lady of the United States. And I'm proud to call her First Lady, and I love to call her wife. And she sends her love too.

I want to thank Randy Kuhl; he served with distinction in the United States Congress. He said, "Look, you've been in my district before; come back up here if you want to be with some just good, down-to-earth people that care about the future of the country." And one of the reasons I'm here is because of Randy's invitation.

I also want to thank Congressman Sherry Boehlert, right next door. I appreciate you being here. Mighty New York Yankee fan, I want you to know—[*laughter*]—fierce baseball—advocate for baseball. Plus, he's a good Congressman.

I want to thank Antonia Novello. Dr. Novello, where are you? She's here—oh, there you are. Good to see you. Appreciate you coming. She's the commissioner of health for the State of New York. I'm honored you're here. I'll tell old 41 I saw you. That's the number for my dad. See, he's the 41st President; I'm the 43d President, so—I'll tell him I saw you.

I want to thank the mayor, who is here—Madam Mayor, where are you? Thanks for coming. Yes, I appreciate you coming. Thanks for your hospitality. It's great to be in your city. I want to thank all the other folks who are State government and local government.

Most of all, I want to thank our panelists. There are different ways to describe an issue that's of concern to the American people. And so one way to describe the issue is to have others help describe it for you, and that's what we're doing. This is a opportunity for me and others to share thoughts about Medicare.

The role of government is to provide good health care for our seniors. We made that commitment, interestingly enough, when Lyndon Baines Johnson was the President. When I got to Washington, I took a look at the Medicare system to determine whether or not Medicare was providing excellent health coverage. If you're going to provide health coverage for somebody, you want to make sure it works. I found a system that was old and stale. It really wasn't a modern health care system. Medicine had changed; Medicare had not changed.

For example, the Government would pay $28,000 for an ulcer surgery for a senior on Medicare but not a dime for the prescription drugs to prevent the ulcer surgery from being needed in the first place. There was a lot of times the cures for disease would lag behind the Government saying it's okay to provide that as a benefit. In other words, it was an old system.

So I worked with the Congress, and we've modernized Medicare. And for the first time, seniors can now get a prescription drug benefit under Medicare. And that's what we're here to talk about—the benefits of such a program; the need for people to, at the very minimum, take a look to see whether or not that program makes sense, and if it does make sense, to sign up on it. You'll hear me make the case: It's a good deal. Now, don't take my word for it. I would hope people would seek advice, seniors seek advice as to whether or not it's a good deal. Twenty-six million seniors so far have taken a look and said, "I think it's worthwhile to sign up."

And so part of the—the main reason I'm here is to talk about the Medicare reform plan, the prescription drug benefit, all aiming to convince people to the very minimum to take a look. I think you're going to like what you see.

One of the things that was necessary in Medicare to make it work better was to have—was to start exercising preventative medicine, to analyze and diagnose disease early, before they become acute. Interestingly enough, in the new Medicare reform law that I signed, for the first time, we're beginning to screen—offer screenings and a free physical for seniors when they sign up for the program. And that's important. Part of making sure health care is modern is to recognize that if you catch disease early, it makes it much easier to cure the problem.

And so not only are we talking about a prescription drug benefit that's important to make sure Medicare and medicine is modern, but we've now got screenings and preventative care—annual screenings and a "Welcome to Medicare" physical. So if you're thinking about signing up, think about having an additional benefit of having a screening or a physical. And that's an important part of making sure that our systems are modern and Government is fulfilling its responsibility to provide good, quality health care for our seniors.

The benefit is really important because it makes sure that seniors have choices as well. See, I've always believed that the consumer has got more options from which to choose, it provides higher quality. I'm one of these people that we ought to—that says, "We ought to trust people; we ought to trust their judgment." So one of the things about the reform plan that went forward is, not only does it provide a prescription drug benefit, but it says seniors ought to have a menu of opportunity, different options from which to choose to meet their needs.

And that created some confusion initially. And I knew it would, as a matter of fact. I knew some seniors on Medicare really didn't want to be confronted with any choice, and that the myriad of options would create a little confusion to begin with. But when people have taken time to look at the options and have sought help—whether it be a son or a daughter, or a community-based organization, or a faith-based organization, or 1–800–MEDICARE—they begin to realize that maybe the system is geared toward them. The more options a senior has to choose from, the more likely it is that the benefit is going to be tailored to his or her needs. And that's important for people to understand.

If you're a low-income senior, the Government is going to pay over 95 percent of your costs. Low-income seniors must take a look at this deal. I'm telling you, it's a good opportunity for you. You know, there was a period of time when seniors had to choose between rent and prescription drugs, and that wasn't right in our country. And this bill I signed is taking care of that problem, so people don't have to make the zero-sum choice. Prescription drugs has become an integral part of health care for a lot of folks, as you know.

The competition is good for consumers; it happens to be good for our taxpayers too. One of the interesting things that has happened is, is that because there are people saying, "I can do a better job for you," if you're a senior, the anticipated premiums for the drug benefit has dropped from $36–$37 a month to $25 a month in a 6-month period of time. In other words, people looked at the bill, and they said, "Well, this is what we think it's going to cost a senior for drug benefits, 37 bucks

a month—not low-income seniors but seniors." And instead, the cost is $25 a month.

The anticipated—in Washington, you know, we spend a lot of time guessing what something is going to cost. And the anticipated cost to the taxpayers for this drug benefit is 20 percent lower in the first year than anticipated. In other words, it matters when people have choice. It matters not only for quality but for price. The average senior on Medicare will get a—will see their prescription drug bills cut in half. If you're a low-income senior, the Government is going to pick up a significant portion of your tab. If you're an average senior—income senior, you're going to see your drug bills cut in half. If you're a taxpayer, the anticipated costs are significantly lower than we thought. It's working. It makes a lot of sense.

Part of my mission here, as I said earlier, was to convince people to find out about the program. If you haven't looked at the new prescription drug benefit, do so. Call 1–800–MEDICARE, or go to medicare.gov on the Internet. We're beginning to see some surveys from people who are actually using the program, and what's interesting is a lot of the seniors are getting information from the Internet. There's—and you'll see it's user-friendly. It's been designed to make it easy for the senior to take advantage of this new program.

If you're interested in the program, get your son or daughter to help you. And if you're a son or daughter and your mom or dad is eligible for Medicare, make sure you at least take time to give your parent the benefit of finding out what's available. If you're an average-income senior, you're going to get one-half of your prescription drugs cut. If you're a poor senior, this Government is going to pay over 95 percent of the cost of your prescription drugs. It makes a lot of sense.

I called upon a fellow named Dr. Mark McClellan to join me in this effort. He's here. That's him right there. He is a—

he's a Ph.D., see. I'm a C student. [*Laughter*] Look who's the President and who's the adviser. [*Laughter*]

Dr. Mark is in charge of what's called CMS. He'll tell you what that means. We use a lot of initials in Washington. The way I like to describe it to you is, he is in charge of making sure the Medicare reform plan is explained, rolled out, and administered properly.

And so, Mark, thanks for coming. Welcome.

Mark B. McClellan. Mr. President, it's great to be here. CMS is——

The President. Ph.D. in what?

Dr. McClellan. In economics, and I'm a physician as well.

The President. See, he spent a lot of time in the classroom. [*Laughter*]

Dr. McClellan. It's great to be part of the team, sir.

The President. We're glad you're here. Tell people what CMS stands for, and tell them what your job description is.

Dr. McClellan. CMS is the Center for Medicare and Medicaid Services. It's the Agency that oversees the Medicare program and also Medicaid. Overall, we're providing health insurance for more than 90 million people. And this is a very important year for us, as the President said. We're making some major improvements in the Medicare program so that seniors will not just think of us as the program that's going to pay the bills when they get sick but the program that's going to help them stay well and live a longer and healthier life. And we're working with States like New York to improve the Medicaid program for people with limited incomes as well.

The President. So we just cranked up. Anytime Washington passes a new law, sometimes the transition period can be interesting. And so we had some early challenges.

Dr. McClellan. That's right. In fact, I was just talking with Diane about this beforehand. Diane is a pharmacist. You're going to hear from her in a minute.

The President. No, I'm the emcee. [*Laughter*] You're the explainer. [*Laughter*] You know how these Ph.D.s are. You know, they kind of—[*laughter*].

[*At this point, Dr. McClellan made further remarks.*]

The President. How about the phone lines? People have——

Dr. McClellan. The phone lines are much better wait times. If you call 1–800–MEDICARE, that 24/7 help line that we make available so seniors can find out exactly what this program means for them, your wait time now is an average of two minutes or less. So you can get through very quickly and find out what this program means for you.

The President. So would you recommend people—a loaded question—kind of leading the witness, and I'm not even a lawyer. [*Laughter*] Why would—why should people sign up for this?

Dr. McClellan. Well, now is a really good time to find out about it. We've got hundreds of thousands of people enrolling each week now, and we're ahead of what I think is going to be a rush towards the end of April and the first part of May as we approach the enrollment deadline. It's a 6-month period that people have to make a decision about the new coverage.

People are finding that they can save typically 50 percent on their prescriptions—or more—compared to not having coverage. And Consumer Reports pointed out recently that if you're willing to look at generic drugs, or other drugs that work in a very similar way to the ones you're taking now, you can save 70 or 80 percent. And if you call 1–800–MEDICARE, go to medicare.gov, or go to one of the many events happening all over the country, including right here in Canandaigua, there are places to go to get face-to-face help right here to find out about what this means for you. You can save literally thousands of dollars on your drug costs, and you can be protected for the rest of your life against high prescription drug costs in the future.

The President. Yes, describe that—the catastrophic care component of Medicare.

Dr. McClellan. Well, the drug benefit will, in most cases, start paying right off the bat. Most seniors who have signed up are already saying they're saving money with the program just 2 months into the benefit. There is what's called catastrophic protection as well. So if you have very high drug expenses, your coverage is never going to run out. For people who have higher—relatively high incomes, if they spend $3,600, Medicare will then pick up as much as 95 percent of all their subsequent drug costs. So no matter what your drug needs are for the rest of your life, you're going to be protected against very high expenses.

And, Mr. President, as you said, for people with limited means, about one in three seniors is living just on a fixed income—they get extra help, so they pay, typically, just a few dollars for each prescription. It's very important help.

The President. People need to take a look. I get out of Washington, people say, "Well, I'm not so sure we can trust the Government all that much." Take a look. One of the reasons I have come is to ask people who are eligible for Medicare just to explore the options. It's a good deal.

For the taxpayers who are here as well, we're doing an—we're providing an important service for our seniors. I repeat to you: The Federal Government has made the commitment to our seniors for good, modern health care. I happen to believe if that's the commitment, we ought to keep it. And the bill that I had the honor of signing keeps that commitment.

And so, Mark, thanks for coming. Stay on it. I'm a results-oriented guy. When I heard that it took a while for people to get on that—call that number and somebody wouldn't answer, I started asking, why? And they're solving it. We're making sure this opportunity for our seniors is done

in a cost-effective, efficient way. We want it to be user-friendly for our seniors.

Again, I repeat: I fully understand some people are perfectly content with life the way it is, and they're not interested in looking at forms and opportunities and choices. I would urge you to get somebody to help you take a look at the opportunities available for you.

Somebody who is helping people understand the opportunities is Susan Wilber. Susan, what do you do? [*Laughter*]

Susan Wilber. Well, I'm an A student, always was, so I became a health care professional. [*Laughter*]

The President. Look, you don't need to rub it in, you know.

[*Ms. Wilber, director, The Brighter Day, made brief remarks.*]

The President. That's good. If you're a church or community-based group or a synagogue, talk to your folks who go to your facility and encourage them to contact 1–800–MEDICARE, medicare.gov, Susan. I mean, there's all kinds of people like Susan.

What have you found to be the response initially, today? Give us a sense for——

Ms. Wilber. Initially, there was a lot of panic and confusion, a lot of new information coming from all directions—the newspaper, the television, the mailings. I think that we're a strong health care system in this community and that we're all well-connected as a health care network, so people were very willing to bring their concerns to us and to ask for help. And that's certainly a confidence that we've instilled in people. And I'm very grateful for that opportunity.

But we've set up individual meetings; we've set up situations where we meet with family members; we've done conference calls with families out of State to help their loved one here. So it's really been quite a collaborative effort to get people signed up.

The President. Thanks. Thirty—26 million people have signed up. That requires a lot of community effort around the country. And I want to thank Susan and others who just make sure the opportunity is at least presented in a way that people can make a choice. And the amazing thing about our country is we've got a lot of really decent souls, like Susan, at the community level who are very concerned about somebody else, that they want to help somebody. And one way to help somebody is to let seniors know about the opportunities available in this Medicare reform.

And you're signing up quite a few people, I understand.

Ms. Wilber. We've had quite a few people sign up initially.

The President. Good. How's it going?

Ms. Wilber. It's going well. There was a little bit of confusion at first, but——

The President. But, I mean, you don't want to recommend somebody to sign up and they say, "Why did you get me to sign up for this?"

Ms. Wilber. For the most part, it's worked very well. We've gotten some excellent feedback from our customers.

The President. Good. Thanks for being here.

Ms. Wilber. Thanks for having me.

The President. My call is, please help. I really hope a son or a daughter takes time on behalf of their mother or father and get on the Internet, medicare.gov, and take a look. You ought to do it. I think it happens to be a duty. If your mother or father is not that interested in getting on the Internet, get on with them. Walk through the steps and take a look at what's available.

We've got with us Diane Lawatsch. Welcome.

Diane Lawatsch. Thank you, Mr. President. I'm happy to be here.

The President. You're gainfully employed?

Ms. Lawatsch. I am gainfully employed.

The President. How? [*Laughter*]

Ms. Lawatsch. Uh-oh. [*Laughter*] I am a pharmacy operations manager for Wegmans Food Markets. I've been a registered pharmacist for almost 18 years. And a pharmacy operations manager helps to oversee the operations in pharmacy. And I have four stores in this region, and the Canandaigua store is one of them.

The President. Good. So give us a feel for how you view the Medicare bill, how it came to be, your reaction. Obviously, you're very much involved in prescription drugs.

[*Ms. Lawatsch made brief remarks.*]

The President. Obviously, pharmacists have got a stake in this. I mean, people show up at the counter, and there's a lot of pharmacists around the country who are saying, "Can we help you?" It's, frankly, in the interest of the pharmacist to give people the opportunity to get a very generous prescription drug benefit from the Government. I don't know if you've seen attitudinal changes yet amongst the people using the program.

Ms. Lawatsch. Well, absolutely. We definitely see customers come in that say, "Gee, I've never had coverage before," and now they have the coverage. One of the things, too, that we did at Wegmans was we started over a year ago preparing and investing in our people and putting our pharmacists and our technicians through training programs. We had four different online training courses so that they were prepared come January, and that helped a great deal.

The President. Good. Thanks. You're on the frontline.

Ms. Lawatsch. Yes, we are.

The President. So we've got Bob and Eleanor with us. Isn't that right?

Bob Wisnieff. Yes, we're here.

The President. So, in my family, the wife starts speaking first. [*Laughter*]

Eleanor Wisnieff. Okay, I'll go first.

[*Mrs. Wisnieff, retiree, made brief remarks.*]

The President. I like the idea of somebody saying, "Here are three choices from which to choose." See, if you give people an opportunity to choose, it means they're more likely to be able to find something that meets their needs. It's a different approach, isn't it? The older—one approach is, "We'll tell you what you need; the Government probably knows a little better than you do, anyway; we'll think on your behalf." What this bill says is, is that let's have some options available so people get to tailor the options to meet their needs. And what ends up happening is, is that there's choice. When we trust seniors with judgment, it helps on price and it helps on quality.

Do you have anything to offer, Bob?

Mr. Wisnieff. Well, I think Eleanor has pretty much got the punch line of my whole thing, so I'll have to be a bit of a Paul Harvey and say "the rest of the story." [*Laughter*]

The President. Pretty good. How long have you all been married?

Mr. Wisnieff. Fifty-two years.

The President. Fifty-two years?

Mr. Wisnieff. Fifty-two happy years. I hope you have the same.

The President. He said 52 happy years, by the way. Thanks for setting a good example.

[*Bob Wisnieff, retiree, made brief remarks.*]

The President. The key is saving a little money in retirement. They're on a fixed income. They've got now a prescription drug benefit. They don't have to make the awful choice between food, electricity, and prescription drugs. And they're actually putting a little extra money in their pocket. If that's true—is that true?

Mr. Wisnieff. That's true.

The President. Okay. If it's true, you ought to look at it. Senior citizens not only here in upstate New York but all across the country ought to look at this plan, ought to look at the opportunities. If you like it, sign up. It's a good deal. If you need help, ask for help. If you want to find out more about it, call 1–800–MEDI-CARE or get on the Internet, medicare.gov.

For the students listening here, one of my jobs is to help explain things to the American people, explain why we make the decisions we make. Today I've tried to explain to you why the Medicare system needed to be changed and some of the principles inherent in the change that benefits our seniors. Part of explaining something is to have people who are actually involved with the program, people that are helping to educate, people that know something about the pharmaceutical industry, people who are benefiting from the plan, to come and share their experience as well. And so I want to thank you all for giving me a chance to come.

One thing I didn't say—I do want to conclude by saying, Dr. Steve Uebbing, who is the superintendent of schools—when I came through the line, he told me about his son Daniel's service in the United States military. I meant to thank a good, proud dad, but more importantly, I want to thank his son for volunteering to serve his country, for volunteering to serve.

And for the students listening, I urge you to find out a way to serve your community. Mentor somebody; help feed the hungry; provide shelter for the homeless. If you're interested in volunteering for the military, that's one way to serve. Peace Corps is a fantastic opportunity to serve your country. Being a teacher is a fantastic way to serve your country. The strength of the United States of America is not the size of our military or the size of our wallets; the strength of the United States of America is found in the hearts and souls of decent, honorable, compassionate people who have heard a call to serve something greater than themselves.

Thank you all for giving me a chance to come by. I ask for God's blessings on you all and on the United States of America. Thank you.

NOTE: The President spoke at 11:45 a.m. in the Canandaigua Academy Theatre. In his remarks, he referred to Stephen J. Uebbing, superintendent, Canandaigua City School District; and Mayor Ellen Polimeni of Canandaigua, NY.

Remarks Following a Visit to Ferris Hills at West Lake Senior Center in Canandaigua
March 14, 2006

The reason I have come is I'm trying to explain to people the benefits of a new Medicare program. Congressman Randy Kuhl asked me to come, and so I did. It shows how influential he is.

I thought the system needed to be changed because it didn't provide a modern form of medicine. A lot of it was good, but some of it was stuck in the past. And so I worked with Congress to get a prescription drug benefit added on to Medicare. The problem is, is that when something changes, people get a little concerned. You know, they say, "Well, I'm not so sure I want to see a change; I'm not so sure change is something that I'm interested in." And I knew that was going to be the case.

But I also knew that if we could convince people who pay attention to take a look and see what options were available, that people would begin to make rational choices, particularly if they had some help. And so I want to thank the Thompson Health Care Group for helping. And as I said at the high school over there, I said,

"If your mom or dad could use a little Medicare, you owe them the opportunity to explain different options and show what's available." But the pharmacists are helping a lot to say, "Look, you ought to take a look at the program."

So we're in your community to urge people to, you know, kind of step back, see what's available, design a program that meets your needs, if that's your interest, and it's going to save some money. That's the key, because this—the benefit is costing less than anticipated, as a result of competition and choice. It's really worthwhile looking at.

I've spent a lot of time, as my administration spends a lot of time, talking about how to get people—information into people's hands. And so that's why we're here. Thank you for giving us a chance to come by and visit with you. It looks like you've got a beautiful facility.

Okay, well, thanks to the press for coming.

NOTE: The President spoke at 1:09 p.m.

Remarks on Medicare Prescription Drug Benefits and a Question-and-Answer Session in Silver Spring, Maryland
March 15, 2006

The President. Listen, thank you all for coming. First of all, I'm proud to be traveling with a Cabinet Secretary. He runs Health and Human Services. His job is to make sure that the Medicare plan works the way it was designed to work.

We've come to answer some questions, if you have any—about any subject.

[*Laughter*] But before I begin, I do want to share some thoughts with you.

First, speaking about Cabinet Secretaries, I know Mary Hill is here. Where's Mary? Oh, hi, Mary. The reason I bring her up is that her daughter is married to one of my Cabinet Secretaries, and she is a fine woman—so is the Cabinet Secretary— [*laughter*]—Norm Mineta, Norm and Deni Mineta.

I want to thank the folks who run this fine facility. Thanks for letting us come by and talk about good health; that's what we're here to talk about. By the way, Laura sends her best. You might remember her; she's the most patient woman in America. I don't know why she didn't come; I should have asked her. I'll ask her. You wanted her to come? Well, listen, that happens to me a lot—[*laughter*]—"You stay home; let Laura come."

But I'm here to talk about Medicare. First of all, when I got to Washington, I took a look at the Medicare system and thought it needed to be improved. When the Government makes a commitment, it ought to make good on its commitment, and it ought to do—make sure we deliver excellence when we say we're going to do something. Lyndon Johnson—nice Texan— signed the Medicare bill, and it was a commitment by the Federal Government to provide health care for our seniors. And my attitude is, if we're going to provide health care for the seniors, let's provide a good system, a modern system.

And so I took a look at it and said that Medicare is doing a lot of good stuff, you know; it really is. It's an important system. But I asked the question, couldn't we do it better? And for example, just to give you an idea, you know, Medicare would pay $28,000 for the surgery for ulcers but wouldn't pay a dime for the medicine to prevent the surgery from being needed in the first place. That didn't sound like a very good system to me. In other words, what had happened was, medicine started to change. You all know what I'm talking

about. Pharmaceuticals became a really important part of the delivery of good health care. But Medicare did not change with medicine.

And so one of the things that we did, we worked with Republicans and worked with Democrats and said, "Let's provide a prescription drug benefit for our seniors to make sure that Medicare is a modern system." Now, I understood that when we began to change Medicare, modernize Medicare, it could create some confusion with people. You know, some people just don't want to change. Some people thought things were just fine and that giving different options or giving people an opportunity to make different decisions could create some confusion.

Now, I understood that. But I also felt it was worth the risk of creating confusion to give people different options from which to choose. And so the Medicare bill—the new Medicare bill does something different. It says there is a prescription drug benefit available for all Americans, special help for the lower income Americans, that seniors have also got the opportunity to make a choice, to design a health care plan that best suits their needs.

And so we started the program. Congress passed the bill. It did provide really good help for low-income seniors. It did provide choices. It did provide a medical examination for people who enroll in Medicare. It does provide for annual screenings. That makes sense, doesn't it? Why don't you— if we screen for disease, it might make it easier for us to solve problems before they become acute.

And so we started saying to the people, "This bill has passed; take a look at it." And so people got on the computers and saw a lot of different options, and said, "Whoa, this may be a little more than I bargained for." And so recognizing that people might need some explanations, we rallied people. We got the churches and the synagogues, and we got the community groups; we got the AARP—we got people all around the country—facilities just like this, as a matter of fact—to start explaining options available to our seniors, so seniors can make the right choice for them.

Since the program got going, 26 million seniors have signed up. That's a lot. Pretty quick period of time—26 million people take a look and signed up for the program. They're signing up by the thousands every week. And so one of the reasons I've come is to encourage people who have not signed up to take a look at Medicare, the new Medicare, take a look at what's available. If you like what you see, sign up. If it doesn't meet your needs, that's fine. But I think you're going to like what you see. Drug bills have been cut in half for the average—for the typical senior. I'm not making it up. I'm just telling you what people who've signed up—realize what the plans available—what it has meant to them.

Drug costs have been cut in half. That's positive news if you're a senior. I was with some folks yesterday in upstate New York, and old Bob got up at a deal like this, and he said in the microphone, he said, "I thought it was too good to be true. It was one of these typical government deals, you know, where they kind of say something is going to happen, and it doesn't." He said, "My drug bills have been cut in half." I think if you—if people pay attention to this program and take a look at it, you'll find that there are some significant cost savings for you.

The other thing that's happened, the tax-payers have got to know, is that it's anticipated—the cost of this is 20 percent lower than anticipated in the first year. In other words, it turns out when people have choices, they get better quality and they get better price. And that's what you're seeing in the Medicare bill.

If you haven't signed up—by the way, I'm not only speaking to you, I'm speaking to the cameras too, by the way—[*laughter*]—because I want people to hear this; it's important. If you haven't signed up, call 1–800–MEDICARE. If you're a—if

you've got—if you're a son or a daughter of a citizen on Medicare, do your parent a favor and get on the Internet and take a look at what's available and help your mom or dad take a look at this new Medicare benefit structure. There are some choices to choose from, no doubt about it. But with more choices to choose from, you can better design a program that meets your needs.

People are signing up by the thousands. There's a May 15th deadline. And so what Mike and I are going to do is travel around the country and hold seminars like this and continue to remind people there's a good opportunity. And I really urge you to take a look. It's a program that does modernize the system. It's a program that says, we trust seniors to make the right choice. It's a program that I think you're going to like a lot.

And that's what I've come to do. Part of my job is to educate the American people about what's available. It's called the educator in chief. [*Laughter*] This is a new program, and it requires a lot of work.

Yesterday I met with a group of concerned citizens from different walks of life—you know, the NAACP and the—some Latino groups, business groups, pharmaceutical groups. I said, look—and they're there for a reason; they wanted to hear my commitment to the program and my encouraging them to go out and find people and encourage them to take a look and sign up.

And so that's what I'm doing here today, and I want to thank you all for giving me a chance to come by and visit with you. If you've got any questions for me, I'll answer them. If they're too hard, I'll turn them over to the Secretary and let him answer them. [*Laughter*] But I'll be glad to answer any questions you've got on any subject on your mind. If you've got something you want to ask about Medicare, you can—any other subject that you care about.

Yes, ma'am.

Private Sector Health Insurance

Q. [*Inaudible*]—subject. First, welcome to the blue State of Maryland.

The President. Thank you. It's good to be here.

Q. Secondly, I am a member of Medicare, of course. I'm also a member of Kaiser Permanente. My medical bills are absolute nothing—90 days or $8. Why does Kaiser have more of a means of putting forth these medications than does the Government of the United States?

The President. See, she is a part of a private program that has provided a benefit that you like, and you don't want to change, and you don't have to change. And that's what we're trying to do. We're trying to give people different options, like the option you have got.

In the old system, they didn't have those options. Matter of fact, they didn't have a prescription drug benefit in the old Medicare system. Now the Medicare system has invited a series of providers—I think there's 34 different providers here in the State of Maryland, if I'm not mistaken—that say, now, I want to give you a chance to be able to come up and have the same satisfaction with the program that you do.

Look, if you're happy with where you are—and it sounds like you're pretty happy about it—don't change.

Q. I'm not going to.

The President. You shouldn't. [*Laughter*] And I don't blame you; I wouldn't either. But if you're—but you ought to take a look. See, people ought to take a look and see. That's all I'm saying. Nobody is making you do anything. I'm just traveling around saying to people, take a look at what's available for you. There's people on this staff here at this facility that will help you. That's all—believe me, it's worth taking a look. It's free.

Yes, ma'am.

Medicare Prescription Drug Benefits

Q. First off, as a resident, I wish to tell you how pleased we are that you took time out to come to Riderwood, because Riderwood beside has a wonderful—you look around at these vibrant, elderly people; you know we have very good health care. And we're looking for good health care.

Now, we have the Advantage—Erickson Advantage is here, which covers Medicare and Part D, which is what you're sponsoring. So we're glad that you're here to explain, even though this is Erickson's health plan. But that doesn't eliminate your Part D.

The President. No, that's right. Yes, I mean, in other words, Erickson is a part of the menu of opportunity.

Q. Right.

The President. Well, I appreciate you bringing it up. You sound like you know a lot on the subject. You ought to be up here speaking. [*Laughter*] No, I appreciate that. Thanks.

Part D—when they hear Part D, that's talking about the prescription drug benefit that's now available. It was not available in Medicare. I signed the bill; it is now available.

Q. Right.

The President. And again, I repeat: If you're a low-income senior, there's a lot of help for you. The Government pays over 95 percent of anything coming your way. And that's important. So you ought to look. That's all we're saying.

Yes, sir. Thanks for wearing the Texas shirt. [*Laughter*]

Health Care for Veterans

Q. I have a grandson here from Houston. He brought it. He gave it to me last Christmas, and I had to wear it today.

The President. I'm honored. Thanks. Yes, kind of reminds me of home. [*Laughter*]

Q. Mr. President, I'm happy to be here at Riderwood. I'm retired military, retired from the Veterans Administration also, and I can get treatment from VA. What is the best thing for a man like me to do? There are many retired military people here who are in the same situation.

The President. Well, I think the Veterans Affairs benefits are a very good package. And Veterans Affairs, one of their major responsibilities is to honor the commitment they've made to you, sir. And they intend to honor it. Again, I don't know all the details of your Veterans Affairs benefit package, but you ought to take a look at all options. It's just a free look. Get your son to get on the Internet with you, and just see whether or not it makes any sense. But I'll bet you'll find the Veterans' benefits are pretty good.

Yes, sir. Thanks for serving, by the way. Appreciate the example you've set.

Yes, sir.

Electronic Medical Records

Q. The people who live here are fortunate to have their health records in a computer—in electronic medical records. Could you talk a little bit about that?

The President. Thank you, sir. [*Laughter*] Yes, well, it's a very good question because part of the issue we face in America is the cost of health care, the rising cost of health care. Part of the rising cost of health care is the result of a really important industry not being a part of the 21st century technology. He asked about medical records, electronic medical records. That means that everybody will have their medical records on a—digitized in a way that can be used over the Internet, for example.

You might remember the old days—and a lot of hospitals are still that way, by the way, or most doctors' offices are that way, when they actually write your prescription or write your procedure on a piece of paper. That's pretty inefficient. One reason is doctors can't write to begin with. [*Laughter*] Are you a doc? Sorry. [*Laughter*]

But carrying your files from one office to the next is not an efficient way to run a system. Files can get lost; people cannot necessarily read what is written; prescriptions can sometimes not be written properly because the handwriting isn't legible. You might—you know, a person transfers from one jurisdiction to the next, and the files may get lost, or the doctor may not exactly understand what the other doctor had talked about in the handwritten files. And that leads to medical errors and a costly health care system.

And so what the good doc is asking is, are we in the process of trying to have medical records like you have here at this facility so that your health care is better delivered and there aren't mistakes? And the answer is, absolutely. I've tasked the Secretary of Health and Human Services to start working on a variety of fronts when it comes to information technology in health care, starting with a common language. The data of medicine is complicated. You can describe different ailments and different diseases in different ways. And so what Mike is doing through his department is coming up with a common language.

And the idea is—I'll give you a practical example of why this is—having medical records is important. When Hurricane Katrina hit, a lot of veterans were displaced. Now, the Veterans Administration has got medical records for people that they're serving. And so you have a person go from New Orleans to Houston, and fortunately, the electronic medical record could go with that person, which then meant the doc in Houston would see a new patient, but the medical records would lay out exactly what needed to be done to take care of the patient.

And that's precisely the kind of vision that we're talking about so that, ultimately, America is using information technology to lower the cost of medicine, but to provide higher quality of medicine for people through medical records. And Mike is in charge of that, and his department is making good progress. Thanks for bringing it up.

The other thing that's really important about medical records, and something my administration is going to be a stickler for, is to make sure that the records are private. We don't want people looking at your medical record if you don't want them looking at your medical record. In other words, it's your record, and there's got to be a certain amount of privacy to that record. And so just because I talk about having electronic medical records, you've just got to understand that there's going to be an important privacy component to making sure that others can't look at your record if you don't want them to.

Good question.

Yes, ma'am.

Medicare Prescription Drug Benefits

Q. Mr. President, I told my mother last night that I was going to be covering the President of the United States on the health—[*inaudible*].

The President. Okay, here you go. She started off saying she talked to her mom last night.

Q. Yes. And you may have some experience with instructions from a forceful mother, sir. [*Laughter*] I got some from mine. [*Laughter*]

The President. Well-spoken.

Q. My mom is 75; she is sick; she's back in New Jersey alone. She didn't know anything about the Part D drug plan until I told her in February, with all the publicity and everything. I'm trying to walk her through it, but she doesn't know what to tell me. I don't know how to help her. I've punched her stuff into medicare.gov. I've got the basics, but it's still too much for her to afford. And I don't know where to tell her to go and get help. She wants to know if you guys will roll back the May 15th deadline.

The President. No. And the reason why is, there's got to be a fixed time for people to sign up. And we want people to realize there is—now is the time. And I'm not exactly sure about your mom's situation. I do want to thank you for helping her. Daughters ought to help their mothers realize what's available.

Now, again, there is a—I'm not sure what the plan—the structure looks like in New Jersey, but rolling back deadlines is not going to help your mom make a good decision. You're going to have to help her make the decision. And a lot of people like your mom were in the same situation—they took a look, said it looks confusing. But there's a lot of help. That's what—one of the reasons I'm here to talk about——

Q. The thing I'm trying to find out is—this is a great system where you have a group like Riderwood—it's a great system in Riderwood, where people can come together, or the church groups. But what do you do with the people who are just sick enough, they can't go out, they don't have help, you know? Do we have a system to knock on doors, to walk——

The President. Absolutely. And that's exactly what our——

Q. Where can I send her?

The President. Well, first of all, I happen to think—and I don't want—look, I'm not going to tell you your business, but I think it's your responsibility to help your mom. And I think a lot of parents—a lot of children should help their moms. And I think you really ought to take a look at the different options for her. I mean, the best grassroots outreach is child to parent. There's other outreach; you're right. The church is outreaching. Again, I don't know the particulars in the neighborhood. I can—if you can get us the area in which she lives, we can find a group that's very much involved in helping people like your mom. I appreciate it.

But that's the whole—her—she's got a great point. In order to—we've got to explain this to as many people as we can. And I fully understand that it's confusing. That's why I started off the talk, "It can be confusing to people." But when you work through the different options and look at the steps and have somebody explain it to you, in the end, it is a really good deal.

Now, if she doesn't choose to be a part of Part D, that's a choice that you and she and others will make. But it is—it has proven to be a cost-effective decision for our seniors. The typical senior has their drug bill cut in half. That's across America. If your mom qualifies, she will get more than 95 percent of her drug bills paid by the Government.

And so thanks for bringing it up.

Health Care Reform

Q. Back here.

The President. Oh, yes.

Q. We still have millions of underinsured or uninsured citizens in the United States, and what are you going to do about that?

The President. Right. No, there's no question that's an issue. And one of the reasons why is because health care costs are going up, and there are ways to address health care costs. One of them is information technology. Another one is legal reform. A lot of doctors are getting sued, and when they get sued, they practice defensive medicine in order to protect them in the courts. And by practicing defensive medicine, it causes costs to go up. Transparency in pricing is another way to make sure consumers have got the capacity to make rational decisions for themselves.

Some of the people who are not insured are younger Americans who choose not to be insured. It's like, I kind of remember that period of time. I thought I was never going to get sick, and so I thought I'd save some money.

A lot of people who are insured—or uninsured are working uninsured, and they tend to work for small businesses. And small businesses have trouble being able to purchase insurance—so they get the insurance. And one idea to help small businesses is to allow them to pool risk across jurisdictional boundaries. In other words, let the restauranteur in Texas and the restauranteur in Maryland join in a risk pool so as to make insurance more affordable for small businesses. Health savings accounts are a way to help small businesses be able to afford insurance.

Now, if you're poor, you're going to get help through Medicaid. There is an insurance plan. If you're a—if you're somebody in this country who needs primary care, we've got community health centers all across America, places where people can get good health care, not in the emergency rooms of our hospitals.

So there is a variety of ways to deal with a very difficult issue. And you're right; it's an issue that the country must address. Thanks for bringing it up.

Yes, sir.

Medicare Prescription Drug Benefits

Q. No one's quite said this, this way, I don't think, sir. Speaking as one resident here, among a very diverse group, that it is an honor and a privilege to be visited by the President of all 300 million of us and the leader of the free world.

The President. Thank you, sir.

Q. Welcome.

The President. Thank you.

Q. I do have a question. When this law was passed with your encouragement—almost immediately after the bill was enacted by Congress, the chief auditor at Medicare came out and spoke on TV and said that he had compiled a projected cost significantly higher than what Congress had been told. And he was threatened with immediate dismissal if he allowed that information to come out. Is that—did that man speak the truth? And if so, why would you not want facts like that to come out to the American people?

The President. Actually, what's happened, sir, is that the estimated cost is 20 percent lower than bodies that tried to estimate the cost. And the reason why is, is because the program has worked better than anticipated, and it has been better than anticipated. And I think you'll be reflected in our budgets.

Well, they estimated, for example, the average premium was going to cost $37 a month, and it's down to $25 a month. In other words, it's working. And I think that's important for people to understand. And there's been a lot of estimates about the cost of the program, but what really matters is the actual costs. And it looks like the dollars are going to be lower than we thought, which is good news—good news—and more importantly, lower to the seniors than we thought. And that's the most important news of all. The most important news to you is, this is a good deal for you, the consumer, the person we're trying to help. And we think it is. And people ought to look at it. I don't know if you've looked at, but you ought to, if you haven't. Thank you.

Yes, ma'am.

Electronic Medical Records

Q. Yes, you mentioned a little while ago about chips—I mean about medical records. Today in The Post, they were talking about people getting chips implanted with their medical records. And it sounded good to me. My dog has one. [*Laughter*] And I bet your dogs have them.

The President. Now, I don't know if our dogs—I don't think—we're not quite that sophisticated yet. Barney might not like it. [*Laughter*]

Q. I guess my question is, in the future, if we want people to have this, would it be possible, or thinking that far ahead, that when a child is born, a chip is implanted and you keep feeding information into it through——

The President. I don't know. That's an interesting question. I, frankly, haven't heard of that. Do you have any—maybe the Secretary—maybe it's time for the Secretary to step in. [*Laughter*]

I think the point is this—I think the point is, is that there is the capacity to carry in a very small object a lot of data that can be downloaded in other medical facilities in order to facilitate a flow of information that enables people to get good health care in a cost-effective way. I don't

know about implantations or not. But nevertheless, I do think that the idea of having a medical chip that is on a card, or it can be anywhere—you got one, doc? No, I thought you were searching for—[*laughter*].

Q. We have one at Erickson.

The President. Yes, sir.

India/Nuclear Energy

Q. Mr. President, I just want to take the opportunity to thank you for your far-sighted policy in India, of assisting them in their civilian nuclear program.

The President. Oh, thank you, sir.

Q. I was at Tarapur 40 years ago, when General Electric inaugurated the first nuclear plant in India. And I think it's going to go a long way towards keeping our friendship with that important country in Asia. Thank you very much.

The President. Well, thanks for bringing that up. He's referring to a trip I just took to India and Pakistan and Afghanistan. And we were working on an agreement with India to encourage India and help India develop its civilian nuclear power industry. And one—a couple of reasons why one would do that: One, when India's demand for fossil fuels goes up, it causes the price of our fossil fuels to go up. And so, therefore, to encourage them to use a renewable source of energy that doesn't create greenhouse gas, this makes a lot of sense.

Secondly, India has been a—is a nonproliferator, has proven to be a nonproliferator for the past 30 years. In other words, they've got a record that, in my judgment, should cause the Congress to pass old law to treat them as a new partner. Thirdly, India wants to be a part of international agreements that will help deal with proliferation.

And so I thank you for your comments. I appreciate you saying that.

Yes, sir.

Pakistan/India

Q. It was particularly courageous, in view of the fact that Pakistan is one of our allies in the war on terrorism, and of course, it's going to affect their attitude to some extent.

The President. Well, I appreciate you saying that. The good news is that, as I said in the speech there in India, we now—I think Indians understand it's good for the United States to be friendly with Pakistan, and the Pakistanis understand it's good for the United States to be friendly with India—which is, as you know, a change of, kind of, the relationship of the United States with those two countries.

I had a good visit with President Musharraf, who is dedicated to routing out Al Qaida if they hide in his country, and we really appreciate his dedication. And at the same time, he's dedicated toward advancing democracy. So it was a great visit. Thanks for bringing it up.

Yes, ma'am—oop, you again. [*Laughter*]

Electronic Medical Records

Q. You mentioned about privacy, Mr. President.

The President. Yes.

Q. It's very well to say privacy on our electronics. You know there's no such a thing as real privacy. Something leaks out all the time somewhere.

The President. I'd say that. [*Laughter*]

Q. Did you ever think, or think in your bill some way that the insurance companies cannot use it against us? Because that's the fear—that's the fear, that an insurance company will say, "Uh-oh, we won't touch you," and you know——

The President. Preexisting conditions——

Q. That's right—or something that you developed along the way.

The President. I think there's laws that protect you on that. It's a different issue from them looking at your records. One is to say, "Well, you've got a preexisting condition; therefore, we won't insure you."

That's different from them taking a look at your records.

Q. Because you get these conditions later on as you go along in life.

The President. Right. I understand. The good news about the current Medicare program is that they'll take care of you as you are.

Q. Here's an electronic card.

The President. Let's see that card. I don't see very well. [*Laughter*]

Q. [*Inaudible*]

The President. They did? Great. Thanks. That's what—the card, yes.

Yes, sir. The mike disappeared on you. Sorry.

Energy/Environment

Q. Thank you. Since we're talking about health care, I wonder if we couldn't address the health care of the world—in particular, the issue of greenhouse gases.

The President. Sure.

Q. The entire—well, I'm one of the scientists who believes that—and many of us do—that the greenhouse gases have been caused by us, and that it's about time that the United States took serious actions on the prevention of further greenhouse gases.

The President. I exactly agree with you, sir, and that's exactly what we're doing. I think you're right. I thought the prescription to the Kyoto plan was the wrong way to go. On the other hand, I do know we can use technologies to achieve exactly that objective.

For example, second-generation nuclear power. It's a renewable resource. It doesn't emit, as you know, greenhouse gases. It's one of the reasons why I work with India and trying to help China, as well, to be able to develop a civilian nuclear power industry without—with guarantees against proliferation, in order to protect the environment.

The other day, in the State of the Union Address, I said, we're too addicted to oil, and we need to get off oil. There are alternative ways to do that. Plug-in hybrid batteries is a new technology that's coming, and I think will help deal with emissions. The use of ethanol—ethanol made from sugar, of course, is a technology that works. But hopefully, we'll be able to have some breakthroughs to be able to use saw grass or wood chips to manufacture ethanol in order to be able to not only make us less dependent on foreign sources of energy but also to be good stewards of the environment.

Ultimately, hydrogen-powered automobiles will help make a huge difference. We're spending about a billion—$200 million or so to research that. Solar technology is another area where there's some great potential breakthroughs. I went to a plant in Michigan the other day and saw these new roofing materials that got photovoltaic cells, a part of them.

And so I agree with you. I think it's very important for us to use technology to help protect the environment and, at the same time, achieve an important economic and national security objective, which is no dependence on oil.

It's a—all right. Yes, sir.

Transparency of Health Costs

Q. Mr. President.

The President. Thank you, sir.

Q. Glad to have you here.

The President. Thanks.

Q. Thank you very much. I have two questions. The first question deals with a resident that's here—was unable to be here, but she's having—the resident is having a problem trying to get enrolled in Medicare B. And all of the time that she's had problems, the person has had a problem getting on the computer, getting anything resolved, and so on and so forth.

The President. Okay.

Q. And that's——

Secretary of Health and Human Services Michael O. Leavitt. I'll get the name, and we'll take care of it.

Q. Okay. The second question——

The President. That's easy. [*Laughter*]

Q. The second question deals with what are we doing at the Federal level to get some uniformity in terms of the billing in hospitals so that we don't have the wide dispersion between hospital billing as a result of someone having insurance and someone who does not have insurance and the whole bit. And that's been going on for years, because I was in a hospital, ran a part of it, and I know that there's a great dispersion in that.

The President. No, I appreciate that. Do you want to take that on, Mike?

Secretary Leavitt. Sure. Last night I was in a hotel, and on the back of the hotel door, there was a price: $449 a night. Now, you'll be pleased to know, Mr. President, that I didn't pay that—[*laughter*]—and we didn't pay that because the Government had created a Government rate. It was only $130 a night, and they slid the bill under the door.

A lot of insurance companies do the same thing and create special prices for the people that are insured with them. What the President has recently done is, he's told every insurance company, every employer, and every provider in the country, "You ought to tell people what you're charging." People deserve, people have a right to know what they're being charged and the kind of quality they're getting. And that's an initiative of the President. And very shortly, I believe you'll start to see that kind of disclosure.

Q. Thank you.

The President. This guy has got a great question because really what he's talking about is transparency in pricing. When you go buy a car, you know exactly what they're going to charge you. [*Laughter*] Well, sometimes you don't know. [*Laughter*] Well, you negotiate with them. [*Laughter*] Well, they put something on the window that says price. [*Laughter*] His point is, is that the more you know about price, the better you can make better decisions, and I appreciate that.

Listen, you're paying me a lot of money to work, and so I think I'm going to have to head back home. But I'm honored. Got any more questions, I'll be glad to answer them.

Electronic Medical Records

Q. I have one.

The President. Okay, yes, please. Thank you.

Q. I'd like to ask you about the medical records. They're not infallible, and we like to have paper backup. Recently had an experience here in Riderwood; went for a blood check. Records were down because the power was down, and they couldn't connect to the computer. They need—most places have paper backup, and I think if you don't have a complete record, it's not going to work as greatly as it does.

The President. No, that's really a kind of redundancy in the process to make sure that if there's a power outage, that there's not an emergency caused by that. No, that's a really good point. Thanks.

Q. Thank you.

The President. I guess, is there a——

Secretary Leavitt. Working on it. [*Laughter*]

The President. Working on it. [*Laughter*] Yes, sir. Working on it. [*Laughter*]

India/Nuclear Technology

Q. Mr. President, there are some—and I guess I would include myself—who have different views about the Indian agreement, because they're concerned about the effect that the agreement will have on the capacity of India to stimulate its own production of nuclear weapons——

The President. No, I understand.

Q. ——by helping them. But I would go beyond that and ask you, while you're still President, to consider one aspect of this whole nuclear question. I guess I'm one of the three standing—left standing Americans who helped—who did the nego-

tiation of the nonproliferation treaty. And the basic bargain there was that other countries would give up their nuclear weapons if we, the nuclear powers, would engage in a program of nuclear disarmament.

Now, I'm aware of all of the agreements that have taken place. I'm aware of the negotiations that you had with Mr. Putin. The point is that we cannot expect that agreement, that basic agreement to hold if the United States, particularly, goes on acting as—and has the position that we might initiate a nuclear war if it is necessary.

And I would ask you just to think about the time—while you're still President, taking the one position that only one American President has taken, and that is President Johnson, to consider a "no first-use" policy to help the prospect of nuclear proliferation in the long run.

The President. Well, thank you. Thank you very much. Thanks for your contribution, by the way. I appreciate it.

Part of the Indian deal is to actually get them to formally join some of the institutions that you helped—your work created. And you're right. I did do an agreement with President Putin—thanks for noticing—where we're—both of us are reducing nuclear stockpiles. But I'll take your words to heart and think about it. Thank you. No commitment standing right here, of course. [*Laughter*]

Well, I'm thrilled to be here. Thank you all for your time. I would hope that people would take a look—just take a look. And if you need help, there are people here who will help you. And if you're watching on TV, ask your son or daughter or ask your neighbor or ask a person that has signed up whether or not it's worthwhile. And I think you'll find this is a program that's—it's a good program.

I appreciate you letting me have a chance to come by and visit with you. Thanks for the town hall meeting. Thanks for the good questions. God bless you all.

NOTE: The President spoke at 1:50 p.m. at Riderwood retirement community. In his remarks, he referred to Richard S. Foster, Chief Actuary, Centers for Medicare & Medicaid Services; President Pervez Musharraf of Pakistan; and President Vladimir V. Putin of Russia.

Remarks at a Celebration of Hungarian Contributions to Democracy
March 15, 2006

Thank you all. Please be seated. Mr. Speaker, thank you for having me here in this beautiful Capitol to celebrate the 50th anniversary of the Hungarian Revolution.

I appreciate being here with the mayor of our city, Mayor Williams. Good to see you, Mr. Mayor. I appreciate Chairman Hyde. Mr. Chairman, it's good to see you. I thank the members of the diplomatic corps, most particularly, Ambassador Walker. I've heard of him before. [*Laughter*] Ambassador Simonyi—thank you all. Members of Congress, most particularly a beacon for—a steadfast beacon for liberty is how I'd like to define my friend Tom Lantos.

I've come today to—not only to thank our strong ally, the Government of Hungary and the people of Hungary, but I've come to thank my friend Tom Lantos, and his wife, Annette, for never letting anybody forget that freedom is precious and necessary in our world.

The Hungarian example is an example of patience and an example of the fact that freedom exists in everybody's soul. It's an example that tyranny can never stamp out the desire to be free. It's an example that— of a country that once becomes free, joins with other freedom-loving countries to keep the peace.

I've come to remind the people of Hungary, they've got a great friend in America. I want to thank, by the way, the Hungarian Americans who are here with us today. You've made a significant contribution to our country.

You know, it's an interesting world in which we live. There's an argument about—in some places—about whether or not freedom is universal, whether or not freedom is okay for some parts of the world but not others. I believe freedom is universal. I believe the example of Hungary proves that freedom is universal. I believe everybody desires to live in freedom. I believe there's an Almighty, and I believe the Almighty God's gift to each person in this world is liberty. And I believe the United States, and I believe Hungary, and I believe other free nations have the responsibility to help other people realize their freedom as well.

You know, one of the interesting examples of Europe that I try to explain to our people is that for 100 years, there were war, where a lot of people lost their lives and a lot of Americans lost their life. But today, Europe is at peace. Europe is whole, free, and at peace. And I believe the reason why is because democracy has taken hold on that continent. And one of the leading lights of democracy has been Hungary.

We thank the Hungarian people for their example. We thank them for their contribution in helping the newly free in Afghanistan and Iraq realize the blessings of liberty. We thank them for being allies in keeping the peace.

Mr. Speaker, thanks for letting me come by and pay my respects to a strong ally and a good friend but also pay my respects to Congressman Tom Lantos, a person who understands the difference between freedom and tyranny, and a person who is willing to speak his mind all times, all places, everywhere.

God bless you all.

NOTE: The President spoke at 5:45 p.m. in Statutory Hall at the U.S. Capitol. In his remarks, he referred to Mayor Anthony A. Williams of Washington, DC; U.S. Ambassador to Hungary George H. Walker III; and Hungary's Ambassador to the U.S. Andras Simonyi.

Remarks Following a Meeting With Members of Congress
March 16, 2006

It's been my pleasure to host Republicans and Democrats from both the House and the Senate here to talk about budget reform. We're talking about the way to—for the executive branch and the legislative branch to work in a cooperative fashion to help make sure that the appropriations bills we pass are—meet priorities, that they are—that the process is transparent, that we're able to say to the American people, "We care about how we spend your money."

Part of the budget reform process is a line-item veto. I want to thank the Members here who have come, who have offered not only constructive advice but practical applications of the line-item veto so that it becomes law. And I listened carefully to some constructive suggestions from both Republicans and Democrats as to how

to get a piece of legislation passed. The American people expect all of us from both parties to work diligently as to how we spend their money. And one way that we can earn the confidence of the people is to pass a line-item veto.

And again, I want to thank the Members for being here. It means a lot that people from both parties are here. I particularly want to thank my opponent in the 2004 campaign, Senator Kerry, for being here. I can remember on the campaign trail, he said that he supported a line-item veto, and he is following through on his word by being here at the table. I'm proud you're here, Senator.

Thank you all for coming.

NOTE: The President spoke at 10 a.m. in the Cabinet Room at the White House.

Remarks on Signing the Stop Counterfeiting in Manufactured Goods Act
March 16, 2006

Thank you. Welcome. Thanks for coming. In a few moments, I will sign a bill that protects the hard work of American innovators, strengthens the rule of law, and helps keep our families and consumers safe. The Stop Counterfeiting in Manufactured Goods Act has earned broad support, and I want to thank all those who helped get this bill passed for being here today. I want

to thank the lawmakers from both political parties for getting this piece of legislation to this desk. I want to thank the consumer protection groups who have joined us as well. Thanks for your hard work on this important piece of legislation.

I want to thank the Attorney General, Al Gonzales, who has joined us; the Secretary of Commerce, Carlos Gutierrez; my

Secretary of Labor, Elaine Chao. Thank you all for being here. I appreciate the chairman of the Judiciary—House Judiciary, Jim Sensenbrenner, for joining us today. I also want to thank the bill's sponsor, Joe Knollenberg from Michigan, as well as Bobby Scott from Virginia. Thank you three Members for being here. The Senators claim they're voting on important legislation; otherwise, they would have been here too. [*Laughter*]

This economy of ours is strong; it's getting stronger. We grew at 3.5 percent last year. The national unemployment rate is 4.8 percent. People are buying homes. The small-business sector is strong. Productivity is up. Our country is productive; it's innovative; it's entrepreneurial. And we've got to keep it that way.

One of the problems we have is that people feel comfortable, at times, in trying to take a shortcut to success in the business world. They feel like they can copy existing products instead of designing their own. In order to keep this economy innovative and entrepreneurial, it's important for us to enforce law, and if the laws are weak, pass new laws to make sure that the problem of counterfeiting, which has been growing rapidly, is arrested, is held in check.

Counterfeiting costs our country hundreds of billion dollars a year. It has got a lot of harmful effects in our economy. Counterfeiting hurts businesses. They lose the right to profit from their innovation. Counterfeiting hurts workers because counterfeiting undercuts honest competition, rewards illegal competitors. Counterfeiting hurts our—counterfeiting hurts consumers because fake products expose our people to serious health and safety risks. Counterfeiting hurts the Government. We lose out on tax revenue. We have to use our resources for law—of law enforcement to stop counterfeiting. Counterfeiting hurts national security because terrorist networks use counterfeit sales to, sometimes, finance their operations.

This administration and Congress have worked together to confront the illegal threat—the real threat of illegal activity such as counterfeiting. And the bill I'm signing today is an important step forward.

The bill helps us defeat counterfeiting in two key ways. First, the bill strengthens our laws against trading counterfeit labels and packaging. In the past, the law prohibited the manufacturing, shipping, and—or selling of counterfeit goods, but it did not make it a crime to ship falsified labels or packaging, which counterfeiters could then attach to fake products.

This loophole helped counterfeiters cheat consumers by passing off poorly-made items as brandname goods. By closing the loophole, we're going to keep honest Americans from losing business to scam artists.

Secondly, the bill strengthens penalties for counterfeiters and gives prosecutors new tools to stop those who defraud American consumers. The bill requires courts to order the destruction of all counterfeit products seized as a part of a criminal investigation. The bill requires convicted counterfeiters to turn over their profits as well as any equipment used in their operations, so it can't be used to cheat our people again. The bill requires those convicted of counterfeiting to reimburse the legitimate businesses they exploited. These commonsense reforms will help law enforcement to crack down on this serious crime. We've got to get the counterfeiters and their products off the streets.

The tools in the bill I sign today will become a part of our broad effort to protect the creativity and innovation of our entrepreneurs. This administration is leading an initiative called STOP—Strategy Targeting Organized Piracy. Nine Federal agencies are coming together in this initiative, including the Department of Justice, which has launched the most aggressive effort in American history to prevent intellectual property violations. We've expanded computer hacking and intellectual property units in U.S. Attorney's offices all across the country. We're posting specially trained prosecutors and FBI agents at American Embassies in Asia and Eastern Europe. We're working with other nations and the World Trade Organization to promote strong intellectual property laws around the globe. We're cooperating with the private sector to raise awareness of counterfeiting so we can help stop fraud before it starts.

These efforts are getting some results. Last year, we dismantled a piracy ring in Massachusetts that was planning to sell more than 30,000 counterfeit hand bags and shoes and necklaces and other items. With partners overseas, we broke up a prescription drug counterfeiting network and seized more than $4 million in phony medicine. With the help of 16 countries on 5 continents, we removed more than a $100 million worth of illegal online software, games, movies, and music. This is a really important effort, and as we call upon folks to send a message to the counterfeiters, "We're not going to tolerate your way of life," that we need to give them all the tools necessary to do their jobs. And this bill I'm going to sign here in 30 seconds does just that.

Again, I want to thank you all for being here to help honor these legislators that crossed the partisan divide to help protect this country from those who feel like they can sell illegal products and counterfeit and steal our—steal intellectual property. Good work. Thanks for coming. Now let's sign the bill.

NOTE: The President spoke at 3:07 p.m. in Room 350 of the Dwight D. Eisenhower Executive Office Building. H.R. 32, approved March 16, was assigned Public Law No. 109–181.

Remarks on the Nomination of Dirk Kempthorne To Be Secretary of the Interior
March 16, 2006

The President. Good afternoon. I'm pleased to announce my nomination of Governor Dirk Kempthorne to be the Secretary of the Interior. The Department of Interior is responsible for managing our national parks and public lands, conserving our natural resources, and pursuing environmentally responsible energy development on Federal lands and waters.

I've nominated Dirk to succeed an outstanding public servant, Gale Norton. As the Secretary of the Interior for the past 5 years, she was instrumental in establishing the Healthy Forests Initiative to protect communities from catastrophic wildfire and to improve the habitat. When Hurricane Katrina devastated the gulf coast region, she helped lead the efforts to restore offshore energy production so that Americans would not suffer further supply disruptions and price increases.

Future generations of Americans will be able to enjoy our great national parks and wildlife refuges because of Gale's untiring work. Gale was one of the original members of my Cabinet and the first woman in American history to hold the post of Secretary of the Interior. I appreciate her dedicated service, and Laura and I wish Gale and John all the best.

Dirk Kempthorne is the right man to build on this progress. As Governor of Idaho, he worked closely with Gale on a variety of important initiatives. They worked together to resolve a longstanding water rights issue, to return responsibility to Idaho for managing the local wolf population, and to make the Healthy Forests Initiative a reality in Idaho.

As Governor, Dirk has been a responsible steward of Idaho's 30 State parks and recreational trailways that serve millions of visitors each year. He has launched the statewide Experience Idaho Initiative, which will fund needed improvements within Idaho's State parks to preserve public spaces and expand recreational opportunities for visitors. Last August, I had a chance to enjoy those recreational opportunities firsthand when Dirk and I biked some of Idaho's trails together.

As Secretary of the Interior, Dirk will continue my administration's efforts to conserve our land, water, and air resources; reduce the maintenance backlog of our national parks; support historic and cultural sites through our Preserve America Initiative; and develop the energy potential of Federal lands and waters in environmentally sensitive ways.

Dirk brings wide experience to these important tasks. He has served at every level of government: as mayor of Boise, as Governor of Idaho, and as a United States Senator. While in the Senate, he chaired the Subcommittee on Drinking Water, Fisheries, and Wildlife, and he chaired the Armed Services Personnel Subcommittee.

He built bipartisan support to enact comprehensive reforms to the Safe Drinking Water Act. Dirk understands that those who live closest to the land know how to manage it best, and he will work closely with State and local leaders to ensure wise stewardship of our resources.

Dirk has had a long and abiding love for nature. When he and his wife, Patricia, were married, they chose to hold the ceremony atop Idaho's Moscow Mountain at sunrise. Dirk said, "I don't think there's a more beautiful cathedral than the outdoors."

I appreciate his willingness to take on this important post, and I ask the Senate to confirm him promptly as the 49th Secretary of the Interior.

Thanks for agreeing to serve.

[Secretary-designate Kempthorne made brief remarks.]

The President. Thank you all.

NOTE: The President spoke at 5:29 p.m. in the Oval Office at the White House. In his remarks, he referred to John Hughes, husband of Secretary of the Interior Gale A. Norton. The transcript released by the Office of the Press Secretary also included the remarks of Secretary-designate Kempthorne.

Statement on House of Representatives Passage of Supplemental Funding Legislation
March 16, 2006

I applaud the House for its quick passage of legislation to provide vital resources for two of our Nation's top priorities. This bill will give our troops in Iraq and Afghanistan tools they need to prevail in the war on terror. The legislation also provides for additional resources for the people of the gulf coast as they continue the work of rebuilding their lives and communities. I urge the Senate to act promptly to pass legislation providing for these critical funds.

Letter to Congressional Leaders Transmitting a Report on Activities in Belarus
March 16, 2006

Dear _____ :

Consistent with the Belarus Democracy Act of 2004 (Public Law 108–347), I hereby transmit a report prepared by my Administration on the Belarusian sale or delivery of weapons and weapons-related technologies and on the personal assets and wealth of the senior Belarusian leadership.

Sincerely,

GEORGE W. BUSH

NOTE: Identical letters were sent to Henry J. Hyde, chairman, and Tom Lantos, ranking member, House Committee on International Relations; and Richard G. Lugar, chairman, and Joseph R. Biden, Jr., ranking member, Senate Committee on Foreign Relations.

Message to the Congress Transmitting a Report on the National Security Strategy of the United States
March 16, 2006

To the Congress of the United States:

Consistent with section 108 of the National Security Act of 1947, as amended (50 U.S.C. 404a), I am transmitting a report prepared by my Administration on the National Security Strategy of the United States.

GEORGE W. BUSH

The White House,
March 16, 2006.

Remarks at a National Republican Congressional Committee Dinner
March 16, 2006

Thank you all. Please be seated. Thank you all for coming. Thank you for the warm welcome. Mr. Speaker, I can't tell you what a joy it is to work with you. America is very fortunate to have Denny Hastert as the Speaker of the House of Representatives. And I want to thank you all for coming tonight to make sure that he remains the Speaker of the House of Representatives.

We're here to not only thank you but to remind you and our fellow citizens, we've got a lot of work to do to lay the foundations for peace, and we've got a lot of work to do to make sure this country remains a prosperous country so that every single citizen can realize the great promise of America.

I bring greetings from the First Lady— that would be Laura. She sends her best regards to the Speaker and the leadership of the House of Representatives. She sends her best regards to you. I'm a lucky guy that she said yes when I asked her to marry me. She is a fabulous woman, a great mom, and she's doing a wonderful job as our Nation's First Lady.

I also bring greetings from the Vice President of the United States, Dick Cheney. You know, mine is an interesting job. I get to make a lot of decisions, and I have to rely on people to give me good, sound, steady advice. And Vice President Dick Cheney gives me good, sound, steady advice. The country is lucky to have him as the Vice President of the United States.

I want to thank my friend Tom Reynolds, Congressman Tom Reynolds from New York, for being the chairman of the NRCC. I thank Buck—and Patricia—for being such a fine chairman and supporting person for this event. This takes a lot of time and a lot of effort to put together a significant event like this. And, Buck, I know you worked hard, and I want to thank you and the entire team of people for making this such a successful event.

I welcome the House majority leader, John Boehner from Ohio. Thank you, John. The House Majority Whip, Roy Blunt from Missouri—I appreciate you being here, Roy. I thank all the leadership team for the House of Representatives who are here tonight. I want to thank all the Members of Congress. Thanks for coming. But most importantly, I thank our distinguished guests.

We've got a lot of work to do. This Nation is a nation at war, and I'm proud to work with Members of the United States Congress who understand that. After September the 11th, I vowed to our country that we would remain firm in defeating an enemy that would try to hurt us again. And I appreciate the strong allies in the House of Representatives who understand the stakes in the world in which we live.

Ours is a nation which is committed to making sure we defeat the terrorists overseas so we do not have to face them here at home. We understand that if somebody harbors a terrorist, feeds a terrorist, houses a terrorist, they're equally as guilty as the terrorist, and they will be held to account. You know, a President, when he says something, he better mean it, and when I told the Taliban, "Cough up Al Qaida, or we will hold you—we will bring you to justice," I meant what I said. Thanks to the United States military, Afghanistan is now free, and America is better off for it.

I know the Members here share the great joy I have in knowing that we liberated 25 million people from the clutches of one of the most barbaric regimes in the history of man. Thanks to defending our Nation, thanks to upholding the doctrine that says if you harbor a terrorist—today, young girls go to school in Afghanistan, women have a chance to succeed. Afghanistan is free, and the world is better off for it.

I appreciate working with Members of the United States Congress who understand that one of the lessons of September the 11th is when this Nation sees a threat, we must take it seriously, before it materializes. I saw a threat in Saddam Hussein. Members of the United States Congress, both Republicans and Democrats, saw a threat. Members of the United Nations Security Council saw a threat. By removing Saddam Hussein from power, America is safer and the world is better off.

We have a strategy for victory in Iraq. Part of that victory means that we will stand by the Iraqi people as a democracy unfolds. I hope you felt the joy in your heart that I felt when millions of Iraqis— 75 percent of voting-age population—defied the terrorists, defied the car bombers, surprised the world, and said loud and clear, "We want to be free."

We've got a comprehensive strategy to help that country rebuild its economy, and we've got a strategy to train Iraqis so they can defend their freedom. We fight a terrorist—an enemy that has got only one weapon. They can't beat us on the battlefield, but they have the capacity and the willingness to kill innocent life. They know full well that our TV screens are full of images of the innocent dying, and they know full well it breaks our heart. The only way the enemy can defeat us, the only way that Iraq will not become a democracy is if we lose our nerve. I will not lose my nerve in the face of assassins and killers.

I thank the Members of the United States Congress understanding that in order to achieve a victory in Iraq, that we will rely upon the wisdom of our commanders on the ground. As Iraqis stand up, we will stand down. And the troop levels in Iraq will not be decided by artificial timetables set in Washington, DC, but by our commanders on the ground.

The work is hard in Iraq, but it's necessary. It's necessary for our security; it's necessary to lay the foundations of peace in a troubled part of the world. We believe that democracy is the right of every man and woman on this world. And we understand that history says loud and clear that democracies do not war.

I want to read a letter from—to you, if you don't mind, from a mother of a courageous American named Sergeant William Scott Kinzer, Jr. I read this letter the other day, and I thought you might like to hear one mother's point of view of what we're doing. William Scott Kinzer was killed last year while securing election sites in Iraq. His mom, Debbie, wrote me. She said: "These words are straight from a shattered but healing mother's heart. My son made a decision to join the Army. He believed that what he was involved in would eventually change Iraq, and those changes would be recorded in history books in years to come. On his last visit home, I asked him what I would ever do if something happened to him in Iraq. He smiled at me, and his blue eyes sparkled as he said, 'Mom, I love my job. If I should die, I would die happy. Does life get any better than that?'"

His mom went on to say: "Please do not let the voices we hear the loudest change what you and Scott started in Iraq. Please do not let his dying be in vain. Do not let my son have given his all for an unfinished job. Please complete the mission." My message to Debbie and the mes-

sage from people here from the United States Congress is the same: We will complete the mission; we will secure this country; we will spread freedom for the sake of peace for our children and our grandchildren.

I thank the Speaker and the leaders of the United States Congress who understand that when we ask our law enforcement officials and intelligence officials to protect us, they must have all the tools necessary to do their job. So we passed the PATRIOT Act right after September the 11th. It's an important act. It's an act that protected the civil liberties of the United States while giving law enforcement the tools necessary to protect us. Parts of the PATRIOT Act expired last year. It came up for reauthorization.

I want to remind the people what the Democrat leader from Nevada said in the United States Senate. He boasted, the "Democrats killed the PATRIOT Act." They didn't kill it for long. Thanks to the leadership of the people up here on this dais, the PATRIOT Act passed, and the homeland is more secure.

The Speaker and I were sitting back there talking about some of the challenges we've faced over the past years. This economy of ours faced some serious challenges. We had a recession, a stock market collapse. There was terrorist attacks, corporate scandals, major natural disasters, rising energy prices. But we acted. We had a plan, an economic recovery plan. And by working together, we passed that plan. And the heart of that plan was this: We believe that when Americans have more money to save and spend or invest, the economy is better off. So we cut the taxes. We cut the taxes on working families; we cut the taxes on family with children; we cut the taxes on small businesses; we cut the taxes on dividends; we cut the taxes on capital gains.

I remember clearly in 2003 when a Democrat leader attacked our economic growth plan and said of the tax relief, it is "reckless and irresponsible;" it's a "reckless and irresponsible tax plan that will undermine opportunity in our country." Today, the United States economy is strong, and it's getting stronger. We grew last year at 3.5 percent, faster than any major industrialized nation. We added 243,000 jobs in February, almost 5 million jobs in the last 2½ years. The unemployment rate across the United States is 4.8 percent—that's lower than the average rate of the 1970s, 1980s, 1990s. Real after-tax income is up for working people. Productivity is high in America. Homeownership are at alltime levels; more minorities own a home today in America than ever before in our Nation's history. The economic recovery plan that we passed works.

Today, many Democrats want the tax relief we passed to expire in a few years. Some even want to repeal it now. If the tax relief is not made permanent, the American people will get a mighty tax increase they do not want and they do not deserve. In order to make sure this economy of ours remains strong, we need to make the tax relief permanent.

We have a plan to cut the deficit in half by 2009. Oh, you'll hear some in Washington say, "Well, let's raise your taxes in order to balance the budget." Folks, that's not the way Washington works. Here's how Washington works: They'll raise your taxes, and they'll figure out new ways to spend your money. The best way to cut the deficit is to keep our progrowth economic policies in place and be wise about how we spend your money. We set priorities in Washington, DC—[applause]. By the way, every single spending program sounds great. They've all got wonderful titles. We believe that it's important to set priorities. So long as we've got any troops in harm's way, they'll have all the equipment, all the support, the best pay, the best housing possible. And I want to thank the Members of the United States Congress who are here for supporting the troops of the United States military.

I thank the Speaker, and I thank the leaders here who've helped us put austere budgets in place, budgets that have cut the rate of growth of nonsecurity discretionary spending every year since 2001. I put out another tight budget for 2007, and I look forward to working with Congress to be wise about how we spend your money, to make sure that the deficit is cut in half by 2009.

I appreciate very much the work on the line-item veto. I look forward to working with the United States Congress, to join with them to make sure that when we spend money, it's money well-spent. Today I met with members of both political parties and both chambers of the United States Congress to strategize about how we can get a line-item veto passed, to my desk, so we can assure the American people their money is going to be spent in a way they want their money spent.

We believe we should not fear the future, but we should shape the future. We believe we ought to put policies in place to make sure that America remains the economic leader of the world. And one way to do that is to make sure we have an economy which is flexible, where regulations are low, as are taxes. And one way to make sure this economy of ours remains strong and vibrant is to continue to work for meaningful, real tort reform.

I know it shocks some of you to hear a Texan say that we're addicted to oil—[laughter]—and we are, and that's a problem. In order to make sure this Nation remains competitive, in order to make sure we're the leader of the world, I look forward to working with the Members of the United States Congress here to pass the Advanced Energy Initiative.

Last year, thanks to the leadership of the Speaker, I was able to sign a comprehensive energy bill. There is more work to be done. We're going to harness technology to make sure the automobiles you drive consume less oil. We believe in plug-in hybrid batteries. It's the wave of the future. We believe in the use of ethanol. I love the fact that when our farmers are growing crops, it makes us less dependent on oil from the Middle East.

Ours is a party that knows you got to challenge the status quo when it comes to energy. In order to make sure this country is less dependent on fossil fuels, we must promote safe and sound nuclear power. We must promote solar energy and clean coal technology and wind energy. Ours is the party that can see into the future. We don't fear it; we welcome it because we intend to continue to lead.

We believe in a health care system that's run by doctors and patients, not by people in Washington, DC. Recently, working with the United States Congress, Members up here on the dias, we have kept a firm commitment to the Nation's elderly. Our Government said, "We're going to take care of the elderly with good health care." And the Medicare system became stagnant and old. It wasn't meeting the requirements of our seniors. So we came together and did something that no Congress had been able to do for years, and that is modernize Medicare. But as we did so, we not only provided prescription drugs for our seniors, but we had a uniquely Republican idea as a part of that bill, and it said that we ought to give our seniors choices. We believe that people ought to be given choices in the marketplace. We believe that Government shouldn't tell people the nature of their health care. We believe that Government ought to say, "Here's some choices from which to choose."

So far, 25 million seniors have signed up for this program. Interestingly enough, because we've injected competition into Medicare, the projected costs for Medicare this year are going to be 20 percent less than projected. Competition works. Trusting people to make the decisions in their lives is the right thing to do. The Medicare modernization plan we passed is good for our seniors, and I'm proud that we're able to get the job done.

We believe in health savings accounts, which puts consumers in charge of their health decisions. We believe in association health plans that enable small businesses to pool risk across jurisdictional boundaries so they can buy insurance at the same rates and same discounts that big companies are able to do. We believe in information technology to help control the cost. And we believe we've got to do something about these frivolous and junk lawsuits that are running good doctors out of practice and running up the cost of medicine for our consumers.

We don't fear the future; we welcome it. And we understand that to make sure this country remains competitive, we've got to stay on the leading edge of technological change. And so therefore, I look forward to working with Congress to double the Federal commitment to the most critical basic research in the physical sciences over the next 10 years. I look forward to working with the United States Congress to make sure the research and development tax credit is a permanent part of our Tax Code. And I look forward to working with the United States Congress to make sure our children have got the skills necessary to become the scientists and engineers and chemists and physicists to keep the jobs of the 21st century right here in the United States of America.

I can stand up here and tell you that we have delivered results for the American people, and we've got an agenda to continue to do so. One of the interesting things about working with these good folks is that they've got a proper perspective of the role of government in our life as well. The way I like to put it is this: Government can hand out money, but it cannot put hope in a person's heart or a sense of purpose in a person's life. We understand that the great strength of America is not in the size of our military force or in the size of our wallets. The great strength of the United States of America lies in the hearts and souls of our citizens who all want to serve something greater than themselves. Ours is a compassionate nation; ours is a loving nation. And we understand the role of government is not to crowd out our faith-based and community-based institutions but to welcome them in the providing of care and love and compassion for our fellow citizens who hurt.

We believe in ushering in the responsibility era, when our citizens understand they are responsible for the decisions they make in life. If you are a mother or a father, you're responsible for loving your child with all your heart. If you're a corporate citizen, you're responsible for being a—for putting something back into our culture, and you're responsible for telling the truth to your shareholders.

If you're a citizen who wants to help change America one heart and one soul at a time, you're responsible for mentoring a child, for feeding the hungry, for providing shelter to the homeless. The great

strength of America is the compassion of America. And I look forward to continue to call people to service, to rally that strength so that every single citizen of our country realizes the great promise and the great hope of the blessed land we call home.

It's an honor to be here. I'm proud to be your President. I'm proud to be working with these Members of the United States Congress. I want to thank you for keeping them in power in Washington. The Nation is better off with Denny Hastert as the Speaker and these leaders running the Congress.

God bless, and God bless America.

NOTE: The President spoke at 7:12 p.m. at the Washington Hilton Hotel. In his remarks, he referred to Patricia McKeon, wife of Representative Howard P. "Buck" McKeon; and former President Saddam Hussein of Iraq.

Remarks at a Saint Patrick's Day Shamrock Presentation Ceremony With Prime Minister Bertie Ahern of Ireland
March 17, 2006

President Bush. Taoiseach, thank you very much. Welcome back.

Prime Minister Ahern. Thank you.

President Bush. Laura and I are delighted to welcome you here to the White House. I'm proud to accept the bowl of shamrocks as a symbol of our friendship.

The friendship between Ireland and the United States has deep roots. Few people fought as hard for American independence as the sons of Erin. At the end of the Revolutionary War, Lord Mountjoy told the House of Commons that, "We've lost America through the Irish." The Irish played a key role in Washington's army. And in the two centuries since, the ties between Ireland and America have only strengthened.

The ties between Ireland and America are reflected in this great house. This house was designed by an Irish architect, and he used as his model the grandest building he knew, Leinster House in Ireland. The affinities between the two buildings are more than just architectural; the White House, built by James Hoban, has been home to every American President since John Q. Adams' father, John. The Dublin building that inspired him now serves as a free parliament in a free and independent Ireland.

The ties between Ireland and America are also reflected in our people. Ireland has one of the fastest growing economies in Europe, and its growth is attracting immigrants. For more than a century, that was a different story. Millions of Irish came to our shores because of war and poverty and famine. Often they arrived with nothing but the faith of their fathers and a willingness to work. These men and women who built our cities were also the soldiers who defended our freedom in every one of our wars. They're the priests and they're the nuns who built a system of parochial schools that provided a decent education for millions of poor immigrants. And they're now doing the same thing for a new generation of African Americans and Latino Americans in our inner cities.

Like Saint Patrick, the Irish in America began their life in their new land as exiles, but came to love it as home. Finally, the ties between Ireland and America are reflected in our common commitment to bring the blessings of liberty to every man and woman and child on this Earth.

In the 20th century, Ireland won its independence and raised up a democracy that offered its people a just and better life. In the 21st century, Ireland is now helping other nations who share the same aspirations for peace and prosperity by fighting hunger and the spread of HIV/AIDS in Africa, by supporting relief efforts

for victims of the tsunami in Asia, and by helping the Afghan people rebuild their lives and their country. Ireland is independent when it comes to foreign policy, but Ireland is not neutral when it comes to the global challenges like hunger and disease and human rights.

Taoiseach, you're making a big contribution to our world, and we appreciate it. The United States appreciates all of Ireland's efforts for peace and freedom. Americans are grateful to our Irish friends, and we are proud of our Irish heritage.

The Census Bureau tells us there are more than 34 million Americans that claim Irish ancestry. On Saint Patrick's Day, I suspect that number jumps a little bit. [*Laughter*] On this special day, we honor the saint who brought the gospel of peace to the Green Isle, and we count ourselves blessed by the warm friendship between his adopted land and our own.

Thanks for coming. Appreciate it.

NOTE: The President spoke at 10:31 a.m. in the Roosevelt Room at the White House. The transcript released by the Office of the Press Secretary also included the remarks of Prime Minister Ahern.

The President's Radio Address
March 18, 2006

Good morning. In recent weeks, Americans have seen horrific images from Iraq: the bombing of a great house of worship in Samarra, sectarian reprisals between Sunnis and Shi'as, and car bombings and kidnapings. Amid continued reports about the tense situation in parts of that country, it may seem difficult at times to understand how we can say that progress is being made. But the reaction to the recent violence by Iraq's leaders is a clear sign of Iraq's commitment to democracy.

I'm encouraged to see that Iraqi political leaders are making good progress toward forming a unity government, despite the recent violence. Our Ambassador to Iraq, Zal Khalilzad, reports that the violence has created a new sense of urgency among these leaders to form a national unity government as quickly as possible. I urge them to continue their work to put aside their differences, to reach out across political, religious, and sectarian lines, and to form a government that can confront the terrorist threat and earn the trust and confidence of all Iraqis.

I also remain optimistic because, slowly but surely, our strategy is getting results. This month, I'm giving a series of speeches to update the American people on that strategy. I'm discussing the progress we are making, the lessons we have learned from our experience, and how we are fixing what has not worked. This past week, I discussed the security element of our strategy. I spoke about our increasingly successful efforts to train Iraqi security forces to take the lead in the fight against the terrorists. And I described our strengthened efforts to defeat the threat of improvised explosive devices, or IEDs.

On Monday, I will give a speech discussing how we are working with all elements of Iraqi society to remove the terrorists and restore order in Iraqi cities, to rebuild homes and communities, and to achieve the stability that can come only from freedom. I will also share some concrete examples of how this approach is succeeding—evidence of real progress that is too often lost amid the more dramatic reports of violence.

Sunday marks the third anniversary of the beginning of Operation Iraqi Freedom. The decision by the United States and our coalition partners to remove Saddam Hussein from power was a difficult decision, and it was the right decision. America and the world are safer today without Saddam Hussein in power. He is no longer oppressing the Iraqi people, sponsoring terror, and threatening the world. He is now being tried for his crimes, and over 25 million Iraqis now live in freedom. This is an achievement America and our allies can be proud of.

These past 3 years have tested our resolve. We've seen hard days and setbacks. After the fall of Saddam Hussein, the terrorists made Iraq the central front in the war on terror, in an attempt to turn that country into a safe haven where they can plan more attacks against America. The fighting has been tough. The enemy has proved brutal and relentless. We have changed our approach in many areas to reflect the hard realities on the ground. And our troops have shown magnificent courage and made tremendous sacrifices.

These sacrifices by our coalition forces—and the sacrifices of Iraqis—have given Iraq this historic opportunity to form a democratic government and rebuild itself after decades of tyranny. In the past 3 years, Iraqis have gone from living under a brutal tyrant to liberation, sovereignty, free elections, a constitutional referendum, and last December, elections for a fully constitutional government. By their courage, the Iraqi people have spoken and made their intentions clear: They want to live in a democracy and shape their own destiny.

In this fight, the American and Iraqi people share the same enemies because we stand for freedom. The security of our country is directly linked to the liberty of the Iraqi people, and we will settle for nothing less than complete victory. Victory will come when the terrorists and Saddamists can no longer threaten Iraq's democracy, when the Iraqi security forces can provide for the safety of their own citizens, and when Iraq is not a safe haven for the terrorists to plot new attacks against our Nation.

More fighting and sacrifice will be required to achieve this victory, and for some, the temptation to retreat and abandon our commitments is strong. Yet there is no peace, there's no honor, and there's no security in retreat. So America will not abandon Iraq to the terrorists who want to attack us again. We will finish the mission. By defeating the terrorists in Iraq, we will bring greater security to our own country. And when victory is achieved, our troops will return home with the honor they have earned.

Thank you for listening.

NOTE: The address was recorded at 7:38 a.m. on March 17 in the Cabinet Room at the White House for broadcast at 10:06 a.m. on March 18. The transcript was made available by the Office of the Press Secretary on March 17 but was embargoed for release until the broadcast. The Office of the Press Secretary also released a Spanish language transcript of this address.

Remarks on Arrival From Camp David, Maryland
March 19, 2006

Progress in Iraq

This morning I had a phone call with our Ambassador to Iraq, and the Ambassador informed me of the progress that the Iraqis are making toward forming a unity government. I encouraged the Iraqi leaders to continue to work hard to get this Government up and running. The Iraqi people voted for democracy last December; 75 percent of the eligible citizens went to the polls to vote. And now the Iraqi leaders are working together to enact a government that reflects the will of the people. And so I'm encouraged by the progress; the Ambassador was encouraged by it.

Today, as well, marks the third anniversary of the beginning of the liberation of Iraq, and it's a time to reflect. And this morning my reflections were upon the sacrifices of the men and women who wear our uniform. Ours is an amazing nation where thousands have volunteered to serve our country. They volunteered to—many volunteered after 9/11, knowing full well that their time in the military could put them in harm's way. So on this third anniversary of the beginning of the liberation of Iraq, I think all Americans should offer thanks to the men and women who wear the uniform and their families who support them.

We are implementing a strategy that will lead to victory in Iraq. And a victory in Iraq will make this country more secure and will help lay the foundation of peace for generations to come.

May God continue to bless our troops in harm's way. Thank you.

NOTE: The President spoke at 12:56 p.m. on the South Lawn at the White House.

Remarks Following Discussions With Secretary General Jakob Gijsbert "Jaap" de Hoop Scheffer of the North Atlantic Treaty Organization
March 20, 2006

President Bush. Fine-looking crowd we've attracted here, fine-looking crowd.

Mr. Secretary General, thanks for coming. We've just had a wide-ranging discussion on a variety of issues, which is what you'd expect when allies and friends come together. We discussed Iraq, and I want to thank NATO for its involvement in helping train Iraqi security forces so they can end up protecting the Iraqi people from the—from those who want to kill innocent life in order to affect the outcome of that democracy.

I want to thank you very much for your strong involvement in Afghanistan. A

NATO presence in Afghanistan is really important. I learned that firsthand when I went to Afghanistan and talked to the— President Karzai and his Government. They were very supportive of the mission and thankful for the mission. NATO is effective, and that's one of the things that's really important for our citizens to understand, that our relationship with NATO is an important part of helping us to win the war on terror.

We also talked about Darfur in the Sudan. I'd called the Secretary General earlier this year. I talked to him about a strategy that would enable NATO to take the lead in Darfur. However, some things have to happen prior to that happening. And the first thing is that the African Union must request from the United Nations a U.N. mission to convert the AU mission to a U.N. mission, at which point if that's done, the—NATO can move in with United States help—inside of NATO—to make it clear to the Sudanese Government that we're intent upon providing security for the people there and intent upon helping work toward a lasting peace agreement.

And so I appreciate your understanding of that. The first time I made the phone call to the Secretary General, he fully understood the challenge, fully understood the need, and it was great to work with a friend in peace to devise a strategy on how to move forward.

So thanks for coming. Looking forward to the meeting later on this year, big NATO summit. And I'm convinced that, like the last summit we had, you'll lead that meeting with the efficiency and professionalism that you're known for.

Secretary General de Hoop Scheffer. Thank you very much, Mr. President. Let me echo what the President has been saying about NATO delivering, about NATO making the difference. In Afghanistan, the fight against terror is an extremely important element there. NATO indeed assists in the African Union in Darfur, and I'm quite sure, as I've told the President, that when the U.N. comes, the NATO allies will be ready to do more in enabling the United Nations force in Darfur.

NATO assisted after Hurricane Katrina. NATO had a major humanitarian operation in Pakistan. NATO is in the Balkans. All 26 NATO allies participate in one way or the other in the training mission in Iraq. Now I want to see NATO-trained Iraqi officers taking their responsibility in fighting the terrorists in their own country.

In other words, NATO is delivering. And in the runup to the NATO summit in Riga at the end of the year, as the President mentioned, we'll make sure—and NATO will make sure that this will be an important event.

In NATO's outreach, let me mention the Middle East, North Africa, Israel, Jordan, the nations of the gulf—NATO's contacts with other nations who share our values— we have Australia, Japan, South Korea— in other words, we'll see to it that the military agenda of NATO and the political agenda of NATO will be very seriously addressed in Riga. And I'm very glad for the support, the permanent support, and the friendship of our most important ally, the United States, and its leader, President Bush.

Thank you very much.

President Bush. Thank you. Yes, good. Thank you.

NOTE: The President spoke at 10:16 a.m. in the Oval Office at the White House. In his remarks, he referred to President Hamid Karzai of Afghanistan.

Remarks to the City Club of Cleveland and a Question-and-Answer Session in Cleveland, Ohio
March 20, 2006

The President. Thank you all. Please be seated. Sanjiv, thanks for the introduction. He called me on the phone and said, "Listen, we believe in free speech, so you're going to come and give us a speech for free." [*Laughter*] Thanks for the invitation; thanks for the warm welcome. It's good to be here at the City Club of Cleveland.

For almost a century, you have provided an important forum for debate and discussion on the issues of the day. And I have come to discuss a vital issue of the day, which is the safety and security of every American and our need to achieve victory in the war on terror.

I want to thank the mayor for joining us. Mr. Mayor, appreciate you being here. It must make you feel pretty good to get the "Most Livable City" award. [*Laughter*] I want to thank all the members of the City Club for graciously inviting me to come. I want to thank the students who are here. Thanks for your interest in your government. I look forward to giving you a speech and then answering questions, if you have any.

The central front on the war on terror is Iraq, and in the past few weeks, we've seen horrific images coming out of that country. We've seen a great house of worship, the Golden Mosque of Samarra, in ruins after a brutal terrorist attack. We have seen reprisal attacks by armed militia on Sunni mosques. We have seen car bombs take the lives of shoppers in a crowded market in Sadr City. We've seen the bodies of scores of Iraqi men brutally executed or beaten to death.

The enemies of a free Iraq attacked the Golden Mosque for a reason: They know they lack the military strength to challenge Iraqi and coalition forces in a direct battle, so they're trying to provoke a civil war. By attacking one of Shi'a Islam's holiest sites, they hoped to incite violence that would drive Iraqis apart and stop their progress on the path to a free society.

The timing of the attack in Samarra is no accident. It comes at a moment when Iraq's elected leaders are working to form a unity government. Last December, 4 short months ago, more than 11 million people expressed their opinion. They said loud and clear at the ballot box that they desire a future of freedom and unity. And now it is time for the leaders to put aside their differences; reach out across political, religious, and sectarian lines; and form a unity government that will earn the trust and the confidence of all Iraqis. My administration, led by Ambassador Zal Khalilzad, is helping and will continue to help the Iraqis achieve this goal.

The situation on the ground remains tense. And in the face of continued reports about killings and reprisals, I understand how some Americans have had their confidence shaken. Others look at the violence they see each night on their television screens and they wonder how I can remain so optimistic about the prospects of success in Iraq. They wonder what I see that they don't. So today I'd like to share a concrete example of progress in Iraq that most Americans do not see every day in their newspapers and on their television screens. I'm going to tell you the story of a northern Iraqi city called Tall 'Afar, which was once a key base of operations for Al Qaida and is today a free city that gives reason for hope for a free Iraq.

Tall 'Afar is a city of more than 200,000 residents, roughly the population of Akron, Ohio. In many ways, Tall 'Afar is a microcosm of Iraq. It has dozens of tribes of different ethnicity and religion. Most of the city residents are Sunnis of Turkmen origin. Tall 'Afar sits just 35 miles from the Syrian border. It was a strategic location for Al Qaida and their leader, Zarqawi.

Now, it's important to remember what Al Qaida has told us, their stated objectives. Their goal is to drive us out of Iraq so they can take the country over. Their goal is to overthrow moderate Muslim governments throughout the region. Their goal is to use Iraq as a base from which to launch attacks against America. To achieve this goal, they're recruiting terrorists from the Middle East to come into Iraq to infiltrate its cities and to sow violence and destruction so that no legitimate government can exercise control. And Tall 'Afar was a key way station for their operations in Iraq.

After we removed Saddam Hussein in April 2003, the terrorists began moving into the city. They sought to divide Tall 'Afar's many ethnic and religious groups and forged an alliance of convenience with those who benefited from Saddam's regime and others with their own grievances. They skillfully used propaganda to foment hostility toward the coalition and the new Iraqi Government. They exploited a weak economy to recruit young men to their cause. And by September 2004, the terrorists and insurgents had basically seized control of Tall 'Afar.

We recognized the situation was unacceptable, so we launched a military operation against them. After 3 days of heavy fighting, the terrorists and the insurgents fled the city. Our strategy at the time was to stay after the terrorists and keep them on the run. So coalition forces kept moving, kept pursuing the enemy and routing out the terrorists in other parts of Iraq.

Unfortunately, in 2004, the local security forces there in Tall 'Afar weren't able to maintain order, and so the terrorists and the insurgents eventually moved back into the town. Because the terrorists threatened to murder the families of Tall 'Afar's police, its members rarely ventured out from the headquarters in an old Ottoman fortress. The terrorists also took over local mosques,

forcing local imams out and insisting that the terrorist message of hatred and intolerance and violence be spread from the mosques. The same happened in Tall 'Afar's schools, where the terrorists eliminated real education and instead indoctrinated young men in their hateful ideology. By November of 2004, 2 months after our operation to clear the city, the terrorists had returned to continue their brutal campaign of intimidation.

The return of Al Qaida meant the innocent civilians in Tall 'Afar were in a difficult position. Just put yourself in the shoes of the citizens of Tall 'Afar as all this was happening. On the one side, you hear the coalition and Iraqi forces saying they're coming to protect you, but they'd already come in once and they had not stopped the terrorists from coming back. You worry that when the coalition goes after the terrorists, you or your family may be caught in the crossfire and your city might be destroyed. You don't trust the police. You badly want to believe the coalition forces really can help you out, but three decades of Saddam's brutal rule have taught you a lesson: Don't stick your neck out for anybody.

On the other side, you see the terrorists and the insurgents. You know they mean business. They control the only hospital in town. You see that the mayor and other political figures are collaborating with the terrorists. You see how the people who worked as interpreters for the coalition forces are beheaded. You see a popular city councilman gunned down in front of his horrified wife and children. You see a respected Sheikh and an Imam kidnaped and murdered. You see the terrorists deliberately firing mortars into playgrounds and soccer fields filled with children. You see communities becoming armed enclaves. If you are in a part of Tall 'Afar that was not considered friendly, you see that the terrorists cut off your basic services like electricity and water. You and your family feel besieged, and you see no way out.

The savagery of the terrorists and insurgents who controlled Tall 'Afar is really hard for Americans to imagine. They enforced their rule through fear and intimidation—and women and children were not spared. In one grim incident, the terrorists kidnaped a young boy from the hospital and killed him, and then they boobytrapped his body and placed him along a road where his family would see him. And when the boy's father came to retrieve his son's body, he was blown up. These weren't random acts of violence; these were deliberate and highly organized attempts to maintain control through intimidation. In Tall 'Afar, the terrorists had schools for kidnaping and beheading and laying IEDs. And they sent a clear message to the citizens of the city: Anyone who dares oppose their reign of terror will be murdered.

As they enforced their rule by targeting civilians, they also preyed upon adolescents craving affirmation. Our troops found one Iraqi teenager who was taken from his family by the terrorists. The terrorists routinely abused him and violated his dignity. The terrorists offered him a chance to prove his manhood by holding the legs of captives as they were beheaded. When our forces interviewed this boy, he told them that his greatest aspiration was to be promoted to the killer who would behead the bound captives. Al Qaida's idea of manhood may be fanatical and perverse, but it served two clear purposes: It helped provide recruits willing to commit any atrocity, and it enforced the rule of fear.

The result of this barbarity was a city where normal life had virtually ceased. Colonel H.R. McMaster of the 3d Armored Cavalry Regiment described it this way: "When you come into a place in the grip of Al Qaida, you see a ghost town. There are no children playing in the streets. Shops are closed and boarded. All construction is stopped. People stay inside, prisoners in their own homes." This is the brutal reality that Al Qaida wishes to impose on all the people of Iraq.

The ability of Al Qaida and its associates to retake Tall 'Afar was an example of something we saw elsewhere in Iraq. We recognized the problem, and we changed our strategy. Instead of coming in and removing the terrorists and then moving on, the Iraqi Government and the coalition adopted a new approach called clear, hold, and build. This new approach was made possible because of the significant gains made in training large numbers of highly capable Iraqi security forces. Under this new approach, Iraq and coalition—Iraqi and coalition forces would clear a city of the terrorists, leave well-trained Iraqi units behind to hold the city, and work with local leaders to build the economic and political infrastructure Iraqis need to live in freedom.

One of the first tests of this new approach was Tall 'Afar. In May 2005, Colonel McMaster's unit was given responsibility for the western part of Nineveh Province where Tall 'Afar is located, and 2 months later, Iraq's national Government announced that a major offensive to clear the city of the terrorists and insurgents would soon be launched. Iraqi and coalition forces first met with tribal leaders and local residents to listen to their grievances. One of the biggest complaints was the police force, which rarely ventured out of its headquarters. When it did venture, it was mostly to carry out sectarian reprisals. And so the national Government sent out new leaders to head the force. The new leaders set about getting rid of the bad elements and building a professional police force that all sides could have confidence in. We recognized it was important to listen to the representatives of Tall 'Afar's many ethnic and religious groups. It's an important part of helping to remove one of the leading sources of mistrust.

Next, Iraqi and Army coalition forces spent weeks preparing for what they knew would be a tough military offensive. They built an 8-foot high, 12-mile long dirt wall that ringed the city. This wall was designed to cut off any escape for terrorists trying to evade security checkpoints. Iraqi and coalition forces also built temporary housing outside the city so that Tall 'Afar's people would have places to go when the fighting started. Before the assault on the city, Iraqi and coalition forces initiated a series of operations in surrounding towns to eliminate safe havens and make it harder for fleeing terrorists to hide. These steps took time, but as life returned to the outlying towns, these operations helped persuade the population of Tall 'Afar that Iraqi and coalition forces were on their side against a common enemy, the extremists who had taken control of their city and their lives.

Only after all these steps did Iraqi and coalition authorities launch Operation Restoring Rights to clear the city of the terrorists. Iraqi forces took the lead. The primary force was 10 Iraqi battalions, backed by 3 coalition battalions. Many Iraqi units conducted their own antiterrorist operations and controlled their own battle space, hunting for the enemy fighters and securing neighborhoods block by block. Throughout the operation, Iraqi and coalition forces were careful to hold their fire to let civilians pass safely out of the city. By focusing on securing the safety of Tall 'Afar's population, the Iraqi and coalition forces begin to win the trust of the city's residents, which is critical to defeating the terrorists who were hiding among them.

After about 2 weeks of intense activity, coalition and Iraqi forces had killed about 150 terrorists and captured 850 more. The operation uncovered weapons caches loaded with small arms ammunition and ski masks, RPG rockets, grenade and machine gun ammunition, and fuses and batteries for making IEDs. In one cache, we found an ax inscribed with the names of the victims the terrorists had beheaded. And the operation accomplished all this while protecting innocent civilians and inflicting minimal damage on the city.

After the main combat operations were over, Iraqi forces moved in to hold the city. Iraqis' Government deployed more than 1,000 Iraqi Army soldiers and emergency police to keep order, and they were supported by a newly restored police force that would eventually grow to about 1,700 officers. As part of the new strategy, we embedded coalition forces with the Iraqi police and with the army units patrolling Tall 'Afar to work with their Iraqi counterparts and to help them become more capable and more professional. In the weeks and months that followed, the Iraqi police built stations throughout Tall 'Afar, and city residents began stepping forward to offer testimony against captured terrorists and inform soldiers about where the remaining terrorists were hiding.

Inside the old Ottoman fortress, a joint coordination center manned by Iraqi Army and Iraqi police and coalition forces answers the many phone calls that now come into a new tip line. As a result of the tips, when someone tries to plant an IED in Tall 'Afar, it's often reported and disabled before it can do any harm. The Iraqi forces patrolling the cities are effective because they know the people, they know the language, and they know the culture. And by turning control of these cities over to capable Iraqi troops and police, we give Iraqis confidence that they can determine their own destiny, and that frees up coalition forces to hunt the high-value targets like Zarqawi.

The recent elections show us how Iraqis respond when they know they're safe. Tall 'Afar is the largest city in western Nineveh Province. In the elections held in January 2005, of about 190,000 registered voters, only 32,000 people went to the polls. Only Fallujah had a lower participation rate. By the time of the October referendum on the Constitution and the December elections, Iraqi and coalition forces had secured Tall 'Afar and surrounding areas. The number of registered voters rose to about 204,000, and more than 175,000 turned out to vote in each election, more than 85 percent of the eligible voters in western

Nineveh Province. These citizens turned out because they were determined to have a say in their nation's future, and they cast their ballots at polling stations that were guarded and secured by fellow Iraqis.

One young teacher described the change this way: "What you see here is hope— the hope that Iraq will become safer and fairer. I feel very confident when I see so many people voting."

The confidence that has been restored to the people of Tall 'Afar is crucial to their efforts to rebuild their city. Immediately following the military operations, we helped the Iraqis set up humanitarian relief for the civilian population. We also set up a fund to reimburse innocent Iraqi families for damage done to their homes and businesses in the fight against the terrorists. The Iraqi Government pledged $50 million to help reconstruct Tall 'Afar by paving roads and rebuilding hospitals and schools and by improving infrastructure from the electric grid to sewer and water systems. With their city now more secure, the people of Tall 'Afar are beginning to rebuild a better future for themselves and their children.

See, if you're a resident of Tall 'Afar today, this is what you're going to see: You see that the terrorist who once exercised brutal control over every aspect of your city has been killed or captured or driven out or put on the run. You see your children going to school and playing safely in the streets. You see the electricity and water service restored throughout the city. You see a police force that better reflects the ethnic and religious diversity of the communities they patrol. You see markets opening, and you hear the sound of construction equipment as buildings go up and homes are remade. In short, you see a city that is coming back to life.

The success of Tall 'Afar also shows how the three elements of our strategy in Iraq— political, security, and economic—depend on and reinforce one another. By working with local leaders to address community grievances, Iraqi and coalition forces helped build the political support needed to make the military operation a success. The military success against the terrorists helped give the citizens of Tall 'Afar security, and this allowed them to vote in the elections and begin to rebuild their city. And the economic rebuilding that is beginning to take place is giving Tall 'Afar residents a real stake in the success of a free Iraq. And as all this happens, the terrorists, those who offer nothing but destruction and death, are becoming marginalized.

The strategy that worked so well in Tall 'Afar did not emerge overnight; it came only after much trial and error. It took time to understand and adjust to the brutality of the enemy in Iraq. Yet the strategy is working. And we know it's working because the people of Tall 'Afar are showing their gratitude for the good work that Americans have given on their behalf. A recent television report followed a guy named Captain Jesse Sellars on patrol and described him as a "pied piper," with crowds of Iraqi children happily chanting his name as he greets locals with the words *"Salaam alaikum,"* which means "Peace be with you."

When the newswoman asks the local merchant what would have happened a few months earlier if he'd been seen talking with an American, his answer was clear: "They'd have cut off my head. They would have beheaded me." Like thousands of others in Tall 'Afar, this man knows the true meaning of liberation.

Recently, Senator Joe Biden said that America cannot want peace for Iraqis more than they want it for themselves. I agree with that. And the story of Tall 'Afar shows that when Iraqis can count on a basic level of safety and security, they can live together peacefully. We saw this in Tall 'Afar after the bombing of the Golden Mosque in Samarra. Unlike other parts of Iraq, in Tall 'Afar, the reaction was subdued, with few reports of sectarian violence. Actually, on the Friday after the attack, more than

1,000 demonstrators gathered in Tall 'Afar to protest the attack peacefully.

The terrorists have not given up in Tall 'Afar, and they may yet succeed in exploding bombs or provoking acts of sectarian violence. The people of the city still have many challenges to overcome, including old-age resentments that still create suspicion, an economy that needs to create jobs and opportunity for its young, and determined enemies who will continue trying to foment a civil war to move back in. But the people of Tall 'Afar have shown why spreading liberty and democracy is at the heart of our strategy to defeat the terrorists. The people of Tall 'Afar have shown that Iraqis do want peace and freedom, and no one should underestimate them.

I wish I could tell you that the progress made in Tall 'Afar is the same in every single part of Iraq. It's not. Though most of the country has remained relatively peaceful, in some parts of Iraq, the enemy is carrying out savage acts of violence, particularly in Baghdad and the surrounding areas of Baghdad. But the progress made in bringing more Iraqi security forces on line is helping to bring peace and stability to Iraqi cities. The example of Tall 'Afar gives me confidence in our strategy, because in this city, we see the outlines of the Iraq that we and the Iraqi people have been fighting for: a free and secure people who are getting back on their feet, who are participating in government and civic life, and who have become allies in the fight against the terrorists.

I believe that as Iraqis continue to see the benefits of liberty, they will gain confidence in their future, and they will work to ensure that common purpose trumps narrow sectarianism. And by standing with them in their hour of need, we're going to help the Iraqis build a strong democracy that will be an inspiration throughout the Middle East, a democracy that will be a partner in the global war against the terrorists.

The kind of progress that we and the Iraqi people are making in places like Tall 'Afar is not easy to capture in a short clip on the evening news. Footage of children playing or shops opening and people resuming their normal lives will never be as dramatic as the footage of an IED explosion or the destruction of a mosque or soldiers and civilians being killed or injured. The enemy understands this, and it explains their continued acts of violence in Iraq. Yet the progress we and the Iraqi people are making is also real. And those in a position to know best are the Iraqis themselves.

One of the most eloquent is the mayor of Tall 'Afar, a courageous Iraqi man named Najim. Mayor Najim arrived in the city in the midst of the Al Qaida occupation, and he knows exactly what our troops have helped accomplish. He calls our men and women in uniform "lionhearts." And in a letter to the troopers of the 3d Armored Cavalry Regiment, he spoke of a friendship sealed in blood and sacrifice, as Mayor Najim had this to say to the families of our fallen: "To the families of those who have given their holy blood for our land, we all bow to you in reverence and to the souls of your loved ones. Their sacrifice was not in vain. They are not dead but alive, and their souls are hovering around us every second of every minute. They will not be forgotten for giving their precious lives. They have sacrificed that which is most valuable. We see them in the smile of every child and in every flower growing in this land. Let America, their families, and the world be proud of their sacrifice for humanity and life." America is proud of that sacrifice, and we're proud to have allies like Mayor Najim on our side in the fight for freedom.

Yesterday we marked the third anniversary of the start of Operation Iraqi Freedom. At the time, there is much to—this time, there's much discussion in our country about the removal of Saddam Hussein from power and our remaining mission in

509

Iraq. The decision to remove Saddam Hussein was a difficult decision. The decision to remove Saddam Hussein was the right decision.

Before we acted, his regime was defying U.N. resolutions calling for it to disarm; it was violating cease-fire agreements, was firing on British and American pilots which were enforcing no-fly zones. Saddam Hussein was a leader who brutalized his people, had pursued and used weapons of mass destruction, and sponsored terrorism. Today, Saddam Hussein is no longer oppressing his people or threatening the world. He's being tried for his crimes by the free citizens of a free Iraq, and America and our allies are safer for it.

The last 3 years have tested our resolve. The fighting has been tough. The enemy we face has proved to be brutal and relentless. We're adapting our approach to reflect the hard realities on the ground. And the sacrifice being made by our young men and women who wear our uniform has been heartening and inspiring.

The terrorists who are setting off bombs in mosques and markets in Iraq share the same hateful ideology as the terrorists who attacked us on September the 11th, 2001, those who blew up the commuters in London and Madrid, and those who murdered tourists in Bali or workers in Riyadh or guests at a wedding in Amman, Jordan. In the war on terror, we face a global enemy, and if we were not fighting this enemy in Iraq, they would not be idle. They would be plotting and trying to kill Americans across the world and within our own borders. Against this enemy, there can be no compromise. So we will fight them in Iraq, we'll fight them across the world, and we will stay in the fight until the fight is won.

In the long run, the best way to defeat this enemy and to ensure the security of our own citizens is to spread the hope of freedom across the broader Middle East. We've seen freedom conquer evil and secure the peace before. In World War II, free nations came together to fight the ideology of fascism, and freedom prevailed. And today, Germany and Japan are democracies, and they are allies in securing the peace. In the cold war, freedom defeated the ideology of communism and led to a democratic movement that freed the nations of Central and Eastern Europe from Soviet domination. And today, these nations are strong allies in the war on terror.

In the Middle East, freedom is once again contending with an ideology that seeks to sow anger and hatred and despair. And like fascism and communism before, the hateful ideologies that use terror will be defeated. Freedom will prevail in Iraq; freedom will prevail in the Middle East. And as the hope of freedom spreads to nations that have not known it, these countries will become allies in the cause of peace.

The security of our country is directly linked to the liberty of the Iraqi people, and we will settle for nothing less than victory. Victory will come when the terrorists and Saddamists can no longer threaten Iraq's democracy, when the Iraqi security forces can provide for the safety of their citizens on their own, and when Iraq is not a safe haven for terrorists to plot new attacks against our Nation. There will be more days of sacrifice and tough fighting before the victory is achieved. Yet by helping the Iraqis defeat the terrorists in their land, we bring greater security to our own.

As we make progress toward victory, Iraqis will continue to take more responsibility for their own security and fewer U.S. forces will be needed to complete the mission. But it's important for the Iraqis to hear this: The United States will not abandon Iraq. We will not leave that country to the terrorists who attacked America and want to attack us again. We will leave Iraq, but when we do, it will be from a position of strength, not weakness. Americans have never retreated in the face of thugs and assassins, and we will not begin now.

Thanks for listening. And I'll be glad to answer some questions, if you have any.

Yes, ma'am.

War on Terror

Q. Thank you for coming to Cleveland, Mr. President, and to the City Club. My question is that author and former Nixon administration official Kevin Phillips, in his latest book, "American Theocracy," discusses what has been called radical Christianity and its growing involvement into government and politics. He makes the point that members of your administration have reached out to prophetic Christians who see the war in Iraq and the rise of terrorism as signs of the apocalypse. Do you believe this, that the war in Iraq and the rise of terrorism are signs of the apocalypse? And if not, why not?

The President. The answer is—I haven't really thought of it that way. [*Laughter*] Here's how I think of it. First I've heard of that, by the way. I guess I'm more of a practical fellow. I vowed after September the 11th that I would do everything I could to protect the American people. And my attitude, of course, was affected by the attacks. I knew we were at a war. I knew that the enemy, obviously, had to be sophisticated and lethal to fly hijacked airplanes into facilities that would be killing thousands of people, innocent people doing nothing, just sitting there going to work.

I also knew this about this war on terror, that the farther we got away from September the 11th, the more likely it is people would seek comfort and not think about this global war on terror as a global war on terror. And that's good, by the way. It's hard to take risk if you're a small-business owner, for example, if you're worried that the next attack is going to come tomorrow. I understand that. But I also understand my most important job, the most important job of any President today—and I predict down the road—is to protect America.

And so I told the American people that we would find the terrorists and bring them to justice, and that we needed to defeat them overseas so we didn't have to face them here at home. I also understood that the war on terror requires some clear doctrine. And one of the doctrines that I laid out was, "If you harbor a terrorist, you're equally as guilty as the terrorist." And the first time that doctrine was really challenged was in Afghanistan. I guess the Taliban didn't believe us—or me. And so we acted. Twenty-five million people are now free, and Afghanistan is no longer a safe haven for the terrorists.

And the other doctrine that's really important, and it's a change of attitude—it's going to require a change of attitude for a while—is that when you see a threat, you got to deal with it before it hurts you. Foreign policy used to be dictated by the fact we had two oceans protecting us. If we saw a threat, you could deal with it if you needed to, you think—or not. But we'd be safe.

My most important job is to protect you, is to protect the American people. Therefore, when we see threats, given the lesson of September the 11th, we got to deal with them. That does not mean militarily, necessarily. Obviously, the first option for a President has got to be the full use of diplomacy. That's what you're watching in Iran right now. I see a threat in Iran. I see it there—I'm kind of getting off subject here, not because I don't want to answer your question, but kind of—I guess that's what happens in Washington; we get a little long-winded. [*Laughter*]

But now that I'm on Iran, the threat to Iran, of course—[*laughter*]—the threat from Iran is, of course, their stated objective to destroy our strong ally, Israel. That's a threat, a serious threat. It's a threat to world peace; it's a threat, in essence, to a strong alliance. I made it clear, and I'll be making it clear again, that we will use military might to protect our ally, Israel, and—[*applause*].

At any rate, our objective is to solve this issue diplomatically. And so our message must be a united message, a message from not only the United States but also Great Britain and France and Germany as well as Russia, hopefully, and China, in order to say, loud and clear, to the Iranians, "This is unacceptable behavior. Your desire to have a nuclear weapon is unacceptable."

And so to answer your question, I take a practical view of doing the job you want me to do—which is, how do we defeat an enemy that still wants to hurt us, and how do we deal with threats before they fully materialize; what do we do to protect us from harm? That's my job. And that job came home on September the 11th, for me—loud and clear. And I think about my job of protecting you every day. Every single day of the Presidency, I'm concerned about the safety of the American people.

Yes, sir.

Intelligence/War on Terror

Q. Mr. President, at the beginning of your talk today, you mentioned that you understand why Americans have had their confidence shaken by the events in Iraq. And I'd like to ask you about events that occurred 3 years ago that might also explain why confidence has been shaken. Before we went to war in Iraq, we said there were three main reasons for going to war in Iraq: weapons of mass destruction, the claim that Iraq was sponsoring terrorists who had attacked us on 9/11, and that Iraq had purchased nuclear materials from Niger. All three of those turned out to be false. My question is, how do we restore confidence that Americans may have in their leaders and to be sure that the information they are getting now is correct?

The President. That's a great question. First, just—if I might correct a misperception, I don't think we ever said—at least I know I didn't say that there was a direct connection between September the 11th and Saddam Hussein. We did say that he was a state sponsor of terror—by the way, not declared a state sponsor of terror by me but declared by other administrations. We also did say that Zarqawi, the

man who is now wreaking havoc and killing innocent life, was in Iraq. And so the "state sponsor of terror" was a declaration by a previous administration. But I don't want to be argumentative, but I was very careful never to say that Saddam Hussein ordered the attacks on America.

Like you, I asked that very same question: Where did we go wrong on intelligence? The truth of the matter is, the whole world thought that Saddam Hussein had weapons of mass destruction. It wasn't just my administration; it was the previous administration. It wasn't just the previous administration. You might remember, sir, there was a Security Council vote of 15 to nothing that said to Saddam Hussein, "Disclose, disarm, or face serious consequences." The basic premise was, "You've got weapons." That's what we thought.

When he didn't disclose and when he didn't disarm and when he deceived inspectors, it sent a very disconcerting message to me, whose job it is to protect the American people and to take threats before they fully materialize. My view is, he was given the choice of whether or not he would face reprisal. It was his decision to make. And so he chose to not disclose, not disarm, as far as everybody was concerned.

Your question, however, the part that's really important, is, how do we regain credibility when it comes to intelligence? Obviously, the Iranian issue is a classic case, where we've got to make sure that when we speak, there's credibility. And so, in other words, when the United States rallies a coalition, or any other country that had felt that Saddam Hussein had weapons of mass destruction is trying to rally a coalition in dealing with one of these nontransparent societies, what do we need to do to regain the trust of not only the American people but the world community?

And so what I did was I called together the Silberman-Robb Commission—Laurence Silberman and former Senator Chuck Robb—to take a full look at what went right and what went wrong on the intelligence, and how do we structure an intelligence network that makes sure there's full debate among the analysts? How do we make sure that there's a full compilation of data points that can help decisionmakers like myself feel comfortable in the decision we make?

The war on terror requires the collection and analysis of good intelligence. This is a different kind of war. We're dealing with an enemy which hides in caves and plots and plans, an enemy which doesn't move in flotillas or battalions. And so therefore, the intelligence gathering is not only important to make a diplomatic case; it's really important to be able to find an enemy before they hurt us.

And so there was a reform process they went through, a full analysis of what—of how the operations worked, and out of that came the NDI, John Negroponte and Mike Hayden. And their job is to better collate and make sure that the intelligence gathering is seamless across a variety of gatherers and people that analyze. But the credibility of our country is essential—agree with you.

Yes, sure.

Spread of Democracy/U.S. Armed Forces

Q. Thank you, Mr. President. Welcome to Cleveland. It's an honor to have you here. I represent the Cleveland Hungarian Revolution 50th anniversary—[*inaudible*].

The President. That's good. I was there, by the way.

Q. Thank you all. [*Laughter*]

The President. At least for the celebration in Capitol with Tom Lantos. But go ahead.

Q. Mr. President, in the interest of free speech, if you'll indulge me, I have to give you a little context of my question. On this third anniversary of your—I consider—courageous initiative to bring freedom and basic human dignity to the Iraqi people, the image of the statue of the tyrant Saddam falling in Baghdad was very reminis-

cent of another statue, another tyrant, Josef Stalin, who fell in Budapest 50 years ago at the hands of many young Hungarian freedom fighters who were seeking to overthrow the tyranny of Soviet communism. Mr. President, just like our brave fighting men and women today and many Iraqi people, those young Hungarian patriots paid a very heavy price for a few days of freedom. But they lit the torch that eventually set the captive nations on the path to achieving liberty. And so, Mr. President, our Cleveland Hungarian community is planning a major event in Cleveland in October—[*laughter*].

The President. The guy seized the moment, you know. He's a——

Q. Right.

The President. I'm not sure what I'm doing in October. Put me down as a maybe. [*Laughter*] Sorry to interrupt.

Q. Just like you came for the Children's Games in 2004, we hope to have you here for that as well. Mr. President, just want to let you know, to win the war on terror, we feel that what was started in 1776 and continued in 1956 must be remembered in 2006.

The President. Thank you. How much more you got?

Q. I'm at the question now. Thanks for your indulgence.

The President. Okay, good. [*Laughter*]

Q. My basic question is, how can we help you, from the grassroots level, how can we help you promote the cause of freedom and liberty for all peoples throughout the world?

The President. I appreciate that. My main job is to make sure I make the case as plainly as I can why it's worth it. And I fully understand—I understand people being disheartened when they turn on their TV screen and see the loss of innocent life. We're compassionate people. Nobody likes beheadings and it—nobody—when innocent children get car bombed. So it's my job, sir, to make it clear about the connection between Iraq and the war on terror.

513

It's my job to remind people that progress is being made, in spite of the violence they see. It's my job to make it clear to the people the stakes.

I've spent time talking about what happens if we were to lose our nerve and Iraq would fall to Al Qaida. And the stakes are high. Look, I understand some don't view that we're in a war against the terrorists. I know that. And therefore, there's a sense that this—9/11 might have been an isolated incident. I just don't agree. And here's what I—here's the basis from which I make decisions. You heard one—is that 9/11 affected the way I think. I know these are like totalitarian fascists. They have an ideology; they have a desire to spread that ideology; and they're willing to use tactics to achieve their strategy.

And one of the tactics—I said early on in the speech the stated objectives of Al Qaida. This isn't my imagination of their strategy; this is what they have told us. And I presume you want the Commander in Chief to take the words of the enemy seriously. And they have told us they believe that we're soft and that with time, we'll leave, and they'll fill the vacuum. And they want to plan and plot and hurt Americans. That's what they have said. And I think it's really important we take their words very seriously.

And so I will continue making the case, sir, but the best way you can help is to support our troops. You find a family who's got a child in the United States military; tell them you appreciate them. Ask them if you can help them. You see somebody wearing a uniform, you walk up and say, "Thanks for serving the country."

Ours is a remarkable country where hundreds—[*applause*]—where we've got thousands of people signing up, volunteering for the United States military, many of them after September the 11th, knowing full well what they were signing up for. And what's amazing about our military is that retention rates are high; people are still signing up. They want to defend the country. And for that, I am grateful.

But my job, sir, is to lay out the strategy and to connect the notion of liberty with peace. And that's hard for some. Sometimes there's a little bit of a—kind of a point of view that says, "Well, maybe certain people can't be free; maybe certain people can't self-govern." I strongly believe that liberty is universal. I believe in the natural rights of men and women. That was part of our founding. And if you believe in that, if you believe in the universality of freedom, then I believe those of us who are free have an obligation to help others become free.

Yes, ma'am. I'm tied up in October, but you know—[*laughter*].

Iraq/Spread of Democracy

Q. I'm a Marine mom.

The President. Okay, good. Thank you. Tell your—[*applause*].

Q. My son signed up after 9/11, and I didn't raise a terrorist. But let's face it; there's a continuum and a lack of clarity about who's violent and who's a terrorist. And we really do want to use the word "enemy" in a meaningful way. I think your speech has been very brave and very important and very clarifying. And in the interest of clarifying the purpose of our country to fight preventive war, which we know does involve violence, it's very important for us to understand what you're saying about your model community in Iraq. And my question is that you are killing the bad guys, and that's very important—that's the entire story of the battle. And we want to know who the bad guys are. Do you feel that Iraq is like a honeycomb, and that we can draw the Al Qaida there so we can stand and fight them there? I'm really asking for clarification.

The President. Sure. I think in Iraq there are three types of folks that are trying to stop democracy. First of all, I think it's very important for people to understand, one reason they're so violent and desperate is because they're trying to stop a society based upon liberty. And you got to ask why. And the reason why is because it's the exact opposite of what they believe.

There are three types. One is Al Qaida, and Al Qaida is headed into there. Al Qaida understands the danger of democracy spreading. And so Zarqawi, this fellow named Zarqawi, is in charge of Al Qaida inside of Iraq, which recruits foreign fighters. And they headed into Iraq because they wanted to fight us. They wanted to stop democracy.

Secondly, there are Saddamists. These were the folks that really enjoyed a life of privilege. These are people that were top of the heap. They were—they represented a minority in the country, but they got all the deal—they got all the goods. And they don't like it—when Saddam was removed. And so they are trying to regroup.

And the third group are rejectionists. These are essentially Sunnis, as well, who really weren't sure as—about whether or not it meant—what it meant to have minority rights, whether or not they'd be protected. You can understand. They didn't— during Saddam, there was no such thing as minority rights. And so as a new society emerged, they were doubtful. And it is those folks that I believe will become marginalized as democracy advances. We're seeing the Sunnis change their mind about things. They barely voted in the first January 2005 elections; they participated overwhelmingly in the December 2005 elections. In just an 11-month period of time, there was a change of attitude to participate in the democratic process.

And the fundamental question that I know people ask is whether or not democracy, one, can take hold in Iraq, and two, will it change people's attitude about the future? And I believe it will. History has proven that democracies can change societies. The classic case I like to cite is Japan. Prime Minister Koizumi is one of my best buddies in the international arena, and when we sit down, we talk the peace. I find it interesting that he is a peacemaker with me on a variety of issues, and yet my dad fought the Japanese. And I'm sure many of your relatives did as well.

Sixty years ago, Japan was the sworn enemy of the United States. Today, they're an ally in peace. And what took place? Well, what took place was a Japanese-style democracy. I can't say I promise you this, but I suspect that if somebody were standing up at the City Club of Cleveland talking about, "Don't worry; someday, Japan is going to be peaceful with the United States, and the 43d President is going to be designing how keep the peace"—they'd say, "Get him off the stage." [*Laughter*] "What's he thinking? They're the sworn enemy." And now they're our ally. So I have faith in the capacity of democracies to help change societies.

And again, I repeat to you, the debate— one of the debates is whether or not certain folks can self-govern. There's kind of a— "Maybe there are some in the world that aren't capable," say the skeptics. I strongly disagree with that. I believe there's—hold on a second—I believe there's a great desire for people to be free. I believe that. And history has proven that democracies don't war with each other. Again, I kind of glossed over this, but particularly for the students here, look at what happened in Europe over a 100-year period, from the early 1900s to today. Europe was at war twice, that cost Americans thousands of lives. Today, they don't war, because the systems of government changed. Democracies are at peace. Europe is whole, free, and at peace.

And that's an important history lesson for those of us—what I'm saying to you, ma'am, is that there is a battle for Iraq now, but it's just a part of the war on terror. It's a theater in the war on terror. Afghanistan was a theater. And we're in a global battle which requires strong alliances, good cooperation, and a constant reminder of the nature of this war. So today I met with the Secretary General of NATO.

And the first subject that came up was the war on terror and how much I appreciated NATO's contribution to helping Afghanistan succeed. But it is—the enemy in this case is disgruntled folks inside of Iraq coupled with an Al Qaida presence there that wants to harm Americans again.

I don't know—is your son still in the military?

Q. Yes, sir.

The President. Thanks. You tell him the Commander in Chief is proud of him. You tell him to listen to his mother too.

Yes. First, and then second; sir, you're next.

National Economy/Education

Q. On behalf of the students here from various high school student leadership programs, we thank you for speaking with us here at the City Club of Cleveland.

The President. Thanks—I hope it's a convenient excuse to skip school, but—[*laughter*].

Q. Mr. President, with the war in Iraq costing $19,600 per U.S. household, how do you expect a generation of young people such as ourselves to afford college at a time like this, when we're paying for a war in Iraq?

The President. Yes. [*Applause*] Well—hold on for a minute. Hold on. We can do more than one thing at one time. And when you grow your economy, like we're growing our economy, there is an opportunity to not only protect ourselves but also to provide more Pell grants than any administration in our Nation's history and increase the student loan program. So if you take a look, I think you'll find that we're robust in helping—at the Federal level, helping people go to college. And it's essential you go to college. It's essential that there be a group of youngsters coming up that are well-educated so that we can maintain our economic leadership position in the world. We've got a robust program to do just that.

But it's also essential that we keep policies in place that keep the economy growing. This economy of ours is strong, and it's—it is, in my judgment, growing stronger. But it is possible to put policy in place that would weaken it, such as raising taxes. I think we got to keep taxes low to keep the economy moving. It's possible to put policy—[*applause*]—it's possible to put policy in place that would hurt this economy, like protectionist policy. It's possible to—if we keep suing our people trying to risk capital, it's conceivable we won't be the leader. That's why we need good tort reform. We got to make sure that—[*applause*].

My point to you is, economic growth enables us to do more than one thing. And that's what we'll continue to do.

Yes, sir. Right. No, no, hold on for a minute. Hold on for a minute.

India/Pakistan

Q. Thank you, Mr. President.

The President. Yes, sir.

Q. Every chief needs Indian on their side. [*Laughter*]

The President. How long were you working on that for? [*Laughter*]

Q. I applaud your vision and foresight to sign a long-term treaty with India. But, sir, I am confused that, on one side, you're helping democratic countries to flourish and establish democracy in the world market, whereas how do we deal with country who has known to harbor terrorism, like Pakistan?

The President. I thought you might be heading there. [*Laughter*] I, obviously, had a trip recently to India and Pakistan and Afghanistan and was able to say in India and in Pakistan both, "It is a positive development for America to be a friend of Pakistan. It's a positive development for India for America to be a friend of Pakistan, and it's a positive development for Pakistan for America to be a friend of India. It's an important accomplishment in order to help keep the peace."

I don't view our relationships with Pakistan and India as a zero-sum relationship. As a matter of fact, I view our relationships with both countries as different sets of issues and the need to nurture both relationships to achieve common objectives. And we're in a position to be able to do so now.

President Musharraf is a friend to the United States. President Musharraf understands that he must help rout out Al Qaida, which is hiding in parts of his country. President Musharraf was reminded of that the four times Al Qaida tried to kill him. He is a—and so I was able to have a very good discussion with the President about our mutual concerns in the war on terror. And it's important that that dialog go on. It's a very important part of our—me doing my most important job, which is to protect you.

He also said in a press conference that he understands that democracy is important. So one of the conversations that I had with him in private—I feel comfortable saying this in public because he himself brought it up—was the need for democracy to advance in Pakistan. History has showed us that democracies don't war.

What's interesting about the relationship between Pakistan and India—and I'll get to India in a minute. I want to say something on India, so thanks for bringing it up—is that when we first—when I first got into office, I remember asking Colin Powell to go get in between India and Pakistan. There was a lot of noise—you might remember, I think it was '01 or '02, where there was deep concerns about—I think '01—deep concerns about a potential nuclear conflict. And so there was shuttle diplomacy, back and forth between India and Pakistan, including not only our—Colin but also Jack Straw, the Foreign Minister of Great Britain. And you never know how dangerous one of these situations can become until it's too late, but nevertheless, we took it very seriously.

And today, you don't see the need for the United States shuffling or Britain shuffling diplomats back and forth, to walk back—walk the two countries back from a potential conflict which would be incredibly damaging for the world. That's positive. In other words, it's—and I give Prime Minister—President Musharraf credit, and I give the Indian Prime Ministers—both Vajpayee and the current Prime Minister—credit for—Prime Minister Singh—for envisioning what is possible, how is it possible to develop a relationship that's a peaceful relationship with our neighbor.

And, sir, I think it's very important for the United States to stay engaged with Pakistan and encourage them. We're trying to negotiate an investment treaty with them, with the hopes of being able to eventually develop more trade with Pakistan, in the belief that trade helps nations develop stability and prosperity is achieved through trade.

India—the visit there was a very important visit. And I want to describe to you right quick, so be careful on the questions. You're going to have to—you'll leave your hand up for a while. I agreed with the Indian Government that India ought to be encouraged to develop a nuclear power industry. And that's a controversial decision on my part, because it basically flies in the face of old cold war attitudes as well as arm control thinking.

Let me just share the logic with you. First of all, in that we live in a global economy, there is a demand for fossil fuels—an increase in the demand for fossil fuels in one part of the world affects the price of gasoline in our world. We're connected. Whether people like it or not, there is an interconnectedness today that affects our economy. Somebody's decision overseas affects whether or not people are going to be able to work here in America. So I think it makes sense for the United States, as we ourselves become less addicted to oil and fossil fuels, which I'm serious about, encourage others to do so as well. And one good way to do so and to protect the environment at the same time is to encourage the use of safe nuclear power. It's in our interests, our economic interests that we work an agreement with India to encourage their expansion of civilian nuclear power.

Secondly, unlike Iran, for example, India is willing to join the IAEA. They want to be a part of the global agreements around nuclear power. Thirdly, India has got a record of nonproliferation. They've had 30 years of not proliferating. Fourthly, India is a democracy and a transparent society. You find out a lot about India because there's a free press. There is openness. People run for office and are held to account. There's committee hearings. It's an open process.

I feel very comfortable recommending to the United States Congress that it's—that they ought to agree with the agreement that Prime Minister Singh and I have reached. It's important—it's important—it's also an important relationship. For too long, America and India were not partners in peace. We didn't deal with each other because of the cold war. And now is the time to set the cold war behind us. It's over, folks. It no longer is. And let's think about the next 30 years.

And so my hope is someday, somebody will be asking a question, "Aren't you glad old George W. thought about entering into a strategic relationship with India?" And I believe it's in our country's interest that we have such a relationship and, at the same time, maintain close relations with Pakistan. And it's possible to do so. And we are doing so.

Yes, sir.

How long do you usually ask questions here for? [*Laughter*]

Terrorist Surveillance Program

Q. Mr. President——

The President. The guy is supposed to smile over there. Yes.

Q. Another theater in the war on terror is domestic. And there's a controversy around warrantless wiretaps domestically.

The President. Yes.

Q. Could you explain why living within the legislation that allowed your administration to get a warrant from a secret court within 72 hours after putting in a wiretap wouldn't be just as effective?

The President. No, I appreciate the question. He's talking about the terrorist surveillance program that was—created quite a kerfuffle in the press, and I owe an explanation to you. Because our people—first of all, after September the 11th, I spoke to a variety of folks on the frontline of protecting us, and I said, "Is there anything more we could be doing, given the current laws?" And General Mike Hayden of the NSA said, "There is." The FISA law—he's referring to the FISA law, I believe—is—was designed for a previous period and is slow and cumbersome in being able to do what Mike Hayden thinks is necessarily—called hot pursuit.

And so he designed a program that will enable us to listen from a known Al Qaida or suspected Al Qaida person and/or affiliate, from making any phone call outside the United States in, or inside the United States out—with the idea of being able to pick up, quickly, information for which to be able to respond in this environment that we're in. I was concerned about the legality of the program, and so I asked lawyers—which you got plenty of them in Washington—[*laughter*]—to determine whether or not I could do this legally. And they came back and said yes. That's part of the debate which you're beginning to see.

I fully understood that Congress needed to be briefed. And so I had Hayden and others brief Members of the Congress, both Republicans and Democrats, House Members and Senators, about the program. The program is under constant review. I sign a reauthorization every—I'm not exactly sure—45 days, say. It's something like that.

In other words, it's constantly being reviewed. There's an IG that is very active at the NSA to make sure that the program stays within the bounds that it was designed.

I fully understand people's concerns about it, but ours is a town, by the way, in Washington, where when you don't connect the dots, you're held up to Congress, and when you do connect the dots, you're held up to Congress. I believe what I'm doing is constitutional, and I know it's necessary. And so we're going to keep doing it.

Domestic Policy

Q. Thank you, Mr. President. Your comments today about Iraq have been, for me, very enlightening. And I greatly appreciate the level of clarity that you've provided. But my question is about domestic policy. Today, in our neighborhoods, there are terrorists. Children cannot play in some of our neighborhoods. Today, we've got— when you see post-Katrina, our country was startled at some of the images around poverty in some of our cities. Can you be as clear about your domestic policy, to address those kinds of things?

The President. Absolutely. Thanks. Let me start with education, which I view as a vital part of providing hope and eradicating poverty. I was disturbed, when I was the Governor of Texas, disturbed about a system that just moved kids through. There was kind of a process-oriented world, that said, "Okay, if you're 10, you're supposed to be here; you're 12, you're supposed to be here," and on through. It was like— without any sense of accountability. If you believe education is one of the cornerstones to a hopeful world, then it seems like to me, it makes sense that we've got to have a system that measures so we know whether or not people are getting educated.

So when I got to Washington, I proposed what's called No Child Left Behind, which passed with both Republican and Democrat votes. And the whole spirit of No Child Left Behind is this: It says in return for increased Federal money, for particularly Title I students, we expect you to measure grades three through eight. We want to see strong accountability because we believe every child can learn, and we expect every school to teach. That's the whole spirit of the No Child Left Behind Act.

If you—it turns out that if you can solve problems early, if you can find out whether or not a curriculum is working or not early on in a child's career, we can correct the problems. And so part of the No Child Left Behind Act is, when you measure and find somebody not up to—measuring to par, not meeting standards, there's extra money called special service money available in the No Child Left Behind Act to make sure that there's early tutoring, to make sure that children are not just simply shuffled through, to make sure an accountability system is used properly—which is to diagnose and solve problems.

The No Child Left Behind Act is beginning to work. You know why? Because we measure. There was an achievement gap in America; that's bad for the country. It's an achievement gap between the difference between some Anglo children and some African American children, particularly inner city. That's beginning to close.

We need to apply the same rigor of No Child Left Behind, particularly in middle [school]* age, for math and science to make sure that we're able to compete for the jobs of the 21st century.

And so step one, in my judgment, to address exactly what you described as true—kind of this enlightenment that, uh-oh, there are parts of our society in which people are, in fact, being completely left behind—is to make sure the education system is rigorously based upon accountability. And when we find the status quo is unacceptable, have the political courage to change, demand high standards and change.

---

* White House correction.

And the cornerstone of demanding change in a system that tends to protect itself is measurement. And I realize there are people in my party who want to undo No Child Left Behind. And I'm sure there are in the other party. But my judgment is, you can't achieve educational excellence unless you measure and correct problems.

Now, there's another aspect to providing a hopeful society, and that is to encourage ownership. One of the interesting things about Katrina, as you well know, is many of the people displaced did not own their own homes, that they were renters. One of the goals that I set for my administration through a variety of pretty simple programs—like helping with downpayment and education programs, recognizing that interest rates drive most of the housing purchases—was to encourage minority home-ownership. It's now at an alltime high.

I believe that the idea of empowering our faith-based institutions—government can help, but government sometimes can't find—well, it just doesn't pass—it's just not a loving organization. And so I believe strongly—I believe strongly in empowering faith-based and community-based programs all throughout America to help achieve certain objectives. Mentoring, for example, mentoring of children in prisoners—whose mother or dad may be in prison is an initiative I started. Drug rehabilitation, giving those who are eligible for drug money a voucher, money themselves, a scrip so they can redeem it at a program that they choose, not that the government assigns them to—in other words, there's a variety of social service programs aimed at lifting people up.

And so I—look, many Americans kind of were—didn't really realize what's taking place in parts of the country that you've described. And Katrina was a wake-up call for many Americans. And now there's an opportunity, in my judgment, to take—well, for people to take notice and put in policy—put policies in place that help those who need help, like community health cen-ters, or—for health care—or expand educational opportunities through rigorous accountability systems, and, I repeat, demanding change where change is due—needed, and promoting ownership.

Thanks. Good question.

Support for the President

Q. ——is no shrinking violet. First of all, I want to commend you on your presentation today. And I tell you I'm 100 percent behind your fight against terrorism. Also——

The President. Why don't you just leave it at that?

Q. Oh, no. Oh, no. [*Laughter*]

I tell you, one of the reasons I'm qualified to say that; you probably heard of Ernie Shavers, the boxer. I trained Ernie Shavers. He fought Muhammad Ali, and Muhammad Ali say he hit him so hard, he woke up his ancestors in Africa. [*Laughter*] So I know a little bit about boxing and things. But I know in boxing—and I taught over 3,300 children over 13 years. Two of them fought for world championships, including Ernie Shavers. I taught them that the best defense is a good offense. That's what you're doing over there now. And I commend you.

My mom and daddy had moved from Alabama to Ohio in the mid-forties. They were the parents of five sons. We all served in the military. I served 8 years, and we all served honorably. So I am a marine. I've also been a Boy Scout and a firefighter. To lead in, the young person spoke about domestic policy. This Wednesday coming, I'll be making my sixth trip to the New Orleans/Mississippi area as a contractor. I'm president of the Ohio Minority Contracting Association. I want to publicly thank Senator Voinovich right now for directing me to Senator Trent Lott, who has directed me to Haley Barbour, the Governor down there, who opened up opportunities.

We got people doing debris removal, putting on roofs. And I got a $600,000 proposal to feed 22,000 workers down there who have been underfed. You've been down there. I have too. People are working 14 and 16 hours a day. And I've never been so proud to be an American, to see the outpouring of people out there helping one another, particularly the faith-based community. So I thank you, appreciate you, and look forward to putting this proposal in your hand. Thank you.

The President. Well, let's see, I got an invitation and a proposal. [*Laughter*]

Yes, sir. Anybody work here in this town? [*Laughter*]

Q. Sorry about that. Mr. President, I just finished Ambassador Paul Bremer's book, and one of the things I just wanted to say to you and to Ambassador Bremer is, thank you for protecting us.

The President. Thanks.

You're next.

Immigration Reform

Q. Okay, my question is——

The President. We have dueling microphones here. Keep firing away.

Q. Okay. My question is, since 9/11, one of the key things that we need is immigration reform, including comprehensive immigration reform that is right now in front of Senator Specter's committee in the Judiciary. There are two principles I'm hoping that you would support: One, the good people, the engineers, the Ph.D.s, the doctors, the nurses, the people in the system who have followed the rules, will go to the head of the line in any form of immigration reform. That's title IV of the bill.

Secondly, the illegals who have not followed the rules—I understand the debate, I appreciate your statements about immigration reform, but isn't it better that we know who they are, have them finger-printed and photographed, and allow some form of 245(i) to come back so——

The President. Tell people what that is. Tell people what 245(i) is.

Q. Okay—245(i) is a partial amnesty program that expired back in 2001, in fact, was going to be voted on on 9/11, unfortu-

nately. But those—it was a small segment of the illegal population where they would pay the $1,000 fine and, for example, coming in illegally, then marrying an American citizen, could somehow legalize their status.

The President. Okay. Let me give you some broad principles on immigration reform as I see them. First of all, we do need to know who's coming into our country and whether they're coming in illegally or not legally—legally or not legally, and whether they're coming in or going out. And part of reforms after September the 11th was a better system of finding out who's coming here.

Secondly, we have a big border between Texas and Mexico that's really hard to enforce. We got to do everything we can to enforce the border, particularly in the South. I mean, it's the place where people are pouring across in order to find work. We have a situation in our own neighborhood where there are ways—disparities are huge, and there are jobs in America that people won't do. That's just a fact. I met an onion grower today at the airport when I arrived, and he said, "You got to help me find people that will pull onions," or pluck them or whatever you do with them, you know. [*Laughter*] There are jobs that just simply aren't getting done because Americans won't do them. And yet if you're making 50 cents an hour in Mexico, and you can make a lot more in America, and you got mouths to feed, you're going to come and try to find the work. It's a big border, of which—across which people are coming to provide a living for their families.

Step one of any immigration policy is to enforce our border in practical ways. We are spending additional resources to be able to use different detection devices, unmanned UAVs, to help—and expand Border Patrol, by the way, expand the number of agents on the border, to make sure we're getting them the tools necessary to stop people from coming across in the first place.

Secondly, part of the issue we've had in the past is, we've had—for lack of a better word, catch-and-release. The Border Patrol would find people sneaking in; they would then hold them for a period of time; they'd say, "Come back and check in with us 45 days later," and then they wouldn't check in 45 days later. And they would disappear in society to do the work that some Americans will not do.

And so we're changing catch-and-release. We're particularly focusing on those from Central America who are coming across Mexico's southern border, ending up in our own—it's a long answer, because it's an important question: How do we protect our borders and, at the same time, be a humane society?

Anyway, step one, focus on enforcing border; when we find people, send them home, so that the work of our Border Patrol is productive work.

Secondly, it seems like to me that part of having a border security program is to say to people who are hiring people here illegally, we're going to hold you to account. The problem is, our employers don't know whether they're hiring people illegally because there's a whole forgery industry around people being smuggled into the United States. There's a smuggling industry and a forgering industry. And it's hard to ask our employers, the onion guy out there, whether or not he's got—whether or not the documents that he's being shown which look real are real.

And so here's a better proposal than what we're doing today, which is to say, if you're going to come to do a job that an American won't do, you ought to be given a fool-proof card that says you can come for a limited period of time and do work in a job an American won't do. That's border security, because it means that people will be willing to come in legally with a card to do work on a limited basis and then go home. And so the agents won't be chasing people being smuggled in 18-wheelers or across the Arizona desert.

They'll be able to focus on drugs and terrorists and guns.

The fundamental question that he is referring to is, what do we do about—there's two questions—one, should we have amnesty? And the answer, in my judgment, is, no, we shouldn't have amnesty. In my judgment, granting amnesty, automatic citizenship—that's what amnesty means—would cause another 11 million people, or however many are here, to come in the hopes of becoming a United States citizen. We shouldn't have amnesty. We ought to have a program that says, you get in line like everybody else gets in line; and that if the Congress feels like there needs to be higher quotas on certain nationalities, raise the quotas. But don't let people get in front of the line for somebody who has been playing by the rules.

And so—anyway, that's my ideas on good immigration policy. Obviously, there's going to be some questions we have to answer: What about the person who's been here since 1987—'86 was the last attempt at coming up with immigration reform—been here for a long period of time? They've raised a family here. And my only advice for the Congress and for people in the debate is, understand what made America. We're a land of immigrants. This guy is from Hungary, you know. And we got to treat people fairly. We've got to have a system of law that is respectful for people.

I mean, the idea of having a program that causes people to get stuck in the back of 18-wheelers, to risk their lives to sneak into America to do work that some people won't do, is just not American, in my judgment. And so I would hope the debate would be civil and uphold the honor of this country. And remember, we've been through these periods before, where the immigration debate can get harsh. And it should not be harsh. And I hope—my call for people is to be rational about the debate and thoughtful about what words can mean during this debate.

Final question, sir. You're paying me a lot of money, and I got to go back to work. [*Laughter*]

Iran

Q. My name is Jose Feliciano.

The President. No.

Q. Yes, it is. [*Laughter*]

The President. Yes—it's like the time I called a guy and said, "Hey, this is George Bush calling." He said, "Come on, quit kidding me, man." [*Laughter*] *Que, Jose? Que quiere decir?*

Q. [*Inaudible*] [*Laughter*]

The President. That's right.

Q. And, actually, I'm chairman of the Hispanic Roundtable—I was going to ask you that same question. However, I'm going to ask you a simple one now, and this relates to preemptive self-defense. How is it, Mr. President, that Iran today is really different from what Iraq was 3 years ago?

The President. Well, first of all, there were 16 Security Council resolutions. The world had spoken with a clear voice, not one time; I think 16—is that right, Stretch [Richard Keil, Bloomberg News], 16? I'm asking a member of the press corps. I like to, like, reverse roles sometimes. [*Laughter*]. Really checking to see if they're paying attention, you know. [*Laughter*] Halfway through, they kind of start dozing off. [*Laughter*]

But the world had spoken by a lot against Saddam Hussein. There was a diplomatic process. You might remember that the Congress, I think in '98, voted a resolution that there should be regime change. My predecessor looked at the same intelligence I looked at and saw a threat. But the difference—one difference was that in Iraq, there was a series of unanimous resolutions that basically held the Iraqi Government to account, which Saddam Hussein ignored. It was, like, resolution after resolution after resolution.

The Iranian issue is just beginning to play out. And my hope, of course, is, as I said earlier, that we're able to solve this issue diplomatically. It's very important that the United States work with our allies—in this case, the lead group of negotiators has been Germany, France, and Great Britain—so that the Iranians hear a unified voice.

Now, the voice sometimes—I mean, if you're one—you're negotiators, probably got some lawyers here who are good negotiators—it's easier to negotiate one person versus six. I'm not suggesting you're a lawyer, you know, but I kind of had the feeling you might have been. [*Laughter*]

And so it's very important for us to continue to make sure that they hear one voice. Nontransparent societies have got an advantage over those of us who are transparent, where every move is in the press, every opinion is aired out. And so it's very important for us to work to make sure that they hear the one voice. Now, you might have read in the newspapers where our Ambassador in Iraq, Zal, has reached out to the Iranians to make it clear to them about our concerns about involvement in Iraq—Iranian involvement in Iraq. It's very important, however for the Iranians to understand that the discussion is limited to Iraq. We feel like they need to know our position.

Ultimately, Iraq-Iranian relations will be negotiated between the Iraqi Government and the Iranian Government. Ours is just—we're using this as an opportunity to make it clear about our concerns of interference within a process that is—a democratic process that is evolving. Our position is still very clearly that the Iraqis—Iranians should not have a program to build a nuclear weapon, and/or the capacity, the knowledge necessary to build something which could lead to a nuclear weapon. And we're working closely with our allies and friends to continue to make that clear to them.

So the issues are different. The issues are different stages of diplomacy.

Listen, I've enjoyed this. I hope you have as well. God bless.

NOTE: The President spoke at 12:25 p.m. at the Renaissance Cleveland Hotel. In his remarks, he referred to Sanjiv K. Kapur, president, City Club of Cleveland; Mayor Frank G. Jackson of Cleveland, OH; senior Al Qaida associate Abu Musab Al Zarqawi; former President Saddam Hussein of Iraq; Prime Minister Junichiro Koizumi of Japan; Secretary General Jakob Gijsbert "Jaap" de Hoop Scheffer of the North Atlantic Treaty Organization; President Pervez Musharraf of Pakistan; former Secretary of State Colin L. Powell; and former Prime Minister Atal Bihari Vajpayee and Prime Minister Manmohan Singh of India. The Office of the Press Secretary also released a Spanish language transcript of these remarks.

Message on the Observance of Nowruz
March 20, 2006

I send greetings to those celebrating Nowruz.

Nowruz is an ancient celebration marking the arrival of the New Year. For millions of people around the world who trace their heritage to Iran, Iraq, Afghanistan, Turkey, Pakistan, India, and Central Asia, Nowruz is a celebration of life and an opportunity to express joy and happiness through visiting family and friends, exchanging gifts, and enjoying the beauty of nature.

Our Nation is blessed by the traditions and contributions of Americans of many different backgrounds. Our diversity has made us stronger and better, and Laura and I send warm regards to all Americans celebrating Nowruz.

Best wishes for peace and prosperity in the New Year.

NOTE: An original was not available for verification of the content of this message.

The President's News Conference
March 21, 2006

The President. Good morning. Yesterday I delivered a—the second in a series of speeches on the situation in Iraq. I spoke about the violence that the Iraqi people had faced since last month's bombing of the Golden Mosque in Samarra. I also said that for every act of violence there is encouraging progress in Iraq that's hard to capture on the evening news.

Yesterday I spoke about an important example of the gains we and the Iraqis have made, and that is in the northern city of Tall 'Afar. The city was once under Al Qaida control, and thanks to coalition and Iraqi forces, the terrorists have now been driven out of that city. Iraqi security forces are maintaining law and order. We see the outlines of a free and secure Iraq that we and the Iraqi people have been fighting for. As we mark the third anniversary of the launch of Operation Iraqi Freedom, the success we're seeing in Tall 'Afar gives me confidence in the future of Iraq.

Terrorists haven't given up; they're tough-minded; they like to kill. There's going to be more tough fighting ahead. No question that sectarian violence must be confronted by the Iraqi Government and a better trained police force. Yet we're making progress, and that's important for the American people to understand.

We're making progress because of—we've got a strategy for victory, and we're making progress because the men and women of the United States military are showing magnificent courage, and they're making important sacrifices that have brought Iraq to an historic moment—the opportunity to build a democracy that reflects its country's diversity, that serves its people, and is an active partner in the fight against the terrorists.

Now Iraq's leaders must take advantage of the opportunity. I was encouraged by the announcement Sunday the Iraqi leaders—that the Iraqi leaders made—are making progress toward a council that gives each of the country's main political factions a voice in making security and economic policies. It's an indicator that Iraq's leaders understand the importance of a government of national unity. Our Ambassador to Iraq, Zal Khalilzad, is very much involved in the process and will encourage the Iraqi leaders to put aside their differences, reach out across sectarian lines, and form a unity government.

Here at home, I'm also encouraged by the strength of our economy. Last year, our economy grew at a healthy 3.5 percent. Over the past 2½ years, the economy has added nearly 5 million new jobs; that's more than Japan and the 25 nations of the European Union combined. The national unemployment rate is 4.8 percent; that's lower than the average rate of the 1970s, the 1980s, and the 1990s. Productivity is strong; inflation is contained. Household net worth is at an alltime high. Real after-tax income is up more than 8 percent per person since the beginning of 2001. The growing economy is a result of the hard work of the American people and good policies here in Washington.

I believe America prospers when people are allowed to keep more of what they earn so they can make their own decisions about how to spend, save, and invest. So I'm going to continue to work with Congress to make the tax relief permanent,

continue to work with Congress to restrain Federal spending, continue to work with Congress to achieve the goal of cutting the deficit in half by 2009.

We cannot take our growing economy for granted, and so I look forward to working with the Congress to make sure we invest in basic research and promote math and science education. I'm going to work with Congress to reduce our dependence on foreign oil. I know it came as a surprise to some of you that I would stand up in front of the Congress and say, "We got a problem; we're addicted to oil." But it is a problem. And I look forward to working with both Republicans and Democrats to advance an agenda that will make us less dependent on foreign oil, an agenda that includes hybrid cars, advanced ethanol fuels, and hydrogen cells. I'm going to look forward to working with Congress to make sure health care is affordable and available.

We're going to work with Congress to make sure we meet our commitments to our fellow citizens who are affected by Katrina. I appreciate the step that the House of Representatives took last week on passing a supplemental appropriations bill that funds gulf coast reconstruction and, of course, supports our men and women in uniform. I look forward to working with the Senate to get that supplemental bill passed and to my desk.

Now I'll be glad to take any questions you have, starting with AP person [Terence Hunt, Associated Press]. [*Laughter*]

Progress in Iraq

Q. Thank you, Mr. President.

The President. That would be you, Terry.

Q. Iraq's Interim Prime Minister said Sunday that violence is killing an average of 50 to 60 people a day and that "if this is not civil war, then God knows what civil war is." Do you agree with Mr. Allawi that Iraq has fallen into civil war?

The President. I do not. There are other voices coming out of Iraq, by the way, other than Mr. Allawi—who I know, by the way, and like; he's a good fellow. President Talabani has spoken. General Casey, the other day, was quite eloquent on the subject—Zal Khalilzad, who I talk to quite frequently. Listen, we all recognize that there is violence, that there's sectarian violence. But the way I look at the situation is that the Iraqis took a look and decided not to go to civil war.

A couple of indicators are that the army didn't bust up into sectarian divisions. The army stayed united. And as General Casey pointed out, they did, arguably, a good job in helping to make sure the country stayed united.

Secondly, I was pleased to see religious leaders stand up. Ayatollah Sistani, for example, was very clear in his denunciation of violence and the need for the country to remain united. The political leaders who represent different factions of the Iraqi society have committed themselves to moving forward on a unity government.

No question that the enemy has tried to spread sectarian violence; they use violence as a tool to do that. They're willing to kill innocent people. The reports of bound Sunnis that were executed are horrific. And it's obviously something we're going to have to deal with. And more importantly, the Iraqis are going to have to deal with it.

But I see progress. I've heard people say, "Oh, he's just kind of optimistic for the sake of optimism." Well, look, I believe we're going to succeed. And I understand how tough it is—don't get me wrong—I mean, you make it abundantly clear how tough it is. I hear it from our troops; I read the reports every night. But I believe the Iraqis—this is a moment where the Iraqis had a chance to fall apart, and they didn't. And that's a positive development.

Steve [Steve Holland, Reuters].

Iran

Q. Thank you. You describe Iran as a threat, yet, you're close to opening talks with them about Iraq. What would be the objective in these talks if they are not negotiations? And is there a risk of getting drawn into the nuclear issue?

The President. Thanks for asking that question. A couple of months ago, I gave Zal, our Ambassador in Iraq, permission to explain to the Iraqi—Iranians what we didn't like about their involvement in Iraq. I thought it was important for them to hear firsthand, other than through press accounts. He asked whether or not it made sense for him to be able to talk to a representative in Baghdad. I said, "Absolutely. You make it clear to them that attempts to spread sectarian violence, or to maybe move parts that could be used for IEDs is unacceptable to the United States."

It is very important for the Iranians to understand that any relationship between Iraq and Iran will be negotiated between those two countries. Iraq is a sovereign government. They have a foreign policy. And when they get their unity government stepped up, they will be in charge of negotiating with the Iranians their foreign policy arrangement. And so this is a way for us to make it clear to them that—about what's right or wrong in their activities inside of Iraq.

Secondly, our negotiations with Iran on the nuclear weapons will be led by the EU–3. And that's important because the Iranians must hear there's a unified voice about—that says that they shall not have a capacity to make a nuclear weapon and/or the knowledge as to how to make a nuclear weapon, for the sake of security of the world.

It's important for our citizens to understand that we have got to deal with this issue diplomatically now. And the reason why is because if the Iranians were to have a nuclear weapon, they could blackmail the world. If the Iranians were to have a nuclear weapon, they could proliferate. This is a country that's walking away from international accords; they're not heading toward the international accords; they're not welcoming the international inspections—

or safeguards—safeguard measures that they had agreed to.

And so our policy for the Iranians, in terms of the nuclear program, is to continue to work with the EU–3, as well as Russia and China. Later on this week, there's going to be a P–5—that's a diplomatic sloganeering for the permanent members of the Security Council plus Germany—and working together to make sure that the message remains unified and concerted.

If you're a nontransparent society, you've got a negotiating advantage over six parties, because all you have to do is kind of try to find a—the weakest link in the negotiating team. And so our job is to make sure that this international will remains strong and united, so that we can solve this issue diplomatically.

Helen [Helen Thomas, Hearst Newspapers]. After that brilliant performance at the Gridiron, I am——

War on Terror

Q. You're going to be sorry. [*Laughter*]

The President. Well, then, let me take it back. [*Laughter*]

Q. I'd like to ask you, Mr. President, your decision to invade Iraq has caused the deaths of thousands of Americans and Iraqis, wounds of Americans and Iraqis for a lifetime. Every reason given, publicly at least, has turned out not to be true. My question is, why did you really want to go to war? From the moment you stepped into the White House, from your Cabinet officers, intelligence people, and so forth—what was your real reason? You have said it wasn't oil, quest for oil—it hasn't been Israel, or anything else. What was it?

The President. I think your premise—in all due respect to your question and to you as a lifelong journalist—is that—I didn't want war. To assume I wanted war is just flat wrong, Helen, in all due respect——

Q. Everything——

The President. Hold on for a second, please.

Q. ——everything I've heard——

The President. Excuse me, excuse me. No President wants war. Everything you may have heard is that, but it's just simply not true. My attitude about the defense of this country changed on September the 11th. We—when we got attacked, I vowed then and there to use every asset at my disposal to protect the American people.

Our foreign policy changed on that day, Helen. You know, we used to think we were secure because of oceans and previous diplomacy. But we realized on September the 11th, 2001, that killers could destroy innocent life. And I'm never going to forget it. And I'm never going to forget the vow I made to the American people that we will do everything in our power to protect our people.

Part of that meant to make sure that we didn't allow people to provide safe haven to an enemy. And that's why I went into Iraq—hold on for a second——

Q. They didn't do anything to you or to our country.

The President. Look—excuse me for a second, please. Excuse me for a second. They did. The Taliban provided safe haven for Al Qaida. That's where Al Qaida trained——

Q. I'm talking about Iraq——

The President. Helen, excuse me. That's where—Afghanistan provided safe haven for Al Qaida. That's where they trained. That's where they plotted. That's where they planned the attacks that killed thousands of innocent Americans.

I also saw a threat in Iraq. I was hoping to solve this problem diplomatically. That's why I went to the Security Council; that's why it was important to pass 1441, which was unanimously passed. And the world said, "Disarm, disclose, or face serious consequences"——

Q. ——go to war——

The President. ——and therefore, we worked with the world, we worked to make sure that Saddam Hussein heard the message of the world. And when he chose to deny inspectors, when he chose not to disclose, then I had the difficult decision to make to remove him. And we did, and the world is safer for it.

Q. Thank you, sir. Secretary Rumsfeld——

Q. Thank you. [*Laughter*].

The President. You're welcome. [*Laughter*] I didn't really regret it. I kind of semi-regretted it. [*Laughter*]

Q. ——have a debate.

The President. That's right. Anyway, your performance at the Gridiron was just brilliant—unlike Holland's, was a little weak, but—[*laughter*].

Sorry.

Progress in Iraq

Q. Secretary Rumsfeld has said that if civil war should break out in Iraq, he's hopeful that Iraqi forces can handle it. If they can't, sir, are you willing to sacrifice American lives to keep Iraqis from killing one another?

The President. I think the first step is to make sure a civil war doesn't break out. And that's why we're working with the leaders there in Baghdad to form a unity government. Obviously, if there is difficulty on the streets, the first line of defense for that difficulty will be the Iraqi forces, which have proved themselves in the face of potential sectarian violence—right after the bombing of the mosque in Samarra. The forces are—part of our strategy for victory is to get the forces the skills and the tools and the training necessary to defend their own country, whether it be against Zarqawi and the killers, or whether it be those who are trying to spread sectarian violence. And they have proven themselves.

And so our position is, one, get a unity government formed, and secondly, prepare the Iraqi troops, and support Iraqi troops, if need be, to prevent sectarian violence from breaking out.

Yes, sir.

War on Terror

Q. Mr. President, I'd like to ask you for your reaction on the latest insurgent attack in Baghdad, 17 police officers killed and a bunch of insurgents freed. I spent a fair amount of time in front of that hotel in Cleveland yesterday, talking to people about the war and saying you were there to talk optimistically. And one woman who said she voted for you, said, "You know what, he's losing me. We've been there too long; he's losing me." What do you say to her?

The President. I say that I'm talking realistically to people. We have a plan for victory, and it's important we achieve that plan. Democracy—first of all, this is a global war on terror, and Iraq is a part of the war on terror. Mr. Zarqawi and Al Qaida, the very same people that attacked the United States, have made it clear that they want to drive us out of Iraq so they can plan, plot, and attack America again. That's what they have said; that's their objective. I think it is very important to have a President who is realistic and listens to what the enemy says.

Secondly, I am confident, or I believe—I'm optimistic we'll succeed. If not, I'd pull our troops out. If I didn't believe we had a plan for victory, I wouldn't leave our people in harm's way. And that's important for the woman to understand.

Thirdly, in spite of the bad news on television—and there is bad news. You brought it up; you said, how do I react to a bombing that took place yesterday—is precisely what the enemy understands is possible to do. I'm not suggesting you shouldn't talk about it. I'm certainly not being—please don't take that as criticism. But it also is a realistic assessment of the enemy's capability to affect the debate, and they know that. They're capable of blowing up innocent life so it ends up on your TV show. And therefore, it affects the woman in Cleveland you were talking to. And I can understand how Americans are worried about whether or not we can win.

I think most Americans understand we need to win, but they're concerned about whether or not we can win. So one of the reasons I go around the country, to Cleveland, is to explain why I think we can win. And so I would say, yes, I'm optimistic about being able to achieve a victory, but I'm also realistic. I fully understand the consequences of this war. I understand people's lives are being lost. But I also understand the consequences of not achieving our objective by leaving too early. Iraq would become a place of instability, a place from which the enemy can plot, plan, and attack.

I believe that they want to hurt us again. And therefore, I know we need to stay on the offense against this enemy. They've declared Iraq to be the central front, and therefore, we've got to make sure we win that. And I believe we will.

Please.

White House Staff

Q. Good morning, sir. Mindful of the frustrations that many Americans are expressing to you, do you believe you need to make any adjustments in how you run the White House? Many of your senior staffers have been with you from the beginning. There are some in Washington who say——

The President. Wait a minute. Is this a personal attack launching over here? [*Laughter*]

Q. Some say they are tired and even tone-deaf, even within your party who say that maybe you need some changes. Would you benefit from any changes to your staff?

The President. I've got a staff of people that have, first of all, placed their country above their self-interests. These are good, hard-working, decent people. And we've dealt with a lot; we've dealt with a lot. We've dealt with war; we've dealt with recession; we've dealt with scandal; we've dealt with Katrina. I mean, they had a lot

on their plate. And I appreciate their performance and their hard work, and they've got my confidence.

And I understand—Washington is a great town for advice. I get a lot of it—sometimes in private, from my friends, and sometimes in public. There are those who like to stand up and say to the President, "Here's what you ought to be doing." And I understand that. This isn't the first time during these 5½ years that people have felt comfortable about standing up, telling me what to do. And that's okay. I take it all in and appreciate the spirit in which it's delivered, most of the time. But—no, look, I'm satisfied with the people I've surrounded myself with. We've been a remarkably stable administration. And I think that's good for the country.

Obviously, there's some times when government bureaucracies haven't responded the way we wanted them to. And like citizens, I don't like that at all. I mean, I think, for example, of the trailers sitting down in Arkansas. Like many citizens, they're wondering why they're down there. How come we got 11,000? So I've asked Chertoff to find out, what are you going to do with them? The taxpayers aren't interested in 11,000 trailers just sitting there; do something with them.

And so I share that sense of frustration when a big government is unable to—sends wrong signals to taxpayers. But our people are good, hard-working people.

Elisabeth [Elisabeth Bumiller, New York Times].

Second-Term Agenda

Q. Can I just follow up on that?

The President. Sure.

Q. But aside from staff, Mr. President, are you listening to suggestions you bring somebody else into the White House, a wise man, a graybeard, some old-time Washington hand who can steady Congress if they're upset about things, Republicans in Congress?

The President. I'm listening to all suggestions. I really am. I mean, I'm listening to Congress. We're bringing Congress down here all the time. And it's interesting to hear their observations. They—they're, obviously, expressing concerns. It's an election year, after all. And it seems like history tends to repeat itself when you're in the White House. I can remember '02 before the elections; there was a certain nervousness. There was a lot of people in Congress who weren't sure I was going to make it in '04, and whether or not I'd drag the ticket down. So there's a certain unease as you head into an election year; I understand that.

My message to them is, please continue to give me advice and suggestions. And I take their advice seriously. But also remember we've got a positive agenda. We've got something to do. It's important for Congress to have confidence in our ability to get things done. We're supporting our troops over the last 12 months. We've got two Supreme Court judges confirmed. We've got the PATRIOT Act reauthorized over the objections of the Democrat leadership in the Senate. We got some tort reform passed. We passed a budget that cut nonsecurity discretionary spending. There's a series of—we got an energy bill passed. We worked to get a lot of positive things done. And now we've got an agenda—continue to keep this economy growing and keep this Nation competitive.

I meant what I said in my speech: We shouldn't fear this future. In other words, we shouldn't allow isolationism and protectionism to overwhelm us. We ought to be confident about our ability to shape the future.

And that's why this Competitiveness Initiative is important. That's why this energy plan that gets us less addicted to oil is important. We got some interesting ideas on health care that we need to continue to press to make sure consumers are actually a part of the decisionmaking process when it comes to health care decisions.

We've got an aggressive agenda that, by working together, will get passed. But I do, I listen.

Yes, Jim [Jim Gerstenzang, Los Angeles Times].

War on Terror/Polls

Q. ——new guy? No new guy?

The President. Well, I'm not going to announce it right now. Look, they've got some ideas that I like and some I don't like. Put it that way.

Q. You've said during your Presidency that you don't pay that much attention to the polls, but——

The President. Correct.

Q. ——there is a handful that have come back, and they all say the exact same thing: A growing number of Americans are questioning the trustworthiness of you and this White House. Does that concern you?

The President. I believe that my job is to go out and explain to people what's on my mind. That's why I'm having this press conference, see. I'm telling you what's on my mind. And what's on my mind is winning the war on terror. And I understand war creates concerns, Jim. Nobody likes war. It creates a sense of uncertainty in the country. The person you talked to in Cleveland is uncertain about our ability to go forward. She's uncertain about whether or not we can succeed, and I understand that. War creates trauma, particularly when you're fighting an enemy that doesn't fight soldier to soldier. They fight by using IEDs to kill innocent people. That's what they use. That's the tool they use. And it creates a sense of concern amongst our people, and that makes sense, and I know that.

And one of the reasons why it's important for me to continue to speak out and explain why we have a strategy for victory, why we can succeed—and I'm going to say it again—if I didn't believe we could succeed, I wouldn't be there. I wouldn't put those kids there. I meet with too many families who's lost a loved one to not be able to look them in the eye and say, we're doing the right thing. And we are doing the right thing. A democracy in Iraq is going to affect the neighborhood. A democracy in Iraq is going to inspire reformers in a part of the world that is desperate for reformation.

Our foreign policy up to now was to kind of tolerate what appeared to be calm. And underneath the surface was this swelling sense of anxiety and resentment, out of which came this totalitarian movement that is willing to spread its propaganda through death and destruction, to spread its philosophy. Now, some in this country don't— I can understand—don't view the enemy that way. I guess they kind of view it as an isolated group of people that occasionally kill. I just don't see it that way. I see them bound by a philosophy with plans and tactics to impose their will on other countries.

The enemy has said that it's just a matter of time before the United States loses its nerve and withdraws from Iraq. That's what they have said. And their objective for driving us out of Iraq is to have a place from which to launch their campaign to overthrow modern governments—moderate governments—in the Middle East, as well as to continue attacking places like the United States. Now, maybe some discount those words as kind of meaningless propaganda. I don't, Jim. I take them really seriously. And I think everybody in government should take them seriously and respond accordingly. And so it's—I've got to continue to speak as clearly as I possibly can about the consequences of success and the consequences of failure and why I believe we can succeed.

Defense Secretary Rumsfeld/Progress in Iraq

Q. Mr. President, Kathleen Koch, CNN. *The President.* Yes.

Q. You said you listen to Members of Congress, and there have been growing calls from some of those Members for the resignation of Defense Secretary Donald Rumsfeld; also from his own former subordinates like U.S. Army Major General Paul Eaton, who described him in a recent editorial as "incompetent and tactically inept." Do you feel that personally you've ever gotten bad advice in the conduct of the war in Iraq? And do you believe Rumsfeld should resign?

The President. No, I don't believe he should resign. I think he's done a fine job of not only conducting two battles, Afghanistan and Iraq, but also transforming our military, which has been a very difficult job inside the Pentagon.

Listen, every war plan looks good on paper until you meet the enemy—not just the war plan we executed in Iraq but the war plans that have been executed throughout the history of warfare. In other words, the enemy changes tactics, and we've got to change tactics too.

And no question that we've had to adjust our tactics on the ground. And perhaps the clearest example is in the training of Iraqi security forces. When we got into Iraq, we felt like we needed to train a security force that was capable for defending the country from an outside threat. And then it became apparent that the insurgents and Zarqawi were able to spread their poison and their violence in a ruthless way, and therefore, we had to make sure that the Iraqi forces were able to deal with the internal threat. And we adjusted our tactics and started spending a lot more time getting the Iraqis up and running, and then embedding our troops with the Iraqis.

And it has been a success. But no question about it, we missed some time as we adjusted our tactics. We had to change our reconstruction strategy. We were—we thought it made sense, initially, when we went in there to build big, grand projects, which turned out to be targets for the insurgents to blow up. And a better strategy was to be spending reconstruction money at the local level, so that local leaders committed to a peaceful and unified Iraq would benefit. In other words, people would see tangible benefits from an emerging democracy, and the leaders would be viewed as people helping to improve their lives.

And so this is a war in which we've changed tactics. It's a war in which we've adjusted and learned lessons in the process of the war.

Yes, sir.

Social Security Reform

Q. Just after the 2004 election, you seemed to—you claimed a really enviable balance of political capital and a strong mandate. Would you make that claim today? Do you still have that?

The President. I'd say I'm spending that capital on the war.

Q. Well, is that costing you elsewhere, then?

The President. I don't think so. I just named 12—I just named an agenda that over the last 12 month was—would be, I suspect, if looked at objectively, would say, well, they got a lot done. And I'd be glad to repeat them if you like, which is— [*laughter*].

Q. ——Social Security——

The President. Wait a minute. Please no hand gestures. [*Laughter*]

Social Security—it didn't get done. You notice it wasn't on the list. [*Laughter*] Let me talk about that, if you don't mind. First of all, Social Security is a really difficult issue for some Members of Congress to deal with because it is fraught with all kind of political peril. As a matter of fact, it's been difficult for a lot of Congresses to deal with. The one time in recent memory that it was dealt with was when there was a near crisis—in other words, when the system was about to fall into the abyss, and people came together and solved it. But they thought it was a fairly long-term fix; it turned out to be a lot shorter fix than they thought.

So I'm disappointed Congress didn't want to go forward with it, but I'm not surprised. Therefore, I tried a new tactic. Last year, the tactic was to believe that once the people saw there was a problem, they would then demand a solution. And we made progress on describing the problem. I think the American people are now beginning to get the picture that if we don't do something, Social Security and Medicare will bust. If we don't do something, future Congresses—not this Congress, but future Congresses—are going to be confronted with some serious decisions about raising taxes enormously or cutting benefits drastically—or other programs drastically.

And so that issue sunk in. Just that—there wasn't that connection with action inside, in the body of the respective chambers—although, there were some noble efforts made by some Members of Congress to get something started.

So the new tactics to get people involved in this process is to try to take the politics out of it and bring members of both parties, both chambers together. There's quiet consultations going on to get this commission—committee together of members that could get something put in place that would have a bipartisan appeal to it. Bipartisanship is hard to achieve in Washington these days. I readily concede that. Yet this issue is one that's going to require a bipartisan approach. It's simply not going to be an issue where one party, without the cooperation of the other party, kind of tries to move a bill. At least, that's how I view it.

But I'm committed to moving the issue. I think it's important. And I'm not deterred by the fact that nothing happened. As a matter of fact, I take great pride in the fact that I was willing to bring up the issue while others might not have. That's the job of the President. The job of the President is not to worry about the short-term attitudes. The job of the President is to confront big issues and to bring them to the front and to say to people, "Let's work together to get it solved." And I'm going to continue working on it.

Carl [Carl Cameron, FOX News].

Terrorist Surveillance Program

Q. Thank you, sir. On the subject of the terrorist surveillance program——

The President. Yes.

Q. ——not to change the tone from all this emphasis on bipartisanship, but there have been now three sponsors to a measure to censure you for the implementation of that program. The primary sponsor, Russ Feingold, has suggested that impeachment is not out of the question. And on Sunday, the number-two Democrat in the Senate refused to rule that out, pending an investigation. What, sir, do you think the impact of the discussion of impeachment and censure does to you and this office and to the Nation during a time of war and in the context of the election?

The President. I think during these difficult times—and they are difficult when we're at war—the American people expect there to be a honest and open debate without needless partisanship. And that's how I view it. I did notice that nobody from the Democrat Party has actually stood up and called for getting rid of the terrorist surveillance program. You know, if that's what they believe, if people in the party believe that, then they ought to stand up and say it. They ought to stand up and say, the tools we're using to protect the American people shouldn't be used. They ought to take their message to the people and say, "Vote for me; I promise we're not going to have a terrorist surveillance program." That's what they ought to be doing. That's part of what is an open and honest debate.

I did notice that, at one point in time, they didn't think the PATRIOT Act ought to be reauthorized—"they" being at least the minority leader in the Senate. He openly said, as I understand—I don't want to misquote him—something along the lines that, "We killed the PATRIOT Act." And if that's what the party believes, they ought to go around the country saying, "We shouldn't give the people on the frontline

of protecting us the tools necessary to do so." That's a debate I think the country ought to have.

Yes, sir.

Progress in Iraq

Q. You mentioned earlier that you were encouraged by some of the discussions going on over a unity government, over the last few days. Do you now have in mind a target date for forming the unity government and——

The President. As soon as possible. Next question.

Public Opinion/Progress in Iraq

Q. How much of a factor do you think that will be, if it's achieved, in turning around, or at least improving the situation in the public opinion?

The President. Here in America?

Q. Right.

The President. That's a trick question, because you want to get me to talk about polls when I don't pay attention to polls.

Q. That was one——

The President. At least that's—after 5½ years, I was able to rout you out. [*Laughter*]

First of all, I have no idea whether or not a—how Americans are going to react to a unity government. There will be a unity government formed; then there could be an attack the next day. And so it's hard for me to predict. I do know a unity government, though, is necessary for us to achieve our objective. I do know that the Iraqi people—11 million of them—voted in an election in December, which was, like, 4 months ago. And the message I received from—that is, I hope, the same message that those who have been in charge with forming a unity government receive, and that is the people have spoken, and they want democracy. That's what they said. Otherwise, they wouldn't have participated. They expect there to be a democracy in place that listens to their demands.

And so I'm—most importantly, I believe a unity government will begin to affect the attitudes of the Iraqis. And that's important for them to get confidence not only in a government but in a security force that will provide them security. It's—confidence amongst the Iraqis is what is going to be a vital part of achieving a victory, which will then enable the American people to understand that victory is possible. In other words, the American people will—their opinions, I suspect, will be affected by what they see on their TV screens. The unity government will affect, first and foremost, the Iraqi people, and that's a very important part of achieving success.

We do have a plan for victory, and victory is clearly stated, and that is that Iraq is not a—becomes a safe haven. And that's important for the American people, that Iraq not be a safe haven for terrorists. Their stated objective is to turn Iraq into a safe haven from which they can launch attacks.

Secondly, part of the plan for victory is for there to be security forces capable of defending and providing security to the Iraqi citizens. And thirdly, that democracy, the government take root to the extent that it can't be overturned by those who want to stop democracy from taking hold in Iraq. These are clear objectives, and they're achievable objectives.

Okay. Mark [Mark Silva, Chicago Tribune].

Deficit Spending

Q. Mr. President, in the upcoming elections, I think many Republicans would tell you one of the big things they're worried about is the national debt, which was $5.7 trillion when you took office and is now nearly $8.2 trillion, and Congress has just voted to raise it to $8.9 trillion. That would be a 58-percent increase. You've yet to veto a single bill, sir—I assume that means you're satisfied with this.

The President. No, I'm not satisfied with the rise of mandatory spending. As you know, the President doesn't have the—doesn't veto mandatory spending increases. And mandatory spending increases are those increases in the budget caused by increases in spending on Medicare and Social Security. And that's why—back to this man's question right here—it's important for—"this man" being Jim—[*laughter*]—sorry, Jim, I've got a lot on my mind these days. That's why it's important for us to modernize and strengthen Social Security and Medicare, in order to be able to deal with the increases in mandatory spending.

Secondly, in terms of discretionary spending, that part of the budget over which Congress has got some control and over which the President can make suggestions, we have suggested that the Congress fully fund the troops in harm's way. And they have, and for that the American people should be grateful.

Secondly, we suggested that Congress fund the reconstruction efforts for Katrina. They have spent now a little more than $100 billion, and I think that's money well-spent, a commitment that needed to be kept.

Thirdly, we have said that other than security discretionary spending, that we ought to, last year, actually reduce the amount of discretionary spending and were able to do so. Ever since I've been the President, we have slowed the rate of growth of non-security discretionary spending and actually cut discretionary spending—nonsecurity discretionary spending.

Last year, I submitted a budget to the United States Congress. I would hope they would meet the targets of the budget that I submitted, in order to continue to make a commitment to the American people. But in terms of the debt, mandatory spending increases is driving a lot of that debt. And that's why it's important to get the reforms done.

National Economy/Line-Item Veto Legislation

Q. Thank you, sir. For the first time in years, interest rates are rising in the U.S., Europe, and Japan at the same time. Is this a concern for you? And how much strain are higher interest rates placing on consumers and companies?

The President. First of all, interest rates are set by an independent organization, which——

Q. ——still, are you concerned about that?

The President. Well, I'm not quite through with my answer yet.

Q. I'm sorry.

The President. I'm kind of stalling for time here. [*Laughter*] Interest rates are set by the independent organization. I can only tell you that the economy of the United States looks very strong. And the reason I say that is that projections for first-quarter growth of this year look pretty decent. That's just projections, that's a guess by some economists, and until the actual numbers come out, we won't know. But no question that the job market is strong. When you have 4.8 percent unemployment—4.8 percent nationwide unemployment, that indicates a strong job market, and that's very important.

One of the measures as to whether or not this economy will remain strong is productivity. And our productivity of the American worker and productivity of the American business sector is rising. And that's positive, because productivity increases eventually yield—eventually yield higher standards of living. Homeownership is at an alltime high. And there has been all kinds of speculation about whether or not homeownership would—home building would remain strong, and it appears to be steady. And that's important.

In other words—and so to answer your question, I feel—without getting into kind of the—kind of microeconomics, from my perch and my perspective, the economy appears to be strong and getting stronger. And the fundamental question that those of us in Washington have to answer is, what do we do to keep it that way? How do we make sure, one, we don't put bad policies in place that will hurt economic growth? A bad policy is to raise taxes—which some want to do. There are people in the United States Congress, primarily on the Democrat side, that would be anxious to let some of the tax relief expire. Some of them actually want to raise taxes now. I think raising taxes would be wrong. As a matter of fact, that's why—and I think it's important for us to have certainty in the Tax Code. That's why I'd like to see the tax relief made permanent.

You know, it's a myth in Washington—for Washington people to go around the country saying, "Well, we'll balance the budget; just let us raise taxes." That's not how Washington works. Washington works—raise in taxes, and they figure out new ways to spend. There is a huge appetite for spending here. One way to help cure that appetite is to give me the line-item veto. You mentioned vetoing of bills—one reason why I haven't vetoed any appropriation bills is because they met the benchmarks we've set. They have—on the discretionary spending, we've said, "Here is the budget." We've agreed to a number, and they met those numbers.

Now, sometimes I didn't—I like the size of the pie; sometimes I didn't particularly like the slices within the pie. And so one way to deal with the slices in the pie is to give the President the line-item veto. And I was heartened the other day when members of both parties came down in the Cabinet Room to talk about passage of a line-item veto. I was particularly pleased that my opponent in the 2004 campaign, Senator Kerry, graciously came down and lent his support to a line-item veto and also made very constructive suggestions about how to get one out of the United States Congress.

Let's see here. They've told me what to say. David [David Jackson, Dallas Morning News].

Spread of Democracy in the Middle East

Q. Mr. President, you've spoken about Iraq as being a beacon for democracy throughout the Middle East. Yet we've had troubles in Iraq, and we've seen aggressiveness from Syria and Iran. Are you concerned that the Iraq experience is going to embolden authoritarian regimes in the Middle East and make it tougher to forge democracy there?

The President. There's no question that if we were to prematurely withdraw and the march to democracy were to fail, the Al Qaida would be emboldened, terrorist groups would be emboldened, the Islamofascists would be emboldened. No question about that.

There are a lot of reformers in the Middle East who would like to see Iraq succeed. And I think that if we were to lose our nerve and leave prematurely, those reformers would be let down. So failure in Iraq—which isn't going to happen—is—would send all kinds of terrible signals to an enemy that wants to hurt us and people who are desperate to change the conditions in the broader Middle East.

The—it's an interesting debate, isn't it, about whether or not this country of ours ought to work to spread liberty. It's—I find it fascinating that—to listen to the voices from around the world as to whether or not it is a noble purpose to spread liberty around the world. And it is a—I think it's—at least, my position is affected by my belief that there is universality when it comes to liberty. This isn't American liberty; this isn't America's possession. Liberty is universal. People desire to be free. And history has proven that democracies don't war. And so part of the issue is to lay peace, is to give people a chance to live in a peaceful world where mothers can raise their children without fear of violence or women are free to be able to express themselves.

Q. But how about the difficulty——

The President. Excuse me a second, David. Excuse me for a second, please.

The—that we ought to pursue liberty. We ought to not be worried about a foreign policy that encourages others to be free. That's why I said in my second Inauguration Address, "The goal of this country ought to be to end tyranny in the 21st century." I meant it. For the sake of—I said that for the sake of peace.

Now, what is your followup yell? [*Laughter*]

Q. I was wondering, have the difficulties of the last 3 years made the job of those reformers more difficult?

The President. Well, if the United States were to lose its nerve, it would certainly make the job of reformers more difficult. If people in Iran, for example, who desire to have a Iranian-style democracy, Iranian-style freedom, if they see us lose our nerve, it's likely to undermine their boldness and their desire.

What we're doing is difficult work. And one—the interesting thing that's happening is, is that imagine an enemy that says, "We will kill innocent people," because we're trying to encourage people to be free. What kind of mindset is it of people who say, "We must stop democracy"? Democracy is based upon this kind of universal belief that people should be free. And yet there are people willing to kill innocent life to stop it. To me, that ought to be a warning signal to people all around the world that the enemy we face is an enemy that ascribes to a vision that is dark and one that doesn't agree with the universal rights of men and women.

As a matter of fact, when given a chance to govern or to have their parasitical government represent their views, they suppressed women and children. There was no such thing as religious freedom. There was no such thing as being able to express yourself in the public square. There was no such thing as press conferences like this.

They were totalitarian in their view. And that would be—I'm referring to the Taliban, of course. And that's how they would like to run government. They rule by intimidation and fear, by death and destruction.

And the United States of America must take this threat seriously and must not—must never forget the natural rights that formed our country. And for people to say, "Well, the natural rights only exist for one group of people," I would call them—I would say that they're denying the basic rights to others.

And it is hard work. And it's hard work, David, because we're fighting tradition. We're fighting people that have said, "Well, wait a minute. The only way to have peace is for there to be tyranny." We're fighting intimidation. We're fighting the fact that people will be thrown in prison if they disagree.

Yes.

Iraq/U.S. Armed Forces

Q. Sir, you said earlier today that you believe there's a plan for success; if you did not, you would pull the troops out. And so my question is, one, is there a point at which having the American forces in Iraq becomes more a part of the problem than a part of the solution? Can you say that you will not keep American troops in there if they're caught in the crossfire in a civil war? And can you say to the American people, assure them that there will come a day when there will be no more American forces in Iraq?

The President. Bob [Bob Deans, Cox Newspapers], the decisions about our troop levels will be made by General Casey and the commanders on the ground. They're the ones who can best judge whether or not the presence of coalition troops create more of a problem than a solution—than be a part of the solution.

Secondly, I've answered the question on civil war. Our job is to make sure the civil war doesn't happen. But there will be—

but if there is sectarian violence, it's the job of the Iraqi forces, with coalition help, to separate those sectarian forces.

Third part of your question?

Q. Will there come a day—and I'm not asking you when, not asking for a timetable—will there come a day when there will be no more American forces in Iraq?

The President. That, of course, is an objective, and that will be decided by future Presidents and future governments of Iraq.

Q. So it won't happen on your watch?

The President. You mean a complete withdrawal? That's a timetable. I can only tell you that I will make decisions on force levels based upon what the commanders on the ground say.

Cannon [Carl Cannon, National Journal].

Same-Sex Marriage

Q. Mr. President——

The President. No, you're not Ken. That Ken. You're Ken [Ken Bazinet, New York Daily News]. Sorry Cannon.

Q. Thank you, sir.

The President. Sorry, you're Ken, according to the chart. You thought I said Cannon——

Q. I thought you said Ken.

The President. Bazinet. [*Laughter*]

Q. Mr. President, 2 years ago, Gavin Newsom, the mayor of San Francisco, heard your State of the Union Address, went back to California, and began authorizing the marriage of gay men and lesbians. Thousands of people got married. The California courts later ruled he had overstepped his bounds. But they were—we were left with these pictures of thousands of families getting married, and they had these children, thousands of children. Now, that might have changed the debate, but it didn't. In light of that, my question is, are you still confident that society's interest and the interest of those children in gay families are being met by government saying their parents can't marry?

The President. I believe society's interest are met by saying—defining marriage as between a man and a woman. That's what I believe.

Immigration

Q. Mr. President, on immigration, yesterday you answered a question from a woman and said, the tough question here is what happens to somebody who has been here since 1987. Will you accept a bill that allows those who have been here a long time to remain in the country permanently?

The President. I also said that—let me make sure, Stephen [Stephen Dinan, Washington Times], that you—first of all, I'm impressed that you're actually paying attention to it. The people I saw in the press pool weren't. They were—like, Elisabeth was half-asleep—[*laughter*]—yes, you were. [*Laughter*]

Q. No, I wasn't.

The President. Okay. Well, the person next to you was. [*Laughter*] They were dozing off. I could see them watching their watches, kind of wondering how long he's going to blow on for. Let's get him out of here so we can go get lunch, is what they were thinking. [*Laughter*] So at least you paid attention. Thanks.

I also went on to say that people who have been here need to get in line, like everybody else who is in line legally. My point is that if we were—first of all, whatever is passed should not say "amnesty." In my judgment, amnesty would be the wrong course of action. We have a way toward legality, in terms of citizenship. In other words, there's a difference between someone who is here legally working and someone who is a citizen. And that's part of the—I maybe didn't make that distinction perfectly clear.

This is going to be a—this could be a fractious debate, and I hope it's not. Immigration is a very difficult issue for a lot of Members, as you know. It's an emotional issue. And it's one that, if not conducted properly, will send signals that I don't think will befit the Nation's history and traditions.

My view is, is that border security starts with a good, solid strategy along the border itself—in other words, Border Patrol agents, technology, the capacity to pass information quickly so that Border Patrol agents will be more likely to intercept somebody coming across the border illegally. There needs to be enforcement mechanisms that don't discourage the Border Patrol agents. They work hard; they get somebody coming in from country X; the person says, "Check back in with us in 30 days"—they don't.

In other words, they end up in society. That has created some despondency—not despondency—it's got to discourage people who are working hard to do their job down there and realize the fruits of their labor is being undermined by a policy that, on the one hand, releases people, kind of, into society, and on the other, doesn't have enough beds to hold people so that we can repatriate them back to their countries. Chertoff has announced the fact that we're getting rid of this catch-and-release program.

Thirdly, there has to be enforcement—employer enforcement of rules and regulations. The problem there, of course, is that people are showing up with forged documents. I mentioned this onion picker that I met yesterday—onion grower—who is worried about having labor to pick his onions. But he's not—I don't think he's in a position to be able to determine whether or not what looks like a valid Social Security card, or whatever they show, is valid or not—which leads to the fact there's a whole industry that has sprung up around moving laborers to jobs that Americans won't do.

It's kind of—when you make something illegal that people want, there's a way around it, around the rules and regulations. And so you've got people, *coyotes*, stuffing people in the back of 18-wheelers or smuggling them across 105-degree desert heat. You've got forgers and tunnel-diggers. You've got a whole industry aimed at using people as a commodity. And it's wrong, and it needs to be—we need to do something about it. And the best way to do something about it is to say that if you're—if an American won't do a job and you can find somebody who will do the job, they ought to be allowed to do it legally, on a temporary basis.

One of the issues I did talk about—the man asked me the question about—don't let people get ahead of the line. So I made that clear. But one of the issues is going to be to deal with somebody whose family has been here for a while, raised a family. And that will be an interesting debate. My answer is, that person shouldn't get automatic citizenship.

Listen, thank you for your time. I've got lunch with the President of Liberia right

now. I'm looking forward to greeting this— the first woman elected on the continent of Africa. Appreciate the opportunity to visit with you all. Look forward to future occasions.

NOTE: The President's news conference began at 10:01 a.m. in the James S. Brady Press Briefing Room at the White House. In his remarks, he referred to former Prime Minister Ayad Allawi of the Iraqi Interim Government; former President Jalal Talabani of the Iraqi Transitional Government; Gen. George W. Casey, Jr., USA, commanding general, Multi-National Force—Iraq; senior Al Qaida associate Abu Musab Al Zarqawi; Grand Ayatollah Ali al-Sistani, Iraqi Shiite leader; and President Ellen Johnson Sirleaf of Liberia.

Remarks Following Discussions With President Ellen Johnson Sirleaf of Liberia
March 21, 2006

President Bush. It has been such an honor to welcome you, Madam President, to the Oval Office. I find that one of the interesting parts of my job is to be able to talk to pioneers, and Madam President, you're a pioneer. You're the first woman elected President to any country on the continent of Africa. And that requires courage and vision and the desire to improve the lives of your people. And I congratulate you on that.

You know, I can remember, it wasn't all that long ago that Laura—that would be Laura Bush—and Condi Rice came back from the inauguration of this good person. I said, "Okay, tell me what kind of person am I going to be dealing with," and they said, "Capable, smart, a person who is a doer, a person committed to a bright future for Liberia." And we welcome you.

The President and I have had a good discussion. We discussed ways that the

United States Government can help this country get on its feet toward a democracy. We talked about education. We talked about security. We talked about—we also talked about the neighborhood. I asked the President her advice on a variety of issues. I told her that part of a friendship is one in which we can speak directly with each other about how best to deal with keeping the peace and making sure that health care initiatives are robust and effective. I also shared with her some of my thoughts about the world beyond the continent of Africa. And so I—we really had a good discussion.

And so, Madam President, thank you. I want to thank your delegation. Laura and I look forward to having you for lunch here in a little bit. But all in all, I think it was a very good first visit.

President Johnson Sirleaf. Mr. President, as I mentioned to you, on behalf of the Liberian people, I would like to thank you—thank you, thank your administration, thank the American people, thank the U.S. Congress—for all the support that our country has received in making this important transition from war to peace.

Our people have new hope. They have new promise in the future as a result of the strong position you took that enabled us to get this opportunity for national renewal. We have taken the necessary first steps to restoring dignity to our people, starting to fix our economy, to get our international credibility and reputation back. And we're confident that Liberian people are ready to do what it takes. They're back at work; our country is open for business. We're beginning to put in all the processes that will enable us to manage our resources that God has been so good to us in giving us, for the good of our people.

We want you to know that Liberia is going to do all it can to justify the confidence that you have given to us. Liberia, we think, has the potential to become the U.S. success story in Africa. We'll be working within our own borders; we'll be working with our neighboring states to bring peace, stability, and development to our subregion. We'll be working with our African leaders to ensure that the example we set on this transition will be one that can fuse many of our—many of other countries and other people in Africa.

As the first democratic-elected woman, I represent the expectations and aspirations of women in Liberia, in Africa and, I dare say, the world. And I must be able to deliver for them. My performance must justify.

Again, we just want to thank you for the encouragement and the support that you have given us to enable us to meet these enormous challenges of development.

President Bush. Thank you, Madam President. Thank you. Good job.

NOTE: The President spoke at 11:58 a.m. in the Oval Office at the White House.

Remarks Following a Meeting With Iraq and Afghanistan Nongovernmental Organizations
March 21, 2006

I want to thank you all for coming. Laura and I have really enjoyed our visit.

We're talking today to people who have decided to try to help improve the lives of folks in Afghanistan and Iraq. And I just marvel at the fact that Americans from around our country have heard a call to help somebody realize the benefits of freedom. And you know, governments can help, and we will help. And obviously, we've got a brave military trying to secure freedom in Afghanistan and Iraq. But one of the real powerful parts of developing civil societies in these two countries is the fact that fellow citizens are willing to interface with citizens in Iraq and Afghanistan.

We've heard stories about Afghan women education programs and Iraqi Fulbright programs and programs to help hospitals and programs to welcome intellectuals, all aimed at helping these societies that were once brutalized by tyrants realize the great benefits and blessings of liberty. And we've got—I'm sure a lot of our citizens don't realize this, but there are thousands of, I would call them, social entrepreneurs, who are figuring out ways to help improve the human condition in these two liberated countries.

And I want to thank you all very much. It's heartening to hear your stories, and it makes me—give me—once again gives me great reason to be proud of our country and the people who live here. So thank you all for coming. God bless your work.

NOTE: The President spoke at 2:56 p.m. in the Roosevelt Room at the White House.

Remarks on the War on Terror and a Question-and-Answer Session in Wheeling, West Virginia
March 22, 2006

The President. Thank you all very much. Please be seated. Thanks for coming. First of all, Terry, thanks for the invitation. My purpose is to share with you what's on my mind, and then I look forward to hearing what's on yours.

I regret only one thing, Terry, and that's that Laura didn't come with me. No, I know, most people generally say, "You should have brought her, and you should have stayed at home." [*Laughter*] They love Laura, and so do I. And she is a fantastic First Lady. She is a great—[*applause*]. And she is a great source of comfort and strength for me, and I wish she were here.

I want to thank the Chamber and the Board of Directors of the Chamber for allowing me to come. You know, I'm—as Terry said, I'm the Commander in Chief; I'm also the educator in chief. And I have a duty to explain how and why I make decisions, and that's part of the reason I'm here.

I want to thank your Governor for being here. Joe Manchin is a—he's a good, decent man. He showed his heart during the mine tragedies. He asked the country—[*applause*]. He represented the best of West Virginia. He showed great compassion, great concern. He asked the Nation to pray on behalf of the families. We still must continue to pray for those who lost their loved ones. Joe is a problem-solver, see. He said, "We're going to deal with this issue head on." And I appreciate you working closely with the Federal Government to make sure that there are safety regulations that work, that the inspection process

works so that the miners here in this important State are able to do their job and their families can be secure in them doing their job.

So, Joe, thank you very much for your leadership. Thanks for bringing Gayle. Like you, I married well too. [*Laughter*]

I appreciate Congresswoman Shelley Moore Capito. Thanks for being here. I appreciate working with you. She's a good one, as we say in Texas. [*Laughter*] I probably shouldn't bring up Texas too much today, given the fact—yeah, I know—[*laughter*]. Never mind. [*Laughter*] I'm a little worried for my Longhorns, though, I tell you that. I'm fully informed that they're going to play a fine team.

I want to thank the mayor for being here. Mr. Mayor, I'm honored that you were at the airport. I appreciate you coming. Thanks for serving your great community. God bless you, sir.

Members of the statehouse greeted me. I appreciate Senator Mike Oliverio. He's here. Mike, I think, did the country a great service when he worked on behalf of Judge Sam Alito to get him approved by the United States Senate. I appreciate your— I want to thank you for that, Mike. I want to thank—Mike said, "Don't hold it against me; I'm a Democrat." I said, "Mike, what we—first and foremost, we're all Americans."

I thank Chris Wakim. He also was out at the airport. It's a little chilly for you all standing out there without your overcoats on, but it's all right. Thanks for being here, Chris. Thanks to all the members of the statehouse and local officials who've joined us today. Thank you for serving your State and your community.

I want to thank John Anderson and Janis LaFont. They're from the—Valley National Gases employees. They presented me with a check for $100,000 for the Katrina Relief Fund. They represent—[*applause*]. I want to thank you all for doing that, and I want to thank the folks you work with for doing that.

It's an amazing country, isn't it, when you think about it, that folks right here in this part of West Virginia care enough about folks in the southern part of our country that they would take some of their hard-earned money and contribute to a relief fund so people can get their lives back together. It means a lot to the people in Louisiana and Mississippi to know that there is love and compassion for their— and concern for their lives, here in West Virginia.

Ours is an incredible nation. And you're going to hear me talk about our military. And if you ask questions about the economy, you'll hear me talk about our economy. But I want to remind everybody that the true strength of America lies in the hearts and souls of our citizens. That's where America is its greatest, and I appreciate you representing that.

I met a woman named Kristen Holloway at the airport. Kristen, where are you? There you go. Gosh, you thought you had a better seat, but nevertheless—[*laughter*]. She came out to say hello. I had a chance to thank her for her being the founder of Operation Troop Appreciation. She has decided to support those who wear our uniform in any way she can. Listen, I understand war is controversial, and I'm going to talk about the war. But America has got to appreciate what it means to wear the uniform today and honor those who have volunteered to keep this country strong.

It doesn't matter whether you agree with my decision or not. But all of us should agree with the fact that we have a remarkable country, when people who know that they're going to be sent into harm's way raise their hand and say, "I volunteer to serve." And no State has presented—had more people volunteering to serve than the great State of West Virginia. Now, they'll say, maybe some States have more people, but they got greater populations. But 75 percent of your National Guard has gone into harm's way, and we appreciate that service. And I want to thank those of you who wear the uniform for your service. I want to thank your loved ones for supporting those who wear the uniform. And I want you to hear loud and clear, the United States of America stands with you and appreciates what you're doing.

The enemy, a group of killers, struck us on September the 11th, 2001. They declared war on the United States of America. And I want to share some lessons about what took place on that day. First of all, I knew that the farther we got away from September the 11th, 2001, the more likely it would be that some would forget the lessons of that day. And that's okay. That's okay, because the job of those of us who have been entrusted to protect you and defend you is really to do so in such a way that you feel comfortable about going about your life, see. And it's fine that people forget the lessons. But one of my jobs is to constantly remind people of the lessons.

The first lesson is, is that oceans can no longer protect us. You know, when I was coming up in the fifties in Midland, Texas, it seemed like we were pretty safe. In the sixties it seemed like we were safe. In other words, conflicts were happening overseas, but we were in pretty good shape here at home. And all that was shattered on that day, when coldblooded killers hijacked airplanes, flew them into buildings and into the Pentagon, and killed 3,000 of our citizens. In other words, they declared war, and we have got to take their declaration of war seriously. The most important responsibility of the Commander in Chief and those who wear the uniform and those who are elected to public office is to defend the citizens of this country. That is our most vital and important responsibility. I have never forgotten that, from September the 11th on. It's just been a part of my daily existence.

Secondly, the best way to defend America is to stay on the offense. The best way to protect you is to rally all the strength of National Government—intelligence and military, law enforcement, financial strength—to stay on the offense against an enemy that I believe wants to hurt us again. And that means, find them where they hide and keep the pressure on and never relent and understand that you can't negotiate with these folks. There is no compromise; there is no middle ground. And so that's exactly what we're doing.

And there's some unbelievably brave troops and intelligence officers working around the clock to keep an enemy that would like to strike us again, on the move and to bring them to justice. And we're making progress about dismantling Al Qaida. Al Qaida, after all, was the enemy that launched the attacks.

The second part of a lesson that we must never forget is the enemy, in that they're not a nation-state—in other words, they don't represent a nation-state like armies and navies used to do—need safe haven. They need places to hide so they can plan and plot. And they found safe haven, as you all know, in Afghanistan. And they were supported by a government that supports their point of view, which is a government that absolutely can't stand freedom. That was the Taliban. If you were a young girl growing up under the auspices of the Taliban, you didn't have a chance to succeed. You couldn't go to school. If you dissented in the public square, you'd be in trouble. If you didn't agree with their dark vision, whether it be religion or politics, you were in trouble. In other words,

they can't—they couldn't stand this concept of a free society—and neither can Al Qaida. See, we're dealing with ideologues. They have an ideology.

Now, I understand some say, "Well, maybe they're just isolated, kind of people that are angry and took out their anger with an attack." That's not how I view them. I view them as people that believe in something; they have an ideological base. They subverted a great religion to meet their needs, and they need places to hide. And that's why I said early on in the war that if you harbor a terrorist, you're equally as guilty as the terrorist—understanding the nature of the enemy and understanding they need safe haven. In order to protect ourselves, we must deny them safe haven.

By the way, if the President says something, he better mean it, for the sake of peace. In other words, you want your President out there making sure that his words are credible. And so I said to the Taliban, "Get rid of Al Qaida, or face serious consequences." They didn't, and they faced serious consequences, and we liberated Afghanistan. We removed the Taliban from power. We've denied Al Qaida safe haven. And that young country, that young democracy is now beginning to grow; 25 million people are liberated as a result of the United States defending itself. And that's important for us to realize, that not only are we defending ourselves, but in this instance, we've given chance to people to realize the beauties of freedom.

There's an interesting debate in the world is whether or not freedom is universal, see, whether or not—let's say, "There's old Bush imposing his values." See, I believe freedom is universal. I believe liberty is a universal thought. It's not an American thought; it is a universal thought. And if you believe that, then you ought to take great comfort and joy in helping others realize the benefits of liberty. The way I put it was, there is an Almighty God. One of the greatest gifts of that Almighty God is the desire for people to be free, is freedom. And therefore, this country and the world ought to say, "How can we help you remain free? What can we do to help you realize the blessings of liberty?"

Remember, as we debate these issues—and it's important to have a debate in our democracy, and I welcome the debate—but remember, we were founded on the natural rights of men and women. That speaks to the universality of liberty. And we must never forget the origin of our own founding as we look around the world.

Afghanistan—I went there with Laura. We had a good visit with President Karzai. I like him—good man. You can imagine what it's like to try to rebuild a country that had been occupied and then traumatized by the Taliban. They're coming around. They got elections. They had assembly elections. He himself was elected. We expect them to honor the universal principle of freedom. I'm troubled when I hear—deeply troubled when I hear the fact that a person who has converted away from Islam may be held to account. That's not the universal application of the values that I talked about. Look forward to working with the Government of that country to make sure that people are protected in their capacity to worship.

There's still a Taliban element trying to come and hurt people. But the good news is, not only do we have great U.S. troops there, but NATO is now involved. One of my jobs is to continue to make sure that people understand the benefits of a free society emerging in a neighborhood that needs freedom. And so I'm pleased with the progress, but I fully understand there's a lot more work to be done.

Another lesson of September the 11th, and an important lesson that really does relate to the topic I want to discuss, which is Iraq, is that when you see a threat now, you got to take it seriously. That's the lesson of September the 11th—another lesson of September the 11th. When you see a threat emerging, you just can't hope it goes away. If the job of the President is to protect the American people, my job then is to see threats and deal with them before they fully materialize, before they come to hurt us, before they come and strike America again.

And I saw a threat in Iraq. I'll tell you why I saw a threat. And by the way, it just wasn't me. Members of the United States Congress in both political parties saw a threat. My predecessor saw a threat. I mean, my predecessor saw a threat and got the Congress actually to vote a resolution that said, "We're for regime change." That's prior to my arrival. The world saw a threat. You might remember, I went to the United Nations Security Council; on the 15-to-nothing vote, we passed Resolution 1441 that said to Saddam Hussein, "Disclose, disarm, or face serious consequences." We saw a threat.

I'll tell you why I saw a threat. I saw a threat because, one, he'd been on the state—he was a state sponsor of terror. In other words, our Government—not when I was President, prior to my Presidency—declared Saddam Hussein to be a state sponsor of terror. Secondly, I know for a fact he had used weapons of mass destruction. Now, I thought he had weapons of mass destruction; Members of Congress thought he had weapons of mass destruction; the world thought he had weapons of mass destruction. That's why those nations voted in the Security Council. I'm finding out what went wrong. In other words, one of the things you better make sure of, is when you're the President, you're getting good intelligence, and obviously, the intelligence broke down. But he had that capacity to make weapons of mass destruction as well. He had not only murdered his own people, but he had used weapons of mass destruction on his own people.

That's what we knew prior to the decision I made. He also was firing on our aircraft. They were enforcing a no-fly zone, United Nations no-fly zone. The world had spoken, and he had taken shots at British and U.S. pilots. He'd invaded his neighborhood. This guy was a threat. And so the world spoke. And the way I viewed it was that it was Saddam Hussein's choice to disclose, disarm, or face serious consequences. And he made the choice, and then I was confronted with a choice. And I made my choice. And the world is better off without Saddam Hussein in power.

The biggest threat America faces is that moment when terror and weapons of mass destruction come together. And if we ever suspect that's happening, we got to take—deal with that threat seriously. Committing our troops into harm's way is the most difficult decision a President can make. I'm going to meet with some—two families of those who lost a loved one. It's my duty to do so. I'm looking forward to being able to hug them, weep with them. And so for anybody out there in West Virginia who thinks it's easy to commit troops—it's hard. It's the last option of the President, not the first option. The first option is to deal with things diplomatically, is to rally the world to send a clear message that the behavior, in this case, of Saddam Hussein, was intolerable. And we did that.

Now the fundamental question is, can we win in Iraq? And that's what I want to talk about. First of all, you got to understand that I fully understand there is deep concern among the American people about whether or not we can win. And I can understand why people are concerned. And they're concerned because the enemy has got the capacity to affect our thinking. This is an enemy who will kill innocent people in order to achieve an objective. And Americans are decent, honorable people; they care. We care about human life. We care about human dignity. We value life. We value the life of our own citizens, and we value the life of other citizens. And so it's easy for an enemy that is willing to kill innocent people to affect us.

The enemy has told us their objectives in Iraq. And I think it's important for the

Commander in Chief to take the words of the enemy very seriously. They have said that they want to spread their philosophy to other parts of the Middle East. They have said that. They have said they want to attack us again. They believe that democracies are soft, that it's just a matter of time for the United States to lose our will and create a vacuum in Iraq, so they can use their terror techniques and their willingness to kill to develop a safe haven from which to launch attacks. That's what the enemy has said. This is—I hope the citizens of this country understand that we have intercepted documents, and we put them out for people to see. And I take the words very seriously.

Iraq is a part of the global war on terror. In other words, it's a global war. We're dealing with a group of folks that want to spread an ideology, and they see a problem developing in Iraq, and so they're heading into Iraq to fight us, because they can't stand the thought of democracy, see. Democracy trumps their ideology every time. Freedom and democracy represent hope; their point of view represents despair. Freedom represents life and the chance for people to realize their dreams; their philosophy says, "You do it my way or else." And so they're trying to fight us in Iraq.

And we have a strategy for victory in Iraq. It's a three-pronged strategy, starting with—it's politics; it is a—it's security; and it's economy. On politics, was to get the people to the polls to see if they even cared about democracy; just give them a chance to vote; see what the people thought. And you might remember the elections; it probably seems like an eternity. It was just a year ago that they started voting—a little more than a year, in January of last year. And the first election round came off okay, but the Sunnis didn't participate. They were a little disgruntled with life there. They liked their privileged status, and they were boycotting the elections. Then they wrote a Constitution, which is a good Constitution. It's a progressive Constitution for that part of the world. More people came out to vote than last December. About 75 percent of the eligible voters said, "I want to be free; I want democracy. I don't care what Mr. Zarqawi and his Al Qaida killers are trying to do to me; I'm going to defy them and go to the polls."

And the people have spoken. And now it's time for a government to get stood up. There's time for the elected representatives—or those who represent the voters, the political parties, to come together and form a unity government. That's what the people want; otherwise, they wouldn't have gone to the polls, would they have?

I spoke to our Ambassador today and General Casey, via video conferencing, and we talked about the need to make it clear to the Iraqis, it's time; it's time to get a government in place that can start leading this nation and listening to the will of the people. It's a little hard. You can imagine what it's like coming out of the—having been ruled by a tyrant. People are—when you spoke out before, no telling what was going to happen to you; it generally wasn't good. And now people are beginning to realize democracy has taken hold.

By the way, if you look at our own history, it was a little bumpy on our road too. You might remember the Articles of Confederation. They didn't work too well. It took us a while from the moment of our Revolution to get our Constitution written, the one that we now live by.

The second part is to help people with their economy. And we had to change our strategy there. We first went in there and said, "Let's build some big plants." The problem was, the big plants served as big targets for those who are disgruntled, the terrorists who are going into Iraq to use it as a safe haven plus some of their allies, the Saddamists. These were Saddam's inner-circle buddies and stuff like that that had received special privileges. They weren't happy that they were no longer

in privileged status. And so they were destroying some of the infrastructure we were building. So we changed our strategy and said, "Look, why don't we go with smaller projects, particularly in the Provinces, so people can begin to see the benefits of what it means to have a democracy unfold."

And the third aspect is security. When we got in there, it became apparent to our troops on the ground that we had a lot of training to do. We had to really rebuild an army to make sure that people had the skills necessary to be able to fight off those who want to stop the march of democracy. First, we trained the army for threats from outside the country. But we realized the true threats were inside the country, whether it be the Saddamists, some Sunni rejectionists, or Al Qaida that was in there torturing and killing and maiming in order to get their way.

And we're making progress when it comes to training the troops. More and more Iraqis are taking the fight. Right after the bombing of the Golden Mosque, for example, is an interesting indication as to whether or not the Iraqi troops are getting better.

The enemy can't defeat us militarily, by the way. They can't beat us on the field of battle. But the only thing they can do is they can either try to stop democracy from moving—they failed on that. Last year, they failed. Their stated objective was just not to let democracy get going, and they flunked the test. Now they're trying to foment a civil war. See, that's the only way they can win. And they blew up the mosque. And there was some awful violence, some reprisals taking place. And I can understand people saying, "Man, it's all going to—it's not working out." But the security forces did a pretty good job of keeping people apart.

In other words, it was a test. It was a test for the security forces, and it was a test for the Iraqi Government. The way I like to put it is they looked into the abyss as to whether or not they want a civil war or not and chose not to.

That's not to say we don't have more work to do, and we do. But it's important for me to continue—look, I'm an optimistic guy. I believe we'll succeed. Let me tell you this—put it to you this way: If I didn't think we'd succeed, I'd pull our troops out. I cannot look mothers and dads in the eye—I can't ask this good marine to go into harm's way if I didn't believe, one, we're going to succeed, and two, it's necessary for the security of the United States.

And it's tough fighting. It's tough fighting, because we got an enemy that's just coldblooded. They can't beat us militarily, but they can try to shake our will. See, remember, I told you, they have said that it's just a matter of time, just a matter of time before the United States loses its nerve. I believe we're doing the right thing, and we're not going to retreat in the face of thugs and assassins. [*Applause*] Thank you.

It's the Iraqis' fight. Ultimately, the Iraqis are going to have to determine their future. They made their decision politically; they voted. And these troops that we're training are going to have to stand up and defend their democracy. We got work, by the way, in '06 to make sure the police are trained as adequately as the military, the army. It's their choice to make. And I like to put it this way: As they stand up, we'll stand down.

But I want to say something to you about troop levels, and I know that's something that people are talking about in Washington a lot. I'm going to make up my mind based upon the advice of the United States military that's in Iraq. I'll be making up my mind about the troop levels based upon recommendations of those who are on the ground. I'm going to make up my mind based upon achieving a victory, not based upon polls, focus groups, or election-year politics.

I talked about a city named Tall 'Afar the other day in a speech I gave in Cleve-

land. Just real quick, it's an important place. It's a place where—close to the Syrian border, where Al Qaida was moving the terrorists from outside the country inside the country, trying to achieve their objective. And right after we removed Saddam Hussein, they started moving in. And I cannot describe to you how awful these people treat the citizens there. I mean, they are—I told a story about a young boy who was maimed, taken to a hospital, was pulled out of the hospital, was killed by the terrorists. His dad went to retrieve him on the side of the road, and they put a bomb underneath him and blew up the family. I mean, Americans cannot understand the nature—how brutal these people are. It's shocking what they will do to try to achieve their objectives.

But it really shouldn't shock us when you think about what they did on September the 11th. It's the same folks, same attitude, same frame of mind. But they're able to lock down cities, particularly those that are worried about their security, and so they basically took control of Tall 'Afar. So our troops went in with Iraqis and cleaned it out. The problem—[*applause*]—oh, not through yet. [*Laughter*] A little early on the clap. [*Laughter*] The problem was, we continued to pursue the enemy, and they moved back in, these killers and murderers moved back in and just created a mess. I mean, they—I said in my speech, they mortared children in a playground. They recruited young kids, abused them, violated them. There's one boy in particular who told our guys, once the city eventually got liberated, his dream was to behead somebody with a—anyway, we started working with the local folks again. This time, though, we had trained more Iraqi Army ready to go.

And the difference in the story between the first time we liberated Tall 'Afar from them and the recent liberation was that the Iraqis were in the lead. And not only were they in the lead, they stayed behind after we left. So our troops are chasing high-value targets and training—and capable Iraqi forces are providing security. And so the day of terror began to change when they saw capable forces and a new mayor and police forces.

I mean, this is—it's hard to put ourselves in their—the shoes of the folks in this town that had been traumatized. But the strategy of clear, hold, and build began to create a sense of confidence. And what's interesting is I can say that—I got one data point that I can share with you—the vote in the January '05 election was the second-lowest vote in the—as percentage of voting population, in the country, and the last vote, 85 percent of the eligible voters voted. In other words, people had a sense of security and hope.

A free Iraq is important for the United States of America. It was important to remove a threat; it was important to deal with threats before they fully materialized. But a free Iraq also does some other things: One, it serves as an amazing example— it will serve as an amazing example for people who are desperate for freedom.

You know, this is, I guess, quite a controversial subject, I readily concede, as to whether or not the United States ought to try to promote freedom in the broader Middle East. Our foreign policy before was just, kind of, if the waters looked calm, great. Problem is, beneath the surface was resentment brewing, and people were able to take advantage of that, these totalitarians, like Al Qaida. So I changed our foreign policy. I said, freedom is universal; history has proven democracies do not fight each other; democracies can yield peace we want, so let's advance freedom. And that's what's happening.

It's a big idea, but it's an old idea. It's worked in the past. I strongly believe that by promoting liberty, we're not only protecting ourselves, but we're laying the foundation of peace for a generation to come. And I'll tell you why I believe that, and then I'll answer questions. Thank goodness

Laura isn't here; she'd be giving me the hook. [*Laughter*]

Two examples that I use that are obviously—well, I'm living one example, and that is my relationship with the Prime Minister of Japan. He is one of my best buddies—I don't know if you're supposed to call them "buddies" in diplomacy or not, but anyway—one of my best buddies in working to keep the peace. I find that a really interesting statement to say to you, knowing my own family's history—18-year-old—my dad, when he was 18, went to fight the Japanese. I think it's really one of the interesting twists of history that I stand here in West Virginia saying to you that Prime Minister Koizumi and I talk about ways to keep the peace, ways to deal with North Korea—he's helping in Iraq— ways to deal with other issues. And 60 years prior to that, when the country called, George H.W. said, "I want to go," just like, I'm sure, relatives of you all. And Japan was a sworn enemy. And there was a lot of bloodshed in order to—remember, they attacked us too. And yet today, the President says, "We're working to keep the peace." And what happened? It's an interesting lesson that I hope people remember. Something happened. What happened was, Japan adopted a Japanese-style democracy.

I believe freedom and liberty can change enemies into allies. I believe freedom has the power to transform societies. It's not easy work; it's difficult work. But we've seen history before. I know you've got relatives who were in World War II. On that continent, hundreds of thousands of Americans lost their lives in two world wars during the 1900s. And yet today, Europe is whole, free, and at peace. What happened? Democracies don't war. And so part of my decisionmaking that I'm trying to explain to you today, about war, about what you're seeing on your TV screens, about the anxiety that a lot of our citizens feel, is based upon, one, the need to protect the American people and my deep reservoir of commitment to doing what it takes—to look at the world realistically, to understand we're in a global war against a serious enemy.

But also my thinking is based upon some universal values and my belief that history can repeat itself and that freedom and liberty has a chance to lay a foundation of peace so that maybe 40 years from now, somebody is speaking here in West Virginia saying, "You know, a bunch of folks were given a challenge and a task, and that generation didn't lose faith in the capacity of freedom to change, and today, I'm able to sit down with the duly elected leaders of democracy in the Middle East, keeping the peace for the next generation to come."

That's what I've come to talk to you about, and that's what's on my mind. And now I'll be glad to answer any questions you got.

Yes, sir. First man up.

Support for the U.S. Armed Forces

Q. Mr. President, I'm going to make your job a little easier on you. To sum it all up, what you're trying to say is, when it comes to fighting terrorism, there is no easy button.

The President. Thank you, sir. I'll be glad to answer any question on any subject, but I always appreciate a good editorial. [*Laughter*]

Q. Mr. President——

The President. Yes, sir. Hold on for a second. We're going to do it a little more orderly here. Right here. Right there. Yes, there you go. Get moving on the mike, please. [*Laughter*] Generally what happens if they don't have a mike, the guy yells the question, and I just answer whatever I want to answer. [*Laughter*]

Q. Mr. President, I have a son that's Special Forces in Iraq. And I have another son that's in the Army. He left college to join the Army. He's out in Hawaii. He's got the good duty right now. [*Laughter*] But I thank God that you're our Commander in Chief. And I wouldn't want my boys—[*applause*].

The President. Okay, thanks.

Q. Again, I thank God you're our Commander in Chief. You're a man for our times. And I'm a supporter of yours, and I think it's good that you come out and tell your story. And I think you need to keep doing more of it, and tell the story and the history of all this. And God bless you, and I thank you for your service.

The President. Well, I appreciate you saying that. A couple of points. First, you tell your kids thanks. The good news is, for moms and dads and husbands and wives and children, that in spite of the debate you're seeing in Washington, that there is a commitment to support our troops when we—when they're in harm's way. There may be an argument about tactics and whether or not we should have done it in the first place; I understand that. But the Congress has stood up, and that's what Congress should do. And take comfort, please, sir, in knowing that the debates that you're seeing will not lessen our Government's support for making sure the people are well-trained, well-paid, well-equipped, well-housed. We owe that. And I'm pleased with the congressional response to supporting troops.

Second, you can e-mail them. It's an interesting war we have, where moms and dads and wives and husbands are in touch with their loved ones by e-mail. It's really interesting.

And I want to thank you very much for saying what you said. I am—as I said, I'm educator in chief, and I'm going to spend a lot of time answering questions and just explaining—explaining to people as clearly as I can about why I made decisions I made and why it is important for us to succeed.

And again, I understand debate. I understand there's differences of opinion, and we should welcome that in America. People should never fear a difference of opinion, particularly on big matters. And war is a big matter, war and peace. And it's healthy for our country for people to be debating, so long as we don't send the wrong signals to our troops, so long as they don't think that we're not behind them, and so long as we don't send mixed signals to the enemy. The enemy believes that we will weaken and lose our nerve. And I just got to tell you, I'm not weak, and I'm not going to lose my nerve. I strongly believe that we're doing the right thing.

Do you want to say something, Joe?

Governor Joe Manchin III. Yes.

The President. How about your Governor? Make it easy.

Alternative Sources of Energy

Gov. Manchin. [*Inaudible*]

The President. Yes, I appreciate it.

Joe talked to me about how do we use the natural resources of the State of West Virginia in such ways to become less dependent on oil. Now, let me talk about that, starting with coal gasification leading to coal liquefaction. I appreciate the subject.

I know it shocked some of you—I know it shocked some of you when I stood up in the State of the Union and said, "We got a problem; we're addicted to oil." Texas, you know, the whole thing—[*laughter*]. I'll tell you why I said it. I'll tell you why I said it. One, because when the demand for fossil fuels goes up, for nonrenewable resources goes up in other parts of the world, it affects the gasoline price here at home. When somebody else's economy starts to boom and they start using more fossil fuel, it affects your price too. It's important for people to understand. And there are some new economies emerging that are growing and that need and use—that are using a lot of hydrocarbons.

Secondly, we get oil from parts of the world that don't like us, is the best way to put it, which creates a national security issue. And therefore, it is in our economic interest and national interest that we get off of our addiction to oil. We import about 60-something percent of our oil from overseas. What Joe is talking about is a different use of resources to help us achieve that objective.

First thing is, we got a lot of coal, 250-year supply of coal, which helps us on our electricity. And we're spending a lot of money on clean coal technology. The whole idea is to use taxpayers' money to develop a technology that will enable us to have zero-emission plants, which will help us achieve a environmental objective, as well as an energy independence objective.

Joe is talking about spending research money on the gasification of coal, which then will lead to the liquefication. In other words, we're able to develop a product that way. And I believe we ought to attack this issue on all fronts, on a variety of fronts. I know we ought to use nuclear power. It is a renewable source of energy that has got zero greenhouse gas effect.

And by the way, I went to a plant that's making solar panels, photovoltaic cells—not bad for a history major. [*Laughter*] Technologies are coming. And to me, it makes sense to work with Congress to spend money on new technologies aiming for a national objective.

The place where we're really going to affect reliance upon oil is changing our automobile—how automobiles are powered. One is, battery technologies are coming around. One of these days, I am told, that if we continue to stay focused in research, you're going to be able to have a pretty good-sized vehicle, plug it in, and it'll be able to drive 40 miles before you need to use any gasoline in your engine. Now, that's not going to help some of you rural folks in West Virginia or Texas, but it's going to help urban people who generally tend not to drive more than 40 miles a day. But imagine if we're able to have battery power where you plug your battery into—when the electricity is down, low usage at night, and they drive 40 miles. That will save—that will reduce demand for gasoline, which reduces demand for crude oil.

Secondly, we're going to be able to drive our cars based upon—with a sugar base or a corn base or saw grass. I said that one day—what the heck is saw grass? It's just grass. It just grows out there, and you bulk it for them. And the idea is to develop technology so that we're using more ethanol. It's happening in the Midwest, by the way. They've got what they call E–85—that's 85 percent ethanol—that's powering automobiles now. A whole new industry is beginning to grow. And the more we use alternative sources of energy, the less dependent we are on oil.

So Joe has been—Joe is always thinking, and he's a practical fellow, which is sometimes not the case in government. [*Laughter*] But what he's saying is, "Can't we use our resources here, in a way, Mr. President, that helps you achieve a grand national objective, which is getting off Middle Eastern oil?" And the answer is, yes, we can.

Yes, you got a question? Are you in school?

Civilian Nuclear Power Program in India/ Iran

Q. Yes.

The President. Good. Did you use me as an excuse to skip school?

Q. Of course. [*Laughter*] Mr. President, I was wondering, actually, how you felt about America's double standard on nuclear energy, as far as countries like Iran, India, and Israel go?

The President. Yes, I appreciate that. I may ask you to clarify your question of "double standard."

Q. Well, how we don't allow Iran to have nuclear energy, yet we're supporting India.

The President. Yes. No, I got it, good, good, good.

Q. And Israel's nuclear weapons——

The President. I wouldn't—I wouldn't necessarily—well, first of all, let me explain the policy, and then you can draw whatever conclusion you want. First of all, it's in our interests that India use nuclear power to power their economic growth because,

as I told you, there is a global connection between demand for fossil fuels elsewhere and price here. And so I went to India, and I said—actually, it's a very sophisticated question, by the way—but I said, we ought to encourage you to use nuclear power.

Now, the difficulty with that issue, and that Congress is going to have to deal with, is that India has heretofore been denied technologies from the United States because of previous decisions they made about nuclear weaponry. My attitude is that over 30 years, they have proven themselves to be a nonproliferator, that they're a transparent democracy. It's in our interest that they develop nuclear power for—to help their economy grow. They need power, and they need energy to do so, and they're willing to go under the safeguards of the IAEA, which is an international forum to make sure that there are certain safeguards.

Iran—the Iranians are a nontransparent society. They're certainly not a democracy. They are sponsors of terrorism. They have joined the IAEA, and yet we caught them cheating. In other words, they weren't upholding the agreements, and they started to try to enrich uranium in order to develop a weapons program. India is heading to the IAEA; the Iranians are ignoring IAEA.

And so to answer your question about potential conflict of civilian energy power, I have said that I support the Russian proposal that says the Iranians should have a civilian nuclear industry; however, Russia and other suppliers would give them the enriched—the product necessarily to power their industry and collect the spent fuel but not enable the Iranians to learn how to enrich in order to develop a weapons programs. That's, I think, how—hold on for a second—oop, oop, oop. [*Laughter*] That's how we addressed the inconsistency on the power side, apparent inconsistency.

However, in that the Iranians are nontransparent, in that they are hostile to the United States and hostile to allies, we've got to be very careful about not letting them develop a weapon. And so we're now dealing with this issue diplomatically by having the Germans and the French and the British send a clear message to the Iranians, with our strong backing, that you will not have the capacity to make a weapon, the know-how to make a weapon. Iran with a nuclear weapon is a threat, and it's dangerous, and we must not let them have a weapon.

Yes.

Voluntarism

Q. Sir, thank you for being in West Virginia. I'm the recruiting commander of the West Virginia Army National Guard. And there are a lot of National Guardsmen here with you in Wheeling today. West Virginians are a proud and very patriotic people. I'd like for you to share with us what you would say to a young person today who would like to join the National Guard, and maybe give some encouraging words in that respect.

The President. Okay, thanks—kind of doing your job for you. All right. [*Laughter*] My statement to all Americans is, serve your country one way or another. I—and service can be done by wearing the uniform. Wearing the uniform is a fantastic way to say, "I want to serve my country." A lot of people have chosen that way, and it's a rewarding experience to wear the uniform. If you want to go to college, it's a good way to gain some skills to help you in your education.

There are also other ways to serve. You can mentor a child, and you're serving America. You can help the Katrina victims, and you're serving America. You can be a Boy Scout troop leader, and you're serving America.

What's really interesting about our country—and I said this early on—is the notion of people coming together to serve a concept greater than themselves. It is—I know it's not unique to America, but it certainly helps define our spirit. De Tocqueville,

who's a French guy, came in 1832 and recognized—and wrote back—wrote a treatise about what it means to go to a country where people associate voluntarily to serve their communities. And he recognized that this—one of the great strengths of America—this is the 1830s—it is still the strength of America. It is a vital part of our society and our communities, the idea of people volunteering to help a neighbor in need.

And one of my jobs is to honor people who are serving our country that way, and to call other peoples to service as well. As you know, one of the interesting and at times controversial proposals was whether or not Government should open up grant money for competitive bidding for faith-based organizations. I'm a big believer in providing grant money available for faith-based organizations, so long as the money doesn't go used—to be used to proselytize, but is used to help serve a purpose, like if your mother or dad is in prison, that it would help to go find a mentor for that child. Or if you're a drug addict or got hooked on alcohol, that you could redeem the Government help at a faith-based institution.

In other words, we in government ought to be asking the question, does the program work? And a lot of times, programs based upon faith do work, that it is—there's nothing better than a faith-based program which exists to love a neighbor like you'd like to be loved yourself. And therefore, one of my jobs is to not only help recruit for the Guard, which—put a plug in there for you—[*applause*]—there you go—but also to call other—to call people to serve, to help change our society one person at a time. And it's happening. It's a remarkable part of the—I'm confident—of this community, just like it is all around the United States. And thanks for your question.

Yes, sir. Yes, the guy in the yellow hat. Give it to the guy on the aisle. Well, no, you're not a guy. [*Laughter*] Right behind you; there you go.

Religious Freedom/Afghanistan

Q. President Bush, I'm a professional firefighter here in Wheeling, West Virginia.

The President. Thank you, sir.

Q. And back during 9/11, I lost over 300 of my brothers in New York. And I was glad that you were our President at that time and took the fight to the terrorists. But as I see, you said earlier about the guy in Afghanistan that is going to convert to Christianity, he may get killed over there for doing that. Do you have an army of sociologists to go over there and change that country, or are you hoping that in a couple decades that we can change the mindset over there?

The President. I appreciate the question. It's a very legitimate question. We have got influence in Afghanistan, and we are going to use it to remind them that there are universal values. It is deeply troubling that a country we helped liberate would hold a person to account because they chose a particular religion over another. And so we are—we will make—part of the messaging just happened here in Wheeling. I want to thank you for that question.

No, I think it's—we can solve this problem by working closely with the Government that we've got contacts with—and will. We'll deal with this issue diplomatically and remind people that there is something as universal as being able to choose religion.

So thank you for the question. I understand your concerns. I share the same concerns.

I had a little guy back here. Yes, sir.

The Presidency

Q. Do you like living in the White House?

The President. Do I like living in the White House? Yes. That's a good, fair question. Your brother has got one too. Do you want to back to back them?

Q. [*Inaudible*]

The President. Okay. Well, I've been the President for 5½ years. I do like living in the White House—it's an interesting question—for some practical reasons. I've got a 45-second commute to my office. [*Laughter*] The food is pretty good. [*Laughter*] It is a—I've enjoyed every second of the Presidency. That's probably hard—like my buddies come up from Texas; one of the things that Laura and I are most proud of—we're proud of a lot—we're most proud of our girls, but we're also very proud of the fact that we had friends prior to being in politics from Texas that will be our friends after we're in politics.

And they come up from Texas, and they're kind of looking at you like, "Man, are you okay?" Yes—you know. [*Laughter*] And I tell them, I say, you know, I can't tell you what an honor it is to do this job. They often ask, "What's the job description?" I say, making decisions. And I make a lot. Obviously, I'm trying to share with you—you may not agree with the decision, but at the very minimum, I want you to understand that I make my decisions based upon some principles I hold dear. In order to make decisions, you have to be enthusiastic about your job, you have to be optimistic about the future, and you have to stand for something. You can't be a President trying to search for what you believe in the midst of all the noise in Washington.

Yes, ma'am. Yes. No, right here. There you go.

Progress in Iraq/Media Coverage

Q. Good afternoon, Mr. President. It is an honor to be here today. Thank you for coming. Greetings from Columbus, Ohio.

The President. There you go.

Q. My husband, who is sitting right here with me——

The President. Actually, my grandfather was raised in Columbus, Ohio—not to change subjects, but——

Q. That's okay, you can do whatever you want to do.

The President. Prescott S. Bush. [*Laughter*]

Q. I have a comment, first of all, and then just a real quick question. I want to let you know that every service at our church you are, by name, lifted up in prayer, and you and your staff and all of our leaders. And we believe in you. We are behind you. And we cannot thank you enough for what you've done to shape our country.

This is my husband, who has returned from a 13-month tour in Tikrit.

The President. Oh, yes. Thank you. Welcome back.

Q. His job while serving was as a broadcast journalist. And he has brought back several DVDs full of wonderful footage of reconstruction, of medical things going on. And I ask you this from the bottom of my heart, for a solution to this, because it seems that our major media networks don't want to portray the good. They just want to focus—[*applause*].

The President. Okay, hold on a second.

Q. They just want to focus on another car bomb, or they just want to focus on some more bloodshed, or they just want to focus on how they don't agree with you and what you're doing, when they don't even probably know how you're doing what you're doing anyway. But what can we do to get that footage on CNN, on FOX, to get it on Headline News, to get it on the local news? Because you can send it to the news people—and I'm sorry, I'm rambling—like I have——

The President. So was I, though, for an hour. [*Laughter*]

Q. ——saying can you use this? And it will just end up in a drawer because it's good, it portrays the good. And if people could see that, if the American people could see it, there would never be another negative word about this conflict.

The President. Well, I appreciate that. No, it—that's why I come out and speak. I spoke in Cleveland, gave a press conference yesterday—spoke in Cleveland

Monday, press conference, here today. I'm going to continue doing what I'm doing to try to make sure people can hear there's—why I make decisions and, as best as I can, explain why I'm optimistic we can succeed.

One of the things that we've got to value is the fact that we do have a media, free media that's able to do what they want to do. And I'm not going to—you're asking me to say something in front of all the cameras here. [*Laughter*] Help over there, will you? [*Laughter*]

I just got to keep talking. And one of the—there's word of mouth; there's blogs; there's Internet; there's all kinds of ways to communicate, which is literally changing the way people are getting their information. And so if you're concerned, I would suggest that you reach out to some of the groups that are supporting the troops, that have got Internet sites, and just keep the word moving. And that's one way to deal with an issue without suppressing a free press. We will never do that in America. I mean, the minute we start trying to suppress our press, we look like the Taliban. The minute we start telling people how to worship, we look like the Taliban. And we're not interested in that in America. We're the opposite. We believe in freedom, and we believe in freedom in all its forms. And obviously, I know you're frustrated with what you're seeing, but there are ways in this new kind of age, being able to communicate, that you'll be able to spread the message that you want to spread.

Thank you for your concerns, and thank you for your prayer. I want to tell you something interesting about the job of President, and, frankly, I didn't anticipate this part of the Presidency, but it's an amazing part of my job to know that millions of people pray for me. It's a—[*applause*]—it really is. It's—think about that. Strangers stand up and say, in front of a couple thousand people, I'm praying for you. And it helps. And I appreciate it, and

I want to thank you for your prayers. It helps do the job; it helps keep perspective.

Yes, sir.

Vision for the Future

Q. I'm a senior at the local high school, Wheeling Park High School, and I just want to know what your views are on what type of America my generation will lead.

The President. Yes, interesting question. First, I hope that your generation will lead—no doubt, your generation will lead. Generations, when called, somehow find the courage to lead. That's step one. Two, I think you'll be dealing in a world in which you will be confronted with making values choices—for example, family, understanding that the family is an important aspect of society. Secondly, the choice of life—for example, you'll be confronted with a very difficult debate between science, on the one hand, and the hopes of science, and life. And it's—that debate is just beginning. In other words, do you destroy life to save life, for example, is one of the very difficult debates that your generation will be confronted with—to what extent does science trump morality, as some see it.

You'll be confronted, hopefully, with a world that has been able to be free enough so that this war that's going on now is—has kind of faded out. This war is not going to stop like that. It's not going to be, like, we'll have the signing ceremony somewhere. But it's a matter of marginalizing those who espouse violence and empowering those who love freedom.

You'll be confronted with a world in which—we're seeing a little bit of it now in America—whether or not we will be bold and confident in our economic policy to shape the future, or will we be worried about competition and retreat within our borders. It's an interesting debate. My attitude is, as I said in the State of the Union, we cannot become an isolationist nation. But you'll be confronted with making that decision. If we're an isolationist nation, it means we'll just say, "Let them—don't worry about them over there; let them deal with it themselves." If it's an isolationist nation, we won't worry about HIV/AIDS on the continent of Africa, which we should worry about. See, I believe to whom much is given, much is required, and that we have an obligation not only to help our folks here at home but also to help save lives elsewhere.

And you'll be confronted with that decision. You'll be confronted with the decision as to whether or not we can confidently compete against nations like India and China on the economic front. And it will be an interesting challenge. We're facing that challenge somewhat now, and in my judgment, this is the beginning of what will be a constant set of decisions that future generations are going to have to make.

You'll be confronted with privacy issues—privacy on the Internet, privacy in electronic medical records that I think ought to happen in order to make sure we save costs in medicine. But you'll be confronted with making sure that these new technologies that we're going to use to help improve, for example, the information of medicine, that it doesn't encroach into your private business, into your life. That will be a confrontation that you'll have to deal with.

Anyway, you'll be confronted with some stuff. Hopefully, our job is to make sure you're confronted with less issues, like being hooked on oil. One of the issues that we're confronting with now that I hope you'll not have to confront with is jobs going elsewhere because our—because we don't have the math and science skills and engineering skills and physics skills that are taught to our children here. One of the really interesting challenges we have is to make sure not only the education of our children focuses on literacy, but there's literacy in math and science and physics and chemistry—where the jobs of the 21st century—the skills necessary for the jobs of the 21st century. Hopefully, we'll have dealt with that. Otherwise, you're going to be confronted with playing catchup. And that's why it's important for us to get that job done.

You're going to be confronted with, unless we act now, a Social Security system and a Medicare system that's gone broke. I want to talk about that right quick, now I thought about it. [*Laughter*] No, I think about it a lot because I see what's coming down the road—a lot of baby boomers like me turning 60 this year. I'll be retirement age in 2 years, in 2008. [*Laughter*] Kind of convenient, isn't it? [*Laughter*] And there's a lot of me—people like me, a lot of people like me, a whole lot of baby boomers. That's one of those statistical facts that people got to pay attention to.

And interestingly enough, my generation has been promised more benefits than the previous generation. People are running for office saying, "Vote for me; I'm going to make sure this next generation gets a better deal than the previous generation." And because there was a lot of folks like me being promised greater benefits who are living longer—I don't know how plan—how other 60-year-olders, how long they plan to live— I plan on kind of stretching her out, you know. And there are fewer people paying in the system per beneficiary. And so we got a problem coming. The system is going to go broke. And I addressed the issue last year, and I'm going to address the issue again and again and again, to call Congress to the table.

My strategy last time was to go around the country and explain the problem, on the belief that once the people heard there was a problem, they would then demand their Representatives do something about the problem. It didn't work. There was no legislation last year. So I got another idea, and that is, I'm going—we're going to set up a group of Members of Congress from both parties, both Chambers, recognizing that nothing can get done on this issue unless it's a bipartisan issue—and say, "Now is the time." That's what we're here for. We have been elected to confront

problems and deal with them. That's what the people expect. And they're tired, by the way, of all the politics in Washington, DC. They expect people to come together, to sit down at the table, and to solve this problem so you don't have to deal with it.

All right, last question. Then I got to go back to work. This isn't work. Yes, go ahead. Hold on for a minute. Please. Like—I can't—okay, two questions. Who yelled the loudest? You did? All right, go ahead. Then you're—you're the last guy. You're next to last. You're last.

Trade

Q. Mr. President, thank you again for coming. My question—I believe that one of our greatest resources is our self-sufficiency. And as you drive down the road, you'll see that our community is dying because of the importation of cheap steel. I'd like to know what your plans are to help alleviate this.

The President. Yes. Well, as you know, right before—right after I got elected, I put a 201 in place that—that was our way of providing breathing space so that the firm could adjust. And I fully understand the problems that the steel mills are going through here. The Governor spent a lot of time briefing me on that, on the way in, as did Shelley Moore. And it's—obviously, it's going to require good energy policy. Your plant can exist if it's got decent energy and reliable supplies at reasonable prices. Your plant can exist if you've got reasonable health care costs. And that's why it's important for us to do a variety of measures to help reduce the cost of health care. I just mentioned one on information technology. Another is to get rid of these junk lawsuits that are running up the cost of medicine.

In order for you to be competitive, we've got to make sure that products are treated fairly. As you know, I'm a free trader, but I also believe that people ought to treat the United States the way we treat them.

If we're letting products coming in here, they ought to let our products in on the same basis. I believe—[*applause*]—I'm aware of the issue you brought up, and thank you bringing it up.

Yes, sir. Final guy. Got to head back home. I hope you understand. Otherwise we'd be here all day. Wouldn't mind being here all day, but I got something else to do. [*Laughter*]

Let her go.

Political Ethics

Q. Mr. President, I want to say it's a privilege and a blessing to be here with you.

The President. Thank you.

Q. And thank you for having integrity since you've been in office, and character.

The President. Thank you, sir.

Q. I'm statewide field director for the campaign for Hiram Lewis for U.S. Senate. And as you close—I appreciate what you had stated earlier about politicians. And as you close today, I did 2 years of volunteer work for the Republican Party while I worked a full-time job, and it paid off for me in this position now. And I see folks that are increasingly discouraged with the status quo, because the difference——

The President. No campaign speeches.

Q. No, sir, I'm not.

The President. Okay.

Q. My only question is, what would you say to those, whether Democrat or Republican—how could you encourage those that are dissatisfied with the status quo?

The President. Right. No, I appreciate that. Look, it is really important for people to at least trust the decisionmaking process of those of us in public office. You may not agree with the decisions. You may not—and look, I understand a lot of people don't agree, and that's fine, that's fine. But they've got to understand, at least in my case, that I'm making my decisions based upon what I think is right, and that making decisions that are the kind that I make, for example, got to be based upon a set of principles that won't change. People got to understand that.

When there's any doubt about the integrity of the public servant, like in Washington there has been recently, they got to clean up—they got to work to clean it up. There's got to be lobby reform in this case. I mean, the truth of the matter is, a couple of Members of the House of Representatives disgraced the process. A person took money in order to put things in appropriations bills. That's unacceptable in our democracy. And it needs to be dealt with in order to be able to earn the confidence of the people.

I worry about lack of voter participation. I'm concerned that people don't participate at the ballot box. And it is something that we've all got to work on, because democracy is—really depends upon the participation of our citizenry. It's really important for high school students. And one of the challenges you'll face is whether or not our democracy is able to continue to get people to say, "I can make a difference in the ballot box."

And so, to answer your question, integrity is a central part of the process. Integrity in decisionmaking, integrity in how we deal with the people's money, integrity of—and part of a system based upon integrity is one that deals with, like in this case, unethical behavior very quickly, with certainty so that people have got confidence in the system.

I appreciate you working in the process. I want to thank you for your question. I wish I could stay longer to answer your questions. I can't; I got to go back to DC. I'm not necessarily saying I'd rather be in DC than here; I'd rather be here than there. But nevertheless, that's what my life dictates. God bless you all.

NOTE: The President spoke at 12:17 p.m. at the Capitol Music Hall. In his remarks, he referred to Terry Sterling, president, Wheeling Area Chamber of Commerce; Gov. Joe Manchin III of West Virginia, and his wife,

Gayle; Mayor Nicholas A. Sparachane of Wheeling, WV; Christopher Wakim, representative, West Virginia State House of Representatives; John Anderson, employee, Wheeling, WV, office, and Janis LaFont, employee, White Plains, MD, office, Valley National Gases, Inc.; President Hamid Karzai of Afghanistan; former President Saddam Hussein of Iraq; senior Al Qaida associate Abu Musab Al Zarqawi; U.S. Ambassador to Iraq Zalmay Khalilzad; Gen. George W. Casey, Jr., USA, commanding general, Multi-National Force—Iraq; and Prime Minister Junichiro Koizumi of Japan.

Memorandum on Designation of Officers of the National Archives and Records Administration
March 22, 2006

Memorandum for the Archivist of the United States

Subject: Designation of Officers of the National Archives and Records Administration

By the authority vested in me as President under the Constitution and laws of the United States of America and pursuant to the Federal Vacancies Reform Act of 1998, 5 U.S.C. 3345 *et seq.* (the "Act"), I hereby order that:

Section 1. Order of Succession.

During any period when both the Archivist of the United States (Archivist) and the Deputy Archivist of the United States (Deputy Archivist) have died, resigned, or otherwise become unable to perform the functions and duties of the office of Archivist, the following officers of the National Archives and Records Administration, in the order listed, shall perform the functions and duties of the office of Archivist, if they are eligible to act as Archivist under the provisions of the Act, until such time as the Archivist or Deputy Archivist is able to perform the functions and duties of the office of Archivist:

Assistant Archivist for Administration

Assistant Archivist for Records Services, Washington, D.C.

Assistant Archivist for Regional Records Services

Assistant Archivist for Presidential Libraries

Assistant Archivist for Information Services

Director of the Federal Register

Director, National Personnel Records Center

Director, Jimmy Carter Library

Sec. 2. Exceptions.

(a) No individual who is serving in an office listed in section 1 in an acting capacity, by virtue of so serving, shall act as Archivist pursuant to this memorandum.

(b) Notwithstanding the provisions of this memorandum, the President retains discretion, to the extent permitted by the Act or other law, to depart from this memorandum in designating an acting Archivist.

Sec. 3. Prior Memorandum Superseded.

This memorandum supersedes the Presidential Memorandum of March 19, 2002, entitled, "Designation of Officers of the National Archives and Records Administration."

GEORGE W. BUSH

Remarks Following a Meeting on Immigration Reform
March 23, 2006

I've just had a very constructive and important dialog with members of the agricultural community, the faith community, the concerned citizen community about immigration. Ours is a nation of law, and ours is a nation of immigrants, and we believe that we can have rational, important immigration policy that's based upon law and reflects our deep desire to be a compassionate and decent nation.

Our Government must enforce our borders; we've got plans in place to do so. But part of enforcing our borders is to have a guest-worker program that encourages people to register their presence so that we know who they are, and says to them, "If you're doing a job an American won't do, you're welcome here, for a period of time, to do that job."

The immigration debate is a vital debate for our country. It's important that we have a serious debate, one that discusses the issues. But I urge Members of Congress and I urge people who like to comment on this issue to make sure the rhetoric is in accord with our traditions. I look around the table and I recognize that we've got people from different backgrounds, different heritages. We all may have different family histories, but we all sit around this table as Americans.

And therefore, when we conduct this debate, it must be done in a civil way. It must be done in a way that brings dignity to the process. It must be done in a way that doesn't pit one group of people against another. It must be done in a way that recognizes our history. I think now is the time for the United States Congress to act to get an immigration plan that is comprehensive and rational and achieves important objectives.

So I want to welcome you all for being here. I want to thank you very much for your involvement in this vital issue. I've assured folks here at the table that I will continue to speak out on the issue. I feel passionately about the need for our country to conduct themselves with dignity and, at the same time, enforce our border and treat people here with respect.

Thank you all very much.

NOTE: The President spoke at 10:37 a.m. in the Roosevelt Room at the White House. The Office of the Press Secretary also released a Spanish language transcript of these remarks.

Remarks on Signing a Bill To Authorize the Extension of Nondiscriminatory Treatment to the Products of Ukraine
March 23, 2006

Thank you. Pleased be seated. Ambassador, good to see you. Please be seated. Welcome. Appreciate you all coming. In a few minutes, I'm going to sign a bill that authorizes permanent normal trade relations between the United States and Ukraine. It's a good bill, and it's going to strengthen our ties with our friend Ukraine.

It's going to create new opportunities, economic opportunities, for both our countries.

I really want to thank the chairman of the Senate Foreign Relations Committee, a man who knows what he's talking about when it comes to the world, and that's Chairman Lugar from Indiana. Thank you for coming, sir. I thank the bill sponsor,

Congressman Jim Gerlach; and his wife, Karen, is here today. Thank you for coming, Mr. Congressman. Congressman Tom Lantos is with us. He's the ranking member of the House International Relations Committee. Congressman Curt Weldon, a cosponsor of the bill, is with us. Congresswoman Candice Miller from Michigan, a cosponsor, is with us, as well as a cosponsor, Congressman Mike Fitzpatrick. Thank you all for being here.

I welcome you all here. I especially welcome the Ambassador from Ukraine, Ambassador Shamshur. Welcome, Mr. Ambassador. Appreciate you coming. This is the third time we've been together in the last 30 days. [*Laughter*] I'm better for it. [*Laughter*]

The bill I sign today marks the beginning of a new era in our history with Ukraine. During the cold war, Congress passed the Jackson-Vanik Amendment as a response to widespread Communist deprivation of human rights. The law made American trade with Communist nations contingent on those countries' respect for the rights of their own people. At the time, the law served an important purpose; it helped to encourage freedom and the protection of fundamental rights and penalized nations that denied liberty to their citizens. Times have changed. The cold war is over, and a free Ukraine is a friend to America and an inspiration to those who love liberty.

The Orange Revolution was a powerful example of democracy for people around the world. The brave citizens who gathered in Kiev's Independence Square demanded the chance to determine their nation's future, and when they got that chance, they chose freedom. In the past 2 years, Ukraine has held free elections, and the people of Ukraine and its President, Viktor Yushchenko, are deeply committed to democratic reform. On Sunday, the Ukrainian people will again have the chance to cast a ballot in parliamentary elections, and they have a chance to continue to shape their own future.

Ukraine is also working to expand its market economy and produce measurable improvements in the lives of the Ukranian people. America supports these efforts, and this bill is an important step. By eliminating barriers to trade between the United States and Ukraine, the bill will help Ukraine grow in prosperity. As we've seen over the past 50 years, trade has the power to create new wealth for whole nations and new opportunities for people around the world. By expanding trade with Ukraine, this bill will open new markets for American products and help Ukrainians continue to build a free economy that will raise the standard of living for families across their land.

As Ukraine embraces democracy and more open trade, our nations' friendship will grow. President Yushchenko has made reforms to increase transparency and provide intellectual property protection and strengthen the enforcement of the rule of law.

These reforms have taken great conviction. And earlier this month, our two nations signed a bilateral agreement that will establish the terms of trade between our nations when Ukraine join the World Trade Organization. We support Ukraine's goal of joining the WTO, and we will help resolve the remaining steps required for entry as quickly as possible. As the Ukrainian Government continues to build on a record of progress at home, we will help Ukraine join the institutions that unite free nations and become a part of Europe that is whole, free, and at peace.

The growth of economic freedom and ownership in countries like the Ukraine reinforces the habits of liberty and democracy and gives citizens a stake in the success of their nation. Ukranian people have shown the world they are committed to the ideals of economic freedom and democratic progress and open trade, and that gives them a promising future.

The United States is proud to call Ukraine a friend, and I'm honored to sign this important piece of legislation into law.

NOTE: The President spoke at 11:01 a.m. in Room 350 of the Dwight D. Eisenhower Executive Office Building. In his remarks, he referred to Ukraine's Ambassador to the U.S. Oleh Shamshur. H.R. 1053, approved March 23, was assigned Public Law No. 109–205.

Memorandum on the National Flood Insurance Program
March 23, 2006

Memorandum for the Secretary of the Homeland Security

Subject: National Flood Insurance Program

Pursuant to the authority vested in me by the Constitution and laws of the United States, including 42 U.S.C. 4016, I have reviewed and hereby approve your request to issue notes to the Secretary of the Treasury in excess of $18.5 billion, but not to exceed $20.775 billion, for the National Flood Insurance Program.

GEORGE W. BUSH

Remarks at a Celebration of Greek Independence Day
March 24, 2006

Thank you. Welcome. Your Eminence, thank you for your kind words. You're a philosopher; you're a wise person; you're an incredibly compassionate soul; and I'm proud to call you friend. Thank you for being here.

Thank you for inviting me to help celebrate the 185th anniversary of Greek Independence. America is a better country because of Greek Americans. It's something about the passion, the verve for life, the willingness to serve. I am blessed by having Greek Americans in my administration, two of the most important of whom have joined us, Your Eminence: John Negroponte, the Director of the National Intelligence, and the Homeland Security Adviser, Frances Fragos Townsend.

Madame Foreign Minister, we are thrilled to have you here. Thank you for coming. Let me just say this, that it is a wise government who relies upon the judgment and advice of a woman as a Foreign Minister or Secretary of State. [*Laughter*] And I look forward to sharing our visit with my mother and dad, who are close to the Minister. And I know they're going to be thrilled to know that you're strong and optimistic in serving your great country with class and dignity.

Mr. Ambassador, thank you as well. Appreciate—good to see you, sir. I appreciate Christos Folias, who is the Deputy Minister of Economy for Greece. Welcome, sir. It's good to see you.

I am really pleased that Senator Paul Sarbanes is with us today. He has served with great distinction in the United States Senate. He has decided to move on to other ventures, and the State of Maryland will miss his leadership. Proud you're here, sir.

I want to thank those who wear the Nation's uniform. Your Eminence, as you know, ours is a remarkable country, where people are willing to volunteer to serve our country in times of war. And our Nation is blessed to have men and women who, in the face of danger, say, "I want to help." So thanks for coming. More importantly, thanks for serving. I know you share the same feeling I share, that it is an honor to serve the United States of America.

I want to thank the other Greek Americans, leaders, and folks who are here. Thanks for coming. Thanks for traveling long distances to be here in Washington.

We honor Greek Independence Day because of the values we share. That's why it's a comfortable event. That's why it's an important event, Your Eminence. The ancient Athenians gave birth to democracy. They entrusted their citizens with the power to govern. That's a powerful concept. It wasn't always that way. In some parts of the world, it still isn't that way. But nevertheless, it is a universal concept, started by the Athenians.

We respect the philosophy that grew out of Greece that honored and respected human dignity and human rights and, as you said, Your Eminence, the belief that there is universality to the concept of liberty. Freedom is not confined to Greece, nor is it confined to America. It is universal in its application, and that's one of the great lessons of Greek Independence Day.

America's Founding Fathers were inspired by the democratic ideals, and it helped form our own Union. Those ideals became implanted in long-lasting documents. But as we watch the world today, we must understand that democracy is difficult at times. It's not easy to take hold. It requires work and diligence and optimism and strength and will. But the Greek lesson, not only in Greece but also here in America, is one that with time and persistence, liberty does take hold because of its universality. It's a lesson we honor on Greek Independence Day.

When the founders of modern Greece claimed their freedom in 1821, they had the strong backing of America. The American people supported that independence. John Adams, Thomas Jefferson, James Madison, all members of the ex-Presidents Club—[*laughter*]—I'm not there yet, Your Eminence—[*laughter*]—all urged support of the Greek cause.

Young Americans volunteered to serve in the new Greek Army. Many more Americans contributed funds to support the Greek people in their struggle for freedom. America stood side by side with those who struggled for liberty in 1821.

It's reminiscent of what's taking place in the 21st century. Our two nations have continued to work together in freedom's cause. Greece was an ally of the United States in major international conflicts of the 20th century. We're allies in the war on terror. In Afghanistan, Greece is a valuable contributor to the NATO-led International Security Assistance Force, and we thank your Government for that. Greece provides security at the Kabul International Airport, and we thank your Government for that as well.

Greece has also been generous in the support for the Afghan people, and the Afghan people thank the Greek Government for that as well. Last month in London, for example, Greece pledged funds to support educational programs. The Greek Government decided to support entrepreneurship, with the full knowledge that education and entrepreneurship can lead to a prosperous and thriving economy so that the people can see the benefits of liberty.

Greece is supporting other efforts in the war on terror. Our two nations remain committed to the security and counterterrorism partnership we put in place during the Olympics in Athens in 2004. By the way, people still marvel at how well those Olympics were run. The Government stood up and, in spite of all the criticism that was taking place, put on some great games. It's a model for other countries to follow.

Greece and the United States are working together to keep our people safe. We'll continue to work together to spread the blessings of liberty because we understand that when we spread the blessings of liberty, it lays the foundation for peace. And that's what we want.

At home, Greek Americans strengthen our communities. Greek entrepreneurs contribute to our country's prosperity. The Greek culture enriches our entire country. The Greek Orthodox Church reflects America's religious diversity. It's a source of strength and unity and inspiration for many Greek Americans.

I also understand that Greek Independence Day is the Feast of the Annunciation in the Orthodox faith, that they're celebrated together because they both represent good news. On Greek Independence Day, Greeks and Americans honor the anniversary of the Greek call for independence and celebrate the universal good news of freedom and liberty. We believe that freedom is God's gift to all people. And we know that by working together, freedom is on the march.

Your Eminence, thank you for inviting me. May God bless you all.

NOTE: The President spoke at 9:59 a.m. in Room 450 of the Dwight D. Eisenhower Executive Office Building at the White House. In his remarks, he referred to Archbishop Demetrios, Primate of the Greek Orthodox Church in America; Minister of Foreign Affairs Theodora Bakoyianni of Greece; and Greece's Ambassador to the U.S. Alexandros Mallias. The Greek Independence Day proclamation of March 17 is listed in Appendix D at the end of this volume.

Remarks at a Reception for Congressional Candidate Michael E. Sodrel in Indianapolis, Indiana
March 24, 2006

Thank you all for coming. Please be seated. Michael, thanks for having me here. Let me start off by telling you it's great to be back in Indiana, the great city of Indianapolis. I'm here because I strongly believe it's in Indiana's interest to send Mike Sodrel back to the United States Congress.

And I want to thank you all for supporting him. Some of you are from his district; some of you aren't, but all of you are wise enough to know a good candidate when you see one.

I'm traveling without the better half of my family. Laura sends her best to the Sodrels; she sends her best to the Governor; she sends her best to the good people of Indiana. I'm a lucky man to be married to Laura Bush, and Mike Sodrel is a lucky man to be married to Keta Sodrel. I'm glad to be here with the Sodrels and the Sodrel family. I like a man in Congress who has his priorities straight, and Michael Sodrel prioritizes his family as a central part of his life.

Governor, I'm proud you're here. I knew Mitch was going to be a fine Governor because, first of all, he's a fine man. He's got a wonderful sense of humor. I like a fellow who doesn't take a—run a poll to tell him what to think. I like somebody who stands up and does what he thinks is right. Give the first lady my best and the four daughters.

I want to thank Congressman Steve Buyer for being here. Buyer, it's good to see you. Thanks for your service in the United States Congress. And Congressman Michael Pence—thanks for coming, Mike. I appreciate you being here. It's a good sign when other Members of Congress come out to support one of their brothers. So thanks for supporting Mike.

You know what I know about him. He's an effective person. He can get things done. He's a reasonable guy. That's what you want in the United States Congress.

In a land of lawyers, it's good to have somebody who is an entrepreneur and started their own business.

I thank the attorney general, Steve Carter, for being here. General, I'm proud you're here; the secretary of State, Todd Rokita—thank you both for coming, and thanks for serving your State. I thank everybody else for coming, particularly those who have worked hard to raise the money. For those of you who are interested in following up on your contributions, get over to Mike's district and help turn out the vote.

And that's why I want to recognize Murray Clark, who's the chairman of the Indiana Republican Party, and his wife, Janet. Get those grassroots moving at the proper time, and we'll send this guy back to the United States Congress.

And finally, I understand the former mayor of Indianapolis, my longtime friend, Steve Goldsmith, is with us today. Stephen, if you're here, thanks for being here; thanks for your service; and thanks for your friendship. He was on the leading edge of the compassionate conservative agenda, which has made an enormous difference in the lives of people, not only here in Indianapolis but around the country.

Let me give you a Mike Sodrel quote. He said, "The first role of the Federal Government is to provide for the defense of the country." It's important to have people in the United States Congress who understand this is a nation at war. I wish I could tell you otherwise. I wish I could say that an enemy which attacked us on September the 11th, 2001, has quit. That is not the reality of the world in which we live. The reality in the world in which we live is there's an enemy which hates those of us who embrace freedom and would like to strike us again. And therefore, it's important to have Members of the United States Congress who understand the stakes in the global war on terror. And Mike Sodrel understands the stakes.

My most important job is to lead our Nation and to protect you. And so I have—want to share with you some of the lessons I learned after September the 11th, 2001, lessons that Members of the United States Congress must have in order for us to do our job. Lesson one is that we must defeat the enemy overseas so we do not have to face them here at home.

Ours is an enemy which has embraced an ideology—an ideology of hatred, an ideology that is totalitarian in nature. They decide if you can worship and how you worship; they decide whether or not your children can go to school; they decide this; they decide that. They stand exactly the opposite of the United States of America. They have expressed their tactics for the world to see. They believe that those of us living in democracies are weak, flaccid. It's just a matter of time, they believe, if they continue to exert pressure, that we will retreat from the world. That's what they want.

It's important to have Members of the United States Congress who understand the stakes and understand the nature of the enemy. They cannot exist without safe haven. And so one of the doctrines and one of the lessons learned after September the 11th is that we must hold people to account for harboring terrorists. If you harbor a terrorist, if you feed a terrorist, if you house a terrorist, you're equally guilty as the terrorists.

Michael Sodrel understands that. He also understands that when the President speaks, he better mean what he says. And I meant what I said when I said that, and that's why I told the Taliban—I said, "Get rid of Al Qaida." They refused. We sent a liberation force into Afghanistan to uphold doctrine, to protect ourselves and, in so doing, liberated 25 million people from the clutches of a barbaric regime.

A lesson of September the 11th is that not only are we facing a brutal enemy that's willing to take innocent life, an enemy which thinks we're soft, an enemy which tries to find safe haven—but a vital lesson of September the 11th that our Nation must not forget is that when we see a threat, we must take it seriously, before it comes to hurt us. You see, before September the 11th, it was assumed by policymakers and people in office that we were safe, that oceans protected us, that we're in good shape when it came to threats. We could see a threat overseas, and we could deal with it if we wanted to, or not.

That changed on September the 11th. From now on, the United States of America, in order to protect our citizens, must deal with threats, must take them seriously to do our most fundamental job, which is to protect the American people. I saw threats in Saddam Hussein. Members of the United States Congress—both Republicans and Democrats—saw a threat in Saddam Hussein. Members of the United Nations Security Council saw threats in Saddam Hussein. The world spoke. They said, "Disarm, disclose, or face serious consequences." The choice was Saddam Hussein's, and removing Saddam Hussein has made this Nation and the world a safer place.

I need Members of Congress who support a plan for victory in Iraq. We've committed brave men and women, volunteers, people who said, "I volunteer to serve the United States of America." And they're in harm's way, and we must have Members of the United States Congress who will not weaken and who will make sure our troops have all the necessary support to achieve the mission. And Mike Sodrel understands that and is a strong supporter of the United States military.

Our strategy is to help rebuild the country. Our strategy is to encourage democracy. I know it's troubled times. I understand the enemy is capable of affecting how we think about the war in Iraq because they're willing to take innocent life. And this turbulence on your TV screens affects the conscious of Americans—I know that, and so does the enemy. But amidst all the turmoil, I want you to remember that progress towards democracy is being made. It wasn't all that long ago—4 months ago— that 11 million Iraqis defied the killers, defied the terrorists, and said loud and clear, "We want democracy." Democracy is on the march in Iraq, and our job as a government is to help them form a unity government, a government around which the country can rally.

The other part of our strategy is to train the Iraqis so they can take the fight to the enemy. The enemy cannot defeat us on the battlefield. They just can't beat us. So what they tried to do is they're trying to create a civil war; that's why they blew up the mosque. But amidst the turmoil and the pictures and the devastation and the reprisal, I want you to know that the Iraqi forces performed. The Iraqi forces we trained were able to bring some sense of stability throughout the country of Iraq. The mission is to train the Iraqis so they can take the fight. The mission is to encourage democracy. As Iraqi troops stand up, we'll stand down.

But I'm going to tell you something about me. I'm not going to make up my mind about Iraq based upon polls and focus groups. I will make up my mind about troops based upon the recommendations of the United States military, not politicians in Washington, DC. [*Applause*] Thank you all.

The only way that we can lose is if we lose our will. It's the only way we can lose. The stakes in Iraq are high. Remember, this is a global war on terror. Iraq is a part of the war on terror. And they're high because the enemy has stated they would like to have a safe haven from which to launch attacks against America again.

I fully understand some in the United States don't believe what the enemy has said. I think you better have a President and Members of Congress who take the enemy seriously. You better have people in Washington, DC, who see the world the way it is, not the way we would like it to be. If our most important job is to protect the American people, we must be diligent and steadfast and never ending in our desire to protect you. Mike understands that, and so do I. Ultimately, the way to defeat the enemy, the way to defeat an ideology of darkness, a totalitarian ideology of darkness, is to defeat it with a philosophy of light. And that philosophy is liberty.

As I make my decisions as to how to protect you, I want you to know I'm guided by this principle: I believe there's an Almighty, and I believe the Almighty's great gift to every man and woman—every man and woman—on the face of the Earth is freedom. Freedom is universal. It is non-negotiable. And as freedom takes hold, the world becomes more peaceful. Democracies don't war.

As you explain what we're trying to do in Iraq—and will do in Iraq—to your friends and neighbors, remind them about the history of Europe. America lost hundreds of thousands of soldiers on the continent of Europe in two world wars. And yet today, Europe is whole, free, and at peace. And the reason why is, democracies don't war.

My dad, as an 18-year-old kid, when the country called, said, "I'm going in to fight the Japanese." I'm sure there's—you've got some relatives of others who went to war with the Japanese in World War II. They were the sworn enemy. They attacked us. They attacked the United States of America. Less people, by the way, died in the Pearl Harbor attack than died on September the 11th, 2001, on our soil.

And yet today, interestingly enough, I sit at a table with the Prime Minister of Japan working on how to keep the peace. Isn't that interesting? Sixty years ago or so, 18-year-old George H.W. Bush volunteered to fight the Japanese as his sworn enemy. And now his son sits at the table to keep the peace with the Japanese.

What happened? What happened was the Japanese adopted a Japanese-style democracy. If we don't lose our nerve, if we stay the course, someday down the road, an American President will be working with democratically-elected leaders in the broader Middle East at the table to keep the peace.

I like working with Mike Sodrel because he understands the role of government is not to create wealth but an environment in which the entrepreneurial spirit can flourish, in which people can realize their dreams, in which people can start with nothing in America and, through hard work and imagination, build assets they call their own.

Mike understands that. By the way, that environment was challenged during my Presidency. We've had a recession; we had a stock market collapse; we had an attack on our country; we have been a nation at war; we've had major natural disasters. But because our party, because Members of the Congress here, people like Mike Sodrel, understand that if people have more of their own money to save and spend and invest, we can recover from difficult economic times.

Oh, I remember the tax debates there in Washington, DC. I remember those Democratic critics who spoke loud and clear. I remember one of them saying, "It's reckless, irresponsible plan that will undermine opportunity in our country." You remember those debates, the loud noises they made about cutting taxes.

Well, let me read to you the statistics. Our economy grew last year at 3.5 percent. The unemployment rate across America is 4.8 percent. In the last 2½ years, we've added nearly 5 million new jobs. The unemployment rate in Indiana is 4.7 percent. Productivity is up. Small businesses are flourishing. More people own a home than ever before in our Nation's history. Cutting taxes for the American people was the right thing to do.

We've got a record to stand on. We've got a record of dealing with some serious economic times. There's a debate, of course, in Washington, DC, about tax cutting, and I want the people of the Ninth Congressional District and districts all across America to understand the difference in our record. Our party and Members of the United States Congress stood squarely for tax relief for everybody who pays taxes.

And the Democratic Party has a clear record. In 2001, more than 90 percent of the congressional Democrats voted against cutting income tax rates. More than 90 percent of the Democrats voted against the bill that provided tax relief for married couples. More than 90 percent of the Democrats voted for [against] * a bill that would have put the death tax on the road to extinction. More than 90 percent of the Democrats voted against a bill that doubled the child credit. More than 95 percent of the congressional Democrats voted against cutting taxes on capital gains.

And recently, during the budget debate, Democrats used the occasion to call for $173 billion in tax hikes and fee increases. The difference is clear: If you want the Government in your pocket, vote Democrat; if you want to keep more of your hard-earned money, vote Republican.

And so the fundamental question confronting us in Washington is, how do we keep this economic recovery going? That's what people ought to be talking about. And we've got some good ideas as to how to keep it going. And the first thing is, make the tax cuts permanent. Oh, I know you've heard the same talk I've heard in Washington, "We've got a problem with the deficit." We do, and we're going to deal with it. But the Democrats have got a good idea, they think, and that's to run up your taxes to make sure the deficit—folks, that's not the way Washington works.

Here's the way Washington works. They'll increase your taxes, and they'll figure out new ways to spend your money. The best way to make sure that we reduce

---

* White House correction.

the deficit is to keep progrowth economic policies in place and be wise about how we spend your money. That's why we need people like Mike Sodrel in the United States Congress.

It's important to set priorities when it comes to our budget. So long as we've got men and women in harm's way, we will make sure they have got that which is necessary to do their job. And I want to thank Mike and the Members of the United States Congress who are here who have prioritized supporting the United States military when it comes into our budget—comes to budget matters.

I don't know if you realize this, but over the past—the last budget cycle, thanks to the good work of Members of the United States Congress, we actually cut nonsecurity discretionary spending. We not only have slowed the growth of nonsecurity discretionary spending every year that I have been the President, last year we cut nonsecurity discretionary spending. And I submitted a budget to the United States Congress to do it again. And the Members in this crowd are supportive of a good, prioritizing, lean budget. And I want to thank you for your support.

The problem we have is that we've got people who want to spend more money in Washington. That's why we need fiscally sound people like Mike Sodrel in the United States Congress. And we also must show some political courage when it comes to the budget. The main reason the budget goes up is because of mandatory spending increases. Those would be your increases in Social Security and Medicare.

And we've got a problem, folks, when it comes to Social Security and Medicare. We've got a whole bunch of us getting ready to retire—that would be baby boomers like me. As a matter of fact—Mitch, you probably don't know this—but I turn 62, which qualifies me for Social Security, in 2008. That's a convenient year to become eligible for retirement. [*Laughter*]

And there's a lot of us, a lot of us baby boomers. I'm kind of scanning out there, and I see quite a few of us. [*Laughter*] And we've been promised greater benefits than the previous generation, and we're living longer. I don't know about you all; I plan on just kind of stretching it out a little bit. [*Laughter*] And there are fewer people paying in the system, and the system is going broke.

I need people in the United States Congress like Michael, who's willing to work with me to reform and modernize these mandatory programs so that a future generation of kids can come up and say, "Thank God for that Congress. Thank God they're willing to do the hard work. Thank God they're willing to take on problems and not pass them on to future Presidents and future generations."

It's a tough issue, but that's why you sent us to Washington, DC, to deal with tough issues. If it were an easy issue, other people would have taken care of it. And I'm looking forward to working with both Republicans and Democrats to modernize both Social Security and Medicare so a young generation will say, "Job well done."

In order to make sure that we're—this economy keeps growing, listen, we can't fear the future. We've got to shape the future. We've got to be confident as a nation. We lead the world today, and I intend to work with Congress to put policies in place so that we can lead the world tomorrow.

And let me share some ideas with you. First of all, in order to lead—be the economic leader of the world, we've got to do something about these frivolous and junk lawsuits that are making it hard to risk capital. You know, it's fine, one thing to be—to have a legitimate lawsuit. It's these frivolous lawsuits and the junk lawsuits—and people are filing lawsuits right and left that are hurting the capacity of this country to realize our full potential. I look forward to working with Congress for meaningful and real tort reform.

I look forward to working with Congress to do something about our energy situation. I know it came as a surprise to you that a fellow from Texas would stand up and say, "We've got a problem; we're addicted to oil." [*Laughter*] But I meant it. It's an economic problem. It's an economic problem because as other economies begin to grow and use more fossil fuels, it affects our price.

It's a national security problem. We're dealing with some countries that don't particularly like us, and they've got a lot of oil. It gives us a national security problem when people threaten to hold oil off the market for geopolitical reasons.

This country needs to come together, do some smart things—particularly when it comes to research and development—smart things about how we change our driving habits. I want people driving with corn extract, ethanol grown right here in the State of Indiana, in order to keep these cars moving. One of these days, they're going to walk in with a crop report to the President and say, "The harvest down there in Indiana is great. We've got us a lot of corn, that means we're less dependent on foreign sources of oil."

We've got to make sure that we continue to invest in battery technologies. Right around the corner is a technology that will enable you to plug in your pickup truck and drive the first 40 miles on electricity. That's not going to help you in parts of rural Indiana, but if you're an urban person—in Indianapolis or Houston, Texas, or anywhere else in America—that first 40 miles means a lot when it comes to your driving. Imagine people being able to drive on electricity, not on gasoline, for the first 40 miles. It will make us less dependent on foreign sources of oil. When it comes to electricity, we've got to be wise about how we use our resources.

We'll continue to invest in clean coal technologies so this abundant resource can be used without fear of polluting our air. We need safe nuclear power if we intend to be an energy dependent and an environmentally conscious country. No, in order to help us remain competitive in the world, we've got to be wise about our energy policy, and I look forward to leading the Congress toward a new day when it comes to consuming, particularly Middle Eastern, oil.

In order to make sure that we're a competitive nation, we shouldn't fear the future; we ought to lead it. And the best way to lead it is to make sure our kids are educated for the jobs of the 21st century. I appreciate what these Governors, like Mitch Daniels, are doing—setting high standards and holding the people to account. I think it makes sense if you're spending a lot of money to say to the school districts, "Why don't you show us whether or not a child can read and write?" It seems like a legitimate question to me.

It doesn't make any sense for the Federal Government to tell you how to teach. We believe in local control of schools. But when you're spending as much money as we do, it seems like we ought to be able to say, "Show us whether or not a child is reading." And if not, correct the problems early, before it's too late. You can't solve a problem unless you diagnose the problem.

And the No Child Left Behind Act believes every child can learn, believes in setting high standards, and says to the local districts, "All we want to know is, can the child learn to read and write and add and subtract? And if not, here's a little extra money to bring them up to speed."

Now, we've got to apply that same rigor and same standards to math and science and at the same time increase Government investment in research and development— and at the same time say to the private sector, "There's certainty when it comes to your budgets." The research and development tax credit should be a permanent part of the Tax Code. In order for the United States of America to be the leader of the world, we must have a job—a set of skills available for youngsters that will able to fill the jobs of the 21st century, and we must be the leader in research and technology.

Mike Sodrel understands that. Mike Sodrel doesn't fear the future because he intends to work with President George W. Bush to shape the future. By being the economic leader in the world, our people will realize a better standard of living. By being the economic leader of the world, we will continue to be able to bring prosperity to corners of our country.

You know, one thing Mike told me, he said, "Just remember one thing, when you're talking about my district, is that we've got a lot of farmers there." All right, I'm going to talk to the farmers in Mike's district. You better have somebody elected to the United States Congress who works to make sure there's markets for you to sell your products. If you're good at something, you want to be able to sell your products in new markets. And Indiana's farmers are very good at a lot of things. They're good at growing. They're good at harvesting, and the United States Government ought to help them sell those products overseas at good prices.

Secondly, if you're a farmer, you better have a Member of the United States Congress who understands the effects of the death tax on the American family farmer. We've got a system today where you farm all your life; you're paying your taxes; and then you pass on—and your heirs get to pay taxes again. And sometimes those inheritance taxes mean you have to liquidate your farm. For the sake of stability in the farm community, we need to get rid of the death tax once and for all.

Most of all, I'm here for Mike Sodrel because he's a good, honest man. He's a decent man. He's a problem-solver. He's a practical fellow. He likes to get things done. He's a patriotic man. He's done a real fine job in the United States Congress, and I look forward to working with him in my last 2 years as President of the United States.

I want to thank you all for coming to support Michael Sodrel. Thanks for your interest. Thanks for your concern about our future. May God bless Indiana. May God continue to bless the United States of America.

NOTE: The President spoke at 2:10 p.m. in the Murat Centre. In his remarks, he referred to Gov. Mitchell E. Daniels, Jr., of Indiana, and his wife, Cheri; and Prime Minister Junichiro Koizumi of Japan.

Message on Freedom Efforts in Belarus
March 24, 2006

I send greetings to those working to return freedom to Belarus and observing the 88th anniversary of the first effort to establish an independent Belarus.

Freedom is the birthright of every human soul and the permanent hope of all mankind. The desire for justice, freedom, human rights, and accountable, representative government is universal. Nations grow by allowing the talents and liberties of their people to flourish, not by suppressing freedom. By upholding the rule of law, limiting the power of the state, holding free and fair elections, and respecting the rights of all people, governments can foster more hopeful societies and empower their citizens.

I appreciate those who labor in the shadows to return freedom to Belarus, and our Nation's thoughts are with those who have been harassed, detained, imprisoned, or beaten for their efforts. The United States condemns the actions by Belarusian security services on the morning of March 24, and we urge all members of the international community to join us in condemning any and all abuses and demanding that Belarusian authorities respect the rights of their own citizens to express themselves peacefully. The United States will continue to stand with the people of Belarus and all those who are working to help Belarus take its rightful place in the community of democracies.

NOTE: An original was not available for verification of the content of this message.

The President's Radio Address
March 25, 2006

Good morning. On Monday, I will attend a naturalization ceremony here in Washington. It's always inspiring to watch a group of immigrants raise their hands and swear an oath to become citizens of the United States of America. These men and women follow in the footsteps of millions who've come to our shores seeking liberty and opportunity, and America is better off for their hard work and love of freedom.

America is a nation of immigrants, and we're also a nation of laws. And our immigration laws are in need of reform. So at Monday's ceremony, I will discuss my vision for comprehensive immigration reform that will secure our borders, improve enforcement of our immigration laws, and uphold our values.

Comprehensive immigration reform begins with securing our borders. Since I took office, we've increased funding for border security by 66 percent, and the Department of Homeland Security has caught and sent home nearly 6 million illegal immigrants. To improve security at the border, we're hiring thousands more Border Patrol agents. We're deploying new technology like infrared cameras and unmanned aerial vehicles to help our agents do their job. And we're installing physical barriers to entry, like fences in urban areas.

We're also working to end the unwise practice of catch-and-release. For decades, many illegal immigrants were released back into society soon after they were caught because we did not have enough detention space. So we're adding more beds so we can hold the people we catch, and we're reducing the time it takes to send them back home. When illegal immigrants know they will be caught and sent home, they will be less likely to break the rules, and our immigration system will be more orderly and secure. We're making good progress, but we have much more work ahead, and we will not be satisfied until we have control of our border.

Comprehensive immigration reform also includes strengthening the enforcement of our laws in America's interior. Since I took office, we've increased funding for immigration enforcement by 42 percent. We're increasing the number of immigration enforcement agents and criminal investigators, enhancing worksite enforcement, and going after smugglers and gang members and human traffickers.

Finally, comprehensive immigration reform requires a temporary-worker program that will relieve pressure on our borders. This program would create a legal way to match willing foreign workers with willing American employers to fill jobs that Americans will not do. By reducing the number of people trying to sneak across the border, we would free up our law enforcement officers to focus on criminals and drug dealers and terrorists and others who mean us harm.

One thing the temporary-worker program would not do is provide amnesty to those who are in our country illegally. I believe that granting amnesty would be unfair, because it would allow those who break the law to jump ahead of people who play by the rules and wait in the citizenship line. Amnesty would also be unwise, because it would encourage waves of illegal immigration, increase pressure on the border, and make it more difficult for law enforcement to focus on those who mean us harm. For the sake of justice and for the sake of border security, I firmly oppose amnesty.

In the coming days, the United States Senate plans to consider proposals on immigration reform. This is an emotional debate. America does not have to choose between being a welcoming society and being a lawful society. We can be both at the same time. As we debate the immigration issue, we must remember, there are hardworking individuals, doing jobs that Americans will not do, who are contributing to the economic vitality of our country.

To keep the promise of America, we must enforce the laws of America. We must also ensure that immigrants assimilate into our society and learn our customs and values—including the English language. By working together, we can meet our duty to fix our immigration system and deliver a bill that protects our country, upholds our laws, and makes our Nation proud.

Thank you for listening.

NOTE: The address was recorded at 7:59 a.m. on March 24 in the Cabinet Room at the White House for broadcast at 10:06 a.m. on March 25. The transcript was made available by the Office of the Press Secretary on March 24 but was embargoed for release until the broadcast. The Office of the Press Secretary also released a Spanish language transcript of this address.

Remarks at a Naturalization Ceremony
March 27, 2006

Thank you all. Thank you very much. It's good to be with you. I am grateful for the chance to witness this joyous and uplifting ceremony. It is inspiring to see people of many different ages, many different countries raise their hands and swear an oath to become citizens of the United States of America.

For some of you, this day comes after a long and difficult journey. For all of you, this is a defining moment in your lives. America is now more than your home; America is your country. I welcome you to this free nation. I congratulate you and your families, and it's an honor to call you fellow Americans.

I appreciate the Attorney General. Dr. Gonzales, thank you, sir. And, Alfonso, it's good to be up here with you. I want to thank the president general of the Daughters of the American Revolution, Ms. Presley Wagoner, for letting us use this fantastic facility for this important ceremony. Thank you for singing the national anthem so beautifully.

It is fitting that we hold this ceremony at the home of the Daughters of the American Revolution. The Daughters of the American Revolution were the daughters of immigrants, because the leaders of our Revolution all had ancestors who came from abroad. As new citizens of the United States, you now walk in the footsteps of millions. And with the oath you've sworn, you're every bit as American as those who came before you.

Our immigrant heritage has enriched America's history. It continues to shape our society. Each generation of immigrants brings a renewal to our national character and adds vitality to our culture. Newcomers have a special way of appreciating the opportunities of America, and when they seize those opportunities, our whole nation benefits.

In the 1970s, an immigrant from Ireland—or the 1790s, an immigrant from Ireland designed the White House, right where Laura and I live. And he helped build the Capitol. In the 1990s, an immigrant from Russia helped create the Internet search engine Google. In between, new citizens have made contributions in virtually every professional field, and millions of newcomers have strengthened their communities through quiet lives of hard work and family and faith.

America's welcoming society is more than a cultural tradition; it is a fundamental promise of our democracy. Our Constitution does not limit citizenship by background or birth. Instead, our Nation is bound together by a shared love of liberty and a conviction that all people are created with dignity and value. Through the generations, Americans have upheld that vision by welcoming new citizens from across the globe, and that has made us stand apart.

One of my predecessors, President Ronald Reagan, used to say this: "You can go to live in France, but you cannot become a Frenchman. You can go to live in Japan, but you cannot become Japanese. But anyone, from any corner of the world, can come to live in America and be an American."

The new Americans we welcome today include men and women from 20 countries on 5 continents. Their ages range from 18 to 59, and they work as teachers and small-business managers and nurses and software engineers and other professions.

One new citizen is Veronica Pacheco. Veronica first came to the United States from Bolivia 15 years ago. In 2000, she moved here permanently and found a job at a catering company in Virginia. Every Friday and Saturday, she spent 5 hours studying English at the local community college. Over the years, she saved enough money to buy her own townhouse. Here's what Veronica says about America: "This is a country of opportunity. If you want to be successful, you can do it. You can have your dreams come true here."

Another new citizen is Maisoon Shahin. Maisoon grew up in Kuwait and moved to the United States with her husband 7 years ago. She enrolled in the community college to improve her English, took a job teaching marines to speak Arabic. Here's what Maisoon said: "The United States is a symbol of justice, freedom, and liberty. I love that. Here they respect people because they are people. I feel I am honored, and I feel that I'm loved."

America is stronger and more dynamic when we welcome new citizens like Maisoon and Veronica to our democracy. With that in mind, I've called on Congress to increase the number of green cards that can lead to citizenship. I support increasing the number of visas available for foreign-born workers in highly skilled fields like science, medicine, and technology. I've signed legislation creating a new Office of Citizenship at the Department of Homeland Security to promote knowledge of citizenship rights and procedures.

And after September the 11th, I signed an Executive order making foreign-born members of our military immediately eligible for citizenship, because those willing to risk their lives for our democracy should be full participants in our democracy. Over the past 4 years, more than 20,000 men and women in uniform have become citizens of the country they serve. They've taken the citizenship oath on the decks of aircraft carriers, on deployments to Afghanistan and Iraq, and at military bases around the world. At Bethesda Naval Medical Center, I watched a brave marine born in Mexico raise his right hand and become a citizen of the country he had defended in uniform for more than 26 years. It's a privilege to be the Commander in Chief of men and women like these, and I'm proud to call them fellow citizens.

All who swear the oath of citizenship are doing more than completing a legal process; they're making a lifelong pledge to support the values and the laws of America. The pledge comes with great privileges, and it also comes with great responsibilities. I believe every new citizen has an obligation to learn the customs and values that define our Nation, including liberty and civic responsibility, equality under God, tolerance for others, and the English language.

Those of us who have been citizens for many years have responsibilities as well. Helping new citizens assimilate is a mission that unites Americans by choice and by birth. I appreciate the work of patriotic organizations like the Daughters of the American Revolution. Some of the new Americans here today might have used DAR's Manual for Citizenship to prepare you for the citizenship test. They obviously did a pretty good job, since you passed. [*Laughter*]

Many other organizations, from churches to businesses to civic organizations, are answering the call to help new citizens succeed in our country. And I am grateful for all those who reach out to people who are going to become citizens.

Government is doing its part to help new citizens succeed as well. The Office of Citizenship has created a new official guide for immigrants. This free publication includes practical advice on tasks like finding housing and jobs or enrolling your children in school or paying taxes.

We're conducting outreach programs with faith-based and community groups to offer civics and English language courses. My administration will continue to pursue policies that open a path to education and jobs, promote ownership, and to give every citizen a chance to realize the American Dream.

Our Nation is now in the midst of the debate on immigration policy, and it's good. Immigration is an important topic. Immigration is also an emotional topic, and we need to maintain our perspective as we conduct this debate. At its core, immigration is a sign of a confident and successful nation. It says something about our country that people around the world are willing to leave their homes and leave their families and risk everything to come to America. Their talent and hard work and love of freedom have helped make America the leader of the world. And our generation will ensure that America remains a beacon of liberty and the most hopeful society the world has ever known.

America is a nation of immigrants, and we're also a nation of laws. All of you are here because you followed the rules and you waited your turn in the citizenship line. Yet some violate our immigration laws and enter our country illegally, and that undermines the system for all of us. America should not have to choose between being a welcoming society and being a lawful society. We can be both at the same time. And so, to keep the promise of America, we must enforce the laws of America.

We must also reform those laws. No one is served by an immigration system that allows large numbers of people to sneak across the border illegally. Nobody benefits when illegal immigrants live in the shadows of society. Everyone suffers when people seeking to provide for their families are left at the mercy of criminals or stuffed in the back of 18-wheelers or abandoned in the desert to die. America needs comprehensive immigration reform.

I've laid out a proposal for comprehensive immigration reform that includes three critical elements: securing the border, strengthening immigration enforcement inside our country, and creating a temporary-worker program. These elements depend on and reinforce one another, and together they will give America an immigration system that meets the needs of the 21st century.

The first element is securing our border. Our immigration system cannot function if we cannot control the border. Illegal immigration puts a strain on law enforcement and public resources, especially in our border communities. Our Nation is also fighting a war on terror, and terrorists crossing the border could create destruction on a massive scale. The responsibility of Government is clear: We must enforce the border.

Since I took office, we've increased funding for border security by 66 percent. We've expanded the Border Patrol to more than 12,000 agents, an increase of more than 2,700 agents. And the budget next year funds another 1,500 new agents. We're helping these dedicated men and women do their jobs by providing them with cutting-edge technology like infrared cameras, advanced motion sensors, and unmanned aerial vehicles. We're installing protective infrastructure, such as vehicle barriers and fencing in urban areas, to prevent people from crossing the border illegally. And we're integrating manpower and technology and infrastructure in more unified ways than ever. Our objective is to keep the border open to trade and tourism and closed to criminals and drug dealers and terrorists.

Our strategy to secure the border is getting results. Since I took office, our agents have apprehended and sent home more than 6 million people entering this country illegally, including more than 400,000 with criminal records. Federal, State, and local and travel enforcement officials are working side by side. Through the Arizona Border Control Initiative, we apprehended more than 600,000 illegal immigrants in Arizona last year. The men and women of our Border Patrol have made good progress, but we have much more work ahead, and we cannot be satisfied until we're in full control of the border.

We're also changing the way we process those we catch crossing the border illegally. More than 85 percent of the illegal immigrants we apprehend are from Mexico, and most are sent back home within 24 hours. We face a different challenge with non-

Mexicans. For decades, Government detention facilities did not have enough beds for the non-Mexican illegal immigrants caught at the border, and so most were released back into society. They were each assigned a court date, but virtually nobody showed up. This practice of catch-and-release is unwise, and my administration is going to end it.

To end catch-and-release, we're increasing the number of beds and detention facilities by 12 percent this year and by another 32 percent next year. We're also expanding our use of a process called expedited removal, which allows us to send non-Mexican illegal immigrants home more quickly.

Last year, it took an average of 66 days to process one of these illegal immigrants. Now we're doing it in 21 days. The goal is to increase the process faster. It's helped us end the catch-and-release for illegal immigrants from Brazil and Guatemala, Honduras, and Nicaragua caught crossing our Southwest border. And since last summer, we've cut the number of non-Mexican illegal immigrants released in society by more than a third. We've set a goal to end catch-and-release over the next year. I look forward to working with Congress to close loopholes that makes it difficult for us to process illegal immigrants from certain countries. And we will continue to press foreign Governments like China to take back their citizens who have entered our country illegally.

When illegal immigrants know they're going to be caught and sent home, they will be less likely to break the rules in the first place. And the system will be more orderly and secure for those who follow the law.

The second part of a comprehensive immigration reform is strengthening enforcement of our laws in the interior of our country. Since I took office, we've increased funding for immigration enforcement by 42 percent, and these resources have helped our agents bring to justice

some very dangerous people: smugglers, terrorists, gang members, and human traffickers. For example, through Operation Community Shield, Federal agents have arrested nearly 2,300 gang members who were here illegally, including violent criminals like the members of MS–13.

Better interior enforcement also requires better worksite enforcement. Businesses have an obligation to abide by the law. The Government has the responsibility to help them do so. Last year, I signed legislation to more than double the resources dedicated to worksite enforcement. We'll continue to confront the problem of document fraud, because hard-working businessowners should not have to act as detectives to verify the status of their workers.

Next month, we're going to launch law enforcement task forces in 11 major cities to dismantle document fraud rings. We're working to shut down the forgers who create the phony documents, to stop the smugglers who traffic in human beings, and to ensure that American businesses are compliant with American law.

The third part of comprehensive immigration reform is to make the system more rational, orderly, and secure by creating a new temporary-worker program. This program would provide a legal way to match willing foreign workers with willing American employers to fill the jobs that Americans are unwilling to do. Workers should be able to register for legal status on a temporary basis. If they decide to apply for citizenship, they would have to get in line. This program would help meet the demands of a growing economy and would allow honest workers to provide for their families while respecting the law.

A temporary-worker program is vital to securing our border. By creating a separate legal channel for those entering America to do an honest day's labor, we would dramatically reduce the number of people trying to sneak back and forth across the border. That would help take the pressure off the border and free up law enforcement to focus on the greatest threats to our security, which are criminals and drug dealers and terrorists.

The program would also improve security by creating tamper-proof identification cards that would allow us to keep track of every temporary worker who is here on a legal basis and help us identify those who are here illegally.

One thing the temporary-worker program should not do is provide amnesty for people who are in our country illegally. I believe granting amnesty would be unfair, because it would allow those who break the law to jump ahead of people like you all, people who play by the rules and have waited in the line for citizenship.

Amnesty would also be unwise, because it would encourage future waves of illegal immigration, it would increase pressure on the border, and make it difficult for law enforcement to focus on those who mean us harm. For the sake of justice and border security, I firmly oppose amnesty.

This week, the Senate plans to consider legislation on immigration reform. Congress needs to pass a comprehensive bill that secures the border, improves interior enforcement, and creates a temporary-worker program to strengthen our security and our economy. Completing a comprehensive bill is not going to be easy. It will require all of us in Washington to make tough choices and make compromises, and that is exactly what the American people sent us here to do.

As we move toward the process, we also have a chance to move beyond tired choices and the harsh attitudes of the past. The immigration debate should be conducted in a civil and dignified way. No one should play on people's fears or try to pit neighbors against each other. No one should pretend that immigrants are threats to American identity because immigrants have shaped America's identity.

No one should claim that immigrants are a burden on our economy because the work and enterprise of immigrants helps sustain our economy. We should not give into pessimism. If we work together, I'm confident we can meet our duty to fix our immigration system and deliver a bill that protects our people, upholds our laws, and makes our people proud.

It's a joyful day for all of you, and it's one you'll always remember. When you came here this morning, I was the President of another country. Now I'm the President of your country, and I'm grateful for that honor. I wish you good luck as citizens of the greatest Nation on the face of the Earth.

May God bless you and your families, and may God continue to bless America. Thank you very much.

NOTE: The President spoke at 10:12 a.m. at the DAR Administration Building. In his remarks, he referred to Alfonso Aguilar, Chief, Office of Citizenship, U.S. Citizenship and Immigration Services. The Office of the Press Secretary also released a Spanish language transcript of these remarks.

Remarks at a Reception for Senatorial Candidate Conrad Burns
March 27, 2006

Senator, thank you. I kind of like being on the same platform as Senator Burns because he makes me sound like Shakespeare. [*Laughter*] I like a plain-talking fellow. The

good thing about Conrad Burns is you know where he stands. That's why the people of Montana respect him and they like him. And I'm here to urge the good people of the State of Montana to send him back to the United States Senate.

I appreciate Phyllis. Phyllis, it's great to see you. Conrad married well. [*Laughter*] So did I. And Laura sends her love to both you all. It was neat to meet daughter Keely and son Garrett, daughter-in-law Kate. But right before we came on, the Senator wanted me to make sure I understood how brilliant and beautiful his granddaughter Ella is. That says something about the man. He's got his priorities straight. He cares deeply about his family. He understands the importance of family in our society, and I appreciate your priorities, Senator.

By the way, he also loves Montana. Every time I see him, he says, "I want you to remember the great State of Montana." He cares deeply about the people there, and he knows the State about as well as anybody could possibly know it. He's traveled the State. He tells people what's on his mind. He is—he's a down-to-earth guy. And the people of Montana have got to understand he can get some things done here in Washington, DC. No, there's a lot of eloquent folks in this town, but it's sometimes short of doers and people who can accomplish some things. I'm here because Senator Burns can get some things done for the good of the people of Montana and the people of the United States of America.

I thank Congressman Denny Rehberg for being here as well. He's a good, down-to-earth guy too. And he's serving the great State of Montana with class and dignity. He is the—he's the leader of the Montana congressional delegation. [*Laughter*]

I appreciate Senator Kit Bond. Senator Bond from Missouri is here tonight. It's nice of him to come by. It's good of you to honor your old buddy, and I'm proud to—I recently said hello to former Senator Don Nickles from Oklahoma. Don, thank you for coming here as well. Montana has elected some fine people—no finer person than Marc Racicot, who I've gotten to know

really well, and I appreciate you being here, Governor. Thanks for coming.

Karl Ohs, who is the chairman of the Republican Party, and Sherri, is with us—Republican Party of Montana, that is. I appreciate you being here, Mr. Chairman. Thanks for coming. I want to thank John Green, who is the finance chair. Thank you all for listening to John's admonition to support this good man. Long word—he's trying to show off here for the folks of Montana. [*Laughter*]

I particularly want to thank the International Union of Painters and Allied Trades for endorsing Conrad Burns tonight. The Painters' general president, Jimmy Williams, is here. Jimmy, thank you for supporting this good man. I'm proud you're here. There's Jimmy over there.

We've got a lot to do in this country. We're in—we're going through historic times, and it's important to have people in the United States Senate who understand the stakes, understand the world in which we live. It's important to have clear-eyed realists working with the administration to lay the foundation for peace. It's really easy to be out there talking about the world the way you'd like it to be, but we can't afford that luxury because we're in a war against some terrorists who would like to harm America again.

Our—over my time—my remaining time here and the time that Senator Burns will have here after he's reelected, we'll be working on making sure that we accomplish our most important objective, and that is to protect the American people from further harm. I know some probably think that, well, this war on terror is isolated to a few angry individuals that got lucky on September the 11th. That's not how I look at the world, and that's not how Conrad Burns looks at the world. After that attack, I vowed that I'd use everything in our national—everything we could, all our national assets to do our most important job, and that is defend the American people, which means we better have some people in the United States Senate who understand the best way to defend the American people is to stay on the offense against an enemy who would do us harm, to defeat an enemy overseas so we do not have to face them here at home.

I appreciate people standing up and supporting the President when he enforces doctrine. I said to the world, "If you harbor a terrorist, you're equally as guilty as the terrorist." And the Taliban didn't take us seriously. So for our own national security and for liberating others, we sent a mighty coalition into Afghanistan to free the people of that country and, at the same time, secure our own. And Conrad Burns stood strong when it came to the liberation of Afghanistan, and I want to thank you for your support.

I want to thank you for your support in Iraq. Iraq is the central front in the war on terror. And one of the lessons of September the 11th is that when this Nation sees a threat, we must take the threat seriously, before it materializes.

And I saw a threat in Saddam Hussein. But it wasn't just me who saw the threat. Members of the United States Senate from both political parties saw the same threat. My predecessor saw the threat. Members of the House of Representatives from both political parties saw the threat. Fifteen members of the United Nations Security Council saw the threat. And the United Nations Security Council said to Saddam Hussein, "Disclose, disarm, or face serious consequences." It was his choice to make. He chose war. And the world is better off without Saddam Hussein in power.

And we need people in the United States Senate who understand the stakes in this theater of the war on terror. The enemy cannot defeat us. They cannot defeat us militarily. The only thing they can do is to use their terror tactics to shake our will. And I'm enjoying working with a United States Senator like Conrad Burns whose

will cannot be shaken because of the actions of thugs and assassins. The United States of America will accomplish our mission. There will be a democratic Iraq that is able to defend itself, sustain itself, and become an ally in the war on terror.

In order to achieve that objective, we must have Senators who support our men and women in combat, and Conrad Burns does. And we must have Senators who will not—who will not—lose their nerve in the face of these terrorist attacks. Conrad Burns is such a man.

I believe liberty and freedom are universal. So does Senator Burns. We believe that there is an Almighty, and the Almighty's gift to each man and woman on the face of this Earth is freedom. The United States of America was formed on the natural rights of men and women. And it should not surprise us when 11 million Iraqis went to the polls in defiance of terrorists and car bombers and assassins and says, "We want to be free." A free Iraq— a free Iraq will help lay the foundation of peace for generations to come.

I like to remind people about this interesting fact of history. My dad—18-year-old kid—raised his arm and said, "I want to volunteer to defend the United States of America against the Japanese." What I find interesting is that some 60 years later, his son, the current President, sits down with the Prime Minister of Japan talking about keeping the peace. We talk about North Korea; we talk about how proud I am that the Japanese have committed forces to help bring security to the people of Iraq so their democracy can develop. Japan is an ally. Japan is a friend in peace.

And what happened between then 18-year-old George H.W. and 59-year-old W.—[*laughter*]—standing here? What happened was, the Japanese adopted a Japanese-style democracy. History has proven people want to be free and democracies yield the peace. And I believe 30 or 40 years from now, an American President will be up here talking—will be talking to people, and they'll be looking back at this moment in history and say, thank God that people like Senator Conrad Burns and Chairman John Warner of the United States Senate and Senator Kit Bond were wise enough to understand about the power of liberty to transform nations into allies. And they'll be keeping the peace with democratically elected leaders in the broader Middle East, starting with Iraq.

These are the stakes. We're laying the foundation of peace, and it's important to have Members of the United States Senate who can look beyond the short term, who have got a strategic view of the world in which we live. And Conrad Burns has that view. Proud to stand with you in laying that foundation.

Here at home, we've been through a lot together. We've had a recession; we've had a stock market correction; we've had corporate scandals; we had an attack on our Nation; we went to war to defend ourselves; we had major natural disasters; we had rising energy prices. But we acted. We put progrowth economic policies in place. We believe that when people have more money in their pockets to save or to spend or to invest, the economy benefits. And so we cut the taxes on the hard-working people of America, and our economy is strong, and it's getting stronger.

People say here in Washington, "Oh, well, these tax cuts didn't make a difference." I can remember all the dire predictions when the debates went on about the ability for taxes to help revitalize our economy and overcome the obstacles we went through. Not Conrad Burns, he understood the basic principle of trusting people with their own money. Today, our economy has grown to 3.5 percent. We have 4.8 percent unemployment nationwide. We've added over 5 million jobs in the last 2½ years. Productivity is up; homeownership is at an alltime high; small businesses are flourishing. The tax cuts we passed are working.

And now the people of Montana are going to be facing a decision as to whether or not they want their taxes to go up or stay low. You see, the Democrat Party showed its true colors during the tax debate. Time in and time out, they voted against cutting the taxes on the American people. And now you hear them talking about, "Well, we need to raise taxes to balance the budget." Conrad and I know better. We've been in Washington long enough to understand how Washington works. Yes, they'll raise your taxes, but they will figure out new ways to spend your money. To keep this economy strong, we must make the tax relief permanent. And I'm proud to have Conrad Burns on the side—[*applause*].

There are a lot of things we need to do during my—the rest of my time here and for Conrad's time as a reelected Senator, starting with making sure we get off foreign oil. In order to make sure this country is competitive over the next 30 to 50 years, in order to make sure we remain the economic leader of the world, we have got to be wise about our energy policy.

Conrad reminded me, walking in here, that we've got plenty of coal in the great State of Montana. And that's why I'm such a strong supporter of clean coal technologies to make sure we can use that coal in environmentally friendly ways and get us off Middle Eastern oil.

But that's just the start. We got to change how we fuel our automobiles. I want it to be said that when there's a good soy crop out of Montana, we got more biodiesel available for people to use in their automobiles. I want it to be said, when we have a technological breakthrough, which we're close to getting to, that we can use saw grass grown in the State of Montana to help grow—to help produce ethanol so we become less dependent on Middle Eastern oil. I want it to be said that this country is imaginative in our use of technology to make us less dependent, for economic security as well as national security.

And Conrad Burns understands that. The people of Montana need to put him back in the United States Senate to join us in making sure we have energy independence.

One of the things that's important for the people of Montana to understand is, you better have somebody here in Washington who's effective when it comes to representing the farmers and ranchers. You know, a lot of times you get the big talkers running for office, but they get here to Washington, and they're unable to deliver. I'd suggest the voters of Montana pay careful attention to the record of this United States Senator when it comes to representing the basic industries and the small-business owners and the hard-working people of the State of Montana.

I remember when I went to Billings, and we sat around and talked to those farmers and ranchers about the threats to their industry and about the opportunities. Conrad was there. He was talking their language. They didn't need a dictionary or a Roget's Thesaurus to figure out what he was saying. [*Laughter*]

He's the kind of person the people of Montana need here. They need somebody who's steadfast when it comes to defending the country; who's wise about how we spend your money; who understands that the money we spend is your money, not the Government's money; who understands good tax policy can keep this economy growing; who knows we've got to have a good, wise energy policy; and who can speak the language of the farmers and the ranchers, right here in Washington, DC.

I'm proud to stand by this man. I strongly urge the people of Montana to reelect Conrad Burns to the United States Senate.

NOTE: The President spoke at 6:07 p.m. at the Madison Hotel. In his remarks, he referred to Phyllis Burns, wife of Senator Burns; former Gov. Marc Racicot of Montana; Sherri Ohs, wife of Montana Republican Party chairman Karl Ohs; John Green, national finance committee chairman, Senator Burns's reelection campaign; and Prime Minister Junichiro Koizumi of Japan.

Interview With Foreign Print Journalists
March 27, 2006

The President. Thanks for coming. I'm looking forward to going down to Cancun. I'm very grateful for President Fox's hospitality. I've never been to Cancun, but I've had a lot of friends who have been to Cancun, and they tell me if I stay too long, I won't return. This is a relatively quick trip. I'm looking forward to going to the Mayan ruins, which will be really exciting. And I'm looking forward to both bilateral and our trilateral discussions.

With Mexico, obviously, there's big issues, particularly immigration right now. But I'll remind people that our relationship is more than just the migration issue. Mexico is our second-largest trading partner. The relationship with Mexico is a strong and vital relationship. Obviously, not only do we have important trade equities, but we've also got common values, and we've got millions of Mexican Americans who take great pride in their heritage. And so Mexico has been and will be a vital issue for future Presidents. And it's very important for us to work on a relationship that has a foundation of mutual benefit as well as openness and candor when it comes to dealing with difficult issues.

And I really value my friendship with President Fox. Obviously, we have been through a lot during my Presidency and his. We've agreed on things, and we haven't agreed, but we've always remained friends, and that's a sign of a vital relationship. I'm, obviously, aware that there is a political season coming up, but until someone is sworn in office, my relationship will be with Vicente Fox as the leader of our important friend to the south. And I'm sure there's going to be all kinds of speculation about whether or not the United States will be involved in the election, and we won't be, pure and simple.

The relationship with Canada is also a vital relationship. Canada is our largest trading partner. This will be my first meeting with the Prime Minister as—with him as the Prime Minister. Obviously, I met him in the past. I'm looking forward to it. This will be the third Prime Minister with which I've dealt as the President. I've had good relations with the previous Prime Ministers, and I'm looking forward to good relations with Stephen Harper.

I'm fully aware of the relationship—the nature of the relationship between Canada and the United States. One, it's a vital relationship, but it's also one in which there is a certain skepticism about the United States, and therefore, I will do my very best to find common ground and to convince—through my relationship with the Prime Minister, convince the people of Canada we genuinely care about our friends and neighbors to the north and will work to resolve different issues in an above-board way that is mutually beneficial.

So it's an important meeting, and it's a way for us to confirm the—and then, eventually, the three of us will get into a room to meet. And it's a very strong signal that the three of us working together are better than each of us working apart, and that whether it be border security or commerce or hearing the values that are important in our neighborhood, we can do a lot together. And I find these meetings to be very useful and very important.

All right, we'll go around a couple of times. Pepe.

Mexico-U.S. Relations

Q. Sir, you mentioned the ties that bind both countries, the U.S. and Mexico. But those ties are also—those issues are extremely politically charged in both countries—trade, immigration, et cetera. So my question would be, where do you expect to lead the U.S.-Mexico relation in the next 3 years?

The President. Appreciate that. First, I think it's very important for both President Fox and myself to explain to both our countries the benefits of $300 million [billion]° two-way trade—well, nearly $300 million [billion]° in the year 2005 of two-way trade. In other words, it's one thing to talk trade, and I fully understand that unless those benefits are translated to more and more people, people begin to wonder whether or not trade is worthwhile.

You'll find that here in America, we're having a debate as well, over trade. I said in my State of the Union that we've got to reject protectionism because I believe that trade, when it's done right, free and fair, is beneficial to the parties. And I strongly believe that the trade between the United States and Mexico has been beneficial for Mexico, as it has for the United States. But as a leader, I've got to continue to explain to people why.

I have a different perspective than many because of the relationship between—because of my time as Governor of Texas, and I remember full well what life was like on the border before NAFTA. And if you go down to the border now, you see vitality on the border, you see that—and vitality on both sides of the border.

There's been—commerce has helped people get jobs, and commerce has helped people realize a better life. And it's important for us to make sure we continue to explain that because if not, there will be

---

° White House correction.

protectionist tendencies that will tend to emerge, not only in our two countries but around the world. And in my judgment, leadership has got to fight off protectionist tendencies. I think that would tend to isolate each other and make it more difficult for us to realize the benefits of our relationship.

There's also going to be an important call for our countries to work together to emphasize the institutions, the democratic institutions that are vital for a functioning and stable society: anticorruption measures; free press; free religion; institutions that sometimes can be challenged in the course of politically—development within our neighborhood and around the world, for that matter.

So the common value theme is a very important theme for me to continue to work with Vicente Fox and whoever were to replace him—obviously, we've got a lot of human issues to deal with. The migration of people across our border is a vital issue that must be done in the same way to protect and honor people's lives. Americans are—I am disgusted by a system in which people are snuck across the border in the bottom of an 18-wheeler. This is inhumane. There's a more humane way to deal with our neighborhood.

There's a lot of big issues that confront us. But in order to make the relationship vital, we've got to explain to people exactly why—you know, the consequences of, for example, not having commerce flow as frequently as we do.

Tell me your papers now. Pepe.

Q. It's El Universal.

Q. La Opinion.

The President. Si. Thank you. Welcome.

Immigration Reform

Q. Over a million people across the country have marched in support of legalization and against H.R. 4437, the Sensenbrenner bill.

The President. In support of what? Legalization, you said?

Q. Legalization, yes. Since you're opposing amnesty, sir, would you agree on a language that puts the undocumented on a path to earn legalization——

The President. Let me tell you what I am for. First of all, there is a—the legislative process is one that—obviously, it goes through the House and then the Senate, and if there are differences, it has got to be resolved. And what people are now doing is reacting to a legislative process. I believe that any immigration bill ought to make sure that we're, one, able to secure the borders. That's what Americans want; that's what any country should want. Your borders ought to be secure.

And I also recognize that part of securing the borders requires a guest-worker program. In other words, the two go hand in hand. I don't believe people who have been here illegally should be granted citizenship status right off the bat. That's amnesty.

Let me finish.

I just, as a matter of fact, gave a speech to a group of citizens that have become U.S. citizens today, in my presence. They had stood in line. And I do not think a country that relies upon law ought to say to somebody who was here illegally, you get to be ahead of the line.

In other words—so therefore, I think that part of a rational worker program is—say you're here on a temporary basis, and if you choose to be a citizen or want to be a citizen, you get in line. But like I said today, I've called upon Congress to increase the number of green cards. To me, that's the most rational way of dealing with the citizenship issue. It's essential that we not have automatic amnesty or legality. First of all, it would send a signal that said, all you've got to do is get here illegally and eventually you get in the head of the line. And that's—I don't think it will work.

Q. But what if they get in line behind those who are waiting for their green cards now?

The President. That's why I said I think one way to deal with this is to increase the number of green cards. And right now part of the problem is that the green cards are limited. And that's why I have spoken before and again reiterated my position that there ought to be a temporary-worker program; people who want to be here should not get—be a citizen should not get ahead of the line but ought to be waiting in line. And if the Congress so desires, they ought to increase the number of green cards in order to take the pressure off the system.

Q. But——

The President. It's a plan that—again, I know people are saying, "Well, the House bill didn't have a temporary-worker program in there," and I think any bill should be a comprehensive bill including a temporary-worker program. I've spoken out on it ever since I've been the President, and I think it is the best way to go, because I realize that, one, it is important to enforcing the border—that being a temporary-worker program; secondly, that it's a humane way to deal with people who are making a contribution to our economy.

In other words, if something is illegal, then people will figure out ways to get around the system. That's what creates the *coyotes*; that's what creates the smugglers; that's what creates the document forgers; that's what creates these places where people are dumped for a period of time and then smuggled across and then told to walk; that's what creates the dangerous predicament for people coming across the desert. And so there's a—and that's why people—that's what causes people to hide in the shadows of our cities.

And there's a much more rational way and much more humane way to deal with people who are doing jobs that Americans won't do. Anyway, that's why I think the work component is a vital part of an immigration policy, and I believe border—I know border security and a guest-worker program go hand in hand. In other words, one supports the other.

U.S. Border/Homeland Security

Q. I guess I wanted to ask you about an issue on the northern border that's of some concern. Your administration has proposed a Western Hemisphere Travel Initiative, which would require passports or passport-like documents for Canadians and Americans coming and going. And there's been some concern in Canada that this will, in effect, do more to harm economic trade and tourism and do little to actually improve security. And I'm wondering, when you're moving towards, sort of, a more integrated approach to security on things like NORAD, why move ahead with something that really amounts to a bit more of a restriction?

The President. Well, I think—first of all, we have the same issue to the south, by the way. How do you come up with a policy where there are thousands of border crossings a day, without—and trying to have a rational approach to determining who's coming in and who's going out of the country, without endangering workforce, tourism, trade? Our goal is to, obviously, consult with our partners to develop, you know, passport and/or passport-like document, you said, and I think that may be the operative word as a plan develops.

There is a desire for a lot of our citizenry—and it's reflected in the Congress—to know, as I said, who's coming in and who's going out and why. And I think that—I'm pretty confident that if we work closely, we can develop such a plan that enables a scanning device or a card that can be dealt with on a scanning device to not stop the flow of traffic of people who make a daily routine of it, and also make sure that we know who's coming in the country.

The purpose is not to impede trade and/or cross-border relations. The purpose is to expedite them in a way that gives both countries, or all three countries, comfort in knowing who's coming across. In Texas, for example, like in El Paso, on a daily basis, there's thousands of people that it's just a part of their daily routine. And the idea would be to develop a document that could be scanned as they just walk across the bridge. It's the same concept for Canada as well.

Q. You couldn't just do it through a driver's license? I mean, that's the——

The President. Well, that's what they're working on. First of all, we have found in our own country that drivers' license aren't necessarily a secure document. I mentioned to you that this is a—the document forgery is a significant problem for our country, primarily for people coming in from the south. And you've got a person looking for somebody to help build an apartment building, and people show up, and they flash a document, and the employer is not equipped to be a document checker. It's not what they do.

And so they say, "Sure, come on and work." And the truth of the matter is, there is a whole industry out there to provide fake documents for people doing work that Americans won't do, because the system needs—the system says—just hasn't been rational, let me just put it to you that way. And therefore, there's a skepticism about certain documents which can be forged. And that's why you're seeing the notion of trying to develop one that is tamper-proof, for not only border crossings but also for working.

And it seems to me to make sense without—again, I understand the sensitivity. I'm very aware, and I'm sure Stephen and Vicente will bring this up. I've already talked to Vicente about the issue in regards to Mexico.

Look, again, this is an issue I'm very familiar with because of my time as the Governor of Texas. Immigration issues and border issues are—it's been a part of our State's history for a long period of time.

Yes, Pepe. You're not going back to migration, are you?

Immigration Reform

Q. Unless you want to go there.

The President. No, but Maribel will. [*Laughter*] I can see it's on the tip of her tongue. No, that's all right. It's a big issue. It's a huge issue. Look—and you should.

Q. The question would be, though—if you excuse me, a few months ago, or a year ago, you said that you would invest political capital in the issue of—the immigration issue.

The President. Yes. You did come back to it. That's good.

Q. Yet in the last couple of weeks, there have been a lot of people in this town talking that your political capital is wasted. So——

The President. Don't underestimate me, Pepe.

Q. No, I don't. But——

The President. Okay. [*Laughter*]

Q. Is this Congress underestimating you? Because——

The President. We'll see. But I will keep speaking out on it. One thing is I'm—I believe it's very important to get this issue—to reform the immigration system. I have spoken out on it before, and I will continue speaking out on it. It's now coming to a head. And I will continue to call Congress to have a comprehensive package that is more than just border security but also enforcement—interior enforcement, as well as a guest-worker program. And I'm going to say it again, that—particularly for the American audience—the two go hand in hand. A temporary-worker program that enables people to cross our border legally to do work Americans won't do takes pressure off of Border Patrol agents who are trying to stop illegal activities, which makes it easier to secure the border.

Government of Mexico/Mexican National Economy

Q. If I may, sir, then what would you expect—or what would you propose or expect or hope that the Mexican Government would do in this case?

The President. No, I appreciate that. I think it's very important for the Mexican Government to continue doing what they have recently done, which is to make it clear to the American people that we have responsibilities on both sides of the border. And I thank President Fox for putting out those statements.

You're aware of, I'm sure, a series of advertisements in our newspapers that said, we have an important relationship with the United States. And it requires the understanding that we will work together on our border—as well as, by the way, working on the southern border of Mexico, because many of the folks that are now coming into our country are coming up from Central America, for example. A lot of folks from Central America have been crossing into Mexico and across. And part of making sure that our borders are secure—all our border, when I say "our borders," I'm talking about Mexico and the United States borders in this case—is that we work hand in glove in the north and also help in the south.

And Vicente has told me he understands that there is an issue on the southern border of Mexico. It's a difficult border to enforce, but it's important.

The truth of the matter is, the long run for the issue is going to be for Mexico's economy to extend its promise beyond just certain regions. Look, I strongly believe most people want to be able to find decent wages at their home, where people are able to provide for their families. And I've told our people ever since I've been involved in this issue that—and the way I like to put it is, family values don't stop at the Rio Grande River. In other words, moms and dads in Mexico are anxious to put food on the table for their children. And therefore, many of them are willing to come great distances and lengths to be able to provide for their families. And I think most people would rather be providing for their families close to their homes.

And so part of a larger strategy has got to be to make sure that we work in concert to develop—to encourage economic growth so that there are meaningful jobs throughout the country. That's why I'm a believer in trade. I believe if we were ever to stop our trade, it would make it harder for prosperity to spread.

And I appreciate Vicente's understanding that education programs are vital. People have got to have a skill set in order to be able to make sure that jobs are—that jobs spread throughout the country. And for a period of time, many people used to come across the border from the border regions, but prosperity, as I mentioned to you, is visible. The life has changed on the border. But the prosperity on the border has caused people from other parts of the country who are looking for work to migrate north, come across the border, and try to find jobs in the United States.

And I believe that the immigrant worker has helped grow our economy. In other words, there's jobs Americans will not do, and it makes sense to have a legal policy that says, if there's a job Americans won't do and people are willing to do it for the sake of their families, we ought to encourage them to do so and make it a legal, temporary experience. And we'll negotiate what the definition of temporary is, and we'll negotiate the kind of documentation necessary to make sure that they're not—there's not a lot of fraud. And we will—and also the issue of citizenship. And again, my own judgment is, is the best way to deal with the citizenship is to not say—to say to somebody, "If you're here illegally, you don't get to take somebody else's place in line who is here legally." The reason we have lines is because of the green card issue. There's a shortage of green cards. And Congress has the right to increase the number of green cards.

Yes, Miss Maribel.

Naturalization/Amnesty

Q. Sir, do you believe there is a difference between amnesty and earned legalization——

The President. What does "earned legalization" mean? Why don't you give me your description, and I will answer your question.

Q. According to Chairman Specter, is they have to pay a fine—the undocumented, I'm talking about—pay a fine, get in line, prove they have a job, that they have paid taxes, that they don't have a criminal record.

The President. Right. But "get in line," you said?

Q. Yes.

The President. That's exactly what I just said. Somebody, in order to become a citizen, must get in line. And amnesty means you're automatically legal and you get ahead. In other words, there is no line; you're just it. You know, you've been here, undocumented; you're legal; boom, you don't have to wait in line.

Getting in line is exactly what I just said. You can call it by any way you want to call it. I would say that it's a system that does not—that rewards and understands people here are doing jobs Americans won't do—take out "rewards"—understands that there are people doing jobs that Americans won't do, but you don't get to be an automatic citizen. You have to get in line.

Q. So you agree with Senator McCain, then.

The President. Look, I'm just telling you exactly what I am for. And what I am for is a program that is not amnesty. In other words, amnesty means you're automatically legal. And there are some that believe that ought to happen, that think that's a rational policy. I disagree. And the reason I disagree was, one, it undermines rule of law. In other words, there's a lot of people here trying to become a citizen that are waiting in line, and all of a sudden—and they're doing it legally, and all of a sudden, you know, by law, it means that those who have been here not legally get ahead of the line.

Secondly, I think it sends a wrong message. In other words, basically, "It's okay; fine, all you have to do is come, come in the country, be undocumented, and in a matter of time, we'll make you legal." And I think that will cause another group of people to come. So therefore, my view is, is that, yes, you can become a citizen, but you have to get in line. In other words, you can't get ahead of those who have been here playing by the rules.

And the bottleneck is the number of green cards the Government issues. And that can be changed, and that's why I called upon Congress to increase the number of green cards.

Now, was that your question? [*Laughter*] You can see, Sheldon, that the migration issue is a consuming issue. And it's an important issue. One of the things that's very important is that this issue be conducted in such a way as it brings dignity to our process, that immigration is emotional and the people who are speaking out on the issue must understand its emotional nature and must not pit neighbor against neighbor, must treat people with respect. After all, we are a nation of immigrants, and I believe has helped—it helps revitalize our soul. I think it's a very important part of our Nation's history. And America should be viewed as a welcoming society that supports its laws, and the two don't necessarily contradict each other.

Trade Relations With Canada

Q. If I could ask you about—a bit of a two-parter. I know you don't like two-parters, necessarily.

The President. It hasn't stopped these people. [*Laughter*] Did it stop you, Nedra [Nedra Pickler, Associated Press], the two-part question, or are you still giving them?

Q. Yes. [*Laughter*]

Q. You mentioned that there's skepticism in Canada about the U.S. And I'm wondering, over the last few years, you've had some——

The President. Let me just make sure that—first of all, I believe most—I believe people on both sides of the border think it's a very important relationship, and there's great friendships. Having said that, the Canadians have, oftentimes, taken independent view of decisions the United States makes. And there is concern about some of the decisions I have made, yes. I just want to make sure that it's not, kind of, universal skepticism—kind of, define it to the proper source.

Q. There's been some personal invective hurled at you over the years by Canadian Parliamentarians. You were the star in one of the former Government's campaign ads.

The President. Did it work?

Q. It didn't work for them.

The President. Okay. [*Laughter*]

Q. I wonder whether that's tarnished your image of Canada at all, and whether— one of the issues that's caused a lot of skepticism——

The President. If it did tarnish my image of Canada, it would also tarnish my image of my own country, because part of being in the political scene is that people—it's the great thing about free societies, people speak their minds. That's what happens here in this country as well.

Q. Well, do you see the opportunity for better relations, and specifically on the issue of softwood lumber? That's an issue that's caused a lot of skepticism.

The President. It has.

Q. People are looking for a strong signal from the President of the United States.

The President. Right. No, I understand. First of all, the relationship is much deeper than softwood lumber. And there will be— I'll comment on softwood lumber in a minute. First of all, I'd like to get the issue solved. So the strong signal is, is that I've told our folks that, let's work hard to bring this issue to conclusion. And we were close to getting it done at one point. And so my strong signal is, yes, let's get this behind us.

I predict, however, that there will be other issues that arise because of our— when we trade as much as we trade, nearly

half-a-billion [half-a-trillion] * two-way trade in '05, there's going to be issues that come up. I can remember the potato issue—I don't know if it had as much impact on thought that softwood lumber did, but it was an important issue. I guess it was mainly confined to the eastern part of the country.

But with as much trade as we've got going for us, there will be other issues that arise. Same with Mexico, by the way. We're dealing with, you know, tomatoes, on occasion, or corn syrup, I think it was—yes, corn syrup. And it's just very important to be in a position to have a relationship such that we can work through these problems. But, no—democracy is what it is. It's a chance for people to express themselves. Sure, there were some harsh words, but— at least from my perspective, the people tend to discount the polemics and the, you know, kind of, just how politics works, and they want to know whether or not there's a genuine commitment to friendship. And there is, between not only America and Canada but also between the United States and Mexico. It's been a long-term relationship.

The migration issue, obviously, as you can see, has created a great deal of, at least, questioning, because it's on people's minds.

Canada-U.S. Relations

Q. Would it help if there was a little more maturity in the relationship, in terms of how Canada deals with the U.S.? Because there's been a perception in Canada that we haven't always been—dealt with you square on issues like missile defense or—you know, there have been a few things.

The President. I don't view—I, frankly, view the relationship as a good and strong relationship. Look, people—face it, part of the problem that we had was because of

---

* White House correction.

my decision to go into Iraq. And the Government of both countries didn't agree, and I understand that. War is terrible. It's an awful thing. And yet we're still able to maintain good relations.

When people are dealing with the subject of war, there is a lot of emotion. And I fully understand that. So I view the relationships both as not only important and vital, but I do view them as mature. As I said, this is the third Prime Minister with whom I will have dealt, and I—there is a certain camaraderie that takes place by virtue of our close ties and close history. And I bear no ill will whatsoever, and I understand the strategic importance of being close to our friends and to have a capacity to talk among ourselves.

As I say, there's a lot we can get done by working together. The great competition for our respective economies, in the long run, will be coming from the Far East. And therefore, the more close our relationships and the more we're able to deal with cross-border issues on trade and other issues, the more we'll be able to work in concert to keep our standard of living high. And Vicente is—you've heard him talk a lot about his worries about China's trade into the hemisphere and his concerns about job losses as a result of competition. And I believe that rather than, kind of, walling

ourselves off, I believe that cooperation, like we have done through the NAFTA process, dealing with disputes in an open-handed way, will enable us to be able to leave in place something beyond our respective times in office, so that future leaders can compete confidently.

And obviously, that's part of a policy. I would like to extend this kind of cooperative spirit beyond just the three of us. That's why the Free Trade Agreement of the Americas—which 28 of 32 members, if I'm not mistaken, supported the Free Trade Agreement of the Americans—that's the concept behind this notion of having a hemisphere that trades freely in order to be competitive—help us be competitive, which will help maintain standards of living. That's, after all, one of the key goals of any government.

Good, we'll see you all down there. Thank you. Looking forward to it.

NOTE: The interview was taped at 11:09 a.m. in the Roosevelt Room at the White House. In his remarks, the President referred to President Vicente Fox Quesada of Mexico; and Prime Minister Stephen Harper of Canada. The transcript was released by the Office of the Press Secretary on March 28. A tape was not available for verification of the content of this interview.

Remarks Announcing the Resignation of Andrew H. Card, Jr., as White House Chief of Staff and the Appointment of Joshua B. Bolten as White House Chief of Staff
March 28, 2006

Earlier this month, Andy Card came to me and raised the possibility of stepping down as Chief of Staff. After 5½ years, he thought it might be time to return to private life, and this past weekend, I accepted Andy's resignation.

Andy Card has served me and our country in historic times: on a terrible day when

America was attacked; during economic recession and recovery; through storms of unprecedented destructive power; in peace and in war. Andy has overseen legislative achievements on issues from education to Medicare. He helped confirm two Justices to the Supreme Court, including a new Chief Justice.

In all these challenges and accomplishments, I have relied on Andy's wise counsel, his calm in crisis, his absolute integrity, and his tireless commitment to public service. Andy is respected by his colleagues for his humility, his decency, and his thoughtfulness. They have looked to him as a leader and a role model, and they, like me, will miss him.

On most days, Andy is the first one to arrive in the West Wing and among the last to leave. And during those long days over many years, I've come to know Andy as more than my Chief of Staff. He is leaving the White House, but he will always be my friend. Laura and I have known Andy and his wife, Kathi, for more than 20 years, and our close friendship will continue.

With me today is Joshua Bolten, who will be the new White House Chief of Staff. Josh is a man with broad experience, having worked on Capitol Hill and Wall Street and the White House staff and for nearly 3 years as a Director of the Office of Management and Budget. Josh is a creative policy thinker. He's an expert on the budget and our economy. He's respected by Members of Congress from both parties. He's a strong advocate for effective accountable management in the Federal Government.

He's a man of candor and humor and directness, who's comfortable with responsibility and knows how to lead. No person is better prepared for this important position, and I'm honored that Josh has agreed to serve.

The next 3 years will demand much of those who serve our country. We have a global war to fight and win. We have great opportunities to expand the prosperity and compassion of America. We've come far as a nation, yet there's a lot on the road ahead. I'm honored to have served with Andrew Card. I've got great confidence in my next Chief of Staff.

Congratulations, Josh.

NOTE: The President spoke at 8:31 a.m. in the Oval Office at the White House. The transcript released by the Office of the Press Secretary also included the remarks of Chief of Staff Card and Chief of Staff-designate Bolten.

Remarks Following a Cabinet Meeting
March 28, 2006

Good morning. We've just finished our third Cabinet meeting of this year. I want to thank my Cabinet members for joining us. We talked about the war on terror. We talked about a war on terror that requires all of us involved in Government to respond and to protect America and help spread freedom.

My Cabinet officials obviously have got many responsibilities in their agencies, but we talked about their need to assume additional responsibilities to make sure that we're using every element of national power to win the war on terror and to secure the peace.

This morning we had briefings from General Abizaid, Ambassador Khalilzad, and General Casey. We heard from the Ambassador about work toward a unity government. I'm pleased to hear from Zal that the Iraqis are now back at the table discussing the formation of a government, the process by which they will conduct a government once a unity government is formed, as well as, obviously, beginning to continue to—or continuing to discuss who will fill the key slots in the government.

We also heard from General Abizaid as well as General Casey, who reported on the ongoing efforts to win this war on terror, to defeat the enemy all around General Abizaid's theater of responsibility, as well as defeat the enemy in the central front in the war on terror, which is Iraq.

I appreciate very much General Pace joining us today as well. These leaders, folks on the ground who know the condition on the ground, recognize this is hard work, but they also report on steady progress that we're making toward meeting our important goals—important goal is to make sure Iraq is a democracy that can sustain herself, defend herself, and is not a safe haven for the terrorists.

Tomorrow I'm going to deliver a third in a series of speeches about the situation in Iraq. During Saddam Hussein's brutal rule, he exploited the ethnic and religious diversity of Iraq by setting communities against one another. And now the terrorists and former regime elements are doing the same; they're trying to set off a civil war through acts of sectarian violence. But the United States and our Iraqi forces cannot be defeated militarily. The only thing the Iraqi insurgents, as well as the terrorists, can possibly do is to cause us to lose our nerve and retreat, to withdraw.

I'm going to discuss how the Iraqi people and our coalition continue to work together to build a stable and free and prosperous Iraq. I'll remind the people we're not going to lose our nerve. The stakes are high; we will complete this mission. Our strategy for rebuilding Iraq is comprehensive, and it includes a commitment from all parts of the Federal Government.

Secretary Rice encouraged our Cabinet members to build relationships with their counterparts in Iraq once the new Iraqi Government is formed, and I expect them to follow through on that—on their commitments. See, by making a broad commitment from the Federal Government, we'll help the Iraqis establish a democracy, we'll help them build the institutions necessary for a stable society, and we'll help defeat the terrorists.

Today was the—today two members of my Cabinet—we had the honor—a chance to honor two members of my Cabinet who won't be with us much longer: Secretary of the Interior Gale Norton and Chief of Staff Andy Card. These two folks have served our country with distinction and honor. I am proud to work side by side with them, and I'm proud to call them friend. Thank you all very much.

NOTE: The President spoke at 10:20 a.m. in the Rose Garden at the White House. In his remarks, he referred to Gen. John P. Abizaid, USA, commander, U.S. Central Command; Gen. George W. Casey, Jr., USA, commanding general, Multi-National Force—Iraq; Gen. Peter Pace, USMC, Chairman, Joint Chiefs of Staff; and former President Saddam Hussein of Iraq. The Office of the Press Secretary also released a Spanish language transcript of these remarks.

Interview With CNN Espanol
March 28, 2006

White House Chief of Staff

Q. Thank you for the interview. A very busy day at the White House, so I have to ask you, you accepted the resignation of Andrew Card today—is this a sign of a major shakeup at the White House?

The President. No, it's a sign of a fellow who has worked 5¼ years. He's here every morning early in the morning; he stays late;

and he put his heart and soul in the job. And he came to me about 2½ weeks ago, or 2 weeks ago and said, "I think it may be time for me to go on; you know, I've given it my all." And I thank him for his service. I consider him an incredibly close friend. And obviously, I picked Joshua Bolten to take his place. And now Josh's job is to design a White House staff that meets the needs of the President, which is one of the key—most important needs, is to make sure I get information in a timely fashion so I can make decisions.

Q. Any more changes coming up?

The President. Well, Josh has just begun to take a look at the White House structure. And I haven't had a chance to talk to him about the future yet. But right now I'm honoring and celebrating the service of Andy Card.

President's Upcoming Visit to Mexico

Q. Let's talk about Cancun. You'll meet with President Fox, Prime Minister of Canada. What do you expect to accomplish in that trip?

The President. Well, I think it's very important for the three of us to continue to commit ourselves to a relationship that—a commercial relationship based upon trade, free and fair trade, a security relationship based upon, kind of, mutual understanding of how we can cooperate. We're going to have a cultural event. We're going to go to the ruins, which will be fantastic, the Mayan ruins.

But the point is, is that the three of us need to be interconnected and work closely together for the good of our respective peoples. I'll remind people that we're not starting anything new. We're really building on what our predecessors left behind. In 2005, there was enormous trade between Mexico and the United States, much more significant than it was, you know, 10 years ago. And I believe both countries benefit from that trade.

But it is also not a given that people in both our countries accept trade. And

therefore, one of the jobs of leadership is to remind people about the benefits, that trade equals jobs, and jobs means people have a chance to realize hopeful dreams.

Immigration Reform

Q. The Government of Mexico recently placed ads in U.S. papers acknowledging their responsibility in the border problem and saying they should have a role in the way the guest-worker program is shaped. Should Mexico have that role? Is that appropriate?

The President. Well, I think, first of all, the fact that they put those ads in the papers talking about joint responsibility in the border makes it easier for those of us who believe in comprehensive migration or immigration reform to get something done. And I appreciate the Government's stand there.

The truth of the matter is, the laws of the United States will be written inside the Congress. Of course, thoughtful suggestions may help. But the job is really to get a bill out of the Senate and eventually the House—or out of a conference committee—that I can sign. And I'm interested in comprehensive immigration reform. That includes not only border security but also a temporary-worker plan that recognizes there are hard-working people here doing jobs Americans won't do. And they ought to be here in such a way so they don't have to hide in the shadows of our society.

The fundamental issue, by the way, it seems like to me, on the guest-worker plan, is should somebody get to the head of the line when it comes to citizenship? And my answer is, no, they ought to get in line, but they don't get to get to the head of the line. And that's where some of the tension about the debate is taking place right now.

Q. The debate is taking place in the Senate. They are discussing a plan, and they're including your guest-worker program that you've requested. But the House said, no.

591

The Sensenbrenner bill doesn't include a guest-worker program.

The President. Well, I wouldn't give up on it yet; we're just starting. For your listeners, this is a process. The House has passed a bill; the Senate, hopefully, will pass a bill; and then they'll get to conference and work something out in conference. And I have called upon both the House and the Senate to pass a comprehensive bill. And a comprehensive bill means, to make sure you include a guest-worker program as part of a comprehensive bill.

I happen to believe a guest-worker program recognizes reality—what's taking place in our economy today. But it also— a guest-worker program is part of border security. I mean, rather than have people sneaking across the border to come and do jobs that Americans won't do, it seems like it makes sense for people to be given an identification card that they can come and use to do a job on a temporary basis, so they can go back and forth freely with this tamper-proof ID card and not have to sneak across, so that our Border Patrol agents on both sides of the border are really dealing with drug smuggling or gun smuggling or terrorists trying to sneak into the country.

Illegal Immigration

Q. So the question is, after those 6 years, if they get the 6 years in this program, how will you enforce sending people back who have to go back who have been living——

The President. Well, you'll have to have a tamper-proof card in order to work. In other words, there will be—it will make it much easier to have employer enforcement in place when there is a card that you know is tamper-proof, in other words, one that can't be forged.

Right now there's a whole document forging industry that has evolved. There are people sneaking across in 18-wheelers or people risking their lives. And the system is inhumane, as far as I'm concerned, and it needs to be reformed.

Border Security

Q. The White House supported the Sensenbrenner bill in the House, making the exception that you were going to pursue a temporary guest-worker program. Now, that bill includes the construction of 700 miles of border, and that is seen not only in Mexico but in many Latin American countries as a sign that the U.S. wants to isolate itself from the region. Is that——

The President. I don't think people ought to read that into it. I think people ought to—first of all, the House is the beginning of the process, as you know. But people shouldn't—it's impractical to fence off the border. But it is also realistic to give our Border Patrol agents tools to be able to do their job. We ought to enforce our borders. That's what the American people expect. I've talked to President Fox about Mexico enforcing her southern border, and he agrees there ought to be border enforcement down there. But he, like I, understand it's difficult to enforce large borders.

And I don't think anybody believes that you could totally fence off the border and be effective. But I do think we ought to be in a position to give our Border Patrol agents better tools, more effective ways to prevent people from smuggling people and/or drugs across our border.

Venezuelan President Chavez

Q. I want to ask you about Venezuela, President Hugo Chavez. He refers to you in very strong terms. He does the same about Secretary Rice. What is your reaction to that, and where do you see—how do you see that affecting relations between your two countries?

The President. I judge the President based upon his honoring of the institutions that make democracy sound in Venezuela. I think it's very important for leaders to honor the freedom to worship, the freedom of the press, contracts, legal—to honor legal contracts, to allow people to express their opinion without fear. And it's very important for leaders throughout the hemisphere, whether they agree with America or not, to honor the tenets of democracy. And to the extent he doesn't do that, then I believe he should be subject to criticism.

Iraq

Q. President—Iraq. You've been telling people the U.S. is going the right way. But the polls—and you've said you don't follow the polls—the polls say people don't agree with you. Could it be that they're right and you're wrong?

The President. History will prove whether I'm right. I think I'll be right because I do believe freedom is universal. I remember it wasn't all that long ago that 11 million Iraqis went to the polls in the face of terrorist threats, in the face of potential assassination, and said, we want to be free. That was last December.

That sentiment still exists in Iraq. The enemy has got—those who want to stop democracy have got one weapon, and that is the ability to kill innocent life to get

on the TV, to shake our will. And my will is not going to be shaken. You cannot have a President make decisions based upon yesterday's polls. You must have a President who believes in certain principles and is willing to lead based upon a vision for a better future.

And I believe my vision for a better future entails having a democratic Iraq as a friend and an ally and to prevent the stated goals of the enemy from taking place. They want us to leave Iraq so they can establish a safe haven from which to launch attacks on our people again. And I take their goal seriously, and I will use all resources at my disposal in order to protect the American people.

Q. *Muchas gracias, Senor Presidente.*

The President. Si, por nada.

NOTE: The interview was taped at 3:08 p.m. in the Map Room at the White House. In his remarks, the President referred to President Vicente Fox Quesada of Mexico; and Prime Minister Stephen Harper of Canada. A tape was not available for verification of the content of this interview.

Statement on the Death of Caspar Weinberger
March 28, 2006

Caspar Weinberger was an American statesman and a dedicated public servant. He wore the uniform in World War II, held elected office, and served in the Cabinets of three Presidents. As Secretary of Defense for President Reagan, he worked to strengthen our military and win the cold

war. In all his years, this good man made many contributions to our Nation. America is grateful for Caspar Weinberger's lifetime of service. Laura and I send our condolences and prayers to the entire Weinberger family.

Interview With CTV
March 28, 2006

Canada-U.S. Relations

Q. Well, first of all, Mr. President, thank you very much for inviting us into your home. We certainly appreciate that.

Before we get on to talking about Canada-U.S. relations, I want to deal a little bit with your personal relations with Canadians. They haven't exactly been a roaring success. Does that matter? Does that matter to you? Does it matter to the relationship?

The President. I think I've had very good relations with the Canadians with whom I've dealt. I mean, Prime Minister Chretien and his successor, Paul Martin, and I got along just fine. We didn't always agree, but I can understand people not agreeing with some of the decisions I made. But that doesn't necessarily mean there's any problems with the relationship.

I guess much has been made about some of the name-calling that went on. That's just part of politics, and it doesn't bother me in the least. If I was bothered about name-calling from Canada, I'd certainly be bothered about name-calling from the United States as well. [*Laughter*]

The relationship between Canada and the United States is really a relationship not necessarily by government only but by the peoples, by the interchange, by the exchanges we have, by the relatives on both sides of the border. And that's what really makes the relationship unique and very strong.

Trade With Canada/Softwood Lumber

Q. In that regard, Prime Minister Harper, the new—I think this is now the third Prime Minister you've gone through——

The President. It is. [*Laughter*]

Q. ——in Canada. He said that of the top priorities that he's got, softwood lumber has to be number one; says it's, in his words, putting a very serious strain on the relationship between the two countries. You've often said that this is something that you want to take care of. I'm giving you an opportunity to make some news here. [*Laughter*]

The President. I may not see that. [*Laughter*]

Q. Okay. [*Laughter*] What would be—is there any one thing that you can do to unblock this issue?

The President. Well, I can tell our people to try to find common ground. I thought we were pretty close to a deal a couple of years ago—I can't remember the exact timing of it, but I know we've been working on softwood lumber for quite a while.

I fully understand how difficult an issue this is, particularly from Canada's perspective, since there's been some rulings. And we want to get it solved. I told that to Stephen Harper, that I understand its importance. I understand its priority. And I'd like to get the issue resolved once and for all myself. The best thing I can do is tell our negotiators that—see if you can find common ground. Again, we were close to an agreement before—maybe that's a place for people to look for common ground.

I know it's not going to get solved if it's done—if these negotiations are public. It's going to require some very quiet consultations to see if we can do what I'd like to see done.

Q. Can it be solved on your watch?

The President. I certainly hope so. This is a difficult issue. I know it creates anxieties in Canada. I really don't want to create anxieties. On the other hand, I do want to be fair to our folks here as well, and I think we can find ground.

Canada-U.S. Border/Homeland Security

Q. Talking about common ground, it seems to me that there's so much that we have in common between these two countries: We've got the world's largest undefended border; we're both countries at war; we've got boots on the ground in Afghanistan. And yet here at home, we're putting more barriers along that Canadian-American border.

You've often said that the reason for this—or what Stephen Harper calls the passport problem—you've said that it's because you want to know who's coming and going across that border. So I guess it begs the question, are the Canadians not telling you who's coming and going? Are we not doing a good enough job?

The President. Oh, I think Canada has been very cooperative, and the relationship between our services is very good. The idea is to have—it doesn't necessarily have to be a passport. It can be a document, a tamper-proof document that will expedite border crossings, not delay border crossings. The idea is to make sure that tourists and trade moves freely and terrorists don't.

And right after September the 11th, obviously, our country took a hard look at the procedures enabling people to come back and forth across our borders, both north and south. And the idea was to come up, as I said, with a tamper-proof document. I know they've been focused on the passport, but surely we can design something—the law doesn't say passport only; the law says, kind of, passport-like, if I'm not mistaken.

But the key is that it be tamper-proof. We've found a lot of, for example, driver's license forgeries throughout the United States that make it difficult to—you know, as best as we can, assure our citizens that we know who's coming in and who's not.

Q. I guess part of the problem for a lot of people in this is they say, look, it's not so much guys like you and me going across—we've all got passports or identity cards. But it's the minor league, peewee hockey team, or the peewee baseball team that won't be able to play in each other's

countries right now because it's too much of a hassle to get this card.

The President. Again, the idea is to make it hassle-free as best as possible. I can understand—I mean, on any change of the status quo, you can always find, kind of, the nightmare scenario that makes life— it makes it feel like life is going to be a lot worse. I don't think it necessarily has to be. I think we can work with our Canadian counterparts to come up with something that's rational and meets the law that has been passed by the Congress and that I signed.

Trade With Canada

Q. Can you foresee—you're going down to Cancun as part of the exercise, I guess, of imagining a new North America and then getting it going. In your vision, can you foresee a day when there would be free travel of people across the borders without identity cards, just free movement of people in North America?

The President. Oh, I don't know. That's probably down the road. But I'm not imagining an important relationship, though, because we're really building on what our predecessors left behind, which is a trading arrangement that has substantially increased trade between the United States and Canada and Mexico.

Canada is our number-one trading partner. I'm a believer that trade helps grow economies. I think free trade is an important part—and fair trade—something that Canadians want and something that Americans want is free and fair trade—benefits both of us. You know, we traded about nearly $500 billion, two-way trade, in 2005, which is very positive for both our economies.

What I'm concerned about is that protectionist tendency and isolationist tendency that could emerge in both our countries as well as in Mexico, which would make it harder for us to realize the benefits of collaboration together, make it harder for us to, kind of, grow together. And that would be not beneficial for the hemisphere, and frankly, it will make it a lot harder for future Americans and Canadians and Mexicans to compete with the Chinese, for example.

And so there is a relationship which exists which needs to be protected and nurtured and streamlined and made more efficient, and that's really what the discussions will be in Cancun.

Canadian Government

Q. A quick last question for you—I don't know if you're going to take the bait on this one.

The President. Probably not.

Q. Okay. [*Laughter*]

The President. Now that you've let me know——

Q. I let the cat out of the bag.

The President. ——let me know there was a hook coming. [*Laughter*]

Q. Are you any happier with the Conservative Government in Canada than a Liberal Government?

The President. I am—I respect the will of the Canadian people, and as I say, you know, this is—there were some tense times when I made the decision to go to war in Iraq, and I understand that. I'm not the—I fully understand why people, not only in Canada but in the United States, expressed deep concern about the use of force to protect ourselves. I stand by the decision. I think it's the right decision. And therefore, I wasn't surprised when I heard, you know, members of political parties in both our countries express deep concern about it.

Having said all that, however, in the midst of turbulent times, my relationships with the two Prime Ministers, prior to Stephen Harper, were good, solid relationships. We had candid discussions; we were friendly toward each other; we shared the same values of human rights and human dignity and freedom to speak and freedom to worship.

So I view the relationship with Canada as a very strong and important relationship for the United States of America. It's a relationship that we should never take for granted, and I'm confident the Canadians won't take our relationship for granted. And it's a relationship that needs attention and care. And there are problems that arise, like softwood lumber. Hopefully, we'll get that solved. But we've also had a BSE issue that came up on my watch, which we solved, as well as potatoes. We had a potato issue when I first became President of the United States that we worked through with Prime Minister Chretien.

Q. Mr. President, you've been very generous with your time, and I appreciate it.

The President. Well, thanks for coming.

Q. Thank you.

The President. Welcome to Washington.

Q. Thank you, sir.

NOTE: The interview was taped at 2:55 p.m. in the Map Room at the White House for later broadcast. In his remarks, the President referred to former Prime Ministers Jean Chretien and Paul Martin, and Prime Minister Stephen Harper of Canada. The transcript was released by the Office of the Press Secretary on March 29.

Remarks Following Discussions With President Olusegun Obasanjo of Nigeria
March 29, 2006

President Bush. Mr. President, welcome back to the Oval Office. We have just had a discussion that covered a lot of topics. Every time I meet with the President, he brings a fresh perspective about the politics and the situation on the continent of Africa, and I want to thank you. I want to thank you for your leadership.

The President and I talked about Darfur and the Sudan, and I made it very clear to him that we're deeply concerned about the humiliation, the rape, the murder that is taking place among the—against the citizens of Darfur. He agreed. And I want to thank you for your compassion.

We talked and strategized about how to move forward, how to make it clear to the Sudanese Government that there will be a international response in working toward a peace. We talked about a dual track, that the rebels must come together and negotiate with the Government, and at the same time, we talked about bolstering the AU peacekeeping force with a blue-helmeted force. And I explained to him my desire to have a NATO overlay to make sure that force is robust.

We talked about economic development. Of course, I brought up energy to the President. He's—he and I talked about the situation in the Nigerian Delta. He talked to me about his strategy to deal with the energy issue.

And finally, I appreciate the decision he made regarding Charles Taylor. In my visit last week with the President of Liberia, we talked about Charles Taylor. The fact that Charles Taylor will be brought to justice in a court of law will help Liberia and is a signal, Mr. President, of your deep desire for there to be peace in your neighborhood.

So welcome to the Oval Office. It's good to have you here, sir.

President Obasanjo. Thank you very much. And as usual, I want to thank you for the warm and hardy reception that you have accorded us.

The areas that I would call the areas of concern, by the time I arrived here last night, seemed to have been definably dealt with by this morning, particularly the issue of Charles Taylor. And as I said to you about a minute—a few minutes ago, Charles Taylor should be landing in Liberia by now, which should start putting the issue of Charles Taylor behind all of us.

I appreciate the understanding of everybody and the way that the issue has been handled. I met the press earlier today to actually give what was our own position and how we were hoping to deal with the issue of Charles Taylor's disappearance. And of course, I do not agree, must disagree that we have been negligent in the way we handled the Charles Taylor issue. If we had been negligent, then Charles Taylor would have got away. He would not have been arrested if there was connivance or condonation on our part.

Having said that, we, of course, talked about the general situation of peace and security in the West Africa subregion, and how West Africa subregion, with Charles Taylor issue behind us, how West Africa subregion is gradually becoming a haven of peace. We have dealt with Togo; we have dealt with Guinea-Bissau; we have dealt with Sierra Leone. Hopefully, we are now dealing with Liberia. And things seem to be going fairly well in Cote d'Ivoire. Well, of course, we are keenly watching the situation in Guinea—Conakry.

Then we looked at the rest of Africa, particularly Democratic Republic of Congo, Ethiopia and Eritrea, and the Great Lakes, generally. Then we talked about the issue of development, particularly security—supplies, security, stability, and also price stability of hydrocarbons from the Gulf of Guinea area, and how we are working hard to establish a Gulf of Guinea commission that will also deal with the issue of reconciling and dealing with ending misunderstanding among those in that—among countries that are in the Gulf of Guinea, how we can protect and how we can monitor what happens in that area, because the hydrocarbon we need for our own development and we need for the economic development and progress of the world. We are moving in this regard not only by ourselves but also by our—with our development partners.

Then, of course, we talked about NEPAD, which is where we work with the G–8 and—politically and individually.

And we—I briefed the President on what we are doing with the Niger Delta, which is very important. And we are very grateful that the measures we are taking, which are essentially socioeconomic measures to address some of the grievances, identified grievances, will resolve the issues of the Niger Delta.

I think these are some of the points. And I think—I want to thank President for remaining his charming self. [*Laughter*]

President Bush. Thank you, sir.

NOTE: The President spoke at 10:30 a.m. in the Oval Office at the White House. In his remarks, he referred to former President Charles Taylor of Liberia, who was arrested on March 29 in Nigeria on United Nations war crimes charges; and President Ellen Johnson Sirleaf of Liberia.

Remarks to Freedom House and a Question-and-Answer Session
March 29, 2006

The President. Thank you. Please be seated. I shouldn't be so instructive to the diplomatic corps. [*Laughter*] Peter, thank you for your warm introduction. Thank you for your commitment to freedom. It turns out freedom runs pretty deep in Peter's family. I don't know if you know this or not, but his son is a Marine First Lieutenant named Elliot Ackerman. He fought in the battle of Fallujah. I know you're proud of your son, and I'm proud to be the Commander in Chief of men and women who volunteer to defend our own freedom.

I appreciate very much the men and women of Freedom House. For more than 60 years, this organization has been a tireless champion for liberty. You've been a clear voice for the oppressed across the world. At Freedom House, you understand that the only path to lasting peace is the expansion of freedom and liberty.

Free societies are peaceful societies. When governments are accountable to their own citizens, when people are free to speak and assemble, when minorities are protected, then justice prevails. And so does the cause of peace.

Freedom House was founded on the principle that no nation is exempt from the demands of human dignity. And you're carrying that message across the world, from Africa to China to Belarus and beyond. At Freedom House, you also understand free societies do not take root overnight, especially in countries that suffer from decades of tyranny and repression. You understand that free elections are an instrument of change, yet they're only the first step. So as you press for democratic change across the world, you're helping new democracies build free institutions they need to overcome the legacies of tyranny and dictatorship.

I want to thank you for your vital work. You're making a significant contribution to the security of our country. I'm also honored that we've got distinguished members of the legislative body with us, particularly Senators—John Warner, who is the chairman of the Armed Services Committee; Senator Dick Lugar, who is the chairman of the Senate Foreign Relations Committee; and, of course, Senator Ted Stevens. I thank the Members from the House and Senate who have joined these distinguished Senators. I appreciate you taking time to come and listen to me. Just listen to me a little more often. [*Laughter*]

I particularly want to pay homage to Ambassador Max Kampelman. Thank you very much. I was telling the Ambassador, right before I came over I was having a little visit with my Chief of Staff-to-be, Josh Bolten. It turns out that Josh's dad and the Ambassador were lifelong friends. And as I came over here, he said, "You make sure that you say hello to one of the finest men our country has ever produced." So, Mr. Chairman, on behalf of a grateful President and a grateful Chief of Staff-to-be, thank you for serving our country.

I appreciate the other members of the Freedom House Board of Trustees. And I thank the diplomatic corps for joining us as well.

We meet at a time of war but also at a moment of great hope. In our world and due in part to our efforts, freedom is taking root in places where liberty was unimaginable a couple of years ago. Just 25 years ago, at the start of the 1980s, there were only 45 democracies on the face of the Earth. Today, Freedom House reports there are 122 democracies, and more people now live in liberty than ever before.

The advance of freedom is the story of our time, and we're seeing new chapters written before our eyes. Since the beginning of 2005, we've witnessed remarkable democratic changes across the globe. The people of Afghanistan have elected their first democratic Parliament in more than a generation. The people of Lebanon have recovered their independence and chosen their leaders in free elections. The people of Kyrgyzstan have driven a corrupt regime from power and voted for democratic change. The people of Liberia have overcome decades of violence and are now led by the first woman elected as a head of state in any African nation. And the courageous people of Iraq have gone to the polls not once, not twice, but three times, choosing a transitional government, a democratic Constitution, and a new Government under that Constitution.

Each of these countries still faces enormous challenges that will take patience and the support of the international community to overcome. Yet Freedom House has declared, the year 2005 was one of the most successful years for freedom since the Freedom House began measuring world freedom more than 30 years ago. From Kabul to Baghdad to Beirut and beyond, freedom's tide is rising, and we should not rest, and we must not rest, until the promise of liberty reaches every people and every nation.

In our history, most democratic progress has come with the end of a war. After the defeat of the Axis powers in World War II and the collapse of communism in the cold war, scores of nations cleared away the rubble of tyranny and laid the foundations of freedom and democracy.

Today, the situation is very different. Liberty is advancing not in a time of peace but in the midst of a war, at a moment when a global movement of great brutality and ambition is fighting freedom's progress with all the hateful violence they can muster. In this new century, the advance of freedom is a vital element of our strategy to protect the American people and to secure the peace for generations to come. We're fighting the terrorists across the world because we know that if America were not fighting this enemy in other lands, we'd be facing them here in our own land.

On September the 11th, 2001, we saw the violence and the hatred of a vicious enemy and the future that they intend for us. That day I made a decision: America will not wait to be attacked again. We will confront this mortal danger. We will stay on the offensive. America will defend our freedom.

We're pursuing the terrorists on many battlefronts. Today, the central front in the war on terror is Iraq. This month, I've given a series of speeches on recent events in Iraq and how we're adapting our approach to deal with the events on the ground. At George Washington University,

I reported on the progress we have made in training the Iraqi security forces, the growing number of Iraqi units that are taking the lead in the fight, the territory we're handing over to them, and the performance they turned in after the bombing of the Golden Mosque in Samarra.

Last week in Cleveland, I told the American people about the northern Iraqi city of Tall 'Afar, which was once a key base of operations for Al Qaida and is now a free city that gives us reason to hope for a free Iraq. I explained how the story of Tall 'Afar gives me confidence in our strategy, because in that city, we see the outlines of the Iraq we've been fighting for, a free and secure people who are getting back on their feet, who are participating in government and civic life, and are becoming allies in the fight against the terrorists.

Today I'm going to discuss the stakes in Iraq and our efforts to help the Iraqi people overcome past divisions and form a lasting democracy, and why it is vital to the security of the American people that we help them succeed.

In the wake of recent violence in Iraq, many Americans are asking legitimate questions: Why are Iraqis so divided? And did America cause the instability by removing Saddam Hussein from power? They ask, after three elections, why are the Iraqi people having such a hard time coming together? And can a country with so many divisions ever build a stable democracy? They ask why we can't bring our troops home now and let the Iraqis sort out their differences on their own.

These are fair questions, and today I'll do my best to answer them. I'll discuss some of the reasons for the instability we're seeing in Iraq, why democracy is the only force that can overcome these divisions, why I believe the vast majority of Iraqis want to live in freedom and peace, and why the security of our Nation depends on the success of a free Iraq.

Today, some Americans ask whether removing Saddam caused the divisions and instability we're now seeing. In fact, much of the animosity and violence we now see is the legacy of Saddam Hussein. He is a tyrant who exacerbated sectarian divisions to keep himself in power. Iraq is a nation with many ethnic and religious and sectarian and regional and tribal divisions. Before Saddam Hussein, Iraqis from different communities managed to live together. Even today, many Iraqi tribes have both Sunni and Shi'a branches. And in many small towns with mixed populations, there's often only one mosque, where Sunni and Shi'a worship together. Intermarriage is also common with mixed families that include Arabs and Kurds and Sunnis and Shi'a and Turkmen and Assyrians and Chaldeans.

To prevent these different groups from coming to challenge his regime, Saddam Hussein undertook a deliberate strategy of maintaining control by dividing the Iraqi people. He stayed on top by brutally repressing different Iraqi communities and pitting them one against the other. He forced hundreds of thousands of Iraqis out of their homes, using expulsion as a weapon to subdue and punish any group that resisted his rule. By displacing Iraqi communities and dividing the Iraqi people, he sought to establish himself as the only force that could hold the country together.

In Saddam's campaign of repression and division, no Iraqi group was spared. In the late 1980s, Saddam Hussein unleashed a brutal ethnic cleansing operation against Kurds in northern Iraq. Kurdish towns and villages were destroyed. Tens of thousands of Kurds disappeared or were killed. In his effort to terrorize the Kurds into submission, Saddam dropped chemical weapons on scores of Kurdish villages. In one village alone, a town called Halabja, his regime killed thousands of innocent men and women and children, using mustard gas and nerve agents. Saddam also forcibly removed hundreds of thousands of Kurds from their homes, and then he moved Arabs into those homes and onto the properties of the people who were forced to leave. As a result of his strategy, deep tensions persist to this day.

Saddam also waged a brutal campaign of suppression and genocide against the Shi'a in the south of Iraq. He targeted prominent Shi'a clerics for assassination. He destroyed Shi'a mosques and holy sites. He killed thousands of innocent men, women, and children. He piled their bodies into mass graves. After the 1991 Persian Gulf war, Saddam brutally crushed a Shi'a uprising. Many Shi'a fled to the marshes of southern Iraq. They hid in the wetlands that could not be easily reached by Saddam's army.

The wetlands, by the way, were also home to the Marsh Arabs, an ancient civilization that traces its roots back 5,000 years. So Saddam destroyed the Marsh Arabs and those who hid in the marshes by draining the marshes where they lived. In less than a decade, the majority of these lush wetlands were turned into barren desert, and most of the Marsh Arabs were driven from their ancestral home. It is no wonder that deep divisions and scars exist in much of the Shi'a population.

Saddam also oppressed his fellow Sunnis. One of the great misperceptions about Iraq is that every Sunni enjoyed a privileged status under Saddam's regime. In truth, Saddam trusted few outside his family and his tribe. He installed his sons and his brothers and his cousins in key positions. Almost everyone was considered suspect, and often those suspicions led to brutal violence.

In one instance, Saddam's security services tortured to death a pilot from a prominent Sunni tribe and then dumped his headless body in front of his family's house. It caused riots that he then brutally suppressed. In the mid-1990s, Saddam rounded up scores of prominent Sunni economists and lawyers and retired army officers and former government officials. Many were never heard from again.

It is hard to overstate the effects of Saddam's brutality on the Iraqi nation. Here's what one marine recalls when he was on the streets of the Iraqi capital. He said, quote, "I had an Iraqi citizen come up to me. She opened her mouth, and she had no tongue. She was pointing at the statue. There were people with no fingers waving at the statue of Saddam, telling us he tortured them. People were showing us scars on their back." Iraq is a nation that is physically and emotionally scarred by three decades of Saddam's tyranny, and these wounds will take time to heal. As one Marsh Arab put it, "Saddam did everything he could to kill us. You cannot recover from that right away."

These are the kinds of tensions Iraqis are dealing with today. They are the divisions that Saddam aggravated through deliberate policies of ethnic cleansing and sectarian violence. As one Middle East scholar has put it, Iraq under Saddam Hussein was "a society slowly and systematically poisoned by political terror. The toxic atmosphere in today's Iraq bears witness to his terrible handiwork."

The argument that Iraq was stable under Saddam and that stability is now in danger because we removed him is wrong. While liberation has brought its own set of challenges, Saddam Hussein's removal from power was the necessary first step in restoring stability and freedom to the people of Iraq.

Today, some Americans are asking why the Iraqi people are having such a hard time building a democracy. The reason is that the terrorists and former regime elements are exploiting the wounds inflicted under Saddam's tyranny. The enemies of a free Iraq are employing the same tactics Saddam used—killing and terrorizing the Iraqi people in an effort to foment sectarian division.

For the Saddamists, provoking sectarian strife is business as usual. And we know from the terrorists' own words that they're using the same tactics with the goal of inciting a civil war. Two years ago, we intercepted a letter to Usama bin Laden from the terrorist Zarqawi, in which he explains his plan to stop the advance of democracy in Iraq. Zarqawi wrote: "If we succeed in dragging the Shi'a into the arena of sectarian war, it will become possible to awaken the inattentive Sunnis as they feel imminent danger. The only solution is for us to strike the religious and military and other cadres among the Shi'a with blow after blow."

The terrorists and Saddamists have been brutal in the pursuit of this strategy. They target innocent civilians; they blow up police officers; they attack mosques; and they commit other acts of horrific violence for the cameras. Their objective is to stop Iraq's democratic progress. They tried to stop the transfer of sovereignty. They tried to stop millions of Iraqis from voting in the January 2005 elections. They tried to stop Sunnis from participating in the October referendum on the Constitution. And they tried to stop millions from voting in the December elections to form a Government under that Constitution.

And in each case, they failed. With every election, participation was larger and broader than the one that came before. And in December, almost 12 million people— more than 75 percent of eligible voters— defied the terrorists to cast their ballots. With their votes, the Iraqi people have spoken and made their intentions clear: They want to live in liberty and unity, and they're determined to chart their own destiny.

Now the elements of a free Iraq are trying to stop the—the enemies of a free Iraq are trying to stop the formation of unity government. They've learned they cannot succeed by facing coalition and Iraqi forces on the battlefield, so they've taken their violence to a new level by attacking one of Shi'a Islam's holiest sites. They blew up the Golden Mosque in Samarra in the hope that this outrageous act would provoke the Shi'a masses into widespread reprisals which would provoke Sunnis to retaliate and drag the nation into a civil war.

Yet despite massive provocations, Iraq has not descended into civil war. Most Iraqis have not turned to violence. The Iraqi security forces have not broken up into sectarian groups waging war against each other. Instead, Sunni, Shi'a, and Kurdish soldiers stood together to protect religious sites, enforce a curfew, and restore civil order.

In recent weeks, these forces passed another important test when they successfully protected millions of Shi'a pilgrims who marched to the cities of Karbala and Najaf for an annual religious holiday. In 2004, the terrorists launched coordinated strikes against the pilgrims, killing scores of innocent worshipers. This year, the pilgrimage was largely peaceful, thanks to the courage and the unity of the Iraqi security forces. In the midst of today's sectarian tension, the ability of Iraqis to hold a peaceful gathering by millions of people is a hopeful sign for the future of Iraq.

In these last few weeks, we've also seen terrible acts of violence. The kidnapings and brutal executions and beheadings are very disturbing. There's no place in a free and democratic Iraq for armed groups operating outside the law. It's vital to the security of a free Iraq that the police are free of militia influence. And so we're working with Iraqi leaders to find and remove leaders from the National Police who show evidence of loyalties to militias. We're partnering U.S. battalions with Iraqi national police to teach them about the role of a professional police force in a democratic society. We're making clear to Iraqi leaders that reining in the illegal militias must be a top priority of Iraq's new government when it takes office.

The violence we're seeing is showing the Iraqi leaders the danger of sectarian division and underscoring the urgency of forming a national unity government. Today, Iraqi leaders from every major ethnic and religious community are working to construct the path forward. Our Ambassador to Iraq, Zal Khalilzad, is helping Iraq's leaders reach out across political and religious and sectarian lines, so they can form a government that will earn the trust and the confidence of all Iraqis.

Putting aside differences to build a democracy that reflects the country's diversity is a difficult thing to do. It's even more difficult when enemies are working daily to stop your progress and divide your nation. Yet Iraqis are rising to the moment. They deserve enormous credit for their courage and their determination to succeed.

Iraqi leaders are coming to grips with an important truth: The only practical way to overcome the divisions of three decades of tyranny is through democracy. Democracy is the only form of government where every person has a say in the governance of a country. It's the only form of government that will yield to a peaceful Middle East. So Iraqis are working to overcome past divisions and build a free society that protects the rights of all its citizens. They're undertaking this progress with just a year's experience in democratic politics.

Many of the institutions and traditions we take for granted here in America—from party structures to centuries' experience with peaceful transitions of power—are new to Iraq, so we should not be surprised if Iraqis make mistakes or face setbacks in their efforts to build a government that unites the Iraqi people.

We're beginning to see the signs of progress. Earlier this month, Iraqi leaders announced they had reached an agreement on the need to address critical issues, such as de-Ba'athification in the operation of security ministries and the distribution of oil revenues, in the spirit of national unity. They agreed to form a new national security council that will improve coordination within the government on these and other difficult issues. This council will include representatives from all major political groups, as well as leaders from Iraq's executive, judicial, and legislative branches. As a result of this council's considered advice, the Iraqi Government that emerges will be more effective and more unified.

Another important sign of progress is that Saddam Hussein is now being called to account for his crimes by the free citizens of a free Iraq. Millions of Iraqis are seeing their independent judiciary in action. At the former dictator's trial, Iraqis recently saw something that's got to be truly amazing to them. When Saddam Hussein stood up and began to give a political speech, the presiding judge gaveled him down. Saddam growled at the judge, declaring, "I'm the head of state." The judge replied, "You used to be the head of the state. And now you're a defendant." Three years ago, any Iraqi who addressed Saddam in this way would have been killed on the spot. Now the former dictator is answering to a judge instead of meting out arbitrary justice, and Iraqis are replacing the rule of a tyrant with the rule of law.

Finally, some Americans are asking if it's time to pull out our troops and leave the Iraqis to settle their own differences. I know the work in Iraq is really difficult, but I strongly feel it's vital to the security of our country. The terrorists are killing and maiming and fighting desperately to stop the formation of a unity government because they understand what a free Iraq in the heart of the Middle East means for them and their ideology. They know that when freedom sets root in Iraq, it will be a mortal blow to their aspirations to dominate the region and advance their hateful vision. So they're determined to stop the advance of a free Iraq, and we must be equally determined to stop them.

The irony is that the enemy seems to have a much clearer sense of what's at stake than some of the politicians here in Washington, DC. One Member of Congress who has proposed an immediate withdrawal of American forces in Iraq recently explained that what would happen after American forces pulled out was this:

He said, "They'll fight each other; somebody will win; they'll settle it for themselves." While it might sound attractive to some, it would have disastrous consequences for American security. The Iraqi Government is still in transition, and the Iraqi security forces are still gathering capacity. If we leave Iraq before they're capable of defending their own democracy, the terrorists will win. They will achieve their stated goal. This is what the terrorists have told us they want to achieve. They will turn Iraq into a safe haven. They will seek to arm themselves with weapons of mass destruction. They will use Iraq as a base to overthrow moderate governments in the Middle East. They will use Iraq as a base from which to launch further attacks against the United States of America.

Mindful of recent history, I ask you to think about what happened in Afghanistan. In the 1980s, the United States helped Afghan freedom fighters drive the Soviet Red Army from Kabul, and once the Soviets withdrew, we decided our work was finished and left the Afghans to defend themselves. Soon the terrorists moved in to fill the vacuum. They took over the country; they turned it into a safe haven from which they planned and launched the attacks of September the 11th.

If we leave Iraq before the job is done, the terrorists will move in and fill the vacuum, and they will use that failed state to bring murder and destruction to freedom-loving nations.

I know some in our country disagree with my decision to liberate Iraq. Whatever one thought about the decision to remove Saddam from power, I hope we should all agree that pulling our troops out prematurely would be a disaster. If we were to let the terrorists drive us out of Iraq, we would signal to the world that America cannot be trusted to keep its word. We would undermine the morale of our troops by betraying the cause for which they have sacrificed. We would cause the tyrants in the Middle East to laugh at our failed re-

solve and tighten their repressive grip. The global terrorist movement would be emboldened and more dangerous than ever. For the security of our citizens and the peace of the world, we will not turn the future of Iraq over to the followers of a failed dictator or to evil men like bin Laden and Zarqawi.

America will leave Iraq, but we will not retreat from Iraq. We will leave because Iraqi forces have gained in strength, not because America's will has weakened. We will complete the mission in Iraq because the security of the American people is linked to the success in Iraq.

We're pursuing a clear strategy for victory. Victory requires an integrated strategy: political, economic, and security. These three elements depend on and reinforce one another. By working with Iraqi leaders to build the foundations of a strong democracy, we will ensure they have the popular support they need to defeat the terrorists. By going after the terrorists, coalition and Iraqi forces are creating the conditions that allow the Iraqi people to begin rebuilding their lives and their country. By helping Iraqis with economic reconstruction, we're giving every citizen a real stake in the success of a free Iraq. And as all this happens, the terrorists, those who offer nothing but death and destruction, are becoming isolated from the population.

I wish I could tell you the violence in Iraq is waning and that all the tough days in the struggle are behind us. They're not. There will be more tough fighting ahead with difficult days that test the patience and the resolve of our country. Yet we can have faith in the final outcome because we've seen freedom overcome the darkness of tyranny and terror and secure the peace before. And in this century, freedom is going to prevail again.

In 1941, the year the Freedom House began its work, the future of freedom seemed bleak. There were about a dozen lonely democracies in the world. The Soviet Union was led by the tyrant Stalin, who massacred millions. Hitler was leading Nazi Germany in a campaign to dominate Europe and eliminate the Jewish people from the face of the Earth. An imperial Japan launched a brutal surprise attack on America. Today, six decades later, the Soviet Empire is no more; Germany and Japan are free nations, and they are allies in the cause of peace; and the majority of the world's governments are democracies.

There were doubters six decades ago who said that freedom could not prevail. History has proved them wrong. In this young century, the doubters are still with us but so is the unstoppable power of freedom. In Afghanistan and Iraq and other nations, that power is replacing tyranny with hope, and no one should bet against it.

One of the greatest forces for freedom in the history of the world is the United States Armed Forces. In the past 4½ years, our troops have liberated more people than at any time since World War II. Because of the men and women who wear our Nation's uniform, 50 million people in Iraq and Afghanistan have tasted freedom, and their liberation has inspired millions more across the broader Middle East to believe that freedom is theirs as well.

This is going to be freedom's century. Thank you for giving me a chance to come and visit with you. May God bless. [*Applause*]

Okay, sit down, please. All right, I'll be glad to answer some questions.

Yes, sir. Yes, please.

Millennium Challenge Account

Q. I have a question. I am from Mali. A couple of years ago, the Millennium Challenge Account was created to help countries that were already on the path to democracy. Looking at a country like Mali in West Africa, where just yesterday we celebrated our 15 years of freedom—we haven't seen any money yet. [*Laughter*]

The President. I like a good lobbyist. [*Laughter*]

Q. Well, isn't it cheaper and easier for people—people from Mali and all throughout Africa, who already are in love with America, and isn't it easier politically to you and show to your critics that, look, in Iraq, maybe we need some [*inaudible*]— we're in there, but in places like Mali that have freedom, we can step in and help them without expecting something back? Thank you.

The President. No, I appreciate that. I— he's referring to a foreign policy initiative of mine called the Millennium Challenge Account. I want to thank the Members of Congress who have been strong supporters of the Millennium Challenge Account. I would hope they would continue to support the Millennium Challenge Account.

The Millennium Challenge Account, the idea behind it was, is that nations are capable of defeating corruption; they are capable of investing in health and education for their citizens; and they are capable about supporting market-oriented economies. If you believe that, then why shouldn't our aid say, you get aid in return for fighting corruption, investing in the health and education of your citizens, and putting market-oriented economic measures in place?

We started the process recognizing that a lot of people would raise their hands, including Mali, by saying we'll start with the poorest nations first. I must confess that our Millennium Challenge Account, while funded in its first year, was a little slow to get going. We've changed the structure to make sure money gets out the door so that other nations such as Mali will be eligible for application and consideration.

I can remember when I first put in the Millennium Challenge Account. People were somewhat aghast that the United States would dare ask for conditions for its money. Those are the defeatists in the world, those who believe that certain people can't fight corruption. We believe opposite of that in America. We believe in high standards, and the taxpayers sure believe in accountability for our foreign dollars.

So thank you for bringing it up. I appreciate a man who is willing to stand up and defend his country in front of the President and all the cameras. [*Laughter*] Yes, sir.

Liberia/Sudan

Q. Mr. President, I'm from The Economist magazine. I understand, Mr. President, you met with President Obasanjo of Nigeria today. I wonder if you could tell us what you discussed and also if——

The President. No, but keep going. [*Laughter*]

Q. Okay. Are you now confident——

The President. I can tell you what I discussed.

Q. Are you now confident that Charles Taylor, the recently recaptured Liberian warlord, will stand trial?

The President. I am much more confident today than I was yesterday. [*Laughter*] This is what we call embedding. [*Laughter*] I talked to the President about a variety of things, one of which, of course, was Charles Taylor. There is a process to get Charles Taylor to the court in the Netherlands. Such a process will require a United Nations Security Council resolution. Secretary Rice, who was in the meeting, told me that she thought that might happen relatively quickly. And so therefore, I think he is headed for where he belongs, which is trial.

I spoke to President Sirleaf about this issue as well. She was deeply concerned that Charles Taylor could be in a position to disturb this young democracy. I must tell you that I was most impressed by the leader from Liberia. I think America is going to be—should be very anxious to work with her and help this country overcome years of violence.

But I do believe that he is headed for trial. We certainly will do our efforts in the diplomatic channels to see to it that that's the case.

We also talked about Sudan. I'm deeply worried about the human conditions in Darfur. Ours is a government that spoke out about genocide, and we meant it. I thanked President Obasanjo for the AU presence in the Sudan. I told him, however, I did not think the presence was robust enough. I do believe there needs to be a blue helmeting of not only the AU forces but additional forces with a NATO overlay. And the reason I believe that NATO ought to be a part of the operation is twofold: one, to provide logistical and command and control and airlift capability but also to send a clear signal to parties involved that the West is determined to help a settlement—to help affect in a settlement, that this is serious business, that we're just not playing a diplomatic holding game, but that when we say "genocide," we mean that the genocide needs to be stopped.

Secondly, we talked about the need for a parallel track, a peace process to go forward, that there needs to be unity amongst the rebel groups. The President told me he has met with the rebel groups, trying to come up with a focused message that can then be used to negotiate with the Government of Sudan. There is a pretty good template to go by, a resource-sharing arrangement. There's a governing structure that, if implemented, would be—in the north/south—because of the north/south agreement, could be a go-by for the Darfur region. But those are the two main things I talked to him about.

Yes, sir. Are you embedded? [*Laughter*]

Environment/Alternative Fuel Sources

Q. From Australia—I've got a question about global warming. A couple of days ago, in the Australian Parliament, Tony Blair called for greater action. And this seems to be something that the U.S. President could make a major difference on. There's a virtual consensus that the planet is warming. If you addressed issues like emissions, fuel efficiency, issues to do with alternative energy in your last few years as President, it could make a significant difference, I think, to the——

The President. I appreciate you bringing that up.

Q. And I suppose I want to know, what is your plan?

The President. Good. We—first of all, there is—the globe is warming. The fundamental debate: Is it manmade or natural? Put that aside. It is in our interests that we use technologies that will not only clean the air but make us less dependent on oil. That's what I said in my State of the Union the other day. I said, look—and I know it came as quite a shock to—for people to hear a Texan stand up and say, "We've got a national problem; we're addicted to oil." But I meant what I said.

Being addicted to oil is a problem for our economy. In a global economy, when burgeoning economies like India and China use more fossil fuels, it affects the price of gasoline here in America. In a world in which sometimes people have got the oil we need, don't like us—kind of a undiplomatic way of putting it—it means we've got a national security issue.

I have—much of my position was defined early on in my Presidency when I told the world I thought that Kyoto was a lousy deal for America. And I tell you why it was a lousy deal for America. It meant that we had to cut emissions below 1990 levels, which would have meant I would have presided over massive layoffs and economic destruction. I believe the best way to put technologies in place that will not only achieve national objectives like less addiction to oil but also help clean the air is to be wealthy enough to invest in technologies and then to share those technologies with parts of the world that were excluded from the Kyoto Protocol.

And so I guess I should have started differently when I first became President, and said, "We will invest in new technologies that will enable us to use fossil fuels in a much wiser way." And what does that mean? Well, it means that we've got

to figure out how to use ethanol more in our cars. Ethanol is produced mainly by cane and corn. But we're near some breakthroughs—that we can use saw grass and biomass to be able to produce ethanol.

It means we got to continue investing in hybrid batteries. Ours is a country where many people live in urban centers, like Washington, DC. And it's possible to have a hybrid battery breakthrough which says that the first 40 miles of an automobile can be used by electricity alone. Right now the hybrid vehicles, as you know, switch between gasoline and electrical power. But that consumes gasoline, which means we're still reliant upon oil. The idea is to get off of oil.

On the electricity front, we need to be using nuclear power more in this country, in my judgment. It is a renewable source of energy that has zero gas emissions. We've got a great natural resource here in America called coal. We have 250-plus years of coal reserves. But we also recognize that by—burning coal causes environmental problems, and so we're spending billions on research to come up with clean coal technologies. And we'd like to share those technologies with other nations of the world that are beginning to grow, so that they are good stewards of the environment as well.

And so I got a comprehensive plan that uses technologies to help this Nation from a national and economic perspective but also will help improve the global economy—the environment from those new, burgeoning economies that are—like China and India, to be exact.

Yes.

Iraq/Syria/Iran

Q. Mr. President, first, thank you for your remarks and your commitment to advance freedom and the courage to use your office to follow through with it. My question is about Iraq. And I wonder if you could tell us, to what degree do you think the insurgency inside Iraq is dependent—

dependent on foreign support, particularly from regional powers——

The President. Yes.

Q. ——and what are we doing, or what could we do more to prevent that?

The President. There are three elements of the insurgency. One are the rejectionists. Those are the Sunnis that didn't feel like they were going to get a fair shake in what they viewed would be a Shi'a-led government. They are slowly but surely recognizing that democracy is their best hope. Then there are the Saddamists. Those are the folks that received enormous privilege under Saddam Hussein, and they're furious that they don't have those privileges. And the last group, of course, is Al Qaida. Now, Al Qaida has stated clearly what I told you during the speech. They have made it abundantly clear that their ambitions are to drive us from the country. They're the ones that we worry about—were receiving foreign assistance—money, as well as safe haven.

The two countries that worry us the most, of course, are the two neighboring countries next to Iraq. That would be Syria and Iran. And we are making it abundantly clear to both that we think it's in their interests to let an Iraqi democracy develop.

Syria has been a—Syria is a complicated issue because of Lebanon. It's not complicated; actually, it's quite clear what needs to be done. Our first focus with Syria, besides stopping cross-border infiltration— that, frankly, has required our—required us to adjust our tactics on the ground and spend a lot of time training people to stop the cross-border infiltration, because there's some doubt as to whether or not we're getting much cooperation on the other side of the border. But we spend a lot of time working with, particularly, France in making it abundantly clear we expect the Syrians to allow the Lebanese democracy to evolve.

I guess it's kind of hard to give up on a country on which you've had a stranglehold. There was a troop withdrawal, as you know. My main concern is to whether or not they withdraw more than just troops, whether they draw intelligence services and people that were in a position to influence the future of the country.

It is very important that there be full cooperation in the investigation of the death of Mr. Hariri. But our message to Bashar Asad is that we expect—if they want to be a welcomed country into the world, that they have got to free Lebanon, shut down cross-border infiltration, and stop allowing Hizballah, PIJ, and other terrorist groups to meet inside the country.

The Iranian issue is more—in dealing with Iran, we're dealing with more than just influence into the formation of a national unity government. I happen to believe that ultimately the Iraqis will say, we want to have our own government. We want to be on our own feet. We've had a little problem with Iran in the past, and therefore, let us, kind of, manage our own affairs. No question, right now we're concerned, however, about influencing the formation of the government, but also, obviously, we're deeply concerned about whether or not the Iranians have the wherewithal and/or the knowledge about building a nuclear weapon.

My negotiation strategy on this issue is that I believe it is better for the Iranians to hear from more than one voice as to whether or not the world accepts them as a viable nation in the international affairs. And so we have asked Germany and France and Great Britain to take the lead, to send a clear message to the Iranian Government.

It's difficult to negotiate with nontransparent societies. It's easier for a nontransparent society to try to negotiate with countries in which there's a free press and a free political opposition and a place where people can express their opinions, because it sometimes causes people to play their cards publicly. In negotiating with nontransparent societies, it's important to keep your counsel.

But I am pleased with the progress we have made on the diplomatic front. As you know, there are now talks of a Presidential letter out of the United Nations, and my Secretary of State, working with Ambassador John Bolton, are constructing such a letter and trying to make sure that there is common consensus, particularly amongst the P–5 plus Germany. As a matter of fact, Condi leaves, I think, today, if not tomorrow, for Europe to sit down with the P–5 plus Germany to continue keeping people knitted up on our strategy. Obviously, there's some cross pressures to some members of the P–5. There's a lot of politics in Europe, there's—which is a good thing, by the way, that people are questioning whether or not it's worth it to try to stop the Iranians from having a nuclear weapon. I just believe strongly it's worth it. Now is the time to deal with these problems before they become acute.

I'm troubled by a nontransparent regime having a weapon which could be used to blackmail freedom-loving nations. I'm troubled by a President who has declared his intentions to destroy our ally, Israel. And we need to take these admonitions and these threats very seriously in order to keep the peace.

So issues around Iraq are complicated and necessary, and that's why my administration spends a lot of time on them.

Yes, sir. You're going to ask me if I read the book. [*Laughter*]

Spread of Democracy/Russia/China

Q. Mr. President, as you noted at the beginning—I'm with Freedom House, and I gave the President a copy of our annual report, "Freedom in the World," before he took the stage. And as you noted, our reports have——

The President. Little print, no pictures. Go ahead. [*Laughter*]

Q. It's the bible of freedom, yes. [*Laughter*]

The President. I'm the funny guy. Go ahead. [*Laughter*]

Q. Our publications have confirmed that freedom is advancing overall in the world during the years of your administration. There is one big, important country, however, in which freedom has declined year by year the last several years, and that's Russia.

The President. Correct.

Q. You have a big summit coming up in July with the G–8 in St. Petersburg. There's been an increasing crackdown on civil society and political parties in Russia. And I'm wondering, if the time between now and the St. Petersburg summit, what you and the administration can do to raise these issues and try to help the defenders of freedom in Russia.

The President. I appreciate that. The G–8 will raise the issue. That's the interesting thing about, kind of, meetings and moments. And I have worked very hard to convince Vladimir Putin that it's in his interest to adopt Western-style values and universal values—rule of law, freedom of religion, the right to people to assemble, political parties, free press.

My strategy with Vladimir Putin is to be in a position where I can talk frankly to him. I've heard some say, "Don't go to the G–8." I think that would be a mistake for the United States not to go to the G–8. I remember very—because I need to be in a position where I can sit down with him and be very frank about our concerns.

I remember meeting with the human rights groups in Russia. And I asked them, "What strategy should I take as the President of the United States? Should I be in a position where I can engage the President in frank discussion? Or should I publicly scold him, in which case he may turn a deaf ear?" And the universal consensus for them kind of played to my own instincts, which is that I think it's important for the United States to be in a position to be able to express our concerns.

Listen, we work with Russia on a variety of issues. Nunn-Lugar is an issue where we work with Russia, for example. But I spend a lot of time with the President making it clear that he should not fear democracy on his border, nor should he fear democracy within his borders. I like to make the case to him that democracies don't war with each other. You don't need to remind him about the brutal history that the Soviet Union went through in World War II. But I do think it's illustrative to point out—like I pointed out in the speech—that Europe is now free, whole, and at peace, and there's a reason why. It's what Americans have got to understand. We tend to forget. Ours is a society where things are, like, instant, so therefore, history almost is, like, so far back it doesn't count. But it counts when you really think about life lost on the continent of Africa and wonder why there's no war today. And there's a reason why there's no war today. And that's because history has proven democracies don't war with each other.

And so in my explanation, to different events that are taking place, to the President, I try to point to historical truths, that it's in an interest of a country like Russia to understand and welcome democracy. It's in an interest for the country to give people the freedom to express themselves.

I do spend time with him in private talking about issues like the NGO law. And as you noticed, they changed laws—obviously now the—it's how laws get implemented matters. But I'm confident that will be a topic of discussion.

I haven't given up on Russia. I still think Russia understands that it's in her interest to be West, to work with the West, and to act in concert with the West. Nobody is saying to Russia, you must look like the United States of America. But we are saying there's just some basic institutions that ought to be adopted. And I will continue making that case.

I do think it's important for me to go to the G–8 so I can make the case. One of the things that I find is that nations oftentimes approach me at these different meetings we go to and say, "Hey, pass the message for me, will you? We need you to pass a message, Mr. President. You're the person who can best make the case." And so I'm pretty confidence in these countries' interest that I be in a position where I'm able to walk into the room with the President of Russia and him not throw me out. And, in fact, that he—you know, we've got a relationship—personal relationships such that there is the possibility for candid conversation.

The other big opportunity for democracy, of course, is China. President Hu Jintao is coming to our country, as you know. I will continue to remind him, ours is a complex relationship and that we would hope that he would not fear a free society, just like it doesn't appear that he's fearing a free market. I happen to believe free markets eventually yield free societies. One of the most pure forms of democracy is the marketplace, where demand causes something to happen. Excess demand causes prices to—the supply causes prices to go up, and vice versa. That stands in contrast to governments that felt like they could set price and control demand.

One of the things that I think should be a part of any foreign policy is to shine the spotlight, is to open societies. You heard me talk about what it's like to deal with nontransparent societies. I think a useful tool of foreign policy for our country is try to let the sun shine in. China has recently read the book on Mao. It's an amazing history of a couple of things: one, about how fooled much of the world was, and how brutal this country was. And yet now there's more transparency into China.

I will make it clear, of course, to the President that our relationship is vital on a variety of fronts. One such front is the economy, and we expect that country to treat us fairly. We expect there to be strong adherence to intellectual property rights. We believe that we grow pretty good crops and grow good beef, and perhaps it's in their interest to open up their markets to our agricultural products. We expect our manufacturers to be treated fairly. We don't believe in state subsidization of industry to give unfair advantage to state-owned enterprise. In other words, there's a variety of things we'll talk about, and one of them is freedom.

I have been—I don't hesitate to talk to him about my visits with the Dalai Lama who is—comes and sees me in the White House; nor do I hesitate to talk about the concerns of the Catholic Church. I'm anxious to talk to him about the evangelicals' concerns inside of China, reminding him that a whole society is one that's just more than open markets; there's institutions and common values that are necessary.

Some, of course—let me say, if I might make a philosophical statement about how I think. As Peter mentioned, there is a philosophical debate taking place in the world—at least I think it is—and that is, whether freedom is universal, or whether, one way to put it, it just applies to only a handful of us. I believe in the universality of freedom. That's what I believe. Much of my foreign policy is driven by my firm belief that everybody desires to be free; that embedded in the soul of each man and woman on the face of the Earth is this deep desire to live in liberty. That's what I believe. I don't believe freedom is confined just to the United States of America, nor do I believe that we should shy away from expressing our deep desire for there to be universal liberty.

You hear the debate, "Well, they're just imposing their values. That's all they're doing." Well, those are the folks who must not think that freedom is universal. They're not American values. There's something universal about the notion of liberty—at least I think it is. And that's what's going to drive my foreign policy. I'll be unabashed about trying to work for more free societies. I believe that's the calling of the 21st century. I meant what I said, that in the 21st century, America ought to work

to end tyranny in our world. It is a noble goal for the United States of America.

I'm concerned about isolationist tendencies in our country that would say, "Well, maybe this isn't—maybe we're not up to this task." Well, if we're not up to this task, who is up to the task? I'm concerned about protectionist policies in our country, which says to me, "We don't have the confidence to compete anymore. Let us withdraw within our borders." I strongly reject isolationism and protectionism. It's not in our country's interest, nor is it in the world's interest.

There's great talk about what you do as the American President with American influence. I believe American Presidents ought to confidently use American influence for the good of the world, and that includes demanding universal liberty and human rights and human dignity.

Yes, sir.

Spread of Democracy/Egypt

Q. Mr. President, I'm from the Public International Law and Policy Group. I'm also from Egypt, and I aspire to one day go back there and join Egyptian politics. So my question is——

The President. Go for President. [*Laughter*]

Q. I'm working on it; I'm working on it—in 2017, everyone. [*Laughter*] But my question is, would you support the regime of Gamal Mubarak if he takes over after President Mubarak?

The President. That's a leading question. [*Laughter*]

Q. ——question.

The President. No. That's a "question I don't answer" question. [*Laughter*] I support a country which does not fear political movements but is willing to compete with political movements. That's the kind of country I support.

There's a—first of all, I appreciate the fact that there were elections in Egypt. That's positive. I think people in positions of responsibility, like mine, ought to say, if there seems to be a movement gaining ground on the streets, the question ought to be why—not how can we repress it, but what is taking place? What is it that's causing somebody to be in favor? What are they saying that I'm not saying, or what are they doing that I'm not doing?

Competition for ideas and the votes of people are very healthy in societies. As a matter of fact, it's one of the ways to defeat the terrorists. Terrorists feed on resentment. When people don't feel their voices are heard, they become resentful, and then they become eligible for recruitment. If people don't feel like they have a chance to express themselves and have a government listen to them, they're likely to turn to people—the false prophets, people who subvert a great religion to play on people's frustrations and then use that false prophecy to kill.

And so I—to answer your question is, is that I support an openness in the political process. I think when—I think Egypt is a—has a chance to be one of the leaders of the freedom movement in the Middle East. And I recognize that not everybody is going to embrace this concept of democracy and freedom as firmly as I'd like them to. But all of us have got to continue to advance progress.

One of the interesting debates we have about the freedom movement is whether or not institutions have to be right before there's elections. So in other words, kind of, one of these interesting philosophical debates that's taking place. My answer—you heard my answer—my answer is, you got to have—you can't wait for perfect, because it's an excuse for the status quo.

Elections start the process; they're not the end of the process. They're oftentimes the beginning of the process. And one of the reasons I respect the Freedom House is because you understand that you follow elections with institution-building and the creation of civil society. But for those who say, "Well, we can't have elections until everything is just right or until we know the outcome of the elections," are those who provide excuse, in my judgment, for a foreign policy which in the past has said, it's okay, just so long as energy is priced okay; and okay, so there's no ruffles on the—the sea looks calm. My problem with that attitude is beneath the surface, there's resentment and anger.

I'll also tell you another—I'm not going to tell you your business in the Freedom House, but I think a movement that must be tapped into in order to advance freedom is the women's movement. I just—there is something universal about the desire to be treated fairly and equally. And therefore, in societies in which women are not being treated fairly and equally—provides great opportunities to advance the cause of freedom. We've got to be wise about how we do it in the United States. Sometimes the stamp of America, obviously, provides those who are trying to resist freedom, giving them an excuse not to; I understand that. But it's—there are great opportunities in the world.

The temptation in today's society is to say, it's not worth it, or certain people can't self-govern. It's really part of the debate in Iraq, isn't it, when you think about it— is, can these people self-govern? And I can understand why some in America say they can't, because all they see is unbelievable violence. And we're a country of deep compassion; we care. One of the great things about America, one of the beauties of our country, is that when we see a young, innocent child blown up by an IED, we cry. We don't care what the child's religion may be or where that child may live; we cry. It upsets us. The enemy knows that, and they're willing to kill to shake our confidence. That's what they're trying to do.

They're not going to shake my confidence, I just want you to know. I understand their tactics, and I know their designs. But I also believe that Iraqis can and want to self-govern. That's what I believe. And so when you see me make decisions or make statements like I make, you've got to understand it's coming from a basic set of beliefs. That's what I believe. And that's what a decisionmaker ought to do. The decisionmaker ought to make decisions based upon deep-seated beliefs. You don't need a President chasing polls and focus groups in order to make tough decisions. You need Presidents who make decisions based upon sound principle.

Now, people may not agree with the decisions; I understand that. But I hope after this talk, those of you who didn't agree at least know I'm making my decisions based on something I believe deep in my soul and something that's worked in the past. Democracies have yielded the peace. I believe 30 years form now, people are going to look back at this moment and say, thank goodness a generation of Americans stood up and said, "We have faith in democracy, faith in democracy to lay the foundation for peace," and an American President will be discussing issues of peace with duly elected leaders in the Middle East, and our children will be better off for it.

And I want to tell you one anecdote now that you've got me wound up. [*Laughter*] I sit down at the table with Prime Minister Koizumi. I tell this story all the time, because one of my jobs is to go out and explain to the American people the consequences of the decisions that I have made and why I think it's in our interests. Koizumi and I are not only good friends, but we're partners in peace. We talk about a variety of issues—North Korea is an issue, we talk—you know, he's got 1,000 troops in Iraq. Isn't that amazing, when you think about it? Because he understands the benefits of democracy in the broader Middle East. We're close friends.

Sixty years ago—it seems like an eternity for a lot of people, I recognize that, but it's not that long ago—my dad fought the Japanese, and so did your relatives. They were the sworn enemy of the United States of America. I find it unbelievable part of history that I am now sitting down at the table with the Prime Minister of Japan talking about the peace, and my dad fought them. And so what happened? What happened was, Japan adopted a Japanese-style democracy. That's what happened. And now they're peaceful. And they sit at the table with their former enemy. I think that's a lesson worth listening to and understanding.

But I bet you after World War II, there were great doubters as to whether or not Harry Truman was doing the right thing to help Japan become a democracy. I see Stevens nodding; he was there. Weren't you? [*Laughter*] Well, I wasn't. [*Laughter*] But I'm reading a lot about it. And I believe it's a lesson for all of us in this— in the 21st century. Spreading democracy is hard work. It's hard to overcome sectarian division and torture. It's hard to overcome that. But it's worth it, for the sake of our children and grandchildren.

Yes. Yes, ma'am. Okay, I'll get you over there. [*Laughter*] You're in the end zone. You're next.

Progress in Iraq

Q. Oh, I'm next.

The President. No, you're not next. She's next. [*Laughter*]

Q. I'm with Creative Associates, and we're one of the small companies that has the honor to work in Iraq, so today is a real honor to be here. As you were mentioning all the steps that we're going to have to go through in the near future, I'm still very concerned that we might not be concentrating on the suffering of the children.

The President. In Iraq?

Q. In Iraq. So I would like to be sure that as the different programs get processed that we don't give up on the children.

The President. Good, thank you very much. Our soldiers are good Samaritans. They're unbelievable. I see pictures all the time from family members of our soldiers in Iraq of their loved one showing compassion to children. No question, I'm concerned about the children in Iraq as well. So our—we've got people in the field who care about the children too. The truth of the matter is, if you care about the children of Iraq, then you would want to make sure that Iraq doesn't slip back into tyranny. Thousands of children lost their parents because of Saddam Hussein.

And so I want to thank you for your work. It's very important for the security situation to improve so that NGOs, people of compassion, are able to help lift lives. But there's a lot of work to be done. There's just a lot of work to be done— same in Afghanistan. First of all, we've rebuilt thousands of schools in Iraq, as we have in Afghanistan as well. And the world is more hopeful as the result of the liberation of these people. Afghanistan—it's obvious—when you have a society in which young girls weren't allowed to go to school because of the Taliban—thought it was, like, against humanity to send girls to school, and now they can, there's an amazing change in that society.

But I readily concede there's a lot of work left to be done. It's—there's no such thing as instant success. I told you that— and by the way, after World War II, Germany and Japan took a while to rebuild, and it took a while for those societies to become stable societies. It just takes a while.

Our march, by the way, between Revolution, liberation, and Constitution wasn't all that smooth either. And frankly, our adhering to the full extent of the liberties embedded in the Constitution and the Declaration of Independence took a while. I realize that when I talk to my Secretary of State. We were—we had people enslaved in the United States for a century. It takes a while. It's hard work. And the fundamental question the American people have to answer is, is it worth it? You've got my position; it absolutely is worth it.

Freedom is contagious, by the way. As liberty begins to spread in the Middle East, more people will demand it. And we should not shirk our duty, nor should we be afraid to encourage reformers. The worst thing that could happen, in my judgment, for the peace of the world is for the United States to lose our nerve and retreat. And there's—anyway. Yes.

Thank you. You've been very anxious. This better be a good one. Yes, you've been waving and yelling over there—[*laughter*]— waving, yelling, stomping your feet. It's a free society. That's what happens. [*Laughter*]

Message to the People of Iraq

Q. I'm Iraqi-American.

The President. Thank you.

Q. Thank you, Mr. President. I think based on what—review over 30 years of Saddam's oppression and the regime in Iraq, and also based on the belief that you have—as an Iraqi mother, Iraqi-American mother and a woman—and I went back 2 years ago without—I worked for a year— there's always that concern and still worrisome. These are beautiful messages, yet there's a big gap that never crosses that ocean. It never gets to the Iraqi, to the simple man, the Iraqis facing despair, disillusionments, all kinds of things. I speak to Iraqi friends and families on daily basis. This is what their message is: We hear of these things, but we don't see it. It doesn't get to us.

The President. Yes, tangible results on the street, right.

Q. But it's not only us, Mr. President. It's not only that. It doesn't reach them in any kind of media, unfortunately. So how can we do that? I've been wondering about this, and you are the only person, I think, who can maybe do something.

The President. Talk to the Iraqi people?

Q. Talk to someone, talk to the Iraqi, relay that message that we are honest, we have great beliefs, and we want to do something.

The President. Well, I appreciate that. First of all, I've got great confidence in the people of Iraq. Iraqis are entrepreneurial; they're well-educated; they're peace-loving. Iraqi mothers want their children to grow up in a peaceful world. That's what mothers want all over the world.

And so I—what my concern is, is that the tangible benefits of democracy aren't reaching into people's pockets yet. I mean, there's got to be a direct correlation with someone's lifestyle, someone's standard of living, and a style of government. And that's one of the things that people who push freedom understand. I mean, there's got to be a—people got to see the direct benefits at some point in time about being free. One direct benefit is that there's not going to be a central government summarily pulling you out of society and killing you if need be. That's the biggest benefit.

But there also has to be tangible benefits on the street. I try to speak to the Iraqi people all the time. Sometimes the message gets through the filters; sometimes it doesn't. I want them to hear a couple of things. I want the Iraqi people to hear I've got great confidence in their capacity to self-govern. I also want to hear—the Iraqi people to hear it's about time you get a unity government going. In other words, Americans understand newcomers to the political arena, but pretty soon, it's time to shut her down and get governing.

I want the Iraqi people to hear that we care deeply about the individuals in Iraq, regardless of their religion. That's what we care about. And we want them to worship freely. I like the fact in Iraq that there's a burgeoning free press; there's a lot of press, which is a positive sign. It's a healthy indication. I also want the Iraqis to hear that while there's a political debate going on here in America, I believe in what we're doing, and we're not going to leave prematurely, that we have got a mission, along with the Iraqis, and that is to secure a country for its democracy and to help them defend themselves, deny Al Qaida a safe haven, and have an ally in the war on terror.

And so I thank you for that admonition for me to speak out to the Iraqi people. I try to do it as much as I possibly can.

Yes, ma'am. No, not—[*laughter*]. Ambassador, you want to ask a question next? Yes, okay, fine.

Immigration Reform

Q. Good afternoon, Mr. President. I'm glad to see you here speaking today. I have a question about the immigration issue that's going on right now. And I'm just curious—the Senate will probably pass a measure; the House has already passed a measure. And I'm curious, what kinds of components are you looking for in an immigration bill that you can support? And how do you reconcile a guest-worker program for undocumented residents who are here, versus those who are on line and in the system waiting 5 and 10 years to get here?

The President. No, that's a great question. Thanks. It's obviously topic du jour and—[*laughter*]. Pretty fancy, huh? Topic du jour? [*Laughter*] I don't want to ruin the image. [*Laughter*]

I believe there ought to be three components to good immigration law. First of all, I hope we get a bill out of the Senate. There's one out of the House. It goes to what's called conference. And here's my suggestions: One, that we're a nation of law, and we ought to enforce our borders. Both the House and the Senate passed good border enforcement measures. We're modernizing or upgrading our border. We recognize that it's important to have more Border Patrol, which we do. But the Border Patrol needs additional tools in order to do their job. We're talking about long borders. It's a subject I'm quite familiar with since I was the Governor of a State that had a long border with Mexico. And so the American people have got to know that we'll enforce law.

Secondly, we've got to enforce—and by the way, part of enforcing law means to make sure that when somebody is caught coming into our country illegally, they're not let back out in society. We had a real issue with detention beds, particularly for non-Mexican illegal people coming in. We'd catch people from Central America. And people worked hard; they spotted people being smuggled across. They were detained—the people being smuggled across. They said, "Check in with your immigration officer in 15 days," and nobody did. And so now we've added the number of detention beds and are working for expedited removal procedures with the countries in Central America. As far as the Mexican folks sneaking in the border, they're sent back very quickly, back into their country. Since 2001, believe it or not, we've stopped 6 million people trying to sneak into our country—an amazing statistic. It's a lot.

Secondly, there's got to be better interior enforcement. But it's very difficult to enforce—get an employer to enforce the law when the employer is uncertain as to whether or not the documentation being presented for the needed worker is legal.

It turns out—what's very interesting is that when you deny—when you make something illegal and there's a demand for it, people find ways around it. That's why you've got a whole smuggling industry called *coyotes*. That's why you've got unbelievable document forging going on. That's why there's tunnels. I mean, there's imaginative ways by people—by unscrupulous people to take advantage of people who are coming here to do an honest day's work.

Thirdly, my judgment is, you cannot enforce the border without having a temporary guest-worker program. The two go hand in hand. There are people doing jobs Americans will not do. Many people who have come into our country are helping our economy grow. That's just a fact of life. And I believe that we ought to say to somebody doing a job an American won't do, here is a tamper-proof identity card that will enable you to be here for a period of time. And if that person wants to become a citizen of the United States, because we're a nation of law, they get at the end of the line, not the beginning of the line.

I also believe—and the Senate is working through different measures to say to the person getting into the line, there's a consequence for being here illegally. Now, if Congress believes that the line is too long or that we should facilitate people's capacity to then get a green card and become a citizen, increase the number of green cards. But people who have been here legally should not be penalized by someone who's been here illegally.

And so I'd like to tell the American people, we are a nation of law but that doesn't preclude us from being a welcoming nation. I think a system which forces people underground and into the shadows of our society, which causes people to have to sneak across our border and risk their life, is a system that needs to be changed.

I also know—and I used to tell this to people down there in Texas—family values don't stop at the Rio Grande River. If you're a mother or a father who's worried about putting food on the table and you're living in an impoverished area and you know there's a job that Americans won't do here, you'll come to do it for the sake of your family. And therefore, I think it makes sense to have a temporary-worker program that says, you're not an automatic citizen, to help, one, enforce the border, and two, uphold the decency of America. If our Border Patrol agents don't have to focus on people trying to sneak across to get a job, they will be able to be more focused on people smuggling drugs, smuggling guns, smuggling terrorists.

And so I look forward to the debate. I'm going to say again what I've said before on this debate. It's very important for all of us in this debate to conduct ourselves with the following principles in mind: One, we're a nation of immigrants; two, our soul is refreshed by newcomers to our society;

three, we love the idea of people starting with nothing and ending up with something in America; four, we value family values, no matter where they may be; and five, we've got to be careful about the language we use when it comes to debating this important subject. People should not pit neighbor against neighbor, group of people against group of people in our country. Ours is a nation that's able to assimilate people because we believe in human rights and human dignity of all.

Final question.

Palestinian Government/Israel

Q. Mr. President——

The President. Okay, two questions. Please, ma'am. You're last. You're the last guy. You're the closer. [*Laughter*] It's a baseball term. Yes, you're the closer. You've been persistent. [*Laughter*]

Q. Thank you, Mr. President, and I think I sprained my arm trying to get your attention. But the main reason for that is because I think I speak for the unheard people. I'm a Palestinian, and I come from a refugee camp, and I'm currently working at the World Bank.

The President. Welcome.

Q. Thank you. What can I say to my cousins, my friends, people in the streets who are asking, why is the United States punishing us and cutting funds for people who choose fair and free elections? I think the National Endowment for Democracy has characterized it as the textbook, fair and free elections. Then why are we punishing the people of—I don't mean the government—the people of Palestine—the refugees, the poor, the malnourished mothers and children?

The President. No, great question. Thank you for asking it. Just to step back, I believe I'm the first President to have articulated the—my desires for there to be a Palestinian state living at peace with Israel. And I still think it's a real possibility for that to happen. I believe democracies don't war with each other, and I believe a Pales-

tinian democracy is in the interests of the Palestinian people, the Israelis, and the rest of the world.

Secondly, I think that aid should go to suffering Palestinians, but nor should it go to a government, however, which has expressed its desire to destroy its neighbor. If the goal of the United States is two states living side by side in peace, and one government elected says, "We want to destroy one of the parties," it makes no sense for us to support that government. We support the election process. We support democracy, but that doesn't mean we have to support governments that get elected as a result of democracy.

Now, Palestinians must make a choice as to whether or not it makes sense for them to have a government that says they want to destroy their neighbor. I don't think it does. As a matter of fact, I think it's important for governments to say, we want to work out our differences in a peaceful way. But I am concerned about the suffering Palestinian people. I think the U.S. Government has got aid that goes directly to people. And I know that we'll continue to call upon governments in the region to support the Palestinian people.

I weep about the suffering of the Palestinians. I particularly weep about the fact that the leadership has let them down for year after year after year. And now is the time for strong leaders to stand up and say, we want the people to decide. And I was pleased that there was an election in the Palestinian Territories, and I agree with you that the elections were good elections. And—but now the government has to make a choice, and we will continue to watch very carefully about the choice they make.

Final question. Then I'm going down to be with the President of Mexico and the Prime Minister with Canada—Cancun. [*Laughter*] No Speedo suit here. [*Laughter*] Thankfully. [*Laughter*]

Progress in Iraq

Q. You ready?

The President. Yes. Sorry to interrupt you. Just testing your concentration. [*Laughter*]

Q. Mr. President, I am on the board of trustees of Freedom House.

The President. Thank you for having me.

Q. And my—you mentioned about Iraq.

The President. Iraq?

Q. About Iraq, the effect of leaving prematurely and the issue it would cause— is there an opportunity right now to perhaps supplement the American forces and perhaps finally to replace them with a strong, large, broad-based troops, security forces of Muslim countries from North Africa, from Middle East, South Asia, Southeast Asia, which could go in there and then perhaps help in the situation? Because Iraq—a disaster in Iraq is a disaster for the whole region.

The President. That's a really good question. I think the preferred strategy is to spend time and efforts on getting the Iraqis stood up so they can defend themselves. At some point in time, the Iraqi citizens are going to have to make the conscious decision that democracy is worth defending. And I appreciate the efforts of some in the Arab world to help train Iraqi police, like the Jordanian academy. There is support for training amongst different Arab nations, as there is from NATO. And the fundamental question is, what will expedite the situation so that the Iraqis are fully prepared to do their job?

So the question—I would reverse your question and say, are we prepared to have others help the Iraqis defend themselves? And the answer is, absolutely. But the Iraqis must be encouraged to continue to take the lead. And that's a measurable part of our progress on the ground, more territories controlled by Iraqis. The march I just described to you was policed by, or guarded by Iraqi units who were in the lead. That Tall 'Afar example I used the other day talked about the Iraqi divisions in the lead that helped secure this city.

The ultimate solution for Iraq is for there to be a unity government which brings people confidence, one that unites different factions, thereby marginalizing the rejectionists, but also making sure the Iraqi Army is prepared to do what it needs to do, as well as a police force.

When we first got in there, we said, "Well, let's prepare an Iraqi Army for an outside threat." It turns out it wasn't necessary. The biggest threat was inside the country. And so we adjusted our strategy and started training Iraqis so that they are prepared to be able to defend sectors of their country. And now the big—Senator Warner came and briefed us at the White House the other day. He said—and this is what the General is telling me as well— we've made good progress in training the Iraqi Army. The problem is the Iraqi police force. And there is a national police force, which is more efficient than local police forces. It still needs to make sure there are coalition troops embedded in the police force to make sure that these police understand that there's—you don't seek reprisal as a police force. You've got to earn the confidence of all people, no matter what their religion is. And we're still working with local police forces.

So in due respect, I think the question is, how do we expedite more Iraqis to earn the confidence of the Iraqi people. We're dealing with a shattered confidence. There's a sense that, well, they may leave us, or our guys aren't prepared to provide security. And the quicker we can get the Iraqis stood up and trained, the faster the Iraqi people will have confidence, not only in their own security situation but in their government.

And so thanks for the suggestion. Listen, I've enjoyed it; I hope you have. God bless.

NOTE: The President spoke at 12:53 p.m. at the Hyatt Regency Capitol Hill. In his remarks, he referred to Peter Ackerman, chairman of the board, Freedom House; President Ellen Johnson Sirleaf of Liberia; Usama bin Laden, leader of the Al Qaida terrorist organization; senior Al Qaida associate Abu Musab Al Zarqawi; President Olusegun Obasanjo of Nigeria; former President Charles Taylor of Liberia, who was arrested on March 29 in Nigeria on United Nations war crimes charges; President Bashar al-Asad of Syria; President Mahmud Ahmadi-nejad of Iran; President Vladimir V. Putin of Russia; President Hu Jintao of China; Prime Minister Junichiro Koizumi of Japan; former President Saddam Hussein of Iraq; President Vicente Fox Quesada of Mexico; and Prime Minister Stephen Harper of Canada. Participants referred to Prime Minister Tony Blair of the United Kingdom; and Gamal Mubarak, son of President Mohammed Hosni Mubarak of Egypt.

Exchange With Reporters in Cancun, Mexico
March 30, 2006

Jill Carroll

Q. Sir, do you have a reaction to Jill Carroll's release?

The President. Thank God.

Q. What do you know about why she is released?

The President. I'm really grateful she's released, and I want to thank those who worked hard for her release, and we're glad she's alive.

It's good to see you all. And I'd like to make sure you work more than you play.

NOTE: The exchange began at 8:07 a.m. at the LeBlanc Spa and Resort. In his remarks, the President referred to American journalist Jill Carroll, who was taken hostage in Baghdad, Iraq, on January 7 and released on March 30.

Remarks Following a Tour of the Chichen-Itza Archaeological Ruins With President Vicente Fox Quesada of Mexico and Prime Minister Stephen Harper of Canada in Chichen-Itza, Mexico
March 30, 2006

[*At this point, President Fox spoke in Spanish, and no translation was provided.*]

President Bush. Mr. President, thank you very much for your hospitality. This is a good start to a very important series of discussions. It is an honor to be here with the Prime Minister of Canada as well. We've got vital relations that will matter to the future of our people. And I look forward to the discussions.

And I want to thank you for letting us begin our very important meetings at this very significant historical site. And I congratulate our guide, and I want to thank those who have worked hard to make sure this important part of history is accessible and is available for people to understand the past, so we can better understand the future.

So, Mr. President, thank you for having us.

[*Prime Minister Harper spoke in French, and no translation was provided. He then continued in English.*]

Prime Minister Harper. And I can repeat the same thing quickly, if you don't mind. Forgive us; that's how we speak Spanish in the north. [*Laughter*] Wonderful to be here. Thank you for the welcome, President Fox. I think we stand here in a historic site, a symbol here of our determination to build a new future for all inhabitants of North America. And I am honored to be with President Bush and President Fox and look forward to our discussions.

President Bush. Gracias, senor.

President Fox. Bienvenidos.

NOTE: The President spoke at 11:15 a.m.

Remarks Following Discussions With President Vicente Fox Quesada of Mexico in Cancun
March 30, 2006

President Fox. We are ready. Good afternoon. I would like to welcome President Bush to Quintana Roo, to Cancun, and to Mexico. It is a great honor to have him here, particularly in this place in Cancun, which is all set and receiving many visitors. But the best visitors are President Bush and Prime Minister Harper, with our working agenda that will be fruitful and positive for the three countries in Latin America.

Some words from Mr. Bush.

President Bush. Mr. President, thank you very much. First of all, thanks for inviting us to Cancun. It's such a beautiful part of the world. The hospitality is magnificent. I know you were hit hard by hurricanes, which reminds me that I need to thank you and the Mexican people for your strong support and help after Hurricane Katrina.

I will never forget being on the—in the gulf coast area of my country, helping people—lift people's spirits. And we went to a school that had been destroyed by Katrina, a little elementary school. And there was the Navy construction team working side by side with members of the Mexican Navy. It was a great sign of cooperation, and it reflects the spirit of friendship that defines the relationship between our two countries and defines our personal relationship.

When you were speaking, I thought about the first time I went to visit you. I was newly elected and flew down to your fantastic ranch. And that started a very important relationship. And I think it's important for the people of our countries to know that while we haven't agreed on every single issue, that nevertheless, we work in the spirit of friendship and cooperation.

Today we had a very important discussion. We discussed border security. The President understands, and I understand, we have an obligation to secure our borders. And I want to thank your Government for sending out such a strong statement about the need for—that the shared responsibility we have. In other words, border security is not just one country's prerogative; it's the prerogative and duty of both countries. And we spent time talking about how to work together to continue to strengthen that cooperation necessary to do our duty.

I also appreciate the President's work to enforce Mexico's southern border. It's a difficult job, but nevertheless, the President shared with me the strategies he's employing to do that job as well.

Obviously, the migration issue came up. I told the President there is a legislative process that's going forward, and that it may look cumbersome to some, but that's how our democracy works. I told the President that I am committed to having a comprehensive immigration bill on my desk. And by "comprehensive" I mean not only border security—a bill that has border security in it, a bill that has interior enforcement in it, but a bill that has a worker permit program in it. And that's an important part of having a border that works.

We don't want people sneaking into our country that are going to do jobs Americans won't do; we want them coming in, in an orderly way, which will take pressure off of both our borders. And I explained to the President my vision of the citizenship issue. I don't believe somebody should be allowed to come into our country and get ahead of the line, the citizenship line.

And so I told President Fox that I think a program that will work is somebody working on a temporary basis with a tamper-proof ID card. And if they want to become a citizen, they can get in line but not the head of the line. And I reminded the President I called for an increase of green cards the other day in Washington, DC, as one way to help manage this issue.

But at any rate, we're in the middle of a legislative process. I'm optimistic we can get a bill done, and I look forward to continuing to work with members of both parties to get a bill done.

We also talked about President Fox's vision of working together in our hemisphere, particularly in Central America. And he's proposed a very innovative set of ideas to help stabilize and help encourage growth in Central America, starting with an energy initiative. And of course we appreciate your leadership on that issue, and I look forward to sending some of our experts down to listen to the ideas being talked about.

One idea, of course, we want to inject in the conversation is the idea of developing alternatives to gasoline that comes from crude oil, that we'd like to see more use of ethanol, and how we can work together to increase the crops necessary to

become the feedstock for an ethanol production.

But at any rate, the point I'm making is, is that we've got a lot to do in our relationship. President Fox is—if people take an objective look at his record, one of the things that I'm most proud of, and I think our country must be most appreciative of, is the stability of the Mexican economy. It's important to have a trade partner that has got a stable economy. And, Mr. President, you've done a fine job of providing stability and increasing the net worth of your citizens, and that's important for the American economy as well. The more net worth there is in Mexico, the more likely it is a Mexican may be wanting to buy a U.S. product—and vice versa, by the way. And so our trade has made a difference in the lives of our citizens, and your leadership has made a difference in the state of your economy.

So it's good to be with you again, sir. Thank you for your warm hospitality.

President Fox. Thank you, President Bush. Thank you. I would like to mention with great satisfaction how productive the relation with the United States has been on bilateral basis, how the NAFTA, the Free Trade Agreement of North America has been, in order to promote development here in Mexico. And all this is part of a commitment and obligation of generating opportunities, making sure that we can build up, create jobs, create greater income, revenues for the families in Mexico, the *maquilla*, the—[*inaudible*]—industry installed in the border of the country.

There is a deficit of 100,000 people. They want to give jobs to 100,000 people due to the great growth that's going on. And not only in this field but in many other fields, in many other areas, we have been working. We might say that something that appeared in the mass media in Mexico—opposition of a state, clearly, very clearly in Mexico of the political parties—the Congress; the house of representatives;

the upper chamber, the Senators; the Executive power, the President of the Republic; the Governors of the States—everybody, everybody has a very clear idea in the topic of our relationship with the United States and, particularly, migration. It is a shared— shared—responsibility, and we understand very clearly here in Mexico all the main characters of the political scenario that we have to work so as to assume our responsibility.

Furthermore, we are working with Central American countries with the same purpose. Let us assume shared responsibilities. It is very clear for us that tomorrow, the Congress of the United States might approve any sort of bill, any sort of matter, migration-wise. It is a sovereign decision, of course, in the United States, but Mexico assumes its responsibilities to work with passion, with commitment, diligently, with our economy and developing opportunities for our people.

Our commitment with the citizenship is very broad. For example, with the United States, we work closely with Homeland Security, with the Ministry of the Interior here in Mexico, with Secretary Abascal. Secretary Abascal has a total support of the President of the Republic, and the possibility of adding the support of all the ministries and all the different Federal agencies that have to do with safety and security, so that we can give steps forward in this topic on the border.

We want to have a safe border for the benefit of our citizens and for the benefit of our relationship with the United States. Likewise, we have intensified our actions with the OASISS project. We are going after the criminals that are trafficking with people, that are, let's say, promoting illegally the movement of citizens to the United States—the alien smugglers. We have stopped more than 120 of these criminals, alien smugglers.

Likewise, in the southern border, as President Bush said, we are very active, very active on what has to do with patrol,

constructions of different stations so as to stop migrants, illegal migrants, people that are coming illegally to the Mexican territory, and sending them back to their own countries, with due respect to human rights. But we're doing an efficient work in that sense.

Now, with the same type of orientation, the idea that we share with President Bush, to consider an important element to thrust development in the Central American economies so that they can grow, they can generate jobs, that through this project and through this program they can generate actual opportunities in these countries, and this is a program of energy.

With this program, we want to achieve the construction of refineries for oil, different docks to build natural gas, sources of electric energy on the other hand, and conversion of natural gas—liquid, fluid gas to natural gas. It is a program that we shall approve next May, the Central American countries and Mexico. And we are cordially inviting the United States to attend, to know, to observe, to see the project, so as to know how can we interact with the strength and the capacity of North America so as to integrate a strong development and solid process in the Central American countries.

We have spoken—we have mentioned about the whole American canal. We have to reactivate the working commission in this area so that we can discuss ideas and give solutions for both parts, as we have always done, worked together, have a dialog, find solutions. And this is what we have proposed in reference to the total or whole American channel.

Thus, I want to thank President Bush for his attendance, for his presence, and for his work, as well as all his team.

Tomorrow in the trilateral meeting, we will be covering other topics—the topic of safety and security and then some other developing topics amongst the three countries, the three partners that belong to this bloc of both economy, trade, and association for our prosperity and security of North America.

Thank you.

NOTE: The President spoke at 4:12 p.m. at the Fiesta Americana Condesa Cancun Hotel. President Fox spoke in Spanish, and his remarks were translated by an interpreter. President Fox referred to Prime Minister Stephen Harper of Canada; and Secretary of Government Jose Carlos Maria Abascal Carranza of Mexico. The Office of the Press Secretary also released a Spanish language transcript of these remarks.

Remarks Following Discussions With Prime Minister Stephen Harper of Canada in Cancun
March 30, 2006

President Bush. Mr. Prime Minister, thank you. This is a—we've had a day full of talks. I had a really good meeting with the Prime Minister on the choppers, flying to the Mayan ruins. We've also had a very good meeting here. We talked about a lot of subjects.

I view the relationship with Canada as a vital relationship for the United States. The relationship, of course, is defined Government-to-Government. It's also defined people-to-people, and there's a lot of people in my country who respect Canada and have great relations with Canadians, and we intend to keep it that way.

The Prime Minister, of course, was—made an emphatic case for softwood lumber. And I appreciate his steely resolve to get something done. And I assured him that our intention is to negotiate in good faith, in a timely fashion, to resolve this issue. And I appreciate your—appreciate you pushing.

We also talked about the mutual values we share: respect for human life and human dignity. And along those lines, I want to thank you very much for two things: one, the quick response that your Government and your country gave to those who suffered by Katrina. It indicates the Canadian people's desire to help humans when they suffer. I appreciate very much your trip to Afghanistan and you and your Government's support of their fledgling democracy, support of people that have been under the brutal thumb of tyrants—so brutal they wouldn't let young girls go to school—and it's representing the great Canadian tradition of really helping restore human dignity in people's lives.

The Prime Minister and I talked about a variety of subjects. We've got a lot of common interests. We've got a lot of trade between our countries—nearly half a billion dollars in—$500 billion in the year 2005. And that trade means jobs on both sides of the border. And it's our intention to make sure that we continue to trade as freely as possible so that our people can benefit. All in all, Mr. Prime Minister, I found today to be a valuable day, and I want to thank you very much for your candor.

Prime Minister Harper. Thank you very much, Mr. President.

[*At this point, Prime Minister Harper spoke in French, and no translation was provided.*]

I'll try to repeat all of that. [*Laughter*] First of all, just to begin by saying that we had a long meeting both this morning and this afternoon, the President and I, discussing particularly global security issues of national and shared security interests.

And as you know, we're cooperating on these things in places like Afghanistan, Sudan, Haiti. Canada and the United States from time to time will disagree on particular courses of action that should be taken, and we may have different perspectives and even different interests, but there should be no doubt that Canada and the United States share very important common values—values like freedom, democracy, human rights, and the rule of law. We believe that these values are important not only for Canada and the United States, but they are the right of every people on the face of the Earth. We may disagree on how we get there, but that's the objective that we share.

We're going to meet later on in the spring to further discuss cooperation on some of these matters. We're also going to be discussing some initiatives—we've taken to task some of our officials to discuss some energy and environmental concerns. We're anxious—we're in a continental security market, and we're anxious to see our officials discuss not just energy security but how we can harness energy, new energy technology, to make real progress on greenhouse gas emissions and also on pollution. So we'll have some discussions in the next few weeks along those lines.

We're going to move quickly to renew— to sign an agreement to renew NORAD, to take that to Parliament in the not-too-distant future.

Of course, we discussed softwood lumber. The President has expressed his desire to see a resolution. I certainly accept at face value the President's commitment to that. I just reminded the President that Canada's position on this is very clear, and if we don't see a resolution, Canada is cer-tainly going to continue to pursue all its legal options as well as enhanced support for our industry through this battle.

We talked about issues like passports, Devil's Lake, BSE, all areas where there remain some difficulties and some—[*inaudible*]—but I think we agreed to work together to seek some collaboration on all these fronts. In particular—and I didn't mention this in French—we've asked— we're going to be asking Secretary Chertoff and Minister Day to meet as soon as possible, at the highest levels, to do what we can to see how we can accommodate congressional legislation on passport travel issues. These present for us some pretty significant challenges, and we are concerned about the disruptions to trade and other travel that this may bring about.

And let me just end by saying, as I think you heard me say a few days ago, I expressed through Ambassador Wilkins, and I've had a chance to do it—[*inaudible*]— how much the Government of Canada appreciates the actions taken by our allies and our friends both in the United Kingdom and in the United States in the liberation of the hostages that were held in Iraq. You know, Iraq, in particular, has been a source of some disagreement—dare I say some tension—between our two peoples, but I think this incident reminds us that when the chips are down, we all pull together and support each other. I hope that's a lesson we keep in mind for the future.

NOTE: The President spoke at 5:40 p.m. at the Fiesta Americana Condesa Cancun Hotel. Prime Minister Harper referred to Minister of Public Safety Stockwell Day of Canada. A portion of these remarks could not be verified because the tape was incomplete.

The President's News Conference With President Vicente Fox Quesada of Mexico and Prime Minister Stephen Harper of Canada in Cancun
March 31, 2006

President Fox. Good morning. Welcome for your interest and your presence and attendance. We have come to an end in this productive meeting, as you well know, with bilateral meetings yesterday and today a trilateral meeting, a very productive one, followed by an enlarged meeting, trilateral-wise, with the attendance of the entrepreneurial community, business, and investment of our three countries. Consequently, we will give you full information.

I would like to ask the Prime Minister of Canada, Stephen Harper, to make some comments.

[*At this point, Prime Minister Harper spoke in French, which was translated as follows.*]

Prime Minister Harper. Thank you. Thank you, President Fox, and ladies and gentlemen. I'd like to thank President Fox first of all. It was a pleasure to meet President Fox and President Bush to discuss issues of importance to our countries and our common will to work together.

In North America, we have an economy that is integrated; it is not necessary to differentiate our products. And we have discussed the progress accomplished in the Security and Prosperity Partnership of North America, and we are committed to considering the private sector. First of all, we believe that it is an engine of competitiveness, made up of members of the private sector, that will allow us to make our economies even more competitive.

Our ministers will be working on this. They will be identifying our priorities, and they will make sure that they are followed up. We will be cooperating on issues of importance—on border security, management of urgent situations, as well as energy security. We will prepare a coordinated and exhaustive way to approach the issues of the bird flu, and we will be guided by common principles. Over the course of the next few months, we will be doing everything possible to ensure the security along our borders and to be able to move our merchandise back and forth. We will be working in the area of energy, the area of research and innovation, to be able to deal with clean technologies.

We are happy with the discussions of our trade ministers on cooperation and of the negotiation of our countries, and we encourage them to follow up with this work.

This meeting has been extremely productive. And Presidents Bush and Fox have accepted my invitation for the next summit meeting, which will take place in Canada in 2007.

[*Prime Minister Harper continued in English.*]

——grateful for our host, President Fox, and to the workers here at the hotel and the Mexican people for their warm hospitality.

Over the past 2 days, I've had the pleasure of meeting with President Fox and President Bush to discuss issues that jointly affect our three nations. I've been encouraged by the common will of our three nations. We are living today in an integrated economy. We cannot afford the politics of isolation.

During my meetings with Presidents Bush and Fox, we reviewed the progress of our Security and Prosperity Partnership, which provides a framework to advance the common interests in areas of security, prosperity, and quality of life.

We committed to further engage the private sector. We've agreed to set up a North American Competitiveness Council, made up of business leaders from all three countries, to advise us on ways to improve the competitiveness of our economies. They will meet with our ministers, identify priorities, and make sure we follow up and implement them.

We agreed to expand our existing cooperation on key issues such as border security, emergency management, and energy security. As an immediate priority, we'll develop a coordinated and comprehensive approach to preparing for a possible avian or pandemic influenza outbreak in North America. Our action will be guided by shared principles. We'll take concrete steps in the coming 24 months to improve the security at our borders and to ensure the smooth and efficient flow of goods and people, particularly—particular discussions with President Bush on the Windsor-Detroit Corridor.

We'll collaborate on energy, especially with respect to innovation and science and technology, with the focus on clean technologies. We also welcome the discussions—the recent discussions by our trade ministers on NAFTA collaboration on trade negotiations with third countries. And we urge that this work be given priority.

These talks were productive. And I'm, of course, very pleased that President Bush and President Fox have accepted my invitation to have the next leaders' meeting in Canada in 2007.

Thank you.

President Fox. President Bush.

President Bush. Thank you for your hospitality. It's a really good choice to pick Cancun—as my press corps will tell you. They're looking forward to staying by the pool after I leave. [*Laughter*] It's a beautiful, beautiful part of the country.

I want to thank you for your friendship as well. It's been a joy discussing very important issues with you over the course of my Presidency. And this is probably one of the most productive meetings we've had. It's been a pleasure to meet with Prime Minister Harper in his official capacity as the Prime Minister of Canada. I find him to be a very open, straightforward fellow.

If he's got a problem, he's willing to express it in a way that's clear for all to understand. And that's the way I like to deal with people.

We've got big goals for this very important relationship. One goal is prosperity. You can't achieve a standard of living increase for your people unless you have a prosperous neighborhood, and it's this prosperity that has been much of a focus on NAFTA. And one of my vows, and I know the other leaders share this goal, is to make sure that people are able to connect the NAFTA relationship with improvement of their own quality of life.

I know there's deep concern about social justice throughout the neighborhood, and social justice can be achieved more likely if people are able to realize their dreams and if there's a prosperous society. And prosperity has been increased as a result of the trade between our nations. And we want to make sure that trade continues in a way that's fair and free but also in a way that enables our countries to be able to compete with the great challenges we face.

And we face prosperity challenges from abroad like never before—the challenge of a growing Chinese economy or the challenge of an Indian economy. And my attitude is we shouldn't fear these challenges; we ought to welcome them and position ourselves so that we can compete. And I think the leaders share that sense of unity when it comes to being a competitive part of the world in the future.

We talked about security. Look, we got long borders, and we got to make sure we work hard to secure the borders. We also have got to make sure we got smart borders. And so the whole vision of our borders has got to be to enhance trade and tourism but to prevent smugglers and terrorists and dope runners from polluting our countries. And I'm confident, with the use of technology and by close collaboration, we'll be able to achieve those objectives.

I want to thank the CEOs and the business leaders from the three countries who are here. I thought we had a very constructive discussion about ways to make sure that there is harmonization between our industries so that the people benefit. And they brought some really good ideas.

We talked about, of course, bird flu, avian flu, and the need to be prepared in case there is an outbreak. We spend a lot of time in my own country preparing for an avian flu outbreak, strategizing as how to coordinate efforts between the Federal, State, and local governments, working to wisely spend money to come up with, hopefully, a vaccine that would then be available for sharing around the world. And I do want to thank Canada for having taken the lead early in this issue and preparing the world for what is possible so that there's good information sharing if the bird flu were to break out in Southeast Asia, for example. But my point is, it's very important for us to share information and data and strategies amongst our three countries so that if this were to happen, there is a focused, coordinated, intelligent response.

We talked about energy. My view of the energy initiative is that we've got to be wise about the resources we have and be smart about the investment for research and development so we can change our energy habits. The truth of the matter is, we'll all be better off if we use alternative sources of energy like ethanol or explore how to use hybrid batteries in a better way. I mean, there's some really interesting things coming down the pike, and I look forward to not only leading my own nation to spend money to be on the leading edge of technological change when it comes to energy but also sharing those technologies and ideas with our counterparts. Because we want to make sure that we've got national security concerns addressed when it comes to energy; we also want to be good stewards of the environment—and we can do both by the use of proper technologies.

It's been a good meeting. I want to thank you for your leadership. I like coming to meetings where people put things on the table and we try to come up with solutions. And this has been such a meeting, Mr. President. Good job. *Es todo.*

President Fox. Thank you. Thank you so much. Undoubtedly, these two days have brought about spaces for meeting of both friends and partners, and undoubtedly, we have made a very good use of time.

The visit to Chichen-Itza was excellent, as well as yesterday evening's dinner, in a relaxed atmosphere but, likewise, creating this association and making a very productive association. Equally important were the different working meetings.

We took advantage of time; we were not working isolated. We touched upon fundamental items in that meeting. First of all, we carried out an evaluation meeting. Then we got information about the development of programs. And then we gave the necessary instructions for the works that should be carried out in the next period of work.

This is a most important thing, and this association has become a dynamic and professional process, a constructive process, a short-term action process, and great vision and perspective in a long term. Consequently, we have concluded that institutionalizing all these mechanisms is of utmost importance so that they will have continuity, so that there will be a followup—a necessary followup, so that they will be fruitful both at a short, middle, and long term.

So we have established the next meeting. The Prime Minister of Canada has suggested and has invited us to Canada. Next June, we shall have, let's say, an information, evaluation, and results study of the work of this association, this Security and Prosperity Partnership. And we have carried out a series of actions that should be integrated in this report.

First of all, I would like to make clear what has been the results of 12 years of joint work in the free trade agreement,

NAFTA. The three nations are fully satisfied of what we have been able to achieve. We have seen the fruits of work through this tool of cooperation, trade, and investment. Nonetheless, we're not fully satisfied. We have to give steps forward. We have many an opportunity and many a challenge.

I want to mention two figures in reference to the results of NAFTA. Mexico has a commercial balance trade of $535 billion, the seventh in size throughout the world. And these would be a direct product of both trade and investment that has been carried out among the three partner countries. And then we should point out that every single State, border States with the United States had per capita income to December as of last year that go beyond to $10,000. The per capita average income has to do with $7,500—the highest in Latin America. Nonetheless, the borderline States are above $10,000 per capita income, and some of them have a per capita rate to $10,000.

We're not talking about small numbers, small figures; we're talking about a concrete result of the efforts and work through trade. It is achieved through investment, and likewise, it is achieved through joint work, everybody's work. Behind all this, there's nothing else but work, work, and work.

Now I would like to mention a couple of items in the goals. First, strengthen and maintain, growing, the free trade agreement, first of all. Benefits are evident, but before the new reality of the 21st century, we have decided to give steps forward and strengthen the relationship. Now we have the alliance both for security and prosperity. One item is as important as the other—shared responsibility an important element—one as important as the other. And that is what the three countries think.

We started with the constitution of the North American Competitiveness Council, so as to consider public and private policies—face a challenge of our region. We want to institutionalize our mechanisms,

have a clear project for the next month of June. It would imply mechanisms by means of which we will give the necessary importance and long-term action, something constant, and continuity should be achieved as well. That has been fruitful, and that can give very good results for our region. We are not renegotiating what has been successful or open the free trade agreement. It's going beyond the agreement, both for prosperity and security.

Summarizing, we have to increase competitiveness of our economies, of our companies, our enterprises, our structures, and likewise, our technological and educational levels so as to face competition of other blocs in the world. We have to homogenize normotivity standards so as to have common standards to facilitate jobs and productivity. We have to make borders much more modern with technology so as to guarantee security but the good flow of commodities and products. We have invested a good amount of time to logistics, efficiency and efficacy in customs, topics that have to do with sharing—sharing these efficiencies.

We are totally aware that we require infrastructure studies in the borderline areas so as to analyze needs, to facilitate both trade and passage of people and goods. This is fundamental; security is fundamental for our future development. It is a problem and a challenge shared by the three countries. Migration can only be solved in that we agree upon under the framework of a legislation that will guarantee our legal order, safe and respectful migration, respecting the rights of people.

We have spoken about the collaboration of the three countries to support development and generation of opportunities for Central American countries and the Caribbean-area countries. We have seen an excellent level of relationships, and these are giving steps forward. They're better and better.

We have more points of coincidence amongst the three countries. I would like to thank the attendance, the presence, in this beautiful port of Cancun in this area of the Riviera Maya. You can see it is dynamic, a beautiful place, as it always has been. We receive millions of tourists every single year, people that come over, and we're proud to receive.

We want to thank President Bush; we want to thank Prime Minister Harper—my acknowledgment, my thanks, and my commitment. We shall be working together, no doubt about it, to give steps forward in the field of prosperity and security. May you have a happy return back home. Thank you.

For the question-and-answer period, we have two questions for the journalists of each country.

Border Security/Trade

Q. Good morning, Presidents and Prime Minister. President Fox, what are the concrete measures that Mexico is implementing to guarantee this indispensable security so as to have a legal, safe, and orderly migration?

For President Bush and President Harper, do you consider that there should be a continuity on the economic policy in Mexico before the change of President in our country? Last but not least, how can the partners of NAFTA—can be competitive before the Asian countries if there are so many differences that are leading us to talk first about security, then productivity? And what are the unilateral decisions on migration matters? Thank you.

President Fox. First, security—many actions have been implemented. Many actions have to do with close cooperation with the security authorities with the United States. This effort, headed by the representative of Homeland Security, Mr. Chertoff, and Minister of the Interior here in Mexico, Mr. Abascal, and the cooperation based upon mutual trust, coresponsibility, and what has to do with security in the borders.

Likewise, we're doing our own work in cases of homicides and crimes among the different Mafias, the drug cartels. We shall continue working on this. There's a presence of Federal forces in the main points in the border, and then a great commitment to win the battle against organized crime and drug trafficking, particularly in the city of Nuevo Laredo. We have programs such as Programma OASISS, OASISS Program, so as to attack the people that are trafficking with people, with migrants. And fortunately, there are more than 120 in jail. And then we have a permanent program, 24 hours a day, so as to achieve this.

We are working in the inner part and in the southern part of the country to stop migration flows that come from Central America that are crossing illegally the southern border of Mexico. And with all due respect to the dignity of these people, respecting their human rights, they are stopped; they remain on temporary bases and stations. They offer them services with dignity, and then we send them back to their communities of origin; 240,000 people—people that were detained, and then they were sent back to Central America.

We are working jointly with the Central American Governments. We have spoken about the fact that the decision of Mexico is not only assuming our responsibilities migration-wise, but we have a firm commitment of generating jobs and employment. We're working jointly with Central America so as to achieve this, so each country will absorb our commitment and our total commitment generating opportunities within our own countries.

And so this program, like the energy initiative for Central America, is one that has the purpose of bringing development and growth to the Central American economies. Thus we're working on a broad spectrum on the issue of security in all of its facets.

President Bush. I don't see how you can be prosperous if you don't have security. I mean, it's—if people are concerned that, for example, the towns along the border aren't secure, it's going to be difficult to keep prosperity alive. And so I appreciate the President's commitment to security along our border, and we've got—we share the same commitment. It's very important to enforce laws. Robust economy depend upon the rule of law, and therefore, when countries enforce law, it kind of creates the conditions for continued economic growth.

When you have robust trade like we have, there are issues that come up. One way to look at it is if we had no trade, there would be no issues. And the more issues there are and the more opportunities there are to discuss them, the likelier it is these economies will continue to grow. And so I don't worry about having to deal with problems. As a matter of fact, I view the problems that have arisen as a result of complex and active trade as positive. And the fundamental question is, can we resolve these issues in a responsible way? And one of the reasons we meet is to put ourselves in a position to do so.

You mentioned something about the elections. I'm not going to talk about them. The only thing I am going to talk about is I love to have a strong, vibrant democracy on our southern border. And I want to thank the President for his strong leadership and his recognition that democracy is a very important legacy of his administration, the previous administration, that we certainly hope there will be a peaceful transition of power, and I'm confident there will be one.

Prime Minister Harper. Obviously, I don't want to get into the issue of Mexican politics, but I can say the same thing that I said yesterday with regard to the leadership of President Fox. We've had both bilateral and multilateral relationships progressively growing and without precedent. I trust that the President is going to leave a stronger economy that is shared, a firm democracy, respect for human rights, and faithfulness to the most important principles for our shared progress, for the Security and Prosperity Partnership of North

America, and all the good results that come from a free market economy.

All of these things lead to more progress, which we hope the next President will be able to build upon, which will benefit all of our countries.

[Prime Minister Harper continued in English.]

And I'll just repeat that I, obviously, do not intend to make any comments or get myself involved in Mexican politics, but I'll just repeat what I said yesterday, which is that President Fox has provided unprecedented leadership for both our bilateral and our trilateral relations, unprecedented progressive leadership.

I believe that the legacy of that leadership will be to leave behind not just the strong democracy that believes in liberty and human rights but also loyalty and adherence to the principles that are—on which the success of our integrated economy is based. And those are the principles of NAFTA, the principles of our security and economic partnership, and, of course, the advantages of free markets from which all of our nations benefit.

Immigration Reform

Q. Thank you. Mr. President, would you veto an immigration bill that did not include a guest-worker program? And how do you counter the angry argument from conservatives on Capitol Hill who are saying that your demand for one could hurt the Republican Party this fall?

President Bush. The migration issue has been a topic of discussion here, as you can imagine. I told the President exactly what I told our country, that, one, I expect the debate to bring dignity to America, in recognition that America is a land of immigrants and people ought to be treated with respect; and this debate ought to be a debate that does not pit neighbor against neighbor; that focuses on three elements. One is that we are a nation of laws and, therefore, must enforce our laws. And that includes enforcing the laws of people coming into our country illegally.

President Fox and I discussed this issue at length. I don't know if people recognize, but his Government, all aspects of the Mexican Government came together to send a clear message to the American people: The Mexican Government understands it has a responsibility, as well, to protect the border. It is a nation of law. You heard the President talk about not only enforcing the northern border but also the southern border.

I also have said to the American people that we must enforce our laws in the interior of the country. Employers must be held to account if they're employing the people in our country illegally. However, part of the problem is—that complicates the lives of our many employers who are providing employment for people who are here illegally, is that there has been a lot of document forgery. There's an industry that has sprung up, and part of that industry is to provide forged documents so that our employers don't know whether a person is in our country legally or not.

I also believe strongly that an important part of securing the border and enforcing our laws is to recognize there are people in our country doing work that Americans will not do. And those people ought to be given a chance to have a tamper-proof card that enables them to work in our country legally for a period of time. That's called a guest-worker program. One of the important issues about a guest-worker program is, what does that mean for someone's desire to become a citizen of our country? I believe if someone has been here in our country illegally, they should not get at the head of the line if they want to become a citizen. In other words, we have a line of people waiting, people who are in our country legally, waiting to become a citizen. And people who have been in our country illegally should not get ahead of the line who are there legally.

A nation of laws can also be a welcoming nation, and I believe a guest-worker program will help us rid the society and the border of these *coyotes* who smuggle people in the back of 18-wheelers. I believe it will help get rid of the document forgers. I believe it will help people on both sides of our border respect the laws of our border and enforce our borders. I believe it is important to bring people out of the shadows of American society so they don't have to fear the life they live. I believe it's important for our Nation to uphold human rights and human dignity. And the plan I've just proposed is one that will do all that and achieve important objectives.

And I'm looking forward to working with the Congress. We're making the—I told the President we're making progress. You know, there's a legislative process. It's—some guy, some wag one time put it, it's like watching people make sausage. It's kind of a—you know, probably appears a little unpleasant from your perspective. [*Laughter*] But we're making progress. And I want a comprehensive bill. And I've made that very clear to the Members of the Congress, and I will continue making it clear to Members of Congress.

Q. [*Inaudible*]

President Bush. So, no answer—I said I want a comprehensive bill. You're presuming there won't be a comprehensive bill; I believe there will be a comprehensive bill.

Canada-U.S. Relations/Border Security

Q. Mr. President, can you explain to Canadians——

President Bush. Which one?

Q. That would be you, Mr. Bush.

President Bush. Me.

Q. Could you explain to Canadians why they'll need to have a passport or an unspecified secure document before they cross over to the United States? And what would the impact be on both of our countries economically if Canada doesn't follow through by the deadline of the end of next year?

President Bush. I appreciate you bringing up this issue. This is an issue, obviously, that affects not only border crossings with Canada, it also affects border crossings with Mexico. The Congress passed the law, and I intend to enforce the law. But the law said there ought to be a passport or a pass-port-like document that, I believe, if properly implemented, will facilitate travel and facilitate trade, not hinder travel and trade. And the reason I believe that is, I think we can be wise about the use of technologies to—envision a card that can be swiped across a reading device that facilitates the movement of people.

It's a—look, I understand this issue has created consternation. Your Prime Minister made it very clear to me that he's very worried that such a implementation of the law on the books will make it less likely people will want to travel between our countries. I've heard from business leaders who are concerned about the bookings for conventions. And so what I've told the Prime Minister and told President Fox, as well, is that we have an obligation to work very closely with our counterparts to provide a set of standards as to what will meet the obligations of the law.

Again, I repeat to you: I believe this can be done in such a way that it makes future travel, future relations stronger, not weaker.

Prime Minister Harper. Maybe I could just add to that. Obviously, we are concerned. I expressed those concerns to President Bush, and I know they've been expressed by Canadian business leaders as well. The President is confronted with legislation passed by Congress and has a responsibility to act upon that legislation, and we understand that. We understand the security concerns that are behind that.

At the same time, we're obviously concerned that if we don't move quickly and properly on this, that this could have effects on trade and movement of people, conven-

tions, you name it, that is not helpful to our economy or to relationships. So we've agreed that Minister Day and Secretary Chertoff will meet as soon as possible to make this their top priority.

Democracy in Mexico

Q. Mr. President Fox, two questions. The first is, our Senate last night passed a law, and I'd like to know what you're going to do. Will you veto that law, or will you leave the legislative packet to the next President of our country? And second, you have spoken and you have warned us Mexicans against populism and the demagogues who exist in campaigns, in Presidential campaigns, and that we are going through a very difficult stage. I'd like to ask if you already forgot the populist language that you used in your own Presidential campaign when you even talked about—[*inaudible*]—and things like that? What about talking about democracy using a populist language in the past, but now you are against candidates doing that.

President Fox. In reference to the first item, the Ministry of the Interior will inform, on behalf of the Federal Government, our position. And I celebrate—I'm glad that both the Congress, the lower chamber and the upper chamber, have exercised their autonomy, their freedom. They have discussed and approved one more of the many laws that have been approved in our country in this last 5 years of democratic and respectful Government—the autonomies and the independence on the other two powers. As never before, we have lived this reality that has been positive, fruitful, in reference to the application of our autonomy and constitutional freedom that all the other powers have.

Now, in reference to the second item, I can only say—and I will say it very clearly—from the second of July and since the second of July of the year 2000, there has been absolute freedom, and that is of utmost importance for all of us. Every single person should express according to his own decision and convenience, by all means, respecting the rights of third parties. But above all this, we have the freedom of both Mexicans, ladies and gentlemen, that work in the mass media: press; newspapers; journals; TV. We have now a freedom that we never had in the past. Every single citizen in our country nowadays exercises this freedom openly. This is one of the great fruits and results of democracy won in the second of July of the year 2000.

Iran

Q. President Bush, Secretary of State Rice is finding common ground with the British today on the view that the next step against Iran could be sanctions. Do you agree that's the way to go if Iran fails to comply with the Security Council's 30-day deadline on its nuclear program?

President Bush. Thanks. First, I do want to offer my country's assistance to the people affected by the recent earthquakes in Iran. We obviously have our differences with the Iranian Government, but we do care about the suffering of Iranian people.

There is common agreement that the Iranians should not have a nuclear weapon, the capacity to make a nuclear weapon, or the knowledge as to how to make a nuclear weapon. And the reason there's common agreement is because the Iranian Government with such a weapon, as is now constituted, would pose a serious threat to world security.

Condoleezza Rice is in Europe today to discuss with the P–5, the permanent members of the U.N. Security Council plus Germany, a strategy to go forward in a unified way that says to the Iranian Government, the world rejects your desires to have a nuclear weapon. Condi is strategizing with those who will be making the U.N. Security Council decisions as to that united front. In other words, we agree on a goal. Now the question is, how do we work together to achieve that goal? And you're watching Secretary of State Rice work with our friends to remind the Iranians on a regular and consistent basis that if they want to be—participate in the international order of things, if they don't want to isolate themselves, they must listen very carefully to what we are saying with unified voice.

Murder Investigation in Cancun

Q. My question is to President Fox, and I wonder if we could prevail upon you, sir, to answer it in English. A few weeks ago, there was a very bloody murder here with the Ianiero family in Cancun. Two young Canadian mothers are very concerned, back in Canada, that Mexican authorities have mistakenly made them suspects amidst concerns, also in Canada, the Mexicans may have bungled this investigation. Can you tell us where this investigation is going, and can you assure those two young women, indeed, they are not suspects?

President Fox. Well, we are absolutely sorry, and we have our, well, feelings that a crime has been carried out here in a hotel in Cancun. The attorneyship office is working, both the Federal one and the local one—they're working on the investigation. When the data is ready and when they finally decide, we can claim which are the guilty people. As of now, that is the only information we have at hand. We're working closely. We are reporting to the Government and the authorities of Canada. Investigation is being carried out. So far we cannot make any further comments. Thank you.

Prime Minister Harper. ——say that we do appreciate the full cooperation of the Mexican Government, Mexican police at all levels. There has been consultation with our officials, and I've spoken to the RCMP, and they assure me that that has been the case, particularly since the commitments made by Secretary Derbez in Ottawa. So we are working together in this; we're fully apprised of the situation. I can just add one small thing, which is that we're told once again, and I think we've been saying this repeatedly for some time, there is no extradition pending—extradition demand pending, nor is there one anticipated in the near future. And that's probably about all I can say.

President Fox. Muchas gracias.

NOTE: The news conference began at 10:45 a.m. in the Fiesta Americana Condesa Cancun Hotel. President Fox spoke in Spanish, and his remarks were translated by an interpreter. Prime Minister Harper referred to Minister of Public Safety Stockwell Day of Canada; and Secretary of Foreign Affairs Luis Ernesto Derbez Bautista of Mexico. President Fox referred to Secretary of Government Jose Carlos Maria Abascal Carranza of Mexico.

Joint Statement by President George W. Bush, Prime Minister Stephen Harper of Canada, and President Vicente Fox Quesada of Mexico—The Security and Prosperity Partnership of North America: Progress *March 31, 2006*

Canada, Mexico and the United States share a continued commitment to enhance the security, prosperity and quality of life of our citizens within North America. We recognize that the success of our countries is enhanced by working cooperatively. The Security and Prosperity Partnership of North America, which celebrates its first anniversary this month, provides a framework for us to advance collaboration in areas as diverse as security, transportation, the environment and public health.

This Partnership has increased our institutional contacts to respond to our vision of a stronger, more secure, and more prosperous region. In June 2005, our three governments released detailed work-plans identifying key initiatives that form an ambitious agenda of collaboration. Since June, we have worked to implement these initiatives. Many will take months or years to be completed, but we already note significant results. We ask our Ministers to build on this momentum.

We have discussed how we can ensure North America is the most economically dynamic region in the world and a secure home for our citizens. Today, we exchanged views with private sector leaders on how to enhance the competitiveness of North America.

Building on existing commitments, we agree that priority initiatives warrant special attention in the coming year:

Strengthening Competitiveness in North America. We are pleased to announce the creation of a North American Competitiveness Council (NACC). The Council will comprise members of the private sector from each country and will provide us recommendations on North American competitiveness, including, among others, areas such as automotive and transportation, steel, manufacturing, and services. The Council will meet annually with security and prosperity Ministers and will engage with senior government officials on an ongoing basis.

We are convinced that regulatory cooperation advances the productivity and competitiveness of our nations and helps to protect our health, safety and environment. For instance, cooperation on food safety will help protect the public while at the same time facilitate the flow of goods. We affirm our commitment to strengthen regulatory cooperation in this and other key sectors and to have our central regulatory agencies complete a trilateral regulatory cooperation framework by 2007.

North American Emergency Management. A disaster—whether natural or man-made—in one of our countries can have consequences across national borders. Our vision for a North American response, relief and recovery strategy would ensure that critical equipment, supplies and personnel can be deployed expeditiously throughout North America. We commit to develop a common approach to critical infrastructure protection, coordinated responses to cross border incidents, and coordinated training and exercises, with the participation of all levels of government in our countries.

Avian and Human Pandemic Influenza. Given the highly integrated nature of our economies, an outbreak of pathogenic avian flu or human pandemic influenza in any one of our countries would affect us all. Today, we have agreed to develop a comprehensive, science-based and coordinated approach within North America to avian influenza and human pandemic influenza management. We have endorsed a set of shared principles to underpin cooperative activities by our Governments in all stages of avian influenza and human pandemic influenza management: prevention; preparedness; response; and recovery. Pursuant to these principles, officials will develop, as an immediate priority, incident management protocols to ensure that we are well prepared in advance of an outbreak in North America. For instance, we have agreed to work together to accelerate research, development, production, and availability of human pandemic influenza vaccines, and develop a strategy to best facilitate the sharing of information to enhance the availability of vaccines to the region. We will also establish a small Coordinating Body of senior officials to ensure follow-up on these commitments.

North American Energy Security. A sustainable, secure and affordable supply of energy is key to fueling the North American economy. Collaboration in the areas of innovation, energy efficiency, and technology development, including moving these technologies to market, promotes energy security. Our governments renew their commitment to trilateral cooperation on clean energy technologies, conservation, and market facilitation as a means to meeting our shared goals of energy security and sustainable development. Officials will also examine how this cooperation can be expanded to further our climate efforts.

North American Smart, Secure Borders. Our vision is to have a border strategy that results in the fast, efficient and secure movement of low-risk trade and travelers to and within North America, while protecting us from threats including terrorism. In implementing this strategy, we will encourage innovative risk-based approaches to improving security and facilitating trade and travel. These include close coordination on infrastructure investments and vulnerability assessments, screening and processing of travelers, baggage and cargo, a single integrated North American trusted traveler program, and swift law enforcement responses to threats posed by criminals or terrorists, including advancing a trilateral network for the protection of judges and officers.

The Security and Prosperity Partnership of North America represents a broad and ambitious agenda. We instruct our Ministers to develop options to strengthen the SPP and present them next June as part of the second report on progress of the SPP.

President Fox and President Bush were pleased to accept, on behalf of their countries, Prime Minister Harper's invitation to host the next trilateral leaders meeting in Canada in 2007.

NOTE: An original was not available for verification of the content of this joint statement.

Joint Statement by President George W. Bush, Prime Minister Stephen Harper of Canada, and President Vicente Fox Quesada of Mexico—The Security and Prosperity Partnership of North America: Next Steps
March 31, 2006

The three leaders of North America agreed to advance the agenda of the Security and Prosperity Partnership of North America (SPP) by focusing on five high priority initiatives:

The North American Competitiveness Council. Increasing private sector engagement in the SPP by adding high-level business input will assist governments in enhancing North America's competitive position and engage the private sector as partners in finding solutions. The Council will:

- Consider issues that could be addressed trilaterally or bilaterally, as improvements in our bilateral relationships enhance North American competitiveness.
- Address issues of immediate importance and provide strategic medium and long-term advice.
- Provide input on the compatibility of our security and prosperity agendas, given the linkages between security and prosperity in a global marketplace.
- Offer ideas on the private sector's role in promoting North American competitiveness.

Advancing Cooperation on Avian and Pandemic Influenza. Leaders agreed to the following principles to guide collaboration on all stages of avian or pandemic influenza management:

- Share information among our governments in an open, timely and transparent manner.
- Adopt an integrated and comprehensive approach that incorporates animal and public health aspects in managing avian influenza and influenza pandemics.
- Ensure coordination within our respective national governments on all aspects of emergency management for an avian influenza outbreak or a human influenza pandemic, by building on existing mechanisms of cooperation and strengthening them as required.
- Coordinate our actions and leverage our respective capacities to ensure rapid and effective steps are taken to deal with avian influenza outbreaks or a human influenza pandemic in North America.
- Advise one another in advance of making any decision that could seriously affect the other countries.
- Base our actions on the best available science and evidence-based decision-making.
- Agree that the imposition and removal of veterinary or public health measures on the movement of people, animals, and goods, under our national laws and international obligations, will not be more restrictive or maintained longer than necessary to achieve the veterinary or public health objective so as to avoid unnecessary interference with the movement of people and goods within North America.
- Ensure that the business continuity plans of our respective governments consider the highly interconnected nature of our economies.
- Strive to utilize clear and consistent messaging to the public and international organizations that is proactive, timely and accurate.

North American Energy Security Initiative. A secure and sustainable energy supply is essential for our economic prosperity in North America. To advance our energy agenda we have agreed to:

- Enhance the development of a diverse energy resource base in North America by increasing collaboration on research, development and commercialization of clean energy-related technologies, and
- Strengthen the North American energy market by improving transparency and regulatory compatibility, promoting the development of resources and infrastructure, increasing cooperation on energy efficiency standards, and supporting other efforts aimed at addressing challenges on the demand side.

North American Emergency Management. The commitments made in the SPP recognize that a disaster—whether natural or man-made—in one North American country can have consequences across national borders, and may demand a common approach to all aspects of emergency management. Recent experience with hurricanes, ice storms, industrial accidents and the like demonstrate our interdependencies, as well as the need for coordination and mutual assistance in protecting and safekeeping our populations. Moving forward we will:

- Develop a common approach to critical infrastructure protection, and response to cross border terrorist incidents and natural disasters, across a number of different sectors including, but not limited to, transportation, energy, and telecommunications.
- Develop and implement joint plans for cooperation for incident response, as well as conduct coordinated training and exercises in emergency response.

Smart, Secure Borders. Leaders agreed to complete the following activities, to contribute to smart and secure borders, over the next twenty-four months:

- Collaborate to establish risk-based screening standards for goods and people that rely on technology, information sharing and biometrics.

- Develop and implement compatible electronic processes for supply chain security that use advanced electronic cargo information to analyze risk and ensure quick and efficient processing at the border;
- Develop standards and options for secure documents to facilitate cross-border travel;
- Exchange additional law enforcement liaison officers to assist in criminal and security investigations; and,
- Develop coordinated business resumption plans at border crossings to ensure legitimate trade continues.

The Security and Prosperity Partnership of North America Key Accomplishments since June 2005

The Security and Prosperity Partnership of North America (SPP), launched by the leaders of Mexico, Canada and the United States in March 2005, aims to promote growth and economic opportunity, increase security, and improve the quality of life of our peoples. In June 2005, lead Ministers issued a joint report outlining steps to achieve these goals. Since then, highlights of accomplishments include:

- To enhance growth and competitiveness in a key sector, the North American Steel Trade Committee developed a new strategy aimed at reducing market distortions, facilitating trade and promoting overall competitiveness through innovation and market development.
- To adapt to changes in sourcing and production methods, the three countries have analyzed ways to liberalize requirements for obtaining NAFTA duty-free treatment. Changes to the rules of origin have been implemented successfully and technical teams are working on additional changes.
- To speed up response times when managing infectious disease outbreaks, save lives, and reduce health care costs, the United States and Canada

signed an agreement to enable simultaneous exchange of information between virtual national laboratory networks (PulseNet).

• To make consumer goods safer, save lives, and prevent injuries, the United States and Mexico signed an agreement for advance notifications when consumer goods violate one country's safety standards or pose a danger to consumers. Canada and the United States signed a similar agreement in June.

• The United States and Canada signed an agreement, which is a milestone in pipeline regulatory cooperation, to allow increased compliance data sharing, staff exchanges and joint training. The sharing of best practices will lead to a more uniform regulatory approach for cross border pipelines.

• The United States and Canada reached a full Open-Skies aviation agreement, removing all economic restrictions on air service to, from, and beyond one another's territory by the airlines of both countries. The agreement will encourage new markets development, lower prices and greater competition.

• The United States and Mexico expanded air service in specific markets by increasing the number of designated passenger airlines per city-pair, and opening cooperative marketing arrangements (code-sharing) to airlines of either country and carriers of third countries.

• In order to increase navigational accuracy across the region, five Wide Area Augmentation System (WAAS) stations were installed in Canada and Mexico in 2005.

• To promote prosperity by reducing the costs of trade, the United States and Canada decreased transit times at the Detroit/Windsor gateway, our largest border crossing point, by 50 percent.

• To support increased trade and expedite secure processing of cross-border trade and travel between Mexico and the United States, six FAST/Express lanes are operating at the US-Mexico border, a new lane in Nogales will open soon, and we are working on a project for a lane in Matamoros. Exclusive lines and schedules will be implemented at nine crossings.

• To allow more efficient examination of rail cargo for hazardous materials and illicit flows of goods, the United States and Mexico have installed gamma ray equipment at key border crossings.

• To speed cargo shipping, the three countries are developing uniform in-advance electronic exchange of cargo manifest data for maritime, railroad and motor carriers.

• To improve air quality and promote a more competitive automotive industry, Mexico implemented an official standard to reduce sulfur in fuels. This will increase supply of low-sulfur fuels in Mexico.

• To increase border security, Mexican and U.S. agencies are harmonizing risk assessment mechanisms, exchanging information, and establishing protocols to facilitate detection of fraud and smuggling.

• To strengthen the integrity and security of asylum and refugee status determination systems, the United States and Canada launched a pilot project to share information on refugee and asylum claimants based on a comparison of fingerprint records.

• To address border violence, United States and Mexico signed an Action Plan to Combat Border Violence and Improve Public Safety. Officials of the two countries in Nogales, AZ-Nogales, Sonora and Laredo, TX-Nuevo Laredo completed protocols on border security and public safety.

- Under the United States-Mexico Voluntary Repatriation Program, more than 35,000 persons, including 20,500 in 2005, were returned to their home in a secure, legal, and humanitarian way.
- To increase maritime security, the United States and Canada completed joint exercises on the St. Clair and Detroit Rivers in September and in February during Super Bowl XL. Officers, who were cross-designated on vessels of the other nation, could authorize pursuit of suspect vessels crossing jurisdictions.
- To advance preparedness to address a cyber incident affecting critical infrastructure, authorities from the United States and Canada completed a multinational exercise, Cyberstorm, in February 2006.
- To enhance aviation security, the United States, Canada, and Mexico completed training on principles to protect aircraft from terrorism threats, on marksmanship skills, and on emergency procedures.
- To enhance port security, Canada and the United States concluded port facility visits at Oakland, CA and Vancouver, BC in October 2005 to facilitate the development of benchmark security standards.
- To ensure food safety while facilitating trade, a Food Safety Coordinating Task Force was formed and is developing a prioritized list of standards to compare for similarities, differences, and scientific bases for the differences. These efforts will facilitate the development of North American standards and, as appropriate, the removal of differences in standards.
- To enhance clarity and compatibility of energy regulation, Canadian, U.S. and Mexican regulators began regular meetings to exchange information on regulatory standards and energy market developments and to discuss bringing gas from Alaska to the North American market.
- To reduce marine air pollution, Canada and the United States have coordinated data collection, marine inventory development and air quality monitoring. The two countries are preparing to approach the International Maritime Organization to designate special areas for controlling sulfur emissions from marine vessels.
- Canada and the United States are developing Mutual Assistance Arrangements, which will enhance our preparedness for cross-border public health emergencies; Mexico has been invited to participate.

NOTE: An original was not available for verification of the content of this joint statement.

Statement on the Earthquakes in Iran
March 31, 2006

On behalf of the American people, Laura and I express our sincere condolences for the loss of life and suffering caused by the series of earthquakes in the Iranian Province of Lorestan. Our thoughts and prayers are with families and individuals who have lost loved ones. The United States stands ready to assist the people of Iran, and we hereby extend an offer of humanitarian assistance.

The President's Radio Address
April 1, 2006

Good morning. As tax day approaches later this month, many American families are now finishing their tax returns. And as you do, an important debate is taking place in Washington that will affect the amount you will pay in the years ahead.

I believe our economy grows when you're allowed to keep more of your hard-earned money and make your own decisions about how to save, spend, and invest. So, working with Congress, we've provided tax relief for all Americans who pay income taxes. We lowered tax rates to let workers keep more of their paychecks. We doubled the child tax credit and reduced the marriage penalty, and we put the death tax on the road to extinction. We also cut taxes on dividends and capital gains and expanded incentives for small businesses to invest so they could grow and create new jobs.

Since 2001, the tax relief we delivered has left $880 billion in the hands of American workers and small businesses and families like yours, and you've used that money to help produce more than 4 years of uninterrupted economic growth. Last year, our economy grew at a healthy 3.5 percent, faster than any other major industrialized nation.

One politician in Washington said in 2003 that our tax cuts were "ruining our economy and costing us jobs." The truth is that since August 2003, America has added almost 5 million new jobs. Our unemployment rate is now 4.8 percent—lower than the average of the 1970s, 1980s, and 1990s. Real after-tax income is up 8 percent per person since the beginning of 2001. More Americans now own their own homes than at any time in our history, and minority homeownership is at record levels. Consumer confidence is at its highest level in nearly 4 years. Productivity has grown

strongly over the past 5 years, and our small-business sector is thriving.

The evidence is overwhelming; the opponents of tax cuts were wrong. Tax relief has helped to create jobs and opportunities for American families, and it's helped our economy grow. By maintaining our progrowth economic policies and practicing spending restraint in Washington, we can keep our economy growing and stay on track to meet our goal of cutting the budget deficit in half by 2009.

The problem is that the tax relief we passed is set to expire over the next few years. Some Democrats in Washington are insisting that we let that happen—or even repeal the tax cuts now. In either case, that would weaken our economy and would leave American families with a big tax hike that they do not expect and will not welcome. Because America needs more than a temporary economic expansion, we need more than temporary tax relief. To keep our economy growing, to keep our businesses investing, and to keep creating jobs, we need to ensure that you keep more of what you earn. So Congress needs to make the tax relief permanent.

Making tax relief permanent includes extending the tax cuts on dividends and capital gains. These tax cuts have been vital to our economic growth. By lowering the cost of capital, this tax relief has given businesses an incentive to invest and expand, and that has helped create jobs and opportunity. I urge the Congress to extend these progrowth tax cuts, so our businesses can plan with confidence and keep creating jobs for American workers.

The debate in Congress over taxes ultimately comes down to this: Who knows best how to use your money, politicians in Washington or you? I believe the money we spend in Washington is your money, not the Government's money. I trust you to make the best decisions about what to do with your hard-earned dollars, because when you do, your family is better off, our economy grows, and prosperity and opportunity spread throughout our great land.

Thank you for listening.

NOTE: The address was recorded at 9:15 a.m. on March 31 at the LeBlanc Spa and Resort in Cancun, Mexico, for broadcast at 10:06 a.m. on April 1. The transcript was made available by the Office of the Press Secretary on March 31 but was embargoed for release until the broadcast. The Office of the Press Secretary also released a Spanish language transcript of this address.

Remarks Following a Meeting on Health Care Initiatives and an Exchange With Reporters
April 4, 2006

The President. America needs a health care system that empowers patients to make rational and smart decisions for themselves and their families, a health care system in which the relationship between the patient and the provider are central, not a health care system where decisions are made by the Federal Government.

So we've been having a discussion here today about how to make sure our health care system meets certain objectives: one, empowering the patients; two, how do we have a system that helps control rising costs in health care?

And one of the interesting and innovative ways to do that is through health savings accounts. Health savings accounts are good for the uninsured; they're good for small businesses; they're good for larger corporations. And people around the table here have been sharing their experiences with how folks are saving money through health savings accounts. And I would urge the small-business owner or the individual who is concerned about his or her health care to take a look at a health savings account.

We talked about the importance of cost savings through these important products, but we also talked about how we can work with the United States Congress to strengthen them, to make them more appealing, to give people more choices in the marketplace, to say to the American people, "We trust your judgment. We trust you to make the right decision for you and your families."

And so I want to thank you all for coming for this most interesting discussion. And I'll be glad to take a couple of questions.

Nedra [Nedra Pickler, Associated Press].

Representative Thomas D. DeLay

Q. Yes, sir. Thank you. I'm wondering if we can get your reaction to Tom DeLay's resignation? Do you think it hurts the Republican Party or your ability to get work done in Congress?

The President. I had a talk last night on my way back from the ball game with Congressman DeLay. He informed me of his decision. My reaction was, it had to have been a very difficult decision for someone who loved representing his district in the State of Texas. I wished him all the very best, and I know he's looking forward to—he's looking to the future.

My own judgment is, is that our party will continue to succeed because we're the party of ideas. And one of the most important ideas is to make sure that health care is available and affordable for the citizens of this country. One way to do so is to trust the patients, trust the American people when it comes to making rational decisions for health care for them and their families. And that's exactly what we've been discussing here at the table.

Caren [Caren Bohan, Reuters].

White House Staff

Q. Thank you, sir. Your new Chief of Staff takes over soon, and I'm wondering, is there likely to be far-reaching changes in the staff at the White House? And is Secretary Snow expected to stay on?

The President. Secretary Snow is here at the table. He's been a part of this discussion. I'm glad you brought him up. He has been a valuable member of my administration, and I trust his judgment and appreciate his service.

I've, as you know, accepted the resignation of Andrew Card, my long-time friend, a person who will go down in the annals as one of the really fine Chiefs of Staff in the history of the White House. I've asked Josh Bolten to take his place. Josh has served us very well as the Director of the Office of Management and Budget. I told Josh that he is—will organize the White House in such a way that he is comfortable with and that meets my needs. And my needs are to have good, crisp information so I can make decisions on behalf of the American people.

And I look forward to Josh's recommendations as to how to get this White House to—for the last 2½ years of my administration, to continue to function in an effective way. And it functioned very effectively under Andy Card, by the way. I'm most proud of his administration and proud of the team that he assembled.

Dick [Richard Stevenson, New York Times].

Iraq

Q. Mr. President, the situation in Iraq continues to be fraught with violence. You have expressed impatience in recent days of the progress towards forming a coalition government. Do you think, as some people on the ground there are saying in the Iraqi political firmament, that it's getting very close to the point of no return?

The President. I believe that people ought to pay attention to the fact that 3 months ago, or a little over 3 months ago, 12 million people went to the polls and said, "I want to live in a democracy." And there is a group of folks in Iraq that want to stop the advance of democracy, and therefore, they're willing to use violence to do so. The one way to help bring confidence to the Iraqi people that those few will not be able to determine the future of that country is for there to be a unity government that steps up and says, "I'm willing to lead."

And so I sent Secretary Rice to Iraq with that message. And the message is, is that the people of Iraq have voted, and now it's time for the elected leaders to stand up and do their job. So we look forward to working with them to put together a unity government, a government that will reject the sectarian violence, will reject the militias, reject Zarqawi and the terrorists that are trying to create enough chaos so that America loses nerve. And I'm not going to lose my nerve as the President, because we're doing the right thing in establishing a democracy in that country. And by establishing a democracy, we're laying the foundation for peace.

And that's what we want. We want there to be peace. We want our children not to have to grow up under the threat of violence coming out of the Middle East. And one of the lessons of September the 11th, 2001, is that—this sense of—that tyranny is okay, but underneath the surface there was resentment—and the way—and anger that became the breeding grounds for these killers. And the best way to defeat that is with the light and hope of democracy. And you bet it's tough in Iraq, and it's tough because people are trying to stop the advance of democracy. And I'm convinced we're making progress there. But

I do urge the folks on the ground to get that unity government in place so that the Iraqi people have confidence in their future.

I thank you all.

NOTE: The President spoke at 10:19 a.m. in the Roosevelt Room at the White House. In his remarks, he referred to senior Al Qaida associate Abu Musab Al Zarqawi. The Office of the Press Secretary also released a Spanish language transcript of these remarks.

Message to the Congress Transmitting a Treaty Between the United States and Uruguay Concerning the Encouragement and Reciprocal Protection of Investment
April 4, 2006

To the Congress of the United States:

With a view to receiving the advice and consent of the Senate to ratification, I transmit herewith the Treaty between the United States and the Oriental Republic of Uruguay Concerning the Encouragement and Reciprocal Protection of Investment, with Annexes and Protocol, signed at Mar del Plata, Argentina, on November 4, 2005. I transmit also, for the information of the Senate, the report prepared by the Department of State with respect to the Treaty.

The Treaty is the first bilateral investment treaty (BIT) concluded since 1999 and the first negotiated on the basis of a new U.S. model BIT text, which was completed in 2004. The new model text draws on long-standing U.S. BIT principles, our experience with Chapter 11 of the North American Free Trade Agreement (NAFTA), and the executive branch's collaboration with the Congress in developing negotiating objectives on foreign investment for U.S. free trade agreements. The Treaty will establish investment protections that will create more favorable conditions for U.S. investment in Uruguay and assist Uruguay in its efforts to further develop its economy.

The Treaty is fully consistent with U.S. policy towards international and domestic investment. A specific tenet of U.S. investment policy, reflected in this Treaty, is that

U.S. investment abroad and foreign investment in the United States should receive national treatment and most-favored-nation treatment. Under this Treaty, the Parties also agree to customary international law standards for expropriation and for the minimum standard of treatment. The Treaty includes detailed provisions regarding the computation and payment of prompt, adequate, and effective compensation for expropriation; free transfer of funds related to investment; freedom of investment from specified performance requirements; and the opportunity of investors to choose to resolve disputes with a host government through international arbitration. The Treaty also includes extensive transparency obligations with respect to national laws and regulations, and commitments to transparency and public participation in dispute settlement. The Parties also recognize that it is inappropriate to encourage investment by weakening or reducing the protections afforded in domestic environmental and labor laws.

I recommend that the Senate give early and favorable consideration to the Treaty and give its advice and consent to ratification.

GEORGE W. BUSH

The White House,
April 4, 2006.

Remarks on Immigration Reform Legislation
April 5, 2006

The United States Senate is debating a very vital issue for our country, and that is immigration reform. I urge the Senators to continue to work toward get a comprehensive bill; a bill that will help us secure our borders; a bill that will cause the people in the interior of this country to recognize and enforce the law; and a bill that will include a guest-worker provision that will enable us to more secure the border, will recognize that there are people here working hard for jobs Americans won't do, and a guest-worker provision that is not amnesty, one that provides for automatic citizenship.

This is a vital debate. I thank the Members who are working hard to get a bill done. I strongly urge them to come to conclusion as quickly as possible and pass a comprehensive bill.

Thank you all very much.

NOTE: The President spoke at 8:55 a.m. on the Colonnade at the White House.

Remarks in a Discussion on Health Care Reform in Bridgeport, Connecticut
April 5, 2006

The President. Thank you all. Darrell, thanks for the invitation. I think you're going to find this an interesting way to discuss a vital issue for our country, and that is, really, how do we stay competitive? How does the United States of America remain the preeminent economic leader in the world?

And one way you do so is you make sure you've got an environment where small businesses can thrive, where people can feel comfortable in having health care that's available and affordable. So thanks for coming and giving us a chance to discuss the issue. You notice I say "us." There's nothing worse than a guy kind of blowing away in a lecture, so I've invited fellow citizens to come and share their experiences about an interesting way to approach affordability and availability in health care.

But before I do that, I want to thank you all very much for taking time out of your day to come and listen. I appreciate very much the Governor, Jodi Rell, joining us. Governor Rell is a—you know, I know something about Governors. I used to be one. She is really a dignified, classy woman who has done a fine job for the State of Connecticut.

I flew down today with Congressman Chris Shays. Shays is a very thoughtful person. He is a friend. He is an independent fellow—[*laughter*]—who speaks his mind. But he does so in a way that gets people to listen to him. And I appreciate his thoughtful approach to a lot of issues. And I appreciate your friendship as well. I'm looking forward to hearing your lecture on the way back to Washington. [*Laughter*]

Mr. Mayor, thank you for joining us. So Laura comes back and says, "I met the mayor of Bridgeport. He's a good guy." I say, "Well, that's great." I don't know what you did, Mayor, but you at least convinced the First Lady you're a good guy. [*Laughter*] And I appreciate your hospitality and your kindness to my wife who—you know, she's really not a politician. She is a really fine woman, great mother, great wife, thoughtful person. And I appreciate your kindness to her. She's also, obviously, got good judgment. Her Chief of Staff, Anita McBride, was raised right here in Bridgeport.

I appreciate other State and local officials who are here, thank all the business leaders. The challenge is whether or not this Nation is going to be a confident nation. Our economy is strong right now. GDP grew at 3.5 percent last year. We're adding jobs. The national unemployment rate is 4.8 percent. I think the unemployment rate here is something less than that, here in the State of Connecticut. People are working. Small businesses are flourishing. Productivity is up. And the fundamental question is, how do we keep it that way? What do we do? Do we lose our confidence and retreat, or do we create the conditions so that capital flows and the entrepreneurial spirit remains strong?

My attitude is that the United States is the leader of the world, and by putting good policies into place, we'll remain the leader of the world. And that's where we should be. And so here are some ideas as to how to do that.

One is to keep taxes low. I believe when people have more money in their pockets it helps the entrepreneurial spirit, causes the economy to grow. One reason we overcame the recession and the stock market collapse and the attacks on our country and the wars we've been through and the natural disasters we've been through is because people have got more money to save and invest and spend. And so I'm looking forward to working with Congress to keep the taxes low and, at the same time, be wise about how we spend the people's money.

I understand we've got an issue with energy. I know it probably came as a shock to some of my fellow citizens here in Connecticut when I stood up in front of the country and said, "We've got a problem; we're addicted to oil." And I meant it. We've got an economic problem being addicted to oil because when fossil fuels— demand for fossil fuels rise in other parts of the world, it causes our energy bills to go up. We've got a national security problem when it comes to oil. When you've got people in the world who don't like us, from which we get supplies of oil, it causes those problems to come into the Oval Office. And therefore, we have to deal with the geopolitics of oil when it comes to securing this country. And we've got an environmental problem relying upon fossil fuels. And so I think there's a better way forward, and I look forward to working with Congress to keep us competitive in the world's stage by diversifying away from the use of oil.

And here are some ideas: Using ethanol in our automobiles is an idea, developing hybrid plug-in batteries so that we can drive the first 40 miles on electricity and not using gasoline, being wise about nuclear power, using solar power. There's a variety of things we need to do together to help us diversify away from hydrocarbons, and I'm intent upon doing that for the sake of the competitiveness of the United States of America.

Another idea I look forward to working with Congress on is to make sure that we are competitive when it comes to having the workforce of the 21st century, and we're going to make good progress on this with Congress. And that is to do something on the research and development tax credit, is double our commitment to the research in the basic sciences in Washington, DC, so that we're technologically competent, that we're on the leading edge of research when it comes to the world's economy, and then make sure our kids have got the skills necessary to fill the jobs by emphasizing math and science, particularly in junior high.

In terms of competitiveness, a big issue, of course, is health care. And in Washington, DC, there is a philosophical debate that rages, and that is how best to implement a health care strategy; what should it look like? And to simplify the debate, it basically says, "Government ought to be the decider. Government ought to drive demand, and Government ought to control supply," versus a system in which individuals are in charge of their own health care decisions. I recognize that it may be oversimplification, but, nevertheless, that's the crux of the debate.

And it's an important debate, and so I've got some ideas as to how this debate ought to go. And it starts with, one, a Federal commitment to certain people within our society, the poor and the elderly. The Medicare plan we passed modernized Medicare for the first time since Lyndon Johnson provided that—signed that bill. It is an important piece of legislation. It is working; 27 million Americans have signed up. If you have not looked at the new Medicare opportunities for you, you ought to do so by calling 1–800–MEDICARE.

Interestingly enough, by providing competition into the system—in other words, giving our seniors choices—the estimated cost for Medicare is dropping significantly. I believe competition works. And I believe Government ought to trust people to make the right decision for their selves and their families. And that's what Medicare has done.

Another important way for health care to work is to expand community health centers. One of the things Shays told me was, he said you've got a good community health center here in Bridgeport. Community health centers are vehicles—places of opportunity for low-income citizens to be able to get primary care, so as to take the stress off of emergency rooms of your hospitals, for example.

We've expanded 800 of them over the years; we intend to expand or open 400 more over the next 2 years. These are wise use of taxpayers' money, to help keep a Federal commitment to helping the poor deal with health care.

And same goes to Medicaid. Medicaid is a very important program. I look forward to working with the Governors to make sure that the Medicaid system works more efficiently, most importantly for those who are getting Medicaid help.

Now, in terms of a lot of other folks, it seems like to me that we ought to be working toward the design of a system that makes health care available and affordable. And let me give you some ideas as to how to do that.

One, many small businesses are having trouble affording health care insurance. One of the reasons why is, they don't have the same pooling opportunity—pooling of risk opportunities that larger companies get. And so I think it makes sense to allow small businesses to pool risk across jurisdictional boundaries so they can afford the same kinds of insurance purchases that big companies get.

For example, a restaurant in Bridgeport ought to be allowed to pool risk with a restaurant in Texas so that there's economies of risk. Today, that can't happen. Association health plans will enable small businesses to better afford insurance. I'm looking forward to working with Congress to get that out of the Congress.

Secondly, one of the cost-drivers for health care are these frivolous lawsuits that are running good doctors out of practice and forces doctors and hospitals to practice defensive medicine. When I first went to Washington I said, "Well, this is just a State issue," Governor. I thought it could be best solved at the State level, until I realized the defensive practice of medicine plus these liability increases through lawsuits costs us about $28 billion a year to the Federal—cost the Federal budget $28 billion. I said, that's a national problem, and it demands a national solution.

The House passed a bill. Of course, it's stuck in the Senate. It needs to get out of the Senate. In order to make health care more affordable and more available, we need comprehensive medical liability reform immediately. You know what's an amazing statistic is, there are 1,700 counties in our country that have no ob-gyn. They got run out of business. And that's not right, and it's not fair, and it's necessary for Congress to act.

The third area we need to work on is information technologies. I know there is a lot of hospital people here. But we've set the goal—and I think you understand what I'm talking about, is to make sure that health care is brought into the 21st century by using information technology in such a way as, on the one hand, we have medical records; on the other hand, we protect patients' privacy. And we can do so.

A classic example of the importance of information technology came down there with Katrina. A lot of veterans were displaced as a result of that hurricane, but they had medical electronic records because the Veterans Administration has begun to modernize. And therefore, they were able to take their medical electronics records to their destination—where they moved to and were able to get immediate health care. The records were there; they were available. The doc that they checked in with was able to access their records on a real-time basis and were able to—so there was no, kind of, loss of care; there was no confusion about what was necessary.

We will save a lot of costs with information technologies, and we'll reduce medical errors with information technologies. And Secretary Leavitt, who is the head of HHS, has got a strong program to encourage the advance of information technology. Some estimate we save 30 percent in health care costs when information technology is spread throughout our society. And so we've got a Federal commitment, and we look forward to working with you to spread that commitment.

And finally, we're here to talk about what's called health savings accounts. It's a really interesting idea that Congress passed in the new Medicare law. It's an idea that it's really important for people— no matter what side of the philosophical

debate you may be on—to at least pay attention to what's available. A health savings account addresses one of the major cost-drivers in our system, and that is, is that a lot of people get health care, but somebody else pays the bill. It's called a third-party payer system.

And when somebody else pays the bill, sometimes you don't pay attention to the cost. You know, when you go out and purchase an automobile, somebody doesn't pay the bill for you; you pay it. And you tend to shop and you look and you try to find out what's best for you. The third-party payer system, which is, you know, an integral part of our health care system today, essentially says, "You sign up for a program, and if you get sick, somebody else will take care of it for you." And I believe that the more the consumer is involved in pricing, the more the consumer is involved in the decisionmaking, the more likely it is people will start making rational decisions for their own needs.

And one way to do that is through the advent of health savings accounts, which is, in essence, health savings account coupled with a high-deductible, catastrophic insurance plan. That's long-word talk for, if you get sick, above a certain amount, your insurance pays for it. If not, you pay for it. But the savings, if you don't spend money, are tax-free. In other words, this is an interesting way of making sure the patient and the provider are the integral deciders in health care decisions. If that's not clear enough, they'll help clear it up for me.

You know, LASIK surgery is an interesting—it's interesting to think about. LASIK surgery is a surgery that helps correct your eyesight. And I don't know how many years ago it was, but LASIK surgery was very expensive. But this happened to be a part of medical—medicine where there really was a market. More people began to provide LASIK surgery. People began to shop for LASIK surgery. And the cost for LASIK surgery has gone down dramatically, and the quality of LASIK surgery has improved dramatically.

A lot of that has to do with the fact that the consumer was the decider. The consumer actually began to look around and decide what was best for him or her in the marketplace. That stands in contrast to a system where somebody else pays the bills.

Health savings accounts really mean that the individual owns and controls their health care. Health savings accounts enable somebody to say, "Look, if I make the right decisions about smoking or drinking or exercising, that I'll end up saving money." Health savings accounts help small businesses more afford health care coverage. Many of the uninsured are people who work for small businesses. They are the working uninsured. And if we have product available for small businesses to better afford insurance, it will help this country remain competitive.

Health savings accounts would be good for young people. A lot of young people feel bulletproof. They don't feel like they need insurance; they don't think they're ever going to get sick. But if a young person starts saving now for future health care costs and the interest compounds on a tax-free basis, it's amazing how much money a person can save.

And so this is an interesting idea. It started off rather slowly. In the marketplace today, there are about 3 million citizens who have got health savings accounts. Interestingly enough, part of the debate in Washington is, they say, "Sure he wants health savings accounts; only the rich will access them." That's not what happened. The uninsured are accessing health savings accounts. Many of the health savings accounts owners are folks with their high school degree. A lot of health savings accounts owners are people with not an extraordinary amount of income. You know, it kind of defies the concept that certain people can't make decisions on their own—

you know, "If you don't have a Ph.D., you shouldn't be allowed to decide things." People are plenty smart when it comes to their own lives and coming to making decisions about health care needs. And I believe we ought to encourage more consumer activism, more involvement in making health care decisions.

So that's what we're here to talk about. And by the way, one other point is you can't make good health care decisions unless there's transparency in the marketplace. People need to see price. One of the things we're trying to encourage is for health care providers to post their prices so people can choose, so people are able to—you know, "This kind of makes sense for me; this doesn't make sense for me." Nontransparency in pricing makes it awfully hard to achieve savings. And after all, one of the national objectives has got to be to have a health care system that is available and affordable. Availability means transparency in prices; affordability means—will be enhanced by transparency in pricing.

And so there's a competing vision from one that says, let's let the Federal Government make decisions. It's one vision I strongly support because I believe—I'm one of these kind of persons that believes that people are plenty capable of making rational decisions and choices.

We're here to talk about this—I mentioned the panel of folks. We'll start with Stephen Glick.

Stephen Glick. Yes, good morning, Mr. President. Welcome to Connecticut.

The President. Yes, it's good to be back here. Was born here, good to be back. [*Laughter*] Educated here. [*Laughter*]

Mr. Glick. We love that.

The President. Yes.

Mr. Glick. Before I make my remarks, I'd like to have my wife, Sally Glick, and partner in the business stand up. She's in the middle of the row up there. Welcome.

The President. That's a pretty good move. Smart guy, you know? Welcome, Sally.

Mr. Glick. Next to her is my son, Aaron, who is finishing his second year of law school—hopefully. [*Laughter*] And next to her is my daughter, Jamie Lombardi. Jamie is part of our team at CIT, and we welcome her.

The President. Why don't you tell everybody what the CIT is.

[*At this point, Mr. Glick, administrator, Chamber Insurance Trust, made brief remarks.*]

The President. Good job. Skip the dating service thing. Anyway—[*laughter*].

Mr. Glick. Do you know——

The President. No, I don't, believe me. [*Laughter*] Look, I'm the funny guy; you're the—[*laughter*].

Mr. Glick. Once in my life. [*Laughter*]

The President. One of the interesting things about society is there's—sometimes people resist change, and part of the reasons I'm doing forums like this and part of the reason Steve does what he does is to help educate people about what's available.

I strongly urge small-business owners to find out more about health savings accounts. I urge young people to find out about health savings accounts. It doesn't hurt to learn. And I think you'll find these to be very interesting opportunities. And one person who knows a lot about them is Dr. Bill West, entrepreneur.

William J. West, Jr. Thank you very much, Mr. President.

The President. Is that a true statement, "entrepreneur"?

Dr. West. Yes, absolutely.

The President. Good. Sometimes "doctor" and "entrepreneur" don't go hand in hand. [*Laughter*]

Dr. West. "Businessman/doctor," don't go hand in hand.

The President. What kind of doctor?

Dr. West. I'm a board-certified practicing ob-gyn, located in Redding, Pennsylvania. I'm actually a third generation——

The President. Have you got a health care crisis in ob-gyns in Redding?

Dr. West. Yes, we do.

The President. A leading question—I knew the answer before he said it. [*Laughter*]

Dr. West. We actually just lost eight more people practicing obstetrics in our hospital as of January 1.

The President. We've got a serious national problem. The Senate needs to get rid of all this, you know, politics and focus on solving this problem. Different subject—go ahead. Sorry about that.

[*Dr. West, president and founder, First HSA, LLC, made brief remarks.*]

The President. So, like, you're making the pitch. What do you tell people about HSAs?

Dr. West. They are not just for the healthy and wealthy; they work for everyone, including the chronically ill. They make total sense for everyone out there. It truly is consumerism.

The President. Tell people why.

Dr. West. Well, basically, you know, right now in the physician marketplace, there is no consumerism. People don't know what the cost of services are, and I don't know what the cost of services are. I might prescribe a drug that I have no clue it costs $20 a tablet, and it's taken every 4 hours. A one-week prescription could cost $600. Why don't I know that? Because I'm not paying for it. And usually the patient is not paying for it because all they have is a copay.

That's the problem with the third-party system. We have a disconnect between the patient, the provider, and the true cost of those health care services. Health savings accounts reconnect the patient and the provider with the true cost. And we start to make wise decisions. We have increased use of generic medications. We shop around for services. Maybe an MRI costs a little bit more at this hospital versus that hospital. And we start to use——

The President. Just to make sure everybody understands—a health savings account is a combination of a high-deductible catastrophic plan, and the deductible is a cash account that earns interest-free. And the cash account is—as you'll hear later on—can be contributed by the individual, contributed by the company, can be contributed a combination of the worker and the company, can be contributed all different ways. But the shopping around is for the cash portion of a person's account.

Dr. West. Absolutely. At First HSA, we provide a checking account which allows unlimited checkbook and Visa debit card access to the funds. Clients get monthly statements; they get the IRS reporting; they have 24-hour telephone banking. And they earn interest on the accounts, and those unused funds rollover from year to year.

So if I had $3,000 in my account and spent 1,000, 2,000 plus interest rolls into the next year, and I can put an additional 3,000 in the following year.

The President. What is important for people to understand is that when you combine the cash contribution plus the premium for the high-deductible insurance, it's less cost than the current insurance plans. That's important for people to understand. That's why we keep—I urge people to take a look. I mean, this is a cost-savings measure that has the additional benefit of connecting the consumer to the provider.

Dr. West. Absolutely. And the consumer benefits from healthy lifestyle choices, as you stated earlier, and they financially benefit from that. As a physician, many times patients will come to me to want to stop smoking, and I'll write a prescription to stop smoking. The first question they're going to ask me is, "Does my health insurance plan cover that?" If the answer is no, they hand the prescription back to me because they're not financially incentivized to do that. In a health savings account, they take that prescription, they go get it filled, and they stop smoking because they're the

ones who are going to benefit from that healthy lifestyle.

The President. And they benefit because they don't spend—ultimately spend money on disease that would drain their savings account. The important thing for people to understand when they listen to the health savings account discussion is that the savings account is owned by the individual, and if a person changed jobs, for example, the savings account goes with the person. It's a part of a person's asset base. It is an integral part of a person's—and will be an integral part of a lot of people's future, to have this money stored up for health care needs, coupled with a high-deductible catastrophic plan in case something disastrous happens.

How's your business going?

Dr. West. It's been phenomenal. There's been exponential growth. I also wanted to let you know that we actually got a union to go 100-percent HSA as one of our clients, and they love the plan. They're really—our clients range from professionals to unions to formerly unemployed, uninsured workers, sole proprietors, entrepreneurs. We have them all.

[*Dr. West made further remarks.*]

The President. Information keeps people involved. Information is an integral part of consumers making rational decisions and choices.

Dr. West. Absolutely. We've developed a personal electronic health record, where they can take this health record with them from doctor to doctor, so they have improved quality.

The President. Explain to people what a personal health record is—an electronic personal health record.

Dr. West. Basically, online, what they have access to is, they can put in all their personal health care information—all their diseases, their medications, past family history, social history—all those things are in the health record. They then can print it out and take that with them, or put it onto their PDA or whatever, and take that with them to the doctor's office. Many times, when we first come into the doctor's office, what do we do? We have to fill out a new form saying, here's all my medical——

The President. Unless you're not a very good writer.

[*Dr. West made further remarks.*]

The President. Things are changing. I think if you listen carefully to the doc, he's describing a different approach to health care that is consumer-centered. Now you've got to—in order to accept that as a rational way of approaching health care, you've got to trust people to make rational decisions. And I think our society should. I think the Federal Government should trust people to make good decisions. And, amazingly, what happens when that starts to happen is, you start seeing the rapid increase of price in health care begin to decline and people watching their—how they treat their bodies better.

So thanks, doc. Thanks for being——

Dr. West. Thank you very much.

The President. Thanks for coming. Greg?

Gregory B. Gravel. Good morning, Mr. President. Thank you. My name is Greg Gravel. I'm the president and chief executive officer of the Whitney Center.

[*Mr. Gravel made brief remarks.*]

The President. The Whitney Center, like you told me earlier, Aunt Marge?

Mr. Gravel. Absolutely.

The President. My grandfather's sister was——

Mr. Gravel. We go back a long ways, sir.

[*Mr. Gravel made further remarks, concluding as follows.*]

Mr. Gravel. We front-ended part of the HSA plan for our employees and continue to do so today.

The President. Tell everyone what that means.

Mr. Gravel. We actually put money into their account. As long as the employee were to contribute a like amount, we put $520 a year into their health savings account.

The President. Right. So in this case, the deductibility is 1,040——

Mr. Gravel. Correct.

The President. Cash into the account that will earn interest tax-free, be withdrawn tax-free, was 1,040, half of which you paid and half of which the employee paid.

Mr. Gravel. Correct. Correct.

[*Mr. Gravel made further remarks.*]

The President. What's the premium on the high-risk deductible plan?

Mr. Gravel. It's about $4,500 for a single covered employee. The difference between 2004 and 2005, we were able to save $78,000 in our premiums; 2005 to 2006, we saw a 1.8 percent increase—1.8 percent, not point—not one-eight—not 18 percent but 1.8 percent increase in our premium. When is the last time you have heard of your health care premium increasing by as little as that amount?

[*Mr. Gravel made further remarks.*]

The President. Good. Lin works with you?

Mr. Gravel. Absolutely.

Lin Onorato. My name is Lin Onorato. I am the assistant director of dining services at the Whitney Center. I am an HSA participant. I have a family plan.

[*Mrs. Onorato made brief remarks.*]

The President. Let me ask you something. People would say, well, you know, you can't possibly make rational decisions. I presume that, kind of, entering in the marketplace as a shopper, consumer is a little daunting at first——

Mrs. Onorato. Definitely.

The President. ——but when somebody is listening out there that says, "I wonder if I ought to try this," how would you encourage—I mean, obviously you're confident enough to talk about it sitting up here with the President—[*laughter*]—and you've gained a certain amount of experience in the process. What would you recommend to somebody who says, "Well, I don't think I've got the capacity to go out and find out what's available"?

Mrs. Onorato. It's real easy. You get from—we use ConnectiCare, and they give us their provider book, and you can go through, and you can ask your doctor questions and, "How much will this cost?" And you can call up different people and get the best price for your money without compromising quality.

The President. See, this is a—change is hard. The old system was, "Well, don't worry; somebody else will take care of it." There is a new opportunity that saves people money, actually earns people money. And I love the idea of Lin being able to say, "I own my account." Notice she emphasized the $800 that was unspent in the cash portion of the account—say, "It's my money; I get to roll it over."

If something terrible were to happen, there is an insurance policy to take care—it's called the catastrophic aspect of this plan. She is in charge of making the decisions for her family. That bothers some people in Washington, DC. They don't believe she's capable of doing so. I do. But the benefit for society as a whole—this helps control costs and makes health care more available and affordable.

And so I want to thank you for having the confidence to share this with us.

Mrs. Onorato. Thank you for the opportunity.

The President. Thank you for being here. Good job.

Verna, are you ready?

Verna Moran. Sure am.

The President. Tell everybody what you do.

Ms. Moran. First of all, I'd like to thank you for allowing me to be here today, Mr. President. And my name is Verna Moran. I'm vice president of human resources for the Seitz Corporation.

[*Ms. Moran made brief remarks.*]

The President. Let me stop you right there, if you don't mind. Sorry.

Ms. Moran. Sure.

The President. A lot of business people, small-business owners, when they're confronted with a 25-percent increase on a relatively high base decide not to offer people insurance anymore. That's why a lot of our citizens who work for small businesses do not have insurance. It's the working uninsured—many of the working uninsured are employees of the small-business company.

What's important, however, is that 70 percent of new jobs in America are created by small-business owners. And therefore, if our small-business sector is weakened because of rising health care costs, it makes this country less competitive.

Sorry to interrupt.

Ms. Moran. Not at all. And with the 25 percent—you can interrupt any time. [*Laughter*]

The President. Maybe here but not at the house. [*Laughter*]

[*Ms. Moran made further remarks.*]

The President. The combination of the high-risk deductible—premium on the high-risk deductible, relative to their cost last year, enabled the savings from their cost last year to be—this company to contribute 100 percent of the cash portion of the health savings accounts for their employee.

Ms. Moran. Correct.

The President. It's a pretty strong benefit for a small company to be able to do.

[*Ms. Moran made further remarks, concluding as follows.*]

Ms. Moran. So a healthy employee could, in fact, at the end of the year, have their whole deductible be rolled over in a future year.

The President. And it's their money.

Ms. Moran. And it's their money.

[*Ms. Moran made further remarks.*]

The President. It's an amazing story, isn't it? One hundred seventy-five employees?

Ms. Moran. One hundred fifty employees, yes.

The President. One hundred fifty employees, I just increased it a little bit. [*Laughter*]

Ms. Moran. Well, that's all right because we plan to increase, so that's okay. [*Laughter*]

The President. Oh, that's good. That's interesting. I bet you're more confident about expanding because all of a sudden, you've got a better handle on your health care costs.

Ms. Moran. Exactly.

The President. And I really strongly urge small-business owners to look at these products. And I find it amazing that Verna is able to describe a plan that is very innovative, employee-centered, and yet at the same time, she can say that we've saved money for the company.

Ms. Moran. Absolutely.

The President. Good job.

Ms. Moran. Thank you. Thank you very much, Mr. President.

The President. We've come to describe one way to approach health care. And it is to take care of the elderly and the poor and to encourage our fellow citizens to become directly involved in making health care decisions.

I urge the Congress to look at ways to strengthen health savings accounts by making the tax deductibility fair, by expanding the size of the contribution levels that people can make, by making sure that health savings accounts are as portable as they possibly can be so that the worker, if he or she chooses to change jobs, can take the full account—insurance plus the savings—with him or her to a new job.

The United States of America is constantly faced with different choices. And there are very important philosophical debates raging. And today you all heard one aspect of a very important part of a philosophical debate taking place, and that is how best to run the health care system. I've made my decision. I'm looking forward to continuing to have a consumer-driven system to be the heart of American health care.

And I appreciate you all sharing your thoughts, and thank you all for letting us come and visit with you.

NOTE: The President spoke at 11:01 a.m. at the Playhouse on the Green. In his remarks, he referred to Darrell Harvey, chair, Business Council of Fairfield County; and Mayor John M. Fabrizi of Bridgeport, CT.

Remarks on the War on Terror and a Question-and-Answer Session in Charlotte, North Carolina
April 6, 2006

The President. Thank you. Firoz, thanks a lot. So I said, "That's an interesting name." He said, "I've lived in seven countries," but he also said he's proud to be an American. And we're proud you're an American. Thank you very much for inviting me.

You know, I was just standing here, listening to Firoz; one of the great things about our country is that you can come, and you can enjoy the great blessings of liberty, and you can be equally American if you've been here for 1 generation or 10 generations. I thought it was neat that somebody who has been—you've been here 27 years though, right? Yes. Well, seven countries, 27 years here, introducing the President, though. I think it says a lot about the United States of America. Thanks for having me.

I'm looking forward to sharing with you what's on my mind. I look forward to hearing what's on yours as well. First thing is, Laura sends her best to the folks of Charlotte. She sends her best, Tony, to you and your bride. Thank you for having us here, to Central Piedmont. I appreciate your involvement in education. I married well; she's a really patient person too. [*Laughter*]

I traveled down here with Congressman Robin Hayes, the Congressman from this district. Congressman, thank you for being here; appreciate it.

I've known your mayor for a long time. He's a man of accomplishment. I know he was particularly proud to land the NASCAR Hall of Fame. Pretty big deal, you know? It's a pretty big deal. Thank you all for coming. I want to thank the others who serve on the city council who are here. The mayor was telling me a lot of the council members are here. I appreciate your service to your city.

I think one of the things I'd like to tell you about is why and how I made some decisions I made. My friends from Texas who, once they get over the shock that I'm actually the President—[*laughter*]—like to ask me what it's like to be President. And I guess the simple job description would be, it is a decisionmaking experience. And I make a lot of decisions. Some of them you see; some of them you don't see. Decisionmaking requires knowing who you are and what you believe. I've learned enough about Washington to know you can't make decisions unless you make them on principle. And once you make a decision based upon principle, you stand by what you decide.

In order to make good decisions, you've got to rely upon good people. People have got to feel comfortable about coming in the Oval Office and tell you what's on their mind. There's nothing worse than people walking in and say, "Well, I'm a little nervous around the guy; I think I'd better tell him what he thinks he needs to hear." You can't do the country justice, you can't make good decisions unless you've got a lot of good, competent people around you, and I do—Condoleezza Rice, Secretary of State; Don Rumsfeld; Vice President.

These are people who have seen good times, and they've seen tough times. But in all times, they're capable of walking in and telling me what's on their mind. That's what you need as the President. And then once you make up your mind, they say, "Yes, sir, Mr. President, I'll get it done."

The biggest decision I've had to make since I've been your President is putting kids in harm's way. It's a decision no President wants to make. It's a decision I wish I did not have to make. But I'd like to share with you why I made the decision I made.

First of all, war came to our shores on September the 11th, 2001. It was a war we did not ask for. It's a war we did not want, but it is a war that I intend to deal with so long as I'm your President. In order to deal with this war on terror, you've got to understand the nature of the enemy. And I'll share my thoughts with—about this enemy we face.

They're an enemy bound together by an ideology. These are not folks scattered around that are kind of angry and lash out at an opportune moment. These are people that are—believe something, and their beliefs are totalitarian in nature. They believe you should not be able to worship freely. They believe that young girls should not go to school. They've got a perverted sense of justice. They believe in the use of violence to achieve their objectives. Their stated objectives, their stated goals are to spread their totalitarian view throughout the Middle East. That's what they want to do.

They have made it abundantly clear that they believe folks who live in America are weak, that we don't have the will to compete with their philosophy. That's what they believe. I'm just telling you what they said. I think it's really important in a time of war for the President to take the words of the enemy very seriously. And I do.

They think that the use of violence will cause us to lose our nerve and retreat. And they have stated that they want safe haven from which to not only topple moderate governments in the Middle East but from which to launch attacks against the United States. Given that in mind, I'd like to share some of the lessons learned. One lesson is the nature of the enemy.

Another lesson is, is that we must defeat the enemy overseas so we don't have to face them here again. And that requires a strategy that is offensive in mind: press the enemy; find the enemy; bring the enemy to justice; never relent; never give them quarter; understand you cannot negotiate with these people; you can't rationalize with these people, that you must stay on the hunt and bring them to justice. This is precisely what we're doing.

One obviously immediate target is to dismantle Al Qaida. They hide in kind of the far reaches of the world. They plot and plan, however, from the far reaches of the world. They're good at communications. They're good at deception. They're good at propaganda. And they want to strike again. We have done a good job of dismantling the operating structure of Al Qaida—Khalid Sheikh Mohammed, Ramzi bin al-Shibh—a series of these folks that have become the operating element of Al Qaida. Obviously, Usama bin Laden and his sidekick Zawahiri is still at large. We understand that. But we're looking, and we're listening, and we're working with allies like President Musharraf of Pakistan, President Karzai of Afghanistan to bring this—to bring the head of Al Qaida to justice.

The second lesson learned is that unlike previous wars, these folks—this kind of terrorist network that is ideologically bound needs safe haven. They need a place to hide. They need a symbiotic relationship with governments that will enable them to plot, plan, and attack.

So early on in the conflict, I not only vowed that we would use our fierce determination to protect this country by staying on the offense, but that we would deny safe haven to these terrorists. And so I said, "If you harbor a terrorist, you're equally as guilty as the terrorist." And one thing that I think is really important for our citizens to understand is that when the President says something, he better mean what he says. In order to be effective, in order to maintain credibility, words have got to mean something. You just can't say things in the job I'm in and not mean what you say.

And I meant what I said. And so we said to the Taliban, "Get rid of the Al Qaida." They chose not to. I made my first decision to send our kids into harm's way and liberate Afghanistan. The decision to liberate Afghanistan was based first and foremost on the need to enforce the doctrine that I thought was necessary to protect the American people. One of the benefits of sending our kids into harm's way was that we liberated 25 million people from the clutches of one of the most barbaric regimes known to the history of man.

Laura and I went over to that fledgling democracy. We went to see President Karzai. It was a remarkable experience. It's hard to describe. You know, I'm not such a good poet. Let me put it to you this way: My spirits were lifted to see people committed to democracy, recognizing that democracy stands in stark contrast to the life these people had to live under the Taliban.

The task now is to continue to fight off the Taliban and Al Qaida that would continue to try to disrupt the march of the new democracy, help this country survive and thrive and grow, and help the Afghan citizens realize the dreams of men and women that they can live in a free and peaceful world. Remember, these folks have voted for a President and voted for a Parliament. I'm proud of the progress we're making there. It's an historic achievement for our country and for our troops. And it was a necessary achievement to enforce the doctrines that we said were necessary to protect our people.

Another lesson—this is an important lesson for the country. It's one that, kind of, sometimes can get obscured in the politics of Washington, but it's one that I'm confident when I tell you it's necessary for this country to adhere to. It's going to be necessary for me or whoever follows me. When we see a threat, we have got to take the threat seriously before it comes to hurt us.

You know, growing up in Midland, Texas, we all felt pretty secure as a kid, mainly because we thought oceans could protect us. Now in my case, we were really far away from oceans too, but nevertheless, it's—when you think about it, though, if you're a baby boomer like me, you think about what it was like growing up. We knew there was a nuclear threat. Of course, we had put forth an interesting sounding strategy called "mutually assured destruction," which provided an umbrella for security and safety.

But nevertheless, we never really felt anybody would invade us, did we? We never felt there would be another attack like Pearl Harbor on our lands. And yet September the 11th changed all that. More people died on September the 11th because of an attack by an enemy on our shore than died at Pearl Harbor. The biggest threat we face is when a terrorist network is able to acquire weapons even stronger than airplanes. If the terrorist network were ever to get weapons of mass destruction, one of their stated objectives, our country and the free world would face a serious threat.

I saw a threat in Iraq. Not only did I see a threat in Iraq; the previous administration saw a threat in Iraq. Not only did the previous—which, by the way, passed a resolution in the United States Congress that said, we ought to have a regime change in Iraq. Not only did the previous administration see a threat in Iraq; members of both political parties, in both Chambers, during my time as President saw a threat in Iraq. And the reason we saw threats is because the intelligence said that Saddam Hussein possesses weapons of mass destruction.

But it wasn't just U.S. intelligence that said that; there was—the worldwide intelligence network felt like he had weapons of mass destruction. After all, when I took the case to the United Nations Security Council, the Security Council voted 15 to nothing to say loud and clear, "Disclose, disarm, or face serious consequences." That's not what the United States said alone. This is what France and Great Britain, China, Russia, and members of the Security Council said, because the world felt like Saddam Hussein had weapons of mass destruction. And after 9/11, it was abundantly clear that a state sponsor of terror, which is what he had been declared by previous administrations, and the idea of weapons of mass destruction and the fact that he was at least, at the very minimum, a stated enemy of the United States of America posed a serious threat for our country.

My biggest job is to protect the American people. That became abundantly clear on September the 11th. It's important to pass good reform for education; it's important to support the community college system; it's important to work for, you know, a Medicare plan that meets the needs. My biggest job is to protect you—at least that's how I see the job. Much of my decision-making, by the way, is based upon what happened on September the 11th. It had an effect on me, just like it had an effect on the country. I've never forgotten that day. I've never forgotten the lessons learned, and so when we saw a threat, we got to take it seriously. Oceans could no longer protect us. The enemy was able to strike us and kill, and they were dangerous.

And before a President ever commits troops, you got to try diplomacy at all costs. I'm going to say to you what I said before: Putting those kids in harm's way is a tough, difficult decision. And nobody should ever want to do it, because I understand fully the consequences of the decision. And so as I told you, I went to the diplomatic route. I was hoping that when the world spoke with that one voice at the United Nations Security Council, Saddam Hussein would see the reason of the free world. But he didn't.

I felt all along the decision was his to make. He said—the world said, "Disclose, disarm." In the meantime, I want you to remember, he was deceiving inspectors. It's a logical question to ask: Why would somebody want to deceive inspectors? I also told you earlier that when America speaks, we got to mean what we said. I meant what we said when we embraced that resolution that said, "Disclose, disarm, or face serious consequences." Words mean something in this world, if you're trying to protect the American people.

I fully understand that the intelligence was wrong, and I'm just as disappointed as everybody else is. But what wasn't wrong was Saddam Hussein had invaded a country. He had used weapons of mass destruction. He had the capability of making weapons of mass destruction. He was firing at our pilots. He was a state sponsor of terror. Removing Saddam Hussein was the right thing for world peace and the security of our country.

Iraq is now the central front on the war on terror. The war on terror is broader than Iraq, but Iraq is the key battlefield right now. And the enemy has made it so.

The advance of democracy frightens the totalitarians that oppose us. Mr. Zarqawi, who is there in Iraq, is Al Qaida. He's

not Iraqi, by the way. He is there representing the Al Qaida network, trying to stop the advance of democracy. It's an interesting question, isn't it. Why would somebody want to stop democracy? Like, what's wrong with democracy; Mister, why are you afraid of it? Are you threatened by the fact that people get to speak and you don't get to dictate? Are you threatened by the fact that people should be able to worship the Almighty freely? What about democracy that bothers—I think it's a legitimate question we all ought to be asking.

But nevertheless, he's tough, and he's mean, and he'll kill innocent people in order to shake our will. They have stated, clearly stated—they being Al Qaida—that it's just a matter of time for the United States to lose its nerve. They recognize they cannot beat us on the battlefield; they cannot militarily defeat the United States of America. But they can affect our conscience. And I can understand why. Nobody likes to see violence on the TV screens. Nobody wants to see little children blown up when a U.S. soldier is trying to give them candy. Nobody likes to see innocent women die at the hands of suicide bombers. It breaks our heart.

The United States of America is an incredibly compassionate nation. We value human life, whether it be here at home or whether it be abroad. It's one of the really noble features of our country, I think. Nobody likes to see that, and the enemy understands that, however. They know that if we lose our nerve and retreat from Iraq, they win.

We've got a strategy for victory in Iraq. It's important for you to know that victory will be achieved with a democracy that can sustain itself, a country that will be able to defend itself from those who will try to defeat democracy at home, a country that will be an ally in the war on terror, and a country that will deny Al Qaida and the enemies that face America the safe haven they want. Those are the four categories for victory. And they're clear, and our command structure and our diplomats in Iraq understand the definition of victory.

And we're moving that way. We're moving that way. We've got a plan to help rebuild Iraq. You know, when we first went in there—by the way, every war plan or every plan is fine, until it meets the enemy. But you've got to adjust. You've got to be able to say on the ground, "Well, this is working; this isn't working." The enemy is not a—they think differently; they make different decisions; they come up with different tactics to try to defeat us. And it's very important for us—for me to say to our commanders and our diplomats, "Devise that strategy on the ground; keep adjusting, so that we achieve the victory that we want."

So when we first got into Iraq, we went with big rebuilding projects. You know, "We're going to help them do this and help them do that," big electricity projects. And the enemy blew them up. And so what we've done now is we've gone to a more rational strategy to provide money for local folks, including our military, to help smaller projects, but projects that are able to connect with the people on the ground. You know, jobs helps a lot if you're trying to say democracy is worth it.

Second aspect of our plan was to promote democracy. And I know 4 months in the way these news cycles work seems like a decade; at least it does to me at times, you know? [*Laughter*] Four months ago, 12 million people went to the polls. It was an amazing event, wasn't it, I mean, really think about it. If you can project back to the amazement, surprise, exhilaration that happened when, given a chance to vote for the third time in one year, the Iraqi people having had suffered under the tyranny of Saddam Hussein said, "I want to be free. That's what we want to be." That's what they said. Twelve million people, in the face of incredible threats and potential suicide bombers—and ugly words

coming out of those who fear democracy—said, "Give me a chance." It was an amazing experience. It was a—in my judgment, a moment that is historic.

Part of the task now is to say to the Iraqis' leaders, "The people said something, now you need to get—you need to act. You need to get a unity government together." And that's what we're watching right now. It takes awhile for people to overcome the effects of tyranny, and there's a lot of politics happening in Iraq. It's a little different from what used to be the place. It's a little different from other countries in that part of the world where one person makes a decision, and everybody kind of either likes it or doesn't like it, but you keep your mouth shut if you don't like it.

Here you're watching people kind of edging for responsibility and working it, and we're very much involved. I know you know Condi went over there the other day, and her message was, let's get moving. The people want there to be a unity government. The people want there to be a democracy, and it requires leadership, for people to stand up and take the lead. And so we're working with them to get this unit government up and running.

And then there's the security side. You can't have a democracy unless the people are confident in the capacity of the state to protect them from those who want to stop the advance of democracy. The enemy for awhile tried to shake our nerve. They can't shake my nerve. They just can't shake it. So long as I think I'm doing the right thing and so long as we can win, I'm going to leave our kids there, because it's necessary for the security of this country. If I didn't think that we could win, I'd pull them out. You just got to know that. I cannot sit with the mothers and fathers of our troops in harm's way and not feel like victory is necessary and victory will be achieved.

Part of my decisionmaking process about whether they're there is based upon whether or not the goal is necessary and attainable. It's necessary to protect this country—I'm going to talk about it a little later—and it is attainable. It's attainable because the Iraqis on the political side have said, "You bet. Give us a chance." They wrote a Constitution; they ratified the Constitution. Twelve million went to the polls. That's a high voter turnout, by the way. On the security side, our goal, our mission is to let the Iraqis take the fight. And as I—I've always been saying, "They stand up; we stand down." That means we train the Iraqis to take the fight to those who want to disrupt their country.

And we're making good progress on the military side. By the way, we had to change our tactics. When we first got there, we said, why don't we train us an army that will be able to protect from an outside threat. It turned out there wasn't much of an outside threat compared to the inside threat. And so now the training mission has adapted to the tactics of the enemy on the ground. We're embedding our guys with the Iraqi Army. They're becoming more efficient. There's over 200,000 trained, and we're constantly monitoring the quality of effort. And as the quality of the forces improves, they take over more territory. The idea is to have the Iraqi face in front, making the—helping the folks get the confidence in their Government.

We lagged in police training. And so General Casey, as he—who is our general on the ground there, told me, he said, "You know, this is going to be the year of training the police so they can bring confidence to people."

The enemy shifted its tactics, as you know, and has tried to create a civil war. And they blew up the—one of the holiest sites in Samarra, trying to get the Sunnis to get after the Shi'a, and vice versa. This has been an objective for awhile. First it was go after coalition troops. There is still danger for our troops, don't get me wrong.

But they really tried to incite a civil war. And what was interesting to watch is to watch the reaction for the—by the Government. The Government, including many of the religious leaders, stood up and said, "No, we don't want to go there; we're not interested in a civil war."

The Iraqi troops did a good job of getting between some mosques and crowds, and they got in between competing elements and stood their ground. And as I put it awhile ago, they said—the Iraqi people looked into the abyss and didn't like what they saw. And it's still troublesome, of course. There's still sectarian violence. You can't have a free state if you've got militia taking the law into their own hands.

Now, remember, this is a society adjusting to being free after a tyranny. And Saddam Hussein's tactics to keep the country in check was to pit one group of people against another and say, "I'm the only stabilizing force for you." He was brutal on Shi'a; he destroyed, with chemical weapons, many Kurds; and he was tough on Sunnis too. But he created a kind of—this sense of rivalry.

And so you can understand why there's revenge after years of this kind of tension he created. Our job and the job of rational Iraqi leaders is to prevent these sectarian reprisal attacks from going on. And it's tough work, but I want you to know, we understand the problem. More importantly, General Casey understands the problem.

We're adjusting our tactics to be able to help these Iraqis secure their country so that democracy can flourish. They want democracy. That's what they've said. The troops, time and time again, have shown that they're better trained than before. And we've got more work to do on that, I readily concede. There's a lot of debate and a lot of questions about what's happening, I understand that.

Again, I repeat to you, I know what violence does to people. First of all, I'm confident—people are saying, "I wonder if these people can ever get their act together and self-govern?" The answer is, I'm confident they can if we don't lose our nerve.

One of the decision—principles—a principle on which I made decisions is this: I believe that freedom is universal. America was founded on the natural rights of men and women, which speaks to the universality of freedom. And if you believe in the universality of freedom, then you have confidence that if given a chance, people will seize that opportunity.

No question the Iraqis need help after living under the thumb of a tyrant. But freedom is embedded, I believe, in the souls of men and women all over the Earth. You know, you don't demand freedom just—more than Methodists demand freedom, let me put it to you that way. I'm a Methodist. [*Laughter*] There's an interesting debate: Is it imposing one's values to encourage others to live in freedom? I argue the answer to that question is, absolutely not, if you believe in the universality of freedom.

And so while thrilled to see the vote, I was—I wasn't shocked. People want to be free. I know you're thinking about, "Well, when's he going to get our troops out of there?" There's a debate going on in Washington, DC, which it should, and it's an important debate about our troop levels. Here's my answer to you: I'm not going to make decisions based upon polls and focus groups; I'm going to make my decisions based upon the recommendations of our generals on the ground. They're the ones who decide how to achieve the victory I just described. They're the ones who give me the information.

I remember coming up in the Vietnam war, and it seemed like that there was a—during the Vietnam war, there was a lot of politicization of the military decisions. That's not going to be the case under my administration. They say, "Well, does George Casey tell you the truth?" You bet he tells me the truth. When I talk to him, which I do quite frequently, I've got all the confidence in the world in this fine

general. He's a smart guy; he's on the ground; he's making incredible sacrifices for our country. And he—if he says he needs more troops, he'll get them, and if he says he can live with fewer troops because the Iraqis are prepared to take the fight, that's the way it's going to be.

There are some in Washington, DC, and around the country who are good folks, legitimate, decent folks, saying, "Pull the troops out." That would be a huge mistake. It would be a huge—[*applause*]—hold on a second—it would be a huge mistake for these reasons: The enemy has said that they want us to leave Iraq in order to be able to regroup and attack us. If the American people—the American Government, not the people—were to leave prematurely, before victory is achieved, it would embolden the enemy.

Now, I recognize some don't see the enemy like I do. There's kind of a different view of the enemy. That's a good thing about America; people can have different points of view, you know. And people should be allowed to express them, which is great.

I see an enemy that is totalitarian in nature, that's clearly stated they want to attack us again, and they want safe haven from which to do so. That's why they're trying to stop democracy in Iraq. If we were to pull out our troops early, it would send a terrible signal to the Iraqis. Twelve million people said, "I want to be free." And they need our help. We're helping the Iraqis achieve freedom. They watch these deals. They listen carefully to the debate in America. They need to watch, by the way; they need to watch this debate, which is good. It's what free societies do; they debate. But they're also listening very carefully about whether or not this country has got the will necessary to achieve the objective.

Thirdly, if we left before the mission was complete, what would it say to our troops and the families, particularly those who have lost a loved one? I spend—let me say this about our military: The Volunteer Army is a necessary part of our society. We need to maintain the Volunteer Army. It is a really—we've got a magnificent group of men and women who serve our country. Do you realize most people who served, are serving today, volunteered after 9/11? They saw the stakes, and they said, "I want to join the United States military." The retention rate is high, which means we've got people serving in uniform who not only volunteered and saw the stakes but have been involved in this conflict and said, "I'd like to stay in the military."

It is a—the military is a vital part of securing this country in the war on terror. Now, if you don't think we're at war, then it probably doesn't matter that much. I not only think we're at war; I know we're at war. And it's going to require diligence and strength and a really—and a military that's well-paid, well-housed, well-trained, where morale is high. And pulling out before the mission is complete would send a terrible signal to the United States military.

I welcome the debate, but I just want people here to know, we're going to complete the mission. We'll achieve victory. And I want to say this to the Iraqi people: We want to help you achieve your dreams. And the United States of America will not be intimidated by thugs and assassins.

I got one more thing to say, then I— [*applause*]—I got one more thing to say. I know I'm getting a little windy. I want to talk to people about why it's important for us to succeed in Iraq, and Afghanistan, for that matter. I told you there's a short-term reason: Deny safe haven and help get allies in the war on terror to prevent this totalitarian movement from gaining a stronghold in places from which they can come hit us.

There's a longer term reason as well, and that is, you defeat an ideology of darkness with an ideology of hope and light. And freedom and liberty are part of an ideology of light. Our foreign policy in the past has been one that said, well, if the waters look calm in parts of the world, even though there may not be freedom, that's okay. The problem with that foreign policy is, below the surface there was resentment and anger and despair which provided a fertile ground for a totalitarian group of folks to spread their poisonous philosophy and recruit.

The way to defeat this notion of—their notion of society is one that is open, that is democratic, that is based upon liberty. This doesn't have to be an American-style democracy. It won't be. Democracy has got to reflect the tradition and the history of the countries in which it takes hold. I understand that. And nobody in the Middle East should think that when the President talks about liberty and democracy, he's saying you got to look just like America or act like America. Nobody is saying that.

I am saying, though, trust your people, give them a chance to participate in society. I believe a society is a whole society in which women are free and are given equal rights. I believe there's a whole society in which young girls are given a chance to go to school and become educated. I believe it's a whole society when government actually responds to people, not dictates to people. That's what I believe. And I believe that it's the best way in the long run to defeat an ideology that feels the opposite way. And we've seen it happen in our history before. It's happened in some of your lifetimes.

One of the ways I like to describe what I'm trying to tell you is about my relationship with Prime Minister Koizumi of Japan. I say this all the time, as the press corps will tell you traveling with me—"When is he ever going to quit saying that?" Well, it's the best example I can give you about what I'm trying to describe is happening today during these historic times. My dad fought the Japanese as an 18-year-old kid— or 19—he went in at 18, I guess. But he was in combat. Many of your relatives fought the Japanese. It's hard to think back and kind of remember the bitterness that we had toward the Japanese. They attacked the United States of America and killed a lot of folks. And we want to war with them, and a lot of people died, and it was a bloody war.

After the war—and by the way, it ended with an old doctrine of warfare, which is, destroy as many innocent people as you can to get the guilty to surrender. That's changed, by the way, with the precision nature of our military and the way we're structured. And the way our troops think is we now target the guilty and spare the innocent. That's another subject if you got a question. But anyway, today, my friend in keeping the peace is Prime Minister of Japan.

Amazing, isn't it? Maybe you take it for granted. I don't. I think it's one of the really interesting parts of—one of the interesting stories of history, that 60 years after we fought the Japanese, I can tell you that I work with Prime Minister Koizumi on a variety of issues. It's amazing, I think. I know 60 seems like a long time. If I were six or seven, it would seem like a long time. At 59, it seems like a long time. [*Laughter*] Maybe when I'm 60, it will seem like a short time.

Anyway, so what happened? What was it that caused something to change, an enemy to become an ally? I believe it's because the Japanese adopted a Japanese-style democracy. And I appreciate the fact that one of my predecessors, Harry S. Truman, had the foresight to see the capacity of freedom, the universal right of people to change the world, to make it so that, eventually, an American President would be able to say, we're working together to keep the peace. They're no longer an enemy; they're a friend. Democracies don't war.

Europe is whole and free and at peace for a reason. We lost thousands of troops on the continent of Africa—on the continent of Europe since World War I. Thousands and thousands of young men and women lost their lives during that war. And today, there's peace. And the reason why is because democracies don't war with each other.

I believe that one day an American President will be talking about the world in which he is making decisions or she is making decisions, and they'll look back and say, "Thank goodness a generation of Americans understood the universality of liberty and the fact that freedom can change troubled parts in the world into peaceful parts of the world."

Is it worth it in Iraq? You bet it is. It's worth it to protect ourselves in the short run, but it's necessary and worth it to lay the foundation of peace for generations to come. And that's what's on my mind these days.

I'll be glad to answer questions. Yes, ma'am.

Federal Budget/National Economy

Q. [*Inaudible*]

The President. Good.

Q. [*Inaudible*]

The President. Good. You're welcome here. [*Laughter*] This is not a political convention. [*Laughter*]

Q. But more importantly, I'm an American, and my husband and I are proud parents of four children and five grandchildren. And I care very deeply, as you, about our future as a country and our place in the world.

The President. Good.

Q. I agree with you completely, that when war came to our borders, that we needed to defend our country against Al Qaida and was completely with you there. I agree that Saddam Hussein is a tyrant, as many are across the world. But I am more concerned about the deficit that we are incurring in this country and the effect that that will have on my children and grandchildren and our present. My colleagues here on the city council and I were just talking about how we can't afford after-school enrichment opportunities for the children of Charlotte because of cutbacks in the community development block grant. And I just——

The President. That's a great question. Thank you.

Q. ——think we need to secure our borders, to protect our ports, and to invest in the people of Charlotte and this country——

The President. Good.

Q. ——for a real national——

The President. I got your question, thank you. It's a good question. She basically—no seriously, it's a legitimate question. What are you doing about the deficit, you know? There are two types of deficits that I want to describe to you. One is the current account deficit. It's the deficit that we're on plan to cut in half by 2009. There's an interesting debate in Washington about how do you deal with a current account deficit.

By the way, we—and the area where we're able to affect the deficit the most is through some of the programs you described called discretionary spending. There's also discretionary sending and mandatory spending. Mandatory spending is a formula-driven spending that happens based upon conditions, not based upon, necessarily, legislation, although you can change mandatory spending through formula adjustment. Mandatory spending in Social Security, mandatory spending Medicare, mandatory spending Medicaid, programs like that; farm program is mandatory spending. Discretionary spending is some of the education programs you described. Discretionary spending is also military spending.

We—I'm going to put this in a little larger context. I promise to answer your question. We were confronted with a series of hurdles to economic growth that we had to deal with in Washington. We had a stock market correction, a quite significant stock market correction, and we had a recession early in '01. And then the enemy attacked us, which hurt our economy. Obviously, my decision to go to war—people don't—you

know, war is an unsettling thing. I fully understand that. Sometimes it's not conducive to risking capital during a time of war. We had a major natural disaster. All of this affected our economy.

I made the decision to cut taxes, as you know. It was a decision based upon the principle that if people had more money in their pocket, they're likely to spend it, save it, or invest it. And therefore, I felt like the best way to address these economic hurdles was to stimulate our economy through progrowth economic policies, starting with a tax cut—and a tax cut, by the way, for everybody. Everybody who paid taxes should get a cut. It's a tax cut that helped our small businesses. I firmly believe by cutting taxes on dividends and capital gains, it stimulated investment.

And our strategy has, I think, been proven by the numbers. We're growing at 3.4 percent—3.5 percent last year. The national unemployment rate is at 4.8 percent—5 million jobs in 2½ years. I mean, I could go on—housing is up. There's a lot of positive economic news. And no question, however, we've been running a deficit.

One reason we're running a deficit is because I'm going to make sure our troops have what it takes to do their job. In the harm's way—when they're in harm's way, you've got to be able to say to their families that we're going to give them all they got. You know, we want to help them.

One of the interesting things about—for this war is that we're saving a lot of lives through a health care system that is phenomenal. And we're pulling these kids off the battlefield and sending them to Walter Reed or Bethesda as quickly as possible, sparing no expense to save lives. But no question, it's been costly.

Katrina—we're up to $100 billion on Katrina. I don't know if you've been over there. You know, it just breaks your heart to see the devastation done in the gulf coast of Mississippi and inside New Orleans. It's a gut-wrenching experience to see the devastation that went on, and the Federal Government has made a strong commitment to provide that money.

That's background for—no question, we have a current account deficit. I have submitted a budget that says we can cut it in half by 2009. Now, there is a debate in Washington. Some of them are saying, "Raise the taxes in order to balance the budget." In all due respect, that's not the way Washington works. Washington will raise the taxes and figure out new ways to spend the money. So my attitude is, let's leave the progrowth economic policies in place, which by the way, yielded a $100 billion-plus more money than anticipated last year, because a growing economy yields more tax revenues, and be tough on the spending.

And I understand it creates some of the conditions you said, and I appreciate you bringing those to my attention. We're now in another budget discussion in Washington. And I submitted another tough budget. Now, people said, "Why don't you veto the budgets?" I'd like to explain that to you. So we sit down from the executive branch and negotiate—we come up with a budget that we think is necessary to meet goals. The goal is to cut the current account deficit in half by 2009, and then we negotiate with the Congress. We say, "Here's the top line; here's what we want you to meet in order to meet the goals we think are necessary."

Thus far, they've hit the top line that we've suggested. Last year, as the councilwoman mentioned, the mayor pro tem mentioned, that there are some cutbacks in CDBG money. It's all aimed at trying to get this deficit under control. And the—and so Congress said last year, you're right. Here's the top line; we made it.

And so the size of the pie was what we thought was necessary to achieve an objective. And so therefore, I'm confronted with a choice. I may not like the slices of the pie, but I like the size. And if I vetoed bills because of the slices, but it

met the size, what would happen during the next budget negotiations? They'd say, "Well, wait a minute; we hit your number; you vetoed the bills. How can we trust you in good faith?"

The job of the President is to set a goal, which is to reduce that deficit in half by 2009. And if people want me to be able to deal with slices of the pie, just give me the line-item veto. And I think that will help make sure that—[*applause*]—let me talk about another thing. I'm sorry—this is a long answer to a very important question. I'm sorry I'm blowing on too much here, but the real deficit—I'll get you in a minute—the real deficit—another real deficit is the deficit inherent in Social Security and Medicare.

There is a massive amount of unfunded liability inherent in those two very important programs. And the reason why is, is that baby boomers like me are getting ready to retire. And there's a lot of us, and we're living longer than the program initially anticipated, and we've been promised greater benefits, and fewer people per retiree paying into the system. And the system is going to go broke, and a lot of people are watching whether or not the United States has the will to address this problem, because if we don't, future Presidents and future Congresses are going to have to raise taxes significantly, reduce benefits significantly, or reduce other programs significantly. This is a significant problem facing a future generation of Americans.

As you know, I took the problem on last year. I might have been the only guy in Washington taking the problem on last year. [*Laughter*] My theory was, go out and explain to the American people we got a problem. And the people now understand we got a problem, and the fundamental question is, how do you translate that to a program that Congress will act on?

And so my second strategy has been—remember, we're always adapting our tactics—was to put together a bipartisan group, which we're in the process of doing, of members from both political parties, from both Chambers, to come up with common ground so we can say to the American people, here is a bipartisan approach to these very serious, unfunded liabilities that face future generations of Americans. It's a short-term account. It's very important, no question, Madam Councilperson. The long-term issue is equally, if not greater of importance, which is the unfunded liabilities inherent in Social Security and Medicare. I'm going to continue to take on the issue. It's a big issue, and I'm confident we can get it solved.

Okay. Yes, sir.

Freedom of Religion

Q. [*Inaudible*]—I want to thank you for coming back to Charlotte again. We certainly enjoyed your wife here a few weeks ago. Okay, thank you. But I just wanted not to ask a question but just to offer you a message of encouragement. I know many men and women in this room and around our region, both Democrat and Republican, continue to pray for wisdom and encouragement for you and strength during these times. So we just want to continue to encourage you.

The President. Thank you. Appreciate you.

I'd like to say one thing about religion—religion and politics, if you don't mind. The United States of America must never lose sight of this beautiful principle: You can worship or not worship, and you're equally American. You're equally American if you're a Christian, Jew, or Muslim, atheist, agnostic. We must never lose sight of that. That's what distinguishes us from the Taliban.

Having said that, I cannot thank you all enough for the prayers. It means a lot to me and Laura. One of the most amazing aspects of the Presidency is to meet total strangers, and they say, "I pray for you." They don't say, "I need a road or a bridge." [*Laughter*] The mayor might have said

that—[*laughter*]—or a museum. They say, "I pray for you, Mr. President." Thank you. Let's see. Yes, ma'am.

The Presidency

Q. A lot of people were betting that I wouldn't get a chance to ask you questions.

The President. Why is that?

Q. Just because there would be, you know, you might not choose me. [*Laughter*] Thank you very much.

The President. Don't bet against yourself is lesson one.

Q. Right. And I wanted to say to you, Mr. President, that on the war on terror, Social Security, the tax cuts, Dubai Ports, immigration, you have shown immense political courage. And I really think that you will be vindicated on all of those positions, as Ronald Reagan was, for example. And also, I wanted to know what else would it take for me to get my picture taken with you? [*Laughter*]

The President. My attitude is, about this job, is just do my job. Say what you think is right. There's an interesting sense about whether this poll or that poll—I'm just going to tell you something about the Presidency. You cannot make decisions based upon polls. [*Applause*] You've got to stand—I'm not trying to elicit applause here; I'm just trying to share with you what it's like, as best I can, to be your President, at least why I do what I do.

And I am—I'm the kind of fellow that—it's like the Social Security issue. You know, they say, "Well, you shouldn't have brought it up," you know. I can't live with myself if I see a problem and not willing to address it. I want, after 8 years, to be able to walk out of that office and say, I did what I thought was right.

Now, you talk—an interesting thing is, I'm reading a lot of history these days, and it's—I've got some books to recommend, if you like them, you know. [*Laughter*] In contrary to what some of them think back there, it's not big print and pictures, either.

[*Laughter*] Yes. Yes, I got you; thank you. [*Laughter*]

I read three books on George Washington. I think it's really interesting, isn't it? Historians are still analyzing the first President of the United States. And history is—sometimes history doesn't record the immediate effects of a Presidency. And you just do what you think is right, and you don't have to—you can't worry about it, you know. If they're still writing about Washington, you know, who knows how long I will be gone before they're writing about me in a way where there's enough time between the day—the Presidency and an objective look of what takes place.

You heard me quoting Harry Truman. I bet you when Harry Truman made the decision to help the Japanese become a democracy, there was some editorialization basically saying, how dare you work with an enemy. You know, I bet there was some of that. I bet there was a lot of skepticism, and I can understand that, you know. I can understand why people are skeptical about whether or not a democracy can take hold in a part of the world like the Middle East. My only point to you, it's necessary for the peace. It has worked in the past, and it's necessary. And we cannot lose confidence in these universal values.

Let's see here. Yes. Yes. No, wait a minute. You're second. Excuse me. [*Laughter*] I beg your pardon.

Voluntarism

Q. [Inaudible]

The President. Young people involved—thank you for that. That's a good question. She asked, what can young people do to get involved? First of all, the fact that you asked the question is an encouraging sign.

I like to tell people that the true strength of America is the hearts and souls of our people. You know, our military might is strong; our wallets are fatter than anybody else's in the world, on an individual—per capita basis. But the true strength of our country is the fact that neighbors love neighbors.

De Tocqueville saw this when he came to the United States in 1830s. He was a traveler, and he came and said, "I'm coming to the land of the rugged individualist." And he discovered something interesting way back in 1832, I think it was, when he wrote his book. He discovered that Americans have a penchant, the desire to form voluntary associations to help a neighbor. And it's that spirit of helping a neighbor that Presidents should foster and encourage because it really is the strength of the United States of America.

When you really think about the community of Charlotte, in spite of the fact that the Federal Government has got influence or the city council has got influence, there are thousands of your fellow citizens teaching a child to read. And it doesn't require one law. There are people feeding the hungry. I bet you've got some of the great food pantry programs in the United States of America here. There are people providing shelter for the homeless. There are thousands of acts of kindness. The Boy Scout troops are active, I bet—the Girl Scouts. These are—the Little League programs, you know, the basketball programs. They—there's thousands of acts of kindness taking place on a daily basis.

To answer your question, involvement can mean a lot of things. It can mean serving in the military; it can mean teaching a child to read; it can mean getting your classmates to volunteer to help feed the hungry. There's thousands of ways to contribute, and the fact that we have millions of Americans doing that is really a remarkable aspect of our country.

One of the principles that has guided me is, to whom much is given, much is required. That's why I'm very proud of our Nation's effort to help lead the effort to solve the HIV/AIDS issue, particularly on the continent of Africa. We're an abundant nation. We're a blessed people in many ways, and yet there's a pandemic raging

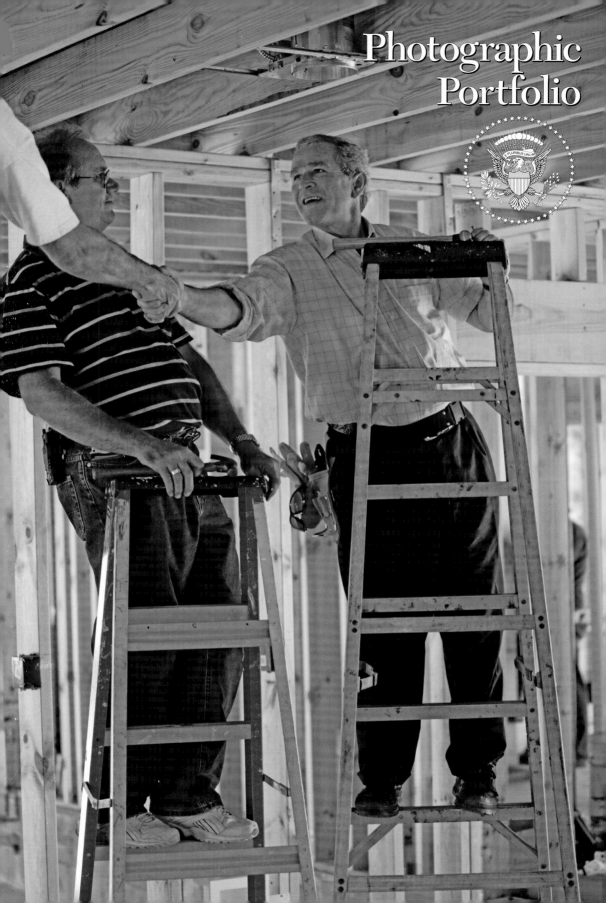

Overleaf: Shaking hands with people helping to rebuild a home destroyed by Hurricane Katrina in Gautier, MS, March 8.

Above left: Delivering remarks on gulf coast reconstruction in Bay St. Louis, MS, Jan. 12.

Left: Delivering the State of the Union Address in the House Chambers of the U.S. Capitol, Jan. 31.

Above: Shaking hands with musician and activist Bono during the National Prayer Breakfast at the Hilton Washington Hotel, Feb. 2.

Right: Greeting newly confirmed U.S. Supreme Court Justice Samuel A. Alito, Jr., at the State of the Union Address in the House Chambers of the U.S. Capitol, Jan. 31.

Above: Walking with President Pervez Musharraf of Pakistan at the Aiwan-e-Sadr in Islamabad, Pakistan, March 4.

Left: Walking with Prime Minister Nuri al-Maliki of Iraq at the U.S. Embassy in Baghdad, Iraq, June 13.

Above right: Greeting President Abdul Kalam and Prime Minister Manmohan Singh of India upon arrival at the Presidential residence in New Delhi, India, March 2.

Right: Cutting the ribbon with President Hamid Zarzai of Afghanistan at a dedication ceremony for the U.S. Embassy in Kabul, Afghanistan, March 1.

Left: Greeting Greece Athena High School senior Jason McElwain and his mother, Debbie, upon arriving in Rochester, NY, March 14.

Below left: Visiting the Chicago Board of Trade in Chicago, IL, Jan. 6.

Right: Attending a cricket clinic with Pakistani youth in the Raphel Memorial Gardens on the grounds of the U.S. Embassy in Islamabad, Pakistan, March 4.

Below: Honoring the 2005 NCAA football champion University of Texas at Austin Longhorns on the South Lawn, Feb. 14.

Overleaf: Attending the annual Peace Officers' Memorial Service at the U. S. Capitol, May 15.

across the continent of Africa that's literally having the potential effect of wiping out a generation of people. And the stories are heartbreaking, and they're devastating to a civilization in many places. And yet our Nation has made the commitment to spend $15 billion over a 5-year period of time to help provide antiretroviral drugs, to help provide prevention, to help the orphans who've been left alone. The program is being administered by the U.S. Government.

And one aspect—there's a Global Fund as well. Another aspect—but the people on the ground, the foot soldiers, many are from the faith community, who have said, "I want to help. What can I do to help a neighbor?" The neighbor could be right around the corner, or the neighbor could be on the continent of Africa, in this case. We are a generous, compassionate people, and it's our true strength.

Let's see here. Yes, sir. Yes, please.

Support for the President

Q. Yes, sir. Actually, I'm bringing a statement to you for a friend, Sahara Bozanis, a young Iraqi woman who just came to America last year. She grew up under Saddam, and she actually worked for the U.S. forces during the war as an interpreter. I talked to her this week. She wanted to make sure that she knew—that you knew that her family that's still there is grateful, that she thinks that even though there may be terrorists still going on, that they are safer now than they ever were before. And her goal is to one day meet you to thank you in person because you have changed their lives. Even though we might not see that in the press, their lives are much better today than they were 3, 4 years ago.

The President. Thank you, sir.

Q. So she wanted to thank you.

The President. Say, wait a minute, I— I will keep my word here. Oh, there you are. Yes, sorry. You thought I forgot, didn't you? I beg your pardon; I did forget.

[*Laughter*] You know how guys near 60, they begin to kind of—[*laughter*].

International Support for the War on Terror

Q. [*Inaudible*]

The President. A civics teacher, great, thank you. Thank you for teaching.

Q. [*Inaudible*]

The President. No, I appreciate—that's a very good question. First of all, thank you for teaching. By the way—as you grow up, the lady behind you—the girl behind you—as you grow up, one way to contribute is to teach, by the way.

The global war on terror requires a global response, and inherent in this woman's question was, what are you doing to make sure that others join the United States, recognizing that we cannot do this alone? And I appreciate the question a lot.

There is a lot of cooperation going on now. One of the great myths is that the United States is alone in the war on terror. Take, for example, Afghanistan. No question, we've got Special Forces there. No question, we've got a viable element of our military there to fight off Al Qaida or Taliban as they either sneak across the border or come from different Provinces to try to do harm, but NATO is very actively involved there as well.

The NATO presence is in the lead in many of the Provinces. There's what's called Provincial Reconstruction Teams. It's kind of along the lines that I talked about earlier, about localizing the reconstruction efforts on a Provincial basis. This is what's happening in Afghanistan, and there's reconstruction—Provincial Reconstruction Teams run by different countries. Germany has got a presence there. France has had— has presence in Afghanistan. In other words, there is a global network there.

In Iraq, as well, there's a lot of coalition forces, some small, some large. Great Britain, of course, is large. The Japanese had a thousand troops there. It's an amazing commitment by Prime Minister Koizumi when you think about the aftermath of World War II. The South Koreans have got a significant force there. The Poles have had a significant force there. There's a big international presence there. Many of the—and the NATO mission, by the way, is present in Iraq, as well, all aimed at helping train. They're very much involved in the training mission to give the Iraqi troops the skills necessary to do their jobs.

The global war on terror is fought on more fronts than just the military front. For example, one of the really important parts of this war on terror is to share intelligence, is to be able to say, "If you hear somebody or see somebody coming that you tell a counterpart in another agency—another intelligence service." And so we spend a lot of time—John Negroponte, for example, or Porter Goss, spends a lot of time with their counterparts constantly figuring out how best to share information.

Again, in old war, people could measure movement by the enemy from—by watching ships and tanks move across plains. Now we're dealing with people that are kind of moving around stealthily. And we've got to be in a position where we can share that intelligence.

The third aspect of the global war on terror is to cut off their money. It turns out, terrorists need money—just like the Federal Government spends money. And it's a—so we're—our Secretary of Treasury, John Snow, and others are constantly working to make sure that *hawalas*, for example, which are kind of a money transmitting entity, doesn't—includes terrorist financing. Or we worked with the Saudi Government to make it clear that the financing of terrorist activities are not in our interest, obviously, or their interest.

By the way, the Saudi Government has been very active in the war on terror. They've got a list of Al Qaida potential killers, and they're bringing them to justice. Pakistan has been a strong ally in the war on terror. You might remember that President Musharraf was one of three coun-

tries—or that Pakistan under President Musharraf was one of three countries that had recognized the Taliban. And so needless to say, after September the 11th, he was—made a choice. Colin Powell did a wonderful job of talking to President Musharraf in a very respectful and dignified way and basically said, "Who are you with?" And he has been an ally in the war on terror.

The interesting thing about President Musharraf is, the enemy has tried to kill him four times. There have been four assassination attempts on him by Al Qaida, which causes him to be a strong ally in the war on terror. [*Laughter*]

And so it's a great question. I'm constantly working to remind people about the stakes. I knew one of the real dangers after 9/11 was that people would tend to forget the lessons learned. And that's normal. And frankly, if you're the President of the United States, you want normalcy. You want people to go back to their life as quickly as possible.

And so it's—my job is to travel the country, like I'm doing a lot of, and saying, "Here are the stakes. Go ahead and live your life and risk capital and raise your families. Let us worry about it." And it's such a different kind of war that we're constantly having to work with our allies, as well, to remind them about the stakes.

The enemy has reminded them about the stakes. Remember that ours isn't the only country that's been attacked. There were attacks in Madrid; there were attacks in London, attacks in Egypt; there's been a series of attacks around the world. Jordan—they go up—Al Qaida goes in and blows up a wedding. These are coldblooded killers, now. These are people that will stop at nothing to achieve their objectives.

And so—no, that's a great question. And the coalition is—it's been a large coalition, and we're constantly working it. Some countries feel comfortable about helping in Afghanistan; some—that same country may not feel comfortable about Iraq. But either way, we're talking about this war on terror on a regular basis.

Yes. Sir.

Progress in Iraq/Lessons Learned in the War on Terror

Q. [*Inaudible*]

The President. Okay, yes. Squeaky wheel? Okay, hold on. [*Laughter*] It'll work.

Q. Mr. President, my name is——

The President. I went with the tall guy first. [*Laughter*]

Q. It's an honor to stand here in front of you and ask you this question. You talked a little bit about your decisionmaking ability, and you've been steadfast as it relates to the global war on terror, which I think is commendable. Another thing I look for in a leader is their ability to look in hindsight, and their ability to be—a degree of humility, and maybe wondering what could have been done differently. I wonder if you look back and go, maybe I should have done this differently. I'd just be curious to hear that.

The President. I appreciate that. I'm constantly looking back to see if things could be done differently or better. A classic example—first of all, I meant what I said on the strategic objective in Iraq. I said in the '04 campaign; I'm going to say it to you again: Knowing what I know today, I'd have made the same decision.

The tactics of going in—one of the interesting questions—you know, for example, the training of troops. We started training a military from ground one, Iraqi military, as if there was going to be a threat from outside its borders, which, in retrospect, we could have done better. After all, the threat was not from outside the borders; the threat was inside the borders as a result of Zarqawi coming in the country.

The police training has now begun in earnest in '06. The fundamental question is, could we have sped that up; could we have done a better job? The strategy, I'm convinced, is right, which is to give the Iraqis the opportunity to defend themselves. The question is, are the tactics—in order to achieve that, could we have done a quicker job and expedited the idea of having the Iraqis standing up and us standing down?

I mentioned the reconstruction projects. Again, these are all necessary to look back to make sure that as we head out into the future, that we're able to adjust quicker and better. And I spent a lot of time reviewing decisions made.

There's a—you know, there's a debate in Washington about the strategic objective, however. That's different from the tactics on the ground. I strongly believe what we're doing is the right thing. If I didn't believe it—I'm going to repeat what I said before—I'd pull the troops out, nor if I believed we could win, I would pull the troops out.

There is a—the military are constantly taking a real-time analysis based upon previous decisions and what they anticipate the needs to be. And so they themselves are constantly evaluating what could have been done differently.

Obviously, one classic case that hurt us that I wish were done differently was Abu Ghraib, the prison. What took place there and the pictures there just represented everything we didn't stand for. And it hurt us. It hurt us in the international arena, particularly in the Muslim world, where they said, look—it gave the enemy a fantastic opportunity to use it for propaganda reasons. "Look at the United States of America. Look what they're doing to these people. They're disgracing—they don't believe in the dignity of each person," and, in fact, we do. I wish that could be done over. It was a disgraceful experience. However, I'm proud to report that the people who made that decision are being brought to justice, and there was a full investigation over why something like that could have happened.

And so, yes, I do. Look, I fully understand there is—I guess, my reputation is, he sticks to his guns and—it's a very legitimate question: Do you ever kind of understand that maybe—that you've got to be somewhat flexible?

I'm not flexible in my principles. I think if you're flexible in your principles, you end up not making sound decision. But I do agree with your question that a President has got to be capable of looking back and learning from how things could have been done differently. Great question. Thank you.

Okay, squeaky wheels. There's three of you up there. Is this like a chorus? [*Laughter*] Would you please decide among yourselves?

Terrorist Surveillance Program

Q. I've got the mike.

The President. Okay, yes, very good. [*Laughter*] Good move.

Q. You never stop talking about freedom, and I appreciate that. But while I listen to you talk about freedom, I see you assert your right to tap my telephone, to arrest me and hold me without charges, to try to preclude me from breathing clean air and drinking clean water and eating safe food. If I were a woman, you'd like to restrict my opportunity to make a choice and decision about whether I can abort a pregnancy on my own behalf. You are——

The President. I'm not your favorite guy. Go ahead. [*Laughter*] Go on, what's your question?

Q. Okay, I don't have a question. What I wanted to say to you is that I—in my lifetime, I have never felt more ashamed of nor more frightened by my leadership in Washington, including the Presidency, by the Senate, and——

Audience members. Boo-o-o!

The President. No, wait a sec. Let him speak.

Q. And I would hope—I feel like, despite your rhetoric, that compassion and common sense have been left far behind during your administration, and I would hope, from time to time, that you have

the humility and the grace to be ashamed of yourself, inside yourself. And I also want to say, I really appreciate the courtesy of allowing me to speak what I'm saying to you right now. That is part of what this country is about.

The President. It is, yes.

Q. And I know that this doesn't come welcome to most of the people in this room, but I do appreciate that.

The President. Appreciate——

Q. I don't have a question, but I just wanted to make that comment to you.

The President. I appreciate it. Thank you. Let me—I'm going to start off with what you first said, if you don't mind. You said that I tap your phones—I think that's what you said. You tapped your phone—I tapped your phones. Yes. No, that's right. Yes. No, let me finish.

I'd like to describe that decision I made about protecting this country. You can come to whatever conclusion you want. The conclusion is, I'm not going to apologize for what I did on the terrorist surveillance program, and I'll tell you why. We were accused in Washington, DC, of not connecting the dots, that we didn't do everything we could to protect you or others from the attack. And so I called in the people responsible for helping to protect the American people and the homeland. I said, is there anything more we could do?

And there—out of this national—NSA, came the recommendation that it would make sense for us to listen to a call outside the country, inside the country from Al Qaida or suspected Al Qaida in order to have real-time information from which to possibly prevent an attack. I thought that made sense so long as it was constitutional. Now, you may not agree with the constitutional assessment given to me by lawyers—and we've got plenty of them in Washington—but they made this assessment that it was constitutional for me to make that decision.

I then, sir, took that decision to Members of the United States Congress from both political parties and briefed them on the decision that was made in order to protect the American people. And so members of both parties, both Chambers, were fully aware of a program intended to know whether or not Al Qaida was calling in or calling out of the country. It seems like to make sense, if we're at war, we ought to be using tools necessary within the Constitution on a very limited basis, a program that's reviewed constantly, to protect us.

Now, you and I have a different—of agreement on what is needed to be protected. But you said, would I apologize for that? The answer is, absolutely not.

Palestinian Elections/Israel

Q. Mr. President—[*inaudible*]—I was raised on a ranch in New Mexico, and my heroes have always been cowboys.

The President. There you go. Thank you, yes. [*Laughter*] I'm not sure I qualify as a cowboy. [*Laughter*]

Q. Thinking about our children's children, if the all-powerful granter of the Presidential request were to visit you this evening and give you one of these three: of ongoing economic growth and security for America, ridding the world of the security threat now posed by North Korea and Iran, or establishing peace between the Israelis and the Palestinians, which one——

The President. Whew. [*Laughter*] Back to back, you know? [*Laughter*] I don't—that's not the way life works. You can do more than one thing at one time. We can achieve peace with the—we can win this war on terror if we're steadfast and strong. It's not going to happen on my watch. It's going to take awhile. We can spread liberty and freedom to create peace. And we can work on the Palestinian-Israeli issue at the same time. I am the first President to have articulated two states living side by side in peace.

And I'm also a President who believed that the Palestinians needed to have elec-

tions. There's an interesting debate in Washington, is do you wait for the conditions to be perfect before elections, that the institutions be in place before there are elections, or do you have elections as a step toward a civil society and a democratic society? As you know, I've taken the latter rather than the former, and encouraged the Palestinian elections.

And what was interesting about those elections is that—and since then, by the way, the Israelis have had elections. The Palestinian elections—let me just step back. I think the Palestinians have been a long-suffering people that deserve better government. The former leadership turned out to be corrupt, like, stole money. And as a result of his leadership, we never got very close to peace. There wasn't a lasting—there weren't lasting institutions in place. I believe democracies don't war.

And so the election was really an interesting one, I think, recently. Guess what the election was based on? Corruption. This is the Palestinian elections. Anticorruption campaigns, "Vote for me; we're not going to steal your money. Vote for me; we'll help educate your kids and provide health care." The dilemma we're in—it's not a dilemma. I made the decision that if you believe in two states living side by side in peace, then one of the parties in the state—one of the parties cannot declare their intentions to destroy the other party. That's not peaceful. That is warlike.

And so our posture at this point in time is to say to the Palestinians, Hamas, get rid of it; get rid of that platform. It's not a peaceful platform. It's a warlike platform. We want there to be two states side by side in peace.

We've also said, we'll help the people but not the Government. You know, somebody said, "Well, you support elections." I said, yes, I do. I don't necessarily have to like who wins. But I do think it was a necessary part of the evolution of the state to have the Palestinian people be able to say, "We're sick of it. We're sick of the status quo. We want something differently. We want a government that's honest, and we want a government that listens to our demands." I thought it was a positive development. And now, I would strongly urge the Hamas Government to change their tune and their rhetoric about Israel and advocate the peace and work toward a civil society that will yield a lasting peace.

Again, this is an issue where I'm—progress is being made, but it requires a steadfast support of our belief that democracies will yield to peace.

I've got to go. I appreciate you. Yes, one last question. Yes, ma'am, I promised you. I'm sorry.

Alternative Fuel Sources

Q. Thank you. Thank you, very much, Mr. President. I am Wilhelmenia Rembert. I serve as vice chair of the Board of County Commission here in Mecklenburg County. I'm joined by my colleague, Commissioner Dumont Clarke, and we welcome you to Mecklenburg County.

The President. Thank you.

Q. I defer my own question to ask you a question of one of my students at Winthrop University—where I'm a professor of social work—asked me to bring to your attention. And that is, what can you, Mr. President, and what will you do to help control the rising cost of fuel, which is really affecting the ability of many students to travel and the rest of us—not just students—to travel back and forth to work and to school? Thank you.

The President. I appreciate that. I wish I could wave a wand and say, we need more gasoline relative to demand. I don't have the capacity to control the market. I do have the capacity to start leading this country away from dependence on oil. And I believe that we need to promote—vigorously promote alternative sources of energy, starting with ethanol, which could help the farmers around here, by the way. There's a lot of ethanol. Ethanol, basically, right now, is produced from corn. In the Mid-

west, a lot of people are using more ethanol—and to promote technologies such as plug-in hybrid batteries. We're close to some significant breakthroughs. By the way, this is where Republicans and Democrats are working together in Washington, DC, to provide the funding necessary for technology to help lead us away from dependency upon oil.

And so this isn't going to help your person tomorrow, I readily concede. But it is going to—it's going to, in the relatively near future, be able to enable people to plug their car in and drive the first 40 miles on battery as opposed to using gasoline.

And so there is a real need—that's why I put this in the State of the Union—a real need for us to diversify away from fossil fuels, not only to protect the environment, Mister, but also for national and economic security reasons. And the—we're making progress.

I was able to make a decision right after Katrina that helped deal with the—what could have been a even stronger rise in the price of gasoline. I was able to suspend EPA rules because of the natural disaster that took place. And by suspending the blended rules, that can create disruption as these—as the seasonal change, there's a disruption in supply. By suspending those rules, it enabled us to import more European gasoline. And that, in turn, provided stability in the marketplace. And so we didn't have significant spikes.

I fully understand the effects of gasoline price raises on people who are working. It's like a tax. Every time it goes up at the pump, people are, like, paying a tax. And the long-term solution is to get off oil. And we are aggressively doing so.

Thanks for your time. God bless.

NOTE: The President spoke at 10:45 a.m. at Central Piedmont Community College. In his remarks, he referred to Firoz Peera, chair, World Affairs Council of Charlotte; P. Anthony Zeiss, president, Central Piedmont

Community College, and his wife, Beth; Mayor Patrick McCrory of Charlotte, NC; Khalid Sheikh Mohammed, senior Al Qaida leader responsible for planning the September 11, 2001, terrorist attacks, who was captured in Pakistan on March 1, 2003; Ramzi bin al-Shibh, an Al Qaida operative suspected of helping to plan the September 11, 2001, terrorist attacks, who was captured in Karachi, Pakistan on September 11, 2002; Usama bin Laden, leader of the Al Qaida terrorist organization; Ayman Al-Zawahiri, founder of the Egyptian Islamic Jihad and senior Al Qaida associate; former President Saddam Hussein of Iraq; senior Al Qaida associate Abu Musab Al Zarqawi; Gen. George W. Casey, Jr., USA, commanding general, Multi-National Force—Iraq; and former Secretary of State Colin L. Powell.

Remarks on Immigration Reform Legislation in Charlotte
April 6, 2006

I'm pleased that Republicans and Democrats in the United States Senate are working together to get a bipartisan comprehensive energy bill—let me start over. I'm pleased that Republicans and Democrats in the United States Senate are working together to get a comprehensive immigration bill.

I want to thank the efforts of those involved in the process. I appreciate their understanding there needs to be a comprehensive immigration bill. I recognize there are still details to be worked out. I would encourage the Members to work hard to get the bill done prior to the upcoming break.

Thank you all.

NOTE: The President spoke at 12:36 p.m. at the North Carolina Air National Guard base at Charlotte-Douglas International Airport.

Remarks Honoring NCAA Championship Teams
April 6, 2006

Thank you all. Welcome. Please sit down. Thanks for coming. It's an honor to welcome outstanding athletes to the White House. I welcome the athletes and their coaches. We offer our congratulations, and we're thrilled to call you national champs.

I'd like to say, champions day is also National Student Athlete Day. It's a chance for us to honor those who excel on the field as well as those in the classroom.

I'm especially pleased to welcome the Members of the United States Congress here, Senators and Congressmen from the States that we're honoring. Thank you all for coming. Proud you're here. I know you'll want to congratulate the coaches and the team members after these brief remarks. We want to welcome the school officials who are here.

Today is the day we recognize that millions have competed in the NCAA, but only a few become champs. And the first champs we honor are the mighty Florida Gators, ably coached by Billy Donovan. People are making hand gestures back there.

I want you all to recognize that the Gators started the season with 17 wins in a row, and they ended with 11 in a row—the most important 11 wins of the season.

They have a following all over the country, including my brother. [*Laughter*] I'm pleased to welcome you here. I'm also pleased to remind the Gator fans the captain of your team, Adrian Moss, was from Humble, Texas. [*Laughter*]

We have three teams today from the great State of Maryland. Perhaps one theme of champions day is: Fear the Turtle.

I want to welcome Brenda Frese and the University of Maryland women's basketball team. They are the NCAA's newest national champions. Less than 48 hours ago, they were cutting down the nets in Boston. Here they are soaking up the sun in the White House. We welcome you here. We marvel at your dramatic overtime win, and we thank you for being such fantastic athletes.

We also welcome the University of Maryland field hockey team. Missy Meharg is with us as well. These women were the number one seed in the NCAA tournament, and they win the NCAA championship. We're proud you're here. It probably gave you a special delight to be able to beat your archrival, Duke.

We want to welcome Sasho Cirovski's University of Maryland men's soccer team. The men's soccer team won its first national championship in almost 40 years. I thought it was interesting that on Times Square, the NASDAQ ticker displayed a message that said, "Go Terps," in honor of the soccer team.

I want to welcome the University of Portland women's soccer team, coached by Garrett Smith. Portland came to celebrate the championship here in the year 2003. I think one of them said to herself, "You know, we'll be back, but I'm not sure if old George W. is going to make it." [*Laughter*] You're back, and so am I. [*Laughter*] I appreciate the fact that the Pilots dominated the season. They did not lose a single game. I appreciate what Father Beauchamp said—he's the university president—"They are Portland's team. They

brought us together as a community." Congratulations, ladies, for the championship.

Jerry Schumacher of the University of Wisconsin men's cross country team is with us today. For 3 years in a row, Wisconsin finished second in the NCAA championships. This year, they broke the pattern, and they come to the White House as national champs. Congratulations.

I welcome Peter Tegen and the Stanford women's cross country team. Stanford won its second women's cross country national championship in the past 3 years. Lauren Centrowitz is with us. She asked me not to mention her name. I kind of mentioned names, but I did it anyway. Sorry, Lauren. And the reason I did is because her dad, Lauren—I mean, Lauren's dad, Matt, won a national cross country championship of his own in 1977. The daughter and the dad on national cross country championship teams—there's nothing better than someone following in a famous father's footsteps. Congratulations to Stanford's team.

Jim McLaughlin and the University of Washington women's volleyball team is here. Congratulations to the Huskies. These women won their first national championship in school history. They weren't supposed to win. They were the underdog. They had low expectations. It's a good thing, is to keep expectations low, by the way. And they brought home a national championship to the University of Wisconsin. Congratulations to you all. I mean, the University of Washington; I beg your pardon.

Now we've got the University of Auburn men's and women's swimming and diving teams. Coach David Marsh is with us. Both the men's swimming and diving teams earned national championships. That's rare to do. And I welcome both teams with us today. It kind of says that, in a year of swimming, this is the year of War Eagle. I want you all to know that the women's swimming team kindly brought me a— [*laughter*].

[*At this point, the President held up a Speedo swimsuit.*]

Awfully thoughtful of you. [*Laughter*] I'm not going to wear it. [*Laughter*]

I welcome the University of Colorado ski team, under Richard Rokos. This is a coed team. The Colorado ski team's motto was "One team, one goal," and you achieved your goal by winning the National Championship. We welcome you. Your coach is an interesting story. He escaped Communist Czechoslovakia. He's a proud American coaching a wonderful group of athletes. Congratulations, and we're glad you're here.

The university—the United States Military Academy men's rifle team is with us. I congratulate the team here today. This is West Point's first championship in any varsity sport in a half a century. Congratulations to you. If you happen to be walking around and run into the Vice President—[*laughter*]—you might give him a few pointers. [*Laughter*] In the meantime, I look forward to coming to see you as your—as the graduation speaker here in May.

The thing I like about these teams is, they're not only great athletes but they also are champs off the field. When you think about the folks here from West Point, they decided to serve our country in a time of war. And I want to thank you for your contributions to our country.

Florida basketball players spent Thanksgiving morning serving hot meals at a local shelter. The Maryland basketball players raised money to support breast cancer research. The Maryland field hockey players worked as counselors in summer camps for girls. They served as mentors. The Mary-land soccer players helped the school canned food drive. The Portland soccer players arranged for the university to donate money for hurricane relief for every goal the team scored. The Wisconsin cross country runners participated in the Frost-bite Road Race to raise money for the local YMCA. The Stanford cross country team visited schools in East Palo Alto to talk about the importance of education and staying off drugs. The Washington volleyball players visited children in hospital. The Auburn swimmers helped raise funds for hurricane relief. The Colorado skiers participated in the Read With the Buff program in elementary schools. What I'm telling you is, we've not only got fine athletes with us; we've got fine Americans with us. Thank you for serving your communities.

Welcome to the White House. God bless.

NOTE: The President spoke at 3:05 p.m. on the South Lawn at the White House. In his remarks, he referred to Billy Donovan, head coach, University of Florida men's basketball team; Gov. Jeb Bush of Florida; Brenda Frese, head coach, University of Maryland women's basketball team; Missy Meharg, head coach, University of Maryland women's field hockey team; Sasho Cirovski, head coach, University of Maryland men's soccer team; Jerry Schumacher, head coach, University of Wisconsin men's cross country team; Peter Tegen, head coach, and Lauren Centrowitz, team member, Stanford University women's cross country team; Jim McLaughlin, head coach, University of Washington women's volleyball team; and Richard Rokos, head coach, University of Colorado women's and men's ski teams.

Letter to the Speaker of the House of Representatives Transmitting Budget Amendments
April 6, 2006

Dear Mr. Speaker:

I ask the Congress to consider the enclosed FY 2007 Budget amendments for the Departments of Agriculture, and State and Other International Programs; the Federal Communications Commission; and the Smithsonian Institution. Overall, the discretionary budget authority in my FY 2007 Budget would not be increased by these requests.

This transmittal also contains FY 2007 Budget amendments for the legislative branch. As a matter of comity, appropriations requests for the legislative branch are commonly transmitted without change.

The details of these proposals are set forth in the enclosed letter from the Director of the Office of Management and Budget.

Sincerely,

GEORGE W. BUSH

Remarks at the National Catholic Prayer Breakfast
April 7, 2006

Thank you all very much. *Gracias, mi Tejano.* Thank you, sir, for your kind words. Thanks for inviting a Methodist. [*Laughter*]

When I first came out here and saw how comfortable these chairs look, I was a little worried you thought I might be giving quite a long speech. [*Laughter*]

I'm so thrilled to be here with cardinals of the Church. Cardinal McCarrick, I know, is here, and Cardinal Bevilacqua. Must make you feel good to see there's not a slice of bacon around. [*Laughter*] My spirits are always uplifted when I'm in the presence of Their Excellencies, and it's great to see you both.

I've been looking forward to this breakfast, but I've got to tell you, I was slightly concerned when I saw the draft of the program went like this: "We will mark the conclusion of the President's speech with the hymn, 'Now Thank We All Our God.' " [*Laughter*]

Laura sends her love and her best. I want to thank the leadership of the National Catholic Prayer Breakfast for having

me and, more importantly, having this chance for all to worship together.

I appreciate so very much the Chief Justice joining us. I'm proud you're here, Chief Justice. I haven't got to the best part of the family yet—[*laughter*]—and Jane.

Secretary Nicholson, I appreciate you being here—Jim Nicholson and Suzanne. As you might recall, he was our Ambassador to the Vatican, and he did a fantastic job.

Other members of the administration, thanks for coming. Don't tarry too long. [*Laughter*] Get back to work. [*Laughter*]

Looking around, I see Members of the United States Senate—Santorum; Members of the House of Representatives. Thank you all for coming. Proud you're here. Thanks for taking time out of your day. Smith, Beauprez, Lungren, I can't—I don't dare name them all.

We needed a hopeful moment for this world of ours. It's a time when more people have a chance to claim freedom that God intended for us all. It's also a time of great challenge. In some of the most advanced parts of our world, some people no longer believe that the desire for liberty is universal. Some people believe you cannot distinguish between right and wrong. The Catholic Church rejects such a pessimistic view of human nature and offers a vision of human freedom and dignity rooted in the same self-evident truths of America's founding.

This morning we ask God to guide us as we work together to live up to these timeless truths. When our Founders wrote the Declaration of Independence, they called liberty an unalienable right. An unalienable right means that freedom is a right that no government can take away because freedom is not government's to give.

Freedom is a gift from the Almighty because it is—and because it is universal, our Creator has written it into all nature. To maintain this freedom, societies need high moral standards. And the Catholic Church and its institutions play a vital role in helping our citizens acquire the character we need to live as free people.

In the last part of the 20th century, we saw the appeal of freedom in the hands of a priest from Poland. When Pope John Paul II ascended to the Chair of Saint Peter, the Berlin Wall was still standing, his native Poland was occupied by a Communist power, and the division of Europe looked like a permanent scar across the continent. Yet Pope John Paul told us, "Be not afraid," because he knew that an empire built on lies was ultimately destined to fail. By reminding us that our freedom and dignity rests on truths about man and his nature, Pope John Paul II set off one of the greatest revolutions for freedom the world has ever known.

Pope John Paul has now been succeeded by one of his closest friends and colleagues, Pope Benedict XVI. Pope Benedict, when he was a Cardinal, and recently—when he was a Cardinal, Laura and I had a chance to meet him, and recently she went back to Rome to see him again. He was such a gracious host, wonderfully kind man.

Like his predecessor, Pope Benedict understands that the measure of a free society is how it treats the weakest and most vulnerable among us. In his Christmas homily, the Pope noted that the Savior came to Earth as a defenseless child, and said that the splendor of that Christmas shines upon every child, born and unborn. Here in the United States, we work to strengthen a culture of life through many State and Federal initiatives that expand the protections of the unborn. These initiatives reflect the consensus of the American people acting through their elected representatives, and we will continue to work for the day when every child is welcome in life and protected in law.

I appreciate the leading role that the Catholic faith-based organizations play in our nation's armies of compassion. And one of the many ways that Catholic faith-based organizations serve their neighbors is by welcoming newcomers and helping them become good citizens.

This Nation of ours is having an important debate about immigration, and it is vitally important that this debate be conducted in a civil tone. I believe that the American Dream is open to all who work hard and play by the rules and that America does not have to choose between being a compassionate society and a society of law.

An immigration system that forces people into the shadows of our society or leaves them prey to criminals is a system that needs to be changed. I'm confident that we can change our immigration system in ways that secures our border, respects the rule of law, and, as importantly, upholds the decency of our country. As the Congress continues this debate, its Members must remember, we are a nation of immigrants, and immigration has helped restore our soul on a regular basis.

In this young century, our Nation has been called to great duties. I'm confident we'll meet our responsibilities so long as we continue to trust in God's purposes. During our time in the White House, Laura and I have been blessed by the prayers of countless Americans, including many in this room. It's really an amazing country where people walk up to you, say, "Mr. President, I pray for you"—expecting to say, "Mr. President, I'd like a bridge." [*Laughter*] But instead, they say, "I pray for you and your family." It uplifts us, and I want to thank you for that from the bottom of our hearts.

I ask for your prayers again, that our Nation may always be an inspiration to those who believe that God made every man, woman, and child for freedom. It is such an honor to be here. May God bless you all, and may God continue to bless our country.

NOTE: The President spoke at 8:30 a.m. at the Washington Hilton Hotel. In his remarks, he referred to Most Rev. Jose H. Gomez, Archbishop of San Antonio, who introduced the President; Theodore E. Cardinal McCarrick, Archbishop of Washington; Anthony J. Cardinal Bevilacqua, Archbishop Emeritus of Philadelphia; Jane M. Roberts, wife of Chief Justice John G. Roberts, Jr.; and Suzanne M. Nicholson, wife of Secretary of Veterans Affairs R. James Nicholson.

Remarks on the National Economy
April 7, 2006

Good morning. This morning's economic report shows that America's growing economy added 211,000 jobs in the month of March. The American economy has now added jobs for 31 months in a row, created more than 5.1 million new jobs for American workers. The unemployment rate is now down to 4.7 pecent; that's below the average rate of the 1960s, 1970s, 1980s, and 1990s.

These millions of new jobs are evidence of an economic resurgence that is strong, broad, and benefiting all Americans. Real after-tax income has grown by more than 8 percent per person since I took office. That means, on average, Americans have an income that is $2,100 higher this year than it was in 2001, after adjusting for inflation.

More Americans own their homes than at any time in history. Minority homeownership has reached record levels. Consumer confidence is at its highest point in nearly 40 years. Productivity is high; inflation is contained; manufacturing activity is growing; and the small-business sector is thriving.

The economy has expanded for 17 straight quarters. And last year, the American economy grew at a healthy rate of 3.5 percent. That's the fastest rate of any major industrialized economy.

These gains are the result of the energy and the effort of American workers, small-business owners, and entrepreneurs. They are also the result of progrowth economic policies. The tax cuts I signed left $880 billion with our Nation's workers, small-business owners, and families. They've used that money to fuel our economic resurgence.

Not everyone in Washington agreed with the decision to let people keep more of their own money. On the day that Republicans in the House and Senate were finalizing the 2003 tax cuts, one Democratic leader said these cuts would, quote, "do nothing to create jobs." Facts have proven the critics wrong 5.1 million times over.

Tax relief has done exactly what it was designed to do. It's created jobs and growth for the American people. Yet some are now proposing that we raise taxes, either by repealing the tax cuts or letting them expire. These are the same politicians who told us that letting Americans—letting America's working families keep more of their own money would be irresponsible, reckless, and shameful. They were wrong then, and they are wrong now. Our economy grows when the American people make the decisions about how to save, spend, and invest their money. To keep our economy creating jobs and opportunity, Congress needs to show its trust in the American people and make the tax relief permanent.

Congress also needs to restrain spending so we can stay on track to cut the deficit in half by 2009. And if necessary, I will enforce spending restraint through the exercise of the veto. The American people expect their leaders to address other key leaders—that directly affect their family budgets and bottom line, especially health care and energy.

When the cost of energy and health care rise, families are squeezed and small businesses suffer. I proposed practical reforms that would make health care more available and affordable. I put forward an energy initiative that will make our dependence on Middle Eastern oil a thing of the past. I've also laid out a plan to make America more competitive by increasing our investment in scientific research, encouraging research and development in the private sector, and improving math and science education.

I urge the Congress to move forward on all these important priorities so we can keep America the economic leader of the world and allow more families and small businesses to realize the American Dream.

Thank you for your time.

NOTE: The President spoke at 9:32 a.m. in the Diplomatic Reception Room at the White House.

The President's Radio Address
April 8, 2006

Good morning. This week, Members of the United States Senate reached a promising bipartisan compromise on comprehensive immigration reform. Unfortunately, this compromise is being blocked by the Senate Democratic leader, who has refused to allow Senators to move forward and vote on amendments to this bill. I call on the Senate minority leader to end his blocking tactics and allow the Senate to do its work and pass a fair, effective immigration reform bill.

Immigration is an emotional issue and a vitally important one. At its core, immigration is the sign of a confident and successful nation. It says something about our country that people around the world are willing to leave their homes, leave their

families, and risk everything to come to America. Their talent, hard work, and love of freedom have helped make America a vibrant, strong nation. And by reforming our immigration laws to meet the realities of the 21st century, we will ensure that America remains a beacon of liberty for generations to come.

I made clear that a comprehensive immigration reform bill must include three elements. First, comprehensive immigration reform must secure our borders. Since I took office, we've increased funding for border security by 66 percent, and Federal agents have apprehended and sent home more than 6 million people entering this country illegally, including more than 400,000 with criminal records. To improve security at the border, we're hiring thousands more Border Patrol agents; we're deploying new technologies like infrared cameras and unmanned aerial vehicles to help our agents do their jobs; we're installing physical barriers to entry, like fences in urban areas. We're making good progress, but we have much more work ahead to gain control of our border. I'll continue to work with Congress to strengthen border security, so we can prevent illegal immigrants from crossing our border and make the immigration system more orderly and secure.

Second, comprehensive immigration reform must strengthen the enforcement of our laws in America's interior. Since I took office, we've increased funding for immigration enforcement by 42 percent, increased the number of immigration enforcement agents and criminal investigators, enhanced worksite enforcement, and gone after smugglers, gang members, and human traffickers. A good immigration bill should enhance our ability to stop document fraud and help employers comply with our laws.

Finally, comprehensive immigration reform must include a temporary-worker program that relieves pressure on our borders while rejecting amnesty. A temporary-worker program would create a legal way to match willing foreign workers with willing American employers to fill jobs that no American is available to do. By creating a legal channel for those seeking temporary work in America, we would reduce the number of people trying to sneak across the border. This would free up law enforcement officers to focus on criminals, drug dealers, terrorists, and others who mean us

harm. A temporary-worker program would also improve security by creating tamper-proof identification cards, so we can keep track of every temporary worker who is here on a legal basis and identify those who are not.

A new temporary-worker program should not provide amnesty. Granting amnesty would be unfair to those who follow the rules and obey the laws. Amnesty would also be unwise, because it would encourage others to break the law and create new waves of illegal immigration. We must ensure that those who break our laws are not granted an automatic path to citizenship. We should also conduct the debate on immigration reform in a manner worthy of our Nation's best traditions.

To keep the promise of America, we must remain a welcoming society and also enforce the laws that make our freedom possible. As we do, our Nation will draw strength from the diversity of its citizens and unity from their desire to assimilate and become one people. By working together, we can fix our immigration system in a way that protects our country, upholds our laws, and makes our Nation proud.

Thank you for listening.

NOTE: The address was recorded at 12:56 p.m. on April 7 in the Cabinet Room at the White House for broadcast at 10:06 a.m. on April 8. The transcript was made available by the Office of the Press Secretary on April 7 but was embargoed for release until the broadcast. The Office of the Press Secretary also released a Spanish language transcript of this address.

Remarks at the Paul H. Nitze School of Advanced International Studies and a Question-and-Answer Session
April 10, 2006

The President. Thank you. Please be seated. Bill, thanks for the kind introduction. I'm pleased to be here at this school, which bears the name of one of America's greatest statesmen. Paul Nitze served as a trusted adviser to six Presidents, from Franklin Roosevelt to Ronald Reagan. He was one of a small group of men who shaped the world that emerged from the Allied victory in World War II. He encouraged our Nation to continue the—its noble and essential role as freedom's defender. He was the principal author of NSC–68, the strategic blueprint for America's victory in the cold war. At a time when some wanted to wish away the Soviet threat, Paul Nitze insisted that the cold war was, in his words, "in fact, a real war in which the survival of the free world is at stake." He helped rally America to confront this mortal danger, and his strategic vision helped secure the triumph of freedom in that great struggle of the 20th century.

At the start of this young century, America is once again engaged in a real war that is testing our Nation's resolve. While there are important distinctions, today's war on terror is like the cold war. It is an ideological struggle with an enemy that despises freedom and pursues totalitarian aims. Like the cold war, our adversary is dismissive of free peoples, claiming that men and women who live in liberty are weak and decadent; they lack the resolve to defend our way of life. Like the cold war, America is once again answering history's call with confidence. And like the cold war, freedom will prevail.

I thank Dr. Bill Brody; I thank Jessica Einhorn. Thank you all for having me here. I appreciate all those who teach here. I appreciate the students letting me come to speak. Glad to provide a convenient excuse to skip class. [*Laughter*] I want to thank Bill Nitze, adjunct professor, son of a great man. I know how you feel. [*Laughter*] I appreciate Mike Chertoff being here. I'm proud to see a lot of folks who wear the Nation's uniform for joining us. Welcome.

I thought I'd give a speech, but a short speech, much to your relief, and then I'll be glad to answer some questions.

Yesterday our Nation marked the third anniversary of a great moment in the history of freedom; it was the liberation of Iraq. Three years ago, coalition forces entered the gates of Baghdad, fought their way into the center of the city, and helped Iraqis pull down the statue of Saddam Hussein. What they found in Baghdad horrified our troops. One marine describes how Iraqis led his unit to a children's prison where more than 100 youngsters were being held. Some of the children had reportedly been jailed because they refused to join the Ba'athist Party Youth Organization. He says, "It was really something. The children just streamed out of the gates, and their parents just started to embrace us."

Under Saddam's brutal regime, the Iraqi people lived lives of fear and desperation. Innocent civilians were executed in public squares; they were massacred and piled into mass graves. Saddam's regime denied people food and medicine while building elaborate palaces from which to rule with an iron hand. Saddam sponsored terrorism; he pursued and used weapons of mass destruction; he fired at U.S. and British air crews patrolling the no-fly zones; he defied more than a dozen U.N. Security Council resolutions. Today, because America and a great coalition acted, the regime is no longer in power, is no longer sponsoring terrorists, is no longer destabilizing the region, is no longer undermining the credibility of the United Nations, is no longer threatening the world. Because we acted, 25 million Iraqis now taste freedom.

The decision by the United States and our coalition partners to remove Saddam Hussein was a really difficult decision. It was the right decision. After September the 11th, America decided that we would fight the war on terror on the offense and that we would confront threats before they fully materialized. Saddam Hussein was a threat to the United States of America. America is safer today because Saddam Hussein is no longer in power.

Coalition forces drove Saddam from power, and a U.S. Army unit, led by a graduate of this school—Colonel James Hickey, class of 1992—captured Saddam when he was hiding in a hole in the ground. Today, thanks to our courageous men and women in uniform, the former Iraqi dictator is sitting in a courtroom instead of a palace, and he's now facing justice for his crimes.

The past 3 years since liberation, the Iraqi people have begun the difficult process of recovering from Saddam's repression. They're beginning to build a democracy on the rubble of his tyranny. They still face brutal and determined enemies: members of the deposed regime who dream of returning to power; other insurgents; and foreign terrorists who dream of turning Iraq into what Afghanistan was under the Taliban, a safe haven from which to plot and plan new attacks against America and our allies. The enemies of a free Iraq are determined to ignite a civil war, put the Iraqi people—to pit the Iraqi people against one another, and to stop the country's democratic progress. Yet the Iraqi people are determined to live in freedom, and America is determined to defeat the terrorists, and we're determined to help the Iraqi people succeed.

America is doing our part to help the Iraqis build a democracy. Our Nation can be proud of what our courageous men and women in uniform have accomplished in the past 3 years. Since liberation, our forces have captured or killed thousands of Al Qaida terrorists and other enemy fighters; we've freed Fallujah and Tall 'Afar and other Iraqi cities from the grip of the terrorists and the insurgents; we've trained Iraqi security forces so they increasingly can take the lead in the fight and eventually assume responsibility for the security of their country.

We've learned from our mistakes. We've adjusted our approach to meet the changing circumstances on the ground. We've adjusted depending upon the actions of the enemy. By pursuing a clear and flexible strategy in Iraq, we helped make it possible for Iraqis to choose their leaders and begin to assume the responsibilities of self-government and self-defense. In the past 3 years, our troops in Iraq have done everything expected of them and more. They've brought freedom to Iraq, security to our country, and pride to the uniform, and they have the gratitude of all Americans.

In the past 3 years, the Iraqi people have done their part. They defied death threats from the terrorists to cast ballots not one time, not twice, but three times, and each election saw larger and broader turnout than the one that came before. Iraqis chose a transitional government, drafted the most progressive Constitution in the Arab world, approved that Constitution in a nationwide referendum, and voted for a new Government under the new Constitution. And in December elections for this Government, despite the threats of violence and efforts to discourage Sunni participation, nearly 12 million Iraqis—that's more than 75 percent of eligible voters—turned out at the polls.

The Iraqi people have begun building a free society, with a thriving free press and hundreds of independent newspapers and magazines and talk radio shows where Iraqis openly debate the future course of their country. The Iraqi people have begun building a free economy, with an independent central bank and thousands of small businesses and a relatively stable currency. Iraqi people have stepped forward to fight for their freedom as well. Despite repeated attacks on military and police recruiting stations, more than 250,000 Iraqis have volunteered to wear their country's uniform. These brave Iraqis are increasingly taking the lead in the fight against the terrorists and the insurgents. Today, there are more than 130 Iraqi Army and police combat battalions in the fight, with more than 70 Iraqi battalions taking the lead. Iraqi units have assumed primary responsibility for more than 30,000 square miles of Iraq. We expect that Iraqi units will control more territory than the coalition by the end of 2006.

Iraqis are fighting bravely, and many have given their lives in the battle for freedom for their country. And by their courage and sacrifice, the Iraqi soldiers and civilians have shown they want to live in freedom, and they're not going to let the terrorists take away their opportunity to live in a free society.

Now it's time for the Iraqi leaders to do their part and finish the job of forming a unity government. The people of Iraq have made their intentions clear. At great personal risk, they went to the polls to choose leaders in free elections. And now the leaders they've elected have a responsibility to come together to form a Government that unifies all Iraqis. Secretary Rice was just in Baghdad, where she delivered a strong message from me: Iraq leaders need to rise to the moment, to put aside their personal agendas, and take charge of their destiny.

Iraqi leaders have taken some important steps forward. They've agreed to an agenda for the new Government to take up once it assumes office, including tough issues such as demobilization of the militias, protecting the rights of women, restoring Iraq's infrastructure, and building national institutions that will effectively represent all Iraqis. Iraqi leaders have also agreed to form a new national security council that includes all major political groups and representatives of the executive and legislative branches. And now they must take the next step and fill key leadership posts so that a new Government can begin its essential work.

I understand that putting aside differences to form a Government is difficult. Pretty hard for our country. Our first governing charter, the Articles of Confederation, failed, and it took us 8 years before we adopted our Constitution and elected our first President under that Constitution. Iraqis are going to make mistakes as well. They are undertaking a difficult process with little democratic experience and with the scars of nearly three decades of Saddam Hussein still fresh on their mind. Moving beyond past divisions to build a strong democracy requires strong leadership, and now is the time for Iraqis to step up and show the leadership.

The Iraqi people have a right to expect it, and so do the American people. Americans have made great sacrifices to help Iraq get to this point. Iraqi voters risked their lives to go to the polls. Iraqi soldiers and police have given their time to make this moment possible. And so Americans and Iraqis alike are waiting and watching to see what this sacrifice will produce, and we both expect results. In the words of one Iraqi newspaper, "The time has come for our politicians to save people from their suffering and crisis. The Iraqi people are more sacred than government positions."

Forming a unity government is critical to defeating the terrorists and securing the peace. The terrorists and insurgents thrive in a political vacuum, and the delay in forming a Government is creating a vacuum that the terrorists and insurgents are working to exploit. The enemies of a free Iraq blew up the Golden Mosque in Samarra in the hope that this outrageous act would provoke reprisals and drag the nation into a civil war. This past Friday, suicide bombers blew up another Shi'a mosque in northern Baghdad. The longer Iraq's leaders delay in forming a unity government, the greater the risk that the terrorists and former regime elements will succeed in their efforts to foment division and to stop the progress of an Iraq democracy.

The terrorists know that the greatest threat to their aspirations is Iraqi self-government. And we know this from the terrorists' own words. In 2004, we intercepted a letter from Zarqawi to Usama bin Laden. In it, Zarqawi expressed his concern about "the gap that will emerge between us and the people of the land." He declared, "Democracy is coming." He went on to say, this will mean "suffocation" for the terrorists. Zarqawi laid out his strategy to stop democracy from taking root in Iraq. He wrote, "If we succeed in dragging the Shi'a into the arena of sectarian war, it will become possible to awaken the inattentive Sunnis as they feel imminent danger. The only solution for us is to strike the religious, military, and other cadres among the Shi'a with blow after blow."

The advance of democracy is the terrorists' greatest fear. It's an interesting question, isn't it: Why would they fear democracy? What is it about freedom that frightens these killers? What is it about a liberty that causes these people to kill innocent women and children? To defeat them, Iraq needs a democratic government that represents all Iraq, that reins in illegal militias, and earns the trust and confidence of all Iraqi communities. When Iraqis have such a government to lead and unite them, they will be in a stronger position to defeat their enemies and secure the future with a free country. When Iraqis have a democratic government in place, it will be a major victory for the cause of freedom. It will be a major defeat for the terrorists' aspirations to dominate the region and advance their hateful vision.

Once a Government is formed, the international community must also do its part to help this young democracy succeed. Iraq needs greater international support, particularly from its Arab neighbors. Arab leaders need to recognize that the choice in Iraq is between democracy and terrorism, and

there is no middle ground. Success of Iraqi democracy is in their vital interests because if the terrorists prevail in Iraq, they will target other Arab nations.

The broader international community has responsibilities as well. So far, other nations and international organizations have pledged more than $13 billion in assistance to Iraq. Iraqis are grateful for the promised aid, and so is the United States. Yet many nations have been slow to make good on their commitments. I call on all Governments that have pledged assistance to follow through with their promises as quickly as possible so that the people of the—across the Middle East will see that democracy leads to a better life and a brighter future. The success of a free Iraq is in the interests of all free nations, and none can afford to sit on the sidelines.

Formation of a unity government is a critical step, but it's not going to bring an immediate end to the violence Americans are seeing on their TV screens. The terrorists are going to continue to spread chaos and carnage in Iraq because they know the images of car bombs and beheadings horrify the American people. They know they can't defeat us on the battlefield and that the only way to win in Iraq is to break our will and force us into an early retreat. Our enemies know what's at stake, and they are determined to stop the rise of a democratic Iraq, and I am equally determined to stop them.

The decision to go to war is one of the most difficult a President can make. And in 3 years since our forces liberated Iraq, we've seen many contradictory images that are difficult for Americans to reconcile. On the one hand, we've seen images of great hope—boys and girls back in school and millions of Iraqis dipping their fingers in purple ink or dancing in the streets or celebrating their freedom. On the other hand, we've seen images of unimaginable despair—bombs destroying hospitals and hostages bound and executed. And this raises the question in the minds of many Americans: Which image will prevail? I'll give you my opinion. I believe that freedom will prevail in Iraq. I believe moms and dads everywhere want their children to grow up in safety and freedom. I believe freedom will prevail because the terrorists have nothing to offer the Iraqi people. I believe freedom will prevail because once people have tasted freedom, they will not accept a return to tyranny.

It's important for Americans to understand the stakes in Iraq. A free Iraq will be an ally in the war on terror. A free Iraq will be a partner in the struggle for peace and moderation in the Muslim world. A free Iraq will inspire democratic reformers from Damascus to Tehran and send a signal across the broader Middle East that the future belongs not to terrorism but to freedom. A free Iraq will show the power of liberty to change the world. And as the Middle East grows in liberty and prosperity and hope, the terrorists will lose their safe havens and recruits, and America and other free nations will be more secure.

Today, Iraq is free and sovereign, and that freedom and sovereignty has come at a great price. Because Americans and Iraqis and troops from 17 other nations gave up their own futures so the Iraqi people could have a future of freedom, this world is better off because of their sacrifice. America will honor their sacrifice by completing the mission in Iraq. And Iraqi leaders have a responsibility to the fallen as well. By working together, we'll build a future of freedom for both our people. We're laying the foundation of peace for generations to come.

I appreciate your attention, and now I'll be glad to answer some questions. Please.

President's Decisionmaking/War on Terror

Q. Mr. President, thank you very much for coming. We appreciate it. I'm a strategic studies concentrator here at SAIS. My question to you, Mr. President—I'll preface it with a comment. Many of us here are aspiring policymakers. Many of us here hope to one day be in positions of leadership. And some of us may be faced with decisions, very difficult decisions on the use of force and engaging in war. I was hoping that from your experience, you could share with us some wisdom or some insight, not necessarily on tactics but something we can take with us through our careers, that we can apply maybe at some point. Thank you.

The President. Thanks. Thanks for the question. I would encourage those of you studying here to be a part of policymaking for our Government. It is a high honor to serve your country. And my first advice is never use force until you've exhausted all diplomacy. I—my second advice is if you ever put anybody in harm's way, make sure they have got all the support of the Government. My third advice is don't make decisions on polls. Stand your ground if you think what you're doing right.

Much of my decision about what we're discussing these days was affected by an event. Look, I—during the 2000 campaign, I don't remember ever discussing with people what—could I handle war, or could my opponent handle war. The war wasn't on our mind. War came unexpectedly. We didn't ask for the attack, but it came. And so much of the statements I make and have made since that war were a result of that attack.

I vowed then that I would use all assets of our power to win the war on terror. That's what I vowed. It—the September the 11th attacks affected me. It affected my thinking deeply. The most important job of the Government is to protect the people from an attack. And so I said, we were going to stay on the offense two ways: One, hunt down the enemy and bring them to justice, and take threats seriously; and two, spread freedom. And that's what we've been doing, and that's what I'm going to continue to do as the President.

I think about the war on terror all the time. Now, I understand there's a difference of opinion in a country. Some view the attack as kind of an isolated incident; I don't. I view it as a part of a strategy by a totalitarian, ideologically based group of people who've announced their intentions to spread that ideology and to attack us again. That's what they've said they're going to do. And the most dangerous—the biggest danger facing our country is whether—if the terrorists get a weapons of mass destruction to use. Now, perhaps some in our country think it's a—that's a pipedream; I don't. I think it is a very real threat and, therefore, will spend my Presidency rallying our assets—intelligence assets, military assets, financial assets, diplomatic initiatives—to keep the enemy off balance and to bring them to justice.

Now, if you're going to be the President or a policymaker, you never know what's going to come. That's the interesting thing about the world in which we live. We're a influential nation, and so therefore, many problems come to the Oval Office. And you don't know what those problems are going to be, which then argues for having smart people around. That's why you ought to serve in Government if you're not going to be the President. You have a chance to influence policy by giving good recommendations to the President.

You got to listen in my line of work, and I listen a lot. Ours is a complex organization that requires a management structure that lets people come into the Oval Office and explain their positions. And I think it's to my interest, by the way, that not everybody agree all the time. You can't make good decisions unless there's a little—kind of a little agitation in there. [*Laughter*] And sometimes we have.

But anyway, good question. I guess my answer to your question is, is that you got to be ready for the unexpected. And when you act, you base your decisions on principles. I'll tell you one principle—I'm not going to filibuster, I promise—but you got me going here, so—[*laughter*]. I want you to understand this principle, and it's an important debate, and it's worth debating here

in this school, as to whether or not freedom is universal, whether or not it's a universal right of all men and women. It's an interesting part of the international dialog today. And I think it is universal. And if you believe it's universal, I believe this country has—should act on that concept of universality. And the reason I do is because I do believe freedom yields the peace.

And our foreign policy prior to my arrival was, "If it seems okay, leave it alone." In other words, if it's nice and placid out there on the surface, it's okay; just let it sit. But unfortunately, beneath the surface was resentment and hatred, and that kind of resentment and hatred provided ample recruitment, fertile grounds for recruiting people that came and killed over 3,000 of our citizens. And therefore, I believe the way to defeat resentment is with freedom and liberty.

But if you don't believe it's universal, I can understand why you say, "What's he doing? Why is he doing that?" If there's no such thing as the universality of freedom, then we might as well just isolate ourselves and hope for the best.

And so—anyway, kind of rambling here. [*Laughter*] Yes.

Iran

Q. Mr. President, thanks very much for your visit today. We're honored by your visit. I'm a first-semester MA student. You mentioned the confluence of terror and weapons of mass destruction as the greatest threat to American security. Will the United States allow Iran to develop nuclear weapons?

The President. Ah—[*laughter*]—we do not want the Iranians to have a nuclear weapon, the capacity to make a nuclear weapon, or the knowledge as to how to make a nuclear weapon. That's our stated goal. It's also the goal, fortunately, of other—of friends and allies, starting with Great Britain, Germany, and France.

One of the decisions I made early on was to have a multinational approach to sending messages, clear messages to the Iranians that if they want to be a part of the—an accepted nation in the world, that they must give up their nuclear weapons ambitions. And we're making pretty good progress.

By the way, if you're studying how to achieve diplomatic ends, it might be worthwhile noting that—I think at least—with the United States being the sole interlocutor between Iran, it makes it more difficult to achieve the objective of having the Iranians give up their nuclear weapons ambitions. It's amazing that when we're in a bilateral position, or kind of just negotiating one on one, somehow the world ends up turning the tables on us. And I'm not going to put my country in that position—our country in that position. Also, I think it's more effective that the three of us—the four of us work closely together.

We've also included Russia into the dialog. A couple of months back, you might remember, there was a discussion about whether or not the Russians should be allowed to build—or encouraged to build a civilian nuclear powerplant, but the fuel of which would be provided and collected by the Russians. I supported that initiative. I thought it was difficult, on the one hand, to say that civilian nuclear power is a sovereign right of a nation, and on the other hand, not to then support the Russian initiative. And I did so. I also did so because I want Russia to be a part of the team, trying to convince the Iranians to give up its nuclear weapons program.

Now, I want to emphasize this point, and that is, is that we're not only making sure they don't have the means to develop the weapon but the knowledge. And that's why I was very strong in saying that they should not have—that there should not be a research component involved with the Russian deal that will enable the Iranians to learn how to better enriched—enrich uranium.

But our objective is to prevent them from having a nuclear weapon. And the good news is, is that many in the world have come to that conclusion. I got out a little early on the issue by saying, "axis of evil." [*Laughter*] But I meant it. I saw it as a problem. And now many others have come to the conclusion that the Iranians should not have a nuclear weapon.

The doctrine of prevention is to work together to prevent the Iranians from having a nuclear weapon. I know here in Washington prevention means force. It doesn't mean force, necessarily. In this case, it means diplomacy. And by the way, I read the articles in the newspapers this weekend. It was just wild speculation, by the way. What you're reading is wild speculation, which is—it's kind of a—happens quite frequently here in the Nation's Capital.

Yes. Please.

Reconstruction in Iraq

Q. Thank you, Mr. President. It's an honor to have you here. I'm a first-year student in South Asian studies. My question is in regards to private military contractors. The Uniform Code of Military Justice does not apply to these contractors in Iraq. I asked your Secretary of Defense a couple months ago what law governs their actions. Mr. Rumsfeld——

The President. I was going to ask him. Go ahead. [*Laughter*] Help. [*Laughter*]

Q. I was hoping your answer might be a little more specific. [*Laughter*] Mr. Rumsfeld answered that Iraq has its own domestic laws which he assumed applied to those private military contractors. However, Iraq is clearly not currently capable of enforcing its laws, much less against—over our American military contractors. I would submit to you that in this case, this is one case that privatization is not a solution. And, Mr. President, how do you propose to bring private military contractors under a system of law?

The President. Yes, I appreciate that very much. I wasn't kidding—[*laughter*]. I was going to—I pick up the phone and say,

"Mr. Secretary, I've got an interesting question." [*Laughter*] This is what delegation—I don't mean to be dodging the question, although it's kind of convenient in this case, but never—[*laughter*]. I really will—I'm going to call the Secretary and say you brought up a very valid question, and what are we doing about it? That's how I work. I'm—thanks. [*Laughter*]

Yes, ma'am.

Public Opinion/Democracy

Q. Hello, Mr. President. I have a followup question on your comments about polls. Your Presidency has been a rather polarizing period in America. And occasionally, your attitude towards protesters and dissenters has been perceived as being dismissive and occasionally, then, cavalier. And I'm wondering how you feel that's contributed to the polarization in politics today and if that approach will change, given that you have fallen somewhat in the polls?

The President. Yes. Well—[*laughter*]—I take protest seriously. I mean, I—by the way, I get protested all the time. [*Laughter*] And I welcome it. I think this is the great thing about a democracy. There needs to be an outlet. If people feel like their government is not listening to them or doesn't agree with them, there ought to be an outlet for their discontent.

And so the protests really don't bother me. I hope that's not viewed as cavalier, but it's just the way I feel. And it's a—in terms of polls, you cannot have a President make decisions based upon the latest political survey. It's just—you got to have people making decisions based upon principle. And my attitude is, I'm going to do what I think is right.

I've got to be able to look at myself, by the way—after the Presidency—in the mirror and say, I didn't come to Washington, DC, to try to chase political opinion; I came to lead this country in a very historic time.

And you heard my discussion about my reaction after 9/11. That's what I believe. And that's what I'm going—those are some of the beliefs on which I'm going to continue to make decisions.

But, no, I hear voices of discontent, and I'm just going to do the best I can do based upon what I think is right. There's too much flattery, too much ego, too much criticism, too much noise, too much politics, too much that, for a President to try to kind of grope his way around looking at the latest public opinion poll. In my judgment, it doesn't serve the Nation well.

A while ago at a press conference, I remember uttering one wonderful piece of wisdom: It's like a dog chasing his tail. It actually didn't fly that good. But nevertheless, my point—[*laughter*]. But thank you; it's a legitimate question. And so to answer your question, yes, I hear the protests. And I can understand why. I can understand why people are concerned about war. Nobody likes war, particularly me. I knew exactly what was going to happen when I committed these troops into harm's way. I knew there would be—people would lose their life. And I knew I'd be trying to comfort mothers and fathers and grieving wives. I knew exactly what was coming. And if I didn't think it was the right thing to do, I wouldn't have sent them. And if I didn't think we could succeed in Iraq, I'd pull them out.

And the good thing about a democracy is people can express themselves. We're fixing to have a huge immigration march today. And it's a sign that there's a—this is a important issue that people feel strongly about. And I repeat to you: I strongly believe that societies in which you're not allowed to express yourself are societies which do breed resentment, and, kind of, bottled-up anxiety causes people to become very frustrated. And that's not healthy for a society.

Yes.

CIA Employee Identity Disclosure Investigation

Q. First, let me say, thank you very much for being here, and thank you for taking questions. I know we appreciate that. I'm a second-year master's student studying international energy policy.

The President. International?

Q. Energy policy.

The President. Oh, good.

Q. Sorry. [*Laughter*] My question, sir, is, well, as Anthony alluded to earlier and as you're aware, we have many students at SAIS who are currently working for or considering working for the State Department, the various intelligence agencies, and such. And how do you respond to recent—the recent report by Prosecutor Fitzgerald that there is, in his words, "a concerted—evidence of a concerted effort by the White House to punish Joseph Wilson," who himself has a distinguished record of Government service?

The President. Yes. No, I—this is—there's an ongoing legal proceeding which precludes me from talking a lot about the case. There's also an ongoing investigation that's a serious investigation. I will say this, that after we liberated Iraq, there was questions in people's minds about the basis on which I made statements, in other words, going into Iraq. And so I decided to declassify the NIE for a reason. I wanted to see—people to see what some of those statements were based on. So I wanted to see—I wanted people to see the truth and thought it made sense for people to see the truth. And that's why I declassified the document.

You can't talk about—you're not supposed to talk about classified information, and so I declassified the document. I thought it was important for people to get a better sense for why I was saying what I was saying in my speeches. And I felt I could do so without jeopardizing ongoing intelligence matters, and so I did.

And as far as the rest of the case goes, you're just going to have to let Mr. Fitzgerald complete his case. And I hope you understand that. It's a serious legal matter that we've got to be careful in making public statements about it.

Yes, please.

Asia-Pacific Countries

Q. Good morning, Mr. President. Thank you for coming here today. I'm a second-year SAIS student studying strategic studies. And I'd like to briefly turn you a moment—turn your attention to the Asia-Pacific, the security situation in Asia right now. Secretary Rice, last March, met with her counterparts in Japan and Australia in a security dialog, discussing security issues in Asia-Pacific. And this made many countries in the region very uncomfortable. They felt that this security dialog may have been an effort to contain the quote unquote "China threat." And mostly our alliance partners in South Korea, Singapore, and Thailand have felt this uneasiness. Could you possibly elucidate for us your administration's strategy towards Asia-Pacific, ahead of President Hu Jintao's visit to Washington? And was the dialog a prelude to a NATO-like security structure in Asia-Pacific?

The President. Thanks for the question. We have worked hard to make sure relations with Japan, China, and South Korea are on firm footing, and they are. First, the Japanese relationship is a close relationship. I'm personally fond of Prime Minister Koizumi. We have a close relationship, and I've worked very closely with him on a variety of matters, starting with making sure our force posture is such that can—that the Japanese are comfortable with.

I don't know if you saw the recent announcements about Okinawa, for example. You're beginning to see a defense relationship and alliance that stays intact but is more attuned to the future. Secondly, he's committed troops into Iraq. He believes, like I believe, that democracy helps keep the peace. We've worked closely in Afghanistan. In other words, we're partners in peace.

The South Korean issue is one, obviously, that's dominated primarily by North Korea. And I made the decision early on in the administration to change the dynamics in that negotiation from the United States and North Korea to the United States, China, Russia, South Korea, and Japan—called the six-party talks, all aiming to get people who have got a stake with North Korea at the table, all aiming, again, to send a united voice to the North Koreans.

I'm a little—the North Korean nuclear issue disturbs me, but also equally disturbs me is the fact that people are being starved to death. And it should disturb the world. It should disturb all of us. The North Korea issue dominates my discussions with South Korea. However, there's a—South Korea and America has committed ourselves to the peace that comes—or the balance that comes with the U.S. force presence there in South Korea, although it's been reduced as well. We did not reduce force; we reduced manpower, as you probably know since you study it.

The issue that is on most Americans' mind, and the issue that really is the issue of the future in many ways, is China. And I would call our relationship with China very positive and complex. It's positive because we do have dialog. It's positive because the Chinese leadership—Hu Jintao and his predecessor—were able to sit down, and we had pretty frank discussions about a variety of issues.

On our agenda, of course, is trade—fairness in trade, as well as human rights and freedom of religion. On their issue—on their agenda has been, in the past, Taiwan, of course, which is a predominate issue. I've worked hard on that issue to make it clear that our position has not changed, and we do not expect either party to unilaterally change the status quo.

And one of the things, of course, we work on is to—would be very helpful if the Japanese and the Chinese had better relations, and the Japanese and the South Koreans. So we're spending time on that issue, as well, to try to bring a sense of—to encourage more dialog with—amongst those parties.

Our presence in the Far East is really important. And so therefore, my administration has been active in making sure we stay active in the region. The visit of Hu Jintao will be an interesting and important visit. He's coming into a country where there's an over $200 billion trade deficit, and a lot of Americans are wondering, where's the equity in trade? And therefore, I think he could help the Americans understand the importance of a free trading world if he were to maybe make a statement on his currency, for example.

I believe it's important for Americans to see a society that goes from being a—have its economic growth driven by exports to one having its economic growth more by consumer demand inside the country. That's an important part of our dialog with China.

It's very important for him to make a declaration on international property rights—IPR. It's difficult for a nation that likes to trade, like ours, to go into a country uncertain as to whether or not patents will be protected or product will be protected from copy. And so it will be a wide agenda.

The Far—the Pacific area is a very important part of our foreign policy. It's one where we've got a very active presence, and we'll continue to keep one. We've got a free trade agreement—you mentioned Singapore—we've got a free trade agreement with Singapore. And it's our—my relationship with these countries is based more than on just trade and commercialism. Mine is to work toward more democracy and freedom, as well, in the region, so that we can keep the peace in the long run.

I keep repeating this, I know, but I firmly believe that one way you lay the foundation for peace is to spread liberty and freedom. And there—again, I understand there's a debate. There's a legitimate debate. I'm just telling you what my position is. And I got something to say about it. Yes.

Human Trafficking

Q. Good morning, President Bush. I also feel very strongly about freedom, although I see it in terms of human trafficking. Your administration takes a very strong stance against prostitution. And because of that, you do not disperse funds to a lot of very effective NGOs around the world who pragmatically combat sex trafficking by working with existing prostitution networks. There's no evidence right now that proves either legalizing prostitution or criminalizing prostitution has any effect in the change of sex-trafficking cases. Have you considered changing your ideas about prostitution for the purposes of helping either save or keep people from being enslaved in sex prostitution?

The President. No, I appreciate it. I'm—it sounds like I'm dodging here, but again, you know more about this subject than I, and I will be glad to call Condi and talk to her about our policy. I thought we had a very robust strategy on exploitation of women and children, particularly around the world. I think I addressed this subject at the United Nations and was the only world leader to do. But as specifically about our position on prostitution, I'm going to have to talk to the Secretary about it. Yes.

Spread of Democracy

Q. Morning, Mr. President. I have a more general question about the United States work to democratize the rest of the world. Many have viewed the United States effort to democratize the world, especially nations in the Middle East, as an imposition or invasion on their sovereign rights.

Considering that it was, in fact, the Prophet Mohammed who established the first known constitution in the world—I'm referring to the constitution he wrote for the city of Medina—and that his life and the principles outlined in his constitution, such as the championing of the welfare of women, children, and the poor, living as an equal among his people, dissolving disputes between the warring clans in Arabia, giving any man or woman in parliament the right to vote and guaranteeing respect for all religions, ironically parallel those principles that we hold most precious in our own Constitution. I'm wondering how might your recently formed Iraq Study Group under the U.S. Institute for Peace explore these striking similarities to forge a new relationship with Iraqis and educate Americans about the democratic principles inherent in Islam?

The President. Great question. I believe that the terrorists have hijacked a peaceful religion in order to justify their behavior. I thank you for bringing that to my attention.

I will pass on your comments to James A. Baker, who is one of the chairmen of the group going to Iraq.

See, you said something really interesting. Initially, you said people view America imposing its beliefs. And I hearken back to what I said earlier—this fellow's question here—that if you believe that freedom is not universal, then it could be viewed as an imposition of beliefs. I'm not saying to countries, "You've got to look like us or act like us," but I am saying, you know, "Give your people a chance to be free." And I think it's necessary for America to take the lead on this issue. I think it is—I think it is vital for our future that we encourage liberty and—in this case, the Middle East. And as you said, it doesn't necessarily run contrary to what the Prophet Mohammed said.

It's a—and so how do you advance freedom? I mean, well, one thing you do is you make sure that the Lebanese have a chance to self-govern freely without Syrian interference. It's one thing you can do.

Another thing you can do is work for the establishment of a Palestinian state, which I'm doing. I believe that there will be a Palestinian state that is at peace with Israel. I believe it's going to have to be a democracy—again, a Palestinian-style democracy—to achieve that. But in my—early in my Presidency, I said, it's in our interest that there be two states, side by side in peace, and we're working toward that end.

You know, part of the debate here that I'm sure you're discussing is whether or not the United States should insist upon elections before everything is right. You hear the—the civil society has to be just right before you can have elections. I disagree strongly with that. I think elections are the beginning of the process, not the end.

And I found the elections that Hamas won very instructive and very interesting. It was—to me, it was a final condemnation of the Arafat era, where people said, "We're sick of corruption. We want better health care and better education; we want—we actually want our leaders to focus on the people, not on their self interests."

And because I believe in two states, side by side in peace, and therefore, expect the Government of both to be peaceful toward each other, we're not going to deal with a Government that has announced that they want to destroy Israel. On the other hand, we will help the Palestinian people. And I believe a democracy will eventually yield the state necessary to be side by side with Israel in peace.

The success of a democracy in Iraq—and as I told you, I think we're going to succeed; as a matter of fact, I know we are, if we don't lose our nerve—will send a powerful signal. Imagine the signal it will send to people in Iran that are not free right now. I believe the women's movement is going to be the leading edge of changing the Middle East. I don't believe women want to live as second-class citizens. I believe it's—I believe there's a universal desire to be treated fairly and equally.

And so I think—look, I'm pleased with the progress. I was reading the other day where Kuwaiti women are running for office. It's a positive sign, you know? We've got to be realistic about what's possible, but we've got to be firm in our belief that freedom is possible and necessary. Otherwise—I'll repeat to you—a system that says, "Okay, let's just tolerate the tyrant so long as everything seems okay," didn't work.

That's one of the lessons of the attack on the United States. You know, the world seemed fine, didn't it? It seemed kind of placid—there was a bubble here, a bubble there. But everything seemed all right. And yet, beneath the surface, there was tremendous resentment. And it's now come to full, and so how do you defeat their—now, if you don't think they have a ideology or a point of view, and/or a strategy to impose it, then I can understand why you think the United States ought not to be as active as we are.

But I believe differently. I believe they're bound—these folks are bound by an ideology. I know that they have got desires. They say it. This is one of—this is a different—this is a war in which the enemy actually speaks out loud. You heard the letter I wrote—read from—they didn't speak out loud on this one, but nevertheless, it's a—we've got to take their word seriously. When the enemy speaks, it makes sense for our military, our intelligence, the President to take the word seriously so we can adapt and adjust.

Anyway, very interesting question. Thanks for bringing that to my attention. Yes, ma'am.

Millennium Challenge Account

Q. Hi, Mr. President. Thank you very much for coming to speak with us. I am studying international development. And you have alluded much to tensions beneath the surface of countries. A lot of times, this comes from economic underdevelopment and lack of economic opportunities. You haven't spoken directly about economic development this morning, and I would like to know where economic development lies on your priority list.

And also, looking at countries that maybe haven't, in your words, gotten everything right in terms of political stability or democratization, is holding development funds—keeping development funds from those countries actually counterproductive? Because if you can help the country to develop economically, maybe some of these underlying tensions might dissipate.

The President. No, it's a great question. First of all, I'm a—matter of fact, I met this morning with Rob Portman, head of the USTR, about the Doha round of—for the WTO. And the reason I did is because I'm a big believer that trade helps lift people out of poverty. As a matter of fact, if you really study the relationship between development aid versus capital and the movement of capital and who—and how a society benefits more, it's because of trade and commerce.

And so we've been very active in this administration. AGOA, for example, is a free trade agreement with Africa. President Clinton passed it. I was more than happy to sign its extension, and we've been very hard in implementing it on the recognition that trade is a vital way for—to help people get their economies up and running.

And so, no question, the economy is important. In the Palestinian Territories, Jim Wolfensohn went over with a plan—prior to the election, by the way—with a plan to help the Palestinians develop their economy on the exact premise that you talk about. Economic development provides hope.

And so, you bet it's an integral of our policy. We give a lot of aid out, by the way. We give aid to countries that may like us, may not like us, except in few instances. I have changed the development program, however, from—let me say, I

added on to the development program through what's called the Millennium Challenge Account. And that is a conditional-based aid program. It's condition-based upon poverty level, but it's also condition-based upon behavior of government.

We should not be—we should insist that governments fight corruption. It seems like to me, it's a rational thing to do with taxpayers' money. And so part of the—one of the criterion for the Millennium Challenge Account, it says, "You don't get money if you don't fight corruption." We should insist that people invest in the health and education of their people. We should insist on marketplace reforms, open markets, so that people have a chance to realize the benefits of a growing economy. And we do. And so we give aid.

But the Millennium Challenge Account is an additional program that is, no question, conditional-based, based upon, I think, rational criterion. I remember having the discussion with some friends of mine from another part of the world. They said, "How can you insist upon conditions for the aid?" I said, "How can you not?" Why does it not make sense to say, get rid of your corruption? Unless you people think—unless people think that maybe the corruption is normal and necessary. It's not. A lot of people—a lot of countries have suffered as a result of governments that didn't care about them.

The other thing we're doing aggressively is to fight hunger and disease. Part of making sure that an economy can take hold is a—for example, for AGOA to be effective, there's got to be—we got to do something about HIV/AIDS, and we are. We're spending about $15 billion—or will have spent $15 billion over 5 years. And it's beginning to make a difference. And I'm real proud of our country, and I'm real proud of our friends and partners on the ground to get antiretroviral drugs to people, to help with prevention, to help take care of the orphans. And we feed a lot of people too. Ours is a generous nation.

So the development program is more than just passing out aid. It is trade. It is insistent upon habits of Government, and it's also fighting disease and hunger.

Yes.

2008 Elections/President's Second-Term Agenda

Q. Thank you, Mr. President, for coming to SAIS today. I'm a first-year master's candidate. In 2 years, the American political system will face a unique moment in its history, for, in fact, a sitting Vice President will decline the nomination for the Presidency. What are the implications for the Republican Party, your legacy, and, if you could choose, who would your successor be? Thank you. [*Laughter*]

The President. I'm not through yet, you know. [*Laughter*] It is—I'm glad my Vice President is not running for President. Not that he would make a great President, but that it certainly changes the dynamics inside the White House. And it is an amazing moment; you're right. I guess it's the most wide-open race ever. Oh, it can't be "ever." "Ever" is too long. [*Laughter*] But in a long time. [*Laughter*]

I am going to spend 2½ years charging as hard as I possibly can—I want to sprint out of office. And I will be a interested observer, and I'm sure I'll be roped into moments after our party nominates a candidate, but I'm just going to let the politics run its course.

And I've got a lot to do. We've got—listen, here are some of the challenges we face. We got to get off Middle Eastern oil, and therefore, we need to stay focused on a research and development initiative that helps us get away from fossil fuels but also helps countries like India diversify away from fossil fuels. And that's why the agreement I reached with India is a very important agreement—I thought that's what you were going to ask. [*Laughter*]

And many of you are—you look a lot younger than me—[*laughter*]—and so therefore, you better be worried about So-cial Security and Medicare. Our balance sheet is, no question, affected by a current account deficit. But a looming issue is the unfunded liabilities inherent in Social Security. And the Government needs to deal with it. The problem is, Washington is so political that it's—so far, it's—well, if somebody looks good, somebody looks bad. And so I'm going to stay focused on that, as well, and hopefully, get a bipartisan solution up on Social Security and Medicare, so that we can say to a younger generation, "We did our duty; we did something that's really hard to do." But we'd better get it done. The system is going broke, and you're going to pay a lot.

The immigration debate is an important debate. I don't—my point is—and I'll be glad to opine on it if you like. I think we need to be a—understand that we're a nation of immigrants, that we ought to be compassionate about this debate and provide a—obviously, we've got to secure the border and enforce the law. But one way to do so is to make sure that people who are coming in here to work have a legal—get a card so they don't have to try to sneak across the border, which takes pressure off our border.

People ought to be here on—be able to work on a temporary basis, and if they want to become a citizen, after a series of steps they got to take—they get in line like everybody else—not at the head of the line but the end of the line. And if Congress wants to say, "Well, we need more people from a certain country," they expand the number of green cards available.

My point to you is I got a lot to do, and you're the beginning—you're the leading edge of what's going to happen. I know—particularly from our friends in the press corps, they're going to be asking these questions a lot, "So-and-so said this; what do you say about that, or so-and-so—who are you for on this?" And I'm going to do my job as the President.

Yes.

Spread of Democracy/Trade

Q. Good morning, Mr. President. Thank you for coming. I agree with your assertion that Iraq is going to serve as a model for reformers, democratic reformers in the Middle East. But at the same time, I believe that whenever the seas are rough, the despots of the Middle East keep their heads down until the winds blow, and then they continue to do the exact same thing they've been doing for generations. I'm wondering, what pressures are we putting—or planning to put on these despots, some of whom are allies?

And one point of correction to Kent—the first constitution was written by Hammurabi in Samaria, modern-day Iraq. [*Laughter*]

The President. I was going to say that, you know, but I wanted to—[*laughter*]. Each President has his own style about how we deal with different leaders. I believe that it's very important for people to be—to listen. And therefore, I'm a person who does a lot of my work in private with these different leaders.

I talk frankly with people, but you can't have a frank discussion with somebody if you—if they feel like you're going to hold them up for public ridicule or public criticism. And so for those of you who are thinking about being President or being involved with diplomacy, you've got to think about how you deal with somebody you don't necessarily agree with and how best to be effective.

And so I just will tell you, however, I'm constantly talking about the need for there to be democracy and reform. And there's plenty of leverage throughout our Government. The President is not the sole voice when it comes to advancing the democracy agenda. You might notice Madam Secretary occasionally is outspoken in her—as she travels the world, which is positive. But there are other ways to send the message, as well, that we believe strongly that countries ought to adapt democratic habits.

I mentioned to you the notion of the women's movement in the Middle East. There is a way where the United States can effectively use NGOs—and I recognize—let me just say, I recognize sometimes if it says "Made in the USA" on it, it makes it more difficult to achieve certain reforms. And so we got to be wise about how we convince others to understand the importance of freedom. But we're—I can just assure you that we're constant dialog.

And I have had a lot of dialog with the leaders that come to see me and reminding them that whole societies are those that recognize the importance of giving people a chance to express themselves. And you'll find in the Middle East, there's—some people will say, "Well, what about such and such a group; they appear to be dangerous."

My answer is, if they've got support on the street, there's a reason. And if I were you, I would listen to the people better than they listen to the people. There's a reason why grass roots movements start. And one thing about democracy is, is that it forces the grass roots movement out in the open so people compete for ideas and for the will of the people in an open forum, not a closed forum. And it's those leaders that say, "I fear the grass root movement," are those that eventually are going to get whipped unless they outcompete them—outcompete them in a good sense, outcompete them for services, outcompete those who are stirring up the anxieties on the street by listening to the people and actually responding.

I know that's a foreign concept at some times, but nevertheless, it's a concept that ends up leading to a more whole society. And it's not easy work. We live in a world today where everything is supposed to happen yesterday. If you really think about Iraq—and it's tough; I fully recognize it's difficult. And I know people are anxious and their hearts break when they see the loss of innocent life. But it was 4 months ago that there was one of the most amazing elections in the history of the Middle East—4 short months ago. It seems like a decade, doesn't it? At least it does to me. [*Laughter*]

And so we're in a world where everything is, like, supposed to happen that way. But that's not the way it works. I believe what we're doing is putting those seeds in the ground. And it's important for future administrations to follow up, it seems like to me. And I said—I thought I laid out a pretty good marker for the United States in my second Inaugural Address, that said, why don't we work to end tyranny—it's a noble goal—under the belief that people desire to be free. And people should live in freedom.

I told you, listen, I'm deeply concerned about societies in which people are starving to death, in which people are ravaged by HIV/AIDS. That's why we've taken the initiative in this country. And it's very important for the American people to feel good about that initiative as well. It's not George Bush's initiative; it's the American people's initiative.

One of the principles that guides my policy is, to whom much is given, much is required. And I believe that's an essential part of the United States foreign policy.

I'll tell you another issue, now that I'm getting wound up, that you better consider and think about as future policymakers, is whether or not this country is going to succumb to protectionism and isolationism. And it's an interesting moment in our country's history. I put it in the State of the Union for a reason. I decided not to go with "here's the 42 things we're going to do to you or for you." [*Laughter*] It's— I talked about—I talked about the themes. I'm serious about this now. And as young policymakers, you need to seriously consider whether or not this country of ours is going to be confident enough to continue to lead. If we become isolationist, then we basically say, "Let them suffer." If we become isolationist, then we say, "It doesn't

matter if people live in freedom or not." If we become protectionist, we say, "Trade is okay, but we're more worried about competing in the world stage than we are helping developed nations grow."

And this is a serious debate that needs to be taken—my position is clear. I'm absolutely for this United States of America staying engaged to the world. And we've got to be confident in the values—listen, we were formed on the natural rights of men and women. Those weren't American rights. They were natural rights. There's something greater in our founding that speaks to, kind of, the universality of liberty.

And we ought to be confident about our ability to compete in trade. And I know it's difficult. I know it's hard if you're living in the Midwest and you lost your job, and somebody tells you, "You lost your job because of free trade." It's difficult for people. I know that. On the other hand, my judgment is if we put up walls and aren't willing to have free and fair trade, it will hurt the world economy, and it will cause people to suffer here at home and abroad.

But this is a defining moment, in my judgment, on these debates. I've got a pretty good antennae. I'm able to—see, I get a pretty good sense of how people are trending. And it's—and I would hope that out of this school comes people who are confident in American values and confident in our ability to compete.

Now, we've got to do smart things, and we've got an economic debate going on here. I think if we run up taxes, it will hurt our economy and make us less competitive. I know we've got to do something about energy to make us competitive in the 21st century. We really have to make sure we've got kids who've got the skill set necessary to fill the jobs of the 21st century. I mean, there are things we've got to do to make sure we remain competitive. It just doesn't happen. But nevertheless, we shouldn't fear it. We shouldn't fear competition. Competition is good.

And so I just hope—I hope—look, I'm not telling you what your curriculum is, but it's something worth talking about. These are—these happen to be the big trends of our society. And it's going to take, in my judgment, a future generation of people standing up, not losing our confidence. Look at the 1920s in our country's history. We shut down immigration; we had huge trade tariffs; and we were isolationist. And it didn't serve our country well, in my judgment.

All right, I've got to go to work. [*Laughter*] This isn't work; this is enjoyable. I want to thank you all for giving me a chance to come by and visit with you. Thanks for considering serving our country. It's a noble calling. It's a noble calling and worthwhile.

God bless you.

NOTE: The President spoke at 10:36 a.m. at Johns Hopkins University. In his remarks, he referred to William R. Brody, president, Johns Hopkins University; Jessica P. Einhorn, dean, Paul H. Nitze School of Advanced International Studies, Johns Hopkins University; Lt. Col. Fred M. Padilla, USMC, commander, 1st Battalion, 5th Marines; senior Al Qaida associate Abu Musab Al Zarqawi; Usama bin Laden, leader of the Al Qaida terrorist organization; Patrick J. Fitzgerald, U.S. Attorney for the Northern District of Illinois and Department of Justice CIA leak investigation special prosecutor; Prime Minister Junichiro Koizumi of Japan; President Hu Jintao of China; James A. Baker III, cochair, Iraq Study Group, U.S. Institute for Peace; and James D. Wolfensohn, Quartet Special Envoy for Gaza Disengagement. A participant referred to former Ambassador Joseph C. Wilson IV, who served as CIA envoy to Niger in February 2002.

Remarks in a Discussion on Medicare Prescription Drug Benefits in Jefferson City, Missouri
April 11, 2006

The President. Thank you all. Thanks for coming. Please be seated. Thank you. Cindy, thanks for the kind introduction. I want to thank the chamber for inviting me here, to what I think you'll find to be an interesting educational event; at least I hope so. As you can see, I mean, there's several ways to have an educational event. One is to put a podium out there and let me blow away for an hour, kind of talk and talk and talk. Another way is to have fellow citizens sit up here and discuss important policy issues. And that's what we're here to do today. We're here to discuss health care, particularly for our seniors. And so I want to thank you all for joining me.

Most important, thank you all for a warm welcome. It's good to be back here in Mis-souri. My only regret is that Laura is not with me. She's actually in Midland, Texas. That's where I was raised and she was born and raised. She's doing a little event there, picking up her mom, bringing her up to Washington. Mother and Dad are coming too, so we're going to have Easter at Camp David. A little family affair which is—[*applause*]. And I'm looking forward to it.

But I've also been looking forward to coming here as well. We just came from the Lutheran Senior Service Center. Carl Rausch—[*applause*]—yes, there you go. Thank you all. And we're about to have one of your fellow workers up here, as you'll note. The reason we were there is we were watching seniors sign up for the new Medicare drug benefit. In other words, we were at a facility where seniors had—

where seniors were, and there were good souls from this part of the world saying to people, "Here's what's available for you if you want to sign up."

What we're here today is to talk about health care for seniors. But before we get there, I do want to recognize Members of the United States Senate who have joined us—first, your senior Senator Kit Bond. Funny thing happened when we were crossing the river. [*Laughter*] He reminded me of how important that Missouri River is for getting farm product to market. I see the hat back there—thank you. Yes, sir. Kind of reminds me of home. [*Laughter*]

And also traveling with us is a fellow who I've come to admire a lot as a straight shooter, Senator Jim Talent—and the Congressman from this district, Kenny Hulshof. Kenny, I appreciate you. Thank you. Peter Kinder, Lieutenant Governor, has joined us; Governor, thanks for being here. Proud you're here. It's good to see you again.

Most of all, thanks for coming. Health care is a vital issue for this country. In my judgment, the best health care plan is one that says, "We'll help the poor; we'll help the elderly; and we'll make sure the doctor-patient relationship is solid for the rest of us." In other words, we don't want the Federal Government—we really don't want the Federal Government telling folks who—what to buy and how to buy it and what price to pay. We want there to be a relationship between doctors and patients. That's what we want.

But our Government made a commitment to our seniors, and it's a commitment that I intended to keep when I went to Washington, DC. In other words, our commitment is our seniors should have first-class health care. That commitment, interestingly enough, was first signed by a fellow citizen from Texas named Lyndon Baines Johnson. And so I came to Washington, DC, and said, "Are we doing as good a job as possible to provide modern medicine for our seniors?" You see, once the Govern-

ment makes a commitment, it ought to be a solid commitment; it ought to be a good commitment. There's no need to have a health care system for our seniors that doesn't meet needs. And one of the things I noticed in the analyzation of the health care system for seniors, analyzation of Medicare, was that medicine had changed but Medicare hadn't.

I'll give you an example. Medicare would pay thousands and thousands and thousands of dollars for ulcer surgery but not a dime for the prescription drugs to help prevent the ulcer from occurring in the first place. That didn't make sense. It certainly didn't make sense for the seniors, did it? In other words, if you're going to have a modern system, you ought to have a system that says, pharmaceuticals have helped change medicine. And it certainly didn't make sense for the taxpayers. After all, if you would spend $50 a month to prevent ulcer surgery, and the surgery costs thousands to begin with, it saves money.

And so I said to the people in Washington, DC, "Let's modernize the system. Let's figure out how to make it work better for our seniors." A commitment made is a commitment we've got to keep. And we finally got a deal done, finally put aside needless politics. I must confess to you, Washington is full of needless politics. We can do a better job.

We need to focus on big problems, and a big problem was that Medicare wasn't living up to its expectations. And I signed the bill, and I proudly signed it. And so this bill helps all seniors afford prescription drugs. It really helps a lot. It gives seniors choices.

I knew this would be a problem at first. Some people just simply don't want to be confronted with choice. You kind of get settled in and everything seems to be going fine, and all of a sudden, up pops a new Medicare plan, and you've got 42 choices to choose from here in Missouri. And that can be a little confusing. I knew that would be the case.

On the other hand, I also knew there were thousands of fellow citizens who would be willing to go out and help people determine what choice suited their needs. See, I believe that people ought to be trusted. I don't think the Government ought to be making every decision on behalf of the citizens. I think the more that people—citizens are given choice in life, the better off it is to meet their needs. See, when you have the Government say, "This is for you," sometimes it doesn't meet a person's needs. When you have a person say, "Here's some options for you to choose from," it means you could design a program to meet your health care needs. And that's what we did in this new Medicare plan.

And thirdly, one of the things the Medicare plan didn't have was catastrophic coverage. One of the things this drug plan says is that something may happen, out of your control, and therefore, you may have a big expenditure. And therefore, it seems to make sense that there would be catastrophic, kind of, stopgap coverage. And so over $3,600, the Government will pay 90 percent in this new plan. To me that makes sense. It gives somebody peace of mind. People say, everything seems to be going okay right now, but if something goes bad, the Government will help you. And so the new drug benefit that we're describing today has got a catastrophic component. And when people sign up, it should give you peace of mind, give your family peace of mind.

Fourthly, it's—I recognize that certain people need help in our society. And therefore, if you're a low-income senior—about a third of the seniors qualify—the Government is going to pay over 90-something percent of your—95 percent of the bill. In other words, we recognize people need help in this society; we're a compassionate society. And so the drug benefit, if you're a low-income senior, is really going to help. It's going to help all seniors. Matter of fact, it's estimated that all seniors' drug bills are

cut in half under this program. And if you're a low-income senior, it's especially beneficial. And that's the way it should be.

I remember the debate in Washington, DC—the language gets a little rugged up there. We had people say, "The prescription drug plan is just simply a hollow promise," or, "The bill will leave millions of seniors worse off." That's not the facts. See, when you cut through all the rhetoric and look at the results, I think people are going to be amazed at what's available.

One the reasons I'm here is that even though 29 million people have signed up, there's still about 7 million people who are qualifying for this program, and they ought to take a look. One way to convince people to take a look is to have others talk about the benefits of the program. They've probably got a little more credibility than I do. [*Laughter*] You don't have to agree with that. [*Laughter*] I'm just telling you, it's a good deal.

As a matter of fact, we estimated the premiums to be $37 a month. They're down to $25 a month for the seniors—for most seniors. When people have choice, the 42 plans helps bring cost-effectiveness into medicine. You got one choice, you don't get cost-effective. You got 42 programs to choose from—it's amazing what happens when somebody kind of competes for your business, that says, "I'm going to try to make the plan attractive for you." And that's the difference between a government-dictated program and a program that trusts seniors to make choice.

We've got up until May 15th for folks to get the best benefits. If you haven't signed up—if you're listening on TV and haven't signed up, please take a look, call 1–800–MEDICARE or go to medicare.gov if you want to find out what's available.

If you're a son—or if you've got a mom or a dad who is eligible for Medicare, a son or a daughter has a duty, in my judgment, to the parent to find out what's available for your mom or dad. That's your duty. This is a good deal. It costs nothing to look at it. I think you're going to find it's an amazing opportunity to really help your mom or dad with prescription drugs, make sure they get modern medicine. Isn't that what a son or a daughter wants, to make sure the mom or dad gets the best possible medicine? Well, here's the plan that will make sure you get the best possible medicine.

If you're a church, in a part of a church or community center, find somebody who's eligible for Medicare and help them. It's not all that hard. It's a pretty simple program. It may be hard for the senior who's not necessarily computer-literate, but if you're computer-literate, it's pretty easy. The steps are easy to follow. And you'll be doing somebody a favor.

If you're a senior wondering whether or not this makes sense, you ought to take a look. It doesn't cost a dime to look, and you're going to save money. Seniors are saving about half on the prescription drug charges already. If you're a poor senior, the Government is going to pay over 95 percent of the deal.

I'm here to, kind of, cut through all the politics and cut through all the rhetoric and help people understand what's available. No better place to come than the State of Missouri, kind of the "Show-Me" State. So we're about to show you. And I'm going to start with Dr. Mark McClellan, fellow Texan. McClellan is an unusual fellow; he's got a lot of degrees.

What are your degrees, McClellan?

Mark B. McClellan. Mr. President, I have a medical degree, also a Ph.D.

The President. Yes. One of the things I like to remind people of is this fact: He's a Ph.D., and I was an okay student. [*Laughter*] Look who the adviser is, and look who the President is. [*Laughter*] I've used it before with him. He's a good sport. His job is—what?

Dr. McClellan. I'm the head of the Medicare and Medicaid programs, and we are working with groups all over the country to help people find out about the most

important new benefit in Medicare in 40 years—that's the drug coverage that you're talking about, sir.

The President. See, we have got a duty at the Federal level to help people find out what's available. That's our duty. Mark is in charge of it. He works with Mike Leavitt, who's the Secretary of Health and Human Services, and they've done a fine job. By the way, when you put 29 million people, right off the bat, into a system, you're going to have glitches, but they've handled the glitches. They're working with your Governor. They're working with the State government to work on dual eligibles. I know you read initially about the issues related to the signups—we're dealing with them. His job is to run them down, find those problems, and solve them.

His job is also to help rally the country, others to help explain the program. And how are we doing? Give us——

Dr. McClellan. Well, now over 29 million people are already participating, hundreds of thousands more seniors and people with a disability are signing up every week. But we want to make sure, Mr. President, that everybody gets the support they need to make a competent decision. Some of the things that we do in that include our Medicare help line. People can call us anytime, day or night, at 1–800–MEDICARE, and get personalized help, finding out about what the drug benefit means for you. If you like to go online, or you've got a son or daughter or grandchildren who do, you can go to medicare.gov and get personalized help as well.

But what we've really found is that events all over the country help us connect with beneficiaries, make sure we're reaching them where they live and work and play and pray, so that they can find out, face to face, what the new drug benefit means for them. We've been working with pharmacists and other health professionals—like at the event that you visited earlier today here in Jefferson City—many advocacy groups that advocate on behalf of seniors, people with a disability——

The President. AARP.

Dr. McClellan. ——AARP, church groups, the NAACP—very diverse range of groups that don't agree on everything, don't agree sometimes on much of anything, but they all agree that seniors and people with a disability should find out about the most important new benefit in Medicare in 40 years.

The President. One thing that's important, that people with disability also qualify—some people do—and they need to make sure that they take a look at what's available.

Give me some of the day—we got a timeframe here we're working in.

Dr. McClellan. That's right. We've got until May 15th—that's the end of the enrollment period. And we're urging people to take a look now so they avoid the rush that's probably going to come as we get very close to that May 15th deadline. This week, there are going to be more than a thousand events all over the country that include many senior officials from your administration, that include health professionals, that include all of these groups that we're collaborating with all over the country to help people find out about the program. We're doing it here in Jefferson City and at events all over the State of Missouri. We're doing it all over the country.

The President. Yes, change isn't easy. It's hard to change, particularly a system that's been in place since the 1960s. And yet we felt it was necessary to encourage change for the sake of our seniors. But we also understand that it requires a massive effort to show people—get it, "show me"—to show people—[*laughter*]—what's available. And old Mark is in charge of it. But it requires an army of compassion to help.

And one thing before we go to Linda, who's a soldier in the army of compassion, by the way—is tell me about the low-income benefit. Describe that to the folks who are listening.

Dr. McClellan. Well, as you said, Mr. President, everybody in Medicare can take advantage of this new drug coverage, whether they've got a retiree plan now—we can help with that—whether they like to get their care through a Medicare Advantage Plan—that's the HMOs or PPOs in Medicare. Lots of people like to get help in different ways. But there is extra help available for people with limited incomes.

And so if you're living month to month on a Social Security check or some other limited fixed income, or if you know someone who is, it's very important to look into the extra help. You apply for this extra assistance. As you said, you can get 95 percent of your drug costs paid for, on average. That's a benefit worth about $3,700 a year on average.

Now, for a typical senior, you're getting about $1,100 worth of help with drug costs on average. So that's important right there. But there's extra help available for people of limited means, and we're making some extra efforts to reach out to people who may not be able to find out about this program otherwise. Here in rural parts of the States, we're working with the Grange; we're working with the USDA to get out into the community and, at a grassroots level, help people find out——

The President. We're working with Heisinger Bluffs Senior Living Center, as well.

Dr. McClellan. That's right.

The President. Weren't we?

Dr. McClellan. That's right; we sure are.

The President. Linda Detring, welcome.

Linda Detring. Good morning, Mr. President.

The President. Thanks for coming. Lutheran Senior Services.

[*At this point, Ms. Detring, vice president of operations, Lutheran Senior Services, made brief remarks, concluding as follows.*]

Ms. Detring. During that time, I also became a Reserve officer in the United States Navy Reserves, as a Nurse Corps officer.

The President. Fantastic, thanks.

Ms. Detring. I retired 2 years ago as a captain.

[*Ms. Detring made further remarks.*]

The President. See, it's interesting; when you listen to what Linda said, she said "educate" about three or four times. And that's what we're doing. That's why I've asked these people to come sit up here with me, which isn't easy, by the way, is it? [*Laughter*] Wait until she speaks; you're not going to believe it. [*Laughter*] Anyway, we want people to know what's available. And I bet you people, when they take a look at the 40-plus choices here in Missouri, get a little nervous at first.

Ms. Detring. This is a little overwhelming at first. But if you help them through it—and I went on the Internet to choose my mother's plan, and it was very simple once I got on there and understood it.

The President. Well, I appreciate you. Thanks.

Ms. Detring. Welcome.

The President. Thanks for serving as a good example two times: one, as a loving daughter, and two, as a person who is involved with the faith community, all extending a helping hand to somebody who needs a little help. Thanks for doing it.

Another person who is involved with senior citizens happens to be Jodie Baker. Isn't that right?

Jodie Baker. Yes, it is.

The President. And what do you do?

Ms. Baker. Thank you, Mr. President. I am a pharmacist. I work here in Jefferson City at Kmart Pharmacy, so I get to see a lot of seniors.

The President. You see people coming to buy—yes, exactly. That's good. So tell us about—tell me about your involvement with the Medicare Part D program.

Ms. Baker. Well, I was very excited to be involved at my place of work in trying to get the word out. And I like to talk. I think most of my customers would agree with that.

The President. We're about to find out, aren't we?

[*Ms. Baker made brief remarks, concluding as follows.*]

Ms. Baker. That's one thing; as a pharmacist, it's heartbreaking to me because I see people come in, and I know their conditions, and I know maybe not all their finances, but the medications are so expensive. I have people ask me, "Can you help me pick which prescription I can get this month?" And that's very hard——

The President. Yes, it's got to be. Listen, there were people literally choosing between the electricity bill and pharmaceuticals.

Ms. Baker. Yes, or food.

The President. And that's not right in this country. And this program fixed it. And one of the things you told me earlier—this, by the way, isn't the first time we've seen each other. Well, it's the first day we've seen each other but not the first time, on the stage. Tell me about what you find with the low-income seniors. And give people a sense—if you're a low-income senior, you need to listen.

[*Ms. Baker made further remarks.*]

The President. Isn't that neat? I appreciate it. There's pharmacists all over the country who, obviously, interface with seniors. And I want to thank those in the pharmaceutical—I mean, in the pharmacist industry who are explaining what's available. And it's an interesting example, isn't it, of somebody who is combining her work with her care for seniors and helping people see what's available.

I appreciate you coming and explaining that.

Ms. Baker. Thank you very much.

The President. Jerry, welcome. Jerry Sooter, thanks for coming.

Gerald "Jerry" Sooter. Thank you, Mr. President.

The President. Appreciate you.

Mr. Sooter. We appreciate you being here very much, and thank you. I retired as a funeral director in June of 2003. I was born and raised in north Missouri, northwest Missouri. And, by the way, my wife and daughter and son-in-law and grandson are here.

The President. Yes. Looking forward to meeting them afterwards.

Mr. Sooter. I'm sure they're looking forward to that too. [*Laughter*]

The President. It would be kind of rough if you said they weren't looking forward— [*laughter*].

[*Mr. Sooter made brief remarks.*]

The President. That's great advice. Isn't it interesting, the society in which we live, word gets out; Jerry gets on the computer and taps into the system which, for some, can be complicated—obviously wasn't for you.

Mr. Sooter. I found it extremely easy, and it's perplexing to me to hear people say it's difficult.

The President. Well, some people are computer-literate, and some aren't, for starters. But I like the self-starter—you're a self-starter. You said, "I'm going to look." People need to take a look. That's what you need to do. Jerry is saving 65 percent on his drugs. That's pretty healthy savings. I bet you could use the savings.

Mr. Sooter. Well, that's correct, because last week, when the computer went out on my automobile, it came in handy. [*Laughter*]

The President. That's good. Well, we appreciate you joining us. Thank you for being willing to tell people your story. You're a lot more credible at telling people your story than I would be. In other words, it's important for people to hear that. Here's Jerry sitting here; he doesn't have anything to—any ax to grind; all he wants to do is tell people what's available. And

that's why we've asked him to come. And you're very articulate about it. Thanks for coming. Looking forward to meeting the grandkids. Appreciate you.

Helen Robinette—isn't that right?

Helen Robinette. Yes, that's right, Mr. President. [*Laughter*]

[*Mrs. Robinette, senior citizen, made brief remarks, concluding as follows.*]

Mrs. Robinette. I save approximately 200 a month on my drugs.

The President. Isn't that interesting?

Mrs. Robinette. Yes, I save approximately 200 a month.

The President. You mean you were paying 300 a month, and now you're paying about 100?

Mrs. Robinette. Yes, yes. It's probably— sometimes it's not even 100. Then also I had——

The President. So your insurance friend laid it out for you?

Mrs. Robinette. Yes.

The President. Explained it?

Mrs. Robinette. Yes, she did. She did. She was very nice, very nice.

The President. Well, she's supposed to be. [*Laughter*]

Mrs. Robinette. We were kind of dense and didn't understand it.

The President. No, listen, but you're not alone. When you're—this can be confusing to folks.

Mrs. Robinette. It is.

The President. And that's why we've asked people to help—step up and help somebody who needs some explanation. Jerry figured it out, but you, fortunately, had somebody who said, "Look, I want to help you see what's available." And you're saving now over $2,000 a year, sounds like.

[*Mrs. Robinette made further remarks.*]

The President. Babying that inhaler.

Mrs. Robinette. I was babying that inhaler. [*Laughter*] And only took it when I couldn't walk across the floor.

The President. I got you.

Mrs. Robinette. And then all my allergies—if the doctor didn't have any samples, I didn't take it because it was very expensive, and I couldn't do that.

The President. Yes.

Mrs. Robinette. So now with your program, my inhaler is $5. And I get to take the allergy medicine too, and I love it. [*Laughter*]

The President. I'm glad you came. Good job.

All right, we're going to end here with Bob Vanderfeltz. Got the Vanderfeltz family here. When I first met him, I said, "I like a guy with a snap-on shirt." [*Laughter*] Tell everybody about yourself right quick.

Bob Vanderfeltz. Your people asked me when they called me, "Are you going to wear a suit?" I said, "No, I'm not going to buy one; I don't have one."

The President. Yes. [*Laughter*] Yes, I wish I didn't have to wear them, believe me. [*Laughter*]

Mr. Vanderfeltz. I wish to acknowledge my family. My beautiful wife and four of my children are here. One of them is a little bit far away. We've got a lieutenant colonel, battalion commander, serving in Iraq at the present time.

The President. Really? Gosh, thank you. Yes, tell him thanks. You tell him. That's great. You know how to e-mail?

Mr. Vanderfeltz. No, sir, I'm one of those illiterate computer boys. I don't even own one.

The President. Yes, well, get one of your sons to e-mail him, and tell him the Commander in Chief is proud.

How do you make a living?

Mr. Vanderfeltz. How do I make a living?

The President. Yes.

Mr. Vanderfeltz. Well, at the present time, I'm retired. I was born and raised right here in central Missouri. The apple didn't fall far from the tree. I live still on the dairy farm I was born and raised on.

The President. Really?

Mr. Vanderfeltz. Yes, sir.

The President. A man of the land. That's great.

Mr. Vanderfeltz. Nothing like it.

The President. You got big hands. [*Laughter*]

Mr. Vanderfeltz. I know how to milk.

The President. Yes, I bet you do. [*Laughter*]

Mr. Vanderfeltz. It's kind of like riding a bicycle. You never forget that. [*Laughter*]

Getting back to what we're here for—[*laughter*]—well, I went about mine a little differently, like I said, being computer-illiterate—well, what did I have to lose; I called my local Social Security office. And surprising to me—I was lucky I knew someone there, and I was talking to them, and in less than 10 minutes, they had me signed up on a program, in less than 10 minutes time. And from that point, I said, well, I'll find out what it is to get into a program, so I attempted to call the 1–800 number in the middle of the day, and I found out that sometimes automated machines work better at nighttime when they aren't so busy. [*Laughter*]

The President. Bring that up with McClellan. [*Laughter*] We did have a problem initially on the 1–800 number. A lot of people were calling, and then they ended up putting a lot more operators on there. Now, I'm not making excuses. Look, I understand. But thank you.

Mr. Vanderfeltz. But I went, like I said, earlier—or later in the evening, at that time, and it was, push the buttons and right straight through.

[*Mr. Vanderfeltz made further remarks.*]

The President. Yes, hear that—$140 a month, now he's paying $7 a month. Here's a guy—he may not be computer-literate, but he's smart enough to call and ask advice for a program that's saving him a lot of money. Isn't that right?

Mr. Vanderfeltz. Right.

The President. You recommend people look at this thing? That's a leading question—I'm not even a lawyer. [*Laughter*]

Mr. Vanderfeltz. No, I appreciate it very much. Needless to say, I didn't have to go to school very far to find out that it saved me money. [*Laughter*]

The President. I bet you're plenty smart; you know what I'm saying? [*Laughter*] I bet you know what you're doing.

I hope you all have found this interesting. You may not believe me, but you'll believe Bob, or you'll believe Helen, or you'll believe Jerry. These are real-life examples of people who said, "I think I'll just take a look." Twenty-nine million Americans have signed up so far. There's 7 million more we're trying to reach. If you're one of the 7 million who have not signed up, at least take a look—take a look at what's available for you.

This Government of ours has modernized Medicare so that we can look seniors in the eye and say, "We're doing the best we can to make sure your medicine is modern." We don't want people choosing between electricity bills or food and their pharmaceuticals, like that was happening a while back.

This program makes sense for our seniors. It makes sense for our taxpayers. Do you realize that because there's choice in the marketplace, because we've trusted seniors to pick a plan that meets their needs, the estimated costs in the first year to the Federal Government are 20 percent less than thought. In other words, one of the things that's important for our society to understand is that when you trust people, good things happen. It happens for them, and it happens for society as a whole.

I'm proud to be here in Missouri. I want to thank you all for giving us a chance to come by and say hello. We're dealing with big issues. We're dealing with health care; we're dealing with keeping the peace; we're helping our small businesses thrive. It is a fantastic opportunity to come and thank you all for really being, however, the—representing the true strength of America. And the true strength of this country is not in the size of our armies or in the size of our wallets; it's in the size of our hearts.

And for those of you who are helping a neighbor in need, helping a child to learn how to read, or providing shelter for the homeless or food for the hungry or advice to the seniors, I want to thank you from the bottom of my heart for helping to make this Nation the greatest nation on the face of the Earth.

Thanks for coming, and God bless.

NOTE: The President spoke at 12:37 p.m. at the Etta and Joseph Miller Performing Arts Center. In his remarks, he referred to Cynthia Brinkley, president, AT&T—Missouri; Carl Rausch, president, Lutheran Senior Services; and Gov. Matt Blunt and Lt. Gov. Peter D. Kinder of Missouri.

Remarks Following a Visit With Senior Citizens in Des Moines, Iowa
April 11, 2006

Senator Grassley and I are thrilled to be here. One of the things that's happening is that people around the country are beginning to realize there's a new prescription drug benefit for folks on Medicare. And it's very important for people to understand that this is a very beneficial program.

And so I'm spending time today and tomorrow, as I have in previous months, reminding people that it doesn't cost anything to look—that people ought to take a look and see what this good program does for people.

I want to thank Senator Grassley. He was very instrumental in getting this important piece of legislation through the Congress. One of the things I remember him saying to me is that "as we pass a Medicare bill, let's make sure that Iowa rural hospitals are taken care of." In other words, he was deeply concerned to make sure Medicare was modernized, so seniors have choices and a prescription drug coverage, but he was also concerned to make sure that rural health was available for the citizens of Iowa and around the country. And Senator Grassley has been a strong leader in this effort.

I strongly urge the seniors here in Iowa to take a look. So far about 29 million seniors have signed up around the country. I met with some folks today that have saved good money. Today, for example, I met with Helen and Debbie. Helen saved $200 a month in her prescription drug coverage, and she convinced her friend, Debbie, to take a look at the Medicare prescription drug plan. Debbie now saves $1,200 a month—saves $1,200 a month.

So I urge people not to listen to the noise and all the politics—just get that out of the system—and see whether or not the prescription drug coverage makes sense. If you're a poor senior, this program will help you a lot. As a matter of fact, the Government pays nearly—over 95 percent of the benefits for poor seniors.

Every senior is saving money, and that's what people have got to know. There is an easy way to find out how the program works, and that's to call 1–800–MEDI-CARE, or you can go on the computer systems at medicare.gov. Here we're seeing some of our fellow citizens reaching out to seniors to explain the program. And this is happening all across the country. I want to thank those who are here for helping our fellow citizens understand what's available. I fully recognize that when you have a variety of choices from which to choose, it can be a little confusing at first. In other words, people get on the computer and say, "Look at all these different options."

But the good thing about the programs and the people who are willing to help is that they can design a program that meets your needs. And that's really important. Now, if you're a son or a daughter whose mom or dad is Medicare-eligible, please help your parent; please do your duty. If you're in a church or a community center, find an elderly citizen who has yet to sign up for Medicare and show him or her what is possible. This is a good program for our seniors. It is a good deal, and it's very important for seniors to sign up prior to May 15th.

And so I'm thrilled to be back in your State, Senator. Iowa has got a special spot in my heart. I bring greetings from the First Lady Bush. And I also, again, encourage the citizens here in Iowa and around the country who are eligible for Medicare, to make sure you look at the program. And again, I remind you of the examples of Helen and Debbie. Debbie's case is an extraordinary case, where she is receiving a lot of help. And that's what we want this program to do, is to provide people with a lot of help.

So thank you very much. The Senator and I look forward to greeting you personally. Appreciate you letting us come by to say hello.

NOTE: The President spoke at 3:20 p.m. at Wesley Acres retirement community. A tape was not available for verification of the content of these remarks.

Remarks at a Reception for Gubernatorial Candidate Jim Nussle in Des Moines
April 11, 2006

Thank you all. Please be seated. Thanks for coming. Governor, I appreciate that introduction. I can't tell you how delighted I am to support Jim Nussle as the next Governor of the State of Iowa. He was there—he was there in Amana. No question about it. He introduced me. What he forgot to tell you was, he actually sang. [*Laughter*] He'll be known as the singing Governor of Iowa. [*Laughter*]

I've gotten to know this man real well. I've seen him when the heat's on. You know, you can judge a person in Washington by how they react to pressure. Jim Nussle stands strong when there's pressure. You need a Governor of Iowa who can take the heat and lead this State to a better future, and that man is Jim Nussle.

He's a proven leader. See, that's what the people of Iowa need. They need somebody to lead. He's proven himself to be a leader. He's got a record, something people can look at. The thing I like about him is when he gives your word, he keeps it. When he looks you in the eye and says, "Mr. President, I'm with you," he means it. What the people of Iowa need is a Governor who looks the people in the eye and says, "This is what I intend to do," and then does what he says he's going to do in office, and that man is Jim Nussle.

I like the fact he's getting Democrat support. I think you need a Governor who can reach across party lines to get things done. I was pleased to see Terry Duggan, the former mayor of Dubuque, is here tonight. He's a Democrat who's switching so he can support his friend Jim Nussle. That's the kind of Governor Nussle will be—he's the kind of person who sets clear agendas and clear goals and brings people together to achieve the goals. People in Iowa, like they are all across the country, are sick and tired of needless politics. What they want is leadership. And they'll get strong leadership in Jim Nussle as the Governor.

And I'm proud to be with his wife, Karen, the next first lady of the State of Iowa. I know something about First Ladies—I'm married to one. [*Laughter*] And Laura sends her love. Nussle came out to the airport, and he said, "Fine, I'm glad to have you here this time of the year, but when we're coming down the stretch, make sure you send the A Team." [*Laughter*] I said, "Which one, Mother or Laura?" [*Laughter*] He said, "Both." [*Laughter*] They both want Jim Nussle to be the Governor of this important State. They know him well, and they admire him and like him. And, Jim, Mother and Laura send their best.

It's also a thrill to be here with your parents, Mark and Lori. You know, there's nothing better than having a strong family, coming down the stretch in a political campaign. And nothing, also, better than having a good runningmate, and it's an honor to be here with Bob Vander Plaats and his wife, Darla. Thank you all for being here. Good luck to you.

I'll never forget campaigning in Iowa, and particularly in the caucuses in 2000. And I had the honor of campaigning with your United States Senator. And so we're driving down the road, and he said, "Old Bill lives in that house, and Jim lives in that house. That's the Smiths' house over there." I've never been with a person who understands the grassroots and the people of Iowa better than Chuck Grassley. Senator, I'm thrilled to be here with you. Oh, there he is.

And so we land at the airport, and Senator Grassley says, "I want you to meet the next member of the statehouse from the 17th District." I said, "I'm looking forward to that, Senator. Who is he?" He said,

"Well, it just happens to be my grandson, Pat Grassley." You're following the footsteps, Pat, of a really fine man in your grandfather. Good luck to you. All I can tell you is they had Grassley in to talk about key issues facing the country, and he said, "Before we talk about the key issues, I just want you to know, my grandson is going to be elected." [*Laughter*] The guy puts his family first, and I appreciate that.

I'm also honored to be here with Congressman Steve King of Iowa. Where are you, Steve? There he is. Thanks for coming. I know when Nussle gets elected to be the Governor, he's going to be smart enough to call upon former Governor Bob Ray for advice. Bob Ray is here—thrilled you're here, Governor. Thanks for coming—one of the real class acts in Iowa politics.

State Senator Jeff Lamberti, who's going to be the next United States Congressman from the Third Congressional District, is with us.

You know, one of the people that has impressed me the most here in Iowa politics is a fellow who's served as a State senator, but he left the party chairmanship of Iowa to go to Iraq. His country called; he said, "Yes, sir, I want to serve"—and that's Chuck Larson.

It's good to see the speaker is here. It's a good sign, Governor. When the speaker starts showing up before the elections, it's always a good sign something is in the air. And by the way, this is a huge crowd for a person running for Governor. And I want to thank you all for coming to support this good man. It's a good sign this early in the campaign to have such a big crowd.

Speaker Chris Rants is here. Thanks for coming, Speaker. And I want to thank Chuck Gipp as well, the majority leader. You're going to have you a Governor you can work with and get some stuff done. I want to appreciate the State auditor—David, thanks for coming. It's proud to be with you again.

I want to thank the party chairman; I want to thank the grassroots activists; I want to thank those who are getting ready to turn out the vote next fall for what you're going to do. You got to help this good man. You got to start manning the phones and putting up the signs at the right time. He's going to count on you to win this election. He cannot do it alone. And I want to thank those of you who have contributed to his campaign. It's hard to have a fundraiser this successful this early in the campaign season. It means you put together a good organization. And I want to thank those who put this fundraising dinner on. You know, it's nothing better than to be a candidate running for office and know that there's a lot of good folks standing with you. It's going to be the kind of thing that empowers the candidacy as it gets closer to the election. The fact that he's had this many folks show up is a good sign. And I want to thank you all for contributing to the next Governor of your State.

You know, I've gotten to see Nussle during some interesting times in our country; we are living in historic times. I wish I could report to you that this was a nation that wasn't at war, but we are. And it's a deadly serious war. It's a war that requires strong leadership and resolve. The war came to us on September the 11th, 2001, and we didn't ask for it, but it came unexpectedly. We lost more people on that day than we lost at Pearl Harbor. It's a day I'll never forget. And it's formulated how I think about foreign policy.

I said to myself on that day that I would use all assets of national power to protect the American people. The most important job Jim and I have in Washington, DC, is to protect our country. And the best way to do that is to stay on the offense, is never relent, is never give in, is never hope for the best but to pursue the enemy until we bring them to justice.

And Iraq is the central front on this broad war on terror. You know, I said this—I gave a speech the other day, and in it, I said something—I said, you know, I wonder why people—what kind of people is it who wants to stop democracy? In our country, we got to think about the nature of the type of person that can't stand liberty. What kind of people is it, when they see a chance for people to live in a free society, they do everything in their power to stop the advance of freedom? I'll tell you what kind of people it is—these are the kind of people who think the opposite of—they adhere to an ideology that's dark and dangerous.

The enemy that we face has got plans. They got ambitions. They believe that democracies are weak. They believe it's a matter of time for the United States to withdraw, and by withdrawing, they would find safe haven from which to launch attacks again. We're not going to be intimidated by thugs and assassins. We will achieve victory in Iraq, and by achieving victory in Iraq, we will make it more secure for a generation of Americans.

They hope that we lose our nerve. We will not lose our nerve. We will stand with the brave freedom fighters and democracy—democrats in Iraq—[*applause*].

These are difficult times for the American people, and I understand that. The enemy cannot defeat us on the battlefield. The only thing they can do is kill innocent life and hope we retreat. We're not going to retreat. Victory in Iraq is vital for our security. We got one powerful weapon going for us besides our brave military, and that is liberty. Jim Nussle and I understand that liberty is universal, that there is an Almighty, and the Almighty's gift to each man and woman on the face of the Earth is freedom, that deep in everybody's soul is the desire to live in a free society. And we understand that as democracy takes hold in parts of the world that is desperate for freedom, we are laying the foundation of peace for a generation to come.

The temptation in Washington, DC, is to try to make decisions based upon polls or focus groups. You cannot lead the Nation, nor can you lead a State, if you rely upon polls to tell you what to think. The thing I like about Jim Nussle is he stands on principle. Principles will be the bedrock for his decisionmaking. You don't have to worry about this man—kind of drift, trying to figure out what he thinks or what he believes. He'll lead this State to a better tomorrow because he's a man willing to stand on principle and make the hard decision and stand by it.

I've got to see him when it comes time to spending your money. And he's pretty good about it. You know, the temptation—every program sounds great in Washington, by the way. And believe me, those appropriators in Washington, they love to appropriate. And that's why it's been important to have an ally on the budget in Jim Nussle. We have passed some lean budgets in Washington, DC, because we want to cut the deficit in half. But he's not going to fall into that trap that you hear coming out of the halls of legislatures all around the country that say, "In order to balance the budget, let's raise taxes." That's what you're going to hear out of Washington, DC. But that's not how Washington works. Yeah, they'll raise your taxes all right, but they'll also figure out ways to spend your money. The best way to balance this budget is to keep your taxes low so this economy grows and be wise about how we spend your money. And Jim Nussle is doing just that as the budget chairman of the House.

He's got a plan to reform the taxes of Iowa. He's got a plan to keep this State on the leading edge of economic vitality. And he's the kind of fellow that can take a plan and put it into action. You know, we were talking about education behind the stage. When I was the Governor of Texas, I used to say, education is to a State what national defense is to the Federal Government. Nussle says, "You bet, education is going to be my number-one priority." And it should be. It's really important to get it right. It's important to have a Governor who's willing to challenge the status quo when he sees failure and mediocrity. It's important to have a Governor set high standards. I love the idea of hearing a Governor-to-be who says, "I'm going to make sure that Iowa is the center of excellence for public education in the United States of America." And there's no doubt in my mind he can get it done.

Senator Grassley and I went over to watch some seniors sign up for Medicare. Jim Nussle and Senator Grassley and I have got a vision for health care for this country, and he's got a good vision for the State. We believe that the Government ought to fulfill its promises to seniors and the poor. But we also believe that Government shouldn't be telling the rest of us who our doctor ought to be and what the procedures ought to be. We believe in the doctor-patient relationship. It's going to be important to have a Governor who understands the power of health savings accounts and association health plans, who understands you can't have good medical care if you're driving good doctors out of the practice of medicine because of frivolous and junk lawsuits.

You know, it's really interesting; I remember coming in the 2002 campaign—we were talking about Medicare, and both Senator Grassley and Congressman Nussle said to me—they said, "If you're going to write that law and modernize Medicare so that seniors have got prescription drug benefits, you make sure we do something about rural health care in Iowa and across the country." They were instrumental in making sure that Iowa hospitals were taken care of. You're about to have yourself a Governor who understands the importance of rural health care in the State of Iowa.

I was trying to find Jim Nussle when I was giving my State of the Union. It's pretty close-in at the State of the Union. It looks like a big hall, but it's not. As a matter of fact, you can look them in the eye when you're giving the speech. And so I was trying to seek him out when I

said, "We got a problem; we're addicted to oil." See, he's been—he and Grassley have both been working on me for a long time about making sure that renewables become the centerpiece of our energy policy. I agree with them wholeheartedly. For the sake of economic security and for the sake of national security, we got to get off of Middle Eastern oil. And the best way to do so is with Iowa corn. [*Applause*]

A couple of corn growers popped up. [*Laughter*] And I'm earnest about this, and I look forward to working with Jim throughout the remainder of this congressional term to make sure we got ample money in our budgets for research and development. And we want to be using corn for ethanol; we want to be using cane; we want to be using biomass. He's got a vision for Iowa that makes sense, and it's a vision that's important for our country as well. And we got to put our mind to it. I'm looking forward to working with this Governor in this important agricultural State. I can't wait for the day for some President to say, "Look, the crop—look at the crop report. We got a lot of corn, which means we're less dependent on foreign sources of energy." It is vital for this Nation to get off oil if we expect to be a competitive nation in the 21st century. And I'm looking forward to working with Jim Nussle.

I think it's important to have you a Governor who understands that every life is precious and works to promote a culture of life in the State of Iowa. And that will be Jim Nussle. And I think it's important to have a Governor who understands the government can't do everything when it comes to helping heal broken hearts. The way I like to put it is government can hand out money, but it can't put hope in a person's heart or a sense of purpose in a person's life. I think it's important to have a Governor who is able to elevate and capture that great compassion of the people of Iowa to help solve seemingly intractable problems. I think it's important to have a Governor who says, "Fine, government has got a role, but a primary responsibility of the citizens is to love a neighbor who hurts, is to feed the hungry, find shelter for the homeless."

I think it's important to have a Governor who is willing to call upon the faith-based institutions of a State to say, "Why don't you help us heal the addicted, find love for the person who needs love?" Governments are law and justice; government isn't love. But fortunately for places like Iowa, there are thousands of loving people who look forward to be called to action, who look forward to rallying behind a Governor who says, "Let us make this State the best

State it can possibly be." And that Governor-to-be is Governor Jim Nussle.

It's an honor to be with this good man. Thank you all for supporting him. God bless.

NOTE: The President spoke at 5:05 p.m. at Hy-Vee Hall. In his remarks, he referred to Robert Vander Plaats, candidate for Lieutenant Governor of Iowa, and his wife, Darla; Christopher Rants, speaker, and Chuck Gipp, majority leader, Iowa State House of Representatives; Iowa Auditor of State David A. Vaudt; and Ray Hoffman, chairman, Republican Party of Iowa.

Message on the Observance of Passover, 5766
April 11, 2006

Say therefore to the people of Israel, "I am the Lord, and I will bring you out from under the burdens of the Egyptians, and I will deliver you from their bondage, and I will redeem you with an outstretched arm and with great acts of judgment."

EXODUS 6:6

I send greetings to those observing Passover, beginning at sundown on April 12.

The story of the Jewish people throughout history reflects the triumph of faith, the importance of family, and the power of hope. During Passover, Jewish people across America and around the world gather together with family and friends to celebrate the liberation of the Children of Israel from slavery. By reading the Hag-

gadah, singing traditional songs, and sharing the Seder meal, Jewish people relive the story of their redemption and ensure that their values and heritage are passed on to future generations.

During this celebration of faith and hope, we are reminded that freedom is the Almighty's gift to every man, woman, and child. We pray for a more peaceful and hopeful world where the blessings of liberty are bestowed upon all mankind.

Laura and I send our best wishes for a blessed Passover.

GEORGE W. BUSH

NOTE: An original was not available for verification of the content of this message.

Remarks Following Discussions With President John Agyekum Kufuor of Ghana
April 12, 2006

President Bush. Mr. President, welcome. It's good to have you back. We just had a wonderful discussion about our bilateral relations and a great discussion about the world. I really enjoy talking to a man of vision and strength and character. President Kufuor has done a fantastic job for Ghana. He's told the people of his country he'd bring honesty to government, and he has. He told the people of his country that he would work on a—create a stable economic platform for—and he has done that as well. And he's a man of peace. He cares deeply about peace in the region.

As a result of his leadership and our confidence in his Government, we're very happy to work with his country to promote what we've called the Millennium Challenge Account. It's a statement of our respect, and it's a statement for our appreciation for somebody who is willing to invest in his people, is willing to fight corruption, who is willing to help a market economy grow.

Mr. President, congratulations on your record of leadership. Thank you for being a man of peace. Thank you for coming to Washington.

President Kufuor. I want to thank the President for understanding Africa. His works, for the past 5 years or so, have done so much in terms of contributing to the fight against HIV/AIDS on two fronts—the fund you set up, $15 billion fund, some of which has helped to, in a way, save and also make life easier for over 400,000 afflicted people.

Then on the education front, I was honored with a visit from Mrs. Bush just about 2 months ago, during which she launched a program towards linking the messages of the United States and Africa, to work out curriculum for primary and basic education, and also for supplying textbooks and education materials for children, and also helping with education for girls.

And then there's AGOA, which Ghana is benefiting from, even though there we need more help. [*Laughter*] And then there's the TIFA, Trade and Investment Framework law. I believe this is a President that is helping Africa help itself. And we count on your support.

On the MCA front, everything going to plan, Ghana and the United States will sign a compact by July. And that would enable Ghana pursue modernized agriculture. We are largely an agricultural country, and these projects that would free hundreds of millions of dollars to help modernize our agriculture would affect as many as 3 million people, help reduce poverty, and also push growth for the economy.

So we see the President as a friend of Ghana's and, I can say, of much of Africa. Thank you.

President Bush. Thank you, Mr. President. Let's go have lunch.

NOTE: The President spoke at 11:57 a.m. on the South Lawn at the White House.

Remarks in a Discussion on Medicare Prescription Drug Benefits in Annandale, Virginia
April 12, 2006

The President. Thanks for coming. I first want to thank Bob Templin, who is the president of Northern Virginia Community College, for hosting us again. This is a place of educational excellence, and what you're about to watch is a seminar on the new Medicare benefit. And the reason why we've got to conduct seminars on education about what's available is because there is a lot of people who haven't signed up yet for the Medicare benefit, and we want people to pay attention to what's available.

And one of the interesting things about this meeting is, I'm trying to show that our Government is reaching out to people from all walks of life and all neighborhoods. And so this is my job. I'm the Commander in Chief, but I'm sometimes the educator in chief, and that's what I am here to do today. So thank you for coming.

As you can see, we've got a different way of doing this—it's not going to be just a speech, but it's going to be—I'm going to rely upon our fellow citizens to help share what's available and why you ought to take a look, if you're eligible for the Medicare program. We want everybody around our country who's eligible for Medicare to take a look and see if it will make your life better. What I'm saying is, it will.

So, Bob, thanks for having us. I want to thank Vellie Dietrich-Hall, the Commissioner of the President's Advisory Commission on Asian Americans and Pacific Islands. Thank you, Vellie. Clayton Fong, who is with us—he is the National Asian Pacific Center on Aging executive director. I want to thank all the community leaders here.

I particularly want to thank the veterans who are here with us today. We have been joined by a special group of people, the veterans from the 442d Regimental Combat Team. By the way, Senator Inouye of Ha-

waii was a member of that very important regimental combat team. And I want to thank you all for being here today, and thanks for serving our country. Welcome.

I also want to thank the Secretary of Labor, Elaine Chao, who is going to have some remarks here.

So we're talking about Medicare. Our Government made a commitment to our seniors to provide health care. My attitude is, if Government makes a commitment, then we better make sure we make a good commitment. And I was worried that the commitment we made to our seniors was not as good as it could be. And so I went to the United States Congress and said, "Let's work together to make sure the medicine we provide for our seniors is modern and is up to date."

One of the things that we didn't do through the Medicare system prior to this reform was, we didn't provide prescription drugs. But prescription drugs was an important part of medicine. I'll give you an example. If you would have ulcer surgery under Medicare, the Government would pay about $28,000, but the Government wouldn't pay one dime for the medicine that would help you prevent the ulcer surgery in the first place. Now that didn't make any sense. It didn't make any sense to not pay $500 to save 28,000.

And so I said, well, we can do better than this. Let's make sure the medicine we deliver to our seniors is modern. Let's make sure the program works as well as it possibly can. And we passed a bill.

And so one of the things that this bill does is it says to seniors, here's a new plan for you to look at. As a matter of fact, in the State of Virginia, there's over 40 plans to look at—40 different options for a senior to choose from. I thought that was very important to have available for seniors. Government tends to say, sometimes, "I'll choose for you." I believe Government ought to say, "We trust you with your choice, and here are some options from which to choose."

The problem with that is that can be confusing to some seniors. Some people reach the stage in life where they just simply don't want a choice. They're happy with the way things are. And I knew that would be the case when we started to bring out the Medicare program. So we put in place—and you'll hear from some people who have been involved with outreach to our senior citizens. That means, we'll go out and explain to people why the different options may make sense to a senior, so a senior can design a program to meet his or her needs, that makes the medicine modern. This program helps all seniors with their drug benefits. That's important to know. This program provides choices for seniors. And although that can be somewhat confusing, it's an important part of the program.

As a matter of fact, it's part of my philosophy. My philosophy is, let's trust the consumer. Let's trust the taxpayer. Let's give people different options from which to choose. Let them design the program, not have the government design the program for them.

By the way, they estimated the cost at something like $34 per month premium for the drug program for the typical senior, because there are choices. It now costs about $25 a month. In other words, choices mean people are going to compete for your business, and that's an important part of helping to hold the cost down for the people we're trying to help, as well as the taxpayers who are paying the bills.

This program provides what's called stopgap insurance. In other words, when you reach $3,600 for drug costs, the Government pays 95 percent of the bills for you. I think that makes sense. It makes sense for a senior to know that he or she doesn't have to worry if something out of the ordi-

nary were to occur; kind of, a catastrophic plan would be available to help. It makes sense for a son or daughter who might be worried about his or her parents' finances. And so this new plan has got what we call catastrophic care or stopgap care which is very important.

And, finally, if you're a low-income senior—about a third of the people eligible for Medicare are low-income—or incomes are such that they qualify, the Government will pay over 95 percent of all the costs. If you're a low-income senior, you really need to look at this program. Any senior needs to look at this program. The average cost savings per senior on the Medicare program, on these pharmaceuticals, is one-half. People's drug bills have been cut by half because they have signed up for this program. And that's really important. It's important for peace of mind. It's important for the person's pocketbook.

Now, I know that sounds too good to be true, but it's happening all across the country. As a matter of fact, 29 million people have signed up for this program. There are 42 million seniors eligible for Medicare, and 29 million people have signed up since January. And that's positive.

And by the way, when 29 million people show up for a new program, there's going to be some glitches. And you're about to hear from a man whose job it is to make sure that he takes care of the glitches. That's what Presidents do—they delegate. [*Laughter*]

We straighten out problems as they occur. Twenty-nine [million] * people have signed up. There are 6 million people who are eligible who have got a job, and they don't need the Medicare. I'm about to talk to a good man in that situation. And there's 7 million people who are eligible who have yet to sign up. And so the reason I've come today is to urge every senior here in the room and around the country who might be listening on TV that if you have not

---

* White House correction.

signed up for the Medicare Part D program, you really need to do it. That's the seminar part. That's trying to educate people.

And by the way, there's a lot of other people helping. It's not just me. We've got the National Asian Pacific Center on Aging helping. We've got the Organization of Chinese Americans helping. AARP is helping seniors realize what's available. The Federation of Korean Associations is helping to sign up people. Other Asian American groups all around the country are helping. Faith-based programs are helping people realize what's available. If you're a son or a daughter whose parent is eligible for Medicare, you need to do your duty. Be a good—be a good, loving child and explain to your parents that which is available for them.

And how do you do it? You can get on the computer, medicare.gov, and look and see whether or not your mom or dad ought to sign up for a program. I'm just telling you what's happening so far. People are saving a lot of money when it comes to their prescription drugs.

By the way, prior to this bill, we had people in this country who had to choose between food and pharmaceuticals, and that wasn't right. We had people who had to choose between paying their utility bill and whether or not they could pay for their prescription drugs. And that's not right.

This bill I signed and this program we're discussing helps change that. If you're eligible—and a third of the seniors are eligible—the Government will pay over 95 percent of your pharmaceuticals. We're a compassionate country. We want our program for Medicare to work well for our seniors.

I fully understand some of the seniors say, "I don't want any choices." And that's okay. But somebody ought to at least help you look. It doesn't cost a dime to look and see whether or not this program is meant for you. It doesn't cost one penny to see whether or not you can save money—and I bet you can. So part of the outreach here is to say to those of you who are helping our senior citizens realize what's available, thank you for what you're doing.

We've set a deadline for May 15th for people to sign up in order to get the discounts involved in the program. And so we're going to spend—"we" being the Government and people involved in the Government—are going to spend a lot of time traveling around the country explaining to our senior citizens, the 7 million who have yet to sign up, take a look. It's a good deal.

So I've got with me today some people who are involved in the program. First, Elaine Chao, she just spoke. She's the Secretary of Labor. She's been in my Cabinet since day one; she's doing a fine job. I'm proud to call her friend. Do you have some words of wisdom here?

Secretary of Labor Elaine Chao. Mr. President, I sure do. Number one, remember—please remember May 15th is the deadline date for the first enrollment. If you don't take advantage of the benefits by May 15th, your premiums will increase if you register by the second date, which is in November. Please remember, May 15th is very important.

Second of all, it's not that difficult to sign up. There are many organizations in your communities that can be of help. Also, call on your children, ask your children to help you sign up. Now, we know that there are many people who speak different languages, so the Department of Health and Human Services has actually toll-free numbers—now, I'm going to see whether I have them here—we have booklets and brochures in all different languages, including Chinese, Spanish, Tagalog, Vietnamese, Japanese. And if you are a non-native speaker and you want some help, let me give you some toll-free numbers as well.

If you speak Chinese—that's Cantonese and Mandarin—the toll-free number is 1–800–582–4218. Don't bother taking it down; there will be these numbers available at the desks, but I do want to tell you now just in case. The Korean number is 1–800–582–4259. And the Vietnamese toll-free number is 1–800–582–4336.

So as the President mentions, this is a good deal. For the majority of people, you're going to save money. So take a look at the Medicare Part D program, and please, do remember, May 15th is the signup date.

The President. Thank you, Madam Secretary. Okay, so here's the way this works. You're the President; you say to the Secretary of Health and Human Services, "Make sure the plan gets implemented." That's called delegation. He then turns to another guy, who happens to be a Texan named Dr. Mark McClellan. He's the administrator of the Centers for Medicare and Medicaid Services. It's a long word for, he's in charge of making sure people know what's available.

So when there's not enough operators to answer the phones—which took place earlier this year; as we said, call 1–800–MEDICARE—a lot of people called 1–800–MEDICARE, and they got a busy signal. So we said, wait a minute, make sure you've got enough operators. We had a problem with dual-eligible citizens, and he worked it out with the States. He's a troubleshooter.

He's also responsible for making sure that enough information gets out so that people can realize what's available. And I want to thank him; I want to congratulate him, even before he talks, for recognizing ours is a diverse nation. And this is an interesting meeting, isn't it, when you think about it. In other words, there are seniors from all walks of life, some of whom require a little special help to learn what's available—maybe a little assistance with the language. Maybe a special group, they've got confidence in a special group that might represent their heritage and their culture, and that group will help explain. We're reaching out to everybody. We want

every senior eligible for Medicare to realize what's available.

Anyway, McClellan, you're doing a fine job. Why don't you explain to me what your responsibilities have been and what you intend to do to make sure people know what's available.

Dr. Mark B. McClellan. Well, thank you, Mr. President. As you said, this is the most important new benefit in the Medicare program in 40 years. And while prescription drug coverage is really important, this is part of making Medicare work in a new way to help people stay well and live longer, and not just pay the bills when they get sick. We can't afford that anymore.

To do that effectively, we need to collaborate. And you talked about delegation; well, what I've done is help—worked together with many partners around the country so that people can find out about what Medicare offers today. We're not just a program to think about when you get sick. Medicare can help you stay well and live much longer through prescription drugs, preventive benefits, and other help.

So we've started a new approach of reaching out at the grassroots level, we're partnering with more than 10,000 organizations around the country to reach all of our diverse beneficiaries where they live and work and play and pray.

That includes groups like the ones represented here, like the National Asian Pacific Center on Aging. Clayton Fong works very closely with me to help provide some of those translation services that you mentioned. It involves many local partners, like the Asian Service Center in Washington, DC, has worked closely with Qien, who is on my staff at CMS, and many of our other partners to help get the word out locally.

We want to make sure people know about this important new benefit, and if they have questions, there are lots of places to go to get the personal information they need to make a good decision and start saving. That includes the medicare.gov web site, which many of the sons and daughters of our beneficiaries are using, as well as the beneficiaries themselves. It includes our 1–800–MEDICARE, 24/7 customer service line, which has around 7,000 trained representatives now and can provide help in multiple languages for people who call in.

And it includes events like this one, that are taking place all over the country, more than 1,000 a week, where people like me, many of your other senior officials, are helping to get the word out and helping people find out about how they can take advantage of this new assistance.

The President. Back me up here on the low-income part of the program.

Dr. McClellan. Well, the benefit for prescription drugs is important for everyone with Medicare. A typical senior can save about $1,100 compared to not having drug coverage. That's more than half of their drug costs. And for people with limited incomes—that's about one in three of our seniors who are living month to month on a fixed income—they can qualify for extra help, they can get their prescriptions for no premium and usually just a few dollars for each drug—paying 95 percent of their drug costs. And that's a very important extra help to sign up for as well. And we can put you touch with the application process and get you into that program as well. It's very important extra help. It's worth about $3,700 a year.

So for people—if you're on Medicare, if you've got a parent who is, someone you care about who is looking into this program between now and May 15th means, literally, $1,100 worth of help, at least; $3,700 worth of coverage if you have a limited income; and protection for the future against those high drug costs that you mentioned earlier, Mr. President.

The President. Yes, this is a good deal. And it's really worth people looking at. I'm going to repeat: If you're a son or a daughter and your mother or dad is eligible for Medicare, you need to help your parent. You really do. You need to get on the

phone or get on the computer, medicare.gov, or 1–800–MEDICARE.

Now, Qien He is with us. Qien, where were you born—yes, I know where you are. [*Laughter*] Where were you born?

Qien He. I was born in China.

The President. Isn't that interesting? Now he is a part of making sure that people realize the opportunities of Medicare. Born whereabouts in China?

Mr. He. Okay. First of all, on behalf of Asian——

The President. No, where were you born in China?

Mr. He. In China, in Beijing.

The President. Beijing. See, I'm asking the questions. [*Laughter*]

Mr. He. Okay.

The President. And you're a doctor?

Mr. He. Yes.

The President. Of what?

Mr. He. Doctor of social linguistics.

The President. Social linguistics. And when did you come to the States?

Mr. He. Nineteen-ninety.

The President. Nineteen-ninety. And here you are sitting on the stage with the President. You're welcome. We're glad you're here.

Mr. He. Thank you.

The President. And so what is your job?

Mr. He. Okay, I'm a health insurance specialist for the Centers for Medicare/Medicaid Services. My office is in Philadelphia.

The President. Your office is in Philadelphia?

Mr. He. Yes.

The President. So you've come all the way from Philadelphia to be here?

Mr. He. Yes, I come here last night. Tomorrow and tonight—I have to come back and organize a similar event tomorrow for seminar for people in Philadelphia. It's called Market Closure Enrollment event, in Philadelphia. Actually, Secretary Chao will go with——

The President. Okay. So your job—one of the jobs is to continue to reach out to people in the Asian American community to convince them to pay attention to this program. So are you having any success?

Mr. He. Well, we have a lot of success. But here, I would like to share some successful stories with you.

The President. Okay, let me hear some.

[*At this point, Mr. He made brief remarks.*]

The President. See, one of the interesting things about America is that there are thousands of people who work in the grassroots to make the communities in which they live a better place. It's really one of the great things about our country, isn't it, when neighbors help neighbors. And what he's really saying is his job is to convince a neighbor to help a neighbor. That's called grassroots. That's what—it's kind of an odd word, maybe, for some to understand. It means at the local level, that people are willing to help somebody who needs help.

And that's what your job is, isn't it?

[*Mr. He made further remarks.*]

The President. Well, thank you. Listen, well, I appreciate it. [*Applause*] Hold on, hold on. Thank you. Save your energy. Thank you very much for that, Qien; thanks for your kind words.

What Qien is saying is, is that we recognize there are some people out there that sometimes aren't able to get the message like other people. And so we want this message to go throughout all the neighborhoods. Here, we're talking to Asian Americans, but we want people in every neighborhood to hear the message.

So, for example, we're working with the AARP to get the word out. The NAACP has been helpful to make sure that certain seniors who are eligible for this program get the message. That's what we want.

And so if you know somebody or if you're listening on TV and know somebody who's eligible for Medicare, make sure you call their attention to the program. And remember, there's a lot of seniors who might be a little confused at first over the number of choices. But convince them to be patient and look at what's available and help them design a plan that meets their needs. And what you will find is there will be savings. People benefit from this program. It's worthwhile to look at.

I'm talking to Dr. Yining Wang. Welcome, Dr. Wang. Thank you for being here, sir. Got to speak into the mike. You're a doc?

Yining Wang. Yes, I'm doctor in the research area.

The President. Where were you born?

Dr. Wang. I'm born in Shanghai.

The President. Shanghai. And here he sits, as well, talking to the President of the United States. We're glad you're here.

Dr. Wang. Yes. Thank you very much, Mr. President.

The President. Proud you're here. When did you come to the United States?

Dr. Wang. Well, it's 1988.

The President. Nineteen eighty-eight.

Dr. Wang. Yes.

The President. That's a fine year.

Dr. Wang. No.

The President. Yes, it was. [*Laughter*] Well, maybe not for you, but for, you know—my dad got elected President in '88. Anyway—[*laughter*]—so you were a doctor. Where did you work?

Dr. Wang. I'm sorry?

The President. Where did you work?

Dr. Wang. I work in the cardiovascular area for the physiology and pathology.

The President. Oh, fantastic. And you're now retired?

Dr. Wang. I'm retired at the end of year 2004.

The President. That's good.

Dr. Wang. That's good. [*Laughter*]

The President. And so what happened? So you hear—how did you hear about the Medicare program?

[*Dr. Wang made brief remarks.*]

The President. Very good. Interesting story, isn't it? So here's a man, he's a well-educated fellow. The first reaction, however, to the program was, "There's so many choices; I don't think I want to get involved." That's a natural reaction, by the way. And yet, nevertheless, as he said it, "patience" was the word I think he used—but somebody helped you understand. AARP gave you some advice.

Dr. Wang. AARP, yes.

The President. You can get good advice from AARP; you can get good advice from somebody who works for the CMS; you can get good advice from somebody from your church; you can get good advice from your son or daughter. There are all kinds of ways to get good advice.

What we're doing here today is explaining to seniors, there's a lot of people willing to give you advice. And it's worthwhile taking a look. And the reason it's worthwhile taking a look is—you just heard the reason. The man said he's going to save about $200 a month. That's good savings.

[*Dr. Wang made further remarks.*]

The President. That's great. You did a good job, doc. Thank you. Very good job.

Dr. Wang. Okay.

The President. I appreciate you. Thank you. Good job, sir.

Dr. Wang. Thank you so much.

The President. Bob Nakamoto, third generation American. Welcome.

Robert Nakamoto. Thank you.

The President. Look, this is a guy still working. Remember I said there's 6 million people still working who get good health care? He's one of the 6 million. Working strong at age 74, and he's not going to slow down a bit.

Mr. Nakamoto. That's right.

The President. Isn't that right? What do you do, Bob?

Mr. Nakamoto. I'm a chairman of a company called Base Technologies. We do IT consulting work, primarily with the Federal and State government, based in McLean, Virginia, and third generation Japanese American.

The President. Congratulations. And how is your company doing?

Mr. Nakamoto. We're doing well. We could do better with your help. [*Laughter*]

The President. Give a man a mike, there's no telling what he's going to say. [*Laughter*] Give us your experience. You took a look at what was going on, didn't you?

Mr. Nakamoto. Pardon?

The President. You took a look at the Medicare.

[*Mr. Nakamoto made brief remarks.*]

The President. See, here's the reason why we've asked Bob—one, is we like to be around successful people, don't we? Secondly, he is a fellow who is eligible, but has chosen to stay on the current program provided by his company, but recognizes that upon leaving the company, there's a good program available. And that's important for people to understand.

Twenty-nine million people have signed up. Here's one right here. There are 6 million people who have not signed up because they're working—and that's Bob. I bet there's somebody out there who represents that part of the 7 million people who are eligible, yet who haven't signed up. And it's really important for you to look.

So you've been looking around at these things, taking a look. You find it okay? I mean, you're a computer guy, so it's a little unfair to say whether—you know, whether or not——

Mr. Nakamoto. We're okay with that.

The President. Using friendly—it's user-friendly?

Mr. Nakamoto. Right.

The President. Yes. See, we try to design this program so it's called user-friendly. That means you can get on there if you're—you don't have to be a computer genius like Bob—and take a look.

Mr. Nakamoto. Right.

The President. Your advice is? Retire and get on it.

Mr. Nakamoto. Right.

The President. Well, not retire, but when retire.

Mr. Nakamoto. Yes. I don't know when that's going to be, but when that time comes, you'll know about it.

The President. There you go. [*Laughter*] Well, listen, I hope you get the feeling for why we're here. We're here to explain a really interesting opportunity for our seniors. If you don't want to sign up, by the way, you don't have to. The Government is not making you do anything you don't want, but what the Government is doing is giving you a lot of opportunities. In the case of Virginia citizens, over 40 opportunities to choose a program that suits your particular needs.

And by that I mean, there's all different kinds of structures for the programs. You might be taking this kind of drug or that kind of drug. You might be taking a lot of drugs a month or no drugs a month. And therefore, you can design a program that says, this is best for me.

I strongly urge our fellow citizens to take a look. I want to thank those of you who are helping our seniors see what's available—and keep doing it up until May 15th and even after May 15th. I repeat: If you're a son or a daughter and your parent is eligible for Medicare, do them a favor and do your duty by getting on medicare.gov or calling 1–800–MEDICARE and find out what's available. Just get people to send the forms to you and look. Ask your parents questions, or ask your parents' doctors questions, or ask your parents' pharmacist questions about what program they need. If you're a senior and you're going to your local pharmacy, many of the pharmacists are helping our seniors design a program that meets their needs.

Is it worth it? I really think it is. If you're a poor senior, the Government will pay most of your drugs. We really don't want to be a society where seniors have to choose between food and medicine. It's worth it even if you're not in that income category because you'll save money.

And saving money is good after you retire. It'll help you. If you're a son or a daughter—again, I repeat: Do your duty. It will give you peace of mind to know that your mom or dad are taken care of.

We worked hard to get this bill passed. It's a good piece of legislation. It's one of those times where people are going to be able to say, "Well, the Government actually did a good thing for us."

And so I want to thank you all for coming. I particularly want to thank our panelists. I want to thank my fellow citizens who've come. I particularly want to, again, thank the vets—veterans who are here. Bob, thanks for your hospitality. Thank you for paying attention.

May God bless you all. Thank you.

NOTE: The President spoke at 2:07 p.m. in the Richard J. Ernst Community Center at Northern Virginia Community College.

Remarks at the Small Business Week Conference
April 13, 2006

The President. Thank you all. Please be seated. Thanks for coming. So I see Eric behind the stage. I said, "Congratulations on being the Small Business Owner of the Year." And he said, "You know, if I thought part of the prize was having to stand in front of those cameras and introduce you, I might not have accepted it." [*Laughter*] But I appreciate your introduction, Eric. Thanks.

I want to thank you all for allowing me to come by to celebrate the Small Business

Week with you. You know, I'm an MBA, but I got to tell you, the most instructive part of my understanding about how the economy works—when I was trying to meet a payroll. The entrepreneurs of this country not only create and run their own businesses, they work hard. But I've learned that it's a calling to run your own business. I mean, there's something special about somebody who stands up and says, "I got a dream; I got a hope."

The great thing about the entrepreneur in the small-business sector of our economy is that you provide great steam and strength to the growth of our economy. And today I want to talk to you about why the small-business owner is at the cornerstone of our progrowth economic policies and what we intend to do to make sure that the environment for taking risk is strong and viable here in this country.

Before I do, I want to say thanks to Eric's wife, as well, for being here. I appreciate my friend Hector Barreto. He's the Administrator of the SBA. Thank you for being here, Hector. Thanks for serving. I also had the honor of congratulating Andrew Field, who is the founder and president of printingforless.com, Livingston, Montana, for being the runner-up; as well as Barbara and Leroy Shatto, owners of Shatto Milk Company, Osborn, Missouri, for also being the runner-up to the SBA Small Business Persons of the Year.

This economy of ours is good. It's strong. It's a good time to be a small-business owner in America. After all, we grew at a healthy rate of 3.5 percent last year. That's the fastest rate of any major industrialized economy. We've now had 17 straight quarters of economic expansion. Real after-tax income has grown by more than 8 percent since 2001. After-tax means money in your pocket, that's what that means. That means, on average, Americans have an income that is $2,100 higher this year than it was the beginning of 2001—that's after adjusting for inflation.

More Americans own a home today than ever before in history; more minorities own a home today than ever before in history. And that's positive news for this economy. Consumer confidence is at its highest point in nearly 4 years. Productivity is high, and it's on the rise. And that's good news for American entrepreneurs and really good news for American workers. Productivity increases improves the lives of our fellow citizens over time. Manufacturing activity is strong. This economy is going well, and the small-business owner is leading the way.

It's really important for our country to understand this fact: Small businesses are vital for our workers. Small businesses create two out of every three new jobs, and they account for nearly half of the country's overall employment. Think about that. Two out of every three new jobs are created by the entrepreneur. That's why it makes sense to have the small business at the cornerstone of a progrowth economic policy.

Recently our economic reports showed that this economy added 211,000 jobs in the month of March. Over the last 2½ years, we've added 5.1 million new jobs. This is the 31st straight month that the American economy has added jobs. The national unemployment rate is down to 4.7 percent. That's lower than the average rate of the past four decades. When small businesses grow, the American economy benefits.

Small businesses are vital for our communities. You sponsor Little League teams, and you donate to local charities and community drives, and you serve on your school boards and hospital boards and different community groups. Without our small businesses and entrepreneurs, our communities would be less vibrant and less welcoming. I appreciate the fact that you're close to your customers. Your hard work and investment is the lifeblood of our cities all across the country.

Small businesses are vital to building a more hopeful future for this country. When you open up a shop or lease a factory or offer a new service, you take a risk. Risk-taking takes vision, and risk-taking takes courage. And it's the risk takers—are people who help define the vibrancy of an economy.

I thought Ronald Reagan put it best when he said, the entrepreneurs are the "explorers of the modern era." Welcome to exploration, and thank you for betting on a brighter future, and thank you for adding optimism into the soul of this country.

Opening a small business is a great opportunity for a lot of folks to realize their dreams. I believe that we should promote an ownership society in America. We want people owning something in this society. Women now own more than one-quarter of the businesses in our country. The number of women-owned businesses is growing strongly. Hispanic Americans are opening their own businesses, and those businesses are opening at a rate—at three times faster than the national average. And those are positive developments for a society.

It's been said that having your own business means working 80 hours a week so you can avoid working 40 hours a week for somebody else. [*Laughter*] Owning your own business is a great responsibility. But there is a strong reward in being independent. And I hope there's a strong reward in your understanding that you're contributing mightily to this great Nation.

And so how do we continue to help people realize this sense of independence? My philosophy of government is this: Government's role is not to create wealth; the job of the government is to create an environment in which people are willing to take risk, in which entrepreneurship flourishes. And that's a strategy I've been pursuing and I'm going to continue to pursue. And so today I want to talk to you about three broad areas where we can continue to work to make sure this environment is good for

the small-business owner. And that includes taxes and spending and health care and expansion of opportunities here and abroad.

First, creating an environment where small businesses can flourish begins with keeping taxes low and spending your money wisely. We've overcome a lot in this economy, and I want to thank you for your hard work in helping us overcome a lot. The history of the past 5 years has—the economic history of the past 5 years has shown this country's capacity to overcome some pretty major hurdles. We've overcome a stock market correction, a recession, a vicious attack on the United States of America. We've overcome war, and we've overcome natural disasters.

I told you what the statistics were about, how fast this economy is growing. It's really amazing when you put it in the context of what you've helped us overcome. And I believe one of the reasons we've overcome these hurdles is because we put progrowth economic policies in place, starting with real, substantial tax cuts.

We cut the taxes for everybody who paid taxes. It wasn't one of these tax deals where, you know, "Okay, you're okay; you're not. Therefore, you get tax relief; you don't." That's—I didn't think that was fair. You might remember, we lowered taxes on families by cutting the rates and by doubling the child credit. We reduced the marriage penalty. It didn't make much sense to tax marriage. [*Laughter*] We passed something else that I think makes a lot of sense for the small-business owner and the farmer and the rancher, is that we put the death tax on the way to extinction.

The problem with that is that it comes back to life in 2011. Congress needs to set aside politics and get rid of the death tax, for the sake of our small-business owners. It makes no sense for you to have to pay taxes while you're alive, and then they pay taxes on the same business after you die.

We cut the taxes on the small-business owners. If you want the small-business sector to grow, if you recognize two-thirds of new jobs are created by small businesses, it makes sense to let small businesses keep more of the money they make. After all, when a small-business owner has got more money in his or her treasury, you're likely to expand your business. You talk to some of these business—the folks who won the business award. I said, "How many jobs—how many employees did you have 5 years ago, and how many do you have today?"

You had how many 5 years ago?

Eric Hoover. Twenty-four.

The President. Twenty-four 5 years ago, and over 100 and——

Mr. Hoover. ——107.

The President. ——107. His business expanded. That's what we want. Two-thirds of new jobs are created by small-business owners, and when small-business owners have more money in their treasuries, they're likely to expand. I also recognize that many small-business owners are either a sole proprietorship or—a small business is a sole proprietorship, or a subchapter S corporation, or a limited partnership, which means that the principals pay tax—the business pays tax at the individual income tax level. So when we reduce taxes on individuals, we are really reducing taxes on small businesses as well.

There's a healthy debate in this town about cutting taxes; I understand that. And some in this town said cutting taxes would ruin the economy. Some of them said, "If you cut taxes, this economy is going to look like the Great Depression." As a matter of fact, on the day when the Republicans in the House and the Senate were finalizing the 2003 tax cuts, one of the Democrat leaders said these tax cuts would do nothing to create jobs. That person was wrong 5.1 million times over in the last 2½ years.

And there's an ongoing debate about the taxes. Some in Washington proposed that we raise your taxes, either by repealing the tax cuts or letting them all expire. These are the same folks who said, "If you keep your own money, that would be irresponsible and reckless policy." Those folks were wrong then, and they're wrong now. To keep the small-business sector strong and creating jobs, Congress needs to make the tax relief permanent.

And they can start when they get back by sending me a bill that extends the tax cuts we delivered on dividends and capital gains, so that our businesses and investors can plan with confidence. Uncertainty in the Tax Code makes it hard for investors to plan. Uncertainty in the Tax Code makes it hard for small-business owners to plan. We need certainty in this Tax Code, and Congress needs to make those tax cuts permanent.

Oh, I know you'll hear the argument that says, "Well, we got to raise your taxes in order to balance the budget." That's not the way Washington, DC, works. I've been here long enough to tell you, it's not going to work that way. What will end up happening is they're going to raise your taxes, and then they're going to figure out new ways to spend your money. The best way to balance this budget, the best way to cut the deficit in half by 2009, is to keep the progrowth economic policies in place and be wise about how we spend your money.

And that starts with setting priorities. I think you know something about setting priorities. When you run your business, you got to set priorities, and we got to set them here in Washington. So long as we've got people in harm's way, so long as we've got men and women in our uniform in a time of war, the number-one priority of this Government is to make sure they got all what it takes to be victorious in the war on terror.

We're making progress on what's called discretionary spending. The last two budgets I've submitted has actually cut discretionary spending, except that which is applied for our military and homeland defense. And that required hard work by the

Congress. But it's not enough, in order to get this deficit cut in half by 2009 and keep this economy growing. One way Congress can help is to pass the line-item veto. It's an important tool to help bring fiscal discipline here to Washington, DC.

And the idea has received bipartisan support. I was very pleased that my opponent in the 2004 campaign, Senator John Kerry, came down to the White House the other day and expressed his support for a line-item veto. He campaigned on a line-item veto, and now he's supporting the administration with a line-item veto. And other Democrats and Republicans must give the President the chance to trim out that part of the budget which does not meet our priorities. And I hope Congress passes this important piece of legislation quickly as a sign of reform.

In the long-term, though, the biggest challenge facing our—facing the budgets of the United States are those inherent in mandatory programs. And that would be Social Security and Medicare. We got a problem in these programs because there's a lot of people just like me getting ready to retire. [*Laughter*] As a matter of fact, my retirement age—my eligibility age for Social Security just happens to come in 2008. [*Laughter*] I hate to admit, I'm turning 60 this year. I can see some other folks out there fixing to turn 60 this year as well. [*Laughter*] And there's a lot of us. There's a lot of baby boomers who are living longer and are promised more benefits than the previous generation. And the system can't be sustained. It's just not going to work.

And there's an unfunded liability problem that faces this generation today, and it's going to be especially acute for a generation coming up. And Congress needs to take my offer to sit down at the table in good faith. We need people from both political parties putting their ideas on the table about how we can deal with Social Security and Medicare, how we can do our job. I tell people, the job of a President

is to confront problems and not to pass them on to future Presidents and future Congresses. And that's what the Congress ought to do—set aside needless politics and do what's right for the American people. And I'm going to work with them to do so.

To create an environment where small businesses flourish means that health care has got to be affordable and available, is a health care system that needs to make sure that we've got high-quality care at reasonable prices for our people. The Federal Government has made a strong commitment to the elderly, and we're going to keep that commitment. And by the way, if you've got a mother or father who's eligible for Medicare, you need to make sure he or she sees the new—the benefits of this new drug—prescription drug coverage we've got. This is a good deal for the American seniors. And we're working hard to make sure that American seniors realize that there is a fine opportunity for them to improve their lot in life.

Listen, I couldn't stand the thought of seniors having to choose between an electricity bill and pharmaceuticals. That didn't make any sense in our country. And if you're a low-income senior listening today, you ought to make sure you get ahold of a representative from Medicare or a friend or a churchmate, or call 1–800–MEDICARE, or get your son or daughter to get on medicare.gov and find out the benefits inherent in this program. If you're one-third of the seniors who are income-qualified, the Federal Government is going to pay 95 percent or more of your prescription drug benefits.

And the Federal Government can keep its commitment to the poor, as well, by making sure Medicaid works well and by continuing to expand community health centers. It makes sense for the taxpayers to help us build community health centers for the poor and the indigent to take the pressure off of our emergency rooms in

America's hospitals—a place where people can get reasonable primary care.

But for the rest of us, we have got to make sure that the system is affordable and available without empowering the Federal Government to make all the decisions for the businessowners and the consumers and the providers. There's a debate here in Washington, DC, about who knows what to do best about health care. And there's some folks who said, "The Federal Government can handle it all," and I'm not one of them. I believe the best health care system has the patient and the doctor central to the decisionmaking of this important industry. And I also understand that small businesses are hit hard by health care costs. As a matter of fact, many of the working uninsured work for small businesses, because small businesses cannot afford the health care they want to provide for their employees.

And so here are some ideas to help. One, I think it's important to, as I said, make sure the patient and the doctor are central to the health care systems. And therefore, I believe strongly in what's called health savings accounts. And I think it's very important for the small-business owners to pay attention to the benefits of a health savings account for your particular company.

Health savings accounts stand in contrast to the traditional insurance system. The traditional insurance system, as you know, the employer provides their employee with a plan that they pay for the deductible and a small copayment, and somebody else pays the bills. It's a third-party payer system. And when somebody else pays the bills, you really don't care about the cost, unless you're having to pay for the rising premium.

Here's the way health savings accounts work. It says that, on the one hand, you buy catastrophic insurance coverage at a low price, and on the other hand, there is a cash account that covers the deductible of the catastrophic plan, that's contributed into the plan by employer, employee, or combination of both, tax-free. And that's—you use that to pay for your ordinary medical expenses, until the catastrophic plan kicks in. If you don't spend the money, the interest on that money is tax-free, and you roll it over to the next year that you—in which you can contribute again.

It turns out that the combination of the contribution—the cash contribution into the tax-free health savings account, plus the premium on the insurance plan, is generally less than third-party payer systems. Small businesses can save money under this plan.

The plan also empowers the employee to make rational decisions about health care. The more the consumer is involved in the quality and price of a product, the more likely it is the product is not going to be increasing at double-digits rates. Consumer involvement is an important aspect of quality health care at affordable prices.

Over the past few years, the number of Americans who own health savings account has gone from 1 million to 3 million. More than a third of those who have chosen HSAs were previously uninsured. You know, if you're a young person feeling relatively healthy, you may decide, "I don't want any health insurance; I'm never going to get sick." You might remember those days. [*Laughter*] Doesn't it make sense to be able to set aside money on a tax-free basis—that you earn tax-free to cover future medical costs? Health savings accounts do just that. Forty percent of those who own an HSA have family incomes below $50,000 a year. It's a really good idea, and I strongly urge you to look into them.

In Connecticut earlier this month, I met a small-business guy who runs a retirement community. He said a third of his employees now have HSAs—health savings accounts. It's given them good coverage, and it saved the company $78,000 on health premiums. Health savings accounts make a lot of sense, and we've got to make them stronger, not weaker here in Washington, DC.

One obstacle to expanding health savings accounts is the Federal Tax Code. Under current law, employers and employees pay no income tax or payroll tax on any health insurance provided through the workplace. But if you buy insurance on your own, you don't get the same tax break. And that means that the self-employed or the unemployed or workers at companies that don't provide health insurance are at a great disadvantage. So Congress needs to end discrimination in the Tax Code and give Americans who buy HSA policies on their own the same tax breaks that those who get their health insurance from their employers.

Another problem with this Tax Code is that it limits the amount you can contribute to your HSA tax-free. The limit is usually tied to your deductible. Buy a high-deductible catastrophic plan, and you can contribute up to the deductible, by current law. But sometimes your out-of-pocket expenses are greater than your deductible. It's especially important for those with chronic illnesses. They often have expenses that go well beyond their deductibles. And so we need to fix the Tax Code by raising the cap on the amount of money you can put into your HSA tax-free. Raising this cap is going to help Americans cover all their out-of-pocket expenses. And equally important, raising this cap will help make sure this product is attractive to people. We want people being able to have different options in the marketplace. We want people directly involved in the decisionmaking of their health care.

And by the way, I got another idea for small businesses, and that is business— small businesses ought to be allowed to pool risk across jurisdictional boundaries so they can buy insurance at the same discount big companies get. So I'm a strong believer in health—association health plans.

Congress needs to act on this idea; it's a good idea for small businesses. I mean, if people want the small-business sector to flourish, then they ought to help small businesses be able to afford health care. This is a rational idea. It makes a lot of sense. The House has done its part, and now the United States Senate needs to do its part as well.

Here's another idea to make sure health care is affordable and available. We got too many junk lawsuits running docs out of business and running up the cost of your medicine. When it looks like you might get sued, if you're a doctor, then you practice what's called defensive medicine. In other words, you prescribe more than you should, more procedures than necessary, because you're constantly thinking about how to make sure you can make your case in front of a jury. These frivolous lawsuits, this plethora of lawsuits, is running up the cost of health care for you. It's not only causing your premiums to go up, but it's causing the cost of medicine to go up, as doctors try to protect themselves against a lawsuit.

And it affects the Federal budget, by the way. As you know, we've got a lot of health care here in Washington. We've got a Medicare system and a Medicaid system and a veterans system. It is anticipated— it is estimated that we spend $28 billion extra a year because of the defensive practice of medicine. And that's why I believe this issue is a Federal problem that requires a Federal response, and the United States Congress needs to pass medical liability reform this year.

A couple of other points I want to make on health care. In other words, we've got a comprehensive strategy that says, "We've got a better vision than having the Federal Government make all the decisions for you." It's a vision that says, "We're going to take care of the elderly, and we're going to help the poor." But it's also a vision that says, "We trust consumers, and we want the marketplace to function, and we want there to be reasonable policy to help deal with the rising cost of health care."

One such way is to promote transparency, so patients know exactly what their options are. When you really think about it, the health care field is not a very transparent place when it comes to price and quality. I mean, how many of you really ever shopped for health care? How many of you have ever actually gotten on the Internet and tried to compare price before you make a health care decision? Not many, because, one, the system has somebody else paying the bills for you, and, two, there's not a lot of transparency. So this Government is going to continue to work with folks in the health care field to make sure that price and quality are available to you as a consumer. It's amazing what happens when people have information at their fingertips before they make decisions.

And another way to help wring out the costs in health care is to help encourage and expand the health care industry to adopt information technology as an integral part of its industry. Many of you have done that. Many of you have used the—information technology to help enhance the productivity of your business. That's generally not the case in health care. I mean, think about the guy who goes to the hospital, and he's carrying the file with him where all the pages are handwritten. It's kind of a problem in health care, since most doctors can't write legibly to begin with. [*Laughter*]

And so I believe we ought to work to make sure we have electronic health records for each individual here in America that, one, protects your safety, but, two, carries your history with you so that we help wring out additional costs in medicine and, at the same time, reduce errors. So there's a comprehensive vision to make sure health care is available and affordable, particularly for our small-business owners.

I want to talk about something else, and that is how to make sure that small businesses can expand here at home and abroad. First, at home, the Small Business Administration is working hard to make it easier for people to start up companies. We understand that sometimes people have

got a good idea, but they're not sure how to get something started. They're a little worried about the startup. And so we've doubled the number of small-business loans out of the SBA since I came to office. And we've increased the number of loans to minority entrepreneurs by 175 percent. I told Hector I want people from all walks of life benefiting from Government programs, and he's done his job, and I appreciate that.

Another important fact is this: We've lowered the cost of running the SBA by more than 20 percent. And so we've increased the amount of our loans to the entrepreneurs by 80 percent. By reducing the cost of granting a loan, it makes the loan less expensive for you.

I'm also going to continue working up markets—working to open up markets overseas. I don't know if you realize this, but we're home to 5 percent of the world's population. That means 95 percent of the potential customers live outside of the United States. If you're good at making something or growing something, it seems like you'd want to make sure your customer base is expanded, that you have an opportunity to be able to access those markets.

Today, small businesses account for about a quarter of this country's exports. I find that to be an encouraging and interesting statistic. The problem is that a lot of small businesses in certain markets find it very difficult to navigate the bureaucracies and paperwork required to sell their good or their service in a particular country. Big businesses have got staffs of people who can do that; small businesses don't. And therefore, I think it is very important for the American citizen to understand that when we work to expand free and fair trade, in one way, we're helping to make sure the small-business sector of this country remains strong. The easier it is for somebody to sell a product in somebody else's market, the more likely it is people will be able to find opportunity here in the United States of America.

When I took office, we had three free trade agreements; now we've got free trade agreements with 11 countries and 18 more pending. I'm also pushing for an ambitious conclusion to the Doha round of the world trade talks so we can lower barriers and reduce regulations to make it easier for people to be able to sell in foreign markets. So we need to be confident in our ability to compete. I believe the United States can outcompete anybody, anytime, anywhere, so long as the rules are fair.

And so one of the places—one country that can show the world that it means to be a trading partner that plays by the rules is China. This coming week, next week, I'm going to meet with President Hu Jintao, and I look forward to welcoming him to the White House. America values China as a trading partner, but we expect China to live up to its commitments. China needs to make itself more transparent. China needs to enforce intellectual property rights. China needs to take additional steps to address the trade imbalance between our countries. And China needs to move to a flexible market-based currency.

This country needs to be confident about the future, and we need to shape the future. And one way we can shape the future is to make sure that we stay on the leading edge of technology and research. And so I've called on Congress to double funding for basic—vital, basic research. I think that's a proper role for the Federal Government, to be involved with helping the basic sciences expand new horizons. Congress needs to make the research and development tax credit a permanent part of the Tax Code to encourage private sector to do its part about making sure this country is technologically advanced and innovative.

And our education system must make sure we set high standards and measure and make sure that we're just not passing kids through the schools that can't read and write. And I'm calling on Congress to encourage school districts to have a special emphasis on math and science. We want our children to be educated so they can lead the world. We want them educated with the skills necessary to fill the jobs of the 21st century.

I also recognize that in order for us to be competitive, we've got to get off oil. I said in my State of the Union that the United States has a problem—we're addicted to oil. Now, I know you probably thought that was kind of weird for a Texan to say. [*Laughter*] But I'm telling you, we've got an economic security problem because of our reliance upon fossil fuels, and we've got a national security problem because of our reliance on fossil fuels.

And I'm looking forward to working with Congress when they get back to make sure we invest wisely in new technologies that will encourage additional use of ethanol to power our automobiles; new technologies that will enable us to develop plug-in batteries so that hybrid vehicles are able to drive the first 40 miles on electricity, without using any gasoline; new technologies that will encourage solar energy; and technologies that will enable us to develop a safe nuclear power industry. We're spending a lot of money right now on clean coal technologies. What I'm telling you is we've got a comprehensive agenda and plan to take this country into a different era when it comes to consuming energy, an era that will make us less dependent on foreign sources of oil, enable us to be wise stewards of the environment.

I want to talk to you about another issue to make sure this country remains competitive, and that's immigration. This is a highly emotional issue; it's a vitally important issue. It's an issue that we need to conduct a debate on in a way that is worthy of this country's best traditions. We are a land of immigrants. Any immigration reform has got to improve the ability to secure our borders and enforce our laws. We are a nation of laws. I don't know if you realize this, but since 2001, we have turned back 6 million folks trying to come into this country illegally. There are a lot of people working hard down on our borders, and we're going to continue to modernize the borders to enable them to do—better do their jobs. But any effective immigration reform must include a temporary-worker program that includes a legal way to match willing foreign workers with willing American employers to fill the jobs Americans will not do.

This immigration program should not provide automatic citizenship or amnesty. It should provide a chance for people to work here legally on a temporary basis. Encouraging people to abide by the law is a necessary part of our country—the history of our country. Recognizing that people are doing jobs here that nobody else will do is important for, perhaps, some of you here in this audience. Making sure there are tamper-proof identification cards so people can't cheat on the system makes sense to me. Treating people with dignity makes sense to me. Making sure the system doesn't force people into the shadows of our society, changing that system for the better—for security and for decency—makes sense to me. And the Congress needs to set aside partisan differences and get a good bill to my desk.

I was encouraged last week when Members of the United States Senate reached a promising bipartisan compromise on comprehensive immigration reform. That was a hopeful sign. Unfortunately, the compromise was blocked by the Senate Democratic minority leader. He refused to allow Senators to move forward and vote for amendments to the bill. It was a procedural gimmick that meant he was singlehandedly thwarting the will of the American people and impeding bipartisan efforts to secure this border and make this immigration system of ours more humane and rational. This town has got too much politics to it. It's time to set aside needless partisan politics and focus on what's right for the United States of America.

I appreciate being with people who are the entrepreneurs of this country. The entrepreneurial spirit of America is strong, and I intend to keep it strong. Look, I can't make you take risk; I can't make you dream. It's up to you. But I can keep your taxes low to make it easier for you to realize your dream. We can do something about health care costs so that you can realize the dream of making sure your employees have got health care coverage. We can open up markets for you. We can make sure the environment is strong, so people continue to realize their dreams.

I love a society in which people are able to pursue their dreams, no matter who they are or where they're from. I think this really speaks to the greatness of the United States of America—a place where a person can start with nothing and end up with something, a place where a small-business owner can grow to be a big-business owner, if that's what he or she desires. A society in which people are able to accomplish their dreams is a whole society and a complete society.

Ours is a remarkable country because of the entrepreneurial spirit of America. And I want to thank you for being a part of this great land of ours. Thanks for what you do. Thanks for expanding the job base. May God bless you, and may God continue to bless your families.

NOTE: The President spoke at 10:46 a.m. at the Ronald Reagan Building and International Trade Center. In his remarks, he referred to Eric Hoover, president and chief executive officer, Excalibur Machine Co., and his wife, Annette; and President Hu Jintao of China. The Office of the Press Secretary also released a Spanish language transcript of these remarks. A portion of these remarks could not be verified because the tape was incomplete.

Message on the Observance of Easter 2006
April 13, 2006

"He is not here; for He is risen, as He said."

MATTHEW 28:6

I send greetings to those observing the joyous holiday of Easter. On Easter, Christians around the world join together with family and friends to celebrate the Resurrection of Jesus Christ and the triumph of love over death. This is a season of renewal, a time for giving thanks and praise and for remembering that hope overcomes despair.

Christ's extraordinary sacrifice and compassion continue to inspire people around the world. His promise of new life gives hope and confidence to His followers. His service and love for His neighbors offer a profound lesson for all people.

During this Easter season, we celebrate God's gifts of freedom and justice. We pray for peace and ask for God's blessings on the brave men and women who wear our Nation's uniform and their families.

Laura and I wish you a Happy Easter.

GEORGE W. BUSH

NOTE: An original was not available for verification of the content of this message.

Statement Supporting Secretary of Defense Donald H. Rumsfeld
April 14, 2006

Earlier today I spoke with Don Rumsfeld about ongoing military operations in the global war on terror. I reiterated my strong support for his leadership during this historic and challenging time for our Nation.

The Department of Defense has been tasked with many difficult missions. Upon assuming office, I asked Don to transform the largest department in our Government. That kind of change is hard, but our Nation must have a military that is fully prepared to confront the dangerous threats of the 21st century. Don and our military commanders have also been tasked to take the fight to the enemy abroad on multiple fronts.

I have seen firsthand how Don relies upon our military commanders in the field and at the Pentagon to make decisions about how best to complete these missions. Secretary Rumsfeld's energetic and steady leadership is exactly what is needed at this critical period. He has my full support and deepest appreciation.

The President's Radio Address
April 15, 2006

Good morning. Monday is tax day, and that means many of you are busy finishing up your tax returns. The good news is that this year, Americans will once again keep more of their hard-earned dollars because of the tax cuts we passed in 2001 and 2003.

An important debate is taking place in Washington over whether to keep these tax cuts in place or to raise your taxes. For the sake of American workers and their families, and for our entrepreneurs, I believe Congress needs to make the tax relief permanent.

Our economy prospers when Americans like you make the decisions on how to spend, save, and invest your money. So the tax relief we passed cut taxes for everyone who pays income taxes. We cut taxes on families by lowering rates and by doubling the child credit. We also reduced the marriage penalty, because our Tax Code should encourage marriage, not penalize it. We cut taxes on small businesses, allowing them to expand and hire more workers. And we worked with Congress to phase out the death tax, because Government should not tax farmers or small-business owners twice—once when you make your money and the second time when you try to pass the fruits of your life's work on to your loved ones.

So far, the tax relief I signed has left $880 billion with America's workers and small-business owners and families, and you have used that money to fuel an economic resurgence. Our economy has added jobs for 31 months in a row, creating more than 5.1 million new jobs for American workers. And the unemployment rate is now down to 4.7 percent, below the average rate for each of the past four decades. Real after-tax income per person has grown by more than 8 percent since I took office. And that means, on average, Americans have an income that is $2,100 higher this year than it was at the beginning of 2001, after adjusting for inflation.

Not everyone agrees that we should let you keep more of your money. Some in Washington said that by cutting taxes, we were ruining our economy. On the day that the House and Senate were finalizing the 2003 tax cuts, one Democratic leader said these cuts would do nothing to create jobs. Since then, the facts have proven that critic wrong—5.1 million times over.

Tax relief has done exactly what it was designed to do: It has created jobs and growth for the American people. Yet some here in Washington are now proposing that we raise taxes, either by repealing the tax cuts or letting them expire. These are the same politicians who told us that letting you keep more of your own money would be irresponsible and reckless and shameful. They were wrong then, and they are wrong now. To keep our economy creating jobs and opportunity, Congress needs to make the tax relief permanent.

There's more to do to maintain America's economic strength. We're working to address rising energy prices and health care costs, which puts pressure on family budgets and the bottom lines of our small businesses. I have proposed practical reforms that would make health care more available and affordable, and I put forward an energy initiative that would make our dependence on Middle Eastern oil a thing of the past. I urge Congress to act on these important priorities, so we can keep America the economic leader of the world and allow more families and small businesses to realize the American Dream.

America's economy is strong and benefiting all Americans. By keeping taxes low and adopting sound policies that help our workers to compete and our businesses to grow and expand, we will keep the economy moving forward and extend prosperity and hope in our country.

Thank you for listening.

NOTE: The address was recorded at 7:36 a.m. on April 13 in the Cabinet Room at the White House for broadcast at 10:06 a.m. on April 15. The transcript was made available by the Office of the Press Secretary on April 14 but was embargoed for release until the broadcast. The Office of the Press Secretary also released a Spanish language transcript of this address.

Remarks Following a Meeting on Taxes and the National Economy in Sterling, Virginia
April 17, 2006

I want to thank Carlos and Owen and Adam for inviting us to their business. I also want to thank the other folks that we had a discussion with for coming over. We've got folks that have benefited from the tax relief, both as a small-business owner and/or an employee—except for Mike; he's a firefighter. And it's been a good discussion.

Here's what I come away with: One, the tax relief helped small businesses a lot. And since small businesses create two-thirds of the new jobs of America, it is no wonder that our job base is expanding. When you help the small-business owner with tax relief, you're helping to create employment. And that's what we're seeing across the country. We've added 5.1 million new jobs in the last 2½ years. A lot of it has to do with the fact that our small-business owners are confident, and they're investing, and they're expanding the job base.

I talked to Shannon Bennett. She's a single mom with one young son who saved about $1,200 or $1,300 on her taxes this past year. And it's important for her family that she has got some additional money. Owen—I mean, Mike has got three children. He's a firefighter. The tax relief helped. In other words, tax relief helped the small-business owner; it's helped our families.

And what's interesting is, the tax relief is set to expire. Actually, there's some Democrats in Congress who would like to raise taxes now. And if that happens, it will be a tax increase no one expects, no one wants. It will be like getting hit by one of these granite rocks.

And so I strongly urge the United States Congress to understand the positive effects of the tax relief and to keep the taxes low—keep the taxes low on the working people, keep the taxes low on these small-business owners, so that we continue—so that we can continue to be the—an economy that leads the world.

And I want to thank you for your time, letting us come by. It's tax day, and it's a day to recommit ourselves to low taxes. It's a day that understands that when these people filing out their forms and writing checks to the Government, that it's the people's money that's coming to Washington, DC. And we intend to let people keep more of their own money, for the sake of the economy and for the sake of our families.

So thanks for letting us come by. Appreciate your hard work. I love the fact that you're living the American Dream.

NOTE: The President spoke at 11:12 a.m. at Europa Stone Distributors, Inc. In his remarks, he referred to Carlos Varela, co-owner and president, Owen Werthmann, co-owner and vice president, and Adam Mahmud, co-owner and vice president, Europa Stone Distributors, Inc.; and Miguel Obleas, firefighter, Fairfax County Fire and Rescue Department.

Remarks on the Nomination of Robert J. Portman To Be Director of the Office of Management and Budget and Susan C. Schwab To Be United States Trade Representative and an Exchange With Reporters
April 18, 2006

The President. Good morning. Today I'm announcing my nomination of two outstanding individuals to serve in my Cabinet and on my economic team.

First, I will nominate Rob Portman to be the Director of the Office of Management and Budget. Rob will replace Josh Bolten, who this week started in his new role as my Chief of Staff. The Office of Management and Budget is one of the most essential agencies of our Government. The OMB has a central responsibility of implementing the full range of my administration's agenda, from defense programs that will keep our people secure, to energy initiatives that will break our dependence on oil, to tax policies that keep our economy growing and creating jobs.

In these and other areas, the job of the OMB Director is to ensure that the Government spends the taxpayers' money wisely or not at all. He is the person in charge of meeting our goal to cutting the budget deficit in half by 2009. And he is responsible for managing Federal programs efficiently. The American people deserve results for every hard-earned dollar they send to Washington.

The job of OMB Director is really an important post, and Rob Portman is the right man to take it on. Rob's talent, expertise, and record of success are well-known within my administration and on Capitol Hill. For the past 11 months, Rob has served as United States Trade Representative. When he took the job, I told him to focus on opening new markets for American exports to ensure that our producers and farmers are treated fairly and to get Congress to pass the Central American-Dominican Republic Free Trade Agreement. He's accomplished those goals.

I signed CAFTA into law last summer, and Rob Portman and his staff completed trade agreements with Bahrain, Oman, Peru, and Colombia. He also re-energized the Doha trade talks at the World Trade Organization. Before joining my Cabinet, Rob represented the Second District of Ohio in the United States Congress for more than a decade. He was a key part of the House leadership. He was an influential member of the Ways and Means Committee, and he served as vice chairman of the Budget Committee.

His legislative achievements range from reforming the Internal Revenue Service, providing tax relief for working families, to encouraging retirement savings. Rob's leadership in Congress was also marked by an ability to work across the aisle and bring people together to get things done. And he's going to bring that same skill to his new post.

As Director of OMB, Rob will have a leading role on my economic team. He will be part of daily senior staff meetings led by Josh Bolten. He will consult often and work closely with legislators on Capitol Hill. He will be a powerful voice for progrowth policies and spending restraint.

Rob is a man of deep integrity. He knows the priorities of my administration; he can get things done. And the Senate should confirm him promptly as Director of the Office of Management and Budget.

I'm also pleased to announce that I'm going to nominate Deputy U.S. Trade Representative Susan Schwab to succeed Rob Portman as the new U.S. Trade Representative.

Trade is one of the most powerful engines of growth and job creation. America accounts for about 5 percent of the world's population, and that means that 95 percent of our potential customers live overseas. So my administration has taken an aggressive agenda to break down barriers to American exports across the world.

When I took office, we had three free trade agreements. Now, we have free trade agreements with 11 countries, and 18 more are pending. Susan will work hard to conclude these agreements and ensure that American goods, services, and crops are treated fairly in overseas markets.

Last year, the countries with which we have free trade agreements represented about 7 percent of the economy abroad but about 42 percent of our exports. Lowering trade barriers to the sale of our goods and services helps provide a level playing field for American workers and farmers and ranchers. And that means more jobs and opportunity, because our workers and ranchers and farmers can compete with anybody, anytime, anywhere, so long as the rules are fair, and Susan Schwab understands that.

As Deputy U.S. Trade Representative for the past 5 months, Ambassador Schwab worked tirelessly to open up new markets, and at the same time, making sure our people were treated fairly. Her trade portfolio covered several continents, and she led USTR efforts in a number of vital policy areas, including intellectual property enforcement.

Susan also worked closely with Ambassador Portman to advance the Doha negotiations. Now she will use her experience to help complete the Doha round and create other new opportunities for American exporters.

Ambassador Schwab started her career as an agricultural trade negotiator in the Office of the U.S. Trade Representative, and she served our Nation overseas as a trade policy officer in our Embassy in Tokyo. In the 1980s, she worked as a trade specialist and then legislative director for Senator Jack Danforth, who chaired a key Senate subcommittee on trade. In the ad-

ministration of former President Bush, she led a staff of more than a thousand as Director General of the U.S. and Foreign Commercial Service. Susan has also served as an executive in the private sector at Motorola and as a professor and administrator at the University of Maryland.

Throughout her distinguished career, Susan has earned the respect of her colleagues, and she has my confidence as well. The Senate should promptly confirm her nomination to be United States Trade Representative.

I appreciate the service that Rob and Susan have given the American people, and I'm really grateful they've agreed to take on new responsibilities. I also thank Rob and Susan's families today. I'm really glad that Rob's wife, Jane, is with us; and it's my pleasure to have welcomed Susan's parents, Gerald and Joan, to the Oval Office and to the Rose Garden. Glad you all are here.

I look forward to the Senate confirming Rob and Susan and welcoming them to be new members of my Cabinet.

Congratulations, and thank you for your willingness to serve.

[*At this point, Director-designate Portman and Ambassador-designate Schwab made brief remarks.*]

Iran

Q. Mr. President.

The President. Hold on for a second, please. I'll take a couple of questions. Nedra [Nedra Pickler, Associated Press], Patsy [Patricia Wilson, Reuters], and Kelly [Kelly O'Donnell, NBC News], in that order.

Q. Thank you, Mr. President.

The President. A little louder, I'm getting older.

Q. Sir, when you talk about Iran and you talk about how you have diplomatic efforts, you also say all options are on the table. Does that include the possibility of a nuclear strike? Is that something that your administration will plan for?

The President. All options are on the table. We want to solve this issue diplomatically, and we're working hard to do so. The best way to do so is, therefore, to be a united effort with countries who recognize the danger of Iran having a nuclear weapon. And that's why we're working very closely with countries like France and Germany and Great Britain. I intend, of course, to bring the subject up of Iranian ambitions to have a nuclear weapon with Hu Jintao this Thursday. And we'll continue to work diplomatically to get this problem solved.

Patsy.

Israel-Palestinian Authority Relations

Q. Sir, are you encouraging Israel to show restraint in reaction to yesterday's Palestinian bombing? Or would a measured military response be appropriate?

The President. I have consistently reminded all parties that they must be mindful of whatever actions they take and mindful of the consequences. Our goal is to have two states living side by side in peace. I strongly deplore the loss of innocent life in the attack on the folks in Israel yesterday. It is unjustified, and it is unnecessary. And for those who love peace in the Palestinian Territories, they must stand up and reject this kind of violence.

Kelly.

White House Staff/Fuel

Q. Morning, Mr. President. Do you expect that there will be some changes that were not voluntary? Today you've highlighted openings in your administration, but will Mr. Bolten ask some people to leave? And would you accept his counsel for Cabinet changes, as well as White House staffers?

The President. I understand this is—you know, this is a matter of high speculation here in Washington. It's the game of musical chairs, I guess you'd say, that people love to follow. My instructions to Josh Bolten was that I expect him to design

the White House structure so that it will function so that he can do his job, function in a way so he's more likely to be able to do his job. And, of course, he will bring different recommendations to me as to who should be here and who should not be here.

And I'm the person who believes in aligning authority and responsibility. I've given him enormous responsibility and authority and expect the White House to work well. And it did under Andy Card, by the way. I'm most proud of his tenure as the Chief of Staff. But with a new man will come some changes. And Josh has got all the rights to make those recommendations to me. And, of course, I listen to advice as to my Cabinet as well. I must tell you that I'm—I've got strong confidence in my Cabinet officials, all of them, and I appreciate the service they've rendered.

But I also understand what happens in Washington. You know, a little flicker of gossip starts moving hard, and people jump all over it. The thing the American people have got to know is we'll structure this White House so it continues to function to deal with major problems. And we're dealing with major problems. We're dealing with a war on terror. We're dealing with high gasoline prices.

And let me remind people that these high gasoline prices are caused by primarily three reasons: one, the increase in the price of crude oil. It's one of the reasons I stood up in front of the Congress and said, we've got to have strong and active research and development to get us to diversify away from crude oil. It's tight supply worldwide, and we've got increasing demand from countries like India and China, which means that any disruption of supply or perceived disruption of supply is going to cause the price of crude to go up. And that affects the price of gasoline.

Secondly, there's increasing demand. At this time of year, people are beginning to drive more, getting out on the highways, taking a little time off, and they're moving around. And that increasing demand is also part of the reason the price of gasoline is going up.

And thirdly, we're switching fuel mixes. The summer fuel mix is different from State to State and is different from what is being used in the winter. And therefore, the combination of these creates higher gasoline prices. And I'm concerned about higher gasoline prices. I'm concerned what it means to the working families and small businesses, and I'm also mindful that the Government has the responsibility to make sure that we watch very carefully and to investigate possible price gouging. And we'll do just that.

Q. Is there going to be rationing, do you think?

The President. No, I don't—that's your word.

Secretary of Defense Donald H. Rumsfeld

Q. Mr. President, you've made it a practice of not commenting on potential personnel moves——

The President. Of course I did.

Q. ——of calling it speculation——

The President. You can understand why, because we've got people's reputations at stake. And on Friday, I stood up and said, I don't appreciate the speculation about Don Rumsfeld; he's doing a fine job; I strongly support him.

Q. But what do you say to critics who believe that you're ignoring the advice of retired generals, military commanders, who say that there needs to be a change?

The President. I say, I listen to all voices, but mine is the final decision. And Don Rumsfeld is doing a fine job. He's not only transforming the military; he's fighting a war on terror. He's helping us fight a war on terror. I have strong confidence in Don Rumsfeld. I hear the voices, and I read the front page, and I know the speculation. But I'm the decider, and I decide what is best. And what's best is for Don Rumsfeld to remain as the Secretary of Defense.

I want to thank you all very much.

NOTE: The President spoke at 9:27 a.m. in the Rose Garden at the White House. In his remarks, he referred to President Hu Jintao of China; and former Senator John C. Danforth of Missouri.

Remarks Following Discussions With Prime Minister Fuad Siniora of Lebanon
April 18, 2006

President Bush. It's been my honor to welcome the Prime Minister of Lebanon to the Oval Office. Prime Minister, thanks for coming.

Prime Minister Siniora. Thank you very much for giving us the opportunity.

President Bush. Well, we just had a really interesting discussion. I told the Prime Minister that the United States strongly supports a free and independent and sovereign Lebanon. We took great joy in seeing the Cedar Revolution. We understand

that the hundreds of thousands of people who took to the street to express their desire to be free required courage, and we support the desire of the people to have a government responsive to their needs and a government that is free, truly free.

We talked about the need to make sure that there is a full investigation on the death of former Prime Minister Hariri, and we'll work with the international community to see that justice is done. We talked about the great tradition of Lebanon to serve as a model of entrepreneurship and prosperity. Beirut is one of the great international cities, and I'm convinced that if Lebanon is truly free and independent and democratic that Beirut will once again regain her place as a center of financial and culture and the arts.

There's no question in my mind that Lebanon can serve as a great example for what is possible in the broader Middle East; that out of the tough times the country has been through will rise a state that shows that it's possible for people of religious difference to live side by side in peace; to show that it's possible for people to put aside past histories to live together in a way that the people want, which is there for to be peace and hope and opportunity.

And so, Mr. Prime Minister, we're really glad you're here. I want to thank you for the wonderful visit we've had, and welcome you here to the White House.

Prime Minister Siniora. Thank you very much, Mr. President. I would like to really thank President Bush for giving us the opportunity to be here at the White House and to discuss matters of mutual interest to the United States and Lebanon and matters that has to do with the developments that have been taking place in Lebanon.

For the past—over 16 or 18 months, Lebanon has been undergoing major

changes. And Lebanon has really been committing itself that we want the change to happen to—in a democratic and a peaceful manner, but at the same time, to really stay course—on course; that we are there to meet the expectations of the people to have a united, liberal, free country and, at the same time, prosperous economy.

So that are the matters that we have discussed with President Bush. And I really would like to seize this opportunity to thank President Bush and the United States for the support that they have been extending to Lebanon throughout the past periods and with all the resolutions that were taken since the assassination of Prime Minister Hariri. The United States has been of great support to Lebanon.

I am really convinced that President Bush and the United States will stand beside Lebanon to have Lebanon stay as a free, democratic, united, and sovereign state. And the United States is really of great importance in this regard, whether this can be done directly or indirectly. So I would like once more to express our great thanks for President Bush and the United States for this.

President Bush. Thank you, sir. Appreciate it.

NOTE: The President spoke at 11:51 a.m. on the South Lawn at the White House.

Remarks at Parkland Magnet Middle School for Aerospace Technology in Rockville, Maryland
April 18, 2006

Thanks for having me. Please be seated. Madam Secretary—I never thought I'd be saying that 10 years ago, I might add. Of course, she never thought I'd be President. [*Laughter*] It is good to be here with you all. Thanks to Parkland Magnet Middle School for having us. We just had an amazing tour. I say "amazing tour" because we

saw what a unique place Parkland is, and we saw a really diverse student body. There's people from all kinds of backgrounds here.

We saw some—three really wonderful teachers, people who are dedicated to their profession, who deeply care about the students they teach. And for all of you here who are teachers, thanks for carrying on a really noble profession. We saw two scientists who are here from NASA. These are good, hard-working folks who said, "I kind of want to lend my expertise to try to convince a child that science is cool." You know, sometimes—you might remember those days, when you were in middle school, people say, you know, "Science isn't cool." Science is not only cool, it's really important for the future of this country. And it's great to have people we call adjunct professors here, to help lend their real-life experiences to stimulate junior high students to the wonders of science.

We saw robotics. When I was in the seventh grade, I don't think we spent much time on robotics. [*Laughter*] Of course, Mr. Jones, the teacher, probably said, "You didn't spend much time paying attention at all, did you, Mr. President." [*Laughter*] We saw people using little devices to look for sun spots. We saw the analysis of a parabola curve for sixth and seventh grade students. We saw a school that is setting high standards in the firm belief that every child can learn. That's what we saw.

And I want to thank the principal, Kevin Hobbs, for welcoming us here today. You know, Kevin skipped a vacation—at least he claimed he skipped a vacation—[*laughter*]—to be here. And I am so grateful you did so, sir. But more importantly, I am grateful that you're a principal. Great schools—the really good schools in our country have at its center an educational entrepreneur who is able to rally a teacher group to set high standards and follow through. And I want to thank you, Kevin. Again, I want to thank all the principals.

I appreciate Chris Van Hollen joining us today. Mr. Congressman, I'm pleased you took time to be here. Thank you so much. It's a joy to be in your district.

I want to thank Nancy Grasmick, who is the Maryland State superintendent of schools. Margaret was telling me coming—I've known Nancy for a while—Margaret was talking about the implementation of

No Child Left Behind—which, by the way, is—I'll talk a little bit about. But it requires people who are dedicated to this firm belief that through accountability, you can determine whether or not every child is getting a good education. And I appreciate Nancy's philosophy and her service to the State of Maryland.

I want to thank—I thank Dr. Jerry Weast, who is the superintendent of schools here in Montgomery County. Jerry, thank you for your—for the tour, and thank you for your service as well—Dr. Charles Haughey, who is the board president. I don't know what's a harder job, Dr. Haughey, President of the United States or board president of a local school. [*Laughter*] Yes, I suspect board president of the Montgomery Country schools. [*Laughter*] Frank Stetson, the community superintendent—I want to thank the other State and local officials. I want to thank the parents who are here.

The truth of the matter is, the parent is really the child's first teacher. And every school I have been to as Governor or President, I have always found that parental involvement makes a significant difference in the quality of the education. So thank you for supporting the teachers and the principal who are here. Thank you for, more importantly, encouraging your children to aim high and work hard.

Here's the question that faces the country: Will we become a nation that is isolationist and fearful of competition from around the world, or will we be—continue to be a bold and innovative country?

We've got a good economy right now. And it's growing at rapid paces, and there's a lot of new jobs being added, and productivity is high, and people are owning homes, and that's all positive. The fundamental question is, how do we make sure that that's the case next year, 5 years, and 10 years from now? That's really what we're confronted with.

As you know, Hu Jintao is coming to Washington—or maybe you don't know—

but the President of China is coming to Washington on Thursday. It's a very important visit. China is a very important strategic friend in many ways, and in many ways, they pose competition to us. It's a growing economy. They've got folks that are beginning to realize the benefits of a marketplace. Their entrepreneurship is strong. And we can either look at China and say, "Let's compete with China in a fair way," or say, "We can't compete with China," and therefore, kind of isolate ourselves from the world.

I've chosen the former route for the United States. I tell our people, we shouldn't fear the future; what we ought to do is shape the future. We ought to be in charge of our future. And the best way to do so is to make sure that we're the most innovative country in the world. We have been the most innovative country in the world for the past decades, and that has helped raise our standard of living. We need to always be on the leading edge of technological change. We need to be the center of research and development.

And so here are two ideas that I intend to work with Congress on to make sure that we're still the technological capital of the world—for the benefit of our people, by the way, so that the standard of living in America continues to improve for everybody. One is that we must increase Federal support for vital, basic research.

I don't know whether you realize it or not, but the Internet began as a Defense Department project to improve military communications. In other words, that was an area where the Federal Government spent research money, and out of that research and development came the Internet, which has substantially changed the way we live. The iPod, interestingly enough, was built on years of Government-funded research in microdrive storage and electrochemistry and signal compression. Isn't that interesting? I find it interesting.

In other words, investment at the Federal level in research has led to practical applications which improve the lives of our citizens. And so I proposed to the Congress that we double the Federal commitment to the most critical basic research programs in physical sciences over the next 10 years. One way to make sure this country is the economic leader of the world so that our people benefit and can find work is for there to be a Federal commitment to research.

A second thing we can do is recognize that most research and development takes place in the private sector. That's about $200 billion a year is spent in private sector research. In other words, we've got some of the leading companies in our country doing research as to how to develop new products that will make sure that not only their company and their shareholders benefit but that it ends up in order to the benefit of the United States.

One way to encourage people to invest corporate funds is through the research and development tax credit. In other words, it's the use of the Tax Code to say, this is in your interest the—by the way, it's in our collective interest as well—but it's in your interest, your corporate interest to invest so that your product line remains modern, so that your scientists that work for your company are able to have funds necessary to continue to think anew.

The problem we have in America is that the research and development tax credit expires on an annual basis. And if you're somebody trying to plan for your—for the next 5 years or the next 10 years, which a lot of smart people do, it's difficult to do so if every year you're wondering whether or not the Congress or the President is willing to stand up and support the research and development tax credit. So another way to make sure that this country of ours is competitive, where we don't have to fear the future because we intend to be the leader, is to make sure that the research and development tax credit is permanent, to add permanency to that in through the Tax Code.

And thirdly—and one of the reasons we're here—is to make it clear to the American people that in order for us to be competitive, we've got to make sure that our children have got the skill sets necessary to compete for the jobs of the 21st century. We live in a global world, and that creates uncertainty in some; I understand that. There's a sense of, well, the world is so big and so connected that it's—maybe we're really not in charge of things here.

In a global economy, for example, if our children do not have the skill sets for the jobs of the 21st century, the jobs are going to go somewhere else. And it's a fact of life. It's a part of the real world we have to deal with. It's a lot different from the 1950s, for example. There wasn't that sense of global competition—at least there wasn't that sense in Midland, Texas, let me put it to you that way. [*Laughter*] But there is today. If you're living in Midland, Texas, or living in Montgomery County, Maryland, it's important to understand, if children don't have those skill sets needed to compete with a child from India or a child from China, the new jobs will be going there.

And so in order to make sure we remain the leader of the world, we have got to continue our focus in education on high standards, accountability, and a new focus—an intense focus on math and science—just like what's happening in this school. I saw the children being taught the skills for the jobs of the 21st century—today. See, it's possible. As a matter of fact, it's happening in a lot of places all across America, just not enough. And this school is the kind of school that we've got to have in neighborhoods throughout the country.

And so here are some things—first of all, let me just remind you that—what the No Child Left Behind Act, as far as I'm concerned, means. It means, one, you believe every child can learn; two, you refuse to accept a system that just shuffles kids through school because they happen to be a certain age. In other words, you use an accountability system—and by the way, we've insisted upon measurement in return for Federal money. We didn't say, "We'll develop the test for you"—you develop your own accountability systems, but we expect there to be results when we spend money. And if you believe every child can learn, then you shouldn't be worried about measuring.

Some of you might remember the old reading curriculum debates, by the way—they were pretty ugly, at least when I was the Governor of Texas. People dug in on both sides of the issue: "I'm right. You're wrong; I'm right." And the best way to determine what works is to measure. So the accountability system, which we should expect, says this: One, we believe every child can learn; therefore, let's measure to make sure every child is learning. And two, we understand there can be differences of opinion on what works and what doesn't work, so let's measure to determine what works. And third, it also makes sense to figure out how we're—how you're doing. How's Parkland doing? Are you doing well compared to other schools in the neighborhood? If not, why? And if so, keep doing what you're doing.

The accountability system is an important tool upholding people to high standards. It makes a lot of sense, as far as I'm concerned. One of the important parts of No Child Left Behind, by the way, particularly in the reading program, if you've fallen behind early, here's extra money to help you catch up. It's called supplemental services. It's a really important part of a program that says every child can read, and when we detect a child not reading, let's correct the problem early, before it's too late. In essence, we've ended social promotion, and we're having high standards. And that's what's going to be necessary to lay the foundation for the skill sets for the jobs of the 21st century. That's important.

And by the way, we're beginning to see marked improvement. How do we know? Because we're measuring. In 2005, America's fourth graders posted the best scores in reading and math in the history of the reading and math tests. And, oh, by the way, I've heard every excuse not to measure—you know, "You're teaching the test." No, you're teaching a child to read so he or she can pass the test, that's what you're doing. Or, "All you do is test." No, good schools are those who've got a curriculum that enables a child to be able to pass a standardized test. That's what we're talking about.

African American fourth graders set record scores in reading and math. That's important, and that's positive. Hispanic fourth graders set records in reading and math. That's important, and that's positive. I'm able to report this to you because we measure. If you didn't measure, you'd just have to guess, right? Maybe they're doing well; maybe they're not doing well. That system didn't work. It doesn't work very well when you end up with a high school kid graduating, who can't read, and you go, "What went wrong? Where did we fail the child? What did we do wrong for the parent?" Measurement is an important way to make sure that children are not left behind.

The National Report Card showed eighth graders earned the best math scores ever recorded; eighth grade Hispanic and African American students achieved their highest math scores ever. We're beginning to make important strides. We're closing an achievement gap in America, an achievement gap that is wrong and important for the future of this country.

But we also know through measurement that our high school students, by the time they reach high school, have fallen behind most of the developed world in math and science. So there's been some positive results that ought to encourage us, but there's some warning signs. If we want to be a competitive nation, if we want our children

to be able to have the jobs of the 21st century, those jobs that are high-paying, high-skilled jobs, we better do something about the fact that we're falling behind in math and science today. Now is the time to act.

And here's some ideas. One, one of the great programs that has been proven to work is Advanced Placement. It is a—I went to an amazing school in downtown Dallas, a really diverse school. It's a school where you walk in—at least you used to walk in, and say, "Well, these kids aren't supposed to do well." They just happen to have set the records for passing AP science and math tests in the United States. Of course, we Texans are always saying we—you know—[*laughter*]. Just telling you, that's what they told me. [*Laughter*] The point is, they're doing well because there's an AP program that helps set high standards and makes a difference.

And so what needs to be done to make Advanced Placement work? Well, one thing, the Federal Government needs to help train 70,000 high school teachers on how to teach AP and how to administer the program and how to make sure it's a viable part of school districts all around the country.

Second, we ought to have 30,000 math and science professionals in our classrooms over the next 8 years. Today I met two; they're called adjunct professors. As I told you earlier, it's really important for students to see firsthand what it's like to be a scientist. Margaret and I didn't do a very good job of teaching what it's like to be a scientist. The two guys from NASA did an excellent job of teaching them what it is like to be a scientist. It is—there's just something that's important for a child to connect with a role model.

And I'm not kidding when I said we need to make sure that people realize math and science are cool subjects. Now, coolness, I think, is—I think it's still prevalent in the junior high, you know? [*Laughter*] Well, there's nothing better than somebody to say, "This is important," than somebody that's actually living it—living the field, living the dream of being a scientist.

And so we've got a goal of 70,000 AP teachers and 30,000 adjunct professors in classrooms. The House of Representatives reauthorized the Higher Education Act, which included the AP program and the adjunct teacher program. And I want to thank them for that. And I look forward to getting the Senate—[*applause*].

I signed an Executive order this morning establishing what is called the national math panel. Let me describe that to you. It's a part of our strategy to make sure that we achieve the objective of laying that foundation for our children in math and science. By January 31st, 2007, the national math panel will report their assessments of the best practices for teaching math. Those experts will come together and help advise school districts about what is working and what's not working, what skills the students need at what grade to master algebra and higher mathematics. In other words, starting to set those—help set realistic standards—the standards and accountability that will be needed to ensure students are learning math. That will be a part of their mandate. They will look at the teaching methods that are most effective for students of different abilities and backgrounds. They will look at the programs and learning materials that work best.

A lot of times, school districts need a little advice on how to—what works. It's—the purchasing, at least it was in my State—there's a lot of different decisionmakers around the State. And I'm pretty confident it will make sense to have a national panel of experts make recommendations—not mandates—but recommendations about how school districts can achieve the objective of making sure math is properly taught and what needs to be used to make sure that it works.

They'll be coming up with recommendations on the most effective ways to train and select and place math teachers, which will be a very important recommendation. I'm not saying all teachers need extra help, but some teachers do. When they get out of a teachers' school, they're going to need the extra—the tools necessary to make sure we meet the goals. And so the math panel will be convening here shortly and reporting back to the country.

And I'm also proposing a new program called Math Now, which will be used to apply the recommendations. And here's what Math Now means: Teachers will be able to use the math panel's recommendations to ensure they're using the best techniques. And there will be money to help. Math Now is similar for No Child Left Behind's Reading First Initiative, which uses scientific findings compiled by the National Reading Panel to help local and State districts achieve their objectives. And by the way—sorry—it's working. The reading initiative is working. It's making an enormous difference in the lives of students from all walks of life.

Math Now for elementary school students will promote research-based practices. Math Now for middle school students will target students struggling with math.

One of the things in Reading First is that, as I told you, we use supplemental services to detect reading problems early and make sure a child gets extra help early, before it's too late. We intend to apply the same rigor in middle school for math students. The tests show we're fine in the fourth grade in math, and we're okay in eighth grade. They start to slip up prior to going to high school. That is the time to intervene in a child's academic career to make sure he or she has that skill set necessary to become the mathematicians or the scientists or the engineers by the time they get out of college.

And so that's what I've come to talk about. It's like setting realistic goals. It's understanding—it is telling this country how important public schools are to the future of our country and working with the public school system to make sure that we achieve a national objective. And that objective is to make sure that the United States of America remains the economic leader of the world, for the good of our people. And it recognizes that we have got to educate our children now for the skill sets necessary for tomorrow. And this is a better place—there's no better place to talk about that—and there is no better place to talk about that right here at Parkland Magnet Middle School for Aerospace Technology.

Thanks for letting us come by. God bless.

NOTE: The President spoke at 2 p.m. The Office of the Press Secretary also released a Spanish language transcript of these remarks.

Statement on the Resignation of H. James Towey as Director of the Office of Faith-Based and Community Initiatives
April 18, 2006

Jim Towey is a dedicated public servant who has served as a vital member of my administration for more than 4 years. Under his leadership, the Office of Faith-Based and Community Initiatives has applied the compassion of America to help solve some of our most challenging problems. His office has held 23 conferences around the country, assisting tens of thousands among America's armies of compassion. Eleven Federal departments and agencies now have Centers for Faith-Based and Community Initiatives that are building upon and expanding their good works in neighborhoods across the country.

Throughout his life, Jim has worked for Democrats and Republicans as an advocate for those in need. He served as Mother Teresa's legal counsel for many years. His work on behalf of the poor and the sick has improved lives. I admire Jim for his compassion, his faith, and his sense of humor. He is a man of great integrity, and I thank him for his service. Laura and I wish Jim, Mary, and the Towey family all the best.

Remarks Following a Meeting With Governors Who Traveled to Kuwait, Iraq, and Afghanistan
April 19, 2006

The President. I just had breakfast with four Governors who have returned from Kuwait, Iraq, and Afghanistan. I invited Secretary Rice and Secretary Rumsfeld, as well as Steve Hadley and Josh Bolten, to breakfast so that we could hear from these Governors.

First of all, I want to thank the four of them for traveling overseas. I particularly want to thank them for going to see our men and women who are helping secure freedom and peace. I thank them for sending a message from home that we care about them—that we care about our troops; that we'll support our troops; that we appreciate the fact that people are willing to make sacrifices.

I assured them that our goal in Afghanistan and Iraq is victory. And victory will be achieved when there is a democracy in both countries that are able to sustain itself and defend itself.

Secretary Rice brought the Governors up to date about a conversation she had with Ambassador Khalilzad. We fully recognize that the Iraqis must step up and form a unity government so that those who went to the polls to vote recognize that a Government will be in place to respond to their needs. In other words, we also recognize that vacuums in the political process create opportunity for malfeasance and harm. And so we assured these Governors that we understand full well that the political process in Iraq must occur soon, and we're working toward that end.

I again want to thank the Governors for coming. I thought—I asked them if they wouldn't mind saying a few words. We— I don't expect everybody to agree with my decision to go into Iraq, but I do want the people to understand—the American people to understand that failure in Iraq is not an option, that failure in Iraq would make the security situation for our country worse, and that success in Iraq will begin to lay the foundation of peace for generations to come.

Governor Daniels.

[*At this point, Gov. Mitchell E. Daniels, Jr., of Indiana, Gov. Joe Manchin III of West Virginia, Gov. Tom Vilsack of Iowa, and Gov. Jeb Bush of Florida made brief remarks.*]

The President. Yes. Again, I want to thank the four Governors for coming. Thank you for your eloquent statements. I appreciate your service to our Nation. I assured the Governors that the United States will complete the mission; that we will honor those who've paid the ultimate price, by completing the mission; that we will help those who desire to live in freedom, and in so doing, we will lay the foundations of peace for a generation to come.

I appreciate you all coming.

NOTE: The President spoke at 9:05 a.m. on the South Lawn at the White House. The transcript released by the Office of the Press Secretary also included the remarks of Governors Daniels, Manchin, Vilsack, and Bush.

Remarks Announcing the Resignation of Press Secretary Scott McClellan
April 19, 2006

Press Secretary McClellan. Good morning, everybody. I am here to announce that I will be resigning as White House Press Secretary.

Mr. President, it has been an extraordinary honor and privilege to have served you for more than 7 years now, the last 2 years and 9 months as your Press Secretary.

The White House is going through a period of transition. Change can be helpful, and this is a good time and good position to help bring about change. I am ready to move on. I've been in this position a long time, and my wife and I are excited

about beginning the next chapter in our life together.

You have accomplished a lot over the last several years with this team, and I have been honored and grateful to be a small part of a terrific and talented team of really good people.

Our relationship began back in Texas, and I look forward to continuing it, particularly when we are both back in Texas.

The President. That's right. [*Laughter*]

Press Secretary McClellan. Although, I hope to get there before you. [*Laughter*]

I have given it my all, sir, and I've given you my all. And I will continue to do so as we transition to a new Press Secretary over the next 2 to 3 weeks. Thank you for the opportunity.

The President. First of all, I thank Scott for his service to our country. I don't know whether or not the press corps realizes this, but his is a challenging assignment dealing with you all on a regular basis. And I thought he handled his assignment with class, integrity. He really represents the best of his family, our State, and our country. It's going to be hard to replace Scott. But nevertheless, he's made the decision, and I accept it.

One of these days, he and I are going to be rocking on chairs in Texas, talking about the good old days and his time as the Press Secretary. And I can assure you, I will feel the same way then that I feel now, that I can say to Scott, "Job well done."

Press Secretary McClellan. Thank you, sir.

NOTE: The President spoke at approximately 9:39 a.m. on the South Lawn at the White House.

Remarks at Tuskegee University in Tuskegee, Alabama
April 19, 2006

Thank you all. Please be seated. Thanks for having me. Mr. President—[*laughter*]—got a nice ring to it. [*Laughter*] I respect President Ben Payton for his commitment to education and his commitment to the United States of America, and I'm proud to be on this campus.

I was telling President Payton that I knew about Tuskegee before I knew about most other universities when I was a kid. When I was growing up, believe it or not, in Midland, Texas, which is way out in the desert, I knew about Tuskegee. I knew Tuskegee was a center of excellence, has been for a long period of time. And I saw firsthand, it is still a center of excellence.

George Washington Carver—you've heard of him; so did I as a young guy. [*Laughter*] Booker T. Washington—when you think Tuskegee, you think Booker T. Washington. And when you hear about Booker T. Washington, you think about Tuskegee—Ralph Ellison, or the music of Lionel Richie. I mean, Tuskegee has been a center for educational excellence and a place for opportunity for a long period of time here in the United States of America.

When I was the Governor of Texas—Governors are heads of the National Guard,

and I had the opportunity and honor to name the person that headed our Guard. And I picked a fellow named Danny James—General Danny James. It just turns out his father was a man named Chappie James. As a matter of fact, Tuskegee—I was in the Chappie James Building a little while ago. You named the building after a fine person.

I appreciate the role that Tuskegee has had in the 20th century to break down racial barriers, to provide hope, and to help build a better America. What I'm here to talk about is the role Tuskegee will continue to play in the 21st century, and it is to prepare our students and our kids for the jobs of the 21st century. Tuskegee is a really important part of making sure the United States of America provides hope and opportunity for all people.

I want to thank Dr. Shaik Jeelani, who is the director for the Center for Advanced Materials. I don't know if you have seen that facility before. I'm sure some of you have who work here, but if you haven't, I strongly urge you to go there. It's a really interesting center of the—where you'll see the future being explored and developed. There's a lot of science going on there.

I appreciate being joined by Governor Bob Riley. Riley is a friend. Riley cares deeply about educating every child. I'm going to talk about the No Child Left Behind Act as part of the foundation to make sure every child gets educated, but in case I forget, Riley is willing to set high standards and hold people to account and provide help so no child gets left behind. And I want to thank you for your leadership.

Margaret Spellings is with us. She's the Secretary of Education. I've known her for a long time. I know this: She's committed to the public school system and the higher education system of the United States of America. I look forward to working with her to make sure that every child gets a good education and every child has a chance to succeed.

I appreciate being here with the Congressman from this district, Congressman Mike Rogers. Thank you for coming, Congressman. I appreciate your service. Although he's not here, we better say something nice about Senator Shelby. [*Laughter*] The reason why is, is that he is the chairman of the Commerce, Justice, and Science Appropriations Committees. And what I'm going to talk about requires appropriations. [*Laughter*] That's why I'm being nice to him. [*Laughter*] Plus, I like him. He's a fine United States Senator—as is Senator Jeff Sessions.

I appreciate all the State folks who are here and the local officials who are here. I want to say something about my friend Johnny Ford. I'm proud that the mayor— there he is—city of Tuskegee mayor. Thank you, Johnny. Thanks for being here. I know you didn't ask me—my advice is, fill the potholes. [*Laughter*] If anybody can get them filled, it's Johnny. [*Laughter*] He's a good man.

Listen, I flew into Montgomery; I choppered over to the airfield. And what I found interesting was, that is the airfield where the Tuskegee Airmen trained. Now, Tuskegee Airmen have led an important part of the reputation of this facility. A lot of people know about the Tuskegee Airmen, and more people are going to know about it when we finish that museum.

With us today is Lieutenant Colonel Herbert Carter, Tuskegee Airman. Where are you, Colonel? Yes, sir. Thank you, sir. Did you bring Mildred? [*Laughter*] Oh, there she is. Hi, Mildred. Thank you for coming. And so is Major Carrol Woods, member of the Tuskegee Airmen. Thank you for coming, Major Woods. Proud you're here. Thank you, sir.

I appreciate the members of the Tuskegee Board of Trustees. I want to thank the university leaders. I particularly want to say something about the faculty. I thank you for teaching. Yours is a noble profession, and yours is an important profession, and I thank you for answering the call. And I want to say something about the students. I hope you're proud of this fine institution. And I know you'll bring honor to it by not only studying hard but by going out and being people of accomplishment after you graduate. And so I thank you for having me. It's such an honor to be here.

So here's the problem we face. The problem is this: Can we compete? Are we going to be a nation in which we can compete in a globalized world? Tomorrow I'm welcoming President Hu Jintao of China to the South Lawn of the White House. Last month, I traveled to India to set the stage for new relations with that important country. These countries are emerging nations. They are growing rapidly, and they provide competition for jobs and natural resources. And it's really an interesting thought, when you think about it. The world has really changed, since at least when I was growing up, where competition might have been around, but it didn't really nearly affect the lives of our citizens as much as it does today.

I'll give you an example of the effects of globalization. When India buys more fossil fuels, it causes the price of crude oil to go up, which causes our price of gasoline to go up. That's an example of globalization. As these new jobs of the 21st century come into being, people are going to hire people with the skill sets. And if our folks don't have the skill sets, those jobs are going to go somewhere else. That's one of the effects of the world in which we live.

And there are several ways to look at the world in which we live. We can say, "We understand the world the way it is, and we're confident in our capacity to shape the future," or, "We don't like the way the world is, and we're going to withdraw and retreat." Withdrawing and retreating is not the right thing to do, in my judgment. America has always been able to compete. As a matter of fact, America should not be afraid of competition; we ought to welcome it and continue to be the leader of the world—the world's economy. We ought to continue to be the leader in research and development. We need to continue to be the leader in higher education. We shouldn't lose our nerve. We shouldn't see the future and fear the future; we ought to welcome the future.

And here are some things we need to do to make sure we shape the future. First is to make sure we're always on the leading edge of research and technology. I saw some amazing things happening today. I was a history major, so maybe they were really amazing because I didn't know what I was looking at. [*Laughter*] It seemed amazing. [*Laughter*] I was at the Center for Biomedical Research—I was really at the Center for Advanced Materials called T–CAM, a sister organization to the Center for Biomedical Research and for the Center for Aerospace Science Engineering. Isn't that interesting, that those three centers exist right here in Tuskegee? I think it's a hopeful part of making sure we're a competitive nation and a confident nation, to be able to say out loud those three centers of excellence, the centers of science right here on this campus.

We spent some time talking about nanotechnology. I don't know if you know much about nanotechnology—[*laughter*]—but I met some students who knew a lot about nanotechnology—Ph.D. candidates who knew a lot about nanotechnology. By the way, Tuskegee produces Ph.D. candidates. I think you produced five last year. You're on your way to five more over the next year or so. That's important.

But also as important is the research that's being done here. It's research that will keep the United States on the leading edge, keep the United States competitive. And that's important for our fellow citizens because so long as we lead, our people are going to have a good standard of living. So long as we're the leader, people will be able to find good work. If we lose our nerve and retreat, it will make it hard for us to be able to provide those jobs people want. The more productive a society is—and by the way, research and development leads to higher productivity—the higher standard of living we'll have. And that's what we want. We want our people to be able to realize their dreams, to be able to get good work.

So here's the first thing that I intend to work with Congress on to make sure that we're on the leading edge of change and technology, and that is to increase Federal support for vital, basic research. I don't know if you realize this, but because of Defense Department spending in the past and because of the research that the Defense Department was doing to enhance communication, to improve military communications, the Internet came to be. In other words, the Defense Department said, "We need to figure out how better to communicate." And therefore, they spent some research dollars at institutions like Tuskegee. And out of that research came the Internet, which has helped change our society in many ways.

Here's another interesting example of where basic research can help change quality of life or provide practical applications for people. The Government funded research in microdrive storage, electrochemistry, and signal compression. They did so for one reason. It turned out that those were the key ingredients for the development of the iPod. I tune in to the iPod occasionally, you know. [*Laughter*] Basic research to meet one set of objectives can lead to interesting ideas for our society. It helps us remain competitive. So the Government should double the commitment to the most basic—critical research programs in the physical sciences over the next 10 years. I look forward to Congress—to doubling that commitment.

Secondly—and by the way, those centers of excellence I went to are funded by—some of them are funded by grants from the Federal Government on this type of research money. So obviously, it helps your institution flourish, but more importantly, it helps our country. It helps our country in two ways. There's no telling what's going to come out of this basic research. As a matter of fact, I saw nanotechnology applied to what could conceivably be the next airplane wing. Boeing is funding research into nanotechnology here at Tuskegee, which may end up yielding a lighter, more firm material which could become the basis for the new airplanes that you fly in. It's lightweight stuff, but it's really strong. It's right here on this campus that people are making research into this—[*applause*].

But you notice I said Boeing. See, the Federal Government has got a role to play, in my judgment, in basic research. But the private sector spends twice as much money on research and development that the Federal Government does. So I think it's important for us to put policy in place to continue that kind of research. If you were to ask the president and the folks involved with the scientific and the engineering departments here, you'll find that private companies are providing research and development money to help meet certain objectives. And one of the things we got to do is continue to provide incentive for cor-

porate America to make these investments. They spend about $200 billion a year. If we want the country to be competitive, if we don't want to fear the future, and shape it, then there needs to be incentive for corporate America to continue to make these research and development investments.

We do that, by the way, through what's called the research and development tax credit. It's fancy words for saying that if you spend the money, there's going to be a—you'll get a credit on your income. It makes sense to me. It makes sense to a lot of other countries, too, by the way. A lot of countries, in trying to be competitive in this global world, are doing the same thing to encourage research and development, because they know what we know, that if you come up with new products and are constantly on the leading edge of change and innovation, the standard of living for the people in the country in which these investments are made goes up.

The problem we have is that the research and development tax credit expires every year. Now, if you're somebody trying to plan an investment strategy and you're uncertain as to whether or not the research and development tax credit is going to be around for the next year, then you're less likely to be aggressive in your research and development spending. It's logical. It makes sense.

So I think Congress needs to make sure there's certainty in the Tax Code, so as to achieve an important social objective—by the way, and an objective which helps Tuskegee—and that is they need to make the research and development tax credit a permanent part of the Tax Code.

Thirdly, and perhaps the most important way that this United States of America can remain the leader when it comes to economic development and opportunity, is to make sure our education systems work well. And so here are some ideas as to how to set in motion a strategy that says, we shouldn't fear the future; we ought to welcome it. We ought to be a nation that says, we can compete. And the way to compete in the 21st century is to make sure that our children have got the skills necessary to fill the jobs of the 21st century.

I said earlier—and this is practical—if we don't get the children the skills in math and science and engineering, those jobs are going elsewhere. That's just the way it is. And therefore, we've got to deal with it head on. We can't hope the world changes. We've got to be confident in our capacity to achieve an objective. And it starts with making sure younger children know how to read and write and add and subtract.

I want to describe to you, if you don't mind, the theory and the strategy and the vision behind the No Child Left Behind Act. And here it is: One, I believe every child can learn; two, I believe it is important for people to show us whether or not every child is learning; and three, if a child is not learning early, there ought to be extra help to make sure he or she does not get left behind. That's the theory behind No Child Left Behind Act.

We spend a fair amount of money at the Federal level, particularly on Title I students. It's money directed toward a certain segment of our population, as it should be. But I think in return for money spent, we ought to—we have said to the States, "You develop an accountability system to let us know whether or not a child can read," for example. All the talk about science and engineering and math matters nothing if the children cannot read. The first step toward making sure our children have the skills of the 21st century is to insist upon a solid reading program that works. How do you know whether a program works or not—really depends on whether or not you're willing to measure.

I was the Governor of Texas; I remember the big debates over the—how to properly teach reading. If you've ever been on a school board, I'm confident you were involved in that debate. And it was quite a philosophical argument. The way to cut through all the rhetoric is to say, "Let's measure and—to see." I've heard every excuse why not to measure, by the way. I don't know if you've heard them, but excuses ranging from, "All you're doing is teaching to test." No. My attitude is, when you teach a third grader to read, he or she can pass the test. "All you do is spend time worrying about tests. It makes me nervous, tests." Well, what ought to make you nervous is a school system that simply shuffles children through without understanding whether or not they've got the basics.

I remember being told that testing is discrimination. I said, no, the system that's discriminatory is one that doesn't care and just says, "If you're so-and-so age, you belong here." I believe a compassionate society is one which says, let us find out early, before it's too late, and provide extra money for after-school tutoring or—help to make sure children get up to grade level.

Now, if you believe certain children can't learn, then it's justifiable that you just pass them through. I believe every child can learn. And therefore, our school systems must make sure we focus on individual children. And so we're beginning to see some improvements, by the way, in the public school systems around America. How do we know? Because we measure.

In 2005, America's fourth graders posted the best scores in reading and math in the history of the test. That's positive. People are beginning to learn. African American fourth graders set records in reading and math. How do we know? Because we measure.

The Federal Government, by the way, didn't design the test. I'm a local-control-of-school guy; I don't think the Federal Government ought to be telling you how to run your schools. And one way to tell you how to run your schools is if the Federal Government designed the test. We said to the Governor, "Design your test, but make sure you measure; make sure we know." It's in your State's interest that people know whether or not the curriculum is working or whether children are learning to read and write.

The Nation's Report Card showed that eighth graders earned the best math scores ever recorded. And that's a positive development if you're worried about making sure our children have the skills to fill the jobs of the 21st century. Eighth grade Hispanic and African American students achieved the highest math scores ever. In other words, there's improvement. It's positive development. But here's the problem: By the time our kids get into high school, we've fallen behind most of the developed world in math and science. In other words, we're closing the achievement gap, and there's improvement in the public school system around America, but what ends up happening is, is that there is a—is we're beginning to fall off. And that's where the challenge exists.

And so how do we make sure that our high school students are coming out of high school so they can go to a place like Tuskegee with a skill set necessary to even go farther, so we remain a competitive nation? Here are some ideas.

First, one of the programs that works well is the Advanced Placement program. I don't know if you've heard of the Advanced Placement program—I hope you've heard of the Advanced Placement program. It is a rigorous course study program. It basically says, it's possible for children from all walks of life to meet high standards. I went to an AP school in Texas, in inner-city Dallas. It wasn't one of these suburban deals; it was inner-city. And there's more children graduating from that high school with—passing AP than any other high school in America—at least, that's what they told me. Texans sometimes, you know, might—[*laughter*]—I believed the principal. [*Laughter*]

But nevertheless, it is important to set high standards, particularly in math and science, and to have rigorous academia.

And a good way to do that is through the Advanced Placement program. Therefore, the Federal Government needs to provide money to train 70,000 high school teachers on how to teach AP. In other words, take a system that's worked and see to it that it's spread all across the United States of America.

Secondly, yesterday Margaret and I went to a high school—a middle school outside of DC, in Maryland, and we met two NASA scientists that were there in the classroom exciting these kids about math and science and engineering. There's nothing better than having somebody in the classroom who actually knows what they're talking about, in terms of the practical applications of science and math and engineering, to excite somebody.

I don't know what it's like now, but when I was coming up, it wasn't too cool to be a chemist—[*laughter*]—or a physicist, or science wasn't exactly—it just didn't ring. We need to make it ring for our kids in high school by having people who know what they're doing. Therefore, part of this program to make sure we're competitive is to bring 30,000 math and science professionals to teach in our classrooms. They're called adjunct professors. I think it's a smart way and a practical way to excite children to take the courses that are necessary to make sure this country is a competitive country.

I want to repeat to you again: If we don't have the skill sets necessary to compete for the jobs of the 21st century, they'll go somewhere else. If our kids do have the skill set necessary to compete for the jobs of the 21st century, the standard of living of our country is going to improve.

And that's the challenge we face. So I set up—recognizing that we need to do better in math and in science, I set up what's called a national math panel. It's a way to analyze—we got experts coming together, and they're going to analyze the best teaching methodology for math, the best curriculum for math. We did the same thing for reading, by the way. We set up a group of experts on reading. And they helped States and local districts understand what works, how best to make sure every child can read. And it's working. I just told you; it's working because we're measuring.

We need to do the same thing for math. We need to make sure that our teachers, our school boards, our principals, our superintendents, our Governors understand what works. You cannot set an objective and achieve that objective unless you have the tactics necessary to do that. And so we're going to call the experts together. They'll be presenting a report to Margaret and myself by January 31st of 2007. It will be a really important study, because, again, it will give—it will help States and local school districts have the methodology, the teaching methods necessary to help achieve an important objective.

And then we're going to implement what's called a Math Now program that will get those recommendations into the teacher's hands. But there's also another interesting aspect of Math Now, which I think is vital, and that is, when we measure and find a child slipping behind in math in the eighth or ninth grade, that child gets extra help. We do that in the third and fourth grades when it comes to reading; we need to apply that same standard of help for a child as they head into the high school.

If you want to deal with the problem of the United States of America falling behind in math and science, you focus on the problem, and you focus on it with what works and money and extra help. And that's exactly what we intend to do to make sure that we begin to lay that foundation for a competitive tomorrow.

I also understand that the Federal Government has a role in helping people go to college, see. It's one thing to make sure the students have got the skill set, but if there's not the financial means to get to a university, then that skill set could conceivably be wasted. And we don't want to

waste it. We want to make sure we've got a strategy that works in the early grades and in the high school, and then make it more likely a child can afford coming to a place like Tuskegee.

Of course, we have helped the Historically Black Colleges and Universities. I want to thank the good doctor for serving on the panel. I pledged a 30-percent increase of Federal help to Historically Black Colleges, and we met that commitment. I also said that it's really—the Pell grant system is a very important program. And since 2001, there have been 1 million additional students on the Pell grant program. So there are now 5 million students across the United States of America on Pell grants, which is an important part of making sure our students get to go to a higher education.

I want to talk about a new program that I hope will interest you. It caught the good president's fancy when I described it to him, and it's this. I've always believed that it's—if you have an objective, like encouraging people to take rigorous courses, particularly in math and science, which lays the foundation for our engineers and our chemists and our physicists of the future, then there ought to be incentives to do that. And Congress this year listened and passed a bill which I signed into law, which Margaret is now going to implement, and it's this: There are two new grants associated with Pell grants. This will be a $4.5 billion program over the next 5 years, and here's the way it works.

One is called the Academic Competitiveness grant, which will provide additional money to first- and second-year students, college students, who have completed a rigorous high school curriculum and have maintained a 3.0 GPA in college. There will be up to 750 for first-year students and up to $1,300 for second-year students. The idea is to encourage rigorous courses and to provide incentive. I'm not talking about impossible; I'm talking about raising the standard—saying to somebody, "Here's your chance. Apply yourself in the fields that we know are necessary to be able to compete in the 21st century, and we'll help you more."

And then third, we've got what's called SMART grants. Now, these grants are for college students, third- and fourth-year college students who have maintained a 3.0 GPA and who major in math, science, or critical foreign languages. What we're trying to do is to make sure that people have got that skill set, and it makes sense to provide incentives for people. And by the way, these grants will be up to an additional $4,000 per person.

So the Federal Government needs to play a vital role. One, a vital role is to set the goals and strategies, to make it clear to the American people we've got a choice to make: Do we compete or do we retreat; do we become isolationists and protectionists as a nation, or do we remain a confident nation and lead the world?

The Federal Government has got a role in making sure that there's research dollars available for places like Tuskegee. The Federal Government has got a role to provide incentive for private corporations to continue to invest in research and development.

I want to remind you that the research being done today in this university will end up somewhere in our society 10, 20, or 30 years from now. That's what's hap-pening. And at the same time, that research is helping a young man or woman realize his or her dream, making sure that person gets the skill sets necessary to become the leaders.

We should never cede any educational territory to anybody anywhere in the world. We need to be the centers of excellence all around the United States. And one way to do that is to continue to provide financial help and to encourage people to take math and science through additional financial help. And another way to do it is to make sure the public school system provides excellent education early in a child's life, laying that foundation for children from all walks of life, all across our country, so that we can continue to be the country of hope.

I am very confident about the future of this country. There's nothing we can't do if we don't put our mind to it. And this is a step in putting our mind to making sure the United States of America is the finest country on the face of the Earth. I'm honored to be at one of the finest institutions in the United States of America to talk about this initiative. Thanks for letting me come. God bless.

NOTE: The President spoke at 12:20 p.m. in the Kellogg Conference Center. In his remarks, he referred to Benjamin Franklin Payton, president, Tuskegee University; and Gov. Bob Riley of Alabama.

Remarks at a Welcoming Ceremony for President Hu Jintao of China
April 20, 2006

Good morning. Laura and I are pleased to welcome President Hu Jintao and his wife, Madam Liu, to the White House.

The United States and China are two nations divided by a vast ocean yet connected through a global economy that has created opportunity for both our peoples.

The United States welcomes the emergence of a China that is peaceful and prosperous and that supports international institutions. As stakeholders in the international system, our two nations share many strategic interests. President Hu and I will discuss how to advance those interests and how China and the United States can cooperate responsibly with other nations to address common challenges.

Our two nations share an interest in expanding free and fair trade, which has increased the prosperity of both the American people and the Chinese people. Trade in goods between our two nations has grown to $285 billion a year, and U.S. exports to China grew nearly 21 percent in last year alone. Our trade relationship can become even stronger as China adopts policies that allow U.S. companies to compete in China with the same freedom that Chinese companies are able to compete here in the United States. So we welcome China's commitments to increase domestic demand, to reform its pension system, to expand market access for U.S. goods and services, to improve enforcement of intellectual property rights, and to move toward a flexible, market-based exchange rate for its currency. These policies will benefit the Chinese people and are consistent with being a responsible member of the international economic system and a leader in the World Trade Organization.

Prosperity depends on security, so the United States and China share a strategic interest in enhancing security for both our peoples. We intend to deepen our cooperation in addressing threats to global security, including the nuclear ambitions of Iran; the genocide in Darfur, Sudan; the violence unleashed by terrorists and extremists; and the proliferation of weapons of mass destruction.

I appreciate China's role as host of the six-party talks, which will be successful only if North Korea makes the right strategic decision: to abandon all its nuclear weapons and existing nuclear programs as pledged to the other five parties. I will continue to seek President Hu's advice and cooperation and urge his nation to use its considerable influence with North Korea to make meaningful progress toward a Korean Peninsula that is free of nuclear weapons.

The natural world also generates threats to international security, and the United States and China share a strategic interest in meeting these challenges as well. We will continue to cooperate to fight avian flu and other pandemic diseases. We will continue to cooperate to respond to natural disasters. We will continue to cooperate to develop alternatives to fossil fuels. New technologies can drive economic growth on both sides of the Pacific and help us become better stewards of our natural resources.

As the relationship between our two nations grows and matures, we can be candid about our disagreements. I'll continue to discuss with President Hu the importance of respecting human rights and freedoms of the Chinese people. China has become successful because the Chinese people are—experience the freedom to buy and to sell and to produce. And China can grow even more successful by allowing the Chinese people the freedom to assemble, to speak freely, and to worship.

The United States will also be candid about our policy toward Taiwan. The United States maintains our "one China" policy based on the three communiques and the Taiwan Relations Act. We oppose unilateral changes in the status quo in the Taiwan Strait by either side, and we urge all parties to avoid confrontational or provocative acts. And we believe the future of Taiwan should be resolved peacefully.

The United States and China will continue to build on our common interests; we will address our differences in a spirit of mutual respect. We have made progress in building a relationship that is candid and cooperative, and President Hu's visit will further that progress.

And so, Mr. President, welcome to the White House. We're really glad you're here. I'm looking forward to our meetings, and I'm so thrilled to welcome Madam Liu as well. Thank you for coming.

NOTE: The President spoke at 9:44 a.m. on the South Lawn at the White House, where President Hu was accorded a formal welcome with full military honors. In his remarks, President Bush referred to Liu Yongqing, wife of President Hu. The transcript released by the Office of the Press Secretary also included the remarks of President Hu.

Remarks Following a Meeting With President Hu Jintao of China and an Exchange With Reporters
April 20, 2006

President Bush. The President and I will make opening statements. We'll be glad to answer two questions from each side.

Mr. President, welcome. We've just had yet another constructive dialog. I enjoy my visits with President Hu. He tells me what he thinks, and I tell him what I think, and we do so with respect.

China has important relations with the United States. We, obviously, have commercial relations that are important. We're working on issues like Iran and Sudan. We've got a mutual interest in seeing that the Korean Peninsula is nuclear weapons-free. We spent time talking about Taiwan, and I assured the President my position has not changed. I do not support independence for Taiwan.

We don't agree on everything, but we're able to discuss our disagreements in a spirit of friendship and cooperation. So it's a very important relationship.

And, Mr. President, thank you for your frankness and for our discussions.

President Hu. To begin with, I would like to thank President Bush for his kind invitation and the generous hospitality accorded to me. And just now I had a pragmatic and constructive dialog with President Bush, and during that meeting, President Bush and I had in-depth exchange of views on the China-U.S. relationship and major regional, as well as international, issues of mutual interest.

We have reached important agreement at the meeting. We both agreed that under the new circumstances, given the international situation here, that China and the United States share extensive, common strategic interests, and there is a broad prospect for the mutually beneficial cooperation between the two countries. A good China-U.S. relationship is of strategic significance to the maintenance and promotion of peace, stability, and development in the Asia-Pacific region and in the world at large.

We both agreed to view and address the bilateral relationship from a strategic and long-term perspective, and we both agreed to comprehensively move forward the constructive and cooperative China-U.S. relationship in the 21st century, to the benefits of the Chinese and American peoples and peoples around the world.

And during the meeting, I stressed the importance of the Taiwan question to Mr. President. Taiwan is an inalienable part of Chinese territory, and we maintain consistently that under the basis of the "one China" principle, we are committed to safeguard peace and stability in the Taiwan Straits, and to the promotion of the improvement and development of the cross-straits relations. We have the utmost sincerity, and we will do this to our utmost, with all sincerity, to strive for the prospect of peaceful reunification. This being said, we will by no means allow Taiwan independence.

President Bush gave us his understanding of the Chinese concerns. He reiterated the

American positions and said that he does not hope that the moves taken by the Taiwan authorities to change the status quo will upset the China-U.S. relationship, which I highly appreciate.

We both agreed to work together to promote the development of the economic ties and trade between the two countries on basis of a mutual benefit in seeking win-win outcomes. As for the differences, or even frictions between the two countries in this regard, we both believe that they may be properly resolved through consultations on an equal footing. Both Mr. President and I spoke highly of the outcomes from the 17th JCCT meeting which was held not long ago.

President Bush and I also agreed that the two countries need to further increase their exchanges and cooperation in the military, law enforcement, science and technology, culture, education, and other fields. We also both agreed to further step up our dialog and cooperation in such fields as counterterrorism, nonproliferation, the prevention and control of the avian influenza, energy, environmental protection, disaster prevention and relief, and other major issues.

Both sides agreed to continue their efforts to facilitate the six-party talks to seek a proper solution to the Korean nuclear issue. And both sides agree to continue their efforts to seek a peaceful resolution of the Iranian nuclear issue.

I assured Mr. President that China is willing to work together with the United States and other countries in the world in a joint endeavor to build a harmonious world featuring enduring peace and shared prosperity.

President Bush. Jennifer [Jennifer Loven, Associated Press].

Chinese Currency/Democracy in China

Q. Thank you, sir. President Hu, when will China become a democracy with free elections?

And President Bush, why have you not been able to persuade China to more quickly revalue its currency?

President Bush. Last July, the Chinese made a major decision on their currency. There's been some appreciation in the currency. We would hope there would be more appreciation in the currency.

Q. President Hu?

President Hu. I don't know—what do you mean by a democracy? What I can tell you is that we've always believed in China that if there is no democracy, there will be no modernization, which means that ever since China's reform and opening up in the late 1970s, China, on the one hand, has vigorously promoted economic reforms, and on the other, China has also been actively, properly, and appropriately moved forward the political restructuring process. And we have always been expanding the democracy and freedoms for the Chinese citizens.

In the future, we will, in the light of China's own national conditions and the will of the Chinese people, continue to move ahead the political restructuring and to develop a socialist democracy. And we will further expand the orderly participation of the Chinese citizens in political affairs so that the Chinese citizens will be in a better position to exercise their democratic rights in terms of democratic supervision, democratic management, and democratic decisionmaking.

President Bush. Do you want to call on somebody from the Chinese side?

China-U.S. Relations/Trade

Q. I have a question for President Hu Jintao. And how do you view the problems and disputes between China and the United States in the field of economic ties and trade? And in your view, what kind of measures shall we take to properly resolve these issues?

President Hu. The economic ties and trade between China and the United States are an important component—the China-

U.S. relationship as a whole. And in this economic ties and trade, I think that mutually beneficial cooperation and win-win outcomes represent the mainstream.

Although the two countries do have different opinions or sometimes even frictions in this relationship, what has happened has proven that all these issues or differences can be properly resolved through consultations on a equal footing and further expansion of the mutually beneficial cooperation.

We understand the American concerns over the trade imbalances, the protection of the intellectual property rights, and market access. We have taken measures, and we'll continue to take steps to properly resolve the issues.

China pursues a policy of boosting domestic demand, which means that we'll mainly rely on domestic demand expansion to further promote the economic growth of the country. We do not pursue a excessively high trade surplus.

We have already launched the reform of the RMB Chinese currency exchange rate regime, which has paid off initially. And in the future, we'll continue to make efforts to improve the RMB exchange rate regime.

We'll continue to expand the market access and increase the import of American products. As a matter of fact, lately, a delegation composed of Chinese businesspeople have been to the United States, and during their trip, they have totally signed 107 commercial contracts or agreements with a total value of over 16.2 billion U.S. dollars.

The U.S. technology products export to China, particularly in the field of the export of high-tech products, are quite incompatible with the economic might of the United States. I hope that the United States Government will be able to relax or ease the restrictions imposed on its export, particularly high-tech export to China. And we also hope that the U.S. Government will be able to create a level playing field for Chinese businesses who want to enter the American market. And this will certainly help bring down the trade deficit of the

United States. And this will also contribute to the further sound and stable growth of the trading ties and economic cooperation between the two countries.

President Bush. Let me say something on this. First of all, it was a very comprehensive answer, and I appreciate that, Mr. President. I am heartened by the President's answer, because he recognizes that a trade deficit with the United States as substantial as it is, is unsustainable.

I appreciate his statement very much, because the American people—all we want to do is be treated fairly in the international marketplace. He's used the word "win-win," and that's a very important concept when it comes to economics that are mutually beneficial. Market access is very important, and I appreciate your commitment to that, Mr. President.

What also is very much important is that for the—as the Chinese society evolves, that it becomes an economy that is not export-driven but consumer-driven. I appreciate the Government's commitment to that evolution, because as there's more consumers and market access, it will mean that U.S. small businesses and businesses and farmers will have a chance to be able to find new markets. Obviously, the Chinese Government takes the currency issue seriously, and so do I. And finally, I want to remind our citizens, as the President said earlier, exports to China are up by 21 percent. And that means jobs.

And so we're going to continue to work on this very important relationship to make sure the playing field is level.

Steve [Steve Holland, Reuters].

Iran/North Korea

Q. Thank you. President Bush, have you presented President Hu to go along with tougher actions against Iran, if necessary, such as sanctions?

And President Hu, is there more you can do to influence North Korea to give up nuclear weapons?

President Bush. The first goal of any dialog with a partner with whom we're trying to create peace is to have a common objective, a stated goal. And we have a common goal, and that is that Iran should not have the nuclear weapon, the capacity to make a nuclear weapon, or the know-how to how to make a nuclear weapon.

And the second goal is to be in a position where we can work on tactics. And one of the tactics that I've been talking to the President about is the use of the United Nations Security Council Chapter VII to send a common message to the Iranians that China and the United States and EU–3 countries, all deeply are concerned about the Iranian ambition.

China is an important voice in international affairs. And I will continue to work with the President to strategize as to how best to achieve our important goal, which is a—an Iran without the capacity, the know-how, or a nuclear weapon.

President Hu. As our friends may know, that the nuclear issue on the Korean Peninsula, China has always been persuading the parties for their reconciliation and promote the talks for peaceful solution. And we have always been making constructive efforts to denuclearize the Korean Peninsula.

It is exactly thanks to the concerted efforts of the parties involved that in September last year, the six parties had their fourth-round talks and successfully concluded a joint statement as a initial result, which has not come easily.

The six-party talks have run into some difficulties at the moment. I hope that the parties will be able to further display flexibility, work together, and create necessary conditions for the early resumption of the talks.

China-U.S. Cultural Exchanges

Q. Mr. President, good morning. I would like to know, what is on your mind and what kind of things you can do to facilitate the people-to-people and cultural exchanges between the two countries?

President Bush. I remember giving—well, the first graduation speech I ever gave as President was to Notre Dame. And I was—I distinctly remember the—a number of Chinese students that were there who had gotten advanced degrees. And it's a vivid reminder that one of the best ways for there to be exchange is for there to be exchange of students. I think the more U.S. students who study in China and the more Chinese students who study in the United States will lead to lasting understanding, which is very important for future relations.

Obviously, there will be exchanges in the arts. There's a great interest in the United States about the Chinese arts and the history of Chinese arts. There's going to be sports exchanges. Yao Ming, I mean, he's a perpetual exchange. He's a great player, and he's here all the time. The Olympics will bring a great opportunity for us to have interchange. There's all kinds of ways for the United States and Chinese people to get to know each other, and I look forward to encouraging those kind of avenues of dialog. Presidents can talk, but sometimes the best way to have lasting friendship is for there to be a lot of people-to-people exchanges.

Thank you very much.

NOTE: The President spoke at 11:16 a.m. in the Oval Office at the White House. In his remarks, he referred to Yao Ming, center, National Basketball Association's Houston Rockets. President Hu and two reporters spoke in Chinese, and their remarks were translated by an interpreter.

Remarks at a Luncheon Honoring President Hu Jintao of China
April 20, 2006

Mr. President, Madam Liu, Laura and I are honored to welcome you to the—and your delegation to the White House. It's a pleasure to have you here, along with our other distinguished guests.

China is home to an ancient civilization, and it is helping to shape the modern world. In a single generation, China's economy has moved from isolation and stagnation to engagement and expansion. As China has grown, our two peoples have come to know one another better.

Thirty-five years ago this month, the Chinese Government welcomed the United States ping-pong team to Beijing. [*Laughter*] It's an event that marked the beginning of renewal—renewed cultural exchanges between our two nations. Today, Chinese athletes compete professionally in the United States, and Americans appreciate the opportunity to see them play.

In 2008, China will welcome athletes from all over the world as your great nation hosts the summer Olympics. Beijing will showcase China's transformation and demonstrate China's commitment to the international institutions that make fair and peaceful competition possible for all nations.

Mr. President, I thank you for the constructive and candid conversations we had this morning. I appreciate the opportunity to expand the dialog between our two great nations. And, Mr. President, I'm pleased to offer a toast to you and to your gracious wife and to the people of China.

NOTE: The President spoke at 1:20 p.m. in the East Room at the White House. In his remarks, he referred to Liu Yongqing, wife of President Hu. The transcript released by the Office of the Press Secretary also included the remarks of President Hu.

Remarks at the President's Environmental Youth Awards Ceremony
April 20, 2006

The President. Thank you. Please be seated. Thanks for coming. Welcome. Glad you're here. Sorry I'm a little late. I just finished having a lunch with President Hu Jintao of China, a very important lunch. I hope you forgive me for running a little late. But thanks for letting us come by to say hello. I'm proud to join Steve Johnson in honoring young Americans who have given time and energy to help make this country a better place. We're really glad you're here.

You're serving as young stewards of the environment, which means you're setting a good example for what it means to be a citizen. It's, like, what we call citizenship

in action. And you're helping make America a wonderful place. And so we're really glad you're here. I'm glad to be a part of the award ceremony.

I want to thank all the Administrators from the EPA who are here, but I particularly want to thank Steve and Debbie for joining us as well. We're here to honor, Steve, in case you don't know it yet—[*laughter*]—49 young Americans who are helping to protect the natural heritage of our country. I appreciate the fact that you're setting good examples too, by the way, and doing what you're doing. You're showing people how to lead and how to be a responsible citizen.

I appreciate the rain gardens that were built in places like Massachusetts and Michigan to catch runoff and prevent it from polluting local rivers and streams. That's a smart idea; thanks for doing it. In New York, folks here have organized volunteers to stencil warnings near neighborhood sewers. That's a good way to help protect the environment, isn't it?

In Pennsylvania, folks here built an environmental demonstration house to showcase environmental products and technologies. It makes a lot of sense to showcase new technologies. After all, technologies are going to help change the world in a positive way so that we can be good stewards of the environment.

As a matter of fact, one of the technologies that are—a part of the technological revolution that we're pushing hard here is to change the way we drive our automobiles. One of these days, we're going to have what they call hybrid plug-in batteries. You'll be able to drive your car for the first 40 miles on electricity. That seems to make sense. It does a couple of things. One, it helps to improve the environment, but it also makes us less dependent on oil. And one of my hopes is that one of these days, the cars you drive won't be using any oil but will be using hydrogen, as a way to protect the environment. So those of you who are working on new technologies, thanks. It's a smart thing to do. That's exactly what this Government needs to be doing more of as well, and will be doing more of.

I'm proud to welcome folks from Georgia and your club called "The Creek Freaks." [*Laughter*] When I first heard the name, I thought it might be like a band or something, you know? [*Laughter*] I welcome the folks from Arkansas, who are clearing trash. By the way, the Creek Freaks are helping to protect wetlands. I don't know if you know this, but we've increased the wetlands by a half a million acres over 2 years. That's a really important initiative. And for those

of you who are helping do that, I want to thank you very much.

In Arkansas you've cleared trash and developed projects to stabilize the banks of a local stream. Thanks for coming, welcome. If you happen to get close to Texas, tell them hello.

In Missouri, you restored a portion of a park—adjacent to a school—to a native prairie. I don't know if you know this or not, but Laura and I are fortunate to own some property in central Texas, near a town called Crawford. You've heard of it, Richard. [*Laughter*] One of our projects is to restore as much of our land as possible to native grasses and wildflowers. We've got buffalo grasses, bluestem—little bluestem grass. And interestingly enough, we've converted about 50 to 60 acres of our land to—so we can provide seed for people so they can then plant little bluestem. And it's a neat project, and I would encourage ranchers and farmers to be able to find ways to help plant native grasses, just like the kids from Missouri have done here.

In Alaska, you built a grated wall that provides access to a local creek. That makes sense, you know. People ought to be allowed to have access to nature, but you want to do it in a way that protects the environment. It's one of the reasons why I proposed that we spend $5 billion on making sure that the maintenance issues in our national parks are improved, and we're on the way to making sure that happens. I believe in national parks, and I believe people ought to have access to national parks. After all, it's the people's parks; it's not a handful of people's parks. It's everybody's park. And the Federal Government has a role to maintain those parks, and we're doing a good job of that.

In California, 8-year-olders here launched a composting and recycling effort called, "The Wonderful Weird World of Worms." [*Laughter*] That's kind of hard for me to say. [*Laughter*]

Got some folks from Utah that built a hybrid land speed racer which he drives to school and races at the nearby salt flats to raise awareness about alternative fuel vehicles. I just talked to you about the hybrid plug-in battery and hydrogen. There's another alternative fuel that we need to use in our vehicles, and that's ethanol. I don't know if you study that in your schools, but it's possible to make fuel for automobiles from corn. As a matter of fact, we're doing quite a bit of that in the Midwest—or sugar. Sugarcane is pretty good for making fuel—ethanol.

But we're close to some breakthroughs, some technological breakthroughs that will enable us to make ethanol from wood chips and compost. And when we hit that, all of a sudden, you're going to see ethanol all across the country. It makes sense to drive our cars from agricultural products, doesn't it, as opposed to oil?

And so thank you for setting such a good example. We're really glad you're here. You know, good environmental policy requires Federal effort, but it also requires State effort and local effort and volunteer effort. All of us need to pitch in to make—to conserve the land and make this country as beautiful as can be. And by being here

today, you're showing a strong commitment for the future of our country. And we're blessed that we've got people like you that are willing to do what you did.

So I want to welcome you. I want to welcome you all; I want to welcome your teachers. Thank you for being here. Thanks for teaching. I want to welcome your parents. I really appreciate you raising such good folks. And I want to welcome the EPA Administrator to announce the awards. God bless; thanks for coming.

[At this point, Administrator of the Environmental Protection Agency Stephen L. Johnson introduced the award recipients from each region, and the President congratulated them.]

The President. Thanks for coming. Congratulations.

NOTE: The President spoke at 2:59 p.m. in Room 450 of the Dwight D. Eisenhower Executive Office Building. In his remarks, he referred to Debbie Johnson, wife of EPA Administrator Johnson; and Richard E. Greene, Environmental Protection Agency Region VI Administrator.

Remarks in a Discussion at Cisco Systems, Inc., in San Jose, California
April 21, 2006

The President. I'm thrilled, John. Thanks for coming. This is going to be an interesting discussion, I hope, for you, because it's going to talk about how America intends to shape our future and not fear the future. That's what we're really here to talk about—interesting challenges facing the country.

Yesterday—one reason you're so nice is because I invited him to lunch at the White House yesterday. [*Laughter*]

John T. Chambers. Thank you.

The President. He and Elaine came, and we had lunch with Hu Jintao, the President

of China. And sitting there during the lunch, I was thinking about people's fears about whether or not we can compete against a country like China. If you really think about a global economy and a global world—there's some folks that say, "Well, maybe we can't compete in the long run." My attitude is just the opposite. Not only can we compete, we must compete and remain a leader of the world.

And that's what we're here to talk about—how you do that. And before we do that, I do want to thank John and the good folks here at Cisco for hosting us.

It's not easy to host the President. [*Laughter*]

Mr. Chambers. That's for sure. [*Laughter*]

The President. Our entourages are quite large. [*Laughter*] But I thank you for having me. I am excited to be at one of America's most innovative companies. And I was asking John—20 years ago, how many employees were there? There were zero. Ten years, maybe 6,000; today, 47,000 highly trained, highly competent, skilled folks that are helping to change America and countries around the world as well. So thanks for having us. It's wonderful to be in entrepreneurial heaven.

I also am honored to be here with the Governor. I cannot thank you enough for coming, Arnold. It's really thoughtful of you to be here. He is a—really an interesting man, a person—[*laughter*]. He didn't have to run for office but chose to do so, and I admire that in you. I admire somebody who doesn't always take the comfortable way in life, in order to serve something greater than himself. And I appreciate your service; I really do.

Traveling with me today is Norm Mineta, a Cabinet Secretary. Mr. Secretary, thank you for coming. Norm Mineta is a person who has been able to—[*applause*]. He said, "I'm glad to fly on Air Force One; I just wished you would have landed at Mineta Field." And his son, David, is here today. More importantly than son David being here, is tomorrow, I think, is David's daughter's birthday. So we've got the grandfather and the father. Thank you all for coming, and thanks for serving the country so well, Norm.

I appreciate Mayor Ron Gonzales of the city of San Jose joining us. Mr. Mayor, thank you for being here. I appreciate your time. I want to thank my friend Floyd Kvamme, who is the cochair of the President's Council of Advisers on Science and Technology, as well as George Scalise, who is with us as well. Thank you all for serving. I appreciate—there is Floyd; thanks for

coming. And Lezlee Westine—it's good to see you, Lezlee. Thank you for coming; appreciate your service in my administration.

Our economy is good. It's real good, and we intend to keep it that way. The fundamental question is, though, can it be that way 5 years from now or 10 years from now? And my answer is, absolutely, if we do some wise things. I happen to believe it's wise to keep taxes low so that people have incentive to invest and save and spend.

I know we're going to have to do something about energy. I aim to be a competitive nation. Part of a competitive agenda means that we have got to deal with problems short-term and long-term, and we've got a problem when it comes to our dependence on oil. I know the folks here are suffering at the gas pump. Rising gasoline prices is like taking a—is like a tax, particularly on the working people and the small-business people.

I pledge to the people here of California that if we find any price gouging, it will be dealt with firmly.

I also recognize that our dependence on oil, and in the fact that we live in a global economy, is causing gasoline prices to go up. And the fundamental strategy to keep us competitive is to get off oil. Tomorrow I'm going to be in Sacramento to talk about your very innovative idea of hydrogen-powered automobiles. I'll be talking about plug-in hybrid automobiles that will enable people to drive on electricity for the first 40 miles. I'm going to be talking about our investment in ethanol to make sure—all of it, by the way, is aimed to making America competitive by changing our driving habits and our dependence upon oil.

We have got to do so for not only economic reasons but for national security reasons as well. It's really important for people to understand that as the Indian economy grows or the Chinese economy grows, they need fossil fuel. And as they buy fossil fuel, it affects our price. And therefore, it's in our national interest to diversify as quickly as possible away from our reliance upon hydrocarbons—particularly oil—when it comes to our automobiles. And I'm convinced we can do so when we put our mind to it.

A flexible economy, an economy that is not overregulated is going to be necessary to keep us competitive. But the most important thing, in my judgment, to keep us competitive is for the United States to remain on the leading edge of technology and to make sure we've got an education system that works.

First, let me talk about technology. I do believe it is a proper use of Federal taxpayer money to double the R&D commitment in—to physical sciences at the Federal level. I believe it makes sense to spend taxpayers' money on research and development out of the Federal Government, because I have seen what expenditure of that kind of money has done in practical ways. And so have you. You may not realize it, but it was investment by the Defense Department that ultimately led to the Internet, which has kind of helped your business a little bit, John. [*Laughter*]

Interestingly enough, tomorrow I'm going to be riding my bike in Napa Valley. I can't wait. I'll be plugged into an iPod. A lot of the reason the iPod exists is because of Federal research dollars. And therefore, I think it makes sense to spend your money on research at the Federal level in the basic sciences to make sure that the United States of America remains the innovative center of the world.

Secondly, I recognize that most money spent on research comes from the private sector. I suspect you spend a lot of money on research.

Mr. Chambers. About $3 billion a year.

The President. Three billion a year. I think it makes sense to encourage the private sector to spend the $200 billion a year we do total—$3 billion right out of Cisco.

One way to do so is through the Tax Code. The research and development tax

credit makes a lot of sense. Interestingly enough, the research and development tax credit expires on a regular basis. And therefore, people have to come, hat in hand, to Congress and say, "Oh, save us." Unfortunately, it is difficult to plan for some companies if you're worried about whether or not the research and development tax credit exists.

Therefore, to keep us on the leading edge of change, to make sure we're the innovative capital of the world, Congress needs to make the research and development tax credit a permanent part of the Tax Code.

People have got to understand that if we don't educate our children in math and science, jobs are going to go to other countries. It's as simple as that. The jobs of the 21st century are going to require a skill level much different from when you and I got out of college. You did get out of college, yes? [*Laughter*] Look, I don't need to be talking; I barely got out myself. [*Laughter*]

I mean, face it, we've got to have a different set of skills. History may not cut it. Math and science are going to be vital to make sure that this country educates the engineers, the chemists, the physicists—the types of folks that John Chambers and Francois are going to be looking for to hire. That's what we're really talking about.

It starts, however, with making sure the public school system does its job in early grades. If I might, I'd just like to take a second to talk about the spirit behind the No Child Left Behind Act. I believe that the Federal Government should continue its role of providing money for Title I students, the poor students. I think that is a good use of your money.

However, I do believe that in return for the expenditure of that money, it makes sense for us to ask whether or not we're getting our money's worth. That means whether or not a child is learning to read and write and add and subtract. I believe strongly that every child can learn, and therefore, I believe there must be an accountability system in place to make sure that every child is learning.

And so we passed the No Child Left Behind Act. Believe it or not, it was a bipartisan measure. Sometimes that can happen in Washington, DC—not enough, I fully concede. But it happened in this case, where we passed the No Child Left Behind Act that says to California or Texas or any other State: "Develop an accountability system in return for this money to show us whether or not a child can read at grade level by the third grade and remain at grade level." That's not too much to ask, is it?

And so measurement is a central part, in my judgment, of holding people to account, of being able to figure out whether curriculum is working. We had all kinds of debates in Texas over the reading curriculum—what worked, what didn't work. The best way to determine what works is to have an accountability system. And that means the Governor or this local school board can say, "We were doing just fine when we compare how we're doing to the school district next door." Or if you're not doing just fine, it gives, at least, parents and those concerned citizens a tool to say, "You've got to change. Mediocrity is unacceptable. We're not going to accept the fact that children can't read by the fourth grade anymore in America."

If you're a reformer—Chambers is a reformer; he is unwilling to accept the status quo; he can't afford to accept the status quo in order to be competitive in this world. The accountability system gives people the opportunity to say, "We demand change."

Interestingly enough, there is an achievement gap in America, but it's narrowing. Our fourth grade African American kids and our fourth grade Hispanic kids are beginning to improve in measurable ways, and that's really positive for the future of the country. And for the teachers who are working hard to meet the challenges of No Child Left Behind, the Governor and I both thank you a lot.

We're doing fine in eighth grade math, by the way, because we measure. But when kids start heading into high school, the position of the United States relative to other countries for our beginning high school kids in math and science is not good enough. Like, we're 15th in the world, or something like that. We don't want to be 15th in the world; we want to be first in the world when it comes to teaching our children math and science.

So here are some ideas. First, we ought to apply the same rigor to math that we've applied to reading. In reading, we measure early, and we've got supplemental service money, which means after-school tutorial money available for children who are not meeting standards. In other words, we measure, and we correct. That makes a lot of sense. We need to do the same thing in junior high math. So the Federal Government is going to make supplemental service money available for students who are falling behind in math right before they get into high school.

That's one way to correct the problem, is to measure, to identify, and to solve. And that's what we intend to do through the new math initiative.

Second, we've got to make sure that we understand what works. And so I put together a national math panel with math experts that will help develop curriculum and teaching tools so that we can say to the States and local school districts, here's what the experts think. Instead of kind of grasping for what might be relevant and might work, we're actually calling people together who know what they're talking about—just like we did in reading—and say, here, here's what you need to try in order to meet the standards.

Thirdly, there are programs which work—and I bet you've got them here in California—and it's called the Advanced Placement program. It's a program that sets high standards and has classroom rigor.

763

One of the problems we have is not enough teachers know how to teach AP. I'm going to ask the Congress to fund enough money to help train 70,000 teachers so they can become prepared to teach Advanced Placement.

I went to a great school in Dallas that— inner-city school; it's not one of these suburban deals; it's inner-city. And the principal claimed that they were the leading high school in the country in terms of kids passing AP. You know, Texans tend to, kind of, put it out there in a way that—[*laughter*]. Whether it's first or not, what mattered was, there was a group of kids from all walks of life, different neighborhoods, all of them passing AP in math and science. They are going to be the leaders of the future. They're going to be our scientists and our chemists and our physicists. And we've got to make sure that that opportunity is available in more classrooms.

Secondly, we went to a school the other day in suburban Maryland. There were two NASA employees there. These guys, as part of their job at NASA, were detailed to junior high classroom. And the reason why is—we call them adjunct professors—and the reason why is, is that sometimes it's not cool to be in the sciences. And these people make it at least seem relevant. And so we're going to attract 30,000 adjunct professors around the country to go into classrooms to say, "This is why science and math are not only cool but are the ticket to a great future for you."

We've expanded our Pell grants. There's now 5 million kids in America getting Pell grants. It's a million more than 5 years ago. And I'm a believer in Pell grants; I think they make sense. But at Tuskegee the other day, I announced a new initiative that provides additional incentive for high school kids who qualify for Pell grants to take rigorous course loads. As a matter of fact, in the first 2 years of college, if you take a rigorous course load in high school and maintain a 3.0 GPA, you'll get $750— up to $750 additional on your Pell grant

and up to $1,500 additional in your second year. If you take math and science or a critical language in college and maintain a 3.0 GPA, you can get up to an additional $4,000 on top of your current Pell grant. And the idea is to say that we believe everybody can learn, and there ought to be tangible incentives to encourage children to get the skills necessary to fill the jobs of the 21st century.

One of the reasons I'm so pleased the Governor is here is because there needs to be a collaborative effort between the Federal Government and the State government and the community college system and the private sector in order for us to achieve this important national objective, and that is for there to be excellence in math and science all throughout our society. And so the Governor is here to talk about California's role in—to making sure that not only California is competitive, but that the country is competitive. When California does things well, it affects the country. And so when you are a part of this competitive initiative, it will help give confidence to others that we're doing the right thing.

And so, welcome. Why don't you share with us some of your thoughts about what you're doing here.

Governor Arnold Schwarzenegger. Well, thank you, Mr. President. First of all, I want to say congratulations on——

The President. On what?

Gov. Schwarzenegger. ——on really paying attention——

The President. Oh. [*Laughter*]

Gov. Schwarzenegger. ——to the competitiveness initiative.

[*At this point, Gov. Schwarzenegger of California made brief remarks.*]

The President. One part of the infrastructure that John Chambers and I talked about today was to make sure that broadband is available, high-speed broadband is available to nearly every American. And we're working it hard; we're making progress. I asked

John today how we're doing. He said, "There is momentum, but we've got a lot of room to catch up in terms of being competitive. Others countries are doing—have done a better job than we have."

We're making progress. And the reason I bring it up is I just want you to know that I know it's important that we've got broadband highways all throughout the country so people can have access to it.

One of the interesting things that the Governor and I just saw was some of the amazing innovation that's taking place here in Cisco. So we get on—we're looking in the camera, and all of a sudden, up comes four people, and it's like they're right here. [*Laughter*] It was an amazing innovation that you're doing. And it just reminded me how important innovation is and why Cisco is doing well—it's because it's an innovative company with innovative people and an innovative CEO.

And so, again, thanks for having me. I'm interested in your thoughts.

Mr. Chambers. Mr. President, I think you said it right. The economy is good; jobs are good; and what we have today is because of our education from before. But we use network academies, and we put them around the world. It's a program that trains young people for getting jobs in the high-tech industry and using it in a practical way.

The President. Network academy—what does that exactly mean? Some guy listening out there isn't going to know——

Mr. Chambers. Well, there's a little bit of sizzle to it. [*Laughter*] What it is, is it trains people to build that highway that you talked about. And it trains people—instead of getting jobs in areas that really don't have much demand, you get jobs where there's a lot of demand. In fact, we can't meet it in this country. And they usually get 30 to 50 percent higher pay because they've done that.

The neat thing is, we're training 100,000 Americans in this area. The challenge is——

The President. Cisco is training——

Mr. Chambers. ——in network academies, with our colleges and high schools—so we generate the program. The challenge, however, is our competition globally is even moving faster on the math and science. China and India graduate 10 times the number of Ph.D.s we do. They have a population four times our size in each of those countries. We all—do the math; that creates a challenge for us. So it's about being the best and brightest in each of our organizations, and we have one of the students here who is just awesome at that. We've got to do better.

The President. Yes. Again, so you took it upon yourself as an interested corporate citizen to provide employees to train others?

Mr. Chambers. Started with a university system, an idea with one single employee, and we wired all of our schools, but nobody maintained it. So we began to train the students to maintain the system. It worked in one area, and then it spread globally.

The President. What John said is really interesting. It is very important for our citizens to understand that education helps you get higher pay.

Mr. Chambers. And jobs.

The President. And a job, yes. It's hard to get higher pay without the job. [*Laughter*]

Mr. Chambers. You got me. [*Laughter*]

The President. I know, you're building—[*laughter*].

Anyway, but people have got to understand that, one, it's not too late to go back to school. And secondly, there's a lot of really interesting opportunities to get the skills necessary to have the jobs that are going to be available in the 21st century. John Chambers just described one such avenue. You're doing 100,000 people—educating 100,000 people here?

Mr. Chambers. In this country—400,000 worldwide.

The President. I appreciate that. One of the interesting things about America is the fact that there are corporate citizens who understand the problem that America faces, and they're doing their part. It's amazing how much training goes on within corporate America, and I appreciate your leadership on this. And I hope others who are interested in making sure this country is competitive do their part, as well, to reach out and train people. Use your skills and your expertise to give people the skills necessary, so we can remain a competitive nation.

I suspect here in Silicon Valley there's a lot of job training going on, which is really important.

Mr. Chambers. There is. We train locally, but we also are taking something, Mr. President, I think you would find extremely interesting. We took the terrible hurricane experience in our gulf coast, and we're working with Mississippi to redo their education system. We're putting $40 million of our own money into building a 21st century education system. We'll start with 52,000 students, 7 school districts, and take one of the States who's probably 49th in terms of math and science and see if we can't make an example of where it goes, with the teachers becoming the innovators, with the students not having—[*inaudible*]. We'll put a wireless mesh over top of the whole community. And, literally, building our students not just to catch up but to lead in math and science.

The President. I appreciate it. It's a great gesture, thanks.

Added value in education can come in all different ways, as I said. And one such place is in our community college system. You've got a great community college system here in California. I know you're a strong supporter. Dr. Fong is with us, who is—tell us what you do, Doc. [*Laughter*]

Bernadine C. Fong. A lot of things.

The President. Well, you're the president of?

Ms. Fong. I'm president of Foothill College in Los Altos Hills. It's right near here.

The President. Right. Close friend, by the way, of Condoleezza Rice.

Ms. Fong. That's right—and Stanford buddies.

The President. She's doing well.

Ms. Fong. Yes, she is. [*Laughter*] Please say hello to her for me. And we'll keep her out of the NFL, if possible.

The President. That's right, yes. Please. [*Laughter*] I need her advice. [*Laughter*]

[*Ms. Fong made brief remarks.*]

The President. Explain the academy, how Cisco works with you. I think people will be interested in this—I'm interested in it. [*Laughter*]

Ms. Fong. The Cisco Academy is basically a degree program, and they will get a degree in network enterprise, and they will also get a Cisco certificate, and it trains individuals. We start, actually, with high school students. You've met two our students today who are Foothill students, but they're actually, currently also enrolled in high school. They want to be computer engineers ultimately, but they wanted to get a head start, so they're in our Cisco Academy.

[*Ms. Fong made further remarks.*]

The President. And it's called Cisco Academy because you helped design the curriculum?

Mr. Chambers. We designed the curriculum, but it's implemented through the colleges and high schools. There is no social promotion. The grades—everyone knows how you compare, both within the States and globally.

The President. See, what's interesting about the community colleges—and I know the Governor knows this—is that they're about as market-oriented as you can get. Community colleges are available; they're very flexible. In other words, the curricula can adjust depending upon the local needs. They're innovative. They're willing to take a Cisco program, implement it in the community college. They're very practical. In other words, they train people for jobs which actually exist.

And it's—*[laughter]*—it's vital, and I appreciate it. And I know the Governor understands that, and we understand at the Federal level. We've got pretty good grant money—$150 million in the '07 budget, coming to help train workers. I just want people to understand that if you're wondering whether or not you're too old to go back to college, you're not. There is plenty of money available to help you go back. And 2 years of additional education can enhance your salary a lot. It makes you more productive, and a more productive worker is one whose standard of living will go up.

The community college system is, I think, one of America's greatest treasures, and I appreciate you, Dr. Fong, for being here. Thanks for your—*[applause]*.

Ms. Fong. Well, the Governor is also a product of our community college system.

The President. Is he?

Gov. Schwarzenegger. Absolutely, yes. Actually, I also want to just add that our community colleges are doing an extraordinary job with career tech and vocational education. It's really amazing the kind of things that they do. Because I think it is so important to recognize that, yes, we want to stress 4-year college, and, yes, we want to inspire kids to go to higher education and all this. But there are many kids that want to do—get into different professions. They want to be a carpenter or plumber, or they want to be a chef or a computer technician or a nurse—great professions with a great future and great salaries and all this. I think that community colleges here in the State are really doing an extraordinary job to prepare them for those jobs.

The President. Good. Thank you. Good job.

Temp Keller.

Temp Keller. Yes, Mr. President.

The President. You know, you probably don't want to answer this question, but, like, how does a guy get named "Temp"? *[Laughter]*

Mr. Keller. She's actually sitting right over there in the third row.

The President. Is she? *[Laughter]* Well, that's a good answer. You know what, I'll just wait and ask her behind the stage. *[Laughter]*

Welcome. Tell people what you do. Tell people what you have done with your program. It's really interesting.

Mr. Keller. It would be my honor, and thank you all for having me.

I'm the founder and president of an organization called RISE: Resources for Indispensable Schools and Educators. And the fundamental idea behind RISE is we are going to revolutionize the way that this country recognizes and retains good, effective teachers in public schools serving low-income communities.

[Mr. Keller made further remarks.]

The President. And so how does your deal work?

Mr. Keller. What we do—two very simple things. We essentially, one, identify good, effective teachers in low-income communities. Now, I'm sure there's a lot of people here in the room and listening that say, "Well, that's not an easy thing to do."

The way that we do it, though, and what makes RISE truly innovative and truly unique is that we ask teachers. We say to them, "How do you know you're any good at what you do? You went into teaching to make a difference. Demonstrate that you're making a difference."

[Mr. Keller made further remarks.]

The President. Nothing better than being around a social entrepreneur. *[Laughter]*

Mr. Keller. That's right.

The President. Here's your chance. How do you raise money? *[Laughter]*

Mr. Keller. Well——

The President. Does corporate California support your program?

Mr. Keller. They do. We have——

The President. It's in corporate California's interest that you succeed.

[*Mr. Keller made further remarks.*]

The President. God, I love a guy who is enthusiastic about what he's doing. [*Laughter*] Thanks. By the way, I also know East Palo Alto—Vermeil, my buddy Vermeil. Actually, the students came to the South Lawn one time. It's a great school. Thanks. Thanks for doing what you're doing.

Francois, step up to the mike here, my man.

[*Francois J. Henley, president and chief executive officer, Silicon Genesis Corporation, made brief remarks.*]

The President. We want people coming here, or who live here, to feel comfortable starting their own business. I love the fact that I am the President of a country where people can start with nothing except an idea and desire and hard work, and end up owning your own business. And Arnold is right—we've got to make sure the environment for entrepreneurship remains strong throughout our country if we want to be on the leading edge.

How fantastic is it that a guy comes from Montreal to realize his dreams? And you're employing people—who knows, you may hit on the thing that makes solar energy the source—I actually believe one of these days, we're going to have homes that become little power generating units unto themselves, and if you don't use electricity, you'll feed it back into the grid. And maybe you're the guy. Maybe one of these days— [*laughter*]. Don't take this marketing too far, you know. [*Laughter*] One camera bank, and he goes crazy. [*Laughter*]

Thanks for coming. I love your story. Good luck. I wish you all the best.

He talked about patents. Basically he's talking about making sure it's easy to protect his ideas. What—also, I want you to know that I talked to President Hu Jintao about—and I know John Chambers says,

as well, over in China—is we expect the same treatment for our products that are patented here in the United States, overseas. Intellectual property rights is a vital part of making sure a trading world is a fair trading world. And I spent time yesterday with the President, in a very respectful way, but a firm way, reminding him that if he's to be a good trading partner with the United States, that when Cisco sells a product there or Francois eventually sells a product there, that property needs to be—that intellectual property inherent in that property needs to be protected and respected.

Final person. We're saving probably the best for the last, wouldn't you say, Arash? [*Laughter*]

Arash Shokouh. Absolutely. Thank you, Mr. President. [*Laughter*] That's right.

The President. You are a dash student?

Mr. Shokouh. Yes.

The President. Where?

Mr. Shokouh. I'm a computer engineering student at San Jose State University. I'm also minoring in mathematics, as well as film acting.

The President. Interesting. [*Laughter*] I got the strategy. [*Laughter*] Why did you major in the first two subjects? [*Laughter*]

Mr. Shokouh. That's the first time I've been asked that. [*Laughter*] Well, I decided to do computer engineering because all my life I've been a complete computer nerd, always playing with computers, electronics, taking them apart, destroying them. I mean, my parents wouldn't really let me go too close to the television without somebody to supervise. But that's basically why. [*Laughter*]

The President. And your dreams?

Mr. Shokouh. I hope to—after I graduate from San Jose State University, I want to go on to pursue an MBA degree and, hopefully, start a small business designing consumer electronics components—plan A. Plan B, to go into a small startup where I can help lead the direction of the product, design the product.

The President. And so when did you start having this kind of notion about where your life would like to go?

[Mr. Shokouh made brief remarks.]

The President. You know what's interesting—why don't you tell folks your family history real quick, if you don't mind.

Mr. Shokouh. Absolutely. I'm an Iranian American, and my parents, who are sitting right back there, are from Iran. My mom and dad came here at around 1980, and me and my sister were born here in San Jose.

The President. I love America, a country that welcomes people. We've got to be a welcoming society. And our soul is renewed when people escape societies that can be really repressive and have a son like Arash, who sits here with the President and the Governor talking about dreams. See, this is a country that has always got to be a place where people can dream big dreams and achieve them.

The question facing America is, will we lose our confidence and become an isolated nation? Will we lose our confidence and our ability to compete in the global marketplace and become a protectionist nation? And the answer is, absolutely not. We will not lose our confidence. And here is part of our strategy to make sure that the United States of America continues to be the leader. And it's important for people to understand that being the economic leader of the world means that it's more likely you'll have a better job, and it's more likely you'll be able to realize your dreams, and it's more likely our standard of living will continue to rise.

And that's the challenge ahead of us. It truly is. And I want to thank those who are here to help make the case why our citizens have got to be confident about the United States of America's place in the world and why we should never relinquish our standing in the world because we fear the future. We welcome it. We welcome competition, and we know we've got to put a strategy in place to be able to deal with that competition. And you're hearing the foundation for that strategy here today.

I want to thank you all for lending your expertise. Thanks for joining me. God bless you all.

NOTE: The President spoke at 1:57 p.m. In his remarks, he referred to John T. Chambers, president and chief executive officer, Cisco Systems, Inc.; George Scalise, member, President's Council of Advisers on Science and Technology; Lezlee Westine, Deputy Assistant to the President and Director of Public Liaison; and Donald E. Vermeil, member, J. William Fulbright Foreign Scholarship Board. The transcript released by the Office of the Press Secretary also included the remarks of Gov. Schwarzenegger.

The President's Radio Address
April 22, 2006

Good morning. This weekend I am traveling in California, where I'm focusing on important issues for our Nation's future, including our economy, energy prices, the war on terror, and immigration reform.

America's economy is strong, and we need to keep it strong in an increasingly competitive world. The talent and innovative spirit of our people have driven America's economic growth. To maintain our economic leadership, our Nation must stay on the leading edge of innovation. So I have proposed the American Competitiveness Initiative.

One important part of this initiative is improving math and science education for our young people, so they have the right skills to succeed in the 21st century economy. On Friday in San Jose, I had the chance to visit Cisco Systems, a company that understands the importance of preparing the next generation for the high-tech jobs of tomorrow.

Through its Networking Academy Program, Cisco is helping to train high school students in math, science, and information technology skills. By ensuring that we have a skilled workforce for the future, companies like Cisco are helping America compete with confidence and keeping our economy growing and creating new jobs for our citizens.

Saturday is Earth Day, and many of you are asking how we can meet our growing energy needs while protecting our environment. The key is technology. So I have proposed the Advanced Energy Initiative to change the way we power our homes, businesses, and cars. I will visit the California Fuel Cell Partnership to take a closer look at hydrogen fuel cells, one of the exciting new technologies supported by my initiative. These fuel cells have the potential to revolutionize the way we power our cars by giving us vehicles that will emit no pollution and will be more efficient than gas-powered cars.

My Advanced Energy Initiative will also help improve hybrid vehicles, cars and trucks that run partly on electricity and help drivers save gas. We're funding research into a new generation of plug-in hybrid vehicles that could be recharged in electrical outlets and could allow many drivers to make their daily commute using no gasoline.

By developing these and other new sources of clean renewable energy like ethanol, we will continue growing our economy, reduce energy prices and protect our environment, and make America less dependent on foreign oil.

Americans are asking about our progress toward victory in the war on terror. I have confidence in the outcome of this struggle

because I know the character of the people who wear our Nation's uniform. On Sunday, I will attend church and have lunch with Marine Corps and Navy personnel and their families at the Twentynine Palms base. I will tell them how honored I am to be their Commander in Chief and express the gratitude of all Americans for their service in the cause of freedom.

Since September the 11th, 2001, the men and women of our military have overthrown a cruel regime in Afghanistan, captured or killed many Al Qaida terrorists, liberated Iraq, and made America more secure from terrorist dangers. We're fighting the terrorists abroad so we do not have to face them here at home. By taking the fight to the terrorists and bringing liberty and hope to a troubled region, our courageous troops are making the world a safer place.

On Monday, I'll visit Irvine, California, to discuss immigration reform with the local community. Immigration is an emotional issue, and it's sparked passionate debate. When we discuss immigration, we're talking about the integrity of our borders, the enforcement of our laws, and the character of our Nation.

Here's what I believe: America does not have to choose between being a welcoming society and being a lawful society. We can be both at the same time. In the coming weeks, I'll press Congress to pass comprehensive immigration reform that secures our border, enforces our laws, meets the needs of our economy, and upholds our highest ideals.

We must also ensure that all immigrants assimilate into our society and learn our customs, our values, and our language. America is a land of immigrants and a nation of laws, and we must stay true to both parts of this great heritage.

As Congress returns from its recess, its Members have important and consequential work before them. I urge them to act on my initiatives to keep America competitive, to promote alternative sources of energy, reform our immigration system, and continue their support of our troops fighting in the global war on terror.

By taking these steps, we'll maintain America's strength. And a strong America will help lead the world to a future of greater freedom and prosperity and peace.

Thank you for listening.

NOTE: The address was recorded at 7:49 a.m. on April 21 in the Cabinet Room at the White House for broadcast at 10:06 a.m. on April 22. The transcript was made available by the Office of the Press Secretary on April 21 but was embargoed for release until the broadcast. The Office of the Press Secretary also released a Spanish language transcript of this address.

Remarks at the California Highway Patrol Academy in Sacramento, California
April 22, 2006

Today the Iraqi people reached an important milestone in their journey on democracy. Iraqi leaders announced agreement on the top leadership posts for a national unity government. This agreement represents compromise and consensus among many different Iraqi groups, and it came after months of patient negotiations.

The agreement reflects the will of the Iraqi people, who defied the terrorists by voting to choose the men and women who will lead their nation forward. And this historic achievement by determined Iraqis will make America more secure.

Iraq is a nation made up of many different ethnic and religious groups, and Iraq's new leaders represent their country's great diversity. The Iraqi people have rejected the terrorists' efforts to divide them, and they have chosen the path of unity for their free nation.

The new Iraqi leadership now has 30 days to finalize the makeup of the Iraqi Cabinet. Once inaugurated, the new Government will hold power for up to 4 years. Unlike the interim and transitional governments that came before, the new Iraqi Government will have full constitutional authority. And because it expresses the will of 12 million Iraqis who went to the polls last December, it will have the popular mandate to address Iraq's toughest long-term challenges.

Iraq's new leaders have important responsibilities to the people who chose them. The new Government has a responsibility to deploy the growing strength of the Iraqi security forces to defeat the terrorists and insurgents and establish control over the militias. The Government has the responsibility to rebuild infrastructure that makes commerce possible and that supports the education and health needs of the Iraqi people. The Government must strengthen the economy and encourage job creation and enforce the rule of law. The new Government must ensure that improvements in prosperity and security occur throughout the country so that all Iraqis share in the benefits of their new democracy.

These are major challenges, and the new Iraqi Government will not face them alone. America is helping Iraq's young democracy move forward. Iraqis and Americans are fighting side by side against a common enemy. We're going to defeat the terrorists in Iraq. We will deny them safe haven. And a free Iraq in the heart of the Middle East will be a powerful blow to the terrorists and a beacon of liberty for people across that region.

Formation of a new Iraqi Government is an opportunity for America to open a new chapter in our partnership with the Iraqi people. The United States and our coalition partners will work with the new Iraqi Government to reassess our tactics, adjust our methods, and strengthen our mutual efforts to achieve victory in this central front in the war on terror.

The new Iraqi Government will assume growing responsibility for their nation's security. And as more Iraqi forces stand up, American forces will stand down. I want to thank all the brave Americans, both in our military and the diplomatic corps, who have served the cause of freedom in Iraq over the past 3 years. I thank their families who have sacrificed time with loved ones serving far from home. I want to thank our wounded service men and women, who have given so much to make this moment possible. And our Nation remembers the fallen heroes who gave their lives to bring liberty to Iraq and security to America. And we will honor their sacrifice by completing this mission.

There's going to be more tough fighting ahead in Iraq, and there will be more days of sacrifice and struggle. Yet the enemies of freedom have suffered a real blow today. And we've taken a great stride on the march to victory. The Iraqi people have defied the terrorist threats; Iraqi soldiers and police have fought with valor for the freedom of their country; and Iraqi leaders have laid the foundations for a democratic government of, by, and for the Iraqi people.

On behalf of all Americans, I congratulate the Iraqi people and their new leaders. The Iraqis are showing the world that democracy is worth the wait, that liberty is worth the sacrifice, and that freedom is the future of every man, woman, and child on this Earth.

Thank you very much.

NOTE: The President spoke at 2 p.m.

Remarks at the California Fuel Cell Partnership in West Sacramento, California
April 22, 2006

Thank you all. Mr. Secretary—I'm really pleased to have Norman Mineta in my Cabinet. He is a really good guy. And I thank you for your service, friend, and thank you for being here to share in this testimony to what technology is going to do for our country to make it a better place for all of us to live.

First of all, happy Earth Day to you. It's a good place to spend Earth Day, here in California. I got to spend the first part of my day riding a mountain bike in Napa Valley. It's a good place to ride—[*laughter*]—a little hillier than I would have liked. [*Laughter*] But it's a spectacular way to commune with nature. And I really appreciate you coming. I want all of us to under-

stand that we have a serious responsibility to be good stewards of our land. And this is a day we unite together to recommit ourselves to be good stewards of our land.

I appreciate the good stewardship—commitment to good stewardship at the heart of the California Fuel Cell Partnership. I bet a lot of our citizens don't understand what goes on here. This is a really interesting collaborative effort between automakers and energy companies and fuel cell technology companies and State and Federal agencies, all united toward a great mission, which is to make hydrogen-powered automobiles and trucks and buses a reality for American drivers. And that will help us be good stewards of the environment, and that will help us become less dependent on foreign sources of oil.

Today I saw cars and buses that run on hydrogen instead of gasoline and that emit pure water instead of exhaust fumes. This Nation does not have to choose between a strong economy and a clean environment; we can have both at the same time. And investing in new technologies like hydrogen will enable this economy to be strong, people to be able to afford fuel, this country's national security not dependent on parts of the world that are unstable. And technology will once again make this country the leader in the world, and that's what we're here to celebrate.

And I want to thank Catherine Dunwoody, the executive director of the California Fuel Cell Partnership. I appreciate your commitment. You know, you can tell when somebody is pretty enthusiastic about what she's doing, a true believer. And she's a believer because she's not only a person with vision, but she is a practical person. And she has seen firsthand the progress being made.

I want to thank Congressman John Doolittle and Julie for being here. And I also want to thank Congressman Dan Lungren. Thank you all for joining us today. I appreciate your interest.

I thank the members and representatives of the California Fuel Cell Partnership. I want to thank the three guys from Ford Motor Company for giving me a tour. One guy was here; he's been 40 years, I think, at Ford. And here he is, describing what it's like to maintain a hydrogen fuel cell vehicle. I bet you didn't think you'd be talking about that 10 years ago, 20 years ago, maybe 5 years ago. Things are changing for the better, and we're here to celebrate this Nation's desire to improve the quality of life.

I would like to report to you on Earth Day that America's air is cleaner, our water is purer, and the land is better cared for. And that's important for people to know. Over the past 5 years, things have improved

with air, land, and water. And we're setting tough standards when it comes to air quality. We're implementing clean air rules that will reduce powerplant pollution by 70 percent. We've established the first-ever national cap on mercury emissions from powerplants, which will result in nearly a 70-percent decrease in those emissions as well.

Two years ago, I announced an important goal, and that is to end the no net loss policy of wetlands in the United States and increase wetlands in this country. I set a goal to restore, improve, and protect at least 3 million acres of wetlands over the next 5 years. So far we've restored, improved, and protected 1.8 million acres of wetlands. We're doing our part in the Federal Government. We have a responsibility to be good stewards of our air and our water and our land.

You know, flying in here, Congressman Lungren pointed out all the different farms. And I want to thank the farmers and ranchers for being good stewards of the land as well. They've got a lot at stake when it comes to being mindful of maintaining good land practices. I don't know if you realize this or not, but in the farm bill we—I signed and Congress passed, we provide about $40 billion over a 10-year period to encourage our farmers and ranchers to protect wildlife and conserve our natural resources.

Flying over the mountain ranges we saw the forests. In Washington, we passed the Healthy Forest Initiative, which will help us clear out dangerous underbrush that will help reduce the risk of catastrophic fires. We've got some commonsense, practical things we're doing in Washington that I think the—I know the American people expect us to do.

You know, riding my bike today in the park reminded me of how important it is to make sure those parks are maintained and accessible to the American people. After all, it's your park system. We pledged 5 billion—$4.9 billion over 5 years to reduce the maintenance backlog in national parks, and we're honoring that commitment.

I'll tell you something I find very interesting. In the 36 years since the first Earth Day, air pollution in America has been reduced by 50 percent—yet our economy has tripled in size during that time. And there's one main reason why, and that's because of technology. We're a technologically competent nation. We must always be on the leading edge of research and development in this country if we expect to be good stewards of the environment and make sure our people are able to find good work. That's the challenge.

And so today we're here to honor a group of folks who are employing technology, using new ideas to help change the face of America. And it's important work we're doing here, because we've got a real problem when it comes to oil. We're addicted, and it's harmful for the economy, and it's harmful for our national security, and we've got to do something about it in this country.

And so I want to try to share some ideas with you about what we can and must do. First of all, I understand the folks here, as well as other places in the country, are paying high gas prices. And you are because the primary component of gasoline is crude oil. And we live in a global marketplace, and when the demand for crude oil goes up in China or India, fast-growing economies, if the corresponding supply doesn't meet that demand, the price of gasoline is going to go up here in America. The American people have got to understand, what happens elsewhere in the world affects the price of gasoline you pay here.

When that price of gasoline goes up, it hurts working people. It hurts our small businesses. And it's a serious problem that we've got to do something about. The Federal Government has a responsibility, by the way, to make sure there is no such—there is no price gouging, and we're watching real careful to make sure that people are treated fairly.

We're going to have a tough summer because people are beginning to drive now during tight supply. The Energy Department predicts gas prices are going to go up. Part of the reason, of course, is the escalating price of crude oil. Another reason why is, we haven't had any refinery capacity in the United States in a long period of time. When you don't have refining capacity and demand goes up, you're going to see a price increase. And so this country has got to be wise about how we permit refineries and encourage additional refining capacity as well as, you well know here in this State, we're changing the fuel mixes from MPBE to ethanol.

It was right to get rid of MPBE—MPBE was polluting water. It's a product that wouldn't biodegrade. It was a—it's a terrible pollutant. And we're replacing that with ethanol, but there's a transition period that has to take place. And all these factors remind us that we got to do something about our dependence on oil. That's what the lessons at the pump say today.

I told you about national security. Let me talk a little bit about that. We get a lot of our oil from places that are unstable, and we get our oil sometimes from people that don't particularly care for us. That's what I mean about national security problems. We do not want to be reliant upon unstable parts of the world. We don't want the lives of our people affected because some nation may not like us.

And so here's a strategy to deal with it: One, we're spending a lot of money at the Federal level to encourage research and development, with the goal of getting away from oil. Spent $10 billion over the last 5 years to develop cleaner and cheaper and more reliable energy sources. The goal is, as I mentioned in my State of the Union, to promote hydrogen and hybrid vehicles and ethanol. In other words, what technology will enable us to do is change our driving habits, is to figure out new ways to utilize fuels so that they're not—so we can get away from oil-based fuels.

I strongly believe hydrogen is the fuel of the future. That's what we're talking about. Hydrogen is used in a fuel cell that can power a car that uses no gasoline, produces no pollution or greenhouse gas emissions. Hydrogen vehicles can be twice as efficient as gasoline vehicles. Hydrogen can be produced from domestic energy sources, which means it has the potential—a vast potential—to dramatically cut our dependence on foreign oil. Hydrogen is clean; hydrogen is domestically produced; and hydrogen is the wave of the future. And the people here at the California Fuel Cell Partnership understand that.

What's interesting is that they're—because of this collaborative effort, there are now 100 hydrogen-powered vehicles on California roads. That may not seem a lot to some of you, but what you're witnessing here is the beginning of a major change in the driving habits of the American people. That's what you're seeing. We're in a facility that is just at the beginning stage of some of the most exciting technological changes this country will ever see. Hydrogen cars are being used by companies like UPS, the governments of San Francisco and Los Angeles, UC-Davis and Irvine.

I met the bus man here and—where is bus man? There he is, yes. He is one enthusiastic guy. [*Laughter*] He is—he truly believes that urban America is going to be transformed in a very positive way because of hydrogen-powered buses. And if you don't believe me, just ask him. [*Laughter*]

We saw a fueling station today where vehicles come—the drivers drive in here to get hydrogen. About 6,000 automobiles have been fueled at this station since it's been up and running. I appreciate Governor Arnold Schwarzenegger's declaration that California plans to build a hydrogen highway. Of all the States in the United States that has been on the leading edge of technological change, it's been California. That's a positive declaration on his part. Basically what he's saying is we want California to continue to lead this country

when it comes to innovative change. And we support him.

I believe that today's children will one day take a driver's test in a hydrogen-powered, pollution-free car. That's the goal of the United States. And it's a big goal, but it's an attainable goal. All you got to do is look at the progress that has been made thus far. In 2003, I pledged that we would spend $1.2 billion over 5 years for hydrogen research and development, and we're on track to meet that goal.

One of the reasons I have come here is because I want the American people to understand that their tax dollars are yielding important results, that we are making progress, that the idea of having a hydrogen-powered automobile is not a foolish dream. It's a reality that is going to come to be. The funding is getting results. Since 2003, researchers have used Federal funding to double the lifetime of the hydrogen fuel cell stacks that power cars. In order for this to work, there has to be longevity—you just can't be changing your fuel cell stacks all the time. There has to be durability in order for this to be a product that people will want to buy.

We've cut the cost of manufacturing hydrogen fuel cells in half. That's pretty rapid progress when you think that the funding started in 2003, and the cost of the fuel cells have been reduced in half. And that is important. In order for this to become a part of life, these fuel cells have to be affordable. People have got to be able to buy them in order for them to be able to function properly. And we're making progress. We're heading for a hydrocarbon economy—from a hydrocarbon economy to a hydrogen economy. And that's a very positive development.

There's another positive development taking place in America today, and that's the advent of the hybrid vehicle. And it's a good way to reduce our oil consumption right now. Hybrid vehicles have both a gasoline-powered engine and an electric battery, and they travel about twice as far on a gallon of fuel as gasoline-only vehicles. We can affect our dependence on oil by encouraging people to purchase hybrid vehicles. And that's why the Federal Government passed a law that says you get a tax credit of up to $3,400 for a hybrid vehicle purchase. In other words, we're trying to make it worthwhile for you to go out and purchase a hybrid vehicle, through the use of a tax credit.

What's really going to be interesting, however, is what's called plug-in hybrid vehicles. And we're spending $31 million annually to speed up research into these battery technologies. And what this means is, is that we're trying to develop a battery that will power your vehicle, where you plug it in at night, and you drive the first 40 miles on electricity alone. Now, think about what that means for big cities. A lot of people don't drive more than 40 miles a day in big cities. So all of a sudden, you've now—we're developing a technology that says, you'll drive by the use of electricity, and you won't use gasoline at all.

And one way to affect consumption is to speed up the development of these plug-in hybrids, and we're doing just that at the Federal level. It's a promising technology that will help people change the way they drive. It'll be a transition to the hydrogen fuel cell batteries.

Finally, I want to talk a little bit about ethanol. I'm a big proponent of ethanol. I like the idea of America's farmers being able to grow fuel. I like the idea of people saying, "My corn crop is up, and therefore, we're less dependent on oil from somewhere." And that's what we're beginning to do. We're beginning to change driving habits of the American people by changing the fuel mix in their cars. Any vehicle can use ethanol with a concentration of less than 10 percent. With minor modifications, cars and trucks can become what's called flex-fuel vehicles that run on a fuel blend called E–85, which is a mix of 85 percent ethanol and 15 percent gasoline.

And there are a lot of E–85 fueling stations now, particularly in the Midwest where they grow a lot of corn. But the idea is to be able to use your money to figure out how to use other materials to be able to manufacture ethanol. And we're close to some interesting breakthroughs. We're close to breakthroughs to be able to make ethanol from wood chips and stalks and switchgrass and other natural materials. And it makes a lot of sense if we're trying to get off oil, and it makes sense to use taxpayers' money to research ways to use switchgrass, for example, to become a fuel for your automobile. I think it does.

Catherine reminded me, however, in my discussions with her, that switchgrass can also be used to manufacture hydrogen. She wanted me to make sure—[*laughter*]—that in my description of what is possible in the United States that we—make sure one technology does not pirate money for another technology. And it's not going to happen. What's going to happen is we'll have research on all fronts to achieve a grand national objective. And there's no doubt in my mind we'll be able to achieve this objective.

We've done a lot of things in this country in the past. We've changed ways of life in—to make life qualitatively better for American people because we're innovators, and we're thinkers, and we get things done. And on this Earth Day, what I wanted to come to California to say is, we're in the process of dreaming big dreams for the American people but dreams that will be accomplished. We can't lose our nerve. We shouldn't lose our vision. We should remember where we've been and where we're going. And we're going to a day— and no doubt in my mind—where the United States of America will not be dependent on oil, will be good stewards of the environment, which will benefit the quality of life of the American people.

Thank you for letting me come by to talk to you. God bless.

NOTE: The President spoke at 2:41 p.m. In his remarks, he referred to Julia Harlow, wife of Rep. John T. Doolittle of California; and Gov. Arnold Schwarzenegger of California.

Remarks at a Republican National Committee Reception in Indian Wells, California
April 22, 2006

Please be seated. Thanks for coming. The lesson of the 1994 fundraiser is I should have had a better chairman. [*Laughter*] I want to thank you all for coming. I really appreciate your support for the Republican Party. We're the party that is the party of ideas, a party of optimism, and a party of people who know how to solve problems, which is exactly what we're doing.

I, first, wish Laura were here; she's not, of course. About four people go through the photo-op line indicated that they kind of would rather have Laura here than me. [*Laughter*] Yes, well—I can understand why. She is really a fine person, and she sends her best to all her friends here.

I thank my friend Brad. You know, one of the great things about our life is that we've had friends before I got into politics, and they're going to be our friends after we're in politics. And Brad Freeman is such a person, and I value his friendship. I want to thank him for organizing this event.

I want to thank all the folks who helped make this a very successful event. One reason why we are successful as a party is because we've got a great party chairman who understands that our message is one that should reach into every neighborhood; ours is one that is inclusive; ours is one that is hopeful—and that's Ken Mehlman. I want to thank you for coming, Ken.

I appreciate Duf Sundheim, party chairman here in California. I saw Duf yesterday at Cisco Systems, saw him here in the desert. What are you doing tomorrow, Duf? [*Laughter*] But thank you for your service; appreciate it very much.

I'm confident that Arnold Schwarzenegger will be reelected to Governor of this important State.

I am always a better person after I've been in the presence of Mary Bono. She is the Congresswoman from this district; she is smart; she's capable; she's doing an excellent job for the constituents here. I don't know if you realize this, but today is Earth Day, and Mary has led the way to make sure that some of the most valuable territory, some of the most valuable country in this part of the world are preserved for generations to come, and I want to thank you for your leadership. I also want to thank you for your strong stand in the war on terror. You're doing a fine job.

Connie Mack, from the great State of Florida, is with us. Congressman, good to see you; thank you for coming. Proud you're here. Good friend of the brothers, and mine too.

Bruce McPherson, the secretary of State is with us. Bruce, thank you for coming. Appreciate you being here, sir. I call him Senator; now we call you Secretary. It's good to see Mary as well.

Chuck Poochigian is with us. Chuck is running for the State attorney general. Chuck, good luck to you. Thank you. My old buddy, proud to see you. Thanks for coming. Thanks for bringing Debbie with you as well.

Steve Poizner is with us, running for the insurance commissioner. Steve—there he is. Good luck to you.

I just said hello to Congressman Brian Bilbray. Where are you, Brian? Thanks for coming. Good luck on your race. We're pulling for you. Finally, Ben Stein is with us. Appreciate you coming, Ben. I think he's with us. Maybe he's not with us.

I'd like to make a couple of points, and then we'll sit down for a second, and then visit some more with you. Today we had an important day in the war on terror. The elected leaders of Iraq came together and formed a unity government for the sake of people—[*applause*]. The formation of a unity government is a blow for the terrorists who have tried to divide Iraq and prevent Iraq democracy from emerging forward.

And the United States of America will continue to stand with the brave citizens of Iraq as this democracy grows. It is in our interests that democracy succeed in Iraq. We must defeat the terrorists by denying them safe haven, and we will defeat the terrorists with an ideology that is hopeful and optimistic and positive, and that's an ideology based upon liberty.

I've also had a wonderful time traveling your beautiful State. Yesterday I talked about a really important initiative for our country, and that is the Competitiveness Initiative. And the reason it's—I started talking about it in my State of the Union is because it is very important for the United States of America to feel confident about our future, and not to fear it.

There are some in our country that feel like we should isolate ourselves from the world. There are some who fear trade with other countries and, therefore, want to throw up walls and protective barriers— not me. I believe the United States, in order to make sure our people have got a standard of living that improves, must be a leader in the world, must not fear competition, must be willing to continue to put policies in place that will mean that other generations of Americans coming up can realize a great quality of life. And it starts with making sure that the United States of America is the leader of research and technology.

And so yesterday at Cisco Systems, I talked about our desire to double Federal funding for the basic sciences so as to continue to make sure we're technologically advanced. I also talked about making sure the research and development tax credit is a permanent part of the Tax Code to encourage private investment when it comes to research.

But I spent a lot of time yesterday talking about education. I proudly signed the No Child Left Behind Act, which changed the way people should view education, from one in which it was okay just to move kids through to one that said we're going to measure, and we're going to hold people to account. We're going to set high standards, and we're going to measure to determine whether our children are learning to read and write and add and subtract. And if we find out they're not able to read and write, we'll correct problems early, before it's too late. I want to extend that same rigor that we've applied in reading to math and science so that our children have got the skills necessary to fill the jobs of the 21st century.

And today I had the honor of being in West Sacramento, after my bike ride, by the way, in Napa Valley, which—good place to ride, by the way. I talked about an issue that I know is on people's minds here in California, and that is high energy prices. And I reminded our folks that we live in a global world, and when China's demand for energy goes up, it affects the gasoline prices here. When India's demand for energy goes up, it affects the gasoline prices here, which says to me, we've got to be smart about using energy—using investment technology to get away from use of oil.

And I talked about plug-in hybrid vehicles, the research going into that, so that one day you'll be driving your first 40 miles on electricity, electric batteries. And I talked about ethanol. But I also talked about hydrogen fuel cells, which I believe will be the wave of the future for how we drive our cars.

What I'm telling you is, ours is a party that has got a vision and a plan to make sure the United States of America is the leader in the world. Our message to the American people is, don't fear the future because we intend to shape the future.

Thanks for coming. I'll answer a few questions in a little bit. Thank you for being here.

NOTE: The President spoke at 6:05 p.m. at the Toscana Country Club. In his remarks, he referred to Bradford M. Freeman, California State finance chairman, Bush-Cheney '04, Inc.; Gov. Arnold Schwarzenegger of California; California Secretary of State Bruce McPherson, and his wife, Mary; Charles S. Poochigian, candidate for California State attorney general, and his wife, Debbie; Brian Bilbray, candidate for Congress in California's 50th Congressional District; and entertainer Ben Stein.

Remarks to Military Personnel and Their Families in Twentynine Palms, California
April 23, 2006

Thanks for the warm welcome. Sergeant Major, thanks for the introduction. It's an honor to be here. I've been really looking forward to coming to Twentynine Palms. The general told me that I'm the first President ever to have come. It's an honor to be the first President, but he also reminded me that my mother beat me to the punch. [*Laughter*]

I want to share some thoughts with you right quick. One, I'm incredibly proud of the United States Marine Corps. You bring honor to our country. You represent the very best of America. You represent men and women who volunteer to serve during dangerous and historic times. And because of your service, we're defeating an enemy overseas so we do not have to face them here at home. Because of your service, we've liberated people from the clutches of a tyrant. And because of your service, we're laying the foundation of peace for a generation of Americans to come. These are historic times, and your service makes me incredibly proud.

And I also want to say something to your families. It's hard when your loved one is overseas. I respect your sacrifice and want to thank you very much for your service to our country as well.

Today I—this morning I was—had three phone calls I think that you might find of interest. I spoke to the President of Iraq, the Speaker of the Iraqi Assembly, and the Prime Minister-designate. It was a remarkable phone call. First, they expressed their deep appreciation for the United States of America and our soldiers. They understand the sacrifices that you are making on their behalf, and they are grateful for those sacrifices. And the reason why they are is because they represent the 12 million people who went to the polls in the face of incredible terrorist threats, and said, "We want to be free; we desire to live in a free society."

I told them—I said that they have awesome responsibilities to their people. They have the responsibility of improving the lives of men and women regardless of their religious status and nature; they have responsibilities to defeat the terrorists; they have a responsibility to unite their country. And I believe they will.

The formation of this Government is an important milestone toward our victory in Iraq. A lot of times people ask me about

779

my attitude about things, and here's my attitude: The only way we can lose in Iraq is if we lose our nerve. And I'm not losing my nerve, and I know that the United States Marine Corps will not lose their nerve, either.

Yesterday was an important day, but I recognize we still have more work to do. Democracy in Iraq will be a major blow for the terrorists who want to do us harm. Democracy in Iraq will deny them safe haven. Democracy in Iraq will set a powerful example for people in a part of the world who are desperate for freedom.

It is such an honor to be here with the mighty United States Marine Corps and their families. May God bless you all, and may God continue to bless our country. Thank you.

NOTE: The President spoke at 12:34 p.m. in the Mess Hall at the Marine Corps Air Ground Combat Center. In his remarks, he referred to Sgt. Maj. James M. Ricker, USMC, and Brig. Gen. Douglas M. Stone, USMC Reserve, commanding general, Marine Air Ground Task Force Training Command; President Jalal Talabani, Speaker of Parliament Mahmoud al-Mashhadani, and Prime Minister-designate Nuri al-Maliki of Iraq. The Office of the Press Secretary also released a Spanish language transcript of these remarks.

Remarks Following a Visit With Former President Gerald R. Ford in Rancho Mirage, California
April 23, 2006

President Bush. It's such an honor to be with President and Mrs. Ford. The country has produced a lot of fine citizens, and there's no two finer people than these two. Thank you for your hospitality, sir.

Former President Ford. We solved all the problems, didn't we? [*Laughter*]

President Bush. That's right; we sure did.

Former President Ford. Well, thank you for stopping by, George.

President Bush. God bless you.

Former President Ford. Same to you, sir.

NOTE: The President spoke at 6:01 p.m. at President Ford's residence.

Remarks on Immigration Reform and a Question-and-Answer Session in Irvine, California
April 24, 2006

The President. Thank you all. Please be seated. Thanks for letting me come by. Tom, thanks for the invitation. What I thought I would do is share some thoughts with you on some issues that kind of, like, may be on the TV screen these days— [*laughter*]—and then answer some of your

questions. I'm interested to know what's on your mind.

First, I've had a fabulous trip to your unbelievably beautiful State. It started off in northern California—Cisco; then I went to Stanford; then I went to Napa Valley. Then I rode my bicycle on Earth Day in

Napa Valley. Then I found out the mountains are a little steep in Napa Valley. [*Laughter*] I then went down and spent a fantastic time in Palm Springs. What an unbelievably diverse State, and it's a fantastic place to end my journey, here in Orange County. I want to thank you for giving me a chance to come by and visit with you.

Laura sends her very best. I, of course, checked in with her this morning before I headed over here, to see if she had any additional instructions for me for the day. [*Laughter*] She said, "Keep it short." [*Laughter*] I'm a lucky man to have Laura as a wife. You can imagine what it's like to be President—there's some pressure on your family, as you can imagine. The good news is I've got a 45-second commute. [*Laughter*] And the better news is I've got a wife who is a fantastic First Lady, who shares a passion with me to do the best we can for our country.

I want to thank Lucy Dunn, as well as thanking Tom for putting this event together. I appreciate the members of the Orange County Business Council. I want to thank Congressman John Campbell for his service; appreciate you. He's the Congressman from this district, by the way. And Catherine is with us. Thank—Congresswoman Mary Bono is with us today. Mary, thank you for being here. I just spent some quality time in her district, and I forgot to tell you that I had the privilege of riding my mountain bike in the desert as well. The national monument that she helped put together to preserve open spaces—she's got a lot of humility; she didn't name the national monument after herself. If I were to name it, I would say, "Really Hard Bike Ride Monument." [*Laughter*]

I want to thank Congressman Ken Calvert for joining us today. Ken, it's good to see you; proud of you. Congressman Gary Miller is with us today. Congressman, thank you. Mayor Beth Krom of city of Irvine—Madam Mayor, thank you for being

here. Thanks for serving. There you are, Mayor. Thank you; appreciate you coming. Thanks for serving. I had—last night—by the way, I had dinner last night with the mayor of Los Angeles and mayor of Long Beach and mayor of Anaheim and some other mayors that came.

Real important for the President to pay attention to people, what's on their mind, and that's what I'm here to do today. I want to share some things that's on my— first of all, Rick Warren, by the way, is here. Where are you, Rick? There you go. I appreciate you. Still got the calendar in the desk. [*Laughter*] Ambassador Argyros— good to see you, George. George served our country as the Ambassador to Spain. Thank you.

I got a lot on my mind these days. I want to share two thoughts with you. First, I want to talk about the war on terror. I wish I could report to you that the war on terror was over. It's not. There is still an enemy that wants to do us harm. And the most important job of the President of the United States is to protect the American people from that harm. That's—and I think about it all the time.

As you know, well, I make a lot of decisions, and at the core of my decisionmaking when it comes to protecting America is the lessons learned from September the 11th, 2001. My job is to use the resources of the United States to prevent such an attack from happening again. And the first lesson of September the 11th, 2001, is that we face an enemy that has no regard for innocent life, an enemy which has hijacked a great religion to suit their political needs.

And therefore, the only way to deal with them is to stay on the offense, to pressure them, and to bring them to justice, which is precisely what the United States of America is doing and will continue to do for the safety of the American people.

The second lesson is we must deny these folks safe haven. They need to find safe haven from which to plot and plan. We denied them safe haven in Afghanistan, and we're denying them safe haven in Iraq.

One of the important things that a President must do is to take the words of the enemy very seriously. And when the enemy speaks—and they speak quite often—we listen carefully. We listen to their aims and their objectives. These are not a kind of isolated, angry people. These are folks bound together by an ideology that is totalitarian in nature. They believe that capitalism produces weak societies. They want to spread their idea of life throughout the Middle East; they have stated so—in word after word. And they believe that with time, they can establish a safe haven in Iraq.

And here's the danger of having an enemy with a safe haven in Iraq: Iraq has got wealth; Iraq has—had weapons of mass destruction and has the knowledge as to how to produce weapons of mass destruction. And the confluence of a terrorist network with weapons of mass destruction is the biggest threat the United States of America faces. They have said it's just a matter of time.

And they've got a powerful weapon, by the way—the enemy does, and that is the willingness and capacity to kill innocent people. And they understand the United States of America is a compassionate nation. They view—I'm sure they view this as a weakness of our country; I happen to view it as a strength, that we value every life, that every person is precious. But they know, and it doesn't take much to realize that when you put carnage on our TV screens, it causes us to weep. It causes people, rightly, to say whether or not the cause is worth it. It's a legitimate question for the American people.

But it's very important for the American people to understand that they're trying to run us out of Iraq for a purpose. And the purpose is to be able to have safe haven from which to launch further attacks. And I understand it. And we've got a strategy in place to achieve victory.

Yesterday I went over to Twentynine Palms—I want to tell you something about the United States military. These young men and women are incredibly dedicated. They are motivated. They understand that we must defeat the enemy over there so we do not have to face them here at home. Most of them raised their hand to volunteer after September the 11th. Many of them have said, "I want to continue to serve our country." We're lucky to have people like them willing to serve. And the United States Government, whether you agree with my policy or not, must stand by our troops. When they're in harm's way, they deserve the best pay, the best equipment, and the best possible support.

And I told them—I told them they didn't have to worry about me. I believe we're going to win in Iraq. And a victory in Iraq will be a major blow to the totalitarian vision of bin Laden and his lieutenants—a major blow. One, it will be a tactical blow. We'll deny them that which they want. But secondly, it will be a major blow because, in the long term, the best way to defeat an ideology of hatred is with an ideology of hope.

I base a lot of my foreign policy decisions on some things that I think are true: One, I believe there's an Almighty; and secondly, I believe one of the great gifts of the Almighty is the desire in everybody's soul, regardless of what you look like or where you live, to be free. I believe liberty is universal. I believe people want to be free. And I know that democracies do not war with each other. And I know that the best way to defeat the enemy, the best way to defeat their ability to exploit hopelessness and despair is to give people a chance to live in a free society.

You know, the Iraqis went to the polls last December for the third time in one year. It seems like a decade ago, doesn't it? It seems like it was just an eternity ago that 12 million people defied terrorists, threats, and said, "We want to be free. We're sick and tired of a society that had been suppressed by a brutal tyrant. We want to go to the polls. We want to be self-governing." I wasn't surprised; I was pleased, but not surprised. If you believe that liberty exists in the soul of each person on the face of the Earth, it shouldn't surprise you that, given the chance, people will say, "We want to be free." And now the role of the United States is to stand by the courageous Iraqis as their democracy develops.

It's not easy work, by the way, to go from tyranny to democracy. We had kind of a round go ourself, if you look back at our history. My Secretary of State's relatives were enslaved in the United States even though we had a Constitution that said all were—that believed in the dignity, or at least proclaimed to believe in the dignity of all. The Articles of Confederation wasn't exactly a real smooth start for our Government to begin. And what you're watching on your TV screens is a new democracy emerging. And I had the privilege of calling the President of Iraq, the new Speaker of Iraq, and the Prime Minister-designee of Iraq, there at—in the comfort of my hotel room in Palm Desert—Palm Springs. And I can't tell you how heartened I was to hear their words.

First of all, they expressed great appreciation for the American people and our troops and the families of our troops. Secondly, to a person—this is a Kurd, a Shi'a, and a Sunni I'm talking to—each one of them said, "We want to have a national unity government. We're sick of the sectarian violence. We believe if you stand with us, we can achieve our objective of becoming a democracy that listens to the people." And I believe them. And I believe them. And I told them—I said, look, it's going to be up to you to make it work, but you can count on the United States of America because we believe in liberty and the capacity of liberty to change lives and to change the neighborhood for a more peaceful tomorrow.

This is a new chapter in our relationship. We had an important milestone when the unity Government was formed, and now there's a new chapter in the relationship, and we're moving forward.

You know, it's really important for people to be able to connect the concept of freedom to our security. And it's hard. It's hard, particularly in a day and age when every act of violence is put in your living room. And I know that. I fully understand the challenge I face as the Commander in Chief to describe to the American people why the sacrifice is worth it.

And perhaps the best way to do so is to share one of my favorite lessons of history with you, and that is that my relationship with Prime Minister Koizumi of Japan is a special relationship. He's an interesting guy. He's a—and he's a friend, and we work to keep the peace. We sit down—when we sit down, we talk about the importance of democracy developing in Iraq. The Japanese had troops, by the way, in Iraq to help this young country. We talked about North Korea. We talk about issues of peace. I find it so interesting and so ironic that those are the conversations I have with him, especially since 60 years ago, my dad and, I suspect, many of your relatives fought the Japanese as the enemy.

And so what happens between 18-year-old George H.W. Bush, Navy fighter pilot, signing up to fight the sworn enemy of Japan and his son sitting down to talk about the peace? What happened was, Japan adopted a Japanese-style democracy. Democracy can help change the world and lay the foundation for peace. And that's what's happening today. These are historic times. My job is to lead this Nation to protect you, and my job is to lay the foundation of peace for generations to come. And that is why I told those marines yesterday that we're going to complete the mission.

I got a lot of other things to talk about. I want to talk about immigration. So I saw my friend Brulte, ex-politician, you know?

Always a friend—he said, "People are wondering why you would come to Orange County to talk about immigration." [*Laughter*] And the answer is because that's what a leader does.

And I want to talk to you, tell you my thoughts about the subject. First of all, I understand it is an emotional subject. And it's really important that those of us who have microphones and can, you know, express ourselves, do so in a respectful way that recognizes we are a nation of immigrants, that we have had a grand tradition in this country of welcoming people into our society. And ours is a society that is able to take the newly arrived, and they become equally American. I believe that immigration has helped reinvigorate the soul of America. I know that when somebody comes to our country because he or she has a dream and is willing to work hard for that dream, it makes America a better place.

Now, first and foremost, the Federal Government has the role to enforce our border. The American people are right in saying to the Government, enforce the border. Listen, I was an old border Governor. I understand it's important to enforce our border, and we are. We got a lot of good people down there working hard on the border to keep people from coming—and contraband, or whatever—from coming into this country illegally. We've increased the number of Border Patrol. And I want to thank the Congresswoman and Congressmen here for being wise about providing resources to increase the number of patrol on the border. But that's not enough.

We've got to have modern equipment to be able to help people find people that are coming across a very long and difficult border—to protect; so we got infrared. Unmanned vehicles are being—aerial vehicles are being—UAVs are being deployed. I mean, we're now beginning to modernize our border so that the people we've asked to enforce the border have got the tools

necessary to do so. In parts of the rural border, there needs to be berms to prevent people from flying across in their SUVs, smuggling people into America. And we're strengthening this border. I'll tell you something that's interesting. Since 2001, 6 million people have been caught illegally trying to get in this country, and turned back—6 million people. So people are working down there, and they're working hard.

And I'm going to continue to work with Congress. I know these people from Congress are interested in providing the Border Patrol and those responsible for enforcing the border the tools necessary to do their job, and I thank you for that.

Secondly, we have got a problem with—we have a problem we're going to solve this year, by the way, of catching people from—non-Mexican illegal immigrants, and just sending them back into society. There wasn't enough detention beds. So you got the people down there working hard and 6 million people caught since 2001 and sent home. Well, most of the Mexican citizens who were caught trying to illegally come in the country just sent back to their country. But if you catch somebody from Central America coming back, you just can't send them back for a while, so there needs to be a place to detain them. We didn't have enough bedspace, and so we had catch-and-release. We're asking people to go down there and do their job, and they find somebody from Central America sneaking in, and they say, "Check back in with us in 45 days; come and see your immigration guy down there." [*Laughter*] And they weren't checking back in after 45 days. [*Laughter*] They were coming to work, see. They wanted to put food on the table for their families, and they weren't interested in checking back in.

And so it meant there was a lot of wasted effort by the Border Patrol. We're going to change that. One of the things that Congress has done, it's done a good job of providing additional money for bedspace and money to make sure that we can send people back home. You got people coming up who want to work, see. They're going broke at home; they want to put food on the table; they go to unbelievable lengths to come and feed their families. We're catching them; we're putting them back in—we're stopping that. Our job is to enforce this border—6 million people have been turned back. And we got a strategy in place to make sure that this border is as tight as it possibly can be.

Secondly, in order to make sure immigration laws work, you got to enforce the laws on the books, see. If it's illegal to hire somebody, then the Federal Government has got to enforce those laws. We're a nation of law. And by the way, you can be a nation of law and a compassionate nation at the same time. You don't have to be— [*applause*].

Now, the problem we have is, is you got some person out there in central Texas needing a worker, and he can't find a worker, an American. And so he says, "Look, is anybody—help me find somebody? I got something to do." This economy is growing, see—4.7 percent unemployment rate nationwide—pretty good numbers. And people are having trouble finding work that's— Americans won't do, and that's a fact of life. And so he says, "Why don't you send somebody over to help me?" And they show up, and they put a Social Security card out there, and it looks real. You know, our small-business owners are not document checkers. These are people trying to get ahead, and it's impossible to—[*applause*]. It's impossible to really effect the enforcement of our laws if people are able to use forged documents.

Now, we've increased the amount of manpower there to hold people to account for hiring illegals, but it is difficult to hold somebody, an employer to account if they're putting false papers on—the truth of the matter is, what's happened is, people are trying to come in this country, and we got smugglers smuggling them in. And

they're putting them in the back of 18-wheelers, stuffing human beings in the back of trucks, because they're come—people are coming to do jobs Americans won't do. They're putting people out in deserts. We've lost a lot of people, a lot of decent, hard-working people, trying to come in this country in the desert—losing their lives. These smugglers are *coyotes*; they're, kind of, preying on innocent life. And they've got a whole document forgery industry going on.

See, we made it such that an underground industry thrives on human beings, people coming to do work that the Americans will not do. And so I think that the best way to enforce our border—and the best way, besides making sure it's modern and we've got manpower and equipment down there, which we do, and it's increasing every week—is to come up with a rational plan that recognizes people coming here to work and let them do so on a temporary basis. That's why I'm for a temporary-worker program that will—that says to a person, "Here is a tamper-proof card that says you can come and do a job an American won't do, fill a need." Tamper-proof card, all of a sudden, makes interior enforcement work. In other words, we now know who's getting the cards, and we know they can't be tampered with. So when somebody—the guy says, "Show me your tamper-proof card before I hire you." And if they do, fine. But if they don't, say, "I'm not hiring you. You got to have the card to get work."

Secondly, we got a lot of people sneaking across the border to do jobs. It is really hard to enforce the border with people sneaking across to do jobs. Doesn't it make sense to have a rational, temporary-worker plan that says, you don't need to sneak across the border; you can come on a temporary basis to do a job Americans won't do? So you don't have to sneak across— so you don't have to pay money to a *coyote* that stuffs you in the back of a truck; so you don't have to burden our borders.

Look, we want our Border Patrol hunting down gun smugglers and dope runners. And it just seems rational to me and logical to me that says, okay, fine, you can come and do a job Americans won't do for a temporary period of time with a tamper-proof card.

All of a sudden, we've kind of taken this smuggling industry and dismantled it through rational policy. All of a sudden, we recognize that we want to treat people with respect. I know this is an emotional debate. And I can understand it's emotional. But one thing we cannot lose sight of is that we're talking about human beings, decent human beings that need to be treated with respect.

Massive deportation of the people here is unrealistic. It's just not going to work. You can hear people out there hollering, it's going to work. It's not going to work. It just—it's—and so therefore, what do we do with people who are here? And this is one of the really important questions Congress is going to have to deal with.

I thought the Senate had an interesting approach by saying that if you've been here for 5 years or less, you're treated one way; and 5 years or more, you're treated another. It's just an interesting concept that people need to think through, about what to do with people that have been here for quite a period of time.

Now, my attitude is this: I think that people ought to be, obviously, here to work on a temporary basis. The definition of temporary will be decided in the Halls of Congress.

Secondly, I believe that a person should never be granted automatic citizenship. And let me tell you why I believe that—that if you've been here, broken the law and have been here working, that it doesn't seem fair, to me, to say you're automatically a citizen, when somebody who has been here legally working is standing in line trying to become a citizen as well. In other words, there's the line for people.

But what I do think makes sense is that a person ought to be allowed to get in line. In other words, pay a penalty for being here illegally, commit him or herself to learn English, which is part of the American system, and get in the back of the line. In other words, there is a line of people waiting to become legal through the green card process. And it's by nationality. And if you're a citizen here, who has been here illegally, you pay a penalty; you learn English; and you get in line, but at the back—not the front. And if Congress wants a shorter line for this—for a particular nationality, they increase the number of green cards. If they want a longer line, they shrink the number of green cards per nationality.

This is an important debate for the American citizens to conduct. It's a debate that requires clear, rational thought. And it's really important for those of us in positions of responsibility to remember that we're a nation of law, a welcoming nation, a nation that honors people's traditions no matter where they're from, because we've got confidence in the capacity of our Nation to make us all Americans, one Nation under God.

And so that's what's on my mind today—got a lot of other things, if you're interested. But I got some time for some—I'd like to answer some questions, if you got any, or hear from you.

Yes, sir.

President's Analysis of First Term

Q. Morning, sir. [*Inaudible*]

The President. Pretty good. I think I'm doing all right, yes. [*Laughter*]

Q. I understand you get a lot of tough questions, and you're very candid person, so assuming that you agree with the fact that no one's perfect——

The President. I agree with that.

Q. Good.

The President. Especially me. [*Laughter*]

Q. I'd like to get your candid response to your perspective from the outside looking in, and now the inside looking out. Before you became President, obviously, you had some perceptions based on your family history, being Governor, what it would be like to be President of the U.S. Now that you are President and you've had a chance to go through the experience and you're in your second term, candidly, if you had it to do over, would there be anything that you'd do differently?

The President. I appreciate it. The fundamental question—the threshold question is, would I run in the first place? That's really the first question that one would ask. Now that I'm here, seeing what it's like, would I do it again? And the answer is, absolutely.

I have enjoyed this experience in a way that's hard for me to describe to you. Listen, there have been some rough moments. But it is an incredible honor to serve our country.

The second threshold question is, would I commit troops to protect the American people? It's really a fundamental question. Knowing what I know today, would I have done anything differently with our troops?

First, you got to know that the hardest decision for a President is to put anybody in harm's way—because I fully understand the consequences of making such a decision. I was at church yesterday in Twentynine Palms. In the pew that I was sitting in was a mother and stepfather grieving for a guy who lost his life, and I knew that I would have to deal with this as best as I possibly can.

I also wanted to let you know that it's before you commit troops that you must do everything you can to solve the problem diplomatically. And I can look you in the eye and tell you, I feel I've tried to solve the problem diplomatically to the max, and would have committed troops both in Afghanistan and Iraq knowing what I know today.

Obviously, as we look back—and every war plan is perfect until it meets the enemy. It's fine on paper until you actually start putting it into practice. And there is a—decisions like preparing an Iraqi Army for a—external threat. Well, it turns out, there may have been an external threat, but it's nothing compared to the internal threat. We got in and started trying to build some big reconstruction projects right off the bat. And it didn't make any sense, because it was easy for—they were—became convenient targets for the enemy. And so we started to decentralize our reconstruction—this kind of—I'm getting down to the minutia. But there are some tactics that—when I look back—that we could have done differently.

The fundamental question on the Iraq theater, though, is, did we put enough troops in there in the first place? That's the debate in Washington. I'm sure you've heard about it. It's a—here, let me just tell you what happened. I called Tommy Franks in with Don Rumsfeld and said, "Tommy, if we're going in, you design the plan, and you got what you need." I said—I remember the era when politicians were trying to run wars, people trying to fine-tune this or fine-tune that. One of the lessons of Vietnam, it seemed like to me—still does—is that you can't—people tried to make decisions on behalf of the military, which, I think, is a terrible precedent to make if you're the Commander in Chief. By the way, you can't run a war, you can't make decisions based upon polls and focus groups, either.

And so I told Tommy, I said, "You know you got what you need." And then it's my—then the fundamental question is, when I'm looking him in the eye, do I think he's comfortable telling the Commander in Chief what's real and isn't real? So I spent a lot of time with Tommy, and the first time I'm with him I'm trying to figure out whether or not he has got the ability to walk in the Oval Office—which can be kind of an intimidating place—and say, "Here's what I think, Mr. President."

I was comforted by the fact that Tommy and I were raised in the same part of the world. He went to Midland Lee High School with Laura, by the way. I felt like that there was kind of a kinship to begin with, and I'm confident, sir, that Tommy told me exactly what was on his mind. I believe that. And so therefore, the troop level that he suggested was the troop level necessary to do the job. And I support it strongly.

And I fully understand people are going to think back and, could you have done something different, or not different? And that's fair, and it's worthwhile. And we still have Members of Congress who are coming in—and they should—are coming in and say, "Mr. President, have you thought about this, or are you going to do that?" And we're constantly adjusting on the ground to meet an enemy which changes. But on the big decisions of sending the troops in, I'd have done it again.

Thank you. Great question.

Yes, sir.

Vision for the Future

Q. Good morning—I'm 14 years old, and I was wondering what America is going to be like in 10 years. [*Laughter*]

The President. Here's what America needs to be like—maybe 20—[*laughter*]—10 to 20. You need to be driving an automobile with hydrogen as the main source of power. And at the very least, with a hybrid—a plug-in battery of a hybrid vehicle that will you get—let you get the first 40 miles without using gasoline. In other words, between 10 to 20 years from now, we got to get off Middle Eastern oil. It's a problem.

You'll be able to see a technology, a technology that will be able—enable you to converse with somebody on long distance, and it seems like the person is right there in the room with you. I saw that at Cisco. It's an amazing technology that will mean that education changes to the better. You can hire a—you've got a—if

you got yourself a State like we got in Texas, that's rural, you can get a chemistry professor from one of the urban centers and put them on the screen, and it's like the professor is right in the room, teaching. There's a way to husband resources.

You'll have the capacity to interface with people around the world in a real-time basis. You'll be able to talk more clearly. Information will become even more powerful than it is today. And the fundamental question is, what do we do with that information? You'll be confronted with very difficult choices when it comes to science. The first choice we all have to deal with right off the bat is whether or not it's okay to destroy life to save life. In other words, as technology progresses, as this country of ours is more technologically advanced, you're going to be confronted with serious ethical choices. It's just—there will be a clash between morality and science that will present some really difficult decisions for people.

You'll be able to have a leader that can go and sit down with a duly elected leader of a major Middle Eastern country, saying, "How can we keep the peace together?" I believe you'll see there's a democracy movement moving across the Middle East over the next 10 years. Much of it's going to be led by women who don't want to be a second-class citizen in any society. I think you'll see a relationship between the United States and other great powers that will enable us to work together to be able to provide a stable platform.

What I hope you don't see is a nation that loses its nerve and becomes isolationist and protectionist. That's one of my concerns, so I put it in the State of the Union. It was such a concern that, instead of going with the—here are the 29 things we're going to do either for you or to you, it was—[*laughter*]—I talked about isolation and protectionism. It's very important for this Nation to be a confident nation and to remain a leader of the world. You cannot win the war on terror if you kind of pull back and say, let somebody else deal with it.

You can't do your duty as a nation that should subscribe to the theory that to whom much is given, much is required—and that duty is to help deal with HIV/AIDS, for example, on the continent of Africa. We have a duty to help feed the hungry, in my judgment.

What I hope you don't see is a nation that loses its confidence in the capacity to trade with countries like China. Hu Jintao was—came to visit, and we had a wonderful visit with him. But I know there are some Americans who wonder whether or not it's worth the effort to try to outcompete with China. They look at the statistics, and they worry about whether or not it is possible to compete with China. I say, you bet it's possible to compete with China. And not only can we compete with China, if we have a level playing field, we'll do just fine.

And so what I'm telling you is, I hope you have a nation that, at home, is one that is able to balance technology and ethical concerns, a nation, by the way—I hope those taxes remain low, see. One of the things you got to make sure—you got to have that proper balance between what Government really needs and money in your pocket.

And anyway—great question, by the way, for a 14-year-old guy. I'm not so sure if I were 14, I'd have been able to get that question out. I might have been a little nervous. [*Laughter*]

Let's see—yes, ma'am.

Community Health Centers

Q. First of all, I want to thank you for coming to Orange County. I don't know who said it wasn't a good idea, but I think it's a great idea. And we love you, so thank you for being here. I very much support your immigration plan. I think it's a good framework. But the one question I have—last year, my daughter fell and broke her hip—she's 12. And it was 5 hours in the emergency room at the hospital before she could see a doctor. And a lot of people in the ER were there because it was their primary medical facility——

The President. Correct.

Q. So in your plan, how do you plan to address health care and schools and so forth that are really impacted?

The President. Community health centers—we—this administration, working with the Congress, has funded the expansion of what's called community health centers. Community health centers are places for the poor and the indigent to get primary care so to do exactly what—to address the problem that you described, which is primary care in emergency rooms are costly. They are—it's not a cost-effective treatment—I guess it is once you get the treatment, but it's not cost-effective overall and, therefore, the advent of community health centers.

And I don't know if you've got them here in Orange County; I hope you do. I bet you do. You don't have any? Well, get to working, Congressman. [*Laughter*] But that's the best way, really, to be able to address the issue, whether it be for an immigrant who is here or anybody else that cannot afford health care. The best place to get primary care is not the emergency rooms. And so we've got a comprehensive strategy. And we're expanding them all across the country, and I'm surprised you don't have one here. I bet you do, and you just don't know it. And therefore, what needs to happen is there needs to be a campaign to explain what's available for people so that they don't go to the emergency rooms.

Yes, sir.

Cuba

Q. Mr. President, I emigrated from Cuba when I was about 9 years old—legally, I might add.

The President. Pedro Pan? Were you Pedro Pan?

Q. No.

The President. No? Okay.

Q. But anyway, besides marrying a wonderful woman and having two great sons, coming to this great land is the best thing that has ever happened to me, and I appreciate your comments on immigration. And my question to you, Mr. President, is that I would like to go to Cuba, to travel, to see—I want to go see my front door that was bullet-riddled when they were fighting Batista's guys. And I can't go there legally. And I don't understand, how can we trade with Vietnam—we lost over 50,000 Americans there—how can we trade with Communist China, we can't even go to Cuba? And I think that if the borders were opened up with Cuba and American enterprise got to go down there, I think Castro would fall like a rock off a cliff. And my question to you, sir, is why can't we open——

The President. Okay, here's why——

Q. Yes.

The President. Here's why: Fidel Castro has got the capacity to arbitrage your dollars to the advantage of his administration. You pay in dollars; he pays in Cuban money and collects the difference. So you go to a hotel in Havana. The money goes to the hotel, which has kind of got a deal with the Government in order to be there in the first place, and the workers get paid in a currency that's worthless compared to the U.S. dollar. And he makes the balance. And so, in all due respect, I have taken the position that trade with the country enables a tyrant to stay in power, as opposed to the opposite. If it's honest disagreement of opinion—I fully recognize—but that's why I made the decision I made. And anyway, my preacher, by the way, at St. John the Divine Church is a guy who came from Cuba at about the same age you did. You look a little younger than he is—but, nevertheless, that's why. That's why.

Yes, sir.

Immigration Reform

Q. As you said, you make a lot of important decisions on a day-by-day basis. I'm interested in the personal, as well as political, aspects of your counsel. Do you know any illegal-status individuals coming from Midland, Texas? What do they feel? And how do they counsel you on this? And also, politically, it's an intensely State-specific issue. Are the States most affected by illegal immigration speaking in a collective voice?

The President. Really good question. No, I don't believe I know anybody who is in Texas illegally. Had I hired somebody who had been here illegally, I guarantee you'd have read about it. [*Laughter*] Isn't that right, Elisabeth [Elisabeth Bumiller, New York Times]?

The interesting thing about this issue is—I want to be respectful in correcting you about the nature of the immigration debate—it is more widespread than you think. It really is. It's a—there's a lot of States who have been affected and maybe impacted in a much more different way than California and Texas has been. Texas and California are—have had a history of Latino presence. It's been a part of our heritage. And there's a—but there are many communities in the United States that for the first time are getting to become acquainted with the Latino heritage. And that probably impacts people even more significantly than parts of California and Texas; it really does. And so there is a universal concern about the issue. And what's really important about this issue is to try to set aside all the emotion and think about how to solve the problem in a rational, calm way.

But, no, it's—people—obviously, if you're from—I was talking to a Congressman from—I don't want to—they'll start trying to find the guy, so I'm not going to give them any hints, but—[*laughter*]. It's a guy. Anyway, but he said, "My town was, like, a small number of minorities, and now it's 50 percent Latino, and we don't know what to do." And this is a new phenomenon. This isn't something that's been around for decades. This is a brand new phenomenon.

And so there is a national concern about this issue; it really is. And obviously, it takes—it reflects the nature of the local community, gets—flares up one way or another around the country. But it's—there's a lot of people talking about it. And it's—we've got to get something done. I want a comprehensive bill. I don't want a—[*applause*].

Yes, sir, back there in the end zone.

Education

Q. Mr. President—for us to compete globally, we need to get better in math and science. What do you see as the role of the Federal Government in that regard?

The President. Yes, thanks. First, the role of the Federal Government is to make sure that we get it right at the early grades. And that's why I worked hard for and was extremely proud to sign the No Child Left Behind Act. And the No Child Left Behind Act starts with these basic premises: One, children can learn, and we ought to expect them to learn. And I know that sounds simple, but that's not the way it was in certain school districts. You look like a vet, and you know full well that in certain school districts—just move them through, man. What mattered was the age, not what—the level of knowledge.

Secondly, that accountability can be used effectively, particularly if it's designed at the local level. In other words, you can use an accountability system to determine whether a curriculum is working, or you can use an accountability system to determine how your school district is doing relative to the school district next door to you. You can use an accountability system to determine whether or not we're closing an achievement gap that needs to be closed if America is going to be a promising place for all people—not just some, but all people.

And so I worked with both Republicans and Democrats—it actually can happen sometimes in Washington that we're able to work together—and passed the No Child Left Behind Act, which said, in return for Federal money—in increasing amounts, by the way—on particularly Title I money, we expect you just to show us. We expect you to measure. You notice I didn't say, we expect you to administer the test we designed. I'm a local-control-of-schools person, and I knew that if a Federal test were designed, it could force people to behave according to the tests. In other words, you can cause people to lose their independence if you're the test designer. And so I said, California, design your own test and measure three through eight and post the results for everybody to see so that concerned citizens, when they saw failure, would have something to say to the—to you: "Change," or, "Thank you for doing what you're doing."

And as a result of measuring, I can report to you that math scores and science scores for fourth graders and reading scores—math and reading scores for fourth graders and eighth graders is on the rise, particularly amongst African American and Latino students.

Things are changing. It's amazing what happens when you say, there's accountability in the system. The problem is, as you know full well, but others may not, is that when a child gets to high school, our math and science skills, relative to other countries in the world, is abysmal. And it's not right. And we're not going to be able to compete successfully for the jobs of the 21st century. So here's the strategy: Apply the same rigor in math that we've applied in reading.

And here's what happens in early grades in reading: If you don't pass the test, there is supplemental service money to enable a child to get up to speed. In other words, we diagnose the problem, and we're actually providing money to solve the problem, and it's paying off. They ought to apply the same rigor to eighth grade math and ninth grade math—measure, find deficiencies, and provide extra money for school districts to make sure children get back up to speed.

Secondly, it is very important for there to be role models in classrooms that basically says, science and math are cool. They weren't too cool when I was going to school, you know. And therefore, one of the things we can do is have adjunct professors in classrooms. I went to a school with Margaret Spellings, who is the Secretary of Education, in Maryland the other day, and there were two NASA scientists there. And part of their job was not only to work at the NASA facility close by but to go into classrooms, to say to children, math and science are really important for you.

Thirdly, AP works—Advanced Placement. I bet you've got some good AP teachers. The Advanced Placement program is the way to set high standards for our children. And so therefore, the Federal Government ought to help train 70,000 AP teachers in classrooms. That says, we believe in setting high standards; we ought not to accept a system that doesn't continue to raise the bar and measure and to hold people to account.

Finally, there's—we've got an additional 1 million students on Pell grants. These are grants to help people who can afford—can't afford college, go to college. And they're very important—it's a very important tool to help people realize dreams. But I think we ought to enhance the Pell grants for those who take rigorous academics in high school for years one and two. And if you maintain a 3.0 grade point average and take science, math, or critical languages in third and fourth year of college, you ought to get an additional $4,000 on top of your Pell grant.

There is a strategy; the strategy of the Federal Government is a part of the strategy. The local school district is an integral part of the strategy. Thanks for being a superintendent; appreciate it.

Yes, sir.

Highway Infrastructure/Levees in California

Q. I'm a civil engineer, and we recently put out a report card for the Nation's infrastructure and—by the American Society of Civil Engineers. It was abysmal, is a word that you've used. And we're really concerned that our Nation is coming to a crisis on its infrastructure. And yet we seem to have problems with the Federal Government coming up with the funds that we need for the various parts of our transportation and our water resources.

The President. Well, I appreciate that very much. We passed a pretty good sized highway bill—like really big. And it's a 6-year bill, and so it's—we've got 5 more years to run on it. But it was a pretty interesting struggle about how much to spend and how much not to spend. And I think if you look at the history of that highway bill, pretty much the bill I signed was more than some thought was necessary.

I did talk to your Governor about an important subject, and that's the levees. And I appreciated his time the other day when I was in—up there in Cisco Systems. And we talked about the levees, and I said, we want to help. He's committed, by the way, to the—to rebuilding the infrastructure of California. It's a good, strong commitment. And it's what Governors do; they lead. But he said, "Look, we need to work together on this," and what he wanted—what they—his office suggested is that we allow the State of California to use the Corps of Engineers to pay the Federal share of levee rebuilding when the water goes down, and then through the budget process, reimburse the State of California. I agreed to that.

In other words, he—the Governor is concerned about being able to get started enough on levee—quick enough on levee repairs so we don't waste time. And part of the concern is there's a sharing arrangement between the Federal Government and the State government. And so I said, advance the State share—advance the Federal share through State money, and we'll reimburse you. That's an important beginning. In other words, the funding match is not an excuse. And secondly, he needs regulatory relief from Federal law and State law in order to be able to take advantage of the dry season to get the levees done. And so we're working with him on that.

And—but, no, I appreciate your concern. It's a—infrastructure is always a difficult issue. It's a Federal responsibility and a State and local responsibility. And I, frankly, feel like we've upheld our responsibility at the Federal level with the highway bill. There are other infrastructures we got to get built. We need a broadband highway all across America if we're going to end up being a competitive nation. I talked about the ability to be able to converse in real-time—speedy and very fast ways. But that requires us to make sure that broadband is effectively distributed all across the country—not just in big cities but out in rural America as well. And we're working hard to—on right-of-way issues and other issues to get broadband extensively spread throughout the country.

Yes, sir.

Immigration Reform

Q. Mr. President, I want to thank you for being here in Orange County. In your first term you came to Santa Ana, if you recall——

The President. Yes.

Q. ——we met with you at the Bowers Museum—it was a wonderful chat we've had with several of the leadership. Your honor, I—I'm calling you "your honor" already—[*laughter*]—anyway, we believe, as you know, the Latino community is America.

The President. Por cierto.

Q. Por cierto, exactamente. And we believe that the effort that you're putting forth as a comprehensive legislation is what we need in this country. We believe that the economy is going to be great. We be-

lieve that the issue that has been raised about the possible changes and possible funding for many infrastructures as well as emergency services will be there, because we're going to make these people to pay taxes, just like you and I. So we thank you for that.

We just want to ask you a question. What is it that we need to do, and you need to do, to make sure Congress will pass this comprehensive immigration bill?

The President. Well, that's starting right here. You know, they've been on vacation and now starting to work the issue. And one way to work it: Stand right here in front of these cameras in California, talking about it in a candid way. And I'm going to do my part to continue to call this Nation to responsible dialog and remind the United States Congress, we need to get a comprehensive bill passed.

The state of play right now is the Senate reached an important compromise, I thought, and it was—they had a chance to get a bill; it just got caught up in, in my judgment, needless politics. One of the problems we face in Washington is we've got too much needless politics. We got people who aren't willing to—they want to play—they want to make the other person look bad, as opposed to make the country look good. And I'm going to continue to call people, whether it be on Social Security reform or immigration reform, to think about the country first and put our political parties aside. And I'm confident, if we can do that, we'll come up with a rational plan that will make the country proud.

I'd like to stay here all day, but I got to go to Vegas. [*Laughter*] Something about what goes on there, stays there—or something like that. God bless you. Thanks for letting me come.

NOTE: The President spoke at 9:14 a.m. at the Hyatt Regency Irvine. In his remarks, he referred to Thomas Phelps, chairman of the board, and Lucetta Dunn, president, chief executive officer, and secretary, Orange

County Business Council; Catherine Campbell, wife of Representative John Campbell; Mayor Antonio R. Villaraigosa of Los Angeles, CA; Mayor Beverly O'Neill of Long Beach, CA; Mayor Curt Pringle of Anaheim, CA; Richard D. "Rick" Warren, pastor, Saddleback Church, Lake Forest, CA; Usama bin Laden, leader of the Al Qaida terrorist organization; President Jalal Talabani, Speaker of Parliament Mahmoud al-Mashhadani, and Prime Minister-designate Nuri al-Maliki of Iraq; former California State Senator James L. Brulte; Gen. Tommy R. Franks, USA, (Ret.), former commander, U.S. Central Command; President Hu Jintao of China; President Fidel Castro of Cuba; and Gov. Arnold Schwarzenegger of California. The Office of the Press Secretary also released a Spanish language transcript of these remarks.

Remarks at a Luncheon for Congressional Candidate Jon C. Porter in Las Vegas, Nevada
April 24, 2006

Thank you all very much. Please be seated. Thank you, Jon, for your kind introduction. First of all, I want to thank you all for supporting Jon Porter. I've gotten to know him well. He's the kind of person who does in office that which he says he's going to do on the campaign trail. He's a straight shooter, plain talker, who is getting the job done for the people of Nevada, and you need to send him back to the United States Congress.

You know, when you find somebody who can get the job done, somebody who focuses on results, somebody who doesn't play that Washington, DC, game of empty rhetoric and harsh talk and severe condemnation, it seems like it makes sense to give him a chance to continue to serve you in the United States Congress. This is a man who has performed while in office. And there's no doubt in my mind, he's one of the rising stars in the United States Congress. Jon Porter deserves to be reelected.

I not only feel that way, but Laura feels that way. She sends her very best. The truth of the matter is Porter said, "Why don't we invite Laura and leave you at home, George W." [*Laughter*] The guy has got good taste. But Laura is doing great. She sends her very best to our friends here in Nevada. I'm a lucky man to have her by my side during these incredibly important times. And I'm lucky to have a fellow like Jon Porter in the United States Congress to work together to make this country more secure, more prosperous, and more hopeful for all our citizens.

So I appreciate the elected officials from this great State being here, starting with your Governor. Governor, it's great to see you. Thanks for serving—Kenny Guinn, good buddy, good friend, who's done a fine job for this important State. I also am proud to be here with the United States Senator, John Ensign. Senator Ensign, I appreciate you being here. Thanks for bringing Darlene. Appreciate you coming, Darlene. Ensign is a straight shooter too. He's a really good man. He deserves to be reelected to the United States Senate from this important State.

Congressman Jim Gibbons from up north—good to see you, Jimmy. Thanks for coming. Proud you're here. The Lieutenant Governor, Lorraine Hunt, is with us. Madam Lieutenant Governor, thank you. The secretary of State, Dean Heller—it's good to see you, Mr. Secretary. Thanks for coming. Former Governor Bob List and his son Robert is here. Governor, thanks for coming. Party Chairman Paul Adams—I'm glad you're here, Mr. Chairman.

I want to thank all the grassroots activists who are here. You're the people who are going to be putting up the signs and making the phone calls and turning out the vote. See, what matters in these elections is, obviously, ability to get yourself on TV, but equally important is the need to make sure people go to the polls. And it's really important to rally those at the grassroots. And I want to thank you for the work that you have done, and I thank you for the work you're going to do to make sure this good man gets reelected to the United States Congress.

I also thank you all very much for contributing to Jon's campaign. Those of us who have run for office know full well that you can't possibly win without the support of people. And I've been blessed to have a lot of good folks here in the State of Nevada support my candidacies, for which I am most grateful. As I look around the room, I see many of you who have been to some of these fundraisers before on my behalf, and I thank you for keeping coming back for Jon's sake. But I really appreciate you helping him. It's not easy to serve in public office these days, but it makes it a lot easier when good folks such as yourself are willing to stand by good people who are willing to run for office. And so thanks for coming. Thanks for supporting Jon.

We've got some things to do. I appreciate a person who runs for office because he wants to get some things done. The most important thing we've got to do is to protect the American people. Our most important job—[*applause*]—as we learned firsthand on September the 11th, there's an enemy that lurks, that would like to destroy America because of what we stand for. And they're tough, and they are vicious. There's no need to try to ration with them or sit down and have discussions with them. The only way to deal with this enemy is to stay on the offense and bring them to

justice, which is precisely why I need Congressmen like Jon Porter by my side.

Today we saw again that the terrorists are willing to try to define the world the way they want to see it. There was bombings today in Egypt. I strongly condemn the killings that took place, the innocent life lost in Egypt. It was a heinous act against innocent civilians. The United States sends our condolences to the families of those who were killed. We keep those who were injured in our thoughts and prayers. And I assure the enemy this: We will stay on the offense; we will not waver; we will not tire; we will bring you to justice for the sake of peace and humanity.

I need people in Congress who understand the nature of this enemy. There are some that kind of feel like maybe these folks are just kind of angry citizens of the world who occasionally lash out. No, these folks are bound by a common ideology. They're totalitarian in nature. They've usurped a great religion to justify their acts of murder. They have territorial ambitions. They have designs. They believe that those of us in free societies are weak, and it's just a matter of time before we lose our nerve and withdraw. I am not going to lose my nerve. I'm going to stay on the offense. I will protect the American people. And I need people like Jon Porter who understand the stakes and stands by my side.

The central front on the war on terror is now Iraq. It is the place that the enemy has decided to fight the forces of freedom and liberty and peace. It's really important for those of us who represent you to take seriously the words of the enemy. The enemy has made it clear that it's just a matter of time before the United States leaves Iraq so that they're able to achieve their objective, which is to have a safe haven from which to launch attacks against moderate Muslim nations, and from which to launch attacks against the United States of America and our allies. That's what they have said.

The bad news for the enemy is that there are thousands and thousands and thousands of Iraqis who want to be free, who want to live in a unified society free of violence so their children can grow up in a hopeful world. I happen to believe—and a lot of my foreign policy is driven by my strong belief that liberty is universal, that all people desire to be free, and that when you free people, it is the best way to defeat an ideology of hate and hopelessness. Free societies will be peaceful societies. Free societies will listen to the hopes and aspirations of their people. And one of the most amazing things that's happening now is that a country that was under the thumb of a brutal tyrant is now emerging as a young, strong democracy. And the United States of America stands with them.

When I was in Palm Springs, I had the opportunity and the privilege to speak to the President of Iraq, the new Speaker of the Iraqi Assembly, and the Prime Minister-designate. One is a Kurd, one is a Sunni, and one is a Shi'a—all three of whom expressed their great appreciation for America and the sacrifices this country has made. All three of them talked about unifying their country to achieve a grand objective, and all three of them talked about the responsibility they have to make sure that the 12 million people who went to the polls are represented by a government of, by, and for the Iraqi people.

We're on our way to victory. The only way that we will lose in this central front on the war on terror is if we lose our nerve, is if we don't understand the great values that can help transform the world. It's important for me to have people in the United States Congress who don't listen to polls and focus groups but stand strong for what they think we're doing right. What we have done in Iraq is right, and we will achieve victory in Iraq, and Jon Porter understands that.

And finally, it's really important to have people in Congress who understand that when we put a man or a woman in harm's way, they deserve the full support of the United States Government. I want to thank Congressman Porter for standing strong for those who wear our uniform. We will make sure our troops have got the best training, the best pay, the best possible equipment so they can achieve their mission. The people of the Third Congressional District of Nevada must make sure you have a Congressman like Jon Porter who understands the obligations of the Government to support the United States military.

We've not only had some big challenges abroad, challenges that we will continue to confront head on, but we've had challenges here at home too. You might remember, although it may seem like a long time ago, but this country's economy has been through a lot. We went through a recession, a stock market correction, corporate scandals, a terrorist attack on our country, a war in Afghanistan and Iraq, major natural disasters. But we acted. Some of them like to talk in Washington, but we acted. We cut the taxes on the American people. We cut the taxes on small-business owners. We understand most jobs are created by small-business owners and that when somebody has more money in their pocket to save, invest, and spend, this economy grows. Our progrowth economic policies are working.

Today, the United States of America is growing faster than any major industrialized nation in the world. Our unemployment rate nationwide is 4.7 percent; the unemployment rate in the State of Nevada is 3.8 percent; 5.1 million new jobs have been added since August 2003. Real after-tax income, the income in the working people's pockets, is up over 8 percent for Americans since 2001. Productivity is high. Small businesses are growing. More people own a home than ever before in our Nation's history. This economy is strong, and we intend to keep it that way.

Oh, you're going to hear all kinds of talk out of Washington, DC, in this campaign— "Oh, don't worry, all we're going to do is just tax the rich." We've heard that kind of rhetoric before. Here's what I think we ought to do to keep this economy growing. I think we need to make the tax cuts we passed permanent, and Jon Porter understands that. You wait till these campaigns get going here around the country—"Well, we need to balance the budget by raising your taxes." That's not the way it works in Washington, DC. Yes, they'll raise the taxes all right, but they'll figure out new ways to spend your money. The best way to balance this budget is to keep progrowth economic policies in place and be wise about how we spend your money, and Jon Porter understands that.

I also want to thank you for helping on the line-item veto. That makes a lot of sense, doesn't it, to give the President the chance to make sure that the taxpayers are well represented in Washington, DC. I need fiscally sound people in our Nation's Capital, and Jon Porter is just such a Congressman.

Let me talk about another issue right quick. I spent a little time in California, which, by the way, was a fantastic experience. One of the problems that I'm concerned about is a nation that loses our nerve—that we become isolationist and protectionist, that we don't want to have any competition with anybody else, that we begin to wall ourselves off. That's not what I think. I think it's really important that we remain the economic leader in the world, for the sake of our folks, that we want to be preeminent when it comes to economic policy.

And so I was spending time talking about two issues that I think you'll find interesting. I know Jon is a strong supporter. One is to make sure that we're the technology country of the world, that we're on the leading edge of change. The Federal Government needs to double its commitment to basic research—research in the basic sciences, so that we're continuing to be the innovative—innovators of the world. We've got to be technologically competent. We've got to continue to lead.

We need to make the research and development tax credit a permanent part of the Tax Code. And we got to make sure that our kids have got the basics in math and science, so that the jobs of the 21st century stay right here in America. And Jon Porter understands the call.

We also got to do something about oil. You know, I know gas prices are high. There's no magic wand to wave. We'll make sure that the energy companies are pricing their product fairly. If we catch them gouging, if we catch them—unfair trade practices, we'll deal with them at the Federal Government. That's what you expect the Federal Government to do. But it's a sign for the American people to understand that we got to do something about our dependence upon oil.

Now, I appreciate Jon supporting the energy bill that we passed, which is a good, comprehensive approach. But there's more to do. I'm absolutely convinced that we're on the breakthrough of major technologies that will enable us to have plug-in batteries and hybrid vehicles that will enable you to drive your first 40 miles without using a drop of gasoline; that we'll be fueling our cars as a result of fuels made from switchgrass—we're already doing it from corn—but from other raw materials; that we'll have hydrogen-powered fuel cells within a 10-year period of time. I need people in the United States Congress who are farsighted, who understand the power of technology to make sure we become less dependent on foreign sources of oil.

Finally, let me talk right quick about health care, and then I'll liberate you. There's a stark choice in Washington, DC, amongst the elected officials there. There's a group of folks up there who believe that the Federal Government ought to make all the decisions for health care. They ought to tell you who the—what doctor you see and what procedures you can get. And they'll pay for it, of course. And that sounds really attractive, but I strongly reject that federalizing medicine will make our health care system better. And Jon joins me in that. The best health care system is one that takes care of the elderly and the poor and leaves the decisions in health care between the patients and the doctors. And that's the kind of health care system we strongly support.

Now, I understand hospitals being crowded, emergency rooms being crowded with people, and that's not a good use of our health care system. And that's why Jon and I are strong supporters of community health care centers. These are really important facilities where the poor and the indigent can get primary care without straining the emergency rooms of the hospitals.

We also understand we got a commitment to our seniors. Listen, the Medicare system was really an important system, but it needed reform; it needed a change. We'd pay $28,000 for ulcer surgery but not a dime for the pharmaceuticals that would prevent the ulcer surgery from being needed in the first place. It made no sense to have a health care system that was stuck in the past when medicine was becoming so modern.

I joined with people like Jon and the other Senators and Congressmen here to modernize the system. And thanks to our leadership, seniors now have got prescription drug coverage in Medicare.

But there are some other—there are practical things we need to do to deal with the cost of health care. One of them is to make sure that information technology becomes a crucial part of our medical systems all across our country. Jon Porter is one of the leaders in helping to modernize medicine. They say that we can probably trim the costs of health care by 30 percent when we bring information tech—now, think about this. We got doctors writing down their words on paper—they don't write very well to begin with—[*laughter*]— and they're passing the paper from one file to the next. Things get lost. Things are illegible. It's a very inefficient system, and we need to introduce information tech-

nology, starting at the Federal Government. And we're doing that, and Jon Porter is leading the way.

Secondly, health savings accounts work. Health savings accounts are a way for small-business companies to be able to afford health care. The uninsured—I remember the debate, Jon, when we were proposing health savings accounts, which are tax-free savings accounts coupled with catastrophic health care—with low-premium catastrophic health care. And they were saying, "This is only good for the rich." It's typical rhetoric out of Washington, of course, you know. It's just everything is kind of trivialized. They said, "Well, this is only good for the rich." Well, as a result of reforming health care, we now have got 3 million people who are now owners of health savings accounts, most of whom have got incomes of $50,000 or less, about a third of those who've signed up. The uninsured are finding a good product and a good way to insure themselves at affordable costs.

Thirdly, we've got to make sure small businesses, many of whom are having trouble paying—getting health care for their employees, have the capacity to pool risk across jurisdictional boundaries so they can buy insurance at the same discount big companies get to do. We're strong supporters of association health plans.

And finally, if you want to have a medical system that is affordable and available, we have got to do something about these junk lawsuits that are running good doctors out of business and running the prices of medicine up.

We got ideas about how to solve our Nation's problems. We do more than just think, though; we act. We get things done. We see problems, and we solve them. And I need people in the United States Congress who get rid of all the silliness in Washington, DC, and focus on solving our Nation's problems, and John Porter is such a man.

Thank you for coming, and God bless.

NOTE: The President spoke at 12:42 p.m. at the Venetian Resort Hotel Casino. In his remarks, he referred to Gov. Kenny C. Guinn of Nevada; Darlene Ensign, wife of Sen. John E. Ensign of Nevada; President Jalal Talabani, Speaker of Parliament Mahmoud al-Mashhadani, and Prime Minister-designate Nuri al-Maliki of Iraq.

Message on Armenian Remembrance Day
April 24, 2006

Today, we remember one of the horrible tragedies of the 20th century—the mass killings and forced exile of as many as 1.5 million Armenians in the final days of the Ottoman Empire in 1915. This was a tragedy for all humanity and one that we and the world must never forget.

We mourn this terrible chapter of history and recognize that it remains a source of pain for people in Armenia and for all those who believe in freedom, tolerance, and the dignity and value of every human life. It is a credit to the human spirit and generations of Armenians who live in Armenia, America, and around the globe that they have overcome this suffering and proudly preserved their centuries-old culture, traditions, and religion.

We praise the individuals in Armenia and Turkey who have sought to examine the historical events of this time with honesty and sensitivity. The analysis by the International Center for Transitional Justice, while not the final word, has made a significant contribution toward deepening our understanding of these events. We encourage dialogues, including through joint commissions, that strive for a shared understanding of these tragic events and move Armenia and Turkey towards normalized relations.

Today, we look with hope to a bright future for Armenia. Armenia's Millennium Challenge Compact reflects our confidence and the importance we place in Armenia making progress on democratic reform and advancement of free markets. We seek to help Armenia bolster its security and deepen its inclusion in the Euro-Atlantic family. We remain committed to securing a peaceful and lasting settlement of the Nagorno-Karabakh conflict and hope the leaders of Armenia and Azerbaijan will take bold steps to achieve this goal.

On this solemn day of remembrance, Laura and I express our deepest condolences to the Armenian people. Our nations stand together, determined to create a future of peace, prosperity, and freedom for the citizens of our countries and the world.

GEORGE W. BUSH

NOTE: An original was not available for verification of the content of this message.

Remarks to the Renewable Fuels Association
April 25, 2006

Thank you all. Bob, thanks for the introduction. It's always good to be introduced by somebody who is referred to as the "promoter in chief." [*Laughter*] For 25 years, the Renewable Fuels Association has been a tireless advocate for ethanol producers. Your advocacy is paying off. Renewable energy is one of the great stories of recent years, and it's going to be a bigger story in the years to come.

I like the idea of talking to people who are growing America's energy security. I like the idea of policy that combines agriculture and modern science with the energy needs of the American people. I'm here to talk to you about the contributions you are making, and I'm here to talk to you about the need for this country to get off our dependency of oil.

And so I want to thank Bob for the invitation. I want to thank Ron Miller, the chairman of the Renewable Fuels Association. I want to thank the board of directors and the members of the Renewable Fuels Association. I thank the members of my administration who are here—Clay Sell is the Deputy Secretary of Energy, who has joined us. I see Members of the United States Congress who are here. I appreciate Jack Kingston of Georgia, Jerry Weller of Illinois, and Gil Gutknecht of Minnesota for joining us. Thank you all for your interest in this very important subject.

Before I talk about energy, I do want to share with you some thoughts about the war on terror. I just got off of a conference—a videoconference with our strong ally Tony Blair, and we were talking about a major development that has taken place in the war on terror. After months of patient negotiations, Iraqi leaders reached an agreement on a unity government. And that's positive. This is a Government—this new leadership reflects the diversity of Iraq, and it reflects the will of the Iraqi people who defied the terrorists and killers and went to the polls last December. This new Government is an important milestone for a free Iraq.

And it's the beginning of a new chapter in our relationship with the Iraqi people. When I was in California over the weekend, I had the opportunity to speak to the three leaders—the President, the Speaker, and the Prime Minister-designate. I congratulated them on their courage and encouraged them to stand strong for the Iraqi people. I reminded them the people had voted, the people had expressed their de-sire for democracy and unity, and now there's a chance for these leaders to stand up and lead.

I told them that they have important responsibilities to their people to rebuild infrastructure and to improve their economy and enhance security. I was pleased with the response I got. It's important for the American people to know that these three leaders appreciate the sacrifice that our troops have made and that our taxpayers have made to help them realize a dream. And the dream is to live in a unified, free society. A free Iraq is in the interest of the United States of America. A free Iraq will be a part of laying the peace for generations to come. And a free Iraq will be a major defeat for the terrorists who still want to do us harm.

We've got good news here at home on the economic front too. This economy of ours is growing, and the entrepreneurial spirit in America is strong. We've cut the taxes for everybody who paid income taxes, and that tax relief is getting results. Last year, our economy grew faster than any major industrialized nation. Since August of 2003, this economy of ours has created 5.1 million new jobs. The unemployment rate nationwide is 4.7 percent. That's lower than the average rate of the sixties, seventies, eighties, and nineties. The American people are working.

Farm income is up. Agricultural exports are growing. Real after-tax income is up over 8 percent per American since 2001. Productivity is high. More people own a home than ever before in our Nation's history. This economy is strong, and we intend to keep it that way. And one way to keep it that way is to make the tax cuts permanent.

Yet amongst this hopeful—these hopeful signs, there's an area of serious concern, and that is high energy prices. And the prices that people are paying at the gas pumps reflect our addiction to oil. Addiction to oil is a matter of national security concerns. After all, today we get about 60 percent of our oil from foreign countries. That's up from 20 years ago where we got oil from—about 25 percent of our oil came from foreign countries. Now part of the problem is, is that some of the nations we rely on for oil have unstable governments or agendas that are hostile to the United States. These countries know we need their oil, and that reduces our influence, our ability to keep the peace in some areas. And so energy supply is a matter of national security. It's also a matter of economic security.

What people are seeing at their gasoline pumps reflects the global economy in which we live. See, when demand for oil goes up in China or India, two fast-growing economies, it affects the price of oil nation—worldwide. And when the price of crude oil goes up, because it's such an important part of the price of gasoline, the average citizen sees the price of gasoline go up at the pump.

Gasoline price increases are like a hidden tax on the working people. They're like a tax on our farmers. They're like a tax on small businesses. Energy prices are—energy experts predict gas prices are going to remain high throughout the summer, and that's going to be a continued strain on the American people.

And so the fundamental question is, what are we going to do? What can the Government do? One of the past responses by Government, particularly from the party of which I am not a member, has been to have—to propose price fixing or increase the taxes. Those plans haven't worked in the past. I think we need to follow suit on what we have been emphasizing, particularly through the energy bill, and that is to encourage conservation, to expand domestic production, and to develop alternative sources of energy like ethanol.

Signing the energy bill was one thing, and I want to thank the Members of Congress for getting a comprehensive energy bill to my desk, but there's a lot more to be done. First thing is to make sure

that the American consumers are treated fairly at the gas pump. Americans understand, by and large, that the price of crude oil is going up and that the prices are going up, but what they don't want and will not accept is manipulation of the market. And neither will I.

The Federal Trade Commission is investigating whether price of gasoline has been unfairly manipulated in any way. I'm also directing the Department of Justice to work with the FTC and the Energy Department to conduct inquiries into illegal manipulation or cheating related to the current gasoline prices. The FTC and the Attorney General are contacting 50 State attorney generals to offer technical assistance, to urge them to investigate possible illegal price manipulation within their jurisdictions. In other words, this administration is not going to tolerate manipulation. We expect our consumers to be treated fairly.

To reduce gas prices, our energy companies have got a role to play. Listen, at record prices, these energy companies have got large cash flows, and they need to reinvest those cash flows into expanding refining capacity or researching alternative energy sources or developing new technologies or expanding production in environmentally friendly ways. That's what the American people expect. We expect there to be strong reinvestment to help us with our economic security needs and our national security needs.

Record oil prices and large cash flows also mean that Congress has got to understand that these energy companies don't need unnecessary tax breaks like the write-offs of certain geological and geophysical expenditures or the use of taxpayers' money to subsidize energy companies' research into deep-water drilling. I'm looking forward to Congress to take about $2 billion of these tax breaks out of the budget over a 10-year period of time. Cash flows are up. Taxpayers don't need to be paying for certain of these expenses on behalf of the energy companies.

Second part of a good plan is to confront high gasoline prices, is to promote greater fuel efficiency. And the easiest way to promote fuel efficiency is to encourage drivers to purchase highly efficient hybrid or clean diesel vehicles which, by the way, can run on alternative energy sources. Hybrid vehicles run on a combination of a traditional engine and an electric battery. The twin sources of power allow hybrid cars and trucks to travel about twice as far on a gallon of fuel as gasoline-only vehicles. When people are driving hybrids, they're conserving energy.

Clean diesel vehicles take advantage of advances in diesel technology to run on 30 percent less fuel than gasoline vehicles do. More than 200,000 hybrid and clean diesel vehicles were sold in the United States last year. It's the highest sales in history. Congress wisely, in the energy bill, expanded a tax credit for purchases of hybrids and clean diesel vehicles up to—as much as up to $3,400 per purchase. That made sense.

If we're trying to conserve energy, if we want to become less dependent on oil, let's provide incentives for consumers to use less energy. The problem is that these tax credits apply to only a limited number of hybrid and clean diesel vehicles for each manufacturer. If the automakers sell more than their limit, new purchasers are not eligible for the full tax credit. And so here's an idea that can—gets more of these vehicles on the road, and that is to have Congress make all hybrid and clean diesel vehicles sold this year eligible for Federal tax credits. We want to encourage people to make wise choices when it comes to the automobiles they drive.

Third part of the plan to confront high gas prices is to boost our supplies of crude oil and gasoline. It makes sense when—the supply-and-demand world, if prices are high, it means demand is greater than supply. One way to ease price is to increase supply. One immediate way we can signal to people we're serious about increasing

supply is to stop making purchases or deposits to the Strategic Petroleum Reserve for a short period of time. I've directed the Department of Energy to defer filling the reserve this summer. Our strategic reserve is sufficiently large enough to guard against any major supply disruption over the next few months. So by deferring deposits until the fall, we'll leave a little more oil on the market. Every little bit helps.

We also need to ensure that there are not needless restrictions on our ability to get gasoline to the pump. Under Federal quality—air quality laws, some areas of the country are required to use fuel blend called reformulated gasoline. Now, as you well know, this year, we're going—undergoing a rapid transition in the primary ingredient in reformulated gas—from MTBE to ethanol. And I appreciate the role the ethanol producers are playing to meet this challenge. You're playing a vital role.

Yet State and local officials in some parts of our country worry about supply disruption for the short term. They worry about the sudden change from MTBE to ethanol—the ethanol producers won't be able to meet the demand. And that's causing the price of gasoline to go up some amount in their jurisdictions.

And some have contacted us to determine whether or not they can ask the EPA to waive local fuel requirements on a temporary basis. And I think it makes sense that they should be allowed to. So I'm directing EPA Administrator Johnson to use all his available authority to grant waivers that would relieve critical fuel supply shortages. And I do that for the sake of our consumers. If Johnson finds that he needs more authority to relieve the problem, we're going to work with Congress to obtain the authority he needs.

Secondly, we also need to confront the larger problem of too many localized fuel blends, which are called boutique fuels. The number of boutique fuels has expanded rapidly over the years, and America

now has an uncoordinated and overly complex set of fuel rules. And when you have
a uncoordinated, overly complex set of fuel
rules, it tends to cause the price to go
up.

And so I'm asking Director—directing
Administrator Johnson to bring the Governors together to form a task force on
boutique fuels. And the mission of this task
force will be to find ways to reduce the
number of boutique fuels and to increase
cooperation between States on gasoline
supply decisions. I want to simplify the
process for the sake of our consumers. And
then I'm asking them to get these recommendations to my desk, and I look forward to working with the United States
Congress to simplify the process.

Listen, we need to expand our refining
capacity. One of the problems we face is
that we've got tight supplies because we
haven't expanded refining capacity. There
hasn't been a new refinery built in 30 years.
If you're worried about the price of gasoline at the pump, it makes sense to try
to get more supply to the market. That
will be beneficial for American consumers,
to get more supply to the market.

Part of the reasons why we haven't expanded or built new refineries to the extent
we need to is because the permitting process in this country is extremely complicated.
Companies that want to upgrade their
equipment or expand their existing refineries or build new ones often have to wade
through long, bureaucratic delays and/or
lawsuits. To make this gasoline supply more
affordable and more secure, Congress
needs to allow refiners to make modifications on their refineries without having to
wait for years to get something—to get
their idea approved. I mean, if we want
more supply, let's reduce the paperwork
and the regulations.

Congress also needs to simplify and
speed up the permitting process for refinery construction and expansion. And so I'm
going to work with Congress. It's important
for Congress to cut through the red tape

and guarantee refinery construction permits
will be processed within a single year.

We also need to be mindful of the fact
that we can find additional crude oil in
our own country in environmentally friendly ways. The technology is such that we're
capable of environmentally sensitive exploration. We got tight crude oil supplies, and
it seems like it makes sense for us to use
our new technologies to find more crude,
particularly crude here at home.

One of the issues that you know, that
has been confronting Congress is ANWR.
And I fully recognize that the passage of
ANWR will not increase the oil supply immediately. But it's also important to understand that if ANWR had been law a decade
ago, America would be producing about a
million additional barrels of oil a day, and
that would increase our current level of
domestic supply by 20 percent. We've got
to be wise about energy policy here in
America. We've got to make sure that we
protect the environment, but we've also got
to make sure that we find additional supplies of crude oil in order to take the pressure off the price of crude, which takes
the pressure off the price of gasoline at
the pump.

And all I've outlined here today are interim strategies—short-term and interim
strategy. The truth of the matter is, the
long-term strategy is to power our automobiles with something other than oil,
something other than gasoline, which is derived from oil.

And we're making progress. In my State
of the Union Address, I talked about the
Advanced Energy Initiative. And this is an
aggressive plan, a wise way of using taxpayers' money to get us off our addiction
to oil. We have a unique opportunity to
continue forward with this plan.

Technology is the way, really, to help
us—to help change America for the better.
Years of investment in fuels like ethanol
have put us on the threshold of major
breakthroughs. And those breakthroughs
are becoming a reality for our consumers.

I set a goal to replace oil from around the world. The best way and the fastest way to do so is to expand the use of ethanol.

The Advanced Energy Initiative is focused on three promising ways to reduce gasoline consumption. One is increasing the use of ethanol; another is improving hybrid vehicles; and finally, one is developing hydrogen technology. All three go hand in hand; all three are an important part of a strategy to help us diversify away from hydrocarbons.

Ethanol is—has got the largest potential for immediate growth. Most people may not know this, but today, most of ethanol produced in America today is from corn. Most vehicles can use 10 percent ethanol—in their automobiles.

What's interesting that Americans don't realize, with a little bit of expenditure, we can convert a—kind of, the standard automobile to what's called a flex-fuel automobile. And that flex-fuel vehicle can use ethanol that is—or fuel that is 85 percent ethanol. It's amazing, isn't it? Without much cost, your automobile can be converted to be able to burn fuel with 85 percent ethanol, or a product made from corn grown right here in America.

Ethanol is a versatile fuel, and the benefits are easy to recognize when you think about it. One, the use of ethanol in our automobiles is good for the agricultural sector. I'm one of these people who believes when the agricultural sector is strong, America is strong. The way I like to put it, it would be a good thing when a President can sit there and say, "Gosh, we've got a lot of corn, and it means we're less dependent on foreign sources of oil."

Years back, they'd say, "Oh, gosh, we've got a lot of corn, worried about the price." Ethanol is good for our rural communities. It's good economic development for rural America. New biorefinery construction creates jobs and local tax revenues. When the farmer—when the family farmer is doing well, it's good for the local merchants.

Ethanol is good for the environment. I keep emphasizing that we can be good stewards of our environment and, at the same time, continue with our economic expansion. And ethanol will help meet that strategy. You don't have to choose between good environment and good economics. You can have both by the use of technology. And ethanol is an example of what I'm talking about. And ethanol is good for drivers. Ethanol is home-grown. Ethanol will replace gasoline consumption. It's a good—ethanol is good for the whole country, and we've been—[applause]. I thought you'd like that. [Laughter]

The ethanol industry is booming. It must be exciting to have worked for as long as you have on encouraging alternative sources of energy and then all of a sudden see the work come to fruition.

Last year, America used a record 4 billion gallons of ethanol. There are now 97 ethanol refineries in our country, and 9 of those are expanding. And 35 more are under construction. The ethanol industry is on the move, and America is better off for it.

Many of these refineries are in the Midwest, the Midwest because that is where the source of that—the feedstock for ethanol comes from. That happens to be corn. But what's really interesting is there are new plants springing up in unexpected areas like the Central Valley of California or Arizona or, of course, in the sugar fields of Hawaii. After all, sugar is also an important—can be used for ethanol. As a matter of fact, it's a very efficient feedstock for ethanol.

Ethanol required our support. In other words, to get this new industry going, it required a little nudge from the Federal Government. Since I took office, we've extended the tax credit to 51 cents per gallon for suppliers. We've created a new 10-cent per gallon tax credit to provide extra help to small ethanol producers and farmers, provided $85 million of loans and grants for the ethanol business ventures.

In other words, this is a collaborative effort. The Federal Government has got a role to play to encourage new industries that will help this Nation diversify away from oil. And so we're strongly committed to corn-based ethanol produced in America. Yet there—you got to recognize there are limits to how much corn can be used for ethanol. After all, we got to eat some, and the animals have got to eat.

And so I am committed to furthering technological research to find other ways, other sources for ethanol. We're working on research—strong research to figure out cellulosic ethanol that can be made from wood chips or stalks or switchgrass. These materials are sometimes waste products and are just simply thrown away. And doesn't it make sense for us—I think it does—to use taxpayers' money to determine whether or not we can use these new—these raw materials to make something out of nothing, so that we continue the advance of ethanol, so the market for ethanol expands throughout the United States.

We're spending—I proposed, and I'm working with these members of the Renewable Caucus—$150 million in next year's budget for research in advanced forms of ethanol. And that's a significant increase over previous levels. I think it makes sense. And surely the prices at the gas pump should say to the taxpayer, it makes sense for this Government to spend money on research and development to find alternative sources of energy.

I also support biodiesel fuel, which can substitute for regular diesel in cars, trucks, buses, and farm equipment. Last year, I went out to see a biodiesel refinery in Virginia that's making clean-burning fuel from soybean oil. And it was a really interesting process to watch. I don't know if you know this or not, but they're able to use waste products like recycled cooking grease to manufacture biodiesel. In other words, research and development has led to new alternative sources of energy like biodiesel. So that's one of the reasons why I signed into law the first ever Federal tax credit for biodiesel producers. In other words, we're interested in addressing our energy security needs on a variety of fronts. It makes sense for the United States to have a comprehensive strategy to help us diversify away from oil.

And so we also have got to understand that we got to research not only to find—to invest in ethanol and biodiesel, but part of a comprehensive strategy is to spend money on researching new battery technologies. And one of the really interesting opportunities available for the American consumer will be the ability to buy a plug-in hybrid vehicle that will be able to drive up to 40 miles on electricity. Seems to make sense to me, if we're trying to get us off gasoline, with crude oil as the main—as its main feedstock, then why wouldn't we explore ways to be able to have vehicles that use less gasoline? And one way to do so is to use electricity to power vehicles.

And we're pretty close to a breakthrough. We believe we're close to a technology that will make it possible to drive up to 40 miles on electricity alone. And then if you have to drive more than 40, then your gasoline kicks in.

But you can imagine what that will mean for a lot of drivers in big cities who, on a daily basis, they don't drive over 40 miles. And so therefore, a lot of drivers that are going back and forth from work in big cities won't be using gasoline. And that's going to help. We've got $31 million in our budget to speed up research and development into advanced battery technologies.

And finally, one other opportunity that is more long-run than ethanol or biodiesel or plug-in hybrid vehicles or encouraging people to buy the hybrids that are on the market today is hydrogen. We're spending about $1.2 billion over 5 years to research the use of hydrogen to power vehicles. And it makes a lot of sense when you think about it, because hydrogen produces zero emissions. The only emission it produces is water. And when I was out there in California, I visited the California Fuel Cell Partnership and saw buses and cars and SUVs that are driving on the highways out there powered by hydrogen. And the research and development money that we have spent has lowered the cost of hydrogen fuel cells; it's helped make them lighter. In other words, there's an industry coming, and it's an industry that will enable consumers to drive to work, just like we're doing today, but not rely on foreign sources of oil.

What I'm describing to you today is a strategy that recognizes the realities of the world in which we live. Our dependency on oil has created economic security issues for us and national security issues for us. And therefore, this country must use our brainpower and entrepreneurial spirit to diversify away from the hydrocarbon economy. You all have known this a lot longer than most Americans. You've known that we've needed to have this strategy, and that's why you're on the forefront of incredible changes that are taking place in this country.

You know, there's no doubt in my mind that one of these days, instead of people driving up to a gas station, they're going to be going up to a fueling station. And they'll be able to have choices to choose

from. Got a hydrogen-powered car, you'll be able to have that choice. If you want 85 percent, maybe someday 100 percent ethanol, that will be an option available too.

We owe it to the American people to be aggressive on price gouging now. We owe it to the American people to be promoting alternative ways to drive their car so as to make us less dependent on foreign sources of oil. We owe it to the American people to be aggressive in the use of technology so we can diversify away from the hydrocarbon society. And that's precisely what we're doing, and I'm glad to stand with you.

I appreciate your work for the United States of America. Thank you for letting me come by and talk to you, and may God bless you.

NOTE: The President spoke at 10:10 a.m. at the Marriott Wardman Park Hotel. In his remarks, he referred to Robert M. Dinneen, president and chief executive officer, Renewable Fuels Association; Prime Minister Tony Blair of the United Kingdom; and President Jalal Talabani, Speaker of Parliament Mahmoud al-Mashhadani, and Prime Minister-designate Nuri al-Maliki of Iraq. The Office of the Press Secretary also released a Spanish language transcript of these remarks.

Remarks Following a Briefing on the War on Terror
April 25, 2006

I want to thank the leadership of the United States Senate for joining me today. We have just been briefed from Baghdad about the formation of the unity Government. Not everybody around this table has agreed with certain aspects of this war on Iraq, but all of us agree that the formation of the unity Government is a very important moment in the history of a new Iraq.

I want to thank the Members for their strong support of our diplomatic mission and the United States military, who are engaged in heroic efforts to help this young country succeed. We're on our way to victory.

We've got more work to do. But the people—our troops need to know, and those working in the field need to know, there is a bipartisan desire for us to be successful in this very important theater in the war on terror.

I want to thank you, Senators, for coming. I appreciate your time. Thank you for your interest in this vital subject.

NOTE: The President spoke at 12:24 p.m. in the Roosevelt Room at the White House. A tape was not available for verification of the content of these remarks.

Remarks on Presenting the Commander in Chief's Trophy to the United States Naval Academy Midshipmen
April 25, 2006

Thank you. Be seated. Welcome to the White House. For you Navy fans, it's welcome to the White House again. [*Laughter*] I am so honored to welcome the Midshipmen from the United States Naval Academy here to the Rose Garden, and I congratulate you for winning your third straight Commander in Chief Trophy.

I also want to announce that Coach Johnson is now a member of the White House Frequent Visitors Club. [*Laughter*]

I appreciate, like a lot of Americans, the football rivalry between our military academies. It's truly one of the country's great traditions.

This season the Midshipmen have pretty well handled that rivalry in good shape, set a good standard by winning their games against the Air Force and the Army. But the greatest achievement for the Midshipmen will be when they join their counterparts from West Point and Colorado Springs to help us win the war on terror. So we're glad you all are here.

I'm particularly pleased to see members of the Naval Academy Board of Visitors who are also in the United States Congress, starting with Congressman Steny Hoyer. Thank you for coming, Steny. Congressman Mike McIntyre, proudly wearing that Navy hat; Congressman John Kline; as well, we have Congressman Ben Cardin. Thank you all for coming; proud you're here.

I appreciate the Secretary of the Navy, Don Winter, is with us. Mr. Secretary, thank you for coming. Admiral Ed Giambastiani—and for those of you who don't speak English too well, we call him Admiral G—happens to be the Vice Chairman of the Joint Chiefs of Staff and a fine man.

Vice Admiral—I mean, Admiral Mike Mullen, Chief of Naval Operations—we're proud you're here, Admiral Mullen. Thanks for the job you're doing. As well as Vice Admiral Rod Rempt—Rod, it's good to see you. Thank you for your service.

I appreciate the members of the Naval Academy football team who are here. I thank the members of the Naval Academy coaching staff who are here, particularly the head coach, who seems to have done a pretty good job. Might deserve a little pay raise if I might make a suggestion, you know what I'm saying? [*Laughter*] I don't know if you agree with that or not, Coach? Yes. [*Laughter*]

This team is a source of great pride for the brigade of Midshipmen and Navy fans everywhere. It will hold a special place in Navy football history. Nothing like making history.

This team showed great resilience. After losing its first two games in heartbreaking fashion, the team went on to win 8 of the next 10, and 5 of those were come-from-behind wins.

It took a little bit to be a Navy fan this year, a little patience, a little faith. But the faith paid off. The Poinsettia Bowl victory in San Diego was the first time a Navy team has ever won bowl games in back-to-back years. And we congratulate you for that feat. Pretty good deal to win big bowls and study hard and prepare to serve your Nation.

I appreciate the fact that the Navy offense led the nation in rushing. And second place to the Navy rushing record was the mighty Texas Longhorn team—[*laughter*]—whose offensive lineman only weighed about 40 pounds per person more.

Seniors on this team have led one of the most dramatic turnarounds in college football history. Navy has won 26 games in the past 3 seasons after winning just 3 games during the previous 3 years. The seniors are the sixth class in Academy history to have beaten Army all 4 years.

The lessons learned on the football field are preparing you all well for your next mission, which is winning the war against the terrorists. Every player on this team works hard to win on Saturday afternoons, but like the rest of your Midshipmen, your top priority is preparing to defend this Nation.

The thing I appreciate about the folks here is that when it came time to serve our country, they said, "I volunteer to serve. I recognize there's something more important than life, than serving myself. I want to serve my nation." And for that the American people are really grateful.

The leadership and discipline and teamwork you have learned not only on the field of play but at the Naval Academy will serve you well as you become commissioned officers in the world's finest military. And I assure you, and I know the Members of Congress assure you, we intend to keep our military the world's finest military.

This Nation is at war, a war we are going to win. And many of your teammates are serving and sacrificing at this very hour. And we send our prayers and best wishes to them. I appreciate the service of people like Marine First Lieutenant Brian Stann, a former Navy linebacker who was awarded the Silver Star last month for his actions and his bravery in Iraq.

Today, there are sailors and marines who are leading vital missions in Afghanistan and in Iraq and around the world. Graduates from the Naval Academy patrol the world's oceans to keep deadly weapons out of the hands of the terrorists and are maintaining America's command of the seas.

You protect our Nation, and equally importantly, you're laying the foundation of peace for a generation of Americans to come. And so we're here to first and foremost honor a really fine football team and present the Commander in Chief Trophy. But as well, we pay tribute to men and women who wear the uniform of the United States and say, thank you from the bottom of our collective hearts for protecting us.

My God bless the Midshipmen, and may God continue to bless our country.

NOTE: The President spoke at 2:05 p.m. in the Rose Garden at the White House. In his remarks, he referred to Paul Johnson, head coach, U.S. Naval Academy football team; and Vice Adm. Rodney P. Rempt, USN, Superintendent, U.S. Naval Academy.

Remarks Following a Meeting With Members of the Senate
April 25, 2006

I want to thank the Members of the United States Senate for joining on a very important discussion, and the discussion was how to get a comprehensive immigration bill out of the United States Senate.

I will report to the American people that there is a common desire to have a bill that enforces the border, a bill that has interior enforcement—in other words, a bill that will hold people to account for hiring somebody who is here illegally but a bill that also recognizes we must have a temporary-worker program, a bill that does not grant automatic amnesty to people but a bill that says, somebody who is working here on a legal basis has the right to get in line to become a citizen.

I thank the Members, both Republicans and Democrats, for taking on this really hard, hard assignment. It's important that we reform a system that is not working. It's important that we uphold the values of the United States of America. It's important that we treat people with dignity.

And I strongly believe that we have a chance to get an immigration bill that is comprehensive in nature to my desk before the end of this year.

And again, I want to thank both the Republicans and Democrats for the spirit of hard work. I particularly want to thank Senator Kennedy and Senator McCain for taking the lead on this important bill on the floor of the United States Senate. And I assured the Members that I look forward to working with them as they try to get a bill out of the Senate by Memorial Day and into conference.

Thank you all.

NOTE: The President spoke at 4:23 p.m. in the Cabinet Room at the White House. The Office of the Press Secretary also released a Spanish language transcript of these remarks.

Letter to the Speaker of the House of Representatives Transmitting a Request for Additional Funds To Support Recovery Efforts in the Gulf Coast
April 25, 2006

Dear Mr. Speaker:

To provide additional resources to assist the greater New Orleans region to continue its recovery from the devastation of Hurricane Katrina, I ask the Congress to consider the enclosed requests for an additional $2.2 billion for the Army Corps of Engineers (Corps), which is in addition to amounts requested on February 16th. This additional amount is offset by a $2.2 billion reduction in the amount requested on February 16th for the Federal Emergency Management Agency's Disaster Relief Fund.

The revised Corps request, which now totals $3.7 billion, replaces the previous supplemental request for the Corps that was submitted on February 16th. This revised request supports the Administration's commitment to further enhance the levee system in parts of the New Orleans area to meet Federal 100-year standards of protection.

I designate these proposals in the amounts requested herein as an emergency requirement.

The details of these requests are set forth in the enclosed letter from the Acting Director of the Office of Management and Budget.

Sincerely,

GEORGE W. BUSH

Remarks Announcing the Appointment of Tony Snow as White House Press Secretary
April 26, 2006

Good morning. I'm here in the briefing room to break some news. I've asked Tony Snow to serve as my new Press Secretary.

Tony already knows most of you, and he's agreed to take the job anyway. [*Laughter*] And I'm really glad he did. I'm confident Tony Snow will make an outstanding addition to this White House staff. I am confident he will help you do your job. My job is to make decisions, and his job is to help explain those decisions to the press corps and the American people.

He understands, like I understand, that the press is vital to our democracy. As a professional journalist, Tony Snow understands the importance of the relationship between Government and those whose job it is to cover the Government. He's going to work hard to provide you with timely information about my philosophy, my priorities, and the actions we're taking to implement our agenda.

He brings a long record of accomplishment to this position. He has spent a quarter of a century in the news business. He's worked in all three major media: print, radio, and television. He started his career in 1979 as an editorial writer for the Greensboro Record in North Carolina. He's going to—went on to write editorials for the Virginian-Pilot in Norfolk. He ran the editorial pages in both the Daily Press of Newport News and the Washington Times. He's written nationally syndicated columns for both the Detroit News and USA Today.

During his career in print journalism, he's been cited for his work by the Society of Professional Journalists, the Associated Press, and Gannett. For 7 years, he served as the host of "FOX News Sunday." Most recently, he reached Americans all across our country as the host of "The Tony Snow Show" on FOX News Radio and "Weekend Live with Tony Snow" on the FOX News Channel.

He's not afraid to express his own opinions. For those of you who have read his columns and listened to his radio show, he sometimes has disagreed with me. I asked him about those comments, and he said, "You should have heard what I said about the other guy." I like his perspective; I like the perspective he brings to this job, and I think you're going to like it too.

Tony knows what it's like to work inside the White House. In 1991, he took a break from journalism to serve as Director of Speechwriting and Deputy Assistant to the President for Media Affairs. He's taught children in Kenya. He belongs to a rock band called Beats Workin'. He's a man of courage; he's a man of integrity; he loves his family a lot. He is the loving husband of a fine wife and the father of three beautiful children.

He succeeds a decent and talented man in Scott McClellan. I've known Scott since he worked for me in Texas. We traveled our State together; we traveled our country together; and we have traveled the world together. We have also made history together. Scott should be enormously proud of his service to our Nation in an incredibly difficult job. I've always—I will always be grateful to him. I will always be proud to call him friend.

I appreciate Scott's offer to help Tony Snow prepare for his new job. And I'm proud to welcome Tony as part of our team.

Tony Snow. Well, Mr. President, I want to thank you for the honor of serving as Press Secretary. And just a couple of quick notes—I'm delighted to be here. One of the things I want to do is just make it clear that I—one of the reasons I took the job is not only because I believe in the

President, because believe it or not, I want to work with you. These are times that are going to be very challenging. We've got a lot of big issues ahead, and we've got a lot of important things that all of us are going to be covering together.

And I am very excited, and I can't wait. And I want to thank you, Mr. President, for the honor, and thank all you guys for your forbearance. And I look forward to working with you.

Thanks.

NOTE: The President spoke at 9:10 a.m. in the James S. Brady Press Briefing Room at the White House. In his remarks, he referred to Jill Snow, wife of Tony Snow, and their children, Kendall, Kristin, and Robbie.

Remarks Honoring the 2006 National and State Teachers of the Year
April 26, 2006

I was going to say, thank you, Laura, for those kind remarks. [*Laughter*] Please be seated. Thank you all. Welcome.

This is one of the great afternoons for Laura and me. We love to recognize our teachers. We really appreciate you coming. Actually, this is an annual event started by Harry Truman. And I'm glad to be a part of a tradition here at the White House, saying thanks to our teachers.

I admire teachers and like teachers so much, I married one. [*Laughter*] Laura is a great advocate for literacy and a strong supporter for America's teachers, and I'm really proud to have her by my side during these unbelievable times and this great experience of serving our country—other than being a fine introducer. [*Laughter*]

The thing I like about teaching is, teaching is such an optimistic profession. I know when teachers look out at their classrooms, you see more than a child at play or at study. You're able to see a child with big dreams and big hopes. You see future doctors and scientists and entrepreneurs and inventors, and I hope you see even a teacher or two.

You dedicated your lives to the formation of young minds. You're giving our children the skills they need to succeed in life and equally important, the courage and the drive to realize those dreams. Our Nation is grateful for your hard work. We appreciate what you do, and we are honored you're here at the White House.

I want to thank our Secretary of Education, Margaret Spellings. She's been a long-time friend. She believes strongly in the classroom teacher, and she believes in the potential of every child.

I'm pleased to recognize Senator Sam Brownback, for the State of Kansas. Welcome. I'm glad you're here—and his wife, Mary; thank you for coming. As well as Congressman Dennis Moore from Kansas and Stephene, thank you all for taking time to honor the teachers who are here.

I appreciate the National Teacher of the Year Finalists: Sam Bennett from Florida— say hello to the Governor—[*laughter*]—Ron Poplau of Kansas—no wonder you all are here—and Susan Barnard of Washington State. We're really glad you're here. Congratulations on setting such a fine example.

Everybody here has been introduced to Kim Oliver, but you haven't met her parents, Vincent and Veronica. Thank you all very much—brothers, cousins, and significant other. [*Laughter*]

I want to thank all the Teachers of the Year from around our country who are here. I really—Laura and I really enjoyed having our picture with you. It's just a brief moment to say thanks. But nevertheless, it's thanks from the bottom of our hearts. And it really means a lot you're here.

I thank Dr. Tom Houlihan, who is the executive director of the Council of Chief State School Officers. That's one of the sponsoring organizations. Thank you for your service, Tom.

Margery Mayer, of the Scholastic Education—Scholastic Inc. I want to thank Margery for being here. That's also a sponsoring organization of this event.

Kathleen Murphy is the president of ING, is here with us, as well as Tom Waldron, who is the executive vice president. These are the sponsoring groups of this important occasion.

I also want to thank the chief state school officers who are with us. Good to see you all. Nice going. Hiring and promoting good teachers is a really important part of your job. I want you to know that we know that being a teacher is difficult work. It's a hard job. It's a job that requires compassion and determination and extraordinary patience. And as Laura hinted, or maybe didn't hint, I was probably one of those kind that tested your patience. [*Laughter*]

You're helping young people to learn the basics of reading and writing and adding and subtracting. You're serving as mentors and, probably most importantly, as role models. You help kindle young imaginations, and you inspire a love of learning. It's a pretty significant job description, when you think about it. And the teachers we honor here today are excelling at that job.

Your daily efforts help young Americans grow into successful adults. In other words, you're building the future for the country. We ask a lot of our teachers, and we owe you a lot in return. Education is my top domestic priority. And when I first came to office, I worked with members of both political parties—believe it or not, it's possible here in Washington to occasionally do that—to increase funding from the Federal level but also to pass the No Child Left Behind Act. The spirit of the No Child Left Behind Act basically says, society has a deep obligation to challenge the soft bigotry of low expectations, that we believe every child can learn, and therefore, we believe it makes sense to determine whether or not every child is learning. And if not, there ought to be extra help so that no child in our society is left behind.

We're beginning to see good results, thanks to our Nation's teachers. The 2005 Nation's Report Card showed America's fourth graders are posting the best scores in reading and math in the history of the test. African American and Hispanic fourth graders set records in reading and math last year. America's eighth graders earned the best math scores ever recorded. Eighth grade Hispanic and African American students achieved their highest math scores ever. We're making really important strides toward closing an achievement gap in America, and I want to thank our teachers for your hard work.

There's more work to be done, obviously. I've recently launched the American Competitiveness Initiative, which will help our students do better in math and science. We need to train 70,000 high school teachers to lead AP courses in math and science. I know we've got some AP teachers here, and I want to thank you for that.

We need to bring 30,000 math and science professionals into our classrooms to send a message to our children: It's okay to be a mathematician or a scientist—as a matter of fact, it's cool. We want to make sure that we help students who struggle with math get extra help to make sure that—to make sure they have a chance to be able to earn the high-wage jobs of the 21st century. If we ensure that America's children have the skills they need to succeed in life, we will make sure America succeeds in the world.

Improving the quality of education for young Americans requires good laws and good policies, but ultimately it depends on good teachers. And that is why we're here on the South Lawn, to honor really good teachers.

The Teacher of the Year, Kim Oliver, teaches kindergarten at Broad Acres Elementary School in Silver Spring, Maryland. Broad Acres is Montgomery County's highest poverty school, a place where 90 percent of the children qualify for federally-subsidized meals and about 75 percent have parents who do not speak English at home.

It's a school filled with the kind of students that inspired Kim Oliver to become a teacher. Kim decided to become a teacher at a young age. It's really interesting for teachers to hear what she said. She said, "As a young child, I loved and admired my day care teacher, Mrs. Chandler. I wanted to be just like her. Mrs. Chandler made me feel special, as if I were the only child in her class."

Kim Oliver had many friends growing up who came from unstable and impoverished homes. She says, "I watched so many of my friends live up to the low expectations that were set for them. To this day, I find myself wondering, what if my disadvantaged friends had 12 years worth of Mrs. Chandlers in their lives?" Kim went on to say, "I chose to become a teacher to motivate and inspire the neediest students, who many have written off, and let them know they can achieve and succeed in life regardless of what the statistics may show."

I love that attitude. I think you're beginning to get the drift of why she's the Teacher of the Year. When Kim Oliver arrived at Broad Acres in 2000, the school was threatened with forced restructuring by the State as a result of poor academic performance. Ms. Oliver took a leadership role at the school. That's what good teachers do; they take the lead. She became a teacher-leader and helped lead a collaborative effort to improve the curriculum, instruction, and assessment. She helped establish instructional planning sessions and formal procedures to examine student work and improve student performance.

She noticed that many parents at the school lacked the language skills to be able to read to their children and to be able to help with their school work. And so she and her colleagues purchased cassette players and recorded books on tape for the students to take home and share with their families, which made it a lot easier for parents who struggle with English to help their children.

Kim Oliver also organized a regular "Books and Supper Night," where families could check out books from the library and read together before sharing a dinner, which fostered learning and family involvement in their children's education. She knows what good teachers know: If you can get the parents involved in the child's education, you have a much better chance of succeeding. She set high expectations. Good teachers set high expectations. She provided needed assistance. She involved families, and she helped turn that school around.

Within 2 years of her arrival, kindergarten students at Broad Acres were mastering early reading skills at higher rates than other schools in the district. After 3 years, Broad Acres students were meeting or exceeding all requirements of the No Child Left Behind Act. There were dramatic increases in reading and math scores for the school's second graders.

The Superintendent of Schools in Montgomery County says this about the impact Kim Oliver has had: "She has a rare gift for touching hearts and minds, inspiring in her students to aim high and believe in their potential." A Broad Acres parent says, "She knows how to talk to the children so they will listen." And all her students know that she cares about them. She made them all feel like they were smart and could learn anything. One of her colleagues says, "When you walk into Ms. Oliver's classroom, one cannot help but notice that this is a special place." She is dedicated to her school community and committed to excellence, and she has been an instrumental force in improving student achievement at her school.

Kim says the reason her students are achieving is simple: "I have high expectations for each of them. I teach them that they can accomplish anything with hard work and persistence."

Kim Oliver understands that the key to helping children succeed is fighting the soft bigotry of low expectations. When a teacher believes that a child can learn, it's amazing what happens; a student believes that he or she can learn.

America is blessed to have teachers like Kim Oliver. We're blessed to have teachers like all those who are gathered here at the White House. We thank you for the love and devotion you've shown our children each day.

May God continue to bless your work, and may God continue to bless our country. Thank you for coming.

NOTE: The President spoke at approximately 1:46 p.m. on the South Lawn at the White House. In his remarks, he referred to Stephene Moore, wife of Congressman Dennis Moore; Gov. Jeb Bush of Florida; Margery W. Mayer, executive vice president and president, Scholastic Education; and Jerry D. Weast, superintendent, Montgomery County Public Schools. The transcript released by the Office of the Press Secretary also included the remarks of the First Lady, who introduced the President.

Message to the Congress Transmitting an Executive Order Blocking Property of Additional Persons in Connection With the National Emergency With Respect to Syria
April 26, 2006

To the Congress of the United States:

Pursuant to the International Emergency Economic Powers Act, as amended (50 U.S.C. 1701 *et seq.*) (IEEPA), I hereby report that I have issued an Executive Order blocking property of persons in connection with the terrorist act in Beirut, Lebanon, on February 14, 2005, that resulted in the assassination of former Lebanese Prime Minister Rafiq Hariri and the deaths of 22 others, and other bombings or assassination attempts in Lebanon since October 1, 2004, that are related to Hariri's assassination or that implicate the Government of Syria or its officers or agents. I issued this order to take additional steps with respect to the national emergency declared in Executive Order 13338 of May 11, 2004, concerning certain actions of the Government of Syria. In Executive Order 13338, I determined that the actions of the Government of Syria in supporting terrorism, continuing its occupation of Lebanon, pursuing weapons of mass destruction, and undermining United States and international efforts in Iraq constituted an unusual and extraordinary threat to the national security, foreign policy, and economy of the United States, and declared a national emergency to deal with that threat.

The United Nations Security Council, in Resolution 1595 of April 7, 2005, established the international independent investigation Commission (the "Commission"), reiterated its call for the strict respect of the sovereignty of Lebanon, and reaffirmed its unequivocal condemnation of the February 14, 2005, terrorist bombing that killed Lebanese Prime Minister Rafiq Hariri and 22 others. The Commission's charter included identifying the bombing perpetrators, sponsors, organizers, and accomplices. United Nations Security Council Resolution (UNSCR) 1636 of October 31, 2005, called upon all States to provide necessary assistance to the Commission concerning its investigation into the February 14, 2005, terrorist bombing and to freeze the assets of those persons designated by the Commission or the Government of Lebanon as suspected of involvement in this terrorist act, upon notification of such designation to, and agreement of, the Committee of the Security Council established by UNSCR 1636. United Nations Security Council Resolution 1644 of December 15, 2005, condemned other terrorist attacks in Lebanon since October 2004 and reaffirmed that all those involved in these attacks must be held accountable for these crimes, and in doing so, authorized the Commission to extend its technical assistance to Lebanese authorities with regard to their investigations regarding the terrorist attacks perpetrated in Lebanon since October 1, 2004.

In view of UNSCR 1636, my new order takes additional steps with respect to the national emergency declared in Executive Order 13338 by blocking the property and interests in property of persons determined by the Secretary of the Treasury, after consultation with the Secretary of State, to be, or to have been, involved in the planning, sponsoring, organizing, or perpetrating of the terrorist act on February 14, 2005, that resulted in the assassination of former Prime Minister Rafiq Hariri and the deaths of 22 others, or any other bombing, assassination, or assassination attempt in Lebanon since October 1, 2004, that is related to Hariri's assassination or that implicates the Government of Syria or its officers and agents, or to have obstructed or otherwise impeded the work of the Commission. The order further authorizes the Secretary of the Treasury, after consultation with the Secretary of State, to designate for blocking those persons determined to have materially assisted, sponsored, or provided financial, material, or technological support for, or goods or services in support of, any such terrorist act, bombings, or assassination attempts, or any person designated pursuant to this order, or to be owned or controlled by, or acting or purporting to act for or on behalf of, directly or indirectly, any person designated pursuant to this order.

I delegated to the Secretary of the Treasury, after consultation with the Secretary of State, the authority to take such actions, including the promulgation of rules and regulations, and to employ all powers granted to the President by IEEPA and the United Nations Participation Act, as amended (22 U.S.C. 287c), as may be necessary to carry out the purposes of my order. The order was effective at 12:01 a.m. eastern daylight time on April 26, 2006.

I am enclosing a copy of the Executive Order I have issued.

GEORGE W. BUSH

The White House,
April 26, 2006.

NOTE: The Executive order is listed in Appendix D at the end of this volume.

Remarks Following a Visit to a Hurricane Damaged Home in New Orleans, Louisiana
April 27, 2006

The President. Mrs. Williams has invited myself and the mayor and the Governor and Congressman into her home, which had been wiped out by the storm. And she went to Texas for a while, and she made it clear to me she was glad to be out of Texas and back home. [*Laughter*]

But the amazing thing that's happened in her home is that there are people from across the country here who are helping to rebuild it. Catholic Charities, in this case, has provided the volunteers to help Ms. Williams reclaim her life. And so I'd like to first start by thanking the volunteers who are here in the home. I want to thank them for setting such a good example.

The man who's running the site here said that they need 2,500 more volunteers to come down to New Orleans to help people get back on their feet. If you're interested in helping the victims of Katrina, if you're interested in helping them get back on their feet, come down here and volunteer. A good place to start is in Catholic Charities. You can get right there on the web page; they'll find work for you. They'll give you a chance to contribute something to your country.

This is National Volunteer Week, and there are people like the good folks standing behind me here who are volunteering all across the country, making a difference. And for those of you who are volunteering, thank you from the bottom of our hearts for making our society a better place.

I had a good visit with the Governor and the mayor as well. One of the things that we're working on is to make sure that we've learned the lessons from Katrina—we've learned lessons at the Federal level and State level and the local level. And we're now working closely together in preparation of the upcoming hurricane season. Secretary Chertoff was down here working with the Governor just to make sure that communications are clear, that equipment will be prepositioned, that the communications system, which failed last time, will be up and running should there be another catastrophic storm.

Listen, all of us in positions of responsibility appreciate those who are working to help us understand how to do our jobs better. And we pray there is no hurricane this coming year, but we are working together to make sure that if there is one, the response will be as efficient as possible.

I'm also talking to the Governor and the mayor about the reconstruction effort going on here in Louisiana. I applaud the Governor for putting forth a housing plan that she'll be submitting to the legislature soon. I call upon the Congress to make sure that the $4.2 billion of CDBG money in the supplemental appropriations is held intact for the people of Louisiana. This money is going to be vital to making sure that the vision of the Governor and the mayor gets implemented as people are able to come back and start reclaiming their lives.

We talked about the levees, and I told the Governor and the mayor earlier on that we would work to have these levees pre-Katrina—better than pre-Katrina by June 1st. We are. There's still money in the supplemental that needs to be passed to make sure that we're able to fulfill our promise, to make sure that the levees, by September of '07, are even better than pre-Katrina. We've got a strategy to help the good folks down here rebuild. Part of it has to do with funding; part of it has to do with housing; and a lot of it has to do with encouraging volunteers from around the United States to come down and help people like Ms. Williams.

So we're proud to be here with you, Ms. Williams, and God bless you.

Ethel Williams. I'm proud to be here, Mr. President. And I won't ever—I can't ever forget you.

The President. You need to forget—remember those people a lot quicker than you're remembering me, because they're the ones who are going to help. She promised to cook me a meal——

Ms. Williams. Oh, yes—[*laughter*]——

The President. Once you get the house up and running.

Ms. Williams. ——and I thank all the volunteers and everybody that is helping to make everything work.

The President. Thank you all very much.

NOTE: The President spoke at 11:58 a.m. on Pauline Street. In his remarks, he referred to Mayor C. Ray Nagin of New Orleans, LA; and Gov. Kathleen Babineaux Blanco of Louisiana.

Remarks During a Visit to the Hands On Gulf Coast Civic Action Center in Biloxi, Mississippi
April 27, 2006

The President. I've come to the conclusion that I'm at a terrific place, where people are here bound by a common desire to show compassion to their neighbors in need. I really thank you. It's a compassion commune—[*laughter*]—where people are united by a singular purpose and setting a great example. Everybody—most people I talk to say, "Well, it makes me feel better." The truth of the matter is, when you volunteer to serve somebody in need, it does make you feel better.

So for all those in our country who are wondering whether or not they can make a difference in somebody's life, the answer is, all you have to do is look at these people here.

Audience member. Volunteer!

The President. All right. Thank you.

NOTE: The President spoke at 3:17 p.m.

Remarks During a Visit to a BP Gas Station in Biloxi
April 27, 2006

Listen, we've got people like this that are working for a living, who are paying higher prices for their gasoline—it's like a tax. And I talked the other day about things we can do. The first thing is to make sure that nobody is getting cheated. One of the roles of the Federal Government is to make sure that you're taken care of.

We need more refining capacity. One of the reasons why you've got high prices is the demand is greater than supply. And when demand is greater than supply, the price goes up. They've got in Pascagoula a really fine refinery. I remember coming over with the Governor, the place was shut down. They got it up and running, and we hope we can put a law in place that will encourage them to expand refining capacity. We've got a problem because we're dependent on oil from overseas. And oil is the main reason—the price of oil is the main thing that drives the cost of gasoline.

One of the things we've got to do is make these trucks run on ethanol—and batteries that won't require gasoline. That's what the future is going to be.

Congress is debating some other ideas. And one idea is to give me the capacity to raise CAFE standards on automobiles. I encourage them to give me that authority. It's an authority that I'd use for light trucks. And I intend to use it wisely, if Congress would give me that authority.

Again, I want to thank you for letting me come by and say hello. It seems like everybody is getting better down here. Thank you.

NOTE: The President spoke at 3:33 p.m. In his remarks, he referred to Gov. Haley Barbour of Mississippi.

Statement on the Framework Agreement With Canada on Softwood Lumber Trade
April 27, 2006

I am pleased that the United States and Canada concluded a framework agreement today to resolve the long-standing dispute on softwood lumber trade. This agreement shows how NAFTA partners can overcome differences and work together. The United States close ties with our good friend and northern neighbor made this agreement possible. I applaud Prime Minister Harper's leadership in resolving this issue, and I am grateful to the lead negotiators on both sides, Ambassador Susan C. Schwab for the United States and Ambassador Michael Wilson of Canada.

Message to the Congress Transmitting an Executive Order Blocking Property of Persons in Connection With the Conflict in Sudan's Darfur Region
April 27, 2006

To the Congress of the United States:

Pursuant to the International Emergency Economic Powers Act (IEEPA), I hereby report that I have issued an Executive Order (the "order") blocking the property of persons in connection with the conflict in Sudan's Darfur region. In that order, I have expanded the scope of the national emergency declared in Executive Order 13067 of November 3, 1997, with respect to the policies and actions of the Government of Sudan, to address the unusual and extraordinary threat to the national security and foreign policy of the United States posed by the actions and circumstances involving Darfur, as described below.

The United Nations Security Council, in Resolution 1591 of March 29, 2005, condemned the continued violations of the N'djamena Ceasefire Agreement of April 8, 2004, and the Abuja Humanitarian and Security Protocols of November 9, 2004, by all sides in Darfur, as well as the deterioration of the security situation and the negative impact this has had on humanitarian assistance efforts. I also note that the United Nations Security Council has strongly condemned the continued viola-tions of human rights and international humanitarian law in Sudan's Darfur region and, in particular, the continuation of violence against civilians and sexual violence against women and girls.

United Nations Security Council Resolution (UNSCR) 1591 determined that the situation in Darfur constitutes a threat to international peace and security in the region and called on Member States to take certain measures against persons responsible for the continuing conflict. The United Nations Security Council has encouraged all parties to negotiate in good faith at the Abuja talks and to take immediate steps to support a peaceful settlement to the conflict in Darfur, but has continued to express serious concern at the persistence of the crisis in Darfur in UNSCR 1651 of December 21, 2005.

Pursuant to IEEPA, the National Emergencies Act, and the United Nations Participation Act (UNPA), I have determined that these actions and circumstances constitute an unusual and extraordinary threat to the national security and foreign policy of the United States, and have issued an Executive Order expanding the scope of the national emergency declared in Executive Order 13067 to deal with this threat.

The order blocks the property and interests in property in the United States, or in the possession or control of United States persons, of the persons listed in the Annex to the order, as well as of any person determined by the Secretary of the Treasury, after consultation with the Secretary of State,

- to have constituted a threat to the peace process in Darfur;
- to have constituted a threat to stability in Darfur and the region;
- to be responsible for conduct related to the conflict in Darfur that violates international law;
- to be responsible for heinous conduct with respect to human life or limb related to the conflict in Darfur;
- to have directly or indirectly supplied, sold, or transferred arms or any related materiel, or any assistance, advice, or training related to military activities to the Government of Sudan, the Sudan Liberation Movement/Army, the Justice and Equality Movement, the Janjaweed, or any person operating in the states of North Darfur, South Darfur, and West Darfur, that is a belligerent, a nongovernmental entity, or an individual; or
- to be responsible for offensive military overflights in and over the Darfur region.

The designation criteria will be applied in accordance with applicable domestic law, including where appropriate, the First Amendment of the United States Constitution.

The order also authorizes the Secretary of the Treasury, after consultation with the Secretary of State, to designate for blocking any person determined to have materially assisted, sponsored, or provided financial, material, or technological support for, or goods or services in support of, the activities listed above or any person listed in or designated pursuant to the order. I further authorized the Secretary of the Treasury, after consultation with the Secretary of State, to designate for blocking any person determined to be owned or controlled by, or acting or purporting to act for or on behalf of, directly or indirectly, any person listed in or designated pursuant to the order. The Secretary of the Treasury, after consultation with the Secretary of State, is also authorized to remove any persons from the Annex to the order as circumstances warrant.

I delegated to the Secretary of the Treasury, after consultation with the Secretary of State, the authority to take such actions, including the promulgation of rules and regulations, and to employ all powers granted to the President by IEEPA and UNPA, as may be necessary to carry out the purposes of the order. All Federal agencies are directed to take all appropriate measures within their authority to carry out the provisions of the order.

The order, a copy of which is enclosed, was effective at 12:01 a.m. eastern daylight time on April 27, 2006.

GEORGE W. BUSH

The White House,

April 27, 2006.

NOTE: The Executive order is listed in Appendix D at the end of this volume.

Remarks Following Discussions With President Ilham Aliyev of Azerbaijan
April 28, 2006

President Bush. Mr. President, welcome. We've just had a really interesting visit. And we talked about the need to—for the world to see a modern Muslim country that is able to provide for its citizens, that understands that democracy is the wave of the future. And I appreciate your leadership, Mr. President.

We, obviously, talked about Iran. I assured the President of my desire to solve this problem diplomatically and peacefully. I appreciate so very much the Government's contribution of support in troops to the new democracy in Iraq. I spent time describing to the President a meeting I had today via video conference with our Ambassador and General Casey—very important for me to bring our ally up to date on the progress that's being made on the ground there. I shared with him my hope that the national unity Government will help achieve the objective we all want, which is peace and democracy.

And we, of course, talked about energy. And I appreciate the vision of the Government and the vision of the President in helping this world achieve what we all want, which is energy security. Azerbaijan has got a very important role to play. And we discussed internal politics, and we discussed politics of the neighborhood as well, particularly relations with Armenia.

I appreciate very much the candid discussion. I thank you for sharing your thoughts with me, and thank you for our alliance. And welcome.

President Aliyev. Thank you very much, Mr. President. I am very grateful for the invitation. I'm very glad to be in Washington and have an opportunity to discuss with you the issues of bilateral relations. I'm sure that our relations of strategic partnership will strengthen in the future.

We covered all the aspects of our bilateral relations. We are very grateful for the leadership of the United States in promotion of the energy security issues in the region, in assisting us to create a solid transportation infrastructure which will allow to develop a full-scale Caspian oil and gas reserves and to deliver them to the international markets.

We are allies in the war on terror. We've been, from the very first day, shoulder to shoulder with the United States in the peacekeeping operations in various parts of the world, and will continue to contribute to the creation of peace and stability in the region.

Of course, the issues of resolution of Armenia and Azerbaijan, Nagorno-Karabakh are also in the center of our discussions. And we—I informed Mr. President with the latest status of the negotiations and expressed my hope that a peaceful settlement of the conflict will happen and will serve to the peace and stability in the whole region.

In general, I'd like to say that I'm very satisfied with my visit, and I consider this as instrumental in the future development of Azerbaijan as a modern, secular, democratic country. We share the same values. We are grateful for United States assistance in promotion of political process, process of democratization of our society, and very committed to continue this cooperation in the future.

Thank you very much, Mr. President.

President Bush. One final word I forgot to mention. I do want to congratulate the President and the First Lady on the marriage of their daughter this weekend. It's a major sacrifice for the President to be here during the planning phases of the wedding. And we wish you and the First Lady all the best, and more importantly, we wish your daughter all the best.

President Aliyev. Thank you, Mr. President.

President Bush. Thank you.

NOTE: The President spoke at 10:49 a.m. in the Oval Office at the White House. In his remarks, he referred to U.S. Ambassador to Iraq Zalmay Khalilzad; Gen. George W. Casey, Jr., USA, commanding general, Multi-National Force—Iraq; and President Aliyev's wife, Mehriban Aliyeva, and daughter, Leyla Aliyeva.

Remarks Following a Meeting With North Korean Defectors and Family Members of Japanese Abducted by North Korea
April 28, 2006

I have just had one of the most moving meetings since I've been the President, here in the Oval Office. I met with a mom and a brother who long to be reunited with her daughter and his sister. They're apart because the North Korean Government abducted the child when she was a teenager. And all the mom wants is to be reunited with her daughter.

It is hard to believe that a country would foster abduction. It's hard for Americans to imagine that a leader of any country would encourage the abduction of a young child. It's a heartless country that would separate loved ones, and yet that's exactly what happened to this mom as a result of the actions of North Korea. If North Korea expects to be respected in the world, that country must respect human rights and human dignity and must allow this mother to hug her child again.

I talked to a family, a young North Korean family that escaped the clutches of tyranny in order to live in freedom. This young couple was about to have a child, and the mom was 5 months pregnant when they crossed the river to get into China. They wandered in China, wondering whether or not their child could grow up and have a decent life. They were deeply concerned about the future of their child; any mother and father would be concerned about their child.

They had to wander because they did not want to have their child grow up in a society that was brutal, a society that did not respect the human condition. By the grace of God, they found safe haven. Their child was born and now safely sits here in the Oval Office.

I talked to a courageous man who escaped from North Korea. He was in the North Korean military. He saw firsthand the brutal nature of the regime, and he couldn't—his heart could no longer take it. He followed his conscience and escaped. He speaks for thousands who have escaped North Korea and thousands who live inside the country; he speaks eloquently about the need for their freedom and for them to be treated decently.

The world requires courage to confront people who do not respect human rights, and it has been my honor to welcome into the Oval Office people of enormous courage: a mom; a mother and dad of a young child; a former soldier; a brother. And so I welcome you here. We're proud you're here. I assure you that the United States of America strongly respects human rights. We strongly will work for freedom so that the people of North Korea can raise their children in a world that's free and hopeful and so that moms will never again have to worry about an abducted daughter.

May God bless you all. Thanks for coming.

NOTE: The President spoke at 11:39 a.m. in the Oval Office at the White House. In his remarks, he referred to Sakie Yokota, mother, and Takuya Yokota, brother, of Megumi

Yokota, who was abducted by North Korean authorities; Kim Guang Choel and Lee Seong Hee, who defected from North Korea, and their daughter, Kim Han Mee; and Chung Seong-san, who defected from North Korea.

The President's News Conference
April 28, 2006

The President. Thank you very much for joining us today. I'm joined by my two top White House economic advisers. The reason why is because we've had some very positive economic news today. The Commerce Department announced that our economy grew at an impressive 4.8 percent annual rate in the first quarter of this year. That's the fastest rate since 2003. This rapid growth is another sign that our economy is on the fast track.

The good news comes on the heels of two other important economic indicators reported earlier this week: New home sales surged forward by nearly 14 percent last month; consumer confidence reached its highest level since May of 2002. This confidence is largely driven by the many jobs being created in our country—5.1 million since August of 2003.

This good news cannot be taken for granted. With gas prices on the minds of Americans, we need to keep our foot on the pedal of this strong economy. The surest way to put the brakes on our economic growth would be to raise taxes or spend too much of the people's money here in Washington. That's why I'm going to continue to work with Congress to make the tax relief that helped spur this economic growth permanent. That's why I'm going to work with Congress to restrain the Federal Government's appetite for spending. And that's why I'm going to work with Congress to make this country less dependent on foreign sources of oil.

I commend America's workers and small-business owners, innovators and educators for contributing to the strong economic health of our Nation. I will continue to pursue progrowth policies so that opportunity reaches every American neighborhood and every American family.

With that, I'll be glad to take a couple of questions.

Q. Mr. President——

The President. Excuse me, please. Jennifer [Jennifer Loven, Associated Press].

Iran

Q. Thank you, sir. The IAEA says that Iran is not in compliance with the Security Council. What sort of sanctions do you—would you like to see and—that could bring Russia and Chinese support?

The President. The IAEA statement is an important statement. It reminds the nations of the world that there is an ongoing diplomatic effort to convince the Iranians to give up their nuclear weapons ambitions. It reminds—it should remind the Iranians that the world is united and concerned about their desire to have not only a nuclear weapon but the capacity to make a nuclear weapon or the knowledge to make a nuclear weapon, all of which we're working hard to convince them not to try to achieve.

I will consult and continue to consult with our allies on this issue. I spoke to Chancellor Merkel this morning about this issue. She will be coming to Washington next week. We will continue discussions about how we can continue to maintain a united front. It's very important for the Iranians to understand there's a common desire by a lot of nations in this world to convince them, peacefully convince them, that they ought to give up their weapons ambitions.

Steve [Steve Holland, Reuters].

Fuel/Energy

Q. Thank you, sir. You mentioned gas prices. Would you go along with an effort by some Senate Republicans that could levy a significant tax on oil companies' profits? And does it bother you that the oil companies are racking up these record profits when people are paying $3 a gallon?

The President. My attitude is that the oil companies need to be mindful that the American people expect them to reinvest their cash flows in such a way that it enhances our energy security. That means pipeline construction for natural gas deliveries. That means expansion of refineries. That means exploration in environmentally friendly ways. It also means investment in renewable sources of energy. And that's what the American people expect. They also expect to be treated fairly at the pump, and that's why the Federal Trade Commission is going to monitor the situation very carefully to make sure the American people are treated fairly.

Q. So "no" to a tax on profits?

The President. Look, the temptation in Washington is to tax everything, and they spend the money—"they" being the people in Washington. The answer is, is for there to be strong reinvestment to make this country more secure from an energy perspective.

Listen, these oil prices are a wake-up call. We're dependent upon oil, and we need to get off oil. And the best way to do so is through technology. And I've been traveling the country talking about the need to develop alternative sources of energy, such as ethanol, and to spend money to advance technologies, such as new battery technology that will enable us to have plug-in hybrid vehicles. We signed a good energy bill a while ago, and that encouraged—for example, one thing it's got in there is a tax credit to encourage people

to purchase hybrid vehicles so that the consumptive patterns of the American people change.

And the American people have got to understand that we're living in a global economy, and so when China and India demand more oil, it affects the price of gasoline at the pump. And therefore, it's important for us to diversify away from oil.

But it's also important for the people to understand that one of the reasons why the price is gasoline is up is there's tight gasoline supplies. And one reason there's tight gasoline supplies is because we haven't built any new refineries since the 1970s. And therefore, Congress needs to provide regulatory relief so people can expand their refineries.

So it's a combination of people investing the cash flows as well as regulatory relief to enhance the ability for people to achieve the objective, which is more gasoline on the market, which will help our consumers.

Dick Keil [Richard Keil, Bloomberg News].

Sudan

Q. Thank you, Mr. President. You have a meeting later today on Darfur, and the Sudanese Government continues to thwart efforts by the U.N. and other multinational organizations to take a firmer control of the situation there. Is there anything you can do to leverage the Sudanese Government, and what's your message to them?

The President. My message to them is, we expect there to be full compliance with the international desire for there to be peace in the Darfur region. We have taken the situation to the United Nations Security Council. My belief is that the AU forces that are on the ground—and by the way, we helped the AU forces get in there in the first place—we think that force needs to be expanded and blue-helmeted with the NATO overlay, with NATO help.

And so therefore, the message to the Sudanese Government is, we're very serious about getting this problem solved. We don't like it when we see women raped and brutalized. And we expect there to be a full effort by the Government to protect human life and human condition.

We also recognize there's a parallel political track taking place, and that we urge the rebels as well as the Government to forge a consensus at Abuja, so that there is a way forward from this—from the impasse, political impasse that has taken place thus far in Sudan. There is a good go-by for people to look at, and that is the north-south agreement that this Government helped fashion under the leadership of Secretary of State Colin Powell as well as Special Envoy Jack Danforth. The north-south agreement shows that political solutions are possible.

And so we expect the Sudanese Government to be good-faith bargainers; we expect the rebels to be good-faith bargainers. But we also expect people to—particularly the Sudanese Government, to make a more concerted effort to control the Janjaweed and protect human life. The meeting today and the rallies around the country are a clear signal that the United States is committed to peace in Darfur.

Mark Smith [Associated Press Radio].

Iran

Q. Mr. President, let's come back to Iran, if we can. The Iranians have said they're going to ignore what happens at the U.N. Security Council. Doesn't that mean the diplomatic options are dwindling?

The President. No, I think the diplomatic options are just beginning. As you might recall, about 6 or 7 months ago, you were asking me questions about the United Nations Security Council vis-a-vis Iran, and now we're headed to the United Nations Security Council. And I look forward to working with all interested parties to make sure that there's a common voice.

Listen, the first thing that has to happen diplomatically for anything to be effective is that we all agree on the goal. And we've agreed on the goal, and that is the Iranians

should not have a nuclear weapon, the capacity to make a nuclear weapon, or the knowledge as to how to make a nuclear weapon. And now that we've got the goal in mind, we're working on the tactics. And today's IAEA report should remind us all that the Iranian Government's intransigence is not acceptable.

David Gregory [NBC News].

Second-Term Agenda

Q. Mr. President, we're seeing some turnover and some change within your administration, and I wonder what it says about what you think is necessary to turn your Presidency around at this point?

The President. I think it's necessary to continue doing—to achieving results for the American people. We've got big challenges for this country, and I've got a strategy to deal with them.

The biggest challenge we face is winning the war on terror and to protect the American people. And we'll continue to keep on the offense, to keep the terrorists off balance, to find them and bring them to justice. And at the same time, we'll continue to work to spread democracy, understanding that democracy is the best way to defeat an ideology of hatred.

At home, it's important to make sure this economy continues to grow, and that's why I'm working with Congress to make the tax cuts permanent. I fully understand there are some here who would like the tax cuts to expire, or raise taxes. In my judgment, that would be bad for the economy. It would hurt small-business formation and hurt the entrepreneurial spirit. So I will continue to work with Congress to make these tax cuts a real part of economic life for a long time coming.

And we've also got to be wise about spending. I issued a veto threat the other day because I was deeply concerned that the supplemental was getting out of hand. And I recognize that in order for us to cut the deficit in half, we've got to keep progrowth economic policies in place, as well as control Federal spending.

I talked about the need for this country not to fear the future but to shape it. In other words, we shouldn't worry about competition from China and India. And because—we can outcompete those countries if we're wise about what we do here at home. And one of the most wise things we can do is to make sure our children have got the skills necessary to fill the jobs of the 21st century.

I've been talking about energy independence for a long period of time. You might remember, last summer, I was urging Congress to pass a comprehensive energy bill so that we could deal with conservation and new technologies and diversification. And so I'm going to keep working hard for the American people to get results.

By the way, we're in the midst of implementing now a Medicare bill which is helping our seniors a lot. And if you—if a senior has not signed up, I urge you to take a look at the Medicare prescription drug program, particularly if you're a low-income senior. It's an enormous benefit, and it's a necessary benefit.

So there's a lot to do today, but we'll continue to be results-oriented.

Martha Raddatz [ABC News].

Q. Sir. I'm sorry, but I asked you about your internal changes and what that says about how you think things need to be changed. They've been very public, your internal changes.

The President. Well, David, I'm a results-oriented person, and my job is to achieve things for the American people, positive results that make us more secure and more prosperous. And of course, I will have people by my side that work toward that objective.

Thank you for your penetrating question.

Q. Thank you.

The President. Plus, I'm not going to hire you, if that's what you were suggesting. [*Laughter*]

Q. I was not suggesting that. [*Laughter*]

The President. I would, except you can't pass the background check. [*Laughter*] Okay, an unnecessary cheap shot; I take it back.

Martha.

Iran/Iraq

Q. You often say Iran is not Iraq.

The President. Yes, I do say that.

Q. There are many people who fear that this will turn into a military confrontation. Why is Iran not Iraq? There's WMD——

The President. Iraq went through 16 different Security Council resolutions. There was resolution after resolution after resolution. Iraq had invaded its neighbors. Iraq was shooting at U.S. aircraft. Iraq had actually used weapons of mass destruction on its people before. There's a difference between the two countries.

Iran's desire to have a nuclear weapon is dangerous, in my judgment. The diplomatic process is just starting.

Q. But when you talk about that, how many resolutions are you going to let go here? How far——

The President. We haven't had one yet.

Q. I know, but how far can you let them go? If you really fear that they're building a nuclear——

The President. Wait until we even get one resolution first, before you ask me about the second resolution. The diplomatic process is just beginning. We're forming a strong coalition of like-minded countries that believe that the Iranians should not have a nuclear weapon. And I've told the American people that diplomacy is my first choice, and it should be the first choice of every American President in order to solve a very difficult problem. There are significant differences between Iran and Iraq.

Kelly [Kelly O'Donnell, NBC News].

Spanish Version of National Anthem

Q. Mr. President, a cultural question for you. There is a version of the national anthem in Spanish now. Do you believe it will hold the same value if sung in Spanish as in English?

The President. No, I don't.

Q. Why, sir?

The President. Because I think the national anthem ought to be sung in English. And I think people who want to be a citizen of this country ought to learn English, and they ought to learn to sing the national anthem in English.

Axelrod [Jim Axelrod, CBS News].

Iran

Q. Mr. President.

The President. Yes.

Q. I just want to follow up one more time on Iran. Mr. Ahmadi-nejad was quoted this morning as saying, those who want to prevent Iranians from obtaining their right should "know that we do not give a damn," his words, sir, "about such resolutions."

The President. Okay.

Q. When you're talking about diplomacy, sir, a question of tactics at this point, not goals. If you have, for instance, Russia saying they don't want a Chapter VII resolution, if you're dealing with a gentleman who uses this kind of rhetoric, what kind of tactics can you possibly come up with?

The President. I guess the first thing I would do is refer those comments to our partners and get their reaction, to see what they say, see how they react to those kind of comments. And I haven't had a chance to do that yet, since it just happened today. But I will continue to work with our friends and allies.

Listen, key—step one is to have a common goal. I know that sounds simple to you, probably, but it wasn't always that way. The world wasn't always of like mind that the Iranians were, you know, headed for a weapon, and that that would be a dangerous course of action. And now we are of like mind. And so we are in the stage now of formulating a strategy to achieve a diplomatic solution to this problem.

Q. But Mr. President, given everything you've been hearing from Mr. Ahmadi-nejad over the past several weeks and months, in your estimation, is this someone you can work with?

The President. That's going to be his choice, eventually. And it's going to be very important for Mr. Ahmadi-nejad to recognize the world is united in our desire, and it's his choice to make.

Carl Cameron [FOX News].

Fuel

Q. Thank you, Mr. President. Good morning.

The President. Thank you.

Q. Back to gas prices just a moment ago. Insofar as you directed some of your Cabinet this week to look into the possibility of price gouging, do you have a suspicion yourself, do you have evidence here at the White House? And should the American consumer believe that you think they're being ripped off?

The President. I have no evidence that there's any rip-off taking place, but it's the role of the Federal Trade Commission to assure me that my inclination and instincts is right. More importantly, it's up to the Federal Trade Commission to assure the American people that they're being treated fairly at the pump.

Let's see—Mark Smith.

Q. Another one?

The President. Oh, you already asked one?

Q. Call on my colleagues.

The President. Did you ask one?

Q. Yes, sir.

The President. Oh, you did ask one. [*Laughter*]

Q. It was a memorable question.

Q. Really a great question. [*Laughter*]

Q. Can I follow up on the energy question, Mr. President?

The President. No, you can't, because I just embarrassed myself by calling on Smith twice. [*Laughter*] That's right; it was that brilliant question. How could I forget?

VandeHei [Jim VandeHei, Washington Post].

Energy/Alternative Fuel Sources

Q. In talking about gas prices, in 2001, when you did your first energy policy and gas prices were about $1.50, a lot of people were saying, you know, you have to push CAFE standards higher for the entire fleet of vehicles; you have to scrutinize oil companies more closely; you have to spend a lot more in alternative fuels than even you were proposing. Do you have any regrets now that gas is $3 that you didn't do enough in your first term to prevent these prices?

The President. As you know, in order for there to be a CAFE standard increase on cars, it requires congressional action. I think it's a good idea to give the President, through the Secretary of Transportation, the opportunity to raise CAFE standards, just like I did on light trucks. And we're spending—I think it's about $10 billion since I've been President on alternative sources of energy, and we're making progress; we're close to some significant breakthroughs.

The point is, is that it's very important for us to diversify away from oil. You might remember, when I first came in, I think the price of oil was like—I know it was below $20, and it's all of a sudden—now that the price of oil is up, alternatives become much more economically viable, and therefore, I think the American people are going to see a lot of technological development happen quickly, which will enable people to have different options and different choices.

The hybrid vehicle has just hit the road recently, as you know. There's a big demand for hybrids. I think it makes sense to have tax credits to encourage people to buy hybrids. Increase in demand will cause producers to produce more. And as you know, that there's limitations on the number of—the amount of tax credit issued per manufacturer. I think we ought to just make sure the tax credit is applied to all people purchasing hybrid vehicles.

Herman [Ken Herman, Austin American-Statesman].

Dubai Holding LLC

Q. Thank you, sir.

The President. Yes. Glad to work you into a national press conference for the first time in a long time.

Q. Proud to be here, sir. Are there inherent and unavoidable risks in allowing the sale of a defense firm to interests owned by Dubai?

The President. That question has been looked at very carefully, has been analyzed by a CFIUS committee. I signed off on it this morning because I'm convinced, at the recommendation of the CFIUS committee, as well as our military, that it's a sale that should go through.

April [April Ryan, American Urban Radio Networks].

Elections in New Orleans, LA

Q. Mr. President, some have questioned your efforts in having every vote count in this Nation, especially after the April 22d New Orleans elections. Now with that, what are you looking to do with the three sections of the Voting Rights Act that are set to expire in 2007? How are you planning to enhance those sections, because we understand that you want to study it prior to any passing of a bill by the Senate.

The President. I think I'm on record— as a matter of fact, I'm pretty clearly on record, particularly at the Rosa Parks— signing of the Rosa Parks bill, that I'm for the extension of the Voting Rights Act, right?

Q. Yes, yes you are on record. But there is word that you want to enhance it, or people within your administration want to look at it to tweak it.

The President. I wanted to make sure the Voting Rights Act is strong and capable. I'm not exactly sure what you're talking about. But my statement is my statement:

The Voting Rights Act ought to be extended. The Voting Rights Act is a very important part of the civil rights legislation. Everybody ought to be encouraged to vote. Voting is a valuable part of democracy, and we want people voting.

Q. Do you think it was valuable in April—for the April 22d elections in New Orleans?

The President. I'm not going to second-guess the Federal judge. I was just down there yesterday; I didn't hear much complaining about it, though, when I was there. And obviously, it's a more difficult election with people scattered around, but the State worked very hard to encourage people to vote. And I was with Mayor Nagin and Governor Blanco, and the subject, frankly, didn't come up. That's not to say it's not on their minds. It's on Mayor Nagin's mind because he wants to win; he wants people voting.

But the State bent over backwards to encourage people to participate in the mayoral election. And it looked like the process, given the circumstances the city had been under, pretty smooth process, which is not necessarily a given.

Yes, sir.

Emergency Management/Gulf Coast Recovery

Q. Mr. President, yesterday Senators Lieberman and Collins said they want to see FEMA abolished. I'd like you to comment on that. But also, with hurricane season only a month away, can you assure the American people that your Government has learned the lessons of Katrina?

The President. Thanks for the question. That was obviously on people's minds when I went down to New Orleans and Mississippi. The lessons of Katrina are very important. We've learned a lot here at the Federal level: One, there needs to be better coordination between local and State governments; secondly, that there needs to be a communications package that will be available to help deal with the situation that

happened last time, which was total destruction of communications capabilities; third, that there needs to make sure that there is a law enforcement alternative in case there's a local—a breakdown of local law enforcement; fourthly, there needs to be a prepositioning of assets so that if a major storm were to come, we'd be able to move equipment in faster.

But most important, there needs to be a coordination and an understanding of the evacuation and relief plans. And I talked to the mayor and both Governors that I met with yesterday about our seriousness in working with them to make sure that the plans are as effective as possible.

The communications, obviously, this time around are a lot better than last time around. And so the lessons are being learned. And my attitude toward the recommendations by Fran Townsend, who is a part of my administration, or the Congress is we ought to take them all seriously. The objective is to respond to these natural disasters as well as we possibly can.

The other issue down there for New Orleans, of course, are the levees. And we've got money in the sup to make sure that these levees are pre-Katrina or better prior to June 1st. I think we'll achieve that objective. Additional money will be spent so that the levees are improved significantly by September of '07. The levees are important—the rebuilding of the levees, or improving of the levees are very important to assure the people of New Orleans that if there is a storm, they're built to pre-Katrina levels, as least in the initial stage. But also, it's important to convince people that it's okay to risk capital in New Orleans.

The amazing thing in the area down there—I don't know if you all went with me—but it was—there's this totally different attitude from when we were there before, early on, obviously, after the storm. People are coming back. Sales taxes along the gulf coast of Mississippi are higher today than they were a year ago this date. And that's positive.

But look, there's still a lot of work to be done, a lot of reconstruction. The CDBG money—and it's very important for the Congress to pass the CDBG money I requested so that the housing issue can get—people can get back to rebuilding their homes. And Mississippi, the CDBG money will be coming out pretty quick; New Orleans, they've still got a little work. The Governor has proposed a plan that will be in front of the legislature, I think, this weekend. It's a very important step to getting this process moving.

And so, got a lot of work to do. But, yes, we're much more ready this time than last time. And we're taking very seriously the lessons learned from Katrina.

Q. Abolish FEMA?

The President. I've looked at all suggestions, but my attitude is, let's make it work. We're about 6 weeks away from—we're getting pretty close.

Who are you again? [*Laughter*]

Q. I got a few more, if you like.

The President. You've had a big day. [*Laughter*]

Q. That's three. That's three.

The President. Butting in once, called on unnecessarily once.

Cooper [Christopher Cooper, Wall Street Journal].

Emergency Response Preparation

Q. Yes, sir, regarding FEMA, do you think that they're prepared for the season? And is there any way to measure that at this point?

The President. I think preparation is—Chris, preparation is preparation at all levels of government. Most Governors will tell you that the main responsibility for disaster relief is at the State level. And the job of the Federal Government is to step in and help. And so Chertoff has been down there. Secretary Chertoff has been down there working with these local governments to review their plans and to analyze where the Federal Government can help if there's any breakdown whatsoever.

One of the key issues, of course, again, in New Orleans, is transportation. We remember those pictures of those buses—people looking to get out, and yet there were these buses in flooded areas. And so one of the areas where Homeland Security Department, working with the State and local governments, is to make sure there's a transportation plan that will work.

It's going to be interesting—let's pray—first of all, pray there's no hurricanes. That would be, like, step one. Step two, if one is coming, I suspect people are going to take hurricane warnings very seriously and that evacuation orders will be heeded very seriously. And so it's going to be a—and therefore, there's a need to make sure that the forecasting is accurate—and this is pretty much the way it is these days, been very accurate forecasting—and that the response by all of us is in a timely fashion to give people time to prepare.

But now is the time to put these plans in place, and we're doing it. And I feel pretty good about the coordination and the sessions that have been taking place down there. And as I understand, Secretary Chertoff will be going back down there again.

And, by the way, the plans are not just for New Orleans and Mississippi; they're for Alabama and Florida and Texas as well. In other words, it's for Hurricane Alley.

Yes. Dallas Morning News man [G. Robert Hillman, Dallas Morning News].

Immigration Reform

Q. Yes, Mr. President. On Monday, several million illegal immigrants, worried about some forms of immigration legislation in the Congress, are going to walk off the job and keep their kids home from schools. What is your view of this call for a national boycott on Monday?

The President. I'm not a supporter of boycotts; I am a supporter of comprehensive immigration. I understand how difficult this issue is for some people here in Washington and around the country, but there is—my judgment, that enforcing our border requires a—and by the way, I think most Americans agree that we've got to enforce our border. I don't think there's any question about that——

Q. Do you think——

The President. Let me finish, please, Bob, thank you—that there needs to be interior enforcement as well. But I recognize it's hard to enforce the border and have interior enforcement if there is a smuggling network that's bringing people across and there's a forgery network that's providing people false documents. And therefore, I believe a temporary-worker program will make it easier to enforce the border, as well as have interior enforcement.

And if somebody is coming across to do a job on a temporary basis, they don't need to sneak across. They don't need a *coyote* to stuff them in the back of an 18-wheeler. They don't need to walk across the desert and risk their lives. And so a rational way to make sure our border is enforced is to have a temporary-worker program. And that's what I support.

I think it's very important for people, when they do express themselves, they continue to do so in a peaceful way, in a respectful way—respectful of the—how highly charged this debate can become. One of the things that's very important is when we debate this issue that we not lose our national soul. One of the great things about America is that we've been able to take people from all walks of life bound as one nation under God. And that's the challenge ahead of us.

And I look forward to working with members of both political parties to get a bill out of the United States Senate and into conference, which would then mean we have a chance to get a comprehensive bill to my desk. And I want a comprehensive bill, one that enforces the border, one that makes sure that we've got interior enforcement procedures in place that actually work, one that provides a temporary-worker process for people, one that does not provide automatic citizenship—I don't think anybody really wants there to be automatic amnesty for people—one that allows somebody here to be able to get in—if they want to be a citizen, to be able to get in line, but not the front of the line but the back of the line.

And that's what I'm for, a comprehensive plan. I think we can get one done if people would set aside politics and focus on what's best for the United States of America.

Thank you for your time. I've enjoyed this. I will see you all tomorrow night, I guess. Looking forward to it. I hope you are as well.

NOTE: The President spoke at 11:47 a.m. in the Rose Garden at the White House. In his remarks, he referred to Edward P. Lazear, Chairman, Council of Economic Advisers; former Secretary of State Colin L. Powell; former Senator John C. Danforth of Missouri; Chancellor Angela Merkel of Germany; President Mahmud Ahmadi-nejad of Iran; Mayor C. Ray Nagin of New Orleans, LA; Gov. Kathleen Babineaux Blanco of Louisiana; and Gov. Haley Barbour of Mississippi.

Remarks Following a Meeting on Sudan
April 28, 2006

I just had an extraordinary conversation with fellow citizens from different faiths, all of who have come to urge our Govern-

ment to continue to focus on saving lives in Sudan. They agree with thousands of our citizens—hundreds of thousands of our citizens that genocide in Sudan is unacceptable.

And there will be rallies across our country to send a message to the Sudanese Government that the genocide must stop. Those rallies will also be an indication that thousands and hundreds of thousands of our citizens urge the world to unite with the United States in concerted action.

We have got AU troops on the ground; those troops need to be augmented and increased through strong United Nations action. And the United States strongly supports a U.N. resolution to do that. I believe it's important for the United States to be involved, and the best way to be involved with the AU troops is through NATO. I've worked with the Secretary General of NATO and our allies in NATO to provide a firm response to the actions that are taking place on the ground. I want the Sudanese Government to understand the United States of America is serious about solving this problem.

I'm proud of our Nation's generosity when it comes to aid, and the American people ought to be proud of the taxpayer dollars that have gone to provide much needed aid for those who suffer. But this Government must understand that we expect the aid to get to the people, and we

expect there to be a solution to this problem.

There will be rallies all across the country. And for those of you who are going out to march for justice, you represent the best of our country. We believe every life is precious, every human being is important. And the signal you send to the world is a strong signal, and I welcome your participation. And I want to thank the organizers for being here.

I want to thank this good man right here; he sits here next to his President, and it wasn't all that long ago that he was a slave inside Sudan. He sits here to represent the thousands of lives who have been affected by a Government that must honor human rights.

And, Simon, I'm proud to have you here as a fellow American, proud to have you here as a friend.

Thank you all for coming.

NOTE: The President spoke at 1:50 p.m. in the Roosevelt Room at the White House. In his remarks, he referred to Secretary General Jakob Gijsbert "Jaap" de Hoop Scheffer of the North Atlantic Treaty Organization; and Simon Deng, founder of the Sudan Freedom Walk.

Letter to Congressional Leaders on the Proposed Acquisition of Ross Catherall US Holdings Inc., by Dubai International Capital LLC
April 28, 2006

Dear Mr. Speaker: (Dear Mr. President:)

Attached is a classified report on my decision to take no action to suspend or prohibit the proposed acquisition of Ross Catherall US Holdings Inc., by Dubai International Capital LLC, a subsidiary of Dubai Holding LLC.

I have made this decision under the authority vested in me as President by section 721 of the Defense Production Act of 1950

(the "Exon-Florio amendment"), 50 U.S.C. App. 2170, and on the basis of the recommendation from senior officials who make up the Committee on Foreign Investment in the United States.

The attached report, prepared by my Administration, is submitted consistent with subsection (g) of that amendment and is subject to the provisions of subsection (c) regarding confidentiality of information.

Sincerely,

GEORGE W. BUSH

NOTE: Identical letters were sent to J. Dennis Hastert, Speaker of the House of Rep-resentatives, and Richard B. Cheney, President of the Senate. An original was not available for verification of the content of this letter.

The President's Radio Address
April 29, 2006

Good morning. Last weekend, the people of Iraq formed a national unity government. This is an important milestone on the road to democracy in Iraq, and it marks the beginning of a new chapter in America's involvement. Last Sunday, I talked to the President, Prime Minister-designate, and Speaker of the new Government. And this week, I sent Secretary of State Rice and Secretary of Defense Rumsfeld to Baghdad to meet face to face with the new Iraqi leadership. We've all been impressed by the Iraqi leaders' commitment to maintain the unity of their country and effectively represent the Iraqi people.

The new Iraqi Government will face many challenges. Iraqi leaders agree that the new Government must continue to build up the Iraqi security forces to defeat the terrorists and must establish control over militias. They also agree that the new Government must rebuild critical infrastructure, strengthen the Iraqi economy, and ensure that all Iraqis benefit as their nation grows in security and prosperity.

During their meetings in Baghdad, Secretaries Rice and Rumsfeld made clear that Iraq will have the continued support of America and our coalition partners as we begin the new chapter in our relationship. We will help the new Iraqi Government assume growing responsibility for the Nation's security. And as Iraqis continue to make progress toward a democracy that can govern itself, defend itself, and sustain itself, more of our troops can come home with the honor they have earned.

The terrorists clearly recognize the threat that the new unity Government poses to their dark plans for Iraq and the broader Middle East. This week, the terrorist Zarqawi, leader of Al Qaida in Iraq, released a video in which he denounced the new Government and promised further acts of terrorist violence. Zarqawi lashed out at what he called "this rotten play of democracy" and declared that Iraq's new Government will become "a poisoned dagger" in the heart of his plans for the Muslim world.

On Wednesday, Iraq's leaders united to strongly condemn Zarqawi's statements. One Iraqi official declared that the terrorists and insurgents, quote, "are feeling this might be the last chance they have to survive. They're fighting everyone in Iraq—every Iraqi. I think that shows how weak they are," end quote. A newly appointed first Deputy Speaker of the Iraqi Parliament said that Zarqawi fears the new Government will unify Shiites and Sunnis and Kurds. He said, quote, "I believe that Zarqawi was caught off guard by the new Government taking shape, because it will be a very strong one representing all Iraqis," end quote.

The new leaders of Iraq are showing great courage in the face of terrorist threats. In recent weeks, terrorists have assassinated three siblings of top Iraqi politicians, but the new leaders of Iraq remain determined to lead their nation toward a future of democracy and peace. These brave leaders deserve our continued support, and I have told them they can count on America to stand with them.

The enemy is resorting to desperate acts of violence because they know the establishment of democracy in Iraq will be a double defeat for them. First, it will deny the terrorists their immediate aim of turning Iraq into what Afghanistan was under the Taliban—a safe haven where they can plot and plan more attacks against free nations. Second, in the long term, a democratic Iraq will be a major blow to the terrorists' hateful ideology, because it will send a powerful message across the region that the future of the Middle East belongs to freedom.

There will be more tough fighting ahead in Iraq and more days of sacrifice and struggle. Yet the enemies of freedom have suffered a real blow in recent days, and we have taken great strides on the march to victory. Iraq's leaders now have laid the foundations for a democratic government of, by, and for the Iraqi people. By helping the Iraqi people build their democracy, America will deal the terrorists a crippling blow and establish a beacon of liberty in the Middle East. And that will make our Nation and the world more secure.

Thank you for listening.

NOTE: The address was recorded at 7:52 a.m. on April 28 in the Cabinet Room at the White House for broadcast at 10:06 a.m. on April 29. The transcript was made available by the Office of the Press Secretary on April 28 but was embargoed for release until the broadcast. In his address, the President referred to President Jalal Talabani, Prime Minister-designate Nuri al-Maliki, Speaker of the Parliament Mahmoud al-Mashhadani, and First Deputy Speaker Khaled Atea of Iraq. The Office of the Press Secretary also released a Spanish language transcript of this address.

Remarks Following a Meeting With Secretary of State Condoleezza Rice and Secretary of Defense Donald H. Rumsfeld
May 1, 2006

I want to thank Secretary Rice and Secretary Rumsfeld. And General Pace, thank you for being here as well. Thank you for joining me this morning.

They came by the Oval Office to brief me on their recent trip to Iraq. First of all, I appreciate them both going over there to send my best wishes to the new Government and to Prime Minister-designate Maliki, as well as the new Speaker and the President. I had spoken to them on the phone, but I thought it was very important for both Secretaries to go firsthand, to be there with the leadership to say we're supporting them. It's very important for these two senior officials to sit down with these new folks and say, "You have our support, and we want you to succeed."

And they brought back interesting impressions from the three new leaders. They said they were optimistic people, that they're full of energy, and they're very eager to succeed. And that's really important for the American people to know, that we've got partners in this effort who are dedicated to a unified Iraq and dedicated to putting a Government together that is one that will represent all the Iraqi people.

This new Government is going to represent a new start for the Iraqi people. It's a Government that understands they've got serious challenges ahead of them. And the three leaders spoke to Secretary Rice and Secretary Rumsfeld about their need to deploy the growing strength of the Iraqi security forces in such a way as to defeat the terrorists and the insurgents. And we will continue to support them in that effort that they talked about: the need to establish control over the militias and other unauthorized armed groups and enforce the rule of law. And we will support them in these efforts to achieve that important objective. They talked about the need to rebuild infrastructure and strengthen their economy, and we agree with that assessment.

And finally, they talked about the need to make sure that all Iraqis share in the benefits of this new democracy. A new Iraqi Government represents a strategic opportunity for America—and the whole world, for that matter. This Nation of ours and our coalition partners are going to work with the new leadership to strengthen our mutual efforts to achieve success, a victory in this war on terror. This is a—we believe this is a turning point for the Iraqi citizens, and it's a new chapter in our partnership.

The Secretaries began building this new partnership during their trip. In other words, the Iraqi leaders saw that we are committed to helping them succeed. They need to know that we stand with them. And the Iraqi people need to know that we stand with them, that we understand the strategic importance of a free Iraq in the Middle East, and that we understand the need to deny safe haven to the terrorists who have caused such turmoil and havoc inside of Iraq.

There's going to be more tough days ahead. These Secretaries know that. They're realistic people. They have brought an assessment of what they saw on the ground, and some of it's positive, and obviously, there's some difficult days ahead because there's still terrorists there who are willing to take innocent life in order to stop the progress of democracy. But this Government is more determined than ever to succeed, and we believe we've got partners to help the Iraqi people realize their dreams.

Last December, the Iraqi people voted to have a free government. I know it seems like a long time ago for the American people, but what we have begun to see now is the emergence of a unity government to represent the wishes of the Iraqi people. Last December, millions of people defied the terrorists and killers and said, "We want to be free; we want a unity government." And now what has happened is, after compromise and politics, the Iraqis have come together to form that Government. And our Secretaries went over there to tell them that we look forward to working with them as partners in peace.

So I want to thank you all for going. I appreciate your dedication to the cause of peace. Thank you.

NOTE: The President spoke at 9:36 a.m. in the Rose Garden at the White House. In his remarks, he referred to Gen. Peter Pace, USMC, Chairman, Joint Chiefs of Staff; and Prime Minister-designate Nuri al-Maliki, Speaker of the Parliament Mahmoud al-Mashhadani, and President Jalal Talabani of Iraq.

Remarks on Presenting the Preserve America Presidential Awards
May 1, 2006

Thank you all. Thanks for the introduction. [*Laughter*] Laura and I welcome you here to the White House. We are privileged to have some of our country's really great community leaders and preservation- ists here in the Rose Garden. This is a fitting place, we think, to honor those who work hard to preserve our Nation's history and protect the natural beauty of the country.

This is a—this Rose Garden is one of America's historic treasures. I spend a lot of time mowing out here. [*Laughter*] The commitment of the folks here to preserve the unique treasures in your own communities means that you celebrate our Nation's history, and you help instill a love of our Nation's natural beauty for future generations. And that's why we have such an event, to encourage people to preserve and instill—preserve what is important and instill love for the—for our natural treasures.

I appreciate not only the First Lady of the United States being here, but I appreciate the first lady of Florida being here— *mi cunada.* Thank you. Give Brother my best. [*Laughter*] Tell him he's doing a fine job. [*Laughter*]

I want to thank Administrator Steve Johnson of the EPA. Thank you for being here, Steve. Lynn Scarlett, who's the Acting Secretary of the Department of Interior; Fran Mainella, who is the Director of the National Park Service; and Senator Craig Thomas of Wyoming—thanks for coming. Appreciate you being here, Senator. Thanks for taking time out of your busy schedule.

I appreciate Bruce Cole, who's the Chairman of the National Endowment for the Humanities, joining us. And it's good to see my old friend John Nau. He's the Chairman of the Advisory Council on Historic Preservation; he's the chairman of the Texas Historical Commission—and he's a fine lad. [*Laughter*] It's good to see Bobbie too. Thanks for coming. And we appreciate all the members of the Advisory Council on Historic Preservation. Thank you for serving. Thank you for your dedication to our country.

Laura and I want every American to have a chance to learn about this country's history, and one of the best ways to do so is to visit our country's great historical landmarks. So in 2003, we created—actually, she created—she told me to create, which I did—[*laughter*]—the Preserve America Presidential Awards, to recognize outstanding contributions to America's cultural

and natural heritage. By the efforts—their efforts, today's award winners have drawn tourists to historic sites and towns; they've revitalized communities and our natural spaces; and they've opened up new opportunities for learning.

The first Preserve America award winner we honor this year is Mission San Luis. It's a project that has reconstructed the former western capital of Spanish Florida in Tallahassee. The mission was burned to the ground over 300 years ago. And the State of Florida, in partnership with local and private groups, successfully recreated nearly every detail of the mission. The reconstruction team used original mission documents to ensure the highest level of historical accuracy. By their painstaking effort, they have helped Mission San Luis rise from the ashes to an educational, cultural, and historical resource reflecting Florida's beginnings. Congratulations, and welcome.

Our second award recipient is the State of Maryland. Through a new program called Maryland Heritage Areas, the State is protecting areas of historical significance and increasing heritage, tourism, and educational opportunities. State and community leaders are investing in projects to highlight special parts of American history, including the location where Harriet Tubman's Underground Railroad helped slaves escape to the North and Fort McHenry, the site that inspired Francis Scott Key to write America's national anthem. And I appreciate the good folks of Maryland for highlighting the amazing sites you've got in your State. And welcome; thank you for coming.

Our third award recipient is a company named Tauck World Discovery, which is helping protect one of America's most precious natural resources. Since 2003, this company has been running an innovative volunteer program in Yellowstone National Park. Under this program, tourists who come to appreciate the scenic landscape can also help keep those vistas beautiful by contributing a good day's work. Pretty interesting concept, isn't it? Since the program began, guests have donated almost 10,000 hours of labor on projects throughout the park. By their good work, the good people at Tauck are inspiring Americans to lend a hand in preservation and making sure that Yellowstone is a natural wonder for the years to come. And we welcome you both. Thank you for coming.

Our fourth award recipient is Hampton Hotels. Probably surprises you, doesn't it? Under their "Save-a-Landmark" program, Hampton Hotels is helping communities rehabilitate roadside attractions along America's great highways. Their efforts have helped preserve landmarks along Route 66, to restore the Jesse Owens Park in Alabama, to refurbish one of the country's classic theme parks in New Jersey, and to save the world's largest Santa Claus in Alaska. [*Laughter*] Each of these landmarks represents a piece of cultural and regional history. By saving them for future generations, they are helping to celebrate the diversity of America and provide educational opportunities for families as they travel across our great land. Thank you very

much; appreciate what you're doing. Congratulations.

All of these award winners set such a wonderful example for our fellow citizens. You've taken the lead in preservation, and we appreciate it. You're showing what is possible when local citizens decide to make a difference in the community in which they live, and your work is preserving America for generations to come.

And so Laura and I welcome you to the Rose Garden. We thank you for your efforts. May God continue to bless our country. Thank you all.

NOTE: The President spoke at 10:22 a.m. in the Rose Garden at the White House. In his remarks, he referred to Columba Bush, wife of Gov. Jeb Bush of Florida; Barbara E. "Bobbie" Nau, wife of Advisory Council on Historic Preservation Chairman John L. Nau III; and Robin Tauck, president and chief executive officer, and Arthur Tauck, chairman of the board, Tauck World Discovery. The transcript released by the Office of the Press Secretary also included the remarks of the First Lady, who introduced the President.

Remarks to the American Hospital Association
May 1, 2006

Thank you very much. It was on this stage 2 nights ago that I had the pleasure of showing up with a George W. Bush look-alike. [*Laughter*] So I walked in, and Dick said, "Is it really you?" [*Laughter*]

Thanks for your introduction, Dick. Thanks for the invitation to be here. I want to, first, thank all the good people of the American Hospital Association. I appreciate the important voice that you provided for our hospitals, but more importantly, I appreciate the compassionate care you give to our citizens.

I have come to talk about a comprehensive health care strategy that will make health care more affordable and available for all our citizens. And I appreciate you giving me a chance to use this forum as an opportunity to discuss our vision for moving forward.

I do want to thank George Lynn, who is the chairman of the American Hospital Association board of trustees. I want to thank all the trustees who are here. I appreciate the leadership of the American Hospital Association. I want to thank the members of the American Hospital Association.

I understand—there he is—my friend Charlie Norwood is here. Good to see you, Congressman. Thank you so much for being here. You're looking pretty good. [*Laughter*] Looking real good, as a matter of fact. [*Laughter*]

This economy of ours is strong, and that's important for health care. It's important for the hospitals. And the economy is getting stronger. We put our trust in the American people by cutting taxes, and the tax relief we passed is saving—is helping people save and spend and invest. And when people save, spend, and invest, it causes our economy to grow. Thanks to tax relief and progrowth economic policies, we're now in our fifth year of uninterrupted economic growth.

In the first quarter of this year, the economy grew at 4.8 percent. We've had 18 straight quarters of economic expansion. Last year our economy grew faster than any other major industrialized nation. Over the past 2½ years, we've created 5.1 million new jobs, and that's more than Japan and the 25 nations of the EU combined. Productivity is high; the unemployment rate is 4.7 percent; consumer confidence is at its highest point ever—in nearly 4 years. The new economic report out today contains good news on income growth.

Things are looking good for this economy, but we cannot be complacent. One of my concerns is that the United States of America loses our nerve, fears competition, and we become an isolated and protectionist nation. And health care plays a vital role in making sure this nation remains competitive.

One of the best ways to make sure that we're a competitive nation is to continue to invest in research and technology. If America wants to be the leader of the world, we've got to remain on the leading edge of change. As many of you know, when I came into office, I pledged to continue the doubling of the funding for the National Institutes of Health, and we kept that commitment. And it's one of the many reasons why our health care system leads the world. And we need to keep—we need to understand the importance of research at the Federal level, and that's why I have proposed that the United States Congress double Federal investment in basic scientific research.

In other words, for this country to be competitive, we've got to invest in the future. See, I don't think we ought to fear the future; I don't think we ought to become protectionists and isolationists. I think we need to continue to lead, and one way to lead is to lead in research and development.

To keep this economy competitive with other nations around the world, we've got to do something about our dependence on oil. Dependency on oil creates an economic problem for us, and it creates a national security problem for us. So I look forward to working with Congress to change—to help speed up research and development so we can change our habits, so we can drive cars fueled by ethanol, or so we can have batteries that enable cars to drive for the first 40 miles on electricity.

To keep this country competitive, we've got to have a health care system that provides our people with good quality care at affordable prices. In other words, you're a part of an industry that must be reformed in order for the United States to continue to be an economic leader.

America has the best health care system in the world, pure and simple. We got the best medicines; we got the best doctors; and we have the best hospitals. And we intend to keep it that way. Yet we are challenged by the fact that health care costs are rising sharply. In the past 5 years, private health insurance premiums have risen 73 percent. And as a result, some businesses have been forced to drop health care coverage for their employees. You know that as well as anybody. Others have been forced to raise copayments and premiums.

Some have been paying increasing health care costs and, therefore, have been unable to give workers the pay raises they need to cope with rising health care costs.

With rising costs, many Americans are concerned. They're concerned they're not going to be able to afford health care. As you well know, millions of our fellow citizens have no health insurance at all. And as you know, that places burdens on our Nation's hospitals. This is unacceptable, for this country to have health care costs rising as fast as they are. If we want to be the leader of the world, we must do something about it. And my administration is determined to do something about it.

To make our health care system work for all Americans, we have to choose between two philosophies: one that trusts government to make the best decisions for the people's health care or one that trusts the people and their doctor to make the best decisions for their health care.

We know from experience which of these systems works best. Other nations that have adopted for bigger government and more centralized control now have long waits for treatment for their people. The quality of care is lower; there's less technological innovation. In America, as you know, we follow a different path. We lead the world in health care because we believe in a system of private medicine that encourages innovation and change.

And the best way to reform this health care system is to preserve the system of private medicine, is to strengthen the relationship between doctors and patients and make the benefits of private medicine more affordable and accessible for all our citizens.

Government has a role to play; don't get me wrong. We're kind of—we're big in the health care field, as you may know. [*Laughter*] We have a major role to play in strengthening and reforming this health care system, but in a way that preserves the doctor-patient relationship.

And that's what I want to talk to you about today. The first goal of our health care strategy is to meet the obligation the Federal Government has made to take care of the elderly and the poor. We have said, as a Federal Government, we will help the elderly and the poor, and I intend to keep that obligation. We're meeting that obligation, that responsibility through Medicare, Medicaid, and community health centers.

More than four decades ago, the Federal Government established Medicare to provide health coverage for older Americans. The bill was signed by Lyndon Baines Johnson. He came from a State I know pretty well. [*Laughter*] When I came into office, I found a Medicare program that was outdated, a Medicare program that was not meeting the needs of America's seniors. The way I tried to explain it to the American people was this: We had a system that would pay $28,000 for an ulcer surgery but not the $500 it would cost for prescription drugs that would prevent the ulcer from being—with taking hold in the first place. And that didn't make any sense—$28,000 for the surgery but not a dime of prescription drugs to prevent the surgery from being needed. To me, that's an outdated system. It's one that's not very cost-effective, and it's one that does not provide quality care for our seniors.

So I decided to do something about it. And I worked with the Congress, and we passed critical legislation that modernizes Medicare and provides seniors with more choices through the private sector and has given our seniors better access to the prescription drugs they need.

The benefit allows seniors to choose from a number of private prescription drug plans to find the one that is right for them. It encourages plan providers to compete for the seniors' business, and that helps lower costs. The new Medicare prescription drug benefit is a good deal for America's seniors. The typical senior will end up spending about half of what he or she used to spend on prescription drugs each year.

In addition, we've provided extra help for low-income seniors. About a third of seniors are eligible for prescription drug coverage that includes low or no premiums, low deductibles, and no gaps in coverage. On average, Medicare will pay for more than 95 percent of the costs of prescription drugs for low-income seniors. I know you shared my concern when we heard the stories of low-income seniors having to choose between food and medicine. And because of this reform, those days are over with.

The Medicare prescription drug benefit went into effect in January. More than 30 million people now have prescription drug coverage through the Medicare program, and hundreds of thousands more are signing up each week. We want every senior who needs coverage to sign up.

The May 15th deadline for seniors to sign up at the lowest cost is approaching. Over the next 2 weeks, this administration will encourage our Nation's pharmacies—pharmacists and doctors and hospitals and others in the medical community to continue to get the word out to seniors about the benefits of this important program. There are some seniors who are risk-adverse; they don't want to change. It is really important for those of us who are involved in health care in this country to get the word out that, at the very minimum, seniors ought to look and see what's available. Americans need to take advantage of this opportunity to choose a plan.

We're also—I also recognize that we got a problem with the long-term viability of Medicare. Today the trustees for our Medicare and Social Security systems will release their annual report. Each year the trustees remind us that these programs are not structured in a way that they will be financially sound for our children and our grandchildren.

The problem is pretty basic. There's a lot of baby boomers like me getting ready to retire—[laughter]—in my case, 2½ years. [Laughter] And there's a lot of baby boomers who are living longer, and there

are fewer workers per beneficiary paying money in the system to support future retirees like me. And so the systems are going broke, and now is the time to do something about it. We've got too much politics in Washington, DC. It's time to set aside politics and restructure Social Security and Medicare for generations to come.

We're honoring our Nation's commitments to take care of the poor by strengthening Medicaid. Medicaid is a program administered in conjunction with the States that provides health care for low-income families with children, poor seniors, and disabled Americans. To help improve Medicaid, earlier this year, I signed legislation to restructure Medicaid and give States more flexibility in designing better programs to cover their citizens.

Under the reforms I signed into law, it's now easier for States to offer alternative benefit plans, provide coverage to more people, and design their Medicaid program to meet their State's needs and budgets. In the coming months, my administration will be encouraging States to adopt commonsense reforms. Our health care system must be guided by the needs of patients, not by rules emanating out of Washington, DC.

Another way we're meeting our commitment to Americans in need is through community health centers. These centers provide primary health care for the poor, so they don't have to go to the emergency room of a hospital to get routine care. This is a really good use of taxpayers' money. It makes a lot of sense to have community health centers so that we can cut down on unnecessary visits to the emergency rooms. Health centers help lower the cost of health care for everyone.

Since I took office, we've funded about 800 new or expanded health centers, bringing our total to more than 3,700 health centers serving more than 13 million Americans a year. And over the next 2 years, we will fund the opening and expanding of 400 more health centers. And Congress needs to fully support these health centers in the budget that I have submitted.

And so we have got a strategy to take care and help our elderly and the poor and the disabled. The second part of our strategy is to make care and coverage more affordable and available for Americans. And here are five key policies to support this goal.

Our first policy is to expand health savings accounts to help improve health care and to help lower costs. Under the current system, as you well know, most Americans have no idea what the actual cost of their treatment is. Third-party insurers pay their bills, so patients have no reason to demand better prices, and the health care industry is under little pressure to lower prices. When somebody else pays the bills, it seems like everything is just fine. The result is that health care costs are skyrocketing. The insurance companies pass these rising costs on to their workers—on to workers and their employees in the form of higher premiums.

Now, health savings accounts transform what I believe is an outdated system by putting patients in control of how their health care dollars are spent. And when patients and consumers see how their health care dollars are spent, they demand more value for their money. The result is better treatment at lower costs.

HSAs have two components: low-cost catastrophic insurance coverage and tax-free savings accounts. The catastrophic coverage protects you and your family in the event of a devastating medical illness. The health savings account allows your—or your employer to contribute to a tax-free account to pay for your routine medical needs. The money that goes into your account is tax-free, the interest earned on your account is tax-free, and the money withdrawn from your account is tax-free. It means that you own your money in your account, and that you can build your savings by rolling over contributions that you do not spend in any given year.

HSAs can help us move toward a health care system that is no longer dominated by third-party payers, to a system in which consumers make their own decisions. And we see strong evidence that HSAs are making health care more affordable and accessible. From March 2005 to January 2006, the number of HSAs tripled from 1 million to more than 3 million. This is a new product. People are getting—taking a look at it. They're beginning to see the merits of a tax-free savings system coupled with catastrophic care.

Forty percent of the people who bought HSAs have family incomes below $50,000. HSAs are making health care more accessible for those without insurance. More than a third of those who bought HSAs on their own had previously been uninsured. HSAs are good for small-business owners. HSAs, in my judgment, will mean that Americans who do not have coverage will be able to get coverage and afford coverage, which is good for America's hospitals. You see, by making health care coverage more affordable, more Americans can afford insurance. And with more Americans insured, fewer people will show up at our Nation's hospitals needing uncompensated care.

HSAs also create an incentive for patients to become more informed about their medical options and more involved in their treatment as they shop for the best value for their health dollar. This involvement strengthens the doctor-patient relationship.

Equally importantly is that HSA owners can see the benefits of changing risky behavior. They can follow doctors' preventative recommendations. The healthier you are, the less money you're going to spend out of your savings account. And there will be a tangible return—more of your own money, tax-free. Some employers are even offering employees financial incentives to get regular checkups and lose weight and get fit. By encouraging preventative medicine, HSAs save lives and save health care dollars.

HSAs will benefit hospitals, doctors, and patients, and they can also benefit hospital workers. Today, only a handful of hospitals offer HSAs to their employees. I encourage the members of the American Hospital Association to consider the benefits of offering health savings accounts to your employees. HSAs will provide your workers with better care and lower your health care costs.

For decades, America's hospitals and health care professionals have led the world in innovation and quality medical care. Now you have an opportunity to help America transform our health care system by choosing the innovation and quality of health savings accounts. As HSAs continue to grow in popularity, my administration is working to expand them to even more Americans.

One way to make HSAs more attractive is to make them portable so they can meet the practical needs of today's workers. Many people are changing jobs, and one of their greatest fears is that they will lose their health care coverage. We believe that no American should have to remain locked in a job to get health insurance. Today, the savings in your health account are portable, and that means you can take your savings accounts from job to job. However, the health insurance within your HSA account is often not portable, and this is because of outdated laws and practices that prevent insurers from offering portable policies. I believe health insurers should be allowed to sell portable HSA policies nationwide.

Another obstacle to expanding HSAs is the Federal Tax Code. Under current law, employers and employees pay no income or payroll tax on any health insurance provided through the workplace. If you buy your own insurance, you do not get the same tax break. That means that the self-employed or the unemployed or workers at companies that do not provide health insurance are at a great disadvantage. Congress needs to end this discrimination in the Tax Code and give Americans who buy HSA policies on their own the same tax breaks as those who get their health insurance from their employers.

The current Tax Code also limits the amount you contribute to your HSA tax-free. The limit is usually tied to your deductible. Sometimes your total out-of-pocket expenses are greater than your deductible. Those with chronic illnesses often have expenses that go well beyond their deductibles. So we need to fix the Tax Code by allowing Americans to cover their out-of-pocket expenses with tax-free dollars and make HSAs even more practical for more American families.

In addition to these efforts to fix the code, I've proposed a refundable tax credit to help low-income Americans purchase health coverage on the individual market. Under my proposal, low-income families can receive up to $3,000 in a refundable tax credit to purchase HSA-qualified insurance. By working together, we can reform our Tax Code and make it easier for American families to get health care.

And this week, Congress takes an important step in these efforts. Congressman Eric Cantor of Virginia will introduce a bill that would end many of the biases in the Tax Code, provide a tax credit of up to $3,000 for low-income families, and make HSAs more attractive. It's a bill called the "Tax-Free Health Savings Act."

I also want to thank Senators Burns and Allen, Ensign, and DeMint for introducing bills to improve HSA options for all Americans and Senators Santorum and Murkowski for introducing legislation supporting the low-income tax credit. Congress needs to pass these reforms and make sure the doctor-patient relationship remains central to our health care system.

The second policy for making health care more affordable and accessible is to increase transparency in our health care system. To be smart consumers, we need to be informed consumers, and this is especially true for patients with HSAs who have an incentive to spend their HSA dollars wisely. They need to know in advance what their medical options are, the quality and expertise of the docs and the hospitals in the area in which they live, and what their medical procedures will cost.

My administration is working with the AHA and other health care associations to provide patients with reliable information about prices and quality on the most common medical procedures. And I want to thank the AHA board for adopting a resolution this week supporting transparency. I appreciate your leadership on this vital issue.

We must work together to get patients the information they need so they can get the best quality care for the best price. If you're worried about increasing costs, it makes sense to have price options available for patients. That's what happens in a lot of our society; it should happen in health care as well. By increasing transparency, the idea is to empower consumers to find value for their dollars and to help patients find better care and to help transform this system of ours to make sure America remains the leader in health care.

Secretary Leavitt has met with leaders in the health care industry in 13 cities to encourage them to work with the Department of Health and Human Services to increase transparency in the marketplace. We're asking doctors and hospitals and other providers to post their walk-in prices to all patients.

I directed the Department of Health and Human Services to make data on Medicare's price and quality publicly available on the Internet. The first data will be available to all Americans by June 1st. We're also asking insurance companies to increase health care transparency by providing their negotiating prices and quality information to their enrollees. And the Federal Government will do the same. My administration will be requiring transparency from insurance plans participating in Federal programs. Beginning this year, the Federal Employees Benefit Program and the military's Tricare system are asking contractors to begin providing price and quality information.

Today I'm asking for your help. Every hospital represented here should take action to make information on prices and quality available to all your patients. If everyone here cooperates in this endeavor, we can increase transparency without the need for legislation from the United States Congress. By working together, transparency—to increase transparency, we can help lower costs.

Third policy is to provide modern information technology to our medical system. Too many doctors' offices and hospitals have the most advanced technology in the 21st century but still use last century's filing systems. Doctors are still writing out files by hand, and that's kind of dangerous because most doctors don't write too well. [*Laughter*] In hospitals, there's more risk of medical error and duplicate tests when records are handwritten on paper instead of cross-checked on a computer.

So in 2004, I set a goal that most Americans would have an electronic health record within 10 years. And we're making good progress toward that goal. The first thing is, we needed to develop a common standard of language so that health care providers in Los Angeles and health care providers in New York knew what the—knew what we are talking about.

Imagine how valuable this access to information will become. If you had someone who had an epileptic seizure outside their hometown and ended up in a hospital in a nearby town, these electronic records would help save lives. Information would be valid and clear. There wouldn't be any confusion amongst those who are working hard to provide compassionate care.

As we develop an information network— nationwide information network, we will make sure that we protect the privacy of a patient's medical record. But make no mistake about it, bringing information technology into our health care system is going to reduce costs and increase quality care for American people.

And I hope you're aggressive on this front. I urge you to work with the AHA to come up with a plan to help develop a nationwide information system that is modern and helps you do your job better.

Fourth policy is to make it easier for small businesses to obtain the same discounts that big companies get when obtaining health care insurance. Unlike big businesses, small companies cannot negotiate lower health insurance rates because they can't spread their risk over a larger pool of employees. So we proposed association health plans that will allow small firms to band together across State lines and buy insurance at the same discounts available to big companies. The House has passed a bill. The Senate hasn't acted, and now it's time for the United States Senate to do something good for the small-business employers of this country.

Our fifth policy to confront high-cost health care and to make sure private medicine is central in the United States is to confront the glut of frivolous lawsuits that are driving good doctors out of practice and driving up the cost of health care. To avoid junk lawsuits, professionals in the health care field are forced to practice defensive medicine. They order tests and write prescriptions that are not necessary so they can protect themselves from trial lawyer lawsuits. One hospital CEO in New York said, "Fear of liability does nothing but threaten patient safety by discouraging open discussion of medical errors and ways to prevent them."

The total cost of defensive medicine to our society is estimated at 60 to a 100

billion dollars a year, and that includes $28 billion billed directly to the American taxpayers through increased costs of Medicare, Medicaid, Veterans Affairs, and other Federal health programs. The costs of frivolous litigation are more than financial; they hurt patients all across America.

Most Americans are shocked when I cite the fact there are nearly 1,500 counties in the United States without an ob-gyn. We want our doctors focused on providing compassionate care, not fighting junk lawsuits. We want our hospitals pursuing innovative and promising ways to heal, not battling lawyers who second-guess them in the courts. This is a national issue that requires a national response. The House of Representatives have passed a good bill; the Senate has done nothing on medical liability reform. For the sake of affordable and accessible health care, we need medical liability reform this year.

I'm looking forward to working with the Congress to enact these reforms. This is a commonsense way of dealing with rising health care costs. And by dealing with rising health care costs, we will strengthen private medicine and fight off the calls of those in Washington, DC, who want the Federal Government making all the decisions for health care.

The story of America's hospitals is a story of America's commitment to be a nation of care and compassion. America's strength and its goodness and prosperity is built on a trust in the extraordinary wisdom and power of the American people. And so I believe that by giving more Americans more control over their health care decisions, we will strengthen the doctor-patient relationship, and we will preserve the system of private medicine that has made our Nation's hospitals and health care the best in the world.

People here in Washington need to trust the people. People here in Washington need to do commonsense things to address the rising costs of health care. And this person in Washington has come to thank you for your compassion and what you do for the communities all around America. May God continue to bless your work, and may God bless our country. Thank you.

NOTE: The President spoke at 1:17 p.m. at the Washington Hilton Hotel. In his remarks, he referred to Richard J. Davidson, president, American Hospital Association.

Remarks to the American Council of Engineering Companies
May 3, 2006

Thanks for the warm welcome. Thanks for inviting me. [*Laughter*] I was looking for something to do this morning. [*Laughter*] I'm really thrilled to be here. I thank you, Mr. Chairman, for letting me come by. I've got something to talk to you about, about the economy. What I'm really thrilled is, is that the American Council of Engineering Companies would allow a history major to come by to speak to you. [*Laughter*]

I want to first say, I appreciate the good work you do for the country. I want you to know that I know how vital your contribution to America is. And it means a lot, and thanks a lot for doing what you're doing. I remember the work you did to help repair the Pentagon after September the 11th. I know full well the work that members of your group do to help construct schools and hospitals in some of the world's newest democracies, particularly Afghanistan and Iraq. And for those of you who encourage your employees to do that or if you've done that yourself, thank you from the bottom of our Nation's collective hearts.

I know that members have been down to help rebuild the communities along the gulf coast. And for those of you who have been down there or may live down there, you know what that storm did. I mean, you talk about wiping out a part of our country; it just flat did. And it makes a difference in people's lives when good-hearted citizens come down and lend their talents and expertise to help rebuild. I've been down there quite a bit; Laura, as a matter of fact, was down in New Orleans last night, and she's there this morning and heading over to Mississippi. And it's amazing what the collective compassion of America has done to help lift the spirits of our fellow citizens. And some of our Nation's engineers were down there helping.

I also want to thank you for helping to build on this country's prosperity. Through your hard work, your vision, your ingenuity, you're helping this economy of ours. You know, I like to remind people that the government's role is not to engineer the economy. The government's role is to create an environment in which people can find work, risk capital, grow their companies, so that, collectively, we all benefit.

I appreciate the entrepreneurial spirit represented here in this room. One of the most important jobs of government is to make sure the entrepreneurial spirit remains strong. We want America to be entrepreneurial heaven, the place where people can come and realize their dreams.

Laura sends her best. I'm a lucky man to have her as my wife. I believe the country is lucky to have her as the First Lady. She is a—[*applause*]—she's pretty busy. She's busy telling me what to do and not what to say. [*Laughter*] It's an interesting life in the White House, as I'm sure you can imagine. There's nothing better, to have somebody by your side who you love, right here in the middle of Washington, DC. [*Laughter*] And Laura is that way. You know, people—my friends from Texas always ask me what it's like to be the President, living in the White House and everything, and it's pretty interesting. I've got a 45-second commute. [*Laughter*] And the good news is, I commute to a house that's warm, and that's because of Laura.

So she sends her very best to you. I wish she were here, but she's, as I said, down in New Orleans helping the people on the gulf coast get their lives back together. As you might remember, she's a librarian, and she's talking about her foundation to help rebuild the libraries down there in the gulf coast of our country. Anyway, she's doing just good. I know you didn't ask, but I'm telling you anyway. [*Laughter*]

I want to thank—not only thank Ed, but I also want to thank the chairman-elect of the ACEC, Jeff Daggett. I want to thank Dave Raymond. I want to thank all the members for letting me come by.

Let me start by telling you, look, I understand there's a lot of, kind of, different opinions about our economy. And you'll hear a lot of different opinions, particularly as the political season approaches. Let me just give you some facts so you can draw your own conclusions, so the American people can draw their own conclusions about whether this economy is strong or not.

In the first quarter of this year, America's economy grew at an impressive rate of 4.8 percent. The strong start follows a strong 2005 when our economy—American economy grew at 3.5 percent. Now, let me put that in perspective for you. Our economy's growth in 2005 was faster than Japan, more than twice as fast as France, and more than three times as fast as Germany.

The American economy is the fastest growing of any major industrialized nation in the world. Productivity has been growing at the highest rate in decades. An economy that is productive is one that will help increase the standard of living for our American people, and we are a productive nation.

We've added jobs for 31 months in a row. We've added more than—[*applause*]—and that's totaled 5.1 million new jobs for the American people, and that's good news. The national unemployment rate has fallen to 4.7 percent. That is lower than the average of any decade since the 1950s. The job market for college graduates is the best it's been in 5 years. The American people are going to work in record numbers, and that's important. Construction spending is at an alltime high. Business confidence is strong, and business investment is growing. Business investment is an indication of confidence in the future. People invest because they think the future is going to be brighter. And when people invest, it helps this country remain productive, and it helps people find work.

Small businesses are flourishing. I know many of you all are small-business owners, and I applaud you for having the courage to start your own business and manage your own business. But small businesses are flourishing in America, and that's important. Most new jobs in America are created by small businesses, and when the small-business sector is strong, it means people are going to find work. The number of Hispanic-owned businesses is growing at three times the national rate, and that's a positive development.

One of the things I try to do is promote an ownership society. We want people owning their own business. There's something that encourages somebody to think about the future of the country when they own their own company. The number of African American-owned businesses is growing at four times the national rate. Real after-tax income has grown by almost 9 percent per person since I took office.

Homeownership recently reached record levels. That's important. I mean, I love the idea, when somebody opens a door to where they live, says, "Welcome to my house; welcome to my piece of property."

It is good for our society to encourage ownership.

Consumer confidence is at its highest point in nearly 4 years. Household wealth is at an alltime high. These are the facts which say to me, this economy is powerful, productive, and prosperous. And we intend to keep it that way.

One of the most important explanations for this strong economy is low taxes. When I came to Washington, taxes were too high, and this economy of ours was headed into a recession. Not only did we have a recession; there was a stock market correction, corporate scandals, an attack on the United States of America. This country went to war to defend ourselves; we had natural disasters. It's amazing the statistics I just read are as strong as they are, given what we've been through. But I believe a lot of the reasons why the statistics are strong is because we let people keep more of their own money under the theory that if you have more of your own money in your pocket to save, invest, or spend, this economy will do just fine.

Part of creating a wealth in which—an environment in which the entrepreneurial spirit is strong is to let people have more of their money, is to unleash the great creative talent of the American people. And that's what we did. I worked with Congress to cut the taxes on everybody who pays taxes. It wasn't one of these tax cuts where, you seem okay, you get a tax cut, and you're not, and you don't. My attitude was, the only fair way to treat people is if you pay taxes, you get tax relief.

So we reduced taxes for every American who pays taxes, and that's more than 110 million people in all. And I want to remind you about the tax relief. First of all, we doubled the child tax credit. We thought it made sense to help people who've got children. Secondly, we put—we reduced the marriage penalty. We did not think it made sense to penalize marriage. We cut the taxes on capital gains and dividends to encourage business investment.

I understand, with more investment, this economy of ours will grow. That's what you want to encourage; you want to encourage people to invest. And it's important for people who watch the economy and try to figure out why we make decisions we make to understand that the more investment there is in the private sector, the more likely it is someone will be able to find work. And so we created incentives in the Tax Code for our small businesses to purchase equipment. We rewarded family businesses and farmers and ranchers by putting the death tax on the way to extinction.

The cumulative effect of these tax cuts left $880 billion in the hands of American workers and businesses. And they have used that money to fuel our economic resurgence. It's the American people, people such as yourself, that used your own money to help make this economy as strong as it is.

There's a business owner today named Gregg Ten Eyck. You know old Gregg. I just named him. Where are you? There he is, right there. [*Laughter*] I hope you're okay with—is that your son? Your son? Yes. Is it okay to mention the old man's name in public? [*Laughter*] Good, because I just did. Gregg is—runs an engineering company in Denver, Colorado. He brought his family. Thank you all for being here. He files as a subchapter S corporation. Most of you know what that means. For those of you who don't, it means that he pays taxes on business income at individual income tax rates.

See, most small businesses are subchapter S corporations or limited partnerships, and therefore, the business pays tax at an individual income tax rate. And so by cutting individual income taxes—rates across the board, we cut taxes on small businesses like Gregg. And there's a reason why you would want to do that. If most new jobs are created by small businesses in the United States and a primary objective is to help people find work, it then makes sense to leave more money in

Gregg's hands so he can spend it to expand his business.

He also took advantage of the new investment opportunities to purchase computers and software that help make him more competitive. Not only did it make him more competitive, but somebody had to make the computers that he purchased. There's an effect throughout the economy when government provides incentives for people to invest. And the fundamental question facing our country is, who do you want making decisions with his own money? Do you want Gregg making the decisions, or do you want somebody in the Halls of Congress? This administration thinks the money is better left in Gregg's hands.

The most important connection for the American people to what I just said about encouraging investment and reducing taxes is this: Gregg's added—Gregg's business added employees for the past 5 years in a row. And this year, he plans to add a few more. Stories like Gregg's prove the tax cuts are doing what we want them to do, and that's to get this economy growing so people can find work. That's what we want.

The problem is that these tax cuts are scheduled to expire in the next few years. So when Congress passed them, they didn't make them a permanent part of the Tax Code. They said, we'll give you some tax relief for a while, but the tax relief is scheduled to go away. And of course, if that were to happen, it means your taxes are going to go up. The prospect of higher taxes, the notion that there's uncertainty in the Tax Code makes it difficult for small-business owners and company execs to plan. How can you plan if you're uncertain about what the future is going to be when it comes to the Tax Code?

Obviously, if you think a big tax crease is incoming—a big tax increase is coming, it will make you less likely to invest. Investment leads to a more productive society; investment leads to job. The lack of invest-

ment will make us less competitive and make it more likely there won't be new jobs created.

And so there's uncertainty in the Tax Code because the Congress made sure that the tax cuts would expire. At a time of high gasoline prices—I know energy prices is on your mind, like a lot of other folks—at a time when there's growing competition in the world, the last thing the American people need is a tax hike. And so my message to the Congress is this: In order to keep this economy strong, Congress needs to make the tax relief permanent.

By the way, there's a struggle here in Washington about who best can spend your money. [*Laughter*] Some are very anxious for the tax cuts to expire; some want to repeal the tax cuts now. Many of those are members of the loyal opposition here in Washington, DC, who've objected to tax relief all along the way. When Congress first cut taxes back in 2001, most of the Democrats in Congress voted against it. One leading Democrat said that tax cuts were a huge mistake. We have a philosophical difference here in Washington; nothing wrong with that. There's nothing wrong with having differences of opinion. Another predicted that the tax cuts would do nothing to create jobs. A year-and-a-half ago, a Democrat Senator informed us the economy may be on the brink of collapse. The Democrats' record of pessimism has been consistent; it's been consistently wrong.

If the people have their way—who want this tax relief to expire—the American people will be hit with $2.4 trillion in higher taxes over the next decade. That's 2.4 trillion that would be taken out of the pockets of firms like Gregg, taken out of the pockets of those who are raising their children. It would be handed over to Government; that's where the money would go. It would be taken out of the economy and given to people here in Washington, DC, to spend. A tax increase would be disastrous for business, disastrous for families, and disastrous for this economy.

Congress has an opportunity to pass a progrowth measure that would keep key elements of the tax relief in place. The House and the Senate are close to completing a bill that would extend the tax cuts on dividends and capital gains for two more years, through 2010. The bill would also extend incentives for small businesses to purchase new equipment. All these provisions have been successful over the past few years. By improving access to capital, the tax cuts on capital gains have led to more investment, more growth, and more job creation.

The tax cuts on the dividends has resulted in more dividend payments to investors and large savings for our seniors who rely on fixed incomes. The small-business expensing incentives have helped many businesses like yours expand and hire new workers. There is no reason for Congress to allow taxes on the job creators to go up. So the House and the Senate have got to resolve their differences and pass progrowth legislation, so I can sign it into law.

Congress also needs to take action on the other side of the ledger as well. And by that I mean, we've got to restrain spending. See, what you'll hear in Washington is, we must balance a budget by raising your taxes. The problem is, that's not the way Washington works. What happens is, they'll raise your taxes and figure out new ways to spend your money. [*Laughter*] The best way to reduce our deficit is to keep progrowth economic policies in place so the economy expands, which will yield more tax revenues, and be wise about how we spend your money.

It's difficult in Washington for people to set priorities when it comes to spending your money. I have set priorities, and our number-one priority is to make sure that the men and women in our uniform have what it takes to defend America and win the war on terror—[*applause*]—which

means we must show discipline in other areas of the budget. You know what that means. You can't spend every—your money on everything you want to spend it on. You have to set priorities. And that's what Congress needs to do.

We're actually making good progress on spending restraint. There are two types of spending: discretionary spending and mandatory spending. Mandatory spending, which I'll talk about a little bit later on, is relief programs that escalate based upon formula. Medicare and Social Security are the two programs that you're most familiar with.

Discretionary spending is where the Congress can decide whether or not to increase or decrease a particular budget. Every year since I took office, we've slowed the growth of discretionary spending that's not related to the military or homeland security. The last two budgets have actually had cuts in this kind of spending. We've reduced the spending.

What we've asked Congress to look at is, we said, look, why don't you analyze whether or not a program is working? See, every program sounds great; they all have got good titles, but sometimes they don't deliver results. And when they don't deliver results, we shouldn't spend taxpayers' money on it. In 2007 budget, we've identified 141 programs that are performing poorly or not fulfilling essential priorities. We've asked Congress to get rid of them. If they're not working, eliminate them.

With a disciplined approach to spending, we're on our way to cutting the deficit in half by 2009, and that's a positive goal. Congress is considering a piece of legislation that will test its commitment to spending restraint. I've requested a bill that would provide emergency funds for the war on terror and hurricane relief. Unfortunately, there are some here in Washington trying to load that bill up with unnecessary spending. This bill is for emergency spending, and it should be limited to emergency measures.

And so I've told the Congress—I'd like to reiterate it here for you—that anything above $92.2 billion for this emergency spending bill, plus the funding to prepare for a pandemic flu emergency, will be vetoed. The Congress needs to hear me loud and clear: If they spend more than 92.2 plus pandemic flu emergency funds, I will veto the bill. It's important for there to be fiscal discipline in Washington, DC, if we want to keep this economy strong.

There are other ways to make sure we're wise about how we spend your money. I'm going to work with Congress to reduce the number of what's called earmarks for special projects. [*Applause*] Sounds like you know what an earmark is. [*Laughter*] Earmarks are often an award of Federal funds to projects without a proper hearing. In other words, people just kind of slide them in there in these bills. And as a result, I don't think the taxpayer gets the best result for their money. It's not—I don't think you can prioritize if you have a system of people just slipping spending in bills without proper hearing.

I appreciate the Senate work on sensible earmark reform. Today the House of Representatives is taking up a measure that includes earmark reform. And I encourage both bodies of Congress to get the job done, to have meaningful, real earmark reform. I look forward to signing such a bill if it comes to my desk.

Congress also can pass the line-item veto. By the way, earmark reform may not require—it's really a matter of Congress having the will to do what's right; same with the line-item veto. A line-item veto would allow me to eliminate wasteful spending items without having to veto the entire bill. And this will be a useful way to help bring fiscal discipline to Washington, DC. The Congress needs to pass a line-item veto quickly. I look forward to working with members of both political parties to achieve budgetary reform so we can do the job you expect us to do.

The biggest problem we've got, however, is—for our budgetary health—is the entitlement spending programs like Social Security and Medicare. If we're wise about keeping progrowth policies in place and fiscal restraint, we can get this deficit down. We're on a trajectory to do so by—cut it in half by 2009. But there's a large problem looming out there, and it's because baby boomers like me and you—[*laughter*]—well, some of you—are getting ready to retire. We're getting to that age where the Government has made us a promise. And there's a lot of us. There's a lot of baby boomers. There's a baby boomer bulge—in more ways than one. [*Laughter*] And we're living longer than anybody thought when they first designed these programs.

And I don't know about you, but I like to get exercise; I'm wise about the choices I make in terms of drinking and all that. And as a result—and medicine has improved—we're living longer lives. So you've got a lot of people getting ready to retire who are going to live longer lives, and we've been promised greater benefits than the previous generation. People running for office say, "Vote for me; I promise to increase your benefits in these entitlement programs." And sure enough, they won and did what they said they were going to do.

But the problem is, is that there are fewer payers per beneficiary into the system than ever before. In other words, there is a heavy burden on a young generation of Americans coming up to pay the promises that Congress has made. And I really, really think that Congress has got to address this issue with me.

I tried last year. I took it on, Social Security in particular, and went around the country saying, "Folks, we got a problem"—on the theory that when the people said we got a problem, Congress would respond. Well, I got half of it right. [*Laughter*] People said, "We got a problem." And it's so political up here that it's difficult at this stage of the game to get people to come together, to come with a bipartisan solution. Look, we don't have to cut programs. It's like making sure you slow your car down to the speed limit. You don't have to put it in reverse. There are common-sense ways to keep the promises to the generation that is fixing to retire but make sure that future generations will have a sound Social Security and Medicare system.

So I just want to assure you this issue is on my mind a lot. I like to remind people that the job of a President is to confront problems, no matter how difficult they may look, and not pass them on to future Presidents. I also believe—[applause]. So we're in the process of working with Democrats and Republicans to come together to forge a bipartisan solution so that we can say we did our duty, that we came and we made the system work better. It's a really important issue.

And so when you hear people talking about the budget, the current account deficit is important; it's really important. But these unfunded liabilities will serve to be a major drag on our economy if we don't do it now. Now is the time to do it. The longer we wait, the more difficult it's going to be for people to come together. So you'll see me working with Democrats and Republicans, hopefully, to come up with a solution that will address this problem.

One of the interesting challenges we face is whether or not this Nation will lose its confidence or not. We live in a global economy, as you well know. And some people in the country really wonder whether it's worth the competition, whether it makes sense to try to compete with these new and growing economies like China and India. I, first of all, know it's important for us to compete and to be confident. If we want to remain the economic leader of the world, which I happen to believe is good for our people, we shouldn't fear the competition. We ought to welcome it, and we ought to develop a strategy so that we can remain the leader. And here's some ideas.

Obviously, we've got to do something about energy. A global economy means that when demand for energy goes up in India and China, which it is, it causes our gasoline prices to go up. When the price of crude goes up, because of international demand increase is greater than the supply, your gasoline prices go up. And so it's—and my attitude about this is to make sure you're not being mistreated at the pump, you're being treated fairly, but also recognize now is the time to spur strong research and development into using other ways to power our cars, such as hydrogen or ethanol or batteries that can give the first 40 miles on electricity, as opposed to gasoline. Now is the time.

And so I look forward to working with Congress to press ahead hard on research and development. And we're close to some amazing breakthroughs. Cellulosic ethanol may be on the verge of becoming commercially viable. We're close to these new battery technologies that will enable people to drive the first 40 miles in a city not using gasoline. Ethanol is on the move. We must, as a nation, in order to stay competitive, diversify away from crude oil. I know it sounds weird for a Texan to say—[laughter]—but I'm telling you, it is essential for our economic security and national security to do so.

We've got a challenge when it comes to making sure our health care is available and affordable. There is a debate here in Washington. There are some who say, "Let's let the Government run it, set the price, set the supply." I'm strongly against that. I believe we've got to empower the doctor-patient relationship. And we put out a lot of good ideas, two that I think will interest you. One is to make sure the small businesses can pool risk across jurisdictional boundaries so they can buy insurance at the same discounts—[applause].

And secondly, do something about these junk lawsuits that are running up the cost of medicine. Do you realize there are over

1,500 counties in America—about, they estimate—that do not have an ob-gyn? That is harmful for our health care system. It's discouraging to the America people. A lot of it is because of these lawsuits. And the lawsuits not only make medicine less accessible, but docs practice defensive medicine. If you think you're going to get sued, you prescribe more drugs than necessary or more procedures than necessary so that you can make your case in a court of law. And this is—these lawsuits harm medicine. It makes the cost of medicine difficult for you, and it makes it hard for you to afford it for your employees.

When I came to Washington, I said, this isn't really a national issue; States ought to deal with it. Then I realized that the cost of defensive medicine and the cost of raising premiums costs our Government—you—about $28 billion a year because of Federal health programs such as Medicare, Medicaid, veterans' benefits. And so I've called upon Congress to get a bill to my desk that is rational, reasonable, and common sense, that does something about these junk lawsuits.

Another initiative I think you'll be interested in is this: To stay competitive, we got to make sure our children have the skill sets necessary to fill the jobs of the 21st century. That skill set happens to be based upon math and science. I think you know what I'm talking about. And as well, in order to be a competitive nation—one that doesn't fear the future, but welcomes the competition and says, look, we can compete, recognizes the importance of research and technology—the research and development tax credit needs to be a permanent part of our Tax Code in order to make sure that people invest in the future, come up with new ideas.

As well, I've committed the Government to double research in basic sciences over the next 10 years. The Government has got a vital role to play. People say to me, why should the Government invest in basic sciences, basic research—research for the

basic sciences? And the answer is, is because it's amazing what happens, what research can bring, such as the Internet. The Internet came to be as a result of Government research monies spent at the DOD. There's unbelievable things that can happen when we unleash the creativity of the American people, and the Federal Government ought to be a rational part of that.

But the other answer—the other real challenge we face is whether or not our kids can compete. And the American people have got to understand that if our children do not have the basics in math and science, they will then not have the skill sets necessary for the jobs of the 21st century. And in a global economy, those jobs will go somewhere else.

And now's the time to get it correct. And we're making pretty good progress, in my judgment. First of all, as people who are results-oriented people, I think you'll appreciate the approach we took in the No Child Left Behind Act, which basically said, in return for spending Federal money, particularly for Title I students, the poor students—which I support—why don't you show us whether or not we're getting results? It's kind of an odd concept, isn't it—[*laughter*]—we spend; you measure.

You notice I didn't say, the Federal Government will design the test. I don't believe in federalizing schools. I believe in local control of schools, but I do believe in accountability. And so therefore, we said to the States, in return for Federal participation, develop accountability systems so we know. There's all kinds of debates that take place in public education. One of them is, does the curriculum work that you're using? The best way to figure it out is to measure.

The second part of this system is that when we find children falling behind early, there's extra money—supplemental service money we call it—to get tutoring so that the children are not left behind. In other words, we're tired of this business about socially promoting students. We want to make sure that people get promoted based upon knowledge. And our system is working.

There's a—there's an achievement gap in America that's got to be closed for the future of this—to make sure this country's future is bright. And we're closing it. How do we know? Because we measure. And we need to apply the same rigor, by the way, that we apply to reading to math and science. It turns out that we're doing fine in fourth grade math, and we're doing fine in eighth grade math, but when kids get into high school, when it comes to the rest of the world, we're falling down. And so therefore, it makes sense to measure in junior high and provide supplemental services for math to make sure that our children have got the skill base necessary to become the engineers and scientists.

AP works—Advanced Placement program works. If it's—if you're involved with your schools in your community, you know what I'm talking about. It's important to set high standards. The Government ought to help train 70,000 teachers to become Advanced Placement teachers to raise the standards for our children. We need 30,000—30,000

scientists and engineers to become adjunct professors, so to speak, in the classrooms to make sure that—[*applause*]. I can go on forever.

Here's the deal, though. Here's what I'm trying to explain to you: We don't need to fear the future because we're going to shape the future. We'll make sure our children are educated. We're going to make sure we do something about these junk lawsuits. We're going to make sure that we do something about energy. Why I wanted to talk to you today, though, is to make sure that you understand that in order for this country to be competitive, in order for us not to fear the future, we got to keep your taxes low.

I appreciate you for what you do for our country. Thanks for letting me come by and share some thoughts with you. God bless you.

NOTE: The President spoke at 11:25 a.m. at the Grand Hyatt Hotel. In his remarks, he referred to Edward J. Mulcahy, chairman, and David A. Raymond, president, American Council of Engineering Companies.

Remarks Following a Meeting With Members of Congress
May 3, 2006

I want to thank the Members of the House and the Senate, members of both parties, for a really constructive and important dialog. We talked about ways to deal with America's energy problem. And we talked about it in a very constructive way, and I want to thank the Members for joining us.

We talked about the need to make sure our consumers are treated fairly, that there be fairness in the marketplace. And there was common consensus that we need to hold people to account if they're not dealing squarely with the American consumer.

We talked about ways to help mitigate demand, and one way to do so is to encourage alternative automobiles, like hybrid automobiles. And there seemed to be an agreement that we ought to extend the tax credit for these kind of automobiles to encourage our consumers to purchase the hybrid automobile.

We talked about ways to—the need to research, to spend money for research and development, to change the fuels that we use in automobiles. One of the great promising sources of fuel is ethanol, and we talked about ways to encourage not only the production of ethanol but the distribution of ethanol.

We talked about the need to continue research and development into new types of batteries so that the American consumer will be able to drive the first 40 miles on electricity. We talked about the need to increase supply of energy. One of the things that is necessary to help relieve price is to increase the amount of gasoline.

We talked about regulatory relief, to see to it that we can expand refining capacity and build new refineries. If the American people want there to be a lower price of gasoline, we need more gasoline on the marketplace.

And so we talked about commonsense ideas. And I really do appreciate the members from both political parties thinking strongly about how we can work together to serve the American consumer and make us less dependent on foreign sources of oil. The prices of gasoline should serve as a wake-up call to all of us involved in public office that we have got an energy security problem and a national security problem, and now is the time to deal with it in a forceful way. And I am heartened by the fact that we were able to have such a constructive dialog, and that there's a commitment to get good legislation out of the Congress.

Thank you all very much for coming.

NOTE: The President spoke at 2:31 p.m. in the Cabinet Room at the White House.

Statement on Zacarias Moussaoui
May 3, 2006

One year ago, Zacarias Moussaoui pled guilty in Federal court to six counts of terrorism, including conspiracy to murder innocent Americans. He openly rejoiced at their deaths. This afternoon the jurors in his sentencing trial concluded that this man should spend the rest of his life in prison.

Our thoughts today are with the families who lost loved ones on September 11th, 2001. Our Nation continues to grieve for the men, women, and children who suffered and died that day. We are still deeply touched by the memory of rescuers who gave all, the passengers who ran a hijacked plane into the ground to prevent an even greater loss of life, and the frightened souls who comforted one another during their final moments on Earth.

The end of this trial represents the end of this case but not an end to the fight against terror. The enemy that struck our shores on September 11th is still active and remains determined to kill Americans. We will stay on the offensive against the terrorists. We will end their ability to plot and plan. We will deny them safe haven and the ability to gain weapons of mass murder. In these 4½ years, with good allies at our side, the United States has killed or captured many terrorists, shut down training camps, broken up terror cells in our own country, and removed regimes that sponsored terror. We have many dedicated men and women fully engaged in this fight— in the military, intelligence, and homeland security; law enforcement personnel; and Federal investigators and prosecutors who gather the evidence, make the case, and ensure that justice is done. They are doing superb work every day to remove this danger and to protect our country.

We have had many victories, yet there is much left to do, and I will not relent in this struggle for the freedom and security of the American people. And we can be confident. Our cause is right, and the outcome is certain: Justice will be served;

evil will not have the final say; this great Nation will prevail.

Remarks Following a Meeting With Chancellor Angela Merkel of Germany and an Exchange With Reporters
May 3, 2006

President Bush. There will be a couple of opening statements and then a couple of questions per side.

Welcome back. Thank you for coming. I've been really looking forward to this visit. Chancellor Merkel has got a very good grasp of the international issues. She's a clear thinker. She speaks very plainly. And I'm honored that you came to visit.

I'm looking forward to taking the Chancellor upstairs to my private residence after this press availability to continue our discussions and to have a dinner that is a continuation of a personal relationship that is developing, where we're able to speak in such a way that we're—can understand our—what we're trying to say and understand our mutual desire to work together to make this world a peaceful place. German-U.S. relations are very important. They're—and I'm just honored you came back.

I do want to mention that we did talk about a couple of very important subjects. Obviously, we spent a lot of time on Iran. After all, we're close allies in trying to make sure that the Iranians do not develop a nuclear weapon. We talked about the WTO round, the Doha round for the WTO, and I appreciated the Chancellor's willingness to work with not only the Europeans but with a country like Brazil and others to see if we can't bring this round to a favorable conclusion.

This evening I'm going to talk to the Chancellor about Sudan and the progress that's being made in Iraq. We've got a lot to talk about because we're friends and allies. And so I welcome you; glad you're here.

Chancellor Merkel. Well, let me say that I am indeed very pleased to be here. And I am also very gratified to know that over the past few months, we have been able to strike up indeed a very, very good rapport, very good relationship, indeed a friendship. And we bolster that friendship mostly by frequent telephone calls; we've been in constant contact.

We addressed a number of issues here today that—of mutual concern, chief among them is Iran, where we are in total agreement, saying that under no circumstances must Iran be allowed to come into possession of nuclear weapons. We are in agreement, also, that a diplomatic solution needs to be found, and we do see good chances for bringing this about. But we also think that it is essential in this context that the clear resolve of the international community is shown by standing united, by showing cohesion on this matter. And what is also essential and indeed crucial in this context is that we try to draw as many partners as possible into the fold and to clearly show to the Iranians that this is unacceptable.

We also addressed the issue of the WTO, the negotiating round, and we said that we want a success of WTO. I explained to the President of the United States that we will use the upcoming EU-Latin American summit in order to get together again with our partners there in bilateral talks and try to impress also the Latin American countries that it is, indeed, necessary for all of us to come to a successful outcome here and that all of these countries need to lend their contribution to bringing that about.

Well—and I trust that this evening we're going to continue discussing other important foreign policy issues. We also, I think, have a number of bilateral issues that we would like to discuss over dinner. Also, because tomorrow one of my stops during this trip will be a stop to New York, where I will meet with representatives of the American business community—so German-American business will also be on the agenda there.

And in conclusion, let me thank you yet again for the very warm and gracious reception here to the White House.

President Bush. Thanks. Deb [Deb Riechmann, Associated Press]. Hold on a second. One at a time. Deb.

Zacarias Moussaoui

Q. Mr. President, are you satisfied with the Moussaoui verdict? He didn't get the death penalty that the Government was seeking. Were you worried that a death sentence might have turned him into a martyr?

President Bush. Mr. Moussaoui got a fair trial; the jury convicted him to life in prison, where he'll spend the rest of his life. In so doing, they spared his life, which is something that he evidently wasn't willing to do for innocent American citizens.

As I think about the trial, I can't help but think about the families who lost a loved one on September the 11th. I think about the rescuers who tried to save lives in the burning buildings. And I know that it's really important for the United States to stay on the offense against these killers and bring them to justice. And those are my thoughts about the Moussaoui trial.

Iran

Q. Mr. President, what kind of sanctions should be taken against Iran, and when?

President Bush. That's the kind of question that allies discuss in private.

Q. You discussed it just this afternoon.

President Bush. Hold on a second. It's very important that the international community send a clear message to the Iranians that a nuclear weapon is unacceptable. We are pleased that the EU–3 has taken such a strong role in this measure. It is part of having a unified message. The United States is actively involved with our partners in achieving this important objective.

The first important thing that must be done in achieving an issue diplomatically is for everybody to share a goal. And the goal is clear, and that is, the Iranians should not have a nuclear weapon or the capacity to make a nuclear weapon. And that in itself is a important diplomatic achievement.

We—the Chancellor and I, of course, obviously, agree on that, but so do other partners in this effort, such as the Russians. They agree that the Iranians should not have a nuclear—it's a good starting point. And now we're talking about the tactics, as to how to achieve that objective. One such tactic is to go to the United Nations Security Council, and today we laid down a resolution. And we will continue to consult with our partners as to how to achieve a diplomatic solution to this issue. And the timing of resolutions and what they should say and—is all—what allies do. And we will come to a common agreement as to how to proceed, because this is a common effort.

And the Iranians must understand that we won't fold, that our partnership is strong, that for the sake of world peace, they should abandon their nuclear weapons ambitions. And we're resolute on that matter. And so that's what Angela and I talk about. We talk about how to make sure this coalition continues to send a common message. And I appreciate her steadfast— and her strength on this issue.

Let's see, we've got Toby [Tabassum Zakaria, Reuters], yes.

Chancellor Merkel. Let me just add one remark. I think in a situation, just as the one that we have now, it is crucial, if one wants to see this matter through to a diplomatic success, to actually do this on a step-by-step basis. Quite often, attempts are being made to rush matters, to actually preempt what should be at the end of the process, and to take the next—the over—next step before the next one. And I really do think that on this one, in order to pursue this diplomatic process successfully, we need to pursue this on a step-by-step basis.

And I mean, it's happening now. We now have an agenda. What is on the agenda now is looking at this matter and then the Chapter VII of the Security Council resolution. And what we need to do further is discuss what we want to pursue further in this process with all of our partners and try to keep them all together.

President Bush. Right. Toby.

Q. Madam Chancellor, do you want the United States to talk directly with Iran on this issue? And did you tell that to President Bush today?

Chancellor Merkel. What I want is to achieve this together, to be successful in this together, in what we are trying to do here, and that is to see to it that Iran is not in possession of a nuclear weapon, persuading them that they will not be allowed to get possession of a nuclear weapon and that they need to abide by international rules.

And I think in this overall process, we have shown that there is very good interaction between us. What we have been doing, we've been doing together, and we shall continue to do so. And I think it is right in this overall process to say, it's important what the European Union has done in this process. They've played a very crucial role. And I must say that I'm fully behind the attempts that have been made by the EU–3, and—together with the United States, because right from the start, we have been in on this together, and we shall continue to be so.

Germany-U.S. Relations

Q. Mr. President——

President Bush. Nice to see you again.

Q. Yes. Thank you very much. Nice to see you too.

President Bush. It's a face a fellow can't forget. [*Laughter*] Okay.

Q. We can talk about this. [*Laughter*] Seriously, we've learned that you have been talking a lot with Madam Merkel, and you've been on the phone for—six times. You've been—you've seen each other a lot. So how has this relation, German-American relation developed since she took office? Are we back into partners in leadership? And when are you planning to come to Germany, maybe to the soccer World Cup?

President Bush. I'm going to come to Germany before the G–8 and—am I supposed to say that? [*Laughter*] Breaking news.

Last time I had a press conference with the Chancellor, I did talk about her predecessor, and, you know, I had a lot of meetings with her predecessor, and I remember them fondly. And I thought our relations—look, the Iraq war made relations difficult. People—it's just—the Government didn't agree, and I understand that.

And the Chancellor is a—I wouldn't call it a new chapter in German-U.S. relations because I did feel we had, you know, we were still writing chapters. But I find the Chancellor to be a—one, a fascinating person who brings a unique perspective. A lot of us who grew up in the West take our liberties for granted, that freedom is something that's just—is prevalent everywhere, and where it's not prevalent, don't worry about it.

Well, I'm talking to a very sophisticated leader who knows what it's like to live in a world that isn't free. And there's just something, to me, that is intriguing and important to have a partner in peace who brings that kind of perspective, who knows the discomfort of what it means to live under the iron hand of a Communist ruler.

So our relationship—the way I view the relationship is, it's growing, and it's strengthening. Any time you have a relationship like this, there has to be a certain degree of trust—and you trust the person when they say something. And I appreciate Chancellor Merkel's straightforward judgment. And I hope that I've created the condition where she tells me what's on her mind, and she expresses her beliefs—and I certainly will express mine—and we're able to find common ground.

And we do disagree, of course. And she—but the disagreements are always in such a way as to make sure that there's a positive relationship, because we both understand relations between Germany and the United States are important for our respective people, important for the relationships in Europe, for the United States. In other words, it enhances the transatlantic relationship. And by working together, we can help solve major problems. And this is a troubled world. We're dealing with Iran. We're dealing with Sudan. And it's very important for diplomacy to work, and it works better when you have a partner in peace, a partner—an ally with—a Germany that understands it can really make a difference in the international community.

And so I value this relationship, and I thank her for her friendship. And I'm looking forward to going to Germany again.

Thank you all.

Chancellor Merkel. Well, to put this in a nutshell, I invited the President to come over before the G–8 summit and to visit me in my constituency, simply because I wanted to show him around and show him a little bit of what has been achieved in what we call the new Linder, to get to know, also, people who, like me, lived on the other side of that wall. And let me say that I'm very much looking forward to his coming over.

Q. When?

Chancellor Merkel. Since the G–8 summit—that was the question as to when you would come over—the G–8 summit is from the 15th through the 17th, so it will, in all probability, be the day before that—the 14th.

President Bush. Yes, somewhere around there. I want to keep it somewhat of a mystery. [*Laughter*] Thank you all.

NOTE: The President spoke at 6:16 p.m. in the Oval Office at the White House. In his remarks, he referred to Zacarias Moussaoui, an Al Qaida operative who was sentenced on May 4 for helping to plan the September 11, 2001, terrorist attacks; and former Chancellor Gerhard Schroeder of Germany. Chancellor Merkel spoke in German, and her remarks were translated by an interpreter.

Remarks on the National Day of Prayer
May 4, 2006

Welcome to the White House. I am really glad you're here. Thanks for coming. And I'm honored to join you for the National Day of Prayer. On this special day, we give thanks for the many ways that America has been blessed, and we acknowledge the Almighty, who is the source of these blessings.

I appreciate the chairman of the National Day of Prayer, Shirley Dobson. I notice

you brought your old husband with you too. [*Laughter*] Thank you for organizing this event here at the White House and around the Nation.

Mrs. Bright, it's good to see you. Thank you; welcome. I'm glad you're back again. Dr. Blackaby, thank you very much, sir, for being the honorary chairman of the National Day of Prayer Task Force. And we welcome Marilynn as well.

I want to thank the members of the Cabinet who are here. Thank you all for coming. Appreciate you taking time out of your day to be here to join.

I'm glad to see my friend Archbishop Demetrios. How are you, sir? Thanks for coming. I appreciate the military chaplains who are here. Thanks for administering to the needs and souls of the men and women who wear the uniform. Yours is an important job, and I'm grateful, as your Commander in Chief, for what you do.

I want to thank Rabbi Ciment, Father Connor, and Jay Dennis for joining us. Thank you for your prayers and your strong statements.

I thank Rebecca St. James for your beautiful music. We're proud you're here. I want to thank those who accompanied you. About the coat—[*laughter*]—your answer is, it's the voice that matters—[*laughter*]—and the spirit behind the voice.

And, Gail, thank you for coming as well. We're proud you're here. Thanks for sharing with us.

America is a nation of prayer. It's impossible to tell the story of our Nation without telling the story of people who pray. The first pilgrims came to this land with a yearning for freedom. They stepped boldly onto the shores of a New World, and many of them fell to their knees to give thanks.

At decisive moments in our history and in quiet times around family tables, we are a people humbled and strengthened and blessed by prayer. During the darkest days of the Revolutionary War, the Continental Congress and George Washington—I call him the first George W.—[*laughter*]—urged citizens to pray and to give thanks and to ask for God's protection.

More than two centuries since our first National Day of Prayer and Thanksgiving, we continue to ask for God's guidance in our own lives and in the life our Nation. Each year, thousands of citizens write letters and send cards to the White House that mention their prayers for this Nation and this Office.

In my travels across the great land, a comment that I hear often from our fellow citizens is, "Mr. President, I pray for you and your family." It's amazing how many times a total stranger walks up and says that to me. You'd think they'd say, "How about the bridge?" or, "How about filling the potholes?" [*Laughter*] No, they say, "I've come to tell you I pray for you, Mr. President."

And the only thing I know to do is to look at them in the eye and say, "That is the greatest gift that a fellow citizen can do for those of us who have been entrusted to lead our country." And for that—[*applause*]. And so I thank thanks—I say thanks to the millions of Americans who pray each day for our Nation, our troops, and our elected leaders.

Prayer is a gift from Almighty God that transforms us, whether we bow our heads in solitude or offer swift and silent prayers in times of trial. Prayer humbles us by reminding us of our place in creation. Prayer strengthens us by reminding us that God loves and cares for each and every soul in His creation. And prayer blesses us by reminding us that there is a divine plan that stands above all human plans.

In the stillness and peace of prayer, we surrender our will to God's will, and we learn to serve His eternal purposes. By opening ourselves to God's priorities, our hearts are stirred, and we are inspired to action—to feed the hungry, to reach out to the poor, to bring aid to a widow or to an orphan or to the less fortunate.

On this day, we also remember that we are a people united by our love for freedom, even when we differ in our personal beliefs. In America, we are free to profess any faith we choose—or no faith at all. What brings us together is our shared desire to answer the call to serve something greater than ourselves.

Over the past 5 years, I have watched the American people answer this call. Some serve their fellow man on distant shores, placing themselves in harm's way so that others might live in freedom. Others serve in our Nation's armies of compassion, bringing comfort and kindness to suffering communities at home and abroad. In millions of acts of service, the American people have shown the good heart of our Nation.

From our Nation's prayerful beginnings, America has grown and prospered. Through prayer, we humbly recognize our continued dependence on divine providence.

I want to thank you all for keeping prayer a part of our national life. May God bless each one of you, and may God continue to bless our Nation.

And now it is my honor to welcome Reverend Jay Dennis.

NOTE: The President spoke at 9:44 a.m. in the East Room at the White House. In his remarks, he referred to James Dobson, husband of National Day of Prayer chairman Shirley Dobson; Vonette Bright, former chairman, National Day of Prayer Task Force; Marilynn Blackaby, wife of Henry T. Blackaby, honorary chairman of the National Day of Prayer Task Force; Archbishop Demetrios Trakatellis, Primate of the Greek Orthodox Church in America; Rabbi Sholom Ciment, director, Chabad Lubavitch of Greater Boynton, Boynton Beach, FL; Father Charles P. Connor, pastor, St. Rose of Lima Church, Carbondale, PA; Rev. Jay Dennis, pastor, First Baptist Church at the Mall, Lakeland, FL; entertainers Rebecca St. James and Gail Richardson. The National Day of Prayer proclamation of May 3 is located in Appendix D at the end of this volume.

Remarks Following Discussions With President Tabare Vazquez of Uruguay
May 4, 2006

President Bush. Bienvenidos. It's been a distinct pleasure to welcome the President to the Oval Office. We've had a very extensive conversation about—we talked about a lot of subjects. We talked about the human condition. We talked about our mutual desire to improve lives through good education and health care. I assured the President that the billions of dollars of aid that we spend in the neighborhood are all aimed at justice and giving people a chance to realize their dreams.

We talked about ways to make sure there's better student exchanges between our countries. It made a lot of sense. After all, the President was educated—or received some education in my home state of Texas, at M.D. Anderson.

We talked about extending our commercial relations. One of the interesting topics that the President brought up was renewable energy, a subject that is very dear to my heart and necessary for our country. And finally, I shared some thoughts with the President about my deep desire to help countries become free, so that this world is more peaceful.

I—in short, it was a very extensive dialog. And finally, he shared with me the joy of being a grandfather. Obviously, he's a good man because he's got such pride in his family.

And so I welcome you here, sir. Thank you for coming.

President Vazquez. Mr. President, thank you very much for your kindest attention. It's, for us, a great opportunity to speak—but I speak Spanish.

President Bush. Si. [Laughter]

President Vazquez. Y tu tambien.

Thank you very much, Mr. President. I want to thank you very much for your welcome. This is one more show of friendship that has been a very deep friendship between our countries from the very beginning.

We've had a very kind and extensive exchange of opinions with President Bush. First of all, we recalled the bilateral investment treaty that was recently signed by our two countries in which we have—and we have now also agreed to work to expand, intensify, and strengthen our trade relations. In fact, our technical people are going to be meeting within the framework of our joint commission in a few months in Montevideo, and we've agreed that we are going to be kicking off work at that time.

I will not extend on the points that have—the items that have already been referred to by the President, but I do want to thank you very much.

And to the Uruguayan people who are listening to me, I want to say to all of you: Without exception, without exclusions, together we will continue to work jointly on this path that we have undertaken in order to further the standard of life with our people, through education, through health care, through more and better jobs, and through decent salaries for all our people, and to truly insert Uruguay on the path of globalization.

Thank you very much.

President Bush. Gracias, senior. Gracias.

NOTE: The President spoke at 11:09 a.m. in the Oval Office at the White House. President Vazquez spoke in Spanish, and his remarks were translated by an interpreter.

Remarks at a Cinco de Mayo Celebration
May 4, 2006

Thank you. Please be seated. *Bienvenidos.* Welcome to the White House. I'm honored to have so many distinguished Hispanic and Mexican American leaders here for the Cinco de Mayo celebration. You may have noticed this celebration is not on the *cinco de Mayo*—[*laughter*]—it's on the *quatro de Mayo*. [*Laughter*] It's such an important holiday, we thought we would start early. [*Laughter*]

I appreciate Hector; good to see you—head of the SBA is with us today. Gaddi Vasquez, thank you for coming. Thank you both for bringing—thank you for bringing your wife, Hector. I want to thank Anna Cabral, who is the Treasurer, and glad you brought Victor. Thanks for coming.

I appreciate the Ambassadors who have joined us. Ambassador *de Mexico* is with us today—*Embajador, gracias—y tambien, mi amigo*, the Ambassador from the United States to Mexico, Antonio Garza. Welcome you both. Glad you're here. I appreciate Eduardo Aguirre, Ambassador to Spain. Thank you for coming, Eduardo—Hans Hertell, the Ambassador to the Dominican Republic. Thank you all very much for coming. Thanks for serving the country, and thanks for serving your country, Ambassador, as well.

I appreciate the military personnel who are here today. We're proud of you. Thanks for wearing the uniform of the United States of America.

Before I introduce our entertainer, I do want to share some thoughts with you about the importance of Cinco de Mayo, for it commemorates a joyful moment in Mexican history. Americans must understand that it was a time when Mexican soldiers won the Battle of Puebla and defended their independence. So obviously,

Cinco de Mayo is a day of special pride for citizens of Mexico, but it is, as well, for Americans. It is a reminder of a proud heritage we share with our neighbor to the south. That's how I view the day.

We pay tribute to that heritage, and we honor the warmth and importance of the friendship between our two nations. The United States and Mexico are united by ties of family and by commerce and by history and by culture and by values. Both nations believe in the rights and the dignity of all people. We share an important trade relationship. We have discovered that trade between our nations is good for our peoples. We believe in the ideals of freedom and independence that Cinco de Mayo represents.

Here in the United States, Mexican Americans have helped build our country and helped shape our culture. Mexican Americans have made our Nation more vibrant and more hopeful *cada dia*. Mexican Americans have enriched the American experience with contributions to business and the arts and music and sports. Latino entrepreneurs are creating jobs across the country; the number of Hispanic-owned businesses is growing at three times the national rate. More Hispanic Americans own their homes than ever before in our Nation's history.

Many Mexican Americans have also shown their devotion to this country by defending it. More than 600,000 of our veterans are of Mexican descent. I see some of our veterans back—I'm sure—we got a lot of veterans here, as a matter of fact. I want to thank you for setting such a good example for those who wear the uniform today.

Many Mexican Americans are wearing the uniform of the United States military, and they're defending our country with valor. They're making America more secure and, at the same time, laying the foundation of peace for generations to come.

I know our citizens have enormous pride in the Mexican heritage, and rightly so. We also know that America has thrived as a nation because we've always welcomed newcomers who, in turn, embrace our values and our way of life. Becoming an American is a great privilege, and it carries with it responsibilities. Those who come here to start new lives in our country have a responsibility to understand what America is about and the responsibility to learn the English language so they can better understand our national character and participate fully in American life. That's what we want. Making this effort is also key to unlocking the opportunities of America, allowing new folks to rise in society and realize the American Dream.

In this country, we're now having an important debate about immigration. And it is really important that we discuss this issue in a way that is worthy of this country's best traditions. Our Nation does not have to choose between being a compassionate society and a lawful society. A lawful society is one that enforces its laws and enforces its border; that's what a lawful society does. A compassionate society rejects a system that treats people as if they're something to be traded, honors human rights and human dignity, helps people out of the shadows of society, treats people in a decent and humane way.

So I support strengthening our borders, and I support a temporary-worker program that would match willing workers with American employers. See, I think we need to create a secure and legal channel for people to come to this country to work. It will reduce the number of people trying to sneak across our border. It will treat people humanely. It will get rid of the *coyotes* and the document forgers. It will affirm our belief that every person has got dignity and every person has got value, and at the same time, it will make it easier for us to be a nation of law and to protect our border.

Immigration reform needs to be comprehensive because all elements of this problem must be addressed together, or none of them will be solved at all. The American people must conduct this debate with dignity. They must remember that we're a nation of immigrants. They must understand—they must remember that throughout our history, people have come to America because this is a place where they can pursue their dreams no matter who they are or where they're from.

Mexican Americans have brought with them a culture based upon faith in God, a deep love for family, and a belief that hard work leads to a better life. Every immigrant who lives by these values makes the United States a better country, makes our future brighter as one nation under God.

Across America tomorrow, there will be many celebrations of Cinco de Mayo. The performances we're going to see today represent some of the very fine talent. It reminds us that we're a nation that is strong because of our diversity. There's going to be a lot of traditional music, a lot of pretty

good Mexican food too, I bet you. [*Laughter*] Kind of reminds us of Texas, doesn't it, Ambassador?

May God continue to bless all of us who are fortunate enough to live in this land, and may God continue to bless our country and the many sons and daughters of Mexico who call our Nation home. Happy Cinco de Mayo. And now it is my pleasure to introduce one of Mexico's great talents, Graciela Beltran.

NOTE: The President spoke at 1:57 p.m. in the East Room at the White House. In his remarks, he referred to Robin Barreto, wife of Small Business Administration Administrator Hector V. Barreto, Jr.; Victor G. Cabral, husband of Treasurer of the United States Anna Escobedo Cabral; Mexico's Ambassador to the U.S. Carlos Alberto de Icaza Gonzalez; and entertainer Graciela Beltran of Mexico. The Office of the Press Secretary also released a Spanish language transcript of these remarks.

Statement on House of Representatives Passage of Port Security Legislation
May 4, 2006

I am pleased that the House of Representatives today passed a bill to enhance the security of our Nation's ports. I look forward to working with Congress on passage of legislation that will make our people safer and facilitate trade.

Remarks at the American Jewish Committee's Centennial Dinner
May 4, 2006

[*The President's remarks are joined in progress.*]

——I want to thank the Members of Congress who are here. I appreciate the members of the diplomatic corps who have joined us today. I want to pay a special tribute to a friend of mine from Texas who

has done a superb job as the Chairman of the U.S. Holocaust Memorial Council, and that's Fred Zeidman.

My administration shares a strong commitment with the AJC to make sure relations between Israel and America remain strong. We have so much in common.

We're both young countries born of struggle and sacrifice. We're both founded by immigrants escaping religious persecution. We have both established vibrant democracies built on the rule of law and open markets. We're both founded on certain basic beliefs: that God watches over the affairs of men and that freedom is the Almighty God's gift to every man and woman on the face of this Earth. These ties have made us natural allies, and these ties will never be broken. America's commitment to Israel's security is strong, enduring, and unshakable.

I'm looking forward to my meeting with Prime Minister Olmert in a couple of weeks. And as he comes to America, I cannot help but think about my friend Ariel Sharon. Ariel Sharon is a friend who remains in our thoughts and prayers. He is a man of courage and a man of peace. And so tonight we pray for his recovery; we rededicate ourselves to the cause to which he devoted his life, the peace and the security of Israel.

As you know, I'm a strong believer in democracy and free elections, but that does not mean we have to support elected officials who are not committed to peace. Hamas has made it clear that they do not acknowledge the right of Israel to exist, and I've made it clear that so long as that's their policy, we will have no contact with the leaders of Hamas. Democratically—leaders cannot have one foot in the camp of democracy and one foot in the camp of terror. Hamas must accept the demands of the international community to recognize Israel, disarm and reject terrorism, and stop blocking the path to peace.

Many of the AJC leaders who have come to know me understand how my thinking was profoundly affected by the attacks on our country on September the 11th, 2001. The security of our Nation is foremost in my mind. I vowed that day and I vow to you today that the United States of America will stay on the hunt and bring the killers to justice.

And one of the lessons of September the 11th is that this Nation must take threats seriously before they fully materialize. And I saw a threat in Saddam Hussein. He had invaded a neighbor; he had used weapons of mass destruction against his own people; he had the capability of making weapons of mass destruction; he harbored terrorists; he was shooting at U.S. aircraft. He was a threat, and the world is better off without Saddam Hussein in power.

Our goal in Iraq is to have an ally in the war on terror and to help that young country establish an Iraqi-style democracy. Last December, 12 million people defied the car bombers and the killers and the terrorists and said that "We want to live in liberty." Recently a unity government has formed in Iraq. They reached an agreement on their top leadership posts. This new Government represents a turning point in Iraq, a new chapter in our engagement there, and an opportunity for progress. We will form a new partnership with these leaders. We will adjust our methods to support their priorities. We will strengthen our mutual efforts to achieve victory.

But I want you to understand that the new Government is yet another blow to those who hate liberty. First, it will deny the terrorists their immediate aim of turning Iraq into a safe haven from which they can plot and plan attacks against the United States and our allies. And secondly, a democratic Iraq will be a major blow to the terrorists' hateful ideology, sending a powerful message across the region that the future of the Middle East belongs to freedom. The only way we can lose in Iraq is if we lose our nerve, and I am not going to lose my nerve.

The AJC, the American Government, and most of the nations of the world are concerned about Iran. We're concerned because the Iranian regime is repressing its people, sponsoring terrorists, destabilizing the region, threatening Israel, and defying the world with its ambitions for nuclear weapons. America will continue to rally the world to confront these threats.

We're making progress. The first goal is to reach a common objective, and the objective amongst America, our European allies, Russia, and China is to deny Iran a nuclear weapon. I spent time with Chancellor Merkel yesterday talking about this important issue. I can assure you we have a strong ally in Chancellor Merkel when it comes to uniting the world to speak with one clear voice.

We will continue to press the Iranian Government to comply with IAEA as well as U.N. Security Council resolutions. America respects and admires the people of Iran. We respect their history and culture. We respect their right to choose their own future and win their own freedom. And America looks forward to the day when our Nation can be closest of friends with a free and democratic Iran.

Before I introduce the Chancellor, I do want to talk about another subject that I know is important to you, and it's important to me, and that's Darfur. Last weekend, thousands rallied on our National Mall to call for justice in Darfur. And among the speakers was a man who understands the meaning of evil. You know him well. Elie Wiesel put it this way: "We refuse to be silent because silent helps the killer, never his victims."

America is not silent. The United States is the only country to have called the crimes taking place in Sudan what they are—genocide. To end these atrocities, we've developed a clear standard. First, there must be a political course. Right now as we speak, we're negotiating to bring a political settlement so that all sides will lay down their arms, a settlement between the

Government and the rebels. These conversations are taking place in Abuja.

But, as well, we must understand that the rape and the murder and the suffering must be stopped. And that's why I believe strongly that we must augment AU forces with a blue-helmeted U.N. force, with a NATO overlay, so that we can send a clear message to the leaders of Sudan: We will not tolerate the genocide taking place in that country.

My remaining time in office, I look forward to working with AJC leaders. I appreciate your steadfast strength when it comes to dealing with terror. I appreciate your strong belief in the power of liberty to transform the world we have. I look forward to working with you to continue to lay the foundations of peace so that generations after our time will look at all of us and say, job well done.

And now it's my pleasure to introduce a leader who understands the importance of freedom. Angela Merkel grew up in East Germany during the dark days of the cold war. She understands what it means to live in a free society. She understands the power of liberty. She's a straightforward person; she tells me what's on her mind. She's a woman of good judgment. She's a strong leader. It's my privilege to welcome her here and to our friends at the AJC.

NOTE: The President spoke at 6:57 p.m. at the National Building Museum. In his remarks, he referred to Prime Minister Ehud Olmert and former Prime Minister Ariel Sharon of Israel; former President Saddam Hussein of Iraq; Chancellor Angela Merkel of Germany; and Nobel prize winner and author Elie Wiesel.

Remarks on the National Economy
May 5, 2006

The President. Listen, I thank you for your hospitality. I'm here to talk about our economy. Today we've got some good news: 138,000 additional Americans found jobs over the last month, which is good. The national unemployment rate is 4.7 percent. This economy is strong.

And one of the hopeful things about our economy is, small businesses are doing well. Small businesses provide most of the job growth in our country. The small-business sector is doing well; so is the American economy.

One thing we've got to make sure is that we keep the people's taxes low to keep this economy growing. Raising taxes will hurt small businesses; raising taxes will hurt consumers; raising taxes will particularly affect working people, now that the price of gasoline has gone up. So one of the things Congress has got to do is be mindful that the economic growth we're seeing, the strong economic growth, is dependent upon good tax policy.

At the same time, Congress should be wise about how they spend the people's money. They've got to make sure the supplemental comes to me at a rate that I'll accept—$92.2 billion—plus money for the pandemic flu.

We've got a plan to make sure this economy keeps growing, but today's news is good news for the American people.

And I want to thank you—let me thank you for coming by here to say hito you.

John Weintraub. All right, I thank you.

The President. It's a good place to shop, by the way. I just spent some of my hard-earned money on Barney. I bought him a couple of toys to chew on—but don't let him know until I get over there; it's a surprise. [*Laughter*] Thanks for letting me come by.

Mr. Weintraub. Okay. Thank you, Mr. President.

NOTE: The President spoke at 10:08 a.m. Participating in the visit was John Weintraub, coowner, Frager's Hardware.

Remarks Announcing the Resignation of Porter J. Goss as Director of the Central Intelligence Agency
May 5, 2006

The President. This morning Director Porter Goss offered his resignation as the Director of the Central Intelligence Agency. I've accepted it.

During the course of his tenure, I've established a very close personal relationship with Porter, which is very important for the Director of the CIA. He's spent a lot of time here in the Oval Office. He's told me—he's given me his candid advice. I appreciate his integrity. I appreciate the

honor in which—that he brought to the job.

Porter's tenure at the CIA was one of transition. He's helped this Agency become integrated into the intelligence community, and that was a tough job. And he's led ably. He's got a 5-year plan to increase the number of analysts and operatives, which is going to help make this country a safer place and help us win the war on terror. He's instilled a sense of professionalism. He honors the proud history of the CIA, an organization that is known for its secrecy in accountability. I am confident that his successor will continue the reforms that he's put in place, and as a result, this country will be more secure.

We've got to win the war on terror, and the Central Intelligence Agency is a vital part of that war. And so I want to thank you for your service.

[*At this point, Director Goss made brief remarks.*]

The President. God bless. Thank you. I appreciate you. Thank you very much.

NOTE: The President spoke at 1:44 p.m. in the Oval Office at the White House. The transcript released by the Office of the Press Secretary also included the remarks of Director Goss.

The President's Radio Address
May 6, 2006

Good morning. Today I want to talk with you about the new Medicare prescription drug coverage that went into effect at the start of this year. Everyone on Medicare is eligible for this new coverage, but the enrollment deadline of May 15th is just over a week away. For those of you with Medicare who have not yet signed up, it is important for you to review your options and choose a plan. By enrolling before the deadline, you can ensure the lowest possible premiums and start saving on your prescription drug bills.

Many of you have already made the wise decision to enroll. Since the new coverage went into effect, more than 30 million Americans now have prescription drug coverage through the Medicare program, and more are enrolling each week. Recent surveys show that the vast majority of seniors are satisfied with the program and for good reason.

Competition in the prescription drug market has been stronger than expected, and costs for seniors are lower than expected. The average premium that seniors pay is a third less than had been expected—just $25 per month instead of $37 per month. The typical person with Medicare who previously had no drug coverage will now spend about half of what he or she used to spend on prescription drugs, saving an average of $1,100 per year.

Low-income seniors receive extra help. For them Medicare will now cover, on average, more than 95 percent of the costs of their prescription drugs. Thanks to this new coverage, America's seniors are now getting the modern medicine they need at prices they can afford.

Prescription drug coverage under Medicare is also giving our seniors more and better choices for their health care. Instead of having to accept a one-size-fits-all plan, seniors are now choosing from a variety of drug plans, and they're finding the one that best fits their needs. Most seniors are able to choose their plans that have low premiums, low or no deductibles, fixed copayments for most drugs, and affordable coverage to fill in coverage gaps.

Medicare prescription drug coverage is a great deal for seniors. So today I am encouraging those of you who still have not enrolled to take a look at your options and sign up before the May 15th deadline, in order to ensure the lowest premiums. Even if you do not have significant drug expenses now, you should consider joining a Medicare drug plan to protect yourself against high prescription drug bills down the road.

There are many ways you can get help to choose a drug plan and enroll. You can ask your doctor or pharmacist for help. You can speak with a Medicare counselor 24 hours a day at 1–800–MEDICARE. You can enroll online by visiting the official Medicare web site at medicare.gov. If you need help enrolling, citizens' groups like AARP and NAACP, faith-based organizations, health professionals, and pharmacies are working to answer questions. Between now and May 15th, events will be held across the country to answer your questions and help you enroll for the new drug coverage. And if you have family or friends on Medicare, you can help too. Helping can be as simple as showing an older neighbor how to fill out a form, helping a senior use the Internet, or making a call for your mom or dad.

I was proud to sign Medicare prescription drug coverage into law. Because we acted, America now has a Medicare system to fit the needs of the 21st century, and millions of American seniors and persons with disabilities are now saving a lot of money and receiving the modern health care they deserve. Over the coming days, we will continue working to make sure that everyone with Medicare has a chance to save money and enjoy the peace of mind that this new drug coverage brings.

Thank you for listening.

NOTE: The address was recorded at 7:50 a.m. on May 5 in the Cabinet Room at the White House for broadcast at 10:06 a.m. on May 6. The transcript was made available by the Office of the Press Secretary on May 5 but was embargoed for release until the broadcast. The Office of the Press Secretary also released a Spanish language transcript of this address.

Commencement Address at Oklahoma State University in Stillwater, Oklahoma
May 6, 2006

Thank you all very much. President Schmidly, thank you. Members of the Oklahoma State faculty and administration; Governor; people in the statehouse; Members of the United States Congress; distinguished guests; parents, friends, family, and, most important, the class of 2006: Thanks for the warm welcome to this great State and to this fine campus. I'm honored to be here.

Laura sends her greetings, and she's disappointed that she couldn't be here with me. She was even more disappointed when she found out I had planned a romantic dinner for two—at Eskimo Joe's. She also said she had one question to ask the students here today: How orange are you? If you read the papers, you know that when some would criticize me, they call me a cowboy. This cowboy is proud to be standing here in the midst of a lot of other cowboys.

I want to thank the moms and dads here for the sacrifice and for the love you've shown your children. I want to thank the faculty for your hard work and dedication. I congratulate the class of 2006. Some of you are graduating with honors that involved much sacrifice and achievement. Others perhaps spent a little less time in the library. [*Laughter*] For all of you, I bring a message of great hope: There's life after English Comp. [*Laughter*] Someday, you'll appreciate what you've learned here; you're going to make your teachers proud. I know the professors who taught me English marvel at my way of words. [*Laughter*]

The last few months before graduation are busy ones. Amid all the excitement, there's one thing that probably eluded a few of you—you haven't had time to find a job. I speak for your parents when I say, now is the time to start looking. Some good news for you: The job market for college graduates is the best it's been in years. The economy of ours is strong, and so you'll have more jobs to choose from than previous classes, and your starting salaries will be higher. And the opportunities beyond are only limited by the size of your dreams.

You're privileged to live in the world's freest country at one of the most hopeful moments in human history. Soon you'll leave this university to take your place in our society. And as you do, you'll witness dramatic changes, and these changes will present you with opportunities and choices and great challenges.

Your generation will enjoy unimagined opportunities because of education. You know, when this university was founded in 1890, it was called the Oklahoma Territorial Agricultural and Mechanical College, one of the Nation's land-grant colleges. And the investment has paid off many times over. Some of the oldtimers remember that after the Dust Bowl hit Oklahoma in the 1930s, this university responded by helping the farmers and ranchers with innovative soil conservation techniques. OSU is still committed to the land-grant mission of high-quality teaching and advanced research and outreach to the communities it serves. But the school has moved far beyond its original focus on agriculture, and Oklahoma State University is now a comprehensive public university with eight degree-granting colleges that offer more than 350 programs to more than 21,000 students.

This fine university has adapted, and to succeed in the 21st century, you're going to have to adapt as well. Your degree marks the successful end of your undergraduate education, and when you leave this university, you're going to enter a dynamic world

and an economy that is constantly creating new opportunities that will require you to learn new skills. I urge you to rise to these challenges. Take charge of your future; be open to new ideas; be willing to take risks. Treat the degree you receive today as the first step in a lifetime of learning, and your lives will be rich in purpose and reward.

Your generation will face unprecedented choices because of technology. When I was in college, we listened to music on 45 rpm records as opposed to the iPod. We used manual typewriters instead of the personal computer. When we made a mistake while writing a paper, we didn't have the luxury of spell check. As a matter of fact, we used something that maybe some of you have heard of—it was big and bulky—it's called a dictionary. [*Laughter*] Technology has helped improve almost every aspect of your life on campus—except maybe the cafeteria food. [*Laughter*]

Just as technology is making life better for college students, it's making all of us more productive. If you take a job in an office, the technology you use will make you more efficient than earlier generations. If you decide to open a small business, technology can help you lower your costs or reach more customers through the Internet. If you're a farmer or a rancher, technology gives you instant access to expert advice from specialists who may live thousands of miles away. By helping each of us do our jobs better, technology is improving life for all of us.

Some of the most exciting advances in technology you'll see will be in the field of energy. When I graduated from school, cars drank gasoline. Last month in California, I saw cars powered by hydrogen that use no gasoline and emit no pollution. Within your lifetime, advances in technology will make our air cleaner and our cars more efficient. The gasoline engine will seem as antiquated as the rotary phone and the black-and-white TV.

Technology holds promise for extending and improving our lives through dramatic breakthroughs in the field of medicine. In recent times, we've gone from x rays to MRIs, from eyeglasses to laser eye surgery, from major operations that would keep you in the hospital for weeks to miracle drugs that can prevent the need for the operation in the first place. In the decades ahead, you're going to witness incredible changes in health care that will even be more revolutionary.

These advances in technology will transform lives, and they will present you with profound dilemmas. Science offers the prospect of eventual cures for terrible diseases and temptations to manipulate life and violate human dignity. With the Internet, you can communicate instantly with someone halfway across the world and isolate yourself from your family and your neighbors. Your generation will have to resolve these dilemmas. My advice is, harness the promise of technology without becoming slaves to technology. My advice is, ensure that science serves the cause of humanity and not the other way around.

Your generation will confront the challenges of a world that is now at our doorsteps. When Oklahoma was settled in the late 19th century, this was America's frontier. Now the whole world is within your reach. You can e-mail friends in Central America, or you can fly nonstop across the Atlantic or Pacific, or you use your Bank of Oklahoma card and withdraw money from an ATM in Australia.

At the same time, we're seeing the rise of new competitors like China and India, and this competition creates uncertainty. Some look at the changes taking place all around us, and they worry about the future. Their reaction is to wall America off from the world and to retreat into protectionism. This is a sure path to stagnation and decline. I ask you to reject this kind of pessimism.

We should welcome competition. We should welcome competition, because it makes our country stronger and more prosperous. Today, the citizens of Oklahoma export wheat to Mexico or pork to Japan or liquid pumps to Russia. For your generation, even more opportunities will come from overseas. Government must help, but it is up to you to take advantage of what you have learned here and meet the future with confidence in your ability to compete and succeed.

A country that shuts itself off from competition will be a country that isolates itself from the duties and opportunities of our world. One of the greatest opportunities of this young century is the advance of human freedom. The advance of liberty is the story of our time, and we're seeing new chapters written before our eyes. Freedom is taking root in places where liberty was once unimaginable. Just 25 years ago, there were only 45 democracies on the face of the Earth. Today, there are 122 democracies, and more people now live in liberty than ever before. The advance of liberty gives us hope in the future because free societies are peaceful societies. As freedom spreads, the threat of tyranny and terror will recede, and the rise of democracy will bring peace to the world and security to the United States of America.

No, this changing world presents you with a lot of exciting opportunities. Yet a changing world also needs the anchor of old-fashioned values and virtues, like courage and compassion. These are the virtues that sustain our democracy and make self-government possible. These virtues are what we will need to build a more hopeful future. And these virtues are present in the Oklahoma State class of 2006.

We see these virtues in an extraordinary young woman named Melissa Unwin. Melissa has been studying in your College of Education. Back in 2001, she was diagnosed with cancer, and the doctors doubted she would ever finish college. If you know anything about educators, you know that when they tell you—when somebody tells them something is impossible, they're going to work harder to prove you wrong. And that's just what Melissa has done. The degree that Melissa has earned today is an example of courage in the face of adversity, and she represents a spirit necessary for your generation to succeed.

We see the spirit of compassion in the members of the class of 2006 who've stepped forward to serve their community. As part of your "Into the Streets" volunteer effort this past fall, one fraternity helped build a playground at the local homeless shelter. They probably realized it was better to help somebody else than go to the bar. [*Laughter*] Other members of your class traveled down the gulf coast after Hurricane Katrina to help clean up debris and deliver comfort and relief. They didn't have to do that, but they felt the calling to go help somebody in need.

I met seniors who have volunteered in a wide variety of ways, upon my landing. They build houses for the underprivileged and visit nursing homes and tutor fellow students. One of these volunteers says this about her service: "I feel I've been very fortunate, and any way I can help other people to have a house to live in, to have food on the table, or even a clean yard, means I'm making a difference."

We see the spirit of service in the members of the class of 2006 who've stepped forward to defend our freedom. In this graduating class, there are 27 new lieutenants who are receiving their Army and Air Force commissions along with their OSU degrees. They're carrying on the proud tradition of service in uniform exemplified by an OSU graduate named Luke James. After earning his commission at OSU in 2002, Luke had the world at his feet; he had a wife and infant son that he adored. Yet Luke had chosen a life of service, and in 2004, Second Lieutenant Luke James, graduate of OSU, was deployed to Iraq as a member of the Army's 82d Airborne. Short-

ly after arriving in that country, Luke was killed while leading his troops on patrol. He was awarded the Bronze Star. He's buried at Arlington National Cemetery.

On the anniversary of her son's death, Luke's mom went to visit her son's grave. And afterward, a young soldier came up to her and thanked her for the way she had raised her son. He said that Lieutenant James had saved his life. Luke's mom says this of her son's service: "All of Luke's life, he was very dedicated to the concept of freedom. While no soldier wants war, he understood the necessity of war, that it can ensure the freedoms we enjoy in America." Luke James is part of a generation who are every bit as selfless and dedicated to liberty as any that has ever come before. And the future of the United States of America is better because of the character of young Americans like Luke James.

In this time of technological change and global competition, ultimately the character of America will be determined by your willingness to serve a cause larger than yourselves. The day will come when you'll be asked, what have you done to build a better America than the one you found? I'm confident that you will answer the call to service. I'm confident that your lives will be more fulfilling and your country more hopeful. And I'm confident that you'll look back and say, "Job well done."

Congratulations to you all. May God bless you, the class of 2006, and may God bless the United States of America.

NOTE: The President spoke at 10:10 a.m. in Boone Picket Stadium. In his remarks, he referred to David J. Schmidly, president, Oklahoma State University; Gov. Brad Henry of Oklahoma; and Arleen James, mother of 2d Lt. Luke S. James, USA, who was killed in Iraq on January 27, 2004.

Interview With Sabine Christiansen of ARD German Television
May 4, 2006

President's Upcoming Visit to Germany

Ms. Christiansen. Thank you very much, Mr. President, for joining us. We feel very honored by this. Mrs. Merkel invited you to Germany, as we heard, this summer, just before the G–8 summit. And we feel very honored in Germany that you would come and visit us. And as I heard, you're going to visit for the first time the former GDR. Are you looking forward to that?

The President. Yes, I am. It was very kind of Chancellor Merkel—who I call Angela, by the way—to invite me to her residence. It's a gesture of friendship that I appreciate. And Laura and I are looking forward to it. And it will give me a chance to continue our dialog on important issues. I'll get to know her a little better, and she'll know me better. It will make the relationship be stronger over time. So I'm looking forward to it, and I really appreciate it.

German Chancellor Angela Merkel

Ms. Christiansen. Your father helped to make German reunification possible. And Chancellor Merkel told me that you've shown a lot of interest in her life, in her former life in the former GDR. What was the point of interest for you?

The President. Well, last night we were sitting around in the private dining room upstairs here, and I thought it would be interesting for her to describe what it was like to grow up in a Communist world. Laura and I certainly don't know what that's like, nor did Condi Rice or Steve Hadley, the members of my team. And I thought it would be good for all of us to hear what it was like.

It was very interesting. She talked about—you know, her dad was a pastor, and she talked about the different pioneer clubs and the schools. It also gave me a chance to get a glimpse into her soul. As I said in the Oval Office yesterday, there's something really refreshing, to work with somebody who understands firsthand what it means to be free. And certainly Angela Merkel has gone from a society which was repressive to a society which is open and free. So I wanted to hear the history, her history, and I also wanted to get a better feel for what she's like and why she thinks the way she thinks.

Germany-U.S. Relations

Ms. Christiansen. That sounds more like a real transatlantic friendship than a partnership—well, with difficulties we had before.

The President. Well, listen, first of all, I had a good relationship with Chancellor Schroeder. The problem was, of course, that there was a disagreement over a very difficult decision I had to make, and that was Iraq.

I fully understand why a government or a people would be, you know, I guess, disappointed in me in a way, and not understand why somebody would commit troops to achieve an objective. And I like to remind people that September the 11th, for us, was a change in our history, and it certainly changed the way I thought. And for others, it was just a moment in passing. So there was a disagreement.

On the other hand, U.S.-German relations were always important, and now we have a chance to turn a new chapter in our relationship, strengthen that alliance, strengthen that relationship, and work on matters that will make this world a better place.

So I'm thrilled with my relationship with Chancellor Merkel. She's a really interesting person. She is—first of all, I found her to be confident, not overconfident, but confident in her beliefs, and that's very important—for me, at least—to be dealing with someone who has got strength of character and confident in her capacity to work to make things better.

Iran

Ms. Christiansen. Now there is Iran on the agenda, and there you seem to be a team that plays together, in that. Are you confident after your meeting with Mrs. Merkel that the Europeans and others will support a resolution that might even open the door to sanctions?

The President. Look, first of all, the most important thing in achieving a diplomatic solution—and I want the German people to understand I want this issue to be solved diplomatically, and I think it can be solved diplomatically. And that—the first objective of trying to get different countries to come together in a diplomatic front is to agree that Iran—in this case, Iran—should not have a weapon. And we've agreed—Germany, France, the United States, certainly agree with that, but so does Russia; so does China. And that's a really important part of putting together a coalition of people saying with a universal voice, or unified voice, "no" to Iran.

Ms. Christiansen. Okay. At the——

The President. Well, that's right.

Secondly, we're working with our allies to—now that the Iranians, by the way, have basically said, "We don't care," what next? And "what next" is to go to the U.N. Security Council. And that's what we're working on now. And we're working on the language of the resolutions and the consequences. And as I told the press yesterday, it's best not to be describing the negotiations amongst ourselves on TV—simply because the Iranians will be listening to everything we say.

But the point is, is that we want a unified front. Iran must hear that the free world is unified in saying, "No weapon, no knowledge of how to build a weapon, no capacity to make a weapon." It's almost a matter of will at this point in time. In other words, they're watching to see whether or not our

coalition will crack, whether or not they can create different factions within our coalition.

And as I've described to people here in this country, is that we must not crack. If we want to solve this diplomatically, there must be a common front with a common strategy to achieve the objective.

Diplomatic Negotiations With Iran

Ms. Christiansen. If this doesn't work with the U.N., you trying to find wide coalition that is going against Iran——

The President. Expand the coalition.

Ms. Christiansen. Exactly. Exactly.

The President. And they're not mutually exclusive. And first of all, I think we ought to assume it can work in the U.N. We want it to work in the U.N. Therefore, the strategy will be to see to it that it does work in the U.N. And that's why—you know, I talked to Putin, President Putin the other day, right before Angela came. And she talked to President Putin in Siberia, as you know. And a lot of our conversations, obviously, revolve around Iran, since this is the most dangerous threat to peace right now.

Ms. Christiansen. And sanctions?

The President. Possibility—absolutely.

Ms. Christiansen. But regarding Russia and China? That will be difficult——

The President. No. It may seem difficult at this point in time, but there's time. As I explained, again, to people in our country, we're at the beginning of the diplomatic process, not the end of the diplomatic process. I know—we live in a world where everything has to be solved instantly. I wish problems could be solved instantly, but that's not how the world works, particularly when you're dealing with a nontransparent regime.

See, they have an advantage—"they" being the Iranians. They don't have a press, like the German press and the United States press, that is constantly reporting.

They don't have democracies that are holding leaders to account. They're nontransparent. So therefore, their negotiating position is much stronger than ours in many ways.

So we must double our efforts, constantly talking to each other, reminding each other about the need to stay unified, and that's what Angela and I spent a lot of time talking about yesterday.

U.S. Role in Diplomatic Negotiations With Iran

Ms. Christiansen. Why isn't Washington talking directly to the Iranians?

The President. Well, because it's much better to have a united front. In other words, we will achieve this diplomatically. If there's more than one country involved—we are very much involved. Yesterday we were part of putting down a U.N. Security Council Resolution. The Iranians know we're involved. But what I don't want to have happen is this unified effort fall apart because everybody depends upon one country to solve the problem.

Ms. Christiansen. If all diplomatic efforts fail, what's worse at the end, a nuclear-armed Iran or an American military action?

The President. You're asking me the classic hypothetical question. I believe we can achieve this diplomatically. And that's what I want to do. I want to achieve this diplomatically, because it's—and it's necessary we do so. And an armed Iran will be a threat to peace. It will be a threat to peace in the Middle East; it will create a sense of blackmail; it will encourage other nations to feel like they need to have a nuclear weapon. And so it's essential that we succeed diplomatically.

Israel

Ms. Christiansen. Are you worried that Israel might not try to solve this diplomatically? Because Mr. Olmert already said, "We can defend ourselves."

The President. Well, if I were an Israeli, I'd be concerned about the combination of a President that said, "I want to wipe Israel off the map," and had a nuclear weapon. And so obviously, Israel is a factor. It's a little country that will defend herself. Again, I keep repeating this, but that's why it's essential we continue to work together, like we're doing now, to convince the Iranians to give up their weapon.

They will be isolated. What they need to understand is that they're going to be isolated from the rest of the world, and that will harm their people, in my judgment. And it's a tough issue, and it's why I ran for office, to solve these problems.

Iraq

Ms. Christiansen. Let's go over to Iraq. Two German hostages who were held in Iraq for months, they just returned home safely, but Iraq remains a major terrorist base. Despite more than, I think, 130,000 U.S. soldiers there, are in the country, what do you say to the many Europeans who feel the Iraq war has made the world a less safer place?

The President. I would say that they need to look at the facts, that Saddam Hussein was a very dangerous person in the world. Saddam Hussein had used weapons of mass destruction. Obviously, we didn't find them like everybody thought we would, but we did know he had the capacity to make them. He had harbored terrorists. He had invaded his neighborhood. And the removal of Saddam Hussein was the right thing to do.

And now there's a new democracy developing. And the best way to defeat the terrorists in the long run is to defeat their ideology with an ideology based upon liberty. And one of the most amazing events in modern history took place in December of last year, when 12 million Iraqis went to the polls. It's just a—it's a joyous moment for them.

Now what's happened is, is there's a unified government formed. Obviously, it took a little longer than we wanted, but nevertheless, they are together. There is a tough

Shi'a as the Prime Minister-designate. There's a Sunni rejectionist who is now reconciled with the country. And what you'll see is a democracy that will grow to be an example for others and a country that will deny safe haven to the terrorists.

I disagree with the assessment that there are more terrorists in Iraq now. As a matter of fact, slowly but surely, we're defeating them. But what's important for people in Germany to listen to is what I listen to, which is the voices of an enemy. Zarqawi and Al Qaida has announced that it's just a matter of time for America and the coalition to leave so we can have our safe haven from which to plot and plan further attacks on America and free nations.

And the only way we can lose Iraq is if we lose our nerve, if we retreat, if we pull out before the job is done. And that's not going to happen so long as I'm the President.

Spread of Democracy

Ms. Christiansen. So the development in Iraq, in Palestine, hasn't made you stop half-way, let's say, in the democratization process——

The President. Oh, quite the contrary. I really believe it's necessary to promote democracy. One of the interesting examples in history is democracies don't fight each other. And Europe today is whole, free, and at peace. You have your disagreements, but those disagreements are not determined on a battlefield anymore.

Japan was a country that my nation fought with, and today, one of my best friends in keeping the peace is the Prime Minister of Japan. What happened between World War II and today is, Japan took on a Japanese-style democracy. What's really interesting is when you go back and look at some of the writings and musings of people after World War II, there was great criticism about trying to help the Japanese become a Japanese-style democracy: "We can't do that; they're the enemy." Well, today, the enemy is the friend. So I think

all the more reason to promote democracy is the elections in Iraq.

I was not pleased that Hamas has refused to announce—its desire to destroy Israel. On the other hand, the elections did say to people in the Palestinian Territories, "We're sick and tired of corruption. We want leaders who don't steal from us. We want leaders who help us educate our children and provide health for our citizens."

And so elections can be good signals of what people are really thinking. I believe that there's still work after elections to be done, but there's no doubt that we've got to spread liberty and freedom if we're going to defeat this ideology that really says, "There should be no rights for women; there should be no religious freedom; and by the way, we'll carry out our foreign policy through acts of violence and murder."

Germany-U.S. Relations/Intelligence

Ms. Christiansen. We Germans seem to be more involved—have been more involved in the Iraq war than anybody else knew—involuntarily, I would like to say. Because the U.S. intelligence services used German airports for secret rendition flights and interrogated, even, German citizens—hardly what you'd expect, I would say, from a friend and ally.

The President. Well, first of all, on intelligence matters, it's my policy not to talk about them; otherwise, they're not intelligence matters anymore. And the questions you ask will be all—in some cases, analyzed through courts, in some cases, through press inquiry. But Germany is a friend.

Ms. Christiansen. But the behavior itself? Is it behavior for an ally——

The President. Well, like, what are you talking about?

Ms. Christiansen. I mean, that you do this, that you don't ask for help for some of the ally, that you don't inform the ally and so on.

The President. On, like, what subject, for example?

Ms. Christiansen. Like these flights, for example.

The President. Well, again, you're asking me to talk about intelligence matters that I'm not going to talk about. And people can say whatever they want to say, but we work closely with Germany on all kinds of fronts in order to protect ourselves.

War on Terror

Ms. Christiansen. Then let me ask you about the image of the United States. Especially for us Germans after the war, the United States stood as the symbol of liberty, for democracy. And then we saw these—we saw Abu Ghraib; we saw Guantanamo. And these seemed, suddenly, to be signals that you're abandoning these values of democracy and liberty. And how do you want to repair them?

The President. Well, first of all, it's absurd to say America is abandoning our values. No question, Abu Ghraib was a disgrace for our country. But I think people ought to take a look at what happened afterwards—and those who are responsible for that disgraceful behavior have been held to account, have been tried, have been, in some cases, dismissed from our military.

We're at war with an enemy, and we've got to protect ourselves. And obviously, the Guantanamo issue is a sensitive issue for people. I very much would like to end Guantanamo; I very much would like to get people to a court. And we're waiting for our Supreme Court to give us a decision as to whether the people need to have a fair trial in a civilian court or in a military court.

But in either case, they will get a trial, which they, themselves, were unwilling to give to the people that they're willing to kill—"they," the enemy.

And so it's—no, listen, our country is strong on human rights and civil rights. That's why we're leading the case in funding for HIV/AIDS in Africa. That's why we're trying to rally the Nation to do something about Darfur—the genocide in Darfur. That's why we provide food for the hungry. That's why we try to liberate people when we find them in the clutches of tyranny.

Ms. Christiansen. So you said you had to do more?

The President. Yes, we are doing a lot.

Iraq

Ms. Christiansen. I understand, like, $320 billion that the Iraq war cost—a lot of people are saying——

The President. It's worth it. It's worth it. I wouldn't have spent it if it wasn't worth it. Any time we put a troop in harm's way, they will get support. We're not going—I'm not going to ask a parent—I'm not going to be able to tell a parent, nor will I tell a parent, "Your son who volunteered or your daughter who volunteered is not going to get the full support of the Federal Government." And so long as we've got people in harm's way, this Government is going to support them.

Dependence on Foreign Sources of Oil/ Gasoline

Ms. Christiansen. Let me ask you another question to the war on terrorism. How do you want, really, to fight terrorism when you are so dependent on Arabian oil?

The President. That's an interesting question. I've never thought of it that way. The first thing we ought to do is get off oil.

Ms. Christiansen. That's what you said.

The President. And I mean that. Yes, I know.

Ms. Christiansen. Do you mean that, really?

The President. Absolutely. Oil has become—it's an economic risk for us. I mean, after all, if the oil—if the demand for oil goes up in India or China, fast-growing economies, it affects the price of gasoline in the United States and in Germany. It's also a national security issue, obviously. Oil comes from unstable parts of the world, so I'm absolutely serious about getting off of oil.

Ms. Christiansen. Because we, in Europe, we asked this when we heard your speech, and we said oil is now——

The President. You don't believe old George W.?

Ms. Christiansen. Gasoline is now, let's say $70 a barrel. And we said, if we look at the United States, your gasoline is still so—I mean, the prices are so low, and we are paying so much money. Why haven't you raise taxes, energy taxes or something, if you really mean it?

The President. Well, because the best way to do it is through technological change. You don't have to tax the working people. And, well, in order—what?

Ms. Christiansen. That's what we do. [*Laughter*]

The President. Well, we don't. We try not to. Listen, the price of gasoline just went up from $2.70 to $3 a gallon, which is about, I guess, 40 percent of what it costs in Germany. And people are screaming, because it's like a tax. And it affects low-income Americans.

And so the best way to solve the problem is to spend money on research and development and come up with alternative ways to drive our automobiles. And we're making interesting progress. We think we're close to a breakthrough, to have a battery in our vehicles that will enable an urban dweller to drive the first 40 miles without using gasoline. So it's that effect of reducing demand for gasoline that will ultimately help our consumers. Obviously, we're trying to do all we can to make sure that supplies of gasoline don't get interrupted in the short term, but in the long term, I can see cars being powered by hydrogen, for example.

Environment/Energy

Ms. Christiansen. Let me ask one more question to that climate topic. After Katrina and after a lot of new evidence of rapid climate change, are you now convinced that this is really a serious problem?

The President. No, I've always said greenhouse gases are a problem. There is an argument there as to whether or not they're naturally made or manmade. And my attitude is, let's just get beyond that argument and do something about it. I believe that we need more nuclear power. If you're really interested in solving greenhouse gas problems, nuclear power is one of the great renewable sources of energy. I know it's controversial.

Ms. Christiansen. Very interesting and controversy debate in Germany as well.

The President. And here in America. But if people are genuinely serious about solving greenhouse gas problems around the world, countries like the United States and India and China ought to be promoting civilian nuclear power.

There's other things we're doing. One, as I just told you, we've got to change our habits when we're driving our cars. One of the real promising areas besides battery research is ethanol research, you know; use corn to be able to fuel automobiles in the United States. Solar energy can work and is becoming more economically feasible. Wind energy is making a marginal difference in the United States but, nevertheless, a difference.

And so my—what I'm saying is, is that we're spending a lot—clean coal technology, for example, we're spending billions of dollars on clean coal technology to figure out how to have zero-emission coal-fired plants. And all this research is going to pay off. And the United States will be able to make sure our economy continues to grow and, at the same time, be good stewards of the environment.

The debate—let me just cut to the chase. I said I didn't support Kyoto, and all of a sudden, everybody said, "Well, George W. Bush doesn't care about clean air"— it's just rubbish. Of course I care about the quality of the air. As a matter of fact, the quality of the air has improved since I've been the President of the United States. But what I didn't want to do is wreck our economy, nor did I think it made sense to sign on to a treaty that didn't include countries like India and China. And so my attitude is, let's get beyond the debate and work in a cooperative fashion to share technologies, to share that which we're researching with each other, and have a new era of energy that is wise about how we treat the environment too.

Russia-U.S. Relations

Ms. Christiansen. I'm very mindful of our time, but I would like to have a look to the G–8 summit and Russia and about the Russian-American friendship as well. Perhaps another question. You had felt quite warm about President Putin, but there is rising criticism from the Vice President, for example, in the moment, and others on a lack of democracy in Russia. Have you talked to Putin directly about this? And will you, perhaps, raise any obstacles regarding the G–8?

The President. Yes, of course, I've talked to him—a lot.

Ms. Christiansen. About this problem?

The President. Oh, absolutely. Yes, a lot.

Ms. Christiansen. What does he say?

The President. Well, first, let me—let me share how I conduct my relations with people. I like Putin, but that doesn't mean I have to agree with some of the decisions he's made. I know this, that if I stand up and constantly criticize Putin publicly, he's not going to be interested in listening to what I have to say—and neither would I. When somebody feels like they can lecture to me publicly and doesn't do me the courtesy of coming to tell me what's on their mind, one-on-one, then I may not be interested in listening to them—if you know what I mean.

So I'm the kind of person that tries to establish a good personal relationship with somebody, and then we can sit down and talk, and I tell them what's on my mind, and they tell me what's on his. And I have expressed our Nation's concerns about—for example, when they shut down parts of the

press corps. I said, "Vladimir, people are wondering why you're making the decision you're making. A free press is an indication of a healthy democracy." And he had an answer.

But nevertheless, as you know, I'm a religious person, and I believe religious liberty is an important part of a society. And I've got friends in the Catholic Church who asked me to talk to him about Catholic bishops being allowed to move in the country and to practice their faith. And so I bring up all these issues with him.

But there's a difference in scolding somebody to try to gain editorial approval, and somebody who is in a position to be effective. I'd much rather be an effective person than a popular person; let me put it to you that way.

Family Values

Ms. Christiansen. As I said, we're very mindful of your time; it's been a great conversation. If you have 2 minutes—because I would like to have two questions, one on women and one on football. Do you agree to that?

The President. Okay, I will.

Ms. Christiansen. Very short ones. [*Laughter*] You seemed to get along very well Angela Merkel, a lot of women, strong women around you, here around the Oval Office. We're—have a big debate in Germany about women working and having children and the family. And your wife, for example, you seem to be a very good team in working together——

The President. Thank you.

Ms. Christiansen. And how do you strike this balance?

The President. Yes. First of all, I have been raised by an incredibly strong woman who I love, and that's my mother. And I'm married to an incredibly strong woman who I love, and that's my wife. I hope that Laura and I have raised two incredibly strong women who will have confidence to go out and explore life and to achieve. I don't think that encouraging my daughters to live life to its fullest means that they can't be good mothers at the same time. As a matter of fact, I think a good mother is somebody who is strong in her own right, confident, and independent.

And one of the things I do try to remind people is that the most important responsibility a person can have is to love their child with all their heart. That is by far the most important thing. I'll never forget—I'll give you one quick—we're fine on time. I'll tell you a quick anecdote. One of my dearest friends in political life is Karen Hughes. She was one of the most powerful women ever in the White House, simply because she had complete access to the President and I trusted her. At the same time, by the way, in an office down the hall was Condoleezza Rice, also a very strong woman who I am very fond of and very close to.

And Karen, one time, came in to see me, and she said, "Mr. President, I'm having trouble at home"—not that she—she wasn't having trouble with her husband or her son—but, "My son is unhappy." And my reaction instantly was, "Karen, do whatever is necessary to make your family happy. That's the most important thing." And so she left, and she went back to Texas, and I missed her dearly. But priorities matter in life, and people are able to set priorities and, at the same time, live life to the fullest.

And Karen is a good example. She got her son squared away; he's now at Stanford University. She's now back in Washington, working with Condi at the State Department. And my only advice is to, one, welcome women in society. I welcome them in the White House. My Presidency is more complete because some of my top advisers are very strong, capable women.

Angela Merkel is somebody who is a joy to deal with. She bring an interesting——

Ms. Christiansen. Why?

The President. Well, because she's got a straightforward manner about herself that is—when she says something, you know she

means it. She is what she is. She's not a fake. And when I sit there talking to Angela, I'm not saying I'm talking to—I don't think gender; I think strength of character. I think reliability. I think clear-headed thinking. I think of a fellow strategist as to how to solve problems.

So, anyway, that's a long answer to a short question.

2006 World Cup

Ms. Christiansen. I think for the two of us, we don't have soccer expert teams sitting here together, but anyway, I think you're a baseball fan——

The President. I am a baseball fan; you're right.

Ms. Christiansen. You are. Do you think you've turned a little bit into a soccer fan? I mean, your team is doing so well at the moment and——

The President. That's what they tell me. I do know a little bit about the World Cup because I read a very interesting article about the German coach. And evidently he's a dynamic—you know, he's spending some time in California. And the World Cup is such a huge event that I think most Americans like me, who weren't raised on soccer, are beginning to pay attention to it. Now, I know that sounds like heresy in Germany.

Ms. Christiansen. In Germany, yes. But think of just—I mean, that the American team could meet the Iranian team.

The President. Yes, could be.

Ms. Christiansen. What then?

The President. Well, I don't view it that way. I view it as, I hope the American team does well. But this is a big event for Germany, and Germany will be a great host for the games. And obviously, I hope the American team does well—they're supposedly a good team.

Ms. Christiansen. If they get world champion, you're coming for the final game?

The President. I don't know. Do you think I possibly would be invited? I don't know.

Ms. Christiansen. We're very happy that you come over in July.

The President. I'm looking forward it, and I want to thank you for this good interview.

NOTE: The interview was taped at 1:21 p.m. in the Diplomatic Reception Room at the White House for later broadcast. In his remarks, the President referred to former Chancellor Gerhard Schroeder of Germany; President Vladimir V. Putin of Russia; President Mahmud Ahmadi-nejad of Iran; former President Saddam Hussein of Iraq; Prime Minister-designate Nuri al-Maliki, and Speaker of Parliament Mahmoud al-Mashhadani of Iraq; senior Al Qaida associate Abu Musab Al Zarqawi; Prime Minister Junichiro Koizumi of Japan; and Jurgen Klinsmann, head coach, Germany's 2006 World Cup men's soccer team. Ms. Christiansen referred to Prime Minister Ehud Olmert of Israel. The transcript was released by the Office of the Press Secretary on May 7. A tape was not available for verification of the content of this interview.

Interview With Kai Diekmann of Bild
May 5, 2006

The President. Have you ever been in the Oval Office before?

Mr. Diekmann. Once, a long time ago——

The President. I'll give you a quick tour before our interview. So the first thing that a President does, which I didn't realize, was pick a rug. I've have no idea about rugs. And so in this job, you've got to delegate. The American President is in a position where there's just unbelievable complexities to the job—Darfur, Iran—a whole lot of issues. So I delegated the decision about the rug to my wife.

The second thing a President has got to do is have a strategic mind. In order to be successful, in my judgment, as the President, you've got to constantly think strategically. And so I said to her, "You pick out the colors; you be the tactical person; but I want it to say, 'optimistic person.' " That's all I wanted it to say. Here is the result. Isn't it beautiful?

Mr. Diekmann. Yes, it is very beautiful.

The President. There's a sense of optimism when you come in here. And there's a reason why. You cannot lead people unless you're optimistic about what you're doing. You've got to believe it in your very soul. One of the interesting things about the Presidency is people watch me like a hawk. They're looking at my moves. And if I'm going to be wringing my hands and if I'm all worried about the decisions I make—are not going to lead to a better tomorrow, they'll figure it out.

And so when you talk to me today, I just want you to know, I not only strongly believe in the decisions I make, I'm optimistic that they're going to work—very optimistic.

These are all Texas paintings. That's west Texas; those are other Texas paintings. At least if you're a Texan, it reflects a way of life and a way of thinking. The interesting thing about Washington is that they want me to change—"they" being the—and I'm not changing, you know. You can't make decisions if you don't know who you are and you flip around with the politics. You've got to stay strong in what you believe and optimistic about that—you'll get good results.

And so—the other thing I want you to know about me is that no matter how pressurized it may seem, I'm not changing what I believe. Now, I may change tactics, but I'm not going to change my core beliefs— a belief that freedom is universal or the belief that private markets work, a belief in ownership—when people own something, society is better off; a belief that there's a role for government, but it's limited in nature. And I'm not changing. I don't care whether they like me at the cocktail parties or not. I want to be able to leave this office with my integrity intact.

That's George Washington, the first President, of course. The interesting thing about him is that I read three—three or four books about him last year. Isn't that interesting? People say, "So what?" Well, here's the "so what." You never know what your history is going to be like until long after you're gone—if they're still analyzing the Presidency of George Washington— [*laughter*]. So Presidents shouldn't worry about the history. You just can't. You do what you think is right, and if you're thinking big enough, that history will eventually prove you right or wrong. But you won't know in the short term.

Lincoln—this is the place on the Oval Office wall where the President puts the most—the best President, and I put Lincoln here, and I don't think there's any question—now, people will have their—but I think he was the most influential President ever. And the reason why is because that in the midst of a difficult Presidency, needless to say—the Civil War, thousands of people dying, with Americans killing Americans—he had a vision of a United States. It's conceivable this country would have ended up being two countries had he not had a clear vision, even though all around him was seemingly falling apart. He was a great President.

That's called "A Charge to Keep," based upon a religious hymn. The hymn talks about serving God. The President's job is never to promote a religion. The great thing about America—and Germany, for that matter—is that you should be able to worship freely. I like to tell people, you're equally American whether you're a Jew, Muslim, Christian, or atheist—you're equally all Americans—and that if we ever lose that, we begin to look like the Taliban.

I understand, in parts of Europe, some scoff at my faith. It doesn't bother me. But I happen to believe, for me at least, faith is one way to make sure that my values stay intact and that I keep life in proper perspective, which is a very important part, in my judgment, of being a good decisionmaker.

Finally, the desk, where we'll have our picture taken in front of is—nine other Presidents used it. This was given to us by Queen Victoria in the 1870s, I think it was. President Roosevelt put the door in so people would not know he was in a wheelchair. John Kennedy put his head out the door.

Mr. Diekmann. Yes, the very famous picture——

The President. That's it—the most famous picture. And then Reagan, interestingly enough, put the bottom on there. He was a big guy; he didn't want to bump his knees under the desk.

Anyway, this is the Oval Office. It's a shrine to democracy. And we treat it that way. When people walk in here, they don't come in here in bathing suits and flip-flops. They come in here dressed like they'd come to a shrine. It is to be respected and honored because the Office of the President is bigger than the person who occupies it. It's one of the great things about a true democracy, is that the institutions outlast the individuals, and therefore, there's stability in the process.

Some Presidents forget that they're not bigger than the Office. But all Presidents must always honor the Office and remember it is a sacred trust to uphold the honor of the Presidency.

Mr. Diekmann. Thank you for taking the time.

The President. Yes, glad to do it.

Mr. Diekmann. Bild has 12 million readers. It's the largest newspaper in Germany. And there's one thing which is really special about our newspaper—every German who wants to work for the newspaper, he has to sign in his working contracts some beliefs—and there's the belief you have to be for reunification; you have to be against totalitarianism from riots on the right side and the left side; and you have to be for the peace and for the understanding with Israel. And since September 11th, we have a new belief—you have to be for partnership with America. Otherwise, you can't work for us, you can't come—you have to sign it in your contract.

The President. My kind of guy. [*Laughter*]

War on Terror

Mr. Diekmann. Okay, so I would like to start. Mr. President, the fifth anniversary of the terrible 9/11 attack is nearing. Has the Western world really learned the right lessons from 9/11?

The President. Yes. The Western world, by and large, understands that we face an enemy that is coldblooded and will kill innocent life to achieve an objective. That killing not only took place on September 11th here in our country, but it has taken place in other countries around the world since then.

Secondly, the governments of the Western world understand that in order to protect our respective peoples, there must be intelligence sharing. We must be willing to converse with each other in ways that might not have happened before. In other words, if we know something is going to happen in Germany, it's very important for the United States Government to call up its counterparts and to share that information. And there's a lot of that information sharing.

Thirdly, we understand that money is what fuels these terror cells. And the idea of sharing intelligence about the movement of money is necessary to make sure we protect our people.

The degree of understanding about September the 11th varies, however. For some people around the world, September the 11th was just a terrible moment. For me and a lot of other people in America, September the 11th was a change of attitude; it was a call to arms in the sense that this is the first—for America—the first battle of the war in the 21st century.

One of the things that I hope people come to understand is that there are two ways to defeat this enemy: One is to bring them to justice so they don't harm people, which means we've got to be constantly on the offense, finding them where they hide and bringing them to justice. And secondly is that the way to defeat their hateful ideology is by the spread of liberty. That notion—some understand that, and some don't. But I want your readers to understand, I fully understand it—that liberty will yield peace that we all want.

And so part of our strategy is to work with countries, particularly in the Middle East, to encourage the spread of liberty and freedom. And we're making progress there.

Mr. Diekmann. But still we see bombs in Tel Aviv——

The President. Yes.

Mr. Diekmann. ——suicide bombers. And just a couple of days ago, even the U.S. Government delivered a warning that there could be attacks and strikes at the World Cup in Germany.

The President. Yes.

Mr. Diekmann. Do you really believe we have a chance to win the war against terrorism?

The President. Absolutely. I know this: That if we don't try to win the war on terrorism, the world will be a lot worse off; that if we believe these are just isolated incidents and people are maybe just temporarily angry, it is an attitude that will ultimately lead to more catastrophe, more danger.

This is an enemy which is—has clearly stated they have ambitions. They want to spread their ideology throughout—starting in the Middle East. They want to topple moderate government. They want to—they believe capitalists and democrats are soft—by democrats, I mean people living in democracies—are soft. They believe it's just a matter of time before the Western world tires. They have stated clearly they want weapons of mass destruction and that they want safe haven from which to launch their attacks. This is what the enemy has said. And I think those of us in positions of responsibility must take the words of the enemy very seriously.

They can be defeated, and they will be defeated, so long as we don't lose our nerve. And so the United States is committed to finding these folks where they hide, to bringing them to justice, which we're doing, and to—but recognizing that the world has changed from the world of the past because of the spread of liberty. Just look at Europe; it's whole, free, and at peace, because democracies live side by side in peace. That's one of the great lessons of the 20th century. And it's a lesson that must be applied to the 21st century.

And so, absolutely, we can win this war on terror. The victory in the war on terror won't come with a signing ceremony. The victory in the war on terror will come as the enemy becomes more and more marginalized. You cannot judge defeat or victory on whether or not a suicide bomber is able to pull off an attack. You can see progress in the war on terror as new democracies take hold around the world and deny—which denies an enemy a safe haven.

And one such democracy that's now evolving and getting stronger is Iraq. Another such new democracy is Afghanistan—50 million people who once lived under the thumb of a tyrant—or two tyrants now are free. And I strongly believe the world is better off for it, and I know that those two democracies are a major defeat for the terrorists.

Relations With the Muslim World

Mr. Diekmann. We have to learn in dealing with the Muslim world. Do we learn the right lessons? Do we have to deal in a different way with the Muslim world?

The President. There is a—there needs to be more understanding between the Muslim world and the Western world. There needs to be a better understanding of the true beliefs of their respective religions. We must understand, words mean things to different people. There's got to be a better way to communicate with ourselves. Sometimes my own messages send signals that I don't mean to send—but stirs up anxieties in the Muslim world.

On the other hand, I take great comfort in knowing that the true Muslim—Islam, itself, is a peaceful religion, and those who adhere to Islam are people that respect the rights of others. And there's common values in the great religions. And what we cannot allow happen is for these totalitarians, these Islamic extremists, to distort a great religion and define the nature of that religion.

And so there's a lot of work that needs to be done between America and the West and the Muslim world, but we can do that work without sacrificing the need to defend ourselves and without condemning people to tyranny.

Europe-U.S. Relations

Mr. Diekmann. How important is the partnership between the United States and Europe when it comes to the war on terror?

The President. The partnership between the United States and Europe is a vital partnership that transcends the war on terror. Part of our relationship is working together in the war on terror, but there are many other areas where we can and will continue to work together.

One such area is, obviously, trade. Europe and the United States benefit from free and fair trade. Another area is to help those who are afflicted with disease, like

HIV/AIDS on the continent of Africa. Another is to deal with suffering that we see in the world. And hopefully, we'll be very strong in our determination to end the genocide in Darfur of Sudan.

But when the United States and Europe cooperate, we can achieve security for our people and enhance the prosperity for our people as well—as well as do our duty. See, I believe there's a duty to help ease the suffering in the world. I believe in the admonition that to whom much is given, much is required. And the United States—the people of the United States have been given a lot. We're a blessed nation—and same for the people of Europe. And we have a duty to work together to help relieve the suffering of those who are less fortunate.

Russia-U.S. Relations/Democracy in Russia

Mr. Diekmann. In this context, is Russia a reliable democratic partner?

The President. Russia is a country in transition. And if you really think about where our fathers, at our age, if they had been sitting around talking about Russia—maybe a little younger—they would have been talking about an enemy, the great Soviet Union. And by the way, that enemy at that point in time bound the relationship between Germany and the United States—at least a part of Germany and the United States—very closely. It gave us a common front.

So Russia no longer is that enemy, and that's a major change. Secondly, Russia is a country that has made some signals that are mixed signals, signals that allow—cause us to question their commitment to whether or not they intend to become a true democracy, where there's a freedom of the press or freedom of religion, all the different freedoms that are inherent in democracy.

I, personally, have a working relationship with Vladimir Putin, and that's very important. I've got a warm relationship with him. It's a relationship where I can sit down

with him and ask him direct questions as to why he's made the decisions he's made. It's a relationship where he questions me about what the intentions of the United States may be. It's one that I value, and I think it's an important relationship not only for the United States to have, but it's an important relationship for countries in Europe, for the United States to have a relationship with Vladimir Putin.

One of our concerns is economic nationalism, to a certain extent, where he's using his oil companies to achieve what appears to be political objectives. And we make our concerns known when someone uses natural gas, for example, to effect—to send signals to government. As you might recall, Secretary Rice was in Europe, and she spoke out loudly about the gas contracts with Ukraine. And the reason she did that is it's—we have a duty to express our concerns, but in such a way that the relationship is one that—where, at my level, I'm able to be comfortable in discussing concerns with Vladimir Putin.

We've got commonality when it comes to dealing with proliferation. It's very important that the United States and Russia work closely to make sure that nuclear materials are stored as safely as possible. We've got commonality when it comes to fighting the war on terror. And we've now got a new, important issue to work together on, as well as working together with Germany and others, and that's Iran.

Germany's Role in the War on Terror

Mr. Diekmann. What role must Germany play in the war on terror?

The President. Germany plays a vital role in the war on terror. Germany is in the heart of Europe. Germany is—whether it's this current administration or the previous administration, we have had a—amongst our intelligence services as well as our law enforcement services—a close coordination and a close discussion. Germany's will is important. When the German Chancellor stands up and says, "The war on terror must be won," or—"is a vital part of the security of our peoples," people around the world listen. Germany plays a very important role.

Iraq

Mr. Diekmann. Taking a look at the past, do the Americans feel that the Germans abandoned them when they went to war with Saddam Hussein?

The President. I've come to realize that the nature of the German people are such that war is very abhorrent, that Germany is a country now that is—no matter where they sit on the political spectrum, Germans are—just don't like war. And I can understand that. There's a generation of people who had their lives torn about because of a terrible war.

I felt like—I made the decision I made based upon my full understanding that threats must be dealt with before they come to fruition. And I fully understood during that period of time not everybody would agree with me. And so we put together a significant coalition and followed through on a difficult decision.

The point now is not what went on in the past; the point now is, how do we work together to achieve important goals? And one such goal is a democracy in Germany. And I appreciate the German Government's—previous Government's support and this Government's support of helping the Iraqis rebuild their lives. Training missions are important. Debt relief was important. Gerhard Schroeder relieved the debt on Iraq. And all those gestures are very important gestures that say that even though people disagreed with the decision to go into Iraq, we now agree that it's important that a democracy in Iraq succeed. And that's how I view the relationship.

Democracy in Iraq

Mr. Diekmann. The dictator is on trial now, but at the same time, the violence in Iraq is getting worse. Is it really a victory? Is the war against Iraq really a success?

The President. Oh, yes, it's going to be a success, absolutely. When 12 million people go to the polls—listen, these people lived under a brutal tyrant. People seem to forget, quickly forget, the nature of Saddam Hussein. This is a man who had used weapons of mass destruction on his own people. He had invaded his neighbors—Kuwait. He was shooting at U.S. aircraft. He was violating sanctions. He had—as we now know, he had been using the Oil-For-Food Programme to enhance his own standing inside the country. We didn't find the weapons of mass destruction that everybody thought he had, but we do know he still had the capacity of making weapons of mass destruction. He had ties to terrorist groups.

Removing Saddam Hussein has made the world a safer place. We found—particularly for Iraqis. We found graves stuffed full of Iraqi men, women, and children. This guy was a brutal, brutal tyrant.

But it is hard work to go from a tyranny to a country based upon liberty. We've been there 3 years. And I think if you look at the history of—in post-World War II, it took a long period of time to recover. And yet we live in a world where there's supposed to be instant success. And my work and the work of those of us in Iraq require patience, and the need is to give the Iraqi people a chance. And they haven't let us down.

Just think about what happened in December: 12 million people voted. That's a lot of people going to the polls in the face of intimidation and threats. These are people that had no chance to express themselves at a ballot box during Saddam Hussein—in free elections. And yet when given a chance, they went to the polls. And now what you're seeing is the formation of a unity government. You've got Shi'a, Sunni, and Kurds, all committed to a unity government, all willing to fight off the terrorists, to get rid of the militias, and to form a government that the Iraqi people can be proud of.

And no question, there's still Al Qaida, which has said they want Iraq as a base from which to attack, willing to recruit suicide bombers. Those are hard to stop. But slowly but surely, the Iraqis, with American help, are reconciling their differences politically, are marginalizing those who are still loyal to Saddam, and are bringing the Al Qaida and the foreign fighters to justice.

Iran

Mr. Diekmann. But Iraq—it's still a long journey to peace, and now there's a new threat. You already mentioned it; that is Iran.

The President. Yes.

Mr. Diekmann. Iran is on the way to a nuclear program. How are we going to prevent them from making true what they threaten us, for example, in destroying Israel?

The President. You know, it's interesting; the world in which we live is one that requires great confidence in our values and strength of purpose. And we are challenged with the Iranian issue. And I want your readers to know that it is my desire and my belief we can solve this diplomatically. And the best way to solve this issue diplomatically is for there to be common purpose amongst the nations of the world.

Any diplomatic solution requires agreement on the goal. And there is solid agreement that the Iranians should not have a nuclear weapon or the knowledge and capacity how to make a nuclear weapon. That agreement—when I say that's the agreement, it's the agreement amongst Germany, France, Great Britain, the United States, Russia, China, and a lot of other nations. We all agree. And that's the most important step. If we didn't agree on the goal, it would be impossible to put together a coalition, a group of nations anxious to say to the Iranians with one voice, "You're not going to have a weapon."

The way forward diplomatically, because of the intransigence of the Iranian Government, is to go into the United Nations Security Council. And that's where we're headed, and we are working closely with our counterparts to develop the tactics to move forward once in the United Nations Security Council. Our message there is, the Iranians have defied the world, and you're now isolated, and it's your choice to make. They must make the choice to give up their weapons.

People have said to me, "Well, why aren't you at the negotiating table?" We are at the negotiating table—in this sense: We're with our partners on a regular basis. I think about this issue a lot. I talk to respective leaders a lot; the United States laid down the Security Council resolution, along with others. I speak to Angela Merkel quite frequently on this subject. It is the number-one item on our agenda when it comes to international coalitions. And the thing that we've got to do is be effective. And what the Iranians are looking forward is weakness among our group. They want to see how firm we are. So one of my jobs is to keep people firm in our resolve. And it's easy, by the way, with your Chancellor. She is firm in her resolve.

Threat of Terror/Iran

Mr. Diekmann. The German Chancellor and the new head of state, Olmert, of Israel, they said the Iranian President is as dangerous as Adolf Hitler. Do you share their view?

The President. I think that it's very important for us to take his words very seriously. When people speak, it is important that we listen carefully to what they say and take them seriously. For example, when Al Qaida speaks, I take their words seriously. When bin Laden says, "We'll bring harm to the West," I take them seriously. When Zarqawi says, "It's just a matter of time for the U.S. to get out of Iraq so we can have safe haven," I take him seriously. Zawahiri, the number-two man in

Al Qaida, he's constantly speaking about their grand designs to spread their ideology.

And when Ahmadi-nejad speaks, we need to take it seriously. And when he says he wants to destroy Israel, the world needs to take that very seriously. It's a serious threat. It's a threat to an ally of the United States and Germany. But what he's also saying is if he's willing to destroy one country, he'd be willing to destroy other countries. And therefore, this is a threat that has got to be dealt with in a way that—where the world—this is an important moment for the world to come together and deal with this in a way that's diplomatic, so that the next person who thinks or the next country that thinks they can threaten will understand that there is an effective response.

Mr. Diekmann. Do you rule out, as a last resort, a military intervention against Iran?

The President. As you know, I have said this on German soil; I've said it on U.S. soil, that my first choice is to solve this diplomatically. I think we can, but all options are on the table.

President's Relationship With Foreign Leaders

Mr. Diekmann. Mr. President, it seems that since Chancellor Angela Merkel took office, the ice age between Washington and Berlin is over. Are good personal ties really so important for the relationship between America and Germany?

The President. I've always felt like it's important to establish personal ties with my counterpart. And the reason why is, is that the role of a President is to be a strategic thinker as well as to be able to understand the tactics necessary to achieve the strategic objectives. And in order to be able to work strategically with my counterparts, I've got to have a personal relationship with them. I've got to be in a position such that when they speak, I listen, and when I speak, they listen, so they know that there is a compatibility to the point where we're comfortable sharing ideas as we try to work together to solve problems.

And this world is full of problems. You're in the Oval Office during this interview—there are—Sudan, North Korea, Iran, Iraq, Israel-Palestine—I mean, that's just to name a few of the problems that come to this desk that I deal with on a regular basis. In order for us to be effective, I've got to have a personal relationship with other leaders so that we can work together to achieve common objectives.

Germany/Leadership

Mr. Diekmann. During a state visit in 1989, your father described Germany as "partner leadership."

The President. Yes.

Mr. Diekmann. Does this statement still apply today?

The President. Absolutely. Absolutely. And it's manifesting itself on the Iranian issue. Chancellor Merkel has been strong. It's very important for the Iranians to know that there is a Germany committed to working with others to send the strong message to the Iranians that their nuclear ambitions, their nuclear weapons ambitions, will cause them isolation in the world in which we live.

President's Upcoming Visit to Germany

Mr. Diekmann. You will visit Germany in July. What would you—did Angela Merkel ask what you would like to see in Germany?

The President. It's really interesting. She felt like it was important for me to go to East Germany—old East Germany. There is no East Germany now—the old East Germany. And, one, I appreciated that a lot. You know, we're all products of how we are raised and, in many ways, where we were raised. If people want to get to know me better, they've got to know my parents and the values my parents instilled in me and the fact that I was raised in west Texas, in the middle of the desert, a long way away from anywhere, hardly.

There's a certain set of values you learn in that experience.

I was very intrigued by dealing with a very strong woman who had been raised in a Communist country and what it meant—what it meant. I spent some time with her upstairs in the private dining quarters here in the White House complex, listening to her. I asked her what it was like to grow up as a child. And the interesting thing—she first described her mother and father, which said a lot to me about the kind of person she is. I thought that was really insightful. She talked about her dad, the pastor, and her mom. She talked about going to school in a Communist system. And she told me she wanted me to come to her home, which, in my part of the world, at least where I'm from, inviting somebody to your home is a gesture of generosity. It's hospitality that is very gracious.

And so I'm really looking forward to going. I'll let her plan my itinerary once I get there. And it's going to be a very fascinating moment for me. And I thank her very much for her invitation.

President's Views on Germany

Mr. Diekmann. Are there things that bother you about the Germans? And are there things that you envy about the Germans?

The President. I am—look, I mean, Germans have always been incredibly efficient, capable businesspeople, and when they make a product, it is always of the highest of quality. The only thing that interests me about Germany is—it's not bothersome, but it's just a challenge for Germany—is the absorption of East and West, and the difficult assignment it is to really help the eastern Germany develop an economy that will be able to give people hope. But, again, I have great respect for Germany.

Trade With Germany

Mr. Diekmann. What kind of role does Germany play in the world?

The President. Germany is vital for the European Union's vitality. And Germany—and that's important for the United States. Listen, we want our trading partners to be strong. If you—if we have trade between one another, it really helps when there's economic vitality with your partner. You want your partner doing well. Trade is not a zero-sum game. Trade is an opportunity for a mutually beneficial relationship. And therefore, we want the European Union's economy as a whole to be doing well. And Germany has a great—when Germany's economy is vibrant, it has a chance to really help all the countries around her to grow well.

National Economy

Mr. Diekmann. The U.S. economy is booming.

The President. Yes, it is, thankfully.

Mr. Diekmann. Yes. It is booming because you made big tax cuts.

The President. True.

Mr. Diekmann. What do you think about the Germans—are you—they acting correctly if they increase taxes now?

The President. We have—our economy is booming for several reasons. One is, no question, the tax cuts help, and I intend to keep our taxes low. Secondly, our work rules are very flexible, and so is our economy.

We've got some issues that put us at a competitive disadvantage, and one is we've got too many lawsuits. And we're trying to do something about that. I am smart enough, however, to allow each country to make its own fiscal decisions as suits the needs of their constituents and the people.

Pope Benedict XVI

Mr. Diekmann. You are a practicing Christian. Does having a German Pope 60 years after World War II have a special meaning to you?

The President. You know, it's interesting that the last two Holy Fathers were from the same neighborhood. The Holy Father who just passed away, who was a great man, came from Poland and really helped rally the spirits of the people to challenge the tyranny of communism. And the current Holy Father came from a country torn asunder by war and is witness to a renewal of a united Germany. And I think it helps the world to have that perspective in a very important position of leadership. I admire the two Popes. These are strong, capable men who challenge the concept of moral relevancy.

The Presidency

Mr. Diekmann. Three last very short questions. What was the most wonderful moment in your terms of being President so far, and what was the most awful moment?

The President. The most awful moment was September the 11th, 2001.

Mr. Diekmann. The famous picture, when somebody gave you the information?

The President. Yes, that. I think, like all of us, it took a while for the—it was more than a moment. It was the event and the aftermath. On a situation like that, it takes a period to understand exactly what was going on. When somebody says, "America is under attack," and—you've got to fully understand what that meant. And the information coming was haphazard at best for a while. We weren't sure if the State Department got hit. I'd heard the White House had got attacked. Of course, I was worried that—my family was here.

And so I would say the toughest moment of all was after the whole reality sunk in, and I was trying to help the Nation understand what was going on, and at the same time, be empathetic for those who had lost lives.

The best moment was—you know, I've had a lot of great moments. I don't know, it's hard to characterize the great moments. They've all been busy moments, by the way. I would say the best moment was when I caught a 7½ pound largemouth bass on my lake. [*Laughter*]

2006 World Cup

Mr. Diekmann. Perfect. Very last question—you're a great sports fan.

The President. Yes, I am.

Mr. Diekmann. How important is the international World Cup in Germany? And what is your personal take on who will be at the end, the world champion?

The President. Listen, the World Cup is a—first of all, most Americans, up until recently, didn't understand how big the World Cup is. And we're beginning to understand. And the reason why is, a lot of us grew up not knowing anything about soccer, like me. I never saw soccer as a young boy. We didn't play it where I was from. It just didn't exist. I can't even—I'm thinking about all the—between age 6, when I can remember sports, and 12 or 13, I just never saw soccer being played.

And so there's a generation of us that really weren't fanatic. There's a new generation of Americans that did grow up on soccer. And there's obviously a huge interest amongst that crowd in the World Cup. And some of us older guys are now beginning to understand the significance of the World Cup around the world. It is the major sporting event worldwide, and it's got to be a great honor for Germany to host the event. And I'm confident that the German people will do a magnificent job of welcoming people from around the world.

And, of course, my team is the U.S. team. They tell me we've got a good team. Now, whether it's good enough to win it all, who knows? But I know they'll try their hardest.

Mr. Diekmann. Mr. President, thank you very much.

NOTE: The interview was taped at 1:55 p.m. in the Oval Office at the White House for later broadcast. In his remarks, the President referred to President Vladimir V. Putin of Russia; former President Saddam Hussein of Iraq; former Chancellor Gerhard Schroeder and Chancellor Angela Merkel of Germany;

Usama bin Laden, leader of the Al Qaida terrorist organization; senior Al Qaida associate Abu Musab Al Zarqawi; and President Mahmud Ahmadi-nejad of Iran. Mr. Diekmann referred to Prime Minister Ehud Olmert of Israel. The transcript was released by the Office of the Press Secretary on May 7. A tape was not available for verification of the content of this interview.

Remarks Announcing the Nomination of General Michael V. Hayden as Director of the Central Intelligence Agency
May 8, 2006

The President. Good morning. Today I'm pleased to nominate General Mike Hayden as the next Director of the Central Intelligence Agency. Mike Hayden is supremely qualified for this position. I've come to know him well as our Nation's first Deputy Director of National Intelligence. In that position, he's worked closely with our Director of National Intelligence, John Negroponte, to reform America's intelligence capabilities to meet the threats of a new century.

Mike has more than 20 years of experience in the intelligence field. He served for 6 years as Director of the National Security Agency and thus brings vast experience leading a major intelligence agency to his new assignment. He also served as Commander of the Air Intelligence Agency, as Director of the Joint Command and Control Warfare Center, and as Deputy Chief of Staff of the United States and U.N. Forces in Korea.

He's held senior positions at the Pentagon, the U.S. European Command, the National Security Council, and served behind the Iron Curtain in our Embassy in Bulgaria during the cold war.

Mike knows our intelligence community from the ground up. He has been both a provider and a consumer of intelligence. He's overseen the development of both human and technological intelligence. He has demonstrated an ability to adapt our intelligence services to the new challenges of the war on terror. He's the right man to lead the CIA at this critical moment in our Nation's history.

It's my honor to welcome Mike's wife, Jeanine, and their family to the Oval Office. I want to thank them for their willingness to support Mike Hayden in his long service to the United States.

With the agreement of the Senate, Mike will succeed a great patriot in Director Porter Goss. Under Porter's leadership, the CIA launched a 5-year plan to strengthen the Agency's human intelligence capabilities. This plan involves increasing the number of operatives and sources in the field and building up the Agency's analytical capabilities, so the hard-working men and women of the CIA have the resources they need to penetrate closed societies and secretive organizations.

Porter also played a vital role in shaping the new relationship between the CIA and the new Director of National Intelligence. And this process benefited greatly from the decades-long friendship between him and Director Negroponte.

Porter took on a critical job at a critical moment in our Nation's history. He instilled a sense of professionalism in the CIA and maintained the high standards of this vital agency at a time of transition and transformation. Throughout his public life, Porter Goss has been a man of accomplishment and integrity, and America appreciates his service.

I'm confident that Mike Hayden will continue the reforms that Porter has put in place and provide outstanding leadership to meet the challenges and threats of a dangerous new century. Mike Hayden was unanimously confirmed by the Senate last year for his current post, and I call on the Senate to confirm him promptly as the Director of the Central Intelligence Agency.

The work of the CIA has never been more important to the security of the American people. America faces determined enemies who struck our Nation on September the 11th, 2001, and who intend to attack our country again. To stop them we must have the best possible intelligence. The men and women of the CIA are working around the clock and around the world in dangerous conditions to gain information that is vital to securing our Nation. I appreciate their dedicated service, and so does Mike Hayden.

In Mike Hayden, the men and women of the CIA will have a strong leader who will support them. He will ensure they have the resources they need to do their jobs. He will enforce the secrecy and accountability that are critical to the security of the American people.

Mike, I appreciate your many years of service to our country. We're grateful that you've agreed to step forward and serve once again. Thank you very much.

[*At this point, Director-designate Hayden made brief remarks.*]

The President. Congratulations, Mike. Thank you very much. Appreciate it.

Thank you all.

NOTE: The President spoke at 9:31 a.m. in the Oval Office at the White House. The transcript released by the Office of the Press Secretary also included the remarks of Director-designate Hayden.

Remarks on a Peace Agreement in Sudan
May 8, 2006

I want to thank the Secretary of State, Condoleezza Rice, for joining me, and I also want to thank Deputy Secretary of State Bob Zoellick. He has just briefed me on his trip to Abuja, where he has played a very important role in setting up a peace agreement between the Government of Sudan and a major rebel group in the Darfur region.

Congratulations on a job well done, Bob. Thank you.

Last week, we saw the beginnings of hope for the people of Darfur. The Government of Sudan and the largest rebel group signed an agreement and took a step toward peace. Many people worked hard for this achievement. I'm particularly grateful for the leadership of President Obasanjo of Nigeria and President Sassou-Nguesso of

Congo. Deputy Secretary Zoellick told me of their really fine work, and I had the honor of calling both of them to thank them over the phone the other day. Their personal hands-on involvement was vital.

We're still far away from our ultimate goal, which is the return of millions of displaced people to their homes so they can have a life without fear. But we can now see a way forward.

Sudan is one of the most diverse nations in Africa and one of the most troubled countries in the world. A 22-year-old civil war between north and south took more than 2 million lives before a peace agreement was made that the United States helped to broker. About the same time, another conflict was raging in the west, and that's in Sudan's vast Darfur region.

Darfur rebel groups had attacked Government outposts. To fight that rebellion, Sudan's regime armed and unleashed a horse-mounted militia called the Janjaweed, which targeted not only rebels but the tribes thought to be supporting them. The Janjaweed murdered men, and they raped women, and they beat children to death. They burned homes and farms and poisoned wells. They stole land to graze their own herds. Hundreds of villages were destroyed, leaving a burnt and barren landscape.

About 200,000 people have died from conflict, famine, and disease. And more than 2 million were forced into camps inside and outside their country, unable to plant crops or rebuild their villages. I've called this massive violence an act of genocide, because no other word captures the extent of this tragedy.

A cease-fire was declared in this conflict in April 2004, but it has been routinely violated by all sides. The Janjaweed continued to attack the camps and rape women who ventured outside the fences for food and firewood. The Government took no effective action to disarm the militias, and the rebels sometimes attacked food convoys and aid workers.

An African Union force of about 7,200 from the region has done all it can to keep order, but they're patrolling an area nearly the size of Texas, and they have reached the limits of their capabilities. With the peace agreement signed on Friday, Darfur has a chance to begin anew. Sudan's Government has promised to disarm the Janjaweed by mid-October and punish all those who violate the cease-fire. The main rebel group has agreed to withdraw into specified areas. Its forces will eventually be disarmed as well, and some of its units will be integrated into the national army and police. The African Union will meet a week from today, urge its members to help implement this new agreement.

Our goal in Darfur is this: We want civilians to return safely to their villages and rebuild their lives. That work has begun and completing it will require even greater effort by many nations. First, America and other nations must act to prevent a humanitarian emergency and then help rebuild that country. America is the leading provider of humanitarian aid, and this year alone, we account for more than 85 percent of the food distributed by the World Food Programme in Sudan.

But the situation remains dire. The World Food Programme has issued an appeal for funds necessary to feed 6 million people over the next several months. The United States has met our commitment, but other major donors have not come through. As a result, this month, the World Food Programme was forced to cut rations by half.

So I proposed in the emergency supplemental before Congress to increase food aid to Sudan by another $225 million. I hope Congress will act swiftly on this true emergency. To get food to Darfur quickly, I've directed USAID to ship emergency food stockpiles. I've directed five ships and ordered them to be loaded with food and proceed immediately to Port Sudan. I've ordered the emergency purchase of another 40,000 metric tons of food for rapid shipment to Sudan. These actions will allow the World Food Programme to restore full food rations to the people of Darfur this summer.

Americans who wish to contribute money to help deliver relief to the people of Darfur can find information about how to do so by going to the USAID web site at www.usaid.gov and clicking on the section marked "Helping the Sudanese People."

Moving forward, we cannot keep people healthy and fed without other countries standing up and doing their part as well. The European Union and nations like Canada, the United Kingdom, the Netherlands, and Japan have taken leadership on other humanitarian issues, and the people of

Darfur urgently need more of their help now.

In addition, the Government of Sudan must allow all U.N. agencies to do their work without hindrance. They should remove the visa and travel restrictions that complicate relief efforts. And all sides must cease attacks on relief workers.

And finally, the United States will be an active participant in the Dutch-led reconstruction and development conference. And it's an important conference. It will take place within the next couple of months, to help the people get back on their feet so they can live normal lives in Darfur.

Second, America and other nations must work quickly to increase security on the ground in Darfur. In the short term, the African Union forces in Darfur need better capabilities. So America is working with our NATO allies to get those forces immediate assistance in the form of planning, logistics, intelligence support, and other help. And I urge members of the alliance to contribute to this effort.

In the longer term, the African Union troops must be the core of a larger military force that is more mobile and more capable, which generates better intelligence and is given a clear mandate to protect the civilians from harm. So I'm dispatching Secretary Rice to address the U.N. Security Council tomorrow. She's going to request a resolution that will accelerate the deployment of U.N. peacekeepers into Darfur. We're now working with the U.N. to identify countries that contribute those troops so the peacekeeping effort will be robust.

I've called on President—I just called President Bashir of Sudan, both to com-mend him on his work for this agreement and to urge the Government to express clear support for a U.N. force. The vulnerable people of Darfur deserve more than sympathy; they deserve the active protection that U.N. peacekeepers can provide.

In recent weeks, we've seen drastically different responses to the suffering in Darfur. In a recent audio tape, Usama bin Laden attacked American efforts in Sudan and urged his followers to kill international peacekeepers in Darfur. Once again, the terrorists are attempting to exploit the misery of fellow Muslims and encourage more death. Once again, America and other responsible nations are fighting misery and helping a desperate region come back to life. And once again, the contrast could not be more clear.

In late 2004 in Darfur, the Janjaweed attacked a village of a woman named Zahara. They raped her, murdered her husband, and set fire to their home. One of the attackers told her, "This year there's no god except us. We are your god now." But you and I know that at all times, in all places, there is a just God who sides with the suffering and calls us to do the same. America will not turn away from this tragedy. We will call genocide by its rightful name, and we will stand up for the innocent until the peace of Darfur is secured.

Thank you.

NOTE: The President spoke at 11:43 a.m. in the Roosevelt Room at the White House. In his remarks, he referred to Usama bin Laden, leader of the Al Qaida terrorist organization.

Statement on Medical Liability Reform Legislation
May 8, 2006

I am disappointed that the Senate has yet again failed to pass real medical liability reform legislation. Unwilling to take on their trial lawyer supporters, the Democrats led this effort to block these much-needed reforms.

Junk lawsuits are driving too many good doctors out of medicine. Women in nearly 1,500 counties are without a single ob-gyn, and frivolous and abusive lawsuits are encouraging the use of defensive medicine, which imposes substantial and unnecessary costs on all Americans.

This is a national problem that deserves a national solution. I have called on Congress to pass responsible medical liability reforms, and the House of Representatives has acted. It is time for the Senate to put the needs of the American people ahead of the interests of trial lawyers and pass meaningful medical liability reform legislation.

Message to the Congress on Continuation of the National Emergency Blocking Property of Certain Persons and Prohibiting the Export of Certain Goods to Syria
May 8, 2006

To the Congress of the United States:

Section 202(d) of the National Emergencies Act (50 U.S.C. 1622(d)) provides for the automatic termination of a national emergency unless, prior to the anniversary date of its declaration, the President publishes in the *Federal Register* and transmits to the Congress a notice stating that the emergency is to continue in effect beyond the anniversary date. In accordance with this provision, I have sent to the *Federal Register* for publication the enclosed notice, stating that the national emergency declared in Executive Order 13338 of May 11, 2004, and expanded in scope in Executive Order 13399 of April 25, 2006, authorizing the blocking of property of certain persons and prohibiting the exportation and reexportation of certain goods to Syria, is to continue in effect beyond May 11, 2006. The most recent notice continuing this emergency was published in the *Federal Register* on May 10, 2005 (70 FR 24697).

The actions of the Government of Syria in supporting terrorism, interfering in Lebanon, pursuing weapons of mass destruction and missile programs, and undermining United States and international efforts with respect to the stabilization and reconstruction of Iraq, pose a continuing unusual and extraordinary threat to the national security, foreign policy, and economy of the United States. For these reasons, I have determined that it is necessary to continue in effect the national emergency authorizing the blocking of property of certain persons and prohibiting the exportation and reexportation of certain goods to Syria and to maintain in force the sanctions to respond to this threat.

GEORGE W. BUSH

The White House,

May 8, 2006.

NOTE: The notice is listed in Appendix D at the end of this volume.

Remarks to Reporters in Coconut Creek, Florida
May 9, 2006

The President. I want to thank you all for joining us. I'm proud to be here with Secretary Leavitt. We're traveling the country reminding people that there's a fantastic opportunity for our seniors, and that is, Medicare now offers a prescription drug benefit that will save people a lot of money.

We just visited with some of our citizens inside there, and they're talking about significant savings. And that's what we want; we want our seniors to be able to have modern medicine. So far a lot of seniors have signed up. It's coming down the stretch toward the May 15th deadline; we want everybody to sign up. We want people to understand that they're going to save a lot of money when it comes to prescription drugs.

And I appreciate Secretary Leavitt's hard work. One of the things that our seniors have got to understand, that if you qualify for extra help in the program, if you're a low-income senior that qualifies for extra help, the May 15th deadline doesn't apply to you; you'll have time to take a look—we want everybody signing up. And if you're a low-income senior, you get—the Government pays about 95 percent or more of your prescription drug benefit. So it's worthwhile for people to look.

I want to thank groups like the AARP, NAACP, many in the faith community, community-based groups, all for working hard to educate seniors as to what's available. This is a good deal for America's seniors, and I'm proud to have signed a law to modernize Medicare, and I'm proud to be working with Michael.

I also want to thank Congressman Foley and Congressman Clay Shaw for joining us. They're strong backers of Medicare reform. They were informing me that a lot of their citizens have signed up. In south Florida, people are taking advantage of this program. And I strongly urge people to take a look and see what's available.

[At this point, Secretary of the Department of Health and Human Services Michael O. Leavitt made brief remarks.]

The President. Thank you all for joining us. Thank you all very much, I appreciate it.

NOTE: The President spoke at 8:53 a.m. at Broward Community College. The transcript released by the Office of the Press Secretary also included the remarks of Secretary Leavitt.

Remarks on the Medicare Prescription Drug Benefit and a Question-and-Answer Session in Sun City Center, Florida
May 9, 2006

The President. Thanks for coming. Please be seated. Thanks for the warm welcome. It's great to be here in Sun City Center. Brother Jeb said, "If you want to come to a really good place, come here." First of all, I think it's a pretty neat deal when you get introduced by your brother, par-

ticularly since he's such a good Governor. We both share the same political adviser—Mom. *[Laughter]* I don't know if Mother is still telling you what to do, Jeb, but she's certainly telling me what to do all the time. *[Laughter]*

And both of us married well. The first lady of Florida is a fantastic woman, and so is the First Lady of the United States. Laura sends her very best. She sends her love. Yesterday she represented us in Costa Rica. They inaugurated a new President, and they sent the word back—please send the best in your family. [*Laughter*] So we sent Laura.

I'm also proud to be joined by Congressman Adam Putnam. Where's Adam? There he is. Thank you. He's a smart guy. He's a smart person, and he's a good guy to work with, and I appreciate you being here, Adam.

I want to thank the WCI Communities' leadership and staff for having me here.

What I thought I would do is spend a little time talking about the new Medicare program. The reason I'm doing this, because I want people to sign up. And then I'll answer some questions, if you have some. And then I'm going to go over to Orlando and do the same thing tomorrow morning—just like I did earlier in south Florida. And the reason why I'm doing this is because we have changed Medicare for the better, but sometimes change creates anxieties. In other words, people say, "Well, maybe I don't want to change. I kind of like it the way things are." And—but we have a duty to educate people and give them a chance to see what's available, and that's what I'm doing. That's what you want your President to do.

First thing, let me give you a little history. As you know, Medicare was signed by one of my predecessors—happened to be from the State of Texas, Lyndon Baines Johnson. And it's a vital program. It's a program that has worked. It's a necessary program. Medicare is a commitment of the Federal Government. And once you make a commitment, it seems like to me, it makes sense to make the commitment a good commitment. In other words, you want it to work. You want it to be a modern, excellent program.

Medicare had done a—provided a lot of comfort for a lot of people, but it was getting old and stale; it needed to be reformed. And one reason it needed to be reformed is because it did not provide prescription drug coverage. And you know that. In other words, Medicare would pay for a surgery, say, like ulcer surgery, for $28,000 but wouldn't pay $500 for the prescription drugs that would have prevented the ulcer in the first place. See, medicine had changed with the advent of prescription drugs, but Medicare hadn't.

So I thought it made sense to make Medicare work better, to keep our commitment to our seniors. And we passed legislation that modernized Medicare, and we are now explaining to people what the modernized system means. Nobody is going to say, "You've got to sign up for this," but I think we have a duty to say to people, "Please take a look at it. Take a look and see what's available."

The first thing that's in the new system I think is important is that every senior now entering Medicare is eligible for a "Welcome to Medicare" physical exam. That wasn't the case prior to the reform. Now it is. And that makes a lot of sense, it seems like to me, to say, "Here's a physical for you." The best way to cure disease is to anticipate it and prevent it from happening in the first place, is to be able to catch illnesses early through screenings. Part of a modern, effective health care says that we'll encourage prevention. Helping to prevent disease is going to be a really important part of a modern system, whether you're on Medicare or not on Medicare; whether you're a guy like me, or whether you're a person who's eligible for Medicare.

There is a new prescription drug coverage in Medicare. And that's important for people to understand. The prescription drug coverage, first of all, helps all seniors pay for prescription drugs, no matter how they've paid before. In other words, everybody should take a look at the prescription drug coverage.

Secondly, what's interesting about the new program is it provides choices for seniors. You know, I knew that when we put—laid out the idea of giving seniors choices, it would create a little confusion for some. I mean, after all, up to now there hadn't been much—many choices in the system. And all of a sudden, a senior who feels pretty good about things says, "Here's old George W. or Mike Leavitt or Jeb or somebody say, 'Take a look.' " And all of a sudden, 40 choices pop up.

The reason why we felt it was necessary to provide choices is because we want the system to meet the needs of the consumer. The more choices you have, the more likely it is you'll be able to find a program that suits your specific needs. In other words, one size fits all is not a consumer-friendly program. And I believe in consumers. I believe in trusting people. I did know that there would be some worries about having to choose from 40 different plans, but I thought it was worth it because I know that 40 different plans here in Florida will mean that each individual can tailor a plan to meet his or her needs. And I thought that was important.

So how do we handle the 40 different programs? Well, we encouraged all kinds of people to help. AARP is helping, NAACP is helping, sons and daughters are helping, faith-based programs are helping people sort through the programs to design a program that meets their needs. I readily concede some seniors have said, "There are so many choices, I don't think I want to participate." My advice is, there is plenty of help for you.

Thirdly, seniors with the highest drug costs are going to get extra help in this modernized Medicare. We have catastrophic protection for the first time. And that's important. Drug costs over $3,600 a year will be—any costs over that will be picked up by 95 percent for the Federal Government. It's called catastrophic care. Part of the reason you modernize medicine this way is to give people peace of mind.

You know that if you sign up for the program and something goes terribly wrong and your prescription drug bills skyrocket, the Government is there to help, after $3,600. And that's important for families and its important for our seniors, to have that notion that there's stopgap insurance, that there's help beyond a certain level of costs.

And third—and fourthly, there's extra help for low-income seniors. If you qualify as a low-income senior—this is about a third of our seniors here in America—the prescription drug coverage includes little or no premiums, low deductibles, no gaps in insurance. On average, the Government will pay more than 95 percent of the cost for prescription drugs for low-income seniors.

It's really important for people to take a look and see whether or not there's a program that meets your needs. A lot of people are signing up. There's about 42 million folks eligible for Medicare in the United States, a little more than that. More than 31 million thus far have signed up. That's a lot. In other words, since January, people have said, "I think I'm going to take a look and get involved in this new program."

There's 6 million more who have an alternative source of coverage. In other words, they're plenty happy with the plans they have. And this program—by the way, nobody forces anybody to do anything. You know, this is our country; you're free to choose. So there's 37 million of the little more than 42 million people that have got coverage, and we're working hard to sign up the remaining eligible seniors. And they're signing up—a lot of people signing up, as we head toward a May 15th deadline.

I want to make this very clear. If you are eligible for extra help, if you're a low-income senior, the May 15th deadline does not apply to you. In other words, you can apply after May 15th without penalty. And that's important for low-income seniors to understand. We want everybody to sign up.

We want people to understand that there are really good benefits for—the average senior is going to save one-half on his or her cost—one-half on the cost of prescription drugs.

We were meeting, as I said, in south Florida earlier, and some of the stories down there for people who signed up were really strong stories—people saving money, people got a little extra money in their pocket. The system is modernized, and it saves you money. And that's what we want. Now, some say, "It's too good to be true." If you haven't looked at the program, take a look. Take a look. I think you're going to find what I said is true.

The other interesting thing that's happened is—just so the people out there who are wondering whether or not this is cost-effective, whether or not this makes sense to do—first of all, I think it makes a lot of sense to do. We don't want seniors choosing between food and medicine. We're a compassionate society. Secondly, because there's competition for you—in other words, somebody said, here's some different options for you, the average premium seniors pay for the prescription drug benefit is $25 a month on average. And that's down from an anticipated cost of $37 a month. In other words, when somebody bids for your business, it tends to be—it helps on price.

In Florida, the lowest cost option is about $10 a month. There are many zero-dollar premium Medicare advantage plans available for our seniors to choose from. The program is saving seniors a lot of money. And as a result of people competing for your business, it's saving the taxpayers money. In other words, people said, "Well, it's going to cost X." Well, it's costing 20 percent less. This is a good deal for America's seniors.

And so over the next week, Secretary Leavitt and myself and others in the administration are reminding people that there's a good opportunity for you. And so I would suggest, if you haven't signed up yet, if you're living in Florida and watching this TV program—or anywhere in the country watching the TV program, I'd call 1–800–MEDICARE, and there's somebody there who'll help you. Or if you've got some—if you're computer-literate or have a friend who's computer-literate, get on the web page, medicare.gov, and take a look—take a look at what's available.

Seniors all across the country are saving money because of this plan. It's—if you're a son or a daughter and your mom or dad is eligible for Medicare and he or she hasn't signed up, I believe the son or a daughter has a duty to help the mom or dad understand what's available. That's what sons and daughters are supposed to do. That's called love. And a loving son or daughter should take a look and help their folks realize what's possible, help design a drug benefit program that meets your mom or dad's needs.

Churches all across the country are reaching out—synagogues, people from different faiths understand that it makes sense to help their parishioners realize the benefits of this plan. I mentioned earlier AARP, NAACP, groups all across the country are out trying to find the folks who haven't signed up yet and encourage them to do so. And so that's why I'm here. I'm here doing my duty as Educator in Chief. [*Laughter*] It's to say to people from around this part of the world and those who may be watching over the airwaves, this is a good deal for the American seniors. And it's the right thing to do for the Government. If the Government makes a promise, we want to make sure that promise lives up to what we've told you. We've said, we're going to get you a modern health care system, and we have.

And that's what I've come to talk about. I'll be glad to answer any questions anybody has on any subject that may be on your mind. But in the meantime, thanks for letting me come by, and God bless.

All righty—[*applause*]—no, no—thank you. I'll be over—we'll get a little picture-taking in a minute. Yes, sir.

Availability of Literature on Medicare Benefits

Q. I find there's a dearth of literature about the new program. I just don't see any pamphlets or books around, which there should be.

The President. True.

Q. Secondly, I want to ask, if you do sign up, and I don't know what it's all about—I'm, truthfully, computer-fearful and so I'm not—I'm computer-illiterate. And I'd like to know, when—if I do sign up, can I quit, can I get out of it?

The President. Yes, you can. [*Laughter*] I think if you sign—first of all, that's a great question. Literature—there's all kind of literature. I can't answer the question as to why——

Q. I haven't seen it.

The President. No, I know, there's not any—you haven't seen it yet, I know. But I will try to find out why you haven't seen any here. Secondly, you're not alone when it comes to saying, "I'm a little frightened about getting on the computer." You're not the only person I've heard say that. And therefore, one of the things that centers such as this do is provide help with people who are computer-illiterate. And it's—with somebody explaining how it works and what you're watching, I think you'll find it to be a lot less intimidating than you think.

And thirdly, I wouldn't sign up, if I were you, unless you were comfortable that it saves you money. This is an add-on to Medicare. It is a part of Medicare. It's called Medicare Part D. In other words, the rest of Medicare exists, but what this does is it provides an additional benefit. And as I said, across the country, people are saving half on their prescription drug bills. People say to me, "Well, I'm feeling pretty healthy, and I'm not taking a lot of prescription drugs; I'm not going to sign up." My advice is, sign up, because you don't know when you're going to have to start taking prescription drugs.

But at the very minimum, take a look. You seem like an inquisitive person, somebody who wants to know the facts, and there should be people here at this center that will help you find the facts out front. And there's going to be some literature, I hope—there is? Brother said there's literature. Now, there had better be literature, because the man—[*laughter*]—the man in the hat is going to walk out there, and if he doesn't see any literature, I'm cooked. [*Laughter*] Good looking hat too.

Yes, sir. Thank you for your question.

Iran

Q. Mr. President, my question concerns the Iranian situation.

The President. Yes.

Q. I'm very worried about it, and I don't think I'm alone. I know that you and Secretary Rice and Ambassador Bolten are doing everything humanly possible to unite the global community in persuading the Iranians that getting the bomb is not in their own interest. And even if you get the Chinese and the Russians to come around eventually on meaningful sanctions, my fear is it's liable to take so long it will be too little and too late. So I assume there's a good possibility, given their attitude, they're going to get the bomb. And my question is, if they do, what next?

The President. Yes. First of all, it's a great question, because he is bringing to the front here a question of international significance. Our objective is not to let them get the bomb, first of all. And I am an optimistic person and, therefore, believe—I'm going to rephrase your question a different way: How are you going to stop them from getting it in the first place—not what are you going to do if they get one.

And the first goal—first of all, all options—the first option and the most important option is diplomacy. As you know, I've made the tough decision to commit American troops into harm's way. It's the toughest decision a President can ever make, but I want you to know that I tried diplomacy. In other words, a President has got to be able to say to the American people, diplomacy didn't work. And therefore, the first choice, and a choice that I think will work with the Iranians, is diplomacy. And I believe we can accomplish this through diplomacy.

Any diplomatic effort must have a common goal. And the common goal here is precisely what you said, sir, which is the Iranians should not have a nuclear weapon or the capacity to make a nuclear weapon.

Now, that wasn't always the case during my Presidency. In other words, people have come together around that goal. And the countries that have come around that goal are not only our allies in Europe but China and Russia agree. So the first step toward good diplomacy is to have different countries agree to a common goal, which is that the Iranians should not have the capacity and/or a nuclear weapon. So that's positive.

Secondly, we're now working on the tactics as to how to convince the Iranians through—to get rid of their ambitions through a united front. And so what you're watching play out—by the way, because we live in a transparent society, everything, of course, is in the newspapers—which is fine; that's healthy. But that's not the case when you're dealing with a nontransparent society.

And so we got six countries—Condi was up there dealing with them last night, sitting around the table saying, how are we going to achieve our common goal? So what you're watching is, of course, all the guessing and speculating about the different positions of the six countries sitting around the table. But I believe that through hard work, we will continue to keep people bound together because there is a common interest to prevent the Iranians from getting that weapon. They understand—the countries understand the danger inherent

with the Iranians having a weapon. They understand the consequences of a nuclear Iran, particularly when you have a President who's threatening people.

And so we're at an early stage of diplomacy at this point in time. And one of the options, of course, is to go to the United Nations Security Council. And once in the United Nations Security Council, we're trying to reach—what does the resolution say. My objective—and thank you for your kinds words about Condi and myself working hard to keep the common front. It's very important for the Iranians to know they will be isolated in the world; that the rest of the world, much of the world, shares the same demands that those of us who are heading the—involved in the negotiations say.

But you're right; this is a very difficult issue. And we will continue to work through diplomatic channels to make it clear that we mean what we say. And obviously, part of making the diplomacy work is, what will be the consequences if the Iranians decide maybe not to listen to the rational demands of the world? And you mentioned one, economic sanctions. But we're—and I'm not going to comment on that, because I think it's very important for good negotiators to keep their cards close to the vest, and then at the appropriate time, make it clear what our intentions are.

This is a serious issue; it's taking a lot of our time, as it should. Ultimately, of course, I would hope that an American President is able to say to the Iranian people, "You're free, and we look forward to having good relations with you." Liberty has got an amazing way of changing the world. I speak to a group of people who know that better than most. You have seen liberty transform the world during your lifetime. You've seen—and one of my favorite ways of explaining the effects of liberty and my belief in what liberty can do is to explain the relationship I have with the Japanese Prime Minister.

I bet I've got some World War II vets here. I'll bet there's some people who know World War II vets, who are here. I bet people are here who know somebody who was called into action to fight the Japanese in World War II. And today I can—I report to you that the Japanese Prime Minister is my friend in keeping the peace. And there's a reason why—is because after World War II, one of my predecessors, Harry S. Truman, had the belief that the United States should help that country, our enemy, become a democracy, not styled—an American-style democracy but a Japanese-style democracy. And because of the faith in the capacity to freedom to change people's way of thinking, because he felt strong to that conviction, today, a Japanese-style democracy is a friend of America.

Freedom has the capacity to change enemies into friends. And so in the long run, the best way to deal with problems such as the Iranian problem is to encourage people to be free. And the fundamental question is, do people want to be free? And the cornerstone of my foreign policy is my strong belief that freedom is universal. People desire to be free.

One of the lessons that your generation has taught our generation is that staying strong to the values that America subscribes to—human rights, human dignity, the universality of freedom—has changed parts of the world in incredible ways. Just look at Europe—this is a long answer—[*laughter*]—to an important question. And the reason I'm framing it this way is I want you to understand how I think about laying the foundation of peace so we can deal with not only the issue that you asked about, sir, but other issues that will inevitably come up during the course of the 21st century.

But freedom has the capacity to lay the foundations for peace, and we must not lose sight of the historical examples. Take Europe, for example—there was two major conflicts in Europe, World War I and World War II. Today, Europe is whole, free, and at peace because democracies don't war. It's one of the historical lessons.

And so in the short term, on the issue you described, we will keep our diplomacy going. We'll be knitted up as best as we possibly can with different—with as many nations as possible—six of them at the table last night in New York, by the way. And in the meantime, it is—we will continue to advance the freedom agenda.

Good question. Yes, sir.

Health Care Reform

Q. Thank you. First, let me say, I think a lot of people will be helped by this program.

The President. They will——

Q. A lot of people will be helped by the Medicare Part D program.

The President. Oh, thank you.

Q. But I think there's major deficiencies in it that I think we'd like to hear some comments from you on. The first major issue—I think the program is going to be a lot more expensive both to the user and to the taxpayer than it needs to be, because we don't allow Medicare to negotiate directly with the pharmaceutical companies. This could wind up costing the taxpayers hundreds of billions of dollars over the next 10 years.

Another thing, the insurance companies are allowed to change their formulary once a person is in the program; a person is not allowed to get out until the end of the year. This is a legalized bait and switch operation by the insurance companies. How many of them are doing it, I don't know, but it's a danger for our seniors.

Third, I have a report here from Families USA indicating that the poorest people that are affected by this program are not being helped.

The President. Well, I just——

Q. Not helped—either they're not signed up, they're not being helped compared to the benefits they were getting under a combination of Medicare and Medicaid.

So, finally, I think there are several major changes that should be made in the program. Number one, let Medicare negotiate with the pharmaceutical companies. Number two, stop the formulary switch. If we do that, by reducing the costs, I think we can possibly reduce the size or even eliminate the doughnut hole that people are exposed to.

The President. Okay, thanks.

Q. And I think—[*laughter*]. One last thing—okay. If we don't bring our costs down this way, we're never going to control health care costs in the U.S. And we're subsidizing the pharmaceutical companies, and we're subsidizing health costs in every other country around the world, because every other country negotiates directly with the pharmaceutical companies.

The President. Yes, I'll be glad to give you some comments. First of all, if a senior takes a look at the program and doesn't think it saves his or her money, they shouldn't sign up.

Secondly, in terms of the low-income seniors, I don't know what the report is that you cite—people cite reports all the time. I will tell you this, that a lot of people are working hard to find the low-income seniors, to give them the chance to sign up for an incredibly beneficial program—including AARP, the NAACP, as I mentioned. I've met with their representatives. They realize this is a good deal for low-income seniors. But if you're premise is right, that the low-income senior won't benefit from the program, they shouldn't sign up to it. I just strongly disagree that this isn't good for low-income seniors.

Thirdly, one of the reasons why—we're trying to make individual choice available for seniors, as opposed to having the Federal Government making the decisions on behalf of seniors. And so the idea of having the Federal Government negotiate price keeps the Federal Government squarely in the middle of the program. There's a philosophical difference, evidently, between me and you. All I can tell you is, is that the program is costing less than anticipated, and this program is going to benefit a lot of seniors because there is more choice for seniors.

Now, the idea of, "This won't help us control health care costs," one, I disagree with that. I think more choices for consumers, the better off we are.

Secondly, health care costs are on the rise. A lot of it has to do with these lawsuits that are driving good doctors out of practice, that are causing people to practice defensive medicine, and running up the premiums for consumers. We need to modernize health care, as well, by introducing information technology so that, kind of, the system of writing files by hand, which leads to errors and inefficiency, is replaced by a modern system of information technology.

Thirdly, we need transparency in pricing. People need to know that which they're purchasing and the quality of that which they purchase so that consumers are able to make more rational decisions.

Fourthly, at the center of the health care needs to be the doctor-patient relationship—not bureaucracy, either government or private bureaucracy. And that's why I'm such a strong believer in health savings account, which are now being—now available for a lot of folks in America.

So I think you and I may have a different vision of health care. I thank you for bringing it up, but, look, if people don't like it, they don't have to sign up for it. People have got the right to pick what they want to pick. And therefore, I know you would agree with me in saying that seniors ought to take a look and see whether or not it meets their needs.

Thank you, sir, very much. I appreciate that.

Yes, ma'am.

Medicare Prescription Drug Benefit May 15th Deadline

Q. Mr. President—[*inaudible*]—to live in this country, and I'm very proud of it.

The President. Good. Where were you from initially?

Q. East Germany.

The President. Very good.

Q. I've been through a lot, and I appreciate this country. And also I just signed up—I belong to AARP supplement, and I just signed up for Medicare Complete Choice Rx United Healthcare with zero monthly premium, and I'm saving 140 some dollars a month.

The President. Good.

Q. Thank you.

The President. How long have you been in the country?

Q. I've been in this country longer than I lived in Germany because I was in East Germany, and we had a lot of problems. You couldn't speak up for anything. My brother was arrested. My sister almost was, for saying something. So I got out pretending I'm performing at the opera house in Nuremberg, and I broke my contract interest, and I stayed in West Germany. And I've been here since 1959. And I'm an American citizen. I'm very proud of it.

The President. Great. Welcome.

Q. Thank you.

The President. Yes, ma'am. By the way, I met with Chancellor Angela Merkel the other day, and she was—she, too, was raised in East Germany. It's interesting to be dealing with a world leader who was raised in a Communist country. She brings an interesting perspective to the idea of people being free. I mean, she understands freedom as well as anybody understands freedom. And she's going to be a—she's a good ally and a good person. When I see her, I'll tell her I saw you. [*Laughter*]

Q. Welcome, Mr. President. Thank you for coming here. One of my questions is, May 15th, I believe, is the sign-up date.

The President. Yes.

Q. If people cannot make a decision by May 15th, will they be penalized, or will there be another time period where they can sign up?

The President. It depends upon whether you're a—eligible for extra benefits, a low-income senior or not. If you're a low-income senior, there will be no penalties. If you're not a low-income senior, sign up before May 15th.

Q. Oh, okay. So then there will be—there will not be another sign-up date?

The President. You can continue to sign up, but there won't be sign-up at the same rates at which you could—the same rates at which you'll get your prescription drug benefits prior to May 15th. Deadlines are important. Deadlines help people understand there's finality, and people need to get after it, you know? And so the idea is, there's the deadline. Now, low-income seniors, as I mentioned to you, will be able to sign up after May 15th without penalty. Let's see—yes, ma'am.

Q. I appreciate everything you've said. I think you're great.

The President. Thank you. Well, we'll leave it at that. [*Laughter*]

Q. No, I'm just like your mother. I do want to suggest—this is a community. Our motto is "Neighbors Helping Neighbors." We're volunteers. There are many, many seniors here who need help. We procrastinated and finally made the decision to sign up through AARP, because you can always change. And if they start increasing costs, we'll change to another one. You can have influence on people you buy from more than if the Government is handling it. And so I appreciate your approach.

However, I would beg, not for myself—because there were logjams; they were shuffling the phone calls directly to Medicare. I got an ID number; my husband got, in the afternoon, a confirmation number. No one knows whether they're actually recorded. The Internet was so bogged down, you couldn't get information, because everyone is doing it at the last minute. Now, when we pay our taxes, there's a deadline. But we can apply for a 6-months reprieve. I think—[*laughter*]——

The President. I think I know where you're headed. [*Laughter*]

Q. All right, I don't have to continue it. We could go out and help our neighbors. There's a Medicare bus—we just found out this week—going to a Catholic church in Tampa to help people sign up. There's a Medicare bus going to a hospital in Sarasota, but we didn't think about getting one to come here for our people, and we need some time to give them some help. Thank you.

The President. Yes, I appreciate that, thanks. In other words, what you're saying is, there's a lot of people beginning to come in at the last minute, and you're afraid they're not going to be able to access the system and/or have their numbers and names filed properly before May 15th. I'll check with the local people to make sure that—see what the strategy is in dealing with that.

Yes, ma'am. There you go.

Medicare Benefits for Individuals With Disabilities

Q. Is this the same Medicare plan——

The President. You're doing fine, just keep cranking it up.

Q. Is this the same Medicare plan for people that are on disabilities?

The President. Disabilities, yes. It applies to people with disabilities as well.

Q. So if you're under 65—then I would have to still go and apply under this?

The President. For the additional help, yes, ma'am.

Q. For additional help on this. And also, I just want to say, thank you very much for the way that you run the Government with the beliefs of—your Christian beliefs and not letting others bring you down when you're standing behind on your beliefs. It's very important. All the Christians stand behind you.

The President. Thank you. Yes, ma'am.

Trade/Energy

Q. ——be able to tell you from the same point of view that I'm very concerned about the growing fields, the products that are now being sent and brought back from other countries, that we've eroded our own economics in America, that we're too trusting of other countries, instead of being able to build up from within. And it's a very great concern, because we live in this area—being Ruskin—a tomato growing area for the State of Florida—going into other countries, other States than Florida. We've lost our fields. We're losing the orange groves. We're losing so much that this whole country was built on, and we're now relying on beef from Australia. We're relying on produce from South America. We're now looking at China to come in and supplement Hewlett Packard and all these other companies that have now said, "We can't afford to keep the Americans employed." This is a very big concern for me, at my age, let alone for the kids who are coming up behind me.

The President. You know, it's an interesting—that's a very interesting question. She—or statement—there's a lot of people that are concerned about a global world in which there is fierce competition. My attitude about this is that I don't think we ought to fear the competition; I think competition is good and healthy. But I think we ought to be smart about how we deal with it. In other words, one of the options to deal with that global fear is to wall ourselves off; is to say, we're not going to accept products; is to go through protectionism; is to say, we'll put high tariffs on products because we don't want other people selling their product in the American market. That's one way to deal with your concern. And it's—I, frankly, think that would lead to economic problems for the country.

I am, as you know, a person who believes in free trade. I also believe in making sure companies treat us fairly—in other words, so that we can compete on a level playing field. And so here's some ideas as to how to deal with it. And by the way, yours is not an isolated concern. It's a legitimate question for policymakers—is, how do you deal—how can you assure us that we can continue to be the economic leader of the world with such competition?

Wait, let me finish. Let me finish my answer. And here's some practical things to do. One, make sure our children have got the job skills necessary—the skills necessary to fill the jobs of the 21st century. One of the things that Brother Jeb has done is he's brought strong accountability in the public schools to make sure that there's high standards and people are measured. And when we find failure, you do something about it, so that we're just not shuffling kids through the system.

And I want to extend those high standards and extra help for Title I students who may not be measuring up to standards in math and science. Because I'm going to tell you what's going to happen in a global world, that if we do not educate our children with the skills necessary to fill the jobs of the 21st century—math, science, engineering—jobs that will help lead this country forward—if we don't do that, the jobs are going to go to other countries. The good, high-paying jobs are going to go to other parts of the world.

So step one is education. Step two is to make sure we're always the leader in innovation and research and development. And the way to do that is to spend Federal money, which we're going to do, in the basic sciences, as well as make sure the research and development tax credit which encourages the private sector to invest in research and technology, make sure that's a permanent part of the Tax Code. In other words, make sure America is the leader in innovation. If we're not the leader in innovation, other countries will be the leader of innovation. So there's competition. We can try to wall ourselves off, but it will still be a competitive world.

Thirdly, we got to do something about energy. The gas prices, as you know, are affecting you; they're high. Part of the reason why they're high is because the price of crude oil is high, and part of the reason the price of crude oil is high is because the demand for crude oil has been outstripping supply. And I'm not sure supply will ever catch up with demand in the short term, so one of the things we need to do is to figure out how to drive our cars differently—different fuels like ethanol grown right here in—the core product of which can be grown right here in Florida.

Hybrid automobiles is the second. And we've got incentives in Federal law that provides incentives for people to buy hybrids. Hybrids mean you're running on a combination of electricity and gasoline. And I'll tell you an interesting breakthrough that's about to come, though, because of research as a result of the Federal Government and private sector, is that we're going to have batteries that will be able to last for the first 40 miles when somebody drives. That's good for urban America, for example. A lot of people don't drive 40 miles in a day. It would be pretty good if they could drive those first 40 without using gasoline.

We got to be wise about our energy policy. I happen to believe in nuclear power. I believe in nuclear power—I know nuclear power is renewable, and it protects the environment. We got to make sure we continue to develop technologies that allow us to burn coal in environmentally friendly ways. Solar technology is becoming more advanced, and the Government is helping with the research there.

My point to you is that on the energy front, we've got to be wise if we're going to compete. We got to do something about junk lawsuits that are making it hard here in America not only for the medical profession but for the business sector, if we want to compete. We got to keep taxes low if we want to compete. If we want to compete in the future, we got to do something about Social Security. Social Security is fine for you. You all are in good shape. It's fine for my generation, but it's not so fine for the people who are going to be trying to pay for my generation. And it's time to put aside all that business—the political business in Washington, DC—and come up with a solution so younger generations of Americans—[*applause*]. My answer to the country is, we shouldn't fear the future; we ought to shape it.

And the alternative is to shut ourselves off, and I think that would be a huge mistake. It's really interesting when you look at the 1920s. During that period of time, the American people became isolated with high protective tariffs, and it eventually was part of the reasons why we had a Great Depression. And I think we always must be mindful of the lessons of history.

Anyway, excellent question. Thanks for giving me a chance—you're not through yet, I take it. [*Laughter*] You want to debate?

Alternative Fuel Sources/Energy

Q. Forty years ago——

The President. Go ahead.

Q. Forty years ago, we had the red flag flying about the oil shortage. We were all told, let's do something. That was 40 years ago. Solar power was supposed to be the future for us. The Government was participating and literally supplying people with the money to put solar power into their homes. It all stopped. Why don't we continue to look at these resources instead of now stopping people because they can't get to their jobs——

The President. No, no, say that again. Look at what now?

Q. Why don't we continue to look at these sources of solar power——

The President. We are.

Q. ——these houses around here, literally, if you put up a solar power panel, somebody is coming up to say, "Hey, wait a minute. It's not okay." Down in Fort Myers, they did it 20 years ago, so it has

been accepted, and it's fine. But 40 years ago, we had these red flags flying——

The President. Yes.

Q. ——why did we waste 40 years? Now we're scared.

The President. No, I appreciate—I actually am not—I don't think "scared" is the right word to describe how I feel. I feel that we need to rise to the challenge. I'll remind you, in 2001, the price of crude oil was like $17 a barrel, is one reason why. In other words, it—the low price of crude oil kind of lulled people into a sense that maybe things we're going to—the supply would be greater than demand. But it also made it more difficult for alternatives to compete.

And I'm not sure what you mean, people aren't encouraged to put up solar panels. I think people can put up solar panels if they want to. But the interesting thing about—and we're spending research money on advanced solar technology. In other words, there's not going to be "a" answer for diversifying away from foreign sources of oil. There's going to be a series of answers on a series of fronts that will enable this country to diversify away from oil, and we need to. I completely agree we need to. And the question is, are we spending money at the Federal level to do so? And the answer is, absolutely. Since I've been President, we've spent about $10 billion on ways to help us diversify away from oil, through research and development.

Yes, sir.

Hurricanes

Q. We put out a patent to control hurricanes, and we sent it to—[*laughter*]—Senator Burr, and he thought it was great, and he——

The President. Give him a mike that works, please. [*Laughter*]

Q. We sent it to Senator Burr, and he thought it was great, and he gave it, I understand, to Karl Rove.

The President. What now? I missed your question, sir.

Q. A patent to control hurricanes.

The President. To control hurricanes?

Q. Right.

The President. Where were you last year? [*Laughter*]

Q. I'm here this year, okay. And Senator Burr thought it was good enough, from North Carolina, and he gave it—I understand it was given to Karl Rove, okay. We want—we tried to get in touch with you, and we hope you get the description of this patent, because we feel sure it's the one thing that can stop hurricanes when they're young and vulnerable, okay. We can get at them, and we're using the coldest thing in the universe to do it. And planes—it's all planned on just how to do it, from MacDill or anywhere. And so we hope you get to read this. I gave it to a guy named Ryan here, that's an associate of yours, and I hope he gives it to you.

The President. Okay, good. What's his name?

Q. My name is Luther Hoffman. We sent you a letter, but I guess it may not have gotten through.

The President. Well, you know—[*laughter*].

Yes, sir.

Gasoline

Q. Yes, sir, can you hear me okay?

The President. Yes, sir.

Q. You mentioned gas prices, and I think everybody understands that this is being driven by economic imperatives. What I don't understand—what seems to violate common sense—is why the oil companies are also reporting record profits. It doesn't seem like people should get rich on somebody else's misery.

The President. Well, my attitude is, is that I believe in the markets; I believe in private enterprise; but I also believe people ought to reinvest. You know, we haven't built a refinery in this country since the early 1970s, not one refinery. And guess what? When you have shortage of supply and demand stays strong, price goes up.

So part of the reasons why we've got high gasoline prices is because the price of crude oil has gone up.

Part of it also is because we're not increasing the supplies of gasoline for the consumers. And so my call to the energy companies is: Reinvest in America; expand refinery capacity; build new ones. Part of the problem, though, is our own fault. We've got a lot of rules and regulations that prevent there to be—that stop people from investing capital in refinery expansion. So one of the things I'm working with Congress is to relax these regulations.

I mean, if we've got a problem, let's address it square on and figure out where the problem is. And there is a bottleneck when it comes to this paperwork. And we've got to be less regulatory in America to increase the supply of gasoline for our people.

We've got another problem, in that in a lot of States, they require different kind of fuel blends, which means that it's hard. When you have to change your gasoline supply on a seasonal basis to have specialized blends, it causes supply disruptions. And disruption in supply causes prices to go up.

And so I don't believe the Federal Government ought to be taking over businesses; I don't believe that. But I do believe that the Federal Government ought to be encouraging people to spend profits here in America, to build pipeline and expand capacity for the sake of consumers.

Yes, ma'am. We're kind of running out of air time, here, because I've got to go to Orlando. Brother, you need to get back to work. They're paying you a lot of money, and you're just sitting there. [*Laughter*]

Arctic National Wildlife Refuge/Oil

Q. First of all, Mr. President, I want you to know that you are in our prayers on a daily basis.

The President. Thank you.

Q. We pray for you and your Cabinet. Secondly of all, I would like to ask one question about the Alaskan pipeline. My understanding is that most of that supply does not come to the United States, and I would like to know why that goes to other countries rather than to where it's needed here, so that we can——

The President. You mean the crude oil coming down the pipeline?

Q. Yes, sir.

The President. I don't know where it goes, to be honest with you. Sorry. I can find out. [*Laughter*]

Q. Okay. Could we just divert a little bit of that our direction, please? [*Laughter*]

The President. I thought you were going to ask, how come we don't have the gas pipeline coming down yet, because there's a lot of untapped oil and gas up there that can be explored in environmentally friendly ways. And I think we ought to be drilling in ANWR—it's called ANWR. I know we can do it and protect the environment at the same time. And I know there's a lot of untapped gas up there that we ought to get down through pipeline as well. I don't know where all the oil goes coming out of the pipeline now. I'll try to find out for you.

Okay, final question. Yes, sir.

Social Security Reform

Q. Morning, Mr. President.

The President. How are you?

Q. I'm a retired New York City fireman.

The President. Yes, sir.

Q. I appreciate the love and affection that you showed New York City after 9/11 on behalf of all them people that passed away at that time——

The President. Yes, thanks.

Q. ——and the 343 firemen, my brother firemen that died there that day. I think you're doing a fantastic job, and we'll always love and respect you.

You said before you'd like a solution for Social Security. I have it right here in my hand, Mr. President.

The President. I'll meet you right there at the corner, and you can hand it to me.

Q. I'd love to. [*Laughter*]

The President. The hurricane guy can show up here with his answer too. [*Laughter*]

Q. I wrote a solution to the Social Security reform a year ago. I sent it to every Congressmen, every Senator, every newscaster, every station throughout this country. I sent 794 letters out, and I got about 5 replies. I think what's happening with Social Security is a disgrace. It's not going to affect us, like you say, but it's going to affect us because we're the parents of the baby boomers.

The President. That's right.

Q. And we're also the grandparents of the boomers' babies. [*Laughter*] And we're worried about them.

The President. Yes. I tell you what. I'm fixing to thank everybody and you stand right there.

Q. Thank you, Mr. President.

The President. And I'm—I tell you what I'm——

Q. Please give me two minutes with this letter.

The President. I'm going to get the photographer to take a picture of you handing me that letter.

Q. Thank you, sir.

The President. And that way I'll remember who you were when you handed it to me. [*Laughter*]

Q. I'll always remember you, Mr. President.

The President. Thanks for being a firefighter.

God bless, everybody. Thank you.

NOTE: The President spoke at 11:09 a.m. at the Kings Point Clubhouse. In his remarks, he referred to Gov. Jeb Bush of Florida, and his wife, Columba; President Oscar Arias Sanchez of Costa Rica; Prime Minister Junichiro Koizumi of Japan; and Chancellor Angela Merkel of Germany. The Office of the Press Secretary also released a Spanish language transcript of these remarks.

Remarks Following a Visit to a Fire Station in Sun City Center
May 9, 2006

The President. Jeb and I just were briefed by the firefighters here about the dry conditions that are creating hazards for the people—and Kelley, I appreciate your briefing. He was in charge of putting out that fire yesterday that consumed 450 acres. They think it was caused by a spark out of one of the utility lines.

I've always been impressed by those who are willing to get out and fight the fires and save lives and save property. I'm surrounded by people who made a career out of that. And I want to thank them for their dedication to service. I want to thank them for the briefing about the threat we find ourselves in; we've got dry and windy conditions.

The good news for the people of Florida is they've got people who are willing to serve and willing to put their lives at risk and willing to fight fires. There's one going on right now, as we speak. Kelley was briefing us on the equipment and manpower that's in place fighting the fire. This is one of these difficult periods for the State of Florida, in dealing with the climatic conditions as they are.

Obviously, the people need to be real careful, they need to be careful about starting fires, they need to be careful about throwing used cigarettes out, and they need to be mindful these are dangerous conditions. And they ought to be thoughtful about how to conduct their lives so they don't put others in the positions where a fire could destroy them or their property.

Do you want to say something, Jeb?

Governor Jeb Bush. Well, other than the fact, as the President said, it's actually right that if someone throws a cigarette out on the Interstate, it could create—first of all, it's a loss of life and property and puts a lot of people at risk. And it's a felony in our State. So we want to make sure that no fires are started because of human error or negligence or malfeasance.

The President. Anyway, I want to thank you all for joining me.

NOTE: The President spoke at 1:59 p.m. at Sun City Center Fire Station No. 28. In his remarks, he referred to Vincent Kelley, captain, Hillsborough County Fire Rescue.

Remarks in a Discussion on the Medicare Prescription Drug Benefit in Orlando, Florida
May 10, 2006

The President. Please be seated. Thank you. Thanks for letting me come by to say hello. I'm thrilled to be back in the State of Florida. Yesterday I checked in with my brother—[*laughter*]—to make sure everything is going all right. I'm real proud of Jeb. He's a good, decent man, and I love him dearly.

I also checked in with Laura this morning, to see how she's doing. She sends her

best to all of you all. She's doing just great, by the way.

I'm here to talk about Medicare. We've got an exciting program and an exciting opportunity for people to improve their lives. So this is an educational forum. This is a chance not only to speak to the folks here but to those who may be watching on TV about a really interesting opportunity for the seniors all around our country to really improve their lives by signing up for a new opportunity in Medicare.

But before I do—and by the way, I've got some interesting helpers here to make the case. I thought it would be better to have others describe what the Medicare program means than me sitting up here just giving a long speech. [*Laughter*] You probably agree with that, but you're too polite to say so. [*Laughter*]

I want to thank Tommy Martinez for welcoming us here. Tommy, thank you. I thank all the good folks who work here. Thanks for helping our seniors to improve their lives. You know, one of the great things about America is there's a lot of citizens who have heard a call to help a neighbor, and there's a lot of people that are willing to, kind of, help educate somebody or help somebody find help. That's what we're really here to honor today, in many ways. We're not only here to talk about a new program for Medicare, but we're here to thank people that have taken time out of their lives to help a senior improve their lives.

I want to thank Sylvia Caceres. She is the central Florida regional director. Thank you, Sylvia. Ramon Ojeda is the president of the Hispanic Chamber of Metro Orlando. Ramon, thank you. Finally, old Rich Crotty, he's here somewhere. Hey, Rich, good to see you, buddy. I was thinking about Rich. You might remember, his son made him famous—[*laughter*]—made me famous too. [*Laughter*] The lad went to sleep in the middle of one of my stemwinders. [*Laughter*] Give him my best, Crotty.

Let me talk real quick about Medicare. First of all, my administration views Medicare as a vital—that Medicare is a vital program. It's an important program that has worked well for many years. And therefore, when I got into office, I said, we're going to not only commit ourselves to Medicare, but we're going to make it better. See, the Federal Government has said to our seniors, "We're going to provide a good health care system for you." And so we started looking at whether or not the Medicare system was delivering as good a health care system as possible. And I determined it wasn't. I said it was good, but it could be better.

And the reason why it wasn't as good as it could be is because the system was not helping seniors with prescription drugs. In other words, medicine had changed a lot since the sixties, obviously—that's an obvious statement—but Medicare itself hasn't changed along with the modernization of medicine. I'll give you a good example. Medicare would pay for ulcer surgery, a surgery which might cost upwards of $25,000, but it would not pay for the prescription drugs that could have prevented the ulcer from happening in the first place. And that didn't make any sense. It didn't make any sense for our seniors, and it didn't make any sense for the taxpayers. And so it seemed like it made sense to me to modernize the system, which we did.

And so we created what's called Part D, and basically Part D is a prescription drug benefit for not only our seniors but those who qualified who are disabled as well. Part D says this: It says that seniors have now got a prescription drug plan available to them. It's your choice to make. One of the interesting things about the strategy we've employed is seniors now have over 40 choices to choose from in Florida. Now, that in itself created a slight problem, because 40 choices can create a sense of uncertainty among people. You know, people say, "I don't think I want all those choices." After all, there had been very little choice up to now. And so the idea of saying, "Well, here are 40 different plans to choose from," I knew was going to create the need to encourage people to get involved to help people make the right choice for them.

I strongly believe that giving seniors choices is important to a good health care system. After all, not everybody's needs are the same. And therefore, the more opportunity there is to pick a program that meets your needs, the better off the health care system will be. That's why choice matters.

It also means there are people actually competing for your business. They're saying, "I want your business; therefore, I'm going to try to make it attractive for you." And the idea of giving choice to people has affected the cost of the plan. When we first got in there, we anticipated the cost for the average senior was going to be $37 a month; now it's down to $25 a month for the average plan. That's positive news. It's positive for our seniors, and it's positive for the taxpayers.

We also believe that peace of mind is important for our seniors. And so inherent in this reform plan is the notion of the Government stepping in after a certain level of expenditures have been made by the average senior. In other words, anything over $3,600 in prescription drug coverage, the Government will pick up 95 percent of it. That's a catastrophic plan. It says that we recognize that we've got to help seniors after a certain level of expenditures, so as to help peace of mind.

That wasn't the case in the old plan, as you might remember. The new plan has got stop-loss; it's got catastrophic care. And that's a very important part of helping make sure the system was modern. The other thing that's important for people to understand is that this program is very generous for low-income seniors. About a third of the seniors qualify for extra help. And that's the way it should be in America, in my judgment. We want to help people who cannot help themselves. And so if you're a low-income senior, this plan will pay nearly 95 percent of all your drug costs, and that's important for our seniors to understand.

We've had good success at signing people up. There's about 42—a little more than 42 million people who are eligible for Medicare in the United States. Up to this point, a little over 31 million have signed up for the new Part D plan. There's about 6 million seniors who don't feel the need to sign up because they're adequately covered elsewhere, and that's okay; I understand that. So there's about 37, more or less, million people have so far signed up since January for this new benefit. And our mission is to reach out for the final 6-plus million, is to encourage people to, at the minimum, take a look at what's available.

There is a May 15th deadline, unless you're a low-income senior, in which case you can sign up after May 15th without any penalty. And that's important for our seniors to understand as well.

And so we're here today to talk about a Medicare plan that I believe is a good deal for America's seniors. It's very important for people to understand that there are significant savings for you involved in this plan. There's—the average senior saves about one-half on his or her drug bills, and that's good news. This is a plan that helps people when there's a catastrophe in their lives, and this is a plan that means our low-income folks won't have to choose between food and medicine. And that's good for America.

Now, we're reaching out to people from all walks of life. First of all, if you're interested in finding out about the program, call 1–800–MEDICARE, and somebody will be there at the other end of the line explaining it to you. If you're computer-literate, call up medicare.gov, and you'll find a program that will help you—it will help explain to you what is available for you.

If you've got a—if you're a son or a daughter, and you've got a mother or dad who is eligible for Medicare and hasn't looked at this program, you have a duty, in my judgment, to be a good son or a daughter and help your mom or dad. You know, some of our seniors aren't that comfortable with using a computer, and I understand that. But your sons and daughters are comfortable, or your grandchildren are comfortable. Get them to help you. Get them to take a look at what's available.

A son or a daughter owes it to their mom and dad to do that. If you're a member of a church group and you've got seniors in your congregation, find help for them. If you're a member of AARP, an active member of AARP, help a friend see what's available. If you're a part of an outreach group such as this, continue doing your duty to give people knowledge.

And that's what we're here to do. We're working with the National Alliance for Hispanic Health, the Hispanic Business Roundtable, the National Coalition of Latino Clergy and Christian Leaders. I mean, we're talking to a lot of groups. We've reached out through Univision and Telemundo and Spanish radio. My point is, is that we're reaching out to all people in all societies. We're working with the NAACP, AARP. There are a lot of people trying to help. And for those of you here who are helping, thank you for doing what you're doing. I hope it makes you feel better. It makes me feel good to know there are millions of Americans who are willing to help a neighbor understand what's available in this important program.

So you're watching the President be Educator in Chief today. [*Laughter*] My job is to go around America and explain that which is available, but I can't do it alone. Yesterday, down in South Florida, Mike Leavitt was with me. He's the Secretary of Health and Human Services. He's doing a fine job. Josefina Carbonell works with Mike. Her title is Assistant Secretary for Aging, Administration on Aging, Department of Health and Human Services—a long title for a fine person. Josefina, tell us what's happening in the Department. Welcome.

Assistant Secretary Josefina Carbonell. Thank you, Mr. President. Yes, I'm known as the Assistant Secretary of Aging, but I've got the great honor to also have been coined in this campaign as "Senora Medicare." [*Laughter*] And we've gone across the country.

It's indeed a wonderful honor to serve you as the Assistant Secretary for Aging, but having worked in the aging field for over 35 years right here in the State of Florida, it is so gratifying and so historic for me personally to see the fine work of individuals and volunteers across this country that have made such a difference. And you'll meet—some of them are with us today, and many in the audience—how important the benefits are.

We've held over 47,000 events like this, assistance and enrollment events and information events. And we've ridden in buses, in our Medicare buses across this country and visited with people in towns small and big, rural and urban communities, in limited English-speaking communities. And we are so proud of the work that our inner-city and our community-based organizations and our volunteers in both the private non-profit sector, civic organizations, the business community, and our municipalities, and most importantly, our volunteers.

We've had a wonderful opportunity to have over 40,000 dedicated volunteers that have served to assist people on one-on-one as a backup to our 1–800–MEDICARE, to, of course, our web site, and our area agencies on aging, our senior centers, our Meals on Wheels programs, our home care agencies. But those 40,000 volunteers have made such a difference. I've been in communities where we've sat around somebody's dining room table in the middle of a little church hall—and being able to assist them one-on-one making that choice.

And that's so important. I know that having worked with seniors for so many years, it is so gratifying to see the difference that this new benefit takes on, not only in cost savings, but the most important thing for me, in many of the minority communities, have been the ability for them to access new preventive benefits—and cardiovascular and diabetes and other chronic conditions that are so prevalent in our minority communities. So that's another very important feature.

911

But help is there. Those that might still be afraid and have not set out—the 1–800–MEDICARE, we've staffed that Medicare line up with 6,000 operators, trained people. We've got volunteers like Sandra, 40,000 across this country, and the area agencies on aging and the elder help lines that are there to assist you. We also have help lines for minority communities. We know that in the Hispanic community, in addition to the 1–800–MEDICARE, we have the 1–800–SU–FAMILIA [1–866–SU–FAMILIA],° run by the National Hispanic Council, the National Hispanic Alliance for Health, which is manned by grassroots organizations across this country, and many, many more that are there to help you.

So seek help. The 15th is the deadline. Don't stay without that very important benefit that not only will give you the prescription drug benefits that you need but, most importantly, will be a lifesaving effort for many, many of our at-risk individuals.

The President. Yes, I knew one of the real challenges, once this bill had passed, was to convince people that change would be in their interests. There's a lot of folks, frankly, at a certain point in their lives, where they're just really aren't interested in change. They're happy with the way things are, and therefore, it would be hard to get people to, kind of, be alert to the new opportunities. And so therefore, we knew we'd have to rally a group of folks who were not political people, but just concerned about their neighbor, so that there was a human touch to convince somebody that change—it's one thing to call a phone number; you're talking to somebody you can't see. But the most important contact is the one-on-one contact that many in this audience have helped others with. And for those of you doing that, I want to thank you.

Josefina also talked about an important part of the reform, and that is that there's now a wellness exam for people entering

---

° White House correction.

Medicare finally. It makes sense to detect problems early so it makes it easier to solve problems. That old Medicare system didn't have, kind of, this sense of prevention as a part of our strategy to help our seniors, and now it does.

But for a senior who hasn't signed up, call but also reach out to somebody. They'll help you. This program is not as complicated as one would initially think. And there's a lot of people that will help you, help you walk through the steps necessary to determine what is best for you.

Now, we've got some folks here who are being served. Pete, Pete Navarro, welcome; thank you for coming.

Peter Navarro. Good morning, Mr. President.

The President. You got to speak into the mike.

Mr. Navarro. Good morning, Mr. President.

The President. Where do you live?

Mr. Navarro. I live in Tavares, Florida.

The President. Very good—right around the corner.

Mr. Navarro. About 45 minutes.

The President. Well, it's a large corner. [*Laughter*] Give people your circumstances, please.

[*At this point, Mr. Navarro, retiree, made brief remarks.*]

The President. One of the things people have got to understand—Pete, by the way, is not eligible for Medicare yet, just in terms of age.

Mr. Navarro. That's correct.

The President. You're 59?

Mr. Navarro. Fifty-nine, yes.

The President. So am I. [*Laughter*] I blame my gray hair on my mother. [*Laughter*] I don't know who you blame yours on. [*Laughter*] I used to think 60 was old, didn't you?

Mr. Navarro. When I was young, I thought that was way out.

The President. Now I think it's young, don't you?

Mr. Navarro. I think so. [*Laughter*]

The President. Yes. Anyway, people on disability can apply for this program as well. You have done so.

Mr. Navarro. I have done so.

The President. You're taking eight different medications a day.

Mr. Navarro. Eight different medications a day.

The President. So you're worried, obviously, about the cost.

Mr. Navarro. I was, and since I have it, I only pay a $2 copay for generics and a $5 copay for the regular drugs.

The President. Right. Are you able to estimate your monthly savings now?

Mr. Navarro. I'm saving between 500 and 600 dollars a month.

The President. I'm not surprised. We hear stories like this all the time, where this program is helping people. The average senior is going to save half on their drug bills. Here's a fellow who is saving a lot more than half.

Mr. Navarro. That's a lot of money.

The President. Yes. And that helps you, obviously—500 or 600 dollars a month gives you a little breathing room.

Mr. Navarro. Oh, yes. It really does. It eliminates that stress that you live when you don't know if you can get it or not.

The President. Yes. Well, I appreciate you sharing your story with us. It's—so, when are you turning 60?

Mr. Navarro. Next January.

The President. Oh, January. You're a lot younger than I am. [*Laughter*] We're baby boomers—[*laughter*]—which really leads to another issue, and that is whether or not the Congress will have the will to help restructure Social Security and Medicare so a young generation, your grandchildren who are going to be paying people like me to retire—whether or not the system is solvent for them. You're fine. I mean, the seniors are in great shape when it comes to Medicare and Social Security. The truth of the matter is baby boomers like old Pete and I here, we're in good shape.

It's just those who are going to be paying for us need to make sure the system is solvent.

It's not exactly the issue, but it is an issue that is of major importance. And, look, I'll work with Congress. Look, we need to just get rid of all the politics in Washington and focus on what's best for the country and do what's right.

All right, Pete, thank you very much.

Gloria Lavergne. Gloria, where do you live?

Gloria S. Lavergne. Good morning, Mr. President.

The President. Yes ma'am, thank you.

Ms. Lavergne. I live here in Orlando.

The President. Fantastic.

Ms. Lavergne. I was born and raised in Puerto Rico.

The President. Que bueno.

Ms. Lavergne. Que bueno. And I moved to Florida in 1982 with my family. I work as a legal assistant for 20 years, and unfortunately, on 2002, I became disabled. And like you, I suffer from that time until 2 months that I'm going to be able to get my supplemental, because I'm paying right now $265 with an insurance. And I would say, when I heard about Medicare Part D, I start my own search. I look at different companies that I receive in the mail and compare, start calling. Don't be afraid to call; get the name of the medication that you are taking—I'm taking six medicines every day. One of them is Lidoderm—it's a patch—that cost me at regular price $175 per month, and I'm paying $28 is my deductible.

The President. Let's slow down for a minute. You're doing great. I just want to make sure everybody understands: This good woman is paying for six different medicines, one of which costs 175—speak in the mike, please—175. You signed up for Medicare Part D, and now it costs you 28?

Ms. Lavergne. My premium is $26.60; my deductibles are $28; and I'm saving $550 per month. That's amazing.

The President. Yes. Now, I know it sounds too good to be true; like, if I had said it, everybody would have said, "Well, I think he's just—you know—just talking." [*Laughter*] So I asked Gloria to be here. It's interesting what she said. She said she took the initiative to see what was available.

Was it that difficult?

Ms. Lavergne. No, it wasn't difficult. I look at the brochures, check with the medication that I was taking, and I enrolled in AARP—for me is one of the best. And I'm very happy. I encourage everybody to join the program.

The President. See, she said—what you just heard her say is, she took the initiative, took a look, and found a program that met her needs. And that's why choice is important. In other words, the Government didn't say, "Here's the program that meets your needs." The Government said, "Here's programs available. You pick the one that meets your needs." It's a little change of attitude, when you think about it—basically empowers the customers.

Now, there are some people, I readily concede, that aren't that confident about picking a program that meets their needs. But there are people out there who are willing to help you. So therefore, please call in and let us know who you are. We're trying to make sure that every senior has a chance to sign up for this program. And there's going to be some people in society that are nervous about the program. They hear all the talk, and they hear this program, and they hear the advertisements, and I know they're nervous. I know they're concerned. But I assure you, it is worth your time to listen to somebody who wants to at least explain what's available for you.

If you're—I repeat, if you're a son or a daughter and your mom hasn't signed up or your dad hasn't signed up, do your duty and—to find out what's available and explain. You just heard the testimony of Gloria; she's saving $500 a month.

Ms. Lavergne. ——$550.

The President. ——$550 a month. Well, that's a lot. And one of the things we want is the program to work, and it works well when people take advantage of the program.

So thank you both for sharing your—you got something else to say? You're welcome—you're through?

Ms. Lavergne. Thank you so much.

The President. Gracias. Good job. Very good job. I told you you'd do a good job. You were great.

We got an interesting fellow here named Ramon Ortiz. Ramon is a pharmacist, as you can see. One of the most important groups of people who are helping our seniors realize what is available are our pharmacists. You can understand why. They're the point of contact for a lot of our seniors.

How long have you been a pharmacist?

Ramon Ortiz. Well, 15 years. I've been 15 years—3 years which I served in the United States Air Force. I was stationed here at Patrick Air Force Base.

[*Mr. Ortiz, pharmacist, CVS Pharmacy, made brief remarks.*]

The President. One of the things he said that's interesting is—CVS took corporate responsibility and said, we now understand—once President George W. signed the bill, we understand that a lot of our customers are now going to be wondering whether or not it makes sense for them to look at it. And the company became a part of the educational outreach by educating first the educators, who happened to be the pharmacists; that's what you're saying.

And then now—so you've got people coming, and saying, hey, Ramon, what's up? Maybe they don't put it that way—[*laughter*]—but they're——

Mr. Ortiz. We knew it was going to be big. And also, we knew that we were going to be providers; we were going to be instrumental in their choices.

[*Mr. Ortiz made further remarks.*]

The President. It's hard for some Americans to believe, but there were seniors who were going out—without their drugs in the past. People had to choose, and that's not right. And this program really helps a lot of low-income seniors. It helps all low-income seniors. We don't want people making that choice between food and medicine. We want the health care system to be modern; we want it to work. If you're going to say to your seniors, "Let's have a good health care system," we need to make it good, and we've done that. And so—keep going; you're on a roll. [*Laughter*] Your mother?

Mr. Ortiz. I also—perhaps one of the most difficult patients that I had was my mom.

The President. Yes, I know the feeling. Does she tell you what to do?

Mr. Ortiz. Yes. For her, I'm the baby; I'm not a pharmacist.

The President. Yes, well, I know the feeling as well. Join the "aggressive mothers club." [*Laughter*]

Mr. Ortiz. So being a pharmacist, seeing how much this program had helped seniors, and I knew, because I was paying for my mom's prescriptions sometimes, and I knew that she was taking—paying over $280 for prescriptions. Recently I called her, yesterday. She told me that she was not even taking some of the medications doctor prescribed because she could not afford it. I said, "Mom, why didn't you call me? I would have paid for your prescriptions."

Finally, I convince her—she's down in Puerto Rico in a small town, Ceiba; she enrolled. And she asked me, tell President Bush—[*laughter*]—this is the greatest thing ever happened. Now my father, at the age of 73, he's looking for retirement. He was working 40 hours just to pay——

The President. To help your mom.

Mr. Ortiz. ——for the prescriptions. Now he can look into retirement. I'm not sure if my mom will allow him to retire. [*Laughter*] They cannot be in the same house. [*Laughter*] True story.

The President. Let's leave it at that, you know? [*Laughter*]

Mr. Ortiz. So I mean, I know there's a lot of complication, and I asked Anna, the first lady that I told you, "Anna, do you really need to understand the Medicare Plan D?" She said, "No, I don't have to; I'm saving money." [*Laughter*] That's what it's all about.

The President. Yes, it is. You know what I come away with? One, I want to thank you for your compassion. There's a lot of people who deeply care—a lot of people who care about our fellow citizens. We really are a compassionate country, aren't we? Here's Ramon. You know, he speaks with passion about people who come to his place of business worried about their health care and worried about their future. Thanks.

The other good lesson is, here's a good son. You know, he takes time to worry about his mom—and dad, by the way. Sons and daughters owe that to their parents. They have received a lifetime of love from a mother or father, and they need to repay it by helping understand what's available in this new program. So if you're—I keep saying this, I know, but I strongly believe it. I believe there's personal responsibility in society, and sons and daughters have a personal responsibility to help their mom or dad, just like Ramon did.

You did a fine job. Thank you. *Gracias.*

Mr. Ortiz. Gracias.

The President. Sandra Johnson. Now, Sandra Johnson works for the Serving Health Insurance Needs of Elders, known as SHINE. Is that right? Explain SHINE.

[*Sandra Johnson, local coordinator, Serving Health Insurance Needs of Elders, made brief remarks.*]

The President. You know what's a blessing? We got people like you in this country, like Sandra. She comes down here, she says, "What can I do to help. How can I help somebody?"

I love your spirit. Thanks for helping. She represents a lot of other people in this area and around the country who are volunteering.

Ms. Bryan. [*Inaudible*]—$22 a month.

The President. There you go. [*Laughter*] From 350 to 22?

Ms. Bryan. Twenty-two.

The President. Testify. [*Laughter*]

Ms. Bryan. [*Inaudible*]

The President. There you go. We're glad you're here, Ms. Bryan. Thank you for coming.

Listen, I hope you've enjoyed this experience. I've asked these good folks to join us to help make the case: One, take a look at what's available; two, help somebody take a look at what's available. That's all we can ask. There's a May 15th deadline coming up, unless you qualify for extra help,

in which case you can sign up after May 15th with no penalty. If you don't quality for extra help, sign up now. Now's the time. This is a good deal. It's the Government doing its duty to provide modern medicine for our seniors.

I want to thank our panelists. You all did a fantastic job. God bless you all, and God bless our country.

NOTE: The President spoke at 9:47 a.m. in the Asociacion Borinquena de Florida Central, Inc. In his remarks, he referred to Gov. Jeb Bush of Florida; Tommy Martinez, president, Asociacion Borinquena de Florida Central, Inc.; Sylvia T. Caceres, southern States regional director, Puerto Rico Federal Affairs Administration; and Mayor Richard T. Crotty of Orange County, FL, and his son, Tyler.

Remarks Following a Meeting With Victims of Identity Theft
May 10, 2006

Identity theft is a serious problem in America. I have just listened to the horror stories from fellow citizens who have had their identities stolen. I listened to their ideas about how the Federal Government can help in the response in not only dealing with those who commit the crime but helping those who have been victimized. And I want to thank you all for joining us. Thanks a lot.

I appreciate Al Gonzales and Chairman Majoras, Deb Majoras, of the FTC for being here, because I just signed an Executive order that has the Attorney General as the Chairman, the Chairman of the FTC as the Vice-Chairman of a coordinating group to make sure that this Government of ours uses our assets in a responsible way, in a good way, to not only put those people who commit identity fraud in jail but to help the victims of identity fraud.

I've signed two pieces of legislation which are important, one of which says that credit companies must issue a credit report once a year free of charge. We're very serious about upholding the law in this administration, and credit companies must look at the spirit and the letter of that law, so that when citizens ask for the free credit report on an annual basis, he or she should be given that free credit report.

I signed law enhancing penalties. Now what we're going to do is make sure that the 13 governmental agencies involved with identity theft have a well-coordinated strategy to help the victims and to put those who commit the theft behind bars.

Again, I want to thank you all very much for helping us understand the issues but, more importantly, telling a story of the emotions and the feelings that you went through during this—difficult periods of your life.

Thank you.

NOTE: The President spoke at 2:27 p.m. in the Roosevelt Room at the White House. A tape was not available for verification of the content of these remarks.

Statement on House of Representatives Passage of Tax Legislation
May 10, 2006

The tax cuts we passed in recent years are working to fuel America's economic expansion. Our progrowth policies have helped the economy create more than 5.2 million jobs since August of 2003, and last year, our economy grew faster than that of any other major industrialized nation. By extending key Capital Gains and Dividends tax relief, the House has taken an important step to continue to help hard-working Americans and to keep our economy strong and growing. I appreciate the House Leadership and Chairman Bill Thomas for their hard work.

I urge the Senate to vote swiftly so that I can sign this bill into law and put a stop to a massive tax hike that would be disastrous for small businesses, our economy, and all working Americans.

Remarks on the Terrorist Surveillance Program
May 11, 2006

After September the 11th, I vowed to the American people that our Government would do everything within the law to protect them against another terrorist attack. As part of this effort, I authorized the National Security Agency to intercept the international communications of people with known links to Al Qaida and related terrorist organizations. In other words, if Al Qaida or their associates are making calls into the United States or out of the United States, we want to know what they're saying.

Today there are new claims about other ways we are tracking down Al Qaida to prevent attacks on America. I want to make some important points about what the Government is doing and what the Government is not doing.

First, our intelligence activities strictly target Al Qaida and their known affiliates. Al Qaida is our enemy, and we want to know their plans. Second, the Government does not listen to domestic phone calls without court approval. Third, the intelligence activities I authorized are lawful and have been briefed to appropriate Members of Congress, both Republican and Democrat. Fourth, the privacy of ordinary Americans is fiercely protected in all our activities.

We're not mining or trolling through the personal lives of millions of innocent Americans. Our efforts are focused on links to Al Qaida and their known affiliates. So far we've been very successful in preventing another attack on our soil.

As a general matter, every time sensitive intelligence is leaked, it hurts our ability to defeat this enemy. Our most important job is to protect the American people from another attack, and we will do so within the laws of our country.

Thank you.

NOTE: The President spoke at 12:03 p.m. in the Diplomatic Reception Room at the White House. The Office of the Press Sec-retary also released a Spanish language tran-script of these remarks.

Commencement Address at Mississippi Gulf Coast Community College in Biloxi, Mississippi
May 11, 2006

Thanks for the warm welcome. President Lott; members of the faculty, staff, and ad-ministration; distinguished guests; family, friends, and, most importantly of all, the graduating class of Mississippi Gulf Coast Community College: This afternoon, we celebrate commencement in a stadium that is still under repair, near streets lined with temporary housing, in a region where too many lives have been shattered, and there has never been a more hopeful day to grad-uate in the State of Mississippi.

I am proud to stand before some of the most determined students at college or uni-versity in America. Over these past 9 months, you have shown a resilience more powerful than any storm. You continued your studies in classrooms with crumbling walls. You lost homes and slept in tents near campus to finish courses. You cleared debris during the day, and you went to class at night. You worked past exhaustion to catch up. By your determination to reach this day, you have sent a message to our Nation and the world: Mississippi is coming back, and it's going to be better than ever before.

You have sent a message, and I've came with a message of my own: This Nation honors your dedication. We're inspired by your optimism, and we're going to help this great State of Mississippi rebuild.

I'm honored to be the first sitting Presi-dent to address a community college com-mencement. Recognizing this is a grand oc-casion, I wanted some tips from the best speaker I know, so I went to the First Lady, Laura. [*Laughter*] I asked her what I should talk about, and she said, "You ought to talk about 15 minutes." [*Laughter*] Listen, I've learned her advice is worth tak-ing. She sends her best to you all.

Today I want to share a few thoughts on the history you've seen this year and the history you will make once you leave this fine college. For some of you, gradua-tion day has been a long time in the mak-ing. Many of you have large responsibilities beyond school, such as jobs and families to care for, and none of those roles are part-time. Others here are taking a first step toward further education at one of Mississippi's fine universities. And on this special afternoon, some of you are fulfilling the dreams of generations by becoming the first person in your family to graduate from college.

This college is also part of a strong mili-tary community, and it's obvious some of you have earned your degree while serving your Nation in uniform. And I'm proud to be your Commander in Chief. There are also military family members in the graduating class, including the Levens fam-ily of Long Beach. Margaret Levens and her son, Matt, are getting their degrees, and they're both carrying pictures of a loved one who they remember today. Ear-lier this year, Donnie Levens, Margaret's son and Matt's brother, was killed in a heli-copter crash while his Marine unit was fighting terrorists near the Horn of Africa. Margaret says Donnie's courage inspired her to complete her studies. She said, "I've never been a quitter. Donnie was never a quitter either. He had a job to do, and he did it well. And I am graduating for him today." America honors the service of Donnie Levens, and we honor the strength and the sacrifice of our military families.

This day of accomplishment would not be possible without the faculty and the staff and the administration of this college. They reopened this school just 17 days after the worst natural disaster in American history struck your campus and your State. All who work at this college have dedicated themselves to this school's stated mission of making "a positive difference in people's lives every day." You have fulfilled that mission and so much more. Your students will always remember your unselfish service in an hour of need, and the United States of America is grateful for your service.

This is my 10th visit to Mississippi since Hurricane Katrina hit. I've seen firsthand the devastation in Gulfport and Gautier, Poplarville and Pascagoula and Pass Christian, Bay Saint Louis and Biloxi. This was the first city in your State I visited after the storm. I remember walking down the street with your fine mayor through a neighborhood where every house had been destroyed. I remember sitting on a doorstep that was surrounded by boards. I remember looking in the eyes of people who were stunned and saddened, longing for all they had lost.

I remember something else too—a quiet, unyielding determination to clear the wreckage and build anew. People who saw their own houses flattened rose to the aid of neighbors. One group of men tied themselves with a rope, dove into a flooded street, and pulled 20 others to safety. Churches and congregations gave to their limit of their resources and then found a way to give more. Thousands lost their homes, their cars, and their businesses, but not their faith in the future. Across this State, a powerful spirit has emerged, a Mississippi spirit that sees hope in adversity and possibility in pain and summons a strength that wind and water can never take away.

And that Mississippi spirit is embodied by your great Governor, Haley Barbour. Haley spoke for the State when he said, "People aren't leaving. They're hitching up their britches and rebuilding Mississippi." That Mississippi spirit is carried to Washington by your superb United States Senators, Trent Lott and Thad Cochran, and by an outstanding congressional delegation. And the Mississippi spirit is sustained daily by your mayors and county officials and local leaders, and many of those leaders are here today. And I appreciate your service, and you can count on a steady partner in my administration.

Over the past 9 months, we have seen what the Mississippi spirit can achieve. The population of coastal Mississippi has returned almost all the way to full strength. Every school district that closed after the hurricane has reopened. More than 90 percent of the debris has been cleared. Highways and bridges are being repaired. Homeowners are rebuilding with the help from the State and the Federal Government. There are more jobs available in Mississippi today than before the storm, and the resurgence of this great State has only begun.

The renewal of the gulf coast is one of the largest rebuilding efforts the world has ever seen, and all of you will play a leading role. Your experience at this college has prepared you to shape the future of your State. I ask you to rise to the challenge of a generation: Apply your skill and your knowledge, your compassion and your character, and help write a hopeful new chapter in the history of the gulf coast.

A hopeful future for the gulf coast will require your skill and your knowledge. The destruction left by Katrina reaches beyond anything we could have imagined. Rebuilding will create an immediate need for workers with a wide range of skills. I appreciate how this college responded, by offering courses in carpentry and plumbing and electrical and drywall and other skills in high demand. Federal funds allowed students to complete these courses for free, and many have moved straight into good jobs with Mississippi companies. When it comes to rebuilding this State, there is no question "if;" it is a matter of "when." Mississippi will rebuild, and you will be the ones to rebuild it.

Ultimately, rebuilding this region will require more than the reconstruction of building and bridges that were destroyed. A renewal of the gulf coast will also require creativity and innovation and enterprise in every aspect of society. The growth and vitality of the gulf coast will come from people who open new stores, design new urban plans, create new jobs, teach children, and care for the sick. The key to unlocking these opportunities is knowledge, and millions who want to gain new knowledge come to community colleges just like the one you're graduating from. In the gulf coast and beyond, community colleges are the centers of hope and the gateways to social mobility. At any stage in life, you can come to a community college, and you can learn something new, and you can put yourself on a course to realize your dreams.

The class of 2006 is filled with people determined to use their knowledge to revitalize the gulf coast. It's full of people determined to realize dreams. Today I met Tracy Malosh, and she's graduating with a degree in nursing. Tracy was born nearby at Keesler Air Force Base, and she has lived in this part of the country for her whole life. She married her high school sweetheart, Charles, 13 years ago, and they have three children who, by the way, are proudly watching their mom graduate today. After Tracy's son Trevor was born with a heart condition, she decided to come to this college to become a pediatric nurse. When Hurricane Katrina hit, Tracy's family lost everything they owned, but she kept coming to class. She was determined. The family is now looking for a new home in the area. Today Tracy gets a degree, and she's planning to work in pediatrics at a local hospital. And here is what she said, "I can't even begin to describe to you how good it feels to finish this. I always knew I'd go back to school, but I never knew I'd face the difficulties that I did—and I conquered this."

Tracy's story is a clear lesson: It's never too late to get a fresh start in life. And people all over the gulf coast are following her lead. Out of the devastation of Katrina will come great opportunities to get a fresh start in life. And for many in this great State, the road to a brighter future will run through a community college.

A hopeful future for the gulf coast will require your compassion and your character. Our whole Nation has been moved by the outpouring of kindness and decency shown by the people of this great State. Neighbors have joined forces to care for the weak and the vulnerable. Strangers have come together to help each other cope. Now you must work to sustain the compassion inspired by this storm long after the damage has been cleared away. I urge you to take the same determination you brought to rebuilding schools and use it to ensure that every school provides a good education. Use that same bravery it takes to rescue people from water to rescue communities from poverty. My hope is that one day, Americans will look back at the rebuilding of Mississippi and say that your work added not only to the prosperity of our country but also to the character as our Nation.

Earlier today I met one of your classmates who represents the character necessary for the gulf coast to succeed. Kendrick Kennedy grew up here in Biloxi. He's a proud graduate of Biloxi High. At age 30, an illness caused Kendrick to go blind, and eventually he lost his job. So he decided to come to this college. He recorded each of his lectures on tape, and he scanned his books into a computer program, provided by the school, that reads them aloud. When the hurricane hit,

Kendrick opened his home to family members in need, and he returned to school as soon as possible. Today this good man is graduating at the top of his class, and he hopes to attend law school one day. Here is what Kendrick said: "I'd be doggoned if I was going to let Hurricane Katrina stop me. I thought, 'You started school when you were blind, and you can overcome this hurricane.'" Kendrick is right, and today we honor his inspiring example.

That same optimism is present in many of the graduates today, and so many others across the gulf coast. And optimism is justified. There is going to be a day when communities across Mississippi sparkle with new homes and businesses bustle with customers and this college is filled with more students than ever before. I plan to return one day to the Biloxi neighborhood I visited on my first trip and see beautiful homes with children playing in the yards. Across this entire region devastated by the storm, new vitality will emerge from the rubble,

and cities from Mobile to Biloxi to New Orleans will be whole again.

It's going to take time for that vision to be realized, and it will demand the skill and knowledge and character of all of you. Yet you can leave this college with confidence in your future and with certainty that you're not going to work alone. In these trying months, we have been aided by a Power that lightens our struggles, reveals our hidden strength, and helps conquer all suffering and loss. We can never know God's plan, but we can trust in His wisdom and in His grace. And we can be certain that with His help, the great State of Mississippi will rise again.

Congratulations to the class of 2006. May God bless you, and may God bless the United States of America.

NOTE: The President spoke at 2:29 p.m. in Mississippi Coast Coliseum. In his remarks, he referred to Willis Lott, president, Mississippi Gulf Coast Community College; and Mayor A.J. Holloway of Biloxi, MS.

Statement on Senate Passage of Tax Legislation
May 11, 2006

I applaud the Senate for passing important tax relief that will help keep our economy strong and growing. This legislation prevents an enormous tax hike that the American people do not want and would not welcome. The bill will extend policies that have helped our economy flourish. We have had 18 straight quarters of growth,

including 4.8 percent growth in the last quarter, and the unemployment rate is 4.7 percent. I appreciate the Senate leadership and Chairman Grassley for their hard work on behalf of American taxpayers and small businesses, and I look forward to signing this important legislation into law.

Remarks Following a Meeting With Military and Diplomatic Leaders
May 12, 2006

I've just completed a second meeting with former Secretaries of State and former

Secretaries of Defense on Iraq. We also discussed the broader Middle East as well.

I want to thank you all very much for sharing your thoughts not only with me but with the Vice President and Secretary Rice and Secretary Rumsfeld. It really means a lot to hear your thoughts and your concerns and your suggestions about the way forward in Iraq. We've had our disagreements in this country about whether or not we should be there in the first place. Now the fundamental question is, how do we achieve our objectives, which is a democracy which can defend itself, sustain itself, a country which is an ally in the war on terror, and a country which serves as a powerful example for others who desire to be free.

Since we last met, there has—a unity government is now in the process of becoming formed. I've got great hopes about this unity Government. We've got a Shi'a as the Prime Minister-designee, a Sunni as the Speaker, a Kurd as the President, all of whom have dedicated themselves to a country moving forward that meets the hopes and aspirations of the Iraqi people.

There are certainly challenges, and the Secretaries here discussed those challenges with us. Perhaps the main challenge is the militia that tend to take the law into their own hands. And it's going to be up for the Government to step up and take care of that militia so that the Iraqi people are confident in the security of their country. It's important to have a secure Iraq in order for people to go about their daily lives. And we understand that.

I also assured the Secretaries here that this Government is committed to success. They've got good people on the ground. We've got brave troops that are working every day to help this country succeed and, at the same time, deny safe haven to Al Qaida.

And again, I want to thank the members for coming—the former Secretaries for coming. I think it's very useful for those of us who are helping to plot the strategies and the tactics to help secure this country, to hear from you. I'm optimistic about our successes. I know this: The only way we will not succeed is if we lose our nerve, we don't have faith in our values, and that we're constantly changing tactics on the ground to achieve our objectives.

So thank you for coming.

NOTE: The President spoke at 10:30 a.m. in the Roosevelt Room at the White House. In his remarks, he referred to Prime Minister-designate Nuri al-Maliki, Speaker of the Parliament Mahmoud al-Mashhadani, and President Jalal Talabani of Iraq. Participating in the meeting were former Secretaries of State Colin L. Powell, Madeleine K. Albright, Warren Christopher, James A. Baker III, and Alexander M. Haig, Jr.; and former Secretaries of Defense William S. Cohen, Frank C. Carlucci, James R. Schlesinger, Melvin R. Laird, and Robert S. McNamara.

Remarks on the Observance of Asian Pacific American Heritage Month and a Presentation of the President's Volunteer Service Awards
May 12, 2006

Thank you all. Welcome. Please be seated. Welcome to the White House. I like to call it the People's House. I'm glad you could join us today to celebrate Asian Pacific American Heritage Month. This is the month we recognize the many accomplishments of Americans who trace their origins to the Asian-Pacific region, and we honor the contributions they make to our great land.

Across our country, Asian Pacific Americans are making their mark in all walks of life, including business and law and politics and education, community service, the arts, and science. Today, more Asian Pacific Americans serve in my administration than in any other administration in history, and two of them serve in my Cabinet. And today—[*applause*]—and I am delighted to recognize Secretary Elaine Chao and Secretary Norm Mineta and thank them for their great work for our country.

I want to thank Ray Pamintuan—he is the Chairman of the President's Advisory Commission on Asian Americans and Pacific Islanders. And I want to thank all the other Commission members who are here. I enjoyed my visit. Thank you for serving.

I want to thank the members of the 442d Regimental Combat Team who are here today. Thank you all for coming. God bless you. Veterans who have set such a fine example for those who wear the uniform today. And I would like to welcome the men and women in uniform who have joined us today. Thank you all for being here. Thank you for your service.

These men and women are on the frontline of defending the United States of America, and in so doing, they're laying the foundation of peace for generations to come. And we are really proud of your service.

Fourteen million Americans can claim ancestry from the Asian-Pacific region. Through a commitment to educational excellence, you help raise standards and show that the American Dream is within reach for all who study hard and persevere. Through your love of family and community, you help unite us as a people. Through entrepreneurship and innovation, you have strengthened our economy, creating jobs for other—and thereby contributing to the opportunity of this Nation.

In 2004, I created the President's Advisory Commission on Asian American and Pacific Islanders to improve the opportunities for small-business development. And to keep this good work moving forward, I signed an Executive order this morning that renews the Commission for another year.

America has thrived as a nation because we've always welcomed newcomers who, in turn, embrace our values and our way of life. Every immigrant who lives by these values makes our country better and makes our future brighter as "one Nation under God."

We're grateful to the many Asian Pacific Americans who serve our Nation in many ways. I just honored those who serve our Nation by wearing the uniform, but there are all kinds of ways to serve America. The President's Volunteer Service Award is the highest honor given in recognition of those who have contributed their time and their talents to those in need.

I created this award because I understand the great strength of the United States of America is not found in our military, and it's certainly not because of the size of our wallets. It's because the strength of America is found in the hearts and souls of generous citizens who answer to a universal call to love a neighbor like you'd like to be loved yourself.

Five folks here today have earned this award by volunteering to improve the communities in which they live and thereby helping our fellow citizens. They've heard that call to serve something greater than themselves. And by the way, by answering the call, they've inspired others to serve; you just don't know it.

Volunteers we recognize have brought care and outreach to veterans and men and women in uniform; they've helped children learn to read; they've extended food and shelter to hurricane victims in our gulf coast; they've helped underprivileged high school students prepare their SATs; and they've aided immigrants who have recently arrived in our country. They have served our Nation in distinct ways and, in so doing, have made America a better place to live.

I am proud of the achievements, the many achievements of our citizens of Asian and Pacific Island heritage. You really have enriched America by your contributions. You've made us a better land. And the five we honor today have done so in a unique way. And so I join all Americans in congratulating you and wishing you continued success of your work. I want to thank you for what you've done. I ask God's blessings on all who are here and their families as well as our great Nation.

And now I ask the commander to please read the citations that will enable me to award the volunteer awards to you.

[*At this point, Lt. Cmdr. Geoff Gagnier, Coast Guard Aide to the President, read the citations, and the President presented the awards.*]

Now you can see why I love an event such as these. [*Laughter*] What a great country we have. And I want to thank you all for being active citizens in the greatest land on the face of the Earth.

May God bless you all.

NOTE: The President spoke at 2:07 p.m. in the East Room at the White House. In his remarks, he referred to Rudy Pamintuan, Chairman, President's Advisory Commission on Asian Americans and Pacific Islanders. The Asian/Pacific American Heritage Month proclamation of April 28 is listed in Appendix D at the end of this volume.

Statement on the Death of G.V. "Sonny" Montgomery
May 12, 2006

Laura and I and the entire Bush family are saddened by the death of a good friend and patriot, Sonny Montgomery. Sonny Montgomery served during World War II and the Korean war, and he was a tireless advocate for America's veterans throughout his three decades in the House of Representatives. He sponsored the Montgomery GI bill, which has helped make

higher education and professional training accessible to millions of our veterans. In 2005, he was awarded the Presidential Medal of Freedom, the Nation's highest civil award, in recognition of his lifetime of service to the United States. We send our condolences and prayers to the Montgomery family.

The President's Radio Address
May 13, 2006

Good morning. This week I nominated General Mike Hayden to be the next Director of the Central Intelligence Agency. The work of the CIA is essential to the security of the American people. The enemies who struck our Nation on September the 11th, 2001, intend to attack us again. And to defeat them, we must have the best possible intelligence. In Mike Hayden, the

men and women of the CIA will have a strong leader who will support them as they work to disrupt terrorist attacks, penetrate closed societies, and gain information that is vital to protecting our Nation.

General Hayden is supremely qualified to lead the CIA. For the last year, he's been our Nation's first Deputy Director of

National Intelligence and has played a critical role in our efforts to reform America's intelligence capabilities to meet the threats of a new century. He has more than 20 years of experience in the intelligence field. He served for 6 years as Director of the National Security Agency and has a track record of success in leading and transforming that large intelligence agency. He also has held senior positions at the Pentagon and the National Security Council, and he served behind the Iron Curtain in our Embassy in Bulgaria during the cold war.

Mike knows our intelligence community from the ground up. He's been both a producer and a consumer of intelligence and has overseen both human and technical intelligence activities, as well as the all-source analysis derived from those activities. Mike was unanimously confirmed by the Senate last year for his current post, and this week members of both parties have praised his nomination. I urge the Senate to confirm him promptly as the next Director of the CIA.

During General Hayden's tenure at the NSA, he helped establish and run one of our most vital intelligence efforts in the war on terror, the terrorist surveillance program. As the 9/11 Commission and others have noted, our Government failed to connect the dots in the years before the attacks of September the 11th. We now know that two of the hijackers in the United States made phone calls to Al Qaida operatives overseas, but we did not know about their plans until it was too late.

So to prevent another attack, I authorized the National Security Agency—consistent with the Constitution and laws—to intercept international communications in which one party has known links to Al Qaida and related terrorist groups. This terrorist surveillance program makes it more likely that killers like the 9/11 hijackers will be identified and located in time. It has helped prevent possible terrorist attacks in the United States and abroad, and it re-

mains essential to the security of America. If there are people inside our country who are talking with Al Qaida, we want to know about it. We will not sit back and wait to be attacked again.

This week new claims have been made about other ways we are tracking down Al Qaida—prevent attacks on America. It is important for Americans to understand that our activities strictly target Al Qaida and its known affiliates. Al Qaida is our enemy, and we want to know their plans. The intelligence activities I have authorized are lawful and have been briefed to appropriate Members of Congress, both Republican and Democrat. The privacy of all Americans is fiercely protected in all our activities. The Government does not listen to domestic phone calls without court approval. We are not trolling through the personal lives of millions of innocent Americans. Our efforts are focused on links to Al Qaida terrorists and its affiliates who want to harm the American people.

Americans expect their Government to do everything in its power under our laws and Constitution to protect them and their civil liberties. That is exactly what we are doing. And so far, we have been successful in preventing another attack on our soil. The men and women of the CIA are working around the clock to make our Nation more secure. I am confident that General Hayden will strengthen the CIA and integrate its vital work with our other intelligence agencies, so we can defeat the terrorists of the 21st century.

Thank you for listening.

NOTE: The address was recorded at 7:50 a.m. on May 12 in the Cabinet Room at the White House for broadcast at 10:06 a.m. on May 13. The transcript was made available by the Office of the Press Secretary on May 12 but was embargoed for release until the broadcast. The Office of the Press Secretary also released a Spanish language transcript of this address.

Statement on the Death of Eusebio Penalver Mazorra
May 13, 2006

Eusebio Penalver Mazorra was a Cuban patriot who spent 28 years in Castro's prisons. His resistance to tyranny is a testament to the moral courage of all Cubans who desire to see freedom return to their beautiful island nation. Laura joins me in sending our thoughts and prayers to his family and friends.

Remarks During a Presentation of White House Trees With Prime Minister John Howard of Australia
May 14, 2006

President Bush. Well, first of all, Ambassador, thanks for having us, and happy birthday.

Ambassador Dennis Richardson. Thank you very much.

President Bush. How old are you?

Ambassador Richardson. Well——

President Bush. Don't say, then. [*Laughter*] It's wonderful to be here with our dear friends the Howards. I think it is interesting that we're planting two trees, and this is a symbol of our enduring friendship. And I can't thank you enough, John, for your strong support for the liberty agenda, deep desire for the world to be a peaceful place. I really enjoy working with you for the common good. Thanks for having us.

Prime Minister Howard. Thank you. Well, George, you and Laura, not only for the offices that you hold but also for the people you are, are very welcome on this piece of Australian soil in Washington. I indicated to the President a moment ago that it was here on this lawn that I addressed a news conference on the 12th of September, 2001, when I said that Australia would stand side by side with the United States in responding to the new threat of terrorism. And that resolve is as strong now as it was on the 12th of September, 2001.

These trees are a wonderful symbol of that friendship. This residence has a lot of history. It was, of course, the very first residence occupied by an Australian envoy to other than a then dominion or Commonwealth country. And when the then Prime Minister, R.G. Menzies, announced it, he said that having an ambassador—a representative or envoy to America represented the first time we were sending one to what he called a foreign country.

There has certainly been nothing foreign in the relationship between our two countries since then, and it's great to have you and Laura with us, and it's a wonderful symbol. The Ambassador has got to look after the trees—[*laughter*]—and to keep his two rottweilers away from them. [*Laughter*]

NOTE: The President spoke at 6:45 p.m. at the Australian Ambassador's residence. Participating in the event was Australia's Ambassador to the U.S. Dennis Richardson.

Remarks at the National Peace Officers' Memorial Service
May 15, 2006

Thank you all very much. Thank you. Thank you for the warm welcome, and thank you for the privilege of being able to join you today.

Every year on this day, our Nation flies flags at half-staff in grateful memory of the officers who have lost their lives in the line of duty. I emphasize the word "grateful," because we're a grateful nation for those who are willing to serve and to protect us all.

Once again, we added names to the National Law Enforcement Officers' Memorial. And once again, we are here to pay our most sincere respects to those whose names have been added.

I appreciate Chuck Canterbury's offer for me to come and speak—I really do—and I want to thank his service to the country by serving as president of the National Fraternal Order of the Police. I want to thank the members of my Cabinet who are here. I appreciate very much the Members of the United States Congress who have joined us, particularly Senator Frist and Senator Leahy. I want to thank Aliza Clark for her speech. I want to thank Ken Ford. I appreciate Vince Gill; he gave the best speech of the day. What a fantastic talent, and thank you for coming, Vince, to help heal the grief.

Family members of the fallen officers, you're welcome here to the Nation's Capital. We're really honored you're here. I wish there was some way I could heal the hurt in your heart. I wish there was a way that we could help dry up the tears. I guess the best way I can help is to say, we love you, and we thank you for the sacrifice of your loved ones. And as we thank you for the sacrifice of your loved ones, we've got to thank those law enforcement officers who are trying to help you deal with your grief.

The really interesting thing about the law enforcement community is there's such a strong bond between those who serve on the frontlines of fighting crime. They sit by your side here in this important event; they hold your hand; they put their arm around you; they're the brothers and sisters who are trying to help you overcome the pain you're going through. I want to thank those who wear the Nation's uniform, who are helping our families who are here deal with the grief, and I thank those who wear the Nation's uniform for working hard to make America a peaceful place for those of us who live here.

I know full well, as do all Americans, that in every community, whether it be a big community or a small community, there's a law enforcement officer on the job watching over the neighborhoods, ready for the next call. Each day in our country, more than 850,000 men and women go to work not knowing what the challenges might bring. Yet each day, they're committed to answering those challenges with courage and decisiveness.

One of those who answered the call was Harvey County, Kansas, Deputy Sheriff Kurt Ford. Though Kurt Ford had left the law enforcement in 2001, his heart really never left it. There's something about the law enforcement officer who is so committed to the job that his or her heart never leaves the job. He returned to service after the terrorist attacks on September the 11th.

In April, he and a team responded to a domestic violence call early on a Saturday morning. When they arrived at the scene, Officer Ford was shot. It turns out, Officer Ford had run toward danger to protect the vulnerable. And today we honor courage of people like Officer Ford.

The call came during the routine parts of the day, as it did to the Columbia, Missouri, Officer Molly Thomas-Bowden. When she was at a traffic stop, Officer Bowden was shot several times. Molly was married to a fellow police officer. She was known to all for her love of horses and her faithful and gentle spirit. Our Nation honors the service of people like Molly for her willingness to serve in making America a better place.

You know, the call can come when it's least expected, as it did for Officer Larry Cox of Chillocothe, Ohio. A 19-year-old veteran of the police force, Officer Cox was off-duty when he stepped up to help fellow officers in pursuit of a suspect. He wasn't even on duty, and yet he knew deep in his soul he needed to help fellow officers in need. And he was shot and killed.

Like many here who wear the uniform, Officer Cox worked with youngsters in the community in which they live. He was a DARE officer. One of the fifth graders he worked with said, "We feel like you're our best friend. We'll always remember you." "You're with God right now," is what the guy went on to say.

These officers are among the names of those we added. Every one represents an extraordinary person. Every one took an oath and carried a badge and committed his or her life to keeping the peace and protecting others. Every one has brought honor to our Nation. And together they live in our national memory as Americans whose courage and commitment has shown the true meaning of heroism.

And so this afternoon, on behalf of all Americans, I offer the respect of a grateful nation and pledge that their courage and sacrifice will never be forgotten.

May God bless you all.

NOTE: The President spoke at 12:43 p.m. on the West Grounds at the U.S. Capitol. In his remarks, he referred to Aliza Clark, president, National Fraternal Order of Police Auxiliary; Kenneth W. Ford, national chaplain, National Fraternal Order of Police; and entertainer Vince Gill. The Peace Officers Memorial Day and Police Week proclamation of May 11 is listed in Appendix D at the end of this volume.

Address to the Nation on Immigration Reform
May 15, 2006

Good evening. I've asked for a few minutes of your time to discuss a matter of national importance, the reform of America's immigration system.

The issue of immigration stirs intense emotions, and in recent weeks, Americans have seen those emotions on display. On the streets of major cities, crowds have rallied in support of those in our country illegally. At our southern border, others have organized to stop illegal immigrants from coming in. Across the country, Americans are trying to reconcile these contrasting images. And in Washington, the debate over

immigration reform has reached a time of decision. Tonight I will make it clear where I stand and where I want to lead our country on this vital issue.

We must begin by recognizing the problems with our immigration system. For decades, the United States has not been in complete control of its borders. As a result, many who want to work in our economy have been able to sneak across our border, and millions have stayed.

Once here, illegal immigrants live in the shadows of our society. Many use forged documents to get jobs, and that makes it difficult for employers to verify that the workers they hire are legal. Illegal immigration puts pressure on public schools and hospitals; it strains State and local budgets and brings crime to our communities. These are real problems. Yet we must remember that the vast majority of illegal immigrants are decent people who work hard, support their families, practice their faith, and lead responsible lives. They are a part of American life, but they are beyond the reach and protection of American law.

We're a nation of laws, and we must enforce our laws. We're also a nation of immigrants, and we must uphold that tradition, which has strengthened our country in so many ways. These are not contradictory goals. America can be a lawful society and a welcoming society at the same time. We will fix the problems created by illegal immigration, and we will deliver a system that is secure, orderly, and fair. So I support comprehensive immigration reform that will accomplish five clear objectives.

First, the United States must secure its borders. This is a basic responsibility of a sovereign nation. It is also an urgent requirement of our national security. Our objective is straightforward: The border should be open to trade and lawful immigration, and shut to illegal immigrants as well as criminals, drug dealers, and terrorists.

I was a Governor of a State that has a 1,200-mile border with Mexico, so I know how difficult it is to enforce the border and how important it is. Since I became President, we've increased funding for border security by 66 percent and expanded the Border Patrol from about 9,000 to 12,000 agents. The men and women of our Border Patrol are doing a fine job in difficult circumstances, and over the past 5 years, they have apprehended and sent home about 6 million people entering America illegally.

Despite this progress, we do not yet have full control of the border, and I am determined to change that. Tonight I'm calling on Congress to provide funding for dramatic improvements in manpower and technology at the border. By the end of 2008, we'll increase the number of Border Patrol officers by an additional 6,000. When these new agents are deployed, we'll have more than doubled the size of the Border Patrol during my Presidency.

At the same time, we're launching the most technologically advanced border security initiative in American history. We will construct high-tech fences in urban corridors and build new patrol roads and barriers in rural areas. We'll employ motion sensors, infrared cameras, and unmanned aerial vehicles to prevent illegal crossings. America has the best technology in the world, and we will ensure that the Border Patrol has the technology they need to do their job and secure our border.

Training thousands of new Border Patrol agents and bringing the most advanced technology to the border will take time. Yet the need to secure our border is urgent. So I'm announcing several immediate steps to strengthen border enforcement during this period of transition.

One way to help during this transition is to use the National Guard. So in coordination with Governors, up to 6,000 Guard members will be deployed to our southern border. The Border Patrol will remain in the lead. The Guard will assist the Border Patrol by operating surveillance systems, analyzing intelligence, installing fences and vehicle barriers, building patrol roads, and providing training. Guard units will not be involved in direct law enforcement activities; that duty will be done by the Border Patrol. This initial commitment of Guard members would last for a period of one year. After that, the number of Guard forces will be reduced as new Border Patrol agents and new technologies come on line. It is important for Americans to know that we have enough Guard forces to win the war on terror, to respond to natural disasters, and to help secure our border.

The United States is not going to militarize the southern border. Mexico is our neighbor and our friend. We will continue to work cooperatively to improve security on both sides of the border, to confront common problems like drug trafficking and crime, and to reduce illegal immigration.

Another way to help during this period of transition is through State and local law enforcement in our border communities. So we'll increase Federal funding for State and local authorities assisting the Border Patrol on targeted enforcement missions. We will give State and local authorities the specialized training they need to help Federal officers apprehend and detain illegal immigrants. State and local law enforcement officials are an important part of our border security, and they need to be a part of our strategy to secure our borders.

The steps I've outlined will improve our ability to catch people entering our country illegally. At the same time, we must ensure that every illegal immigrant we catch crossing our southern border is returned home. More than 85 percent of the illegal immigrants we catch crossing the southern border are Mexicans, and most are sent back home within 24 hours. But when we catch illegal immigrants from another country, it is not as easy to send them back home. For many years, the Government did not have enough space in our detention facilities to hold them while the legal process unfolded. So most were released back into our society and asked to return for a court date. When the date arrived, the vast majority did not show up. This practice, called catch-and-release, is unacceptable, and we will end it.

We're taking several important steps to meet this goal. We've expanded the number of beds in our detention facilities, and we will continue to add more. We've expedited the legal process to cut the average deportation time. And we're making it clear to foreign governments that they must accept back their citizens who violate our immigration laws. As a result of these actions,

we've ended catch-and-release for illegal immigrants from some countries. And I will ask Congress for additional funding and legal authority so we can end catch-and-release at the southern border once and for all. When people know that they'll be caught and sent home if they enter our country illegally, they will be less likely to try to sneak in.

Second, to secure our border, we must create a temporary-worker program. The reality is that there are many people on the other side of our border who will do anything to come to America to work and build a better life. They walk across miles of desert in the summer heat or hide in the back of 18-wheelers to reach our country. This creates enormous pressure on our border that walls and patrols alone will not stop. To secure the border effectively, we must reduce the numbers of people trying to sneak across.

Therefore, I support a temporary-worker program that would create a legal path for foreign workers to enter our country in an orderly way for a limited period of time. This program would match willing foreign workers with willing American employers for jobs Americans are not doing. Every worker who applies for the program would be required to pass criminal background checks. And temporary workers must return to their home country at the conclusion of their stay.

A temporary-worker program would meet the needs of our economy, and it would give honest immigrants a way to provide for their families while respecting the law. A temporary-worker program would reduce the appeal of human smugglers and make it less likely that people would risk their lives to cross the border. It would ease the financial burden on State and local governments by replacing illegal workers with lawful taxpayers. And above all, a temporary-worker program would add to our security by making certain we know who is in our country and why they are here.

Third, we need to hold employers to account for the workers they hire. It is against the law to hire someone who is in this country illegally. Yet businesses often cannot verify the legal status of their employees because of the widespread problem of document fraud. Therefore, comprehensive immigration reform must include a better system for verifying documents and work eligibility. A key part of that system should be a new identification card for every legal foreign worker. This card should use biometric technology, such as digital fingerprints, to make it tamper-proof. A tamper-proof card would help us enforce the law and leave employers with no excuse for violating it. And by making it harder for illegal immigrants to find work in our country, we would discourage people from crossing the border illegally in the first place.

Fourth, we must face the reality that millions of illegal immigrants are here already. They should not be given an automatic path to citizenship. This is amnesty, and I oppose it. Amnesty would be unfair to those who are here lawfully, and it would invite further waves of illegal immigration.

Some in this country argue that the solution is to deport every illegal immigrant, and that any proposal short of this amounts to amnesty. I disagree. It is neither wise nor realistic to round up millions of people, many with deep roots in the United States, and send them across the border. There is a rational middle ground between granting an automatic path to citizenship for every illegal immigrant and a program of mass deportation. That middle ground recognizes there are differences between an illegal immigrant who crossed the border recently and someone who has worked here for many years and has a home, a family, and an otherwise clean record.

I believe that illegal immigrants who have roots in our country and want to stay should have to pay a meaningful penalty for breaking the law: to pay their taxes; to learn English; and to work in a job for a number of years. People who meet these conditions should be able to apply for citizenship, but approval would not be automatic, and they will have to wait in line behind those who played by the rules and followed the law. What I've just described is not amnesty; it is a way for those who have broken the law to pay their debt to society and demonstrate the character that makes a good citizen.

Fifth, we must honor the great American tradition of the melting pot, which has made us one Nation out of many peoples. The success of our country depends upon helping newcomers assimilate into our society and embrace our common identity as Americans. Americans are bound together by our shared ideals: an appreciation of our history; respect for the flag we fly; and an ability to speak and write the English language. English is also the key to unlocking the opportunity of America. English allows newcomers to go from picking crops to opening a grocery; from cleaning offices to running offices; from a life of low-paying jobs to a diploma, a career, and a home of their own. When immigrants assimilate and advance in our society, they realize their dreams, they renew our spirit, and they add to the unity of America.

Tonight I want to speak directly to Members of the House and the Senate. An immigration reform bill needs to be comprehensive because all elements of this problem must be addressed together, or none of them will be solved at all. The House has passed an immigration bill. The Senate should act by the end of this month so we can work out the differences between the two bills, and Congress can pass a comprehensive bill for me to sign into law.

America needs to conduct this debate on immigration in a reasoned and respectful tone. Feelings run deep on this issue, and as we work it out, all of us need to keep some things in mind. We cannot build a unified country by inciting people to anger or playing on anyone's fears or exploiting the issue of immigration for political gain. We must always remember that real lives will be affected by our debates and decisions, and that every human being has dignity and value, no matter what their citizenship papers say.

I know many of you listening tonight have a parent or a grandparent who came here from another country with dreams of a better life. You know what freedom meant to them, and you know that America is a more hopeful country because of their hard work and sacrifice. As President, I've had the opportunity to meet people of many backgrounds and hear what America means to them. On a visit to Bethesda Naval Hospital, Laura and I met a wounded marine named Guadalupe Denogean. Master Gunnery Sergeant Denogean came to the United States from Mexico when he was a boy. He spent his summers picking crops with his family, and then he volunteered for the United States Marine Corps as soon as he was able. During the liberation of Iraq, Master Gunnery Sergeant Denogean was seriously injured. And when asked if he had any requests, he made two: a promotion for the corporal who helped rescue him and the chance to become an American citizen. And when this brave marine raised his right hand and swore an oath to become a citizen of the country he had defended for more than 26 years, I was honored to stand at his side.

We will always be proud to welcome people like Guadalupe Denogean as fellow Americans. Our new immigrants are just what they've always been, people willing to risk everything for the dream of freedom. And America remains what she has always been—the great hope on the horizon, an open door to the future, a blessed and promised land. We honor the heritage of all who come here, no matter where they come from, because we trust in our country's genius for making us all Americans—one Nation under God.

Thank you, and good night.

NOTE: The President spoke at 8:01 p.m. in the Oval Office at the White House. The Office of the Press Secretary also released a Spanish language transcript of this address.

Remarks at a Welcoming Ceremony for Prime Minister John Howard of Australia
May 16, 2006

Good morning. Laura and I are honored to welcome Prime Minister John Howard and his wife, Janette, back to the White House.

Australia and the United States share timeless values. On opposite sides of the Pacific, our peoples created lands of opportunity and offered millions the hope of new beginnings. As frontier peoples, we cherish the spirit of discovery. We believe that men and women who dream big and work hard can create a better world.

Australians and Americans also believe in the power of freedom. Our two nations were once remote outposts of liberty, lands where those escaping tyranny could find a better life. Today, freedom is on the move. Australians and Americans celebrate freedom's advance, because nations that respect the rights and dignity of their own people are the best partners for peace and the strongest anchors of stability in every region of the world.

Freedom has enemies, and for more than 100 years, Australians and Americans have joined together to defend freedom. Together we fought the Battle of Hamel in World War I. Together we fought in World War II from the beaches of Normandy to the waters of the Coral Sea. Together we fought in Korea and Vietnam. And together we're fighting and winning the global war on terror.

Prime Minister Howard, you and I stood together here at the White House the day before September the 11th, 2001. And our nations have stood together on every day afterwards. The American people know that Australia is a strong ally. We admire your courage, and we appreciate your sacrifice.

We share your grief over the loss of your own countrymen who were brutally attacked in Bali. We share your determination to defeat those who murder the innocent to promote their ideology of hatred. To defeat the terrorists, we must stay on the offensive, and Australia has been on the frontlines of every offensive in the war on terror.

In Afghanistan, the first casualty among American allies was an Australian. In Iraq, Australian Special Operation forces were among the first coalition units on the ground. The bravery and skill of the Australian military have helped the people of these two nations claim their freedom and deny the terrorists safe havens from which to launch further attacks.

War has reaffirmed the strength of our alliance, yet our alliance is only one component of our broad partnership. Australia and the United States signed a free trade agreement in 2004 because we recognize that open markets create greater prosperity for both our peoples. We're cooperating to expand trade worldwide. In the Doha negotiations, Australia and America speak with one voice. We continue to urge all parties to reduce global trade barriers that keep millions in the developing world mired in poverty.

Our two nations accept other global responsibilities as well. We helped to build the Asia-Pacific Partnership on Clean Development and Climate, so we can make the latest energy technologies available to all to increase efficiency and reduce pollution.

We've pooled our resources to help the victims of natural disasters, and we're working together to meet the threat of pandemic disease. We share a common approach to security issues, including Iran and North Korea. Our two nations are closer than ever, and Americans admire Australia's strong leader. Prime Minister John Howard has affirmed our common values. He's strengthened our alliance. He's built on our long history of partnership. I value his counsel. I admire his courage.

Mr. Prime Minister and Mrs. Howard, thank you for making the long journey. We welcome you with the honor due to a valiant nation and with the warmth of close friends. Welcome to America.

NOTE: The President spoke at 9:16 a.m. on the South Lawn at the White House, where Prime Minister Howard was accorded a formal welcome with full military honors. The transcript released by the Office of the Press Secretary also included the remarks of Prime Minister Howard.

The President's News Conference With Prime Minister John Howard of Australia
May 16, 2006

President Bush. Thank you all. It's my honor to welcome the Prime Minister of Australia here to the East Room for a press briefing. I'm going to feed him tonight— before I feed him tonight, I'm going to feed him to you. [*Laughter*]

We just had a really interesting discussion about a lot of issues. First, I admire

John Howard's understanding that the war on terror still goes on and that we've got to be steadfast and firm if we intend to succeed in defeating the terrorists.

Secondly, I appreciate very much his understanding and discussions about the way forward in Iraq. We spent quite a bit of time talking about the new Government. I described to him as best as I could my feelings about the Prime Minister-designee, who I believe is a firm and decisive person that is going to make a difference in that country's future.

I thanked him very much for the commitment of Australian troops. We, of course, talked about the Iraqi security forces' capacity to defend themselves. I reported to him that we're pleased with the progress being made but that the United States will make decisions about our troop levels based upon conditions on the ground.

We talked about Afghanistan. Again, I want to thank the Prime Minister for his support there for this fledgling democracy. We talked about North Korea. We talked about Iran. We talked about a lot. And that's what you'd expect when you're talking to an ally and a friend and a good strategic thinker.

The Prime Minister is capable of not only seeing the problems for today; he's capable of looking down the road. And I appreciate his advice and his judgment on national security matters, as well as in talking about issues like energy and trade. We've got a good relationship with Australia, and we intend to keep it that way.

I always remind my friends who talk to me about countries around the world, I say, I can't think of a country more like— a place more like Texas than Australia. And that's a compliment—[*laughter*]—except for some of these people over here. [*Laughter*] The people of Australia are independent-minded; they're smart; they're capable; they're hard-working. And I really enjoy my relationship with the Prime Minister.

So Mr. Prime Minister, welcome. Thanks for coming, and the floor is yours.

Prime Minister Howard. Well, thank you very much, Mr. President. Again, can I thank you very warmly for the great hospitality that you have extended to me. It was a real privilege to sit around the Cabinet table and talk to your Cabinet officers, which followed a very extensive discussion between the two of us about all of those issues of which you spoke.

We remain a steadfast ally of the United States in the war against terror. I've made that clear on every occasion I've spoken here in the United States. The war against terror will go on for a long time; I think we have to accept that. Progress is being made. The challenge remains very, very strong, and there needs to be a continued commitment. And we admire and respect the leadership given by you and by the United States in that war, and it's a war that confronts us all. Those who imagine that somehow or other you can escape it by rolling yourself into a little ball and going over in the corner and hoping that you're not going to be noticed are doomed to be very, very uncomfortably disappointed.

We did have an opportunity to talk extensively about some of the challenges in our immediate region. And I spoke about the situation in East Timor and the Solomon Islands and the importance of the role of Indonesia, the symbolism and also the practical consequence of Indonesia being the largest Islamic country in the world. And therefore, the success and prosperity of moderate Islamic leadership in that country is itself a very important factor in the long-term success of the fight against terrorism, because the fight against terrorism is not only a military and physical one; it is also an intellectual one. And it's a question of providing within the Islamic world a successful democratic model as an alternative to the fanaticism of those who would obscenely invoke the sanction of Islam to justify what they seek to do.

Can I finally say that of the many ties that bind Australia and the United States, as I said on the lawn earlier today, none are more important, of course, than the shared values and the beliefs that both of our countries have—that the spread of democracy around the world is an important goal and an important responsibility. It's been a privilege for our two peoples to enjoy democracy in an uninterrupted fashion for so long that we tend to take it for granted, and we forget its liberating impact on those who taste and experience it for the first time. And both of our societies have a responsibility in expanding the opportunities for democracy, and that, of course, lies very much at the heart of much of what our two societies do.

Mr. President, thank you very, very much for the honor you've done me and the courtesy and friendship that you've extended to me and all of the traveling party. We appreciate it very, very deeply, indeed. Thank you.

President Bush. Two questions a side. Terry [Terence Hunt, Associated Press].

Terrorist Surveillance Program

Q. Thank you, Mr. President. Mr. President, you've said that the Government is not trolling through the lives of innocent Americans, but why shouldn't ordinary people feel that their privacy is invaded by the NSA compiling a list of their telephone calls?

President Bush. What I have told the American people is, we'll protect them against an Al Qaida attack, and we'll do so within the law. I've been very clear about the principles and guidelines of any program that has been designed to protect the American people.

I've also been clear about the fact that we do not listen to domestic phone calls without court approval and that this Government will continue to guard the privacy of the American people. But if Al Qaida is calling into the United States, we want to know, and we want to know why.

For the Australian press friends here, we got accused of not connecting dots prior

to September the 11th, and we're going to connect dots to protect the American people, within the law. The program he's asking about is one that has been fully briefed to Members of the United States Congress in both political parties. They are very aware of what is taking place. The American people expect their Government to protect them, within the laws of this country, and I'm going to continue to do just that.

Prime Minister Howard. Australian press. Mr. Curry.

Australian Prime Minister Howard

Q. Mr. President, your relationship with Mr. Howard is obviously very close, personally. And I was wondering, first, could you just expand a little on that chemistry? And secondly, sir, do you think you would be able to work effectively with a future Australian leader, be it either a successor of Mr. Howard from his own party or from their opposition?

President Bush. Well, I suspect he's going to outlast me, so that is a moot point—[*laughter*]—probably a question you ought to ask him. Somebody said, "You and John Howard appear to be so close. Don't you have any differences?" And I said, "Yes, he doesn't have any hair." [*Laughter*]

Look, ours is a world in which sometimes people tell you something and they don't mean it. In order to work together to make difficult decisions—decisions of war and peace, decisions of security, decisions of trade—you've got to have somebody you talk to that tells you straight up what's on their mind. You know, politics sometimes produces people that will tell you one thing and don't mean it. It's really hard to be making rational decisions if somebody you're talking to just doesn't level with you.

And that's what I like about John Howard. He may not be the prettiest person on the block—[*laughter*]—but when he tells you something, you can take it to the bank. He is a reliable partner. And we don't agree on 100 percent, of course. But the interesting thing, talking to John Howard, is that you can trust the man. And that's what is a necessary ingredient to be working together for the common good.

And I also appreciate a person who is capable of standing by a decision. I remember the campaign—as a matter of fact, your campaign was right before my campaign—and John Howard stood strong. And I remember telling somebody—and the polls didn't look all that good, I guess, at one point in time—and I remember saying to somebody, "This man is going to be rewarded at the ballot box because the people of Australia want somebody who is consistently strong, not somebody who tries to waffle around trying to figure out where to end up for political expediency."

People may not agree with his position on every issue, but people have got to agree with the fact that he's a man of conviction. And that's the essence of leadership—courage and conviction. And so we've got a relationship that is based upon respect, and I respect him. I've seen him in action. I've seen what it means to have him being pressured—probably by your newspaper. But I've seen him stand strong, and that's what's needed in this world.

Holland [Steve Holland, Reuters], yes.

Immigration Reform

Q. Thank you, sir. On immigration, some worry that the U.S. military is stretched too thin. How effective can these National Guard troops be if they're shuttling in and out of the border area every two or three weeks? And how are you going to turn around these House Members who seem to be unswayed by your argument on the guest-worker program?

President Bush. The program to put Guard on the border is one that will enable the Border Patrol to do its job better. It's very important for the American people to know it's the Border Patrol that's going to be on the frontline of apprehending people trying to sneak into our country. And the

Guard will be doing a variety of functions, which I outlined last night.

Secondly, the Guard is—the up to 6,000 Guard in the first year of operation really is not going to put a strain on our capacity to fight and win the war on terror, as well as deal with natural disasters. And, of course, we'll be working in conjunction with Governors to make sure that that's not the case, that it doesn't put an unnecessary strain on other functions of the Guard.

Thirdly, the Pentagon is briefing today—how the program is going to work. There are Guard troops in Arizona and New Mexico and Texas that can be used by the Governors down there to work with the Border Patrol, that they'll be reimbursed for. And there's also training missions that can be used to help complement the Border Patrol. We're going to have double the Border Patrol agents since 2001, by 2008. And what the Guard is doing, the Guard is providing an interim service until those Border Patrol agents get stood up.

I made it clear to the country last night that we're not going to militarize our border. Mexico is a friend. But what we are going to do is use assets necessary to make sure that we can assure the American people that the border is secure.

Now in order to secure the border, it's important for people up here in Washington to understand that there's got to be a temporary-worker program. Border security and a temporary-worker program are really important because—let me say, a temporary-worker program is really important to border security, because we don't want people trying to sneak into the country. It seems rational to me to say, "If you're coming to work, come to work in a legal way, on a temporary basis, so you're not trying to sneak across." So the temporary-worker program goes hand in hand with border security. In order for there to be a—in order for us to solve the problem of an immigration system that's not working, it's really important for Congress to understand that there needs a—that the elements I described all go hand in hand.

And so I'll continue to work with them. Look, this is a hard issue for many people.

Q. Would you go along with border protection only and a guest-worker program— [*inaudible*].

President Bush. I said I want a comprehensive bill because I understand there needs to be a comprehensive bill in order to make—in order for us to achieve the objective.

And the objective is, on the one hand, protect our borders, and on the other hand, never lose sight of the thing that makes America unique, which is, we're a land of immigrants and that we—we're not going to discriminate against people. Now, we don't think there ought to be an automatic path to citizenship; that's called amnesty. Amnesty would be wrong. Amnesty would say that somebody that stood in line legally is—is mistreated, as far as I'm concerned. Amnesty would mean that more people would try to come and sneak into our country in the hopes that they would be granted automatic citizenship.

But there ought to be a way for somebody to pay a fine or learn English or prove that they've been here for a long time working and be able to get in line—not the head of the line but the back of the line—in order to become a citizen.

You know, there are some in our country who say, "Let's just deport everybody." It's unrealistic. It may sound attractive to some. You can't deport people who have been in this country for a long period of time— millions of people that have been here.

And so we've got to be rational about how we move forward. And part of my appeal last night was to say to people, let's don't get so emotional that we forget who we are. We're a land of immigrants, and when we welcome somebody to our country who is here legally, willing to work and willing to realize a dream, it helps restore our soul.

So this is a difficult debate for Members. I'm going to continue working with them. Part of my job is to lead, and I did last night. I said, here's how we get to where we need to be.

Australia's Wheat Market/Trade

Q. Mr. President, American wheat growers are angry that hundreds of millions of dollars in bribes were paid to Saddam's Iraq to protect Australia's wheat market. Do you share their anger, and do you sympathize with the push on Capitol Hill to investigate this further in America? And Mr. Prime Minister, I'd be interested in your comments on a possible Capitol Hill inquiry into this.

President Bush. My own judgment is, is that the Howard administration is pretty capable of investigating what took place, and I look forward to seeing the results of the investigation.

Prime Minister Howard. For my part, you are aware of what the Australian Government has done. Australia is the only country in the world that has responded to the bulk of findings with a public inquiry with the powers of a royal commission. And you are aware that the commission has probably completed its public hearings, and we're likely to have a report by the 30th of June.

What the United States Congress does in relation to this is a matter for the United States Congress. And, clearly, if it decides to do something, then we will respond in the appropriate fashion. But for our part, in Australia, we have been open, transparent that we do not approve in any way, shape, or form of the payment of bribes, and if a finding is to that effect, then the full processes of Australian law should be brought to bear. You can't be more transparent than that, and I think that is understood in the United States.

But obviously, just as we have responsibilities within Australia, the legislators of this country, where I'm a guest, have responsibilities in this country. And if it discharges those in a particular fashion, the way it thinks fit—well, that's its right, and we will respond in what is also the appropriate fashion. I don't think I can add anything more to that, and we have been patently transparent and open. And let me just repeat again, Australia is the only country in the world that has established a public inquiry with the powers of the royal commission.

President Bush. Thank you, sir.

NOTE: The President's news conference began at 11:43 a.m. in the East Room at the White House. In his remarks, he referred to Prime Minister-designate Nuri al-Maliki of Iraq.

Remarks Honoring the 2005 Women's National Basketball Association Champion Sacramento Monarchs
May 16, 2006

Thank you. Please be seated. It is a beautiful day to welcome the Monarchs to the White House. I want to first congratulate the 2005 WNBA champs, the Sacramento Monarchs. We're glad you're here. Thanks for coming, and congratulations to you.

I was thinking about a little one-on-one here on the South Lawn. [*Laughter*] Then I reconsidered. Laura said, "You might as well stick to your mountain bike; don't try to take on these athletes." But we're really glad you're here.

I want to congratulate Coach John Whisenant on being such a fine coach. Congratulations, sir. Glad you're here. Thanks for coming. Glad you brought Joyce. Welcome.

I want to thank my Cabinet Secretary, Alphonso Jackson. Welcome, A.J.—thanks for coming. I knew you were a sports fan, and I knew you appreciated excellence on the court, so I'm not surprised you're here.

I want to thank Doris Matsui, Congresswoman Matsui—thanks for coming—from the Sacramento area, as well as John Doolittle. I really appreciate you all being here. Thanks for taking time to honor these champs.

I appreciate Donna Orender, the president of the WNBA. Thanks for coming.

Proud you're here. I want to thank John Thomas of Maloof Sports & Entertainment for coming. John, congratulations for putting together a good franchise. Good job. It's not easy to field a championship team, but you've done so.

I'm also proud to be up here with Yolanda Griffith, the WNBA Finals MVP. Congratulations, Yolanda—[*applause*]—popular member of the team, as you can tell. I want to welcome all the other Monarch players who are here. I'm honored to be up here with you. I can't thank you enough for coming by to give us a chance to pay a proper tribute to your championship run.

I also want to welcome members of the local Junior WNBA program; glad you all are here. Welcome to the White House. This is the—interestingly enough, the 10th year of the WNBA, and I don't know if you can remember, but I certainly do, when a lot of people were speculating that the WNBA wouldn't last. "They couldn't possibly make it," they were saying. Well the truth of the matter is, the WNBA has not only lasted; it's thrived. And American sports are better for it.

A lot of fans are coming to see the games, which is a good indication. The WNBA broadcasts are seen now in 193 countries in 31 different languages. That means a lot of people are paying attention to what you're doing on the courts. And we appreciate it.

And I appreciate the team. I appreciate a team that's figured out how to, kind of, meld stars together for the common good. You know, there are a lot of teams with stars on them. I'm sure you've run into a few of them with some pretty good stars. But a lot of times, teams aren't able to work together, and this team was able to do so. They were tough on defense. They had an attitude—a positive attitude all the way throughout the season. In other words, they didn't think they could get beat. As a matter of fact, they only lost two games on their home court. It's a pretty good— it's called the home court advantage— [*laughter*]—15 and 2 in Arco Arena.

I know the city of Sacramento is really proud of you, and I know that if the mayor were here and the citizens that are, kind of, serving the folks of Sacramento were here, they'd be saying, "We really like the Monarchs. We're really proud that you brought a championship team to our city."

So one of the things I'd like to say to you is thanks for being team players; thanks for setting high goals; and thanks for working together to achieve those goals.

I also appreciate the fact that you've got players from China and Portugal and Mali, as well as a lot of different States here in the United States. I think it's pretty neat, isn't it, for people who—from different backgrounds, different cultures are able to figure out a way to win. I think it's a great example for the world; I really do. I think it's important for people to come together for a common cause. I know you view yourself only as athletes, but I view you as diplomats as well.

I also want to thank you for the example you've set. It's one thing to be called champs on the court; it's another thing to

be called champs in life. One of the things you've done is you've set a great example for young women athletes. As the father of twin daughters who had trouble finding the backboard, I might add—[*laughter*]— sorry, girls—I love the fact that there are role models, though, for young women, that somebody can look up to and say, "Gosh, I want to be like her. I want to realize my dreams by being like Yolanda."

So it's great to be able to play basketball as well as you play, but it's also really important to know that you're setting a good example for people watching your every move.

I was impressed by the fact that you're working on Read to Achieve. You know, I oftentimes call on fellow citizens to serve our country by helping somebody else. One way you can really help somebody is to teach somebody to read. What a wonderful gift. And the fact that pro athletes were willing to take time out of your busy schedule to help inspire a young reader means a lot to the country.

I appreciate very much your honoring breast cancer survivors, helping to lift somebody's spirits. Thanks for entering the annual Race for the Cure. I used to be able to run. [*Laughter*] But thanks for running while you're young. I know you didn't have to do it, but you set a good sign for people. All in all, I'm honored to be up here with some champs. It's a delight to welcome you here to the White House.

May God bless you and your families, and may God continue to bless our country. Welcome.

NOTE: The President spoke at 1:27 p.m. in the East Garden at the White House. In his remarks, he referred to John Whisenant, head coach, Sacramento Monarchs, and his wife, Joyce; John Thomas, president, Sacramento Monarchs; and Mayor Heather Fargo of Sacramento, CA.

Remarks at a State Dinner Honoring Prime Minister John Howard of Australia
May 16, 2006

Mr. Prime Minister, Mrs. Howard, distinguished guests: Welcome to the White House. This is going to be a joyous occasion because we're honoring two really good friends. We wish you a warm welcome. We thank the Howards for making a long journey, and thanks for spending so much time with us here in the States.

Our partnership is broad, and it's deep. Australia and America are working together to expand trade and to counter threats of nuclear proliferation, to make the latest energy technologies available to all nations. In the global war on terror, we have no better ally than Australia and John Howard. And in the spread of freedom to create lasting peace, we have no better friend than Australia and John Howard.

Mr. Prime Minister, we value your courage and your faithfulness and your strength, and I value your friendship. Laura and I have cherished every visit with you and Janette. We really appreciated the chance to plant those trees yesterday at the Australian Embassy. [*Laughter*] We wanted to bring a Texas tree up, but they don't grow too well here in Washington. [*Laughter*] But

I know those trees are going to grow strong and sturdy, just like our friendship has grown strong and sturdy.

I was thinking about how to really describe John Howard and his leadership in Australia, and I thought I would remind everybody what Ronald Reagan used to say: it was "morning in America." And Mr. Prime Minister, that's still true for our country. We're really an optimistic people, and we firmly believe the best days are ahead for our country. I know you feel the same way about Australia. It's also comforting to know that on the other side of the world, it's already morning in Australia. [*Laughter*]

Mr. Prime Minister, Laura and I offer a toast to you and Janette, to our allies, and to the great people of Australia.

NOTE: The President spoke at 8:07 p.m. in the State Dining Room at the White House. In his remarks, he referred to Janette Howard, wife of Prime Minister Howard. The transcript made available by the Office of the Press Secretary also included the remarks of Prime Minister Howard.

Remarks Honoring the United States Winter Olympic and Paralympic Teams
May 17, 2006

Thank you all very much. Please be seated. Laura and I are so honored to welcome the 2006 winter Olympic and Paralympic teams to the White House. It is such a joy to have you all here, and congratulations for being champs.

I appreciate the Members of the Congress who are here: Senator Thomas and Congressmen Shays, Buyer, Hastings, and

Ryun. Thank you all for coming. Thanks for honoring these great Olympians—Congressman Ted Poe from Texas as well.

I want to thank all the athletes who've taken time to come. We really appreciate your giving us a chance to pay respects to your athleticism and your character. I want to thank the coaches and the team leaders and the U.S. Olympic staff. I particularly want to thank the members of the Texas A&M Singing Cadets for joining us today. Thanks for coming to provide the— [*applause*].

I wish I could have been at the games there in Turin, but fortunately we do have TVs here in the White House. [*Laughter*] It was such a thrill to watch you all compete. Laura represented our country and really enjoyed getting to know you all. She came back and talked about the kindness and the integrity of our athletes. I appreciate the fact that you treated her with such respect. More importantly, I appreciate the fact that you represented our country with such nobility and dignity.

I thank you for the example you set. I don't know if you know this or not, but there's all kinds of people watching our Olympic and Paralympic athletes, wondering whether or not it's possible for them to be able to achieve the same level of accomplishments that you all achieved. The fact that you compete hard and train hard and set high goals and succeed is a really important part of encouraging others to follow in your footsteps. Being a champ means that you've got enormous responsibilities, and I thank you for upholding those responsibilities with the class that you've showed as athletes in Turin.

Thanks for creating so many lasting memories for the American people. We love our athletes. We follow your successes. We love it when the "Star Spangled Banner" is played. We also understand that not everybody is going to win the gold, but we appreciate so much the fact that you competed so hard and in such a way that brought honor to our country.

The memories are such that we remember the—America's first medal in ice dancing in 30 years with Tanith and Ben. Congratulations to you both. We appreciate the courage of Lindsey Kildow, who overcame a terrible crash in the training run and then decided to continue to compete. That kind of courage stirs our hearts. It's such a great example for people.

We appreciate Joey Cheek, who won the gold and then turned around and donated $40,000 to help the refugee children of Sudan. What a wonderful example for all of us here in America to know that with our personal victories comes the responsibility of helping those who suffer and those who need help.

We're honored that "the Flying Tomato" represented our country. And we want to thank all the dudes and dudesses of the snowboarders who are here. [*Laughter*]

America's Paralympians overcame incredible odds to earn 12 medals for our Nation. Laurie Stephens was born with spina bifida; she won two golds and the silver medal in Alpine skiing. What a strong example for people to look at Laurie and realize that "I can achieve dreams too."

Steve Cook, he lost part of his right leg in a tractor accident, but that didn't stop him. He's gone on to earn seven medals in cross-country skiing, including two golds and a bronze in this year's Paralympics. Steve, I appreciate your courage, and I appreciate the example you have shown for others.

Lonnie Hannah is with us; she had breast [he had skin]° cancer last year and came back to help the U.S. sled hockey team win the bronze in a really thrilling game against Germany.

All of our successes in the Olympics and Paralympics required unbelievable skill and determination, and they also required the support of a lot of people in your lives. The honors you've won are a tribute to, of course, your coaches and trainers but also to your parents and to your brothers and sisters and your friends and supporters who continue to cheer you. I know all of you join me in thanking those who supported you.

At the games, you showed the best values of our country. You were humble in

---

° White House correction.

victory and gracious in defeat. You made us proud. And so here on the White House South Lawn, I want to thank you for being such great ambassadors to our country. Welcome, and may God bless you all.

NOTE: The President spoke at 10:16 a.m. on the South Lawn at the White House. In his remarks, he referred to Tanith Belbin and Benjamin Agosto, ice dancers, Lindsey Kildow, Alpine skier, Joey Cheek, speed skater, and Shaun "the Flying Tomato" White, snowboarder, U.S. Olympic Team.

Remarks on Signing the Tax Increase Prevention and Reconciliation Act of 2005
May 17, 2006

Thank you all. Please be seated. Good afternoon, and welcome to the White House. It's nice to see so many Members of Congress at this end of Pennsylvania Avenue. [*Laughter*] And you've come for a really good reason. This is a good day for American workers and families and businesses. You have passed a bill that will keep our taxes low and keep our economy growing. And I'm really pleased to be able to sign this vital piece of legislation. Thank you for your leadership.

I'm glad you're here, and so is the Vice President. I'm proud to be up here with Vice President Cheney. I couldn't have picked a better person to be the Vice President of the United States. I appreciate Secretary John Snow for his leadership on this issue. Mr. Secretary, you have made a difference. I'm proud of your leadership. Thank you.

I want to thank the Speaker of the House, Denny Hastert. Mr. Speaker, welcome back to the White House. Thank you for your leadership. And I want to thank Senator Bill Frist, the Senate majority leader. Both these men have shown fine leadership capabilities on an important issue for the American people.

I want to thank Mitch McConnell, Jon Kyl, Kay Bailey Hutchison from the United States Senate. I want to thank John Boehner, Deborah Pryce, Eric Cantor. I particularly want to pay my respects to the chairman of the Senate Finance Committee and the chairman of the House Ways and Means Committee; Chuck Grassley and Bill Thomas are incredibly able legislators. They've done a fantastic job on behalf of the American people, and our Nation owes them a debt of gratitude. I appreciate all the Members being here today.

This economy of ours is hitting full stride. In the first quarter of this year, our economy grew at an annual rate of 4.8 percent. This follows a vigorous 2005, when the American economy grew at 3.5 percent. The past 2½ years, we've added more than 5.2 million new jobs. Productivity over the last 5 years has grown at the fastest rate in decades. Higher productivity leads to higher wages for the American workers. Hourly compensation grew at an annual rate of 5.7 percent in the first quarter of this year. American workers are taking home bigger paychecks, and their standard of living is on the rise. The American economy is powerful, productive, and prosperous, and we're going to keep it that way.

Economic growth begins with the hard work of the American people and good policies in Washington, DC. Over the past few years, our economy has faced a lot of challenges. We've been through a recession, a stock market decline, corporate scandals, an attack on our country, high energy prices, and major natural disasters.

But we acted. We believe that our economy prospers when the American people make their own decisions about how to save and spend and invest their own money. And starting in 2001, we delivered the largest tax relief since Ronald Reagan was in the White House.

We reduced taxes for every American who pays income taxes. We doubled the child tax credit, reduced the marriage penalty, created new incentives for small businesses to invest. We put the death tax on the road to extinction. The American people have used their money better than the Government ever could have. They've used the tax relief to provide for their families and create jobs and help the American economy become the envy of the industrialized world.

Our progrowth policies stand in stark contrast to those in Washington who believe you grow your economy by raising taxes and centralizing power. They are wrong. Our progrowth economic policies are working for all Americans.

One of the most important decisions we made was to cut the taxes on dividends and capital gains. These cuts were designed to lower the cost of capital and to encourage businesses to expand and hire new workers. And these tax cuts are doing exactly what we expected. When these cuts were passed in 2003, business investment had been dropping for several years. Since then, business investment has been growing at more than 9 percent a year. Spending on equipment and software has hit record levels. And businesses have hired millions of new workers to fill the jobs that this investment creates.

The cuts on dividends and capital gains are reaching families and businesses alike. About half the households in America, 57 million in all, have some investment in the stock market. They either own shares in individual companies or through mutual funds. Sometimes they own these shares through their retirement plans. By cutting the taxes on dividends and capital gains, we helped add about $4 trillion in new wealth to the stock market.

If you have a mutual fund for your family, these tax cuts made you better off. If you have an IRA or a 401(k), these tax cuts will help provide a better retirement. If you're a senior who depends on dividend income to make ends meet, these tax cuts have led to a better check each month. At all levels of income, the tax cuts on dividends and capital gains are letting Americans keep more of their own money and live a better life.

The danger was that the tax cuts on dividends and capital gains were set to expire in 2008. That's created great uncertainty, because businesses and investors couldn't plan for the future without worrying about a big tax increase around the corner. That uncertainty discourages investment and expansion. It reduces opportunities for workers and families. The bill you passed helps to address this problem by extending the tax cuts on dividends and capital gains. By reassuring businesses that their taxes will not be going up any time soon, the bill increases confidence for our job creators. It will help millions of American families who are saving for the future.

Part of our strategy to cut our deficit in half is to continue to grow this economy. Tax relief has helped a growing economy, which means more tax revenue for the Federal treasury—2005 tax revenues grew by $274 billion, an increase of nearly 15 percent over the previous year. This year, the economy is still growing, and tax revenues are growing with it. So far, tax revenues are 11 percent higher than they were at the same point last year, which is better than projected. More than a quarter of these tax revenues come from corporations who pay more because they're growing with the economy.

By growing this economy, we're staying on track to meet our goal of cutting the deficit in half by 2009. But to meet that goal, we must be strong on controlling the Federal appetite for spending. Every year since I took office, we've slowed the growth of discretionary spending that's not related to the military or homeland security. My last two budgets have actually cut this kind of spending.

Congress is now considering an emergency supplemental bill that can show the American people we're determined to be fiscally sound with their money. I've set a clear limit on spending that I'll accept for this legislation, and if this bill goes over the limit or includes nonemergency or wasteful spending, I'll veto it.

For the past 50 years, Republicans and Democrats have had many differences, but they've often been able to agree that the American people should keep more of their own money. Presidents like John F. Kennedy and Ronald Reagan proposed and cut taxes with strong bipartisan support, and in each case, the economy prospered and grew.

The tax cuts we passed in 2001 and 2003 have also helped the economy grow and prosper. Opponents of these tax cuts were wrong when they voted against them the first time. They've been wrong to oppose extension of tax relief in the face of overwhelming evidence that the tax cuts have helped grow the economy and create millions of new jobs.

With this bill, we're sending the American people a clear message about our policy. We're going to continue to trust the American people with their own money. We'll continue to be wise with the people's money in Washington. We'll continue to work and to make sure the tax cuts are permanent. And the bill I sign today is a victory for the American taxpayers, and it's a strong lift for our economy. Congratulations on a job well done.

It's now my honor to sign the Tax Increase Prevention and Reconciliation Act of 2005.

NOTE: The President spoke at 1:58 p.m. on the South Lawn at the White House. H.R. 4297, approved May 17, was assigned Public Law No. 109–222.

Remarks at a Republican National Committee Gala
May 17, 2006

The President. Thank you all. Thanks for the warm welcome. Thanks for being here at the RNC Gala. I can't thank you enough for helping our party succeed. It's such an honor to be here. I am, first, really proud of the Republican Party. We're a party, over the past 5 years, that has made a significant difference for the American people. We have defended freedom at home and abroad, and by doing so, we've done our duty to make this Nation safer. And we've trusted the people, and as a result, America is a stronger and more prosperous nation.

I want to thank my friend Ken Mehlman for leading our party. When I talked to him about leading the Republican Party, I said, "I want to be a party that welcomes everybody, from all walks of life, a party based upon principles, a party that trusts the people, a party that stands strong in a time of historic challenge." And Ken is doing a fine job of reaching out. Our party is strong, and it's getting stronger.

Laura sends her love. She's a fabulous First Lady. She's got to be the most patient woman in America. [*Laughter*]

Audience member. She's hot!

The President. Yes—well, wait a minute. [*Laughter*] *Muy caliente.* [*Laughter*] I hope she's not watching, you know? [*Laughter*]

I appreciate the members of my Cabinet who are here. I thank you all for coming. Thanks for serving. I also want to thank my friend Bill Frist, majority leader of the United States Senate, who is here with us. The Speaker is rounding up votes right now, but like Senator Frist, the Speaker is doing a fabulous job for the American people. And we intend to keep Denny Hastert Speaker of the House and Bill Frist majority leader of the Senate. I want to thank all the other Members of the House and the Senate who are here. Thank you all for coming.

I appreciate Jo Ann Davidson, who is the cochairman of the RNC. I appreciate her leadership and her friendship. I want to thank Dwight and Martha Schar; he's the finance chairman for the RNC. You've done a great job tonight. Appreciate you making Schar look good. I want to thank the Gala chairs, Sam Fox, Jack Oliver, Bob and Suzy Pence, and Bill Paxon. I want to thank all the people who have worked to make this such a successful event. I particularly want to thank Diamond Rio for their fantastic singing.

We're just kind of warming up for these off-year elections. [*Laughter*] Tonight is part of the process to make sure that when our candidates take it to the voters, they're able to do so in a way where people can hear them loud and clear. You know, elections are all about choices. And our party is a party that has built a vision based upon solid principle, a vision which is inclusive, a vision which does not shy away from certain truths and values. We're the party of the future, and our candidates will be running against the party of the past, a party that offers no new ideas like the Republican Party, a party that can only offer opposition. The Republican Party is the party of the future because we believe it is our job to take on the challenges of our time and not to pass them on to future Congresses or future generations.

Ours is an optimistic party. We know we don't need to fear the future, because we intend to shape the future for the American people. We believe in the power of freedom, and we trust in the American

people. We're going to make our choice—make these choices very clear to the voters come November. And I'm confident the American people will realize the difference between positive and negative, optimistic versus pessimistic, and reelect Republican majorities to the United States Congress.

And I'm just getting warmed up. [*Laughter*] These are historic times in which we live, and we're in a war. We're in a war against an enemy that is ruthless, an enemy which adheres to an ideology of hatred, a backward ideology, an ideology that can't stand freedom. Ours is a nation that loves freedom and will never back down.

People have a choice to make, between folks who want to stay on the offense and protect the American people and people who lose their nerve.

We learned some lessons from September the 11th, lessons that I'll never forget. First lesson is, is that in order to protect the American people, which is our most important job, the United States of America must stay on the offense. And that's exactly what your Nation is doing. We will find the terrorists and bring them to justice before they can hurt the American people again.

We had a second lesson learned on September the 11th, and that is, if we find somebody harboring a terrorist, they're just as guilty as the terrorists. And when I said that, I meant what I said. When your President speaks, he must speak clearly and mean what he says. And when I said, "If you harbor a terrorist, you're as guilty as the terrorists," the Taliban didn't take me seriously. But we acted. We upheld doctrine to protect the American people, and because of our actions, 25 million people are no longer in the clutches of one of the most barbaric regimes in the history of mankind.

A serious lesson of September the 11th is that we must take threats seriously before they come to hurt us. And I saw a threat, and members of both political parties saw a threat, in Iraq. Iraq was run by a dictator who was killing his own people, who had used weapons of mass destruction, invaded his neighbors, was shooting at our aircraft, harbored terrorists. The world is better off without Saddam Hussein in power.

We have a plan for victory in Iraq. There's a political track taking place. I know it seems like a decade ago, but it wasn't all that long ago that 12 million people defied car bombers and assassins and terrorists and said loud and clear, "We want to be free." Democracy is on the march in Iraq, and the United States of America will help these brave people achieve their objective.

A new government is being formed in that country, made up of a Kurd and a Shi'a and a Sunni, people who are brave and dedicated, people who understand that the people of their country desires to be free. It shouldn't surprise us that they want to be free, because we firmly understand that the desire to be free is in every human heart. There is an Almighty, and one of the greatest gifts of the Almighty is freedom, and the United States of America will never forget that lesson.

It's tough work. It's tough work to help a young country go from tyranny to democracy. But it's worth it. Free countries are peaceful countries. Free countries will lay the foundation of peace for our children and grandchildren.

The enemy cannot defeat us in Iraq, and they can't defeat us anywhere else in the world. The only way we can be defeated is if we lose our nerve, and the Republican Party will not lose its nerve.

We understand the power of freedom to transform our world. I want to remind you that this Nation lost thousands and thousands of young men and women during World War II and World War I, and yet today, the continent of Europe is whole, free, and at peace. Why? Because democracies do not war.

One of the interesting lessons of history comes home to me every time I meet with my friend the Prime Minister of Japan.

Prime Minister Koizumi is a good friend. Sixty years ago, the United States was embroiled in a terrible war with Japan. My predecessor Harry Truman had the wisdom, however, to recognize the power of freedom to transform societies. Today, I sit down at the table with the Prime Minister of a former enemy and talk about how to keep the peace in North Korea. They've committed troops in Iraq because he understands democracy can make the world a better place.

Something happened between the time World War II ended and George W. was able to sit down with Prime Minister Koizumi, and what happened was, Japan assumed a Japanese-style democracy. One of these days, an American President will be sitting down with a duly elected leader from Iraq talking about keeping the peace, and a generation of Americans will be better off for it.

Our party has worked hard to protect the American people. It's our most important duty. And we passed the PATRIOT Act. You might remember the debates of the PATRIOT Act. Senator Harry Reid, Democrat of the Senate, boasted, quote, he "killed the PATRIOT Act." Because the Republican Party stood strong, our law enforcement have the tools necessary to protect the American people.

There's a lot of debate in Washington, DC, about connecting the dots. My job is to protect you. My job is to defend the civil liberties of the American people. My job is to act within the confines of the Constitution and the law. And that's precisely what I'm doing when it comes to making sure we understand the intent of the enemy. Let me tell you this: If Al Qaida is making phone calls in the United States, we need to know why. We're not going to sit around and wait for another attack.

These are historic times, and I'm proud to be working with Republican Members of the Senate and the House who are making sure we do our duty, and that's to defend the American people. And we're doing our duty here at home as well. We've got clear choices when it comes to our economy. People are going to be able to choose between a party that's going to keep your taxes low to keep the economy growing and a party that's going to run your taxes up. It's a stark choice, and I'm going to keep talking about it, because we've got a record to run on. This economy of ours is strong, and it's getting stronger.

And the amazing thing is, we've overcome incredible obstacles. Think about the history of this economy. We've been through a recession and corporate scandals and an attack on the United States of America and high energy prices, and we've been through natural disasters. And yet this economy is roaring along, and we intend to keep it that way.

You know, right after the attacks came, right after I got elected and then the attacks, I worked with the United States Congress to pass a progrowth economic policy. It was based on a principle that is profound and works, and that—it says when the American people have more of their own money to save, invest, and spend, the economy grows. The progrowth tax cuts we passed are working. The United States economy grew last year at 3.5 percent. That's faster than any major industrialized nation in the world. Since 2003, we've created 5.2 million new jobs. The national unemployment rate is 4.7 percent. Real after-tax income is 8 percent for Americans since 2001. That means, on average, Americans have an income that is more than $2,300 higher this year than it was at the beginning of 2001, adjusting for inflation. Consumer confidence has been at its highest point in nearly 4 years. Productivity is high. Manufacturing activity is up. People are owning homes. More minority own a home than ever before in our Nation's history. This economy is strong, and we're going to keep it strong for the American people.

I want to remind you, we cut taxes on American families; we cut taxes on everybody who pays taxes. We cut taxes on the small businesses of America; we cut taxes on dividends; we cut taxes on capital gains. We've put the death tax on the road to extinction.

And that stands in stark contrast to the Democrat Party. Here in Washington, DC, most congressional Democrats voted against cutting income tax rates. Most voted against a bill that provided tax relief for married couples. Most voted against a bill that doubled the child credit. Most Democrats voted against a bill to put the death tax on the road to extinction. In 2003, most congressional Democrats voted against cutting taxes on dividends and capital gains. They continue to block our efforts to make the tax cuts permanent. If we want to keep this economy roaring and strong, we have got to make the tax cuts permanent.

The elections this year offer the American people a clear choice: If you want to send more of your paycheck to Washington, DC, vote Democrat. [*Laughter*] If you want to keep more of your paycheck for your family, vote Republican.

We're also going to cut the deficit in half by 2009. You know, there's a myth in Washington, DC, that says we can cut the deficit by raising your taxes. When you're out there helping people get elected, you might remind people, that's not the way Washington works. Sure, they'll raise your taxes, but they're going to figure out new ways to spend your money. The best way to cut that deficit is to keep progrowth economic policies in place by keeping your taxes low and be wise about how we spend your money.

Let me make sure you've got the record about what's taken place in Washington, DC, over the last couple of years. We've cut the rate of growth on nonsecurity discretionary spending. That's discretionary spending other than for the military and the homeland security.

Last year, we had a cut in that discretionary spending. I proposed another budget to do so. The Democrats don't like that idea. They're trying to figure out new ways to spend your money. But the best way to cut that deficit in half is for the United States Congress to join with this administration, set priorities, and be wise about how we spend your money.

I sent a supplemental up to the United States Congress recently to make sure our troops—what they have they need to be able to do their jobs, and to make sure we provide important emergency relief for Katrina. The number was $92.2 billion. And if the United States Congress sends me a bill that includes nonemergency measures that exceed the number I've put out there, I will veto it.

Monday night I gave a speech of real importance for this country. The Republican Party needs to lead on this issue of immigration. The immigration system is not working, and we need to do something about it now. America can be a lawful society and a welcoming society, and we don't have to choose between the two.

And so I talked about a five-point plan to make this country's immigration system work. And the first part of the plan is for the United States of America to secure its borders. I understand something about borders; you might recall I was the Governor of the great State of Texas. We've got a long border with Mexico. I'm very aware of the issue. I know how important it is to secure the borders.

I also know how important it is to treat people with dignity. We've increased funding for border security by 66 percent since I've been the President. We've expanded our Border Patrol from about 9,000 to 12,000 agents. Our Border Patrol folks are doing good work under difficult circumstances. Over the past 5 years, we have caught and returned 6 million people trying to come into our country.

But our border is not yet secure, and there's more work to be done. And that's

what I explained to the American people the other night. And so we're going to increase the Border Patrol agents by another 6,000 by the year 2008. And at the same time, we're going to make sure that we put the most modern technology on our border to make sure our Border Patrol agents can do the job.

And until those 6,000 agents are up and running, I think it's very important for us to help our Border Patrol by providing 6,000 Guard troops. It's really important that we help the men and women in our Border Patrol do their job, so the American people know that we're using manpower, technology, and equipment to do our duty to protect the border of the United States of America.

We're ending a policy called catch-and-release. Eighty-five percent of the folks coming across are from Mexico, and they're sent back within 24 hours. But a lot of people are coming from other countries. The problem with that is we haven't had enough bedspace. So they come in, and a Border Patrol agent finds them, and they say, "Why don't you check back for your court date?" [*Laughter*] A lot of them aren't checking back for the court date. [*Laughter*] So I'm going to work with Congress to expand the number of detention beds, speed up the deportation process, make sure countries know that we're very serious about them taking the people that we catch trying to come into our country illegally. We're going to end catch-and-release.

Secondly, to secure this border, you have got to understand there are people coming to work. They want to put food on the table for their families, and they'll do—they'll go to unbelievable means to come here. They walk across our deserts in the 100-degree heat. They get stuffed in the back of an 18-wheeler to come. They want to come and work. In order to secure this border, we must have an orderly way for people to come, on a temporary basis, who are doing jobs Americans aren't doing.

We must have a rational plan that says, if you're going to come and work, you're allowed to do so, on a temporary basis—you've got to pass a criminal background check, but you ought to be able to come in an orderly way, so you're not having to sneak across. In order to enforce this border, we want people coming to work jobs Americans aren't doing, on a temporary basis, in a legal way.

Secondly—thirdly, in order to make this plan work, we've got to make sure our employers are held to account. It's illegal for somebody to employ somebody here illegally. But the problem we face is that there's a lot of document fraud. See, people are showing up with IDs that an employer can't verify. So in order to make sure we secure our border and do our duty and treat people with dignity, we need to develop a tamper-proof ID card that uses biometrics, and that way, an employer will know whether or not they're hiring somebody who's illegally here. And when the word gets out, you've got to have a tamper-proof card, and you don't have one, it's likely you're not going to come to the United States at all.

Fourthly, you got to understand, in this country, there's a lot of people who have been here for a long period of time—decent, hard-working, honorable people. I oppose amnesty, and the United States Congress ought to oppose amnesty. Amnesty would be harmful for those who have waited in line to become a citizen legally, and amnesty would encourage others to come in the hopes that they, too, would become automatically a citizen. In this debate, we must make sure we distinguish between those who have been here for a while and those who are newly arrived. For those who are newly arrived, they've got to get a temporary-worker card, finish out their time, and go back home.

But for those who have been here for a while, it is unrealistic to deport them. What is realistic is to say, "Pay a fine; learn the English language; prove that you've been working here for a while; and get in line—but the back of the line, not the front of the line."

And fifthly, to make sure we have an immigration system that upholds our values and speaks to the decency of America, we must help people assimilate into our country. And the best way to assimilate is to help folks learn to speak the English language.

When you learn to speak the English language, and you're a hard worker, you're likely to go from somebody who's picking crops to owning a grocery, somebody who's cleaning offices to working in an office. You know, one of the great things about America is we have been a welcoming society. People come to this country because they want to realize the great American Dream. They want to be able to say, "I'm putting food on the table for my family. I want to own my own home." Every immigrant who comes and works hard lifts the spirit of this country. We're a land of immigrants, and we're better for it. We always got to have confidence in our ability to be one Nation under God.

Ours is a party that recognizes we're too dependent on oil, and we intend to do something about it.

Audience member. All right! [*Laughter*]

The President. I signed a good energy bill, supported by the Republicans. The bill encourages conservation, encourages exploration for oil and gas in environmentally friendly ways, so we become less dependent on foreign sources of oil. And it's a bill that encourages alternative sources of energy. I firmly believe it makes sense for us to encourage use of ethanol. We want our farmers growing energy and—not trying to buy energy from parts of the world that don't like us.

We're on our way for breakthroughs for automobiles that will be able to drive the first 40 miles on electricity without using a drop of gasoline. The party of Lincoln has been active about spending your money on research and development to find new ways to power automobiles, to find better ways to burn coal, to be able to use solar energy. My point to you is we understand, as a Republican Party, that it's in our economic interests, in our national interests, national security interests, to get off our addiction to foreign oil.

Ours is a party that's doing something about the cost of health care. The other ones are good about talking about it; we're actually doing something about it. You know, we have a duty, in my judgment, to help the poor and the elderly. That's a commitment our country has made, and it's a commitment the Republican Party is keeping. I want to remind you that for years, the Democrats have promised our seniors a stronger Medicare system. But we delivered. You see, it didn't make any sense to have a Medicare system where decisions were made out of Washington, DC, and that would pay $25,000 for an ulcer surgery but not one single dime for the prescription drugs that would have prevented the surgery from being needed in the first place.

And so we reformed Medicare. We said to our seniors, "We trust you; we trust you to make decisions that meets your needs." Do you realize in the State of Florida, there's over 40 different plans from which a senior can choose a prescription drug benefit? See, Republicans believe in choice. We believe that when you're able to make a choice in the marketplace, it helps affect cost and quality at the same time.

You know, the Medicare drug benefit really does help our low-income seniors. I don't know about you, but I didn't like those stories about some of our seniors having to choose between food and medicine. We stepped up and delivered a Medicare bill, and no longer do poor seniors in America have to make that choice.

Ours is a party that understands the best health care system is when the doctor-patient relationship is central to decision-making. That's why we're strong believers in health savings accounts. That's why we

believe in transparency in pricing. That's why we believe in information technology.

We also understand that small businesses have trouble buying insurance so they can afford it for their employees. And so we believe small businesses ought to be able to pool risk across jurisdictional boundaries so they can buy insurance at the same discount big businesses get.

We also fully understand that junk lawsuits are driving good doctors out of practice and driving up the cost of medicine. Ours is a party that supports medical liability reform. And when you're out there talking to your friends, I want you to remind them that last week, Senate Democrats defeated the opportunity for small businesses to pool risk and once again defeated our ability to provide medical liability reform so that health care is available and affordable to the American citizens.

Finally, ours is a party that will continue to work to build a culture of life where every human—every human—is respected. You know, I passed—we passed and I signed a ban on partial-birth abortion. It is the right thing to do for the American people, to recognize the value and worth of every human being in our society.

Ours is a party that understands government can pass out money but it cannot put love in a person's heart. And so we make sure that faith-based and religious charities are treated on an equal basis when it comes to providing compassion for those who need help.

Ours is a political party that understands we need to have people on the bench who understand the difference between legislating and being a good judge. I was proud to nominate Chief Justice John Roberts and Justice Sam Alito, and I want to thank the United States Senate for passing—for confirming these two good men.

I've also successfully appointed 44 courts of appeal judges, which is about 25 percent of all the Federal appeal court judges in our Nation. I'm going to continue working with Members of the Senate to make sure my judges get a timely hearing, and I'm going to continue nominating good, conservative judges who will interpret the law and not legislate from the bench.

Ours is a party that believes in the sanctity of marriage, and ours is a party that believes in strong families. We got something to run on. We got something other than rhetoric to run on. We're going to run on principles and a strong record. And I'm confident, with your help, we'll continue to maintain our majorities in the United States Senate and the United States House, and America will be better off for it.

I'm looking forward to the contest. [*Laughter*] I'm looking forward to getting out there among the people again, talking about what I believe in. I believe that because of Members of the House and the Senate working with the administration, that this country is more secure. I believe we're laying the foundation of peace; I truly believe that. I believe history is going to look back at this time and say, thank good-

ness we had people in the United States Congress and the House of Representatives, good strong Republicans, people that stay true to our values, that when the times got tough, we didn't try to take the easy course, that we understood that there's universal truths and we didn't back off of them, and that we understood to keep this economy strong and America hopeful, that government must always trust the American people.

It is a joy to be your President. I'm proud to be here with you. May God bless you all, and may God bless our country.

NOTE: The President spoke at 6:58 p.m. at DAR Constitution Hall. In his remarks, he referred to Martha Schar, wife of Dwight Schar, finance chairman, Republican National Committee; and former President Saddam Hussein, President Jalal Talabani, Prime Minister-designate Nuri al-Maliki, and Speaker of the Parliament Mahmoud al-Mashhadani of Iraq.

Remarks Following a Tour of the Border in Yuma, Arizona
May 18, 2006

Thank you all very much for allowing me to come by and say hello. It's good to be here in Yuma. I'd never been to Yuma before. [*Laughter*] I'd like to come back. It's a hospitable place with good weather. [*Laughter*] Remember, I was raised in west Texas. [*Laughter*]

I've come down here to first of all thank the men and women of the Border Patrol for doing a fine job on behalf of the American people. A lot of time, you don't get the credit you deserve, but there's a lot of folks who understand how hard you work. And we really appreciate it. So on behalf of a grateful nation, thanks for doing an important job.

I'm down here to talk about the immigration issue. And this is an important issue. It really is. It's an important debate our country is having. We need to have—we need to secure our border, and we need fair and effective immigration laws. The other night I spoke to the country about the way I see it, and I'm looking forward to working with the United States Congress to get something done.

There's a lot of politics in Washington, DC. And it's time to get rid of all the politics and do what's right for the United States of America and help you do your job. And that's why I've come to this part of the world. I wanted to hear firsthand from David and Ronald Colburn what they need to get the job done and where we're making progress and where we aren't making progress.

I think it helps to have the President out here, seeing the part of the area of the country that one time was overrun by people coming in here—that's beginning to get settled down because of a strategy that's being employed. And so I really want to thank you all for greeting me. Plus, I liked riding in the dune buggy. [*Laughter*]

I appreciate very much your Governor for being here. Governor Napolitano is with us today. Thank you very much for coming. I'm honored you're here. She's an important person as part of helping to implement this strategy; after all, she's the commander in chief of the Arizona National Guard. And I'm going to talk a little bit about the Guard's presence here on the border to help the Border Patrol do its job.

But I also want to thank the Members of the United States Congress who flew out here with me. It's a good bunch, a little rambunctious at times, but they're—I enjoy being with them. I call them friends. Congressmen Kolbe, Hayworth, Shadegg, Flake, and Franks—appreciate you guys taking time out of your day to come down. You care a lot about your State, and you care a lot about this issue. And I appreciate you being here.

I want to thank Senator Ken Bennett. He's the president of the Arizona Senate. Senator, you didn't need to come down here, but I'm grateful you did. And I also want to thank Speaker Weiers for being here as well. I appreciate your interest in the subject. The mayor, Mayor Larry Nelson, is with us. Mr. Mayor, thank you for coming.

I want to thank all the other State and local officials. I want to thank Major General David Rataczak. He's the head of the Arizona National Guard. We're going to be working with our Guard. Don't go overboard for the guy. [*Laughter*] We're going to be working closely with our Guard around the country to help the Border Patrol do its job.

I want to thank all the folks who are here for taking time out of your day to give me a chance to come and visit. I particularly want to thank the local law enforcement officials as well.

I understand that illegal immigration is a serious problem. And one of our jobs in public office is to fix problems, is to deal with a problem in a rational way and not pass them on to other people. And I spoke to the country the other night because I want to fix the problem. And I want to work with people in Washington to do so. People here know firsthand that illegal immigration puts big pressure on our local communities, puts pressures on the schools, puts pressures on the hospitals, puts pressure on the State and local budgets, puts pressures on your penal system. I know that.

Our country is a country of laws, and we've got to enforce our laws. But we're also a nation of immigrants, and we've got to remember that proud tradition as well, which has strengthened our country in many ways. These are not contradictory goals: to remember our heritage and uphold our laws. America can be a lawful society and a welcoming society at the same time.

There's a debate in Washington, and the House started the debate by passing a strong enforcement bill last December. And now the Senate is debating. And I do want to compliment the Senators from this State—Senator McCain and Senator Kyl—for taking the lead. They understand the importance of getting this issue solved, and they're on the floor of the Senate debating a good immigration bill. And they've offered thoughtful proposals, for which I am grateful.

The Senate needs to get the bill out, and get it to what they call the conference committee so we can work hard to iron out the differences between the House and the Senate. I support, strongly support a comprehensive reform bill though. It needs to have five key elements to it.

First, as I mentioned to you, we're going to secure our borders. That is the duty of our country. It's a sovereign responsibility. We want the border to be open to trade and lawful immigration, and we want our borders shut to illegal immigrants as well as criminals and drug dealers and terrorists. That's the objective.

You might remember, I was the Governor of a border State, so I understand how big the border is. I would suggest to Members of Congress, as they debate this issue, that they ought to come down and take a look at the border, see what it's really like. It requires an intense focus of resources and assets in order to secure this border. It also requires a comprehensive strategy as well.

Since I became the President, we've increased funding for our border security by 66 percent. That's helped upgrade equipment, infrastructure. Border Patrol agents have gone from 9,000—about 9,000 to nearly 12,000, a significant increase of Border Patrol agents, so that we can have more people in the frontlines of doing our duty.

Here, we've added about—more than 100 Border Patrol agents in the Yuma Sector in the last year. In other words, people are beginning to see, those on the frontline of protecting the border are beginning to see additional agents coming on board. That's about an increase of 20 percent, to more than 660 agents. This border—this sector was overwhelmed at one time from people coming across illegally. I understand that. And one way to help deal with that problem is to increase the number of agents on the frontline, which is what the leadership of the Border Patrol has done.

We saw some new fencing taking place. It makes sense to use fencing along the border in key locations in order to do our job. We saw lighting. I just saw the cameras in place where we're beginning to install—modernize the border, is what I'm telling you. We're in the process of making our border the most technologically advanced border in the world.

Interestingly enough, I don't think most Americans know this, but over the past 5 years, Federal agents, like our Border Patrol agents, have apprehended and sent home about 6 million people—6 million people since 2001 coming into this country illegally. I mean, we've got some people working hard.

Last year, agents in the Yuma Sector apprehended more than 70,000 illegal entrants. That's up from 14 percent. People's work is making a difference, but we do not have full control of the border. And that's what I want you all to understand—I realize, and a lot of people in Congress realize.

And so here's the part—here's the strategy: We're going to increase our Border Patrol by another 6,000 agents. That will have doubled the Border Patrol from 2001. We should have those agents on line by 2008. We're going to make sure we continue to be wise about how we enable you to do your job better, with technologies and high-tech fences in urban corridors and patrol roads and barriers in rural areas and motion sensors, infrared cameras, unmanned aerial vehicles. All the equipment is aimed to enable the Border Patrol to do their job. We're adding additional equipment which will enable the 18,000 Border Patrol agents we'll have in place to be able to effectively control this border.

It's going to take time to get the technology in place, and it's going to take time to train the Border Patrol agents. And yet the need to enforce the border is urgent, and that's why, in coordination with our Governors, we're going to send 6,000 National Guard troops to be deployed on the southern border.

Now, the reason why I think this strategy is important is because deploying the 6,000 troops to complement the work of the Border Patrol will get immediate results. And it's time to get immediate results. And so I want to thank Governors like Janet for her understanding about the need to utilize assets to do our job to enforce the border.

The Guard is going to support border control efforts. And the Border Patrol, of course, will be in the lead. The Guard will operate surveillance and communications systems. They will install fences and vehicle barriers. They're going to help build patrol roads. They'll analyze intelligence. They will help spot people. But the Border Patrol will be involved in direct law enforcement. The Guard is going to free up agents to be in direct contact with those trying to sneak across. It is—the Guard is complementary. The Guard makes it easier for the Border Patrol to do its job.

And the initial commitment will last for about a year for the 6,000—for the Guard, and after that, the forces will be reduced as new Border Patrol agents and new equipment comes on line.

There are more than 400 Guard members deployed along the Southwest border. In other words, this is something we've tried; this isn't anything new. The Governor has deployed Guard down here before. We've got Guard already helping the Border Patrol right now. The missions are directly related to their specific skills. In this sector, men and women from the Arizona Guard are assisting with communications and intelligence. Guard personnel from Pennsylvania and Ohio are helping install new infrastructure and technology. So the strategy I'm announcing—I announced last Monday has already started to work.

State and local law enforcement in border communities are also a part of the strategy. And so we're going to draw on their expertise and provide new resources. We're going to increase Federal funding for State and local authorities assisting the Border Patrol on targeted law enforcement missions. The Federal Government isn't telling you what to do, but we are saying that if you choose to help the Border Patrol, that you'll be reimbursed for targeted enforcement missions. And we're going to help—we'll give State and local authorities

specialized training to help Federal officers apprehend and detain illegal immigrants.

As we catch more people crossing the border illegally, we got to make sure they're all returned home. And one of the problems we've had here in the border, that Border Patrol agents will tell you, is the problem of catch-and-release. Now, more than 85 percent of illegal immigrants caught—who get caught crossing the border are from Mexico. And they're sent home within 24 hours, and that's good. Part of having a secure border is people have got to understand when you're caught, you're sent home.

But the problem is, is that it's not so easy to send home illegal immigrants from other countries. For many years, we didn't have enough space in detention facilities. You all know that. And so what would happen is somebody would get caught; the Border Patrol would do their job. They'd work hard to enforce the border, and some of the—a judge would say, "Show back up; we'll see you back here in 30 days." Well, guess what? There was nobody back in 30 days. They went and headed into society. We've got to stop that practice. In order to make sure the Border Patrol is effective and do their jobs—I can't think of, frankly, anything more discouraging than to be out there doing—working as hard as you possibly can, apprehend somebody, and the next thing you know, they're let back out.

And so we're going to add detention facilities. We'll continue to—we've added some already; we're going to continue to add more. We're going to expedite the legal process to cut the average deportation time. And the State Department, along with the White House, is going to continue to work with Governments to say, "Look, we want you to take these folks back. You've got to make sure that when we start sending them back that you take them back."

And we're making some pretty good progress. We've caught—we've ended catch-and-release for illegal immigrants from some countries. And so I'm going to ask Congress for funding and legal author-ity to end catch-and-release at the southern border once and for all, for all countries.

I strongly believe that to have—secure the border, we need to have a temporary-worker program. And the reason why I do is I understand there are many people on the other side of the border who will do anything to come and work. And that in-cludes risking their life crossing your desert or being willing to be stuffed in the back of an 18-wheeler. I believe in order for the Border Patrol to be able to effectively do their job, we've got to have a plan in place that will reduce the people who are trying to sneak across.

A temporary-worker program would cre-ate a legal path for foreign workers to enter a country in an orderly way for a limited period of time. A temporary-worker pro-gram would reduce the number of people trying to sneak across. A temporary-worker program would reduce the appeal of human smugglers. There's a whole industry that has sprung up that traffics in human beings, that degrades the human soul. *Coyotes*—that's a familiar word here in this part of the world. A lot of people around the coun-try don't understand what a *coyote* is, but they're somebody who, for money, will smuggle people into the United States so they can work.

We want to know who is coming in the country and who is not coming in the coun-try. And so I think it makes sense to say, if someone is willing to do a job Americans aren't doing, here's a temporary way to come and work. Here's a tamper-proof card, so you don't have to sneak across the border. You could walk across the bor-der, and you can do that work, and when your time is up, you go home.

Now, these people are going to have to pass a criminal background check, but we've got to recognize there are people here doing jobs Americans aren't doing. You know it as well as anybody in this part of the world. And it seems like to me, there ought to be an orderly way, a

rational way, to deal with those workers—with a temporary-work plan.

And by the way, issuing a card, a tamper-proof card, will make it easier for us to enforce the law in the interior of our coun-try. It is against the law for an employer to hire somebody who is here illegally. That's the law of the United States. We're a nation of laws; we'll uphold the laws. But how can you ask employers to uphold the laws when they're not sure whether the documents they're looking at are fraud-ulent?

So not only has the current immigration system caused a whole smuggling industry to come up, but there's also a document forgery industry. We want our employers to be able to be confident about who they're hiring. That's why we need a tam-per-proof ID card based upon modern bio-metrics.

Fourth, it is important to resolve the sta-tus of million illegal immigrants who are here already. First of all, in this debate, there should be—nobody should be given an automatic citizenship—that's called am-nesty. I oppose amnesty. Amnesty would be unfair to those who are here lawfully, to those who have played by the rules. Am-nesty would undermine the rule of law, and amnesty would invite a further wave of illegal immigrants.

There are some in this country who be-lieve we ought to deport everybody who has been here. I just don't think it's going to work. I don't think it makes sense. And so I believe there's a rational middle ground between automatic citizenship and a program of mass deportation.

And here it is. First, it's important for the law to distinguish between someone who has crossed the border illegally—re-cently—and someone who has worked here for many years and has a home and raised a family and has a clean record. For that person, the person who has got roots in our country, I believe that person should pay a meaningful fine, pay their taxes, learn English, prove they've worked in a job for a number of years, and then that person should be able to apply for citizenship—but would not be granted an automatic citizenship, but instead would be at the end of the citizenship line.

In other words, people have been here legally, somebody who pays their dues, pays their taxes, pays a fine, proven to be a good citizen, they get at the end of the line. Someone said, well, that's amnesty—that's not amnesty. Amnesty is automatic citizenship. This is a rational way to deal with people who are God-fearing, decent people, and respect their dignity at the same time.

Fifth, we've got to honor the great American tradition of the melting pot. Americans are bound together by shared ideals and appreciation of our history, of respect for our flag and ability to speak the English language. There's certain things that unite us, no matter where we're from or what our background has been.

I want people to understand, as we go through this debate, that I fully understand English is the key to unlocking opportunity in America. Part of the greatness of America is that we've been able to help assimilate people into our society, people from all kinds of backgrounds who have come here to seek a better life and become American, because we have the capacity to assimilate.

And part of that assimilation process is English. I believe this: If you learn English and you're a hard worker and you have a dream, you have the capacity from going from picking crops to owning the store or from sweeping office floors to being an office manager. That's been the greatness of America, when you think about it. People have come here with a dream and have worked hard and realized that dream.

And yet because we're from different backgrounds, we've all been able to be one America, one Nation under God. And so part of a rational immigration plan has got to remember that helping people assimilate into our society is a really important part of making sure we have an immigration system that works.

I strongly believe that Congress needs to pass a comprehensive immigration bill, because you cannot secure the border unless you have all elements of a comprehensive plan in place. Doing our duty to secure the border requires a comprehensive approach. The United States Senate needs to end by the act—act by the end of this month. They need to do their duty and get a bill out so we can get on about the business of getting a comprehensive bill to my desk.

We have a duty in Washington, DC, to conduct this debate with dignity and honor. Immigration is an emotional issue. Sometimes people get carried away on the issue, and they—in doing so, they forget the greatness of our country, that we are a land of immigrants, that we've always been a haven for better opportunity, that we welcome people who are willing to abide by our laws and work hard and raise their family and trust in the Almighty. America's greatness has been and always will be the fact that we are one Nation under God.

Thanks for letting me come by.

NOTE: The President spoke at 12:51 p.m. at the Yuma Sector Border Patrol Headquarters. In his remarks, he referred to David V. Aguilar, Chief, and Ronald S. Colburn, Chief Patrol Agent, U.S. Border Patrol; Gov. Janet A. Napolitano of Arizona; and James P. Weiers, speaker, Arizona State House of Representatives. The Office of the Press Secretary also released a Spanish language transcript of these remarks.

Statement on House of Representatives Passage of Federal Budget Legislation
May 18, 2006

The House's vote to pass a responsible budget marks a positive step toward controlling Federal spending. This Budget Resolution helps enforce spending discipline and moves us in the right direction to fund our Nation's key priorities. I congratulate Chairman Nussle, the House leadership, and all Members of the House who voted for this budget for their hard work and commitment to spending restraint.

Message to the Congress on Continuation of the National Emergency Protecting the Development Fund for Iraq and Certain Other Property in Which Iraq Has an Interest
May 18, 2006

To the Congress of the United States:

Section 202(d) of the National Emergencies Act (50 U.S.C. 1622(d)) provides for the automatic termination of a national emergency unless, prior to the anniversary date of its declaration, the President publishes in the *Federal Register* and transmits to the Congress a notice stating that the emergency is to continue in effect beyond the anniversary date. In accordance with this provision, I have sent the enclosed notice to the *Federal Register* for publication. This notice states that the national emergency declared in Executive Order 13303 of May 22, 2003, as expanded in scope by Executive Order 13315 of August 28, 2003, and modified in Executive Order 13364 of November 29, 2004, is to continue in effect beyond May 22, 2006. The most recent notice continuing this emergency was published in the *Federal Register* on May 20, 2005 (70 *FR* 29435).

The threats of attachment or other judicial process against (i) the Development Fund for Iraq, (ii) Iraqi petroleum and petroleum products, and interests therein, and proceeds, obligations, or any financial instruments of any nature whatsoever arising from or related to the sale or marketing thereof, or (iii) any accounts, assets, invest- ments, or any other property of any kind owned by, belonging to, or held by, on behalf of, or otherwise for the Central Bank of Iraq create obstacles to the orderly reconstruction of Iraq, the restoration and maintenance of peace and security in the country, and the development of political, administrative, and economic institutions in Iraq. Accordingly, these obstacles continue to pose an unusual and extraordinary threat to the national security and foreign policy of the United States. For these reasons, I have determined that it is necessary to continue the national emergency protecting the Development Fund for Iraq, certain other property in which Iraq has an interest, and the Central Bank of Iraq, and to maintain in force the sanctions to respond to this threat.

GEORGE W. BUSH

The White House,

May 18, 2006.

NOTE: The notice is listed in Appendix D at the end of this volume.

957

Message to the Congress on Continuation of the National Emergency With Respect to Burma
May 18, 2006

To the Congress of the United States:

Section 202(d) of the National Emergencies Act (50 U.S.C. 1622(d)) provides for the automatic termination of a national emergency unless, prior to the anniversary date of its declaration, the President publishes in the *Federal Register* and transmits to the Congress a notice stating that the emergency is to continue in effect beyond the anniversary date. I have sent the enclosed notice to the *Federal Register* for publication, which states that the Burma emergency is to continue beyond May 20, 2006, for publication. The most recent notice continuing this emergency was published in the *Federal Register* on May 18, 2005 (70 *FR* 28771).

The crisis between the United States and Burma arising from the actions and policies of the Government of Burma, including its policies of committing large-scale repression of the democratic opposition in Burma, that led to the declaration of a national emergency on May 20, 1997, has not been resolved. These actions and policies are hostile to U.S. interests and pose a continuing unusual and extraordinary threat to the national security and foreign policy of the United States. For this reason, I have determined that it is necessary to continue the national emergency with respect to Burma and maintain in force the sanctions against Burma to respond to this threat.

GEORGE W. BUSH

The White House,
May 18, 2006.

NOTE: The notice is listed in Appendix D at the end of this volume.

Letter to the Speaker of the House of Representatives Requesting Additional Funds for Border Security
May 18, 2006

Dear Mr. Speaker:

On May 15th, I outlined to the Nation a comprehensive immigration reform initiative with five objectives. As part of my first objective to secure our Nation's borders, I ask the Congress to consider the enclosed requests for an additional $1.9 billion for the Departments of Defense, Justice, and Homeland Security, which is in addition to supplemental funding requested on February 16th for the Global War on Terror and the consequences of Hurricane Katrina. This additional amount is offset by a $1.9 billion reduction in the amount requested on February 16th for the Department of Defense.

The revised request for the Department of Homeland Security will support my Administration's commitment to gain full control of the borders through the deployment of additional Border Patrol agents, infrastructure, and technology (such as hundreds of miles of new roads, vehicle barriers, tactical communications, and aerial surveillance).

The request for additional resources, coupled with additional legal authority from the Congress, will end the practice of catch and release along our southern border once and for all by increasing detention, transportation, and removal capabilities.

The revised request for the Department of Defense will support the deployment, in coordination with the Governors, of up to 6,000 National Guard members to the southern border. There, they will assist the Border Patrol by operating surveillance systems, building infrastructure, analyzing intelligence, and providing training until new Border Patrol agents and technologies come online. The request increases funding for training and other assistance for State and local authorities to support the Border Patrol on targeted enforcement missions. The request for the Department of Justice will provide additional resources for the prosecution and adjudication of illegal immigration cases.

I designate these proposals in the amounts requested herein as an emergency requirement. I urge the Congress to act expeditiously to address the security needs along the Nation's borders.

The details of these requests are set forth in the enclosed letter from the Acting Director of the Office of Management and Budget.

Sincerely,

GEORGE W. BUSH

Message on the Observance of Cuban Independence Day, 2006
May 18, 2006

I send greetings to those celebrating the 104th anniversary of Cuban Independence.

The hope of freedom is found in every heart, and it is the future of every land. The United States is committed to advancing the values that sustain liberty and helping establish a just and peaceful government in Cuba. On this anniversary of Cuba's independence, we look forward to the day when Cuba embraces democracy and human rights for all her people.

This anniversary also is an opportunity to recognize the generations of Cuban Americans who have contributed to the vitality, success, and prosperity of our great Nation. Through their devotion to faith, family, and freedom, they have helped make our country stronger and better.

Laura and I send our best wishes. May God bless the people of Cuba.

GEORGE W. BUSH

NOTE: This message was released by the Office of the Press Secretary on May 19. An original was not available for verification of the content of this message.

Remarks on American Competitiveness in Highland Heights, Kentucky
May 19, 2006

The President. Thanks. Please be seated. Geoff, thanks for the introduction. He said I was the last sitting President—the last sitting President to be here before me was a Texan. [*Laughter*] I don't know what took the other ones so long to get here—[*laughter*]—but I'm proud to be here; particularly proud to be in NKU, Northern Kentucky University. Thank you very much for letting me come by.

It's a good place to come to, to make sure that America understands we don't need to fear the future because we can shape it. That's what I want to talk to you about today, is the need for the United States of America to remain the leader of the world. And one way you remain the leader is you have places like excellence—centers like Northern Kentucky University where you've got innovative curriculum, high standards, the willingness to work in your community—all aimed at making sure our kids have got the skills necessary to compete. And that's why I'm here.

So I want to thank the president—Mr. President, thanks for having me. [*Laughter*] He'd probably rather be called doctor. But, Jim, thank you for having us. Thank the faculty for letting me come. I appreciate you teaching; teaching is a noble profession. For the students who are here, one career path you ought to think about is being a teacher. And one thing you've always got to remember is the child's first teacher is a mother and a father.

I bring my RSVPs from Laura. She is giving a graduation speech tomorrow—she just didn't get the invitation to come to NKU to give the graduation speech here. [*Laughter*] If you had been wise, you would have had her and not me. [*Laughter*] She sends her best. She is really, really a good person, and I'm proud to—[*applause*]—I'm proud to call her wife. She's got to be the most patient woman in America. [*Laughter*] She's doing great; she sends her best.

I appreciate very much Congressman Geoff Davis. He's an interesting person. He served his country in the United States military. He didn't have to run for the United States Congress; chose to do so—I think sets a good example for people to understand, public service is a noble calling. And I want to thank you for inviting me here, Geoff.

I appreciate Senator Jim Bunning being here as well. So I was asking him what it was like to face the Cincinnati Reds. [*Laughter*] You might remember those days—[*laughter*]—at least I do. He's not only a fine Senator, he's a wonderful person. And his wife, Mary, reminded me she came here to NKU just a couple of years ago. [*Laughter*] She had the same kind of career my mother did. Got in, got out without a degree, but nevertheless loved the experience. [*Laughter*]

I appreciate very much State Senator David Williams, president of the State senate. Thanks for coming. Make sure they got plenty of money to run this university, Senator. I've known Williams long enough where I can tell him that, see. [*Laughter*] It's great to see you. It's good to see the Judge as well. I appreciate Katie Stine—is with us today. Senator Stine, thanks for coming.

I want to thank the mayor—I want to thank Mayor Roettger, who is the mayor of Highland—the city of Highland Heights. Thanks for being here, Mr. Mayor. I want to thank all the local and State officials here. I want to thank Gary Toebben, who is the president of the Northern Kentucky Chamber. Thanks for having me here. I met Dr. Ed Hughes. If you don't know Ed, Ed is the founding president and CEO of Gateway Community and Technical College.

I want to say a quick word about community colleges. They're a really important part of making sure the United States is able to compete. People around here, if you've got a growing economy and are looking for labor, you need to support your community colleges. They're one of the really important institutions of the United States. And so for the community college students who are here, welcome; thanks for coming. Appreciate you taking advantage of the opportunities available to you.

We're living in historic times. They are exciting times. If you're a student getting ready to graduate from NKU, you've got a job available for you that's paying better than a lot of other college graduates have ever been able to get. This is a good time to be getting out of college.

On the other hand, these are difficult times in some ways, when you think about it. I mean, we're at war. And war is unsettling to people. War puts a strain on the

United States of America. War causes people to think about the future in different ways.

These are times of globalization. In other words, we're all connected now. Competition is coming at the United States from different places around the world. These are times of change. Technology changes so rapidly that it can create a sense of concern amongst our citizens.

I don't know if you know this or not, but by the time somebody gets 30 in this job market, people have changed jobs several times. That stands in stark contrast to the days when previous generations would go to work and stay at the job all their life. Pension funds are different now. We've got 401(k), defined contribution plans as opposed to defined benefit plans. These are changing times. And the fundamental question facing any nation, but particularly ours, is how do we adjust to those times? What do we do about it?

The temptation during changing times and unsettling times, for some, is to retreat and say, you know, it's really not worth it. We've been through this period in our Nation's history, a time when people would look abroad or look afar and say, "Well, these just seem such difficult problems that it's probably best that we don't take them on," or that, "Competition in the economic sphere is such that the best way to deal with that kind of competition is just to wall ourselves off."

Those two tendencies, which have happened in our Nation's history—tenants of thought—would be called isolationism and protectionism. And I'm here to talk today about why it is really important for us to reject those two notions—that the United States of America must not wall ourselves off from the world and must not forget our duty to help lead the world to be a better place.

Now there's a practical reason why we shouldn't isolate ourselves, and that is, there's an enemy that still wants to hurt us. And it's important for you all to know

that everyday that I wake up I think about the war on terror. I knew that after September the 11th—and many of the decisions I make are based upon what happened on that day, September the 11, 2001. My job is to do everything I can to protect the American people. And I knew that after the attacks there would be a tendency by people to say, well, maybe there's not a war, maybe that's just an isolated incident. Part of my job, by the way, was to say to the American people, "Go about your business; create jobs; go to school; raise your families—let us worry about it in Washington, DC."

But I think about this all the time. I know that in order for us to be able to defend ourselves, we have got to be active in the world. Another way to put it is, we will stay on the offense and bring the terrorists to justice before they hurt us again.

What's unsettling about these times for some is that we face a determined enemy. Let me tell you what I think about the enemy. The enemy is—they're coldblooded killers, the best way to describe them. They will take innocent life to achieve a tactical and strategic objective. These are people that are bound by an ideology. See, they're driven by an ideological fervor. In other words, they're not just isolated angry people; they're people that have got a point of view.

Perhaps the best way to describe the point of view is to remind people what life was like under the Taliban in Afghanistan. There's no freedom to dissent, no freedom to worship; if you're a woman, you were a second class citizen; if you were a young girl, you had no chance, very little chance to be educated. In other words, they had a view of the world which is 100 percent opposite of us. And that's the ideology of these people. And they believe it. They strongly believe that they should distort a great religion and convert it to meet their means. It's totalitarian in nature. It's something akin to dealing with fascism and communism but with a different flavor to it.

Now, I recognize some in our country don't believe that, and that's okay. The great thing about our country is, we all have different views. But I believe it. And I know that if we were ever to retreat and isolate and say it's just too difficult to get involved, that ideology would flourish. After all, they've told us what their ambitions are, through intercepted communications and the different ways of finding out information. They have made it clear in their communications with each other that democracies are soft, capitalism is a failed system, and that it's just a matter of time before the United States of America were to lose its nerve.

That's what they believe. They believe if they can make life painful enough, that we will retreat from the battlefield, that we will give them safe haven—allow them to get safe haven. They want to reestablish roots in a country like they did in Afghanistan so they can help topple moderate governments in the Middle East as well as launch attacks against the United States of America. That's what they have said. As your Commander—as your President and as the Commander in Chief, it's probably pretty wise that I take the words of the enemy seriously, which I do.

And so therefore, for those who think it's probably best to let the world kind of drift off without American leadership or American involvement, they really don't see the world the way—at least the way I see it. And I understand some would like to see the world the way they hope it would be. But you've got to have a President who sees the world the way it is. And the way it is, is a dangerous place that requires the United States of America to be on the offense. And so we're waging the global war on terror.

And the global war on terror has a variety of fronts. The two most notable fronts, of course, are Afghanistan and Iraq. In Afghanistan, I said if you harbor a terrorist,

you're as guilty as a terrorist. I know full well that when the President says something, he better mean it. I meant it. And when the Taliban didn't believe us, we liberated the country. And today, there's a new democracy in the world, and that's important, particularly for the students to understand, because eventually I'm going to tie in democracy and peace. But there is a new democracy, and we're helping that democracy survive and grow.

Secondly, I said if you see a threat, you've got to take threats seriously. I saw a threat. Now, I don't want to rehash the history of the decisionmaking that went on in the runup to the war of Iraq. I would just remind people that people in both political parties and people all around the world saw a threat. And I feel strongly that the world is better off without Saddam Hussein in power.

And no matter what your position was on the issue of war in Iraq—and I can understand why good people differ about my decision—but we've got to make sure we don't retreat from the world and allow the good work that has gone on to collapse so that the enemy is able to gain a safe haven from which to create havoc and launch attacks. And so therefore, we have developed a plan for victory. It's not a plan for retreat; it's a plan for victory.

And the definition of victory is to support the Iraqis so they can sustain themselves, govern themselves, defend themselves, be an ally in the war on terror, and deny safe haven to Al Qaida. That's the goal.

The work is difficult work. It's hard to help a society go from a tyranny to a democracy. You see, the people who lived under the thumb of Saddam Hussein were terrorized by him. He divided the society up. He pitted groups of people against each other. He was ruthless in his administration of his so-called justice, and as a result, there's a lot of scarred emotions and distrust.

And yet something amazing happened in December of last year—admittedly it seems like an eternity ago—but 12 million Iraqis defied car bombers, killers, and terrorists and declared in unity, "We want to be free." It's an amazing moment in the history of freedom. They've said to their Government and said to the people, "Look, we want to live in a free society. We want to be able to express ourselves. We want to be able to elect our officials." And so the political process is one that's now moving forward to honor that request, to honor the 12 million who voted.

There's a government forming in Iraq. This is a new process for them. You might remember, we had a little trouble getting our own Constitution up and running; we weren't a perfect democracy in our beginnings either. But nevertheless, what particularly the students now are seeing is, as a result of active involvement—not only to defend ourselves but adherence to some basic beliefs—a new democracy in the heart of the Middle East is emerging.

We're training these Iraqis so they can take the fight to the enemy. I have said clearly to the American people, as the Iraqi forces step up, we will step down. But it's really important for us to understand that if we leave too early, the new democracy will falter. It's in the Nation's interest that democracy prevail, because democracies help yield the peace.

A nation that becomes isolationist will be one that doesn't understand that democracy can change the world, is one that says, well, let's just get out of there before we complete the mission; let's just not worry about what takes place in parts of the world other than, perhaps, our own neighborhood. But to me, that's a bad choice, because, you see, during a period of time when we thought everything was calm, there was resentment and bitterness growing, which enabled an enemy to recruit suiciders who were willing to launch an attack on our Nation, which has caused more people to lose their life than in Pearl Harbor.

And so therefore, I really think it's important for the American Government to work with allies to stay on the leading edge of change, to not lose our nerve, and to remember the lessons of history.

One of the interesting lessons of history is to look at Europe. We had World War I and World War II in a pretty quick period of time, and we lost a lot of troops there. And today, Europe is whole and at peace. So what happened? What caused the world to change? What caused the world to change was, Europe established democracies, and history has proven democracies don't war with each other.

I love to tell the story about my relationship with Prime Minister Koizumi. You know, my dad was a young guy; right before he went to college, he joined up in the United States Navy just like a lot of others did—and I'm sure some of your relatives did the same thing—to fight the Japanese. Yet today, I sit down at the peace table with Koizumi. We talk about North Korea; we talk about Iraq; we talk about how allies can work to keep the peace.

I find it really interesting that that's taking place. And what happened was, was that between the time that the United States fought the Japanese and the time old George W. sitting down there at the table with the Prime Minister, Harry Truman said, let's help the Japanese develop a Japanese-style democracy. See, it's really important for the students here to understand that liberty and freedom have got the—have proven the capacity to convert enemies into allies. And if you're interested in keeping the peace, it's important for the United States of America to lead.

There's something universal about freedom. I believe in the universality of freedom. I believe everybody desires to be free. I don't believe freedom is only owned by America; I don't believe only Methodists can be free. I believe everybody desires to be free, and the United States of America must lead the world to be more free.

But our concern shouldn't just be in winning the war on terror and changing the conditions that enable folks to recruit—in other words, battling the ideology of hatred with the ideology of hope. An active nation is one that also works hard in places like the Sudan, where ours is the only nation in the world that has condemned what's going on in Darfur as genocide. The United States must lead to make sure—[*applause*]. A confident nation that does it's duty in the international community is one that does what we're doing now in Darfur. We provide over 85 percent of the food aid to help the refugees in this area. We're taking the lead in the United Nations to call the world to account.

I believe to whom much is given, much is required. And therefore, it's important for the United States to continue to lead in the fight against HIV/AIDS in places like the continent of Africa. I believe that when we see starvation, this great Nation of ours should lead the world to help feed the hungry. I believe when we see devastation, the United States must continue to be willing to use assets to help people such as those whose lives were turned upside down by the tsunamis or the earthquakes in Pakistan. You see, a confident nation—a nation confident in its ideals and confident in its capacity must continue to lead and not isolate ourselves from the world.

We've got a good economy right now. And that's good news. Unemployment rate is 4.7 percent nationwide. We've got—productivity is up; homeownership is up; after-tax—real after-tax income is up by over 8 percent since 2001. Things are rocking along. The entrepreneurial spirit is strong. And yet when you think about it—when some think about it, they look at our economic future, and they're very worried. They're troubled. See, they're troubled by competition from places like China and India. And I can understand that. These are vast labor markets that are just beginning to grow.

And the response, in some instances, is to say, "Let's just don't—let's don't take them on; let us kind of pull back and wall ourselves off through protectionist policy." For those of you who've studied history, you might remember, we've had this kind of—we've had these decisions before in our Nation's history.

How about the 1920s? You might remember the 1920s, at least through your history books, at least—and that is, is that we were an isolationist nation. We said, "Let them figure it out in Europe; we'll let them work out their differences over there. We don't need to be involved." And we had high protective tariffs—and, by the way, really high taxes. And as a result, there's a worldwide depression. I'm not saying all of it was caused by those tendencies; I'm saying some of it was caused by those tendencies. So we've been through a period of time where we said let's—we lose our confidence; let's not be bold in our willingness to do the right things at home so that we can compete.

My attitude is this about America: We shouldn't fear the future, I told you. And I want to talk to you about some ways that we can shape the future in order to make sure America remains the leader. I'm not only talking about the leader for peace, but I'm also talking about the economic leader of the world. It's in our interests that that be the case. When our Nation leads and remains the most productive place in the world, it means a higher standard of living for our people. It means better wages, better quality of life. It means you're more likely to realize your dream. If we wall ourselves off and stagnate as an economy, it's going to be harder for this great American Dream to continue to renew itself.

And so here are some ideas for you as to how to make sure we continue to shape the future. One is to keep taxes low. The reason why it's important to keep taxes low is because in a global economy, capital will tend to flow where taxes are low. And the other reason why is, is that you want money in the hands of the entrepreneurs.

You might remember, we've been through a lot in the last 5 years: recession; stock market collapse; corporate scandals; attacks on the country; natural disasters; high energy prices. Yet, we're growing; we're strong. And one of the reasons why is, is because we let the people keep more of their own money. See, the theory is, is that when somebody has more of their own money to spend, save, or invest, the economy grows. And so if we're going to be competitive, we've got to make sure that we keep money in the people's pockets. That's how the entrepreneurial spirit remains strong.

It's really important for our citizens to remember that 70 percent of new jobs in America are created by small-business owners. And the more money they have in their coffers, the more likely it is they're going to create jobs for the American people.

Secondly, we want this always to be the best place for entrepreneurship. We want people in our country saying, you know, "If I've got a good idea and willing to work hard, I'm going to take a risk because I want to own my own business." There's nothing better than meeting somebody who says, you know, "I started my business recently, Mr. President, and I'm doing just fine—and by the way, thanks for the tax relief so I can keep some more money to expand."

You'll hear, in Washington, people saying, "Well, we've got to raise the taxes in order to balance the budget." That's not the way Washington works. If we were to raise your taxes, Washington would figure out new ways to spend your money. And it might sound good; the titles of the programs will sound just fine, but we've got to make sure we set priorities with your money. My number-one priority is this: So long as we've got a troop in harm's way, a man or woman in uniform who's risking their lives for the security of America,

they're going to get whatever it takes to do their job. [*Applause*] Thank you all.

But we can cut this deficit in half if we're wise about how we spend your money, by setting priorities. And we will. The interesting thing about progrowth economic policies, coupled with fiscal sanity in Washington, is that when the economy grows, it creates more revenues for the Treasury. Last year, we've got about $100 billion more revenues to our Treasury than anticipated. And this year, there's 11 percent ahead of where we were last year. And so if you hold your spending down by setting priorities and grow your economy, the deficit shrinks. And that's one way to control your budget.

But the real budget problems we face beyond the current account is—of the budget—is the unfunded liabilities inherent in Social Security and Medicare. If this Nation wants to be competitive, we have got to make sure that we reform Medicare and Social Security. And here's the problem, and this is—I'm addressing this particularly for the ones coming up, the people getting ready to get in the workplace, because the truth of the matter is, Social Security is fine for people who are eligible today. And Social Security is in pretty good shape for baby boomers. As a matter of fact, we're the problem. [*Laughter*] We're getting ready to retire—just so happens I turn 62 in 2008, which is a convenient age. [*Laughter*]

But there's a lot of us, see, and we're living longer than anybody anticipated. I'm riding that mountain bike because I'm trying to retard the aging process. [*Laughter*] But a lot of my—baby boomers are more conscious of their health. In other words, we're mindful that if you smoke, it's going to shorten your lifetime, or if you're drinking too much, it will affect you. And so there's been a—there's a health consciousness among my generation. There's a lot of us, and there's fewer people paying into the system, and we've been promised greater benefits, which means we're on a collision course for our younger workers. And you're paying into this system that's going to be broke. And it's going to affect our ability to compete. That's what I'm telling you.

And so Congress has got to listen to this. Let's get rid of all the politics once and for all up there and come together and put a bipartisan solution to Social Security and Medicare so that we can say to a young generation of Americans, "We did our duty." And by doing our duty, by solving a problem that, admittedly, is down the road—but the longer we wait, the more acute the problem is going to be. Now is the time to fix it to make sure the United States of America remains the economic leader of the world. [*Applause*] Thank you all.

I was just getting warmed up, and we're running out of oxygen in here. [*Laughter*]

Trade is an interesting issue. One way to determine whether the Nation has lost its confidence is whether or not the Nation is willing to trade, be a free trading nation. And I can understand people's concerns about imports coming in from China and imports coming in from India. But I don't think we ought to allow those concerns to close down markets. As a matter of fact, I feel very strongly that the United States of America must do the right things internally and also open up markets so that we can keep competition in a global way.

Here's the thing: My job is to make sure that we're treated fairly, that with opening markets—our own markets and getting other people to open their markets, that they treat us the way we treat them, because I strongly believe, one, trade is good for the world; two, it's a good way to alleviate poverty; three, it's important for creating jobs. Northern Kentucky, by the way, benefits from trade. One reason your job base is strong is because we're selling goods made here, elsewhere.

The way I like to tell the American people—it's like China, for example. I was with President Hu. I said, "Mr. President, it's fine for you, selling your goods here, but you've got to understand something about the American people: We just want to be treated fairly. So intellectual property rights, if you have a product here, we're not going to steal the patent—steal the intellectual property rights from you; don't steal it from us. If you—treat our manufacturers well; make sure your currency moves like our currency moves. That's all we want, Mr. President." The American people are fair. And the reason I'm confident in talking about why opening markets will be good for us, because I firmly believe we can compete with anybody, anytime, anywhere. And America must never, never lose that thought.

So I know I shocked some people the other day when I got up and said, we're addicted to oil and that's a problem. But if we're really interested in being a competitive nation, we're going to have to do something about our reliance upon oil—now. So I'm working with Congress to promote what's called this Advanced Energy Initiative. And we're working on a variety of fronts. First, one thing we can do is make sure we promote clean coal technology. We've got a lot of coal—like, 250-some odd years worth of coal. We also care about our environment here in America. And we've also got the capacity to make sure that we develop the technologies that will enable us to use this coal. One way to get off oil and hydrocarbons is to use our coal in an environmentally friendly way, and I believe we'll be able to do so. We're spending a lot of money in Washington, by the way, on clean coal technology, and I think it's a proper use of taxpayers' money to do so.

We're also investigating coal-to-liquid technology. In other words, we'll be able to use our coals to be able to provide liquids that we'll be able to use, as well as an energy source. But there's some other interesting ideas going on. For example, I like the idea of our farmers being able to provide energy to power automobiles; it's called ethanol.

But there will be some technological breakthroughs that allow us to use switchgrass. Somebody said, what is it? Well, it's grass that looks like a switch—[*laughter*]—that grows in dry climate. See, that makes sense, doesn't it, to be able to investigate whether or not we can convert that kind of material to energy? I think we'll be able to. Wood chips—now all of this sounds fanciful to some, which the Internet seemed fanciful at one point in time.

And so we're spending money at the Federal level to investigate ways to be able to diversify. One of the interesting technologies that's now on the market is hybrid automobiles. But there's new battery technology being developed, and I'm told we're close to breakthroughs in this technology that will enable you to drive your first 40 miles on electricity alone. That's a pretty good deal, if we're able to achieve that kind of breakthrough. Particularly in big cities—a lot of people in big cities aren't going to drive 40 miles a day. They may not drive 40 miles a week. But nevertheless, when you start taking that amount of demand off the market, for gasoline, it starts to begin to affect our national and economic security.

In terms of electricity, we have got to move forward with nuclear power. Nuclear power is clean—and we're spending money on solar energy and wind energy. There's not going to be a single breakthrough; there's going to be a variety of sources, of new renewable energy sources that are going to enable us to be able to say to the next generation coming, we're less reliant on oil. It's in our economic interests and it's in our national security interests that we spend money now to develop the technologies that will get us off oil so we can leave behind an America that's com-

petitive, that will be able to compete in the global economy.

I'm now getting to the reason I came here—[*laughter*]—and that is that this country of ours, in order to be competitive, must always be on the leading edge of technological change and, therefore, must be always the best at research and development and, at the same time, must educate our children so they have the skills necessary to fill the jobs of the 21st century.

NKU has got some really innovative programs, kind of a seamless transition from high school to college. You've got math and science fairs. You're focusing a lot of your attention on making sure the skill sets that you teach your children are relevant, that will actually keep us competitive.

Let me talk about research and development right quick. I believe there's a proper Federal role for basic research. The reason why is, there has been some Federal research projects which have made a difference in your lives. People here probably don't understand it, but at least understand this. But the Defense Department spent a lot of money on figuring out ways to communicate, out of which came the Internet. See, the Internet came to be as a result of Federal research dollars being spent. I like to mountain bike; I like to put a little country and western music on my iPod. [*Laughter*] The iPod came to be because of Federal research into microdrive storage and different technologies. And so therefore, in order to make sure America is competitive and that we're the leader of the world, I believe we ought to double the amount of money we spend in basic research at the Federal level.

Secondly, what's interesting is, most research money is spent by the private sector. One of the great things about our system is it encourages people to—encourages corporations to invest so they can remain productive and be able to compete. One of the tools that we've used to encourage people to invest in research and development is the research and development tax credit.

Curiously enough, it expires on a regular basis, which then causes uncertainty. If you're not sure the tax thing is going to be around, you may not want to invest. And so in order to make sure we continue to get the $200 billion a year we get from private sector into research and development, we need to make the research and development tax credit permanent.

Thirdly, if our children don't have the skills necessary to fill the jobs of the 21st century, the jobs are going somewhere else; make no mistake about that. In a global economy, whether we like it or not, whether we're protectionists or confident, the jobs will go somewhere else. And so therefore, it's really important that the United States of America focus hard on the math and sciences. And by the way, we made a pretty good start with No Child Left Behind. And the reason why is, is that we're beginning to change the attitudes towards one of the real keys to success, and that is measurement.

So I go to Washington, and I said, we'll be strongly committed to helping Title I students in particular with additional money, but I want the States and the local governments to show us whether or not the kids are learning. I didn't think that was too much of a request to ask.

We didn't say, "Here, you do this curriculum." We didn't say that. We didn't say, "You've got to hire so-and-so or run your schools this way," because I believe in local control in schools. But we did say, "Why don't you show us—measure." Let's stop guessing in America. Let us know for certain whether or not our children are going to be able to compete in the 21st century, starting with making sure every child learns to read. I don't think that's too much to ask, to make sure every child can read. If you can't read, you're not going to be a scientist or an engineer. You won't be able to fill the jobs of the 21st century.

And so we started No Child Left Behind, and I want to appreciate the State of Kentucky for implementing the No Child Left Behind standards. It says we're going to raise standards—we're not going to tell you how to run your schools, but you need to measure. And by the way, if you find that a child can't read at grade level, here's a little extra money to help. In other words, we use the accountability system to be able to diagnose problems early and solve them before it's too late.

In the old days—you might remember those days—we just kind of shuffled the kids through. And guess who got shuffled through? Inner-city African American kids, just move them through; it's so much more easy; just let them go. Kids whose parents don't speak English as a first language, they're too tough; just move them through. But that's not fair, and it's not right, and it's going to mean America will not be able to compete. And so we shut that practice down, and America is better for it.

And so let me read you some interesting statistics—I'm able to read these to you because we measure. [*Laughter*] In 2005, America's fourth graders posted the best scores in reading and math in the history of the test. In other words, there's a norming test to determine whether or not the local accountability system—standards or systems are making a difference. African American fourth graders set records in reading and math. The Nation's Report Card showed eighth graders earned the best math scores recorded ever. Eighth grade Hispanic and African American students achieved the highest math scores ever.

In other words, we've had an achievement gap in our country, and because we focus on each child and measure and insist that curriculum work, that achievement gap is growing—in order for this country—is shrinking. In order for this country to be competitive, all our students have got to get a good education. Everybody must be drilled in the basics. And now it's time to add. It's time to add math—focus on math and science. This college is going to—this university will benefit by making sure that we've got high school students— junior high and high school students coming out of our—these institutions with the capacity to be interested in math and the skill set necessary to be able to take on some of the really interesting courses being taught here.

And so why am I concerned about math? Well, we also know that by the time a student gets to high school, most of our students have fallen behind the rest of the developed world in math and science. You're able to measure. And that's not good enough for America. It's a warning signal, it seems like to me. If we're going to be a confident nation that doesn't wall ourselves off from the world, that competes and leads, we better make sure the next generation of children coming up not only are good readers but have got the ability to be skillful in math and science and engineering and physics and chemistry.

And here's some ideas for us. First, I believe we ought to expand Advanced Placement programs around the country by providing money to train 70,000 high school teachers over the next 5 years to teach AP. Now, AP is an interesting program. Some of you probably know what it is. Here's the way I like to describe it: We're going to set high standards, and we're going to expect the best. And we're going to have teachers with that skill set necessary to convince students it's in their interest to learn AP. I went to an interesting AP school in Dallas, Texas, and they said it's graduating more AP students than any other high school in the country. Of course, you know how Texans are. Anyway—[*laughter*].

But I walked into a classroom and had a young Latino—guy had a pony tail on, and he said, "I want to be an astrophysicist, Mr. President." And it was child after child—because they had an AP teacher raise those standards—say, I want to be a chemist; I want to be a physicist. We can do this in America. And one way to start is to make sure that AP classes flourish.

Secondly, we're going to have a program that has 30,000, what we call, adjunct professors. These will be math and science professionals who will go into classrooms— one way to say this strategy is to say, "Look, it's okay to be a math—and scientist; it's cool." But we need—I went to a classroom outside of Maryland, and there was a NASA engineer in there, and he could make science really seem interesting to these kids.

Thirdly, we've got to make sure that we have the same rigorous examination of our math curriculum that we did with our reading curriculum. See, we went through a whole process of helping local districts determine whether or not the reading curriculum they were using was going to work. By the way, one way to determine is you measure.

And so Secretary of Education Spellings has established what's called the national math—I signed, through Executive order, her recommendation—the national math panel. They met this week earlier. They're 17 expert panelists and 6 members from other Government agencies. They're going to help design standards and accountability, as well as teaching methods. In other words, we're going to get focused on this, and we expect our States to join us and to focus on math and science. It is really important that we start laying that skill set now for the next generation of Americans if we're going to be confident.

And by the way, in the eighth grade, if you start falling behind in math, you ought to get that supplemental service money, that extra help, just like we provide for third and fourth graders in reading when they begin to fall behind.

Obviously, some are saying, "Well, that sounds great, Mr. President, how about helping those of us who can't go to college, go to college." I'm a big believer in Pell grants. Pell grants are a very important part of making sure American education lays that foundation for excellence. We've increased the number of Pell grants since

I've been your President by a million. We've got 5 million kids now getting Pell grants, and the maximum grant has gone from 3,750 to 4,050. If you qualify, you get 4,050. But I think we ought to provide additional incentives to the Pell grant program. We call them enhanced Pell grants—and we're working with Congress—they've actually just passed the two ideas that I think make sense.

One is that if you're a graduate with a 3.0 and you've taken a rigorous high school curriculum—if you take a rigorous high school curriculum and you go to college and maintain a 3.0 in college for your first 2 years, your Pell grant increases 750 for the first year, 1,300 for the second year. The purpose of this is to say to high schools, keep raising that standard. Keep providing rigorous courses in math and science, and for the students that qualify, there will be a reward. And by the way, once you get into college, there will be an additional $4,000, on top of the Pell grant, for third and fourth year students who have maintained 3.0 and who major in math, science, or a critical foreign language.

And so here are some incentives to build on this strategy to make sure America competes. So before you all pass out, I want to say one other thing—[*laughter*]. Laura said, whatever you do, don't go over to Kentucky and get a little long-winded. I obviously didn't listen. [*Laughter*]

I feel passionately about our country's future. I am optimistic about America. I've got a unique perspective. I am able to see America in a different way from you all. I am able to see these unbelievable acts of kindness that take place on a regular basis here in our country, people willing to say, I want to serve my country by loving a neighbor. I also understand that our value system, our belief in human liberty is just a powerful motivator for good. And I know the entrepreneurial spirit is a way to make sure people are able to realize dreams.

And so what I really want to share with you is I understand that there's some uncertainty and worries because of circumstances today, but you've got a President whose—I've got no doubt in my mind that the world is headed toward peace and that this country is going to remain the economic leader of the world. We just can't lose our confidence. America shouldn't fear the future, because we're going to shape the future.

Thanks for letting me come by.

NOTE: The President spoke at 3:30 p.m. at Northern Kentucky University. In his remarks, he referred to James C. Votruba, president, Northern Kentucky University; Kentucky State Senator Katie Kratz Stine; Mayor Charles W. Roettger III of Highland Heights, KY; Prime Minister Junichiro Koizumi of Japan; and President Hu Jintao of China.

Remarks at a Reception for Congressional Candidate Geoffrey C. Davis in Florence, Kentucky
May 19, 2006

The President. Thank you all very much. Geoff, thanks very much for your kind introduction; thanks for your service. I'm here because there's no doubt in my mind, Geoff Davis is the right candidate for the Fourth Congressional District.

I've gotten to know him. I got to know the kind of person he is. And you know, when you find somebody who is full of integrity, somebody who prioritizes his faith and his family above all else is somebody you need to send back to Washington, DC.

He came and campaigned hard here, and he told you what he was going to do, and he has done what he said he's going to do. Geoff Davis needs to be reelected to the United States Congress for the good of this district and for the good of the United States of America.

You know, one of the interesting things about Washington is we've got plenty of lawyers up there. [*Laughter*] I'm not one. [*Laughter*]

Congressman Davis. Me, neither.

The President. Neither is the Congressman. [*Laughter*] Seems like when you've got somebody who has got the kind of experience we need in Washington—I'm talking about experience outside of politics—that you ought to keep him up there. See, he's a fellow who's a small-business owner. This is a really vibrant part of our country, right here in northern Kentucky. It's a part of the world where the entrepreneurial spirit is strong. And it makes sense to have somebody in the United States Congress who has lived the life that many of our entrepreneurs have lived.

And we're a nation that is at war. And I need allies in the United States Congress, people who understand what the military is all about. This man wore the uniform of the United States of America. Send him back to the United States Congress.

Davis really wanted—he really wanted Laura. He said, "You stay at home, Mr. President." [*Laughter*]

Audience member. Next time.

The President. Yes, next time. Unfortunately, she was tied up. But she's a believer. She wants me to tell you all, thanks very much for supporting this good fellow. I bring a message from her, and I bring a message from myself: Any time when you find somebody who is willing to run, that's making a sacrifice, it means a lot to have the support of the people. And so thank you all for coming today. Thanks for contributing to this man's campaign.

And I want to remind you that money is one thing, but he's also going to need people out working those coffee shops, working the neighborhoods. And so I'm going to thank you not only for what you have done; I want to thank you for what you're going to do, which is turn out the vote to make sure he gets back to Washington, DC.

Anyway, Laura sends her best. And old Geoff is like me; he married well. [*Laughter*] All you've got to do is—if your six kids were 21, it would be a landslide. [*Laughter*]

But we flew down on Air Force One together. We talked about two things, I think, that will interest you. You can get to know a person pretty well when you're with them for a while and nobody else is around listening and there's not any—not any cameras and not any agenda papers. And so guess what he wanted to talk about? First, he wanted to talk about his children. I thought that was interesting. He could have talked about anything. He could have said bridges, or how about——

Congressman Davis. We did talk about— [*laughter*].

The President. How about this, Mr. President? Or why don't you tell them this, Mr. President? Presidents get a lot of advice. Some of it is solicited, and some of it is unsolicited. [*Laughter*] He wanted to talk about his family, how proud he was of his family. He wanted me to make sure I understood that he had six children and that one of them is going to NKU and one of them is 6. [*Laughter*] He wanted me to know how much he loved his wife and how much he respects her. I think that says something about the nature of the man. And I think the voters of this district ought to pay attention to the values of the candidates who are running for office. This is a man who's got strong values, the kind of values we need in the public arena.

Then he wanted to talk about the military. He wanted to share some thoughts. See, he went to West Point.

Audience member. Hey!

The President. Yes.

Congressman Davis. His son went to West Point.

The President. I'm glad somebody appreciates it. [*Laughter*] He wanted to share his experience with me as an officer, a West Point grad who—he's got friends out in the trenches still fighting for America. I think it's interesting to have a Congressman who feels comfortable enough to talk to the President about the command structure, the decisions we make that influence the troops in the field. See, we need people in Congress who understand that once you commit somebody into harm's way, they deserve all the support of the Federal Government. They not only deserve monetary support, they need strong moral support of our Government.

I'm proud also that Jim Bunning is with us today. He's a fine United States Senator, good man. That big right-hander is big enough to be able to see all way in the back. And his wife, Mary, is with him as well. Thank you, Mary. Thank you all for coming.

I want to thank State Senator Dan Kelly, the senate majority floor leader, for being here. Senator, thanks for coming. You make sure you turn out to help this guy turn out the vote.

You know, one of the interesting things about—one of the things I learned in Texas politics is the importance of the—we call them "county judges;" you call them "country judge executives"—"county judge-dash-executive." [*Laughter*] I remember campaigning for my dad in 1964. He was running against—yes, he's a good old boy. [*Laughter*] And he said, "Your job is to go tell them you'll pass out the literature in the courthouse." Then I got in the courthouse, and of course, it was completely empty. [*Laughter*] The courthouses were dominated in those days by the Democrat Party.

Good politics starts at the courthouse. You can tell whether a person is going to do well politically if he can get the court-

house crowd going for him, because that's—local politics always is the base of support. So I'm honored to welcome today Gary Moore, Ralph Drees, and Steve Pendery. These are the county judge executives of Boone County, Kenton County, and Campbell County. And we're glad you're here. Thanks for coming.

I want to thank the grassroots activists who are here. Somebody who is a grassroots activist is somebody who gets on the telephone at the right time and says, "I know Geoff Davis, and it's in our interest, our mutual interest, for you to go vote for him." A grassroots activist is somebody who does the tedious tasks of stuffing envelopes full of mailers that say, here's a good man with a good record. A grassroots activist is somebody who goes to their place of worship and says, "Oh, by the way, we have a duty to vote, and we've got a good man running here; don't let him down." That's what a grassroots activist is. And for those of you who are grassroots activists, thanks very much for being involved in campaigns; thank you for turning out the vote.

Let me talk about a couple of issues that are important. You win elections based not only on your values but what you believe and what you do. See, there's an interesting debate in Washington right now. There's a lot of anger in Washington. But anger is not a philosophy. Anger is not a set of principles. Anger is—you can't win elections by being angry. You win elections by being optimistic and hopeful and leading. That's how you win elections.

And we're in the lead. And I want to thank Geoff for joining this Nation as we lead the world toward peace. Our biggest challenge in Washington is to protect the American people. That's the biggest calling we have. It's the most important responsibility. When somebody says, "Name your most important responsibility, Mr. President," it's easily, "To protect you." I learned that lesson on September the 11th, 2001. It's a lesson I'll never forget as your President, that my most solemn duty is to protect the American people. And therefore, it's important to have allies like Geoff Davis who are willing to stand strong in observing and honoring that duty.

I learned some lessons on September the 11th, and one of them is we face an enemy that is full of hate, that adheres to an ideology that is backwards, an ideology that's the opposite of freedom. An ideology, nevertheless, is one that can bind people together. I learned that these are folks you can't negotiate with; you can't hope for the best. You, kind of, can't sit back and say, well, maybe they'll change their mind. The only way to protect the American people and do our duty is to stay on the offense and bring them to justice. And it's important to have people in the United States Congress who understand that. And Geoff understands that.

Another lesson I learned is that it's really important to make sure this enemy can't find safe haven, can't hide in places so they can plot and plan in order to attack us. See, they have stated their objectives clearly. They want to spread their ideology, and they want us to retreat from the world. They think we will. They think it's just a matter of time for the United States to lose our nerve and to be—and to withdraw.

But they don't understand me, and they don't understand people in the United States Congress, like Geoff Davis. We understand our duty. I said, "If you harbor a terrorist, you're equally as guilty as the terrorist." Just as an aside, when the President says something, he better mean what he says. When a member of Congress says something, they better mean what they say, as well. I meant what I said, and the Taliban no longer is in power, and now 25 million people are free.

One of the interesting lessons of September the 11th, in this world in which we live, is that the United States cannot be complacent when we see a threat. If we see a threat, we must deal with that threat before it comes home to hit us. It used to be, we could see a threat, and

we'd say, wait a minute, we're okay; we've got oceans protecting us—you know, we're fine, because we're pretty well insulated from those kind of threats.

That changed on September the 11th. And I saw a threat. Matter of fact, people in both political parties saw the same threat I saw. Countries from around the world saw the same threat I saw. And the threat was a dictator who had killed millions of his people—killed hundreds of thousands of his people, used weapons of mass destruction, had invaded his neighborhood, declared the United States an enemy, harbored terrorists.

The President must use diplomacy before he ever commits troops into harm's way. We—worked as hard as I could to solve the issue of Iraq peacefully. When we couldn't do so, Saddam Hussein had a choice to make: disclose and disarm, or face serious consequences. He made the choice. The world is better off without Saddam Hussein in power.

And we have a plan for victory in Iraq. And a victory in Iraq is a country that can sustain itself, govern itself, and defend itself, an ally in the war on terror, and someone who will deny that which the enemy has declared they want, which is a safe haven from which to launch further attacks. And we're on our way. And it's really important to have Members in the United States Congress who understand the power of freedom to transform societies, the ability of our fighting forces—if given the proper equipment—to be able to achieve an objective, and not cut and run before the mission is complete.

These are difficult times for the American people. War is tough, particularly when you face an enemy that is able to put bloodshed on our TV screens on a regular basis. See, these people have no conscience; they have no sense of justice; they will take innocent lives in order to drive us out. That's what they're trying to do. And I need allies in Congress who are willing to understand the stakes, who know that there is no option other than victory; that we're not going to retreat; that we're not going to allow the enemy to be able to have a safe haven in Iraq. And we will not abandon the 12 million people who defied car bombers and terrorists and said to the world, we want to be free.

We're going to succeed. We're going to succeed. You know, there are some interesting lessons in history—Geoff and I were talking about them as well. It's important for those of us in Washington to study history and to learn from history. One of the interesting lessons of history is the power of liberty to transform societies. It's happened. It's happened in recent times. World War I was a terrible war; World War II, also a terrible war. Both of them took place on the continent of Europe. And yet there are no wars on Europe today. Europe is free and whole, at peace because democracies don't war with each other. That's one of the lessons of history.

One of my better buddies in the world is Prime Minister Koizumi of Japan. That's probably not much of interest, until you realize my dad—or think about the fact that my dad fought the Japanese. One of the really interesting things that I think about when I visit with Prime Minister Koizumi—and, by the way, when I'm visiting with him, we're talking about the peace; we're talking about how to help democracy in Iraq; we're talking about what to do about the man in North Korea; we're talking about how to work together as strong allies to lay the foundation of peace. I find it interesting, and I think the American people ought to listen carefully to that lesson of history, that because Japan adopted a Japanese-style democracy, an enemy, a sworn enemy of the United States is today an ally in keeping the peace.

The same thing is going to happen in the broader Middle East. As democracy takes hold in the broader Middle East, we will have an ideology that defeats the ideology of terror in place, and someday an American President is going to be sitting down with a duly elected leader of Iraq saying, how do we keep the peace? We're laying the foundation for peace, and I need allies like Geoff Davis who understand the stakes.

Government doesn't create wealth; government creates the environment in which people are willing to take risk to realize their dreams. And there is a fundamental difference in Washington, DC, on how to run this economy. We believe that the best way to run the economy is to let the people run the economy by keeping more of their own money.

This economy of ours is strong: 3.5 percent GDP growth last year; 4.7 percent unemployment rate across the Nation; 5.2 million new jobs in 2½ years. Productivity is on the rise; small businesses are flourishing; more people own a home today than ever before in our Nation's history. More minorities own a home today than ever before in our Nation's history. And the reason it's strong is because of the tax cuts we passed.

And I know what's going to happen if the other party runs the United States Congress; they're going to run up your taxes. Make no mistake about it; their view on how to grow this economy is to take more money out of your pocket. Our view on how to grow the economy is to let you keep more money. The tax cuts need to be made permanent.

Oh, you hear a lot of talk about the deficit in Washington, and the other side will say, well, here's how you solve the deficit—raise your taxes. See, it becomes a convenient excuse. That's not how it works in Washington. And Geoff understands that—that it doesn't work that way, to raise your taxes and balance the budget. No, what happens is, they're going to raise your taxes, and they're going to figure out new ways to spend your money. That's how Washington works.

The best way to balance the budget is to keep progrowth economic policies in place which generate more revenue for the

Federal Treasury and hold down Federal spending. And that's why I need allies like Geoff Davis who are fiscally responsible with the people's money. We're on our way to cutting that deficit in half by 2009.

And by the way, if the United States Congress sees that supplemental I sent up there—that supplemental, by the way, aimed to make sure our troops have the combat equipment necessary to win this war on terror and to help the people down in Katrina—if they bust a 92.2 barrier I put on it, I'm going to veto the bill.

In order to make sure that we're a competitive—I just—by the way, I had a fantastic experience at NKU. I really enjoyed myself there. And it's a wonderful institute here. And I was talking about how to keep America competitive. That's one of the things we need. We need forward-thinking people in Washington, DC, who don't fear the future, because we intend to shape the future. We intend to make sure that we put policies in place that keep us the most competitive nation in the world.

And one thing we need to do in order to be the most competitive nation in the world is to get off our addiction to oil. In order to make sure America has the economic security for the future and the national security that we need, is we've got to do something about oil, and we've got to diversify away from it.

Here's some ideas: one, clean coal technology. We're going to spend research and development money to make sure we can use the coal—250 years worth of coal and burn it in an environmentally friendly way. We can do that. We'll be able to do that.

Secondly, we need to use coal to help get liquid fuels, see. And one of the things about Davis, he understands that. And he put, in the defense bill, $5 million to help us make sure we can extract liquids from coal. In other words, it's a different way to make us less dependent on foreign sources of oil.

We need to change how we drive our cars. I want Kentucky farmers growing the fuel for the future. I'm a big believer in ethanol. We've got battery technology going on that would mean that you can drive your first 40 miles on electricity and your thing doesn't have to look like a golf cart. [*Laughter*]

We're working on new solar technologies. We're working on wind technologies. We're investing in hydrogen so the little fellow here will be driving his car, not driven by gasoline but powered by hydrogen. I need——

Audience member. Good——

The President. I was about to say, this man is a nuclear power guy, and so am I. [*Laughter*] The best way to protect the environment and to have renewable sources of energy is through nuclear power.

And so I need allies in the United States Congress who understand that we have got to diversify away from oil. It's in our national interest and our economic interest that we develop a broad-based energy strategy that will get the job done.

Finally, I do want to talk about the importance of people in Congress who understand that values are important. One of the areas where we're making progress is promoting the culture of life. I think it's really important for our society to be a welcoming society, a society that recognizes everybody has worth, born and unborn.

Geoff Davis is an ally in promoting a culture of life. He's an ally—look, he didn't get to vote on these deals. He's in the House. But I can assure you, he supports my nominees for the Supreme Court and for the circuit court. These are people who will not legislate from the bench, people who are solid constructionists, strict constructionists.

It's really important to have people in Washington who understand that government can hand out money, but government can't put hope in a person's heart. That's done when a loving soul says, "I love you, brother. What can I do to help you?" Some of the most intractable problems in our country cannot be solved by money.

One of the things that we've initiated in Washington is the Faith-Based and Community-Based Initiative, which says to people of faith, you can apply for Federal grant money so that you can help heal broken hearts, and you don't have to lose the core of your mission. And we ought to have people in the United States Congress who understand that in order to solve problems, problems of the heart, that requires a higher power than the United States Government sometimes to do so. Geoff Davis understands that.

You know, de Tocqueville came to America in the 1830s. He came to America and observed that America was such a unique place because of the voluntary associations all across our country, where people would show up to help a neighbor in need. That spirit is still alive in America today, by the way. We've got people doing millions of acts of kindness on a daily basis, and there hasn't been one law that says you've got to do it, except for a higher calling. And the power of government must not stand in the way of those trying to practice their faith to heal open hearts, but to stand side by side with them, and Geoff Davis understands that.

So I've come to northern Kentucky to support this good man and to ask you to continue to support him. He's making a difference in the United States Congress. He understands the challenges of the world in which we face, and he shares the same sense of optimism that I share, that this great country of ours can solve any problem when we put our mind to it. Send him back to the United States Congress and you'll be better off for it.

Thank you, and God bless.

NOTE: The President spoke at 5:34 p.m. at the Hilton Greater Cincinnati Airport. In his remarks, he referred to Pat Davis, wife of Representative Davis; former President Saddam Hussein of Iraq; Prime Minister Junichiro Koizumi of Japan; and Chairman Kim Jong Il of North Korea.

The President's Radio Address
May 20, 2006

Good morning. Earlier this week, I spoke to you from the Oval Office to lay out my vision for reforming our Nation's immigration system. And on Thursday, I went to Arizona to visit with the men and women of the Border Patrol. I wanted to get an update on their efforts because a secure America depends on a secure border.

I believe America can be a lawful society and a welcoming society at the same time. We must enforce our laws while honoring our proud immigrant heritage. So I support comprehensive immigration reform that will accomplish five clear objectives.

First, America must secure its borders. Since I became President, we've increased funding for border security by 66 percent, hired thousands more Border Patrol agents, and caught and sent home about 6 million illegal immigrants. Yet we have much more work to do.

So this week, I asked Congress to provide funding for dramatic improvements in manpower and technology at the border. We'll hire thousands more Border Patrol agents. And to help these agents do their jobs, we will deploy advanced technologies such as high-tech fences in urban areas, infrared cameras, and unmanned aerial vehicles. We'll also draw on the expertise of State and local law enforcement in our border communities and give them new resources and training so they can help secure our border.

Putting these new resources in place will take time. To help during this transition, up to 6,000 National Guard members will be deployed to our southern border. They will assist the Border Patrol by operating surveillance and communication systems, installing fences and vehicle barriers, building patrol roads, and analyzing intelligence. The support of Guard personnel will allow Border Patrol agents to use their skills to focus on securing the border.

Second, to secure our border, we must create a temporary-worker program that provides foreign workers a legal and orderly way to enter our country for a limited period of time. This program would reduce pressure on the border, meet the needs of our economy, and allow honest immigrants to provide for their families while respecting the law. And it will help us make certain we know who is in our country and why they are here.

Third, we need to hold employers to account for the workers they hire by creating a better system for verifying documents and work eligibility. The system should include a new tamper-proof identification card for every legal foreign worker. This card would help us enforce the law and leave employers with no excuse for breaking it. And by making it harder for illegal immigrants to find work in our country, we would discourage people from crossing the border illegally in the first place.

Fourth, we must resolve the status of millions of illegal immigrants who are already here. They should not be given an automatic path to citizenship. This is amnesty, and I oppose it. Amnesty would be unfair to those who are here lawfully, and it would invite further waves of illegal immigration.

Some people think any proposal short of mass deportation is amnesty. I disagree. There's a rational middle ground between automatic citizenship for every illegal immigrant and a program of mass deportation. Illegal immigrants who have roots in our country and want to stay should have to

pay a meaningful penalty, pay their taxes, learn English, and work in a job for a number of years. People who meet these conditions should be able to apply for citizenship, but approval will not be automatic, and they will have to wait in line behind those who played by the rules and followed the law.

Fifth, we must honor the great American tradition of the melting pot by helping newcomers assimilate into our society. Americans are bound together by our shared ideals: an appreciation of our history; respect for our flag; and the ability to speak and write in English. We will work to ensure that every new citizen fully embraces our common culture. When immigrants assimilate, they will advance in our society, realize their dreams, renew our spirit, and add to the unity of America.

Congress is now considering legislation on immigration reform. That legislation must be comprehensive. All elements of this problem must be addressed together or none of them will be solved at all. The House started the debate by passing an immigration bill. Now the Senate should act by the end of this month, so we can work out the differences between the two bills, and Congress can pass a bill for me to sign into law.

We should approach this debate with confidence. America has shown before that we can enforce our laws and uphold our values, and we will do it again. Our Nation honors the heritage of all who've come here because we trust in our country's genius for making us all Americans, one Nation under God.

Thank you for listening.

NOTE: The address was recorded at 7:45 a.m. on May 19 in the Cabinet Room at the White House for broadcast at 10:06 a.m. on May 20. The transcript was made available by the Office of the Press Secretary on May 19 but was embargoed for release until the broadcast. The Office of the Press Secretary also

released a Spanish language transcript of this
address.

Statement on the Formation of Iraq's Government
May 20, 2006

I congratulate Prime Minister Maliki on
the formation of Iraq's new unity Government. Iraqis now have a fully constitutional
government, marking the end of a democratic transitional process in Iraq that has
been both difficult and inspiring. This
broadly representative unity Government
offers a new opportunity for progress in
Iraq.

The new Government reflects Iraq's diversity and opens a new chapter in that
country's history. Iraq's new leaders know
the period ahead will be filled with great
challenge. But they also know that they and
their great country will not face them
alone. The United States and freedom-loving nations around the world will stand

with Iraq as it takes its place among the
world's democracies and as an ally in the
war on terror.

Today, as Iraqis look to their new Government, they can be proud that in 3 years,
they have progressed from the oppression
of a brutal dictator who fomented sectarian
divides to an elected government in which
all Iraqis have a voice. As Iraq's leaders
work together to chart the future of their
nation, bringing freedom and security to
the Iraqi people, they make the world a
safer place for all of us. The sacrifices of
many of our country's noblest and bravest
have helped make this day possible. We
will not forget their contribution to our security and Iraq's democracy.

Remarks on the Formation of Iraq's Government
May 21, 2006

The formation of a unity government in
Iraq is a new day for the millions of Iraqis
who want to live in freedom. And the formation of the unity Government in Iraq
begins a new chapter in our relationship
with Iraq.

This morning I called the President, the
Prime Minister, and the Speaker to congratulate them on working together to form
the unity Government. I assured them that
the United States will continue to assist
the Iraqis in the formation of a free country, because I fully understand that a free
Iraq will be an important ally in the war

on terror, will serve as a devastating defeat
for the terrorists and Al Qaida, and will
serve as an example for others in the region
who desire to be free.

Thank you.

NOTE: The President spoke at 8:33 a.m. in
the Diplomatic Reception Room at the
White House. In his remarks, he referred to
President Jalal Talabani, Prime Minister Nuri
al-Maliki, and Speaker of the Council of Representatives Mahmoud al-Mashhadani of
Iraq.

Remarks on the War on Terror and a Question-and-Answer Session in Chicago, Illinois
May 22, 2006

The President. Thank you all very much. Thanks for the warm welcome. It's great to be back in Chicago, home of the mighty Chicago White Sox, world champs. I said that because the mayor is here—[*laughter*]—who, by the way, is one of the finest mayors in our country. Mayor Daley, thank you for being here. He's a huge Chicago White Sox fan. When I had the White Sox to the White House to congratulate them on the world championship—winning the world championship trophy, there was the mayor, beaming.

The other team here isn't doing quite so well these days. [*Laughter*] As a matter of fact, I had the honor, though, of throwing out the first pitch in the Chicago Cubs home opener against Cincinnati, and they won that game 16 to 7. You know, when you're President, sometimes you get blamed for a lot of things. [*Laughter*] So I want to assure all the Cubs fans here that the last time I saw them play, they were undefeated. [*Laughter*]

I really appreciate being invited here by the National Restaurant Association. Thanks for having me. You know, Laura and I don't eat out as much as we used to. [*Laughter*] But we do appreciate your industry's contribution to the country.

I appreciate your leadership in Washington on really important issues like tort reform and tax relief and immigration reform. I'm going to spend a little time today talking about immigration reform. But the main reason I've come today is to talk to you about a watershed event that took place this weekend in Iraq. On Saturday, in Baghdad, Iraqis formed a new Government, and the world saw the beginning of something new—constitutional democracy at the heart of the Middle East.

And if you like, after my remarks, I'd like to answer some of your questions. So be thinking of them.

But before I get there, I do want to thank Ed Tinsley. He's a west Texan, and like me, he married a woman from Midland, Texas. It's the best decision Tinsley ever made, and it's the best decision I ever made. Laura sends her greetings to you all. She's a fine First Lady, and I'm lucky she said yes when I asked her to marry me.

I appreciate Steven Anderson, the President and CEO of the National Restaurant Association. I appreciate sharing the stage with Denny Hastert. He is an excellent Speaker of the House. He is dependable, reliable, smart, capable. Do you realize that he will have served, come June 1st, longer than any other Republican Speaker in our Nation's history? And the reason why, he knows what he's doing.

And I appreciate Congressman Ray LaHood and Congresswoman Judy Biggert for joining us as well, today. They're here looking for a ride back to Washington on Air Force One. [*Laughter*] I appreciate all the State and local officials for coming too.

Our economy is strong, and it's growing. And the restaurant industry plays a vital role in this prosperity. National unemployment is 4.7 percent. That's lower than the average of the 1970s, 1980s, and 1990s. People are working. We've added over 2 million jobs in the last 2½ years. And one of the main reasons why is because the National Restaurant Association members are employing people. The NRA—National Restaurant Association—estimates that more than 12.5 million people work at 925,000 restaurants across our country. That makes restaurants the largest private employer in our land.

You not only help people put food on the table, but you provide many Americans with their first job, with a start. You teach people the importance of showing up on time and working hard and meeting the needs of our customers. You're also America's largest employer of immigrants, and you know how essential it is that we have an immigration system that is safe, orderly, and fair. And I agree with you, and that's why I laid out a vision for comprehensive immigration reform that would accomplish five key goals.

First, the United States will secure our borders by deploying thousands of new Border Patrol agents and giving those agents the best technology available to do their job.

Secondly, you can't secure our border with thousands trying to sneak in. And therefore, this country needs a temporary-worker program that will allow foreign workers to enter our country legally on a temporary basis to meet the needs of our economy and take the pressure off our border.

Third, we must create a reliable system for verifying documents and work eligibility so we can better enforce our immigration laws at the workplace.

Fourth, we will find a rational middle ground to resolve the legal status of the millions of people who have been here for quite a while, without granting amnesty.

And fifth, we will uphold the great American tradition of the melting pot so America can remain what it always has been, one Nation under God.

The reforms I proposed regarding guest workers are really important for your industry. Your association estimates that restaurants will add—will need 1.9 million new workers over the next 10 years, which means that you need workers—your need for workers will be growing faster than the American labor force. So you understand why effective immigration reform must include a practical and lawful way for businesses to hire foreign workers when they can't fill those jobs with Americans. The restaurant industry has first-hand experience with immigrants and immigration law. And I appreciate your strong stand on Capitol Hill for comprehensive reform.

And here's where we are. The House passed a bill last—an immigration bill last December, and the Senate is working hard on its version of the bill. The Senate needs to complete its bill now so that the House and Senate can work out their differences and pass a comprehensive reform bill that I can sign into law.

We face challenges at home, and we face challenges abroad. So I've come to talk to you about an historic event that took place halfway around the world this weekend. This Saturday in Baghdad, the new Prime Minister of Iraq announced a national unity Government. This is a free Government under a democratic Constitution, and its formation marks a victory for the cause of freedom in the Middle East.

In three elections last year, millions of Iraqis cast their ballot in defiance of the terrorists. And now they have a Government of their own choosing under a Constitution that they drafted and they approved. As this new unity Government takes office, it carries with it the hopes of the Iraqi nation and the aspirations of freedom-loving people across a troubled region.

The unity Government has strong leaders that will represent all of the Iraqi people. I called them this weekend to congratulate them. I thanked them for being courageous and strong and standing for the belief that liberty will help transform their troubled nation.

The new Government is led by Prime Minister Maliki. He's a Shi'a. He's an Iraqi patriot who, for years, was part of the resistance to Saddam Hussein. He's shown courage and wisdom by surrounding himself with strong leaders who are committed to serving all the people. Prime Minister Maliki said this weekend, "Just as we did away with the tyrant and the days of oppression and despotism, we will do away with terrorism and sabotage, backwardness, poverty, and ignorance." The Iraqi people are blessed to have a leader like Prime Minister Maliki, and I'm proud to call him ally and friend.

Iraq's new Government has another strong leader in its President, President Talabani. He's a Kurd who distinguished himself by his service in the transitional government and in his long fight against Saddam Hussein. He's proved that he's not afraid to take the lead. He's made clear that a democratic Iraq must reject sectarian violence as strongly as it rejects terrorism. He says, "It's our duty, all of us, to work hand in hand to protect our people and to support Iraqi unity."

Iraq's new Government has another able leader in Speaker Mashhadani. He'll preside over Iraq's new Council of Representatives. The Speaker is a Sunni who originally opposed America's presence in Iraq. He rejects the use of violence for political ends. And by agreeing to serve in a prominent role in this new unity Government, he's demonstrating leadership and courage. It was said to me that he wouldn't have taken my phone call a year ago. He's now taken it twice. He says Iraq's new leaders must govern by common vision. This common vision is critical to the new Government's success.

Although Iraq's new leaders come from many different ethnic and religious communities, they've made clear they will govern as Iraqis. They know that the strategy of the terrorists and the insurgents is to divide Iraq along sectarian lines. And the only way the enemy will be defeated is if they stand and act as one.

The Government is still a work in progress, and overcoming longstanding divisions will take time. Iraq's new leaders know they have a great deal of work ahead to broaden the base of their Government and to unite the people. They also understand that representing all Iraqis and not just narrow sectarian interests, they will be able to make a decisive break with the past and make a future of progress and opportunity for all their people a reality. The unity Government must now seize this moment and pursue a common agenda for the future.

This weekend Prime Minister Maliki laid out his plan for a new Iraq. He promised to work for a sovereign Iraq that will assume responsibility for the security of its people. He committed himself to a free Iraq that will uphold international standards of human rights and respect the role of women in Iraqi society. He pledged to work for a prosperous Iraq that welcomes foreign investments and accelerates reconstruction and lays the foundations for economic growth and opportunity. He declared he would lead a transparent Iraq where Government is open and accountable and corruption is not tolerated. And he vowed to work for a peaceful Iraq that is the enemy of terror, a friend to its neighbors, and a reliable partner in the community of nations.

The Prime Minister promised that he will soon fill the remaining positions in his Government and announced the details of his plans to build his new country, his new Iraq. As his Government moves forward, it can draw on many strengths of the Iraqi nation. Iraqis are among the most highly educated and skilled people in the Middle East. They have abundant natural resources, including fertile soil, abundant water, and large reserves of oil. And they're rich in cultural and historical and religious sites that one day could draw millions of tourists and pilgrims from across the world. Iraq's new leaders understand that so long as they remain united, there is no limit to the potential of their country.

The unity Government opens a new chapter in the relationship between the United States and Iraq. The new Iraqi Government does not change America's objectives or our commitment, but it will change how we achieve those objectives and how we honor our commitment. And the new Iraqi Government—as the new Iraqi Government grows in confidence and capability, America will play an increasingly supporting role. To take advantage of this moment of opportunity, the United States and our coalition partners will work with the new Iraqi Government to adjust our methods and strengthen our mutual efforts to achieve victory over our common enemies.

At my direction, the Secretaries of State and Defense recently traveled to Baghdad to meet with the Prime Minister and other leaders. And now the new Government has been formed, I've instructed those Secretaries to engage Iraq's new leaders as they assess their needs and capabilities, so we will be in the best position to help them succeed. Iraqis are determined to chart their own future. And now they have the leadership to do it. And this unity Government deserves American support, and they will have it.

Our Nation has been through three difficult years in Iraq. And the way forward will bring more days of challenge and loss. The progress we've made has been hard-fought, and it's been incremental. There have been setbacks and missteps—like Abu Ghraib—that were felt immediately and have been difficult to overcome. Yet we have now reached a turning point in the struggle between freedom and terror.

Two years ago, Al Qaida's leader in Iraq wrote a letter that said, "Democracy is coming," and this would mean "suffocation" for Al Qaida and its allies. The terrorists fought this moment with all their hateful power—with suicide attacks and beheadings and roadside bombs—and now the day they feared has arrived. And with it has come a moment of great clarity: The terrorists can kill the innocent, but they cannot stop the advance of freedom.

The terrorists did not lay down their arms after three elections in Iraq, and they will continue to fight this new Government. And we can expect the violence to continue, but something fundamental changed this weekend. The terrorists are now fighting a free and constitutional Government. They're at war with the people of Iraq. And the Iraqi people are determined to defeat this enemy, and so are Iraq's new leaders, and so is the United States of America.

The path to freedom is always one of struggle and sacrifice. And in Iraq, our brave men and women in uniform have accepted the struggle and have made the sacrifice. This moment would not be possible without their courage. The United States of America is safer because of their success, and our Nation will always be grateful to their service.

For most Iraqis, a free, democratic, and constitutional Government will be a new experience. And for the people across the broader Middle East, a free Iraq will be an inspiration. Iraqis have done more than form a government; they have proved that the desire for liberty in the heart of the Middle East is for real. They've shown diverse people can come together and work out their differences and find a way forward. And they've demonstrated that democracy is the hope of the Middle East and the destiny of all mankind.

The triumph of liberty in Iraq is part of a long and familiar story. The great biographer of American democracy, Alexis de Tocqueville, wrote: "Freedom is ordinarily born in the midst of storms. It is established painfully among civil discords, and only when it is old can one know its benefits." Years from now, people will look back on the formation of a unity Government in Iraq as a decisive moment in the story of liberty, a moment when freedom gained a firm foothold in the Middle East and the forces of terror began their long retreat. Thank you for having me. [*Applause*]

Thank you all very much. Thank you. Thank you all. I'll be glad to answer some questions, if you've got some. Tinsley said it would be helpful if I answered some questions. [*Laughter*]

The President. Let's see, you got one? Yes, sir.

Tax Reform

Q. I was just wondering, being a small-business owner, one of the things we really appreciate about your administration was the tax cuts for small business. And I was just wondering, are those going to be permanent, and are we taking action to make them permanent?

The President. His question is about tax cuts and whether they'll be permanent. First of all, a lot of Americans don't really understand that when you cut taxes on individuals, you cut taxes on a lot of small businesses. Many small businesses are subchapter S corporations or limited partnerships, which end up paying their taxes based upon the individual income tax rates. And so when you reduce taxes on everybody who pays taxes, you're really helping the small-business sector. And why that's—that's an important part of our economic recovery policy, because small businesses create 70 percent of the new jobs in America.

So thank you for recognizing the—thank you for reminding people here the importance of those tax cuts for small business. And also, by the way, there was some incentives in our economic recovery package that encourage you to buy equipment. And when you buy equipment, somebody has got to make the equipment. When somebody makes the equipment, it means somebody is more likely to be able to find a job not only at your place of work but the equipment manufacturer's place of work.

And so his question was, are you going to allow the tax cuts to expire? See, they weren't permanent. My answer is, in order to make sure this economic recovery is lasting and real, the tax cuts need to be made permanent. And the Speaker agrees with me, you'll be happy to hear. It's important for Congress to understand that when there is any uncertainty in the Tax Code, it will

make it less likely someone is willing to invest in a small business and expand their businesses. Uncertainty in the Tax Code creates uncertainty in the investment community or when people make investments.

So we're absolutely committed to making the tax cuts permanent. The argument you'll hear is, well, how can you possibly balance the budget if you make the tax cuts permanent? I guess the reverse of that is, "We want to raise your taxes to balance the budget." Unfortunately, that's not the way Washington works. The way Washington works is they will raise your taxes and figure out new ways to spend the money and not balance the budget.

The best way to balance the budget is to keep progrowth economic policies in place. I think you're going to find a report coming out this summer to be very interesting. In other words—last year, by the way, we exceeded the estimated revenues by about $100 billion. The economy is cranking. When the economy works, people are employing people, and when people are making money, they pay more taxes. Right now it looks like that the revenues coming into our Treasury are greater than anticipated this time around too.

And so the best way to reduce our deficit is to keep progrowth economic policies in place—hence, permanent tax cuts—as well as being wise about how we spend your money. And the best way to be wise about how we spend your money is to set priorities. And my priority is to make sure our troops have what it takes to defend the United States of America.

Voluntarism

Q. Mr. President, my daughter's name is Jamie. She's a 16-year-old girl. What advice or recommendations would you give to her and to other youth of our country to help make our country a better place?

The President. Thank you. I would say that—to Jamie, listen carefully to that universal admonition to love a neighbor like you'd like to be loved yourself. You know,

I get an interesting perspective of America. I, of course, get to see the incredible folks who wear our Nation's uniform. It's unbelievably inspiring to meet men and women who have volunteered to serve our country in a time of war. And not only do I get to meet them, I get to meet their families. I also get to meet the entrepreneurs of America, people who are willing to risk time, effort, and money to grow a business. And as a result, we've got a great—we've got fat wallets relative to the rest of the world.

But the true strength of the country lies in the hearts and souls of our citizens. That's the really unbelievable strength of America. I get to meet people all the time. I met two youngsters today, Chinese Americans, who volunteered to go down to help the Katrina victims. Nobody told them to do it. There was no government law that said, "You're going to go down and love your neighbor." They heard the call.

And so my advice is to tell your daughter that she can be a part of a changing America by helping somebody who hurts; feed the hungry; find shelter for the homeless. America's strength lies in the armies of compassion that exist all across the United States of America.

And so I thank you for your question. Yes.

Health Care Reform

Q. Thank you, Mr. President. First, I want to tell you, thank you—how much we love your brother in the State of Florida.

The President. I had nothing to do with it. [*Laughter*] Thank my mother. [*Laughter*]

Q. He has been very good to the restaurant industry.

The President. He has been eating a lot, I noticed. [*Laughter*]

Q. You said that, not me. [*Laughter*] Mr. President, with mandated health care beginning to sweep the Nation, and we're seeing it pop up on the State level, do you see the association health plan passing,

hopefully, before you're out of office? And where do you see mandated health care going for the business industry?

The President. First of all, I think that the Government has a—the Federal Government has a responsibility, particularly on two fronts, when it comes to health care. One is to take care of the elderly. Lyndon Johnson signed that bill, and it said the Federal Government will provide health care for the elderly, called Medicare. And thanks to the Speaker's leadership and others here, we reformed Medicare so it actually meets the needs of our seniors.

My attitude is, if you made a commitment to the seniors, make it a good commitment; make it work. And we didn't have prescription drug benefits as a part of Medicare. And yet we're willing to pay for the surgery for an ulcer, for example, but not the drugs to prevent the ulcer from happening in the first place.

Secondly, we got to—made a commitment to the poor, and that's through Medicaid as well as community health centers. These are facilities—and the Speaker and I have been working on this—to expand community health centers throughout America so the poor and the indigent can get primary care in these facilities and not at your local emergency rooms.

Now, I also believe—[*applause*]—but I believe the best health care system beyond that means making sure we strengthen the doctor-patient relationship. And that is—that's not a mandate; that's just a practical way to view medicine.

And so how can you do that? Well, one is to promote health savings accounts, which we are doing. Health savings accounts are unique products that enable a small-business owner and/or an individual to be able to purchase a catastrophic plan—low-premium catastrophic plan, high-deductible catastrophic plan—coupled with a tax-free savings account. Now, that's important because it means that you're in control of your account. The person, the customer, the consumer is in control of making health care decisions.

One of the problems we have when it comes to cost is that we have the third-party payer system. Somebody else pays the bills, and therefore, there is no consumerism, so to speak, involved in health care.

Secondly, we got to recognize that certain individuals don't have the capacity to be able to buy health insurance like big companies can do, and therefore, it erodes the capacity of small businesses to be able to maintain their purchasing power. In other words, if it costs you a lot of money to buy the insurance plan, you're not going to pay for your insurance, see. And right now our small businesses are being penalized because they're not allowed to pool risk across jurisdictional boundaries. A solution to that is association health plans. The Speaker got it passed out of the House. It got killed by the trial lawyers in the United States Senate.

To answer your question, yes, I hope to get it out. It's a practical way of making sure that small businesses aren't mandated but have got choice in the marketplace. That's what I'm trying to tell you. I believe in choices in the marketplace. I believe in empowering people to make rational choices. In order to have a health care system that helps control costs and where people can make rational decisions, there needs to be transparency in pricing.

I know when I go to restaurants, I got a menu, see, and they say, here's what it costs you. That's not the case in most health care decisions, is it? I don't—I haven't seen a lot of price postings. So we're working—we're using Federal leverage through Medicare and the Veterans Administration, for example, to say, if you're doing business with the Federal Government, post your prices and the quality of service you're getting, so consumers can start making rational decisions in the marketplace. When you've got rational decisionmaking based upon price, it's going to

help control cost, which is very important for your industry.

Third, this is an industry—the health care industry is one that's kind of lagging behind when it comes to information technology—the docs are still writing out prescriptions with longhand. Or sometimes when you're in a hospital and you're going from place to place, you're carrying files, right? And they've been written out in longhand. Well, it's not a very efficient use of a person's time; plus, most doctors can't write. [*Laughter*] And therefore, costs are higher than they should be in medicine. So we're working to make sure that information technology is spread throughout the medical industry.

Again, the Federal Government has got a good chance to help leverage our position. We're a major provider of health care. And therefore, we ought to be using our position to start off helping the industry write a common language. Part of the problem in medicine is that there's not a common language, and therefore, it's hard to have a smooth information technology system throughout the medical industry. Our goal, by the way, is for every American to have a electronic medical record, and—but, by the way, with a guarantee of privacy.

And finally, one reason why you're having trouble buying health care is because these lawsuits are running good docs out of practice. Do you realize there are over 1,500 counties in America without an ob-gyn? And part of the argument is we got a health care system that is accessible and affordable—then we got to do something about these junk lawsuits. Again, the Speaker got a good medical liability bill out of the House of Representatives, but the trial lawyers defeated it in the United States Senate. And if you really want to help the country and make sure you've got affordable health care, get ahold of your United States Senators who are voting against meaningful medical liability reform, and help us get a bill passed.

That's a long answer—it's a long answer because I wanted to show you we've got a comprehensive plan that runs the opposite of Federal Government being the decider at all costs. I don't believe we ought to federalize medicine; I believe we ought to localize medicine. And the most local medicine is between the doctor and the patient.

Canada-U.S. Relations/Border Security

Q. Good morning, Mr. President—from Toronto, Canada, and my question is regarding border restrictions between our two countries. Given the impact on tourism, do you feel that it's necessary to continue increasing border restrictions between Canada and the U.S.?

The President. What he's referring to is right after 9/11, the Congress passed legislation that said there will be a new—border—an identification card between—travel between our countries. And you can understand why our Nation reacted the way—I hope you can understand the way our Nation reacted the way we did after 9/11. I mean, we were—we analyzed all aspects of our security. We were—we said we were going to do everything we can within the law to protect ourselves. And Congress passed some new laws to make sure that we knew who was coming in the country and who was leaving the country. And I supported those laws.

And now we're working with your Government to make sure that the identification cards that will be used between our two borders are compatible not only with our needs but your needs. I spoke to Prime Minister Harper about this subject. He's very aware and worried about a identification card that would be difficult to get into the hands of Canadians; it would make it difficult for Canada to continue to attract conventions. And so to answer your question, yes, we ought to have a system that is compatible with both our countries' needs.

The difference between—and by the way, it's very important for the Canadians to understand, there's a difference in the debate going on between the northern border and the southern border. The southern—and by the way, it's important for Americans to understand, the language of this debate must never say that Canada and/or Mexico are the enemies of the United States. They're friends of the United States. They're our friends and neighbors.

And so the issue this gentleman is referring to really is, how do we make sure we have a system that enables the legal people to come back and forth, I guess, is the best way to describe it. And we're working on it, to make sure that whatever documents are needed will not be restrictive, but nevertheless, informational, I guess is the best way to put it.

Thanks.

Yes, sir. Okay, you're next after that. Yes.

Fuel/Energy

Q. President Bush—from Crown Point, Indiana. First of all, I want to say, you're doing a fine job.

The President. Well, leave it at that, will you? Thank you. That kind of makes your question not very credible when you say something like that. [*Laughter*] But I'll accept it anyway.

Q. My question is, is there a realistic yet aggressive timetable and strategy to get our reliance off of Middle East oil and go to a different fuel source or ways that the United States can prosper?

The President. No, that's a great question. One of the things that should be evident to the American people now is that we live in a global world, and when demand for hydrocarbons increases in places like China and India, it causes our gasoline prices to go up. In other words, a global economy is such that when demand rises faster than international supply, the price of crude goes up—which is the feedstock for gasoline. And so the American people see firsthand what it means to be in a global world which is dependent upon fossil fuels, hydrocarbon.

And so the realistic timetable is as soon as possible. And I do think it's realistic. And here's—what he's saying is, how quick can we get off oil, all right? Well, most oil is consumed in America because of our automobiles. And the question then is, how quickly can we diversify the automobile fleet from one that is gasoline-only to one that becomes a mix, for example, of gasoline and ethanol? And we're making pretty good progress. If you really think about, for example, the penetration of ethanol in the Midwest, it's been amazing over the last couple of years. Indiana people—you're beginning to get E–85 pumps. E–85 means 85 percent of the fuel you buy at an E–85 pump is ethanol. We've put tax incentives in place to encourage the construction of ethanol refineries, and they're beginning to grow quite dramatically.

Some people say, well, you've got ethanol pumps, but doesn't it make it difficult to use it because the cars are not compatible? That's not true. There are 5 million automobiles on the road today that are flex-fuel vehicles. In other words, they can use ethanol and/or gasoline or a combination of the both. So the technologies to make our automobiles ethanol-compatible are around. As a matter of fact, you may have a flex-fuel vehicle and just don't know it.

The question then is, how do we—do we have enough feedstock into the ethanol business to be able to really get major penetration? And that's where we're spending some money. Because we got corn all right, but sometimes you got to eat corn. And sometimes your pigs and cows have got to eat corn. And so pretty soon, we're going to run into a bind when it comes to corn for ethanol and corn for other means and other needs. And so we're spending quite a bit of money at the Federal level, and have been for a couple of years, to see whether or not we can develop new tech-

nologies to make ethanol out of other feedstocks like switchgrass or wood chips.

They say we're getting pretty close to that. I can't give you a specific timetable. I know we're getting close to a battery that can go into a hybrid vehicle. Hybrid vehicles are good things—that switches between electricity and gasoline. And the next breakthrough is going to come to a vehicle that doesn't switch between electricity and gasoline until you've driven your first 40 miles. In other words, you'll have a battery that will be able to last for 40 miles before your car has to kick into gas—gasoline. And that's going to help save a lot of—that will help reduce demand for oil.

Longer term—and this is—this is a longer term—that's within 5 years, they tell me, as well. But over the next 10 years, my hope is that we have hydrogen become a technology that is commercial and applicable, so you're really driving automobiles with hydrogen as fuel source, not gasoline. And we're spending a lot of money on that. We're spending over a billion dollars to accelerate technologies to do that.

In the short term, in order to—by the way, it doesn't answer your question, how do you get off oil. But it does answer, how do we help consumers in America. I view rising gasoline prices as like a tax. It certainly affects small businesses. And one way to do it is to make sure we've got ample supplies of gasoline available. You realize, we haven't built a new refinery since the 1970s. If Congress is that concerned about the price of gasoline, it seems like they ought to give us flexibility so we can permit expansions and/or new refineries so that we can keep the price—[*applause*]. It's a long-winded answer, but it's a problem that requires a strategy in which we spend money on research and development and on a variety of fronts.

Another example is clean coal technologies. It's conceivable that relatively— well, within a period of time—it's not— in my lifetime; let's put it that way—that we can have coal-fired plants that have got zero emissions. Now, that's important for people to know, that it's possible. We've spent about billions there, as well, to achieve this breakthrough, because we've got 250-some odd years of coal reserves in the United States.

I think we ought to be using nuclear power. It is renewable, and it produces no emissions. We're spending money on technologies to make sure we can reprocess spent fuels. In other words, we're working on a variety of fronts. I don't know the timetable—as soon as possible. And the reason why is, is that our national security issues oftentimes rest with countries that have got oil, and they don't like us, see.

And so the faster we're off oil, the better off we're going to be from an economic security perspective and a national—and I probably surprised you when I got up at my State of the Union and said, "We've got a problem; we're addicted to oil." You know, I'm from Texas and all that. But I believe it, and I know it. And so I'm going to work with members from both political parties to expedite research and development so we've got new technologies to achieve this important objective.

Yes, ma'am.

U.S. Relations With Latin America

Q. Thank you—Westport, Connecticut. Speaking of oil-producing countries that are not friendly to the United States right now, I'm very concerned about what's going on in Venezuela and Bolivia and all—the coalition of Hugo Chavez. I wondered what your strategy was going to be, or what you're working on in that respect.

The President. Thank you. I am going to continue to remind our hemisphere that respect for property rights and human rights is essential for all countries in order for there to be prosperity and peace. I'm going to remind our allies and friends in the neighborhood that the United States of America stands for justice; that when we see poverty, we care about it, and we

do something about it; that we care for good—we stand for good health care.

I'm going to remind our people that meddling in other elections is—to achieve a short-term objective is not in the interests of the neighborhood. I will continue to remind people that trade is the best way to help people be lifted from poverty; that we can spend money—and we do in the neighborhood—but the best way for there to be growth is to encourage commerce and trade and prosperity through the marketplace.

I want to remind people that the United States stands against corruption at all levels of government, that the United States is transparent. The United States expects the same from other countries in the neighborhood, and we'll work toward them.

We'll continue to work with forces like the Central—countries like the Central American countries, where we passed a free trade agreement called CAFTA, to remind the people in that area that relations with the United States will be beneficial to their people. There's a lot of things we're doing.

Thank you very much. I'm concerned— let me just put it bluntly—I'm concerned about the erosion of democracy in the countries you mentioned.

Trust in Government

Q. Hi—Orlando, Florida. Let me first say, it's an honor to hear you speak. And I'm a proud supporter. I just had a quick question. Yesterday, at the keynote address, Ted Koppel mentioned that there is a growing lack of trust between government and the American people. How would you address this statement?

The President. He said there's a growing lack of trust between our Government and the American people?

Q. Yes, he did.

The President. Well, I think I would say that there's an unease in America now, and the reason why is because we're at war. And war is difficult—particularly this kind of war, where it's on our TV screens every day. And I can understand why people are uneasy. Americans care about human life. We have a great compassion for people all around the world. And so when people read or see that the enemy has run a suicide bomber into a village or a marketplace and innocent people died, it breaks our heart. So there is an unease about America.

Hey, listen, we got an amazing economy—it's strong, and yet there's an uneasiness. And that's what happens in war. And let me just share my thoughts about this with you. If I didn't think we'd succeed, I wouldn't stay. And if I didn't think it was important that we succeed, I wouldn't stay. And the reason it's important is that we must understand that we're in a global war against a totalitarian group of people who will kill innocent life, there or here, in order to achieve an objective. That's just the lessons of September the 11th that I refuse to forget.

In Iraq, the enemy has made it clear—this is their words, not mine; I quoted the man—the Al Qaida guy in Iraq—those weren't my—I didn't make up those quotes. That's what he said. And by the way, you need your President and your Commander in Chief to take the words of the enemy seriously. And they have said it's just a matter of time—[*applause*]. They have said it's a matter of time for the United States to leave, that democracies are soft, that capitalist societies are weak. And their view is that if they kill enough innocent people, we will tire and leave. That's what they said.

They've also said, "We're going to stop the elections." They will try to sow sectarian violence in order to make it difficult for a democracy to succeed in Iraq. And the reason why they want us to leave is because they want safe haven from which to launch attacks—not only against the United States but modern Muslim nations in the Middle East. That's what they want to do.

Their vision—they have a vision. They have an ideology that is the opposite of ours. They don't believe in freedom to dissent and freedom to worship. Matter of fact, they've taken a great religion and, in my judgment, have twisted it to meet their own needs.

If somebody said, "Well, what do you think life would be like with these folks?", just remind them what life was like in Afghanistan under the Taliban. There was no dissent, and if you did, you were whipped. Young girls didn't go to school. They have a backward vision of the world, but they do have a vision, and they want to spread that vision. And we stand in the way of spreading that vision—we and a coalition of nations that have bound together to promote democracy and freedom. That's what—and democracy worries them.

My quote in the speech was this guy's words—democracy will be a setback. That's why I said, the formation of this Government, under a Constitution drafted and approved by the Iraqis, is a setback, because it's—they've said, "We will defeat this democracy." But they're not going to defeat the democracy. The only way they defeat the democracy is if we let them defeat the democracy, we don't stand with this young Government.

Again, I know that—I know there's concern about—from the American people that we can't win. See, most Americans want us to win. Most Americans want to succeed. And there's questions about whether or not the strategy will do so.

And I can understand why people are concerned about whether or not our strategy can succeed, because our progress is incremental. Freedom is moving, but it's in incremental steps. And the enemy's progress is almost instant, on their TV screens. And of course, I get briefings from our commanders on the ground. I want to assure you that the information—I make my mind up based not upon politics or political opinion polls but based upon what the commanders on the ground tell me is going on.

I do want to share with you—thanks for bringing this up. It's not exactly the question. [*Laughter*] I'll share with you some of my thoughts about why it's important to have a democracy—liberty prevail in the Middle East. You know, our policy up until now was, let's just hope everything's fine. If it looked okay on the surface, then let's just don't rock the boat. Let's get our energy sources and everything will be all right.

But that's not what was happening. Beneath the surface, there was a—discontent and hopelessness and despair was beginning to take hold. And as a result, this group of killers sprung up, and they were able to recruit and train sophisticated suiciders. And they killed over 3,000 of our people.

I felt it was important for us to address not only the short-term needs of the country—which means, stay on the offensive and bring them to justice before they hurt us again—but also the longer term needs of the country, by addressing the root cause of the resentment and hatred. And in my judgment, the best way to defeat the totalitarian vision of the enemy is with an ideology that has worked, that is bright and it's hopeful, called freedom and liberty, expressed through democracy.

Now, I know there are some people in our country who say, why worry? Well, the reason "why worry" is because we have a duty to lay the foundation of peace for a generation to come. And I'm confident we can succeed. And I will tell you two examples of this—of why I'm confident. One, think of all the lives lost in Europe during World War I and World War II, American lives lost. You all know some of them. You know neighbors who had a grandfather or a father who went over—called up, went overseas to—and fought in Europe and lost their lives. But today, after nearly a century of violence and death and destruction, Europe is whole, free, and at peace. And it's important for America to ask the question, why is that the case? Well, democracies don't war with each other, and democracies have taken hold in Europe.

The second example I like to bring up is from World War II as well, and that is what's happened to our former enemy, the Japanese. Prime Minister Koizumi is coming to our country soon. I'll be sitting down at the table with a friend talking about issues like North Korea or thanking him for having 1,000 troops in Iraq or worrying about the spread of pandemic disease or talking about how we can help the young democracy, Afghanistan. And I find it amazing that the President of the United States is sitting down talking about peace with the head of a country that my dad went to war with and your dads and grandads went to war with.

And what happened between the brutal attack on our country—that, by the way, killed fewer people at Pearl Harbor than we lost on September the 11th—and today, when we're talking about keeping the peace? Japan adopted a Japanese-style democracy. One thing history teaches—and by the way, if you look back at some of the written word, when Harry Truman had the vision of helping this country recover from the war and become a democracy, a lot of people were saying, it's a waste of his time; hopelessly idealistic, they would say. But he had faith in certain fundamental truths. One truth is, everybody desires to be free. Freedom is universal. It's not just a right for America.

And the second truth is, proven after 60 years of time, that freedom has the capacity to convert an enemy to a friend. And as I said in my remarks, I believe that this is an historic moment in Iraq, and that someday people will be looking back on this period of time saying, thank goodness the United States of America didn't lose its faith in certain fundamental values and we laid the foundation of peace.

And it's hard work. It's hard work to go from a tyranny to a democracy. And I understand why people are concerned; I understand it. Listen, I meet with—the hardest job of the President is to meet with families of the fallen. And it's a—it's my duty. But almost to a person, they say, "Whatever you do, Mr. President, complete the mission; lay the foundation of peace so my child had not died in vain." And I give them that assurance every time I'm with them.

Yell it.

Federal Response to Catastrophic Events

Q. I'm from Munster, Indiana. I was wondering, sir, if we were to be attacked by a biological weapon or if there was an outbreak of the avian flu, would we be prepared?

The President. Good question. We are working to be prepared. His question is, if there is a catastrophic event that is beyond the magnitude of a natural event, such as a biological attack and/or a attack of pandemic flu, would we be prepared?

Well, first step is to recognize that it's a possibility and start preparing, which we're doing at the Federal level. Yes, we've got a good strategy—now, whether or not it would work to perfection, you hope you never have to find out.

One of the classic cases—one of the classic dilemmas we're trying to resolve is that most—it's against the law to put Federal troops in to enforce the law. It's posse comitatus, you know? I'm not a lawyer, but nevertheless, that's what the lawyers tell me. However, States can use their Guard to do law enforcement activities. And the fundamental question is, if there's an event big enough, should the Federal Government be able to prevent State authority— should there be an automatic declaration of a state of emergency that will enable me to rally Federal troops to keep the law?

We haven't resolved that issue yet, but that's one of the dilemmas on a catastrophic event that ends up exceeding the boundaries of—that would make it not a local event. But we're working hard on it. We've spent a lot of time on pandemic flu, which, by the way, has got the same—

a biological attack would have the same applications as to how you—how do you isolate the incident; how do you isolate the spread of disease; how do you rally local authorities to make the right decisions about public facilities.

Mike Leavitt is in charge of this, the health aspect of this response. He's been traveling the country, working with local and State response plans, and it's a big job to get ready for it. I appreciate your question.

Q. From Arlington, Texas.

The President. Oh, yes.

Q. Home of your Texas Rangers.

The President. Mighty Rangers. They never—they still don't have——

Q. They're in first place; that's good. My question is about——

The President. I thought with change of ownership they'd go all the way, you know? [*Laughter*]

Health Care Reform/Global Warming

Q. My question is about health care reform.

The President. Yes.

Q. You mentioned health care reform, catastrophic health care reform, Americans with disabilities as well. Under the umbrella of that, it doesn't seem that there is much addressed in terms of dental care, even though that is part of health care, I would think.

And the second part of that question is, will you see Al Gore's new movie? [*Laughter*]

The President. Doubt it. [*Laughter*] But I will say this about the environmental debate, that my answer to the energy question also is an answer to how you deal with the greenhouse gas issue, and that is, new technologies will change how we live and how we drive our cars, which all will have the beneficial effect of improving the environment.

And in my judgment, we need to set aside whether or not greenhouse gases have been caused by mankind or because of natural effects and focus on the technologies that will enable us to live better lives and, at the same time, protect the environment.

Not sure how to answer your question on dentistry, frankly. I'll take a look at it. Yes, drop your address off.

Chef, how are you doing, buddy?

Q. Doing very good. I'm doing very good, sir.

The President. You know how I could tell you were chef?

Q. I don't know. [*Laughter*]

The President. Yes.

Q. Thank you. On behalf of—I'm from Tampa, Florida. And on behalf of all the cooks and chefs in our country, I have to say, you're running the country the way a chef would run the country, and we're proud of you, first of all.

The President. Thank you, sir.

Governor Jeb Bush of Florida/Public Service

Q. You have created a lot of jobs, and our industry is just, like you said, it's cranking, and we're loving every minute of it. My biggest concern, sir, is 2008 is coming. Do you have a plan for—to keep your policies in place and keep them going?

And would Jeb ever consider—we like him—even though we're the home of the Tampa Bay Devil Rays—we don't have everything, but would Jeb ever consider——

The President. Playing for the Tampa Bay Devil Rays?

Q. Hell no. [*Laughter*] For our country—for our country, sir.

The President. You better ask Jeb. Look, I said something about it the other day. Somebody asked me about him. I said, look, I think he'd be a great President. But it's—he said he's not going to run in 2008, and I think you've got to take him for his word. He's been in public life now for 8 years, and I think he wants a breather.

But thank you for your kind words. You go back and write him a letter, you know.

He's a good man. Look, my—here's the thing about Washington that—the rhetoric needs, in my judgment, toned down up there so that we're able to attract good people, both Republican and Democrat, to run for public office. You know, it's one thing to disagree, but it's another thing to disparage people. And we just—we don't need that kind of language, in my judgment—in order to attract good people to public service.

And there's too much politics in Washington these days. There really is. And so my worry is, not so much about Jeb, but when people take a look at Washington and say, "Why mess with it? Why do I want to put my family through it all?" And my advice to them is, one, it's worth it. But my advice, also, to all of us in public office is not to demean somebody because you don't agree with them. At least, in the debate, be considerate of the other person's point of view.

And the immigration debate is one where America needs to start, in my judgment. I'm very worried about the tone of this debate. We are a land of immigrants. One of the great things about America is we've been able to assimilate people from all around the world into becoming Americans. And that debate—if that debate tends to divide this country or cause people to wonder about their worth as an individual, it will be a debate of—it will be a debate that will be harmful.

Now, I understand the emotions of this issue. It's a tough issue for Members to vote on. I happen to believe my comprehensive plan is the way to go. But if somebody doesn't agree with me, I'm not going to debase them in the public arena. And so whether the debate is immigration or tax or Iraq, it's really important, in my judgment, for us to conduct this debate with dignity. And that will help answer your question as to whether or not people are going to be wanting to run for office.

You know, my buddies in Texas take a look at Washington and say, "Why are you even up there, man? Come on home." [*Laughter*] "What are you doing that for?" My answer is, I love my country. Public service is noble and necessary. I'm glad I ran for President. And I'll try to do my part to elevate the tone and hold people— and treat people with respect whether they agree with me or not.

I've got to go back to Washington. God bless. Thanks for coming.

NOTE: The President spoke at 10:37 a.m. at the Arie Crown Theater at Lakeside Center—McCormick Place. In his remarks, he referred to Mayor Richard M. Daley of Chi-

cago, IL; Edward R. Tinsley III, chairman of the board of directors, National Restaurant Association, and his wife, Meredith; Prime Minister Nuri al-Maliki, former President Saddam Hussein, President Jalal Talabani, and Speaker of the Council of Representatives Mahmoud al-Mashhadani of Iraq; senior Al Qaida associate Abu Musab Al Zarqawi; Prime Minister Stephen Harper of Canada; and Prime Minister Junichiro Koizumi of Japan. Participants referred to President Hugo Chavez Frias of Venezuela; Ted Koppel, former anchor, ABC News; and former Vice President Al Gore.

Statement on the Death of Lee Jong-wook
May 22, 2006

Laura and I were saddened to learn of the death of Dr. Lee Jong-wook. As the world's top health official, Dr. Lee worked tirelessly to improve the health of millions of people, from combating tuberculosis and HIV/AIDS to his aggressive efforts to eradicate polio. He provided tremendous leadership to the international community as it

confronted the challenges of the 21st century, including the threat of an influenza pandemic. Dr. Lee's outreach to world leaders and entities increased awareness of potentially devastating public health dangers. We send our deepest condolences to his family.

The President's News Conference With Prime Minister Ehud Olmert of Israel
May 23, 2006

President Bush. Thank you. Mr. Prime Minister, welcome. I'm particularly pleased to welcome Mrs. Olmert to the White House as well. Thanks for coming.

The Prime Minister and I have known each other since 1998, when he was the mayor of Jerusalem and I was the Governor of Texas. And I remember you greeting me in your office there, and you probably thought you were going to be the Prime

Minister—I wasn't sure if I was going to be the President. [*Laughter*]

We've just had a really productive meeting. We reaffirmed the deep and abiding ties between Israel and the United States. And those ties include our commitment to democracy and our strong belief that everybody has the right to worship freely. The ties include growing trade and economic relationships. The ties include important educational exchange programs that allow

Israeli students to study at American colleges and universities and American students to travel and study in Israel.

In our meeting, the Prime Minister and I recalled the great contributions to peace made by Ariel Sharon. I asked the Prime Minister to convey my very best wishes to Ariel Sharon's sons.

Prime Minister Olmert and I discussed peace and security in the Middle East, which the people of Israel seek and the American people support. In 2002, I outlined my vision of two democratic states, Israel and Palestine, living side by side in peace and security. Prime Minister Olmert told me that he and his Government share this vision. The international community seeks to realize this goal to the roadmap, which calls for a comprehensive settlement that resolves all outstanding issues between Israelis and Palestinians. I believe, and Prime Minister Olmert agrees, that a negotiated final status agreement best serves both the Israelis and the Palestinians and the cause of peace.

Palestinian Authority President Abbas favors and speaks out for peace and negotiations. Yet the Hamas-led Palestinian Government does not. Hamas needs to make a strategic choice for peace. The United States and the international community have made clear that Hamas must recognize Israel's right to exist, must abandon terror, and must accept all previous agreements between the Palestinian Authority and Israel. No country can be expected to make peace with those who deny its right to exist and who use terror to attack its population.

Today Prime Minister Olmert shared with me some of his ideas; I would call them bold ideas. These ideas could lead to a two-state solution if a pathway to progress on the roadmap is not open in the period ahead. His ideas include the removal of most Israeli settlements, except for the major Israeli population centers in the West Bank. This idea would follow Prime Minister Sharon's decision to remove all settlements in Gaza and several in the West Bank.

I look forward to learning more about the Prime Minister's ideas. While any final status agreement will be only achieved on the basis of mutually agreed changes, and no party should prejudice the outcome of negotiations on a final status agreement, the Prime Minister's ideas could be an important step toward the peace we both support. I'm encouraged by his constructive efforts to find ways to move the peace process forward.

And finally, the Prime Minister and I shared our concerns about the Iranian regime's nuclear weapons ambitions. The United States and the international community have made our common position clear: We're determined that the Iranian regime must not gain nuclear weapons.

I told the Prime Minister what I've stated publicly before: Israel is a close friend and ally of the United States, and in the event of any attack on Israel, the United States will come to Israel's aid. The United States is strongly committed, and I'm strongly committed, to the security of Israel as a vibrant Jewish state.

I look forward to our continuing discussions after this press conference. I'm not sure the delegations realize this yet, but we're going to shed ourselves of our delegations, and the Prime Minister and I are going to go up to the Residence and sit down and have a continued dialog. And if we decide to brief our delegations on what we discuss, we will do so. But if not, they're going to have to guess. [*Laughter*] And then I'm looking forward to dinner.

Welcome.

Prime Minister Olmert. Thank you, Mr. President. I thank you for your kind invitation to visit Washington and for the opportunity to meet with you and discuss the many issues on our common agenda. Our meeting was enlightening, and I look forward to working closely with you in the coming years to deepen the friendship, understanding, and bilateral ties between the United States and Israel.

I also recall our meeting in the city hall when you and I were strolling around the beautiful building, at the terrace on the sixth floor, watching the walls of the city of Jerusalem. At that time, you were the Governor; I was the mayor. And I think none of us thought that the day would come that I will have the honor and the privilege of being hosted by you, as President of the United States and Prime Minister of Israel.

I could sense then your deep connection to the Holy Land and your friendship and commitment to the State of Israel. I must say, Mr. President, that my instincts did not fail me. I, and the entire people of Israel, appreciate your true friendship and unwavering commitment to Israel's security and its well-being as a vibrant Jewish state.

Your involvement in the Middle East and personal contribution to the efforts towards resolving the Israel-Palestinian conflict has been significant. The vision, which you outlined in your historic speech of June 2002, of two democratic states living side by side in peace and security, is the basis of any progress towards the solution in this region. Your unreserved support of the disengagement plan and your letter of April 14, 2004, to Prime Minister Ariel Sharon—and I join you in praying for his recovery—were the basis for the success of its implementation. What you immediately recognized to be an historic step was later adopted by all those who were skeptical in the beginning.

I intend to exhaust every possibility to promote peace with the Palestinians according to the roadmap, and I extend my hand in peace to Mahmoud Abbas, the elected President of the Palestinian Authority. I hope he will take the necessary steps which he committed to in order to move forward.

Unfortunately, the rise of Hamas, a terrorist organization which refuses to recognize Israel's right to exist and regards terrorism as a legitimate tool, severely undermines the possibility of promoting a genuine peace process. As you stated, Mr. President, the Palestinian Authority headed by Hamas Government must abandon the path of terrorism, dismantle the terror infrastructure, honor agreements, and recognize Israel's right to exist. By doing so they will find us a willing partner in peace. However, we will not enter into any kind of partnership with a party which refuses to recognize our right to live in peace and security.

Despite our sincere desire for negotiations, we cannot wait indefinitely for the Palestinians to change. We cannot be held hostage by a terrorist entity which refuses to change or to promote dialog. If we come to the conclusion that no progress is possible, we will be compelled to try a different route.

I presented to the President ideas which I believe could help advance his vision and prevent a political stalemate. According to these ideas, we will remove most of the settlements which are not part of the major Israeli population centers in Judea and Samaria. The settlements within the population centers would remain under Israeli control and become part of the State of Israel as part of the final status agreement. This process of realignment would reduce friction between Israelis and Palestinians, ensure territorial contiguity for the Palestinians, and guarantee Israel's security as a Jewish state with the borders it desires.

The implementation of these ideas would only be possible with the comprehensive support of the United States and the international community. I anticipate working with you to explore ways to advance this.

We discussed the Iranian issue. The Iranian regime, which calls for Israel's destruction, openly denies the Holocaust, and views the United States as its enemy, makes every effort to implement its fundamentalist religious ideology and blatantly disregards the demands of the international community. The Iranian threat is not only a threat to Israel, it is a threat to the stability of the Middle East and the entire world. And it could mark the beginning of a dangerous and irresponsible arms race in the Middle East.

Mr. President, we appreciate your efforts to curb Iran's nuclear ambitions, including through the U.N. Security Council. They are of crucial importance. The international community cannot tolerate a situation where a regime with a radical ideology and a long tradition of irresponsible conduct becomes a nuclear weapons state. This is a moment of truth. It is still not too late to prevent it from happening.

I thank you again for your gracious hospitality and for our discussions. I look forward to continue working with you, Mr. President. Thank you very much.

President Bush. We'll take two questions a side, starting with Steve Holland [Reuters].

Middle East Peace Process

Q. You mentioned that the West Bank plan could be an important step. Doesn't this sweep away the U.S. principle of a negotiated two-state solution? And should the Palestinian side approve any plan that would establish Israel's final borders?

President Bush. You just heard the Prime Minister say that he's going to exhaust all options to negotiate, that he wants to reach out a hand to President Abbas. And I agree. I said in my opening statement that the best solution is one in which there's a negotiated final status. And we discussed—we spent ways—we spent some time discussing about how it's important to get a Palestinian President to the table. And the Prime Minister says he looks forward to discussing the issue.

And so our preferred option, of course, is there to be a negotiated settlement. On the other hand, as the Prime Minister said, that if he's unable to find a partner in peace, if nothing can go forward, he is willing to think about ways to advance the process forward.

And in order to solve this problem, there needs to be willingness to take the lead and creativity and the desire to follow through on the vision. The most important aspect about peace is to have a vision for peace. And I appreciate the Prime Minister's vision of two states side by side— two democratic states side by side in peace. That's possible.

And so what I come away from the meeting with is that the Prime Minister, one, has a vision; two, willing to reach out to determine whether or not that vision exists with the Palestinian President, which I think it does; three, is willing to work to see whether or not it is possible for two sides to come together, and if not, is still willing to consider other ways to move the process forward. That's, to me, a very positive statement.

Q. You said you wanted to hear more. Is there anything that worries you about this plan?

President Bush. No, the only thing that worries me about the plan is that Hamas has said they want to destroy Israel. And the reason that worries me is how can you have two states side by side in peace if one of the partners does not recognize the other state's right to exist? It's illogical for somebody to say, I'm for a state side by side with another state, and yet I don't want the state to exist. And so we spent time talking about Hamas, and I assured the Prime Minister that our position is steady and strong, that Hamas must change.

Now, we care about the Palestinian people—and I say, "we," both of us—he can speak for himself on this issue—but we are trying to set up a mechanism that supports the Palestinian people. Our beef is not with the Palestinian people. Our beef is with the Government that—a group in the Government that says they don't recognize Israel. And so the United States, we're working with the Europeans—Condi's people in the State Department are working with the Europeans to come up with a mechanism to get food and medicine and aid to the Palestinians.

You may want to comment on it yourself, Mr. Prime Minister.

Prime Minister Olmert. Thank you, Mr. President. Indeed, the Government, Sunday, decided to spend 50 million shekels buying medical equipment—50 million shekels, about $11 million—for the time being, to buy medical equipment and drugs needed for the hospitals in Gaza. And as I said during the Cabinet meeting, we will spend any amount of money needed in order to save lives of innocent Palestinians suffering from the indifference of their Government. We will not hesitate to do it. We will use the revenues that we have collected, and more if necessary. We will make arrangements, together with our friends, so that the supplies will arrive directly to those who need them.

This is a humanitarian commitment. We are absolutely committed to help innocent people that suffer from the brutality and the intransigence of their own Government, and we will continue to do it at all times.

Thank you, Mr. President.

Iran

Q. Mr. Prime Minister, are you satisfied from what you have learned out of your meeting with the President with regard of the Iranian issue? And what's your message to the Israeli public about this issue?

And, Mr. President, with your permission, there is a military option, from your point of view, to solve the threat of the Iranian problem, their work on—to getting nuclear weapons?

Prime Minister Olmert. The Iranian issue was discussed, indeed, between the President and myself. And we'll continue to talk about it later. Obviously, there is a major threat posed, as I've said already and the President said, by the Iranians and their attempts to have nonconventional capabilities and also to build up delivery systems and the ballistic missiles that can hit major

centers all across Europe, not just in the Middle East.

This is something that needs to be stopped. We discussed this issue at length, and there is a total agreement and understanding between the President and myself that there is a need to stop it. And we reviewed the different ways how to do it, and I am very satisfied with what I heard from the President and on what we agreed that we would continue to do in order to achieve this goal.

President Bush. Our primary objective is to solve this problem diplomatically. I've told the American people that I will, on all issues, will try diplomacy first and exhaust diplomacy. And I explained to the Prime Minister that—about our diplomatic efforts—the most important thing in diplomacy is that there be a shared goal and—in other words, you have to have a common objective, a common goal in order to get people to come together around it. And now we have got a common goal throughout most of the world, and that is, Iran should not have a nuclear weapon. And that's important, and we are now working the diplomatic front around that goal.

We have a variety of options, one of which, of course, is the United Nations Security Council, if the Iranians aren't willing to show progress toward that goal. We're working very closely with what's called the EU–3. That's Germany, England, and France. And I've been pleased and Secretary of State Rice has been pleased about their willingness to stay tough on the goal, of achieving the goal. Sometimes when you've got a variety of negotiating parties, it's easier for one—a nontransparent negotiator to pick off a weak link. And yet they've been firm, and that's important for Israel to know. It's important for me to praise our partners for that strength of purpose.

Obviously, there's other parties we have to work with, including Russia and China. In other words, you can't get anything out of the U.N. Security Council unless there's an agreement that the Iranians are not negotiating in good faith and aren't willing to go forward. And so we're spending a lot of time working with our Russian friends, in particular, to make it clear to them that Iran is showing no good faith.

And one of the interesting issues that the Iranians have tossed out in this debate is that they believe they have the sovereign right for civilian nuclear power. And my position has been, fine, it's just you just don't get to enrich the fuel necessary for the plant. And so we provided a—I thought—a very interesting opportunity for them—to say, if you want civilian nuclear power, you can have your plant and the international consortium will provide the fuel for the plant. And we'll pick up the spent fuel from the plant. And this was a very realistic and reasonable approach—and has been rejected by the Iranians.

And so I say to our friends in our consortium, I'm not so sure these people really do want a solution, and therefore, let us make sure that we're willing to be working together in the U.N. Security Council. That's where we are. We're headed—we're on the cusp of going to the Security Council. And I repeat to your question, obviously, we'd like to solve this issue peacefully and diplomatically. And the more the Iranians refuse to negotiate in good faith, the more countries are beginning to realize that we must continue to work together.

Martha [Martha Raddatz, ABC News]. Yes, you.

Progress in Iraq

Q. If we can switch to Iraq, sir.

President Bush. Iraq. Okay.

Q. I know that this is something you're leaving up to your commanders, but from what you've heard from your commanders, how confident are you that you can start drawing down troops by the end of the year?

President Bush. First of all, we are making progress in achieving our objective of training the Iraqis to take the fight to the enemy. And the reason I know that is because I talk to our commanders quite frequently. And we're making good political progress, as the world saw in the formation of a unity government. The Government has yet to get their full Cabinet in place, although we think that will happen relatively quickly. And then this sovereign Government is going to assess their security situation and their security forces and their needs and work with our commanders. We haven't gotten to the point yet where the new Government is sitting down with our commanders to come up with a joint way forward.

However, having said that, this is a new chapter in our relationship. In other words, we're now able to take a new assessment about the needs necessary for the Iraqis. And when I get that report from our commanders, I'll share it with others and you.

Q. Sir, can I just add——

President Bush. Please——

Q. The U.S. has the most powerful military in the world, and they have been unable to bring down the violence in any substantial way in several of the Provinces. So how can you expect the Iraqis to do that?

President Bush. If one were to measure progress on the number of suiciders, if that's your definition of success, I think it gives—I think it will—I think it obscures the steady, incremental march toward democracy we're seeing. In other words, it's very difficult—you can have the most powerful army of the world—ask the Israelis what it's like to try to stop suiciders—it is a difficult task to stop suicide bombers. That's the—but that's one of the main—that's the main weapon of the enemy, the capacity to destroy innocent life with a suicider.

And so I view progress as, is there a political process going forward that's convincing disaffected Sunnis, for example, to participate? Is there a unity government that says, it's best for all of us to work together to achieve a common objective, which is democracy? Are we able to meet the needs of the 12 million people that defied the car bombers? To me, that's success. Trying to stop suiciders—which we're doing a pretty good job of on occasion—is difficult to do. And what the Iraqis are going to have to eventually do is convince those who are conducting suiciders who are not inspired by Al Qaida, for example, to realize there's a peaceful tomorrow. And those who are being inspired by Al Qaida, we're just going to have to stay on the hunt and bring Al Qaida to justice. And our Army can do that and is doing that right now.

Israel's Disengagement Plan/Middle East Peace Process

Q. Mr. President, the Prime Minister just said that the settlement blocks, the major population centers will be part of Israel, annexed to Israel in the future. Do you support that? Would the United States sanction that?

And, Mr. Prime Minister, can you give us some assessment of the time that you are willing to wait for the emergence of a Palestinian partner?

President Bush. My answer to your question is, refer to my April 14, 2004, letter. I believed it when I wrote it, and I still believe it. [*Laughter*]

Q. [*Inaudible*]

President Bush. ——rare that I wrote the letter, or rare that I believed what I wrote? [*Laughter*]

Prime Minister Olmert. First of all, I want to emphasize again what I said before—and what I said before the elections and immediately after the elections in Israel and when my Government was inaugurated in the Knesset just a couple of weeks ago. I said that we will make a genuine effort to negotiate with the Palestinian side on the basis of the roadmap, which is the framework for future negotiations towards, hopefully, a peace agreement between us and the Palestinians.

I meant precisely what I said. I'll make every possible effort. And in order to exam-

ine it carefully and seriously, I will certainly meet with the elected President of the Palestinian Authority, Mahmoud Abbas. We haven't yet decided about the timing. It will be in the near future. And I will do everything that I can in order to help create the necessary circumstances for such negotiations to take place, providing, of course, that the Palestinian partner will have to not just to make a public commitment but to be able to deliver on the basic requirements of the roadmap and the Quartet decisions, namely to recognize the State of Israel and its right to exist as a Jewish state, to unarm the terrorist organizations, and to implement all the obligations of the agreement signed between the State of Israel and the Palestinian Authority.

So we will make an effort. And I say time and again that we accept the sincerity of Mahmoud Abbas as the elected President of the Palestinian Authority. He is genuine; he is sincere; and we hope that he will have the power to be able to meet the requirements necessary for negotiations between us and the Palestinians. How soon it will be? The sooner the better. I don't want to prejudge it at this point. I think it's too early. And I didn't come with a timetable to meet with the President of the United States.

We shared our observations. I entirely agree with the vision of the President as it was outlined so brilliantly in the famous speech in June of 2002, which really set the course for all the developments that took place in the Middle East since then and created the possibility for, ultimately, the disengagement, which was a turning point in the history of the Middle East. And we are grateful to the President for the courage that he manifested then in presenting this outline and in being the first to support the disengagement, and carry on in spite of the difficulties and the skepticism and the question marks posed by different countries at the beginning. Most of them joined in later.

So we are anxious to have negotiations. And we will look and find every possible avenue to help establish a process of negotiations on the basis of these conditions. However, as I said, we will not wait indefinitely. If we will reach the conclusion that in spite of all these efforts, it is impossible to implement the principles of the roadmap through a negotiating process, we'll look for other ways to implement these principles and to ultimately create a situation where there are secured borders for the State of Israel with the population centers in the territories as part of a State of Israel and with a contiguous territory that will allow the Palestinians to establish their own Palestinian state alongside the State of Israel. And hopefully, this is something that will happen within the next 3 to 4 years.

Again, I am grateful to the President for the efforts that he was making and for his willingness to examine together with me these new ideas—as he called them, bold ideas—in the event that all other options will not be possible.

Thank you.

President Bush. Good job.

NOTE: The President's news conference began at 5:05 p.m. in the East Room at the White House. In his remarks, he referred to Aliza Olmert, wife of Prime Minister Olmert; former Prime Minister Ariel Sharon of Israel, and his sons, Omri and Gilad; and President Mahmoud Abbas (Abu Mazen) of the Palestinian Authority.

Statement on the Death of Lloyd M. Bentsen, Jr.
May 23, 2006

Laura and I and the entire Bush family are saddened by Lloyd Bentsen's death. Lloyd Bentsen served in the House of Representatives for 6 years, and he represented the people of Texas in the United States Senate for 22 years. During his time in Congress, he was known for his integrity and for seeking bipartisan solutions to issues facing our Nation. He later became Secretary of the Treasury in President Clinton's administration.

As a young man, Lloyd Bentsen served our country in battle in the United States Army Air Forces, and he was awarded the Distinguished Flying Cross. In 1999, in recognition of his lifetime of service to the United States, he received the Presidential Medal of Freedom, the Nation's highest civil award. Lloyd Bentsen was a man of great honor and distinction. We send our condolences and prayers to B.A. and the Bentsen family.

NOTE: The statement referred to Beverly Ann "B.A." Bentsen, wife of Lloyd M. Bentsen, Jr.

Remarks on Energy in Pottstown, Pennsylvania
May 24, 2006

Thank you all. Please be seated. Thanks for the warm welcome. If I talk too long, it's going to be even warmer. [*Laughter*] I really appreciate the chance to come to the Limerick Generating Station. I'm glad to see it in action. More importantly, I was glad to see the people working here, glad to meet them, glad to get to know them.

I appreciate their strong dedication to safe-ty. I appreciate their dedication to the con-sumers you serve.

This plant serves 2 million homes in the area, and it does so in a way that does not require us to pollute the air. It's a perfect example of how we can grow our economy and protect our environment at the same time. And so thanks for receiving me. I'm honored to be here.

I thank John Rowe for introducing me, and thanks for coming over from Chicago. Appreciate you being here. I want to thank Chris Crane. I want to thank Ron DeGregorio. Thank you for having me, Ron. I want to thank the mayor, Sharon Valentine-Thomas, of the Borough of Potts-town. Thanks for coming, Madam Mayor. I appreciate you being here. I want to thank all the folks from the local govern-ment—sorry about clogging the neighbor-hoods coming through, but thanks. [*Laugh-ter*] Appreciate you letting me come by.

I want to talk about how the United States of America can continue to be the economic leader of the world. First of all, I think it's important that we're the eco-nomic leader of the world, because when you're the leader, it helps the folks who live in your country. See, it matters if we're on the cutting edge of change. It matters to people working every day in America if we're creating strong economic growth.

Today, we are creating strong economic growth. I mean, this economy of ours is moving forward with a full head of steam—fifth year in a row of uninterrupted growth. Our economy grew faster than any other major industrialized nation in the world. We added 5.2 million new jobs since Au-gust of 2003. The national unemployment rate is 4.7 percent. Productivity is high, and that's important. A productive society will yield a higher standard of living for our people. Hourly compensation grew at an annual rate of 5.7 percent in the first quar-ter of this year. Our workers are taking bigger—home bigger paychecks. The stand-

ard of living is on the rise. After-tax income is up. Things are good.

And the fundamental question is, can you keep them that way, see? And there's a lot of competition in the world that creates some uncertainty and anxiety amongst our people. And the temptation for some is to say, "Well, we can't compete anymore so let's protect ourselves and let's withdraw; let's become isolationists." I think that would be a wrong approach by our country. See, we ought not to fear the future; we ought to shape the future. We ought to be confident in our ability to be able to compete and to remain the most innovative country in the world.

And so here are some ideas. First, if we want to be the economic leader in the world so our people can prosper, we need to keep taxes low. We need to be able to be a society that says, you get to earn more of that which you earn.

As you might recall, we went through a pretty tough time in this country over the past 5 years. We had a recession, cor-porate scandals, a stock market correction, a attack on our country. We went to war to defend ourselves; we've had high energy prices; and we had natural disasters. And yet this economy of ours is strong. And I believe the reason why is, is because of the tax cuts we passed in Washington, DC.

We believe that if you have more money in your pocket to save, spend, or invest, the economy grows. And so one way to make sure that we're the economic leader in the world is to make sure the tax cuts we passed are permanent. Now, people say, "Well, if you make the tax cuts permanent, you can't balance the budget." Well, let me talk a little bit about how Washington works. I've been there long enough to be able to give you an accurate report. [*Laugh-ter*]

Don't believe it when they say they're going to raise your taxes to balance the budget. They're going to raise your taxes and figure out new ways to spend the money. The best way to balance the budget is to keep progrowth economic policies in place. And, by the way, last year, because our economy was growing, we generated $100 billion more for the Treasury than we thought. And this year, because of the economy growing strong, we're generating better rates than we did last year.

And so the best way to balance the budget is to keep growing the economy so we collect more tax revenues and be wise about spending your money. See, in Washington, everything sounds good there; every program sounds fantastic. But Government, in order to be wise about spending your money, has got to learn to set priorities. And my priority is this: So long as we have a soldier in harm's way, he or she will have what it takes to achieve victory and secure America.

We're on our way to cutting the deficit in half by 2009. Congress is now debating a supplemental bill. It's money to help fund our troops in Iraq, as well as helping the victims in Katrina. And I've made it very clear that I intend to participate with them in keeping the spending down. And if they exceed the $92.2 billion request, plus monies for avian flu, I'm going to veto the bill. See, that's one way you keep fiscal discipline in Washington, DC.

We'll be competitive if we keep taxes low and be wise about how we spend your money. We'll be competitive, by the way, if we're smart about improving education for our people. See, this is a global economy, whether people like it or not. And the jobs of the 21st century will be either here in America or wherever the workforce is trained to fill those jobs. And therefore, it's important for us to make sure we educate our children early and emphasize math and science so our kids have got the skills necessary to fill those jobs.

We changed how we view public education in Washington. We passed the No Child Left Behind Act, see. It basically said, we're going to make sure we fulfill our commitment to Title I students, but we're starting to ask some questions—questions that I'm sure are asked at this plant: Are you meeting objectives, for example? If you set a goal, are you meeting those goals? And so we set some goals: How about every child learning to read at grade level by the third grade? That didn't seem like an unrealistic goal to me. As a matter of fact, it was a necessary goal.

And then we said to the States, you measure. We're going to get you some money, but you measure to show us whether or not we're meeting the goal. And if you're not meeting the goal, figure out why. See, you can't solve a problem unless you diagnose the problem. And so the No Child Left Behind Act basically says, we're going to diagnose problems early and solve them, before it's too late. This business about shuffling kids through the school—through our schools, based upon age, didn't work. It wasn't fair. It wasn't right. And so the No Child Left Behind Act says, we're going to measure early, and we're going to help children who have fallen behind in reading early, and then we're going to extend that to math.

See, one of the interesting things is because we measure, we know that we're doing fine in math in the eighth grade. But children get to high school—relative to other countries, we're not doing fine in math. And we better do something about it now if we want to be the economic leader of the world.

So we've got a plan to, one, make sure the same standards applied to reading for early grades are applied to math. If we measure in the eighth grade or ninth grade and you're falling behind, you're going to get extra help.

Secondly, advanced placement programs work. I bet I'm looking at some folks out here who took AP when they were in high school. AP means high standards. But we don't have enough teachers around the country to teach AP, so we've got a plan to train 70,000 Advanced Placement teachers to keep raising those standards.

We want to have 30,000 adjunct professors in our classrooms in high school and junior—sometimes it's not cool to be involved with science—and yet it is cool. And we need people who are on the frontlines of science explaining that. I went to a school in Maryland the other day, and there was a NASA scientist there, explaining to junior high kids why the sciences matter and why it's fun to be in science.

We're going to make sure our Pell grants—which, by the way, have expanded by a million kids since I've been the President—continue to have incentives in there for children to take rigorous academics coming out of high school and the first 2 years of college, and then if they maintain a 3.0 average or are taking math, science, or critical language, there's an additional $4,000 on top of their Pell grant. In other words, this is an effort to make sure that we have a workforce that can compete in a global economy so we remain the economic leader of the world.

I want to talk about energy, see. If we don't get it right in energy, we can have the most educated workforce in the world, but we're not going to be able to compete. We can have the lowest taxes in the world, the least regulations, the fewest lawsuits, but if we haven't done something about our energy situation, we're not going to be able to compete in the world.

And so that's why I've come to this important powerplant, to talk about how the United States can have a diversified energy policy that makes us less dependent on foreign sources of oil and more dependent on renewable sources of energy.

Now, one of the things I want to start off by telling the—telling you all, and I hope others are listening, is that over the past 30 years, our economy has grown three times faster than our energy consumption. Isn't that interesting statistics? In other words, we're becoming more technologically advanced. And during that same period of time, we created more than 55 million jobs while cutting air pollution by 50 percent.

So what I believe the American people should understand is that we can put policies in place that encourage economic growth so you've got a better standard of living and, at the same time, become less dependent on energy from overseas and protect the environment.

So what do we need to do? Well, the first thing we got to do is understand that we've got to change our driving habits over time. You've seen the price of gasoline going up. One of the reasons why your price of gasoline is going up is because demand for oil is increasing in places like India and China, and the supply for oil is not meeting that demand. And the key ingredient for gasoline is crude oil. So when the Chinese economy is growing or the Indian economy is growing, and that demand is going up, so is your price at the pump.

One way to make sure the price at the pump doesn't go up as global demand increases for hydrocarbons is to figure out how to drive our cars with different kinds of fuels, such as ethanol. One of the really interesting developments that's taking place now in America is the use of corn-based ethanol—pretty cool deal, isn't it, for the President to be able to say, you know, we're growing a lot of corn—[*laughter*]—and we're less dependent on foreign sources of oil. It's coming—particularly in the Midwest right now, there's a lot of ethanol pumps and plants being developed there to manufacture ethanol from corn.

We've got to do more, though, if we're going to become less dependent on foreign sources of oil, when it comes to ethanol. And so we're spending a lot of your money to develop technologies that will enable us to be able to manufacture ethanol from wood chips or switchgrass. Somebody said, "What is switchgrass?" I said, "Well, it's grass that looks like a switch that grows in dry country." In other words, there's all kinds of opportunities to manufacture ethanol, and we're exploring ways to do so. America has always been on the leading edge of technology and research and development, and here's an area where we've got to stay on the leading edge of change.

Another way to help reduce our use of gasoline is through hybrid vehicles. They're coming; they're coming on the market. As a matter of fact, the energy bill I signed actually will pay you—give you a tax credit if you buy a hybrid. We're trying to stimulate demand through the Tax Code. It makes sense. But there's going to be an additional breakthrough—or additional breakthroughs—when it comes to hybrid vehicles, starting with the development of a battery that will enable you to drive your first 40 miles on electricity. And the Federal Government is very much involved in this research. We're spending your money, again, on research to help fund breakthroughs for battery technologies that will enable you to drive a plug-in hybrid battery.

And, oh, by the way, on ethanol, just one thing I forgot to tell you is that there are 5 million flex-fuel vehicles on the road today. Flex-fuel means you can either have gasoline or ethanol or a combination of the two. You've probably got one and you don't even know it. The technology—the barrier to change is not the automobile; it is the ability to make the fuel in quantities—economic quantities so we can get them to you at the pump.

And same with hybrid batteries; they're coming. Hybrid, plug-in hybrid vehicles with new batteries, they're coming your way. And one of the reasons why is because the Government has entered into research partnerships with the private sector to accelerate these technologies, all aimed at making us less dependent on oil.

A third way to help this country remain an economic leader when it comes to the cars you drive is hydrogen. We spend about a—over a billion dollars of research to bring hydrogen to the marketplace. One fellow reminded me, wisely, it costs—it takes quite a bit of power to make hydrogen. An interesting way to make hydrogen on an economic basis would be through nuclear power, see. But we're spending money and time and effort, all aimed at making sure that the automobiles of the future will require less crude oil. And we're close to some significant breakthroughs.

It's going to take time to move away from the hydrocarbon economy to the hydrogen economy, and in the meantime, it seems like it makes sense to me to do something about the refinery capacity of the United States. Like, if you're worried about the price of gasoline—you don't like it when your price got over $3—and I don't blame you—you might want to ask the question, how come the Government isn't working hard to expand refinery capacity so that there's more gasoline? If you have more gasoline on the market relative to demand, guess what—it takes the pressure off price.

We haven't built a new refinery in the United States since the 1970s. The regulatory burden is a lot. You're kind of used to that here in this industry. And so we got to cut through all that business. If we're serious about helping our consumers and getting more gasoline to the market, we got to have regulatory relief. I suggested to Congress that we put new refineries on abandoned military facilities. It seemed to make sense to me. And so we need to be wise about these policies so that we can say to the American people, we're on our way out of the hydrocarbon era. But in the meantime, let's be thoughtful of the consumers here in the United States.

We're also going to need a lot of electricity in the future. Electricity demand is projected to increase by nearly 50 percent over the next 25 years. That's a lot. And we better be wise about how we implement a strategy to meet that demand; otherwise, we're not going to be the economic leader; otherwise, our people aren't going to be having the good jobs that we want them to have; otherwise, your children and my children, our grandchildren are not going to have the bright, hopeful America that we want for them.

Now, one of the things that people have got to understand is that we get our—we generate our electricity from four sources: coal—it's about 50 percent; nuclear power—about 20 percent; natural gas—18 percent; and then other renewable sources like hydroelectric, solar, and wind power. And that's the mix; that's the energy mix.

Coal is by far the most abundant and affordable energy resource. We got about 240 years at current rates of consumption. It's a valuable asset for the United States. The problem is, coal isn't—when you burn it, it isn't clean. It doesn't meet our standards. It's not—it doesn't enable us to say, you can grow your economy and, at the same time, protect the environment like we want.

And so we're developing clean coal technology. We're spending over $2 billion in a 10-year period to be able to say to the American people that we're using the money wisely to determine whether or not we can have zero-emissions coal-fired powerplants. It's in our interests that we do that. It makes sense. About 2012, under the FutureGen Initiative, we think we will build the first powerplant to run on coal and remove virtually all pollutants.

Natural gas is an important commodity. By the way, we can explore for natural gas in environmentally friendly ways. And we ought to be exploring for natural gas in the ANWR, as well as off the gulf coast of the United States.

Here's another interesting way to help make sure there's enough natural gas for this economy to grow—by the way, natural gas, as you know, is not just used for power. It's used for fertilizers, a variety of uses. You can liquefy natural gas; you can put it in a ship, and you can send it long distances and still have an economic product. And there are places in this world where there's a lot of natural gas—a lot.

And they're building liquefied production facilities. And they put them on these ships—but we don't have any places to offload it in the United States. We got some, but not enough.

If we're really interested in diversifying our energy sources and making sure the American people have got enough energy to watch this economy grow, we have got to have LNG sites to offload the gas from abroad. And so what we've done is, I signed a new bill, energy bill, that clarifies Federal authority to license new sites, that reduces the bureaucratic obstacles to opening up the terminals and streamlines the development. It's in your interest that we enable liquefied natural gas to come into our country so that we can help take the burden off some of the pricing pressures that we're inevitably going to feel with demand going up and not enough electricity supply.

Thirdly, about 6 percent of the continental U.S. is highly suitable for the construction of wind turbines. And this is a really interesting opportunity for the country—they ought to put one big one in Washington, DC. [*Laughter*] They say—the experts tell me that this area alone has the potential to supply up to 20 percent of our Nation's electricity. I think that's an interesting opportunity. I don't know if it's true or not, but it's certainly worth trying to find out, in order to make sure this country has got a bright future. And so we got $44 million for wind energy research. And the goal is to expand the use and lower the cost of wind turbine technology.

In other words, we're constantly researching and looking. I don't know if you know this or not, but the Federal Government does spend money on research in a variety of fronts, and it should. And I intend to double the basic—the budget for basic research over the next 10 years. The iPod—like, I like to ride my mountain bike and plug in the iPod. The technology for the iPod came as a result of Federal research. The Internet came about because of defense money research.

So we're spending money on research. The reason I keep repeating that is not only is it going to help us diversify our energy sources and make us competitive in the world, but it also helps make sure America is always on the leading edge of technological change.

Solar energy—the dream in solar energy is to develop technology so that someday your house is like a little generating plant, and if you don't use the power, you feed it back into the grid. It's possible, but it's not going to be possible if we don't spend money on research and development. So we're spending $150 million to combine Government money with private research money in solar technologies to see if we can't help foster technologies that will be able to capture the sun, feed it into your house, generate enough electricity, and if you've got a little excess, feed it back into the grid. I think that's a pretty interesting idea, and it's certainly one worth exploring.

Finally, I want to talk about nuclear power—a subject you all are very familiar with. It is a really important way to meet our goals, which is to have abundant, affordable, clean, and safe sources of energy. The important thing for the American people to understand is this concept: One, nuclear power is abundant and affordable. In other words, you have nuclear powerplants, you can say, we've got an abundant amount of electricity. And once you get the plant up and running, the operating costs of these plants are significantly lower than other forms of electricity plants, which means the energy is affordable.

As I mentioned, nuclear power—it's the second leading source of electricity here. We have 100 nuclear powerplants that operate in 31 States. Now, we haven't built one in a long period of time.

People in our country are rightly concerned about greenhouse gases and the environment, and I can understand why; I

am too. As a matter of fact, I try to tell people, let's quit the debate about whether greenhouse gases are caused by mankind or by natural causes; let's just focus on technologies that deal with the issue. Nuclear power will help us deal with the issue of greenhouse gases. Without nuclear energy, carbon dioxide emissions would have been 28 percent greater in the electricity industry in 2004. Without nuclear power, we would have had an additional 700 million tons a year of carbon dioxide, and that's nearly equal to the annual emissions from 136 million passenger cars. Nuclear power helps us protect the environment.

And nuclear power is safe. It is safe because of advances in science and engineering and plant design. It is safe because the workers and managers of our nuclear powerplants are incredibly skilled people who know what they're doing.

For the sake of economic security and national security, the United States of America must aggressively move forward with the construction of nuclear powerplants. Other nations are. Interestingly enough, France has built 58 plants since the 1970s and now gets 78 percent of its electricity from nuclear power. I think that's an interesting statistic, isn't it? The United States hasn't ordered a plant since the 1970s, and yet France has not only ordered them, they built 58 plants. And 78 percent of their electricity comes from nuclear power. They don't have to worry about natural gas coming from somewhere else. They worry about it, but they don't have to worry about it to the extent that we do.

China has 9 nuclear plants in operation, and they got—plan to build 40 more over the next two decades. They understand that in order to be an aggressive nation, an economic nation that is flourishing so their people can benefit, they better do something about their sources of electricity. They see it. India—I just came from India—they're going to build some nuclear powerplants.

To maintain our economic leadership, we got to do it again. And so here's the strategy. First, in the energy bill I signed in 2005, there are loan guarantees, production tax credits, Federal risk insurance for the builders of new plants. In other words, we said, this is an industry that hadn't got much going since the seventies. It's an overregulated industry. It's highly risky because of the regulations to try to build a plant. People don't know this, but you get yourself a design for a nuclear powerplant; you start spending money for plans and engineering plans and everything; you get building; and all of the sudden, somebody can shut you down. And that makes it awfully difficult to take risk, if a lawsuit can cause you to spend enormous sums of money and have no productive use of the money spent.

And so we got together with the Congress and said, "Well, how—what can we do to create incentives to show the industry that we're serious about moving forward?" Well, one is loan guarantees, and that gives investors confidence that this Government is committed to the construction of nuclear powerplants. Secondly is production tax credits, and those credits will reward investments in the latest advanced nuclear power generation.

In other words, there's incentives—loan guarantee is an incentive, tax credits are incentives, Federal risk insurance. What the Federal risk insurance says—is offered for the first six new powerplant—nuclear powerplants. And the insurance helps protect builders of the plants against lawsuits or bureaucratic obstacles and other delays beyond their control. We have got what's called the Nuclear Power 2010 Initiative, which is a $1.1 billion partnership between the Federal Government and the industry to facilitate new plant orders. In other words, I have said, we need more nuclear powerplants, and here's a strategy to get them going, see. Here's a way to say to the industry, we're serious about this.

This time last year, only two companies were seeking to build nuclear powerplants. Now 16 companies have expressed an interest in new construction, and they're considering as many as 25 new plants, trying to get these plants—construction started by the end of this decade. I want it to be said that this generation of folks had the foresight necessary to diversify our—or to continue to diversify electricity supply and recognize that nuclear power is safe, and we did something about it. We just didn't mark our time. We actually did something about it so a generation of Americans coming up will be able to have a better America.

I understand the issue of waste, and we've got to do something about it. We've got to be wise about nuclear waste. I'm a believer that Yucca Mountain is a scientifically sound place to send the waste, and I would hope that the United States Congress would recognize that as well.

I also recognize that we can do something on a reprocessing front. And so I got our administration to commit to the Global Nuclear Energy Partnership. I think you'll find this interesting; at least I did. Under the partnership, America is going to work with nations that have already got an advanced civilian nuclear energy program, such as France and Japan and Russia, and we're going to use new technologies that effectively and safely recycle spent nuclear fuel. In other words, we're coming together to say, how can we do a better job of reprocessing and recycling fuel?

And the reason that's important, at least for our fellow citizens to understand, is it will reduce the amount of the toxicity of the fuel and reduce the amount we have to store. To me, it's a smart way to combine with others to reduce storage requirements for nuclear waste by up to 90 percent. It's a good way to work with other nations that are spending money on research and development as well. It's a way to, kind of, leverage up an investment. We're going to—I've asked Congress to spend $250 million on this partnership. I hope they follow through with it. It is a necessary expenditure of money to make sure that the nuclear power industry can move forward with confidence, and the American people move forward with confidence as well.

And so here are some ideas—not only ideas; this is what we're doing; this has gone from idea to action. What I'm telling you is, is that I understand the need to get off oil. I understand the need to work on renewable sources of energy. And I'm pleased to report we're working with Congress to do it. We're spending your money on research and development to find interesting technologies. You know, I hope that when my grandchildren and some of your children start taking their driver's test, they'll be cranking up a hydrogen-powered automobile, with hydrogen produced from electricity generated from plants such as these.

We have a duty to think about the problems this country is going to face. Listen, this economy is good, and I want to keep it that way; but I also want to make sure it's good 10 years from now. And I want

to make sure that this global economy, this world that is becoming more connected, is one that doesn't cause us to fear and to neglect our duties, but that we put policies in place that enable us to remain confident, that we're an entrepreneurial society, that we're well-educated people, that we're willing to work hard to raise our families and put bread on the table. And we've got to make sure we have a good energy policy to do that.

I want to thank you for giving me the chance to come and share with you today what the country is doing right now. I want to thank you very much for showing what is possible. I appreciate your hard work here.

May God bless you all.

NOTE: The President spoke at 3:29 p.m. at the Limerick Generating Station. In his remarks, he referred to John W. Rowe, chairman, president, and chief executive officer, Christopher M. Crane, senior vice president, and Ronald J. DeGregorio, site vice president of Limerick Generating Station, Exelon Corporation.

Remarks at a Pennsylvania Congressional Victory Committee Dinner in Philadelphia, Pennsylvania
May 24, 2006

Thank you all. Thanks for coming. I want to thank you for joining the Pennsylvania Congressional Victory Committee. I am so honored to be standing by two of the young stars of the United States Congress. You know, I've been up there long enough to be able to spot talent, and Jim Gerlach and Mike Fitzpatrick are really talented Congressmen, and they deserve to be reelected to the United States Congress.

I appreciate Karen. It's good to see you again, Karen. Thanks for coming. Katie, Rob, Joel, Jay, and Katelyn are also here.

[*Laughter*] All you got to do is register them to vote, and it's a landslide. [*Laughter*]

And I appreciate Kathy Fitzpatrick and Jimmy for being here as well. And by the way, Mike's mother [father], * James, and mom, Mary, is with us. So it's good to have the Fitzpatrick family well represented to pay honor to this good man here.

I appreciate all the local officials who are here and the grassroots activists. See,

_____

* White House correction.

you win campaigns by being able to raise money—and we've raised a lot tonight, and thank you for that. But you also win campaigns by convincing people to put up the signs and make the phone calls and go to the coffee shops and go to your houses of worship and tell people, when you've got somebody who's decent, honest, and honorable, put them back in office. And we've got people who are decent, honest, and honorable representing the Sixth and Eighth Congressional Districts here from Pennsylvania.

And so thank you for what you have done and what you're going to do coming down the stretch of the elections. We're just kind of getting warmed up. [*Laughter*] We're in the jumping-jack phase of the political season. [*Laughter*] We're getting ready to run and win. And one of the interesting things about politics, you can't win without a good candidates, and we've got two really fine candidates standing right up here on the stage.

Jim Gerlach is an experienced leader. He's been involved for 16 years in the political process. He is a—he's an independent voice, which is good. It's good for the people of this congressional district. He believes in low taxes. I appreciate his strong stand on national security. He's a member of the Transportation and Infrastructure Committee, and that's important for people in his congressional district because he's helped to improve traffic and roads, and he's promoted open spaces as well. He's a good, thoughtful Member of the United States Congress. And the people in his district are lucky to have him there, as far as I'm concerned.

Mike Fitzpatrick—I don't know what it's like in local politics here, but the county commissioner is somebody who generally knows the feelings of the people, and Mike was a county commissioner. And he's pretty—it means he was close to the constituents; he knows what they think. It's important to have people in Washington who don't lose touch with the constituents. And

Mike Fitzpatrick certainly didn't lose the touch.

He is an Eagle Scout, and interestingly enough, he continually goes to Eagle Scout ceremonies. You know why? He wants to help some other youngster set high values and understand the importance of achievement, but he also wants to thank the parents and those involved in the Scout troops for reaching out to help somebody.

I like Mike a lot. He's an honorable fellow who is for low taxes, good environmental policy; he cares a lot about health care. The people of his congressional district are really lucky to have him representing them.

We're going to win the elections in November of 2006. The reason why is we get things done on behalf of the American people. We've been given some challenges, and we've responded to meet those challenges. I spend the most time as your President working on ways to secure our country. The biggest challenge we face is to make sure that we prevent another attack on the American people. Much of my thinking about the presidency was formed on September the 11th, 2001. It's a day, of course, I will never forget; it's a day that all of us should never forget; it's a day in which our standing in the world changed dramatically. Because you see, we grew up thinking oceans could protect us, and we realized that there's an enemy out there that will do incredible harm to the American people. I'm proud to have allies in the United States Congress who understand that our most important job in Washington is to protect the American people.

We face an enemy that is totalitarian in nature. They've taken a great religion and have hijacked it to suit their own needs. They're Islamo-fascists. They will kill innocent life to achieve an objective. They have made it clear they'd like to hurt America again. They would like to drive us out of regions of the world so they could establish safe haven. They would like to mate their terrible ambitions with weapons of mass destruction. These are their words, not mine. They believe this country is soft, and it's just a matter of time before we lose our nerve. And I'm proud to have two Members of the United States Congress standing up here who understand the stakes and who are strong in the support of the men and women who wear our uniform and strongly support our efforts to bring the enemy to justice before they hurt us again.

A battlefront in the war on terror is, of course, Iraq. And people in our country are unsettled because of the war, and I understand that. I fully understand why people in America are disquieted about what they're seeing on their TV screens. There's a concern about whether or not we can win. There's no doubt in my mind we will win. And our objective is to have an Iraq that can govern itself, sustain itself, and defend itself; an ally in the war on terror, and an example for others in a region that is desperate for freedom.

The enemy cannot defeat us on the battlefield, but what they can do is put horrible images on our TV screens. And it's really important for those who wear our uniform and the enemy and the people of Iraq to know that the United States of America will complete the mission, and in so doing, will make our country more secure and will be laying the foundation for peace.

I appreciate working with Members of Congress who understand the lessons of history. And one of the really interesting lessons of history, one way I'd like to describe what's taking place in the world today, is my relationship—I describe my relationship with the Prime Minister of Japan, Koizumi. He's a good friend of mine, personally. He's an interesting fellow. He loved Elvis. [*Laughter*] Still does. [*Laughter*] You know what's interesting, though, about my talks with the Prime Minister—and by the way, when I sit down at the table with him, we talk about how we can keep the peace. We talk about how

to deal with North Korean and the fact that he's trying to develop a weapon of mass destruction and, at the same time, creating starvation inside his country. We talk about the young democracy of Iraq, where Japan has 1,000 troops. We talk about a fledgling democracy in Afghanistan and how we can work together to help this young, new democracy grow and flourish.

It's really interesting, isn't it? What makes it even more interesting is the fact that 60 years ago or so, my dad went to war with the Japanese. And something happened between the 19-year-old Navy pilot, George H.W. Bush, and George W. Bush sitting at the table talking about the peace. And what happened was, my predecessor—one of my predecessors—Harry S. Truman, believed in what I believed in, the universality of freedom, the capacity of people to be—to take on democracy, and the knowledge that democracy yields the peace.

And so what you're seeing today is tyranny going to democracy, is people who demanded freedom—12 million people said, "I want to be free"—learning what it means to self-govern. Someday an American President is going to be able to tell the story of our generation. They're going to be able to tell the story of those of us who've been honored to serve our country and say, "Thank goodness they believed in the capacity of freedom to take a troubled country and convert it into an ally." Someday an American President is going to be sitting down with a duly elected leader from Iraq, working to keep the peace, and our children and grandchildren are going to be better off.

Here at home, we've got a strong economy. You know, the economy grew at 3.5 percent last year. That is faster than any other major industrialized nation in the world. The national unemployment rate is 4.7 percent, which happens to be the unemployment rate here in the State of Pennsylvania. We created 5.2 million new jobs since August of 2003. People are working. After-tax real income is up more than 8 percent per American since 2001. Productivity is on the rise; homeownership is high; small businesses are flourishing. This economy is strong, and we intend to keep it that way.

I think it's amazing to be able to tell you how strong the economy is, given through—what we have been through, however. We've been through a recession; we've been through corporate scandals; we've been through a stock market correction; we've been through an attack on our country; we've been through wars; we have been through natural disasters; we've been through high energy prices. Yet we have got a strong economy. You know why? Because we cut the taxes on the American people.

Our progrowth economic policies work. The three of us believe that when you have more of your own money in your pocket to save, invest, or spend, the economy grows. We would rather you spend your money than the Federal Government spends your money.

Now, you'll hear them in the campaign, they'll be talking about the deficit. I'm confident they'll be yelling about the deficit at these two Congressmen. Let me just set the record straight for you. See, they're going to say, "We're going to run up your taxes to balance the budget." That's not the way Washington, DC, works. They're going to run up your taxes, and they're going to figure out new ways to spend your money on new programs, and there will still be a deficit.

The best way to reduce the deficit is to keep progrowth economic policies in place and be wise about how we spend your money, which is exactly what we're doing in Washington. We're on our way to cut the deficit in half by 2009.

One of my concerns is that the United States will lose our nerve and fear competition and become an isolated place. You know, when you see the global competition these days from China and India, some in our country say, "Well, I don't think we

want to try to compete with them." And so they worry about protectionism—they think about protectionism, or they're isolators—that's not my attitude, and I know it's not the attitude of these Congressmen. We have nothing to fear about the future, because we intend to shape it, see. We intend to make America the most competitive nation in the world.

So I'm going to work with these two Congressmen to pass what we've called the American Competitive Initiative, which says that we will be the most—we'll lead the world when it comes to research and development. The Federal Government should double its commitment to basic research in physical sciences over the next 10 years. People say, "Why would the Federal Government be investing?" Well, I'll give you why—the Internet. The Internet came to be because of Federal research dollars—iPods—got one? I got one, you know—[*laughter*]—as a result of Federal research. It's important for the United States to be the most technologically advanced nation in the world.

And that's why I've called for Congress to make the research and development tax credit a permanent part of our Tax Code. And that's why I look forward to working with these Congressmen to make sure that our schools are adept at teaching people the skills necessary to fill the jobs of the 21st century, which means strong math and science curriculum.

So today I went out to one of the most advanced nuclear powerplants in the world—at least in our country. And I did so because I wanted to make this point: In order for us to be a competitive nation, in order for us to keep a high standard of living, we have got to get off of our addiction to oil. And I'm looking forward to working with these Congressmen to do that.

And so I talked today, and I'm going to work with the Congressmen to continue to spend your money on research and development; for example, to speed up new battery technology so that the hybrid—we'll have plug-in hybrid batteries, which means, in Philadelphia, you'll be driving the first 40 miles per day on electricity, not on gasoline; or more advanced uses of ethanol so we can be using crops grown here in America rather than oil from the Middle East to power our automobiles. Eventually, we'll be firing up our automobiles using hydrogen.

I went to the powerplant today. It's estimated that demand for electricity is going to increase by 50 percent over young people's lifetimes, which means we better have the capacity to generate electricity and protect our environment at the same time. And a really good way to do so is through nuclear power.

I'm also going to work with the Congressmen to continue to spend research money on clean coal technology. We've got 240 years worth of coal; let's burn it cleanly. Let's use it in a way that says we can protect our environment and make sure we maintain our standard of living.

We'll continue to invest in solar technology. Here's the dream of solar technology—and by the way, we've got $150 million in my budget for solar technology. The dream is, is that every house will have a solar roof to it. And if you do not use all the power generated that day from the sun, you feed it back into the grid. It's like your little powerplant. [*Laughter*] You become a generator of electricity. It's coming.

And we intend to lead the charge to change our habits when it comes to energy to protect our environment, on the one hand, and to make sure the United States is a competitive nation on the other.

I want to talk about health care. For years, Democrats have been talking about Medicare, see, how they're going to make it work better. They never did—they never got the job done. So we came along. We modernized Medicare for our seniors. We said, "If you make a pledge to the seniors of the United States, make it a good

pledge; make it work." You see, the Government would pay $25,000 for an ulcer surgery but not a dime for the prescription drugs to prevent the surgery from being needed in the first place. What I'm telling you is, medicine had become modern, but Medicare hadn't.

And so we changed it. And today, more than 32 million seniors have enrolled in Part D of Medicare, which means there's a prescription drug benefit. The average senior saves one-half on his or her drug bills. And if you're a poor senior—about a third of those eligible for Medicare—the Federal Government is going to pay 95 percent of your drug bills. The days of a senior having to choose between food and medicine are gone, thanks to the Republican Party.

But we also understand that we don't want the Federal Government running your health care. The best health care system is one where the patient-doctor relationship is central to the decisionmaking, and that's why we're for transparency, information technology in the health care field. That's why we're strong believers in health savings accounts, which will help the uninsured and the small-business owners. We're believers in association health plans that will allow small businesses to pool risk across jurisdictional boundaries so they can buy insurance at the same discounts that big businesses get to do.

I'll tell you what else we're for: We understand that frivolous and junk lawsuits run good doctors out of practice and runup the cost of your medicine. And you got a problem here in Pennsylvania. You got ob-gyns leaving your State. You got specialists who are fearful of practicing medicine. And you need people like these two Congressmen who are willing to stand up to the trial lawyers and promote good, strong medical liability reform.

Finally, although they're not in the Senate, I appreciate them supporting me in picking judges, the right kind of judges, judges who will not legislate from the bench but judges who will strictly interpret the Constitution. I am proud to have nominated Chief Justice John Roberts and Justice Sam Alito, and I'm even prouder they got confirmed by the United States Senate.

Ours is a philosophy that trusts people. We'd rather you have your money. We believe you can spend it wisely. We believe you can make the right decisions when it comes to medicine. We believe our seniors should be given modern medicine, and we delivered on our promises. The other bunch, they get angry, and they yell and they, you know, scream and holler. We just go about and get the job done. We're people who can deliver results on behalf of the American people.

I've signed a Medicare reform bill; I've signed an energy bill; I've signed tax cuts; I've signed bills to make sure those who

wear the uniform get the full support of the United States Government. And I'm proud to have these two accomplished men serving in Washington, DC. The people of Pennsylvania have got two good Congressmen in these two, and you need to send them back. They're serving this State with dignity, and they're serving our country with honor, and I'm proud to call them friends.

NOTE: The President spoke at 5:46 p.m. at the Sheraton Philadelphia City Center. In his remarks, he referred to Karen Gerlach, wife of Representative Jim Gerlach; Kathleen Fitzpatrick, wife of Representative Michael G. Fitzpatrick; Prime Minister Junichiro Koizumi of Japan; and Chairman Kim Jong Il of North Korea.

Remarks at the Change of Command Ceremony for the Commandant of the United States Coast Guard
May 25, 2006

Thank you all. Thank you for the warm welcome. I'm delighted to be here with you at Fort McNair. I'm pleased to join you in celebrating an historic moment for the United States Coast Guard. This morning we mark a change of command at the helm of America's oldest continuous maritime service.

Our Nation thanks a fine patriot, Admiral Tom Collins, for his leadership these past 4 years. And we thank his wife, Nancy, and their family for joining us today. We also congratulate Admiral Thad Allen, as he begins his duties as the 23d Commandant of the United States Coast Guard. And we appreciate the love and support of his wife, Pam, and their fine family as well.

I want to thank Michael Chertoff for his distinguished service to our country. I appreciate the other members of my Cabinet

who have joined to celebrate Thad Allen's beginning his duties as the Commandant: Secretary Elaine Chao and Secretary Norm Mineta and Secretary Sam Bodman and Acting Secretary Lynn Scarlett.

I'm honored to be on stage with General Pete Pace, Chairman of the Joint Chiefs, and I welcome his wife, Lynne, as well. I want to thank the Members of Congress who have joined us today. I appreciate Master Chief Frank Welch, who is the Master Chief Petty Officer of the United States Coast Guard. I want to thank Captain Wilbur Douglass for his fine invocation. I appreciate the members of the diplomatic corps who are here. Thank you all for coming.

The history of the Coast Guard dates back more than two centuries to the Revenue Cutter Service, established by Alexander Hamilton during the presidency of

George Washington, or as I call him, the first George W. [*Laughter*]

Through the generations, the men and women of the Coast Guard have stepped forward to defend our Nation, to protect our waterways and ports, to enforce maritime law, to safeguard commerce and natural resources, and to rescue those in peril on the seas. Now the Coast Guard is carrying out those missions during a new kind of war. The Coast Guard is vital to our Nation's security, and the American people are grateful to stand behind your shield of freedom.

The Coast Guard is also the world's premier lifesaving service, and the whole world saw your skill and bravery during the hurricanes last year. They saw Coast Guard rescuers plunging from helicopters, lifting people from rooftops, hoisting them to safety. In all, more than 4,000 Coast Guard personnel came to the aid of their fellow Americans and rescued more than 33,000 citizens. One of those saved said this about her rescuers: "They're my guardian angels. I couldn't be here if it wasn't for them."

Countless others who lived through last year's hurricanes feel the same way. When Americans were at their most desperate, they looked to the skies for help, and they knew their prayers were answered when they saw those rescue choppers from the United States Coast Guard. The Coast Guard performed with courage and distinction, and your response to Hurricane Katrina will go down as one of the finest hours in the Coast Guard's 216-year history.

In all your work over the past 4 years, the Coast Guard has benefited from a superb leader in Admiral Tom Collins. Admiral Collins assumed his duties as Commandant shortly after September the 11th, 2001, and has worked tirelessly to transform the Coast Guard for this war on terror. Admiral Collins has led the men and women of this service with honor and respect and devotion to duty. And he's made recruitment and retention a top priority.

Thanks to his leadership, recruitment is up, and the Coast Guard's retention rate is at its highest level since World War II.

Admiral Collins has a right to be proud of all that he accomplished in his time as Commandant. Now he has the right to take some time off. [*Laughter*] Maybe even spend a few afternoons at Fenway Park. [*Laughter*] Today Admiral Collins will mark the end of a distinguished 38-year career in the Coast Guard. He retires with the admiration and gratitude of the United States, and Laura and I wish him and Nancy all the best in the next chapter of their lives.

In a few moments, Admiral Collins will pass the duties of Commandant to an outstanding successor in Admiral Thad Allen. I came to know Admiral Allen well last September when he directed recovery efforts after Hurricanes Katrina and Rita. We surveyed damage together. We sat one evening on the deck of the USS *Iwo Jima* talking about how we could help the folks in that region recover. He gave me regular updates on what was taking place—an incredibly devastated part of our country.

It didn't take long to recognize his ability or his integrity or his ability to lead. I knew I could count on Admiral Allen to give me candid judgment. I relied on his steady nerves and his presence of mind in trying conditions. I was impressed by his compassion and his determination to help those who had lost so much.

Admiral Allen brings his experience with Hurricane Katrina to his new post, and he brings much more. The Admiral is a graduate of the Coast Guard Academy, where he was a star football player—he still looks like he could hold his own on the gridiron. [*Laughter*] He spent his life around the Coast Guard officers and enlisted personnel. Admiral Allen's father, Clyde, with us today, served in the Coast Guard. That means Thad followed in his father's footsteps; I see nothing wrong with that. [*Laughter*]

At every stage of his career, Admiral Allen has inspired those around him with energy and dedication to service. One of his former colleagues likened Admiral Allen to the Energizer bunny. [*Laughter*] Another said, "He brings out the best in people, especially in times of crisis." I want to thank Admiral Allen for his willingness to take on this incredibly important responsibility, and I look forward to calling him Commandant of the Coast Guard.

One of Admiral Allen's most important tasks as Commandant will be to help ensure that the Federal Government is ready for the hurricane season, which begins a week from today. The Coast Guard performed heroically during last year's hurricanes, and other agencies of our Government can look to you for example.

We're determined to learn the lessons of Katrina, and we're doing everything possible to be prepared for the next storm. The Department of Homeland Security has reviewed emergency plans for all 50 States and America's 75 largest cities. The Department is working closely with communities to identify any weaknesses in their plans and to find ways to improve them now.

Secretary Chertoff has taken steps to reform FEMA, improve partnerships with the Red Cross and the Department of Defense, expand the amount of supplies the Federal Government has on hand. We're also making it clear that all able-bodied Americans should have the resources necessary to sustain themselves for 48 to 72 hours after a disaster so that emergency personnel can focus on saving those who cannot help themselves.

I appreciate the many dedicated Americans who are working to prepare for this hurricane season. And I'm confident that if danger arrives, whether from nature or man, the United States Coast Guard will be ready.

The Coast Guard has always been ready to defend our people and our freedom, and I thank you for your dedicated service. *Semper Paratus*.

And now, in recognition of your exceptional service during Hurricane Katrina, I will present the Presidential Unit Citation to the United States Coast Guard.

May God bless you all.

NOTE: The President spoke at 11:12 a.m. at Fort Lesley J. McNair. In his remarks, he referred to Capt. Wilbur C. Douglass III, USN, chaplain of the Coast Guard.

Statement on House of Representatives Passage of Energy Legislation
May 25, 2006

I applaud the House of Representatives for passing the energy and water appropriations bill. I am grateful for the House leadership's work on it. This bill marks a critical first step toward realizing my American Competitiveness Initiative, and it fully funds my request for the Energy Department's Office of Science. I appreciate the leadership of Chairman Hobson and Chairman Lewis in working to keep our economy the most competitive in the world. This bill also will support my Advanced Energy Initiative and help make America more secure and less dependent on foreign sources of energy. I urge the Senate to join the House in supporting these important initiatives.

NOTE: The statement referred to H.R. 5427.

Statement on the National Economy
May 25, 2006

America's economy is on the fast track. Today's revised report by the Commerce Department indicates our economy grew at 5.3 percent for the first quarter of this year. That is the fastest growth in 2½ years and another clear sign that our economy is powerful, productive, and prosperous. I commend America's workers, small-business owners, and innovators for contributing to this strong economic growth. I will continue to work to pursue progrowth policies, make the tax cuts permanent, and restrain Government spending so that opportunity reaches every American neighborhood and every American family.

Statement on the Department of Justice's Handling of Representative William J. Jefferson's Materials
May 25, 2006

Over the last several days, the House of Representatives and the Department of Justice have attempted to resolve a dispute over the execution of a search warrant on the Capitol Hill office of Congressman William Jefferson, who is under criminal investigation.

The Department of Justice's search was part of an important investigation of alleged public corruption. At the same time, the bipartisan leadership of the House of Representatives believes this search violated the constitutional principle of separation of powers and the Speech or Debate Clause of the Constitution. They note these principles must be adhered to, even in the pursuit of a legitimate criminal investigation.

I recognize these are deeply held views. Our Government has not faced such a dilemma in more than two centuries. Yet after days of discussions, it is clear these differences will require more time to be worked out.

So today I am directing the Department of Justice to seal all the materials recovered from Congressman Jefferson's office for the next 45 days and not to allow access to anyone involved in the investigation. I am also ordering the sealed materials to remain under the custody of the Solicitor General, who heads a separate office within the Justice Department and is not involved in the investigation.

This period will provide both parties more time to resolve the issues in a way that ensures that materials relevant to the ongoing criminal investigation are made available to prosecutors in a manner that respects the interests of a coequal branch of Government. The Justice Department and the House of Representatives should continue their discussions and resolve this matter as quickly as possible.

Let me be clear: Investigating and prosecuting crime is a crucial executive responsibility that I take seriously. Those who violate the law—including a Member of Congress—should and will be held to account. This investigation will go forward, and justice will be served.

Memorandum on Handling of Materials Held by the Department of Justice Following Execution of a Search Warrant
May 25, 2006

Memorandum for the Attorney General and the Solicitor General of the United States
Subject: Handling of Materials Held by the Department of Justice Following Execution of a Search Warrant

After taking appropriate account of the respective constitutional functions of the House of Representatives and of the executive branch, including important law enforcement interests, the protections afforded those functions under the Constitution, and the need for comity between the executive and legislative branches in the service of the American people, I direct that, with respect to the materials taken pursuant to the warrant dated May 18, 2006, and captioned "In the Matter of the Search of Rayburn House Office Building Room Number 2113," including any copies thereof or items derived in whole or in part therefrom:

(1) The Attorney General, acting through the Solicitor General of the United States who shall for this purpose be subject to no supervision by any officer of the Department of Justice other than the Attorney General, shall (a) preserve and seal the materials, (b) ensure that no use is made of the materials, and (c) ensure that no person has access to the materials, except that Office of the Solicitor General personnel under the direct supervision of the Solicitor General may have the minimum physical access to the materials essential to the preservation of the materials.

(2) The Attorney General shall endeavor, and the House of Representatives is respectfully encouraged to endeavor, to resolve any issues relating to the materials through discussions between them in good faith and with mutual institutional respect and, if it should prove necessary after exhaustion of such discussions, through appropriate proceedings in the courts of the United States.

The Attorney General shall keep me informed of discussions to which this memorandum refers and proceedings relating to the materials. This memorandum shall expire on July 9, 2006.

GEORGE W. BUSH

cc: The Speaker of the House of Representatives

NOTE: An original was not available for verification of the content of this memorandum.

Statement on Senate Passage of Immigration Reform Legislation
May 25, 2006

I commend the Senate for passing bipartisan comprehensive immigration reform before the Memorial Day deadline set by its leaders. I appreciate the hard work of the leadership and Senators on both sides of the aisle. An effective immigration reform bill will protect our borders, hold employers to account for the workers they hire, create a temporary-worker program to take pressure off our border and meet the needs of our growing economy, address the issue of the millions of illegal immigrants already in our country, and honor America's great tradition of the melting pot. The House of Representatives began a national dialog by passing an immigration bill last year. Now that the Senate has acted, I look forward to working together with both the House of Representatives and the Senate to produce a bill for me to sign into law.

NOTE: The statement referred to S. 2611. The Office of the Press Secretary also released a Spanish language transcript of this statement.

Statement on House of Representatives Passage of Energy Legislation
May 25, 2006

I applaud today's vote in the House to allow for environmentally responsible energy exploration in a small part of the Arctic National Wildlife Refuge. A reliable domestic supply of energy is important to America's security and prosperity. This project will keep our economy growing by creating jobs and ensuring that businesses can expand. And it will make America less dependent on foreign sources of energy, eventually by up to a million barrels of crude oil a day—a nearly 20 percent increase over our current domestic production. I thank the House leadership and Chairman Pombo for their hard work on this issue. I urge the Senate to join the House in passing ANWR legislation.

NOTE: The statement referred to H.R. 5429.

Statement on Signing the Coastal Barrier Resources Reauthorization Act of 2005
May 25, 2006

Today I have signed into law S. 1869, the "Coastal Barrier Resources Reauthorization Act of 2005." This Act provides for digital mapping in support of the coastal barrier resources system and authorizes appropriations through fiscal year 2010 for implementation of the Coastal Barrier Resources Act.

Section 3(c)(2) and section 4(c)(3)(C) and (D) purport to require executive branch officials to submit legislative recommendations to the Congress. The executive branch shall construe such provisions in a manner consistent with the Constitution's commitment to the President of the authority to submit for the consideration of the Congress such measures as the President judges necessary and expedient and to supervise the unitary executive branch.

GEORGE W. BUSH

The White House,
May 25, 2006.

The President's News Conference With Prime Minister Tony Blair of the United Kingdom
May 25, 2006

President Bush. Thank you all. Good evening. I want to thank Prime Minister Tony Blair for coming to Washington to discuss his recent visit to Iraq. The Prime Minister met with key leaders of the new Iraqi Government that represents the will of the Iraqi people and reflects their nation's diversity. As Prime Minister Blair will tell you, Iraqi Prime Minister Maliki outlined an aggressive agenda to bring security to the Iraqi people, to improve electricity and other essential services, and to pursue a strategy for national reconciliation.

The agenda that Prime Minister Maliki has outlined demonstrates that Iraq's new Government understands its duty to deliver real improvements in the daily lives of the Iraqi people. The formation of a new government represents a new beginning for Iraq and a new beginning for the relationship between Iraq and our coalition. The United States and Great Britain will work together to help this new democracy succeed. We'll take advantage of this moment of opportunity and work with Iraq's new Government to strengthen its young democracy and achieve victory over our common enemies.

As we celebrate this historic moment, it's important to recall how we got there and take stock on how far we've come over the last 3 years. The violence and bloodshed in Iraq has been difficult for the civilized world to comprehend. The United States and Great Britain have lost some of our finest men and women in combat. The car bombings and suicide attacks and other terrorist acts have also inflicted great suffering on the Iraqi people. And Iraqis have increasingly become the principal victims of terror and sectarian reprisal.

Yet in the face of this ongoing violence, each time the Iraqi people voiced their opinion, they chose freedom. In three different elections, millions of Iraqis turned out to the polls and cast their ballots. Because of their courage, the Iraqis now have a government of their choosing, elected under the most modern and democratic Constitution in the Arab world.

The birth of a free and democratic Iraq was made possible by the removal of a cruel dictator. The decision to remove Saddam Hussein from power was controversial. We did not find the weapons of mass destruction that we all believed were there, and that's raised questions about whether the sacrifice in Iraq has been worth it. Despite setbacks and missteps, I strongly believe we did and are doing the right thing. Saddam Hussein was a menace to his people; he was a state sponsor of terror; he invaded his neighbors. Investigations proved he was systematically gaming the Oil-For-Food Programme in an effort to undermine sanctions, with the intent of restarting his weapons programs once the sanctions collapsed and the world looked away. If Saddam Hussein were in power today, his regime would be richer, more dangerous, and a bigger threat to the region and the civilized world. The decision to remove Saddam Hussein was right.

But not everything since liberation has turned out as the way we had expected or hoped. We've learned from our mistakes, adjusted our methods, and have built on our successes. From changing the way we train the Iraqi security forces to rethinking the way we do reconstruction, our commanders and our diplomats in Iraq are constantly adapting to the realities on the ground. We've adapted our tactics, yet the heart of our strategy remains the same: to support the emergence of a free Iraq that can govern itself, sustain itself, and defend itself.

All our efforts over the past 3 years have been aimed towards this goal. This past weekend, the world watched as Iraqis stood up a free and democratic government in the heart of the Middle East. With our help, Iraq will be a powerful force for good in a troubled region and a steadfast ally in the war on terror.

With the emergence of this Government, something fundamental changed in Iraq last weekend. While we can expect more violence in the days and weeks ahead, the terrorists are now fighting a free and constitutional government. They're at war with the people of Iraq, and the Iraqi people are determined to defeat this enemy, and so are Iraq's new leaders, and so are the United States and Great Britain.

It is vital that Iraq's new Government seize this opportunity to heal old wounds and set aside sectarian differences and move forward as one nation. As Prime Minister Maliki has made his priorities clear, we have learned they're the right priorities. He's said he will focus on improving the security situation in Baghdad and other parts of the country. He has declared he will use maximum force to defeat the terrorists. He's vowed to eliminate illegal militias and armed gangs. He wants to accelerate the training of the Iraqi security forces so they can take responsibility from coalition forces for security throughout Iraq. He wants to improve health care and housing and jobs, so the benefits of a free society will reach every Iraqi citizen.

Our coalition will seize this moment as well. I look forward for continued indepth discussions with Tony Blair, so we can develop the best approach in helping the new Iraqi Government achieve its objectives. The new Government of Iraq will have the full support of our two countries and our coalition, and we will work to engage other nations around the world to ensure that constitutional democracy in Iraq succeeds and the terrorists are defeated.

Mr. Prime Minister.

Prime Minister Blair. Thank you, Mr. President, and can I say what a pleasure it is to be with you again at the White House. And thank you for your welcome.

As everyone knows, I was in Iraq earlier in this week, in Baghdad. And I was able to discuss with the new leaders of Iraq, firsthand, their experience and their hopes and expectations for the future. And I came away thinking that the challenge is still immense, but I also came away more certain than ever that we should rise to it. And though it is at times daunting, it is also utterly inspiring to see people from all the different parts of the community in Iraq—the Sunni, the Shi'a, the Kurds—sitting down together, all of them democratic leaders—democratically elected by their people—elected for a 4-year term, elected and choosing to come together as a government of national unity, and completely determined to run their country in a different way for the future.

Anybody who studies the program of the Iraqi Government can't fail to see the similarities with the type of program that any of us would want to see for our countries. And what is remarkable about it is that they put the emphasis, of course, on the issues to do with economic recovery and reconstruction and all the problems of infrastructure that they have in their country, but they also very clearly commit themselves to reconciliation between the different parts of the country, to the fight against sectarianism, and to the defeat of terrorism.

And I think what is important now is to say that after 3 years, which have been very, very difficult indeed, and when, at times, it looked impossible for the democratic process to work—I think after these 3 years and the democratic process working and producing this Government, then it is our duty, but it is also the duty of the whole of the international community, to get behind this Government and support it, because the other thing that came across to me very strongly from talking to them was that the reason there is bloodshed and violence in Iraq is that the very forces that we are confronting everywhere, including in our own countries, who want to destroy our way of life, also want to destroy their hope of having the same type of life. In other words, the very forces that are creating this violence and bloodshed and terrorism in Iraq are those that are doing it in order to destroy the hope of that country and its people to achieve democracy, the rule of law, and liberty.

And I think there is a pattern here for us in the international community. I know the decision to remove Saddam was deeply divisive for the international community and deeply controversial. And there's no point in rehearsing those arguments over and over again. But whatever people's views about the wisdom of that decision, now that there is a democratic Government in Iraq, elected by its people, and now they are confronted with those whose mission it is to destroy the hope of democracy, then our sense of mission should be equal to that, and we should be determined to help them defeat this terrorism and violence.

And I believe very, very strongly indeed—even more so having talked to the leaders there and now coming back and examining our own situation and how we help—I'm more than ever convinced that what is important for them in Iraq is to know that we will stand firm with them in defeating these forces of reaction.

I believe the same, incidentally, is true of the struggle in Afghanistan, where again, exactly the same forces of terrorism and reaction want to defeat the hopes of people for progress. I would also like to think—and this is something the President and I were discussing earlier—we will carry on discussing over tonight and tomorrow—and that is the importance of trying to unite the international community behind an agenda that means, for example, action on global poverty in Africa and issues like Sudan; it means a good outcome to the

world trade round, which is vital for the whole of the civilized world, vital for developing countries but also vital for countries such as ourselves; for progress in the Middle East; and for ensuring that the global values that people are actually struggling for today in Iraq are global values we take everywhere and fight for everywhere that we can in our world today.

So I would like to pay tribute also to the work that our forces do there. I think both our countries can be immensely proud of their heroism and their commitment and their dedication.

But one very interesting thing happened to me when I was there and talking to some of our Armed Forces and talking, also, to the Iraqi soldiers that were working alongside them, and that is, for all the differences in culture and background and nationality, both of them were working together in a common cause, and that was to help a country that was once a brutalized dictatorship become a country that enjoys the same rights and the same freedoms that we take for granted here and in the United Kingdom. And for all the hardship and the challenge of the past few years, I still think that is a cause worth standing up for.

Thank you, Mr. President.

President Bush. Terry [Terence Hunt, Associated Press].

Timetables for Iraq

Q. Mr. President, Pentagon officials have talked about prospects for reducing American forces in Iraq to about 100,000 by year's end. Does the formation of a unity government in Iraq put you on a sound footing to achieve that number?

And, Mr. Prime Minister, is it realistic to think that Iraqi forces will be able to take control of all Iraq by the end of next year as Mr. Maliki suggests?

President Bush. First of all, we're going to work with our partners in Iraq, the new Government, to determine the best way forward in achieving an objective, which is an Iraq that can govern itself and sustain itself and defend itself.

I have said to the American people, as the Iraqis stand up, we'll stand down. But I've also said that our commanders on the ground will make that decision. And I have—we'll talk to General Casey once he is—conferred with the new Government of Iraq. They don't have a defense minister yet; they're in the process of getting a defense minister. So it probably makes a lot of sense for our commander on the ground to wait until their defense structure is set up before we discuss with them, and he with me, the force levels necessary to achieve our objective.

Q. So the 100,000——

President Bush. That's some speculation in the press that I—they haven't talked to me about. And as the Commander in Chief, they eventually will talk to me about it. But the American people need to know that we'll keep the force level there necessary to win. And it's important for the American people to know that politics isn't going to make the decision as to the size of our force level; the conditions on the ground will make the decision. And part of the conditions on the ground, Terry, is a new government, and we believe the new Government is going to make a big difference in the lives of the Iraqi people.

I told you earlier that when you attack an Iraqi now, you're at war with an Iraqi Government that's constitutionally elected. And that's a different attitude from the way it's been in the past.

Prime Minister Blair. I think it's possible for the Iraqi security forces to take control progressively of their country. That's exactly the strategy we've outlined at the beginning. And I think it's possible to happen in the way that Prime Minister Maliki said. For that to happen, obviously, the first thing that we need is a strong government in Baghdad that is prepared to enforce its writ throughout the country. My very strong feeling, having talked to the leaders

there, is that they intend theirs to be such a government.

Secondly, what they intend is to come down very hard on those people who want to create the circumstances where it's difficult for the Iraqi forces to be in control. And the truth of the matter is, there is no excuse now for anyone to engage in violence in Iraq. I mean, if people's worry is to do with being excluded from the political process, everybody has got their place in the political process today. And obviously, there are still issues to do with the capability of the Iraqi forces, but all the time they are building up, both in number and in capability, and we've got to support that all the way through.

But I'll tell you one interesting thing from talking to all the different groups—because sometimes, certainly in our country, the impression is given that the Iraqi people wish that we were gone from Iraq and weren't there any longer in support of the Iraqi Government or the Iraqi forces. Not a single one of the people I talked to, not one of the political leaders from whatever part of the spectrum, in Iraq, that I talked to—and these are all people from all the different communities elected by their people—not one of them wanted us to pull out precipitately. All of them wanted us to stick with it and see the job done.

Now, of course, they want to take back control of their own country fully, and we want them to do that. But when the Prime Minister, Maliki, talked about an objective timetable, what he meant was a timetable governed by conditions on the ground. And we will be working with them now over the coming period of time to see how we can put that framework together. But they have a very, very clear sense of what they want the multinational force to do. They want us there in support until they've got the capability, and then they want us to leave and them to take full charge of their country. And I believe that can happen.

Yes, Adam.

United Nations

Q. One gets a clear sense of your mutual relief that a Government has now been formed, an elected Government has been formed in Iraq. But, nonetheless, the current Secretary-General of the United Nations has said that he believes that the invasion of Iraq was probably illegal. When you look at your legacy and you look ahead to the reforms of the United Nations you want to see, are you really saying that what you'd actually like to see is a United Nations which could take preemptive action legally?

Prime Minister Blair. I think what we need to do is to recognize that there are threats in our world today that require us to act earlier and more effectively. And I think we can debate the institutional structure within which that should happen in the United Nations and elsewhere. But I also think that when we look at this global terrorism that we face, there is—to me, at any rate—a very clear link between the terrorism that is afflicting virtually every country in the Western world, either in actuality or potentially, the terrorism that is happening all over different countries of the Middle East and in Asia and elsewhere, and the terrorism that is there in Iraq and Afghanistan.

And one of the things, I think, certainly for our people, they find most difficult to understand is, they will say, "Well, is it—can it be worth everything that we are doing? I mean, it's such a huge sacrifice that is being made. Can it be worth it?" And I think the answer to that is, it is worth it to those engaged in this violence and terrorism to try to stop us, and we should have the same faith and confidence in our determination to succeed as they have in their determination to make us fail.

And I think that is an issue for the whole of the international community, because I've got no doubt at all that if we do succeed, as I believe that we will in Iraq, difficult though it will be, and we succeed

in Afghanistan, then the whole of this global terrorism will suffer a defeat. And that's why I think we need an international community that's capable of recognizing these problems and acting on them.

President Bush. I'd like to see a United Nations that's effective, one that joins us in trying to rid the world of tyranny; one that is willing to advance human rights and human dignity at its core; one that's an unabashed organization—is unabashed in their desire to spread freedom. That's what I'd like to see, because I believe that freedom will yield the peace. I also believe freedom is universal. I don't believe freedom is just a concept only for America or Great Britain; it's a universal concept. And it troubles me to know that there are people locked in tyrannical societies that suffer. And the United Nations ought to be clear about its desire to liberate people from the clutches of tyranny. That's what the United Nations ought to be doing, as far as I'm concerned.

Yes, Steve [Steve Holland, Reuters].

Iran

Q. Thank you, Mr. President. How close are you to an agreement on a package of incentives for Iran? And what does Iran stand to gain if it were to give up its enrichment program? And why are you ignoring these recent back-channel overtures from Iran?

President Bush. We spent a great deal of time talking about the Iranian issue, and one of the goals that Tony and I had was to convince others in the world that Iran with a nuclear weapon would be very dangerous, and therefore, we do have a common goal. And this fundamental question is, how do you achieve that goal, obviously. We want to do it diplomatically.

Right now we, as a matter of fact, spent a lot of time upstairs talking about how to convince the Iranians that this coalition we put together is very serious. One option, of course, is through the United Nations Security Council. And we strategized about how do we convince other partners that the Security Council is the way to go if the Iranians won't suspend like the EU–3 has asked them to do. The Iranians walked away from the table. They're the ones who've made the decision, and the choice is theirs. Now, if they would like to see an enhanced package, the first thing they've got to do is suspend their operations, for the good of the world. It's incredibly dangerous to think of an Iran with a nuclear weapon.

And therefore, Steve, to answer your questions, of course, we'll look at all options, but it's their choice right now. They're the folks who walked away from the table. They're the ones who said that, "Your demands don't mean anything to us."

Now, in terms of—you said back channels——

Q. Back-channel overtures.

President Bush. Well, I read the letter of the President, and I thought it was interesting. It was, like, 16 or 17 single-spaced typed pages of—but he didn't address the issue of whether or not they're going to continue to press for a nuclear weapon. That's the issue at hand.

And so it's—we have no beef with the Iranian people. As a matter of fact, the United States respects the culture and history of Iran, and we want there to be an Iran that's confident and an Iran that answers to the needs of the—we want women in Iran to be free. At the same time, we're going to continue to work with a government that is intransigent, that won't budge. And so we've got to continue to work to convince them that we're serious, that if they want to be isolated from the world, we will work to achieve that.

Q. Should this enhanced package include a light-water reactor and a security guarantee?

President Bush. Steve, you're responding to press speculation. I've just explained to you that the Iranians walked away from the table, and that I think we ought to be continuing to work on ways to make

it clear to them that they will be isolated. And one way to do that is to continue to work together through the United Nations Security—if they suspend and have the IAEA in there making sure that the suspension is real, then, of course, we'll talk about ways forward, incentives.

United Nations/Iran

Q. Prime Minister, you've both talked a little about the U.N. I know that you believe the U.N. needs vigorous leadership, and you're going to pick up on these themes in your speech tomorrow. Is that a job application? And if not——

President Bush. Wait a minute. [*Laughter*]

Q. ——do you both have a sense—do you have someone in mind? And if not, how are you going to get the reform of the U.N. you want to see?

Prime Minister Blair. No, no, and I'm not sure—[*laughter*]—is the answer to those ones. Look, what we want to do is to make sure that the U.N. is an effective instrument of multilateral action. That's what everyone wants to see. And the fact is, there are multiple problems in the world; they require the international community to respond on a collective basis, but you've got to have an effective set of multilateral institutions to do that. And that's true whether you're tackling global poverty or trying to resolve disputes or, indeed, when you're dealing with issues like Iran.

The whole point about the international community today is that these problems are urgent; they need to be tackled. If they're not tackled, the consequences are very quickly felt around the world, and you've got to have institutions that are capable of taking them on and tackling them and getting action taken.

Now, we were just talking about Iran a moment ago. I mean, we want to have this resolved through the process of the multilateral institutions. There's a way we can do this. I mean, after all, we are the ones saying the Atomic Energy Authority—their duties and obligations they lay upon Iran should be adhered to. And we've got absolutely no quarrel with the Iranian people. The Iranian people are a great people; Iran is a great country. But it needs a government that is going to recognize that part of being a great country is to be in line with your international obligations and to cease supporting those people in different parts of the world who want, by terrorism and violence, to disrupt the process of democracy.

So I think that our position with Iran is a very reasonable one. And we want to see how we can make progress and help them to do the things that we believe that they should do, but they must understand that the will of the international community is sure and is clear, and that is that the obligations that are upon them have got to be adhered to.

President Bush. Stretch [Richard Keil, Bloomberg News].

Secretary of the Treasury John W. Snow/ National Economy

Q. Thank you, Mr. President.

President Bush. I call him Stretch.

Q. And I've been called worse. [*Laughter*] Has Treasury Secretary Snow given you any indication that he intends to leave his job any time soon?

President Bush. Secretary of Treasury Snow?

Q. Has he given you any indication he intends to leave his job any time soon? And related to that, Americans—macroeconomic numbers are indeed good, but many Americans are concerned, increasingly concerned about rising health care costs, costs of gasoline. And does that make it hard for your administration, Treasury Secretary Snow, and everyone else to continue to talk up the economy?

President Bush. No, he has not talked to me about resignation. I think he's doing a fine job. After all, our economy is—it's strong. We grew at 3.5 percent last year;

a good, strong first quarter this year. We added five—2.5 million new jobs; we've got 4.7 percent unemployment rate nationwide. Productivity is up; homeownership is high; small businesses are doing well. He's done a fine job.

And our—obviously, people are concerned about rising fuel prices—all the more reason to get off oil and to promote alternatives, such as ethanol or battery technologies that will enable us to drive the first 40 miles on electricity. We're spending about $1.2 billion over the next 10 years to develop hydrogen fuel cells. We want—we need to get away from hydrocarbons here in America for economic security, for national security, and for environmental reasons as well.

One way we could help alleve gasoline prices here in America is for the Congress to pass some regulatory relief so we can actually expand refining capacity. We haven't built a new refinery here since the 1970s. And curiously enough, when demand for a product goes up with tight supply, price follows. And so we put out some logical ways for Congress to work with the administration to relieve price pressures on gasoline.

As far as health care goes, there are some practical ways to deal with health care costs, and one of the most practical ways is to get rid of these junk lawsuits that are running good doctors out of practice and running up the price of medicine. Passed it out of the House; they can't get it out of the Senate because the lawyers won't let it out. But we put forth a commonsense practice to deal with rising health care costs as well.

Progress in Iraq

Q. You both presented the Iraqi Government as a substantial vindication of the conflict. Do you also accept, as a matter of harsh political reality, that the Iraq conflict has also left both of you politically weakened and, whether justly or unjustly, less able to give the kind of moral leadership that you're discussing today?

President Bush. No question that the Iraq war has created a sense of consternation here in America. I mean, when you turn on your TV screen and see innocent people die, day in and day out, it affects the mentality of our country.

But here's what they're asking in America; they're asking, "Can we win?" That's what they want to know. Do we have a strategy for victory? And so the talk about the unity Government—you might remember, there was some—a lot of speculation as to whether there would even be a unity government. A couple of months ago, people were saying, "Well, they can't even get a unity government going." But we have a unity government—a Kurd President, a Prime Minister who is a Shi'a, a Speaker who is a Sunni. These are strong leaders. It's an indication that progress is being made.

Part of progress, of course, is on the political track. You know, we had elections in Iraq; 12 million people voted last December. Now, it seems like an eternity ago, I know, like a decade. But that's not all that long ago in the larger scope of things. Twelve million people said, we want to be free. It was an astounding moment. And this unity Government is now formed as a result of those elections, under a Constitution approved by the Iraqi people. That's progress. It's certainly a far sight from the days of a tyrant who killed hundreds of thousands of his own people and used weapons of mass destruction and threatened the neighborhood. I mean, that is progress.

No question, however, that the suiciders and the killers and the IEDs and the deaths have an effect on the American people. But one of the reasons that I appreciate Tony coming is that he brings a fresh perspective of what he saw. And the American people need to know, we are making progress toward a goal of an Iraq that can defend itself, sustain itself, and govern itself; that will deny the terrorists a safe haven.

You know, Al Qaida has made it clear what their intentions are in Iraq. I'm sure you've read some of the intercepts that are laid out there for people to see. And they have made it clear that it's just a matter of time for countries like Great Britain and the United States to leave. In other words, if they make life miserable enough, we'll leave. And they want us to leave because they want a safe haven from which to launch attacks, not only on us but on moderate Muslim governments as well. These people are totalitarians. They're Islamic fascists. They have a point of view; they have a philosophy; and they want to impose that philosophy on the rest of the world. And Iraq just happens to be a—one of the battles in the war on terror.

And Tony brings up a good point: Why are they resisting so hard; what is it about democracy they can't stand? Well, what they can't stand about democracy is this: Democracy is the exact opposite of what they believe. They believe they can impose their will; they believe there's no freedom of religion; they believe there's no women's rights. They have a dark vision of the world, and that's why they're resisting so mightily.

So, yes, I can understand why the American people are troubled by the war in Iraq. I understand that. But I also believe the sacrifice is worth it and is necessary. And I believe a free Iraq is not only going to make ourselves more secure, but it's going to serve as a powerful example in the Middle East.

You know, foreign policy, for a while, just basically said, if it seems okay on the surface, just let it be. And guess what happened? There was resentment and hatred that enabled these totalitarians to recruit and to kill, which they want to continue to do to achieve their objectives. And the best way to defeat them in the long run is through the spread of liberty.

And liberty has had the capacity to change enemies to allies. Liberty has had the capacity to help Europe become whole, free, and at peace. History has proven that freedom has got the capacity to change the world for the better, and that's what you're seeing.

You know, the amazing thing about dealing with Prime Minister Blair, has never once has he said to me on the phone, we better change our tactics because of the political opinion polls. And I appreciate that steadfast leadership. And I appreciate somebody who has got a vision, a shared vision for how to not only protect ourselves in the war on terror but how to make the world a better place.

Prime Minister Blair. I don't really think it's a matter of our vindication. I think, in a way, that's the least important part of it. But I do think that occasionally, we should just take a step back and ask, why are we doing this? Why is it so important?

Saddam was removed from power 3 years ago. Since then, incidentally, our forces have been there with the United Nations mandate and with the consent of the Iraqi Government itself—the Iraqi Government becoming progressively more the product of direct democracy.

So whatever people thought about removing Saddam—you agree with it, you didn't agree with it—for these last 3 years, the issue in Iraq has not been, these people are here without any international support, because we haven't had any United Nations resolution governing our presence there. The issue is not, you're there, but the Iraqi people don't want you there, because the Iraqi Government and now this directly elected Iraqi Government has said they want us to stay until the job is done.

So why is it that for 3 years, we have had this violence and bloodshed? Now, people have tried to say, it's because the Iraqi people—you people, you don't understand; you went in with this Western concept of democracy, and you didn't understand that their whole culture was different;

they weren't interested in these types of freedom. These people have gone out and voted—a higher turnout, I have to say—I'm afraid to say, I think, than either your election or mine. These people have gone out and voted——

President Bush. Depends on which one, 2000 or 2004? [*Laughter*]

Prime Minister Blair. I think both of them.

President Bush. I think you're right. [*Laughter*]

Prime Minister Blair. They have gone out and voted despite terrorism, despite bloodshed, despite literally the prospect of death for exercising their democratic right. So they have kept faith with the very democratic values that we say we believe in, and the people trying to wrest that democracy from them are opposed to absolutely everything we stand for and everything the Iraqi people stand for.

So what do we do in response to this? And the problem we have is very, very simple. A large part of the perspective with which we look at this is to see every act of terrorism in Iraq, every piece of ghastly carnage on our television screens, every tragic loss of our own forces—we see that as a setback and as a failure, when we should be seeing that as a renewed urgency for us to rise to the challenge of defeating these people who are committing this carnage. Because over these past 3 years, at every stage, the reason they have been fighting is not, as we can see, because Iraqi people don't believe in democracy; Iraqi people don't want liberty. It is precisely because they fear Iraqi people do want democracy; Iraqi people do want liberty.

And if the idea became implanted in the minds of people in the Arab and Muslim world that democracy was as much their right as our right, where do these terrorists go? What do they do? How do they recruit? How do they say, America is the evil Satan? How do they say, the purpose of the West is to spoil your lands, wreck your religion, take your wealth? How can they say that? They can't say that.

So these people who are fighting us there know what is at stake. The question is, do we?

President Bush. Must say, that was a great answer. [*Laughter*]

Prime Minister Blair. Yours was pretty good too. [*Laughter*]

Q. You have your chance now. [*Laughter*]

President Bush. Another chance, good. Well, thank you, Martha [Martha Raddatz, ABC News].

Troop Levels in Iraq

Q. Mr. President, you have said time and time again, and again tonight, when Iraqi forces stand up, coalition forces can start standing down.

President Bush. Right.

Q. But the fact is, you have been standing up Iraqi forces in great numbers. The administration says you have hundreds of thousand trained and equipped, tens of thousand leading the fight. And yet during the same period they've been standing up, there has not been a substantial decrease in U.S. and coalition forces. So what does that tell us about how meaningful the figures are on Iraqi troops? And what does that tell us about a potential for a drawdown?

President Bush. It tells you that the commanders on the ground are going to make the decision, that's what that tells you. And when they feel comfortable in recommending to me fewer troops, I will accept that. But they're going to make that recommendation based upon the conditions on the ground. I know I keep saying that, and it probably bores you that I keep giving the same answer, but I haven't changed my opinion.

I talk to our commanders all the time. They feel strongly that the Iraqi Army is getting better. It's hard to have a command and control system with an Iraqi Army when you don't have a defense minister.

And so Mr. Maliki is going to have to pick one soon. And then our commanders will gauge as to whether or not the command and control structure is sufficient to be able to enable the Iraqis to take more of the fight. They are taking more of the fight, by the way. They're in more Provinces than ever before. They're taking over more territory. They're taking over more missions. There are some gaps that we need to continue to work on to fill. The transportation issue is going to need to be dealt with over time.

All I can report to you is what General Casey—in whom I have got a lot of confidence—tells me, and that is, the Iraqis are becoming better and better fighters. And at some point in time, when he feels like the Government is ready to take on more responsibility and the Iraqi forces are able to help them do so, he will get on the telephone with me and say, "Mr. President, I think we can do this with fewer troops." We've been up to 165,000 at one point; we're at about 135,000 now.

Q. [*Inaudible*]

President Bush. Hold on for a second. Actually, he moved some additional troops from Kuwait into Baghdad. Conditions on the ground were such that we needed more support in Baghdad, to secure Baghdad, so he informed me, through Donald Rumsfeld, that he wanted to move troops out of Kuwait into Baghdad.

So these commanders—they need to have flexibility in order to achieve the objective. You don't want politicians making decisions based upon politics. You want the Commander in Chief making decisions based upon what the military thinks is the right way to achieve the objective. I've set the objective; it's clear for everybody—a country that can sustain itself, defend itself, and govern itself. And we're making progress on all fronts. But as to how many troops we have there will depend upon the generals and their commanders saying, "This is what we need to do the job, Mr. President." And that's the way it's going to be so long as I'm standing here as the Commander in Chief, which is 2½ more years.

Prime Minister Blair. I spoke to General Casey and to our own General Fry in Baghdad on Monday. We sat down and talked this very issue through. And I think what you will find is that progressively, there will be more and more parts of Iraq that are policed by the Iraqi security forces themselves, and their capability is improving. But I also think you will find, probably over the next few months, there will be a real attempt by the antidemocratic forces to test them very, very strongly. And remember, a lot of the attacks are now happening not on the multinational force, although those attacks continue, of course, but actually on the Iraqi forces themselves, on their police, on their army, and so on. And the purpose, of course, of that is to deter them from the very buildup of capability that we want to see.

But over the course of the next few months, you will see progressively those Provinces in Iraq coming under Iraqi control, and then, of course, it will be for the Iraqis to sort out that responsibility.

President Bush. One thing, Martha, is that we want to make sure we complete the mission, that we achieve our objective. A loss in Iraq would make this world an incredibly dangerous place. Remember, there is not only sectarian violence, a hangover from Saddam's era, but there is an Al Qaida presence in the form of Zarqawi, who wants to sow as much havoc as possible to cause us to leave before the mission is complete.

Listen, I want our troops out; don't get me wrong. I understand what it means to have troops in harm's way. And I know there's a lot of families making huge sacrifices here in America. I'll be going to a Memorial Day ceremony next Monday, paying tribute to those who have lost their life. I'm sure I will see families of the fallen. I fully understand the pressures being placed upon our military and their families.

But I also understand that it is vital that we do the job, that we complete the mission. And it has been tough. It's been really tough, because we're fighting an unconventional enemy that is willing to kill innocent people. There are no rules of war for these people. But make no mistake about it, what you're seeing in Iraq could happen all over the world if we don't stand fast and achieve the objective.

No, I had the followup answer; you can't have a followup question. Nice try, though.

Prime Minister Blair

Q. Prime Minister, this is possibly your last official visit to Washington as Prime Minister——

President Bush. Wait a minute. [*Laughter*] Back-to-back disses.

Q. At least the beginning of the end of your particular special relationship. Will you miss the President? What will you miss about him? [*Laughter*]

And for the President, what will you miss about Tony Blair, and what are you looking for in an eventual replacement?

President Bush. I'll miss those red ties, is what I'll miss. [*Laughter*] I'll say one thing—he can answer the question—don't count him out; let me tell it to you that way. I know a man of resolve and vision and courage. And my attitude is, I want him to be here so long as I'm the President.

Prime Minister Blair. Well, what more can I say? [*Laughter*] Probably not wise to say anything more at all. [*Laughter*]

You guys, come on, I want you to—the British delegation, ask a few serious questions. [*Laughter*]

President Bush. Right.

Prime Minister Blair. Or we'll go on to one of you guys. [*Laughter*]

President Bush. Plante [Bill Plante, CBS News].

Iraq

Q. Perhaps I can change the mood. Mr. President, you talk about setting the objective. But our people, my colleagues on the ground in Iraq, say that when they talk to American troops, the rank and file, they say they don't believe that they've had enough to do the job. They say further that while the Iraqi Army may be improving, there is absolutely no way to depend upon the police, who they say are corrupt and aligned with militias. All of this going on—what reason is there to believe that the new Government can do any better with these people than we've been able to do so far?

President Bush. There are several tracks, Bill. One is the political track. I think it's very important for the Iraqi people to have a government that has been elected under a Constitution they approved. In other words, the political track has been a vital part of having a country that can govern itself and defend itself.

There's a security track. And there's no question that there are a lot of Iraqis trained to fight, and many of them are good fighters—117,000 have been trained and equipped. There needs to be more equipment; no question about that. The Iraqis—I think if you were to get a—at least the assessment I get, is that the Iraqi Army is moving well along and they're taking more and more of the territory over in order to defend their country.

No question, we've got a lot of work to do on the police. General Casey has said publicly that year 2006 is the year that we'll train the police up and running. Perhaps the place where there needs to be the most effective police force is in Baghdad. I just told you, we're moving more troops in. There's a—General Casey met today with the Prime Minister to talk about how to secure Baghdad. It's really important that Baghdad—that capital city become more secure. And there's plans to deal with the contingencies on the ground. All I can

tell you is, is that we're making progress toward the goal.

Prime Minister Blair. Can I just—and I'd like to say something, again, out of the discussions I had on Monday. I think that what is important is, try and get a sense of balance in this. Look, it would be completely foolish for us to say, there are no problems with either the police or the army; you've got a full force capability in the way that we want. And nobody is actually saying that.

It would also be wrong to turn it around the other way, though, even in respect to the police. I had quite a detailed discussion, not, in fact, with the generals, but some of the ordinary soldiers who—British soldiers there, up in Baghdad, and also with some of the people who are working with the police at the moment. And what they said to me is, yes, there are real problems to do with corruption in parts of the police force, but actually, there is also another side to it, which there are people who are really dedicated and really committed to a nonsectarian Iraq, who also are playing their part.

Now, I think the whole question is whether this new Government can then grip this in the way, in a sense, that only they can. You see, I think this is where, inevitably, over time, we have to transfer responsibility. And that is, of course, what we wish to do, and part of that is because it is easier for an Iraqi interior minister, who is the product of an Iraqi-elected Government, to go in and take the really tough measure sometimes that is necessary to sort some of these issues out.

But I can assure you of two things: First of all, there is another, more positive side to the Iraqi forces—both the army and in parts of the police as well; and secondly, the Iraqi Government knows that this is the absolute prerequisite of success for them. It's just—one of the ministers said to me, he said, "You should understand, our state was a completely failed state." The police—people didn't go to the police in Iraq if they had a problem under Saddam. They had a problem if they were in contact with the police because of the way the state was run.

And so you're talking about literally building the institutions of a state from scratch. And I don't think it's, in one sense, very surprising that it is both difficult and taking time. But I think that they do know that this is of vital importance for them to succeed. And I think you may find that it is easier for Iraqis to do this themselves and take some of these measures necessary, than it is for us, although we would be there, obviously, in support of what they're doing.

Lessons Learned in the War on Terror

Q. Mr. President, you spoke about missteps and mistakes in Iraq. Could I ask both of you which missteps and mistakes of your own you most regret?

President Bush. Sounds like kind of a familiar refrain here—saying "bring it on," kind of tough talk, you know, that sent the wrong signal to people. I learned some lessons about expressing myself maybe in a little more sophisticated manner—you know, "wanted dead or alive," that kind of talk. I think in certain parts of the world it was misinterpreted, and so I learned from that. And I think the biggest mistake that's happened so far, at least from our country's involvement in Iraq, is Abu Ghraib. We've been paying for that for a long period of time. And it's—unlike Iraq, however, under Saddam, the people who committed those acts were brought to justice. They've been given a fair trial and tried and convicted.

Prime Minister Blair. I think inevitably, some of the things that we thought were going to be the biggest challenge proved not to be, and some of the things we didn't expect to be challenges at all proved to be immense. I think that probably in retrospect—though at the time it was very difficult to argue this—we could have done

the de-Ba'athification in a more differentiated way than we did.

I think that the most difficult thing, however, has been the determination of people to move against the democratic process in Iraq in a way that, I think—as I was saying a moment or two ago—indicates our opponents' very clear view from a very early stage that they have to stop the democratic process working. And I think it's easy to go back over mistakes that we may have made, but the biggest reason why Iraq has been difficult is the determination of our opponents to defeat us. And I don't think we should be surprised at that.

Maybe in retrospect, when we look back, it should have been very obvious to us, and is obvious still in Afghanistan, that for them, it is very clear. You know, they can't afford to have these countries turned round, and I think that probably, there was a whole series of things in Iraq that were bound to come out once you got Al Qaida and other groups operating in there to cause maximum destruction and damage. And therefore, I'm afraid in the end, we're always going to have to be prepared for the fall of Saddam not to be the rise of democratic Iraq, that it was going to be a more difficult process.

President Bush. Mr. Prime Minister, can I buy you dinner?

Prime Minister Blair. Certainly.

NOTE: The President's news conference began at 7:31 p.m. in the East Room at the White House. In his remarks, the President referred to Prime Minister Nuri al-Maliki, former President Saddam Hussein, President Jalal Talabani, and Speaker of the Council of Representatives Mahmoud al-Mashhadani of Iraq; Gen. George W. Casey, Jr., USA, commanding general, Multi-National Force—Iraq; President Mahmud Ahmadinejad of Iran; and senior Al Qaida associate Abu Musab Al Zarqawi. Prime Minister Blair referred to Lt. Gen. Sir Robert Fry, Royal Marines, deputy commander, Multi-National

Force—Iraq. A reporter referred to Secretary-General Kofi Annan of the United Nations.

Statement on Senate Confirmation of Michael V. Hayden as Director of the Central Intelligence Agency
May 26, 2006

I commend the Senate for confirming Michael Hayden as Director of the Central Intelligence Agency by a bipartisan majority. Winning the war on terror requires that America have the best intelligence possible, and his strong leadership will ensure that we do. General Hayden is a patriot and a dedicated public servant whose broad experience, dedication, and expertise make him the right person to lead the CIA at this critical time. I look forward to working with Ambassador Negroponte, General Hayden, and the other leaders of our intelligence community as we continue to address the challenges and threats we face in the 21st century. I congratulate General Hayden and his family on his confirmation and thank him for his continued service to our Nation.

Statement on Senate Confirmation of Brett M. Kavanaugh as a United States Circuit Judge for the District of Columbia
May 26, 2006

I applaud the Senate's vote to confirm Brett Kavanaugh to the U.S. Court of Appeals for the District of Columbia Circuit. Brett Kavanaugh is superbly qualified for the Court of Appeals and will be a brilliant, thoughtful, and fair-minded judge. I appreciate his distinguished service in the executive branch for the last 5 years, as Associate Counsel and then Senior Associate Counsel to the President, and since July 2003 in the vital role of Staff Secretary. I congratulate Brett and his family on today's confirmation and thank him for his continued service to the law and our Nation.

Statement on Senate Confirmation of Dirk Kempthorne as the Secretary of the Interior
May 26, 2006

I applaud the Senate for confirming Dirk Kempthorne as Secretary of the Interior. Dirk has an abiding love of nature and the outdoors and is dedicated to conserving our natural resources. He will continue my administration's efforts to effectively manage our national parks, support historic and cultural sites through our Preserve America Initiative, and pursue environmentally responsible energy development on Federal lands and waters. He will also work to maintain good relations with Native American tribes and will play a leadership role in my cooperative conservation approach to environmental stewardship. I congratulate

Dirk and his family on today's confirmation and thank him for his continued service to our Nation.

Statement on Senate Confirmation of Robert J. Portman as Director of the Office of Management and Budget
May 26, 2006

I commend the Senate for confirming Rob Portman as Director of the Office of Management and Budget. In this key position, Rob will have a leading role on my economic team and will help ensure that the Government spends the taxpayers' money wisely, or not at all. In addition, Rob will be in charge of implementing my goal of cutting the budget deficit in half

by 2009 while funding our priorities. The American people deserve results for every hard-earned dollar they send to Washington. Rob is a man of character and will perform his duties with dedication and integrity. I congratulate Rob and his family on today's confirmation and thank him for his continued service to our Nation.

Joint Statement by President George W. Bush and Prime Minister Tony Blair of the United Kingdom
May 26, 2006

The United States has no closer ally than the United Kingdom. U.S. and U.K. forces are fighting terror in Afghanistan, Iraq, and around the globe. The Prime Minister and the President discussed ways to strengthen defense cooperation.

The two leaders are pleased to announce that the United States and United Kingdom recently signed an agreement that allows appropriately cleared British and U.S. personnel to use the same computer network to access military and intelligence information and other planning tools to support joint military operations in the defense of freedom.

Additionally, the leaders recognize that as American and British soldiers, sailors, airmen, and marines are right now standing together in harm's way, we must plan for the future capabilities that will enhance our

ability to cooperate. Both governments agree that the UK will have the ability to successfully operate, upgrade, employ, and maintain the Joint Strike Fighter such that the UK retains operational sovereignty over the aircraft. Further, both governments agree to protect sensitive technologies found within the Joint Strike Fighter program. Together, we are working out the details, while remaining committed to these principles.

Finally, the President and Prime Minister have a shared view that we need to continue to strengthen and deepen the relationship between our defense establishments to achieve fully interoperable forces and to leverage the respective strengths of U.S. and U.K. industries. The Prime Minister and President look forward to new ways we can achieve that goal.

NOTE: An original was not available for verification of the content of this joint statement.

Commencement Address at the United States Military Academy in West Point, New York
May 27, 2006

Thank you for the warm welcome—General Lennox, Secretary Harvey, Members of the United States Congress, Academy staff and faculty, distinguished guests, proud family, and, most importantly, the class of 2006.

On the way in, General Lennox showed me what you did to his car. [*Laughter*] I told him, "That's a fine looking vehicle"— [*laughter*]—"but you need to stay away from Marine One." [*Laughter*]

I see a lot of "Gray Hogs" out there— a few "Century Men" too. During your 4 years at this Academy, I'm told, there are about 18,000 opportunities to be late for class, drill, march, or inspection, and many of you availed yourselves of those opportunities. [*Laughter*] Others got written up just for having bad haircuts. No matter what reason you got slugged, help is on the way. In keeping with longstanding tradition, I hereby absolve all cadets who are on restriction for minor conduct offenses. I leave it to General Lennox to define exactly what "minor" means. [*Laughter*]

It's a privilege to stand before the future leaders of the United States Army. You have worked hard to get to this moment. You've survived the hardest Beast on record, the "best summer of your lives" in Buckistan, countless hours in the House of Pain. In 4 years, you've been transformed from "bean-heads" to "yuks" to "cows" and "Firsties." And today you will become proud officers of the greatest army in the history of the world. Your teachers are proud of you; your parents are proud

of you; and so is your Commander in Chief. Congratulations on a fantastic achievement.

This Academy has shaped your minds and bodies for the challenges that lie ahead. You worked hard in the classroom and on the playing field to prepare for the rigors of combat. One cadet described the West Point attitude this way: "First I'll beat Navy and Air Force, and then I'll beat the enemies of freedom on the battlefield."

The field of battle is where your degree and commission will take you. This is the first class to arrive at West Point after the attacks of September the 11th, 2001. Each of you came here in a time of war, knowing all the risks and dangers that come with wearing our Nation's uniform. And I want to thank you for your patriotism, your devotion to duty, your courageous decision to serve. America is grateful and proud of the men and women of West Point.

The reality of war has surrounded you since your first moments at this Academy. More than 50 of your fellow cadets here at West Point have already seen combat in Afghanistan and Iraq. And 34 times since your class arrived, you have observed a moment of silence in Washington Hall to honor a former cadet fallen in the war on terror. Each loss is heartbreaking, and each loss has made you even more determined to pick up their mantle, to carry on their fight, and to achieve victory. We will honor the memory of those brave souls. We will finish the task for which they gave their lives. We will complete the mission.

West Point has adapted to prepare you for the war you're about to enter. Since the attacks of September the 11th, 2001, this Academy has established a new combating terrorism center, a new minor in terrorism studies, with new courses in counterinsurgency operations, intelligence, and homeland security, and winning the peace. West Point has expanded Arabic language training, has hired new faculty with expertise in Islamic law and culture, brought in members of the 101st and 82d Airborne to train you and share their experiences on the frontlines in Iraq and Afghanistan. And each of you endured grueling Saturday training events where you practiced identifying IEDs, conducting convoy operations, and running checkpoints. By changing to meet the new threats, West Point has given you the skills you will need in Afghanistan and Iraq and for the long war with Islamic radicalism that will be the focus of much of your military careers.

This Academy went through a similar period of change six decades ago, at the end of World War II. Some of West Point's greatest graduates—men like Eisenhower and Bradley, Patton and MacArthur—had just brought our Nation victory in Europe and Japan. Yet almost immediately, a new threat appeared on the horizon, the threat of imperial communism. And West Point, like America, had to prepare for a long struggle with a new adversary, one that would require the determination of generations of Americans.

In the early years of that struggle, freedom's victory was not obvious or assured. In 1947, Communist forces were threatening Greece and Turkey; the reconstruction of Germany was faltering; mass starvation was setting in across Europe. In 1948, Czechoslovakia fell to communism; France and Italy appeared to be headed for the same fate; and Berlin was blockaded on the orders of Josef Stalin. In 1949, the Soviet Union exploded a nuclear weapon, giving our new enemy the ability to bring catastrophic destruction to our homeland. And weeks later, Communist forces won their revolution in China and claimed the

world's most populous nation for communism. And in the summer of 1950, seven North Korean divisions poured across the border into South Korea, marking the start of the first direct military clash of the cold war. All of this took place in just the first 5 years following World War II.

Fortunately, we had a President named Harry Truman, who recognized the threat, took bold action to confront it, and laid the foundation for freedom's victory in the cold war. President Truman set a clear doctrine. In a speech to Congress, he called for military and economic aid to Greece and Turkey and announced a new doctrine that would guide American policy throughout the cold war. He told the Congress, "It must be the policy of the United States to support free peoples who are resisting attempted subjugation by armed minorities or by outside pressures." With this new doctrine, and with the aid to back it up, Greece and Turkey were saved from communism, and the Soviet expansion into Southern Europe and the Middle East was stopped.

President Truman acted boldly to confront new adversaries. When Stalin tested America's resolve with a blockade of Berlin, President Truman launched the Berlin Airlift, delivering supplies to the besieged city, forcing the Red Army to back down, and securing the freedom of West Berlin. Later, Truman again responded to Communist aggression with resolve, fighting a difficult war in Korea. Korean war saw many setbacks and missteps and terrible losses. More than 54,000 Americans gave their lives in Korea. Yet in the end, Communist forces were pushed back to the 38th Parallel, and the freedom of South Korea was secure.

President Truman acted boldly to help transform old adversaries into democratic allies. In Asia, his administration led the effort to help Japan change from a nation that had launched a surprise attack on America into a thriving democracy and steadfast ally. In Europe, he launched the

Marshall plan, an unprecedented effort to help Germany and other nations in Europe recover from war and establish strong democracies. The Marshall plan cost about 100 billion in today's dollars, and it helped to save Western Europe from Soviet tyranny and led to the emergence of democratic allies that remain indispensable to the cause of peace today.

President Truman transformed our alliances to deal with new dangers. After World War II, he led the effort to form the North Atlantic Treaty Organization, the first peacetime alliance in American history. NATO served as a military bulwark against Communist aggression and helped give us a Europe that is now whole, free, and at peace.

President Truman positioned U.S. forces to deal with new threats. Despite enormous pressure to bring our troops home after World War II, he kept American forces in Germany to deter Soviet aggression and kept U.S. forces in Japan as a counterweight to Communist China. Together with the deployment of U.S. forces to Korea, the military footprint Truman established on two continents has remained virtually unchanged to this day and has served as the foundation for security in Europe and in the Pacific.

President Truman launched a sweeping reorganization of the Federal Government to prepare it for a new struggle. Working with Congress, he created the Department of Defense, established the Air Force as a separate military service, formed the National Security Council at the White House, and founded the Central Intelligence Agency to ensure America had the best intelligence on Soviet threats.

President Truman made clear that the cold war was an ideological struggle between tyranny and freedom. At the time when some still wanted to wish away the Soviet threat, he brought Winston Churchill to Missouri to deliver his famous "Iron Curtain" speech. And he issued a Presidential directive called NSC–68, which de-

clared that America faced an enemy "animated by a new fanatic faith" and determined to impose its ideology on the entire world. This directive called on the United States to accept the responsibility of world leadership and defend the cause of freedom and democracy, and that's exactly what the United States did.

By the actions he took, the institutions he built, the alliances he forged, and the doctrines he set down, President Truman laid the foundation for America's victory in the cold war. As President Truman put it towards the end of his Presidency, "When history says that my term of office saw the beginning of the cold war, it will also say that in those 8 years, we set the course that can win it." His leadership paved the way for subsequent Presidents from both political parties—men like Eisenhower and Kennedy and Reagan—to confront and eventually defeat the Soviet threat.

Today, at the start of a new century, we are again engaged in a war unlike any our Nation has fought before. And like Americans in Truman's day, we are laying the foundations for victory. The enemies we face today are different in many ways from the enemy we faced in the cold war. In the cold war, we deterred Soviet aggression through a policy of mutually assured destruction. Unlike the Soviet Union, the terrorist enemies we face today hide in caves and shadows and emerge to attack free nations from within. The terrorists have no borders to protect or capital to defend. They cannot be deterred—but they will be defeated. America will fight the terrorists on every battlefront, and we will not rest until this threat to our country has been removed.

While there are real differences between today's war and the cold war, there are also many important similarities. Like the cold war, we are fighting the followers of a murderous ideology that despises freedom, crushes all dissent, has territorial ambitions, and pursues totalitarian aims. Like the cold war, our enemies are dismissive of free peoples, claiming that men and women who live in liberty are weak and lack the resolve to defend our way of life. Like the cold war, our enemies believe that the innocent can be murdered to serve a political vision. And like the cold war, they're seeking weapons of mass murder that would allow them to deliver catastrophic destruction to our country. If our enemies succeed in acquiring such weapons, they will not hesitate to use them, which means they would pose a threat to America as great as the Soviet Union.

Against such an enemy, there is only one effective response: We will never back down; we will never give in; and we will never accept anything less than complete victory. Like previous generations, history has once again called America to great responsibilities, and we're answering history's call with confidence. We're confronting new dangers with new determination and laying the foundations for victory in the war on terror.

In this new war, we have set a clear doctrine. After the attacks of September the 11th, I told a joint session of Congress, "America makes no distinction between the terrorists and the countries that harbor them. If you harbor a terrorist, you are just as guilty as the terrorists, and you're an enemy of the United States of America." In the months that followed, I also made clear the principles that will guide us in this new war: America will not wait to be attacked again; we will confront threats before they fully materialize; we will stay on the offense against the terrorists, fighting them abroad so we do not have to face them here at home.

In this new war, we have acted boldly to confront new adversaries. When the Taliban regime in Afghanistan tested America's resolve, refusing our just demands to turn over the terrorists who attacked America, we responded with determination. Coalition forces drove the Taliban from power, liberated Afghanistan, and brought freedom to 25 million people.

In Iraq, another tyrant chose to test America's resolve. Saddam Hussein was a dictator who had pursued and used weapons of mass destruction. He sponsored terrorists, invaded his neighbors, abused his people, deceived international inspectors, and refused to comply with more than a dozen United Nations resolutions. When the United Nations Security Council gave him one final chance to disclose and disarm, or face serious consequences, he refused to take that final opportunity. So coalition forces went into Iraq and removed his cruel regime. And today, Iraq's former dictator is on trial for his crimes, and America and the world are better off because Saddam Hussein is no longer in power.

In this new war, we have helped transform old adversaries into democratic allies. Just as an earlier generation of Americans helped change Germany and Japan from conquered adversaries into democratic allies, today, a new generation of Americans is helping Iraq and Afghanistan recover from the ruins of tyranny. In Afghanistan, the terror camps have been shut down; women are working; boys and girls are going to school; and Afghans have chosen a President and a new parliament in free elections.

In Iraq, the people defied the terrorists and cast their ballots in three free elections last year. And last week, Iraqis made history when they inaugurated the leaders of a new Government of their choosing, under a Constitution that they drafted and they approved. When the formation of this unity Government—with the formation of this unity Government, the world has seen the beginning of something new: a constitutional democracy in the heart of the Middle East. Difficult challenges remain in both Afghanistan and Iraq. But America is safer and the world is more secure because these two countries are now democracies—and they are allies in the cause of freedom and peace.

In this new war, we have forged new alliances and transformed old ones for the challenges of a new century. After our Nation was attacked, we formed the largest coalition in history to fight the war on terror. More than 90 nations are cooperating in a global campaign to dry up terrorist financing, to hunt down terrorist operatives, and bring terrorist leaders to justice. Nations like Pakistan and Saudi Arabia that once turned a blind eye to terror are now helping lead the fight against it. And since September the 11th, 2001, our coalition has captured or killed Al Qaida managers and operatives in over two dozen countries and disrupted a number of serious Al Qaida terrorist plots, including plots to attack targets inside the United States. Our Nation is more secure because we have rallied the world to confront this threat to civilization.

The greatest threat we face is the danger of terrorists armed with weapons of mass destruction. To confront this danger, we launched the Proliferation Security Initiative, a coalition of more than 70 nations that are working together to stop shipments of weapons of mass destruction on land, at sea, and in the air, and to stop them from falling into terrorist hands. And building on the legacy of Harry Truman, we launched the most dramatic transformation of the NATO alliance since its founding in 1949. Working with allies, we created a new NATO Response Force that will allow NATO to deploy rapid reaction forces on short notice anywhere in the world. And together we transformed NATO from a defensive alliance focused on protecting Europe from Soviet tank invasion into a dynamic alliance that is now operating across the world in the support of democracy and peace.

For five decades, NATO forces never deployed outside of Europe. Today, NATO is leading security operations in Afghanistan, training Iraqi security forces in Baghdad, delivering humanitarian relief to earthquake victims in Pakistan, and training peacekeepers in Sudan. An alliance some said had lost its purpose after the cold war is now meeting the challenges of the 21st century.

In this new war, we're positioning our forces to meet new threats. For more than a half a century, American forces essentially had remained in the same places that President Truman deployed them. So 2 years ago, I announced the largest transformation of our global force posture since the start of the cold war. Over the coming decade, we will move U.S. forces from cold war garrisons in Europe and Asia and reposition them so they can surge quickly to trouble spots anywhere. We will deploy advanced military capabilities that will increase U.S. combat power across the world, while bringing home between 60,000 and 70,000 troops now stationed overseas. By taking these steps, we will reduce stress on our military families, raise the pressure on our enemies, and ensure that when you put on the uniform of the United States Army, you are ready to meet any threat.

In this new war, we've undertaken the most sweeping reorganization of the Federal Government since the start of the cold war. We created a new Department of Homeland Security, merging 22 different Government organizations into a single department with a clear mission: to protect America from future attacks. We created the new Director of National Intelligence, which has led a broad restructuring of our Nation's intelligence agencies for the threats of the 21st century. We have transformed the FBI into an agency whose primary focus is stopping terrorism, and reorganized the Department of Justice to help us meet this new threat. We passed the PATRIOT Act, which broke down barriers that prevented law enforcement and intelligence agencies from sharing vital information on terrorist threats.

At the Department of Defense, we created a new Northern Command responsible for homeland defense, a new Strategic

Command responsible for defending America against long-range attacks. We transformed the Special Operations Command, more than doubling its budget, adding thousands of new troops, and making it the lead command in the global war on terror. And we're undertaking the largest transformation of the Army in more than 100 years. Since the turn of the last century, the Army has been organized around the division structure designed by Napoleon. Today, we're replacing that division structure with a 21st century Army built around modular brigade combat teams that will be interchangeable and available to work for any division commander. These brigades will make our Army faster and lighter and more agile and more lethal, and it will make you more effective in the defense of freedom.

We have made clear that the war on terror is an ideological struggle between tyranny and freedom. When President Truman spoke here for the 150th anniversary of West Point, he told the class of 1952, "We can't have lasting peace unless we work actively and vigorously to bring about conditions of freedom and justice in the world." That same principle continues to guide us in today's war on terror. Our strategy to protect America is based on a clear premise: The security of our Nation depends on the advance of liberty in other nations. On September the 11th, 2001, we saw that problems originating in a failed and oppressive state 7,000 miles away could bring murder and destruction to our country. And we learned an important lesson: Decades of excusing and accommodating the lack of freedom in the Middle East did nothing to make us safe. So long as the Middle East remains a place where freedom does not flourish, it will remain a place where terrorists foment resentment and threaten American security.

So we are pursuing a forward strategy of freedom in the Middle East. I believe the desire for liberty is universal, and by standing with democratic reformers across a troubled region, we will extend freedom to millions who have not known it and lay the foundation of peace for generations to come.

We're still in the early stages of this struggle for freedom, and like those first years of the cold war, we've seen setbacks and challenges and days that have tested America's resolve. Yet we've also seen days of victory and hope. We've seen people in Afghanistan voting for the first democratic parliament in a generation. We have seen jubilant Iraqis dancing in the streets, holding up ink-stained fingers, celebrating their freedom. We've seen people in Lebanon waving cedar flags and securing the liberty and independence of their land. We've seen people in Kyrgyzstan drive a corrupt regime from power and vote for democratic change. In the past 4 years alone, more than 110 million human beings across the world have joined the ranks of the free, and this is only the beginning. The message has spread from Damascus to Tehran that the future belongs to freedom, and we will not rest until the promise of liberty reaches every people and every nation.

Now the class of 2006 will enter the great struggle, and the final outcome depends on your leadership. The war began on my watch, but it's going to end on your watch. Your generation will bring us victory in the war on terror. My call to you is this: Trust in the power of freedom, and be bold in freedom's defense; show leadership and courage, and not just on the battlefield; take risk; try new things; and challenge the established way of doing things; trust in your convictions; stay true to yourselves—and one day, the world will celebrate your achievements.

I have confidence in the final outcome of this struggle, because I know the character and determination of the men and women gathered before me. We see that character and determination in a cadet named Patrick Dowdell. It was Patrick's dream to attend West Point, and he applied straight out of high school, but he did not get in on his first try. After being turned down, he wondered if he was cut out for the Academy. His father, New York Fireman Kevin Dowdell, encouraged Patrick to apply again. Kevin wrote letters to his Congressman on behalf of his son. And he spent long hours working with Patrick on his application—right up to September the 9th, 2001. Two days later, Kevin Dowdell raced across the Brooklyn Bridge with his fire rescue unit to the burning World Trade Towers, and he never returned.

After the attack, Patrick spent months digging at Ground Zero looking for his dad—and thinking about the dream that they had shared about his future. He was determined to fulfill that dream. And in the summer of 2002, Patrick arrived here at West Point as a new cadet, and today he will receive his degree and his commission.

A few weeks ago, Patrick's mom, RoseEllen, attended another graduation ceremony, at the New York City Fire Academy, where her other son, James, followed his father's footsteps as one of New York's bravest. And today RoseEllen is with us to see Patrick join the ranks of America's bravest, as an officer in the United States Army.

We live in freedom because young Americans like Patrick and all the cadets here today have stepped forward to serve. You have chosen a difficult and dangerous vocation, and America is grateful for that choice. Today you will accept a sacred trust: You will lead America's sons and daughters on the battlefield in a time of war. Our Nation is counting on you as we count on no other group of young leaders in our country. The last 4 years have tested you in ways you never imagined, and you leave here well prepared for the challenges you will face.

There's a saying at West Point, that much of the history you teach here was made by the people you taught here. Now the class of 2006 will leave for the battlefield, and you will make history. Never falter; never quit. Bring honor to the uniform and pride to your country. May God bless you and the class of 2006.

NOTE: The President spoke at 9:33 a.m. in Michie Stadium. In his remarks, he referred to Lt. Gen. William J. Lennox, Jr., USA, superintendent, U.S. Military Academy at West Point; former President Saddam Hussein of Iraq; and President Hamid Karzai of Afghanistan.

The President's Radio Address
May 27, 2006

Good morning. This Memorial Day weekend, Americans pay tribute to those who have given their lives in service to our Nation. America is free because generations of young Americans have been willing to sacrifice to defend the country they love, so their fellow citizens could live in liberty.

This weekend, I am visiting some of the brave men and women who will soon take their own place in the defense of our freedom, the 2006 graduating class at West Point. This was the first class to arrive at West Point after the attacks of September the 11th, 2001. Each of them came to West Point in a time of war, knowing all the risks and dangers that come with wearing our Nation's uniform. And the reality of that war has surrounded them since their first moments at the Academy. Thirty-four times since they arrived at West Point they have observed a moment of silence to honor a former cadet fallen in the war on terror.

One of those former cadets was First Lieutenant Rob Seidel, a 2004 West Point graduate who gave his life in Iraq earlier this month. Rob grew up in Maryland, and as a child, he and his family made frequent visits to the Civil War battlefield at Gettysburg, and from his earliest days, he dreamed of serving in the U.S. Army. He deployed to Iraq with the 10th Mountain Division and was killed by a bomb in Baghdad. His father says this about Rob: "He loved his family and believed in God, and he loved his country, and he was willing to pay the ultimate sacrifice on behalf of his country."

We live in freedom because of young Americans like Lieutenant Rob Seidel. And in recent days in Iraq, we've seen what their sacrifices have made possible. A week ago, the new Prime Minister of Iraq announced the formation of a national unity government. British Prime Minister Tony Blair recently visited Baghdad to meet with Prime Minister Maliki and Iraq's new leaders, and this week, he came to the United States to give me his impressions. Prime Minister Blair told me that Iraq's new leaders are determined to rid their country of terrorism, unite Iraqis as one people, and deliver peace and prosperity for all their citizens.

The formation of a democratic government in Iraq marks a victory for the cause of freedom in the Middle East. It is a victory for millions of Iraqis, who defied the terrorists and cast their ballots in three elections last year. It is a victory for the Iraqi security forces, who fought and bled for this moment and now have a democracy worthy of their sacrifice. And it is a victory for the American, British, and other coalition forces who removed a murderous dictator who threatened the world. Because of their courage and sacrifices, Iraq has a free government that will be a strong and capable ally in the global war on terror.

The new Government in Iraq is also a defeat for the terrorists, who fought the arrival of a free and democratic Iraq with all the hateful power they could muster. Now a day that they feared has arrived. The terrorists can kill the innocent, but they cannot stop the advance of freedom. We can expect the terrorists to continue bombing and killing, but something fundamental has changed: The terrorists are now fighting a free and constitutional government. They are at war with the people of Iraq. The Iraqi people and their new leaders are determined to defeat this enemy, and so is the United States of America.

This Memorial Day weekend, we remember First Lieutenant Seidel and the brave Americans of every generation who have given their lives for freedom, liberated the oppressed, and left the world a safer and better place. And the best way to honor America's fallen heroes is to carry on their fight, defend our freedom, and complete the mission for which they gave their lives.

Thank you for listening.

NOTE: The address was recorded at 7:50 a.m. on May 26 in the Cabinet Room at the White House for broadcast at 10:06 a.m. on May 27. In his address, the President referred to Prime Minister Nuri al-Maliki and former President Saddam Hussein of Iraq. The transcript was made available by the Office of the Press Secretary on May 26 but was embargoed for release until the broadcast. The Office of the Press Secretary also released a Spanish language transcript of this address.

Statement on the Earthquake in Indonesia
May 27, 2006

On behalf of the American people, Laura and I send our deepest sympathies to the families and friends of those who lost their lives in the devastating earthquake in Indonesia. Our thoughts and prayers are with the Indonesian people as they comfort all those affected by this terrible disaster.

Through financial and material support, the United States is assisting with recovery efforts in coordination with Indonesian authorities, and we stand prepared to provide additional assistance as needed.

Remarks at a Memorial Day Ceremony in Arlington, Virginia
May 29, 2006

Thank you all. Laura and I are honored to join you today. Thank you for coming. Mr. Secretary, thank you for your kind words. Members of my Cabinet, General Pace, Members of Congress, members of the United States military, veterans, honored guests, and the loved ones of the fallen: A few moments ago, I placed a wreath at the Tomb of the Unknowns. I was honored to do so on behalf of the American people, as a sign of our solemn gratitude and our deep respect. The names of those buried there are known only to God, yet their souls have entered into the spirit of America, and they will never be forgotten by our Nation.

In this place where valor sleeps, we acknowledge our responsibility as Americans to preserve the memory of the fallen. On this Memorial Day, we look out on quiet hills and rows of white headstones and we know that we are in the presence of greatness. The markers here record the names of more than 296,000 men and women. Each of the soldiers, sailors, airmen, and marines buried here answered the call to serve and stepped forward to protect the nation they loved.

All who are buried here understood their duty. They saw a dark shadow on the horizon and went to meet it. They understood that tyranny must be met with resolve and that liberty is always the achievement of courage. Here, in the presence of veterans they fought with and loved ones whose pictures they carried, the fallen give silent witness to the price of our liberty, and our Nation honors them this day and every day.

In this place where valor sleeps, we are reminded why America has always gone to war reluctantly—because we know the costs of war. We have seen those costs in the war on terror we fight today. These grounds are the final resting place for more than 270 men and women who have given their lives in freedom's cause since the attacks of September the 11th, 2001. With us here are veterans who fought alongside them and who have come today to pay their respects. They are joined by veterans of World War II, Korea, Vietnam, and other conflicts across the globe, whose friends and comrades also lie in this sacred ground. As we pray for their fallen friends, we also remember those who went to war and are still missing, and we are determined to account for them all.

In this place where valor sleeps, we find strength in knowing that those serving freedom's cause have acted with principle and steadfast faith. Second Lieutenant Jack Lundberg was killed 2 weeks after D-Day.

At the end of World War II, he wrote his Mom and Dad a letter to be opened in the event he did not come home. He wrote, "I am sorry to add to your grief, but we of the United States have something to fight for—never more fully have I realized that. The United States of America is worth the sacrifice."

That same feeling moves those who are now fighting the war on terror. First Lieutenant Mark Dooley was killed by a terrorist bomb last September in the Iraqi city of Ramadi. Before he left for his tour, he gave his parents a last letter, just in case. He wrote, "Remember that my leaving was in the service of something that we loved, and be proud. The best way to pay respect is to value why a sacrifice was made."

Last week, the family of Lieutenant Colonel Joseph Fenty, Junior, gathered here at Arlington to pay their last respects to the husband, son, and father they loved. Colonel Fenty was killed with nine of his fellow soldiers in a helicopter crash in Afghanistan earlier this month. Hours before that crash, he had spoken to his wife, Kristin, about their newborn daughter he was waiting to meet. Someday she will learn about her dad from the men with whom she served—he served. And one of them said this about her father: "We all wanted to be more like Joe Fenty. We were all in awe of him." I am in awe of the men and women who sacrifice for the freedom of the United States of America.

Our Nation is free because of brave Americans like these, who volunteer to confront our adversaries abroad so we do not have to face them here at home. Our Nation mourns the loss of our men and women in uniform. We will honor them by completing the mission for which they gave their lives—by defeating the terrorists, by advancing the cause of liberty, and by laying the foundation of peace for a generation of young Americans. Today we pray that those who lie here have found peace with their Creator, and we resolve that their sacrifice will always be remembered by a grateful nation.

May God bless the United States of America.

NOTE: The President spoke at 11:26 a.m. in the Amphitheater at Arlington National Cemetery. In his remarks, he referred to Secretary of Defense Donald H. Rumsfeld, who introduced the President; and Gen. Peter Pace, USMC, Chairman, Joint Chiefs of Staff.

Remarks Announcing the Nomination of Henry M. Paulson, Jr., To Be Secretary of the Treasury
May 30, 2006

The President. Good morning. Welcome to the White House. I'm pleased to announce that I will nominate Henry Paulson to be the Secretary of the Treasury.

For the past 8 years, Hank has served as chairman and chief executive officer of the Goldman Sachs Group. It's one of the most respected firms on Wall Street. He has a lifetime of business experience. He has an intimate knowledge of financial markets and an ability to explain economic issues in clear terms. He's earned a reputation for candor and integrity. And when he is confirmed by the Senate, he'll be a superb addition to my Cabinet.

The Secretary of the Treasury has one of the most important jobs in the Federal

Government. The Treasury Secretary is responsible for recommending and implementing policies dealing with taxes, financial markets, Federal spending, trade, and other issues affecting the health and competitiveness of the American economy. The Treasury Secretary oversees the minting of U.S. currency, the management of public finances, and the enforcement of important laws, including our efforts to crack down on terrorist financing. The Treasury Secretary is the leading force on my economic team and the chief spokesman for my economic policies.

For the past 3 years, Secretary John Snow has shown strong leadership in carrying out these responsibilities. John answered the call to public service in a time of uncertainty for our economy, and under his leadership, we have seen a broad and vigorous economic resurgence. He's been a steady advocate for small-business entrepreneurs and working families, and he's helped deliver jobs and opportunity for the American people. I appreciate his years of service to our country. I wish you, John, and your family all the very best.

When he's confirmed by the Senate, Hank will build on John's fine work. He takes this new post at a hopeful time for American businesses and workers. In the first quarter of 2006, the U.S. economy grew at an annual rate of 5.3 percent, the fastest growth in 2½ years. We added 5.2 million new jobs since August of 2003. The national unemployment rate is down to 4.7 percent. Productivity is high, and that's leading to higher wages and a higher standard of living for the American people. Hourly compensation grew at an annual rate of 5.7 percent in the first quarter this year.

The American economy is powerful, productive, and prosperous, and I look forward to working with Hank Paulson to keep it that way. As Treasury Secretary, Hank will be my principal adviser on the broad range of domestic and international economic issues that affect the well-being of all Americans. Hank shares my philosophy that the economy prospers when we trust the American people to save, spend, and invest their money as they see fit.

The tax relief we delivered has helped set off the economic expansion that we're seeing today. And one of Hank's most important responsibilities will be to build on this success by working with Congress to maintain a progrowth, low-tax environment.

Hank also understands that the Government should spend the taxpayers' money wisely or not at all. He will work closely with Congress to help restrain the spending appetite of the Federal Government and keep us on track to meet our goal of cutting the deficit in half by 2009.

Hank will also be an important representative of the United States on the international scene. As an investment banker, he understands the importance of opening new markets for American exports. He will insist on fair treatment for American businesses, workers, and farmers. He will help ensure that our trading partners play by the rules, respect intellectual property rights, and maintain flexible, market-based exchange rates for their currencies.

To all these tasks, Hank brings a record of achievement and excellence. He grew up on a farm in Illinois. He went to college at Dartmouth. He starred on the field as an All-Ivy football player and in the classroom as a Phi Beta Kappa student. He earned an MBA from Harvard. He served in the Pentagon and here at the White House. He started at Goldman Sachs in 1974 and rose to its top office after 24 years of distinguished work at the firm. He has a lifelong passion for nature, and he's served as chairman of the Nature Conservancy, where he has promoted conservation both at home and abroad.

As one of America's most prominent business executives, Hank has been a strong and consistent voice for corporate accountability. When the corporate scandals broke, Hank showed his leadership and character by calling for reforms that would strengthen the way America's public companies are governed and improve their accounting practices. And as Treasury Secretary, Hank will bring those high standards to one of the most important posts in Washington.

I want to thank Hank for his willingness to leave one of the most rewarding jobs on Wall Street to serve the American people. Hank will follow in the footsteps of Alexander Hamilton and other distinguished Treasury Secretaries who used their talents and wisdom to strengthen our financial markets and expand the reach of the American Dream.

Hank is going to make an outstanding Secretary of the Treasury, and I call on the United States Senate to promptly confirm him.

Mr. Secretary.

[*At this point, Secretary of the Treasury John Snow made brief remarks.*]

The President. Thank you, Mr. Secretary. Thank you very much.

[*Secretary-designate Paulson made brief remarks.*]

NOTE: The President spoke at 9:14 a.m. in the Rose Garden at the White House. The transcript released by the Office of the Press Secretary also included the remarks of Secretary Snow and Secretary-designate Paulson.

Remarks on Receiving Diplomatic Credentials From Ambassador Samir Shakir al-Sumaydi of Iraq
May 30, 2006

President Bush. It is my honor and pleasure to welcome the papers from Iraq's Ambassador to the United States. Mr. Ambassador, congratulations.

Ambassador al-Sumaydi. Thank you, Mr. President.

President Bush. You're now officially the Ambassador. I look forward to working with you, Mr. Ambassador, and the new Government, to help Iraq become a country that can govern itself and sustain itself and defend itself. I'm confident in the future of liberty in Iraq because I believe the people of Iraq want to live in a free society. And although there's been some very difficult times for the Iraqi people, I am impressed by the courage of the leadership, impressed by the determination of the people, and want to assure you, sir, that the United States stands ready to help the Iraqi democracy succeed.

So welcome here to the Oval Office. Thank you for coming.

Ambassador al-Sumaydi. Thank you, Mr. President. I am honored and privileged to serve as the Ambassador of free Iraq, after 16 years of isolation, to represent my country to this great country, to have a voice for the new elected Iraqi Government, and communicate directly with this administration and with the people of the United States, to express our ambitions and desire to live in peace and remove the scourge of terrorism from our land and help others remove it from theirs.

The President said a couple of days ago in his radio address that the terrorists can kill innocent people, but they cannot stop the march of freedom. I echo those words and say that the terrorists can target the innocent and the weak and the vulnerable, but they will never stop us establishing a democratic and free country.

I'm proud to represent this country to you, Mr. President.

President Bush. Thank you, Ambassador. Very well done. Thank you.

NOTE: The President spoke at 11:15 a.m. in the Oval Office at the White House. A por- tion of these remarks could not be verified because the tape was incomplete.

Remarks Following Discussions With President Paul Kagame of Rwanda and an Exchange With Reporters
May 31, 2006

President Bush. I want to welcome the President of Rwanda to the Oval Office again. He was here last year, and I'm honored to welcome you back.

The President is—he's a man of action; he can get things done. I'm proud of your leadership. We have talked about a lot of issues. We talked about the Sudan, and I want to thank the President for committing troops in the AU mission to help deal with what I have called a genocide. We strategized about how we can go forward to resolve the situation. I thank you for your wisdom; I thank you for your concern.

One of the interesting things about President Kagame's Government is there is more women in his Government than anywhere else in Africa, which I think speaks to the man's character and understanding about how societies remain strong and whole. I appreciate his commitment to education. And I want to thank you, Mr. President, for your understanding that the best way for an economy to develop is to welcome private capital. He's been working hard with companies here in America. Many companies are taking a good look at Rwanda because they realize it's a country where they will be treated fairly, and there is a transparent society. And he's had some success, which will help people find work. And that's, to me, a sign of leadership. So welcome back.

I, finally, want to thank you for your commitment to fighting HIV/AIDS. This Government has done a really good job of using some of the monies that we provided to save lives. And I've always told people that it's one thing for the American

Government—and the American people, more importantly—to generously write checks to help, but it requires strong leadership at home. And you provided that leadership.

So I welcome you back to the Oval Office, and thank you for your friendship.

President Kagame. Thank you, President. It's a great honor for me to be here, President, and I appreciate the discussion we have had on a wide range of issues—starting with bilateral discussions we have had about United States Government has been very helpful in its support of Rwanda in different areas—dealing with HIV/AIDS, to supporting the private sector to invest in our country, to dealing with infrastructure programs. And also the support we have had during the period we were working under the African Union mission to send our troops to Darfur. The United States Government, with your support, Mr. President—we have had our forces, our troops airlifted by the United States military to Darfur and continued support for the African Union mission.

We are very grateful for—generally, the support in the area will bring peace to the Great Lakes region and to supporting the efforts in Sudan and, ultimately, that process of supporting my country to be able to develop and continue building on the foundation we have laid in the last 12 years. So we appreciate that, Mr. President.

President Bush. Welcome. The President and I will take two questions a side, starting with the Americans. Nedra [Nedra Pickler, Associated Press].

Iraq/U.S. Armed Forces

Q. Mr. President, what have you been told about the killings at Haditha? And are you worried about the impact it could have on the situation in Iraq?

President Bush. I am troubled by the initial news stories. I am mindful that there is a thorough investigation going on. If, in fact, the laws were broken, there will be punishment. I know this: I've talked to General Pete Pace about the subject, who is a proud marine, and nobody is more concerned about these allegations than the Marine Corps. The Marine Corps is full of men and women who are honorable people who understand rules of war. And if, in fact, these allegations are true, the Marine Corps will work hard to make sure that that culture, that proud culture will be reinforced, and that those who violated the law, if they did, will be punished.

Rwanda

Q. I'll ask a question—I'm a journalist from Rwanda.

President Bush. Welcome.

Q. Can I ask you a question on the genocide of Rwanda? It's been 13 years after the genocide of Rwanda, but many perpetrators of the genocide, many people who did it, who carried out the genocide are still at large. One estimate is about over 50 of them in Europe and the U.S., others in the Congo. What's the U.S. going to do to help run—to get these people to——

President Bush. The interesting thing about Rwanda today is that you have a President who understands that part of a successful society is for people to work hard on reconciliation. There's no question the genocide in Rwanda was a real tragedy. It's one of the most significant tragedies in modern history. And yet your President and his Government has worked hard to reconcile, help people reconcile the tragedy at all levels of society.

To the extent that he wants our help in finding certain perpetuators of crimes, we'll be glad to do so. But the way I look at the situation is that Rwanda can serve as an example for other societies that are troubled. As you know, we're working hard in Iraq to bring a democracy—to help a democracy grow there. And yet there's still sectarian violence. People are still using violence to achieve either revenge or political means. And the Rwanda example shows what's possible when people work hard on reconciliation.

That's why I support Prime Minister Maliki's desire to have reconciliation moves. And the President actually offered to help, and it may be at some point in time it makes sense for the new Government in Iraq to do that. But I'm very proud of the accomplishments that Rwanda has made over 13 years—13 years after the genocide.

Kelly [Kelly O'Donnell, NBC News].

Iran

Q. Mr. President, Secretary Rice is outlining a change in U.S. position toward Iran today, after so many years of not engaging directly with them. Why now? And will you respond directly to the letter from the President?

President Bush. I believe it's very important that we solve this issue diplomatically, and my decision today says that the United States is going to take a leadership position in solving this issue. And our message to the Iranians is that, one, you won't have a weapon, and two, that you must verifiably suspend any programs, at which point we will come to the negotiating table to work on a way forward.

I thought it was important for the United States to take the lead, along with our partners, and that's what you're seeing. You're seeing robust diplomacy. I believe this problem can be solved diplomatically, and I'm going to give it every effort to do so.

I've talked on the telephone in the last couple of days with Jacques Chirac and Angela Merkel, and I spoke to Tony Blair when he was here about this issue; I spoke to Prime Minister Koizumi. I'm on the phone a lot talking to—and President Putin, by the way—and I'm on the phone a lot talking to our folks that share the same concern I share, and say, "Look, let's get this solved diplomatically," but there must be a united international front that shares the same message, and that is, is that we will work collaboratively to prevent the Iranians from developing a nuclear weapon.

I also want to make it very clear that we have—we respect the Iranian people, and we respect their heritage and their history, and we hope their Government listens to the international demands and doesn't isolate itself from the world and doesn't foolishly spend money on a weapons program that takes away the capacity—the ability for the Iranian economy to grow so people are able to put food on the table and find work.

Final—anybody else from Rwanda?

Situation in Sudan

Q. Yes, Mr. President, I come from Rwanda. I heard the President of Rwanda thanking you for the assistance you are giving on Darfur, but in spite all that you've been doing, it has persisted. Are you planning to up your support in that regard, Mr. President?

President Bush. To support the Rwanda troops in Darfur? I will. As a matter of fact, we had a very good discussion about this subject. The President is concerned about whether or not the United States will honor its commitments. We will honor our commitments, but the United States

Congress must pass the supplemental with the money in there for the Sudan. See, part of the money in a supplemental request that's working its way through a conference committee now is to help repay a country like Rwanda that's putting troops on the ground.

And so I told the President that sometimes the Congress doesn't move as quickly as I'd like on issues, but I'm confident they'll get the supplemental passed when they come back from their Memorial Day break. That supplemental must, one, meet the financial conditions that I talked about—in other words, I'm going to veto the bill if they spend more money than I requested—and it's got to set—it's got to meet priorities as well. And one of the priorities is our own troops who are in harm's way. And another priority is helping the Katrina victims. And a third priority in that bill that we've submitted is to help in Sudan. I told the President I'm confident they'll pass that bill and that his troops will get reimbursed.

Thank you all very much.

NOTE: The President spoke at 11:43 a.m. in the Oval Office at the White House. In his remarks, he referred to Gen. Peter Pace, USMC, Chairman, Joint Chiefs of Staff; Prime Minister Nuri al-Maliki of Iraq; President Mahmud Ahmadi-nejad of Iran; President Jacques Chirac of France; Chancellor Angela Merkel of Germany; Prime Minister Tony Blair of the United Kingdom; Prime Minister Junichiro Koizumi of Japan; and President Vladimir V. Putin of Russia.

Remarks at a Swearing-In Ceremony for Michael V. Hayden as Director of the Central Intelligence Agency in Langley, Virginia
May 31, 2006

Thank you. Thanks for the warm welcome. It's great to be back with the really

fine people here at the Central Intelligence Agency.

I'm honored to be here at the swearing-in of Mike Hayden as America's new Director of the CIA. He's such a good man, we're going to swear him in twice—yesterday—[*laughter*]—and today.

Mike is a patriot; he's a reformer; he's one of our Nation's finest intelligence professionals. I know firsthand how good this guy is; I've worked with him on some really important issues related to the security of the United States. He brings more than two decades of experience in the intelligence field. He is going to be a superb leader for the dedicated men and women of the CIA.

I appreciate Ambassador Negroponte being with us today, the Director of National Intelligence. I want to thank Attorney General Al Gonzales for joining us and the Director of the FBI, Bob Mueller, for joining us as well. But most importantly, thank you all for coming.

I'm proud to serve with you. It is such an honor to serve the United States of America, and I appreciate your serving along my side to make America secure. The role of the CIA is critical to the security of the United States. This Agency is helping to lead the intelligence war against the terrorists who attacked us on September the 11th, 2001. They continue to plot attacks, and together, we are going to stop them.

The role of the CIA is vital to my doing my job. I cannot do my job without the Central Intelligence Agency. This Agency remains the principal provider of intelligence analysis to the President, to the Director of National Intelligence, and to senior national security officials in my administration. As Director of the CIA, Mike will continue the reforms needed. America's leaders are going to have the best possible intelligence, and Mike Hayden is going to work with you to see that that's the case.

I've asked Mike to continue to develop the human intelligence capabilities of the CIA, which are essential to understanding the plans and intentions of dangerous re-gimes and terrorist organizations around the world. I've asked Mike to continue improving the analytical skills of the CIA, which apply the best minds to interpret the intelligence that we gather. I'm confident that under Mike's leadership, the CIA will help us stay ahead of America's enemies and win the war on terror.

The men and women who work here at the CIA have got a tough job and a really important job. You must penetrate closed societies and secretive organizations. You must master foreign languages and deal with unfamiliar cultures. Much of your work is secret, and American lives depend on that work remaining secret. America appreciates the good work you're doing, and so do I.

And in Mike Hayden, you have a leader who recognizes your talents, who understands your challenges and will ensure that you remain the finest intelligence agency in the world.

In his new position, Mike will build on the good work of Director Porter Goss. Nearly 2 years ago, I asked Porter to take on a tough assignment, the transformation of the CIA. Porter carried out that assignment with skill and determination. He upheld the high standards and proud tradition of the Agency, and he leaves behind a CIA that's stronger than the one he found. And Laura and I wish Porter and his family well as they begin a new chapter in their lives.

Mike Hayden succeeds Porter Goss at a time of great change in the world and great challenge for our intelligence community. Under the leadership of John Negroponte, our intelligence community is growing more integrated and more effective every day. And under the leadership of Mike Hayden, the Central Intelligence Agency will continue to play a critical role in our Nation's intelligence enterprise. Mike understands that the CIA must transform to confront new dangers and do so without slowing the high tempo at which it already operates, to protect this country.

I'm confident that with Mike Hayden at the helm, the CIA will succeed and continue to make important contributions to the security of the American people.

As Mike takes on this important assignment, he has my trust, my full trust, and he has the support of a loving family. I'm glad to see his wife, Jeanine, his children and grandchildren, and his father, Harry, and all the other members of the Hayden family who have joined us as well today.

I want to thank Mike for agreeing to serve our Nation once again. And I look forward to continuing to work with him to do our duty to protect the American people.

Thank you all for coming today. May God bless Mike Hayden; may God bless you all; and may God continue to bless America.

NOTE: The President spoke at 2 p.m. at CIA Headquarters. The transcript released by the Office of the Press Secretary also included the remarks of Director Hayden.

Remarks at a Reception for Gubernatorial Candidate Robert L. Ehrlich, Jr., in Baltimore, Maryland
May 31, 2006

Thanks for coming tonight. Thank you all. So he just gave my speech. [*Laughter*] You know, when you have somebody who accomplishes positive things—he's got a record of accomplishment for everybody—not just a handful, but everybody—you need to send him back as the Governor of the State of Maryland.

So in our line of work, there's a lot of big talkers. [*Laughter*] And sometimes you find a doer, somebody who knows how to set an agenda and lead people to accomplish that agenda. Bob Ehrlich is a doer; he's a great leader; and he needs to be reelected Governor of the State of Maryland.

So the one thing he didn't take credit for was—I think he should have—was the Maryland women's basketball team. He can't even touch the net. [*Laughter*] Well, that's not true.

We both married really well. [*Laughter*] He married a fabulous woman; the first lady of Maryland is doing a wonderful job. Laura and I are very fond of Kendel and Bob. We consider them friends. We invited them to come to Camp David once, which is, after all, in the State of Maryland. So

he arrived—as did about 10 feet of snow. [*Laughter*] So I said, "Come on back in the summer." [*Laughter*] But Laura sends her love to the Ehrlichs.

And just a word on Laura. She's down in New Orleans today. She is a fabulous First Lady. She is really—I'm really proud of the job she does for our country.

I'm also proud to be here with Bob's parents, Bob and Nancy. Thank you all for coming. I'm sure Nancy—[*applause*]—I'm sure one of the reasons why your son is so successful as the Governor is because you keep telling him what to do. [*Laughter*] And obviously, he's wise enough to listen. [*Laughter*] I've got the same problem in my family. [*Laughter*]

Mr. Chairman, thank you for your leadership. I want to thank you all for supporting the Victory Committee. I want to thank you for giving of your money to help this good man and the party succeed. And I want to thank you in advance for what you're going to do when we come down the stretch in October/November, and that is, turn out the vote.

So I want to thank all the grassroots activists who are here. There's a couple of you out there, you know, stuffing the envelopes, making the phone calls, putting up the signs. That's how you win. When you've got somebody as good as Governor Ehrlich, you need to get on the streets and go to the coffee shops and houses of worship and tell the people, you've got a good man; you've got a good man who has done a fabulous job for the people of Maryland. By the way, when you're getting him in as Governor, make sure you put Michael Steele into the United States Senate.

One of the things it's important to have in a chief executive officer, whether it be at the State level or the Federal level, is somebody who's willing to take on problems, to confront problems. You know, a lot of times in the political arena, it's easy just to shuffle them along. You know, you see a problem and say, "Well, let's just not deal with it; let's let somebody else take care of it." I like Bob Ehrlich because he's not afraid to take on problems. He understands that our jobs are to solve problems. Bob Ehrlich is a problem-solver. He sets agendas; he makes decisions based upon principles; he doesn't worry about polls and focus groups; and he leads. And he's the right guy to be reelected to the State of Maryland.

We're living in historic times. These are times that require steadfast conviction. I just want to share some thoughts with you about the war on terror. First of all, I want to thank the Governor for his strong support for the men and women who wear the uniform of the United States. As the Commander in Chief of a military full of incredibly fine people, it is important to have people in elected office like the Governor who know what it means to have—to be able to say strong words of support. These kids need our support. They're doing hard work on our behalf.

My most important job and the most important job of the Governor is to protect the American people. And that job came home, became very clear to us on September the 11th of 2001. It's a day that I'll never forget. Many of the decisions that I have made as your President are based upon the lessons I learned on that day. The first lesson I learned on that day is, there are evil people in the world who want to do harm to the American citizens. I learned that you can't negotiate with these people; you can't rationalize with them; you can't hope for the best. That we must—in order to protect the country, we must bring them to justice before they do harm again.

I learned that when a President speaks, he better mean what he says. I understand to protect this country that we must deny safe haven to these terrorists who'd like to do us harm. And so I said, "If you harbor a terrorist, you're equally as guilty as the terrorists." I meant what I said. I gave the Taliban an opportunity to hand over Al Qaida. They refused to do so. And because of the bravery of our troops and coalition troops, Afghanistan is liberated and free and is no longer a threat to the United States of America.

I learned on September the 11th a lesson I'm never going to forget, that we've got to take threats seriously before they come home to hurt us. It's really important, if you think our duty is to protect the folks, to take every threat seriously. You see, when we grew up, or some of us grew up, baby boomers grew up, we felt pretty confident that America could be secure from a foreign attack, except maybe by missile. And then that attitude changed dramatically when we realized oceans couldn't protect us. And so when we see a threat, we've got to take them seriously.

I saw a threat. As a matter of fact, the world saw a threat with Saddam Hussein. See, he was a state sponsor of terror; he had used weapons of mass destruction; he had the capacity to make weapons of mass destruction; he invaded his neighbors; he was shooting at U.S. pilots. He was given a lot of United Nations Security Council resolutions, to change. He refused to change. He chose war, and the world is better off without Saddam Hussein in power.

And now we're doing the hard work of helping people who were suppressed by a tyrant, to understand the blessings of liberty. But we shouldn't be discouraged when you see the car bombings and killings. It saddens us. But remember that last December, 12 million Iraqis went to the polls in defiance of car bombers and killers and terrorists, and said, "We want to be free. We want to be free." We understand that freedom is a universal principle. It is universal—I believe in an Almighty, and I believe one of the great gifts of the Almighty is freedom. Freedom isn't just, you know, for Methodists or Texans or Americans; freedom is for everybody. And it shouldn't surprise us when 12 million people are free.

And it shouldn't surprise us that there are killers and terrorists who are trying to stop democracy. See, their ideology is the exact opposite of a free society. They don't believe in dissent. They don't believe in the freedom to worship. They don't believe women should have rights. Their ideology is dark and backwards. And yet freedom brings light and hope. What you're seeing is an historic—is history being made as societies are—as two societies, Afghanistan and Iraq, have found the beauty of freedom, and they're establishing constitutional Governments of and by and for the people.

We're going to succeed in Iraq. We will succeed because we've got a great military, full of decent and honorable people. We will succeed because the Iraqi people want us to succeed. And we will succeed because the terrorists and killers offer no hope, whatsoever.

I want to tell you something about what's going on. I just talked today to my buddy Prime Minister Koizumi, on the phone. And we were talking about peace. And every time I meet with him, we sit down at the table and talk about peace. We talk about North Korea. He's got a thousand troops in Iraq because he understands the power of democracy to make the world a better place. Yet that wasn't necessarily going to happen after World War II. My dad fought the Japanese—I'm sure relatives of yours fought the Japanese. They were the sworn enemy of the United States. I think it's amazing—don't you—that the President of the United States sits at the table talking about peace with the leader of an enemy, former enemy. You know what happened? Japan adopted a Japanese-style democracy after World War II. Fortunately, one of my predecessors, Harry S. Truman, believed in the power of freedom to transform an enemy into an ally.

Someday, an American President will be sitting down with duly elected leaders of Iraq, keeping the peace. Freedom causes people to reach for hope. Freedom brings light into society. Democracies don't war. What you're seeing today is the hard work of changing a society that was under the brutal thumb of a dictator into one that is free. And we're laying the foundation of peace for generations to come.

At home, if you're looking for work, you can find a job. Bob Ehrlich and I believe that the role of Government is not to create wealth but to create an environment in which the entrepreneurial spirit flourishes. That's the principle by which we make decisions. And you might remember, we've been through some pretty difficult times in this country when it came to our economy. We've been through a recession and a stock market correction, an attack on our country; we've been to war to defend ourselves; we had some terrible natural disasters; energy prices are up. Yet our economy is strong, and it's getting stronger.

And the reason why our economy grew at 3.5 percent last year—it grew at 5.3 percent in the first quarter of this year—the reason why the national unemployment rate is 4.7 percent and we've added 5.2 million new jobs since August of 2003, is because we cut the taxes. We believe that when someone has more money to save, spend, or invest, the economy grows.

Bob Ehrlich and I understand this fact: 70 percent of new jobs in America are created by the small-business owners—70 percent. And so if you can stimulate small-business growth, you stimulate job growth. And by cutting the taxes, individual tax rates, we cut taxes on subchapter S's and limited partnerships and sole proprietorships. The tax cuts we passed have helped make our small-business sectors strong and robust, and America is better off for it.

Ehrlich is going to fight to keep taxes low. It's not just low on some; it's low on everybody. See, we're not these kind of people who say, "Let's have selective tax cuts." We believe if you're going to cut taxes, you cut taxes on everybody who pays taxes. Tax cuts are good, strong economic policy.

And then there's the other thing in Washington, which Bob knows only too well, that says, "Well, look, you got to raise the taxes to balance the budget." But that's not the way Washington works. I suspect it's not the way Annapolis works. They're going to raise your taxes, but they're going to figure out new ways to spend your money. [*Laughter*] That's the way Washington works. I bet that's the way the statehouse works too. That's why you've got to have a fiscally sound Governor as the Governor of the State of Maryland.

And so the best way to cut the deficit, at least in Washington, is to keep your taxes low so the economy grows. When the economy grows, it generates more tax revenues for the treasury—and then be wise about how we spend your money.

We're going to cut the deficit in half by 2009. I told the Congress, I said, "Look, if you bust the supplemental we've got coming up there, if you're greater than 92.2 billion and—plus some for the pandemic flu, I'm going to veto the bill." I'm serious about it, you know. They've got to understand that we're going to cut this deficit in half by 2009 by being wise about how we spend your money and keeping progrowth economic policies in place.

Bob Ehrlich steps into office, as he told you—you took some of my speech away from me—[*laughter*]—but the people of Maryland have got to understand, he shows up in office, and they have a $4 billion deficit, see. When he shows up, you're in the hole $4 billion. Now he's standing up here asking for reelection, and he's able to say to the people of Maryland, "We've got us a $2 billion surplus." Don't you want that kind of guy back in office?

Sometimes the temptation, when you get into government, is to grow it. And a good place to look is at the office of the Governor; see, that's a good place to start to determine whether or not you've got yourself a Governor who knows how to manage. See, the chief executive officer not only has got to set an agenda and call people to achieve the agenda; he's also got to be a manager. He's got to be able to do a lot with less, if you're dealing with the taxpayers' money.

Interestingly enough, he's decreased the size of Maryland's executive branch by 7 percent. See, he's in charge of the executive branch. And so the voters of Maryland—I don't care whether you're Republican or Democrat or independent—need to say to yourself, "Who best to manage the executive branch of the State of Maryland?" Bob Ehrlich has got a strong record.

The other thing that's interesting that probably doesn't get discussed a lot here in Maryland, but should, is what could have happened had he not been the Governor. See, we've discussed what he did as the Governor. We know what happened since he's the Governor. The question is, what would have happened? Well, I'll tell you what would have happened. The legislature would have raised $7.5 billion in tax increases had you not had this man as the Governor of the State of Maryland.

I'll talk about three things real quick: one, education. I used to say when I was the Governor of Texas, education is to a State what national defense is to the Federal Government. I think it's by far the most important—should be the most important priority of any Governor. I know it's a really important priority of Governor Bob Ehrlich. You know why? I've been to schools here in Maryland. I've seen him firsthand come into classrooms and talk to teachers and parents. And he generally cares about making sure the public school system—the public school system does what it's supposed to do, and that's educate everybody.

We had—when I came to Washington, I was very concerned about a system that just kind of shuffled people through—social promotion. You know we'd say, oh, you're supposed to be—you're X age; you're supposed to be here. You know what happened under that system? Impoverished kids, inner-city black kids, or kids whose parents don't speak English as a first language just got moved through. That's the easiest thing to do. And so we changed the attitude. And I'm proud to have a partner in Bob Ehrlich who understands, one, you've got to set high standards, see; you've got to believe every child can learn; and secondly, in return for money, we expect people to measure.

Now, I believe in local control of schools, and so does Bob. I'm a strong believer in local control of schools. But I said, in return for increasing Federal money, particularly for poor students, I want to know. I want to know whether a child can read and write and add and subtract. And I want to know early.

And so we worked with Governor Ehrlich. He put in a very strong accountability system—that's uncomfortable for some people. Oh, I've heard every excuse—you know, teaching the test, or you're testing too much. I don't accept that and neither does Governor Ehrlich. You can't have a good education system unless you determine early whether a child can read by grade level, and whether or not, if you find a child not reading by grade level, you've got courage enough to change the curriculum and make sure that child gets extra

help. No Child Left Behind Act is working in the State of Maryland because you've got a strong education leader in Bob Ehrlich.

And how do we know? We're measuring. You know, there's an achievement gap. So you've got a Governor like Governor Ehrlich, who recognizes what I recognize: You can't have an achievement gap in America and have America be a hopeful place. You can't have certain kids reading at the fourth grade level and other kids not, and you have a bright future for your country. You just can't. And he understands that, and so do I. And so he said, "The achievement gap is narrowing." Do you know why? Do you know? Because we're measuring. High standards, strong accountability, local control of schools, demanding change where you find the status quo is unsatisfactory is the key to success, and Maryland has an education Governor in Bob Ehrlich.

Why are charter schools important? They're important because if the status quo is unacceptable, you need to give parents alternatives. And that's what the charter school movement is all about. It says, "You don't trust government to make decisions for people when it comes to education; you trust the parents to make the decisions for the children." And if parents are not happy with the status quo, they ought to be given other options. The charter school movement is going to put Maryland on the leading edge of educational excellence, and Governor Bob Ehrlich gets a lot of credit for being the pioneer of the charter school movement in this State.

Our party is one that has proven that you can have economic growth and sound environmental policy at the same time. Environmental policy and economic growth are not zero-sum. As a matter of fact, I happen to believe that in order to have a good environment, you've got to have a strong economy so you can afford that which is necessary to protect the environment. Bob Ehrlich has got a very, very strong record of conservation.

He signed the most important legislation to clean up the Chesapeake Bay—ever. That's leadership. Some of them talk a good game—I'm sure they're spouting all kinds of stuff about how—[*laughter*]. This man has delivered. The Chesapeake Bay Restoration Act—the Bob Ehrlich "I'm going to protect the Chesapeake Bay" Act—upgrades the State's 66 largest waste water treatment plants, upgrades sewage systems to increase nitrogen removal.

The Ehrlich-Steele administration has preserved nearly 60,000 acres of fields, forests, and open space and farmland. This man has got a record to run on. And if you care about the environment here in the State of Maryland, you need to put Bob Ehrlich back in as the Governor.

Finally, I proudly wear the label of compassionate conservative, and so does Bob Ehrlich. Let me tell you what I think that means. I think it means that government has got to recognize its limits in providing compassionate care. See, Government can hand out money, but it can't put hope in a person's heart or a sense of purpose in a person's life.

If you find somebody who hurts in society, it's best to rally a person who's heard a universal call to love a neighbor like you'd like to be loved yourself. There's nothing better than somebody putting their arm around a lonely person and saying, "How can I help you, brother or sister?" There's nothing better than having a church or a synagogue or a mosque take up the cause of feeding the hungry and finding shelter for the homeless. Government should not fear the involvement of faith in our society; we ought to welcome faith in order to help solve some of society's most intractable problems.

Ehrlich's got the Office of Community Initiatives. He's got a way to make sure that bureaucracy gets out of the way of helping people who have heard a universal call to help. I oftentimes remind the American people that—who look at our country and say, "Well, our strengths are our military"—and it's part of our strength, but that's not the greatest strength for America. The size of our wallets, that's important. We're a wealthy nation, and we can do a lot with our wealth—which we're doing, by the way. We're leading the world when it comes to feeding the hungry. We're helping fight HIV/AIDS on the continent of Africa. This is a generous nation. We believe to whom much is given, much is required. But the greatest strength of this country lies in the hearts and souls of our citizens.

Alexis De Tocqueville recognized that when he came to America in 1832. He recognized that one of the really unusual things about our society, characteristics of our society, was the voluntary organizations all aimed at helping someone who is down and out. That's what he recognized. Our job is—my job as President and Bob's job as the Governor is to recognize that strength and to rally that strength and to call people to serve; is to help those who need help, by calling on a fellow citizen to love a neighbor like they'd like to be loved themselves.

You've got a good man as your Governor in the State of Maryland, and you need to put him back in office, for the good of the people. Thanks for coming. God bless.

NOTE: The President spoke at 6:25 p.m. at the BWI Airport Marriott. In his remarks, he referred to John M. Kane, chairman, Maryland Republican Party; Michael S. Steele, Lieutenant Governor of Maryland and former Senatorial candidate; former President Saddam Hussein of Iraq; and Prime Minister Junichiro Koizumi of Japan.

Remarks to the United States Chamber of Commerce
June 1, 2006

Thank you all. I told Michael to keep it short—[*laughter*]—and he did. Thanks for having me. Speaking about short, it's a short commute from where I work and live to this place. Thanks for having me, Tom.

I'm honored to be back here at the chamber. I'm proud to be with some of America's finest entrepreneurs, job creators, risk takers. And I'm also proud to be with leaders from the national Citizen Corps. I thank you all for joining us today. I thank you for representing the true strength of America, which are those who are willing to volunteer in our communities to make the country a better place. We got people from the Citizen Corps from all different backgrounds—from business associations to government agencies to community groups to schools to non-profits to advocates for the disabled and emergency responders.

Citizen Corps is making a significant difference in our country. When the hurricanes hit our gulf coast last year, members of the Citizen Corps played a critical role in the relief efforts. I want to thank you for answering the call to service. Congress needs to provide the Citizen Corps with the funding you need to keep our communities safe and prepared for emergencies.

Today I want to talk about immigration, talk about the need for this country to have a comprehensive immigration reform. I'm going to spend a little time on making sure that workforce enforcement is effective and an integral part of making sure we have a comprehensive immigration reform.

Before I do, I want to thank the chamber very much for your strong advocacy of comprehensive immigration reform. I want to thank you and I want to thank your members for being an articulate, rational voice in the immigration debate.

I want to thank Chertoff for his service to our country—excuse me—Secretary Chertoff. Sometimes if you're from west Texas, you get a little familiar. [*Laughter*] Still adjusting to the protocols here in Washington. [*Laughter*] Of course, he knew what I was talking about.

I want to thank Ralph Basham, the Commissioner of the U.S. Customs and Border Protection. Thank you for being here, Ralph. Thanks for your service. Ralph ran the Secret Service so ably, did such a fine job, I asked him to serve in this capacity. And he'll do a fine job there.

I want to thank David Aguilar. He's the Chief of the U.S. Border Patrol. David, it's good to see you. David and I recently went down to the border, and we took a good look at this long border. It gave me a chance to see firsthand what's taking place down there. It also gave me a chance to thank the Border Patrol agents, men and women who are working every day to do our job. And I want to thank you for your leadership.

I thank Julie Myers, Assistant Secretary for U.S. Immigration and Customs Enforcement. I want to thank Tracy Henke, Assistant Secretary, Office of Grants and Training for DHS. She is the chair of the National Citizen Corps Council. And again, thank you all for letting me come by.

One of the jobs of the Government is to encourage entrepreneurship. We've done so in this administration, and as a result, America's risk takers are—and businessowners, both small and large, are hiring people. If you want a job in America, you can find a job in America. This economy of ours is growing, at 3.5 percent last year, 5.3 percent in the first quarter of this year. The national unemployment rate is 4.7 percent; 5.2 million new jobs have been created since August of 2003. Small businesses are flourishing; productivity is high; after-tax income is up; homeownership is at an alltime level. This economy of the United States is strong, and we intend to keep it that way.

And the U.S. Chamber has been a strong supporter in making sure that Congress has sensible policies to keep this economy strong. And one of the most sensible things the United States Congress can do is to make the tax cuts we passed permanent. You'll hear talk in Washington that says, "Well, you've got to raise taxes on people in order to balance the budget." That's not how Washington works. They're going to raise your taxes, and they're going to figure out new ways to spend your money. The best way to balance this budget is to keep progrowth economic policies in place and be fiscally wise about how we spend your money.

Progrowth economic policies generate additional revenues for our Treasury. Last year, revenues exceeded expectations by about $100 billion. This July, we're going to find out whether it happened again. I hope it does. I think it might, because we're growing this economy. When the economy grows, people pay taxes. And so the fundamental question is not whether or not we're going to have more revenues; the fundamental question is if we're going to have rational spending in order to balance this budget.

I told the United States Congress to get a $92.2 billion supplemental to my desk. It's money needed to fund our troops. It's money needed to help the people down there in—that we're affected by the hurricanes. It's money to do important other measures. But if they bust the 92.2, I'm going to veto it. It's important for Washington to have fiscal sanity in order to balance this budget.

The fundamental question facing this country is, do we fear the future or do we intend to shape it? I intend to shape the future so America remains the economic leader in the world, which means we've got to have a good legal policy. I

want to thank the chamber for being on the leading edge opposing—and enabling me to sign meaningful tort reform. We don't need junk lawsuits running good people out of business. We don't need junk lawsuits running good doctors out of practice. What this country needs is a rational legal system that is fair and balanced. So I'm going to continue to work for tort reform in the Halls of Congress.

We need a health care system that takes care of the elderly and the poor, but also recognizes that the best health care system is one in which the decisions are made by doctors and patients, not by bureaucrats right here in Washington, DC.

We need energy policy that's wise. We got a problem in America: We're too dependent on oil from parts of the world where people may not necessarily like us. So I proposed an Advanced Energy Initiative, and I want to thank the chamber for supporting me on helping this country diversify away from hydrocarbons.

Today I want to talk about immigration, because the chamber of commerce understands that in order for this country to be an economic leader, in order for this country to be a country that upholds our values, we've got to have an immigration system that is secure and orderly and fair.

For decades, this country has not been in control of its borders. Yet we have an obligation to the American people to secure our borders. That's a solemn obligation of the Federal Government. And as a result of not securing our borders, many who want to work in this economy have been able to sneak across.

This is an issue I'm familiar with, since I was the Governor of Texas. You got to understand, there are people in our neighborhood who are desperate to put food on the table for their families. And if they, say, make $7 in America versus 50 cents where they live, and they want to support their families, guess what? They're going to try to sneak across the border. And many have been able to do so. And that illegal immigration has put pressure on our schools and hospitals; it's strained State and local budgets; and in some instances, bring crime to our neighborhood.

Yet we have got to remember that the vast majority of illegal immigrants are decent people. They're hard-working people. They're people who love their families, people of faith, and people who lead responsible lives. They're part of American life, and they are vital to our economy, and yet they're beyond the reach and protection of American law.

This Nation is a nation of laws. And we're going to enforce our laws. That's what the American people expect. But we're also a nation of immigrants. And we must uphold that tradition, which has strengthened this Nation in so many ways. These aren't contradictory goals. America can be a lawful society and America can be a welcoming society at the same time.

Congress is moving forward on immigration reform. The House started this debate by passing a bill that focuses on border security and interior enforcement. Then the Senate had its debate, and it passed a comprehensive bill that also includes a temporary-worker program and a plan to resolve the status of illegal immigrants who are already in this country. And now the two versions must be worked out in a conference committee.

The House and Senate bills will require effort and compromise on both sides. It's a difficult task, yet the difficulty of this task is no excuse for avoiding it. The American people expect us to meet our responsibility and deliver immigration reform that fixes the problems in the current system, that upholds our ideals and provides a fair and practical way forward.

The United States Congress needs to pass a comprehensive bill, one that will accomplish five objectives. First, a comprehensive reform bill must help us secure our borders. The border should be open to trade and lawful immigration and shut to illegal immigrants as well as criminals, drug dealers, and terrorists.

Since I became President, we've increased funding for border security by 66 percent. We've expanded the Border Patrol from about 9,000 to 12,000 agents. As I told the folks down there, David, in Yuma, I am proud of the Border Patrol, and so should the American people. Do you realize that over the past 5 years, the men and women of the Border Patrol, working under incredibly difficult circumstances, have apprehended and sent home about 6 million people entering this county illegally? There's some people working hard down there on our behalf.

Despite the progress, despite the fact that they've turned back 6 million people in 5 years, we don't have full control of this border. And I'm determined to change that. I called on Congress to provide funding for dramatic improvements in manpower and technology on the border. And so by the end of 2008, we'll increase the number of Border Patrol agents by an additional 6,000. In other words, we will have doubled the size of the Border Patrol during my Presidency.

That's not going to be enough to do our job of securing the border. That's what you've got to understand. And so these Border Patrol agents need help. And the best way to help the Border Patrol is to construct high-tech fences in urban areas, urban corridors, to build patrol roads and barriers in rural areas. We're going to create a virtual fence that employs motion detectors and infrared cameras and unmanned aerial vehicles to detect and prevent illegal crossings. What I'm telling you is that we're going to have a border that is smart and secure.

And the best way to do that is to have Border Patrol agents, and then give them the most advanced technology so they can do their job. Training thousands of new Border Patrol agents and deploying the most advanced technology is going to take time. Yet the need to secure this border is urgent. And so I'm acting.

This month, National Guard units will deploy to the border to set up headquarters that will help coordinate Guard operations that will support the Border Patrol. In other words, we'll be training 6,000 additional agents, but in the meantime, I'm going to send 6,000 National Guard down there. These forces are the first of 6,000 members that are going to assist the Border Patrol. They're going to operate surveillance systems and analyze intelligence, and install fences and vehicle barriers, and build patrol roads, and provide training. In other words, they're going to be a complement to the Border Patrol.

The Guard units will not be involved in direct law enforcement activities. That's the job of the Border Patrol. The United States is not going to militarize our border. What we're going to do is support those who we hire to do the job of enforcing the border.

As new Border Patrol agents and technologies come on line, the Guard forces are going to be reduced. The Federal Government is working to conclude formal agreements with California and Arizona and New Mexico and Texas that will define the roles and responsibilities of National Guard units deploying to the southern border. We're going to work closely with the Governors of those States to secure this border. Also in touch with the chief of the National Guard Bureau, General Blum, to make sure that we get those 6,000 Guard down there to help the Border Patrol do their job.

I also recognize the role of local and State enforcement authorities to help David and his people do the job. And so we'll increase Federal funding for State and local authorities assisting our Border Patrol on targeted enforcement missions. As well, we're going to give specialized training to certain State and local folks so they can complement the Border Patrol.

One of the problems we have down there is we got people working hard to find people, and in some instances, they apprehend somebody; then they head right into our society. That's frustrating for the Border Patrol agents. We got people working long, long hours down there, and they catch somebody sneaking into our country, and they say, "Hey, go over here to this legal proceeding, and since the courts are full, just check back with us in 45 days." The problem is, a lot of people who want to put food on the table or want to do other things don't check back. That's a program that needs to end.

See, most of the people we catch at the border trying to enter illegally are Mexicans, and 85 percent of them are sent right back home within 24 hours. But the real problem we've had is when we catch illegal immigrants from other countries trying to come in. It's easy to send people back into Mexico; it's hard to send somebody to a country south of Mexico, for example.

One of the problems we've had is we didn't have enough detention space. So we've got the Border Patrol agents working hard; they catch somebody from a country other than Mexico coming into our country, and there's no place to put them. And so part of our strategy is to end catch-and-release by expanding the number of beds in detention facilities along the border. We've added some, and we're going to add more. We're going to add enough to be able to end catch-and-release.

We've also expedited the legal process to cut the average deportation time. I've been in touch, as has my administration, with foreign governments, where we tell them, "You got to take your citizens back. When we catch one of your citizens coming in, you have an obligation to take that person back into your society." We've ended catch-and-release for illegal immigrants from the key Central American countries; now Congress needs to provide additional funding and legal authority so we can end catch-and-release at the southern border once and for all.

The strategy is this: We're going to enforce our border. When we catch you, we're going to send you home—so that the message is very clear, and that is, you're going to be sent home if we catch you, illegally, which means don't try to come in in the first place, illegally.

Second, in order to have a comprehensive reform bill, we have to have a temporary-worker program. Part of securing this border is a temporary-worker program. You see, there are people who will do anything to come into this country to work. That's what you got to understand. People are motivated by a desire, in many cases—in most cases, to support the family. I used to tell people in Texas, family values do not stop at the Rio Grande. And so therefore, it shouldn't surprise you when people hike across the hot desert to—and risking their lives to come and work or are willing to get stuffed in the back of an 18-wheeler to come and do a job others won't do here in America.

The fact that people are willing to take those risks puts enormous pressure on our border, so much pressure that walls and patrols aren't going to stop it. In other words, you got people saying, "I'll do anything to come and work; just give me a chance." And we can put up—we can have a lot of patrols and a lot of walls, and it's not going to stop that flow. It will put a dent in it. But if the job is to secure this border, it seems like to me, we got to stop the number of people who are trying to sneak across in the first place. And the best way to do that is to make a temporary-worker program a part of immigration reform. Program would create a legal path for foreign workers to enter this country in an orderly way for a limited period of time. It would match willing foreign workers with willing American employers for jobs Americans are not doing.

Every worker who applies for the program would be required to pass a criminal background check. Temporary workers must return to their homes at the conclusion of their stay. A temporary-worker program would meet the legitimate needs of American employers, and it would give an honest immigrant a chance to contribute to our economy and, at the same time, provide for their families. A temporary-worker program would reduce the appeal of human smugglers and make it less likely people would have to risk their lives to cross this border. A temporary-worker program would ease the financial burden on State and local Governments by replacing illegal workers with lawful taxpayers. And above all, the temporary-worker program would add to the security of this country by making certain we know who is coming into this country and why they're here.

Third, a comprehensive reform bill must hold employers to account for the workers they hire. It is against the law to hire someone who is in this country illegally. Those are the laws of the United States of America, and they must be upheld.

To ensure our laws are enforced, we've increased funding for immigration enforcement inside this country by 42 percent since I took office. Last year, I signed a bill that doubled Federal resources for worksite enforcement. We've launched law enforcement task forces in 11 major cities to dismantle criminal rings that are producing fake documents. Not only do we have a whole industry that's evolved to smuggle people in—you ever hear of the word *coyote*; these are these folks that are willing to use human life as a commodity, to make money off of somebody. We've also got document forgers too. See, there's a whole industry that's sprung up as a result of enforcement—an immigration system that isn't working. And so we're out to bust those document forgers.

Most American businesses want to abide by the law. Many are unable to determine whether their workers are legal, however, because of this document fraud. Today, there's an industry that's making these IDs and fraudulent Social Security numbers. See, American employers who check these documents often discover that the names of their workers don't match their Social Security numbers. So then we've got people trying to verify, doing what they're expected to do under the law. But when this happens, the employer receives a "no match" letter from the Social Security Administration, yet under current law, the immigration enforcement agents at the Department of Homeland Security are not informed of these mismatches. The system isn't working.

See, we need to address problems and ensure that agents can enforce the law. Businessowners should not have to act as detectives to verify the legal status of their workers. And so the Federal Government has the responsibility to ensure that businesses have a clear and reliable way to check work documents. We have that responsibility. If we expect people to adhere to the law that you're not supposed to hire somebody illegally, we have a responsibility here in Washington, DC, to help you verify documents.

One thing we've done is we've launched what's called Basic Pilot. Basic Pilot is a voluntary online verification system that allows employers to confirm the eligibility of new hires by checking the information they provide against Federal databases. If there's a mismatch, the applicant then has 8 working days to contest the finding. By giving employers a quick and practical way to verify Social Security numbers, Basic Pilot gives employers confidence that their workers are legal, improves the accuracy of wage and tax reporting, and helps ensure that those who obey our laws are not undercut by illegal workers.

Basic Pilot, just a while ago, was only available in six States; now it's nationwide. As I told you, the program is optional. And the truth of the matter is, most employers do not participate. Now, the House and the Senate immigration bills would require employers to use Basic Pilot. I think this

is sensible. I think if we want to enforce our laws, people ought to be required to check to see whether or not names and numbers match. Homeland Security, by the way, in order for it to work, needs more money to make sure that the program is up and running.

Now, the other thing we need to do besides good verification procedures is to develop a new identification card for every legal foreign worker. The card should be tamper-proof. It ought to use biometric technology such as digital fingerprints. We got the technology to do this. It makes sense to have somebody who's going to be here legally, working on a temporary basis, to have a card that will allow American employers to know that the foreign job applicant is who he or she says she is, or he is. A tamper-proof card is going to be a vital tool to enforce the law, and it's got to be a part of a comprehensive immigration reform package.

Improving enforcement for immigration laws also requires stiffening the penalties for those violating the laws. Today, the fine for a business that fails to check an employee's ID can be as low as $100. You might as well pay a speeding ticket. A penalty for knowingly hiring an illegal immigrant can be as low as $250 and can't exceed $2,000. These low penalties, frankly, provide little incentive for dishonest businesses to obey the law. And so we're going to increase the penalties. If we want to be smart about worksite enforcement, we got to say to somebody who's breaking the law, "There's going to be a cost, and it's more than $250." And so the fines need to be larger.

The whole point and purpose of what I've just described to you is to assure the American people that we've got a plan in place that says to the employers, this is going to help you determine whether or not who you're hiring should be here in the first place. Secondly, it's going to help get rid of document fraud. I repeat: We don't want our employers becoming document experts. That's not their—they're trying to get a job done.

And thirdly, we want to make sure that when we catch you, there's a consequence. You know, most American businesses are law-abiding. They really do want to uphold the law. They understand there's a responsibility to be an American, and that is to uphold the laws of the land. And yet we've got to recognize there are some unscrupulous folks who want to take advantage of low-cost labor. Illegal workers can be paid less than the market rate, see. And guess what? When you're illegal and you're worried about being detected, you can be exploited. And that's not the American way. We don't like people living in the shadows of our society. We're a nation of the rule of law, and we want people to be treated with respect. And so people who—businesses that knowingly employ illegal workers undermine this law and undermine the spirit of America. And we're not going to tolerate it in this country.

Fourthly, a comprehensive reform bill has got to address the reality that millions of illegal immigrants are here already. Now, these folks should not be given an automatic path to citizenship. That is called amnesty. I oppose amnesty. I opposed amnesty because it would be unfair to those people who are here lawfully, and I oppose amnesty because it would invite further waves of illegal immigrants.

One of the difficult tasks before the House and the Senate is deciding how American law will treat the illegal immigrants now in our country. Some Members of Congress argue that no one who came to this country illegally should be allowed to continue living and working in our country and that any plan that allows them to stay equals amnesty, no matter how many conditions we impose. Listen, I appreciate the Members are acting on deeply felt principles; I understand that. Yet I also believe that the approach they suggest is wrong and unrealistic. There's a rational middle ground between granting an automatic path to citizenship for every illegal immigrant and a program that requires every illegal immigrant to leave. The middle ground recognizes there are differences between an illegal immigrant who crossed the border recently, and someone who has worked here for many years who's got a home, a family, and a clean record.

My position is clear: I believe that illegal immigrants who have roots in our country and who want to stay should have to pay a meaningful penalty for breaking the law, to pay their taxes, to learn English, and to work in a job for a number of years. People who meet these conditions should be eventually permitted to apply for citizenship like other foreign workers. But approval would not be automatic. They would have to wait in line behind those who played by the rules and followed the law. This isn't amnesty. It is a practical and reasonable way for those who have broken the law to pay their debt to society and demonstrate the character that makes a good citizen.

Fifth, a comprehensive bill must honor the great American tradition of the melting pot, which has made us one Nation out of many peoples. This debate is an interesting debate. It gets quite emotional, and sometimes an emotion—in all the emotions, we forget we are a land of immigrants. Success of this country has depended and will depend upon helping newcomers assimilate into our society and help folks embrace our common identity as Americans.

Americans are bound together by our shared ideals: an appreciation of our history; respect for the flag we fly; and an ability to speak and write the English language. As businessowners and community leaders, you know that English is the key to unlocking the opportunity of America. See, English allows a newcomer to go from picking crops to opening a grocery store. English allows a newcomer from sweeping an office floor to running that office. English allows someone to go from a low-paying job to a diploma, a career, and homeownership. When immigrants assimilate and advance in our society, they realize their dreams. And as they do, they renew our spirit, and they add to the unity of our country.

As the chamber, you appreciate the great contributions immigrants have made to America's freedom and prosperity, and you know their importance for the future of this Nation. And so you're helping this country reach consensus by conducting the debate on immigration in a reasoned and respectful tone. And I appreciate that a lot.

I urge our fellow citizens to understand that harsh language, unnecessary politics, sends the wrong message about who we are as a nation. I appreciate the fact you're working for an immigration bill that is comprehensive. That makes a lot of sense, because you know that all the elements of this problem must be addressed together or none of them will be solved at all.

Throughout our long history, America has prospered because we welcome people who abided by our laws and worked hard and raised their families and trusted in the Almighty. I believe we must be guided by that history as we reform our immigration system. I trust in our country's genius for making us all Americans, one Nation under God. And I'm confident that the United States Congress will do its duty and pass an immigration bill that secures our borders, strengthens our laws, and upholds the promise of the United States of America.

May God bless you all.

NOTE: The President spoke at 8:50 a.m. at the U.S. Chamber of Commerce. In his remarks, he referred to Secretary of Homeland Security Michael Chertoff, who introduced the President; Thomas J. Donohue, president and chief executive officer, U.S. Chamber of Commerce; and Lt. Gen. H. Steven Blum, chief, National Guard Bureau. The Office of the Press Secretary also released a Spanish language transcript of these remarks.

Remarks Following a Cabinet Meeting and an Exchange With Reporters
June 1, 2006

The President. I want to thank the members of my Cabinet who came today. We had a really good discussion about a variety of important issues. We talked about the war against terror, and I reminded our Cabinet Secretaries that we all have a responsibility to help us win this war, including sending members of our administration to Iraq to help this new democracy succeed.

We talked about the hurricane season that's upon us, and the work we're doing to help local governments and State governments prepare for the hurricane season.

I talked about the immigration issue. I talked about how strongly I feel for this country to have comprehensive immigration reform.

And then we heard from Secretary Snow about the strength of this economy and what we intend to do to keep it strong. One thing we intend to do is to continue to work with the United States Congress to make sure the tax cuts we passed are permanent. It turns out, our progrowth economic policies have worked, and the best way to make sure that the recovery we have is sustainable is to keep those taxes low. The Secretary briefed us on the fact that revenues coming into our Treasury look very robust. The best way to balance the budget is to keep progrowth economic policies in place and, at the same time, work with our Cabinet Secretaries to keep spending down.

And so I'm very pleased with the progress on our economy. And I want to, again, thank my Cabinet Secretaries for being here.

And now I'll answer a couple of questions. Jennifer [Jennifer Loven, Associated Press].

Iran

Q. Thank you, sir. Do you have either China or Russia on board with Iran?

The President. Yesterday, Secretary Rice, at my instructions, said to the world that we want to solve the problem of the Iranian nuclear issue diplomatically. And we made it very clear publicly that we're willing to come to the table, so long as the Iranians verifiably suspend their program. In other words, we said to the Iranians, the United States of America wants to work with our partners to solve the problem.

I spoke to the President of Russia and explained my position clearly to him, and that is, the choice is up to the Iranians whether or not they're going to listen to the world demand, and if they do, we've got something to talk to them about. And if they don't, we expect Russia to participate in the United Nations Security Council. We'll see whether or not they agree to do that. I got a positive response from the President. He said he understands our strategy, and he agrees we want to solve this issue diplomatically.

I also spoke to President Hu Jintao this morning. I laid out to him why I instructed Secretary Rice to do what she did. And now it's going to be up to the Iranians to make their decision, and if they choose not to verifiably suspend, we have laid the groundwork for an effective international response.

Q. Was the response from President Hu positive?

The President. They understood our strategy, and they understood—the most positive thing about all the conversations

I had is there is uniform agreement that the Iranians should not have a nuclear weapon. And we'll discuss tactics and strategies to make sure that the international community speaks with one clear voice if the Iranians choose not to verifiably suspend. And so we'll see what their decision is. My decision is to be robust in trying to solve this problem diplomatically.

Matthew [Matt Spetalnick], Reuters. Yes, there you are.

Q. But the Iranian Foreign Minister, today, has already—while welcoming the offer of talks, has rejected the idea that they would first suspend uranium enrichment. How do you react to that, and is it now——

The President. My reaction is, the choice is theirs. And we'll see whether or not that is the firm position of their Government. If that's what they decide to do, then the next step, of course, will be to—for our coalition partners to go to the United Nations Security Council. And the choice is up to the Iranians. And they've already said, by the way, that they're willing to suspend. And this gives them a second chance to make their words mean something.

I want to solve this problem diplomatically, and I want to solve it peacefully. And the best thing for the Iranians to understand is that if they choose not to suspend in a verifiable—if they continue their obstinance, if they continue to say to the world, "We really don't care what your opinion is," then the world is going to act in concert. The next step of acting in concert is to go to the United Nations Security Council.

Ann [Ann Compton, ABC News].

Iraq/U.S. Armed Forces

Q. Why do American forces in Iraq need retraining on core values, as the military puts it?

The President. Our troops have been trained on core values throughout their training, but obviously there was an incident that took place in Iraq. It's now being investigated. And this is just a reminder for troops either in Iraq, or throughout our military that there are high standards expected of them and that there are strong rules of engagement. The Haditha incident is under investigation. Obviously, the allegations are very troubling for me and equally troubling for our military, especially the Marine Corps. I've spoken to General Pace about this issue quite a few times. And he's troubled by the allegations, because he understands that the Marine Corps has got a proud tradition of upholding rules of engagement.

One of the things that happens in a transparent society like ours is that there is—there will be a full and complete investigation. The world will see the full and complete investigation. It also is a reminder to our commanders that they must constantly enforce the proud tradition of our military, and that's what they're doing.

Q. Have you gotten updates on the situation?

The President. Well, I'm not involved with the investigation, and you shouldn't expect me to be. I expect this investigation to be conducted independent of the White House, with a full and thorough investigation. And I'm confident.

Listen, the Marine Corps wants to get to the bottom of this. If anybody wants to make sure that they know the facts and to correct problems, if they do exist, it's the United States Marine Corps. They are run by—the Marines are run by an incredibly proud group of men and women who understand the history and tradition of the Marines. And they'll get to the bottom of this.

And if there is wrongdoing, people will be held to account. And at the same time, what you're seeing is the Marine Corps reminding our troops about what it means to be a marine, what it means to uphold the honor of that Corps, and what it means to adhere to the rules of engagement that we expect our soldiers to adhere to. The United States of America has got a willingness to deal with issues like this in an upfront way, in an open way, and correct problems. And that's what you're going to see unfold.

Thank you all.

NOTE: The President spoke at 11:01 a.m. in the Cabinet Room at the White House. In his remarks, he referred to President Vladimir V. Putin of Russia; President Hu Jintao of China; and Gen. Peter Pace, USMC, Chairman, Joint Chiefs of Staff. A reporter referred to Minister of Foreign Affairs Manuchehr Motaki of Iran.

Remarks at a Swearing-In Ceremony for Brett Kavanaugh as a United States Circuit Judge for the District of Columbia
June 1, 2006

Please be seated. Thanks for coming. Welcome to the Rose Garden where, in a few moments, Brett Kavanaugh will be sworn in as a judge on the United States Court of Appeals for the District of Columbia Circuit.

Today, a court that is often considered the second highest in our land gains a brilliant and talented new member. The staff of the White House celebrates a friend they admire and a colleague they will miss. I congratulate a good man and a fine public servant on a job well done.

I'm especially pleased to be with Brett's wife, Ashley—[*laughter*]—whose face I know well and whose marriage was the first lifetime appointment I arranged for Brett. [*Laughter*]

We welcome Brett's parents, Martha and Ed, and his mother-in-law and father-in-law, Nancy and John Estes from Abilene, Texas.

I welcome the star of Brett's most recent televised hearing, Margaret Murphy Kavanaugh. [*Laughter*] Margaret has his mother's—has her mother's good looks and her dad's preference for hearings that do not last too long. [*Laughter*]

We're honored this afternoon by the presence of Justice Anthony Kennedy, who hired Brett as a law clerk more than a decade ago. He now welcomes him as a fellow judge. And I'm also pleased that Mary Kennedy is with us today. Thanks for coming.

The Vice President has joined us. Mr. Vice President, welcome. Appreciate Al— Attorney General Al Gonzales for being here, and former Attorney General John Ashcroft is with us as well. I want to extend a warm welcome to Brett's new colleagues on the DC Court of Appeals. Thank you all for coming.

The power to nominate judges is one of the most serious responsibilities the Constitution gives the President. Our Founders thought carefully about the role they wanted judges to play in the American Republic. They decided on a court system that would be free of political and public pressure, with judges who are prudent in exercising judicial power and firm in defending judicial independence.

When a President chooses a judge, he owes it to the Constitution and to the country to choose with care, and I have done so in choosing Brett Kavanaugh. I chose Brett because of the force of his mind, his breadth of experience, and the strength of his character.

Brett grew up in Maryland. In high school, he distinguished himself both in academics and athletics. He graduated from Yale with honors. What did that feel like?

[*Laughter*] He stayed at Yale to earn his law degree. Brett was an editor of the Yale Law Review and impressed all around him with his mastery of the law and his strong work ethic.

After Yale, he embarked on a law career that has spanned judicial—on a career that has spanned the judicial branch, the executive branch, and the private sector. He clerked for Judges Walter Stapleton and Alex Kozinski on the Federal appellate courts and for Justice Kennedy on the Supreme Court. He served in the Solicitor General's Office and in the Office of the Independent Counsel. He was a partner in a leading national law firm. For the past 5 years, he has served in the White House as Associate Counsel, a senior Associate Counsel, and as Staff Secretary.

Over his career, he's argued cases before the Supreme Court, appellate courts, and trial courts. He has given his time and talent to provide legal services for those in need. He's earned a reputation for integrity and independence. Brett's abilities and professionalism have been recognized by members of both political parties. After I nominated Brett, a bipartisan group of his law school classmates wrote a letter of support saying Brett would bring credit to the distinguished court to which he has been nominated.

Brett's nomination also earned the backing of many leaders of the bar, including former Attorney Generals of both parties. And in three separate evaluations by the American Bar Association, all 42 reviewers rated him as well-qualified or qualified to serve on the Federal bench.

In the history of the DC Circuit, no judge has undergone a more thorough and rigorous confirmation process. And all who watched this process saw what I know: that he's a man of fairness, humility, and a reverence for the laws and the Constitution of our country.

Brett Kavanaugh is one of the many highly qualified men and women I've nominated to the Federal courts. These nominees come from many different backgrounds, and they bring different experiences to the bench. Yet they all have met the same high standards of legal ability, temperament, and judgment. I'll continue to fulfill my responsibility to nominate men and women of character and integrity who administer the law and not legislate from the bench. And I call upon the United States Senate to meet its responsibility to give every nominee a fair hearing and a timely up-or-down vote.

When Brett Kavanaugh takes his oath this afternoon, he will carry on a fine family tradition. His mother, Martha, was a public school teacher in the District of Columbia and went on to serve as a prosecutor and a State judge in Maryland. Martha instilled in her son a passion for service and raised

him to be true to the motto of his Jesuit high school: "Men for Others."

Throughout his life, Brett has used his many talents to serve others, and today he walks a new path of service: to administer justice equally, impartially, without fear or favor. Our Nation is fortunate that Brett Kavanaugh has accepted these responsibilities, and I'm proud to stand with Brett as he takes his place as a judge on the DC Circuit Court of Appeals.

And now I ask Justice Kennedy to administer the oath.

NOTE: The President spoke at 1:06 p.m. in the Rose Garden. In his remarks, he referred to Mary Kennedy, wife of U.S. Supreme Court Associate Justice Anthony M. Kennedy. The transcript released by the Office of the Press Secretary also included the remarks of Judge Kavanaugh.

Letter to Congressional Leaders Transmitting Designations Under the Foreign Narcotics Kingpin Designation Act
June 1, 2006

Dear _____ :

This report to the Congress, under section 804(b) of the Foreign Narcotics Kingpin Designation Act, 21 U.S.C. 1901–1908 (the "Kingpin Act"), transmits my designations of the following three foreign persons and two foreign entities for sanctions under the Kingpin Act, and reports my direction of sanctions against them under that Act:

Dawood Ibrahim
Fahd Jamil Georges
Ali Naway
Dawood Ibrahim Organization
Amezcua Contreras Organization
Sincerely,

GEORGE W. BUSH

NOTE: Identical letters were sent to Pat Roberts, chairman, Senate Select Committee on

Intelligence; Arlen Specter, chairman, Senate Committee on the Judiciary; Richard G. Lugar, chairman, Senate Committee on Foreign Relations; John W. Warner, chairman, Senate Committee on Armed Services; Charles E. Grassley, chairman, Senate Committee on Finance; Susan M. Collins, chairwoman, Senate Committee on Homeland Security and Governmental Affairs; Peter Hoekstra, chairman, House Permanent Select Committee on Intelligence; F. James Sensenbrenner, Jr., chairman, House Committee on the Judiciary; Henry J. Hyde, chairman, House Committee on International Relations; Duncan Hunter, chairman, House Committee on Armed Services; William M. Thomas, chairman, House Committee on Ways and Means; and Peter T.

King, chairman, House Committee on Homeland Security.

Remarks at a Swearing-In Ceremony for Robert J. Portman as Director of the Office of Management and Budget
June 2, 2006

Please be seated. Good morning. Welcome to the White House. Today I'm pleased to witness the swearing-in of Rob Portman as the new Director of the Office of Management and Budget. We welcome Rob's wife, Jane, as well as his brother, Wym, and other family members here with us today. I want to thank you all for supporting Rob.

As the OMB Director, Rob will not be racking up the frequent flyer miles that he did as America's Trade Representative. I think that's going to be a relief for Jane and his children. [*Laughter*]

I appreciate the Vice President being here. I want to thank Carlos Gutierrez for joining us as well, the Secretary of the Department of Commerce; John Walters, Office of National Drug Control Policy. Congressman Mike Turner, it's awfully kind for you to come back to witness the swearing-in of your friend. I appreciate the former Secretary, Don Evans, for being here as well.

The job of the OMB Director is one of the most important in our Federal Government. The OMB Director is a critical member of my Cabinet. He plays a vital role in every aspect of my administration's agenda, from securing the homeland to winning the war on terror to growing our economy and creating jobs.

For the past 3 years, these responsibilities have been carried out by a talented public servant, Josh Bolten. At my direction, Josh has pursued clear goals at OMB. He's worked to implement progrowth economic policies and ensure that taxpayers' money is spent wisely or not at all. He's

improved the management of Federal programs so that when we do spend taxpayer money, they deliver real results for the American people. He's put us on track to cut the deficit in half by 2009.

Now that Josh is serving as my Chief of Staff, I've turned to another outstanding public servant to take up these important responsibilities, and that's Rob Portman. Rob has served for more than a decade in the United States Congress, where he was vice chairman of the House Budget Committee, a member of the Ways and Means Committee, and a member of the House leadership. In Congress, Rob earned a reputation as an effective legislator who worked with members of both political parties.

For the past year, Rob has served his country as United States Trade Representative. He worked tirelessly to open new markets for American exports and to ensure that American workers, farmers, and small businesses are treated fairly overseas. He's reenergized the Doha round trade talks at the World Trade Organization. He completed trade agreements with Bahrain, Oman, Peru, and Colombia and launched new trade agreement negotiations with the Republic of Korea and Malaysia. His leadership was critical to the passage of the landmark Central American-Dominican Republic Free Trade Agreement last summer.

Rob assumes his responsibilities as OMB Director at a really important time for our economy. This morning's economic report shows that America's national unemployment rate is down to 4.6 percent because we added 75,000 jobs in the month of May.

The American economy has now added jobs for 33 months in a row and has created more than 5.3 million new jobs. In the first quarter of 2006, the U.S. economy grew at an annual rate of 5.3 percent—that's the fastest growth in 2½ years. Productivity is high, and that is leading to higher wages and a higher standard of living for the American people. The American economy is powerful. It is productive, and it is prosperous, and we intend to keep it that way.

I've given Rob a clear agenda. We'll continue to pursue progrowth economic policies. The tax relief we delivered has helped set off the economic expansion that we're seeing today. And Rob will build on this success by working with Congress to maintain a progrowth, low-tax environment.

Tax relief is important to families, workers, and entrepreneurs, and it is also vital to our efforts to reduce the budget deficit. When I came to office, taxes were too high, our economy was headed into a recession, and tax revenues were on the decline. By cutting taxes, we've helped produce a strong economic recovery, and that economic growth is producing more tax revenues. In 2005, tax revenues grew by a record $274 billion, an increase of nearly 15 percent over the previous year. This year, the economy has continued to grow, and tax revenues are growing with it. These increased revenues are helping us to meet our goal of cutting the deficit in half by 2009.

To meet this goal, we must also control the Federal appetite for spending. Every year since I took office, we've slowed the growth of discretionary spending that's not related to the military or homeland security. My last two budgets have actually cut this kind of spending. And with Rob's leadership, we will continue to cut unnecessary spending and show respect for the taxpayers' money.

To cut unnecessary spending, I need the line-item veto. I've sent Congress a line-item veto proposal that has strong bipar-

tisan support. And Rob will work with his former colleagues on Capitol Hill to get a bill to my desk so I can sign it into law.

Rob will also work with Congress to pass reforms that will help us reduce earmarks and wasteful spending in the Federal budget. Congress is now considering an emergency supplemental bill that can show the American people we're determined to be responsible with their money. I've set a clear limit on spending that I will accept in this legislation, and if this bill goes over that limit, I'll veto it.

In the long run, the biggest challenge to our Nation's budgetary health is entitlement spending on programs such as Social Security and Medicare. Entitlement programs are growing much faster than our ability to pay for them. To keep these programs solvent, we need to slow their growth to a level we can afford. It's not a cut. It's the difference between slowing your car down to the speed limit and putting your car in reverse. Every American family and business has to set priorities and live within a budget, and so should the United States Congress.

My administration is committed to fiscal discipline and economic growth, and these policies will have a strong champion in Rob Portman. As OMB Director, Rob now assumes one of the most important posts in Washington. I'm pleased that he's agreed to serve our country once again. I look forward to working with him to keep America's economy the envy of the world, to create jobs and opportunity for all our citizens, and deliver results for the American taxpayer.

Congratulations.

NOTE: The President spoke at 11:05 a.m. in the Rose Garden at the White House. In his remarks, he referred to former Secretary of Commerce Donald L. Evans. The transcript released by the Office of the Press Secretary also included the remarks of Director Portman.

Remarks Honoring the 2006 Super Bowl Champion Pittsburgh Steelers
June 2, 2006

Thank you all for coming. Please be seated. It sounds like some people have been drinking some Iron City beer here. [*Laughter*] It's such an honor to welcome the Pittsburgh Steelers here to the White House. Congratulations on being the champs. You had a ring for every finger; now you've got one for the thumb.

I want to thank all the fans who've gathered here. I want to thank Senators Specter and Santorum for joining us, and Congressman Tim Murphy. I appreciate you all being here. It's good to see former U.S. Attorney Dick Thornburgh, former Governor of Pennsylvania.

The team probably doesn't recognize him, but they got quite a huge following here in Washington, DC, including in my administration. As a matter of fact, you have no greater fan than the new Director of the Central Intelligence Agency. So he came in for one of these briefings, see—he was going to keep the President abreast of what's going on in the world. And he was wearing a "terrible towel." [*Laughter*] Back in his school days in Pittsburgh, Mike spent a lot of time on the football field. Most of the Steeler fans know that Dan Rooney is a team owner, but Mike Hayden is able to call him coach. Mr. Rooney was Mike's coach. And you coached him well.

I want to—look, I was a Texas Cowboy fan, you know—[*laughter*]—Dallas Cowboy fan—and—yes, I know, I know. It's kind of hard for me to admit, but the Steeler franchise is one of the really great franchises in football history. And one of the reasons why is because of the Rooney family.

You know, I used to be in baseball, and I know the ability of an owner to affect the culture of the team, to be able to instill the habits necessary to win. And a class franchise starts with class ownership. And the Rooneys—Mr. Dan Rooney and Mr.

Art Rooney—are classy people. And I welcome you here to the White House.

I tested Mr. Rooney's sense of humor. See, I'm an early-morning riser, and of course, I saw the Super Bowl and got up early and was there in the Oval Office, and I just couldn't—I couldn't hold back. And so I said to the operator, "Get Mr. Rooney on the phone. I've got something I want to say to him." Unfortunately, I had gone to bed relatively early, and he had gone to bed relatively late. [*Laughter*] So he took my phone call after about 3 hours of sleep. And he was a gentleman then, when I apologized for waking him up; he's a gentleman today. Again, I want to publicly apologize—[*laughter*]—for routing you out of your sack. [*Laughter*] Except I'm pretty sure you were happy to get the phone call. [*Laughter*]

I want to congratulate all the coaches and the folks who make the franchise run. I particularly want to say something about those in the training room and those who pick up the laundry. Those are the folks that generally don't get a lot of credit, but I know the players will give you credit, and I know the ownership gives you credit, and I know Bill Cowher gives you credit. He is a—he's an amazing coach. He's got the most unusual expressions on the sideline. [*Laughter*] So I told the Vice President I was going to be able to congratulate Coach Cowher in person, and he said, "Well, get him to give me some tips on his scowl." [*Laughter*] You can't win a Super Bowl unless you've got a great coach. And the Pittsburgh Steelers have a great coach. And congratulations. Proud you're here.

I want to congratulate the players and their families. The country is proud of the way you played football. You've got some amazing characters on your team. You got a "Bus." You got a "Longhorn." [*Laughter*]

We used to pump iron together. [*Laughter*] His took; mine didn't. [*Laughter*] You got a "Big Ben." And you got a man known for his swagger; I've been looking forward to Joey Porter's new dance. [*Laughter*] He's a great player, and I'm proud to have him here at the White House. You're welcome to be here. Thanks for coming. I appreciate you.

Coach Cowher said this before the Super Bowl: "You play as a team, and you're going to walk away as champions." And this team played as a team. You may have some interesting characters on the team, but one thing the Pittsburgh Steelers learned to do was play as a unit. And that's why you're standing right here. It was a tough brand of football. It wasn't always flashy, but you learned how to win. And you're the kind of team Pittsburgh Steeler fans like to watch—hard-nosed football.

About halfway through the season, a lot of people were counting the Steelers out. They said you didn't have a chance. I kind of know the feeling. [*Laughter*] But you won eight games in a row, including three on the road in the playoffs, and of course Super Bowl XL in Detroit. You had some amazing unexpected players step up to help you play. You had the quarterback make an important tackle, and you had yourself a receiver make an important pass.

Super Bowl XL included other entries in the record book—"Fast" Willie Parker, 75-yard touchdown, the longest run in Super Bowl history. Looking sharp too. [*Laughter*] Your quarterback was the youngest quarterback in history to win an NFL title. But the most amazing thing about the victory, it seemed like to me, and for a lot of other fans, was you had

a fine man, a man you call "The Bus," retire in his home city of Detroit with the Lombardi Trophy in his arms. It was a touching moment for football fans.

There's a great responsibility with being in the spotlight and being champions, and I appreciate the acts of kindness the Pittsburgh Steelers do to help improve the community in which you live. I appreciate Jerome Bettis's The Bus Stops Here Foundation that helps underprivileged children in inner-cities. I appreciate Hines Ward, Super Bowl MVP, who traveled to his mother's home country of South Korea to inspire children of multiracial backgrounds speak out against discrimination. I thought that was an act of a champion. I appreciate the players who participated in Play Ball for Kids to raise money to help somebody who needs help.

You know, one of the great admonitions of all time is to love a neighbor like you'd like to be loved yourself. And true champs do that. So it's an honor to have champions on the field and off the field here at the White House. It is a joy for me to welcome you. Congratulations. Play hard. I'll be around here next year to see you come back. [*Laughter*]

NOTE: The President spoke at 1:40 p.m. in the East Room at the White House. In his remarks, he referred to Daniel M. Rooney, chairman, Arthur J. Rooney II, president, Bill Cowher, head coach, Jerome Bettis, former running back, Casey Hampton, nose tackle, Ben Roethlisberger, quarterback, Joey Porter, linebacker, Willie Parker, running back, and Hines Ward, wide receiver, Pittsburgh Steelers.

The President's Radio Address
June 3, 2006

Good morning. Next week, the United States Senate will begin debate on a constitutional amendment that defines marriage in the United States as the union of a man and woman. On Monday, I will meet with a coalition of community leaders, constitutional scholars, family and civic organizations, and religious leaders. They're Republicans, Democrats, and independents who've come together to support this amendment. Today I want to explain why I support the marriage protection amendment and why I'm urging Congress to pass it and send it to the States for ratification.

Marriage is the most enduring and important human institution, honored and encouraged in all cultures and by every religious faith. Ages of experience have taught us that the commitment of a husband and a wife to love and to serve one another promotes the welfare of children and the stability of society. Marriage cannot be cut off from its cultural, religious, and natural roots without weakening this good influence on society. Government, by recognizing and protecting marriage, serves the interests of all.

In our free society, people have the right to choose how they live their lives. And in a free society, decisions about such a fundamental social institution as marriage should be made by the people, not by the courts. The American people have spoken clearly on this issue, both through their Representatives and at the ballot box. In 1996, Congress approved the Defense of Marriage Act by overwhelming bipartisan majorities in both the House and Senate, and President Clinton signed it into law. And since then, voters in 19 States have approved amendments to their State constitutions that protect the traditional definition of marriage. And today, 45 of the 50 States have either a State constitutional amendment or statute defining marriage as the union of a man and a woman. These amendments and laws express a broad consensus in our country for protecting the institution of marriage.

Unfortunately, activist judges and some local officials have made an aggressive attempt to redefine marriage in recent years. Since 2004, State courts in Washington, California, Maryland, and New York have overturned laws protecting marriage in those States. And in Nebraska, a Federal judge overturned a State constitutional amendment banning same-sex marriage.

These court decisions could have an impact on our whole Nation. The Defense of Marriage Act declares that no State is required to accept another State's definition of marriage. If that act is overturned by activist courts, then marriages recognized in one city or State might have to be recognized as marriages everywhere else. That would mean that every State would have to recognize marriages redefined by judges in Massachusetts or local officials in San Francisco, no matter what their own laws or State constitutions say. This national question requires a national solution, and on an issue of such profound importance, that solution should come from the people, not the courts.

An amendment to the Constitution is necessary because activist courts have left our Nation with no other choice. The constitutional amendment that the Senate will consider next week would fully protect marriage from being redefined, while leaving State legislatures free to make their own choices in defining legal arrangements other than marriage. A constitutional amendment is the most democratic solution to this issue, because it must be approved by two-thirds of the House and Senate and then ratified by three-fourths of the 50 State legislatures.

As this debate goes forward, we must remember that every American deserves to be treated with tolerance, respect, and dignity. All of us have a duty to conduct this discussion with civility and decency toward one another, and all people deserve to have their voices heard. A constitutional amendment will put a decision that is critical to American families and American society in the hands of the American people, which is exactly where it belongs. Democracy, not court orders, should decide the future of marriage in America.

Thank you for listening.

NOTE: The address was recorded at 7:30 a.m. on June 2 in the Cabinet Room at the White House for broadcast at 10:06 a.m. on June 3. The transcript was made available by the Office of the Press Secretary on June 2 but was embargoed for release until the broadcast. The Office of the Press Secretary also released a Spanish language transcript of this address.

Remarks Following Discussions With President Denis Sassou-Nguesso of the Republic of the Congo
June 5, 2006

President Bush. It's been my honor to welcome the President of the Congo here to the Oval Office. Mr. President, welcome. Thank you for coming. I welcome you not only as the President of your country but as a leader of the African Union.

We had a very constructive discussion about a variety of issues. We talked about our common commitment to help end the genocide in Darfur. I appreciate the President's leadership in helping negotiate a peace agreement, and I appreciate his leadership in working with the United Nations so we can get the AU forces blue-helmeted as quickly as possible.

And one of my interests, of course, is to join with African nations in combating HIV/AIDS, and I want to congratulate the President for the low infection rate in Congo. Thank you for your leadership on that issue.

We've had a very good visit here, and I look forward to seeing you in St. Petersburg, Russia, where we can continue our discussions. So, welcome.

President Sassou-Nguesso. I, first of all, thank you, Mr. President, and I want to say to everyone that I'm very happy and

honored to be here, actually for the second time, because in 1990, President Bush— father of President Bush now—welcomed me to this house on a state visit. So I'm very happy to be here, Mr. President.

Indeed, President Bush is absolutely right; we discussed a lot of issues that we're all interested in: peace, security, and not just in Africa, but beyond Africa, in the world. We talked about terrorism; we talked about the Iranian nuclear issue; we talked about the dialog that's about to open up, I hope, and that will bring good results to that problem.

And on behalf of all of Africa, I thank President Bush for his commitment in fighting AIDS, the commitment of the United States in the fight against HIV/ AIDS. As you know, we had a special meeting on AIDS at the United Nations General Assembly, and as you know also, Africa is the continent that suffers the most from this scourge.

And we also talked about African development issues. We talked about the situation in the Gulf of Guinea and the Congo Basin, the NEPAD, Project for African Development in Africa. And I was happy to see President Bush give his entire support to the development of Africa.

And I'm, again, very happy with this very useful meeting that we had with President Bush here. And I'm very happy for the fact that we're going to see each other in St. Petersburg, because President Putin invited me to come to the G–8 summit as a representative for Africa.

I thank President Bush for his very friendly and warm welcome. And I'm very happy to be here, back in the White House.

NOTE: The President spoke at 9:51 a.m. in the Oval Office at the White House. President Sassou-Nguesso spoke in French, and his remarks were translated by an interpreter. President Sassou-Nguesso referred to President Vladimir V. Putin of Russia.

Remarks Following Discussions With President Manuel Zelaya Rosales of Honduras
June 5, 2006

President Bush. Mr. President, welcome. It's good to have you here. We've had a very good discussion, as you would expect amongst friends. We discussed our common interests, and one of our common interests is expanded commercial opportunity. And CAFTA gives us a chance to realize those opportunities. We talked about our common desire to make sure the democracies in the region are strong.

We talked about the immigration issue. The President is very concerned about the immigration issue. I assured him that my administration supports a comprehensive immigration bill that treats people with respect and, at the same time, upholds our laws. And over lunch, I will give him our strategy to continue to press for a comprehensive bill that will enforce our borders but allow people to come to our country in a legal way to work on a temporary basis.

So, Mr. President, thank you. The people of America respect your country and appreciate our close ties. And we're sure glad you're here.

President Zelaya. I have expressed my appreciation to the President. I'd like to reiterate my thanks to him for the frankness with which he has spoken about the solutions to the common problems we face in the Western Hemisphere.

And we come to this meeting with President Bush with great enthusiasm. And in coming here, we have asked for God's blessing so that this is a meeting that will truly strengthen the fraternal ties that join us in trying to achieve peace in our day.

I thank you very much, Mr. Bush. Your trust makes both of our nations strong.

President Bush. Thank you, sir. Thank you all.

NOTE: The President spoke at 11:51 a.m. in the Oval Office at the White House. President Zelaya spoke in Spanish, and his remarks were translated by an interpreter.

Remarks on a Proposed Constitutional Amendment To Protect Marriage
June 5, 2006

Thank you all. Please be seated. Good afternoon, and welcome to the White House. It is a pleasure to be with so many fine community leaders, scholars, family organizations, religious leaders, Republicans, Democrats, independents. Thank you all for coming.

You come from many backgrounds and faith traditions—yet united in this common belief: Marriage is the most fundamental institution of civilization, and it should not be redefined by activist judges. You are here because you strongly support a constitutional amendment that defines marriage as a union of a man and a woman, and I am proud to stand with you.

This week, the Senate begins debate on the marriage protection amendment, and I call on the Congress to pass this amendment, send it to the States for ratification so we can take this issue out of the hands of over-reaching judges and put it back where it belongs, in the hands of the American people.

The union of a man and woman in marriage is the most enduring and important human institution. For ages, in every culture, human beings have understood that marriage is critical to the well-being of families. And because families pass along values and shape character, marriage is also critical to the health of society. Our policies should aim to strengthen families, not undermine them. And changing the definition of marriage would undermine the family structure.

America is a free society which limits the role of government in the lives of our citizens. In this country, people are free to choose how they live their lives. In our free society, decisions about a fundamental social institution as marriage should be made by the people.

The American people have spoken clearly on this issue through their elected Representatives and at the ballot box. In 1996, Congress approved the Defense of Marriage Act by large bipartisan majorities in both the House and the Senate, and President Clinton signed it into law. And since then, 19 States have held referendums to amend their State constitutions to protect the traditional definition of marriage. In every case, the amendments were approved by decisive majorities with an average of 71 percent.

Today, 45 of the 50 States have either a State constitutional amendment or statute defining marriage as a union of a man and a woman. These amendments and laws express a broad consensus in our country for protecting the institution of marriage. The people have spoken. Unfortunately, this consensus is being undermined by activist judges and local officials who have struck down State laws protecting marriage and made an aggressive attempt to redefine marriage.

Since 2004, State courts in Washington and California and Maryland and New York have ruled against marriage laws. Last year, a Federal judge in Nebraska overturned a State constitutional amendment banning same-sex marriage, an amendment that was approved by 70 percent of the population. And at this moment, nine States face lawsuits challenging the marriage laws they have on the books.

Some argue that defining marriage should be left to the States. The fact is, State legislatures are trying to address this issue. But across the country, they are being thwarted by activist judges who are overturning the expressed will of their people. And these court decisions can have an impact on our whole Nation.

The Defense of Marriage Act declares that no State is required to accept another State's definition of marriage. If that act is overturned by the courts, then marriage recognized in one city or State may have to be recognized as marriages everywhere else. That would mean that every State would have to recognize marriage as redefined by judges in, say, Massachusetts or local officials in San Francisco, no matter what their own State laws or their State constitutions say.

This national question requires a national solution. And on an issue of such profound importance, that solution should come not from the courts but from the people of the United States. An amendment to the Constitution is necessary because activist courts have left our Nation with no other choice. When judges insist on imposing their arbitrary will on the people, the only alternative left to the people is an amendment to the Constitution, the only law a court cannot overturn.

The constitutional amendment that the Senate will consider this week would fully protect marriage from being redefined. It will leave State legislatures free to make their own choices in defining legal arrangements other than marriage. A constitutional amendment is the most democratic process by which our country can resolve this issue. In their wisdom, our Founders set a high bar for amending the Constitution. An amendment must be approved by two-thirds of the House and the Senate and then ratified by three-fourths of the 50 State legislatures. This process guarantees that every State legislature and every community in our Nation will have a voice and a say in deciding this issue.

A constitutional amendment would not take this issue away from the States, as some have argued. It would take the issue away from the courts and put it directly before the American people.

As this debate goes forward, every American deserves to be treated with tolerance and respect and dignity. On an issue of this great significance, opinions are strong and emotions run deep. And all of us have a duty to conduct this discussion with civility and decency toward one another. All people deserve to have their voices heard, and a constitutional amendment will ensure that they are heard.

I appreciate you taking an interest in this fundamental issue. It's an important issue for our country to debate and to resolve. And the best way to resolve this issue is through a constitutional amendment, which I strongly support. God bless.

NOTE: The President spoke at 1:48 p.m. in Room 450 of the Dwight D. Eisenhower Executive Office Building.

Remarks on Immigration Reform and a Swearing-In Ceremony for W. Ralph Basham as Commissioner of Customs and Border Protection in Artesia, New Mexico
June 6, 2006

Thank you all. Please be seated. Pete, thanks for your kind words, and thanks for your leadership. New Mexico has got a fine senior Senator in Pete Domenici. All he talks about is New Mexico when I'm with him. Now I'm afraid all he's going to talk about is FLETC. [*Laughter*]

It's good to be in Artesia. Some people probably think I've never heard of Artesia. You forgot I grew up in Midland. Home of the Mighty Bulldogs, Artesia is. The land where the sky is big and the people are friendly. I knew I was in pretty good country when I saw all the cowboy hats, and I think I saw one guy spitting in a can. [*Laughter*] But I'm thrilled to be here, I really am, and I appreciate a chance to be here at the Border Patrol Academy, here at the Federal Law Enforcement Training Center.

I want to—the reason I'm here is because I want the country to pay attention to what you're doing. And I want you to understand, those of you who are training to become Border Patrol agents and those of you who are training the trainees, I want you to understand that I really appreciate your contribution to the United States of America, and so do the American people.

What you're learning to do here is important. It's important for the security of our Nation. And I want to thank you for volunteering. At this academy, new agents undergo 19 weeks of training, and by the looks of it, it isn't all that easy. It's practical experience. It's the kind of experience that's going to put you in pretty good stead when it comes to doing the job that we expect you to do.

You're taking courses in counterterrorism and immigration law. You're taking courses in antidrug trafficking and firearms. You're taking courses in motor vehicle operations. And for those of you who don't know how to speak Spanish, you're learning how to speak Spanish. Those are all very important parts of your training.

Look, I'm not here to give you a lecture, but I am here to thank you. I want to appreciate what you're doing; I appreciate your service. I look forward to seeing you out there on the border doing the job we expect you to do. And in a little while, I'm going to tell you, you expect something from us too. But the first thing you can expect is the full support of the Federal Government, and you have it.

I appreciate—[*applause*]—Pete Domenici is keeping pretty good company today with Senator Jeff Bingaman. It's good to see the Senator. Thanks for coming. I'm proud you're here as well. I flew down with two Members of the United States Congress, Congressman Tom Udall—he's from the northern part of the State—and Congressman Steve Pearce—he's here from the eastern part of New Mexico. It's good

to see you all. Pearce has got that umbrella up because he's bald-headed. [*Laughter*] He's also a fine Congressman.

I want to thank the Governor of the great State of New Mexico, Governor Bill Richardson. Governor, I'm proud you're here. Thank you for taking the time. I know what it's like to be the Governor of a border State. And I know Governor Richardson counts on the Federal Government to pass a good piece of legislation that will enable him and the people of this State who are working with you to do their jobs. And I'm proud you're on the lead of comprehensive immigration reform, Bill.

I want to thank Secretary Mike Chertoff for joining us. I want to thank other members of my administration, starting with Ralph Basham, who is the Commissioner of the U.S. Customs and Border Protection, and his wife, Judy. We're fixing to swear Ralph in. Part of this ceremony is for you to witness the swearing-in of your boss. I think that's a good way for us to make it clear that those of us who are in Washington, DC—in my case, on a temporary basis, I want to emphasize—[*laughter*]—we know you're out here, see, and we care about the job you're doing. I thought it made sense to swear in the new Commissioner in your presence, as a way of making it clear for us to say, he may have an office in Washington, but his heart is right here with the Border Patrol agents.

I appreciate very much Connie Patrick, who's the Director of the Federal Law Enforcement Training Center. I want to thank David Aguilar; he's the Chief of the Border Patrol. For those of you fixing to join the Border Patrol, you need to know, you've got a Chief who knows what he's talking about. See, he did exactly what you've done. Plus, he's a Texan. [*Laughter*] I appreciate Jay Ahern; he's Assistant Commissioner of Field Operations for the U.S. Customs and Border Protection.

I just had a tour given to me by Charlie Whitmire. Maybe you've heard of Charlie. [*Laughter*] He's a no-nonsense kind of guy.

See, he's the kind of guy you want running a facility like this. He's got one thing in mind, and that is to give you the tools necessary to do the job. Whitmire, I appreciate your service, and thanks for your leadership. Thanks for the tour.

I appreciate all the State and local officials who have taken time out of your day to come and say hello, and I particularly want to thank the mayor, Manuel Madrid, for being here as well. Mr. Mayor, thank you for coming; proud you're here. Thanks for your time.

Most of all, I want to thank you all, and I want you to thank your families on behalf of a grateful nation. You need to tell your wives and children, mothers and fathers how much we appreciate what you're doing. So you've got my permission to take a little time off this afternoon—[*laughter*]—and let them know. This is a family deal. You're here training for a very important mission, a mission that's sometimes dangerous. And I understand how important it is to have the support of somebody in your house.

See, I got support from a great lady too, like many of you who are married. I'm fortunate to be married to Laura Bush, who sends her very—[*applause*]—she sends her best to all the good folks out here in eastern New Mexico. Her mother is living right across the border, so we stay in touch with how people are thinking out here.

And it's—I can't tell you how—a joy it is to be out here where the air is dry and fresh and the people are down-to-earth and decent—people who love our country and people who expect us to handle this immigration debate with dignity and to get something done. That's what they expect. The people of Artesia want something done on the immigration issue, and the people all across our country want something done on this important issue. So I want to talk to you today about the debate we're having in Washington, DC.

The first thing is, illegal immigration is a serious problem. The first thing we got

to understand as a country is that illegal immigration undermines the rule of law. It creates an underground economy. It can danger our national security. And therefore, we need to do something about it.

Illegal immigration makes it tough on local communities. It puts a strain on public schools and strains State and local budgets, brings crime to some of our communities. And we need to do something about it.

We've also got to remember this though, during this debate, that illegal immigration is a problem, but we need to remember that immigrants have been one of the great strengths of the United States of America. For generations, immigrants to this country have risked everything because of the dream of freedom. And they've assimilated into our society. And they've contributed to our economy. And they've contributed to the greatness of America. During this debate, this important debate on illegal immigration, we've got to remember we're a land of immigrants, and therefore, conduct this debate with dignity.

The United States is a nation of laws, and we're going to enforce our laws. We're also a nation of immigrants, and we're going to uphold that tradition. And these are not contradictory goals. America can be a lawful society, and America will be a welcoming society at the same time.

So I'm going to work with Congress to fix our immigration problems, and I'm going to work with Congress to pass a comprehensive bill I can pass into law. And we're making progress. I know you're following the debate in Washington, but we're making progress toward a comprehensive bill.

When I visited the border last fall, Congress was still debating whether to take any action at all. See, last fall there was a doubt as to whether or not Congress was going to act on the immigration bill. The last time I visited the border last month, the House had passed a bill focusing on border security and interior enforcement. Now the

Senate has passed a bill, and it's a more comprehensive approach that includes a temporary-worker program and a plan to resolve the status of illegal immigrants inside our country. And the next step is for the House and the Senate to reconcile its difference and agree on legislation that both houses can agree on. And I believe that legislation needs to be comprehensive in nature, which I'm going to talk about here in a minute.

I know when you watch your television or listen to the radio, it seems like there's nothing but disagreement on immigration policy in Washington. Yet there's a growing consensus among all parties and all regions of the country that fundamental reforms are needed. In other words, people are coming to the conclusion we got to do something about a system that isn't working. And while the differences grab the headlines, the similarities in approaches are striking.

We all agree we need to control our borders. There's a common agreement that the Federal Government has a responsibility to control the borders, so that every illegal immigrant caught at the border needs to be sent home. We agree with that. Secondly, we agree that the Government needs to crack down on businesses that hire illegal workers. In other words, in order to help you do your job, we all agree that if someone is hiring somebody who is an illegal immigrant, they've broken the law, and we need to crack down on that.

We all agree we must reduce the incentives for foreign workers to cross the border illegally. See, there's agreement on that in Washington. We agree that it's unacceptable to have millions of illegal immigrants living in our country beyond the reach of law and the protection of the law. And we all agree that immigrants to America must assimilate into our society. They must embrace our values and learn to speak the English language. See, there's common agreement; there's a consensus. And we

need to act on that broad consensus and deliver comprehensive reform that makes our system orderly, secure, and fair.

We all agree we've got to enforce the borders. Since 2001, I've worked with the United States Congress to increase border security funding by 66 percent. I want to thank the Members of Congress for working on that. Border Patrol has been expanded from about 9,000 agents to 12,000 agents, and we're building new infrastructures on the border.

Federal agents like you have apprehended and sent home about 6 million people entering America illegally since 2001. It's an amazing statistic, isn't it? Most American people have no earthly idea how hard our Border Patrol agents are working. Six million people since 2001 have been caught trying to come into this country illegally and sent home. And that's why I tell you, I'm grateful for your hard work. People are doing an outstanding job.

But we got to make sure that we give you more to secure the border. Congress needs to fund dramatic increases in manpower and additional technology that will help you build on the successes. See, there's more work to be done. We're going to increase the size of the Border Patrol by additional 6,000 agents by the end of 2008. You're going to be busy here at this facility. See, our goal is to have doubled the Border Patrol to about 18,000 Border Patrol agents. That's what they tell me is going to work. I said, "Fine, get it done." And your classes here are part of that doubling of the Border Patrol. And when these agents that are trained here are deploying, we're going to give them what's necessary in terms of technology to be able to do their jobs.

See, we need to add new technologies to the new manpower we're training, so we can tell the American people we're doing our best we possibly can to secure our border. Americans expect us to secure the border. It's an important job of the Federal Government. And so we're going to double your size, and we're going to get you new technologies.

We're going to build high-tech fences in urban corridors. For the agents here who've been on the frontlines of enforcing our border, you understand how important those high-tech fences are so you can do that job. We're going to make sure you got new patrol roads. We can't ask these new Border Patrol agents that we're training to do their job and not have adequate patrol roads to be able to go up and down the border. We're going to build virtual fence that employs motion detectors and infrared cameras and unmanned aerial vehicles to prevent illegal crossings. See, we're going to leverage technology so you can better do your job.

Proposals to boost manpower and upgrade technologies have the support of Republicans and Democrats in the House and the Senate. In other words, there's consensus on that. We're going to get this part of the job done. And I understand and you understand, it takes time to get technology and Border Patrol agents in place.

The training you do here takes 19 weeks, as it should. We don't want to rush you through the academy. See, when we put you on the frontline of doing your job, we want you to be as well-trained as you possibly can be. That's what your families expect, that's what your Government expects, and that's what your trainers want. They want to use their skills to give you the skills necessary to do the job.

But it takes the time, and yet we don't have time to get this border enforced. And so therefore, I decided to work with our State Governors, Republicans and Democrats, to move 6,000 National Guard troops on the border to help the current Border Patrol do the job until the new agents are trained. That makes sense to me, doesn't it? If we've got a problem, let's address it square on. And if part of the problem is we're waiting to get new Border Patrol agents trained, and we can't wait, let's move some troops in—National Guard

troops that will be able to help those of you on the frontlines of securing our border do your job better.

Guard members are arriving at the border, and they're going to set up a headquarters to support Border Patrol operations. You see, you notice I said "support the Border Patrol." The Border Patrol is in the lead; that's why they're going through significant training. The Border Patrol is the primary law enforcement agency on the border. And so the Guard units are down there to support your job; they're to make it easier for you to do your job. Our Guard units will not be involved in direct law enforcement activities. That's not what they're going to go down there for. The United States of America will not militarize our border. We're going to make sure that the Border Patrol is the—is directly involved in law enforcement activities. That's what you're trained to do. The Guard is going to free up Border Patrol to focus on stopping illegal immigrants coming in. They're going to be building the roads, and they're going to be doing the support.

When I was down in Yuma, I saw the Guard working side by side with Border Patrol, and what they're doing is, they're freeing up the Border Patrol to be on the frontlines. And I want to thank Governor Richardson and Governor Perry and Governor Schwarzenegger, Governor Napolitano for working with the Federal Government to prepare the way for the arrival of the Guard troops. And as soon as you get the Border Patrol agents trained, these Guard troops will be going home. But until that time, I want them down here helping you do the job that the American people expect us to do.

We've got to stop catch-and-release. Perhaps the people of Artesia, New Mexico, know what I'm talking about; a lot of Americans don't. What happens is, these Border Patrol agents work hard; they find somebody coming back—coming into our country; they say, "The rules say you check in with the officer here, in the court; come back in about 20 days when we've got time for you to show up," and they don't show up. So you've got somebody working hard to find somebody, and we let them back out in society, and guess what? They disappear. And we're going to end that practice.

Eighty-five percent of the illegal immigrants caught crossing the border are Mexican citizens, so they get sent back quickly. Within 24 hours they're sent back across the country, and that's important for people to know; if you get caught, you get sent home. It means it's less likely you're going to try to come in, in the first place.

Unfortunately, it wasn't that easy to send home illegal immigrants from other countries, Central American countries, for example, and so they were released back into our society. It had to be frustrating for you Border Patrol agents who were on the frontlines. You work hard, you find somebody who is trying to sneak in from Central America, you do your job; next thing you know you hear, "Oops, they're somewhere in society." So we're going to end that practice.

And the way you end it is, you build more detention facilities. See, part of the problem was, we didn't have a place to hold these folks. And so now I'm working with Congress to increase the number of detention facilities along our borders, to make sure that when we catch somebody from a place other than Mexico, there's a place to hold them until such time as we send them back to their country.

I'm also talking to leaders of those countries from which these people are coming, and I'm saying, "You have a responsibility to take them back as quickly as possible." And our mission is to end catch-and-release once and for all on the southern border of the United States, and we intend to do just that.

In order to make sure this Border Patrol strategy works, this strategy of securing the border, we all agree in Washington that employers must be held to account for the workers they hire. I spoke to the Chamber of Commerce last week, and I made it clear that the United States is not going to tolerate employers who violate our immigration laws. See, it's against the law to hire someone who is here illegally. That's what the law says. We're a nation of laws, and we expect people to abide by the laws.

Most businesses want to comply with the law; they really do. Most people are good, law-abiding citizens who want to comply, but they have trouble verifying the legal status of their employees because of widespread problem of fake IDs and fraudulent Social Security numbers. See, there's a problem here. We got people sneaking into our country, and there's a whole document forgery ring supplying them with fake documents. And it's hard to expect some small-business person in Artesia, New Mexico, to be in a position to be a document checker.

And the Federal Government can help. So we're working on an effective system for verifying work eligibility so the businesses can better comply with the law, and then we'll be in a position to say, "If you don't comply with the law, you deserve to be punished. If we catch you cheating right now, you'll be punished." But we got to make sure that small businesses and large businesses have got the capacity to verify whether a person is here legally or not.

Congress needs to give Federal agents the authority they need to enforce the law when job applicants submit fraudulent Social Security numbers. Congress needs to make it mandatory for employers to check information provided by job applicants against Federal databases. Right now it's voluntary. In other words, you getting ready to hire somebody, you need to check against the Federal database to make sure the numbers on the cards aren't forged, are real. But what really Congress needs to do is to use a biometric technology to create a new tamper-proof identification card for every legal foreign worker. That's what we need; we need a tamper-proof card. It says, if you're here legally working, here's your card, and you got to show it. And the businessowner has got to call for it. And if they hire somebody without the tamper-proof card, they're in violation of the law and will be fined.

We've got to reduce the incentives for foreign workers to sneak across the border. That's what we agree on in Washington. If I were a Border Patrol agent, I'd be asking, "What are you trying to do about the people trying to sneak in here to work? How come you don't have a temporary way for them to come work on the jobs Americans aren't doing?" See, I believe that we need to understand that there are people coming across this border to put food on the table for their family, and they'll do anything to make it into America to do work. That's what you got to understand. A lot of people in Artesia, New Mexico, know what I'm talking about. There are people coming to do work Americans aren't doing. They're working in the dairy farms; they're working the crops; they're laying tile; they're putting roof on in August.

And therefore, it seems like to me, if we want to protect this border, we ought to recognize they're coming and give them a temporary-worker card. They can come if they pass a criminal background check, for a limited period of time, and after they do their time, they go back home.

If you want to secure this border, you got to make it so people don't feel like they got to sneak across the border. The people these people catch are coming into this country to do jobs. We ought to recognize that and say, "Here is a legal way for you to come on a temporary basis for jobs that Americans aren't doing. And when you finish your time, when your time is up with the temporary-worker card, you go back home." And one way to secure that border is to have people not trying to sneak across the border, is to give them a chance to come here legally on a temporary basis.

You know, I was out in Yuma, and they were describing one of the techniques for people coming here to work. You got a couple of Border Patrol agents out on a part of the world—a part of the road there, and a hundred people rush them. A hundred people coming to do work rush right across the border, and you got three agents trying to stop them. And it's impossible. So the way to stop them is to do what we're doing out there: add Border Patrol agents, add new double-fencing in that part of the border. But it seems like to me, it's logical to say, "You can come over; you don't need to rush the Border Patrol. Just come over here in a legal way, if you pass a background check, for a temporary period of time, and do work Americans aren't doing." That's called a temporary-worker plan. And, in my judgment, any comprehensive bill that will work requires a temporary-worker plan.

We all agree we've got to resolve the status of millions of illegal immigrants who are here already. And this is the toughest part of the bill for the Congress. Now, I believe there's widespread agreement that we should not have an automatic path to citizenship, which is called amnesty. I'm against amnesty. I'm against amnesty because it's unfair to those people who are standing in line to become a citizen and who have been here lawfully. And I'm against amnesty because I think if you grant amnesty, it invites a further wave of illegal immigrants to try to come in this country. So whatever plan we do should not be viewed as amnesty.

In other words, some say, "Well, the way to solve this problem is to say, you're here; you're automatically a citizen." I disagree strongly with that. Now, there is a debate and honest disagreement who believe that immigration policy should force every illegal immigrant to return home for good. That's what some people in Washington think. And obviously, there are those at the other end who believe that every illegal immigrant should be granted automatic citizenship. Neither of those plans are going to work. I just described why one wouldn't work. And trying to find 10 million people who have been here for a long period of time and rout them out of our society and send them home is just impractical. It may sound good; it's not going to work.

Our job is to put something on paper that will work, so these Border Patrol agents can get their job done. Our job is to be practical and to use common sense. And so here's a commonsense middle ground between those two polarized positions. First of all, we've got to recognize that people who—the difference between people who have been here for a while and people here newly arrived. Those who have been here newly arrived ought to be given a temporary-worker card, and they work their time and go home.

But we've got to recognize that there are people who have been here for years, and they've got a home and a clean record, and they've been paying taxes. And so I believe if they want to stay here, that they ought to pay a fine, first and foremost. They've broken our law, and they ought to pay a fine for breaking the law. Secondly, I believe they've got to pay taxes and make sure that they pay their taxes. Thirdly, I believe they ought to speak English. And fourthly, I believe they have to prove they've been working for a job for a number of years. In other words, there's a consequence. And then—and then—they can apply for citizenship, but they don't get at the head of the line; they get in the back of the line. You get behind the people who have been here legally.

In other words, you've got somebody who has been here for a while; they've been a good citizen; they've been working hard; and they pay a penalty for being here illegally. But if they want to choose to be a citizen, they get behind those people who have been here legally and who haven't broken the law. And if Congress is worried about the number of people getting in, they

can decrease the number of green cards. You can control the size of the line by the number of green cards you issue. If you want a longer line for people, issue fewer green cards. If you want to shorten the line, issue more green cards. But here is a rational way to make sure that we treat people with dignity without granting automatic citizenship, which is called amnesty.

And finally, whatever our views on the issue, we've got to agree that we've got to uphold the great American tradition of the melting pot. You know, we are one Nation under God for a reason, and that is because we appreciate our history, and we share ideals, we respect the flag we fly, and we're bound together by a common language.

I believe English is the key to unlocking opportunity in America. It's been what it takes to help somebody go from picking crops to owning a grocery store or from cleaning the floors of an office building to running that office. It's what we call assimilation, as part of assimilating to be Americans. When immigrants assimilate into this society, they realize their dreams. A lot of people have come here to this country over the decades with a dream, some of them just as simple as, "I'd like to own my own house," or, "I want to work hard so my child can go to college."

I'll never forget being the Governor of Texas and going to schools like UTEP, University of Texas at El Paso. One of the most amazing parts of that ceremony is when the president of the university stood up, and she said, "How many of you are first-generation graduates from college," and you see the students—a lot of them stood up. And you see their proud parents who've worked all their life to help a child go to college. There's something about America where people can work hard and realize dreams. That has, I think, made us a unique nation. And as we go through this debate, we've got to understand that people who have dreams and work hard to achieve those dreams renews the spirit of the country, gives us a uniqueness and the capacity to say, we're all Americans.

So here are the elements for a comprehensive immigration bill—and I believe strongly this: That if we don't address all the elements together, none of it is going to be solved at all. The reason I called for a comprehensive bill is because I understand that in order for these good folks to do their job, we've got to link all five aspects together. We've got to be realistic about what it takes to enforce the border. So I look forward to working with Congress on this important issue.

I'll make you this pledge: My tone in this debate is going to be respectful. The language I use in this debate is going to remember the values and ideals of America. The language I use in this debate is to remember we're from different backgrounds, different religions, different cultures, but ultimately we're united under the great ideals of the United States of America. And I expect everybody else in this debate to carry that same tone as well.

And so I want to thank you for giving me a chance to share my thoughts with you. I feel passionately about this issue. I feel like one reason the people send us to Washington, DC, is to solve difficult problems. That's what you send us to do. You didn't send us up there to kind of shove them aside and hope that they go away. This one is not going away. This one needs to be solved right now.

And I also came to thank those who are getting ready to serve the Border Patrol for serving this great country of ours.

You're an important part of securing America, and I want to thank you for your dedication to our country.

I want to congratulate the new Commissioner for U.S. Customs and Border Protection, Ralph Basham. Ralph has a long and distinguished record of service in Federal law enforcement. He joined the Secret Service during the Presidency of Richard Nixon. Some of you all weren't even born during that period of time. [*Laughter*] He served as Special Agent in Charge of the Secret Service Offices in Cleveland and in Washington. He rose all the way to the position of Secret Service Director in 2003. I know he made it to that position because I put him there, and I put him there for a reason. He knows what he's doing. He can get the job done.

Ralph served as Chief of Staff for the Transportation Security Administration and Director of Federal Law Enforcement Training Center. That's where he came to know the Border Patrol Agency—Academy. He's a decent man. I trust him deeply, and he's going to be a superb leader for Customs and Border Protection.

And now it's my honor to witness his swearing-in.

NOTE: The President spoke at 10:45 a.m. at the Federal Law Enforcement Training Center. In his remarks, he referred to Charlie Whitmire, acting chief, Border Patrol Academy; Mayor Manuel Madrid of Artesia, NM; Gov. Rick Perry of Texas; Gov. Arnold Schwarzenegger of California; and Gov. Janet A. Napolitano of Arizona.

Remarks at the Laredo Border Patrol Sector Headquarters and an Exchange With Reporters in Laredo, Texas
June 6, 2006

The President. Well, it's good to be in my home State with my home Governor.

Governor Perry understands, like I understand, the need to enforce this border. He also understands what I understand—that in order to do so, we've got to have a comprehensive plan.

I started my day earlier in New Mexico, where I saw the training facility that is going to put out enough Border Patrol to be able to tell the American people, we will have doubled the Border Patrol since 2001. And that's a really important part of our strategy, is to train more Border Patrol agents to help those that are working hard already to do their job. But we need to make the border technologically advanced as well.

We just saw some of the remote cameras that are in place that will help the Border Patrol be able to do its job better. But more than that, we've got to have a comprehensive approach. And that includes a temporary-worker plan that says, "You can come and do a job Americans aren't doing if you pass a criminal background check, for a period of time. And then once you finish that time, you go home."

We also have got to make sure that we deal with the problem of people who have been here for a long period of time. Some people say, "Throw them out of the country." That doesn't make any sense. You just can't throw them out of the country. Others say, "Give them amnesty." And that doesn't make any sense. And the reason why giving them automatic citizenship doesn't make any sense, it will encourage others to come. So what we ought to do is say to somebody who's been here for a while, if you pass a background check, criminal background check, you've shown that you've worked here for a while, you paid a penalty—that you can apply for citizenship, but you get at the back of the line, the citizenship line, not at the front.

A comprehensive plan is necessary to help these good folks do their job. And I'm going to keep calling on Congress to think about a comprehensive plan. We agree on a lot of stuff. A lot of the elements of this plan have got common agreement. And now it's time for folks to set

aside politics and get the job done on behalf of the American people.

Nedra [Nedra Pickler, Associated Press], you got a question?

Iran

Q. Yes, sir. Can you respond to Iran's initial reaction to the incentives package today?

The President. Why don't you tell me what it was?

Q. Well, the top negotiator said——

The President. As you know, I've been in Artesia.

Q. Right. I was. But the top negotiator said that the package contained positive steps, but there were some ambiguities, but the talks were constructive.

The President. I think that's positive. I want to solve this issue with Iran diplomatically. And I think that—I appreciate Javier Solana carrying a message to the Iranians that America, Russia, China, Britain, France, and Germany—the main group of negotiators—wants this problem to be solved. And so we will see if the Iranians take our offer seriously.

The choice is theirs to make. I have said, the United States will come and sit down at the table with them so long as they're willing to suspend their enrichment in a verifiable way. Sounds like a positive response to me.

Steve [Steve Holland, Reuters].

Somalia

Q. Sir. In Somalia, sir, it appears to have fallen to Islamic militants. Is there a need for international peacekeepers there, or what do you think has happened there?

The President. Well, I talked to Secretary of State Rice about this subject yesterday. And obviously, when there's instability anywhere in the world, we're concerned. There is instability in Somalia. The first concern, of course, would be to make sure that Somalia does not become an Al Qaida safe haven; that it doesn't become a place from which terrorists can plot and plan. And so we're watching very carefully the developments there, and we will strategize more when I get back to Washington as how to best respond to the latest incident there in Somalia.

Yes.

Immigration Reform

Q. President Bush——

The President. Where are you from, here?

Q. Laredo Morning Times.

The President. It's nice to be back here. Thank you.

Q. Very nice to meet you too.

The President. Rick and I were talking about the first time I came here after I had won Governor—he had already been in office for a while—was the Washington day parade, and I remember it fondly. It's good to be back in Laredo.

Q. It's good to have you here, sir. Are you all—are you hoping to—a lot of people say that the answer for immigration is to—well, one group is saying that the quotas need to be raised for the amount of legal documented workers that can come in. Is that part of your proposal?

The President. Well, I think the framework I've outlined recognizes that Congress has got the right to regulate what they call green cards. And if Congress thinks that the line for citizens from Mexico is too long, they can increase the number of green cards. If they think it's—or they can shorten—increase the number of green cards. If they think it's too short, they can eliminate the number of green cards. In other words, they can control the flow of people from a particular part of the country.

What I want is people who have been here for a while to be able to have the choice—if they pay a fine, if they learn the English language, if they've proven they worked—to be able to get in the citizenship—in the potential citizenship line—but at the back of it. See, they don't get to be in the front. The people who have been here legally are in the front of the line. They get to wait in line. And if Congress wants to shorten the line, they increase the number of green cards.

Q. And I guess for those that haven't been here that long, do you favor deportation of those?

The President. Well, I believe that—as I've said in my remarks—that there ought to be a difference between those folks who have been here for a period of time and—like for those who own a home or have got a family established or have had a job for a long period of time and—and those who have arrived recently. Those people ought to be given a temporary-worker card for a limited period of time. And when the time is up, they need to go home. That's what a temporary worker is—it's not a permanent-worker card; it's a temporary-worker card.

And Congress needs to determine the length—the proper length of time. Right now, one consideration is 3 years with a 3 year renewal. And what that will do is that will help people who are looking for somebody to do a job Americans aren't doing find workers. It'll also mean that somebody doesn't have to sneak across the border. See, we've got Border Patrol agents chasing down people who are trying to sneak across and do work Americans aren't doing. So it seems like it makes sense to me that—"Here, you can come to our country on a temporary basis to do a job, and when the time is up, you get to go home." That's how you enforce the border. You enforce the border with more Border Patrol agents, better technology, and a rational way to treat people who are coming here to do work Americans aren't doing.

That's one of the reasons I've come down here to Laredo, as well as Artesia, is I want to talk to these Border Patrol agents. And I want to assure them that we're listening to what they need to get their job done. Our job in government is to say to people who are risking their lives and working hard is, "What do you need to get the job done?" And that's why I've been coming down here, and we'll keep coming down here. And Congress needs to get a bill done.

Yes, sir.

Congressional Action on Immigration Legislation

Q. Mr. President, you spoke about progress earlier today in Artesia. You said that you feel it's progress that both the Senate and the House have both taken up the issue of immigration. What concrete progress can you point to, in terms of winning over the conservatives in your party who still stand pretty firmly against the idea of any path to citizenship for immigrants?

The President. Well, one thing is, it's conceivable you could have been asking me, "How come you can't get any Chamber in Congress to pass a bill?" And so progress—what I'm telling the American people is, is that from last fall to now, we've got two bills out there. That's progress.

What else is progress is a common understanding. One, we've got to enforce the border; two, that people need to be treated with respect; three, that there needs to be assimilation; four, that we need to hold employers who break the law to account; five, there needs to be some way to deal with people who are here to work on a temporary basis; and six, ultimately, we're going to have to do something about people who've been here for a long period of time. In other words, people understand those are the principles that we've got to work on.

There's no question this is a difficult issue for some in Washington, DC. But my job is to continue calling people to account and say, "We've got to work together to get a bill done." And one way to do it is to come right down here on the frontlines of border enforcement and say to the United States Congress, "There are people working hard on behalf of this country, and we owe them a comprehensive

piece of legislation so they can do their job." And I'm going to keep doing it.

Yes, ma'am. Where are you from?

Q. ABC News.

The President. ABC News? I'd suggest getting a little sunblock——

Q. Sunblock. Yes. [*Laughter*]

The President. Yes. Always looking out for my fellow citizens. [*Laughter*]

Q. Thank you. Last summer, you set a deadline for Congress before their August recess to pass things like the energy bill. Are you going to put such a deadline on an immigration bill——

The President. My attitude is, is that in order for these people to be doing their job, they need a bill as soon as possible. I'm looking forward to getting that conference, seeing the conference get together. You know, people—there are people making statements, and that's important for people to set out there, say things, and kind of set their markers. The conferences have a way of working things out. And I'm going to be continuing to urge people to work things out in conference.

They haven't yet sat down as a conference yet, but they will pretty soon. And that will give us a pretty good feel for whether or not attitudes are hardened to the point nothing can get done. I don't think so. I think the people want something done in America. If you look at the—you know what people are saying. They're saying, "Let's get something done in a comprehensive way." And I believe we can get something done. No question, it's hard work, but that's all the more reason to work hard to get it done. I recognize some people in Washington would rather duck the hard issue, but that's not the way I am, and that's not the way most people in Congress are. They want to get the job done, so we should keep working on it.

Okay, thank you all, unless you want to stand out here a little longer. [*Laughter*] You're back again.

Trade With Mexico

Q. Mr. President, I'm sorry, one last question.

The President. That's fine. I'm glad to be working with the local press.

Q. Thank you so much. Some people say that Mexico needs to do a whole lot more to just create more jobs that pay a more decent wage for its people, and that America should help Mexico by investing more or providing more development funds. Is that—what do you think about that, and do you have any kind of proposals for that?

The President. I think the people that say that the long-term solution to immigration is for people to be able to find work in Mexico, they're right. And that's why I've been a strong supporter of NAFTA.

One of the interesting things about the border here that I don't think a lot of Americans are aware, but I know those of us who grew up in Texas are aware of, is that this part of the world used to be really poor. Up and down the Rio Grande Valley, there was a lot of impoverished people. Laredo is a booming town—I mean, it's thriving. It has really changed a lot, and one of the main reasons why is because of trade with Mexico. On the other side of the border, the border States are prosperous States.

And so to answer your question, the first thing is to promote free and fair trade between Mexico and the United States. Trade enhances wealth; it provides opportunities for people. The problem is in Mexico is that the opportunities you can find here on the border don't extend to the south of the country. And so therefore, a lot of the Mexicans that we're finding at the border are people coming up from the south trying to find work so they can put food on the table. And I've talked to President Fox about this very issue, and I know Rick has talked to President Fox about this issue. And that is, what more can we do with Mexico to encourage economic development south of the northern tier States?

President Fox, the last time I saw him, said that there are 100,000 vacant jobs in northern Mexican States. I think that's really interesting. And I said, "What are we going to do about it?" And the issue is education. The issue is to make sure that people in the interior and the south of the country have got enough education, enough skills so they can fill those 100,000 jobs.

And so to answer your question, economic development works through free and fair trade, as well as helping put an education system in place that makes sense. And that's Mexico's responsibility; that's their job. But we can help, and we work with Mexico all the time. I know Texas has got all kinds of collaborative programs with Mexico to help their education system.

Yes, Steve. You enjoying the heat? [*Laughter*]

Immigration Reform

Q. It's not so bad.

The President. It's because you've got a fine looking hat on there. [*Laughter*]

Q. Thanks, sir. The word "amnesty"— the critics seem to be able to just label this an amnesty and get away with it. I mean, are you having trouble fighting back that impression? Is it sinking in to people that this isn't amnesty and it's going——

The President. Look, if you're one of these types of people that basically say, we got to, you know, throw them out, then you just use the word "amnesty," just toss it around. You know, amnesty is something nobody is for in America. I'm not for it. But in order to frighten people, you just say the word "amnesty."

On the other hand, you can't kick people out of this country. You can stop people from coming in, but there have been people here in this part of the world, for example, been here for a decade—honest, hardworking citizens doing jobs Americans aren't doing, providing for their families.

They own their home. And the fundamental question is, how do you treat them with respect and, at the same time, have a system that's fair and orderly and respects our laws?

And so my attitude is on that, if a person wants to apply for a citizenship, they've got to pay a fine first. They have broken the laws of the United States, and they need to pay a fine. Then they've got to prove they've got a clean criminal record, paid their taxes, and worked. And then they can apply for citizenship, but they're at the back of the line. See, there's a line of people waiting to become a citizen, and they need to get at the back of the line, not at the front of the line. And that's how I think we can have an orderly system. That's not amnesty.

Amnesty is, "Okay, everybody who is here, you're a citizen." That's amnesty, and I'm not for that. I think it would be a mistake. And the reason I'm not for—and I recognize some people are for that. The reason I think it's a mistake is that, one, there are people who played by the rules here in America, law abiding citizens who've applied for citizenship, who are in line to become a citizen. They've adhered to all our laws. They're here legally, and they're in line, and they ought to be at the head of the line. And if you say to somebody who has been here illegally, "You're an automatic citizen," then that means they're not the head of the line—

it means somebody jumped in front of them who had broken our laws.

Secondly, if people are granted amnesty—in other words, the Government would say, "You're automatically a citizen"—there's going to be another 8 million people trying to get in this country, because a lot of people want to be citizens of the United States. It's a great honor to be a citizen of this country. It's a great tribute to our country, by the way, that people are willing to come here to work and to live. We're the land of the free; we're the land of the opportunity. And yet we've got to control our border. And so therefore, to say to some group of people, "You're an automatic citizen," would increase the likelihood of a lot of other people trying to come back in here so they can become a citizen automatically. And therefore, I'm against amnesty.

And I understand words in politics and words trying to frighten people. But the comprehensive approach I've outlined, when people think about it, makes a lot of sense, and you can't—all five need to go together in order to be able to do the job of enforcing the border.

I've enjoyed this, and I hope you have. Thank you.

NOTE: The President spoke at 3:23 p.m. In his remarks, he referred to Gov. Rick Perry of Texas; Secretary General Javier Solana of the Council of the European Union; and President Vicente Fox Quesada of Mexico.

Remarks on Immigration Reform in Omaha, Nebraska
June 7, 2006

Thanks for the warm welcome. It's great to be back in Omaha. I'm a little—I just wish the timing were a little better—[*laughter*]—Senator. If I'd only delayed my trip, we'd have been able to watch the College World Series again. [*Laughter*]

But I couldn't delay it, for this reason: This country is debating an important issue. It's an issue about our soul and our character. It's an issue that relates to people that are in our country. It's the immigration issue. And I don't think this issue can wait for a baseball game or a baseball tournament; it needs to be addressed now. And I'm honored to be here in Omaha, Nebraska, right here in the middle of our country, to talk about a vital issue that affects us all.

Before I came here to give the speech, I went to the Juan Diego Center. It's right down the road, if you haven't been there. It's run by Catholic Charities. By the way, Catholic Charities is one of the most important battalions in the army of compassion. It's full of—[*applause*]—it's a center of love and compassion. It's a place where volunteers come to reach out to somebody who could use a little extra help, and those volunteers ask nothing in return.

I saw a place where people are learning to speak English and learning the civic lessons of what it means to be an American citizen. I sat around a table with entrepreneurs, people from different countries, all of whom are bound by a common dream of owning their own business; people who are willing to work hard to put food on the table for their families and to realize a dream. It was such an inspiring conversation for me.

One such person I met was Salvador Pina. He's a new American citizen who had a dream; he wanted to own his own business. And Salvador went to the Juan Diego Center and said, "Can anybody here help me?" For some of us, we take it for granted that it's easy to understand what forms to fill out or what worker compensation means or how do you pay your sales tax. But for some, they need a little extra help. They don't need to be inspired to dream big dreams, but they need help to realize those dreams.

He—Salvador received a $10,000 loan from Catholic Charities. That's not exactly a microloan, but it's help. In other words, he said, "Can you help me? I'll work hard for whatever you do to help me, but can you give me—lend me a hand, brother?" And Catholic Charities did, and today he owns his own business. He's the proud

owner of Pina Auto Repair. By the way, if you're looking for a good man to fix your car—[*laughter*]—give old Salvador a chance.

So what's it like? He said, "I've been working hard." I said, "Do you employ anybody?" He said, "Yes, I've started with just me, and now I've got three employees." That's what America is all about, isn't it, one person with a dream helping others to provide an employment opportunity. Salvador owns his own building. That's what we want in America. We want to encourage an ownership society, where a person like Salvador who started with nothing can say, "Welcome to my business, and I own my building; come on into the building I own, and here are the three people I'm employing."

When you hear people like me talk about assimilation, that's what we're talking about, helping people assimilate into America, helping us remain one Nation under God. So I want to thank Catholic Charities for their good work, and I want to thank a dreamer like Salvador for coming here, obeying the law, and working hard to achieve the American Dream.

When I get back to Washington, I'm going to sign an Executive order creating a task force on the new Americas. This task force is going to be led by our Secretary of Homeland Security, Chertoff. It's going to work to help people at the grassroots level expand the teaching of English and civics and history instruction programs to help others assimilate into America.

We want to—I'm going to create—I've also signed legislation creating an Office of Citizenship at the Department of Homeland Security to promote knowledge of citizens' rights and responsibilities. In other words, one aspect of making sure we have an immigration system that works, that's orderly and fair, is to actively reach out and help people assimilate into our country. That means, learn the values and history and language of America. And for those of you who are wondering how you can help our country, volunteer to be a part of such an assimilation process, just like the volunteers at Catholic Charities are doing.

I appreciate the Governor being here. Mr. Governor, thank you and Sally for coming. You're kind to take time out of your schedule to say hello to the old President. [*Laughter*] Getting older by the minute, by the way. [*Laughter*] I'm not supposed to talk about myself, but in a month, I'm turning 60. For you youngsters, I want to tell you something. When I was your age, I thought 60 was really old. [*Laughter*] It's all in your mind. It's not that old; it really isn't. Right, Senator Hagel? [*Laughter*]

I want to thank Chuck Hagel for his leadership on this issue, this immigration issue. You see, you can make the choice in Washington, DC, whether you want to be a leader or whether you want to kind of lay back and see how things work out and then take a position. You can go to Washington to solve problems, or you can go to Washington to hope those problems go away. Senator Hagel is one of the type of people that said, "I'm going to go to Washington to take a lead on this issue." This problem isn't going away; it needs to be fixed now, and I want to thank Chuck Hagel for his leadership on this important issue.

I'm proud to be here with one of the most decent men in the United States Congress, a man who's got a huge heart, a compassionate fellow, a person who didn't have to go into public service, but said, service to a nation you love and a State you care about is an important lesson for others to realize, and Tom Osborne is one of the fine, fine Americans.

I want to thank the Lieutenant Governor, Rick Sheehy, and the secretary of State, John Gale. Thank you all for coming today.

I'm glad we're at a community college. And I thank Jody McDowell and the board and the teachers who are here, welcoming me here. This is a—[*applause*]. I don't know if the people of Omaha realize what

an important asset you have in your community college system. I certainly understand it. Community colleges are a really important part of making sure America remains a competitive nation.

I remind our fellow citizens, particularly those who look to the future and get nervous and say, "Well, we can't compete," or, "There's no way for America to be the economic leader of the world. There's just too much competition"—I simply just don't believe that. I tell people, "Let's don't fear the future; let's shape it." And one way we can shape the future is to make sure people have the skills necessary to fill the jobs of the 21st century, and one of the best places for people to learn the skills of the 21st century is at a community college.

Community colleges are practical. They design curriculum that meets the needs of today's world. So when people come here, they come here to learn a set of skills so they can go out and get a job and be a contributor to our society. Maybe the best way for me to describe how important a community college is, is to tell you a quick story about Heather Fowler. Where is Heather? There you are. You got a lousy seat, but that's okay. [*Laughter*] She should have had a better seat because she's the president of the community college. Heather has got, I think, the toughest job in America, and that is being a single mother raising two children. It's particularly tough since one of her daughters is nearly 16. [*Laughter*] I know what it's like.

She's the president. She had been out of school for 16 years. She had been working to raise her family, but she realized that she needed to come back to enhance her skills. So guess where she came—right here. And she's graduating with a nursing degree. See, she had the initiative to say, "I may have been dealt a tough hand, but I'm going to play it with all my strength and all my might, and I'm going to take advantage of that which is available." The community colleges makes advantages available to people.

Heather, I want to thank you for your dedication; I want to thank you for your example. If anybody is listening out there and you're wondering whether or not you can find a place to enhance your skills so you can get a higher paying job, so you can become a more productive worker, which means more pay for you, take the heart of the president of this school—take the lesson to heart. Heather Fowler shows what's possible here at the community college system. And I'm honored, Heather, you let me use you as an example to encourage others to come to this fine place of learning.

I want to thank Scot Adams. He tolerated me. He's the fellow who is the executive director of Catholic Charities who took me on the tour—great tour guide.

I want to thank—I've got two messages for you from Washington, one from the Secretary of Agriculture—[*laughter*]—Johanns; he's doing fine. [*Laughter*] He's doing really good. As a matter of fact, he remembers where he came from. That's an important part of Washington; it's important that you go up there and serve but never forget where you came from. And Mike Johanns knows where he came from, and he's doing an excellent job as the Secretary of Agriculture.

And Laura sends her best, by the way. She's a—I checked in with her this morning. I'm an early riser, maybe a little too early for her in this case. But she's doing good, really good. And I'm proud to call her wife, and I hope you all are proud to call her First Lady. She's a fine person.

We talked about the importance to help people assimilate into our society. This is what's happened throughout the ages here in America. People have learned to assimilate. You know, I like to remind people, when we think about this immigration debate, the first thing people have got to remember is we are a nation of immigrants, that we've had this debate before in Amer-

ican history. This isn't the first time the United States of America has had to take a look at our nature and our soul and our history.

I'm here to talk about a comprehensive immigration reform package, one part of which is to help people assimilate. The reason I want a comprehensive reform package is because I want whatever we do to work. And in my judgment, the definition of "work" is: We want a border that's safe and secure; we want rule of law to prevail; and we want the American Dream to flourish. We're a nation of laws, and we want to uphold those laws. We're also a compassionate nation that treats people decently, and the two are not in conflict. That's what's important for our fellow citizens to understand. The two are not in conflict.

I know you probably look at Washington and think it's impossible to develop a consensus in Washington, DC. It probably seems that way, doesn't it, when you pay attention to all the sharp elbows being thrown and the people opinionating and screaming and hollering and calling each other names. But there is a consensus emerging on this issue. I remind the folks, I was down—one reason I'm red-faced is I was down on the border yesterday in Laredo. It was about 106. But I reminded people that last fall, when I moved around the country on this issue, there wasn't any legislation at all. As a matter of fact, it was in doubt as to whether or not people even wanted to talk about the issue. You could hear them saying in Washington, "Two thousand-six is an election year; maybe we don't want to take on this issue."

But some of us in Washington said, "Well, you got to take on the issue." There's a problem. It's not working. The system is not working; the borders aren't secure; we got people living in the shadows of our society, and that's not right. People don't have trust in the border. The Federal Government is doing its job on the border, and at the same time, we got a whole industry sprung up of smugglers and document forgers and people who are using people like chattel, and that's not fair, and that's not right, either.

And so since then, since when I was—went down there to the border for the first time to bring up the issue, the House passed a bill. And then I mentioned the Senate passed a bill with Chuck's leadership there. So there's progress. You can't get a piece of legislation out that I can sign unless you get both bodies to move.

And so now we're in what's called a conference committee, and there's a consensus developing. Listen, all of us in America agree we've got to secure our border. That's the job of a Federal Government. You want to know who's coming into your country and why; that's what you want to know. We have a responsibility to enforce the border.

And we're making good steps toward that. First thing is, you've got to have Border Patrol agents to enforce the border. And by 2008, we will have doubled the number of Border Patrol agents to 18,000 Border Patrol agents. And these are people who are highly trained people, whose job it is to respect the law, to be able to ascertain if somebody's coming into this country illegally or not. See, their job is to make sure the border is open for tourism and legal traffic and shut down for drugs and narcotics and smugglers.

And I was out there to the training plant in Artesia, New Mexico, by the way, yesterday, and there's some fine people serving our country. They really are hard-working, decent folks who volunteered and said, "I want to serve the United States of America in the Border Patrol." And since 2001, we've apprehended and sent back 6 million people trying to get in the country.

People are working hard to defend our border, and so therefore, we're going to double the number of Border Patrol agents. And until we get them stood up, in my judgment, it made sense to send some National Guard folks down there, not to be the law enforcement arm of the Border Patrol but to man the phones and radars and help build the roads, to complement the Border Patrol so that the Border Patrol stays on the frontline of enforcing the border. And once we get the Border Patrol up and running, the Guard can go back to doing what they're doing. But it makes sense to tell the American people that we understand our obligation, and we're going to do our job of enforcing the border.

This is a long border. I mean, it's hard to enforce. And therefore, we need to have good technology down there—cameras and infrared devices and unmanned aerial vehicles and high-tech—high-density corridors, some fencing—just so the Border Patrol can do its job. That's what the American people expect, and we're going to modernize our border, and Congress agrees on that.

The other problem we got along the border is that when people get stopped who are illegally trying to come in the border, a lot of them just get sent back into society. That's not a good system. There's something wrong with this system. In other words, you got people down there enforcing the law, and somebody gets apprehended, and they send them to an immigration holding deal, and they say, "Look, check back after 45 days, with us, please." Well, they're not checking back after 45 days. That's called catch-and-release.

Most of the people we catch are Mexican citizens, and they're sent back to their country immediately. But a lot of folks from Central America, for example, are caught, and since we didn't have enough detention beds, places to hold them until they're able to be sent back to their country, people were let out in society. And that demoralized our Border Patrol. It basically said to the American people, "We're not serious about enforcing our border."

And so we're ending the practice of catch-and-release by increasing the number of facilities for people to be compassionately held until they're able to be sent back to their countries. And I'm working with the countries to encourage their leaders to accept back those who have been caught trying to sneak into our country.

Look, the strategy is this: The strategy is to say, once people understand that they can't come into our country illegally and they'll be sent home when they try to, then they're not going to try in the first place. That's part of the strategy.

However, I want you to know that I don't believe we can enforce our border without having a rational way for people to come here to do work that Americans are not doing. It's called a temporary-worker plan. A temporary-worker plan recognizes that—two things: One, there are jobs Americans aren't doing—they're just not—and yet there's a need. We got employers who are looking for employees to do a certain kind of work. And the second aspect is, you've got to understand family values don't stop at the Rio Grande River. There are a lot of hard-working, decent people who want to put food on the table for their families. And therefore, they're willing to get in the back of an 18-wheeler or walk across a hot desert to work.

And that's part of the phenomenon you're seeing, you see, and you can't enforce the border like the American people expect us with just Border Patrol and technology alone. So long as there's that strong desire for people to improve their lives, to do whatever it takes to come to America to work, it's going to make it really hard to enforce that border. And so the best way to do it is to have a plan so people don't feel like they got to sneak in. We ought to have a plan that says, "You can come in legally for a limited period of time; you can come in and do work Americans are not doing, and then you go home. But you can take that money you made and help your family." That's what we ought to have.

See, when people are trying to sneak across the border, it makes it hard to enforce the border. When people can come here in a rational way that saves their lives as well as takes pressure off the border, it will enable us to be able to tell the American people we got a better way of doing the job they expect us to do, which is enforce the border.

I strongly support a temporary-worker program. I think most people in Congress understand the rationality of a temporary-worker program. I guarantee you, many employers here in the State of Nebraska, people in the agricultural sector, people in the hospitality sector, understand the need to have a rational plan that will enable them to have somebody here on a temporary basis to do the jobs Americans aren't doing.

We all agree that we need to uphold the law when it—oh, by the way, in order to get one of these cards, something I'm about to describe to you, you got to pass a criminal background check. In other words, we want to know who's coming into the country and why they're coming in the country, and we want to help meet an economic need as well as a humanitarian need.

I repeat to you, America should not tolerate a system that has encouraged *coyotes* to flourish. *Coyotes* are the unscrupulous that take a human being who desires to improve his or her life and stuffs them in the back of an 18-wheeler. And in my judgment, a temporary-worker program would put *coyotes* out of business, and society would be better off without them.

We agree in Washington that we need to enforce laws when it comes to hiring illegal workers. See, it's against the law in America to hire an illegal worker. That's what the law says. You can't hire—you can't uphold the law, however, when people are showing up with forged documents. How can you expect your employers to say, you're here legally or not legally, when employers are not document verifiers? And so therefore, a temporary-worker program has got to have a tamper-proof identification card that shows somebody is here legally and so the employer knows that they're not breaking the law.

It makes sense to me to say to our employers, "Sure, you ought to be able to hire somebody, but just make sure they're legally here. And here's a system that encourages you to be able to know that you're hiring somebody who is legally here."

The big issue facing Washington is what to do with people that have been here for quite a while. That's really, I think, the ultimate stumbling block, when you think about it. There's serious disagreement on the issue around the country. First of all, we've got to recognize that there are people who have been here that are newly arrived, and then there are people who have been here for, say, a decade, who have paid their taxes and built a home and raised a family. So the question is, what do you do, what do you do as a society?

The debate really—much of the debate I'm sure you're hearing from is either amnesty or deportation, both of which I'm against. Amnesty means you're automatically a citizen. I don't think that makes sense. It's not fair to those who have waited legally. We got a lot of people waiting to be citizens here, and they've done—they've adhered to our laws, and they're in line— they're in the citizenship line. And I think it would be unfair to those who have been here legally to say to those who have been here illegally that these folks get ahead of you in line. That doesn't make any sense to me, if we're a country that's going to uphold laws.

On the other hand, it makes no sense at all to say we can find people and run them out of the country. For some, I guess that sounds appealing. It's impractical. It's not going to work, and it's not necessary, in my judgment. It's not the right thing to do.

The right thing to do is to recognize that if you've been here illegally, that there ought to be a cost for doing so, but also recognize there are decent, hard-working people that have contributed to our society at the same time. And so I believe here's a way to work out—work through this problem. One is to say, you got to pay a fine for being here illegally. You've got to learn the English language. In other words, you got to pay—repay a debt to society and learn the skills necessary to assimilate into our society. Show us you've been working hard. In other words, there's a way to verify your contributions to our society. And then, if you want to be a citizen, you can get in line to be a citizen, but not at the head of the line—you get to get at the back of the line.

And to me, that is a humane, decent way of addressing a very difficult problem that Congress is going to have to wrestle with. I believe we ought to differentiate between those who've been here for a long period of time and those who are newly arrived. I know we need to treat people with respect and dignity. I think the best way to assure the American people that we're a nation of laws and a compassionate nation at the same time is to say, "Pay your debt to society, and if you choose to be a citizen, you can; just you wait in line at the back, not in the beginning."

See, there are lines for people who want to become a citizen, and they're based upon nationality. And Congress can determine the length of the line if they want. If the line is too long for Irish people or people from different countries or Mexicans, then increase the number of green cards. If the people are worried about the number of citizens all of a sudden becoming eligible for citizenship, you can decrease the number of green cards. But in the meantime, we need to treat people with respect.

This is a tough debate for America; it really is. It's a tough debate because it's one in which the language can sometimes send the wrong signals about what we're about. People are very emotional about this issue. And my admonition to people who are concerned about the immigration debate is to remember that language can send signals about who we are as a nation, that harsh, ugly rhetoric on the debate tends to divide our country. It tends to forget the values that have made us great.

The values that made us great is that we're a nation that have been united by common ideals, proud of our history, proud of our flag, understanding of the need to have a common language, and at the same time, a society whose soul has been uplifted constantly by the fact that people have come to our country to realize a dream: the dream of working hard and improving their lot in life, the dream of putting food on the table, and at the same time, hoping the child goes to college, the dream of owning their own businesses. That's uniquely American. It enables me to say to the American people that "one Nation under God" means something. And we must never lose that spirit.

For people in Washington, DC, now's the time to get something done. It's important for our elected leaders to understand, if you're going to address the issue of immigration, you've got to address all aspects of the immigration. It's got to be a comprehensive bill if we want there to be an effective bill.

People say, "Well, you know, Mr. President, it looks impossible that something's going to happen." I disagree. American people want something to happen. They expect us as people elected to office to work together to get something done in a positive way. That's what they expect of us. And I'm going to continue traveling this country reminding the people that we have got an opportunity to put together a comprehensive package to reform the system to make it work, a system that will enforce our border and a system that will reinforce our values.

I want to thank you for giving me a chance to come and talk to you about this important issue. I'm really glad to be back in Omaha, Nebraska. May God bless you all, and may God continue to bless our country.

NOTE: The President spoke at 8:32 a.m. at the Metropolitan Community College— South Omaha Campus. In his remarks, he referred to Gov. Dave Heineman of Nebraska and his wife, Sally; and Jo Ann C. "Jody" McDowell, president, and Heather Fowler, student ex officio, Metropolitan Community College.

Remarks at a Swearing-In Ceremony for Dirk Kempthorne as Secretary of the Interior
June 7, 2006

Thank you all. Please be seated. Welcome to the White House. Laura and I are thrilled you are here to witness the swearing-in of Dirk Kempthorne as our Nation's 49th Secretary of the Interior.

We welcome Dirk's family, particularly his wife, Patricia, and his children, Heather and Jeff. Thank you all for being here. I'm really happy Dirk's dad, Jim, is with us. I sure appreciate you being here, Mr.

Kempthorne. I want to thank all the other friends of the Kempthorne family and members of the family who have joined us here today.

I found it interesting that when Dirk and Patricia were married, they chose a wedding ceremony at sunrise high atop Idaho's Moscow Mountain. It's an interesting commitment to make, isn't it? [*Laughter*] And an interesting place to make the commitment. It shows a love of—Dirk's love for his wife and their mutual love for nature. And one of the reasons I picked Dirk Kempthorne is because of his love of the beautiful country that we are fortunate to call America. That's why I picked him.

I want to appreciate the Vice President joining us today. Mr. Vice President, welcome. Thank you for being here, sir. I want to thank Justice Scalia for joining us, to administer the oath of office.

Dirk, you must be given a lot of these, kind of, swearing-in ceremonies, and we generally don't have a man of such esteem join us in a situation like this. [*Laughter*]

I appreciate Lynn Scarlett, the Deputy Secretary of the Interior, joining us, as well as all those who work for the Secretary of the Interior. I want to thank members of my Cabinet for being here. Thank you all for coming. Appreciate you taking time out of your day to be here, and I know Dirk does as well. I appreciate Members of the United States Senate who join us, starting with the Senate President pro tem, Ted Stevens. Thank you, Senator, proud you're here—as well as the two Senators from Idaho, Larry Craig and Mike Crapo. Thank you both for joining us. We have the House majority whip with us, Roy Blunt. I see former colleagues of Dirk Kempthorne have joined us as well. Thank you all for coming.

We have the privilege of living in a land of unparalleled beauty. We've got vast mountain ranges and mighty rivers and open plains and spectacular coastlines. These open spaces are shared—are the shared heritage of everybody. They just don't belong to a few people; they belong to all of us. It's the job of the Secretary of the Interior to manage these natural resources in such a way that we can pass them on to future generations, in good shape. That's Dirk's job. There's no doubt in my mind he'll be able to do it well.

Dirk Kempthorne is uniquely qualified for this important position. He is the first Secretary of the Interior to serve as a Governor, a Senator, and a mayor. And each of these positions prepared Dirk well for his new responsibilities.

As Governor of Idaho, Dirk was responsible for managing Idaho's 30 State parks and recreational trails. He proved himself to be an outstanding steward of his State's open spaces. He launched a statewide initiative to fund improvements in the State's parks and public spaces. He created the Idaho Department of Environmental Quality. He established the Governor's Office of Species Conservation. He's a true conservationist, with a track record to prove it.

As a United States Senator, Dirk chaired the Subcommittee on Drinking Water, Fisheries, and Wildlife, and built bipartisan support to enact comprehensive reforms to the Safe Drinking Water Act.

As a former mayor of Boise, Dirk understands that those who live closest to the land know how to manage it best. He understands that while people here in Washington may care deeply about the land, it's the people that's closest to the land that we're going to rely upon to manage those resources. We're going to work closely with local and State leaders to ensure our natural resources are managed wisely.

Dirk takes up his new responsibilities at an important time in our Nation's history, and he follows an outstanding Secretary of the Interior in Gale Norton. Gale was instrumental in establishing the Healthy Forests Initiative to safeguard our forests and woodlands against fire damage. And thanks to her leadership, our administration has reduced the danger of fires by treating or removing hazardous fields from 11 million acres of Federal land so far. Gale also led the effort in Washington to improve our national parks and reduce the park maintenance backlog that we found when we came into office. Dirk is going to continue focusing on our national parks.

After Hurricane Katrina devastated our Nation's gulf coast, Gale helped lead the effort to restore offshore energy production. She worked tirelessly to prevent a massive energy disruption that could have crippled our economy. America is a better place because of Gale Norton's leadership.

Dirk Kempthorne is going to build upon the strong foundation left by Gale Norton. He's going to continue my administration's effort to conserve our land and water and air resources. He's going to work to improve our national parks. He's going to preserve our Nation's historic and cultural sites. He'll carry forward our approach of cooperative conservation by encouraging conservation on both public and private lands in close collaboration with local communities. As we work to reduce our dependence on foreign sources of energy, he

will make sure that any exploration on Federal lands and in Federal waters is done in an environmentally sensitive way. As the Secretary of the Interior, Dirk Kempthorne will make certain that our Nation's natural spaces are cleaner and safer and more productive.

I want to thank Dirk for agreeing to serve our country again. I want to thank his family for supporting him. And now it's my honor to witness the swearing-in of Dirk Kempthorne.

NOTE: The President spoke at 3 p.m. on the South Lawn at the White House. The transcript released by the Office of the Press Secretary also included the remarks of Justice Antonin Scalia and Secretary Kempthorne.

Statement on Senate Passage of Marriage Protection Legislation
June 7, 2006

Today's Senate vote on the marriage protection amendment marks the start of a new chapter in this important national debate. I thank the Senators who supported this amendment, but I am disappointed the Senate did not achieve the necessary number of votes to move the amendment process forward. Our Nation's founders set a high bar for amending our Constitution, and history has shown us that it can take several tries before an amendment builds the two-thirds support it needs in both

houses of Congress. My position on this issue is clear: Marriage is the most fundamental institution of our society, and it should not be redefined by activist judges. The people must be heard on this issue. And as this debate continues, each American deserves to be treated with tolerance, respect, and dignity.

NOTE: The statement referred to S.J. Res. 1.

Statement on Congressional Passage of Broadcast Decency Enforcement Legislation
June 7, 2006

I applaud the Congress for passing S. 193, the Broadcast Decency Enforcement Act. I believe that Government has a responsibility to help strengthen families. This

legislation will make television and radio more family friendly by allowing the FCC to impose stiffer fines on broadcasters who air obscene or indecent programming. I look forward to signing this important legislation into law.

Statement on Congressional Passage on Mine Safety Legislation
June 7, 2006

I am pleased that the Congress has acted in a bipartisan way to pass important mine safety legislation. This legislation will complement the Mine Safety and Health Administration's efforts to enhance mine safety training, improve safety and communications technology, and provide emergency caches of breathable air for miners. The bill also increases penalties for those who violate mine safety laws. America's miners and their families can be confident that their Government is committed to taking measures that will help prevent accidents and save lives. I look forward to signing this bill into law.

NOTE: The statement referred to S. 2803.

Remarks on the Death of Senior Al Qaida Associate Abu Musab Al Zarqawi
June 8, 2006

Good morning. Last night in Iraq, United States military forces killed the terrorist Al Zarqawi. At 6:15 Baghdad time, Special Operation forces, acting on tips and intelligence from Iraqis, confirmed Zarqawi's location and delivered justice to the most wanted terrorist in Iraq.

Zarqawi was the operational commander of the terrorist movement in Iraq. He led a campaign of car bombings, assassinations, and suicide attacks that has taken the lives of many American forces and thousands of innocent Iraqis. Usama bin Laden called this Jordanian terrorist "the prince of Al Qaida in Iraq." He called on the terrorists around the world to listen to him and obey him. Zarqawi personally beheaded American hostages and other civilians in Iraq. He masterminded the destruction of the United Nations headquarters in Baghdad. He was responsible for the assassination of an American diplomat in Jordan and the bombing of a hotel in Amman.

Through his every action, he sought to defeat America and our coalition partners and turn Iraq into a safe haven from which Al Qaida could wage its war on free nations. To achieve these ends, he worked to divide Iraqis and incite civil war. And only last week, he released an audio tape attacking Iraq's elected leaders and denouncing those advocating the end of sectarianism.

Now Zarqawi has met his end, and this violent man will never murder again. Iraqis can be justly proud of their new Government and its early steps to improve their security. And Americans can be enormously proud of the men and women of our Armed Forces, who worked tirelessly with their Iraqi counterparts to track down this brutal terrorist and to put him out of business.

The operation against Zarqawi was conducted with courage and professionalism by the finest military in the world. Coalition and Iraqi forces persevered through years of near misses and false leads, and they never gave up. Last night their persistence and determination were rewarded. On behalf of all Americans, I congratulate our troops on this remarkable achievement.

Zarqawi is dead, but the difficult and necessary mission in Iraq continues. We can expect the terrorists and insurgents to carry on without him. We can expect the sectarian violence to continue. Yet the ideology of terror has lost one of its most visible and aggressive leaders.

Zarqawi's death is a severe blow to Al Qaida. It's a victory in the global war on terror, and it is an opportunity for Iraq's new Government to turn the tide of this struggle. Two minutes ago, I spoke to Prime Minister Maliki. I congratulated him on close collaboration between coalition and Iraqi forces that helped make this day possible. Iraq's freely elected Prime Minister is determined to defeat our common enemies and bring security and the rule of law to all his people.

Earlier this morning, he announced the completion of his Cabinet appointments with the naming of a new Minister of Defense, a new Minister of the Interior, and a new Minister of State for National Security. These new ministers are part of a democratic government that represents all Iraqis. They will play a vital role as the Iraqi Government addresses its top priorities: reconciliation and reconstruction and putting an end to the kidnapings and beheadings and suicide bombings that plague the Iraqi people. I assured Prime Minister Maliki that he will have the full support of the United States of America.

On Monday, I will meet with my national security team and other key members of my Cabinet at Camp David to discuss the way forward in Iraq. Our top diplomats and military commanders in Iraq will give me an assessment of recent changes in the political and economic and security situation on the ground. On Tuesday, Iraq's new Ambassador to the United States will join us, and we will have a teleconference discussion with the Prime Minister and members of his Cabinet. Together we will discuss how to best deploy America's resources in Iraq and achieve our shared goal of an Iraq that can govern itself, defend itself, and sustain itself.

We have tough days ahead of us in Iraq that will require the continued patience of the American people. Yet the developments of the last 24 hours give us renewed confidence in the final outcome of this struggle, the defeat of terrorism threats, and a more peaceful world for our children and grandchildren.

May God bless the Iraqi people, and may God continue to bless America.

NOTE: The President spoke at 7:31 a.m. in the Rose Garden at the White House. In his remarks, he referred to Prime Minister Nuri al-Maliki, Minister of Defense Abd al-Qadir al-Mufriji, Minister of the Interior Jawad al-Bulani, and Minister of State for National Security Shirwan al-Waili of Iraq; Usama bin Laden, leader of the Al Qaida terrorist organization; and Iraq's Ambassador to the U.S. Samir Shakir al-Sumaydi.

Remarks at the National Hispanic Prayer Breakfast
June 8, 2006

Thank you very much, Luis. Thanks for your introduction. Right before we came in, I said, "Luis, how's your school doing?"

See, I got to first know Luis when I went into inner-city Philadelphia, and he said, "I'm starting a school." I said, "How's your school doing?" He said, "Oh, pretty good." He said, "Last year, we had 69 of the 70 graduates from our school go to college."

Luis's school is doing better than pretty good; it's doing great. And we hold out hope to some kid, you know, that it's amazing what results we can achieve in a society when you raise the bar and you say, "I have hope for you; I love you." It's amazing what our country can achieve. And so, Luis, thank you very much for your leadership, and thanks for having me here at the National Hispanic Prayer Breakfast.

I think it is fitting we come together to recognize the importance of prayer and the importance of faith. You see, Americans are a people of faith. And for millions of our citizens, prayer is a daily part of life. In prayer we give thanks for the many blessings bestowed upon us by our Creator. We're blessed with courageous young men and women willing to defend us in time of war. We're blessed with a growing economy and material prosperity. And we're blessed by the diversity and creativity of millions of Hispanic Americans who enrich our great country.

We've got plenty of blessings to give thanks for, and I'm blessed by the fact that millions of Americans, many of whom I've never seen face to face, pray for me and my family. It's one of the great blessings of America, to be President of a land of prayer. So this morning we come together to give our thanks for all our blessings and recognize our Nation's continuing dependence on Divine Providence.

I appreciate the sponsors of this breakfast. It's an important breakfast. This is a time for us to come together in common purpose to say, we're humble enough to be on bended knee. I appreciate my friend Attorney General Al Gonzales for joining us today. It's good to see you, *mi general.* The Director of the Peace Corps, Gaddi Vasquez—thank you for coming, Gaddi. Appreciate you being here. I see Senator Brownback—I think—yes, there he is. [*Laughter*] I know there are other Mem-

bers of the Senate and the Congress who are here. Thank you all for coming today. It's really important that you're here. And I know the participants of this breakfast are glad you're here as well. I appreciate all the pastors and community leaders who are with us here today too. Thanks for coming.

In America, we are a people who profess many different faiths, with some of our citizens embracing no faith at all. In America, all are welcome. No citizen stands above another. In America, what unites us all is our dedication to freedom, and what brings us together today as men and women of faith is our belief that we're all equal and precious in the eyes of the Almighty.

I like to tell people that my job as the President is to promote the fact that people are free to worship however you choose. See, that's what distinguishes us from the Taliban or Al Qaida, that we're free to worship and that we're all equally American. If you're a Christian, Jew, or Muslim, you're equally American. If you choose not to worship, you're equally American.

But I've also said, from my personal perspective, I rely upon the Almighty for strength and comfort. The daily example of our Hispanic communities reminds us that strong faith and strong families can build a better future for all. We are more— we're a more hopeful society because men and women of Hispanic descent have put their faith and values into action.

More than 200,000 Hispanic Americans serve with courage and honor in our military, some of whom are with us today. And we thank you for your service. Our Government is enriched and strengthened by the Latinos who serve here in Washington, DC. Across America, Hispanic leaders are serving on the frontlines of our armies of compassion, reaching out to change the lives of brothers and sisters in need, changing this great country one heart, one soul at a time.

I like to remind people that government can hand out money, but government cannot put faith in a person's heart or a sense of purpose in a person's life. The best way to strengthen this country is for people such as yourself to continue to reach out to a neighbor in need, to listen to the universal call to love a neighbor just like you'd like to be loved yourself, to mentor to a child who needs to learn to read, to feed the hungry, to provide shelter for the homeless.

And that's precisely what the leaders in this room do. You're inspired by prayer; you move to action. And America is better off when you go into our neighborhoods to reach out to those who hurt, to provide comfort for those who are sick, to say loud and clear to a brother and sister in need, "We love you, and what can we do to help you?" On behalf of a grateful nation, I thank you for being soldiers in the armies of compassion and for making America a hopeful place for more of our citizens.

Speaking about a hopeful place, it is important for us in this important debate on immigration to remember that we've always been a hopeful nation. We are a land of immigrants. We're a country when people—we're a compassionate people. We're also a nation of laws, and being a nation of laws is not contradictory with being a compassionate country. We can enforce our laws. And we can treat people with respect and treat people with dignity and remember our heritage as a nation.

The immigration system isn't working today, and it needs to be fixed. Our borders need to be secure. The American people from all walks of life expect the Government to secure our border, and we will do that.

The system isn't fixed—the system is broken because we've got too many citizens, too many people here, too many people living in our country, living in the shadows of our society, beyond the reach of the law. That's not the America I know. The America I know is one in which people

are treated with respect; the America I know is one in which when we see something broken, we fix it.

So we'll secure our borders. We'll make sure people who hire people illegally pay a fine. But I want our fellow citizens to understand, you cannot secure our borders and you cannot be a compassionate society unless we provide a legal channel for people to work in America. We've got people coming across our borders who want to come and work and put food on the table for their families.

When I was Governor of Texas, I reminded people, family values do not stop at the Rio Grande River. There are people who are coming to our country who are doing jobs Americans are not doing. And we need a legal and orderly system. If we want to enforce the border, we must have a system that says, "You don't have to sneak across our border in order to find work. You don't need to risk your life."

So therefore, I strongly support and call upon the Congress to support the temporary-worker program that says, "You can come into our country legally"—so that we can match willing worker with willing employer, doing jobs Americans are not doing—"and you can come for a period of time, and you can work, and then you can go home in an orderly way as well."

The other part of this debate that's really important is what do we do with the folks that are here. See, there's a difference between those who have newly arrived that are doing work and those who have been here for quite a period of time. We've got people in this country who have paid their taxes, own a home, whose children are becoming valedictorians in high schools and colleges—people have been working hard.

This debate is—there's a heated debate on this subject here in Washington. There are some who say, "Well, best thing to do is just call them citizens right off the bat." I disagree with that. It's called amnesty. I don't think that would be fair to those who are legally here and are waiting in line to become a citizen. You probably know many such citizens. They're here legally, and they say, "We want to be a citizen of your country," and we said, "Fine, get in line and wait." Granting amnesty to those folks who have been here illegally would be unfair to those who have been here legally. We're a nation of laws, and we must uphold the laws.

And then there are those here in Washington who say, "Why don't we just find the folks and send them home." That isn't going to work. That's not a good idea. It sounds simple; it's impractical. There's a reasonable middle ground. There's a reasonable way to uphold our laws and treat people with respect, and that is this: If you've paid your taxes, you've been here for awhile, you can prove that you've been working, you've got a clean background; if you want to become a citizen, you pay a fine, you learn English, you learn the values and ideals of America that have made us one Nation under God. And then if you want to be a citizen, you can get in line,but in the back of the line, not the front of the line. You can wait in line like those who have been legally here in America. We don't have to choose between the extremes. There's a rational middle ground.

I call upon Congress to enact commonsense immigration reform that enforces our border, that upholds our laws, that treats people with respect, and remembers the greatness of America is the fact that we've been able to come from different backgrounds, united under the common ideals of our country, and we live one Nation under God.

For centuries, people have come to this Nation because it is the land of promise. It's a place where people can realize their dreams. Yesterday I was in Omaha, Nebraska, at a Catholic Charities institute that was helping people learn English and learn the ideals of our country. I remember walking into a civics class, and the people were slightly startled to see the President walk in. I guess it's kind of the ultimate civics

lesson. [*Laughter*] But I was proud to be there. I really was.

And we sat down with a group of folks at a table to discuss entrepreneurship. And I went around the room asking, how long have you been here, and what are you doing? And I remember coming to the fellow, Pina—I think his name was Federico Pina. He said he started a couple years ago a automobile maintenance business. He said it was a dream of his to have his own business. I said, "How's it going?" He said, "Well, I've employed three people, and I own my own building." Here's a man who came to our country with a dream, and he's realizing that dream.

And what our citizens have got to understand is that if you're able to maintain a sense of hope in the United States, and people work hard to realize that hope, it inspires our Nation as a whole. It lifts our spirit. It reinvigorates what America is all about.

We have a great opportunity here in Washington to remember the traditions and history of the United States of America and to uplift that sense that America is a welcoming society, a country of law, but a country that also says, "If you work hard and dream big dreams, you can realize your dreams." And many of those who are in our country who are working hard to realize their dreams also rely upon a higher power to help them realize those dreams. And so I'm here to say thank you for your prayers, thank you for your example, thank you for helping your fellow citizens, and thank you for being great citizens of the United States of America.

Que Dios les bendiga.

NOTE: The President spoke at 8:08 a.m. at the J.W. Marriott Hotel. In his remarks, he referred to Rev. Luis Cortes, Jr., president and chief executive officer, Esperanza USA, who introduced the President; and Salavador Pina, owner, Pina's Auto Repair in Omaha, NE.

Remarks Following a Meeting With Governors on the Line-Item Veto
June 8, 2006

Appreciate some of our Nation's finest Governors joining us today. We talked about a couple of things. The first thing I did was bring the Governors up to date on recent successes we've had in Iraq. I talked about my discussion with Prime Minister Maliki, about the fact that he's completed his cabinet. I also told them that I had talked to our commanders and congratulated them on bringing Mr. Zarqawi to justice.

I thanked our Governors for being such strong commanders in chief. I hope they take a message back to their respective Guard units, how much our country appreciates their service, and I hope they also take the message back that we appreciate the service of their families.

We also talked about fiscal discipline, how the executive branch can have certain tools to work with the legislative branch to make sure that they're—responsible spending. Every one of these Governors have got a line-item veto, and they've used it wisely, and they shared their experiences with me. And the reason they did so is because we're urging Congress to give this President and future Presidents the opportunity to be able to have what is very much similar to a line-item veto. And the American people expect their money to be spent wisely. The President needs to have a tool to be able to work with the Congress so that that money is spent wisely.

I appreciate the support of both Republicans and Democrats on the Hill in supporting the bill that we've submitted. I urge the Congress to pass this type of legislation so that we can work together to get our deficit cut in half by 2009, but, more importantly, assure the American people that we're being wise about how we use their money.

I thank you all very much. Thank you all for coming. I appreciate it.

NOTE: The President spoke at 10:50 a.m. in the Roosevelt Room at the White House. In his remarks, he referred to Prime Minister Nuri al-Maliki of Iraq; and senior Al Qaida associate Abu Musab Al Zarqawi, who was killed in Baquba, Iraq, on June 7.

Remarks Following Discussions With President Michelle Bachelet Jeria of Chile
June 8, 2006

President Bush. It is such an honor for me to welcome to the Oval Office the President of Chile. Madam President, welcome.

President Bachelet. Thank you.

President Bush. I was told ahead of time that I was to meet a very charming person, and my briefers were right. I appreciate very much your dedication to values that are important: human rights and human decency, the right for people to be able to speak freely and to vote. I admire your personal story. I also thought it was very interesting that the President, before she came to see me, went by a middle school where she had been educated. It shows that she's dedicated to education and the welfare of the people.

I assured her that the United States of America shares her same sense of social justice and that our desire is to help, when we can, people to become educated so they can realize their dreams.

We talked about the neighborhood. She shared with me her strategy to encourage there to be peaceful development and prosperous development. I assured the President that I'm very interested in her points of view. I look forward to working with you. The neighborhood is very important to the United States of America; it's very important for our country to be engaged and working with friends and allies to help others. And so I've been looking forward to this meeting for quite a while. We've got very good relations with Chile, and I intend to keep them that way.

And Madam President, you're welcome. I'm really glad you're here.

President Bachelet. Thank you, Mr. President.

[*At this point, President Bachelet spoke in Spanish, and no translation was provided.*]

President Bachelet. I am very glad to be here, and as President Bush has said, Chile and the United States have very good relationships, and we'll continue that way. And we have political, commercial relationships,

and we have been—we really are happy of how our relations have developed. And we have talked and shared opinions about how we can build peace, how can we fight together against poverty, for social justice, how we can help strengthen democracy in the region. And how we also can look at the issues as energy innovation, education, health, and so on.

It's for me an honor to be here. And as I live here as a child and then as an adult, it's always for me a wonderful possibility to be in a country where I have learned to love the American people, where I learned to—some experiences as how you can live in a country with difference, with different cultures, tradition, the different ethnic groups, and that's possible, and how you can integrate. And we want to integrate more in the region; we want to continue developing the best relationships with the United States, with the Government; and we hope we succeed in this covenant.

Thank you; Mr. President.

President Bush. Thank you, appreciate it.

NOTE: The President spoke at 11:50 a.m. in the Oval Office at the White House.

Joint Statement Between the United States of America and the Republic of Chile
June 8, 2006

Presidents George W. Bush and Michelle Bachelet underscored the increasingly strong and close ties that Chile and the United States enjoy, based on common values and objectives, including the promotion of democracy, development, economic growth, hemispheric integration, trade liberalization, international security, and combating terrorism. They recognized the link among development, peace, security, human rights, and social justice. They reaffirmed their commitment to further

strengthen the bilateral relationship based on these principles and to deepen the two nations' ongoing strategic dialogue on democracy and regional development, and other key shared priorities.

They agreed that Chile and the United States, like all the peoples of the Americas, are united by ties, and by common aspirations, expressed in the founding Charter of the Organization of American States, which says: "The historic mission of America is to offer man a land of liberty and a favorable environment for the development of his personality and the realization of his just aspirations."

They agreed that the important measure of governments is whether they are committed in principle and in practice to the core conditions of democracy: to govern justly, to advance economic freedom, and to invest in their people. They agreed that a consensus in support of democratic governance unites our hemisphere and is enshrined in the Inter-American Democratic Charter, which declares that the people of our hemisphere have a right to democracy and that their governments have a responsibility to protect and promote that right, and that democracy is essential for the social, political, and economic development of the people of the Americas.

They agreed that the success of democracy in the Americas has produced increased expectations, and that in free societies citizens rightly insist that people should not go hungry, that every child deserves the opportunity for a decent education, and that hard work and initiative should be rewarded. The Presidents agreed that if democracy is to answer popular demands for development, if it is to help reduce poverty and inequality, then democratic institutions must be effective and responsive; that institutions like political parties, the police, and an independent judiciary must be representative of and accountable to the people; that institutions must be reformed to fight corruption and to function transparently; and that every democracy must have the strength to create opportunities for improved health and education for all of its citizens. For men and women who are committed to freedom, who work hard and play by the rules, democratic governments must eliminate policies and practices that interfere with opportunities to rise as high as their talents will take them. That is how we define social justice.

The Presidents recognized that the democracies of the Americas have now forged a consensus on the vital link between security and prosperity as well as democracy and prosperity. They agreed that in a hemisphere that is becoming more democratic, the central security issue in the Americas is no longer one of state-to-state or military-to-military security, but how we face nontraditional threats such as organized crime, terrorism, delinquency, gangs, natural disasters, pandemics, weapons proliferation, and drug trafficking.

The Presidents agreed to work to make democracy a force for inclusion and empowerment, for effective institutions that will better people's lives in real ways, especially for the most disadvantaged and marginalized, while also recognizing that political and economic freedoms are not quick fixes, but are in fact lasting fixes.

They agreed to partner globally through the U.N. Democracy Fund and the Community of Democracies to support specific democracy promotion initiatives, particularly those aimed at improving democratic governance and strengthening institutions, promoting civil society participation, and sharing regional and trans-regional best practices and experiences. They further agreed to work together to support efforts to strengthen the capacity of the OAS and the Secretary-General to respond effectively to threats to democracy in the region and to help countries implement the provisions of the Charter.

The Presidents also reaffirmed their commitment to working to ensure a successful and ambitious conclusion of the Doha Round in the near future. In this context, President Bachelet welcomed President Bush's reaffirmation that the United States is ready to eliminate all tariffs, subsidies, and other barriers to the free flow of goods and services as other nations do the same.

Reaffirming the WTO Agreement on Trade-Related Aspects of Intellectual Property Rights (TRIPS), they acknowledged that the protection and enforcement of intellectual property rights should contribute

to the promotion of technological innovation to the mutual advantage of producers
and users of technological knowledge and
in a manner conducive to social and economic welfare. The leaders agreed to promote innovation and technological advancement by providing strong intellectual property protection and effective enforcement
of intellectual property rights.

The Presidents acknowledged that economic growth and job creation are vital to
reducing poverty and inequality and advancing human development, and that free
trade is the key and their vision remains
a Free Trade Area of the Americas, in the
world's largest free trade community. The
Presidents noted the importance of continuing efforts to promote trade liberalization and reaffirmed their commitment to
the FTAA. They also observed that efforts
toward economic and trade integration in
the Americas are important tools for the
promotion of prosperity, stability, and democracy in the region. They welcomed
agreement by the IMF and World Bank
to provide 100 percent debt relief for the
poorest countries in our hemisphere. In addition, they agreed that the Inter-American
Development Bank also should act to reduce the debt burden on the poorest countries. Collectively, these actions will ensure

that more resources are available to invest
in health and education.

The Presidents expressed their commitment to ensure that political stability, democracy, and development take firm root
in Haiti. They welcomed, as hemispheric
partners in this effort to support democracy, the successful outcome of presidential
and legislative elections held in February
and April and expressed support for the
new Government's efforts to respond to urgent social needs while aiming to achieve
sustainable growth and poverty reduction.

The Presidents noted with satisfaction
the activities of our continuing cooperation
in the areas of economic growth, trade, cultural, people-to-people, and military exchanges. The Presidents agreed to intensively explore opportunities for people-to-
people exchanges, including graduate doc-
toral education and English language education.

The Presidents reaffirmed their friendship and their commitment to further
strengthening ties between the two nations
to foster freedom, democracy, security, and
prosperity.

NOTE: The transcript was released by the Office of the Press Secretary on June 9. An
original was not available for verification of
the content of this joint statement.

The President's News Conference With Prime Minister Anders Fogh Rasmussen of Denmark at Camp David, Maryland
June 9, 2006

President Bush. Good day. Welcome to
Camp David. More importantly, welcome
to Camp David to the Prime Minister and
his wife. Mr. Prime Minister, we're glad
you're here. Welcome.

The invitation to come to Camp David
is an expression of my high regard for
Prime Minister Rasmussen and our friendship between our two countries. You know,

I think—I was checking back; I think it's
been over 2 years since we've had a foreign
leader come and visit us here. And thanks
for bringing such good weather. It's important to have good weather today, because
the Prime Minister is going to give me
a mountain biking lesson after this news
conference.

A couple of thoughts, and then he's going to speak, and then we'd be glad to answer some questions.

First, I appreciate the Prime Minister's belief that freedom can help change the world and that freedom is universal. We had a really important discussion about our desire to help others realize the great blessings of liberty, particularly in Iraq and Afghanistan. Prime Minister Rasmussen has been a strong believer in supporting the Iraqi Government's desire to live in democracy. I thank you for your courage; I thank you for your country's commitment of troops that are helping make a difference.

We talked about the new Government in Iraq. The Prime Minister has met Prime Minister Maliki; I have not, and so it was very useful for me to hear from him first-hand about the Prime Minister's determination to succeed. I appreciate his understanding of the Prime Minister's desire to set priorities, starting with electricity in Baghdad, security in Baghdad, and dismantling militia groups that are creating havoc.

We discussed our common strategies in Iraq. One of the most important strategies is to make sure that the police force in Iraq is capable of inspiring the population who they're supposed to be protecting. And I believe we took a long—we took a big step toward that when the Prime Minister selected a new Minister of the Interior and—as well as a new Defense Minister.

And so we spent time on that, and we spent time on Afghanistan as well. Prime Minister Rasmussen shared his thoughts with me about President Karzai. We both agree that he's a patriot, that he's the kind of person that we can back and that we will back as this new democracy begins to develop.

We spent time on Iran. We shared thoughts about how to diplomatically solve the problem. And the problem is, the Iranians want to have a nuclear weapon, and they shouldn't have one.

We spent time talking about Darfur, our desire to help the AU forces achieve stability in Darfur. I've spoken out on this subject a lot. I believe there's genocide taking place, and I believe we have a responsibility to work together to bring some security to the poor folks that are being harassed and raped and murdered in the far reaches of Darfur.

The Prime Minister and I share values, and he spent time making sure that I understood his strong belief that when we fight the war on terror and we help new democracies, that we've got to uphold the values that we believe in. And he brought up the Guantanamo issue. And I appreciate the fact that the Prime Minister is concerned about the decisions that I made on—toward Guantanamo. I assured him that we would like to end the Guantanamo. We'd like it to be empty. And we're now in the process of working with countries to repatriate people.

But there are some that, if put out on the streets, could create grave harm to American citizens and other citizens of the world. And therefore, I believe they ought to be tried in courts here in the United States. We will file such court claims once the Supreme Court makes its decision as to whether or not—as to the proper venue for these trials. And we're waiting on our Supreme Court to act.

We talked about bilateral relations. I am impressed by the fact that the Prime Minister is off to the west coast with a message of new technologies and the desire for Denmark to work with some of our venture capitalists and businesses to promote energy independence, for example, and to come up with technologies that will enable a country like ours to become less reliant upon foreign sources of energy.

All in all, we had a very constructive visit, which will be continued over lunch after the bike ride and—presuming he doesn't ride me into the ground. [*Laughter*]

So, Mr. Prime Minister, welcome. Glad you're here.

Prime Minister Rasmussen. Thank you very much, Mr. President. Let me first of all express my gratitude for inviting me to Camp David. I'm very honored to be here. And one could hardly imagine a better venue to spend time for work and pleasure with close friends. So thank you very much.

We have had a very productive meeting this morning at this wonderful setting. First we talked about Iraq. A few weeks ago, I met with the new Iraqi Government, as the President pointed out. It was with a particular sense of respect, I heard the views of the first permanent democratically elected Government in Iraq. I would say that our efforts have not been in vain.

Democracy is what it is all about. We agree on the very reason for being engaged in Iraq: to put an end to oppression and to promote freedom, democracy, and human rights. These are the very values we want to defend. That also gives us strong obligation to live up to those values in every step we take. When unacceptable events happen in Abu Ghraib and when allegations are made about horrific events in Haditha, it is not only a tragedy for the victims; it is damaging to our own efforts and an offense to our very own values. The President has assured me that all allegations will be investigated, and if there has been wrongdoing, then the responsible will be prosecuted.

We are committed to remain in Iraq as long as the Iraqi Government and the U.N. request our assistance and as long as we can make a positive difference.

As the President mentioned, we had also a discussion on Iran. I am pleased that the United States, under the President's leadership, has joined his European allies in presenting a package to the Iranians. It's now up to the Iranians to take advantage of this window of opportunity.

Secondly, we touched upon energy. I strongly share the President's view that energy is a major strategic challenge. I think that transatlantic cooperation can contribute to ensuring energy security and sustainable development. It could, for instance, be in-strumental in developing new energy technologies.

In Denmark, this issue has been a high priority for 30 years. We have focused on renewable energy and energy efficiency, and we are among the leading countries when it comes to developing technologies in that field. It is part of the reason for our strong economy and competitiveness. And in Denmark, we have managed to combine economic growth with energy efficiency. Over the last 25 years, the Danish economy has grown by 50 percent without increasing the use of energy.

I think it's fair to say that Danish companies are at the edge in developing new technologies, and they are already engaged in the United States. Some of them are traveling with me to the west coast on Monday.

Which brings me to my final point on our bilateral economic relations. Trade and investment between the United States and Denmark is flourishing at impressive growth rates. The United States is now the biggest foreign investor in Denmark. Likewise, Danish companies have turned their attention towards the United States. Our top five companies have created more than 20,000 jobs in the United States, and they have engaged in a vast number of subcontractors. I think that the broad range of subjects demonstrates the vitality and closeness of our relations.

Mr. President, the health experts tell us that we need daily exercise. So before we even start thinking about lunch, I'm looking forward to exploring Camp David in even greater detail on bike. It's going to be hard work; I know that. But I will do my very best to keep up with you, Mr. President. [*Laughter*]

So once again, thank you very much for your hospitality. Meeting with you at Camp David has indeed been a great symbol of the close and very warm relations between our two countries. Thank you.

President Bush. I'll take a couple of questions. Deb [Deb Riechmann, Associated Press].

Iraq/Abu Musab Al Zarqawi

Q. Mr. President, after meeting with the Danish Prime Minister last month, Maliki said he thought he could stand up the Iraqi security forces in about a year-and-a-half. And with Zarqawi's death, do you think this is realistic?

President Bush. I think it is—we'll get a realistic appraisal about the capacity for standing up Iraqi troops as this new Government begins to function as a government. It wasn't until just a couple of days ago that they didn't had a Defense Minister. Now they've got a Defense Minister, which will give us time to assess their command and control, their capacity to be able to send an order from the top to the bottom of their organization—a Defense Ministry that will be independent from politics, hopefully.

Once we make those assessments, then I think I'll be able to give the American people a better feel for what "stand up/stand down" means. And one of the reasons we're coming here—I'm coming here Monday, by the way, Mr. Prime Minister, with a lot of my Cabinet members to discuss the way forward in Iraq, to analyze the new Government, to look carefully at what their blueprint for the future looks like, and to figure out how we can help. And of course, I will share our thoughts with the Prime Minister, because he's a very important part of our coalition.

Zarqawi's death helps a lot. Zarqawi was bin Laden's main advocate, outside of some remote parts of the world. He was the operator. He was the person that had made the declaration that it's just a matter of time for America and other democracies to leave, so that we could then—so that they could then develop safe haven from which to launch further attacks. He beheaded people; he was a coldblooded killer; he masterminded the bombing of the hotel in Jordan; he masterminded the bombing of the U.N. headquarters early on in the liberation of Iraq.

Removing Zarqawi is a major blow to Al Qaida. It's not going to end the war, and it's certainly not going to end the violence. But it's going to help a lot.

One of the goals of Al Qaida was to encourage sectarian violence inside that country; it was to pit Sunni against Shi'a and Shi'a against Sunni in order to be able to stop democracy. His whole ambition was to stop the advance of democracy in Iraq. And our troops—who performed brilliantly, by the way, in bringing this man to justice—did the Iraqis and the Americans and anybody else who loves freedom a great service by bringing him to justice.

Iraqi Government

Q. Can I ask you a followup?
President Bush. Probably not.
Q. How long will——
President Bush. Yes.
Q. You said you'd have to reassess with the new Government these various things. How long do you think that that assessment is going to take?
President Bush. See, part of the issue I deal with is people want to know with certainty when certain things are going to happen, and I understand that; it's a legitimate question. It's like, when are you going to withdraw troops? And the answer is, when conditions on the ground——
Q. I didn't ask that.
President Bush. No, I know, but I'm—you asked the question; I answer them. The answer is, as to when we'll be able to stand up Iraqis and stand down, when we'll be able to analyze the situation, depends upon how these people react—how they react to pressure, how they react to forming their Government. This is a brand new democracy. And the problem with the war we have is it requires a certain degree of patience in order to succeed. And we have to be patient here, as this new democracy

begins to flourish and has to deal with people like Zarqawi who is trying to stop their advance.

And so, as soon as possible. I've told the American people I'd like to get our troops out as soon as possible. But the definition of "as soon as possible" is depending upon victory in Iraq. And victory in Iraq is a country that can sustain itself, govern itself, and defend itself. That's the definition of victory, and we're making progress toward that goal.

Here you go.

Iran

Q. Mr. President, Mr. Prime Minister, last week, we saw a major change in the policy towards Iran. And although you don't want to talk about timetables, the Prime Minister talked about a window of opportunity for the Iranians. How do you see that window of opportunity? What is the timetable, and what will be the next step in the procedure when we talk about Iran?

President Bush. Thank you. Actually, you saw a shift in tactics but not a shift in strategy. I've always felt like we needed to solve this problem diplomatically. And I always felt it was essential that when the Iranians looked out at the world, they see a common, united group of nations saying, "No nuclear weapon."

Part of the change in tactics was to do two things: One, say to the Iranians, "The choice is yours to make," see. "You have said you're going to verifiably suspend your program. Now we're going to see whether or not you really mean it. And if you do, by the way, the United States will come to the table." And I said to our friends and partners, "If they choose not to come back—to suspend verifiably, there must be a consequence." There must be a sense of urgency on our part to send a common message to them. And I applaud my Secretary of State for effectively delivering that message.

And so to answer your question, we've given the Iranians a limited period of time—weeks, not months—to digest a proposal to move forward. And if they choose not to verifiably suspend their program, then there will be action taken in the U.N. Security Council.

Caren [Caren Bohan, Reuters].

Abu Musab Al Zarqawi

Q. Thank you, Mr. President. Your initial public comments on the death of Zarqawi have been described as more cautious than other developments, such as the capture of Saddam Hussein. Are you more cautious now? And, if so, why?

President Bush. Well, let me make sure everybody understands, I'm thrilled that Zarqawi was brought to justice. And I am so proud of our troops and intelligence officers who brought him to justice. This man had a lot of blood on his hands. He killed a lot of people. And it's a big deal to have brought him to justice. Having said that, I don't want the American people to think that a war is won with the death of one person that—we have still more work to do.

I am confident that Al Qaida will try to regroup and kill other people in order to say, "Well, we haven't lost our way." I believe that. I also know that there are criminal elements and irritated people inside of Iraq who will try to stop the progress of the Government; they will continue to bomb.

The problem we have in this war is that all they've got to do is kill some innocent people by a car bomb, and it looks like they're winning, see. It takes a major event like an election or the death of Zarqawi to understand that we're making progress. And so one of the things I'm trying to be is realistic with the American people and say, there's still going to be tough days ahead because the enemy has got the capacity to get on our TV screens with death and destruction. That's what they've got the capacity to do.

In the meantime, however, the political process—remember, a government that can sustain itself and govern itself and defend itself. Well, the governance aspect, as the Prime Minister will attest, is making progress under Prime Minister Maliki. It's a new type of government. It's a unity Government that represents the Iraqi people under a Constitution which they ratified, which is a remarkable feat, by the way, in the Middle East. A government that can defend itself, and that is, a government with an army that's well-trained, with a chain of command that's responsive to civilian leadership.

And finally, a government that can sustain itself is one that not only has an economic—a bright economic future for its people, but one in which the internal security is such that people have confidence in their Government. And frankly, that's the area where we need a lot of work, which is in the police forces. The Interior Minister was dominated by politicians that wanted to seek revenge, as opposed to provide blanket security. And as General Casey has said, "The—training our troops—training the police is the mission of our troops for 2006." And I want to thank the Prime Minister for his great contribution through NATO and the police training academies that we're helping to run.

But we're making progress. But I don't want—I want the people to understand that our progress will be viewed as incremental progress. If I didn't think we would succeed, I wouldn't stay. And if I didn't think it was necessary for peace, I wouldn't have put our troops there in the first place. And I told that to the Prime Minister. I said you can count on America for standing by this new Government, because we're doing the right thing. And people are going to look back at this moment in history and say a democracy in Iraq helped change the world for the better and helped provide security. It certainly helped address the simmering resentment that exists in a part of a region that for too long has been ignored, see.

And some say, I understand, that liberty isn't universal; therefore, we shouldn't worry about freeing people of Iraq. I strongly disagree with that. Liberty is universal. And not only in our attempts to defend ourselves—we also have got to understand that to help win hearts and minds, freedom is an avenue that will help do that. We've got to be confident in our belief in freedom and confident in our knowledge that freedom has the capacity to yield the peace we want.

Abu Ghraib Prison/Situation in Iraq

Q. Mr. President and Mr. Prime Minister, in previous meetings, you have discussed Guantanamo, Abu Ghraib, and now Haditha, and possibly other crimes have been added to that list.

Mr. President, how did you try to convince the Prime Minister today that that kind of violations of human rights will stop and guilty will be prosecuted? And for Mr. Prime Minister, are you today convinced that violations of human rights will stop so that these violations are not undermining the war for democracy in Iraq? Thank you.

President Bush. You know, the last time—I think it was in Denmark, we talked about Abu Ghraib, if I'm not mistaken. Yes. I told the people in Denmark—on your soil—that it was a disgusting event. It soiled our soul. It's not what America stands for. I also—I'm not sure I put it this way, but I understand humans make mistakes, but there needs to be accountability. And since then, those involved with the Abu Ghraib have been brought to justice. And that's what happens in transparent societies— which, by the way, stood in stark contrast to the society that Saddam Hussein ran, where there was no justice, where there was no transparency, where people weren't given a chance to take their case in front of an impartial court. But that's what's happened here in America.

I'm like the Prime Minister; I understand that these incidents run contrary to what we believe; I know that. But I also want to assure—I assured the Prime Minister that they'll be dealt with. That's what societies like ours do. I can't guarantee success all across the front, but I can guarantee there will be justice.

Prime Minister Rasmussen. I'm very much in line with that. What we have seen in Abu Ghraib is not, was not what we are standing for. If the allegations concerning Haditha show up to be true, it is definitely not what the coalition, what America, what Denmark stands for. On the contrary, we are in Iraq to promote freedom, democracy, respect for human rights. And, of course, we should comply with these basic principles in all our behavior.

I can give no guarantee, but just like the President, I can give the guarantee that in free and open societies, the whole process will be transparent. And if there are wrongdoings, the responsible will be prosecuted. That's a guarantee you can give in a free and open society based on the rule of law.

The President. Bret [Bret Baier, FOX News].

Abu Musab Al Zarqawi/War on Terror

Q. Mr. President——

President Bush. Fine looking shoes you've got on there. [*Laughter*]

Q. Thank you, sir. Mr. President, what are your top commanders telling you, in the last 48 hours, about the possible impact of Zarqawi's death? And how does that affect what you are trying to accomplish in these strategy meetings here in Camp David, Monday and Tuesday?

President Bush. First, we had the strategy meetings scheduled before Zarqawi's death, interestingly enough. I haven't spoken to our commanders yet, except to call General Casey and McChrystal and congratulate them but, more importantly, for them to congratulate the troops and the intel groups that were working on finding Zarqawi.

I suspect they will tell you what I just said, answered to Caren, and that is that

it's a big deal, but it's certainly not the end of conflict. We had some—we believed that Al Qaida was stirring up violence inside of Baghdad. And one of the things the Prime Minister told the Prime Minister and me by phone, that the security of Baghdad is a central part of having a strategy that shows the Iraqi people that the Government is capable of governing and achieving objectives. And therefore, if Al Qaida was a part of—not the sole source, but a part of the violence inside of Baghdad, it helps to get rid of their commander.

It's also a—General Abizaid, whose job it is to think beyond just Iraq—he's the CENTCOM; he's the theater commander—will tell you that the upper management of Al Qaida was counting on Zarqawi to help implement their vision beyond Iraq.

See, it's really important for the American people to understand that Al Qaida has got an ideology and a strategy to impose that ideology. And part of the strategy is to create turmoil in moderate Muslim nations. And they want to overthrow moderate Muslim nations. They want to have their view of the world. I call it totalitarian, Islamo-fascism. Whatever you want to call it, it is extreme, and it's real. And Zarqawi was the implementer of that strategy, and he can no longer implement. And that is helpful in winning the war on terror.

Iraq is a theater in the war on terror; it's not the war on terror. It's a part of the war on terror. And Zarqawi was a general inside of Iraq, and he was a part of their strategy outside of Iraq. And I suspect General Abizaid—I don't mean to be putting words into one of our top commanders, but I would suspect he would say this was a major blow to Al Qaida.

The death of Zarqawi was very important for the people of Iraq. He was sowing incredible violence inside of Iraq. He promoted spectacular death. And by the way, he talked about human rights abuses, and we definitely need to be held to account. But the world needs to hold to account terrorists for civil rights abuses too. The killing of innocent people to achieve a military objective is the cornerstone of Al Qaida's military strategy. And this world of ours—it's no question we ought to be concerned about what the United States does. But I expect the free world, as well, to unite in condemnation of terrorist activities around the world. See, there ought to be a universal condemnation. We ought not to excuse that kind of behavior.

And yesterday's action—or a couple of days ago action, expressed our disdain for that kind of killing of innocent life. And bringing him to justice is a positive thing.

It's important for the Iraqi people to see progress in the death of Zarqawi. There's no question progress toward more stable— it's not going to solve all problems. And I'm sure, as I mentioned to you, there's going to be some who step up and say, "We will teach you a lesson, and we will continue to send suiciders into neighborhoods just to show that we've still got power." But they've lost their general. They've lost the person that the top management of Al Qaida was counting on. And it's a positive development.

Upcoming Meeting on Iraq

Q. Is there specific goals for Monday and Tuesday?

President Bush. Specific goals for Monday and Tuesday is to review the Iraqi strategy, the Iraqi way forward. In other words, the Prime Minister has put forward a strategy as to how to achieve his objectives, which coincide with our objectives— a nation that can sustain itself, govern itself, and defend itself. And we want to review all aspects of that strategy. I felt that Camp David is a good place to do it because it can be distracting down in Washington, with phone calls and all those kinds of stuff; we can make sure the people involved in senior levels of Government stay focused on the task at hand.

I will be talking to Zal and our commanders just to get assessment. One question I'll ask is precisely the question you

asked. I want to get a feel for their view of the Iraqi Government's plans and how we can help Iraq achieve the objectives they want. And then the next day, we're going to have the Ambassador from Iraq to the United States up to talk with him, as well as have a Cabinet meeting between my government and the Maliki Government via secure video. And I think that will be a very interesting moment for the Iraqi Government, to see that we're concerned and interested about their plans for success. And I think it will be interesting for us to be able to get a sense for the type of people that the Prime Minister has attracted.

Ask Anders a question, will you? He's feeling a little defensive. [*Laughter*]

Central Intelligence Agency

Q. I'm sorry, I have one for you, Mr. President. This week, a report from the European Council talked about some CIA flights, illegal CIA flights with the prisoners in Europe, and illegal CIA presence also in some European countries. Have these flights taken place, and did you discuss this in your meeting today?

President Bush. We haven't discussed it yet. I suspect we will now that you brought it up. I would just—I can tell you what I'll tell the Prime Minister, is that in cases where we're not able to extradite somebody who is dangerous, sometimes renditions take place. It's been a part of our Government for quite a period of time—not just my Government, but previous administrations have done so in order to protect people. And as we do so, we protect the sovereign rights of nations that we're involved with.

Okay, thanks for the press conference. Enjoy yourselves. Get out of here. [*Laughter*] Welcome, glad you all are here.

Q. Are you guys going to race?

President Bush. No, we're old—one of us is old. [*Laughter*] I'm taking a lesson.

NOTE: The President's news conference began at 10:43 a.m. In his remarks, he referred to Anne-Mette Rasmussen, wife of Prime Minister Rasmussen; Prime Minister Nuri al-Maliki, Minister of the Interior Jawad al-Bulani, Minister of Defense Abu al-Qadir al-Mufriji, and former President Saddam Hussein of Iraq; President Hamid Karzai of Afghanistan; senior Al Qaida associate Abu Musab Al Zarqawi, who was killed in Baquba, Iraq, on June 7; Usama bin Laden, leader of the Al Qaida terrorist organization; Gen. George W. Casey, Jr., USA, commanding general, Multi-National Force—Iraq; Lt. Gen. Stanley A. McChrystal, USA, commander, Joint Special Operations Command, U.S. Central Command Forward, U.S. Special Operations Command; Gen. John P. Abizaid, USA, commander, U.S. Central Command; U.S. Ambassador to Iraq Zalmay Khalilzad; and Iraq's Ambassador to the U.S. Samir Shakir al-Sumaydi.

The President's Radio Address
June 10, 2006

Good morning. This was a good week for the cause of freedom. On Wednesday night in Iraq, U.S. military forces killed the terrorist Zarqawi.

The killing of Zarqawi is an important victory in the global war on terror. This Jordanian-born terrorist was the operational commander of Al Qaida in Iraq. He led a campaign of car bombings and kidnapings and suicide attacks that has taken the lives of many American forces, international aid workers, and thousands of innocent Iraqis. Zarqawi had a long history of murder and bloodshed. Before September the 11th, 2001, he ran a camp in Afghanistan that trained terrorists, until coalition forces destroyed that camp. He fled to Iraq, where he received medical care and set up operations with terrorist associates.

After the fall of Saddam, Zarqawi went underground and declared his allegiance to Usama bin Laden, who called him the "Prince of Al Qaida in Iraq" and instructed terrorists around the world to "listen to him and obey him." Zarqawi personally beheaded American hostages and other civilians in Iraq. He masterminded the destruction of the United Nations headquarters in Baghdad, and he was responsible for the assassination of an American diplomat in Jordan and the bombing of hotels in Amman. His goals in Iraq were clear: He wanted to stop the rise of democracy, drive coalition forces out, incite a civil war, and turn that country into a safe haven from which Al Qaida could launch new attacks on America and other free nations. Instead, Zarqawi died in the free and democratic Iraq that he fought so hard to prevent, and the world is better off because this violent man will never kill again.

Iraqis can be justly proud of their new Government and its early steps to improve their security. And Americans can be enormously proud of the men and women of our Armed Forces and the intelligence officers who support them. In the past 3 years, our troops have overthrown a cruel dictator, fought the terrorists and insurgents house to house, and trained Iraqi forces to defend their new democracy. All the while, they stayed on the trail of this brutal terrorist, persevering through years of near misses and false leads and never giving up hope. This week, they got their man. And all Americans are grateful for their remarkable achievement.

Zarqawi is dead, but the difficult and necessary mission in Iraq continues. In the weeks ahead, violence in Iraq may escalate. The terrorists and insurgents will seek to prove that they can carry on without

Zarqawi. And coalition and Iraqi forces are seizing this moment to strike the enemies of freedom in Iraq at this time of uncertainty for their cause. The work ahead will require more sacrifice and the continued patience of the American people.

I'm encouraged by Prime Minister Maliki's determination to defeat our common enemies and bring security and rule of law to all Iraqis. This week, he took another major step toward this objective when he completed the formation of his Cabinet, naming a new Minister of Defense, a new Minister of the Interior, and a new Minister of State for National Security. These new leaders will help the Government address its top priorities: reconciliation, reconstruction, and putting an end to the kidnapings, beheadings, and suicide bombings.

As they pursue these goals, they will have America's full support. On Monday, I will convene my national security team and other key members of my Cabinet at Camp David to discuss the way ahead in Iraq. On Tuesday, Iraq's new Ambassador to the United States will join us, and we will have a teleconference discussion with Prime Minister Maliki and members of his Cabinet. Together we will determine how to best deploy America's resources in Iraq and achieve our shared goal of an Iraq that

can govern itself, sustain itself, and defend itself.

There's still difficult work ahead in Iraq. Yet this week, the ideology of terror has suffered a severe blow. Al Qaida has lost its leader in Iraq; the Iraqi people have completed a democratic government that is determined to defend them; and freedom has achieved a great victory in the heart of the Middle East.

Thank you for listening.

NOTE: The address was recorded at 1:45 p.m. on June 8 in the Cabinet Room at the White House for broadcast at 10:06 a.m. on June 10. The transcript was made available by the Office of the Press Secretary on June 9 but was embargoed for release until the broadcast. In his address, the President referred to senior Al Qaida associate Abu Musab Al Zarqawi, who was killed in Baquba, Iraq, on June 7; Usama bin Laden, leader of the Al Qaida terrorist organization; former President Saddam Hussein, Prime Minister Nuri al-Maliki, Minister of Defense Abd al-Qadir al-Mufriji, Minister of the Interior Jawad al-Bulani, and Minister of State for National Security Shirwan al-Waili of Iraq; and Iraq's Ambassador to the U.S. Samir Shakir al-Sumaydi. The Office of the Press Secretary also released a Spanish language transcript of this address.

Remarks Following a Meeting With the Interagency Team on Iraq at Camp David, Maryland
June 12, 2006

I want to thank Generals Abizaid and Casey, as well as Ambassador Khalilzad for the last—for the briefing for the last 3 hours. I thought your assessment of the situation in Iraq was very realistic. I think your recommendations to us on how to win in Iraq, to have an Iraq that can govern itself, sustain itself, and defend itself are—your recommendations are valid.

I look forward to continuing to visit with you later on this afternoon about how we can help this new Government succeed. Zal, you've been—I just want to thank you all very much for remaining in theater and working as hard as you are. You're making a significant difference.

And again, please give my best congratulations to the troops on the ground for bringing Zarqawi to justice. I fully recognize that's not going to end the war. On the other hand, it was a major blow to Al Qaida and the killers and terrorists that are trying to spread violence and suffering and stop the emergence of a new democracy.

Zal, we left off where you were talking about the way forward in Iraq and your perception of this new Government.

NOTE: The President spoke at 12:33 p.m. In his remarks, he referred to Gen. John P. Abizaid, USA, commander, U.S. Central Command; Gen. George W. Casey, Jr., USA, commanding general, Multi-National Force—Iraq; U.S. Ambassador to Iraq Zalmay Khalilzad; and senior Al Qaida associate Abu Musab Al Zarqawi, who was killed in Baquba, Iraq, on June 7. A portion of these remarks could not be verified because the tape was incomplete.

Remarks Following Meetings on Iraq and an Exchange With Reporters at Camp David
June 12, 2006

The President. We just had a meaningful day. We have spent a lot of time talking to our team in Baghdad about the way forward in Iraq. We've spent time talking about the security situation in Iraq and what we intend to do to help the Iraqi Government bring security to neighborhoods in Baghdad and Basra. We talked about the economic situation in Iraq. We talked about the energy situation in Iraq. We talked about a variety of matters with Ambassador Khalilzad and General Casey and General Abizaid.

As you can see, I not only have my national security team here, I've got members of my Cabinet as well. We all agree that we have got to continue to help this new Government move forward. Success in Iraq will depend upon the capacity of the new Government to provide for its people. We recognize that. We're encouraged by the formation of a unity government, and we recognize our responsibilities to help that new Government.

And tomorrow we'll be meeting with the new Government via SVTS, and that will be a very interesting experience for all of us, to be able to talk to our respective counterparts.

The message to the Iraqi Government is, is that we stand with you, that what you're doing is important, that democracy in Iraq is not only important to the 12 million people that went to the polls and their families, but democracy in Iraq is important in the war on terror. It's important that we succeed in Iraq in order to make America more secure and the world a better place.

So I want to thank my Cabinet Secretaries for being with me today, and other members of my team, to really have this very vital and important discussion.

I'll answer a couple of questions.

U.S. Troop Levels in Iraq

Q. You said that you were going to listen to your U.S. commanders on the ground about the troops. And, you know, General Casey has said now that he thinks that gradual U.S. troop reductions could be made in the coming months. So do you agree with this?

The President. Well, as I also said the last time you asked me this question—which was a couple of days ago—that we were going to make sure that we fully understand the Iraqi capability to be able to take the fight to the enemy and secure its country. And the Iraqi Defense Minister is just in office. And General Casey, of course, will be making those assessments, as he told us today via the teleconference—that he will make the proper assessments and come back to us and make recommendations to us.

Whatever we do will be based upon the conditions on the ground. And whatever we do will be toward a strategy of victory. And so this is a process of getting to know the—understand the Iraqi capabilities, particularly the command and control structure, and what our need—we need to do to help them achieve victory.

Abu Musab Al Zarqawi/War on Terror

Q. Mr. President, what do you think of the successor to Zarqawi that was named by Al Qaida? And how do you stop an insurgency that is still able to recruit people and continue to threaten attacks?

The President. I think the successor to Zarqawi is going to be on our list to bring to justice.

What was the second part of your question?

Q. How do you stop an insurgency that continues to be able to recruit people and continues to threaten attacks and carry them out?

The President. The best way to win this war against an insurgency is to stand up a unity government which is capable of defending itself but also providing tangible benefits to the people. The Iraqis have got some wonderful assets. They've got energy, which they can use to the benefit of their people. They're entrepreneurial. They've got a stable currency. They've got a small-business sector that's growing. And, ultimately, the Iraqi people are going to have to make up their mind: Do they want to live in terror, or do they want to live in peace? And the United States and our coalition will help them realize their ambitions if they choose to live in peace and hope, which we believe they will.

Remember, it wasn't all that long ago that 12 million people went to the polls and said, "We want to live in a free society." No question, the fighting is tough. No question, the enemy is violent and mean. But the enemy doesn't stand for anything. They have no message of hope. They have no positive philosophy. All they can do is kill and hope that the Government splits up or that the American people lose their will. And I keep reminding the American people that the stakes are worth it. It is worth it to help Iraq succeed. It is worth it to have a democracy in the Middle East. It is worth it to show other reformers and people who want to live in a free society what is possible.

Q. Mr. President

The President. Yes.

International Support for Iraq

Q. Are you satisfied with what Iraq's neighbors and the international community are doing to help this new Government, or would you like to see them do more, and what should it be?

The President. Iraq's neighbors ought to do more to help them. And we're constantly working with our friends in the neighborhood to encourage them to support this new democracy. And I recognize that there's some concerns about a Shi'a Prime Minister and a—from different countries where there's Sunni representation, Sunni leadership. But our message is, is that Iraq will show that it's possible for people of all faiths to live together. After all, they've got the most modern Constitution in the history of the Middle East.

We expect our friends who have made commitments, $13 billion, to honor those commitments. Many of those countries are outside of the Middle East. And so we'll continue—we discussed that today, as to how to continue to rally not only the neighborhood, Iraq's neighbors, to the cause of the new democracy, but how to help others who have made a pledge to honor their pledge.

Yes.

Energy/Foreign Sources of Oil

Q. Mr. President, did you talk about oil production and maybe getting it back to prewar levels, or anything?

The President. We did. We spent a lot of time in talking about energy and oil. The oil belongs to the Iraqi people. It's their asset. It is one of the—it's—the capacity to generate wealth from the ground distinguishes Iraq from Afghanistan, for example. It's something that I view as a very positive part of Iraqi future. And we talked about how to advise the Government to best use that money for the benefit of the people.

Secondly, obviously, we spent time figuring out how to help strategize with the new ministries as to how to get oil production up. And recently, they've had oil production as high as a little over 2 million barrels a day, which is extremely positive. The oil sector is very much like the rest of the infrastructure of Iraq: Saddam Hussein let it deteriorate. There wasn't much reinvestment or not much modernization. After all, he was using money for his own personal gain, and he wasn't spending the people's money on enhancing the infrastructure. And the oil infrastructure collapsed and deteriorated. And as a result, there's a lot of work that needs to be done on, for example, work-overs, that is, to help old wells become revitalized, see, just a standard maintenance procedure. So there's a maintenance program on to help the Iraqi people get their production up.

There's some unbelievably interesting exploration opportunities. And the new Government is going to have to figure out how best to lease the people's lands in a fair way. My own view is, is that the Government ought to use the oil as a way to unite the country and ought to think about having a tangible fund for the people, so the people have faith in central government.

Listen, thank you all for coming today. And tomorrow is going to be a fascinating day, and I'm looking forward to having discussions with our counterparts via SVTS. Thank you.

NOTE: The President spoke at 3:40 p.m. In his remarks, he referred to U.S. Ambassador to Iraq Zalmay Khalilzad; Gen. George W. Casey, Jr., USA, commanding general, Multi-National Force—Iraq; Gen. John P. Abizaid, USA, commander, U.S. Central Command; Minister of Defense Abd al-Qadir al-Mufriji, Prime Minister Nuri al-Maliki, and former President Saddam Hussein of Iraq; and senior Al Qaida associate Abu Musab Al Zarqawi, who was killed in Baquba, Iraq, on June 7.

Remarks Following Discussions With Prime Minister Nuri al-Maliki of Iraq in Baghdad, Iraq
June 13, 2006

Mr. Prime Minister, thank you for this opportunity to visit with your Cabinet. I have expressed our country's desire to work with you, but I appreciate you recognizing the fact that the future of this country is in your hands. The decisions you and your Cabinet make will be determinate as to whether or not a country succeeds that can govern itself, sustain itself, and defend itself. I'm impressed by the Cabinet that you've assembled. You've assembled people from all parts of your country, representing the different religions and different histories and traditions.

And yet the Cabinet here represents the entire Iraqi people, and I appreciate your commitment to representing the people of Iraq. I'm impressed by the strength of your character and your desire to succeed. And I'm impressed by your strategy. We've discussed—I discussed earlier with the Prime Minister and here with his Cabinet and with members of my Cabinet the strategy necessary to have a country that is capable of answering to the needs of the people.

We discussed the security strategy. We discussed an economic strategy, a reconstruction strategy. And all of it makes sense to me. And so I've come to not only look you in the eye, I've also come to tell you that when America gives its word, it will keep its word; that it's in our interests that Iraq succeed. It's not only in the interests of the Iraqi people, it's in the interests of the American people and for people who love freedom.

Iraq is a part of the war on terror. Iraq is a central front on that war, and when Iraq succeeds in having a government of and by and for the people of Iraq, you will have dealt a serious blow to those who have a vision of darkness, who don't believe in liberty, who are willing to kill the innocent in order to achieve a political objective.

And so, Mr. Prime Minister, I want to thank you for giving me and my Cabinet a chance to hear from you personally and a chance to meet the members of this team you've assembled. It's an impressive group of men and women, and if given the right help, I'm convinced you will succeed, and so will the world.

NOTE: The President spoke at approximately 6:36 p.m. at the U.S. Embassy.

Remarks to United States Military Personnel in Baghdad
June 13, 2006

Thank you all. Thank you for the warm welcome. Thought I'd stop in to say hello. [*Laughter*] I bring greetings from a grateful nation. I thank you for your sacrifice; I thank you for your service; I thank you for making history.

You know, one of the things I try to do is put good people in place who accomplish hard jobs. And I can't think of two better leaders than Zal Khalilzad and General Casey to lead this important effort. I thank you all very much for your service to our country. Your sacrifice is noble, and your sacrifice is important.

I understand long deployments are tough; they're tough on you, and they're tough on your families. And so the first thing I want to tell you is the American people are incredibly grateful for what you do, and I bring their greetings and their thanks for the sacrifices you and your family make.

These are historic times. The mission that you're accomplishing here in Iraq will go down in the history books as an incredibly important moment in the history of freedom and peace, an incredibly important moment of doing our duty to secure our homeland.

You know, right after September the 11th, I knew that some would forget the dangers we face. Some would hope that the world would be what it's not—a peaceful place in which people wouldn't want to do harm to those of us who love freedom. I vowed that day, after September the 11th, to do everything I could to protect the American people. And I was able to make that claim because I knew there were people such as yourself who were willing to be on the frontline in the war on terror.

Baghdad and Iraq is a front in the war on terror. It is a part of our mission to help make sure that the world is a better place. I truly believe the work that you're doing here is laying the foundation of peace for generations to come, and I thank you from the bottom of my heart.

The progress here in Iraq has been remarkable when you really think about it. The people of this country suffered under the hands of a brutal tyrant. And thanks to the United States forces and coalition forces, the people are liberated from the clutches of Saddam Hussein. America is safer, the world is better off, and the Iraqi people have a chance to realize the great blessings of liberty because Saddam Hussein is no longer in power.

Thanks to your hard work, the Iraqi people have been given a chance to go to the polls—not once but three different times—to elect a government that is dedicated to the will of the people. Today I have come to not only thank you but to look Prime Minister Maliki in the eyes, to determine whether or not he is as dedicated to a free Iraq as you are, and I believe he is.

I met with the Cabinet officials from all walks of life here in Iraq and came away with the distinct impression that they are unified in serving the people of Iraq. They want to succeed. The faith and future of Iraq is in their hands, and our job is to help them succeed—and we will.

I have come today to personally show our Nation's commitment to a free Iraq. My message to the Iraqi people is this: Seize the moment; seize this opportunity to develop a government of and by and for the people. And I also have a message to the Iraqi people, that when America gives a commitment, America will keep its commitment.

Our work is not done with the formation of a unity government. This Government is just getting started. And the enemies of a free Iraq will do everything they can to stop the progress. That should tell us something about the enemies of a free Iraq. Who wouldn't want the people's will to be

expressed? Who wouldn't want a government to be able to meet the needs of the people? Those who kill the innocent lives or those who have no concept of liberty have no sense of justice, have no respect for human rights and human dignity.

But I believe the Iraqi Government that's formed does respect human rights and human dignity. It will respond to the will of the people. There are going to be tough days ahead and more sacrifice for Americans as well as Iraqis. But I come here—come away from here believing that the will is strong and the desire to meet the needs of the people is real and tangible.

You know, one of the things that we've got to realize—"we," the world, have got to realize, is that Iraqi women want their children to grow up in a peaceful world. They want their sons and daughters to be well educated. They want to live in peace and harmony. They want to be able to realize their hopes and aspirations. It's a common desire, and is one that you all are helping the Iraqis realize. It's important work; it's vital work; and it's historic work.

Our military will stay on the offense. We will continue to hunt down people like Mr. Zarqawi and bring them to justice. We will continue to train the Iraqis so they can help the unity Government secure the peace. I've told the American people that as the Iraqis stand up, we will stand down, and I appreciate all the military folks here who are working hard to help the Iraqi forces become capable and able to do the job the Iraqi people expect them to do. Those of you who are not in the military, the civilians, have got a really important job to do as well, and I want to thank you for the job you're doing.

It is clear that Saddam Hussein destroyed many of the institutions necessary for this society to succeed. It is clear that he was a selfish, brutal leader who was willing to sacrifice infrastructure and civil society in order to meet his narrow objectives. And it is clear to me that our job is to help the Prime Minister and his Government implement his strategy and his plan to restore infrastructure and education and health and agricultural society so that people have the confidence in their new Government. Yours is hard work, but it's necessary work, and the Government of the United States stands strongly beside you.

The stakes are high, and what happens here in Iraq reaches far beyond the borders of Iraq. The war on terror really will be addressed by strong actions by our intelligence and military services to bring to justice those who would do us harm. I've told the American people we will defeat the enemy overseas so we do not have to face them here at home.

Ultimately, the victory in the war on terror, the victory in a struggle against those who have no ideology—well, they've got an ideology, but it's an ideology that is dark and dismal. It's one that doesn't respect human dignity. It's an ideology that doesn't believe in the freedom to worship. It's an ideology that doesn't respect the role and rights of women in society. It's an ideology that has no hope. The way to defeat that ideology is with an ideology of light. I believe in the universality of freedom. I believe deep in everybody's soul is the desire to be free.

We don't expect the Iraqi Government to look like the American Government. We expect an Iraqi government to honor its traditions and its histories and its religious faiths. But we do expect the Iraqi Government to honor the right of every man, woman, and child to live in a free society. And when Iraq succeeds—and it will—the rest of the world, particularly in the Middle East, will see such a hopeful example of what's possible.

I told you earlier, we were laying the foundation of peace for generations to come, and we are, because we go with confidence, knowing that liberty is the desire of every soul. When Iraq succeeds, reformers and people who desire to live in a free society will see such a hopeful example, and they'll begin to demand the same rights and the same conditions and the same hopeful society.

And that's why I tell you, what you're doing is historic in nature. People will look back at this period and wonder whether or not America was true to its beginnings; whether we strongly believed in the universality of freedom and whether we were willing to act on it. Certainly we acted in our own self-interest right after September the 11th, and now we act not only in our own self-interests but in the interests of men, women, and children in the broader Middle East, no matter what their religion, no matter where they were born, no matter how they speak.

This is a moment—this is a time where the world can turn one way or the other, where the world can be a better place or a more dangerous place. And the United States of America and citizens such as yourself are dedicated to making sure that the world we leave behind is a better place for all.

It is such an honor to be here. It is such an honor to be with you. May God bless you all; may God bless your work; may God bless your families; and may God continue to bless the United States of America.

NOTE: The President spoke at approximately 8:32 p.m. at the U.S. Embassy. In his remarks, he referred to U.S. Ambassador to Iraq Zalmay Khalilzad; Gen. George W. Casey, Jr., USA, commanding general, Multi-National Force—Iraq; former President Saddam Hussein, and Prime Minister Nuri al-Maliki of Iraq; and senior Al Qaida associate Abu Musab Al Zarqawi, who was killed in Baquba, Iraq, on June 7. A tape was not available for verification of the content of these remarks.

The President's News Conference
June 14, 2006

The President. Good morning. Thank you. I've just returned from Baghdad, and I was inspired to be able to visit the capital of a free and democratic Iraq.

It was a pleasure to meet face to face with the Prime Minister. I talked to him on the phone a couple of times, but I thought it was important to sit down with him and talk to him in person. I saw first-hand the strength of his character and his deep determination to succeed, to build a country that can sustain itself, govern itself, and defend itself.

I also had the pleasure of meeting with people who work for the U.S. Government, our Embassy staff, the intelligence community, and I had a chance to thank them. Theirs is a tough job, and they're far away from home, and obviously, they miss their families. And it was an honor to say to them, I appreciate their hard work, and so do the American people.

And I met with our troops. I had a chance to congratulate those that were responsible for bringing Zarqawi to justice. You know, when you're in a theater like that, it's important to hear words of congratulations sometimes, to hear that their efforts are appreciated—and doing hard work. And I got to do that.

General Casey briefed me on the operations that followed the death of Zarqawi. He told me that Iraqi and coalition forces are still on the offense, that they launched a series of raids on terrorist targets across Iraq. We've got new intelligence from those raids which will enable us to continue to keep the pressure on the foreigners and local Iraqis that are killing innocent lives to stop the advance of a country that can sustain itself and govern itself and defend itself.

Obviously, the raids aren't going to end terrorism. I understand that, and the American people understand that, and the Iraqi people understand that. But the terrorists are vulnerable, and we will strike their network and disrupt their operations and continue to bring their leaders to justice.

Prime Minister Maliki and I held a joint meeting of our two Cabinets—members of my Cabinet participating by video, some of whom were slightly surprised to see me from afar. I told the Prime Minister how impressed I was to meet the team he assembled. These are good people from different walks of life. I appreciated very much the agenda he's laid out. In other words, he's got a plan to succeed. And I appreciated their determination—it's not just his determination but their Cabinet's determination to succeed. In other words, part of the success in Iraq depends upon the Iraqis and their will and their desire. The Iraqi people have expressed their desires, and now it's up to the Government to follow through.

The Prime Minister briefed us on immediate steps he's taken in three key areas: to improve security; to build up the Iraqi economy so they can see—the Iraqi people can see real progress, real economic progress; and he's reaching out to the international community to help secure support for this new Government. We discussed ways that my administration can help the Prime Minister accomplish these objectives. The policy of the United States Government is to stand with this new Government and help them succeed, and we will do what it takes to help them succeed.

The Prime Minister is taking immediate action to implement a plan to improve security, and his top priority is around Baghdad. Operation Together Forward started this morning. This operation is a joint effort to restore security and rule of law to high-risk areas in the capital city. It will be carried out by some 26,000 Iraqi soldiers, some 23,000 Iraqi police, backed up by over 7,200 coalition forces. Iraqi troops will increase the number of checkpoints, enforce a curfew, and implement a strict weapons ban across the Iraqi capital. Baghdad is a city of more than 6½ million residents, and we've got to recognize that it's going to take time for these operations to take hold.

Iraqi and coalition forces are also working to restore security in Ramadi, the capital of Anbar Province. The Prime Minister's plan to bring militias and other armed groups under Government control is moving forward, and we talked about that plan. He understands how important it is to rein in these militias. Many militia members will be demobilized and integrated into the Iraqi security forces, where they'll be dispersed among different units and, obviously, monitored closely by the Government. I've directed General Casey and our Ambassador to work with the Prime Minister on this really important effort, so he can make clear: Illegal militias have no future in a free Iraq.

Prime Minister Maliki is working to build confidence in the Iraqi security forces, and he has a plan to do that. To assist him, we'll continue embedding coalition transition teams in Iraqi Army and police units. We've deployed advisory teams to assist Iraq's new ministries of—Ministers of Defense and Interior, both of whom I met. We want to help them build the command and control capacity of their ministries. In other words, you can't have an effective army unless you've got command and control coming out of Government.

We want to establish an internal affairs bureau to root out corruption. No question, this Government has got to deal with corruption at all levels in order to earn the confidence of the people. And, of course, we will encourage them and help them investigate and punish human rights violations in order to earn the confidence of all Iraqis.

Part of the Prime Minister's plan is to improve the Iraqi judicial system. And to assist him, I've directed the Attorney General and the Secretaries of State and Defense to work together on a new rule-of-law initiative. Under this initiative, we'll help train Iraqi judges, increase security so they can do their jobs, improve Iraqi prison capacity, and help the Iraqi Government provide equal justice for all its citizens.

Prime Minister Maliki is promoting reconciliation among the Iraqi people. And during my discussions with his Cabinet and others, the concept of reconciliation kept coming up. People know they've got to reconcile the past in order to have a bright future. He told us he's going to soon appoint a reconciliation committee that will focus on resolving specific concerns of different Iraqi communities. We will support his efforts to bring the Iraqis together by encouraging leaders from countries like South Africa to share their experiences with this new Government to help them reconcile the past.

Secondly, the Prime Minister has a plan to revitalize the Iraqi economy. He understands that the people have got to feel benefits from the new Government. I mean, it's a simple concept, but it's a profound one. I've directed our Secretary of Treasury and—or the Treasury Department to send teams of experts to Iraq to help the Government create a public finance system that is accountable and transparent. These advisers will help Iraqis develop an economic framework that promotes growth and job creation and opportunity. I've directed the Secretaries of Commerce and Agriculture to travel to Iraq as soon as possible to meet with their counterparts.

To revitalize the Iraqi economy, the Prime Minister is working to increase oil and electricity production. We spent a lot of time talking about energy in Iraq. I reminded the Government that that oil belongs to the Iraqi people and the Government has the responsibility to be good stewards of that valuable asset and valuable resource.

We have—we're working with the Iraqi Government on measures to protect key infrastructure from insurgent attacks. There's rapid-repair teams that are being established that will quickly restore oil and electricity production if and when attacks do occur.

I've directed the Secretary of Energy to travel to Iraq to meet with his counterpart and identify ways we can provide additional support. It's up to the Iraqis to pass a hydrocarbon law, which they're now debating. It's up for the Iraqi Government to decide what to do with the people's asset. Our advice is to be careful and to develop it with the people's interest in mind.

Finally, the Prime Minister has taken immediate action to engage the international community, and we're going to help him. Earlier, the international community pledged about $13 billion to help this new Government, and they've only paid about 3 billion. And so we're going to help encourage those who've made a pledge to pay up to help the new Government succeed. Plus, he's working to develop what he's calling an international compact. Under this compact, Iraq will take a series of steps in the political, economic, and security areas. And then the international community will provide more robust political and economic support.

I told the Prime Minister, I'll designate Deputy Treasury Secretary Bob Kimmitt to lead our efforts on behalf of our country and the people of this country. He'll be supported by State Department Counselor Phil Zelikow and other senior officials, and they will soon travel to the United Nations and then to Baghdad for consultations. And then they're going to travel across Europe and Asia and the Middle East to discuss the compact and secure support from Governments for this new Government.

I was impressed with the Prime Minister, and I'm impressed by his team. I told him that America is a nation that meets its commitments and keeps its word. And that's what we're going to do in Iraq. It's in our interest that Iraq succeed. More importantly, it's in the interest of the Iraqi people. The challenges that remain are serious, and they will require more sacrifice and patience. And our efforts are well worth it.

By helping this new Government succeed, we'll be closer to completing our mission, and the mission is to develop a country that can govern itself, sustain itself, and defend itself, and a country that is an ally in the war on terror. We'll seize this moment of opportunity to help the Prime Minister. We'll defeat our common enemies. We'll help build a lasting democracy in the heart of the Middle East, and that will make Americans and Iraqis and the world more secure.

I'll now take your questions. Nedra [Nedra Pickler, Associated Press].

Support for the Iraqi Government

Q. Thank you, Mr. President. You said yesterday that a standard of no violence in Iraq is an impossible standard to meet, but do you believe that there needs to be a reduction in violence for U.S. troops to begin to draw down? And if so, how much?

The President. Yes, I said that if people say, "Well, there's got to be no violence in order for this to be a successful experience," then it's not going to happen. All that does is give the power of—a handful of murderers to determine success. Obviously, we'd like violence to go down, and that's what the operation in Baghdad is intending to do, starting in the capital, is to reduce violence. And the reason why it's important for violence to be reduced, obviously, is, one, to save lives, but, two, give confidence to the Iraqi people that their Government will be able to sustain itself and govern itself and meet the needs of the people.

This is a tough struggle, and the reason why is because the rules of warfare as we used to know them are out the window. I mean, there's no rule of warfare. It's just, if you can kill innocent life in order to shake somebody's will or create consternation in society, just go ahead and do it. And so it's a tough task, no question about it.

But I'm confident that this Government will succeed in meeting that task. And the reason why I said that we shouldn't use the level of—have a zero-violence expectation is because there are other measures to determine success, starting with political measures. I mean, this is a government which is now a unity government, formed under a Constitution that the people voted for. That's success. The question is, can this Government sustain itself, and that will be determined if—whether or not they're be able to get electricity and use their oil resources wisely. Can it defend itself? One way to measure whether it can defend itself is through the strength of their army and their police. And so that's what I said.

And the second part of your question?

Q. Do you have a specific target for how much you want that violence to be reduced?

The President. Enough for the Government to succeed. In other words, the Iraqi people have got to have confidence in this unity Government, and reduction in violence will enable the people to have confidence.

And you said something about troop levels. Our policy is stand up/stand down; as the Iraqis stand up, we'll stand down. But if we stand down too soon, it won't enable us to achieve our objectives. And we will support this Iraqi Government—that's what I went to tell them. We'll do what it takes to support them. And part of that support is the presence of coalition forces.

Guantanamo Bay Detainees/Abu Ghraib Prison

Q. Thank you, Mr. President. You expressed serious concern when you learned about the Guantanamo suicides, and you and your aides immediately called allies. I'm wondering, how concerned are you about the U.S. image abroad, based on this incident and the ongoing investigation in Haditha and Abu Ghraib and other incidents? And also, why shouldn't Guantanamo be closed now?

The President. I'd like to close Guantanamo, but I also recognize that we're holding some people that are darn dangerous and that we better have a plan to deal with them in our courts. And the best way to handle—in my judgment—handle these types of people is through our military courts. And that's why we're waiting on the Supreme Court to make a decision.

Part of closing Guantanamo is to send some folks back home, like we've been doing. And the State Department is in the process of encouraging countries to take the folks back. Of course, sometimes we get criticized for sending some people out of Guantanamo back to their home country because of the nature of the home country. It's a little bit of a catch-22. But we're working through this.

No question, Guantanamo sends a signal to some of our friends, provides an excuse, for example, to say, the United States is not upholding the values that they're trying to encourage other countries to adhere to. And my answer to them is, is that we are a nation of laws and rule of law. These people have been picked up off the battlefield, and they're very dangerous. And so we have that balance between customary justice, the typical system, and one that will be done in the military courts. And that's what we're waiting for.

Eventually, these people will have trials, and they will have counsel, and they will be represented in a court of law. I say "these people," those who are not sent back to their mother countries. You know, we've sent a lot of people home already. I don't think the American people know that, nor do the citizens of some of the countries that are concerned about Guantanamo.

You mentioned Abu Ghraib. No question, it's set a terrible example. I was asked at a press conference in the East Room with Tony Blair, mistakes. Abu Ghraib was a terrible mistake. I was asked that question, by the way, about Abu—very same question you asked, by a member of the Iraqi Cabinet. And I told her, I said that where there's allegations, we will investigate. And I reminded her that ours is a transparent society where people will see and follow these investigations, and people will be held to account according to our laws.

But I also want the people to understand, here and around the world, that 99.9 percent of our troops are honorable, decent people who are serving our country under difficult conditions, and I'm proud of them. I'm proud of the United States military. And that's a message our military and their families must consistently hear, that they're doing fine work. I understand the politics and all that. But I'm going to continue to remind them that, set politics aside, this Nation owes you a debt of gratitude.

So we'll deal with these incidents, and we'll deal with them in an upfront way. But I'm not going to let these incidents stain the reputation of our military. They're good people; they really are.

Yes, sir. Roger [Roger Runningen, Bloomberg News].

National Economy

Q. Thank you, sir.

The President. Roger, Roger.

Q. Thank you, sir. Mr. President, you've said that you trust the markets to guide you, but stock and bond markets are telling us that inflation is a growing concern. Is there a threat that inflation is going to derail the economic expansion?

The President. There are a lot of indicators about the strength of our economy, starting with job creation, productivity increases, small—the entrepreneurial spirit is strong. There's a lot of positive things. And obviously, the Fed is watching the signals for inflation very carefully. They'll make decisions independent of the White House.

On fiscal policy, though, I would strongly urge the Congress to recognize why we have grown the way we have grown, why we're—have got strong economic growth in the first quarter of this year, why we've added over 5 million new jobs in a—in 2¾ years, and that's because the tax cuts are working, and they need to make the tax cuts permanent. Progrowth economic policies work. And that's why I've been calling for permanence in the Tax Code.

And so there will be monetary policy; we'll pay attention very carefully to signs, inflationary signs. That's Ben Bernanke's job. Our job is to work with Congress to have wise fiscal policy. And wise fiscal policy means not only keeping revenues low, but it also means being wise about how we spend the people's money. I called Chairman Lewis this morning to congratulate him on getting a good supplemental out of the House of Representatives. It's a supplemental that meets our numbers and meets the requirements for a good bill. And evidently, it's going to be voted on in the Senate here pretty quick, and I look forward to signing that piece of legislation, should it make it to my desk.

Let's see here. Jake Tapper [ABC News]. Yes, filling in, huh?

Progress in Iraq/Natural Resources

Q. How are you doing, sir?

The President. I'm doing all right. Thank you. A little jetlagged, as I'm sure you can imagine—nearly 60.

Q. I can, sir. Thank you.

The President. Good. I'm not sure you possibly can empathize—[*laughter*]—but nevertheless——

Q. Jetlag, I understand jetlag.

The President. Okay, good.

Q. What are your feelings about discussions, in the new Iraqi Government, of amnesty for insurgents?

And regarding the oil resources in Iraq that you discussed, do you support guaranteeing the Sunnis a percentage of the oil profits, either through a new law or through a constitutional provision?

The President. Yes, that's not a bad question for a substitute guy. [*Laughter*] I believe that the Iraqi Government—first of all, the decision on what to do with their resources is their decision, not mine. And so this is advisory. These are people that are elected and under a Constitution. My advice to them is to use their energy assets as a way to unite the country. And by that I mean that people will have—they may not have oil resources in their Provinces, but they would have a stake in how the resources are developed elsewhere in the country.

One option I laid out the other day for them to consider—I must confess, this isn't probably the best way to convince a government to do something, is to put it out through the press—but I did suggest a royalty trust on behalf of the Iraqi people. Other countries have tried that; the state of Alaska has tried that. To me, it's an interesting idea for them to consider, to basically say that no matter where you live in the country, you have a stake in the future of your country because of your ownership in energy assets.

Other part of the question?

Q. Possible amnesty for insurgents.

The President. Yes—I talked to the Prime Minister about—his question is, possible amnesty. The Prime Minister, I think, would say "reconciliation." This is an issue that is on the minds of a lot of the folks there in Iraq. In other words, they're trying to figure out how to reconcile an ugly past with a hopeful future. And part of that is reconciliation. I'm not exactly sure how you would—what you mean by—if somebody has committed a crime, I don't know whether or not they'll be that lenient, frankly.

But I do recognize that—I mean, they recognize that, for example, Ba'ath Party membership in order to secure a job or to be able to get an advanced degree should be a part—shouldn't be held against

a person. And I think they're willing to balance the difference between terror and—"expediency" isn't the right word, but terror and membership of a party to advance one's life. And I was impressed. I was impressed by their—the sophisticated nature of that discussion and their recognition that it's really important to do the best they can to reconcile the past.

One of the things I was looking for was—first of all, I'm convinced this Government will succeed. And one of the reasons I am is because there is a sense of hopefulness. If you're a person stuck in the past, you tend to be bitter and look for ways to seek revenge. I didn't sense that. I did have a strong sense that they're really happy to get rid of Saddam Hussein, to a person. They believe he wrecked their country in more ways than one. It was clear he wrecked their infrastructure. And it is clear that he wrecked a lot of lives. But I didn't have that great sense of people being so bound up in bitterness that they weren't willing to think positively about the future. And I think that's important. I really do.

Gregory [David Gregory, NBC News], fine-looking scarf—not scarf, what do you call that thing?

Progress in Iraq

Q. Thank you very much.

The President. It's strong.

Q. Thank you. [*Laughter*] Mr. President, you've made a public point recently of soliciting outside advice about the way forward in Iraq and retooling your strategy. I wonder, what idea from a critic or somebody outside your administration that you've concluded should be part of the strategy going forward?

The President. Well, I think—I've gotten a lot of advice from people. You know, one of the interesting debates from the outside community is troop levels. I've got people who say, "You need to increase the number of forces—now." I've gotten people that said, "Well, the role of the United

States ought to be more indirect than it has been," in other words, in a supporting role. To those folks, I say, "Look, I'm going to rely upon General Casey." But I did share with him the philosophies that were reflected in a conversation we had over lunch at Camp David.

I've had people come in and say, "You better make sure that the Iraqi forces are well-tooled to do their job." In other words, there's people who have gone over there and taken a hard look, have felt like that the Iraqi forces were not equipped well enough to be able to stand up as we stand down. I asked that question of General Casey, and the area where he agrees with the critics is that they don't quite have the capability to move themselves around the country. In other words, they need more mobility. And he recognizes that and is working toward an Iraqi Army that has more mobility.

Obviously, there has been criticism about our reconstruction plan, that we started with big projects that were sometimes blown up or sometimes didn't get off the ground like we'd hoped. And that's why we morphed a lot of our aid into a PRT approach, where local commanders had the capacity to get money out more quickly.

But I appreciate people's advice, and I appreciate their candor. I am going to meet this afternoon with a group of folks put together by the Peace Institute. They're going to take a look at Iraq. And the reason I bring that up to you is that it's important for people to share their advice with this administration. It's an important business. And it's not easy. It's a complex task to help a society go from tyranny to freedom.

But the American people have got to understand, I believe we're going to succeed. That's why we're there. And my message to the Iraqis is, we're going to help you succeed. My message to the enemy is, don't count on us leaving before we succeed. My message to our troops is, we support you 100 percent; keep doing what you're doing. And my message to the critics

is, is that we listen very carefully and adjust when needed to adjust.

This policy will be driven by the people on the ground. Those are the folks who are going to ultimately make the recommendation that I'll accept. It's important to get advice; I share the advice with our commanders and with Zal. They're the folks who are right there. These are very competent, capable people who understand the Iraqi situation well. And their judgment is important, and I listen very carefully to it—along the same way.

Sheryl [Sheryl Gay Stolberg, New York Times]. Welcome. Got a couple of newcomers today, sitting next to Tapper.

2006 Midterm Elections/Democratic Party

Q. Thank you, Mr. President. I'm pleased to be here. Mr. President, polls show that the public thinks Democrats can do a better job of running the country than Republicans. Are you concerned that Republicans will lose control of Congress in November? And do you think there's anything you could have done differently to put them in a better position, coming up in the midterms?

The President. I remember 2004. At one point, people—you would have stood up and said, "You know, there's no way you can get reelected," if you had been listening to those polls. I can't remember; I was probably down double digits at some point. And they said, "How can you possibly stand here and tell us you're going to get reelected?" Listen, the elections are a long way off. What's going to matter is who has got the plan that will enable us to succeed in Iraq and keep the economy growing. And I look forward to the campaign. And I believe we're going to hold the House and the Senate, because our philosophy is one that is forward-looking and optimistic and has worked. We've got a record to run on.

There's an interesting debate in the Democrat Party about how quick to pull out of Iraq. Pulling out of Iraq before we accomplish the mission will make the world a more dangerous place. It's bad policy. I know it may sound good politically; it will endanger our country to pull out of Iraq before we accomplish the mission.

See, Iraq is a part of the global war on terror. It's not the global war on terror; it's a theater in the global war on terror. And if we fail in Iraq, it's going to embolden Al Qaida types. It will weaken the resolve of moderate nations to stand up to the Islamic fascists. It will cause people to lose their nerve and not stay strong.

And so I look forward to taking the debate—that's not quite right—kind of getting warmed up as a result of your question—the timing is not right for me to get out there yet. But I think the Democrat economic policy of raising people's taxes isn't going to work either. I know they'll couch it in all kinds of language, but really what they're saying is, we're going to raise your taxes.

So, you know, Sheryl, thanks for your question. I don't necessarily buy your premise. I feel confident we will hold the House and the Senate.

Let's see here. Peter [Peter Baker, Washington Post].

CIA Employee Identity Disclosure Investigation

Q. Thank you, Mr. President. Mr. President, when you ran for office for the first time, you said you would hold the White House to a higher ethical standard. Even if Karl Rove did nothing illegal, I wonder whether you can say now whether you approve of his conduct in the CIA leak episode, and do you believe he owes Scott McClellan or anyone else an apology for misleading them?

The President. I appreciate the job that the prosecutor did. I thought he conducted himself well in this investigation. He took a very thorough, long look at allegations and rumors. And I, obviously, along with others in the White House, took a sigh of relief when he made the decision he

made. And now we're going to move forward. And I trust Karl Rove, and he's an integral part of my team.

There's an ongoing trial, Peter, and I know the temptation is—not the temptation, you'll keep asking questions during the course of the trial. We're not going to comment beyond that.

Yes. Jim Axelrod [CBS News].

Progress in Iraq/War on Terror

Q. Good morning, Mr. President. You seem quite energized by this moment of opportunity.

The President. No, I'm just fighting off fatigue.

Q. I know the feeling, sir. I'm wondering, though, if there are ever moments of doubt about your decisions and strategy in Iraq. Do you ever have a moment where you feel this just won't end well, that no matter how many Zarqawis are killed, the insurgents are just never going to give up?

The President. Well, one of the reasons I went to Iraq was to be able to sit down with an Iraqi Government to determine whether or not they have the will to succeed.

Success in Iraq depends upon the Iraqis. If the Iraqis don't have the will to succeed, they're not going to succeed. We can have all the will we want; I can have all the confidence in the ability for us to bring people to justice, but if they choose not to take the—make the hard decisions and to implement a plan, they're not going to make it. And so one of the things I went to Iraq to do was to, as best as I possibly can, expel any doubt in my mind as to whether or not we have a partner that is going to do the hard work.

One of the interesting things that—and by the way, I believe we will have a partner to do the hard work. I made it clear to the Government there that it's up to them to succeed. It's really up to them to put a plan in place and execute it. We'll help, but it's—they were elected by the people; they're living under a Constitution that the people endorsed; and they have to follow through.

And that's why I was most interested in hearing the Prime Minister's plans on electricity and energy and security. As I mentioned to you, there's an operation now going on in Baghdad that he helped put together, that we're helping him on. He recognizes that the capital city of a country sends important signals to the rest of the country—the security of the capital city—to the country and the world. He knows that. And that's why he has worked out a robust plan, with our help.

And so doubts about whether or not this Government can—has got the will to go forward was expelled. That's why I went. In other words, sitting here in America, wondering whether or not these people have got what it takes can create uncertainty. I've eliminated that uncertainty. I was able to sit with the man and talk to him.

I was also pleased to meet with his Cabinet. You might remember, it wasn't all that long ago that there were some doubts in people's minds as to whether or not this Government had the capacity to put a unity government—as a matter of fact, there was doubts after the first election as to whether or not a portion of the population would even participate in the elections. And last December a lot of folks voted, from all different aspects of society, and the Government reflects that. And that was important for me to see firsthand as well.

The enemy has an advantage in this war, because they can get on our TV screens every day. And of course, it upsets me when I see the loss of innocent life, and it upsets me to know that our service men and women are losing their lives. I'm like most Americans, it is—death affects my way of thinking. But I also understand the stakes of this war, see. I understand how important it is to defeat the enemy. Now, I recognize some in the country don't feel that same sense of urgency I do. But Al Qaida is real; their philosophy is a real phi-

losophy; they have ambitions. Their stated goal is to drive us out of Iraq before a government can defend itself and govern itself and sustain itself, so they can have safe haven from which to launch further attacks. And my most important job is to protect the American people from harm. And I understand the stakes of this war, and I understand this battlefront in Iraq.

And I want to repeat something: Iraq is not the only part of this war. It's an essential part, but it's not the only part of the war on terror. And so the decisions I make are all aimed at protecting the American people and understanding the vast stakes involved. If the United States of America leaves before this Iraqi Government can defend itself and sustain itself and govern itself, it will be a major blow in the war on terror. Al Qaida will benefit. And make no mistake about it, they still want to do innocent people harm, whether it be in the Middle East or whether it be here in the United States of America. The stakes are high in Iraq.

And my trip over there gave me confidence that we have a partner that is capable of setting priority and developing a plan to meet those priorities, and then following through to see that those priorities are met. And my assurances to him were, you get good plans and you have the desire to follow through; we'll help you. We'll help you. We will do what it takes to help you succeed. It's in our national interest to do so.

Let's see here. Bret [Bret Baier, FOX News].

Iraqi Government

Q. Thank you, Mr. President. Could you characterize the worry you heard from Iraqi leaders about U.S. troop levels that you first mentioned on the flight home from Iraq? And here in the Rose Garden a week ago, you said that Zarqawi's death is an opportunity for Iraq's new Government to turn the tide in this struggle. After your visit, do you truly believe that the tide is turning in Iraq?

The President. First part of the question? I'm sorry.

Q. About the worry that you——

The President. Yes. No question, there are concerns about whether or not the United States will stand with this Government. And I can understand why. You know, ours is a society that encourages debate, and people are free to express themselves. And they do so; they say, "Look, this is my view of how we ought to go forward; this is what I think." And the willingness of some to say that "If we're in power, we'll withdraw on a set timetable," concerns people in Iraq, because they understand our coalition forces provide a sense of stability, so they can address old wrongs and develop their strategy and plan to move forward. They need our help, and they recognize that. And so they are concerned about that.

And I'm concerned that an enemy will hear the wrong message. And then I'm also concerned that there are people inside Iraq who have yet to make up their mind as to whether or not they want to help this Government succeed, or maybe, or just maybe America will lose its nerve and, therefore, something else, a new team may show up. And so I made it very clear to the Iraqis, and I'm going to make it clear to them again right here that we're going— we'll stay with them and help them succeed.

I know there is a lot of discussion about troop levels. Those troop levels will be decided upon by General Casey. He will make the recommendations, in consultation with an Iraqi government. But whatever decision General Casey makes, the message is going to be, "We stand with you." In other words, if you're more capable, it requires less troops, but nevertheless, we're still with you.

Other part?

Q. Is the tide turning in Iraq?

The President. I think—tide turning— see, as I remember—I was raised in the desert, but tides kind of—it's easy to see a tide turn—did I say those words?

Q. [*Inaudible*]

The President. Yes, I probably ought to then reflect on those words and think that—I sense something different happening in Iraq. The progress will be steady toward a goal that has clearly been defined. In other words, I hope there's not an expectation from people that, all of a sudden, there's going to be zero violence—in other words, it's just not going to be the case. On the other hand, I do think we'll be able to measure progress. You can measure progress in capacity of Iraqi units. You can measure progress in megawatts of electricity delivered. You can measure progress in terms of oil sold on the market on behalf of the Iraqi people. There's ways to determine whether or not this Government's plans are succeeding.

But I know there's a tangible difference between the Government that is now in place and previous governments, and the reason why is because this is a government that's formed under elections and a Constitution. And it's a unity government, and so people have a sense of—they're pulling for their Government to succeed. And the reason why is, by far, the vast majority of Iraqis want a normal life. They want their children to be able to go out in the street and play. They want there to be a good education system. They want to be able to have their business—their little storefront business flourish without fear of bombing. That's what they want.

And so they're pulling for this Government to succeed. And it's a government that they elected. It's not a government that we appointed; it's a government that they elected. They have a vital stake in the future of this Government. And so there is a noticeable change. And whoever said it's a tide turning and all that needs— never mind. [*Laughter*]

Elaine [Elaine Quijano, Cable News Network].

President's Visit to Iraq

Q. Thank you, Mr. President. What kind of signal do you think it sends to the Iraqi people that your administration notified the leader of Iraq's sovereign Government only 5 minutes beforehand of your arrival? And was there a specific security concern about either Prime Minister Maliki's inner circle or others that led you to make that decision?

The President. No, I think—look, it's a security concern because I'm a high-value target for some. And Iraq is a dangerous place. The American people have got to know that I will take precautions when I travel somewhere. I'm not going to put our Government at risk to achieve a very important trip. And therefore, we were—a lot of people didn't know about it. Half my Cabinet didn't know about it. Does that mean I'm going to run them off? No. I just—we want to make sure we're extra secret about this deal. And the reason why is, Iraq is dangerous. It's a dangerous place. And I think if there was ample notification that I was coming, perhaps it would have given somebody a chance to plan, and we just didn't want to take that risk.

There is no question about Prime Minister Maliki's—when he walked in, I never—I didn't fear. I was happy to see him, and he was happy to see me. But you should expect the President to be—to take precaution. I take precaution when I go somewhere here in the United States. Obviously, not to that extent, but nevertheless, we're careful. And that's what the people expect, us to be careful.

I appreciate the efforts that went into this trip. There are a lot of people that worked hard to make sure this worked. And it worked well. It was a good trip. And it was an exciting trip, by the way. I was up there in the cockpit of that airplane coming into Baghdad, watching Colonel Tillman steer us in. It was an unbelievable, unbelievable feeling. And walking into that ballroom there in Saddam's old palace, to see our—see our people on the frontlines of changing history was an exciting moment for me. It's a thrill to be able to shake their hands and look them in the eye and tell them America appreciates what they're doing. I really, really appreciated the fact that I was able to go and—no matter how secret it was.

McKinnon [John McKinnon, Wall Street Journal].

Progress in Iraq

Q. Thank you, sir. You just mentioned that you think the United States will be able to measure progress in terms of electricity and oil and violence. And I'm wondering if you can say how you're going to measure that in terms of time. In other words, are you going to put a 6-month timeframe on this, or a 12-month timeframe on this?

The President. John, I know—look, I understand the pressures to put timetables out there on everything. And my answer to you is, is that we will work with the Iraqi Government to do what's realistic. And the people on the ground will help me understand what is realistic. We will know whether or not the Government is capable of following through because we're going to help them follow through.

The answer to electricity is, sooner the better. It's hot over there, and it would be helpful if people had the capacity to cool their homes. It would be a pretty good signal that the Government is making a difference in somebody's life.

There are certain projects that are easier to achieve than others. Fixing the infrastructure of the northern Iraq oil fields is going to be more difficult to do. It's old; it's tired; it's been destroyed by an enemy. And it's going to take a while to get that done, and so we've got to be realistic with this Government. There is a—but, nevertheless, I do believe that it makes sense to develop, with them, benchmarks, so we can measure progress. And once those are in place, and to the extent they are, we'll be glad to share them with you.

Part of my visit yesterday was a strategy session, to sit down with a partner, the Prime Minister, Maliki, to figure out how to move forward, to listen to his plans and how we can help his plans. The important thing for me to hear from him is, "Here's what I intend to do," he says; not, "Here's what we want you to do," like the oil suggestion. I really meant what I said; it was just a suggestion. It wasn't, "You must do this." And same with the electricity. And he made a point to have his Electricity Minister brief my Cabinet, because he wanted us to know that he has a plan to put in place. The guy, by the way, said, "I need your help." And we'll provide the help as best as we can.

You know, the ultimate judge about whether this Government is making a difference is going to be the Iraqi people, and these elected officials know that. That's the great thing about being elected; you get a sense if people don't, kind of, like what you're doing—or not. And democracy causes you to respond to the people's needs. Tyrants don't have to. They don't have—sometimes they may have to, but they always have got kind of an interesting way of helping suppress dissent. This elected Government is going to have to respond to the people, and that's a big change.

Remember that Saddam did a really good job of milking the society to keep himself in power. In other words, the infrastructure is destroyed, or a lot of it is destroyed and dilapidated. We heard that over and over again in Baghdad. People said, "You've got to understand how backward we are compared to where we want to be." And he divided society and pitted people against each other in order to justify his own presence. And we're having to deal with that. The Iraqis are having to deal with that.

And I was impressed by their willingness to be up front about the past. And it's going to be difficult work, no question about it. There are still resentments and bitterness and people wondering, does the future belong to them. The Sunni—I was impressed, by the way, by the Speaker— Denny Hastert told me I'd like him; Denny met with him. And I was impressed by him. He's a fellow that had been put in prison by Saddam and, interestingly enough, put in prison by us. And he made a decision to participate in the Government. And he was an articulate person. He talked about running the parliament. It was interesting to see a person that could have been really bitter talk about the skills he's going to need to bring people together to run the parliament. And I found him to be a hopeful person.

They tell me that he wouldn't have taken my phone call a year ago—I think I might have shared this with you at one point in time—and there I was, sitting next to the guy. And I think he enjoyed it as much as I did. It was a refreshing moment. And the Deputy Speaker was there as well.

Let's see here. Ann [Ann Compton, ABC News].

Iraqi Government

Q. Thank you, Mr. President. Yesterday while you were gone, Senator Kerry, who was your challenger in the last election——

The President. I remember that.

Q. You remember that. [*Laughter*] He said he now regrets his votes on the war. And, actually, I think Senator Clinton, at the same meeting, actually heard some boos when she said that she did not support a timetable for withdrawal. Do you see, as some of your critics do, a parallel between what's going on in Iraq now and Vietnam?

The President. No.

Q. Why?

The President. Because there's a duly elected government; 12 million people voted. They said, "We want something different from tyranny; we want to live in a free society." And not only did they vote for a Government, they voted for a Constitution. Obviously, there is sectarian violence, but this is, in many ways, religious in nature, and I don't see the parallels.

You know, look—I thought you were going to ask, do I regret what I did. Absolutely not. I made the right decision in Iraq. It's the right thing to get rid of Saddam Hussein. And now it's the right thing to stand with this Government when they build a new democracy. And I reminded the Iraqi people, their democracy doesn't have to look like us. It's their country, and the Government ought to reflect their traditions and their history. All we expect is people to be treated with respect and there to be self-governance in a way that tolerates differences of opinion.

Yes, Peter [Peter Wallsten, Los Angeles Times]. Are you going to ask that question with shades on?

CIA Employee Identity Disclosure Investigation

Q. I can take them off.

The President. I'm interested in the shade look, seriously.

Q. All right, I'll keep it then.

The President. For the viewers, there's no sun. [*Laughter*]

Q. I guess it depends on your perspective. [*Laughter*]

The President. Touche. [*Laughter*]

Q. Following up on the other Peter's question about Karl Rove, you said you were relieved with what happened yesterday. But the American public, over the course of this investigation, has learned a lot about what was going on in your White House that they didn't know before, during that time, the way some people were trying to go after Joe Wilson, in some ways. I'm wondering if, over the course of this investigation, that you have learned anything that you didn't know before about what was going on in your administration. And do you have any work to do to rebuild credibility that might have been lost?

The President. I think that—first of all, the decision by the prosecutor speaks for itself. He had a full investigation. Karl Rove went in front of the grand jury like—I don't—a lot of times. More times than—they took a hard look at his role.

Secondly, as I told the other Peter, I'm going to tell you that there's an ongoing trial; it's a serious business. And I've made the comments I'm going to make about this incident, and I'm going to put this part of the situation behind us and move forward.

Let's see here—yes, sure. Richard [Richard Benedetto, USA Today].

Public Opinion on Iraq/War on Terror

Q. Mr. President, the death of Zarqawi and the formation of the new Government in Iraq has given you a chance to reengage the American people on Iraq. A majority of the people still say that the war was a mistake. Do you think that the people have turned off on Iraq? Or do you think they're still winnable back, to consider that it was worth it?

The President. I think the people want to know, can we win? That's what they want to know. Listen, admittedly, there are a group of people in our country that say, "It wasn't worth it; get out now." And that opinion is being expressed. As these campaigns start approaching, you'll hear more people say, I suspect, "It's a mistake; Bush shouldn't have done what he did; pull out." And that's a legitimate debate to have in America, and I look forward to the debate. I will remind the American people, if we pull out before we achieve our objective, the world will be a lot more dangerous and America will be more at risk.

Then there are some in the country that say, "We understand the stakes, but do they have a plan to win, can they possibly win?" And I will continue to explain to the American people, winning means a government that can sustain itself, defend itself, and govern itself, and an ally in the war on terror. And we will help this Government do that. And one of the reasons I went to Iraq was to determine whether or not we have a partner which is capable of making the tough decisions necessary to achieve our objective.

The American people have got to understand that Iraq is a part of the war on terror. Now, Richard, I fully understand how people might have made the decision that America is no longer under threat or the lessons of September the 11th were just momentary lessons. I can understand that. But I have a responsibility to lay out what I believe. And the lessons learned from September the 11th are still an integral part of my thinking, and I'll continue to make decisions based upon the lessons.

And I know there is an international jihadist movement that desires to do us harm, and they have territorial ambitions. The reason I know that is, that's what they've told us. And part of their territorial ambition is to have safe haven in Iraq. That's what they've said. That's what the enemy has clearly said. And it seems like to me that the Commander in Chief ought to listen to what the enemy says. And they believe capitalists and democratic societies are soft, and it's a matter of time before we pull out.

And that's why one message that I will continue to send to the enemy is, don't count on us leaving before the mission is complete. Don't bet on it; don't bet on American politics forcing my hand, because it's not going to happen. I'm going to make decisions not based upon politics but based upon what's best for the United States of America.

But I understand why people, Richard, are concerned, because progress is hard to see. You know, it's one thing to say, "We've got Zarqawi;" that's progress. It's another thing to say, "I met with the man, and I believe he can make the right decisions." And so somebody is going to say, "Sure, well, show me." And I understand that. And I understand how tough it is for the American people to reconcile death on

their TV screens with the President saying, we're making incremental progress toward an important goal. But what I hope they understand is how important it is we succeed in Iraq, that the country is more dangerous if we don't—the world is more dangerous if we don't succeed.

And so I'm going to keep talking about it and talking about—because I believe passionately we're doing the right thing. And I've told the American people this: If I didn't think we could succeed and if I didn't think it was worth it, I'd pull our troops out. And I mean that.

And one reason I went to Iraq yesterday, no matter how secretive the trip was, was to get a firsthand feel for how those people are thinking over there, what are they like. I understand leadership. Leadership requires determination. You've got to be determined to do something in order to be able to lead, particularly in difficult circumstances. You've got to have will. You've got to have desire to succeed, and you've got to have a plan. And that's what I found in Iraq.

It's really important that the Iraqi people have no doubt in their mind that we will help this Government succeed. It's important for them to understand that. And I know there's going to be different voices, and there should be different voices out of America. That's where we're great. That's what makes us interesting and great; people can say whatever they want to say as they try to attract votes. But my voice—what you hear from me, no matter what these polls and all the business look like, is that it's worth it, it is necessary, and we will succeed.

Thank you all very much.

NOTE: The President's news conference began at 9:45 a.m. in the Rose Garden at the White House. In his remarks, he referred to Prime Minister Nuri al-Maliki, Minister of Defense Abd al-Qadir al-Mufriji, Minister of the Interior Jawad al-Bulani, Minister of Electricity Karim Wahid al-Hasan, Speaker of the Council of Representatives Mahmoud al-Mashhadani, and Deputy Speaker of the Council of Representatives Khaled Atea of Iraq; senior Al Qaida associate Abu Musab Al Zarqawi, who was killed in Baquba, Iraq, on June 7; Gen. George W. Casey, Jr., USA, commanding general, Multi-National Force—Iraq; U.S. Ambassador to Iraq Zalmay Khalilzad; Deputy Secretary of the Treasury Robert M. Kimmit; Prime Minister Tony Blair of the United Kingdom; Patrick J. Fitzgerald, U.S. Attorney for the Northern District of Illinois and Department of Justice CIA leak investigation Special Prosecutor; and Col. Mark Tillman, USAF, commander, Presidential Airlift Group. A reporter referred to former Ambassador Joseph C. Wilson IV, who served as CIA envoy to Niger in February 2002.

Remarks Following Discussions With President Alvaro Uribe Velez of Colombia
June 14, 2006

President Bush. Thank you all for coming. It's my honor to welcome back to the Oval Office *mi amigo el Presidente.* Mr. President, we're glad you're here. This is my first chance to be able to congratulate the President for a very strong victory. I asked him what it's like to win with a lot of votes. [*Laughter*] He was obviously a good campaigner that had a message that the Colombian people appreciated. So first of all, congratulations for a grand victory.

President Uribe is a personal friend. I'm able to talk very frankly with him about a variety of subjects. I told him that one of the things I admire is he's a strong believer in democracy, human rights, human dignity. He's got a tough job in dealing with narcoterrorist groups in his country, but he's committed to dealing firmly with narcoterrorism. He's committed to helping reconcile past differences. He's committed to helping people get back into society. And I appreciate those commitments. He's committed to human rights.

We talked about trade. We negotiated a free trade agreement. We've still got some details to work out, but we committed ourselves to working out those details and try to get this done as quickly as we can. I will submit the agreement to Congress once it gets done, and I would hope members of both political parties understand the importance of a free trade agreement with this vital ally of ours.

We talked about the neighborhood. We talked about—he came from a meeting with some of the Andean neighbors, and he brought messages, and he shared some thoughts with me. I appreciate strategizing with the President about how to make sure our neighborhood is a peaceful and hopeful place.

I told President Uribe that one of the things I will do a better job of is communicating to the people of South America and Central America my country's desire to promote justice and education and health. We spend about $1.6 billion a year in Central and South America. I want the people to understand that money is meant to help them, to help improve their lives. I want the people to understand America is a considerate country, that we care about justice.

And so, Mr. President, I am really pleased you're here. It's good to see you again. And again, congratulations on a great victory.

President Uribe. Thank you, Mr. President. I want to repeat my gratitude to your Government, to you personally, to your Congress, to the U.S. public opinion, for the permanent support of my country. I appreciate your friendship, your permanent advice, and we have many challenges before us.

One challenge is that Colombia can overcome this long nightmare of terrorism. I understand the mandate my fellow country citizens have given me to work harder and with better results for my country to get peace, and the United States cooperation is necessary.

In the last 2 years, we have not gotten the—[*inaudible*]—result in dropping the areas with illegal drugs. One point we have studied this morning with President Bush is how to speed up the eradication of drugs, because we need to show better results in this area.

And of course, as President Bush has informed to you, we spoke about our free trade agreement and some pending points. And we spoke about the necessity in Colombia and in all the Central American and South American countries to improve social cohesion. For I thank President Bush, he's willing—his willingness and determination to help us in education, in social issues, because we need to conduct hand in hand our fight against terrorism with our fight to create social cohesion, not only in Colombia but in the whole region as well.

President Bush. Gracias, amigo. Thank you very much.

NOTE: The President spoke at 12:06 p.m. in the Oval Office at the White House. The Office of the Press Secretary also released a Spanish language transcript of these remarks.

Remarks Following a Meeting With the Iraq Study Group
June 14, 2006

I want to thank a distinguished group of Americans, led by Jim Baker and Lee Hamilton, for your willingness to look at the way forward in Iraq and to provide advice to the administration, to the Congress, and to the American people about the proper strategies and tactics to achieve success.

Iraq is a complex situation. It is vital that we succeed. And the fact that you all are willing to lend your expertise to help chart the way forward means a lot. And I can't thank you enough. We've got Republicans at the table; we've got Democrats at the table; we've got people who've served in the administration, administra-tions past, our court system, and the legislative branch. And you bring a lot of expertise and a lot of knowledge, and the fact that you're willing to lend your expertise and knowledge to help our country means a lot.

Once again, you've been called to serve, and once again, you are serving, and we thank you for that a lot. Appreciate you very much.

NOTE: The President spoke at 2:36 p.m. in the Roosevelt Room at the White House. In his remarks, he referred to James A. Baker III and Lee H. Hamilton, cochairs, Iraq Study Group.

Remarks at the Initiative for Global Development's 2006 National Summit
June 15, 2006

Thank you all. Whatever successes this administration has had in combating global poverty, Colin Powell gets a lot of credit. I will spend some time talking about our responsibility as government to address global poverty. It's a responsibility we take seriously, and it's a responsibility that Colin Powell carried out in his distinguished tenure as the Secretary of State of our country. I want to thank you for being a friend, and thank you for your service to the country. He's a good man.

Thank you all for allowing me to come by to speak. I appreciate the cofounders and the leaders of the Global Development effort. I want to thank you for having this summit. Thank you for being what I call social entrepreneurs, people who care about the plight of other people.

The facts are these: Across the globe, more than a billion people live on less than a dollar a day. That should be a troubling statistic to all Americans. They lead lives of hunger; they lead lives of desperation. Every day is a struggle just to survive. That struggle ought to inspire us here in America. It's inspired you; it ought to inspire all our citizens.

I want to thank you for lending your expertise and your funds to address problems alongside your Government. Colin said, "You know, this is not a governmental effort; it's not a business effort; it's not an NGO effort; it's a combined effort by a lot of compassionate hearts to address a significant problem." And so I'm here to thank you for your commitment and to let you know, we're pleased to stand with you.

I want to thank Susan Schwab, who traveled with me today. Maybe you don't know who she is, but you will soon, because she just got sworn in as the new Trade Representative for the United States. So who do you pick to be the Trade Minister?

Well, you pick somebody who is a good negotiator, for starters, somebody who understands that opening markets is in our national interest and that when you open a market, you make sure—as we open our markets, you make sure you're treated fairly. That's what we want. That's all we want. We want to be able to tell the American people that free trade is good for our country, but fair trade means that it's responsible. And so she understands that. She'll be a good, hard negotiator, but she also understands something I understand, and that is, trade is one of the best ways to help lift people out of poverty. I'm going to talk about that in a little bit.

I'm sorry Laura couldn't be with me here. She's a—she is a person who cares deeply about the suffering in places like the continent of Africa. When she travels, she brings the message to the people there that a lot of Americans care deeply about AIDS or care deeply about hunger or malaria. She sends her greetings. I'm lucky she said yes when I asked her to marry me. I think this country is lucky to have her as an ambassadress for the good hearts of the American people.

I thank Bill Clapp and General Shalikashvili, former Senator Dan Evans, Bill Ruckelshaus, cofounders of the Initiative for Global Development. Thank you for being farsighted. Thank you for calling people to action. I thank the members who are here as well.

I appreciate Ambassador Randy Tobias. He had a pretty easy job there in Indianapolis at one time. [*Laughter*] I asked him to—I asked him—I said, "Look, Randy, you've got management skills, and you care; why don't you serve your country, see; why don't you come here to Washington, DC, and put up with all the rhetoric and the noise and the sharp elbows and do something for people around the world?" And he did. He ran the—he ran our HIV/AIDS initiative, and he did a really good job.

America is on the leading edge of fighting HIV/AIDS, and one of the reasons we're effective is because of Randy Tobias. So I'm confident he wanted to leave—"See, I got a place in Montana where I can fish." I think you got one in Montana, don't you? Yes, he started talking about his fishing place in Montana. My answer was, "You're not through yet." [*Laughter*] I said, "You need to run USAID." It's an important part of helping deal with global poverty. It's an important part of our strategy. I want to thank you for staying on, and I want to thank you for your hard work and your vision. You represent the very best of corporate America. You get your skills; you make a living; and then you come and serve your fellow countrymen and the world. Randy, I really thank you for the inspiration and the example you've set.

I'm going to talk about the Millennium Challenge Account. Colin mentioned it. The head of it is here today, John Danilovich. We were really kind of bureaucratic when we first got the thing set up. Like, we weren't moving money out the door, and Congress began to get nervous. I remember Colin was coming to the Oval saying, "Look, it's a great idea, but we got to show some results here pretty quick." Danilovich understands the job is to be less bureaucratic and more forward-leaning when it comes to implementing the Millennium Challenge Account strategy. I want to thank you for taking on this important job.

And I also want to thank my friend Rob Mosbacher, fellow Texan, who's running OPIC. Appreciate you serving the country. Thanks for coming up from Houston to serve.

Here's what I believe: I believe to whom much is given, much is required. This country has been given a lot. We've got a great system; we've got wonderful entrepreneurs; and we're wealthy. We're wealthy because of the ingenuity of the American people. We're wealthy because there's risk takers. We're wealthy because we've got a fiscal system that encourages the private sector to flourish. We're wealthy because we're a country of rules and laws.

I also believe that with prosperity comes an enormous responsibility. We have a moral duty to care for those who hurt here at home, and we have a moral duty to care for those—as best as we can for those abroad. That's part of the foreign policy of our country. It's a foreign policy that Secretary of State Powell helped implement—helped form and implement. We believe every person, no matter their income or economic status, bears the image of a Creator. That's what I believe. I believe every person, no matter their income or their status or where they live, has dignity of matchless value. And we believe that those who live in the most extreme poverty deserve this country's help.

Fighting global poverty reflects this country's values. It serves our Nation's interests as well. It's the country's economic interest that we fight global poverty, because as developing nations grow in prosperity, they create better lives for their citizens and markets for U.S. products. It's in our security interests that we fight global poverty, because weakened, impoverished states are attractive safe havens for terrorists and tyrants and international criminals. We believe that young people without opportunities are susceptible to ideologies of hatred. And so by helping poor nations create a more hopeful future, we can not only build prosperity; we reduce the appeal of radicalism.

Our values and our interests draw us to the same conclusion: The reduction of extreme poverty in our world must be a key objective of American foreign policy. And it is. And so today I want to talk to you about the need for us to expand trade, to promote freedom, and to reform the programs that we have in place, in order to achieve results, in order to say that—to the

American taxpayer, the money is not only being spent; it's being spent wisely.

First, the strategy to defeat extreme poverty begins with trade. That's sometimes hard for some people to connect with. It's kind of a—people don't quite understand why that's the case. One way to describe it, the value of trade, is this: The value of trade is more than 10 times the value of foreign investment and foreign aid combined. In other words, prosperity as a result of trade is more likely, 10 times more likely, to have a positive effect on somebody living in a poor society than just investment and grants.

History has shown what I'm talking about. Take the example of South Korea. It's probably hard for some to remember, back in the fifties, particularly if you were born in the sixties—[*laughter*]—but South Korea was one of the poorest nations in Asia. South Korea reformed its economy and opened its markets to the world. And today, export growth—the capacity for people to find work in South Korea, for products that are sold elsewhere—has made this country the tenth largest economy in the world.

India, for a long period of time, had restricted its markets. India opened its markets to global trade 15 years ago. It has doubled the size of its economy since then and created a middle class which is larger than the entire population of the United States.

I don't believe these are isolated examples. The World Bank study found that developing nations that lowered their trade barriers in the 1990s grew three times faster than those that did not. Economic growth is one important way to reduce poverty. It's the most effective way to reduce poverty. The best way to help millions mired in poverty is to expand the benefits of global trade. That's part of this administration's strategy.

I asked Congress, and Congress granted trade promotion authority. It took a lot of work, as you recall, Mr. Secretary, but it

was a necessary part of our capacity to expand trade. And since then, we've completed negotiations on free trade agreements with 15 nations on 5 continents with a combined population of 200 million people.

We've built on the success of the African Growth and Opportunity Act. For those of you who follow the economic vitality of Africa, you know that AGOA has been a very effective policy. It was put in place by my predecessor, President Clinton. And we signed into law the AGOA Acceleration Act. In other words, we took the step that President Clinton took and took it farther.

And it's worked. That's what's important for our citizens to understand. Trade helps lift people out of poverty. Since AGOA's inception, U.S. imports from Africa have increased by 114 percent. Last year, over 98 percent of U.S. imports from AGOA-eligible countries entered this country duty-free. When somebody is able to sell a product into the United States, it means somebody is working. It means somebody has got a job. It means that people aren't reliant upon the Government to help them realize their dreams. This is like—AGOA has created new opportunities. Americans have got to understand that when we talk about trade, we're not only talking about enhancing economic growth and vitality; we're helping people get out of poverty. Trade is an important part of making sure that we implement this strategy.

You know, the AGOA showed that bipartisan cooperation here in Washington is possible. And one thing you can help is to make sure that bipartisan cooperation on other trade agreements is possible in Washington, DC. If you're genuinely serious about reducing poverty, you need to help us make sure this Nation does not become a protectionist nation. The tendencies are to say, "Let's just wall ourselves off from competition." But if we become a protectionist nation, if we lose our confidence and our capacity to compete in the global economy, it will make it much harder to achieve the common goal of reducing global poverty.

Now we're confronted with a really good opportunity, by the way, to deal with global poverty, and that is to complete the Doha round of the WTO negotiations. And it's tough sledding right now. You know, national interests seem to be kind of more important than a—than reducing barriers and tariffs across the world. You know, local politics has a lot to do with whether or not this Doha round is going to get completed, and I understand that. And I knew that going into the negotiations.

And that's why at the United Nations last year, I made this pledge on behalf of the American people: We're ready to eliminate all tariffs and subsidies and other barriers to free flow of goods and services, and we expect other nations to do the same. That's what I said to get the Doha round moving. See, we're ready to make the move on agriculture and services and manufacturing, but we expect other nations to do the same thing. We expect other nations to give us market access. I want to be able to go to people here in the United States, producers, and say, "We got you market access so you can compete fairly." And that's why we're going to get rid of the subsidies that now exist on the books.

The Doha negotiations are at a critical moment. It is—in my view, countries in Europe have to make a tough decision on farming. And the G–20 countries have to make a tough decision on manufacturing. And the United States is prepared to make a tough decision along with them. That's my message to the world.

Susan's going to carry that message. I'm going to carry it to Europe next week at the EU summit. Now is the time for the world to come together and make this world a free trading world, not only for the benefit of our own economies but as an important part of the strategy to reduce poverty around the world.

I think we have to expand freedom in order to reduce poverty. Free nations produce the vast majority of the world's economic output. Many of the worst dictatorships are some of the world's most poorest nations. I believe there's a correlation between prosperity and freedom. And this country of ours will continue to pursue an agenda that understands that human liberty is universal. It's just not a U.S. thing; it's its own—liberty is something that everybody yearns for. And freer the world becomes, the more prosperous the world becomes and the more likely people will not be mired in poverty.

Nations that build institutions that secure the rule of law and respect human dignity also are more likely to create an economic climate that fosters investment and growth. And so we support the rise of free and democratic societies across the world. And the story of freedom is one of the really, really interesting chapters of the 21st century, when you think about it. From Afghanistan to Iraq to Lebanon to Georgia to Ukraine to Kyrgyzstan, people have gone to the polls and elected their leaders. In the last 5 years, more than 110 million people have joined the ranks of the free. That's an astonishing development when you think about it. And it's a positive development for those of us who care deeply about global poverty.

As more people gain their freedom, they will also gain the opportunity to build a better life. That's a fact of life. And so this country has got to be confident in our willingness, in our desire to help people—to help free people from the clutches of tyrants. I said in my second Inaugural speech, "The goal of this country ought to be to end tyranny in the 21st century." I could have easily have said, "One way to reduce global poverty is to reduce tyranny in the 21st century."

Free peoples need to do more than cast their ballots. We recognize that. Going to the polls is not the kind of freedom necessary to reduce global poverty. It's just the beginning of a process to reduce global poverty. And so the United States has an obligation to help others build the institutions necessary—in a civil society—necessary to be able to deal in a—with the advent of freedom. And so we're helping new democracies build free institutions that are responsive to the people's needs. And we're doing so through organizations like the National Endowment of Democracy. We've worked to double its budget over the past 5 years. Those funds support programs that will help form civic organizations. We're helping dissidents become legislators. We're helping businesses in new market economies organize trade associations and chambers of commerce. It's the things we take for granted here in America, these funds are meant to do.

It's one thing to promote trade; it's one thing to promote freedom, but we've got to recognize that our own aid programs have got to help complement those objectives. In other words, we want results from the money we spend. That's what the American people expect, by the way. See, when we talk about foreign aid, they expect the foreign aid to mean something. You know, I travel around a lot. I think about people out there that are working hard for a living, and they say, "You know, you're spending this money overseas. Why?" And the answer is, because not only do we have a moral duty, it's in our national interest to do so.

But I've got to be able to tell them, as well, and anybody in elected office has got to be able to say, "We're making a difference with the money, see; it's actually producing results." For decades, we provided aid with good intentions. We didn't always ask if we were getting good results. One of the great reforms of Colin Powell's tenure as Secretary of State is, he started asking, "What are the results of the programs; what are we achieving?"

Since 2002, we've committed to increase the resources we devote to fighting poverty across the world. As Colin mentioned, since

taking office, we more than doubled assistance around the world from 10 billion to 27½ billion. It's the largest increase, by the way, of foreign aid since the Marshall plan. And you get a lot of credit for that, Mr. Secretary. I remember you coming into the Oval Office saying, "Let's put our hearts out there for people to see." And one way to do it is by increasing our budgets.

I want to remind you what we're doing with that money. We're fighting HIV/AIDS, and we're helping countries fight malaria. We're expanding education for women and girls. We're rewarding developing nations that move forward with economic and political reform. And by the way, shortchanging these efforts—Congress has got to understand, in shortchanging these efforts, if they choose to do so in the appropriations process, they would undercut our long-term security and dull the conscience of our country. I urge Congress to serve the interests of America by showing the compassion of America and approve my full funding request for foreign assistance this year.

And as we increase the resources, we'll increase accountability for those who have received American aid. In many poor countries, it's really important for all of us who are involved in this program to admit that corruption runs deep. And a lot of times, the assistance we have provided has been wasted or put in the pockets of corrupt officials. I know that's unpleasant for some to hear, but it's a fact. If we expect the people to support us in our efforts to be robust in our compassion overseas, then we've got to recognize that sometimes that money gets stolen and people don't get the results for the money that they expect.

And so we decided to do something about it. We decided that our foreign policy ought to recognize true compassion as measured by real improvements, not just by the amount of money spent. And real improvement is the goal of our assistance.

And so we've set up the Millennium Challenge Account. And it was set up under the—in the State Department when Colin was there. And here's what it says, it says, "We want to grant you money. We want to give assistance, but you've got to be responsible. You, the recipient, have got to be responsible for fighting corruption, embracing democratic government, encouraging free markets, and investing in the health and education of your people."

I remember when we put that out, it was a little controversial, as you remember. I don't see what's controversial in that. I don't see what's wrong with saying to a nation, "You don't get any money if you're corrupt." Because we believe countries are capable of getting rid of corruption. I don't see what's wrong with saying, "You've got to show real investment in education and health care in order to receive our money." I think that's a wise thing to ask. I think if part of the goal is to encourage economic development, we ought to say to countries, in return for U.S. aid, open your markets so you can enhance the prosperity of your citizens. Every nation that applies for a Millennium Challenge grant develops its own priorities and develops its own strategies. But one of the things we do—and this is what Danilovich does and his staff does—they develop clear goals that are measurable. So we say, "This is what you're going to do? Fine. Show us as time goes on that you're doing it."

So far, eight nations have compacts in place that's worth over $1½ billion. Additional 15 countries are now negotiating with the Millennium Challenge Account. And we're going to get the money out the door so long as they meet the criterion.

But the point I'm trying to make to you is that wise use of Government monies can help us achieve objectives which lead to the reduction of global poverty. And so we're just through spending the money without asking for results.

We're an optimistic nation. We believe countries have got the capacity to change; that's what we believe. We refuse to accept the status quo. It is time for other countries

around the world to demand anticorruption regimes. If we're truly interested in reducing global poverty, those of us who are granting money need to stand up with a united voice and say, "We're not going to tolerate corruption."

One of the things Randy Tobias and others are going to do at the State Department, they're going to apply the same principle I've just described to you to all our development aid. We're going to insist upon transparency and performance and accountability. We're going to ensure that every American aid dollar encourages developing nations to build institutions necessary for long-term success. And we're going to help developing nations achieve economic independence. That's what we're going to do. We're going to get away from this notion about, kind of, just analyzing monies based upon percentage of this, that, or the other. We're going to be generous in our contribution and demand results in return.

Now, what's interesting about the goal of eliminating poverty is that about 85 percent of American resources to the developing world come from the private sector. It's one thing for me to talk, and now I'm changing from what we're doing to encouraging you to continue doing what you're doing.

The truth of the matter is, our generous Nation is—the generosity of our Nation is reflected in the private sector a lot. I think that's what makes us such a unique country. You know, government helps, and government does a lot. As I said, we've doubled aid, but what our private sectors do is—it's unbelievable, when you think about it.

And corporate America has a responsibility. And for those of you who represent the NGOs and faith-based groups, thank you for joining the cause as well. This is a collaborative effort. Some of the best work in fighting poverty is accomplished in partnership with private institutions. The

Global Development Alliance has successfully built 400 worldwide alliances. That's good. You've leveraged about 1.4 billion of taxpayers' dollars to over $4.6 billion. In other words, you've taken the money we're spending as kind of a—I wouldn't call it a downpayment, but it's part of a way to really leverage your generosity.

And you're making a difference in the lives of millions of people. I'm grateful for you. That's what I've really come to say. I've come to assure you that the effort to eliminate global poverty is an integral part of our foreign policy. And I think it needs to be a foreign—part of foreign policy after 2½ years, by the way. I think it needs to be a—I think it needs to be part of the calling of the United States in the 21st century.

One of the moral objectives of our time—the great moral objectives of our time is to reduce poverty. I like what Alexis de Tocqueville said about America. He's a pretty interesting observer. Back in 1832, he captured a lot of the spirit of this country. He said this, he said, "When an American needs the assistance of his fellows, it's very rare that it be refused. When some unexpected disaster strikes a family, a thousand strangers willingly open their purses."

That was the America he saw in the 1830s. It's still got to be the America of the 21st century as well, but not only to help our fellow citizens here at home but for our national interests and our economic interests, and just to answer the call of our hearts, it ought to be our foreign policy. It ought to be the center of our foreign policy and the center of the social entrepreneurs in America.

I want you to know that when disaster strikes, we move. We moved hard for the tsunamis, with a military presence that helped organize relief. When the earthquake came in Pakistan, we didn't hesitate; we moved. We know that when a neighbor needs assistance, that we have an obligation to help provide it.

My assurance to you is that we will continue to stand with our brothers and sisters who are poor, to help as best as we possibly can, and I want to thank you for helping as well. God bless your efforts, and may God bless our country.

NOTE: The President spoke at 9:55 a.m. at the Willard InterContinental Washington.

Remarks on Signing the Broadcast Decency Enforcement Act of 2005
June 15, 2006

Thank you all. Please be seated. Thank you all for coming. In a few moments, I will sign the Broadcast Decency Enforcement Act. This is a good bipartisan bill. It's going to help American parents by making broadcast television and radio more family-friendly.

I appreciate the many citizens groups who are here, and I want to thank the Members of Congress who worked hard to get this bill passed. And I'm looking forward to signing it into law.

I want to thank Kevin Martin, who's the Chairman of the Federal Communications Commission, and I want to thank the other Commissioners who are here today.

I appreciate Senator Bill Frist joining us. He's the majority leader of the United States Senate. I want to thank Senator Ted Stevens for joining us as well. I thank Senator Sam Brownback, Senator George Allen. I want to thank the House majority leader, John Boehner, for being here. I want to thank Joe Barton, chairman of the House Energy and Commerce Committee.

The bill sponsor is with us, Fred Upton from the State of Michigan. Thank you for coming, Fred. I appreciate Congressman Bobby Rush from the State of Illinois, Chip Pickering from Mississippi, and Joe Pitts from Pennsylvania.

Every day, our Nation's parents strive to raise their children in a culture that too often produces coarse, vulgar, and obscene entertainment. In our free society, parents have the final responsibility over the television shows that their children watch or the web sites they visit or the music they listen to. That's a responsibility of moms and dads all across the country, to make sure their children are listening to or watching the right kind of programming.

The best way to do that is for parents to be vigilant, pay attention to what their children are doing. One thing they can do if they're worried about people watching a bad program is turn off the TV. That's why they put the on/off button there. [*Laughter*] Parents are the first line of defense, but broadcasters and the electronics industry must play a valuable role in protecting our children from obscene and indecent programming.

They provide the tools that empower parents to make good decisions, such as voluntary rating systems and the V-chip. And we applaud those. Broadcasters also have a duty to respect common decency, to take into account the public interest, and to keep the public airwaves free of indecent material, especially during the hours when children are most likely to be watching and listening.

Unfortunately, in recent years, broadcast programming has too often pushed the bounds of decency. One study found that during the hours between 8 and 9 p.m.— that's the time when most families are watching television—the use of profanity on television shows increased vulgar language by 95 percent from '88 to—1988 to 2002. In other words, the language is becoming coarser during the times when it's more likely children will be watching television.

It's a bad trend, a bad sign. Since 2000, the number of indecency complaints received by the FCC has increased from just hundreds per year to hundreds of thousands. In other words, people are saying, "We're tired of it, and we expect the Government to do something about it."

And so we believe we have a vital role to play. We must ensure that decency standards for broadcasters are effectively enforced. That's the duty of the FCC. That's why we've got the Chairman standing right here, which he understands. [*Laughter*] It's the duty of the FCC to impose penalties on broadcasters and stations that air obscene or indecent programming. It's one of their responsibilities. People expect us to adhere to our responsibilities. He's a part of the executive branch. And since I'm the head of the executive branch, I take responsibility, as well, for putting people in place at the FCC who understand, one of their jobs, and an important job, is to protect American families.

The problem we have is that the maximum penalty that the FCC can impose under current law is just $32,500 per violation. And for some broadcasters, this amount is meaningless. It's relatively painless for them when they violate decency standards. And so the Congress decided to join the administration and do something about it.

And so the bill I'm about to sign, the Broadcast Decency Enforcement Act, increases tenfold the penalty that the FCC can impose, to $325,000. The Congress got serious, and I appreciate their hard work on this measure.

The legislation does not change the broadcast decency standards that are already on the books. What the legislation does is it gives the FCC the means to enforce them more effectively. By allowing the FCC to levy stiffer and more meaningful fines on broadcasters who violate decency standards, this law will ensure that broadcasters take seriously their duty to keep the public airwaves free of obscene, profane, and indecent material. American families expect and deserve nothing less.

And so I'm going to ask the Members of Congress who have worked hard on this piece of legislation to join me. I congratulate you for your good work. Thank you for coming. May God bless you.

NOTE: The President spoke at 11:07 a.m. in Room 350 of the Dwight D. Eisenhower Executive Office Building. S. 193, approved June 15, was assigned Public Law No. 109–235.

Remarks on Signing the MINER Act
June 15, 2006

Thanks for coming. Welcome to the White House, and thank you for witnessing this bill signing ceremony. In a few moments, I'm going to sign into law the most sweeping overhaul of Federal mine safety law in nearly three decades. The MINER Act of 2006 has strong support of mine workers and the mining industry, and it was overwhelmingly passed by the Congress. I want to thank the Members of the United States Congress who have joined us here for their hard work on this important measure.

I thank the Secretary of Labor, Elaine Chao, who has joined us. I appreciate the Governors from three important coal mining States, Joe Manchin, Ernie Fletcher, and Ed Rendell for joining us here as well. I was struck by how the Governors handled the tragedies of the mine incidents. I thought they were able to convey a deep sense of compassion in an attempt to heal hearts, and I thank them for their courage.

I appreciate Bill Frist, who has joined us, and Mitch McConnell, Members of the United States Senate, as well as Mike Enzi, Senator Ted Kennedy. I'm particularly thrilled that Senator Robert Byrd is here. I don't know if you know this, but last Monday he achieved a milestone, and that is, he has served longer in the United States Senate than any other Senator in our Nation's history, and he's served with distinction. And we're glad you're here, Senator. Thank you for coming.

I thank Majority Leader John Boehner for joining us, as well as Congressman Buck McKeon and Shelley Moore Capito, Hal Rogers, Rick Boucher from Virginia. I appreciate all the Members of Congress who've joined us.

I appreciate the leaders of the mining industry. I appreciate the workers who are here. Thanks for taking time in your day to come.

I want to welcome the families of those—who mourn the loss of life. We share in your grief, and we honor the memories of your loved ones. I know it's hard. It's really hard for you, but we welcome you here, and we're honored you took time to be here.

I appreciate members of my administration who have joined us as well today. The hard work of American miners provides us with really important fuel. This economy is growing because of the work of our miners. Coal is an important part of our Nation's present and future.

Thanks to modern technology and equipment, we've come a long way from the days when a miner would take a canary into the coal mines. Passage—and since the passage of the Mine Safety and Health Act in '77—1977, America has seen significant decreases of injuries and fatal mining accidents.

Yet events in recent months have reminded us that mining is dangerous work. That's what we've seen. This year alone, accidents have taken the lives of 33 miners in our country. Just last month, five miners were killed in a mine explosion in Harlan County, Kentucky. And in January, Americans watched and prayed—a lot of Americans prayed with the people of West Virginia for the 13 miners that were trapped underground by the explosion in the Sago mine. Only one man came out, and he's with us today—Randal McCloy, and his wife, Anna. And we welcome you all.

And we know—we know, and I hope you know that your fallen mining brothers are with us here today in spirit. They're with us today with their loved ones here, eyes wet with tears but proud of their accomplishments. We're glad you're here.

We honor the memory of all lost miners today; that's what we're doing signing this bill. We make this promise to American miners and their families: We'll do everything possible to prevent mine accidents and make sure you're able to return safely to your loved ones.

The bill I'm about to sign is an important part of the effort. The MINER Act will build on the Mine Safety and Health Administration's ongoing efforts to enhance mine safety training, to improve safety and communications technology for miners, and provide more emergency supplies of breathable air along escape routes.

This new legislation will require mine operators to report any life-threatening accident no later than 15 minutes after they know that one has occurred. And to ensure compliance with the law, the MINER Act will increase the maximum penalty for flagrant violations of mine safety regulations nearly fourfold.

To implement this new legislation, we need effective and experienced leadership at the Mine Safety and Health Administration. Last month, I named, or nominated Richard Stickler of the State of West Virginia to be the head of MSHA. He's got experience. He served for 6 years as the Director of Pennsylvania's Bureau of Deep Mine Safety. He was a miner, mine shift foreman, a superintendent, and a manager, and the Senate needs to confirm Richard Stickler to this key position.

America's miners work hard every day to support their families and support this country. It's hard work. You deserve the best training, the best equipment, and safeguards that we can provide to protect the lives. And this good legislation I'm signing today is an important part of honoring that commitment.

May God bless you all. May God bless our miners and their families, and may God continue to bless our country. And now it's my honor to sign the MINER Act into law.

NOTE: The President spoke at 11:23 a.m. in Room 450 of the Dwight D. Eisenhower Executive Office Building. In his remarks, he referred to Gov. Joe Manchin III of West Virginia; Gov. Ernie Fletcher of Kentucky; and Gov. Edward G. Rendell of Pennsylvania. S. 2803, approved June 15, was assigned Public Law No. 109–236.

Remarks on the Establishment of the Northwestern Hawaiian Islands Marine National Monument
June 15, 2006

Thank you all. Please be seated. Pretty good deal when you get introduced by your wife. [*Laughter*] I really am glad Laura is here, because she is a champion of our Nation's cultural and natural resources. It's an honor to share this important day with her at the podium. And I want to thank you all for coming.

As I was walking in here, I actually saw Theodore Roosevelt's portrait over there. What's interesting is that we are here to fulfill a legacy of conservation that was first begun by Theodore Roosevelt. In 1909, President Roosevelt established the Hawaiian Island Reservation, and he did so to protect native sea birds from being hunted. His Executive order was the first of many Presidential efforts to protect the life and waters of Northwestern Hawaiian Islands.

In a few moments, I will sign a proclamation to designate the waters in this region a national monument. This action will create the Northwestern Hawaiian Islands Marine National Monument, the largest single conservation area in the history of our country and the largest protected marine area in the world.

As a marine national monument, the waters of the Northwestern Hawaiian Islands will receive our Nation's highest form of marine environmental protection. We will protect a precious natural resource. We will show our respect for the cultural and historical importance of this area. And we will create an important place for research and learning about how we can be good stewards of our oceans and our environment.

I can't thank the Governor for being here enough, Governor Linda Lingle. She's—as I'll mention a little later on, we've been in close consultation with the Governor. And when did you leave yesterday? [*Laughter*] We're sure honored you're here representing your great State.

I want to thank Senator Daniel Akaka for joining us as well. I want to thank Congressman Ed Case, and I know that Congressman Neil Abercrombie will be here shortly for the signing of this important proclamation. Sherry Boehlert is here from the great State of New York—a strong conservationist. Welcome, Congressman. I'm glad you're here. I appreciate Senator Fred Hemmings from—he's a minority leader, by the way, of the Hawaiian State Senate. Thanks for coming. I'm glad you're here.

I appreciate Secretary Dirk Kempthorne, Secretary Carlos Gutierrez. I want to thank Vice Admiral Conrad Lautenbacher of NOAA. Thanks for coming. Appreciate your hard work on this issue. As you will hear a little later on, NOAA will be playing an important part of this national monument.

I want to thank Jean-Michel Cousteau for joining us. He just showed me a picture of another President—well, two fathers kind of gathered together. And it's proud for two sons to be carrying on the legacy of conservation. He's made a really important movie that I hope people watch about the Northwestern Hawaiian Islands. I think the American people will understand better about why I made the decision I made when they see the movie that Jean-Michel has produced.

I want to thank Sylvia Earle. She's a marine biologist. She's explorer in residence of the National Geographic Society. It was during the showing of the movie that she sat me down and gave me a pretty good lecture about life. [*Laughter*] She actually invited me to spend a week with her under the seas. [*Laughter*] There's some in Congress who would like me to spend my lifetime under the seas. [*Laughter*]

I want to thank Mike Nussman; he's the president and CEO of American Sportfishing Association. Thanks for coming, Mike. I want to thank the guests from the environmental community who are here today. Thanks for your hard work on this vital issue.

The vibrant beauty of the oceans is a blessing to our country, and it's a blessing to the world. The oceans contain countless natural treasures. They carry much of our trade; they provide food and recreation for billions of people. We have a responsibility, a solemn responsibility to be good stewards of the oceans and the creatures who inhabit them.

In 2004, my administration released an Ocean Action Plan to promote an ethic of responsible use and stewardship for our oceans and coastal resources. By establishing this new national monument, we implement an important part of our plan, and we accomplish three goals for the nation: First, this new national monument will honor our commitment to be good stewards of America's natural resources.

Our duty is to use the land and seas wisely or, sometimes, not use them at all. Good stewardship of the environment is not just a personal responsibility, it is a public value. Americans are united in the belief that we must preserve our natural heritage and safeguard the environment. This belief has affirmed our laws, and today we reaffirm that commitment once again.

The Northwestern Hawaiian Islands are a beautiful and special place. The 10 islands and atolls stretch over 1,400 miles. That's the distance from Chicago to Miami. In the tropical waters surrounding the archipelago, there are more than 4,500 square miles of coral reef habitat thriving under the surface. Think about that—4,500 square miles of coral reef. These undersea forests and mountain ranges comprise the largest remote reef system in the world. And this region holds the largest and healthiest untouched coral reef system in the United States. And we're going to preserve it.

These reefs burst with life, great predators like the white tip reef shark and the spinner dolphins and the Trevally jacks. The archipelago is home to more than 7,000 marine species. That's a quarter of which are found nowhere else on the world. The Northwestern Hawaiian Islands are also the primary home for nearly 1,400 surviving Hawaiian monk seals. That's virtually the entire population of this critically endangered species. They are the breeding grounds for approximately 90 percent of the threatened Hawaiian Island green sea turtle population.

I think you're beginning to get a feel for why I made the decision I made. The national monument we're establishing today covers nearly 140,000 square miles. To put this area in context, this national monument is more than 100 times larger than Yosemite National Park, larger than 46 of our 50 States, and more than 7 times larger than all our national marine sanctuaries combined. This is a big deal.

We will preserve access for native Hawaiian cultural activities. As part of the proclamation, the Department of the Interior and the Department of Commerce will work with the State of Hawaii and the public to develop a plan to manage the monument. This proclamation will also charge NOAA to use its expertise to oversee the new marine areas and the Fish and Wildlife Service to apply their skills to the wildlife refuge areas.

Within the boundaries of the monument, we will prohibit unauthorized passage of ships; we will prohibit unauthorized recreational or commercial activity; we will prohibit any resource extraction or dumping of waste. And over a 5-year period, we will phase out commercial fishing as well. For sea birds and sea life, this unique region will be a sanctuary for them to grow and to thrive. And for the American people, it will be a place that honors our responsibility to protect our natural resources.

This new monument shows what cooperative conservation can accomplish. My administration is committed to working in a spirit of respect and cooperation with those seeking to protect our land and sea and sky. We believe cooperative conservation is the best way to protect the environment. This means we must focus on the needs of States and respect the unique knowledge of local authorities and welcome the help of private groups and volunteers.

Through cooperative conservation, we're moving away from the old environmental debates that pit one group against another and towards a system that brings citizens of every level of government together to get results. In the northwest Hawaiian Islands, we have worked with Governor Lingle and State officials and native Hawaiian leaders to ensure, first and foremost, that they wanted the monument and, secondly, to make sure that we protect the cultural and historical heritage of these islands.

For more than 1,000 years, native Hawaiians sailed these waters and visited these islands as part of sacred journeys. The islands are dotted with archeological treasures and traditional sites of worship. This monument will protect the cultural ties that native Hawaiians have to these lands and waters. We respect these natives' beliefs, and this monument will safeguard both the natural and spiritual treasures of the region. And for this reason, we will consult with native Hawaiian leaders to give this monument a native Hawaiian name.

Protecting the Northwestern Hawaiian Islands, volunteers play an important part. Jean-Michel taught us that in his movie. Through a major Federal-State partnership, volunteer divers work together to remove nets and gear that have been abandoned by fishermen. In one year alone, divers removed more than 120 tons of this derelict fishing gear. To fight the destructive effects of abandoned nets and other debris, the Ocean Action Plan directed the Coast Guard and EPA and NOAA and the State Department and the Interior Department to coordinate efforts to improve how the Federal Government tracks, prevents, and cleans up maritime waste. And we've got more work to do. And I expect these agencies to be robust in our efforts to prevent this kind of debris from polluting our—polluting this sanctuary, this monument.

We're going to work together with volunteers to make our oceans safer for marine life. And to give this remote and special place our Nation's highest level of protection—as we give it this kind of protection, we're also reminded of our responsibility to be wise managers of marine resources living off every coast. And that's why we're working to end overfishing. Overfishing is harmful. It's harmful to our country, and it's harmful to the world.

To protect our marine ecosystem and the future fishing of all kinds, the Ocean Action Plan calls for Congress to reauthorize the Magnuson-Stevens Fishery Conservation and Management Act. They need to get that done. This act would provide enhanced authority to work with regional fish councils to build an improved market-based system to restore our fisheries. I like to fish, and I expect this Government of ours to protect the fisheries so sports people can fish and get a good catch. That's why I'm glad the sportsmen are here—sportfishing people are here. You know, you just got to understand, we're going to listen to you. It's in the Nation's interest that we have a robust recreational fishing industry.

Congress needs to move forward with my administration's plan to build a well-managed system of offshore aquaculture. Aquaculture or "fish farming" uses pens in the ocean—open ocean to feed and grow shrimp, shellfish, and many other types of fish. And when we get this right, these farmed fish can provide a healthy source of food and reduce pressure on the ocean ecosystems.

In the Northwest Hawaiian Islands, we're also preserving an historic landmark of great importance. Near the northern edge of these islands lies Midway Island, the site of one of the most decisive battles of World War II. On this atoll, there's a memorial to the sacrifice and valor of those who fought in the Pacific theater during World War II. This national monument will have special access area around Midway Island. That's what we want. We want people to go and pay homage to those who sacrifice for our freedom.

Third, the new national monument creates a new opportunity for ocean education and research for decades to come. Successful ocean stewardship depends on informed policy makers and an informed public. One of the key priorities of the Ocean Action Plan is promoting ocean education. Jean-Michel put it this way, he said, "How can we protect what we don't understand?"

Ninety-five percent of our planet's oceans have yet to be explored. We're just beginning to appreciate what the seas have to offer humanity. The waters of this new national monument will be a living laboratory that offers new opportunities to discover new life, that helps us better manage our ocean ecosystems, and allows us to pursue advances in science.

You know, in America, there's a great consensus that we have an obligation to be good stewards of the environment. Success of a generation is not defined by wealth alone. We also will be measured by the respect we give to the precious creatures of our natural world.

We have great choices before us in this country. And with the designation of the Northwestern Hawaiian Island Marine National Monument, we are making a choice that will leave a precious legacy.

I want to thank you all for joining us today. It's an historic moment. Thank you all for your leadership. And may God bless the country.

NOTE: The President spoke at 2:34 p.m. in the East Room at the White House. In his remarks, he referred to Gov. Linda Lingle of Hawaii; and oceanographer Jean-Michel Cousteau.

Statement on Congressional Passage of Appropriations Legislation
June 15, 2006

I applaud those Members of Congress who came together in a fiscally responsible way to provide much-needed funds for the war on terror and continued Hurricane Katrina recovery, as well as for securing our border and protecting against a possible avian flu pandemic. Responding to these critical needs in a timely way is not easy, but it must be done if we are to fight terrorism, defend our homeland, enforce our borders, and fulfill our moral obligation to help our fellow Americans in need. I am pleased that Congress has addressed these urgent national priorities within the spending limits I set. House and Senate leadership and Chairmen Cochran and Lewis deserve great credit for working together to pass a fiscally responsible bill. The statement referred to H.R. 4939.

Statement on Signing the Emergency Supplemental Appropriations Act for Defense, the Global War on Terror, and Hurricane Recovery, 2006
June 15, 2006

Today, I have signed into law H.R. 4939, the "Emergency Supplemental Appropriations Act for Defense, the Global War on Terror, and Hurricane Recovery, 2006." The Act provides additional resources needed to fight the war on terror, help citizens of the Gulf States recover from devastating hurricanes, and protect Americans from a potential influenza pandemic.

Sections 1209 and 2202 of the Act prohibit use of certain funds appropriated in the Act to initiate new start programs unless the congressional defense committees receive advance written notice. The Supreme Court of the United States has stated that the President's authority to classify and control access to information bearing on the national security flows from the Constitution and does not depend upon a legislative grant of authority. Although the advance notice contemplated by sections 1209 and 2202 can be provided in most situations as a matter of comity, situations may arise, especially in wartime, in which the President must act promptly under his constitutional grants of executive power and authority as Commander in Chief of the Armed Forces while protecting certain extraordinarily sensitive national security information. The executive branch shall construe these sections in a manner consistent with the constitutional authority of the President.

Subsection 1304(a) of the Act amends section 550 of Public Law 109–102 to purport to require the President to consult with committees of the Congress prior to exercising authority granted to the President by section 550. Subsection 1304(b) purports to require the Secretary of State to consult such committees prior to exercising authority under that provision. Because the President's constitutional authority to supervise the unitary executive branch and take care that the laws be faithfully executed cannot be made by law subject to a requirement to consult with congressional committees or to involve them in executive decision-making, the executive branch shall construe the references in the provisions to consulting to require only notification.

The provision under the heading, "Joint Explosive Device Defeat Fund," Department of Defense-Military, that calls for the reporting to congressional committees of information that may include highly sensitive and classified national security information, will be construed consistently with the President's constitutional responsibility to control the dissemination of such information.

The executive branch shall construe the provision in the Act under the heading "Disaster Relief," Federal Emergency Management Agency, Department of Homeland Security, that purports to require the Secretary of Homeland Security to submit a housing proposal and expenditure plan for congressional committee approval as calling solely for notification, as any other construction would be inconsistent with the constitutional principles enunciated by the Supreme Court of the United States in *INS v. Chadha*.

Sections 7030 through 7033 of the Act, inclusive, purport to make changes in or in relation to statements of managers that accompanied various appropriations bills reported from House-Senate conferences in the past. Also, a provision in chapter 9 of the Act under the heading "Emergency Relief Program," Federal Highway Administration, Department of Transportation, purports to give binding effect to a document not presented to the President. The executive branch shall construe these provisions in a manner consistent with the bicameral passage and presentment requirements of the Constitution for the making of a law.

GEORGE W. BUSH

The White House,
June 15, 2006.

NOTE: H.R. 4939, approved June 15, was assigned Public Law No. 109–234.

Letter to Congressional Leaders Reporting on Deployments of United States Combat-Equipped Armed Forces Around the World
June 15, 2006

Dear Mr. Speaker: (*Dear Mr. President:*)

I am providing this supplemental consolidated report, prepared by my Administration and consistent with the War Powers Resolution (Public Law 93–148), as part of my efforts to keep the Congress informed about deployments of U.S. combat-equipped Armed Forces around the world. This supplemental report covers operations in support of the war on terror, Kosovo, and Bosnia and Herzegovina.

The War on Terror

Since September 24, 2001, I have reported, consistent with Public Law 107–40 and the War Powers Resolution, on the combat operations in Afghanistan against al-Qaida terrorists and their Taliban supporters, which began on October 7, 2001, and the deployment of various combat-equipped and combat-support forces to a number of locations in the Central, Pacific, and Southern Command areas of operation in support of those operations and of other operations in our war on terror.

I will direct additional measures as necessary in the exercise of the U.S. right to self-defense and to protect U.S. citizens and interests. Such measures may include short-notice deployments of special operations and other forces for sensitive operations in various locations throughout the world. It is not possible to know at this time either the precise scope or duration of the deployment of U.S. Armed Forces necessary to counter the terrorist threat to the United States.

United States Armed Forces, with the assistance of numerous coalition partners, continue to conduct the U.S. campaign to pursue al-Qaida terrorists and to eliminate support to al-Qaida. These operations have been successful in seriously degrading al-Qaida's training capabilities. United States Armed Forces, with the assistance of numerous coalition partners in Combined Forces Command, Afghanistan, ended the Taliban regime and are actively pursuing and engaging remnant al-Qaida and Taliban fighters in Afghanistan. Approximately 200 U.S. personnel also are assigned to the International Security Assistance Force (ISAF) in Afghanistan. The U.N. Security Council authorized the ISAF in U.N. Security Council Resolution 1386 of December 20, 2001, and has reaffirmed its authorization since that time, most recently for a 12-month period beginning October 13, 2005, in U.N. Security Council Resolution 1623 of September 13, 2005. The mission of the ISAF under NATO command is to assist the Government of Afghanistan in creating a safe and secure environment that allows reconstruction and the reestablishment of Afghan authorities. Currently, all 26 NATO nations contribute to the ISAF. Ten non-NATO contributing countries also participate by providing military and other support personnel to the ISAF.

The United States continues to detain several hundred al-Qaida and Taliban fighters who are believed to pose a continuing threat to the United States and its interests. The combat-equipped and combat-support forces deployed to Naval Base, Guantanamo Bay, Cuba, in the U.S. Southern Command area of operations since January 2002 continue to conduct secure detention operations for the approximately 460 enemy combatants at Guantanamo Bay.

The U.N. Security Council authorized a Multinational Force (MNF) in Iraq under unified command in U.N. Security Council Resolution 1511 of October 16, 2003, and reaffirmed its authorization in U.N. Security Council Resolution 1546 of June 8, 2004. In U.N. Security Council Resolution 1637 of November 8, 2005, the Security

Council, noting the Iraqi government's request to retain the presence of the MNF, extended the MNF mandate for a period ending on December 31, 2006. Under Resolutions 1546 and 1637, the mission of the MNF is to contribute to security and stability in Iraq, as reconstruction continues. These contributions have included assisting in building the capability of the Iraqi security forces and institutions as the Iraqi people drafted and approved a constitution and established a constitutionally elected government. The U.S. contribution to the MNF is approximately 131,000 military personnel.

In furtherance of our efforts against terrorists who pose a continuing and imminent threat to the United States, our friends and allies, and our forces abroad, the United States continues to work with friends and allies in areas around the globe. These efforts include the deployment of U.S. combat-equipped and combat-support forces to assist in enhancing the counterterrorism capabilities of our friends and allies. United States combat-equipped and combat-support forces continue to be located in the Horn of Africa region, and the U.S. forces headquarters element in Djibouti provides command and control support as necessary for military operations against al-Qaida and other international terrorists in the Horn of Africa region, including in Yemen. In addition, the United States continues to conduct maritime interception operations on the high seas in the areas of responsibility of all of the geographic combatant commanders. These maritime operations have the responsibility to stop the movement, arming, or financing of international terrorists.

NATO-Led Kosovo Force (KFOR)

As noted in previous reports regarding U.S. contributions in support of peacekeeping efforts in Kosovo, the U.N. Security Council authorized Member States to establish KFOR in U.N. Security Council Resolution 1244 of June 10, 1999. The mis-

sion of KFOR is to provide an international security presence in order to deter renewed hostilities; verify and, if necessary, enforce the terms of the Military Technical Agreement between NATO and the Federal Republic of Yugoslavia (which is now Serbia); enforce the terms of the Undertaking on Demilitarization and Transformation of the former Kosovo Liberation Army; provide day-to-day operational direction to the Kosovo Protection Corps; and maintain a safe and secure environment to facilitate the work of the U.N. Interim Administration Mission in Kosovo (UNMIK).

Currently, there are 24 NATO nations contributing to KFOR. Eleven non-NATO contributing countries also participate by providing military personnel and other support personnel to KFOR. The U.S. contribution to KFOR in Kosovo is about 1,700 U.S. military personnel, or approximately 11 percent of KFOR's total strength of approximately 16,000 personnel.

The U.S. forces have been assigned to the eastern region of Kosovo. For U.S. KFOR forces, as for KFOR generally, maintaining a safe and secure environment remains the primary military task. The KFOR operates under NATO command and control and rules of engagement. The KFOR coordinates with and supports the UNMIK at most levels; provides a security presence in towns, villages, and the countryside; and organizes checkpoints and patrols in key areas to provide security, protect minorities, resolve disputes, and help instill in the community a feeling of confidence.

In accordance with U.N. Security Council Resolution 1244, UNMIK continues to transfer additional competencies to the Kosovar Provisional Institutions of Self-Government, which includes the President, Prime Minister, multiple ministries, and the Kosovo Assembly. The UNMIK retains ultimate authority in some sensitive areas such as police, justice, and ethnic minority affairs.

NATO continues formally to review KFOR's mission at 6-month intervals. These reviews provide a basis for assessing current force levels, future requirements, force structure, force reductions, and the eventual withdrawal of KFOR. NATO has adopted the Joint Operations Area plan to regionalize and rationalize its force structure in the Balkans. The UNMIK international police and the Kosovo Police Service (KPS) have full responsibility for public safety and policing throughout Kosovo. The UNMIK international police and KPS also have begun to assume responsibility for guarding patrimonial sites and established border-crossing checkpoints. The KFOR augments security in particularly sensitive areas or in response to particular threats as needed.

NATO Headquarters in Bosnia and Herzegovina

Pursuant to the June 2004 decision made by NATO Heads of State and Government, and in accordance with U.N. Security Council Resolution 1575 of November 22, 2004, NATO concluded its Stabilization Force operations in Bosnia-Herzegovina and established NATO Headquarters-Sarajevo to continue to assist in implementing the Peace Agreement in conjunction with a newly established European Force. The NATO Headquarters-Sarajevo, to which approximately 250 U.S. personnel are assigned, is, with the European Force, the legal successor to SFOR. The principal tasks of NATO Headquarters-Sarajevo are providing advice on defense reform and performing operational supporting tasks, such as counterterrorism and supporting the International Criminal Tribunal for the Former Yugoslavia.

I have directed the participation of U.S. Armed Forces in all of these operations pursuant to my constitutional authority to conduct U.S. foreign relations and as Commander in Chief and Chief Executive. Officials of my Administration and I communicate regularly with the leadership and other Members of Congress with regard to these deployments, and we will continue to do so.

Sincerely,

GEORGE W. BUSH

NOTE: Identical letters were sent to J. Dennis Hastert, Speaker of the House of Representatives, and Richard B. Cheney, President of the Senate.

Remarks at the Congressional Picnic
June 15, 2006

Thank you all for coming. Welcome to the South Lawn. Laura and I are thrilled you're here. This is called "Rodeo on the South Lawn." [*Laughter*] And we've—first of all, I want to thank all the Members of the Congress and the Senate who are here. Thanks for serving the country.

I always take this opportunity to thank your families on your behalf. I know you do it all the time, but I know you couldn't serve without the support of your loved ones. And so, for all the family members who are here, the wives and the husbands and the children and the grandchildren, welcome. Thanks for serving the country too.

We got some interesting entertainment for you tonight. We got some people who can play music and some people who think they can play music. [*Laughter*] We got three bands, one—the first band will be called The Compassionates. The leader of that band is my Chief of Staff, Josh Bolten.

Yes. Then we've got—The Second Amendments will be playing tonight. That would be Congressman Collin Peterson, Dave Weldon, Kenny Hulshof, Thaddeus McCotter—he's that rock-and-roll dude, Thaddeus McCotter—and Congressman Jon Porter. Once you get through those two bands, then a real group of musicians will be here, and we're fortunate Riders in the Sky will be playing for you tonight.

I hope you enjoy this as much as Laura and I enjoy it. We're really glad you're here. God bless you all, and God bless our great country. Please welcome The Compassionates.

NOTE: The President spoke at 6:50 p.m. on the South Lawn at the White House.

Message on the Observance of Juneteenth
June 12, 2006

I send greetings to all those observing Juneteenth.

President Lincoln called the Emancipation Proclamation of 1863 the "central act" of his administration and "the greatest event of the nineteenth century." The joyous news of freedom did not reach Galveston, Texas, until two and a half years after emancipation when Major General Gordon Granger arrived and announced that the Civil War was over and all slaves were free. Ever since, Americans have marked June 19th with special celebrations and traditions commemorating this historic moment.

On this day, we honor the vision of President Lincoln, and we will keep striving to build a Nation where the dignity of every person is respected, where people are judged by the content of their character, and where the hope of the American dream reaches every neighborhood and every citizen. Together, we can continue to advance the ideals of liberty and justice that make our country strong and help more Americans realize the full promise of this great Nation.

Laura and I send our best wishes on this special occasion. May God bless you, and may God continue to bless the United States of America.

GEORGE W. BUSH

NOTE: This message was released by the Office of the Press Secretary on June 16. An original was not available for verification of the content of this message.

Remarks at a Reception for Congressional Candidate Heather Wilson in Albuquerque, New Mexico
June 16, 2006

Thank you very much. Thanks for coming. It's great to be back in New Mexico again. It just seemed like I was here the other day. [*Laughter*] This time I've come because I cannot tell you how important it is to reelect Heather Wilson to the United States Congress.

I have spent enough time in Washington, DC, to be able to distinguish between the real, genuine person and those who are just up there to mark time. Heather Wilson is honest; she is capable. She has gone to Washington, DC, to do a job on behalf of the citizens of New Mexico, and she deserves to be reelected to the United States Congress.

And I thank you for helping her. This has been a successful event. So I want to thank the organizers and the phone callers and the people that encouraged you to come, and then I want to thank you for being here. When you find somebody who is a decent soul willing to sacrifice time with her family, willing to travel the long distances between New Mexico and Washington, DC, willing to do the hard work on behalf of the citizens of Albuquerque and the surrounding area, you need to support her. And I want to thank you for supporting her.

When Heather tells you something, she means it. And you don't have to worry about her disgracing the office of the United States Congress. You know, I like strong women. [*Laughter*] I was raised by one; I married one; and I hope we're raising two. [*Laughter*] And sometimes a strong woman—sometimes they—they all listen, and sometimes they do what you ask them to do, and sometimes they don't. [*Laughter*] See, Heather Wilson is an independent soul. That's what you want from a person from this district. You want somebody who is strong in her beliefs, strong in her convictions, but strong, first and foremost, to the people of this district. The way I like to describe her is: She's compassionate; she's smart; she's independent-minded; and she can get the job done. And that's why she needs to go back to the United States Congress.

Laura sends her best. In the photo line, the guy said, "Where's Laura?" It didn't hurt my feelings, you know. [*Laughter*] Kind of like, you know, "How come you're here and she's not?" [*Laughter*] But Laura knows talent and strength of character when she sees it; Heather Wilson is one of her favorite people in Washington, DC.

And she sends her love to Heather and sends her thanks to you all for helping this fine lady get reelected to the United States Congress.

By the way, I lucked out when she said yes. [*Laughter*] We were raised, as you know, right across the border, so I have a pretty good feeling about the values and the thinking of the people of New Mexico. And so does Laura. And there's no doubt in her mind and my mind that Heather Wilson is the right person to represent you in the United States Congress. And again, I want to thank you. I forgot to ask you to do one thing, though, and that is thanks for giving of your hard-earned money; make sure that you turn out the vote coming down the stretch.

She's going to win. No doubt in my mind, she's going to win. I want to thank her family, Jay, Joshua, and Caitlin. I was telling Joshua and Caitlin coming over—I spent some quality time with Heather on Air Force One; it's amazing what people do to get on Air Force One, by the way. [*Laughter*] I said to Joshua and Caitlin, "I know a lot about you." They kind of looked at me like, you know, "Huh?" [*Laughter*] I said, "That's all your mother talked about for half the leg." [*Laughter*] I love a person who values her family, who places her family at the center of her life. We need people in the United States Congress who understand the importance of family in our society. Heather Wilson not only talks about family, she acts on her love of her family. And I want to thank Jay and Josh and Caitlin for being here today. And thank you for supporting your mom and your wife for her hard work doing the job.

I want to thank Allen Weh—[*applause*]—yes, he's a good fellow. I want to thank the grassroots activists who are here. I want to thank those of you who, a lot of time, don't get credit for making phone calls—there's one right there—[*laughter*]—and people who put up the signs and go to the rallies and stuff the envelopes, the people who really turn out to be the wind at the candidate's back. And you're going to make the difference coming down the stretch for Heather. So thank you in advance for what you're fixing to do.

We're dealing with some big issues. We really are. These are historic times. And one of the reasons I feel so strongly that Heather needs to be reelected is, she understands the stakes of the world in which we live. See, we need people who see the world the way it is, not the way we would hope it would be. And the world we live in is a dangerous world because there's still enemies that would like to strike the United States of America.

We need clear-eyed realists in Washington, DC. Heather Wilson is a clear-eyed realist. She brings a lot of experience to the job. By the way, she's on the Intelligence Committee; I'm probably not supposed to talk about it. [*Laughter*] The reason she's on it is because she's a clear-eyed realist. It's a very, very important job. She helps make sure this country has the best intelligence possible. And the reason that's important is because our most important job, the most important priority of the President and the Congress, is to protect the American people. And the best way to protect the American people is to stay on the offense and bring the killers to justice so they don't hurt the American people again.

And in order to stay on the offense, we've got to have good intelligence, and we've got to have smart, capable people helping this Government find these terrorists. In order to protect the American people, I need people in the United States Congress who understand the importance of supporting the men and women who wear the uniform of the United States of America, and Heather Wilson understands that.

We're fighting a global war on terror. Now, I know most of the attention is focused on Iraq, but I want to remind you, that is just a battlefield in the global war on terror. It's a part of the war on terror.

I need people in the United States Congress like Heather, who understands that the war on terror is not just Iraq but it's Afghanistan, and it's places where people plan and plot their attacks on the United States of America.

I just came back from Baghdad. It's a remarkable experience to, first and foremost, meet the leaders of a new Government, people that are in office because 12 million people are able to vote because we threw out a tyrant that was so brutal and so ruthless that—not only to kill his own people by the thousands, that he invaded his neighbors, that he threatened the United States of America, that he harbored terrorists. And now they have a chance to vote, and they did, and now there's a Government formed under one of the most modern constitutions ever written in the Middle East. And it was refreshing to see these people that are anxious to fulfill the will of the people of Iraq.

And it's hard work. But I went to take the measure of the person. I went to say this to him: "It's up to you; here's your chance; here's your chance to succeed; here's your chance to liberate people; here's your chance to make history; here's your chance to spread the peace; here's your chance to help us fight those who want to destroy your hopes and aspirations." And I also told him this, that "When the United States of America gives a commitment, we will keep our word. We will not cut and run." It's important to have people in the United States Congress who understand the stakes of the fight in Iraq and complete the mission. And Heather Wilson is such a person.

We're going to succeed in Iraq. We will succeed. And when we do, they will be an ally in the war on terror, and they'll be an example for others to see. You see, I base a lot of my decisions upon this belief: There is an Almighty, and one of the great gifts of the Almighty to men and women from all faiths and all walks of life is freedom. Freedom is universal. Freedom is not owned just by people in the United States of America, it's universal; all people desire to be free. And free societies turn out to be peaceful societies. Free societies figure out ways to keep the peace. And so, in our fight against the terrorists, not only will we bring them to justice and stay on the hunt to protect the American people, but at the same time, we will act on the universal principle of freedom and help others become free.

People say, "What do you mean by that, Mr. President?" Well, I'll give you an example. Two weeks from today, I'll be meeting with the Prime Minister of Japan, Prime Minister Koizumi. He's coming. We'll have a visit in Washington, DC. It turns out he's an Elvis fan, so he and I are then going to go to Graceland. [*Laughter*] Think about that, though. Think about the American President traveling to Graceland—[*laughter*]—with the Prime Minister of Japan. Let me ask you something—60 years ago, would you have thought that would be possible? [*Laughter*] Think about it.

See, my dad and, I bet, your relatives too—some of you had relatives who fought the Japanese. They were the sworn enemy of the United States of America in a bloody, bloody conflict. And 60 years later, I'll be sitting down at the table with the Prime Minister talking about North Korea, how to keep the peace there. I'll be talking about the fact that their country has contributed 1,000 troops to help this young democracy in the heart of the Middle East. He understands that freedom can help change a neighborhood that's been full of hatred.

What happened? What happened was Japan adopted a Japanese-style democracy. They had a different form of government. They became—they adopted a different style of governing themselves. Democracies have the capacity to convert enemies into allies. And what's happening today is we're after the terrorists not only by staying on the hunt, but we're after them with an

ideology of hope, an ideology of light, an ideology that recognizes human rights and human dignity. And one of these days, somebody is going to be sitting down— a duly-elected leader from Iraq sitting down at the table with a future U.S. President talking about how to keep the peace. We're laying the foundation of peace for generations to come, and Heather Wilson understands the stakes.

Our economy is strong. And one of the reasons it's strong is because we put policies in place that recognize that if you have more money in your pocket to save, invest, or spend, this economy is going to grow. See, there's a philosophical debate in Washington, DC: Who best can spend your money? [*Laughter*] We like—Heather and I like for you to spend your own money. We believe if you have more money in your pocket, the economy—[*applause*]. We believe if you're a small-business owner and you got more money in your treasury, your more likely to hire somebody. That's what we believe.

The other crowd believes they need to run up your taxes, because they think they can spend your money better than you can. You might remember, we've had some tough economic times in this country. We had a recession, a stock market correction, corporate scandals, an attack on the United States of America, two wars to defend ourselves, major natural disasters, and high energy prices—and yet this economy is going strong. And we intend to keep it strong. [*Applause*]

And the reason it's strong is because we cut the taxes. We let you keep more of your own money. Now, you'll hear them in Washington say, "Well, what we need to do is balance the budget by raising the taxes." That's not the way Washington works; it's just not the way. It may sound attractive to some here in Albuquerque, "Oh, we'll just tax a certain number of people, and we'll balance the budget that way." No, the way Washington works is, they will raise your taxes, and they will figure out new ways to spend your money. The best way to balance the budget is to set priorities when it comes to spending the people's money, to be strong on those priorities, and to keep progrowth economic policies in place so we get more tax revenues coming into the Treasury because this economy is growing. That's how you balance the budget.

Make no mistake about it, if the other bunch gets in control of the Congress, you'll be paying higher taxes. And that's why we're going to win this November. People understand they're taxed enough. What they want is fiscal sanity in Washington, DC. That's what they want.

You know something? One of the things that we're going to run on as a party and Heather can really run on is, she's delivered. Take Medicare, for example. That's a program—it's an important program. It was signed by Lyndon Baines Johnson in 1965. It's really an important deal. The Federal Government has made a commitment to help our elderly when it comes to health care. And our attitude is, if you make a commitment, you want to make sure you have a modern health care system. There's no need to make a commitment and have a lousy health care system. And Medicare had done a lot of good work, but it was getting old, and it needed to be reformed. Medicine was changing, but Medicare wasn't.

And so we got together and decided we're going to do something on behalf of the seniors. We're going to fulfill our promise to the seniors of the United States of America. The other bunch had been talking about it, year after year. We did—we got something done. What we did is, we provided prescription drugs as an integral part of Medicare.

People say, why was that important? Well, I'll give you one reason. Medicare would pay for heart surgery but would not pay one dime for the prescription drugs that could prevent the heart surgery from being needed in the first place. Medicine

had been modernizing; Medicare had not. And thanks to the leadership of Heather Wilson, I was able to sign a modern Medicare bill. And if you're a poor senior in Albuquerque, New Mexico, this Government is going to help you with your prescription drugs. And the days of you having to choose between medicine and food are over, thanks to Heather Wilson.

I could keep talking all day long about her—[*laughter*]—but I might miss my dinner with Laura. [*Laughter*] But I do want to talk about her love of the young people. You might remember, she served in the cabinet here as the Secretary of Children, Youth, and Family. She was—she said, "Look, I want to serve my State by helping young people, helping the disadvantaged." In other words, she's got a good heart.

And she took that heart to Washington and helped us pass the No Child Left Behind Act. Let me tell you something about the No Child Left Behind Act. It said, we're going to increase money, particularly for poor students. I think that's a good use of money. I really do. But instead of just accepting mediocrity in our schools, we said, "We're going to challenge the soft bigotry of low expectations." Here's the truth. In some schools, it's just as easy to pass somebody who looks hard to educate along. "If you're at such-and-such an age, you're supposed to be here; we'll just move you there."

See, Heather and I believe every child can learn, no matter if you're—how you were raised, no matter your heritage. We believe you can learn to read. You know, if your mom and dad don't speak English as their primary language, we still believe you can learn. And not only we believe you can learn, we expect the school to teach you to learn. That's what we want. We expect the schools to teach you how to read and write and add and subtract.

And so we worked to raise the standards and said to States, "You measure, because we want to know." We want to know early, before it's too late. The No Child Left Behind Act that Heather was a strong supporter of has helped change America for the better. It says, if we find a child struggling with reading early, we're going to make sure there's extra money to help that child, because we don't want one child left behind in America.

There is an achievement gap in America. There really is. When you look at the fourth grade results, there's a—the Anglo students are here, and Latino students are here, and the African American—that's not right. That's not what this country is all about. This country is about equal opportunity. This country is about making sure every child, no matter what her—his or her background is, gets a great education. And the No Child Left Behind Act is challenging mediocrity, and it's challenging failure, and that achievement gap is closing. And Heather Wilson gets credit for being a strong supporter of good schools in New Mexico.

You know, there's a lot of problems that rise—rise up for a State like New Mexico. You've got very important labs, and these labs make a difference for the United States of America. But it's not a given the labs will be there. You need people in the

Congress that understand how to get things done.

It seems like to me the people of this district would want somebody to be able to pick up the phone and call the President of the United States and have the President of the United States answer the phone. I'm close to Heather, you know. As I told you, she's independent. But that doesn't mean I don't hold her in the highest—highest regard and deep respect, which I do. I love her integrity. And when she calls me on the phone, I answer. And guess what— guess what she's generally talking about? The people of this congressional district. She loves of the people of this district. She's serving the people of this district. And I urge the people of this district, for their own sake, for their own good, and for the good of the United States of America, to send Heather Wilson back to the United States Congress.

Thanks for coming. God bless.

NOTE: The President spoke at 4:40 p.m. at the Hyatt Regency Albuquerque. In his remarks, he referred to Allen Weh, chairman, Republican Party of New Mexico; Prime Minister Nuri al-Maliki and former President Saddam Hussein of Iraq; and Prime Minister Junichiro Koizumi of Japan.

The President's Radio Address
June 17, 2006

Good morning. Earlier this week, I traveled to Baghdad to visit the capital of a free and democratic Iraq. It was an incredible feeling to stand in the cockpit of Air Force One and watch the pilot steer us in toward Baghdad.

After we landed, I had the pleasure of meeting with our dedicated Embassy staff and intelligence officers serving far from home under dangerous circumstances. And I was honored to meet with some of our

troops, including those responsible for bringing justice to the terrorist Zarqawi. It was a privilege to shake their hands, look them in the eye, and tell them how much the American people appreciate their daily courage and how much we appreciate the sacrifices that they and their families are making.

On my trip, I also met with the new Iraqi Prime Minister Maliki, and I was able to see firsthand his strong character and his determination to succeed. We held a joint meeting of our two Cabinets, with members of my Cabinet participating by video teleconference from Camp David. The Prime Minister briefed us on his plan to take immediate steps in three key areas: improving security; building up Iraq's economy so Iraqis can see real progress in their lives; and reaching out to the international community to secure support for Iraq's new Government. Then we discussed how my administration can help the Prime Minister accomplish these vital objectives.

His top priority is securing Baghdad, so coalition and Iraqi forces have launched Operation Together Forward, a joint effort to restore security and the rule of law to high-risk areas of the city. To help the Prime Minister improve security, we will continue embedding coalition transition teams in Iraqi Army and police units, and we will help the new Iraqi Ministers of Defense and Interior improve their command and control, root out corruption, and investigate and punish human rights violations. We will also support the Prime Minister as he works to rein in illegal militias, build a judicial system that will provide equal justice to all, and promote reconciliation among the Iraqi people.

To aid the Prime Minister in revitalizing Iraq's economy, we will send additional experts to help the Iraqi Government develop an economic framework that will promote job creation and opportunity for all Iraqis. We will also help the Prime Minister increase oil and electricity production by working together on ways to protect key infrastructure from attacks and to quickly restore oil and electricity production when attacks do occur.

Finally, America will help the Prime Minister engage the international community in Iraq's success. We will encourage other nations to fulfill the monetary pledges they have already made to help the new Iraqi Government succeed. We will also support the Prime Minister's efforts to forge a new international compact. Under

this compact, Iraq will take a series of steps in the political, economic, and security areas, and in return, the international community will provide Iraq with more robust political and economic support.

During my trip, I was impressed with the Prime Minister, the team he has assembled, and the plan he has set for his Government. I appreciate his determination and the determination of his Cabinet to make his agenda work. I told them that the future of Iraq is in their hands. And I told them that America is a nation that keeps its word, and America will stand with them as we work toward our shared goal: a free Iraq that can govern itself, sustain itself, and defend itself. By seizing this moment of opportunity, we will defeat our common enemies and build a lasting democracy in the heart of the Middle East, and that will make Americans, Iraqis, and the world more secure.

I traveled to Baghdad to personally show our Nation's commitment to a free Iraq, because it is vital for the Iraqi people to know with certainty that America will not abandon them after we have come this far. The challenges that remain in Iraq are serious. We face determined enemies who remain intent on killing the innocent, and defeating these enemies will require more sacrifice and the continued patience of our country. But our efforts in Iraq are well worth it. The mission is necessary for the security of our country, and we will succeed.

Thank you for listening.

NOTE: The address was recorded at 7:10 a.m. on June 16 in the Cabinet Room at the White House for broadcast at 10:06 a.m. on June 17. The transcript was made available by the Office of the Press Secretary on June 16 but was embargoed for release until the broadcast. In his address, the President referred to senior Al Qaida associate Abu Musab Al Zarqawi, who was killed in Baquba, Iraq, on June 7; and Prime Minister Nuri al-Maliki, Minister of Defense Abd al-Qadir al-Mufriji, and Minister of the Interior Jawad al-Bulani of Iraq. The Office of the Press Secretary also released a Spanish language transcript of this address.

Commencement Address at the United States Merchant Marine Academy in Kings Point, New York
June 19, 2006

The President. Thank you for the warm welcome, if you know what I mean. [*Laughter*] Admiral Stewart, Secretary Mineta, Members of the United States Congress, Academy staff and faculty, distinguished guests, proud family members, and most importantly, the class of 2006: I'm honored to be the first President to address the United States Merchant Marine Academy. I know that a Presidential visit to Kings Point has been a long time in coming, and, Admiral, I hope it's worth the wait. [*Laughter*]

This is a proud moment for the class of 2006. You have worked hard for this day. You sweated through the hardest indoc in Academy history; you braved the Jamaican beef patties of Delano Hall. [*Laughter*] You spent a year when your classroom was a ship and your campus the seven seas. You've made it through endless drills on the Grinder; you've survived the restriction musters that come with missing the train back from Manhattan. This fall, your football team brought home the Secretaries Cup by beating the Coast Guard. You've rung the bell outside Wiley Hall. And the words etched in your class ring affirm your commitment to teamwork: "Not for you, not for me, but for us." Your parents are proud of you; your teachers are proud of you; and this Academy is proud of you. On behalf of the American people, I congratulate you on a fine achievement, and I thank you for choosing to serve the United States of America.

This morning I flew here on Air Force One with my friend Andy Card. You might remember Andy; he was my former chief of staff, and he attended this Academy in the 1960s. It just so happens, when he was a plebe, he was stuffed in a duffel bag and run up the flagpole. [*Laughter*] I know he appreciates the much warmer welcome he received here today. [*Laughter*]

Secretary Card also reminded me that the President of the United States has the authority to lift all demerits and restrictions. So I bring you a graduation present. [*Laughter*] In keeping with the longstanding tradition at our Nation's service academies, I hereby absolve all midshipmen who are on restriction for minor conduct offenses; I leave it to Admiral Stewart to define exactly what "minor" means. [*Laughter*]

Life at this Academy is demanding, and it is meant to be. America is a great maritime power, and our merchant marine has a vital role to play. In times of peace, the merchant marine helps ensure our economic security by keeping the oceans open to trade. In times of war, the merchant marine is the lifeline of our troops overseas, carrying critical supplies, equipment, and personnel. For more than six decades, the mission of this Academy has been to graduate highly skilled mariners to serve America's economic and national security needs. To train you for these responsibilities, this Academy sharpens your mind; it strengthens your body and builds up your character. The Academy has made you strong and instilled respect for the Kings Point motto: *Acta Non Verba*, "Deeds, Not Words."

"Deeds, Not Words" was the hallmark of this Academy in World War II. In the early years of the war, America's efforts to supply our allies in Europe were threatened by the U-boats that were sinking American ships faster than we could build them. The need to arm and defend our merchant ships was urgent, and King Pointers answered the call. And one of them was an 18-year-old named Edwin O'Hara, whose statue stands not far from here. In September 1942, Cadet O'Hara was serving on the USS *Stephen Hopkins* when it came under attack from two Nazi raiders. After the entire guncrew of the *Hopkins* was killed by enemy fire, O'Hara singlehandedly served and fired the last five shells in the ready box, scoring direct hits on the German warship *Stier*. Cadet O'Hara was mortally wounded in the action, but not before he helped send the *Stier* to the bottom of the South Atlantic.

Edwin O'Hara is one of 142 Academy graduates who gave their lives in the Second World War. Today, Kings Point is still the only one of our five service academies that sends its students into the theaters of war—and for that reason, it is the only Academy authorized to fly a battle standard.

"Deeds, Not Words" was your response on the morning of September the 11th, 2001. From this campus, every man and woman could see the black smoke rising from the Twin Towers. Within hours, your midshipmen were working side by side with the Coast Guard and Marine Division of the New York City Fire Department. Over the next 9 days, you moved firefighters and police and emergency response teams into Ground Zero. You moved tons of food and water and supplies. The heroic response to that terrible day showed the spirit of America and the spirit of this fine Academy, and I thank you for your service.

"Deeds, Not Words" defines the Academy's role in the global war on terror. Your cadets are forward-deployed in the Middle East, where they're supporting operations in Afghanistan and Iraq. Your Global Maritime and Transportation School is providing advanced training in areas from marine engineering to port security for military units like the Navy Seabees and Surface Warfare Officers. And your graduates are serving our Nation in every branch of our Armed Services, as sailors projecting American combat power across the Earth, as marines and soldiers leading platoons from Khandahar to Tikrit, as Coast Guard officers securing our homeland, and as airmen delivering justice to terrorists hiding in safe houses and caves. In the global war on terror, the men and women of this Academy are making a difference on every front, and the American people are grateful for your service.

To win the war on terror, we will continue to build and strengthen ties with our friends and allies across the world. America's alliance with Europe is a key pillar of our strategy for victory. And tomorrow Laura and I will depart on my 15th trip to Europe since I have taken office. This visit comes at a critical moment for America and our allies. We have important decisions to make that will affect the prospects for peace and prosperity across the world. And today I'm going to talk to you about the objectives I will pursue on this important trip.

My first stop will be Vienna, where I will attend the annual summit between the United States and the European Union. And then I'm going to travel to Budapest to commemorate the 50th anniversary of the Hungarian Revolution. And I'm really looking forward to the trip. Americans have strong ties to the European people. We have warm friendships with European nations. And on my trip this week, we will strengthen our close and growing partnership with the European Union.

America's partnership with the European Union grows from sturdy roots—our common love of freedom and our commitment to democratic principles. Those of you graduating today have grown up with a Europe whose major powers are at peace with one another. Yet in the sweep of history, this is a dramatic change. There was a time in the history when Europe was the site of bloody conflicts and bitter rivalries. As recently as the last century, Europe was the site of two devastating world wars. Now, because generations have sacrificed for liberty and built strong democracies, the nations of Europe are partners in common union and neighbors on a continent that's whole, free, and at peace.

A free and peaceful Europe is one of the great achievements of the past century. My generation and yours will be judged by what comes next. So America and Europe must work together to advance freedom and democracy. We will cooperate to expand trade and prosperity. We will strengthen our efforts to combat terrorism. And we will stand together to stop the proliferation of weapons of mass destruction.

Our work begins with a common commitment to extending the reach of freedom and democracy. On Prime Minister Blair's recent visit to America, he said, "The governments of the world do not all believe in freedom, but the people of the world do." As people who have secured our own freedom, America and Europe have a duty to help others do the same. We're fulfilling that duty together in Belarus, where we support the reformers seeking to erase the stain of dictatorship from Europe. We're fulfilling that duty together in Georgia and the Ukraine, where we stand with brave people striving to consolidate democratic gains. We're fulfilling that duty together in the Balkans, where people who have suffered so much have made a choice to live in liberty and should be welcomed as a part of Europe in the 21st century.

As we saw on September the 11th, 2001, the actions of a repressive regime thousands of miles away can have a direct impact on our own security. In this new century, the loss of freedom anywhere is a blow to freedom everywhere. And when freedom advances, people gain an alternative to violence, and the prospects for peace are multiplied, and all nations become more secure. So America and Europe have launched bold initiatives to aid democratic reformers across the world, especially in the broader Middle East. We've worked with the United Nations to end the Syrian occupation of Lebanon, and we will not rest until the Lebanese people enjoy full independence. We're determined to end the conflict in the Holy Land and bring about a solution with two democratic states, Israel and Palestine, living side by side in peace and security.

Our shared commitment to extending freedom and democracy is clear in Afghanistan and Iraq. Together America and Europe have helped bring about a historic transformation in those countries. Two of the world's most dangerous regimes have been removed from power, and the world is better off for it. Al Qaida's training camps have been closed in Afghanistan. Al Qaida's leader in Iraq has been killed. Two violent dictatorships are being replaced with growing democracies that answer to their people, that respect their neighbors, and that serve as allies in the war on terror. Afghanistan and Iraq are taking their rightful place in the free world, and America and Europe must work tirelessly to help them succeed.

One week ago today, I left Camp David and flew to the capital of a free and democratic Iraq. In Baghdad, I met with Prime Minister Maliki and members of his Cabinet. The Prime Minister is a man of strong character. He has a clear and practical plan to lead his country forward. He briefed me on the immediate steps he's taking to improve security in Baghdad, to build up Iraq's economy, and to reach out to the international community.

The formation of a new Government, successful raids on Al Qaida targets in Iraq have created a moment of opportunity. Iraqis must seize this moment, and we will help them succeed. I assured the Prime Minister that when America gives a commitment, America will keep its word. By helping Prime Minister Maliki's new Government achieve its aims, we will expand opportunity for all the Iraqi people, we will inflict a major defeat on the terrorists, and we will show the world the power of a thriving democracy in the heart of the Middle East.

A free and sovereign Iraq requires the strong support of Europe. And some of the most important support for Iraqis is coming from European democracies with recent memories of tyranny, Poland and Hungary and Romania and Bulgaria and the Czech Republic and Slovakia, Georgia, Ukraine, Latvia, Lithuania, and Estonia. Others in Europe have had disagreements with our decisions on Iraq. Yet we've all watched the Iraqi people stand up for their freedom, and we agree that the success of a democratic government in Baghdad is vital for the Iraqis and for the security of the world.

The European Union has been the world's most—among the world's most generous financial donors for reconstruction in Iraq. And Europe and America will encourage greater international support to help Prime Minister Maliki implement his plans for recovery. The international community has pledged about $13 billion to help this new Government. Yet only $3½ billion has been paid. This is a critical time for Iraq's young democracy, and assistance from the international community will make an immediate difference. All nations that have pledged money have a responsibility to keep their pledges, and America and Europe will work together to ensure they do so.

America and Europe also stand together in our determination to widen the circle of prosperity. We're cooperating on projects to develop clean, secure energy sources, especially alternatives to fossil fuel. On the continent of Africa, we're working to strengthen democracy, relieve debt, fight disease, and end the genocide in Darfur. At the World Trade Organization, we're working to lower trade barriers by con-

cluding the Doha talks. America has made a bold proposal to eliminate trade-distorting agricultural subsidies and tariffs, and I call on Europe to join us, so we can set an example of free and fair trade for the world. By spreading prosperity, America and Europe will create new opportunities for our people to help alleviate poverty and deliver hope and dignity and progress to millions across the world.

Together America and Europe are laying the foundations for a future of peace and prosperity. And yet the terrorists are threatening this progress. So at our summit this week, we'll take new steps to strengthen our cooperation on counterterrorism, to improve transportation security, and to crack down on terrorist financing. And we will renew our commitment to support the voices of peace and moderation in the Muslim world, to help provide a hopeful alternative to radicalism. America and Europe must stand united in this war on terror. By being steadfast and by being strong, we will defeat the enemies of freedom.

America and Europe are also united on one of the most difficult challenges facing the world today, the behavior of the regime in Iran. The leaders of Iran sponsor terror, deny liberty and human rights to their people, and threaten the existence of our ally, Israel. And by pursuing nuclear activities that mask its efforts to acquire nuclear weapons, the regime is acting in defiance of its treaty obligations, of the United Nations Security Council, and of the International Atomic Energy Agency. Nuclear weapons in the hands of this regime would be a grave threat to people everywhere.

I've discussed the problem of the Iranian regime extensively with leaders in Europe, particularly in Great Britain and Germany and France. I've also consulted closely with the Presidents of Russia and China. We've all agreed on a unified approach to solve this problem diplomatically. The United States has offered to come to the table with our partners and meet with Iran's representatives, as soon as the Iranian regime fully and verifiably suspends its uranium enrichment and reprocessing activities. Iran's leaders have a clear choice. We hope they will accept our offer and voluntarily suspend these activities, so we can work out an agreement that will bring Iran real benefits. If Iran's leaders reject our offer, it will result in action before the Security Council, further isolation from the world, and progressively stronger political and economic sanctions.

I've a message for the Iranian regime: America and our partners are united. We have presented a reasonable offer. Iran's leaders should see our proposal for what it is, an historic opportunity to set their country on a better course. If Iran's leaders want peace and prosperity and a more hopeful future for their people, they should accept our offer, abandon any ambitions to obtain nuclear weapons, and come into compliance with their international obligations.

I've a message for the Iranian people: The United States respects you and your country. We admire your rich history, your vibrant culture, and your many contributions to civilization. When Cyrus the Great led the Iranian people more than 2,500 years ago, he delivered one of the world's first declarations of individual rights, including the right to worship God in freedom. Through the centuries, Iranians have achieved distinction in medicine and science and poetry and philosophy and countless other fields.

In the 21st century, the people of Iran, especially the talented and educated youth, are among the world's leaders in science and technology. Iranians have a large presence on the Internet and a desire to make even greater progress, including the development of civilian nuclear energy. This is a legitimate desire. We believe the Iranian people should enjoy the benefits of a truly peaceful program, to use nuclear reactors to generate electric power. So America supports the Iranian people's rights to develop nuclear energy peacefully, with proper international safeguards.

The people of Iran, like people everywhere, also want and deserve an opportunity to determine their own future, an economy that rewards their intelligence and talents, and a society that allows them to pursue their dreams. I believe Iranians would thrive if they were given more opportunities to travel and study abroad and do business with the rest of the world. Here in the United States, Iranian Americans have used their freedom to advance in society and make tremendous contributions in areas from business to medicine to academics.

To help provide more opportunities for the people of Iran, we will look for new ways to increase contact between Americans and Iranians, especially in education and culture, sports, and tourism. We'll provide more than $75 million this year to promote openness and freedom for the Iranian people. These funds will allow us to expand and improve radio and television broadcasts to the people of Iran. These funds will support Iranian human rights advocates and civil society organizations. And these funds will promote student and faculty exchanges, so we can build bridges of understanding between our people.

Americans believe the future of Iran will be decided by the people of Iran, and we believe that future can be one of progress and prosperity and achievement. We look forward to the day when our nations are friends and when the people of Iran enjoy the full fruits of liberty and play a leading role to establish peace in our world.

The advance of freedom is the calling of our time, and the men and women of the United States Merchant Marine Academy are answering that call. In a few moments, you will walk through Vickery Gate and leave the Academy that's been your home. You leave with a bachelor's degree, a license as a merchant marine officer, and a commission in one of the branches of our Armed Services. And you leave with something else: The great truth that duty and honor and courage are not just words; they are virtues that sustain a free people, people who are determined to live under self-government. They're the virtues that will be your anchor and compass in a life of purpose and service. These are the virtues that America demands of those entrusted with leading her sons and daughters in uniform. And these are the virtues that America has come to expect from the blue and gray.

We see the devotion to duty and honor and country in the life of one of this Academy's finest graduates, Aaron Seesan. Aaron was an Ohio boy who grew up dreaming of being a soldier. He brought that dream with him to this Academy, and when he walked through these gates 3 years ago, he carried on his shoulders the gold bar of a second lieutenant in the United States Army. After entering the Army, Lieutenant Seesan trained as a combat engineer. And he was serving at Fort Lewis, Washington, when a group of soldiers who were based at that fort were struck by a suicide bomb in Iraq. Two of the men were killed. And that's when this young lieutenant volunteered to go to Iraq to take the place of a wounded platoon leader.

When Lieutenant Seesan arrived in Iraq, some of his fellow soldiers wondered, "What was the Army thinking?" His platoon sergeant said, "I didn't know what the hell a merchant marine graduate was doing here in the 73d Engineering Company." The sergeant quickly changed his mind when he saw Lieutenant Seesan in action, taking care of his men as they patrolled the most dangerous roads in and around Mosul. In May 2005, he was leading a routine sweep of a city street when a bomb exploded and hit the fuel tank of his Humvee. Those who were with him recall his last words: "Take charge, Sergeant Arnold, and take care of the others."

He died on May 22, on National Maritime Day. For his act of bravery, Lieuten-ant Seesan was awarded the Bronze Star. And the campus memorial that bears his name will remind all who come here of Kings Point commitment to service above self.

Aaron Seesan gave his life freely. While still in high school, he wrote a poem that now seems prophetic. He wrote, "Mourn not my terrible death, but celebrate my cause in life." Aaron's cause in life was freedom, and as you take your place as officers in our Armed Forces, I ask you to celebrate the freedom for which Aaron fought and died.

America has invested in you, and she has high expectations. My call to you is this: Trust your instincts, and use the skills you were taught here to give back to your Nation. Do not be afraid of mistakes; learn from them. Show leadership and character in whatever you do. The world lies before you. I ask you to go forth with faith in America and confidence in the eternal promise of liberty.

In all that lies ahead, I wish you fair winds and following seas. As I look out at the men and women before me, I will leave here knowing that you will bring honor to our Nation and to this Academy that has prepared you for the challenges you will face.

May God steer thee well, Kings Point. And may God bless America.

NOTE: The President spoke at 10:07 a.m. on the Captain James Harvey Tomb Field at Brooks Stadium. In his remarks, he referred to Vice Adm. Joseph D. Stewart, USMS, superintendent, U.S. Merchant Marine Academy; Prime Minister Tony Blair of the United Kingdom; senior Al Qaida associate Abu Musab Al Zarqawi, who was killed in Baquba, Iraq, on June 7; Prime Minister Nuri al-Maliki of Iraq; President Vladimir V. Putin of Russia; and President Hu Jintao of China.

Message to the Congress on Blocking Property of Certain Persons Undermining Democratic Processes or Institutions in Belarus
June 19, 2006

To the Congress of the United States:

Consistent with subsection 204(b) of the International Emergency Economic Powers Act, 50 U.S.C. 1703(b)(IEEPA), and section 301 of the National Emergencies Act, 50 U.S.C. 1631 (NEA), I hereby report that I have issued an Executive Order (the "order") blocking the property of persons in connection with the situation in Belarus. In that order, I declared a national emergency with respect to the policies and actions of certain individuals in Belarus, to address the unusual and extraordinary threat to the national security and foreign policy of the United States posed by the actions and circumstances involving Belarus, as described below. This action follows the issuance of Proclamation 8015 of May 12, 2006, "Suspension of Entry as Immigrants and Nonimmigrants of Persons Responsible for Policies or Actions That Threaten the Transition to Democracy in Belarus," in which I determined that it is in the interest of the United States to suspend the entry into the United States of members of the government of Alyaksandr Lukashenka and others who formulate, implement, participate in, or benefit from policies or actions, including electoral fraud, human rights abuses, and corruption, that undermine or injure democratic institutions or impede the transition to democracy in Belarus.

The United States, the European Union, and other allies and partners around the world have repeatedly expressed support for the democratic aspirations of the Belarusian people and condemned the Belarusian government's human rights abuses, assaults on democracy, and corruption. The Belarusian authorities have resorted to intense repression in an attempt to preserve their power, including the disappearances of four regime critics in 1999

and 2000, which the authorities have failed to investigate seriously despite credible information linking top government officials to these acts.

The undemocratic 2006 presidential election was only the latest example of the Belarusian government's disregard for the rights of its own citizens. Hundreds of civic and opposition activists were arrested—and many beaten—both before and after the vote for exercising their rights. The authorities forcibly dispersed peaceful post-election demonstrations. There is simply no place in a Europe whole and free for a regime of this kind.

The order also takes an important step in the fight against public corruption, which threatens important United States interests globally, including ensuring security and stability, the rule of law and core democratic values, advancing prosperity, and creating a level playing field for lawful business activities. As noted in Proclamation 8015, the persistent acts of corruption by Belarusian government officials in the performance of public functions has played a significant role in frustrating the Belarusian people's aspirations for democracy. This order authorizes the Secretary of the Treasury to block the assets of senior-level officials of the Government of Belarus, their family members, or those closely linked to such officials engaged in such corruption.

Thus, pursuant to IEEPA and the NEA, I have determined that these actions and circumstances constitute an unusual and extraordinary threat to the national security and foreign policy of the United States, and I have issued the order to deal with this threat.

The order blocks the property and interests in property in the United States, or in the possession or control of United States persons, of the persons listed in the

Annex to the order, as well as of any person determined by the Secretary of the Treasury, after consultation with the Secretary of State:

- to be responsible for, or to have participated in, actions or policies that undermine democratic processes or institutions in Belarus;
- to be responsible for, or to have participated in, human rights abuses related to political repression in Belarus;
- to be a senior-level official, a family member of such official, or a person closely linked to such an official who is responsible for or has engaged in public corruption related to Belarus.

The order also authorizes the Secretary of the Treasury, after consultation with the Secretary of State, to designate for such blocking any person determined to have materially assisted, sponsored, or provided financial, material, or technological support for, or goods or services in support of, the activities listed above or any person listed in or designated pursuant to the order. I further authorized the Secretary of the Treasury, after consultation with the Secretary of State, to designate for such blocking any person determined to be owned or controlled by, or acting or purporting to act for or on behalf of, directly or indirectly, any person listed in or designated pursuant to the order. The Secretary of the Treasury, after consultation with the Secretary of State, is also authorized to remove any persons from the Annex to the order as circumstances warrant.

I delegated to the Secretary of the Treasury, after consultation with the Secretary of State, the authority to take such actions, including the promulgation of rules and regulations, and to employ all powers granted to the President by IEEPA, as may be necessary to carry out the purposes of the order. All executive agencies are directed to take all appropriate measures within their authority to carry out the provisions of the order.

The order, a copy of which is enclosed, was effective at 12:01 a.m. eastern daylight time on June 19, 2006.

GEORGE W. BUSH

The White House,
June 19, 2006.

NOTE: The Executive order is listed in Appendix D at the end of this volume.

Message to the Congress on Continuation of the National Emergency With Respect to Weapons-Usable Fissile Material in the Russian Federation
June 19, 2006

To the Congress of the United States:

Section 202(d) of the National Emergencies Act (50 U.S.C. 1622(d)) provides for the automatic termination of a national emergency unless, prior to the anniversary date of its declaration, the President publishes in the *Federal Register* and transmits to the Congress a notice stating that the emergency is to continue in effect beyond the anniversary date. In accordance with this provision, I have sent the enclosed notice to the *Federal Register* for publication, stating that the emergency declared with respect to the accumulation of a large volume of weapons-usable fissile material in the territory of the Russian Federation is to continue beyond June 21, 2006. The most recent notice continuing this emergency was published in the *Federal Register* on June 20, 2005 (70 FR 35507).

It remains a major national security goal of the United States to ensure that fissile material removed from Russian nuclear weapons pursuant to various arms control and disarmament agreements is dedicated to peaceful uses, subject to transparency measures, and protected from diversion to activities of proliferation concern. The accumulation of a large volume of weapons-usable fissile material in the territory of the Russian Federation continues to pose an unusual and extraordinary threat to the national security and foreign policy of the United States. For this reason, I have determined that it is necessary to continue the national emergency declared with re-

spect to the accumulation of a large volume of weapons-usable fissile material in the territory of the Russian Federation and maintain in force these emergency authorities to respond to this threat.

GEORGE W. BUSH

The White House,
June 19, 2006.

NOTE: The notice is listed in Appendix D at the end of this volume.

Remarks at the President's Dinner
June 19, 2006

Thank you all very much. Thank you. Please be seated. Thanks for the warm welcome.

Jim, thanks very much for your introduction. Thanks for your leadership for this incredibly successful dinner. Thank you all for coming.

I told Laura, I said, "I'm going to the President's Dinner." She said, "Cook it yourself." [*Laughter*] She's doing great, by the way. She is a—I'm a lucky man that she said yes when I asked her to marry me. She is a fabulous mom, a great wife, and she's doing a wonderful job as the First Lady of the United States.

She sends her best. She, like me, understands that we're going to keep the House and we're going to keep the Senate thanks to you all. And there's a reason why we got to keep the House and the Senate. We got a fabulous Speaker and leadership team in the United States House of Representatives and a great leader in Bill Frist in the United States Senate.

We're here for a reason. We're here to solve problems and not pass them to future Congresses and future Presidents. We're making a difference for the people of the United States of America. When we see problems, we solve them. The Democrats

are good talkers; we're good doers. We get the job done. We understand the stakes to the world in which we live. We understand the most important responsibility we have in Washington is to defend the people of the United States, and that's exactly what we're doing.

I appreciate the members of my Cabinet here tonight. Thank you all for coming. Don't stay too long; you got to get back to work. [*Laughter*]

I'm thrilled that Speaker Denny Hastert is here, and Leader Bill Frist. [*Applause*] I want to thank the—must have a lousy seat. [*Laughter*] I want to thank Elizabeth Dole and Lamar Alexander. I want to thank Congressman Tom Reynolds. I want to thank Mitch McConnell. I want to thank John Boehner. I want to thank all the Members of the House and the Senate who've joined us tonight. I appreciate your service to our country, and I'm proud to serve with you.

These are historic times in which we live, and these are times that require people to make hard decisions. I'm proud to be serving with people, here in Washington, DC, who make decisions on what's right, not what the focus groups say and what the polls say. And what is right is doing what it takes to defend the United States of America from attack again.

I'm proud to be serving with people who understand the lessons of September the 11th. And here's what I've learned. I've learned that we must look at the world the way it is, not the way we hope it is. I've learned that in order to do our duty to protect the American people, we must understand the nature of the enemy we face. We face coldblooded killers who would like nothing more than to strike the United States of America again, and the only way to defeat them is to stay on the offense and bring them to justice before they hurt America again.

When the President speaks, he better mean what he says, and when I said, "If you harbor a terrorist, you're equally as guilty as the terrorist," I meant exactly what I said. And when the Taliban refused to cough up Al Qaida, we acted. In the United States Congress, we're strong supporters of upholding that doctrine. And as a result of our action, America is safer, Al Qaida no longer has training camps, and 25 million people now live in freedom.

I'm proud to be working with a Speaker and the leader of the Senate and Republican Members of the House and the Senate who understand the stakes of the world in which we live. I am proud to be working with clear-eyed realists who understand that we can give no quarter to an enemy that would like to do us harm again.

One of the lessons of September the 11th is that when this country sees a threat, we must deal with it before it fully materializes. When a lot of us were coming up, we thought oceans could protect us from harm, but the lesson of September the 11th is, oceans can no longer protect the United States.

The best way to protect the United States is to take care of threats before they come to hurt us. In Iraq, Republicans and Democrats saw a threat. We saw Saddam Hussein who terrorized his neighbors, Saddam Hussein who killed his own people,

a Saddam Hussein who used weapons of mass destruction, a Saddam Hussein who had funded terrorists, Saddam Hussein who defied U.N. resolution after U.N. resolution. And when he defied his last U.N. resolution, we removed him from power, and the world is better off for it.

And I'm proud to be serving with Members of the United States Congress and the United States Senate who stand by their convictions, who don't try to change history in the midst of hard work. And that's what this world requires; it requires hard work by the United States of America. And right now we're doing hard work in Iraq. Iraq is the central front on the war on terror. And it's important we succeed.

You know I just recently went to Baghdad, had an interesting experience there. I met the new Prime Minister and the new Cabinet of a unity government. And here's what I saw: I saw people dedicated to living out the—to living out the desires of the 12 million people who went to the polls in defiance of the car bombers and the killers. I saw people from different groups in that country coming together to say, "We want to succeed." And I saw people wondering whether the United States would have the nerve to stay the course and help them succeed.

I went to Iraq, and I said, "It's up to you. It's up to you to seize this moment." But I also told them this, "When America gives its word, America will keep its word." And we will help this good country of Iraq become a thriving democracy in the heart of the Middle East.

Now, we're going to win the war on terror if we don't lose our nerve. We will win the war on terror by bringing the terrorists to justice. We will win the war on terror by defeating the terrorists in Iraq, and we will win the war on terror by defeating their hateful ideology with freedom.

You see, I want you to understand something loud and clear. I make my decisions based upon principles that just aren't going to change, and I'm proud to be standing with Members—Republican Members of the House and Senate who stand on the very same principles. We believe in the universality of freedom. We believe everybody desires to be free. And we believe that the spread of freedom will yield the peace this world wants. It is important to have Members of the United States Congress who will not wave the white flag of surrender in this war on terror.

There is a debate here in Washington, and there should be. And I welcome the debate, and we should welcome the debate. But I want to remind you of the consequences if those who want to withdraw from Iraq happen to prevail in the debate. An early withdrawal would be a defeat for the United States of America. An early withdrawal would embolden the terrorists. Talk about a deadline before we've done the job sends chills throughout the spines of Iraqi citizens who are wondering whether or not the United States has the capacity to keep its word.

An early withdrawal would embolden Al Qaida and bin Laden. An early withdrawal, before we completed the missions, would say to the United States military, "Your sacrifices have gone to vain." There will be no early withdrawal so long as we run the Congress and occupy the White House.

I want to thank the Members of Congress, Republican Members of Congress, for supporting the United States military. It's really important for our military to know that the United States of America supports them in Iraq. I'll tell you one of the things that just struck me when I was there in Baghdad. I looked in the eyes of our civilians who were there and I looked in the eyes of our troops, and I saw brave and honorable and decent and courageous souls. I saw the best of America. And this Congress and this White House will give them what it takes to win the war on terror.

And here at home, Republicans in the House and the Senate, working with the White House, have dealt with some pretty tough times for our economy. I know it

seems like a long time ago, but it wasn't all that long ago that we had to deal with a recession and a stock market correction and corporate scandals and attacks on our country and two wars and two major invasions as a part of the war on terror and natural disasters and high energy prices. Yet instead of talking, we acted, and we acted on principle.

We Republicans believe that when you have more of your own money in your pocket to save, spend, or invest, it can overcome tough economic times. We believe that we ought to trust you with your money, and not trust Government on how to spend your money. And as a result of our progrowth economic policies, this economy is strong, and we intend to keep it strong.

Our economy grew at 3.5 percent last year, and that's faster than any other major industrialized nation in the world. We added 5.3 million new jobs since August of 2003. The national unemployment rate is 4.6 percent. That's below the average for every decade since the 1960s. The entrepreneurial spirit is strong in America because of Republican progrowth economic policies.

And there is a clear record on this issue. And as people start going to the polls next November, I want them to remember who cut the taxes and who was against the tax cuts. Every single tax cut was opposed by the Democrat leadership, every tax cut: tax cuts for child—children, families with children; tax cuts to get rid of the death tax; tax cuts on capital gains and dividends; tax cuts for everybody who pays taxes; tax cuts for small businesses. We're the party of tax cuts, and we're the party of economic growth. And we intend to keep it that way by making the tax cuts permanent.

If you want your taxes raised, vote Democrat. If you want your taxes low, keep Denny Hastert and Bill Frist as leaders of the House and the Senate.

Oh, you hear all kinds of excuses for raising taxes here in Washington. The classic is, "We need to raise the taxes to balance the budget." That's not how Washington works. I've been here 5½ years; I can tell you how it works. See, they're going to raise your taxes, and then they'll figure out new ways to spend your money.

The best way to balance the budget is to be fiscally wise with your money and to keep progrowth economic policies in place, which is exactly what we're going to do. We're on our way to cutting this deficit in half by 2009, because our economy is strong as a result of low taxes and because we're working together to make sure we're wise about how we spend your money. I'll tell you one thing about spending your money, though. So long as we have got any soldier in harm's way, I look forward to working with the Congress to make sure he or she gets all the equipment, all the training, all the pay necessary to win this war on terror.

We're willing to deal with tough issues, and we got a tough issue with immigration. This is an important debate for the United States of America, but I want all of us to remember one thing: We are a nation of immigrants, and we will treat people with respect, no matter what country they're from.

The American people expect us to secure our borders, and we will. We will increase the number of Border Patrol agents, and I want to thank the Congress for passing strong measures to do just that. We will provide new technologies for our borders, to help our Border Patrol agents. We will end catch-and-release, so when we catch somebody trying to sneak in our country, they're going to go back home. We will send a clear message to people trying to sneak across our borders: The United States will secure our borders. But I also want you to understand that to secure our borders, we need a comprehensive immigration plan.

We need a plan that says, instead of trying to sneak across our borders, you can come and work in our borders—in our country, on a temporary basis, for jobs Americans aren't doing. We need a temporary-worker plan in order to make sure this border of ours is secure. We need to give those temporary workers a chance to come here and then go back home after they work, and give them a card, see. They need to have a tamper-proof card. And that's how you begin to have true enforcement.

It's against the law to hire somebody who's here—who is illegally here, and we intend to make sure we uphold the laws against employers who are hiring illegal immigrants. We oppose amnesty. Amnesty is wrong for the United States of America. Amnesty sends the wrong signal to people here by—playing by the rules. On the other hand, it is unrealistic to expect the United States of America can deport 11 million people. And so my plan is, is that if you pay your fine, pay your dues, learn English, you can get at the end of the citizenship line, not ahead of those who are here legally.

And finally, during this debate I want us to remember that this country has had an amazing capacity to assimilate people from different walks of life, and so a part of a comprehensive plan will not only be to secure our borders but to have an orderly work plan to be responsible on how we treat people who have been here—but as well as to help people learn English and learn the customs and habits of the United States of America.

I love a country where someone can go from picking onions to owning the grocery store, when somebody can go from sweeping the floor of an office to running the office. I love a country where somebody can come and work in a small business and own the small business. America is one Nation under God, and the Republican Party must always stand for that.

You know, ours is the party that came here to Washington, DC, and saw a Medicare system that wasn't working. The Democrats were great about talking about making Medicare work; they could never get anything done. And we did. People say, "What did you care about Medicare for?" I cared about it because the Government has made a commitment to the elderly to provide good health care. And once—my view is, once you make a commitment, you got to honor the commitment. And I saw a Medicare system that wasn't working, and so did a lot of the Republicans in the United States Congress.

I'll give you an example of why it wasn't working. We had a Medicare system that would pay $25,000 for surgery but not one single dime for the prescription drugs that could prevent the surgery from being needed in the first place. The system was old. It was tired. It wasn't working. And Republicans came together to make sure we had a Medicare system that delivered modern medicine for our seniors. And if you're a poor senior in America, we give you help. The days from choosing between an electricity bill and medicine are over, thanks to the Republican Party.

There is more work to be done when it comes to making sure health care is available and affordable. That's why we support association health plans to help small businesses be able to afford health insurance. That's why we support health savings accounts, so you're in control of the health decisions. That's why we support the advent of information technology to help bring excess costs out of the systems. And in order to make sure health care is available and affordable, we strongly support medical liability reform. We got to make sure these junk lawsuits stop running good doctors out of practice and stop running up your bills.

Ours is the party that understands we got to have a comprehensive energy plan to make us less dependent on foreign sources of oil. We strongly support conservation measures. We strongly support clean coal technologies and nuclear power. We strongly support hybrid vehicles, new battery technologies, ethanol. Ours is a party that is willing to work hard to say to the American people, soon, that we're less dependent on foreign sources of oil, and that's good for national security, and that is good for economic security.

What I'm telling you is, we stand for some things, and we get things done for the American people. We stand on principles. We believe in human dignity of each and every person. We stand for a culture of life. We strongly stand for families in America. And we believe it is essential to make sure that we have a judiciary that understands its proper role in society.

I want to thank the United States Senate for confirming two fantastic Supreme Court Justices in John Roberts and Sam Alito. And our pledge to you is that I will continue to nominate good judges, good honorable men and women, who will interpret the law and not legislate from the bench.

Ours is a party that understands that Government can hand out money but cannot put hope in a person's heart or a sense of purpose in a person's life. And therefore we strongly support—we strongly believe in supporting faith-based and community programs that all exist to put an arm around a brother who is lost or a sister who needs help, and says, "I love you." We strongly believe that Government ought to support programs of faith in order to help lift the souls and the spirits of those who need something much greater than Government can provide.

Ours is a party that believes in limited government and empowering the people of the United States. There's no question that this country of ours can accomplish anything we set our minds to. We can win the war on terror, and we will. We can make sure people are able to find work all around our country. We can help the homeless, help the addicted. We can help feed the hungry. We can lift up the souls of every person who is lucky enough to be a citizen of this great country, and we will.

I want to thank you for your help. I want to thank you for giving us a chance to lead this great country. I want to thank you for helping make sure that Denny Hastert and Bill Frist remain in their positions in the Senate and the House, and I assure you of this: We will continue to lead this country with an optimistic, hopeful, positive vision that says to every Amer-

ican, opportunity belongs to you as much as your neighbor.

May God bless you all, and may God bless the United States of America.

NOTE: The President spoke at 7:50 p.m. at the Washington Convention Center. In his remarks, he referred to Rep. James O. McCrery III of Louisiana; Prime Minister Nuri al-Maliki of Iraq; and Usama bin Laden, leader of the Al Qaida terrorist organization.

Message to the Senate Transmitting a Report on Additional Geneva Convention Amendments
June 19, 2006

To the Senate of the United States:

With a view to receiving the advice and consent of the Senate to ratification, I transmit herewith: the Protocol Additional to the Geneva Conventions of 12 August 1949, and relating to the Adoption of an Additional Distinctive Emblem (the "Geneva Protocol III"), adopted at Geneva on December 8, 2005, and signed by the United States on that date; the Amendment to Article 1 of the Convention on Prohibitions or Restrictions on the Use of Certain Conventional Weapons Which May be Deemed to be Excessively Injurious or to Have Indiscriminate Effects (the "CCW Amendment"); and the CCW Protocol on Explosive Remnants of War (the "CCW Protocol V"). I transmit, for the information of the Senate, the report of the Department of State concerning these treaties.

Geneva Protocol III. Geneva Protocol III creates a new distinctive emblem, a Red Crystal, in addition to and for the same purposes as the Red Cross and the Red Crescent emblems. The Red Crystal is a neutral emblem that can be employed by governments and national societies that face challenges using the existing emblems. In addition, Geneva Protocol III will pave the way for Magen David Adom, Israel's na-

tional society, to achieve membership in the International Red Cross and Red Crescent Movement. Legislation implementing Geneva Protocol III will be submitted to the Congress separately.

CCW Amendment. The amendment to Article 1 of the CCW, which was adopted at Geneva on December 21, 2001, eliminates the distinction between international and non-international armed conflict for the purposes of the rules governing the prohibitions and restrictions on the use of certain conventional weapons. It does not change the legal status of rebel or insurgent groups into that of protected or privileged belligerents.

CCW Protocol V. CCW Protocol V, which was adopted at Geneva on November 28, 2003, addresses the post-conflict threat generated by conventional munitions such as mortar shells, grenades, artillery rounds, and bombs that do not explode as intended or that are abandoned. CCW Protocol V provides for the marking, clearance, removal, and destruction of such remnants by the party in control of the territory in which the munitions are located.

Conclusion. I urge the Senate to give prompt and favorable consideration to each of these instruments and to give its advice and consent to their ratification. These treaties are in the interest of the United States, and their ratification would advance the longstanding and historic leadership of the United States in the law of armed conflict.

GEORGE W. BUSH

The White House,
June 19, 2006.

NOTE: This message was released by the Office of the Press Secretary on June 20. An original was not available for verification of the content of this message.

The President's News Conference With European Leaders in Vienna, Austria
June 21, 2006

Chancellor Wolfgang Schuessel. So, ladies and gentlemen, let me first start by saying that this was—is the 15th journey of President of the United States, George Bush, to Europe. And I'm really happy that this journey leads—it's a kind of an Austria-Hungarian journey—leads George Bush and his team to Vienna.

We had a summit, a very fruitful and a positive summit touching a broad range of subjects, from economy—quite obvious—America and Europe, we are the E–2, the economic big two powers of the world, and we spoke about common trade, foreign investment in both directions. Of course, we touched some problems, but don't forget that 99 percent of our trade volume is done without any problems. It's, per date, a sum of around $2 billion traded above the Atlantic Ocean.

And we touched foreign policy issues; we touched Iran; we touched Iraq; Balkan issues; global issues like global warming, climate change, et cetera.

Although we might have different approaches in some aspects, this should never overshadow the depth and quality of our cooperation. We covered, as I said it, a wide range of issues during our talks, from foreign policy and economic cooperation. The energy security was high on our agenda, the protection of intellectual property rights, the cooperation in the fight against terror, and the protection of human rights around the world.

In our common responsibility to promote stability and security for our citizens and the world, the European Union and United States successfully work together. There are recent examples for our good cooperation, as I mentioned, just Iran, Middle East, and Iraq.

And in one of the topics we intensively discussed today, our efforts to keep Iran from producing nuclear weapons. We have come to a crossroad on the Iranian nuclear issue. Iran has to make the right choice. And we welcome a U.S. involvement, in particularly, recent historic signal that U.S. is ready to join negotiations talks if conditions for resuming negotiations are met. And this signal greatly contributed to the credibility of a united position between the key players. And I told President George Bush how much we appreciate his constructive role in this particularly sensitive situation.

The situation in Middle East is still complex. There's no doubt that the Palestinian Government has to accept the basic principles of the peace process—nonviolence, recognition of Israel, acceptance of existing agreements, the so-called roadmap. On the other hand, both America and Europe consequently argue against any unilateral steps by Israel. The escalation of armed confrontation during the recent days and weeks show the lack of a political perspective. The solution to this conflict can only be a political one based on negotiations and the principles of the roadmap.

In Iraq, we welcome the formation of the new Iraqi national unity Government on 20th of May. We strongly condemn terrorist acts, the continuing campaign of violence against the Iraqi people and their constitutionally elected Government. At the European Council last week, we stressed our encouragement for enhanced institutional and international engagement and underlined our willingness for continued supporting U.N. role in Iraq.

On Balkans, we informed President Bush on the European strategy. We have opened negotiations last week with Croatia. Macedonia is a candidate. We signed an agreement for stabilization association with Albania. We have now Montenegro independent. Bosnia is integrated, and we are, all the time, involved in positive talks with Serbia. Of course, there are open questions, and we discussed them in detail. In Kosovo, negotiations under the chairmanship of Martti Ahtisaari and Albert Rohan are taking place here in Vienna. The office of Ahtisaari is here, and we do our utmost to help and to ease.

Strong bilateral ties between Europe and USA are absolutely important. We are the most important economic partners for each other. The summit highlights only some topics. Progress made in many other areas should not be overlooked.

Today we signed an agreement on higher education and vocational training that will last for a longer period of time than the previous one, engage us in a larger quantity of programs and funds, and will reach more students and teachers—three times more students than before.

Given the worldwide increase in energy demands and, at the same time, limited resources, security of supply is of strategic importance. And therefore, we welcome the establishment of a strategic cooperation between America and Europe. And we are committed to develop a coherent energy strategy that not only emphasizes security of supply but also efficiency, sustainability, and climate protection.

This is my first statement. I now invite the President of the United States, George Bush, to take the floor, and then the President of the Commission.

President Bush. Mr. Chancellor—I call him, Wolfgang; he calls me, George W.— Jose, it's good to see you. Thank you very much for your hospitality. I also want to thank President Fischer for his hospitality as well. I've really been looking forward to this trip. I have never been to your beautiful country. I need to come back. It is—and your hospitality has been grand. I really appreciate it a lot.

We did have a very engaged and fruitful conversation, as we should. We're close partners in peace and prosperity. I've always believed that when America and the EU work together, we can accomplish big deeds. And this world needs us to work together, because there's a lot of challenges.

We talked about democracy and new democracies, and I want to thank the European Union for its strong support of Afghanistan and Iraq. Look, I fully understand we've had our differences on Iraq, and I can understand the differences. People have strong opinions on the subject. But what's past is past, and what's ahead is a hopeful democracy in the Middle East. And I want to thank your leadership, both of your leaderships, on this important issue. I believe the Maliki Government is going to succeed. I know the Government needs our help, and the European Union has stood up to help, and I can't thank you enough for that.

We talked about Lebanon and the need for Lebanon to be free from Syrian influence. We worked very closely together at the United Nations to send that clear message to the Syrians: Leave Lebanon alone;

let them be; let them be a free democracy—which is a necessary part of laying the foundation for peace in the Middle East.

We talked about Israel and Palestine. I assured the leaders here that my position is firm, and that is, I envision two states living side by side in peace. And we want to help. On the other hand, we're not going to deal with a Government that has made the destruction of Israel one of its key policy platforms. How can you be side by side in peace if part of your platform is the destruction of one of the countries you're supposed to be at peace with? And I appreciate Europe being strong on that issue as well.

We talked about the Balkans, and I assured the Chancellor that Austria's role in the Balkans and the European Union's role in the Balkans is essential, and we look forward to supporting your role. In essence, the EU, particularly under the Chancellor's guidance, is in the lead on the Balkans. And we want to help. We want to be a participant in helping bring peace to that region.

I think the European Union is a vital part of helping solve the issue of the Balkans. After all, aspirations to the EU causes people to adopt the habits necessary for there to be a democracy and peace. And so we're very strongly supportive of the EU's role in the Balkans and applaud your strong role as well, Mr. Chancellor.

We talked about development and prosperity. Listen, we're trading partners, and we've got to make sure that commerce and trade and capital continues to flow freely between the EU and America. And we talked about some of the impediments to capital flows, and we discussed our desire to make sure that we continue to trade as freely as possible.

Obviously, the Doha round of the WTO was a big subject. And it's a tough subject because we're trying to make difficult adjustments to our own internal policy in order to satisfy a—in order to reach an

agreement that's fair for all of us. But the good news is, is that we were very frank in our discussion with each other. I mean, the Europeans have problems with the U.S. position; we have problems with the European position; we both have problems with the G–20 position. But the point is, we're committed to a successful round. And it's going to take hard work. There's a ministers meeting here at the end of this month, and my pledge to our European counterparts is, we'll do the very best we can to reach an agreement that is—that satisfies all parties' desires.

But make no mistake about it, it's hard work. My view is, is that we can't let this round fail. A failed WTO round would be missed opportunity, particularly to help people in the impoverished—who are impoverished. The best way to help lift people out of poverty is trade. You can give all the money you want—and my Government has been very generous on the continent of Africa. We're joining with the Europeans to fight HIV/AIDS and to deal with hunger. But if you're really interested in development, the best way to do it is to have a successful round at the WTO. And I understand that, and we're committed to working for success in that round.

We talked about energy. I kind of startled my country when, in my State of the Union, I said, "We're hooked on oil, and we need to get off oil." That seemed counterintuitive for some people to hear a Texan say. But the truth of the matter is, we got to diversify away from oil. And the best way to do it is through new technologies. And we agreed we would share technologies between our nations and between the EU and the United States. The EU needs to get diversified as well. And so this is going to be a very interesting period for us as new technologies develop, and we're willing to share those technologies.

We talked about our efforts to continue to defeat the terrorists. I reminded my fellow leaders here that the terrorists still want to strike, and they want to do harm, and we have an obligation to work very closely together.

And obviously, they brought up the concern about Guantanamo. And I understand their concerns. But let me explain my position. First, I'd like to end Guantanamo; I'd like it to be over with. One of the things we will do is we'll send people back to their home countries. We've got about 400 people there left—200 have been sent back—400 are there, mainly from Saudi Arabia, Afghanistan, and Yemen. And I explained to the two leaders here our desires to send them back. Of course, there's international pressure not to send them back. But, hopefully, we'll be able to resolve that when they go back to their own country.

There are some who need to be tried in U.S. courts. They're coldblooded killers. They will murder somebody if they're let out on the street. And yet we believe there's a—there ought to be a way forward in a court of law, and I'm waiting for the Supreme Court of the United States to determine the proper venue in which these people can be tried.

So I understand the concerns of the leaders. They expressed the concerns of the European leaders and the European people about what Guantanamo says. I also shared with them my deep desire to end this program, but also, I assured them that we will—I'm not going to let people out on the street that will do you harm. And so we're working through the issue. And I appreciate your interest and appreciate your questions.

Finally, we talked about Iran. It's very important for the leadership in Iran to look at the world and say, Europe and the United States and Russia and China are united in our common desire to make sure that Iranians do not develop a nuclear weapon. And step one of achieving a diplomatic success is to share a goal. And there's no question we share the goal of Iran not having the capacity and/or a nuclear weap-

on. It would be a terrible situation if they developed a weapon.

And so the second phase of a diplomatic strategy is to have a common front, a common diplomatic front that says clearly to the Iranians, here is a way forward for it, but you get to choose. And so I said to the—I said to our—my counterparts here that we'll come to the table to negotiate, so long as the Iranians verifiably end any enrichment activities. The Iranians have said that they will end uranium enrichment activities before; that's what they told the EU–3. We're just asking them to do what they already said they would do.

But it's their choice to make. And I'm convinced that when they look and see that we're working very closely together, that they will see the seriousness of our intent to resolve this in a diplomatic and peaceful way.

And so the discussions were wide-ranging, which is a positive sign of a healthy relationship. We shared tactics and strategies, which is a sign of a healthy relationship. We disagreed in an agreeable way on certain issues, but we're bound to work together for the good of our respective peoples. And this meeting has been a great success, Mr. Chancellor, and I appreciate you running it. And again, I want to thank you for your hospitality.

Chancellor Schuessel. Thank you. Jose.

President Jose Manuel Durao Barroso. Thank you. Thank you very much. I think there is a very good spirit in European Union and United States relations, and we're building on that today. And as President Bush just said, it was not just a working meeting for very concrete results, but also, we were thinking aloud; we were discussing together some possible strategies for the future. And this is precisely that spirit that relations between partners like the United States and European Union should be established.

But let me just concentrate on concrete results of this summit that were already presented by Chancellor Schuessel, but I want to highlight some of them. First, we are entering into strategic cooperation on energy to promote energy security for producers, consumers, and transit countries alike. I think this is important, strategic cooperation on energy between the United States and Europe. Second, we have agreed to establish a European Union and United States high-level dialog on climate change, clean energy, sustainable development. This will address ways to deliver cost-effective emission cuts, development and employment of new technologies, efficiency and conservation, renewable fuels, and other environmental issues such as biodiversity.

We have also discussed how to deliver an ambitious and balanced conclusion to the Doha development agenda. These negotiations are at a crucial phase. European Union and the United States have a joint responsibility to help deliver an agreement which promotes growth and opportunity, especially for the poorest. We look for a similar determination from other WTO members. And after the good exchange of views we had today during this summit, I'm convinced, I'm really convinced that it's possible to have a successful outcome of the Doha talks. And it's crucially important from a trade point of view, from a global economic point of view, but also from a development point of view.

Third, we have endorsed today a strategy for the enforcement of intellectual property rights in third countries. For the first time, we have named the countries and regions which cause most concern. They will be the focus of concrete actions to reduce global piracy and counterfeiting. Proper protection of intellectual property is vital for our industry and for our consumers.

Fourth, we also agreed on the need for open investment regimes, fighting all protectionist tendencies that can happen in some of our circles. We need to boost growth, jobs, and get best control of our very dynamic transatlantic economy. Two-way investment benefits our economies. In this context, I hope we will see the finaliza-

tion of the European Union-United States Air Transport Agreement, if possible by the end of the year.

We also addressed the issue that is very important in European Union of this—for establishment of reciprocal visa-free travel for all European Union citizens to the United States. I also believe this is good for our citizens; this is good for our economies.

Finally, the point I want to highlight, I want to emphasize our shared commitment to promoting democracy, freedom all over the world. The very enlargement of the European Union has been one of the greatest achievements in terms of promotion of democracy from Southern Europe, West Europe, to Eastern Europe, North Europe, from the Iberian Peninsula in the eighties to the Baltic countries, now most recently. European Union is a great success story in terms of promoting democracy. And we want to do it also globally, and we are doing it globally. And that's one of the fields where I see that the United States and European Union can do, and should do, even more together.

One thing is sure, the world now is very complex. Even together we are not sure that we will solve all issues. But if we don't—aren't working together, it will be much more difficult to face global challenges. I believe this summit was very helpful for having this closer relationship between the United States and Europe so that together, we can do our best to make the world a better place.

Chancellor Schuessel. Thank you.

President Bush. Jennifer [Jennifer Loven, Associated Press].

North Korea

Q. Thank you, Mr. President. Could you explain why the world should care that North Korea is test-firing a long-range missile? And what sort of penalties do you think are in order if they do so?

And to the Chancellor, if I might, where does the EU stand on possible penalties for such a test?

President Bush. The North Koreans have made agreements with us in the past, and we expect them to keep their agreements— for example, agreements on test launches. We think it would be in the world's interest to know what they're testing, what they intend to do on their test. It should make people nervous when nontransparent regimes that have announced that they've got nuclear warheads fire missiles.

And so we've been working with our partners, particularly in that part of the world, to say to the North Koreans that this is not the way you conduct business in the world; this is not the way that peaceful nations conduct their affairs.

I was pleased to see that the Chinese spoke out to the North Korean Government and suggested they not fire—whatever it is on—their missile. And we'll see whether or not the North Koreans listen. One of our strategies in North Korea has to make sure we include other countries as a part of our consortium to deal with this nontransparent regime. And China is an integral part of what we've called the six-party talks, and I am pleased that they're taking responsibility in dealing with the leader of North Korea. I think it's a very positive sign.

I've talked to President Putin about this subject. I know that we're reaching out to the Japanese, all aimed at saying to the North Koreans, this is not a—in order to be an accepted nation, a nonisolated nation, there are certain international norms that you must live by. And we expect them to live by those norms.

Chancellor Schuessel. I couldn't agree more with the question of North Korea, and the compliance with the international rules and the international standards are always a matter of great concern, always high on the priority list of foreign policy matters within the European Union. And if this happens, there will be a strong state-ment and a strong answer from the international community. And Europe will be part of it. So there's no doubt. We discussed it, by the way, in our debate, what to do when and if, and there will be a strong response on that.

Nuclear Proliferation/Energy

Q. A question to President Barroso and President Bush. Thank you. Do you actually share the view that Russia is using its energy resources to oppress other countries? And in what respect does your cooperation help you now to position yourselves against that?

And if I may, to President Bush, you've got Iran's nuclear program, you've got North Korea, yet most Europeans consider the United States the biggest threat to global stability. Do you have any regrets about that?

President Bush. That's absurd. There's my statement. The United States is—we'll defend ourselves, but at the same time, we're actively working with our partners to spread peace and democracy. So whoever says that is—it's an absurd statement.

President Barroso. Yes. On energy, as you know, that energy is a geostrategic question. That's why in January, President Bush called for an end to American oil addiction. That's why in February, in Washington, I asked for partnership between United States and European Union in matters of energy. That's why today we are agreeing on key principles to guarantee energy security. I also welcome the high-level—the agreement on a high-level dialog between European Union and United States on climate change, sustainable development.

These are central challenges to all of us globally. So our agreement is not against anyone, by the way, we expect the G-8 summit to be a very important point, to be a success. And we wish President Putin success at that G-8 summit. We believe it should be an occasion to reinforce our message for an open, stable, nondiscriminatory, transparent market on energy. So energy is a global issue, and it should be tackled globally.

President Bush. Steve [Steve Holland, Reuters].

Iran

Q. Mr. President. Thank you, sir. If Iran says it will respond to the offer in late August, is that a suitable timeframe? And I would ask all of you, Iran's Foreign Minister says some kind of negotiations can start before a final answer is given; are you willing to do that?

President Bush. Well, our position, Steve, is that we'll come to the table when they verifiably suspend, period. And we expect them to verifiably suspend. This is what they said they would do, to the EU–3.

Secondly, the August 22d date—is that part of your question? Yes. It seems like an awful long time for a reasonable answer—for a reasonable proposal, a long time for an answer. And we look forward to working with our partners. We just got word of this statement as we walked in here, but it shouldn't take the Iranians that long to analyze what is a reasonable deal.

Q. [*Inaudible*]

President Bush. Well, I said weeks, not months. And I believe that's the view of our partners—weeks, not months.

Chancellor Schuessel. We agree. We spoke about Iran in length, and it is really one of the fruits of a well-balanced partnership and cooperation that we were able to offer a bold package of incentives to Iran, to the Iranian Government and to the Iranian people. And as President Bush said, it's better to agree as soon as possible. The time is limited, and I think we should not play with time.

This is—we discussed it for months and months, and I think time—there is in Greek language, there is—and I learned ancient Greek—there is a fantastic word, kairos. Kairos means "the right moment." The right moment—it's not only time; it's

the right moment. And I think now is the right moment for Iran to take this offer, to grab it and to negotiate. This is a well-balanced—we got advice from everybody from the international scene—United Nations, ElBaradei here, the International Atomic Energy organization, a lot of experts, of scientists that convinced us—of course, the EU–3 and America, Russia, and China are on board. So this is their kairos. Take it. This is my advice.

Spread of Democracy/American Influence Worldwide/War on Terror

Q. Chancellor Schuessel, the European public is deeply worried by these secret prisoners that the CIA has been transporting, is transporting through Europe. Did you get the assurance today from the President that this is not going to happen anymore, that there won't be anymore in the kidnaping of terror suspects in Europe, that this is a thing of the past?

And to the President, Mr. President, you said this is "absurd," but you might be aware that in Europe, the image of America is still falling, and dramatically in some areas. Let me give you some numbers. In Austria, in this country, only 14 percent of the people believe that the United States, what they are doing is good for peace; 64 percent think that it is bad. In the United Kingdom, your ally, there are more citizens who believe that the United States policy under your leadership is helping to destabilize the world than Iran. So my question to you is, why do you think that you've failed so badly to convince Europeans, to win their heads and hearts and minds? Thank you.

President Bush. Well, yes, I thought it was absurd for people to think that we're more dangerous than Iran. It's a—we're a transparent democracy. People know exactly what's on our mind. We debate things in the open. We've got a legislative process that's active. Look, people didn't agree with my decision on Iraq, and I understand that.

For Europe, September the 11th was a moment; for us, it was a change of thinking. I vowed to the American people I would do everything I could to defend our people, and will. I fully understood that the longer we got away from September the 11th, more people would forget the lessons of September the 11th. But I'm not going to forget them. And therefore, I will be steadfast and diligent and strong in defending our country.

I don't govern by polls, you know. I just do what I think is right. And I understand some of the decisions I made are controversial. But I made them in the best interest of our country and, I think, in the best interest of the world. I believe when you look back at this moment, people will say, it was right to encourage democracy in the Middle East. I understand some people think that it can't work. I believe in the universality of freedom; some don't. I'm going to act on my beliefs so long as I'm the President of the United States. Some people say, it's okay to condemn people for—to tyranny. I don't believe it's okay to condemn people for—to tyranny, particularly those of us who live in the free societies.

And so I understand, and I'll try to do my best to explain to the Europeans that, on the one hand, we're tough when it comes to the war on terror; on the other hand, we're providing more money than ever before in the world's history for HIV/AIDS on the continent of Africa. I'll say, on the one hand, we're going to be tough when it comes to terrorist regimes who harbor weapons; on the other hand, we'll help feed the hungry. I declared Darfur to be a genocide because I care deeply about those who have been afflicted by these renegade bands of people who are raping and murdering.

And so I will do my best to explain our foreign policy. On the one hand, it's tough when it needs to be; on the other hand, it's compassionate. And we'll let the polls figure out—people say what they want to say. But leadership requires making hard choices based upon principle and standing by the decisions you make, and that's how I'm going to continue to lead my country.

Thank you for your question.

Chancellor Schuessel. And let me add something. I think Austria is a really a good example to show that America has something to do with freedom, democracy, prosperity, development. Don't forget, I was born in '45. At that time, Vienna and half of Austria laid in ruins. I mean, without the participation of America, what fate would have Europe? Where would be Europe today? Not the peaceful, prosperous Europe like we love it and where we live.

Nothing—I will never forget that America fed us with food, with economic support. The Marshall plan was an immense aid and incentive to develop industry, agriculture, tourism. And by the way, I said it to the President, the Marshall Fund is still working in Austria. It's now transformed into a kind—in a fund for research and development—still working.

The American people—at that time, the American Government invested billions of dollars in Europe to develop the former enemy. And now we are a partner. So I think it's grotesque to say that America is a threat to the peace in the world compared with North Korea, Iran, other countries.

Of course, we—and I thank you very much for the question on human rights and the overflights and the secret prisons and Guantanamo. And it was quite interesting to see how the debate was going on in—this morning—the President started, himself. He didn't wait that we raise the question. He came up and said, "Look, this is my problem; this is where we are." And I think we should be fair from the other side of the Atlantic. We should understand that what September 11th meant to the American people. It was a shock—for the first time, a real shock. A society values were attacked—American values, international values, European values were attacked in the home country of the President and all Americans. And we should not be naive. We Europeans are also attacked. We had bomb attacks in Madrid; hundreds of people were killed. We had bomb attacks in London subway; buses were blown up. We had detected some terrorists who tried to shoot down an Israeli plane. So we should not be naive.

And since September 11th—and I think this is important to underline—that since September 11th, we are now able to define our targets, to fight against terror and terrorists, to cut off their financial supplies, to share information, to secure our citizens, our people. This is the ultimate goal: not creating enemies, virtual enemies, but to secure our people and to secure peace in the world and to stabilize our societies.

The problem is—and I will be very frank on that, and I said it the same way like we did it here, and we say it now—we are only—we can only have a victory in the fight against terror if we don't undermine our common values. It cannot—it can never be a victory, a credible victory over terrorists if we give up our values: democracy, rule of law, individual rights.

This is important to know. And our discussion with all the European Parliament, the European governments, I personally—we are calling for the closure of Guantanamo. But our discussion today went far beyond the closing Guantanamo, because we have—we have a legal problem; we have gray areas. And there should be no legal void, not in the fight against terrorists, but also not in—for individuals to be guaranteed in their individual rights, in their freedom.

And it's quite interesting to see how the President reacted. I welcome, of course, your statement saying that you're looking forward to close Guantanamo, and it depends on the Supreme Court's decision. And we got clear, clear signals and clear, clear commitments from the American

side—no torture, no extraordinary or extraterritorial positions to deal with the terrorists all—the McCain amendment, for instance. All the legal rights must be preserved.

But we have to help if we're to find a way-out strategy, to help countries to take back the prisoners, either to charge them or to release them. And there are international organizations which could help and could assist. And we discussed this in detail. And I think it's important to know that although there are differences in the legal perception, it was possible to have such a statement.

And I really want to add, after my visit to you in December '05, last December, we established a very good cooperation between John Bellinger, the leading adviser of the State Department, and the Austrian Volkerrechtsburo Bureau, the Department for International Law. And this is working. We are really working in a precise, professional way on that. So thank you very much.

Let me say, Mr. President, I'm really happy that you are here, that you were here in Vienna. Come back, if possible. You will find a little bit more from our town and from the possibilities of our city. And don't let us wait for another nearly 30 years for the next visit. All the best. Thank you.

President Bush. Good job. Thank you, sir.

NOTE: The President's news conference began at 2:50 p.m. in Zeremoniensaal Hall at the Hofburg Palace. Participating in the event were Chancellor Wolfgang Schuessel of Austria and President Jose Manuel Durao Barroso of the European Commission. President Bush referred to President Heinz Fischer of Austria; Prime Minister Nuri al-Maliki of Iraq; Chairman Kim Jong Il of North Korea; and President Vladimir V. Putin of Russia. Chancellor Schuessel referred to Martti Ahtisaari, U.N. Special Envoy for the Future Status Process for Kosovo; Albert Rohan, U.N. Deputy Special Envoy for the

Future Status Process for Kosovo; and Director General Mohamed ElBaradei of the International Atomic Energy Agency. A re-porter referred to Minister of Foreign Affairs Manuchehr Motaki of Iran.

Joint Statement: United States-European Union Summit Declaration
June 21, 2006

We, the leaders of the United States of America and the European Union (EU), met today in Vienna to respond to the concerns of our citizens for peace, security, stability and prosperity in an increasingly globalize world.

We welcome that over the past year our Transatlantic Partnership has delivered real results as shown by the political and economic Progress Reports we issued today. We remain committed to finding common or complementary lines of action in many areas. Over the last year, there have been many examples of how productive our relationship is in the Middle East, Iran, the Western Balkans, Belarus, on the frozen conflicts, and Sudan, as well as in our efforts to promote transatlantic trade and investment under last Summit's Economic Initiative.

We have decided to further strengthen our strategic Partnership by adopting a number of priority actions to support our cooperation in the following four areas:

- Promoting peace, human rights and democracy worldwide;
- Confronting global challenges, including security;
- Fostering prosperity and opportunity;
- Promoting strategic cooperation on energy and energy security, climate change and sustainable development.

Promoting Peace, Human Rights and Democracy Worldwide

We recognize that the advance of democracy is a strategic priority of our age. We will intensify our efforts to promote peace, democracy, freedom, the rule of law and respect for human rights in the world to make it more secure, safe, and prosperous for all mankind. Noting the need for tolerance of diverse cultures, beliefs and religions and the importance of dialogue while emphasizing respect for universal human rights, we will sustain our efforts to advance democracy.

We will work with the United Nations and international and regional organizations, civil society, NGOs and dedicated individuals committed to human rights, democracy and the rule of law. We will work to ensure that the newly created Human Rights Council becomes an effective and efficient body committed to the promotion and protection of human rights and fundamental freedoms for all. We underline our shared commitment to UN-Reform and we welcome the establishment of and give our backing to the Peacebuilding Commission and the UN Democracy Fund. We will continue to support reform in the Mediterranean region and the Middle East and will promote greater participation of civil society in the reform process through our respective efforts, including the Barcelona Process, the European Neighbourhood Policy, the Middle East Partnership Initiative, and our joint actions through the Broader Middle East and North Africa Initiative and the Foundation and Fund for the Future.

We will continue to closely cooperate in the Middle East, notably through the Quartet. We welcome the temporary international mechanism to deliver assistance directly to the Palestinian people. We will continue to deliver humanitarian assistance and promote Palestinian democracy and civil society. Whilst recalling President Abbas' commitment to a platform of peace, we will continue to urge the new Palestinian government to commit to non-violence, recognize Israel's right to exist and accept existing agreements and obligations. We will continue to call on Israel to ease restrictions on access and movement and to take additional steps including with respect to the Palestinian tax and customs revenues, to improve the humanitarian situation of the Palestinian people. We remind both sides of their obligations under the 15 November 2005 Agreement. We will continue to promote a negotiated solution to the Israeli-Palestinian conflict on the basis of the Roadmap in order to advance a just, viable and lasting two-state solution and we call on both parties to avoid unilateral measures that prejudice final status issues. We call on the Palestinian Authority government to implement policies that will permit the international community to provide greater support to and review its policies on contact with the Palestinian Authority.

We will strongly urge Syria to implement UNSC Resolutions 1559, 1595, 1636, 1680 and 1686 and to prevent its territory from being used to support violence in Iraq, and end cross-border transit and support for terrorist groups. Similarly, Syria must end its support for Lebanese and non-Lebanese militias, and prevent the smuggling of arms and other support to these groups. We will work together to increase support for human rights and democracy, and secure the release of political prisoners in Syria. We will strongly urge Syria to refrain from any attempt at destabilizing Lebanon.

We will jointly support political, economic and institutional reforms in Lebanon, as well as its sovereignty, democracy, territorial integrity, unity and political independence. We will strengthen efforts to coordinate assistance to Lebanon, and we support the reform plan of the Lebanese government and seek to work towards an international Core Group conference. We

support the efforts of the Lebanese government to disarm and disband Lebanese and non-Lebanese militias, as called for in UNSCR 1559 and 1680, and we will support the call expressed by the UN Security Council to halt the flow of arms and funds to terrorist groups and militias. We support UNSCR 1686 and the continuation of the investigation of the assassination of former Lebanese Prime Minister Rafiq Hariri.

We support progress by the Government of Egypt towards ensuring fundamental freedoms, and building multi-party democracy. We will continue to encourage the Egyptian government to proceed with the fundamental political and constitutional reforms it announced particularly by replacing the emergency law with a counterterrorism law in conformity with international human rights standards.

We will support the newly constitutionally elected government of Iraq and call upon it to continue the policies of inclusiveness as a means to overcome divisions within Iraq. We will continue to assist in building an independent, stable, secure, democratic, prosperous and united Iraq at peace with its neighbors and the international community. We call on the international community to show its support for the new government in particular by increasing development, rule of law, and security assistance, offering capacity building support, providing generous debt relief on terms equivalent to the Paris Club Agreement and extending its local presence keeping in mind the security situation.

Over the past year our cooperation on Iran has reached a new level. We have worked closely together at every stage of the ongoing attempts to address the question of Iran's nuclear program. We have agreed on a set of far-reaching proposals as a basis for discussion with Iran. We believe that they offer Iran the chance to reach a negotiated agreement based on cooperation, if Iran is willing to make that choice. The United States has made clear that it is prepared to join the negotiations should Iran resume full and verifiable suspension of all enrichment related and reprocessing activities as required by the IAEA. We have agreed that if Iran decides not to engage in negotiations, further steps would be taken in the Security Council. We urge Iran to take the positive path.

Building on the success of the London January 2006 conference on Afghanistan, we will support Afghan efforts to build a democratic, accountable and sustainable state. We will pay particular importance to governance, human rights, reform of the public administration, the judiciary and security sector, counter-narcotics as well as an Afghan-led process of reconciliation and justice.

Recognizing the next year to be a crucial period for the Western Balkans we will build on the experience of our successful transatlantic cooperation by cooperating to stabilize the countries in the region, support their European and Euro-Atlantic perspectives and to combat organized crime and corruption. We will continue to work with NATO as well as the OSCE to ensure the security and prosperity of the region. On Kosovo in particular, we will continue to ensure the convergence of our positions on the ongoing talks in order to promote a lasting status that respects the Contact Group principles. We will develop our relations with Montenegro as a sovereign, independent State and call on both Serbia and Montenegro to pursue a direct and constructive dialogue on their future relations.

Ukraine has made remarkable progress in democratic and economic reforms. Building on the March 2006 elections, we will support Ukraine's development as a democratic, prosperous and secure country. We will help Ukraine pursue economic reforms, combat corruption and reform the energy sector.

We will continue to support the democratic aspirations of the people of Belarus and work together to strengthen democratic institutions, assist civil society, and promote independent media. We condemn the use of violence in Belarus and the repression of the democratic opposition and we urge the authorities of Belarus to release all political detainees. The travel ban imposed on President Lukashenko and others, as well as the freezing of assets of individuals responsible for violations of international election standards and human rights abuses are good examples of our broad cooperation and coordination. We remain resolved to help the people of Belarus achieve their aspirations for a better future.

We will contribute to finding a solution to the Transnistrian conflict that assures Moldova's territorial integrity. We will work with all relevant parties to resolve through peaceful, negotiated settlements the frozen conflicts in the Southern Caucasus and encourage the democratic processes in Armenia, Azerbaijan and Georgia.

We will work together to promote democratic and economic reforms, human rights, freedom of expression and the press, the rule of law in Central Asia to promote international security and stability. We continue to call upon Uzbekistan government to facilitate an independent international investigation into the tragic events of Andijon.

We attach great importance to our relationship with Russia and are pursuing deeper cooperation on a range of issues of common interest, including some important foreign policy issues, non-proliferation and counterterrorism. We are concerned about some recent developments in Russia and the region and will work with Russia to promote energy security, the application of the rule of law, an independent judiciary and full respect for human rights, including free and independent media and a vibrant civil society, and a resolution of frozen conflicts in the region. We will make constructive use of the OSCE as an important forum for cooperative and comprehensive security and call on Russia to fulfill all Istanbul and OSCE commitments.

Regarding our respective relations with Latin America and the Caribbean, we recognize the need for greater collaboration to promote stable and effective democracies, as well as market economies that contribute to greater social cohesion. We will actively engage NGOs and civil society, and we will support access to information, establishment of rule of law and independent media where this is not provided. Where necessary, we call on countries in the region to provide coherent and effective support and protection to individuals, organizations or institutions working for the promotion and protection of human rights and democracy. We express our deep concern about the human rights situation in Cuba, and urge the Cuban government to take rapid steps to improve the situation. We welcome the reestablishment of the constitutional order in Haiti, support the renewal of the UN Stabilization Mission's mandate, and welcome police and troop contributions to the mission.

We will jointly work towards rapid implementation of the Darfur Peace Agreement. We will work with the United Nations and other international and regional partners and organizations, including NATO, to strengthen the African Union Mission in Sudan (AMIS) with the assistance required, and UN authorization to "bluehat" the AMIS force by September. We will continue to support the Comprehensive Peace Agreement in Sudan and will continue to mobilize resources for humanitarian needs.

We will seek to ensure successful elections on 30 July 2006 in the Democratic Republic of Congo, and will continue our support for the building of government institutions, training programs, and security sector reform. In the post-transition the United States and the EU will prioritize support for improved governance, the rule of law and security sector reform.

In Somalia, we reiterate our support to the efforts of the Transitional Federal Institutions (TFI) in pursuing dialogue, reconciliation and stable governance. We will assist the transition and the establishment of viable and inclusive institutions in order to promote stability in Somalia and the region.

We will further coordinate our respective efforts on humanitarian and democracy assistance to address the worsening plight of the population in Zimbabwe. We call on the Government of Zimbabwe to restore democratic freedoms and the rule of law, and to respect human rights. We are ready, as soon as significant action in this direction is taken, to reconsider the restrictive measures now in place against Zimbabwe. We also call for measures by the Government of Zimbabwe needed to reverse the economic collapse.

We will enhance our joint efforts in conflict prevention and crisis management by increasing consultations on current and potential crises, identifying ways to strengthen cooperation in crisis management and post-conflict reconstruction, and coordinating efforts to improve international crisis management capacities.

Confronting Global Challenges, including Security

Since no single nation can efficiently and effectively deal with global challenges such as climate change, counter-terrorism, non-proliferation, pandemics and natural disasters on its own, we commit ourselves to strengthening our cooperation to address these challenges.

Consistent with our common values, we will ensure that measures taken to combat terrorism comply fully with our international obligations, including human rights law, refugee law and international humanitarian law. We attach great importance to our ongoing in-depth dialogue on our common fight against terrorism and our respective domestic and international legal obligations.

We will step up our cooperation against terrorism, including through denying resources (financing, travel, and other material support) and shelter to terrorists, and we will co-ordinate efforts to prevent a new generation of recruits from emerging by countering radicalization and recruitment, and promoting tolerance, including by co-operating on developing regional strategies and by implementing—and encouraging others to implement—steps required by UNSCR 1624. In particular, we will work to enhance our border security cooperation by improving lost and stolen passport data sharing with Interpol, coordinating the implementation of biometric standards based on ICAO recommendations. We will co-operate to block terrorism financing, in particular in the informal financial sector, by developing improved procedures for information sharing and a more pro-active use of financial investigations implementing FATF Special Recommendations, among others by enforcing cash declaration regulations for travelers, optimizing the use of financial intelligence and controls, and engaging the private sector to develop partnerships to enhance protection of financial institutions.

We will strengthen our cooperation by completing negotiations on a U.S.-Eurojust cooperative agreement and we will step up our coordination to improve counterterrorism capacity building in third countries. We welcome the signature of bilateral agreements by EU member states and the United States to accompany the U.S.-EU Mutual Legal Assistance Treaty and Extradition Agreements, and will aim to bring them into force as soon as possible. We intend to agree without delay on a Comprehensive UN Convention on International Terrorism, and on a universally accepted definition of terrorism and we will work with others towards a targeted UN strategy on combating terrorism. We take note of the "Vienna Initiative", initialed on 4th May, on possible future tripartite cooperation in the field of justice and home affairs between the EU, the Russian Federation and the United States.

We will strengthen our efforts to prevent access by terrorists to weapons of mass destruction (WMD) and their means of delivery. We will work together to further implement our Program of Work on the Non-Proliferation of WMD, in particular by reinforcing our support for the Nuclear Non-Proliferation Treaty and we will continue to work together to strengthen it, stressing the importance of compliance and promoting its universality.

Our cooperation will include the full implementation of UNSC Resolution 1540, including by conducting joint demarches, where appropriate, to urge all countries to fully implement their obligations under UNSCR 1540, and by assisting States to meet their obligations. In implementing UNSC Resolution 1540, we will also address the issue of financing of proliferation-related activities and develop our cooperation in that regard by seeking to identify, track, seize or freeze assets associated with the proliferation trade, in accordance with national legislation and consistent with international law, and consider further actions against proliferation finance.

We will support the rapid opening and conclusion of negotiations on a Fissile Material Cut-Off Treaty at the Conference on Disarmament and emphasize that, pending the conclusion of the Treaty and the Treaty's entry into force, all states should declare publicly and observe a moratorium on the production of fissile material for use in nuclear weapons. We will continue to work together in the Nuclear Suppliers Group framework on proposals to develop transfer restrictions on enrichment and reprocessing (ENR) technology and to support multilateral mechanisms for reliable fuel supply assurances for States that have chosen not to pursue ENR.

We will coordinate efforts in preparing for the Biological Toxins and Weapons Convention Review Conference with a view to promote a productive outcome, the universality of the convention and the implementation by all States Parties through national laws and regulations in order to put these obligations into practice. We reaffirm our commitment to the Chemical Weapons Convention and its full implementation.

We reiterate our support for multilateral efforts to improve prevention and combat global health threats such as the spread of pandemics, including HIV/AIDS, Malaria and Tuberculosis, and other communicable diseases like SARS and Hepatitis. We agree that priority should be given to promoting effective control measures in animal health as a means to reduce outbreaks of H5N1 in birds. We will further increase regional and global cooperation between states, international organizations and civil society in mitigating and preparing for a pandemic, to which input by the International Partnership on Avian and Pandemic Influenza is welcome. We will further improve coordination of our response to natural disasters that have cost the lives of hundreds of thousands of people.

Fostering Prosperity and Opportunity

We reiterate our strong commitment to reaching an ambitious conclusion to the Doha Development Agenda by the end of 2006. These negotiations are at a critical phase and we call on all WTO members to demonstrate the political will and courage necessary to achieve an ambitious and balanced agreement that will help strengthen global economic growth, improve living standards, and alleviate poverty. We recognize the need for trade ministers to make substantial progress on core negotiating areas over the next few weeks in order to ensure that this historic opportunity to liberalize trade is not missed. As responsible leaders, we will continue to work in cooperation with other WTO members towards an agreement that is worthy of the objectives identified in launching the Doha Development Agenda in 2001.

We will increase our partnership with developing countries to promote growth globally for the benefit of all. This will help us to realize the internationally agreed development goals and objectives, including the Millennium Development Goals and

the objectives and commitments of the Monterrey Consensus, which have helped to galvanize efforts towards poverty eradication through development co-operation and economic growth.

We will redouble our efforts to promote economic growth and innovation and reduce the barriers to transatlantic trade and investment by implementing all aspects of the Transatlantic Economic Initiative, in line with the Work Program agreed at the U.S.-EU Economic Ministerial Meeting in November 2005, and to be updated and reviewed at a second U.S.-EU Economic Ministerial meeting later this year.

We endorse the new Action Strategy for the enforcement of intellectual property rights against piracy and counterfeiting. Implementation has already started with concrete actions aimed at promoting strong and effective enforcement in third countries, strengthening cooperation to reduce global piracy and counterfeiting, and offering public-private partnerships to protect intellectual property. We will enhance our dialogue to promote a more efficient international patent system.

We will build on the progress of the High Level Regulatory Cooperation Forum and associated dialogues, and expand implementation of our Regulatory Cooperation Roadmap to address new topics and sectors and initiate targeted exchanges of regulatory experts. As part of our Innovation Initiative, we will work to measure innovation performance, its impact on the economy, and to understand better each other's innovation policies. We will implement the U.S.-EU plan on e-accessibility with the goal of reaching a coherent approach on our policies in this area. We will work on an implementing arrangement on environment research and eco-informatics under our Agreement on Scientific and Technological Cooperation. We will continue to work together through the U.S.-EU Financial Markets Regulatory Dialogue and the Policy Dialogue on Border and Transportation Security.

We pledge to keep our investment regimes open and to build on existing investment flows to boost growth and create jobs
in the transatlantic economy. We will address obstacles to transatlantic investment
with a view to promoting closer economic
integration.

We will redouble our efforts to conclude
a first stage Air Transport Agreement in
2006. The United States and the EU will
cooperate closely on the legal framework
governing the transfer of air passenger data
following the European Court of Justice
ruling of 30 May 2006.

We will work together to ensure implementation of phase I of the Wine Agreement, and, as mutually agreed, pursue negotiations on phase II in September.

We have signed today a new Agreement
on Higher Education and Vocational Training under which our respective educational
institutions will inaugurate innovative joint
study programs, promote exchanges of students, teachers, and other professionals,
strengthen the Fulbright-Schuman Program
and encourage greater institutional collaboration in tertiary education.

We recognize the need for tangible
progress to be made towards the establishment of reciprocal visa-free travel for all
EU citizens to the United States, as part
of our efforts to promote the economic and
social benefits of increased travel while
keeping borders secure.

*Promoting Strategic Cooperation on Energy
and Energy Security, Climate Change and
Sustainable Development*

We recognize the strategic role of security of supply, competitiveness and sustainability in the energy sector. In this connection, we strongly reaffirm our commitment
to the energy security principles enunciated
by the International Energy Agency. We
have agreed to reinforce our strategic energy cooperation to:
- support diversification of energy
  sources and supplies;
- secure our energy infrastructure;

- promote market-based energy security
  policies that ensure competition, transparency, respect for contracts, and
  non-discriminatory trade, transit, and
  access;
- speed development of new lower-pol-
  lution and lower carbon technologies;
- accelerate investment in cleaner, more
  efficient use of fossil sources and renewable sources in order to cut air
  pollution harmful to human health and
  natural resources, and reducing greenhouse gases associated with the serious
  long-term challenge of global climate
  change.

We will cooperate to ensure sufficient,
reliable and environmentally responsible
supplies of energy at prices reflecting market fundamentals, facilitating sustained
global economic growth as well as expanding access to energy in developing countries. Thus, we agree to:
- Improve energy security by enhancing
  the dialogue with the main transit, producer and consumer countries and by
  promoting diversification of energy
  sources and supply routes worldwide
  and notably in the Caspian Sea region,
  Middle East, continental Africa and
  Latin America;
- Analyze geopolitical implications of the
  worldwide energy situation as it develops, its impact on our external policies
  and to develop mutually reinforcing
  policies where appropriate;
- Promote energy security policies in key
  third countries by encouraging a gradual transition to market pricing and behavior, and co-ordinate capacity-building assistance to emerging economies,
  including to increase energy efficiency,
  adopt clean technologies and build
  strategic stocks;
- Support maintenance and improvement of pipeline infrastructure to ensure uninterrupted deliveries and facilitate diversification investments in

large trans-national projects by ensuring convergence of legal and regulatory frameworks and supporting collaboration among energy regulatory authorities, notably with Ukraine;

- Coordinate where appropriate technical assistance to improve energy legal and regulatory frameworks and investment climates in third countries;
- Improve the security of global energy networks and develop standards for physical security of critical energy infrastructure;
- Facilitate development of Liquefied Natural Gas (LNG);
- Increase our coordination within international fora, notably the G8, the International Energy Agency (IEA) and the International Energy Forum (IEF);
- Use energy in a more efficient and environmentally responsible manner, and in particular cooperate on improving the efficiency of world-wide traded products. In this context we have just initialed a new Energy Star Agreement;
- Make more and better use of renewable energy sources and reinforce technological cooperation and partnerships, notably on environmentally-friendly low emission power generation technologies, hydrogen energy, carbon sequestration, cutting gas flaring and biofuels;
- Promote diversification of fuel sources in transportation sector, including through increase use of biofuels;
- Continue cooperation through the International Partnership for a Hydrogen Economy and increase collaboration over regulatory, standards and trade issues affecting alternative fuels and emerging technologies, especially hydrogen;
- Cooperate on developing efficient, transitional transport technologies, and

fuel standards, such as plug-in hybrids or efficient diesel engines;
- Continue scientific exchanges among U.S. and EU research and development organizations focused on energy efficiency in buildings;
- Promote, consistent with national energy policies, safety standards in the production of nuclear energy.

To monitor and guide this process, we will conduct an annual strategic review of U.S.-EU energy cooperation.

We also agreed to promote energy security worldwide by applying the following Energy Security Principles:

a. Contractual commitments should be upheld and market-based principles should prevail at all stages of the energy supply chain.

b. Diversifying sources of energy and modes/routes of transit, and ensuring non-discriminatory third-party access to transit infrastructure will improve the functioning of energy markets worldwide.

c. Open, transparent, non-discriminatory and stable legal conditions that ensure fair and equitable treatment for energy investment and trade are essential to helping producing and transit countries meet market demands.

d. Further development of production and export capacities in producer countries in a safe and secure environment, and the upgrading of existing and development of new energy transportation infrastructures by producer and transit countries as well as further development of refinery capacity in all countries are critical.

e. Bolstering and ensuring the highest levels of physical and environmental security and safety of energy infrastructures, as well as the highest level of nuclear safety, is crucial to the durability and sustainability of the global energy system.

f. We should encourage the most economic and efficient use of energy worldwide notably through the use of market-based instruments to minimize negative environmental consequences, and should promote in particular the use of cleaner and more efficient use of fossil fuels and the development of economically competitive non-fossil energy sources based on appropriate policies and market-based instruments.

g. We should promote continued research, development and deployment of alternative energy sources and the facilitation of technological and industrial co-operation.

h. Supporting effective implementation of transparency and data sharing initiatives, such as the Joint Oil Data Initiative (JODI), including on the evaluation of oil reserves, and the Extractive Industries Transparency Initiative (EITI) will improve transparency and predictability of the market for all stakeholders.

i. Addressing energy poverty endured by many of the world's poorest people who will still lack access to modern energy services is a priority.

We will work more closely to address the serious and long-term challenge of climate change, biodiversity loss and air pollution and will act with resolve and urgency to reduce greenhouse gas emissions. We will continue our dialogue and efforts under the UN Framework Convention on Climate Change (UNFCCC), including work on long-term cooperative action in the process established in Montreal in December 2005. To this end, we have agreed to establish an U.S.-EU High Level Dialogue on Climate Change, Clean Energy and Sustainable Development to build on existing bilateral and multilateral initiatives and further advance implementation of the G–8 Gleneagles Plan of Action for Climate Change, Clean Energy and Sustainable Development. This dialogue will be guided by the ultimate objective of the UNFCCC and will initially meet in fall 2006 in Helsinki. Among topics of importance for this dialogue will be experience with different market-based mechanisms to promote cost-effective reductions in greenhouse gas emissions; advancing the development and deployment of existing and transformational technologies that are cleaner and more efficient, producing energy with significantly lower emissions; efficiency and conservation; renewable fuels; clean diesel; capture of methane; lower emitting agricultural operations and energy production and distribution systems, as well as other environmental issues.

NOTE: An original was not available for verification of the content of this joint statement.

Remarks in a Discussion With Foreign Students in Vienna
June 21, 2006

The President. It's always important to wait on your wife. [*Laughter*] Please sit down. Here's what we're going to do. I'm going to give a statement, then answer a couple of questions. Then we'll get the press out of here and have a dialog. Is that okay? Yes. Let them get set up.

This will take a little bit of time and then we'll—first of all, I want to thank our Ambassador for setting this up, and thank you all very much for joining Laura and me. We're the parents of 25-year-old twin daughters who have dreams and aspirations just like I'm sure you do. And one of the things that I hope we're able to accomplish today is I want to learn about you and your dreams and aspirations, and I want you to ask me questions about our country and, you know, the decisionmaking process that I go through. I'll answer any question you have.

I just want to assure you of one thing, that I believe that freedom is universal. I don't think freedom is just a right for American citizens. I don't think it's just a right for people who practice religion one way. I think it is the right of everybody who lives everywhere. I believe that free societies end up yielding peace and hope. And that's the cornerstone of my foreign policy.

I've had to make some very difficult decisions, as you know, and I made the decisions based upon what I think is in the best interest of my country, the security of my country. But I also believe the decisions I have made will end up helping people realize the great blessings of liberty. I believe people ought to be able to worship freely or not worship at all, but you're equally a citizen of the world. I believe that poverty and hopelessness in the spirit can be changed. I believe the United States has got an obligation to help others.

And we're doing so. We've got a very robust foreign policy. One part of the foreign policy you hear about is, obviously, my determination to defend ourselves. But we're also actively working with people who are suffering from HIV/AIDS in Africa. I'm deeply concerned about the Sudan and the situation in Darfur. I believe that it's very important for the United States to work with friends and allies to accomplish our objectives.

And so the purpose of my visit here to Vienna has been to work with my European Union counterparts to join in a common alliance for the good of mankind. And so thank you for giving me a chance to come by and visit. I'll answer a couple of questions. If anybody has any thoughts or questions and wants to be the lead-off person,

please step up and do so. Don't be shy. [*Laughter*] Any questions or thoughts?

Yes, sir. Please. State where you're from so everybody knows.

Kosovo

Q. Mr. President, Mrs. Bush, and Ambassador McCaw, I just wanted—first of all, I wanted to say that I'm really honored to have been given this opportunity to participate in this breathtaking occasion. I would like—first of all, I would like to give thanks to Ambassador McCaw for the very friendly invitation to the Embassy and for choosing me as a student of this country that has been chosen here, among so many countries in the world. And want to thank also President Bush, American Government, and the American people, especially, for giving a continuous contribution and help to a country that was having, and is having, a tough time. Therefore, I have reason to believe that tough times never last, that tough people do.

The President. Do you mind if I use that sometime? [*Laughter*]

Q. It's not original from me. So long live America and its people. And thank you. And the following question is concerning my country. So I would like to ask you, since the peaceful people of Kosovo has put its trust to America and since the people of Kosovo believe in American power and American democracy, what will the American contribution be for the independence of Kosovo? And furthermore, to what extent is America as a superpower—to what extent is it ready to take on burden and responsibility for solving the problem of Kosovo and to contribute in its progress and democracy, economy and education and freedom?

The President. Yes, thank you very much. Is it Niser? Niser is from Kosovo. And yours is a country which is a part of the world which has got our attention. As you know, we've got U.S. troops stationed there with the intention of helping provide stability so that there can be a peaceful resolution to the issue between Serbia and Kosovo.

We believe that dialog between Serbia and those who aspire for an independent country in Kosovo need to be ongoing, in such a way that there is a resolution that meets the needs of the majority and, at the same time, enhances minority rights inside Kosovo. To this end, we're working with our European partners to try to just bring a sense of stability and a sense of calm so that a rational solution can be worked out and so that the people, the Kosovars can realize dreams.

The ultimate political solution is going to require a buy-in by both sides. And I think the proper role of the United States is to encourage this kind of dialog. The Prime Minister of Serbia will be coming to the United States shortly, and we will work with him to urge him to listen to the needs of the Kosovars and, at the same time, assure him that our policy is to guarantee minority rights.

Thank you for your question. One of the things that—you asked what else we can do. One of the things that is very important for our country is to have exchanges with students such as yourself. I hope that some of you, as you consider your future, will come to the United States to study. And the reason why I say that is because I want you to get to see America the way it is, not the way, necessarily, sometimes it's portrayed through a robust and free media around the world. You'll find the people there to be very understanding, very respectful of traditions. After all, we are a country of immigrants. One of the interesting things about our country is that we've been able to accept people from around the world and, as a result of common values and—that people become Americans. And it is that capacity to help people assimilate into our society that I'd like for you to see firsthand. I think you'll

find there to be a very open society, one that honors freedom for all.

Yes, ma'am. Where are you from?

Foreign Investment/Life at the White House

Q. Hello—I'm from Kosovo as well. And first of all, I can say it's an honor to meet you, the President, the First Lady, and the Ambassador McCaw. Mr. President, I want wholeheartedly thank you, your Government, and the people of the United States for working for a stable, free, and democratic Kosovo and the region.

I wanted to say one thing. The intervention of 1999 of the American troops along with NATO partners has enabled me to be a participant today at this roundtable. Otherwise, most of all, I would have had the tragic fate of my father, a prominent university professor and minister of agriculture, as well, who was murdered in the war.

I have two questions. For Mr. President, do you believe that an independent Kosovo will attract foreign investments, consequently improve the economy and enable Kosovo to slowly gain financial independence by supporting their infrastructure and slowly decreasing the need for international financial aid?

And the other question goes to Mrs. Bush. Can you please describe a family day at the White House? [*Laughter*]

The President. Let me start, please. No matter what government I talk about, in order to attract capital, there must be some basic considerations—first of all, rule of law. In order for there to be capital and investment in any society, people have to be assured that their investment will be treated fairly, and therefore, there has to be consistent and constant law. What you can't do is have contracts, for example, that are broken—summarily broken, without an adequate court system to protect that kind of investment.

Secondly, in order for people to feel comfortable investing, there has to be a society which shuns corruption. Capital looks at a country and says, well, maybe my money will end up being stolen, or maybe I have to bribe my way in, or maybe I have to make concessions in order to get my capital to be properly invested. And therefore, it's important that any society that wants to attract capital must have strong anticorruption measures.

Thirdly, capital needs a rate of return. In other words, if somebody invests in a society, they expect there to be a return on their investment. And that means rational tax policy and monetary policy by the host government. What I'm saying to you is, is that there are certain, just basic standards that must be met in order to attract capital. On the other hand, you're absolutely right. The investment into a society far outweighs the grants and aid, for example. A society that's capable of handling investment in a proper way is a society which will grow and prosper and enable people to be able to realize dreams.

The word I like to use in America is "entrepreneurial spirit." And how do you enhance that entrepreneurial spirit? Well, you do it through good law, good practice, and anticorruption.

The First Lady. Okay, a day at—a typical day at the White House. Well, I'll give you a workday first. We get up about 5:30 a.m.—the President gets up and goes in and gets the coffee and brings it back to me in bed. [*Laughter*] Very nice of him.

The President. Record that, please. [*Laughter*]

The First Lady. Then, we have three animals that get up at the same time, and they have to go out—two dogs and a cat. The cat actually doesn't have to go out, but the two dogs do. So then we read the newspapers and drink coffee until we finally get up. We eat breakfast about 6:30 a.m. The President goes to work at the West Wing, which is right there; we live where we work. It's sort of like living above the shop—and goes to the West Wing to work at 7:00.

Usually, I don't go to work until later, around 9 o'clock, unless I'm traveling in the U.S. The President's offices are in the West Wing of the White House; my offices are in the East Wing. And my chief of staff happens to be here with me, right now, Anita McBride. I think there are about 18 people on my staff, and we— I have a lot of initiatives that we're working on.

We travel the country to work on issues that have to do with what we can do to help young people, especially boys, because right now boys in the United States are not going to college—not as many boys go to college. More boys drop out of school; more boys, obviously, get in trouble and are arrested. So we have an initiative that we've been working on where I visit programs around the country that help young people.

Sometimes we meet with—at the same time that I'm meeting with people—I meet with Afghan teachers, for instance, that are being trained in the United States—and the President, of course, is meeting with world leaders over there in the West Wing—also going out and traveling. And then, usually about 5:30 or 6, we're back in the Residence of the White House.

We have dinner. A lot of times our girls come over to have dinner with us. One of them was just living with us, but she just has moved out. The other one lives in an apartment and is teaching school; she's a third grade schoolteacher. So sometimes they'll come over and have dinner with us. Sometimes we'll watch a movie in the White House theater. But we do go to bed early. And so that's sort of the typical day.

The President. Thank you all.

NOTE: The President spoke at 4:33 p.m. at the Austrian National Library. In his remarks, he referred to U.S. Ambassador to Austria Susan Rasinski McCaw; and Prime Minister Vojislav Kostunica of Serbia.

Statement on Senate Passage of Fisheries Management Legislation
June 21, 2006

I applaud the Senate for passing a stronger Magnuson-Stevens Act by unanimous consent. By emphasizing the important role of ecosystem-based approaches to fisheries management and strengthening penalties for overfishing and other violations, this legislation will be vital to ensuring that we remain good stewards of our marine environment. I congratulate Chairman Stevens and Cochairman Inouye for their work on this important bipartisan bill that embraces my priorities of ending overfishing and rebuilding our Nation's fish stocks through more effective, market-based management methods.

Since my administration released the Ocean Action Plan in 2004, we have been making great strides in our efforts to make our oceans, coasts, and lakes cleaner, healthier, and more productive. Last week, I established the Northwestern Hawaiian Islands Marine National Monument, the largest single conservation area in the history of our country and the largest protected marine area in the world. Enactment of a stronger Magnuson-Stevens Act is one of the top priorities of the Ocean Action Plan, and Senate passage of this bill is an important milestone on the way to another significant bipartisan ocean policy achievement.

I urge the House of Representatives to join the Senate in passing this important initiative.

NOTE: The statement referred to S. 2012.

Remarks at a Welcoming Ceremony in Budapest, Hungary
June 22, 2006

President Laszlo Solyom of Hungary. Mr. President, may I welcome you to Sandor Palace. Thank you very much for coming to Budapest to commemorate the 50th anniversary of the 1956 Hungarian Revolution and freedom fight.

Mr. President, your visit is a rarity and signifying prelude to the celebration later this year, which will be attended by more than 50 heads of state and government here in Budapest.

Your visit today here in Hungary underlines the importance of 1956, how important it was from the point of view of global history. At the same time, it also highlights the importance of those values for which the Hungarians and Hungary fought in 1956. These are freedom, liberty, democracy, human rights, and national self-determination.

And both the United States of America and Hungary belong to the same community of common values. This is the foundation of the fact that now we are allies. And this is also—gave a foundation to the fact that after crushing 1956, the United States of America admitted more than 35,000 Hungarian refugees. For that, Mr. President, I wish to express my sincere thanks.

These values constitute the foundation of our alliance. It also means obligation for us, and it also means that we have got to represent that in an authentic way. And that was also the secret to Hungary's successful process of democratization and the fact that even under the extraordinary international circumstances made no—[*inaudible*]—and insisted on observing the Constitution and the law.

It is my firm belief that our common responsibilities, duty now is to fight terrorism. This fight against terrorism can be successful only if every step and measures taken are in line with international law. That is why it is my special pleasure to welcome the Vienna declaration.

We are aware of the fact and the various help and of the system that the United States of America contributed and helped this country and the countries of this region, that democracy should be able to take root.

There are many examples, many of these examples are not even known to the general public. In the course of our discussions, Mr. President, I would like to give you a couple of examples for that and also would like to speak about our common responsibility for the future generation and also sustainable global growth and also mention a few words about the visa.

Thank you very much.

President Bush. Listen, I'm thrilled to be here, Mr. President. Thank you for your hospitality, and thank you for your personal contribution to your country's democracy.

I am here to celebrate the 1956 Revolution, the idea of a revolution that celebrated the notion that all men and women should be free. I'm also here to confirm the friendship between Hungary and the United States.

I bring greetings from thousands of Hungarian Americans who are very proud of their homeland and their heritage. I also bring greetings from a nation that admires your courage and your desire to continue to do the hard work necessary for democracy to take hold.

I thank you for your grand hospitality, and I too look forward to our discussions.

NOTE: The President spoke at approximately 9:40 a.m. in the Maria Therese Salon at Sandor Palace. President Solyom spoke in Hungarian, and his remarks were translated by an interpreter.

Remarks Following Discussions With Prime Minister Ferenc Gyurcsany of Hungary in Budapest
June 22, 2006

Prime Minister Gyurcsany. First of all, I'd like to thank from the depth of my heart to the President of the United States for his visit today to Hungary, on the 50th anniversary of the '56 Revolution. We consider this visit to be a tribute to be a point to perseverance of the Hungarian people for freedom.

We also see this as a confirmation of our joint effort that freedom and democracy must not only be preserved but also spread around the world in every region and every country, wherever necessary. Now this work that we started must not and cannot be completed, but it must be continued, because the world is the way how you shape it.

The alliance of the United States and Hungary is based on values and interests at the same time. There are no major unsolved or painful issues, open issues in the relations of our two countries. There are challenges, and there are tasks to be solved, but that's just the way how it is.

As a European country, I believe that we should finally end with preconception that Europe represents morality and the United States represents efficiency. And if we are democrats, then we believe that morale and power must go hand in hand. And we are democrats on both sides of the Atlantic. Now, in terms of practical matters, of course, we just cannot avoid talking about the visa issue whenever we meet. We are well aware of each other's standpoints. We cannot pose much surprises to each other. But because we know that this is a long road, this is a long path that we must go down, so we must look for other areas where we can be more successful.

However, an important step on this road is that within a couple of months, finally, the building, the Tancsics was captured was kept—the building known as the Tancsics prison will return to Hungarian ownership. Let me tell you quite frankly that the President showed much more understanding for the importance and the meaning of this issue. And just within this circle, I can say that he promised, and if he did that, it will happen.

So, by and large, this is what we talked about.

President Bush. Mr. Prime Minister, thank you. I'm honored to be here. As I recall, this trip started back when you invited me to come when you were visiting the Oval Office. I thank you for the invitation. I'm proud to be here. I'm impressed by the beauty of this city. I'm honored to be able to speak to the people of Hungary tonight when I talk about the unbelievable thirst for freedom that was exhibited in 1956. And that spirit of freedom still exists in the world today. And I thank you for your troops who are working through NATO to help Iraq and the PRT that we're working on for Afghanistan. And thank you for your commitment to help others be free.

It is also my pleasure to congratulate you on being reelected. It's not easy to win a second opportunity to serve, but you have done so. And I appreciate the courage you're showing not only in foreign policy but in domestic policy. We have a very good relationship, which means the Prime Minister is comfortable in bringing up the visa issue. Look, I understand this is a difficult issue, and we have developed a roadmap to work through this issue, so the people of your good country will understand that you're doing your best and I'm doing my best to meet U.S. laws, and you're doing your best to represent the people of Hungary to get this issue solved.

And so thank you for bringing up a lot of issues, and thank you for your leadership. And we are very proud of our friendship and alliance with Hungary. Thanks for the invitation.

Prime Minister Gyurcsany. Thank you, Mr. President.

NOTE: The President spoke at approximately 11:40 a.m. in the Parliament Building. Prime Minister Gyurcsany spoke in Hungarian, and his remarks were translated by an interpreter.

Remarks at a Luncheon Hosted by President Laszlo Solyom and Prime Minister Ferenc Gyurcsany of Hungary in Budapest
June 22, 2006

President Solyom. Mr. President, Mrs. Bush, distinguished guests, it is indeed a great honor and great privilege to have the President of the United States of America here in Hungary on the occasion of the commemoration of the 50th anniversary of the 1956 Revolution and freedom fight.

This visit demonstrates that community of shared values that is a very strong bond between us. It was freedom, democracy, self-determination, and human rights—were the values for which so many people sacrificed their lives in Hungary in 1956.

This year, in March, in the Capitol, President Bush said, on the occasion of the commemoration, that the Hungarian Revolution was an example of patience and is a value which is deeply rooted in everybody's soul. We were, indeed, very patient. We carried this value in the heart of our hearts for 35 years, and not only in the heart, and finally, after 35 years, it became reality.

This set of values is a must for us, to authentically represent it all over the world. During our bilateral meetings, we were able to exchange views on the various techniques that can help people to have these values take deep roots in the hearts of the people.

Only a few of us know, though, the great importance of the practice of the Supreme Court of the United States, especially in the field of human rights, the lesson we learn from them and started to exercise them, and then radiate the lesson to the neighboring countries in east-central Europe and even beyond that, down to South Africa. And these techniques are just as important as is another important initiative by the father of President Bush, who initiated the establishment of environmental center, which radiated an impact and influence all over the region.

In the course of our bilateral relations, I reiterated our commitment to fight and enhance sustainable economic growth in the world. We touched upon several foreign political issues as from the Balkans down to Iraq, Iran, and Russia. We agreed that there are vast opportunities to further expand our bilateral cooperation, and our two respective countries have their own role to play. And Hungary, because of its geopolitical situation and tradition, can help a lot to materialize our common goals and objectives.

In the spirit of this common cooperation, may I propose a toast to the health of Mr. President, Mrs. Bush, and the cooperation between our two respective countries.

President Bush. Mr. President, Mr. Prime Minister, Laura and I thank you and your wives for such gracious hospitality in this beautiful country. It is a joy to be in Hungary. It is an honor to be here.

I bring the greetings from my country. I bring the greetings from Hungarian Americans who are so proud of their heritage. I bring the thanks of the American people for supporting the freedom movement. I'm looking forward to sharing some thoughts about the unbelievable events that took place in 1956. And all of us who have the blessings of freedom must remember the spirit that took place then and must never take freedom for granted.

I congratulate your political leaders for doing the hard work necessary to make sure democracy takes hold. And I assure the Hungarian people that we're proud to be your friend and ally. And so it is in the spirit of respect and friendship that I would like to offer a toast to the people of Hungary.

Prime Minister Gyurcsany. Mr. Presidents, ladies and gentlemen, freedom and love, these are the two things I need. That's how we Hungarians, many Hungarians sing but this is also how Americans or anybody else in the world could sing and celebrate like we do here in Hungary all the time. Freedom and love really link together the two basic conditions for public and private happiness. Neither of these can exist without enthusiasm. Neither of these can tolerate selfishness. And both of these require unselfishness and sacrifice. So we are prepared to do our best for a better world, unselfishly and with some self-sacrifice sometimes.

And we know that this better world needs more democracy, more understanding, and sometimes, perhaps, more love. Well, this is perhaps where we are linked together, Europe and the United States, Hungary and the United States, in this effort, in this struggle. Sometimes we might have debates; we might have discussions; but after all, we know that we must work together and fight together for the objectives that we have together.

So, welcome, Mr. President. Let's make this a better world, better Hungary, and better United States.

NOTE: The President spoke at approximately 12:20 p.m. in Hunter Hall at the Parliament Building. In his remarks, he referred to Erzsebet Solyom, wife of President Solyom; and Klara Dobrev, wife of Prime Minister Gyurcsany. President Laszlo and Prime Minister Gyurcsany spoke in Hungarian, and their remarks were translated by an interpreter.

Remarks in Budapest
June 22, 2006

Thank you very much. *Jo napot kivanok.* Thank you for your warm welcome. I first want to thank the President for his gracious hospitality and the chance to visit Sandor Palace. It's a beautiful site, and I know you're proud of it. I also want to thank your Prime Minister for his hospitality and the chance to go to the Parliament Building. Laura and I particularly liked to see the Holy Crown of St. Stephen. It was beautiful. It's a grand reminder of the great history of Hungary.

I thank the Hungarian people for their gracious reception. Laura and I are honored to visit your great nation. Hungary sits at the heart of Europe. Hungary represents the triumph of liberty over tyranny, and America is proud to call Hungary a friend.

I appreciate the opportunity to stand here on Gellert Hill, which offers a striking view of your beautiful city. Fifty years ago, you could watch history being written from this hill. In 1956, the Hungarian people suffered under a Communist dictatorship and domination by a foreign power. That fall, the Hungarian people decided they had enough and demanded change. From this spot, you could see tens of thousands of students and workers and other Hungarians marching through the streets. They called for an end to dictatorship, to censorship, and to the secret police. They called

for free elections, a free press, and the release of political prisoners. These Hungarian patriots tore down the statue of Josef Stalin and defied an empire to proclaim their liberty.

Twelve days after the Hungarian people stood up for their liberty, the Communists in Moscow responded with great brutality. Soon the streets of Budapest were filled with Soviet tanks. The Red Army killed many who resisted, including women and children. The Soviets threw many more into prison. They crushed the Hungarian uprising but not the Hungarian people's thirst for freedom.

Some 200,000 Hungarians fled into exile in search of liberty. Many found refuge in the United States. These immigrants have contributed to my country in countless ways, and America will always be glad that we opened our doors to Hungarians that were seeking freedom. Fifty years later, the sacrifice of the Hungarian people inspires all who love liberty. Some of those who faced those tanks are here today. I had the honor of meeting three such gentlemen at lunch. I was proud to be in their presence. America honors your courage. We've learned from your example, and we resolve that when people stand up for their freedom, America will stand with them.

In 1989, a new generation of Hungarians returned to the streets to demand their liberty and boldly helped others secure their freedom as well. By giving shelter to those fleeing tyranny and opening your border to the West, you helped bring down the Iron Curtain and gave the hope of freedom to millions in Central and Eastern Europe. Because you had the courage to lead, Hungary became the first Communist nation in Europe to make the transition to democracy.

Hungary has continued to move forward. You regained your independence, held free elections, and established a free economy. Hungary is now a valued member of NATO and the European Union. You know that the democratic journey is not easy, but you continue to make the tough decisions that are necessary to succeed. America admires your perseverance; we welcome your progress; and America values our alliance with the free people of Hungary.

You believe that free nations have an obligation to help others realize the benefits of freedom. So last year, you launched the International Center for Democratic Transition here in Budapest. You set that center up to help others learn from your country's experiences. Hungary was also an early contributor to the United Nations Democracy Fund, which supports emerging democracies with legal and technical and financial assistance. And together America and Hungary helped launch the Foundation for the Future, which supports democratic reformers, independent journalists, women's groups, and human rights advocates throughout the Middle East. Hungary is making a difference in our world, and I thank you for your leadership in freedom's cause.

Hungary is also showing courage in freedom's cause. In Kosovo, Hungarian soldiers are helping to secure the peace. Your work is aiding the rise of democracy in a region that has endured violence and tyranny for many decades. By your efforts, you're helping the people of the Balkans establish free and democratic societies, and you're paving the way for their membership in the institutions of a united Europe.

Hungarian troops are also defending freedom's cause in the war on terror. In Afghanistan, your soldiers have rebuilt schools and a medical center. They've helped train Afghan police to enforce the rule of law and to protect the Afghan people. In Iraq, Hungarian troops played a vital role in Operation Iraqi Freedom by providing security and delivering food and medical supplies to coalition forces. Today, Hungarian soldiers are helping to train Iraqi security forces. This is important work. By supporting these two young democracies, you are strengthening two new allies in the war on terror, and you're bringing hope to millions of people in a vital region of the world.

Last week, I traveled to Baghdad. I was impressed by what I saw. Americans and Hungarians and other coalition partners can be proud of what we have achieved in partnership with the Iraqi people. I met with Iraq's new Prime Minister and was able to see firsthand his strong character, his commitment to freedom, and his determination to succeed. Hungarians will recognize this spirit. Prime Minister Maliki is committed to the democratic ideals that also inspired Hungarian patriots in 1956 and 1989. He has a sound plan to improve security, to unify his people, and to deliver a better life for the citizens of Iraq. The success of the new Iraqi Government is vital to the security of all nations, and so it deserves the support of the international community. We will continue to help the Iraqi Government establish free institutions, to achieve its goals, and we will continue to help Iraq take its rightful place alongside America and Hungary as beacons of liberty in our world.

Iraq's young democracy still faces determined enemies, people who will use violence and brutality to stop the march of freedom. Defeating these enemies will require sacrifice and continued patience, the kind of patience the good people of Hungary displayed after 1956. We will help them rebuild a country destroyed by a tyrant. We'll help the Iraqis defeat the enemies of freedom. Our commitment is certain; our objective is clear. The new Iraqi Government will show the world the promise of a thriving democracy in the heart of the Middle East.

The Hungarian people know well the promise of freedom. Many of you lived through the nightmare of fascism or communism or both. Yet you never lost hope. You kept faith in freedom. And 50 years after you watched Soviet tanks invade your beloved city, you now watch your grandchildren play in the streets of a free Hungary.

The lesson of the Hungarian experience is clear: Liberty can be delayed, but it cannot be denied. The desire for liberty is universal, because it is written by our Creator into the hearts of every man, woman, and child on this Earth. And as people across the world step forward to claim their own freedom, they will take inspiration from your example and draw hope from your success.

Earlier today Laura and I laid a bouquet of flowers at the 1956 Memorial Monument across the river. It was our privilege to do so. It was a moving moment for us. Kossuth Square is named for the father of Hungarian democracy and honors more than a century-and-a-half of Hungarian sacrifice in freedom's cause. A bust of this great leader stands in the United States Capitol. It affirms that those who fight for liberty are heroes not only in their own land but of all free nations. All who love liberty are linked together across the generations and across the world.

Your great poet, Petofi, said this: "Here is the time, now or never! Shall we be slaves or free? This is the question; answer! By the God of the Hungarians we swear: We swear to be slaves no more!"

These words were addressed to the Hungarian people, yet they speak to all people in all times. This is the spirit that we honor today. I appreciate the opportunity to come to this great country and to celebrate the Hungarian example—the courage, the sacrifice, the perseverance that has led to this democracy.

On behalf of all Americans, *Koszonom.* May God bless you all. Thank you very much.

NOTE: The President spoke at 4:38 p.m. on Gellert Hill. In his remarks, he referred to President Laszlo Solyom and Prime Minister Ferenc Gyurcsany of Hungary; and Prime Minister Nuri al-Maliki and former President Saddam Hussein of Iraq.

Statement on House of Representatives Passage of Legislative Line-Item Veto Legislation
June 22, 2006

I commend Members of the House who voted today in support of the Legislative Line Item Veto Act of 2006. I also applaud the House Republican leadership, Congressman Paul Ryan and Congressman Mark Udall, for successfully steering this bill to passage. Controlling the Federal appetite for spending and protecting taxpayer dollars are shared responsibilities of the legislative and executive branches and require a bipartisan approach. I appreciate those Democrats who have supported the line-item veto in the past and did so again today. The line-item veto is a critical tool that will help rein in wasteful spending and bring greater transparency to the budget process.

Forty-three Governors have a line-item veto, and we need similar authority at the Federal level to control spending. Working with Congress, this tool can be used to help reduce the budget deficit and discourage the practice of earmarking Federal funds for projects that are wasteful, duplicative, or unnecessary. I urge the Senate to also pass the line-item veto legislation, so Congress and my administration can begin using this important tool to help enforce fiscal discipline.

NOTE: The statement referred to H.R. 4890.

Message to the Congress on Continuation of the National Emergency With Respect to the Western Balkans
June 22, 2006

To the Congress of the United States:

Section 202(d) of the National Emergencies Act (50 U.S.C. 1622(d)) provides for the automatic termination of a national emergency unless, prior to the anniversary date of its declaration, the President publishes in the *Federal Register* and transmits to the Congress a notice stating that the emergency is to continue in effect beyond the anniversary date. In accordance with this provision, I have sent the enclosed notice to the *Federal Register* for publication, stating that the Western Balkans emergency is to continue in effect beyond June 26, 2006. The most recent notice continuing this emergency was published in the *Federal Register* on June 24, 2005, 70 FR 36803.

The crisis constituted by the actions of persons engaged in, or assisting, sponsoring, or supporting (i) extremist violence in the Republic of Macedonia, and elsewhere in the Western Balkans region, or (ii) acts obstructing implementation of the Dayton Accords in Bosnia or United Nations Security Council Resolution 1244 of June 10, 1999, in Kosovo, that led to the declaration of a national emergency on June 26, 2001, in Executive Order 13219 has not been resolved. Subsequent to the declaration of the national emergency, I amended Executive Order 13219 in Executive Order 13304 of May 28, 2003, to address acts obstructing implementation of the Ohrid Framework Agreement of 2001 in the Republic of Macedonia, which have also become a concern. The acts of extremist violence and obstructionist activity outlined in Executive Order 13219, as amended, are hostile to U.S. interests and pose a continuing unusual and extraordinary threat to the national security and foreign policy of the United States. For these reasons, I have determined that it is necessary to continue the national emergency declared with respect to the Western Balkans and maintain in force the comprehensive sanctions to respond to this threat.

GEORGE W. BUSH

The White House,
June 22, 2006.

NOTE: This message was released by the Office of the Press Secretary on June 23. The notice is listed in Appendix D at the end of this volume.

Remarks at Opening Day of 2006 White House Tee-Ball
June 23, 2006

The President. Seth, thank you very much. Good job. Welcome to the South Lawn. Laura and I are thrilled you're here for opening day. It is an honor for me and the commissioner, General Pete Pace, to welcome you all here for what is going to be an exciting ball game between the Yankees from McGuire Air Force Base— [*applause*]—yes, right from New Jersey. Welcome. Glad you all are here. And they're going to be playing the Dolcom Little League Indians from Groton, Connecticut, representing the Naval Submarine Base of New London. Thank you all for coming. Welcome.

We want to welcome the coaches and the players. We want to welcome the moms and dads and grandparents here to this historic ballpark. And we're glad you're here to help us kick off the 2006 Tee-Ball on the South Lawn season. General Pace and I expect there to be some pretty good competition today.

I do want to welcome the mayor of Groton, Connecticut, Mayor Harry Watson. Mr. Mayor, thank you for coming; proud you're here. Thanks for serving. Thanks for joining us. I welcome Captain Sean Sullivan, who will be the first base coach. Captain, thanks for serving. Proud you're here. Good luck. You've got some awesome duties today. And Colonel Rick Martin from McGuire, good to see you, Colonel. Thanks for coming, Colonel. Proud you're here.

We're proud to welcome Steve Keener, who is the president and CEO of Little League International, and his wife, Cheryl. Steve, thanks for coming back. Thanks for helping. For those of you who want to be a Major League player, Mike O'Connor is with us, from the mighty Washington Nationals. Mike, thank you for coming, buddy. Mike is a pitcher for the Nationals. Glad you're here, Mike. We welcome Seth Fallon. We just heard from Seth. Thanks.

And I want to thank the Navy Sea Cadets Corps, who happen to be the color guard.

Zane Ellingwood is about to put the first ball on the first tee for the first game. But not quite yet. I do want to welcome Tim Brant. Where are you, Tim? There he is. Tim, thanks for coming, buddy.

Announcer Tim Brant. Thank you, pal.

The President. A national baseball announcer here to call opening day. We really appreciate you coming. Thanks.

And finally, I do want to welcome representatives from the Armed Forces Foundation, the Fisher House, and our military kids. Thank you for serving our families. After the game, it's my honor to be able to present the balls to each of the players on the team. And I will also be able to welcome Dave Erbe, who is a youth volunteer. He volunteers to help the wounded and injury—military personnel at Walter Reed. David, thank you in advance for doing what you're doing. Thanks for serving your generation and our country. You're a good man.

And now, before we put the first ball on the tee, I do want you to join me in the Little League Pledge. Are you ready? All players ready? Doesn't look like it. [*Laughter*] Are you ready?

[*At this point, the pledge was recited.*]

The President. Play ball.

NOTE: The President spoke at 1:05 p.m. on the South Lawn at the White House. In his remarks, he referred to Seth Fallon, member, Maryland State Boychoir, who sang the national anthem; Gen. Peter Pace, USMC, Chairman, Joint Chiefs of Staff, in his capacity as 2006 commissioner of White House tee-ball; Capt. Sean P. Sullivan, USN, commanding officer, Naval Submarine Base New London, who served as first base coach; Col. Frederick H. Martin, USAF, commander,

McGuire Air Force Base, who served as third base coach; and youth volunteer Zane Ellingwood.

Statement on the Proliferation Security Initiative
June 23, 2006

Today members of the international community are gathered in Warsaw, Poland, to share their experiences and develop new approaches to countering the trafficking of weapons of mass destruction through the Proliferation Security Initiative (PSI). Since the initiative was launched in Krakow, Poland, on May 31, 2003, the PSI has grown from a handful of nations to a global partnership of more than 70 countries from all around the world.

The PSI is dedicated to stopping all aspects of the proliferation trade and to denying terrorists, rogue states, and their supplier networks access to WMD-related materials and delivery systems. Together, we are working to disrupt the financial activities of networks that support proliferation, as called for in United Nations Security Council Resolutions 1540 and 1673. Together, we are shutting down front companies and proliferation networks and interdicting cargo carrying these dangerous materials, whether transported by land, air, or sea. With renewed determination, PSI supporters have come to Warsaw to further enhance our ability to counter WMD proliferation.

I join President Lech Kaczynski in welcoming PSI supporters to Warsaw, including our newest partners from the Persian Gulf and Central Asia. I commend all member nations for their readiness in taking on this vital task, and I urge all responsible states to join this global effort to end the WMD proliferation trade.

NOTE: The statement referred to President Lech Kaczynski of Poland.

Statement on the Resignation of Norman Y. Mineta as Secretary of Transportation
June 23, 2006

Norman Mineta has served America with integrity, dedication, and distinction. He leaves his position as the longest serving Secretary of Transportation in our Nation's history.

Norm's life is a story of determination, courage, and service. As a child, he lived in an internment camp. As a young man, he wore his country's uniform in Korea and Japan. From there, he went on to become a mayor, a Congressman, and a Cabinet Secretary under two Presidents.

As my Secretary of Transportation, Norm performed a crucial role on September 11, 2001, leading the successful effort to bring tens of thousands of passengers aboard commercial aircraft to safe landings. His leadership was vital to strengthening the security of America's seaports and airports. Norm worked hard to help eliminate red tape and liberalize the commercial aviation market. After Hurricane Katrina, Norm and his team were able to rapidly repair and reopen the region's major highways, airports, seaports, and pipelines. He also oversaw important changes in fuel economy standards that will save fuel, save lives, and save jobs.

Norm is an inspiration to all of us and has earned the admiration of a grateful Nation. I am honored that he agreed to serve in my Cabinet. Laura and I wish Norm, Deni, and their children all the best.

The President's Radio Address
June 24, 2006

Good morning. This past week, I traveled to Austria and Hungary, where I had productive meetings with our European allies. We discussed the challenges and opportunities we share, including the importance of spreading prosperity at home and around the world. It's good to be back home, and I'm pleased to report that our economy is strong, growing, and delivering prosperity to more of our people.

Let me give you a few facts. In the first quarter of 2006, our economy grew at an impressive annual rate of 5.3 percent. Since August of 2003, America has created more than 5.3 million new jobs, more than all 25 nations of the European Union combined. Productivity is growing, and wages are beginning to rise. And because taxes are low, workers are keeping more of the money they earn.

Our economy is heading into the summer on the fast track, and one of the best ways to keep our momentum going is to restrain spending in Washington, DC. Earlier this month, Congress took an important step by passing an emergency spending bill that stayed within the strict spending limits I set. The bill included necessary funding for high priorities, such as equipping our military and rebuilding the gulf coast, and it showed discipline in other areas. Congress deserves credit for meeting my spending limits, and I was pleased to sign the emergency spending bill into law.

As Members of Congress show restraint on spending bills, they also need to make reforms in the spending process. Under the current system, many lawmakers are able to insert funding for pet projects into large spending bills. This process is called earmarking, and it often results in unnecessary spending. For example, a bill to fund our military can be loaded up with unjustified earmarks and other spending that may not add to our national security.

This leaves Members of Congress with two bad options: They can either vote against the whole bill, including all the worthwhile spending, or they have to accept the whole bill, including the wasteful spending. The President is left with the same dilemma: Either he has to veto the entire bill or sign the bill and approve the unnecessary spending.

There's a smarter way to handle taxpayer dollars, and it begins with granting the President a tool called the line-item veto. A line-item veto would allow the President to remove wasteful spending from a bill while preserving the rest of the legislation. Forty-three of our Nation's 50 Governors have line-item veto authority, and they have used that authority to remove needless spending from otherwise good bills.

Ten years ago, Members of Congress from both parties voted to grant President Clinton the line-item veto. However, the Supreme Court ruled that version of the line-item veto unconstitutional because it took too much spending authority away from the Congress. I proposed a new version of the line-item veto that fixes the problem and gives the President a clear and constitutional way to cut wasteful spending. Under my proposal, the President would identify a list of unnecessary items that should be removed from a larger spending bill. Congress would then be required to hold a prompt up-or-down vote on the list.

A line-item veto would give the President a way to insist on greater discipline in the budget. A line-item veto would reduce the incentive for Congress to spend wastefully because when lawmakers know their pet projects will be held up to public scrutiny, they will be less likely to suggest them in the first place. Most importantly, a line-item veto would benefit American taxpayers by ensuring greater respect for their hard-earned dollars.

This past Thursday, the House of Representatives passed a bill granting line-item-veto authority. This was a victory for the taxpayers and for spending restraint. I call on the Senate to show a bipartisan commitment to fiscal discipline by passing the line-item veto so we can work together to cut wasteful spending, reduce the deficit, and save money for American taxpayers.

Thank you for listening.

NOTE: The address was recorded at 7:50 a.m. on June 23 in the Cabinet Room at the White House for broadcast at 10:06 a.m. on June 24. The transcript was made available by the Office of the Press Secretary on June 23 but was embargoed for release until the broadcast. The Office of the Press Secretary also released a Spanish language transcript of this address.

Remarks Following a Meeting With Organizations That Support the United States Military in Iraq and Afghanistan and an Exchange With Reporters *June 26, 2006*

The President. I have just had a remarkable discussion with some of my fellow citizens who have dedicated their lives to making sure our troops know that this country supports them as they help secure our country and spread freedom.

One of the amazing things about America is that people are desirous of coming together to support a neighbor in need. And we've got kids who are overseas defending this country, and we've got people at this table who are supporting their families, their loved ones, and most importantly, the troops who are in harm's way.

There's an organization called America Supports You. I would hope my fellow citizens would look on the web page americasupportsyou.mil to determine how you can help support our troops if you so

desire. I would urge Americans to do that, and around the table are leaders of the different organizations that make up this umbrella group. We've heard from people that are helping families of the wounded. We're talking to people who are using their position in different fields, like the entertainment field, to go over and provide hope for our troops. We're talking to moms and wives of those who have volunteered to serve our country.

But I want to thank you all for joining us, and thank you for serving your country. I told the folks here that the politics in Washington can be rough. But make no mistake about it, I am determined to succeed. And we will implement a plan to achieve victory, which is necessary, and that they need to tell the troops that no matter how tough it looks here in the Nation's Capital, that I know we're doing the right thing, and I know we will win.

I'll take a couple of questions. Terry [Terence Hunt, Associated Press].

Iraq/U.S. Armed Forces

Q. Mr. President, General Casey saw you on Friday, and it's been reported that he's talked about withdrawing two brigades from Iraq by this year. Can you tell us what he recommended to you?

The President. First of all, I did meet with General Casey, and I met with him because it's very important for me, as well as Secretary Rumsfeld, to meet with our commander on the ground. I've told the American people our commanders will be making the decisions as to how to achieve victory, and General Casey, of course, is the lead person. So we had a good visit with him.

And we talked about a lot of things. The first thing we talked about was the joint operations with the Iraqi forces to secure Baghdad and how that's going. We talked about the actions we're taking in Ramadi. The coalition is in the lead in Ramadi, and we're trying to make sure Ramadi does not become a safe haven for Al Qaida. And so he explained to me the tactics on the ground, what we're doing to secure that city and to run the Al Qaida-types out.

We talked about the Iraqi training mission. And as you well know, our standards are, as Iraqis stand up, the coalition will be able to stand down. And he talked about that kind of progress.

But in terms of our troop presence there, that decision will be made by General Casey, as well as the sovereign Government of Iraq, based upon conditions on the ground. And one of the things that General Casey assured me of is that whatever recommendation he makes, it will be aimed toward achieving victory. And that's what we want. And victory means a free Government that is able to sustain itself, defend itself. It's a Government that will be an ally in the war on terror. It's a Government that will be able to fight off Al Qaida and its desires to have a safe haven.

And so I did visit with General Casey, and I came away once again with my trust in that man. I've told the people here around the table that the decisions that I will make will be based upon the recommendations of people like General George Casey.

Toby [Tabassum Zakaria, Reuters].

North Korea

Q. Mr. President, how much closer do you believe North Korea is to launching the long-range missile, and how concerned are you about this? What if they just launch a satellite——

The President. Toby, I have said that the North Koreans should notify the world of their intentions, what they have on top of that vehicle and what are their intentions. We have not heard from the North Koreans, so I can't tell you what their intentions are. I have made clear to our partners on this issue—that would be Japan and South Korea and China and Russia—that we need to send a focused message to the North Koreans in that this launch is provocative. And I was pleased to hear that the Chinese have delivered that message to the North Koreans, and we would hope that the leader in North Korea listened to the Chinese.

So we don't know; we don't know. That's part of the problem. It's a nontransparent society that ought to be sharing its intentions with the rest of the world.

Hutch [Ron Hutcheson, Knight Ridder].

Environment

Q. I know you are not planning to see Al Gore's new movie, but do you agree with the premise that global warming is a real and significant threat to the planet that requires action——

The President. I think—I have said consistently that global warming is a serious problem. There's a debate over whether it's manmade or naturally caused. We ought to get beyond that debate and start implementing the technologies necessary to enable us to achieve a couple of big objectives: one, be good stewards of the environment; two, become less dependent on foreign sources of oil for economic reasons and for national security reasons.

That's why we're pressing for clean coal technology. That's why the hydrogen initiative is robust. In other words, we want our children being able to drive cars not fueled by gasoline but by hydrogen. That's why I've been a strong advocate of ethanol as an alternative source of fuel to run our cars. I strongly believe that we ought to be developing safe nuclear power. The truth of the matter is, if this country wants to get rid of its greenhouse gases we've got to have the nuclear power industry be vibrant and viable. And so I believe in—and I've got a plan to be able to deal with greenhouse gases.

April [April Ryan, American Urban Radio Networks].

Voting Rights Legislation

Q. Mr. President, what are you doing to ensure that the Voting Rights Act is reauthorized by the midterm elections, as you're saying that's one of your top priorities? And also, do you support foreign ballots—foreign language ballots?

The President. I am working very carefully with Members of Congress to implement that which I said when I signed the proclamation for Rosa Parks, is I want this Voting Rights Act extended. And so we're working with Members of the United States Congress to see if we can't get it done.

Bank Records/War on Terror

Q. Sir, several news organizations have reported about a program that allows the administration to look into the bank records of certain suspected terrorists. My questions are twofold: One, why have you not gone to Congress to ask for authorization for this program, 5 years after it started? And two, with respect, if neither the courts nor the legislature is allowed to know about these programs, how can you feel confident the checks and balances system works?

The President. Congress was briefed. And what we did was fully authorized under the law. And the disclosure of this program is disgraceful. We're at war with a bunch of people who want to hurt the United States of America, and for people to leak that program and for a newspaper to publish it, does great harm to the United States of America. What we were doing was the right thing. Congress was aware of it, and we were within the law to do so.

The American people expect this Government to protect our constitutional liberties and, at the same time, make sure we understand what the terrorists are trying to do. The 9/11 Commission recommended that the Government be robust in tracing money. If you want to figure out what the terrorists are doing, you try to follow their money. And that's exactly what we're doing. And the fact that a newspaper disclosed it makes it harder to win this war on terror.

Thank you.

NOTE: The President spoke at 10:41 a.m. in the Roosevelt Room at the White House. In his remarks, he referred to Gen. George W. Casey, Jr., USA, commanding general, Multi-National Force—Iraq; and Chairman Kim Jong Il of North Korea.

Remarks at a Reception for Black Music Month
June 26, 2006

Glad you're here. Thank you all. Welcome to the White House, and thank you for joining us as we celebrate Black Music Month.

I wish Laura were here, but she's got a good excuse. She's in New Orleans. She went down there to talk to the American Library Association's Annual Conference, and she spoke about the importance of rebuilding school libraries up and down the gulf coast of our country. She sends her best. I wish she could be here to hear the music. I know she's going to love it as much as I will love it.

I'm looking forward to introducing our artists here in a second. I do want to recognize Alphonso Jackson, who's a member of my Cabinet. Thank you for coming, and thank you for bringing us here. And it's good to see the Federal coordinator for the gulf coast rebuilding effort, Don Powell. Thank you for being here, sir. I welcome Chip Pickering from Mississippi and Congresswoman Marsha Blackburn from Tennessee. Thank you both for coming. I'm proud you're here.

It is always a special treat to be in the presence of Dr. Dorothy Height. Good to see you, Dr. Height.

And with us we have two great athletes, Alana Beard—thank you for coming, Alana—and Kareem Abdul-Jabbar. Proud you're here. I don't know whether you know this, but Kareem Abdul-Jabbar is a jazz expert, and he is working on a documentary about the connection between jazz and basketball. [*Laughter*] Pretty good combination. [*Laughter*]

During this month, we recognize the great contributions that black music has made to our Nation. That's why we're here. We express our gratitude to the artists whose works have inspired our Nation and have brought such beauty into the world.

Black music was often born of great pain, from the music of slaves who sang to warn others that the master was coming to the music of faith that helped African Americans endure tremendous suffering and overcome injustice. Black music is a really important part of our Nation's history and culture, and that's why we're celebrating it here today.

Some of the finest performances by black musicians have been heard right here in the White House, and we're going to continue that tradition today. During—in 1878, during the administration of Rutherford B. Hayes, soprano Marie Selika became the first black artist to perform here in the White House. A few years later, the Jubilee Singers of Fisk University became the first black choir to perform here. They moved President Chester Arthur to tears with a rendition of "Safe in the Arms of Jesus." Like the man they sang about, the Jubilee Singers could not find an inn that would welcome them here in Washington, DC. Those times have changed, thank goodness.

In more recent times, the White House has been graced by performances by artists like Louis Armstrong and Pearl Bailey, Ella Fitzgerald, Aretha Franklin, Shirley Caesar, Duke Ellington, and Lionel Hampton. These men and women created some of the greatest music America has ever produced, and they honored our country by sharing their gifts right here in the people's house. We're about to have the same type of performances here, if I can ever quit talking. [*Laughter*]

This year, Black Music Month celebrates the music of our Nation's gulf coast, soul and blues and jazz. And I'm honored that we've got three tremendous performers who represent the best of these three great traditions.

1213

Patti Austin is one of America's most talented singers and songwriters. Her extraordinary career began at the age of 4 when she made her debut alongside her godmother, Dinah Washington, at Harlem's famed Apollo Theater. Since then, she's recorded 16 solo albums featuring everything from soul to standards. Recently Patti earned her sixth Grammy nomination with her tribute to Ella Fitzgerald. Patti is an incredible artist. Laura and I have been privileged to see her perform at the Kennedy Center. I think you're going to like her a lot. [*Laughter*]

She's sung at the White House for every President since Ronald Reagan. When she was rehearsing her performance for President Reagan, Patti was singing so powerfully the piece of molding fell from the ceiling here in the East Room. [*Laughter*] Be forewarned. [*Laughter*] When Patti sings, she brings down the house. [*Laughter*] I'm proud to join the distinguished line of Presidents who have welcomed her here to the White House.

With us today is B.B. King, "King of the Blues." B.B. was raised in the Mississippi Delta, where he picked cotton for 35 cents a day, and then he played after work on the street corners for dimes. He says that when he sang gospel songs, "They'd pat me on the head but wouldn't ever put anything in the hat." [*Laughter*] So he would change, "my Lord" to "my baby"—[*laughter*]—and then they always gave him a tip. [*Laughter*]

One night in the 1950s, B.B. King was playing in an Arkansas town called Twist when two men got in a fight over a woman and knocked over a kerosene stove and set the whole place on fire. B.B. got out, but then he realized he had left his guitar behind. And so he went back inside; he braved the flames; and he rescued the guitar. Later, he learned that the lady who had inspired the brawl was named Lucille. So that's what he named his guitar.

Since then, B.B. and Lucille have played more than 10,000 shows. They have thrilled audiences all over the world. B.B. has notched an incredible 74 entries on the Billboard charts, and his work has influenced virtually every major guitar player over the last half-century. He remains gracious and humble, what folks in Mississippi call "free-hearted."

B.B. says this about his career: "I'm trying to get people to see that we are our brother's keeper." He went on to say, "Red, black, brown, yellow, rich, and poor, we all have the blues." It's hard to have the blues when you're about to hear B.B. King perform. At 80, this ageless star is still going strong, and we are thrilled to welcome him back to the White House.

We're also pleased to welcome Irvin Mayfield. Irvin is the cultural ambassador of New Orleans and artistic director of the New Orleans Jazz Orchestra. At just 28 years old, Irvin has already become one of America's finest trumpet players, in the great New Orleans jazz tradition. He's more than a musician; he's a decent, big-hearted man.

Last year, as Hurricane Katrina roared through New Orleans, the rising water took his dad, Irvin, Sr. The pain of losing his father was suddenly unimaginable. Yet in his father's name, Irvin pushed back his grief, and he went to work. He pulled out his trumpet; he pulled together his orchestra and started performing to help others who had lost homes and loved ones. He helped dry New Orleans's tears through the inspiring power of his music, and he hasn't stopped.

He's using his God-given talent to help rebuild his beloved homeland—his hometown, one brick and one note at a time. After the storm, Irvin made this solemn vow: No breached levee will wash away the culture of New Orleans.

There's a wonderful and unique tradition in New Orleans called the jazz funeral. The funeral procession parades slowly through the streets followed by a band playing a mournful dirge as it moves to the cemetery. Once the casket has been laid in place and the mourners have moved out of the cemetery, the music begins to speed up and the procession is joined by a joyful second line, with crowds of people dancing and celebrating the triumph of spirit over death.

Today Irvin Mayfield will play a song in the great tradition called "Just a Closer Walk With Thee." It's the first song he learned from his dad. He played it at his dad's—in his dad's memory after Hurricane Katrina, and then he retired the song. We're honored that he's decided to play it one last time, right here in the White House.

Irvin, we thank you for your personal courage and your dedication to others in a time of adversity. I have no doubt that with every good deed you perform and every note you play, your dad is smiling down on you. God bless you, Irvin.

Ladies and gentlemen, please welcome Irvin Mayfield.

NOTE: The President spoke at 5:23 p.m. in the East Room at the White House. In his remarks, he referred to civil rights leader Dorothy I. Height; Alana Beard, guard and forward, Women's National Basketball Association's Washington Mystics; and Kareem Abdul-Jabbar, former National Basketball Association center. The Black Music Month proclamation of May 25 is listed in Appendix D at the end of this volume.

Statement on the 10th Anniversary of the Terrorist Attack on the Khobar Towers in Saudi Arabia
June 26, 2006

Ten years ago yesterday, in an attack on the Khobar Towers apartment complex in Dhahran, Saudi Arabia, 19 members of our Armed Forces were killed and hundreds of other Americans were injured by terrorists who we believe were working with Iranian officials. We honor the courage of those who paid the ultimate price in defending our country. America will carry on the legacy of these fallen heroes by continuing the mission for which they gave their lives: defeating tyranny, defending freedom, and protecting their fellow citizens.

Laura and I offer our prayers and the gratitude of this great Nation to the families who lost loved ones in that brutal attack. These families can know that their loved ones will always be remembered and that we will remain determined in our efforts to bring to justice those responsible for this attack.

In remembrance of those who lost their lives 10 years ago, I ask Americans to keep their families in your hearts and your prayers.

Message to the Congress Transmitting Legislation To Implement the United States-Oman Free Trade Agreement
June 26, 2006

To the Congress of the United States:

I am pleased to transmit legislation and supporting documents to implement the United States-Oman Free Trade Agreement (FTA). This FTA enhances our bilateral relationship with a strategic friend and ally in the Middle East region. The FTA will benefit the people of the United States and Oman, illustrating for other developing countries the advantages of open markets and increased trade.

In negotiating this FTA, my Administration was guided by the objectives set out in the Trade Act of 2002. Congressional approval of this FTA will mark another important step towards creating a Middle East Free Trade Area. Like our FTA with Bahrain that the Congress approved in Decem-

ber 2005, and our FTA with Morocco that was approved in July 2004, this FTA offers another important opportunity to encourage economic reform in a moderate Muslim nation. Oman is leading the pursuit of social and economic reforms in the region, including by selling state-owned businesses, encouraging foreign investment connected to broad-based development, and providing better protection for women and workers. It is strongly in our national interest to embrace these reforms and do what we can to encourage them.

GEORGE W. BUSH

The White House,

June 26, 2006.

Remarks to the Manhattan Institute for Policy Research
June 27, 2006

Thank you very much. Thanks for letting me come by to say a few words. Larry, thanks for the introduction. I do want to congratulate the Manhattan Institute for being a think tank for new ideas and better ways for our Nation to handle some of the problems we face. I appreciate your thought; I appreciate your works. For those of you who support the Manhattan Institute, I thank you for supporting them. For those of you who serve on the Board of Trustees, thanks for helping. And thanks for inviting me here today.

I want to talk about our economy. I want to talk about ways that we can—the executive branch can work with the Congress to convince the American people we're being wise about how we spend our money. One of the things I want to assure you

is that I believe that this country ought not to fear the future; I believe we ought to put good policy in place to shape the future. And by that I mean we shouldn't fear global competition. We shouldn't fear a world that is more interacted. We should resist temptations to protect ourselves from trade policies around the world. We should resist the temptation to isolate ourselves. We have too much to offer for the stability and peace and welfare of the world than to shirk our duties and to not accept an international community.

I know some in our country are fearful about our capacities to compete. I'm not. I believe that we can put policies in place that will make sure we remain the most entrepreneurial country in the world, that we're capable of competing in the world.

And one way to do so is to keep progrowth economic policies in place and be wise about how we spend the people's money. And that's what I want to talk about.

I do want to thank my Director of Office of Management and Budget, Rob Portman, who has joined us today. He has done a spectacular job as the person partially responsible for tearing down trade barriers and to making sure our Nation was treated fairly in the trade arena when he was head of USTR. And now I've asked him to come over and manage OMB. It's a powerful position. The person who knows how the money is being spent is generally the person who's got a lot of influence in government. So I put a good friend in there to make sure we're able to work with the Congress to bring some fiscal austerity to the budget.

I want to thank Senator Thad Cochran, who is the chairman of the Senate Appropriations Committee. It's awfully generous of the Senator to be here today. He's a good fellow and a fine United States Senator, and we're proud to have him in our midst.

I want to thank Senator Judd Gregg, who's the chairman of the Senate Budget Committee. I've known Judd a long time. I've had to—when I was running for President, I was asked to debate my opponent a couple of times, and one of the things you do prior to debating your opponent is you have somebody serve as the opponent, and that happened to be Judd Gregg in both elections. [*Laughter*] And I had to kind of reconcile myself with the fact that he whipped me in—every time we debated. [*Laughter*] He's a good man who's just introduced some interesting ideas onto the floor of the United States Senate about how to deal with some of the fiscal problems and financial problems this Nation faces.

I'm proud to be here with John McCain—speaking about debates—[*laughter*]—we had a few. But one thing we agree upon is that this country needs to have

a line-item veto. And I'm proud the Senator is here, and I appreciate you coming. I might add, one of the many things we agree upon.

I'm proud to be here with Congressman Paul Ryan, who's the House bill sponsor of the line-item veto, as well as Congressman Mark Udall. Thank you both for being here. Congratulations on getting that bill out of the United States House of Representatives. I'm also honored that Congressman Mike Castle, Congresswoman Marilyn Musgrave, and Congressman Henry Cuellar from the great State of Texas, has joined us. Thank you all for coming.

For those of you who are working the Halls of Congress to get a line-item veto out, thanks for doing what you're doing. One of the reasons I've come to give you a speech on the line-item veto is to encourage you to continue working hard with members of both political parties to get the job done.

We're growing. This economy of ours is strong. And that's good news. It's amazing where we've come from, if you really think about it. We've been through a recession; we've been through a stock market correction; we've been through corporate scandals; we've been through an attack on our country; we've been through two major operations to defend the United States of America; and we've been through amazing natural disasters and high energy prices. And yet we're growing. We're the envy of the industrialized world. The growth in the last year was 3.5 percent; it was 5.3 percent in the first quarter of this year. That's good news. It means the entrepreneurial spirit is strong, that people are investing and people are making wise decisions with their money. And as a result of the growing economy, the national unemployment rate is 4.6 percent. That's low. That means your fellow citizens are going to work. That means people are having a chance to put food on the table. And that's a positive indication of how strong our economy is.

We're a productive nation. Productivity is on the increase. That's a result of investments that are being made in the private sector. A productive economy is one that will yield higher wages for the American people. The more productive you are, the more likely it is your wages will go up, which means a higher standard of living for the American people. And I want to thank the Manhattan Institute's support for progrowth economic policies, policies that really send a clear signal that we are still the land of dreamers and doers and risk takers.

The cornerstone of our policy has been to keep taxes low, see. We believe, and you believe, that the more money a person has in their pocket, the more likely it is this economy is going to grow. We trust people to make the right decisions on how to spend, save, and invest. That's certainly not necessary—necessarily the common policy here in Washington. There's some good and decent folks who think they can spend your money better than you can. I just don't agree with them. And one of the reasons why this economy is strong is because we cut the taxes on everybody who pays taxes in the United States. If you have a child, you got extra money. If you're married, we did something about the marriage penalty. It doesn't make any sense, by the way, to penalize marriage. Society ought to be encouraging marriage.

If you're an investor, you got tax relief because we cut the taxes on the dividends and capital gains. If you're a small business, it's likely that you pay taxes at the individual income tax rate because you're more likely than not to be a sole proprietorship or a subchapter S corporation. Seventy percent of new jobs in America are created by small business, and it made sense to let our small-business entrepreneurs keep more of their own money to save and invest and expand their businesses. The tax relief we passed is working, and the Congress needs to make the tax relief we passed permanent.

One of the benefits of keeping taxes low and growing your economy is that you end up with more tax revenues in the Federal Treasury. I know that seems counterintuitive to some people. You'll hear people say, "Let's balance the budget by raising taxes." By the way, that's not the way Washington works. They'll raise your taxes and figure out new ways to spend your money.

It turns out that when you encourage economic vitality and growth, the Treasury benefits from it. In 2005, tax revenues grew by almost $274 billion, or 15 percent. That's the largest increase in 24 years. The economy is continuing to grow, and tax revenues are growing with it. So far this year, tax revenues are more than 11 percent higher than they were at the same point last year, which is significantly better than projected. These increased tax revenues are part of how we intend to cut the deficit in half by 2009. In other words, Rob Portman will be giving a report to the Nation about how we're doing on the tax revenues; I think you're going to find that progrowth economic policies means that more revenues are coming into the Treasury than anticipated, which makes it easier to deal with a current account budget deficit.

But there's a second part of the equation to dealing with the current account budget deficit, and that is, how we spend your money. Now, I'm going to talk about discretionary spending in a minute, but I just want you to understand that a significant problem we face is in our mandatory programs. And I know you know that. Those would be programs called Medicare and Social Security and Medicaid.

As you might recall, I addressed that issue last year, focusing on Social Security reform. I'm not through talking about the issue. I spent some time today in the Oval Office with the United States Senators, and they're not through talking about the issue either. It's important for this country. I know it's hard politically to address these issues. Sometimes it just seems easier for people to say, "We'll deal with it later on." Now is the time for the Congress and the President to work together to reform Medicare and reform Social Security so we can leave behind a solvent balance sheet for our next generation of Americans.

If we can't get it done this year, I'm going to try next year. And if we can't get it done next year, I'm going to try the year after that, because it is the right thing to do. It's just so easy to say, "Let somebody else deal with it." Now is the time to solve the problems of Medicare and Social Security, and I want your help. I need the Manhattan Institute to continue to agitate for change and reform. You've got a big voice. You got creative thinkers, and if you don't mind, I'd like to put this on your agenda and let you know the White House and Members of the Senate and the House are anxious to deal with this issue and get it done once and for all.

In the meantime, we've got to do everything we can to control the spending that Congress votes on and approves every year. That's called discretionary spending. My administration is doing its part on discretionary spending. Every year since I took office, we've reduced the growth of discretionary spending that is not related to the military or homeland security. And the reason why we haven't reduced the growth on spending for the military is because so long as we've got troops in harm's way, they're going to have whatever it takes to win the war on terror.

We will not shortchange the people who wear the uniform of the United States military. As the Commander in Chief of this fine group of men and women, I have got to be able to look in the eyes of their loved ones and say, one, "The mission is worth it," and two, "This Government and the people of the United States support your loved ones with all we got." And that's exactly how I'm going to continue to conduct this war on terror.

But apart from defending our country, the last two budgets have cut nonsecurity discretionary spending—have cut the nonsecurity discretionary spending. And that's not easy. It's not easy to do that, but the Congress delivered, at least on last year's appropriations bills. And they're working on this year's appropriations bills. Our view is, taxpayers' dollars should be spent wisely or not at all. One of Rob Portman's jobs is to analyze programs that are working or not working. Look, every program sounds good, I know. But we're focusing on the results of the programs. Are they achieving the objectives that we expect?

One of the first tests of this year on whether or not the administration can work with the Congress on fiscal restraint was on a supplemental spending bill. That's a bill that was passed to provide emergency spending for our troops overseas and for citizens that had been hit by Katrina and to prepare for the dangers of a pandemic flu. I felt those were important priorities that needed to be a part of the supplemental bill, and so we sent that bill up.

Obviously, there was some noise coming out of the Congress at first; people had different opinions. And that's a good thing about democracy; you'll find there's all kinds of different opinions here in Washington, DC. People had different views about what ought to be in that bill.

Part of my job is to help bring some fiscal discipline to Washington. So I said that if the Congress exceeded a limit that I thought was wise, I would veto the bill. Congress acted responsibly. And it was hard work, and I applaud Senator Cochran for his hard work on this measure. He brought the House together with the Senate, and they took out $15 billion in spending that had been added to the bill. It came under the spending limit I had set. And it's a good example of fiscal restraint set by the Congress. I appreciate so very much your leadership on that issue, Mr. Chairman. Thanks for working with us.

I believe another crucial test for the Congress is to whether or not the Congress will pass a line-item veto. And that's what I want to talk to you about today. A line-item veto would be a vital tool that a President could use to target spending that lawmakers tack on to the large spending bills. That's called earmarking, and that's become quite a controversial subject here in Washington, DC.

I happen to believe that, a lot of times, earmarking results in unnecessary spending. See, part of the job of the President and the leaders in the Congress is to set priorities with the people's money. If you don't set priorities, the tendency is to overspend. And sometimes, a lot of times, the earmark doesn't fit into the priorities that have been set through the budgetary process. A lot of times earmarks are inserted into bills at the last minute, which leaves no time, or little time, for debate. Part of the process—a good process is one in which Members are able to debate whether or not spending meets a priority, whether it makes sense. Earmark sponsors are often not required to provide their colleagues with a reasoned justification for proposed spending. And not surprisingly, the process often results in spending that would not have survived had it not been subject—subjected to closer scrutiny. Part of a good legislative process is for Members to take a good look at whether or not a spending request meets a priority or not.

And the process has changed. And according to the Congressional Research Service, the number of earmarks has increased from about 3,000 to 13,000 over the last decade. In other words, this process is taking place more and more often. I don't think that's healthy for the process. Matter of fact, I think it's circumventing the process. Now, that's up—obviously, up for the Legislature to determine whether I'm right or not. The President proposes, and the legislative body disposes, and I'm proposing a way to help deal with this

problem. And that way is to pass a line-item veto.

Now, here's why it's necessary. First of all, part of the problem with the line-item veto is that it's oftentimes deemed to be unconstitutional. As a matter of fact, I know there are people in this room that helped pass the line-item veto in 1996. President Clinton was the President then, and the Congress—in my judgment—wisely gave him the line-item veto. And yet shortly thereafter, when he started using the line-item veto, the Supreme Court struck it down because they concluded that it unconstitutionally permitted the President to unilaterally change a law passed by the Congress. In other words, the bill didn't pass constitutional muster.

And so we dealt with this issue. We figured out that, obviously, any line-item veto would again be challenged to our highest Court. And so we proposed the following type of legislation: When the President sees an earmark or spending provision that is wasteful or unnecessary, he can send it back to the Congress. And Congress is then required to hold a prompt up-or-down vote on whether to retain the targeted spending. In other words, the Congress is still in the process.

The line-item veto submitted would meet the Court's constitutional requirements. And that's important. Members of Congress need to know that we've thought carefully about this, and we've worked with them to make sure that that which is passed is constitutional.

The other thing the line-item veto needs to do is it will shine the light of day on spending items that get passed in the dark of the night, and that will have—in my judgment—a healthy—it will send a healthy signal to the people that we're going to be wise about how we spend their money.

The bill I submitted will be an effective tool for restraining Government spending because it will address a central dilemma created by unwarranted earmarks. And here's the dilemma: When Members of

Congress are faced with an important bill that includes wasteful spending in the bill, they have two bad options. On the one hand, they can vote against the whole bill, including the worthwhile spending, or they can vote for the whole bill, including the wasteful spending. When such a bill comes to the President, it creates a dilemma. I've negotiated year after year on a top-line budget number. And Congress has met that top-line budget number, which means it's very difficult for the President, then, to veto the appropriations bills that have met the top-line budget number, because the next year's budget negotiations will be meaningless. You can imagine Members of the United States House or Senate walking into the President's office and saying, "Wait a minute; we met your number last year, and you vetoed the bill, so forget negotiations."

I want to be a part of the budgetary process. It's an important part of the President's working with Congress, and I'm not going to deal myself out of the budgetary process. So my point is, they can meet the size of the pie, but I may not like some of the slices of the pie. And therefore, what do we do about it? And one way to deal with it is the line-item veto. The President could approve the spending that is necessary, could redline spending that is not, and then let the Congress decide whether or not the President is right. It's a fair process; I believe it's a necessary process.

Many Members in Congress, I know, want to do the right thing. And so one of the interesting things about the line-item veto is it will help deal with that dilemma I described, either all or nothing when it comes to voting for appropriations bills. You know, sometimes a Member of Congress gets a special project for the district, and they go back and tout the project. Then you have Members who don't agree with earmarking, and they don't have any special project to tout to the district. And yet the people in their district are voting for the special project for the other per-

son's district. And I think the line-item veto—I know the line-item veto would help resolve this dilemma.

You see, if there's an opportunity for the President to redline certain programs and hold them up to the light of day, it will probably mean Members of Congress are less likely to propose the earmarks in the first place. Rather than being able to move a special project into the bill without hearing, this—the President would have the opportunity to say, "Wait a minute; this doesn't make much sense; it doesn't seem to fit into the priorities. This special project, this unusual study"—[*laughter*]—"or this particular project, this doesn't make sense."

I believe that part of a budgetary reform program is the line-item veto, the opportunity to put the light on such programs. And that will help Members resolve the dilemma of either voting for an important bill with bad items in it or being a part of trying to put bad items in it in order to justify their existence in the Congress.

The good thing about the line-item veto, it has bipartisan support. We've got a Democrat Member from the United States Congress who supported that bill strongly. Governors have had the line-item veto. I met with Senator Ben Nelson earlier this morning in the Oval Office; he talked about what an effective tool it was to have the line-item. Did you have it, Engler, when you were Governor? Engler had it. It's an important part of relating with the legislative process. And by the way, these aren't just Republican Governors with the line-item veto; they're Democrat and Republican Governors who are using that line-item veto effectively.

The line-item veto has bipartisan support in the Congress. Thirty-five Democrats joined more than 200 Republicans in the House to get the bill passed. That's a good sign. I was disappointed, frankly, though, that more Democrats didn't vote for the bill, especially those who are calling for fiscal discipline in Washington, DC. I mean, you can't call for fiscal discipline on the one hand and then not pass a tool to enhance fiscal discipline on the other hand. You can't have it both ways, it seems like to me.

Now the Senate is going to take up the measure. And again, I want to thank the Senators who are here for strategizing on how we can get the bill moving. Senator Frist is committed to getting the bill moving. Senator McCain is one of the important cosponsors, as is Senator John Kerry. I remember campaigning against him in 2004, and I remember him talking about the line-item veto, and I appreciate the fact that he's living up to the political promises he made. It's a good sign, and I applaud Senator Kerry for taking the lead on the line-item veto. And I hope members of his party listen to his justifications for that important piece of legislation.

What's really interesting is we've had Senators on record for the line-item veto. After all, the Senate passed a line-item veto in 1996. And for those Senators who passed the line-item veto in 1996, I hope they still consider it an important vote in 2006. Ten years hasn't made that big a difference. It was good enough 10 years ago; it's good enough today, for those who voted for the line-item veto.

Oh, I know this town is full of all kinds of politics, but we ought to set politics aside. We need to set politics aside when it comes to reforming Social Security and Medicare, and we need to set politics aside so that the President can work with the Congress to bring fiscal discipline to our budgets. That's what the taxpayers expect from those of us who are honored to serve.

So that's my opinion on the line-item veto. I hope you can feel—tell I feel strongly about it. I think it makes sense, no matter who the President may be. I think it makes sense for a Republican President to have a line-item veto, and I think it makes sense for a Democrat President to have a line-item veto. And I urge the United States Senate to pass this important legislation so we can reconcile whatever differences there are between the House and the Senate version and show the people that we are serious about being responsible with their money.

Thanks for letting me come by and say hello.

NOTE: The President spoke at 10:58 a.m. at the JW Marriott Hotel. In his remarks, he referred to Lawrence J. Mone, president, Manhattan Institute for Policy Research; and former Gov. John Engler of Michigan.

Remarks Following a Meeting With the National Endowment for Democracy Award Recipients
June 27, 2006

It has been my honor to welcome four amazing individuals to the Oval Office. These four folks are from the continent of Africa. They're here to receive the National Endowment for Democracy's award, which is an award to honor courage and fortitude and strength in promoting freedom.

And we have had an amazing discussion. My spirits are enriched by talking to free-dom lovers and freedom fighters. We've got a man from the Sudan who talked eloquently about free press. We had a doctor from Zimbabwe who talked about the human condition and the need for the United States to make sure we stay engaged with the democracy movements and help people who are hungry.

I talked to two really unusual ladies, one from the Democratic Republic of Congo.

She is very concerned about free elections, and she wants to make sure people in the rural part of her country are represented in free elections.

And then we had an amazing discussion with a lady from Sierra Leone but who's working in Liberia. And one of the most amazing stories is when she recounted the fact that she was escaping Liberia in the mid-1990s and had to get on a fishing boat to escape the authorities who wanted to bring—to do her harm because she expressed her desire for people to be free.

Again, I want to thank all of you for doing what you have done. I'm proud to be in your company. I'm proud to have you here in the Oval Office. I thank you for being witness to this universal fact: that

liberty is universal in its application; that people everywhere desire to be free; that freedom is not just—belongs to the American citizens, freedom belongs to everybody. And you're courageous in your fight and your desire to spread the concept of freedom.

Congratulations on winning a very important award. Congratulations on being so courageous. Thank you all for coming.

NOTE: The President spoke at 2:22 p.m. in the Oval Office at the White House. In his remarks, he referred to National Endowment for Democracy's 2006 Democracy Award recipients Alfred Taban Logune, Reginald Matchaba-Hove, Immaculee Birhaheka, and Zainab Hawa Bangura.

Remarks During a Run With Staff Sergeant Christian Bagge
June 27, 2006

The President. So I first met Christian when I went to Walter Reed—Brooke Army, San Antonio, Texas. And he said, "I want to run with you." He was in bed. He had lost both legs. I looked at him, like, you know, there's an optimistic person. But I could tell in his eyes that he meant it. And after a lot of hard work and a lot of compassionate care, this fine man is here on the South Lawn running with the President. And he ran the President into the ground, I might add. [*Laughter*]

But I'm proud of you. I'm proud of your strength. I'm proud of your character. Thank you for your service.

It's an amazing sight for me to be running with a guy who, last time I saw him,

was in bed wondering whether or not— I was wondering whether or not he'd ever get out of bed. There was no doubt in his mind that he would.

Thanks for your service.

S. Sgt. Bagge. Your welcome, Mr. President.

The President. Good man. God bless you.

S. Sgt. Bagge. It's a privilege.

The President. We're not through running yet. Get out of the way. [*Laughter*]

NOTE: The President spoke at 4:02 p.m. on the South Lawn at the White House. S. Sgt. Christian Bagge, USA, was injured in Iraq in June 2005 while serving in the Oregon National Guard.

Statement on Senate Passage of a Proposed Constitutional Amendment To Prohibit Desecration of the American Flag
June 27, 2006

Today a bipartisan majority of United States Senators voted to protect our Nation's most important symbol through a constitutional amendment to authorize Congress to prohibit the desecration of the American flag. Unfortunately, the final count fell short of the votes needed to send this important proposed amendment to the States for ratification.

By showing respect for our flag, we show reverence for the ideals that guide our Nation and we show appreciation for the men and women who have served in defense of those ideals.

I commend the Senators from both parties who voted to allow the amendment ratification process to protect our flag to go forward and continue to believe that the American people deserve the opportunity to express their views on this important issue.

NOTE: The statement referred to S.J. Res. 12.

Letter to the Speaker of the House of Representatives Transmitting Budget Amendments for International Assistance Programs
June 27, 2006

Dear Mr. Speaker:

I ask the Congress to consider the enclosed FY 2007 Budget amendments for International Assistance Programs. The total discretionary budget authority in my FY 2007 Budget would not be increased by these requests.

The details of this proposal are set forth in the enclosed letter from the Director of the Office of Management and Budget.

Sincerely,

GEORGE W. BUSH

Remarks Following a Meeting With Military Personnel in St. Louis, Missouri
June 28, 2006

I want to thank you all for coming. I just had a discussion with fellow citizens in the Guard, Reserve, and active duty who have been in both Iraq and Afghanistan. I want to thank you for sharing your insights with me. Thank you for your service to the country.

I told these men and women that their service is necessary for the security of the United States of America and that they're serving in historic times. And one day, their children will be able to look back and say, "My dad or my mom went to Iraq and Afghanistan and helped a young country become a democracy, and therefore, the world is more peaceful for it."

One of the things I am going to do is I'm going to meet with the family members of these good people and express our country's gratitude for their service as well. A lot of times military families don't get proper thanks, and I can't wait to meet your loved ones and tell them firsthand that the country appreciates your service.

One thing I told these good folks is that this country stands with the people wearing our Nation's uniform. We're with you. We know the work is hard, but the work is necessary. And we're winning, and we're winning. And the world is going to be better off because of your courageous service, and I thank you for it.

Thanks for letting me come by and visit. I appreciate it.

NOTE: The President spoke at 3:41 p.m. at VFW Overland-St. Ann Memorial Post 3944.

Remarks at a Dinner for Senatorial Candidate James M. Talent in St. Louis
June 28, 2006

The President. Thanks for coming. Thanks a lot. Thanks for the warm welcome.

Audience Member. Four more years! [*Laughter*]

The President. No more wife. [*Laughter*]

Thanks for supporting Jim Talent. He is a decent, honorable, can-do man who deserves to be reelected to the United States Senate.

Laura and I are very fond of Jim and Brenda. Jim is very fond of Laura, to the point where he was hoping she would be the keynote speaker. [*Laughter*] But the Senator and I both married very well. You know, you cannot succeed in this line of work unless you've got a supportive family. It's really important. And the Talents have the right priorities: their faith and their family and their country. And that's another reason why he's a great United States Senator. So not only do I want to thank Jim for his service, I do want to thank Brenda for being such a fabulous partner to Jim. And I also want to welcome Michael and Chrissy, the Talent children. Thanks for coming.

Laura sends her best. She not only sends her best to the Talents, she sends her best to Uncle Bucky and Aunt Patty. She sends her best to all our friends here in St. Louis.

She is a fabulous First Lady, and I am proud to call her—proud she's my wife.

I want to thank your Governor for joining us, Matt Blunt, and Melanie. Thank you for serving. Governors can make a big difference in the States—the State in which they live, and you are doing just that.

Where's Branch? Yes. He was afraid he couldn't make it through the speech. [*Laughter*] It's good to see old Branch. I think I remember getting to know Branch kind of before Branch became Branch—[*laughter*]—during the 2004 campaign. But thank you all for coming, and thanks for your service. I'll tell your old man you're doing all right. [*Laughter*]

I thank the Lieutenant Governor, Peter Kinder, for being here. Governor, it's good to see you again. Thanks for your service. I thank all the statehouse folks who are here. Thanks for serving. It's not an easy job to serve the communities in which you live, but it's important jobs. And so thanks for setting a good example.

I appreciate so very much my friend Jack Oliver, who happens to be the finance chairman for this effort. And Rachel—thanks for coming, Rachel. It's a pretty big sacrifice for you to be here tonight. Is there a doctor in the house? [*Laughter*]

I want to thank you all for—for those of you who organized this event. This is a big, successful event, and it takes a lot of hard work. So for all of those who have helped organize this event, thanks a lot. It's important. You can't win without friends. And the Talent for Senate race is a vital race for the United States of America, and you're helping him.

I want to thank the grassroots activists who are here. You're the folks who make the phone calls and put up the signs and turn out the vote. I want to thank you in advance for what you're going to do when we're coming down the stretch, which is to make sure that Jim Talent is not only backed financially but backed with your hard work and labor. He deserves your support. He has got a record to run on. He has made the people of Missouri proud, and he needs to be sent back to Washington, DC, for 6 more years.

These are historic times in which we live, and it is essential that we have people in the United States Senate who are clear-eyed realists who see the world the way it is, not the way we would hope it would be. And the reason why it's important to have clear-eyed realists is because it's essential we do not forget the lessons of September the 11th, 2001. And one lesson is, is that in order to secure the homeland, we must defeat the enemy overseas so they do not hurt us here at home. And therefore, we must have a United States Senate who understands that we must stay on the offense in order to protect America.

The second lesson is that when you see a threat, you must deal with that threat before it fully materializes. What that means is, is that oceans can no longer protect us, and if there's an enemy out there that's willing to do us harm, we must have United States Senators who are willing to take action to protect the homeland. And Jim Talent understands the world in which we live.

Oh, I know some of them in Washington are trying to rewrite history. But we all saw a threat in Saddam Hussein. See, he had threatened his neighbors; he invaded

his neighbors. He was a sworn enemy of the United States of America. He harbored terrorists. He had used weapons of mass destruction. He was hoping the world would look the other way so he could manufacture weapons of mass destruction, at the very least. He defied U.N. resolution after U.N. resolution. Republicans and Democrats looked at the same intelligence and saw a threat. And when he defied the U.N., we removed Saddam Hussein, and America and the world are better off for it.

Iraq is a central front in the war on terror; it's not the only front. Today I went to the VFW hall and was able to thank in person men and women who have served in both Afghanistan and Iraq, two crucial fronts in the war on terror. But Iraq is now the central front, and we've got a plan to succeed, a plan for victory, a plan that will enable a new ally in the war on terror to govern itself, sustain itself, and defend itself as a free nation. The stakes are vital, and it is important that Missouri send a United States Senator who understands that retreat is not an option for the United States of America.

One thing about old Jim Talent, he understands what I understand, is that when you put a man or woman in uniform and ask them to go into harm's way, they deserve the full support of the United States Government. We will complete the mission, and I will make my judgments as to the troop levels necessary to achieve victory not based upon political polls or focus groups but based upon the measured judgment of our commanders on the ground.

Make no mistake about it: There's a group in the opposition party who are willing to retreat before the mission is done. They're willing to wave the white flag of surrender. And if they succeed, the United States will be worse off, and the world will be worse off. These are historic times. We will defeat the enemy by, one, bringing them to justice before they hurt us again, and we will defeat the enemy—we will defeat their hateful ideology by spreading liberty.

There's an interesting debate in the world today; it's an interesting debate as to whether or not liberty is universal or not. Jim Talent and I understand there's an Almighty; we understand a great gift of the Almighty is freedom for every man, woman, and child on this Earth. I'm not talking about just for Methodists or Texans. [*Laughter*] I'm talking about the universality of freedom. Everybody wants to be free, and everybody is desirous to be free. And freedom yields the peace we're looking for. The way to win this war on terror is not only to defeat the enemy abroad, but it's also to defeat them by spreading a hopeful ideology, an ideology which has worked in the past.

You see, tomorrow I'm going to have an interesting day; every day is interesting when you're the President. [*Laughter*] I'm going to welcome Prime Minister Koizumi from Japan. And so we'll have the deal tomorrow, which is going to be a lot of fun, there on the South Lawn. And then we'll meet and have the press conference and a nice dinner. And then on Friday— Friday, we're going to Graceland. [*Laughter*] The Prime Minister, my dear friend, loves Elvis. [*Laughter*] So what better place to go.

Isn't it interesting, though, when you think about this moment in history compared to what life was like 60 years ago. You see, I guarantee you there's some folks here whose relatives were in combat against the Japanese, the sworn enemy of the United States, a nation which had launched an attack on our country, killing—by the way, we lost more on September the 11th than we did on Pearl Harbor. But, nevertheless, it was an attack on the Nation, and our Nation responded with force. President Roosevelt understood when you're going after an enemy, you use all your assets. That's what I understand too. If you're going to commit your military,

you commit it, so we can achieve victory. That's what he understood.

And yet 60 years later, I'm meeting with the Prime Minister of the former enemy. I find that to be really interesting. One reason why I'm able to is because a fellow from Missouri named Harry S. Truman had faith in the universality of liberty. He understood that people desire to be free. And the reason I'm able to call Prime Minister Koizumi friend and ally is because Japan became a democracy in her own image, a democracy that recognizes the traditions and history of the Japanese people. Democracies don't fight each other. Democracies work together to yield the peace. Liberty has the capacity to change an enemy into a friend.

And what you're seeing today in the Middle East is the spread of liberty. And it's hard work. It's hard work to replace tyranny with democracy, but it's necessary work. We're laying the foundations for peace. Someday, an Iraqi leader will be coming to America to sit down and to help keep the peace, and generations of America will be safer for it. And Jim Talent understands the stakes.

I also appreciate the fact that he understands the nature of the enemy, and he understands we've got to be smart about how we defend the homeland. I've sworn to uphold the Constitution, and I will. I'm also expected to defend the United States of America. And when we think somebody from Al Qaida is calling in to somebody in the United States from out of the country, we want to know why. We want to know why somebody is talking to Al Qaida, in order to protect the United States of America.

I told the American people we would defend ourselves. I remember all the kind of recommendations that we were getting, by the way, after 9/11. The 9/11 Commission took a look and said, "You need to do more on cutting off the money of the terrorist organizations." Newspapers editorialized: Make sure you do what you need to do to cut off their funding. One way to win the war on terror is to starve the enemy of money. I thought that made a lot of sense.

And so the Treasury Department launched a program to track the flow of terrorist money. See, we wanted to watch the money that the terrorists were moving around. It's one way to help protect the American people. It's one way for us to do the job that you've expected us to do. The program we put in place is legal. We got a lot of lawyers in Washington who scrutinize that which we do. It's legal. It has been briefed to the United States Congress. Like the terrorist surveillance program, this program of chasing terrorist financing was briefed to Members of Congress. We want them to understand what we're doing. We have an obligation in the executive branch to work with the legislative branch.

This program has been a vital tool in the war on terror. Last week, the details of this program appeared in the press. There can be no excuse for anyone entrusted with vital intelligence to leak it, and no excuse for any newspaper to print it.

The American people expect the Government to protect them. That's what you expect. It's our most important job. Jim Talent understands, our most important job is to protect the American people. And they want our people to have the tools necessary to achieve victory in the war on terror and to do our job. The disclosure of this valuable program makes it harder for us to identify terrorist cells and their activities. It makes it harder for us to build international cooperation. It makes it harder to protect the American people. It's tough enough to fight the terrorists; we shouldn't have to worry about news organizations revealing important information that makes it more important—makes it more difficult to protect our country.

We'll uphold our values; we'll follow the law; and I will do everything in my power to protect the American people. And it's important to have a United States Senator like Jim Talent who understands the stakes.

One of the issues in this campaign is going to be who best to spend your money, you or the Federal Government. [*Laughter*] That's right. You know, it's amazing, I would hope people, when they go to the polls, would take a look at the economic record that we've achieved, a record that is really pretty remarkable when you think about what the economy has been through. We've been through a recession, a stock market correction, corporate scandals, an attack on the United States of America, two major theaters in the war on terror to defend ourselves, natural disasters, and high energy prices. And yet the economic growth of the United States is the envy of the industrialized world. The national unemployment rate is 4.6 percent. We've created millions of new jobs in the last couple of years. The entrepreneurial spirit is high. Small businesses are flourishing. More people own a home than ever before in our Nation's history. Productivity is high.

This economy is strong, and we intend to keep it that way. And one reason it's strong is because we cut the taxes on the American people. We didn't cut just some taxes; we cut taxes for everybody who pays taxes. Talent and I don't believe we use the Tax Code to play political favorites. We said, "If you're paying taxes, you deserve tax relief." And guess who benefits? People with children; investors, because we've reduced the dividend—the taxes on dividends and capital gains; small businesses—most small businesses pay tax at the individual income tax rate because they're sole proprietorships or subchapter S's. When you hear them talking about, "Oh, we're just going to tax the rich," what Talent's opponent is really saying is, "We're going to tax small businesses," and that's bad for job creation in Missouri. Jim and I believe we need to get rid of the death tax once and for all.

You know, it's amazing when you listen to the debate up there in Washington about the budget. We've got a plan to cut the budget in half by—the deficit in half by 2009, and we're on our way to doing that. You know what's amazing is, when you cut the taxes, it causes the economy to grow. And when the economy grows, it yields more tax revenues than you anticipated. That's what's happening. That's what progrowth economic policies do for your budget.

The problem in Washington is, is that sometimes they take those revenues and don't apply it to the deficit; they apply it to additional programs, see. And so one of the reasons I like Talent so much is, he understands that to get the deficit cut in half, you got to be wise about spending your money. And we're doing a fine job on it.

Now, I recognize that the budgets have gone up, but for this reason: So long as we have a troops in harm's way, we're going to spend what is ever necessary to get he or she the equipment, the training, and the pay to win the war on terror. That's what we owe the folks. That's what we owe their families.

But we have cut nonsecurity discretionary spending, last year, and we intend to do it again this year. And that's hard to do because every program sounds good. But if you listen to the debate about—the other side, how they want to balance the budget, they say, "Let's just raise some taxes to balance the budget." That's not the way Washington works. If the other side gets in power, they will raise your taxes, and I promise you, they will figure out new ways to spend your money. The best way to balance the budget is to keep the taxes low and to set priorities with the people's money and to be wise and fiscally sound, just like Jim Talent is.

And I need this tool to be able to do my job: the line-item veto. And Jim Talent is one of the Senate sponsors and leaders on the line-item veto.

Health care is an issue. And so we took a look at the Medicare program. My attitude is this, and I know Jim agrees with me: If you're going to provide health care for our seniors, let's make sure it's modern. Makes sense for the taxpayers and certainly makes sense for the seniors. And the Medicare system—which was signed by Lyndon Baines Johnson, by the way—had become stale and old. I will give you an example. Our system would pay for a ulcer surgery— 20, $15,000, whatever it costs—but not a dime for the medicine that would prevent the ulcer surgery from being needed in the first place. In other words, medicine was changing, but Medicare didn't.

And so we got together and said, "How can we improve this for the seniors? How can we make it work?" And we also added another feature to a new and improved Medicare. We said, "If you're poor, you shouldn't have to choose between medicine and food." We said, "If you're a poor senior, you shouldn't have to make that difficult choice of the medicine necessary to keep you going or the food necessary to keep you going."

And so we modernized Medicare. We improved the system. We delivered on behalf of the seniors. And Jim Talent gets a lot of credit for modernizing Medicare. And he's running against a person who said she would have voted against the bill, this bill that is positive for seniors, was necessary for our seniors. And I am proud to have signed it, and I am proud to have worked with Jim Talent to make the Medicare work better.

We have got a national security and economic security problem when it comes to energy. We've got to do something about our addiction to oil. I know it sounds odd for some to think—a Texan to say, but that's the way I feel. [*Laughter*] I understand the consequences of living in a global economy. When the demand for hydrocarbons goes up in China and India, it affects the price of gasoline here in St. Louis, Missouri. That's the way it works. I'm worried about a situation where sometimes we get our hydrocarbons from people that don't like us, and that creates a national security problem.

I'm proud to be standing side by side with Jim Talent and his efforts to promote alternative sources of energy like ethanol. He led the renewable fuel standard in the Halls of the United States Senate. He is more than a talker; he's a doer. He's getting stuff done for Missouri and the American people.

I appreciate his work on methamphetamine eradication. He's a leader in the United States Senate. You've got a problem in Missouri, and we've got a problem around the country in methamphetamines. Jim Talent is working hard to deliver positive legislation and decent appropriations to fight methamphetamines. And I want to thank you for your fight and thank you for your struggle.

He gets things done. There's a lot of noise in Washington. But, you know, when you find somebody who is a positive person, who is able to accomplish things, you've got to send him back to Washington, DC. Talent can deliver for the people of Missouri and for the people of the United States. He's got a proven track record. He deserves to be reelected. I love his values.

I love the fact that he understands the judiciary needs to be filled with people who aren't going to legislate from the bench but will strictly interpret the Constitution of the United States. I'm proud that he stood up strong for Judge Roberts and Judge Alito, two really fine members of the Supreme Court. It's another issue in this campaign. Who do you want in the Senate to be able to confirm and battle for what kind of judges? You want judges that are—that understand the limitation of the judiciary. We got plenty of legislators in Washington. That's not the role of a judge. The judge is to interpret the Constitution of the United States. Jim Talent understands this. Most Missouri citizens understand the proper role of the judiciary. He's in tune with Missouri.

He's in tune with Missouri when it comes to taxes. He understands the farm issue. He understands small businesses. He is in tune with the elders and seniors of Missouri. He's a good man who's delivered a lot for the people of this State. He stands on solid moral ground. You don't have to worry about his honesty. You never have to worry about his integrity. He's a decent, honorable person that deserves reelection to the United States Senate. Thanks for coming, and God bless.

NOTE: The President spoke at 5:24 p.m. at the Ritz-Carlton. In his remarks, he referred to Melanie Anderson Blunt, wife of Gov. Matt Blunt of Missouri, and their son, William Branch Blunt; Rachel Oliver, wife of John L. Oliver III, finance chair, Jim Talent for U.S. Senate; former President Saddam Hussein of Iraq; and Prime Minister Junichiro Koizumi of Japan.

Statement on Senate Confirmation of Henry M. Paulson, Jr., as Secretary of the Treasury
June 28, 2006

I commend the Senate for moving swiftly to confirm Henry Paulson as Secretary of the Treasury. I look forward to working with Hank to keep our economy and financial markets strong and to continue our efforts to choke off sources of terrorist financing. I thank Chairman Grassley, Senator Baucus, and Senator Schumer for their leadership during the confirmation process. I congratulate Hank and his family on his confirmation and thank him for his service to our Nation.

Letter to the Speaker of the House of Representatives Requesting Additional Funds for the Department of Veterans Affairs
June 28, 2006

Dear Mr. Speaker:

I ask the Congress to consider expeditiously the enclosed fully offset FY 2006 request for the Department of Veterans Affairs (VA) to address the security of personal information of veterans and service personnel.

I am requesting these additional resources for VA to cover the increased costs to the VA information technology account in FY 2006 as a result of providing credit monitoring and fraud watch services for veterans and service members impacted by a security breach that occurred on May 3, 2006. The total cost of this effort, estimated to be $160.5 million in FY 2006, is fully offset.

The details of these proposals are set forth in the enclosed letter from the Director of the Office of Management and Budget.

Sincerely,

GEORGE W. BUSH

Remarks at a Welcoming Ceremony for Prime Minister Junichiro Koizumi of Japan
June 29, 2006

President Bush. Good morning. Laura and I are welcome—are proud to welcome and honored to welcome our friend Prime Minister Koizumi back to the White House. Japan and the United States have built a strong alliance and a close friendship. Decades ago, our two fathers looked across the Pacific and saw adversaries, uncertainty, and war. Today, their sons look across that same ocean and see friends and opportunity and peace.

The friendship between our two nations is based on common values. These values include democracy, free enterprise, and a deep and abiding respect for human rights. These values have created a better life for both our peoples, a firm alliance between our two nations, and a common approach to our engagement with the world.

These values are under attack by terrorist networks that bring death and destruction to all who oppose their hateful ideology, so the United States and Japan are working together to defend our shared values and win the war on terror.

Japanese naval vessels have refueled hundreds of coalition ships as part of Operation Enduring Freedom. Japan is now the third largest donor nation for reconstruction efforts in Afghanistan. In Iraq, Japanese Self-Defense Forces have helped improve the lives of citizens in a key Iraqi Province that will soon return to Iraqi control. And Japan continues to provide critical airlift support to coalition forces in Iraq. The people of Japan can be proud of the contribution their Self-Defense Forces have made in the war on terror, and Americans are proud to serve alongside such courageous allies.

Japan and the United States are cooperating to address other threats to our security. Our two nations are working together through the six-party talks, insisting that North Korea meet its pledge to abandon all nuclear weapons and its existing nuclear programs. Japan and the United States are also founding members of the Proliferation Security Initiative that is working to keep dangerous weapons from rogue states and terrorist groups. And our two nations are repositioning our forces to counter the emerging threats of the 21st century.

As we meet threats to our security, we're also working together to improve the lives of our people and address common challenges. Our two economies are the largest in the world, and we are working to expand trade and investment opportunities for both our peoples. Japan and the United States are working together for a successful conclusion to the Doha negotiations, which would add to the prosperity of our nations and help lift millions in the developing world out of poverty.

With prosperity comes responsibility. So our two nations helped build the Asian-Pacific Partnership on Clean Development and Climate, so we can make the latest energy technologies more widely available, reduce pollution, and increase energy efficiency.

Americans cherish our friendship with the Japanese people and value our alliance with the nation of Japan. And we honor the leadership of Japan's Prime Minister Koizumi. He's a man of vision; he's a man of integrity. And I'm proud to call him my friend. I thank the Prime Minister for coming to the White House. And I'm looking forward to joining him tomorrow at Graceland. [*Laughter*] Officially, he's here to see the President, but I know the highlight of his visit will be paying his respects to "the King." [*Laughter*]

Mr. Prime Minister, thank you for your leadership, and welcome back to America.

Prime Minister Koizumi. Good morning.

Audience Member. Good morning.

Prime Minister Koizumi. Our Japan children very good. [*Laughter*] You can learn both Japanese and English. In the future, it's useful to you all.

First of all, allow me to express my heartfelt gratitude to President Bush, the Government, and the people of the United States for putting on such a splendid welcome ceremony for me.

In Japan, I am known as "Lucky Man." And I feel that I am lucky in the United States as well. Look at this fine weather; I feel that this weather is also welcoming me.

I believe it is no exaggeration to say that over the past 5 years, there has been no world leader, alongside Mr. Bush—President Bush, among the world leaders with whom I have felt so much heart to heart, felt so deep a friendship and trust, and have cooperated with.

And I believe having personal and good relations between the two leaders is good not just for the two friends, the two of us. From now on, I'll engage in the discussions with President Bush on—as Japan and the United States are allies on various matters, not simply of bilateral relations but on the questions of how best we, our two countries, could cooperate together as allies in addressing various international issues.

I sincerely hope that my visit this time will enable our two countries to continue to cooperate and develop together and, as allies in the international community, make even greater contributions to the numerous challenges in the world community.

And in concluding, I would like to express my heartfelt wishes for further prosperity of the Government and the people of the United States of America.

Thank you again. Such a wonderful hospitality. Thank you.

NOTE: The President spoke at 9:11 a.m. on the South Lawn at the White House, where Prime Minister Koizumi was accorded a formal welcome with full military honors. Prime Minister Koizumi spoke partly in Japanese, and those portions of his remarks were translated by an interpreter.

The President's News Conference With Prime Minister Junichiro Koizumi of Japan
June 29, 2006

President Bush. Thank you all. Please be seated. Mr. Prime Minister, as I said on the South Lawn, we are delighted to have you here in Washington. The Prime Minister and I have got a very friendly relationship. We've just had 2 hours of discussions. We talked about a lot of areas of mutual concern. I've reminded the Prime Minister—the American people, Mr. Prime Minister, over the past months, that it was not always a given that the United States and America [Japan]* would have a close relationship. After all, 60 years we were at war—60 years ago, we were at war, and today we talked about North Korea and Iran and Iraq and trade and energy cooperation.

It's an amazing fact that we're able to have these discussions. To me it shows the power of liberty and democracy to transform enemies to allies and to help transform the world. And one thing about the Prime Minister is he understands that. He's a firm believer that—in universal values. He believes in freedom, and he's willing to act on those beliefs. And we have been a strong partner in peace, Mr. Prime Minister.

You've had a remarkable tenure as the Prime Minister of your country. You have led with courage. You have made hard decisions. You've helped us change our relationship so that Japan and the United States will be able to work even closer together in the 21st century. You made the hard decision to help realign our troops in your part of the world to better accommodate the needs of the Japanese people and, at the same time, keep in position a relationship that will be necessary for peace and stability.

---

* White House correction.

I want to thank you for opening your markets to U.S. beef. I think the Japanese people are going to like the taste of U.S. beef. As a matter of fact, I had a good slice of beef last night, and you told me you did as well, and you look like you're feeling pretty good. [*Laughter*]

Prime Minister Koizumi. Very good. [*Laughter*]

President Bush. Right, good. We had an interesting discussion about energy. And one of the things that Japan and the United States can do is we can help provide technologies that will improve the climate as well as reduce our dependence on hydrocarbons. We discussed the Nuclear Suppliers Group that we're a part of and our contributions to some research and development that will help speed up fast breeder reactors and new types of reprocessing so that we can help deal with the cost of globalization when it comes to energy; make ourselves more secure, economically, as well as make us less dependent on hydrocarbons from parts of the world that may not agree with our policies.

As I mentioned, we discussed Iraq and Afghanistan. By the way, the Japanese defense forces did a really good job when they were in Iraq. And they're able to leave because they did such a good job. And now the Iraqis will be running the Province in which the Japanese forces used to be. Nevertheless, the Prime Minister, as he mentioned in the comments, will continue to provide airlift capacity and naval help.

The North Korean issue is one, obviously, that's got everybody's attention now. And we discussed this issue in length. We both agree that it's very important for us to remain united in sending a clear message to the North Korean leader that, first of all, launching the missile is unacceptable. There have been no briefings as to what's on top of the missile. He hasn't told any-body where the missile is going. He has an obligation, it seems like to me and the Prime Minister, that there be a full brief-ing—to those of us who are concerned about this issue—as to what his intentions are. It makes sense, doesn't it? It's a rea-sonable thing for somebody to do.

We talked about the six-party talks, and to make sure we remain bound up in send-ing a clear message to the leader of North Korea. I also talked about one of the most touching moments of my Presidency, when the mom of the abducted daughter came to the Oval Office and talked to me about what it was like to have a young daughter abducted by the North Koreans. And it really broke my heart. I told the Prime Minister it was a moving moment for me. I just could not imagine what it would be like to have somebody have taken, you know, my daughter—one of my daugh-ters—and never be able to see her again. And the woman showed such great cour-age, Mr. Prime Minister, when she came and shared her story with me. It took ev-erything I could not to weep, listening to her.

It also reminded me about the nature of the regime: what kind of regime would kidnap people, just take them offshore, you know; what kind of person would not care about how that woman felt.

And so we talked about the need to work together to bring a resolution to this issue about nuclear weapons. And I reminded the Prime Minister—he didn't need re-minding, but I'm going to share with him once again my deep concern about the human condition inside North Korea. He shares that condition—after all, he's the Prime Minister of a country that has suf-fered a lot as a result of abductions. So we spent time talking about abductions.

All in all, it was a visit that I knew was going to be a good one, because I know the man; I know what he's like. He's a good thinker; he's a strategic thinker; he's a clear speaker. And plus, as you all know,

it's become quite well-known that we're going to end the visit at Graceland tomor-row. He's an Elvis fan. Laura and I gave him a jukebox as a gift, and I can't—what was the first song you put on? It wasn't "Hound Dog;" it was——

Prime Minister Koizumi. "I Want You, I Need You, I Love You."

President Bush. See, he loves Elvis, and I couldn't think of a better way to honor my friend, by going to Graceland. But it also sends a signal about how close our relationship is.

And so, Mr. Prime Minister, we're glad you're here. Thanks for your friendship; thanks for your alliance; and thanks for your leadership.

Prime Minister Koizumi. Thank you very much. With President Bush, I had a very candid exchange of views. Over the past 5 years, I've really had a close friendship with President Bush, and thanks to that, we've been able to have a very candid ex-change of views. And I believe this is not just limited to close relations between us, personally, but I believe this close relation-ship is necessary in the future between Japan and the United States as well.

Japan and the United States is in a Japan-U.S. alliance in the world, and we reconfirmed that we can cooperate with each other on various challenges, maintain Japan's security and deterrence, and reduce burdens on local communities. On these points we were able to have a very impor-tant agreement, and we're most grateful for that.

In the meeting, we discussed not just Japan-U.S. bilateral relations but numerous challenges that the world community faces today—Afghanistan, North Korea, poverty reduction—reduced poverty for people who suffer from various diseases. We shared a common perception, and by doing so, we'll be able to cooperate with each other.

Now, Japan, in a way different than the U.S., has been supporting the nation-build-ing in Iraq by the Iraqis themselves. The ground self-defense forces stationed in

Samawa, having accomplished their mission, will be withdrawing. But as a responsible member of the international community, through cooperation with various countries concerned and through cooperation with the United Nations, Japan will continue provide support and help the Iraqis get back on their feet.

With regard to North Korea, we spent a lot of time, and I expressed my views, and President Bush also expressed his thoughts. President Bush was kind enough to meet with Mrs. Sakie Yokota. And he told me he was very moved on that occasion. Anyone, if one's daughter is abducted, naturally will be grieved. And this feeling need to be shared by Americans and Japanese. We discussed that sort of thing.

We do have the six-party talks framework. Japan and the United States, I believe, need to maintain close coordination and encourage North Korea to become a responsible member of the international community.

With regard to Iranian nuclear proliferation, Japan also is concerned about this problem. The United States attaches importance to cooperation with EU and other countries concerned. Japan certainly supports that U.S. stance of seeking resolution through a dialog regarding the nuclear proliferation issue. The Iranian issue remains a grave issue for the entire world economy, and Japan wishes to cooperate with the United States and other countries concerned on this matter as well.

On U.N. reforms, building on the results achieved so far, we would like to work out with the G–4 a proposal that can be supported by the United States and achieve reforms of the United Nations and the Security Council. Japan and the United States will maintain close coordination, partnership. We need to do that and address various challenges.

The Japan-U.S. alliance is not just an alliance for our two countries; it is an alliance for the world. And in the interest of the world, we were able to confirm that we need to cooperate with each other. And I think this was a very substantive, fruitful meeting. And I would like to thank President Bush and the U.S. for a very warm, hospitable welcome.

President Bush. We've agreed to take two questions a side. Walking in, I reminded the Prime Minister of one of Elvis's greatest songs, "Don't Be Cruel"—[*laughter*]. So keep that in mind, Hunt [Terence Hunt, Associated Press], when you ask your question.

Hamdan v. Rumsfeld

Q. Thank you, Mr. President. You've said that you wanted to close the prison at Guantanamo Bay, but you were waiting for the Supreme Court decision that came out today. Do you intend now to close the Guantanamo Bay quickly? And how do you deal with the suspects that you've said were too dangerous to be released or sent home?

President Bush. Thank you for the question on a court ruling that literally came out in the midst of my meeting with the Prime Minister—and so I haven't had a chance to fully review the findings of the Supreme Court. I, one, assure you that we take them very seriously; two, that to the extent that there is latitude to work with the Congress to determine whether or not the military tribunals will be an avenue in which to give people their day in court, we will do so.

The American people need to know that this ruling, as I understand it, won't cause killers to be put out on the street. In other words, there's not a—it was a drive-by briefing on the way here; I was told that this was not going to be the case. At any rate, we will seriously look at the findings, obviously. And one thing I'm not going to do, though, is I'm not going to jeopardize the safety of the American people. People have got to understand that. I understand we're in a war on terror, that these people were picked up off of a battlefield. And I will protect the people and, at the same time, conform with the findings of the Supreme Court.

Q. Do you think the prison will close?

President Bush. Well, I haven't had a chance to fully review what the Court said, Terry. I wish I had, and I could have given you a better answer. As I say, we take the findings seriously. And again, as I understand it—now please don't hold me to this—that there is a way forward with military tribunals in working with the United States Congress. As I understand, certain Senators have already been out expressing their desire to address what the Supreme Court found, and we will work with the Congress. I want to find a way forward.

In other words, I have told the people that I would like for there to be a way to return people from Guantanamo to their home countries, but some of them—people need to be tried in our courts. The Hamdan decision was the way forward for that part of my statement, and again, I would like to review the case. And we are; we've got people looking at it right now to determine how we can work with Congress, if that's available, to solve the problem.

North Korea

Q. On North Korea, I'd like to ask a question of both of you, Prime Minister and President. On North Korea, I understand you spent a lot of time to exchange views. It is said that the North Koreans are preparing to launch Taepodong-2. To resolve this missile issue, what kind of cooperation do you think is possible between Japan and the United States? And also, did you discuss possibly referring the matter to the U.N. Security Council?

On the abduction issue and human rights issue, I understand, Mr. President, you've shown deep concern for the resolution of the abduction issue. What sort of cooperation do you think is possible between the U.S. and Japan?

President Bush. Do you want to go? Yes, please.

Prime Minister Koizumi. The North Koreans—I believe, in the first place, we need to try and approach the North Koreans not to launch Taepodong-2, through various efforts, and should they ever launch the missile, that will cause various pressures—we would apply various pressures. And we discussed that. I believe it is best that I do not discuss what specific pressures we were talking about.

As we approach the North Koreans, we shall maintain close cooperation and coordination with the United States, including the abduction issue.

President Bush. ——all kinds of opportunities, and the U.N. is an opportunity to express our common concern. You know, another interesting opportunity is, over time, to work on missile defenses. The Japanese cannot be—afford to be held hostage to rockets. And neither can the United States or any other body who loves freedom. And so one really interesting opportunity is for—to share and cooperate on missile defenses.

You know, the leader of North Korea is just going to have to make a decision: Does he want to be isolated from the world, or is he interested in being an active participant in, kind of, the nations of the world who care about their people and desire peace? It's his choice to make. We've made our choice. We believe it's important for nations such as Japan and the United States to be active participants in the world in a positive way. And that's what we're doing.

You know, a lot of the focus of our relationship is based upon, obviously, Iraq and Afghanistan, but the truth of the matter is, Japan and the United States make mighty contributions to end suffering because of disease and hunger. And that's why I appreciate the Prime Minister's leadership. He understands that with economic might comes serious responsibilities in the world. And the United States takes those responsibilities seriously, and so does Japan. Matt [Matt Spetalnick, Reuters].

Hamdan v. Rumsfeld

Q. Yes, Mr. President. We can assume you've at least been given some of the broad strokes of the Supreme Court's decision on Guantanamo——

President Bush. No, I just gave you the answer on that. I'll be glad to answer another question—I gave you the broad strokes I've been given.

Q. Right, but this—can you comment on what looks like a judicial repudiation of your administration's policy on the treatment of terror suspects post-9/11?

President Bush. Matt, I can't—I wish I could comment, and would, obviously. I'm a person who generally comments on things. I haven't been briefed enough to make a comment on it, except for the following things. I'm sorry you had to waste your question, but we will conform to the Supreme Court. We will analyze the decision. To the extent that the Congress has given any latitude to develop a way forward using military tribunals, we will work with them.

As I understand, a Senator has already been on TV. Haven't seen it; haven't heard what he said, but as—they briefed me and said he wants to devise law in conformity with the case that would enable us to use a military tribunal to hold these people to account. And if that's the case, we'll work with him.

I can't comment any more than I have just done in the first question; otherwise, I would have. I just haven't been fully briefed enough to answer your question, Matt.

Japan-U.S. Relations

Q. Over the past 5 years, Prime Minister Koizumi and President Bush have built up the best sort of relationship between the two of you in the history of Japan and the United States. Now, what is the greatest reason for having maintained this policy of attaching greatest importance to Japan-U.S. relations?

And a question for President Bush. Various problems have occurred after 9/11. And in the Prime Minister Koizumi's policy of attaching importance to Japan-U.S. relations, what was the case—instance where you were most appreciative of Prime Minister Koizumi's position? And what sort of impact has it had on your feeling and stance toward Japan?

Prime Minister Koizumi. Well, attaching importance to our relations with the United States—well, after the Second World War, throughout—over the past 6 years, Japan has maintained that policy. We've recognized the importance of a Japan-U.S. alliance and also maintain a stance of international cooperation and coordination. It's because we have learned the lessons of World War II, we took up this policy in believing that this was good for Japan. In the past, today, and the future, as well maintain Japan-U.S. alliance and international cooperation. This is a very important fundamental policy of Japan that should never change.

Last year, President Bush visited Kyoto in Japan and had one-on-one meeting. Some seem to think that the—to the extent Japan-U.S. relations is undermined, that could be complemented by better relations with Asia and other countries. And I've said I do not subscribe to that view. The better the Japan-U.S. relations, my view is that we will be able to have better relations with China and other countries in Asia.

Now, some in the mass media took up on that and misinterpreted my position. In other words, they thought that I was saying, to the extent Japan-U.S. relations remain good, I couldn't care less what Japan's relations would be with other countries. That is not at all what I said. I've been saying that there is no country in the world that has as important bilateral relations as Japan-U.S. bilateral relations. But I have no view such as having better relations with the United States at the expense of relations with other countries.

My view is that by having better relations with the United States, I can have better relations with other countries. And from that perspective, in the post-war years, Japan has achieved remarkable growth and development. It is because we've learned lessons from the past in our relations with the United States and determined to maintain friendly relations with the United States. And that is what we have done to date.

In the future as well, Japan-U.S. alliance is something that will be—contribute to the resolution of various challenges in the world—by maintaining friendly ties between Japan and the United States. Attaching importance to our relations with the United States does not sacrifice our views and our relations with other countries. Please do not misunderstand.

President Bush. It's a pretty tricky question. I hate to point out one area where that has influenced my thinking about Japan's contributions for fear of diminishing the contributions in other areas. Because the truth of the matter is, we live in a very complex world, and by—cooperating to solve problems makes the world a better place. However, since you asked, I'll answer. I would think it is the Prime Minister's understanding of the capacity for democracies to help change the conditions of the world. And therefore, his strong support for helping a new Afghanistan democracy grow and his willingness to do something a lot of other leaders in Japan have been unwilling to do, which is to commit Self-Defense Forces to help the growth of a new democracy.

And I tell the American people this: I use the Prime Minister all the time in my speeches, as the press corps will tell you, incredibly bored of hearing. But nevertheless, I do share the example with the people about my relationship with the Prime Minister. It is just—it strikes me as just amazing. A lot of people take it for granted. I don't, because 60 years ago, we were at war. And something happened between our visit to Graceland and when our respective fathers looked at each other with deep suspicion. And what happened was, Japan developed a Japanese-style democracy based upon shared values. And today, we're able to discuss peace. It is a remarkable transformation of a relationship. We just happen to be the beneficiaries of that transformation. I also believe, however, that there are people who are coming up who have shedded the bonds of tyranny are also the benefits of this relationship.

And so Japan is making a mighty contribution to new democracy, which I strongly believe is in our Nation's interests and I strongly believe will yield peace. And I firmly believe that the example that we show today will be repeated over the decades, particularly with newly elected leaders in the Middle East. And the Prime Minister understands that. And I'm grateful for the contribution of the Japanese people to the cause of peace.

Mr. Prime Minister, thank you.

Prime Minister Koizumi. Thank you very much, American people, for "Love Me Tender." [*Laughter*]

NOTE: The President's news conference began at 11:33 a.m. in the East Room at the White House. In his remarks, he referred to Chairman Kim Jong Il of North Korea; and Sakie Yokota, mother of Megumi Yokota, who was abducted by North Korean authorities. Prime Minister Koizumi and some reporters spoke in Japanese, and their remarks were translated by an interpreter.

Joint Statement by President George W. Bush and Prime Minister Junichiro Koizumi of Japan: The Japan-U.S. Alliance of the New Century
June 29, 2006

President George W. Bush of the United States of America hosted Prime Minister Junichiro Koizumi of Japan for an Official Visit to the White House on June 29, 2006, that celebrated their close personal friendship and the deep and increasing ties between the American and Japanese people.

The two leaders agreed that the U.S.-Japan partnership stands as one of the most accomplished bilateral relationships in history. They reviewed with great satisfaction the broadened and enhanced cooperation achieved in the alliance under their joint stewardship, and together heralded a new U.S.-Japan Alliance of Global Cooperation for the 21st Century.

The U.S.-Japan Alliance Based on Universal Values and Common Interests

The United States and Japan stand together not only against mutual threats but also for the advancement of core universal values such as freedom, human dignity and human rights, democracy, market economy, and rule of law. These values are deeply rooted in the long historic traditions of both countries.

The United States and Japan share interests in: winning the war on terrorism; maintaining regional stability and prosperity; promoting free market ideals and institutions; upholding human rights; securing freedom of navigation and commerce, including sea lanes; and enhancing global energy security. It is these common values and common interests that form the basis for U.S.-Japan regional and global cooperation.

Bilateral Political, Security and Economic Cooperation

The President and Prime Minister welcomed the tremendous progress in the U.S.-Japan security relationship achieved during their tenures. Bilateral security cooperation has deepened as a result of ballistic missile defense cooperation and legislation in Japan to deal with contingencies.

The two leaders welcomed the establishment of common strategic objectives of February 2005 as well as the conclusion of watershed agreements to transform the alliance for the future. These agreements, including the most significant realignment of U.S. and Japanese forces in decades, constitute historic steps forward that make the U.S. military presence more enduring and effective, and ensure the capabilities necessary for the alliance to cope with diverse challenges in the evolving security environments. The two leaders agreed that full and prompt implementation of these agreements is necessary, not only for Japan and the United States, but also for peace and stability of the Asia-Pacific region.

Asia's historic transformation is underway, creating a region that increasingly embraces the universal values of democracy, freedom, human rights, market economy, and rule of law. The two leaders pledged to work together to shape and support this transformation. In this regard, the two nations will continue to work on common challenges in the region such as (a) promoting individual freedoms; (b) increasing transparency and confidence in the political, economic, and military fields; and (c) protecting human dignity, and resolving humanitarian and human rights problems including the abduction issue.

The two leaders affirmed that robust U.S.-Japan cooperation embraces the dynamism of China, and helps to maintain peace and tranquility in Northeast Asia. They reaffirmed the importance of advancing strategic dialogues with friends and allies in the region such as Australia. They called on North Korea to fulfill denuclearization pledges made in the September 2005 Joint Statement of the Six Party Talks and to continue to adhere to its missile test moratorium. They discussed the need for the few isolated regimes in the region to respect human rights and democratic principles including an inclusive political dialogue.

The two leaders reaffirmed their common efforts on a wide range of global activities including recent successes in the war on terrorism, support for the new government in Iraq, and cooperation on counter-proliferation activities, including on Iran. The President praised Japan's humanitarian and reconstruction assistance in Afghanistan and Iraq as well as Japan's support provided to coalition forces operating in the Indian Ocean.

Mindful of Japan's significant role and contributions at the U.N., Japan and the United States will intensify their cooperation, and work together in realizing Japan's permanent membership at the Security Council.

They pledged to continue close cooperation under the Strategic Development Alliance and to work together on other global challenges such as capacity-building for natural disaster response and prevention and response to avian/pandemic influenza. They also agreed to work on the interrelated challenges of energy security, clean development, reducing pollution, and climate change.

Building upon the progress achieved over the last five years under the U.S.-Japan Economic Partnership for Growth, the two

leaders agreed to explore ways to further deepen the mutually-beneficial bilateral economic relationship as well as to enhance cooperation on regional and global economic issues.

Such an expanded partnership would include: promoting growth and economic reform; promoting and maintaining open markets; ensuring efficient movement of legitimate goods, services, people, and investments, while tackling threats from terrorism; strengthening intellectual property rights protection and enforcement; enhancing global energy security; and fostering transparent and favorable business climates in both countries.

The two leaders also affirmed their commitment to make a strong contribution to ensure a successful and ambitious outcome for the WTO Doha Development Agenda negotiations by the end of 2006 that opens markets and achieves a balanced outcome across the board. They expressed their determination to work together to strengthen the Asia-Pacific Economic Cooperation (APEC) forum, recognizing its crucial role in promoting stability, security, and prosperity in the region.

The two leaders shared the view that the U.S.-Japan global alliance remains a constant and positive force. They shared the expectation that the U.S.-Japan friendship and global cooperation shall continue to grow stronger.

NOTE: An original was not available for verification of the content of this joint statement.

Statement on House of Representatives Passage of Scientific Research Legislation
June 29, 2006

I commend the House for approving full funding of the basic research component of the American Competitiveness Initiative

through the Science, State, Justice and Commerce appropriations bill. With this funding, the House has shown that it is committed to supporting the work of our Nation's most brilliant scientists as they study promising areas such as new energy technologies, supercomputing, and nano-technology.

I appreciate the support of Chairman Lewis and the tireless and effective efforts of Chairman Wolf, and I commend the House leadership's work to move quickly on the centerpiece of our innovation agenda. I urge the Senate to join the House in passing this important legislation.

Remarks at a Dinner Honoring Prime Minister Junichiro Koizumi of Japan
June 29, 2006

Mr. Prime Minister and distinguished guests, Laura and I thank you for joining us tonight, and we welcome you to the White House. This room has hosted many honored guests, and tonight it also hosts a treasured friend.

Mr. Prime Minister, our strong friendship has grown out of the strong alliance between our two nations. Japan and America share a common belief in the power of freedom to bring hope to millions who have not known it. And we share a common commitment to meet the challenges of our time and lay the foundations of peace for generations to come.

In our meetings today, you have once again demonstrated the qualities of character that both the Japanese people and the American people admire. You have an optimistic view of the world. You welcome hard work and big challenges, and you are determined that your great nation will con-tinue to make a positive contribution to our world.

Mr. Prime Minister, more than 25 years ago, the White House welcomed another distinguished visitor who shared much in common with you. Like you, he had great hair. [*Laughter*] Like you, he was known to sing in public. [*Laughter*] And like you, he won admirers in countries far from home. That man was Elvis. [*Laughter*] And Laura and I are looking forward to joining you tomorrow in our visit to his home in Memphis.

But tonight, Mr. Prime Minister, it's my honor to offer a toast to you and to our friends and allies, the people of Japan.

NOTE: The President spoke at 8:05 p.m. in the State Dining Room at the White House. The transcript released by the Office of the Press Secretary also included the remarks of Prime Minister Koizumi.

Remarks With Prime Minister Junichiro Koizumi of Japan in Memphis, Tennessee
June 30, 2006

President Bush. It is such a joy to be here to Graceland. It's my first visit.

Prime Minister Koizumi. My first visit too.

President Bush. The Prime Minister's first visit.

Prime Minister Koizumi. It's like a dream, with President Bush and Presley's daughter.

President Bush. Thank you all for greeting us. You're awfully kind to be here.

Prime Minister Koizumi. You look like Elvis.

[*At this point, the late entertainer Elvis Presley's daughter, Lisa Marie, spoke in Japanese, and no translation was provided.*]

President Bush. The visit here is an indication of how well-known Elvis was around the world. A lot of people are still singing Elvis Presley songs here in the States, and there's a lot of people who love Elvis Presley in Japan, including the Prime Minister. This visit is also a way of reminding us about the close friendship between our peoples.

And, Mr. Prime Minister, thank you for agreeing to come here. A lot of Americans are thrilled you're here, particularly to Graceland. It means a lot to our country that you would be that interested in one of America's icons, Elvis Presley.

Prime Minister Koizumi. My birthday is the same as Elvis's.

President Bush. You and Elvis were born on the same day?

Prime Minister Koizumi. January 8th. Even now, I often listen to Elvis CDs.

President Bush. Still listen to Elvis CDs?

Prime Minister Koizumi. Sure.

President Bush. You're a pretty good Elvis singer.

Prime Minister Koizumi. I'm not impersonator.

[*Prime Minister Koizumi sang an Elvis song.*]

President Bush. I thought you were going to do "Blue Suede Shoes." Thank you.

NOTE: The President spoke at 10:38 a.m. at Graceland.

Remarks Following a Tour of Graceland With Prime Minister Junichiro Koizumi of Japan in Memphis
June 30, 2006

President Bush. First of all, the Prime Minister and I would like to thank Priscilla and Lisa for their gracious hospitality. And we thank the Graceland staff as well for arranging this unusual experience. First of all, my presence here shows it's never too late to come to Graceland. Laura and I are—we've known Elvis Presley since we were growing up. He's obviously a major part of our music history. He had an international reputation. His reputation was so strong that he attracted the attention of the now Prime Minister of Japan.

I was hoping the Prime Minister would want to come to Graceland. I knew he loved Elvis; I didn't realize how much he loved Elvis. He not only knows Elvis's history, he can sing a pretty good Elvis song. This visit here shows that not only am I personally fond of the Prime Minister, but the ties between our peoples are very strong as well.

And so, again, to the Presleys, thank you all. And Mr. Prime Minister, glad you joined us. Want to say a few comments?

Prime Minister Koizumi. It's like a dream. I never expected Mr. President come with me to visit Graceland. There's Elvis song: "To Dream Impossible." [*Laughter*]

[*At this point, Prime Minister Koizumi sang an Elvis song.*]

Prime Minister Koizumi. My dream came true. So thank you very much for—[*inaudible*]—thank you. Thank you very much for treating me nice. That's an Elvis song.

[*Prime Minister Koizumi sang another Elvis song.*]

Prime Minister Koizumi. Thank you.

President Bush. We're going to go have some barbeque. Thank you.

NOTE: The President spoke at 11:44 a.m. on the front lawn at Graceland. In his remarks, he referred to the late entertainer Elvis Presley's wife, Priscilla, and daughter, Lisa Marie.

Appendix A—Digest of Other White House Announcements

The following list includes the President's public schedule and other items of general interest announced by the Office of the Press Secretary and not included elsewhere in this book.

January 1

In the morning, the President traveled from the Bush Ranch in Crawford, TX, to San Antonio, TX, where, at Brooke Army Medical Center, he visited wounded soldiers and their family members and presented Purple Heart medals to nine soldiers.

In the afternoon, the President and Mrs. Bush returned to Washington, DC.

January 2

In the morning, the President had an intelligence briefing.

January 3

In the morning, the President had an intelligence briefing and a briefing on the situation in Tallmansville, WV, where 13 coal miners were trapped underground in the I.C.G. Sago Run Mine following an accident. Later, in the Roosevelt Room, he met with the Homeland Security Council to discuss the USA PATRIOT Act.

Later in the morning, the President met with Lt. Gen. Keith W. Dayton, USA, U.S. security coordinator to Israel and the Palestinian Authority.

Also in the morning, the President had a telephone conversation with Gov. Joe Manchin III of West Virginia to discuss the situation in the Sago Run Mine.

In the afternoon, in the Private Dining Room, the President had lunch with Vice President Dick Cheney. Later, in the Oval Office, he met with Secretary of State Condoleezza Rice.

January 4

In the morning the President had an intelligence briefing. Later, in the Oval Office, he had a telephone conversation with Gov. Joe Manchin III of West Virginia to discuss the situation in the Sago Run Mine. He then traveled to Arlington, VA, where, at the Pentagon, he participated in a briefing on the war on terror.

In the afternoon, the President returned to Washington, DC. Later, he had a meeting and participated in a photo opportunity with White House Fellows.

The President announced his intention to nominate Patricia A. Butenis to be Ambassador to Bangladesh.

The President announced his intention to nominate Robert M. Couch to be President of the Government National Mortgage Association.

The President announced his intention to nominate John A. Simon to be Executive Vice President of the Overseas Private Investment Corporation.

The President announced his intention to appoint Robert J. Creighton as a member of the Medal of Valor Review Board (Emergency Services).

The President announced his intention to appoint Robert George Hayes as a member of the International Commission for the Conservation of Atlantic Tunas (Sport Fishing Representative).

The President announced his intention to appoint Randi Parks Thomas as a member of the International Commission for the Conservation of Atlantic Tunas (Commercial Fishing Representative).

The President announced his intention to appoint Howard H. Li as a member of the President's Advisory Commission on Asian Americans and Pacific Islanders.

The President announced his intention to designate Myrna Blyth as chairman of the President's Commission on White House Fellowships.

The President announced the recess appointment of Floyd Hall and Enrique J. Sosa as members of the AMTRAK Reform Board.

The President announced the recess appointment of Nadine Hogan and Roger W. Wallace as members of the Board of Directors of the Inter-American Foundation (Private Representatives).

1245

The President announced the recess appointment of Gordon England as Deputy Secretary of Defense.

The President announced the recess appointment of Benjamin A. Powell as General Counsel of the Office of the Director of National Intelligence.

The President announced the recess appointment of Ronald E. Meisburg as General Counsel of the National Labor Relations Board.

The President announced the recess appointment of Julie L. Myers as Assistant Secretary of Homeland Security (Bureau of Immigration and Customs Enforcement).

The President announced the recess appointment of Tracy A. Henke as Executive Director of the Office of State and Local Government Coordination and Preparedness at the Department of Homeland Security.

The President announced the recess appointment of Arthur F. Rosenfeld as Federal Mediation and Conciliation Director at the Federal Mediation and Conciliation Service.

The President announced the recess appointment of Ellen R. Sauerbrey as Assistant Secretary of State (Population, Refugees, and Migration).

The President announced the recess appointment of Dorrance Smith as Assistant Secretary of Defense (Public Affairs).

The President announced the recess appointment of Robert D. Lenhard, Steven T. Walther, and Hans von Spakovsky as members of the Federal Election Commission.

The President announced the recess appointment of Peter N. Kirsanow as a member of the National Labor Relations Board.

The President announced the recess appointment of Stephen Goldsmith as a member of the Board of Directors of the Corporation for National and Community Service.

The President declared a major disaster in Minnesota and ordered Federal aid to supplement State and local recovery efforts in the area struck by a severe winter storm from November 27–29, 2005.

The President declared a major disaster in North Dakota and ordered Federal aid to supplement State and local recovery efforts in the area struck by a severe winter storm from November 27–30, 2005.

January 5

In the morning, the President had a telephone conversation with United Nations Secretary-General Kofi Annan. Later, he had an intelligence briefing. He then had a telephone conversation with Coach Mack Brown of the University of Texas Longhorns football team to congratulate him on the team's Rose Bowl victory.

Later in the morning, in the Oval Office, the President participated in a photo opportunity with Secretary of State Condoleezza Rice, Secretary of Defense Donald H. Rumsfeld, and former Secretaries of State and Defense.

In the afternoon, in the Oval Office, the President participated in a bill signing ceremony for H.R. 3402, the Violence Against Women and Department of Justice Reauthorization Act of 2005.

January 6

In the morning, the President had an intelligence briefing. He then traveled to Chicago, IL, where, upon arrival, he met with USA Freedom Corps volunteer Erin Green. Later, he participated in a tour of the Chicago Board of Trade.

In the afternoon, the President returned to Washington, DC.

The President announced his intention to nominate Richard T. Miller to be U.S. Representative in the Economic and Social Council of the United Nations, with the rank of Ambassador, and Alternate U.S. Representative to the Sessions of the United Nations General Assembly.

The President announced his intention to nominate Jackie W. Sanders to be Alternate U.S. Representative for Special Political Affairs in the United Nations, with the rank of Ambassador, and Alternate U.S. Representative to the Sessions of the United Nations General Assembly.

The President announced his intention to nominate Mark D. Wallace to be U.S. Representative to the United Nations for Management and Reform, with the rank of Ambassador, and Alternate U.S. Representative to the Sessions of the United Nations General Assembly.

The President announced the recess appointment of John Gardner as a Governor of the Board of Governors of the U.S. Postal Service.

January 7

During the day, the President traveled to Camp David, MD, where he had an intelligence briefing.

January 8

In the afternoon, the President returned to Washington, DC.

January 9

In the morning, in the Private Dining Room, the President had breakfast with Supreme Court Associate Justice-designate Samuel A. Alito, Jr. Later, he had an intelligence briefing.

Later in the morning, the President had a telephone conversation with Vice President Dick Cheney to wish him well after his brief hospital visit earlier that morning. He and Mrs. Bush then traveled to Glen Burnie, MD, where they visited with students at North Glen Elementary School. They then returned to Washington, DC.

In the evening, in the Cabinet Room, the President met with Vice President Cheney, members of the Joint Chiefs of Staff, and combatant commanders to discuss U.S. military operations around the world. Later, in the Residence, he hosted a reception and dinner for members of the Joint Chiefs of Staff and combatant commanders.

The President announced his designation of the following individuals as members of a Presidential delegation to Astana, Kazakhstan, to attend the inauguration of President Nursultan Nazarbayev on January 11:

Mike Johanns (head of delegation);
John M. Ordway;
Josette Sheeran Shinger; and
Timothy D. Adams.

The President announced the recess appointment of Steven Kent Mullins as U.S. Attorney for the District of South Dakota.

January 10

In the morning, the President had an intelligence briefing.

In the afternoon, the President had lunch with Vice President Dick Cheney. Later, in the Oval Office, he participated in a photo opportunity with the 2005 Little League Softball World Series champions.

The President declared a major disaster in Oklahoma and ordered Federal aid to supplement State and local recovery efforts in the area struck by an extreme wildfire threat on December 1, 2005, and continuing.

January 11

In the morning, the President had an intelligence briefing. Later, he met with Secretary of State Condoleezza Rice. Then, in the Oval Office, he participated in a bill signing ceremony for H.R. 4340, the U.S.-Bahrain Free Trade Agreement.

Later in the morning, the President traveled to Louisville, KY, where, upon arrival, he met with USA Freedom Corps volunteer Bob Manning.

In the afternoon, at the Kentucky International Convention Center, the President met with family members of a soldier killed in Iraq. Later, he returned to Washington, DC.

The President declared a major disaster in Texas and ordered Federal aid to supplement State and local recovery efforts in the area struck by an extreme wildfire threat beginning on December 1, 2005, and continuing.

January 12

In the morning, the President had a telephone conversation with Acting Prime Minister Ehud Olmert of Israel to express his concern for the health of Prime Minister Ariel Sharon of Israel and to wish the Acting Prime Minister well. Later, he had an intelligence briefing.

Later in the morning, the President traveled to New Orleans, LA. While en route aboard Air Force One, he had a telephone conversation with Supreme Court Associate Justice-designate Samuel A. Alito, Jr., to discuss the judge's Senate confirmation hearing. Upon arrival in New Orleans, he met with USA Freedom Corps volunteer Daisy VanDenburgh.

In the afternoon, the President traveled to Waveland, MS, where, upon arrival, he met with a group of first-responders. Later, he traveled to Palm Beach, FL, where, upon arrival, he met with USA Freedom Corps volunteer Yirela Alcantara.

In the evening, at a private residence, the President attended a Republican National Committee reception. Later, he returned to Washington, DC.

The President announced his intention to nominate Gale A. Buchanan to be Under Secretary of Agriculture for Research, Education, and Economics.

The President announced his intention to nominate Donald T. Bliss to be U.S. Representative on the Council of the International Civil Aviation Organization with the rank of Ambassador.

January 13

In the morning, the President had an intelligence briefing. Later, he had a telephone conversation with President Elias Antonio Saca Gonzalez of El Salvador to discuss bilateral issues. Then, in the Oval Office, he met with Chancellor Angela Merkel of Germany.

In the afternoon, the President had a working lunch with Chancellor Merkel. Later, in the Oval Office, he met with business leaders to discuss natural disaster relief and reconstruction efforts in Central America.

Later in the afternoon, in the Oval Office, the President participated in a photo opportunity with the U.S. Solheim Cup women's golf team. He and Mrs. Bush then traveled to Camp David, MD.

The White House announced that the President will welcome Prime Minister Shaukat Aziz of Pakistan to the White House on January 24.

The President announced his designation of a Presidential delegation to attend the inauguration of President Ellen Johnson-Sirleaf of Liberia on January 16:

Laura Bush (head of delegation);
Condoleezza Rice;
Donald E. Booth;
Jendayi E. Frazer;
Cindy Courville; and
Barbara P. Bush.

January 14

In the morning, the President had an intelligence briefing.

January 15

In the afternoon, the President returned to Washington, DC.

January 16

In the morning, the President had an intelligence briefing.

January 17

In the morning, the President had an intelligence briefing. Later, in the Oval Office, he met with Secretary of Veterans Affairs R. James Nicholson, American Legion National Com-

mander Tom Brock, and John Summer, executive director of the Washington office of the American Legion.

In the afternoon, in Room 350 of the Dwight D. Eisenhower Executice Office Building, the President met with members of the Foreign Intelligence Service Advisory Board and participated in a swearing-in ceremony for the board.

The White House announced that the President will welcome President Lech Kaczynski of Poland to the White House on February 9.

The President announced his intention to nominate Richard A. Boucher to be Assistant Secretary of State for South Asian Affairs.

The President announced his intention to nominate Tyler D. Duvall to be Assistant Secretary of Transportation (Transportation Policy).

The President announced his intention to nominate Preston M. Geren to be Under Secretary of the Army.

The President announced his intention to nominate James B. Gulliford to be Assistant Administrator for Toxic Substances at the Environmental Protection Agency.

The President announced his intention to nominate Roger Shane Karr to be Assistant Secretary of Transportation (Governmental Affairs).

The President announced his intention to nominate Nicole R. Nason to be Administrator of the National Highway Traffic Safety Administration.

The President announced his intention to nominate David L. Norquist to be Chief Financial Officer at the Department of Homeland Security.

The President announced his intention to nominate David C. Sanborn to be Administrator of the Maritime Administration of the Department of Transportation.

The President announced his intention to nominate James S. Simpson to be Federal Transit Administrator at the Department of Transportation.

The President announced his intention to nominate Ben S. Bernanke to be U.S. Alternate Governor of the International Monetary Fund.

The President announced his intention to appoint John N. Etchart as a member of the Advisory Board of the National Air and Space Museum.

The President announced his intention to appoint Valencia Campbell, Raymond Paul Caldiero, and James T. Dyke, Jr., as members of the Board of Governors of the United Service Organization, Incorporated.

The President announced his intention to designate David L. Dunn as Acting Under Secretary of Education.

The President announced the recess appointment of C. Boyden Gray as U.S. Representative to the European Union with the rank and status of Ambassador.

The President announced the recess appointment of Dennis P. Walsh as a member of the National Labor Relations Board.

January 18

In the morning, the President had an intelligence briefing followed by a meeting with Secretary of Defense Donald H. Rumsfeld. Later, he had a telephone conversation with Chancellor Angela Merkel of Germany to discuss the situation in Iran.

January 19

In the morning, the President had an intelligence briefing. He then had a telephone conversation with President-elect Michelle Bachelet Jeria of Chile to congratulate her on her election victory. Later, he traveled to Sterling, VA.

Later in the morning, the President returned to Washington, DC.

The President announced his intention to nominate Randall L. Tobias to be Administrator of the U.S. Agency for International Development.

The President announced his intention to nominate Thad W. Allen to be Commandant of the U.S. Coast Guard.

January 20

In the morning, the President had an intelligence briefing followed by a National Security Council meeting. Later, he met with Secretary of State Condoleezza Rice.

In the afternoon, the President and Mrs. Bush traveled to Camp David, MD.

The President declared a major disaster in South Carolina and ordered Federal aid to supplement State and local recovery efforts in the area struck by a severe ice storm from December 15–16, 2005.

January 21

In the morning, the President had an intelligence briefing.

January 22

In the afternoon, the President and Mrs. Bush returned to Washington, DC.

January 23

In the morning, the President had an intelligence briefing. Later, he traveled to Topeka, KS, where, upon arrival, he met with USA Freedom Corps volunteer Janet Dunn. He then traveled to Manhattan, KS.

In the afternoon, the President met with family members of a soldier killed in Afghanistan. He then returned to Washington, DC. Later, in the Oval Office, he participated in a photo opportunity with members of the U.S. Walker Cup team.

In the evening, the President and Mrs. Bush hosted a retirement dinner for Federal Reserve Chairman Alan Greenspan.

January 24

In the morning, the President had an intelligence briefing. Later, he met with Senator Norm Coleman of Minnesota and Senator Mark Pryor of Arkansas, cochairs of the National Prayer Breakfast, to discuss preparations for the breakfast.

In the afternoon, in the Old Family Dining Room, the President had a working lunch with Prime Minister Shaukat Aziz of Pakistan. Later, on the South Lawn, he participated in a photo opportunity with NASCAR Nextel Cup champion Tony Stewart and members of his racing team.

During the day, in the Oval Office, the President met with Gov. Joe Manchin III of West Virginia.

The President announced his designation of the following individuals as members of a Presidential delegation to Pristina, Kosovo, to attend the funeral of President Ibrahim Rugova of Kosovo on January 26: Alphonso R. Jackson (head of delegation); Philip S. Goldberg; and Frank Wisner.

The President announced his intention to nominate Thomas J. Barrett to be Administrator of the Pipeline and Hazardous Materials Safety Administration at the Department of Transportation.

The President announced his intention to nominate Rajkumar Chellaraj to be Assistant Secretary of State for Administration.

The President announced his intention to appoint Margaret L. Kripke as a member of the President's Cancer Panel (Scientist).

The President announced his intention to designate Mary K. Bush as chair of the Helping to Enhance the Livelihood of People (HELP) Around the Globe Commission.

January 25

In the morning, in the Oval Office, the President had a telephone conversation with Prime Minister-elect Stephen Harper of Canada to congratulate him on his election victory. Later, he had an intelligence briefing. He then participated in an interview with the Wall Street Journal.

Later in the morning, in the Roosevelt Room, the President met with Members of the Senate to discuss the war on terror and the strategy for victory in Iraq.

In the afternoon, the President traveled to Fort Meade, MD, where, at the National Security Agency, he made remarks to employees. He then participated in a tour of the National Security Agency. Later, he returned to Washington, DC.

The President announced his designation of the following individuals as members of a Presidential delegation to Tegucigalpa, Honduras, to attend the inauguration of President Jose Manuel Zelaya Rosales of Honduras on January 27:

Alberto R. Gonzales (head of delegation);
Charles A. Ford;
Cresencio Arcos;
Miguel A. Estrada; and
Redmond James Hogan.

January 26

In the morning, the President had an intelligence briefing.

The President declared a major disaster in Kansas and ordered Federal aid to supplement State and local recovery efforts in the area struck by a severe winter storm from November 27–28, 2005.

The President declared a major disaster in Nebraska and ordered Federal aid to supplement State and local recovery efforts in the area struck by a severe winter storm from November 27–28, 2005.

January 27

In the morning, the President had an intelligence briefing. Later, in Room 350 of the Dwight D. Eisenhower Executive Office Building, he met with the Senate Republican Conference to discuss legislative priorities.

In the afternoon, the President participated in an interview with Bob Schieffer of CBS News.

The President announced his intention to nominate Thomas P. D'Agostino to be Deputy Administrator for Defense Programs in the National Nuclear Security Administration at the Department of Energy.

The President announced his intention to nominate Randall S. Kroszner to be a member of the Board of Governors of the Federal Reserve System for the Fifth District.

The President announced his intention to nominate Boyd Kevin Rutherford to be Assistant Secretary of Agriculture (Administration).

The President announced his intention to nominate Kevin M. Warsh to be a member of the Board of Governors of the Federal Reserve System for the Second District.

The President announced his intention to designate Mary M. Rose as Vice Chairman of the Merit Systems Protection Board.

January 28

In the morning, the President had an intelligence briefing.

In the evening, at the Capital Hilton Hotel, the President and Mrs. Bush attended the Alfalfa Club Dinner.

January 29

In the afternoon, the President participated in a speech preparation session for his January 31 State of the Union Address.

January 30

In the morning, the President had an intelligence briefing. Later, in the Family Theater, the President participated in a speech preparation session for his January 31 State of the Union Address.

In the afternoon, in the Oval Office, the President participated in a signing ceremony for a Presidential proclamation in honor of the fourth anniversary of the USA Freedom Corps.

The President announced his intention to nominate W. Ralph Basham to be Commissioner of Customs at the Bureau of Customs and Border Enforcement in the Department of Homeland Security.

The President announced his intention to nominate Paul DeCamp to be Administrator of the Wage and Hour Division at the Department of Labor.

The President announced his intention to nominate Edward P. Lazear to be a member of the Council of Economic Advisers and, upon appointment, to designate him as Chairman.

The President announced his intention to nominate Jeffrey L. Sedgwick to be Director of the Bureau of Justice Statistics at the Department of Justice.

The President announced his intention to appoint Mark Sullivan as Director of the U.S. Secret Service at the Department of Homeland Security.

The President announced his designation of the following individuals as members of a Presidential delegation to the 2006 Olympic Games in Turin, Italy:

Laura Bush (head of delegation);
Ronald P. Spogli;
Barbara P. Bush;
Roland Betts;
Brad Freeman;
Dorothy Hamill;
Eric Heiden;
Kerri Strug;
Debi Thomas; and
Herschel Walker.

January 31

In the morning, the President had an intelligence briefing. Later, in the Roosevelt Room, he met with Samuel A. Alito, Jr., to congratulate him on being confirmed by the Senate as an Associate Justice of the U.S. Supreme Court.

In the afternoon, in the Old Family Dining Room, the President had lunch with television correspondents.

February 1

In the morning, the President had a telephone conversation with President Vladimir V. Putin of Russia to discuss the situation in Iran. Later, he had a telephone conversation with President Evo Morales of Bolivia to congratulate him on his election victory and inauguration. He then had an intelligence briefing.

Later in the morning, in the Oval Office, the President and Mrs. Bush participated in a signing ceremony for a Presidential proclamation in honor of American Heart Month. He and Mrs. Bush then traveled to Nashville, TN, where, upon arrival, he met with USA Freedom Corps volunteer Suzanne Bingham.

In the afternoon, the President and Mrs. Bush returned to Washington, DC.

February 2

In the morning, the President had an intelligence briefing. Later, he traveled to Minneapolis, MN, where, upon arrival, he met with USA Freedom Corps volunteer Anna Edlund. He then traveled to Maplewood, MN, where he toured 3M Headquarters.

In the afternoon, the President traveled to Albuquerque, NM, where, upon arrival, he met with USA Freedom Corps volunteer Mike Martin.

February 3

In the morning, the President had an intelligence briefing. Later, the President traveled to Dallas, TX, where, upon arrival in the afternoon, he met with USA Freedom Corps volunteer Sharon Randolph.

Later in the afternoon, the President traveled to the Bush Ranch in Crawford, TX.

The White House announced that the President will welcome King Abdullah II of Jordan to the White House on February 8.

The White House announced that the President will welcome Secretary-General Kofi Annan of the United Nations to the White House on February 13.

The President announced his intention to nominate Benedict S. Cohen to be General Counsel of the Department of the Army.

The President announced his intention to nominate Robert M. McDowell to be a Commissioner on the Federal Communications Commission.

The President announced his intention to nominate Mauricio J. Tamargo to be Chairman of the Foreign Claims Settlement Commission of the U.S. at the Department of Justice.

The President announced his intention to nominate Armando J. Bucelo to be a director of the board of directors of the Securities Investor Protection Corporation (Public).

The President announced his intention to nominate Todd S. Farha to be a director of the board of directors of the Securities Investor Protection Corporation (Public) and, upon appointment, to designate him as vice chairman.

The President announced his intention to appoint Douglas DeMaster as Deputy U.S. Commissioner on the International Whaling Commission.

The President announced his intention to appoint William Hogarth as U.S. Commissioner on the International Whaling Commission.

The President announced his intention to appoint William B. Keleher as a member of the Board of Directors of the Valles Caldera Trust (Expert in Cultural and Natural History).

The President announced his intention to appoint Michael R. Oestreicher as a member of the Advisory Committee for Trade Policy and Negotiations.

The President announced that he has appointed Kevin J. Bergner as Special Assistant to the President and Senior Director for Iraq.

The President announced that he has appointed Scott Jennings as Special Assistant to the President and Deputy Director of Political Affairs.

The President announced that he has appointed Jeffrey F. Kupfer as Special Assistant to the President for Economic Policy.

The President announced that he has appointed Elisabeth Millard as Special Assistant to the President and Senior Director for South and Central Asian Affairs.

The President announced that he has appointed Luis A. Reyes as Special Assistant to the President for Presidential Personnel.

The President declared a major disaster in Nevada and ordered Federal aid to supplement State and local recovery efforts in the area struck by severe storms and flooding from December 31, 2005, to January 4, 2006.

The President declared a major disaster in California and ordered Federal aid to supplement State and local recovery efforts in the area struck by severe storms, flooding, mudslides, and landslides from December 17, 2005, through January 3, 2006.

February 4

In the morning, the President had an intelligence briefing.

The White House announced that the President and Mrs. Bush will attend the funeral of Coretta Scott King on February 7.

February 5

In the morning, the President and Mrs. Bush returned to Washington, DC.

February 6

In the morning, the President had an intelligence briefing followed by a National Security Council meeting. Later, he had a telephone conversation with Daniel M. Rooney, chairman of the Pittsburgh Steelers football team, to congratulate him on the team's Super Bowl victory on February 5. He then had a telephone conversation with Amir Sabah al-Ahmad al-Jabir al-Sabah of Kuwait to offer his condolences on the death of his brother, Amir Jabir al-Ahmad al-Jabir al-Sabah, to wish him well as he takes the position, and to invite him to the White House at his convenience.

In the afternoon, in the Family Dining Room, the President and Mrs. Bush had lunch with former President Jose Maria Aznar of Spain and his wife, Ana Botella.

In the evening, in the East Room, the President and Mrs. Bush attended a performance honoring the Dance Theatre of Harlem.

February 7

In the morning, the President had a working breakfast with Attorney General Alberto R. Gonzales. Later, he had an intelligence briefing.

Later in the morning, the President and Mrs. Bush traveled to Lithonia, GA. While en route aboard Air Force One, he had a telephone conversation with Prime Minister Anders Fogh Rasmussen of Denmark to discuss the recent violence against Danish and other diplomatic facilities and the importance of religious tolerance and freedom of the press.

In the afternoon, the President and Mrs. Bush returned to Washington, DC.

In the evening, the President had a working dinner with King Abdullah II of Jordan and Members of Congress.

The President announced his intention to nominate Patricia P. Brister to be the U.S. Representative on the Commission on the Status of Women of the Economic and Social Council of the United Nations, with the rank of Ambassador.

The President announced his intention to appoint Sander R. Gerber as a member of the Board of Trustees of the Woodrow Wilson International Center of Scholars (Public).

The President announced his intention to appoint Tamala L. Longaberger as a member of the Board of Trustees of the Woodrow Wilson International Center of Scholars (Government Representative).

The President announced his intention to designate Peter Jon Thomas as Acting Assistant Secretary of Agriculture for Administration.

The President announced his intention to designate David E. Jeremiah, Arthur B. Culvahouse, and Donald L. Evans as members of the Intelligence Oversight Board.

February 8

In the morning, the President had an intelligence briefing. Later, he traveled to Manchester, NH, where, upon arrival, he met with USA Freedom Corps volunteer Vernette Reimel.

In the afternoon, the President returned to Washington, DC. Later, in Room 350 of the Dwight D. Eisenhower Executive Office Building, he dropped by a meeting of CEOs from the Business Roundtable. Then, in the Cabinet Room, he had a meeting with Republican congressional leaders to discuss legislative priorities.

February 9

In the morning, the President had a telephone conversation with Chancellor Angela Merkel of Germany to discuss foreign policy issues and the situation in the Middle East. Later, he had an intelligence briefing.

In the afternoon, in the Old Family Dining Room, the President had lunch with President Lech Kaczynski of Poland. Later, he participated in a meeting and photo opportunity with members of the Major Cities Chiefs Association and the Major County Sheriff's Association.

The White House announced that the President will welcome President Elias Antonio Saca Gonzalez of El Salvador to the White House on February 24.

The President announced his intention to nominate Andrew B. Steinberg to be Assistant Secretary of Transportation for Aviation and International Affairs.

The President announced his intention to appoint Julianna M. Cellini as a member of the Abraham Lincoln Bicentennial Commission.

The President announced his intention to appoint Trung Dung and Richard J. Wall as members of the Board of Directors of the Vietnam Education Foundation.

February 10

In the morning, the President had breakfast with Secretary of State Condoleezza Rice. Later, he had an intelligence briefing. Then, in the Oval Office, he met with Rebecca Garang, Minister of Transportation, Roads, and Bridges of the Government of Southern Sudan.

Later in the morning, the President traveled to Cambridge, MD.

In the afternoon, the President returned to Washington, DC.

February 11

In the morning, the President had an intelligence briefing.

February 13

In the morning, the President had an intelligence briefing followed by a National Security Council meeting. Later, he participated in a signing ceremony for the 2006 Economic Report of the President and a photo opportunity with members of the Council of Economic Advisers.

In the afternoon, the President had lunch with Vice President Dick Cheney.

In the evening, at a private residence, the President made remarks at a National Republican Senatorial Committee reception.

The President announced his designation of the following individuals as members of a Presidential delegation to attend the closing ceremonies of the 2006 Olympic Games in Turin, Italy:

Rudolph W. Giuliani (head of delegation);
Ronald P. Spogli;
Mario Andretti; and
A. Kenneth Ciongoli.

The President announced his intention to nominate Robert Irwin Cusick, Jr., to be Director of the Office of Government Ethics.

The President announced his intention to nominate James Lambright to be President of the Export-Import Bank of the U.S.

The President announced his intention to nominate Jon T. Rymer to be Inspector General of the Federal Deposit Insurance Corporation.

The President announced his intention to nominate Dennis R. Spurgeon to be an Assistant Secretary of Energy (Nuclear Energy).

The President announced his intention to appoint the following individuals as members of the President's Committee on the National Medal of Science:

Oliver K. Baker;
Sally K. Mason;
Robert Y. Moore; and
Harvey S. Rosen.

The President announced his intention to appoint Samuel K. Lessey, Jr., John S. Rainey, and William H. Strong as members of the Board of Visitors of the U.S. Military Academy.

The President announced his intention to appoint the following individuals as members of the President's Council on Service and Civic Participation:

Raymond G. Chambers;
Darrell Green;
Michelle Nunn;
Sara Evans Schelske; and
Mark G. Yudof.

February 14

In the morning, the President had an intelligence briefing.

In the afternoon, in the Oval Office, the President met with the President's Council on Service and Civic Participation.

In the evening, in the State Dining Room, the President and Mrs. Bush attended a Valentine's Day dinner. Later, in the East Room, they attended a Valentine's Day performance.

February 15

In the morning, the President had breakfast with congressional leaders to discuss legislative priorities. Later, he had an intelligence briefing. He then met with Secretary of State Condoleezza Rice.

Later in the morning, the President traveled to Columbus, OH, where, upon arrival, he met with USA Freedom Corps volunteer Suraj Hinduja, before traveling to Dublin, OH. Then, in the employee break room at Wendy's International, Inc., Corporate Headquarters, he participated in a meeting on health savings accounts.

In the afternoon, the President returned to Washington, DC. Later, in the Oval Office, he participated in a bill signing ceremony for H.R. 4636, the Federal Deposit Insurance Reform Conforming Amendments Act of 2005.

February 16

In the morning, the President had an intelligence briefing. Later, he had a meeting with health insurance and business leaders to discuss health care transparency issues. He then participated in a briefing on the war on terror in Iraq with Republican Members of Congress.

In the afternoon, at the historic Evermay house, the President attended a Republican National Committee luncheon.

The President announced his intention to nominate Linda Avery Strachan to be Assistant Secretary of Agriculture for Congressional Relations.

The President announced his intention to appoint Lee J. Styslinger III as a member of the President's Export Council.

The President announced his intention to appoint Joyce A. Silverthorne and Arthur W. Zimiga as members of the National Advisory Council on Indian Education.

February 17

In the morning, the President had an intelligence briefing. He then had a telephone conversation with Secretary General Jakob Gijsbert "Jaap" de Hoop Scheffer of the North Atlantic Treaty Organization to discuss the situation in Darfur, Sudan.

Later in the morning, the President traveled to Tampa, FL, where, at MacDill Air Force Base, he met with USA Freedom Corps volunteer Joe MacDougald. Later, he participated in a briefing on the war on terror with commanders of U.S. Central and Special Operations Commands.

In the afternoon, the President met with family members of a soldier killed in Iraq. Later, he traveled to Orlando, FL, where, upon arrival, he met with USA Freedom Corps volunteer Shauna Clark. He then traveled to Lake Buena Vista, FL.

In the evening, at Disney's Contemporary Resort, the President attended a Republican Party of Florida dinner. He then returned to Washington, DC.

February 18

In the morning, the President had an intelligence briefing.

February 20

In the morning, the President had a telephone conversation with President Gloria Macapagal-

Arroyo of the Philippines to offer condolences for the loss of life during massive mudslides in St. Bernard and to pledge continued U.S. disaster relief assistance. He then had an intelligence briefing. Later, he had a telephone conversation with President Vicente Fox Quesada of Mexico to discuss border security, immigration reform, and other issues.

Later in the morning, the President traveled to Milwaukee, WI, where, upon arrival, he met with USA Freedom Corps volunteer Beverly Christy-Wright. He then toured the Johnson Controls Battery Technology Center.

In the afternoon, the President traveled to Selfridge Air National Guard Base in Macomb County, MI, where, upon arrival, he met with USA Freedom Corps volunteer Brian Willingham. He then traveled to Auburn Hills, MI, where, at United Solar Ovonic, he participated in a briefing on alternative energy sources. Later, he traveled to Buckley Air Force Base in Aurora, CO, where, upon arrival, he met with USA Freedom Corps volunteer Delmar "Pete" Beverly before traveling to Englewood, CO.

February 21

In the morning, the President had an intelligence briefing. Later, he traveled to Golden, CO, where he participated in a tour of the National Renewable Energy Laboratory.

In the afternoon, the President returned to Washington, DC.

The President announced his designation of the following individuals as members of a Presidential delegation to attend the closing ceremonies of the 2006 Olympic Games in Turin, Italy:

Rudolph W. Giuliani (head of delegation);
Ronald P. Spogli;
Mario Andretti;
Lawrence E. Auriana; and
A. Kenneth Ciongoli.

February 22

In the morning, the President had an intelligence briefing. Later, he met with Secretary of Defense Donald H. Rumsfeld.

In the afternoon, the President had lunch with Vice President Dick Cheney. Later, in the Oval Office, he participated in a photo opportunity with crew members of the Space Shuttle *Discovery* and their families.

In the evening, in the Family Theater, the President and Mrs. Bush hosted a screening of "Glory Road" followed by a dinner.

The White House announced that the President will host Prime Minister Silvio Berlusconi of Italy at the White House on February 28.

February 23

In the morning, the President had a telephone conversation with President-elect Rene Garcia Preval of Haiti to congratulate him on his election victory. Later, he had an intelligence briefing. He then traveled to Mishawaka, IN, where, at Bethel College Indiana, he met with a soldier wounded in Iraq.

In the afternoon, the President traveled to Cincinnati, OH.

In the evening, at a private residence, the President attended a Mike DeWine for U.S. Senate reception. He then returned to Washington, DC.

The President announced his intention to nominate John G. Emling to be Assistant Secretary of Commerce for Legislative and Intergovernmental Affairs.

The President announced his intention to appoint William M. Murphy as a member of the Nuclear Waste Technical Review Board.

The President announced his intention to appoint Gail A. Jaquish, A.J. Scribante, and Jackie Winters as members of the Board of Visitors to the U.S. Air Force Academy.

The President announced his intention to appoint Antonio Falcon, Bruce D. San Filippo, and Cecilia Rosales as members of the U.S. Section of the United States-Mexico Border Health Commission.

February 24

In the morning, the President had an intelligence briefing followed by a National Security Council meeting on Iraq.

In the afternoon, in the Oval Office, the President met with President Elias Antonio Saca Gonzalez of El Salvador.

The White House announced that the President will host Prime Minister Mikulas Dzurinda of Slovakia at the White House on March 13.

The President declared an emergency in Maine and ordered Federal aid to supplement State and local recovery efforts in the area struck by record snow from December 25–27, 2005.

February 25

In the morning, the President had an intelligence briefing.

February 27

In the morning, the President had an intelligence briefing followed by a National Security Council meeting. Later, in the Oval Office, he met with widows of prodemocracy advocates who disappeared in Belarus.

Also in the morning, the President had a telephone conversation with President Alvaro Uribe Velez of Colombia to discuss the conclusion of bilateral free trade negotiations.

The President announced his intention to nominate William Ludwig Wehrum, Jr., to be Assistant Administrator of the Environmental Protection Agency for Air and Radiation.

The President announced his intention to appoint the following individuals as members of the President's Council of Advisers on Science and Technology:

F. Duane Ackerman;
Paul M. Anderson;
Robert A. Brown;
Nance K. Dicciani;
Richard H. Herman;
Martin C. Jischke;
Fred Kavli;
Daniel A. Reed;
Hector de Jesus Ruiz;
Stratton D. Sclavos;
John Brooks Slaughter;
Joseph M. Tucci;
Robert E. Witt; and
Tadataka Yamada.

The President announced his intention to designate Susan Schanlaber Barnes as Vice Chairman of the Advisory Council on Historic Preservation.

The President announced his intention to designate Jeffrey William Runge as Acting Under Secretary of Homeland Security for Science and Technology.

The President declared a major disaster in Idaho and ordered Federal aid to supplement State and local recovery efforts in the area struck by severe storms and flooding from December 30, 2005, through and including January 4, 2006.

February 28

In the morning, the President had an intelligence briefing.

In the afternoon, the President and Mrs. Bush traveled to Kabul, Afghanistan, arriving the following day.

In the evening, while en route to Afghanistan, the President and Mrs. Bush stopped over at Shannon International Airport in Shannon, Ireland, where they greeted U.S. Marines being deployed to Iraq.

March 1

In the morning, aboard Air Force One, the President had an intelligence briefing.

In the afternoon, at the Presidential Palace in Kabul, Afghanistan, the President had a working lunch with President Hamid Karzai of Afghanistan. Later, he and Mrs. Bush traveled to New Delhi, India, where, upon arrival, they were greeted by Prime Minister Manmohan Singh of India and his wife, Gursharan Kaur.

March 2

In the morning, the President had an intelligence briefing. Later, at Rashtrapati Bhavan, the official residence of the President of India, he and Mrs. Bush participated in an arrival ceremony with President A.P.J. Abdul Kalam and Prime Minister Manmohan Singh of India and his wife, Gursharan Kaur. They then participated in a wreath-laying ceremony at the Mahatma Gandhi Memorial.

In the afternoon, at the Taj Palace Hotel, the President and Mrs. Bush had lunch with Prime Minister Singh and his wife, Gursharan Kaur. Later, at Roosevelt House, he greeted U.S. Embassy personnel and their families. Then, at the Maurya Sheraton Hotel and Towers, he participated in separate meetings with Indian Opposition Leader Lal Krishna Advani and Indian National Congress Party chairman Sonia Gandhi.

In the evening, at Rashtrapati Bhavan, the President paid a courtesy call on President Kalam.

The President announced his designation of the following individuals as members of a Presidential delegation to attend the inauguration of President Michelle Bachelet Jeria of Chile on March 11: Condoleezza Rice (head of delegation); Craig A. Kelly; and Karen P. Hughes.

The President announced his designation of the following individuals as members of a Presidential delegation to attend the inauguration of President Anibal Cavaco Silva of Portugal on March 9: George H.W. Bush (head of delegation); Al Hoffman; and John D. Stufflebeem.

The President announced his designation of the following individuals as members of a Presidential delegation to attend the opening ceremonies of the IX Paralympic Winter Games in Torino, Italy:

Margaret Spellings (head of delegation);
Ronald P. Spogli;
Kirk Bauer;
Chad Colley; and
Nancy Starnes.

March 3

In the morning, the President had an intelligence briefing. Later, he and Mrs. Bush traveled to Hyderabad, India. He then visited Acharya N.G. Ranga Agriculture University.

In the afternoon, the President and Mrs. Bush returned to New Delhi.

In the evening, the President and Mrs. Bush traveled to Islamabad, Pakistan.

The President announced that he has nominated John W. Cox to be Chief Financial Officer at the Department of Housing and Urban Development.

The President announced that he has nominated George McDade Staples to be Director General of the Foreign Service at the Department of State, and his intention to appoint him as Chairman of the Board of the Foreign Service.

The President announced that he has nominated Mickey D. Barnett and Katherine C. Tobin to be Governors of the Board of Governors of the U.S. Postal Service.

The President announced that he has designated of William Ludwig Wehrum, Jr., as Acting Assistant Administrator for Air and Radiation at the Environmental Protection Agency.

The President announced that he has designated Sean O'Hollaren as Deputy Assistant to the President for Legislative Affairs.

The President announced that he has designated Lisa E. Epifani as Special Assistant to the President for Economic Policy.

The President announced that he has designated Brian V. McCormack as Special Assist-

ant to the President and Deputy Director of Public Liaison.

March 4

In the morning, at the U.S. Ambassador's residence in Islamabad, Pakistan, the President had an intelligence briefing. Later, at the Aiwan-e-Sadr, the President of Pakistan's residence, he and Mrs. Bush participated in an arrival ceremony with President Pervez Musharraf of Pakistan. Then, in the Pink Room at the Aiwan-e-Sadr, he met with President Musharraf.

Later in the morning, in the Reception Hall at the Aiwan-e-Sadr, the President participated in a briefing on the Pakistani earthquake and reconstruction efforts.

In the afternoon, in the President's Dining Room at the Aiwan-e-Sadr, the President and Mrs. Bush had lunch with President Musharraf and his wife, Sehba Musharraf. Later, at the U.S. Embassy in Islamabad, the President greeted U.S. Embassy staff. Then, in the Raphel Memorial Gardens of the U.S. Embassy, he participated in a cricket clinic with Pakistani youth.

In the evening, in the Reception Hall at the Aiwan-e-Sadr, the President and Mrs. Bush attended a performance. Later, they returned to Washington, DC, arriving the following morning.

March 6

In the morning, the President had an intelligence briefing. Later, in Room 350 of the Dwight D. Eisenhower Executive Office Building, he dropped by a meeting of the Academic Competitiveness Council.

In the afternoon, the President participated in a briefing on Hurricane Katrina recovery and rebuilding efforts along the gulf coast.

The White House announced that the President will welcome President Alejandro Toledo of Peru to the White House on March 10.

March 7

In the morning, the President had an intelligence briefing.

In the afternoon, in the Oval Office, the President met with Minister of Foreign Affairs Sergey V. Lavrov of Russia. Later, he and Mrs. Bush traveled to Crawford, TX.

The President announced his intention to nominate Jerry Gayle Bridges to be Chief Financial Officer at the Corporation for National and Community Service.

The President announced his intention to nominate Richard Capka to be Administrator of the Federal Highway Administration.

The President announced his intention to nominate Robert F. Godec to be Ambassador to Tunisia.

The President announced his intention to nominate Philip D. Moeller and Jon Wellinghoff to be members of the Federal Energy Regulatory Commission.

The President announced his intention to nominate Michael E. Ranneberger to be Ambassador to Kenya.

The President announced his intention to nominate Warren W. Tichenor to be the U.S. Representative to the European Office of the United Nations and other international organizations with the rank of Ambassador.

The President announced his intention to appoint Scott G. Kriens as a member of the President's National Security Telecommunications Advisory Committee.

The President announced his intention to appoint the following individuals as members of the Advisory Commission on Drug-Free Communities:

James R. Aiona, Jr. (State Organization);
Sandra Heverly (National Organization);
Keith N. Humphreys (Public);
Patricia J. Kempthorne (Public);
Charles W. Larson, Jr. (State Organization);
Darren L. Myles (National Organization); and
Camille Q. Solberg (Public).

The President announced his intention to designate William McCabe as Acting Chief Financial Officer of the Department of Education.

The President made additional disaster assistance available to areas of Mississippi impacted by Hurricane Katrina.

March 8

In the morning, the President and Mrs. Bush traveled to New Orleans, LA. While en route aboard Air Force One, he had an intelligence briefing, and then he and Mrs. Bush participated in a briefing on hurricane recovery and rebuilding efforts in New Orleans and other parts of Louisiana. Upon arrival in New Orleans, he met with USA Freedom Corps volunteer Theo Richards.

Later in the morning, aboard Marine One, the President and Mrs. Bush participated in an aerial tour of hurricane damaged areas of New Orleans followed by a walking tour of damaged areas and reconstruction efforts in New Orleans, including the Lower Ninth Ward and Industrial Levee Canal. During the tour, they stopped in at Stewart's Diner in the Lower Ninth Ward. They then traveled to Gautier, MS, where they toured hurricane damaged areas.

In the afternoon, the President and Mrs. Bush returned to Washington, DC.

March 9

In the morning, the President had a telephone conversation with Chancellor Angela Merkel of Germany to discuss foreign policy issues. Later, he had an intelligence briefing. He then participated in a photo opportunity with the National and Distinguished Principals of the Year.

Later in the morning, the President met with Republican congressional leaders to discuss legislative priorities. Later, on the North Portico, he participated in a photo opportunity with U.S. Senate Youth Program students.

In the afternoon, the President met with bipartisan Members of Congress to discuss his proposed Advanced Energy Initiative.

In the evening, the President traveled to College Park, GA. Later, he returned to Washington, DC.

The White House announced that the President will travel to Cancun, Mexico, to meet with President Vicente Fox Quesada of Mexico and Prime Minister Stephen Harper of Canada on March 30–31.

March 10

In the morning, the President had breakfast with Secretary of State Condoleezza Rice. Later, he had an intelligence briefing. He then participated in a National Security Council meeting on Iraq.

In the afternoon, the President and Mrs. Bush had lunch with President Alejandro Toledo of Peru. Later, in the Oval Office, he and Mrs. Bush met with members of military service organizations that have participated in the Department of Defense's America Supports You program.

The White House announced that the President will welcome Prime Minister Bertie Ahern of Ireland to the White House on March 17 and that he and Prime Minister Ahern will meet with Secretary of State for Northern Ireland

Peter Hain of the United Kingdom and Northern Ireland community peace activists.

The President announced his intention to nominate Robert D. McCallum, Jr., to be Ambassador to Australia.

March 11

In the morning, the President had an intelligence briefing.

In the evening, at the Capital Hilton Hotel, the President and Mrs. Bush attended the Gridiron Club dinner.

March 13

In the morning, the President had an intelligence briefing. Later, in the Old Indian Treaty Room of the Dwight D. Eisenhower Executive Office Building, the President participated in a photo opportunity with the Intel Science Talent Search finalists.

In the afternoon, the President received diplomatic credentials from newly appointed Ambassadors to the United States.

The President announced his intention to nominate Kenneth L. Wainstein to be an Assistant Attorney General and, upon appointment, to designate him as Assistant Attorney General for National Security.

The President announced his intention to nominate Jonann C. Chiles to be a member of the Board of Directors of the Legal Services Corporation.

The President announced his intention to nominate J.C.A. Stagg to be a member of the Board of Trustees of the James Madison Memorial Fellowship Foundation (Academic).

The President announced his intention to appoint John Cornyn and Edward M. Kennedy as members of the Board of Trustees of the James Madison Memorial Fellowship Foundation.

March 14

In the morning, the President had an intelligence briefing. Later, he traveled to Rochester, NY, where, upon arrival, he met with USA Freedom Corps volunteer Father Joseph M. Champlin.

In the afternoon, in a hangar at the Greater Rochester International Airport, the President met with family members of soldiers killed in Iraq and Afghanistan. Later, he returned to Washington, DC. Then, in the Roosevelt Room, he met with members of organizations involved in educating and enrolling seniors in Medicare prescription drug benefit plans.

March 15

In the morning, the President had an intelligence briefing. Later, he met with Secretary of Defense Donald H. Rumsfeld. He then met with Republican congressional leaders to discuss legislative priorities.

In the afternoon, the President traveled to Silver Spring, MD. Later, he returned to Washington, DC.

The President announced his intention to nominate Andrew C. von Eschenbach to be Commissioner of Food and Drugs at the Department of Health and Human Services.

The President announced his intention to nominate Mark C. Minton to be Ambassador to Mongolia.

The President announced his intention to nominate John A. Rizzo to be General Counsel of the Central Intelligence Agency.

The President announced his intention to designate Thomas E. McNamara as Program Manager of the Information Sharing Environment.

March 16

In the morning, the President met with Members of Congress who had recently visited the Darfur region of Sudan. Later, he had an intelligence briefing.

In the afternoon, at the U.S. Capitol, the President attended a St. Patrick's Day luncheon. Later, in the Oval Office, the President participated in a photo opportunity with recipients of the Public Safety Officer Medal of Valor.

The White House announced that the President will welcome President Ellen Johnson Sirleaf of Liberia to the White House on March 21.

The President declared a major disaster in Missouri and ordered Federal aid to supplement State and local recovery efforts in the area struck by severe storms, tornadoes, and flooding during the period of March 11–13.

March 17

In the morning, the President had an intelligence briefing. Later, in the Oval Office, he met with Prime Minister Bertie Ahern of Ireland. Then, he and Prime Minister Ahern met with community leaders from Northern Ireland and attended a St. Patrick's Day reception.

In the afternoon, the President participated in a briefing on avian influenza. Later, he and Mrs. Bush traveled to Camp David, MD.

The White House announced that the President will host NATO Secretary General Jakob Gijsbert "Jaap" de Hoop Scheffer at the White House on March 20.

The President announced his intention to nominate Michael D. Kirby to be Ambassador to Moldova.

The President announced his intention to appoint Floyd E. Bloom and Nicholas Eberstadt as members of the President's Council on Bioethics.

The President announced his intention to appoint Raymond Jardine, Jr., Samuel Metters, and William Gregory Rothman as members of the National Veterans Business Development Corporation.

The President announced his intention to designate Thomas E. Harvey as Acting Assistant Secretary of Veterans Affairs (Congressional Affairs).

March 18

In the morning, the President had an intelligence briefing.

March 19

In the afternoon, the President returned to Washington, DC.

March 20

In the morning, the President had an intelligence briefing. Later, he met with Secretary of State Condoleezza Rice. He then traveled to Cleveland, OH, where, upon arrival, he met with USA Freedom Corps volunteer Lois Hagood.

In the afternoon, the President returned to Washington, DC.

The President declared a major disaster in Oregon and ordered Federal aid to supplement State and local recovery efforts in the area struck by severe storms, flooding, landslides, and mudslides from December 18, 2005, through and including January 21, 2006.

March 21

In the morning, the President had an intelligence briefing.

In the afternoon, the President and Mrs. Bush had lunch and attended a performance with President Ellen Johnson Sirleaf of Liberia.

March 22

In the morning, the President had an intelligence briefing followed by a National Security Council meeting on Iraq. Later, he traveled to Wheeling, WV, where, upon arrival, he met with USA Freedom Corps volunteer Kristen Holloway.

In the afternoon, at the Capitol Music Hall, the President met with family members of soldiers killed in Iraq. Later, he returned to Washington, DC.

The White House announced that the President will welcome President Hu Jintao of China to the White House on April 20.

March 23

In the morning, the President had an intelligence briefing.

In the afternoon, the President had lunch with Vice President Dick Cheney. Later, in the Oval Office, he participated in a photo opportunity with the 2006 White House News Photographers Association "Eyes of History" winners.

In the evening, in the Blue Room, the President and Mrs. Bush hosted a social dinner to honor the 300th anniversary of the birth of Benjamin Franklin. Following the dinner, in the East Room, they attended a performance.

The President announced his designation of the following individuals as members of a Presidential delegation to Tallinn, Estonia, to attend the funeral of former President Lennart Meri of Estonia on March 26: David A. Sampson (head of delegation); Aldona Zofia Wos; and Daniel Fried.

March 24

In the morning, the President had an intelligence briefing.

In the afternoon, the President traveled to Indianapolis, IN, where, upon arrival, he met with USA Freedom Corps volunteer Marvin Bardo. Later, he traveled to Pittsburgh, PA, where, upon arrival, he met with USA Freedom Corps volunteer Edy Hope. He then traveled to Sewickley Heights, PA, where, at a private residence, he attended a Santorum 2006 reception.

In the evening, the President returned to Washington, DC.

The White House announced that the President will welcome President Olusegun Obasanjo of Nigeria to the White House on March 29.

March 25

In the morning, the President had an intelligence briefing. Later, he and Mrs. Bush traveled to Camp David, MD.

March 26

In the afternoon, the President and Mrs. Bush returned to Washington, DC.

March 27

In the morning, the President had an intelligence briefing.

In the afternoon, the President had lunch with Vice President Dick Cheney.

The President announced his intention to nominate Ronald S. Cooper to be General Counsel of the Equal Employment Opportunity Commission.

The President announced his intention to nominate Harry R. Hoglander and Peter W. Tredick to be members of the National Mediation Board.

The President announced his intention to nominate Molly A. O'Neill to be Assistant Administrator of the Environmental Protection Agency for Environmental Information.

The President announced his intention to appoint the following individuals as members of the Advisory Council on Historic Preservation:

John Nau (General Public);
D. Franklin Arey III (General Public);
Alan Autry; and
Matt Blunt.

The President announced his intention to appoint Marilyn Castor Mashon Pattillo and Frank Jao as members of the Board of Directors of the Vietnam Education Foundation.

The President announced his intention to appoint the following individuals as members of the President's Committee for People with Intellectual Disabilities:

Ricardo Barraza, Jr.;
Herbert Bartlett;
Sharman Word Dennis;
Carmela Vargas Gonzales;
Harris N. Hollin;
Casey Patrick O'Halloran;
Thomas J. Reilly;
Steven C. Rhatigan;
Neil Romano; and
Dallas Rob Sweezy.

March 28

In the morning, the President had an intelligence briefing. Later, he had a telephone conversation with outgoing Prime Minister Percival James Patterson of Jamaica to commend him for his distinguished service. He then had a telephone conversation with Prime Minister-designate Portia Simpson Miller of Jamaica to congratulate her on taking office.

In the afternoon, the President met with Members of Congress who had recently visited Iraq.

During the day, the President met with President-elect Rene Garcia Preval of Haiti.

The President declared a major disaster in Illinois and ordered Federal aid to supplement State and local recovery efforts in the area struck by tornadoes and severe storms on March 11–13.

March 29

In the morning, the President had a telephone conversation with Acting Prime Minister Ehud Olmert of Israel to congratulate him on his party's success in the recent election. Later, he had an intelligence briefing.

In the afternoon, the President met with Republican congressional leaders to discuss legislative priorities. Later, he participated in a photo opportunity with Spring 2006 White House interns. He then traveled to Cancun, Mexico.

March 30

In the morning, the President had an intelligence briefing. Later, he traveled to Chichen-Itza, Mexico, where he toured the Chichen-Itza archaeological ruins. He then returned to Cancun, Mexico.

In the evening, at the Fiesta Americana Condesa Cancun Hotel, the President had dinner with President Vicente Fox Quesada of Mexico and Prime Minister Stephen Harper of Canada.

The President announced his nomination of Daniel L. Cooper to be Under Secretary for Benefits of the Department of Veterans Affairs.

March 31

In the morning, the President had an intelligence briefing. Later, at the Fiesta Americana Condesa Cancun Hotel, he participated in a meeting with American, Canadian, and Mexican chief executive officers to discuss the North

American economy. He then traveled to the Bush Ranch in Crawford, TX.

The President announced that he has appointed Dana M. Perino as Deputy Assistant to the President and Deputy Press Secretary.

The President announced that he has appointed Kenneth A. Lisaius as Special Assistant to the President and Deputy Press Secretary.

The President announced that he has appointed Christopher G. Michel as Special Assistant to the President for Speechwriting.

The President announced that he has appointed Blain Rethmeier as Special Assistant to the President for Communications.

April 1

In the morning, the President had an intelligence briefing.

April 3

In the morning, the President had an intelligence briefing. He then had a telephone conversation with Chancellor Angela Merkel of Germany. Later, he traveled to Cincinnati, OH, where, upon arrival, he met with USA Freedom Corps volunteer Eugene Goss and Keith and Carolyn Maupin, parents of Sgt. Keith Matthew Maupin, USA, who disappeared after being captured by insurgents in Iraq on April 9, 2004.

In the afternoon, at Great American Ball Park, the President greeted Major League Baseball officials and visited the Chicago Cubs and Cincinnati Reds team clubhouses. Later, he participated in pregame ceremonies with soldiers wounded in Iraq and Afghanistan and with John Prazynski, whose son, Lance Cpl. Taylor B. Prazynski, USMC, was killed in Afghanistan on May 9, 2005. He then threw out the first pitch for an opening day game between the Cubs and the Reds and watched the game.

Later in the afternoon, the President returned to Washington, DC. While en route aboard Air Force One, he had a telephone conversation with Representative Tom DeLay of Texas to thank him for his service and wish him well in his retirement.

The President announced his designation of the following individuals as members of a Presidential delegation to attend the inauguration of President Thomas Yayi Boni of Benin on April 6:

Karen P. Hughes (head of delegation);
Wayne E. Neill;

Ruth A. Davis; and
Ward Brehm.

April 4

In the morning, the President had an intelligence briefing.

In the afternoon, at the historic Evermay house, the President made remarks at a Republican National Committee finance luncheon. Later, he met with Republican Members of the Senate to discuss legislative priorities.

The President announced his intention to nominate Eric M. Bost to be Ambassador to South Africa.

The President announced his intention to nominate Lisa Bobbie Schreiber Hughes to be Ambassador to Suriname.

The President announced his intention to nominate David M. Robinson to be Ambassador to Guyana.

The President announced his intention to nominate Earl Anthony Wayne to be Ambassador to Argentina.

The President announced his intention to appoint the following individuals as members of the Board for International Food and Agricultural Development:

Catherine Ann Bertini;
Allen C. Christensen;
Robert A. Easter; and
Timothy A. Rabon.

April 5

In the morning, in the Oval Office, the President had breakfast with Republican congressional leaders to discuss legislative priorities. Later, he had an intelligence briefing. He then traveled to Bridgeport, CT, where, upon arrival, he met with USA Freedom Corps volunteer Amargeet Singh.

In the afternoon, the President returned to Washington, DC. Later, he met with Republican Members of Congress.

In the evening, the President and Mrs. Bush hosted a screening of the film "Voyage to Kure."

The White House announced that the President will welcome President John Agyekum Kufuor of Ghana to the White House on April 12.

The President declared a disaster in Tennessee and ordered Federal aid to supplement State and local recovery efforts in the area struck by severe storms and tornadoes on April 2–3.

The President declared a disaster in Missouri and ordered Federal aid to supplement State and local recovery efforts in the area struck by severe storms, tornadoes, and flooding from March 30 to April 3.

April 6

In the morning, the President had an intelligence briefing. Later, he traveled to Charlotte, NC, where, upon arrival, he met with USA Freedom Corps volunteer Michelle Cornellier.

In the afternoon, the President returned to Washington, DC.

The President announced his intention to nominate John A. Cloud, Jr., to be Ambassador to Lithuania.

The President announced his intention to nominate Lurita Alexis Doan to be Administrator of General Services.

The President announced his intention to nominate R. David Paulison to be Under Secretary for Federal Emergency Management at the Department of Homeland Security.

The President announced his intention to nominate John Clint Williamson to be Ambassador at Large for War Crimes Issues.

The President announced his intention to appoint Raymond Richard Geddes, Stephen Odland, and Mary E. Peters as members of the National Surface Transportation Policy and Revenue Study Commission.

April 7

In the morning, the President had an intelligence briefing. Later, he participated in a National Security Council meeting on Iraq. He then participated in an interview with business and financial journalists.

In the afternoon, the President had lunch with Vice President Dick Cheney.

April 8

In the morning, the President had an intelligence briefing.

April 10

In the morning, the President had an intelligence briefing. Later, he participated in a photo opportunity with recipients of the Presidential Rank Award of Distinguished Executive.

In the afternoon, the President attended a Homeland Security Council meeting.

The White House announced that the President will welcome Prime Minister Fuad Siniora of Lebanon to the White House on April 18.

The White House announced that the President will welcome President Ilham Aliyev of Azerbaijan to the White House on April 28.

April 11

In the morning, the President had an intelligence briefing. Later, he traveled to Columbia, MO, where, upon arrival, he met with USA Freedom Corps volunteer Doris Hickman. He then traveled to Jefferson City, MO, where he visited Lutheran Senior Services at Heisinger Bluffs retirement community during a Medicare prescription drug plan enrollment session for senior citizens.

In the afternoon, the President traveled to Des Moines, IA, where, upon arrival, he met with USA Freedom Corps volunteer Anjana Chandran. He then visited Wesley Acres retirement community during a Medicare prescription drug plan enrollment session for senior citizens.

In the evening, the President returned to Washington, DC.

April 12

In the morning, the President met with Vice Premier Wu Yi of China to discuss the results of the recent Joint Commission on Commerce and Trade session. Later, he had an intelligence briefing. He then met with Secretary of State Condoleezza Rice.

In the afternoon, in the Yellow Oval Room, the President and Mrs. Bush hosted a social lunch for President John Agyekum Kufuor of Ghana and his wife, Theresa.

Later in the afternoon, the President traveled to Annandale, VA. Later, he returned to Washington, DC.

In the evening, the President and Mrs. Bush hosted a retirement dinner for former U.S. Supreme Court Associate Justice Sandra Day O'Connor and her husband, John.

The White House announced that the President will welcome Chancellor Angela Merkel of Germany to the White House on May 3.

The President declared a major disaster in Arkansas and ordered Federal aid to supplement State and local recovery efforts in the area struck by severe storms and tornadoes from April 1–3.

April 13

In the morning, the President had an intelligence briefing. Later, he had a telephone conversation with President Alejandro Toledo of Peru to congratulate him on the signing of a U.S.-Peru trade agreement.

In the afternoon, the President had lunch with Vice President Dick Cheney. Later, he and Mrs. Bush traveled to Camp David, MD.

The President announced his intention to nominate Anita K. Blair to be Assistant Secretary of the Air Force for Manpower and Reserve Affairs.

The President announced his intention to nominate Anne E. Derse to be Ambassador to Azerbaijan.

The President announced his intention to nominate Robert S. Ford to be Ambassador to Algeria.

The President announced his intention to nominate Mark V. Rosenker to be Chairman of the National Transportation Safety Board.

The President announced his intention to nominate Leslie V. Rowe to be Ambassador to Papua New Guinea, the Solomon Islands, and Vanuatu.

The President announced his intention to nominate Daniel S. Sullivan to be Assistant Secretary of State for Economic and Business Affairs.

The President announced his intention to appoint Craig J. Duchossois and Robert Pacheco as members of the Board of Visitors to the U.S. Naval Academy.

The President declared a major disaster in Kansas and ordered Federal aid to supplement State and local recovery efforts in the area struck by severe storms, tornadoes, and straight-line winds on March 12 and 13.

The President declared a major disaster in Oklahoma and ordered Federal aid to supplement State and local recovery efforts in the area struck by severe storms and tornadoes on March 12.

April 14

In the morning, the President had an intelligence briefing.

April 15

In the morning, the President had an intelligence briefing.

In the afternoon, the President and Mrs. Bush had Easter lunch with family members.

April 16

In the morning, at the Evergreen Chapel at Camp David, MD, the President, Mrs. Bush, and family members attended an Easter Sunday service. Later, he met with U.S. military personnel.

In the afternoon, the President and Mrs. Bush returned to Washington, DC.

April 17

In the morning, the President had an intelligence briefing. Later, on the State Floor, he and Mrs. Bush attended a White House Easter Egg Roll breakfast reception. They then participated in the White House Easter Egg Roll on the South Lawn.

Later in the morning, the President traveled to Sterling, VA, where, upon arrival, he toured Europa Stone Distributors, Inc.

In the afternoon, the President returned to Washington, DC.

The President announced his intention to nominate Paul A. Denett to be Administrator for Federal Procurement Policy at the Office of Management and Budget.

The President announced his intention to appoint the following individuals as members of the U.S. Holocaust Memorial Council:

Debra Abrams;
Esther Jungreis;
Norma Lerner;
Marvin A. Pomerantz;
Alan Neil Rechtschaffen;
J. Philip Rosen;
Elie Wiesel;
Bradley David Wine; and
Judith Yudof.

April 18

In the morning, the President had an intelligence briefing. Later, he traveled to Rockville, MD, where, at the Parkland Magnet Middle School for Aerospace Technology, he met with students and teachers.

In the afternoon, the President returned to Washington, DC.

The President announced his intention to nominate Robert J. Portman to be Director of the Office of Management and Budget.

The President announced his intention to nominate Susan C. Schwab to be U.S. Trade Representative, with the rank of Ambassador.

April 19

In the morning, the President had an intelligence briefing. Later, he met with a children's soccer team from Iraq. He then traveled to Tuskegee, AL, where, upon arrival, he met with USA Freedom Corps volunteer Vester Marable.

Later in the morning, at Tuskegee University, the President participated in a demonstration of nanotechnology research.

In the afternoon, the President returned to Washington, DC.

The President announced that he has appointed Joel D. Kaplan as Assistant to the President and Deputy Chief of Staff for Policy.

The President announced the recess appointment of John L. Palmer and Thomas R. Saving as members of the Boards of Trustees of the Federal Old-Age and Survivors Insurance Trust Fund, the Federal Disability Insurance Trust Fund, the Federal Hospital Insurance Trust Fund, and the Federal Supplementary Medical Insurance Trust Fund.

The President announced the recess appointment of Bertha K. Madras as Deputy Director for Demand Reduction at the Office of National Drug Control Policy.

The President announced the recess appointment of James F.X. O'Gara as Deputy Director for Supply Reduction at the Office of National Drug Control Policy.

April 20

In the morning, the President had an intelligence briefing.

In the afternoon, in the East Room, the President and Mrs. Bush hosted a social lunch and entertainment for President Hu Jintao of China and his wife, Liu Yongqing.

April 21

In the morning, the President had an intelligence briefing. Later, he met with Secretary of State Condoleezza Rice. He then traveled to Moffett Federal Airfield, CA, where, upon arrival, he met with USA Freedom Corps volunteer Joe Russo. While enroute aboard Air Force One, he had in a telephone conversation with Prime Minister-elect Romano Prodi of Italy to congratulate him on his election victory.

Later in the morning, the President traveled to San Jose, CA.

In the afternoon, the President traveled to Stanford, CA, where, at a private residence, he

met with Hoover Institution Fellows. Later, the President had dinner at a private residence.

In the evening, the President traveled to St. Helena, CA.

The White House announced that the President will host Prime Minister Anders Fogh Rasmussen of Denmark at Camp David, MD, on June 9.

April 22

In the morning, the President had an intelligence briefing. Later, in the Los Posados State Forest, he bicycled with the Travis Air Force Base cycling team.

In the afternoon, the President traveled to West Sacramento, CA, where he toured the California Fuel Cell Partnership. Later, he traveled to Palm Springs, CA, where, upon arrival, he met with USA Freedom Corps volunteer Liridon Leti. He then traveled to Indian Wells, CA.

In the evening, the President traveled to Rancho Mirage, CA.

April 23

In the morning, the President had separate telephone conversations with President Jalal Talabani, Speaker of Parliament Mahmoud al-Mashhadani, and Prime Minister-designate Nuri al-Maliki to congratulate them on their new positions and to pledge continued support for democracy in Iraq. The President also had a telephone conversation with U.S. Ambassador to Iraq Zalmay Khalilzad.

Later in the morning, the President traveled to Twentynine Palms, CA, where, in the Protestant Chapel of the Marine Corps Air Ground Combat Center, he attended a church service.

In the afternoon, in the Mess Hall of the Marine Air Ground Combat Center, the President had lunch with Marine Corps and Navy personnel and their family members. Later, he returned to Rancho Mirage, CA.

In the evening, the President met and had dinner with local officials.

April 24

In the morning, the President had an intelligence briefing. Later, he traveled to Santa Ana, CA, where, upon arrival, he met with USA Freedom Corps volunteer Laura Chanan. He then traveled to Irvine, CA.

Later in the morning, the President traveled to Las Vegas, NV, where, upon arrival, he met with USA Freedom Corps volunteer Patty Murphy.

In the afternoon, the President returned to Washington, DC.

The White House announced that the President will welcome President Tabare Vazquez of Uruguay to the White House on May 4.

April 25

In the morning, the President had a telephone conversation with President Mohamed Hosni Mubarak of Egypt to offer condolences for the loss of life due to recent terrorist attacks in Egypt. Later, he had an intelligence briefing. Then, in the Roosevelt Room, he met with Senators to discuss the situation in Iraq.

The President announced his intention to nominate April H. Foley to be Ambassador to Hungary.

The President announced his intention to nominate Tracey Ann Jacobson to be Ambassador to Tajikistan.

The President announced his intention to nominate Kevin J. Martin to be a Commissioner of the Federal Communications Commission and, upon appointment, to designate him as Chairman.

The President announced his intention to nominate Sue C. Payton to be Assistant Secretary of the Air Force for Acquisition, Research, and Development.

The President announced his intention to nominate Steven C. Preston to be Administrator of the Small Business Administration.

The President announced his intention to nominate Gaddi H. Vasquez for the rank of Ambassador during his tenure of service as U.S. Representative to the United Nations Agencies for Food and Agriculture.

The President announced his intention to nominate Lawrence A. Warder to be Chief Financial Officer of the Department of Education.

The President announced his intention to appoint Ralph B. Marquez as a member of the Joint Public Advisory Committee of the Commission for Environmental Cooperation.

The President announced his intention to appoint David A. Ullrich as a Commissioner of the U.S. Section of the Great Lakes Fishery Commission.

The President announced his intention to designate Robert H. Foglesong as Cochairman of the U.S.-Russian Joint Commission on POW/MIAs.

April 26

In the morning, the President had an intelligence briefing. Later, in the Roosevelt Room, he met with Members of Congress to discuss the situation in Iraq.

In the afternoon, the President had lunch with Vice President Dick Cheney. Later, he met with John J. Danilovich, Chief Executive Officer of the Millennium Challenge Corporation. Then, in the Yellow Oval Room, he met with Republican Senators.

In the evening, the President and Mrs. Bush hosted a reception for Republican Members of Congress.

April 27

In the morning, the President had a telephone conversation with Prime Minister Ferenc Gyurcsany of Hungary to congratulate him on his election victory. Later, he had an intelligence briefing. He then traveled to New Orleans, LA, where, upon arrival, he met with USA Freedom Corps volunteer Tris Coffin, Jr.

In the afternoon, on North Roman Street, the President participated in a Habitat for Humanity house rebuilding project. Later, he traveled to Biloxi, MS, where he toured the Hands On Network Gulf Coast Civic Action Center. He then returned to Washington, DC.

The President announced his intention to nominate Robert Anthony Bradtke to be Ambassador to Croatia.

The President announced his intention to nominate Dale Klein to be a Commissioner of the Nuclear Regulatory Commission and, upon appointment, to designate him as Chairman.

The President announced his intention to nominate James B. Lockhart III to be Director of the Office of Federal Housing Enterprise Oversight.

The President announced his intention to nominate the following individuals to be members of the Internal Revenue Service Oversight Board:

Paul Cherecwich, Jr.;
Donald V. Hammond;
Catherine G. West; and
Deborah L. Wince-Smith.

The President announced his intention to appoint the following individuals as members of the President's Council on Physical Fitness and Sports:

John Burke (and, upon appointment, to designate him Chairman);

Dorothy Gay Richardson (and, upon appointment, to designate her Vice Chairman);

Denise Austin;

James N. Baird;

Paul Carrozza;

William Greer;

T.L. Mitchell;

Charles H. Moore, Jr.;

Catherine M. Baase;

Kirk M. Bauer;

Steven Bornstein;

Susan Lieberman Dell;

Lillian Rachelle Green-Chamberlain;

Donna Richardson Joyner;

Edward R. Laskowski;

Elisha Nelson Manning;

Jerry V. Noyce;

Mary Lou Retton;

Andrew Roddick; and

W. Edgar Welden.

The President announced his intention to designate James B. Lockhart III as Acting Director of the Office of Federal Housing Enterprise Oversight.

April 28

In the morning, the President had an intelligence briefing.

April 29

In the morning, the President had an intelligence briefing.

In the evening, at the Washington Hilton Hotel, the President and Mrs. Bush attended the White House Correspondents' Association dinner.

May 1

In the morning, the President had a telephone conversation with President Vladimir V. Putin of Russia. Later, he had an intelligence briefing.

During the day, the President had a telephone conversation with President Umar Hassan Ahmad al-Bashir of Sudan to discuss peace efforts in Sudan.

The President announced his intention to nominate Sheila C. Bair to be Chairman of the Board of Directors of the Federal Deposit Insurance Corporation.

The President announced his intention to nominate John M.R. Kneuer to be Assistant Secretary of Commerce for Communications and Information.

The President announced his intention to nominate Dawn M. Liberi to be Ambassador to Mauritania.

The President announced his intention to nominate William B. Taylor, Jr., to be Ambassador to Ukraine.

The President announced his intention to nominate Michael Wood to be Ambassador to Sweden.

The President announced his intention to appoint the following individuals as members of the Committee for Purchase From People Who Are Blind or Severely Disabled:

Perry E. Anthony;

Robert J. Henke;

Andrew D. Houghton; and

James House.

May 2

In the morning, the President had a telephone conversation with President Hamid Karzai of Afghanistan. Later, he had an intelligence briefing.

In the afternoon, in the Private Dining Room, the President had lunch with Vice President Dick Cheney. Later, in the Oval Office, he met with Republican congressional leaders to discuss legislative priorities.

The President announced his designation of the following individuals as members of a Presidential delegation to San Jose, Costa Rica, to attend the inauguration of President Oscar Arias Sanchez of Cost Rica on May 8: Laura Bush (head of delegation); and Mark Langdale.

The President declared an emergency in Connecticut and ordered Federal aid to supplement State and local recovery efforts in the area struck by record snowfall from February 11–12.

The President declared a major disaster in Hawaii and ordered Federal aid to supplement State and local recovery efforts in the areas struck by severe storms, flooding, landslides, and mudslides from February 20 to April 2.

May 3

In the morning, the President had an intelligence briefing. Later, in the Oval Office, he met with Secretary of Defense Donald H. Rumsfeld.

In the afternoon, on the South Portico, the President participated in a photo opportunity with recipients of the 2005 Presidential Award for Excellence in Mathematics and Science Teaching.

In the evening, at the Residence, the President and Mrs. Bush hosted a dinner for Chancellor Angela Merkel of Germany.

The White House announced that the President will travel to Vienna, Austria, to participate in the U.S.-European Union summit on June 21.

The President announced his intention to nominate Mark Myers to be Director of the U.S. Geological Survey at the Department of the Interior.

The President announced his intention to nominate the following individuals to be members of the National Museum and Library Services Board:

Katherine M.B. Berger;
Karen Brosius;
Ioannis N. Miaoulis;
Sandra Pickett;
Christina Orr-Cahall; and
Kevin Owen Starr.

The President announced his intention to designate James Manning as Acting Assistant Secretary for Postsecondary Education at the Department of Education.

May 4

In the morning, the President had an intelligence briefing. Later, he had a telephone conversation with Prime Minister Abdullah bin Ahmad Badawi of Malaysia.

In the afternoon, the President dropped by a meeting between Secretary of the Security Council of Russia Igor S. Ivanov and National Security Adviser Stephen J. Hadley.

May 5

In the morning, the President had breakfast with Secretary of State Condoleezza Rice. Later, he had an intelligence briefing followed by a National Security Council meeting on Iraq. Then, in the Library, he participated in an interview with Larry Kudlow of CNBC.

In the afternoon, in the Oval Office, the President met with Quartet Special Envoy for Gaza Disengagement James D. Wolfensohn to thank him for his service.

In the evening, at the Marine Barracks, the President and Mrs. Bush participated in a photo opportunity with U.S. Marine Corps Non-commissioned Officers of the Year. They then met with marines wounded in the war on terror. Later, they participated in a briefing by Col. Terry Lockard, USMC, commanding officer, Marine Barracks, Washington.

Later in the evening, the President and Mrs. Bush participated in the evening parade.

May 6

In the morning, the President had an intelligence briefing. Later, he traveled to Stillwater, OK, where, upon arrival, he met with USA Freedom Corps volunteer William O'Connor. While en route aboard Air Force One, he had separate telephone conversations with President Olusegun Obasanjo of Nigeria and President Denis Sassou-Nguesso of the Republic of the Congo to discuss the peace process in Darfur, Sudan. Later, at Oklahoma State University, he met with family members of a soldier killed in Iraq.

Later in the morning, the President returned to Washington, DC, arriving in the afternoon.

May 8

In the morning, the President had an intelligence briefing.

In the afternoon, the President traveled to Fort Lauderdale, FL, where, upon arrival, he met with USA Freedom Corps volunteer David Tompkins. Later, at a private residence, he made remarks at a Friends of Clay Shaw reception.

The White House announced that the President will welcome Prime Minister John Howard of Australia to the White House on May 16.

The President announced the designation of the following individuals as members of a Presidential delegation to Port-au-Prince, Haiti, to attend the inauguration of President Rene Garcia Preval of Haiti on May 14: Jeb Bush (head of delegation); Janet Ann Sanderson; and M. Rony Francois.

The President announced his intention to nominate Troy R. Justesen to be Assistant Secretary for Vocational and Adult Education at the Department of Education.

The President announced his intention to nominate Eric Solomon to be Assistant Secretary of the Treasury for Tax Policy.

The President announced his intention to nominate W. Stuart Symington IV to be Ambassador to Djibouti.

The President announced his intention to nominate Ellen C. Williams to be a Governor of the Board of Governors of the U.S. Postal Service.

The President announced his intention to nominate the following individuals to be members of the National Council on Disability:

John R. Vaughn;
Victoria Ray Carlson;
Chad Colley; and
Lisa Mattheiss.

The President announced his intention to appoint Sean M. Healey as a member of the President's Export Council.

May 9

In the morning, the President had an intelligence briefing. Later, he traveled to Coconut Creek, FL.

Later in the morning, the President traveled to Tampa, FL, where, upon arrival, he met with USA Freedom Corps volunteer Julie Whitney. He then traveled to Sun City Center, FL.

In the afternoon, the President traveled to Orlando, FL, where, upon arrival, he met with USA Freedom Corps volunteer Dick Stipe.

May 10

In the morning, the President had an intelligence briefing. Later, at Norman's Restaurant, he participated in an interview with representatives of Florida's print media.

Later in the morning, the President returned to Washington, DC, arriving in the afternoon.

May 11

In the morning, the President had an intelligence briefing. Later, in the Yellow Oval Room, he met with Chinese human rights activists Li Baiguang, Wang Yi, and Yu Jie.

In the afternoon, the President traveled to Biloxi, MS, where, upon arrival, he met with USA Freedom Corps volunteer Deeneaus Polk.

Later in the afternoon, the President met with family members of soldiers killed in the war on terror. Later, he returned to Washington, DC, arriving in the evening.

The President announced his intention to nominate Gayleatha Beatrice Brown to be Ambassador to Benin.

The President announced his intention to nominate Peter R. Coneway to be Ambassador to Switzerland and Liechtenstein.

The President announced his intention to nominate Christina B. Rocca for the rank of Ambassador during her tenure of service as U.S. Representative to the Conference on Disarmament.

The President announced his intention to nominate William H. Tobey to be Deputy Administrator for Defense Nuclear Nonproliferation in the National Nuclear Security Administration at the Department of Energy.

The President announced his intention to appoint Arthur E. Johnson and Walter B. McCormick, Jr., as members of the President's National Security Telecommunications Advisory Committee.

The President announced his intention to appoint the following individuals as members of the Commission on Presidential Scholars:

Robert A. Gleason, Jr.;
Richard R. Kilgust;
J. Bryan Pickens;
Linda O. Shaw; and
Harvey W. Schiller.

The President announced his intention to appoint the following individuals as members of the Commission for the Preservation of America's Heritage Abroad:

Linda Leuchter Addison;
Ronald H. Bloom;
David A. Burke;
Mordechai E. Gobioff;
Andrew M. Klein;
Elizabeth May Stern;
Robert Zarnegin;
Martin Berson Gold; and
Harley Lippman.

May 12

In the morning, the President had an intelligence briefing.

In the afternoon, the President and Mrs. Bush traveled to Camp David, MD.

May 13

In the morning, the President had an intelligence briefing.

May 14

In the afternoon, the President and Mrs. Bush returned to Washington, DC.

In the evening, at the residence of Australia's Ambassador to the U.S. Dennis Richardson, the

President and Mrs. Bush had dinner with Prime Minister John Howard of Australia and his wife, Janette.

May 15

In the morning, the President had an intelligence briefing followed by a National Security Council meeting on Iraq. Later, in the Oval Office, he participated in a photo opportunity with recipients of the 2006 MATHCOUNTS National Competition Award.

In the afternoon, in the Oval Office, the President received diplomatic credentials from newly appointed Ambassadors to the United States.

The White House announced that the President will welcome Prime Minister Ehud Olmert of Israel to the White House on May 23.

May 16

In the morning, the President had an intelligence briefing.

During the day, the President had separate telephone conversations with Speaker of the House of Representatives J. Dennis Hastert and Senate Majority Leader Bill Frist.

In the evening, in the State Dining Room, the President and Mrs. Bush hosted a state dinner for Prime Minister John Howard of Australia and his wife, Janette, followed by entertainment in the East Room.

The President announced his intention to nominate John Ray Correll to be Director of the Office of Surface Mining Reclamation and Enforcement at the Department of the Interior.

The President announced his intention to nominate John H. Hill to be Administrator of the Federal Motor Carrier Safety Administration.

The President announced his intention to nominate R. Hunter Biden and Donna R. McLean to be members of the Amtrak Reform Board.

The President announced his intention to appoint Norman Y. Mineta as a member of the Amtrak Reform Board.

May 17

In the morning, the President had an intelligence briefing. Later, he participated in a photo opportunity with the Texas A&M Singing Cadets.

The President declared a major disaster in Washington and ordered Federal aid to supple-

ment State and local recovery efforts in the area struck by severe storms, flooding, tidal surge, landslides, and mudslides from January 27 to February 4.

May 18

In the morning, the President had an intelligence briefing. Later, he traveled to Yuma, AZ, where, upon arrival, he toured the Yuma Sector of the U.S.-Mexico border.

In the afternoon, at the Yuma Sector Border Patrol Headquarters, the President participated in a briefing on border security. Later, the President participated in interviews with television networks.

Later in the afternoon, at the Yuma Marine Corps Air Station, the President greeted U.S. military personnel. Later, he returned to Washington, DC, arriving in the evening.

The President announced his intention to nominate Kathleen L. Casey to be a Commissioner of the Securities and Exchange Commission.

The President announced his intention to nominate Donald L. Kohn to be Vice Chairman of the Board of Governors of the Federal Reserve System.

The President announced his intention to appoint Carl E. Schneider as a member of the President's Council on Bioethics.

The President announced his intention to appoint Alan Austerman as a U.S. Commissioner on the U.S. Section of the North Pacific Anadromous Fish Commission (Alaska State Representative).

The President announced his intention to appoint Gary Thomas Smith as a U.S. Commissioner on the U.S. Section of the North Pacific Anadromous Fish Commission (Washington State Representative).

The President announced his intention to appoint Joseph Albert Cirillo, Elizabeth Ann Stewart, and John Charles Wyvill as members of the Architectural and Transportation Barriers Compliance Access Board.

The President announced his intention to appoint the following individuals as members of the Advisory Committee on the Arts at the John F. Kennedy Center for the Performing Arts:

Brittain Bardes Cudlip;
Jody Dow;
Fred Wiehl Lazenby;
Robert D. Leebern, Jr.;

Carole J. McNeil;
Robert Frank Pence;
Larry Ruvo;
Mark S. Siegel;
Stephanie Spencer Tellefsen;
David Carl Weinstein;
Nancy R. Williams; and
Ilene Zatkin-Butler.

The President announced his intention to designate LaSalle Doheny Leffall, Jr., as Chairman of the President's Cancer Panel.

May 19

In the morning, the President had an intelligence briefing. Later, he met with Minister of Foreign Affairs Saud al-Faysal bin Abd al-Aziz Al Saud of Saudi Arabia. He then traveled to Virginia Beach, VA.

In the afternoon, at a private residence, the President attended a Thelma Drake for Congress reception. Later, he traveled to Highland Heights, KY, where, upon arrival, he met with USA Freedom Corps volunteer David Trinh. He then traveled to Florence, KY.

In the evening, the President returned to Washington, DC.

The President announced his intention to appoint Malik M. Hasan as a member of the Advisory Committee on the Arts at the John F. Kennedy Center for the Performing Arts.

The President announced his intention to designate Steven D. Aitken as Acting Administrator of the Office of Information and Regulatory Affairs at the Office of Management and Budget.

May 20

In the morning, the President had an intelligence briefing.

May 21

In the afternoon, the President had a telephone conversation with Mayor C. Ray Nagin of New Orleans to congratulate him on his election victory.

May 22

In the morning, the President had an intelligence briefing. Later, he traveled to Chicago, IL, where, upon arrival, he met with USA Freedom Corps volunteers Barry and Tanya Jeong.

In the afternoon, the President returned to Washington, DC.

May 23

In the morning, the President had an intelligence briefing.

In the evening, the President had a working dinner with Prime Minister Ehud Olmert of Israel.

The White House announced that the President will welcome Prime Minister Tony Blair of the United Kingdom to the White House on May 25.

The White House announced that the President will welcome President Manuel Zelaya Rosales of Honduras to the White House on June 5.

The President announced his designation of the following individuals as members of a Presidential delegation to attend the inauguration of President Ahmed Abdallah Mohamed Sambi of Comoros on May 26: Frederick W. Schieck (head of delegation); and James David McGee.

The President announced his intention to nominate Richard E. Hoagland to be Ambassador to Armenia.

The President announced his intention to nominate Clifford M. Sobel to be Ambassador to Brazil.

May 24

In the morning, the President had an intelligence briefing. Later, in the Rose Garden, he participated in a photo opportunity with members of the President's Council on Physical Fitness and Sports.

In the afternoon, the President traveled to Pottstown, PA, where he participated in a tour of the Limerick Generating Station. Later, at the Saratoga Court Elder Care Center, he greeted residents of Pottstown. He then traveled to Philadelphia, PA, where, upon arrival, he met with USA Freedom Corps volunteer Reggie Waller.

In the evening, the President returned to Washington, DC.

The White House announced that the President and Mrs. Bush will welcome Prime Minister Junichiro Koizumi of Japan to the White House on June 29.

The President announced his intention to nominate Robert O. Blake, Jr., to be Ambassador to Sri Lanka.

The President announced his intention to nominate Elizabeth Dougherty to be a member of the National Mediation Board.

The President announced his intention to nominate Patrick W. Dunne to be Assistant Secretary of Veterans Affairs for Policy and Planning.

The President announced that he has appointed Karl Zinsmeister as Assistant to the President for Domestic Policy.

May 25

In the morning, the President had an intelligence briefing.

In the afternoon, on the South Lawn, the President participated in an arrival ceremony for Prime Minister Tony Blair of the United Kingdom.

The White House announced that the President will welcome President Paul Kagame of Rwanda to the White House on May 31.

The President declared a major disaster in Maine and ordered Federal aid to supplement State and local recovery efforts in the area struck by severe storms and flooding beginning on May 13 and continuing.

The President declared a major disaster in Massachusetts and ordered Federal aid to supplement Commonwealth and local recovery efforts in the area struck by severe storms and flooding beginning on May 12 and continuing.

The President declared a major disaster in New Hampshire and ordered Federal aid to supplement State and local recovery efforts in the area struck by severe storms and flooding beginning on May 12 and continuing.

May 26

In the morning, the President had an intelligence briefing.

In the afternoon, the President and Mrs. Bush traveled to Camp David, MD.

The White House announced that the President will welcome Prime Minister Stephen Harper of Canada to the White House on July 6.

May 27

In the morning, the President had an intelligence briefing. Later, he traveled to Newburgh, NY, where, upon arrival, he met with USA Freedom Corps volunteer Heather DiSilvio. He then traveled to West Point, NY.

Later in the morning, the President returned to Camp David, MD.

In the evening, the President had a telephone conversation with President Susilo Bambang Yudhoyono of Indonesia to express his condolences for the loss of life following the earthquake in Java.

May 28

In the afternoon, the President and Mrs. Bush returned to Washington, DC.

May 29

In the morning, the President had an intelligence briefing. Later, in the Oval Office, he participated in separate bill signing ceremonies for H.R. 1499, the Heroes Earned Retirement Opportunities Act, and H.R. 5037, the Respect for America's Fallen Heroes Act.

In the evening, the President had a private dinner with King Abdullah II of Jordan.

May 30

In the morning, the President had an intelligence briefing. Later, he had a meeting with public policy experts on Iraq.

Later in the morning, the President had separate telephone conversations with President Vladimir V. Putin of Russia, President Jacques Chirac of France, and Chancellor Angela Merkel of Germany to discuss the situation in Iran.

In the evening, in the Family Theater, the President and Mrs. Bush hosted a screening of the film "United 93."

The President announced his intention to nominate Henry M. Paulson, Jr., to be Secretary of the Treasury.

May 31

In the morning, the President had an intelligence briefing. Later, he had separate telephone conversations with President Hamid Karzai of Afghanistan, Prime Minister Junichiro Koizumi of Japan, and Prime Minister Ehud Olmert of Israel.

In the afternoon, the President traveled to CIA Headquarters in Langley, VA. Later, he returned to Washington, DC. He then traveled to Baltimore, MD.

During the day, the President participated in a swearing-in ceremony for Mark J. Sullivan as Director of the U.S. Secret Service.

In the evening, the President returned to Washington, DC.

The President announced his appointment of Raul F. Yanes as Assistant to the President and Staff Secretary.

June 1

In the morning, the President had a telephone conversation with President Hu Jintao of China to discuss the situation in Iran. Later, he had an intelligence briefing.

In the afternoon, the President had lunch with Vice President Dick Cheney.

The White House announced that the President will welcome President Denis Sassou-Nguesso of the Republic of the Congo to the White House on June 5.

The President announced his intention to nominate David H. Laufman to be Inspector General of the Department of Defense.

The President announced his intention to nominate Charles D. Nottingham to be a member of the Surface Transportation Board and, upon confirmation, to designate him as Chairman.

The President announced his intention to nominate Charles Darwin Snelling to be a member of the Board of Directors of the Metropolitan Washington Airports Authority.

The President announced his intention to appoint George Nesterczuk as a member of the Federal Salary Council for Labor Relations and Pay Policy and, upon appointment, to designate him as Vice Chairman.

The President announced his intention to appoint Dallas Rob Sweezy as a member of the President's Committee for People With Intellectual Disabilities and, upon appointment, to designate him as Chair.

The President announced his intention to appoint R. Todd Gardenhire as a member of the Advisory Committee to the Pension Benefit Guaranty Corporation (Employer Representative).

The President announced his intention to appoint Nelson W. Wolff as a member of the Advisory Committee to the Pension Benefit Guaranty Corporation (Public Representative).

June 2

In the morning, the President had an intelligence briefing. Later, he had a telephone conversation with Prime Minister John Howard of Australia to discuss the situations in Iran and East Timor. Then, in the Oval Office, he met with Senior Minister Goh Chok Tong of Singapore.

Later in the morning, the President participated in a photo opportunity with members of the American Society of the Italian Legions of Merit.

The White House announced that the President will welcome President Michelle Bachelet Jeria of Chile to the White House on June 8.

June 3

In the morning, the President had an intelligence briefing.

June 5

In the morning, the President had a telephone conversation with President Vladimir V. Putin of Russia. Later, he had an intelligence briefing. Then, in the Dwight D. Eisenhower Executive Office Building, he met with Chinese Leadership Program Fellows.

The President declared a major disaster in California and ordered Federal aid to supplement State and local recovery efforts in the area struck by severe storms, flooding, landslides, and mudslides from March 29 to April 16.

The President declared a major disaster in Minnesota and ordered Federal aid to supplement State and local recovery efforts in the area struck by flooding from March 30 to May 3.

The President declared a major disaster in North Dakota and ordered Federal aid to supplement State and local recovery efforts in the area struck by severe storms, flooding, and ground saturation from March 30 to April 30.

The President declared a major disaster in South Dakota and ordered Federal aid to supplement State and local recovery efforts in the area struck by a severe winter storm from April 18–20.

June 6

In the morning, the President had an intelligence briefing. Later, he traveled to Artesia, NM, where he participated in a tour of the Federal Law Enforcement Training Center.

In the afternoon, the President traveled to Laredo, TX, where he participated in a tour of the Laredo Border Patrol Sector Headquarters. Later, he visited with staff and students of Mary Help of Christians School. He then visited the Cotulla Style Pit Bar-B-Que restaurant.

Later in the afternoon, the President traveled to Omaha, NE, where, upon arrival, he met with USA Freedom Corps volunteer John "Buzz" Garlock.

The White House announced that the President will travel to St. Petersburg, Russia, to attend the G–8 summit on July 15–17.

The President announced his intention to nominate Wayne Cartwright Beyer to be a member of the Federal Labor Relations Authority.

The President announced his intention to nominate Cesar Benito Cabrera to be Ambassador to Mauritius and the Seychelles.

The President announced his intention to nominate Robert L. Sumwalt III to be a member of the National Transportation Safety Board and, upon confirmation, to designate him as Vice Chair.

The President announced his intention to nominate Colleen Conway-Welch and C. Thomas Yarington, Jr., to be members of the Board of Regents of the Uniformed Services University for Health Sciences.

The President announced his intention to designate Lt. Gen. Ronald L. Burgess, Jr., as Acting Principal Deputy Director of National Intelligence.

June 7

In the morning, the President had an intelligence briefing. Later, he visited Catholic Charities—Juan Diego Center, where he participated in a microbusiness networking breakfast and a U.S. citizenship class.

Also in the morning, the President had separate telephone conversations with President Elias Antonio Saca Gonzalez of El Salvador and President-elect Alan Garcia Perez of Peru.

In the afternoon, the President returned to Washington, DC. Later, he met with Republican congressional leaders. He then met with Members of Congress who had recently traveled to Iraq.

In the evening, National Security Adviser Stephen J. Hadley briefed the President on the death of senior Al Qaida associate Abu Musab Al Zarqawi in Baquba, Iraq, following U.S. airstrikes.

The White House announced that the President will welcome President Alvaro Uribe Velez of Colombia to the White House on June 14.

The White House announced that the President will host Prime Minister Janez Jansa of Slovenia at the White House on July 10.

June 8

In the morning, the President had separate telephone conversations with Prime Minister Tony Blair of the United Kingdom and Prime Minister Nuri al-Maliki of Iraq to discuss the death of Abu Musab Al Zarqawi in Baquba, Iraq, on June 7. Later, he had an intelligence briefing.

In the afternoon, the President had lunch with President Michelle Bachelet Jeria of Chile. Later, in the Roosevelt Room, he met with President Vaira Vike-Freiberga of Latvia. He and Mrs. Bush then traveled to Camp David, MD.

The White House announced that the President will travel to Budapest, Hungary, on June 22, following his participation in the U.S.-European Union summit in Vienna, Austria.

June 9

In the morning, the President had an intelligence briefing.

In the afternoon, the President and Mrs. Bush had lunch with Prime Minister Anders Fogh Rasmussen of Denmark and his wife, Anne-Mette.

The President announced his intention to nominate Randall M. Fort to be Assistant Secretary of State for Intelligence and Research.

The President announced his intention to nominate Margo M. McKay to be Assistant Secretary of Agriculture for Civil Rights.

The President announced his intention to nominate Stephen S. McMillin to be Deputy Director of the Office of Management and Budget.

The President announced his intention to nominate Drue Pearce to be Federal Coordinator for Alaska Natural Gas Transportation Projects.

The President announced his intention to nominate Marc Spitzer to be a member of the Federal Energy Regulatory Commission.

June 10

In the morning, the President had an intelligence briefing.

June 11

In the afternoon, the President returned to Washington, DC.

June 12

In the morning, the President had an intelligence briefing. Then, on the North Portico, he participated in a photo opportunity with members of the World Cup youth delegation.

Later in the morning, the President traveled to Camp David, MD.

In the evening, the President traveled to Baghdad, Iraq, arriving the following afternoon.

June 13

In the morning, while en route to Baghdad, Iraq, the President had an intelligence briefing.

In the afternoon, at the U.S. Embassy in Baghdad, the President met with Prime Minister Nuri al-Maliki of Iraq. Later, he met with Prime Minister Maliki, the Iraqi Cabinet, and the President's Cabinet, participating from Camp David, MD, through video teleconference. He then had separate meetings with President Jalal Talabani and Speaker of the Council of Representatives Mahmoud al-Mashhadani of Iraq and Iraqi business, cultural, and education leaders.

In the evening, the President returned to Washington, DC, arriving the following morning. While en route aboard Air Force One, he participated in an interview with radio and television reporters.

The White House announced that the President and Mrs. Bush will accompany Prime Minister Junichiro Koizumi of Japan to Memphis, TN, on June 30 following Prime Minister Koizumi's visit to the White House on June 29.

June 14

In the morning, the President had an intelligence briefing.

June 15

In the morning, the President had an intelligence briefing. Later, in the Oval Office, he participated in a swearing-in ceremony for U.S. Trade Representative Susan C. Schwab. Then, in the Dwight D. Eisenhower Executive Office Building, he met with Randal L. McCloy, Jr., the only survivor of a January mining accident in Sago, WV, and his wife, Anna.

In the afternoon, the President had lunch with Vice President Dick Cheney.

The President announced his intention to nominate Geoffrey S. Bacino to be a member of the Board of Directors of the Federal Housing Finance Board.

The President announced his intention to nominate Michael V. Dunn to be a Commissioner of the Commodity Futures Trading Commission.

The President announced his intention to nominate Thomas C. Foley to be Ambassador to Ireland.

The President announced his intention to nominate Nancy Montanez-Johner to be Under Secretary of Agriculture for Food, Nutrition, and Consumer Services and a member of the Board of Directors of the Commodity Credit Corporation.

The President announced his intention to nominate the following individuals to be members of the National Council on the Humanities:

Josiah Bunting III;
Mary Habeck;
Robert S. Martin;
Wilfred M. McClay;
Manfredi Piccolomini;
Jay Winik; and
Kenneth R. Weinstein.

The President announced his intention to nominate the following individuals to be members of the National Science Board of the National Science Foundation:

Mark R. Abbott;
Camilla Persson Benbow;
John T. Bruer;
Patricia D. Galloway;
Jose-Marie Griffiths;
Karl Hess;
Thomas N. Taylor; and
Richard F. Thompson.

The President announced his intention to appoint the following individuals as members of the President's Council on Service and Civic Participation:

Janine L. Gauntt;
Angela Baraquio Grey;
Kelly Perdew; and
Daniel C. Wuerffel.

The President announced his intention to designate Jean M. Case as Chairman of the President's Council on Service and Civic Participation.

The President announced his intention to designate Daniel Pearson as Chairman of the U.S. International Trade Commission.

The President announced his intention to designate Shara L. Aranoff as Vice Chairman of the U.S. International Trade Commission.

June 16

In the morning, the President had an intelligence briefing. Later, he traveled to Seattle, WA, where, upon arrival at the Boeing Field/King County International Airport, he met with USA Freedom Corps volunteer Norma McQuiller. He then traveled to Medina, WA, where, at a private residence, he attended a reception for congressional candidate David G. Reichert and the Washington State Republican Party.

In the afternoon, the President traveled to Albuquerque, NM, where, upon arrival, he met with USA Freedom Corps volunteer Patricia Ortiz. Later, he traveled to the Bush Ranch in Crawford, TX.

June 17

In the morning, the President had an intelligence briefing.

June 18

In the afternoon, the President and Mrs. Bush returned to Washington, DC.

June 19

In the morning, the President had an intelligence briefing. Later, he traveled to New York City, NY, where, upon arrival, he met with USA Freedom Corps volunteer Christopher Branning. He then traveled to Kings Point, NY.

In the afternoon, the President returned to Washington, DC.

The White House announced that the President will welcome President Mikheil Saakashvili of Georgia to the White House on July 5.

June 20

In the morning, the President had an intelligence briefing. Later, he and Mrs. Bush traveled to Vienna, Austria, arriving in the evening.

The President announced his intention to nominate William B. Wark and William E. Wright to be members of the Chemical Safety and Hazard Investigation Board.

The President announced his intention to nominate Robert L. Wilkie to be Assistant Secretary of Defense for Legislative Affairs.

The President announced his intention to nominate Warren Bell, Chris Boskin, and David H. Pryor to be members of the Board of Directors of the Corporation for Public Broadcasting.

The President announced his intention to appoint Edmund G. Archuleta, David Michael Cote, and James B. Nicholson as members of the National Infrastructure Advisory Council.

The President announced his intention to appoint Susan Schanlaber Barnes as a member of the the Advisory Council on Historic Preservation and, upon appointment, to designate her Vice Chair.

The President announced his intention to appoint Rhonda Bentz as a member of the Advisory Council on Historic Preservation.

The President announced his intention to appoint Benjamin K. Homan and David A. Williams as members of the Helping To Enhance the Livelihood of People (HELP) Around the Globe Commission.

The President announced his intention to appoint the following individuals as members of the Community Development Advisory Board:

Jennings David Colbert (Native American Tribal Development Representative);

J. French Hill (Insured Depository Institution Representative);

Farah M. Jimenez (Community Development Representative);

Jack Lund (Consumer/Public Interest Organization Representative); and

L. Raymond Moncrief (Community Development Financial Institution Representative).

The President announced his intention to designate Michael W. Smith as Vice Chair of the President's Council on Service and Civic Participation.

June 21

In the morning, the President had an intelligence briefing. Later, in the Johann Strauss Ballroom of Hofburg Palace, he and Mrs. Bush greeted U.S. Embassy personnel. Then, in the Hunting Room, he met with President Heinz Fischer of Austria.

Later in the morning, in the Mittlere Lounge of Hofburg Palace, the President met with Chancellor Wolfgang Schuessel of Austria. He then met with European Union leaders. Later, in the Grosser Redoutensaal Room at Hofburg Palace, he participated in the U.S.-European Union summit.

In the afternoon, the President had a working lunch with European Union leaders. Later, he and Mrs. Bush toured the Austrian National Library, where they watched a performance by the Vienna Boys Choir.

In the evening, the President and Mrs. Bush traveled to Budapest, Hungary.

June 22

In the morning, the President had an intelligence briefing. Later, he greeted U.S. Embassy personnel. Then, at Sandor Palace, he and Mrs. Bush participated in an arrival ceremony.

Later in the morning, in the conference hall of the Parliament Building, the President had separate meetings with Speaker of Parliament Katalin Szili and Hungarian political party leaders.

In the afternoon, the President and Mrs. Bush participated in a wreath-laying ceremony at the 1956 Memorial Monument.

In the evening, the President and Mrs. Bush returned to Washington, DC.

The President announced his intention to nominate Linda Mysliwy Conlin to be First Vice President of the Export-Import Bank of the United States.

The President announced his intention to nominate J. Joseph Grandmaison to be a member of the Board of Directors of the Export-Import Bank of the United States.

The President announced his intention to nominate Thomas E. Harvey to be Assistant Secretary of Veterans Affairs for Congressional Affairs.

The President announced his intention to nominate Roger L. Hunt, John E. Kidde, and John Peyton to be members of the Board of Trustees of the Harry S. Truman Scholarship Foundation.

June 23

In the morning, the President had an intelligence briefing. Later, he met with experts on Russia.

In the afternoon, the President met with Gen. George W. Casey, Jr., USA, commanding general, Multi-National Force—Iraq.

The President announced that he has appointed John Emling as Special Assistant to the President for Legislative Affairs.

The President announced that he has appointed Julie Goon as Special Assistant to the President for Economic Policy.

The President announced that he has appointed Hunter Moorhead as Special Assistant to the President for Agriculture, Trade, and Food Assistance.

The President announced that he has appointed John M. Smith as Associate Counsel to the President.

June 24

In the morning, the President had an intelligence briefing.

June 25

In the evening, the President and Mrs. Bush attended the Ford's Theatre Gala, where he made remarks for television broadcast on July 4.

June 26

In the morning, the President had an intelligence briefing. Later, in the East Room, he participated in a photo opportunity with the 2006 Presidential Scholars.

In the afternoon, at the historic Evermay house, the President made remarks at a Republican National Committee finance luncheon.

June 27

In the morning, the President had an intelligence briefing. Later, he met with Senators to discuss proposed line-item veto legislation.

In the afternoon, in the Oval Office, the President participated in a photo opportunity with S. Sgt. Christian Bagge, USA, who was wounded in Iraq in June 2005.

The President announced his intention to nominate Jay M. Cohen to be Under Secretary for Science and Technology at the Department of Homeland Security.

The President announced his intention to nominate Sean T. Connaughton to be Administrator of the Maritime Administration at the Department of Transportation.

The President announced his intention to nominate the following individuals to be members of the National Institute for Literacy Advisory Board:

Carmel Borders;
Donald D. Deshler;
Blanca E. Enriquez;
Patricia Mathes;
Eliza McFadden; and
Timothy Shanahan.

June 28

In the morning, the President had an intelligence briefing. Later, he met with Secretary of Defense Donald H. Rumsfeld.

In the afternoon, the President traveled to St. Louis, MO, where, upon arrival, he met with 2006 Presidential Scholar J. Andrew Benecke and USA Freedom Corps volunteer Susan Reese.

In the evening, the President returned to Washington, DC.

The White House announced that the President will travel to Stralsund and Trinwillershagen, Germany, on July 13 to meet with Chancellor Angela Merkel of Germany.

June 29

In the morning, the President had an intelligence briefing.

In the evening, in the Grand Foyer, the President and Mrs. Bush participated in a photo opportunity with Prime Minister Junichiro Koizumi of Japan. Later, in the State Dining Room, he and Mrs. Bush hosted an official dinner for Prime Minister Koizumi, followed by entertainment in the East Room.

The President made additional disaster assistance available to areas of Louisiana impacted by Hurricane Katrina.

The President made additional disaster assistance available to areas of Mississippi impacted by Hurricane Katrina.

June 30

In the morning, the President had an intelligence briefing. Later, he and Mrs. Bush traveled with Prime Minister Junichiro Koizumi of Japan to Memphis, TN, where they participated in a tour of Elvis Presley's Graceland mansion.

In the afternoon, at the Rendezvous restaurant, the President and Mrs. Bush had lunch with Prime Minister Koizumi.

Later in the afternoon, the President met with USA Freedom Corps volunteer Sandi Langley before traveling to Columbus, OH, where, at a private residence, he attended a Mike DeWine for U.S. Senate reception.

In the evening, the President traveled to Camp David, MD.

The President announced his intention to appoint Lynette Boggs McDonald as a member of the Board of Visitors to the U.S. Naval Academy.

The President announced his intention to appoint Jason Edward Allen and William S. Gates as members of the Board of Trustees of the Christopher Columbus Fellowship Foundation.

The President announced that he has nominated Frank R. Jimenez to be General Counsel of the Department of the Navy.

The President announced that he has nominated Donald C. Johnson to be Ambassador to Equitorial Guinea.

The President announced that he has nominated Bruce I. Knight to be Under Secretary of Agriculture for Marketing and Regulatory Programs and a member of the Board of Directors of the Commodity Credit Corporation.

The President announced that he has nominated Charles E. McQueary to be Director of Operational Test and Evaluation at the Department of Defense.

The President announced that he has nominated Frederic S. Mishkin to be a member of the Board of Governors of the Federal Reserve System (1st District).

The President announced that he has nominated Edmund C. Moy to be Director of the Mint.

The President announced that he has nominated Nathaniel F. Wienecke to be Assistant Secretary of Commerce for Legislative and Intergovernmental Affairs.

The President announced that he has designated Paul J. Hutter as Acting Assistant Secretary of Veterans Affairs for Policy and Planning.

The President declared a major disaster in Pennsylvania and ordered Federal aid to supplement Commonwealth and local recovery efforts in the area struck by severe storms, flooding, and mudslides beginning on June 23 and continuing.

Appendix B—Nominations Submitted to the Senate

The following list does not include promotions of members of the Uniformed Services, nominations to the Service Academies, or nominations of Foreign Service officers.

Submitted January 18

Ben S. Bernanke,
of New Jersey, to be U.S. Alternate Governor of the International Monetary Fund for a term of 5 years, vice Alan Greenspan.

Donald T. Bliss,
of Maryland, for the rank of Ambassador during his tenure of service as Representative of the United States of America on the Council of the International Civil Aviation Organization.

Richard A. Boucher,
of Maryland, a career member of the Senior Foreign Service, class of Career Minister, to be Assistant Secretary of State for South Asian Affairs, vice Christina B. Rocca.

Gale A. Buchanan,
of Georgia, to be Under Secretary of Agriculture for Research, Education, and Economics, vice Joseph J. Jen, resigned.

Patricia A. Butenis,
of Virginia, a career member of the Senior Foreign Service, class of Minister-Counselor, to be Ambassador Extraordinary and Plenipotentiary of the United States of America to the People's Republic of Bangladesh.

Robert M. Couch,
of Alabama, to be President, Government National Mortgage Association, vice Ronald Rosenfeld.

Tyler D. Duvall,
of Virginia, to be an Assistant Secretary of Transportation, vice Emil H. Frankel.

Preston M. Geren,
of Texas, to be Under Secretary of the Army, vice R.L. Brownlee, resigned.

James B. Gulliford,
of Missouri, to be Assistant Administrator for Toxic Substances of the Environmental Protection Agency, vice Stephen L. Johnson, resigned.

Roger Shane Karr,
of the District of Columbia, to be an Assistant Secretary of Transportation, vice Nicole R. Nason.

Nicole R. Nason,
of Virginia, to be Administrator of the National Highway Traffic Safety Administration, vice Jeffrey William Runge.

David L. Norquist,
of Virginia, to be Chief Financial Officer, Department of Homeland Security, vice Andrew B. Maner.

David C. Sanborn,
of Virginia, to be Administrator of the Maritime Administration, vice William Schubert.

Jackie Wolcott Sanders,
of Virginia, to be an Alternate Representative of the United States of America to the Sessions of the General Assembly of the United Nations during her tenure of service as Alternate Representative of the United States of America for Special Political Affairs in the United Nations.

Jackie Wolcott Sanders,
of Virginia, to be Alternate Representative of the United States of America for Special Political Affairs in the United Nations, with the rank of Ambassador.

John A. Simon,
of Maryland, to be Executive Vice President of the Overseas Private Investment Corporation, vice Ross J. Connelly, resigned.

James S. Simpson,
of New York, to be Federal Transit Administrator, vice Jennifer L. Dorn.

Mark D. Wallace,
of Florida, to be Alternate Representative of the United States of America to the Sessions

of the General Assembly of the United Nations, during his tenure of service as Representative of the United States of America to the United Nations for U.N. Management and Reform.

Mark D. Wallace,
of Florida, to be Representative of the United States of America to the United Nations for U.N. Management and Reform, with the rank of Ambassador, vice Patrick Francis Kennedy.

Withdrawn January 18

Eugene Hickok,
of Pennsylvania, to be a member of the National Council on the Humanities for the remainder of the term expiring January 26, 2008, vice Sidney McPhee, which was sent to the Senate on October 17, 2005.

Submitted January 25

Thomas J. Barrett,
of Alaska, to be Administrator of the Pipeline and Hazardous Materials Safety Administration, Department of Transportation (new position).

Steven G. Bradbury,
of Maryland, to be an Assistant Attorney General, vice Jack Landman Goldsmith III, resigned.

Vanessa Lynne Bryant,
of Connecticut, to be U.S. District Judge for the District of Connecticut, vice Dominic J. Squatrito, retired.

Renee Marie Bumb,
of New Jersey, to be U.S. District Judge for the District of New Jersey, vice William H. Walls, retired.

Michael A. Chagares,
of New Jersey, to be U.S. Circuit Judge for the Third Circuit, vice Michael Chertoff, resigned.

Rajkumar Chellaraj,
of Texas, to be an Assistant Secretary of State (Administration), vice William A. Eaton, resigned.

Brian M. Cogan,
of New York, to be U.S. District Judge for the Eastern District of New York, vice Frederic Block, retired.

Thomas M. Golden,
of Pennsylvania, to be U.S. District Judge for the Eastern District of Pennsylvania, vice Franklin Van Antwerpen, elevated.

S. Pamela Gray,
of the District of Columbia, to be an Associate Judge of the Superior Court of the District of Columbia for the term of 15 years, vice Susan Rebecca Holmes, retired.

Andrew J. Guilford,
of California, to be U.S. District Judge for the Central District of California, vice Dickran M. Tevrizian, Jr., retired.

Noel Lawrence Hillman,
of New Jersey, to be U.S. District Judge for the District of New Jersey, vice William G. Bassler, retired.

Brett M. Kavanaugh,
of Maryland, to be U.S. Circuit Judge for the District of Columbia Circuit, vice Laurence H. Silberman, retired.

Gray Hampton Miller,
of Texas, to be U.S. District Judge for the Southern District of Texas, vice Ewing Werlein, Jr., retired.

Richard T. Miller,
of Texas, to be an Alternate Representative of the United States of America to the Sessions of the General Assembly of the United Nations during his tenure of service as Representative of the United States of America on the Economic and Social Council of the United Nations.

Richard T. Miller,
of Texas, to be Representative of the United States of America on the Economic and Social Council of the United Nations, with the rank of Ambassador.

Susan Davis Wigenton,
of New Jersey, to be U.S. District Judge for the District of New Jersey, vice John W. Bissell, retired.

Submitted January 27

Thomas P. D'Agostino,
of Maryland, to be Deputy Administrator for Defense Programs, National Nuclear Security Administration, vice Everet Beckner, resigned.

Randall S. Kroszner,
of New Jersey, to be a member of the Board of Governors of the Federal Reserve System for the unexpired term of 14 years from February 1, 1994, vice Edward M. Gramlich, resigned.

Boyd Kevin Rutherford,
of Maryland, to be an Assistant Secretary of Agriculture, vice Michael J. Harrison, resigned.

Kevin M. Warsh,
of New York, to be a member of the Board of Governors of the Federal Reserve System for the unexpired term of 14 years from February 1, 2004, vice Ben S. Bernanke, resigned.

Submitted January 31

W. Ralph Basham,
of Virginia, to be Commissioner of Customs, Department of Homeland Security, vice Robert C. Bonner, resigned.

Paul DeCamp,
of Virginia, to be Administrator of the Wage and Hour Division, Department of Labor, vice Tammy Dee McCutchen, resigned.

Edward P. Lazear,
of California, to be a member of the Council of Economic Advisers, vice Ben S. Bernanke.

Jeffrey L. Sedgwick,
of Massachusetts, to be Director of the Bureau of Justice Statistics, vice Lawrence A. Greenfeld, resigned.

Submitted February 6

Armando J. Bucelo, Jr.,
of Florida, to be a director of the Securities Investor Protection Corporation for a term expiring December 31, 2008 (reappointment).

Benedict S. Cohen,
of the District of Columbia, to be General Counsel of the Department of the Army, vice Steven John Morello, Sr., resigned.

Todd S. Farha,
of Florida, to be a director of the Securities Investor Protection Corporation for the remainder of the term expiring December 31, 2006, vice William Robert Timken, Jr., resigned.

Todd S. Farha,
of Florida, to be a director of the Securities Investor Protection Corporation for a term expiring December 31, 2009 (reappointment).

Robert M. McDowell,
of Virginia, to be a member of the Federal Communications Commission for a term of 5 years from July 1, 2004, vice Kathleen Q. Abernathy, resigned.

Mauricio J. Tamargo,
of Florida, to be Chairman of the Foreign Claims Settlement Commission of the United States for a term expiring September 30, 2009 (reappointment).

Submitted February 8

Patricia P. Brister,
of Louisiana, for the rank of Ambassador during her tenure of service as the Representative of the United States of America on the Commission on the Status of Women of the Economic and Social Council of the United Nations.

Sandra Segal Ikuta,
of California, to be U.S. Circuit Judge for the Ninth Circuit, vice James R. Browning, retired.

Michael Brunson Wallace,
of Mississippi, to be U.S. Circuit Judge for the Fifth Circuit, vice Charles W. Pickering, Sr., retired.

Submitted February 10

Gordon England,
of Texas, to be Deputy Secretary of Defense, vice Paul D. Wolfowitz, resigned, to which position he was appointed during the last recess of the Senate.

Stephen Goldsmith,
of Indiana, to be a member of the Board of Directors of the Corporation for National and Community Service for a term expiring October 6, 2010 (reappointment), to which position he was appointed during the last recess of the Senate.

C. Boyden Gray,
of the District of Columbia, to be Representative of the United States of America to the European Union, with the rank and status of Ambassador Extraordinary and Plenipotentiary, vice Rockwell A. Schnabel, resigned, to which

position he was appointed during the last recess of the Senate.

Floyd Hall,
of New Jersey, to be a member of the Reform Board (Amtrak) for a term of 5 years (reappointment), to which position he was appointed during the last recess of the Senate.

Tracy A. Henke,
of Missouri, to be Executive Director of the Office of State and Local Government Coordination and Preparedness, Department of Homeland Security, vice C. Suzanne Mencer, resigned, to which position she was appointed during the last recess of the Senate.

Nadine Hogan,
of Florida, to be a member of the Board of Directors of the Inter-American Foundation for a term expiring June 26, 2008 (reappointment), to which position she was appointed during the last recess of the Senate.

Peter N. Kirsanow,
of Ohio, to be a member of the National Labor Relations Board for the term of 5 years expiring August 27, 2008, vice Ronald E. Meisburg, to which position he was appointed during the last recess of the Senate.

Robert D. Lenhard,
of Maryland, to be a member of the Federal Election Commission for a term expiring April 30, 2011, vice Danny Lee McDonald, term expired, to which position he was appointed during the last recess of the Senate.

Ronald E. Meisburg,
of Virginia, to be General Counsel of the National Labor Relations Board for a term of 4 years, vice Arthur F. Rosenfeld, term expired, to which position he was appointed during the last recess of the Senate.

Julie L. Myers,
of Kansas, to be an Assistant Secretary of Homeland Security, vice Michael J. Garcia, resigned, to which position she was appointed during the last recess of the Senate.

Benjamin A. Powell,
of Florida, to be General Counsel of the Office of the Director of National Intelligence (new position), to which position he was appointed during the last recess of the Senate.

Arthur F. Rosenfeld,
of Virginia, to be Federal Mediation and Conciliation Director, vice Peter J. Hurtgen, resigned, to which position he was appointed during the last recess of the Senate.

Ellen R. Sauerbrey,
of Maryland, to be an Assistant Secretary of State (Population, Refugees, and Migration), vice Arthur E. Dewey, resigned, to which position she was appointed during the last recess of the Senate.

Dorrance Smith,
of Virginia, to be an Assistant Secretary of Defense, vice Victoria Clarke, resigned, to which position he was appointed during the last recess of the Senate.

Enrique J. Sosa,
of Florida, to be a member of the Reform Board (Amtrak) for a term of 5 years (reappointment), to which position he was appointed during the last recess of the Senate.

Hans von Spakovsky,
of Georgia, to be a member of the Federal Election Commission for a term expiring April 30, 2011, vice Bradley A. Smith, resigned, to which position he was appointed during the last recess of the Senate.

Roger W. Wallace,
of Texas, to be a member of the Board of Directors of the Inter-American Foundation for a term expiring October 6, 2008 (reappointment), to which position he was appointed during the last recess of the Senate.

Dennis P. Walsh,
of Maryland, to be a member of the National Labor Relations Board for the term of 5 years expiring December 16, 2009 (reappointment), to which position he was appointed during the last recess of the Senate.

Steven T. Walther,
of Nevada, to be a member of the Federal Election Commission for a term expiring April 30, 2009, vice Scott E. Thomas, term expired, to which position he was appointed during the last recess of the Senate.

Andrew B. Steinberg,
of Maryland, to be an Assistant Secretary of Transportation, vice Karan K. Bhatia.

Submitted February 13

Robert Irwin Cusick, Jr.,
of Kentucky, to be Director of the Office of
Government Ethics for a term of 5 years, vice
Amy L. Comstock, resigned.

Donald J. DeGabrielle, Jr.,
of Texas, to be U.S. Attorney for the Southern
District of Texas for the term of 4 years, vice
Michael Taylor Shelby.

James Lambright,
of Missouri, to be President of the Export-Import Bank of the United States for a term expiring January 20, 2009, vice Philip Merrill, resigned.

Dennis R. Spurgeon,
of Florida, to be an Assistant Secretary of Energy (Nuclear Energy) (new position).

Submitted February 14

Jerome A. Holmes,
of Oklahoma, to be U.S. District Judge for the
Northern District of Oklahoma, vice Sven E.
Holmes, resigned.

Jon T. Rymer,
of Tennessee, to be Inspector General, Federal
Deposit Insurance Corporation, vice Gaston L.
Gianni, Jr.

Milan D. Smith, Jr.,
of California, to be U.S. Circuit Judge for the
Ninth Circuit, vice A. Wallace Tashima, retired.

Frank D. Whitney,
of North Carolina, to be U.S. District Judge
for the Western District of North Carolina, vice
H. Brent McKnight, deceased.

Submitted February 17

Linda Avery Strachan,
of Virginia, to be an Assistant Secretary of Agriculture, vice Mary Kirtley Waters.

Randall L. Tobias,
of Indiana, to be Administrator of the U.S.
Agency for International Development, vice Andrew S. Natsios, resigned.

David F. Kustoff,
of Tennessee, to be U.S. Attorney for the Western District of Tennessee for the term of 4
years, vice Terrell Lee Harris, resigned.

John Charles Richter,
of Oklahoma, to be U.S. Attorney for the Western District of Oklahoma for the term of 4
years, vice Robert Garner McCampbell, resigned.

Amul R. Thapar,
of Kentucky, to be U.S. Attorney for the Eastern
District of Kentucky for the term of 4 years,
vice Gregory F. Van Tatenhove, resigned.

Submitted February 27

John G. Emling,
of Pennsylvania, to be an Assistant Secretary
of Commerce, vice Brett T. Palmer, resigned.

Timothy Anthony Junker,
of Iowa, to be U.S. Marshal for the Northern
District of Iowa for the term of 4 years, vice
John Edward Quinn.

Patrick Carroll Smith, Sr.,
of Maryland, to be U.S. Marshal for the Western
District of North Carolina for the term of 4
years, vice Gregory Allyn Forest, resigned.

William Ludwig Wehrum, Jr.,
of Tennessee, to be an Assistant Administrator
of the Environmental Protection Agency, vice
Jeffrey R. Holmstead, resigned.

Submitted March 2

Mickey D. Barnett,MDNM
of New Mexico, to be a Governor of the U.S.
Postal Service for a term expiring December
8, 2013, vice Robert F. Rider, term expired.

John W. Cox,
of Texas, to be Chief Financial Officer, Department of Housing and Urban Development, vice
Carin M. Barth, resigned.

George McDade Staples,
of Kentucky, a career member of the Senior
Foreign Service, class of Minister-Counselor, to
be Director General of the Foreign Service, vice
W. Robert Pearson, resigned.

Katherine C. Tobin,
of New York, to be a Governor of the U.S.
Postal Service for a term expiring December
8, 2012, vice S. David Fineman, term expired.

Submitted March 7

Jerry Gayle Bridges,
of Virginia, to be Chief Financial Officer, Corporation for National and Community Service, vice Michelle Guillermin, resigned.

Richard Capka,
of Pennsylvania, to be Administrator of the Federal Highway Administration, vice Mary E. Peters, resigned.

Robert F. Godec,
of Virginia, a career member of the Senior Foreign Service, class of Counselor, to be Ambassador Extraordinary and Plenipotentiary of the United States of America to the Republic of Tunisia.

Philip D. Moeller,
of Washington, to be a member of the Federal Energy Regulatory Commission for the term expiring June 30, 2010, vice Patrick Henry Wood III, resigned.

Michael E. Ranneberger,
of Virginia, a career member of the Senior Foreign Service, class of Minister-Counselor, to be Ambassador Extraordinary and Plenipotentiary of the United States of America to the Republic of Kenya.

Jon Wellinghoff,
of Nevada, to be a member of the Federal Energy Regulatory Commission for the term expiring June 30, 2008, vice William Lloyd Massey, term expired.

Withdrawn March 7

James Hardy Payne,
of Oklahoma, to be U.S. Circuit Judge for the Tenth Circuit, vice Stephanie K. Seymour, retired, which was sent to the Senate on September 29, 2005.

Submitted March 13

Jonann C. Chiles,
of Arkansas, to be a member of the Board of Directors of the Legal Services Corporation for a term expiring July 13, 2008, vice Robert J. Dieter, resigned.

Robert D. McCallum, Jr.,
of Georgia, to be Ambassador Extraordinary and Plenipotentiary of the United States of America to Australia.

J.C.A. Stagg,
of Virginia, to be a member of the Board of Trustees of the James Madison Memorial Fellowship Foundation for a term expiring November 17, 2011, vice Jay Phillip Greene, term expired.

Kenneth L. Wainstein,
of Virginia, to be an Assistant Attorney General (new position).

Submitted March 15

Mark C. Minton,
of Florida, a career member of the Senior Foreign Service, class of Minister-Counselor, to be Ambassador Extraordinary and Plenipotentiary of the United States of America to Mongolia.

John A. Rizzo,
of the District of Columbia, to be General Counsel of the Central Intelligence Agency, vice Scott W. Muller, resigned.

Warren W. Tichenor,
of Texas, to be Representative of the United States of America to the Office of the United Nations and Other International Organizations in Geneva, with the rank of Ambassador, vice Kevin E. Moley.

Andrew von Eschenbach,
of Texas, to be Commissioner of Food and Drugs, Department of Health and Human Services, vice Lester M. Crawford, resigned.

Submitted March 27

Ronald S. Cooper,
of Virginia, to be General Counsel of the Equal Employment Opportunity Commission for a term of 4 years, vice Eric S. Dreiband, resigned.

Harry R. Hoglander,
of Massachusetts, to be a member of the National Mediation Board for a term expiring July 1, 2008 (reappointment).

Michael D. Kirby,
of Virginia, a career member of the Senior Foreign Service, class of Minister-Counselor, to be Ambassador Extraordinary and Plenipotentiary

of the United States of America to the Republic of Moldova.

Molly A. O'Neill,
of Virginia, to be an Assistant Administrator of the Environmental Protection Agency, vice Kimberly Terese Nelson.

Peter W. Tredick,
of California, to be a member of the National Mediation Board for a term expiring July 1, 2007, vice Edward J. Fitzmaurice, Jr., term expired.

Withdrawn March 27

Henry W. Saad,
of Michigan, to be U.S. Circuit Judge for the Sixth Circuit, vice James L. Ryan, retired, which was sent to the Senate on February 14, 2005.

David C. Sanborn,
of Virginia, to be Administrator of the Maritime Administration, vice William Schubert, which was sent to the Senate on January 18, 2006.

Submitted March 30

Daniel L. Cooper,
of Pennsylvania, to be Under Secretary for Benefits of the Department of Veterans Affairs for a term of 4 years (reappointment).

Gary D. Orton,
of Nevada, to be U.S. Marshal for the District of Nevada for the term of 4 years, vice Richard Zenos Winget.

Withdrawn March 30

Daniel P. Ryan,
of Michigan, to be U.S. District Judge for the Eastern District of Michigan, vice Patrick J. Duggan, retired, which was sent to the Senate on February 14, 2005.

Submitted April 5

Eric M. Bost,
of Texas, to be Ambassador Extraordinary and Plenipotentiary of the United States of America to the Republic of South Africa.

Lisa Bobbie Schreiber Hughes,
of Pennsylvania, a career member of the Senior Foreign Service, class of Counselor, to be Ambassador Extraordinary and Plenipotentiary of

the United States of America to the Republic of Suriname.

David M. Robinson,
of Connecticut, a career member of the Senior Foreign Service, class of Minister-Counselor, to be Ambassador Extraordinary and Plenipotentiary of the United States of America to the Cooperative Republic of Guyana.

Earl Anthony Wayne,
of Maryland, a career member of the Senior Foreign Service, class of Career Minister, to be Ambassador Extraordinary and Plenipotentiary of the United States of America to Argentina.

Submitted April 6

John A. Cloud, Jr.,
of Virginia, to be Ambassador Extraordinary and Plenipotentiary of the United States of America to the Republic of Lithuania.

Lurita Alexis Doan,
of Virginia, to be Administrator of General Services, vice Stephen A. Perry, resigned.

R. David Paulison,
of Florida, to be Under Secretary for Federal Emergency Management, Department of Homeland Security, vice Michael D. Brown, resigned.

John Clint Williamson,
of Louisiana, to be Ambassador at Large for War Crimes Issues.

Withdrawn April 6

Robert M. Duncan,
of Kentucky, to be a member of the Board of Directors of the Corporation for National and Community Service for a term expiring June 10, 2009, vice Juanita Sims Doty, term expired, which was sent to the Senate on April 4, 2005.

Submitted April 24

Gustavo Antonio Gelpi,
of Puerto Rico, to be U.S. District Judge for the District of Puerto Rico, vice Hector M. Laffitte, retired.

Philip S. Gutierrez,
of California, to be U.S. District Judge for the Central District of California, vice Terry J. Hatter, Jr., retired.

Daniel Porter Jordan III,
of Mississippi, to be U.S. District Judge for the Southern District of Mississippi, vice Tom S. Lee, retired.

Erik C. Peterson,
of Wisconsin, to be U.S. Attorney for the Western District of Wisconsin for the term of 4 years, vice J.B. Van Hollen, resigned.

Anita K. Blair,
of Virginia, to be an Assistant Secretary of the Air Force, vice Michael L. Dominguez.

Paul A. Denett,
of Virginia, to be Administrator for Federal Procurement Policy, vice David Safavian.

Anne E. Derse,
of Maryland, a career member of the Senior Foreign Service, class of Minister-Counselor, to be Ambassador Extraordinary and Plenipotentiary of the United States of America to the Republic of Azerbaijan.

Robert S. Ford,
of Maryland, a career member of the Senior Foreign Service, class of Counselor, to be Ambassador Extraordinary and Plenipotentiary of the United States of America to the People's Democratic Republic of Algeria.

Dirk Kempthorne,
of Idaho, to be Secretary of the Interior, vice Gale Ann Norton, resigned.

Mark V. Rosenker,
of Maryland, to be Chairman of the National Transportation Safety Board for a term of 2 years, vice Ellen G. Engleman, term expired.

Leslie V. Rowe,
of Washington, a career member of the Senior Foreign Service, class of Minister-Counselor, to be Ambassador Extraordinary and Plenipotentiary of the United States of America to Papua New Guinea, and to serve concurrently and without additional compensation as Ambassador Extraordinary and Plenipotentiary of the United States of America to the Solomon Islands and Ambassador Extraordinary and Plenipotentiary of the United States of America to the Republic of Vanuatu.

Daniel S. Sullivan,
of Alaska, to be an Assistant Secretary of State (Economic and Business Affairs), vice Earl Anthony Wayne.

Withdrawn April 24

John G. Emling,
of Pennsylvania, to be an Assistant Secretary of Commerce, vice Brett T. Palmer, resigned, which was sent to the Senate on February 27, 2006.

Submitted April 25

April H. Foley,
of New York, to be Ambassador Extraordinary and Plenipotentiary of the United States of America to the Republic of Hungary.

Tracey Ann Jacobson,
of the District of Columbia, a career member of the Senior Foreign Service, class of Counselor, to be Ambassador Extraordinary and Plenipotentiary of the United States of America to the Republic of Tajikistan.

Kevin J. Martin,
of North Carolina, to be a member of the Federal Communications Commission for a term of 5 years from July 1, 2006 (reappointment).

Sue C. Payton,
of Virginia, to be an Assistant Secretary of the Air Force, vice Marvin R. Sambur.

Steven C. Preston,
of Illinois, to be Administrator of the Small Business Administration, vice Hector V. Barreto, Jr., resigned.

Frances Marie Tydingco-Gatewood,
of Guam, to be Judge for the District Court of Guam for the term of 10 years, vice John S. Unpingco, term expired.

Gaddi H. Vasquez,
of California, for the rank of Ambassador during his tenure of service as U.S. Representative to the United Nations Agencies for Food and Agriculture.

Lawrence A. Warder,
of Texas, to be Chief Financial Officer, Department of Education, vice Jack Martin, resigned.

Submitted April 27

Robert Anthony Bradtke,
of Maryland, a career member of the Senior Foreign Service, class of Minister-Counselor, to be Ambassador Extraordinary and Plenipotentiary of the United States of America to the Republic of Croatia.

Robert J. Portman,
of Ohio, to be Director of the Office of Management and Budget, vice Joshua B. Bolten.

Dale Klein,
of Texas, to be a member of the Nuclear Regulatory Commission for the term of 5 years expiring June 30, 2011, vice Nils J. Diaz, term expiring.

James B. Lockhart III,
of Connecticut, to be Director of the Office of Federal Housing Enterprise Oversight, Department of Housing and Urban Development for a term of 5 years, vice Armando Falcon, Jr., resigned.

Submitted May 1

Paul Cherecwich, Jr.,
of Utah, to be a member of the Internal Revenue Service Oversight Board for a term expiring September 14, 2009, vice Charles L. Kolbe, term expired.

Donald V. Hammond,
of Virginia, to be a member of the Internal Revenue Service Oversight Board for a term expiring September 21, 2010, vice Robert M. Tobias, term expired.

John M.R. Kneuer,
of New Jersey, to be Assistant Secretary of Commerce for Communications and Information, vice Michael D. Gallagher, resigned.

Dawn M. Liberi,
of New York, a career member of the Senior Foreign Service, class of Minister-Counselor, to be Ambassador Extraordinary and Plenipotentiary of the United States of America to the Islamic Republic of Mauritania.

William B. Taylor, Jr.,
of Virginia, to be Ambassador Extraordinary and Plenipotentiary of the United States of America to Ukraine.

Catherine G. West,
of the District of Columbia, to be a member of the Internal Revenue Service Oversight Board for a term expiring September 14, 2008, vice Karen Hastie Williams, term expired.

Deborah L. Wince-Smith,
of Virginia, to be a member of the Internal Revenue Service Oversight Board for a term expiring September 14, 2010, vice Larry L. Levitan, term expired.

Michael Wood,
of the District of Columbia, to be Ambassador Extraordinary and Plenipotentiary of the United States of America to Sweden.

Submitted May 2

Sheila C. Bair,
of Kansas, to be a member of the Board of Directors of the Federal Deposit Insurance Corporation for the remainder of the term expiring July 15, 2007, vice Donald E. Powell, resigned.

Sheila C. Bair,
of Kansas, to be a member of the Board of Directors of the Federal Deposit Insurance Corporation for a term expiring July 15, 2013 (reappointment).

Sheila C. Bair,
of Kansas, to be Chairperson of the Board of Directors of the Federal Deposit Insurance Corporation for a term of 5 years, vice Donald E. Powell, resigned.

Submitted May 3

Mark Myers,
of Alaska, to be Director of the U.S. Geological Survey, vice Charles G. Groat, resigned.

Susan C. Schwab,
of Maryland, to be U.S. Trade Representative, with the rank of Ambassador Extraordinary and Plenipotentiary, vice Robert J. Portman.

Submitted May 4

Valerie L. Baker,
of California, to be U.S. District Judge for the Central District of California, vice Consuelo B. Marshall, retired.

Jerome A. Holmes,
of Oklahoma, to be U.S. Circuit Judge for the Tenth Circuit, vice Stephanie K. Seymour, retired.

Charles P. Rosenberg,
of Virginia, to be U.S. Attorney for the Eastern District of Virginia for the term of 4 years, vice Paul J. McNulty, resigned.

Withdrawn May 4

Jerome A. Holmes,
of Oklahoma, to be U.S. District Judge for the Northern District of Oklahoma, vice Sven E. Holmes, resigned, which was sent to the Senate on February 14, 2006.

Submitted May 5

Katherine M.B. Berger,
of Virginia, to be a member of the National Museum and Library Services Board for a term expiring December 6, 2010, vice Nancy S. Dwight, term expired.

Karen Brosius,
of South Carolina, to be a member of the National Museum and Library Services Board for the remainder of the term expiring December 6, 2006, vice Thomas E. Lorentzen, resigned.

Karen Brosius,
of South Carolina, to be a member of the National Museum and Library Services Board for a term expiring December 6, 2011 (reappointment).

Ioannis N. Miaoulis,
of Massachusetts, to be a member of the National Museum and Library Services Board for a term expiring December 6, 2010, vice Terry L. Maple, term expired.

Christina Orr-Cahall,
of Florida, to be a member of the National Museum and Library Services Board for a term expiring December 6, 2010, vice Maria Mercedes Guillemard, term expired.

Sandra Pickett,
of Texas, to be a member of the National Museum and Library Services Board for a term expiring December 6, 2010 (reappointment).

Kevin Owen Starr,
of California, to be a member of the National Museum and Library Services Board for a term expiring December 6, 2009, vice David Donath, term expired.

Submitted May 8

General Michael V. Hayden,
U.S. Air Force, to be Director of the Central Intelligence Agency, vice Porter J. Goss, resigned.

Troy R. Justesen,
of Utah, to be Assistant Secretary for Vocational and Adult Education, Department of Education, vice Susan K. Sclafani.

W. Stuart Symington, IV,
of Missouri, a career member of the Senior Foreign Service, class of Counselor, to be Ambassador Extraordinary and Plenipotentiary of the United States of America to the Republic of Djibouti.

Submitted May 9

Victoria Ray Carlson,
of Iowa, to be a member of the National Council on Disability for a term expiring September 17, 2007, vice Joel Kahn, term expired.

Chad Colley,
of Florida, to be a member of the National Council on Disability for a term expiring September 17, 2007, vice David Wenzel, term expired.

Lisa Mattheiss,
of Tennessee, to be a member of the National Council on Disability for a term expiring September 17, 2007, vice Carol Hughes Novak, term expired.

Eric Solomon,
of New Jersey, to be an Assistant Secretary of the Treasury, vice Pamela F. Olson, resigned.

John R. Vaughn,
of Florida, to be a member of the National Council on Disability for a term expiring September 17, 2007, vice Lex Frieden, term expired.

Ellen C. Williams,
of Kentucky, to be a Governor of the U.S. Postal Service for the remainder of the term expiring December 8, 2007, vice John S. Gardner.

Submitted May 10

Neil M. Gorsuch,
of Colorado, to be U.S. Circuit Judge for the Tenth Circuit, vice David M. Ebel, retired.

Submitted May 11

Thomas D. Anderson,
of Vermont, to be U.S. Attorney for the District of Vermont for the term of 4 years, vice Peter W. Hall, resigned.

Gayleatha Beatrice Brown,
of New Jersey, a career member of the Senior Foreign Service, class of Counselor, to be Ambassador Extraordinary and Plenipotentiary of the United States of America to the Republic of Benin.

Peter R. Coneway,
of Texas, to be Ambassador Extraordinary and Plenipotentiary of the United States of America to Switzerland, and to serve concurrently and without additional compensation as Ambassador Extraordinary and Plenipotentiary of the United States of America to the Principality of Liechtenstein.

Christina B. Rocca,
of Virginia, for the rank of Ambassador during her tenure of service as U.S. Representative to the Conference on Disarmament.

William H. Tobey,
of Connecticut, to be Deputy Administrator for Defense Nuclear Nonproliferation, National Nuclear Security Administration, vice Paul Morgan Longsworth, resigned.

Submitted May 16

Francisco Augusto Besosa,
of Puerto Rico, to be U.S. District Judge for the District of Puerto Rico, vice Juan M. Perez-Gimenez, retired.

R. Hunter Biden,
of Delaware, to be a member of the Reform Board (Amtrak) for a term of 5 years, vice Michael S. Dukakis, term expired.

John Ray Correll,
of Indiana, to be Director of the Office of Surface Mining Reclamation and Enforcement, vice Jeffrey D. Jarrett.

John H. Hill,
of Indiana, to be Administrator of the Federal Motor Carrier Safety Administration, vice Annette Sandberg, resigned.

Donna R. McLean,
of the District of Columbia, to be a member of the Reform Board (Amtrak) for a term of 5 years, vice John Robert Smith, term expired.

Submitted May 18

Kathleen L. Casey,
of Virginia, to be a member of the Securities and Exchange Commission for a term expiring June 5, 2011, vice Cynthia A. Glassman, resigned.

Donald L. Kohn,
of Virginia, to be Vice Chairman of the Board of Governors of the Federal Reserve System for a term of 4 years, vice Roger Walton Ferguson, resigned.

Martin J. Jackley,
of South Dakota, to be U.S. Attorney for the District of South Dakota for the term of 4 years, vice Steven Kent Mullins.

Kimberly Ann Moore,
of Virginia, to be U.S. Circuit Judge for the Federal Circuit, vice Raymond C. Clevenger III, retired.

Bobby E. Shepherd,
of Arkansas, to be U.S. Circuit Judge for the Eighth Circuit, vice Morris S. Arnold, retiring.

Submitted May 23

Richard E. Hoagland,
of the District of Columbia, a career member of the Senior Foreign Service, class of Minister-Counselor, to be Ambassador Extraordinary and Plenipotentiary of the United States of America to the Republic of Armenia.

Clifford M. Sobel,
of New Jersey, to be Ambassador Extraordinary and Plenipotentiary of the United States of America to the Federative Republic of Brazil.

Submitted May 24

Patrick W. Dunne,
of New York, to be an Assistant Secretary of Veterans Affairs (Policy and Planning), vice Claude M. Kicklighter, resigned.

Submitted May 25

Anna Blackburne-Rigsby,
of the District of Columbia, to be Associate Judge of the District of Columbia Court of Appeals for the term of 15 years, vice Frank Ernest Schwelb, retiring.

Robert O. Blake, Jr.,
of Maryland, a career member of the Senior Foreign Service, class of Minister-Counselor, to be Ambassador Extraordinary and Plenipotentiary of the United States of America to the Democratic Socialist Republic of Sri Lanka, and to serve concurrently and without additional compensation as Ambassador Extraordinary and Plenipotentiary of the United States of America to the Republic of Maldives.

Elizabeth Dougherty,
of the District of Columbia, to be a member of the National Mediation Board for a term expiring July 1, 2009, vice Read Van de Water, term expiring.

Phyllis D. Thompson,
of the District of Columbia, to be Associate Judge of the District of Columbia Court of Appeals for the term of 15 years, vice John A. Terry, retired.

Submitted June 5

David H. Laufman,
of Texas, to be Inspector General, Department of Defense, vice Joseph E. Schmitz, resigned.

Charles D. Nottingham,
of Virginia, to be a member of the Surface Transportation Board for a term expiring December 31, 2010, vice Roger P. Nober, term expired.

Charles Darwin Snelling,
of Pennsylvania, to be a member of the Board of Directors of the Metropolitan Washington Airports Authority for a term expiring May 30, 2012 (reappointment).

Submitted June 6

Cesar Benito Cabrera,
of Puerto Rico, to be Ambassador Extraordinary and Plenipotentiary of the United States of America to the Republic of Mauritius, and to serve concurrently and without additional compensation as Ambassador Extraordinary and Plenipotentiary of the United States of America to the Republic of Seychelles.

Wayne Cartwright Beyer,
of New Hampshire, to be a member of the Federal Labor Relations Authority for a term of 5 years expiring July 1, 2010, vice Othoniel Armendariz.

Colleen Conway-Welch,
of Tennessee, to be a member of the Board of Regents of the Uniformed Services University of the Health Sciences for a term expiring May 1, 2011, vice L.D. Britt, term expired.

Marcia Morales Howard,
of Florida, to be U.S. District Judge for the Middle District of Florida, vice Harvey E. Schlesinger, retired.

Leslie Southwick,
of Mississippi, to be U.S. District Judge for the Southern District of Mississippi, vice William H. Barbour, Jr., retired.

Robert L. Sumwalt III,
of South Carolina, to be a member of the National Transportation Safety Board for the remainder of the term expiring December 31, 2006, vice Richard F. Healing, resigned.

Robert L. Sumwalt III,
of South Carolina, to be a member of the National Transportation Safety Board for a term expiring December 31, 2011 (reappointment).

C. Thomas Yarington, Jr.,
of Washington, to be a member of the Board of Regents of the Uniformed Services University of the Health Sciences for a term expiring May 1, 2011, vice Ikram U. Khan, term expired.

Submitted June 7

Gregory Kent Frizzell,
of Oklahoma, to be U.S. District Judge for the Northern District of Oklahoma, vice Sven E. Holmes, resigned.

Submitted June 9

R. Alexander Acosta,
of Florida, to be U.S. Attorney for the Southern District of Florida for the term of 4 years, vice Marcos D. Jimenez.

Troy A. Eid,
of Colorado, to be U.S. Attorney for the District of Colorado for the term of 4 years, vice John W. Suthers, resigned.

Phillip J. Green,
of Illinois, to be U.S. Attorney for the Southern District of Illinois for the term of 4 years, vice Ronald J. Tenpas, resigned.

George E.B. Holding,
of North Carolina, to be U.S. Attorney for the Eastern District of North Carolina for the term of 4 years, vice Frank DeArmon Whitney.

Sharon Lynn Potter,
of West Virginia, to be U.S. Attorney for the Northern District of West Virginia for the term of 4 years, vice Thomas E. Johnston, resigned.

Brett L. Tolman,
of Utah, to be U.S. Attorney for the District of Utah for the term of 4 years, vice Paul Michael Warner, resigned.

Submitted June 12

Randall M. Fort,
of Virginia, to be an Assistant Secretary of State (Intelligence and Research), vice Thomas Fingar, resigned.

Margo M. McKay,
of Virginia, to be an Assistant Secretary of Agriculture, vice Vernon Bernard Parker.

Stephen S. McMillin,
of Texas, to be Deputy Director of the Office of Management and Budget, vice Joel David Kaplan.

Drue Pearce,
of Alaska, to be Federal Coordinator for Alaska Natural Gas Transportation Projects for the term prescribed by law (new position).

Marc Spitzer,
of Arizona, to be a member of the Federal Energy Regulatory Commission for the term expiring June 30, 2011, vice Nora Mead Brownell, resigned.

Lisa Godbey Wood,
of Georgia, to be U.S. District Judge for the Southern District of Georgia, vice Dudley H. Bowen, Jr., retiring.

Submitted June 16

Mark R. Abbott,
of Oregon, to be a member of the National Science Board, National Science Foundation, for a term expiring May 10, 2012, vice Jane Lubchenco, term expired.

Geoffrey S. Bacino,
of Illinois, to be a Director of the Federal Housing Finance Board for a term expiring February 27, 2013, vice Franz S. Leichter, term expired.

Camilla Persson Benbow,
of Tennessee, to be a member of the National Science Board, National Science Foundation, for a term expiring May 10, 2012, vice Warren M. Washington, term expired.

John T. Bruer,
of Missouri, to be a member of the National Science Board, National Science Foundation, for a term expiring May 10, 2012, vice John A. White, Jr., term expired.

Josiah Bunting III,
of Rhode Island, to be a member of the National Council on the Humanities for a term expiring January 26, 2012, vice Wright L. Lassiter, Jr., term expired.

Michael V. Dunn,
of Iowa, to be a Commissioner of the Commodity Futures Trading Commission for a term expiring June 19, 2011 (reappointment).

Thomas C. Foley,
of Connecticut, to be Ambassador Extraordinary and Plenipotentiary of the United States of America to Ireland.

Patricia D. Galloway,
of Washington, to be a member of the National Science Board, National Science Foundation, for a term expiring May 10, 2012, vice Diana S. Natalicio, term expired.

Jose-Marie Griffiths,
of Pennsylvania, to be a member of the National Science Board, National Science Foundation, for a term expiring May 10, 2012, vice Nina V. Fedoroff, term expired.

Mary Haybeck,
of Maryland, to be a member of the National Council on the Humanities for a term expiring January 26, 2012, vice James R. Stoner, Jr., term expired.

Karl Hess,
of Illinois, to be a member of the National Science Board, National Science Foundation, for the remainder of the term expiring May 10, 2008, vice Delores M. Etter, resigned.

Robert S. Martin,
of Texas, to be a member of the National Council on the Humanities for a term expiring January 26, 2012, vice Jeffrey D. Wallin, term expired.

Wilfred M. McClay,
of Tennessee, to be a member of the National Council on the Humanities for a term expiring January 26, 2012 (reappointment).

Nancy Montanez-Johner,
of Nebraska, to be Under Secretary of Agriculture for Food, Nutrition, and Consumer Services, vice Eric M. Bost.

Nancy Montanez-Johner,
of Nebraska, to be a member of the Board of Directors of the Commodity Credit Corporation, vice Eric M. Bost.

Manfredi Piccolomini,
of New York, to be a member of the National Council on the Humanities for a term expiring January 26, 2012, vice Andrew Ladis, term expired.

Thomas N. Taylor,
of Kansas, to be a member of the National Science Board, National Science Foundation, for a term expiring May 10, 2012, vice Daniel Simberloff, term expired.

Richard F. Thompson,
of California, to be a member of the National Science Board, National Science Foundation, for a term expiring May 10, 2012, vice Mark S. Wrighton, term expired.

Kenneth R. Weinstein,
of the District of Columbia, to be a member of the National Council on the Humanities for a term expiring January 26, 2012, vice David Hertz, term expired.

Jay Winik,
of Maryland, to be a member of the National Council on the Humanities for a term expiring January 26, 2012, vice Nathan O. Hatch, term expired.

Submitted June 19

Henry M. Paulson, Jr.,
of New York, to be Secretary of the Treasury, vice John W. Snow, resigned.

Submitted June 26

Warren Bell,
of California, to be a member of the Board of Directors of the Corporation for Public Broadcasting for a term expiring January 31, 2012, vice Kenneth Y. Tomlinson, resigned.

Chris Boskin,
of California, to be a member of the Board of Directors of the Corporation for Public Broadcasting for a term expiring January 31, 2012, vice Katherine Milner Anderson, resigned.

Linda Mysliwy Conlin,
of New Jersey, to be First Vice President of the Export-Import Bank of the United States for a term expiring January 20, 2009, vice April H. Foley, term expired.

J. Joseph Grandmaison,
of New Hampshire, to be a member of the Board of Directors of the Export-Import Bank of the United States for a term expiring January 20, 2009 (reappointment).

Thomas E. Harvey,
of New York, to be an Assistant Secretary of Veterans Affairs (Congressional Affairs), vice Pamela M. Iovino, resigned.

Roger L. Hunt,
of Nevada, to be a member of the Board of Trustees of the Harry S. Truman Scholarship Foundation for a term expiring December 10, 2009, vice Scott O. Wright, term expired.

John E. Kidde,
of California, to be a member of the Board
of Trustees of the Harry S. Truman Scholarship
Foundation for a term expiring December 10,
2011, vice Frederick G. Slabach, term expired.

John Peyton,
of Florida, to be a member of the Board of
Trustees of the Harry S. Truman Scholarship
Foundation for a term expiring December 10,
2011, vice Patrick Lloyd McCrory, term expired.

David H. Pryor,
of Arkansas, to be a member of the Board of
Directors of the Corporation for Public Broadcasting for a term expiring January 31, 2008,
vice Christy Carpenter, term expired.

William B. Wark,
of Maine, to be a member of the Chemical
Safety and Hazard Investigation Board for a
term of 5 years, vice Rixio Enrique Medina,
resigned.

Robert L. Wilkie,
of North Carolina, to be an Assistant Secretary
of Defense, vice Daniel R. Stanley.

William E. Wright,
of Florida, to be a member of the Chemical
Safety and Hazard Investigation Board for a
term of 5 years, vice Gerald V. Poje, term expired.

Submitted June 28

John Preston Bailey,
of West Virginia, to be U.S. District Judge for
the Northern District of West Virginia, vice
Frederick P. Stamp, Jr., retiring.

Mary O. Donohue,
of New York, to be U.S. District Judge for the
Northern District of New York, vice Frederick
J. Scullin, Jr., retired.

John Alfred Jarvey,
of Iowa, to be U.S. District Judge for the Southern District of Iowa, vice Ronald E. Longstaff,
retiring.

Robert James Jonker,
of Michigan, to be U.S. District Judge for the
Western District of Michigan, vice Gordon J.
Quist, retired.

Kent A. Jordan,
of Delaware, to be U.S. Circuit Judge for the
Third Circuit, vice Jane R. Roth, retired.

Raymond M. Kethledge,
of Michigan, to be U.S. Circuit Judge for the
Sixth Circuit, vice James L. Ryan, retired.

Debra Ann Livingston,
of New York, to be U.S. Circuit Judge for the
Second Circuit, vice John M. Walker, Jr., retiring.

Paul Lewis Maloney,
of Michigan, to be U.S. District Judge for the
Western District of Michigan, vice Richard Alan
Enslen, retired.

Stephen Joseph Murphy III,
of Michigan, to be U.S. Circuit Judge for the
Sixth Circuit, vice Susan Bieke Neilson, deceased.

Janet T. Neff,
of Michigan, to be U.S. District Judge for the
Western District of Michigan, vice David W.
McKeague, elevated.

Carmel Borders,
of Kentucky, to be a member of the National
Institute for Literacy Advisory Board for a term
expiring November 25, 2008 (reappointment).

Jay M. Cohen,
of New York, to be Under Secretary for Science
and Technology, Department of Homeland Security, vice Charles E. McQueary, resigned.

Sean T. Connaughton,
of Virginia, to be Administrator of the Maritime
Administration, vice William Schubert, resigned.

Donald D. Deshler,
of Kansas, to be a member of the National Institute for Literacy Advisory Board for a term expiring January 30, 2008, vice Phyllis C. Hunter,
term expired.

Blanca E. Enriquez,
of Texas, to be a member of the National Institute for Literacy Advisory Board for a term expiring January 30, 2009 (reappointment).

Patricia Mathes,
of Texas, to be a member of the National Institute for Literacy Advisory Board for a term expiring November 25, 2007, vice Mark G. Yudof, resigned.

Eliza McFadden,
of Florida, to be a member of the National Institute for Literacy Advisory Board for a term expiring January 30, 2009, vice Douglas Carnine, term expired.

Timothy Shanahan,
of Illinois, to be a member of the National Institute for Literacy Advisory Board for a term expiring November 25, 2007, vice Jean Osborn, term expired.

Submitted June 29

Frank R. Jimenez,
of Florida, to be General Counsel of the Department of the Navy, vice Alberto Jose Mora, resigned.

Donald C. Johnson,
of Texas, a career member of the Senior Foreign Service, class of Minister-Counselor, to be Ambassador Extraordinary and Plenipotentiary of the United States of America to the Republic of Equatorial Guinea.

Bruce I. Knight,
of South Dakota, to be Under Secretary of Agriculture for Marketing and Regulatory Programs, vice William T. Hawks, resigned.

Bruce I. Knight,
of South Dakota, to be a member of the Board of Directors of the Commodity Credit Corporation, vice William T. Hawks, resigned.

Charles E. McQueary,
of North Carolina, to be Director of Operational Test and Evaluation, Department of Defense, vice Thomas P. Christie, resigned.

Frederic S. Mishkin,
of New York, to be a member of the Board of Governors of the Federal Reserve System for the unexpired term of 14 years from February 1, 2000, vice Roger Walton Ferguson, Jr., resigned.

Edmund C. Moy,
of Wisconsin, to be Director of the Mint for a term of 5 years, vice Henrietta Holsman Fore, resigned.

Nathaniel F. Wienecke,
of New York, to be an Assistant Secretary of Commerce, vice Brett T. Palmer, resigned.

Peter D. Keisler,
of Maryland, to be U.S. Circuit Judge for the District of Columbia Circuit, vice John G. Roberts, Jr., elevated.

Appendix C—Checklist of White House Press Releases

The following list contains releases of the Office of the Press Secretary which are not included in this book.

Released January 3

Transcript of a press briefing by Press Secretary Scott McClellan

Released January 4

Transcript of a press briefing by Press Secretary Scott McClellan

Statement by the Press Secretary on the death of Shaykh Maktoum bin Rashid Al Maktoum, Vice President and Prime Minister of the United Arab Emirates and Ruler of Dubai

Statement by the Press Secretary on disaster assistance to Minnesota

Statement by the Press Secretary on disaster assistance to North Dakota

Released January 5

Transcript of a press briefing by Press Secretary Scott McClellan

Statement by the Press Secretary announcing the the President signed H.R. 3402

Released January 6

Transcript of a press gaggle by Assistant Press Secretary Trent Duffy and Chairman of the National Economic Council Allan B. Hubbard

Statement by the Press Secretary announcing the the President signed H.R. 1815

Fact sheet: Economic Growth Continues—Unemployment Falls Below 5 Percent

Fact sheet: President Bush's Agenda for Job Creation and Economic Opportunity

Released January 9

Transcript of a press briefing by Press Secretary Scott McClellan

Fact sheet: No Child Left Behind—Strengthening America's Education System

Released January 10

Transcript of a press briefing by Press Secretary Scott McClellan

Statement by the Press Secretary announcing that the President signed H.R. 972

Statement by the Press Secretary announcing that the President signed H.R. 2017, H.R. 3179, H.R. 4501, and H.R. 4637

Statement by the Press Secretary on disaster assistance to Oklahoma

Fact sheet: Progress and the Work Ahead in Iraq

Released January 11

Transcript of a press gaggle by Press Secretary Scott McClellan

Statement by the Press Secretary: Signing of H.R. 4340, U.S.-Bahrain Free Trade Agreement

Statement by the Press Secretary announcing that the President signed H.R. 4340

Statement by the Press Secretary on disaster assistance to Texas

Fact sheet: The Asia-Pacific Partnership on Clean Development and Climate

Released January 12

Transcript of a press gaggle by Press Secretary Scott McClellan

Transcript of a press briefing by Office of Management and Budget Deputy Director Joel D. Kaplan on the effects of gulf coast recovery costs on the Federal budget

Fact sheet: A Commitment to Continued Recovery and Rebuilding in the Gulf Coast

Released January 13

Transcript of a press briefing by Press Secretary Scott McClellan

Statement by the Press Secretary: Visit of Pakistani Prime Minister Shaukat Aziz

Transcript of a press briefing by Office of Management and Budget Deputy Director Joel D. Kaplan and Deputy Assistant Secretary of Defense for Public Affairs Bryan Whitman on funding related to ongoing operations in Iraq

Released February 3

Transcript of a press gaggle by Press Secretary Scott McClellan

Statement by the Press Secretary: Condolences for the Victims in the Sinking of an Egyptian Ferry in the Red Sea

Statement by the Press Secretary: Visit by King Abdullah II of Jordan to Washington

Statement by the Press Secretary: Visit by United Nations Secretary-General Kofi Annan

Statement by the Press Secretary announcing that the President signed H.R. 4659

Statement by the Press Secretary on disaster assistance to California

Statement by the Press Secretary on disaster assistance to Nevada

Fact sheet: Economic Growth Continues—Unemployment Rate Falls to 4.7 Percent

Released February 4

Statement by the Press Secretary announcing that the President and Mrs. Bush will attend the funeral of Coretta Scott King to be held on Tuesday in Atlanta

Statement by the Press Secretary on the burning of the Danish and Norwegian Embassies in Damascus, Syria

Released February 6

Transcript of a press briefing by Press Secretary Scott McClellan

Transcript of a press briefing by Office of Management and Budget Director Joshua B. Bolten on the President's fiscal year 2007 budget

Transcript of a press briefing by Director of the Office of Faith-Based and Community Initiatives H. James Towey and Assistant to the President for Domestic Policy Claude Allen on the President's fiscal year 2007 budget and low-income programs

Fact sheet: Highlights of the President's FY 2007 Budget

Released February 7

Transcript of a press gaggle by Press Secretary Scott McClellan

Released February 8

Transcript of a press gaggle by Press Secretary Scott McClellan

Fact sheet: President Bush Signs the Deficit Reduction Act

Released February 9

Transcript of a press briefing by Press Secretary Scott McClellan

Transcript of a press briefing by Assistant to the President for Homeland Security and Counterterrorism Frances Fragos Townsend on the west coast terrorist plot

Statement by the Press Secretary: Visit by President Elias Antonio Saca Gonzalez of El Salvador

Released February 10

Statement by the Press Secretary announcing that the President signed H.R. 4519

Released February 13

Transcript of a press briefing by Press Secretary Scott McClellan

Transcripts of press briefings by Council of Economic Advisers members Katherine Baicker and Matthew Slaughter on the 2006 Economic Report of the President

Advanced text: Remarks by Assistant to the President for Homeland Security and Counterterrorism Frances Fragos Townsend on national preparedness to the NEMA Conference

Released February 14

Transcript of a press briefing by Press Secretary Scott McClellan

Released February 15

Transcript of a press gaggle by Press Secretary Scott McClellan

Statement by the Press Secretary announcing that the President signed H.R. 4636

Released February 16

Transcript of a press briefing by Press Secretary Scott McClellan

Transcript of a press briefing by Office of Management and Budget Deputy Director Joel D. Kaplan, Under Secretary of Defense Tina W. Jonas, State Department Senior Adviser for Foreign Assistance Maria Raphael, State Department Senior Advisor for Iraq James F. Jeffrey on the FY 2006 emergency supplemental request for the global war on terror

Fact sheet: President Requests $72.4 Billion for the Global War on Terror

Fact sheet: President Bush Requests $19.8 Billion for Hurricane Recovery

Released February 17

Transcript of a press gaggle by Deputy Press Secretary Trent Duffy

Fact sheet: President Bush Receives Briefing From Military Commanders

Released February 18

Statement by the Press Secretary announcing that the President signed H.R. 4745

Released February 20

Transcript of a press gaggle by Press Secretary Scott McClellan

Released February 22

Transcript of a press briefing by Press Secretary Scott McClellan

Statement by the Press Secretary: Visit of Prime Minister Silvio Berlusconi of Italy

Fact sheet: The United States-UAE Bilateral Relationship

Fact sheet: The CFIUS Process and the DP World Transaction

Released February 23

Transcript of a press gaggle by Deputy Press Secretary Dana Perino

Transcript of a press briefing by Assistant to the President for Homeland Security and Counterterrorism Frances Fragos Townsend

Fact sheet: The Federal Response to Hurricane Katrina: Lessons Learned

Released February 24

Transcript of a press briefing by National Security Adviser Stephen J. Hadley on the President's visit to India and Pakistan

Statement by the Press Secretary: Visit of Prime Minister Mikulas Dzurinda of the Slovak Republic

Statement by the Press Secretary on disaster assistance to Maine

Released February 27

Transcript of a press briefing by Press Secretary Scott McClellan

Statement by the Press Secretary announcing that the President signed S. 1989

Statement by the Press Secretary on disaster assistance to Idaho

Released February 28

Transcript of a press gaggle by Secretary of State Condoleezza Rice and National Security Adviser Stephen J. Hadley

Released March 1

Transcript of a press briefing by Press Secretary Scott McClellan and Deputy Press Secretary Joseph W. Hagin

Released March 2

Transcript of a press briefing by National Security Adviser Stephen J. Hadley

Transcript of a press briefing by Under Secretary of State for Political Affairs R. Nicholas Burns

Fact sheet: United States and India: Strategic Partnership

Released March 3

Transcript of a press briefing by Assistant Secretary of State for South and Central Asia Richard A. Boucher and National Security Council Senior Director for South and Central Asia Elisabeth Millard

Released March 4

Transcript of a press gaggle by Press Secretary Scott McClellan

Transcript of a press briefing by Secretary of State Condoleezza Rice on the President's visit to South Asia

Fact sheet: United States and Pakistan: Long-Term Strategic Partners

Released March 6

Transcript of a press briefing by Press Secretary Scott McClellan

Transcript of a press briefing by Lt. Gen. Carl Strock, commander and chief of engineers, U.S. Army Corps of Engineers, on recovery efforts in the gulf coast

Transcript of a press briefing by Office of Management and Budget Director Joshua B. Bolten on the President's line-item veto legislation

Statement by the Press Secretary: Visit by President Alejandro Celestino Toledo Manrique of Peru

Statement by the Press Secretary announcing that the President signed S. 1777

Fact sheet: President Submits Line Item Veto Legislation to Congress

Released March 7

Transcript of a press briefing by Press Secretary Scott McClellan

Statement by the Press Secretary on disaster assistance to Mississippi

Released March 8

Transcript of a press gaggle by Press Secretary Scott McClellan

Fact sheet: India Civil Nuclear Cooperation: Responding to Critics

Fact sheet: Gulf Coast Update: Hurricane Relief, Recovery, and Rebuilding Continues

Released March 9

Transcript of a press briefing by Press Secretary Scott McClellan

Statement by the Press Secretary: Visit of Prime Minister Ahern of Ireland

Statement by the Press Secretary: President Bush To Travel to Cancun, Mexico

Statement by the Press Secretary announcing that the President signed H.R. 3199

Fact sheet: Compassion in Action: Producing Real Results for Americans Most in Need

Fact sheet: Safeguarding America: President Bush Signs Patriot Act Reauthorization

Released March 10

Fact sheet: Economic Growth Continues—Almost 5 Million Jobs Created Since August 2003

Released March 13

Transcript of a press briefing by Press Secretary Scott McClellan

Statement by the Press Secretary announcing that the President signed S. 449

Fact sheet: Strategy for Victory: Defeating the Terrorists and Training Iraqi Security Forces

Released March 14

Transcript of a press gaggle by Press Secretary Scott McClellan

Statement by the Press Secretary: Death of Former President of Estonia Lennart Meri

Statement by the Press Secretary announcing that the President signed S. 4515

Fact sheet: The Medicare Prescription Drug Benefit: Helping Seniors and Reducing Costs

Released March 15

Transcript of a press briefing by Press Secretary Scott McClellan

Released March 16

Transcript of a press briefing by Press Secretary Scott McClellan

Transcript of a press briefing by Deputy National Security Adviser Jack D. Crouch II on the national security strategy

Statement by the Press Secretary: Visit by President Ellen Johnson Sirleaf of the Republic of Liberia

Statement by the Press Secretary announcing that the President signed H.R. 32

Statement by the Press Secretary on disaster assistance to Missouri

Fact sheet: President Bush Signs the Stop Counterfeiting in Manufactured Goods Act

Fact sheet: The President's National Security Strategy

Released March 17

Transcript of a press briefing by Press Secretary Scott McClellan

Statement by the Press Secretary: Visit of NATO Secretary General Jaap de Hoop Scheffer

Released March 18

Fact sheet: Operation Iraqi Freedom: Three Years Later

Released March 20

Transcript of a press gaggle by Press Secretary Scott McClellan

Statement by the Press Secretary announcing that the President signed H.J.Res. 47 and S. 1578

Statement by the Press Secretary announcing that the President signed H.R. 1287, H.R. 2113, H.R. 2346, H.R. 2413, H.R. 2630, H.R. 2894, H.R. 3256, H.R. 3368, H.R. 3439, H.R. 3548, H.R. 3703, H.R. 3770, H.R. 3825, H.R. 3830, H.R. 3989, H.R. 4053, H.R. 4107, H.R. 4152, H.R. 4295, S. 2089, and S. 2320

Statement by the Press Secretary on disaster assistance to Oregon

Fact sheet: Strategy for Victory: Clear, Hold, and Build

Released March 22

Transcript of a press gaggle by Press Secretary Scott McClellan

Statement by the Press Secretary: Visit of President Hu Jintao of the People's Republic of China

Released March 23

Transcript of a press briefing by Press Secretary Scott McClellan

Released March 24

Statement by the Press Secretary: Visit by President Olusegun Obasanjo of the Republic of Nigeria

Statement by the Press Secretary announcing that the President signed H.R. 1053, H.R. 1691, S. 2064, and S. 2275

Statement by the Press Secretary announcing that the President signed H.R. 4826, S. 1184, and S. 2363

Released March 27

Transcript of a press briefing by Press Secretary Scott McClellan

Fact sheet: Comprehensive Immigration Reform: Securing Our Border, Enforcing Our Laws, and Upholding Our Values

Released March 28

Transcript of a press briefing by Press Secretary Scott McClellan

Statement by the Press Secretary on disaster assistance to Illinois

Released March 29

Fact sheet: Strategy for Victory: Freedom in Iraq

Released March 30

Transcript of a press briefing by National Security Council Senior Director for Western Hemisphere Affairs Daniel W. Fisk on the President's visit to Mexico

Statement by the Press Secretary on China's treatment of Kim Chun-Hee

Released April 1

Statement by the Press Secretary announcing that the President signed H.R. 4911

Released April 3

Transcript of a press gaggle by Press Secretary Scott McClellan

Released April 4

Transcript of a press briefing by Press Secretary Scott McClellan

Released April 5

Transcript of a press gaggle by Press Secretary Scott McClellan

Statement by the Press Secretary: Visit by President John Kufuor of the Republic of Ghana

Statement by the Press Secretary on disaster assistance to Missouri

Statement by the Press Secretary on disaster assistance to Tennessee

Fact sheet: Health Savings Accounts: Affordable and Accessible Health Care

Fact sheet: Health Savings Accounts: Myth vs. Fact

Text: Statement by Chairman James L. Connaughton of the Council on Environmental Quality on levee repairs in California

Released April 22

Fact sheet: Earth Day 2006: Developing New Transportation Technology

Released April 23

Transcript of a press gaggle by Press Secretary Scott McClellan

Released April 24

Transcripts of press gaggles by Press Secretary Scott McClellan

Statement by the Press Secretary: Visit of Uruguayan President Tabare Vazquez

Fact sheet: Comprehensive Immigration Reform: Securing Our Border

Released April 25

Transcript of a press briefing by Press Secretary Scott McClellan

Transcript of a press briefing by National Economic Council Director Allan B. Hubbard on the President's four-point energy plan

Fact sheet: President Bush's Four-Part Plan To Confront High Gasoline Prices

Released April 26

Transcript of a press briefing by Press Secretary Scott McClellan

Fact sheet: The National Teacher of the Year: A Commitment to Education Excellence

Released April 27

Transcript of a press gaggle by Press Secretary Scott McClellan

Statement by the Press Secretary: U.S.-Targeted Sanctions on Persons in Connection With the Conflict in Sudan's Darfur Region

Released April 28

Statement by the Press Secretary on proposed acquisition of Ross Catherall US Holdings, Inc., by a subsidiary of Dubai Holding LLC

Fact sheet: CAFE Reform for Passenger Cars

Released May 1

Transcript of a press briefing by Press Secretary Scott McClellan

Fact sheet: Making Health Care More Affordable and Accessible for All Americans

Released May 2

Transcript of a press briefing by Press Secretary Scott McClellan

Statement by the Press Secretary on disaster assistance to Connecticut

Statement by the Press Secretary on disaster assistance to Hawaii

Released May 3

Transcript of a press briefing by Press Secretary Scott McClellan and Assistant to the President for Homeland Security and Counterterrorism Frances Fragos Townsend

Statement by the Press Secretary announcing the President's upcoming visit to Vienna, Austria, to participate in the annual U.S.-EU summit on June 21

Fact sheet: Advancing the Nation's Preparedness for Pandemic Influenza

Fact sheet: Growing Our Economy: Keeping Taxes Low and Restraining Spending

Released May 4

Transcript of a press briefing by Press Secretary Scott McClellan

Released May 5

Transcript of a press briefing by Press Secretary Scott McClellan

Statement by the Press Secretary: Darfur Peace Agreement

Fact sheet: Economic Growth Continues—More Than 5.2 Million Jobs Created Since August 2003

Released May 6

Advanced text: Remarks by the President to Oklahoma State University

Released May 8

Transcript of a press briefing by Director of National Intelligence John D. Negroponte on the nomination of Gen. Michael V. Hayden,

USAF, to be Director of the Central Intelligence Agency

Statement by the Press Secretary: Visit by Prime Minister John Howard of Australia

Fact sheet: Brett M. Kavanaugh: Nominee to the U.S. Court of Appeals for the DC Circuit

Fact sheet: Darfur Agreement: A Step Toward Peace

Fact sheet: General Michael V. Hayden: The Right Leader for the CIA

Released May 9

Transcript of a press gaggle by former Press Secretary Scott McClellan

Fact sheet: General Michael V. Hayden: Extremely Well Qualified To Lead the CIA

Fact sheet: Medicare Prescription Drug Coverage: Saving Beneficiaries Money, and Getting Them the Drugs They Need

Released May 10

Fact sheet: The President's Identity Theft Task Force

Released May 11

Transcript of a press gaggle by Deputy Press Secretary Dana Perino

Advanced text: The President Delivers the Commencement Address to Mississippi Gulf Coast Community College

Released May 12

Transcript of a press briefing by Press Secretary Tony Snow

Released May 15

Transcript of a press briefing by Press Secretary Tony Snow, Counselor to the President Daniel J. Bartlett, Assistant to the President for Homeland Security and Counterterrorism Frances Fragos Townsend, and Assistant to the President and Deputy Chief of Staff for Policy Joel D. Kaplan on the President's speech on immigration

Statement by the Press Secretary: Visit by Prime Minister Ehud Olmert of Israel

Fact sheet: Overview: Comprehensive Immigration Reform

Excerpts of the President's address to the Nation on immigration

Advance text of the President's address to the Nation on immigration

Released May 16

Transcript of a press briefing by Press Secretary Tony Snow

Transcript of a press briefing by Secretary of Homeland Security Michael Chertoff, Border Patrol Chief David Aguilar, Immigrations and Customs Enforcement Assistant Secretary Julie L. Myers, Assistant Secretary of Defense Paul F. Mchale, and Chief of the National Guard Bureau Lt. Gen. H. Steven Blum on the President's immigration reform plan

Released May 17

Transcript of a press briefing by Press Secretary Tony Snow

Statement by the Press Secretary on disaster assistance to Washington

Fact sheet: Extending the President's Tax Relief: A Victory for American Taxpayers

Released May 18

Transcript of a press gaggle by Press Secretary Tony Snow

Transcript of a press briefing by Department of Homeland Security Deputy Secretary Michael P. Jackson, National Guard Bureau Comptroller Christopher Gardner, and Office of Management and Budget Executive Associate Director Austin Smythe on the President's supplemental appropriation request

Statement by the Press Secretary: Denial of the Appeal of Egyptian Politician Ayman Nour

Statement by the Press Secretary announcing that the President signed H.J. Res. 83 and S. 1382

Fact sheet: President Requests Funds To Strengthen Border Security

Released May 19

Transcript of a press gaggle by Press Secretary Tony Snow

Fact sheet: The American Competitiveness Initiative: A Commitment to Education, Research, and Innovation

Released May 22

Transcript of a press gaggle by Press Secretary Tony Snow

Released May 23

Transcript of a press briefing by Press Secretary Tony Snow

Statement by the Press Secretary: Visit of British Prime Minister Tony Blair

Statement by the Press Secretary: Visit by President Zelaya of Honduras

Released May 24

Transcript of a press gaggle by Press Secretary Tony Snow

Statement by the Press Secretary: Official Visit of Prime Minister Junichiro Koizumi of Japan

Fact sheet: The Advanced Energy Initiative: Ensuring a Clean, Secure Energy Future

Released May 25

Transcript of a press briefing by Press Secretary Tony Snow

Statement by the Press Secretary: Visit by President Kagame of Rwanda

Statement by the Press Secretary announcing that the President signed S. 1165

Statement by the Press Secretary on disaster assistance to Maine

Statement by the Press Secretary on disaster assistance to Massachusetts

Statement by the Press Secretary on disaster assistance to New Hampshire

Released May 26

Statement by the Press Secretary congratulating the Government of Nigeria on supporting democracy by calling for national elections in 2007

Statement by the Press Secretary: Visit by Prime Minister Harper of Canada

Released May 29

Statement by the Press Secretary announcing that the President signed H.R. 1499 and H.R. 5037

Released May 30

Transcript of a press briefing by Press Secretary Tony Snow

Released May 31

Transcript of a press briefing by Press Secretary Tony Snow

Statement by the Press Secretary announcing that the President signed S. 1736

Released June 1

Transcript of a press briefing by Press Secretary Tony Snow

Statement by the Press Secretary: Presidential Designation of Foreign Narcotics Kingpins

Statement by the Press Secretary: Visit by President Denis Sassou-Nguesso of the Republic of the Congo

Fact sheet: Comprehensive Immigration Reform: Improving Worksite Enforcement

Released June 2

Transcript of a press briefing by Press Secretary Tony Snow

Statement by the Press Secretary: Visit by President Michelle Bachelet of Chile

Fact sheet: Economic Growth Continues—More Than 5.3 Million Jobs Created Since August 2003

Released June 5

Transcript of a press briefing by Press Secretary Tony Snow

Statement by the Press Secretary on disaster assistance to California

Statement by the Press Secretary on disaster assistance to Minnesota

Statement by the Press Secretary on disaster assistance to North Dakota

Statement by the Press Secretary on disaster assistance to South Dakota

Released June 6

Transcript of a press gaggle by Press Secretary Tony Snow

Statement by the Press Secretary: President Bush To Attend 2006 Group of Eight (G–8) Summit

Released June 7

Transcript of a press gaggle by Press Secretary Tony Snow

Transcript of a press gaggle by Press Secretary Tony Snow

Statement by the Press Secretary on the murder of four Russian diplomats in Iraq

Released June 27

Transcript of a press briefing by Press Secretary Tony Snow

Fact sheet: The Legislative Line-Item Veto: Constitutional, Effective, and Bipartisan

Released June 28

Transcript of a press briefing by Press Secretary Tony Snow

Statement by the Press Secretary: 50th Anniversary of the Poznan Uprising

Statement by the Press Secretary: President To Visit Germany

Released June 29

Transcript of a press briefing by Press Secretary Tony Snow

Statement by the Press Secretary on disaster assistance to Louisiana

Statement by the Press Secretary on disaster assistance to Mississippi

Released June 30

Transcript of a press gaggle by Press Secretary Tony Snow

Statement by the Press Secretary announcing that the President signed H.R. 5603

Statement by the Press Secretary on disaster assistance to Pennsylvania

Appendix D—Presidential Documents Published in the Federal Register

This appendix lists Presidential documents released by the Office of the Press Secretary and published in the Federal Register. The texts of the documents are printed in the Federal Register (F.R.) at the citations listed below. The documents are also printed in title 3 of the Code of Federal Regulations and in the Weekly Compilation of Presidential Documents.

PROCLAMATIONS

PROCLAMATIONS—Continued

EXECUTIVE ORDERS

OTHER PRESIDENTIAL DOCUMENTS

OTHER PRESIDENTIAL DOCUMENTS—Continued

OTHER PRESIDENTIAL DOCUMENTS—Continued

Subject Index

Name Index

Document Categories List